HE O'LEARY SERIES

Microsoft®
Office 2013:
A Case Approach

Timothy J. O'Leary

*Professor Emeritus,
Arizona State University*

Linda I. O'Leary

McGraw-Hill
Irwin

McGraw-Hill
Irwin

THE O'LEARY SERIES MICROSOFT® OFFICE 2013: A CASE APPROACH
Published by McGraw-Hill/Irwin, a business unit of The McGraw-Hill Companies, Inc., 1221 Avenue of the
Americas, New York, NY, 10020. Copyright © 2014 by The McGraw-Hill Companies, Inc. All rights reserved.
Printed in the United States of America. No part of this publication may be reproduced or distributed in any
form or by any means, or stored in a database or retrieval system, without the prior written consent of The
McGraw-Hill Companies, Inc., including, but not limited to, in any network or other electronic storage or
transmission, or broadcast for distance learning.

Some ancillaries, including electronic and print components, may not be available to customers outside the
United States.

This book is printed on acid-free paper.

1 2 3 4 5 6 7 8 9 0 RMN/RMN 1 0 9 8 7 6 5 4 3

ISBN   978-0-07-351937-1
MHID   0-07-351937-5

Senior Vice President, Products & Markets: *Kurt L. Strand*
Vice President, Content Production & Technology Services: *Kimberly Meriwether David*
Director: *Scott Davidson*
Senior Brand Manager: *Wyatt Morris*
Executive Director of Development: *Ann Torbert*
Development Editor II: *Alaina G. Tucker*
Digital Development Editor: *Kevin White*
Marketing Manager: *Tiffany Russell*
Project Manager: *Marlena Pechan*
Senior Buyer: *Michael R. McCormick*
Designer: *Jana Singer*
Senior Content Licensing Specialist: *Jeremy Cheshareck*
Media Project Manager: *Brent dela Cruz*
Media Project Manager: *Cathy L. Tepper*
Typeface: *11/13 Times LT Std Roman*
Compositor: *Laserwords Private Limited*
Printer: *R. R. Donnelley*

All credits appearing on page OFC.1 or at the end of the book are considered to be an extension of the
copyright page.

Library of Congress Cataloging-in-Publication Data

O'Leary, Timothy J., 1947-
    Microsoft Office 2013: a case approach / Timothy J. O'Leary, Professor Emeritus, Arizona State
University, Linda I. O'Leary.
      pages cm.—(The O'Leary series)
      Includes index.
      ISBN 978-0-07-351937-1 (alk. paper)
      ISBN 0-07-351937-5 (alk. paper)
      1. Microsoft Office. 2. Business—Computer programs. I. O'Leary, Linda I. II. Title.
    HF5548.4.M525O446 2014
    005.5—dc23

                                                                                    2013007267

The Internet addresses listed in the text were accurate at the time of publication. The inclusion of a website does
not indicate an endorsement by the authors or McGraw-Hill, and McGraw-Hill does not guarantee the accuracy
of the information presented at these sites.

www.mhhe.com

Brief Contents

LAB 3 · CREATING REPORTS AND TABLES WD3.1

WORKING TOGETHER: COPYING, LINKING, AND EMBEDDING BETWEEN APPLICATIONS   *WDWT.1*

EXCEL

LAB 1   CREATING AND EDITING A WORKSHEET   *EX1.1*

LAB 2 ENHANCING THE WORKSHEET WITH GRAPHICS AND CHARTS EX2.1

LAB 3 MANAGING AND ANALYZING A WORKBOOK EX3.1

WORKING TOGETHER: LINKING AND EMBEDDING BETWEEN WORD 2013 AND EXCEL 2013 *EXWT.1*

ACCESS

LAB 1 CREATING A DATABASE *AC1.1*

**MODIFYING AND
FILTERING A TABLE AND
CREATING A FORM** AC2.1

**QUERYING TABLES
AND CREATING
REPORTS**   AC3.1

POWERPOINT

LAB 1   CREATING A PRESENTATION   *PP1.1*

Acknowledgments

We would like to extend our thanks to the instructors who took time out of their busy schedules to provide us with the feedback necessary to develop the 2013 Edition of this text. The following instructors offered valuable suggestions on revising the text:

Anne Acker
Jacksonville University

Jack Alanen
California State University–Northridge

Ken Araujo
Francis Marion University

Tahir Aziz
J. Sargeant Reynolds Community College

Lois Blais
Walters State Community College

Bob Clary
Patrick Henry Community College

Robert Doyle
Dona Ana Community College

Michael Dunklebarger
Alamance Community College

Jeffrey Finch
Kanawha Valley Community & Technology College

Kimberly Fish
Butler County Community College

Bob Forward
Texarkana College

Terry Griffin
Midwestern State University

Dexter Harlee
York Technical College

Tina Johnson
Midwestern State University

Dee Joseph
San Antonio College

Philip Kim
Walsh University

Ben Martz
Northern Kentucky University

Theresa McDonald
Texarkana College

David McNair
Jefferson College

Barb Norstrom
Kaskaskia College

Terry Rooker
Germanna Community College

Victor Suich
Walters State Community College

Lakeisha Vance
Alamance Community College

Barbara Wells
Central Carolina Technical College

Jensen Zhao
Ball State University

We would like to thank those who took the time to help us develop the manuscript and ensure accuracy through painstaking edits: Barbara Norstrom of Kaskaskia College, Robert Doyle of Dona Ana Community College, Candice Spangler of Columbus State Community College, and Kate Scalzi.

Finally, we would like to thank team members from McGraw-Hill, whose renewed commitment, direction, and support have infused the team with the excitement of a new project. Leading the team from McGraw-Hill are Wyatt Morris, Senior Brand Manager; Tiffany Russell, Marketing Manager; and Alaina Tucker, Developmental Editor II.

The production staff is headed by Marlena Pechan, Project Manager, whose planning and attention to detail have made it possible for us to successfully meet a very challenging schedule; Jana Singer, Designer; Michael McCormick, Senior Buyer; Kevin White, Digital Developmental Editor; Jeremy Cheshareck, Senior Content Licensing Specialist; Betsy Blumenthal and Chet Gottfried, copy editors; Sharon O'Donnell and Peter DeLissovoy, proofreaders—team members on whom we can depend to do a great job.

Excel

Kathleen Stewart has authored Access and Excel textbooks for McGraw-Hill's Professional Approach series (later the Lesson Approach) since its inception. She has a master's degree in Education as well as an MBA. After several years teaching at a suburban high school, Kathleen became Department Chairperson and Professor of Information Management Systems at Moraine Valley Community College in suburban Chicago, working with students with many interests, skill levels, and backgrounds. In addition, as president of her own training and consulting company, she and her staff delivered individual and classroom instruction and help-desk support in the public and private sectors. Kathleen is retired from her position at the college but remains active in Illinois with organizations that address higher education issues.

Access

Paula Gregory was influenced at an early age by her mother, who had enrolled in computer classes at the local community college in the early 1980s. When her mother brought home a computer made by Radio Shack, the cassette-driven TRS-80, Paula became hooked on technology and learning. Paula has since majored in computer science and received an associate's degree with honors in 1990 from Yavapai College. Thereafter, she began teaching and helping people one-on-one with computers, receiving her teaching certification in 1998. Paula is MCAS-certified in Microsoft Word and Access, as well as ACA-certified in Adobe Photoshop. Now teaching full time at Yavapai College, Paula loves helping students learn all about computers and software, in particular the Microsoft Office and Adobe Creative suites. Also being an artist and a writer, Paula enjoys combining all her skills to develop material that engages the audience and makes learning fun.

Bonnie Gundlach is employed as an independent technical writer, instructor, and voice messaging consultant. Possessing many years' experience in developing and delivering comprehensive technical training, system design, and voice messaging solutions to clients, Ms. Gundlach holds a BA in Elementary Education from the University of South Florida, as well as a post-baccalaureate certificate in Information Systems from Virginia Commonwealth University. As an instructor with Asheville-Buncombe Technical Community College, she has worked teaching computer skills to new and returning adult students. Residing in Asheville, North Carolina, she enjoys life with her husband and treasured feline companions.

The 20th century brought us the dawn of the digital information age and unprecedented changes in information technology. There is no indication that this rapid rate of change will be slowing—it may even be increasing. As we begin the 21st century, computer literacy is undoubtedly becoming a prerequisite in whatever career you choose.

The goal of the O'Leary Series is to provide you with the necessary skills to efficiently use these applications. Equally important is the goal to provide a foundation for students to readily and easily learn to use future versions of this software. This series accomplishes this by providing detailed step-by-step instructions combined with careful selection and presentation of essential concepts.

Times are changing, technology is changing, and this text is changing too. As students of today, you are different from those of yesterday. You put much effort toward the things that interest you and the things that are relevant to you. Your efforts directed at learning application programs and exploring the web seem, at times, limitless.

On the other hand, it's easy to be shortsighted, thinking that learning the skills to use the application is the only objective. The mission of the series is to build upon and extend this interest not only by teaching the specific application skills but by introducing the concepts that are common to all applications, providing students with the confidence, knowledge, and ability to easily learn the next generation of applications.

Instructor's Resource Center

The Online **Instructor's Resource Center** contains access to a computerized Test Bank, an Instructor's Manual, Solutions, and PowerPoint Presentation Slides. Features of the Instructor's Resource are described below.

- **Instructor's Manual**   The Instructor's Manual, authored by the primary contributor, contains lab objectives, concepts, outlines, lecture notes, and command summaries. Also included are answers to all end-of-chapter material, tips for covering difficult materials, additional exercises, and a schedule showing how much time is required to cover text material.

- **Computerized Test Bank**   The test bank, authored by the primary contributor, contains hundreds of multiple choice, true/false, and discussion questions. Each question will be accompanied by the correct answer, the level of learning difficulty, and corresponding page references. Our flexible EZ Test software allows you to easily generate custom exams.

- **PowerPoint Presentation Slides**   The presentation slides, authored by the primary contributor, include lab objectives, concepts, outlines, text figures, and speaker's notes. Also included are bullets to illustrate key terms and FAQs.

Online Learning Center/Website

Found at **www.mhhe.com/oleary**, this site provides additional learning and instructional tools to enhance the comprehension of the text. The OLC/website is divided into these three areas:

- **Information Center** Contains core information about the text, supplements, and the authors.

- **Instructor Center** Offers the aforementioned instructional materials, downloads, and other relevant links for professors.

- **Student Center** Contains data files, chapter competencies, chapter concepts, self-quizzes, additional web links, and more.

SimNet Assessment for Office Applications

SimNet Assessment for Office Applications provides a way for you to test students' software skills in a simulated environment. SimNet is available for Microsoft Office 2013 and provides flexibility for you in your applications course by offering:

Pretesting options
Post-testing options
Course placement testing
Diagnostic capabilities to reinforce skills
Web delivery of tests
Certification preparation exams
Learning verification reports

For more information on skills assessment software, please contact your local sales representative, or visit us at **www.mhhe.com**.

Computing Concepts

Computing Essentials 2014 offers a unique, visual orientation that gives students a basic understanding of computing concepts. *Computing Essentials* encourages "active" learning with exercises, explorations, visual illustrations, and screen shots. While combining the "active" learning style with current topics and technology, this text provides an accurate snapshot of computing trends. When bundled with software application lab manuals, students are given a complete representation of the fundamental issues surrounding the personal computing environment.

Tim and Linda O'Leary live in the American Southwest and spend much of their time engaging instructors and students in conversation about learning. In fact, they have been talking about learning for over 25 years. Something in those early conversations convinced them to write a book, to bring their interest in the learning process to the printed page. Today, they are as concerned as ever about learning, about technology, and about the challenges of presenting material in new ways, in terms of both content and method of delivery.

A powerful and creative team, Tim combines his 30 years of classroom teaching experience with Linda's background as a consultant and corporate trainer. Tim has taught courses at Stark Technical College in Canton, Ohio, and at Rochester Institute of Technology in upstate New York, and is currently a professor emeritus at Arizona State University in Tempe, Arizona. Linda offered her expertise at ASU for several years as an academic advisor. She also presented and developed materials for major corporations such as Motorola, Intel, Honeywell, and AT&T, as well as various community colleges in the Phoenix area.

Tim and Linda have talked to and taught numerous students, all of them with a desire to learn something about computers and applications that make their lives easier, more interesting, and more productive.

Each new edition of an O'Leary text, supplement, or learning aid has benefited from these students and their instructors who daily stand in front of them (or over their shoulders). The O'Leary Series is no exception.

Dedication

We dedicate this edition to our parents, Irene Perley Coats, Jean L. O'Leary, and Charles D. O'Leary, for all their support and love. We miss you.

Introduction to Microsoft Office 2013

Objectives

After completing the Introduction to Microsoft Office 2013, you should be able to:

1. Describe the Office 2013 applications.

2. Start an Office 2013 application.

3. Use the Ribbon, dialog boxes, and task panes.

4. Use menus, context menus, and shortcut keys.

5. Use the Backstage.

6. Open, close, and save files.

7. Navigate a document.

8. Enter, edit, and format text.

9. Select, copy, and move text.

10. Undo and redo changes.

11. Specify document properties.

12. Print a document.

13. Use Office 2013 Help.

14. Exit an Office 2013 application.

What Is Microsoft Office 2013?

Microsoft's Office 2013 is a comprehensive, integrated system of programs designed to solve a wide array of business needs. Although the programs can be used individually, they are designed to work together seamlessly, making it easy to connect people and organizations to information, business processes, and each other. The applications include tools used to create, discuss, communicate, and manage projects. If you share a lot of documents with other people, these features facilitate access to common documents. Additionally, Office 2013 allows you to store and share files in the cloud on SkyDrive or SharePoint. The **cloud** refers to any applications and services that are hosted and run on servers connected to the Internet. This version is designed to work with all types of devices, including desktops, laptops, tablets and hybrid tablet/laptops.

Microsoft Office 2013 is packaged in several different combinations of programs or suites. The major programs and a brief description are provided in the following table.

Program	Description
Word 2013	Word processor program used to create text-based documents
Excel 2013	Spreadsheet program used to analyze numerical data
Access 2013	Database manager used to organize, manage, and display a database
PowerPoint 2013	Graphics presentation program used to create presentation materials
Outlook 2013	Desktop information manager and messaging client
OneNote 2013	Note-taking and information organization tools

The four main components of Microsoft Office 2013—Word, Excel, Access, and PowerPoint—are the applications you will learn about in this series of labs. They are described in more detail in the following sections.

Word 2013

Word 2013 is a word processing software application whose purpose is to help you create text-based documents such as letters, memos, reports, e-mail messages, or any other type of correspondence. Word processors are one of the most flexible and widely used application software programs.

WORD 2013 FEATURES

The beauty of a word processor is that you can make changes or corrections as you are typing. Want to change a report from single spacing to double spacing? Alter the width of the margins? Delete some paragraphs and add others from yet another document? A word processor allows you to do all these things with ease.

Edit Content

Word 2013 excels in its ability to change or **edit** a document. Basic document editing involves correcting spelling, grammar, and sentence-structure errors and revising or updating existing text by inserting, deleting, and rearranging areas of text. For example, a document that lists prices can easily be updated to reflect new prices. A document that details procedures can be revised by deleting old procedures and inserting new ones. Many of these changes are made easily by cutting (removing) or copying (duplicating) selected text and then pasting (inserting) the cut or copied text in another location in the same or another document. Editing allows you to quickly revise a document, by changing only the parts that need to be modified.

To help you produce a perfect document, Word 2013 includes many additional editing support features. The AutoCorrect feature checks the spelling and grammar in a document as text is entered. Many common errors are corrected automatically for you. Others are identified and a correction suggested. A thesaurus can be used to display alternative words that have a meaning similar or opposite to a word you entered. The Find and Replace feature can be used to quickly locate specified text and replace it with other text throughout a document. In addition, Word 2013 includes a variety of tools that automate the process of many common tasks, such as creating tables, form letters, and columns.

Format Content

You also can easily control the appearance or **format** of the document. Perhaps the most noticeable formatting feature is the ability to apply different fonts (type styles and sizes) and text appearance changes such as bold, italics, and color to all or selected portions of the document. Additionally, you can add color shading behind individual pieces of text or entire paragraphs and pages to add emphasis. Other formatting features include changes to entire paragraphs, such as the line spacing and alignment of text between the margins. You also can format entire pages by displaying page numbers, changing margin settings, and applying backgrounds.

To make formatting even easier, Word 2013 includes Document Themes and Styles. Document Themes apply a consistent font, color, and line effect to an entire document. Styles apply the selected style design to a selection of text. Further, Word 2013 includes a variety of built-in preformatted content that helps you quickly produce modern-looking, professional documents. Among these are galleries of cover page designs, pull quotes, and header and footer designs. While selecting many of these design choices, a visual live preview is displayed, making it easy to see how the design would look in your document. In addition, you can select from a wide variety of templates to help you get started on creating many common types of documents such as flyers, calendars, faxes, newsletters, and memos.

Insert Illustrations and Videos

To further enhance your documents, you can insert many different types of graphic elements. These include drawing objects, SmartArt, charts, pictures, clip art, screenshots, and videos. The drawing tools supplied with Word 2013 can be used to create your own drawings, or you can select from over 100 adjustable shapes and modify them to your needs. All drawings can be further enhanced with 3-D effects, shadows, colors, and textures. SmartArt graphics allow you to create a visual representation of your information. They include many different layouts such as a process or cycle that are designed to help you communicate an idea. Charts can be inserted to illustrate and compare data. Complex pictures can be inserted in documents by scanning your own, using supplied or purchased clip art, or downloading images from the web. Additionally, you can quickly capture and insert a picture, called a screenshot, from another application running on your computer into the current document. Finally, you can easily find and insert videos from different online sources to enhance your document.

Collaborate with Others

Group collaboration on projects is common in industry today. Word 2013 includes many features to help streamline how documents are developed and changed by group members. A comment feature allows multiple people to insert remarks in the same document without having to route the document to each person or reconcile multiple reviewers' comments. You can easily consolidate all changes and comments from different reviewers in one simple step and accept or reject changes as needed. Finally, if you save your documents online, you can review and edit simultaneously with others. The changes are accessible to the entire group. If someone does not have Office installed on his or her computer, you can send the individual a link to your document allowing him or her to follow along in a browser.

Two documents you will produce in the first two Word 2013 labs, a letter and flyer, are shown here.

A letter containing a tabbed table, indented paragraphs, and text enhancements is quickly created using basic Word features

January 9, 2015

Dear Adventure Traveler:

Imagine camping under the stars in A
Costa Rica, or following in the footsteps of the
Picchu. Turn these thoughts of an adventure i
Tours on one of our four new adventure tours

To tell you more about these exciting
These presentations will focus on the features
places you will visit and activities you can part
attend one of the following presentations:

Date	Time
February 5 ------ 7:00 p.m.-----
February 18----- 7:30 p.m.-----
March 7---------- 1:00 p.m.-----

In appreciation of your past patronag
the new tour packages. You must book the tri
letter to qualify for the discount.

Our vacation tours are professionally
everything in the price of your tour while givir
these features:

➢ All accommodations and meals
➢ All entrance fees, excursions, transfer
➢ Professional tour manager and local g

We hope you will join us this year on
Travel Tours each day is an adventure. For res
Travel Tours directly at 1-800-555-0004.

Adventure Travel Tours

NEW ADVENTURES

Attention adventure travelers! Attend an Adventure Travel presentation to learn about some of the earth's greatest unspoiled habitats and learn how you can experience the adventure of a lifetime. This year Adventure Travel Tours is introducing four new tours that offer you a unique opportunity to combine many different outdoor activities while exploring the world.

Safari in Tanzania

India Wildlife Adventure

Costa Rica Rivers and Rainforests

Inca Trail to Machu Picchu

Presentation dates and times are January 5 at 7:00 p.m., February 3 at 7:30 p.m., and March 8 at 7:00 p.m. All presentations are at convenient hotel locations. The hotels are located in downtown Los Angeles, in Santa Clara, and at the LAX airport.

Call Adventure Travel Tours at 1-800-555-0004 for presentation locations, a full color brochure, and itinerary information, costs, and trip dates. Student Name will gladly help with all of your questions.

Visit our Web site at www.adventuretraveltours.com

A flyer incorporating many visual enhancements such as colored text, varied text styles, and graphic elements is both eye-catching and informative

Excel 2013

Excel 2013 is an electronic spreadsheet, or **worksheet**, that is used to organize, manipulate, and graph numeric data. Once used almost exclusively by accountants, worksheets are now widely used by nearly every profession. Nearly any job that uses rows and columns of numbers can be performed using an electronic spreadsheet. Once requiring hours of labor and/or costly accountants' fees, data analysis is now available almost instantly using electronic spreadsheets and has become a routine business procedure. This powerful business tool has revolutionized the business world. Typical uses include the creation of budgets and financial planning for both business and personal situations. Marketing professionals record and evaluate sales trends. Teachers record grades and calculate final grades. Personal trainers record the progress of their clients.

EXCEL 2013 FEATURES

Excel 2013 includes many features that not only help you create a well-designed worksheet, but one that produces accurate results. The features include the ability to quickly edit and format data, perform calculations, create charts, and print the worksheet. Using Excel 2013, you can quickly analyze and manage data and communicate your findings to others. The program not only makes it faster to create worksheets, but it also produces professional-appearing results.

Enter and Edit Data

The Microsoft Excel 2013 spreadsheet program uses a workbook file that contains one or more worksheets. Each worksheet can be used to organize different types of related information. The worksheet consists of rows and columns that create a grid of cells. You enter numeric data or descriptive text into a cell. These entries can then be erased, moved, copied, or edited.

Format Data

Like text in a Word document, the design and appearance of entries in a worksheet can be enhanced in many ways. For instance, you can change the font style and size and add special effects such as bold, italic, borders, boxes, drop shadows, and shading to selected cells. You also can use cell styles to quickly apply predefined combinations of these formats to selections. Additionally, you can select from different document themes, predefined combinations of colors, fonts, and effects, to give your workbooks a consistent, professional appearance.

Unlike the Word application, Excel includes many formatting features that are designed specifically for numeric data. For example, numeric entries can be displayed with commas, dollar signs, or a set number of decimal places. Special formatting, such as color bars, can be applied automatically to ranges of cells to emphasize data based on a set of criteria you establish and to highlight trends.

Analyze Data

The power of a spreadsheet application is its ability to perform calculations from very simple sums to the most complex financial and mathematical formulas. Formulas can be entered that perform calculations using data contained in specified cells. The results of the calculations are displayed in the cell containing the formula. Predefined formulas, called functions, can be used to quickly perform complex calculations such as calculating loan payments or performing a statistical analysis of data.

Analysis of data in a spreadsheet once was too expensive and time-consuming. Now, using electronic worksheets, you can use what-if or sensitivity analysis by changing the values in selected cells and immediately observing the effect on related cells in the worksheet. Other analysis tools such as Solver and Scenarios allow you to see the effects of possible alternative courses of action to help forecast future outcomes.

Chart Data

Using Excel, you also can produce a visual display of numeric data in the form of graphs or charts. As the values in the worksheet change, charts referencing those values automatically adjust to reflect the changes. You also can enhance the appearance of a chart by using different type styles and sizes, adding three-dimensional effects, and including text and objects such as lines and arrows.

Two worksheets you will produce using Excel 2013 are shown below.

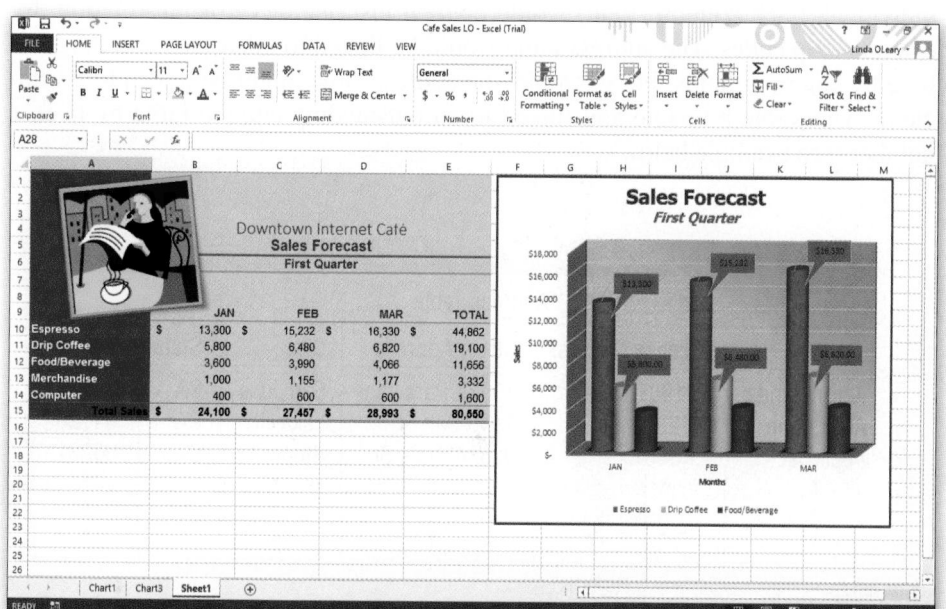

A worksheet showing the quarterly sales forecast containing a graphic, text enhancements, and a chart of the data is quickly created using basic Excel 2013 features

A large worksheet incorporating more complex formulas, conditional formatting, and linked worksheets is both informative and attractive

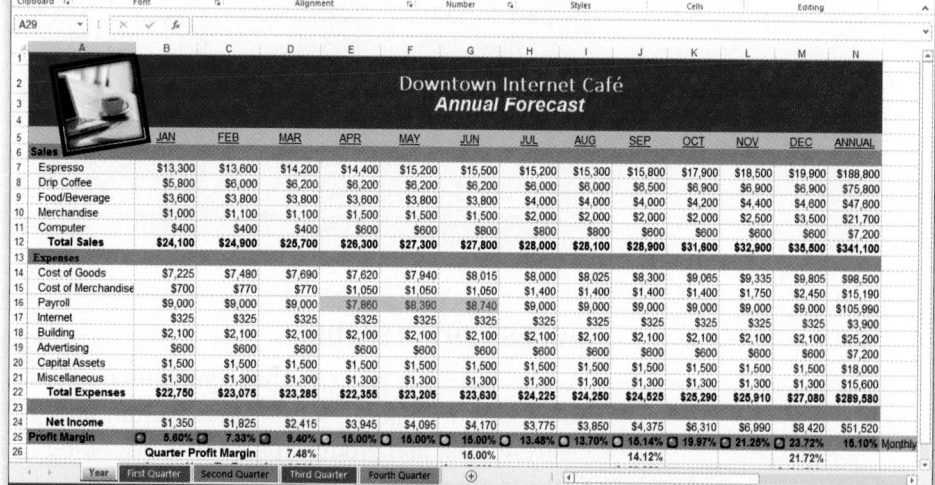

Access 2013 is a relational database management application that is used to create and analyze a database. A **database** is a collection of related data. **Tables** consist of columns (called **fields**) and rows (called **records**). Each row contains a record, which is all the information about one person, thing, or place. Each field is the smallest unit of information about a record.

In a relational database, the most widely used database structure, data is organized in linked tables. The tables are related or linked to one another by a common field. Relational databases allow you to create smaller and more manageable database tables, since you can combine and extract data between tables.

For example, a state's motor vehicle department database might have an address table. Each row (record) in the table would contain address information about one individual. Each column (field) would contain just one piece of information, for example, zip codes. The address table would be linked to other tables in the database by common fields. For example, the address table might be linked to a vehicle owner's table by name and linked to an outstanding citation table by license number (see example below).

Address Table

Name	License Number	Street Address	City	State	Zip
Aaron, Linda	FJ1987	10032 Park Lane	San Jose	CA	95127
Abar, John	D12372	1349 Oak St	Lakeville	CA	94128
Abell, Jack	LK3457	95874 State St	Stone	CA	95201
⋮	⋮	⋮	⋮	⋮	⋮

key fields linked

key fields linked

Owner's Table

Name	Plate Number
Abell, Jack	ABK241
Abrams, Sue	LMJ198
Abril, Pat	ZXA915
⋮	⋮

Outstanding Citation Table

License Number	Citation Code	Violation
T25476	00031	Speed
D98372	19001	Park
LK3457	89100	Speed
⋮	⋮	⋮

ACCESS 2013 FEATURES

Access 2013 is a powerful program with numerous easy-to-use features including the ability to quickly locate information; add, delete, modify, and sort records; analyze data; and produce professional-looking reports. Some of the basic Access 2013 features are described next.

Find Information

Once you enter data into the database table, you can quickly search the table to locate a specific record based on the data in a field. In a manual system, you can usually locate a record by knowing one key piece of information. For example, if the records are stored in a file cabinet alphabetically by last name, to quickly find a record, you must know the last name. In a computerized database, even if the records are sorted or organized by last name, you can still quickly locate a record using information in another field.

Add, Delete, and Modify Records

Using Access, it is also easy to add and delete records from the table. Once you locate a record, you can edit the contents of the fields to update the record or delete the record entirely from the table. You also can add new records to a table. When you enter a new record, it is automatically placed in the correct organizational location within the table. Creation of forms makes it easier to enter and edit data as well.

Sort and Filter Records

The capability to arrange or sort records in the table according to different fields can provide more meaningful information. You can organize records by name, department, pay, class, or any other category you need at a particular time. Sorting the records in different ways can provide information to different departments for different purposes.

Additionally, you can isolate and display a subset of records by specifying filter criteria. The criteria specify which records to display based on data in selected fields.

Analyze Data

Using Access, you can analyze the data in a table and perform calculations on different fields of data. Instead of pulling each record from a filing cabinet, recording the piece of data you want to use, and then performing the calculation on the recorded data, you can simply have the database program perform the calculation on all the values in the specified field. Additionally, you can ask questions or query the table to find only certain records that meet specific conditions to be used in the analysis. Information that was once costly and time-consuming to get is now quickly and readily available.

Generate Reports

Access includes many features that help you quickly produce reports ranging from simple listings to complex, professional-looking reports. You can create a simple report by asking for a listing of specified fields of data and restricting the listing to records meeting designated conditions. You can create a more complex professional report using the same restrictions or conditions as the simple report, but you can display the data in different layout styles, or with titles, headings, subtotals, or totals.

A database and a report that you will produce using Access 2013 are shown on the next page.

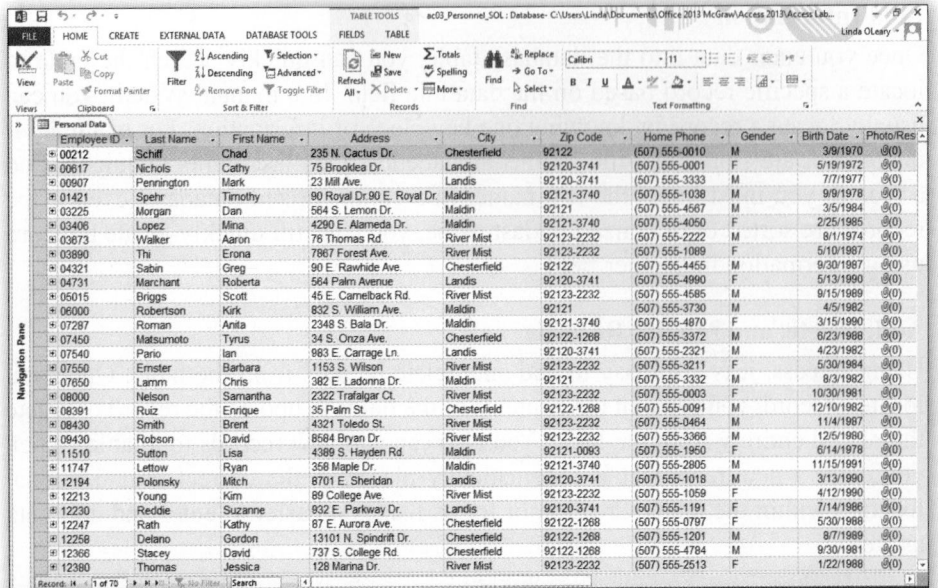

A relational database can be created and modified easily using basic Access 2013 features

Job Position Report
For Landis

Employee ID	First Name	Last Name	Position
12703	Jeff	Bader	Fitness Instructor
12389	Jennifer	Blackman	Sales Associate
05015	Scott	Briggs	Personal Trainer Director
12501	Elizabeth	DeLuca	Personal Trainer
12855	Kimberly	Fachet	Sales Associate
13484	Stephanie	Franklin	Food Service Server
12914	Alfonso	Gomez	Cleaning
22469	Ryan	Hogan	Personal Trainer
13303	Chris	Jensen	Greeter
13027	Kimberly	Kieken	Food Service Server
07650	Chris	Lamm	Sales Director
22085	Kristina	Lindau	Child Care Provider
13635	Juan	Martinez	Fitness Instructor
03225	Dan	Morgan	Food Service Director
99999	Student	Name	Human Resources Administrator
12420	Allison	Player	Maintenance
13005	Emily	Reilly	Assistant Manager
22297	Patricia	Rogondino	Greeter
07287	Anita	Roman	Child Care Director
12918	Carlos	Ruiz	Assistant Manager
00212	Chad	Schiff	Club Director
12583	Marie	Sullivan	Greeter

Page 1 of 2

A professional-looking report can be quickly generated from information contained in a database

WWW.MHHE.COM/OLEARY

PowerPoint 2013 is a graphics presentation program designed to help you produce a high-quality presentation that is both interesting to the audience and effective in its ability to convey your message. A presentation can be as simple as overhead transparencies or as sophisticated as an on-screen electronic display. Graphics presentation programs can produce black-and-white or color overhead transparencies, 35 mm slides, onscreen electronic presentations called **slide shows**, web pages for web use, and support materials for both the speaker and the audience.

POWERPOINT 2013 FEATURES

Although creating an effective presentation is a complicated process, PowerPoint 2013 helps simplify this process by providing assistance in the content development phase, as well as in the layout and design phase. PowerPoint includes features such as text handling, outlining, graphing, drawing, animation, clip art, and multimedia support. In addition, the programs suggest layouts for different types of presentations and offer professionally designed templates to help you produce a presentation that is sure to keep your audience's attention. In addition, you can quickly produce the support materials to be used when making a presentation to an audience.

Develop, Enter, and Edit Content

The content development phase includes deciding on the topic of your presentation, the organization of the content, and the ultimate message you want to convey to the audience. As an aid in this phase, PowerPoint 2013 helps you organize your thoughts based on the type of presentation you are making by providing both content and design templates. Based on the type of presentation, such as selling a product or suggesting a strategy, the template provides guidance by suggesting content ideas and organizational tips. For example, if you are making a presentation on the progress of a sales campaign, the program would suggest that you enter text on the background of the sales campaign as the first page, called a **slide**; the current status of the campaign as the next slide; and accomplishments, schedule, issues and problems, and where you are heading on subsequent slides.

Design Layouts

The layout for each slide is the next important decision. Again, PowerPoint 2013 helps you by suggesting text layout features such as title placement, bullets, and columns. You also can incorporate graphs of data, tables, organizational charts, clip art, and other special text effects in the slides.

PowerPoint 2013 also includes professionally designed themes to further enhance the appearance of your slides. These themes include features that standardize the appearance of all the slides in your presentation. Professionally selected combinations of text and background colors, common typefaces and sizes, borders, and other art designs take the worry out of much of the design layout.

Deliver Presentations

After you have written and designed the slides, you can use the slides in an onscreen electronic presentation or a web page for use on the web. An onscreen presentation uses the computer to display the slides on an overhead projection screen. As you prepare this type of presentation, you can use the rehearsal feature that allows you to practice and time your presentation. The length of time to display each slide can be set and your entire presentation can be completed within the allotted time. A presentation also can be modified to display on a website and run using a web browser. Finally, you can package the presentation to a CD for distribution.

A presentation that you will produce using PowerPoint 2013 is shown below.

A presentation consists of a series of pages or "slides" presenting the information you want to convey in an organized and attractive manner

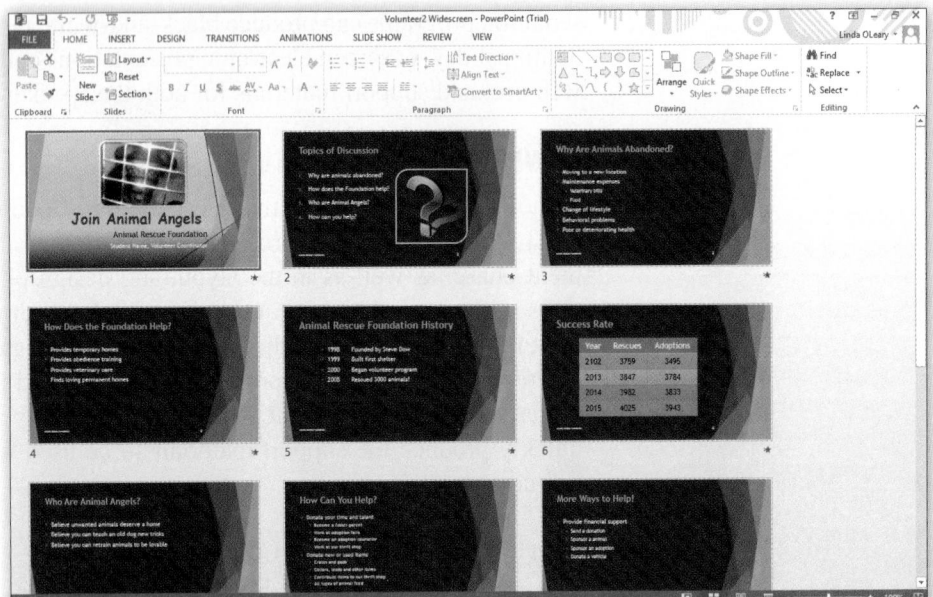

When running an on-screen presentation, each slide of the presentation is displayed full-screen on your computer monitor or projected onto a screen

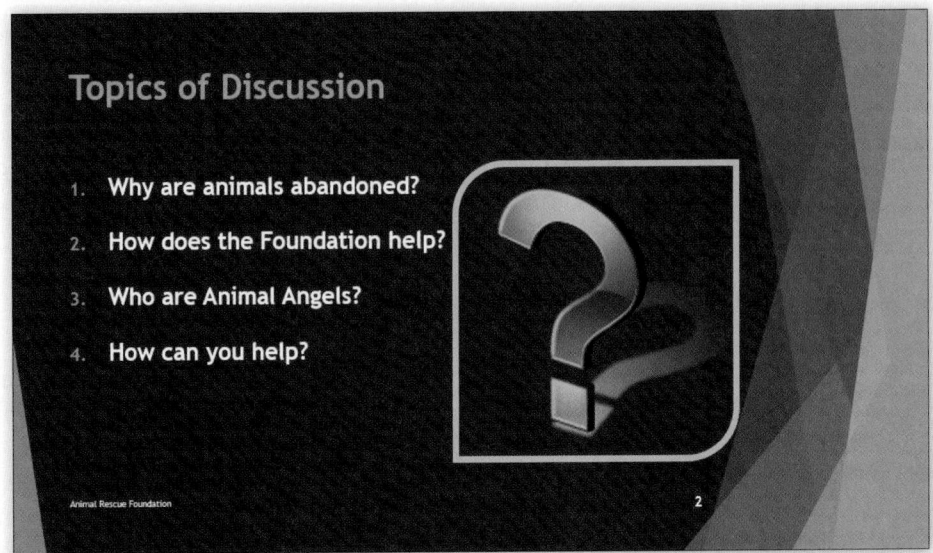

Instructional Conventions

As you follow the directions in the upcoming hands-on section and in the application labs, you need to know the instructional conventions that are used. Hands-on instructions you are to perform appear as a sequence of numbered steps. Within each step, a series of bullets identifies the specific actions that must be performed. Step numbering begins over within each topic heading throughout the lab.

COMMANDS

Commands that are initiated using a command button and the mouse appear following the word "Click." The icon (and the icon name if the icon does not include text) is displayed following "Click." If there is another way to perform the same action, it appears in an Another Method margin note when the action is first introduced as shown in Example A.

Example A

1

- Select the list of four tours.

- Open the Home tab.

- Click **B** Bold in the Font group.

> **Another Method**
> The keyboard shortcut is Ctrl + B.

Sometimes, clicking on an icon opens a drop-down list or a menu of commands. Commands that are to be selected follow the word "Select" and appear in black text. You can select an item by pointing to it using the mouse or by moving to it using the directional keys. When an option is selected, it appears highlighted; however, the action is not carried out. Commands that appear following the word "Choose" perform the associated action. You can choose a command by clicking on it using the mouse or by pressing the Enter key once it is selected. (See Example B.)

Example B

1

- Click **A ▾** Font Color in the Font group of the Home tab.

- Select Green.

- Choose Dark Blue.

FILE NAMES AND INFORMATION TO TYPE

Plain green text identifies file names you need to select or enter. Information you are asked to type appears in blue and bold. (See Example C.)

Example C

1

- Open the document wd01_Flyer.

- Type **Adventure Travel presents four new trips**

Now that you know a little about each of the applications in Microsoft Office 2013, you will take a look at some of the features that are common to all Office 2013 applications. In this hands-on section you will learn to use the common user interface and application features to allow you to get a feel for how Office 2013 works. Although Word 2013 will be used to demonstrate how the features work, only features that are common to all the Office applications will be addressed.

COMMON INTERFACE FEATURES

All the Office 2013 applications have a common **user interface**, a set of graphical elements that are designed to help you interact with the program and provide instructions as to the actions you want to perform. These features include the use of the Ribbon, Quick Access Toolbar, task panes, menus, dialog boxes, and the File tab.

Starting an Office 2013 Application

To demonstrate the common features, you will start the Word 2013 application. There are several ways to start an Office 2013 application. The most common method is to click a tile on the Windows 8 Start screen for the program if it is available.

Additional Information

The procedure to start Excel, Access, and PowerPoint is the same as starting Word, except that you must select the appropriate application tile.

Having Trouble?

If you are using Windows 7, click 🪟 Start and choose Word 2013. If you

do not see the program name on the Start menu, select All Programs, choose Microsoft Office 2013, and then choose Word 2013.

❶

Click the 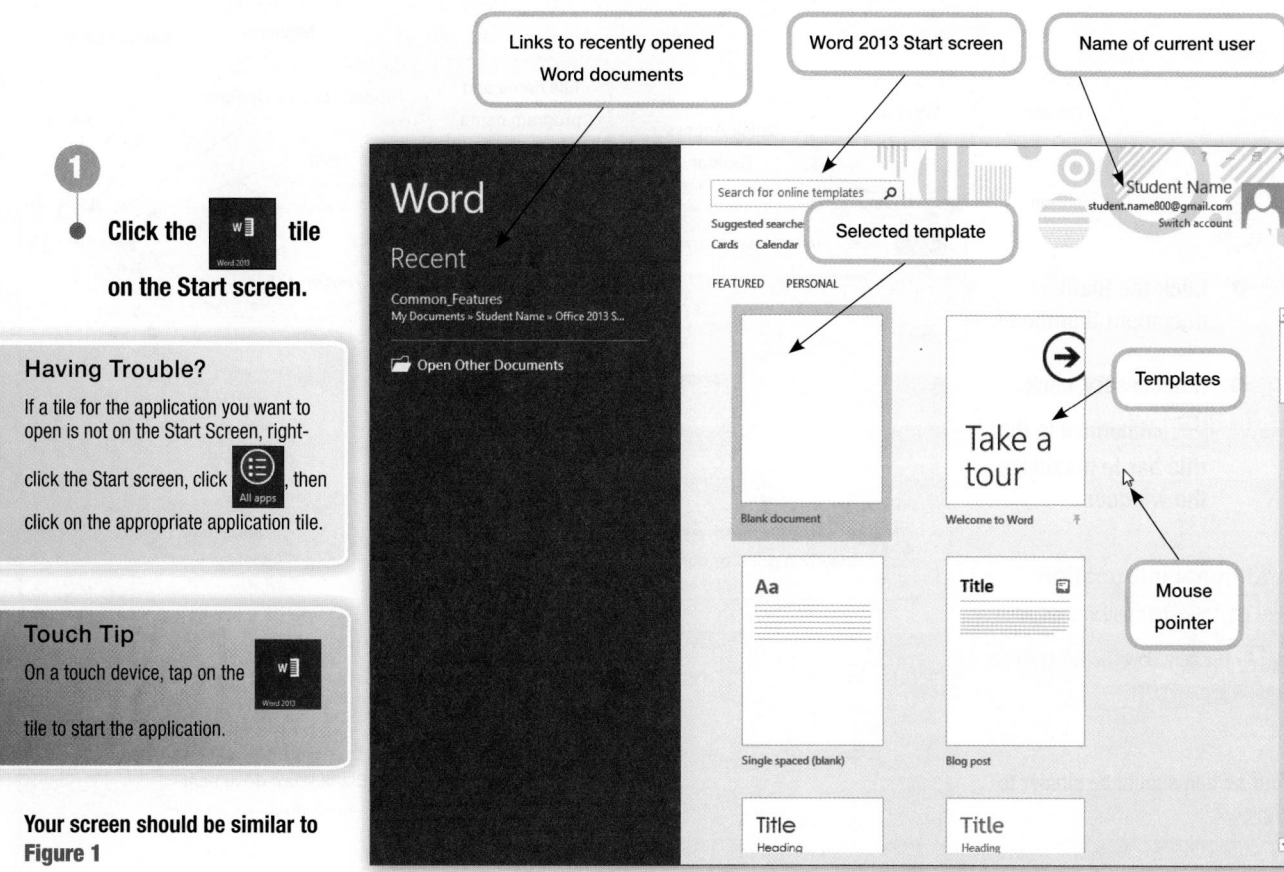 **tile on the Start screen.**

Having Trouble?

If a tile for the application you want to open is not on the Start Screen, right-click the Start screen, click [All apps], then click on the appropriate application tile.

Touch Tip

On a touch device, tap on the [Word 2013] tile to start the application.

Your screen should be similar to Figure 1

Links to recently opened Word documents

Word 2013 Start screen

Name of current user

Selected template

Templates

Mouse pointer

Figure 1

The Word 2013 program is started and the Start screen is displayed in a window on the desktop. A list of links to recently opened Word documents is displayed in the left column. A gallery of thumbnail images of available templates is displayed in the main window area. A **template** is a professionally designed document that is used as the basis for a new document. The Blank document thumbnail is selected by default and is used to create a new Word document from scratch.

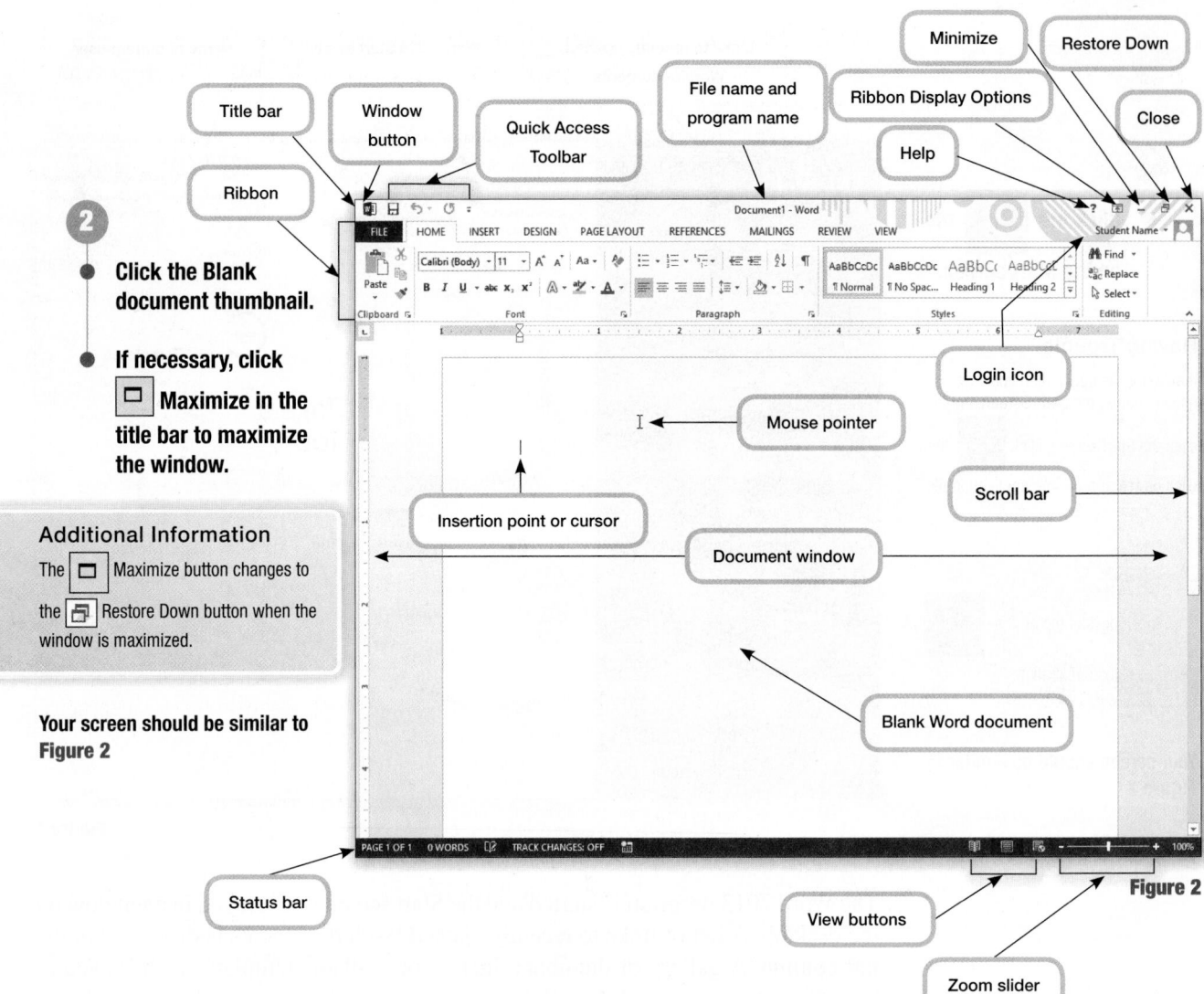

2

● **Click the Blank document thumbnail.**

● **If necessary, click** ☐ **Maximize in the title bar to maximize the window.**

Additional Information

The ☐ Maximize button changes to the ⧉ Restore Down button when the window is maximized.

Your screen should be similar to Figure 2

Figure 2

Additional Information

Application windows can be sized, moved, and otherwise manipulated like any other windows on the desktop.

The blank document template is open and displays in the Word 2013 application window. The center of the title bar at the top of the window displays the file name followed by the program name, in this case Word. Both ends of the title bar contain **buttons**, graphical elements that perform the associated action when you click on them using the mouse. At the left end of the title bar is the ▩ Window button. Clicking this button opens a menu of commands that allow you to size, move, and close the window. To the right of the ▩ Window button is the **Quick Access Toolbar** (QAT), which provides quick access to frequently used commands. By default, it includes the ▤ Save, ↶ Undo, and ↻ Repeat buttons, commands that Microsoft considers to be crucial. It is always available and is a customizable toolbar to which you can add your own favorite buttons. The right end of the title bar displays five buttons. The ? Help button accesses the program's Help system. The ⌅ Ribbon Display Options button controls the display of the tabs and ribbon, allowing more content to be displayed in the application window. The last three buttons are shortcuts to the ▩ Window button menu commands that are used to size, move, and close the application window. The buttons on the title bar are the same in all the Office 2013 programs: ▬ Minimize, ◰ Restore Down/◻ Maximize, and ✕ Close.

Below the title bar is the **Ribbon**, which provides a centralized location of commands that are used to work in your document. The Ribbon has the same basic structure and is found in all Office 2013 applications. However, many of the commands found in the Ribbon vary with the specific applications. You will learn how to use the Ribbon shortly. At the right end of the Ribbon is the login icon that indicates if you are logged into Microsoft's online services for file storage and collaboration. It consists of your user name and Microsoft account photo. You can click the photo to adjust your account settings, swap in a new picture, or even switch accounts.

Additional Information

You will learn about opening existing files shortly.

The large center area of the application window is the **document window** where open application files are displayed. In this case, because you selected the Blank document template, a new blank Word document named Document1 (shown in the title bar) is open, ready for you to start creating a new document. In Excel, a new, blank workbook named Book1 would be opened and in PowerPoint a new, blank presentation file named Presentation1 would be opened. In Access, however, a new blank database file is not opened automatically. Instead, you must create and name a new database file or open an existing database file.

Additional Information

You will learn about other mouse pointer shapes and what they mean as you use the specific application programs.

The **cursor**, also called the **insertion point**, is the blinking vertical bar that marks your location in the document and indicates where text you type will appear. Across all Office applications, the mouse pointer appears as an I I-beam when it is used to position the insertion point when entering text and as a ⇱ when it can be used to select items. There are many other mouse pointer shapes that are both common to and specific to the different applications.

On the right of the document window is a vertical scroll bar. A **scroll bar** is used with a mouse to bring additional information into view in a window. The vertical scroll bar is used to move up or down. A horizontal scroll bar is also displayed when needed and moves side to side in the window. The scroll bar is a common feature to all Windows and Office 2013 applications; however, it may not appear in all applications until needed.

At the bottom of the application window is another common feature called the **status bar**. It displays information about the open file and features that help you view the file. It displays different information depending upon the application you are using. For example, the Word status bar displays information about the number of pages and words in the document, whereas the Excel status bar displays the mode of operation and the count, average, and sum of values in selected cells. All Office 2013 applications include **View buttons** that are used to change how the information in the document window is displayed. The View buttons are different for each application. Finally, a **Zoom Slider**, located at the far right end of the status bar, is used to change the amount of information displayed in the document window by "zooming in" to get a close-up view or "zooming out" to see more of the document at a reduced view.

Displaying ScreenTips

You are probably wondering how you would know what action the different buttons perform. To help you identify buttons, the Office applications display Screen-Tips when you point to them.

1 ● Point to the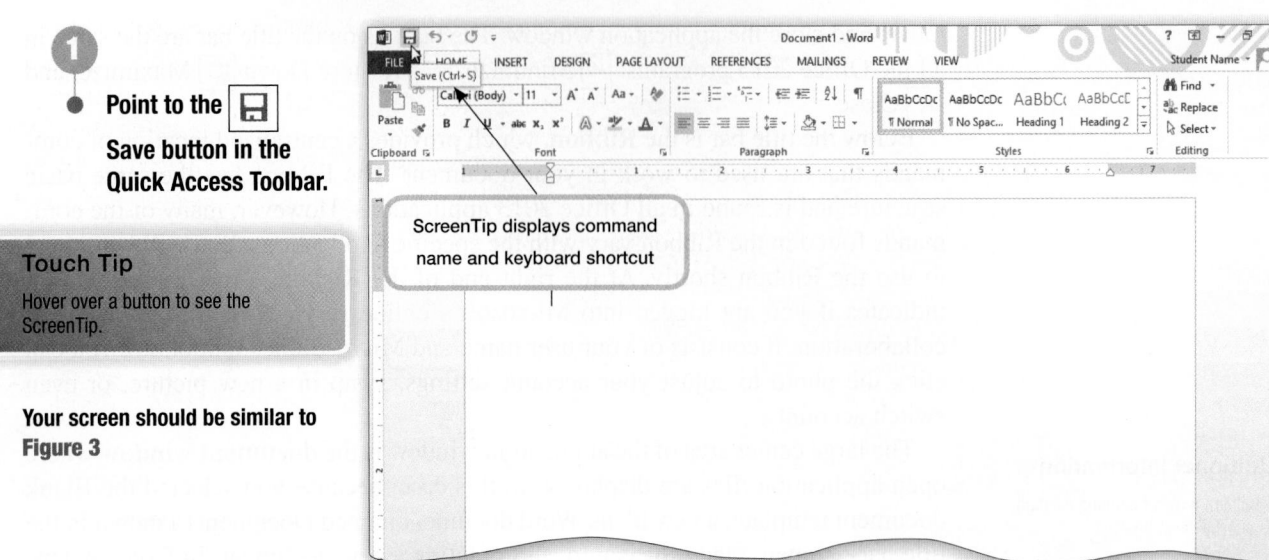
Save button in the
Quick Access Toolbar.

Your screen should be similar to
Figure 3

Figure 3

A **ScreenTip**, also called a **tooltip**, appears displaying the command name and the keyboard shortcut, Ctrl + S. A **keyboard shortcut** is a combination of keys that can be used to execute a command in place of clicking the button. In this case, if you hold down the Ctrl key while typing the letter S, you will access the command to save a file. ScreenTips also often include a brief description of the action a command performs.

Using Menus

Notice the small button ⤓ at the end of the Quick Access Toolbar. Clicking this button opens a menu of commands that perform tasks associated with the Quick Access Toolbar.

1 ● Point to the ⤓
button at the end of
the Quick Access
Toolbar to display the
ScreenTip.

● Click ⤓ to open the
menu.

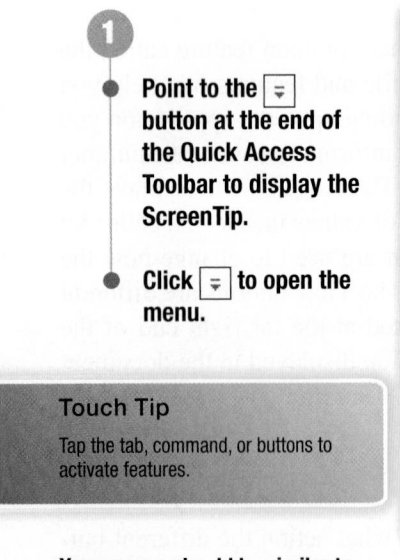

Your screen should be similar to
Figure 4

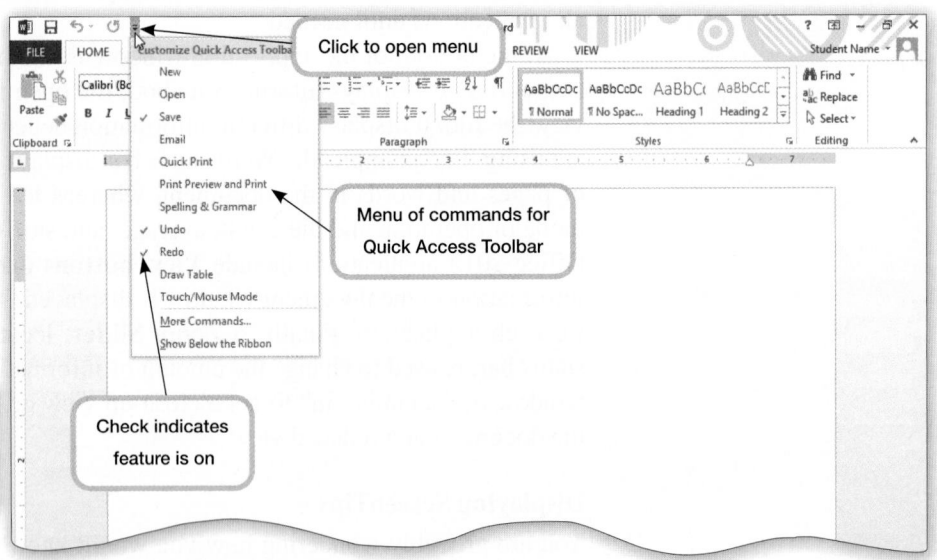

Figure 4

The first 11 items in the menu allow you to quickly add a command button to or remove a command button from the Quick Access Toolbar. Those commands that are already displayed in the Quick Access Toolbar are preceded with a checkmark.

The last two commands allow you to access other command features to customize the Quick Access Toolbar or change its location.

Once a menu is open, you can select a command from the menu by pointing to it. As you do the selected command appears highlighted. Like buttons, resting the mouse pointer over the menu command options will display a ScreenTip. Then to choose a selected command, you click on it. Choosing a command performs the action associated with the command or button. You will use several of these features next.

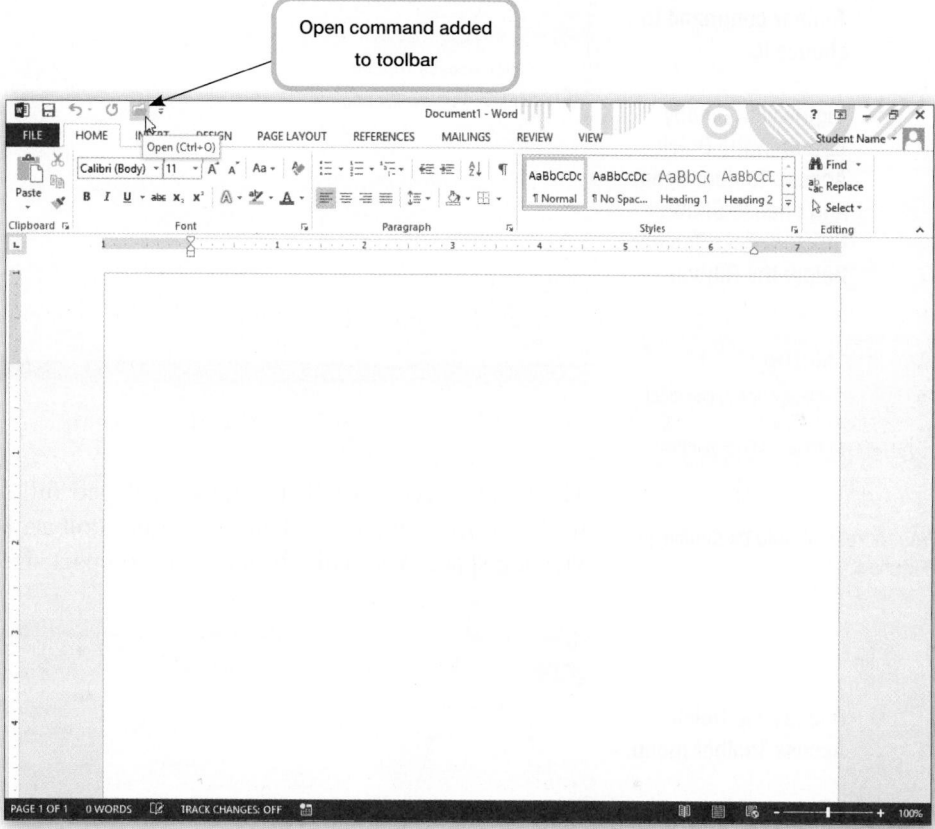

2

● Point to the commands in the Quick Access Toolbar menu to select (highlight) them and see the ScreenTips.

● Click on the Open command to choose it and add it to the Quick Access Toolbar.

● Point to the ⬜ Open button on the Quick Access Toolbar to display the ScreenTip.

Your screen should be similar to Figure 5

Open command added to toolbar

Figure 5

The command button to open a document has been added to the Quick Access Toolbar. Next, you will remove this button and then you will change the location of the Quick Access Toolbar. Another way to access some commands is to use a context menu. A **context menu**, also called a **shortcut menu**, is opened by right-clicking on an item on the screen. This menu is context sensitive, meaning it displays only those commands relevant to the item or screen location. For example, right-clicking on the Quick Access Toolbar will display the commands associated with using the Quick Access Toolbar and the Ribbon. You will use this method to remove the Open button and move the Quick Access Toolbar.

3

- Right-click on the Open button on the Quick Access Toolbar to display the context menu.

- Click on the Remove from Quick Access Toolbar command to choose it.

- Right-click on any button in the Quick Access Toolbar again and choose Show Quick Access Toolbar Below the Ribbon.

Another Method

You also can type the underlined letter of a command to choose it or press Enter to choose a selected command.

Your screen should be similar to Figure 6

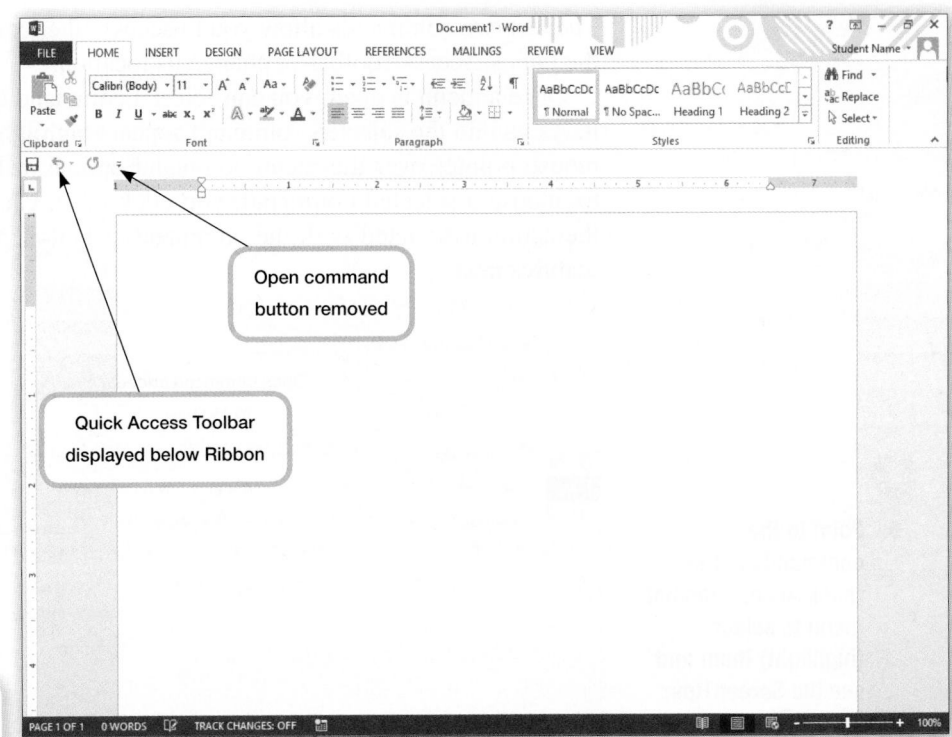

Open command button removed

Quick Access Toolbar displayed below Ribbon

Figure 6

The Quick Access Toolbar is now displayed full size below the Ribbon. This is useful if you have many buttons on the toolbar; however, it takes up document viewing space. You will return it to its compact size.

4

- Display the Quick Access Toolbar menu.

- Choose Show Above the Ribbon.

Your screen should be similar to Figure 7

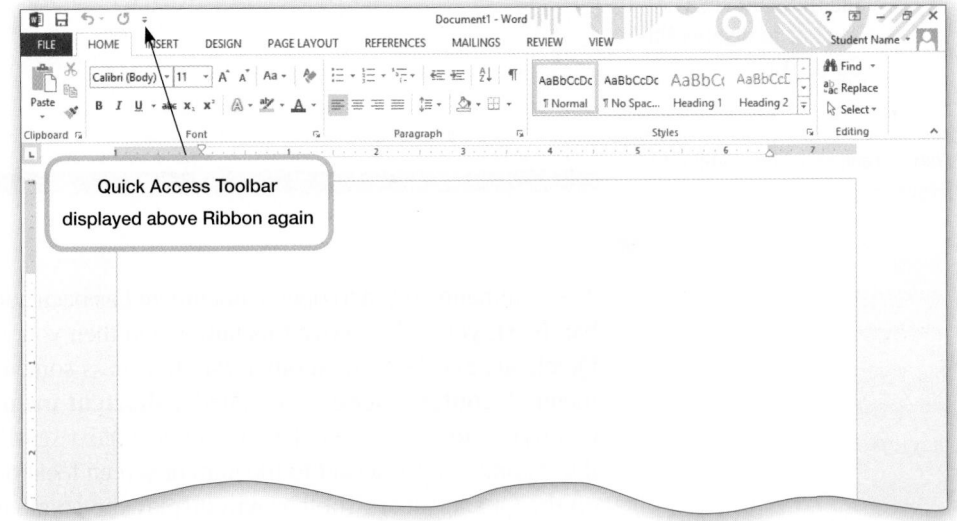

Quick Access Toolbar displayed above Ribbon again

Figure 7

The Quick Access Toolbar is displayed above the Ribbon again.

Using the Ribbon

The Ribbon has three basic parts: tabs, groups, and commands (see Figure 8). **Tabs** are used to divide the Ribbon into major activity areas. Each tab is then organized into **groups** that contain related items. The related items are **commands** that consist of command buttons, a box to enter information, or a menu. Clicking on a command button performs the associated action or displays a list of additional options.

The Ribbon tabs, commands, and features vary with the different Office applications. For example, the Word Ribbon displays tabs and commands used to create a text document, whereas the Excel Ribbon displays tabs and commands used to create an electronic worksheet. Although the Ribbon commands are application specific, many are also common to all Office 2013 applications. In all applications, the Ribbon also can be customized by changing the built-in tabs or creating your own tabs and groups to personalize your workspace and provide faster access to the commands you use most.

Opening Tabs

The Word application displays the File tab and eight Ribbon tabs. The Home tab (shown in Figure 7), consists of five groups. The tab name appears in blue and is outlined, indicating it is the open or active tab. This tab is available in all the Office 2013 applications and because it contains commands that are most frequently used when you first start an application or open a file, it is initially the open tab. In Word, the commands in the Home tab help you perform actions related to creating the text content of your document. In the other Office 2013 applications, the Home tab contains commands related to creating the associated type of document, such as a worksheet, presentation, or database. To open another tab you click on the tab name.

1

Click on the Insert tab.

Your screen should be similar to Figure 8

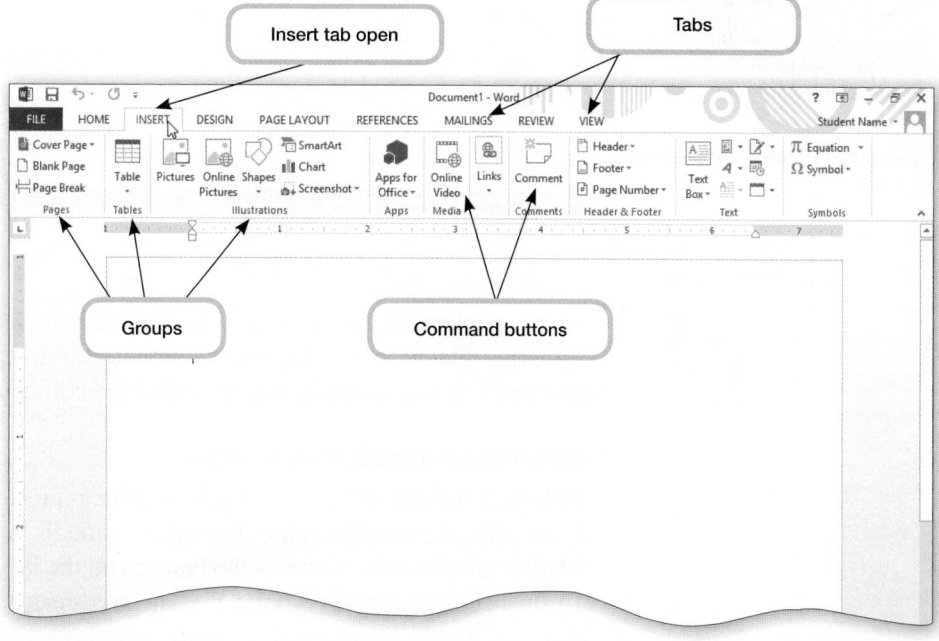

Figure 8

This Insert tab is now open and is the active tab. It contains 10 groups whose commands have to do with inserting items into a document. As you use the Office applications, you will see that the Ribbon contains many of the same tabs, groups, and commands across the applications. For example, the Insert tab is available in all applications except Access. Others, such as the References tab in Word, are specific to the application. You also will see that many of the groups and commands in the common tabs, such as the Clipboard group of commands in the Home tab, contain all or many of the same commands across applications. Other groups in the common tabs contain commands that are specific to the application.

To save space, some tabs, called **contextual tabs** or **on-demand tabs**, are displayed only as needed. For example, when you are working with a picture, the Picture Tools tab appears. The contextual nature of this feature keeps the work area uncluttered when the feature is not needed and provides ready access to it when it is needed.

2

Click on each of the other tabs, ending with the View tab, to see their groups and commands.

Additional Information

If you have a mouse with a scroll wheel, pointing to the tab area of the Ribbon and using the scroll wheel will scroll the tabs.

Touch Tip

On a touch device you can swipe the Ribbon tab to scroll the tabs.

Your screen should be similar to Figure 9

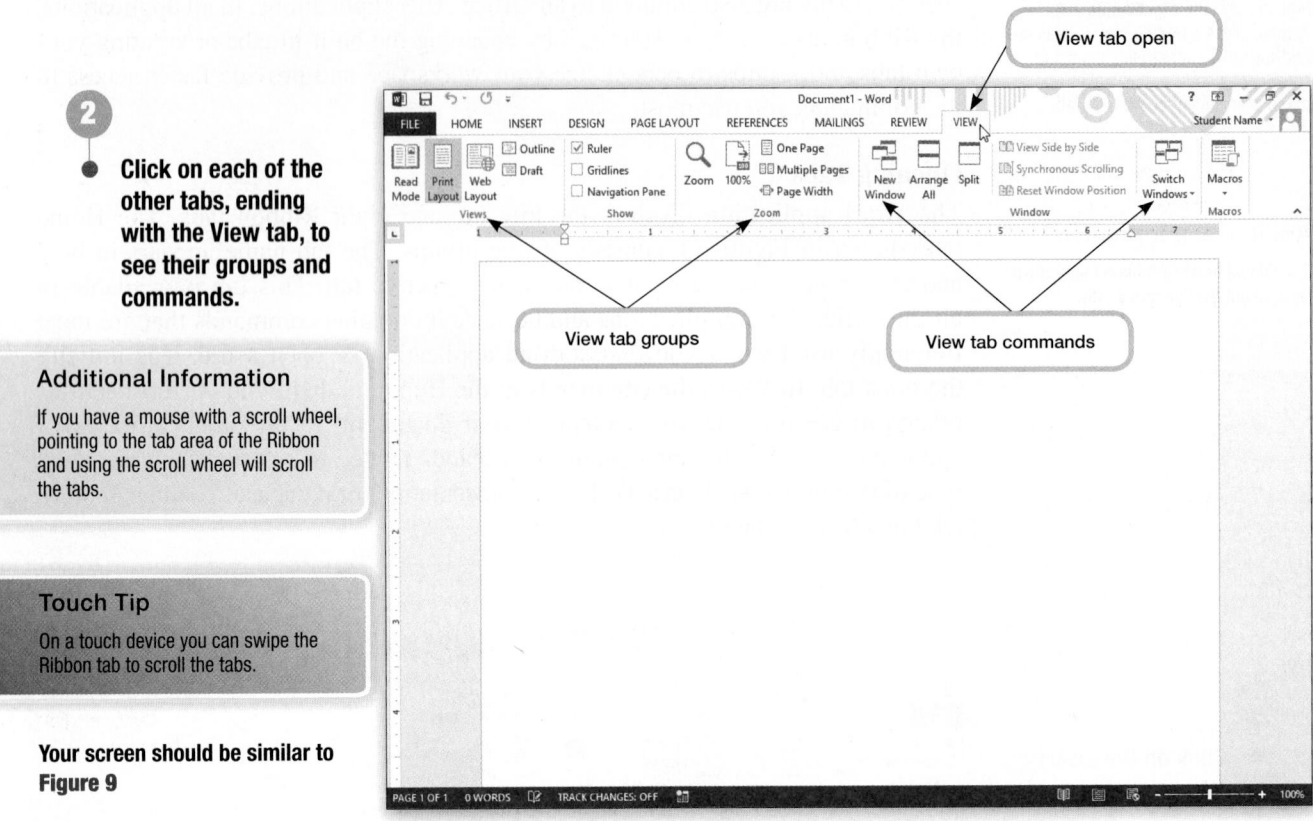

View tab open

View tab groups

View tab commands

Figure 9

Each tab relates to a type of activity; for example, the View tab commands perform activities related to viewing the document. Within each tab, similar commands are grouped together to make it easy to find the commands you want to use.

Displaying Enhanced ScreenTips

Although command buttons display graphic representations of the action they perform, often the graphic is not descriptive enough. As you have learned, pointing to a button displays the name of the button and the keyboard shortcut in a ScreenTip. To further help explain what a button does, many buttons in the Ribbon display **Enhanced ScreenTips**. For example, the ▢ Paste button in the Clipboard group of the Home tab is a two-part button. Clicking on the upper part will immediately perform an action, whereas clicking on the lower part will display additional options. You will use this feature next to see the Enhanced ScreenTips.

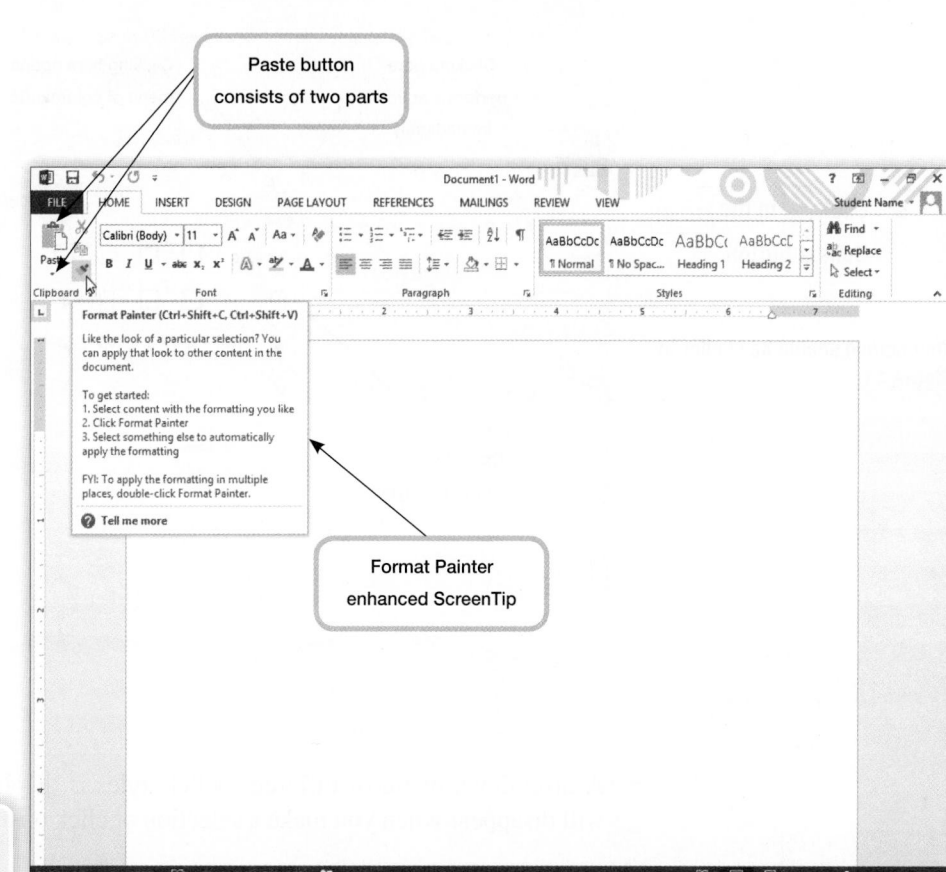

Paste button consists of two parts

Format Painter enhanced ScreenTip

Figure 10

1

- **Click on the Home tab to open it.**

- **Point to the upper part of the** 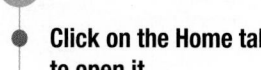 **Paste button in the Clipboard group.**

- **Point to the lower part of the** Paste **button in the Clipboard group.**

- **Point to** Format **Painter in the Clipboard group.**

Additional Information

Depending upon your screen resolution and size, the ✦ button may appear as ✦ Format Painter .

Your screen should be similar to Figure 10

Additional Information

Not all commands have keyboard shortcuts.

Additional Information

You will learn about using Help shortly.

Touch Tip

On a touch device, it may be difficult to touch the arrow only. To add space between buttons, turn on Touch Mode from the Quick Access toolbar.

Because the Paste button is divided into two parts, both parts display separate Enhanced ScreenTips containing the button name; the keyboard shortcut key combination, Ctrl + V; and a brief description of what action will be performed when you click on that part of the button. Pointing to Format Painter displays an Enhanced ScreenTip that provides more detailed information about the command including steps on how to use the feature. Enhanced ScreenTips help you find out what the feature does without having to look it up using Office Help, a built-in reference source. If a feature has a Help article, you can automatically access it by pressing F1 while the Enhanced ScreenTip is displayed or by choosing "Tell me more."

Using Command Buttons

Clicking on most command buttons immediately performs the associated action. Some command buttons, however, include an arrow as part of the button that affects how the button works. If a button includes an arrow that is separated from the graphic with a line when you point to the button (as in Bullets), clicking the button performs the associated default action and clicking the arrow displays a menu of options. If a button displays an arrow that is not separated from the graphic with a line when you point to it (as in Line and Paragraph Spacing), clicking the button immediately displays a menu of options. To see an example of a drop-down menu, you will open the Bullets menu.

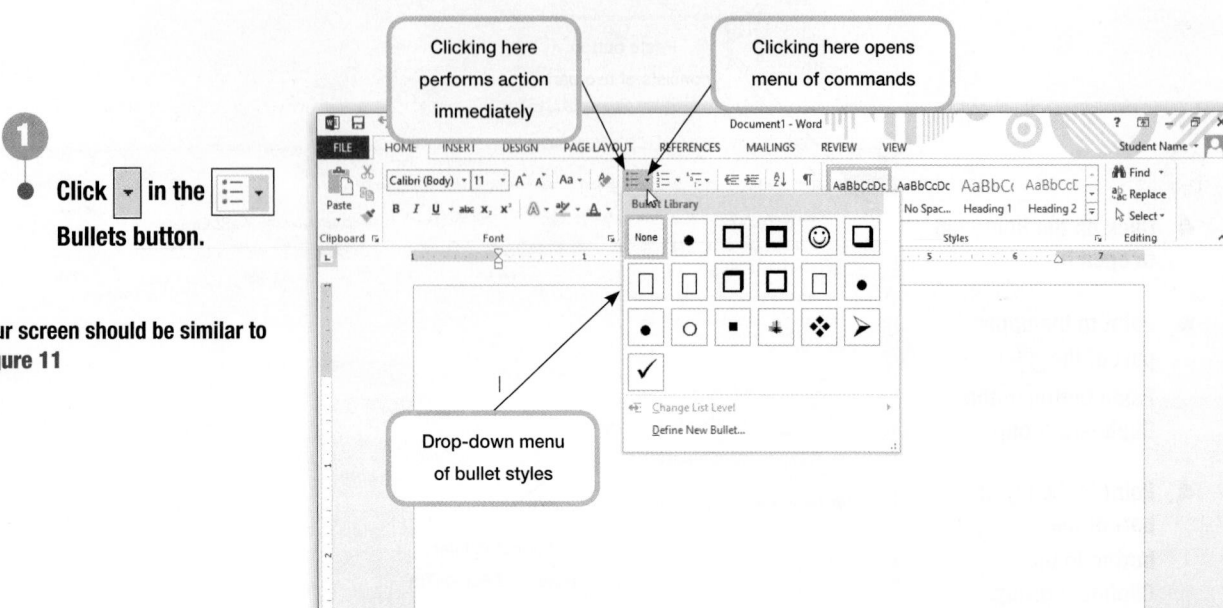

1

● Click ▾ in the
Bullets button.

Your screen should be similar to
Figure 11

Figure 11

A drop-down menu of different bullet styles is displayed. The drop-down menu
will disappear when you make a selection or click on any other area of the window.

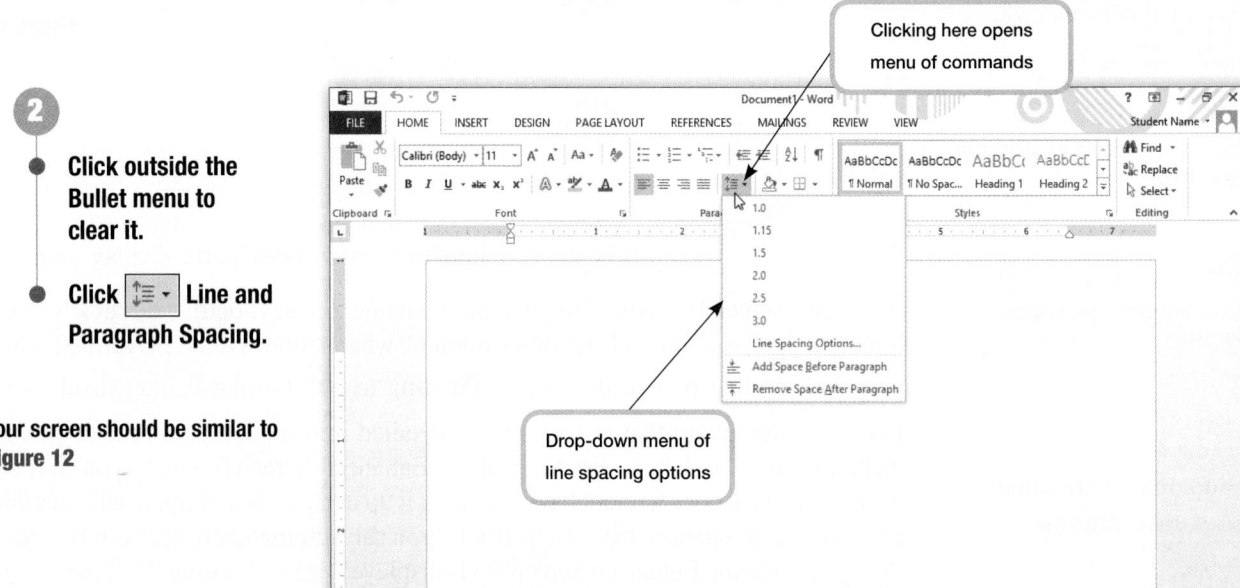

2

● Click outside the
Bullet menu to
clear it.

● Click ▾ Line and
Paragraph Spacing.

Your screen should be similar to
Figure 12

Figure 12

Another Method

You also can open tabs and choose
Ribbon commands using the access key
shortcuts. Press [Alt] or [F10] to display
the access key letters in KeyTips over
each available feature. Then type the
letter for the feature you want to use.

The menu of options opened automatically when you clicked ▾ Line and Paragraph Spacing.

Using the Dialog Box Launcher

Because there is not enough space, only the most used commands are displayed in the Ribbon. If more commands are available, a ⬛ button, called the **dialog box launcher**, is displayed in the lower-right corner of the group. Clicking ⬛ opens a dialog box or task pane of additional options.

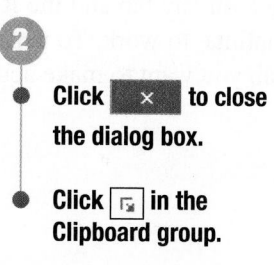

- Click outside the Line and Paragraph Spacing menu to clear it.

- Point to the ⬛ of the Paragraph group to see the ScreenTip.

- Click ⬛ of the Paragraph group.

Your screen should be similar to Figure 13

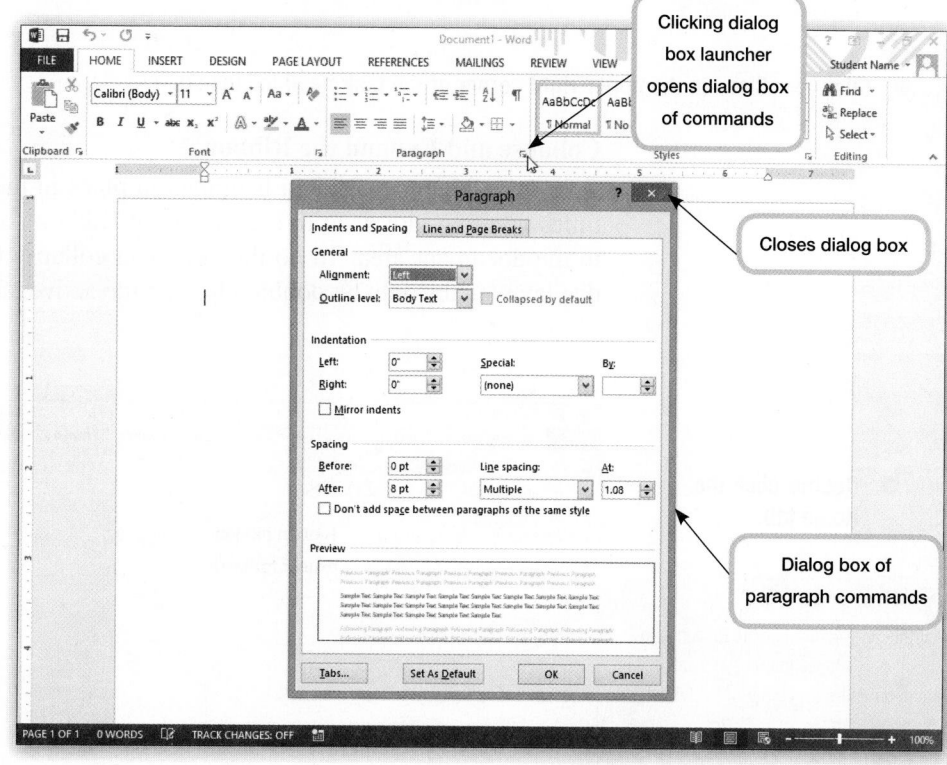

Figure 13

The Paragraph dialog box appears. It provides access to the more advanced paragraph settings options. Selecting options from the dialog box and clicking [OK] will close the dialog box and apply the options as specified. To cancel the dialog box, you can click [Cancel] or [×] Close in the dialog box title bar.

- Click [×] to close the dialog box.

- Click ⬛ in the Clipboard group.

Your screen should be similar to Figure 14

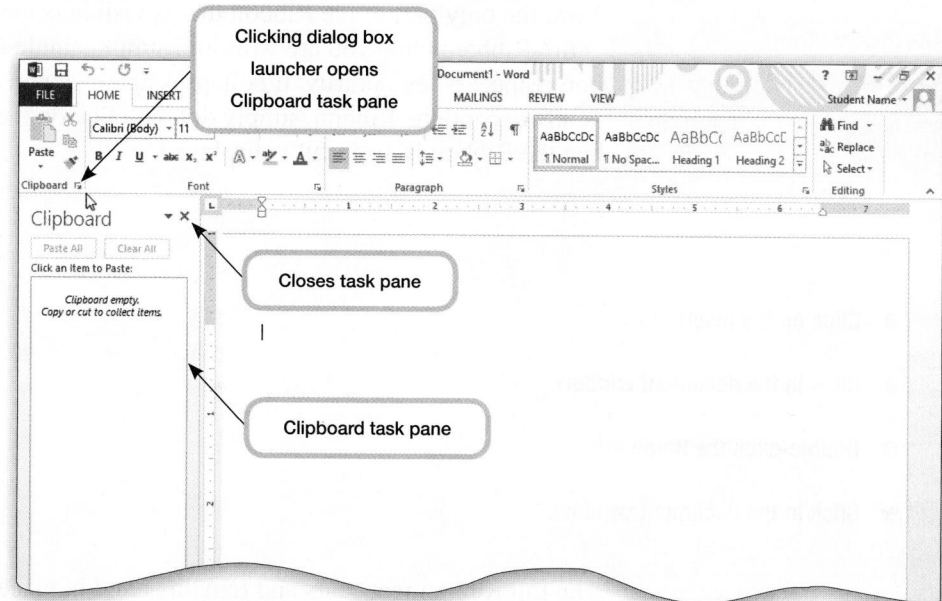

Figure 14

A **task pane** is open (see Figure 14) that contains features associated with the Clipboard. Unlike a dialog box, a task pane is a separate window that can be sized and moved. Generally, task panes are attached or docked to one edge of the application window. Also, task panes remain open until you close them. This allows you to make multiple selections from the task pane while continuing to work on other areas of your document.

● Click ☒ Close in the upper-right corner of the task pane to close it.

Collapse and Expand the Ribbon

Currently, the entire Ribbon is pinned in place in the application window. Sometimes you may not want to see the entire Ribbon so that more space is available in the document area. To do this, you can collapse the Ribbon to minimize it to display the tabs only by double-clicking the active tab.

● **Double-click the Home tab.**

Your screen should be similar to Figure 15

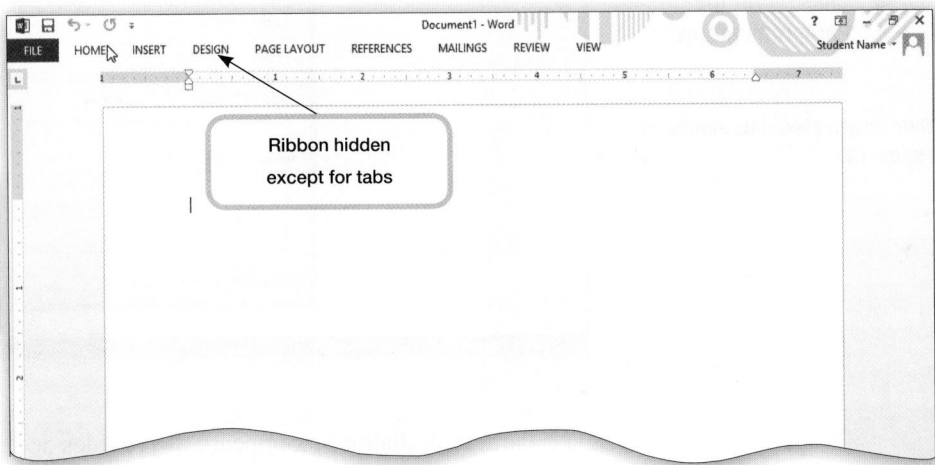

Ribbon hidden except for tabs

Figure 15

Now, the only part of the Ribbon that is visible is the tab area. Then, to access the entire Ribbon while you are working, simply single-click on any tab and the Ribbon reappears temporarily. It collapses again as you continue to work. To permanently expand the Ribbon, simply double-click on the tab you want to make active and the Ribbon is again fully displayed.

● **Click on the Insert tab.**

● **Click in the document window.**

● **Double-click the Home tab.**

● **Click in the document window.**

The full Ribbon reappears and remains fixed in place and the Home tab is active.

Using the Office Backstage

To the left of the Home tab in the Ribbon is the File tab. Unlike the other tabs that display a Ribbon of commands, the File tab opens the Office Backstage. The Office **Backstage** contains commands that allow you to work *with* your document, unlike the Ribbon that allows you to work *in* your document. The Backstage contains commands that apply to the entire document. For example, you will find commands to open, save, print, and manage your files and set your program options. The File tab is common to all the Office 2013 applications, although the options may vary slightly.

1

- Click the File tab to open the Backstage.

- Click Info in the list of sidebar options.

Your screen should be similar to Figure 16

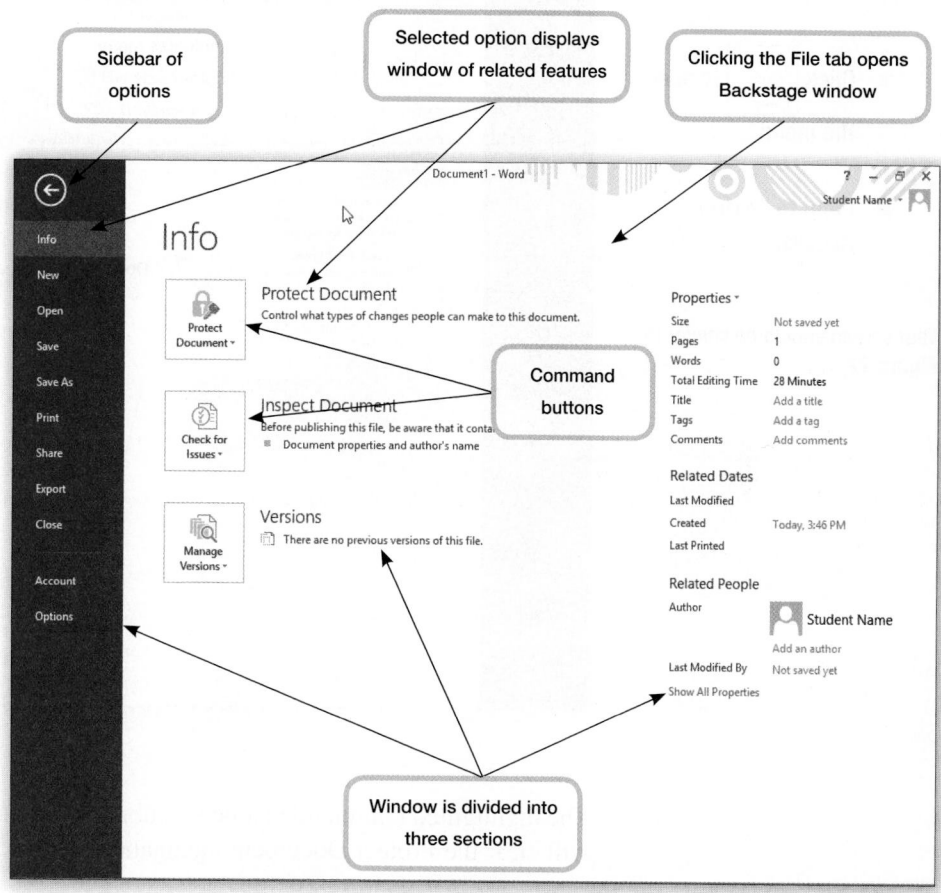

Figure 16

Another Method

You also can use the directional keys to move up, down, left, or right within Backstage and press Enter to choose a selected option or command.

The Backstage window is open and completely covers the application window. The left side of the window displays a list of options in a sidebar. Pointing to an option selects it and it appears highlighted. Clicking an option chooses it and displays related commands and features in the right side. Choosing some options opens a dialog box or immediately performs the associated action. The last two options in the sidebar are used to change account and program settings.

The Info window is open and displays information about the current document. The three command buttons are used to control changes that can be made to the document, check for issues related to distribution, and manage document versions for the current document. A description of these buttons and the current document settings is shown to the right of the button. Notice that the buttons display a ▭. This indicates that a menu of commands will be displayed when you click the button. The right side of the window displays a list of settings, called **properties**, associated with the document. The current properties displayed in the Info window show the initial or **default** properties associated with a new blank document.

Additional Information

You will learn more about document properties shortly.

2

● Click 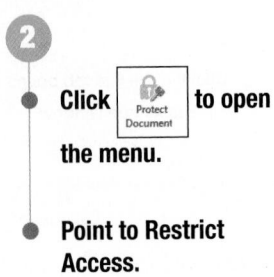 to open the menu.

● Point to Restrict Access.

Your screen should be similar to Figure 17

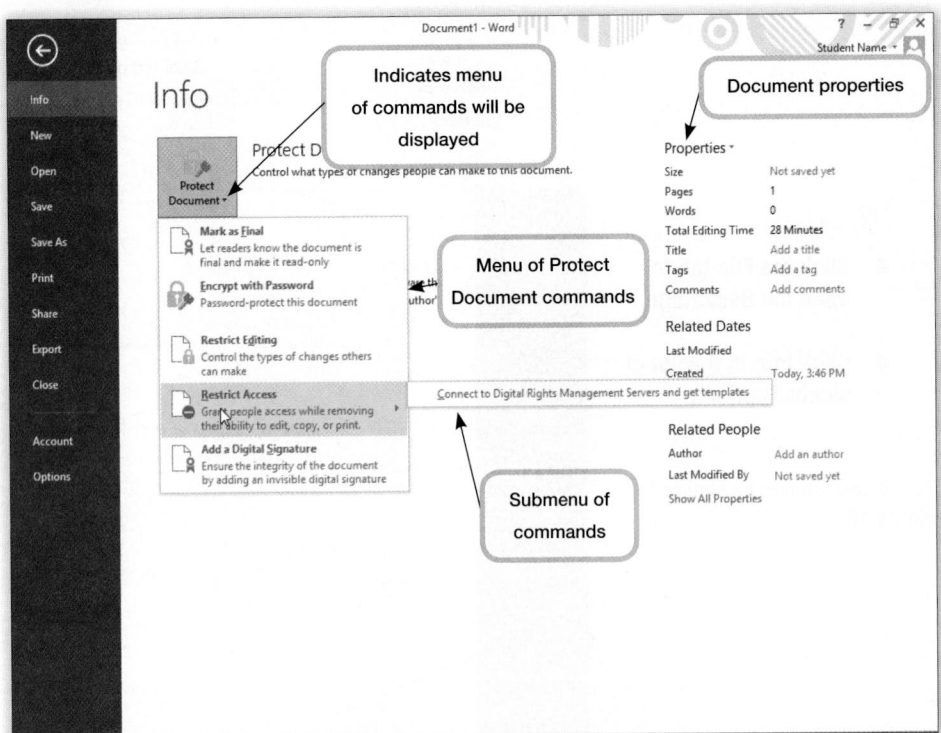

Figure 17

The highlighted command displays a submenu of additional commands. Next, you will clear the Protect Document menu and open the New window in Backstage.

3

Click  again to clear the submenu.

Click the **New option** in the sidebar.

Your screen should be similar to Figure 18

New window displays options to create new documents

Template files

Figure 18

The Backstage window now displays options for creating a new document. It is very similar to the Start screen that appears when you first start Word 2013.

4

Click ← at the top of the sidebar.

Backstage is closed and the document window is displayed again.

Another Method

You also can press Esc to close the Backstage window.

COMMON APPLICATION FEATURES

So far you have learned about using the Office 2013 user interface features. Next, you will learn about application features that are used to work in and modify documents and are the same or similar in all Office 2013 applications. These include how to open, close, and save files; navigate, scroll, and zoom a document; enter, select, edit, and format text; and document, preview, and print a file. To do this, you will open a Word document file and make a few changes to it. Then you will save and print the revised document. Once you have gained an understanding of the basic concepts of the common features using Word, you will be able to easily apply them in the other Office applications.

Opening a File

In all Office 2013 applications, you either need to create a new file using the blank document template or another template or open an existing file. Opening a file retrieves a file that is stored on your computer hard drive or an external storage location and places it in RAM (random-access memory) of your computer so it can be read and modified.

1

- **Click the File tab to open the Backstage.**

- **Click the Open option in the sidebar.**

Your screen should be similar to Figure 19

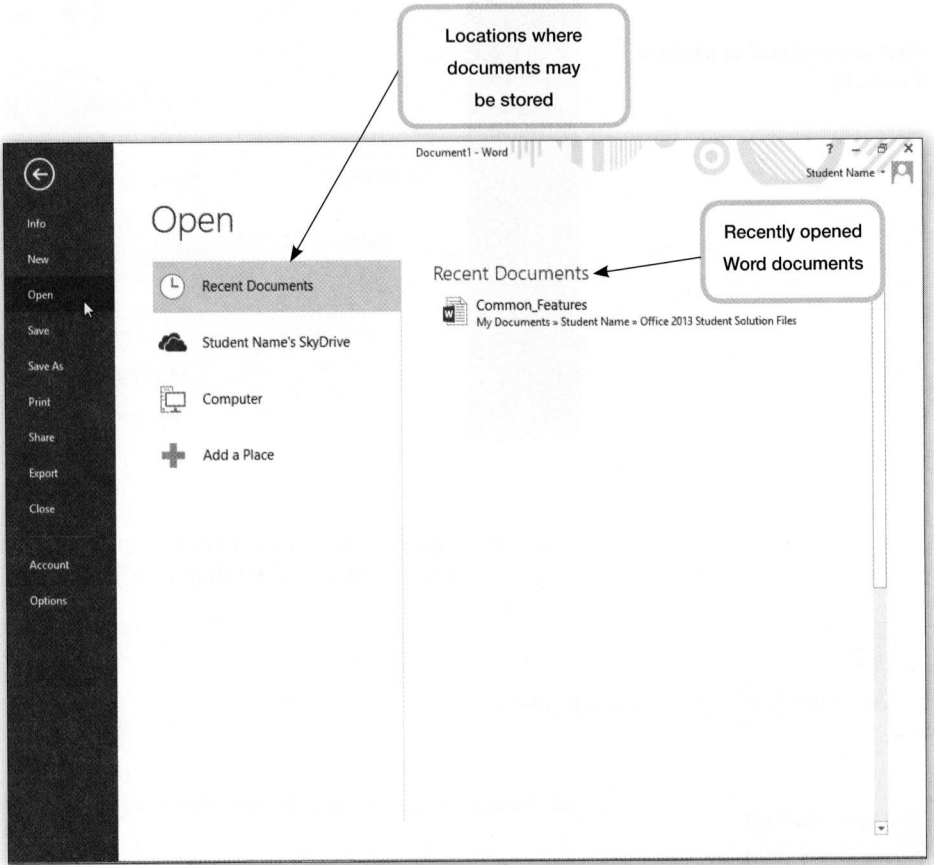

Figure 19

The left side of the Open window displays locations where the file you want to open is stored. The location may be the hard drive of your computer, an external storage device, a local network, or in the cloud on SkyDrive or SharePoint. The **cloud** refers to any applications and services that are hosted and run on servers connected to the Internet. The Recent Documents option is selected by default and displays a list of file names of documents that have been recently opened in Word 2013 in the Recent Documents pane. Below the file name the path location of the file is displayed. If the file you want to open appears in the Recent Documents list, clicking on the file immediately opens it.

First you need to change to the location where your data files for completing these labs are stored.

Additional Information

Microsoft SkyDrive and SharePoint are subscription file storage services that you can access anytime you are online.

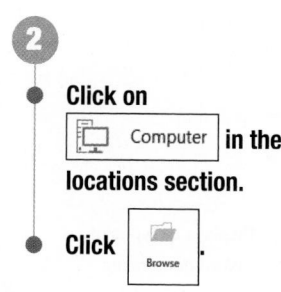

2

• **Click on** 📺 Computer **in the locations section.**

• **Click** 📁 Browse **.**

Your screen should be similar to Figure 20

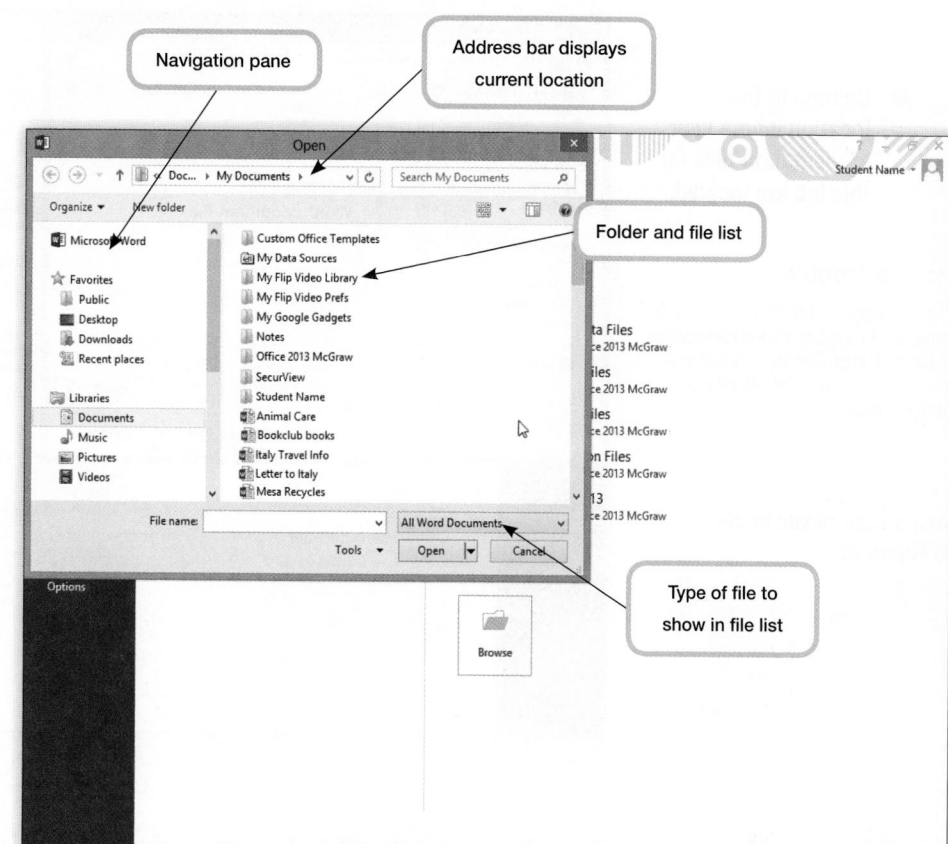

Navigation pane

Address bar displays current location

Folder and file list

Type of file to show in file list

Figure 20

Additional Information

The Open dialog box is common to all programs using the Windows operating system. Your dialog box may look slightly different depending on the current View setting.

The Open dialog box is displayed in which you specify the location where the file you want to open is stored and the file name. The location consists of identifying the hard drive of your computer or an external storage device or a remote computer followed by folders and subfolders within that location. The Address bar displays the default folder as the location to open the file. The file list displays folder names as well as the names of any Word documents in the current location. Only Word documents are listed because All Word Documents is the specified file type in the File Type list box. In Excel and PowerPoint, only files of that application's file type would be displayed.

Additional Information

You will learn about the different file types shortly.

There are several methods that can be used to locate files. One is to use the Address bar to specify another location by either typing the complete folder name or path or by opening the drop-down list of previously accessed locations and clicking a new location. Another is to use the features in the Navigation pane, to choose a link to a Favorite item or location, to search the folders and files in the Libraries or to navigate through the hierarchical structure of drives and folders on your computer. Clicking a link or folder from the list displays files at that location in the file list. Then, from the file list, you can continue to select subfolders until the file you want to open is located.

You will open the file IO_Common Features that is supplied with your student data files for this lab.

3 ● Change to the location where your student data files for this lab are located.

Having Trouble?

The text assumes the location is on your computer in a folder named Introduction to Office. If your files are in a different location, your instructor will provide further directions.

Your screen should be similar to Figure 21

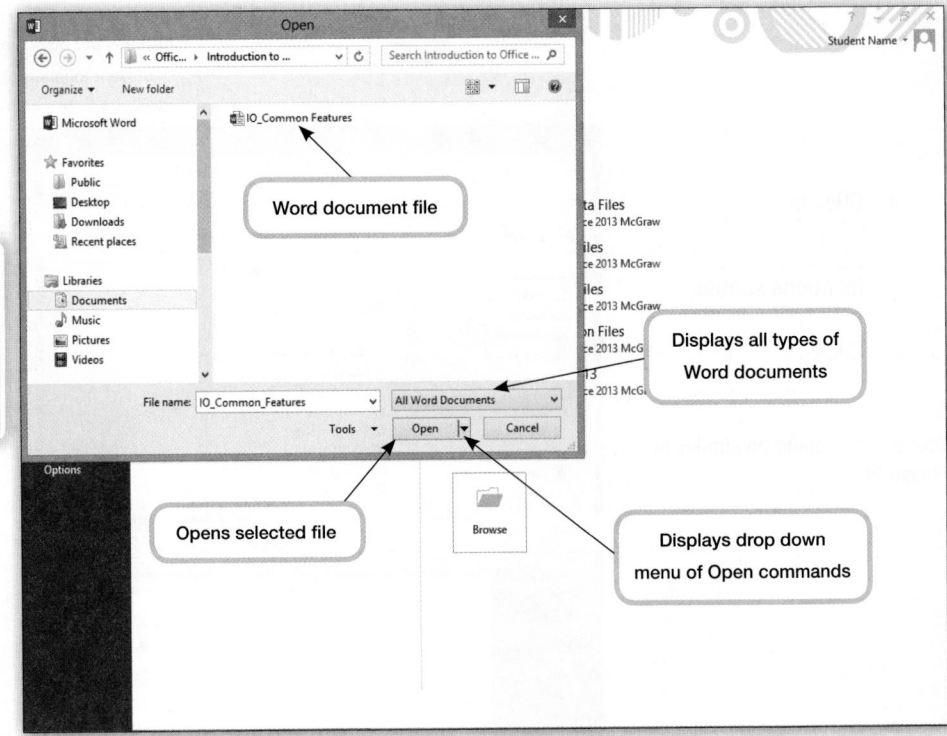

- Word document file
- Displays all types of Word documents
- Opens selected file
- Browse
- Displays drop down menu of Open commands

Figure 21

Now the file list displays the names of all Word files at that location. Next, you open the file by clicking on the file name to select it and clicking the ☐ Open ▾ button. In addition, in the Office applications you can specify how you want to open a file by choosing from the ☐ Open ▾ drop-down menu options described in the following table.

Open Options	Description
Open	Opens with all formatting and editing features enabled. This is the default setting.
Open Read-only	Opens file so it can be read or copied only, not modified in any way.
Open as Copy	Automatically creates a copy of the file and opens the copy with complete editing capabilities.
Open in Browser	Opens HTML type files in a web browser.
Open with Transform	Opens certain types of documents and lets you change it into another type of document.
Open in Protected View	Opens files from potentially unsafe locations with editing functions disabled.
Open and Repair	Opens file and attempts to repair any damage.

Another Method

You could also press [Enter] to open a selected file or double-click on the file name.

You will open the file IO_Common Features. Clicking the ☐ Open ▾ button opens the file using the default Open option so you can read and edit the file.

4

● **Select** IO_Common
Features.

● **Click** Open ▾.

Your screen should be similar to Figure 22

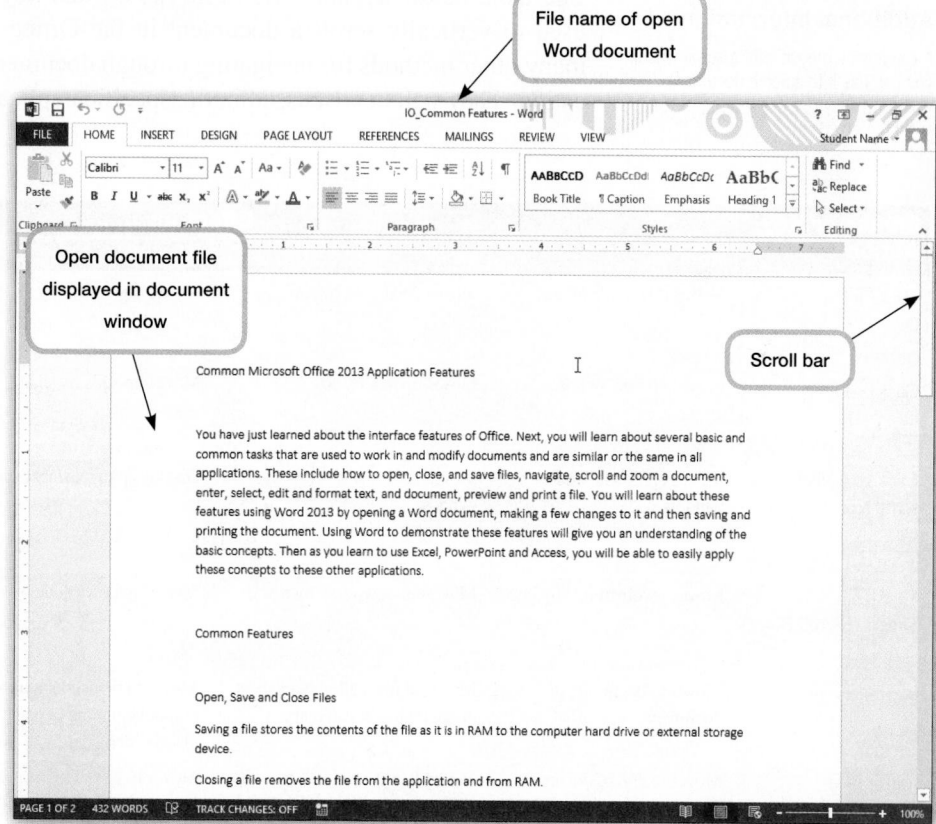

File name of open Word document

Open document file displayed in document window

Scroll bar

Common Microsoft Office 2013 Application Features

You have just learned about the interface features of Office. Next, you will learn about several basic and common tasks that are used to work in and modify documents and are similar or the same in all applications. These include how to open, close, and save files, navigate, scroll and zoom a document, enter, select, edit and format text, and document, preview and print a file. You will learn about these features using Word 2013 by opening a Word document, making a few changes to it and then saving and printing the document. Using Word to demonstrate these features will give you an understanding of the basic concepts. Then as you learn to use Excel, PowerPoint and Access, you will be able to easily apply these concepts to these other applications.

Common Features

Open, Save and Close Files

Saving a file stores the contents of the file as it is in RAM to the computer hard drive or external storage device.

Closing a file removes the file from the application and from RAM.

Figure 22

A Word document file describing the common Microsoft Office application features is displayed in the document window.

Scrolling the Document Window

As documents increase in size, they cannot be easily viewed in their entirety in the document window and much time can be spent moving to different locations in the document. All Office 2013 applications include features that make it easy to move around and view the information in a large document. The basic method is to scroll through a document using the scroll bar or keyboard. Both methods are useful, depending on what you are doing. For example, if you are entering text using the keyboard, using the keyboard method may be more efficient than using the mouse.

Additional Information

Scroll bars are also found in task panes and dialog boxes and operate similarly.

Touch Tip

With a touch device, you can touch the document and slide it up and down.

Additional Information

If you have a mouse with a scroll wheel, you can use it to scroll a document vertically.

The table below explains the basic mouse and keyboard techniques that can be used to vertically scroll a document in the Office 2013 applications. There are many other methods for navigating through documents that are unique to an application. They will be discussed in the specific application text.

Mouse or Key Action	Effect in:			
	Word	**Excel**	**PowerPoint**	**Access**
Click ▼ Or ↓	Moves down line by line.	Moves down row by row	Moves down slide by slide	Moves down record by record
Click ▲ Or ↑	Moves up line by line.	Moves up row by row	Moves up slide by slide	Moves up record by record
Click above/below scroll box Or Page Up / Page Down	Moves up/down window by window	Moves up/down window by window	Displays previous/next slide	Moves up/down window by window
Drag Scroll Box	Moves up/down line by line	Moves up/down row by row	Moves up/down slide by slide	Moves up/down record by record
Ctrl + Home	Moves to beginning of document	Moves to first cell in worksheet or beginning of cell entry	Moves to first slide in presentation or beginning of entry in placeholder	Moves to first record in table or beginning of field entry
Ctrl + End	Moves to end of document	Moves to last-used cell in worksheet or end of cell entry	Moves to last slide in presentation or to end of placeholder entry	Moves to last record in table or end of field entry

Additional Information

You also can scroll the document window horizontally using the horizontal scroll bar or the → and ← keys.

You will use the vertical scroll bar to view the text at the bottom of the Word document. When you use the scroll bar to scroll, the actual location in the document where you can work does not change, only the area you are viewing changes. For example, in Word, the cursor does not move and in Excel the cell you can work in does not change. To move the cursor or make another cell active, you must click in a location in the window. However, when you scroll using the keyboard, the actual location as identified by the position of the cursor in the document also changes. For example, in Word the cursor attempts to maintain its position in a line as you scroll up and down through the document. In Excel the cell you can work in changes as you move through a worksheet using the keyboard.

1

- Click ⬇ in the vertical scroll bar 10 times.

- Click at the beginning of the word Scroll in the Common Features section to move the cursor.

- Press ⬇ 10 times to scroll the window and move the cursor down 10 lines.

Your screen should be similar to Figure 23

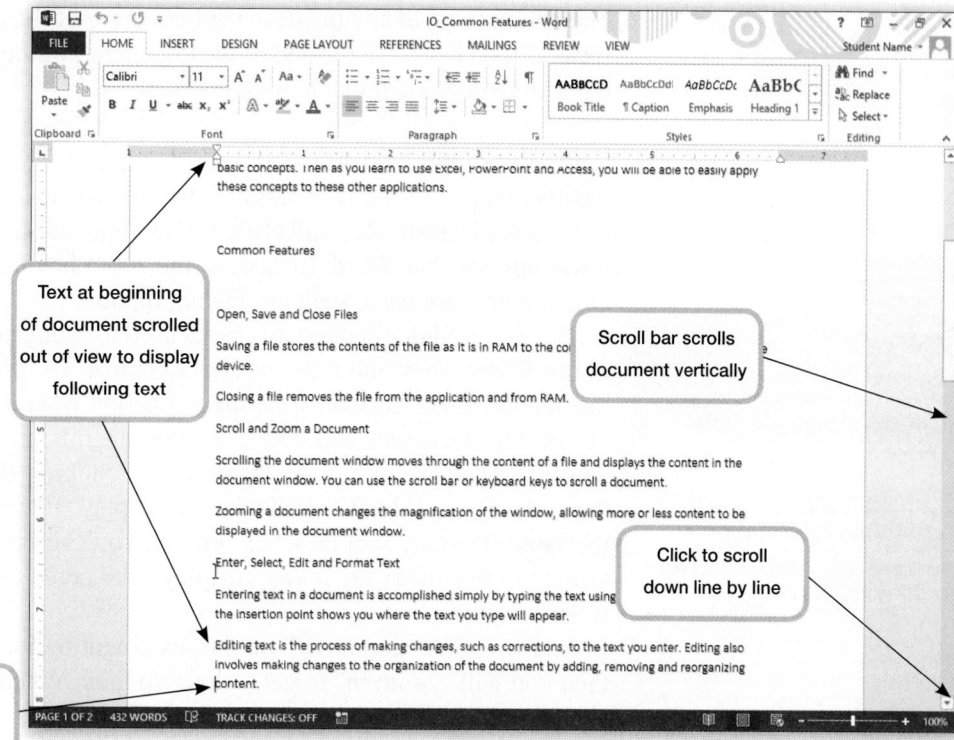

Text at beginning of document scrolled out of view to display following text

Scroll bar scrolls document vertically

Click to scroll down line by line

Cursor moves when scrolling using the keyboard

Figure 23

Having Trouble?

If your screen scrolls differently, this is a function of the type of monitor you are using.

The text at the beginning of the document has scrolled line by line off the top of the document window, and the following text is now displayed. In a large document, scrolling line by line can take a while. You will now try out several additional mouse and keyboard scrolling features that move by larger increments through the document.

2

- Click below the scroll box in the scroll bar.

- Press ⌈Ctrl⌋ + ⌈End⌋ to move to the end of the last line of the document.

- Drag the scroll box to the top of the scroll bar.

Your screen should be similar to Figure 24

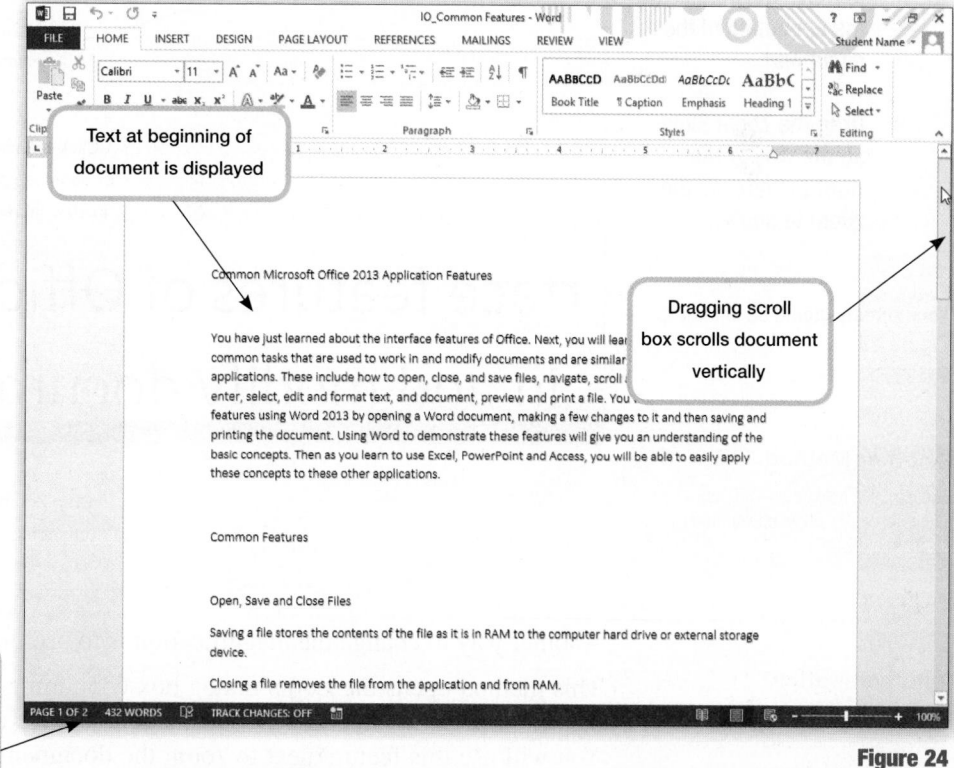

Text at beginning of document is displayed

Dragging scroll box scrolls document vertically

Cursor still on page 2 at end of document because it does not move when scrolling using the scroll bar

Figure 24

The document window displays the beginning of the document; however, the cursor is still on page 2 at the end of the document. Using these features makes scrolling a large document much more efficient.

Using the Zoom Feature

Another way to see more or less of a document is to use the zoom feature. Although this feature is available in all Office 2013 applications, Excel and PowerPoint have fewer options than Word. In Access, the zoom feature is available only when specific features are used, such as viewing reports.

The Zoom Slider in the status bar is used to change the magnification. To use the Zoom Slider, click and drag the slider control. Dragging to the right zooms in on the document and increases the magnification whereas dragging to the left zooms out on the document and decreases the magnification. You also can change the zoom percentage by increments of 10 by clicking the ➕ or ➖ on each end of the slider control. In Word, the default display, 100 percent, shows the characters the same size they will be when printed. You can increase the onscreen character size up to five times the normal display (500 percent) or reduce the character size to 10 percent.

You will first "zoom out" on the document to get an overview of the file, and then you will "zoom in" to get a close-up look. When a document is zoomed, you can work in it as usual.

Touch Tip

With a touch device, you can zoom in by stretching two fingers apart and zoom out by pinching two fingers together.

Additional Information

The degree of magnification varies with the different applications.

1

- Click ➖ in the Zoom Slider five times to decrease the zoom percentage to 50%.

- Press [Ctrl] + [Home] to move the cursor to the beginning of the document.

- Drag the Zoom Slider all the way to the right to increase the zoom to 500%.

Your screen should be similar to Figure 25

Another Method

You can also hold down [Ctrl] while using the scroll wheel on your mouse to zoom a document.

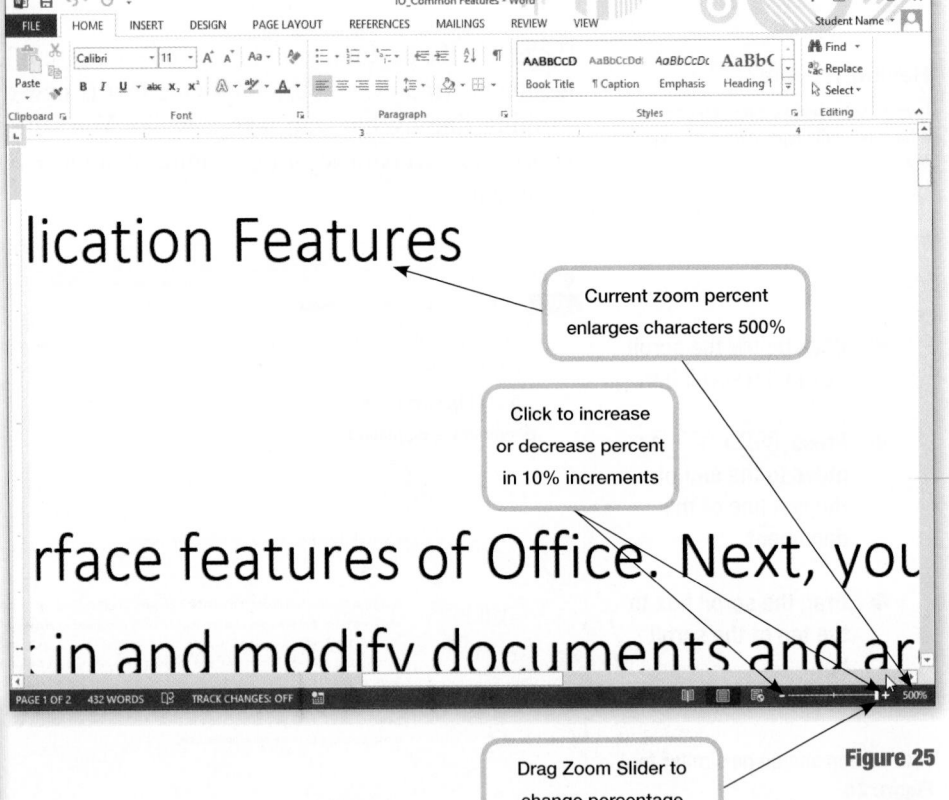

Figure 25

Another way to change the magnification is to use the 🔍 Zoom button in the View tab. This method opens the Zoom dialog box containing several preset zoom options, or an option that lets you set a precise percentage using the Percent scroll box. You will use this feature next to zoom the document. This method is available in Word only.

Another Method

You can also click on the zoom percentage in the status bar to open the Zoom dialog box.

2

- Open the View tab.

- Click 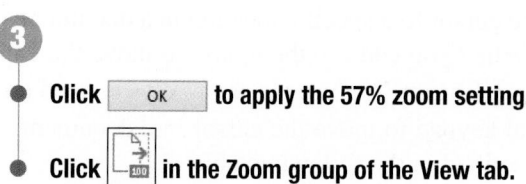 in the Zoom group.

- Click Whole Page and note that the percent value in the Percent text box and the preview area reflect the new percentage setting.

- Click the ▲ scroll button in the Percent scroll box to increase the zoom percentage to 57.

Your screen should be similar to Figure 26

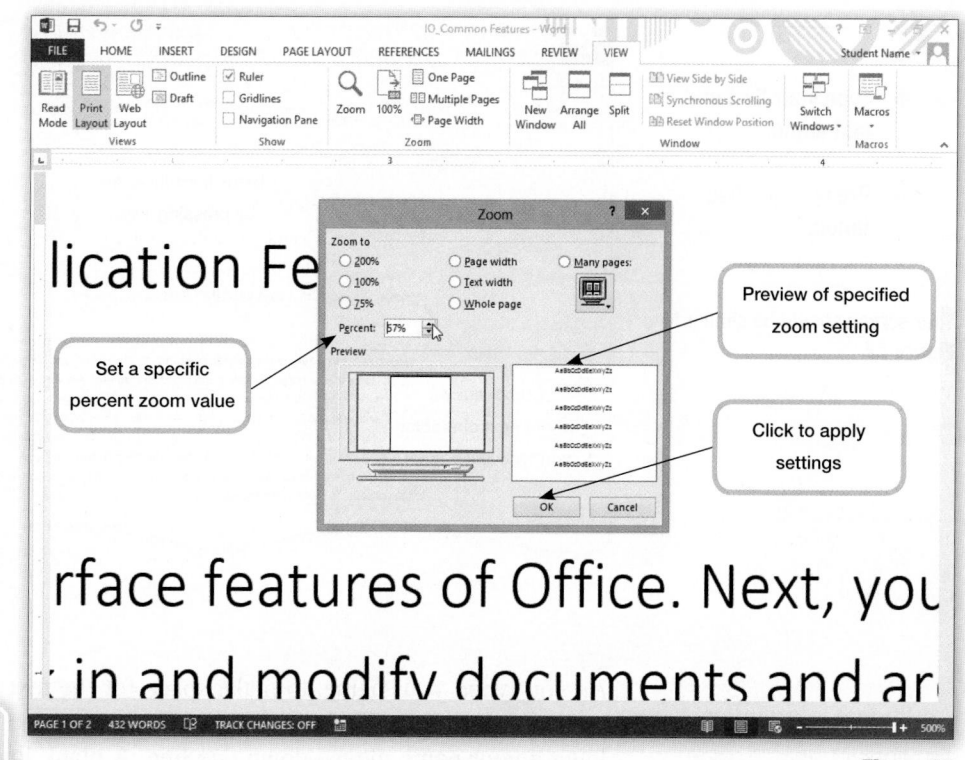

Figure 26

The Zoom dialog box preview areas show how the document will appear on your screen at the specified zoom percent. Not until you complete the command by clicking [OK] will the zoom percent in the document actually change. You will complete the command to apply the 57% zoom setting. Then, you will use the [100%] button in the Zoom group to quickly return to the default zoom setting.

3

- Click [OK] to apply the 57% zoom setting.

- Click [100%] in the Zoom group of the View tab.

The document is again at 100% magnification.

Entering and Editing Text

Now that you are familiar with the entire document, you will make a few changes to it. The keyboard is used to enter information into a document. In all applications, the location of the cursor shows you where the text will appear as you type. After text is entered into a document, you need to know how to move around within the text to edit or make changes to the text. Again, the process is similar for all Office applications.

Currently, in this Word document, the cursor is positioned at the top of the document. You will type your name at this location. As you type, the cursor moves to the right and the characters will appear to the left of the cursor. Then you will press [Enter] to end the line following your name and press [Enter] again at the beginning of a line to insert a blank line.

1

● Type your first and last name.

● Press ⌅Enter⌅ two times.

Your screen should be similar to Figure 27

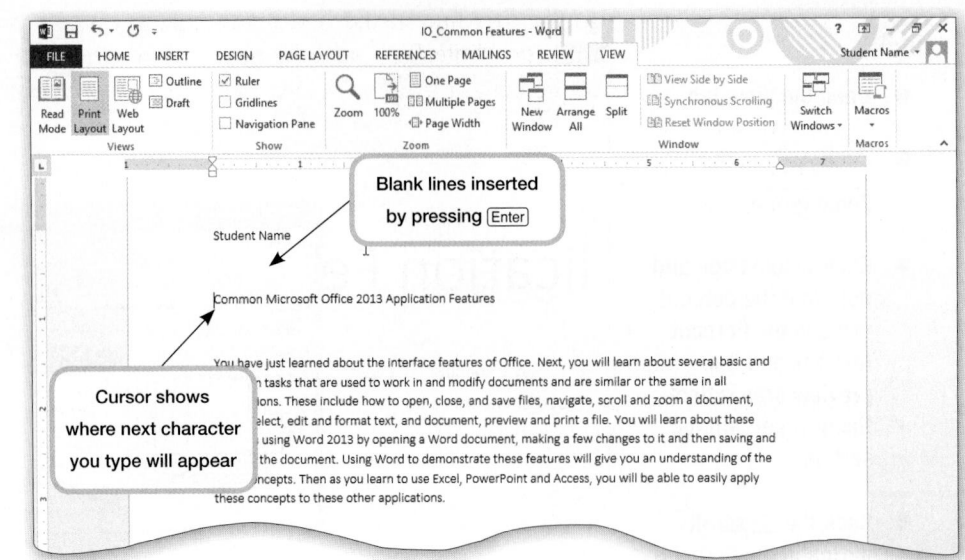

Blank lines inserted by pressing ⌅Enter⌅

Student Name

Common Microsoft Office 2013 Application Features

You have just learned about the interface features of Office. Next, you will learn about several basic and tasks that are used to work in and modify documents and are similar or the same in all ions. These include how to open, close, and save files, navigate, scroll and zoom a document, lect, edit and format text, and document, preview and print a file. You will learn about these using Word 2013 by opening a Word document, making a few changes to it and then saving the document. Using Word to demonstrate these features will give you an understanding of the ncepts. Then as you learn to use Excel, PowerPoint and Access, you will be able to easily apply these concepts to these other applications.

Cursor shows where next character you type will appear

Figure 27

Additional Information

You can use the directional keys on the numeric keypad or the dedicated directional keypad area. If using the numeric keypad, make sure the Num Lock feature is off; otherwise, numbers will be entered in the document. The Num Lock indicator light above the keypad is lit when on. Press ⌅Num Lock⌅ to turn it off.

Touch Tip

With a touch device, tap in the text to place the cursor.

As you typed your name, to make space for the text on the line, the existing text moved to the right. Then, when you pressed ⌅Enter⌅ the first time, all the text following your name moved down one line. A blank line was inserted after pressing ⌅Enter⌅ the second time.

Next, you want to add a word to the first line of the first paragraph. To do this, you first need to move the cursor to the location where you want to make the change. The keyboard or mouse can be used to move through the text in the document window. Depending on what you are doing, one method may be more efficient than another. For example, if your hands are already on the keyboard as you are entering text, it may be quicker to use the keyboard rather than take your hands off to use the mouse.

You use the mouse to move the cursor to a specific location in a document simply by clicking on the location. When you can use the mouse to move the cursor, the mouse pointer is shaped as an Ⅰ I-beam. You use the arrow keys located on the numeric keypad or the directional keypad to move the cursor in a document. The keyboard directional keys are described in the following table.

Key	Word/PowerPoint	Excel	Access
→	Right one character	Right one cell	Right one field
←	Left one character	Left one cell	Left one field
↑	Up one line	Up one cell	Up one record
↓	Down one line	Down one cell	Down one record
Ctrl + →	Right one word	Last cell in row	One word to right in a field entry
Ctrl + ←	Left one word	First cell in row	One word to left in a field entry
Home	Beginning of line	First cell in row	First field of record
End	End of line		Last field of record

Additional Information

Many of the keyboard keys and key combinations have other effects depending on the mode of operation at the time they are used. You will learn about these differences in the specific application labs as they are used.

In the first line of the first paragraph, you want to add the word "basic" before the word "interface" and the year "2013" after the word "Office." You will move to the correct locations using both the keyboard and the mouse and then enter the new text.

2

- **Click at the beginning of the word You in the first paragraph.**

- **Press → four times to move to the beginning of the second word.**

- **Press Ctrl + → five times to move to the beginning of the seventh word.**

Additional Information

Holding down a directional key or key combination moves quickly in the direction indicated, saving multiple presses of the key.

- **Type basic and press Spacebar.**

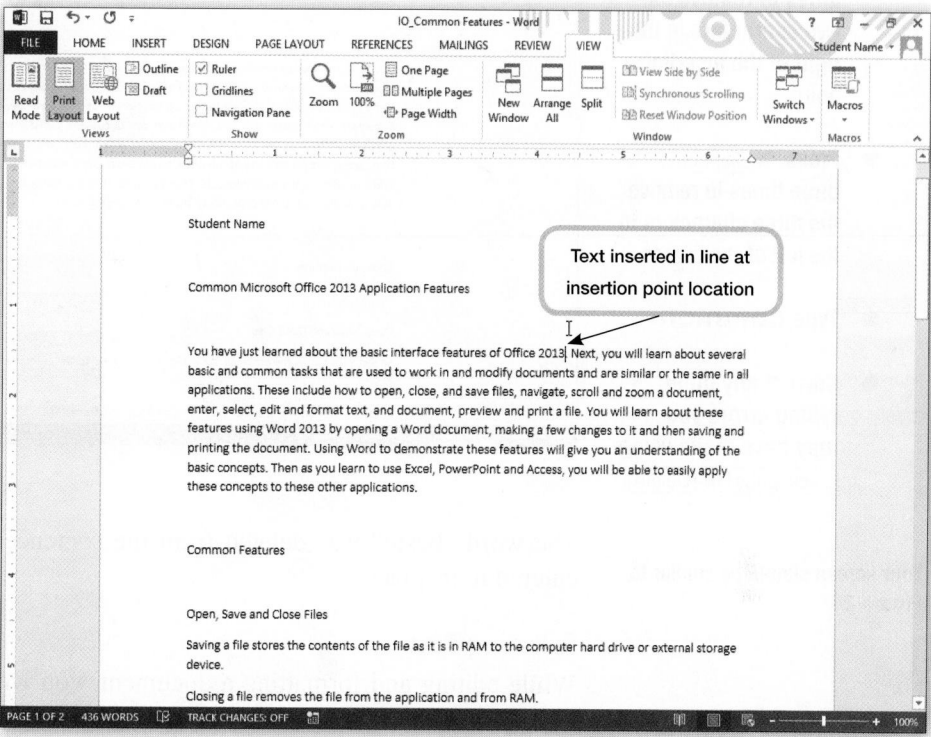

Figure 28

Having Trouble?

Do not be concerned if you make a typing error; you will learn how to correct them next.

- **Position the I-beam between the e in Office and the period at the end of the first sentence and click.**

- **Press Spacebar and type 2013**

Your screen should be similar to Figure 28

Next, you want to edit the text you just entered by changing the word "basic" to "common." Removing typing entries to change or correct them is one of the basic editing tasks. Corrections may be made in many ways. Two of the most basic editing keys that are common to the Office applications are the Backspace and Delete keys. The Backspace key removes a character or space to the left of the cursor. It is particularly useful when you are moving from right to left (backward) along a line of text. The Delete key removes the character or space to the right of the cursor and is most useful when moving from left to right along a line.

   You will use these features as you make the correction.

3

- Move the cursor between the s and i in "basic" (in the first sentence).

- Press Delete two times to remove the two characters to the right of the insertion point.

- Press Backspace three times to remove the three characters to the left of the cursor.

- Type **common**

- Correct any other typing errors you may have made using Backspace or Delete .

Your screen should be similar to Figure 29

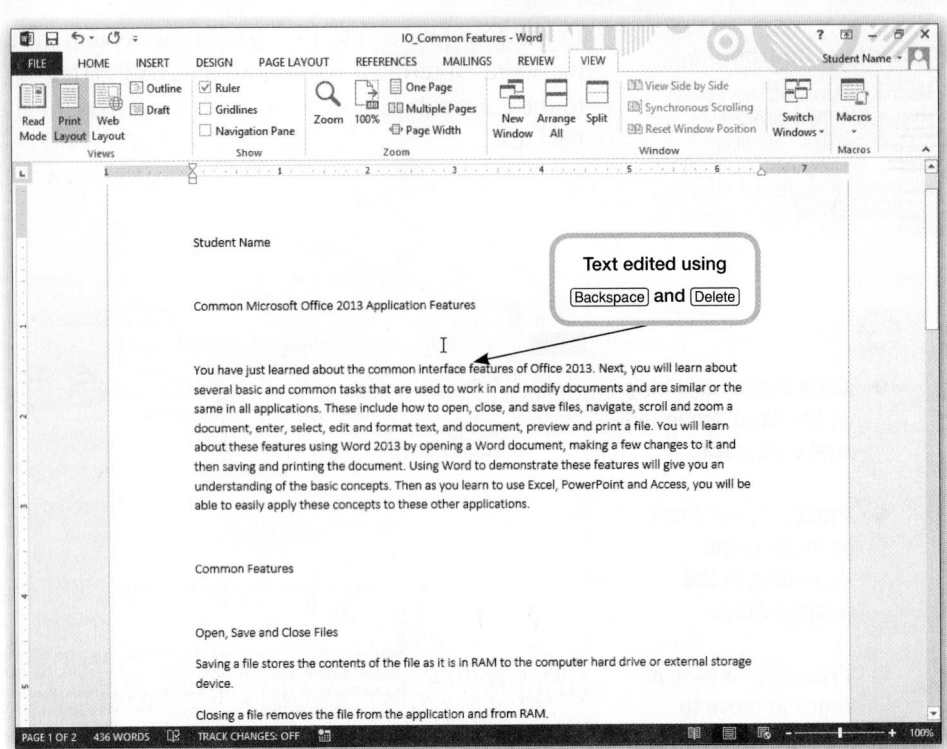

Figure 29

Additional Information

The capability to select text is common to all Office 2013 applications. However, many of the features that are designed for use in Word are not available in the other applications. Some are available only when certain modes of operation are in effect or when certain features are being used.

Touch Tip

With a touch device, tap in the text to place the cursor and drag the selection handle to select.

The word "basic" was deleted from the sentence and the word "common" was entered in its place.

Selecting Text

While editing and formatting a document, you will need to select text. Selecting highlights text and identifies the text that will be affected by your next action. To select text using the mouse, first move the cursor to the beginning or end of the text to be selected, and then drag to highlight the text you want selected. You can select as little as a single letter or as much as the entire document. You also can select text using keyboard features. The following table summarizes common mouse and keyboard techniques used to select text in Word.

To Select	Mouse	Keyboard
Next/previous space or character	Drag across space or character.	Shift + →/Shift + ←
Next/previous word	Double-click in the word.	Ctrl + Shift + →/Ctrl + Shift + ←
Sentence	Press Ctrl and click within the sentence.	
Line	Click to the left of a line when the mouse pointer is ⟁.	
Multiple lines	Drag up or down to the left of a line when the mouse pointer is ⟁.	
Text going backward to beginning of paragraph	Drag left and up to the beginning of the paragraph when the mouse pointer is ⟁.	Ctrl + Shift + ↑
Text going forward to end of paragraph	Drag right and down to the end of the paragraph when the mouse pointer is ⟁.	Ctrl + Shift + ↓
Paragraph	Triple-click on the paragraph or double-click to the left of the paragraph when the mouse pointer is ⟁.	
Multiple paragraphs	Drag to the left of the paragraphs when the mouse pointer is ⟁.	
Document	Triple-click or press Ctrl and click to the left of the text when the mouse pointer is ⟁.	Ctrl + A

Having Trouble?

If you accidentally select the incorrect text, simply click anywhere in the document or press any directional key to clear the selection and try again.

You want to change the word "tasks" in the next sentence to "application features". Although you could use Delete and Backspace to remove the unneeded text character by character, it will be faster to select and delete the word. First you will try out several of the keyboard techniques to select text. Then you will use several mouse features to select text and finally you will edit the sentence.

- Move the cursor to the beginning of the word "basic" in the second sentence.

- Press Shift + → five times to select the word basic.

- Press Shift + Ctrl + → to extend the selection word by word until the entire line is selected.

- Press Shift + Ctrl + ↓ to extend the selection to the end of the paragraph.

Your screen should be similar to Figure 30

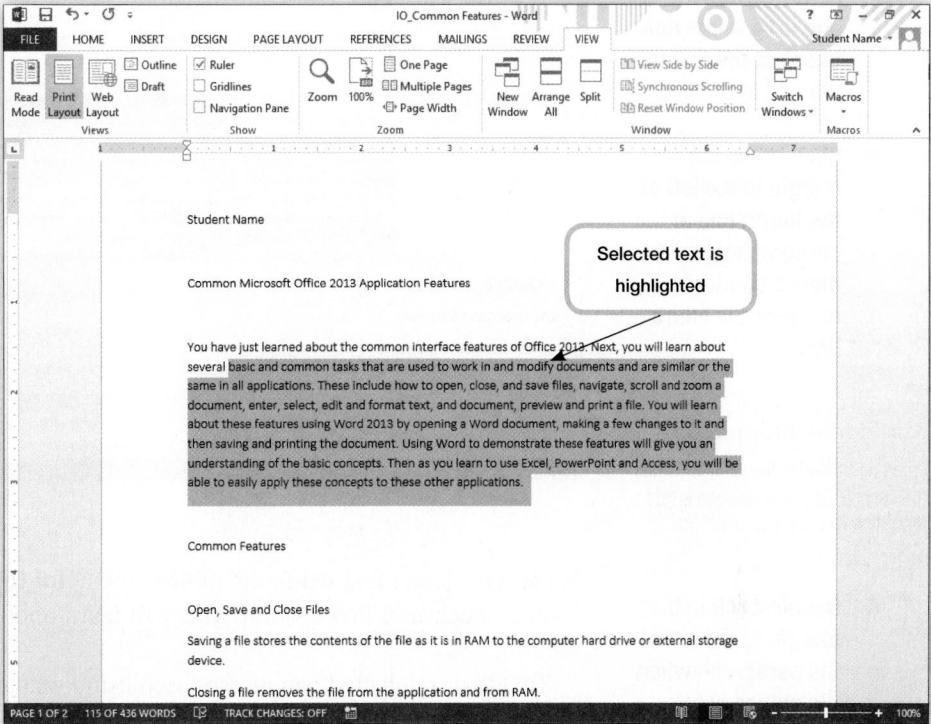

Figure 30

The text from the cursor to the end of the paragraph is selected. Next, you will clear this selection and then use the mouse to select text.

2

● Click anywhere in the paragraph to clear the selection.

● Click at the beginning of the word "basic" and drag to the right to select the text to the end of the line.

● Click in the left margin to the left of the fourth line of the paragraph when the mouse pointer is 📐 to select the entire line.

Additional Information

When positioned in the left margin, the mouse pointer shape changes to 📐, indicating it is ready to select text.

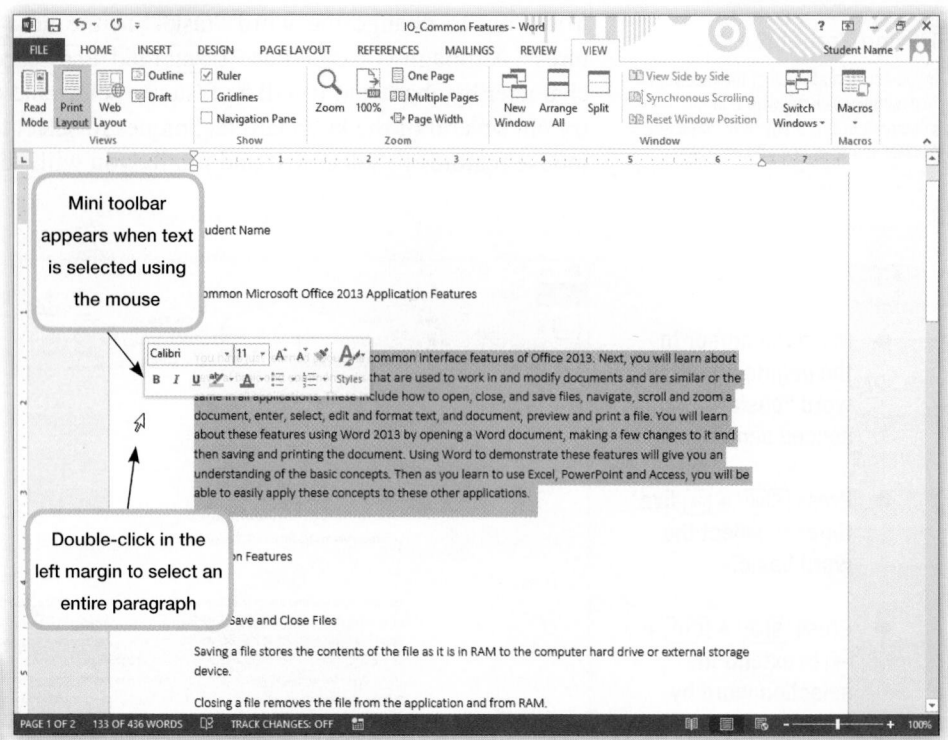

Mini toolbar appears when text is selected using the mouse

Double-click in the left margin to select an entire paragraph

Figure 31

When you select text using the mouse, the **Mini toolbar** appears automatically in Word, Excel, and PowerPoint. You will learn about using this feature in the next section.

Text that is selected can be modified using many different features. In this case, you want to replace the word "tasks" in the second sentence with "application features".

● Double-click in the margin to the left of the paragraph when the mouse pointer is 📐 to select the paragraph.

Your screen should be similar to Figure 31

3

● Double-click on the word "tasks" in the second sentence.

● Type **application features**

Your screen should be similar to Figure 32

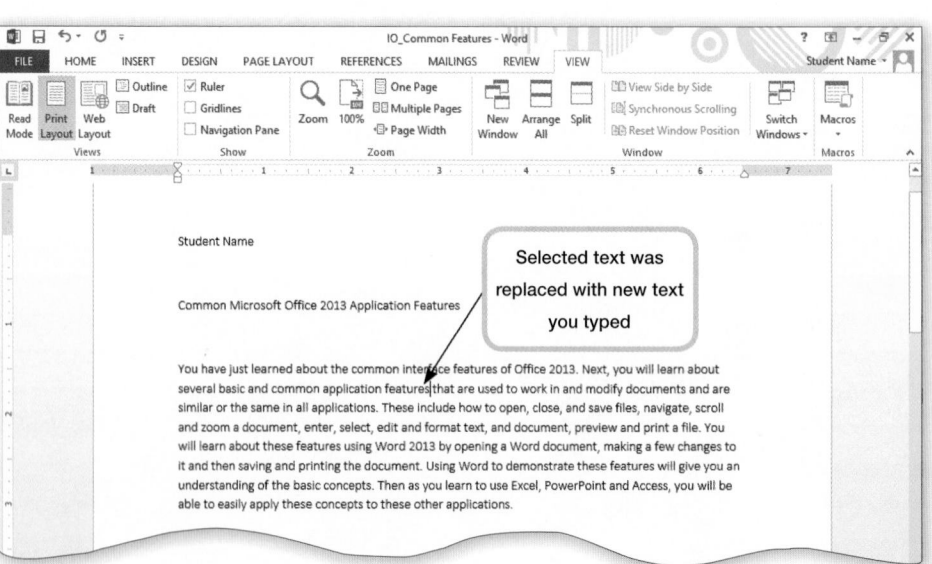

Selected text was replaced with new text you typed

Figure 32

As soon as you began typing, the selected text was automatically deleted. The new text was inserted in the line by pushing the existing text to the right. Any text that could not fit on the line moved to the beginning of the next line. This is the **word wrap** feature. Although this feature is used mostly in Word, it is also used in the other applications.

Formatting Text

An important aspect of all documents you create using Office 2013 is the appearance of the document. To improve the appearance you can apply many different formatting effects. The most common formatting features are font and character effects. A **font**, also commonly referred to as a **typeface**, is a set of characters with a specific design. The designs have names such as Times New Roman and Courier. Each font has one or more sizes. **Font size** is the height and width of the character and is commonly measured in points, abbreviated "pt." One point equals about 1/72 inch. **Character effects** are enhancements such as bold, italic, and color that are applied to selected text. Using font and character effects as design elements can add interest to your document and give readers visual cues to help them find information quickly.

First you want to change the font and increase the font size of the title of this document.

1

● Click in the left margin next to the title line when the mouse pointer is ⇗ to select it.

● Open the Home tab.

● Open the Calibri ▾ **Font** drop-down menu in the Font group.

● Point to the Arial Black font option in the menu.

Your screen should be similar to Figure 33

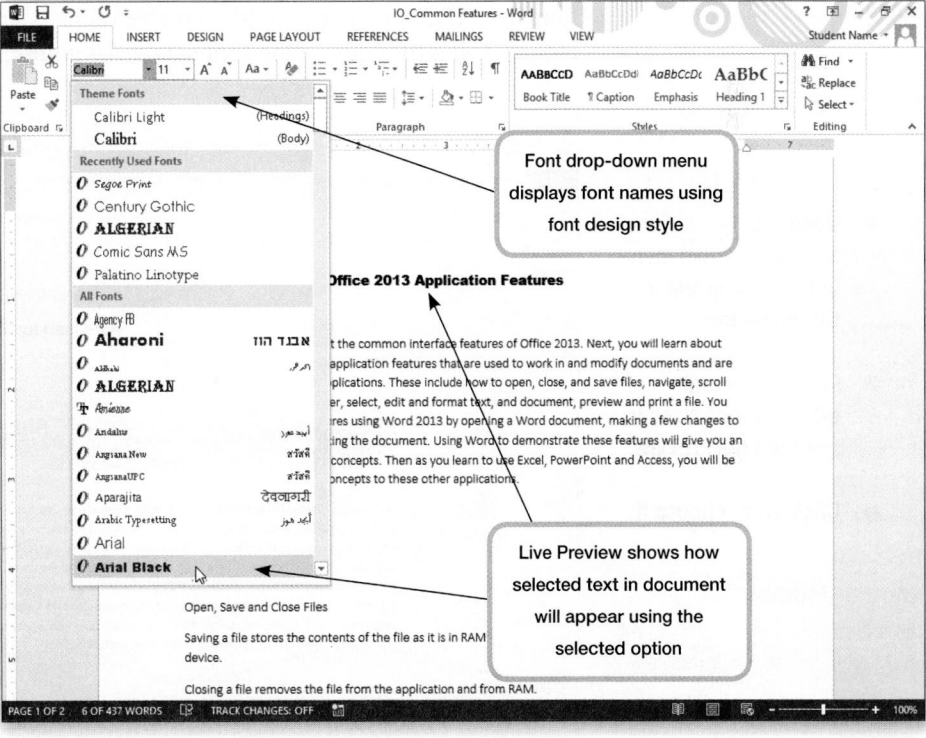

Figure 33

As you point to the font options, the **Live Preview** feature shows you how the selected text in the document will appear if this option is chosen.

2

- Point to several different fonts in the menu to see the Live Preview.

- Scroll the menu and click Segoe Print to choose it.

Additional Information

Font names are listed in alphabetical order.

Having Trouble?

If this font is not available on your computer, choose a similar font.

Your screen should be similar to Figure 34

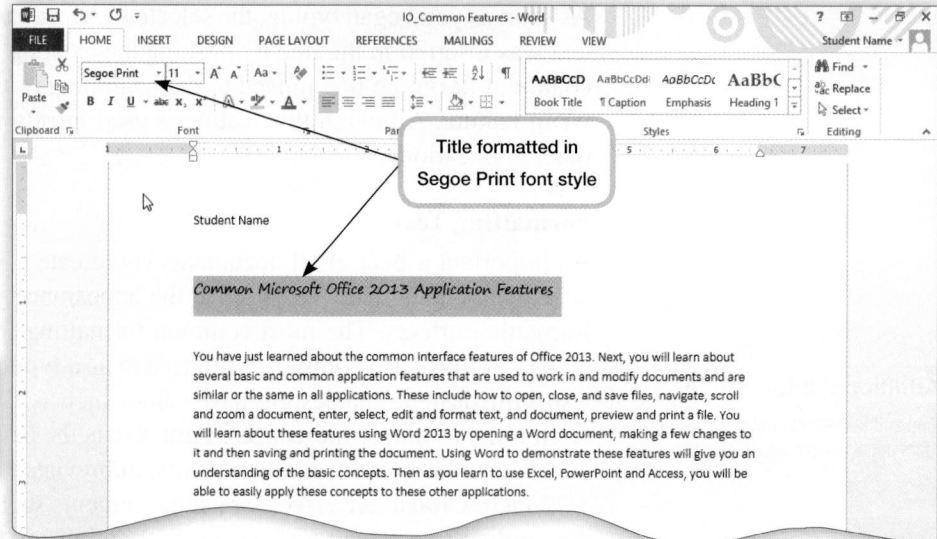

Figure 34

The title appears in the selected font and the name of the font used in the selection is displayed in the Segoe Print Font button. Next you want to increase the font size. The current (default) font size of 11 is displayed in the 11 Font Size button. You will increase the font size to 16 points.

3

- Open the 11 Font Size drop-down menu in the Font group of the Home tab.

- Point to several different font sizes to see the Live Preview.

- Click 16 to choose it.

Another Method

The keyboard shortcut is Ctrl + Shift + P.

Your screen should be similar to Figure 35

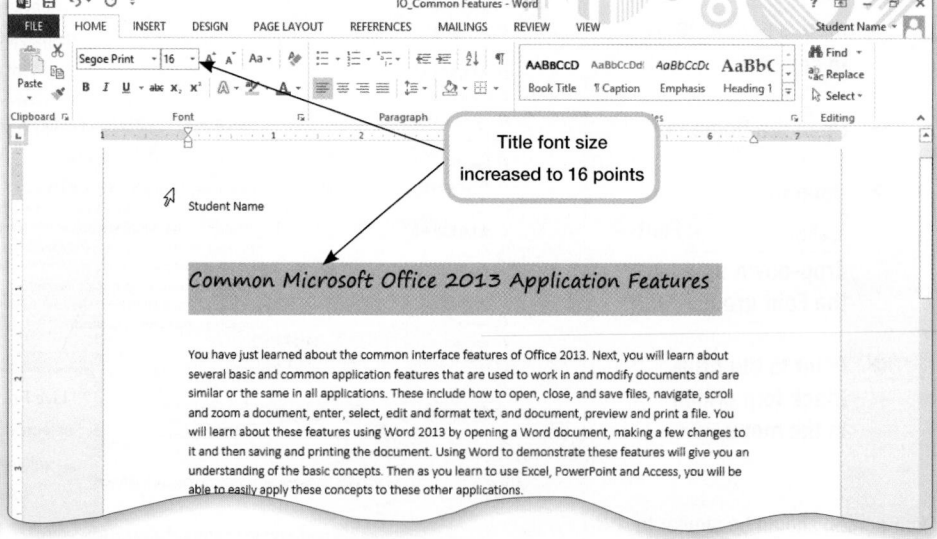

Figure 35

Touch Tip

With a touch device, tap on the selected text, then tap on the formatting option.

Now the title stands out much more from the other text in the document. Next you will use the Mini toolbar to add formatting to other areas of the document. As you saw earlier, the Mini toolbar appears automatically when you select text. Initially the Mini toolbar appears dimmed (semi-transparent) so that it does not interfere with what you are doing, but it changes to solid when you point at it. It displays command buttons for often-used commands from the Font and Paragraph groups that are used to format a document.

4

- Select the line "Common Features" and point to the Mini toolbar.

- Click 11 ▾ Font Size and choose 14.

- Click **B** Bold.

- Click *I* Italic.

- Click U̲ Underline.

Your screen should be similar to Figure 36

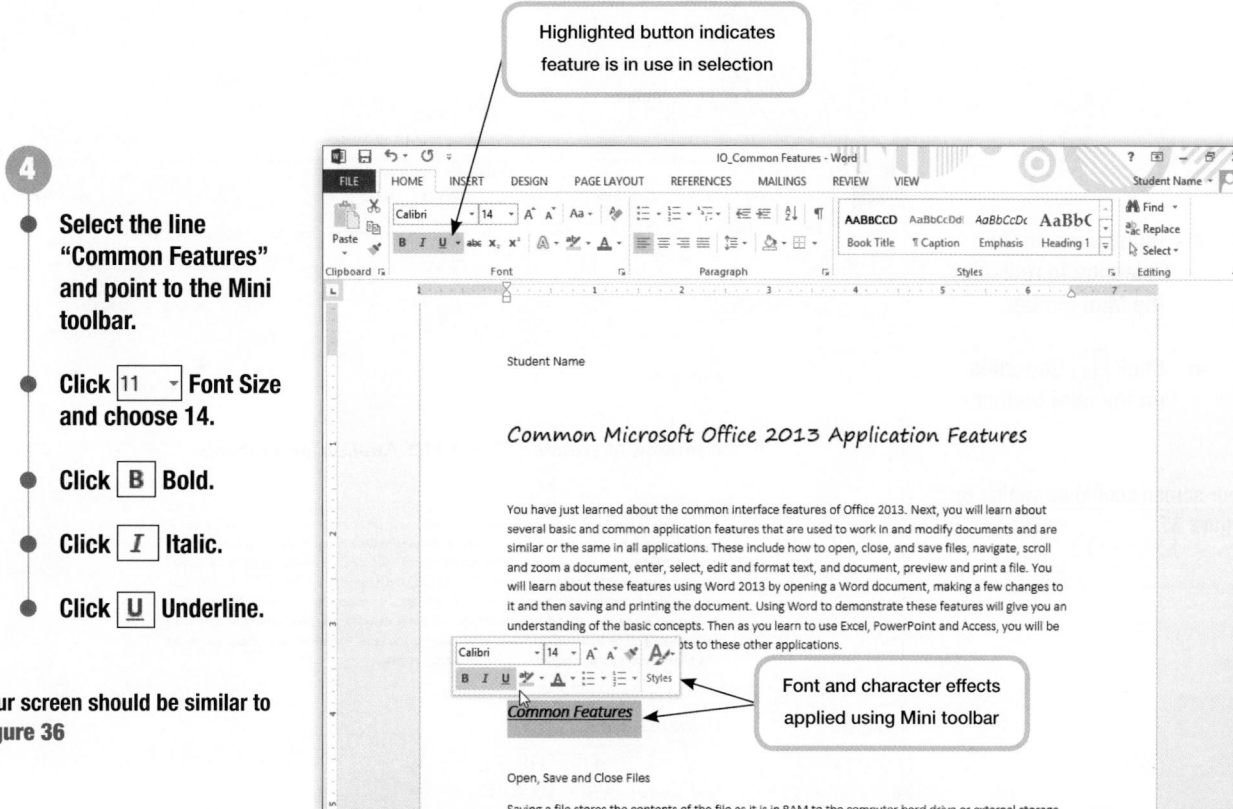

Highlighted button indicates feature is in use in selection

Font and character effects applied using Mini toolbar

Figure 36

The increase in font size as well as the text effects makes this topic heading much more prominent. Notice the command button for each selected effect is highlighted, indicating the feature is in use in the selection.

Using the Mini toolbar is particularly useful when the Home tab is closed because you do not need to reopen the Home tab to access the commands. It remains available until you clear the selection or press Esc. If you do nothing with a selection for a while, the Mini toolbar will disappear. To redisplay it simply right-click on the selection again. This will also open the context menu.

You will remove the underline effect from the selection next.

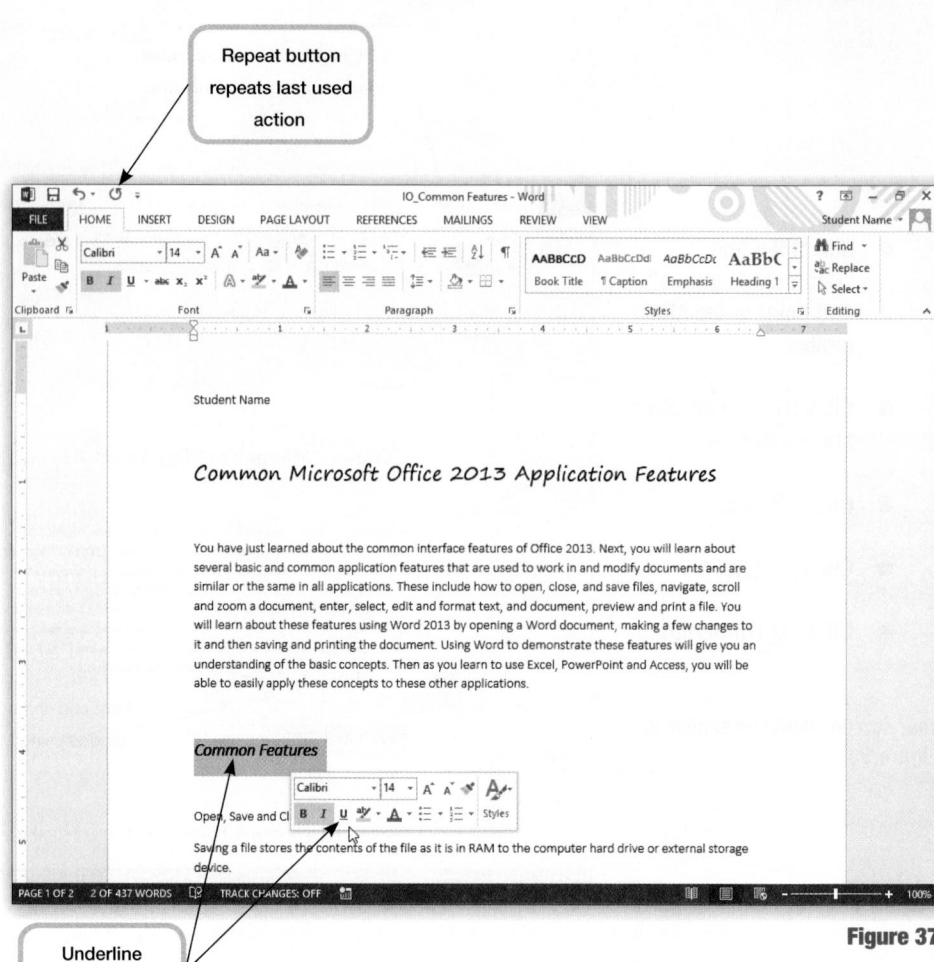

Repeat button repeats last used action

5

● **Right-click on the selection to redisplay the Mini toolbar.**

● **Click U Underline on the Mini toolbar.**

Your screen should be similar to Figure 37

Underline effect removed

Figure 37

The context menu and Mini toolbar appeared when you right-clicked the selection. The context menu displayed a variety of commands that are quicker to access than locating the command on the Ribbon. The commands that appear on this menu change depending on what you are doing at the time. The context menu disappeared after you made a selection from the Mini toolbar. Both the Mini toolbar and context menus are designed to make it more efficient to execute commands.

Also notice that the ⟳ Redo button in the Quick Access Toolbar has changed to a ⟳ Repeat button. This feature allows you to quickly repeat the last-used command at another location in the document.

Undoing and Redoing Editing Changes

Instead of reselecting the U Underline command to remove the underline effect, you could have used ↺ Undo to reverse your last action or command. You will use this feature to restore the underline (your last action).

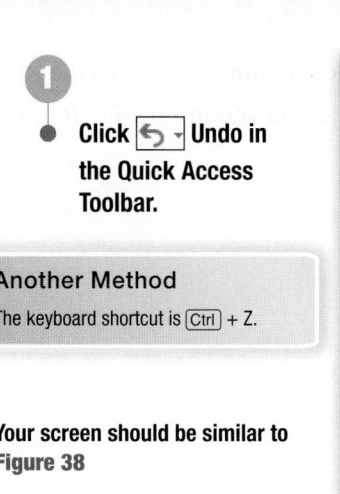

1

Click ↺ Undo in the Quick Access Toolbar.

Another Method

The keyboard shortcut is Ctrl + Z.

Your screen should be similar to Figure 38

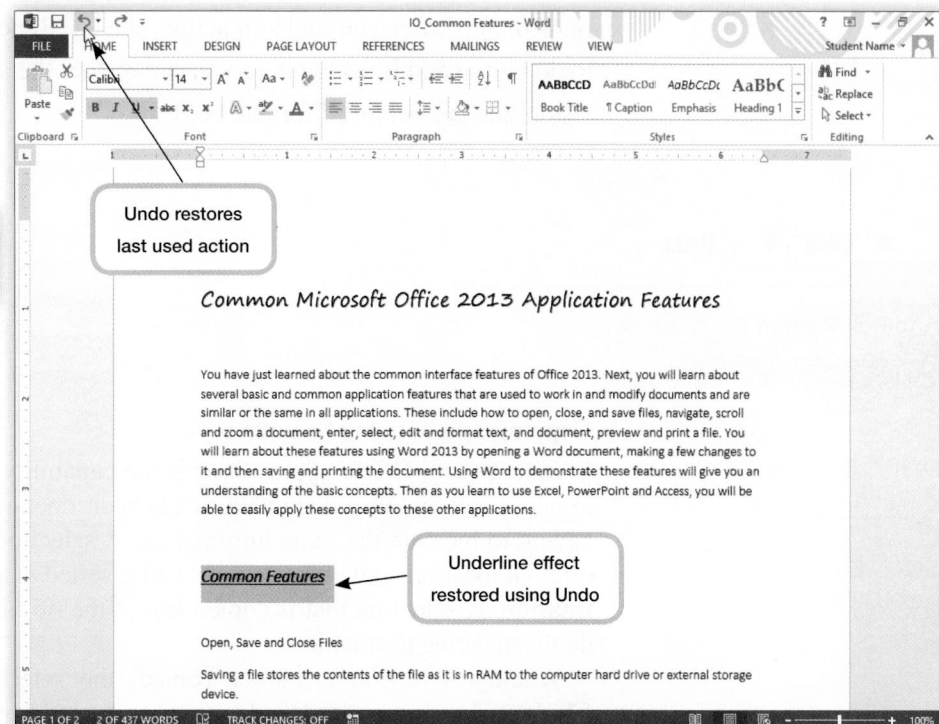

Undo restores last used action

Underline effect restored using Undo

Figure 38

Undo reversed the last action and the underline formatting effect was restored. Notice that the ↺ button includes a drop-down menu button. Clicking this button displays a menu of the most recent actions that can be reversed, with the most-recent action at the top of the menu. When you select an action from the drop-down menu, you also undo all actions above it in the menu.

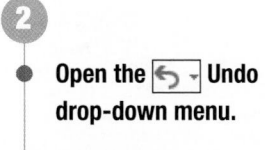

2

Open the ↺ Undo drop-down menu.

Choose Bold.

Your screen should be similar to Figure 39

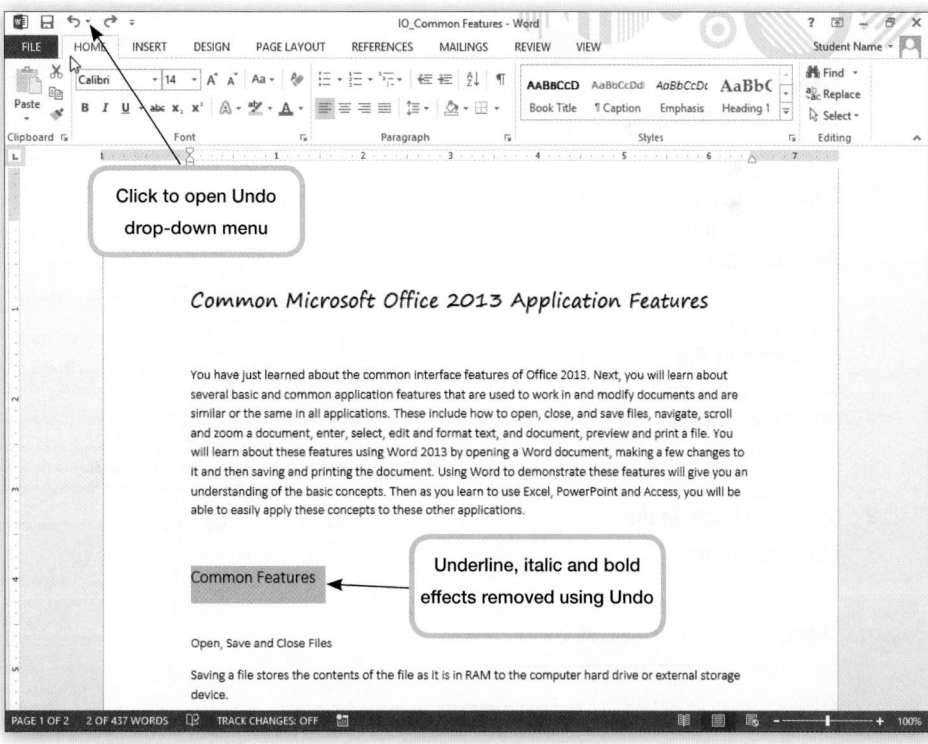

Click to open Undo drop-down menu

Underline, italic and bold effects removed using Undo

Figure 39

The underline, italic, and bold effects were all removed.

Immediately after you undo an action, the  Repeat button changes to the ⟳ ⫶ Redo button and is available so you can restore the action you just undid. You will restore the last-removed format, bold.

3
● Click ⟳ ⫶ Redo.

Another Method
The keyboard shortcut is Ctrl + Y.

Copying and Moving Selections

Common to all Office applications is the capability to **copy** and **move** selections to new locations in a document or between documents, saving you time by not having to recreate the same information. A selection that is moved is cut from its original location, called the **source**, and inserted at a new location, called the **destination**. A selection that is copied leaves the original in the source and inserts a duplicate at the destination.

When a selection is cut or copied, the selection is stored in the system **Clipboard**, a temporary Windows storage area in memory. It is also stored in the **Office Clipboard**. The system Clipboard holds only the last cut or copied item, whereas the Office Clipboard can store up to 24 items that have been cut or copied. This feature allows you to insert multiple items from various Office documents and paste all or part of the collection of items into another document.

First, you will copy the text "Office 2013" to two other locations in the first paragraph.

Additional Information
You will learn about using the Office Clipboard in the individual application texts.

1
● Select the text "Office 2013" in the title line.

● Click 📋 Copy in the Clipboard group of the Home tab.

● Move to the beginning of the word "applications" (third line of first paragraph).

● Click 📋 Paste in the Clipboard group.

Another Method
The Copy keyboard shortcut is Ctrl + C.
The Paste keyboard shortcut is Ctrl + V.

Your screen should be similar to Figure 40

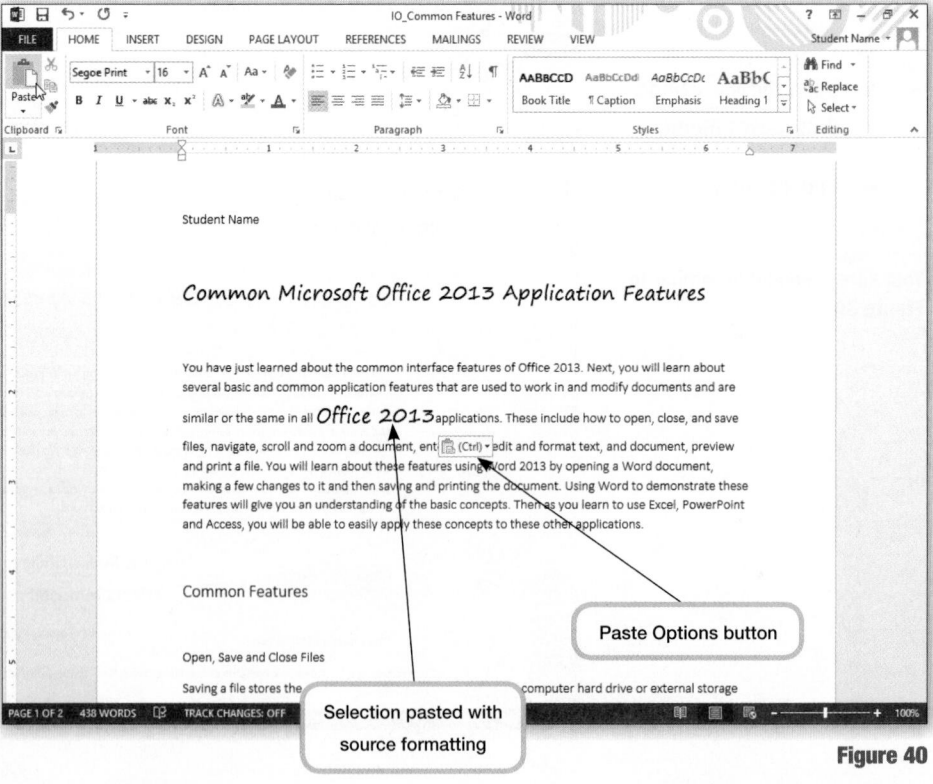

Figure 40

The copied selection is inserted at the location you specified with the same formatting as it has in the title. The 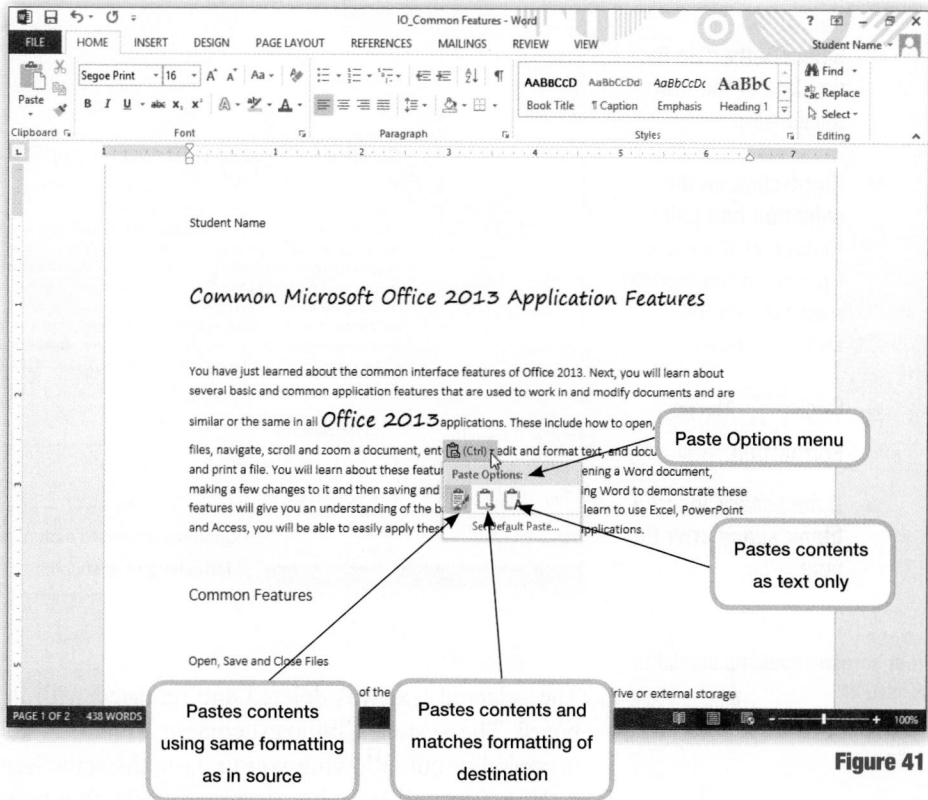 (Ctrl) ▾ Paste Options button appears automatically whenever a selection is pasted. It is used to control the format of the pasted item.

2

● Click the ▢ (Ctrl) ▾ Paste Options button.

● If necessary, insert a blank space after the year.

Your screen should be similar to Figure 41

Figure 41

Paste Options menu

Pastes contents as text only

Pastes contents using same formatting as in source

Pastes contents and matches formatting of destination

Additional Information

The Paste Options vary with the different applications. For example, Excel has 14 different Paste Options. The Paste Options feature is not available in Access and Paste Preview is not available in Excel.

The Paste Options are used to specify whether to insert the item with the same formatting that it had in the source, to change it to the formatting of the surrounding destination text, or to insert text only (from a selection that is a combination of text and graphics). The default as you have seen is to keep the formatting from the source. You want to change it to the formatting of the surrounding text. As you point to a Paste Options button, a **Paste Preview** will show how that option will affect the selection. Then you will copy it again to a second location.

③

- Click 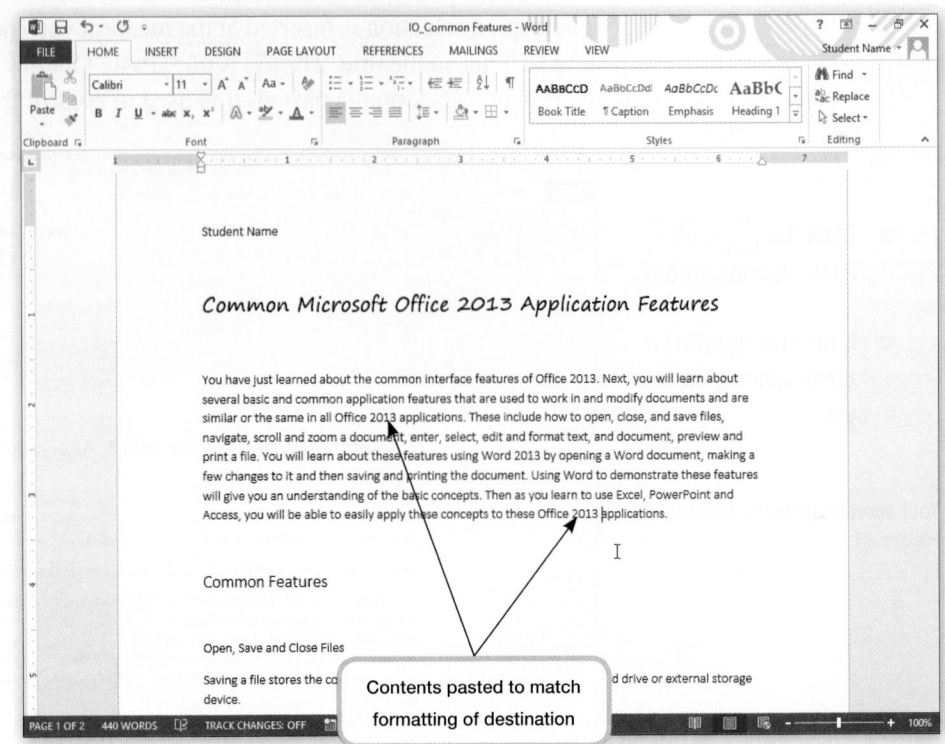 Merge Formatting.

- Select "other" in the last line of the first paragraph.

- Right-click on the selection and point to each of the Paste Options in the context menu to see the Paste Preview.

- Click Merge Formatting.

- If necessary, insert a blank space after the year.

Figure 42

Your screen should be similar to Figure 42

The selected text was deleted and replaced with the contents of the system Clipboard. The system Clipboard contents remain in the Clipboard until another item is copied or cut, allowing you to paste the same item multiple times.

Now you will learn how to move a selection by rearranging several lines of text in the description of common features. You want to move the last sentence in the document, beginning with "Opening a file", to the top of the list. The Cut and Paste commands in the Clipboard group of the Home tab are used to move selections.

4
- Scroll to see the end of the document.

- Double-click in the left margin next to the last sentence in the document to select it.

- Click ✂ **Cut** in the **Clipboard group.**

Your screen should be similar to Figure 43

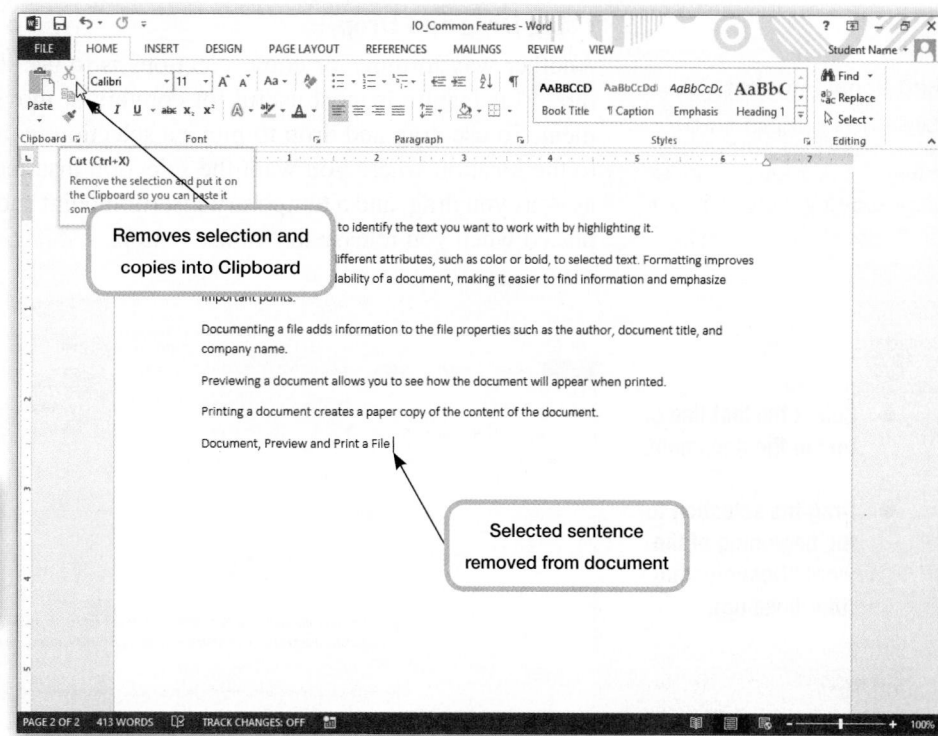

Figure 43

The selected paragraph is removed from the source and copied to the Clipboard. Next, you need to move the cursor to the location where the text will be inserted and paste the text into the document from the Clipboard.

5
- Move to the beginning of the word "Saving" at the top of the Common Features list.

- Press Ctrl + V.

Your screen should be similar to Figure 44

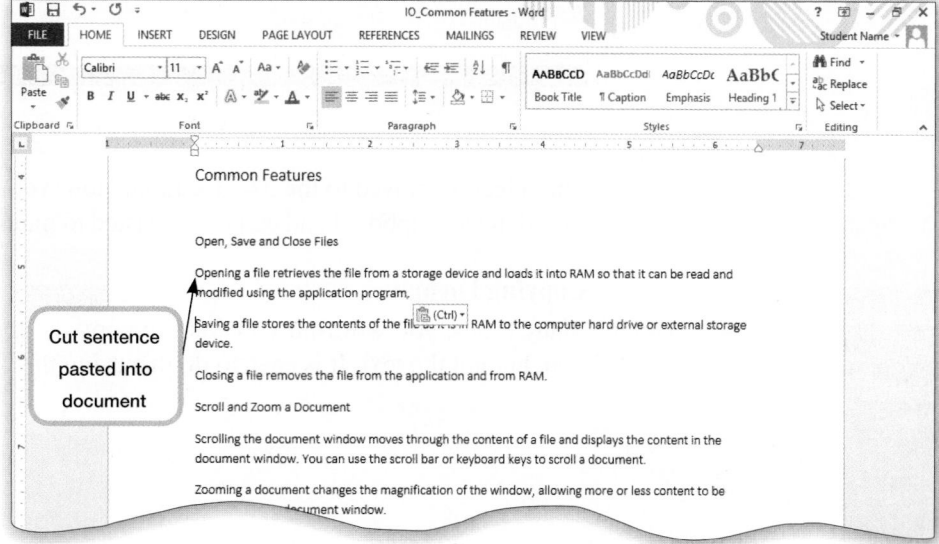

Figure 44

The cut sentence is reentered into the document at the cursor location. That was much quicker than retyping the whole sentence! Because the source has the same formatting as the text at the destination, the default setting to keep the source formatting is appropriate.

Using Drag and Drop

Another way to move or copy selections is to use the drag-and-drop editing feature. This feature is most useful for copying or moving short distances in a document. To use drag and drop to move a selection, point to the selection and drag it to the location where you want the selection inserted. The mouse pointer appears as 🔖 as you drag, and a temporary insertion point shows you where the text will be placed when you release the mouse button.

1

- **Select the last line of text in the document.**

- **Drag the selection to the beginning of the word "Documenting" (four lines up).**

Touch Tip

With a touch device, tap in the selection and then slide or drag the selection to move it.

Your screen should be similar to Figure 45

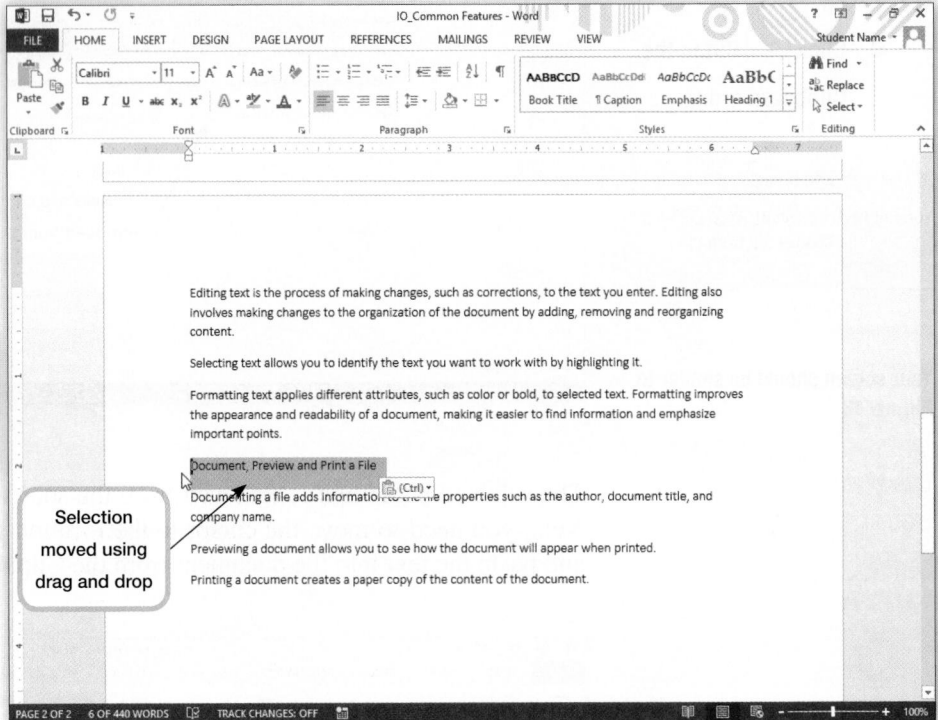

Figure 45

The selection moved to the new location. However, the selection is not copied and stored in the Clipboard and cannot be pasted to multiple locations in the document.

Copying Formats

Many times, you will find you want to copy the formats associated with a selection, but not the text. It is easy to do this using the **Format Painter** tool.

1

- Apply bold and italic effects and increase the font size to 14 for the currently selected text.

- Click [🖌] **Format Painter** in the Clipboard group.

- Scroll the document up and select the topic line of text "Enter, Select, Edit and Format text".

Your screen should be similar to Figure 46

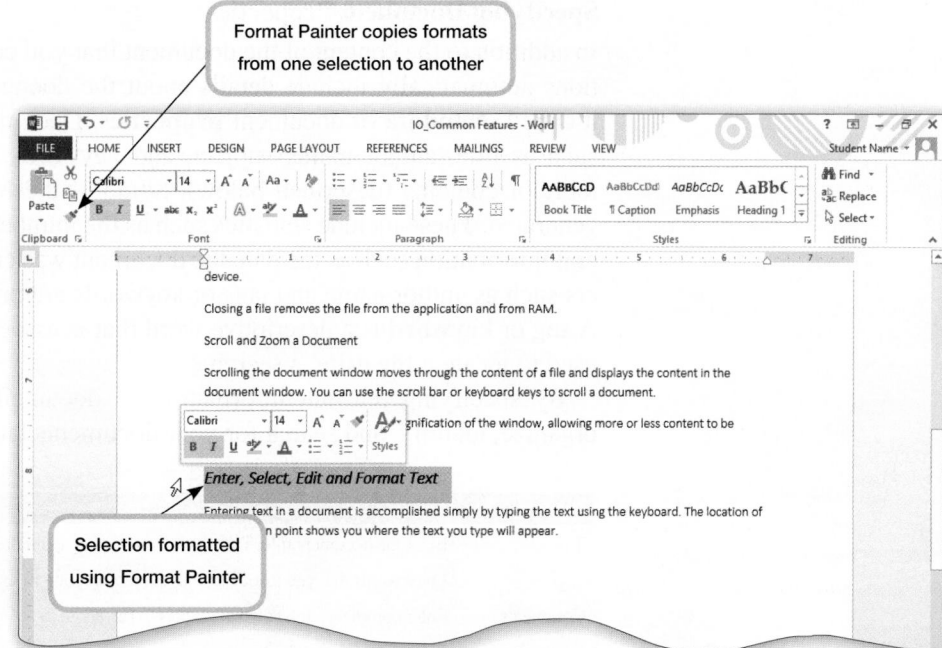

Format Painter copies formats from one selection to another

Selection formatted using Format Painter

Figure 46

The text you selected is formatted using the same formats. This feature is especially helpful when you want to copy multiple formats at one time. Next, you want to format the other topic heads in the Common Features list using the same formats. To do this, you can make the Format Painter "sticky" so that it can be used to copy the format multiple times in succession.

2

- Double-click [🖌] **Format Painter** in the Clipboard group.

- Select the remaining two topic heads in the Common Features list:

  Scroll and Zoom a Document

  Open, Save and Close Files

- Click [🖌] **Format Painter** to turn off this feature.

- Clear the selection.

Your screen should be similar to Figure 47

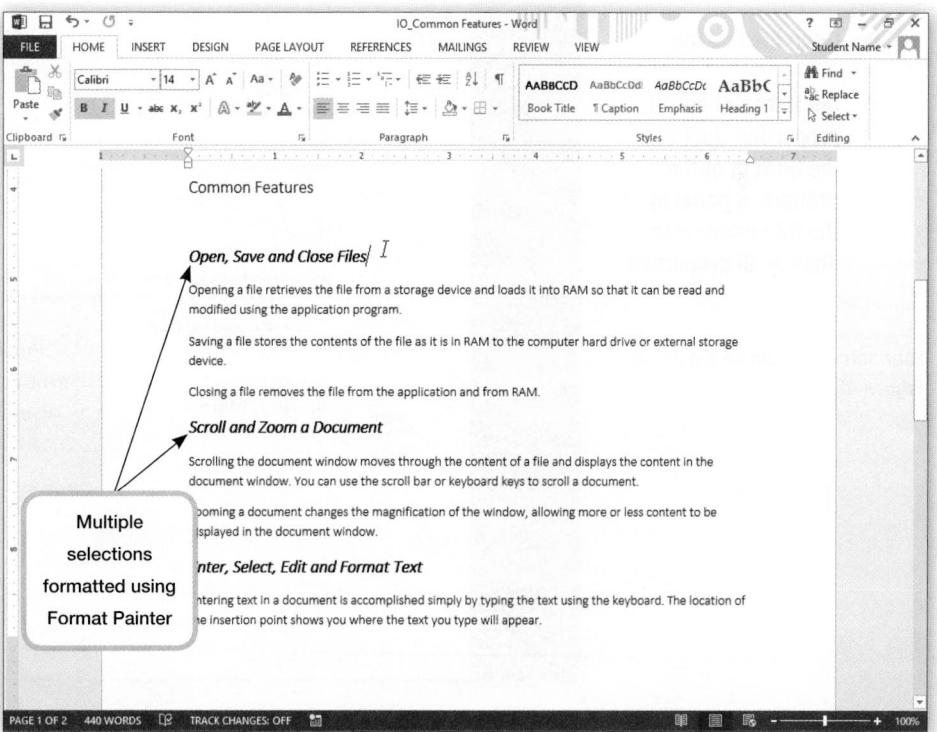

Multiple selections formatted using Format Painter

Figure 47

Specifying Document Properties

In addition to the content of the document that you create, all Office 2013 applications automatically include details about the document that describe or identify it called **metadata** or document **properties**. Document properties include details such as title, author name, subject, and keywords that identify the document's topic or contents (described below). Some of these properties are automatically generated. These include statistics such as the number of words in the file and general information such as the date the document was created and last modified. Others such as author name and tags or keywords are properties that you can specify. A **tag** or **keyword** is a descriptive word that is associated with the file and can be used to locate a file using a search.

By specifying relevant information as document properties, you can easily organize, identify, and search for your documents later.

Property	Action
Title	Enter the document title. This title can be longer and more descriptive than the file name.
Tags	Enter words that you associate with the presentation to make it easier to find using search tools.
Comments	Enter comments that you want others to see about the content of the document.
Categories	Enter the name of a higher-level category under which you can group similar types of presentations.
Author	Enter the name of the presentation's author. By default this is the name entered when the application was installed.

You will look at the document properties that are automatically included and add documentation to identify you as the author, and specify a document title and keywords to describe the document.

1

● **Open the File tab.**

● **Click the "Show all properties" link at the bottom of the Properties panel in the Info window to display all properties.**

Your screen should be similar to Figure 48

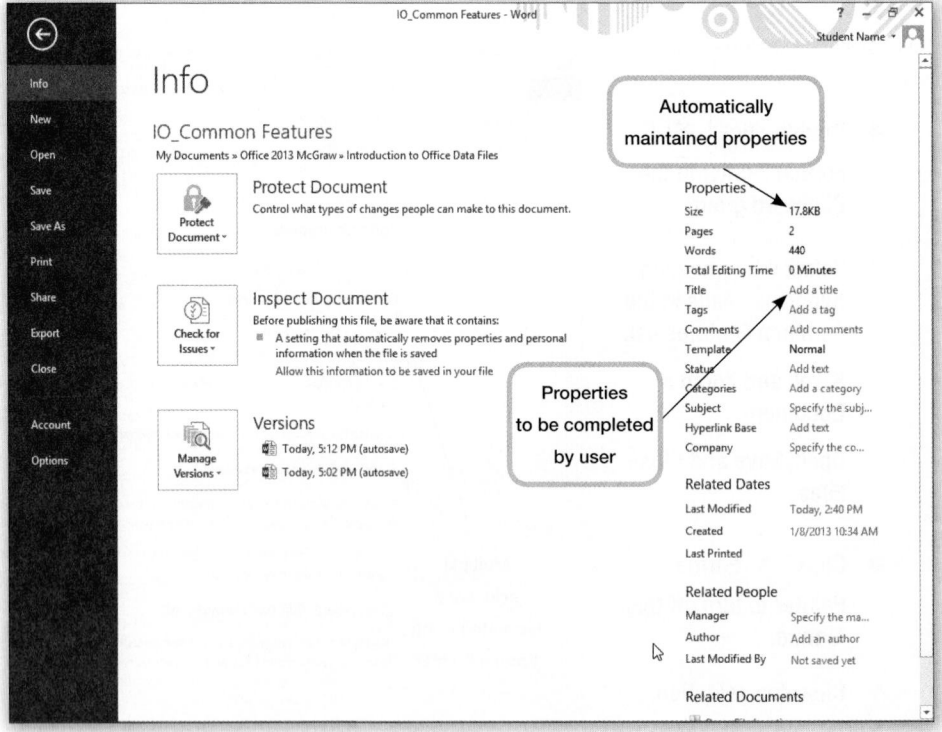

Figure 48

The Properties panel in the right section of the Info tab is divided into four groups and displays the properties associated with the document. Properties such as the document size, number of words, and number of pages are automatically maintained. Others such as the title and tag properties are blank waiting for you to specify your own information.

You will add a title, a tag, and your name as the author name.

- Click in the Title text box and type **Common Office Features**

- In the same manner, enter **common, features, interface** as the tags.

- Click in the Add an Author text box and enter your name.

- If necessary, click outside the search results box to clear it.

Your screen should be similar to Figure 49

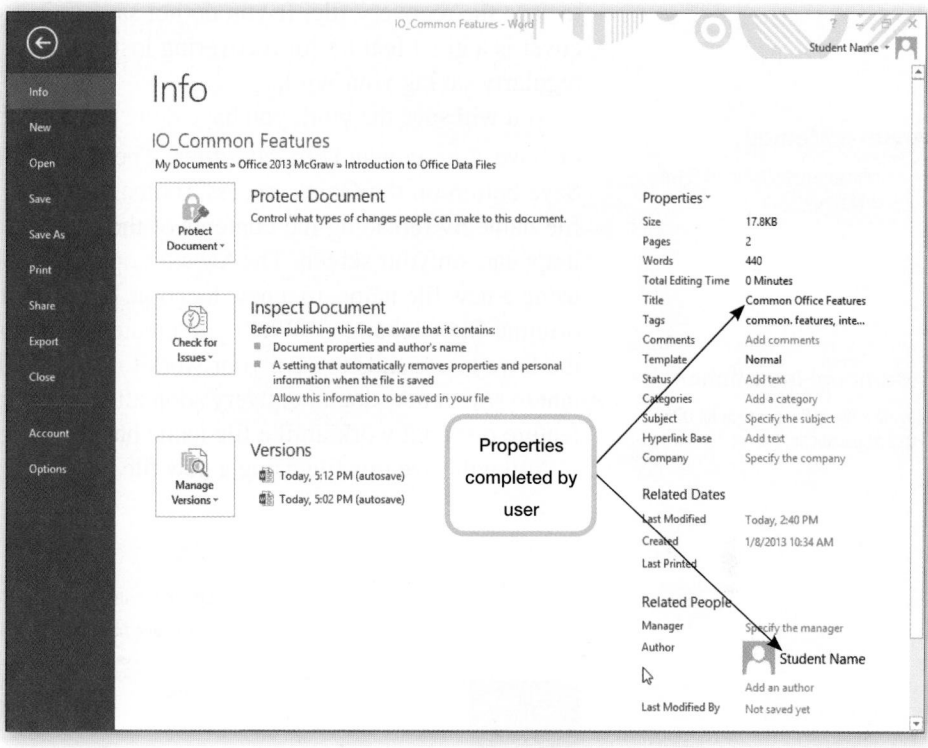

Figure 49

Once the document properties are specified, you can use them to identify and locate documents. You also can use the automatically updated properties for the same purpose. For example, you can search for all files created by a specified user or on a certain date.

Saving a File

As you enter and edit text to create a document in Word, Excel, and PowerPoint, the changes you make are immediately displayed onscreen and are stored in your computer's memory. However, they are not permanently stored until you save your work to a file on a disk. After a document has been saved as a file, it can be closed and opened again at a later time to be edited further. Unlike Word, Excel, and PowerPoint, where you start work on a new document and then save your changes, Access requires that you name the new database file first and create a table for your data. Then, it saves your changes to the data automatically as you work. This allows multiple users to have access to the most up-to-date data at all times.

Additional Information

You can specify different AutoRecover settings by choosing Options/Save in the Backstage and specifying the AutoRecover settings of your choice.

As a backup against the accidental loss of work from power failure or other mishap, Word, Excel, and PowerPoint include an AutoRecover feature. When this feature is on, as you work you may see a pulsing disk icon briefly appear in the status bar. This icon indicates that the program is saving your work to a temporary recovery file. The time interval between automatic saving can be set to any period you specify; the default is every 10 minutes. After a problem has occurred, when you restart the program, the recovery file is automatically opened containing all changes you made up to the last time it was saved by AutoRecover. You then need to save the recovery file. If you do not save it, it is deleted when closed. AutoRecover is a great feature for recovering lost work but should not be used in place of regularly saving your work.

Another Method

The keyboard shortcut for the Save command is Ctrl + S.

You will save the work you have done so far on the document. You use the Save or Save As commands to save files. The Save option on the File tab or the 💾 Save button on the Quick Access Toolbar will save the active file using the same file name by replacing the contents of the existing disk file with the document as it appears on your screen. The Save As option on the File tab is used to save a file using a new file name, to a new location, or as a different file type. This leaves the original file unchanged. When you create a new document, you can use either of the Save commands to save your work to a file on the disk. It is especially important to save a new document very soon after you create it because the AutoRecover feature does not work until a file name has been specified.

Additional Information

Saving a file is the same in all Office 2013 applications, except Access.

You will save this file using a new file name to your solution file location.

1

- **Click Save As in the sidebar of the Backstage.**

Your screen should be similar to Figure 50

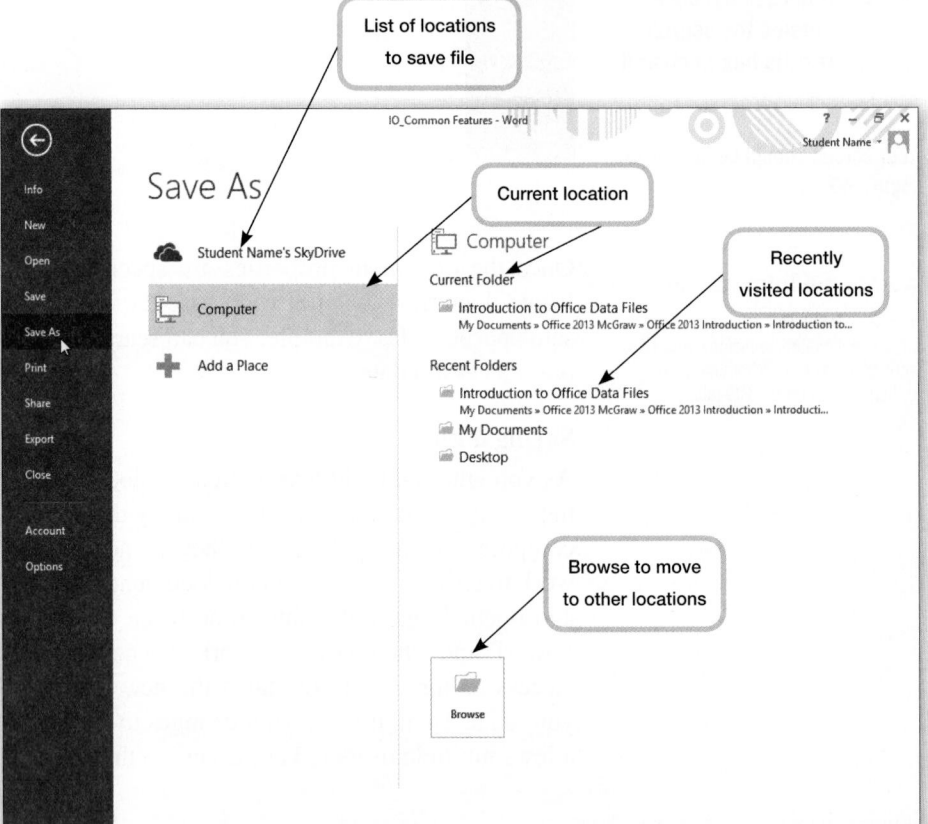

Figure 50

The Save As window is displayed in which you select the location where you want to save the file. Just as in the Open window, the location may be the hard drive of your computer, an external storage device, a local network, or in the cloud on SkyDrive or SharePoint. The location where the file was opened is the current location in the list. A list of current and recent folders is displayed in the right section. If the current folder location is where you want to save the file, clicking on the folder immediately opens it. If you need to open a different folder, click on it in the Recent Folders list or click [Browse] to locate the folder.

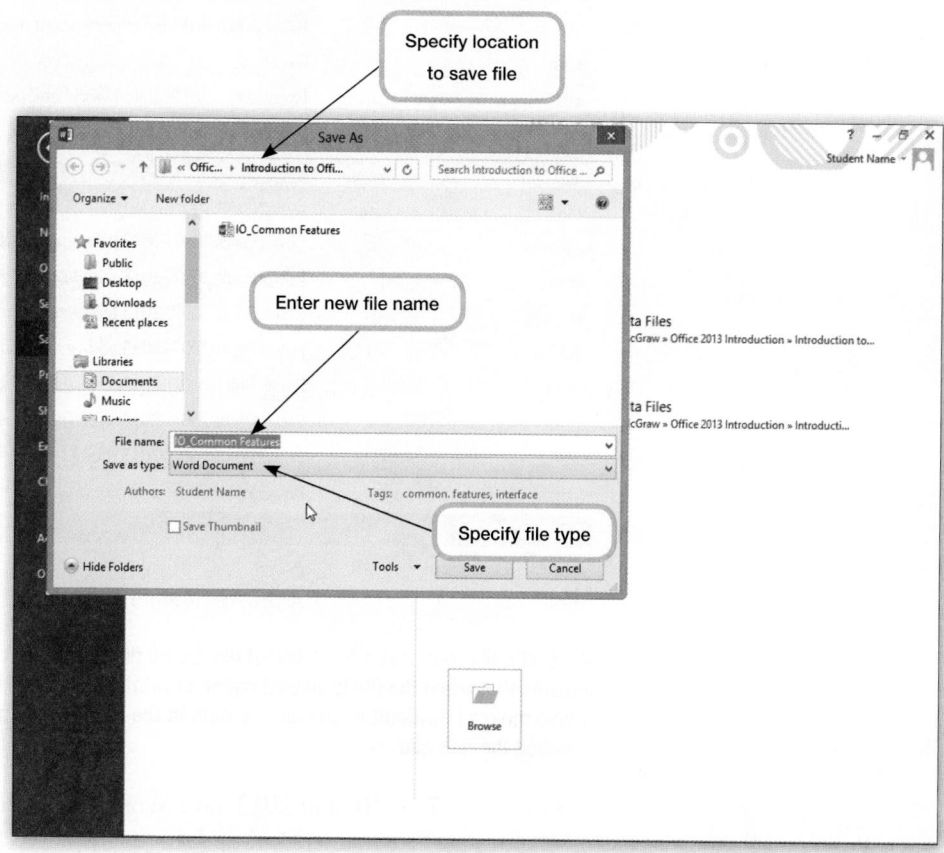

2

- If necessary, select a different location from the list of locations.

- Select the folder from the Current Folder or Recent Folders list or click [Browse].

Your screen should be similar to Figure 51

Figure 51

Having Trouble?

Do not be concerned if your Save As dialog box Save location and file details such as the size, type, and date modified are different. These features are determined by the Folder and dialog box settings on your computer.

Additional Information

You can set a default location to save a file by choosing Options/Save in the Backstage and specifying the default save location.

The Save As dialog box is used to specify the location where you will save the file and the file name. The Address bar displays the current folder location and the File name text box displays the name of the open file. The file name is highlighted, ready for you to enter a new file name. The Save as type box displays "Word Document" as the default format in which the file will be saved. Word 2013 documents are automatically saved using the file extension .docx. The file type you select determines the file extension that will be automatically added to the file name when the file is saved. The file types and extensions for the four Office 2013 applications are described in the following table.

Extensions	File Type
Word 2013	
.docx	Word 2007–2013 document without macros or code
.dotx	Word 2007–2013 template without macros or code
.docm	Word 2007–2013 document that could contain macros or code
.xps	Word 2007–2013 shared document (see Note)
.doc	Word 95–2003 document
Excel 2013	
.xlsx	Excel 2007–2013 default workbook without macros or code
.xlsm	Excel 2007–2013 default workbook that could contain macros
.xltx	Excel 2007–2013 template without macros
.xltm	Excel 2007–2013 template that could contain macros
.xps	Excel 2007–2013 shared workbook (see Note)
.xls	Excel 97–2003 workbook
PowerPoint 2013	
.pptx	PowerPoint 2007–2013 default presentation format
.pptm	PowerPoint 2007–2013 presentation with macros
.potx	PowerPoint 2007–2013 template without macros
.potm	PowerPoint 2007–2013 template that may contain macros
.ppam	PowerPoint 2007–2013 add-in that contains macros
.ppsx	PowerPoint 2007–2013 slide show without macros
.ppsm	PowerPoint 2007–2013 slide show that may contain macros
.thmx	PowerPoint 2007–2013 theme
.ppt	PowerPoint 2003 or earlier presentation
Access 2013	
.accdb	Access 2007–2013 database
.mdb	Access 2003 or earlier database

NOTE XPS file format is a fixed-layout electronic file format that preserves document formatting and ensures that when the file is viewed online or printed, it retains exactly the format that you intended. It also makes it difficult to change the data in the file. To save as an XPS file format, you must have installed the free add-in.

Office 2007, 2010, and 2013 save Word, Excel, and PowerPoint files using the XML format (Extensible Markup Language) and a four-letter file extension. This format makes your documents safer by separating files that contain macros (small programs in a document that automate tasks) to make it easier for a virus checker to identify and block unwanted code or macros that could be dangerous to your computer. It also makes file sizes smaller by compressing the content upon saving and makes files less susceptible to damage. In addition, XML format makes it easier to open documents created with an Office application using another application.

Previous versions of Word, Excel, and PowerPoint did not use XML and had a three-letter file extension. If you plan to share a file with someone using an Office 2003 or earlier version, you can save the document using the three-letter file type; however, some features may be lost. Otherwise, if you save it as a four-letter file type, the recipient may not be able to view all features. There also may be loss of features for users of Office 2007 (even though it has an XML file type) because the older version does not support several of the new features in Office 2013. Office 2013 includes a feature that checks for compatibility with previous versions and advises you what features in the document may be lost if opened by an Office 2007 user or if the document is saved in the 2003 format.

If you have an Office Access 2007 (.accdb) database that you want to save in an earlier Access file format (.mdb), you can do so as long as your .accdb database

Additional Information

Depending upon your Office 2013 setup, a prompt to check for compatibility may appear automatically when you save a file.

Additional Information

Using Save As in Access creates a copy of the open database file and then opens the copy. Access automatically closes the original database.

does not contain any multivalued lookup fields, offline data, or attachments. This is because older versions of Access do not support these new features. If you try to convert an .accdb database containing any of these elements to an .mdb file format, Access displays an error message.

First you may need to change the location to the location where the file will be saved. The same procedures you used to specify a location to open a file are used to specify the location to save a file. Then, you will change the file name to Common Features using the default Word document type (.docx).

3

- If necessary, select the location where you save your solution files.

- If necessary, drag in the File Name text box to highlight the existing file name.

- Type **Common Features**

- Click [Save].

Your screen should be similar to Figure 52

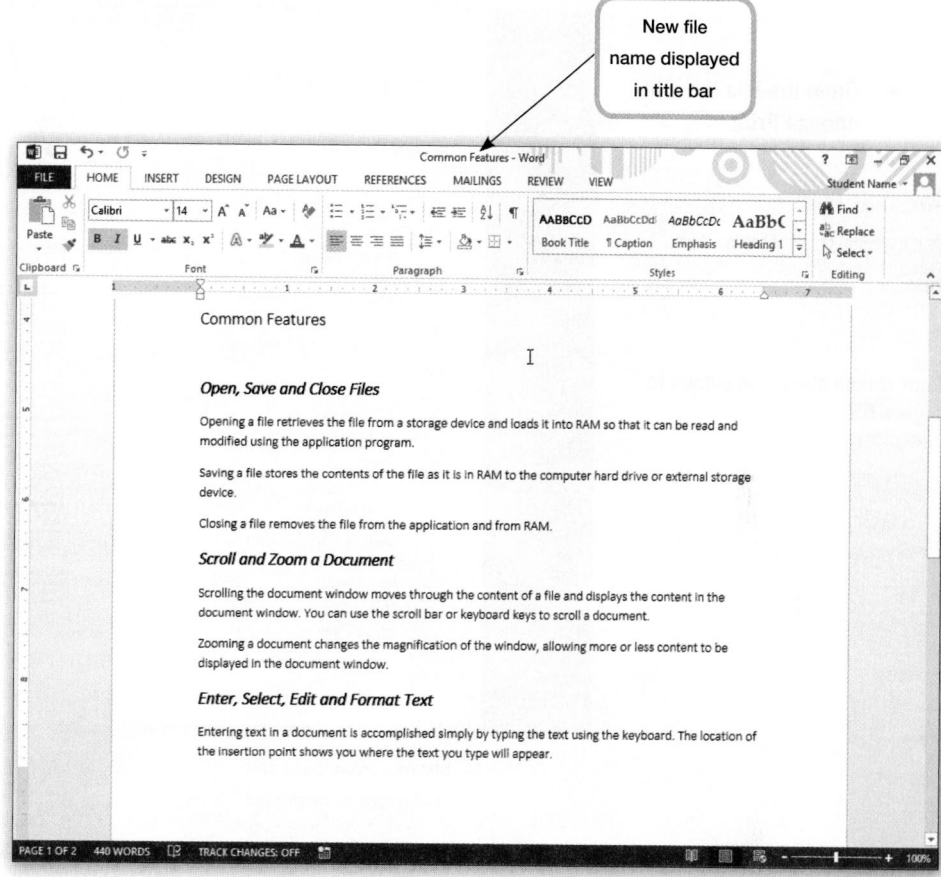

New file name displayed in title bar

Figure 52

The document is saved as Common Features.docx at the location you selected, and the new file name is displayed in the Word application window title bar. Depending upon your Windows setup, the file extension also may be displayed in the title bar.

Printing a Document

Once a document appears how you want, you may want to print a hard copy for your own reference or to give to others. All Office 2013 applications include the capability to print and have similar options. You will print this document next.

- **Open the File tab and choose Print.**

Another Method

The keyboard shortcut for the Print command is Ctrl + P.

Your screen should be similar to Figure 53

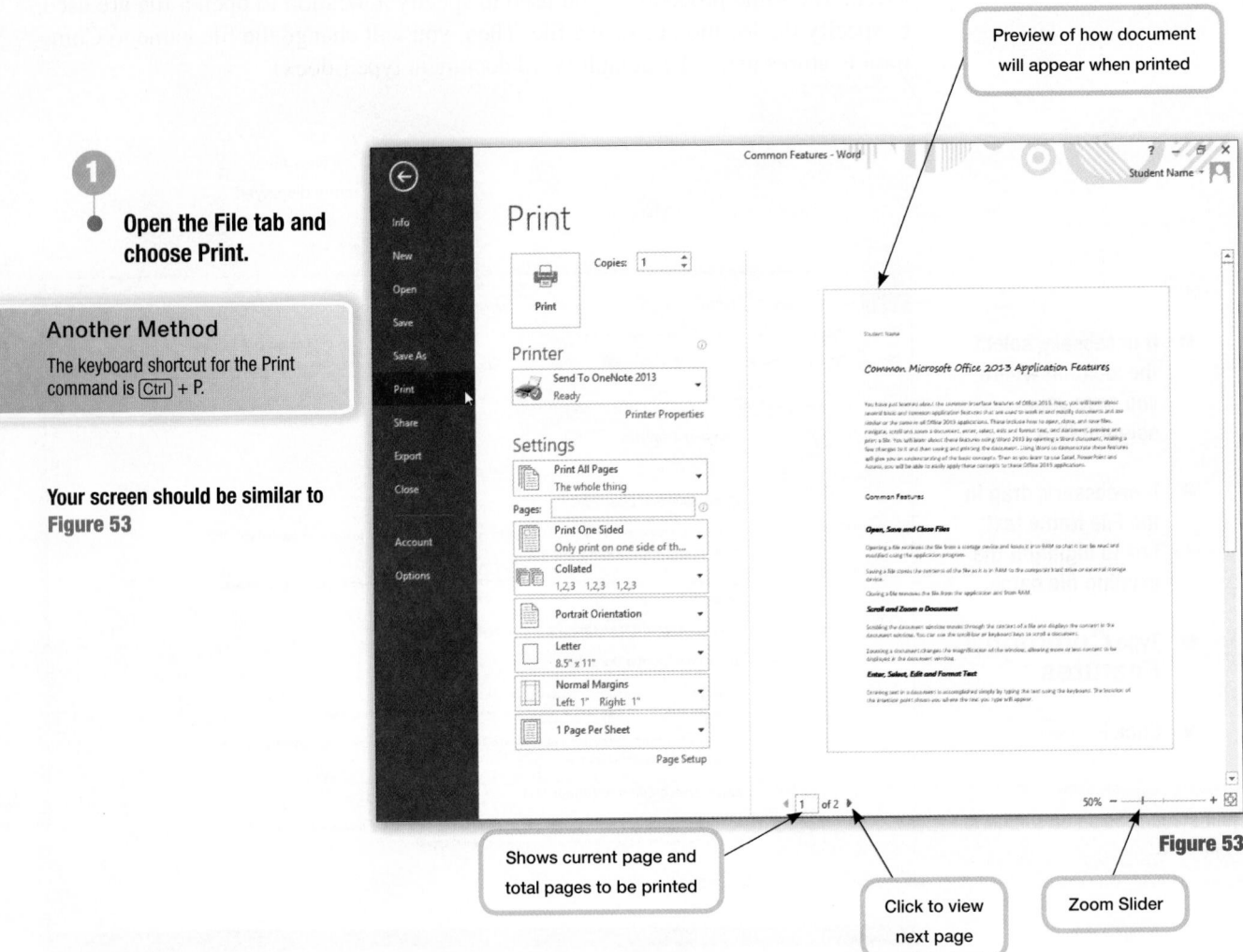

Preview of how document will appear when printed

Shows current page and total pages to be printed

Click to view next page

Zoom Slider

Figure 53

The right section of the Print page displays a preview of the current page of your document. To save time and unnecessary printing and paper waste, it is always a good idea to preview each page of your document before printing. Notice below the preview, the page scroll box shows the page number of the page you are currently viewing and the total number of pages. The scroll buttons on either side are used to scroll to the next and previous pages. Additionally, a Zoom Slider is available to adjust the size of the preview.

- Click ▶ to view the second page of the document.

- Increase the zoom to 70%.

Your screen should be similar to Figure 54

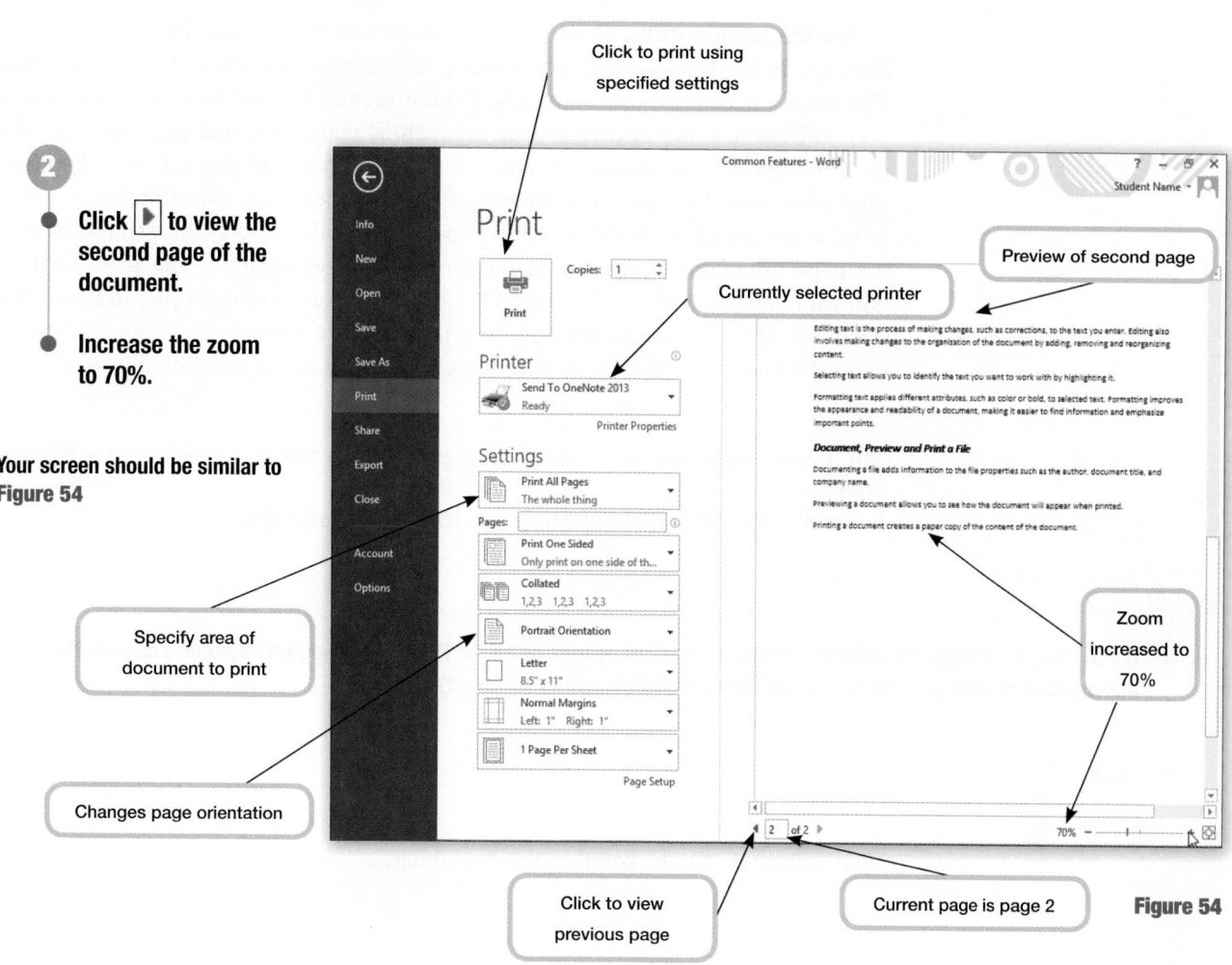

Click to print using specified settings

Preview of second page

Currently selected printer

Specify area of document to print

Changes page orientation

Zoom increased to 70%

Click to view previous page

Current page is page 2

Figure 54

If you see any changes you want to make to the document, you would need to close the File tab and make the changes. If the document looks good, you are ready to print.

The left section of the Print page is divided into three areas: Print, Printer, and Settings. In the Print section you specify the number of copies you want printed. The default is to print one copy. The Printer section is used to specify the printer you will use and the printer properties such as paper size and print quality. The name of the default printer on your computer appears in the list box. The Settings area is used to specify what part of the document you want to print, whether to print on one or both sides of the paper or to collate (sort) the printed output, the page orientation, paper size, margins, and sheet settings. The print settings will vary slightly with the different Office applications. For example, in Excel, the options to specify what to print are to print the entire worksheet, entire workbook, or a selection. The differences will be demonstrated in the individual labs.

NOTE Please consult your instructor for printing procedures that may differ from the following directions.

You will print the document using the default print settings.

3

- If you need to change the selected printer to another printer, open the Printer drop-down menu and choose the appropriate printer (your instructor will tell you which printer to select).

- Click  .

Your printer should be printing the document.

Closing a File

Finally, you want to close the document.

Open the File tab and choose Close.

Another Method

The keyboard shortcut is Ctrl + F4.

Your screen should be similar to Figure 55

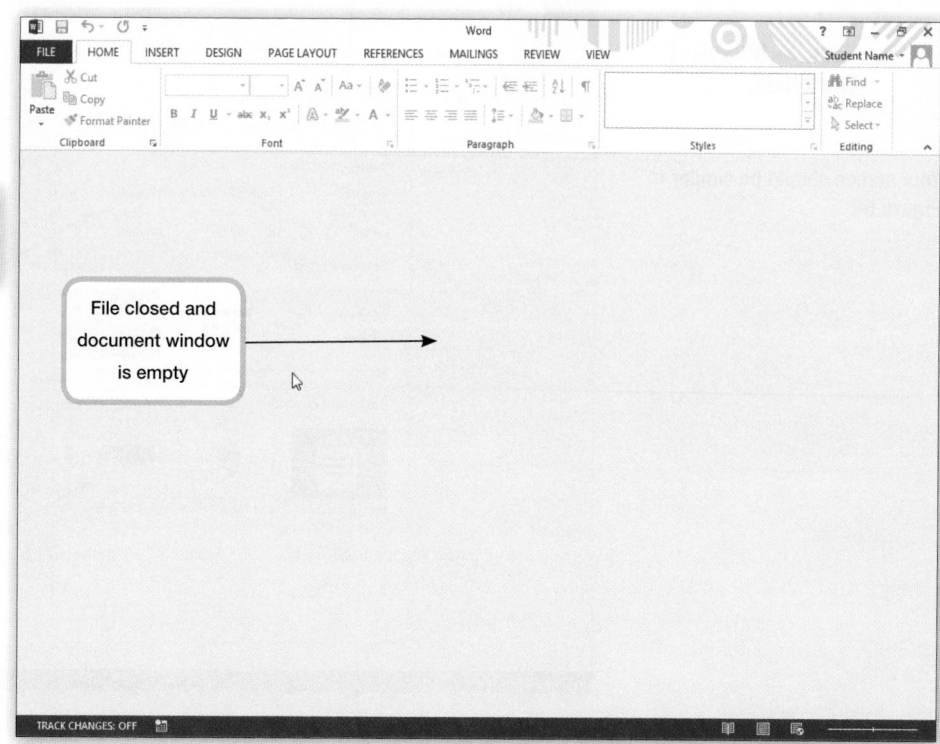

File closed and document window is empty

Figure 55

Additional Information

Do not click ✕ Close in the window title bar as this closes the application.

Now the Word window displays an empty document window. Because you did not make any changes to the document since saving it, the document window closed immediately. If you had made additional changes, the program would display a dialog box asking whether you wanted to save the file before closing it, to close the file without saving the changes or to cancel the action. This prevents the accidental closing of a file that has not been saved first.

USING OFFICE HELP

Another Method

You also can press F1 to access Help.

The ? in the upper-right corner of the Ribbon is used to access the Microsoft Help system. This button is always visible even when the Ribbon is hidden. Because you are using the Microsoft Word 2013 application, Microsoft Word Help will be accessed.

Click ? Microsoft Word Help.

Your screen should be similar to Figure 56

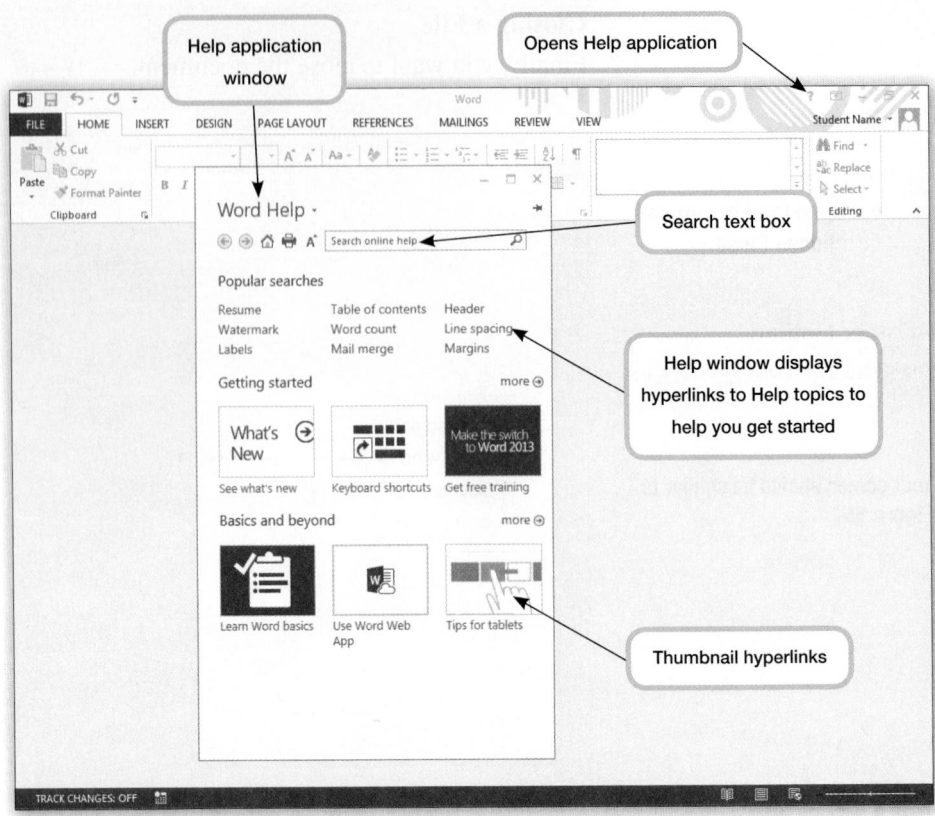

Help application window

Opens Help application

Search text box

Help window displays hyperlinks to Help topics to help you get started

Thumbnail hyperlinks

Figure 56

Additional Information

Because Help is an online feature, the information is frequently updated. Your screens may display slightly different information than those shown in the figures in this lab.

The Word Help feature is a separate application and is opened and displayed in a separate window. If you are connected to the Internet, the Microsoft Office Online website, Office.com, is accessed and help information from this site is displayed in the window. If you are not connected, the offline help information that is provided with the application and stored on your computer is located and displayed. Generally, the listing of topics is similar but fewer in number.

Selecting Help Topics

Additional Information

Depending on the size of your Help window, you may need to scroll the window to see all the Help information provided.

The Home window is displayed and provides several ways you can get help. The first is to type in the Search text box a word or phrase about a topic you want help on. A second is to select a topic from the Popular searches list. Each topic is a **hyperlink** or connection to the information located on the Office.com website or in Help on your computer. When you point to a hyperlink, it appears underlined and the mouse pointer appears as 🖑. Clicking the hyperlink accesses and displays the information associated with the hyperlink. A third method is to click one of the thumbnail hyperlinks in the Getting Started or Basics and beyond sections to access information about these topics.

1

- Click the "Learn Word basics" thumbnail.

- Scroll the Help window to see the "Choose a template" topic.

Your screen should be similar to Figure 57

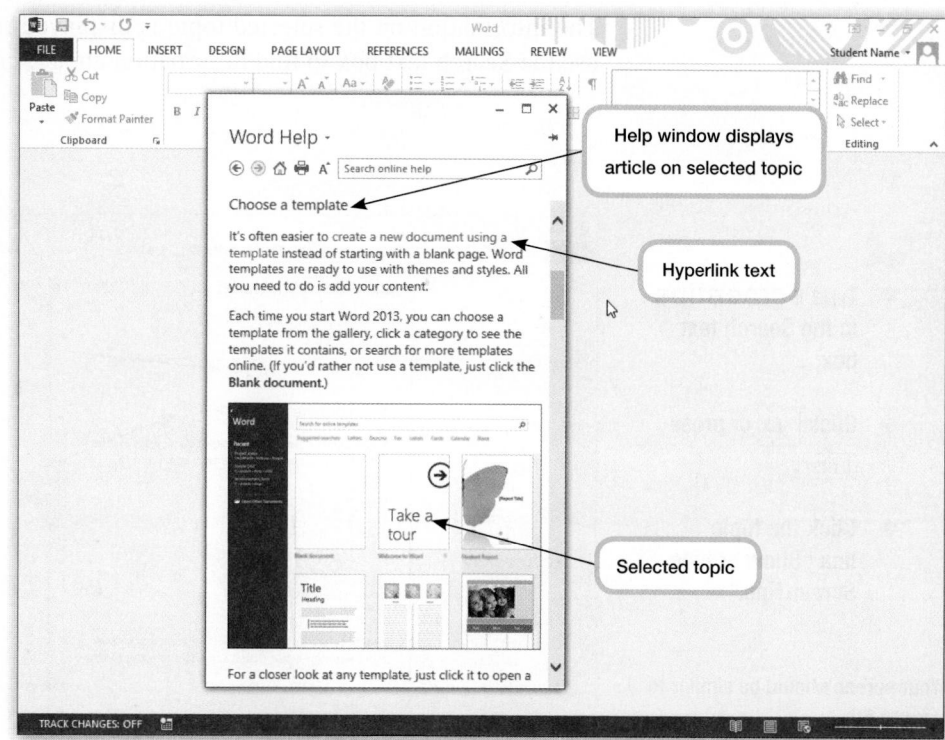

Figure 57

An article containing information about basic features of Word 2013 is displayed. Notice the colored text "create a new document using a template." This indicates the text is a hyperlink to more information about this topic.

2

- Click "create a new document using a template."

- Scroll the window and read the information about this topic.

- Scroll back to the top of the window.

Your screen should be similar to Figure 58

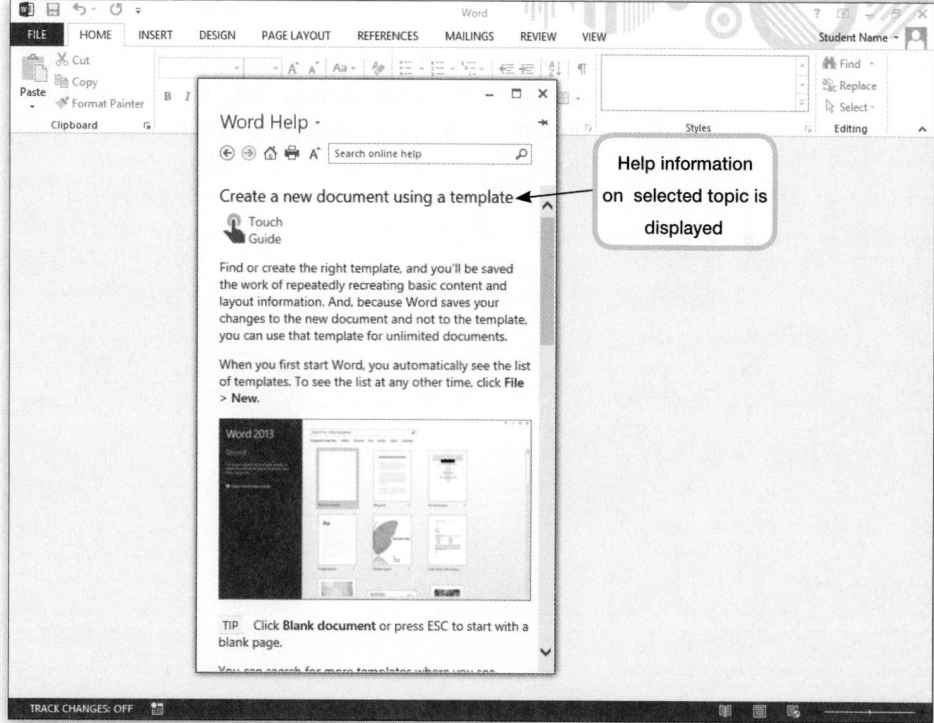

Figure 58

The information on the selected topic is displayed in the window. Next, you will use the Search text box to find information about ScreenTips.

3

● Type **screentips** in the Search text box.

● Click [🔍] or press [Enter].

● Click the topic link "Show or hide ScreenTips."

Your screen should be similar to Figure 59

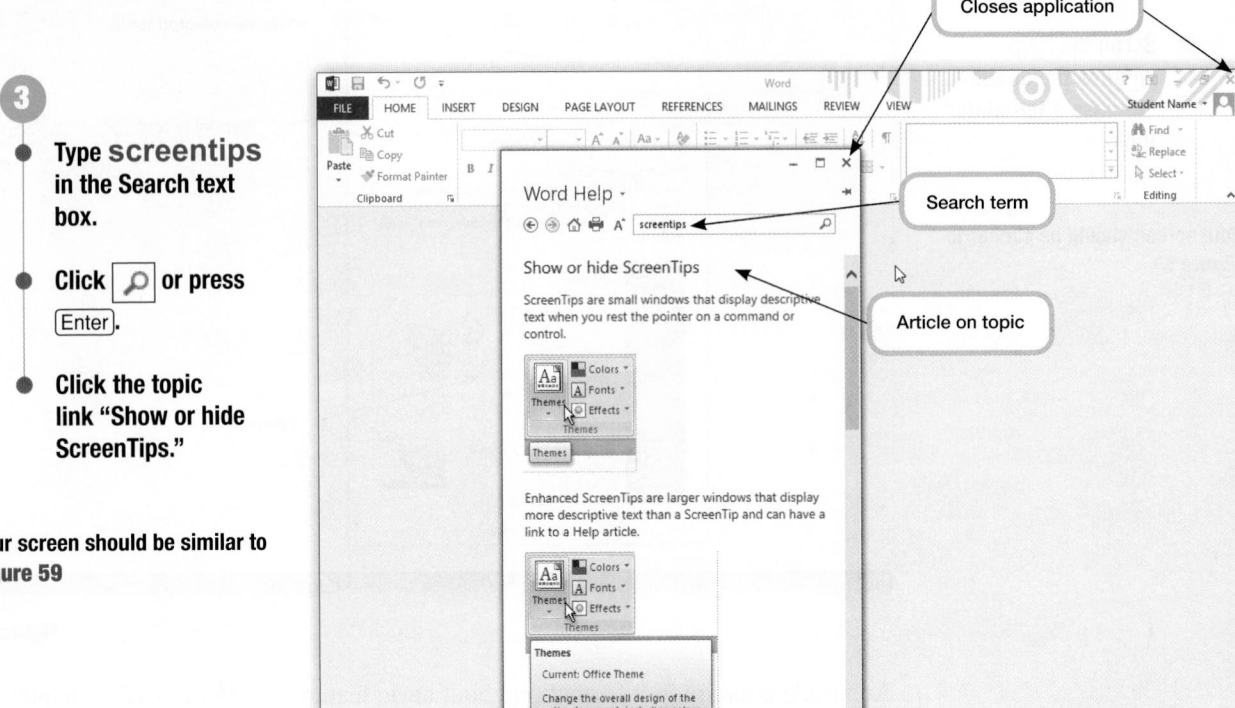

Figure 59

Now information about ScreenTips is displayed in the Help window. To move through previously viewed Help topics, you can use the ⊙ Back and ⊙ Forward buttons in the Help toolbar. You can quickly redisplay the opening Help window using ⌂ Home on the Help toolbar.

4

● Click ← Back two times to display the last two previously viewed topics.

● Click 🏠 Home in the Help window toolbar.

Your screen should be similar to Figure 60

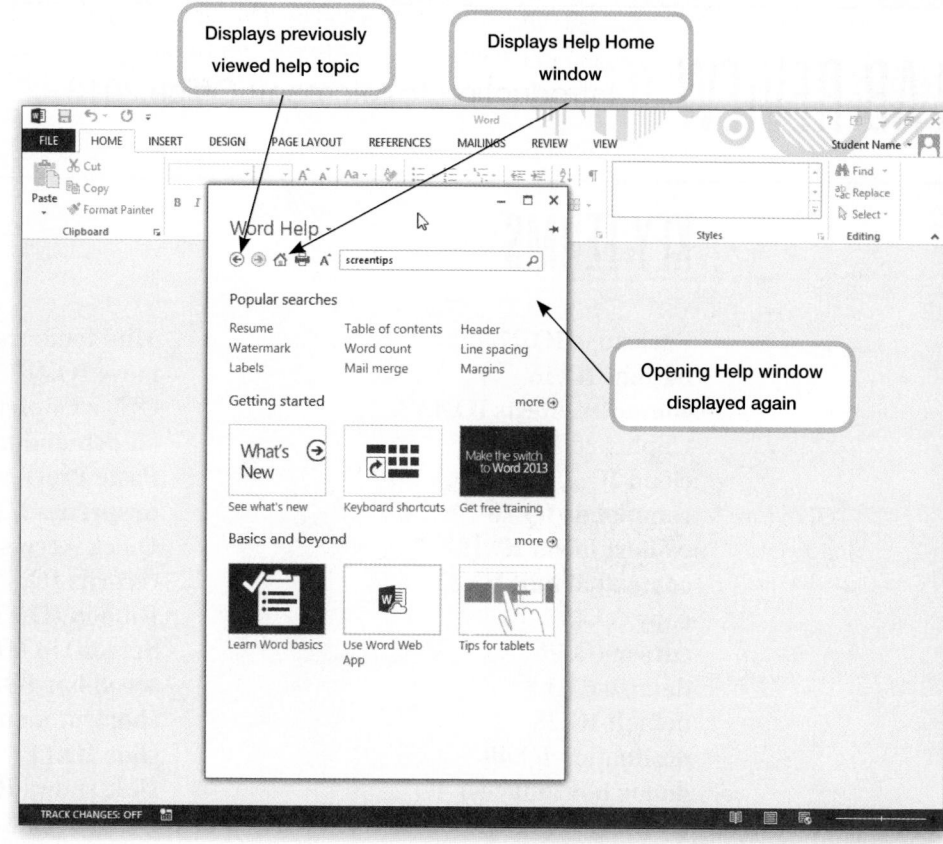

Displays previously viewed help topic

Displays Help Home window

Opening Help window displayed again

Figure 60

The Help Home window is displayed again.

EXITING AN OFFICE 2013 APPLICATION

Now you are ready to close the Help window and exit the Word program. The ✗ Close button located on the right end of the window title bar can be used to exit most application windows. If you attempt to close an application without first saving your document, a dialog box appears asking if you want to save your work before exiting the application, not to save your latest changes to the document or to cancel the action. If you do not save your work and you exit the application, any changes you made since last saving it are lost.

● Click ✗ Close in the Help window title bar to close the Help window.

● Click ✗ Close in the Word window title bar to exit Word.

Another Method

The keyboard shortcut for the Exit command is Alt + F4.

The program window is closed and the Windows desktop is visible again.

KEY TERMS

Backstage IO.27	Mini toolbar IO.42, IO.44
buttons IO.16	move IO.48
character effects IO.43	Office Clipboard IO.48
Clipboard IO.48	on-demand tabs IO.22
cloud IO.3, 30	Paste Preview IO.49
commands IO.20	properties IO.28, 54
context menu IO.19	Quick Access Toolbar IO.16
contextual tabs IO.22	records IO.8
copy IO.48	Ribbon IO.17
cursor IO.17	ScreenTip IO.18
database IO.8	scroll bar IO.17
default IO.28	shortcut menu IO.19
destination IO.48	slide IO.11
dialog box launcher IO.25	slide shows IO.11
document window IO.17	source IO.48
edit IO.3	status bar IO.17
Enhanced ScreenTips IO.22	tables IO.8
fields IO.8	tabs IO.20
font IO.43	tag IO.54
font size IO.43	task pane IO.26
format IO.4	template IO.15
Format Painter IO.52	tooltip IO.18
groups IO.20	typeface IO.43
hyperlink IO.64	user interface IO.14
insertion point IO.17	View buttons IO.17
keyboard shortcut IO.18	word wrap IO.43
keyword IO.54	worksheet IO.6
Live Preview IO.43	Zoom Slider IO.17
metadata IO.54	

COMMAND SUMMARY

Command/Button	Shortcut	Action
Quick Access Toolbar		
↺ ▾ Undo	Ctrl + Z	Restores last change
↻ ▾ Redo	Ctrl + Y	Restores last Undo action
↻ Repeat	Ctrl + Y	Repeats last action

COMMAND SUMMARY (CONTINUED)

Command/Button	Shortcut	Action
W▢		Displays a menu of commands to open, close, and size the application window.
? Microsoft Word Help	F1	Opens Microsoft Help
File tab		
Info		Displays document properties
New		Starts a new document file
Open	Ctrl + O	Opens existing file
Save	Ctrl + S or 💾	Saves document using same file name
Save As	F12	Saves document using a new file name, type, and/or location
Print	Ctrl + P	Prints document using specified settings
Close	Ctrl + F4 or ✕	Closes document
View tab		
Zoom group 🔍 Zoom		Changes magnification of document
Home tab		
Clipboard group 📋 Paste	Ctrl + V	Inserts copy of Clipboard at location of cursor
✂ Cut	Ctrl + X	Removes selection and copies to Clipboard
📑 Copy	Ctrl + C	Copies selection to Clipboard
🖌 Format Painter		Duplicates formats of selection to other locations
Font group Calibri ▾ Font	Ctrl + Shift + F	Changes typeface
11 ▾ Font Size	Ctrl + Shift + P	Changes font size
B Bold	Ctrl + B	Adds/removes bold effect
I Italic	Ctrl + I	Adds/removes italic effect
U Underline	Ctrl + U	Adds/removes underline effect

STEP-BY-STEP

EXPLORING EXCEL 2013

1. In this exercise you will explore the Excel 2013 application and use many of the same features you learned about while using Word 2013 in this lab.

    a. Start Office Excel 2013 and choose Blank workbook.

    b. What shape is the mouse pointer when positioned in the document window area? _____

    c. Excel has _____ tabs. Which tabs are not the same as in Word? _____

    d. Open the Formulas tab. How many groups are in the Formulas tab? _____

    e. Which tab contains the group to work with charts? _____

    f. From the Home tab, click the Number group dialog box launcher. What is the name of the dialog box that opens? _____ How many number categories are there? _____ Close the dialog box.

    g. Display ScreenTips for the following buttons located in the Alignment group of the Home tab and identify what action they perform.

    h. Open the Excel Help window. From the Help window choose "Learn Excel Basics" and then choose "Enter data manually in worksheet cells" and answer the following:

    • What is the definition of worksheet? Hint: Click on the hyperlinked term "worksheet" to view a definition.

    _____

    • What four types of data can be entered in a worksheet? _____, _____, _____, _____

    i. Read the topic "Quick Start: Edit and enter data in a worksheet." If you have an Internet connection, click the Watch the video link and view the video. Close your browser window.

    j. Enter the term "formula" in the Search text box. Look at several articles and answer the following question: All formula entries begin with what symbol? _____

    k. Redisplay the "Enter data manually in worksheet cells" topic. Return to the Home page.

    l. Close the Help window. Exit Excel.

EXPLORING POWERPOINT 2013

2. In this exercise you will explore the PowerPoint 2013 application and use many of the same features you learned about while using Word 2013 in this lab.

   a. Start PowerPoint 2013 and choose Blank presentation.
   b. PowerPoint has _____ tabs. Which tabs are not the same as in Word?

   _____

   c. Open the Animations tab. How many groups are in this tab? _____
   d. Which tab contains the group to work with themes? _____
   e. Click on the text "Click to add title." Type your name. Select this text and change the font size to 72; add italic and bold. Cut this text. Click in the box containing "Click to add subtitle" and paste the cut selection. Use the Paste Options to keep the source formatting.
   f. Click on the text "Click to add title" and type the name of your school. Select the text and apply a font of your choice.
   g. Open the PowerPoint Help window. From the Help window, choose "Learn PowerPoint Basics." Read the information in this article:

   • In the "Insert a new slide" topic, click the link to "Add, rearrange, and delete slides."

   • What is a layout?

   _____

   h. Enter the term "menus" in the Search text box. What do the commands in the Animations tab do?

   _____

   i. Display the Help Home window again. Close the Help window. Exit PowerPoint and do not save the changes you made to the presentation.

LAB EXERCISES

EXPLORING ACCESS 2013

3. As noted in this Introduction to Microsoft Office 2013, when you start Access 2013 you need to either open an existing database file or create and name a new database. Therefore, in this exercise, you will simply explore the Access 2013 Help information without opening or creating a database file.

   a. Use the Start menu to start Office Access 2013.

   b. Click [**?**] Help in the Access Start window.

   c. Choose the topic "Basic tasks for an Access 2013 desktop database."

   • In the first paragraph, what are three examples of kinds of information that can be stored in a database?
   _____, _____, and _____.

   d. In the Search box enter "table." Choose the topic "Introduction to tables" and from the Overview answer the following questions:

   • What is a database?
   _____

   • What are the three parts of a table?
   _____, _____, and _____.

   • A field is also commonly called a _____.

   • Each row in a table is also called a _____.

   e. Close the Help window. Exit Access.

ON YOUR OWN

USING TOUCH IN OFFICE

1. In addition to the Help information you used in this lab, Office 2013 Help also includes online tutorials. Selecting a Help topic that starts a tutorial will open the browser program on your computer. You will use one of these tutorials to learn more about using touch features.

   Start Word 2013. Open Help and choose "Learn Word basics" from the Help Home window. Click on the Touch Guide. The Office Touch Guide web page is opened in your browser. Read the information in this article. When you are done, close the browser window, close Help, and exit Word 2013.

Creating and Editing a Document Lab 1

Objectives

After completing this lab, you will know how to:

1. Enter and edit text.

2. Insert and delete text and blank lines.

3. Use spelling and grammar checking.

4. Use AutoCorrect.

5. Cut and copy text.

6. Change fonts and type sizes.

7. Bold and color text.

8. Change alignment.

9. Insert, move, and size pictures.

10. Change picture layout.

11. Print a document.

12. Use a template.

CASE STUDY

Adventure Travel Tours

As a recent college graduate, you have accepted a job as advertising coordinator for Adventure Travel Tours, a specialty travel company that organizes active adventure vacations. The company is head-quartered in Los Angeles and has locations in other major cities throughout the country. You are responsible for coordination of the advertising program for all locations. This includes the creation of many kinds of promotional materials: brochures, flyers, form letters, news releases, advertisements, and a monthly newsletter. You are also responsible for distributing this information by using traditional mail, by e-mail, and through the company website.

Adventure Travel Tours is very excited

about four new tours planned for the upcoming year. It wants to promote them through informative presentations held throughout the country. Your first job as advertising coordinator will be to create a flyer advertising the four new tours and the presentations. The flyer will be modified according to the location of the presentation.

The software program you will use to create the flyer is the word processing application Microsoft Office Word 2013. It helps you create documents such as letters, reports, and research papers. In this lab, you will learn how to enter, edit, and print a document while you create the flyer (shown on the next page) to be distributed to Adventure Travel Tours clients.

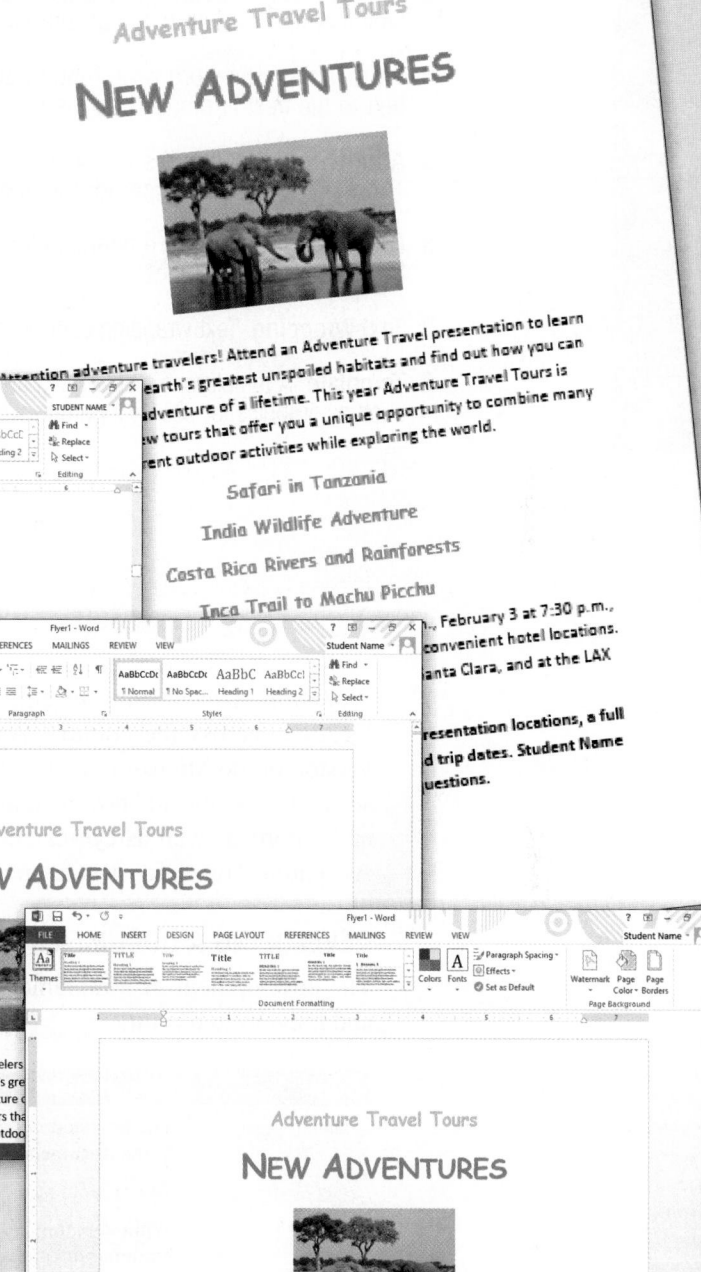

Entering and editing text is simplified with many of Word's automated features.

Formatting enhances the appearance of a document.

Pictures add visual interest to a document.

The following concepts will be introduced in this lab:

1 Grammar Checker The grammar checker advises you of incorrect grammar as you create and edit a document, and proposes possible corrections.

2 Spelling Checker The spelling checker advises you of misspelled words as you create and edit a document, and proposes possible corrections.

3 AutoCorrect The AutoCorrect feature makes basic assumptions about the text you are typing and, based on these assumptions, automatically corrects the entry.

4 Word Wrap The word wrap feature automatically decides where to end a line and wraps text to the next line based on the margin settings.

5 Alignment Alignment is the positioning of text on a line between the margins or indents. There are four types of paragraph alignment: left, centered, right, and justified.

6 Graphics A graphic is a nontext element or object such as a drawing or picture that can be added to a document.

7 Text Wrapping Text wrapping controls how text wraps around a graphic object.

8 Template A template is a document file that stores predefined settings and other elements such as graphics for use as a pattern when creating documents.

Creating New Documents

Adventure Travel Tours recently upgraded its computer systems at many of its locations across the country. As part of the upgrade, it has installed the latest version of the Microsoft Office 2013 suite of applications. You are very excited to see how this new and powerful application can help you create professional letters and reports as well as eye-catching flyers and newsletters. Your first project with Adventure Travel Tours is to create a flyer about four new tours.

DEVELOPING A DOCUMENT

The development of a document follows several steps: plan, enter, edit, format, and preview and print.

Step	Description
Plan	The first step in the development of a document is to understand the purpose of the document and to plan what your document should say.
Enter	After planning the document, you enter the content of the document.
Edit	While creating a document, you will **edit** it to correct typing, spelling, and grammar errors. You will also revise the document by adding and deleting information and by reorganizing it to make the meaning clearer.
Format	**Formatting** enhances the appearance of the document. This is usually performed when the document is near completion, after all edits and revisions have been completed. It includes many features such as boldfaced text, italics, and bulleted lists.
Preview and Print	The last step is to preview and print the document. When previewing, you check the document's overall appearance and make any final changes before printing.

You will generally follow the steps in the order listed in the table for your first draft of a document. However, you will probably retrace steps such as editing and formatting as the final document is developed.

During the planning phase, you spoke with your manager regarding the purpose of the flyer and the content in general. The primary purpose of the flyer is to promote Adventure Travel Tour's new tours. A secondary purpose is to advertise the company.

You plan to include specific information about the new tours in the flyer as well as general information about Adventure Travel Tours. The content also needs to include information about the upcoming new tour presentations. Finally, you want to include information about the Adventure Travel Tour's website.

EXPLORING THE WORD 2013 WINDOW

You will use the word processing application Microsoft Office Word 2013 to create a flyer promoting the new tours and presentations.

Having Trouble?

See "Common Interface Features," on page IO.14, for information on how to start the application and use features that are common to all Office 2013 applications.

1

- Start Word 2013.

- Choose Blank document from the Start screen.

- If necessary, maximize the Word 2013 application window.

Your screen should be similar to Figure 1.1

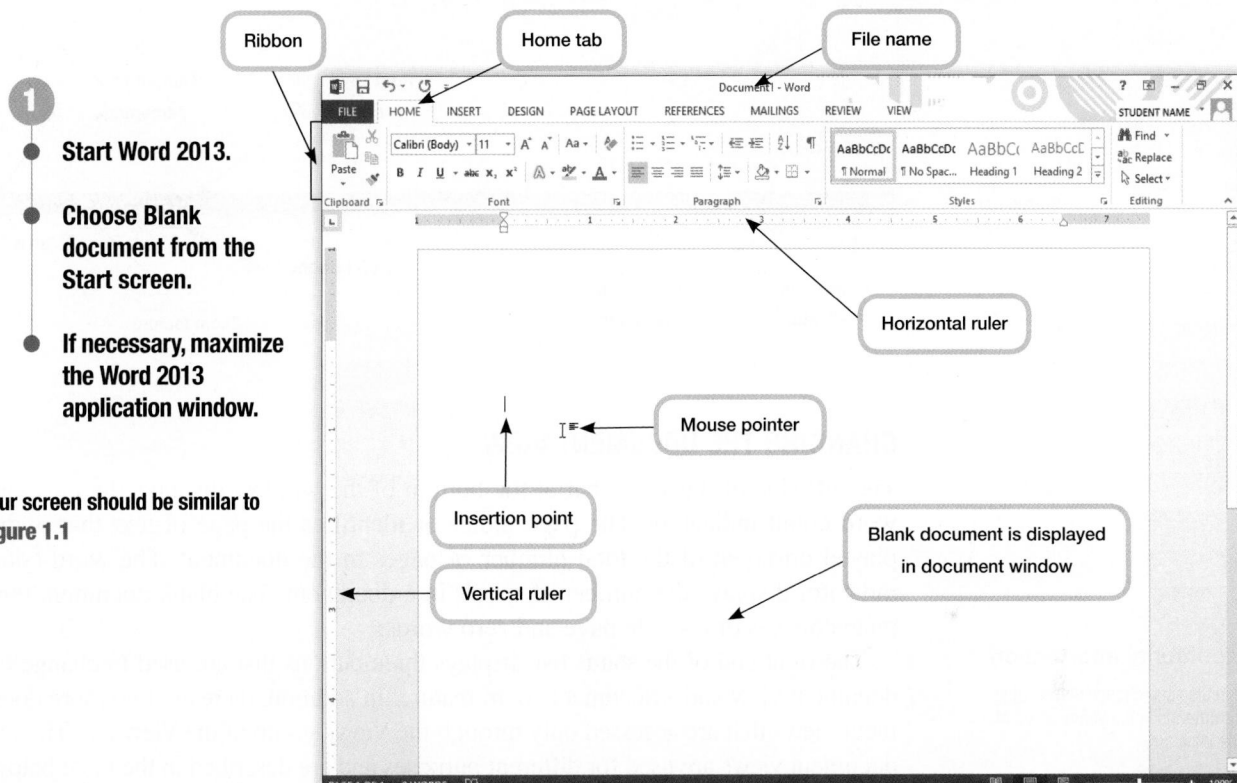

Figure 1.1

Additional Information

The Ribbon may display additional tabs if other application add-ins associated with Office are enabled.

Additional Information

If the rulers are not displayed, open the View tab, and click the Ruler check box.

Additional Information

The mouse pointer also may appear in other shapes, depending upon the task being performed.

The Word 2013 Ribbon is located below the title bar and displays tabs that provide access to commands and features that are used to create and modify a document.

The area below the Ribbon is the **document window**. It currently displays a blank Word document. The insertion point, or cursor, identifies your location in the document. A vertical and horizontal **ruler** may be displayed along both edges of the document window. The horizontal ruler at the top of the document window shows the line length in inches and is used to set margins, tab stops, and indents. The vertical ruler along the left edge shows the page length in inches and shows your line location on the page.

The mouse pointer may appear as an I-beam (see Figure 1.1) or a left- or right-pointing arrow, depending on its location in the window. When it appears as an I-beam, it is used to show your location in the text, and when it appears as an arrow, it is used to select items.

2

- Move the mouse pointer into the left edge of the blank document to see it appear as ⟨.

- Move the mouse pointer to the Ribbon to see it appear as ⟨.

Your screen should be similar to **Figure 1.2**

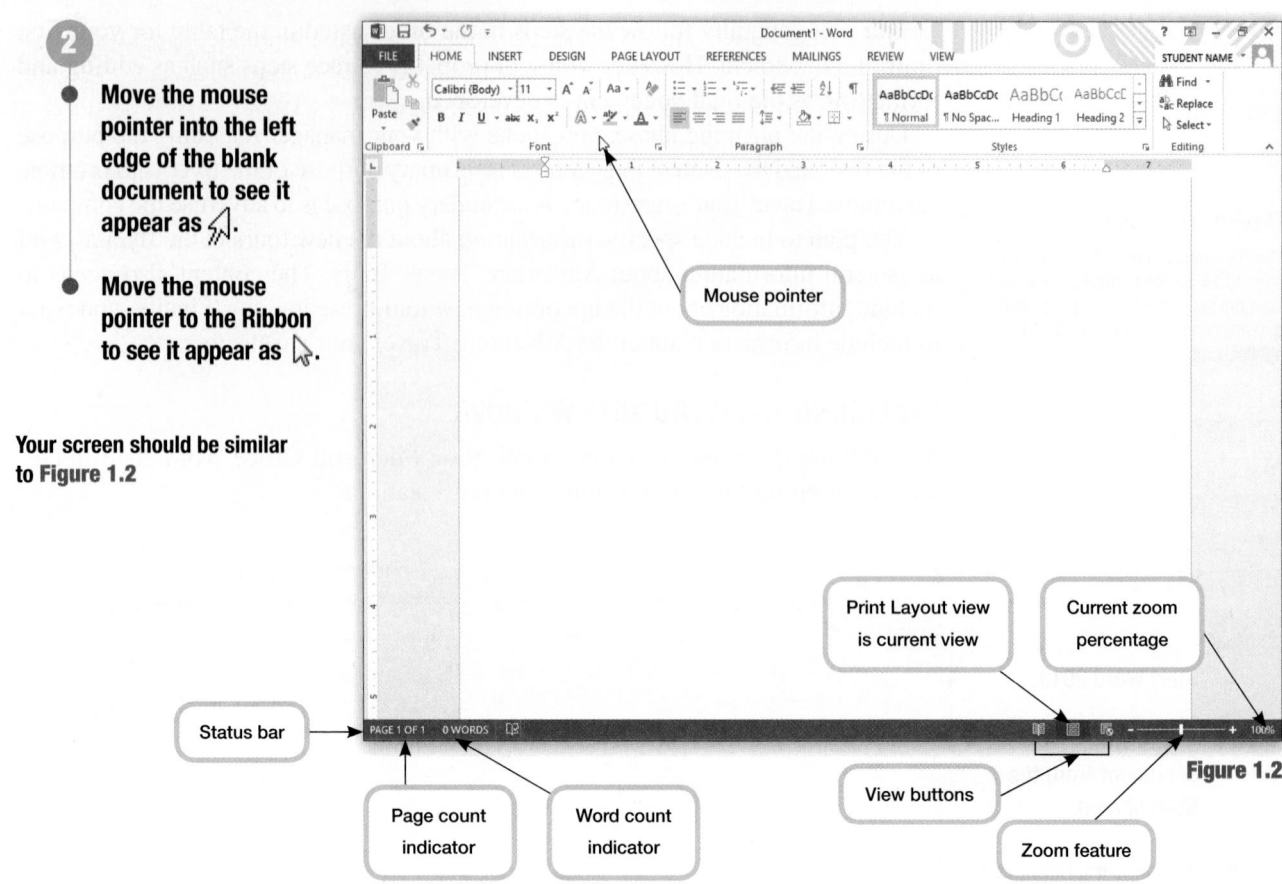

Figure 1.2

CHANGING THE DOCUMENT VIEW

The left side of the status bar at the bottom of the window displays the page and word count indicators. The page indicator identifies the page of text that is displayed onscreen of the total number of pages in the document. The word count indicator displays the number of words in a document. The blank document template consists of a single page and zero words.

The right end of the status bar displays three buttons that are used to change the document view and a document zoom feature. In addition, there are two more document views that are accessed only through the Views group of the View tab. The five document views are used for different purposes and are described in the table below.

Document View	Button	Effect on Text
Read Mode		Shows the document only, without Ribbon, status bar, or any other features. Useful for viewing and reading large documents. Use to review a document and add comments and highlighting.
Print Layout		Shows how text and objects will appear on the printed page. This is the view to use when adjusting margins, working in columns, drawing objects, and placing graphics.
Web Layout		Shows the document as it will appear when viewed in a web browser. Use this view when creating web pages or documents that will be displayed on the screen only.
Outline	Outline	Shows the structure of the document in outline form with the content as bulleted points. This is the view to use to plan and reorganize text in a document.
Draft	Draft	Shows just the text in the document without headers and footers or other objects and is useful for quick editing.

Print Layout view is the view you see when you open a blank new document. You can tell which view is in use by looking at the view buttons. The button for the view that is in use appears highlighted (see Figure 1.2). The zoom setting for each view is set independently and remains in effect until changed to another zoom setting. Initially the zoom percentage for Print Layout view is 100%. At this percentage, the document appears as it will when printed.

You will "zoom out" on the document to see the entire page so you can better see the default document settings.

1

Drag the Zoom slider to the left to reduce the zoom until the entire page is visible.

Your screen should be similar to Figure 1.3

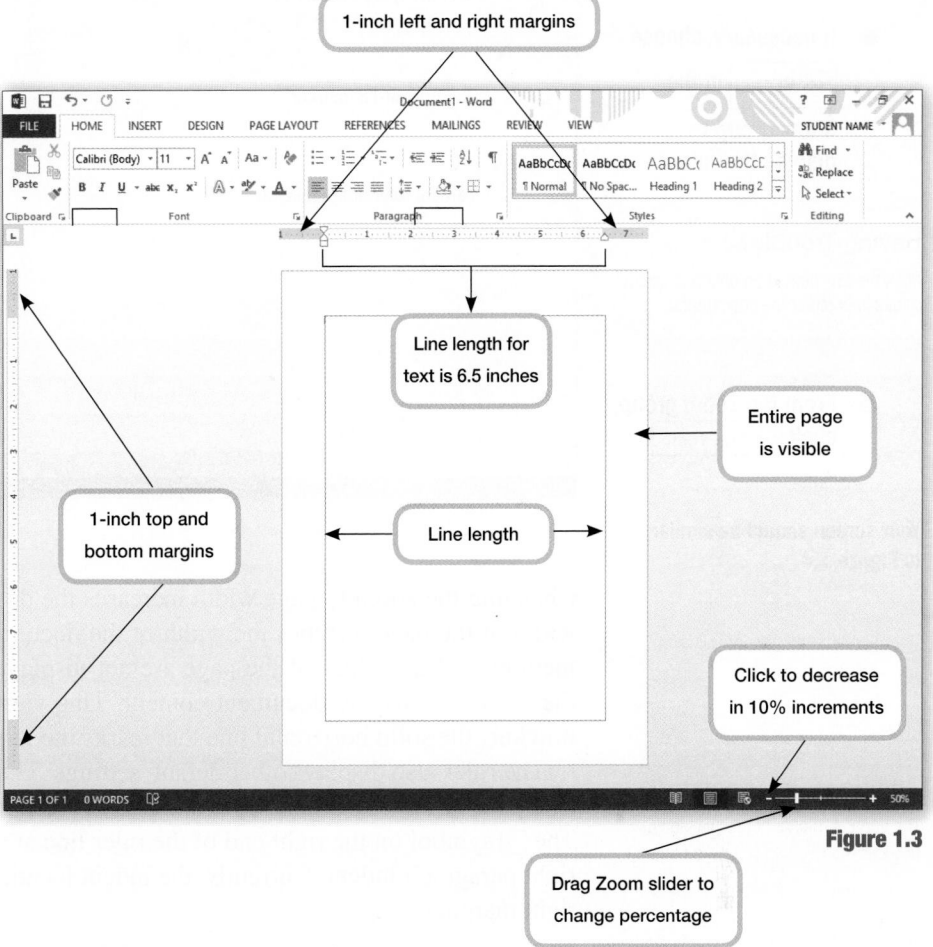

Figure 1.3

At this zoom percentage, the entire page is displayed and all four edges of the paper are visible. It is like a blank piece of paper that already has many predefined settings. These settings, called **default** settings, are generally the most commonly used settings. The default settings include a standard paper-size setting of 8.5 by 11 inches, 1-inch top and bottom margins, and 1-inch left and right margins.

You can verify many of the default document settings by looking at the information displayed in the rulers. The shaded area of the ruler identifies the margins and the white area identifies the line length or page length. The line length measures 6.5 inches of the page. Knowing that the default page size is 8.5 inches wide, this leaves 2 inches for margins: 1 inch for equal-sized left and right margins. The vertical ruler shows the entire page height is 11 inches with 1-inch top and bottom margins, leaving 9 inches of page length.

You will use Draft view to create the flyer about this year's new tours. You will use the View tab to change to this view. You will also change the document zoom level using the Zoom group on the View tab.

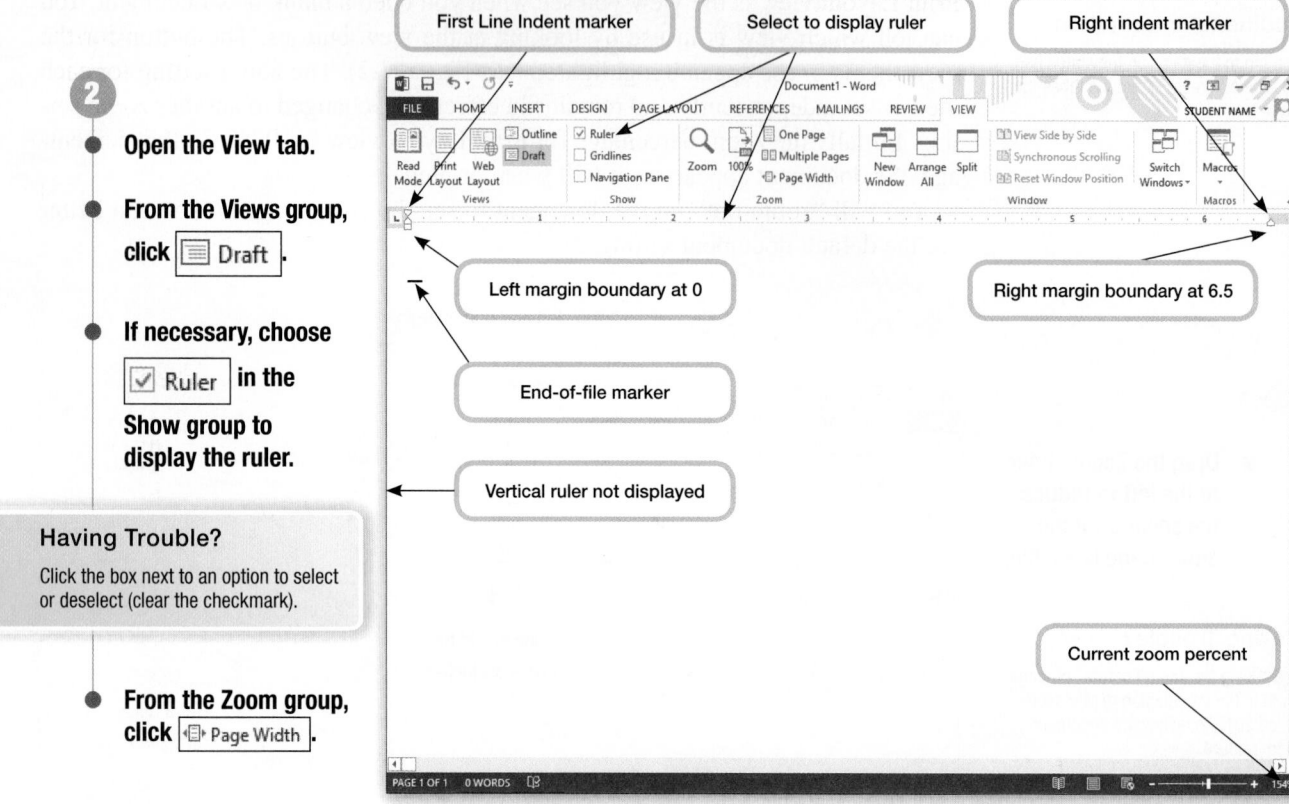

First Line Indent marker

Select to display ruler

Right indent marker

Left margin boundary at 0

Right margin boundary at 6.5

End-of-file marker

Vertical ruler not displayed

Current zoom percent

2

● **Open the View tab.**

● **From the Views group, click [≡ Draft].**

● **If necessary, choose [✓ Ruler] in the Show group to display the ruler.**

Having Trouble?

Click the box next to an option to select or deselect (clear the checkmark).

● **From the Zoom group, click [⊞ Page Width].**

Your screen should be similar to Figure 1.4

Figure 1.4

Changing the zoom to page width increases the document magnification until the width of the page matches the width of the document window. In Draft view, the margins and the edges of the page are not displayed. This allows more space on the screen to display document content. This view also displays the **end-of-file marker**, the solid horizontal line that marks the last-used line in a document.

The ruler also displays other default settings. The symbol ▽ at the zero position is the First Line Indent marker and marks the location of the left paragraph indent. The △ symbol on the right end of the ruler line at the 6.5-inch position marks the right paragraph indent. Currently, the indent locations are the same as the left and right margin settings.

Additional Information

The vertical ruler is not displayed in Draft view.

Entering Text

Now you are ready to start the second step in document creation, entering the text. As you type, you will probably make simple typing errors. Word includes many features that make entering text and correcting errors much easier. These features include checking for spelling and grammar errors, auto correction, and word wrap.

TYPING TEXT

As you enter the first line of the text, it will include the intentional error identified in italic.

- **Type Adventure Traveel (do not press Spacebar after typing the last letter).**

Having Trouble?

To review the basics of moving the insertion point and editing a document, refer to the "Entering and Editing Text" section on page IO.37 of the Introduction to Microsoft Office 2013.

Your screen should be similar to Figure 1.5

Additional Information

The status bar also can display additional information such as the horizontal position of the insertion point on the line and the line number. To customize the status bar, right-click the status bar and select the features you want displayed from the status bar context menu.

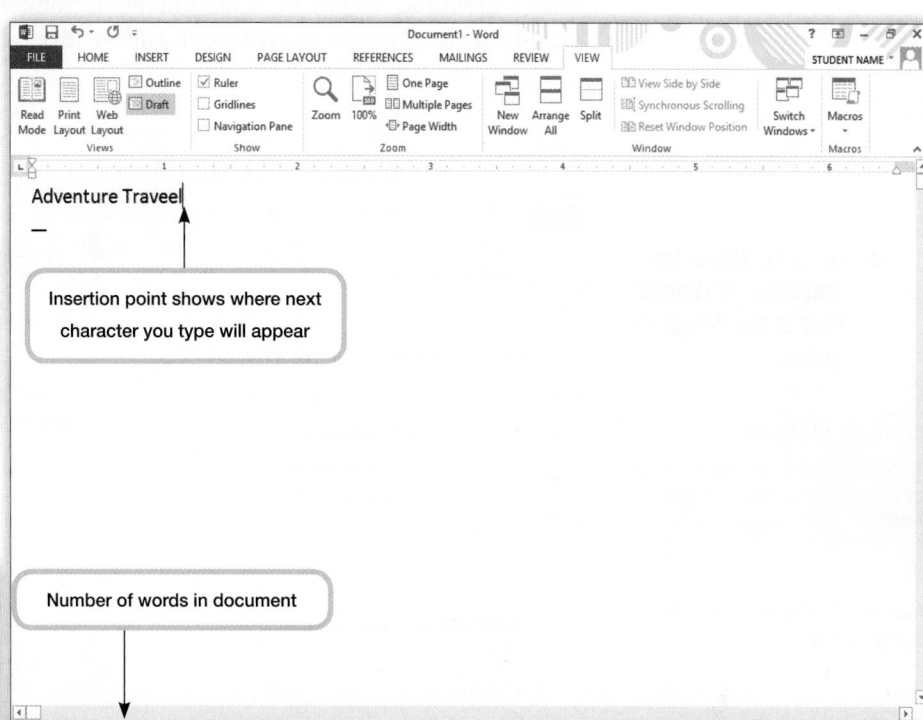

Figure 1.5

Notice that the status bar now tells you that there are two words in the document.

Next, you need to correct the typing error by deleting the extra "e" in the word "travel." Then you will complete the first line of the flyer.

- **Press ← or position the I-beam between the "e" and "l" and click.**

- **Press Backspace to remove the extra "e."**

- **Press → or click at the end of the line.**

- **Press Spacebar.**

- **Type Tours four new adventures and correct any typing errors using Backspace or Delete.**

- **With the insertion point positioned at the end of the line, press Enter 3 times.**

Your screen should be similar to Figure 1.6

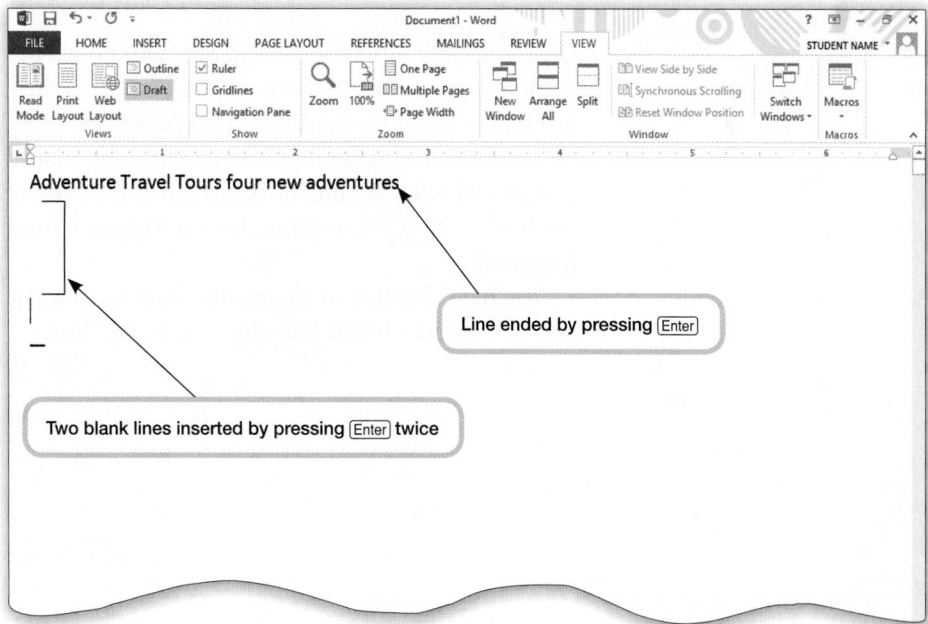

Figure 1.6

Pressing Enter once ended the first line of text and inserted a blank line. The next two times you pressed Enter inserted blank lines.

REVEALING FORMATTING MARKS

While creating a document, Word automatically inserts formatting marks that control the appearance of your document. These marks are not displayed automatically so that the document is not cluttered. Sometimes, however, it is helpful to view formatting marks to assist with editing text.

- **Open the Home tab and click ¶ Show/Hide in the Paragraph group.**

Another Method

You also can use the keyboard shortcut Ctrl + * to show and hide formatting marks.

Your screen should be similar to Figure 1.7

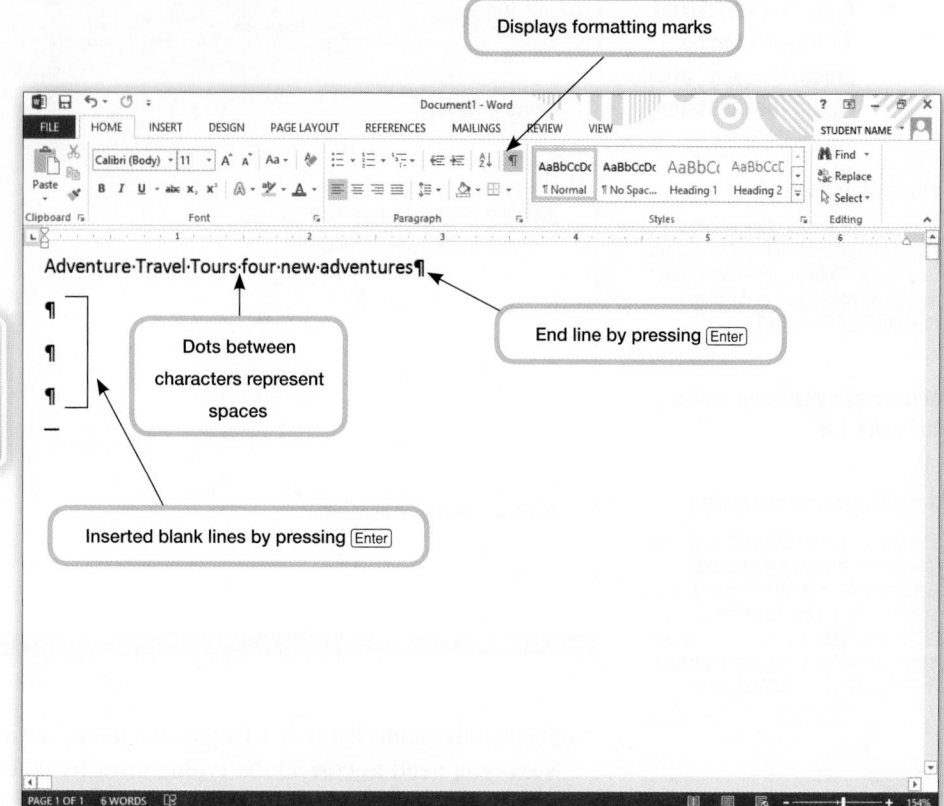

Figure 1.7

Once formatting marks display, you will notice that a dot appears between words. Each dot represents a space. When you press the Enter key, a paragraph mark is inserted in the document. The first paragraph mark ended the line of text, and the second and third paragraph marks represent blank lines. Formatting marks do not appear when the document is printed and do not interfere with inserting and editing text. The ¶ Show/Hide button toggles between showing and hiding formatting marks.

You have decided to change the flyer heading to a two-line heading. To do this, you will insert a blank line after the word "Tours".

2

- Click to the left of the dot after the "s" in "Tours".

- Press Enter 2 times.

- Press ↓.

- Return to the beginning of line 3 and press Delete to remove the space.

Your screen should be similar to **Figure 1.8**

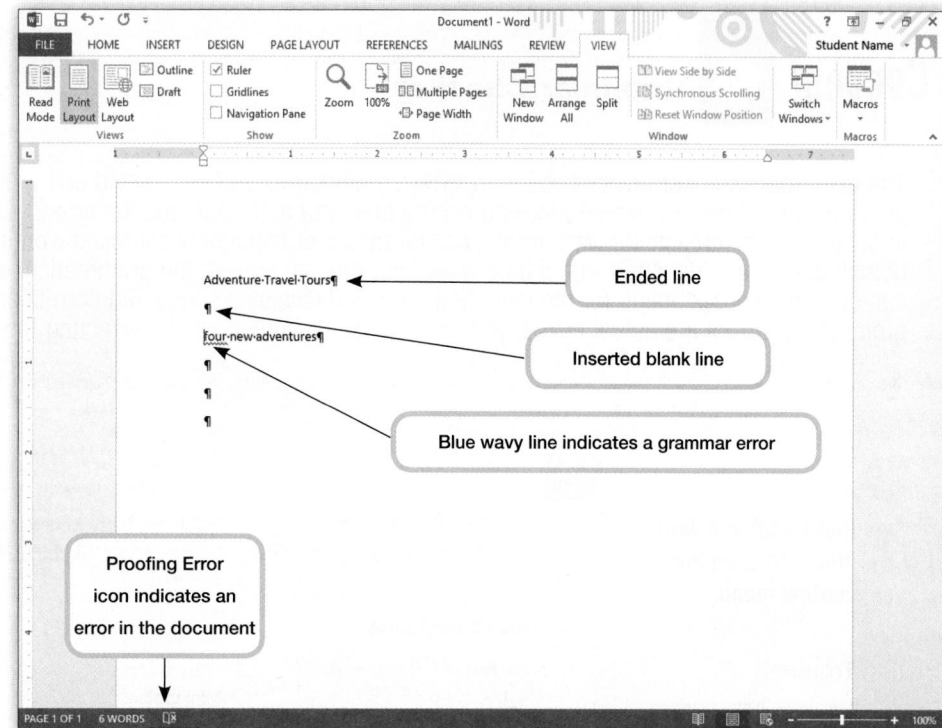

Ended line

Inserted blank line

Blue wavy line indicates a grammar error

Proofing Error icon indicates an error in the document

Figure 1.8

All the text to the right of the insertion point moved to the beginning of the next line when you pressed the Enter key.

Identifying and Correcting Errors Automatically

Having Trouble?

If the wavy underline is not displayed, open the File tab, choose Options/Proofing, and select the "Check spelling as you type", "Mark grammar errors as you type", and "Check grammar with spelling" options.

Notice that a blue wavy line appears under the word "four." This indicates an error has been detected.

As you enter text, Word constantly checks the document for spelling and grammar errors. The Proofing Error icon in the status bar displays an animated pencil icon 🖉 while you are typing, indicating Word is checking for errors as you type. When you stop typing, it displays either a checkmark ✓, indicating the program does not detect any errors, or an X ✗, indicating the document contains an error.

In many cases, Word will automatically correct errors for you. In other cases, it identifies the error by underlining it. The different colors and designs of underlines indicate the type of error that has been identified. In addition to identifying the error, Word provides suggestions as to the possible correction needed.

CHECKING GRAMMAR

In addition to the blue wavy line under "four," the Proofing Error icon appears as ✗ in the status bar. This indicates that a spelling or grammar error has been located. A blue wavy line below the error indicates it is a grammar, style, or contextual error. A red wavy line under a word indicates a potential spelling error.

Concept  Grammar Checker

The **grammar checker** advises you of incorrect grammar as you create and edit a document, and proposes possible corrections. Grammar checking occurs after you enter punctuation or end a line. If grammatical errors in subject–verb agreements, verb forms, capitalization, or commonly confused words, to name a few, are detected, they are identified with a blue wavy line. You can correct the grammatical error by editing it or you can open the context menu for the identified error and display a suggested correction. Because not all identified grammatical errors are actual errors, you need to use discretion when correcting the errors.

● **Right-click the word "four" to open the context menu.**

Having Trouble?

Review context menus in the "Common Office 2013 Features" section on page IO.19 in the Introduction to Microsoft Office 2013. If the wrong context menu appears, you probably did not have the I-beam positioned on the error with the wavy line. Press Esc or click outside the menu to cancel it and try again.

Your screen should be similar to Figure 1.9

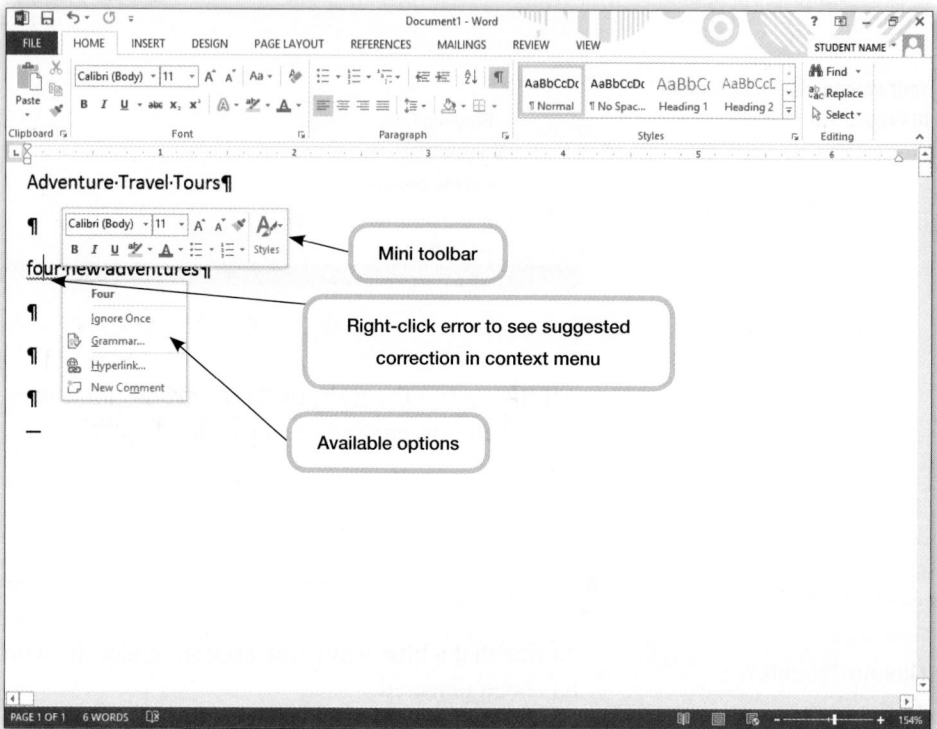

Figure 1.9

Additional Information

You will learn about using the Mini toolbar shortly.

The Word Mini toolbar and a context menu containing commands related to the grammar error are displayed. The first item on the menu is the suggested correction, "Four." The grammar checker indicates you should capitalize the first letter of the word because it appears to be the beginning of a sentence. It also includes the Ignore Once and Grammar options. Ignore Once instructs Word to ignore the grammatical error. The Grammar option opens the Grammar task pane and displays an explanation of the error.

To make this correction, you could simply choose the correction from the menu and the correction would be inserted into the document. Although, in this case, you can readily identify the reason for the error, sometimes the reason is not so obvious. In those cases, you can open the Grammar task pane to learn more information.

2

● Choose Grammar from the context menu.

Your screen should be similar to Figure 1.10

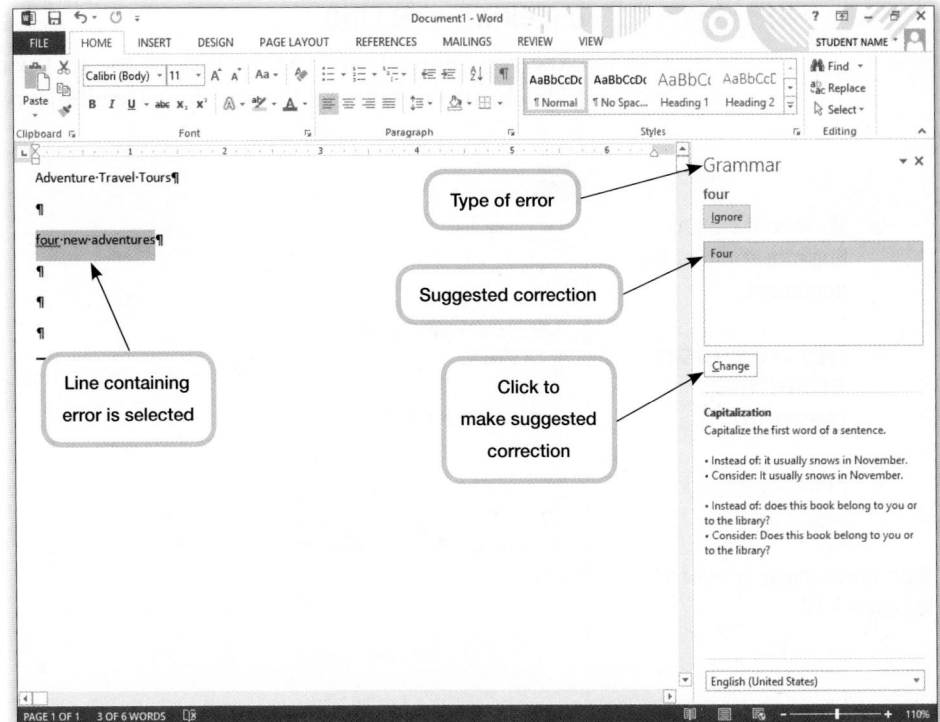

Figure 1.10

The Grammar task pane identifies the type and location of the grammatical error and the suggested correction. The line in the document containing the error is also highlighted (selected) to make it easy for you to see the location of the error.

3

● Click  .

Your screen should be similar to Figure 1.11

Additional Information

Moving the insertion point using the keyboard or mouse deselects or removes the highlight from text that is selected.

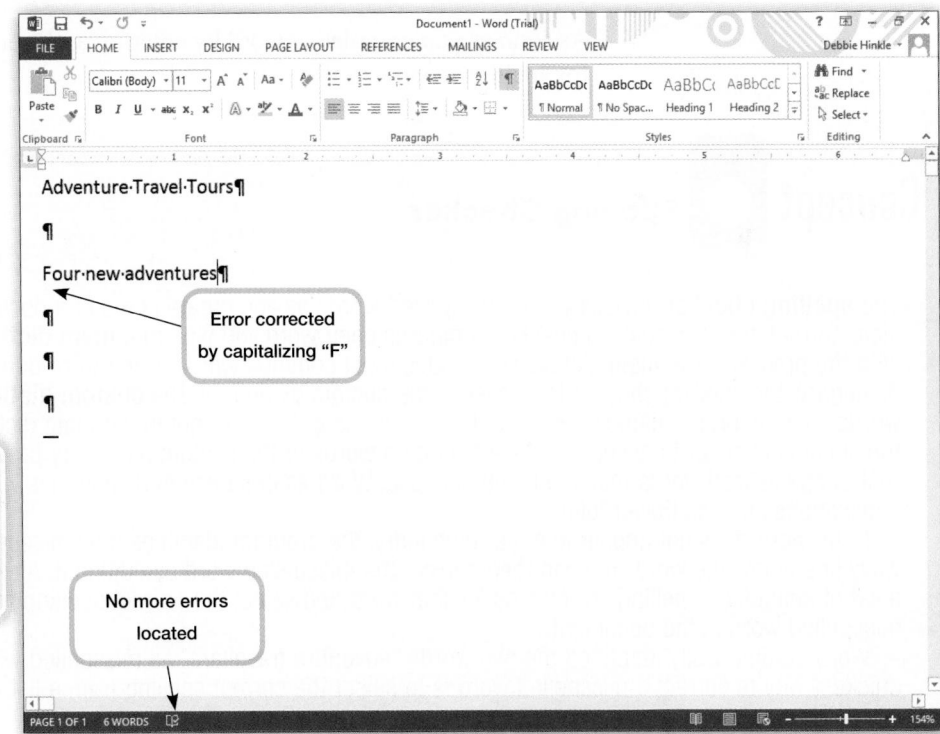

Figure 1.11

The error is corrected, the wavy line is removed, the Grammar task pane is closed, and the Proofing Error icon returns to ⬛.

CHECKING SPELLING

Now you are ready to type the text for the first paragraph of the flyer. Enter the following text, including the intentional spelling errors.

- **Move to the blank line at the end of the document.**

- **Type Attention adventire travellars!**

- **Press** Spacebar.

Your screen should be similar to **Figure 1.12**

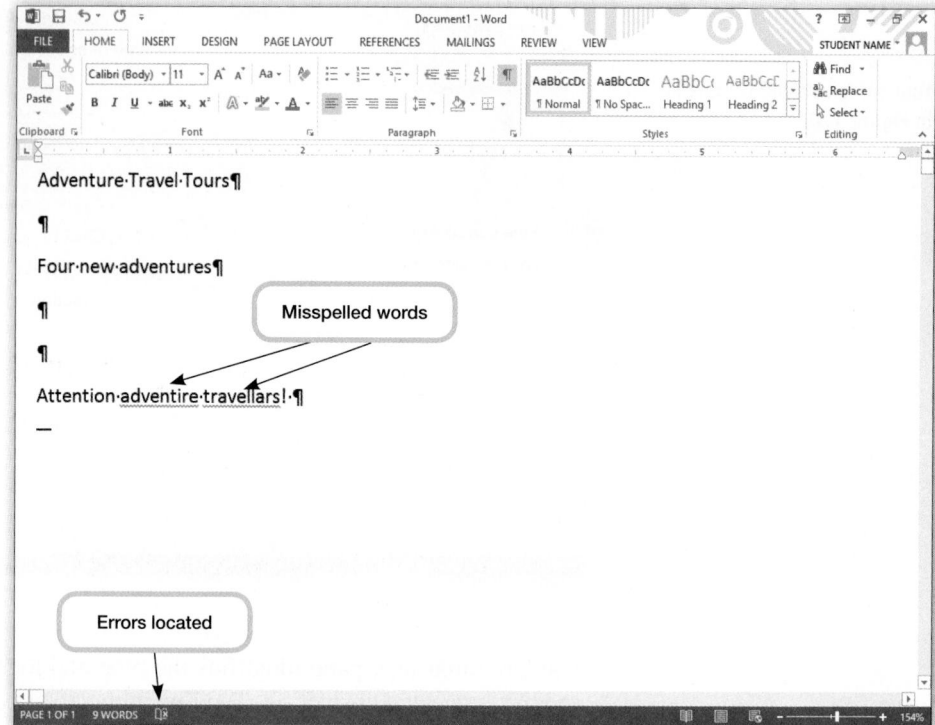

Figure 1.12

As soon as you complete a word by entering a space, the program checks the word for spelling accuracy.

Concept ② Spelling Checker

The **spelling checker** advises you of misspelled words as you create and edit a document, and proposes possible corrections. The spelling checker compares each word you type to a **main dictionary** of words supplied with the program. The main dictionary includes most common words. If the word does not appear in the main dictionary, the spelling checker then checks the custom dictionary. The **custom dictionary** consists of a list of words such as proper names, technical terms, and so on that are not in the main dictionary and that you want the spelling checker to accept as correct. Adding words to the custom dictionary prevents the flagging as incorrect of specialized words that you commonly use. Word shares custom dictionaries with other Microsoft Office applications such as PowerPoint.

If the word does not appear in either dictionary, the program identifies it as misspelled by displaying a red wavy line below the word. You can then correct the misspelled word by editing it. Alternatively, you can display a list of suggested spelling corrections for that word and select the correct spelling from the list to replace the misspelled word in the document.

Word automatically identified the two words "adventire travellars" as misspelled with a red wavy line. The quickest way to correct a misspelled word is to select the correct spelling from a list of suggested spelling corrections displayed on the context menu.

2 Right-click "adventire" to display the context menu.

Your screen should be similar to **Figure 1.13**

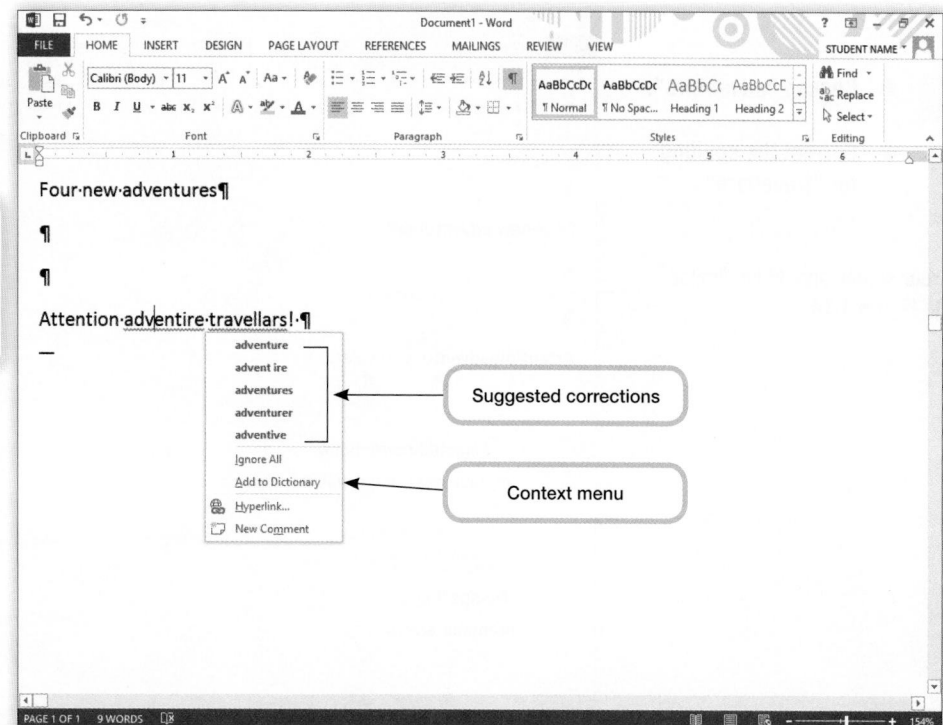

Figure 1.13

A context menu containing suggested correct spellings is displayed. The context menu also includes options to Ignore All and Add to Dictionary. The Ignore All option instructs Word to ignore the misspelling of this word throughout the rest of the document. The Add to Dictionary option adds the word to the custom dictionary list. When a word is added to the custom dictionary, Word always accepts that spelling as correct.

Sometimes there are no suggested replacements because Word cannot locate any words in its dictionary that are similar in spelling; or the suggestions are not correct. If this occurs, you need to edit the word manually. In this case, the first suggestion is correct.

3

- Choose "adventure".

- Correct the spelling for "travellars".

Your screen should be similar to **Figure 1.14**

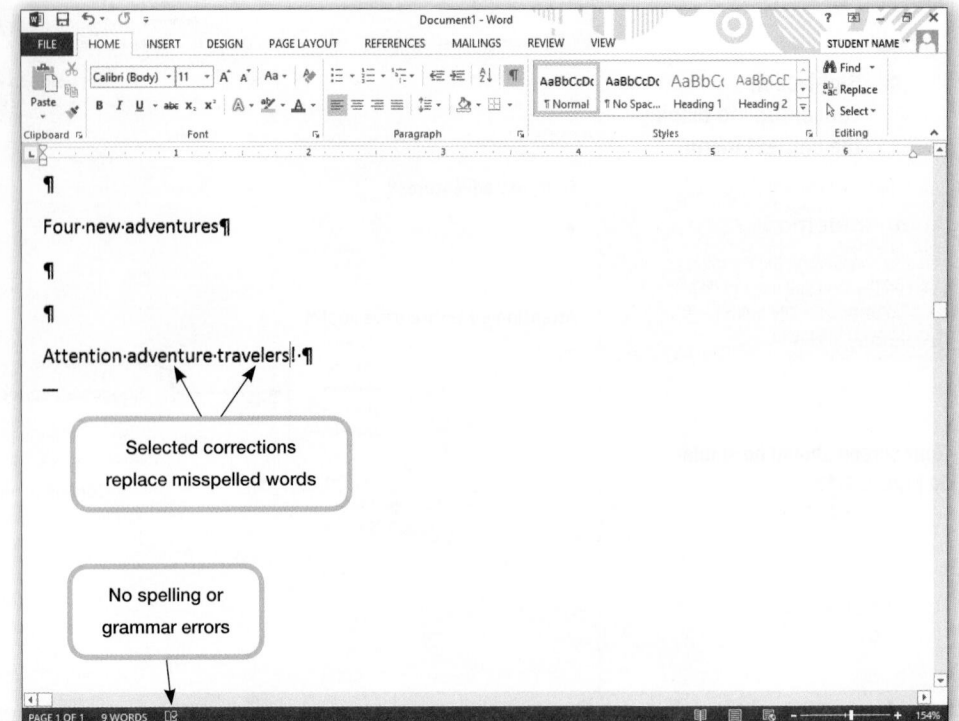

Four·new·adventures¶

Attention·adventure·travelers|·¶

Selected corrections replace misspelled words

No spelling or grammar errors

Figure 1.14

The spelling corrections you selected replace the misspelled words in the document. The Proofing Error icon returns to ▣, indicating that, as far as Word is able to detect, the document is free from errors.

USING AUTOCORRECT

As you have seen, as soon as you complete a word by entering a space, the program checks the word for grammar and spelling accuracy. Also, when you complete a sentence and start another, additional checks are made. Many spelling and grammar corrections are made automatically for you as you type. This is part of the AutoCorrect feature of Word.

Concept ③ AutoCorrect

The **AutoCorrect** feature makes basic assumptions about the text you are typing and, based on these assumptions, automatically corrects the entry. The AutoCorrect feature automatically inserts proper capitalization at the beginning of sentences and in the names of days of the week. It also will change to lowercase letters any words that were incorrectly capitalized because of the accidental use of the [Shift] key. In addition, it also corrects many common typing and spelling errors automatically.

One way the program automatically makes corrections is by looking for certain types of errors. For example, if two capital letters appear at the beginning of a word, Word changes the second capital letter to a lowercase letter. If a lowercase letter appears at the beginning of a sentence, Word capitalizes the first letter of the first word. If the name of a day begins with a lowercase letter, Word capitalizes the first letter. When Spelling Checker provides a single suggested spelling correction for the word, the program will automatically replace the incorrect spelling with the suggested replacement.

Another way the program corrects text is by checking all entries against a built-in list of AutoCorrect entries. If it finds the entry on the list, the program automatically replaces the error with the correction. For example, the typing error "withthe" is automatically changed to "with the" because the error is on the AutoCorrect list. You also can add words to the AutoCorrect list that you want to be automatically corrected.

Enter the following text, including the errors (identified in italics).

1

- **Press** [End] **to move to the end of the line.**

- **Press** [Enter].

- **Type attend a presentaation to lern aboutthe**

- **Press** [Spacebar].

Your screen should be similar to Figure 1.15

Having Trouble?

The "Capitalize first letter of sentences" and "Replace text as you type" AutoCorrect features must be selected. Open the File tab, choose Options/ Proofing, click [AutoCorrect Options...], and select these options if necessary.

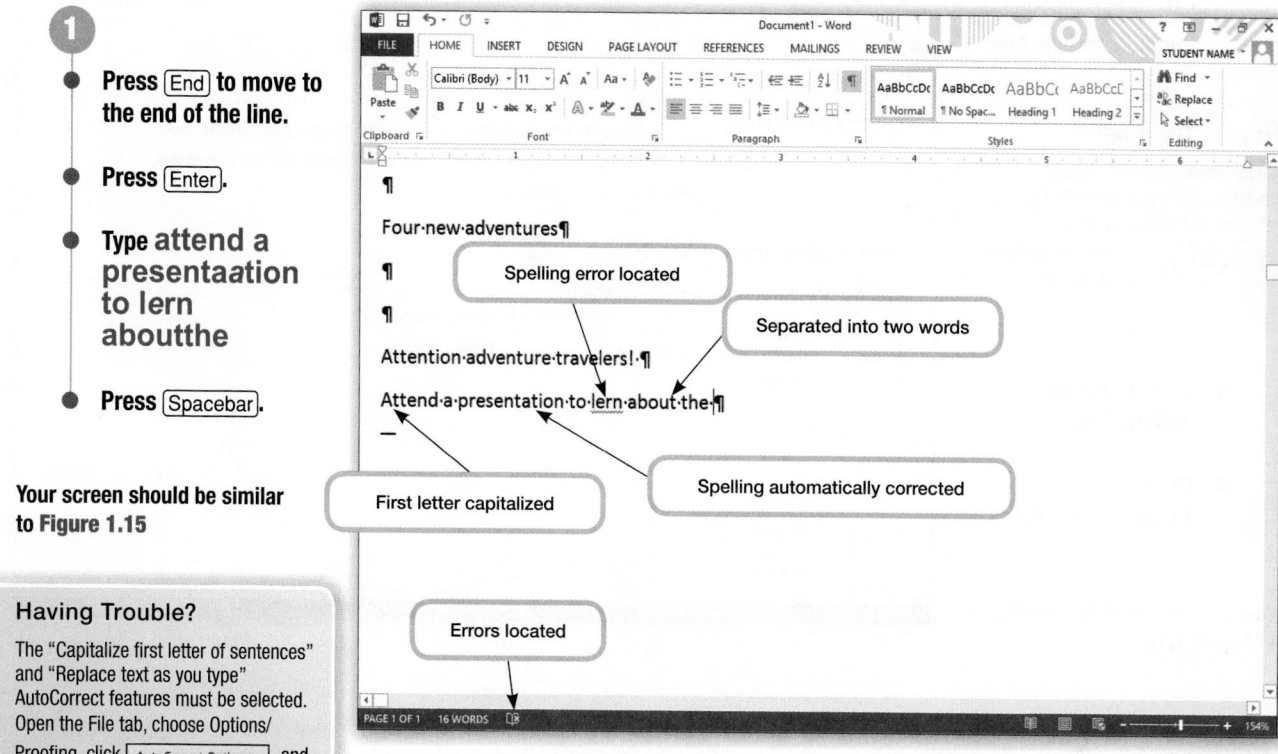

Figure 1.15

The first letter of the word "attend" was automatically capitalized because, as you were typing, the program determined that it is the first word in a sentence. In a similar manner, it corrected the spelling of "presentation" and separated the words "about the" with a space. The AutoCorrect feature corrected the spelling of "presentation" because it was the only suggested correction for the word supplied by the Spelling Checker. The word "lern" was not corrected because there are several suggested spelling corrections.

When you rest the mouse pointer near text that has been corrected automatically or move the insertion point onto the word, a small light-blue box appears under the first character of the word. The blue box is an options box that indicates there are other options available. It changes to the [⬛] AutoCorrect Options button when you point to it.

Point to the word "Attend" to display the blue options box.

Point to the blue options box.

Click ✏ ▾ AutoCorrect Options.

Your screen should be similar to Figure 1.16

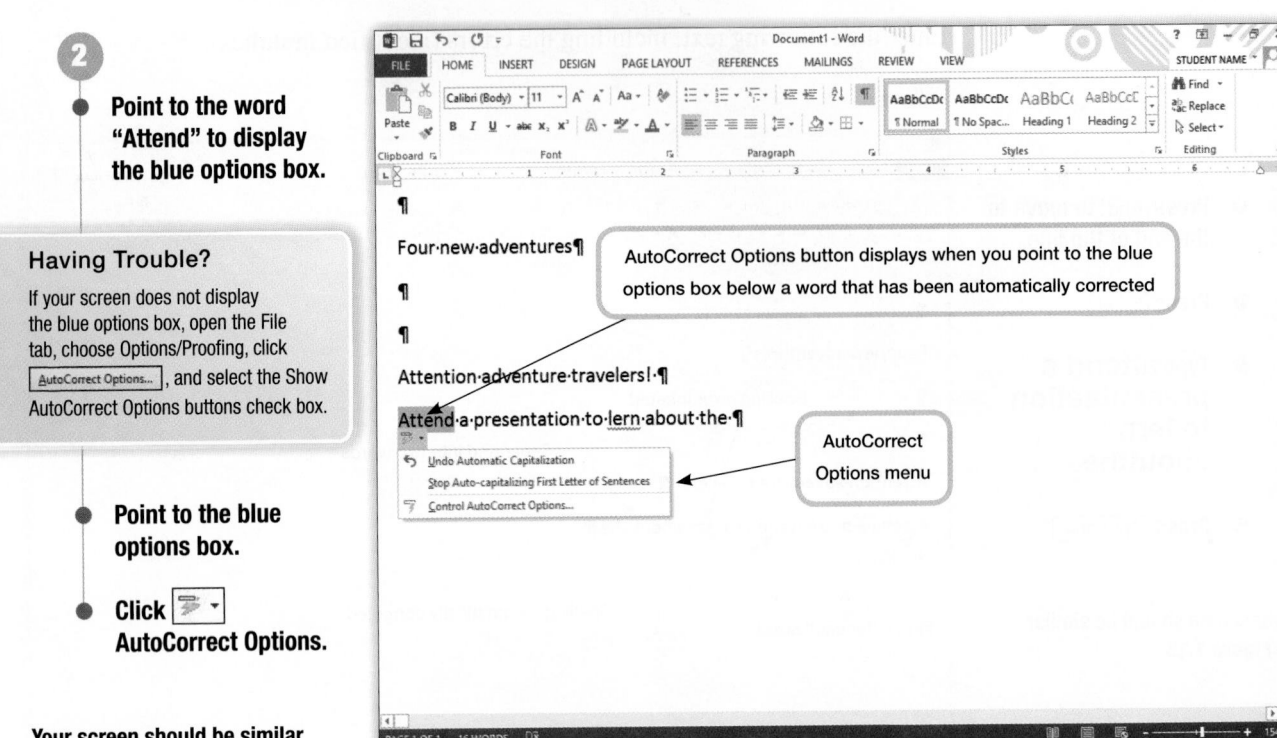

Figure 1.16

Each time Word uses the AutoCorrect feature, the AutoCorrect Options button is available. The AutoCorrect Options menu allows you to undo the AutoCorrection or to permanently disable the AutoCorrection for the remainder of your document. The Control AutoCorrect Options command is used to change the settings for this feature. In some cases, you may want to exclude a word from automatic correction. You can do this by adding the word to the exceptions list so the feature will be disabled for that word. If you use Backspace to delete an automatic correction and then type it again the way you want it to appear, the word will be automatically added to the exceptions list.

3

Click outside the menu to close it.

Open the spelling context menu for "lern" and choose "learn".

The spelling is corrected, and the Proofing Error icon in the status bar indicates that the document is free of errors.

Using Word Wrap

Now you will continue entering the paragraph text. As you type, when the text gets close to the right margin, do not press Enter to move to the next line. Word will automatically wrap words to the next line.

Concept ④ Word Wrap

The **word wrap** feature automatically decides where to end a line and wrap text to the next line based on the margin settings. This feature saves time when entering text because you do not need to press [Enter] at the end of a full line to begin a new line. The only time you need to press [Enter] is to end a paragraph or to insert blank lines. Remember, a paragraph is any line ending with [Enter]. In addition, if you change the margins or insert or delete text on a line, the program automatically readjusts the text on the line. Word wrap is common to all word processors.

Enter the following text to complete the sentence.

1

- Press [End] to move to the end of the line.

- Type **earth's greatest unspoiled habitats and find out how you can experience the adventure of a lifetime.**

- Correct any spelling or grammar errors that are identified.

Your screen should be similar to **Figure 1.17**

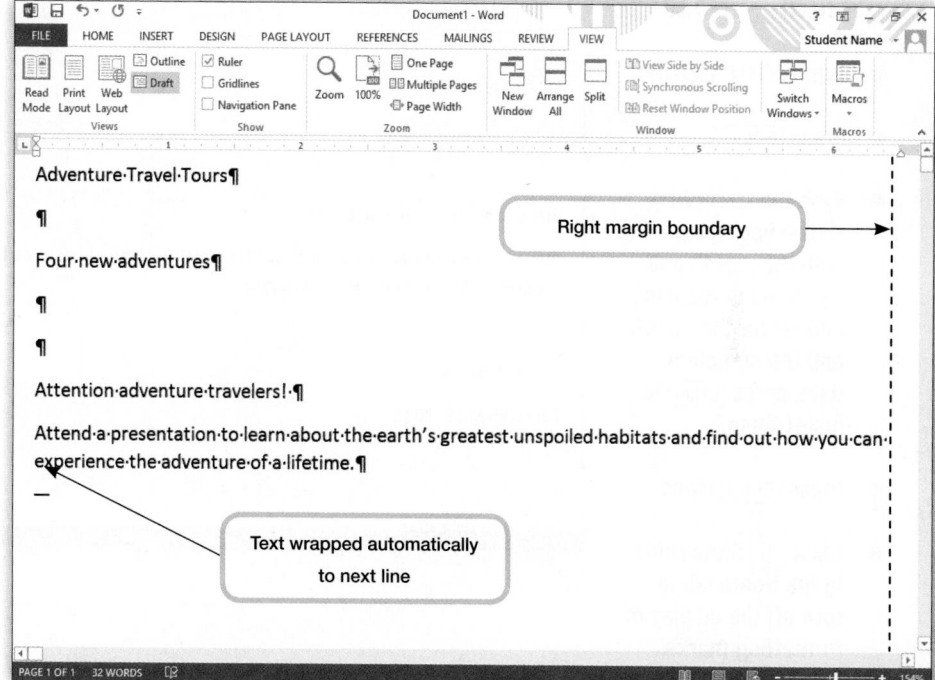

Figure 1.17

The program has wrapped the text that would overlap the right margin to the beginning of the next line.

You have a meeting you need to attend in a few minutes and want to continue working on the document when you get back. You decide to add your name and the current date to the document. As you type the first four characters of the month, Word will recognize the entry as a month and display a ScreenTip suggesting the remainder of the month. You can insert the suggested month by pressing Enter. Then enter a space to continue the date and another ScreenTip will appear with the complete date. Press Enter again to insert it.

Additional Information

You can continue typing to ignore the date suggestion.

2

- **Move to the end of the sentence and press Enter twice.**

- **Type your name**

- **Press Enter.**

- **Type the current date beginning with the month and when the ScreenTips appear for the month and the complete date, press Enter to insert them.**

- **Press Enter twice.**

- **Click ¶ Show/Hide in the Home tab to turn off the display of formatting marks.**

Your screen should be similar to Figure 1.18

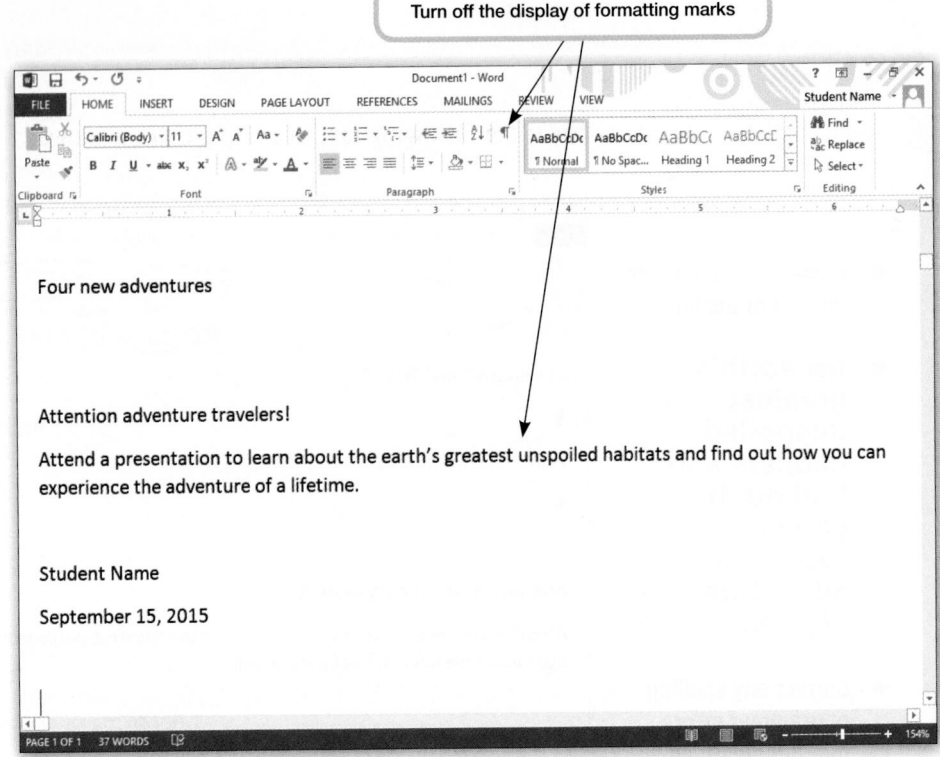

Turn off the display of formatting marks

Four new adventures

Attention adventure travelers!

Attend a presentation to learn about the earth's greatest unspoiled habitats and find out how you can experience the adventure of a lifetime.

Student Name

September 15, 2015

Figure 1.18

Having Trouble?

Review saving files in the "Saving a File" section on page. IO.55 in the Introduction to Microsoft Office 2013.

As you have seen, in many editing situations, it is helpful to display the formatting marks. However, for normal entry of text, you will probably not need the marks displayed. Now that you know how to turn this feature on and off, you can use it whenever you want when entering and editing text.

Next, you will save your work to a file. You will name the document Flyer and use the default document type (.docx).

3

- Click 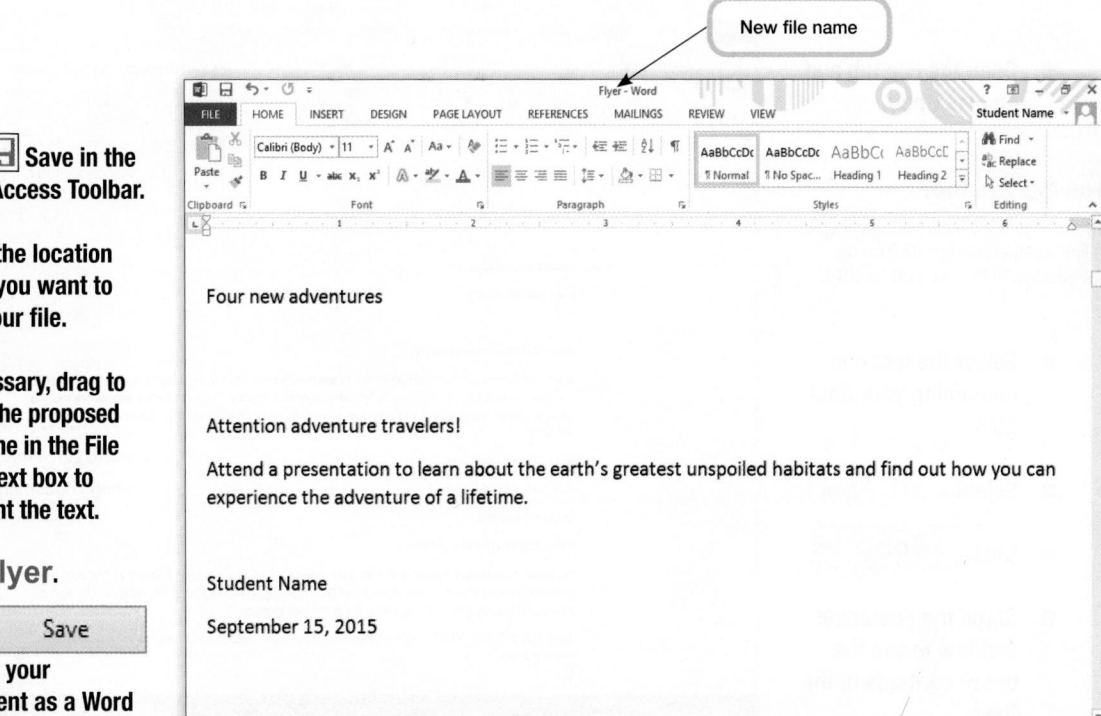 Save in the Quick Access Toolbar.

- Select the location where you want to save your file.

- If necessary, drag to select the proposed file name in the File Name text box to highlight the text.

- Type **Flyer**.

- Click **Save** to save your document as a Word document.

Four new adventures

Attention adventure travelers!

Attend a presentation to learn about the earth's greatest unspoiled habitats and find out how you can experience the adventure of a lifetime.

Student Name

September 15, 2015

Figure 1.19

Your screen should be similar to Figure 1.19

The document is saved as Flyer.docx at the location you selected, and the new file name is displayed in the Word title bar.

Finally, you want to close the document while you attend your meeting.

4

- Open the File tab and choose Close.

Now the Word window displays an empty document window.

Having Trouble?

Review closing files in the "Closing a File" section on page. IO.62 in the Introduction to Microsoft Office 2013.

Editing Documents

While you were away, your assistant added more text to the Flyer document. You will open the revised file and continue working on the flyer.

①

Open the File tab and choose Open.

Having Trouble?

Review opening files in the "Opening a File" section on page IO.30 in the Introduction to Microsoft Office 2013.

Select the location containing your data files.

Select wd01_Flyer1.

Click Open ▼ .

Scroll the document window to see the entire contents of the flyer.

Click anywhere in the last line to move the insertion point.

Your screen should be similar to Figure 1.20

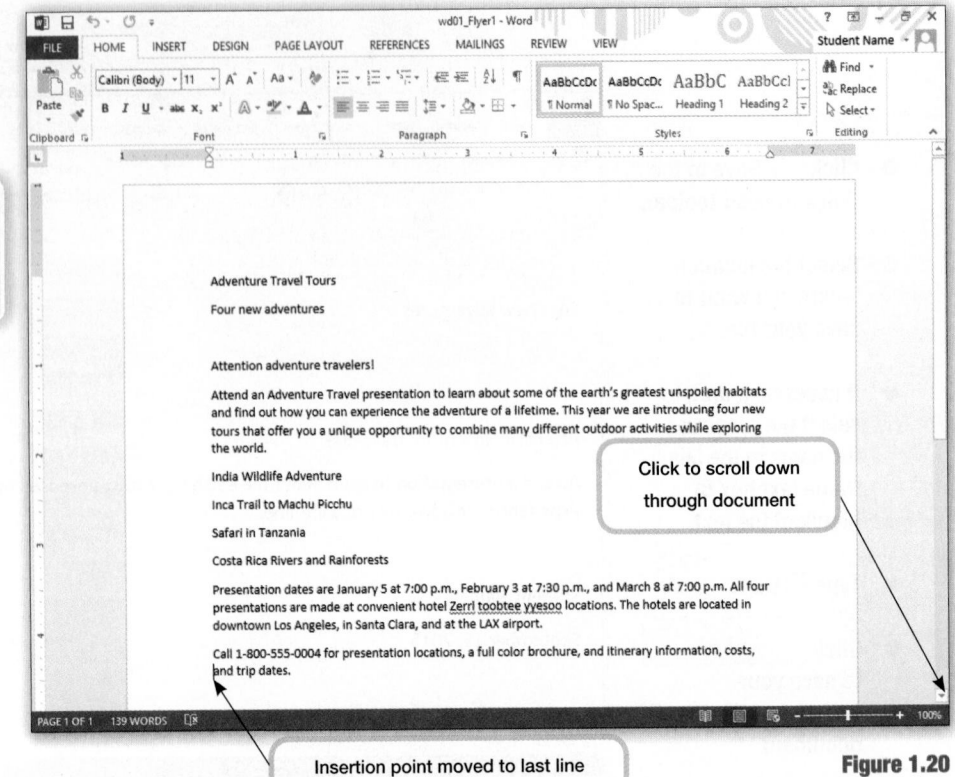

Figure 1.20

After looking over the changes that were made by your assistant to the flyer, you have identified several errors that need to be corrected and changes you want to make to the content. The changes you want to make are shown below.

Having Trouble?

Review how to navigate a document in the "Scrolling the Document Window" section on page IO.33 of the Introduction to Microsoft Office 2013.

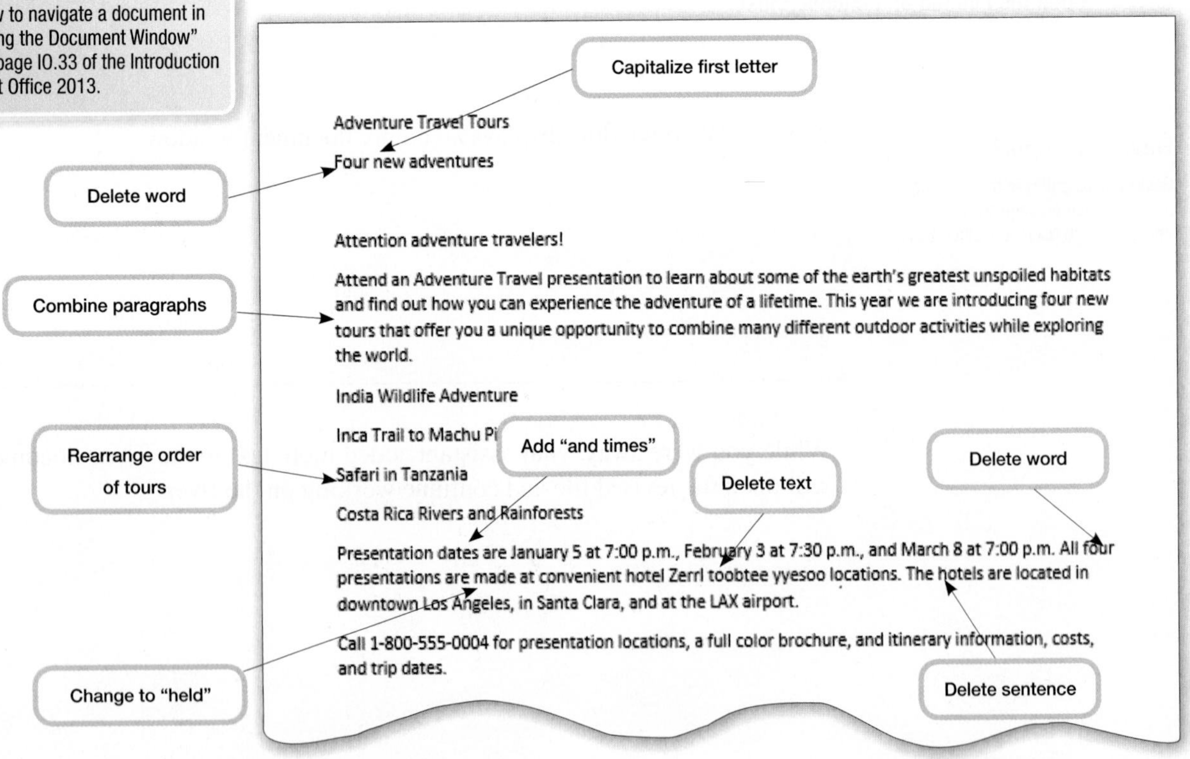

INSERTING AND REPLACING TEXT

As you check the document, you see that the first sentence of the paragraph below the list of trips is incorrect. It should read: "Presentation dates and times are. . . ." The sentence is missing the words "and times." In addition, you want to change the word "made" to "held" in the following sentence. These words can easily be entered into the sentence without retyping the entire line. This is because Word uses **Insert mode** to add new characters to existing text. Existing text moves to the right to make space for the new characters.

Additional Information

You can replace existing text using Overtype mode, in which each character you type replaces an existing character. This feature is turned on by opening the File tab, choosing Options, Advanced, and then selecting Use overtype mode.

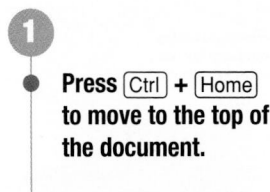

- **Press** Ctrl + Home **to move to the top of the document.**

- **Move the insertion point to the left of the "a" in "are" in the first sentence of the paragraph below the list of tours.**

Additional Information

Throughout these labs, when instructed to move to a specific letter in the text, this means to move the insertion point to the left side of the character.

- **Type** and times

- **Press** Spacebar.

Your screen should be similar to Figure 1.21

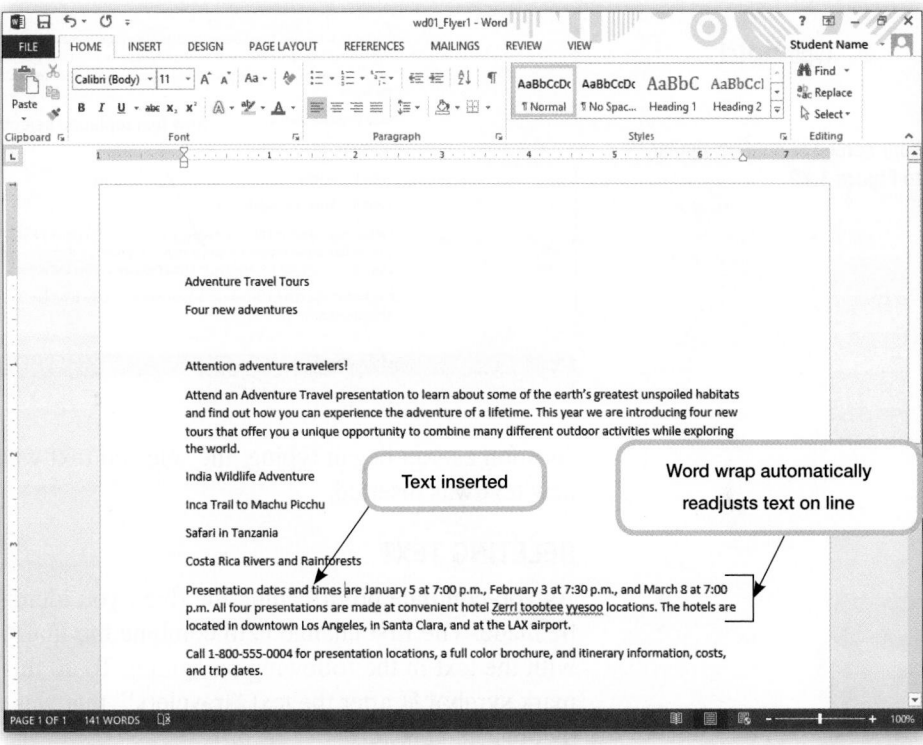

Figure 1.21

The inserted text moves the existing text on the line to the right, and the word wrap feature automatically readjusts the text on the line to fit within the margin settings.

In the second sentence, you want to change the word "made" to "held." You could delete this word and type the new word, or you can select the existing text and type the new text.

Having Trouble?

Review how to select text in the "Selecting Text" section on page IO.40 of the Introduction to Microsoft Office 2013.

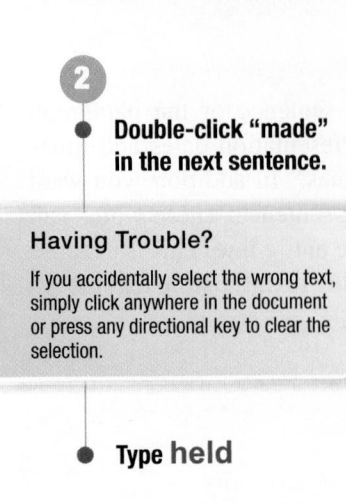

2

- Double-click "made" in the next sentence.

Having Trouble?

If you accidentally select the wrong text, simply click anywhere in the document or press any directional key to clear the selection.

- Type **held**

Your screen should be similar to **Figure 1.22**

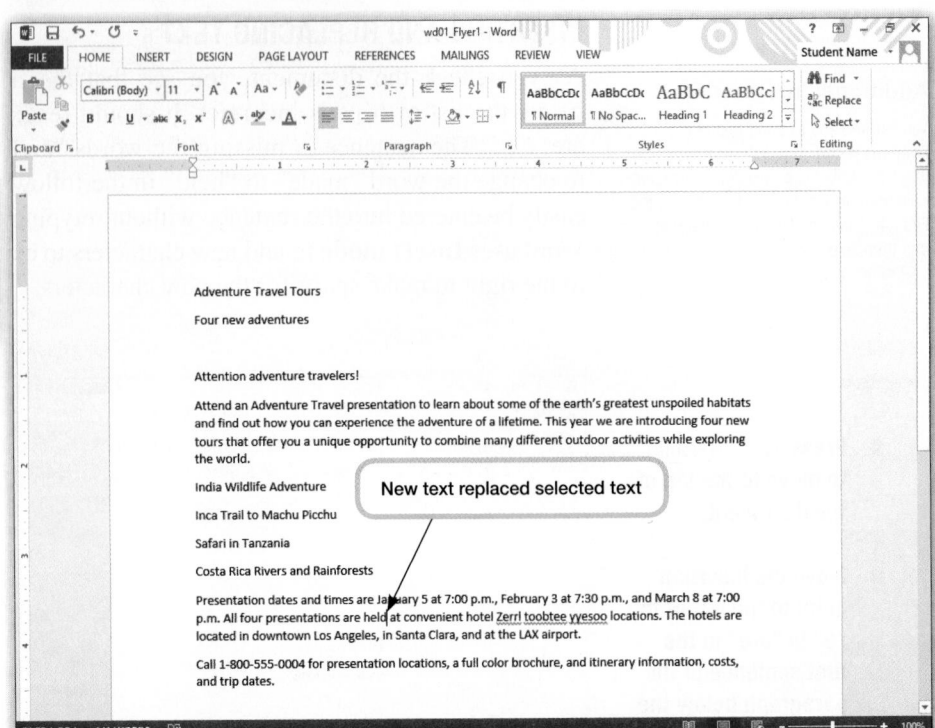

New text replaced selected text

Figure 1.22

As soon as you began typing, the selected text was automatically deleted and the new text was inserted.

DELETING TEXT

As you continue proofreading the flyer, you identify several changes that need to be made. The first change is to combine the line "Attention adventure travelers!" with the text in the following paragraph. To do this, you will delete the paragraph mark symbol ¶ after the text "travelers!" that was added when you ended the line by pressing ⏎Enter.

1

- Move to the beginning of the paragraph that begins "Attend an Adventure."

- Press ⏎Backspace⏋.

Your screen should be similar to **Figure 1.23**

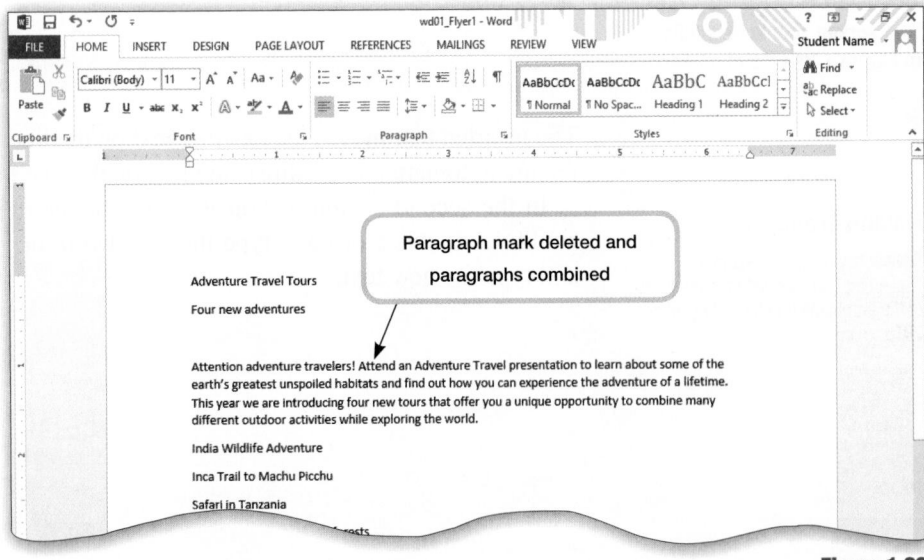

Paragraph mark deleted and paragraphs combined

Figure 1.23

Deleting the ¶ that ended the previous paragraph combines the two paragraphs.

You next want to delete the word "four" from the second sentence in the paragraph below the list of tours. The Ctrl + Delete key combination deletes text to the right of the insertion point to the beginning of the next group of characters. In order to delete an entire word, you must position the insertion point at the beginning of the word.

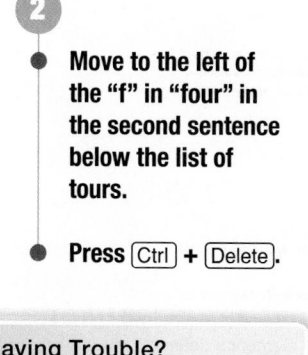

2

- **Move to the left of the "f" in "four" in the second sentence below the list of tours.**

- **Press Ctrl + Delete.**

Having Trouble?

Hold down Ctrl while pressing Delete.

Your screen should be similar to Figure 1.24

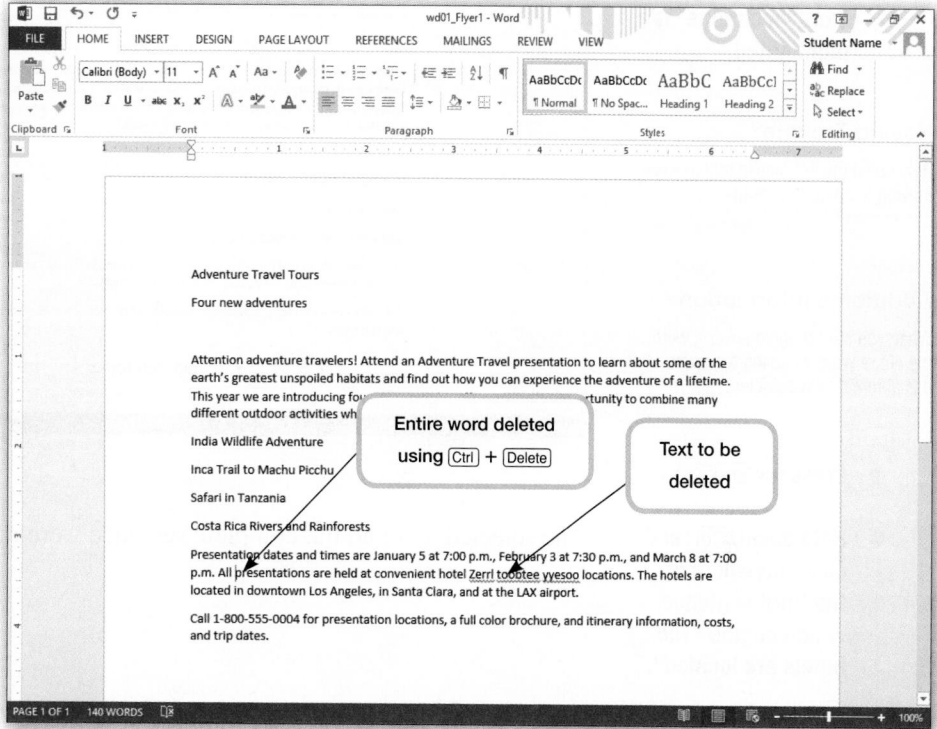

Adventure Travel Tours

Four new adventures

Attention adventure travelers! Attend an Adventure Travel presentation to learn about some of the earth's greatest unspoiled habitats and find out how you can experience the adventure of a lifetime. This year we are introducing fou... ...rtunity to combine many different outdoor activities wh...

India Wildlife Adventure

Inca Trail to Machu Picchu

Safari in Tanzania

Costa Rica Rivers and Rainforests

Presentation dates and times are January 5 at 7:00 p.m., February 3 at 7:30 p.m., and March 8 at 7:00 p.m. All presentations are held at convenient hotel Zerrl tooƄtee yyesoo locations. The hotels are located in downtown Los Angeles, in Santa Clara, and at the LAX airport.

Call 1-800-555-0004 for presentation locations, a full color brochure, and itinerary information, costs, and trip dates.

> Entire word deleted using Ctrl + Delete

> Text to be deleted

Figure 1.24

You see that the end of the same sentence contains a section of unnecessary characters. To remove these characters, you could use Delete and Backspace to delete each character individually, or Ctrl + Delete or Ctrl + Backspace to delete each word or group of characters. A quicker method, however, is to select the text to be deleted and then press Delete.

You will use this method to remove the unnecessary text as well as the entire last sentence of the paragraph.

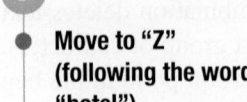

3

- Move to "Z" (following the word "hotel").

- Drag to the right until all the text including the space before the word "locations" is highlighted.

Having Trouble?

Hold down the left mouse button while moving the mouse to drag.

Additional Information

When you start dragging over a word, the entire word including the space after it is automatically selected.

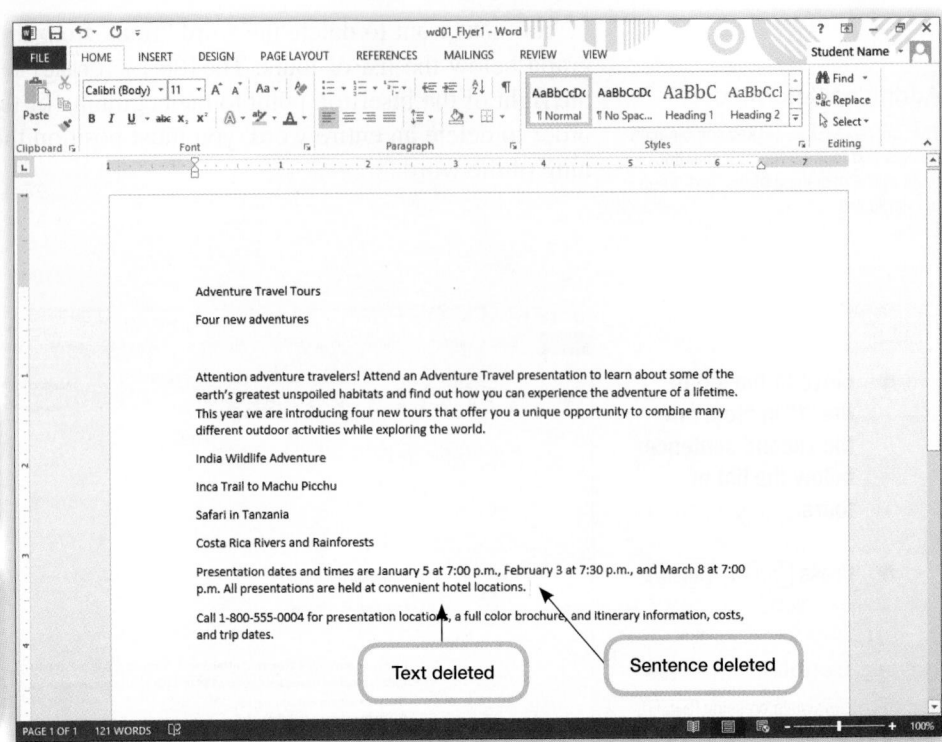

Figure 1.25

- Press Delete.

- Hold down Ctrl and click anywhere in the third sentence, which begins "The hotels are located".

- Press Delete.

The selected text and the complete sentence were removed from the flyer.

Your screen should be similar to Figure 1.25

Having Trouble?

Review the Undo feature in the "Undoing Editing Changes" section on page IO.46 of the Introduction to Microsoft Office 2013.

UNDOING EDITING CHANGES

After removing the sentence, you decide it should be reinserted. To quickly restore this sentence, use ↺ Undo to reverse your last action or command. Notice that the Undo button includes a drop-down list button. Clicking this button displays a list of the most recent actions that can be reversed, with the most recent action at the top of the list. When you select an action from the drop-down list, you also undo all actions above it in the list.

Another Method

The keyboard shortcut for the Undo command is Ctrl + Z.

1

● **Open the** 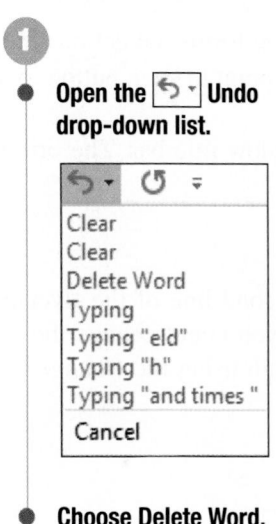 **Undo drop-down list.**

● **Choose Delete Word.**

Your screen should be similar to Figure 1.26

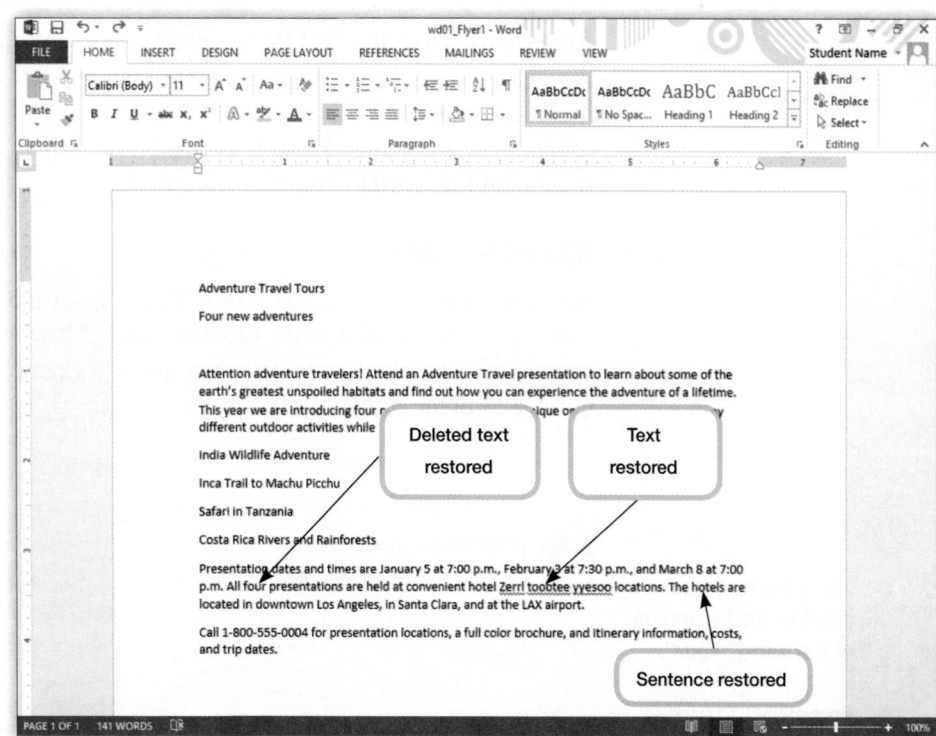

Figure 1.26

The deleted sentence, extra characters, and the word "four" are restored. You will restore two of your corrections and then save the changes you have made to the document to a new file.

2

● **Click** **Redo 2 times.**

Another Method

The keyboard shortcut is Ctrl + Y.

● **Open the File tab and choose Save As.**

● **Save the document as** Flyer1 **to your solution file location.**

Your screen should be similar to Figure 1.27

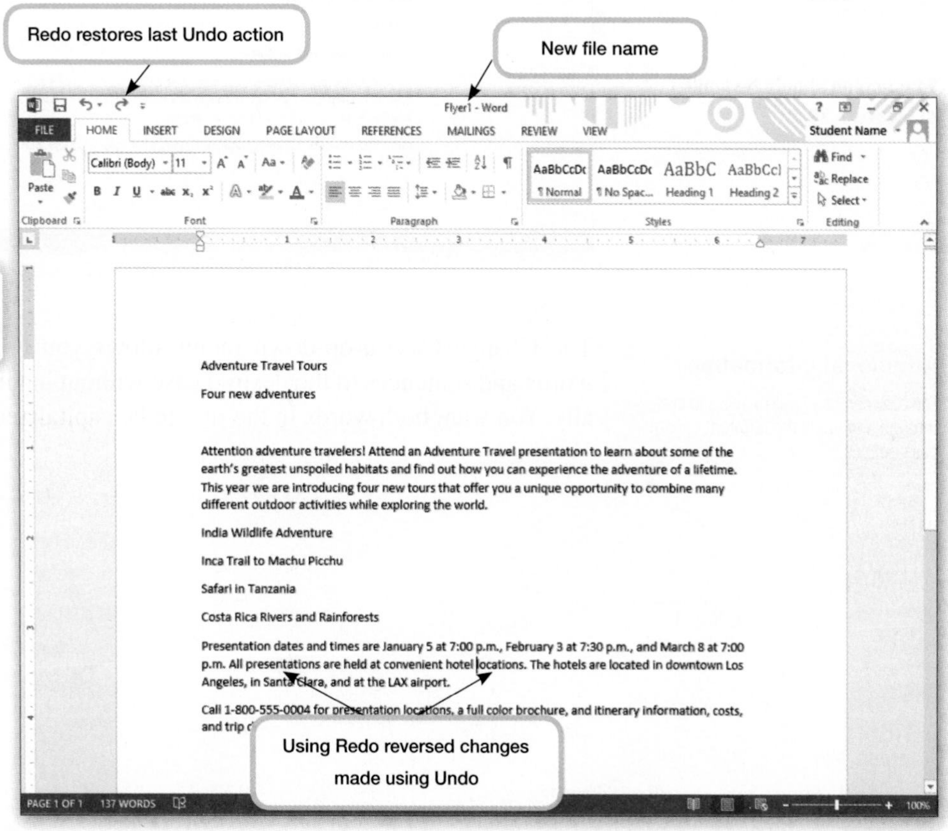

Redo restores last Undo action

New file name

Using Redo reversed changes made using Undo

Figure 1.27

Repeatedly using the ⤺ Undo or ⤻ Redo buttons performs the actions in the list one by one. To see what action will be performed, point to each button to see the ScreenTip.

The new file name, Flyer1, is displayed in the window title bar. The original document file, wd01_Flyer1, is unchanged.

CHANGING CASE

You also want to delete the word "Four" from the second line of the flyer title and capitalize the first letter of each word. Although you could change the case individually for the words, you can quickly change both using the Change Case command in the Font group.

1 ● **Move the insertion point to the beginning of the word "Four".**

● **Press** Ctrl + Delete.

● **Click in the left margin to select the entire title line.**

● **From the Font group, click** Aa ▾ **Change Case.**

Your screen should be similar to Figure 1.28

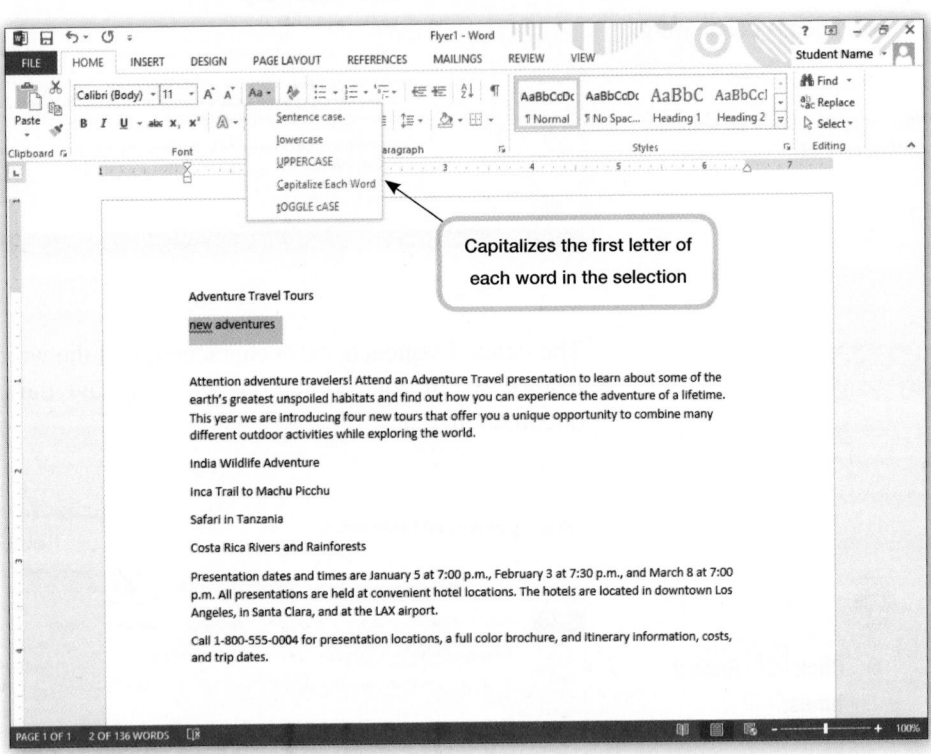

Capitalizes the first letter of each word in the selection

Figure 1.28

Additional Information

You also can use Shift + F3 to cycle through and apply the different change case options.

The Change Case drop-down menu allows you to change the case of selected words and sentences to the desired case without having to make the change manually. You want both words in the title to be capitalized.

- Choose Capitalize Each Word.

- Click anywhere to deselect the title line.

Your screen should be similar to Figure 1.29

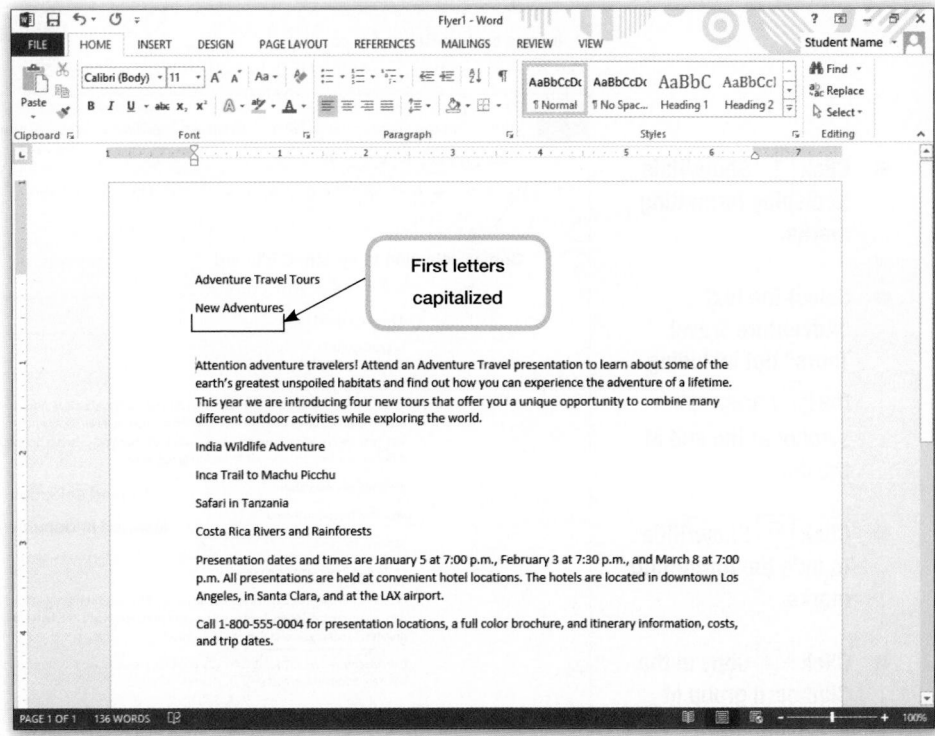

Figure 1.29

Copying and Moving Selections

After looking over the letter, you decide to add the company name in several other locations and to change the order of the list of tours. To make these changes quickly, you can copy and move selections.

USING COPY AND PASTE

Having Trouble?

Review how to copy and move selections in the "Copying and Moving Selections" section on page I0.48 of the Introduction to Microsoft Office 2013.

You want to include the company name in the last paragraph of the letter. Because the name has already been entered on the first line of the document, you will copy the name instead of typing the name again. Before you copy the text, it is helpful to display formatting marks to make sure you're copying exactly what you want.

1

- **Click ¶ Show/Hide to display formatting marks.**

- **Select the text "Adventure Travel Tours" not including the ¶ paragraph symbol at the end of the line.**

- **Click ¶ Show/Hide to hide the formatting marks.**

- **Click 📋 Copy in the Clipboard group of the Home tab.**

- **Move the insertion point to the left of "1" in the phone number (last paragraph).**

- **Click 📋 Paste in the Clipboard group.**

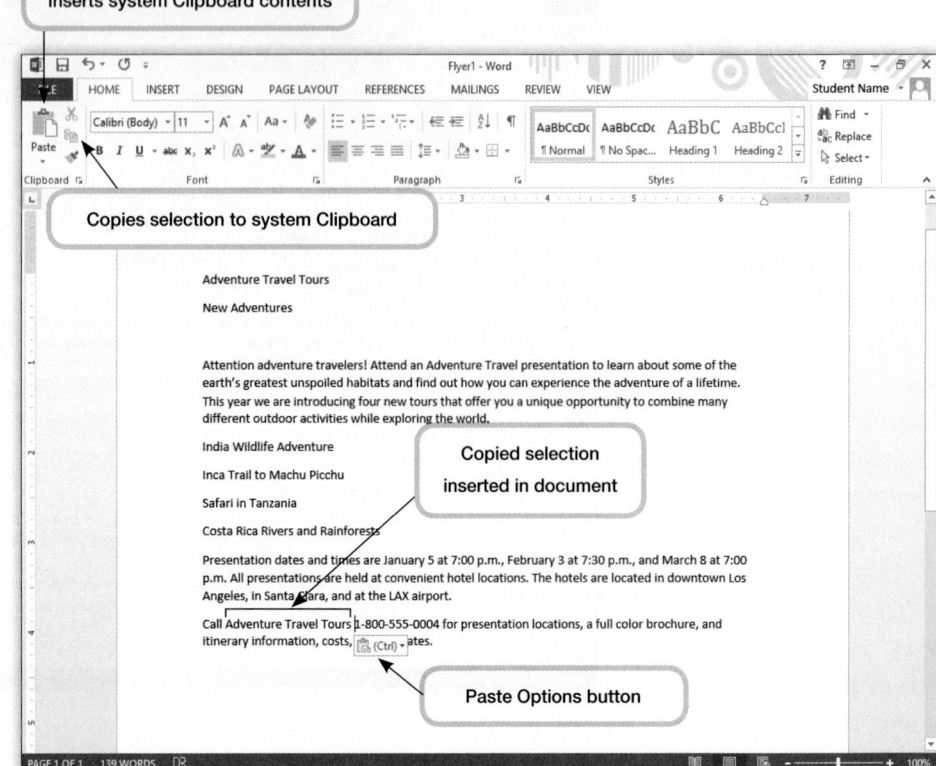

Figure 1.30

Another Method

The Copy keyboard shortcut is [Ctrl] + C. The Paste keyboard shortcut is [Ctrl] + V.

Your screen should be similar to Figure 1.30

The copied selection is inserted at the location you specified. The 📋 (Ctrl) ▾ Paste Options button appears automatically whenever a selection is pasted. It is used to control the format of the pasted item. By default, pasted items maintain the original formatting from the source.

2

Click the  (Ctrl) ▾
Paste Options button.

Your screen should be similar
to **Figure 1.31**

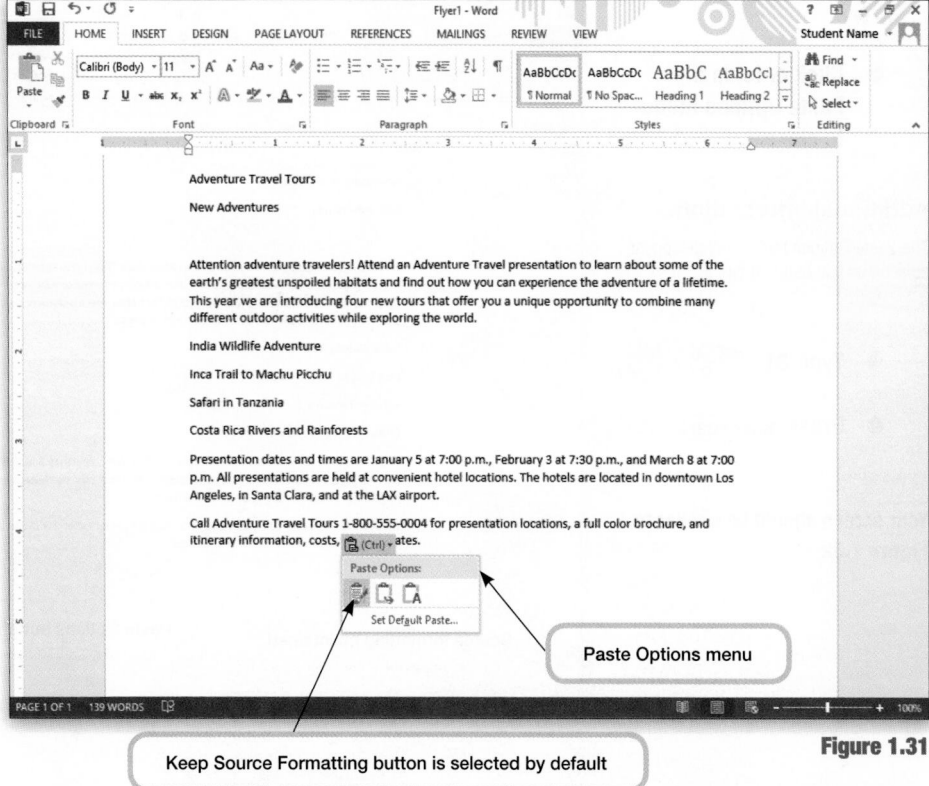

Adventure Travel Tours

New Adventures

Attention adventure travelers! Attend an Adventure Travel presentation to learn about some of the
earth's greatest unspoiled habitats and find out how you can experience the adventure of a lifetime.
This year we are introducing four new tours that offer you a unique opportunity to combine many
different outdoor activities while exploring the world.

India Wildlife Adventure

Inca Trail to Machu Picchu

Safari in Tanzania

Costa Rica Rivers and Rainforests

Presentation dates and times are January 5 at 7:00 p.m., February 3 at 7:30 p.m., and March 8 at 7:00
p.m. All presentations are held at convenient hotel locations. The hotels are located in downtown Los
Angeles, in Santa Clara, and at the LAX airport.

Call Adventure Travel Tours 1-800-555-0004 for presentation locations, a full color brochure, and
itinerary information, costs, ates.

Paste Options menu

Keep Source Formatting button is selected by default

Figure 1.31

The following table describes the options on the Paste Options menu.

Paste Option	Description
Keep Source Formatting 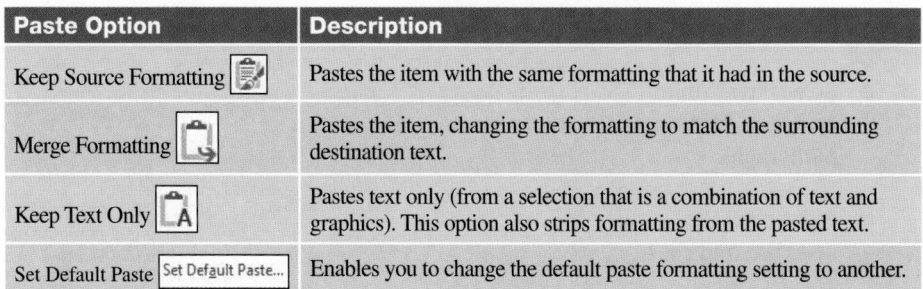	Pastes the item with the same formatting that it had in the source.
Merge Formatting	Pastes the item, changing the formatting to match the surrounding destination text.
Keep Text Only	Pastes text only (from a selection that is a combination of text and graphics). This option also strips formatting from the pasted text.
Set Default Paste	Enables you to change the default paste formatting setting to another.

Since the selection was pasted correctly using the same formatting it had in the
source, you will close the Paste Options menu without changing the selection.

● **Click outside the Paste Options menu to close it.**

● **Type at**

● **Press** [Spacebar].

Your screen should be similar to **Figure 1.32**

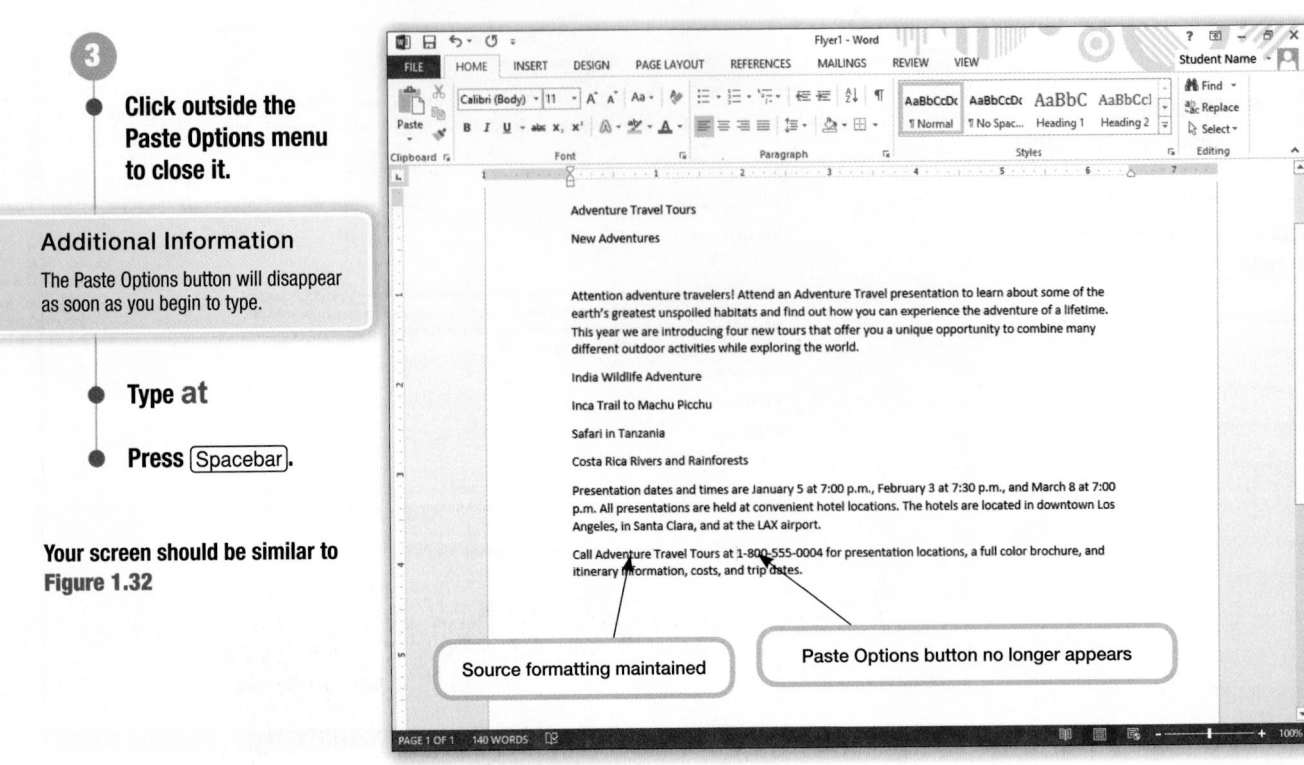

Source formatting maintained

Paste Options button no longer appears

Figure 1.32

Next, you want to insert the company name in place of the word "we" in the first paragraph and then change the word "are" to "is".

4

● **Select "we" (third sentence, first paragraph).**

● **Right-click the selection and click** 📋 **Keep Source Formatting from the context menu.**

● **Change "are" in the same sentence to "is".**

Your screen should be similar to **Figure 1.33**

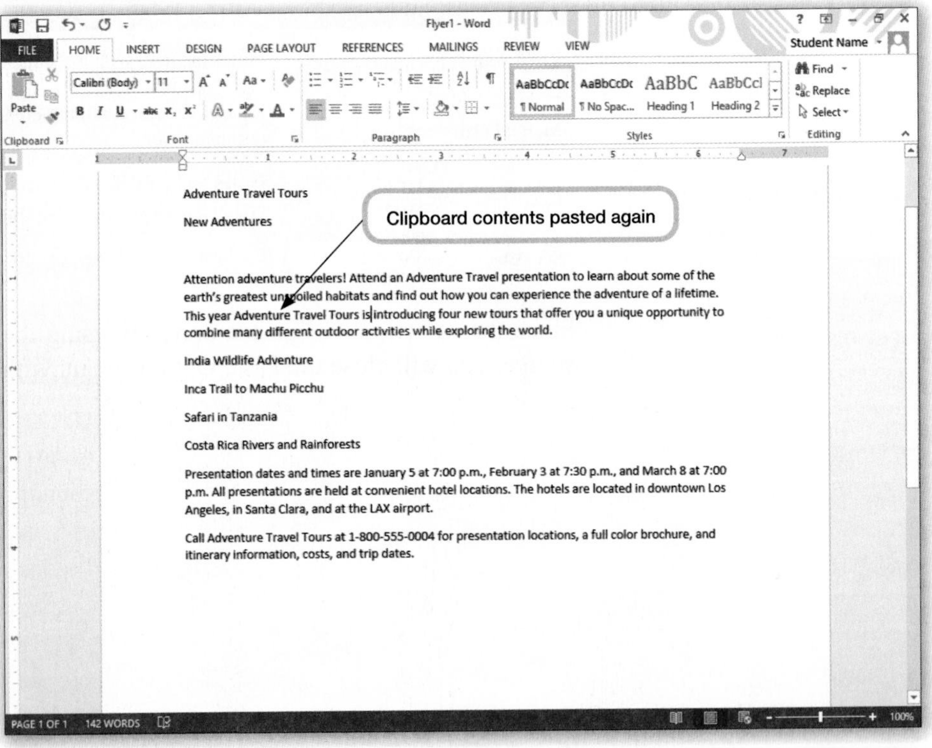

Clipboard contents pasted again

Figure 1.33

The selected text was deleted and replaced with the contents of the system Clipboard. The system Clipboard contents remain in the Clipboard until another item is copied or cut, allowing you to paste the same item multiple times.

USING CUT AND PASTE

You've decided to move the Costa Rica Rivers and Rainforests tour name to the second position in the tour list. To do this, you will use the Cut and Paste commands.

1

- Select the text "Costa Rica Rivers and Rainforests" including the space at the end of the line.

- Click ✂ Cut in the Clipboard group.

- Move to the beginning of the line "Inca Trail to Machu Picchu".

- Press Ctrl + V.

Your screen should be similar to Figure 1.34

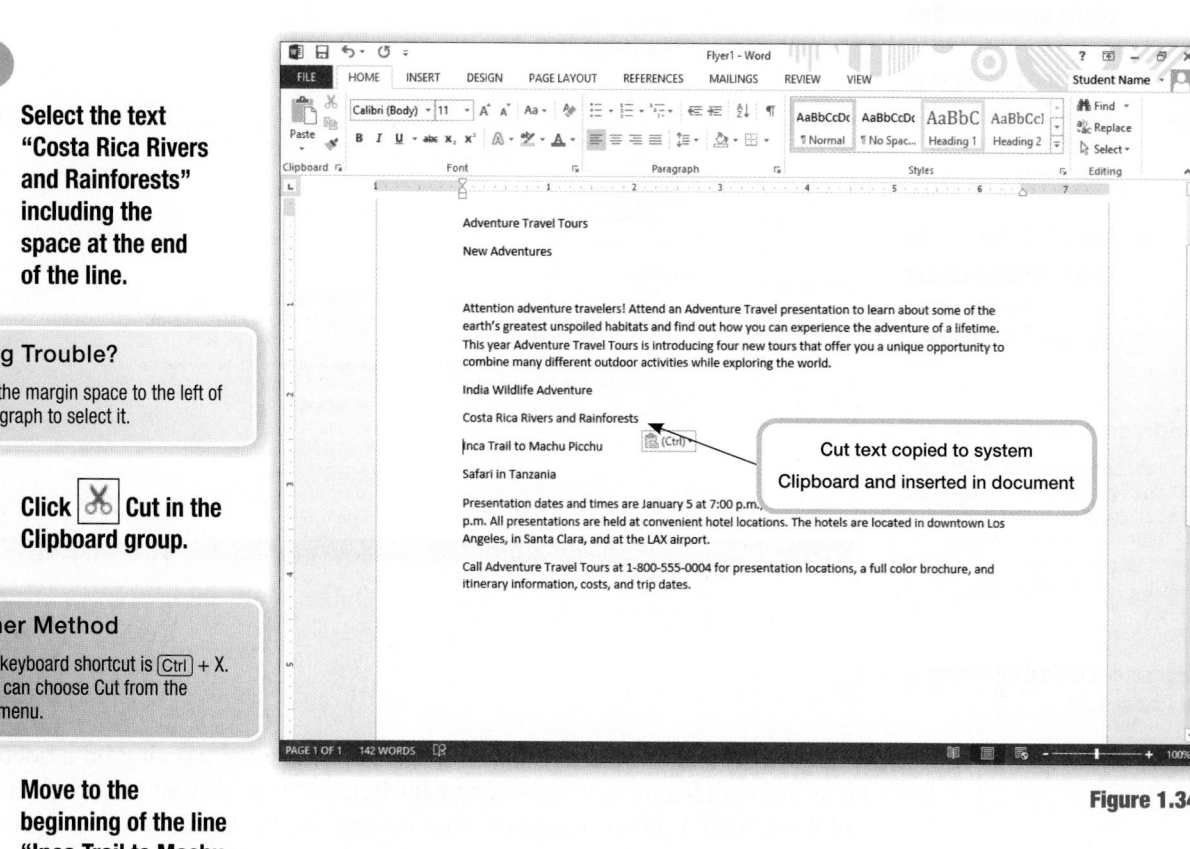

Figure 1.34

The selected text was removed from the source and copied to the Clipboard. Then it was reentered into the document at the insertion point location.

USING DRAG AND DROP

Finally, you also decide to move the tour name "Safari in Tanzania" to first in the list. Rather than use Cut and Paste to move this text, you will use the drag-and-drop editing feature. This feature is most useful for copying or moving short distances in a document.

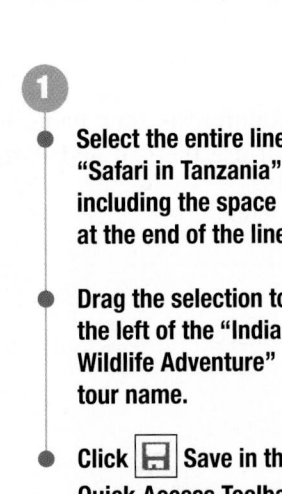

- **Select the entire line "Safari in Tanzania", including the space at the end of the line.**

- **Drag the selection to the left of the "India Wildlife Adventure" tour name.**

- **Click** 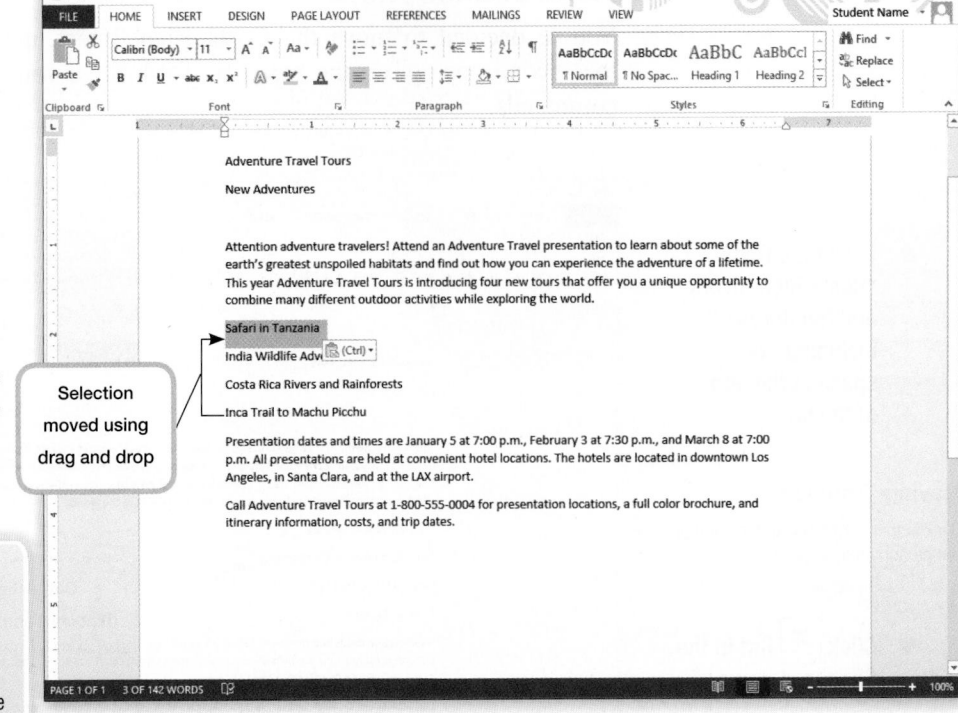 **Save in the Quick Access Toolbar to save the file using the same file name.**

Selection moved using drag and drop

Additional Information

You also can move or copy a selection by holding down the right mouse button while dragging.

When you release the mouse button, a context menu appears with the available move and copy options.

Figure 1.35

Your screen should be similar to Figure 1.35

The selection is moved to the new location. As you are working on a document, it is a good idea to save your document frequently to prevent the accidental loss of work from a power outage or other mishap. While AutoRecover is a great feature for recovering lost work, it should not be used in place of regularly saving your work.

Formatting a Document

Because this document is a flyer, you want it to be interesting and easy to read. Applying different formatting to characters and paragraphs can greatly enhance the appearance of the document. **Character formatting** consists of formatting features that affect selected characters only. This includes changing the character style and size, applying effects such as bold and italics to characters, changing the character spacing, and adding text effects. Paragraph formatting features affect an entire paragraph. A paragraph consists of all text up to and including the paragraph mark. **Paragraph formatting** features include how the paragraph is positioned or aligned between the margins, paragraph indentation, spacing above and below a paragraph, and line spacing within a paragraph.

CHANGING FONTS AND FONT SIZES

The first formatting change you will make is to use different fonts and font sizes in the flyer. Using fonts as a design element can add interest to your document and give readers visual cues to help them find information quickly.

Having Trouble?

Review font and font size in the "Formatting Text" section on page IO.43 in the Introduction to Microsoft Office 2013.

WWW.MHHE.COM/OLEARY

Two basic types of fonts are serif and sans serif. **Serif fonts** have a flair at the base of each letter that visually leads the reader to the next letter. They are generally used for text in paragraphs. Two common serif fonts are Roman and Times New Roman. **Sans serif fonts** don't have a flair at the base of each letter and are generally used for headings. Arial and Calibri are two common sans serif fonts. A good practice is to use only two fonts in a document, one for text and one for headings. Using too many different font styles can make your document look cluttered and unprofessional.

Several common fonts in different sizes are shown in the table below.

Font Name	Font Type	Font Size
Arial	Sans serif	This is 10 pt. This is 16 pt.
Calibri	Sans serif	This is 10 pt. This is 16 pt.
Times New Roman	Serif	This is 10 pt. This is 16 pt.

To change the font before typing the text, use the command and then type. All text will appear in the specified setting until another font setting is selected. To change a font setting for existing text, select the text you want to change and apply a format. If you want to apply font formatting to a word, simply move the insertion point to the word and the formatting is automatically applied to the entire word.

First you want to increase the font size of all the text in the flyer to 14 points to make it easier to read. Currently, you can see from the Font Size button in the Font group that the font size is 11 points.

1

● **Triple-click in the left margin when the mouse pointer is 𝒜 to select the entire document.**

Another Method

The keyboard shortcut is Ctrl + A.

● **From the Font group, open the 11 ▾ Font Size drop-down list.**

Another Method

The keyboard shortcut is Ctrl + Shift + P.

Your screen should be similar to Figure 1.36

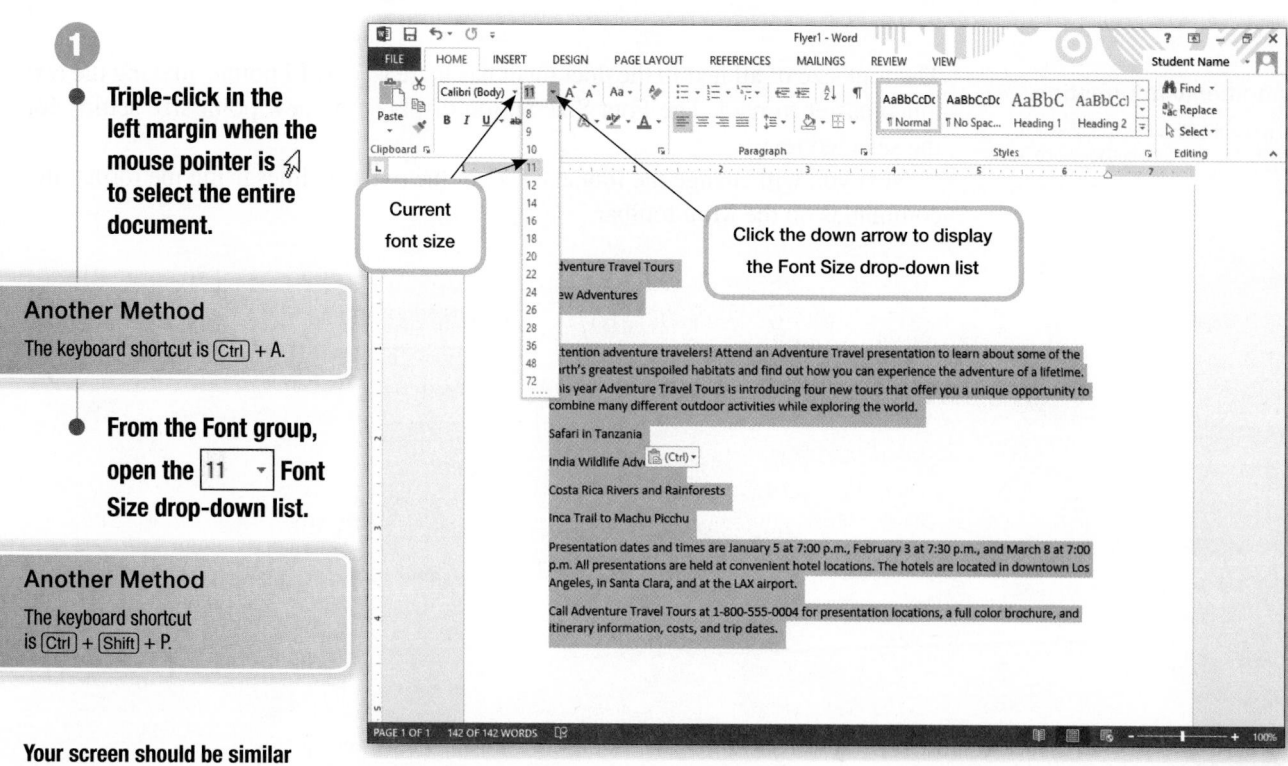

Current font size

Click the down arrow to display the Font Size drop-down list

Figure 1.36

Formatting a Document   **WD1.35**

Having Trouble?

Review the Live Preview feature in the section "Formatting Text" on page IO.43 in the Introduction to Microsoft Office 2013.

The current (default) font size of 11 is selected. As you point to the size options, the Live Preview feature shows how the selected text in the document will appear if chosen.

2

- **Point to several different point sizes in the list to see the Live Preview.**

- **Click 14 to choose it.**

Your screen should be similar to Figure 1.37

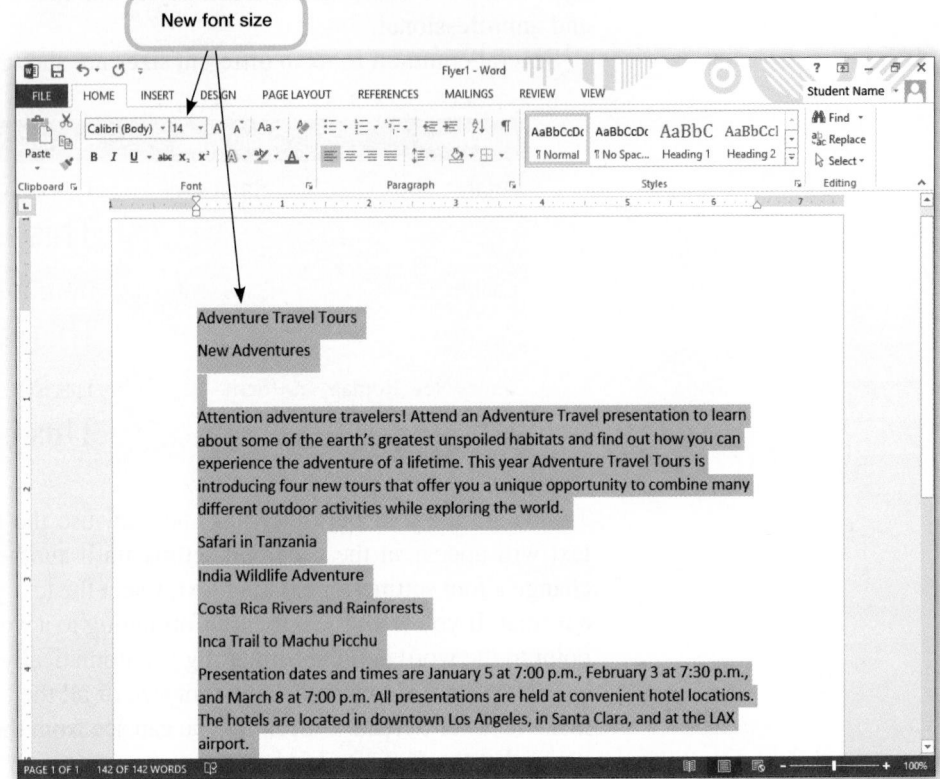

New font size

Figure 1.37

Additional Information

If a selection includes text of various sizes, the Font Size button will be blank.

The font size of all text in the document has increased to 14 points, making the text much easier to read. The Font Size button displays the new point size setting for the selected text.

Next you will change the font and size of the two title lines using the formatting commands on the Mini toolbar.

3

- **Select the two title lines and point to the Mini toolbar.**

- **Open the** Calibri (Body) ▾ **Font drop-down menu in the Mini toolbar.**

- **Scroll the list and choose Comic Sans MS.**

Additional Information

Font names are listed in alphabetical order. If a font was recently used, it appears in the Recently Used Fonts section at the top of the list.

Having Trouble?

If this font is not available on your computer, choose a similar font.

Your screen should be similar to Figure 1.38

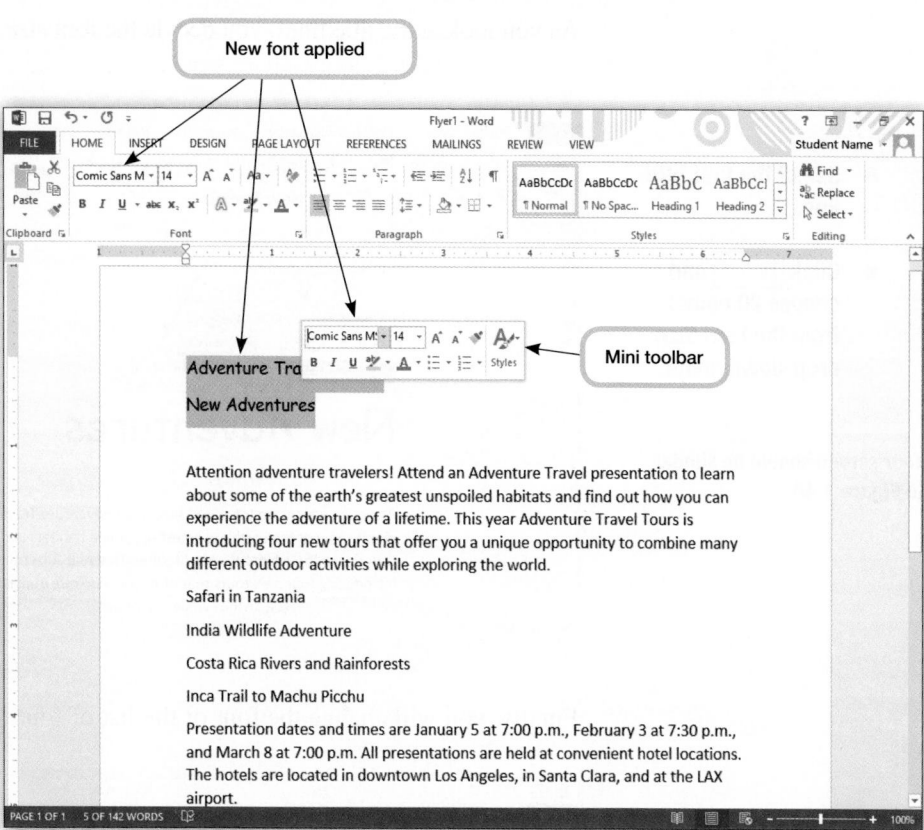

Figure 1.38

Using the Mini toolbar to apply the formats is a quick and convenient alternative to using the Ribbon.

4

- **Open the** 14 ▾ **Font Size drop-down menu in the Mini toolbar.**

Having Trouble?

If needed, right-click on the selection to redisplay the Mini toolbar.

- **Choose 36.**

Your screen should be similar to Figure 1.39

Another Method:

You also can type the name of the font in the Font text box or the size in the Font size text box to change it.

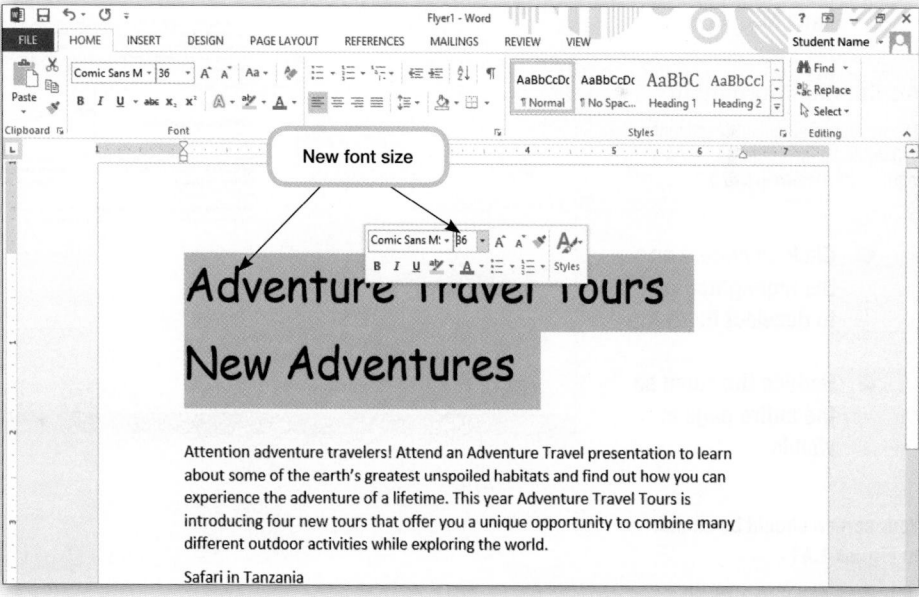

Figure 1.39

The Font and Font Size buttons reflect the settings in use in the selection.

As you look at the title lines, you decide the font size of the first title line is too large.

5

● Select the first title line.

● Click 36 ▾ and choose 20 points from the Font Size drop-down menu.

Your screen should be similar to Figure 1.40

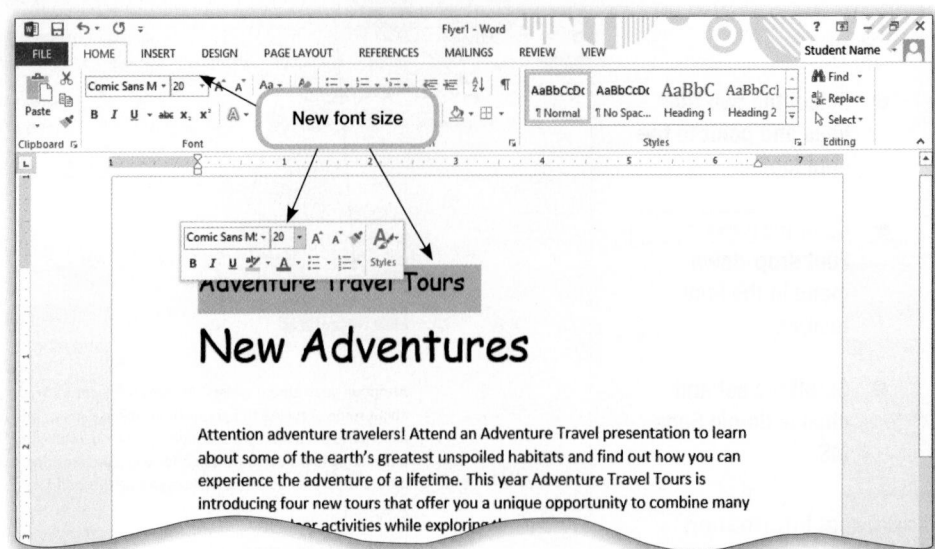

Figure 1.40

Finally, you will change the font of the list of four tours.

6

● Select the list of four tours.

● Click Calibri (Body) ▾ Font in the Mini toolbar and change the font to Comic Sans MS.

Additional Information

Theme fonts and recently used fonts appear at the top of the list. You will learn about themes in Lab 3.

● Click anywhere on the highlighted text to deselect it.

● Reduce the zoom so the entire page is visible.

Your screen should be similar to Figure 1.41

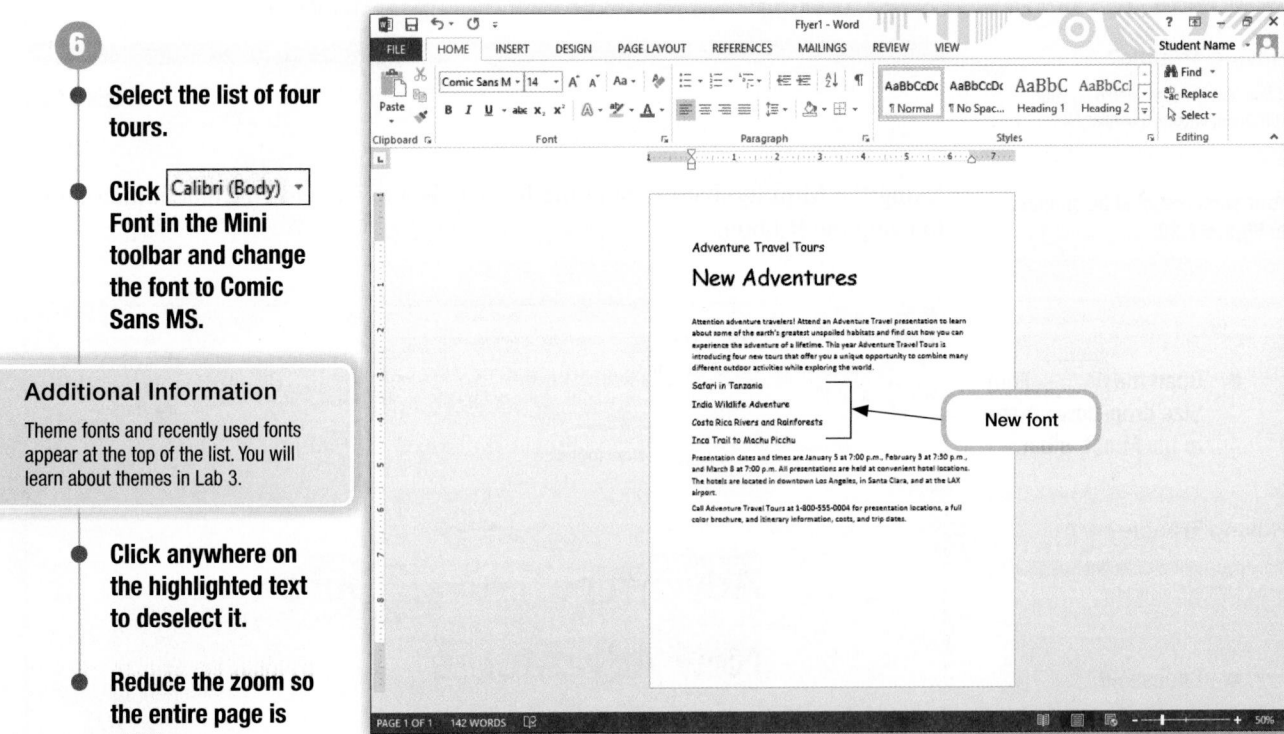

Figure 1.41

The changes you have made to the font and font size have made the flyer somewhat more interesting. However, you want to further enhance the document.

APPLYING CHARACTER EFFECTS

Next you want to liven up the flyer by adding character effects such as color and bold to selected areas. The table below describes some of the effects and their uses.

Format	Example	Use
Bold, italic	**Bold** *Italic*	Adds emphasis.
Underline	Underline	Adds emphasis.
Strikethrough	~~Strikethrough~~	Indicates words to be deleted.
Double strikethrough	Double Strikethrough	Indicates words to be deleted.
Superscript	"To be or not to be."[1]	Used in footnotes and formulas.
Subscript	H_2O	Used in formulas.
Shadow	Shadow	Adds distinction to titles and headings.
Outline	Outline	Adds distinction to titles and headings.
Reflection	Reflection	Adds distinction to titles and headings.
Glow	Glow	Adds distinction to titles and headings.
Small caps	SMALL CAPS	Adds emphasis when case is not important.
All caps	ALL CAPS	Adds emphasis when case is not important.
Hidden		Prevents selected text from displaying or printing. Hidden text can be viewed by displaying formatting marks.
Text highlight color	Text highlight color	Makes text stand out by applying a bright color over selection.
Font color	Color Color **Color**	Adds interest.

First you will add color and bold to the top title line. The default font color setting is Automatic. This setting automatically determines when to use black or white text. Black text is used on a light background and white text on a dark background.

1

- **Return the zoom to 100%.**

- **Select the first title line.**

- **Open the** 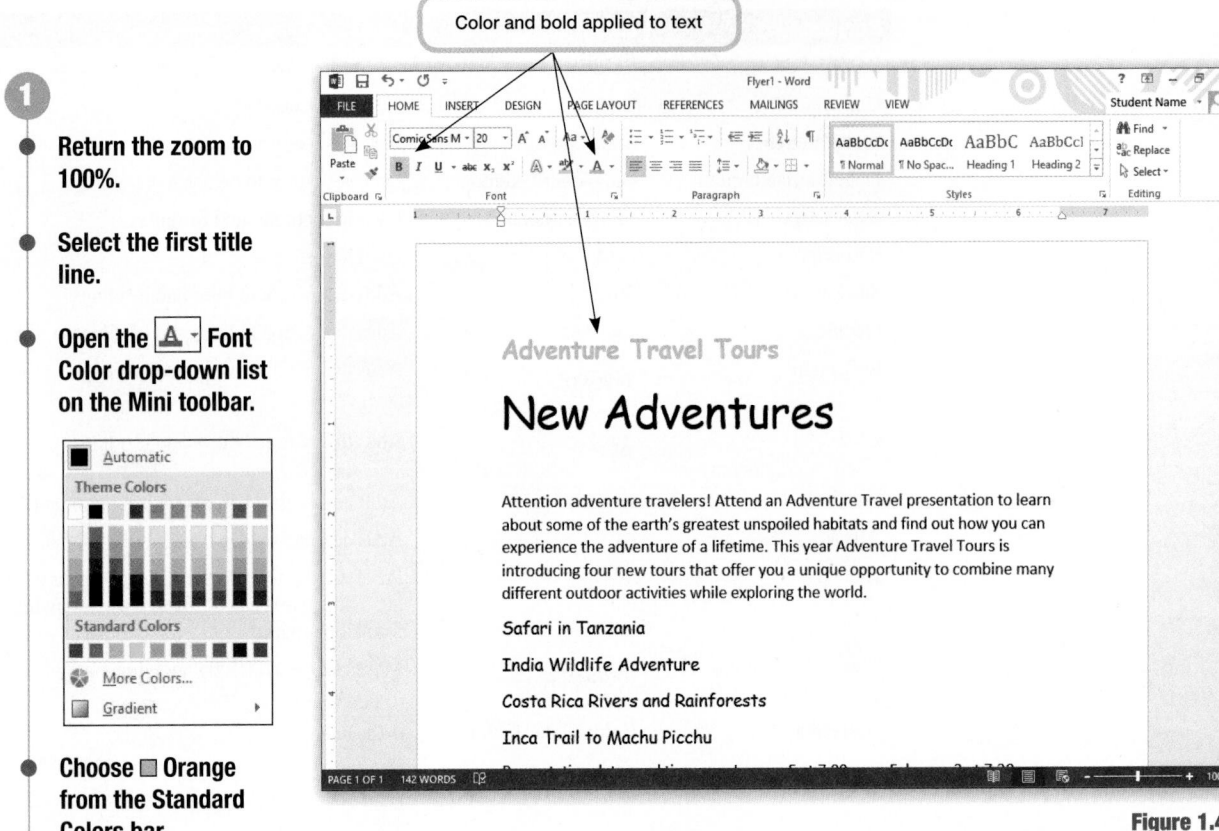 **Font Color drop-down list on the Mini toolbar.**

- **Choose ▢ Orange from the Standard Colors bar.**

Color and bold applied to text

Figure 1.42

The Bold button appears highlighted to show the bold effect is associated with the text at the insertion point. The Font Color button appears in the last selected color. This color can be quickly applied to other selections now simply by clicking the button.

Additional Information

A ScreenTip displays the name of the color when selected.

- **Click B Bold on the Mini toolbar.**

Another Method

The keyboard shortcut is Ctrl + B.

- **Click the title line to clear the selection.**

Your screen should be similar to Figure 1.42

Next you will add color and bold to several other areas of the flyer.

2

- Select the second title line.

- Using the Mini toolbar, change the font color to Green in the Standard Colors bar.

- Add bold to the selected title.

- Select the list of four tours.

- Using the Mini toolbar, click **A** Font Color to change the color to green.

Additional Information

The currently selected font color can be applied to the selection simply by clicking the button.

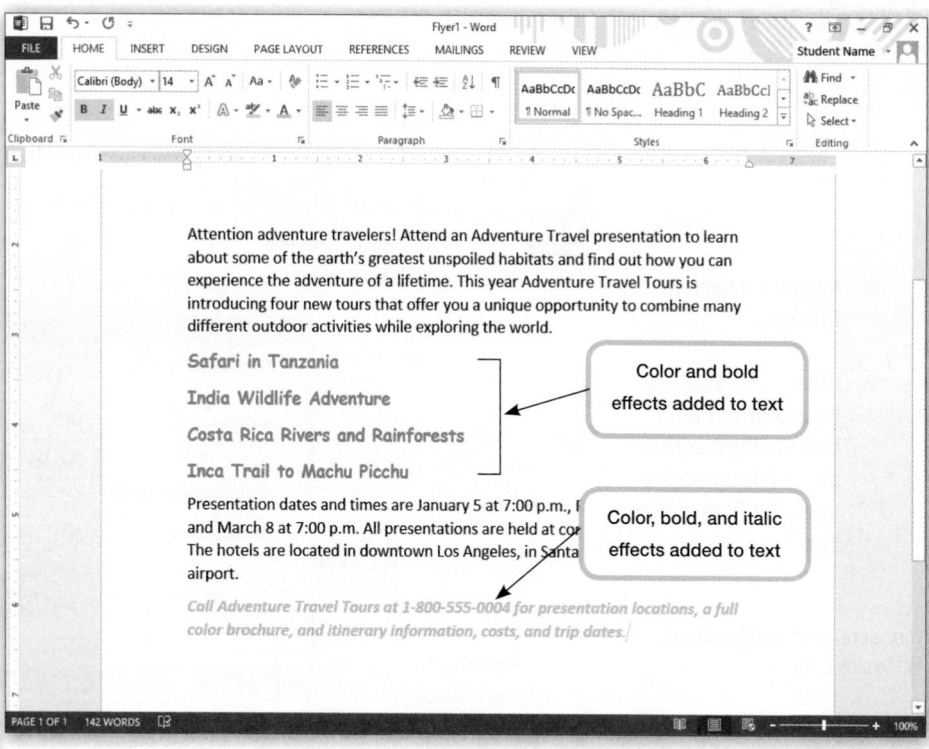

Figure 1.43

- Click **B** Bold, **I** Italic.

- Click **I** Italic again to remove the italic effect.

Additional Information

Many formatting commands are toggle commands. This means the feature can be turned on and off simply by clicking on the command button.

- Using any method, apply bold, italic, and orange font color to the last sentence of the flyer.

- Click in the last sentence to deselect the text.

Your screen should be similar to Figure 1.43

The character formatting effects you added to the flyer make it much more interesting.

Having Trouble?

Review the Dialog Box Launcher feature in the "Using the Dialog Box Launcher" section on page IO.25 of the Introduction to Microsoft Office 2013.

The next formatting change you will make is to apply the Small Caps effect to the second title line. Since the Ribbon does not display a button for this feature, you need to open the Font dialog box using the Dialog Box Launcher to access this feature.

3

• **Select the second title line.**

• **Click Dialog Box Launcher in the bottom-right corner of the Font group to open the Font dialog box.**

Your screen should be similar to Figure 1.44

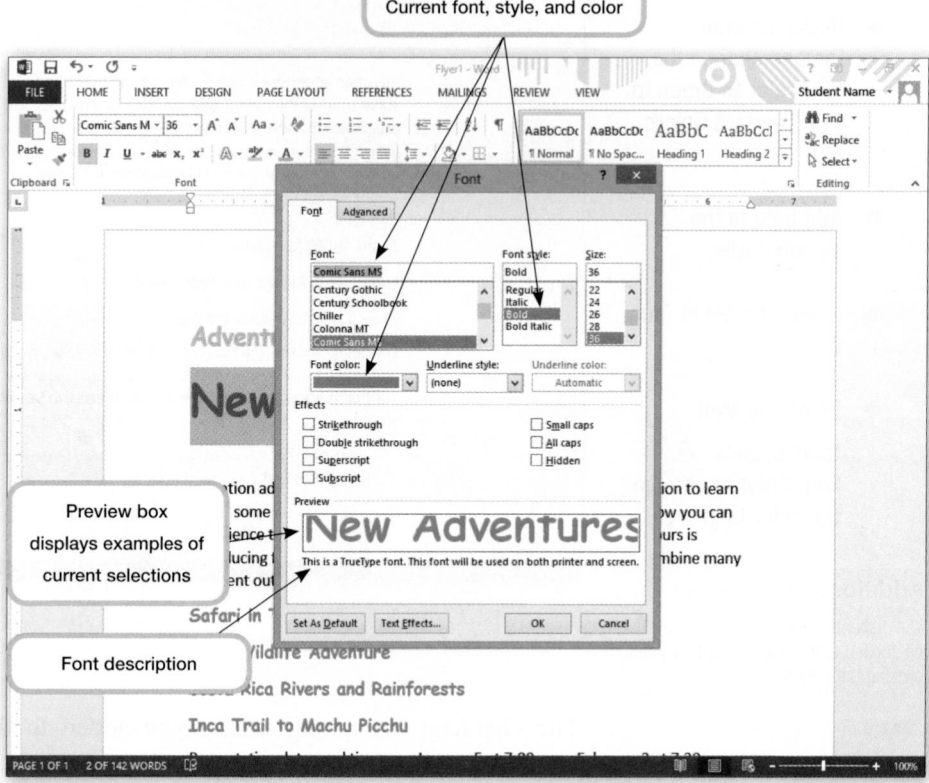

Figure 1.44

Additional Information

If parts of the selection include different character effects, the Preview box shows only those that are common to the selection.

The Font dialog box contains all of the Font commands in the Font group and more. The font and font style used in the selected text are identified in the list boxes.

The Preview box displays an example of the currently selected font settings. Notice the description of the font below the Preview box. It states that the selected font is a TrueType font. **TrueType** fonts are fonts that are automatically installed when you install Windows. They appear onscreen exactly as they will appear when printed. Some fonts are printer fonts, which are available only on your printer and may look different onscreen than when printed.

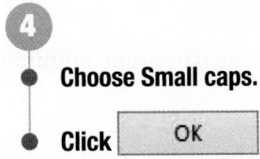

● **Choose Small caps.**

● **Click** OK .

Your screen should be similar to Figure 1.45

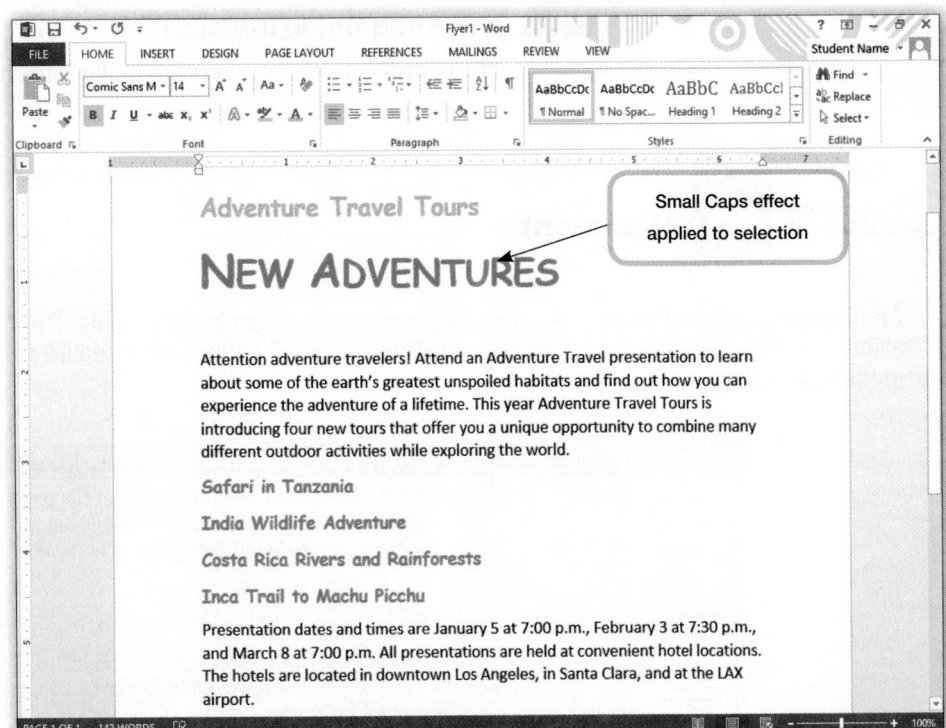

Small Caps effect applied to selection

Figure 1.45

The Small caps effect has been applied to all text in the selection and adds additional emphasis to the title.

SETTING PARAGRAPH ALIGNMENT

The final formatting change you want to make is to change the paragraph alignment.

Concept 5 Alignment

Alignment is the positioning of text on a line between the margins or indents. There are four types of paragraph alignment: left, centered, right, and justified. The alignment settings affect entire paragraphs and are described in the table below.

Alignment	Effect on Text Alignment
Left	Aligns text against the left margin of the page, leaving the right margin ragged or uneven. This is the most commonly used paragraph alignment type and is the default setting.
Center	Centers each line of text between the left and right margins. Center alignment is used mostly for headings or centering graphics on a page.
Right	Aligns text against the right margin, leaving the left margin ragged. Use right alignment when you want text to align on the right side of a page, such as a chapter title or a header.
Justify	Aligns text against the right and left margins and evenly spaces the words by inserting extra spaces, called **soft spaces**, that adjust automatically whenever additions or deletions are made to the text. Newspapers commonly use justified alignment so the columns of text are even.

The paragraph alignment buttons in the Paragraph group and their keyboard shortcuts are shown in the following table.

Alignment	Keyboard Shortcut	Button
Left	Ctrl + L	≡
Center	Ctrl + E	≡
Right	Ctrl + R	≡
Justify	Ctrl + J	≣

You will change the alignment of all paragraphs in the flyer from the default of left-aligned to centered.

1

Triple-click in the left margin to select the entire document.

Click ▤ Center in the Paragraph group.

Reduce the zoom so the entire page is visible.

Your screen should be similar to Figure 1.46

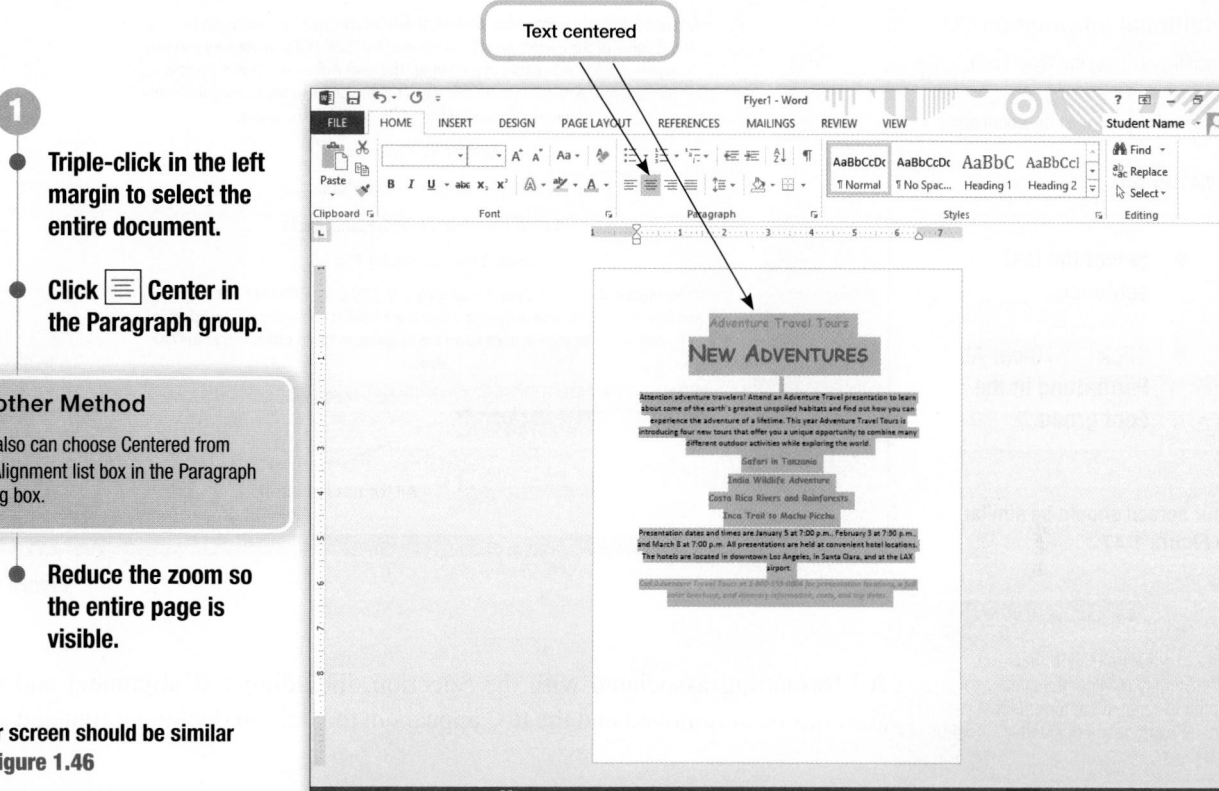

Text centered

Figure 1.46

Each line of text is centered evenly between the left and right page margins.

CLEARING FORMATS

As you look at the entire flyer, you decide the last line is overformatted. You think it would look better if it did not include italics and color. Since it has been awhile since you applied these formats, using Undo would remove many other changes that you want to keep. Instead, you will quickly clear all formatting from the selection and then apply only those you want.

1

Increase the zoom to 100%.

Additional Information

In addition to using the Zoom slider, you can click ![100%] in the Zoom group of the View tab.

Select the last sentence.

Click ![Clear All] **Clear All Formatting in the Font group.**

Your screen should be similar to Figure 1.47

Another Method

Instead of clearing all formats, you could simply reselect the command button to remove the formats that you did not want or select another format to replace it.

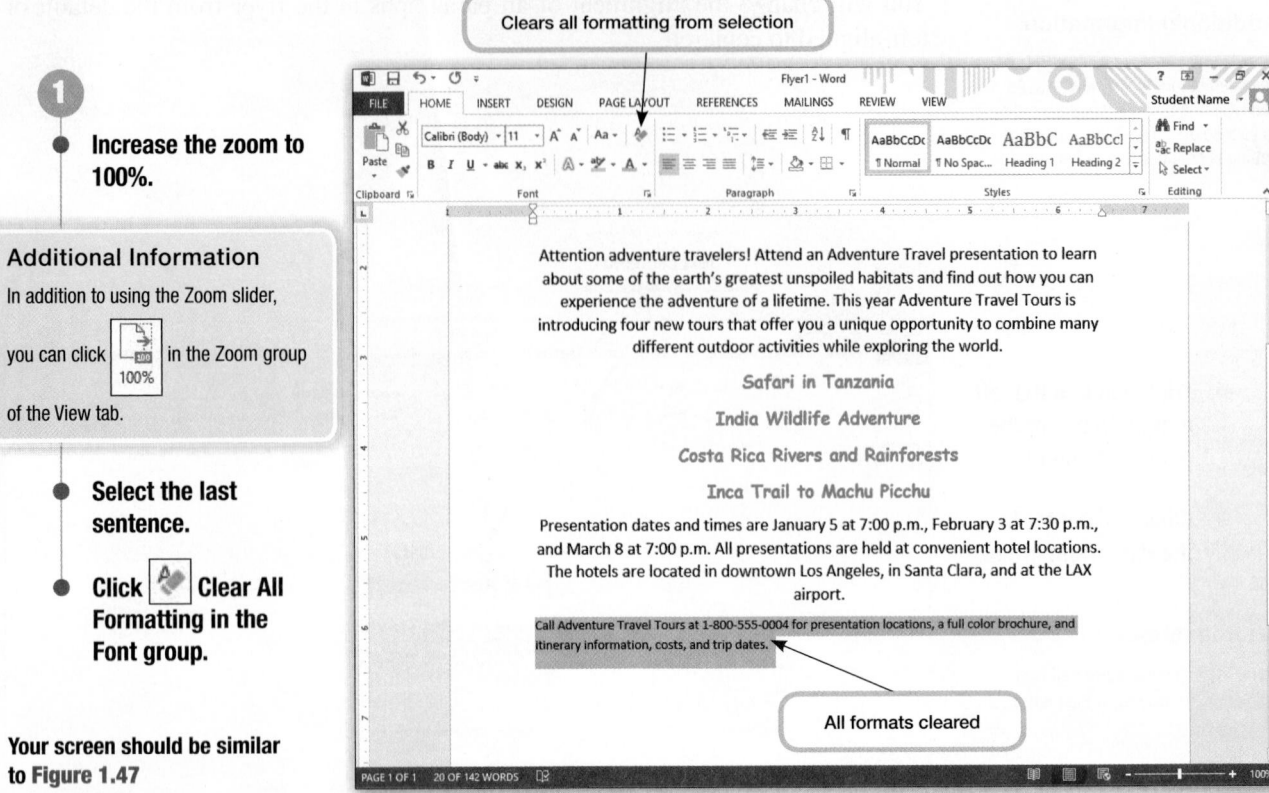

Clears all formatting from selection

All formats cleared

Figure 1.47

All formatting associated with the selection, including text alignment and font size, has been removed and the text appears in the default document font and size.

2

Format the last sentence to bold, centered, and a font size of 14.

Move to the top of the document.

Click ![Save] **Save in the Quick Access Toolbar to save the file using the same file name.**

Working with Graphics

Finally, you want to add a graphic to the flyer to add interest.

Concept  6   Graphics

A **graphic** is a nontext element or object such as a drawing or picture that can be added to a document. An **object** can be sized, moved, and manipulated.

A graphic can be a simple **drawing object** consisting of shapes such as lines and boxes. Many simple drawing objects can be created using Word. A **picture** is an illustration such as a graphic illustration or a scanned photograph. Pictures are graphics that were created using another program and are inserted in your Word document as **embedded objects**. An embedded object becomes part of the Word document and can be opened and edited from within the Word document using the **source program**, the program in which it was created. Any changes made to the embedded object are not made to the original picture file. Several examples of drawing objects and pictures are shown below.

Drawing object

Graphic illustration

Photograph

Add graphics to your documents to help the reader understand concepts and to add interest.

Additional Information

You also can scan a picture and insert it directly into a Word document without saving it as a file first.

Digital images created using a digital camera are one of the most common types of graphic files. You also can create picture files using a scanner to convert any printed document, including photographs, to an electronic format.

Pictures can be obtained from your computer or a computer network and a variety of online sources. All types of pictures, including clip art, photographs, and other types of images, can be found on the Internet. Keep in mind that any images you locate on the Internet may be copyrighted and should be used only with permission. You also can purchase CDs containing graphics.

INSERTING A PICTURE FROM YOUR COMPUTER

You will add a picture you have saved on your computer to the flyer below the two title lines. To insert a picture, first move to the location in the document where you want it to be displayed.

1

- Move the insertion point to the left of the "A" in Attention at the beginning of the first paragraph below the second title line.

- Open the Insert tab.

- From the Illustrations group, click 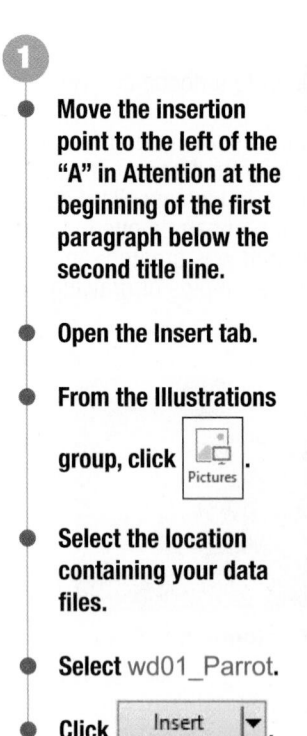.

- Select the location containing your data files.

- Select wd01_Parrot.

- Click Insert ▼.

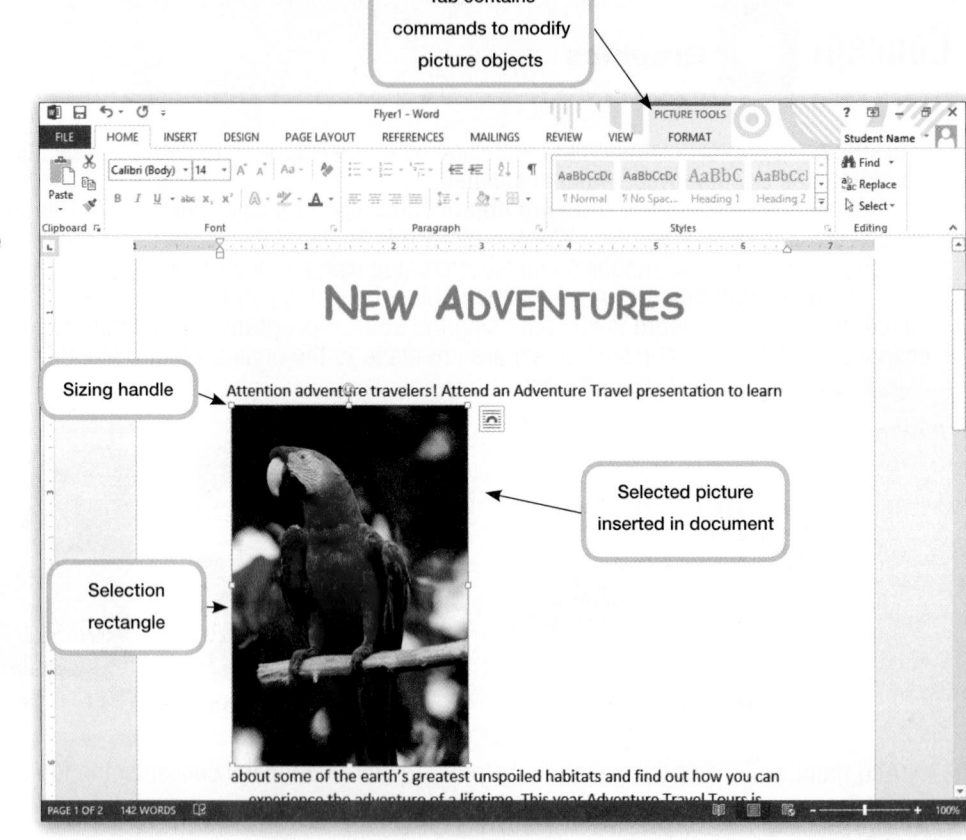

Figure 1.48

Your screen should be similar to Figure 1.48

Additional Information

You will learn more about the Picture Tools Format tab options in later labs.

A copy of the picture is inserted in the document at the location of the insertion point. Notice the picture is surrounded by a **selection rectangle** and eight squares, called **sizing handles**, indicating it is a selected object. When selected, it can be deleted, sized, moved, or modified. The Picture Tools Format tab that automatically appears is used to modify the selected picture object.

INSERTING A PICTURE FROM ONLINE SOURCES

Although you like the picture of the parrot, you want to check online sources for pictures of elephants.

1

- Click outside the parrot graphic to deselect it.

- Move the insertion point to the left of the "A" in "Attention".

- Open the Insert tab.

- From the Illustrations group, click [Online Pictures].

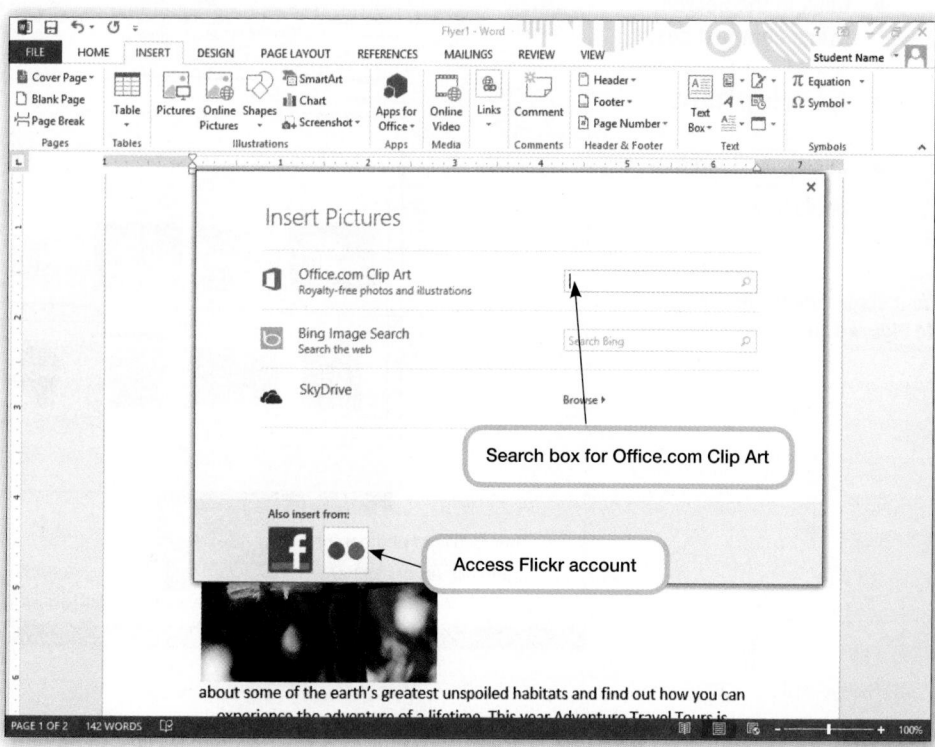

Figure 1.49

Having Trouble?

If you do not have an Internet connection, you will not be able to complete this section. Insert the picture wd01_Elephant from your data file location and skip to the Deleting a Graphic section.

Your screen should be similar to Figure 1.49

Additional Information

You also can enter multiple search words separated by a comma to find graphics that have all of the keywords.

The Insert Pictures window provides several methods to locate online graphics. The first is to use Microsoft's Office.com Clip Art website. The second is to use Microsoft's search engine Bing to search the web. A third is to access your SkyDrive account to locate pictures you have stored at that location. Finally, you can access Flickr, an online photo management and sharing website, for pictures you have uploaded to an account with the website.

You will use the Office.com website to search for elephant pictures by entering a word or phrase that describes the picture you want to locate in the Search Office.com text box. Enter a specific search term to get fewer results that are more likely to meet your requirements.

2

- **Click in the Search Office.com text box.**

- **Type** elephant

- **Click** 🔍 **Search or press** Enter.

Your screen should be similar to Figure 1.50

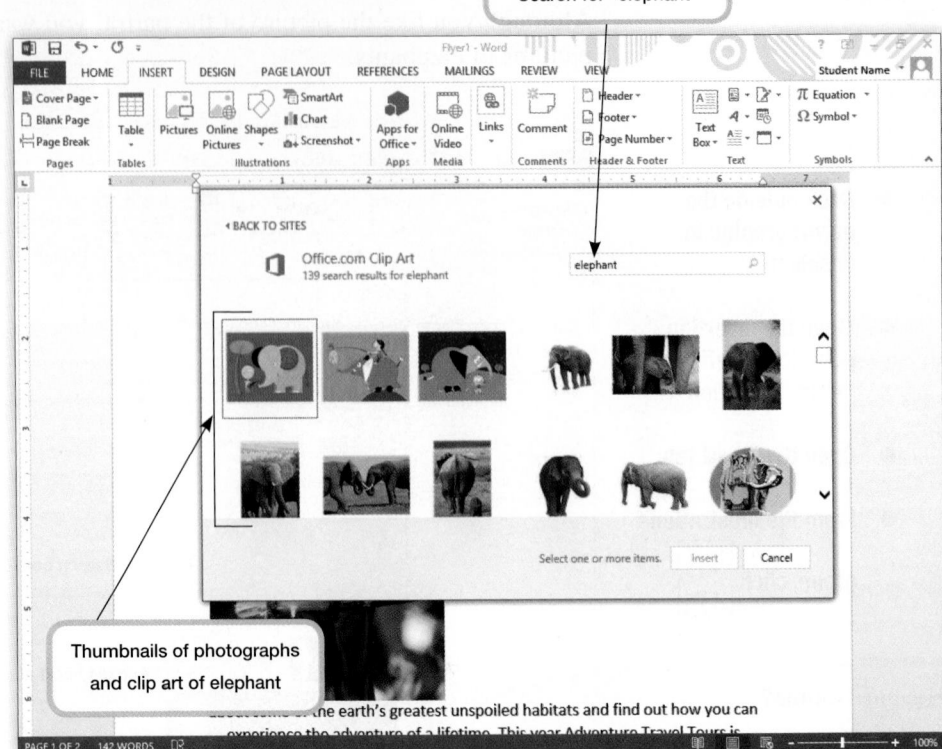

Search for "elephant"

Thumbnails of photographs and clip art of elephant

Figure 1.50

Having Trouble?

Your Office.com results may display different pictures than shown in Figure 1.50.

The program searches the Office.com Clip Art gallery for clip art and graphics that match your search term and displays **thumbnails**, miniature representations of pictures, of all located graphics. Pointing to a thumbnail displays a ScreenTip containing a title or the keywords associated with the picture. The keywords and picture size are also displayed in the bottom line of the window. Additionally, because it is sometimes difficult to see the detail in a graphic, you can preview it in a larger size by clicking 🔍 View Larger.

- Scroll the list to view additional images.

- Point to the thumbnail of the image shown in Figure 1.51 to see a ScreenTip.

- Click on View Larger.

Your screen should be similar to Figure 1.51

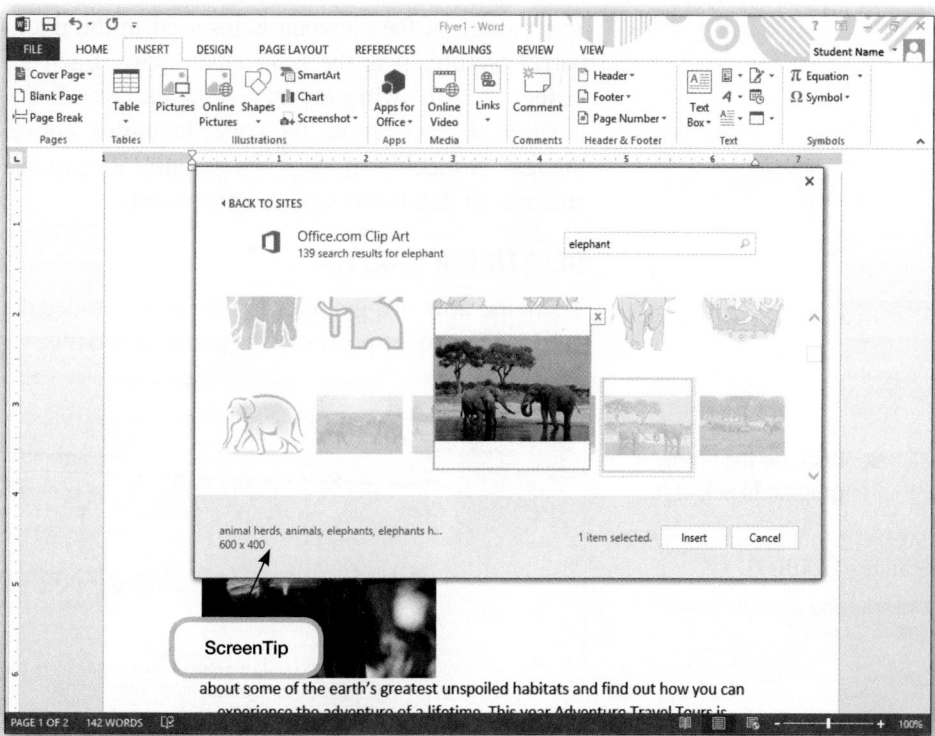

Figure 1.51

Each graphic has several keywords associated with it. All the displayed graphics include the keyword "elephant." The selected graphic is larger so it is easier to see. You think this looks like a good choice and will insert it into the document.

4

- Click [Insert] to insert the graphic in the flyer.

Another Method

You also could double-click the image to insert it.

- Scroll the document, if necessary, to view the pictures in their entirety.

Your screen should be similar to Figure 1.52

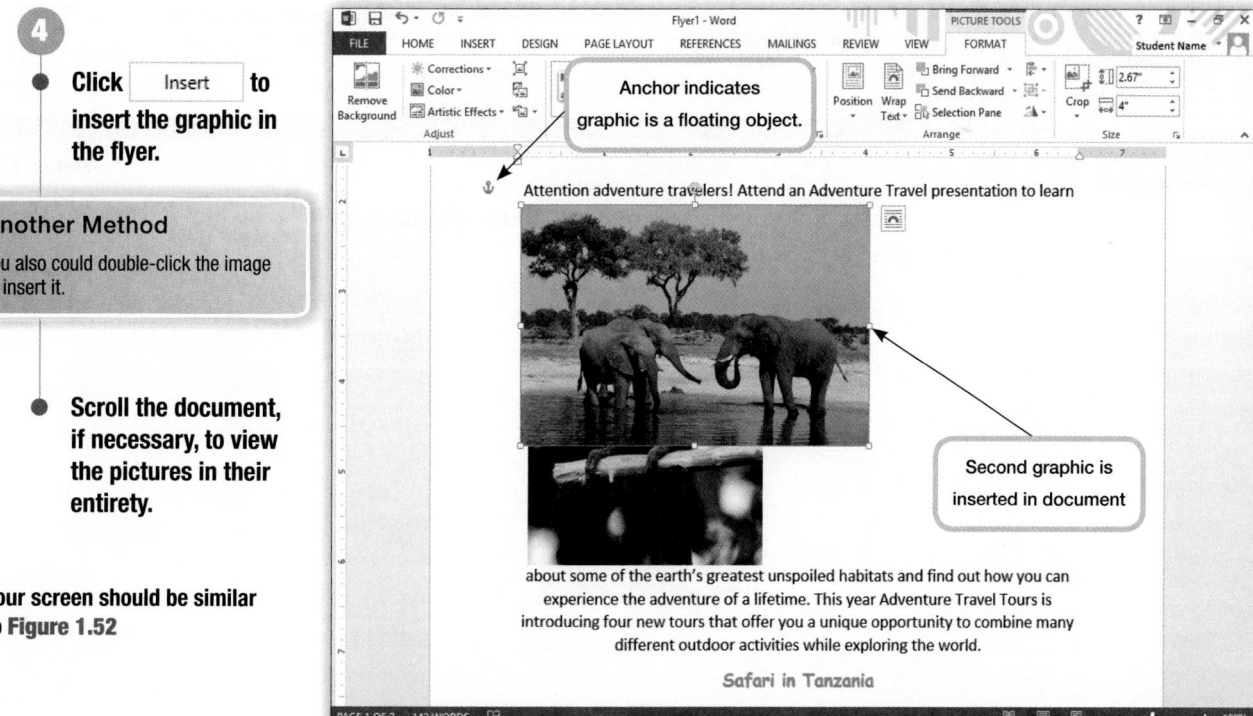

Figure 1.52

The picture of the elephant is inserted in the document and appears on top of the parrot picture. It is the selected graphic. Each graphic is inserted as a **floating object** on a **drawing layer**, a separate layer from text that allows graphics to be positioned precisely on the page, including above and below other graphics and the text. Notice the ⚓ near the graphic. This indicates it is a floating object that is attached to that location in the document.

DELETING A GRAPHIC

There are now two graphics in the flyer. You decide to use the elephant graphic and need to remove the picture of the parrot. To do this, you select the graphic and delete it.

● **Click on the parrot graphic to select it.**

Having Trouble?

Click the visible area of the parrot graphic to select it.

● **Press** Delete.

Your screen should be similar to Figure 1.53

Additional Information

Sometimes a picture may be hidden behind text or another graphic. To locate and select the picture, click ⬚ Select ▾ in the Editing group of the Home tab and choose Selection Pane from the menu in the Selection Pane, then click the picture.

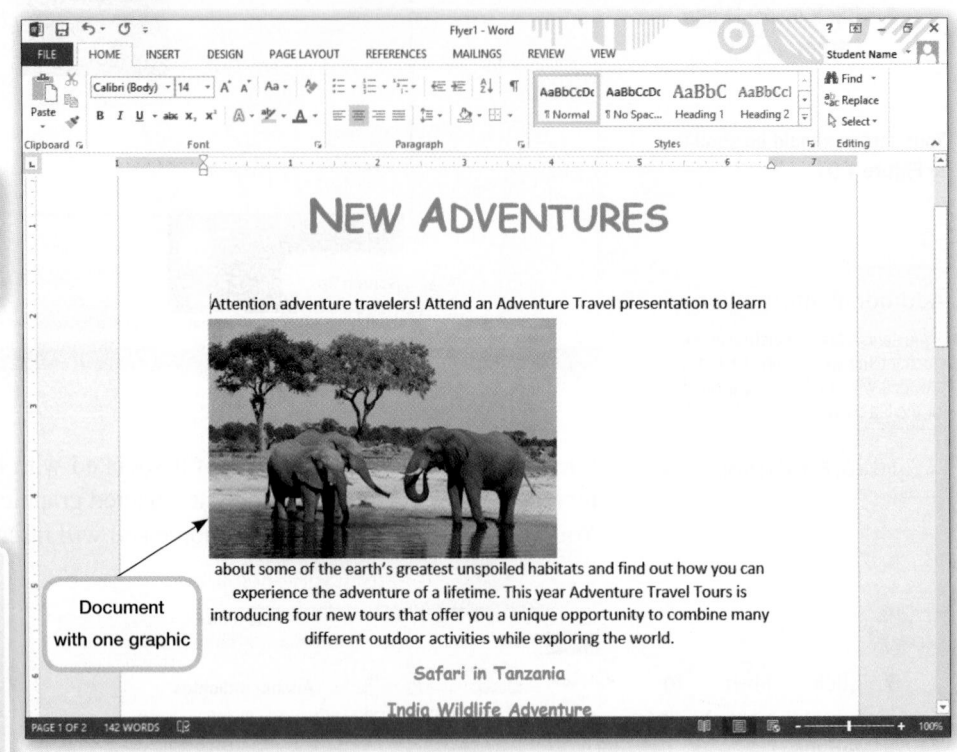

Document with one graphic

Figure 1.53

The parrot graphic is removed and the elephant graphic is aligned at the left margin between the lines of text.

CHANGING THE LAYOUT

Notice the picture is positioned at the left margin between lines of text. The layout position of a graphic in a document is controlled by the text wrapping style associated with the object.

Concept  Text Wrapping

Text wrapping controls how text wraps around a graphic object. Examples of the eight text wrapping styles are shown below.

| In Line with Text | Square | Tight | Through | Top and Bottom | Behind Text | In Front of Text |

All the text wrapping styles except In Line with Text are floating objects. The In Line with Text style is an **inline object** and is treated as a character in the paragraph. It is part of the text and moves around like any other character in the paragraph when text is inserted or deleted before it. Floating objects can be changed to inline objects by choosing the Inline with Text wrapping style.

Additionally, each floating graphic is anchored to the paragraph that is closest to the top of the picture. When you move a picture, the picture attaches to the next closest paragraph. You can lock an **anchor** to ensure that the object is always attached to the same paragraph and on the same page as the picture anchor. The point of attachment is indicated by a small anchor icon.

Another Method

You also can use the 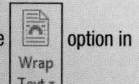 option in the Picture Tools Format tab.

You will try out several different wrapping styles using the [icon] Layout Options icon that appears whenever a graphic object is selected.

1

- If necessary, select the elephant picture.

- Click the 🔲 Layout Options icon to the right of the selected graphic.

- Click 🔲 Square (first option below With Text Wrapping).

- Click 🔲 Behind Text (fifth option below With Text Wrapping).

- Click 🔲 In Line with Text.

Your screen should be similar to Figure 1.54

Having Trouble?

If the anchor icon is not displayed, use File/Word Options/Display and turn on the Object Anchor option.

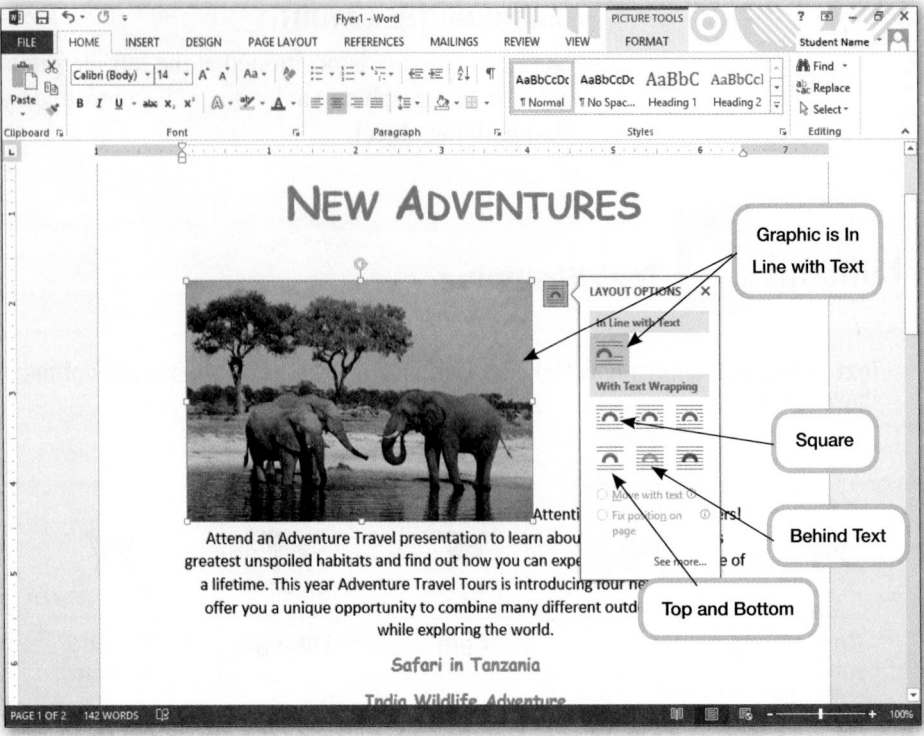

Figure 1.54

The square layout wrapped the text around the graphic on all sides. The Behind Text option shows the graphic behind the text. The In Line with Text option positions the graphic as part of the text in the paragraph. In this layout the ⚓ is not displayed, indicating the graphic is not a floating object. The Layout Options gallery stays open to allow you to preview the effect of the different layout options. When you close the Layout gallery, the last selected option will remain in effect.

Since you want to position the graphic between the second title line and the first paragraph, you will return the layout to the Top and Bottom style.

2

- Click 🔲 Top and Bottom (fourth option below With Text Wrapping).

- Click ❌ Close to close the Layout Options gallery.

Another Method

You also can size a graphic by entering exact values in the Shape Height and Shape Width text boxes in the Size group of the Picture Tools Format tab.

Having Trouble?

If the alignment guides do not appear, open the Picture Tools Format tab, click 🔲 Align Object in the Arrange group, and choose Use Alignment Guides to turn on this feature.

SIZING AND MOVING A GRAPHIC

Usually, when a graphic is inserted, its size and position on the page will need to be adjusted. To size a graphic, you select it and drag the sizing handles to increase or decrease the size of the object. The mouse pointer changes to ↘ when pointing to a handle. The direction of the arrow indicates the direction in which you can drag to size the graphic. The easiest way to move a graphic is to drag the picture anywhere on the page, including in the margins or on top of or below other objects, including text if it is a floating object. The only places you cannot place a graphic object are into a footnote, endnote, or caption. When you move an object, green alignment guides appear to show when you reach a margin or the vertical or horizontal center of the page to help you position the graphic on the page. You will size and move the image and lock the anchor.

- Click on the graphic to select it.

- Point to the upper-right corner handle.

Additional Information

Hold down (Shift) while dragging a corner handle to maintain the original proportions of the graphic.

- With the pointer as a 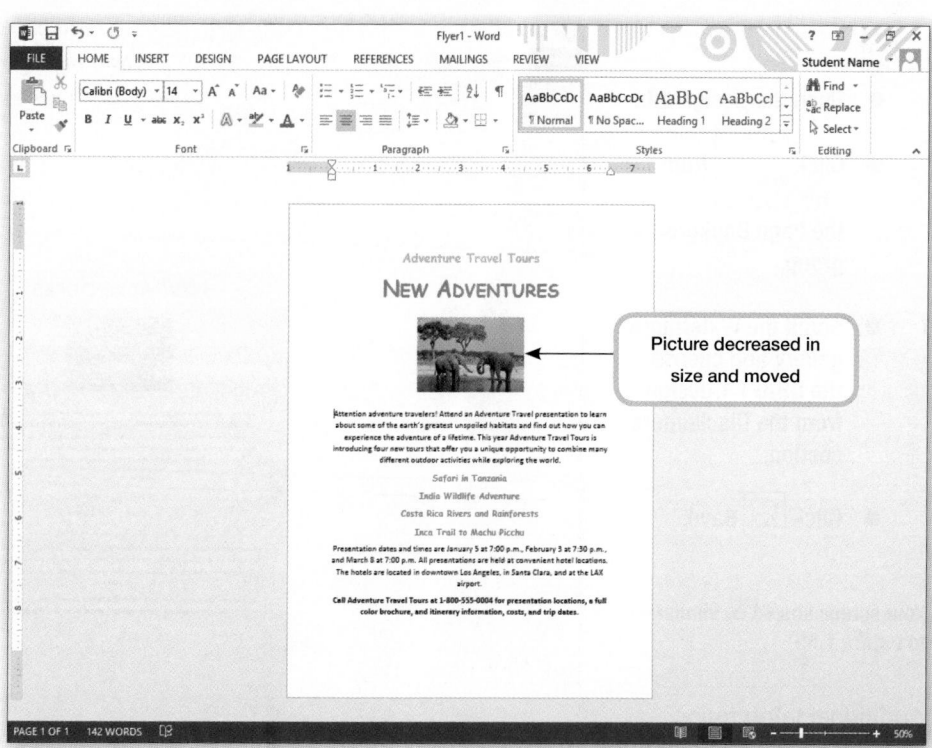, drag inward to decrease the size to approximately 2.5 inches wide by 1.5 inches high (use the ruler as a guide and refer to Figure 1.55).

- Drag the picture up to below the New Adventures title, center it vertically between the title and the paragraph, and drop it in place when the vertical green guide appears.

- Click Layout Options and choose Fix position on page.

- Click anywhere in the document to deselect the graphic.

- Reduce the zoom to 50%.

Your screen should be similar to Figure 1.55

Additional Information

You also can move a picture in small increments using the arrow keys; however, the alignment guides do not appear.

Figure 1.55

ADDING A WATERMARK

The final change you want to make to the flyer for now is to add a watermark in the page background identifying the document as a draft. **Watermarks** are text or pictures that appear behind document text. You can insert a predesigned watermark from a gallery of watermark text, or you can insert a watermark with custom text.

- **Open the Design tab.**

- **Click from the Page Background group.**

- **Scroll the Watermark gallery and choose the DRAFT 1 design from the Disclaimers section.**

- **Click 💾 Save.**

Your screen should be similar to Figure 1.56

Additional Information

You can see watermarks only in Print Layout view and Read Mode view or in a printed document.

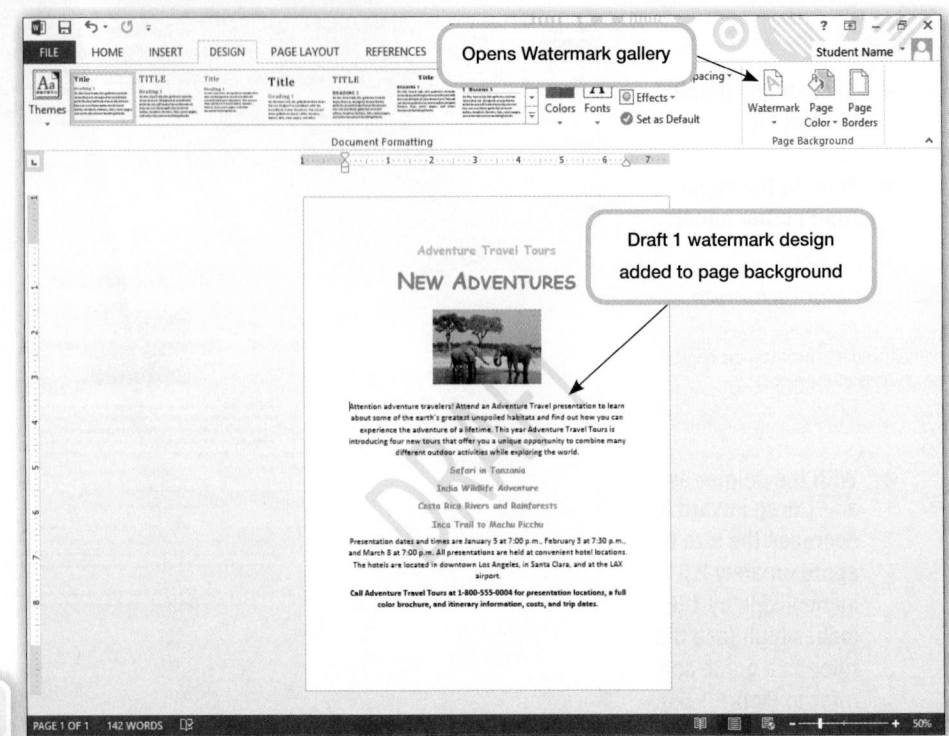

Opens Watermark gallery

Draft 1 watermark design added to page background

Figure 1.56

Additional Information

Choose Remove Watermark from the menu to remove a watermark.

The DRAFT watermark appears diagonally across the background of the page. Watermarks appear on every page of a document except on a page that is a designated title page.

MODIFYING DOCUMENT PROPERTIES

Before printing the document for your manager, you will add a sentence to the flyer that includes your name and edit the document properties.

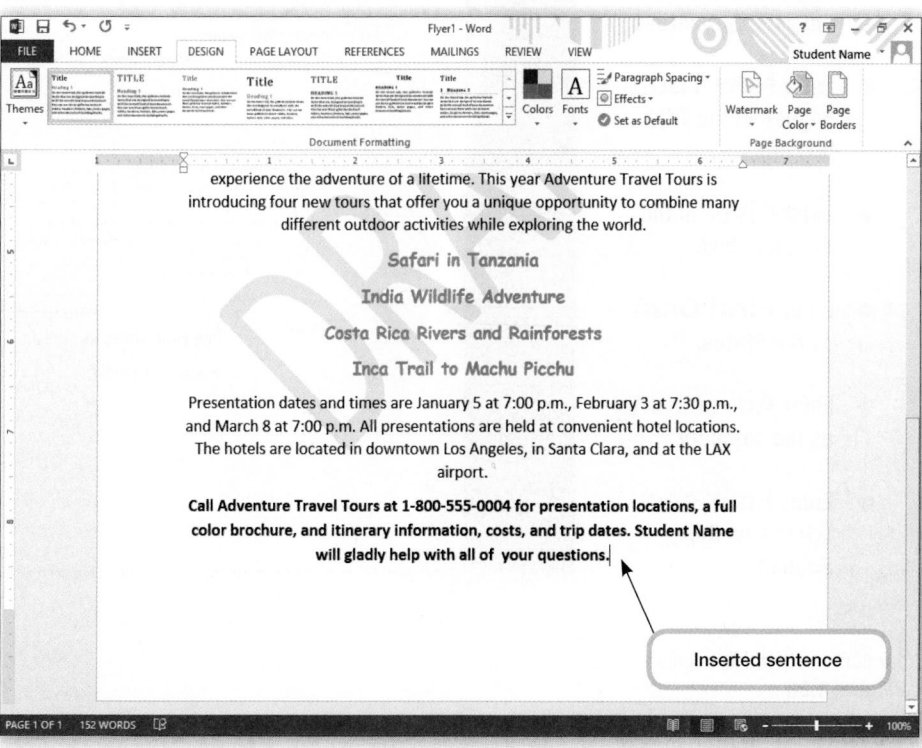

Figure 1.57

Next, you will look at the document properties that are automatically included with the Flyer1 file. You also will add documentation to identify you as the author, and specify a document title and keywords to describe the document.

2

- Open the File tab and click the Show All Properties link below the list of properties.

- Enter **New Tours Flyer** in the Title text box.

- Enter **Flyer** in the Tags text box.

- Enter **First Draft** as the Status.

- Enter **Advertising** as the category.

- Enter **Four new tours** as the Subject.

Figure 1.58

Your screen should be similar to Figure 1.58

Printing a Document

Although you still plan to make several formatting changes to the document, you want to give a copy of the flyer to your manager to get feedback regarding its content and layout.

PREVIEWING THE DOCUMENT

As part of the printing process, Word automatically displays a preview image of your document, showing exactly how the document will appear when printed.

Additional Information

Review previewing and printing in the "Printing a Document" section on page IO.60 of the Introduction to Microsoft Office 2013.

1

- If necessary, make sure your printer is on and ready to print.

- Choose Print on the File tab.

Your screen should be similar to Figure 1.59

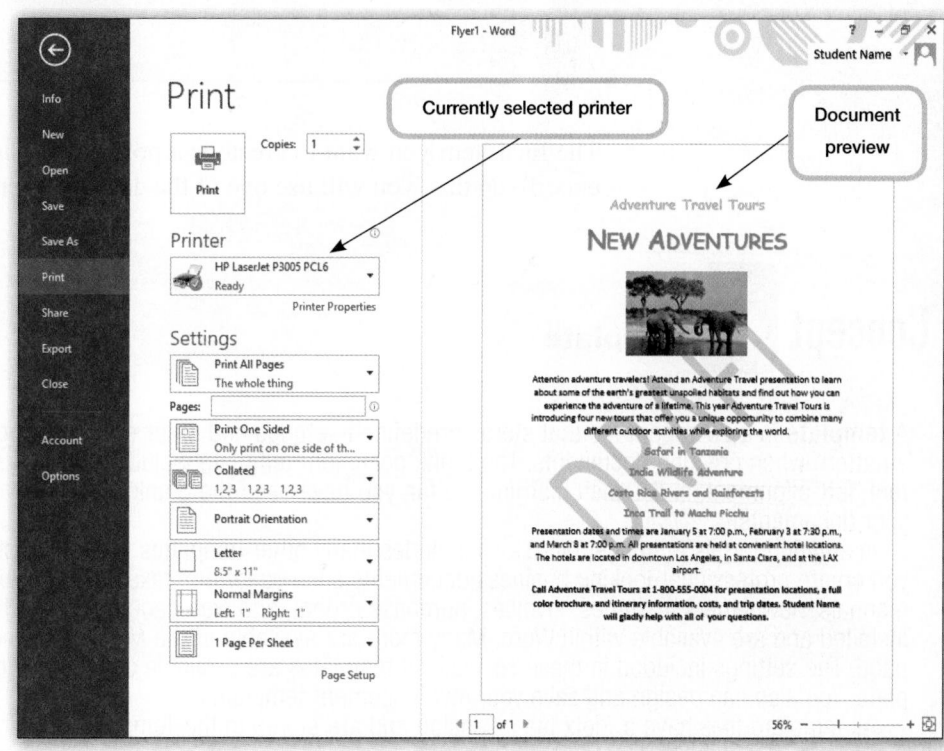

Figure 1.59

A preview image of your document displays on the right side of your screen. This image of the flyer should be similar to the document shown in the Case Study at the beginning of the lab.

NOTE Please consult your instructor for printing procedures that may differ from the following directions.

2

- If you need to change the selected printer to another printer, open the Printer drop-down list box and select the appropriate printer (your instructor will tell you which printer to select).

- Click .

Your printer should be printing the document.

You are finished working on the flyer for now and want to save the properties you entered.

3

- Click 🖫 Save.

- Open the File tab and choose Close.

The flyer is saved and the document window is empty.

Working with Templates

The final item you want to create is a postcard version of the flyer to send to clients. To do this, you will use one of the document templates included in Word.

Concept 8 Template

A **template** is a document file that stores predefined settings and other elements such as graphics for use as a pattern when creating documents. The Blank document template includes settings such as a Calibri 11-point font, left-alignment, and 1-inch margins. So far, you have used the Blank document template only as a basis for your documents.

In addition to this template, Word also includes many other templates that are designed specifically to help you create professional-looking business documents such as letters, faxes, reports, brochures, press releases, manuals, newsletters, resumes, invoices, purchase orders, and web pages. Many of the templates are already installed and are available within Word. Many more are available at the Microsoft Office Online Templates web page. The settings included in these specialized templates are available only to documents based on that template. You also can design and save your own document templates.

All template files have a .dotx file extension and are stored in the Templates folder. The Normal document template, for example, is named Normal.dotx. When you create a new document from a template file, a copy of the file is opened and the file type changes to a Word document (.docx). This prevents accidentally overwriting the template file when the file is saved.

You will now start a new document using one of Word's memo templates. This template file is available at the Microsoft Office.com website.

1

- Open the File tab and choose New to display the available templates.

Your screen should be similar to Figure 1.60

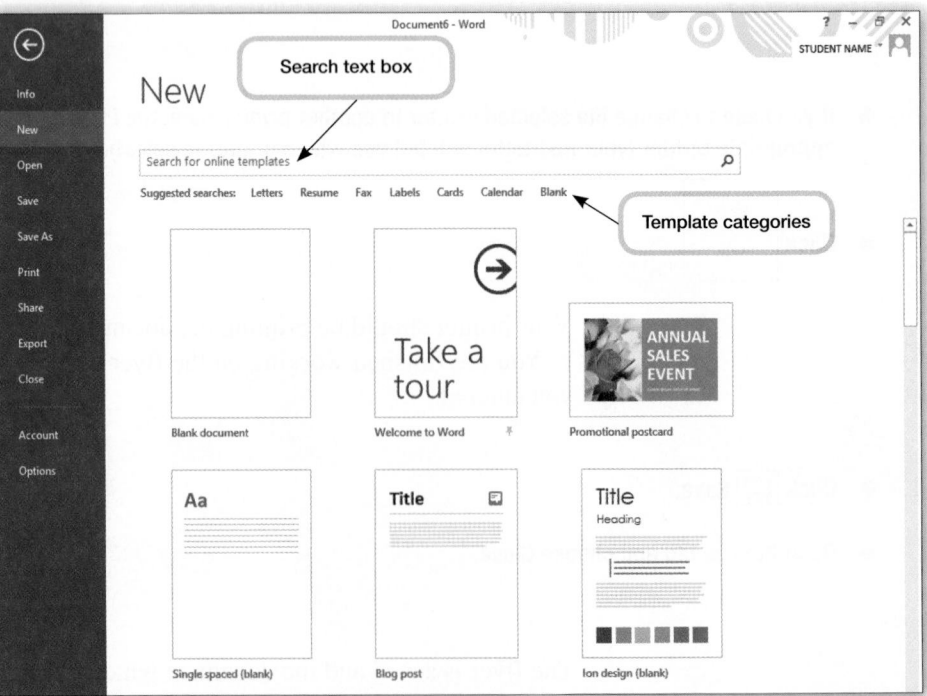

Figure 1.60

The New window displays a variety of templates as well as a search text box and a row of suggested searches. You will use the search text box to locate postcard templates.

● **Type** postcard **in the Search online templates text box, and press** Enter **or click** 🔍 **Start Searching.**

● **Scroll the displayed template thumbnails and click the Promotional postcard thumbnail to select it.**

● **Click** ▶ **to see the backside of the postcard.**

Your screen should be similar to Figure 1.61

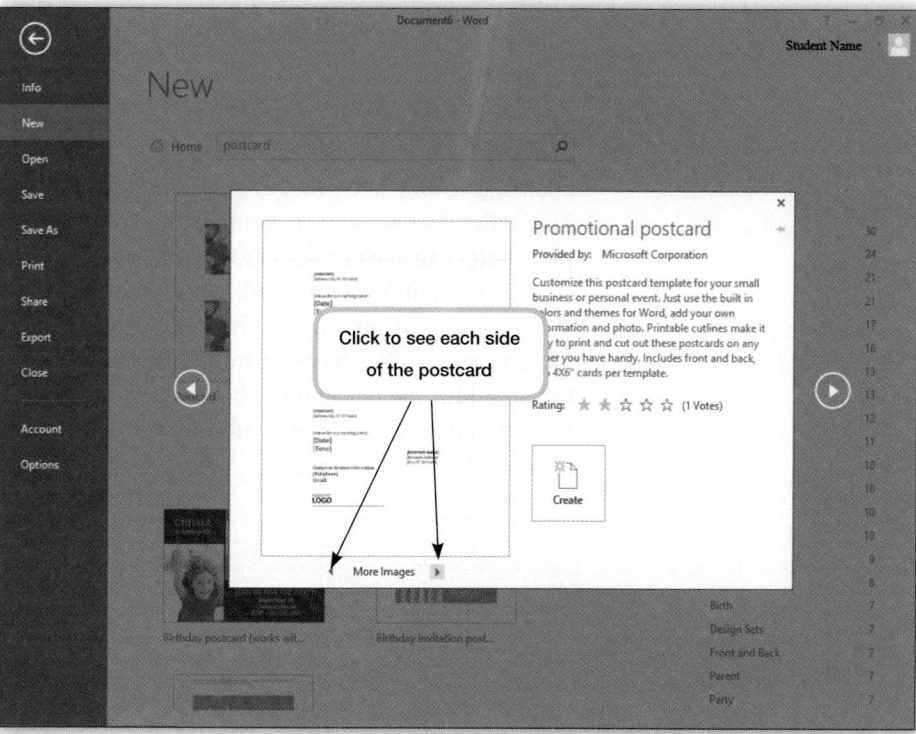

Figure 1.61

The template consists of two postcards per page with a front and back design. You think the design of this postcard will work well and will download it from the Office Online website to your computer. It will then open automatically for you in Word.

● **Click**  .

● **Change the zoom to 70% to see the fronts of both postcards.**

Your screen should be similar to Figure 1.62

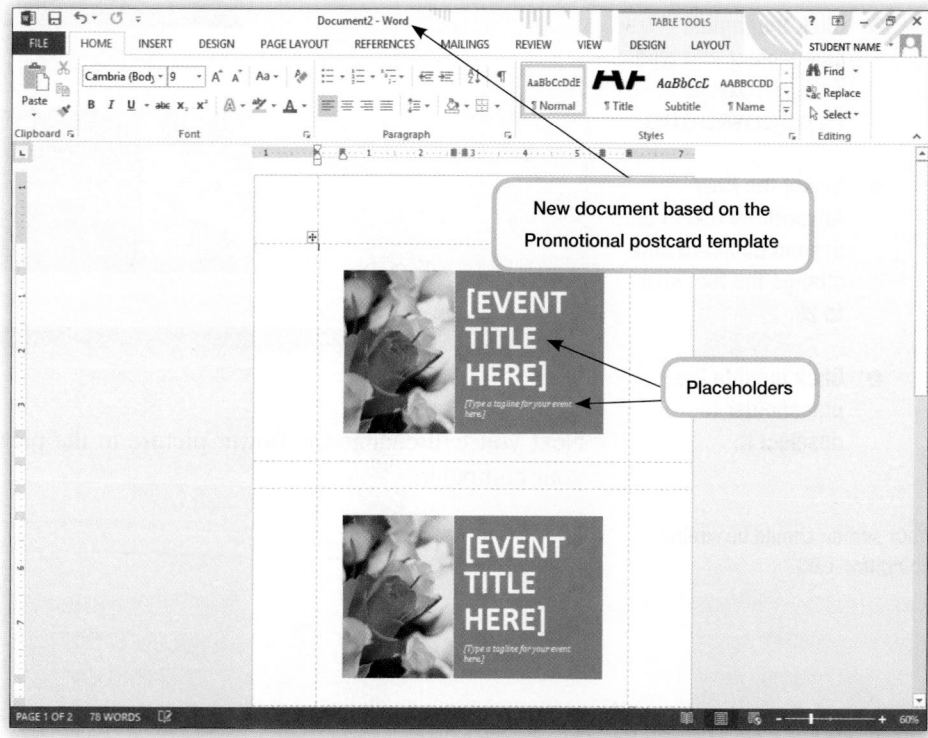

Figure 1.62

Additional Information

During a Word session as new documents are opened, they are named Document followed by a sequential number.

A copy of the Promotional postcard template is opened as a new Word document and is displayed in Print Layout view. The file name Document2 appears in the title bar, indicating that the current document hasn't yet been saved. The template itself, however, is saved to your computer so that you can open and use it again without having to download it again.

REPLACING PLACEHOLDERS

Templates often include **placeholders**, which are graphic elements, commonly enclosed in brackets, that are designed to contain specific types of information. You edit placeholders to contain the information you want by clicking on the placeholder to select it and then typing the new information.

The Promotional postcard template contains several formatted placeholders. When you enter text in placeholders, it may be necessary to change the font size, alignment, or other types of formatting to ensure the typed text is not too large or too small for the placeholder boundaries. You will modify the front of the postcard first by entering a title and subtitle. As you enter text in the first postcard, it will also appear in the second.

1

- **Click the Event Title Here placeholder.**

- **Type New Adventures**

- **Select the text and change the font size to 28.**

- **Click the tagline placeholder and type Travelogue Presentations**

- **Select the New Adventures text in the second postcard and change the font size to 28.**

- **Click outside the placeholder to deselect it.**

Your screen should be similar to Figure 1.63

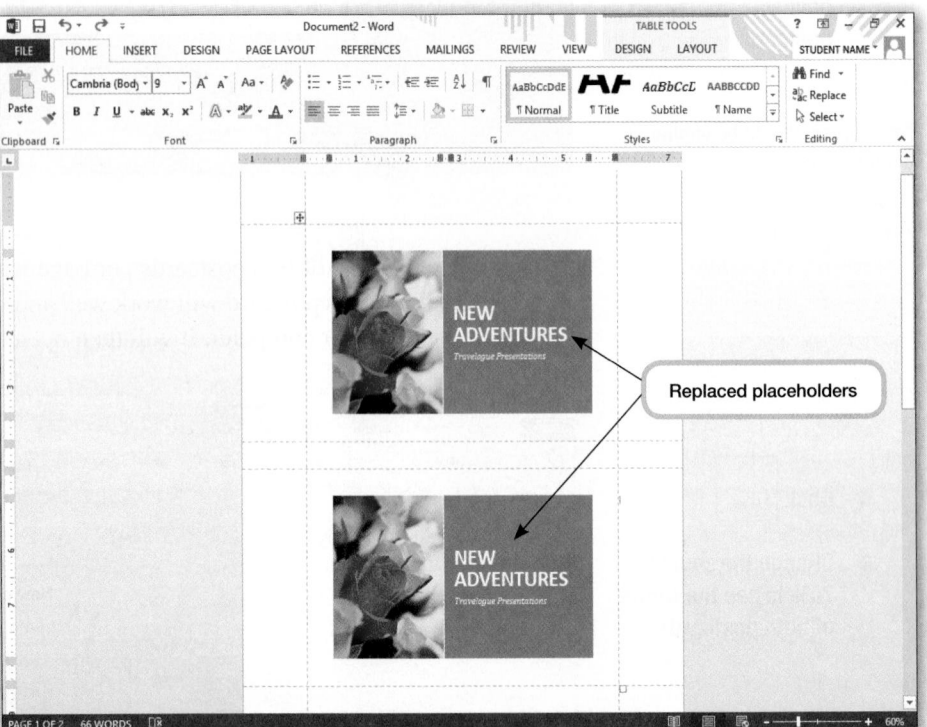

Figure 1.63

Next you will change the flower picture to the picture of the parrot you have on your computer.

2

- Click on the flower picture to select it and press [Delete].

- Insert the picture wd01_Parrot from your data file location on your computer.

- Adjust the size of the picture as in Figure 1.64.

- Replace the flower picture in the second postcard with the parrot picture and size it appropriately.

Your screen should be similar to **Figure 1.64**

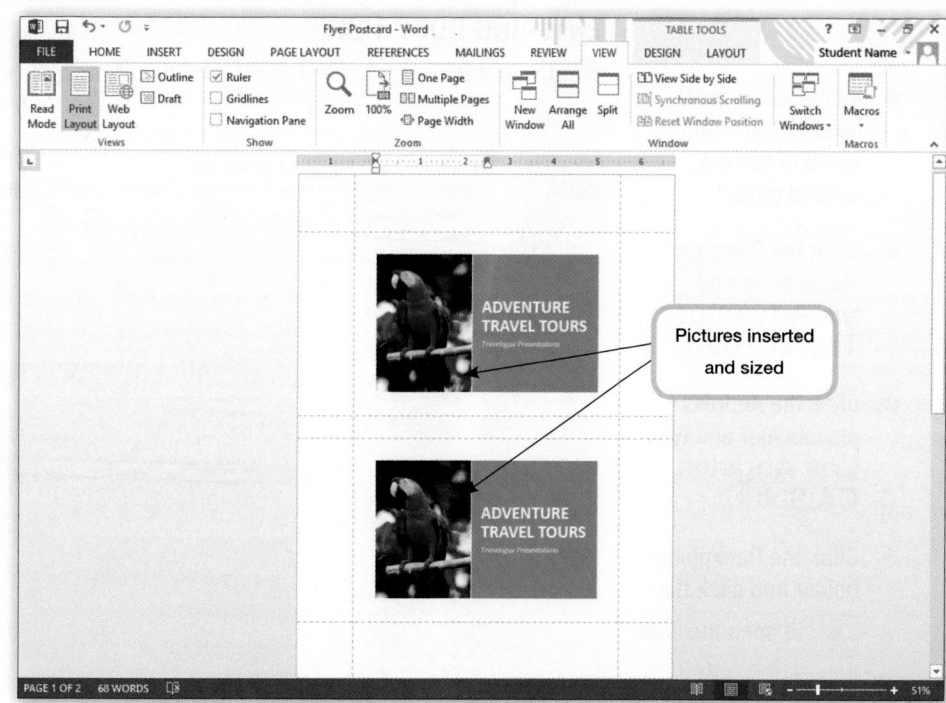

Figure 1.64

ENTERING BODY TEXT

Next you will type the text for the back side of the postcard.

- Increase the zoom level to 100% and scroll to see the second page.

- Click the Company placeholder and type **Adventure Travel Tours**

- Click the Address placeholder and type **Los Angeles, CA 90007**

- Click the Date placeholder and click the ▼ to open the date picker.

- Click **Today**.

- Click the Time placeholder and type **7 p.m.**

- Click the Telephone placeholder and type **1-800-555-0004**

- Click the Email placeholder and type the company website: **www.adventuretraveltours.com**

- Select the Logo placeholder and press Delete.

- Scroll to see the back of the second card and delete the Logo placeholder.

- Select the Recipient Name and Address placeholders for both postcards and enter **your name** and **school address**

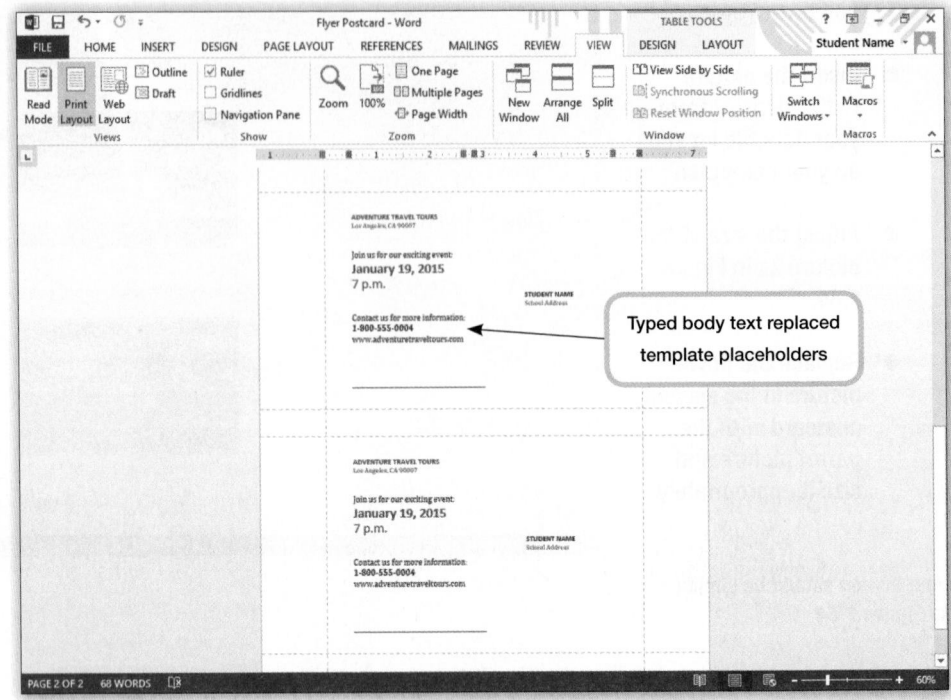

Figure 1.65

Your screen should be similar to **Figure 1.65**

The text you typed replaced the postcard placeholders in both parts of the postcard with the exception of the recipient name and address to allow you to enter different recipient information for each postcard.

Exiting Word

Additional Information

Review exiting in the "Exiting an Office 2013 application" section on page IO.67 of the Introduction to Microsoft Office 2013.

You want to save the postcard and exit the Word application. The Close command in the File menu or the ☒ Close button in the application window title bar is used to quit the Word program. If you attempt to exit the application without first saving your document, Word displays a warning asking if you want to save your work. If you do not save your work and you exit the application, any changes you made since last saving it are lost.

1

- **Open the File tab and choose Close.**

- **Click** [S̲ave] **and select your solution file location.**

- **In the File name text box, change the proposed file name to** Flyer Postcard.

- **Click** [S̲ave] **.**

The postcard is saved as Flyer Postcard.docx to the location you selected and the document is closed.

2

- **Click** ☒ **to exit the Word 2013 application.**

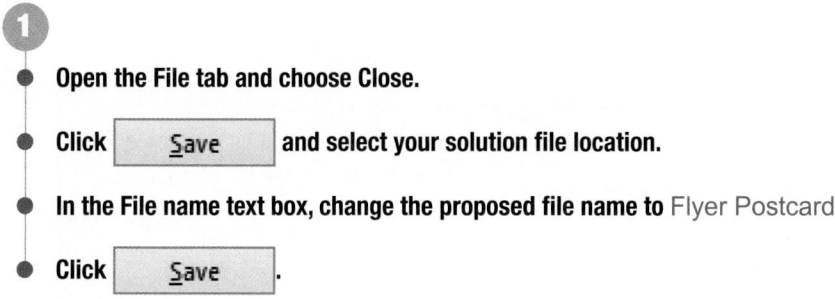

)CUS ON CAREERS

EXPLORE YOUR CAREER OPTIONS

Food Service Manager

Have you noticed flyers around your campus advertising job positions? Many of these jobs are in the food service industry. Food service managers are traditionally responsible for overseeing the kitchen and dining room. However, these positions increasingly involve administrative tasks, including recruiting new employees. As a food service manager, your position would likely include creating newspaper notices and flyers to attract new staff. These flyers should be attractive and error-free. The median annual salary for a food service manager is $48,130.

Grammar Checker (WD1.12)

The grammar checker advises you of incorrect grammar as you create and edit a document, and proposes possible corrections.

Spelling Checker (WD1.14)

The spelling checker advises you of misspelled words as you create and edit a document, and proposes possible corrections.

AutoCorrect (WD1.16)

The AutoCorrect feature makes basic assumptions about the text you are typing and, based on these assumptions, automatically corrects the entry.

Word Wrap (WD1.19)

The word wrap feature automatically decides where to end a line and wrap text to the next line based on the margin settings.

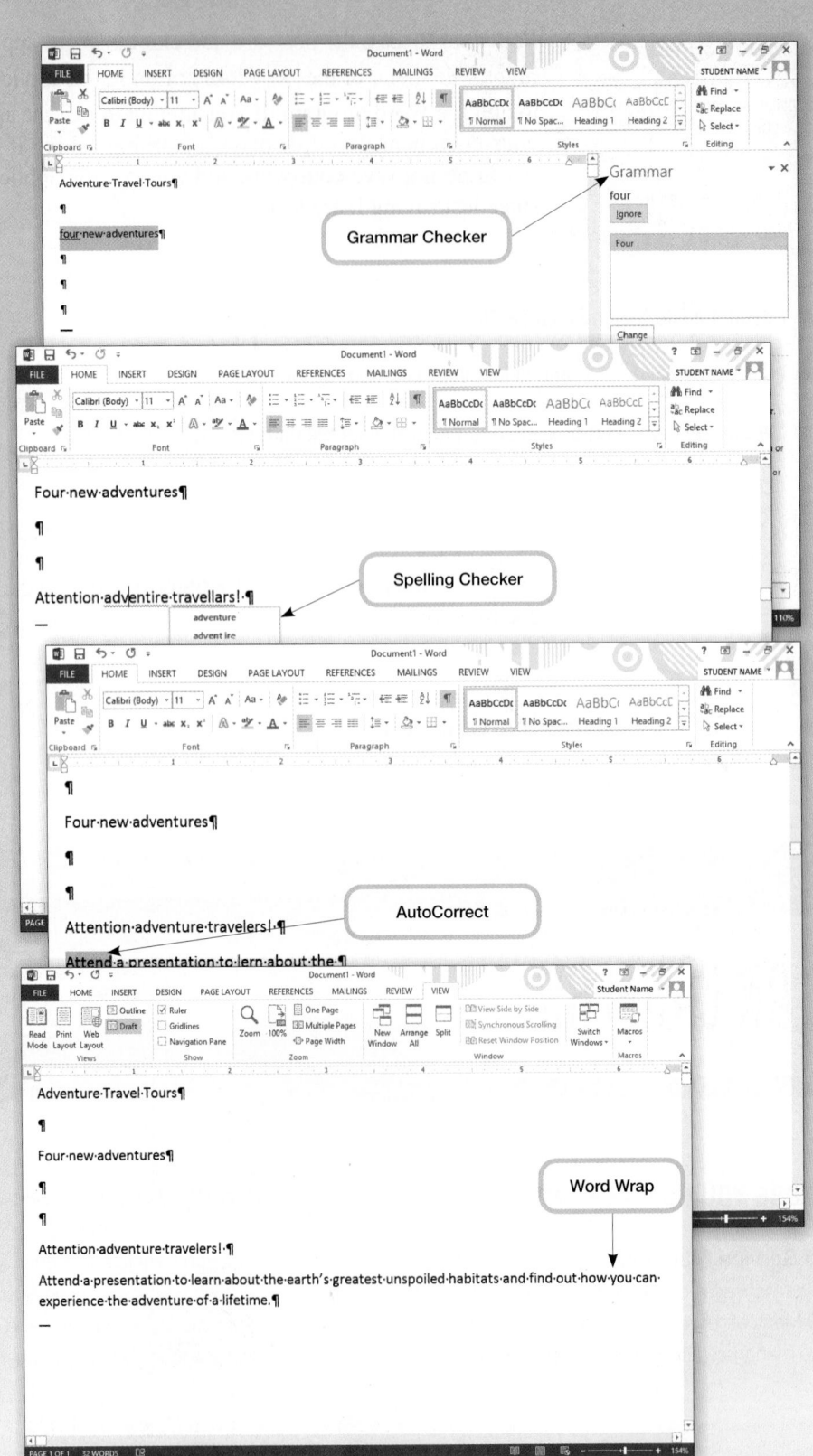

Alignment (WD1.44)

Alignment is the positioning of text on a line between the margins or indents. There are four types of paragraph alignment: left, centered, right, and justified.

Graphics (WD1.47)

A graphic is a nontext element or object such as a drawing or picture that can be added to a document.

Text Wrapping (WD1.53)

Text wrapping controls how text wraps around a graphic object.

Template (WD1.60)

A template is a document file that stores predefined settings and other elements such as graphics for use as a pattern when creating documents.

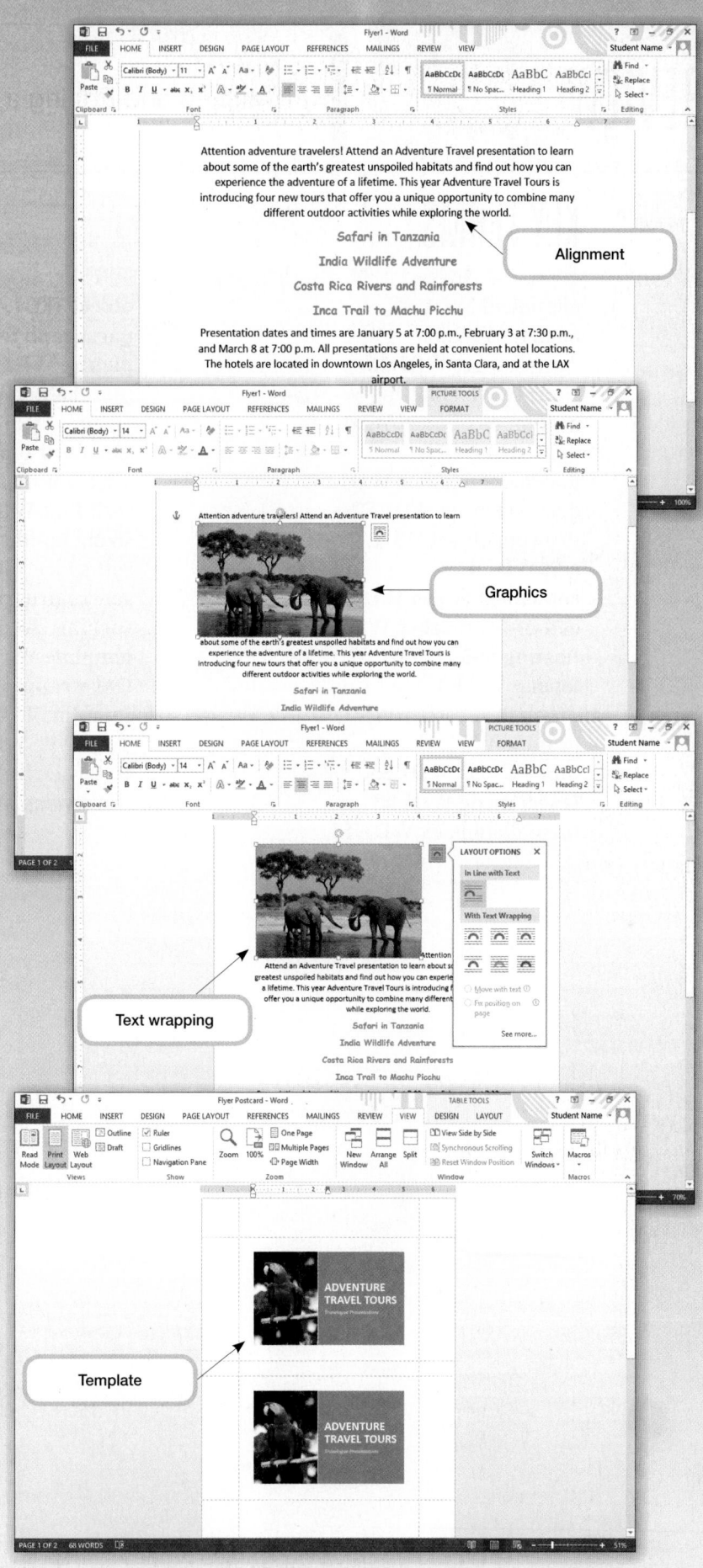

KEY TERMS

alignment WD1.44
anchor WD1.53
AutoCorrect WD1.16
character formatting WD1.34
custom dictionary WD1.14
default WD1.7
document window WD1.5
drawing layer WD1.52
drawing object WD1.47
edit WD1.4
embedded object WD1.47
end-of-file marker WD1.8
floating object WD1.52
format WD1.4
grammar checker WD1.12
graphic WD1.47
inline object WD1.53
Insert mode WD1.23
main dictionary WD1.14

object WD1.47
paragraph formatting WD1.34
picture WD1.47
placeholder WD1.62
ruler WD1.5
sans serif font WD1.35
selection rectangle WD1.48
serif font WD1.35
sizing handles WD1.48
soft space WD1.44
source program WD1.47
spelling checker WD1.14
template WD1.60
text wrapping WD1.53
thumbnail WD1.50
TrueType WD1.42
watermark WD1.55
word wrap WD1.19

COMMAND SUMMARY

Command	Shortcut	Action
Quick Access Toolbar		
🖫 Save	Ctrl + S	Saves document using same file name
↶ Undo	Ctrl + Z	Restores last editing change
↷ Redo	Ctrl + Y	Restores last Undo or repeats last command or action
File tab		
New	Ctrl + N	Opens new blank document or specialized template
Open	Ctrl + O	Opens existing document file
Save	Ctrl + S	Saves document using same file name
Save As	F12	Saves document using a new file name, type, and/or location
Print	Ctrl + P	Prints document
Close	Ctrl + F4	Closes document
Options		Change options for working with Word
Home tab		
Clipboard group		
📄 Copy	Ctrl + C	Copies selection to Clipboard
✂ Cut	Ctrl + X	Cuts selection to Clipboard
📋 Paste	Ctrl + V	Pastes items from Clipboard
Font group		
Calibri (Body) Font		Changes typeface
11 ▾ Font Size		Changes font size
🅰 Clear Formatting		Removes all formatting from selection

LAB REVIEW

COMMAND SUMMARY (CONTINUED)

Command	Shortcut	Action
B Bold	Ctrl + B	Adds/removes bold effect
I Italic	Ctrl + I	Adds/removes italic effect
Aa ▾ Change Case	Shift + F3	Changes case of selected text
A ▾ Font Color		Changes text to selected color
Paragraph group		
¶ Show/Hide	Ctrl + *	Displays or hides formatting marks
Align Text Left	Ctrl + L	Aligns text to left margin
Center	Ctrl + E	Centers text between left and right margins
Align Text Right	Ctrl + R	Aligns text to right margin
Justify	Ctrl + J	Aligns text equally between left and right margins
Insert Tab		
Illustrations group		
Pictures		Inserts selected picture
Online Pictures		Inserts online clips
Design Tab		
Page Background group		
Watermark ▾		Inserts watermark behind page content

COMMAND SUMMARY (CONTINUED)

Command	Shortcut	Action
View Tab		
Views group		
Print Layout	▣	Shows how text and objects will appear on printed page
Read Mode	📖	Displays document only, without application features
Web Layout	🌐	Shows document as it will appear when viewed in a web browser
Outline		Shows structure of document
Draft		Shows text formatting and simple layout of page
Show group		
☑ Ruler		Displays/hides ruler
Zoom group		
Zoom		Opens Zoom dialog box
100%		Zooms document to 100% of normal size
One Page		Zooms document so an entire page fits in window
Page Width		Zooms document so width of page matches width of window
Picture Tools format		
Wrap Text ▾		Controls how text wraps around a graphic object

LAB EXERCISES

SCREEN IDENTIFICATION

1. In the following Word screen, letters identify important elements. Enter the correct term for each screen element in the space provided.

Possible answers for the screen identification are:

Proofing Error icon	Show/Hide	A. _____	L. _____
Scroll bar	Center	B. _____	M. _____
Bold	Scrolls down	C. _____	N. _____
Graphic	Redo	D. _____	O. _____
Save	Tab mark	E. _____	P. _____
Ruler	Status bar	F. _____	Q. _____
Close	Draft view	G. _____	R. _____
Font	Ribbon	H. _____	S. _____
Undo	Paragraph mark	I. _____	
Zoom	Print Layout view	J. _____	
Font color		K. _____	

MATCHING

Match the item on the left with the correct description on the right.

1. alignment   _____ a. reverses last command
2. inline object   _____ b. moves to the top of the document
3. point   _____ c. feature that automatically begins a new line when text reaches the right margin
4. sans serif   _____ d. simplifies the creation of new documents
5. template   _____ e. shows dialog box
6. word wrap   _____ f. object treated as a character in the paragraph
7. ⌐   _____ g. font size measurement
8. 🖫   _____ h. controls paragraph positioning between the margins
9. ↺ ▾   _____ i. saves a document using the same file name
10. Ctrl + Home   _____ j. font without a flair at the base of each letter

TRUE/FALSE

Circle the correct answer to the following questions.

1. All text wrapping styles are floating objects.   **True**   **False**
2. A selected picture is surrounded by a selection rectangle and eight moving handles.   **True**   **False**
3. A red wavy line indicates a potential spelling error.   **True**   **False**
4. Font sizes are measured in inches.   **True**   **False**
5. Hard spaces are used to justify text on a line.   **True**   **False**
6. The AutoCorrect feature automatically identifies and corrects certain types of errors.   **True**   **False**
7. The automatic word wrap feature checks for typing errors.   **True**   **False**
8. The default document settings are stored in the Normal.docx file.   **True**   **False**
9. The Delete key erases the character to the right of the insertion point.   **True**   **False**
10. The drawing layer is a separate layer from text that allows graphics to be positioned precisely.   **True**   **False**

LAB EXERCISES

FILL-IN

Complete the following statements by filling in the blanks with the correct terms.

1. A(n) _____ is a miniature representation of all located graphics in the Office.com Clip Art window.

2. A(n) _____ object is anchored to the paragraph that is closest to the top of the picture.

3. A small blue box appearing under a word or character indicates that the _____ feature was applied.

4. The _____ at the top of the window contains commands that are organized into related groups.

5. The default document settings are stored in the _____ template file.

6. The _____ feature displays each page of your document in a reduced size so you can see the page layout.

7. The _____ feature shows how your formatting choices will appear on selected text.

8. To size a graphic evenly, click and drag the _____ in one corner of the graphic.

9. Use _____ when you want to keep your existing document with the original name and make a copy with a new name.

10. Word 2013 documents are identified by the _____ file extension.

MULTIPLE CHOICE

Circle the correct response to the questions below.

1. A(n) _____ is text or pictures that appear behind document text.
   a. embedded object
   b. graphic
   c. thumbnail
   d. watermark

2. A set of characters with a specific design is called a(n) _____.
   a. AutoFormat
   b. design
   c. font
   d. style

3. Document development follows these steps.
   a. design, enter, edit, format, preview, and print
   b. enter, edit, format, preview, and print
   c. plan, enter, edit, format, preview, and print
   d. plan, edit, enter, format, preview, and print

4. Font sizes are measured in _____.
   a. bits
   b. inches
   c. pieces
   d. points

5. The _____ feature shows how various formatting choices would look on selected text.
   a. Actual Preview
   b. Active Preview
   c. Live Preview
   d. Real Preview

6. The _____ text wrapping option is treated as a character in the paragraph.
   a. in line with text
   b. square
   c. tight
   d. top and bottom

7. This feature makes basic assumptions about the text entered and automatically makes changes based on those assumptions.
   a. AutoChange
   b. AutoCorrect
   c. AutoFormat
   d. AutoText

8. When text is evenly aligned on both margins, it is _____.
   a. centered
   b. justified
   c. left-aligned
   d. right-aligned

9. Words that are not contained in the main dictionary can be added to the _____ dictionary.
   a. additional
   b. custom
   c. supplemental
   d. user-defined

10. Words that may be spelled incorrectly in a document are indicated by a _____.
    a. blue wavy line
    b. green wavy line
    c. purple dotted underline
    d. red wavy line

STEP-BY-STEP

ASKING FOR INPUT FLYER ★

1. The Lifestyle Fitness Club is planning to perform maintenance work on its facilities in the near future. You have been asked to solicit suggestions from existing customers about what changes they would like to see made to the club. You decide to send all of the current club members a flyer asking them for their input. Your completed flyer will be similar to the one shown here.

   a. Open a blank Word 2013 document and enter the following in Draft view.

   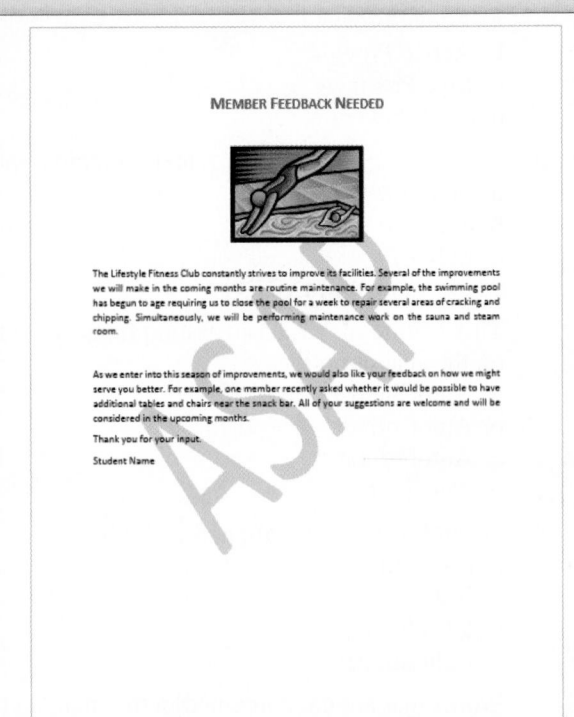

   Member Feedback Needed

   The Lifestyle Fitness Club constantly strives to improve its facilities. Several of the improvements we will make in the coming months are routine maintenance. For example, the current swimming pool has begun to age, requiring us to close the pool for a week to repair several areas of cracking and chipping. We will be performing maintenance work on the sauna and steam room. As we enter into this season of improvements, we would also like your feedback on how we might serve you better. For example, one member recently asked whether it would be possible to have additional tables near the snack bar. All of your suggestions are welcome and will be considered in the upcoming months.

   Thank you for your input.

   b. Correct any spelling and grammar errors that are identified.

   c. Turn on the display of formatting marks. Check the document and remove any extra blank spaces between words or at the end of lines.

   d. Save the document as Member Feedback in your solution file location.

   e. Switch to Print Layout view.

   f. At the beginning of the fourth sentence of the paragraph (that begins "We will be"), insert the word "Simultaneously" followed by a comma. Change the following "W" in "We" to lowercase. In the second to last sentence of the paragraph, insert the words "and chairs" after the word "tables". Delete the word "current" from the third sentence.

   g. Start a new paragraph beginning with the fifth sentence. Add two blank lines below the title and one blank line between paragraphs.

   h. Change the font size for the entire document to 12 pt and the alignment to justified. Apply 20 pt, bold font color of your choice, and small caps to the flyer title. Center the title.

i. Turn off the display of formatting marks.

j. Insert the picture of a swimming pool from the file wd01_Pool supplied with your data files. Size it appropriately and display it centered below the title.

k. Add an ASAP1 watermark.

l. Enter your name on the last line of the flyer. Include your name in the document properties as author and the file name as the title.

m. Save the document again and submit the document.

PROMOTING CELEBRATE BIKES SUNDAY ★★

2. You are the program coordinator for the city of Westbrook's Parks and Recreation Department. In next week's newspaper, you plan to run an article to promote bike riding in the community through the Celebrate Bikes Sunday event. Your completed article will be similar to the one shown here.

a. Enter the following information in a new Word 2013 document. Press [Enter] at the end of each paragraph.

Celebrate Bicycling!

May is traditionally National Bike Month, so take out your bicycle, tune it up, and get a breath of fresh air! Plan to take part in Celebrate Bikes Sunday on 5/8 to learn about the benefits of bike riding.

As part of the activities on this day, the Westbrook Parks and Recreation Department is sponsoring a bike ride from the West Avenue YMCA to the Main Street Park beginning at 11 a.m.

Businesses and organizations participating in the event are all "related to biking in Westbrook and most of them are involved in the development of the trail system," says event director Mary Jo Miller.

At the end of the bike ride, the riders are encouraged to stay for fun and informative activities in the

CELEBRATE BICYCLING!

May is National Bike Month, so take out your bicycle, tune it up, and get a breath of fresh air! Plan to take part in Celebrate Bikes Sunday on *May 8* to learn about the benefits of bike riding and bicycle safety.

Businesses and organizations participating in the event are all "related to biking in Westbrook and most of them are involved in the development of the trail system," says event director Mary Jo Miller.

As part of the activities on this day, the Westbrook Parks and Recreation Department is sponsoring a bike ride from the West Avenue YMCA to the Main Street Park. The ride begins promptly at *11 a.m.*

At the end of the bike ride, stay for fun and informative activities in the park. Activities include a bike safety program, entertainment, and food booths. The Safe Route to School program will work with parents and children to find the safest route to either walk or bike to school.

Registration is free and availability by calling *(603) 555-0113*, visiting the YMCA during regular business hours, or beginning at 10 a.m. on Sunday at the YMCA.

Student Name

[Current Date]

park. Activities include a bike safety program, entertainment, and food booths. The Safe Route to School program will work with parents and children to find the safest route to either walk or bike to school.

Registration is free and available by calling (603) 555-0113, visiting the YMCA during regular business hours, or beginning at 10 a.m. on Sunday at the YMCA.

b. Correct any spelling or grammar errors. Save the document as Bike Event.

c. Turn on the display of formatting marks. Check the document and remove any extra blank spaces between words or at the end of lines.

d. In Print Layout view, center the title. Change the title font to Britannic Bold (or a font of your choice), 36 pt, and light blue font color. Apply small caps to the title.

e. In the first paragraph, delete the word "traditionally" and change the number 5/8 to "May 8". Add the text "and bicycle safety" to the end of the second sentence in this paragraph.

f. Locate the text "Main Street Park" in the second paragraph. Insert a period after "Park". Change the following sentence to "The ride begins promptly at 11 a.m."

g. Delete the phrase "the riders are encouraged to" from the first sentence of the fourth paragraph.

h. Move the paragraph beginning with "Businesses and organizations" to the second paragraph, with "As part of the activities" becoming the third paragraph.

i. Add italics, bold, and light blue font color to the date in the first paragraph, the time in the third paragraph, and the phone number in the last paragraph.

j. Justify the paragraphs.

k. Increase the font size of the paragraphs below the title to 12 pt. Change the font of the paragraphs below the title to Times New Roman.

l. Insert a blank line below the title.

m. With the insertion point on the blank line, insert a clip art graphic of your choice of a child riding a bike by searching on the keyword "bike" or use the graphic file wd01_Child on Bike. Change the width of the graphic to approximately 2.5 inches. If necessary, change the wrapping style to Top and Bottom. Center the picture below the title. If necessary, insert a blank line before or after the picture.

n. Add your name and the current date on separate lines several lines below the last line. Left-align both lines. Turn off the display of formatting marks.

o. Review the document and, if necessary, adjust the size of the graphic to fit the document on a single page.

p. Include your name in the file properties as author and the file name as the title.

q. Save the document again. Submit the document.

ANNOUNCING MONTHLY MUSIC PERFORMANCES ★★

3. The Downtown Internet Café combines the relaxed atmosphere of a coffee house with the fun of using the Internet. The café will now be hosting monthly performances featuring local musicians. You want to create a flyer about the monthly music performances that you can distribute to local businesses. Your completed flyer will be similar to the one shown here.

   You will also create a coupon for a discount at the café using a Word template.

   a. Open a new Word document and enter the following text, pressing [Enter] where indicated.

   Monthly music performances every fourth Sunday!
   [Enter]

   Downtown Internet Cafe [Enter] (2 times)

   Come enjoy an excellent dark Italian Roast coffee, premium loose teas, blended drinks, and quality light fare of sandwiches, pitas and salads. [Enter]

   Your favorite coffeehouse has recently added a superb sound system composed of quality speakers and amplifiers. Starting Sunday, January 24 at 3 p.m., we will be hosting performances by local musicians. Come by every fourth Sunday and be entertained! [Enter]

   Cafe Hours: Sunday - Thursday 8 a.m. to 9 p.m. Friday and Saturday 8 a.m. to 12 a.m. [Enter]

   2314 Telegraph Avenue [Enter]

   b. Correct any spelling and grammar errors that are identified.

   c. Save the document as Music Performances.

   d. Turn on the display of formatting marks. Center the document title lines.

   e. Capitalize each word of the first line. Change the case of the text "Downtown Internet Café" to small caps.

Monthly Music Performances Every Fourth Sunday!

DOWNTOWN INTERNET CAFÉ

Your favorite coffeehouse has recently added a superb sound system composed of quality speakers and amplifiers. Starting Sunday, January 24, at 3 p.m., we will be hosting performances by local musicians. Come by every fourth Sunday and be entertained.

February 28, West Coast Bluegrass Experience

March 28, Vocal String Quartet

April 25, International Guitar Night

Come enjoy an excellent dark Italian Roast coffee, premium loose teas, blended drinks, and quality light fare of sandwiches, pitas, and salads.

2314 Telegraph Avenue

Café Hours:

Sunday – Thursday 8 a.m. to 9 p.m.

Friday and Saturday 8 a.m. to 12 a.m.

Student Name, Current Date

Downtown Internet Café | discount coupon

Receive a blonde roast coffee when you buy one of equal or less value

Redeemable at any participating Downtown Internet Café
Expires: December 31, 2015

www.downtowninternetcafe.biz

Downtown Internet Café | discount coupon

Receive a blonde roast coffee when you buy one of equal or less value

Redeemable at any participating Downtown Internet Café
Expires: December 31, 2015

www.downtowninternetcafe.biz

Downtown Internet Café | discount coupon

Receive a blonde roast coffee when you buy one of equal or less value

Redeemable at any participating Downtown Internet Café
Expires: December 31, 2015

www.downtowninternetcafe.biz

wntown Café | count coupon

LAB EXERCISES

f. Using drag and drop, move the second paragraph, including the paragraph mark, to the left of "C" of "Come" in the previous paragraph.

g. Using cut and paste, move the street address, including the following paragraph mark, to the left of the "C" of "Café Hours".

h. Insert the following three lines of text between the first and second paragraphs:

February 28, West Coast Bluegrass Experience

March 28, Vocal String Quartet

April 25, International Guitar Night

i. Change the first title of the document to a font color of dark red, font type of Arial Black or a font of your choice, and size of 24 pt.

j. Change the text "Downtown Internet Café" to a font color of blue, font type of Arial Narrow or a font of your choice, and size of 28 pt.

k. Select all the remaining text in the document and increase the font size to 14 pt.

l. Change the three date lines below the first paragraph to a font color of purple and a font size of 16 pt. Center the three lines. Change the last two lines (address and hours) to a font color of dark blue. Add bold to the selection. Center the address and operating hours. Position the insertion point after "Cafe Hours:" and press Enter. Position the insertion point after "9 p.m." and press Enter.

m. Insert the graphic file wd01_Saxophone (from your data files) on the blank line below the title Downtown Internet Café at the top of the document. Size the graphic to be approximately 2 by 2 inches using the ruler as a guide. Select the graphic and drag to center the saxophone horizontally.

n. Add your name and the current date, left-aligned, on one line, below the last line.

o. If a paragraph mark is displayed to the right of the date, delete it.

p. Turn off the display of formatting marks.

q. If necessary, reduce the size of the graphic so the entire flyer fits on one page.

r. Include your name in the file properties as author and the file name as the title. Save, submit, and then close the flyer document.

s. Locate and download the Coupon template.

t. Replace the [Company Name] placeholder with "Downtown Internet Cafe".

u. Replace the [Promotion] placeholder with "a blonde roast coffee".

v. Using the [Date] placeholder enter "December 31, 2015".

w. Replace the [Website] placeholder with "www.downtowninternetcafe.biz".

x. Save the completed document as Cafe Coupon.

y. Print or submit the document as directed by your instructor.

PREPARING A NEWSLETTER ARTICLE ★★★

4. The Mountain View Camera Club meets on the second and fourth Thursdays each month at 7 p.m. in the Arts Center. A monthly newsletter is published for members and club visitors. Each month an article is written to answer questions that have been submitted to the newsletter committee. This month's newsletter will include an article on photographing animals.

   a. Open the Word document wd01_Photographing Animals.

   b. Correct any spelling and grammar errors that are identified. Save the document as Photographing Animals.

   c. Format the title using Century Gothic font, 14 pt, bold, and small caps.

   d. Change all text below the title to 11 pt, Palatino Linotype.

   e. Select the four topic headings "Setting," "Composition," " Telephoto Lens," and "Lens Hood." Apply 12 pt, bold, italic, and small caps formatting.

   f. Select the title and the four topic headings and apply a font color of your choice.

   g. Select the Composition heading, the paragraph that follows, and the blank line. Move the selected paragraphs above the Setting heading.

   h. Move to the beginning of the paragraph that begins "Animals have". Use Office.com to insert a picture of a dog of your choice. If you do not have Internet access, insert the picture wd01_Dog from your data file location.

   i. Size the picture so that the picture height is approximately 1 inch. Change the text wrap to Tight and align the picture on the left margin. Size the graphic if necessary so that the height of the graphic is equal to the height of the paragraph text.

   j. Add your name and the current date on separate lines two lines below the last line. Right-align the text. If needed, reduce the size of the graphic to fit the entire document on one page.

   k. Include your name in the file properties as author and the document title as the title. Save the document. Submit the document.

PHOTOGRAPHING ANIMALS

When photographing animals, consider the assignment a challenge. Whether you are shooting pets, animals in a zoo, or animals in the wild, patience and time are critical for taking great pictures.

Animals have their own personality, and it is important to know your subject. Learn the behavior patterns of your subject so that you will know when it is resting or active and then choose the time of day to begin shooting. Also, you may need to consider the season of the year so you can choose an appropriate background. When photographing a pet, try to get on the pet's level. Get as close as possible to your subject, but keep a safe distance.

COMPOSITION
Composition is the arrangement of elements in a photograph. Composition includes foreground and background objects so it important to have a main subject. Be careful to keep the subject as the center of attention. Animals should not be centered in the frame. Use the rule of thirds to position the subject off-center. Determine if you want to photograph the entire body of the animal or just the facial features. Fill the frame, and use the eyes for the focal point. Avoid using a flash when photographing animals.

SETTING
Lighting is an important factor when photographing animals. There are three basic types of lighting: front lighting, back lighting, and side lighting. Take photos using all types of lighting and determine which type is best for your photo subject. Many photographers prefer to take pictures in the early morning or in the late afternoon when the light source is considered warm. Shooting at noon places the subject in direct sunlight and may wash out the colors of the photo. Shooting on an overcast day eliminates shadows and intensifies colors.

TELEPHOTO LENS
A telephoto lens enables you to focus on a subject that is far away. When purchasing a telephoto lens, buy a lens with auto-focusing (AF) and image stabilization (IS). Image stabilization is designed to prevent blurring when the camera moves. Check the weight, size, and cost of a lens before buying. It may be too large, too heavy, and too expensive.

LENS HOOD
Attach a lens hood to your lens to reduce glare.

Student Name
Current Date

LAB EXERCISES

WRITING AN ARTICLE ON THE HISTORY OF ICE CREAM ★★★

5. Each month the town's free paper prints a fun article on the history of a topic people are familiar with but might not know anything about. You researched the topic online and found the information you needed about the history of ice cream from the International Dairy Foods Association's website at www. idfa.org/news--views/media-kits/ice-cream/the-history-of-ice-cream. Your completed article will be similar to the one shown here.

   a. Open the file named wd01_History of Ice Cream.

   b. Correct any spelling and grammar errors. (Hint: Click ⧉ Next in the status bar to move to each error.) Save the document as Ice Cream History.

   c. Enter the following headings at the location shown in parentheses.

      History of Ice Cream (above first paragraph)

      The Evolution of Ice Cream (above second paragraph)

      Ice Cream in America (above third paragraph)

   d. Center the title "History of Ice Cream". Change the font to Lucida Sans with a point size of 24, and add the small caps effect. Add a color of your choice to the title.

   e. Change the other two headings to bold with a type size of 14 pt. Use the same color as in the title for the headings.

   f. Move The Evolution of Ice Cream heading and paragraph to below the second Ice Cream in America paragraph.

   g. Undo the move operation you performed in the last step.

   h. Change the alignment of the first paragraph to justified.

   i. Add a blank line below the main title of the article and insert the picture wd01_Ice Cream (from your data files) at this location.

   j. Size the picture to be 1 inch wide (use the ruler as a guide). Use the square text wrapping option, and drag the picture to the middle of the the two paragraphs below the Ice Cream in America heading.

   k. Add a Draft watermark.

l. Add your name and the current date below the last line of the article. View the whole page and, if necessary, reduce the size of the graphic so the entire article fits on one page.

m. Include your name in the file properties as author and the document title as the title. Save the document again. Submit the document.

ON YOUR OWN

CREATING A FLYER ★

1. Adventure Travel Tours is offering a great deal on a Day of the Dead Bicycle Tour in Mexico. Research the Day of the Dead celebration using the web as a resource. Then, using the features of Word you have learned so far, create a flyer that will advertise this tour. Use at least two colors of text, two sizes of text, two kinds of paragraph alignment, a sans serif font for the headings, and a serif font for the body text. Include a graphic from Office.com. Include your name at the bottom of the flyer. Include your name in the file properties as author and the file name as the title. Save the document as Mexico Adventure.

CREATING A FAX COVERSHEET ★★

2. You work at the community pool and have been asked by your boss (Anna Najarian) to fax information to Asher Hayes at the local high school describing the rules swimmers should follow when using the pool. Create a new document using the Fax (Equity theme) template. Edit the template to include the following recipient information: **Asher Hayes** (To:), **650-555-0198** (Fax:) **650-555-0197** (Phone:), **Pool Rules** (Re:). Include the following sender information: **Your Name** (From:), **1** (Pages:), **Today's Date** (Date:), and **Anna Najarian** (CC:). Select the For Review check box by clicking it. (The box should appear shaded.)

   Edit the Type Comments: placeholder to include the five most important rules to follow while swimming at the pool. Use the web as a resource for obtaining pool safety information. Place each rule on a separate line. Insert a clip art from Office.com after the list of rules. Size the image if necessary so that the document remains one page in length. Include your name in the file properties as author and the file name as the title. Save the document as Pool Rules.

ASTRONOMY CLASS MEMO ★★★

3. The city of Gilbert, Arizona, recently built a $100,000 observatory that includes a $20,000 telescope in a local park. The observatory is open evenings for small groups of five to six people to take turns looking through the 16-inch telescope's eyepiece. The use of the observatory is free.

   The city has decided to offer classes for the community to learn how to use the telescope and to teach astronomy. As a trial run, the class will first be offered to city employees and their families. You want to notify all employees about the observatory and the class by including a flyer with their paycheck. Using

LAB EXERCISES

Step-by-Step Exercise 1 as a model, provide information about when and where the class will be held. Include information about how people can sign up for the class and an appropriate graphic. Include your name as the last line of the flyer. Include your name in the file properties as author and the file name as the title. Save the flyer as Astronomy Basics.

VOLUNTEER OPPORTUNITIES ★★★

4. Many community groups, hospitals, libraries, and churches are looking for volunteers to assist in their programs. Volunteering has rewards for both the volunteer and the community. Using the web as a resource, research volunteer opportunities in your community. Then write a one-page report that includes information about two volunteer groups for which you would like to volunteer. Include information about what the organization does for the community. List the types of jobs/activities available for volunteers, times, and number of hours. Also include the skills you have to offer and the amount of time you can commit as a volunteer. Include a title at the top of the document and your name and the current date below the title. Center the title lines. Use at least two colors of text, two sizes of text, and two kinds of paragraph alignment. Include a graphic from Office.com. Include your name in the file properties as author and the file name as the title. Save the document as Volunteer Opportunities.

WRITING A NATIONAL PARK REPORT ★★★

5. Using the library or the web, research information on a national park in the United States. Write a one-page report including the following information: location of the park, best time to visit the park, general facts and statistics, special events, wildlife, and activities such as hiking, photography, and biking. At the top of the document, add a title. Format the title attractively. Add a picture to the document. Size and position the picture appropriately. Add at least two subheadings, and format the headings using 14 pt, bold, and small caps. Add your name and current date at the end of the document. Include your name in the file properties as author and the file name as the title. Save the document as National Park.

Revising and Refining a Document   Lab 2

Objectives

After completing this lab, you will know how to:

1. Use the Spelling and Grammar and the Thesaurus tools.

2. Work with multiple documents.

3. Control document paging.

4. Find and replace text.

5. Insert the current date.

6. Change indents, line spacing, and margins.

7. Create a tabbed table.

8. Add color highlighting and underlines.

9. Create numbered and bulleted lists.

10. Create and use Building Blocks.

11. Insert and modify a shape.

12. Add a page border.

13. Secure content.

14. E-mail a document.

15. Prepare and print envelopes.

Adventure Travel Tours

After creating the rough draft of the new tours flyer, you showed the printed copy to your manager at Adventure Travel Tours. Your manager then made several suggestions for improving the flyer's style and appearance. In addition, you created a letter to be sent to clients along with the flyer. The letter briefly describes Adventure Travel Tour's four new tours and invites clients to attend an informational presentation. Your manager likes the idea but also wants the letter to include information about the new Adventure Travel Tours website and a 10 percent discount for early booking.

In this lab, you will learn more about editing documents so you can reorganize and refine both your flyer and a rough draft of the letter to clients. You also will learn to use many more of the formatting features included in Office Word 2013 so you can add style and interest to your documents. Formatting features can greatly improve the appearance and design of any document you produce so that it communicates its message more clearly. The completed letter and revised flyer are shown here.

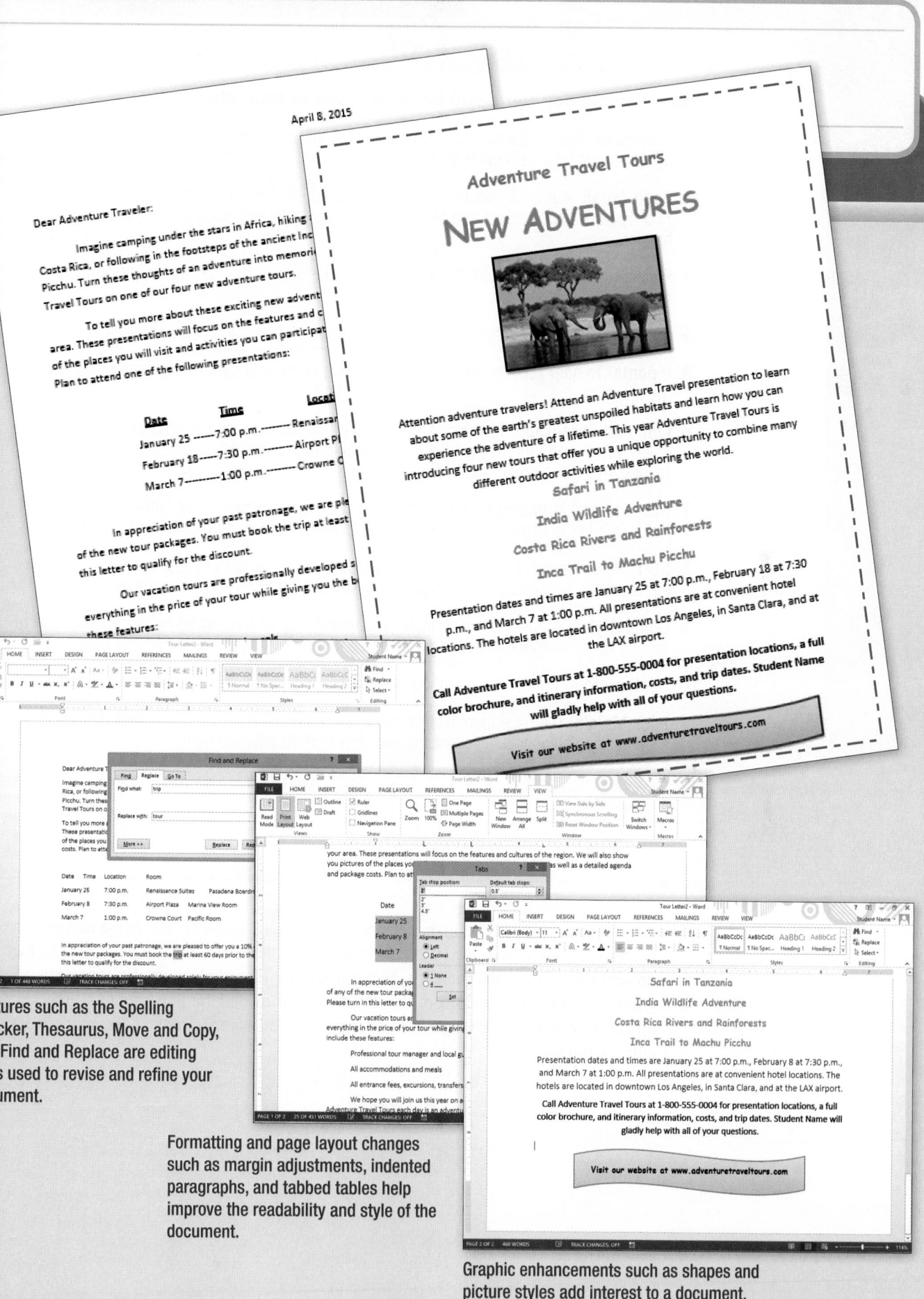

...tures such as the Spelling ...cker, Thesaurus, Move and Copy, ... Find and Replace are editing ...s used to revise and refine your ...ument.

Formatting and page layout changes such as margin adjustments, indented paragraphs, and tabbed tables help improve the readability and style of the document.

Graphic enhancements such as shapes and picture styles add interest to a document.

The following concepts will be introduced in this lab:

1 Thesaurus Word's Thesaurus is a reference tool that provides synonyms, antonyms, and related words for a selected word or phrase.

2 Page Break A page break marks the point at which one page ends and another begins. Two types of page breaks can be used in a document: soft page breaks and hard page breaks.

3 Find and Replace You use the Find and Replace feature to find text in a document and replace it with other text as directed.

4 Field A field is a placeholder that instructs Word to insert information into a document.

5 Indents To help your reader find information quickly, you can indent paragraphs from the margins.

6 Line and Paragraph Spacing Adjusting the line spacing, or the vertical space between lines of text, and increasing or decreasing spacing before and after paragraphs improve readability of document text.

7 Bulleted and Numbered Lists Whenever possible, add bullets or numbers before items in a list to organize information and to make your writing clear and easy to read.

8 Sort Word can quickly arrange or sort text, numbers, or data in lists or tables in alphabetical, numeric, or date order based on the first character in each paragraph.

9 Quick Styles Applying a quick style, a named group of formatting options, allows you to quickly apply multiple formats to a text selection or an object in one simple step.

10 Section To format parts of a document differently, you divide a document into sections.

11 Page Margin The page margin is the blank space around the edge of the page. Standard single-sided documents have four margins: top, bottom, left, and right.

Revising a Document

After speaking with the manager about the letter's content, the basic topics that need to be included in the letter are to advertise the new tours, invite clients to the presentations, describe the early-booking discount, and promote the new website. After creating a rough draft of the letter, you proofread the document and marked up the printout with changes and corrections you want to make. The marked-up copy is shown here.

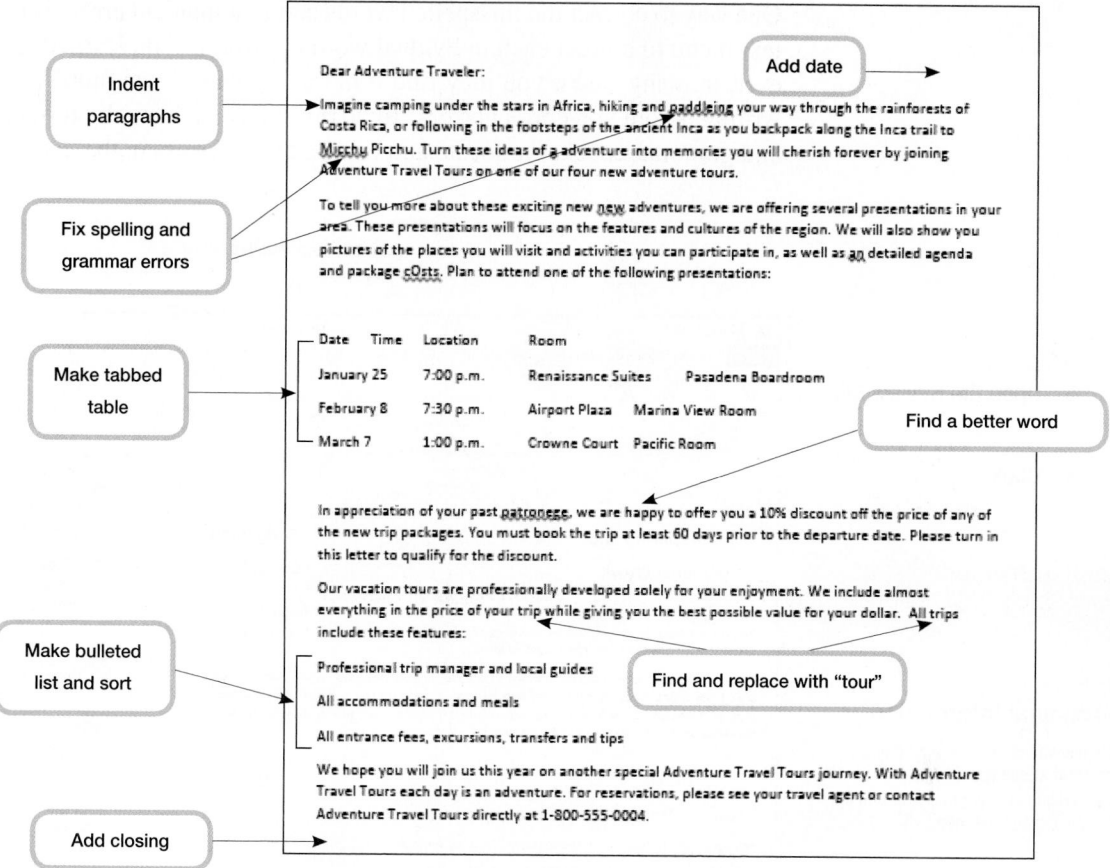

SPELL-CHECKING THE ENTIRE DOCUMENT

The first correction you want to make is to fix the spelling and grammar errors that Word has identified.

1

- Start Microsoft Word 2013 and open the file wd02_Tour Letter.

- If necessary, change to Print Layout view at 100% zoom.

Your screen should be similar to Figure 2.1

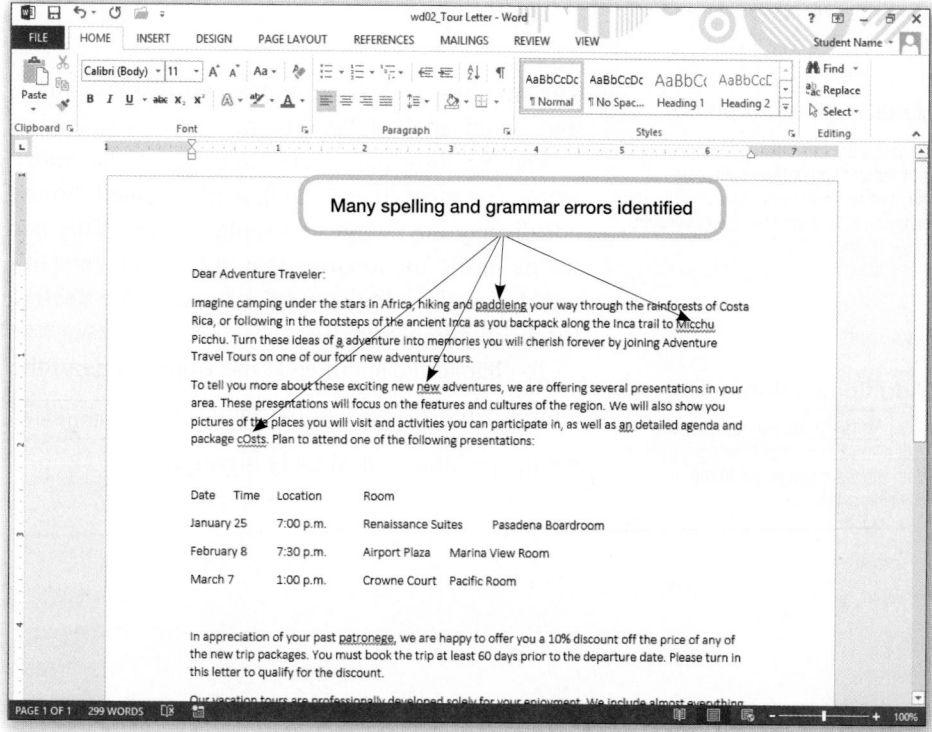

Figure 2.1

One way to correct the misspelled words and grammatical errors is to use the context menu to correct each individual word or error, as you learned in Lab 1. However, in many cases, you may find it more efficient to wait until you are finished writing before you correct errors. To do this, you can manually turn on the spelling and grammar checker to locate and correct all the errors in the document at once.

2

● **Open the Review tab.**

● **Click** Spelling & Grammar.

Another Method

The keyboard shortcut is F7.

Additional Information

You also can click the Spelling and Grammar status icon to move to the next spelling or grammar error and open the spelling context menu.

Your screen should be similar to Figure 2.2

Additional Information

The definitions will vary with the installed dictionary on your system.

Additional Information

Because the contents of the list are determined only by spelling, any instances of terms that seem inappropriate in context are completely coincidental.

Additional Information

The Change All option replaces the same word throughout the document with the word you select in the Spelling pane.

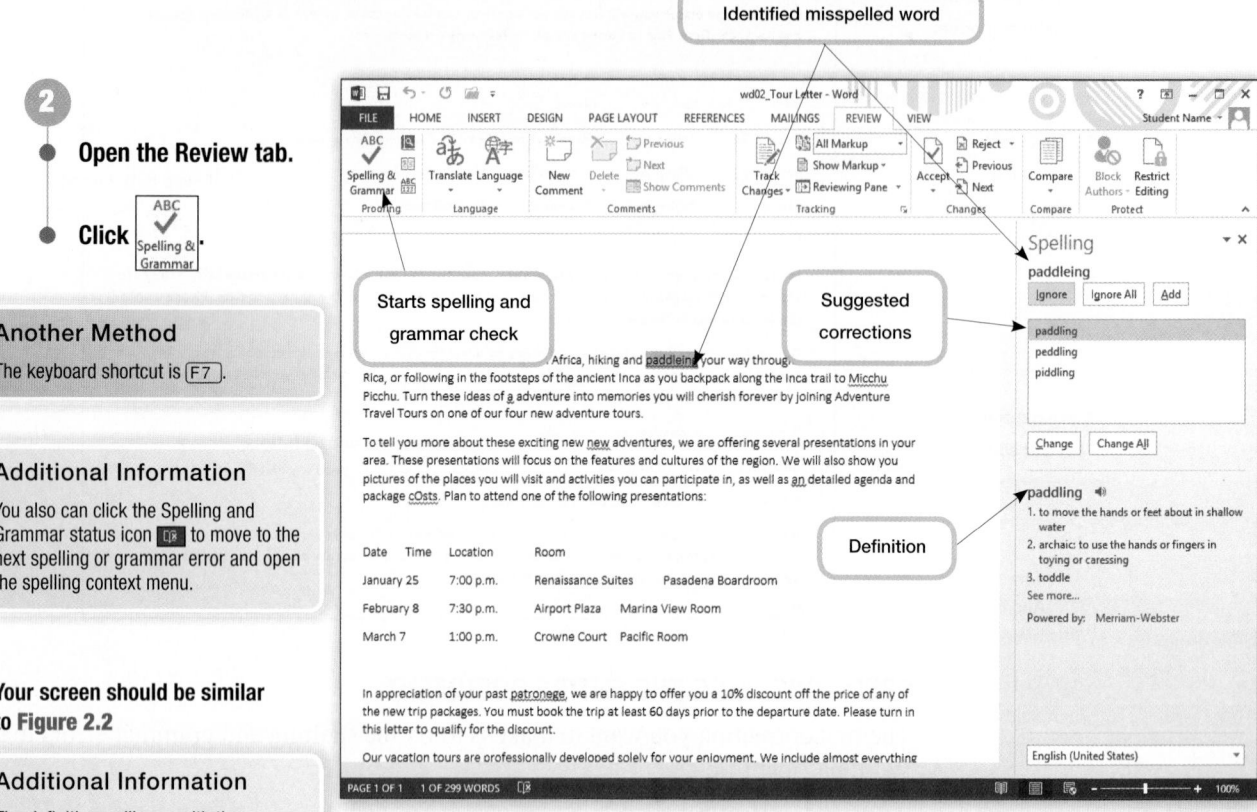

Figure 2.2

The Spelling task pane opens and displays the first word it has identified that may be misspelled, "paddleing." The word is highlighted in the document.

The Spelling pane lists suggestions that most closely match the misspelled word. The most likely match is highlighted. Sometimes the spelling checker does not display any suggested replacements. This occurs when it cannot locate any words in the dictionaries that are similar in spelling. If no suggestions are provided, you can edit the word manually. The Spelling pane also displays definitions for the highlighted word.

To change the spelling of the word to one of the suggested spellings, select the correct word in the list and then click Change. In this case, the correct replacement, "paddling," is already highlighted.

3

Click Change.

Your screen should be similar to Figure 2.3

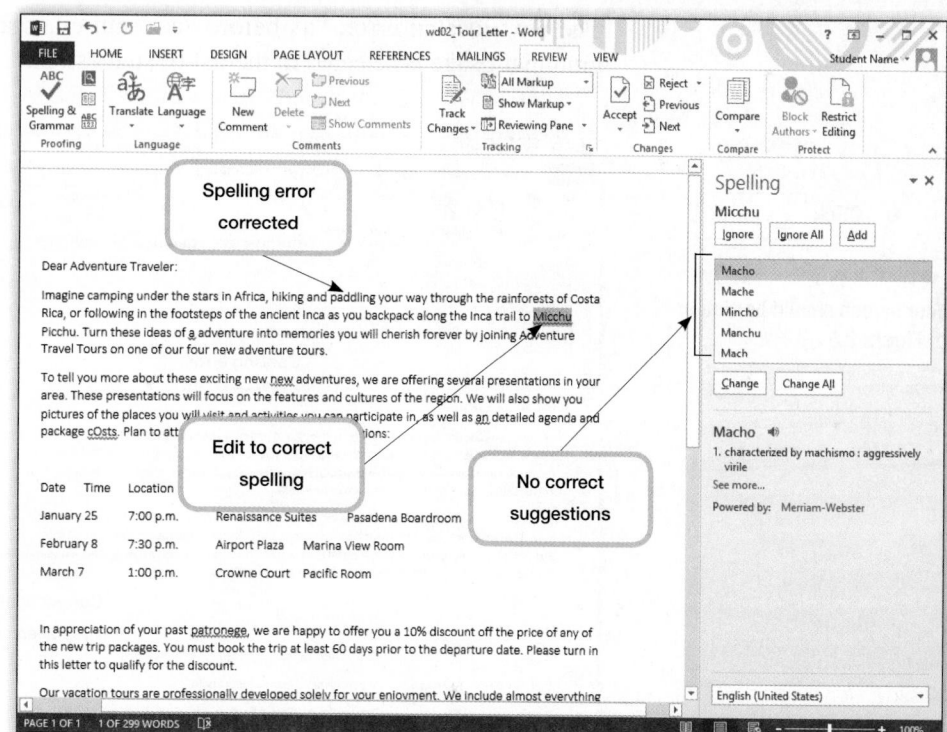

Spelling error corrected

Edit to correct spelling

No correct suggestions

Figure 2.3

Additional Information

On your own computer system, you would want to add words to the custom dictionary that you use frequently and that are not included in the standard dictionary.

The spelling checker replaces the misspelled word with the selected replacement and highlights the next possible error. This time the error is the name of the Inca ruins at Machu Picchu. "Micchu" is the incorrect spelling for this word; there is no correct suggestion, however, because the word is not found in the dictionary. You will correct the spelling of the word by editing it in the document.

4

• Click on the highlighted word in the document.

• Edit the spelling of the word to Machu

• Click Resume in the Spelling pane.

Your screen should be similar to Figure 2.4

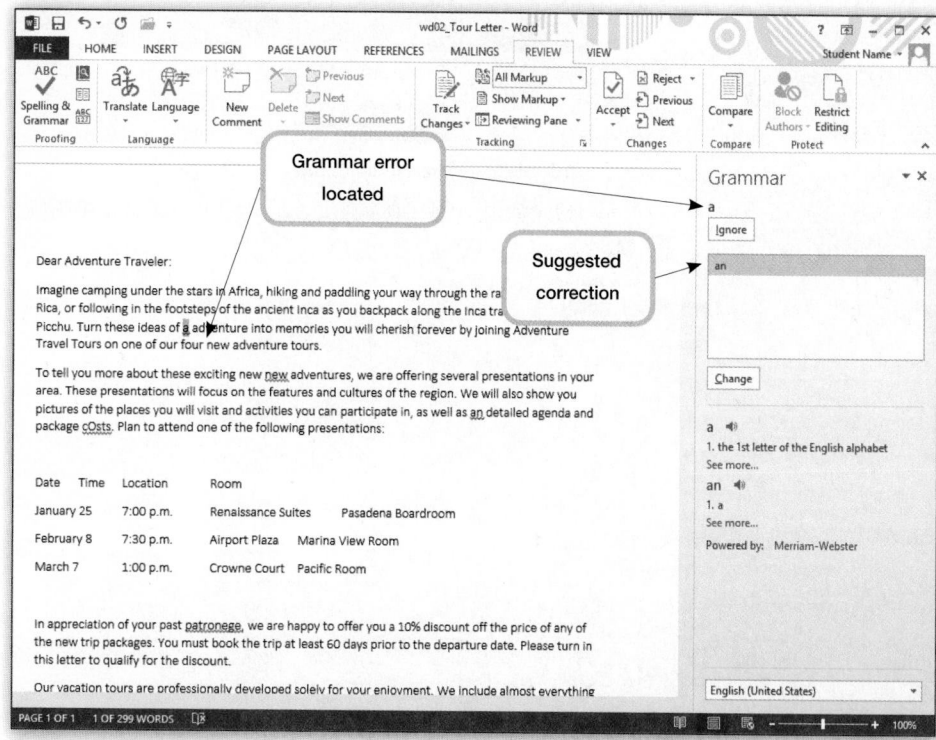

Grammar error located

Suggested correction

Figure 2.4

The next located error, "a" before "adventure," is a grammar error. The correct grammar usage is selected in the list of suggestions.

● Click Change.

Your screen should be similar to Figure 2.5

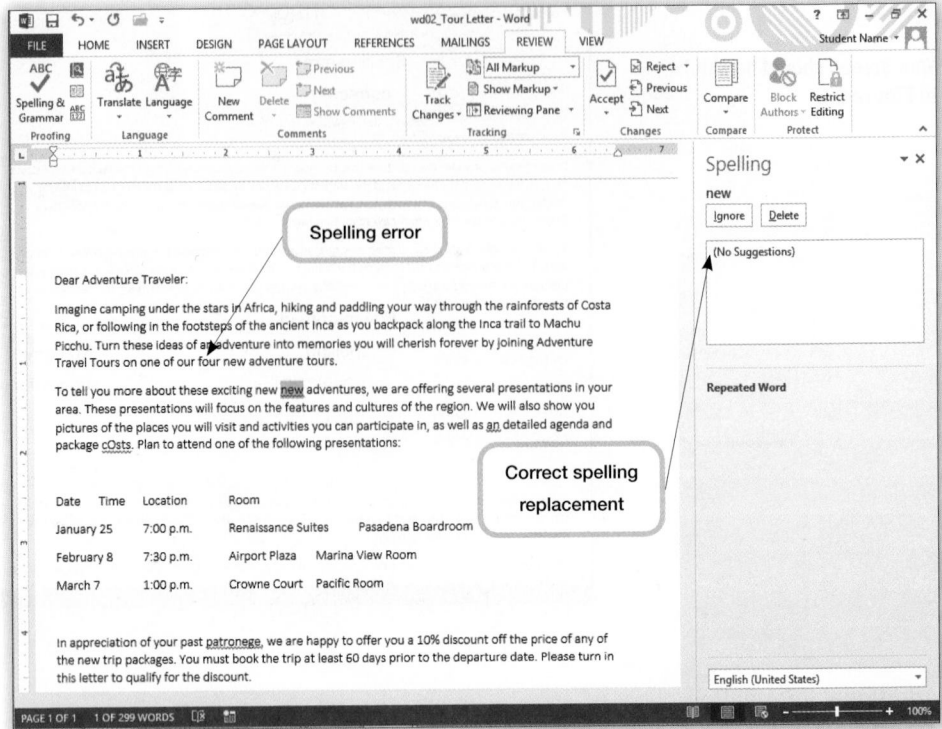

Figure 2.5

The next four errors that will be identified and their causes are shown in the following table:

Identified Error	Cause	Action	Result
new	Repeated word	Delete	duplicate word "new" is deleted
cOsts	Inconsistent capitalization	Change	costs
an detailed	Grammatical error	Change	a
patronege	Spelling error	Change	patronage

6

● Respond to the spelling and grammar checker by taking the actions in the table on the previous page for the identified errors.

● Click **OK** in response to the message telling you that the spelling and grammar check is complete.

● Move to the top of the document.

Your screen should be similar to Figure 2.6

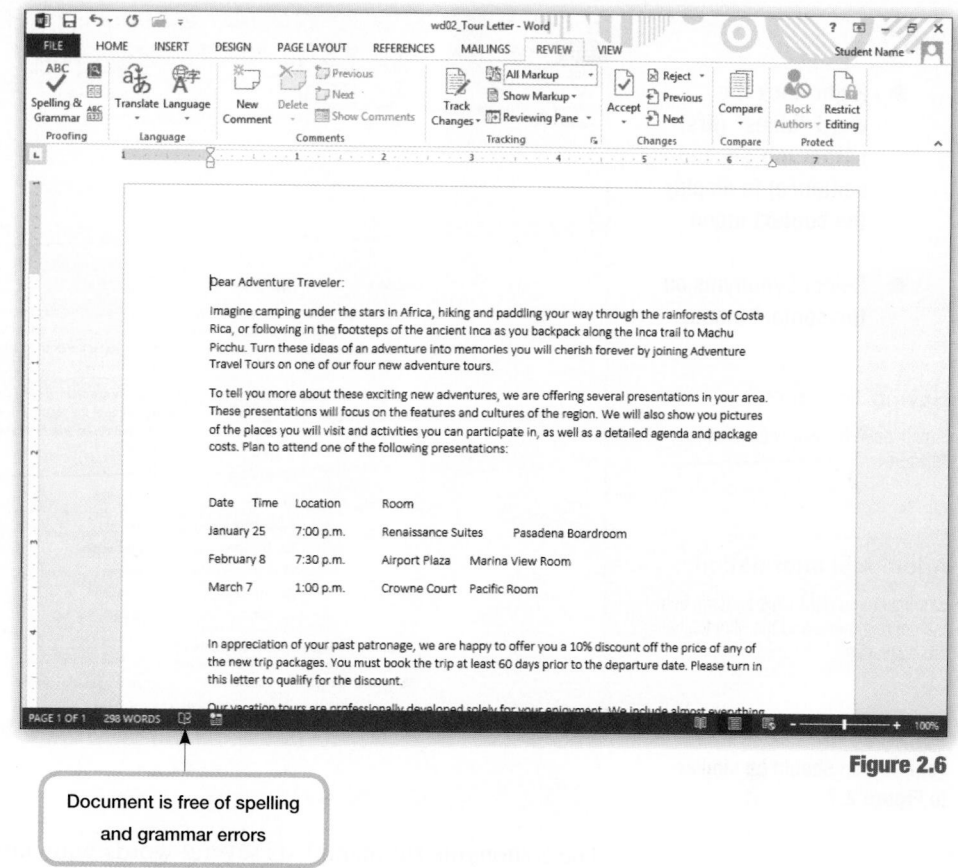

Figure 2.6

Document is free of spelling and grammar errors

USING THE THESAURUS

The next text change you want to make is to find a more descriptive word for "ideas" in the first paragraph and "happy" in the second paragraph. To help find a similar word, you will use the Thesaurus tool.

Concept ① Thesaurus

Word's **Thesaurus** is a reference tool that provides synonyms, antonyms, and related words for a selected word or phrase. **Synonyms** are words with a similar meaning, such as "cheerful" and "happy." **Antonyms** are words with an opposite meaning, such as "cheerful" and "sad." Related words are words that are variations of the same word, such as "cheerful" and "cheer." Using the Thesaurus tool can help improve your document by adding interest and variety to your text.

First you need to identify the word you want changed by moving the insertion point on the word. Then you use the Thesaurus to suggest alternative words. The quickest way to find synonyms is to use the context menu for the word you want to replace.

1

- **Right-click the word "ideas" (first paragraph, second sentence) to display the context menu.**

- **Select Synonyms on the context menu.**

Having Trouble?

Simply point to the menu option to select it.

Additional Information

Whenever you right-click an item, both the context menu and the Mini toolbar are displayed.

Your screen should be similar to Figure 2.7

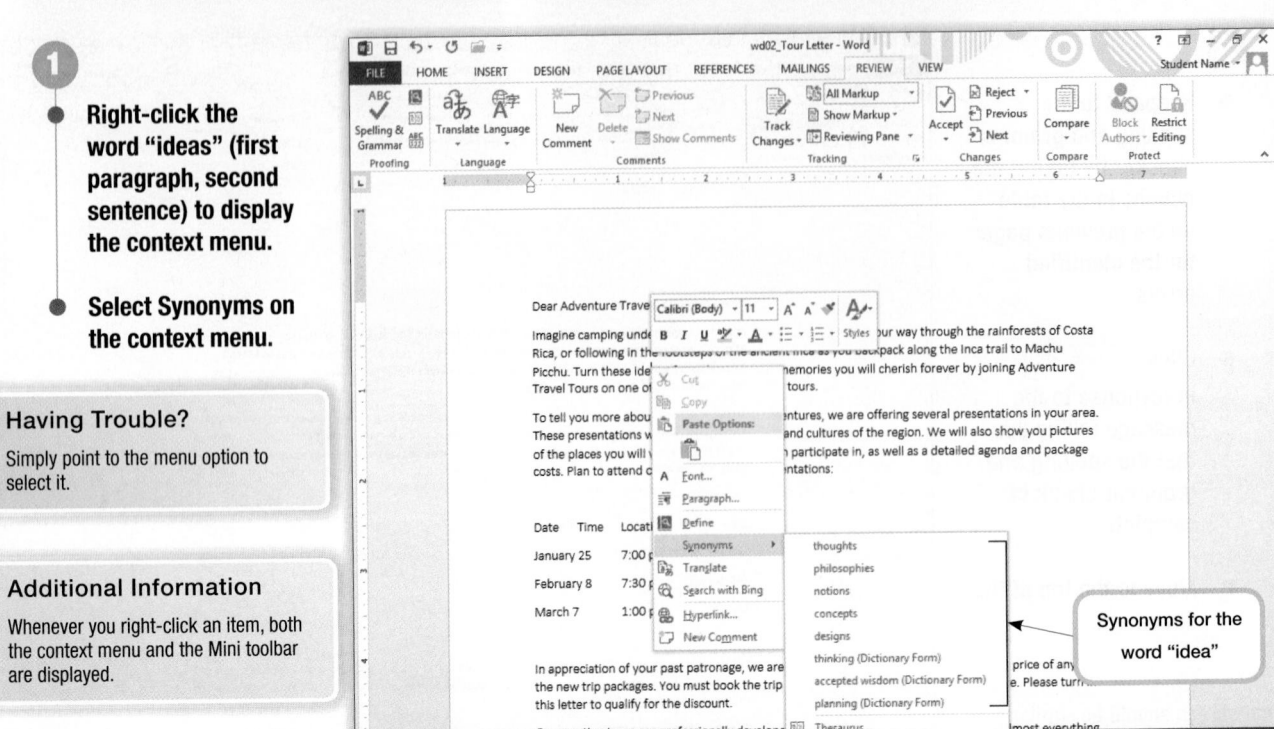

Synonyms for the word "idea"

Figure 2.7

The Synonyms submenu lists several words with similar meanings. You decide to replace "ideas" with "thoughts." Then you will use the Thesaurus to locate synonyms for "happy."

2

- **Choose "thoughts".**

- **Click on the word "happy" (first sentence in the paragraph below the presentation dates).**

- **Click 📖 Thesaurus in the Proofing group of the Review tab.**

Another Method

The keyboard equivalent is Shift + F7.

Your screen should be similar to Figure 2.8

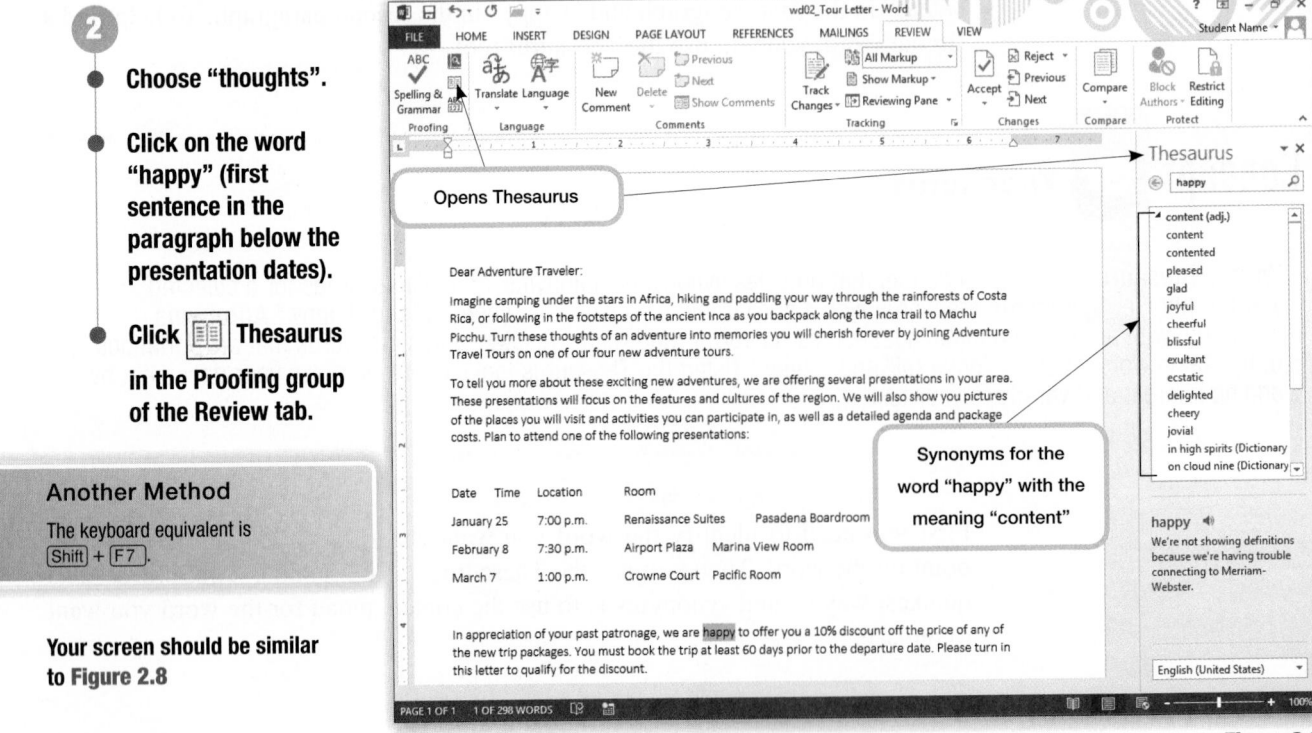

Opens Thesaurus

Synonyms for the word "happy" with the meaning "content"

Figure 2.8

The Thesaurus task pane displays the selected word "happy" in the text box. The suggestions list box displays synonyms for the word "happy" with a meaning of "content (adj.)." The most likely choice from this list is "pleased." To see whether any other words are closer in meaning, you will look up synonyms for the word "pleased."

● Click "pleased".

Your screen should be similar to Figure 2.9

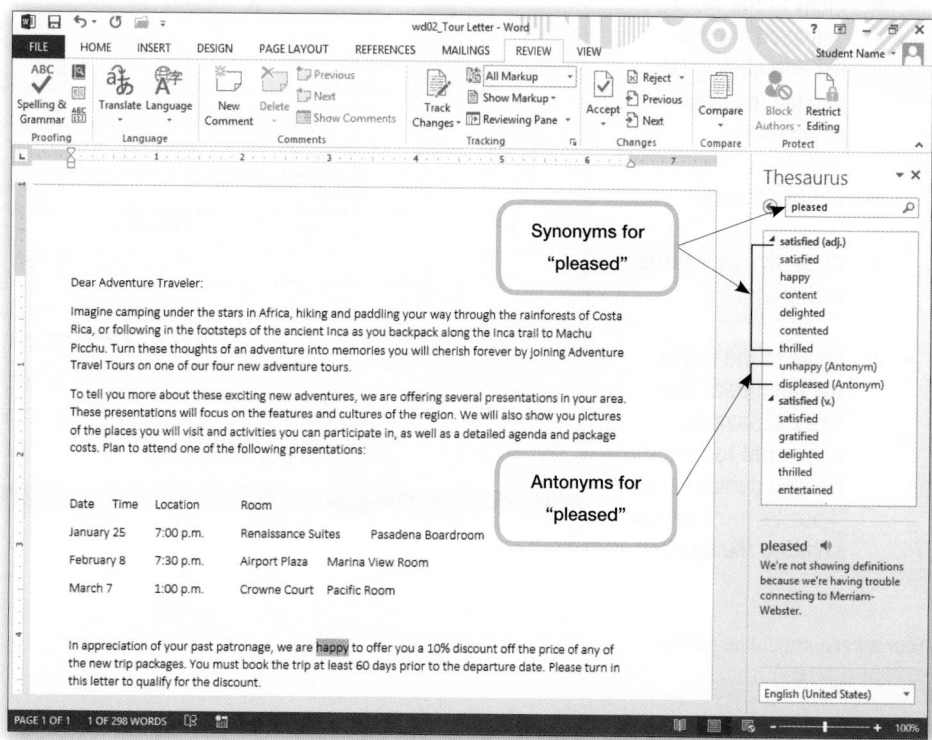

Figure 2.9

The word "pleased" is entered in the text box and the suggestions list displays synonyms, as well as a few antonyms, for this word. You decide to use "pleased" and will return to the previous list to insert the word into the document.

4

● Click ⬅ **Back** to display the list for the word "happy."

● Point to the word "pleased" in the list and click ▾ to display the drop-down menu.

● Choose **Insert.**

● Close the Thesaurus task pane.

● Move to the top of the document and use the **Save As** command to save the revised document as Tour Letter2 to your solution file location.

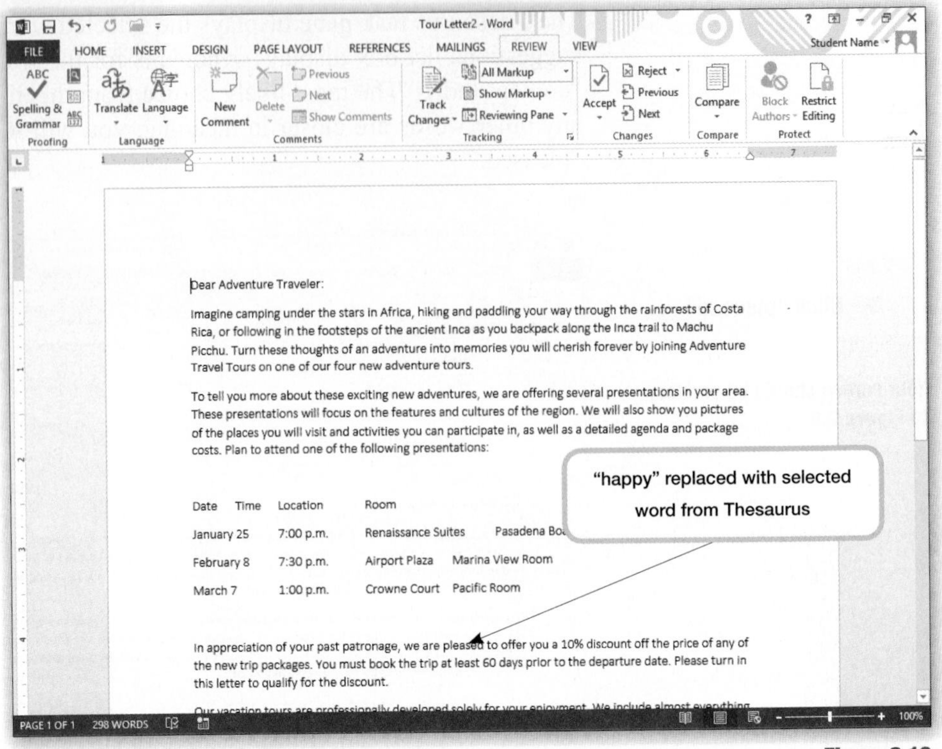

Your screen should be similar to Figure 2.10

Dear Adventure Traveler:

Imagine camping under the stars in Africa, hiking and paddling your way through the rainforests of Costa Rica, or following in the footsteps of the ancient Inca as you backpack along the Inca trail to Machu Picchu. Turn these thoughts of an adventure into memories you will cherish forever by joining Adventure Travel Tours on one of our four new adventure tours.

To tell you more about these exciting new adventures, we are offering several presentations in your area. These presentations will focus on the features and cultures of the region. We will also show you pictures of the places you will visit and activities you can participate in, as well as a detailed agenda and package costs. Plan to attend one of the following presentations:

Date	Time	Location	Room
January 25	7:00 p.m.	Renaissance Suites	Pasadena Boa...
February 8	7:30 p.m.	Airport Plaza	Marina View Room
March 7	1:00 p.m.	Crowne Court	Pacific Room

"happy" replaced with selected word from Thesaurus

In appreciation of your past patronage, we are pleased to offer you a 10% discount off the price of any of the new trip packages. You must book the trip at least 60 days prior to the departure date. Please turn in this letter to qualify for the discount.

Our vacation tours are professionally developed solely for your enjoyment. We include almost everything

Figure 2.10

Working with Multiple Documents

You plan to enclose the flyer with the letter to be mailed to clients. To do this, you will open the flyer document and copy it into the letter document file. All Office 2013 applications allow you to open and use multiple files at the same time. This feature makes it easy to compare documents or to move or copy information between documents.

ARRANGING AND SCROLLING WINDOWS

You have made several changes suggested by your manager to the flyer, including changing the font colors and removing the watermark.

Open the wd02_
Flyer2 **document.**

**Your screen should be similar
to Figure 2.11**

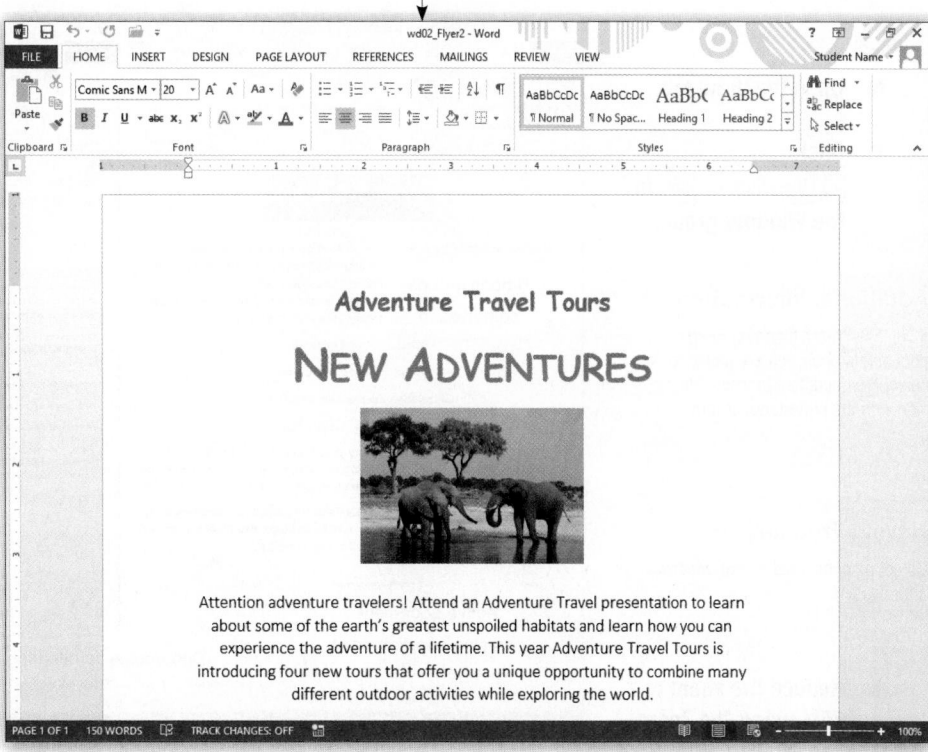

Figure 2.11

The flyer document opens and displays in a separate Word 2013 application
window. You revised the flyer slightly by changing the font colors, updating the
presentation dates, and removing the watermark. You would like to see both documents in the window at the same time.

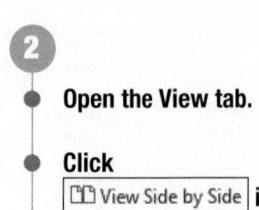

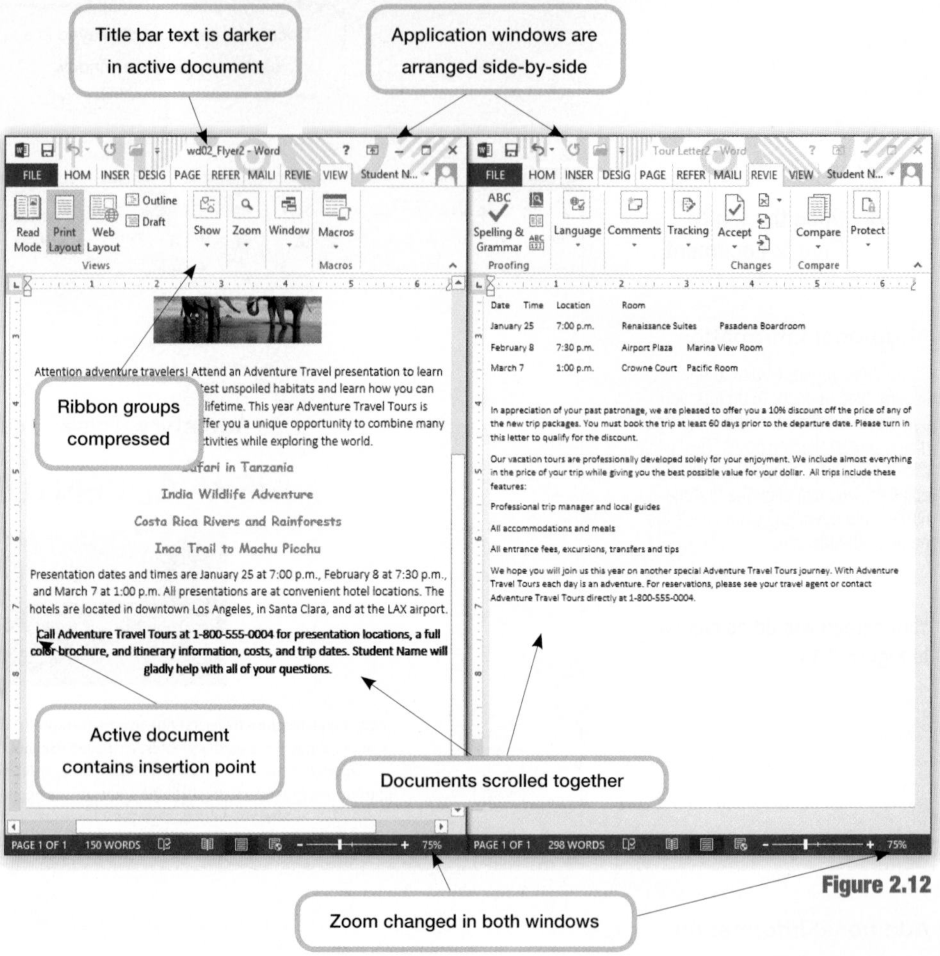

Title bar text is darker in active document

Application windows are arranged side-by-side

2

- Open the View tab.

- Click ⊡ View Side by Side in the Window group.

Ribbon groups compressed

Active document contains insertion point

Documents scrolled together

Zoom changed in both windows

Figure 2.12

Additional Information

If you have more than two Word documents open, you are asked to select the document to view side-by-side with the current document.

Having Trouble?

Do not be concerned if your windows are reversed.

- Reduce the zoom to 75% using the Zoom slider for the wd02_Flyer2 **window.**

- Scroll to the bottom of the wd02_Flyer2 window.

- Move to the beginning of the last paragraph.

Your screen should be similar to Figure 2.12

Additional Information

Using ⊞ Arrange All arranges all open windows horizontally on the screen.

Additional Information

You may see more or less of the document in the window depending on the size of your monitor.

Now, the two Word application windows are arranged side by side on the screen and the zoom percentage has automatically adjusted to display each document in Page Layout view in the new window size. The flyer contains the insertion point, which indicates that it is the **active window**, or the window in which you can work. Simply click the other document to make it active. Because the windows are side by side and there is less horizontal space in each window, the Ribbon groups are compressed. To access commands in these groups, simply click the group button and the group commands appear.

Did you notice when you scrolled the document that both documents scrolled together? This is because the windows are **synchronized**, meaning both windows will act the same. When synchronized, the documents in both windows will scroll vertically and horizontally together so you can compare text easily. If you are not comparing text, this feature can be turned off so that they scroll independently.

3

Click 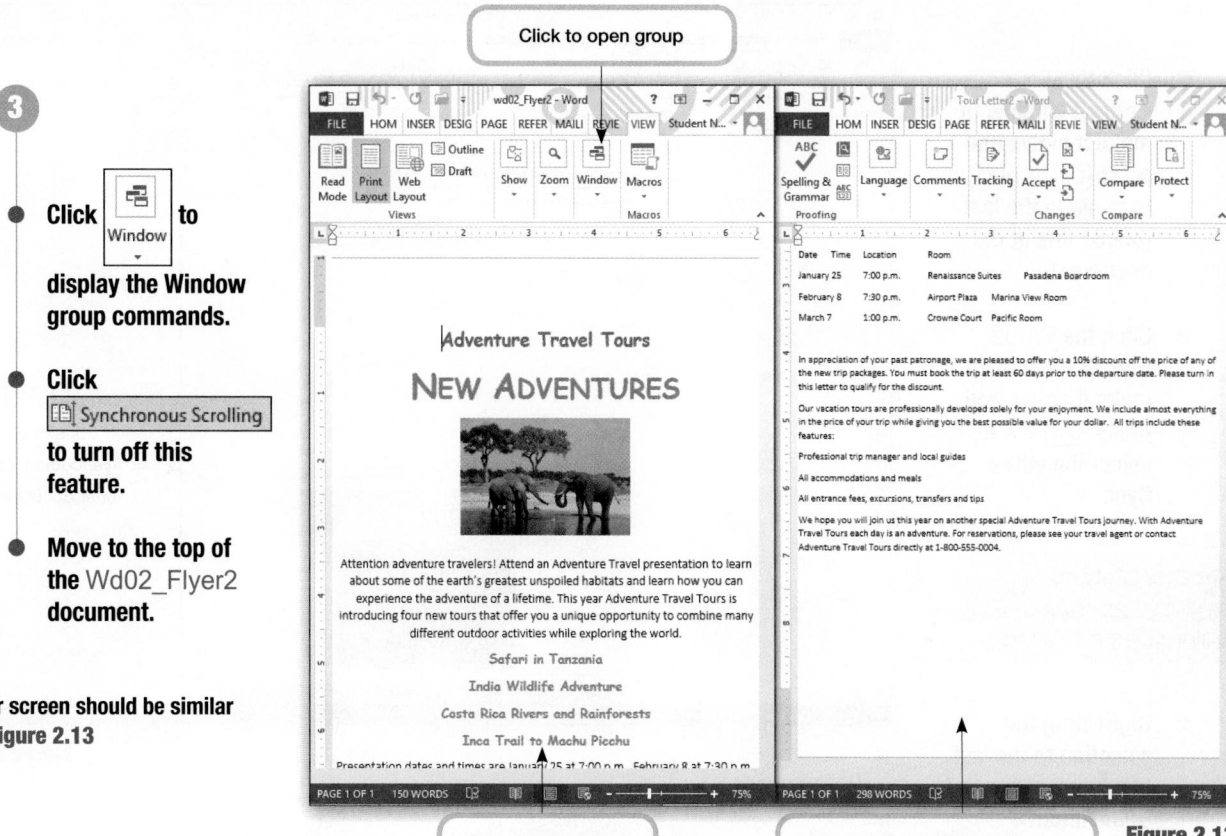 to display the Window group commands.

Click 🖹 Synchronous Scrolling to turn off this feature.

Move to the top of the Wd02_Flyer2 document.

Your screen should be similar to Figure 2.13

Click to open group

Document scrolled

Document remained stationary

Figure 2.13

The flyer document scrolled while the letter document remained stationary.

COPYING BETWEEN DOCUMENTS

You plan to enclose the flyer with the letter to be sent to clients. Since the document windows are displaying side by side, you can simply copy the entire flyer to the bottom of the letter document using drag and drop. To copy between documents using drag and drop, hold down the right mouse button while dragging. When you release the button, a context menu appears where you specify the action you want to perform. If you drag using the left mouse button, the selection is moved by default.

1

- Click the Tour Letter2 window to make it active and press `Ctrl` + `End` to move to the last (blank) line of the document.

- Click the Wd02_Flyer2 window to make it active and press `Ctrl` + A to select the entire flyer.

- Right-drag the selection to the last blank line at the end of the letter.

- Release the mouse button and choose Copy Here from the context menu.

- Click 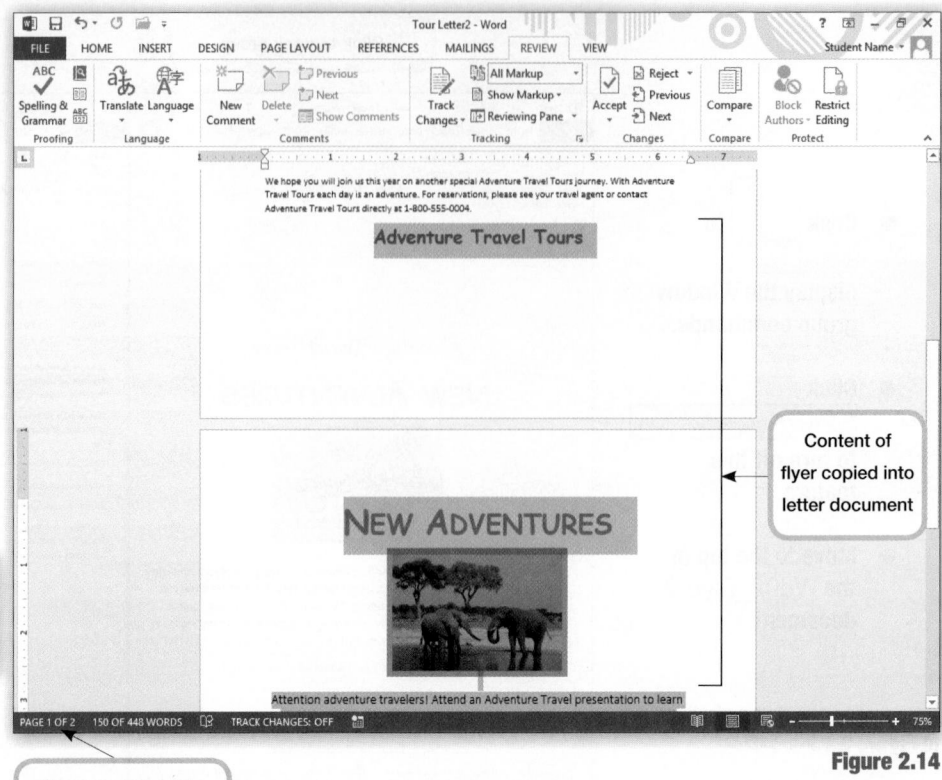 Maximize in the Tour Letter2 title bar to maximize the application window.

- Scroll the window to see the bottom of page 1 and the top of page 2.

Your screen should be similar to **Figure 2.14**

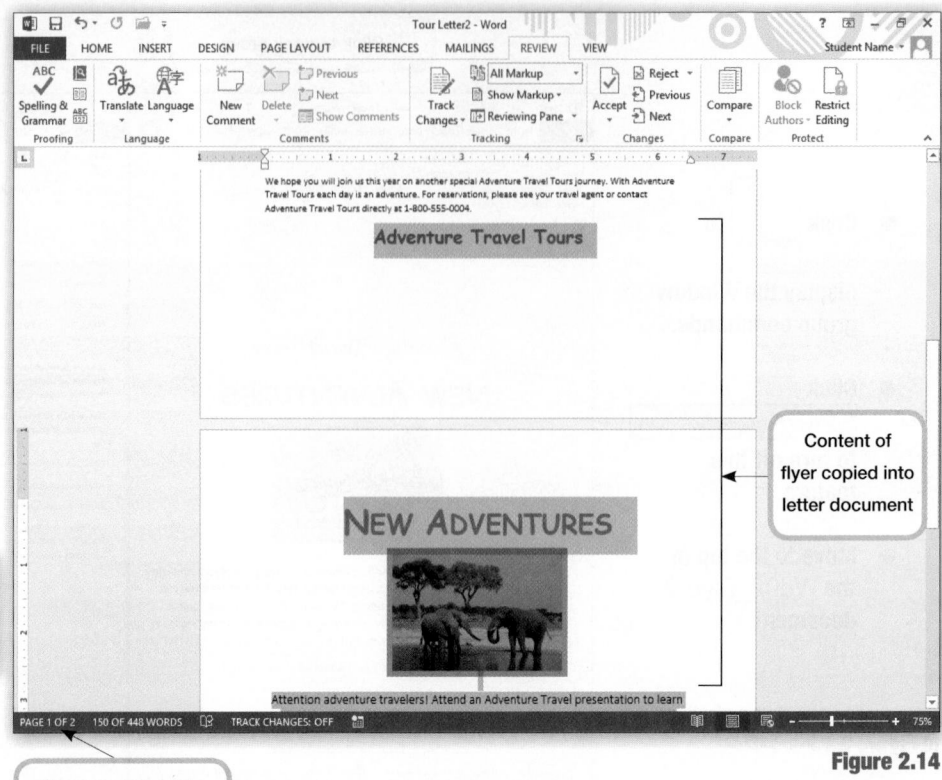

Content of flyer copied into letter document

Document consists of 2 pages

Figure 2.14

The letter now consists of two pages. Notice the status bar shows the insertion point location is on page 1 of 2 pages.

Since you no longer need to use the Wd02_Flyer2 document, you will close it.

● **Point to**  **on the Windows taskbar.**

Having Trouble?

If your Windows taskbar is hidden, point to the bottom of the window to display it.

● **Right-click** Wd02_Flyer2 **and choose Close from the shortcut menu.**

Having Trouble?

If your taskbar displays separate buttons for each open document, simply right-click the Wd02_Flyer2 button and choose Close from the shortcut menu.

● **If prompted to save your document, click** Don't Save .

● **Scroll to the bottom of the** Tour Letter2 **document and replace Student Name with your name in the last sentence.**

● **Move the insertion point to the top of the document and then save the document.**

The Tour Letter2 document is now the only open document.

CONTROLLING DOCUMENT PAGING

As text and graphics are added to a document, Word automatically starts a new page when text extends beyond the bottom margin setting. The beginning of a new page is identified by a page break.

Concept ② Page Break

A **page break** marks the point at which one page ends and another begins. Two types of page breaks can be used in a document: soft page breaks and hard page breaks. As you fill a page with text or graphics, Word inserts a **soft page break** automatically when the bottom margin is reached and starts a new page. As you add or remove text from a page, Word automatically readjusts the placement of the soft page break.

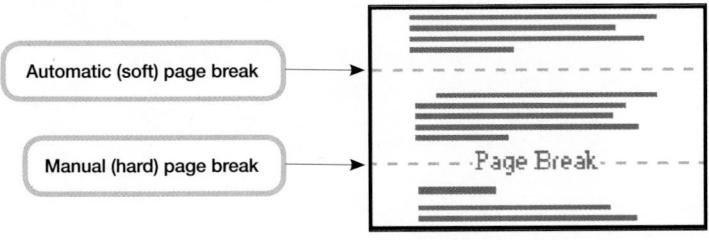

Many times, however, you may want to force a page break to occur at a specific location. To do this you can manually insert a **hard page break**. This action instructs Word to begin a new page regardless of the amount of text on the previous page. When a hard page break is used, its location is never moved regardless of the changes that are made to the amount of text on the preceding page. All soft page breaks that precede or follow a hard page break continue to adjust automatically. Sometimes you may find that you have to remove the hard page break and reenter it at another location as you edit the document.

In Print Layout view, the page break is identified by a space between pages. However, you cannot tell if it is a hard or soft page break. You will switch to Draft view to see the soft page break that was entered in the document. Also notice that graphics are not shown in Draft view.

1

● **Switch to Draft view at 100% zoom.**

● **If necessary, scroll the document to see the soft page break line.**

Your screen should be similar to Figure 2.15

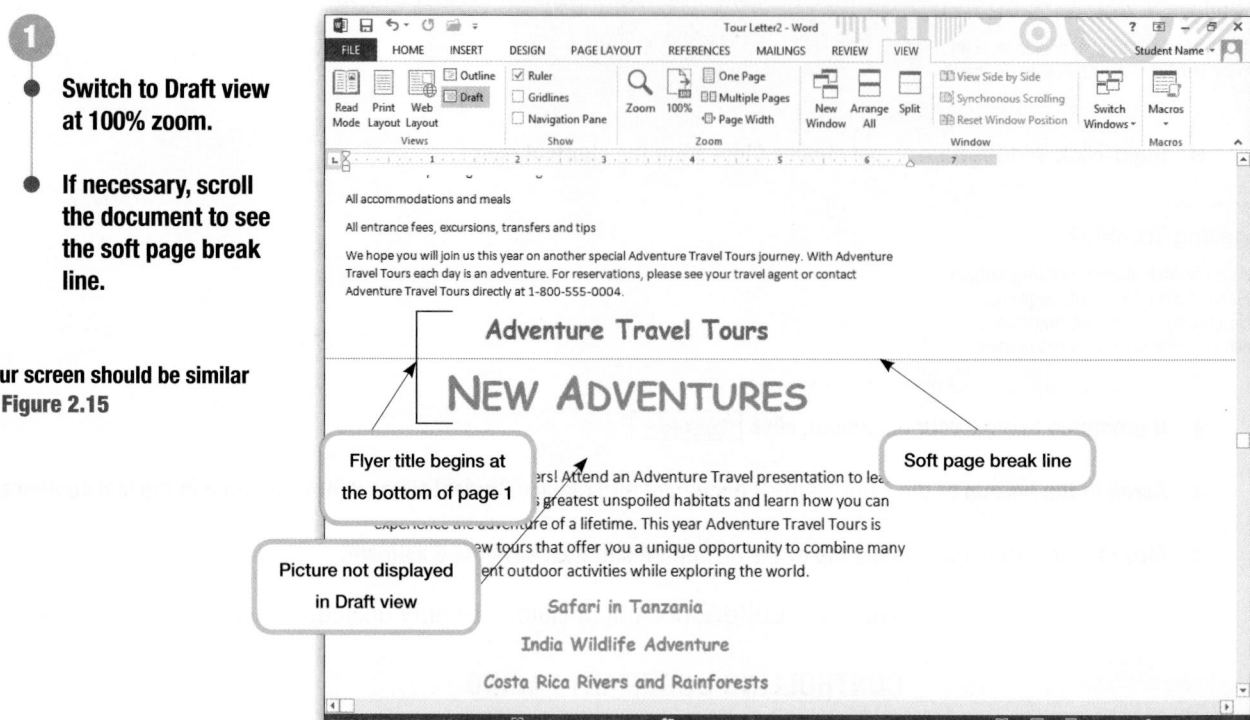

Figure 2.15

To show where one page ends and another begins, Word displays a dotted line across the page to mark the soft page break.

INSERTING A HARD PAGE BREAK

Many times, the location of the soft page break is not appropriate. In this case, the location of the soft page break displays the flyer title on the bottom of page 1 and the remaining portion of the flyer on page 2. Because you want the entire flyer to print on a page by itself, you will manually insert a hard page break above the flyer title.

1

- Move to the beginning of the first line of the flyer text, "Adventure Travel Tours."

- Display formatting marks in the document.

Having Trouble?

Click ¶ in the Paragraph group of the Home tab or press Ctrl + * to display and hide formatting marks.

- Press Ctrl + Enter to insert a hard page break line.

Another Method

The Ribbon equivalent is Insert/ Page Break or Page Layout/ Breaks ▾ /Page.

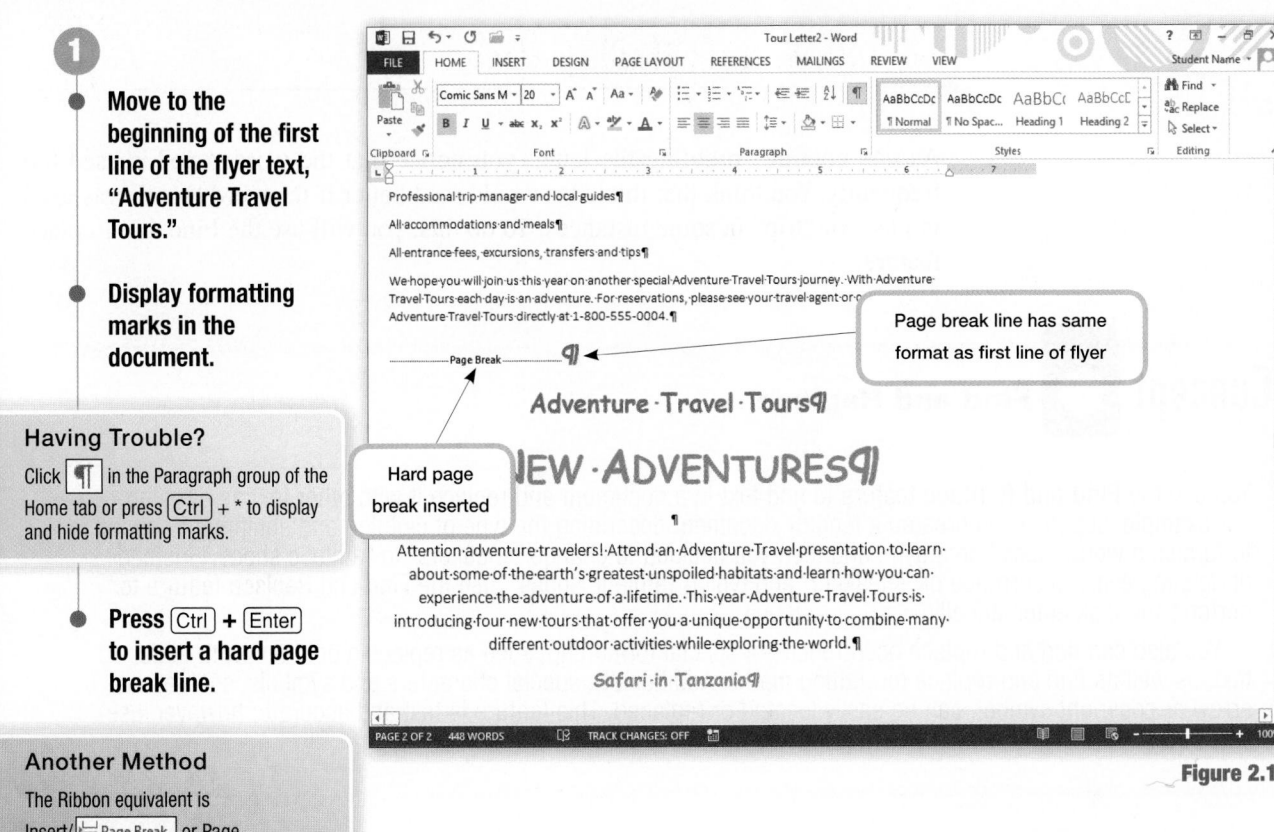

Page break line has same format as first line of flyer

Hard page break inserted

Figure 2.16

Your screen should be similar to Figure 2.16

Additional Information

To remove a hard page break, simply select the hard page break line and press Delete.

A dotted line and the words "Page Break" appear above the flyer title, indicating that a hard page break was entered at that position. Also notice the page break line has the same format as the first line in the flyer. You will clear the formats from the page break line so that it has the same format as the text on this page and does not interfere with changes you may want to make later.

2

- If necessary, open the Home tab.

- Select the page break line and click 🔲 Clear All Formatting in the Font group.

- Turn off the display of formatting marks.

- Switch to Print Layout view at 100% zoom.

- Save the document again.

As you continue proofing the letter, you notice that the word "trip" is used too frequently. You think that the letter would read better if the word "tour" was used in place of "trip" in some instances. To do this, you will use the Find and Replace feature.

Concept ③ Find and Replace

You use the **Find and Replace** feature to find text in a document and replace it with other text as directed. For example, suppose you created a lengthy document describing the type of clothing and equipment needed to furnish a world-class home gym, and then you decided to change "sneakers" to "athletic shoes." Instead of deleting every occurrence of "sneakers" and typing "athletic shoes," use the Find and Replace feature to perform the task automatically.

You also can find and replace occurrences of special formatting, such as replacing bold text with italicized text, as well as find and replace formatting marks. Additionally, special characters and symbols, such as an arrow or copyright symbol, can be easily located or replaced. This feature is fast and accurate; however, use care when replacing so that you do not replace unintended matches.

FINDING TEXT

First, you will use the Find command to locate all occurrences of the word "trip" in the document.

Move the insertion point to the top of the document.

Another Method

Reminder: Use Ctrl + Home to quickly move to the top of the document.

Click 🔍 Find ▾ **in the Editing group.**

Another Method

You also can open the Navigation pane by clicking page count in the status bar or by using the keyboard shortcut Ctrl + F.

Your screen should be similar to Figure 2.17

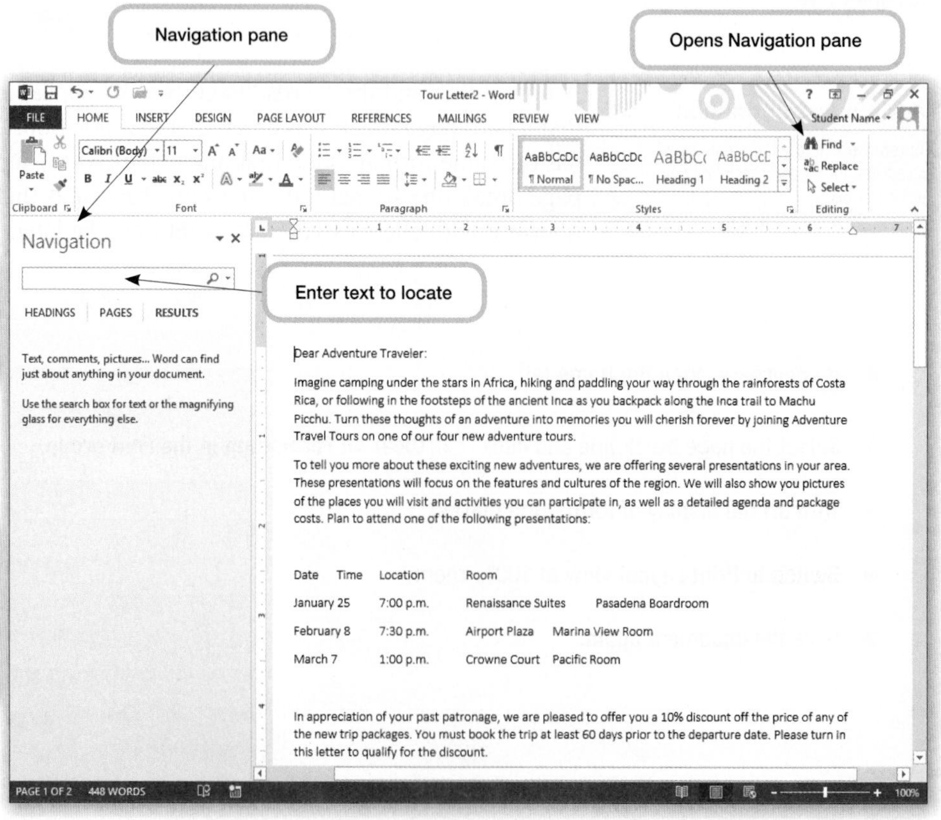

Navigation pane

Opens Navigation pane

Enter text to locate

Figure 2.17

The **Navigation pane**, located to the left of your document, provides a convenient way to quickly locate and move to specified text. The Search document text box at the top of the Navigation pane is used to specify the text you want to locate. As you type each letter of the search text in the Search document box, the Navigation pane displays and narrows the search results.

2

● **Click in the Search document text box and type trip**

Your screen should be similar to **Figure 2.18**

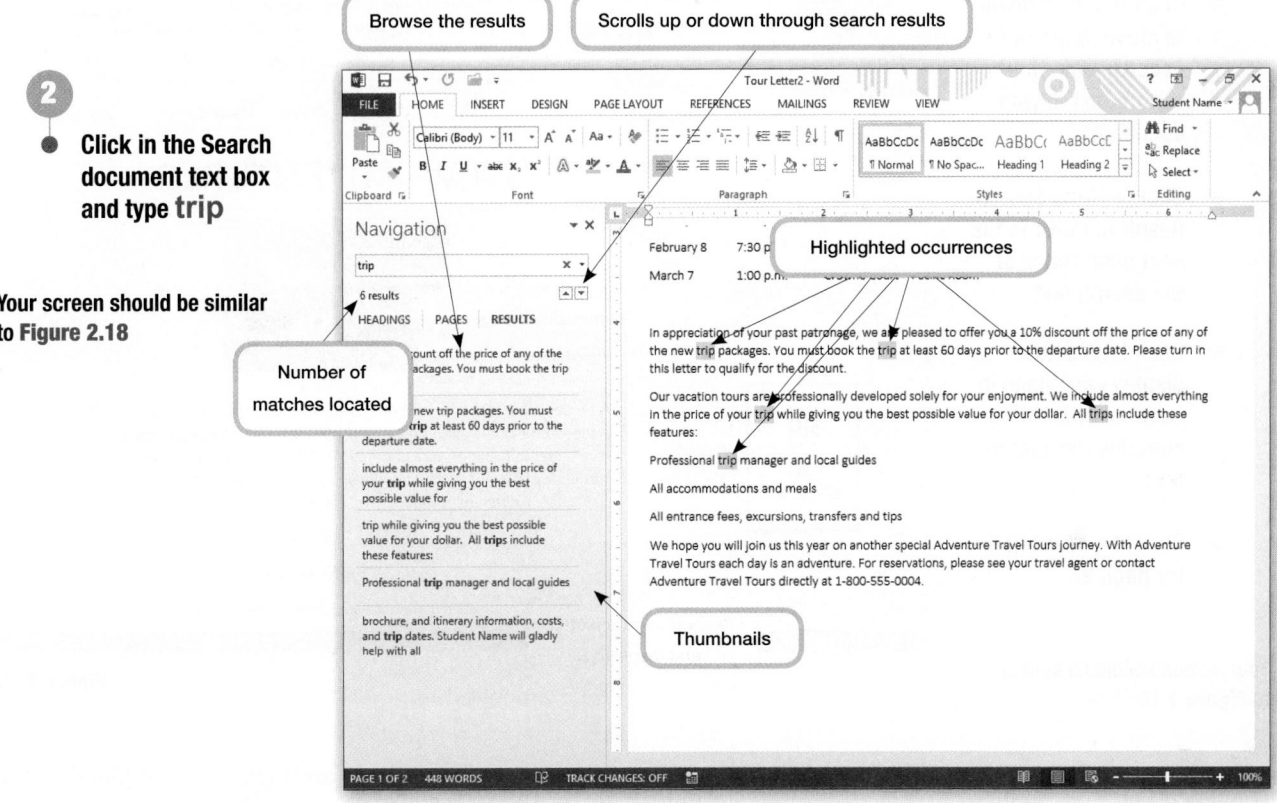

Browse the results

Scrolls up or down through search results

Highlighted occurrences

Number of matches located

Thumbnails

Figure 2.18

Word searches for all occurrences of the text to find beginning at the insertion point and locates the word "trip" six times in the document. The search results are displayed in the Navigation pane and the first five search results are highlighted in your document. The last use of the word "trip" is on the last line of the flyer. By clicking a search result in the Navigation pane, you can move to that location in your document. You can also scroll through your search results using the ▲ Previous Search Result and ▼ Next Search Result buttons located to the right of the tabs in the Navigation pane.

Unless you specify otherwise when you use the Find command, the RESULTS view is displayed in the Navigation pane. Alternatively, the PAGES view when selected displays thumbnails of each page containing the search text, and the HEADINGS view displays all the headings in your document and highlights any headings in yellow that contain the search text. The PAGES and HEADINGS views are especially useful when working with longer documents because they provide an overview of where search text has been found.

You will use several of these features to browse through the search results.

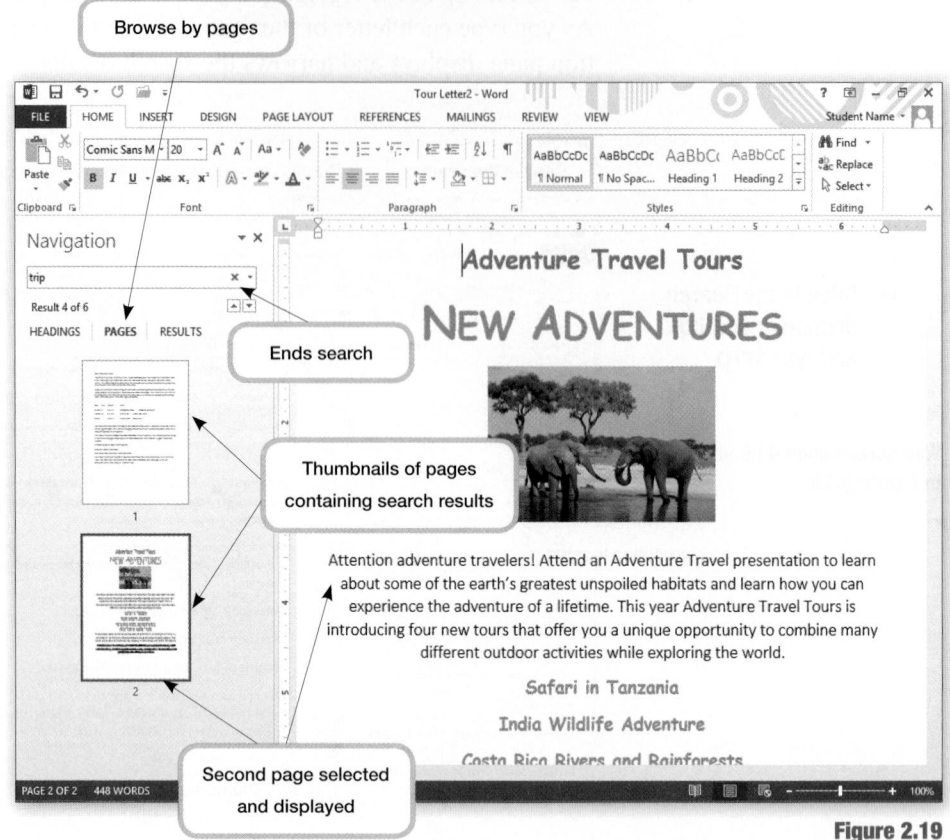

Figure 2.19

3

- Click the third result to move to the third occurrence of the search text in your document.

- Click ⬇ Next Search Result to move to the next occurrence of the search text.

- Click PAGES to display each page in your document that contains the search text.

- Click the thumbnail for page 2.

Your screen should be similar to Figure 2.19

The top of the second page is displayed and the search text is highlighted at the bottom of the current page. To see the highlighted text, you would have to scroll down in your document. If you look closely, you can even see the search terms highlighted in the thumbnails.

There may be cases when you need to refine the method Find uses to locate the search text. Clicking 🔍 ▾ Find Options at the right end of the search box opens a drop-down menu of commands that accesses options for customizing your search as well as options for searching for other types of document elements including graphics and tables.

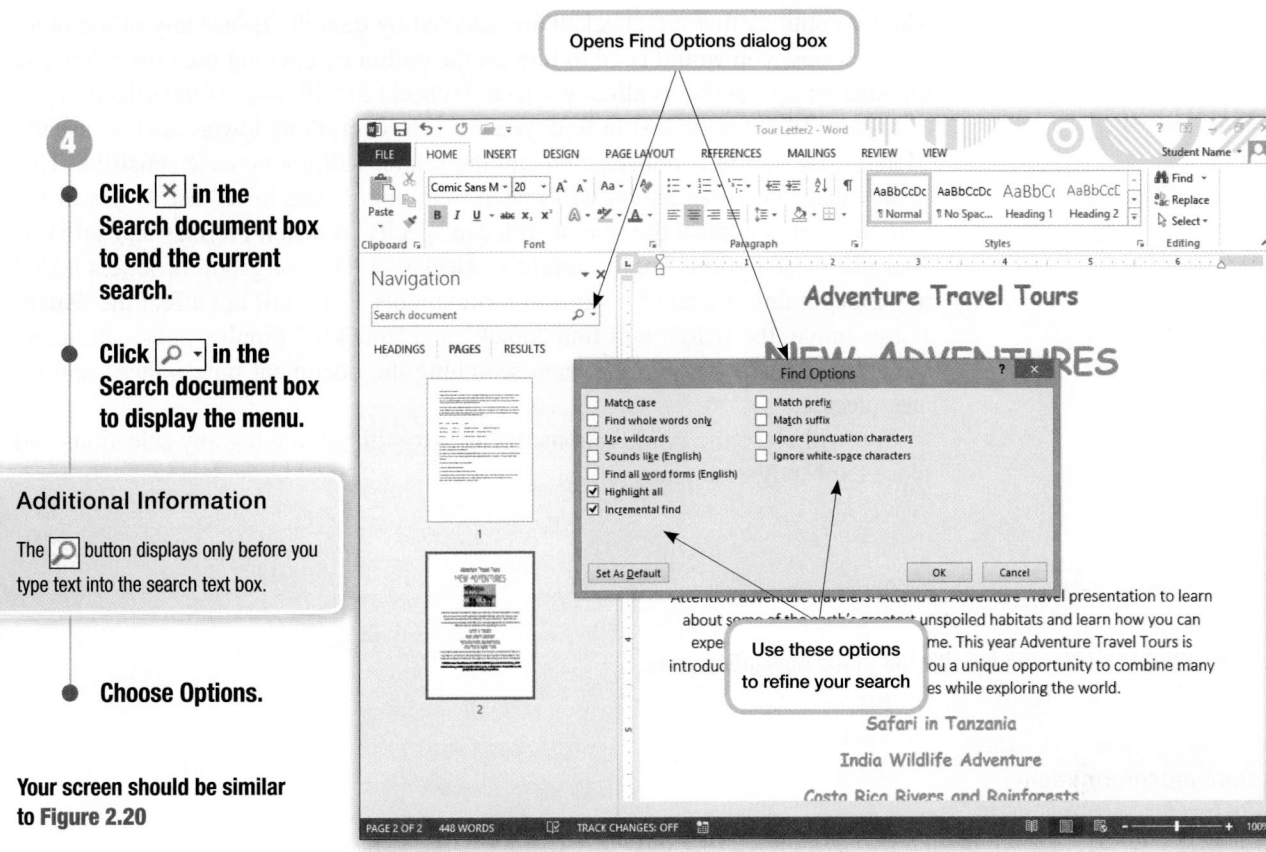

4

- Click ☒ in the Search document box to end the current search.

- Click 🔍 ▾ in the Search document box to display the menu.

Additional Information

The 🔍 button displays only before you type text into the search text box.

- Choose Options.

Your screen should be similar to Figure 2.20

Figure 2.20

The Find Options dialog box displays 11 search options that can be combined in many ways to help you find and replace text in documents. They are described in the table below.

Option	Effect on Text
Match case	Finds only those words in which the capitalization matches the text you typed.
Find whole words only	Finds matches that are whole words and not part of a larger word. For example, finds "cat" only and not "catastrophe."
Use wildcards	Refines a search; for example, c?t finds "cat" and "cot" (one-character matches), while c*t finds "cat" and "court" (searches for one or more characters).
Sounds like (English)	Finds words that sound like the word you type; very helpful if you do not know the correct spelling of the word you want to find.
Find all word forms (English)	Finds and replaces all forms of a word; for example, "buy" will replace "purchase," and "bought" will replace "purchased."
Highlight all	Highlights all matches in your document.
Incremental find	Finds and refines your search incrementally with each letter you type in the search box.
Match prefix	Finds all words that begin with the same letters you type.
Match suffix	Finds all words that end with the same letters you type.
Ignore punctuation characters	Finds words that are similar to your search text, but that might contain punctuation, such as a hyphen (-) or apostrophe ('), in it.
Ignore white-space characters	Finds text that is similar to your search text but that may also contain spaces.

The two options that are checked are selected by default. To use any of the other Find options, you would need to turn on the option by clicking the box. Likewise, clicking an option that is already selected (checked) will turn off the selection.

When you enter the text to find, you can type everything lowercase because the Match Case option is not selected and the search will not be **case sensitive**. This means that lowercase letters will match both upper- and lowercase letters in the text. To further control the search, you can specify to match prefixes and suffixes. Because these options aren't currently selected, a letter or group of letters added at the beginning or end of a word to form another word will not affect the search. For example, the search will find "quick" and "quickly." Finally, punctuation and white spaces will be ignored when searching the document unless these options are selected.

You will close the Find Options dialog box without making any selections and close the Navigation pane.

5

- Click [Cancel] **in the Find Options dialog box.**

- Click [×] **Close in the title bar of the Navigation pane.**

Additional Information

The [▼] Task Pane Options button in the title bar of the Navigation pane lets you move, size, and close the pane.

REPLACING TEXT

You decide to replace several occurrences of the word "trip" in the letter with "tour" where appropriate. You will use the Find and Replace feature to do this.

Opens Find and Replace dialog box

1

- **Move to the top of the document.**

- Click [ab̶ac Replace] **in the Editing group.**

Your screen should be similar to Figure 2.21

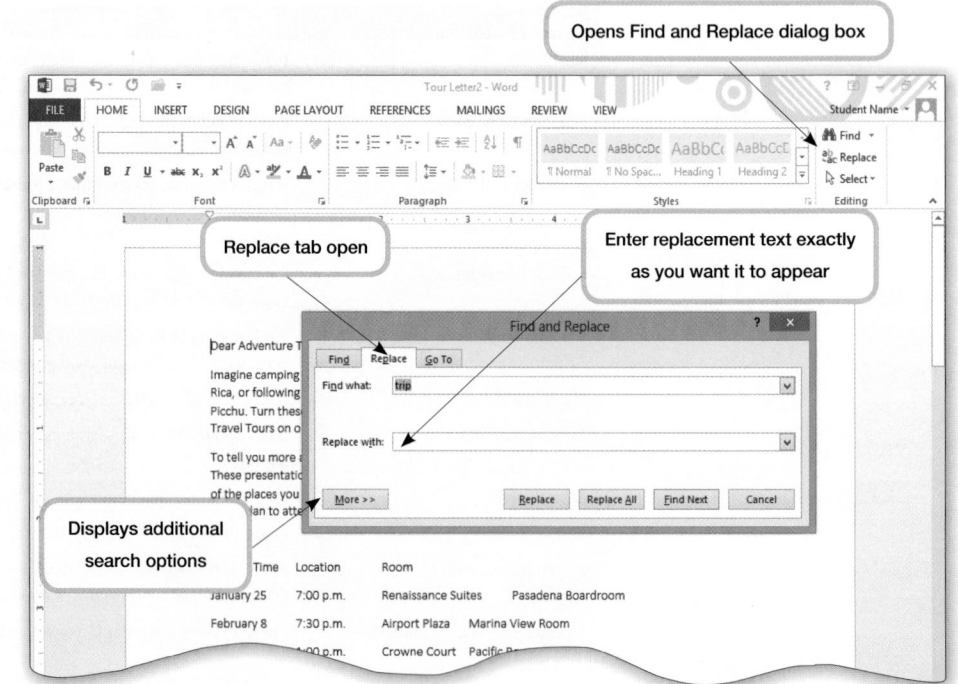

Replace tab open

Enter replacement text exactly as you want it to appear

Displays additional search options

Figure 2.21

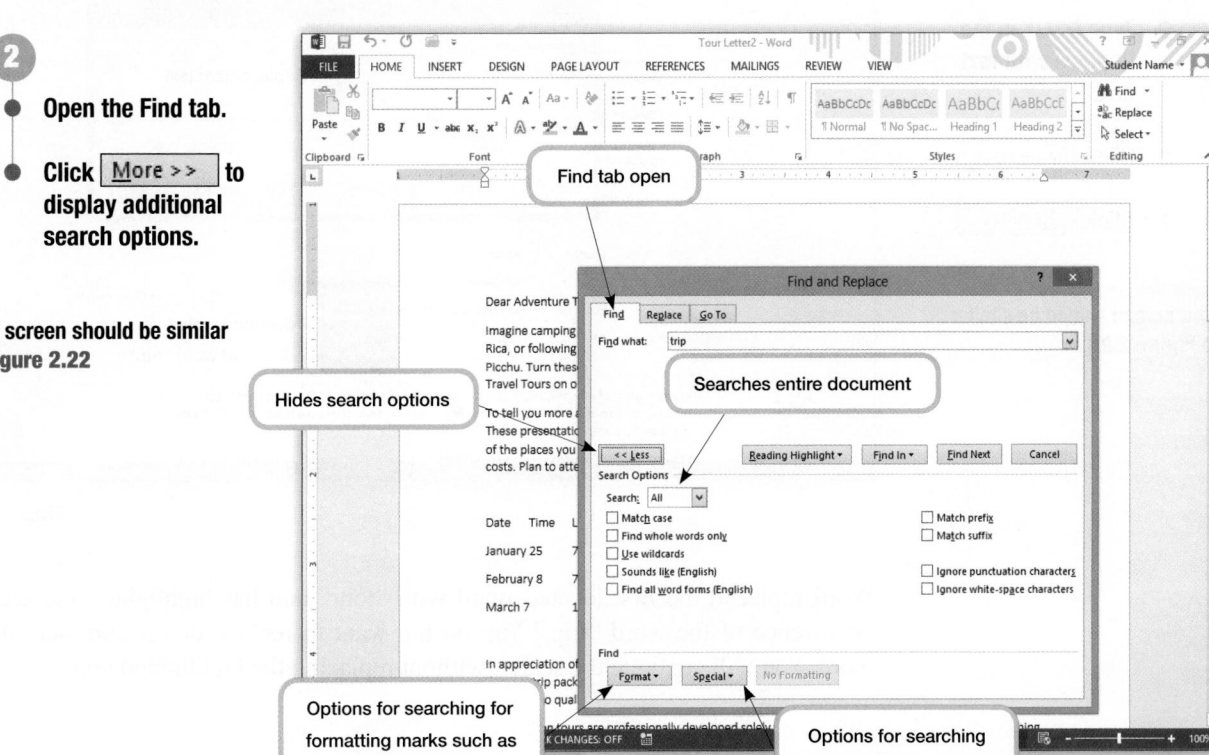
The Find and Replace dialog box is open and displays the search text "trip" that you had entered in the Navigation pane Search document text box in the Find what text box. You want to find and replace selected occurrences of the word "trip" with "tour." Again, you can refine how the search is conducted by accessing the Find options from the Find and Replace dialog box.

2

- **Open the Find tab.**

- **Click** More >> **to display additional search options.**

Your screen should be similar to Figure 2.22

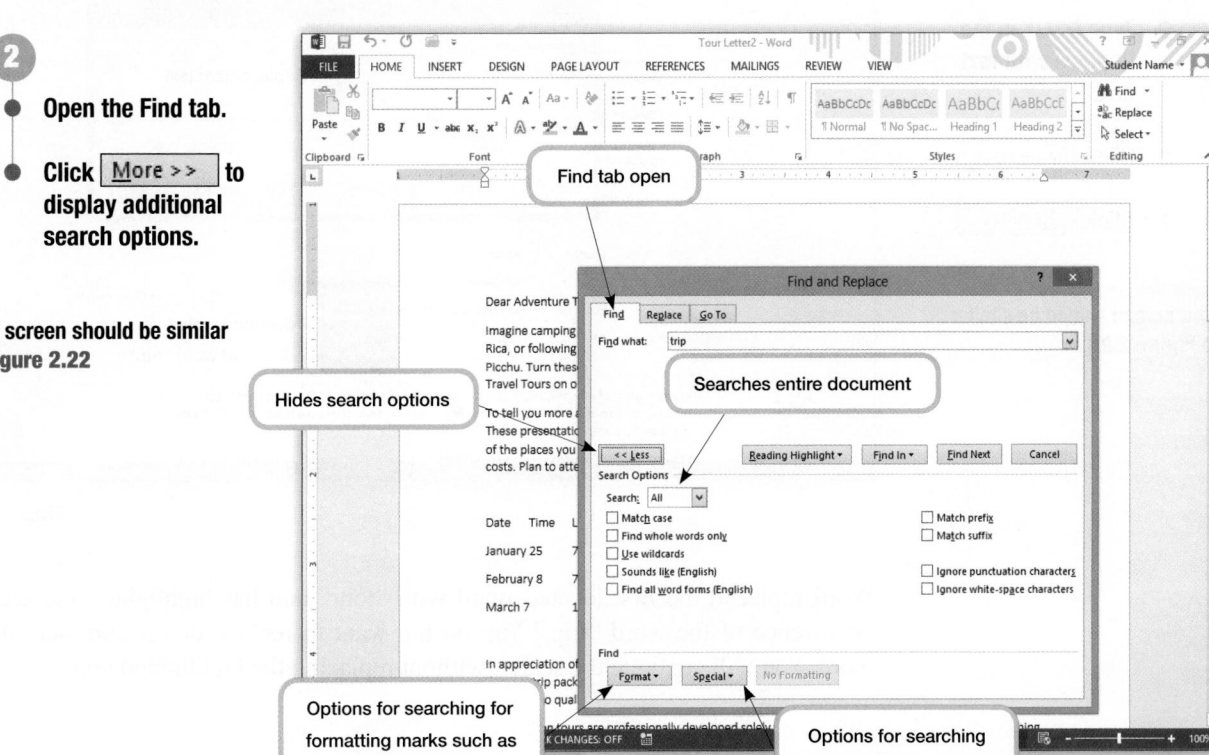

Find tab open

Hides search options

Searches entire document

Options for searching for formatting marks such as bold or italics

Options for searching for document symbols

Figure 2.22

The Find tab provides another method for finding text in a document. The same Find options that are available in the Navigation pane are available in the Find and Replace dialog box. Note that the Search option is set to All. This means that by default Word will search the entire document, including headers and footers. You also can choose to search Up to the top of the document or Down to the end of the document from your current location in the document. These options search in the direction specified but exclude the headers, footers, footnotes, and comments from the area to search. Because you want to search the entire document, All is the appropriate setting.

Next, you will open the Replace tab again and enter the replacement text in the Replace with text box. This text must be entered exactly as you want it to appear in your document. The Replace tab also displays the Search options that you opened in the Find tab. You will hide the search options and enter the replacement text. Then you will replace the first located match with the replacement text.

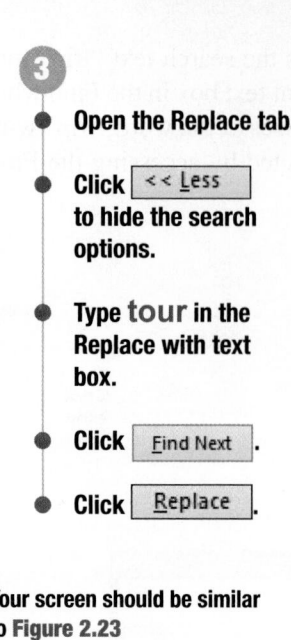

3

- Open the Replace tab.

- Click << Less to hide the search options.

- Type tour in the Replace with text box.

- Click Find Next .

- Click Replace .

Your screen should be similar to Figure 2.23

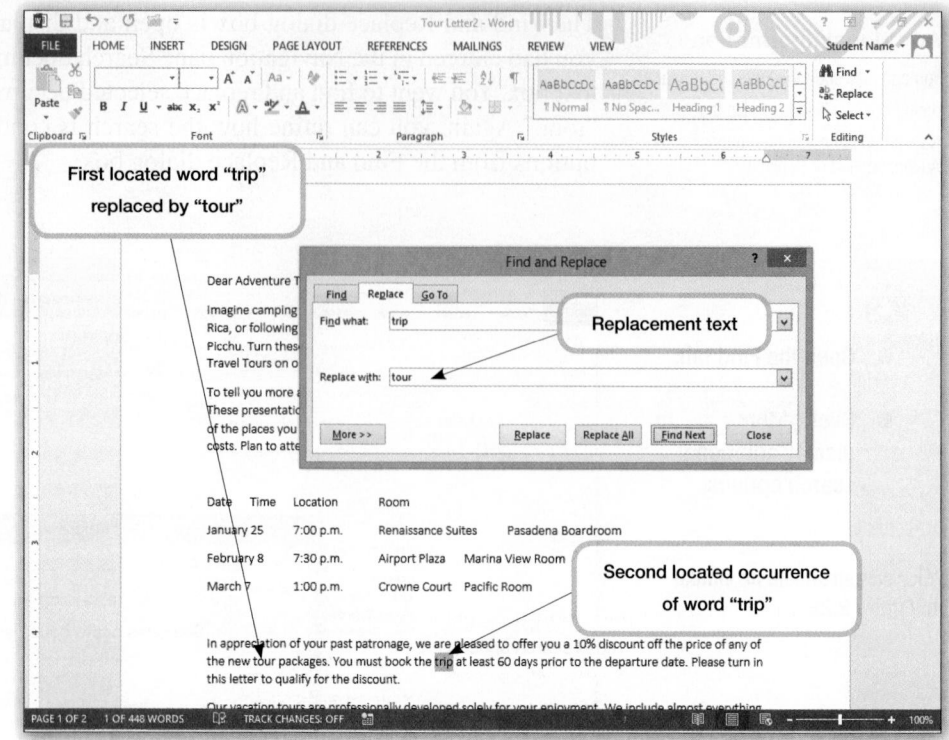

First located word "trip" replaced by "tour"

Replacement text

Second located occurrence of word "trip"

Figure 2.23

Word replaced the first located word with "tour" and has highlighted the second occurrence of the word "trip." You do not want to replace this occurrence of the word. You will continue the search without replacing the highlighted text.

4

- Click [Find Next] to skip this occurrence and locate the next occurrence.

- Replace the next located occurrence.

- Continue to review the document, replacing all other occurrences of the word "trip" with "tour," except in the final paragraph of the flyer.

- Click [Find Next].

- Click [OK] to close the information dialog box.

- Click [×] to close the Find and Replace dialog box.

- Save the document.

Your screen should be similar to Figure 2.24

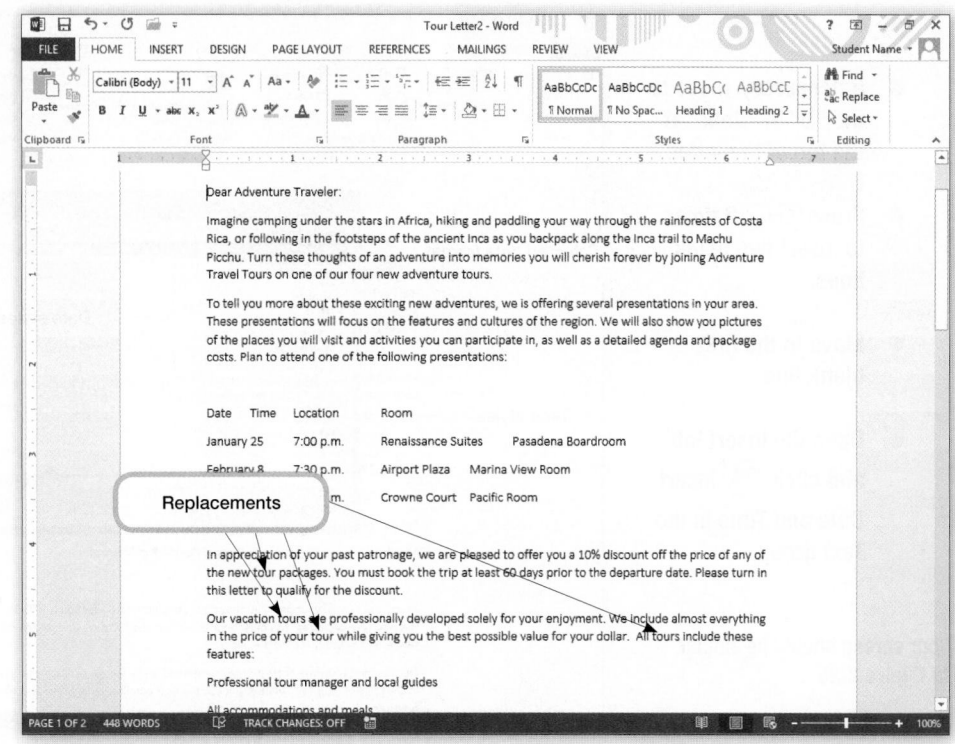

Dear Adventure Traveler:

Imagine camping under the stars in Africa, hiking and paddling your way through the rainforests of Costa Rica, or following in the footsteps of the ancient Inca as you backpack along the Inca trail to Machu Picchu. Turn these thoughts of an adventure into memories you will cherish forever by joining Adventure Travel Tours on one of our four new adventure tours.

To tell you more about these exciting new adventures, we is offering several presentations in your area. These presentations will focus on the features and cultures of the region. We will also show you pictures of the places you will visit and activities you can participate in, as well as a detailed agenda and package costs. Plan to attend one of the following presentations:

Date	Time	Location	Room
January 25	7:00 p.m.	Renaissance Suites	Pasadena Boardroom
February 8	7:30 p.m.	Airport Plaza	Marina View Room
	m.	Crowne Court	Pacific Room

Replacements

In appreciation of your past patronage, we are pleased to offer you a 10% discount off the price of any of the new tour packages. You must book the trip at least 60 days prior to the departure date. Please turn in this letter to qualify for the discount.

Our vacation tours are professionally developed solely for your enjoyment. We include almost everything in the price of your tour while giving you the best possible value for your dollar. All tours include these features:

Professional tour manager and local guides

All accommodations and meals

PAGE 1 OF 2   448 WORDS   TRACK CHANGES: OFF

Figure 2.24

When using the Find and Replace feature, if you wanted to change all the occurrences of the located text, it is much faster to use [Replace All]. Exercise care when using this option, however, because the search text you specify might be part of another word and you may accidentally replace text you want to keep. If this happens, you could use Undo to reverse the action.

Inserting the Current Date

The last text change you need to make is to add the date to the letter. The Date and Time command on the Insert tab inserts the current date as maintained by your computer system at the location of the insertion point. You want to enter the date on the first line of the letter, five lines above the salutation.

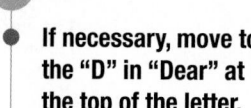

- If necessary, move to the "D" in "Dear" at the top of the letter.

- Press [Enter] 2 times to insert two blank lines.

- Move to the first blank line.

- Open the Insert tab and click  Insert Date and Time in the Text group.

Your screen should be similar to Figure 2.25

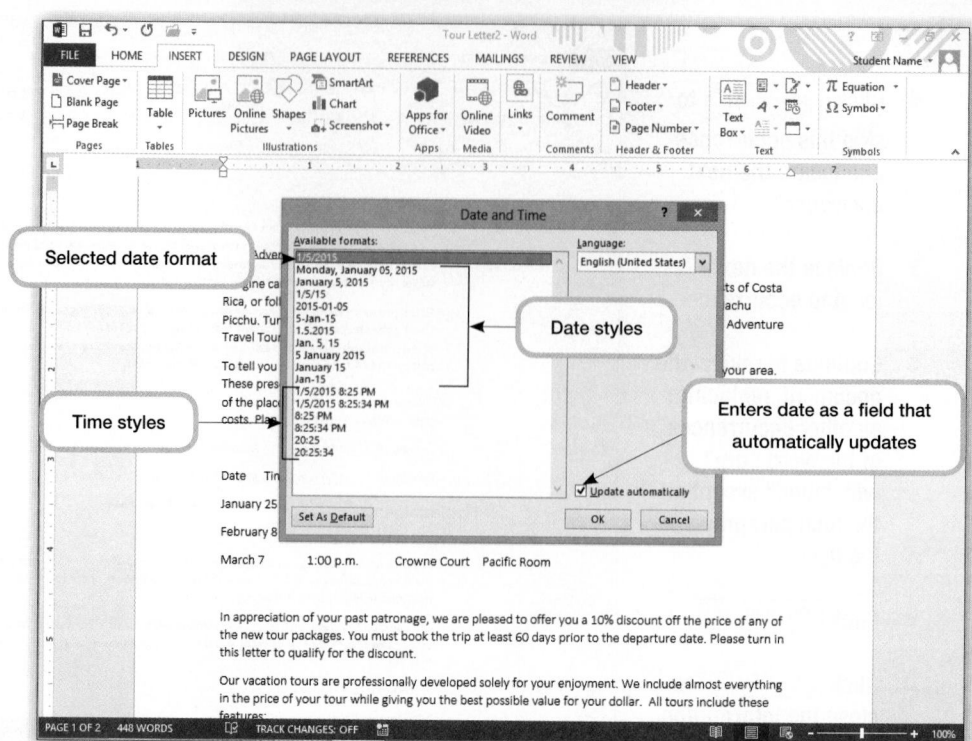

Figure 2.25

Additional Information

The current time also can be inserted into a document using the same procedure.

From the Date and Time dialog box, you select the style in which you want the date displayed in your document. The Available Formats list box displays the format styles for the current date and time. You want to display the date in the format Month XX, 2XXX, the third format setting in the list.

You also want the date to be updated automatically whenever the letter is opened or printed. You use the Update Automatically option to do this, which enters the date as a field.

Concept 4 Field

A **field** is a placeholder that instructs Word to insert information into a document. The **field code** contains the directions as to the type of information to insert or action to perform. Field codes appear between curly brackets {}, also called braces. The information that is displayed as a result of the field code is called the **field result**. Many field codes are automatically inserted when you use certain commands; others you can create and insert yourself. Many fields update automatically when the document changes. Using fields makes it easier and faster to perform many common or repetitive tasks.

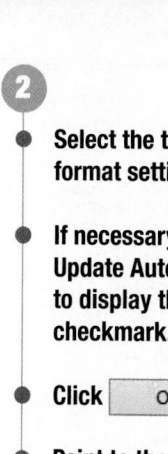

- Select the third format setting.

- If necessary, select **Update Automatically** to display the checkmark.

- Click [OK].

- Point to the date.

- Click the date.

- If necessary, scroll the window up slightly to better see the field.

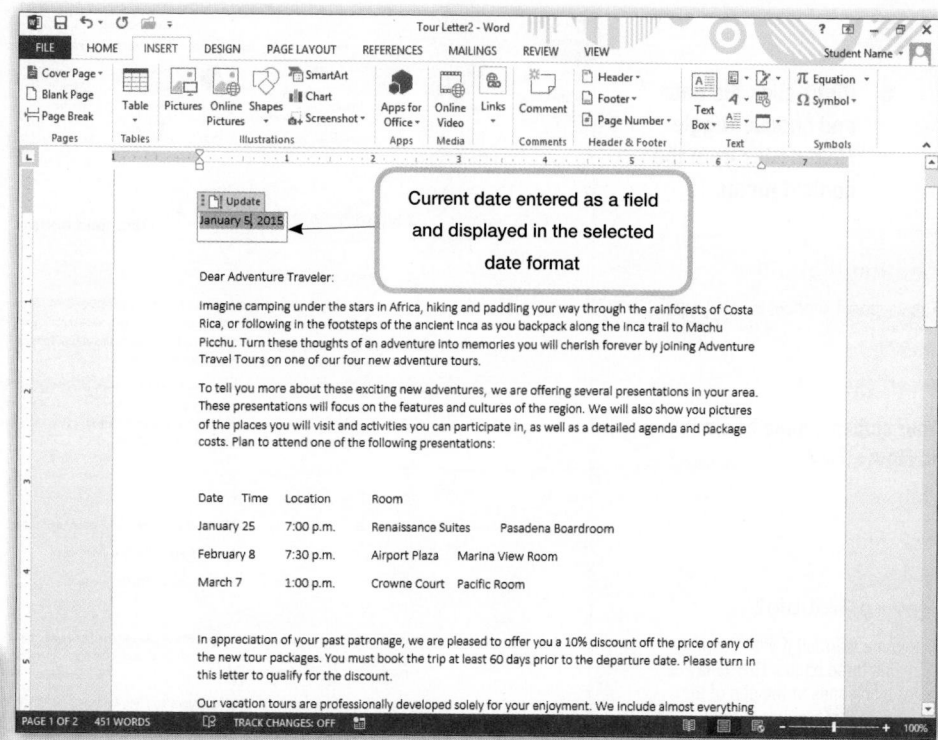

Figure 2.26

Your screen should be similar to Figure 2.26

The current date is entered in the document in the format you selected. When you point to a field, the entire entry is shaded to identify the entry as a field. When the insertion point is positioned in a field entry, the entire entry is highlighted, indicating it is selected and can be modified.

The date is the field result. You will display the field code to see the underlying instructions.

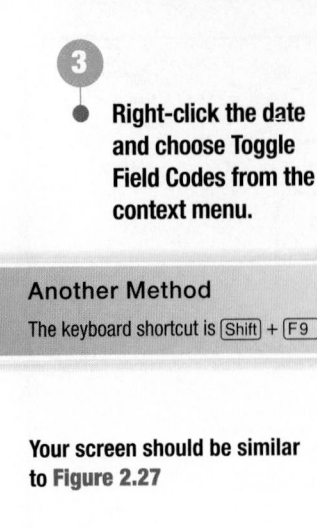

③ Right-click the date and choose Toggle Field Codes from the context menu.

Your screen should be similar to Figure 2.27

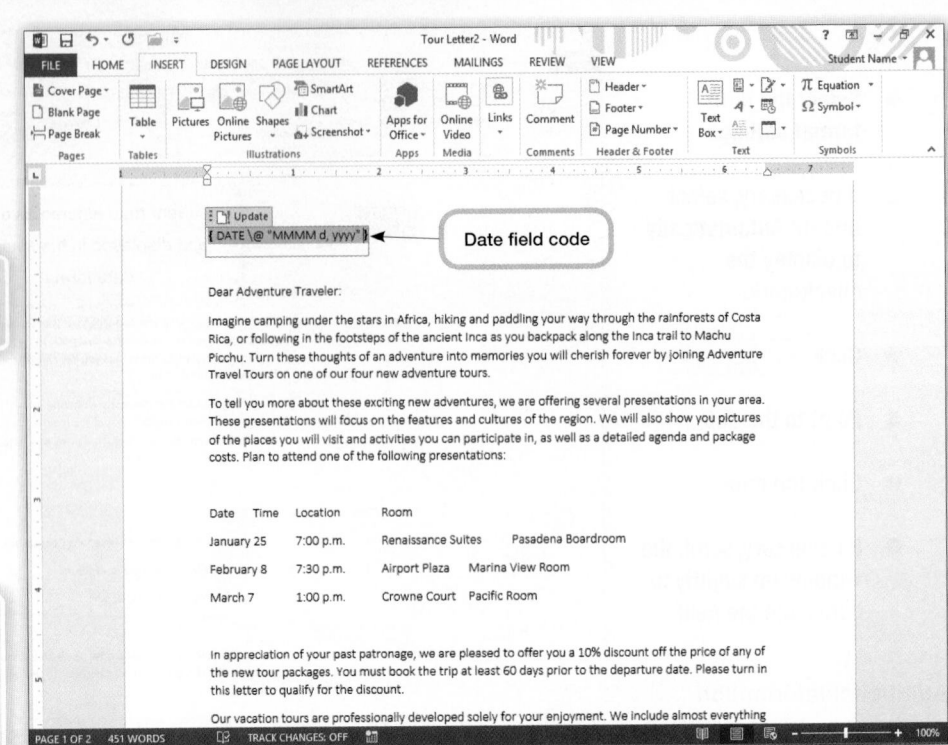

Figure 2.27

The field code includes the field name "DATE", followed by the field properties, which in this case controls how the date will be formatted. Whenever this document is printed, Word will print the current system date using this format.

If you want to change the date format, you can edit a field manually or choose another format from the Field dialog box. To try both methods, you will choose another date format from the Field dialog box and then edit it manually.

(4)

- Right-click the date field, and choose Edit Field to open the Field dialog box.

- Select the second date format in the Field properties area (dddd, MMMM dd, yyyy).

- Click [OK].

- Display the date field code again.

- Click to the left of the first "d" in the field code, and delete dddd, and the space before MMMM.

- Right-click and choose Toggle Field Codes from the context menu.

- Delete the first "d" after MMMM in the field code.

- Press F9 to update the field.

Another Method

You could also choose Update Field from the context menu.

Your screen should be similar to Figure 2.28

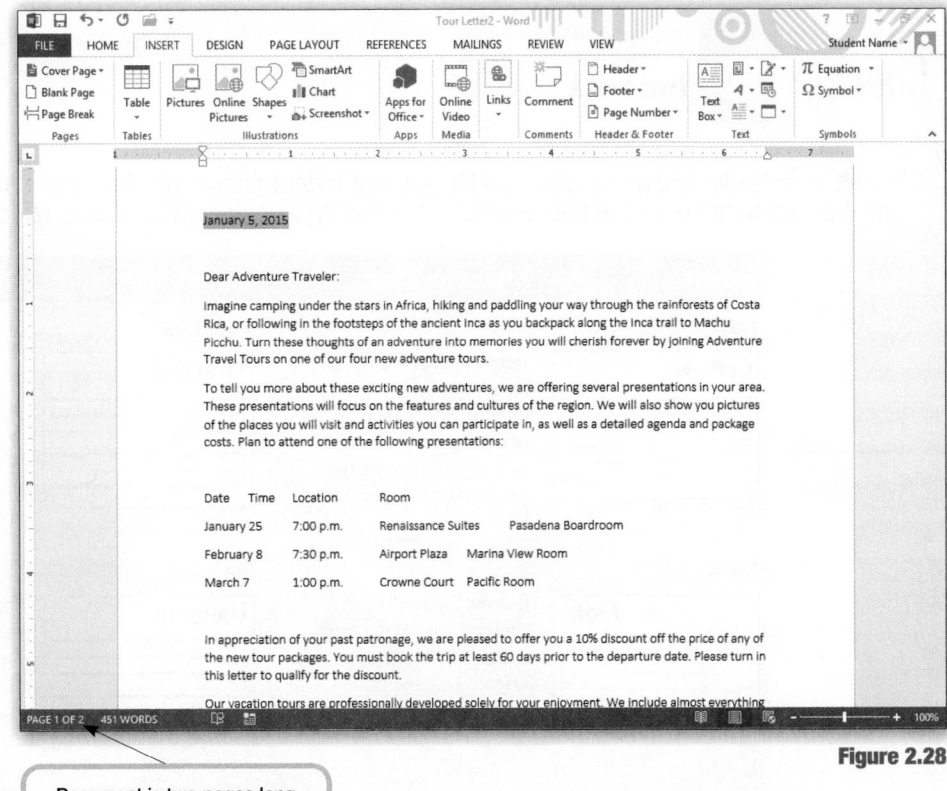

Figure 2.28

Document is two pages long

When you edit field codes manually, you must be absolutely sure you have the correct syntax. After you edit the field code, remember to update the field. It is usually best to make changes to the field format by using the Field dialog box unless you need to use a format that is not available in the Field dialog box.

Modifying Page Layout

Next the manager has suggested that you make several changes to improve the overall appearance of the letter and flyer. Two common page layout features are paragraph settings, such as indents and line spacing, and page margin settings. Other page layout features include page background colors, themes, vertical alignment, and orientation of text on a page.

To give the document more interest, you can indent paragraphs, use tabs to create tabular columns of data, and change the line spacing. These formatting features are all paragraph formats that affect the entire selected paragraph.

INDENTING PARAGRAPHS

Business letters typically use a block layout style or a modified block style with indented paragraphs. In a block style, all parts of the letter, including the date, inside address, all paragraphs in the body, and closing lines, are evenly aligned with the left margin. The modified block style indents certain elements such as the date, all paragraphs in the body, and the closing lines.

Concept 5 Indents

To help your reader find information quickly, you can **indent** paragraphs from the margins. Indenting paragraphs sets them off from the rest of the document. The four types of indents and their effects are described below.

Indent	Effect on Text	Indent	Effect on Text
Left Left→ ⟶ (text block with lines)	Indents the entire paragraph from the left margin. To "outdent," or extend the paragraph into the left margin, use a negative value for the left indent.	**First Line** First line (text block with first-line indented lines)	Indents the first line of the paragraph. All following lines are aligned with the left margin.
Right ←Right (text block with lines)	Indents the entire paragraph from the right margin. To outdent, or extend the paragraph into the right margin, use a negative value for the right indent.	**Hanging** Hanging (text block with hanging indented lines)	Indents all lines after the first line of the paragraph. The first line is aligned with the left margin. A hanging indent is typically used for bibliographies and for bulleted and numbered lists.

You want to change the letter style from the block style to the modified block style. You will begin by indenting the first line of the first paragraph. The quickest way to indent the first line of a paragraph is to press Tab when the insertion point is positioned at the beginning of the first line. Pressing Tab indents the first line of the paragraph to the first tab stop from the left margin. A tab stop is a marked location on the horizontal ruler that indicates how far to indent text each time the Tab key is pressed. The default tab stops are every 0.5 inch.

Change the zoom to Page Width.

Move to the beginning of the first paragraph on page 1.

Press Tab.

Your screen should be similar to Figure 2.29

First line indent marker positioned at 0.5-inch location on ruler

First line indented 0.5 inch

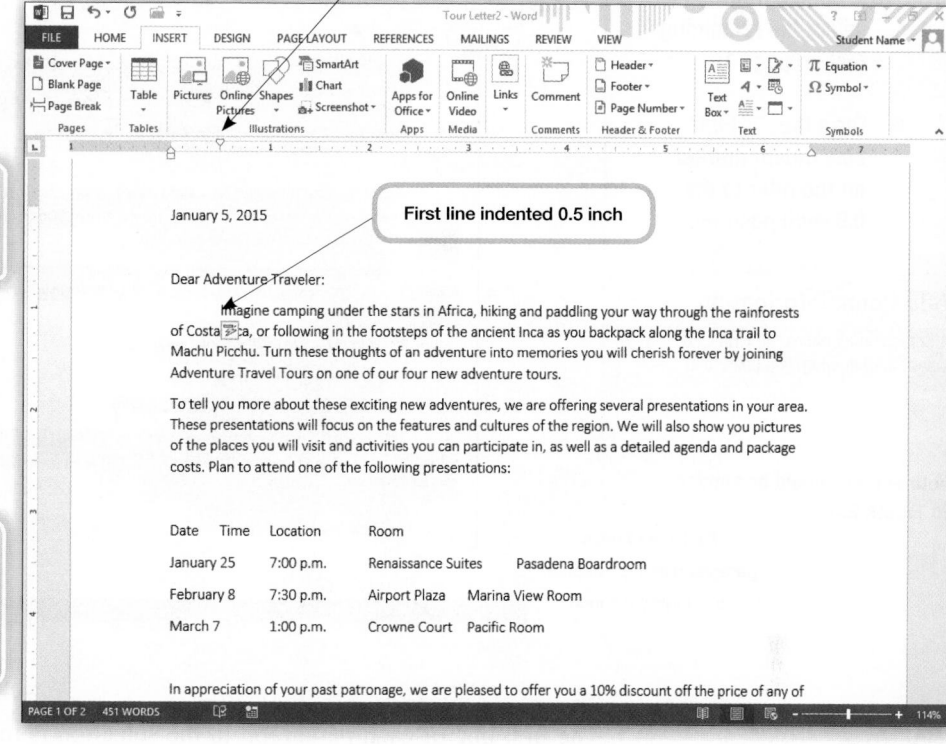

Figure 2.29

The first line of the paragraph indents a half inch from the left margin. The text in the paragraph wraps as needed, and the text on the following line begins at the left margin. Notice that the ▽ First Line Indent marker on the ruler moved to the 0.5-inch position. This marker controls the location of the first line of text in the paragraph.

If the insertion point was positioned anywhere else within the line of text, pressing Tab would move the text to the right of the insertion point to the next tab stop and the indent marker would not move.

You can indent the remaining paragraphs individually, or you can select the paragraphs and indent them simultaneously by dragging the ▽ First Line Indent marker on the ruler.

2

- Beginning with the second paragraph, select the remaining text on page 1.

- Drag the ▽ First Line Indent marker on the ruler to the 0.5-inch position.

Additional Information

A ScreenTip identifies the First Line Indent marker when you point to it.

Your screen should be similar to Figure 2.30

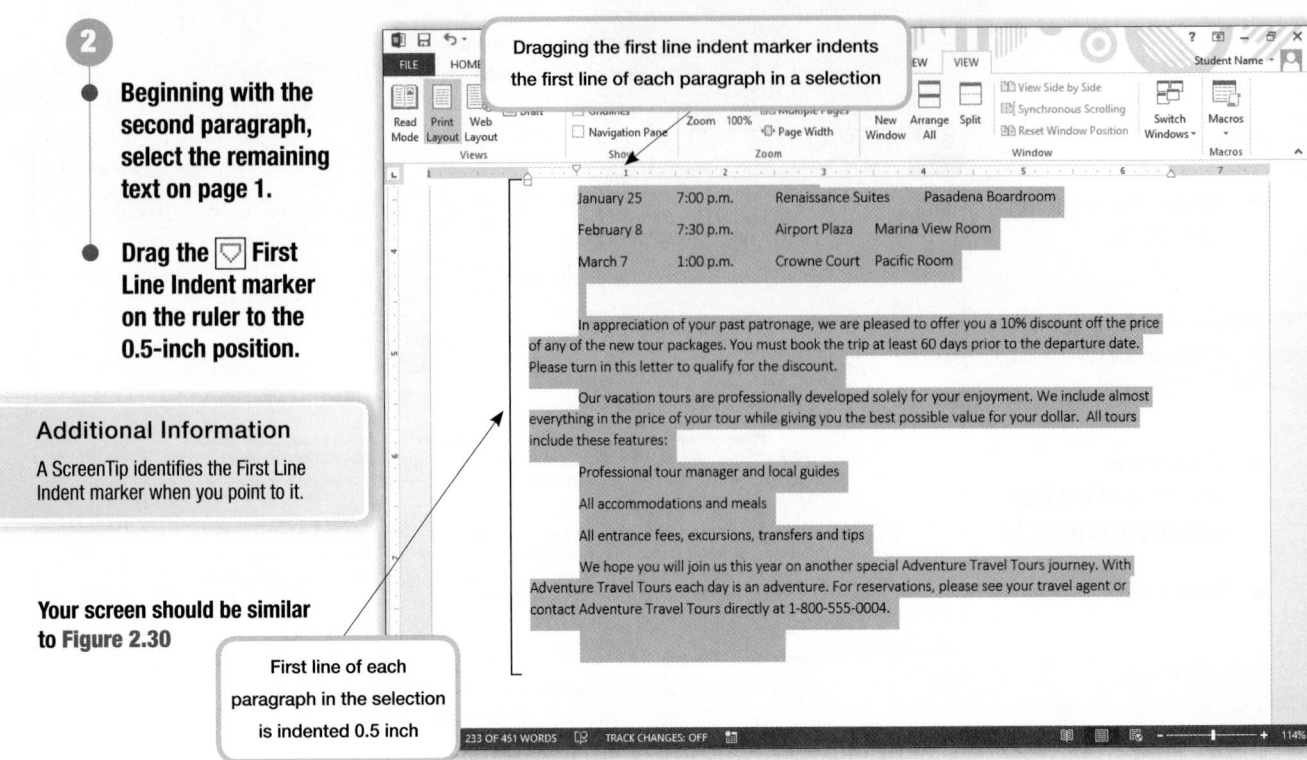

Dragging the first line indent marker indents the first line of each paragraph in a selection

First line of each paragraph in the selection is indented 0.5 inch

Figure 2.30

The first line of each paragraph in the selection is indented. Notice that each line of the presentation date and time information and the list of tour features also are indented. This is because Word considers each line a separate paragraph (each line ends with a paragraph mark). You decide to further indent the date and time information to the 1-inch position.

3

- Select the line of table headings and the three lines of data.

- Drag the ▽ First Line Indent marker on the ruler to the 1-inch position.

Having Trouble?

If the selection does not move to the 1-inch position, repeat dragging the ▽ First Line Indent marker to the 1-inch position.

Your screen should be similar to Figure 2.31

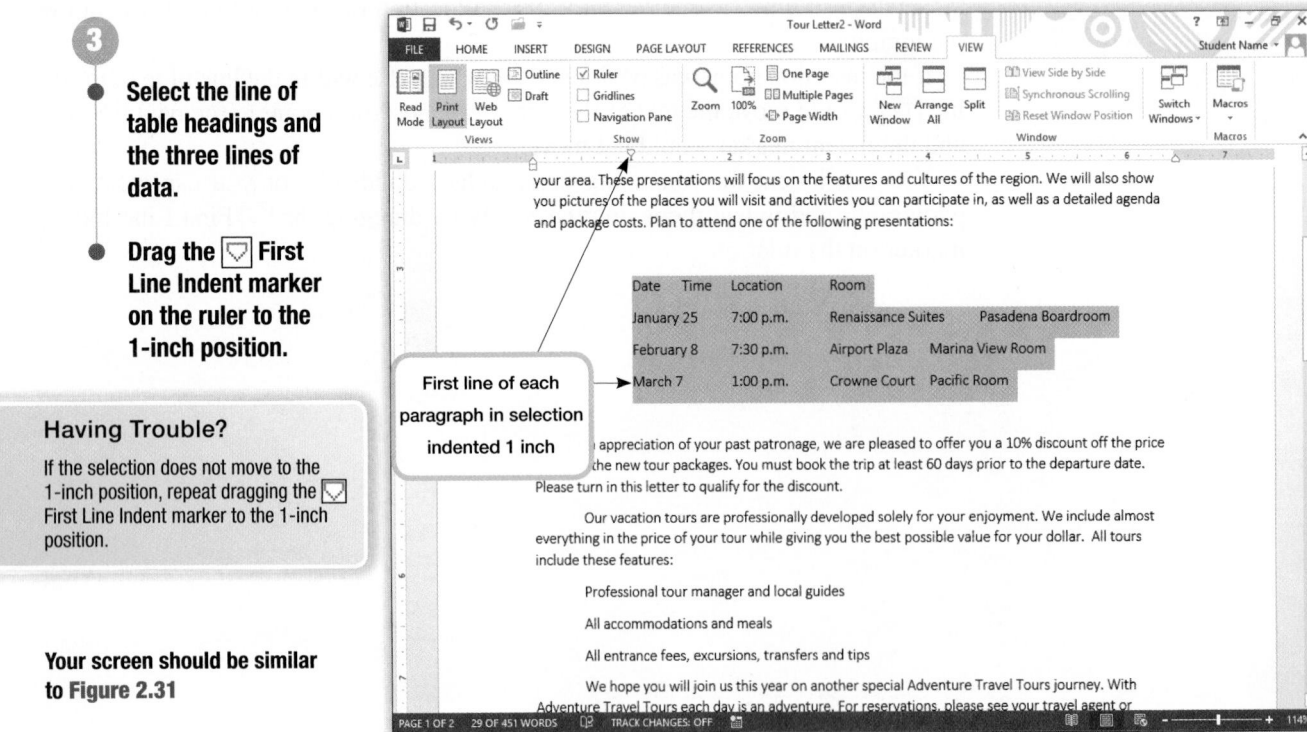

First line of each paragraph in selection indented 1 inch

Figure 2.31

SETTING TAB STOPS

Next you want to improve the appearance of the list of presentation times and dates. The date and time information was entered using the Tab key to separate the different columns of information. However, because the default tab stops are set at every 0.5 inch, the columns are not properly aligned. To improve the appearance of the information, you will set manual **tab stops** to align the information in evenly spaced columns. You also can select from five different types of tab stops to control how characters are positioned or aligned with the tab stop. The following table explains the five tab types, the tab marks that appear in the tab selector box (on the left end of the horizontal ruler), and the effects on the text.

Tab Type	Tab Mark	Effects on Text	Example
Left	L	Extends text to right from tab stop	left
Center	⊥	Aligns text centered on tab stop	center
Right	⌐	Extends text to left from tab stop	right
Decimal	⊥.	Aligns text with decimal point	35.78
Bar	I	Draws a vertical line through text at tab stop	|

You want to reformat the list of presentation times and dates to appear as a tabbed table of information so that it is easier to read, as shown below.

Date	Time	Location	Room
January 25	7:00 p.m.	Renaissance Suites	Pasadena Boardroom
February 8	7:30 p.m.	Airport Plaza	Marina View Room
March 7	1:00 p.m.	Crowne Court	Pacific Room B

Additional Information

The default tab stops are visible on the ruler as light vertical lines below the numbers.

To align the information, you will set three left tab stops at the 2-inch, 3-inch, and 4.5-inch positions. You can quickly specify manual tab stop locations and types using the ruler. To select a type of tab stop, click the tab selector located directly above the vertical ruler to cycle through the types of tabs. Then, to specify where to place the selected tab stop, click the ruler at the appropriate location.

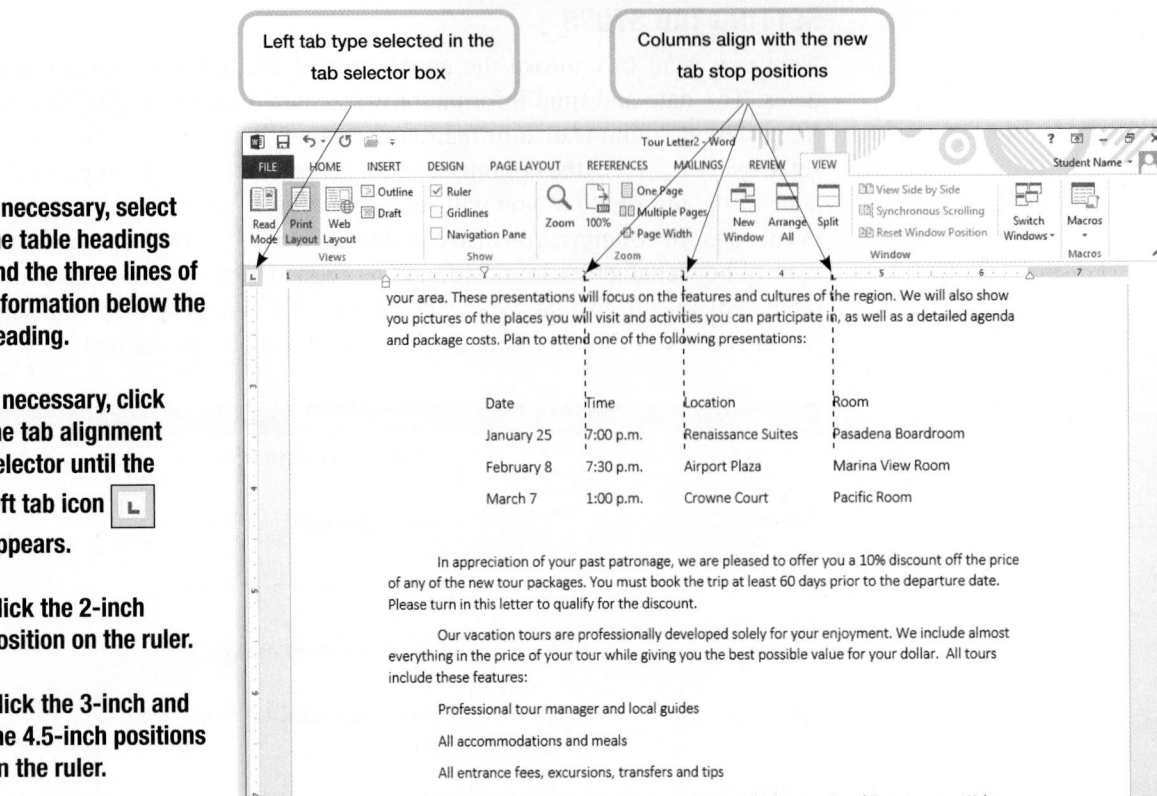

1

- If necessary, select the table headings and the three lines of information below the heading.

- If necessary, click the tab alignment selector until the left tab icon ⌊L⌋ appears.

- Click the 2-inch position on the ruler.

- Click the 3-inch and the 4.5-inch positions on the ruler.

- Click anywhere in the table to deselect it.

Left tab type selected in the tab selector box

Columns align with the new tab stop positions

Figure 2.32

Your screen should be similar to Figure 2.32

Additional Information

The tab selector box also can be used to insert first line or hanging indents by selecting ▽ First Line Indent or △ Hanging Indent.

The three tabbed columns appropriately align with the new tab stops. All default tabs to the left of the manual tab stops are cleared. The column headings would look better centered over the columns of information. To make this change, you will remove the three left tab stops for the heading line and then add three center tab stops.

Manual tab stops can be removed by dragging the tab stop up or down off the ruler. They also can be moved by dragging them left or right along the ruler. In addition the Tabs dialog box can be used to make these same changes. You will first drag a tab stop off the ruler to remove it and then you will use the Tabs dialog box to clear the remaining tab stops.

Center tab type selected

Headings center-aligned at tab stop positions

- **Position the insertion point in the table heading line.**

- **Drag the 2-inch tab stop marker down and off the ruler.**

- **Double-click any tab stop to open the Tabs dialog box.**

- **Click** Clear All **to remove the remaining two tab stops.**

- **Click** OK **.**

- **Click the tab alignment selector until the center tab icon ⊥ appears.**

- **Set center tab stops at the 1.25-inch, 2.25-inch, 3.5-inch, and 5-inch positions.**

Your screen should be similar to Figure 2.33

Date heading not centered aligned at tab

your area. These presentations will focus on the features and cultures of the region. We will also show you pictures of the places you will visit and activities you can participate in, as well as a detailed agenda and package costs. Plan to attend one of the following presentations:

Date	Time	Location	Room
January 25	7:00 p.m.	Renaissance Suites	Pasadena Boardroom
February 8	7:30 p.m.	Airport Plaza	Marina View Room
March 7	1:00 p.m.	Crowne Court	Pacific Room

In appreciation of your past patronage, we are pleased to offer you a 10% discount off the price of any of the new tour packages. You must book the trip at least 60 days prior to the departure date. Please turn in this letter to qualify for the discount.

Our vacation tours are professionally developed solely for your enjoyment. We include almost everything in the price of your tour while giving you the best possible value for your dollar. All tours include these features:

Professional tour manager and local guides

All accommodations and meals

All entrance fees, excursions, transfers and tips

We hope you will join us this year on another special Adventure Travel Tours journey. With Adventure Travel Tours each day is an adventure. For reservations, please see your travel agent or

Figure 2.33

The Time, Location, and Room headings are appropriately centered on the tab stops. However, the Date heading still needs to be indented to the 1.25-inch tab stop position by pressing Tab.

3

- If necessary, move to the left of the "D" in "Date."

- Press Tab.

Your screen should be similar to Figure 2.34

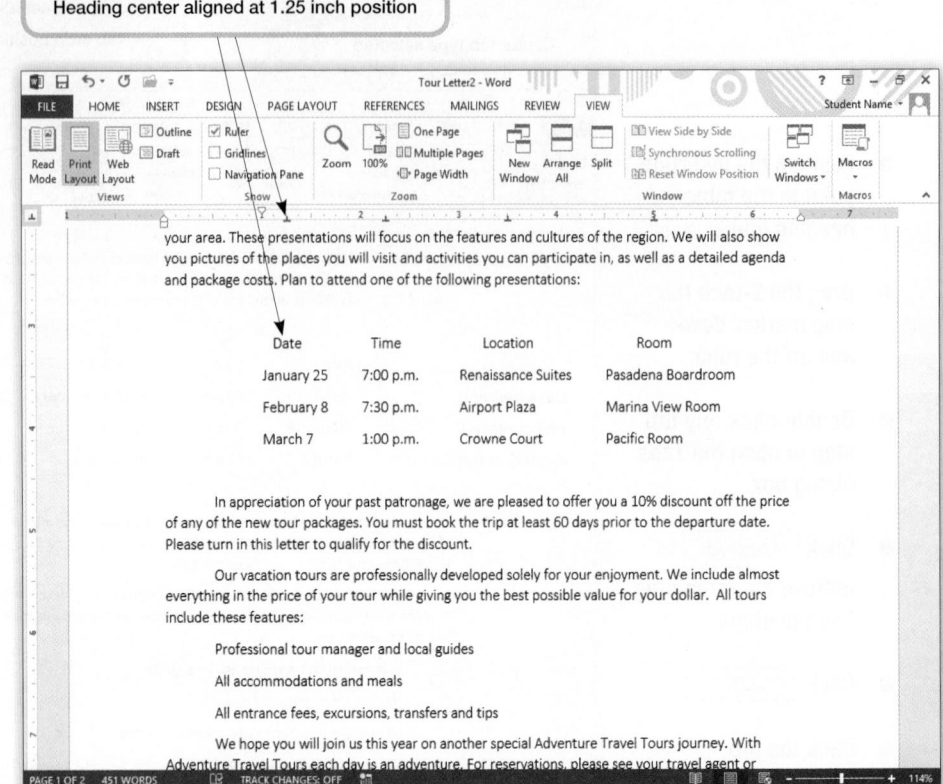

Heading center aligned at 1.25 inch position

your area. These presentations will focus on the features and cultures of the region. We will also show you pictures of the places you will visit and activities you can participate in, as well as a detailed agenda and package costs. Plan to attend one of the following presentations:

Date	Time	Location	Room
January 25	7:00 p.m.	Renaissance Suites	Pasadena Boardroom
February 8	7:30 p.m.	Airport Plaza	Marina View Room
March 7	1:00 p.m.	Crowne Court	Pacific Room

In appreciation of your past patronage, we are pleased to offer you a 10% discount off the price of any of the new tour packages. You must book the trip at least 60 days prior to the departure date. Please turn in this letter to qualify for the discount.

Our vacation tours are professionally developed solely for your enjoyment. We include almost everything in the price of your tour while giving you the best possible value for your dollar. All tours include these features:

Professional tour manager and local guides

All accommodations and meals

All entrance fees, excursions, transfers and tips

We hope you will join us this year on another special Adventure Travel Tours journey. With Adventure Travel Tours each day is an adventure. For reservations, please see your travel agent or

PAGE 1 OF 2   451 WORDS   TRACK CHANGES: OFF

Figure 2.34

As you can see, setting different types of tab stops is helpful for aligning text or numeric information vertically in columns. Using tab stops ensures that the text will indent to the same set location. Setting manual tab stops instead of pressing Tab or Spacebar repeatedly is a more professional way to format a document, as well as faster and more accurate. It also makes editing easier because you can change the tab stop settings for several paragraphs at once.

ADDING LEADER CHARACTERS

To make the presentation times and location information even easier to read, you will add leader characters before each of the tab stops. **Leader characters** are solid, dotted, or dashed lines that fill the blank space between tab stops. They help the reader's eye move across the blank space between the information aligned at the tab stops. To do this, use the Tabs dialog box.

1

- **Select the three lines of presentation information, excluding the heading line.**

- **Double-click any tab stop on the ruler.**

Another Method

You could also open the Paragraph dialog box and click `Tabs...`.

Your screen should be similar to Figure 2.35

Having Trouble?

If you do not double-click fast enough, you may add an extra tab.

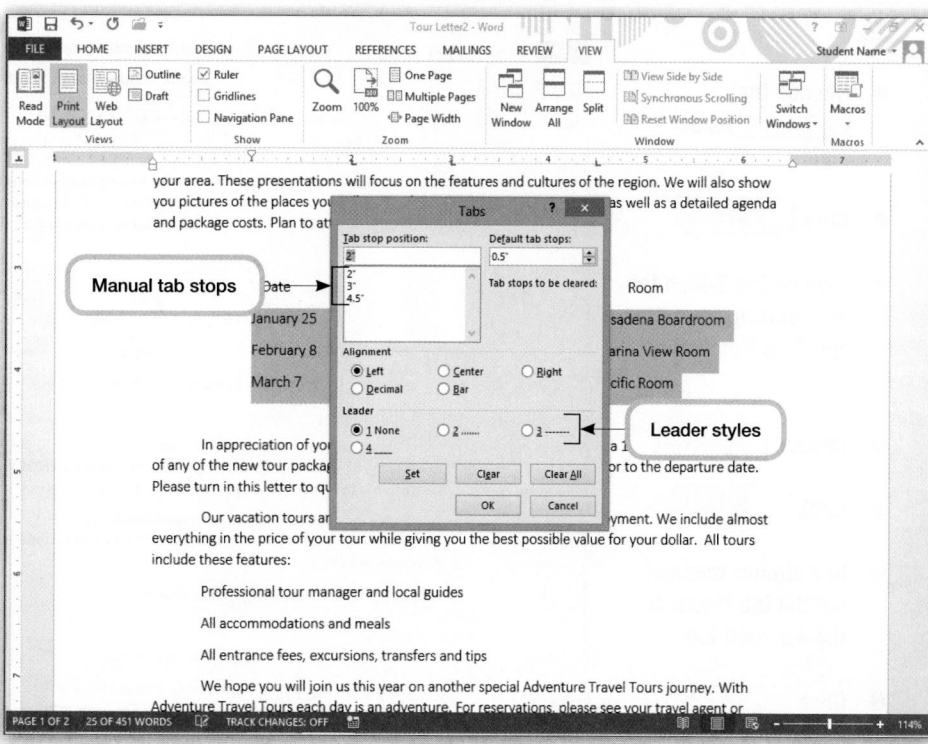

Figure 2.35

Additional Information

The Tabs dialog box can be used to set more precise tab stops than can be set using the ruler.

Notice that the Tabs dialog box displays the manual tabs you set using the ruler. You also can set tab stops using the Tabs dialog box by entering the tab positions in the text box and selecting the tab alignment. You can clear an individual tab stop by selecting the tab stop position from the list and clicking `Clear`.

The 2-inch tab stop appears in the Tab Stop Position text box, indicating it is the tab stop that will be affected by your actions. The Leader setting is None for the 2-inch tab stop. You can select from three styles of leader characters. You will use the third leader style, a series of dashed lines. The leader characters fill the empty space to the left of the tab stop. Each tab stop must have the leader style individually set.

2

- Choose the ⊙ 3 ------- leader style.

- Click [Set].

- Choose the 3-inch tab stop setting from the Tab Stop Position list box.

- Choose ⊙ 3 -------.

- Click [Set].

- In a similar manner, set the tab leader for the 4.5-inch tab.

- Click [OK].

- Click in the table to deselect the text.

Your screen should be similar to Figure 2.36

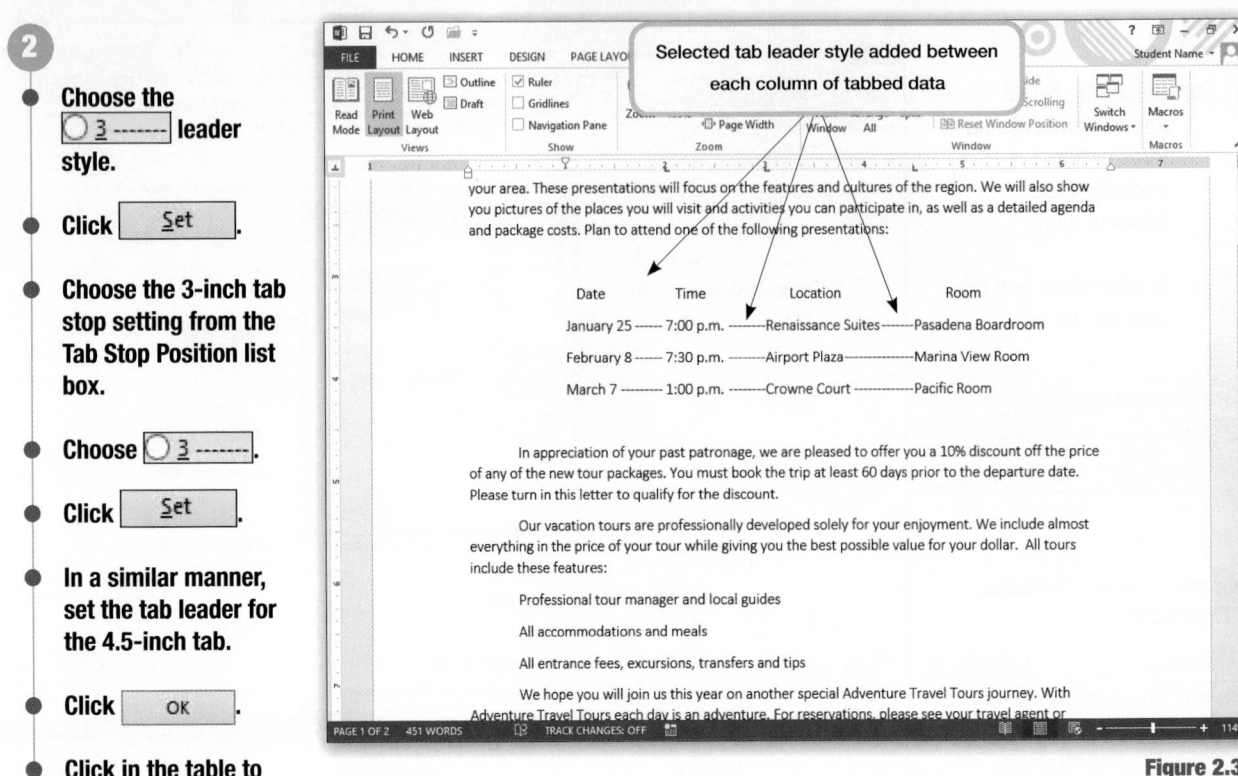

Figure 2.36

The selected leader style has been added to the blank space between each column of tabbed text.

CHANGING LINE AND PARAGRAPH SPACING

Next, you will adjust the paragraph spacing above and below the table as well as the spacing between the lines in the table.

Concept  6   Line and Paragraph Spacing

Adjusting the **line spacing**, or the vertical space between lines of text, and increasing or decreasing spacing before and after paragraphs improve readability of document text. If a line contains a character or object, such as a graphic, that is larger than the surrounding text, the spacing for that line is automatically adjusted. Additional line spacing settings are described in the table below.

Spacing	Effect
Single	Accommodates the largest font in that line, plus a small amount of extra space; the amount of extra space varies with the font that is used.
1.5 lines	Spacing is one and a half times that of single line spacing.
Double (2.0)	Spacing is twice that of single line spacing.
At least	Uses a value specified in points as the minimum line spacing that is needed to fit the largest font or graphic on the line.
Exactly	Uses a value specified in points as a fixed line spacing amount that is not adjusted, making all lines evenly spaced. Graphics or text that is too large will appear clipped.
Multiple	Uses a percentage value to increase or decrease the spacing from single spacing. For example, 1.3 will increase the spacing by 33 percent.

The default line spacing for a Word 2013 document is set to multiple with an 8 percent increase (1.08) over single spacing.

In addition to changing line spacing within paragraphs, you also can change the spacing before or after paragraphs. The default paragraph spacing adds a small amount of space (8 pt) after a paragraph and no extra space before a paragraph.

Additional Information

You also can change the paragraph spacing for the entire document using Paragraph Spacing ▾ in the Document Formatting group of the Design tab.

The ⬚ ▾ Line and Paragraph Spacing command in the Paragraph group of the Home tab can be used to specify standard spacing settings, such as double and triple spacing. It also adds or removes the extra spacing between paragraphs.

- **Select the table including the blank lines above and below it.**

- **Open the [≡▾] Line and Paragraph Spacing drop-down menu in the Paragraph group of the Home tab.**

- **Choose Line Spacing Options.**

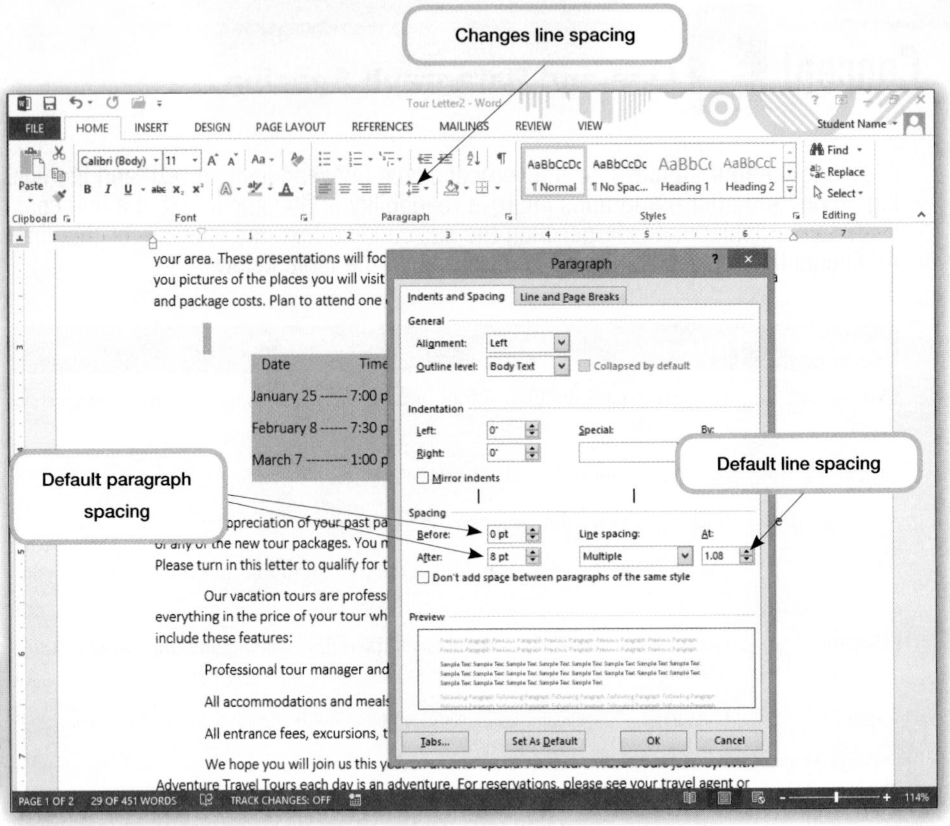

Another Method

You also could click [▫] in the Paragraph group to open the Paragraph dialog box to access this feature.

Another Method

You also can use [Ctrl] + 1 or 2 to change the line spacing to single- or double-spaced.

Your screen should be similar to Figure 2.37

Figure 2.37

The default document line spacing setting, multiple at 1.08; before paragraph spacing of 0 pt; and after paragraph spacing of 8 pt are displayed in the Spacing section of the Paragraph dialog box.

You want to decrease the spacing between each line of the table. Because Word considers each line of the table and the blank lines above and below it as separate paragraphs, you can decrease the Spacing After paragraph setting to achieve this effect. You also will change the line spacing to single to remove the 8 percent spacing increase. As you make these changes, the Preview box will show a preview of the change.

- **Choose Single from the Line Spacing drop-down menu.**

- **Click the down scroll button of the After box to decrease the spacing to 6 pt.**

- **Click** OK .

Your screen should be similar to **Figure 2.38**

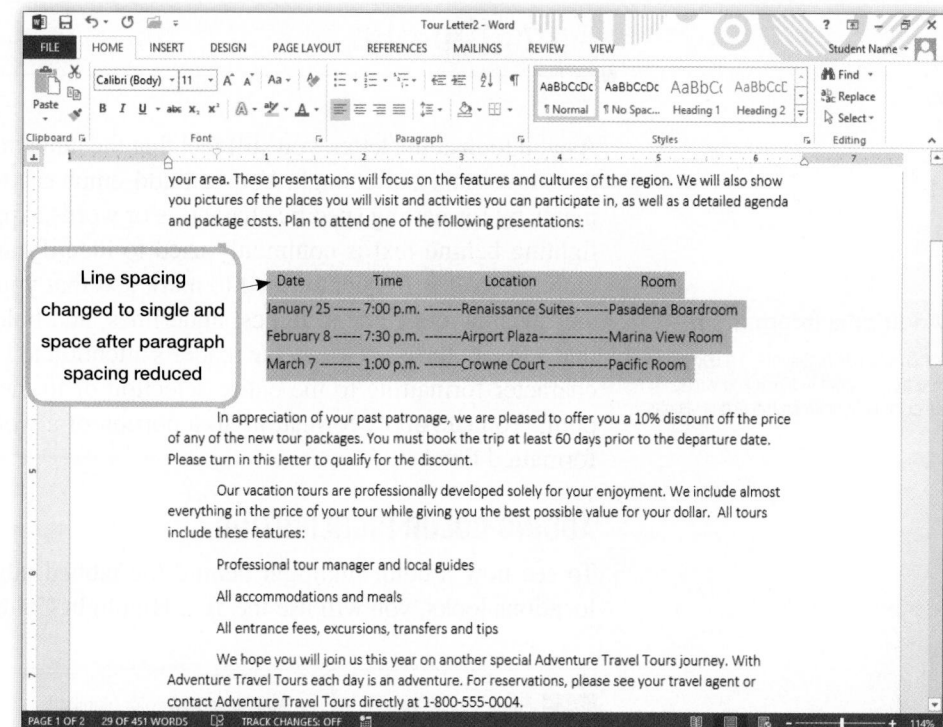

Line spacing changed to single and space after paragraph spacing reduced

Figure 2.38

Changing the line and paragraph spacing improves the appearance of the table and makes the information stand out more from the other text in the letter. You will make this same change to the list of tour features using a different method.

- **Select the list of three tour features.**

- **Click** ☰ ▾ **Line and Paragraph Spacing and choose 1.0.**

- **Select the first two items in the tour feature list.**

- **Open the Page Layout tab.**

- **Reduce the** ⬍ After: 8 pt **Spacing After setting in the Paragraph group to 6 pt.**

Your screen should be similar to **Figure 2.39**

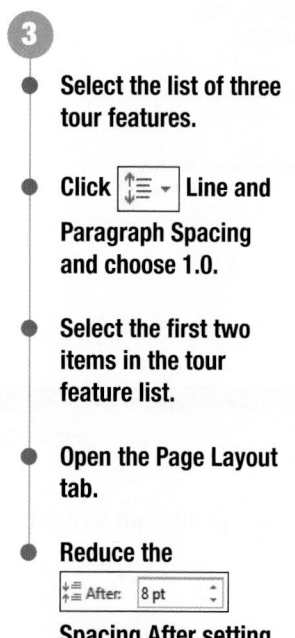
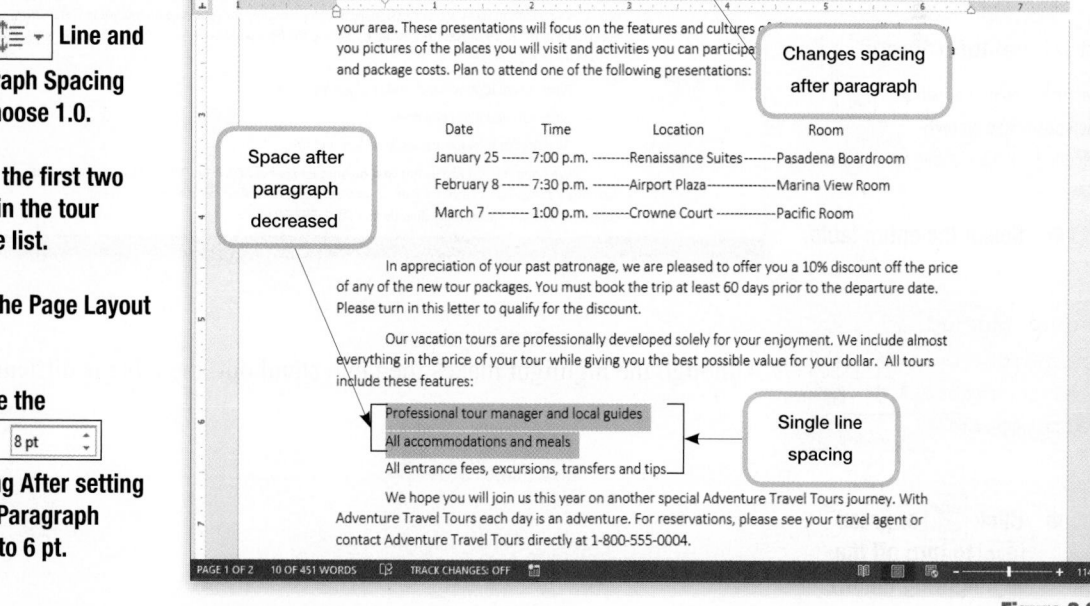

Changes spacing after paragraph

Space after paragraph decreased

Single line spacing

Figure 2.39

As you look at the letter, you still feel that the table of presentation dates and times does not stand out enough. You can add emphasis to information in your documents by formatting specific characters or words. Applying color shading or highlighting behind text is commonly used to identify areas of text that you want to emphasize. It is frequently used to mark text that you want to locate easily as you are revising a document. Italics, underlines, and bold are other character formats that add emphasis and draw the reader's attention to important items. Word applies character formatting to the entire selection or to the entire word at the insertion point. You can apply formatting to a portion of a word by selecting the area to be formatted first.

Additional Information

When you use highlights in a document you plan to print in black and white, select a light color so the text is visible.

ADDING COLOR HIGHLIGHTING

To see how a color highlight behind the tabbed table of presentation times and locations looks, you will use the Text Highlight Color command.

1

- Click anywhere in the table.

- Open the [aby] **Text Highlight Color** palette in the Font group of the Home tab.

- Choose the turquoise color from the color palette.

Additional Information

The mouse pointer appears as [✐] when positioned on text, indicating the highlighting feature is on.

- Select the entire table.

Another Method

You also can select the area you want to highlight first and then click [aby ▾] to select and apply a color.

- Click [aby] or press Esc to turn off the highlighting feature.

Your screen should be similar to Figure 2.40

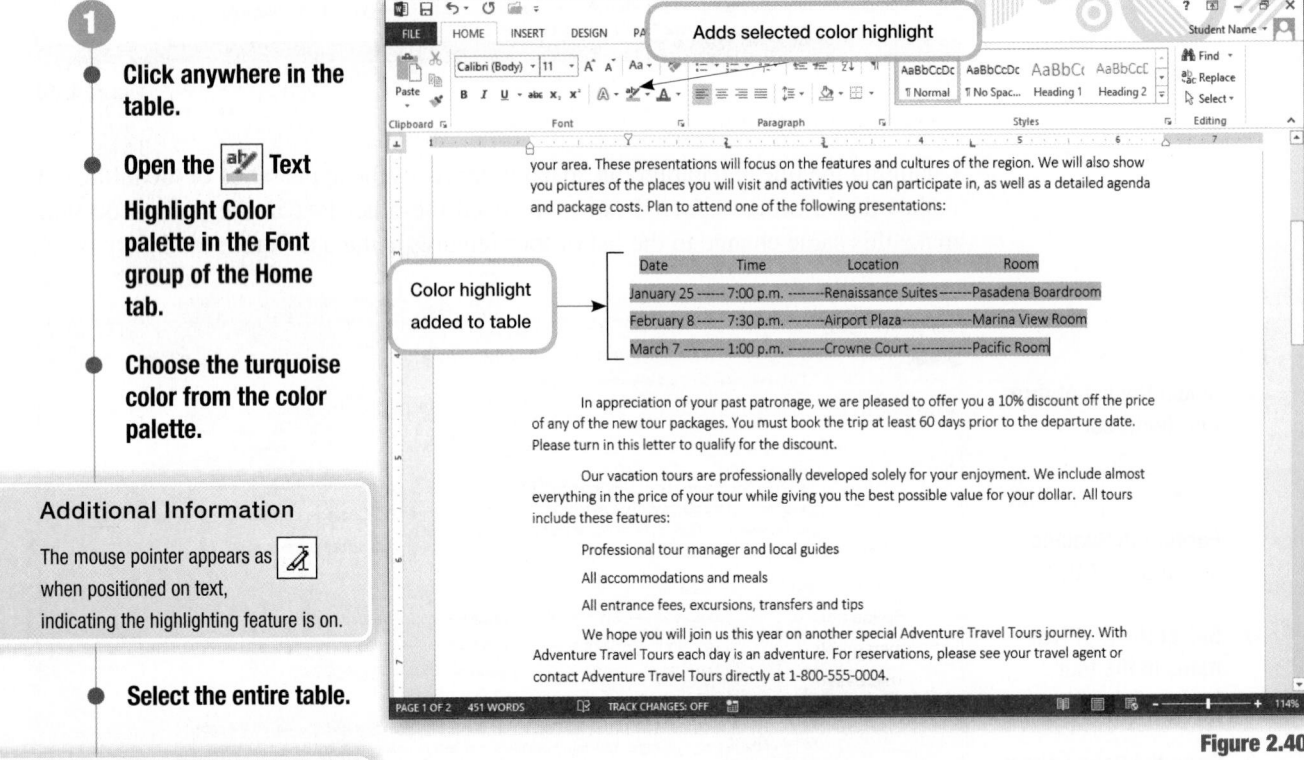

Figure 2.40

Although the highlight makes the table stand out, the table is difficult to read.

UNDERLINING TEXT

Instead, you decide to bold and underline the headings. The default underline style is a single black line. In addition, Word includes 15 other styles of underlines.

1

- Click ↶ Undo.

- Select the table heading line.

- Click **B** Bold from the Mini toolbar.

- Click **U** Underline from the Mini toolbar.

Your screen should be similar to Figure 2.41

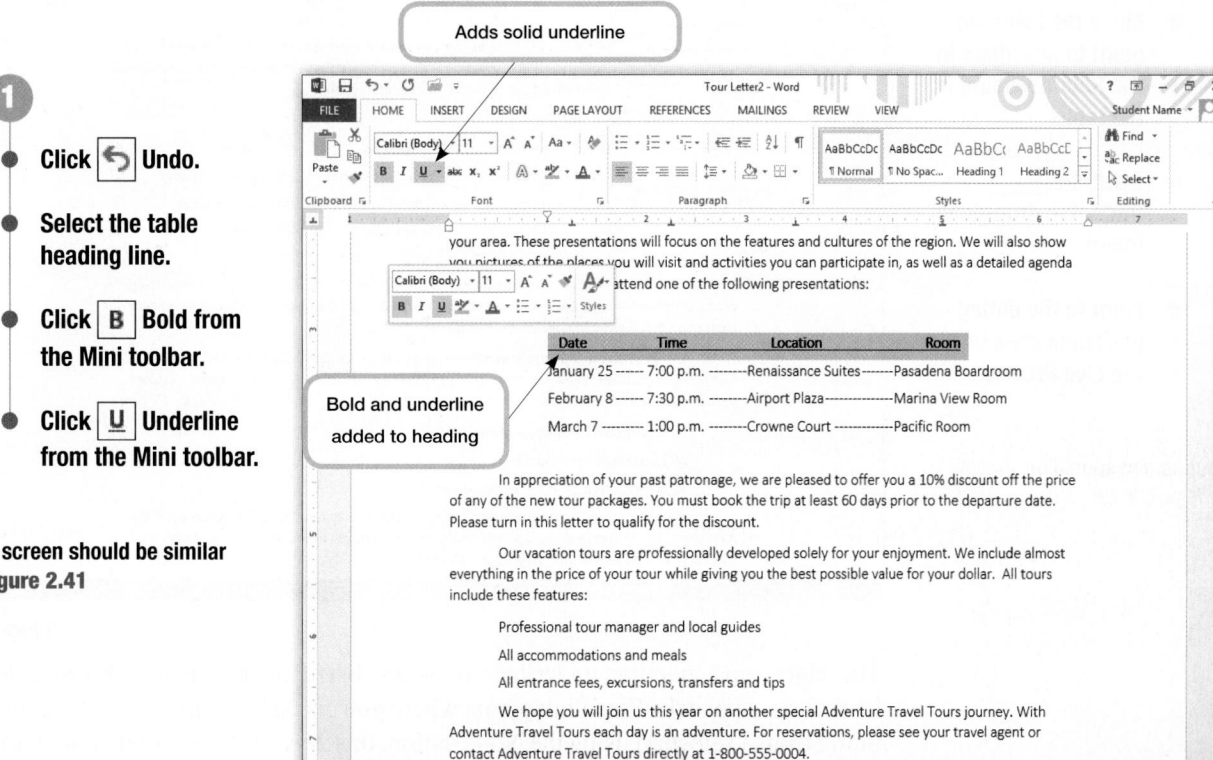

Figure 2.41

All the words are bold, and a single black underline has been added below the headings. To change the underline style to appear under each word only, you will select another underline style and apply the underline to the word individually. When the insertion point is positioned on a word, the selected underline style is applied to the entire word.

2

● Click Undo to remove the underline.

● Move the insertion point to anywhere in the Room heading in the table.

● Open the **U** ▾ Underline drop-down menu.

● Point to the dotted underline style to see the Live Preview.

Your screen should be similar to Figure 2.42

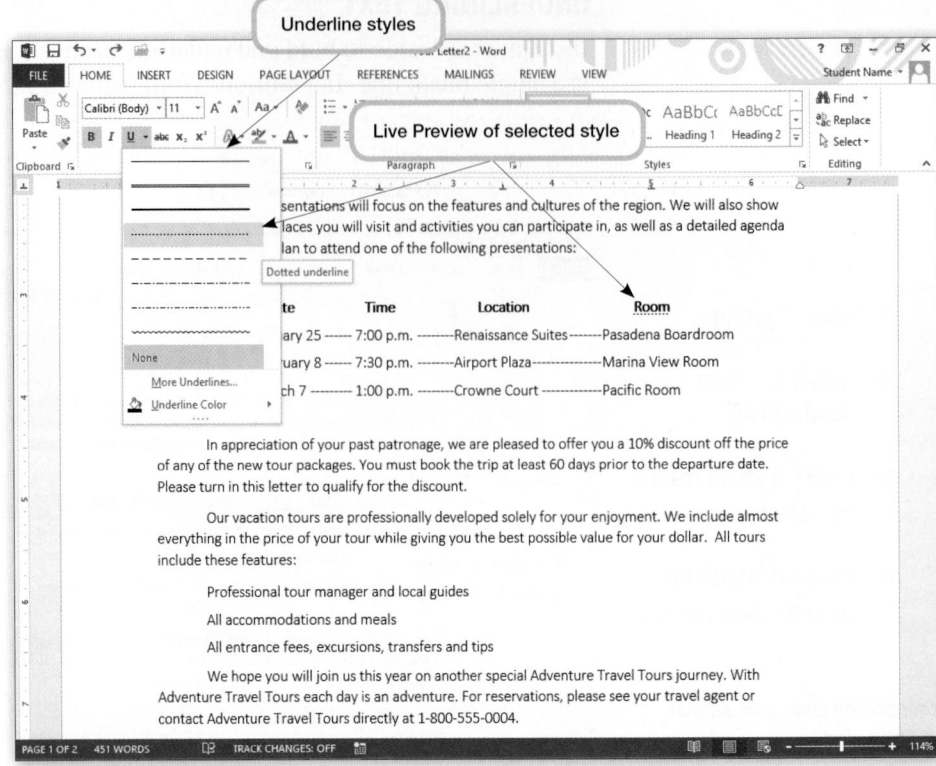

Figure 2.42

The eight most popular underline styles are listed in the menu. Choosing More Underlines opens the Font dialog box, where you can select other styles, clear underlining from a selection using the None option, or select the Words Only option to display a single underline below words in the selection, not under the spaces between words. Live Preview shows you how the selection will appear in the document.

3

● Select several other underline styles and see how they appear in the Live Preview.

● Choose the double underline style.

Additional Information

Using the keyboard shortcut Ctrl + U adds the default single underline style.

Your screen should be similar to Figure 2.43

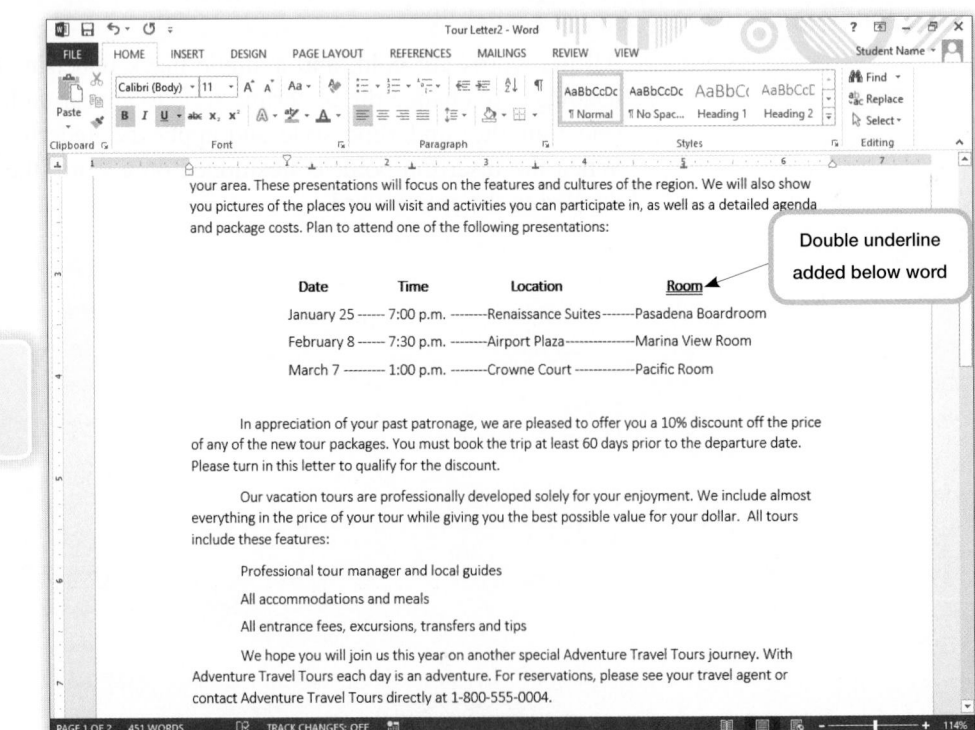

Figure 2.43

The selected word is underlined using the double underline style.

COPYING FORMATS WITH FORMAT PAINTER

To apply the same formats to the other headings, you will use the **Format Painter**. This feature applies the formats associated with the current selection to new selections. If the selection is a paragraph (including the paragraph mark), the formatting is applied to the entire paragraph. If the selection is a character, the format is applied to a character, word, or selection.

To use this feature, move the insertion point to the text whose formats you want to copy and click the 🖌 Format Painter button. Then select the text to which you want the formats applied. The format is automatically applied to an entire word simply by clicking the word. To apply the format to more or less text, you must select the area. Clicking 🖌 Format Painter once formats one selection, clicking the button twice formats multiple selections until you turn off this feature by clicking 🖌 Format Painter again or pressing Esc.

Additional Information

When Format Painter is on, the mouse pointer appears as 🖌I.

1

- **If necessary, move the insertion point to anywhere in the Room heading.**

- **Double-click 🖌 Format Painter in the Clipboard group.**

- **Click the Date, Time, and Location headings.**

- **Click 🖌 to turn off Format Painter.**

Another Method

You can press Esc to turn off Format Painter.

- **Save the document again.**

Your screen should be similar to Figure 2.44

Additional Information

A list can be used whenever you present three or more related pieces of information.

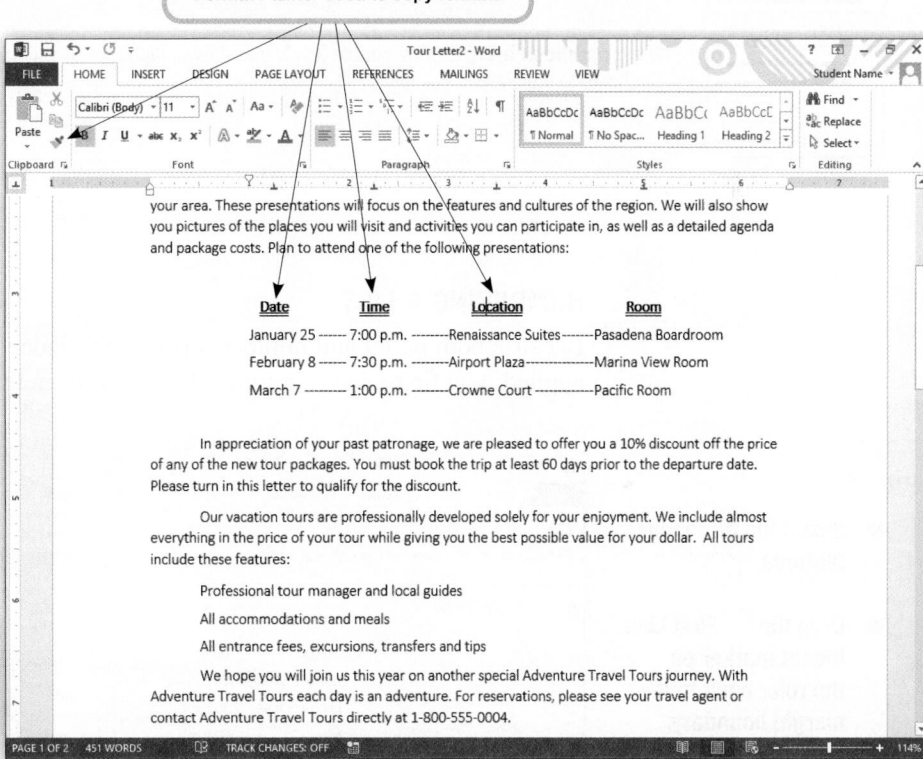

Figure 2.44

Creating Lists

The next change you want to make is to use the bullets or numbering feature to display the three lines of information about tour features as an itemized list.

Concept  Bulleted and Numbered Lists

Whenever possible, add bullets or numbers before items in a list to organize information and to make your writing clear and easy to read. Word includes many basic bullets, a dot or other symbol, and number formats from which you can select. Additionally, there are many picture bullets available. If none of the predesigned bullet or number formats suits your needs, you also can create your own customized designs.

(bulleted list icon)	Use a **bulleted list** when you have several items in a paragraph that logically make a list. A bulleted list displays one of several styles of bullets before each item in the list. You can select from several types of symbols to use as bullets, and you can change the color, size, and position of the bullet.
(numbered list icon)	Use a **numbered list** when you want to convey a sequence of events, such as a procedure that has to follow a certain order. A numbered list displays numbers or letters before the text. Word automatically increments the number or letter as you start a new paragraph. You can select from several different numbering schemes to create numbered lists.
(multilevel list icon)	Use a **multilevel list** to display outline levels that show a hierarchical structure of the items in the list. There can be up to nine levels.

NUMBERING A LIST

Because both bullet and number formats will indent the items automatically when applied, you first need to remove the indent from the three tour features.

1

- Select the three tour features.

- Drag the ▽ First Line Indent marker on the ruler back to the margin boundary.

- Right-click the selection and open the ▤ ▾ Numbering drop-down menu in the Mini toolbar.

Another Method

The Ribbon equivalent is ▤ ▾ Numbering in the Paragraph group.

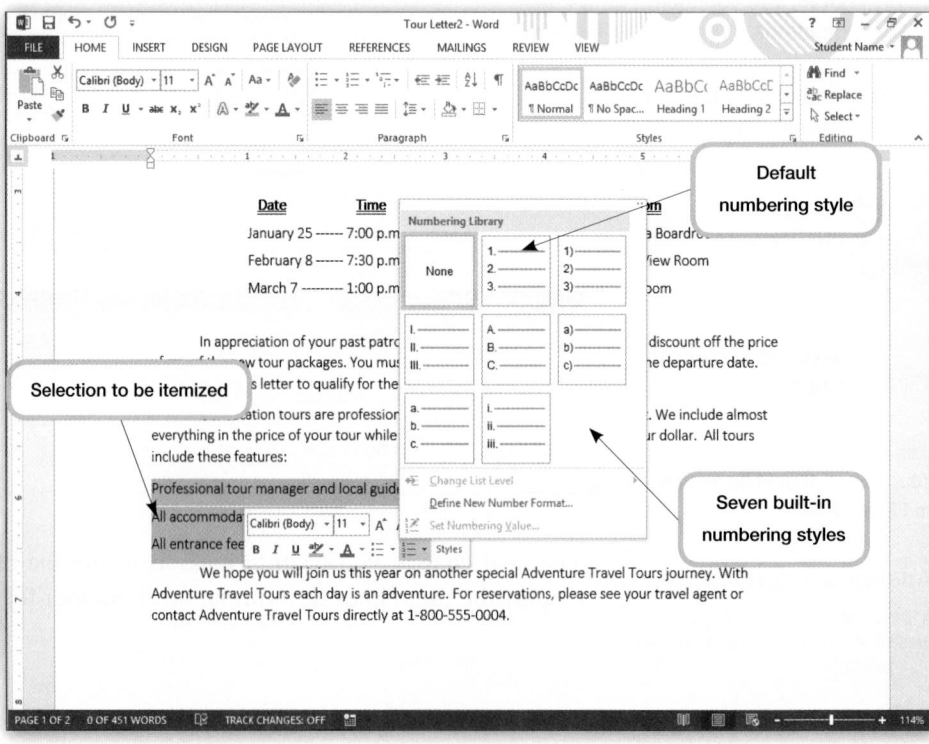

Your screen should be similar to **Figure 2.45**

Figure 2.45

The Numbering gallery displays examples of seven built-in numbered list formats in the Numbering Library category. The None option is used to remove an existing numbering format. Numbers followed by periods is the default style that is applied when clicking ⊞ Numbering. However, if another style has been used since starting Word, the last-used numbering format is inserted.

The Numbering gallery may include a Recently Used category if this feature has already been used since Word 2013 was started. If the document contains another numbered list, the gallery will display the used number style in a Document Number Formats category.

The three options at the bottom of the menu are used to change the indent level of the items, to customize the appearance of the built-in formats, and to set a start number for the list (1 is the default). For example, you could increase the indent level of the list, change the color of the numbers, and start numbering with 3 instead of 1.

2

Click the 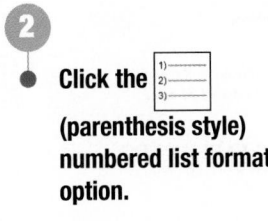 **(parenthesis style) numbered list format option.**

Your screen should be similar to **Figure 2.46**

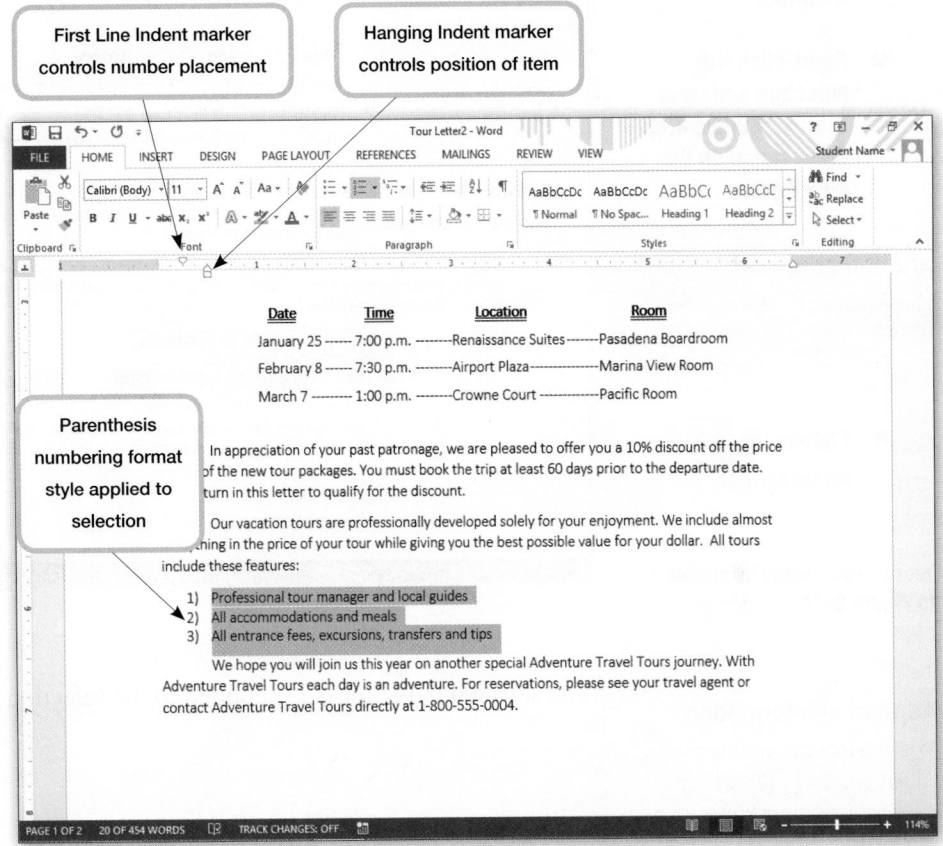

Figure 2.46

A number is inserted at the 0.25-inch position before each line, and the text following the number is indented to the 0.5-inch position. In an itemized list, the First Line Indent marker on the ruler controls the position of the number or bullet, and the Hanging Indent marker controls the position of the item following the number or bullet. If the text following each bullet were longer than a line, the text on the following lines would also be indented to the 0.5-inch position. Additionally, the extra space between the lines was removed because the feature that adds space between paragraphs of the same style was automatically turned off.

BULLETING A LIST

After looking at the list, you decide it really would be more appropriate if it were a bulleted list instead of a numbered list. The solid round bullet format is the default when clicking ▤ Bullets. However, if another style was previously used since starting Word 2013, that style is inserted. The bullet submenu is divided into the same three groups as the Numbering submenu and has similar options.

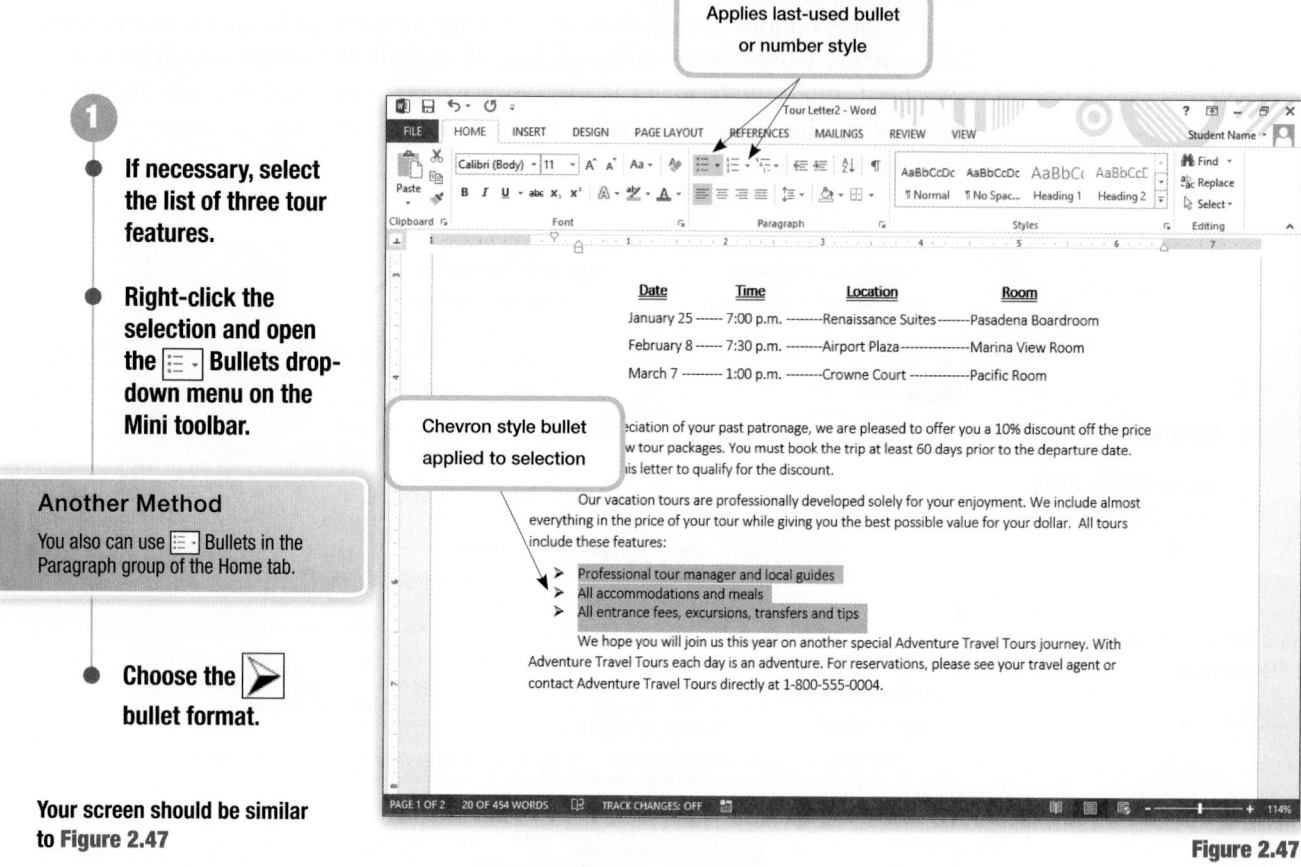

- **1**

  • **If necessary, select the list of three tour features.**

  • **Right-click the selection and open the ▤ ▾ Bullets drop-down menu on the Mini toolbar.**

Another Method

You also can use ▤ ▾ Bullets in the Paragraph group of the Home tab.

  • **Choose the ➤ bullet format.**

Your screen should be similar to Figure 2.47

Figure 2.47

Additional Information

To remove bullets or numbers, select the text, open the ▤ ▾ Bullets drop-down menu, and select None, or click ▤ Bullets again.

The selected bullet format is applied to the selection.

SORTING A LIST

As you look at the bulleted list, you decide you want the three items to appear in alphabetical order. To make this change quickly, you can sort the list.

Concept 8 Sort

Word can quickly arrange or **sort** text, numbers, or data in lists or tables in alphabetical, numeric, or date order based on the first character in each paragraph. The sort order can be ascending (A to Z, 0 to 9, or earliest to latest date) or descending (Z to A, 9 to 0, or latest to earliest date). The following table describes the rules that are used when sorting.

Sort by	Rules
Text	First, items beginning with leading spaces and punctuation marks or symbols (such as !, #, $, %, or &) are sorted.
	Second, items beginning with numbers are sorted. Dates are treated as three-digit numbers.
	Third, items beginning with letters are sorted.
Numbers	All characters except numbers are ignored. The numbers can be in any location in a paragraph.
Date	Valid date separators include hyphens, forward slashes (/), commas, and periods. Colons (:) are valid time separators. If unable to recognize a date or time, Word places the item at the beginning or end of the list (depending on whether you are sorting in ascending or descending order).
Field results	If an entire field (such as a last name) is the same for two items, Word next evaluates subsequent fields (such as a first name) according to the specified sort options.

When a tie occurs, Word uses the first nonidentical character in each item to determine which item should come first.

You will use the default Sort settings that will sort by text and paragraphs in ascending order.

1

- If necessary, select the entire bulleted list.

- Click ⬆⬇ Sort in the Paragraph group.

- Click [OK] to accept the default settings.

- Click the document to clear the highlight.

- Select the third list item and increase the space after to 12 pt.

- Save the file.

Your screen should be similar to Figure 2.48

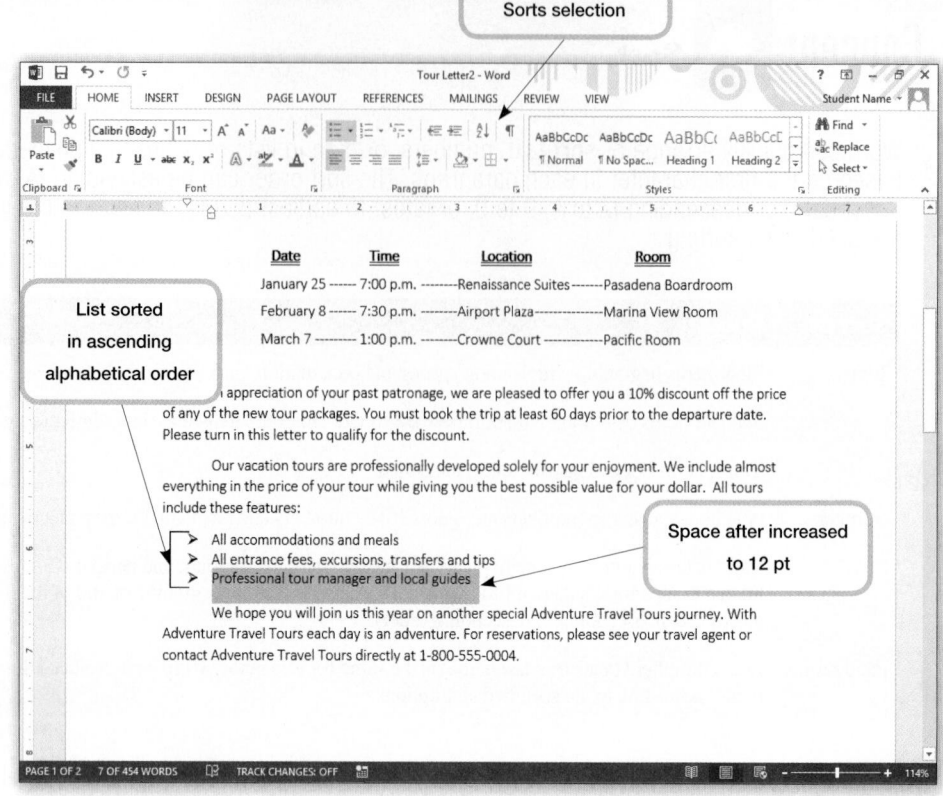

Figure 2.48

The three items in the list now appear in ascending sorted order.

Using Quick Parts

While looking at the letter, you realize that the closing lines have not been added to the document. You can quickly insert text and graphics that you use frequently using the Quick Parts feature. The **Quick Parts** feature includes reusable pieces of content or document parts, called **building blocks**, that give you a head start in creating content such as page numbers, cover pages, headers and footers, and sidebars. In addition to the supplied building blocks, you also can create your own custom building blocks.

USING SUPPLIED BUILDING BLOCKS

You will create the closing for the letter using the Author and Company building blocks that access information from the file's document properties.

Adds selected building block

1

- Move to the end of the last line of the letter and press [Enter] to insert a blank line.

- Return the indent to the left margin.

- Type **Best Regards,**

- Press [Enter].

- Open the Insert tab and click [≡] ▼ **Explore Quick Parts** in the Text group.

- Select **Document Property** and choose **Author** from the submenu.

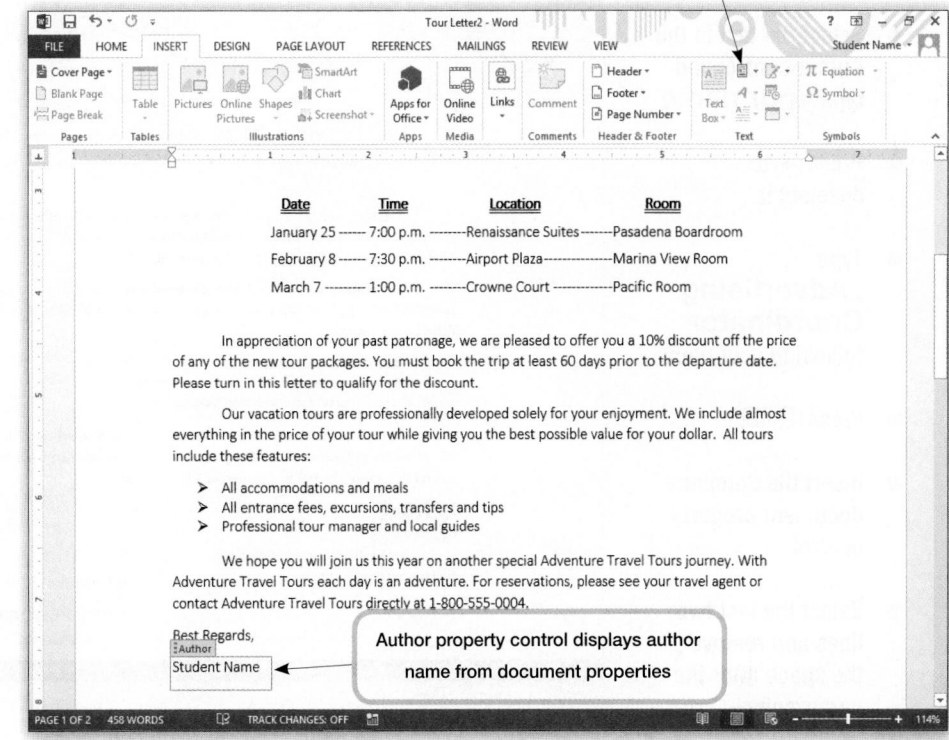

Date	Time	Location	Room
January 25 ------ 7:00 p.m. --------Renaissance Suites -------Pasadena Boardroom			
February 8 ------ 7:30 p.m. --------Airport Plaza----------------Marina View Room			
March 7 --------- 1:00 p.m. --------Crowne Court -------------Pacific Room			

In appreciation of your past patronage, we are pleased to offer you a 10% discount off the price of any of the new tour packages. You must book the trip at least 60 days prior to the departure date. Please turn in this letter to qualify for the discount.

Our vacation tours are professionally developed solely for your enjoyment. We include almost everything in the price of your tour while giving you the best possible value for your dollar. All tours include these features:

➤ All accommodations and meals
➤ All entrance fees, excursions, transfers and tips
➤ Professional tour manager and local guides

We hope you will join us this year on another special Adventure Travel Tours journey. With Adventure Travel Tours each day is an adventure. For reservations, please see your travel agent or contact Adventure Travel Tours directly at 1-800-555-0004.

Best Regards,
:Author
Student Name ◄——— Author property control displays author name from document properties

PAGE 1 OF 2   458 WORDS   TRACK CHANGES: OFF

Figure 2.49

Your screen should be similar to Figure 2.49

An Author property control containing the name that is currently stored in the file's Author document property is inserted in the document. A **control** is a graphic element that is a container for information or objects. Controls, like fields, appear shaded when you point to them.

You can update or modify the information displayed in a property control by editing the entry. Any changes you make in the property control are automatically updated in the document's properties. You will change the information in the Author property to your name and then continue to create the closing.

2

- Select the text in the Author control and type **your name**

- Press ⭢ to deselect it.

- Type **, Advertising Coordinator** following your name.

- Press ⟨Enter⟩.

- Insert the Company document property control.

- Select the last two lines and remove the space after the paragraphs.

- Increase the spacing after the Best Regards line to 18 pt to make space for a signature.

Your screen should be similar to Figure 2.50

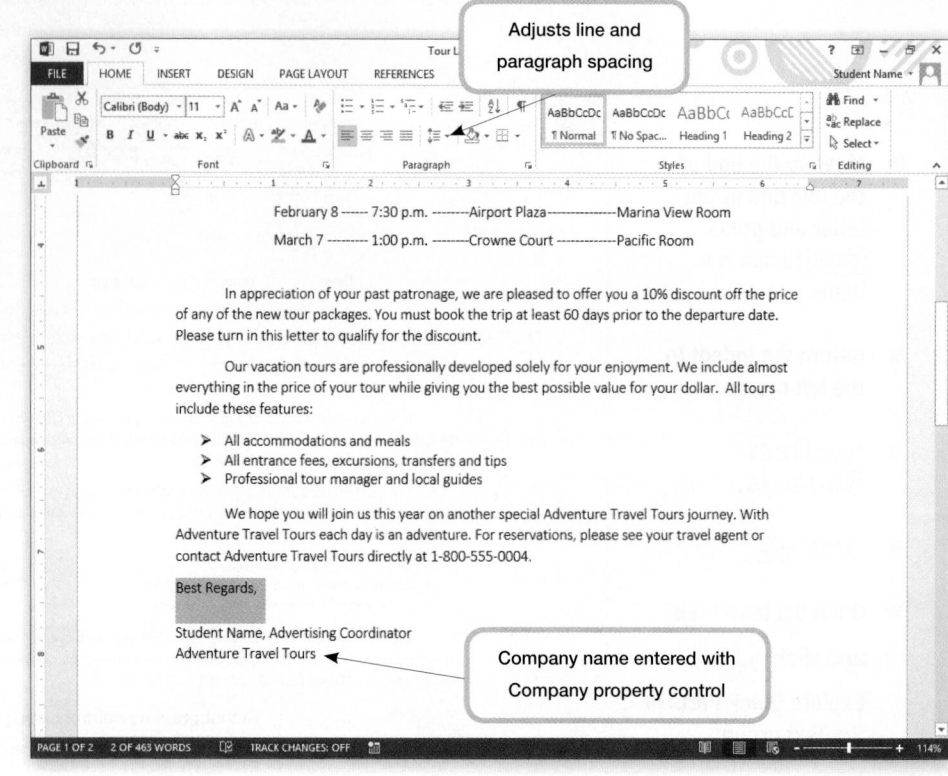

February 8 ------ 7:30 p.m. --------Airport Plaza----------------Marina View Room

March 7 --------- 1:00 p.m. --------Crowne Court -------------Pacific Room

In appreciation of your past patronage, we are pleased to offer you a 10% discount off the price of any of the new tour packages. You must book the trip at least 60 days prior to the departure date. Please turn in this letter to qualify for the discount.

Our vacation tours are professionally developed solely for your enjoyment. We include almost everything in the price of your tour while giving you the best possible value for your dollar. All tours include these features:

- All accommodations and meals
- All entrance fees, excursions, transfers and tips
- Professional tour manager and local guides

We hope you will join us this year on another special Adventure Travel Tours journey. With Adventure Travel Tours each day is an adventure. For reservations, please see your travel agent or contact Adventure Travel Tours directly at 1-800-555-0004.

Best Regards,

Student Name, Advertising Coordinator
Adventure Travel Tours ◄

> **Company name entered with Company property control**

> **Adjusts line and paragraph spacing**

Figure 2.50

The closing is now complete and the document properties now include your name as the author. Using document property controls in a document is particularly helpful when the same information is used multiple times. When a control is updated or edited, all controls of the same type throughout the document are automatically updated.

CREATING A CUSTOM BUILDING BLOCK

In addition to the supplied building blocks, you can create your own. In this case, because you frequently use the same closing when creating correspondence, you will create a building block that you can use to quickly insert this information.

1

- Turn on the display of formatting marks.

- Select the entire closing (excluding the Page Break line).

- Open the Insert tab and click 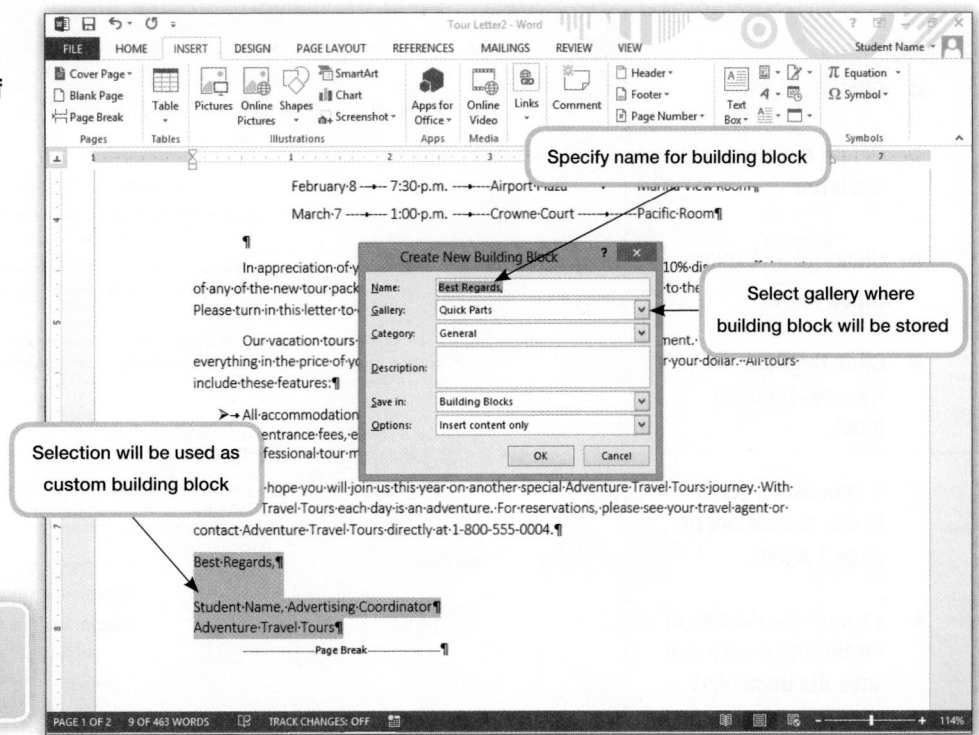 ▾ Explore Quick Parts.

- Choose Save Selection to Quick Part Gallery.

Your screen should be similar to Figure 2.51

Figure 2.51

In the Create New Building Block dialog box, you define the properties for the building block. This includes entering a unique name for the building block, specifying the gallery where you want the building block stored, and providing other information that is needed to identify and use the building block.

You will use the proposed name, Best Regards, and store it in the Quick Parts gallery. All the other default settings for this building block are appropriate. After saving the building block, you will erase the closing you typed in the letter and then reinsert it using the stored Quick Part.

2

- Click [OK].

- Delete the closing in the letter.

- Click [icon] ▾ Explore Quick Parts.

- Click the Best Regards building block.

- If necessary, scroll to see the bottom of page 1 again.

- Turn off the display of formatting marks and save the document again.

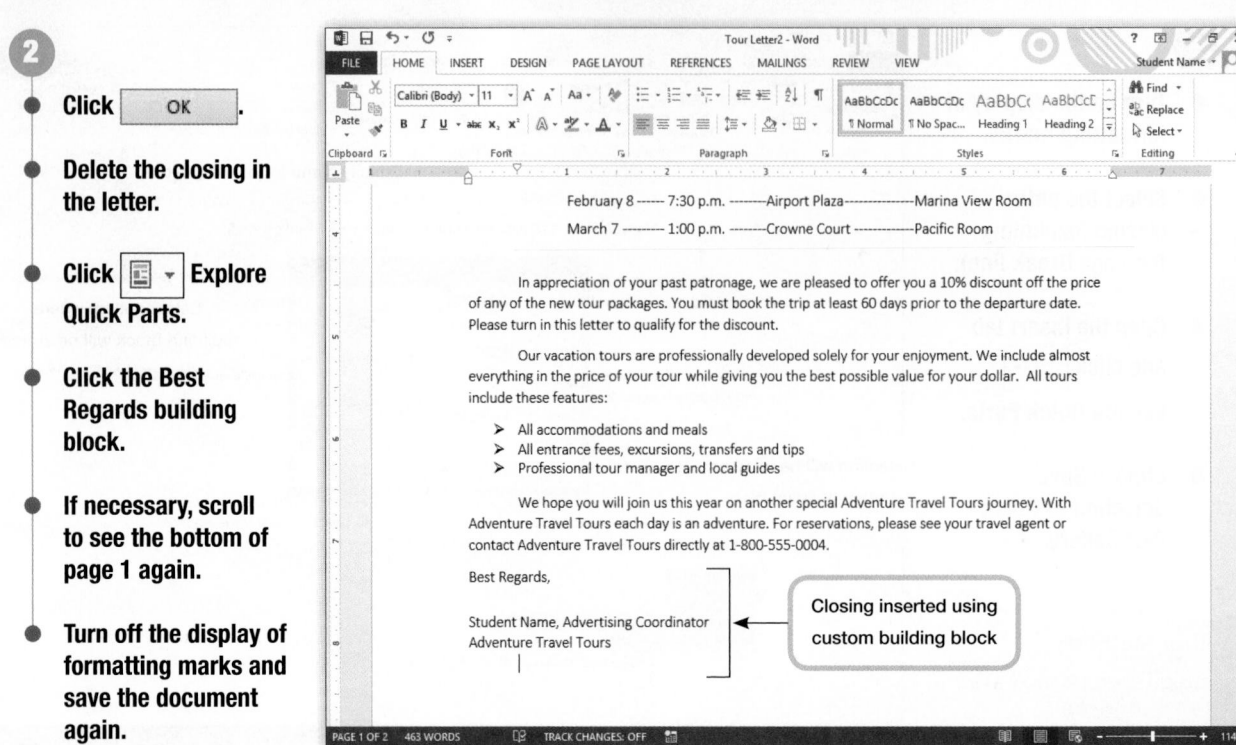

Figure 2.52

Your screen should be similar to Figure 2.52

The custom building block you created appeared as a gallery item at the top of the Quick Parts menu, making it easy for you to access and use. The selected block was inserted into the document at the location of the insertion point. As you can see, using Quick Parts was much quicker than typing the closing.

Adding and Modifying Shapes

You also want to add a special graphic to the flyer containing information about the company website to attract the reader's attention. To quickly add a shape, you will use one of the ready-made shapes that are supplied with Word. These include basic shapes such as rectangles and circles, a variety of lines, block arrows, flow-chart symbols, stars and banners, and callouts. You also can combine shapes to create more complex designs. To see and create shapes, use Print Layout view. In Draft view, shapes are not displayed. If you are using Draft view when you begin to create a shape, the view will change automatically to Print Layout view.

INSERTING A SHAPE

You want to add a graphic of a banner to the bottom of the flyer.

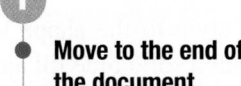

1

- Move to the end of the document.

- Open the Insert tab.

- Click 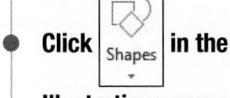 in the Illustrations group.

- From the Stars and Banners group, point to the Wave shape.

Your screen should be similar to **Figure 2.53**

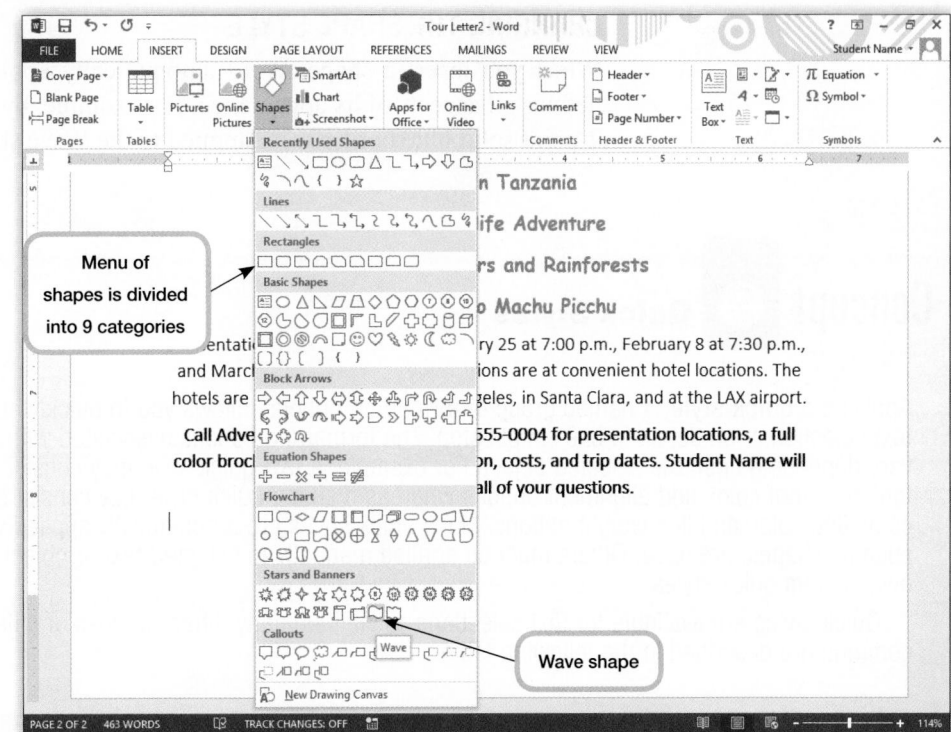

Menu of shapes is divided into 9 categories

Wave shape

Figure 2.53

The Shapes menu displays nine categories of shapes. Pointing to a shape displays the shape name in a ScreenTip. The recently selected shapes appear at the top of the menu. You will insert the Wave shape at the end of the flyer.

2

- Click the Wave shape.

- Click below the last line of the flyer to insert the shape.

- Drag the sizing handles to obtain a shape similar to that shown in Figure 2.54.

Additional Information

To maintain the height and width proportions of a shape, hold down [Shift] while you drag.

Your screen should be similar to **Figure 2.54**

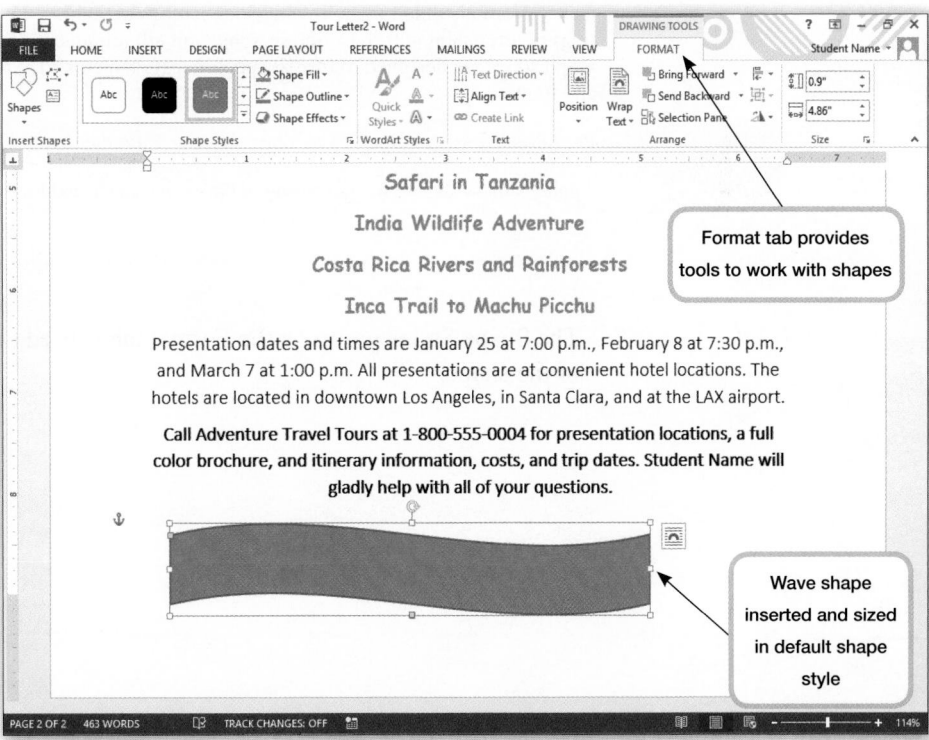

Format tab provides tools to work with shapes

Wave shape inserted and sized in default shape style

Figure 2.54

The Wave shape is inserted in the document as a floating object. It is a selected object and can be modified using the Drawing Tools Format tab.

CHANGING THE SHAPE STYLE

When you insert a shape, Word automatically applies a style to the shape that defines all aspects of its appearance. For example, by default a solid blue fill and a 2-point solid blue border were applied to the Wave shape you inserted.

Concept  9 Quick Styles

Applying a **quick style**, a named group of formatting options, allows you to quickly apply multiple formats to a text selection or an object in one simple step. The formatting options associated with the different quick styles vary depending upon the selected object. For example, a text quick style may consist of a combination of font, font size, font color, and alignment options whereas a shape quick style may consist of a combination of fill color, line color, and line weight options. Many quick styles are automatically applied when certain features, such as shapes, are used. Others must be applied manually to selected text or object. You also can create your own custom quick styles.

Quick styles are available for text selections as well as many different types of objects. Some of the most common are described in the following table.

Type of Style	Description
Shape	Affects all aspects of a graphic object's appearance, including fill color, outline color, and other effects.
Text	Affects selected text within a paragraph, such as the font and size of text, and bold and italic formats.
Paragraph	Controls all aspects of a paragraph's appearance, such as text alignment, tab stops, and line spacing. It also can include character formatting. The default paragraph style is named Normal, which includes character settings of Calibri, 11 pt, and paragraph settings of left indent at 0, 1.15 line spacing, and left alignment. In addition, many paragraph styles are designed to format specific text elements such as headings, captions, and footnotes.
Table	Provides a consistent look to borders, shading, alignment, and fonts in tables.
List	Applies similar alignment, numbering or bullet characters, and fonts to lists.

The Shape Styles group on the Format tab is used to easily change the default style of the shape.

- **Click ▾ More in the Shape Styles group to open the Shape Styles gallery.**

- **Point to several of the styles to see the Live Preview.**

- **Click the Light 1 Outline, Colored Fill - Orange, Accent 2 style to apply it to the Wave shape (third row, third column).**

Your screen should be similar to Figure 2.55

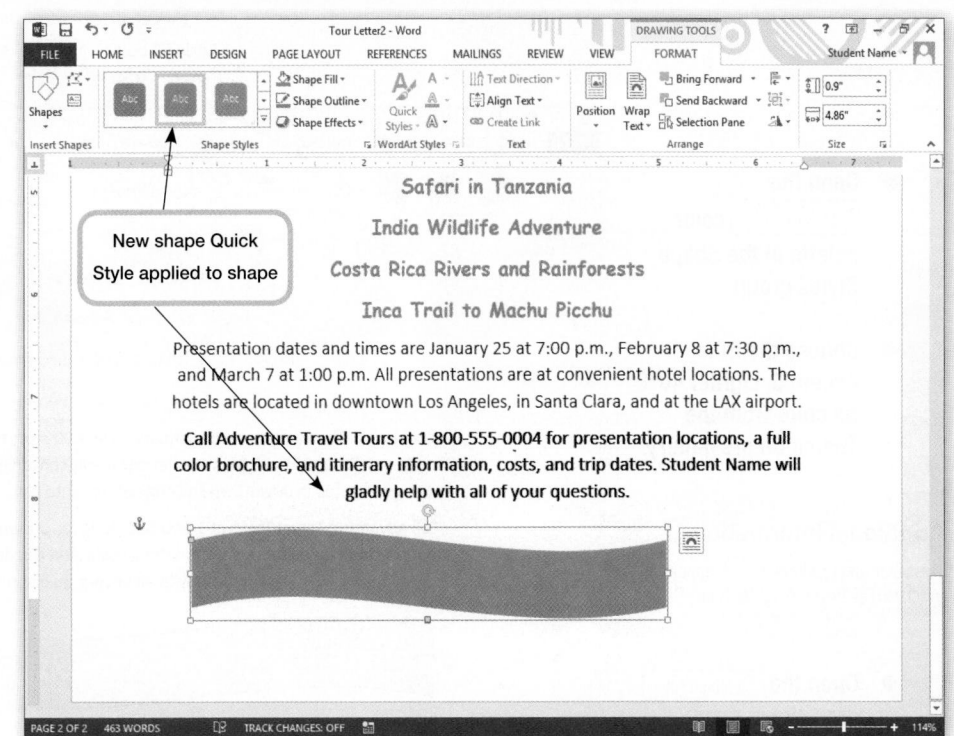

Figure 2.55

FILLING THE SHAPE WITH COLOR

You decide to change the fill color of the Wave shape to match the text color used in the flyer. You can easily customize shapes using many of the features on the Format tab, such as adding a background fill color, gradient, and line color. A **gradient** is a gradual progression of colors and shades, usually from one color to another, or from one shade to another of the same color.

1

- Open the 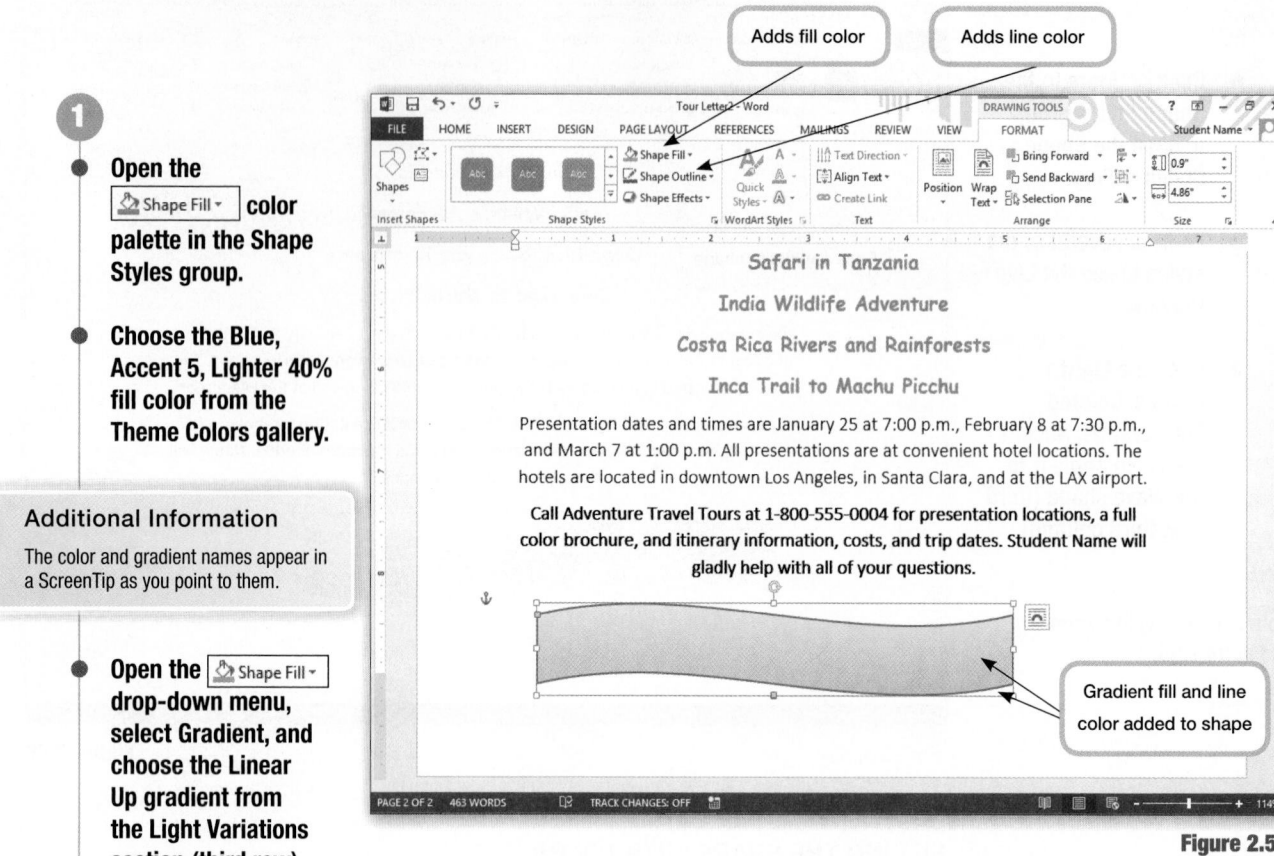Shape Fill ▾ color palette in the Shape Styles group.

- Choose the Blue, Accent 5, Lighter 40% fill color from the Theme Colors gallery.

- Open the Shape Fill ▾ drop-down menu, select Gradient, and choose the Linear Up gradient from the Light Variations section (third row).

- In the same manner, open the Shape Outline ▾ menu and choose Blue, Accent 5 from the Theme Colors bar.

Your screen should be similar to Figure 2.56

Figure 2.56

ADDING TEXT TO A SHAPE

Next you will add information about the company's website to the shape. It will include the website's address, called a **URL** (Uniform Resource Locator). Word automatically recognizes URLs you enter and creates a hyperlink. A **hyperlink** is a connection to a location in the current document, another document, or a website. It allows the reader to jump to the referenced location by clicking the hyperlink text when reading the document on the screen.

1

● Right-click the shape to open the context menu.

● Choose Add Text.

● Type Visit our website at www.adventuretraveltours.com and press [Spacebar].

● If necessary, adjust the shape size to fully display the text.

● Click outside the shape to deselect it.

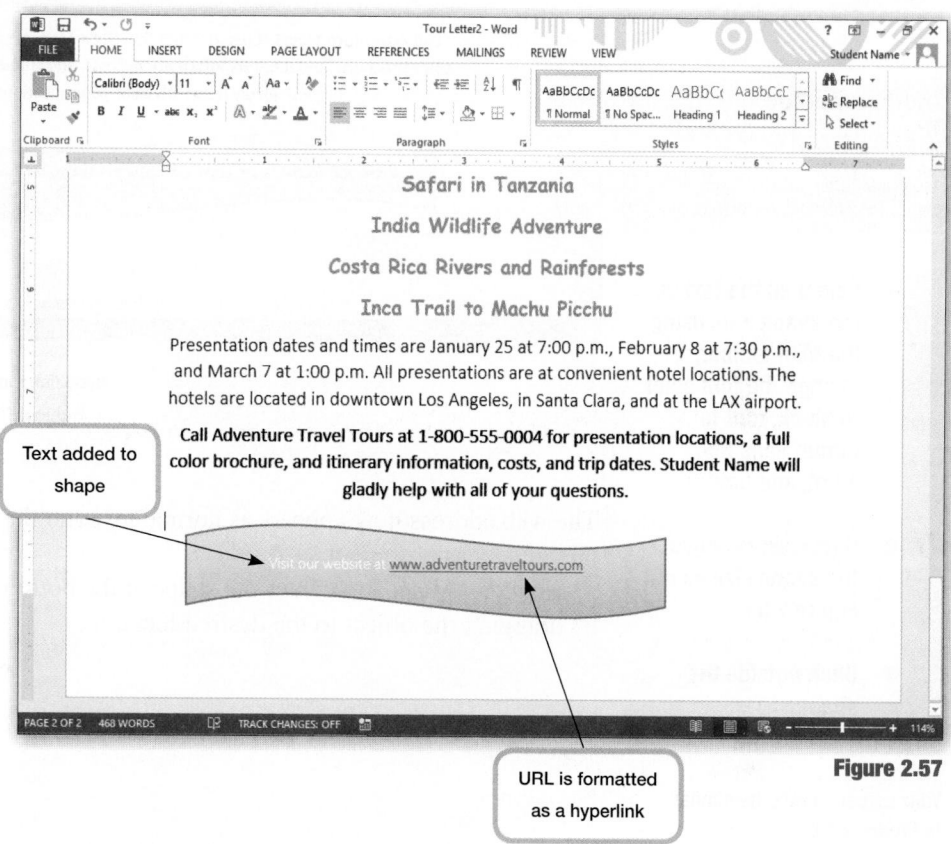

Figure 2.57

Your screen should be similar to **Figure 2.57**

The text appears in the default font settings. The text color is white because the default font color setting is Automatic. The Automatic setting changes the text color to black if the background fill color is light and white if the fill color is dark.

The web address is automatically formatted in blue and underlined, indicating the entry is a hyperlink. The AutoFormat feature automatically formats a web address, replaces ordinals (1st) with a superscript (1st) and fractions (1/2) with fraction characters (½), and applys a bulleted list format to a list if you type an asterisk (*) followed by a space at the beginning of a paragraph. AutoFormat features can be turned off if the corrections are not needed in the document.

Because this is a document you plan to print, you do not want the text displayed as a link. Since the hyperlink was created using the AutoFormat feature, you can undo the correction or turn it off using the AutoCorrect Options button. You also can choose Remove Hyperlink from the hyperlink's context menu.

Additional Information

You can turn off the AutoFormat feature so the hyperlinks are not created automatically. To do this, open the File tab, Options, choose Proofing, AutoCorrect Options. Next, open the AutoFormat tab and clear the Internet and network paths with hyperlinks option.

Right-click the hyperlink and choose Remove Hyperlink from the context menu.

Additional Information

A ScreenTip appears when you point to a hyperlink with instructions on how to follow a link.

Another Method

You also could click ↶ Undo immediately after entering a URL to remove the hyperlink formatting.

Select all the text in the shape and, using the Mini toolbar, change the font color to black, font to Comic Sans MS, 12 pt, and bold.

If necessary, adjust the shape size as in Figure 2.58.

Click outside the shape.

Your screen should be similar to **Figure 2.58**

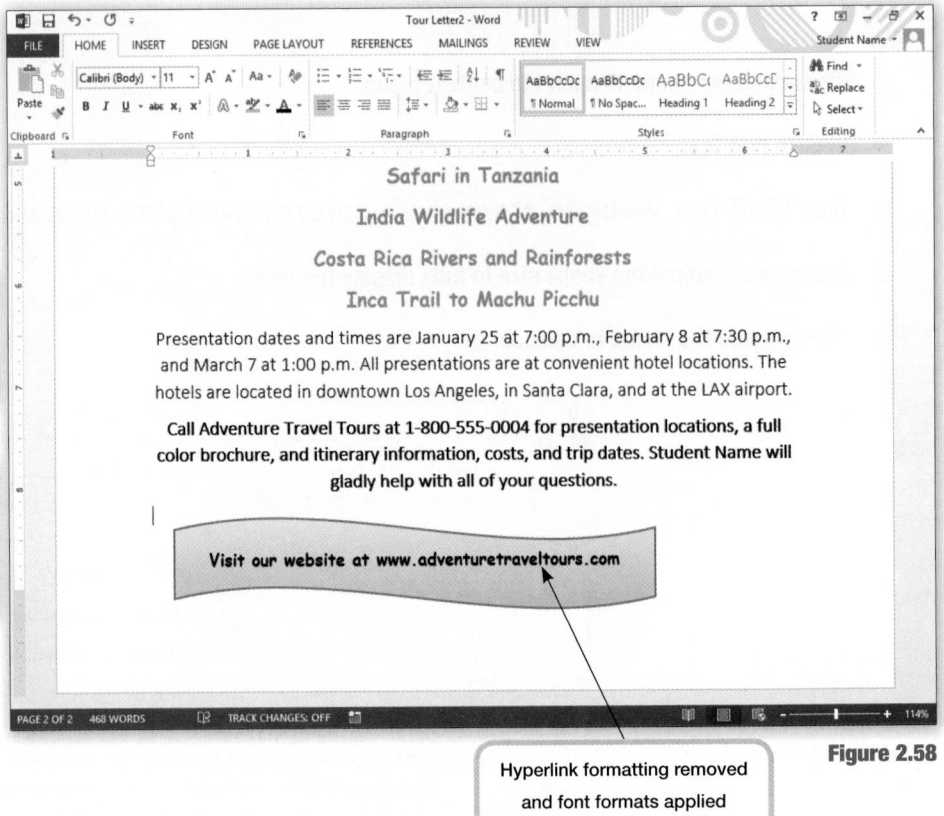

Safari in Tanzania

India Wildlife Adventure

Costa Rica Rivers and Rainforests

Inca Trail to Machu Picchu

Presentation dates and times are January 25 at 7:00 p.m., February 8 at 7:30 p.m., and March 7 at 1:00 p.m. All presentations are at convenient hotel locations. The hotels are located in downtown Los Angeles, in Santa Clara, and at the LAX airport.

Call Adventure Travel Tours at 1-800-555-0004 for presentation locations, a full color brochure, and itinerary information, costs, and trip dates. Student Name will gladly help with all of your questions.

Visit our website at www.adventuretraveltours.com

Hyperlink formatting removed and font formats applied

Figure 2.58

The web address now appears as normal text and the font changes make the entire line much easier to read.

Finally, you need to center the shape at the bottom of the flyer. You will do this by dragging the object to the desired location.

3

● Drag the shape and use the alignment guide to center it, as shown in Figure 2.59.

Having Trouble?

Review the section Sizing and Moving a Graphic in Lab 1 for help with using the alignment guide.

● Click outside the shape to deselect it.

● Save the document again.

Your screen should be similar to Figure 2.59

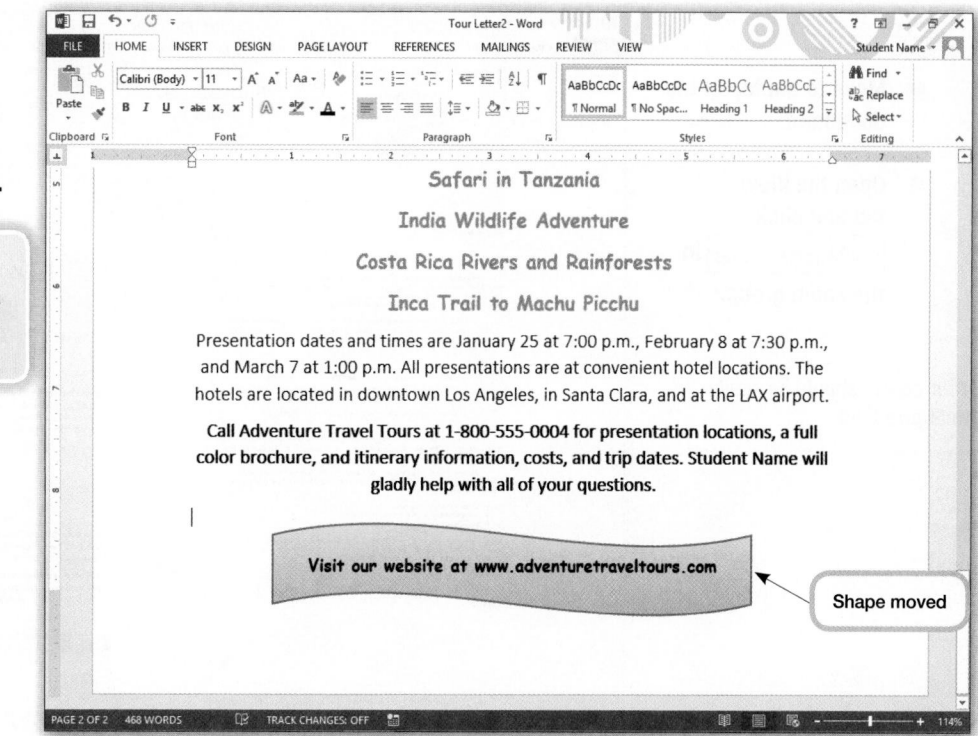

Figure 2.59

The banner complements the colors used in the flyer and adds the needed information about the website.

Finalizing the Document

Next you will check out the layout of the document and make any final changes to the letter and flyer before printing it.

VIEWING THE ENTIRE DOCUMENT

First, you want to display both pages of your document at the same time in the window.

1

- Move to the top of the document.

- Open the View tab and click 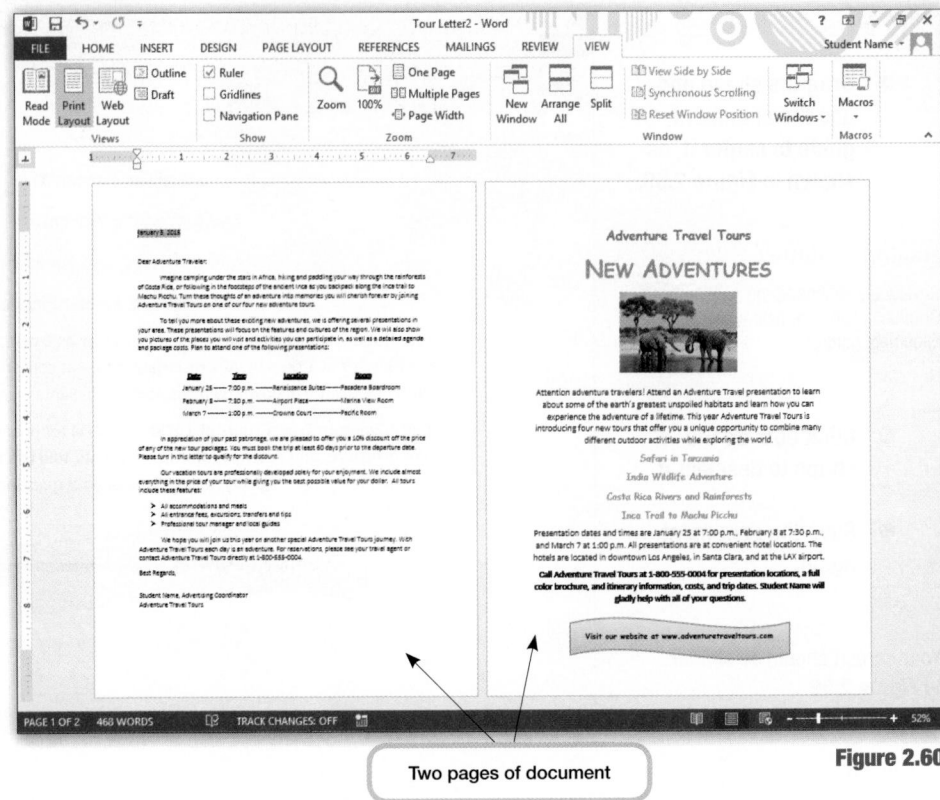 Multiple Pages in the Zoom group.

Your screen should be similar to **Figure 2.60**

Two pages of document

Figure 2.60

Now that you can see the entire letter, you decide to indent the date and closing to the 3.5-inch tab position. You will select both these items at the same time and then change the indent. To select nonadjacent areas in a document, hold down Ctrl while selecting each additional area.

2

- Select the date.

- Hold down Ctrl and select the closing.

- Drag the ▽ First Line Indent marker to the 3.5-inch position.

Your screen should be similar to **Figure 2.61**

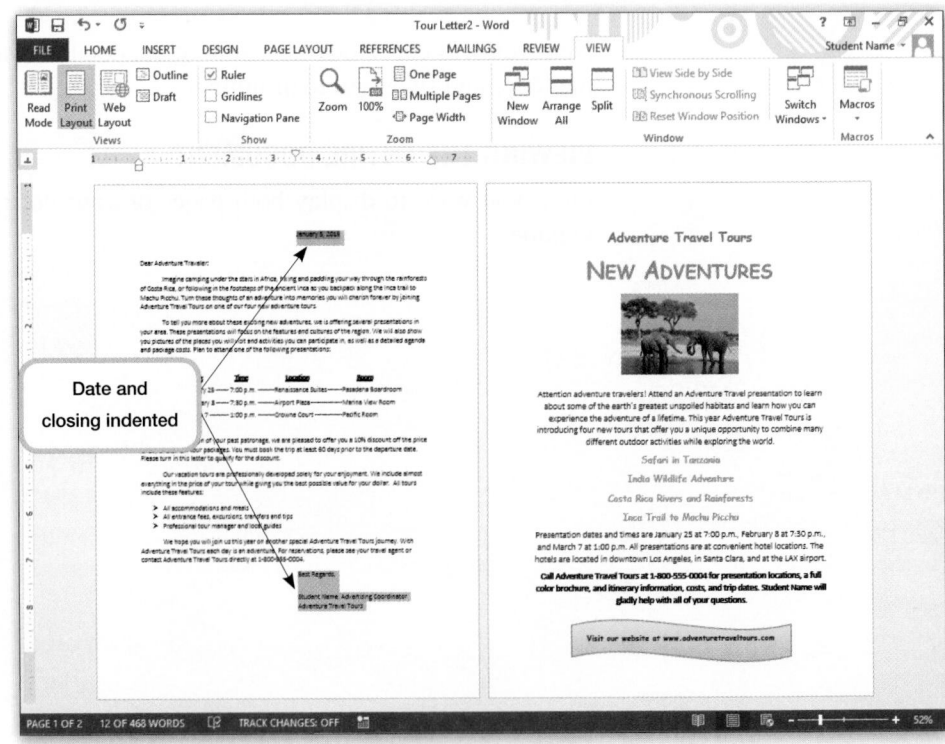

Date and closing indented

Figure 2.61

While looking at the document, you decide to emphasize the list of tour features by adding bold. You also want to decrease the space between the tour names in the flyer.

3

- **Select the three bulleted items.**

- **Click** **B** **Bold on the Mini toolbar.**

Having Trouble?

If the date at the top of the document moved back to the left margin, select the date and then repeat dragging the First Line Indent marker to the 3.5-inch position.

- **Select the list of four tours in the flyer.**

- **Change the line spacing to Single.**

- **Move to the beginning of the following paragraph, click** **≡** **Line and Paragraph Spacing, and choose Add Space Before Paragraph.**

Your screen should be similar to **Figure 2.62**

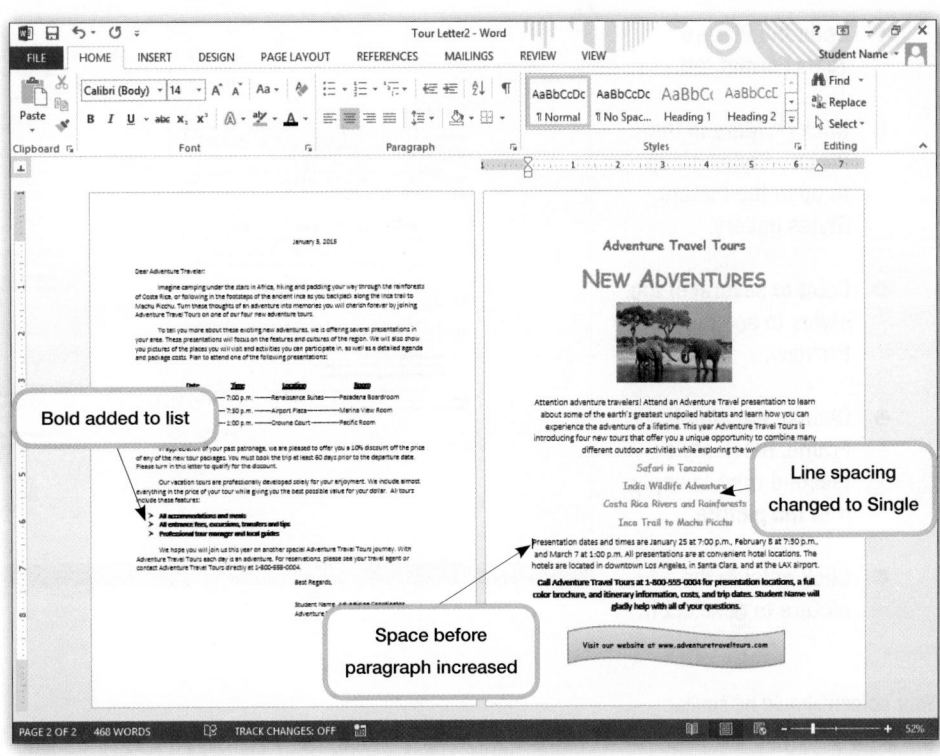

Figure 2.62

APPLYING A PICTURE STYLE

Additional Information

You can also customize many other individual aspects of a picture using the 🖼 Picture Border ▾ and 🖼 Picture Effects ▾ buttons on the Picture Tools Format toolbar. In addition, the Format Picture dialog box, which you can access from the picture's context menu, provides even more options for enhancing your pictures.

While looking at the document, you decide to enhance the picture in the flyer using a picture style. Picture styles change the appearance of a picture's border and apply special effects such as a shadowed or beveled edge.

- ● Click the elephant picture to select it.

- ● Open the Picture Tools Format tab.

- ● Click ⯆ More in the Picture Styles group to open the Picture Styles gallery.

- ● Point to several of the styles to see the Live Preview.

- ● Choose the Simple Frame, Black style (second row) to apply it to the picture.

- ● Click outside the picture to deselect it.

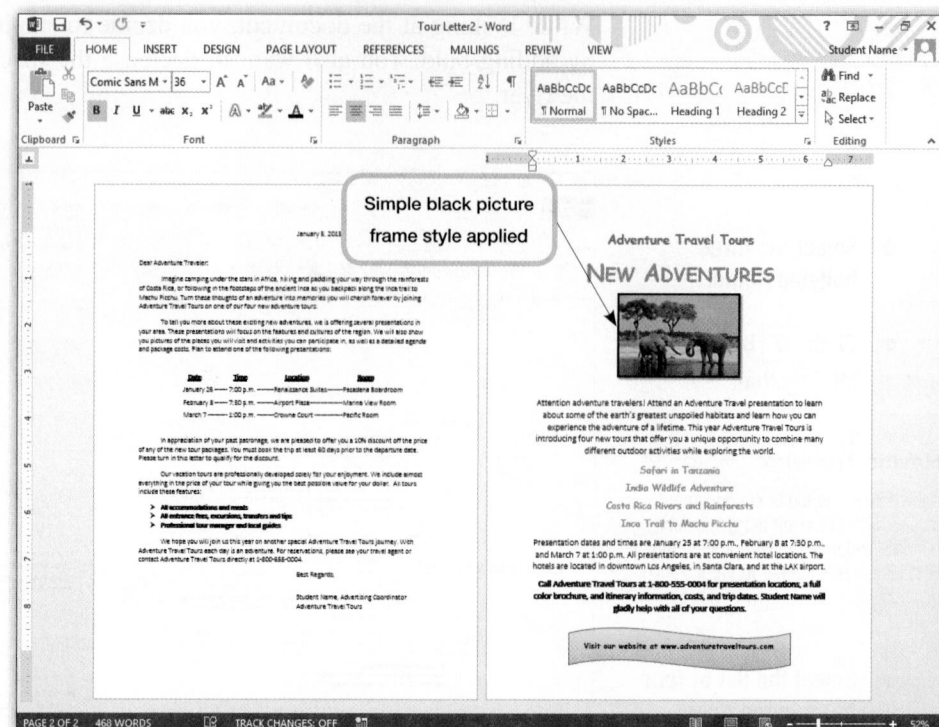

Figure 2.63

Your screen should be similar to Figure 2.63

INSERTING A SECTION BREAK

Next you will make the margins of the letter only narrower. Many format and layout settings, including margin settings, when applied affect an entire document. To apply layout or formatting changes to a portion of a document, you need to create separate sections in the document by inserting section breaks.

Concept 10 Section

To format parts of a document differently, you divide a document into sections. Initially a document is one section. To separate a document into different parts, you insert section breaks. **Section break** identifies the end of a section and stores the document format settings associated with that section of the document. Once a document is divided into sections, the following formats can be changed for individual sections: margins, paper size and orientation, paper source for a printer, page borders, vertical alignment, headers and footers, columns, page numbering, line numbering, and footnotes and endnotes.

The three types of section breaks, described below, control the location where the text following a section break begins.

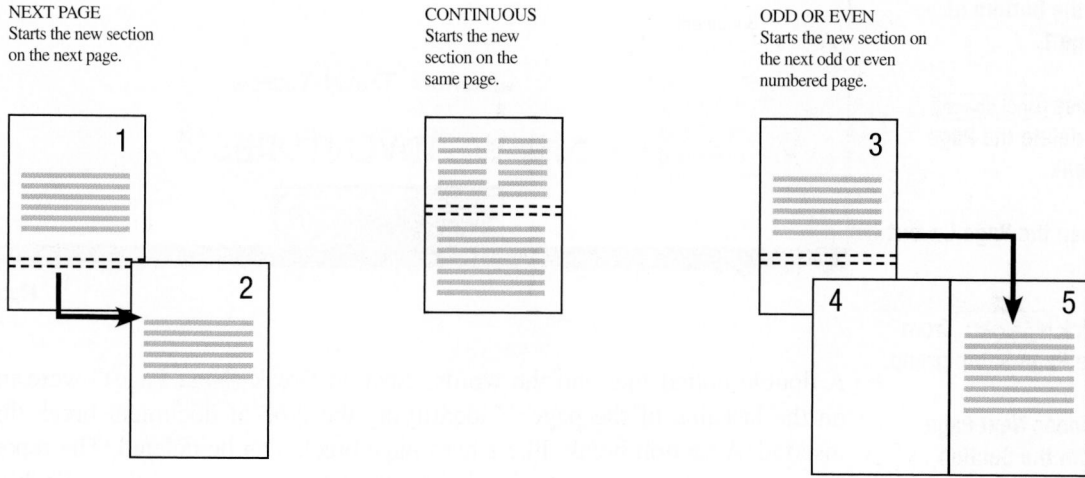

NEXT PAGE
Starts the new section
on the next page.

CONTINUOUS
Starts the new
section on the
same page.

ODD OR EVEN
Starts the new section on
the next odd or even
numbered page.

If you delete a section break, the preceding text becomes part of the following section and assumes its section formatting.

Additional Information

You can right-click on the status bar and select the Section option to display document section information in the status bar.

Because you do not want the new margin settings to affect the flyer portion of your document, you will divide the document into two sections. To do this, you will delete the Page Break code located at the bottom of page 1 and insert a Next Page section break at the same location.

- Turn on the display of paragraph marks.

- Increase the zoom to 100% and then scroll to view the bottom of page 1 and the top of page 2.

- Position the insertion point to the right of the Page Break line at the bottom of page 1.

- Press [Backspace] to delete the Page Break.

- Open the Page Layout tab.

- Click [Breaks ▾] from the Page Setup group.

- Choose Next Page from the Section Breaks category.

- Press [Delete] to delete the paragraph mark located at the top of page 2.

- Save the document.

Your screen should be similar to Figure 2.64

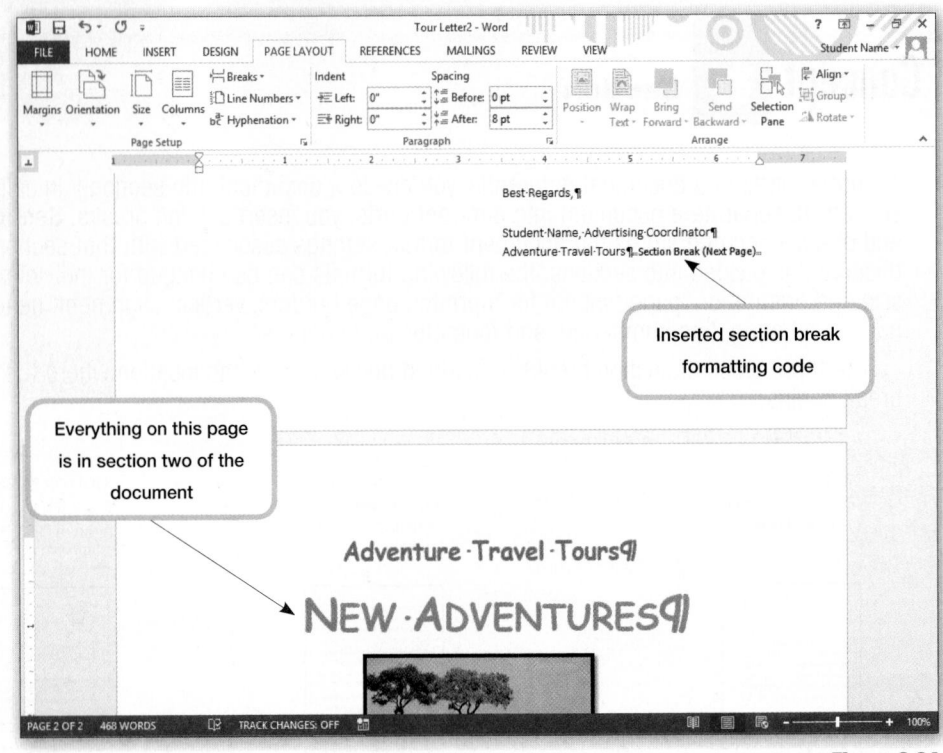

Figure 2.64

A double dotted line and the words "Section Break (Next Page)" were inserted on the last line of the page 1, identifying the type of document break that was inserted. A section break, like a hard page break, can be deleted. The report now contains one section break that divides the letter into two sections. Each section can be formatted independently.

SETTING PAGE MARGINS

The default document setting for the left and right margins is 1 inch. You would like to see how the document would look if you decreased the size of the right and left margin widths for just the letter portion of the document (page 1). Because a section break appears at the bottom of page 1, you can format page 1 independently of page 2.

Concept 11 Page Margin

The **page margin** is the blank space around the edge of a page. Generally, the text you enter appears in the printable area inside the margins. However, some items can be positioned in the margin space. You can set different page margin widths to alter the appearance of the document.

Standard single-sided documents have four margins: top, bottom, left, and right. Double-sided documents with facing pages, such as books and magazines, also have four margins: top, bottom, inside, and outside. These documents typically use mirror margins in which the left page is a mirror image of the right page. This means that the inside margins are the same width and the outside margins are the same width. (See the illustrations below.)

You also can set a "gutter" margin that reserves space on the left side of single-sided documents, or on the inside margin of double-sided documents, to accommodate binding. There are also special margin settings for headers and footers. (You will learn about these features in Lab 3.)

Single-sided with gutter

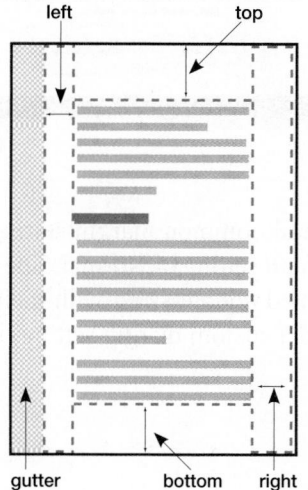

Double-sided with facing pages

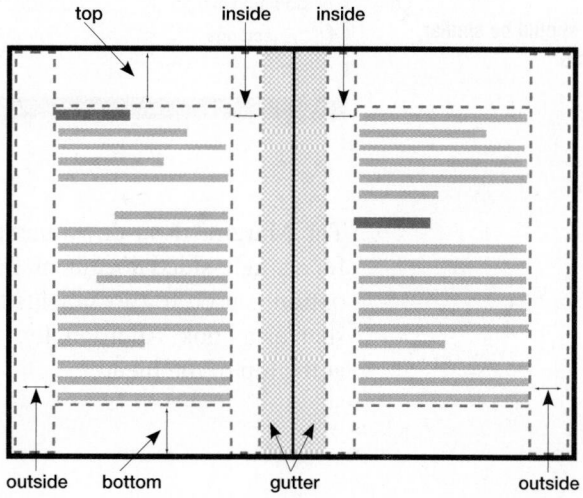

The Page Setup group is used to change settings associated with the layout of the entire page.

Reduce the zoom to 55% and turn off the display of paragraph marks.

Move the insertion point to anywhere on page 1.

Open the Page Layout tab.

Click Margins **in the Page Setup group.**

Your screen should be similar to Figure 2.65

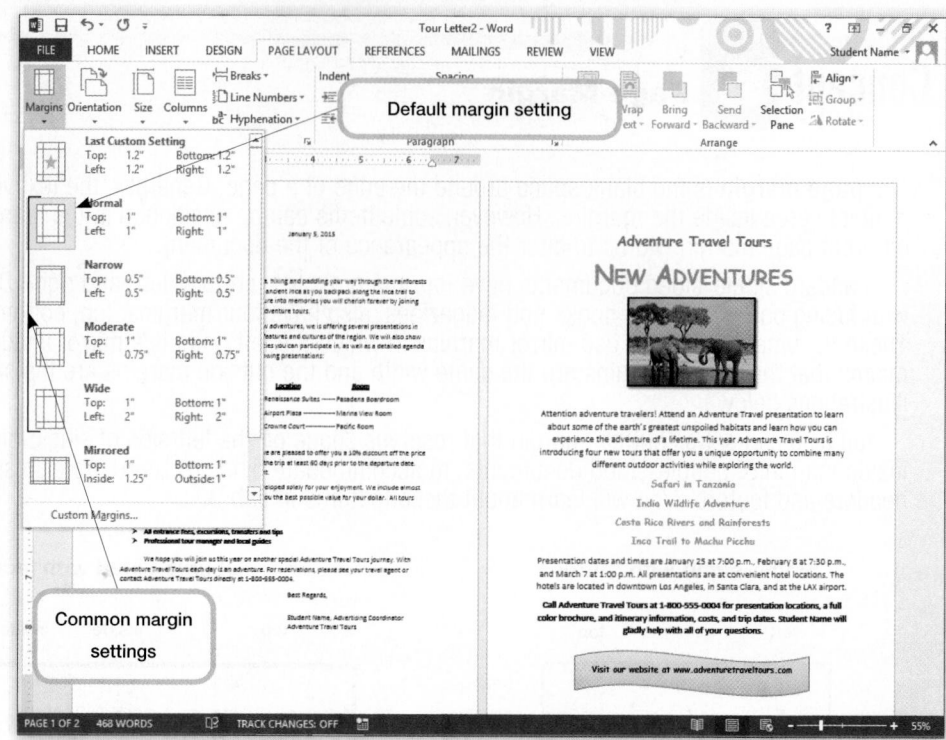

Figure 2.65

The Margins drop-down menu displays several common margin setting options for a single-sided document, including the default setting of Normal. The Mirrored option is used for documents that will be printed double-sided with facing pages, such as a book. Additionally, if you have used a custom margin setting, it appears at the top of the menu.

2
● **Choose Narrow.**

**Your screen should be similar
to Figure 2.66**

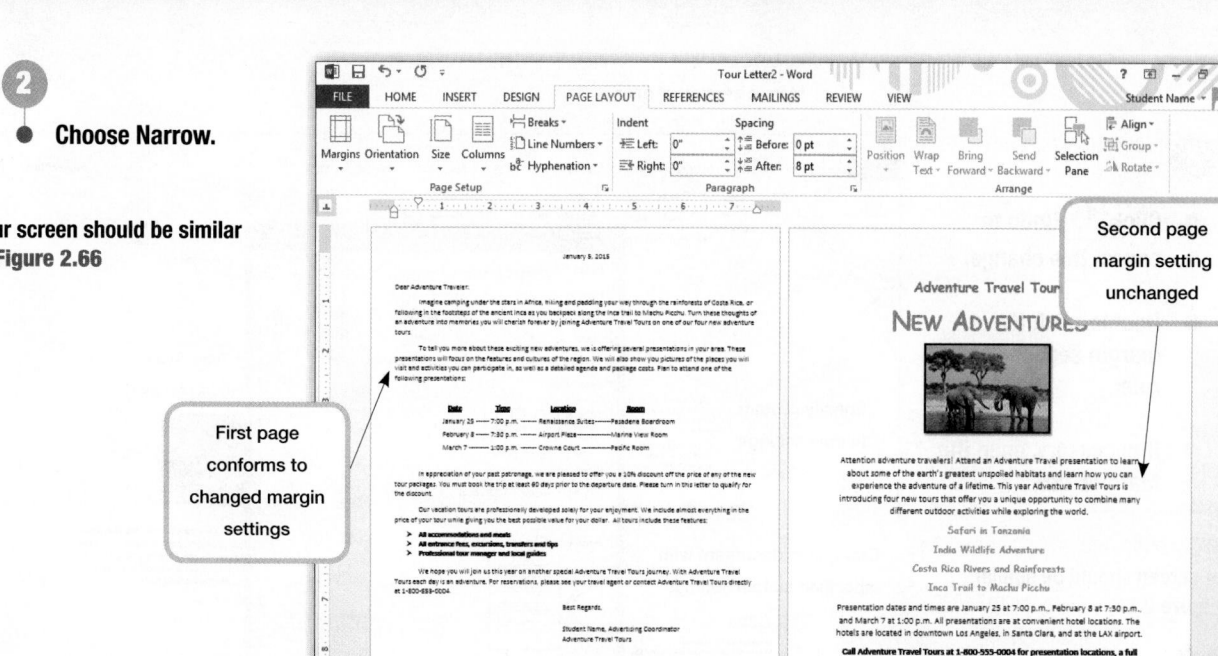

First page
conforms to
changed margin
settings

Second page
margin setting
unchanged

Figure 2.66

The first page of the document was reformatted to the narrow margin settings, however, the second page remains unchanged. It remains unchanged because the margin setting affects only the current section, which in this case consists of page 1. If you hadn't inserted the section break, the entire document would conform to the narrow margin settings.

You do not like this setting and will undo the change. Then you will create a custom setting to change the first page of the document to have 1.2-inch margins all around. Custom margin settings are specified using the Custom Margins option on the Margins drop-down menu. You also can double-click the margin section of the ruler to access this feature.

Additional Information

Use the Custom Margins option if you want the new margin settings to be saved for future use.

- Click 🔄 Undo to cancel this change.

- Double-click the margin section of the ruler.

- If necessary, open the Margins tab.

Your screen should be similar to Figure 2.67

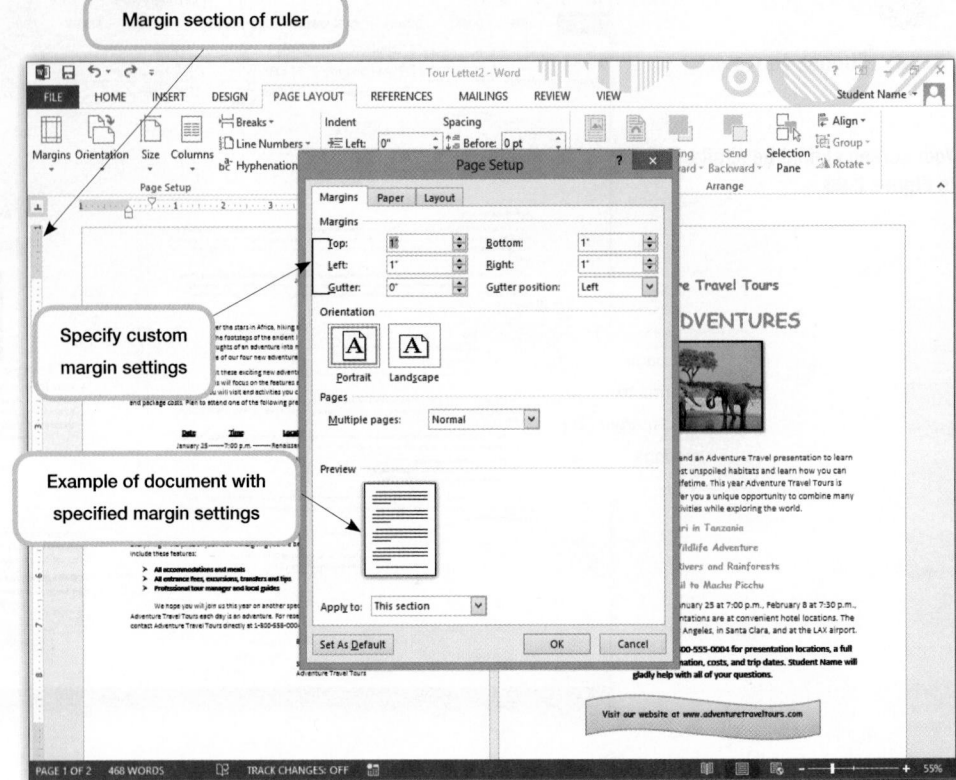

Margin section of ruler

Specify custom margin settings

Example of document with specified margin settings

Figure 2.67

The Margins tab of the Page Setup dialog box displays the default margin settings for a single-sided document. The Preview box shows how the current margin settings will appear on a page. New margin settings can be entered by typing the value in the text box, or by clicking the ▲ Up and ▼ Down scroll buttons or pressing the ↑ or ↓ key to increase or decrease the settings by tenths of an inch.

- **Using any of these methods, set the top, bottom and side margins to 1.2 inch.**

- **Click** OK **.**

Your screen should be similar to Figure 2.68

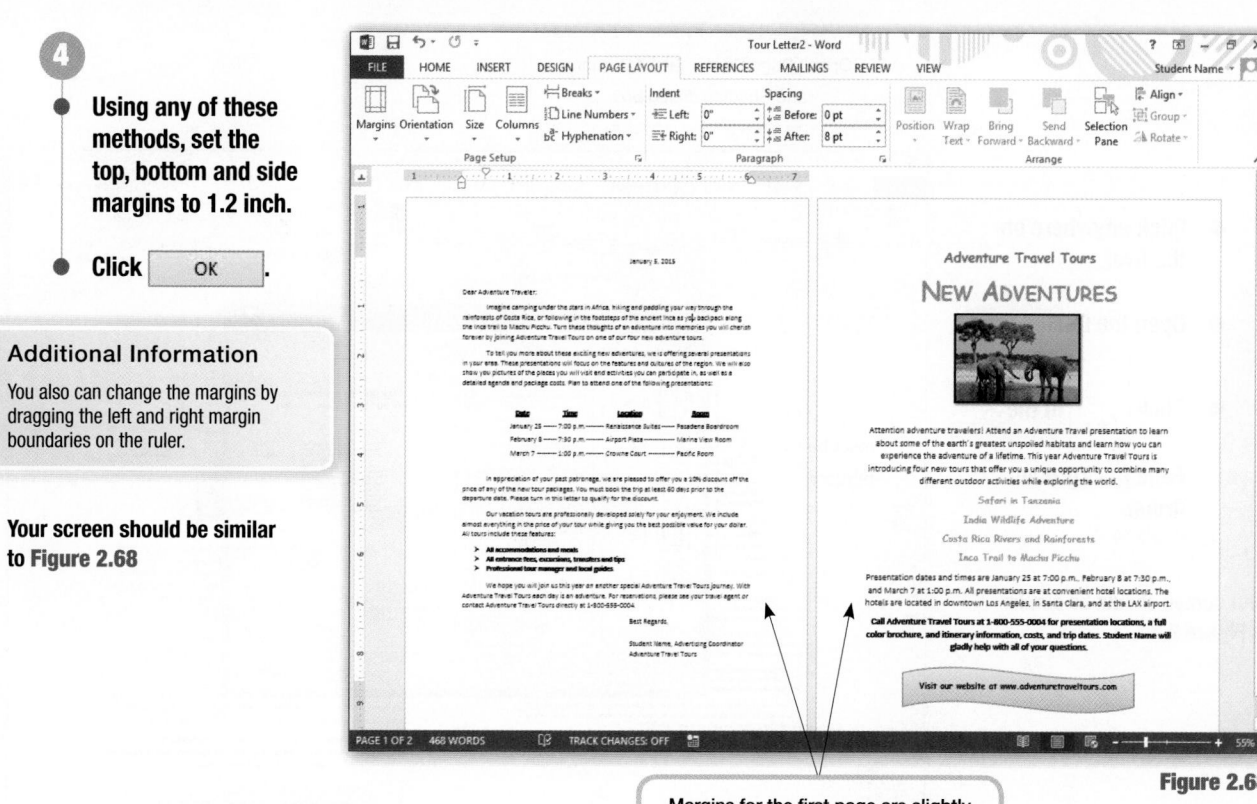

Figure 2.68

Margins for the first page are slightly larger than those for the second page

Although the text is difficult to read, you can easily see the layout of the pages and that the margin settings for the first page have been changed slightly. The margins for the flyer have not changed.

ADDING A PAGE BORDER

Finally, you want to add a decorative border around only the flyer to enclose it and enhance its appearance.

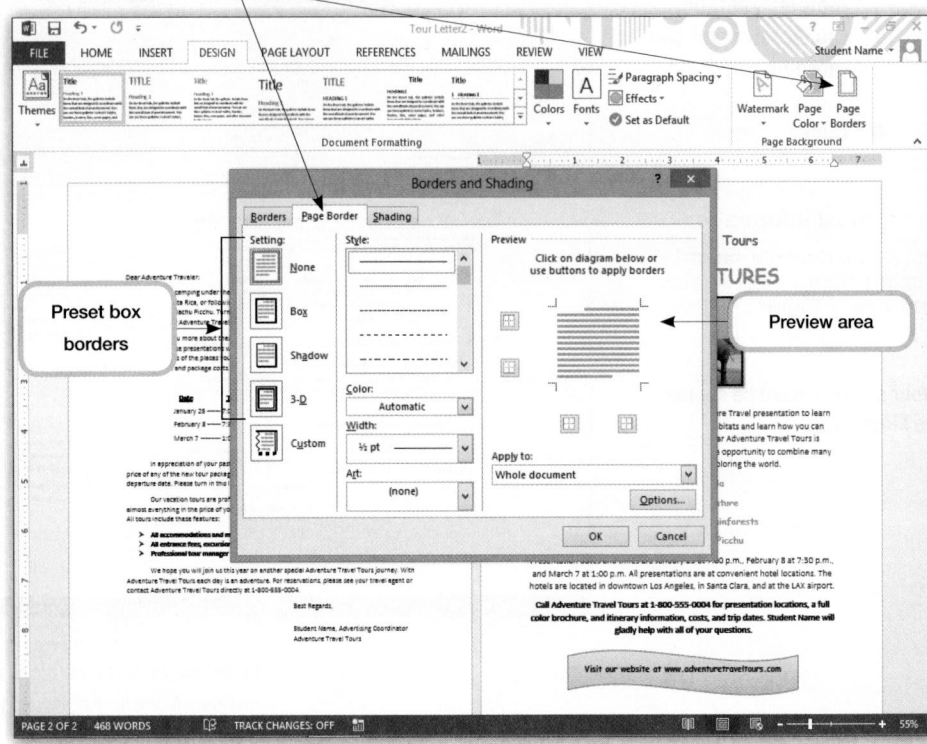

Opens Page Border tab of Borders and Shading dialog box

1

- Click anywhere on the flyer.

- Open the Design tab.

- Click [Page Borders] in the **Page Background group.**

Your screen should be similar to Figure 2.69

Preset box borders

Preview area

Figure 2.69

Additional Information

There are also a variety of graphical borders available in the Art drop-down list.

From the Page Border tab of the Borders and Shading dialog box, select either a preset box border or a custom border. Then specify the style, color, weight, and location of the border. A page border can be applied to all pages in a document, to all pages in the current section, to the first page of a section, or to every page except the first page of a section.

You want to create a box border around the entire page of text. As you specify the border settings, the Preview area will reflect your selections.

2

● Choose Box in the Setting area.

● From the Style list box, select

┌─────────────┐
│ ─ ─ ─ ─ ─ ─ │
└─────────────┘
.

● Open the Color gallery and select Blue from the Standard Colors bar.

● From the Width drop-down list box, choose 3 pt.

Your screen should be similar to Figure 2.70

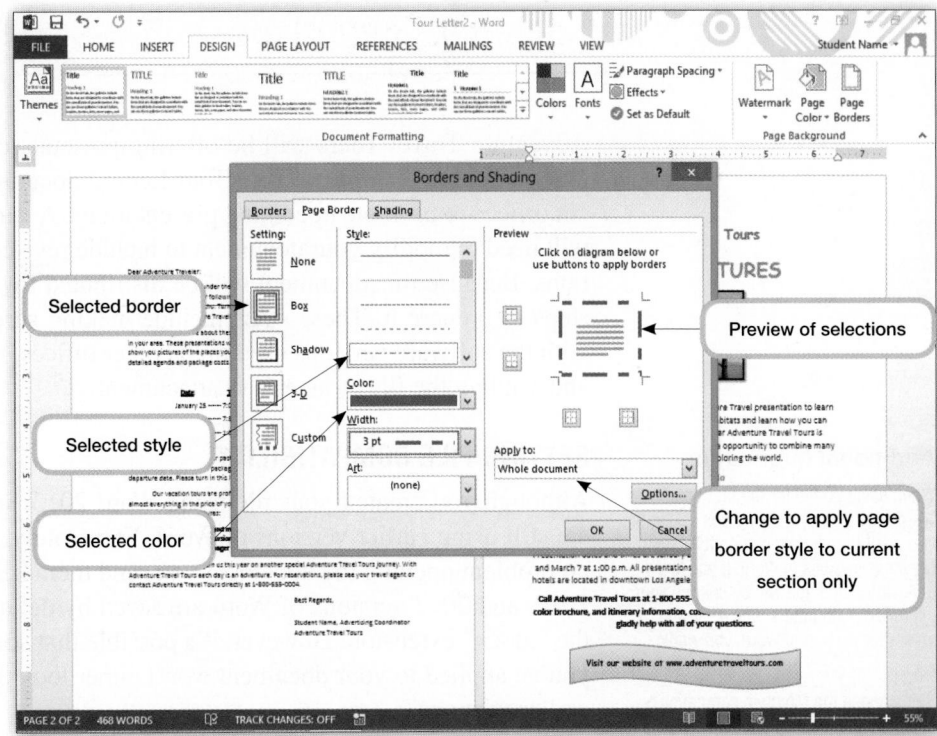

Figure 2.70

Having Trouble?

Use the None option to remove all border lines, or remove individual lines by selecting the border location again.

The Preview area shows how the box page border will appear in the style, color, and point size you selected. The default selection of Whole Document needs to be changed since you want the border setting to affect only page 2 of the document (the current section).

3

● Choose "This section" from the Apply To drop-down list.

● Click OK.

● If necessary, reposition or resize the Wave shape so that it is not touching the page border, and then click outside the shape to deselect it.

Having Trouble?

If your document extends to a third page, reduce the size of the graphic until it fits on two pages.

● Save the document.

Your screen should be similar to Figure 2.71

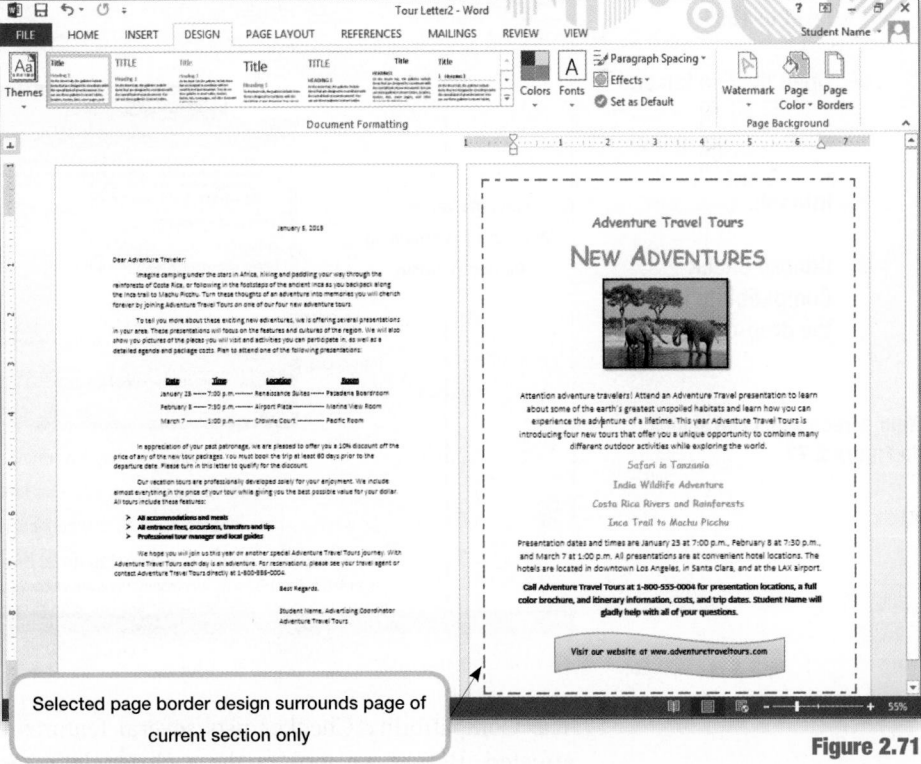

Figure 2.71

The selected page border appears around only the second page of the document.

Securing Content

Adventure Travel Tours will be offering presentations around the country in the cities where it has offices. Your Tour Letter2 document will be used by the different offices to promote upcoming presentations. A staff member in each ATT office will need to modify your document to include revised presentation dates and locations. Because this document will be distributed for use, you need to take several steps to prepare it. These steps include making sure that your file is compatible with the software versions used in the other offices, removing private information, and sending the file as an e-mail attachment.

SETTING FILE COMPATIBILITY

Additional Information

When saving a file for the first time, Word may display a dialog box asking if you want to maintain compatibility with previous versions of Word. If you know in advance that you will be sharing your document with others who are using an earlier version of Word, you would click [Cancel] in this dialog box and then choose the Maintain compatibility check box. If you don't do this, some formatting features of your 2013 document may appear somewhat different in Word 2003, 2007, and 2010.

Although you created your file using Word 2013, some of the other ATT offices are still using earlier versions of Word. Fortunately, your co-workers should have no problem opening the document you send them because documents in the 2007, 2010, and 2013 versions of Word are saved by default to a file format defined by the ".docx" extension. However, it's possible that some of the Word 2013 features you've applied to your document won't either look the same or be available in the earlier versions.

You want to make sure that those co-workers who are using earlier versions of Word will be able to see all the features you've included in the document you send them. The **Compatibility Checker** lists any features that aren't compatible with the previous versions of Word and the number of occurrences in the document.

1

- Change the zoom level to 100%.

- Open the File tab and click 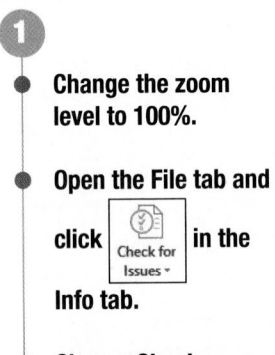 in the Info tab.

- Choose Check Compatibility from the drop-down list.

Your screen should be similar to Figure 2.72

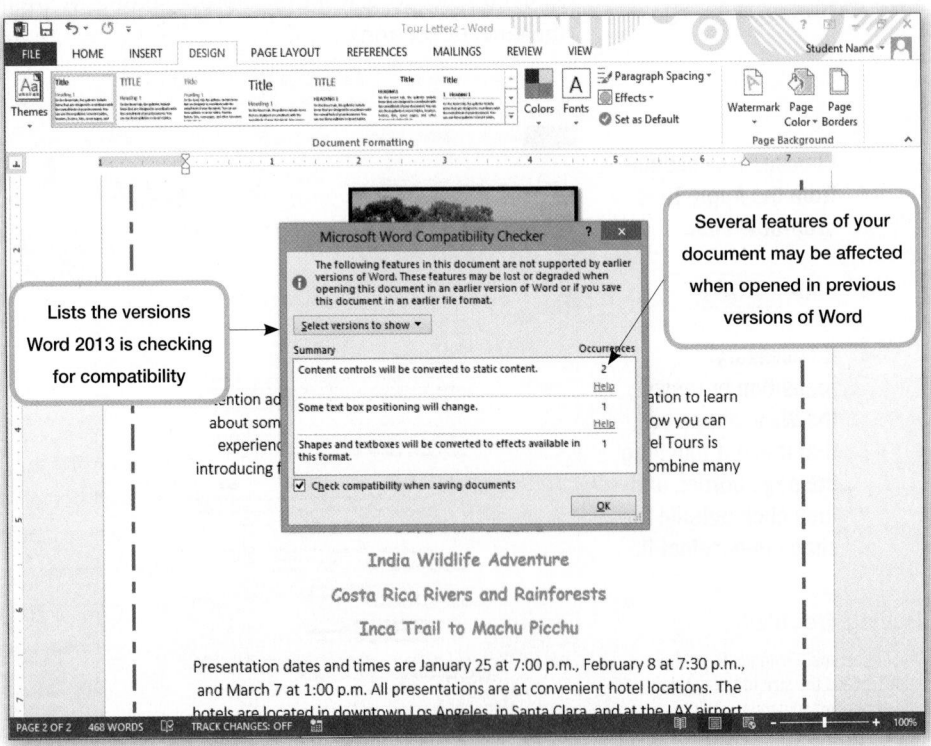

Figure 2.72

The Compatibility Checker lists several features of your document that may be affected. Before we look at these closer, let's see if these problems will affect Word 2007 and 2010 users.

2

- Click  to open the drop-down list.

- Deselect Word 97-2003.

Your screen should be similar to Figure 2.73

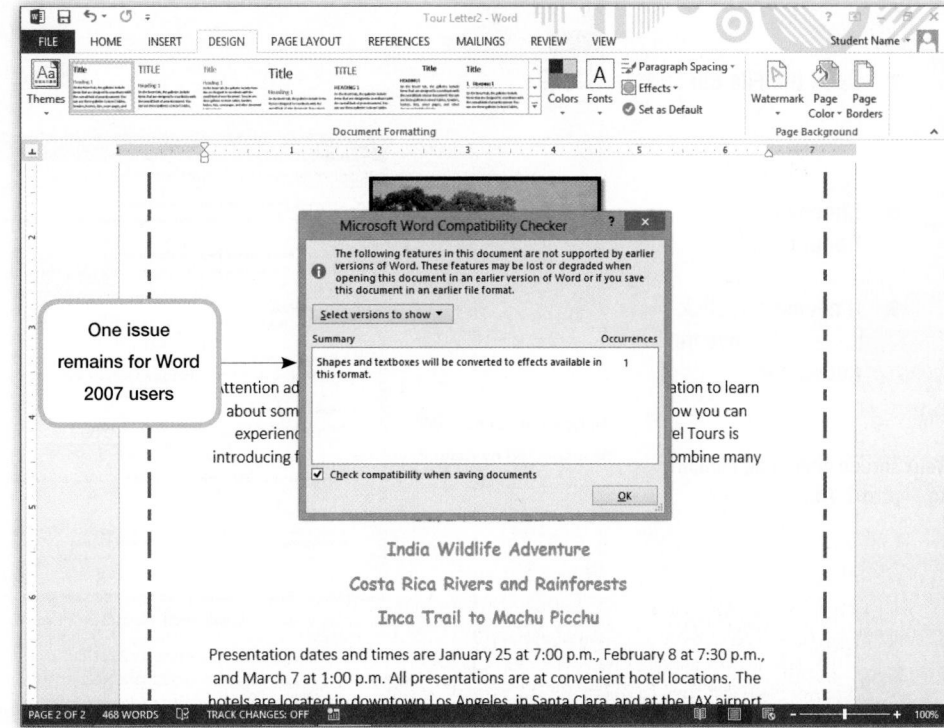

One issue remains for Word 2007 users

Figure 2.73

The dialog box indicates that the shapes and textboxes in your Word 2013 document might not look exactly the same in these versions. As a result, the Wave shape might appear somewhat different to your co-workers when they open the document.

3

- Click ___OK___.

CHECKING FOR PRIVATE INFORMATION

Before you give a file to another user, it is a good idea to check the document for hidden data or personal information that may be stored in the computer itself or in the document's properties that you may not want to share. To help locate and remove this information, you can use the Document Inspector.

Additional Information

It is a good idea to save a backup copy of a document before using Document Inspector, as it is not always possible to restore data that was removed by this feature.

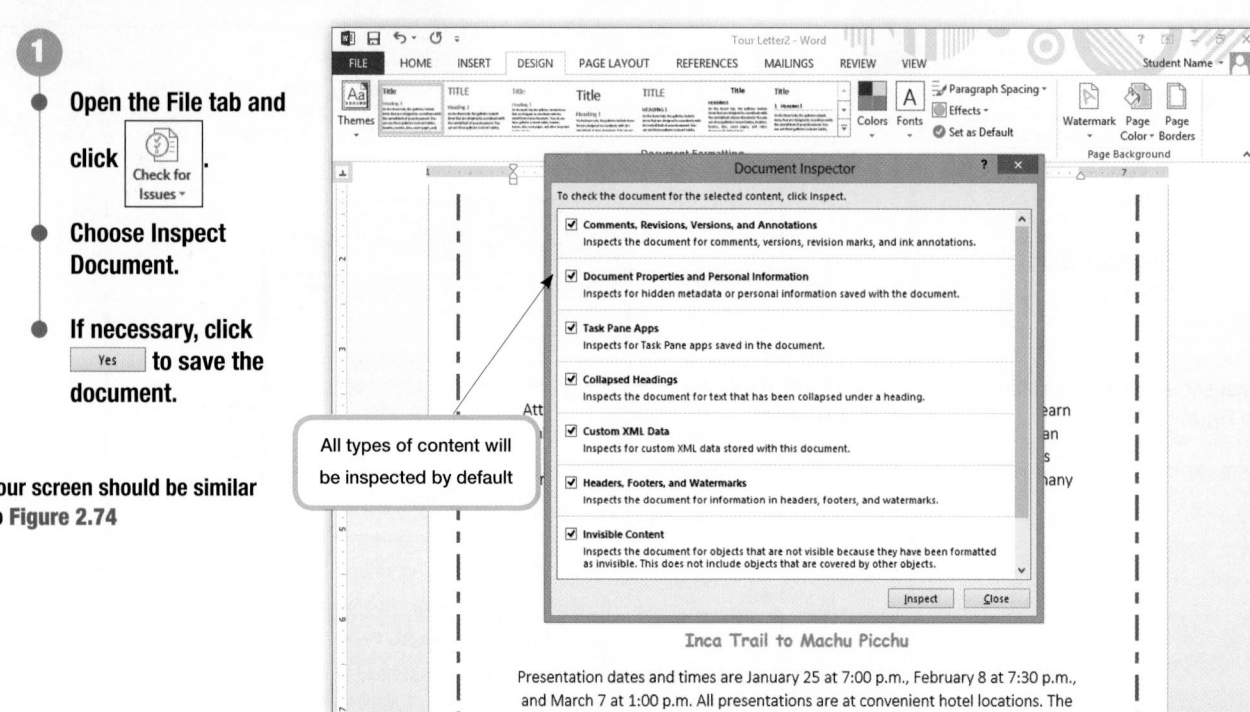

1

- Open the File tab and click [Check for Issues].

- Choose Inspect Document.

- If necessary, click [Yes] to save the document.

Your screen should be similar to Figure 2.74

All types of content will be inspected by default

Figure 2.74

Using the Document Inspector dialog box, you can specify the type of content you want inspected by checking each of the types described in the following table.

Type	Removes
Comments, Revisions, Versions, and Annotations	Comments, tracked changes revision marks, document version information, and ink annotations.
Document Properties and Personal Information	All document properties, including statistical information, e-mail headers, routing slips, send-to-review information, document server properties, content type information, user name, template name.
Task Pane Apps	Task pane apps saved in the document.
Collapsed Headings	Text that has been collapsed under a heading.
Custom XML Data	All custom XML data that was stored within the document.
Headers, Footers, and Watermarks	All information in headers and footers as well as watermarks.
Invisible Content	All content that has been formatted as invisible.
Hidden text	Any text that was formatted as hidden.

You will inspect the Tour Letter2 document for all types of information.

● **If necessary, select all eight types of content to check.**

● **Click** Inspect **.**

Your screen should be similar to Figure 2.75

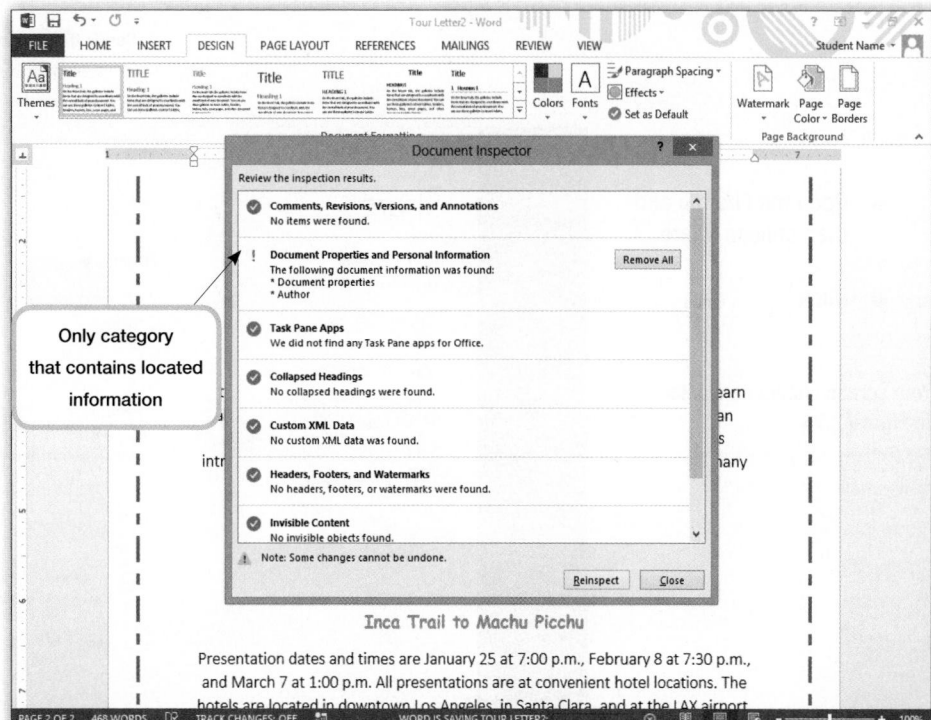

Only category that contains located information

Figure 2.75

The Inspector results show that only Document Properties and Personal Information were located. For any located items, you have the option of removing the information. To remove any located information, you would click Remove All next to each item in the list; otherwise, the information is maintained. You want to maintain your name and the company name in the document properties and will close the Document Inspector without removing this information.

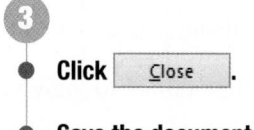

● **Click** Close **.**

● **Save the document.**

NOTE Skip this section if you do not have an e-mail program installed on your system and an Internet connection.

E-mailing a Document

You will send the document to your co-workers via e-mail.

Next, you want to provide a copy of the document to the other Adventure Travel Tours offices. Word provides several methods for sharing your document, as described in the table below.

Share Option	Description
Invite People	Document can be shared with others once it is saved to a SkyDrive location.
Email	Sends the document via your e-mail program.
Present Online	Creates a link to the document that makes it available to anyone while you are presenting in a web browser through the Office Presentation service.
Publish as Blog Post	Publishes your document to the web as a blog post.

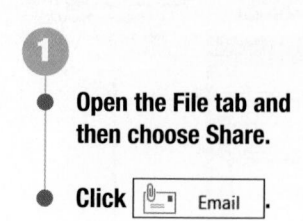

Open the File tab and then choose Share.

Click [📧 Email].

Your screen should be similar to Figure 2.76

Sends the current document as an attachment

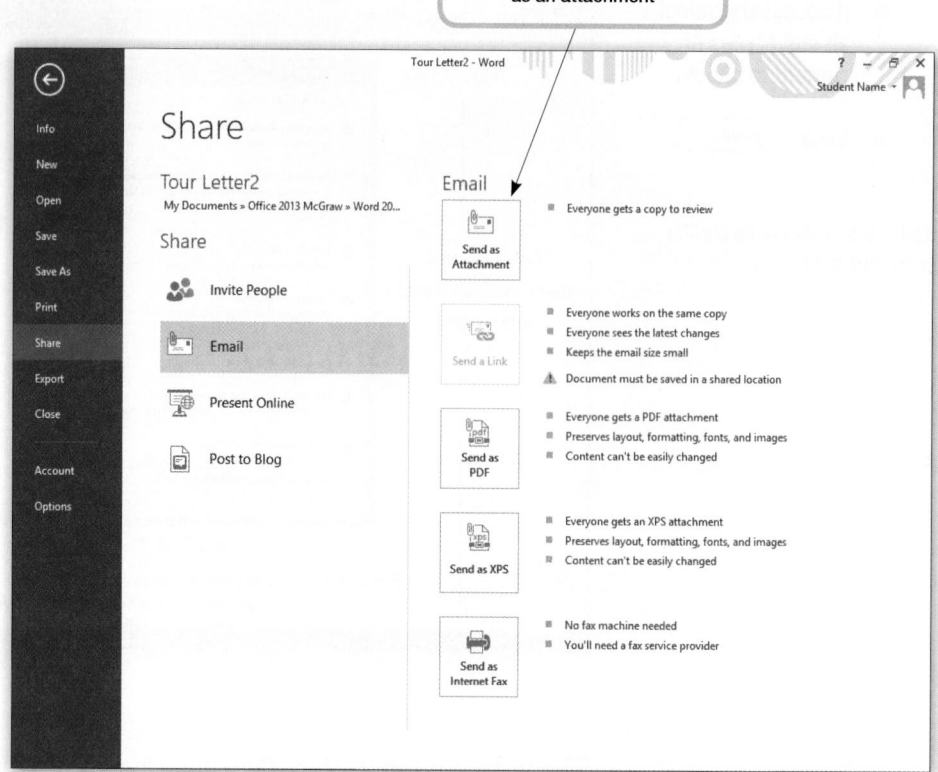

Figure 2.76

When using e-mail to share your document, Word provides several options. You can send the document as an **attachment**, which is a file that is sent with the e-mail message but is not part of the e-mail text. You can attach the document in a Word format using [📧 Send as Attachment], in a PDF format using [📄 Send as PDF], or in an XPS format using [📄 Send as XPS]. The PDF and XPS formats allow others to view your document but not make changes to it. Alternatively, if your document is saved on a shared storage device, such as on a SharePoint server, you can include a hyperlink in your e-mail message that references your document using [🔗 Send a Link]. Finally, if you subscribe to an Internet fax service, you can choose to send your document as a fax using [🖨 Send as Internet Fax]. You will send your document as an e-mail attachment.

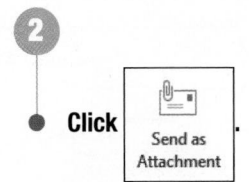

● **Click** [Send as Attachment]

Your screen should be similar to Figure 2.77

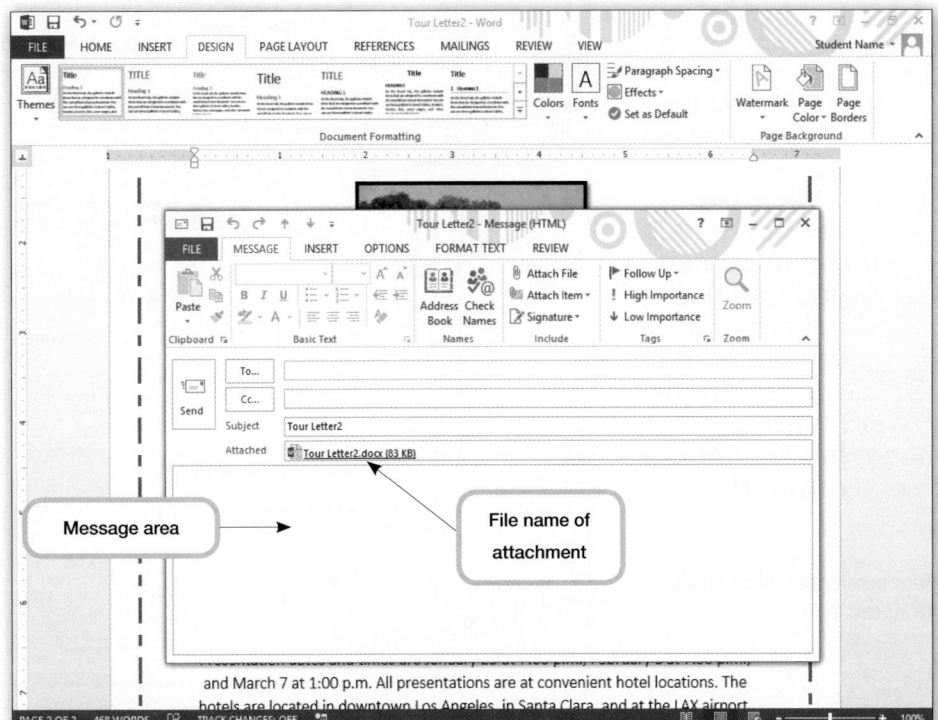

Message area →

File name of attachment

Figure 2.77

Having Trouble?

Your e-mail message window may look different than that shown in Figures 2.76 and 2.77 depending on the e-mail program on your computer.

An e-mail window is displayed in which you can address your e-mail message. Notice that the Subject and the Attached fields display the file name of the attached document. The file extension indicates the application in which the file will open, which is helpful to know.

3

● In the **To** field, type your e-mail address.

● In the message area, type **Here is the document you can use to advertise your upcoming ATT presentations. I hope you have a good turnout!**

Your screen should be similar to Figure 2.78

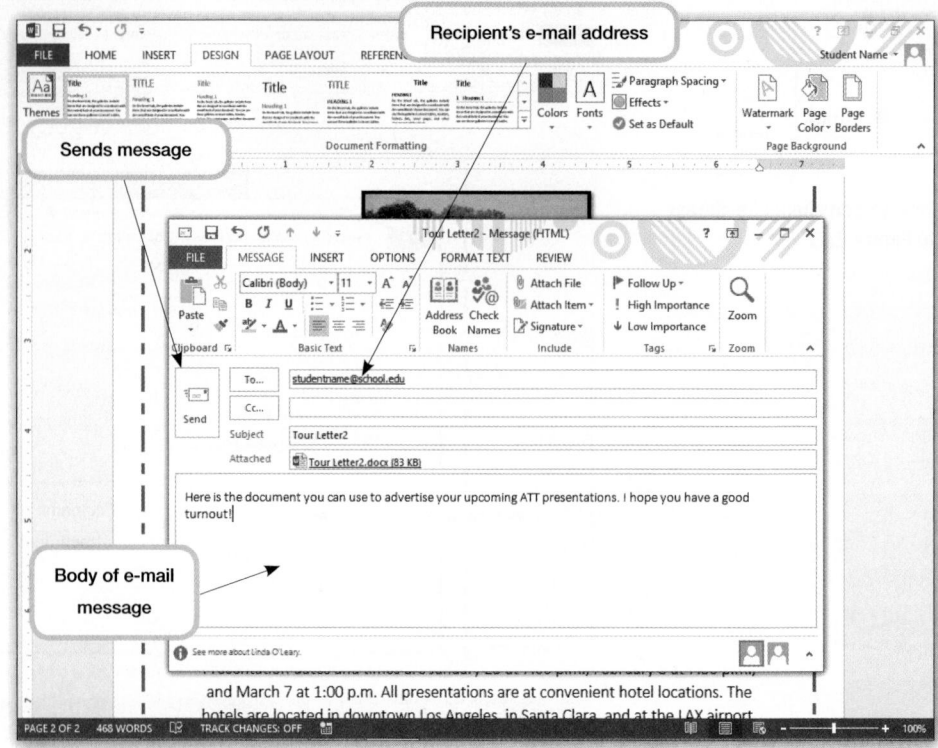

Figure 2.78

Now you are ready to send the message. If you have access to the Internet, you will send the message; otherwise, you will save it to be sent at a later time.

4

● If you have Internet access, click 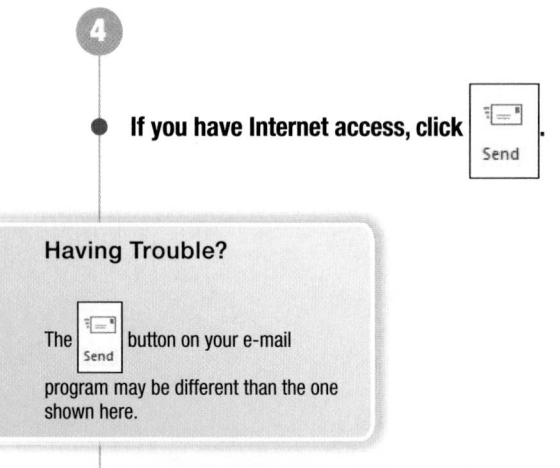.

Having Trouble?

The [Send] button on your e-mail program may be different than the one shown here.

● If you do not have Internet access, save the message as Tour Letter2 E-Mail to your solution files location.

● Close the e-mail window.

● Close the Word document.

The recipient of the e-mail message will be able to open the attached file in Word 2013, 2010, or 2007 and view and make changes to it like any other document.

Preparing and Printing Envelopes

You plan to mail out the letter and flyer to the ATT clients in your area. Before doing this, you decide to see how Word's envelope feature works.

1

- **Start a new blank document.**

- **Open the Mailings tab.**

- **Click** Envelopes **in the Create group.**

- **Type your name and address into the Delivery Address text box.**

Your screen should be similar to Figure 2.79

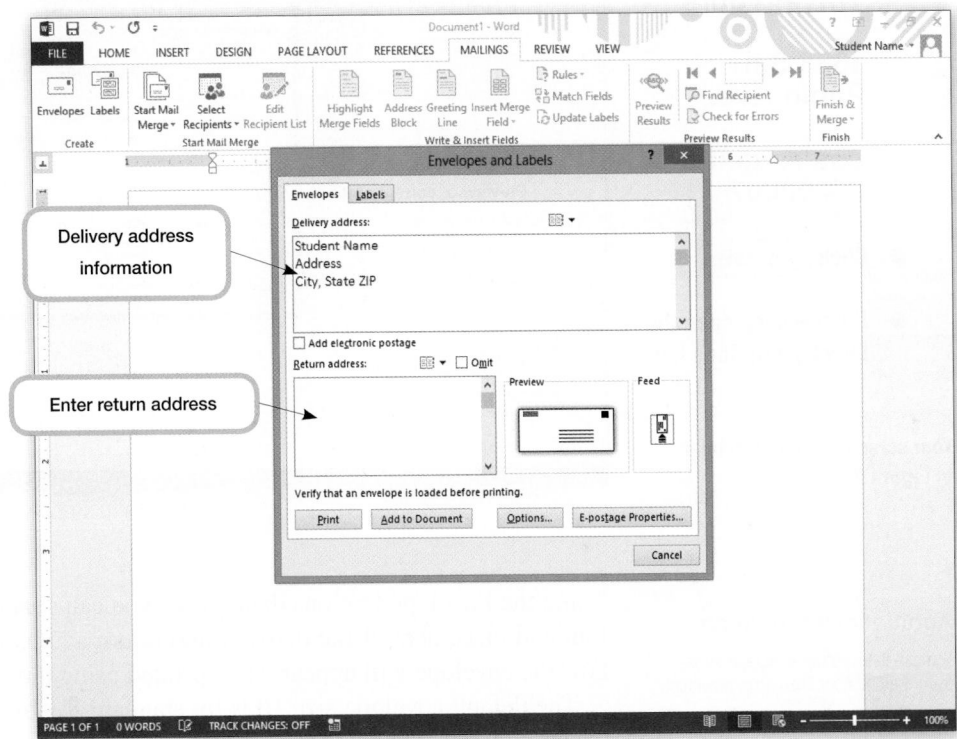

Figure 2.79

Additional Information

You also can copy an address into the Delivery Address text box.

Additional Information

The Labels tab is used to create a mailing label rather than to print the address directly on the envelope. This feature is accessed by clicking Labels.

To complete the information for the envelope, you need to add the return address. Then you will check the options for printing and formatting the envelope.

2

Type the following in the Return Address text box:

Adventure Travel Tours

1338 San Pablo Ave.

Los Angeles, CA 90007

Click Options... **.**

If necessary, open the Envelope Options tab.

Your screen should be similar to Figure 2.80

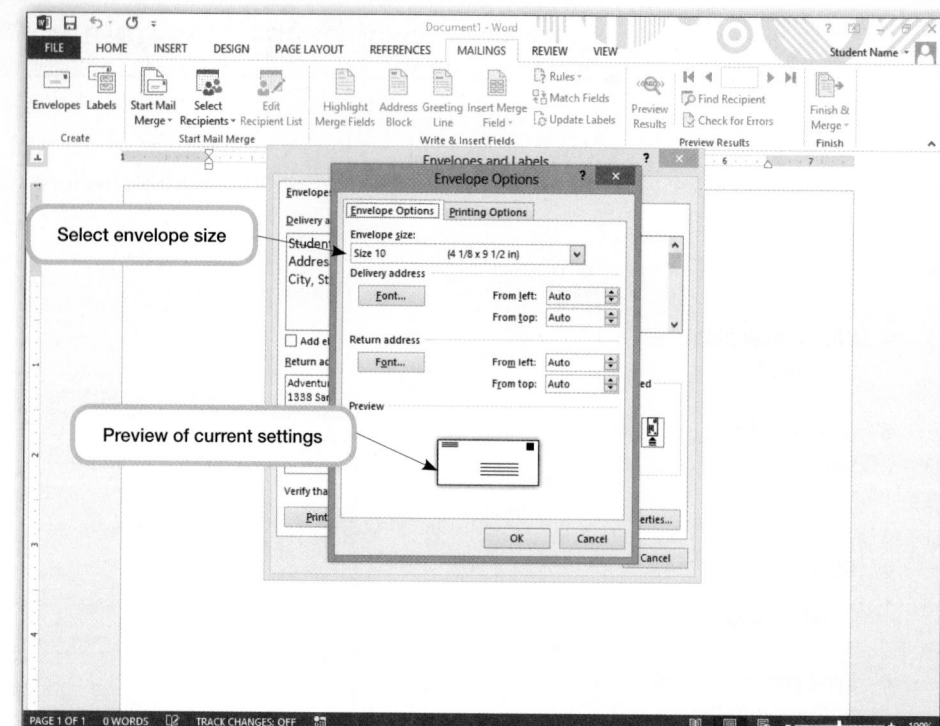

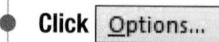

Figure 2.80

Additional Information

You can select other envelope sizes from the Envelope Size drop-down list.

Using the Envelope Options dialog box, you can change the envelope size and the font and placement of the delivery and return addresses. The Preview area shows how the envelope will appear when printed using the current settings.

The default envelope size 10 is for standard 8½-by-11-inch letter paper. This is the appropriate size for the letter. Next, you will check the print options.

3

Open the Printing Options tab.

Additional Information

Depending on your default printer, the envelope printing option may be different than shown here.

Your screen should be similar to Figure 2.81

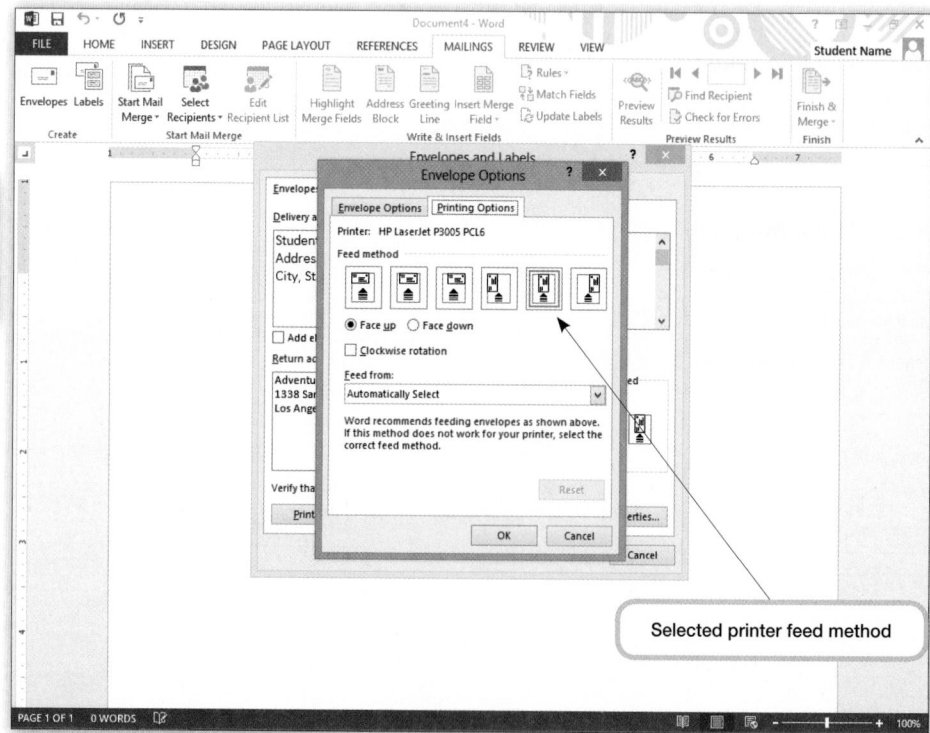

Figure 2.81

The options in this tab are used to specify how the envelope is fed into the printer. Word automatically selects the best option for the selected printer. You do not need to change any of the envelope options. If you were printing an actual envelope, you would need to insert the correct-size envelope in the printer at this time. However, you will simply print it on a sheet of paper.

4

● Close the Envelope Options dialog box.

Additional Information

Use [Add to Document] to add the envelope to the beginning of the active document so that you can print the envelope at the same time you print the document.

● Click [Print].

● Click [No] in response to the prompt to save the return address as the default.

Additional Information

Responding [Yes] displays that address automatically whenever envelopes are printed.

● Close the document window without saving it.

● Exit Word 2013.

)CUS ON CAREERS

EXPLORE YOUR CAREER OPTIONS

Assistant Broadcast Producer

Have you wondered who does the background research for a film or television broadcast? Or who is responsible for making sure a film production runs on schedule? Assistant producers are responsible for background research and the daily operations of a shooting schedule. They also may produce written materials for broadcast. These written materials are often compiled from multiple documents and sources. The typical salary range for an assistant broadcast producer is $30,000 to $50,000. Demand for those with relevant training and experience is expected to continue.

Thesaurus (WD2.9)

Word's Thesaurus is a reference tool that provides synonyms, antonyms, and related words for a selected word or phrase.

Page Break (WD2.17)

A page break marks the point at which one page ends and another begins. Two types of page breaks can be used in a document: soft page breaks and hard page breaks.

Find and Replace (WD2.20)

You use the Find and Replace feature to find text in a document and replace it with other text as directed.

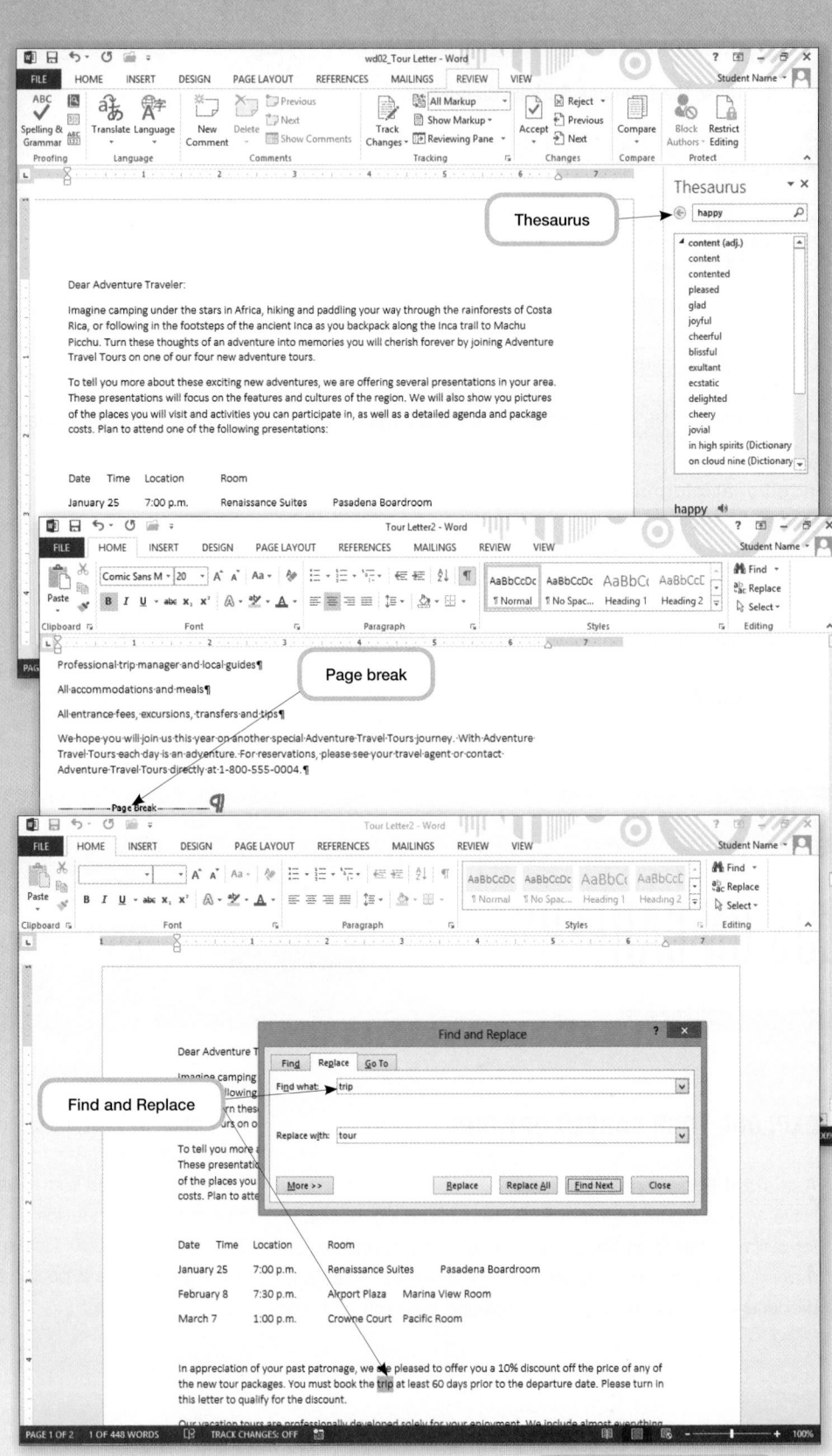

Field (WD2.28)

A field is a placeholder that instructs Word to insert information into a document.

Indents (WD2.32)

To help your reader find information quickly, you can indent paragraphs from the margins.

Line and Paragraph Spacing (WD2.41)

Adjusting the line spacing, or the vertical space between lines of text, and increasing or decreasing spacing before and after paragraphs improve readability of document text.

Bulleted and Numbered Lists (WD2.48)

Whenever possible, add bullets or numbers before items in a list to organize information and to make your writing clear and easy to read.

Sort (WD2.51)

Word can quickly arrange or sort text, numbers, or data in lists or tables in alphabetical, numeric, or date order based on the first character in each paragraph.

Quick Styles (WD2.58)

Applying a quick style, a named group of formatting options, allows you to quickly apply multiple formats to a text selection or an object in one simple step.

Section (WD2.67)

To format parts of a document differently, you divide a document into sections.

Page Margin (WD2.69)

The page margin is the blank space around the edge of the page. Standard single-sided documents have four margins: top, bottom, left, and right.

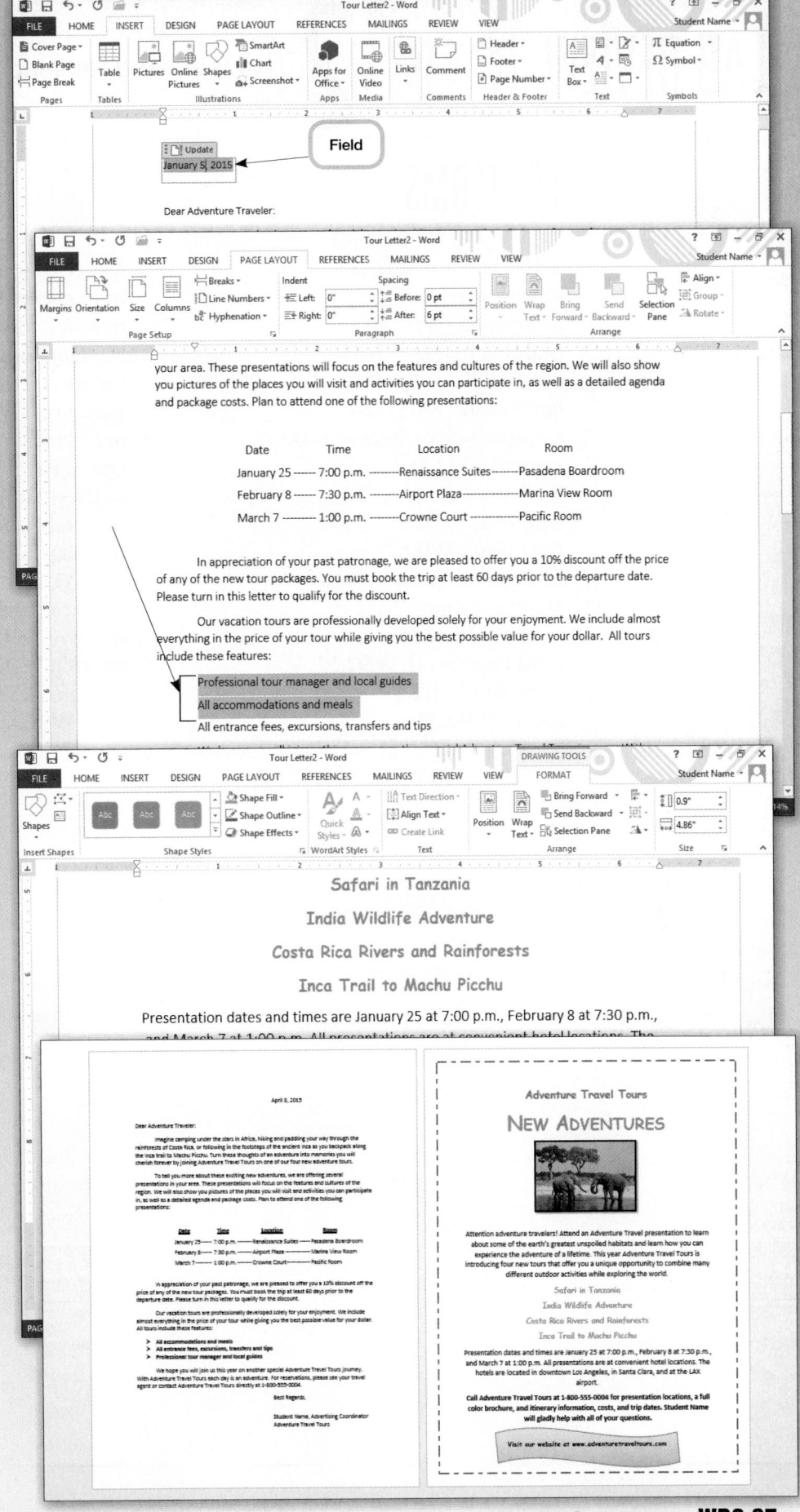

KEY TERMS

active window WD2.14
antonym WD2.9
attachment WD2.80
building blocks WD2.52
bulleted list WD2.48
case sensitive WD2.24
Compatibility Checker WD2.76
control WD2.53
field WD2.28
field code WD2.28
field result WD2.28
Find and Replace WD2.20
Format Painter WD2.47
gradient WD2.59
hard page break WD2.17
hyperlink WD2.60
indent WD2.32

leader character WD2.38
line spacing WD2.41
multilevel list WD2.48
Navigation pane WD2.21
numbered list WD2.48
page break WD2.17
page margin WD2.69
Quick Parts WD2.52
quick style WD2.58
section break WD2.67
soft page break WD2.17
sort WD2.51
synchronized WD2.14
synonym WD2.9
tab stop WD2.35
Thesaurus WD2.9
URL WD2.60

COMMAND SUMMARY

Command	Shortcut	Action
File tab		
[icon] Check for Issues /Inspect Document		Checks your document for hidden data or personal information
[icon] Check for Issues /Check Compatibility		Checks your document for features that aren't compatible with previous versions
Share/Email/ [icon] Send as Attachment		Sends a document as an e-mail attachment
Home tab		
Clipboard group		
[icon] Format Painter		Duplicates formats of selection to other locations
Font group		
[icon] Underline	Ctrl + U	Underlines selected text with single line
[icon] Text Highlight Color		Provides color highlight behind text
Paragraph group		
[icon] Bullets		Creates a bulleted list
[icon] Numbering		Creates a numbered list
[icon] Sort		Rearranges information in a list in alphabetical order
[icon] Line and Paragraph Spacing	Ctrl + 1 or 2	Changes spacing between lines of text
[icon] / Tabs...		Specifies types and positions of tab stops
[icon] /Indents and Spacing/ Special/First Line	Tab	Indents first line of paragraph from left margin
[icon] /Indents and Spacing/ Line Spacing	Ctrl + 1 or 2	Changes the spacing between lines of text

LAB REVIEW

COMMAND SUMMARY (CONTINUED)

Command	Shortcut	Action
Editing group		
🔍 Find ▾ Find	Ctrl + F	Locates specified text
🔤 Replace	Ctrl + H	Locates and replaces specified text
Insert tab		
Pages group		
Page Break	Ctrl + Enter	Inserts hard page break
Illustrations group		
Shapes		Inserts graphic shapes
Text group		
Explore Quick Parts		Inserts Building Blocks
Insert Date and Time		Inserts current date or time, in selected format
Design tab		
Document Formatting group		
Paragraph Spacing ▾		Changes the paragraph spacing for the entire document
Page Background group		
Page Borders		Inserts and customizes page borders
Page Layout tab		
Page Setup group		
Margins		Sets margin sizes
Breaks ▾		Inserts page and section breaks
Mailings tab		
Create group		
Envelopes		Prepares and prints an envelope

COMMAND SUMMARY (CONTINUED)

Command	Shortcut	Action
Review tab		
Proofing group		
ABC ✓ Spelling & Grammar	F7	Starts Spelling and Grammar Checker
Thesaurus	Shift + F7	Opens Thesaurus Tool
View tab		
Window group		
Switch Windows ▾		Switches between open document windows
Arrange All		Arranges all open windows horizontally on the screen
View Side by Side		Displays two document windows side by side to make it easy to compare content
Synchronous Scrolling		When viewing two documents side by side, scrolls the documents together
Picture Tools Format tab		
Picture Styles group		
Picture Border ▾		Customizes a picture's border
Picture Effects ▾		Adds special effects to a picture
Drawing Format tab		
Shape Styles group		
▾ More		Opens the Shape Styles gallery
Shape Fill ▾		Adds colors, gradients, and textures to shapes
Shape Outline ▾		Adds colors and other effects to a shape's outline

LAB EXERCISES

MATCHING

Match the item on the left with the correct description on the right.

1. field   _____ a. inserts a hard page break
2. leader character _____ b. placeholder that instructs Word to insert information into a document
3. line spacing   _____ c. arranges selection in sorted order
4. soft page break _____ d. displays all open windows horizontally on the screen
5. synonyms   _____ e. copies formatting to another place
6. ［A Z↓］   _____ f. indents first line of paragraph
7. ［Ctrl］ + ［Enter］ _____ g. words with similar meaning
8. ［Arrange All］   _____ h. solid, dotted, or dashed lines between tab stops
9. ［Tab］   _____ i. vertical space between lines of text
10. ［🖌］   _____ j. automatically starts a new page when a previous page is filled with text

TRUE/FALSE

Circle the correct answer to the following questions.

1. A hyperlink is a connection to a location in the current document, to another document, or to a website.   **True**   **False**
2. By default the Find capability is case sensitive.   **True**   **False**
3. Draft view does not display graphics.   **True**   **False**
4. Indents are used to move text to the left or to the right of the document margins.   **True**   **False**
5. Press ［Shift］ + ［Home］ to move to the top of the document.   **True**   **False**
6. Styles are collections of formatting characteristics.   **True**   **False**
7. The Find and Replace feature is used to locate misspelled words in a document.   **True**   **False**
8. The Quick Parts feature can be used to quickly insert text and graphics.   **True**   **False**
9. The Thesaurus identifies synonyms for common words.   **True**   **False**
10. When sorting text, text beginning with numbers is sorted before text beginning with letters.   **True**   **False**

FILL-IN

Complete the following statements by filling in the blanks with the correct terms.

1. A(n) _____ code instructs Word to insert the current date in the document using the selected format whenever the document is printed.

2. A(n) _____ is a gradual progression of colors and shades.

3. _____ are reusable pieces of content that can be quickly inserted in a document.

4. Double-sided documents with facing pages typically use _____ margins.

5. In a(n) _____ style letter, all parts are aligned with the left margin.

6. The _____ checks a document for hidden data or personal information that may be stored in your document's properties.

7. The _____ displays the features that will be disabled in previous versions of Word.

8. To select multiple adjacent files from the Open dialog box, click the first file name, press _____, and click the name of the last file.

9. Two types of page breaks that can be used in a document are _____ and _____.

10. Windows that are _____ scroll together.

LAB EXERCISES

MULTIPLE CHOICE

Circle the correct response to the questions below.

1. A _____ marks the point at which one page ends and another begins.
   a. leader character
   b. selection point
   c. field code
   d. page break

2. A(n) _____ is a website address.
   a. URL
   b. RUL
   c. WSL
   d. ULR

3. A predefined set of formatting characteristics is called a(n) _____.
   a. attachment
   b. margin
   c. style
   d. section break

4. _____ is a feature that applies the formats associated with a selection to another selection.
   a. Format Painter
   b. Find and Replace
   c. AutoFormat
   d. Format Designer

5. The blank space around the edge of the page is called the _____.
   a. gutter
   b. indent
   c. margin
   d. white space

6. The field _____ contains the directions that identify the type of information to insert.
   a. results
   b. code
   c. placeholder
   d. format

7. The information that is displayed as a result of a field is called a _____.
   a. field code
   b. field result
   c. quick part
   d. wildcard

8. The _____ is a reference tool that provides synonyms and antonyms.
   a. Find and Replace feature
   b. research
   c. Thesaurus
   d. Clipboard

9. The _____ option replaces the same word throughout the document with the word you select in the Spelling pane.
   a. Change
   b. Change All
   c. Replace
   d. Replace All

10. Word includes preformatted content, called _____, to insert content such as page numbers, cover pages, headers and footers, and sidebars.
    a. drag and drop
    b. Format Painter
    c. building blocks
    d. AutoContent

LAB EXERCISE   Hands-On Exercises

STEP-BY-STEP

CREATING A HANDOUT ★

1. You work as an intern for the local county government and today's assignment is to create a handout for use in the County Agriculture Resources Center. The county has experienced an ever-increasing gardening audience and is interested in recruiting volunteers to meet the public demand for horticulture information. The text of the handout has been prepared, but it is not formatted. Your completed document will be similar to the one shown here.

   a. Open the file wd02_ Master Gardener. Spell-check the document.

   b. Select the entire document and change the line spacing to single and the spacing after to 12 points. Change the font to 12 pt Palatino Linotype.

   c. Position the insertion point at the top of the document, and type Master Gardener and press Enter.

   d. Select the title and apply the following format: Tahoma font, 28 pt, bold, small caps, 36 points spacing before, and 24 points spacing after.

   e. Select the text "Qualifications for a Master Gardener" and format the text using 14 pt, small caps, bold, italic, and Tahoma font.

   f. Use the Format Painter to copy the format from the Qualifications line to the lines beginning "Core Classes" and "Volunteer Activities."

   g. Select all lines of text below the Volunteer Activities and apply the solid, black square bullet. Sort the list.

   h. Repeat the format applied in the previous step to the lines of text below the Core Classes heading. Sort the list.

MASTER GARDENER

The Master Gardener program is an Agriculture Extension education program that utilizes volunteers to assist the gardening public.

QUALIFICATIONS FOR A MASTER GARDENER

General qualifications for a master gardener include a strong interest in horticulture, written and oral communication skills, and a willingness to share knowledge with community residents. Completing training sessions and serving as a volunteer are also requirements of the Master Gardener program.

Specific qualifications for master gardeners include the following:

   A. Attend a minimum of 40 hours of instruction.
   B. Provide a minimum of 50 hours of volunteer service.
   C. Score 80 percent on a final exam.

Upon successful completion of the extensive training in horticulture, a certificate is awarded. The certificate is restrictive and is only issued for one year. Master Gardeners are required to complete 8 hours of continuing education and volunteer 20 hours.

CORE CLASSES IN THE MASTER GARDENER PROGRAM

- Botany
- Communications
- Disease Control
- Entomology
- Insect management
- Lawns
- Ornamental trees and shrubs
- Plant nutrition
- Plant Pathology
- Propagation
- Pruning
- Soils and composting
- Vegetable and Flower Gardening
- Water conservation

i. Apply a numbered list format to the text below the paragraph beginning "Specific qualifications." Use an alphabetic format (A, B, C).

j. Position the insertion point at the paragraph that begins "Specific qualifications," and insert a picture related to gardening using Office.com. Size the picture to approximately 2 inches high, and apply square text wrapping. Drag the picture to the right margin.

k. Open the Shapes gallery and choose the first option in the Lines group. Draw a horizontal line under the title from the left margin to the right margin. Select the line, if necessary, and display the Drawing Tools Format tab. Click the Shape Outline button and choose Weight. Select 2¼ pt. Change the shape outline to black.

l. Apply a shadow page border to the document. Choose a solid line style and a 2¼ pt width.

m. Change the bottom margin to 0.5 inch.

VOLUNTEER ACTIVITIES

- Create educational exhibits
- Diagnose plant, insect, and disease problems
- Greet visitors and answer questions
- Lecture on gardening topics
- Manning garden hotlines
- Prepare newsletters and displays
- Present workshops and demonstrations
- Schedule plant clinics

FOR MORE INFORMATION:
CONTACT YOUR LOCAL AGRICULTURE RESOURCES CENTER

Student Name
Current Date

n. Add a shape at the end of the document. Choose the Frame option from the Basic Shapes group. Center the shape horizontally using the Alignment Guide. Format the frame shape using the Shape Fill, Shape Outline, and Shape Styles buttons.

o. Add the following text to the shape:

For more information:
Contact your local Agriculture Resources Center

p. Format the text using the Tahoma font and small caps.

q. Review the document and apply formatting changes where necessary.

r. Type your name and date at the end of the document.

s. Add document properties. Save the document as Master Gardener and submit it.

DOG PARK RULES ★★

2. You are a part-time city employee and have been asked to create a document that lists the rules dog owners must follow before using any of the city's five dog parks. You started the document a few days ago and you need to apply formatting. You also want to check the document to make sure others in your department who are using previous versions of Word will be able to open it for review. Your completed document will be similar to that shown below.

    a. Open the document wd02_ Dog Park Rules. Spell- and grammar-check the document.
    b. Replace all occurrences of the word "canine" with the word "dog".
    c. Insert the current date on a separate line below the title using the Date and Time command. Pick the date format of your choice.
    d. Select the title and date and change the spacing before and after the selection to 0 pt.
    e. Center the title and date. Change the font to Arial Black with a point size of 24. Add a color of your choice to the title.
    f. Select the remainder of the document and change the spacing before and after each paragraph to 6 pt.
    g. Use the Format Painter to apply the same formatting from the title to the third line in the document describing the hours of operation. Change the font size to 14 pt. Increase the spacing after for this line to 24 pt.
    h. Select the remainder of the document and change it to a numbered list using the numbering format of your choice.

Dog Park Rules
April 8, 2015

Hours: Sunrise to Sunset

1. Dogs must be current on all vaccinations
2. Dogs must have a current dog license. Dogs should also wear an owner identification tag at all times.
3. Dogs must be leashed when entering and exiting the Dog Park.
4. Aggressive dogs are not permitted on the premises. Dogs must be removed at the first sign of aggression.
5. Dog owners must be in the park and within view of their dogs at all times.
6. All off-leash dogs must be under voice control of their owners. If you cannot control your dog off leash, keep your pet leashed at all times.
7. Dog owners must keep their leash in hand at all times.
8. Please do not bring dog food into the park.
9. Owner must clean up dog feces. Seal waste in the provided plastic bags before disposing in designated receptacles.
10. Fill any holes your dog digs.
11. Proof of a current rabies vaccination and license is required upon request of a police or animal control officer. Tags may serve as proof.
12. Failure to abide by the park rules may result in loss of privileges or owners may be ticketed.

Follow the rules to help keep our dog parks safe!

Contact Student Name if you have questions.

    i. Save the document using the file name Dog Park Rules.
    j. Change the top and bottom margins to 1.25 inch. Change the right and left margins to 1.5 inch.
    k. Insert the Double Wave shape at the bottom of your document. Size it to span from the left to the right margin and apply the shape style of your choice.
    l. Add the following text to the shape: Follow the rules to help keep our dog parks safe! Contact Student Name if you have questions. Increase the font size of the shape text to 16 pt. If necessary, change the size of the shape so that the text displays on two lines. Apply formatting, such as color

and bold, of your choice to this line. Fill the shape with a gradient color. Change the font color if necessary.

m. Add a page border of your choice to the document.

n. Use the Document Inspector to check the document for hidden properties or personal information. Remove any items that are found.

o. Run the Compatibility Checker to see what items might be affected in previous versions of Word, and then close the dialog box.

p. Add document properties. Save, submit, and then close the document.

PROMOTING NEW FITNESS CLASSES ★★

3. The Lifestyle Fitness Club has just started a new series of informal classes for the members and their families. You want to spread the word by creating a flyer for club members to pick up at the front desk. You have created a Word document with the basic information that you want to include in the flyer. Now you just need to format it. Your completed flyer will be similar to the one shown here.

a. Open the file wd02_ Fitness Fun.

b. Find each occurrence of "class" and replace it with "Class" where appropriate. Be sure to use the match case and whole words only options. Find and replace all occurrences of "mins" with "minutes."

c. Use the spelling and grammar checker to correct the identified errors.

d. Save the document as Fitness Fun Flyer.

e. Change the title font to Lucida Sans (or a font of your choice), 48 pt, and a color of your choice. Center the title.

f. Justify the introductory paragraph and set line spacing to 1.0.

Fitness Fun!

Need a break from the everyday stresses of life? Interested in exploring new and exciting activities with the whole family? Try one of Lifestyle Fitness Club's new informal classes. Come and dance with a spouse or friend. Spend some quality time with the kids. Or come alone and decompress.

CLASS DESCRIPTIONS

MOVE TO MOVIES
Soundtracks, movie clips, and scene participation make this course something special! Sing along, dance along, and act along to movie classics suitable for the whole family.

TAI CHI
An introduction to Chen style movements that are practiced slowly in a relaxed manner coordinated with deep breathing.

FAMILIES IN MOTION
An exercise class for the whole family, this course offers something for moms, dads, and kids.

DADS AND LADS CLASS
This course is a father/son workout featuring batting and putting practice, plus strength training.

WATER DANCE
This truly unique workout is a graceful, low-impact course. Learn some of the basics of synchronized swimming under the stars.

HIP-HOP AND SWING
Hip-Hop Dance instructors share the basics in this high-energy exciting class.

OCTOBER CLASS SCHEDULE

Day	Class	Time	Length of Class
Sunday	Tai Chi	6:30	60 minutes
Monday	Families in Motion	6:00 and 7:00	50 minutes
Tuesday	Water Dance	7:00	50 minutes
Wednesday	Dads and Lads	6:00 and 7:00	50 minutes
Thursday	Hip-Hop and Swing	7:00	50 minutes
Friday	Move to Movies	7:00	90 minutes
Saturday	Move to Movies	6:00 and 7:00	90 minutes

[Author] April 8, 2015

Fun for the whole family!

LAB EXERCISES

g. Use Format Painter to format the Class Descriptions heading the same as the title. Reduce the font size to 14, apply small caps, and left-align it. Add space before the paragraph.

h. Increase the font size of the rest of the document to 12.

i. Format the eight class titles using Lucida Sans font, bold, small caps, and 6 pt spacing before.

j. Delete the class title and description for Beginning Ballroom Dance as well as the scheduling information (at the bottom of the document) because you do not have an instructor for this month.

k. Set the margins to Narrow.

l. Use drag and drop to move the Tai Chi class title and description below the Move to Movies description.

m. Create a tabbed table of the schedule. Add left tab marks at 1.5, 3, and 5 inches. Bold, add color, and underline the words only of the table heads: Day, Class, Time, and Length of Class. Move the tab marker from the 5-inch position to the 4.5-inch position for the entire table. Change the tab at the 3-inch position to a center tab stop at the 3.5-inch position. Add space after the heading line only of the tabbed table.

n. Above the table, add the heading October Class Schedule. Format it the same as the Class Descriptions heading. Insert a hard page break above the table heading.

o. Add the shape "Explosion 2" from the Stars and Banners section below the Line Dancing description at the bottom of page 1. Add the text Fun for the whole family! Bold and size the text to 12 pt. Add fill color and font color of your choice to the shape. Move and size the shape to fit in the bottom right of the flyer.

p. Delete the Line Dancing class title and description. Delete the hard page break.

q. Increase the left and right margins to 1 inch. Reposition and size the shape as needed.

r. Add a 6 pt page border to the flyer.

s. Use the Document Inspector to check the document for hidden properties or personal information. Remove any items that are found.

t. Add your name using the Author quick part and the current date (as a field) on the last line on the page. Adjust the line spacing as needed to fit the document on one page.

u. Run the Compatibility Checker to see what items might be affected in previous versions of Word, and then close the dialog box.

v. Add a title to the document properties. Save and submit the document.

ENERGY CONFERENCE ANNOUNCEMENT ★★★

4. The Energy Conservation Council is actively seeking volunteers to help with an upcoming conference on alternative energy sources. You are preparing the information that will appear on the website and the flyer that will be distributed to local businesses. Your completed document will be similar to the one shown here.

a. Open a new document and set the margins to Moderate.

b. On the first line, type the title ECC Needs Your Help! Increase the font to 36 points and apply formats of your choice.

c. Several lines below the title, type the following paragraphs:

The Energy Conservation Council needs volunteers to help with our upcoming conference.

Registration and Hospitality

We need help at registration throughout the meeting, assembling packets several days prior to the meeting, and with answering questions and giving directions at hospitality tables.

Education: Session Moderators

We need help in preparing rooms for presentations, assisting and introducing speakers, collecting evaluation sheets, assisting with poster session.

Special Events

We need help greeting, collecting tickets, loading buses, and decorating.

If you are interested in serving in any of these areas, please contact:

[Your Name], Volunteer Coordinator at (800) 555-8023

ECC Needs Your Help!

The Energy Conservation Council needs volunteers to help with our upcoming conference.

Registration and Hospitality

We need help at registration throughout the conference, assembling packets several days prior to the conference, and with answering questions and giving directions at hospitality tables.

Education: Session Moderators

We need assistance in preparing rooms for presentations, assisting and introducing speakers, collecting evaluation sheets, assisting with poster session.

Special Events

We need help greeting, collecting tickets, loading buses, and decorating.

VOLUNTEER TIMES AVAILABLE

Day	Date	Time
Monday	May 8	10 a.m. to 1 p.m.
Tuesday	May 9	7 p.m. to 9 p.m.
Saturday	May 13	10 a.m. to 7 p.m.
Sunday	May 14	9 a.m. to 4 p.m.

If you are interested in serving in any of these areas, please contact:

[Your Name], Volunteer Coordinator at (800) 555-8023

Visit **www.ecc.com** for more information.

d. Spell-check the document. Use the Thesaurus to find a better word for "help" in the Education: Session Moderators paragraph.

e. Find and replace all occurrences of "meeting" with "conference."

f. Save the document as Conference Volunteers.

g. Increase the font size of all the text in the document to 12, not including the title. Add bold and font color to the three headings. Indent the paragraphs below each heading 0.5 inch. Apply 12 pt spacing before to each of the headings.

h. Below the Special Events paragraph that begins "We need," enter the title Volunteer Times Available. Use the same formatting as the main title with a font size of 14 points bold, small caps, aligned at the left margin.

i. Below this heading, you will create a table describing when help is needed with upcoming special events. Place center tab stops at 1, 2.5, and 4.25 inches on the ruler. Enter the word Day at the first tab stop, Date at the second tab stop, and Time at the third tab stop.

LAB EXERCISES

j. Press [Enter], then clear the tab stops. Create a left tab at 0.75 and 2.25 and a right tab stop at 5. Enter the schedule information shown here into the table.

Monday	May 8	10 a.m. to 1 p.m.
Tuesday	May 9	7 p.m. to 9 p.m.
Saturday	May 13	10 a.m. to 7 p.m.
Sunday	May 14	9 a.m. to 4 p.m.

k. Apply the same color as the title to the table headings. Add an underline style of your choice to the table headings. Center the two lines of text below the tabbed text.

l. Create a shape of your choice and add the text Visit www.ecc.com for more information! using a font size of 16 points, and bold. Move and size the shape appropriately. Remove the hyperlink format from the URL. Add color to the URL. Apply a shape style of your choice to the shape.

m. Add a page border to the document.

n. Add document properties. Save and submit the document.

ADVERTISING WEEKLY SPECIALS ★★★

5. In addition to monthly music concerts at the Downtown Internet Café, the owner wants to continue to attract new and repeat customers by offering weekly specials. You want to create a flyer describing the coffee varieties and specials for the week. Your completed flyer will be similar to the one shown here.

a. Open a new document.

b. Enter the title Downtown Internet Cafe on the first line. Add four blank lines. Change the font of the title to Lucida Sans.

c. Enter Italian Market Reserve on line 4 followed by two blank lines.

d. On line 7, place a left tab stop at 0.5 and center tabs at 3.25 and 5.75 inches.

e. Enter the word Coffee at the first tab stop, Description at the second tab stop, and Cost/Pound at the third tab stop.

f. On the next line, clear all the tab stops and enter the rest of the information for the table shown below using left tabs at 0.5, 2, and 5.5.

Original	Our Signature Coffee! With Old World charm	$10.49
Decaffeinated	All the original has to offer—decaffeinated natural	$13.49
Reduced Caffeine	All the original has to offer with half of the caffeine	$13.49

g. Remove the space after each line in the table.

h. Right-align the first title line and change the font color to blue with a font size of 24 pt.

i. Center the text "Italian Market Reserve" and change it to blue with a font size of 20 pt.

j. Increase the font of the table headings to 14 pt. Add bold, color, and an underline style of your choice to the table headings.

k. Save the document as Weekly Specials.

l. Open the file wd02_Coffee Flyer. Display the document windows side by side. Copy the title and first two paragraphs from wd02_Coffee Flyer and insert them above "Italian Market Reserve" in the Weekly Specials document.

m. Spell-check the Weekly Specials document. Use the Thesaurus to find better words for "desire" and "giant" in the first paragraph.

n. Use Find and Replace to replace all occurrences of "java" with "coffee" (except the one following "high-powered").

o. Right-align the words "Weekly Specials" below the title. Use the same font as the title, and select a color of your choice.

p. Format the paragraph that begins with "Tired" justified, Cambria font, and 12 pt, and set the line spacing to 1.5. Add dark red color to the URL.

q. Increase the font size of the line above "Italian Market Reserve" to 14 pt. Center the text. Change the font to Cambria.

r. Copy the remaining paragraph from the wd02_Coffee Flyer document and insert it at the bottom of the Weekly Specials document. Include two blank lines between the table and the paragraph. Close the wd02_Coffee Flyer document.

s. Bold and center the final paragraph. Remove the hyperlink format from the URL. Format the URL as italic and dark red. Change the paragraph font to Cambria.

t. Create the Explosion 1 shape from the Stars and Banners group. Enter the text **Coffee Sale!** and change the font size to 22 pt. Add a fill color of your choice. Move the shape to the left of the title. Size the shape appropriately.

u. Adjust the line spacing and formatting of the document as needed to improve its appearance. Add an attractive page border.

v. Add your name using the Author quick part and the current date (as a field) on a single line below the final paragraph. Left-align this line.

w. Add the title "Weekly Specials Flyer" to the document properties. Save and submit the document.

Downtown Internet Café

Weekly Specials

Coffee Sale!

Tired of brewing a wimpy cup of coffee that just doesn't have the punch you crave? Then point your Web browser to www.somecoffee.com for our huge sale, and have our high-powered java delivered right to your front door. You'll never buy bland supermarket coffee again.

Through January, take $2 off the regular coffee prices shown below.

Italian Market Reserve

Coffee	Description	Cost/Pound
Original	Our Signature Coffee! With Old World charm	$10.49
Decaffeinated	All the original has to offer—decaffeinated natural	$13.49
Reduced Caffeine	All the original has to offer with half of the caffeine	$13.49

You can also order online at www.somecoffee.com today, and get coffee delivered right to your door! But hurry, our sale won't last forever.

[Author]   April 8, 2015

LAB EXERCISES

ON YOUR OWN

REQUESTING A REFERENCE ★

1. Your first year as a business major is going well and you are looking for a summer internship with a local advertising firm. You have an upcoming interview and want to be prepared with a letter of reference from your last position. Write a business letter directed to your former supervisor, Kevin Westfall, at R & A Publishing requesting a reference. Use the modified block letter style shown in the lab. Be sure to include the date, a salutation, two paragraphs, a closing, and your name as a signature. Spell-check the document, save the document as Reference Letter, and submit it.

CELL PHONE RATES ★

2. MyRatePlan.com provides comparative pricing information for a variety of products. For example, it posts up-to-date rate information on cell phone rates and available minutes at each price break. Using your web browser, go to myrateplan.com/wireless_plans and then type your ZIP Code. Scroll down to view the rates offered by different wireless carriers. Create a tabbed table of this rate plan information. Bold and underline the column heads. Add style 2 tab leaders to the table entries. Above the table, write a paragraph explaining the table contents. Include your name and the date below the table. Save the document as Cell Phone Rates and submit the document.

YARD SALE ★★

3. Create a flyer to advertise a yard sale you plan for Saturday morning. Include the following features on your flyer:
   - Two different fonts in different sizes, colors, and styles.
   - Bulleted or numbered list.
   - Indents.
   - A shape with appropriate text.
   - A graphic.
   - A tabbed table with tab leaders.

   Include your name as the contact information. Save the document as Yard Sale Flyer and submit it.

WYOMING RELOCATION ★★

4. You work for the Department of Tourism for the State of Wyoming. You have been asked to produce a relocation packet to assist people planning to move to the state. This packet includes information on state history, the weather, geography, major cities, population statistics, and so forth. Research information on the web about Wyoming and create a one-page fact sheet of your findings. Your completed project should include an introductory paragraph on relocation, graphics, a table with the average weather statistics, a bulleted list of attractions, and shapes. Include your name as the contact and save the file as Wyoming Facts. Submit the file.

DEVELOP A FAMILY DISASTER PLAN ★★★

5. Severe weather threatens thousands of people each year, and it is important to prepare a family disaster plan to protect your family and property during an emergency. Use the Internet to research family disaster plans, and create a document listing critical information to include in the plan. Study the following topics:
    - Type of disasters that are most likely to happen in your area.
    - How to prepare for each type of disaster.
    - Community warning system.
    - Special requirements for people who are elderly or disabled.
    - Special requirements for children.
    - Special requirements for pets and whether emergency shelters can accommodate pets.
    - List of two places to meet after a disaster: outside the home and outside the neighborhood.
    - List of emergency telephone numbers.
    - List of contents for an emergency supply kit and other supplies.

    Save the document as Family Disaster Plan and submit the file.

Creating Reports and Tables Lab 3

Objectives

After you have completed this lab, you will know how to:

1. Use Read Mode.

2. Apply and customize styles.

3. Navigate by browsing headings and pages.

4. Create a cover page.

5. Apply and customize document themes.

6. Create and update a table of contents, table of figures, and an index.

7. Add citations and create a bibliography.

8. Add footnotes, captions, and cross-references.

9. Find, insert, and play video.

10. Create and format a table.

11. Add headers, footers, and page numbers.

CASE STUDY

Adventure Travel Tours

Adventure Travel Tours provides information on its tours in a variety of forms. Travel brochures, for instance, contain basic tour information in a promotional format and are designed to entice potential clients to sign up for a tour. More detailed regional information packets are given to people who have already registered for a tour, so they can prepare for their vacation. These packets include facts about each region's climate, geography, and culture. Additional informational formats include pages on Adventure Travel's website and scheduled group presentations.

Part of your responsibility as advertising coordinator is to

gather the information that Adventure Travel will publicize about each regional tour. Specifically, you have been asked to provide background information for two of the new tours: the Tanzania Safari and the Machu Picchu trail. Because this information is used in a variety of formats, your research needs to be easily adapted. You will therefore present your facts in the form of a general report on Tanzania and Peru.

In this lab, you will learn to use many of the features of Word 2013 that make it easy to create an attractive and well-organized report. A portion of the completed report is shown here.

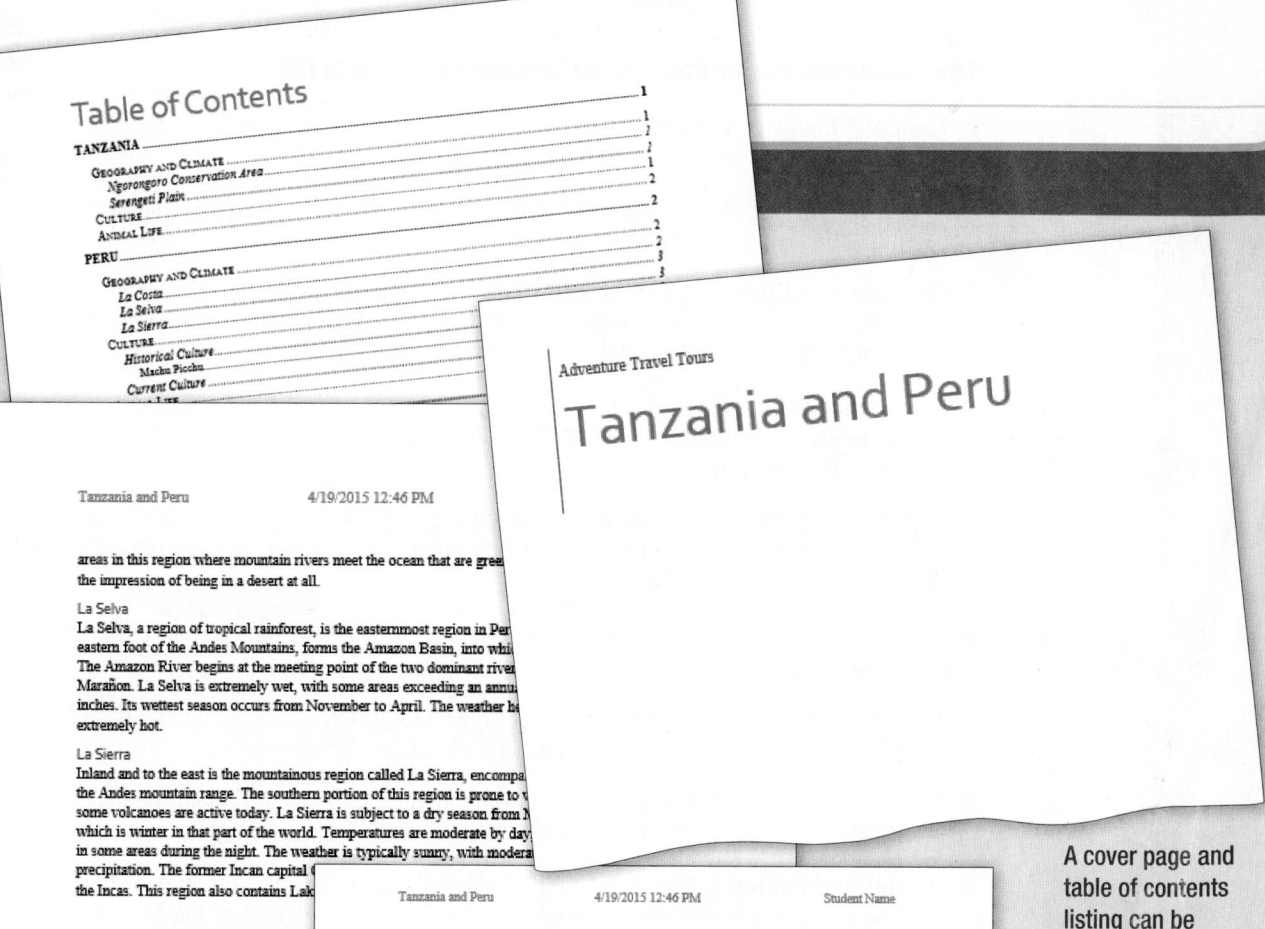

Table of Contents

Adventure Travel Tours

Tanzania and Peru

Tanzania and Peru   4/19/2015 12:46 PM

areas in this region where mountain rivers meet the ocean that are gre[...]
the impression of being in a desert at all.

La Selva
La Selva, a region of tropical rainforest, is the easternmost region in Per[...]
eastern foot of the Andes Mountains, forms the Amazon Basin, into whi[...]
The Amazon River begins at the meeting point of the two dominant river[...]
Marañón. La Selva is extremely wet, with some areas exceeding an annu[...]
inches. Its wettest season occurs from November to April. The weather h[...]
extremely hot.

La Sierra
Inland and to the east is the mountainous region called La Sierra, encompa[...]
the Andes mountain range. The southern portion of this region is prone to v[...]
some volcanoes are active today. La Sierra is subject to a dry season from [...]
which is winter in that part of the world. Temperatures are moderate by day[...]
in some areas during the night. The weather is typically sunny, with modera[...]
precipitation. The former Incan capital C[...]
the Incas. This region also contains Lak[...]

Region	Annu...
La Costa	
La Selva	
La Sierra	

Table 1: Peru Climate

Culture
Historical Culture
Peru is where the Incas built their home[...]
Sierra until around 1300 CE, when they [...]
built their empire, overrunning and assi[...]
into a socialist-type theocracy under an [...]
The Inca Empire reached its maximum [...]

In 1532 the Spanish explorer Francisco [...]
seizing the empire because of the rich g[...]
superior armament. This opened the doo[...]

³ Lake Titicaca is 12,507 feet above sea level.

3

Tanzania and Peru   4/19/2015 12:46 PM   Student Name

conquistadors to join in the pursuit, who brought with them both modern weaponry and
smallpox, which ultimately led to the demise of most of the Inca government. Civil disorder and
rioting followed in what remained of the empire, and the Spanish used this as leverage to seal
their victory.

Machu Picchu
Though the Incas are no more, their culture can still be seen in the ruins of their great cities and
architecture. Rising from the Sacred Valley of the Incas, Machu Picchu is the Incas' stunning
hilltop citadel, a complex of vine-shrouded temples, baths and stairways. Machu Picchu
constitutes the end of the Inca Trail, connecting it to Cuzco, the former Inca capital. The trail
sprawls across three mountain passes and dense tropic jungle. Machu Picchu is enshrouded in
mystery, which attracts much speculation on its cultural significance. It is not believed to be a
city itself, but rather a religious retreat or royal estate. Its inaccessibility further supports this
belief. For the same reason, Machu Picchu has fortunately survived in all its former
magnificence. When the conquistadors invaded other Incan cities, they typically destroyed them,
using their stone bricks to build cathedrals and marketplaces for the Spaniards. The
conquistadors never discovered Machu Picchu, however. It was forgotten for 400 years, an
unblemished icon of Incan innovation and culture.

Current Culture
Today Peru consists largely of Native Americans who account for approximately 45 percent of
the population. The remaining population consists of 37 percent Mestizo (mixed Native
American and European ancestry), 15 percent white, and 3 percent other (primarily Black and
Asian). The official language is Spanish, and the predominant religion is Roman Catholic.

Animal Life
Peru is home to many exotic animals, but is particularly known for its large
population of birds. More than 1,700 species can be found, including
parakeets, toucans, and Amazon parrots. Many extremely rare families of
birds also live here. Each geographical region of Peru boasts its own distinct
habitat, and som[...]

The popular Ma[...]
unbroken Peruvi[...]
ocelot, alligators[...]
of the best place[...]
monkey, named [...]

Figure 2: Peruvian Flamingos

Tanzania and Peru   4/19/2015 12:46 PM   Student Name

Works Cited

Camerapix. *Spectrum Guide to Tanzania*. Brooklyn: Interlink Books, 2002.

Country Studies US. *Peru*. 2003-2005. 16 April 2015. <http://countrystudies.us/peru/23.htm>.

Wikipedia: The Free Encyclopedia. *Tanzania*. 25 October 2012. 16 April 2015.
    <http://en.wikipedia.org/wiki/Tanzania>.

A cover page and table of contents listing can be created quickly using Word's built-in features.

Tables, footnotes, cross-references, and headers and footers are many standard features that are quick and easy to include in a report.

Wrapping text around graphics, adding figure captions, and applying a document theme are among many features that can be used to enhance a report.

A bibliography can be quickly generated from cited sources.

The following concepts will be introduced in this lab:

1 Theme A theme is a predefined set of formatting choices that can be applied to an entire document in one simple step.

2 Table of Contents A table of contents is a listing of the topic headings that appear in a document and their associated page numbers.

3 Citations and Bibliography Parenthetical source references, called citations, give credit for specific information included in the document. Complete source information for citations is included in a bibliography at the end of the report.

4 Footnotes and Endnotes Footnotes and endnotes are used in documented research papers to explain or comment on information in the text, or provide source references for text in the document.

5 Captions and Cross-References A caption is a numbered label for a figure, table, picture, or graph. A cross-reference is a reference from one part of a document to related information in another part.

6 Table A table is used to organize information into an easy-to-read format of horizontal rows and vertical columns.

7 Table of Figures A table of figures is a list of the figures, tables, or equations used in a document and their associated page numbers.

8 Index An index appears at the end of a long document as a list of major headings, topics, and terms with their page numbers.

9 Header and Footer A header is a line or several lines of text in the top margin of each page. A footer is a line or several lines of text in the margin space at the bottom of every page.

Using Heading Styles

After several days of research, you have gathered many notes from various sources including books, magazines, and the web. You have created a document using these notes; however, you find it difficult to read because all the text seems to run together, making it difficult to identify topics.

USING READ MODE

You organized the report into two main topics, Tanzania and Peru, and many sub-topics. You decide to use Read Mode view to quickly look over the document. This view displays pages of your document on the screen in a larger font size and easy-to-read columns.

- **Open the** wd03_ Tour Research **data file.**

- **Click** 📖 **Read Mode in the status bar.**

Another Method

Alternatively, you can switch to the Read Mode view by clicking

📖 Read Mode on the View tab.

- **If necessary, click View in the menu bar, select Column Width, and choose Default.**

Having Trouble?

Do not be concerned if your screen displays more or fewer pages than in Figure 3.1. The size of your monitor affects how the document is displayed.

- **Click ▶ twice to move forward two pages in the document.**

- **Click ◀ to move backward in the document.**

Another Method

In Read Mode you can also press the Pg Up and Pg Dn keys, the Spacebar and ←Backspace, or the arrow keys to move forward and backward. You can also use the scroll wheel on your mouse. On a touch device, you can swipe left or right.

Your screen should be similar to Figure 3.1

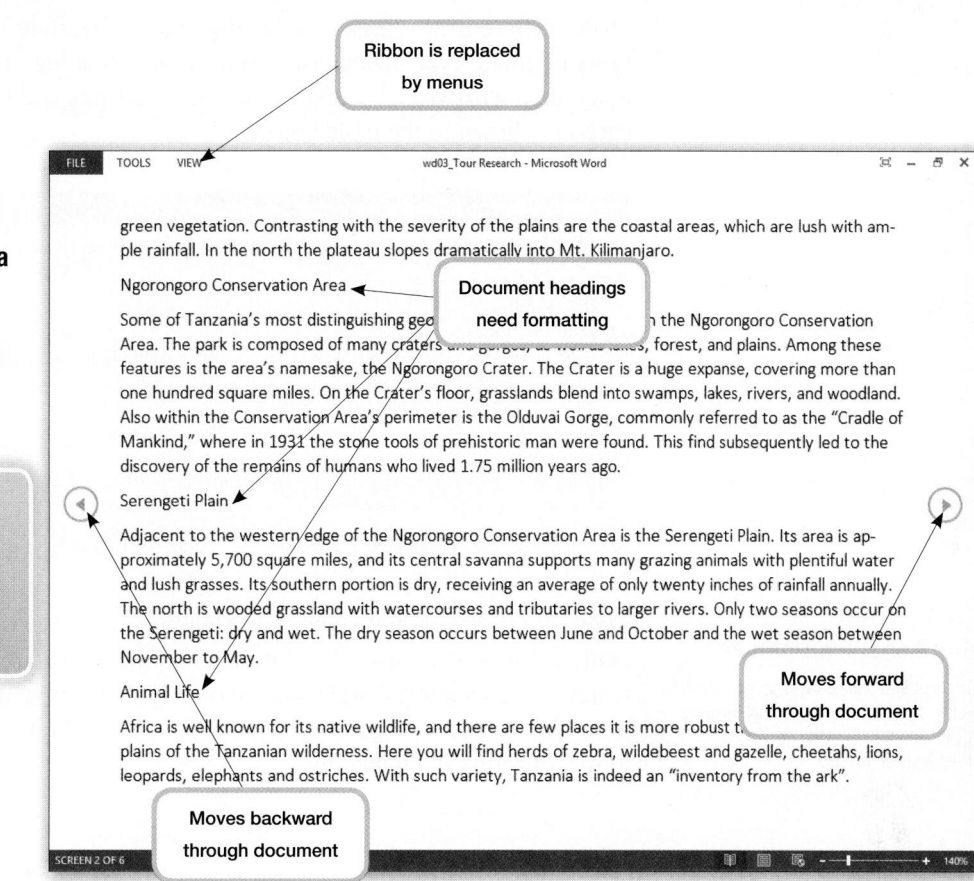

Figure 3.1

In Read Mode, the Ribbon and tools used to edit a document are not displayed. This allows more space for the pages to be displayed. However, tools that are used for reading, such as adding comments or zooming in and out on graphics, are included in the menus. The column width and a larger font size are automatically adjusted to the size of the screen.

When you exit Read Mode, your location in the document is the same as your location in Read Mode. If you reopen the document at a later time, Word remembers where you were in Read Mode, so you can keep reading where you left off.

APPLYING HEADING STYLES

As you scrolled through the document, you may have noticed that the headings in the document are not formatted. Adding formatting to headings makes it easier to identify where a new topic begins. Rather than apply individual sets of formats to the topic headings, you will use Word's **heading styles** to change the appearance of the different headings in your document. Heading styles consist of combinations of fonts, type sizes, color, italics, and spacing. The heading styles that are associated with Word's default document settings and the formats associated with each are shown in the table below:

Heading Level	Appearance
Heading 1	Calibri Light, 16 pt, left align, spacing 12 pt before, 0 pt after, blue
Heading 2	Calibri Light, 13 pt, left align, spacing 2 pt before, 0 pt after, blue
Heading 3	Calibri Light, 12 pt, left align, spacing 2 pt before, 0 pt after, blue
Heading 4	*Calibri Light, 11 pt, italic, left align, spacing 2 pt before, 0 pt after, blue*
Heading 5	Calibri Light, 11 pt, left align, spacing 2 pt before, 0 pt after, blue

Additional Information

Only the first five heading styles appear in the Styles gallery. Additional heading styles appear when the previous heading level is used.

There are nine heading styes. The Heading 1 style is the largest and most prominent and should be used for the major points in your document. Subheadings are assigned the Heading 2 style, and so on. Headings give the reader visual cues about how information is organized in your document. You will apply a Heading 1 style to the Tanzania main heading.

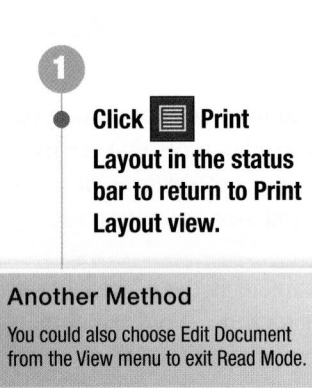

1

- Click [ ] Print Layout in the status bar to return to Print Layout view.

Another Method

You could also choose Edit Document from the View menu to exit Read Mode.

- Move to the Tanzania heading at the beginning of the document.

- If necessary, open the Home tab.

- Click [ ] More in the Styles group to open the Styles gallery.

Another Method

You also can scroll the list of styles.

Your screen should be similar to
Figure 3.2

Figure 3.2

The Styles gallery displays 19 style options, including the five heading styles. The current style, Normal, is selected as this is the style applied to the Tanzania text. Each style is named and displays a sample of the style formatting above the name. The formatting of the different styles reflects a selection of colors, fonts, and effects. When you point to a style, the document displays a Live Preview of how that style would appear if selected.

- **Point to several styles to see how they would look.**

- **Choose Heading 1.**

Having Trouble?

If you accidentally apply the wrong style, simply select the correct style.

Your screen should be similar to Figure 3.3

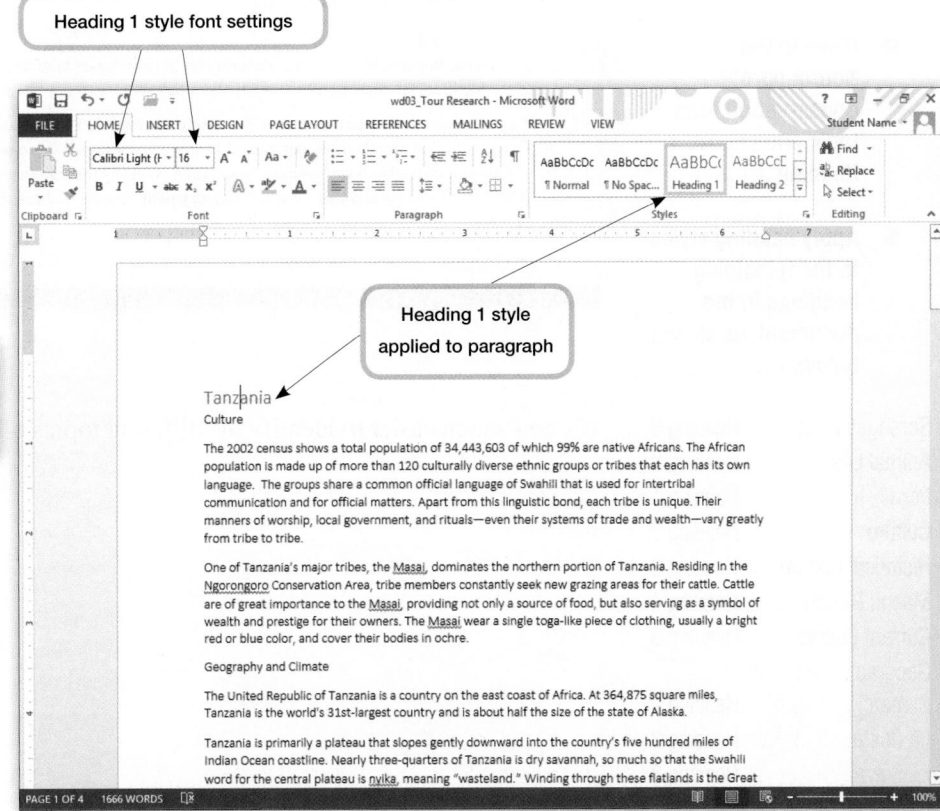

Figure 3.3

Notice that the entire title appears in the selected style. This is because the Heading 1 style is a paragraph style, affecting the entire paragraph at the insertion point. The Heading 1 style includes font settings of Calibri Light, 16 pt, in blue.

You will now apply heading styles to the remaining headings in the document. You can choose from the displayed styles in the Ribbon without opening the Styles gallery. You also can click ⊡ to scroll through the gallery.

- Move to the Culture topic.

- Choose Heading 2 from the Styles gallery.

- Move to the Geography and Climate topic and choose Heading 2.

- Move to the Ngorongoro Conservation Area topic and choose Heading 3.

- Apply heading styles to the remaining headings in the document, as shown below.

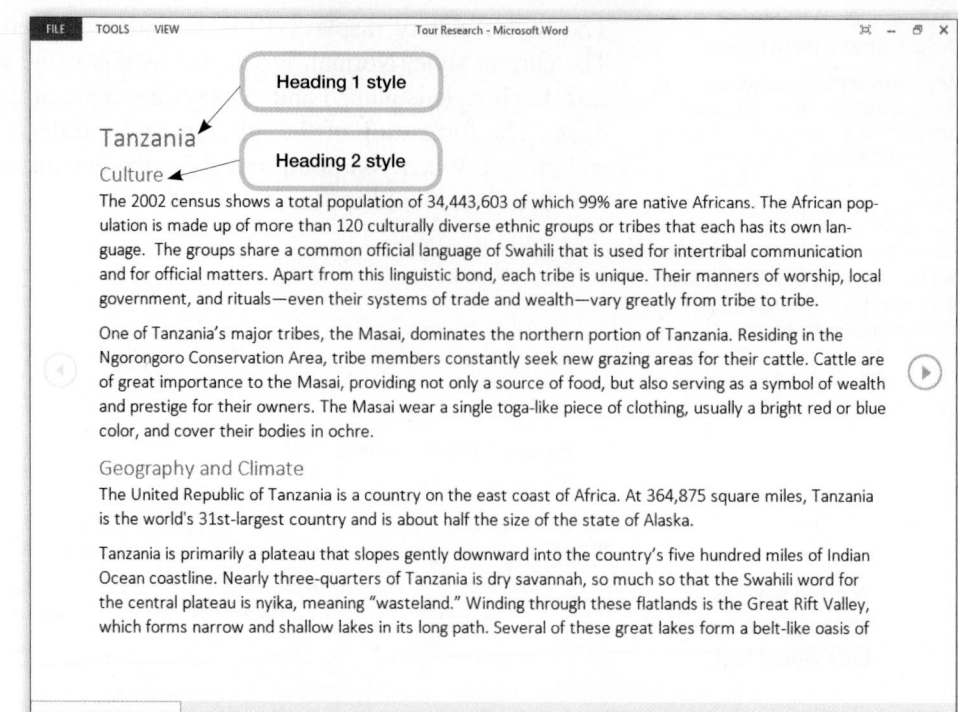

Figure 3.4

Serengeti Plain	Heading 3
Animal Life	Heading 2
Peru	Heading 1
Culture	Heading 2
Historical Culture	Heading 3
Machu Picchu	Heading 4
Current Culture	Heading 3
Geography and Climate	Heading 2
La Costa	Heading 3
La Selva	Heading 3
La Sierra	Heading 3
Animal Life	Heading 2

It's now much easier to identify the different topics of information in the document.

- Save the document as Tour Research to your solution file location.

- Move to the top of the document and display the document in Read Mode.

Your screen should be similar to Figure 3.4

UPDATING THE NORMAL STYLE

Another change you would like to make to the document to make it easier to read is to increase the font size of all the body text from 11 points to 12 points. The body text in your document is determined by the Normal style, which currently specifies an 11-point font. The easiest way to increase the point size of all the body text in the document is to first increase the point size of a paragraph of body text and then update the Normal style to match that text.

1

- Change to Print Layout view.

- Select the first paragraph below the Tanzania and Culture headings and increase the font size to 12 points.

- Right-click the paragraph and click 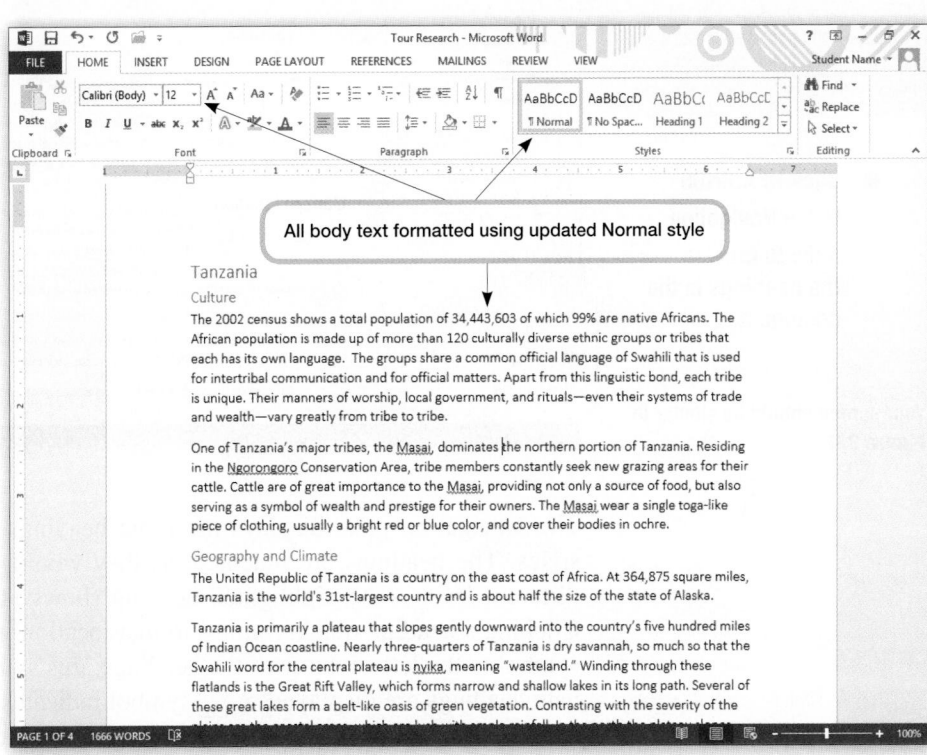 on the Mini toolbar.

- Right-click the Normal style and choose Update Normal to Match Selection.

- Click in the document to clear the selection.

Your screen should be similar to Figure 3.5

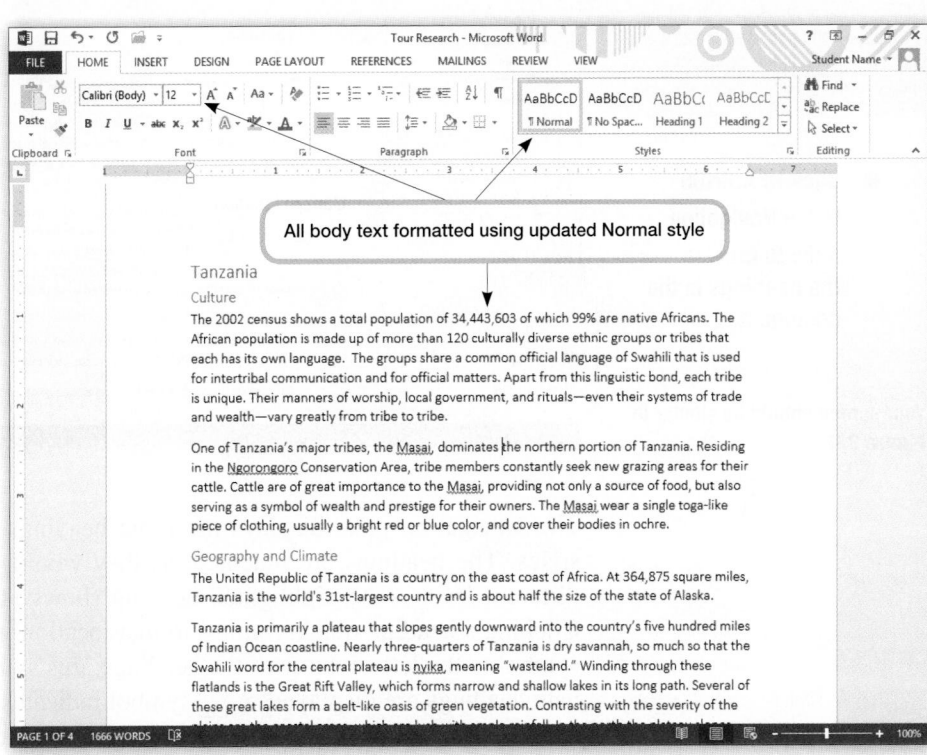

All body text formatted using updated Normal style

Figure 3.5

All body text in the document that uses the Normal style has been immediately updated to the new font size of 12 points. The new Normal style settings affect this document only and will not affect the Normal style in any other document.

Navigating a Document

In a large document, locating and moving to an area of text you want to view can take a lot of time. However, after headings are applied, there are several features that make navigation easier. For example, when scrolling by dragging the scroll box, a ScreenTip identifies the topic heading in addition to the page number that will be displayed when you stop dragging the scroll box. Even more convenient, however, is to use the Navigation pane to jump to a selected location.

BROWSING BY HEADINGS

The Navigation pane is used to quickly view and browse document headings, expand and collapse headings, change heading levels, and move topics.

1

Press Ctrl + F to display the Navigation pane.

Another Method

You also can click the Find button in the Editing group of the Home tab, select Navigation pane from the View tab, or click page count in the status bar to open the Navigation pane.

Click HEADINGS in the Navigation pane to browse the headings in the document.

Your screen should be similar to Figure 3.6

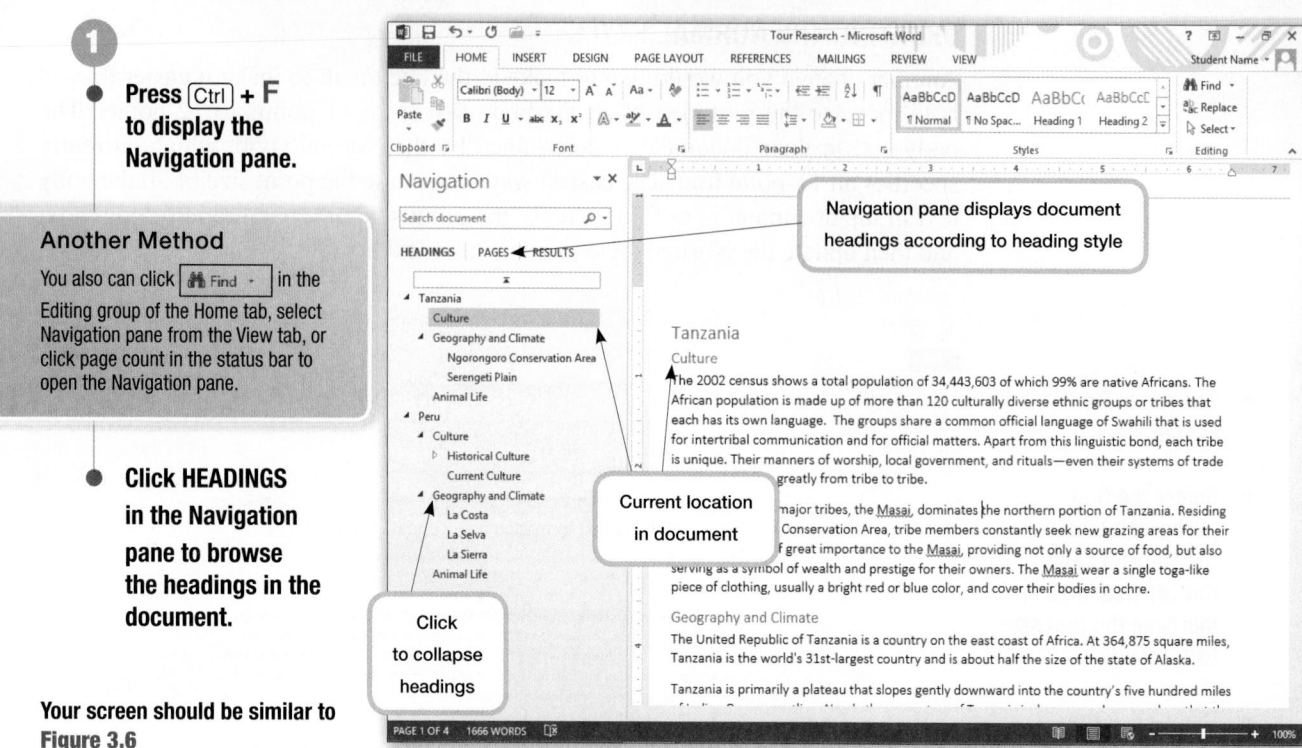

Figure 3.6

The Navigation pane displays the topic headings you identified using heading styles. The headings are indented, as they would be in an outline, to show the different levels. The highlighted heading shows your location in the document. Clicking a heading quickly jumps to that location in the document. Notice the ◢ symbol to the left of many of the headings; this symbol indicates that all subordinate headings are displayed. A ▷ symbol indicates that subordinate headings are not displayed. Clicking these buttons expands or collapses the subordinate headings in the Navigation pane.

2

Click the Peru heading in the Navigation pane.

In the Navigation pane, click ◢ in the Peru topic to collapse the headings.

Your screen should be similar to Figure 3.7

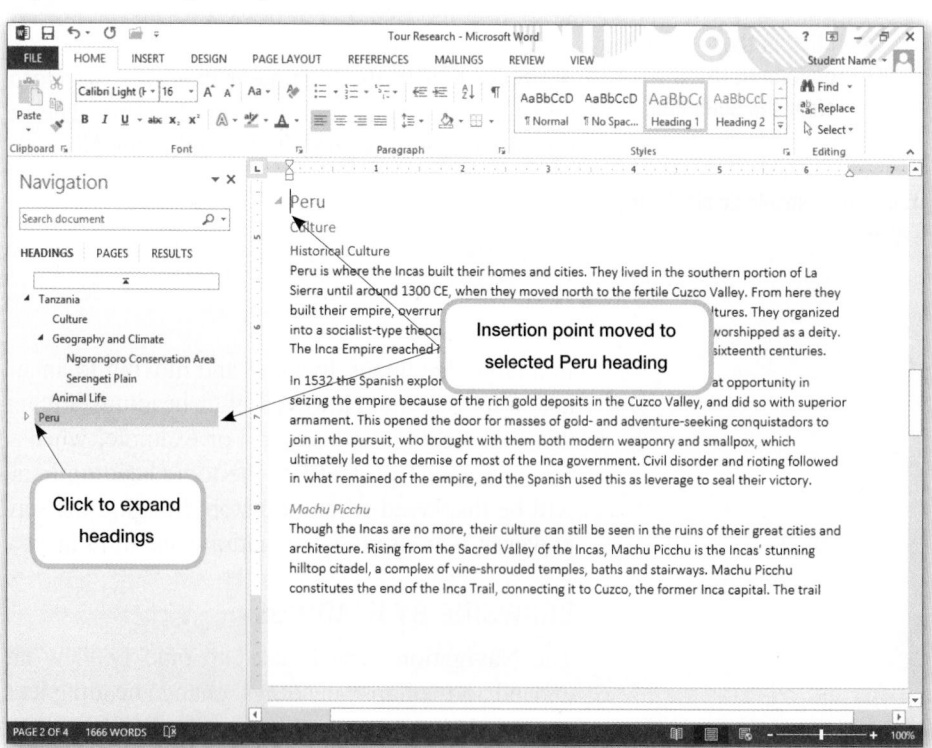

Figure 3.7

The selected topic appears at the top of the window. The subtopics below Peru are hidden in the Navigation pane; however, the document itself still displays the Peru content. Collapsing headings in the Navigation pane is particularly helpful when navigating a long document.

Additional Information

You can also double-click a heading in the Navigation pane to expand and collapse the headings.

3

- Click ▷ again in the Peru topic to expand the headings.

- On your own, practice expanding and collapsing headings.

- Expand all headings again so that your screen looks similar to Figure 3.6.

As you look at the organization of the report, you decide to move the discussion of culture in the Tanzania section so that it follows the Geography and Climate section. Moving headings using the Navigation pane quickly selects and moves the entire topic, including subtopics and all body text.

4

- Click the Culture heading in the Tanzania section and drag it down to above the Animal Life heading in the same section.

Additional Information

A solid line will display showing where the topic will be moved.

- Click the Culture heading in the Peru section and drag it down to above the Animal Life heading in the same section.

- Click the Culture heading again in the Peru section.

- Save the document.

Your screen should be similar to Figure 3.8

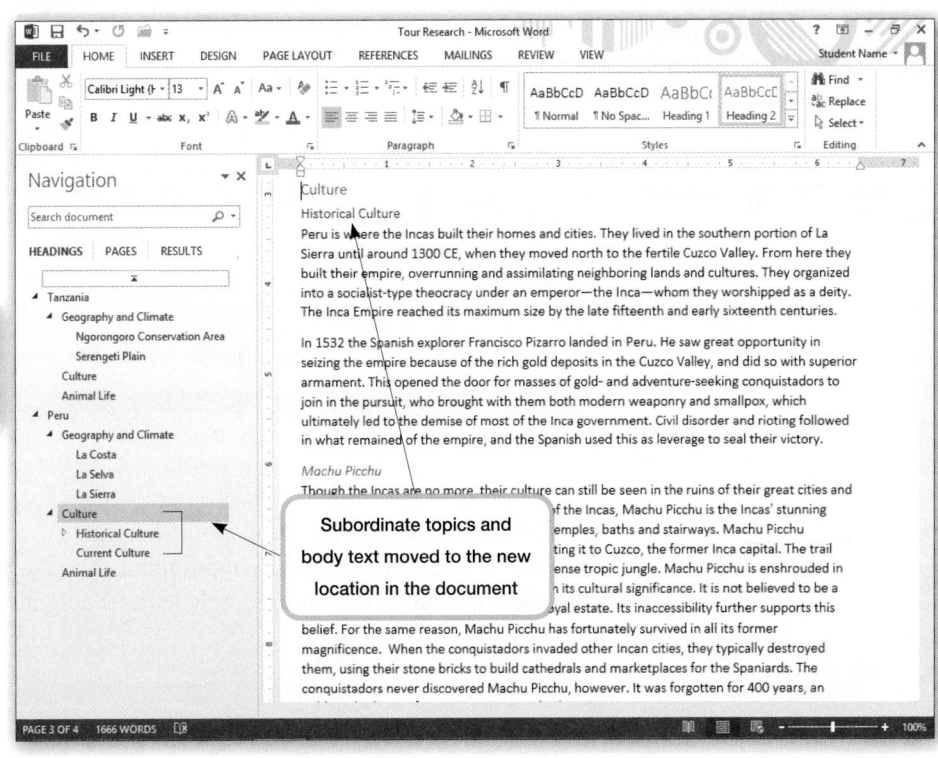

Figure 3.8

Additional Information

There may be times when you want to change the level of a heading in your document. For example, you might want to turn a Heading 1 into a Heading 2 heading. To do this, right-click the heading in the Navigation pane and then choose ← Promote or → Demote.

In the Navigation pane, the subtopics appear below the heading you moved. When you move or change the level of a heading that includes subordinate headings and body text, the headings and text are also selected. Any changes you make to the heading, such as moving, copying, or deleting, also affect the subordinate text.

BROWSING BY PAGES

The Navigation pane also can display thumbnails of each page in your document. Clicking on a thumbnail moves directly to that page.

1

- **Click PAGES in the Navigation pane.**

- **Click on the page 4 thumbnail in the Navigation pane.**

- **Scroll to the top of the Navigation pane and click the page 2 thumbnail.**

Your screen should be similar to Figure 3.9

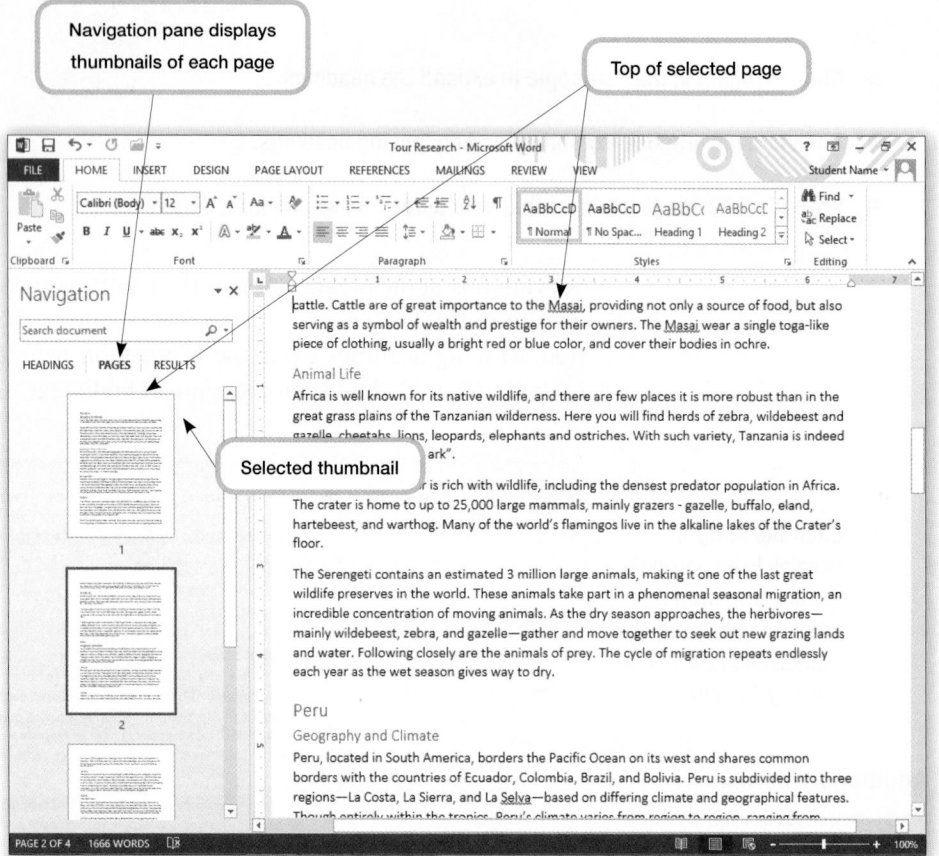

Figure 3.9

In the document, the insertion point has moved to the top of the selected page and the selected thumbnail is highlighted. The Navigation pane remains open in the view you are using until you close the Navigation pane or close the document window.

COLLAPSING AND EXPANDING PARTS OF A DOCUMENT

In addition to collapsing and expanding headings in the Navigation pane, you can use the small triangles that appear when you move the insertion point over a heading to collapse or expand content in the document window.

- **Click the thumbnail for page 1 and change to HEADINGS view in the Navigation pane.**

- **Point to the Tanzania heading in the document window.**

- **Click ◢ to collapse the entire Tanzania section.**

Your screen should be similar to Figure 3.10

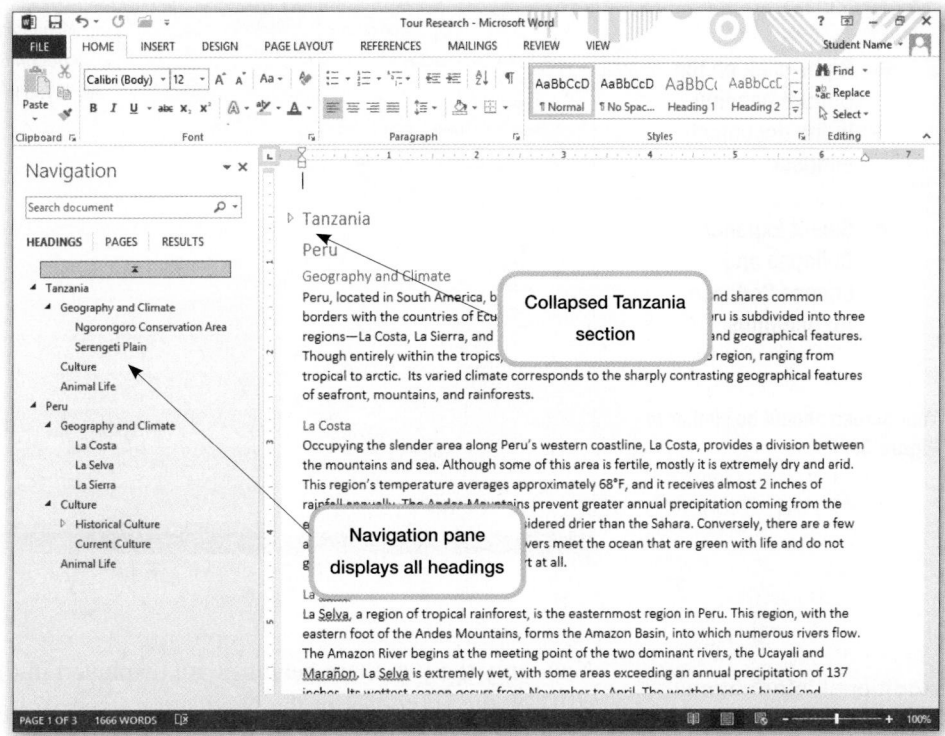

Figure 3.10

All the content below the Tanzania heading is collapsed and hidden from view. The Navigation pane, however, still shows all the heading levels for Peru. This makes it easy to quickly expand the content in the document window again and at the same time move to the selected topic. When you right-click on a heading, the Expand/Collapse option displays in the context menu. The submenu includes options to Expand or Collapse a Heading or to Expand or Collapse All Headings.

2

- Click **Culture** in the Tanzania section in the Navigation pane.

- Right-click on the **Culture** heading in the document window.

- Select **Expand/ Collapse** and choose **Collapse All Headings**.

Your screen should be similar to Figure 3.11

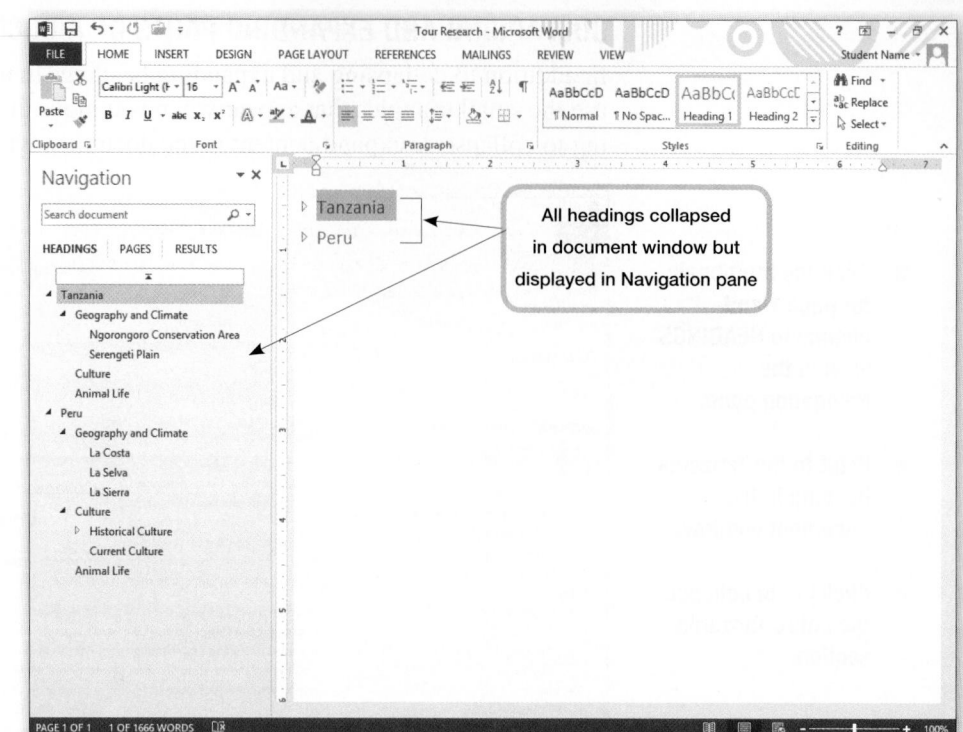

All headings collapsed in document window but displayed in Navigation pane

Figure 3.11

Additional Information

The solid ▲ indicates that all subtopics are expanded and the ▷ indicates the subtopics are collapsed.

Now only the two main headings are displayed in the document window. You can still see the subtopics in the Navigation pane. You also can expand and collapse headings in the document window using the triangles.

3

- Close the Navigation pane.

- Click the triangle ▷ beside Peru.

- Click the triangle ▷ beside Tanzania.

- Right-click the Tanzania heading, select Expand/Collapse, and choose Expand All Headings.

You were easily able to expand headings without using the Navigation pane and now the entire document is visible again.

Creating a Cover Page

Now you want to add a title or cover page. Generally, this page includes information such as the report title, the name of the author, and the date.

When preparing research reports, two styles of report formatting are commonly used: MLA (Modern Language Association) and APA (American Psychological Association). Although they require the same basic information, they differ in how this information is presented. For example, MLA style does not include a separate title page, but APA style does. The report you will create in this lab will use many of the style requirements of the MLA. However, because this report is not a formal report to be presented at a conference or other academic proceeding, some liberties have been taken with the style to demonstrate Word 2013 features.

INSERTING A COVER PAGE

Word 2013 includes many preformatted building blocks that help you quickly create professional-looking documents. The preformatted content includes cover pages, pull quotes, and headers and footers. They are fully formatted and include placeholders where you enter the title, date, and other information. Regardless of the location of the insertion point in a document, a cover page is always automatically inserted at the beginning of the document.

1

● **Open the Insert tab.**

● **Click** 📄 Cover Page ▾ **in the Pages group.**

● **Scroll the gallery and choose the Whisp cover page design.**

● **Change the zoom to display two pages.**

Having Trouble?

Use the Zoom slider or ⊞ Multiple Pages on the View tab.

Your screen should be similar to Figure 3.12

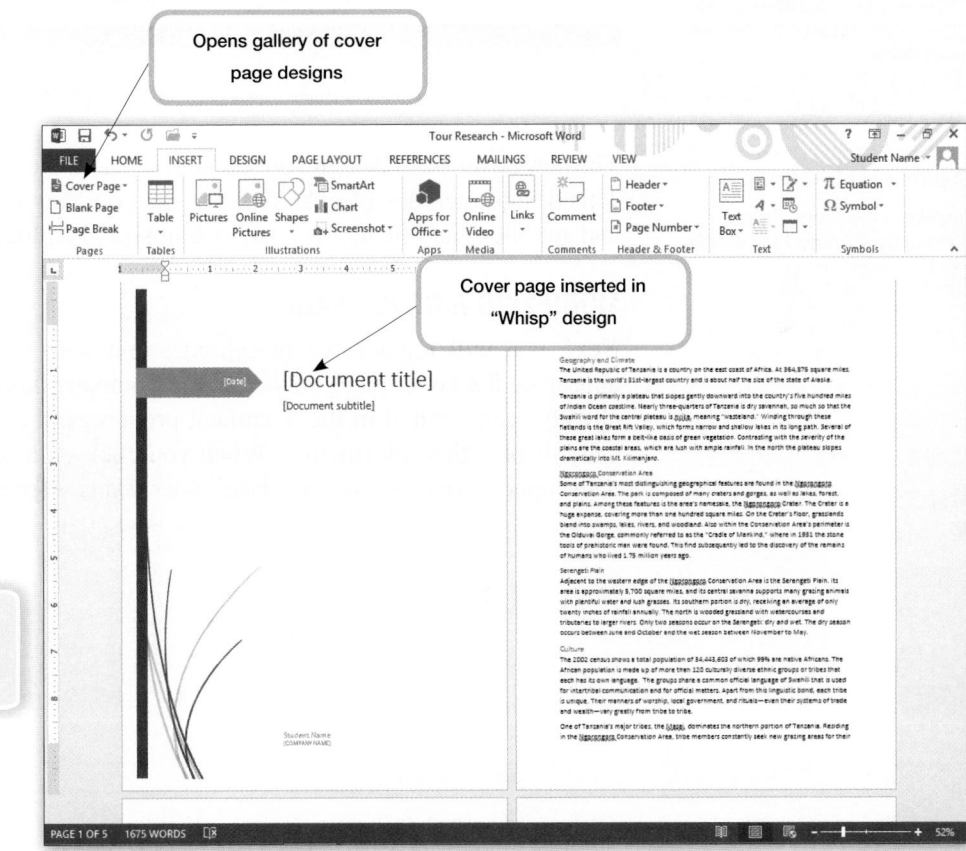

Opens gallery of cover page designs

Cover page inserted in "Whisp" design

Figure 3.12

A new page is inserted at the beginning of the document with the selected cover page design.

After looking at this design, you decide to change it to a more traditional cover page look.

2

- **Click** [Cover Page ▾] on the Insert tab.

- **Choose the Sideline design.**

Your screen should be similar to Figure 3.13

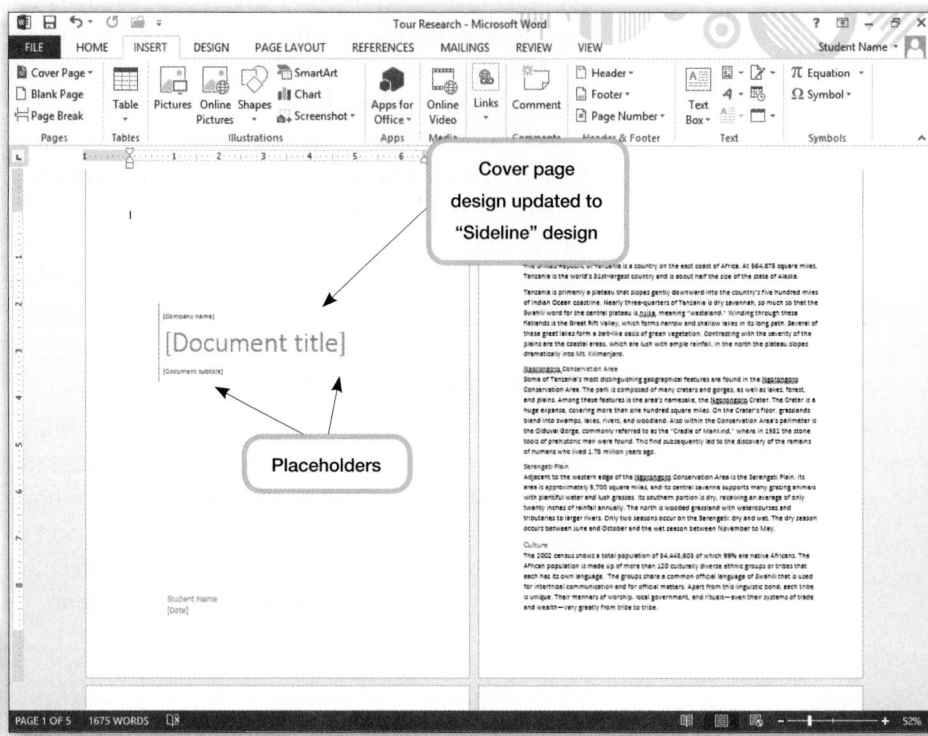

Cover page design updated to "Sideline" design

[Company name]

[Document title]

[Document subtitle]

Placeholders

Student name
[Date]

Figure 3.13

The new cover page design you selected replaces the first cover page you inserted. This design includes placeholders for the company name and the document title and subtitle. The title text is a larger font size and blue.

MODIFYING A COVER PAGE

Next, you will replace the placeholder text with the information you want to appear on the cover page. If the author, company name, and document title have already been entered in the document properties, the placeholders will automatically display this information. When you click on a placeholder, the placeholder name appears in a tab and the placeholder text is selected and ready to be replaced.

- Increase the zoom to 70%.

- Scroll the window to see the placeholders at the bottom of the cover page.

- Click the Company name placeholder and type **Adventure Travel Tours**

- Click the Document Title placeholder, and type **Tanzania and Peru**

Your screen should be similar to Figure 3.14

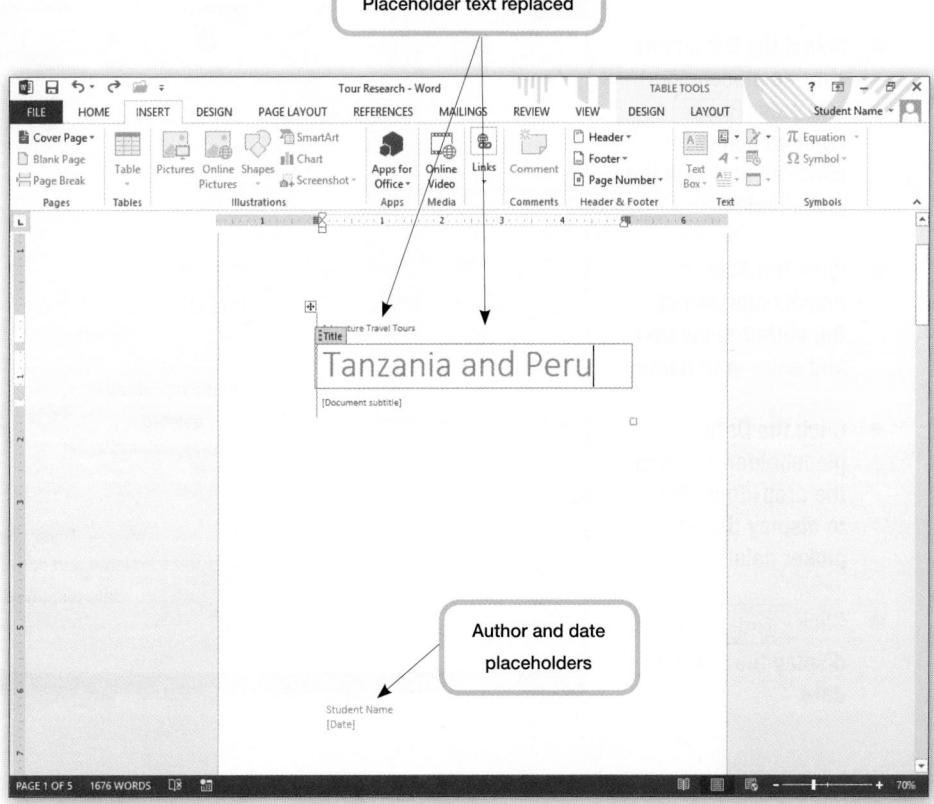

Placeholder text replaced

Author and date placeholders

Figure 3.14

The placeholder text was replaced with the text you typed. Additionally, the company name and title information you entered have been automatically added to the document properties.

Finally, you will delete the Company subtitle placeholder and add your name as author and the current date. Notice Student Name appears as the Author because this is the name that is stored in the document properties. Since the name is not placeholder text, you will need to select it before replacing it with your name. When you click the Date placeholder, you will use the date picker feature to quickly enter the current date from the pop-up calendar.

- Select the Document subtitle placeholder and press (Delete) twice to delete the contents and then the placeholder.

- Click the Author placeholder, select the author name text, and enter your name.

- Click the Date placeholder and open the drop-down list to display the date picker calendar.

- Click [Today] to display the current date.

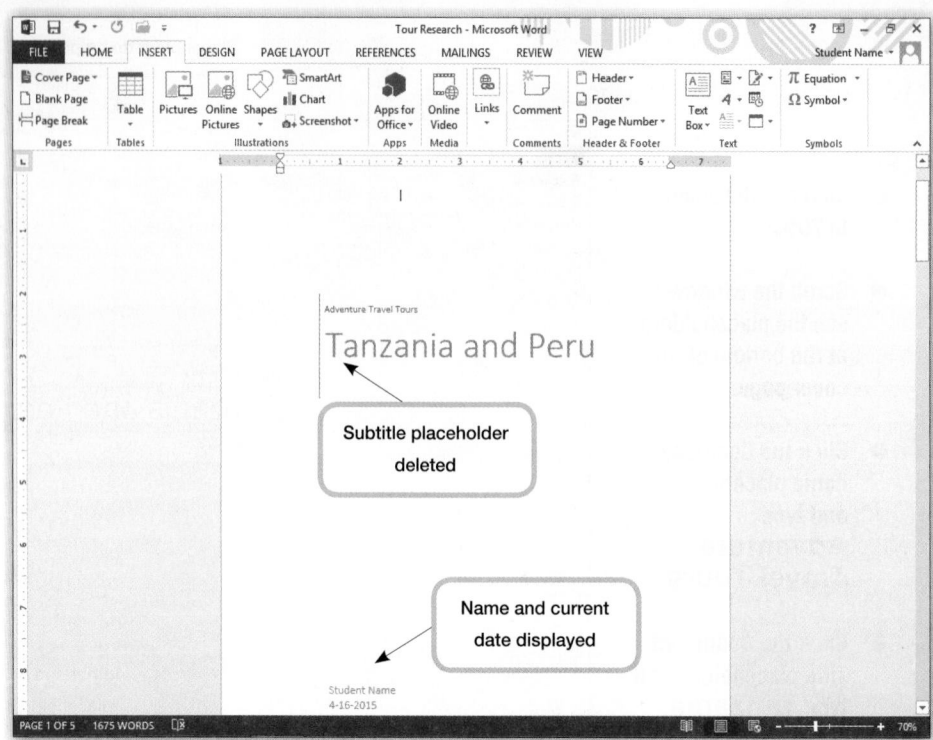

Figure 3.15

- Click outside the placeholder.

- Save the document.

Your screen should be similar to Figure 3.15

Using Document Themes

Because color and design are important elements of documents, Word includes a collection of built-in document themes.

Concept ① Theme

A **theme** is a predefined set of formatting choices that can be applied to an entire document in one simple step. Heading styles and other effects available to your document are determined by the current theme. Word includes several named built-in document themes. Each document theme includes three subsets of themes: colors, fonts, and effects. Each color theme consists of 12 colors that are applied to specific elements in a document. Each fonts theme includes different body and heading fonts. Each effects theme includes different line and fill effects. You also can create your own custom themes by modifying an existing document theme and saving it as a custom theme.

The Blank document template (Normal.dotm) uses the Office theme. If you change the current theme, style choices that you've previously made will be updated to match settings in the new theme. However, colors that you've selected from the standard colors gallery will remain the same.

Using themes gives your documents a professional and modern look. Because document themes are shared across 2013 Office applications, all your office documents can have the same uniform look.

APPLYING A THEME

Next, you will apply a different document theme to the report.

①
- **Change the zoom to display two pages.**

- **Open the Design tab.**

- **Click** [Themes] **from the Document Formatting group.**

Your screen should be similar to Figure 3.16

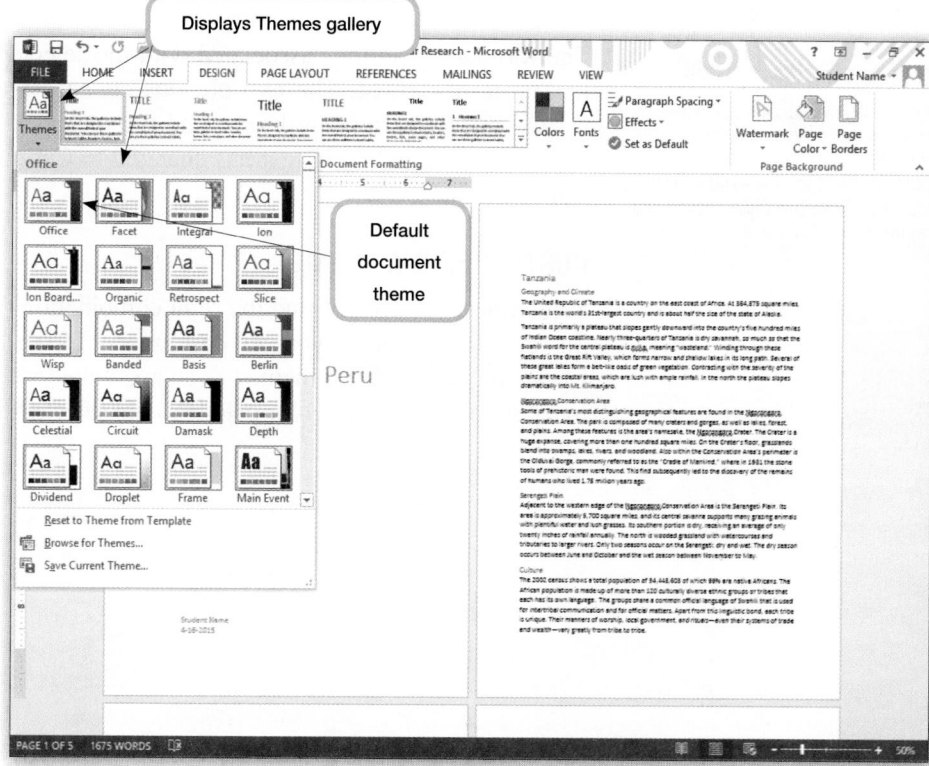

Figure 3.16

A gallery of built-in named themes is displayed. A sample shows the color and font effects included in each theme. The Office theme is the default theme and is the theme that is used in this document. Pointing to each theme will display a Live Preview of how it will appear in the document.

- Point to several themes to preview them.

- Choose the Slice theme.

Your screen should be similar to Figure 3.17

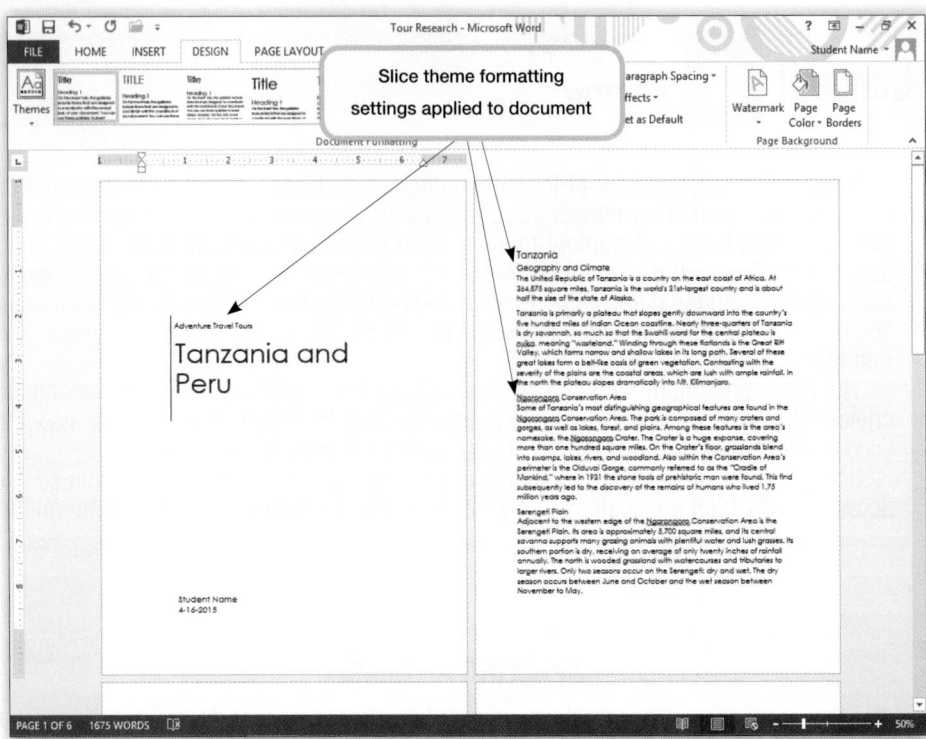

Figure 3.17

If you made manual changes to text, for example, by increasing the font size of the body text, or changing the font and font size of the title as opposed to applying a Title style, these changes are not updated to the new theme design.

The formatting settings associated with the selected theme have been applied to the entire document. The two obvious changes are the color and font changes for the titles and heading levels, and the increased line spacing. The font of all heading styles and body text has changed to Century Gothic from the default of Calibri Light.

CUSTOMIZING A THEME

Sometimes, you cannot find the right combination of features in a built-in theme. To solve this problem, you can customize a theme by changing the color palette, fonts, and effects. Each theme has an associated set of colors that you can change by applying a different color palette to the selected theme.

1

Click Colors .

Your screen should be similar to
Figure 3.18

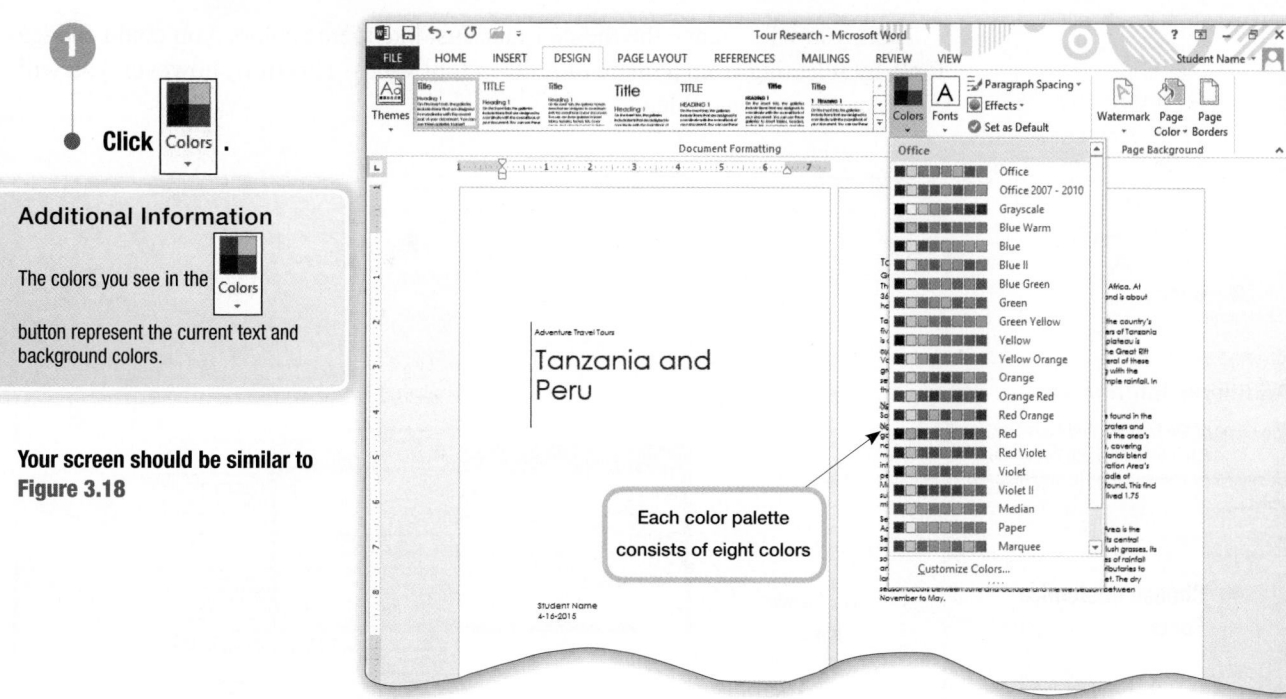

A drop-down list of 23 built-in color palettes is displayed. Each palette consists of eight colors that represent the text, background, accent, and hyperlink colors. Pointing to a color palette will display a Live Preview of the selection. You want to see how the Green color palette would look.

2

Point to several color palettes to preview them.

Choose Green.

Your screen should be similar to
Figure 3.19

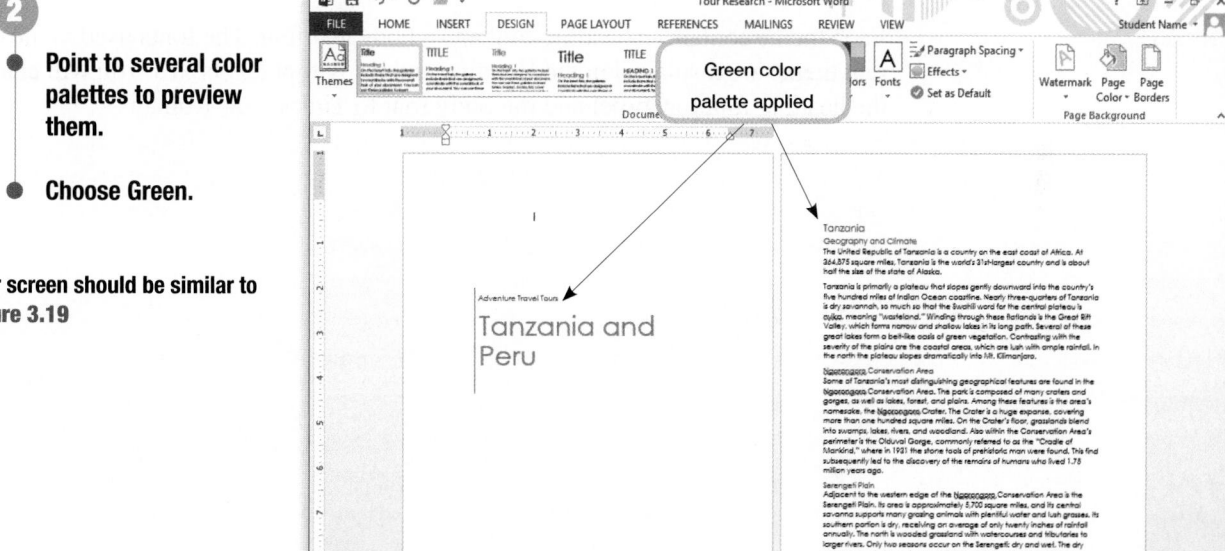

The new color palette has been applied to different elements such as the headings. All other aspects of the Slice theme are unchanged.

Next, you will change the theme fonts. Just like theme colors, you could change fonts by selecting from a menu of built-in font styles. This time, however, you will create a custom font style.

3

Click [A Fonts] .

Additional Information

The name of the heading and body text fonts for each theme appears below the Theme Fonts name in the Theme Fonts gallery.

• Choose Customize Fonts.

Your screen should be similar to Figure 3.20

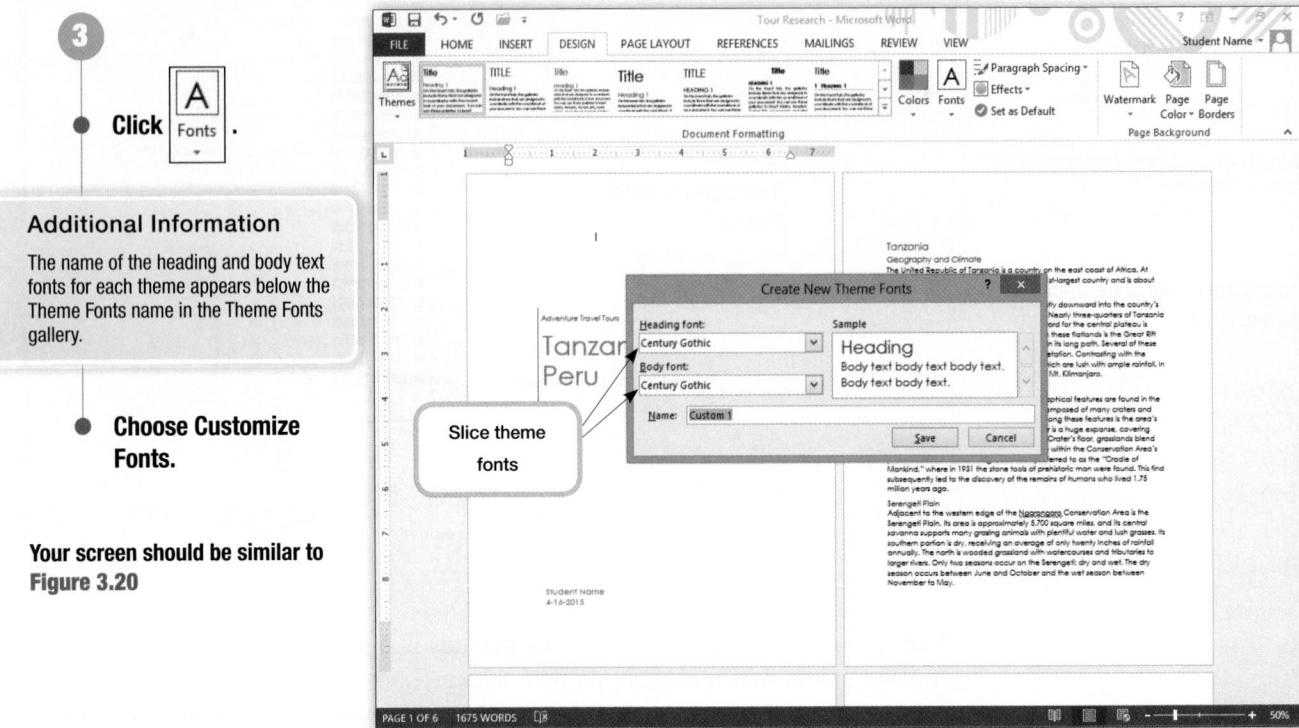

Figure 3.20

Each theme contains a heading font and a body text font. The fonts used in the current theme are displayed in the Heading and Body font text boxes. You will change the heading font to Corbel and the body font to Times New Roman.

- **From the Heading font: drop-down list, choose Corbel.**

- **From the Body font: drop-down list, choose Times New Roman.**

- **Replace the default name with Report Font**

- **Click** Save .

- **Click** Fonts .

Your screen should be similar to Figure 3.21

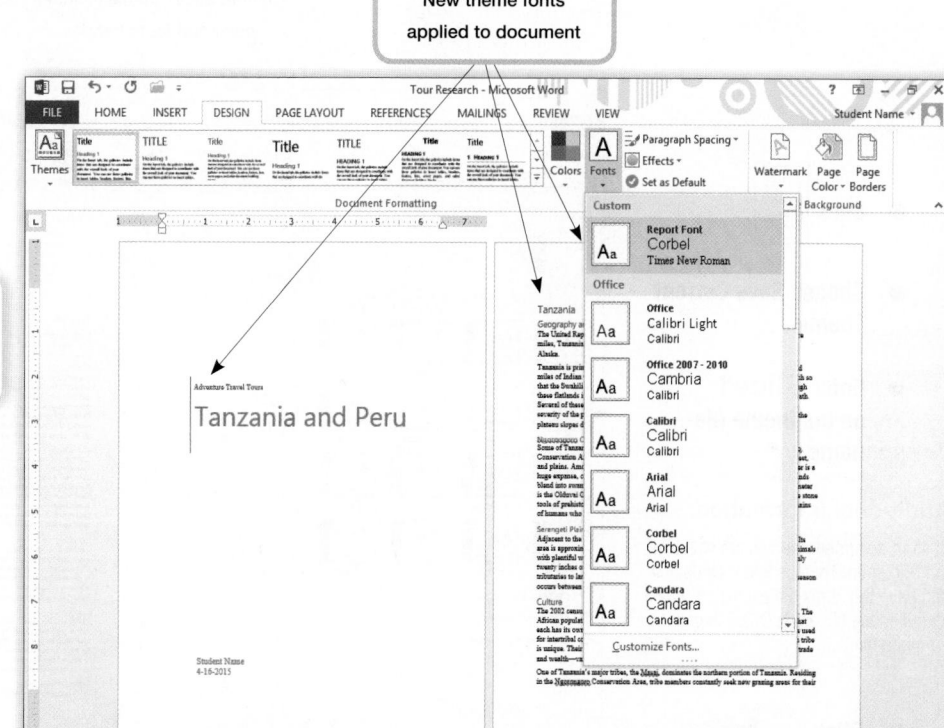

Figure 3.21

The name of the custom theme font appears at the top of the Theme Fonts gallery list and could be applied simply by selecting it from the list. As you add other features to the document, they will be formatted using the customized Slice theme colors and fonts.

SAVING A CUSTOM THEME

After making changes to the Slice theme, you decide to save the changes as a custom theme. Custom theme settings can be applied to another document in the future.

Custom Slice1 theme includes
color and font changes

- **Click** Themes.

- **Choose Save Current Theme.**

- **Enter** Slice1 as the theme file name.

Additional Information

Custom document themes are saved in the Document Themes folder by default and have the .thmx file extension, which identifies the file as an Office theme template file.

- **Click** Save.

Having Trouble?

If the Slice1 custom theme already exists, click **Yes** to replace it.

- **Click** Themes.

Your screen should be similar to Figure 3.22

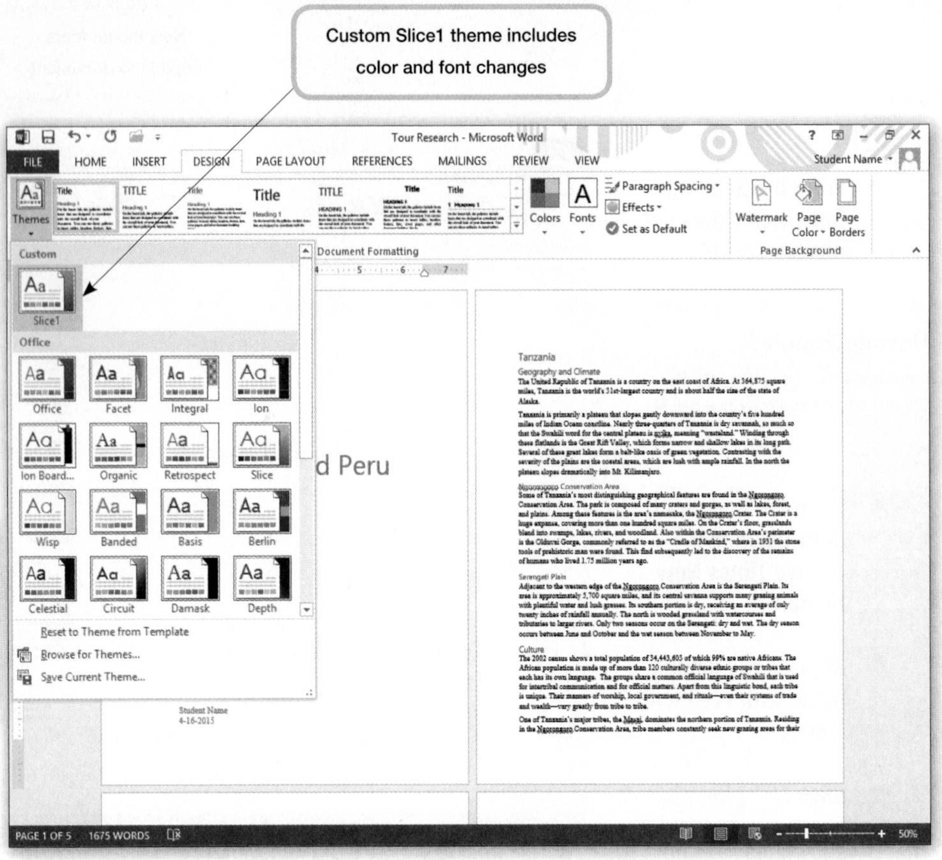

Additional Information

To remove a custom theme, choose Delete from the theme's shortcut menu.

Additional Information

You can quickly return a document back to the default style using Reset to Theme from Template on the Themes menu.

Figure 3.22

The custom theme you created appears at the top of the Themes gallery. Now you can quickly reapply this entire theme in one step to another document.

CHANGING THE STYLE SET

Another way to quickly change the look of the entire document is by selecting a Style Set. Style Sets are built-in combinations of font and paragraph properties that are applied to the body and headings of the entire document. The colors in the Style Set reflect the selected theme colors.

1

• Click ⏷ in the Document Formatting group to open the Style Set gallery.

• Point to several Style Sets to preview their effect on the document.

• Choose the Modern Style Set.

Having Trouble?

If the Modern Style Set is not available, choose Fancy.

Your screen should be similar to Figure 3.23

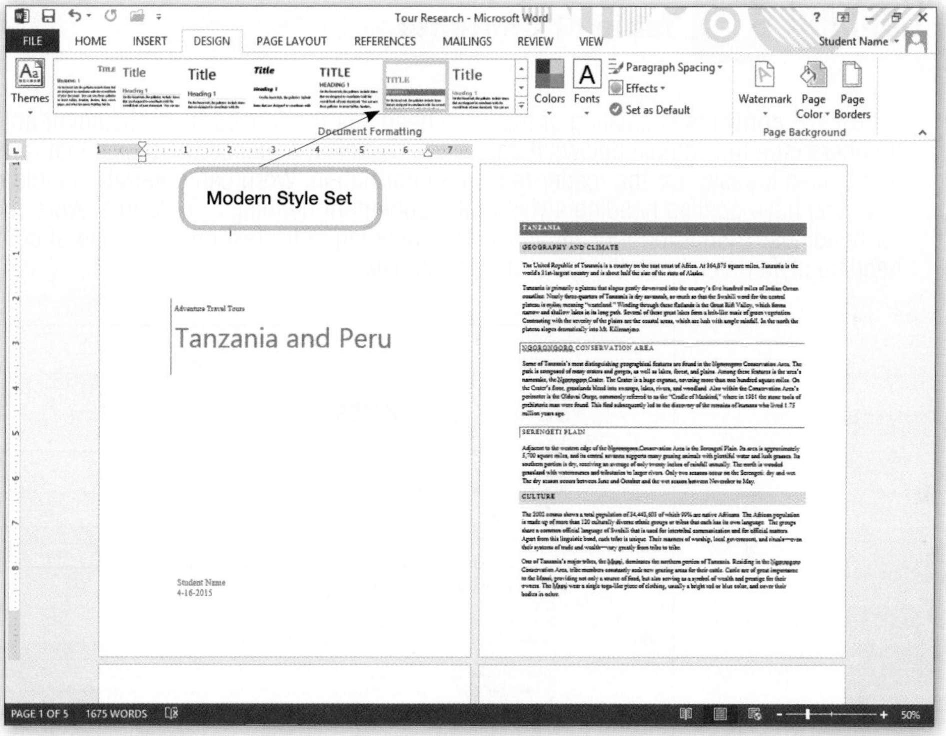

Figure 3.23

In addition to font and paragraph setting changes, this Style Set adds highlight bars and horizontal lines to further differentiate heading levels. You decide to undo this change and keep the previous settings.

2

• Click ↶ Undo to remove the Style Set.

• Save the document.

Creating a Table of Contents

Next you will create the table of contents for the report.

Concept 2 Table of Contents

A **table of contents** is a listing of the topic headings that appear in a document and their associated page numbers (see the sample below). It shows the reader at a glance the topics that are included in the document and makes it easier for the reader to locate information. Word can generate a table of contents automatically after you have applied heading styles to the document headings. To do this, Word first searches the document for headings. Then it formats and inserts the heading entry text into the table of contents. The level of the heading style determines the table of contents level.

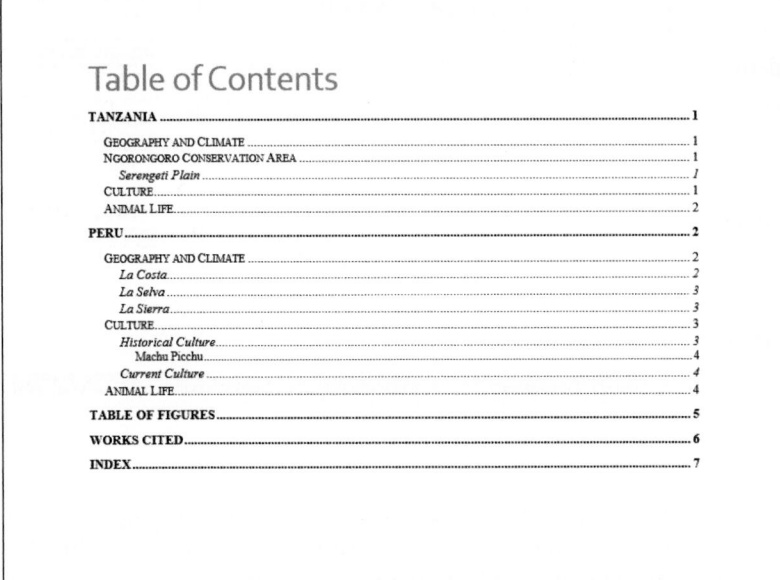

The table of contents that is generated is a field that can be easily updated to reflect changes you may make to the document after the list is generated. Additionally, each entry in the table is a hyperlink to the heading in the document.

INSERTING A BLANK PAGE

Since a table of contents appears at the beginning of a document, you will need to insert a blank page after the title page.

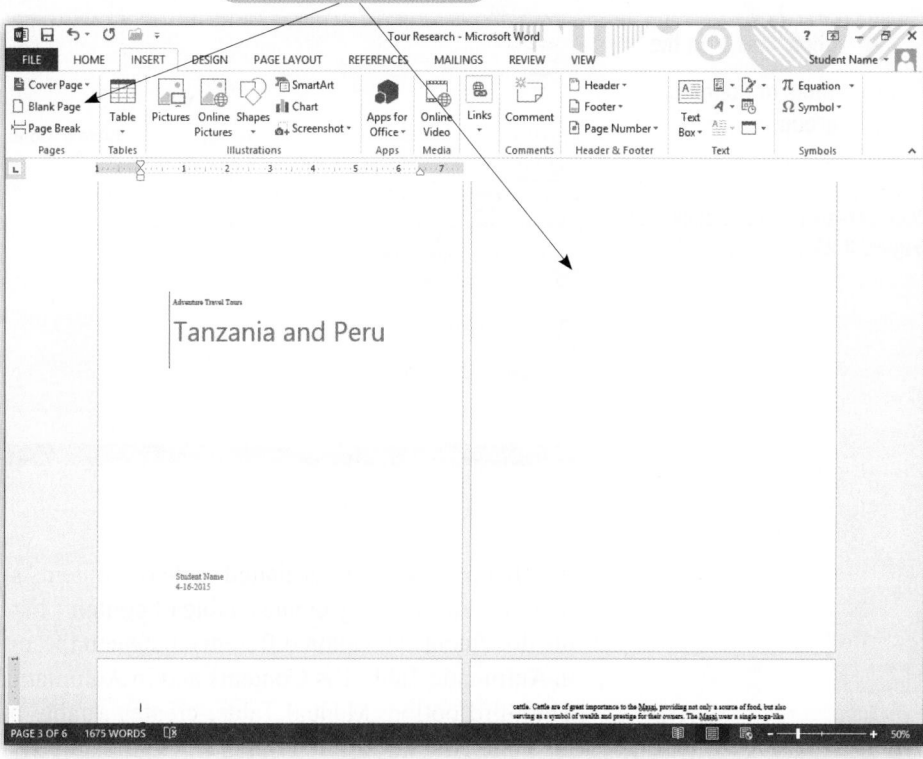

> Inserts blank page above location of insertion point

1

- **Move to the blank line above the Tanzania heading at the top of page 2.**

- **Open the Insert tab and click Blank Page in the Pages group.**

Another Method

You also could press Ctrl + Enter to insert a blank page.

Your screen should be similar to Figure 3.24

Figure 3.24

Having Trouble?

If a second blank page is also inserted, change to Draft view and delete one of the hard page break lines.

Additional Information

MLA and APA styles do not use a table of contents.

A blank page has been inserted in the document at the location of the insertion point.

GENERATING A TABLE OF CONTENTS

The document already includes heading styles to identify the different topics in the report. Now, all you need to do is select the style you want to use for the table of contents.

1

- **Move to the top of the newly inserted page (see Figure 3.25).**

- **Open the References tab.**

- **Click** Table of Contents **in the Table of Contents group.**

Your screen should be similar to Figure 3.25

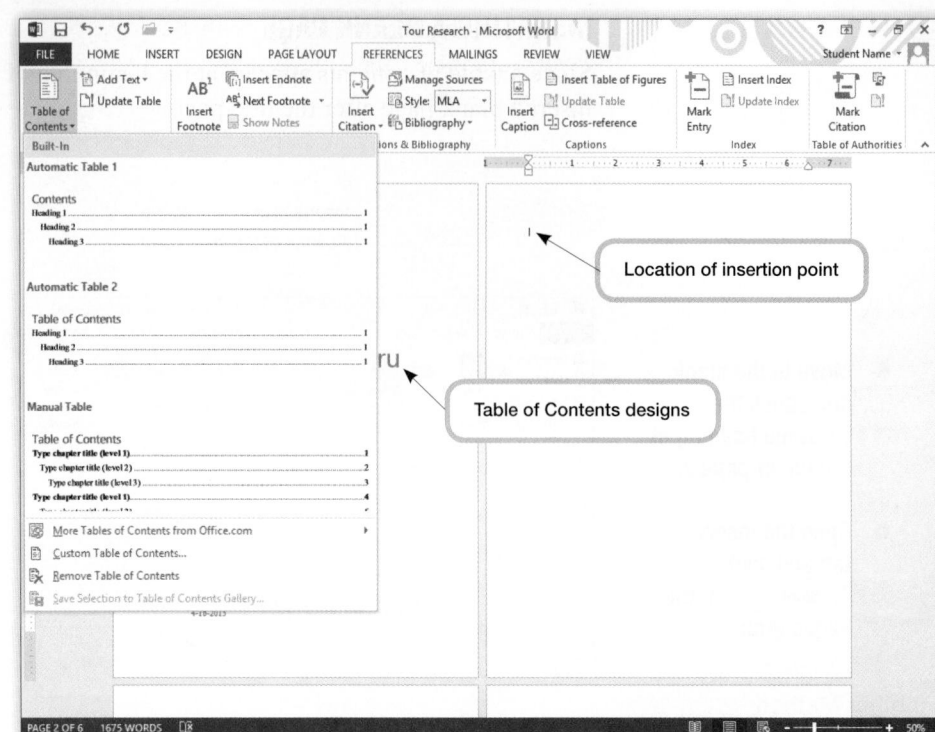

Location of insertion point

Table of Contents designs

Figure 3.25

A gallery of three preformatted table of contents styles is displayed. The first two options automatically create a table of contents list using the Heading 1–3 styles in the document. The main difference between these two options is that the title used in Automatic Table 1 is Contents and in Automatic Table 2 it is Table of Contents. The third option, Manual Table, creates a table of contents that you can fill out independent of the content in the document.

2

- **Choose Automatic Table 2.**

- **Increase the zoom to 100% and then scroll upward to see the table of contents.**

- **Click anywhere in the table of contents to select it.**

Your screen should be similar to Figure 3.26

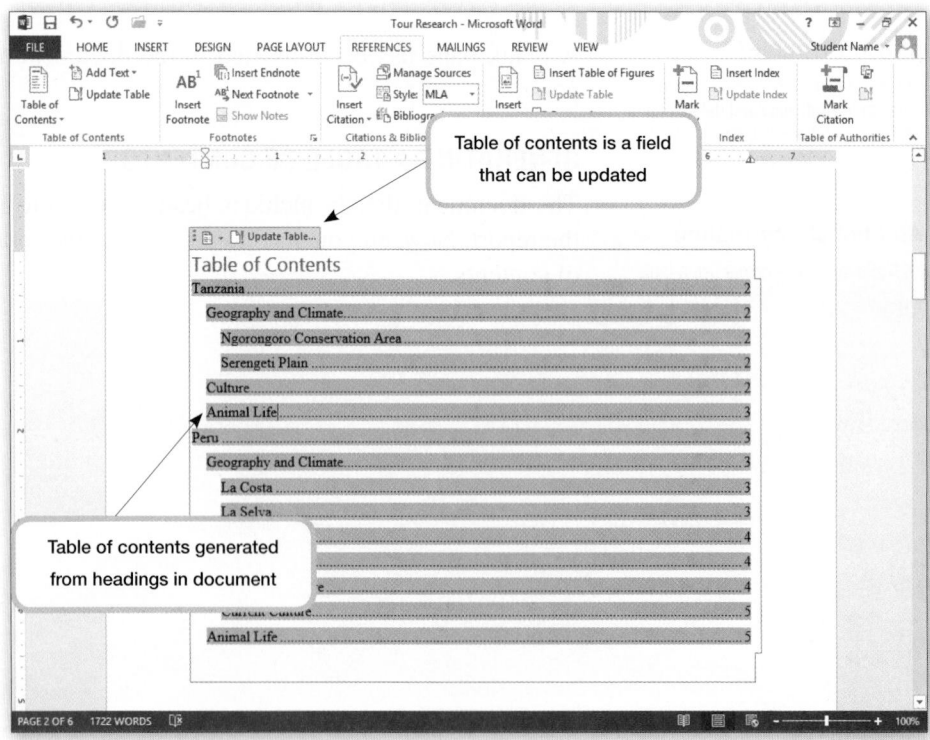

Table of contents is a field that can be updated

Table of contents generated from headings in document

Figure 3.26

WWW.MHHE.COM/OLEARY

Word 2013

Word searched for headings with the specified styles, sorted them by heading level, referenced their page numbers, and displayed the table of contents using the selected style in the document. The headings that were assigned a Heading 1 style are aligned with the left margin, and subordinate heading levels are indented as appropriate. The table of contents displays the page numbers flush with the right margin with a dotted-line tab leader between the heading entry and the page number. It includes all entries in the document that are formatted with Headings 1, 2, and 3.

The table of contents is a field that is highlighted and enclosed in a box when selected. The field tab provides quick access to the Table of Contents menu by clicking Table of Contents and the Update Table... command button. Because it is a field, the table of contents can be easily updated to reflect changes you may make to the document after the list is generated.

MODIFYING A TABLE OF CONTENTS

You want the table of contents to include topics formatted with the Heading 4 style. Additionally, you want to change how the Table of Contents heading is formatted. To do this, you need to modify the table of contents settings.

From the References tab, click 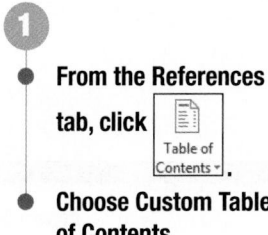 **Table of Contents.**

Choose Custom Table of Contents.

Your screen should be similar to Figure 3.27

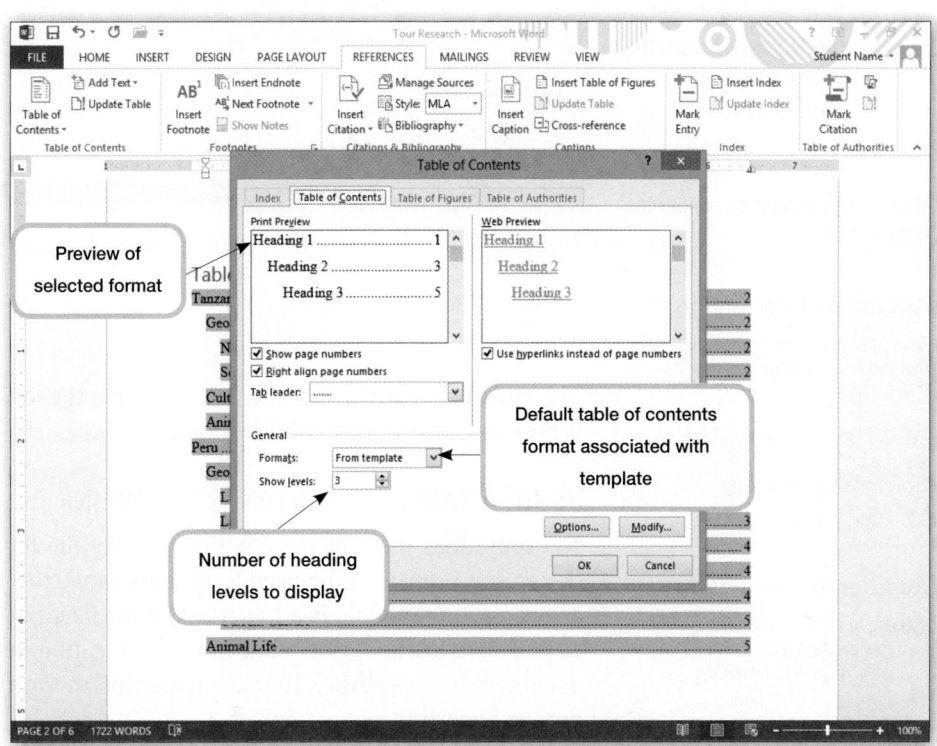

Figure 3.27

From the Table of Contents dialog box, you select the format (style) of the table and the number of levels to show. The default style is determined by the Normal template and the number of levels to show is set to three. The two Preview boxes display an example of how the selected format will look in a printed document or in a document when viewed in a web browser.

You will change the format to another and the level to four. You also will apply the Title style to the table of contents title.

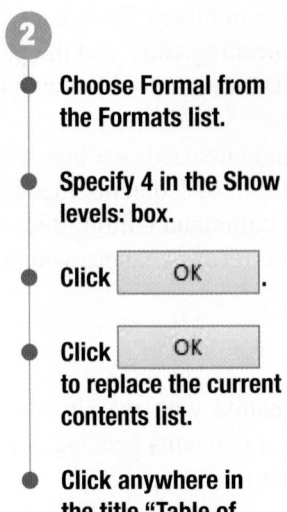

2

- Choose Formal from the Formats list.

- Specify 4 in the Show levels: box.

- Click OK .

- Click OK to replace the current contents list.

- Click anywhere in the title "Table of Contents" and apply the Title style from the Styles group on the Home tab.

Your screen should be similar to Figure 3.28

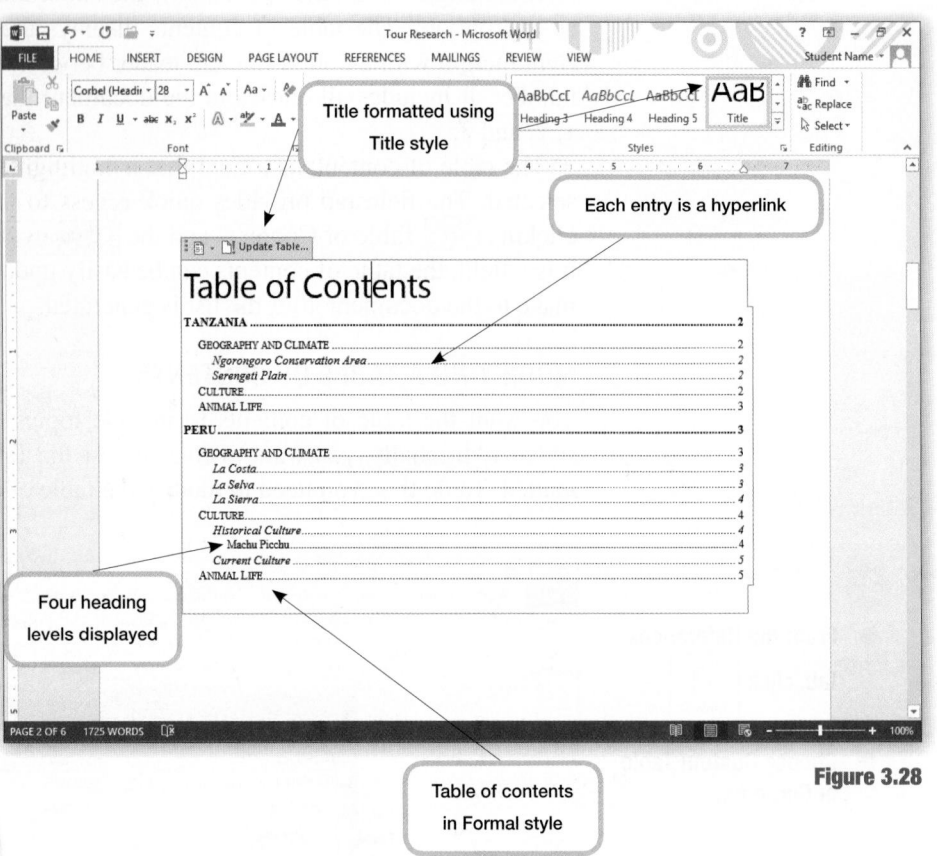

Figure 3.28

Figure 3.28

Additional Information

To remove a table of contents, choose Remove Table of Contents from the

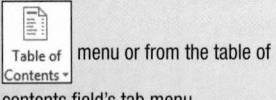

Table of Contents ▾ menu or from the table of contents field's tab menu.

Additional Information

Pointing to an entry in a table of contents displays a ScreenTip with directions on how to follow the hyperlink.

The table is updated using the new style and the level 4 heading for Machu Picchu is now displayed in the table of contents.

USING A TABLE OF CONTENTS HYPERLINK

Not only does the table of contents display the location of topic headings in the report, but it also can be used to quickly move to these locations. This is because each entry in the table is a hyperlink to the heading in the document. A hyperlink, as you have learned, is a connection to a location in the current document, another document, or a website. To use a hyperlink in Word, hold down Ctrl while clicking the hyperlink.

1

Hold down Ctrl **and click the Peru table of contents hyperlink.**

Additional Information

The mouse pointer shape changes to a 🖑 when holding down Ctrl and pointing to a hyperlink.

Your screen should be similar to Figure 3.29

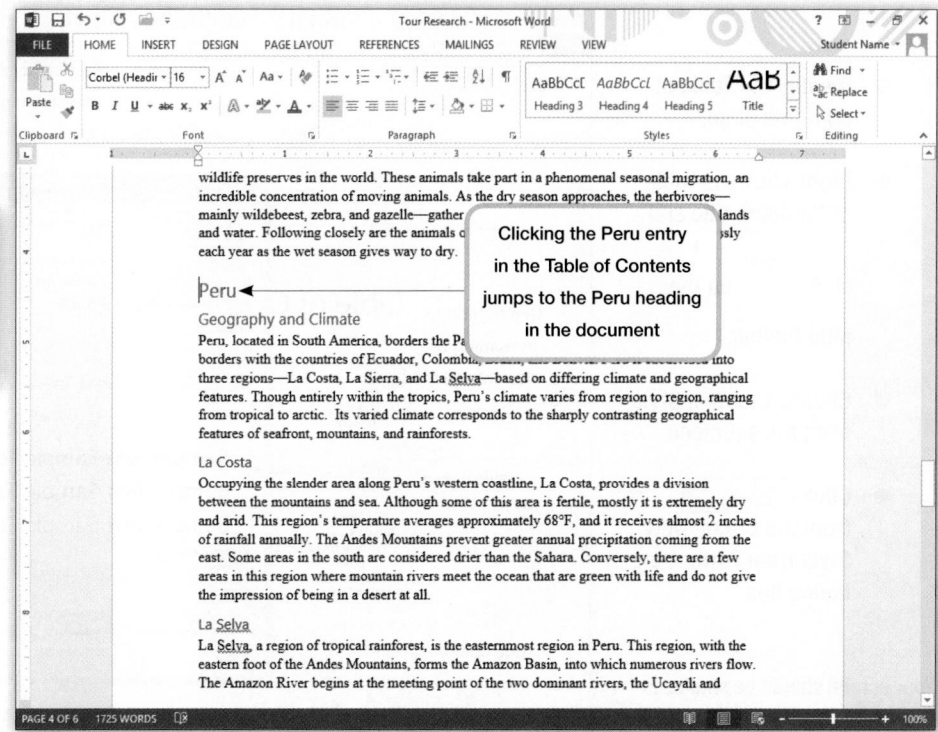

wildlife preserves in the world. These animals take part in a phenomenal seasonal migration, an incredible concentration of moving animals. As the dry season approaches, the herbivores—mainly wildebeest, zebra, and gazelle—gather ... lands and water. Following closely are the animals o ... sly each year as the wet season gives way to dry. ...

Peru ◄

Geography and Climate

Peru, located in South America, borders the Pa... borders with the countries of Ecuador, Colombia, ... into three regions—La Costa, La Sierra, and La Selva—based on differing climate and geographical features. Though entirely within the tropics, Peru's climate varies from region to region, ranging from tropical to arctic. Its varied climate corresponds to the sharply contrasting geographical features of seafront, mountains, and rainforests.

La Costa

Occupying the slender area along Peru's western coastline, La Costa, provides a division between the mountains and sea. Although some of this area is fertile, mostly it is extremely dry and arid. This region's temperature averages approximately 68°F, and it receives almost 2 inches of rainfall annually. The Andes Mountains prevent greater annual precipitation coming from the east. Some areas in the south are considered drier than the Sahara. Conversely, there are a few areas in this region where mountain rivers meet the ocean that are green with life and do not give the impression of being in a desert at all.

La Selva

La Selva, a region of tropical rainforest, is the easternmost region in Peru. This region, with the eastern foot of the Andes Mountains, forms the Amazon Basin, into which numerous rivers flow. The Amazon River begins at the meeting point of the two dominant rivers, the Ucayali and

Clicking the Peru entry in the Table of Contents jumps to the Peru heading in the document

PAGE 4 OF 6   1725 WORDS

Figure 3.29

The insertion point jumps to the Peru heading in the document. Now, however, the table of contents is no longer visible. If you wanted to jump to a different topic, you would need to return to the table of contents page and select another hyperlink or use the Navigation pane.

CREATING A CUSTOM STYLE

Although the Title style you applied to the table of contents title looks good, you decide instead that you want the title to be the same color as the title on the cover page. To do this, you will modify the Title style and then save the modified design as a custom style so you can quickly apply the style in the future.

- Display the Table of Contents page.

- Right-click the Table of Contents title and click 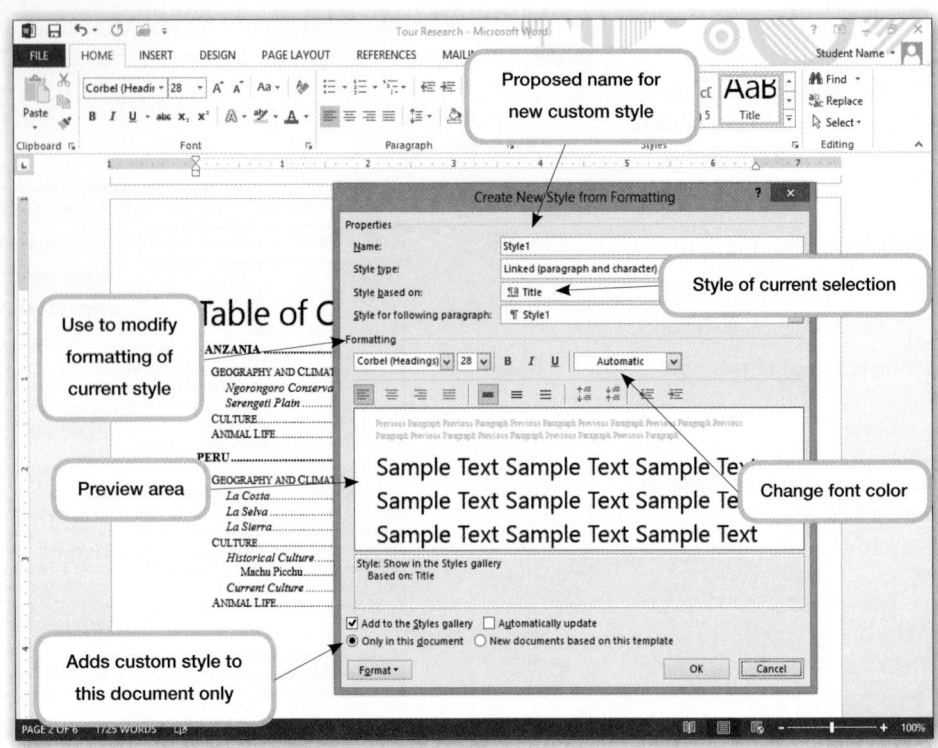 Styles on the Mini toolbar.

- Choose Create a Style from the submenu.

- Click Modify... from the Create New Style from Formatting dialog box.

Your screen should be similar to Figure 3.30

Figure 3.30

Additional Information

If you wanted a custom style to be available in future documents, you would use the New documents based on this template option.

The Create New Style from Formatting dialog box displays the settings associated with the current selection. You will change the font color associated with the Title style and then give the custom style a descriptive name.

- Open the Font Color drop-down menu and choose the Green, Accent 1 theme color.

- In the Name text box, replace the default name with **TOC Title**

- Click OK.

- Save the document.

Your screen should be similar to Figure 3.31

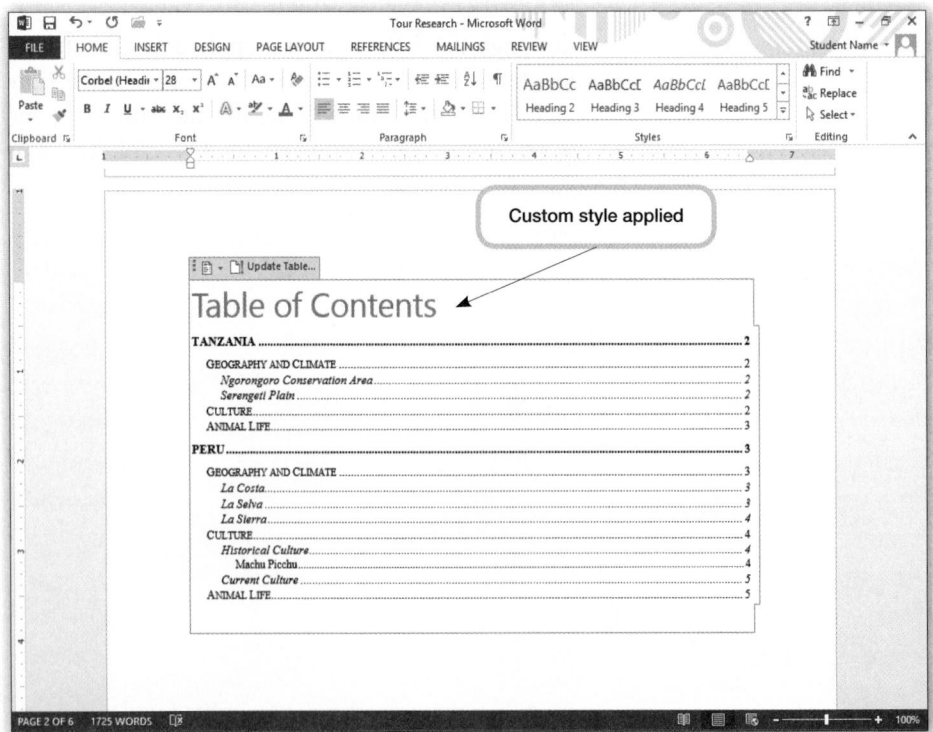

Figure 3.31

The new TOC Title style is applied to the selection and added to the Styles gallery. If you ever need to change a style back to the default document style, you can easily clear the style by moving to the text whose style you want removed and choosing Clear Formatting from the Styles gallery or clicking  Clear Formatting in the Font group.

Including Source References

Documented research papers typically provide credit for the sources of information that were used in developing the document. These sources are cited both within the text of the document and in a bibliography.

Concept 3 Citations and Bibliography

Parenthetical source references, called **citations**, give credit for specific information included in the document. Complete source information for citations is included in a **bibliography** at the end of the report. Citations and bibliographies must be entered using the appropriate reference style, such as MLA or APA style. Word includes a feature that will automatically format citations and bibliographies according to different reference styles. This saves you the time it would take to learn the style from the documentation manuals, and of entering the citations and bibliographies using the correct format.

As you insert citations, Word asks for the bibliography information for each source. Once a source is created, it is stored in two places: a Master List and a Current List. The Master List is a database of all sources ever created. The Current List includes all of the sources that will be used in the current document. The purpose of the Master List is to save you from retyping and reentering information about sources that you commonly use. One advantage of the Master List is the ability to select and copy sources in your Master List to add them to your Current List.

Word uses the information in the Current List to quickly generate a complete bibliographic list (similar to the sample shown here) of the information for each source according to the selected reference style.

> Works Cited
>
> Camerapix. *Spectrum Guide to Tanzania*. Brooklyn: Interlink Publishing Group, 2002.
>
> Country Studies US. *Peru*. 2003-2005. 4 October 2015. <http://countrystudies.us/peru/23.htm>.
>
> Wikipedia: The Free Encyclopedia. *Tanzania*. 25 October 2012. 8 February 2015.
> <http://en.wikipedia.org/wiki/Tanzania>.

Both citations and bibliography entries are inserted as fields in the document. This means that any changes you may make to the source information is automatically updated in both the citation and the bibliography.

SELECTING A REFERENCE STYLE

You have been following the MLA reference style guidelines. You can change the reference style at any point while working on your document and your citations and bibliography will be automatically updated to reflect the new style.

● **Open the References tab.**

● **If necessary, open the** [⊞ Style: APA ▾] **drop-down list in the Citations & Bibliography group and choose MLA Seventh Edition from the drop-down list.**

Now, as you enter citations and create a bibliography, they will be formatted using the MLA style guidelines.

CREATING CITATIONS

Research papers using the MLA style require citations to include the author's last name and a page number or range within parentheses. The first citation that needs to be included in the document is to credit the source of the geography statistics about Tanzania. The source of this information was from the Wikipedia website.

To create a citation, move to the end of the sentence or phrase in the document that contains the information you want to cite. Then enter the bibliography information for the source.

- Open the Navigation pane and click **HEADINGS**.

- Click the Tanzania Geography and Climate heading.

- Move to the end of the first paragraph (before the period after "Alaska") of the Geography and Climate section.

- Open the References tab, if necessary, and click [Insert Citation] in the Citations & Bibliography group.

- Choose Add New Source.

- Choose the Show All Bibliography Fields option to see additional fields.

Your screen should be similar to **Figure 3.32**

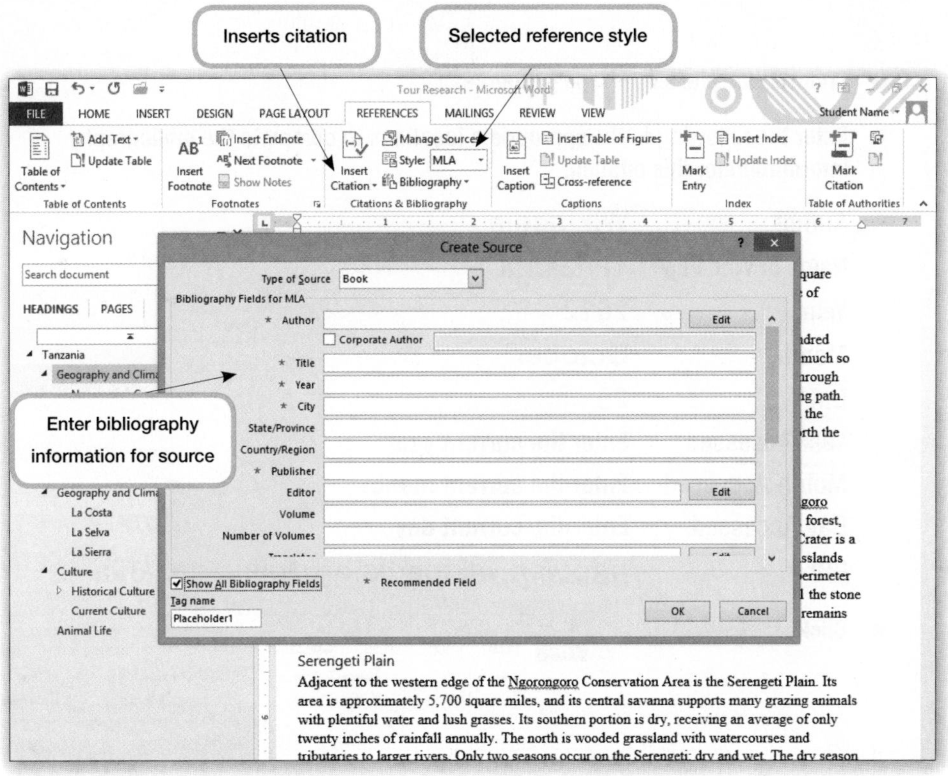

Inserts citation

Selected reference style

Enter bibliography information for source

Figure 3.32

In the Create Source dialog box, select the type of source, for example, a book, a journal article, or a website. Then enter the bibliography information for the source in the appropriate text boxes for the selected source type. The red asterisks indicate fields that are recommended to be completed. The fields vary with the type of source.

②

- Choose **Web site** as the type of source.

- Enter the following in the appropriate locations to complete the bibliography information for this citation.

Author	Wikipedia
Name of Web Page	Tanzania
Year	2012
Month	October
Day	25
Year Accessed	Enter the current year
Month Accessed	Enter the current month
Day Accessed	Enter the current day
URL	http://en.wikipedia.org/wiki/Tanzania

- **Click** OK .

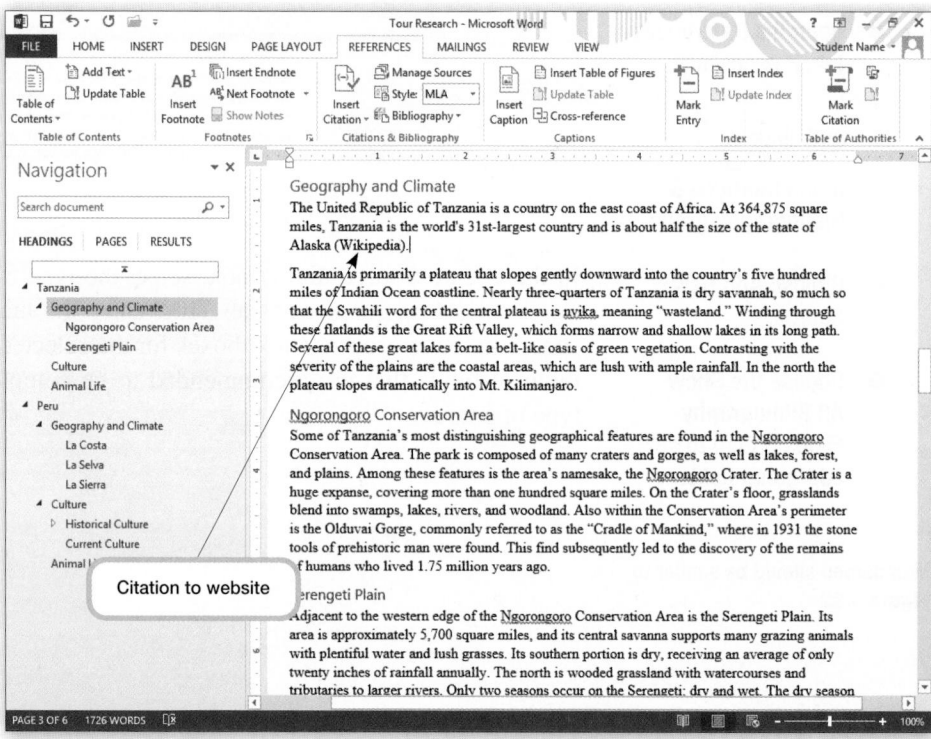

Figure 3.33

Your screen should be similar to **Figure 3.33**

Additional Information

You also can create a citation placeholder to mark the place in a document where you need to add a citation. You can then complete the bibliographic information later by editing the citation. The default citation placeholder tag is "Placeholder" followed by a number. You can use the default placeholder tag names or you can enter whatever you want.

The citation is inserted at the location of the insertion point. It is a field that is linked to the source information. The source information is now stored in both the Master List and the Current List.

The next citation is also to the Wikipedia website. Once source information has been specified, it is easy to insert the citation again. This is because the Insert Citation drop-down menu displays a brief bibliographic entry for each source in the Current List. You will insert another citation for the same source in the report and add a citation for the quote at the end of the first paragraph of the Tanzania Animal Life topic. This quote was found on page 252 of a book that was compiled by Camerapix Publishers International. Because this citation is to a quote, the page number must be included in the citation. You will enter the source information and then edit the citation to include the page.

3

- Click the Tanzania Culture heading in the Navigation pane.

- Move to the end of the third sentence (after the word "matters" and before the period) in the first paragraph of the Culture section.

- Click [Insert Citation ▾] and choose the Wikipedia entry from the Citation list.

- Click the Tanzania Animal Life heading in the Navigation pane, and move to the end of the first paragraph (before the period) of the Animal Life section.

- Click [Insert Citation ▾] and choose Add New Source.

- From the Type of Source drop-down list choose Book.

- Enter the following in the appropriate locations to complete the bibliography information for this citation.

Corporate Author	Camerapix
Title	Spectrum Guide to Tanzania
Year	2002
City	Brooklyn
Publisher	Interlink Publishing Group

- Click [OK].

- Click the citation and open the drop-down menu.

- Choose Edit Citation.

- Enter 252 as the page number.

- Click [OK].

Book citation includes page number

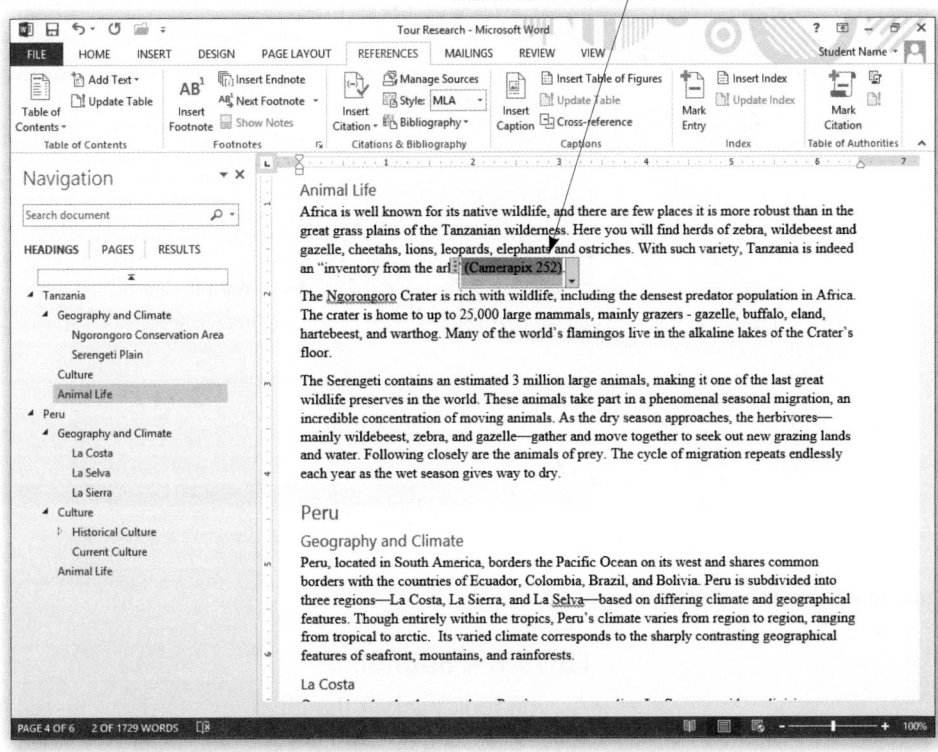

Figure 3.34

Your screen should be similar to Figure 3.34

The last citation you will complete for now is to credit the source of the geography statistics about Peru. The source of this information was from the Country Studies website. This website contains the online versions of books that were published by the Federal Research Division of the Library of Congress as part of the Country Studies/Area Handbook series.

4

- Click the Peru Geography and Climate heading in the Navigation pane, and move to the end of the second sentence (after the word "features" and before the period) in the first paragraph in the section.

- Insert a Web site citation using the following source information:

Corporate Author	Country Studies US
Name of Web Page	Peru
Year	2003-2005
Year Accessed	Enter the current year
Month Accessed	Enter the current month
Day Accessed	Enter the current day
URL	http://countrystudies.us/peru/23.htm

Having Trouble?

Click the Show All Bibliography Fields check box to see the URL field.

- Click [OK].

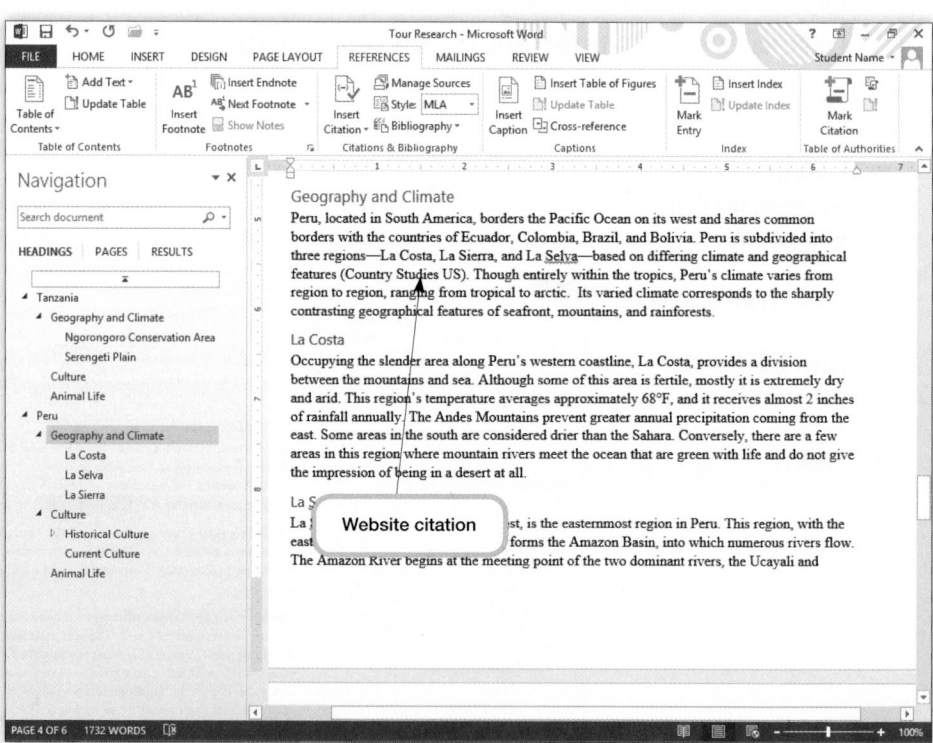

Figure 3.35

Your screen should be similar to Figure 3.35

EDITING A SOURCE

As you look back at the citations you just entered, you realize the author for the Wikipedia website should have been entered as a corporate author, not an individual author. Additionally, the website name is incomplete. You will quickly return to this citation using the Go To feature and edit the source.

1

- Click 🔍 (at the end of the Search box) in the Navigation pane and then choose **Go To**.

Another Method

You also can click on the page count indicator in the status bar to open the Go To dialog box.

- Choose **Field** from the Go to What list.

- Click **Previous** three times to search backward through the document.

- Click **Close** when the Wikipedia citation is located.

Having Trouble?

You may need to move the dialog box to see the document text.

- Choose **Edit Source** from the citation's drop-down list.

- Click **Corporate Author** to move the information in the Author text box to the Corporate Author text box.

- Type **:The Free Encyclopedia** following Wikipedia in the Corporate Author box.

- Click **OK**.

- Click **Yes** to update both the Master and Current Lists.

Your screen should be similar to Figure 3.36

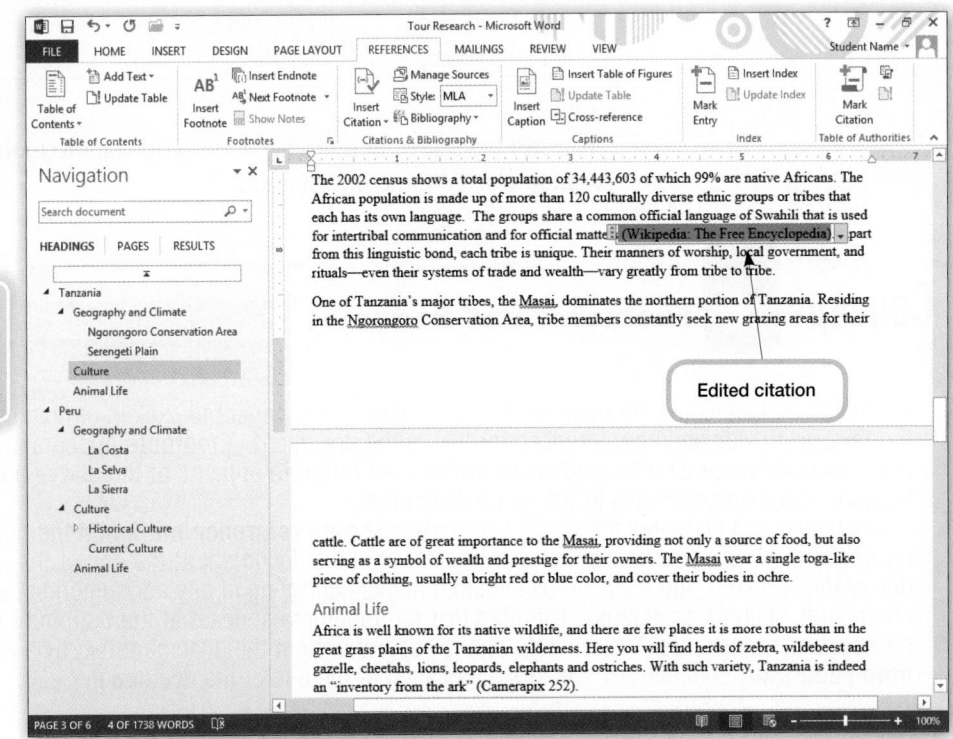

Figure 3.36

The information for the source is now correct and both citations to this source have been updated appropriately.

Including Footnotes

You still have several reference notes you want to include in the report as footnotes to help clarify some information.

Concept 4 Footnotes and Endnotes

Footnotes and endnotes are used in documented research papers to explain or comment on information in the text, or provide source references for text in the document. A **footnote** appears at the bottom of a page containing the material that is being referenced. An **endnote** appears at the end of a document. You can have both footnotes and endnotes in the same document.

Footnotes and endnotes consist of two parts, the **note reference mark** and the note text. The default note reference mark is a superscript number appearing in the document at the end of the material being referenced (for example, text [1]). You also can use custom marks consisting of any nonnumeric character or combination of characters, such as an asterisk. The note text for a footnote appears at the bottom of the page on which the reference mark appears. The footnote text is separated from the document text by a horizontal line called the **note separator**. Endnote text appears as a listing at the end of the document.

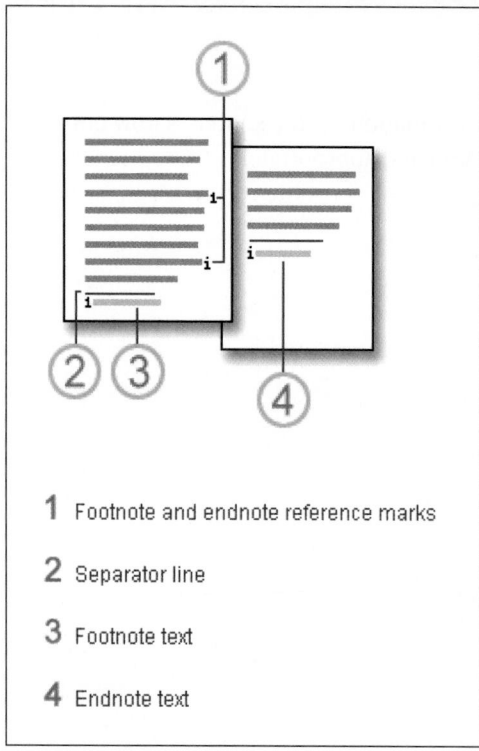

1 Footnote and endnote reference marks

2 Separator line

3 Footnote text

4 Endnote text

Note text can be of any length and formatted just as you would any other text. You also can customize the appearance of the note separators.

INSERTING FOOTNOTES IN DRAFT VIEW

The first footnote reference you want to add is the height of Mt. Kilimanjaro. This note will follow the reference to the mountain at the end of the second paragraph in the Geography and Climate section for Tanzania. To create a footnote, you first need to move to the location in the document where you want the footnote reference mark to be displayed. Then enter the footnote text. You want to create numbered footnotes, so the default settings are acceptable.

1

- Using the Navigation pane, move to the Tanzania Geography and Climate heading.

- Switch to Draft view.

- Move to the end of the second paragraph.

- Open the References tab.

- Click **Insert Footnote** from the Footnotes group.

Another Method
The keyboard shortcut to insert a footnote using the default settings is Alt + Ctrl + F.

Your screen should be similar to Figure 3.37

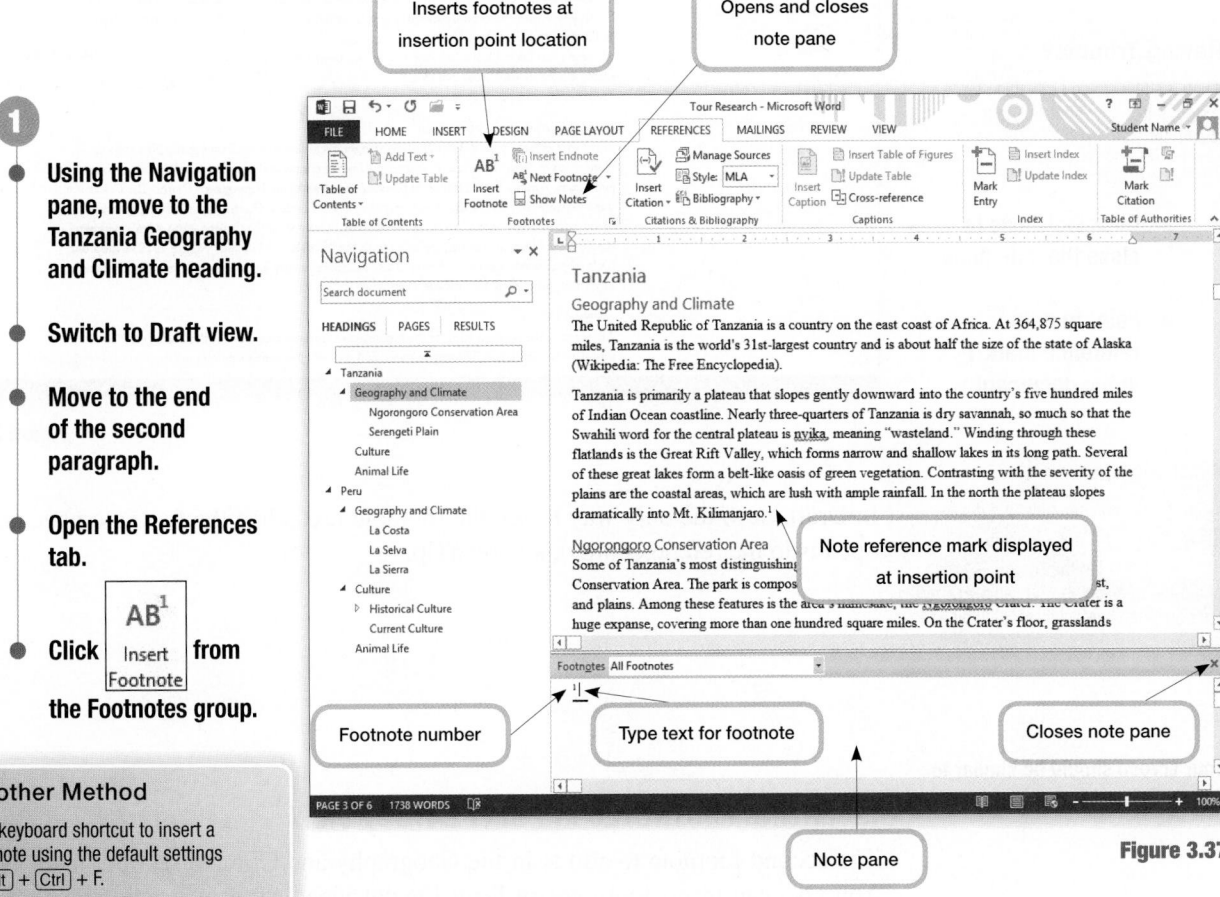

Inserts footnotes at insertion point location

Opens and closes note pane

Note reference mark displayed at insertion point

Footnote number

Type text for footnote

Closes note pane

Note pane

Figure 3.37

The document window is now horizontally divided into upper and lower panes. The report is displayed in the upper pane. The note reference mark, 1, appears as a superscript in the document where the insertion point was positioned when the footnote was created. The note pane displays the footnote number and the insertion point. This is where you enter the text for the footnote.

When you enter the footnote text, you can insert, edit, and format it like any other text.

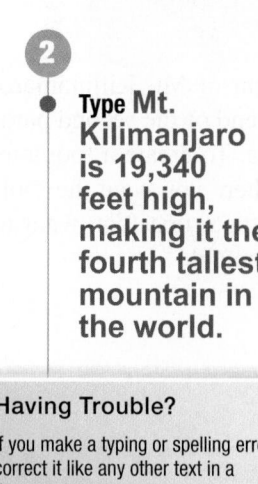

2

- Type **Mt. Kilimanjaro is 19,340 feet high, making it the fourth tallest mountain in the world.**

Having Trouble?

If you make a typing or spelling error, correct it like any other text in a document.

- Click ☒ **Close** to close the note pane.

- Point to note reference mark 1 in the document.

Another Method

In Draft view, you can hide and display the note pane anytime by using

⊟ Show Notes in the Footnotes group of the References tab. You can also open the note pane by double-clicking on a note reference mark in the document.

Your screen should be similar to Figure 3.38

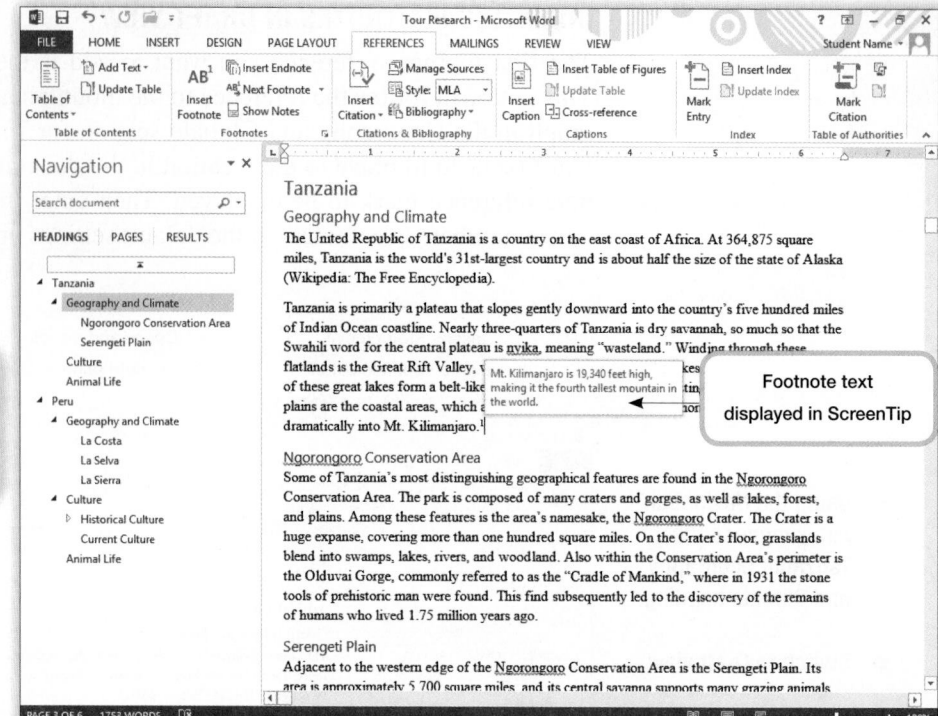

Figure 3.38

In Draft view, the only way to see the footnote text when the footnote pane is not open is in the reference mark's ScreenTip.

INSERTING FOOTNOTES IN PRINT LAYOUT VIEW

The second footnote to add is in the Geography and Climate section under Peru. You also can insert footnotes in Print Layout view. After using the command to insert a footnote, the footnote number appears in the footnote area at the bottom of the page, ready for you to enter the footnote text.

①

- Switch to Print Layout view at 100% zoom.

- Using the Navigation pane, move to the La Sierra heading in the Peru Geography and Climate section.

- Click at the end of the paragraph in the La Sierra section after the word "lake."

- Click **Insert Footnote** .

- Type **Lake Titicaca is 12,507 feet above sea level.**

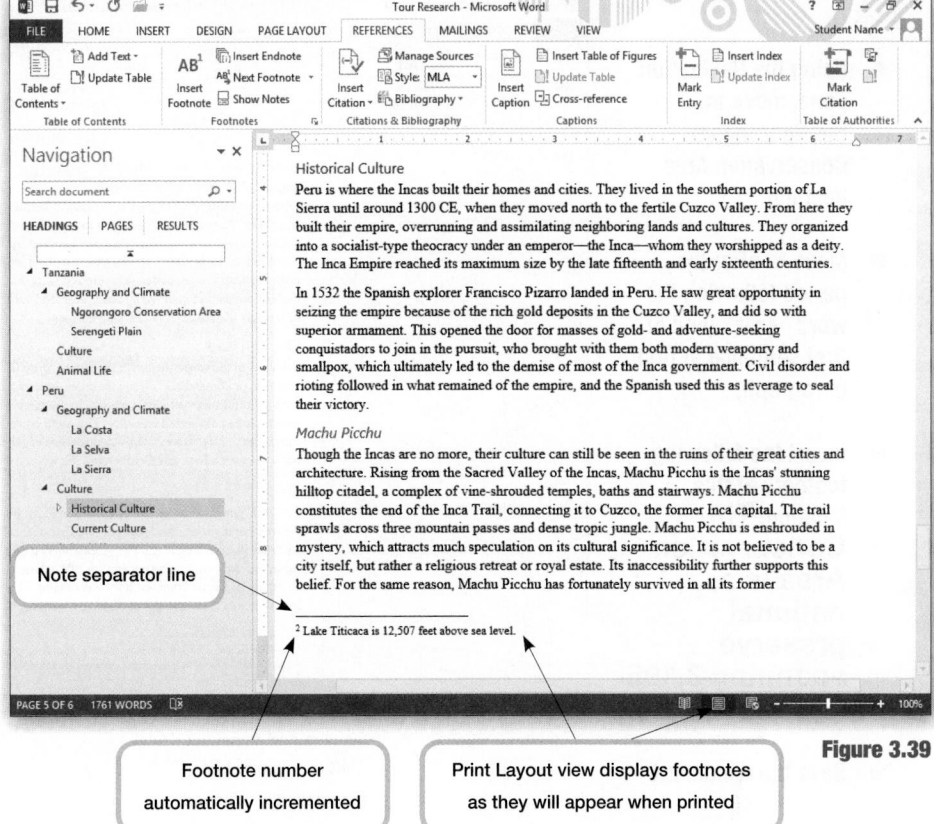

Figure 3.39

- Note separator line
- Footnote number automatically incremented
- Print Layout view displays footnotes as they will appear when printed

Your screen should be similar to Figure 3.39

Your screen should be similar to Figure 3.39

Additional Information

A footnote or endnote can be copied or moved by selecting the note reference mark and using Cut or Copy and Paste. You also can use drag and drop to copy or move a note.

Additional Information

In Print Layout view, you also can display the footnote text in a ScreenTip by pointing to the note reference mark.

The footnote number 2 was automatically entered at the location of the insertion point in the text and the footnote text is displayed immediately above the bottom margin separated from the text by the note separator line. Footnotes are always displayed at the bottom of the page containing the footnote reference mark. Print Layout view displays footnotes as they will appear when the document is printed.

Next, you need to enter a footnote earlier in the document, on page 2.

2

- Using the Navigation pane, move to the Ngorongoro Conservation Area heading.

- Move to after the period following the word "Area" (end of first sentence of first paragraph).

- Insert the following footnote at this location: The Conservation Area is a national preserve spanning 3,196 square miles.

- Save the document.

Your screen should be similar to Figure 3.40

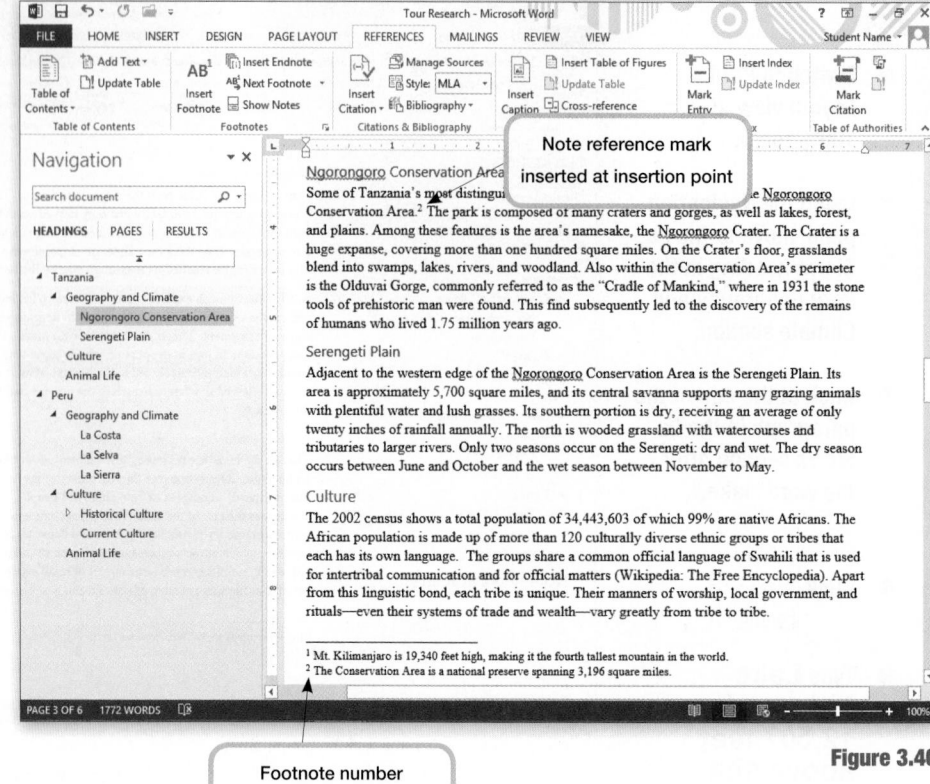

Note reference mark inserted at insertion point

Footnote number automatically adjusted

Figure 3.40

Additional Information

To delete a footnote or endnote, highlight the reference mark and press Delete. The reference mark and associated note text are removed, and the following footnotes are renumbered.

Notice that this footnote is now number 2 in the document. Word automatically adjusted the footnote numbers when the new footnote was inserted.

Footnotes can quickly be converted to endnotes and vice versa by right-clicking on the note you want to convert and choosing Convert from the context menu.

Adding a Web Video

Having Trouble?

If you do not have an Internet connection, skip this section. Insert the picture wd03_Mt Kilimanjaro. Size and position it as in Figure 3.43.

In addition to inserting pictures, you also can insert videos from online sources directly in a Word document.

You can search online sources to locate, preview, and insert video clips. Once a video is inserted, it behaves just like a picture. Then you can quickly play the video inside the Word document.

FINDING AND INSERTING VIDEO

You will insert a video about Tanzania next to the second paragraph on page 3.

1

- Use the Navigation pane to move to the Geography and Climate heading under Tanzania.

- Close the Navigation pane.

- Move to the beginning of the second paragraph.

- Open the Insert tab and click 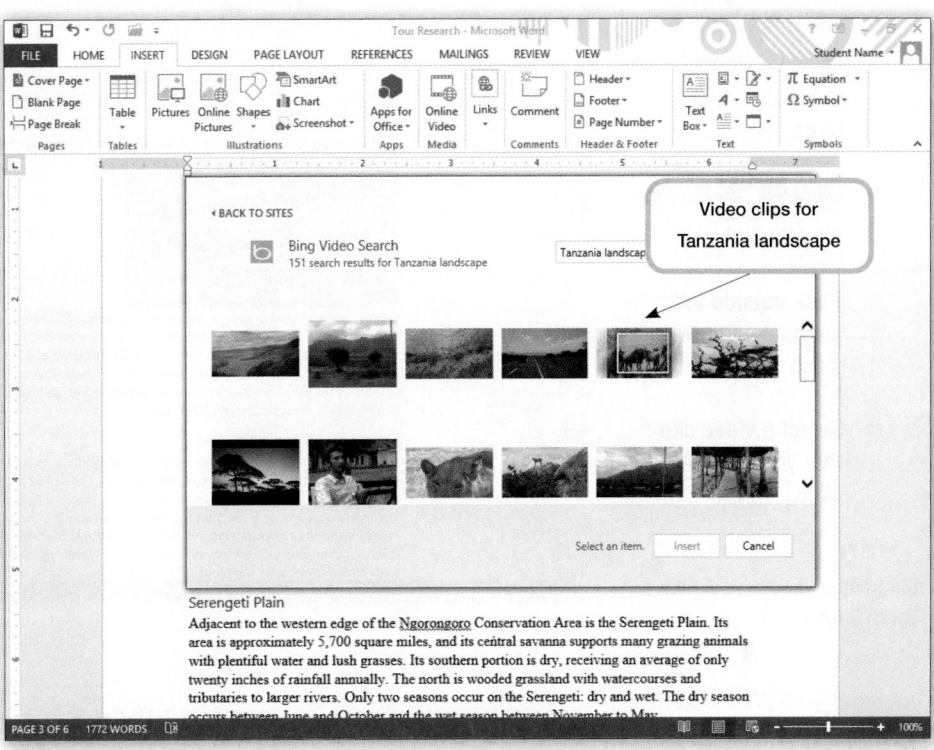 in the Media group.

- Enter Tanzania landscape in the Bing Video Search text box and press Enter.

Your screen should be similar to Figure 3.41

Figure 3.41

The Bing search engine has located many videos about Tanzania and displays the results as thumbnail images. Pointing to the thumbnail will show the title of the video, the source (for example, YouTube), and its length. Before inserting a video in a document, you will want to preview and play it to make sure it is the one you want to use.

- Point to any video clip thumbnail and click 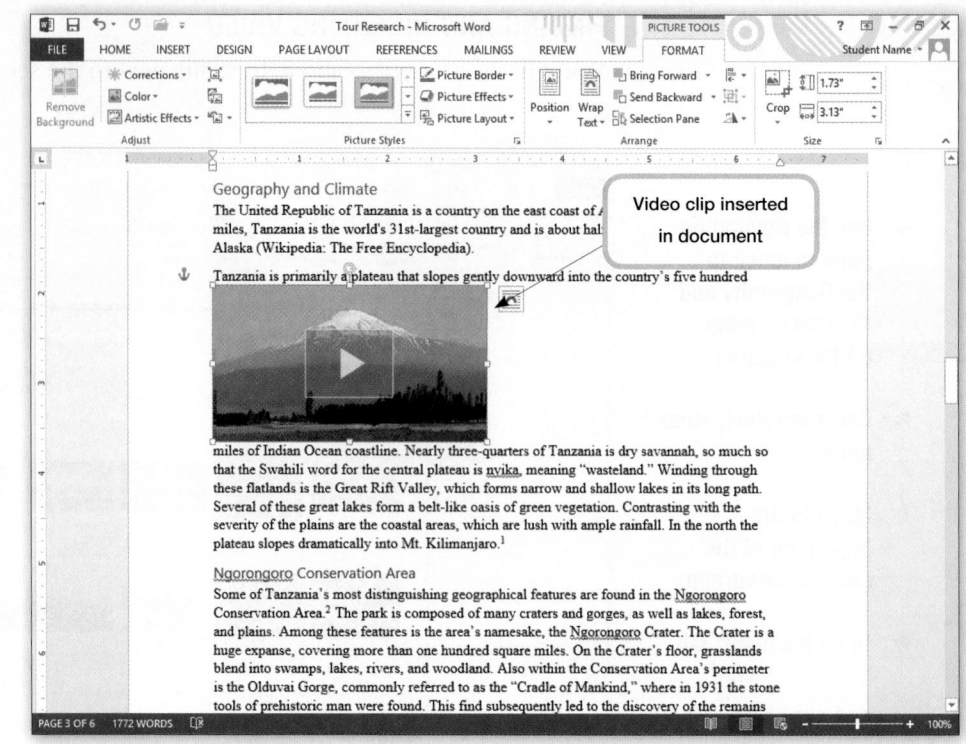 View Larger to preview it in a larger size.

- Click ▶ Play to play the video.

- Click outside the preview window to close it.

- Select a video clip that you like, and click [Insert].

Your screen should be similar to Figure 3.42

Figure 3.42

MANIPULATING AND PLAYING A VIDEO

Having Trouble?

Refer to the "Working with Graphics" section in Lab 1 to review working with graphic files.

The thumbnail image of the selected video is displayed in the document. It is an object that can be manipulated like any other graphic object including moving, sizing, and changing the layout.

1

- Change the text wrap layout to Square.

- Align the video object with the left margin and top of the paragraph and size it to approximately 2 inches high by 2.5 inches wide.

- Point to the video object.

Your screen should be similar to Figure 3.43

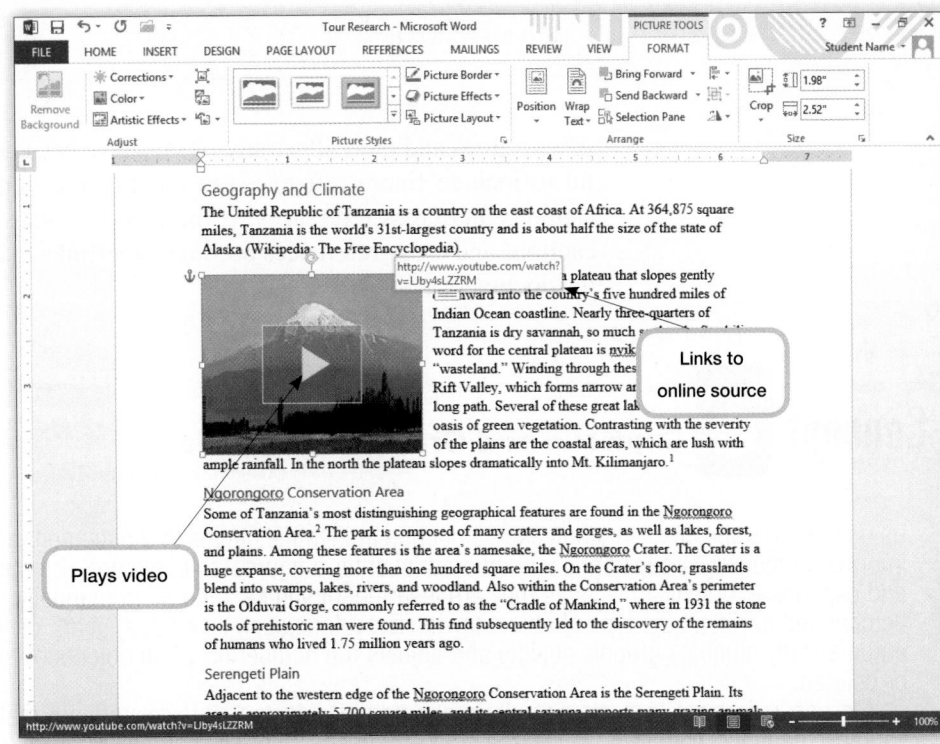

Geography and Climate
The United Republic of Tanzania is a country on the east coast of Africa. At 364,875 square miles, Tanzania is the world's 31st-largest country and is about half the size of the state of Alaska (Wikipedia: The Free Encyclopedia).

http://www.youtube.com/watch?v=Uby4sLZZRM ... a plateau that slopes gently ... ward into the country's five hundred miles of Indian Ocean coastline. Nearly three-quarters of Tanzania is dry savannah, so much ... word for the central plateau is nyik ... "wasteland." Winding through thes ... Rift Valley, which forms narrow ar ... long path. Several of these great lak ... oasis of green vegetation. Contrasting with the severity of the plains are the coastal areas, which are lush with ample rainfall. In the north the plateau slopes dramatically into Mt. Kilimanjaro.[1]

Links to online source

Plays video

Ngorongoro Conservation Area
Some of Tanzania's most distinguishing geographical features are found in the Ngorongoro Conservation Area.[2] The park is composed of many craters and gorges, as well as lakes, forest, and plains. Among these features is the area's namesake, the Ngorongoro Crater. The Crater is a huge expanse, covering more than one hundred square miles. On the Crater's floor, grasslands blend into swamps, lakes, rivers, and woodland. Also within the Conservation Area's perimeter is the Olduvai Gorge, commonly referred to as the "Cradle of Mankind," where in 1931 the stone tools of prehistoric man were found. This find subsequently led to the discovery of the remains of humans who lived 1.75 million years ago.

Serengeti Plain
Adjacent to the western edge of the Ngorongoro Conservation Area is the Serengeti Plain. Its area is approximately 5,700 square miles, and its central savanna supports many grazing animals

Figure 3.43

The video thumbnail is a link to the online source hosting the video. The Screen-Tip displays the web address of the video and instructions on how to go to the source location. Unlike pictures, a copy of the video is not inserted in the document, only a link to the online source hosting the video is saved. Therefore, the reader of the document must have Internet access to play the video. If the website was not available or the video was removed from the site, it also could not be accessed. The advantage to linking to the source is that the document file size will not increase significantly.

The video thumbnail displays a large Play button that invites readers to view the video.

2

- Click the 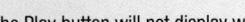 Play button to start the video.

- Click the ▶ Play button to test the video.

- Return to the document by clicking the document text.

- Save the document.

The video opened and played in its original size in a separate small window.

Referencing Figures

After figures and other illustrative items have been added to a document, it is helpful to include figure references to identify the items. Figure references include captions and cross-references. If the reader is viewing the document online, the captions and cross-references become hyperlinks to allow the reader to navigate in the document.

Concept 5 Captions and Cross-References

Using captions and cross-references in a document identifies items in a document and helps the reader locate information quickly. A **caption** is a numbered label for a figure, table, picture, or graph. Word can automatically add captions to graphic objects as they are inserted, or you can add them manually. The caption label can be changed to reflect the type of object to which it refers, such as a table, chart, or figure. In addition, Word automatically numbers graphic objects and adjusts the numbering when objects of the same type are added or deleted.

A **cross-reference** is a reference from one part of a document to related information in another part. Once you have captions, you also can include cross-references. For example, if you have a graph in one part of the document that you would like to refer to in another section, you can add a cross-reference that tells the reader where the graph is located. A cross-reference also can be inserted as a hyperlink, allowing you to jump to another location in the same document or in another document.

ADDING A FIGURE CAPTION

Next, you want to add a caption below the video of Tanzania.

- Select the video thumbnail object of Tanzania in the Tanzania section.

- Open the References tab.

- Click **Insert Caption**.

Your screen should be similar to Figure 3.44

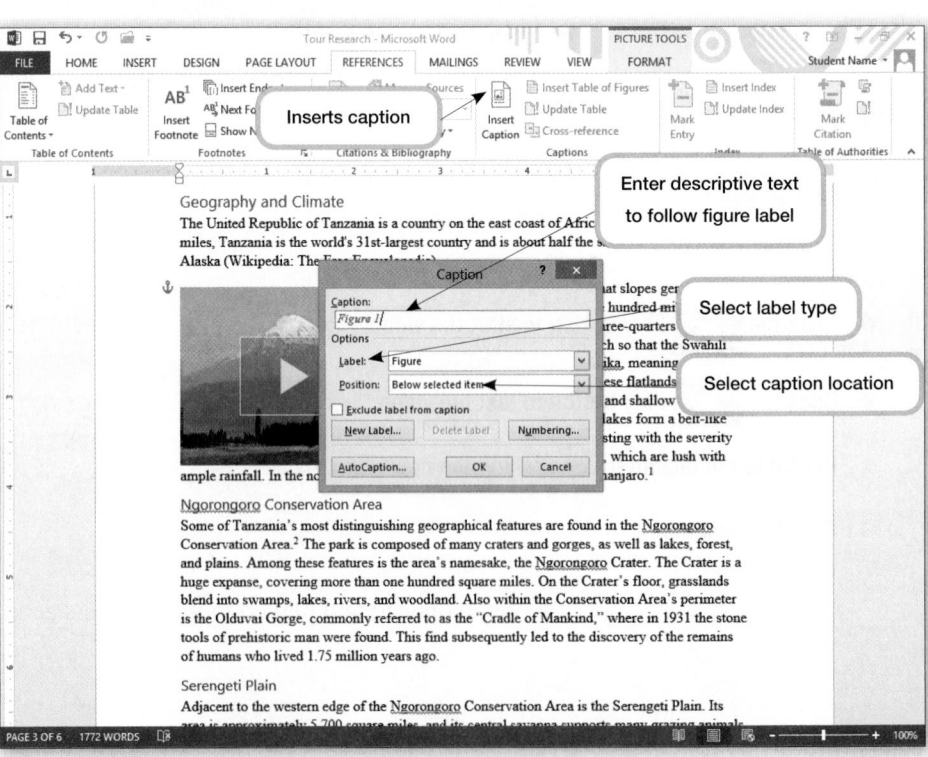

Figure 3.44

The Caption options are described in the following table.

Option	Description
Label	Select from one of three default captions: Table, Figure, or Equation.
Position	Specify the location of the caption, either above or below a selected item. When an item is selected, the Position option is available.
New Label	Create your own captions.
Numbering	Specify the numbering format and starting number for your caption.
AutoCaption	Turns on the automatic insertion of a caption (label and number only) when you insert selected items into your document.

The default caption label is Figure 1. You will use this caption and add additional descriptive text. The default setting of "Below selected item" is also correct.

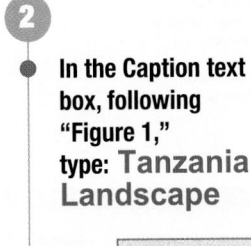

In the Caption text box, following "Figure 1," type: Tanzania Landscape

Click OK .

Size and position the video thumbnail and caption as in Figure 3.45.

Your screen should be similar to Figure 3.45

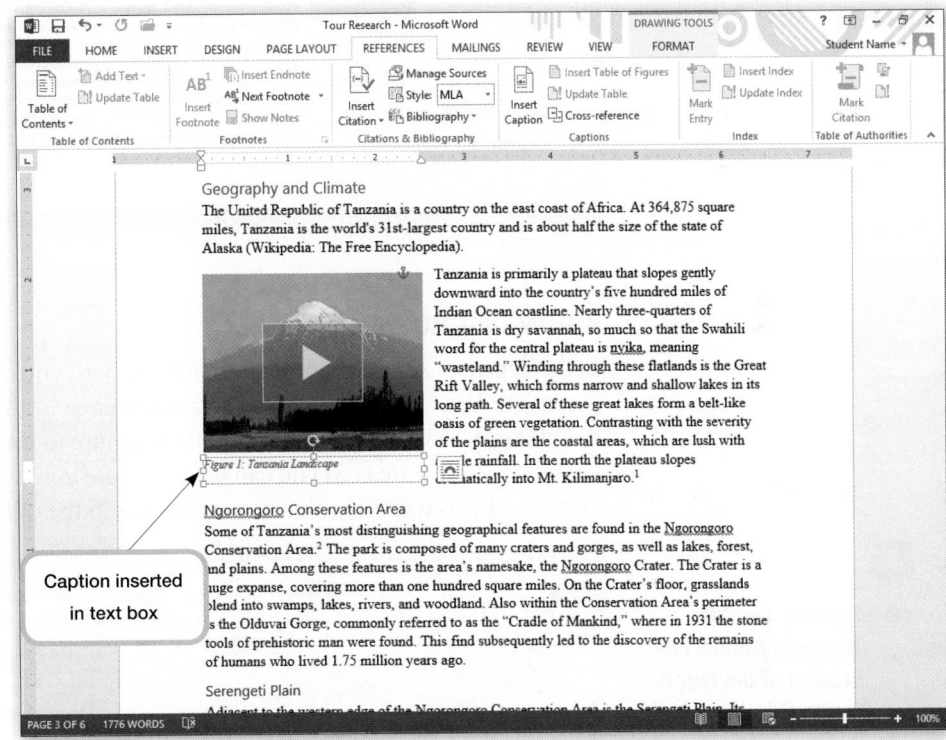

Caption inserted in text box

Figure 3.45

The caption label appears below the figure. It is formatted using the caption style associated with the selected theme. The figure number is a field that will update automatically as you add or delete captions in the document. The caption is contained in a **text box**, a container for text and other graphic objects that can be moved like any other object.

3

In a similar manner, add a **Figure 2: Peruvian Flamingos** caption below the flamingos picture on page 6.

Size and position the picture and caption as in Figure 3.46.

Your screen should be similar to Figure 3.46

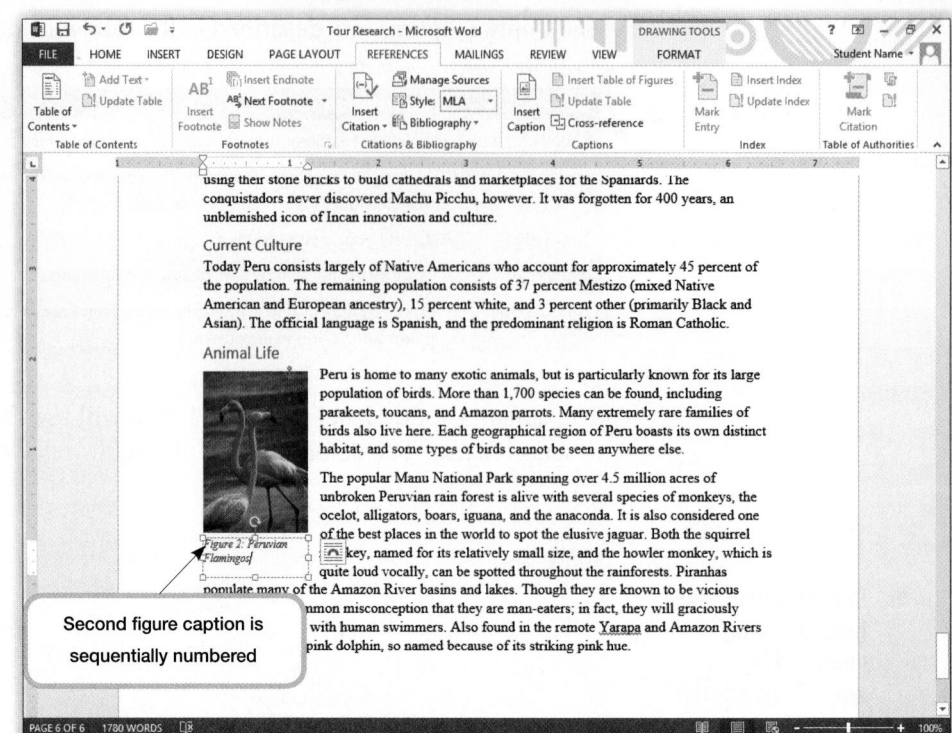

Second figure caption is sequentially numbered

Figure 3.46

ADDING A CROSS-REFERENCE

In the Tanzania Animal Life section of the report, you discuss the animals found in the Serengeti. You want to include a cross-reference to the video at this location. While doing this, you will use the **split window** feature to divide the document window into separate viewing areas so you can see the figure you will reference in one area and the text where you will enter the cross-reference in the other area.

1

Scroll to see the Tanzania Animal Life section of the report (page 4) in the middle of the window.

Open the View tab.

Click 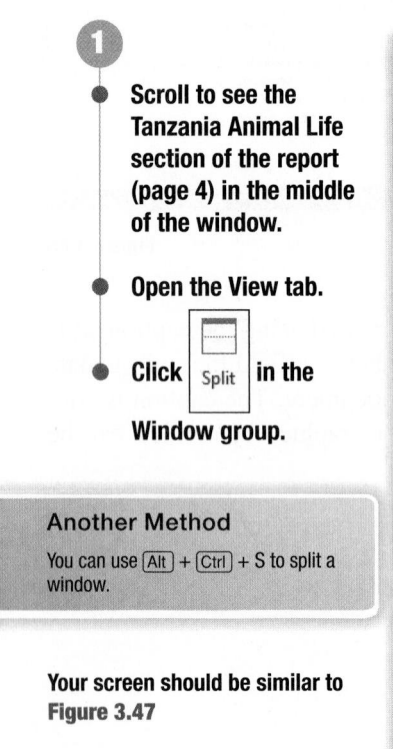 in the Window group.

Another Method

You can use [Alt] + [Ctrl] + S to split a window.

Your screen should be similar to Figure 3.47

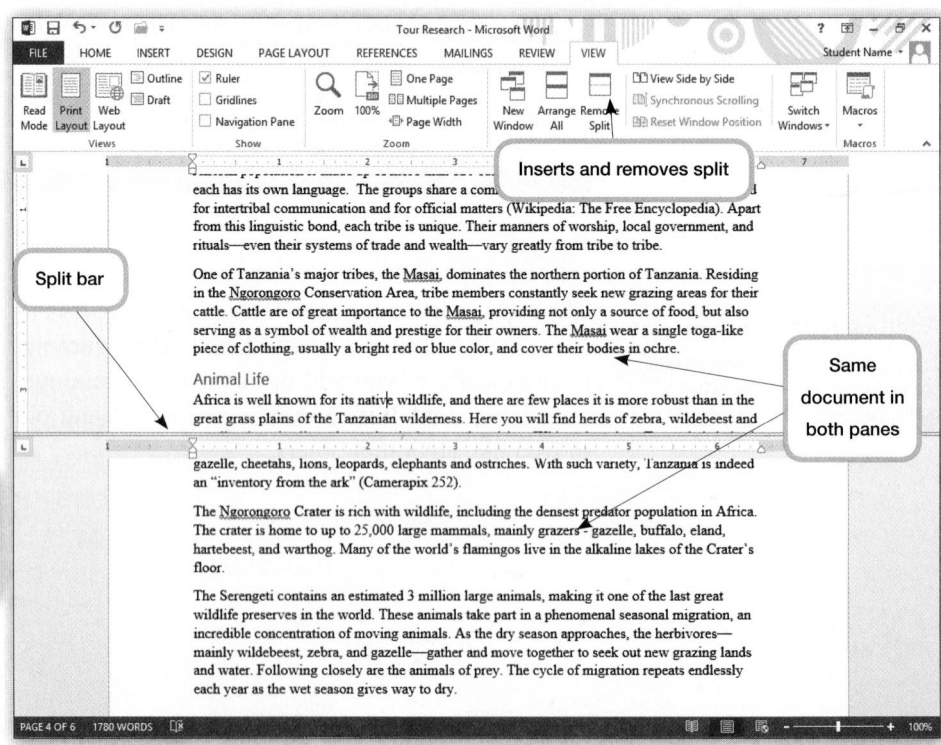

Inserts and removes split

Split bar

Same document in both panes

Figure 3.47

The document area is divided into two horizontal sections by a split bar. You can drag the split bar to any position in the window to display more or less of the document in each pane. Each section is displayed in a pane that can be scrolled and manipulated independently.

Next, you will scroll the document in the panes to display the areas you want to view. While using panes, the insertion point and the ruler are displayed in the active pane or the pane in which you are currently working.

2

- Click in the upper pane and scroll the pane to display the Figure 1 caption below the video thumbnail.

- Scroll the lower pane to display the third paragraph in the Tanzania Animal Life section (page 4).

Your screen should be similar to Figure 3.48

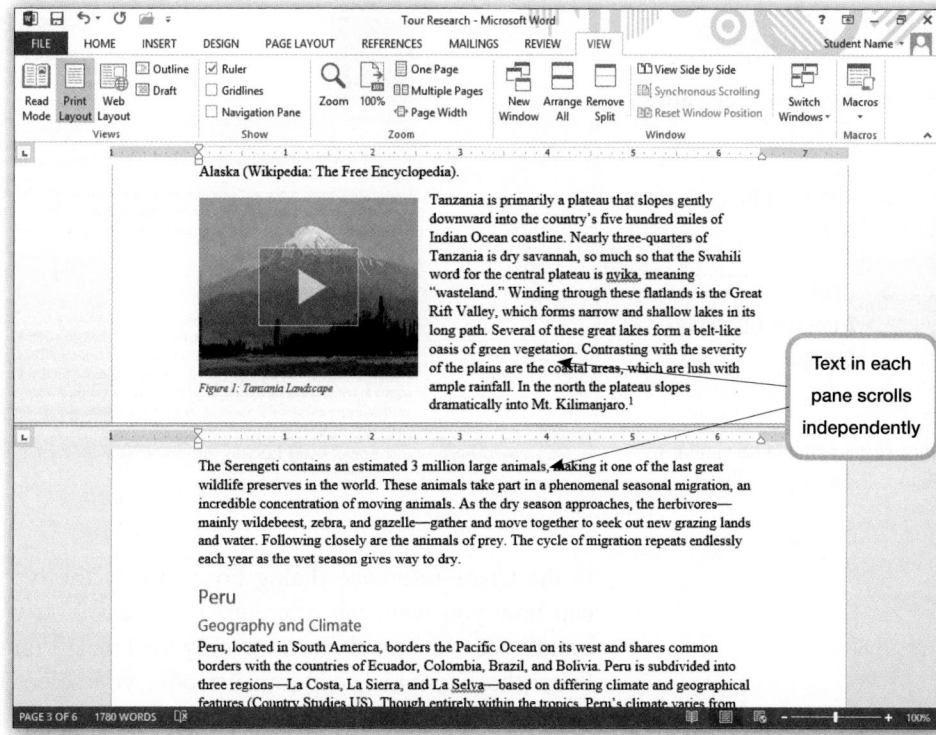

Figure 3.48

The text in each pane scrolls independently. Now you can conveniently see both areas of the document while you enter the cross-reference.

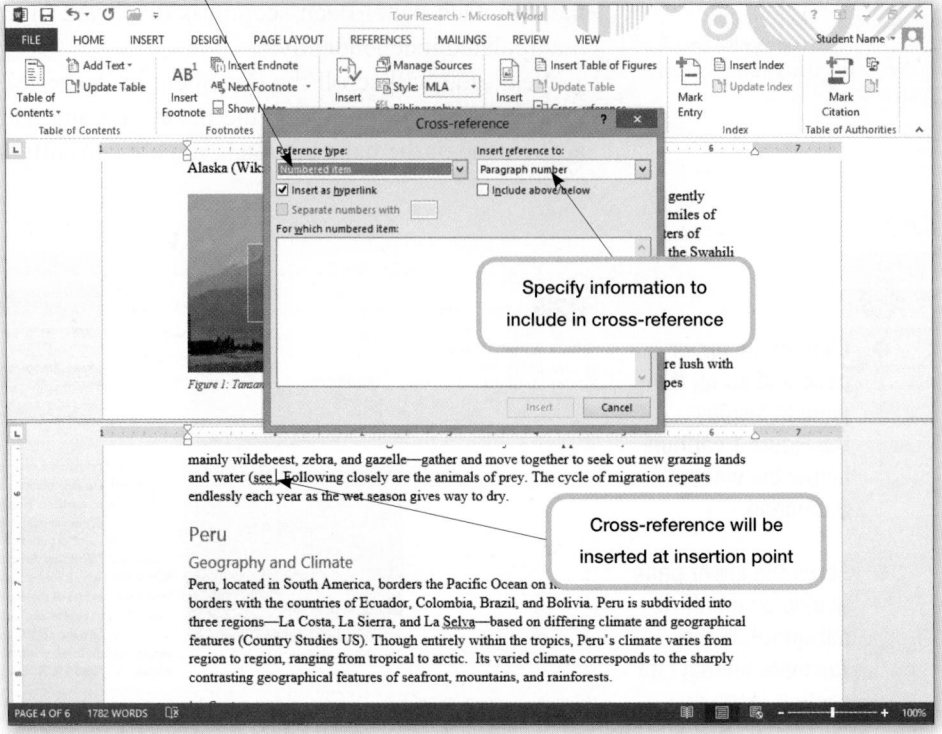

3

- Move to the word "water" (before the period) in the third paragraph in the Tanzania Animal Life section.

- Press Spacebar.

- Type (see and press Spacebar.

- Open the References tab.

- Click 🔲 Cross-reference from the Captions group.

Your screen should be similar to Figure 3.49

Select type of item to be referenced

Specify information to include in cross-reference

Cross-reference will be inserted at insertion point

Figure 3.49

In the Cross-reference dialog box, specify the type of item you are referencing and how you want the reference to appear. You want to reference the Tanzania Landscape video, and you want only the label "Figure 1" entered in the document. From the For which caption: list box, you select the figure you want to reference from the list of all figure captions in the document. Notice that the Insert as Hyperlink option is selected by default. This option creates a hyperlink between the cross-reference and the caption. The default setting is appropriate.

4

- **From the Reference type: drop-down list box, choose Figure.**

- **From the Insert reference to: drop-down list box, choose Only label and number.**

- **If necessary, from the For which caption: list box, select Figure 1: Tanzania Landscape.**

- **Click** Insert **.**

- **Click** Close **.**

- **Type) after the Figure 1 cross-reference.**

- **Click on the Figure 1 cross-reference.**

Your screen should be similar to Figure 3.50

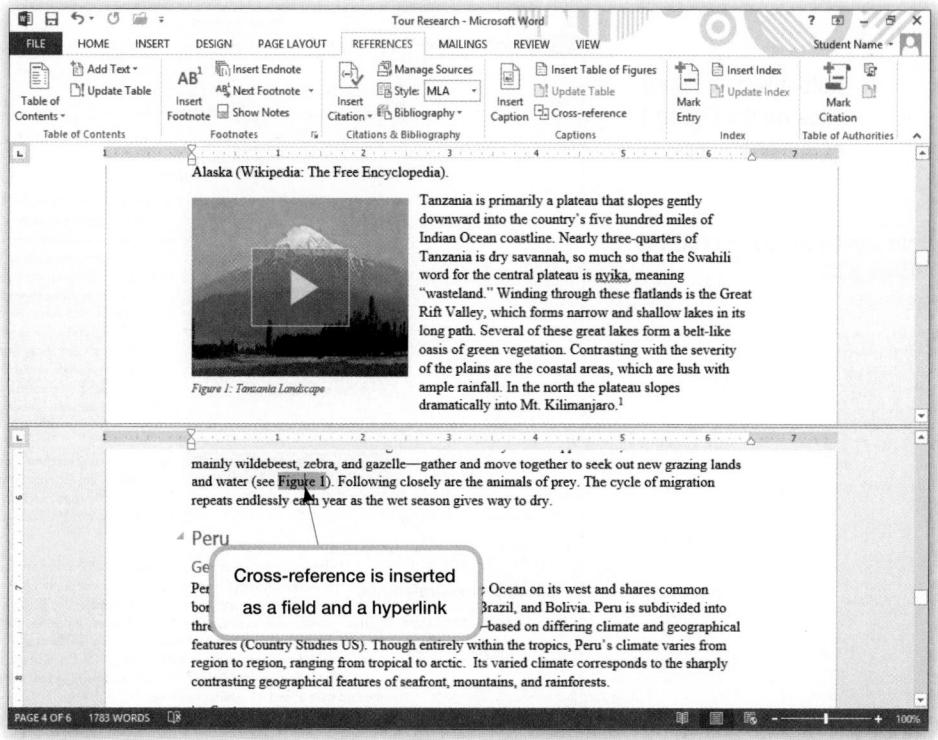

Figure 3.50

The cross-reference to Figure 1 is entered into the document as a field. Therefore, if you insert another picture or item that is cross-referenced, the captions and cross-references will renumber automatically. If you edit, delete, or move cross-referenced items, you should manually update the cross-references using Update Field. When you are working on a long document with several figures, tables, and graphs, this feature is very helpful.

USING A CROSS-REFERENCE HYPERLINK

The cross-reference field is also a hyperlink and, just like a table of contents field, can be used to jump to the source it references.

1 Hold down Ctrl and click on the Figure 1 cross-reference.

Your screen should be similar to Figure 3.51

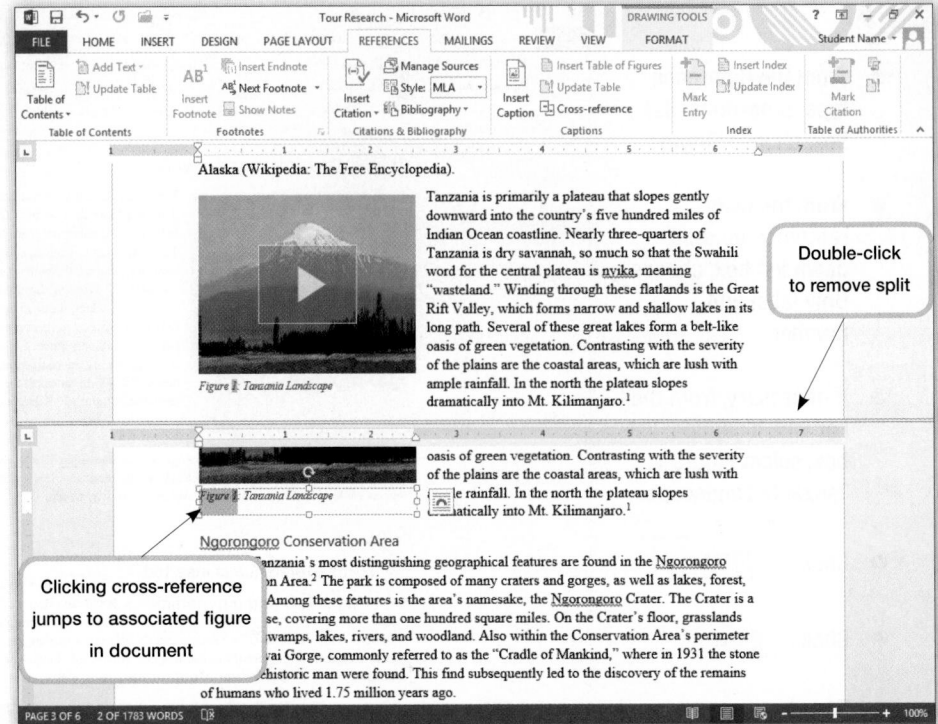

Figure 3.51

The document in the lower pane jumped to the caption beneath the figure. You will clear the split and save the document next.

2 Double-click the split bar to remove the split.

Save the document.

Another Method

You also can click [Remove Split] in the Window group of the View tab, drag the split bar to the top of the document window, or use Alt + Ctrl + S to remove the split.

The split is removed and the document window returns to a single pane. As you can see, splitting the document window is most useful for viewing different sections of the document at the same time and allows you to quickly switch between panes to access information in the different sections without having to repeatedly scroll to the areas.

Creating a Simple Table

Next, you want to add a table comparing the rainfall and temperature data for the three regions of Peru.

Concept 6 Table

A **table** is used to organize information into an easy-to-read format of horizontal rows and vertical columns. The intersection of a row and column creates a **cell** in which you can enter data or other information. Cells in a table are identified by a letter and number, called a **table reference**. Columns are identified from left to right beginning with the letter A, and rows are numbered from top to bottom beginning with the number 1. The table reference of the top-leftmost cell is A1 because it is in the first column (A) and first row (1) of the table. The second cell in column 2 is cell B2. The fourth cell in column 3 is C4.

A	B	C	D	E
(A1)	Jan	Feb	Mar	Total
East	7 (B2)	7	5	19
West	6	4	7	17
South	8	7 (C4)	9	24
Total	21	18	21	60

Tables are a very effective method for presenting information. The table layout organizes information for readers and greatly reduces the number of words they have to read to interpret the data. Use tables whenever you can to make your documents easier to read.

The table you want to create will display columns for regions, rainfall, and temperature. The rows will display the data for each region. Your completed table will be similar to the one shown below.

Region	Annual Rainfall (Inches)	Average Temperature (Fahrenheit)
La Costa	2	68
La Selva	137	80
La Sierra	35	54

INSERTING A TABLE

Word includes several methods to create tables. One method will quickly convert text that is arranged in tabular columns into a table. Another uses the Draw Table feature to create any type of table, but it is most useful for creating complex tables that contain cells of different heights or a varying number of columns per row. Another method inserts a preformatted table containing sample data that you replace with your data.

The last method, which you will use, creates a simple table consisting of the same number of rows and columns.

Move to the end of the paragraph on La Sierra, to the right of the numbered footnote.

Press Enter **twice to insert two blank lines.**

Open the Insert tab.

Click Table .

Point to the boxes in the grid in the drop-down menu and drag to select a 3 by 3 table.

Click the lower-right corner of the selection to insert it.

Your screen should be similar to Figure 3.52

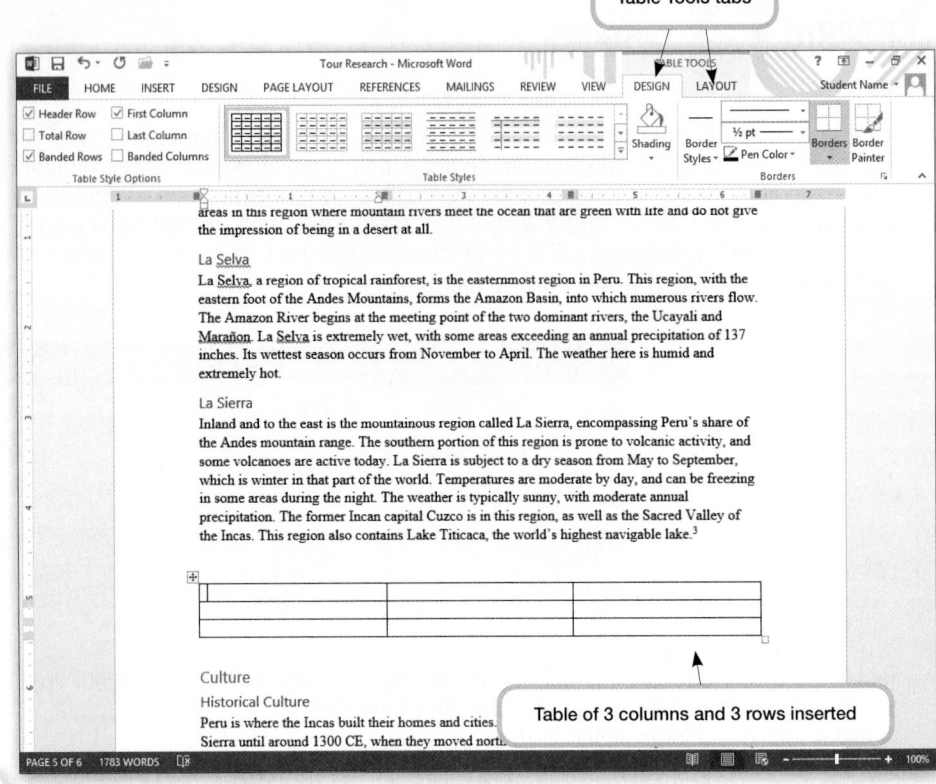

Table Tools tabs

Table of 3 columns and 3 rows inserted

Figure 3.52

A table the full width of the page is inserted. It has equal-sized columns and is surrounded by a black border. The Table Tools tab is automatically open and includes a Design tab and a Layout tab that are used to work with the table.

ENTERING DATA IN A TABLE

Now you are ready to enter information in the table. Each cell contains a single line space where you can enter data. You can move from one cell to another by using the arrow keys or by clicking on the cell. The insertion point appears in the cell that is selected. In addition, you can use the keys shown in the table below to move around a table.

To Move to	Press
Next cell in row	Tab
Previous cell in row	⇧Shift + Tab
First cell in row	Alt + Home
Last cell in row	Alt + End
First cell in column	Alt + Page Up
Last cell in column	Alt + Page Down
Previous row	↑
Next row	↓

The mouse pointer also may appear as a solid black arrow when pointing to the table. When it is a ↓, you can click to select the entire column. When it is a ↗, you can click to select a cell. You will learn more about this feature shortly.

You will begin by entering the information for La Costa in cells A1 through C1. You can type in the cell as you would in the document.

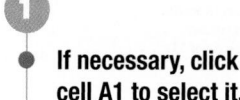

- If necessary, click cell A1 to select it.

- Type La Costa

- Press Tab.

- In the same manner, type 2 in cell B1 and 68 in cell C1.

- Continue entering the information shown below, using Tab to move to the next cell.

Cell	Entry
A2	La Sierra
B2	35
C2	54
A3	La Selva
B3	137
C3	80

Your screen should be similar to Figure 3.53

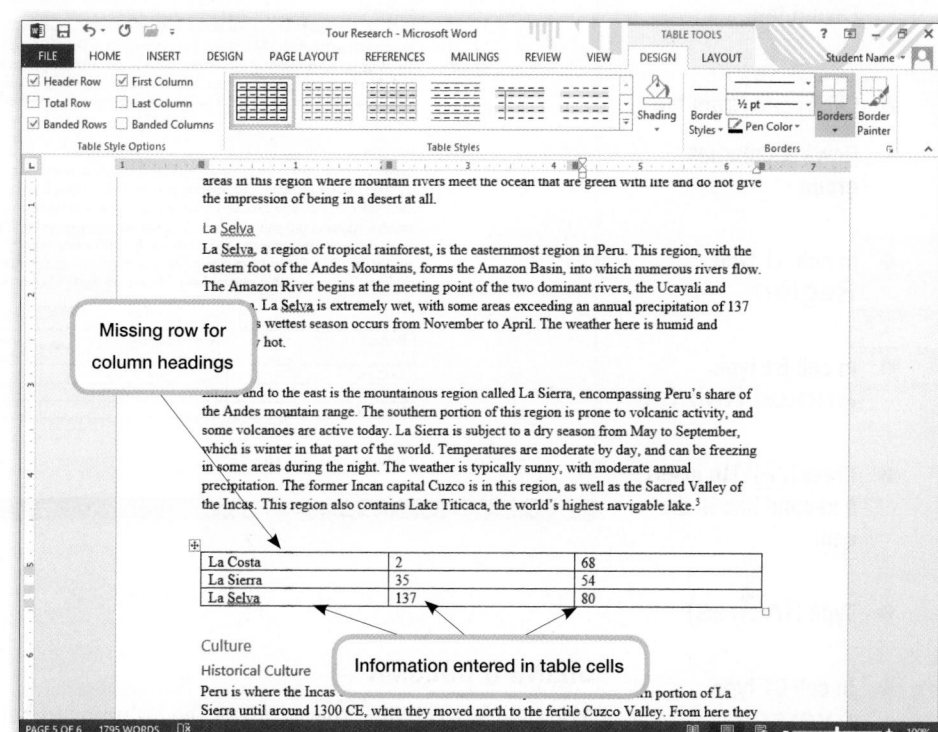

Figure 3.53

INSERTING A ROW

After looking at the table, you realize you need to include a row above the data to display the descriptive column headings. To add a row, simply click in any cell above or below the location where you want to add the row and then use the appropriate command to insert a row. Alternatively you can insert rows by clicking on the insert controls (the plus and double line) that appear when you point to the left edge of the table between two existing rows. This method can be used in all cases except when inserting a new top row. Once the row is inserted, you will enter the column headings in the cells.

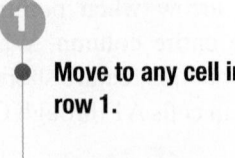

1

- Move to any cell in row 1.

- Open the Table Tools Layout tab.

- Click Insert Above from the Rows & Columns group.

- In cell A1 type **Region**

- In cell B1 type **Annual Rainfall**

- Press Enter to insert a second line in the cell.

- Type **(Inches)**

- In cell C1 type **Average Temperature** on the first line and **(Fahrenheit)** on the second.

Your screen should be similar to Figure 3.54

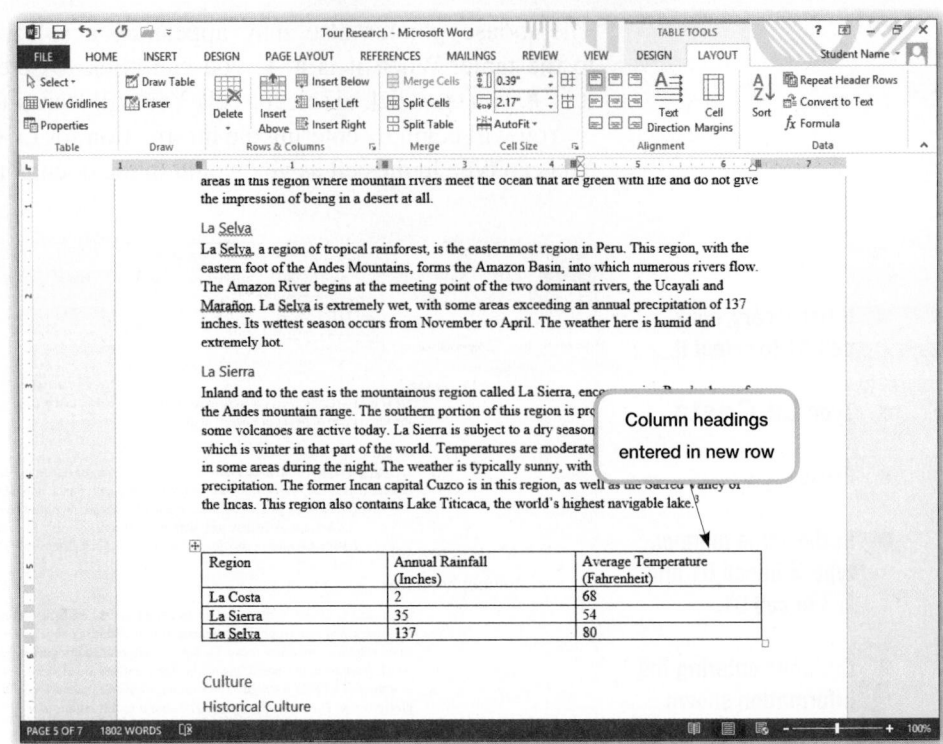

Figure 3.54

SIZING A COLUMN

You decide to change the width of the columns to better fit the data. To change the width of a column you simply point to the vertical divider until the mouse pointer looks like ↔. Then drag the divider to the left or right, depending on whether you want to narrow or widen a column.

Additional Information

Row height can be changed using the same method.

1

- Point to the vertical divider between the first and second columns until the mouse pointer looks like +‖+.

- Using the ruler as your guide, narrow the column by dragging the column divider to position 1.5 inches.

- Drag the divider between the second and third columns to position 3.5 inches.

- Drag the right edge of the table to position 6 inches.

Your screen should be similar to Figure 3.55

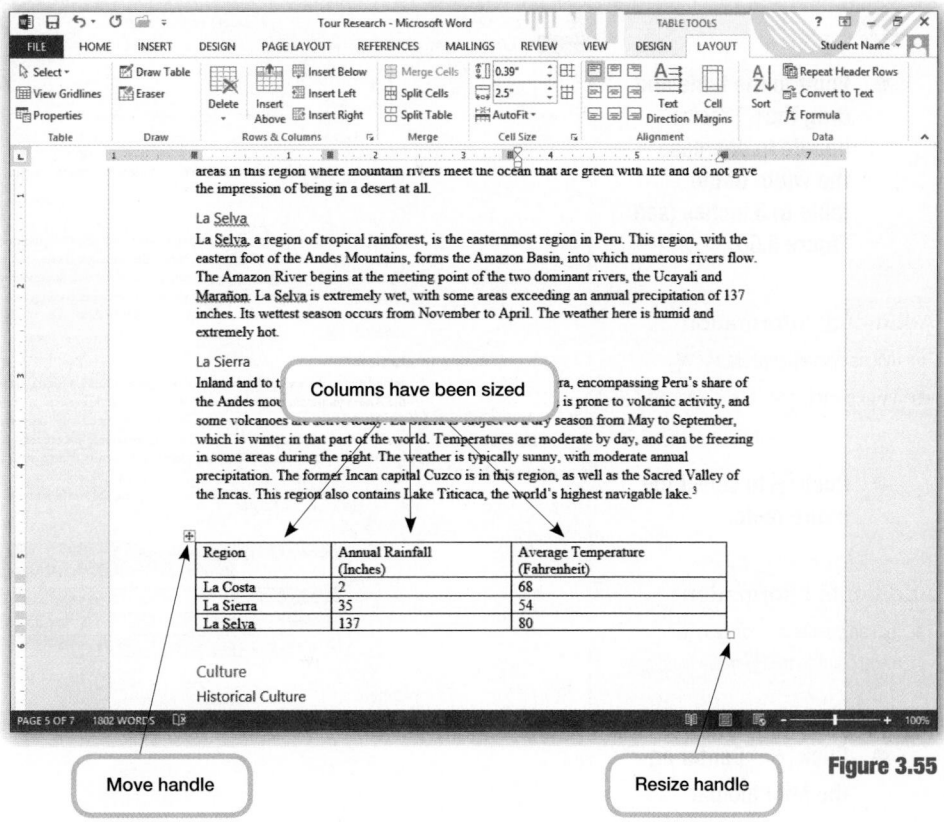

Move handle

Resize handle

Figure 3.55

SIZING A TABLE

The table is still wider than it needs to be. To quickly reduce the overall table size, you can drag the resize handle □. This handle appears in the lower-right corner whenever the mouse pointer rests over the table. Once the table is smaller, you will select the entire table by clicking the ⊕ move handle and center it between the margins.

See Concept 8: Sort in Lab 2 to review this feature.

1

● **Point to the table and drag the ☐ resize handle to decrease the width of the table to 5 inches (see Figure 3.56).**

Additional Information

The mouse pointer appears as ⬉ when you point to the ☐ resize handle.

● **Click ⊞ to select the entire table.**

Additional Information

The mouse pointer appears as ✛ when you point to the ⊞ move handle.

● **Click ≡ Center on the Mini toolbar.**

Your screen should be similar to Figure 3.56

Another Method

You also can drag the ⊞ move handle to move the table to any location or click ⊞ Center in the Table Properties dialog box.

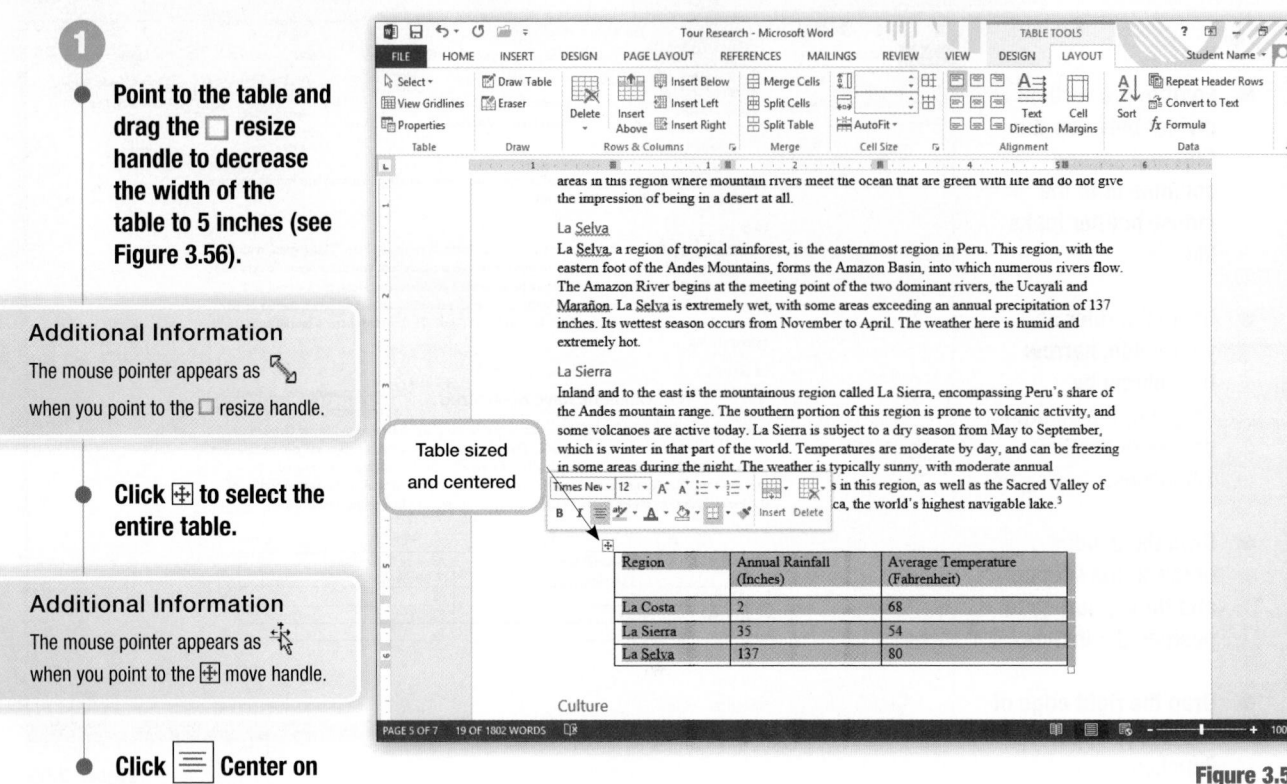

Figure 3.56

SORTING A TABLE

Next you decide you want the three regions to appear in alphabetical order as they are presented in the report. To make this change quickly, you can **sort** the table. The process is similar to sorting a list.

You will use the default Sort settings that will sort by text and paragraphs in ascending order. Additionally, when sorting a table, the program assumes the first row of the table is a header row and uses the information in that row for you to select the column to sort on. The default is to sort on the first column. In this case, this is acceptable because you want to sort the table by Region.

Having Trouble?

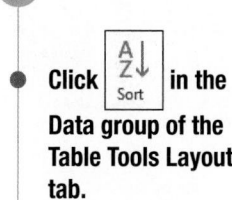

- Click in the Data group of the Table Tools Layout tab.

- Click OK to accept all the default settings.

- Click in the table to clear the highlight.

Your screen should be similar to Figure 3.57

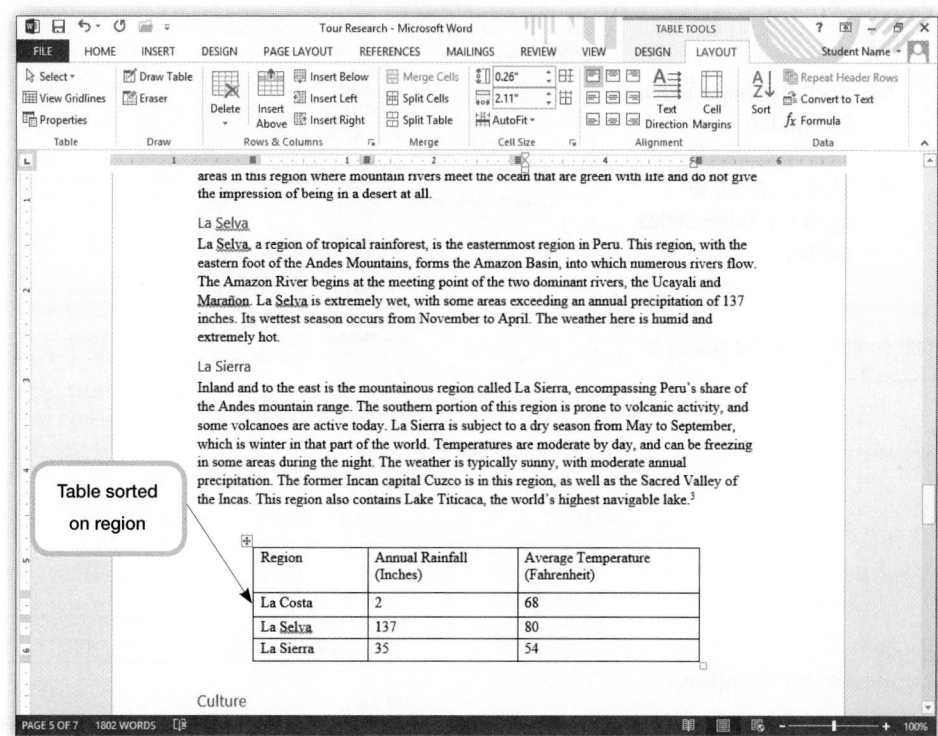

Table sorted on region

Region	Annual Rainfall (Inches)	Average Temperature (Fahrenheit)
La Costa	2	68
La Selva	137	80
La Sierra	35	54

Figure 3.57

The three regions now appear in ascending sort order in the table.

FORMATTING A TABLE

To enhance the appearance of the table, you can apply many different formats to the cells. This process is similar to adding formatting to a document, except that the formatting affects the selected cells only or the entire table.

The quickest way to apply formats to a table is to use a table quick style. This feature includes built-in combinations of formats that consist of different fill or background colors, patterns, borders, fonts, and alignment settings.

Having Trouble?

Refer to Concept 9 Quick Styles in Lab 2 to review this feature.

Open the Table Tools Design tab.

Click ⌄ More to open the Table Styles gallery.

Your screen should be similar to Figure 3.58

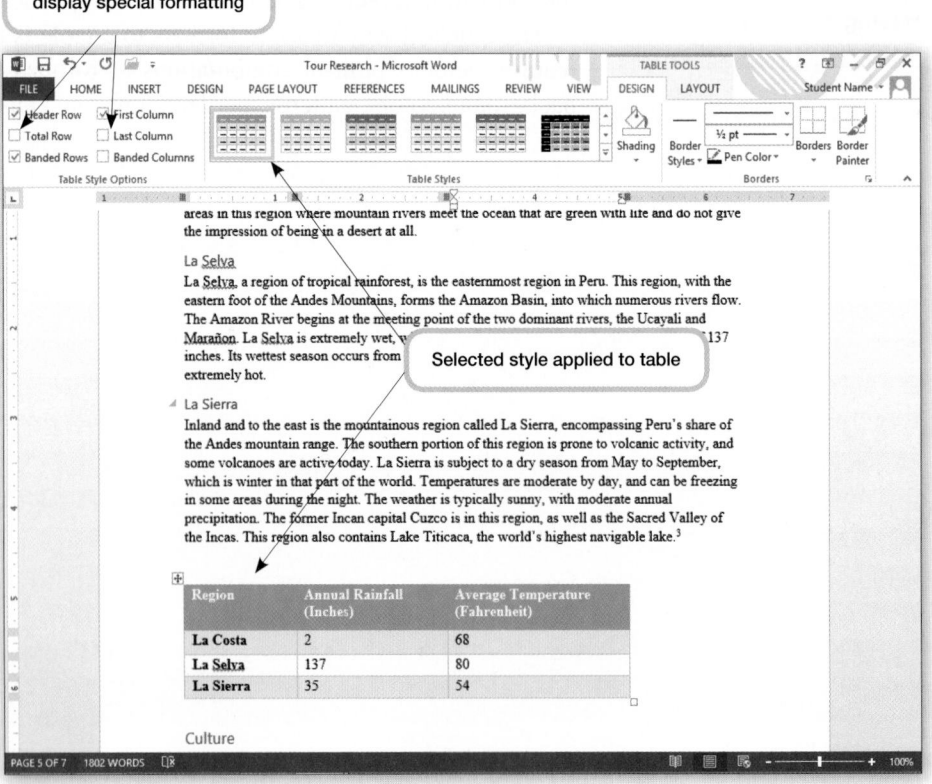

Default table style

Table styles gallery

Grid Table 4 - Accent 2

Figure 3.58

From the Table Styles gallery, select the table design you want to use. As you point to a style, the style name appears in a ScreenTip and Live Preview shows how the table will look.

Select areas of table to display special formatting

Choose Grid Table 4 - Accent 2 (4th row, 3rd column).

Your screen should be similar to Figure 3.59

Selected style applied to table

Figure 3.59

The entire table is reformatted to the new design. It includes banded shades of color for the table data. In addition, the first column and row heading text are bold. Notice that the table is no longer centered; however, the table size was not changed. The table alignment was changed because the new design includes left alignment. Using a table style was much faster than applying these features individually.

Even after applying a table style, you may want to make additional changes. For example, the selected table style applies bold formatting to the header row and first column. It also uses a banded row effect for the table data. If you do not want one or all of these features, you can turn them off using the quick styles options.

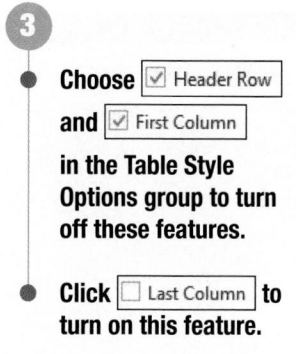

Choose ☑ Header Row **and** ☑ First Column **in the Table Style Options group to turn off these features.**

Click ☐ Last Column **to turn on this feature.**

Your screen should be similar to Figure 3.60

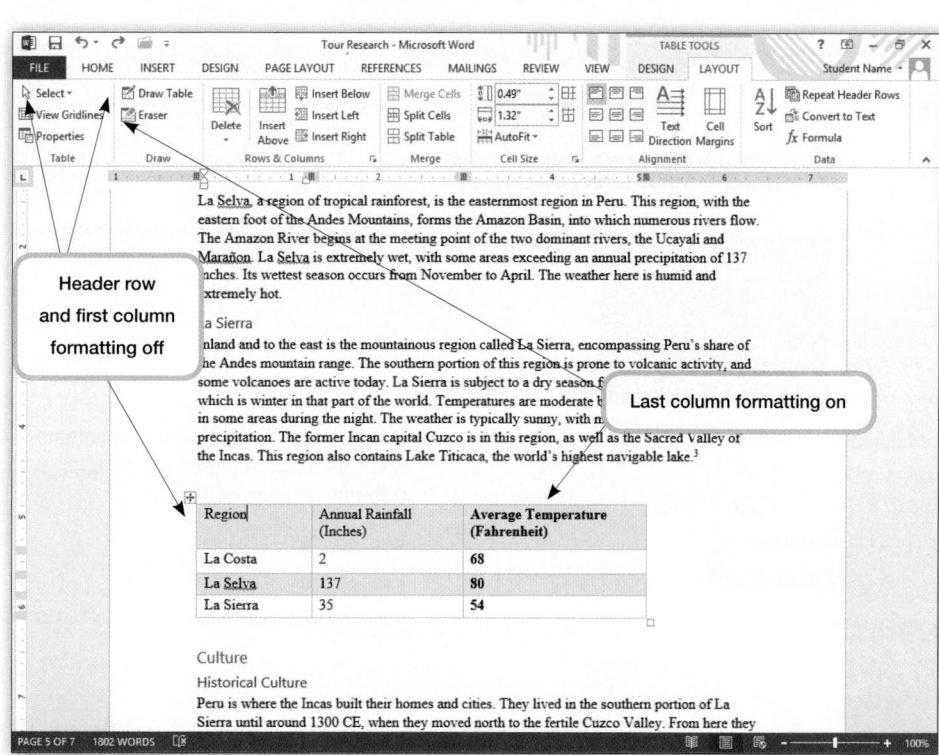

Figure 3.60

Additional Information

The gallery of table styles also reflects the changes in the style options.

The background of the first row is now shaded because of the Banded Rows setting and the bold effect was removed from the column and row headings. Bold was added to the last column to emphasize the data. As you can see you can quickly emphasize different areas of the table by selecting areas of the table to display special formatting.

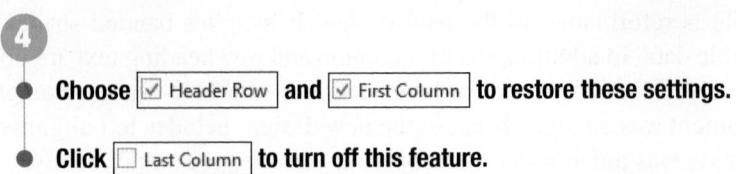

4

● **Choose** ☑ Header Row **and** ☑ First Column **to restore these settings.**

● **Click** ☐ Last Column **to turn off this feature.**

As you continue to modify the table, many cells can be selected and changed at the same time. The table below describes the procedures to select information in a table.

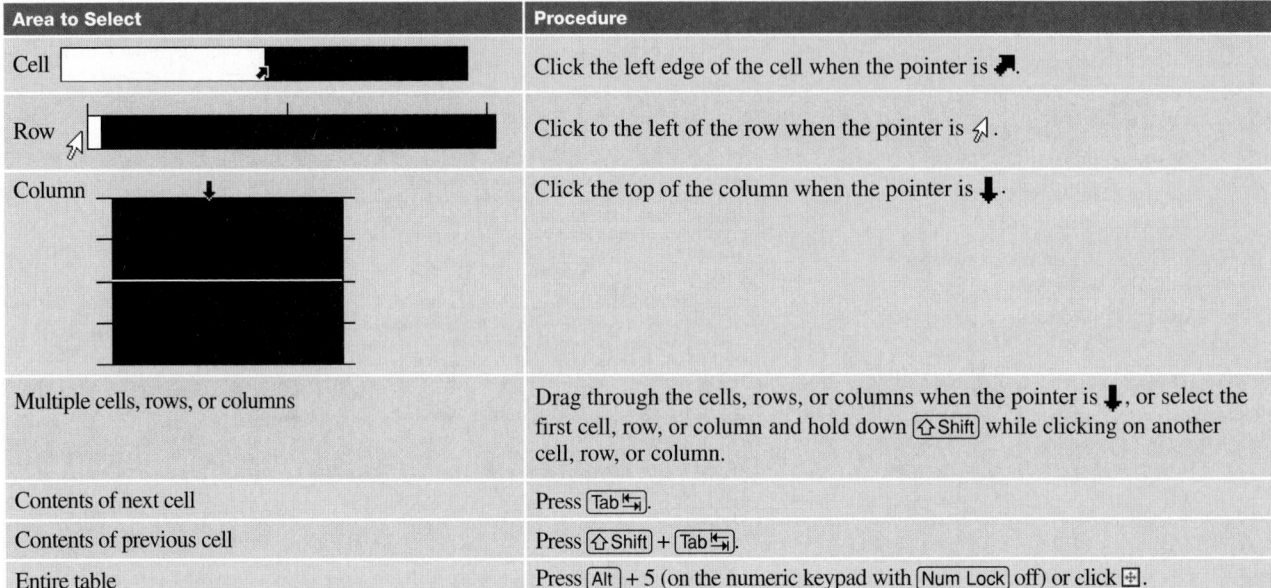

Area to Select	Procedure
Cell	Click the left edge of the cell when the pointer is ➚.
Row	Click to the left of the row when the pointer is ⟋.
Column	Click the top of the column when the pointer is ↓.
Multiple cells, rows, or columns	Drag through the cells, rows, or columns when the pointer is ↓, or select the first cell, row, or column and hold down ⇧ Shift while clicking on another cell, row, or column.
Contents of next cell	Press Tab↹.
Contents of previous cell	Press ⇧ Shift + Tab↹.
Entire table	Press Alt + 5 (on the numeric keypad with Num Lock off) or click ⊞.

You want the entries in the header row (cells A1 through C1), and the table data in cells B2 through C4, to be centered in their cell spaces. You also want to increase the font size of the header text. Finally, you will add a caption below the table.

5

- Select cells A1 through C1 containing the table headings.

- Open the Table Tools Layout tab.

- Click 🗔 Align Top Center from the Alignment group.

- In the same manner, center cells B2 through C4.

- Select the header row again.

- Click A⃗ Increase Font Size in the Mini toolbar.

- Select the table and center it again.

- Add the caption **Table 1: Climate** below the table.

Having Trouble?

Follow the same steps for adding a figure caption, except choose Table as the caption label.

- Insert a blank line below the caption.

- Save the document.

Your screen should be similar to Figure 3.61

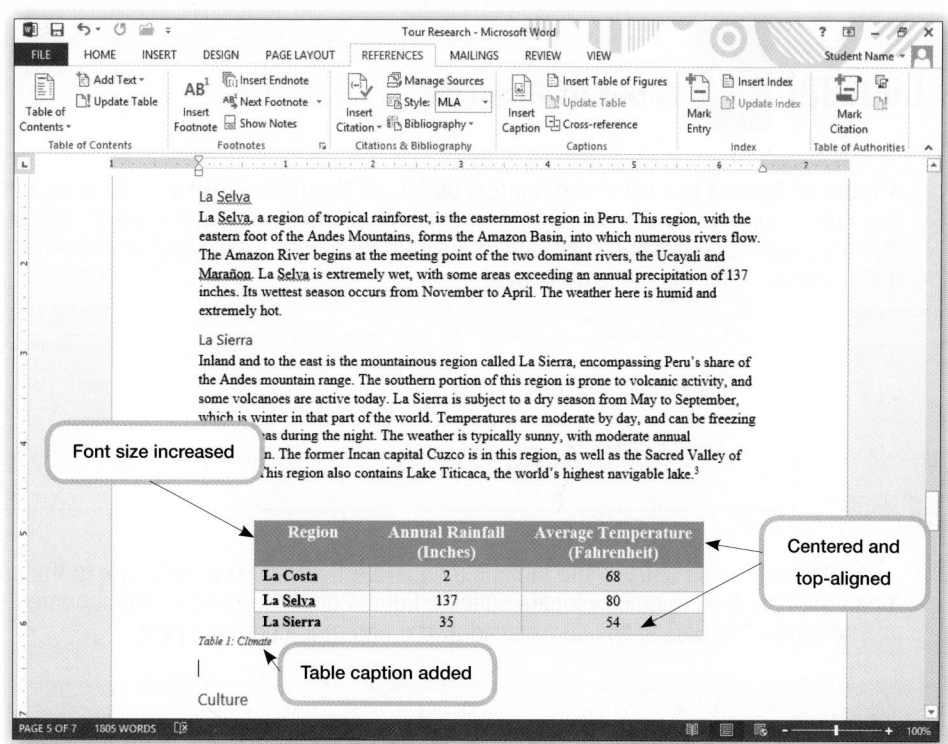

Figure 3.61

Including a Table of Figures

The report is near completion and you want to add a table of figures to the report.

Concept (7) Table of Figures

A **table of figures** is a list of the figures, tables, or equations used in a document and their associated page numbers, similar to how a table of contents lists topic headings. The table of figures is generated from captions that are included in the document and is a field that can be easily updated to reflect changes you may make to the document after the list is generated.

> ## Table of Figures
>
> *Figure 1: Tanzania Landscape* *1*
> *Table 1: Peru Climate* *3*
> *Figure 2: Peruvian Flamingos* *4*

Additionally, each entry in the table is a separate field that is a hyperlink to the caption in the document. It can then be used to quickly locate specific figures or other items in the document.

The table of figures is typically placed at the end of a long document.

CREATING A TABLE OF FIGURES

Because you have already added captions to several items in the report, creating a table of figures will be a simple process.

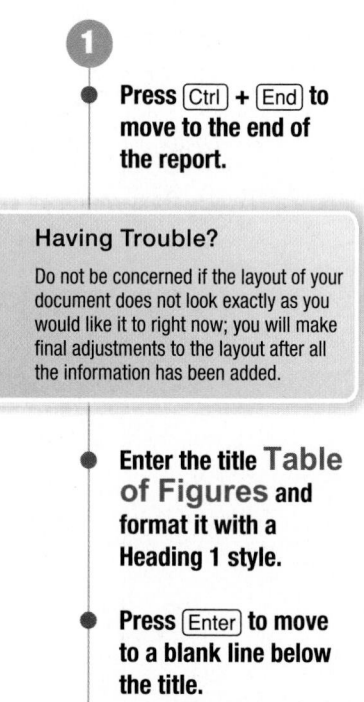

1

- Press Ctrl + End to move to the end of the report.

Having Trouble?

Do not be concerned if the layout of your document does not look exactly as you would like it to right now; you will make final adjustments to the layout after all the information has been added.

- Enter the title **Table of Figures** and format it with a Heading 1 style.

- Press Enter to move to a blank line below the title.

- Open the References tab and click [Insert Table of Figures] in the Captions group.

Your screen should be similar to Figure 3.62

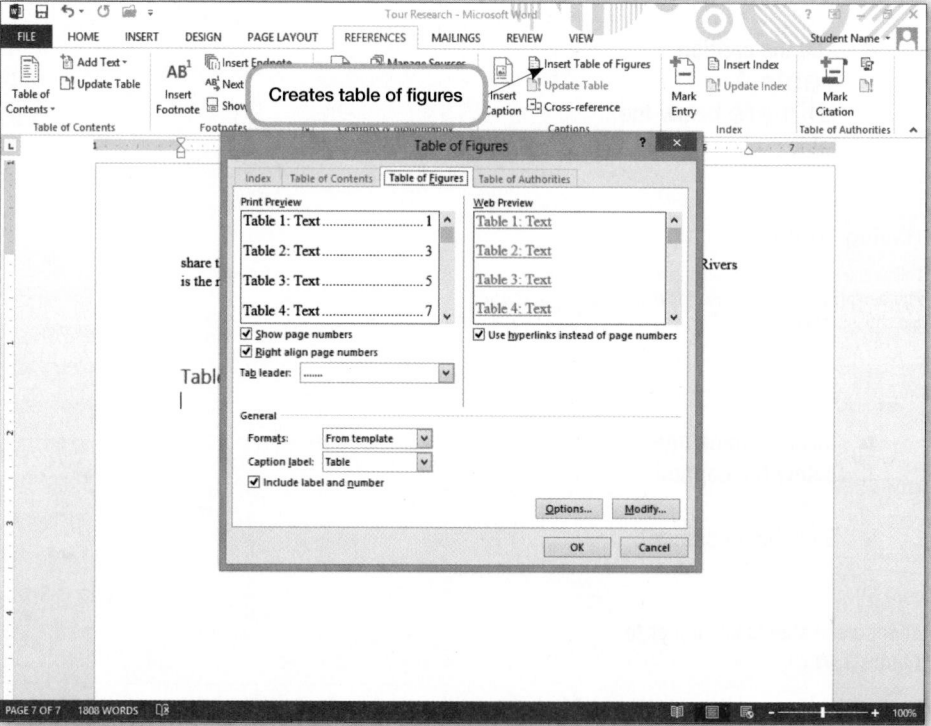

Figure 3.62

WWW.MHHE.COM/OLEARY

Word 2013

The Table of Figures dialog box options are very similar to those in the Table of Contents dialog box. The default options to show and right-align page numbers are appropriate as well as the use of the tab leaders. The Formats box is used to select a design for the table of figures. The default design is the design included in the Normal template and is displayed in the Preview boxes. In the Caption label box, you select the type of caption label you want to compile in the table of figures. The default is to display Table caption labels. You will change the Format to another style and the caption label to compile figures.

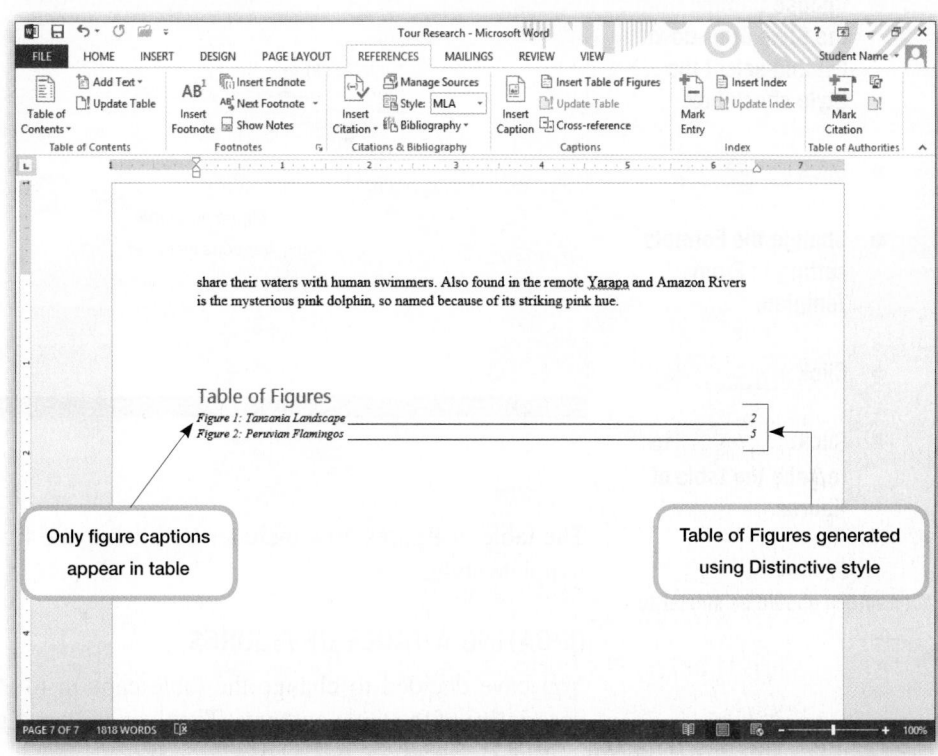

2

● **Choose Distinctive from the Formats drop-down list.**

● **Choose Figure from the Caption label drop-down list.**

● **Click** OK **.**

Your screen should be similar to Figure 3.63

Figure 3.63

The program searches for all figure captions in the document and displays them in the table of figures in sorted order by number. The table appears formatted in the selected style.

MODIFYING A TABLE OF FIGURES

You also want to include the table references in the table of figures. To do this, you could create a second table of figures to display the table references only. Alternatively, you can modify the table of figures to display all types of captions in a single table. You decide, since there are only three captions, to use one table. You also decide that you do not like how the Distinctive format looks and will use the default template formatting instead.

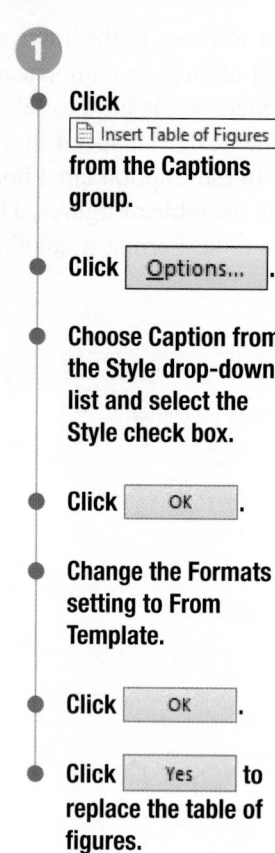

1

- **Click** ⬚ Insert Table of Figures **from the Captions group.**

- **Click** Options... .

- **Choose Caption from the Style drop-down list and select the Style check box.**

- **Click** OK .

- **Change the Formats setting to From Template.**

- **Click** OK .

- **Click** Yes **to replace the table of figures.**

Your screen should be similar to Figure 3.64

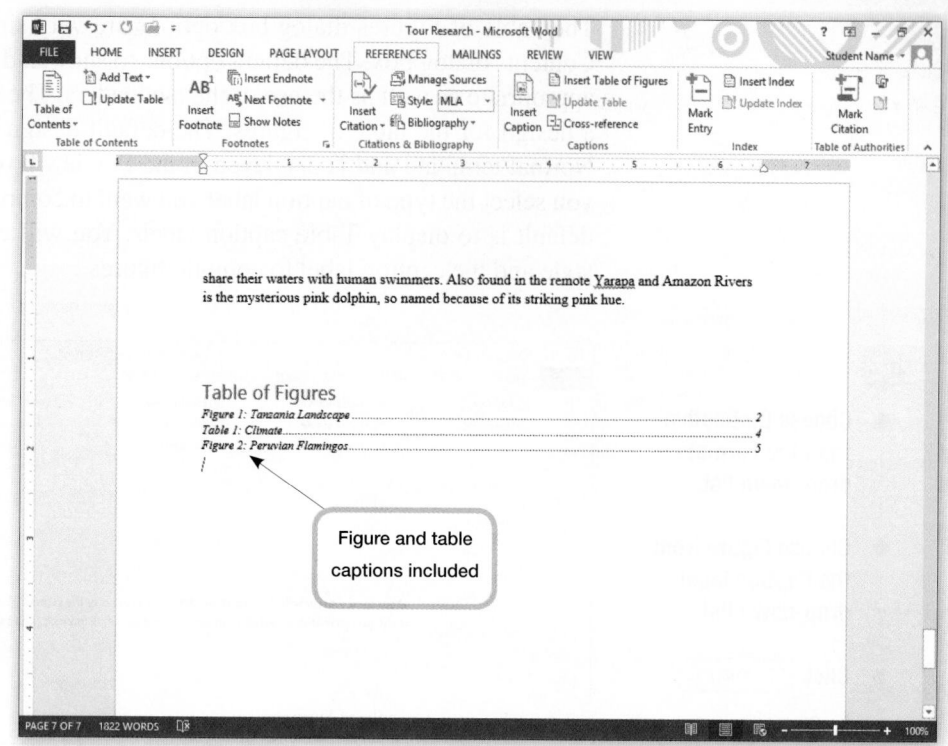

Figure 3.64

The table of figures now includes both table and figure captions using the default template style.

UPDATING A TABLE OF FIGURES

You have decided to change the table caption to Peru Climate to make it more descriptive of the table contents. Then you will update the table of figures to reflect this change.

Updates selected table

1

- Use the Table 1: Climate hyperlink in the table of figures to jump to that location in the document.

- Click in the caption before the word Climate, type **Peru**, and press Spacebar.

- Move back to the end of the document and click on the table of figures to select it.

- Click 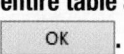 in the Captions group.

- Choose Update entire table and click **OK**.

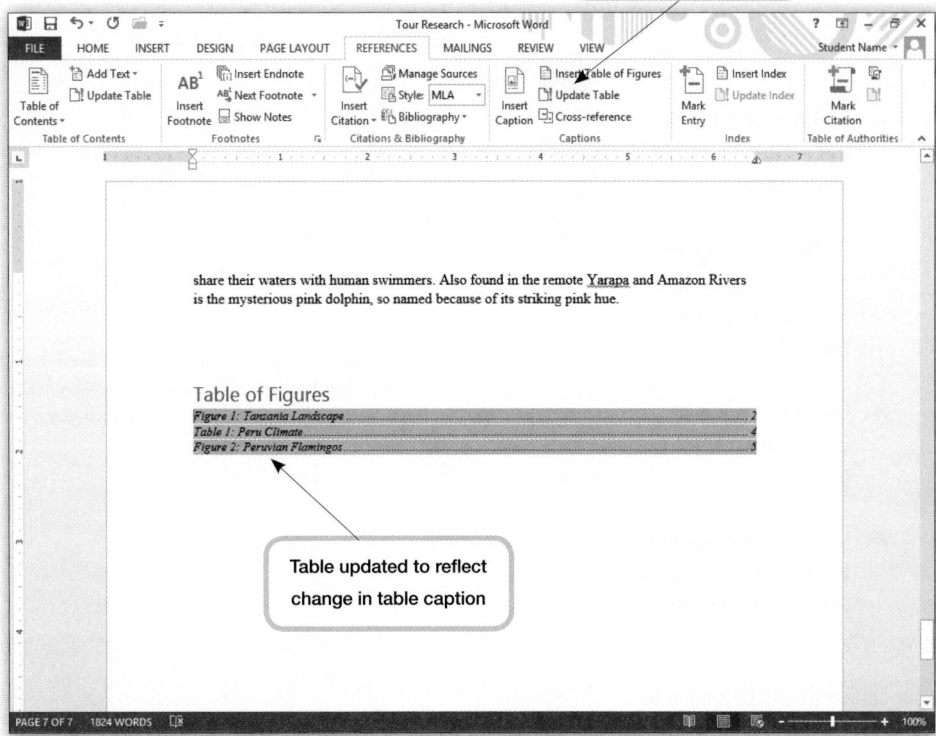

share their waters with human swimmers. Also found in the remote Yarapa and Amazon Rivers is the mysterious pink dolphin, so named because of its striking pink hue.

Table of Figures

Table updated to reflect change in table caption

Figure 3.65

Another Method

You also could press F9 to update the table of figures or choose Update Field from the table's context menu.

The entry for the table is updated in the table of figures to reflect the change you made to the table caption.

Your screen should be similar to Figure 3.65

Creating a Bibliography

Finally, you are ready to create the bibliography for the report (see Concept 3). Word makes the process of creating a bibliography effortless by automatically generating a bibliography using the selected report style from the source information you entered when creating citations.

GENERATING THE BIBLIOGRAPHY

The requirements for formatting a bibliography vary depending on the report style used. The MLA style requires that each work directly referenced in the paper be listed in alphabetical order by author's last name on a separate page with the title "Works Cited."

Additional Information

Word can automatically generate a complete bibliography that lists all sources associated with the document or an abbreviated bibliography that lists only those sources that have been cited.

Because you have already specified the MLA reference style, the Works Cited bibliography entries will automatically appear using the selected reference style.

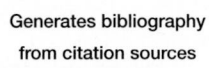
Generates bibliography from citation sources

- Insert a new blank page after the table of figures.

- Click ⬚ Bibliography ▾ in the Citations & Bibliography group of the References tab.

- Choose the Works Cited option from the gallery.

- If necessary, scroll to the top of the page to see the bibliography.

Your screen should be similar to Figure 3.66

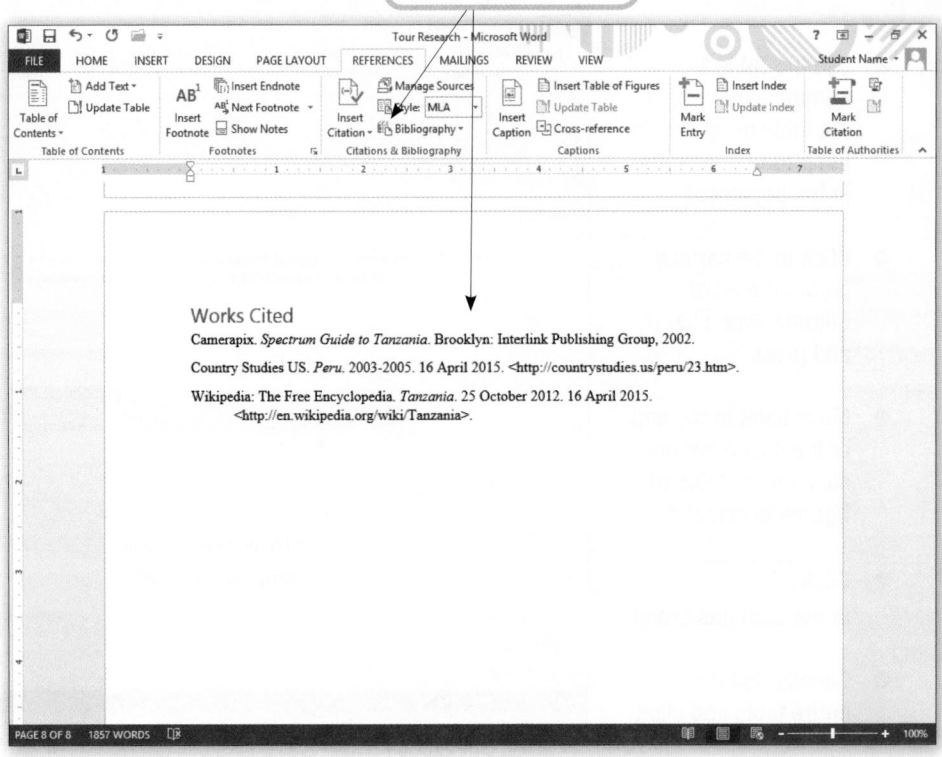

Works Cited

Camerapix. *Spectrum Guide to Tanzania*. Brooklyn: Interlink Publishing Group, 2002.

Country Studies US. *Peru*. 2003-2005. 16 April 2015. <http://countrystudies.us/peru/23.htm>.

Wikipedia: The Free Encyclopedia. *Tanzania*. 25 October 2012. 16 April 2015. <http://en.wikipedia.org/wiki/Tanzania>.

Figure 3.66

The Works Cited bibliography is formatted using the selected MLA documentation style. The page is labeled with a Works Cited heading and each citation source is listed in ascending alphabetical order.

UPDATING A BIBLIOGRAPHY

Now, as you look at the Works Cited list, you believe you entered the wrong publisher information for the Camerapix source. Even though the bibliography has been generated, it can easily be updated to reflect additions and modifications to the sources. This is because the bibliography is a field that is linked to the sources in the Current List. You will fix the source information and update the bibliography. Rather than return to the citation in the document for this source to edit it, you will use the Source Manager.

Click

🗐 Manage Sources

in the Citations &
Bibliography group.

Your screen should be similar to
Figure 3.67

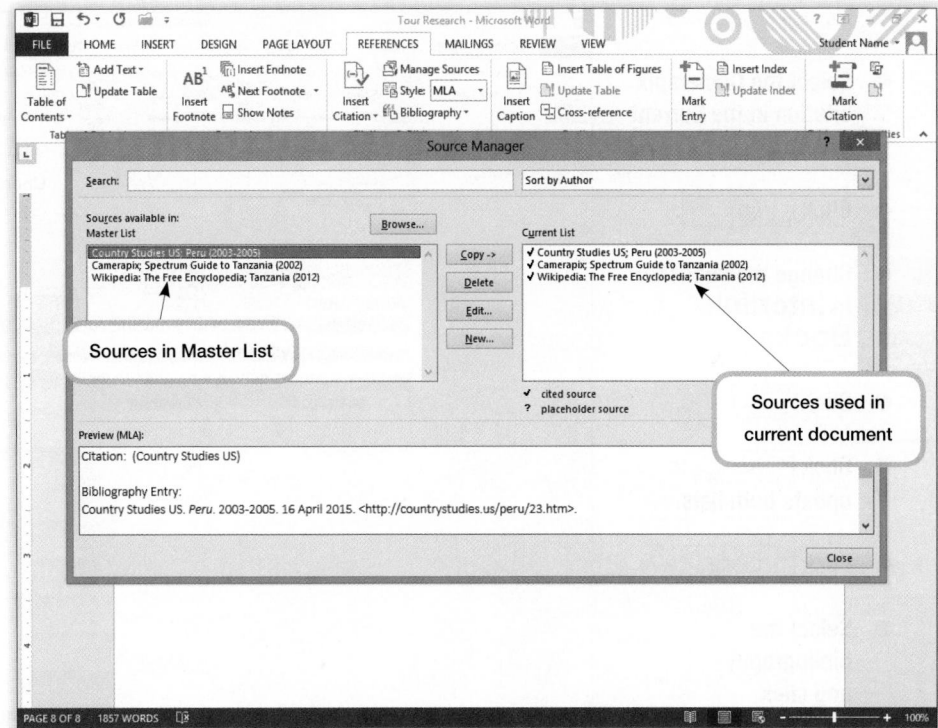

Sources in Master List

Sources used in
current document

Figure 3.67

Additional Information

The master list may display additional
sources if they have been entered
previously using this computer.

The Source Manager dialog box displays the three sources you entered in both the
Master and Current List boxes. It is used to add, copy, delete, and edit sources.
Notice that the items in the Current List are preceded with checkmarks. This indi-
cates they have all been cited in the document. All items in the Current List will
appear in the bibliography when it is generated. If a source appears in the Master
List that you want to appear in the bibliography, you can select it and copy it to the
Current List.

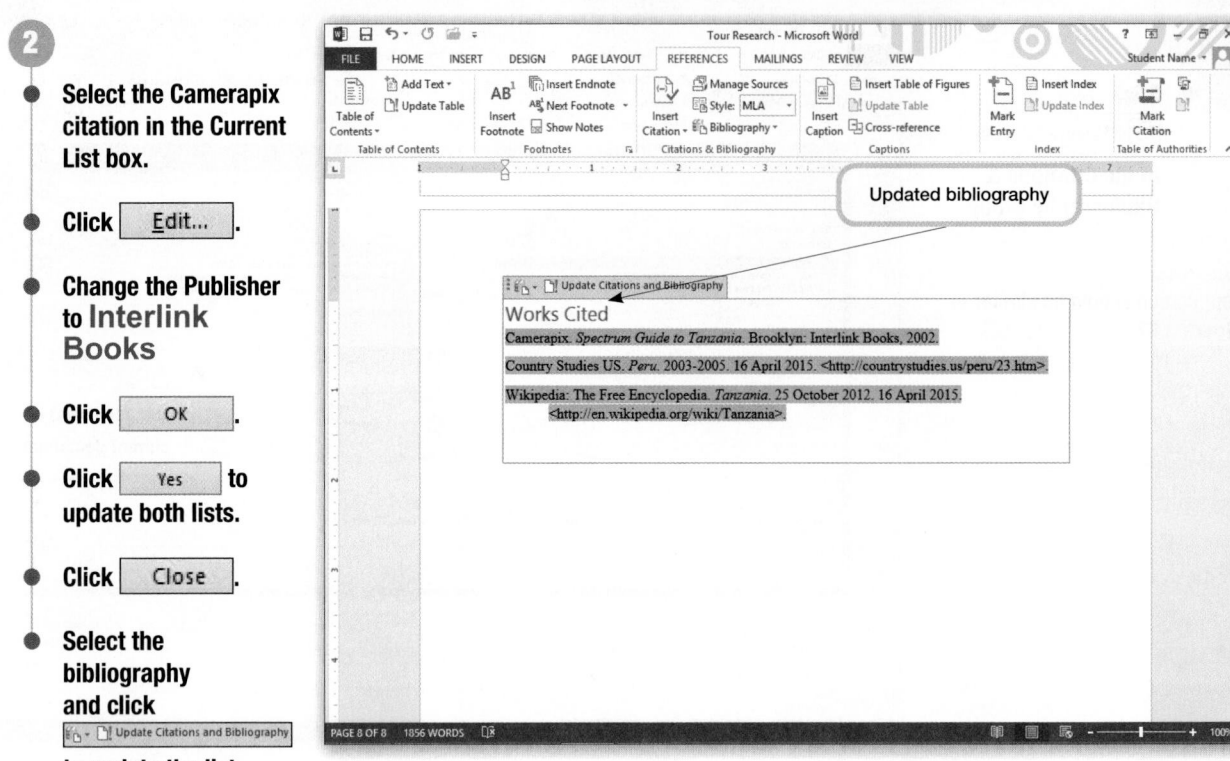

2

- Select the Camerapix citation in the Current List box.

- Click ⟨ Edit... ⟩.

- Change the Publisher to **Interlink Books**

- Click ⟨ OK ⟩.

- Click ⟨ Yes ⟩ to update both lists.

- Click ⟨ Close ⟩.

- Select the bibliography and click ⟨ Update Citations and Bibliography ⟩ to update the list.

Figure 3.68

Your screen should be similar to Figure 3.68

The bibliography information for the Camerapix source is now correct and the Works Cited list has been appropriately updated.

MODIFYING A BIBLIOGRAPHY

Finally, you will modify the format of the Works Cited page to more closely meet the MLA requirements. The page title should be centered at the top of the page. The bibliography entries must be formatted as hanging indents—the first line is even with the left margin and subsequent lines of the same work are indented 0.5 inch. MLA formatting for the Works Cited page also requires that it should be double-spaced, as is the entire report.

In addition to centering the title at the top of the page, you decide to change the style of the title to the same as the table of contents title.

1

- **Move to the Works Cited title.**

- **Choose TOC Title from the Styles group of the Home tab.**

- **Click ☰ Center.**

Your screen should be similar to Figure 3.69

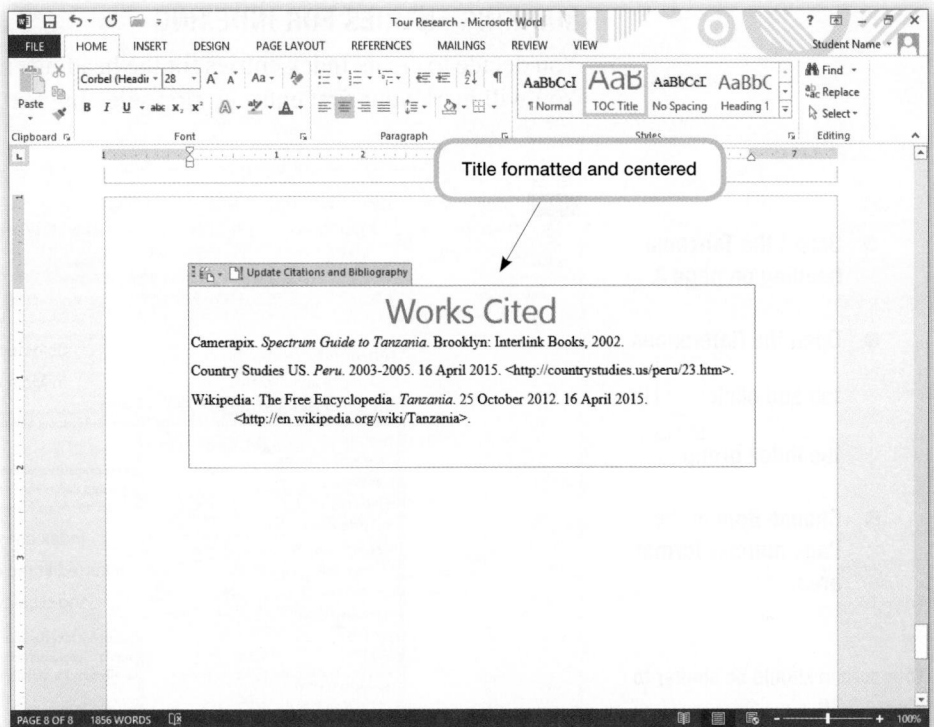

Title formatted and centered

Works Cited

Camerapix. *Spectrum Guide to Tanzania*. Brooklyn: Interlink Books, 2002.

Country Studies US. *Peru*. 2003-2005. 16 April 2015. <http://countrystudies.us/peru/23.htm>.

Wikipedia: The Free Encyclopedia. *Tanzania*. 25 October 2012. 16 April 2015.
     <http://en.wikipedia.org/wiki/Tanzania>.

Figure 3.69

Creating an Index

In a long document, a reader may remember seeing a particular item or term but not remember on which page to find it. To help your readers locate information quickly, you will create an index for your document.

Concept 8 Index

An **index** appears at the end of a long document as a list of major headings, topics, and terms with their page numbers. Word generates an index by compiling all of the entries and references to entries that you have previously marked in the content of your document, alphabetizing the list, and then assigning page numbers to the entries. An index subentry item is used to further define or explain the first index item. Once you've marked index entries in your document, you compile the entries into an index. The diagram below shows the relationship between index entries and subentries.

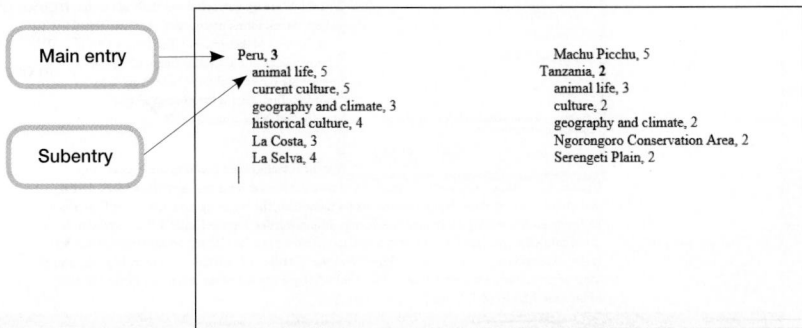

Main entry → Peru, **3**
     animal life, 5
Subentry → current culture, 5
     geography and climate, 3
     historical culture, 4
     La Costa, 3
     La Selva, 4

Machu Picchu, 5
Tanzania, **2**
     animal life, 3
     culture, 2
     geography and climate, 2
     Ngorongoro Conservation Area, 2
     Serengeti Plain, 2

MARKING ENTRIES FOR INDEXING

You decide to create index entries for the headings in the Tour Research document. You will mark your first entry by first selecting text.

1

● Select the Tanzania heading on page 3.

● Open the References tab and click [Mark Entry] in the Index group.

● Choose Bold in the Page number format area.

Your screen should be similar to Figure 3.70

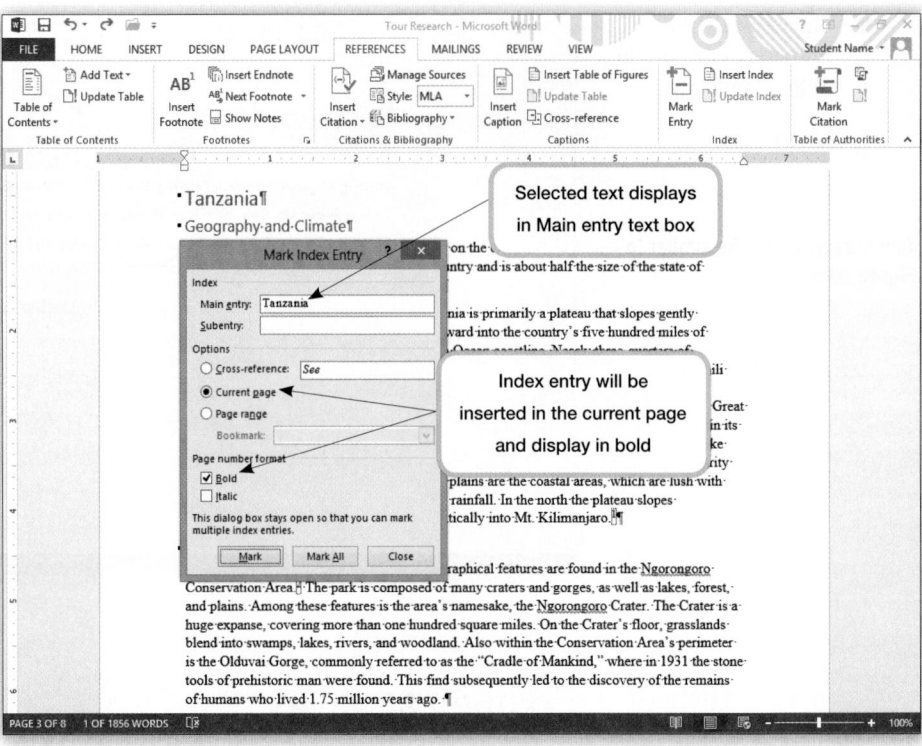

Figure 3.70

The selected text, Tanzania, is automatically displayed in the Main entry text box. The page number for this entry will be bold.

2

● Click  .

Your screen should be similar to Figure 3.71

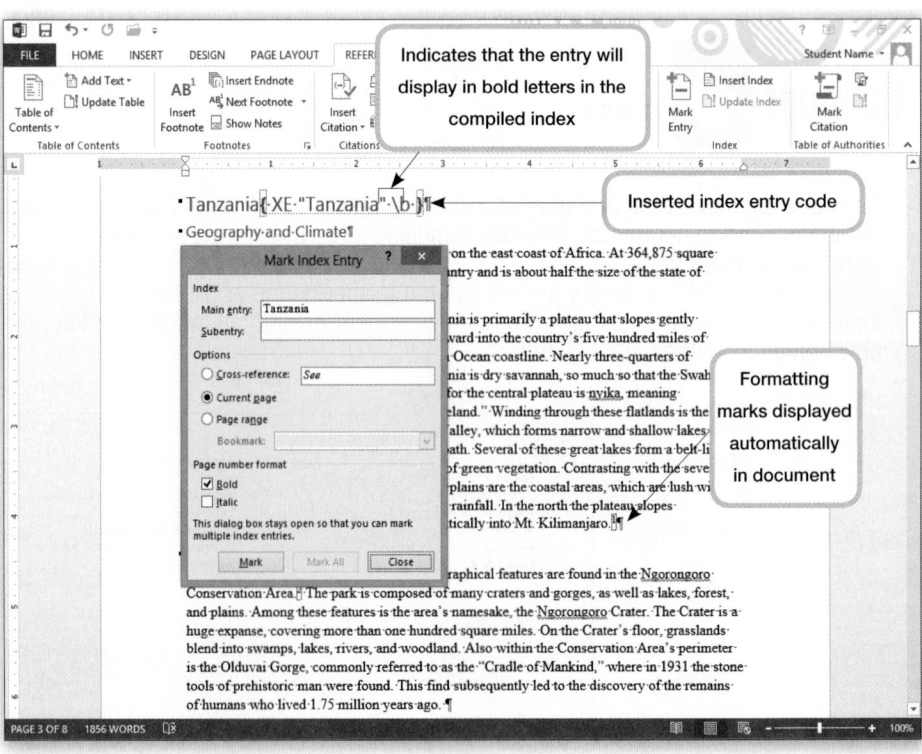

Figure 3.71

Notice that Word automatically turned on the display of formatting marks in your document and has inserted the field code "XE" with curly braces { } after the Tanzania heading. The XE field code will not print but will be used by Word later when generating the index. The Mark Index Entry dialog box is still open so that you can mark additional entries. Next you will create an index entry for the Geography and Climate heading by typing it in directly.

3

- If necessary, move the Mark Index Entry dialog box to the right side of your screen so that you can see more of your document.

- Click to the right of the Geography and Climate heading on page 3.

- Click in the Main entry text box and type **Tanzania**

- Type **geography and climate** in the Subentry text box.

- Click the Bold check box to remove the checkmark.

- Click [Mark].

Your screen should be similar to Figure 3.72

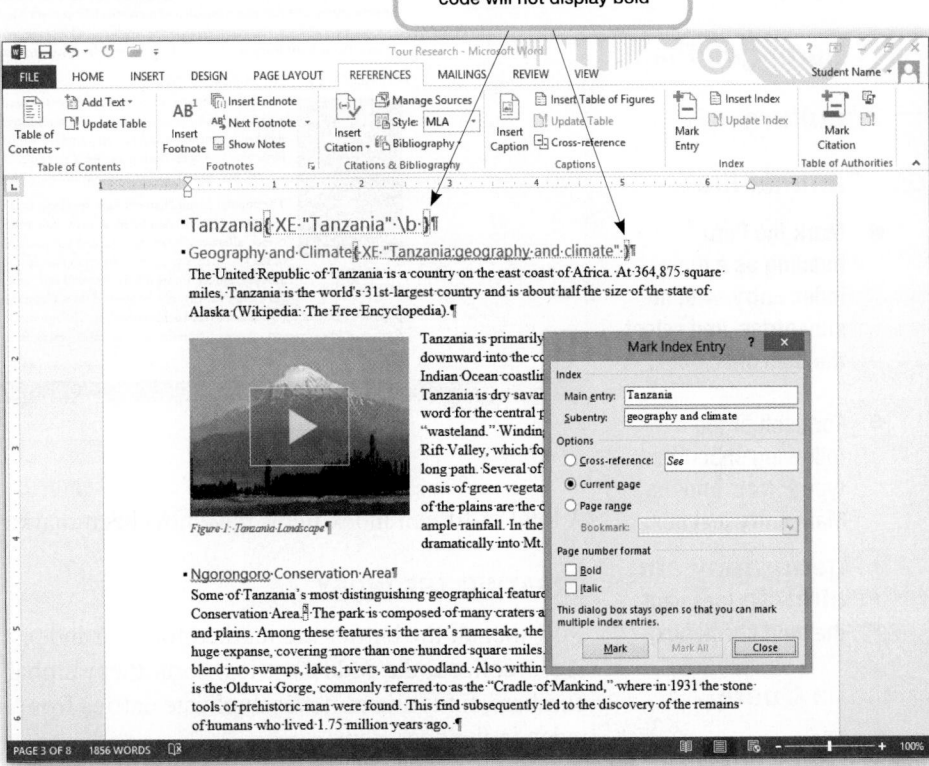

Second inserted index entry code will not display bold

Figure 3.72

Another XE field code was inserted in the document. There was no need to capitalize the words "geography and climate" because they are not proper nouns. These words will be indented without bold letters below the Tanzania topic in the compiled index.

You will now mark thirteen additional index entries, all headings, in the Tour Research document. As you work, you may have to move the Mark Index Entry dialog box to another location on your screen to see the document text. Also, when marking subentries, it is usually easier to click to the right of the heading you want to include in your index before marking it. If you select the text instead, the selected text will appear in the Main entry text box and you will need to delete it.

4

- **For each of the following subentries, type Tanzania into the Main entry text box:**

  Ngorongoro Conservation Area

  Serengeti Plain

  culture

  animal life

- **Mark the Peru heading as a main index entry, with no subentries, and select the bold check box.**

- **For each of the following subentries, type Peru into the Main entry text box:**

  geography and climate (deselect the bold check box)

  La Costa

  La Selva

  La Sierra

  historical culture

  Machu Picchu

  current culture

  animal life

- **Close the Mark Index Entry dialog box.**

Your screen should be similar to Figure 3.73

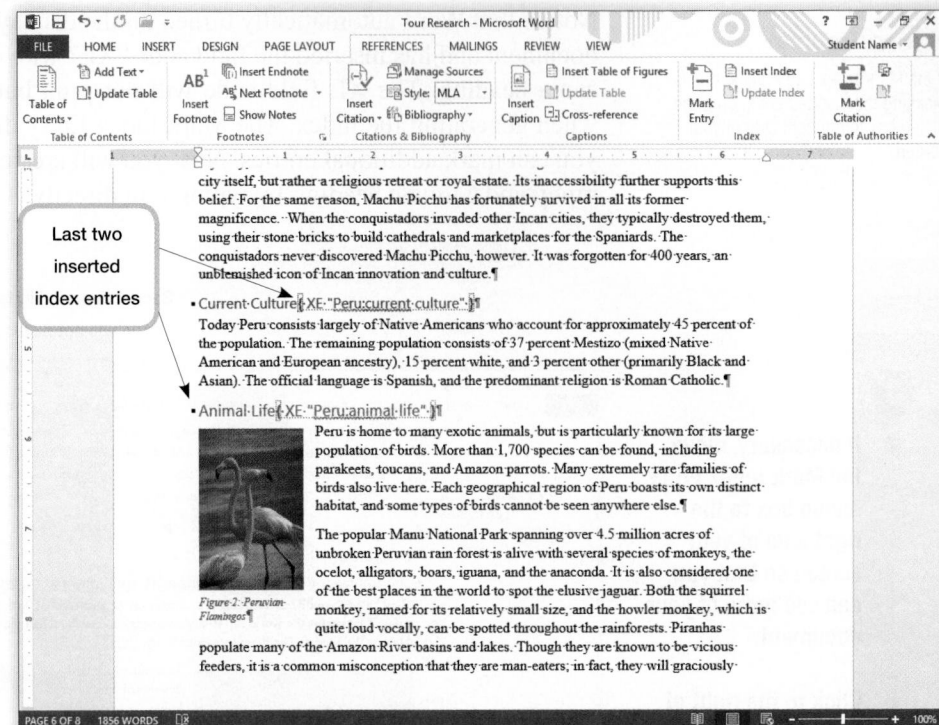

city itself, but rather a religious retreat or royal estate. Its inaccessibility further supports this belief. For the same reason, Machu Picchu has fortunately survived in all its former magnificence. When the conquistadors invaded other Incan cities, they typically destroyed them, using their stone bricks to build cathedrals and marketplaces for the Spaniards. The conquistadors never discovered Machu Picchu, however. It was forgotten for 400 years, an unblemished icon of Incan innovation and culture.

Current Culture{ XE·"Peru:current·culture"· }

Today Peru consists largely of Native Americans who account for approximately 45 percent of the population. The remaining population consists of 37 percent Mestizo (mixed Native American and European ancestry), 15 percent white, and 3 percent other (primarily Black and Asian). The official language is Spanish, and the predominant religion is Roman Catholic.

Animal·Life{ XE·"Peru:animal·life"· }

Peru is home to many exotic animals, but is particularly known for its large population of birds. More than 1,700 species can be found, including parakeets, toucans, and Amazon parrots. Many extremely rare families of birds also live here. Each geographical region of Peru boasts its own distinct habitat, and some types of birds cannot be seen anywhere else.

Figure 2: Peruvian Flamingos

The popular Manu National Park spanning over 4.5 million acres of unbroken Peruvian rain forest is alive with several species of monkeys, the ocelot, alligators, boars, iguana, and the anaconda. It is also considered one of the best places in the world to spot the elusive jaguar. Both the squirrel monkey, named for its relatively small size, and the howler monkey, which is quite loud vocally, can be spotted throughout the rainforests. Piranhas populate many of the Amazon River basins and lakes. Though they are known to be vicious feeders, it is a common misconception that they are man-eaters; in fact, they will graciously

Last two inserted index entries

PAGE 6 OF 8   1856 WORDS

Figure 3.73

A total of fifteen index items have now been marked in your document.

CREATING THE INDEX

Now that all the entries are marked for your index, it is time to generate the index. Word collects the index entries, sorts them alphabetically, references their page numbers, finds and removes duplicate entries from the same page, and displays the index in the document.

- **Turn off the display of formatting marks and then move to the end of the report.**

- **Insert a new blank page.**

- **Enter the title Index and format it with a Heading 1 style.**

- **Press** [Enter] **to move to a blank line below the title.**

- **Click** [📄 Insert Index] **in the Index group of the References tab.**

- **Click** [OK] .

Your screen should be similar to Figure 3.74

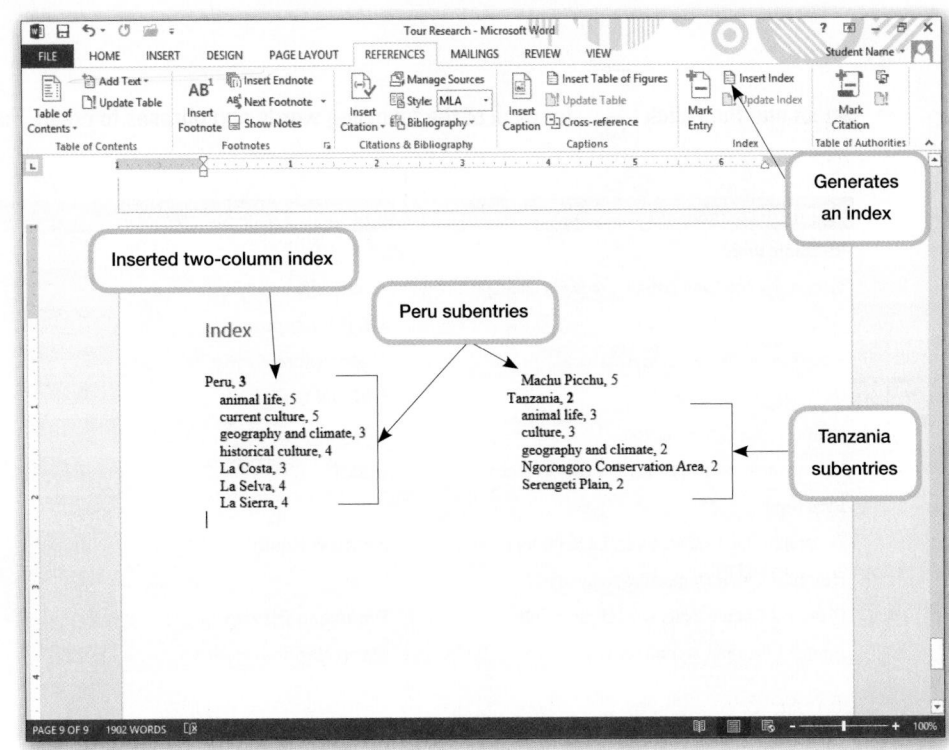

Figure 3.74

Word has generated a two-column index with the entries you marked in the document. Notice that the page numbers for the main entries Tanzania and Peru are bold. Each subentry appears indented below its corresponding main entry.

UPDATING AND MODIFYING THE INDEX

Next, you want to include items in the index from the body text of the Tour Research document. For example, you want the index to include a reference to Mt. Kilimanjaro, the Olduvai Gorge, and several other sites. An index, like a table of contents, is a field that can easily be updated if you add, edit, format, or delete index entries after the index is generated.

1

Select and then click  Mark Entry for each of the following words and phrases to create main index entries.

Location	Main Entry
Tanzania topic	
Geography and Climate topic, second paragraph	**Great Rift Valley**
	Mt. Kilimanjaro
Ngorongoro Conservation Area topic	**Ngorongoro Crater**
	Olduvai Gorge
Culture topic, first paragraph	**Swahili**
Culture topic, second paragraph, first sentence	**Masai**
Peru topic	
Geography and Climate topic, La Selva topic	**Amazon Basin**
Historical Culture topic, first paragraph	**Incas**
Historical Culture topic, second paragraph	**Francisco Pizarro**
Animal Life topic, second paragraph	**Manu National Park**

Additional Information

You may find the need to edit, format, or delete an index entry. To edit or format an existing index entry, click in the XE field in your document, and then change the text inside the quotation marks. Any formatting you apply to the text in the XE field will also be reflected in the compiled index. To delete an index entry, select the entire XE field, including the braces ({}), then press Delete.

- **Close the Mark Entry dialog box.**

- **Click on the index at the end of the document and press F9 to update the table.**

- **Turn off the display of formatting marks, and then click outside the index.**

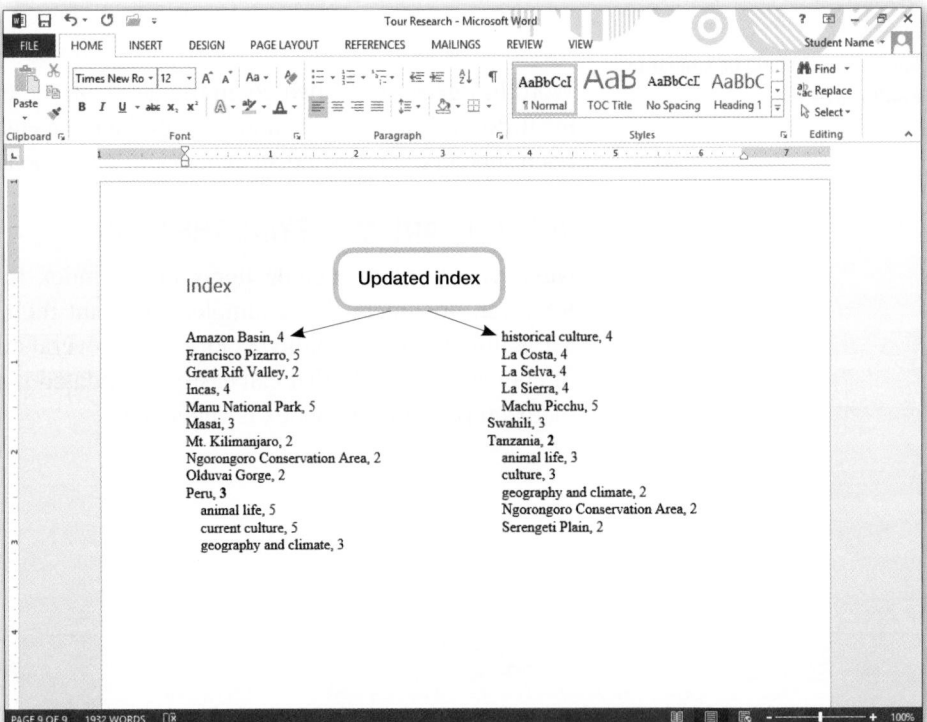

Figure 3.75

Your screen should be similar to Figure 3.75

The index includes all the newly added index entries. Finally, you want to modify the design of the index so that the entries appear in a single column.

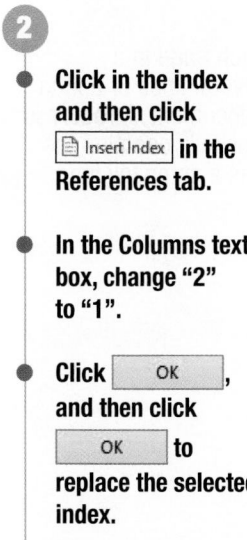

2

- Click in the index and then click [Insert Index] in the References tab.

- In the Columns text box, change "2" to "1".

- Click [OK], and then click [OK] to replace the selected index.

- Save the document.

Your screen should be similar to Figure 3.76

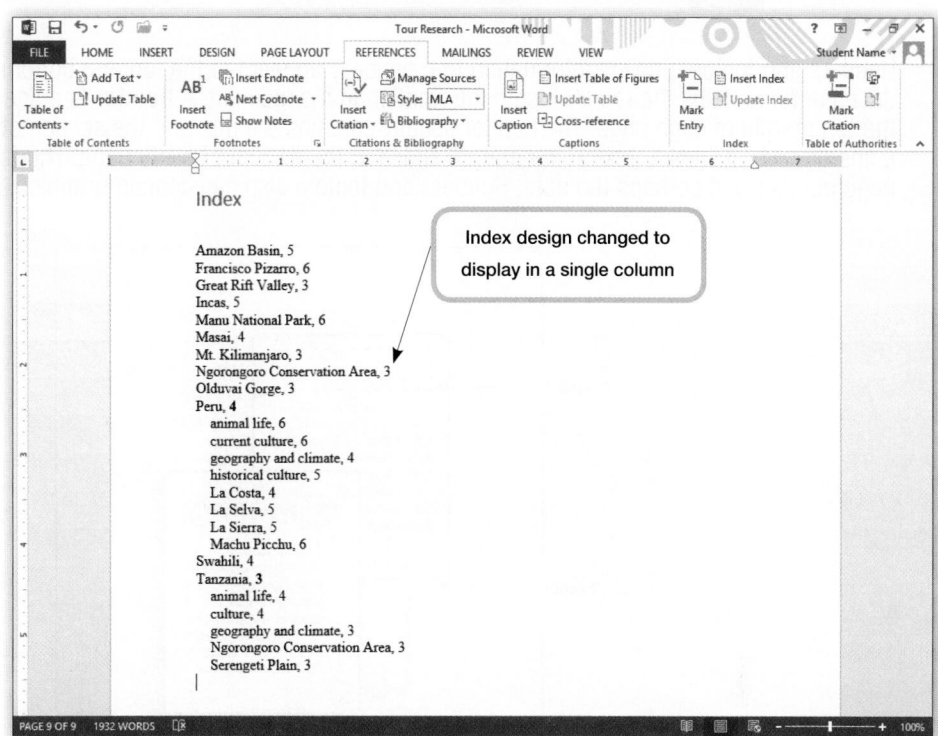

Figure 3.76

Creating Headers and Footers

Next you want to add information in a header and footer to the report.

Headers and footers provide information that typically appears at the top and bottom of each page in a document and helps the reader locate information in a document. A **header** is a line or several lines of text in the top margin of each page. The header usually contains the title and the section of the document. A **footer** is a line or several lines of text in the margin space at the bottom of every page. The footer usually contains the page number and perhaps the date. Headers and footers also can contain graphics such as a company logo.

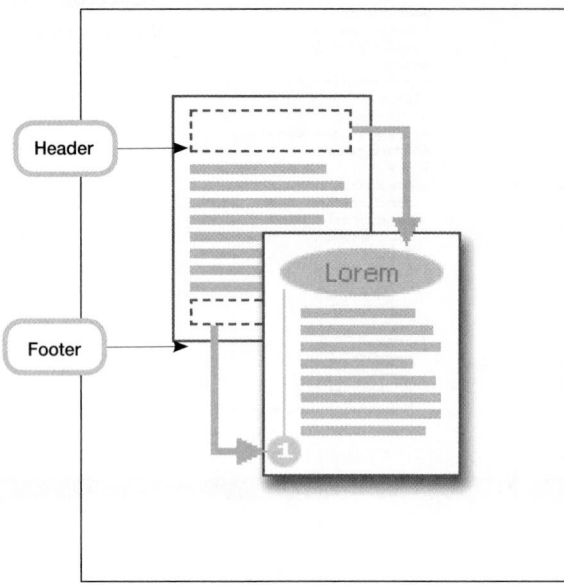

The same header and footer can be used throughout a document, or a different header and footer can be used in different sections of a document. For example, a unique header or footer can be used in one section and a different one in another section. You also can have a unique header or footer on the first page, or omitted entirely from the first page, or use a different header and footer on odd and even pages.

USING A PREDESIGNED HEADER

Word includes many features that help you quickly create attractive headers and footers. Among these features are predesigned built-in header and footer designs that include placeholders for entering information.

Because you do not want headers and footers on the first two pages of the document, you will divide the document into two sections. You replace the hard page break that you inserted when creating the table of contents page with a Next Page section break.

Additional Information

MLA style requires that headers and footers be placed 0.5 inch from the top and bottom of the page. This is the default layout for Word documents. Headers are to include the page number preceded by the author's last name, right-aligned.

- Move to the table of contents page.

- Turn on the display of formatting marks.

- Select the hard page break line below the table of contents and press Delete to remove it.

- At this location, insert a Next Page section break.

Having Trouble?

If you're having trouble inserting a Next Page section break, refer to the Inserting a Section Break topic in Lab 2.

- Turn off the display of formatting marks.

- Open the Insert tab and click ☐ Header ▾ in the Header & Footer group.

- From the gallery of header designs, choose Ion (Light).

- Choose ☐ View Gridlines from the Table group of the Table Tools Layout tab.

Your screen should be similar to Figure 3.77

Additional Information

You can hide the display of the document text while working with headers and footers by deselecting ☑ Show Document Text in the Options group of the Design tab.

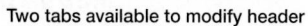
Two tabs available to modify header

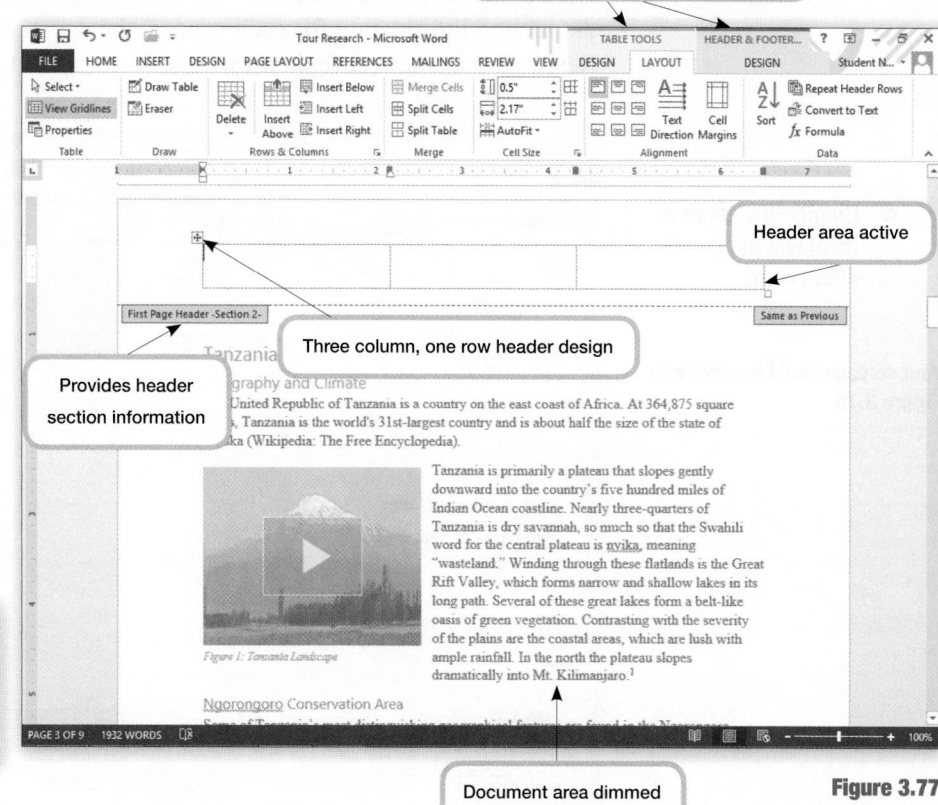

Header area active

First Page Header -Section 2-

Three column, one row header design

Provides header section information

Same as Previous

Document area dimmed and inactive

Figure 3.77

The document area dims and the header area, above the dashed line, is active. The Header & Footer Tools Design tab is automatically displayed. Its buttons are used to add items to the header and footer and to navigate between headers and footers.

In addition, the Table Tools tab is displayed. This is because the Ion (Light) header design is contained in a one row, three-column layout table that is used to control the placement of items. The page number appears in the third cell and is right-aligned.

MODIFYING HEADER SETTINGS

Notice the tab on the left below the dashed line of the header. This tab identifies the section information for each page of the document. Both sections of the Tour Research document have their own header areas that can be formatted differently.

Change the zoom to display 3 pages at 40% zoom.

Your screen should be similar to Figure 3.78

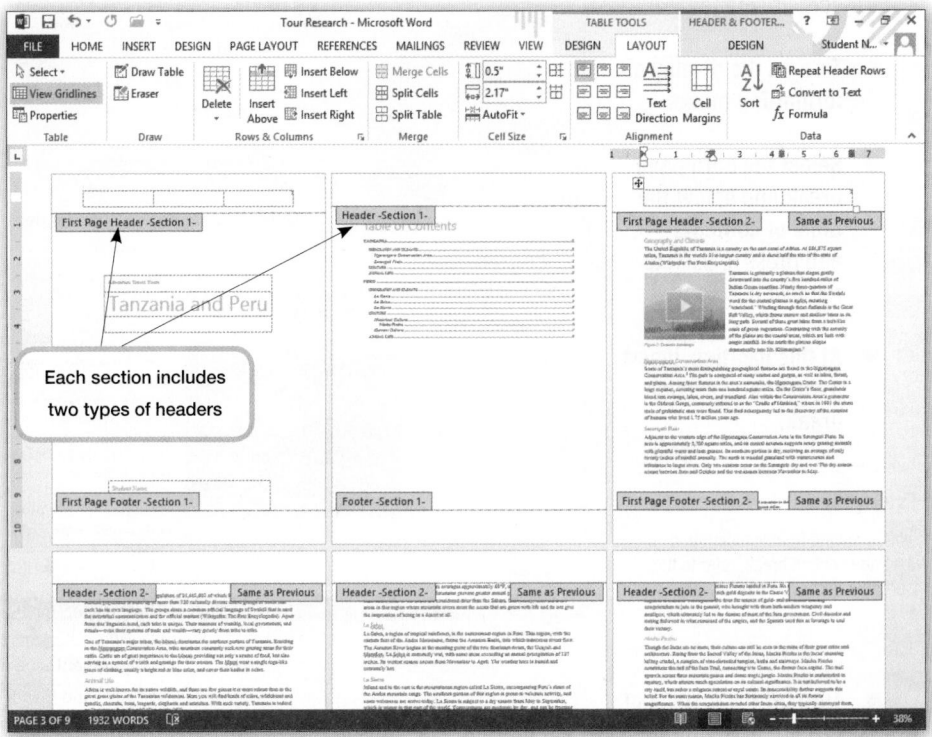

Figure 3.78

Now you can see that the document contains two types of headers: "First Page Headers" and running "Headers." First page headers appear on the first page of each section and running headers appear on all subsequent pages in a section. Notice the Ion (Light) design has been inserted only in the "First Page Header" headers and that the headers on the following pages of the same section are blank. This is because the option to use a different header on the first page is on by default.

Since it is not necessary to have a separate First Page Header in section 2, you will remove it and then insert the Ion (Light) design again for the running header of that section.

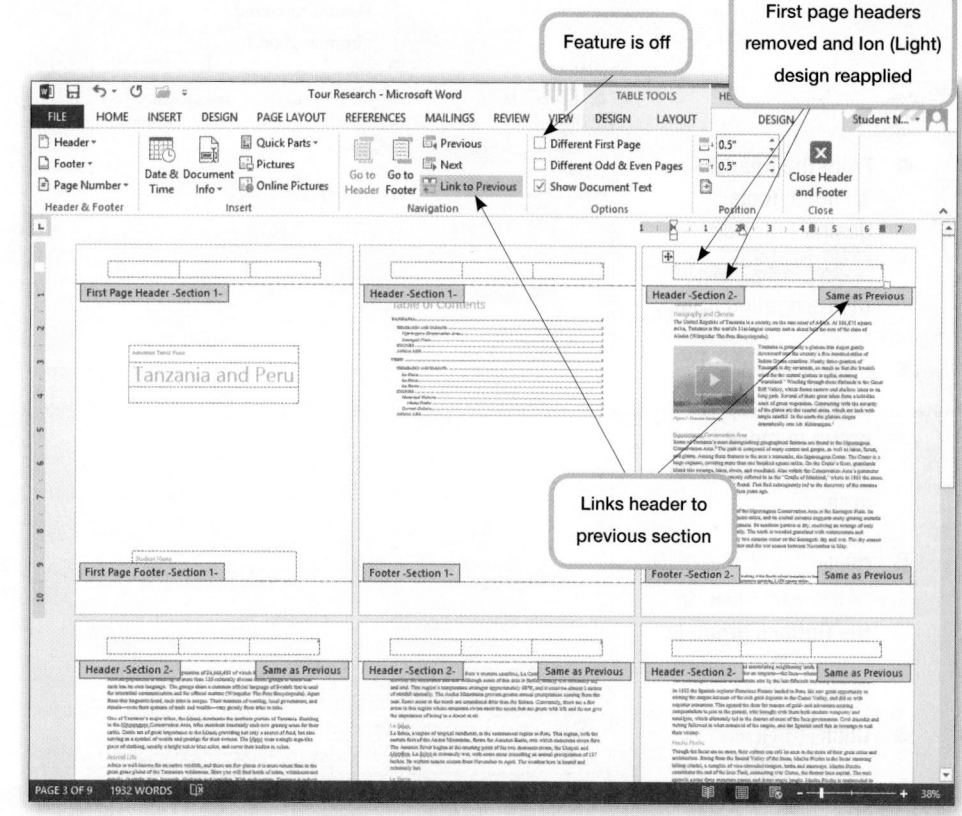

2

- Click the "First Page Header-Section 2" tab below the dotted header line on page 3.

- Click ☑ Different First Page in the Options group of the Design tab to turn off this feature for section 2.

- Click ☐ Header ▾ in the Header & Footer group, and choose Ion (Light).

Your screen should be similar to Figure 3.79

Feature is off

First page headers removed and Ion (Light) design reapplied

Links header to previous section

Figure 3.79

Now all the headers in both sections of the document are formatted using this design. The same design was applied to both sections because the headers are initially linked even though the document is divided into sections. Notice the tab on the right displays "Same as Previous." When this setting is on, the header in the previous sections will have the same settings as the header in the section you are defining. Because you do not want the title or contents pages in section 1 to display information in the header, you will break the connection between sections 1 and 2 by turning off this option. Then you will remove the header from section 1.

3

- **From the Header & Footer Tools Design tab click** `Link to Previous` **in the Navigation group.**

- **Click** `Previous` **in the Navigation group to move to the section 1 header area.**

- **Click** `Different First Page` **in the Options group to turn off this feature.**

- **Click** `Header ▾`.

- **Choose Remove Header.**

Header removed from section 1

Link to previous section removed

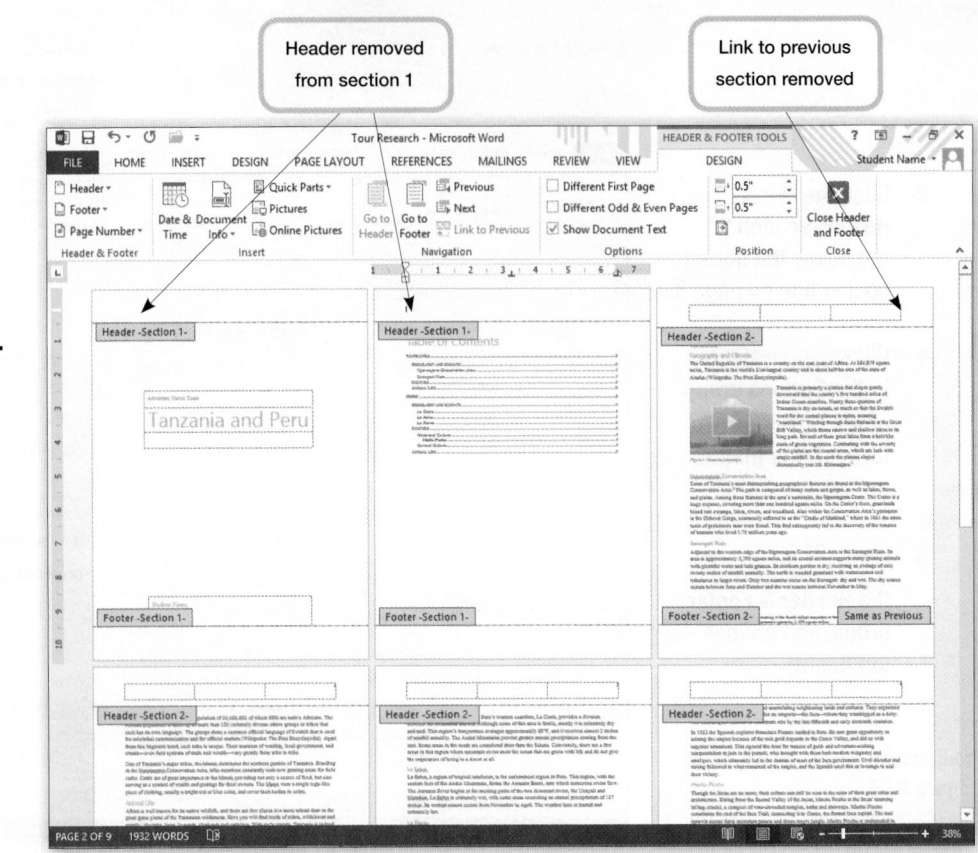

Figure 3.80

Your screen should be similar to Figure 3.80

The header information is removed from section 1.

ADDING HEADER CONTENT WITH QUICK PARTS

The page number in the third table cell is a field that updates automatically. You want to delete this field and replace it with the Author Quick Part.

1

- From the Design tab click [📑 Next] in the Navigation group to move to the Section 2 header area.

- Increase the zoom to 100%.

- Select the page number field in the third cell and press [Delete] to remove it.

- Click [📋 Quick Parts ▾] in the Insert group.

- Select Document Property and choose Author.

Your screen should be similar to Figure 3.81

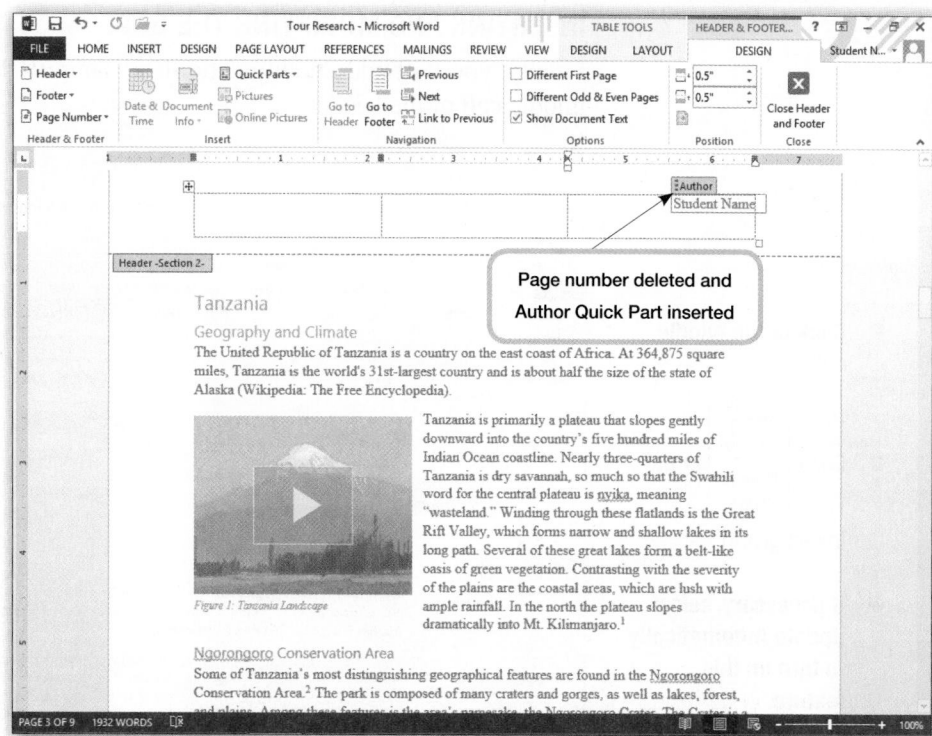

> Page number deleted and Author Quick Part inserted

Figure 3.81

The page number field was deleted and the Author Quick Part displays your name because this information is stored in the document properties. You will display the report title in the left table cell next.

2

- Click the left table cell.

- Click 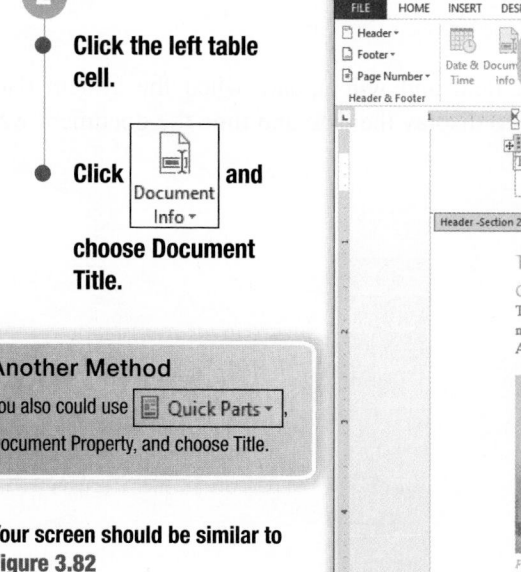 and choose Document Title.

Another Method

You also could use [📋 Quick Parts ▾], Document Property, and choose Title.

Your screen should be similar to Figure 3.82

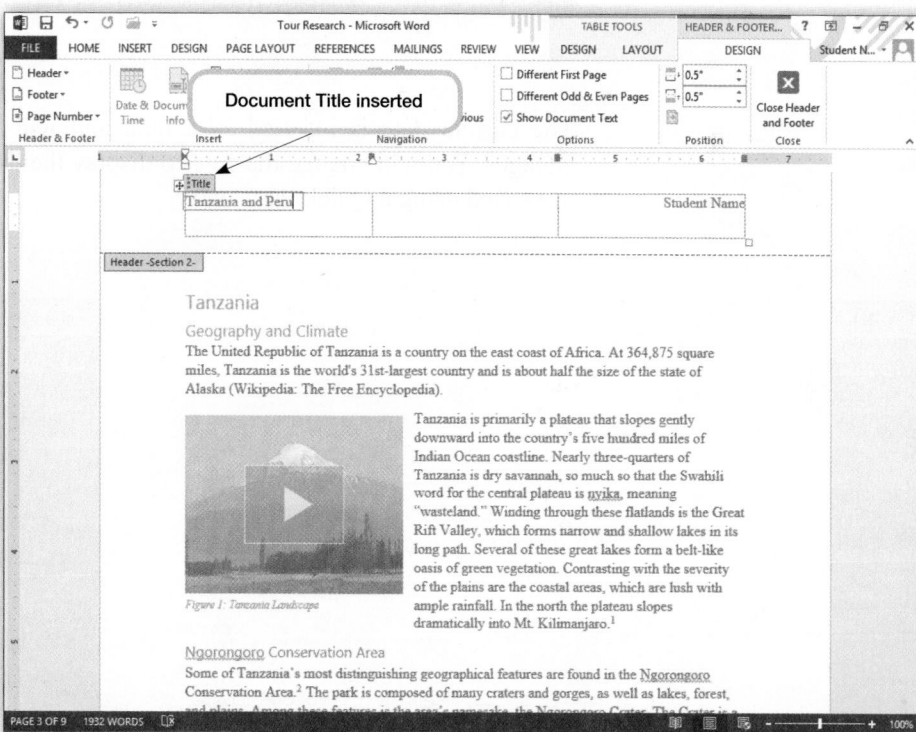

> Document Title inserted

Figure 3.82

The report title is displayed left-aligned in the table cell. The font size, color, and alignment of cell entries is part of the Ion (Light) Header design.

INSERTING AND MODIFYING THE DATE

Finally, you will add an automatic date stamp to display the current date in the middle cell of the header.

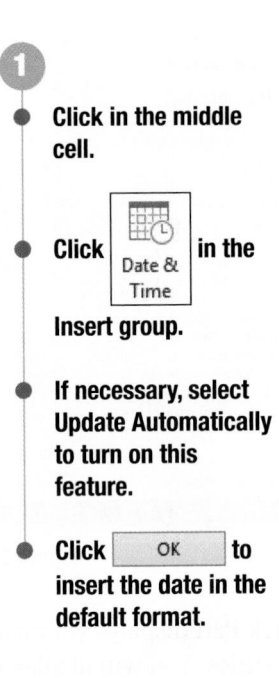

- **Click in the middle cell.**

- **Click** [Date & Time] **in the Insert group.**

- **If necessary, select Update Automatically to turn on this feature.**

- **Click** [OK] **to insert the date in the default format.**

Your screen should be similar to Figure 3.83

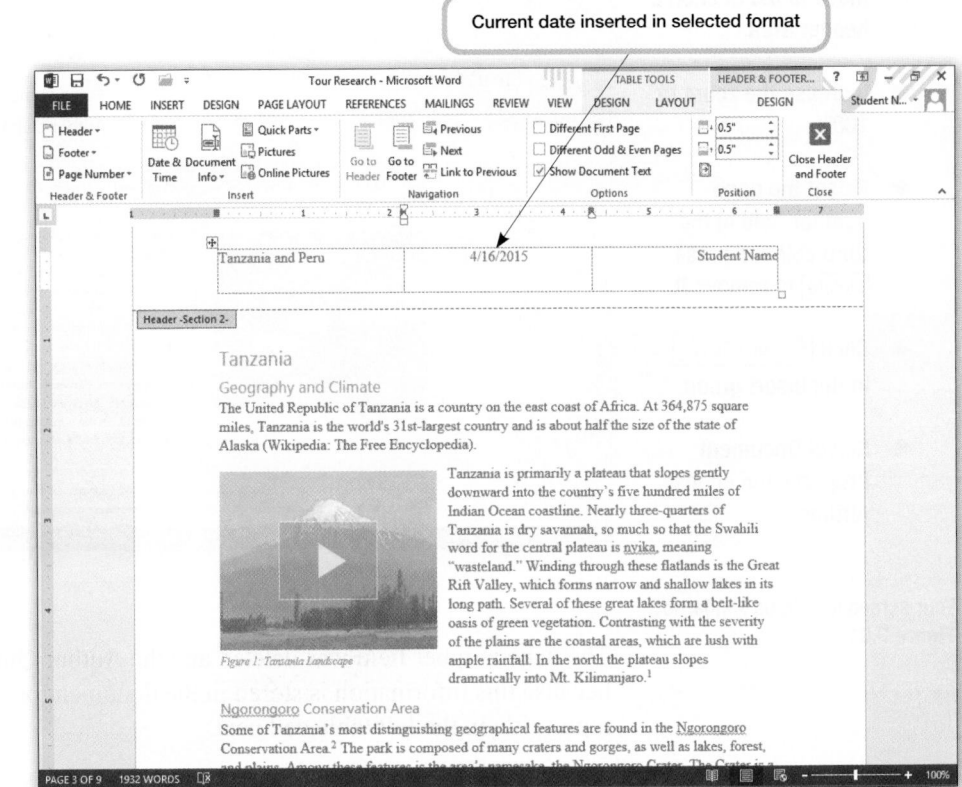

Current date inserted in selected format

Figure 3.83

The current date is inserted as a field and will update when the system date changes. You will change the date to display the date and time the document was last saved using a Quick Parts entry.

2

- Select and delete the date placeholder.

- Click 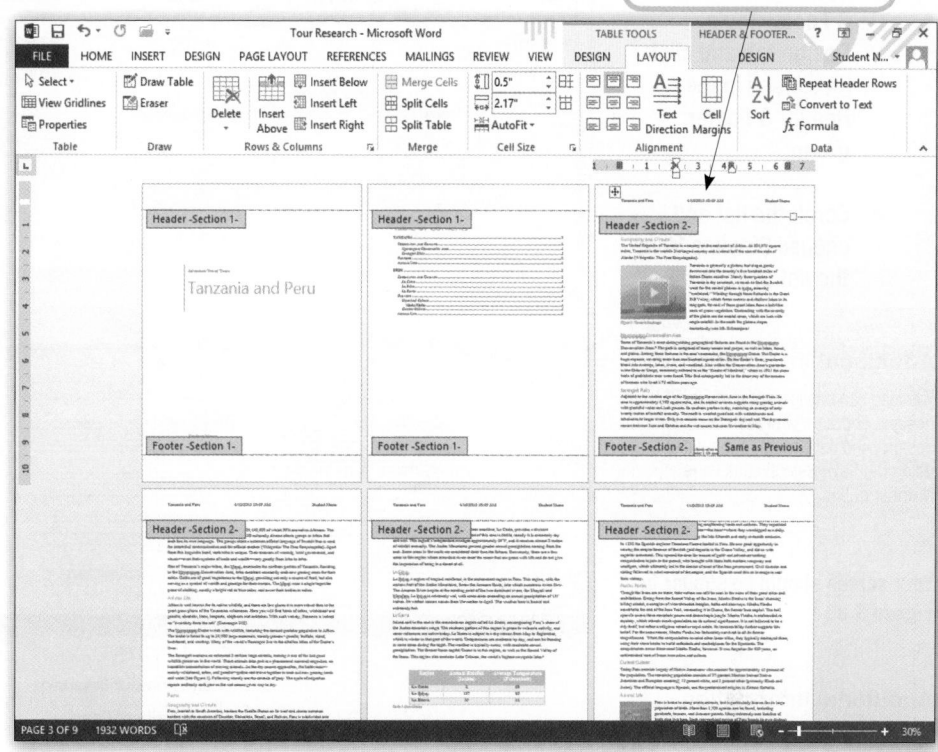 Quick Parts ▾ and choose Field.

- Choose Date and Time from the Categories list.

- Choose SaveDate from the Field Names list.

- Choose the M/d/yyyy h:mm am/pm date and time format (1/9/2015 4:05 PM).

- Click OK.

- Click View Gridlines on the Table Tools Layout tab to hide the table's gridlines.

- Reduce the zoom to 30%.

Your screen should be similar to Figure 3.84

File save date and time inserted using Quick Parts

Figure 3.84

The date and time reflect the date and time the file was last saved. It can be updated when you save the file again.

INSERTING AND MODIFYING PAGE NUMBERS

Next, you will add information to the footer. You want the footer to display the page number. Page numbers can be added to the top, bottom, or side margins of the page. Word includes many built-in page number designs that include formatting and graphic elements to help you quickly create attractive page numbers. You will add the number to the bottom of the page, which inserts it in the footer.

1

- **Open the Header & Footer Tools Design tab and click** Footer ▾ **in the Header & Footer group.**

- **Scroll the list and choose Sideline from the list of styles.**

Your screen should be similar to Figure 3.85

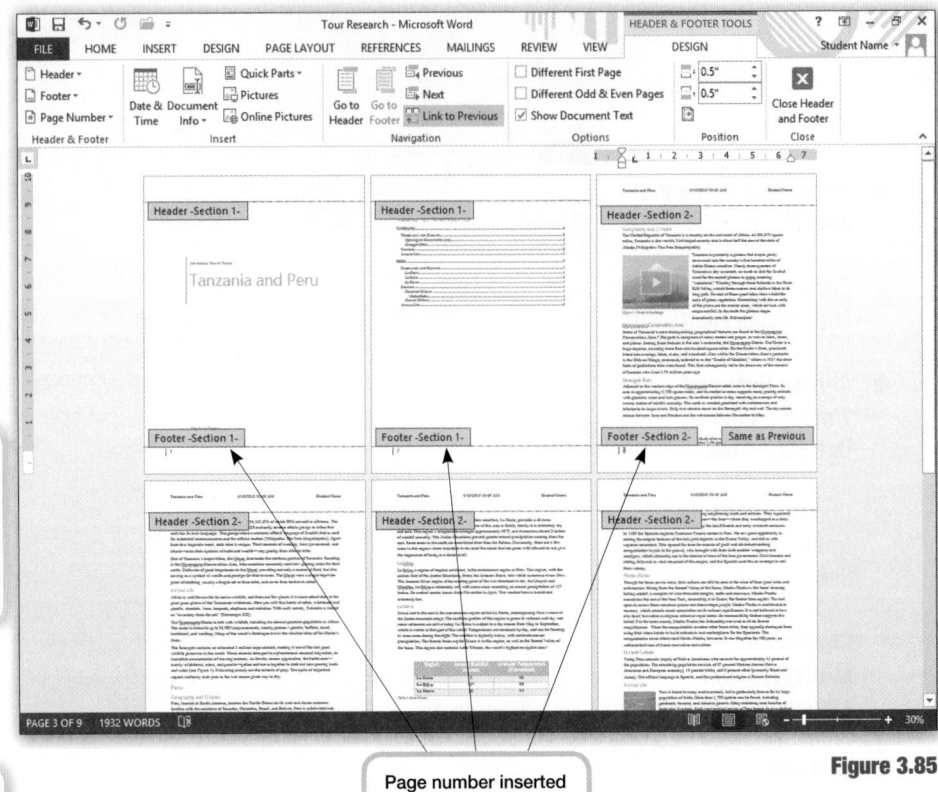

Page number inserted for all sections

Figure 3.85

The footer area is active and the page number appears aligned on the left margin. The number is a field that updates to reflect the document page. By default, when you insert sections, page numbering continues from the previous section. Because you do not want the title or contents pages in section 1 to display the footer information, you will break the connection between sections 1 and 2 by turning off this option. Then you will remove the footer from section 1 and begin page numbering with section 2.

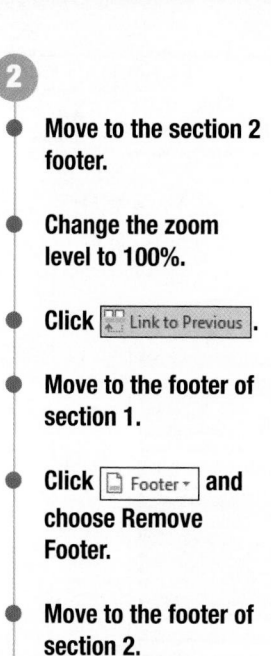

2

- Move to the section 2 footer.

- Change the zoom level to 100%.

- Click 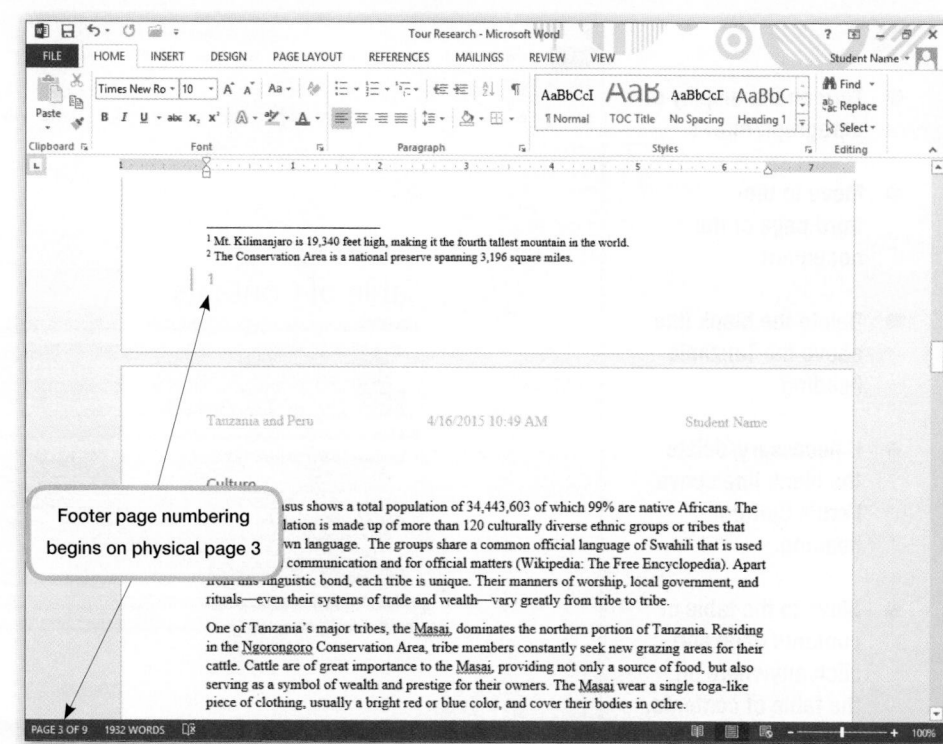 Link to Previous.

- Move to the footer of section 1.

- Click ☐ Footer ▾ and choose **Remove Footer**.

- Move to the footer of section 2.

- Click # Page Number ▾ in the Header & Footer group.

- Choose **Format Page Numbers**.

- Choose **Start At**.

Additional Information

The default Start At setting begins numbering with 1.

- Click [OK].

- Double-click outside the footer area to close the header and footer areas.

- Scroll the document so that your screen appears similar to Figure 3.86.

Your screen should be similar to Figure 3.86

Additional Information

You also can use ☐ Footer ▾ on the Insert tab or the Header & Footer Tools Design tab to insert a predesigned footer with placeholders for items such as the date and page number.

Footer page numbering begins on physical page 3

Figure 3.86

The section 2 footer now displays "1" as the current page number.

Updating a Table of Contents

You have made many modifications to the report since generating the table of contents, so you want to update the listing. Because the table of contents is a field, if you add or remove headings, rearrange topics, or make other changes that affect the table of contents listing, you can quickly update the table of contents. In this case, you have added pictures, a table, a bibliography, a table of figures, and an index that have affected the paging and content of the document.

You will first review the overall layout of your document, and then update the table of contents to ensure that the page references are accurate and that any new content is included. You will also update the table of figures and the index to ensure that the correct page numbers are displaying.

- **Turn on the display of paragraph marks.**

- **Move to the third page of the document.**

- **Delete the blank line above the Tanzania heading.**

- **If necessary, delete the blank line above Peru's Culture heading.**

- **Move to the table of contents page and click anywhere on the table of contents.**

- **Click** `Update Table...` **in the field tab.**

- **Choose Update entire table.**

- **Click** `OK` .

- **Turn off the display of paragraph marks.**

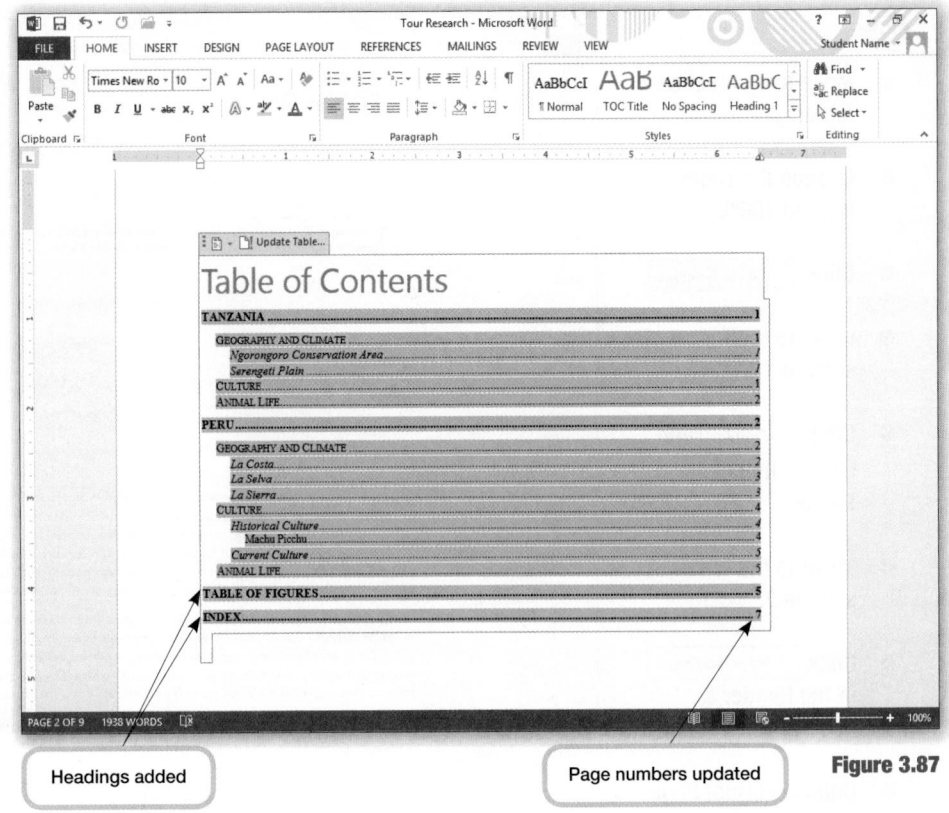

Headings added   Page numbers updated   **Figure 3.87**

The page numbers referenced by each table-of-contents hyperlink have been updated as needed and the Table of Figures and Index headings have been added to the list. However, the Works Cited page is not included. This is because the Works Cited page title is formatted using the TOC Title style, not a heading style. You will add the Works Cited page to the table of contents listing by marking the individual entry.

Another Method

You also can use `Update Table` on the References tab, or choose Update Field from the table of contents context menu, or press `F9` to quickly update a table of contents field.

Your screen should be similar to Figure 3.87

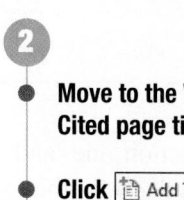

2

- Move to the Works Cited page title.

- Click Add Text ▾ in the Table of Contents group of the References tab.

- Choose Level 1 as the level for the heading.

- Click 📄 Update Table in the Table of Contents group.

- Choose Update entire table.

- Click OK .

- Move back to the table of contents page.

Your screen should be similar to Figure 3.88

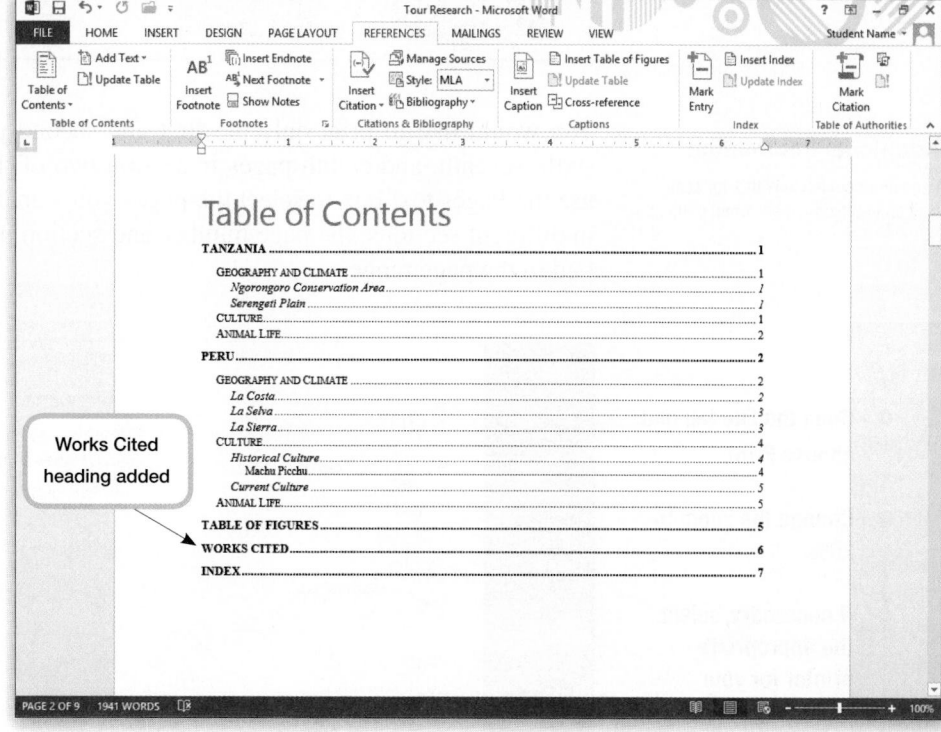

Table of Contents

Works Cited heading added

PAGE 2 OF 9   1941 WORDS

Figure 3.88

The listing now includes a hyperlink to the Works Cited page. Finally, you will update the table of figures and the index.

3

- Use the Table of Figures link in the table of contents to quickly navigate to the table of figures.

- Right-click the table of figures and then choose Update Field.

- Choose Update entire table and then click OK .

- In a similar manner, update the index at the end of the document.

- Move to the beginning of the document and save the document.

The document has now been updated with the correct page numbers.

Printing Selected Pages

Additional Information

Page numbers begin with 1 for each section in the document when printing.

You would like to print only the first and second pages in section one, and the sixth, seventh, and eighth pages in section two of the document. To do this, you use the Pages text box to select the pages you want to print. When printing pages in different sections, the page number and section number (p#s#) must be identified in the page range.

- **Open the File tab and choose Print.**

- **Change the zoom to 20%.**

- **If necessary, select the appropriate printer for your computer system.**

- **Type p1s1, p2s1, p6s2-p8s2 in the Pages text box.**

Your screen should be similar to Figure 3.89

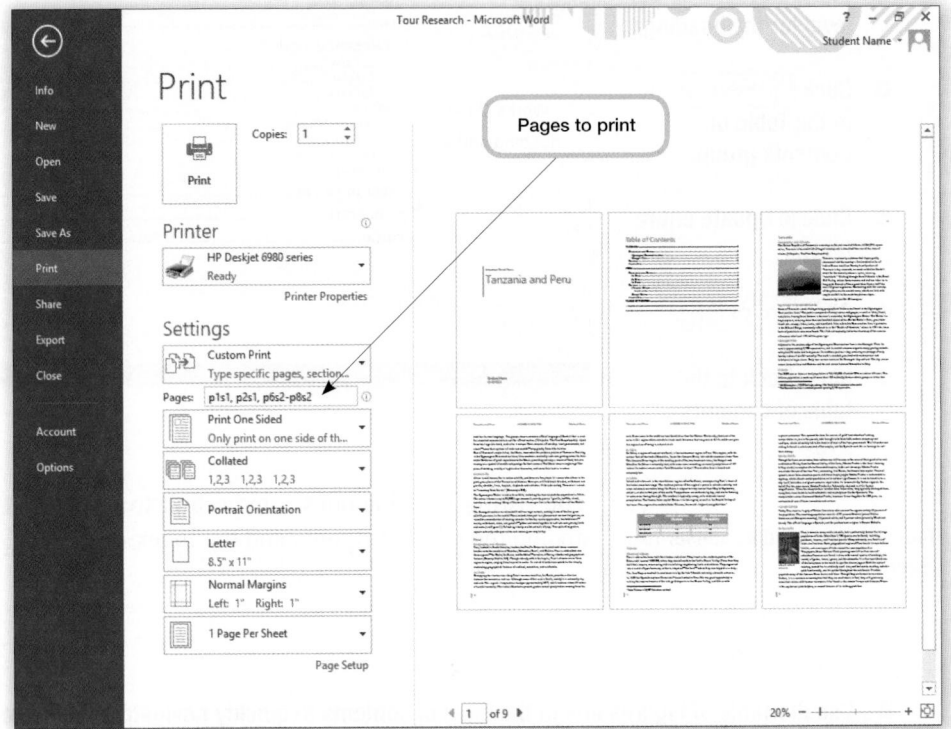

Figure 3.89

2

● Click 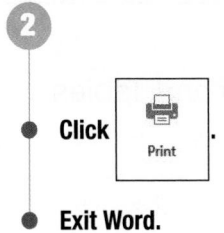 .

● Exit Word.

Your printed output should be similar to that shown in the Case Study at the beginning of the lab.

CUS ON CAREERS

EXPLORE YOUR CAREER OPTIONS

Market Research Analyst

Have you ever wondered who investigates the market for new products? Ever thought about the people who put together phone surveys? Market research analysts are responsible for determining the potential sales for a new product or service. They conduct surveys and compile statistics for clients or their employer. These reports usually include report features like a table of contents, cross-references, headers and footers, and footnotes for references. Market research analysts may hold positions as faculty at a university, work for large organizations, or hold governmental positions. The average salary range for an entry-level market research analyst is $60,570, with demand higher in a strong economy.

Theme (WD3.19)

A theme is a predefined set of formatting choices that can be applied to an entire document in one simple step.

Table of Contents (WD3.26)

A table of contents is a listing of the topic headings that appear in a document and their associated page numbers.

Citations and Bibliography (WD3.33)

Parenthetical source references, called citations, give credit for specific information included in the document. Complete source information for citations is included in a bibliography at the end of the report.

Footnotes and Endnotes (WD3.40)

Footnotes and endnotes are used in documented research papers to explain or comment on information in the text, or provide source references for text in the document.

Captions and Cross-References (WD3.48)

A caption is a numbered label for a figure, table, picture, or graph. A cross-reference is a reference from one part of a document to related information in another part.

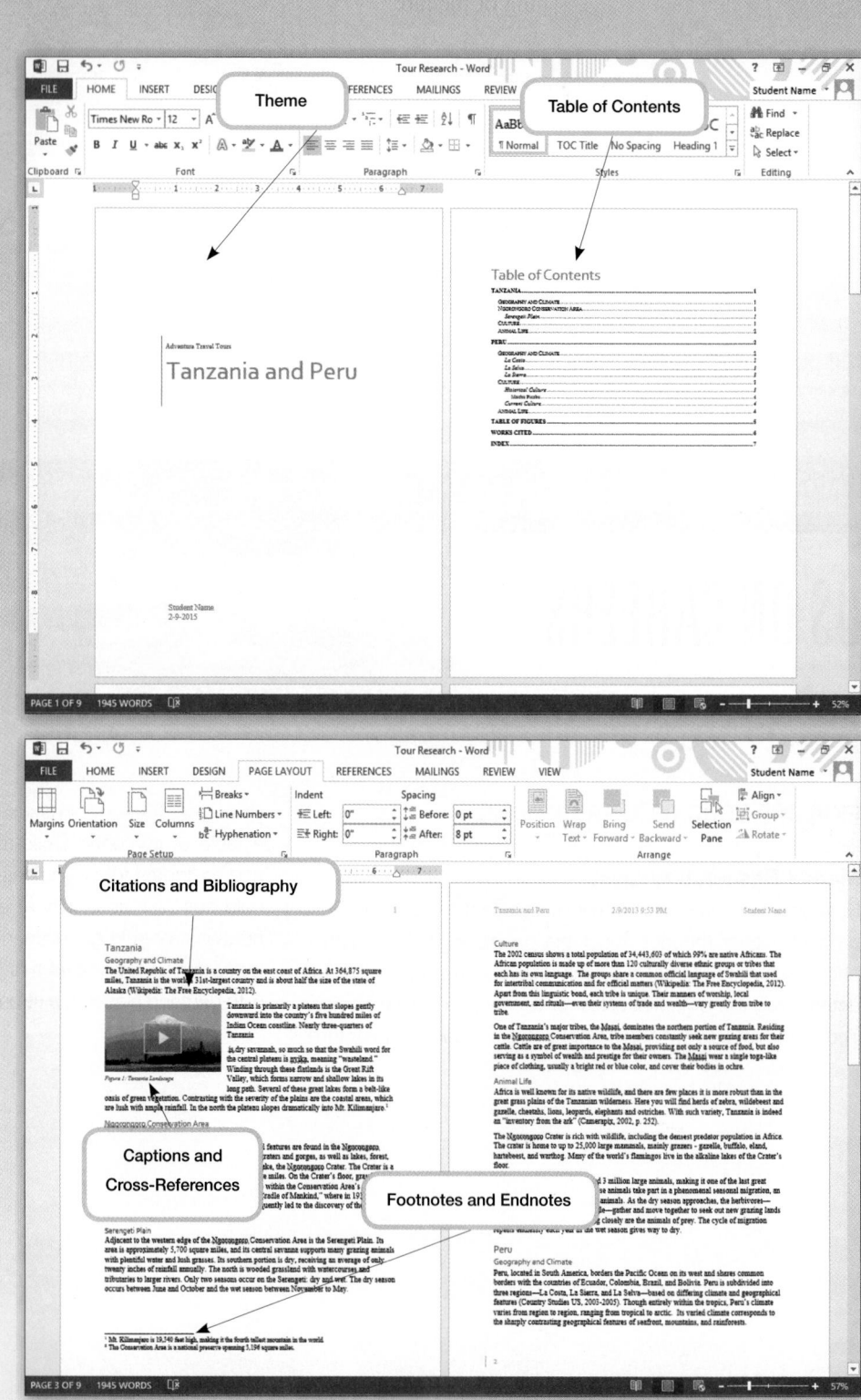

Table (WD3.55)

A table is used to organize information into an easy-to-read format of horizontal rows and vertical columns.

Table of Figures (WD3.66)

A table of figures is a list of the figures, tables, or equations used in a document and their associated page numbers.

Index (WD3.73)

An index appears at the end of a long document as a list of major headings, topics, and terms with their page numbers.

Header and Footer (WD3.80)

A header is a line or several lines of text in the top margin of each page. A footer is a line or several lines of text in the margin space at the bottom of every page.

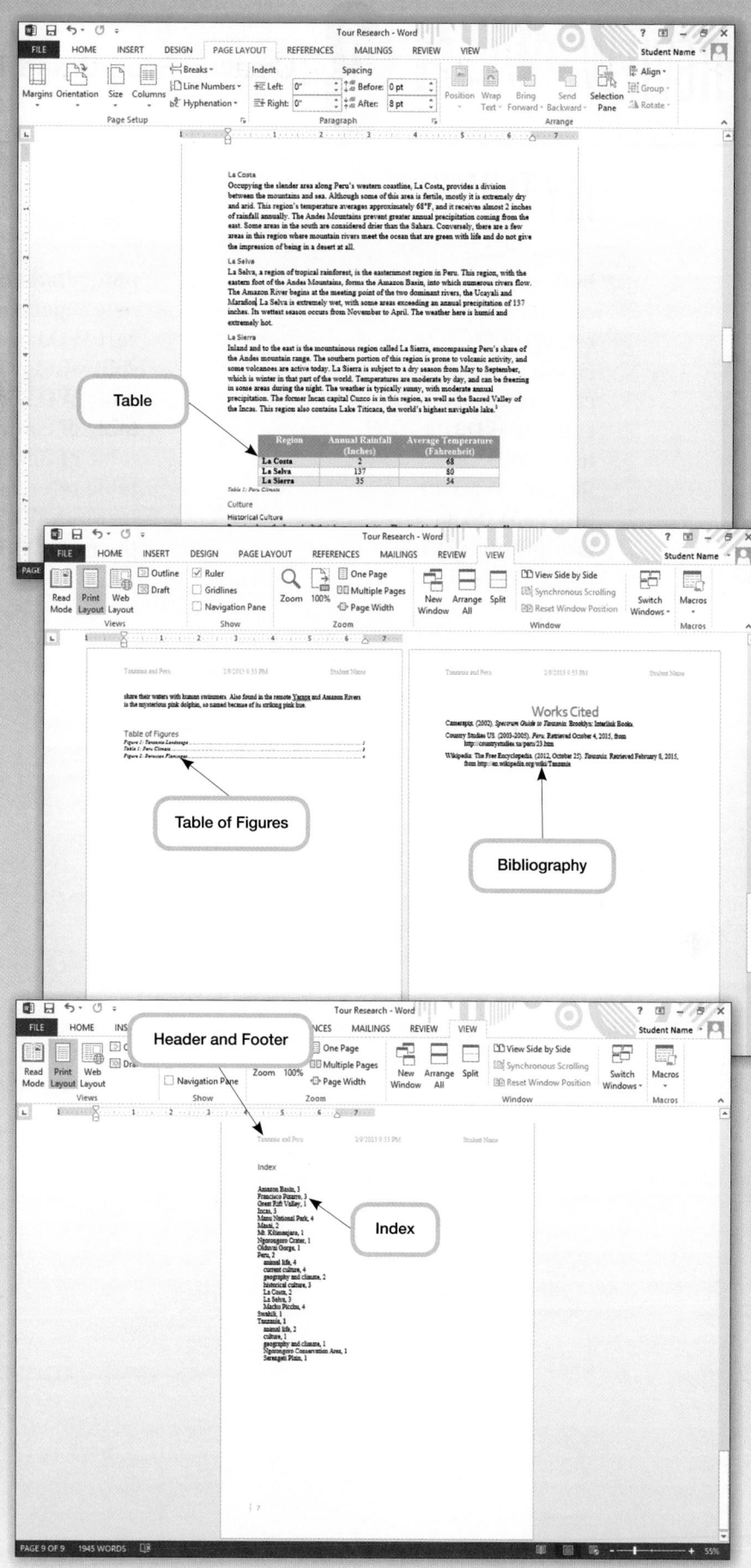

KEY TERMS

bibliography WD3.33	note reference mark WD3.40
caption WD3.48	note separator WD3.40
cell WD3.55	sort WD3.60
citations WD3.33	split window WD3.50
cross-reference WD3.48	table WD3.55
endnote WD3.40	table of contents WD3.26
footer WD3.80	table of figures WD3.66
footnote WD3.40	table reference WD3.55
header WD3.80	text box WD3.49
heading style WD3.5	theme WD3.19
index WD3.73	

COMMAND SUMMARY

Button/Command	Shortcut	Action
File tab		
Print		Prints document
Options/Proofing		Changes settings associated with Spelling and Grammar checking
Insert Tab		
Pages group		
Cover Page ▾		Inserts a preformatted cover page
Blank Page		Inserts a blank page
Tables group		
Table		Inserts table at insertion point
Media group		
Online Video		Inserts online video
Header and Footer group		
Header ▾		Inserts predesigned header style
Footer ▾		Inserts predesigned footer style
Design tab		
Document Formatting group		
Themes		Applies selected theme to document
Colors		Changes colors for current theme
Fonts		Changes fonts for current theme
References tab		
Table of Contents group		
Table of Contents ▾		Generates a table of contents
Add Text ▾		Adds selected text as an entry in table of contents
Update Table...	F9	Updates the table of contents field

LAB REVIEW

COMMAND SUMMARY (CONTINUED)

Button/Command	Shortcut	Action
Footnotes group		
AB Insert Footnote	Alt + Ctrl + F	Inserts footnote reference at insertion point
Show Notes		Displays footnote pane when in Draft view
Citations & Bibliography group		
Insert Citation		Creates a citation for a reference source
Manage Sources		Displays list of all sources cited
Style: MLA		Sets the style of citations
Bibliography		Creates a bibliography list of sources cited
Captions group		
Insert Caption		Adds a figure caption
Insert Table of Figures		Inserts a table of figures
Update Table	F9	Updates table of figures field
Cross-reference		Creates figure cross-references
Index Group		
Mark Entry		Marks an index entry
Insert Index		Inserts an index at the insertion point
View tab		
Window group		
Split	Alt + Ctrl + S	Divides a document into two horizontal sections
Table Tools Design tab		
Table Style Options group		
Header Row		Turns on/off formats for header row
First Column		Turns on/off formats for first column
Last Column		Turns on/off formats for last column
Table Styles group		
More		Opens Table Styles gallery

COMMAND SUMMARY (CONTINUED)

Button/Command	Shortcut	Action
Table Tools Layout tab		
Table group		
▦ View Gridlines		Displays table gridlines
Rows & Columns group		
Insert Above		Inserts a new row in table above selected row
Cell Size group		
AutoFit ▾		Automatically resizes column width in tables.
Alignment group		
Align Top Center		Aligns text at top center of cell space
Data group		
A↓ Z↓ Sort		Rearranges items in a selection into ascending alphabetical/numerical order
Header & Footer Tools Design tab		
Header & Footer Group		
Header ▾		Inserts predesigned header style
Footer ▾		Inserts predesigned footer style
# Page Number ▾		Inserts page number in header or footer
Insert group		
📅		Inserts current date or time in header or footer
Document Info ▾		Inserts document information in header or footer
/Document Property		Inserts selected document property into header or footer
/Field		Inserts selected field Quick Part
Navigation group		
Previous		Moves to previous header or footer
Next		Moves to next header or footer
Link to Previous		Turns on/off link to header or footer in previous section
Options group		
☑ Different First Page		Specifies a unique header and footer for the first page
☐ Different Odd & Even Pages		Specifies different header or footer on odd and even pages
☑ Show Document Text		Shows/hides document text when working on header or footer

LAB EXERCISES

MATCHING

Match the item on the left with the correct description on the right.

1.	bibliography	____ a.	letter and number used to identify table cells
2.	caption	____ b.	set of formatting instructions for the entire document
3.	citation	____ c.	parenthetical source reference
4.	collapse	____ d.	a line or several lines of text that display in the top margin of each page
5.	cross-reference	____ e.	lists major headings, topics, and terms with their page numbers
6.	document theme	____ f.	hides content below heading from view
7.	header	____ g.	combination of fonts, type sizes, bold, and italics used to identify different topic levels in a document
8.	heading style	____ h.	reference from one part of the document to related information in another part
9.	index	____ i.	numbered label for a figure, table, picture, or graph
10.	table reference	____ j.	complete list of source information that identifies references consulted or cited in a report

TRUE/FALSE

Circle the correct answer to the following questions.

1.	A document theme is applied to selected characters and paragraphs.	True	False
2.	A table of contents and an index are fields.	True	False
3.	A table of contents hyperlink is used to jump directly to a specific location in a document.	True	False
4.	A table of figures lists figures and tables included in a document and associated page numbers.	True	False
5.	Citations give credit for specific information included in the document.	True	False
6.	Footnotes must be manually renumbered as you move text around in a document.	True	False
7.	Indexes are used for compiling complete source information for citations.	True	False
8.	Information that appears at the top of every page is referred to as an endnote.	True	False
9.	Once heading styles are applied to a document's titles, it becomes easier to navigate the document.	True	False
10.	To use the Sort command, the document must be in Draft view.	True	False

FILL-IN

Complete the following statements by filling in the blanks with the correct terms.

1. A(n) _____ is a number or other symbol marking text that is accompanied by a footnote or endnote.

2. A(n) _____ is a placeholder that instructs Word to insert information into a document.

3. A(n) _____ is a line or several lines of text at the top of each page in a document.

4. A(n) _____ is a set of predefined formatting that is assigned a name and can be quickly applied to an entire document.

5. A(n) _____ is used to identify topics and their associated page numbers in a document and appears at the end of a document.

6. A(n) _____ is used to organize information into horizontal rows and vertical columns.

7. The _____ appears to the left of a document and provides a convenient way to locate text or to move text in a document.

8. The _____ for a footnote appears at the bottom of the page on which the reference mark appears.

9. When a video object is inserted in a document, a(n) _____ image links to the online source.

10. The intersection of a row and a column creates a(n) _____.

LAB EXERCISES

MULTIPLE CHOICE

Circle the correct response to the questions below.

1. _____ are lines of text at the top and bottom of a page outside the margin lines.
   a. Headings and paragraphs
   b. Headers and footers
   c. Styles and themes
   d. Tables and charts

2. A _____ displays information in horizontal rows and vertical columns.
   a. chart
   b. header
   c. table
   d. theme

3. A _____ is a line of text that describes the object that appears above it.
   a. caption
   b. citation
   c. cross-reference
   d. footnote

4. A _____ is a reference from one part of a document to related information in another part of the same document.
   a. caption
   b. citation
   c. cross-reference
   d. heading

5. A(n) _____ is a predesigned set of formats that can be applied to an entire document.
   a. AutoFormat
   b. style
   c. theme
   d. Quick Part

6. A(n) _____ is inserted at the end of a document listing headings and topics with their associated page numbers.
   a. bibliography
   b. caption list
   c. index
   d. table of figures

7. The _____ feature allows you to see two parts of the same document at the same time.
   a. Navigation pane
   b. note pane
   c. section
   d. split window

8. The _____ feature automatically chooses a width for columns in a table.
   a. AutoCorrect
   b. AutoFit
   c. AutoFormat
   d. AutoText

9. Which of the following inserts a video clip in a document?
   a. Insert tab, Hyperlinks
   b. Insert tab, Online Pictures
   c. Insert tab, Online Video
   d. Insert tab, Links

10. Which of the following would you insert at the end of a report to identify the sources you used when conducting research for a report?
    a. bibliography
    b. caption
    c. citation
    d. table of figures

STEP-BY-STEP

IMPROVING A REPORT ★

1. You have become the local composting expert in your community. Many of your friends and neighbors have asked you for more information about composting, so you've put together some information in a Word document. The document is in need of formatting to help your readers to more easily identify topics and lists. You would also like to add a picture to the document and a footer. Your completed document is similar to the one shown here:

   a. Open the file wd03_Composting.

   b. Apply the Heading 1 style to the title "Basic Information." Change the spacing before this heading to 0.

   c. Insert a line after the title that includes the following text: **Compiled by Student Name**. Center the first two lines of the document.

   d. Apply the Heading 2 style to the following text: "Did You Know That Compost Can . . ." on page 1, "Organic Materials" on page 1, "What to Compost—The IN List" at the bottom of page 1, and "What Not to Compost—The OUT List" on page 2.

   e. Apply bullets using the style of your choice to the list of items in the "Did You Know That Compost Can . . ." section. Apply this same bullet style to the list of items in the "What to Compost—The IN List" and "What Not to Compost—The OUT List" sections, not including the "Note" at the bottom of the page.

   f. Save the document as Composting Information.

BASIC INFORMATION

Compiled by Student Name

Compost is organic material that can be used as a soil amendment or as a medium to grow plants. Mature compost is a stable material with a content called humus that is dark brown or black and has a soil-like, earthy smell. It is created by: combining organic wastes (e.g., yard trimmings, food wastes, manures) in proper ratios into piles, rows, or vessels; adding bulking agents (e.g., wood chips) as necessary to accelerate the breakdown of organic materials; and allowing the finished material to fully stabilize and mature through a curing process.

Natural composting, or biological decomposition, began with the first plants on earth and has been going on ever since. As vegetation falls to the ground, it slowly decays, providing minerals and nutrients needed for plants, animals, and microorganisms. Mature compost, however, includes the production of high temperatures to destroy pathogens and weed seeds that natural decomposition does not destroy.

DID YOU KNOW THAT COMPOST CAN...

- Suppress plant diseases and pests.
- Reduce or eliminate the need for chemical fertilizers.
- Promote higher yields of agricultural crops.
- Facilitate reforestation, wetlands restoration, and habitat revitalization efforts by amending contaminated, compacted, and marginal soils.
- Cost-effectively remediate soils contaminated by hazardous waste.
- Remove solids, oil, grease, and heavy metals from storm water runoff.
- Capture and destroy 99.6 percent of industrial volatile organic chemicals (VOCs) in contaminated air.
- Provide cost savings of at least 50 percent over conventional soil, water, and air pollution remediation technologies, where applicable.

ORGANIC MATERIALS

Yard trimmings and food residuals together constitute 23 percent of the U.S. waste stream, as documented by EPA. An estimated 56.9 percent of yard trimmings were recovered for composting or grass cycled in 2000, a dramatic increase from the 12 percent recovery rate in 1990. Accompanying this surge in yard waste recovery is a composting industry that has grown from less than 1,000 facilities in 1988 to nearly 3,800 in 2000. Once dominated by public sector operations, the composting industry is increasingly entrepreneurial and private-sector driven, led by firms that add value to compost products through processing and marketing. Compost prices have been as high as $26 per ton for landscape mulch to more than $100 per ton for high-grade compost, which is bagged and sold at the retail level.

While yard trimmings recovery typically involves leaf compost and mulch, yard trimmings can also be combined with other organic waste, such as food residuals, animal manure, and bio solids to produce a variety of products with slightly different chemical and physical characteristics. In contrast to yard trimmings recovery, only 2.6 percent of food waste was composted in 2000. The cost-prohibitive nature of residential food waste separation and collection is the primary deterrent to expanding food waste recovery efforts. Yet in many communities, edible food residuals are donated to the needy, while inedible food residuals are blended into compost or reprocessed into animal feed. In some areas, composting operations are working with high-volume commercial and institutional food producers to recover their food byproducts, saving these firms significant disposal costs.

† All the information in this document comes from the United States Environmental Protection Agency website at http://www.epa.gov/osw/conserve/rrr/composting/basic.htm

①

g. Display the headings in the document using the Navigation pane. Using the Navigation pane, move the What to Compost—The IN List heading and associated text to after the What Not to Compost—The OUT List section.

h. Move the Note paragraph located at the end of the What Not to Compost—The OUT List section and the following blank line to the end of the document.

i. Insert the current page number in a footer using the Circle style.

j. Insert a footnote to the right of the word "Compiled" on the second line of the document that includes the following text: **All the information in this document comes from the United States Environmental Protection Agency website at http://www.epa.gov/wastes/conserve/composting/index.htm**.

k. Remove the formatting from the hyperlink.

l. Use the Office.com Clip Art gallery to insert a picture related to composting at the beginning of the "Did You Know That Compost Can . . ." section. Size the picture appropriately.

NOTE: Finished compost can be applied to lawns and gardens to help condition the soil and replenish nutrients. Compost, however, should not be used as potting soil for houseplants because of the presence of weed and grass seeds.

m. Apply the Square or Tight wrapping style to the picture. Drag to position the picture.

n. Apply the Organic theme to the document. Display the footer area, and change the Shape Fill and the Shape Outline colors to coordinate with the theme.

o. Increase the spacing after to 12 pt for each paragraph below the Compiled line and each paragraph below the Organic Materials heading.

p. Insert a page break at the beginning of the heading "What Not to Compost—The OUT List."

q. Format the side headings with 14 pt, bold, small caps. Select the title and apply 18 pt, bold, small caps.

LAB EXERCISES

r. Add a page border. Review the document and check to see if the page number graphic interferes with the page border. If so, display the footer pane and resize the page number graphic to 0.5 inch for the height and width. Drag the graphic above the page border.

s. On page 2, insert a video on composting. Size and position the video clip and add a picture style.

t. Save, submit, and then close the file.

CREATING A TABLE ★

2. You work for the Animal Rescue Foundation and are compiling a list of contact information. You would like to display the information in a table. Your completed document will be similar to the one shown here.

a. Open a new document and enter the title **Animal Rescue Foundation** left-aligned at the top of the document on the first line and **Telephone Contacts** on the second line. Apply the Title style to the first line and the Subtitle style to the second line.

b. Enter the following introductory paragraph left-aligned below the subtitle.

> This listing of direct-dial telephone numbers will make it easy for you to contact the appropriate ARS department. If you are unsure of your party's extension, please dial the main number, (803) 555-0100. You will be greeted by an automated attendant, which will provide you with several options for locating the party with whom you wish to speak.

c. Two lines below the paragraph, insert a simple table with 3 columns and 7 rows. Enter the following information into the table:

Pet Adoption	Jack Rogers	803-555-0158
Behavior Helpline	Rachel Howard	803-555-0132
Education Department	Jon Willey	803-555-0122
Therapeutic Programs	Samantha Wilson	803-555-0146
Volunteer Services	James Thomas	803-555-0173
Job Hotline	Gavin Smith	803-555-0133
Membership & Giving	Mike Miller	803-555-0166

Animal Rescue Foundation

Telephone Contacts

This listing of direct-dial telephone numbers will make it easy for you to contact the appropriate ARS department. If you are unsure of your party's extension, please dial the main number, (803) 555-0100. You will be greeted by an automated attendant, which will provide you with several options for locating the party with whom you wish to speak.*

Department	Contact	Telephone Number
Behavior Hotline	Rachel Howard	803-555-0132
Education Department	Jon Willey	803-555-0122
Job Hotline	Gavin Smith	803-555-0133
Membership & Giving	Mike Miller	803-555-0166
Pet Adoption	Jack Rogers	803-555-0158
Therapeutic Programs	Samantha Wilson	803-555-0146
Volunteer Services	James Thomas	803-555-0173

* If you need operator assistance, simply press "0" at any time.

STUDENT NAME

d. Insert a new row above the first entry and enter the following headings:

Department   Contact   Telephone Number

e. Change the sort order of the table so that it is sorted by department in ascending order.

f. Select a document theme and then apply a table style of your choice to the table.

g. If necessary, size the table to display the data in each row on a single line. Center the table.

h. Position the insertion point after the period that follows "speak" in the first paragraph. Insert the footnote **If you need operator assistance, simply press "0" at any time.** Click the Footnotes dialog box launcher and locate the Number format text box. Click the down arrow and choose the format that begins with an asterisk (*).

i. Add a footer to the document using the Ion (Dark) design. Delete the Document Title placeholder and then type your name in the Author placeholder on the right margin.

j. Save the document as ARS Department Contacts.

k. Submit the document.

CREATING AN INFORMATIONAL SHEET ★★

3. You are the manager of Justice Bike Shop, a small bike repair and retail shop. Lately, you've had to repair many bikes due to accidents on the local college campus. As a result, you've decided to prepare an informational sheet about bike safety, and to then post it around town and on campus. The information sheet will also be posted on the Justice Bike Shop website. Your completed document will be similar to the one shown here.

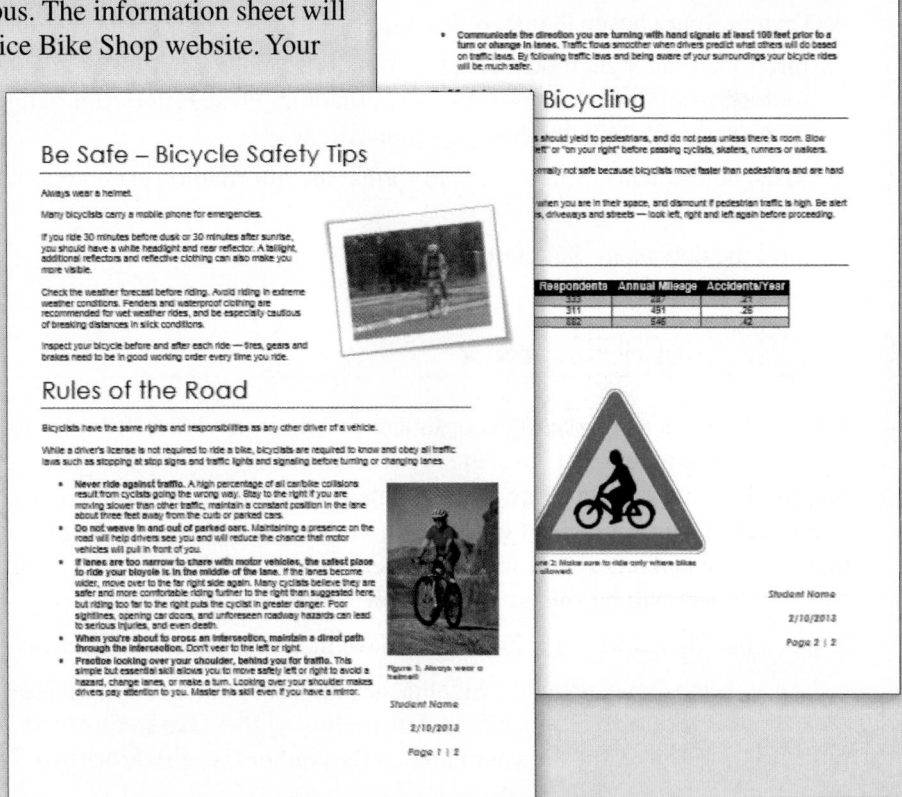

a. Open the file wd03_ Bike Safety.

b. Apply the Title style to the document's three titles.

c. Create a bulleted list in the Rules of the Road section beginning with the third paragraph (Never ride), selecting a bullet design of your choice.

d. Select a document theme of your choice. Save the document as Bike Safety.

LAB EXERCISES

e. Add the heading **Statistics** to the end of your document and then format it using the Title style. Enter the following information in a table below the Statistics heading:

1-Gear	333	287	.21
3-Gear	311	491	.26
5-15 Gear	882	546	.42

f. Insert a new row above the first entry and enter the following headings:

Gears	Respondents	Annual Mileage	Accidents/Year

g. Select the table text, and change the space after paragraphs to 0. Apply a table style of your choice. Turn off the first column style effect. Center-align all the text in the table. Increase the font size of the column headings to 12 points. Size the table to the contents, keeping each row to a single line, and center the table.

h. Locate a clip art image showing a biker wearing a helmet and insert it in the Rules of the Road section of the document. Size and position the image by referring to the completed document. Add the following caption below the graphic: **Figure 1: Always wear a helmet!**

i. Locate the clip art image shown at the end of the completed document and then size and position it accordingly. Add the following caption to the image: **Figure 2: Make sure to ride only where bikes are allowed.**

j. Insert an online video on bicycle safety on page 1 in the Be Safe section.

k. Change your chosen theme, if desired, to better match the inserted images.

l. Insert the Grid style footer. Display formatting marks and type your name on the first line of the footer. Press Enter and insert the date as a field. Press Enter. Right-align the footer text. Select the footer text and apply the Intense Emphasis style.

m. Make adjustments, if necessary, to format the information sheet to look similar to the one pictured at the beginning of this exercise.

n. Save the document. Submit the document.

CREATING A BROCHURE ★★★

4. Your next project as marketing coordinator at Adventure Travel Tours is to create a brochure promoting three new adventures. You have already started working on the brochure and have added most of the text content. Because this brochure is for clients, you want it to be both factual and attractive. Additionally, you want to include a table of contents on the second page of the document, several pictures, a table of tour dates, and an index. You will also insert a video for the online version of the brochure. Your completed brochure will be similar to that shown here.

a. Open the file wd03_ATT Brochure. Save the document as ATT Brochure.

b. Create a cover page using the Sideline design. Enter the title **Three New Adventures** and subtitle **Alaska Railroads Scenic Rail Tour, Hiking the Great Eastern Trail, Kayaking the Blue Waters of Mexico**. Add your name as the Author. Type **Adventure Travel Tours** in the Company placeholder.

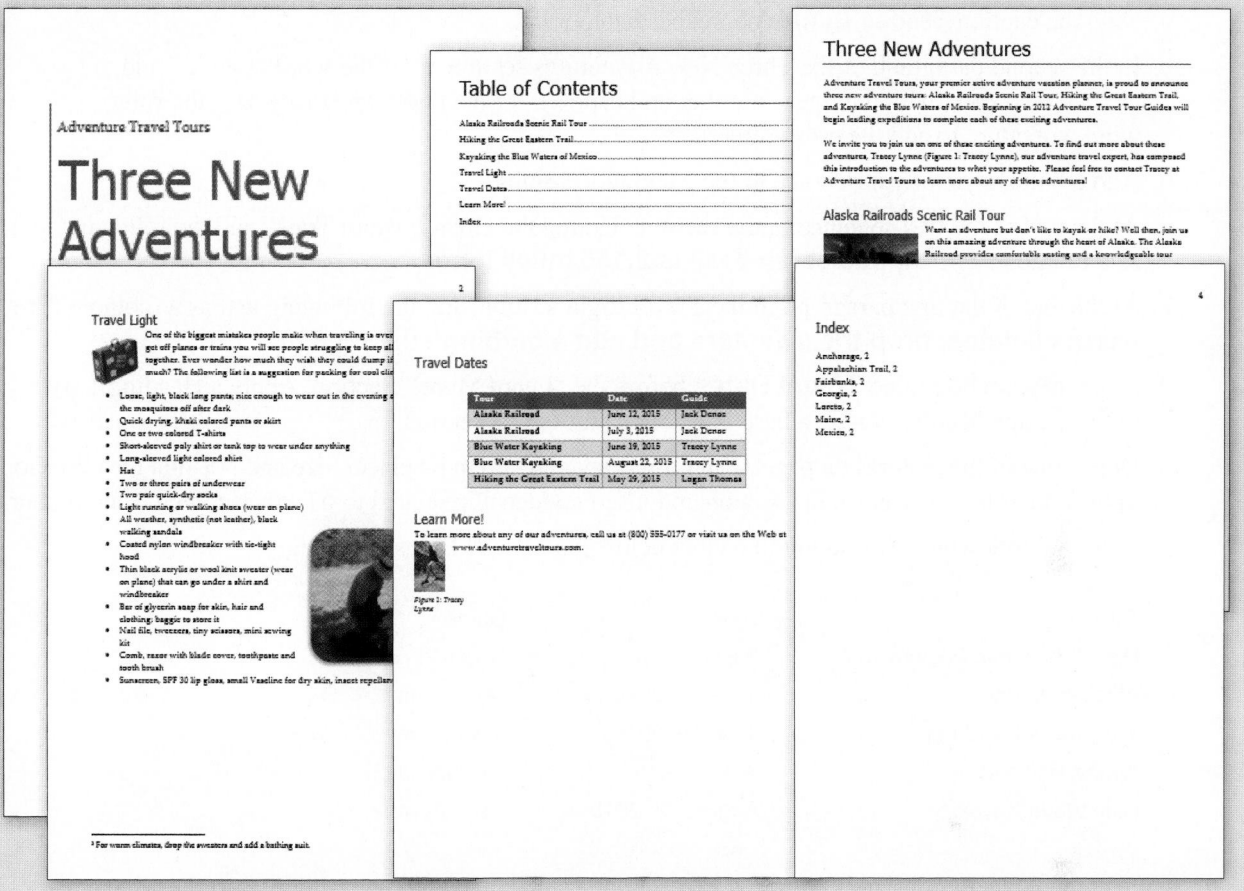

c. Create a custom document theme that includes custom colors and fonts for the brochure. Add a coordinating color to the title and subtitle on the cover page.

d. Apply the Title style to the first topic heading line. Apply the Heading 1 style to the remaining five topic headings.

e. Insert a new page as page 2 and insert a Contents listing. Apply the Title style to the Table of Contents heading.

f. In this step, you will insert several graphics. For each of these, size the graphic appropriately. Wrap the text around the picture using a text wrapping style of your choice.

- Search Office.com Clip Art for a picture related to the railroad, or insert the graphic wd03_Train to the left of the paragraph in the Alaska Railroads Scenic Rail Tour section.

- Search Office.com Clip Art for a picture related to hiking, or insert the graphic wd03_Hiking to the left of the first paragraph of the Hiking the Great Eastern Trail section.

- Search Office.com Clip Art for a picture related to kayaking, or insert the graphic wd03_Kayaking to the left of the first paragraph of the Kayaking the Blue Waters of Mexico section.

- Insert a picture from the Office.com Clip Art gallery in the Travel Light section.

- Insert wd03_Tracey to the left of the last paragraph in the last section of the report.

LAB EXERCISES

g. Add the caption **Tracey Lynne** below her photograph.

h. In the second paragraph of the Three New Adventures section, after the word "Lynne," add a cross-reference, with the figure number and caption, for the photo of Tracey. Use the split window feature to add the cross-reference.

i. Add a bullet style of your choice to the packing list items.

j. At the end of the first sentence in the section "Hiking the Great Eastern Trail," add the following text as a footnote: **The Appalachian Trail is 2,155 miles long**.

k. At the end of the first paragraph in the Travel Light section, add the following text as a footnote: **For warm climates, drop the sweaters and add a bathing suit**.

l. Add a new section titled **Travel Dates** before the "Learn More!" section. Apply a Heading 1 style to the section heading. Insert a hard page break above this section.

m. Delete one of the pictures on page 1, and insert a video clip in its place. Size and position the clip. Go to the end of the "Travel Light" section and insert a video clip related to packing for an adventure tour.

n. Enter the following information in a table below the "Travel Dates" heading.

Tour	Date	Guide
Hiking the Great Eastern Trail	May 29, 2015	Logan Thomas
Alaska Railroad	June 12, 2015	Jack Denae
Blue Water Kayaking	June 19, 2015	Tracey Lynne
Alaska Railroad	July 3, 2015	Jack Denae
Blue Water Kayaking	August 22, 2015	Tracey Lynne

o. Size the table appropriately. Apply formatting of your choice to the new table. Sort the table in ascending sort order by tour. Center the table.

p. Switch to Read Mode and review the document. Then, switch to Print Layout view.

q. Mark the following items as main entry index items:

Mexico and Loreto (Kayaking section)

Appalachian Trail and Georgia and Maine (Hiking section)

Anchorage and Fairbanks (Alaska Railroads section)

r. Insert a few extra lines at the end of the document. Type **Index** on the first line and then apply the Heading 1 style. Generate the index in a single column below the heading. Insert a page break to place the index on a separate page.

s. Add a header that includes a right-aligned page number. The header should not display on the cover page or the table of contents page.

t. Update the table of contents and adjust the document's formatting as needed.

u. Save the document. Submit the report.

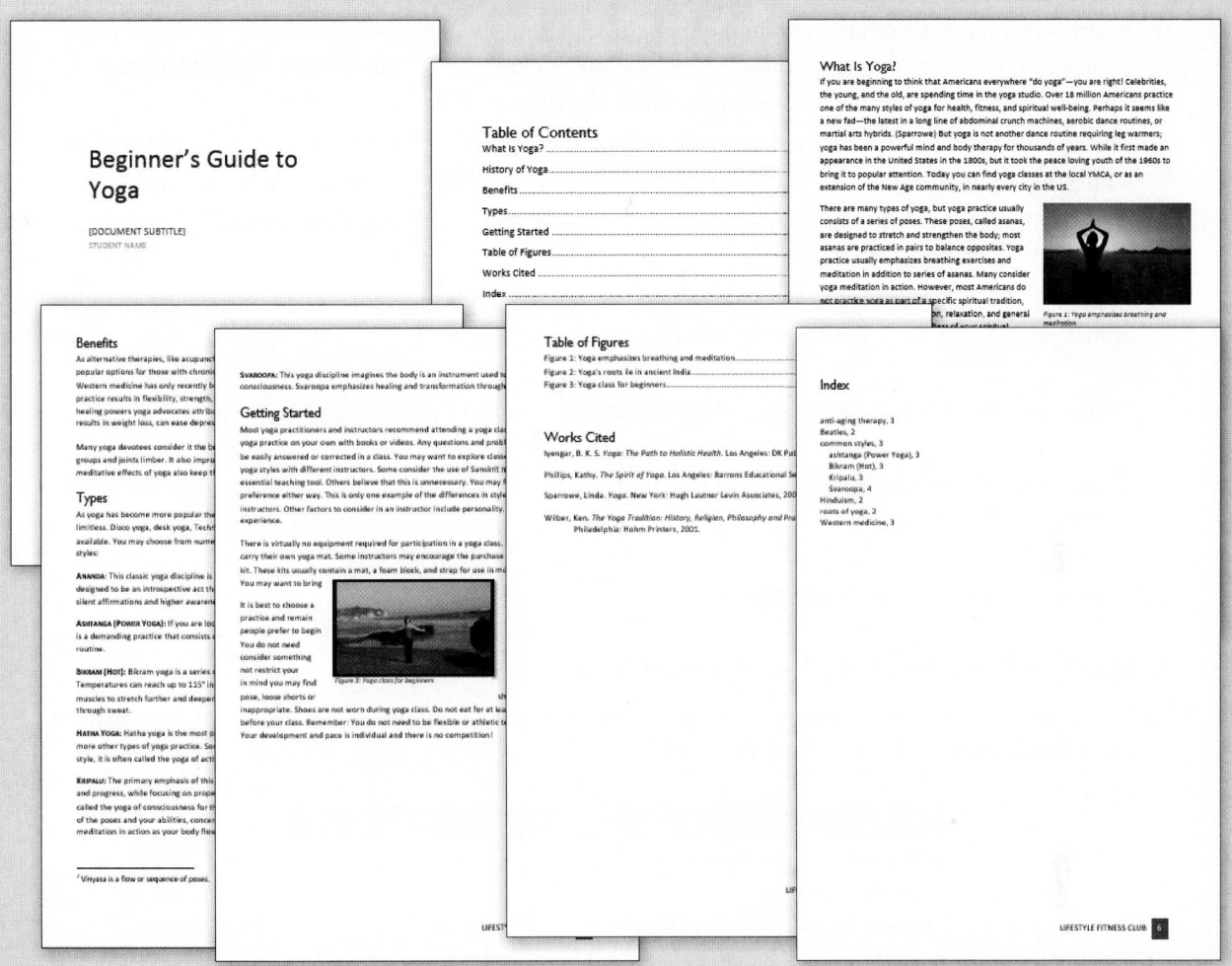

WRITING A REPORT ★★★

5. As a senior trainer at Lifestyle Fitness Club, you are responsible for researching new fitness trends and sharing your findings with other trainers and clients. You have written a Beginner's Guide to Yoga for this purpose. Pages 2 and 3 contain the body of your report. You still need to add several pictures, footnotes, and citations to the report. Your completed report will be similar to that shown here.

a. Open the file wd03_Yoga Guide. Save the document as Yoga Guide.

b. Create a cover page using a design of your choice. Include the report title **Beginner's Guide to Yoga**, your name as the author, and the current date. Remove any other placeholders.

c. Apply a Heading 1 style to the five topic headings.

d. Create a table of contents on a separate page after the cover page.

e. Insert a yoga graphic from Office.com to the right of the second paragraph in the What Is Yoga? section as shown in the example. Size the graphic appropriately and use the square text wrapping style. Include the figure caption **Yoga emphasizes breathing and meditation** below the graphic.

f. Insert a second yoga-related graphic to the left of the first two paragraphs in the History of Yoga section. Size the graphic appropriately and use the square text wrapping style. Include the figure caption **Yoga's roots lie in ancient India** below the graphic.

g. Locate a beginner's instructional yoga video clip and place the clip in the Getting Started section. Apply square text wrap, and size and position the graphic. Add an appropriate figure caption.

h. Apply a document theme of your choice for the report. Remove the underline from the yoga type paragraphs, and apply bold and small caps formatting.

i. In the History of Yoga section, move to the end of the second sentence in the first paragraph after the word "poses" and add the following text as a footnote:

Ancient ceramics found in the caves of Mojendro-Daro and Harappa depict recognizable yoga positions.

j. In the Ashtanga (Power Yoga) description, move to the end of the second sentence after the word "style" and add the following text as a footnote:

Vinyasa is a flow or sequence of poses.

k. Display the six types of yoga in alphabetical order.

l. Using MLA style, enter citations in the text at the locations specified below using the information in the following four reference sources:

Location	Source
First paragraph, end of third sentence	Sparrowe
End of third paragraph	Wilber
Fifth paragraph, end of third sentence	Iyengar
End of second paragraph	Phillips

Type	Author	Title	Year	City	Publisher
Book	Linda Sparrowe	Yoga	2002	New York	Hugh Lautner Levin Associates
Book	B. K. S. Iyengar	Yoga: The Path to Holistic Health	2001	Los Angeles	DK Publishing
Book	Kathy Phillips	The Spirit of Yoga	2002	Los Angeles	Barrons Educational Series
Book	Ken Wilber	The Yoga Tradition: History, Religion, Philosophy and Practice Unabridged	2001	Philadelphia	Hohm Printers

m. At the end of the document, on a new blank page, create a table of figures and a Works Cited bibliography. Add a title above the table of figures formatted using the Heading 1 style.

n. Add a title below the Works Cited section named Index. Apply the Heading 1 style. Mark the following index entries:

Main Entries	Subentries	Location
roots of yoga		History of Yoga section
Hinduism		
Beatles		
Western medicine		Benefits section
anti-aging therapy		
common styles		Types section, first paragraph
	Ananda	
	Ashtanga	
	Bikram	
	Hatha	
	Kripalu	
	Svaroopa	

o. Generate a single-column index below the Index title. Insert a page break to place the Index on a separate page.

p. Update the table of contents and adjust any formatting in the document as necessary.

q. Use the Integral footer design and delete the Author Quick Part. Use the document Quick Part to add the company name, **Lifestyle Fitness Club**. Do not display the footer on the cover page.

r. Start the page numbering with "1" on the table of contents page.

s. Review the layout of the document and make adjustments as needed. Then, update tables and your index so that the correct page numbers display.

t. Save the document. Submit the report.

LAB EXERCISES

ON YOUR OWN

DESIGNING A FLYER ★

1. The Sports Company is introducing a new line of kayaking equipment. It is holding a weekend promotional event to familiarize the community with paddling equipment. You have already started designing a flyer to advertise the event, but it still needs additional work.

- Open the file wd03_Kayaking Flyer.
- Create the following table of data below the " . . . boat giveaway!" paragraph. Use an appropriate table style.

TIME	EVENT
12:00 p.m.	Freestyle Whitewater Panel Discussion
1:15 p.m.	Kids Canoe Relay Race
1:30 p.m.	Becky Andersen & Brad Ludden Autographed Boats Charity Auction
2:30 p.m.	Drawing for Extrasport Joust Personal Flotation Device
3:00 p.m.	Team Dagger Autograph Session
5:00 p.m.	Free BBQ dinner

- Insert the picture wd03_Kayaking from your data files to the right of the text "Meet Team Dagger." Size and position the graphic appropriately.
- Add a caption below the image.
- Add formatting and styles of your choice to the document.
- Make any editing changes you feel are appropriate.
- Enter your name and the date centered in the footer.
- Save the document as Kayaking Flyer.
- Submit the document.

CREATING A REPORT FROM AN OUTLINE ★★

2. You are working on the Downtown Internet Café website and want to include information about coffee characteristics, roasting, grinding, and brewing. You have created an outline that includes information on these topics. Open the file wd03_Coffee Outline and, using the web as your resource, complete the report by providing the body text for the topics in the outline. Include the following features in your report:

- Create a cover page and table of contents.
- Select a document theme.
- Locate a video clip and insert the clip. Apply square or tight text wrapping. Size and position the clip.
- The body of the report should include at least three footnotes and two cross-referenced images.
- Include three citations. Generate a bibliography of your sources.

- Create an index that includes at least five main entries and three subentries.
- Add page numbers to the report, excluding the title page.
- Include your name, file name, and the date in the footer.

  Save the report as Coffee Report. Preview and submit the title page, the first page, the works cited page, and the index page.

PREPARING A REPORT ★★

3. You have been asked to prepare a handout for clients of Adventure Travel Tours to help them plan for international travel. Select one of the following tours.
   - Safari in Tanzania.
   - India Wildlife Adventure.
   - Costa Rica Rivers and Rainforests.
   - Inca Trail to Machu Picchu.

   Prepare a report with two sections. The first section will include general information on international travel. The second section will include specific information on the country to be visited.
   Include the following information in the general information section:
   - Define and explain the procedure to obtain a passport, visa, and work permit.
   - List immunization requirements for international travel.
   - Research the procedure to enroll in the Smart Traveler Enrollment Program; investigate the Consular Information Program.
   - Determine items to leave at home (copy of itinerary, passport, unneeded credit cards, social security card, etc.).
   - List the items to pack (telephone numbers and addresses of destinations, prescriptions, foreign language dictionary, adapters, flashlight, currency exchange information, etc.).

   Include the following information in the second section:
   - Select destination (country to visit) and include a description of the country.
   - Research the entry/exit requirements.
   - List customs restrictions to the foreign destination (what you cannot take to the country) and what travel documents are required.
   - List U.S. customs restrictions (what you cannot bring back).
   - What is the procedure to contact the embassy?

   Include the following features in the report:
   - There should be a minimum of two levels of headings. Apply appropriate styles.
   - Apply a document theme and customize the heading and body fonts.
   - Insert at least one table and three pictures. Add a caption to each. If appropriate, insert a video clip.
   - Add a minimum of three footnotes and three citations.

LAB EXERCISES

- Add a header to include the document title aligned at the right margin.
- Add a footer to include your name on the left margin and a page number on the right margin.
- Create a cover page, table of contents, table of figures, index, and bibliography.

  Save the report as International Travel. Submit the report.

WRITING A RESEARCH PAPER ★★★

4. Adventure Travel Tours is working with the National Park Service and National Geographic to plan and coordinate travel to several national parks with an emphasis on outdoor photography. Prepare a photography handout for beginning photographers. The report should include information on the following topics (emphasis on outdoor photography using a digital SLR):

- Shutter speed.
- Aperture or f-stop (lens opening).
- Focal length and depth of field.
- ISO.
- Night photography.
- Winter photography (snow).
- Summer photography (sand/water).
- Photographing wildlife.
- Landscape photography.
- Recommended equipment (list of lenses, types of filters, lens hood, tripod/monopod, light meter, cable release, extra memory cards, batteries, etc.)

  Include the following features in the report:

- There should be a minimum of two levels of headings. Apply appropriate styles.
- Apply a document theme and customize the heading and body fonts.
- Insert at least one table and three pictures. Add a caption to each. If appropriate, insert a video clip.
- Add a minimum of three footnotes and three citations.
- Add a header to include the document title aligned at the right margin.
- Add a footer to include your name on the left margin and a page number on the right margin.
- Create a cover page, table of contents, table of figures, index, and bibliography.

  Save the report as Outdoor Photography. Submit the report.

RESEARCHING VIRUS HOAXES ★★★

5. There are many computer viruses that can seriously damage or destroy your computer. Some users ignore all virus warning messages, leaving them vulnerable to a genuine, destructive virus.

   Use the web as a resource to learn more about virus hoaxes. Write a brief report defining virus hoaxes. Describe three hoaxes, how they are perpetuated, and the effect they could have if the receiver believes the hoax. The report must include the following features:

   - A cover page that displays the report title, your name, and the current date.
   - A table of contents.
   - At least two levels of headings and a minimum of two footnotes and three citations in the body of the paper.
   - At least one picture with a caption and cross-reference.
   - A table of information with a caption.
   - A table of figures.
   - A bibliography page of your reference sources.
   - The page numbers, file name, and date in a header and/or footer. Do not include this information on the cover page or table of contents page.

   Save the document as Computer Viruses. Submit the document.

Working Together: Copying, Linking, and Embedding between Applications

CASE STUDY

Adventure Travel Tours

Each year you prepare a report for the regional manager showing the sales figures for the four major tours for the past three years. You have started to create a table of the sales information in a Word document; however, you decide it would be easier to maintain and update the sales data each year in an Excel worksheet and then copy the Excel information into the Word document when needed. Because you have created a table in Word already, you will copy the information from the Word table into an Excel workbook. Then you will update the Word document with the sales data from Excel.

A second project you are working on is to provide a monthly status report to the regional manager showing the bookings for the four new tours. You

maintain this information in an Excel worksheet and want to include the worksheet of the tour status in a memo each month. You will link the worksheet data to the memo.

The final project you need to do is to create a report to the regional manager that shows the sales from the four new tours. Because the manager also wants a copy of the file, you will embed the worksheet data in the report.

You will learn how to share information between applications as you create the Excel worksheet and the reports.

NOTE This lab assumes that you are familiar with the basic features of Excel 2013.

Linking an Excel worksheet to a Word document allows the Word document to be quickly updated when data in the worksheet changes.

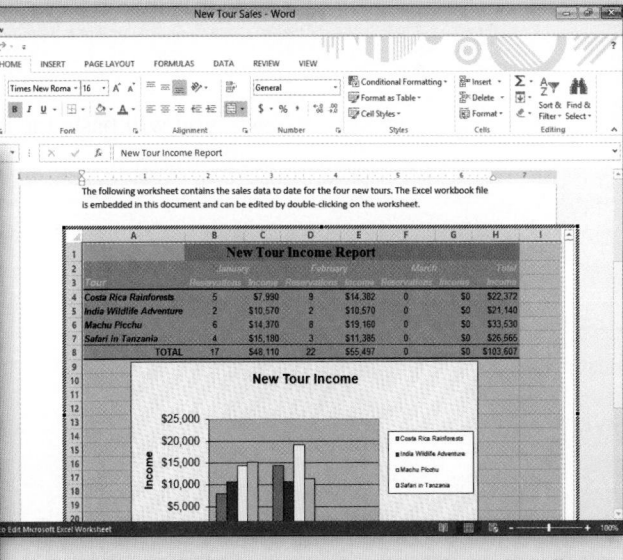

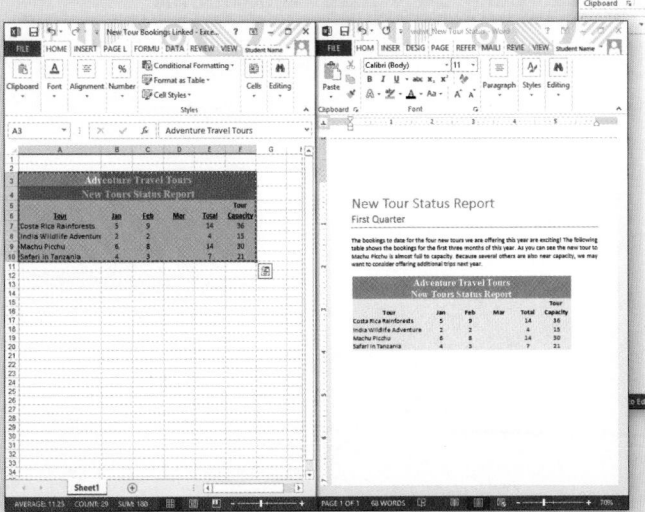

Embedding an Excel worksheet in a Word document allows the worksheet to be used from within the Word document.

Copying between Applications

All Microsoft Office 2013 applications have a common user interface such as similar Ribbons and commands. In addition to these obvious features, they have been designed to work together, making it easy to share and exchange information between applications. For example, the same procedures that are used to copy information within a Word 2013 document are used to copy information to other Office applications such as Excel 2013. The information is pasted in a format the application can edit, if possible. Information also can be copied as a linked object or an embedded object. You will use each of these methods to copy information between Word 2013 and Excel 2013.

First you will copy the sales data for the four major tours that you entered in a table in a Word 2013 document.

1

- **Start Word 2013 and open the document** wdwt_Annual Tour Sales.

- **Select the entire table.**

- **Click** 📋 **Copy.**

Your screen should be similar to Figure 1

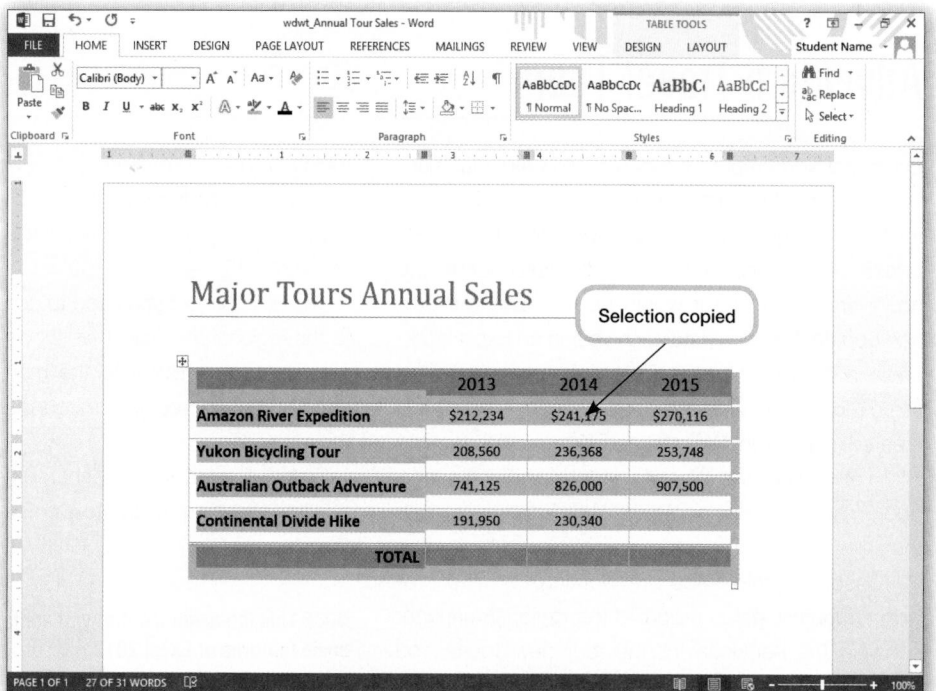

Figure 1

Next, you will paste the information into a new Excel workbook file.

- **Start Excel 2013 and open a blank new workbook.**

- **If necessary, maximize the workbook and sheet window.**

- **Click cell A4 of the worksheet.**

Your screen should be similar to Figure 2

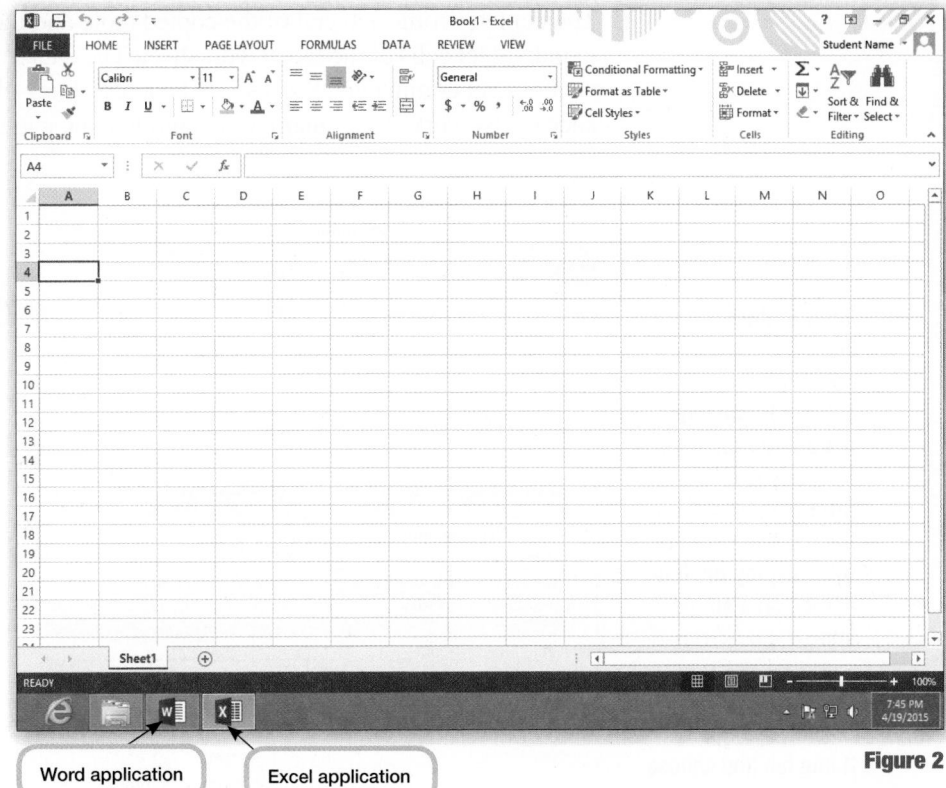

Figure 2

Word application

Excel application

There are now two open applications, Word and Excel, and both application buttons are displayed in the taskbar. You are now ready to paste the table into the worksheet. While using Word, you have learned how to use cut, copy, and paste to move or copy information within and between documents. You also can perform these operations between files in the same application and between files in different Office applications.

- **Click** 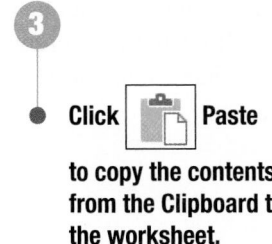 **Paste to copy the contents from the Clipboard to the worksheet.**

Your screen should be similar to Figure 3

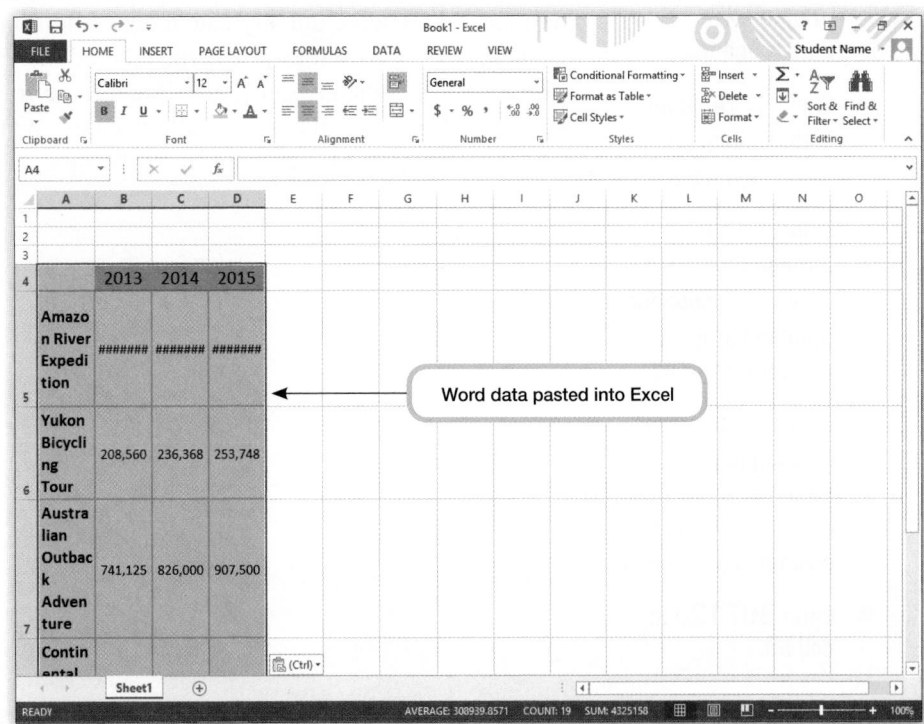

Word data pasted into Excel

Figure 3

Copying between Applications · · · · · **WDWT.3**

The content from each cell of the copied table and the formatting has been inserted in individual cells of the Excel worksheet. The data can now be edited and formatted using Excel commands. You will make a few quick changes to improve the appearance of the worksheet, enter the remaining data, and total the worksheet values.

4

- Point to the divider line between column A and column B and when the pointer changes to ↔, drag to the right to increase the column width to fully display the tour names on a single line.

- Click 📊 Format ▾ in the Cells group on the Home tab and choose **AutoFit Column Width** to adjust the size of the other columns.

- Click 📊 Format ▾ in the Cells group and choose **AutoFit Row Height** to adjust the size of all the rows.

- Drag to select cells B9 through D9.

- Click Σ **AutoSum** in the Editing group on the Home tab.

- Select cells B5 through D9 and click $ **Accounting Number Format** in the Number group.

- Click .00 **Decrease Decimal** in the Number group twice and adjust the column widths again.

- Enter 307120 in cell D8.

Your screen should be similar to Figure 4

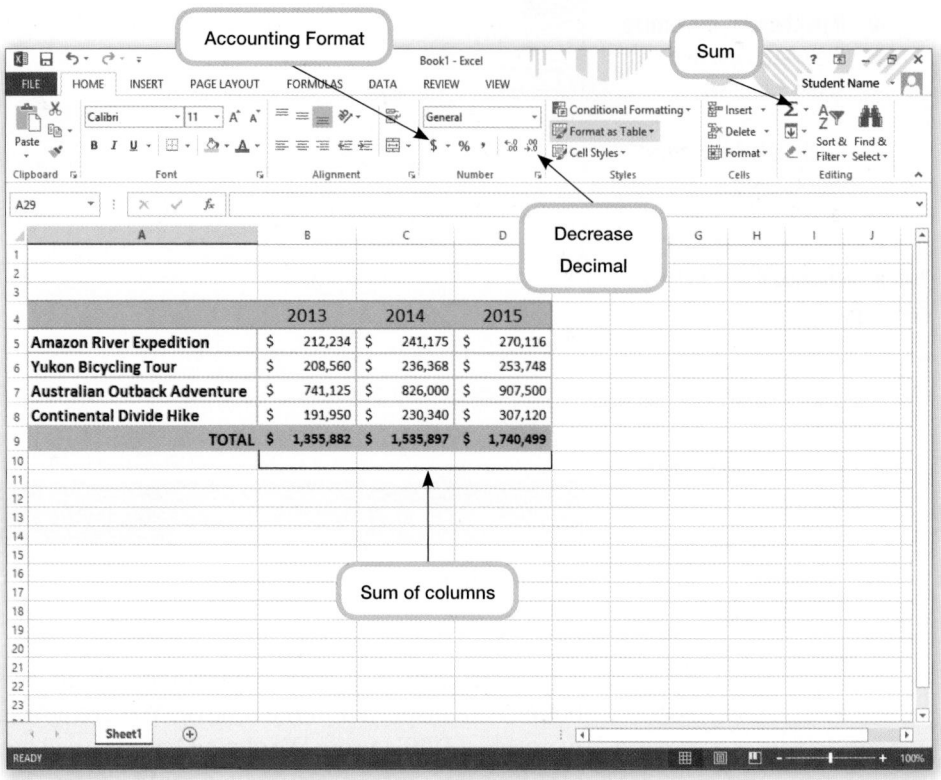

Figure 4

A formula to sum the values in the selected cells was entered in the Total cells and the total values were quickly calculated. Additionally, the formula automatically recalculated the 2015 total when you entered the value in cell D8 in the referenced cell range. It is much easier to use Excel to perform and update calculations than Word. Finally, you will copy the title from the Word document.

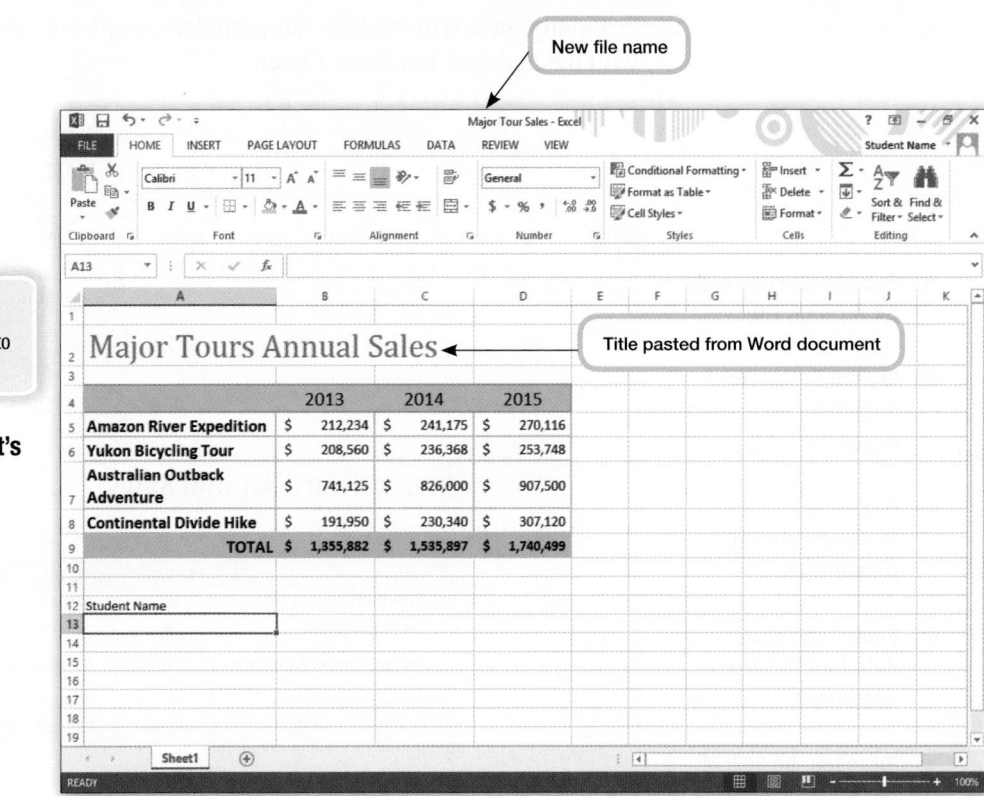

Figure 5

5

- Switch to the Word document.

Having Trouble?

Click on the taskbar button to switch to the Word window.

- Select the document's title text.

- Click 📋 Copy.

- Switch to Excel.

- Paste the title into cell A2.

- Enter your name in cell A12.

- Save the Excel file as Major Tour Sales to your solution file location.

Your screen should be similar to Figure 5

Copying the information from the Word table to an Excel worksheet was much quicker than entering all the data.

Finally, you will replace the partially completed table in the Word document with the updated data from Excel.

6

- Select and copy cells A4 through D9.

- Switch to the Word document and select the entire table.

- Right-click on the table and choose Delete Table.

- Paste the Excel data into the Word document.

- Increase the size of the table to display the data on a single line.

- Enter your name below the table.

- Save the document as Annual Tour Sales to your solution file location.

- Submit the document.

Your screen should be similar to Figure 6

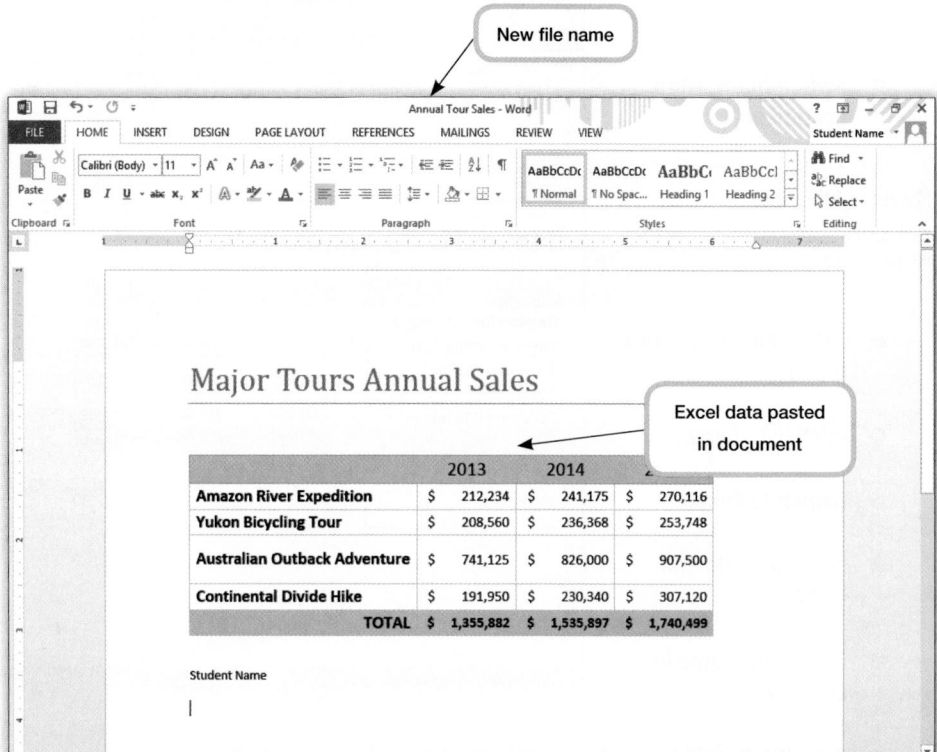

Figure 6

The Excel worksheet is copied into the document as a table that can be edited using Word features. Only the values in the Total cells, not the formulas, were copied.

Linking between Applications

The second project is to create a quarterly report for the manager showing the reservation status for the four new tours. This information is maintained in an Excel worksheet. You have already entered the body of the report and need to add the Excel worksheet data to it.

You will open the Word document and the Excel workbook files and display the two open application windows side by side to make it easier to see and work with both files.

1

- **Close the** Annual Tour Sales **file.**

- **Open the file** wdwt_ New Tour Status.

- **Switch to Excel and close the** Major Tour Sales **file.**

- **Open the workbook file** wdwt_New Tour Bookings.

- **Save the file as** New Tour Bookings Linked **to your solution file location.**

- **Display the two open windows side by side.**

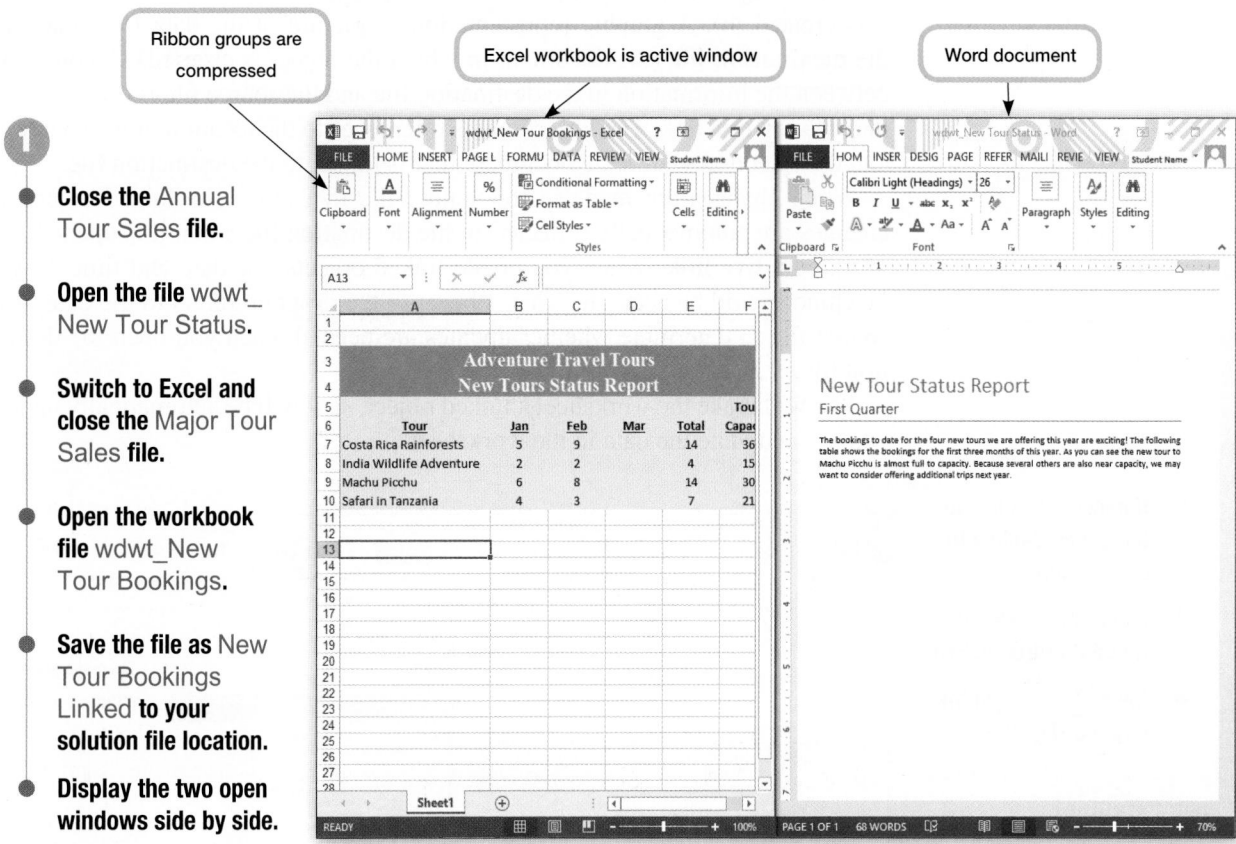

Figure 7

Having Trouble?

Choose Show windows side by side from the taskbar shortcut menu or manually size and place the windows side-by-side.

Your screen should be similar to Figure 7

The active window is the window that displays the cursor and does not have a dimmed title bar. It is the window in which you can work. Because the windows are side-by-side and there is less horizontal space in each window, the Ribbon groups are compressed. To access commands in these groups, simply click on the group button and the commands appear in a drop-down list.

You will insert a copy of the worksheet in the document as a **linked object**. A linked object is information created in one application that is inserted in a document created by another application while maintaining a link between the files. When an object is linked, the data is stored in the **source file** (the document it was created in). A graphic representation or picture of the data is displayed in the **destination file** (the document in which the object is inserted). A connection between the information in the destination file and the source file is established by the creation of a link. The link contains references to the location of the source file and the selection within the document that is linked to the destination file.

When changes are made in the source file that affect the linked object, the changes are automatically reflected in the destination file when it is opened. This is called a **live link**. When you create linked objects, the date and time on your machine should be accurate. This is because the program refers to the date of the source file to determine whether updates are needed when you open the destination file.

You will make the worksheet a linked object, so it will be automatically updated when you update the data in the worksheet.

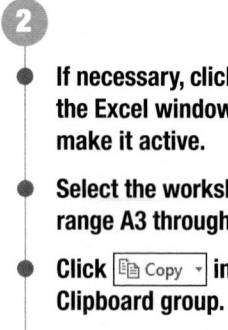

- If necessary, click in the Excel window to make it active.

- Select the worksheet range A3 through F10.

- Click 🖹 Copy ▾ in the Clipboard group.

Having Trouble?

Click  to open the group.

- Click on the Word document window to make it active.

- Move to the blank space below the paragraph.

- Open the Paste drop-down menu and choose Paste Special.

- Choose Paste link.

Your screen should be similar to Figure 8

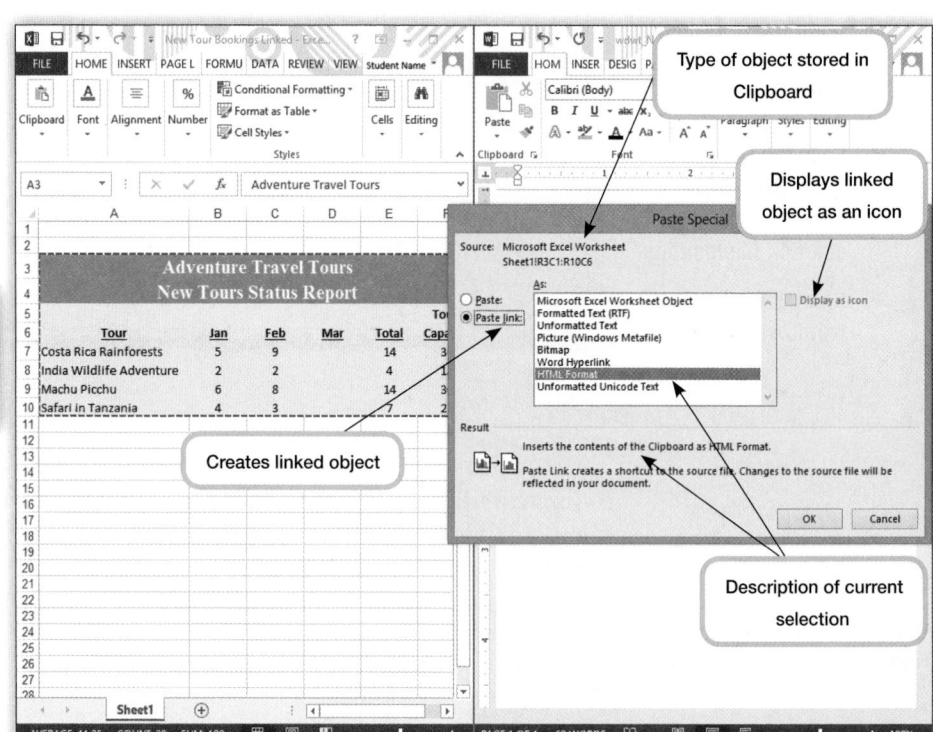

Figure 8

The Paste Special dialog box displays the type of object contained in the Clipboard and its location in the Source area. From the As list box, you select the type of format in which you want the object inserted in the destination file. There are many different object types from which you can select. It is important to select the appropriate object format so that the link works correctly when inserted in the destination file.

Additional Information

Using Paste inserts the worksheet in Word as a table that can be manipulated within Word.

The Result area describes the effect of your selections. In this case, you want to insert the object as an Excel Worksheet Object, and a link will be created to the worksheet in the source file. Selecting the Display as Icon option changes the display of the object from a picture to an icon. Then, to open or edit the object, you would double-click the icon. You need to change the type of format only.

3

● Choose Microsoft Excel Worksheet Object.

● Click OK.

● Reduce the zoom of the Word window to 70% and the Excel window to 80%.

Your screen should be similar to Figure 9

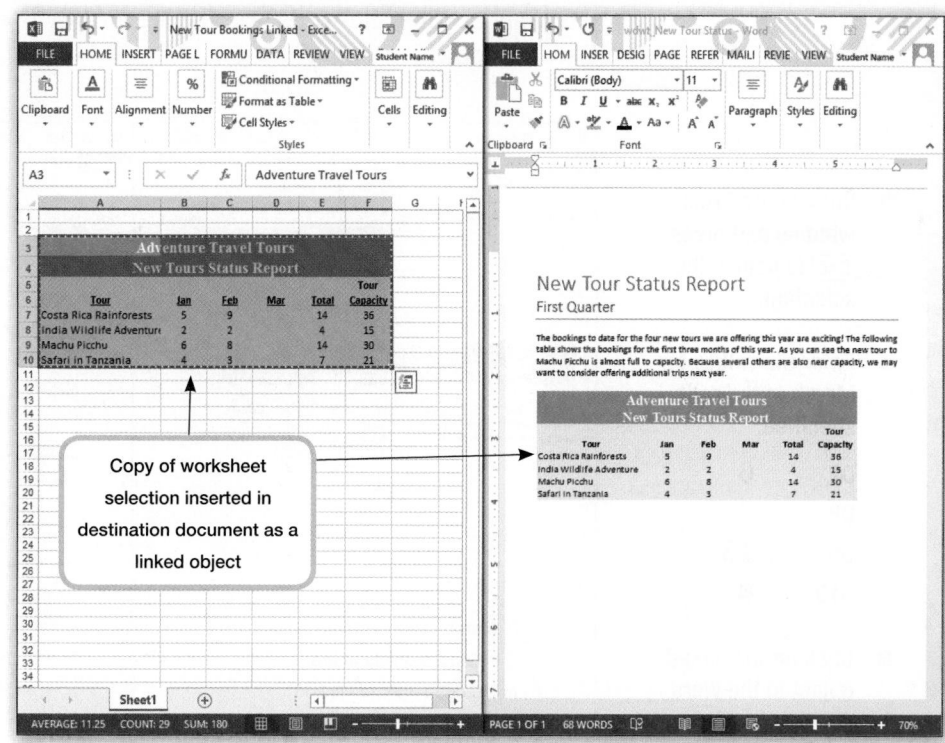

Figure 9

A copy of the worksheet selection was inserted in the Word document as a linked object.

UPDATING A LINKED OBJECT

While preparing the report, you received the tour bookings for March and will enter this information in the worksheet. To make these changes, you need to switch back to Excel. Double-clicking on a linked object quickly switches to the open source file. If the source file is not open, it opens the file for you. If the application is not open, it opens both the application and the source file. Because the Excel application and worksheet file are already open, you will just switch to the Excel window.

1

● **Click in the Excel window and press** Esc **to cancel the selection.**

● **Enter the values for March in the cells specified.**

D7	6
D8	4
D9	13
D10	8

● **Click on the linked object in the Word document to select it, and press** F9 **to update the link.**

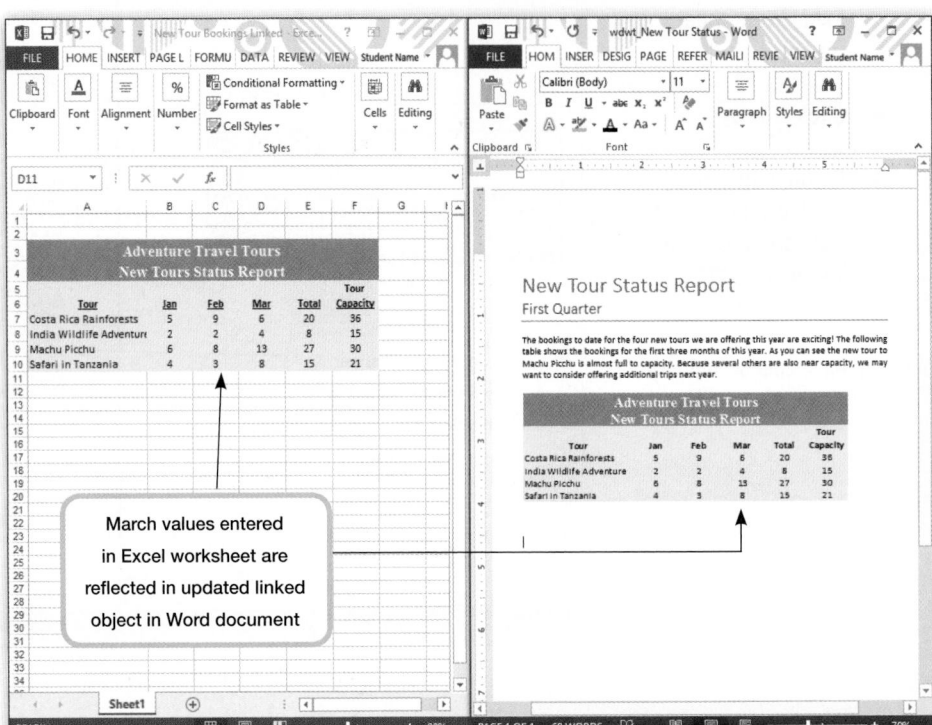

Figure 10

Another Method

You also could choose Update Link from the object's shortcut menu.

Your screen should be similar to Figure 10

The worksheet in the report reflects the changes in data. This is because any changes you make to the worksheet in Excel will be automatically reflected in the linked worksheet in the Word document.

EDITING LINKS

Whenever a document is opened that contains links, the application looks for the source file and automatically updates the linked objects. If there are many links, updating can take a lot of time. Additionally, if you move the source file to another location or perform other operations that may interfere with the link, your link will not work. To help with situations like these, you can edit the settings associated with links. You will look at the links to the worksheet data created in the Word document.

1

• **If necessary, switch to the Word document.**

• **Right-click the linked object, select Linked Worksheet Object, and choose Links.**

Your screen should be similar to Figure 11

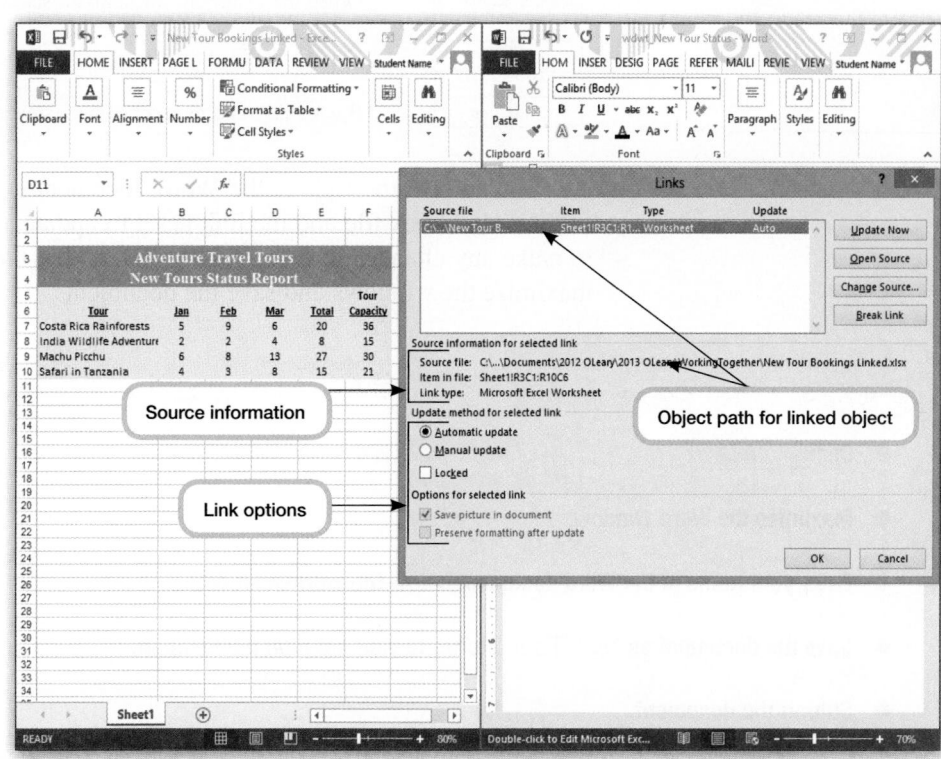

Figure 11

The Links dialog box displays the object path for all links in the document. This includes the path and name of the source file, the range of linked cells or object name, the type of file, and the update status. Below the list box, the details for the selected link are displayed.

The other options in this dialog box are described in the table below.

Option	Effect
Automatic update	Updates the linked object whenever the destination document is opened or the source file changes. This is the default.
Manual update	The destination document is not automatically updated and you must use the Update Now command button to update the link.
Locked	Prevents a linked object from being updated.
Open Source	Opens the source document for the selected link.
Change Source...	Used to modify the path to the source document.
Break Link	Breaks the connection between the source document and the active document.

As you can see, the link in the Word document is to the New Tour Bookings Linked workbook file and the link is set to update automatically. You do not need to make any changes to these settings. Now that the report is complete, you will maximize the windows and save the documents.

2

- Click Cancel.

- Maximize the Word window.

- Enter your name in the Word document below the worksheet data.

- Save the document as New Tour Status to your solution file location.

- Submit the document.

- Close the document.

- Switch to Excel, maximize the window, and close the worksheet, saving the changes.

Linking documents is a very handy feature, particularly in documents whose information is updated frequently. If you include a linked object in a document that you are giving to another person, make sure the user has access to the source file and application. Otherwise the links will not operate correctly.

Embedding an Object in Another Application

The final project you need to work on is to create a report to the regional manager that shows the sales from the four new tours. Because the manager also wants a copy of the file, you will embed the worksheet data in the report. An object that is embedded is stored in the destination file and becomes part of that document. The entire file, not just the selection that is displayed in the destination file, becomes part of the document. This means that you can modify it without affecting the source document where the original object resided.

1

● Open the Word
document wdwt_
New Tour Sales.

● If necessary, change
the zoom to 100%.

● Replace "Student
Name" with your
name.

● Save the document
as New Tour Sales.

● Switch to Excel and
open the workbook
file wdwt_New
Tour Income.

● If necessary, change
the zoom to 100%.

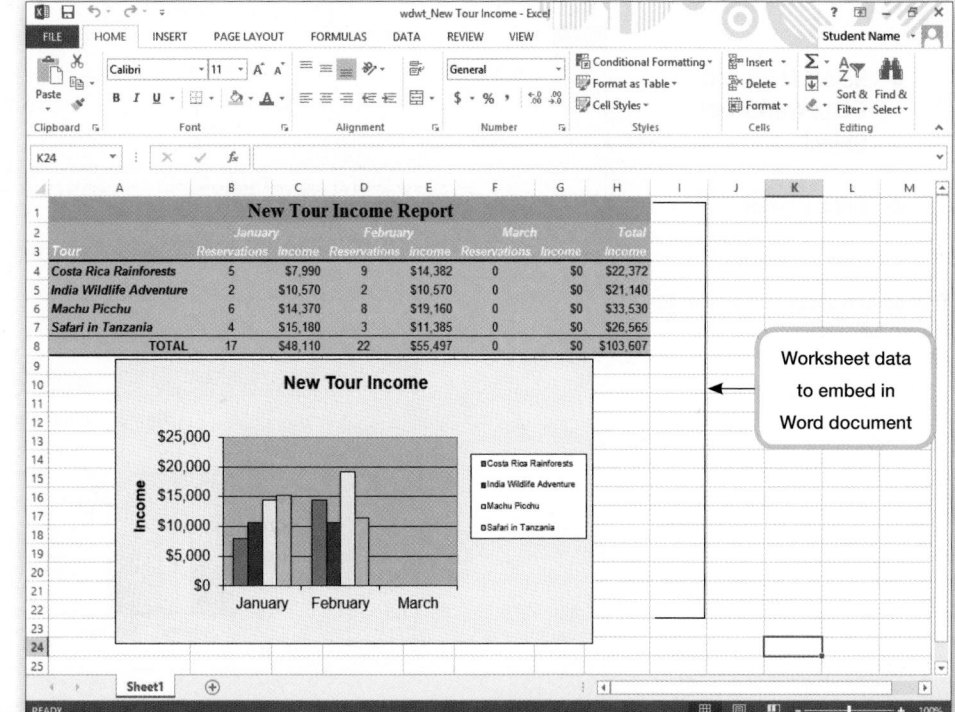

Figure 12

Your screen should be similar to
Figure 12

You will embed the worksheet in the Word document.

2

● Copy the range A1
through H24.

● Switch to the Word
document window.

● Move to the second
blank line below the
paragraph.

● Open the Paste
drop-down menu and
choose Paste Special.

Your screen should be similar to
Figure 13

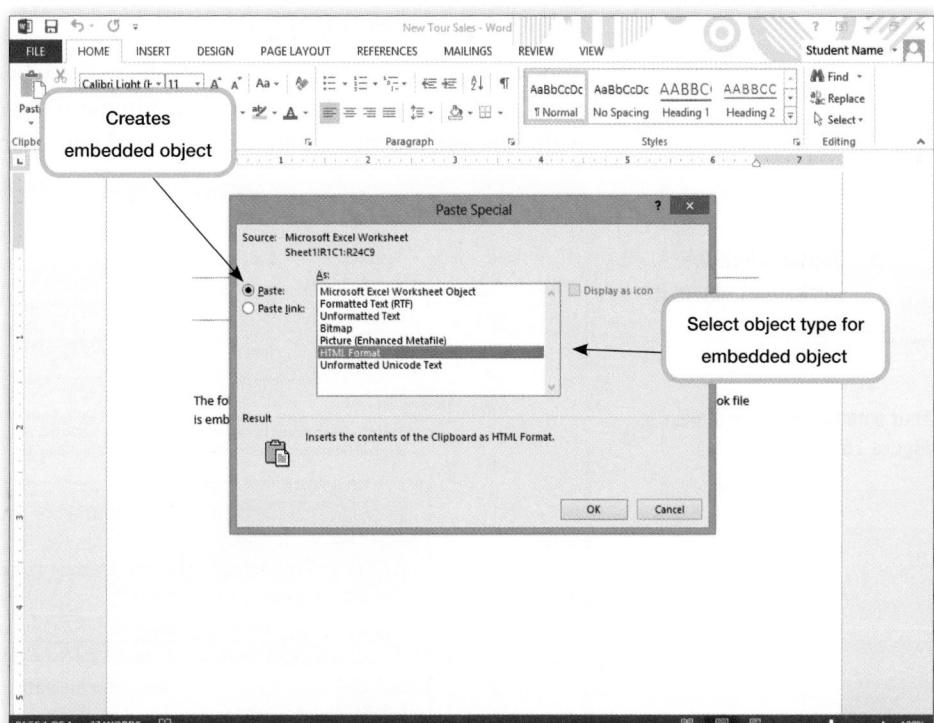

Figure 13

The Paste option inserts or embeds the Clipboard contents in the format you specify from the As list box. In this case, you are embedding a Microsoft Excel Worksheet Object.

Embedding an Object in Another Application   **WDWT.13**

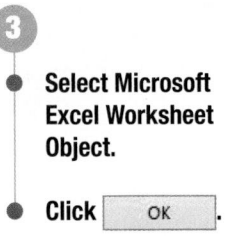

3
● Select Microsoft Excel Worksheet Object.

● Click OK.

Your screen should be similar to Figure 14

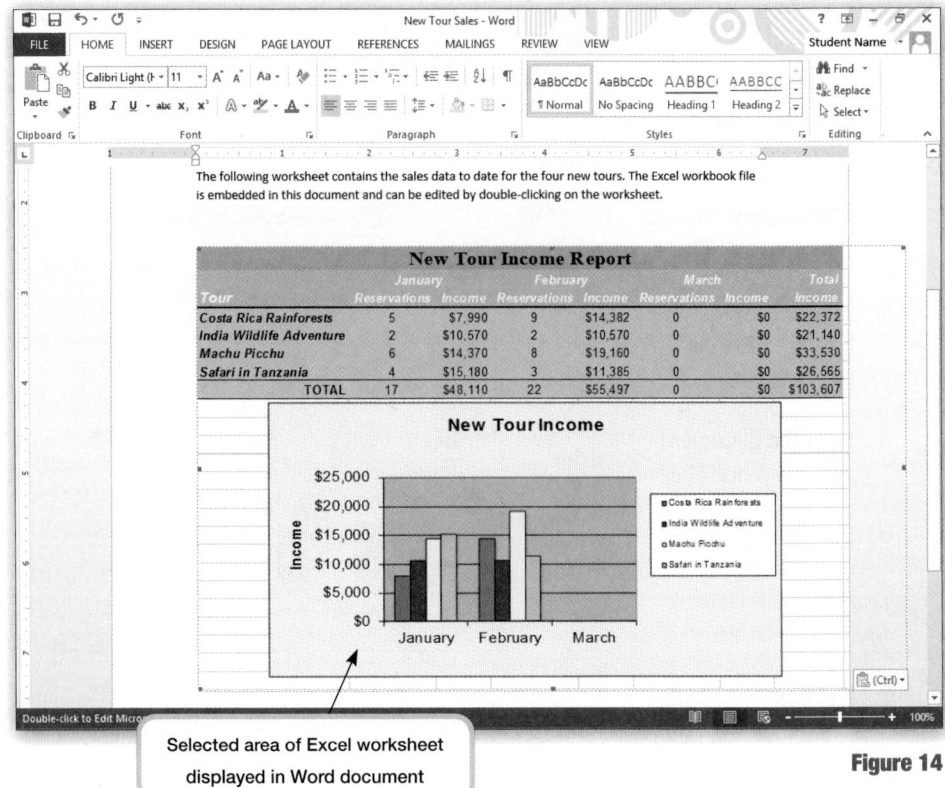

Selected area of Excel worksheet displayed in Word document

Figure 14

The selected portion of the worksheet is displayed in the memo at the location of the insertion point.

UPDATING AN EMBEDDED OBJECT

You want to add the March reservations to the worksheet. Because the worksheet is embedded, you can do this from within the Word document. To open Excel from within the document, double-click the embedded object.

1
● Double-click the worksheet object in Word.

Your screen should be similar to Figure 15

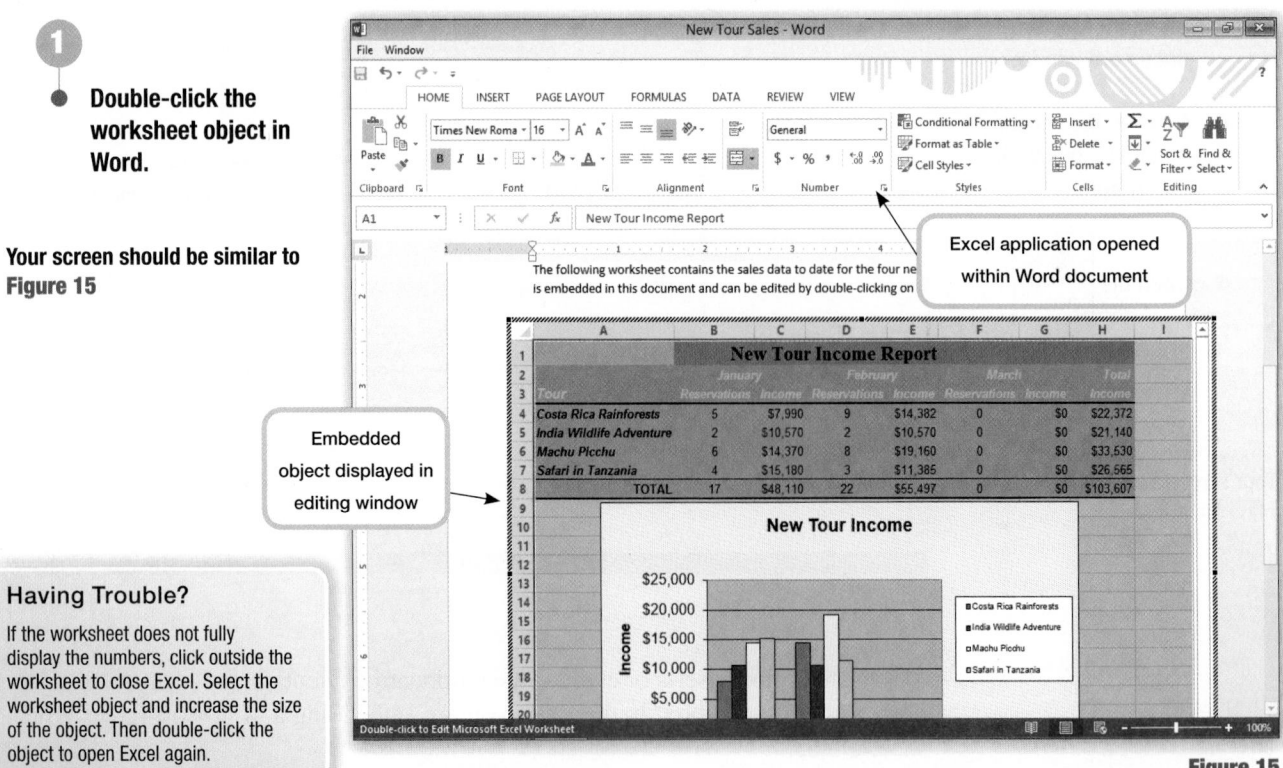

Excel application opened within Word document

Embedded object displayed in editing window

Figure 15

Having Trouble?

If the worksheet does not fully display the numbers, click outside the worksheet to close Excel. Select the worksheet object and increase the size of the object. Then double-click the object to open Excel again.

The associated application, in this case Excel, is opened. The Excel Ribbon replaces the Ribbon in the Word application window. The selected portion of the embedded object is displayed in an editing worksheet window. Now you can use the Excel commands to edit the object.

2

- **Enter the values for March in the cells specified.**

  F4   6
  F5   4
  F6   13
  F7   8

- **Close the embedded application by clicking anywhere outside the object.**

- **Scroll the window, if necessary, to display the entire worksheet object.**

- **Submit and save the document.**

Your screen should be similar to Figure 16

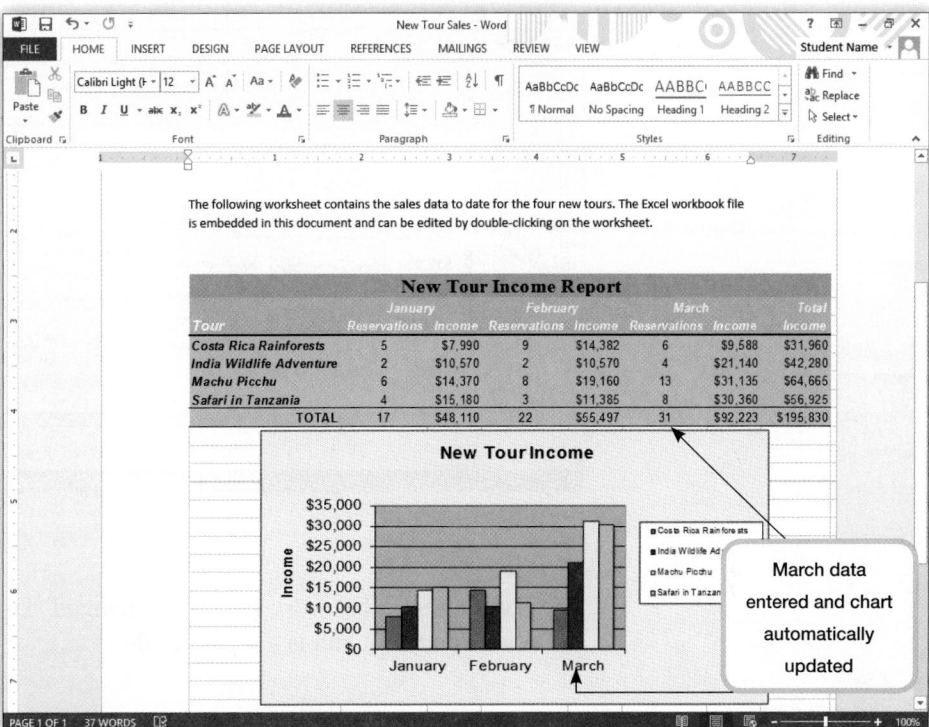

Figure 16

The embedded object in the report is updated to reflect the changes you made. Notice the chart also updated to reflect the addition of the March data.

3

● **Switch to the Excel window.**

Your screen should be similar to
Figure 17

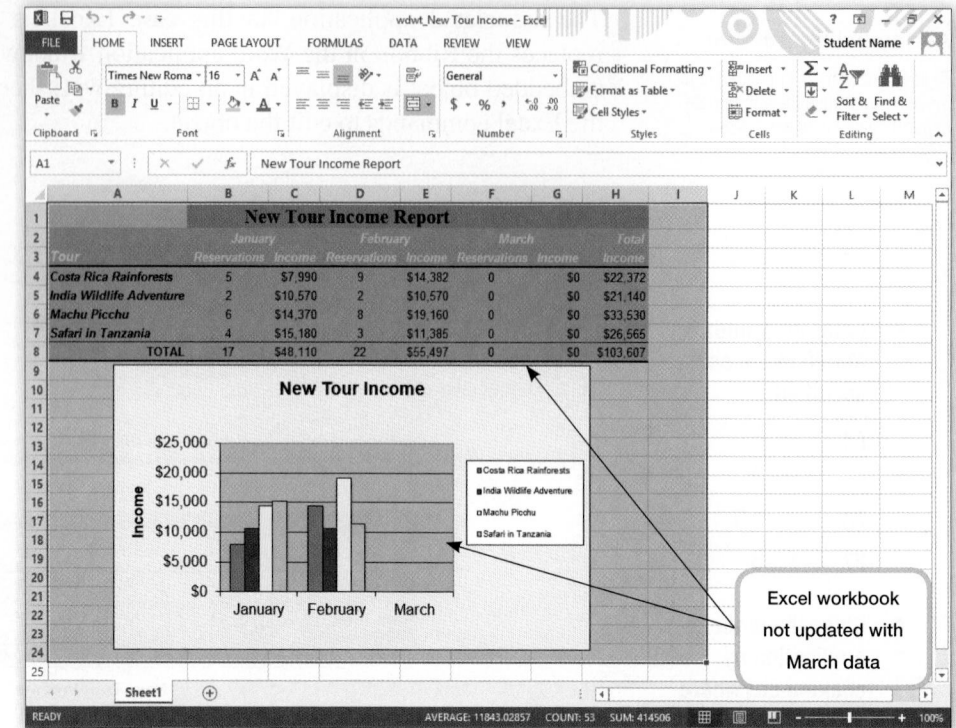

Figure 17

The data in the Excel worksheet is unchanged. This is because it is not linked to the Word document and is a separate file.

4

● **Enter the March reservation data as you did in the report.**

● **Save the workbook as** New Tour Income **to your solution file location and exit Excel.**

● **Exit Word.**

KEY TERMS

destination file   WDWT.8   live link   WDWT.8
linked object   WDWT.8   source file   WDWT.8

COMMAND SUMMARY

Command	Shortcut	Action
Home tab		
Clipboard group		
/Paste Special/Paste link		Pastes contents of Clipboard as a linked object
/Paste Special/Paste		Embeds contents of Clipboard as selected type of object

STEP-BY-STEP

SALES ANALYSIS REPORT ★

1. Tamira Jones manages the Animal Rescue Foundation's new retail store. The Foundation director has requested a summary of the sales and expenses for the board of directors. Tamira has completed the report and has been asked to fax the summary to the director. The completed fax document should be similar to that shown here.

   a. Start Word and open the document wdwt_Animal Angels Sales.

   b. Enter the following information in the fax header:

      To: Sam Johnson

      From: Student Name

      Re: Biannual Sales Review

      Cc: Sally Laney

      Fax: 814-555-7071

      Date: Current Date

      Pages: 1

      Delete the address placeholder.

   c. Start Excel and open the workbook file wdwt_AA Sales. Copy the worksheet data and paste it just below the paragraph in the Word document. Size and format the table using a table design style of your choice.

   d. Save the Word document as AA Sales Report to your solution file location. Preview and submit the document.

   e. Exit Word and Excel.

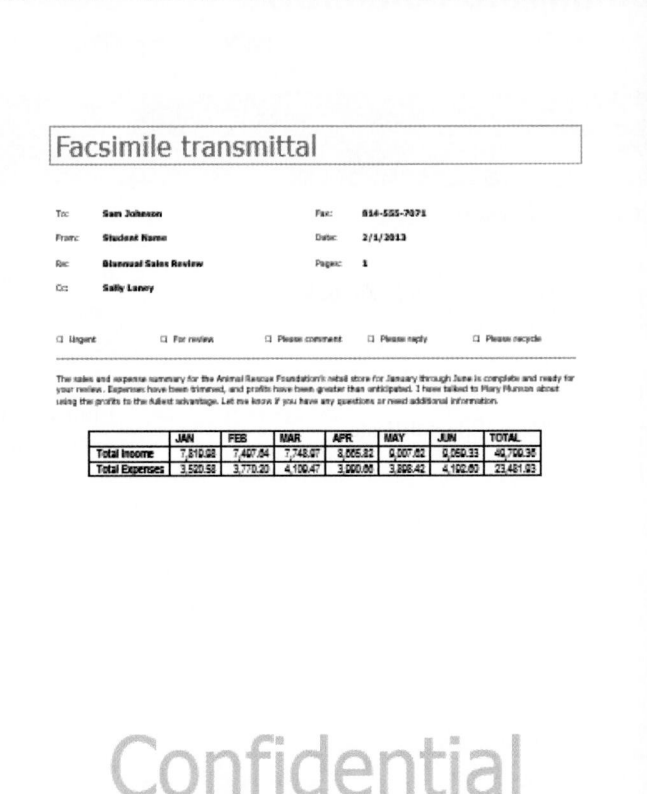

PAYROLL DEPARTMENT REPORT ★★

2. Karen works in the payroll department for a large hotel chain and has recently created a new time sheet for tracking hours. She has been asked to prepare a handout listing the payroll changes for the next department managers' meeting. The completed handout should be similar to that shown here.

a. Start Word and open the document wdwt_Time Sheet Report.

b. Start Excel and open the workbook file wdwt_Time Sheet. Copy the range containing the time sheet and paste it as a linked object just below the first paragraph in the Word report. Center the time sheet in the report.

c. You still need to complete the sample by entering the hours worked on Saturday. In Excel, enter **4** as the Total Hours and Regular Hours worked on Saturday.

d. Save the Excel workbook as Time Sheet to your solution file location. Exit Excel.

e. Update the linked worksheet object in the Word document.

f. Save the Word document as Time Sheet Linked to your solution file location. Preview and submit the document. Exit Word.

PAYROLL CHANGES

The payroll department is implementing two changes starting with the next payroll period.

- Department managers are to record each employee's hours on the new time sheet form.
- Time sheets are due by 9 a.m. the Monday after each period ends.

SAMPLE TIME SHEET

Time Sheet

	Total Hours	Regular Hours	Overtime Hours	Adjusted Total Hours
Employee Name:				
Week of:				
Day				
Monday	10	8	2	10
Tuesday	8	8	0	8
Wednesday	9	8	1	9
Thursday	9	8	1	9
Friday	8	8	0	8
Saturday	4	4	0	4
Weekly Total:				48

LAB EXERCISES

OPERA DONORS REPORT ★★★

3. The City Opera Foundation has decided to hold a spring fund-raising event and would like to extend invitations to the top donors. You have been asked to prepare a list of the donors and to create a letter for the chairman of the board. Your completed letter should be similar to that shown here.

   a. Start Word and open the document wdwt_Opera Donors.

   b. Start Excel and open the workbook wdwt_COF Donors.

   c. Copy the range containing the donations and paste it as an embedded object into the Word document below the first paragraph in the letter. Center the worksheet.

   d. You received a report that contains anticipated donation information that has not yet been entered in the Excel worksheet. Include the following text at the end of the report: **Please note that the 2015 donation listed for Palmquist Equipment has not been finalized, but Mary assures me that this donation has been promised and "is in the works."**

   e. From the Word document, open the embedded Excel worksheet and enter **12670** as the Palmquist Equipment 2015 donation.

   f. Save the Word document as Opera Donors2 to your solution file location. Preview and submit the document. Exit Word. Exit Excel.

[Current Date]

Mr. Steven Veritz
City Opera Foundation Board
5888 Peach Street
Erie, PA 16509

Dear Mr. Veritz:

I have finished reviewing the Foundation records and have compiled the donation information you requested. The names of corporations and individuals that have contributed over $50,000 are listed in the following table.

Donors	2012	2013	2014	2015 Total Donations
T. W. B Foundation	24,558	25,994	22,198	28,005	100,755
Red Finch Antiques	10,384	15,832	14,892	13,855	54,963
Café Trocadero	13,765	14,593	12,854	12,844	54,356
Fulton Farms	16,524	17,485	18,933	16,693	65,915
Palmquist Equipment	15,330	14,832	17,005	12,670	59,837
Total	80,901	80,006	85,882	83,067	388,826

Please note that the 2015 donation listed for Palmquist Equipment has not been finalized, but Mary assures me that this donation has been promised and "is in the works."

Please let me know if you need additional information.

Sincerely,

Student Name

Creating and Editing a Worksheet Lab 1

Objectives

After completing this lab, you will know how to:

1. Create new worksheets.

2. Enter and edit data.

3. Modify column widths and row heights.

4. Use proofing tools.

5. Copy and paste cell contents.

6. Create formulas.

7. Insert and delete rows and columns.

8. Format cells and cell content.

9. Hide and unhide rows and columns.

10. Create a basic chart.

11. Format values as a date.

12. Preview and print a worksheet.

13. Display and print formulas.

14. Change worksheet orientation and scale content.

Downtown Internet Café

You are excited about your new position as manager and financial planner for a local coffeehouse. Evan, the owner, has hired you as part of a larger effort to increase business at the former Downtown Café. Evan began this effort by completely renovating his coffeehouse and installing a wireless network. He plans to offer free WiFi service for customers to use with their own laptop computers. In addition, he has set up several computer kiosks for customers to use who do not have laptops and has provided a printer and copier for all customers to use. He also has decided to rent an MP3 download kiosk for customers who may want to update the music on their iPods or PDAs. Finally, to reflect the new emphasis of the café, he has changed its name to the Downtown Internet Café.

You and Evan expect to increase sales by attracting techno-savvy café-goers, who you hope will use the Downtown Internet Café as a

place to meet, study, work, or download music for their iPods and PDAs. You also believe the rental computers will be a draw for vacationers who want to check e-mail during their travels.

Evan wants to create a forecast estimating sales and expenses for the first quarter. As part of a good business plan, you and Evan need a realistic set of financial estimates and goals.

In this lab, you will help with the first quarter forecast by using Microsoft Office Excel 2013, a spreadsheet application that can store, manipulate, and display numeric data. You will learn to enter numbers, perform calculations, copy data, and label rows and columns as you create the basic structure of a worksheet for the Downtown Internet Café. You will then learn how to enhance the worksheet using formatting features and by adding color as shown here.

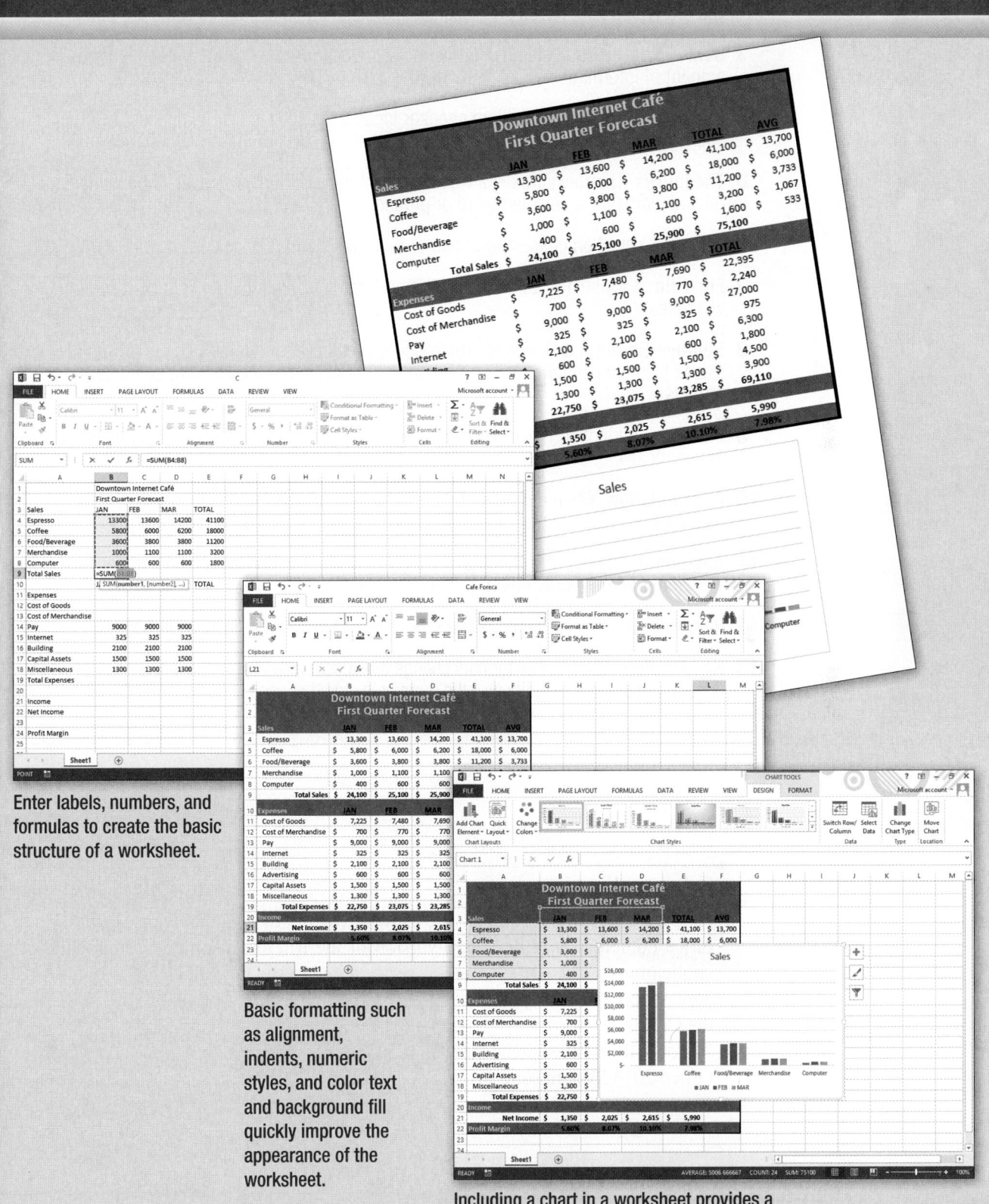

Enter labels, numbers, and formulas to create the basic structure of a worksheet.

Basic formatting such as alignment, indents, numeric styles, and color text and background fill quickly improve the appearance of the worksheet.

Including a chart in a worksheet provides a visual representation of the worksheet data.

The following concepts will be introduced in this lab:

1 Data The basic information or data you enter in a cell can be text or numbers.

2 AutoCorrect The AutoCorrect feature makes some basic assumptions about the text you are typing and, based on these assumptions, automatically corrects the entry.

3 Column Width The column width is the size or width of a column and controls the amount of information that can be displayed in a cell.

4 Spelling Checker The spelling checker locates misspelled words, duplicate words, and capitalization irregularities in the active worksheet and proposes the correct spelling.

5 Thesaurus The thesaurus is a reference tool that provides synonyms, antonyms, and related words for a selected word or phrase.

6 Range A selection consisting of two or more cells on a worksheet is a range.

7 Formula A formula is an equation that performs a calculation on data contained in a worksheet.

8 Relative Reference A relative reference is a cell or range reference in a formula whose location is interpreted in relation to the position of the cell that contains the formula.

9 Function A function is a prewritten formula that performs certain types of calculations automatically.

10 Recalculation When a number in a referenced cell in a formula changes, Excel automatically recalculates all formulas that are dependent upon the changed value.

11 Alignment Alignment settings allow you to change the horizontal and vertical placement and the orientation of an entry in a cell.

12 Row Height The row height is the size or height of a row measured in points.

13 Number Formats Number formats change the appearance of numbers onscreen and when printed, without changing the way the number is stored or used in calculations.

Creating a Workbook

As part of the renovation of the Downtown Internet Café, Evan upgraded the office computer with the latest version of the Microsoft Office System suite of applications, Office 2013. You are very excited to see how this new and powerful application can help you create professional budgets and financial forecasts for the Café.

You will use the spreadsheet application Excel 2013 included in the Microsoft Office 2013 System suite to create the first quarter forecast for the Café.

Start Excel 2013.

Choose Blank workbook from the Start screen.

If necessary, maximize the Excel application window.

Your screen should be similar to Figure 1.1

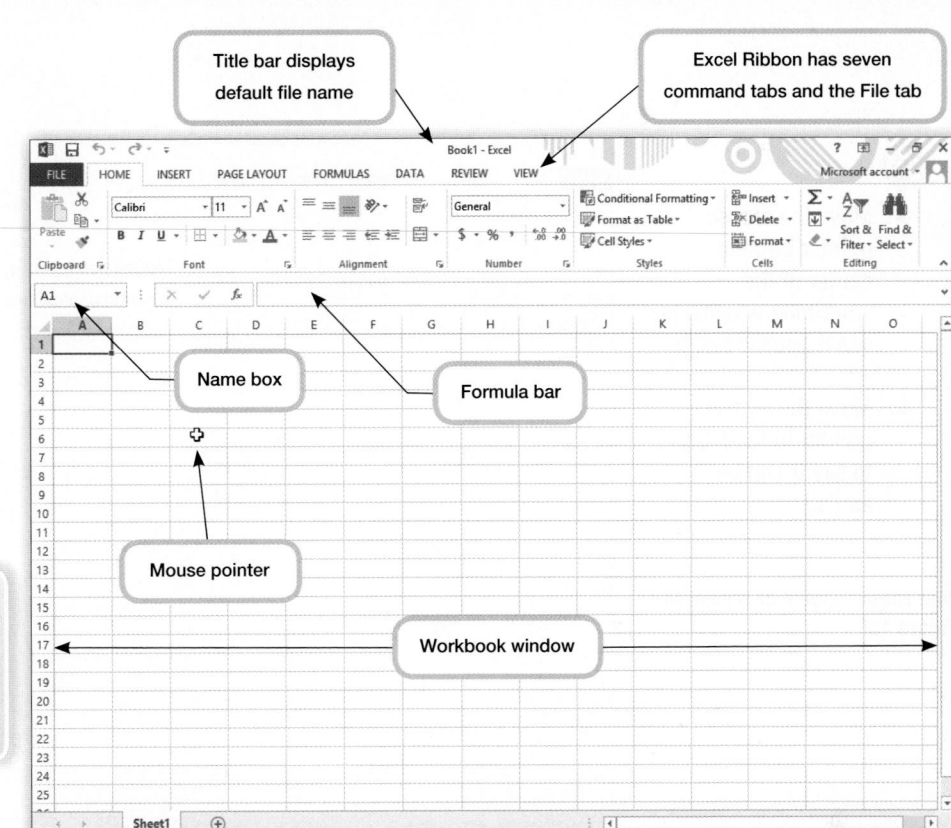

Figure 1.1

Title bar displays default file name

Excel Ribbon has seven command tabs and the File tab

Name box

Formula bar

Mouse pointer

Workbook window

After a few moments, the Excel application window is displayed. Because Excel remembers many settings that were in use when the program was last closed, your screen might look slightly different.

The Excel application window title bar displays the default file name, Book1, and program name. The Ribbon below the title bar consists of seven tabs that provide access to the commands and features you will use to create and modify a worksheet and the File tab for managing printing, saving, and sharing workbooks.

Below the Ribbon is the formula bar. The **formula bar** displays entries as they are made and edited in the workbook window. The **Name box**, located at the left end of the formula bar, provides information about the selected item.

The large center area of the program window is the **workbook window**. A **workbook** is an Excel file that stores the information you enter using the program. You will learn more about the different parts of the workbook window shortly.

The mouse pointer can appear as many different shapes. The mouse pointer changes shape depending upon the task you are performing or where the pointer is located on the window. Most commonly it appears as a ▷ or ✛. When it appears as a ✛, it is used to move to different locations in the workbook window; when it appears as a ▷, it is used to choose items, such as commands from the Ribbon.

2

- Move the mouse pointer into the center of the workbook window to see it appear as ⊕.

- Move the mouse pointer to the Ribbon to see it appear as ▷.

Your screen should be similar to Figure 1.2

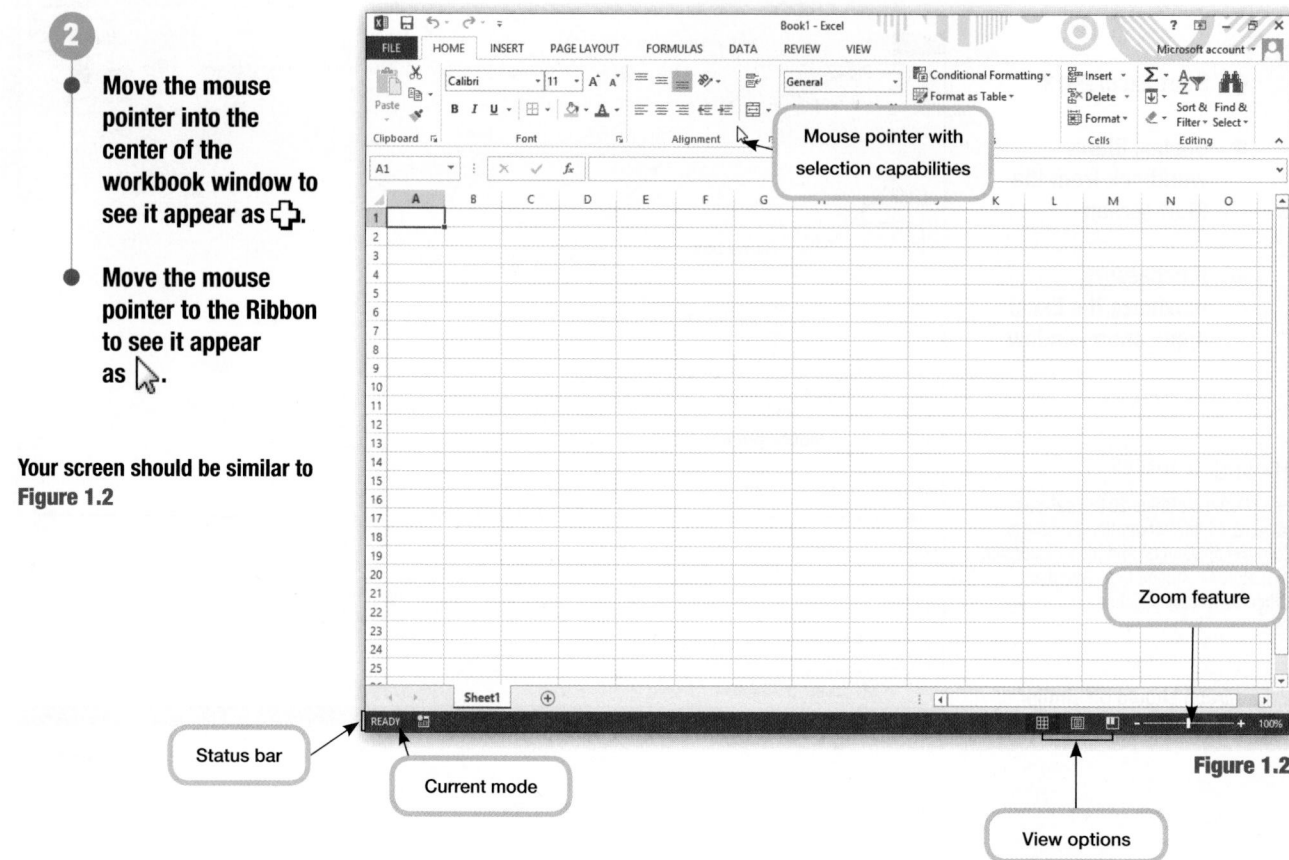

Mouse pointer with selection capabilities

Zoom feature

Status bar

Current mode

View options

Figure 1.2

The status bar at the bottom of the Excel window displays information about various Excel settings. The left side of the status bar displays the current mode or state of operation of the program, in this case, Ready. When Ready is displayed, you can move around the workbook, enter data, use the function keys, or choose a command. As you use the program, the status bar displays the current mode. The right side of the status bar contains buttons to change the view and a zoom feature.

Exploring the Workbook Window

When you open a blank workbook from the Start screen, the new workbook includes basic default settings. These settings include font style and size, column width and row height, and a single blank worksheet. A **worksheet,** also called a **sheet,** is used to store and work with different types of information, such as financial data or charts. It is a rectangular grid of **rows** and **columns** used to enter data. It is always part of a workbook and is the primary type of sheet you will use in Excel. The worksheet is much larger than the part you are viewing in the window. The worksheet actually extends 16,384 columns to the right and 1,048,576 rows down.

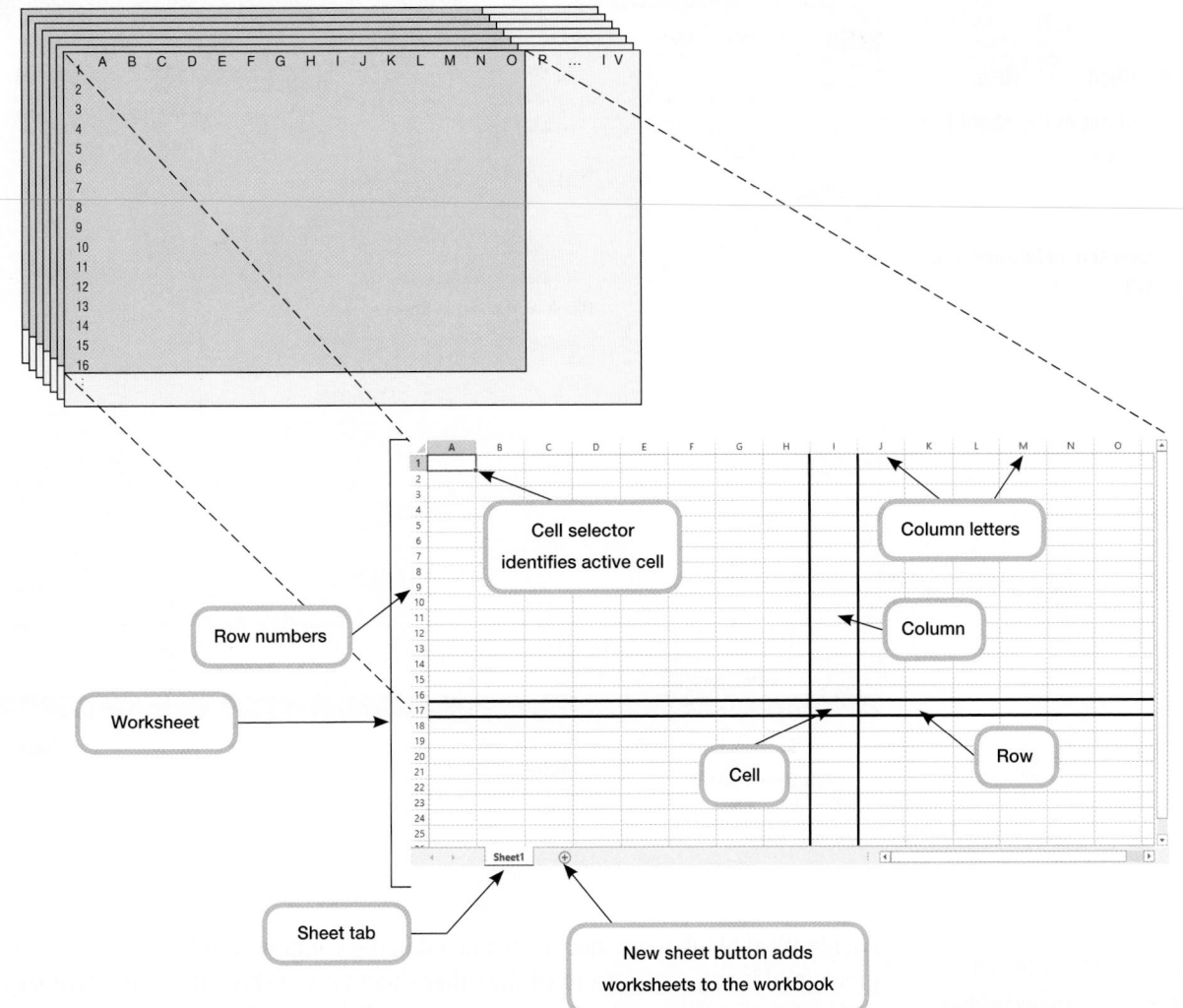

The **row numbers** along the left side and the **column letters** across the top of the workbook window identify each worksheet row and column. The intersection of a row and column creates a **cell**. Notice the green border, called the **cell selector**, surrounding the cell located at the intersection of column A and row 1. This identifies the **active cell**, which is the cell your next entry or procedure affects. Additionally, the Name box in the formula bar displays the **cell reference**, consisting of the column letter and row number of the active cell. The reference of the active cell is A1.

Each sheet in a workbook is named. The first blank sheet in a workbook is named Sheet1. As additional sheets are added to the workbook they are named Sheet2, and so on. The sheet names are displayed on **sheet tabs** at the bottom of the workbook window. The name of the **active sheet**, which is the sheet you can work in, appears bold green. The currently displayed worksheet in the workbook window, Sheet1, is the active sheet. You will use the ⊕ New Sheet button to add a second sheet to the workbook.

1
● Click ⊕ **New sheet** in the sheet tab area.

Your screen should be similar to Figure 1.3

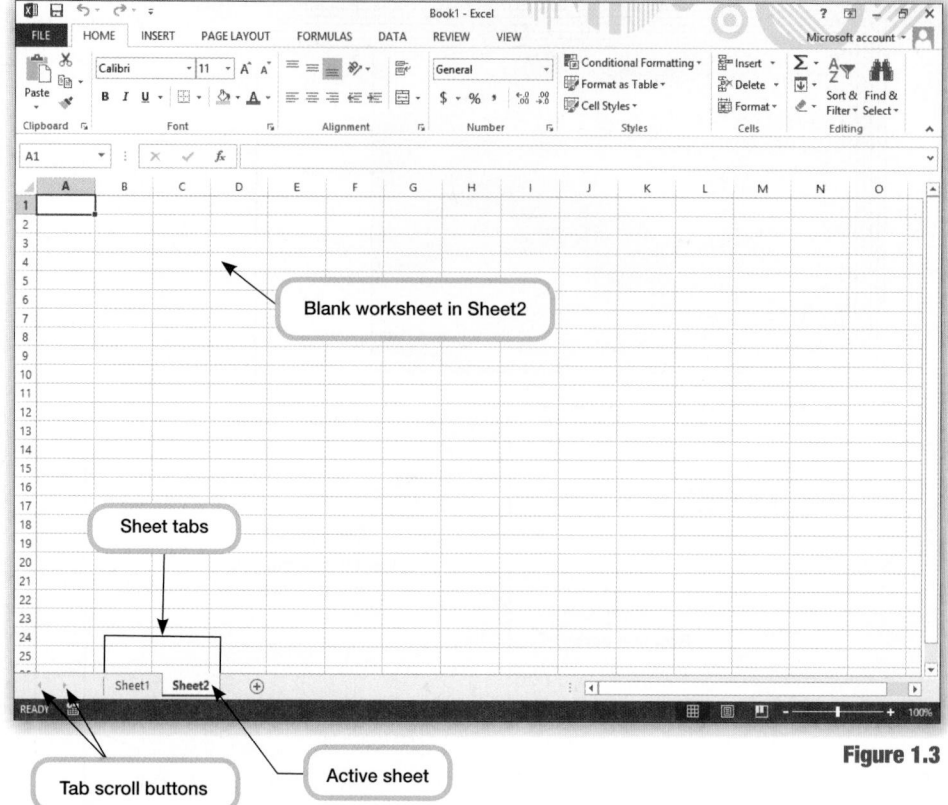

Blank worksheet in Sheet2

Sheet tabs

Tab scroll buttons

Active sheet

Figure 1.3

An identical blank worksheet is displayed in the window. The Sheet2 tab letters are green, and it appears in front of the other sheet tabs to show it is the active sheet.

The sheet tab area also contains **tab scroll buttons**, which are used to scroll tabs right or left when there are more sheet tabs than can be seen. You will learn about these features throughout the labs.

MOVING AROUND THE WORKSHEET

The mouse or keyboard commands can be used to move the cell selector from one cell to another in the worksheet. To move using a mouse, simply point to the cell you want to move to and click the mouse button. Depending upon what you are doing, using the mouse to move may not be as convenient as using the keyboard, in which case the directional keys can be used. You will make Sheet1 active again and use the mouse, then the keyboard, to move in the worksheet.

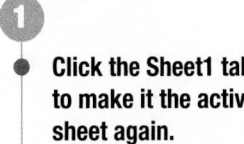

1

● **Click the Sheet1 tab to make it the active sheet again.**

Another Method

You also can press Ctrl + Page Down to move to the next sheet and Ctrl + Page Up to move to the previous sheet.

● **Click cell B3.**

● **Press → (3 times).**

● **Press ↓ (4 times).**

Your screen should be similar to Figure 1.4

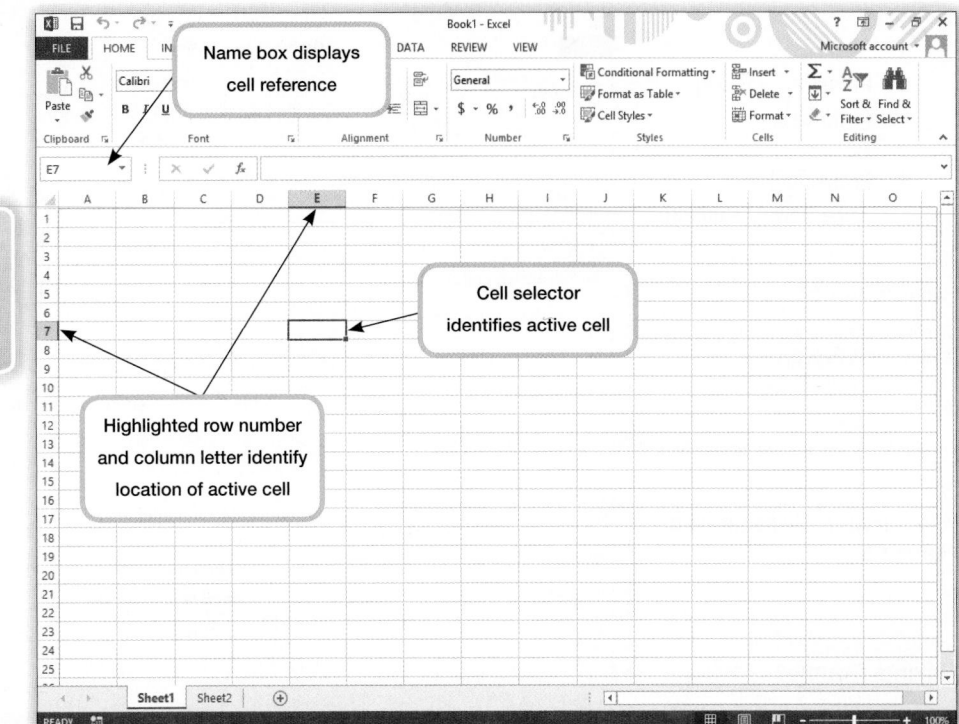

Figure 1.4

Cell E7 is outlined in green, indicating this cell is the active cell. The Name box displays the cell reference. In addition, the row number and column letter are gray to further identify the location of the active cell.

As you have learned, the worksheet is much larger than the part you are viewing in the window. To see an area of the worksheet that is not currently in view, you need to scroll the window. The keyboard procedures shown in the table that follows can be used to move around the worksheet.

Having Trouble?

Refer to the "Scrolling the Document Window" section of the Introduction to Office 2013 for more keyboard and mouse procedures.

Keyboard	Action
Alt + Page Down	Moves right one full window.
Alt + Page Up	Moves left one full window.
Home	Moves to beginning of row.
Ctrl + Home	Moves to upper-left corner cell of worksheet.
Ctrl + End	Moves to last-used cell of worksheet.
End →	Moves to last-used cell in row.
End ↓	Moves to last-used cell in column.

Touch Tip

Another way to scroll is to touch the worksheet or scroll bar with your finger and slide it up or down.

In addition, if you hold down an arrow key, the Alt + Page Up or Alt + Page Down keys, or the Page Up or Page Down keys, you can quickly scroll through the worksheet.

You will scroll the worksheet to see the rows below your current last row and the columns to the right of your current last column.

Press Page Down
(3 times).

Press Alt +
Page Down **(3 times).**

Having Trouble?

Do not use the numeric keypad
Page Up and Page Down keys,
as this may enter a character
in the cell.

**Your screen should be similar to
Figure 1.5**

Having Trouble?

Your screen may display more or fewer
rows and columns and the active cell
may be a different cell. This is a function
of your screen and system settings.

Additional Information

If you have a mouse with a scroll wheel,
rotating the wheel forward or back
scrolls up or down a few rows at a time.

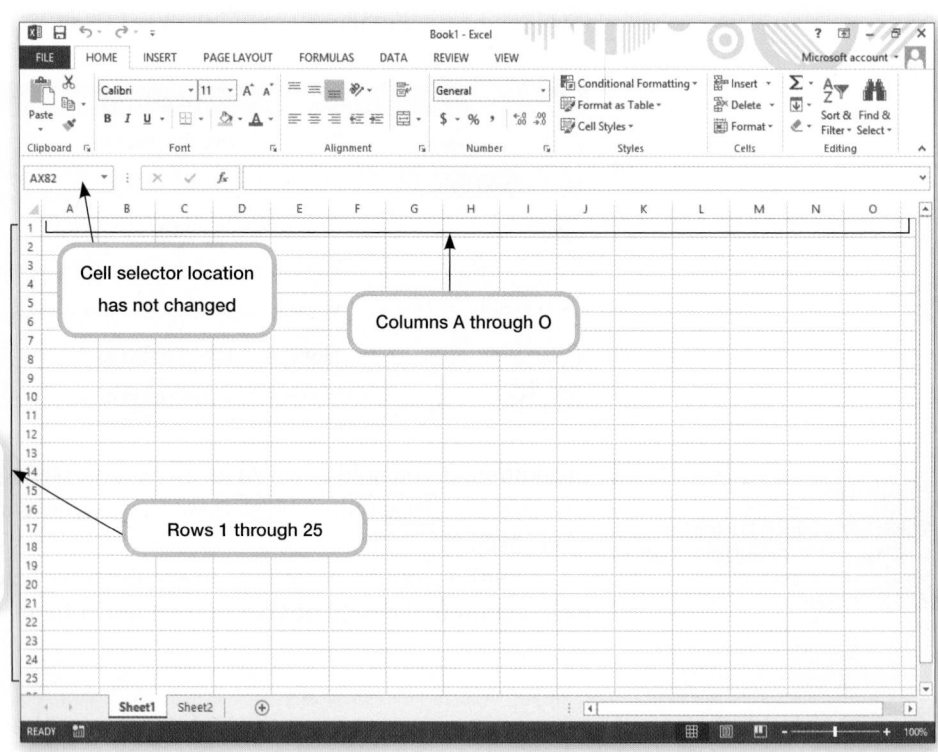

Figure 1.5

The worksheet scrolled downward and left three full windows, The cell reference
of your active cell depends on the screen resolution set at your computer. As you
scroll the worksheet using the keyboard, the active cell also changes.

It is even more efficient to use the scroll bar to move long distances.

**Slowly drag the
vertical scroll box up
the scroll bar until
row 1 is displayed.**

**Slowly drag the
horizontal scroll box
left along the scroll
bar until column A is
displayed.**

Additional Information

As you scroll, the scroll bar identifies
the current row position at the top of the
window or column position at the left
side of the window in a ScreenTip.

**Your screen should be similar to
Figure 1.6**

Figure 1.6

Another Method

You also can type a cell address in the Name box and press ←Enter to move to that location.

The beginning rows and columns are displayed again. Notice that the Name box displays the same active cell location. When you use the scroll bar to scroll the worksheet, the active cell does not change until you click on a cell that is visible in the window.

- **Practice moving around the worksheet using the keys presented in the table on page EX1.9.**

Additional Information

The Ctrl + End key presented in the table will not change the worksheet location until the worksheet contains data.

- **Press Ctrl + Home to move to cell A1.**

You can use the mouse or the keyboard with most of the exercises in these labs. As you use both the mouse and the keyboard, you will find that it is more efficient to use one or the other in specific situations.

DEVELOPING A WORKSHEET

Now that you are familiar with the parts of the workbook and with moving around the worksheet, you are ready to create a worksheet showing the forecast for the first three months of operation for the Downtown Internet Café.

Worksheet development consists of four steps: planning, entering and editing, testing, and formatting. The objective is to create well-designed worksheets that produce accurate results and are clearly understood, adaptable, and efficient.

Step	Description
1. Plan	Specify the purpose of the worksheet and how it should be organized. This means clearly identifying the data that will be input, the calculations that are needed to achieve the results, and the output that is desired. As part of the planning step, it is helpful to sketch out a design of the worksheet to organize the worksheet's structure. The design should include the worksheet title and row and column headings that identify the input and output. Additionally, sample data can be used to help determine the formulas needed to produce the output.
2. Enter and edit	Create the structure of the worksheet using Excel by entering the worksheet labels, data, and formulas. As you enter information, you are likely to make errors that need to be corrected or edited, or you will need to revise the content of what you have entered to clarify it or to add or delete information.
3. Test	Test the worksheet for errors. Use several sets of real or sample data as the input, and verify the resulting output. The input data should include a full range of possible values for each data item to ensure the worksheet can function successfully under all possible conditions.
4. Format	Enhance the appearance of the worksheet to make it more readable or attractive. This step is usually performed when the worksheet is near completion. It includes many features such as boldface text, italic, and color.

As the complexity of the worksheet increases, the importance of following the design process increases. Even for simple worksheets like the one you will create in this lab, the design process is important. You will find that you will generally follow these steps in the order listed above for your first draft of a worksheet. However, you will probably retrace steps such as editing and formatting as the final worksheet is developed.

During the planning phase, you have spoken with the Café manager, Evan, regarding the purpose of the worksheet and the content in general. The primary purpose is to develop a forecast for sales and expenses for the next year. First, Evan wants you to develop a worksheet for the first quarter forecast and then extend it by quarters for the year. After reviewing past budgets and consulting with Evan, you have designed the basic layout for the first quarter forecast for the Café, as shown below.

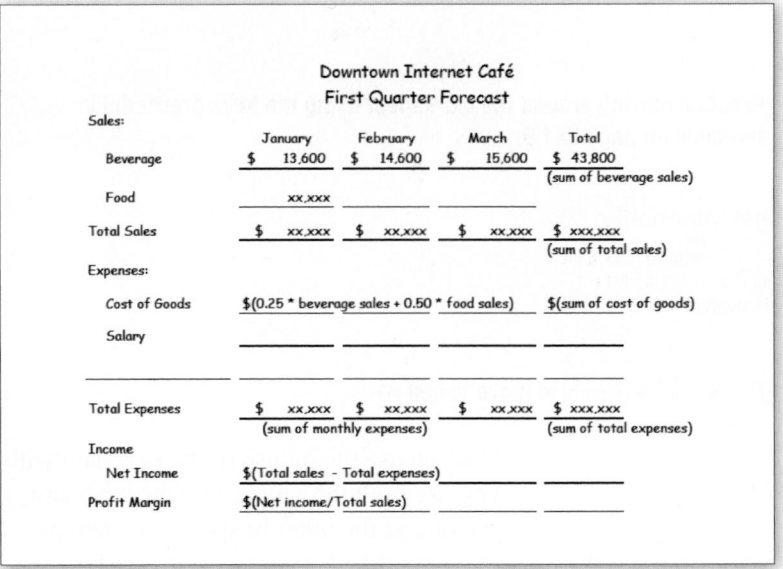

Entering and Editing Data

Now that you understand the purpose of the worksheet and have a general idea of the content, you are ready to begin entering the data. Each worksheet is like a blank piece of paper that already has many predefined settings. You will use the blank Sheet1 worksheet with the default settings to create the worksheet for the Café.

As you can see, the budget you designed above contains both descriptive text entries and numeric data. These are two types of data you can enter in a worksheet.

Concept  Data

Basic information or **data** you enter in a cell can be text, numbers, dates, or times. **Text** entries can contain any combination of letters, numbers, spaces, and any other special characters. **Number** entries can include only the digits 0 to 9 and any of the special characters + – ( ) , . / $ % ? =. Number entries can be used in calculations.

Text and number entries generally appear in the cell exactly as they are entered. However, some entries such as formulas direct Excel to perform a calculation on values in the worksheet. In these cases, the result of the formula appears in the cell, not the formula itself. You will learn about formulas later in the lab.

Adding Text Entries

You enter data into a worksheet by moving to the cell where you want the data displayed and typing the entry using the keyboard. First, you will enter the worksheet headings. Row and column **headings** are entries that are used to create the structure of the worksheet and describe other worksheet entries. Generally, headings are text entries. The column headings in this worksheet consist of the three months (January through March) and a total (sum of entries over three months) located in columns B through E. You will begin by entering the column heading for January in cell B2.

1

- **Click on cell B2 to move to it.**

- **Type January**

Having Trouble?

Do not be concerned if you make a typing error. You will learn how to correct it shortly.

Your screen should be similar to Figure 1.7

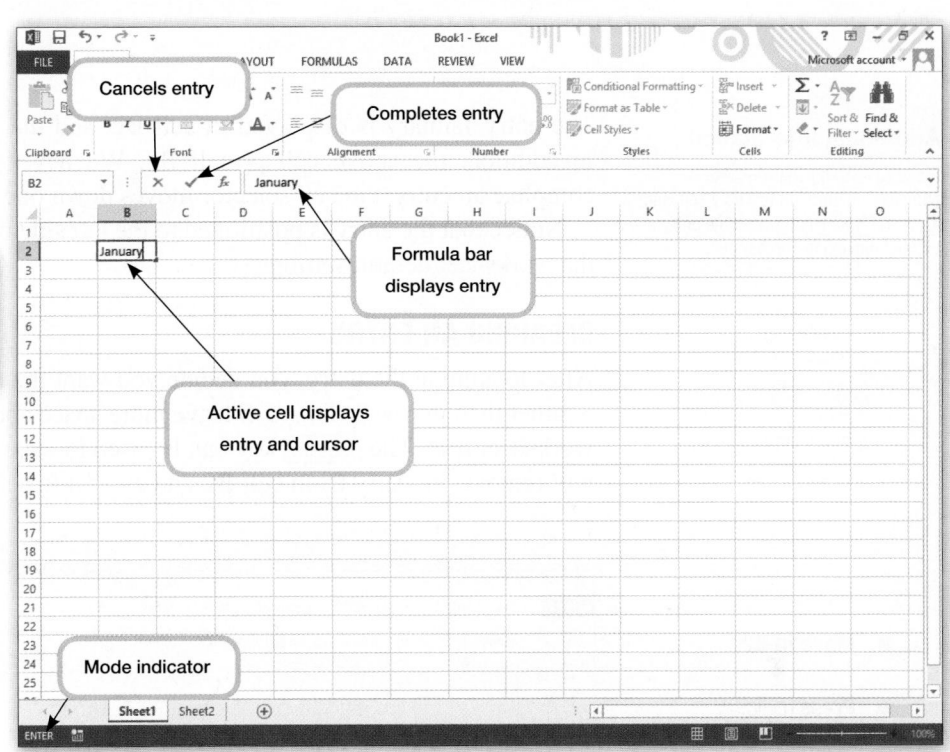

Figure 1.7

Several changes have occurred in the window. As you type, the entry is displayed both in the active cell and in the formula bar. The cursor appears in the active cell and marks your location in the entry. Two new buttons, $\times$ and $\checkmark$, appear in the formula bar. They can be used with a mouse to cancel your entry or complete it.

Notice also that the mode displayed in the status bar has changed from Ready to Enter. This notifies you that the current mode of operation in the worksheet is entering data.

Although the entry is displayed in both the active cell and the formula bar, you need to press the ⟵Enter or Tab key, click $\checkmark$, or click on any other cell to complete your entry. If you press Esc or click $\times$, the entry is cleared and nothing appears in the cell. Since your hands are already on the keyboard, it is quicker to press ⟵Enter or Tab than it is to use the mouse.

2 ● Press ⏎Enter .

Your screen should be similar to Figure 1.8

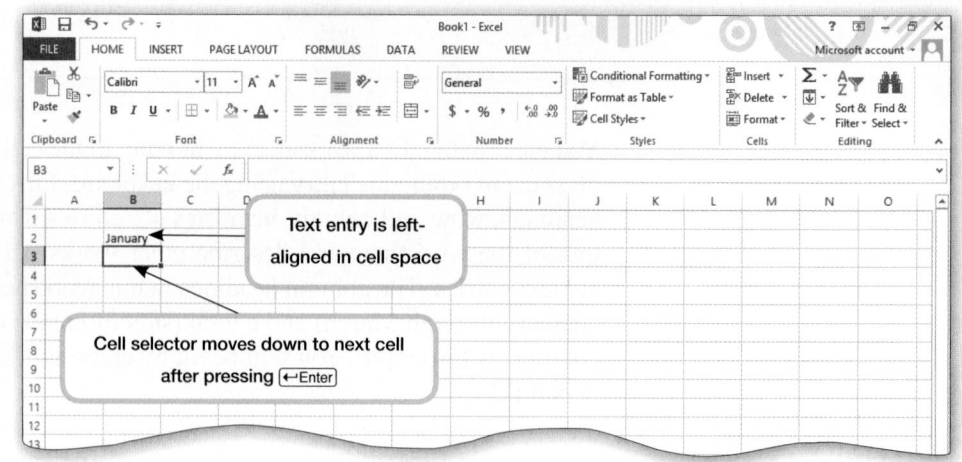

Text entry is left-aligned in cell space

Cell selector moves down to next cell after pressing ⏎Enter

Figure 1.8

The entry January is displayed in cell B2, and the mode has returned to Ready. In addition, the active cell is cell B3. Whenever you use the ⏎Enter key to complete an entry, the cell selector moves down one cell.

Notice that the entry is positioned to the left side of the cell space. This is one of the worksheet default settings.

CLEARING AN ENTRY

After looking at the entry, you decide you want the column headings to be in row 3 rather than in row 2. This will leave more space above the column headings for a worksheet title. The Delete key can be used to clear the contents from a cell. You will remove the entry from cell B2 and enter it in cell B3.

1 ● Move to B2.

● Press Delete .

Another Method

You also can use 🧽 ▾ Clear/Clear Contents in the Editing group of the Home tab.

● Move to B3.

● Type January

● Click ✓ Enter.

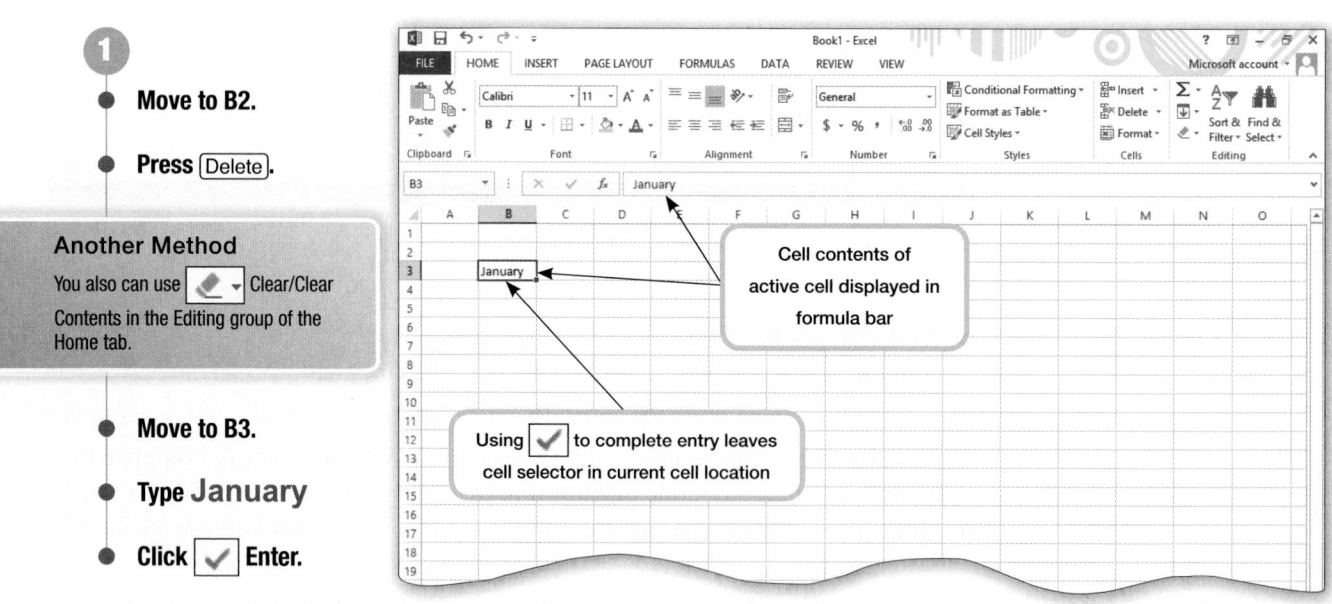

Cell contents of active cell displayed in formula bar

Using ✓ to complete entry leaves cell selector in current cell location

Figure 1.9

Your screen should be similar to Figure 1.9

The active cell does not change when you click ✓ to complete an entry. Because the active cell contains an entry, the cell content is displayed in the formula bar.

EDITING AN ENTRY

Next, you decide to change the heading from January to JAN. An entry in a cell can be entirely changed in the Ready mode or partially changed or edited in the Edit mode. To use the Ready mode, you move to the cell you want to change and retype the entry the way you want it to appear. As soon as a new character is entered, the existing entry is cleared.

Generally, however, if you need to change only part of an entry, using the Edit mode is quicker. To change to Edit mode, double-click on the cell whose contents you want to edit.

Touch Tip

If you're using a touch screen, you can change a cell to Edit mode by double-tapping it.

1 • Double-click B3.

Having Trouble?

The mouse pointer must be 🔆 when you double-click on the cell.

Another Method

Pressing the F2 key also will change to Edit mode. The cursor is positioned at the end of the entry.

Your screen should be similar to Figure 1.10

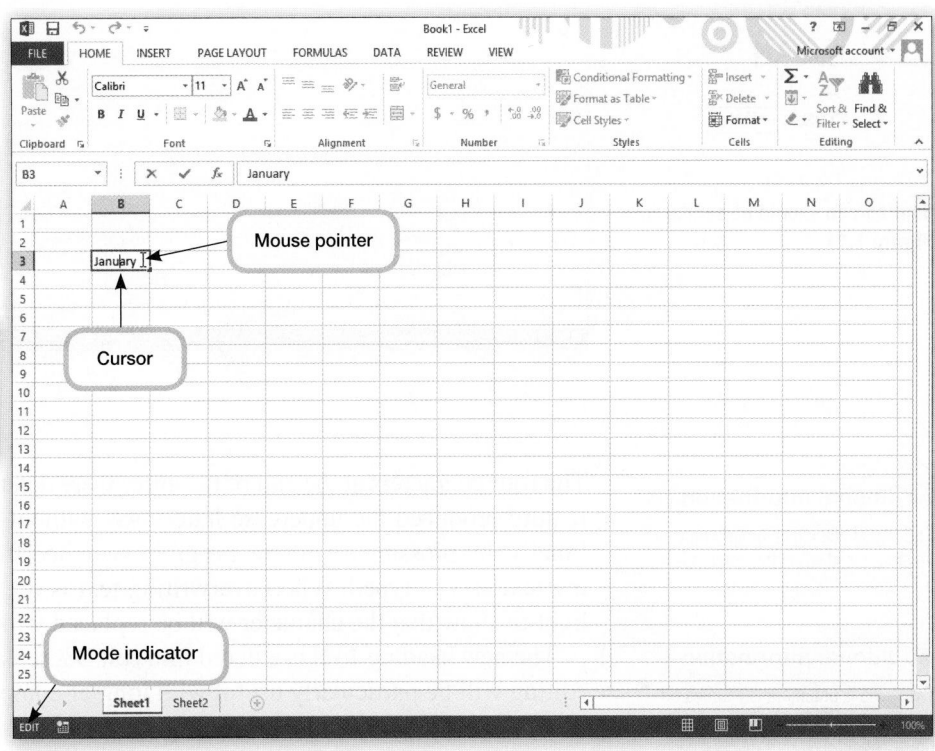

Figure 1.10

The status bar shows that the new mode of operation is Edit. The cursor appears at the location you clicked in the entry, and the mouse pointer changes to an I-beam when positioned on the cell. Now you can click again or use the directional keys to move the cursor within the cell entry to the location of the text you want to change.

After the cursor is appropriately positioned, you can edit the entry by removing the incorrect characters and typing the correct characters. To do this, you can use the Backspace and Delete keys to delete text character by character and enter the new text, or you can select the text to be changed and then type the correction. You will change this entry to JAN.

Having Trouble?

Refer to the "Entering and Editing Text" and "Selecting Text" sections of the Introduction to Office 2013 to review these features.

Additional Information

You also can use Ctrl + Delete to delete everything to the right of the cursor in the active cell.

Adding Text Entries   **EX1.15**

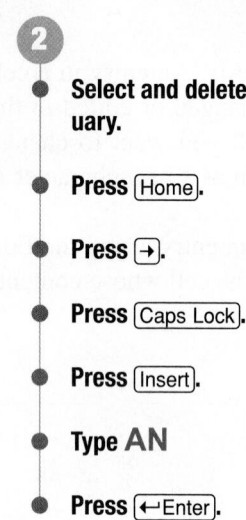

● **Select and delete uary.**

● **Press** Home.

● **Press** →.

● **Press** Caps Lock.

● **Press** Insert.

● **Type AN**

● **Press** ←Enter.

Your screen should be similar to Figure 1.11

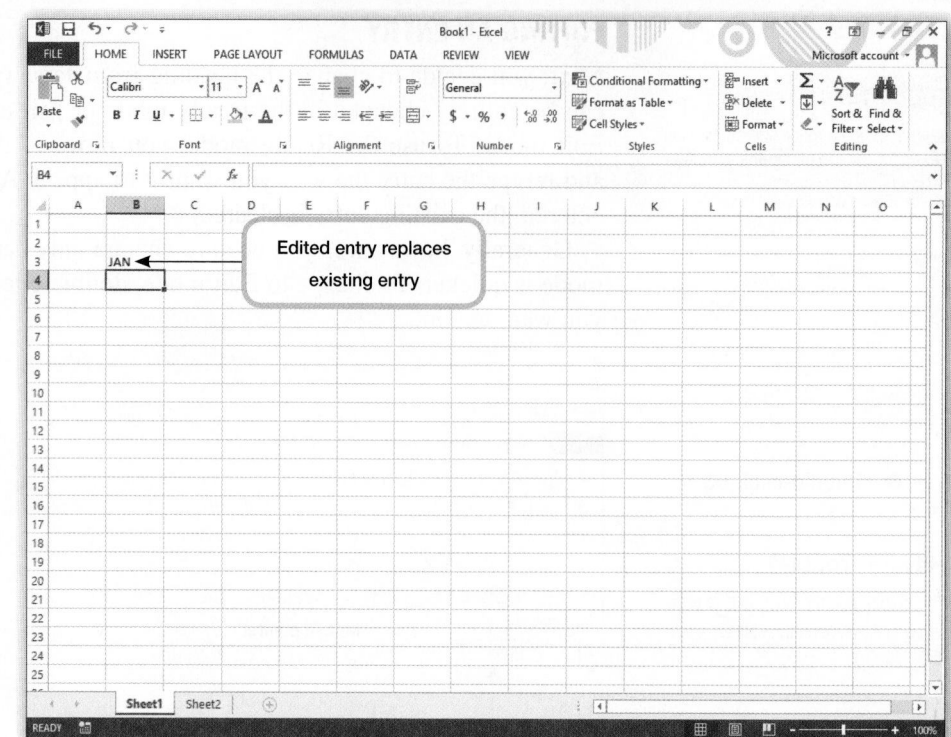

Edited entry replaces existing entry

Figure 1.11

Additional Information

The Caps Lock indicator light on your keyboard is lit when this feature is on.

Additional Information

Overwrite is automatically turned off when you leave Edit mode or you press Insert again.

The four characters at the end of the entry were deleted. Turning on the Caps Lock feature produced the uppercase letters AN without having to hold down ⇧Shift. Finally, by pressing Insert, the program switched from inserting text to overwriting text as you typed. When overwriting text is on, the cursor changes to a highlight to show that the character will be replaced with the new text you type.

The new heading JAN is entered into cell B3, replacing January. As you can see, editing will be particularly useful with long or complicated entries.

Next, you will enter the remaining three headings in row 3. Because you want to move to the right one cell to enter the next month label, you will complete the entries using → or Tab⇄.

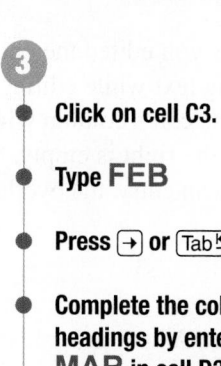

3

- Click on cell **C3**.

- Type **FEB**

- Press → or Tab ↹.

- Complete the column headings by entering **MAR** in cell D3 and **TOTAL** in cell E3.

Having Trouble?

Remember to press ←Enter, Tab ↹, or an arrow key or click in another cell to complete each entry.

- Press Caps Lock to turn off this feature.

Your screen should be similar to Figure 1.12

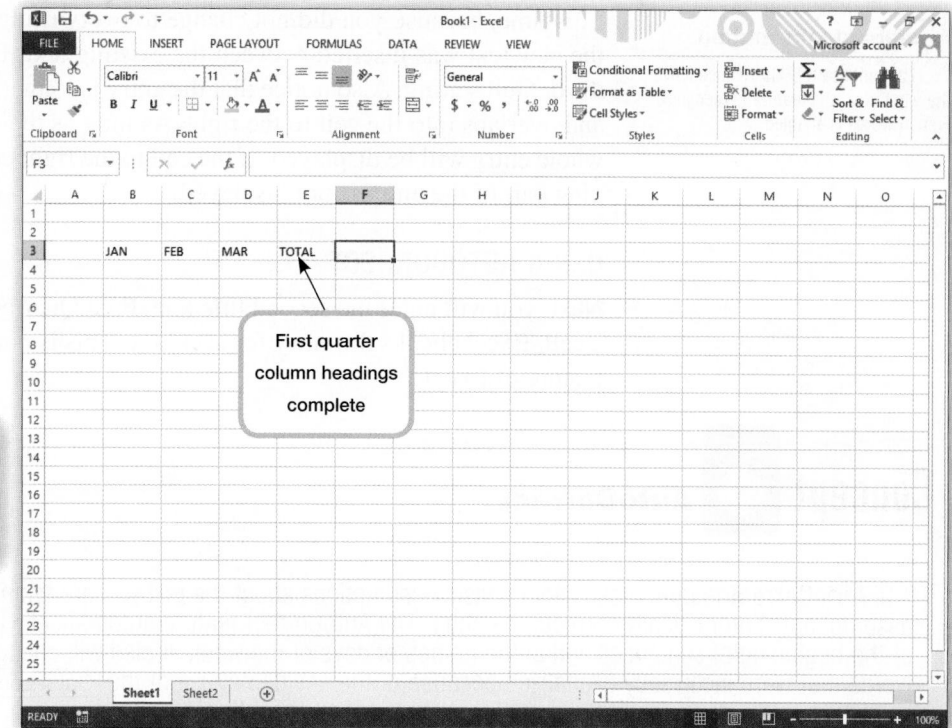

First quarter column headings complete

Figure 1.12

The column headings are now complete for the first quarter. Above the column headings, you want to enter a title for the worksheet. The first title line will be the café name, Downtown Internet Café.

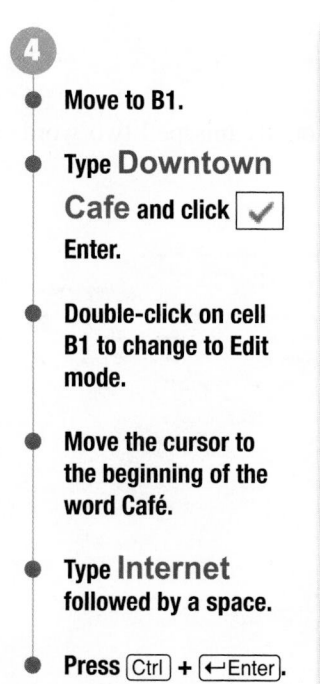

4

- Move to **B1**.

- Type **Downtown Cafe** and click ✓ Enter.

- Double-click on cell **B1** to change to Edit mode.

- Move the cursor to the beginning of the word Café.

- Type **Internet** followed by a space.

- Press Ctrl + ←Enter.

Your screen should be similar to Figure 1.13

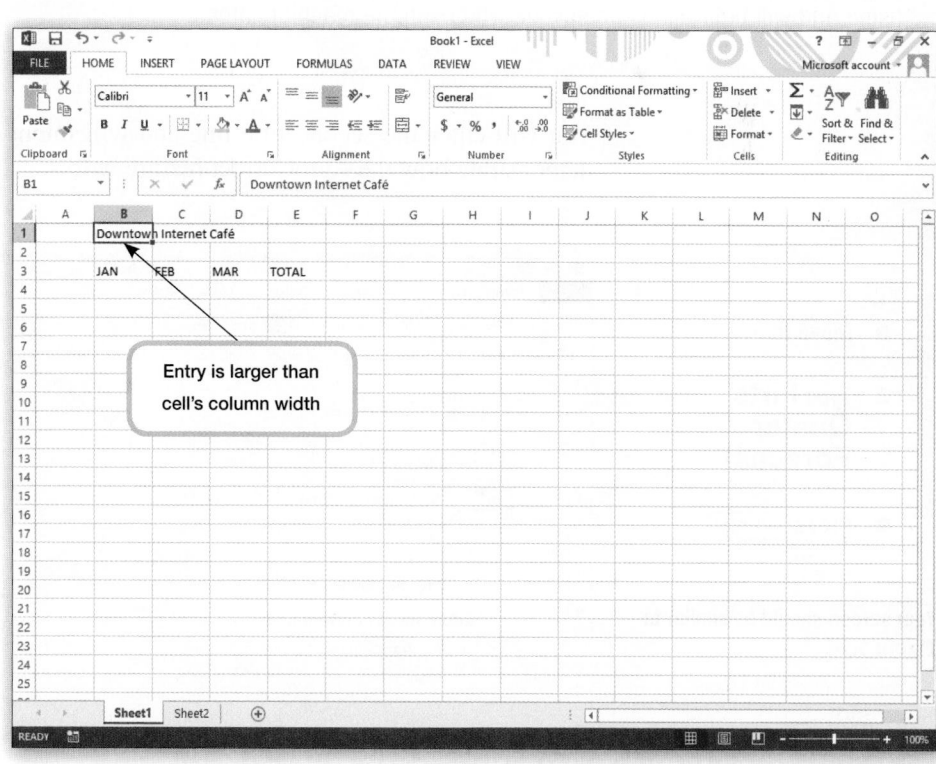

Entry is larger than cell's column width

Figure 1.13

Adding Text Entries   **EX1.17**

This time, because you did not change to overwriting text as you edited the entry, the new text was inserted between the existing text. Inserting text while editing is the default setting. Also notice that the entry is longer than the cell's column width and overlaps into the cell to the right. As long as the cell to the right is empty, the whole entry will be displayed. If the cell to the right contains an entry, the overlapping part of the entry is not displayed.

USING AUTOCORRECT

Next, you will enter the second title line, First Quarter Report. As you enter text in a cell, Excel checks the entry for accuracy. This is part of the automatic correcting feature of Excel.

Concept 2 AutoCorrect

The **AutoCorrect** feature makes some basic assumptions about the text you are typing and, based on these assumptions, automatically corrects the entry. The AutoCorrect feature automatically inserts proper capitalization at the beginning of sentences and in the names of days of the week. It also will change to lowercase letters any words that were incorrectly capitalized because of the accidental use of the [Caps Lock] key. In addition, it also corrects many common typing and spelling errors automatically.

One way the program automatically makes corrections is by looking for certain types of errors. For example, if two capital letters appear at the beginning of a word, the second capital letter is changed to a lowercase letter. If a lowercase letter appears at the beginning of a sentence, the first letter of the first word is capitalized. If the name of a day begins with a lowercase letter, the first letter is capitalized.

Another way the program makes corrections is by checking all entries against a built-in list of words that are commonly spelled incorrectly or typed incorrectly. If it finds the entry on the list, the program automatically replaces the error with the correction. For example, the typing error "aboutthe" is automatically changed to "about the" because the error is on the AutoCorrect list. You also can add words that you want to be automatically corrected to the AutoCorrect list. Words you add are added to the list on the computer you are using and will be available to anyone who uses the machine later.

You will enter the second title line and will intentionally misspell two words to demonstrate how the AutoCorrect feature works.

- Move to B2.

- Type **Firts Quater Forecast**

- Press (←Enter).

Your screen should be similar to Figure 1.14

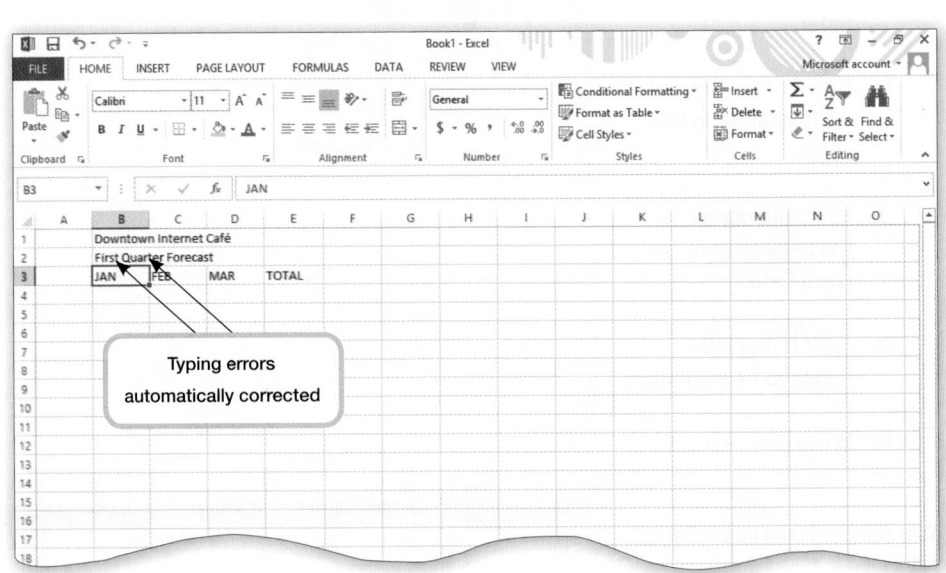

Figure 1.14

The two typing errors were automatically corrected as soon as you completed a word by pressing the spacebar. If the entry was a single word, it would be checked as soon as you completed the entry.

Next, the row headings need to be entered into column A of the worksheet. The row headings and what they represent are shown in the following table.

Heading	Description
Sales	
Espresso	Income from sales of espresso-based drinks
Coffee	Income from drip coffee sales
Food/Beverage	Income from sales of baked goods, sandwiches, salads, and other beverages
Merchandise	Income from sales of mugs, books, magazines, candy, etc.
Computer	Income from computer rental usage, printing, copier use, and MP3 downloads
Total Sales	Sum of all sales
Expenses	
Cost of Goods	Cost of espresso, coffee, and food items sold
Cost of Merchandise	Cost of merchandise other than food and beverage
Wages	Manager and labor costs
Internet	WiFi access, MP3 kiosk rental, etc.
Building	Lease, insurance, electricity, water, etc.
Capital Assets	Equipment leases, interest, depreciation
Miscellaneous	Maintenance, phone, office supplies, outside services, taxes, etc.
Income	
Net Income	Total sales minus total expenses
Profit Margin	Net income divided by total sales

2

● Complete the row headings for the Sales portion of the worksheet by entering the following headings in the indicated cells.

Cell	Heading
A3	Sales
A4	Espresso
A5	Coffee
A6	Food/Beverage
A7	Merchandise
A8	Computer
A9	Total Sales

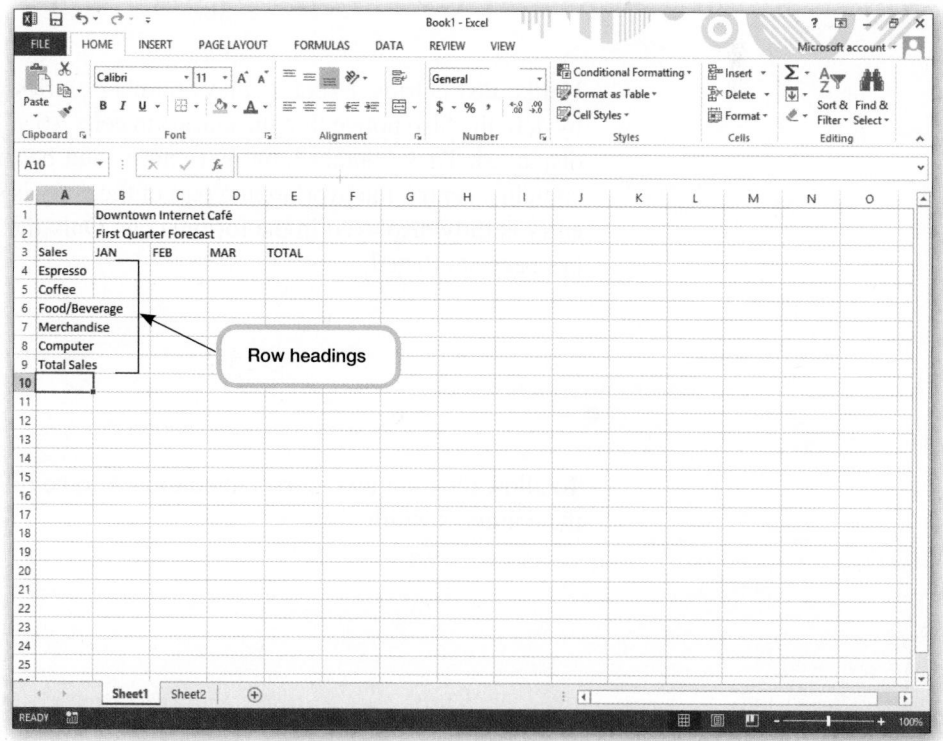

Your screen should be similar to Figure 1.15

Figure 1.15

ADDING NUMBER ENTRIES

Next, you will enter the expected sales numbers for January into cells B4 through B8. As you learned earlier, number entries can include the digits 0 to 9 and any of these special characters: + − ( ) , . / $ % ? =. When entering numbers, it is not necessary to type the comma to separate thousands or the currency ($) symbol. You will learn about adding these symbols shortly.

Additional Information

You can use the number keys above the alphabetic keys or the numeric keypad area to enter numbers. If you use the numeric keypad, the [Num Lock] key must be on.

- **Move to B4.**

- **Type 13300 and press [←Enter].**

- **In the same manner, enter the January sales numbers for the remaining items using the values shown below.**

Cell	Number
B5	5800
B6	3600
B7	1000
B8	600

Your screen should be similar to Figure 1.16

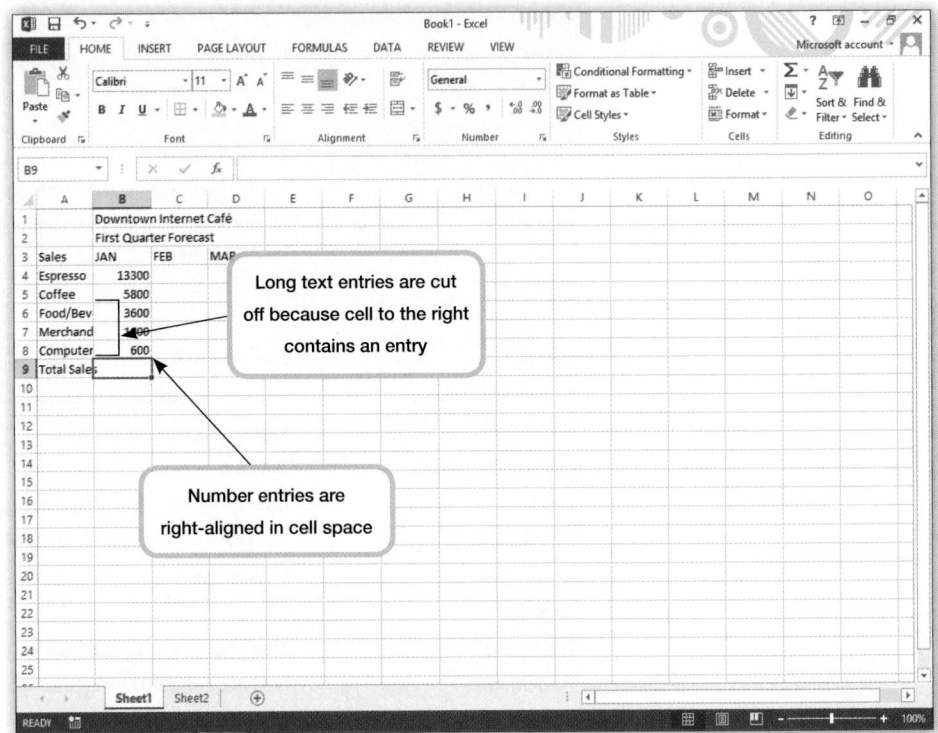

Figure 1.16

Unlike text entries, Excel displays number entries right-aligned in the cell space by default. Also notice that the entries in cells A6 and A7 are no longer completely displayed. They contain long text entries and because the cells to the right now contain an entry, the overlapping part of the entry is shortened. However, the entire entry is fully displayed in the formula bar. Only the display of the entry in the cell has been shortened.

Modifying Column Widths

To allow the long text entries in column A to be fully displayed, you can increase the column's width.

Concept ③ Column Width

The **column width** is the size or width of a column and controls the amount of information that can be displayed in a cell. A text entry that is larger than the column width will be fully displayed only if the cells to the right are blank. If the cells to the right contain data, the text is interrupted. On the other hand, when numbers are entered in a cell, the column width is automatically increased to fully display the entry.

The default column width setting is 8.43. The number represents the average number of digits that can be displayed in a cell using the standard type style. The column width can be any number from 0 to 255. If it is set to 0, the column is hidden.

When the worksheet is printed, it appears as it does currently on the screen. Therefore, you want to increase the column width to display the largest entry. Likewise, you can decrease the column width when the entries in a column are short.

There are several ways to change the column width. Using the mouse, you can change the width by dragging the boundary of the column heading. You also can set the column width to an exact value or to automatically fit the contents of the column.

DRAGGING THE COLUMN BOUNDARY

The column width can be quickly adjusted by dragging the boundary line located to the right of the column letter. Dragging it to the left decreases the column width, while dragging it to the right increases the width. As you drag, a temporary column reference line shows where the new column will appear and a ScreenTip displays the width of the column.

1

- Point to the boundary line to the right of the column letter A, and when the mouse pointer changes to ↔, click and drag the mouse pointer to the right.

- When the ScreenTip displays 24.00, release the mouse button.

Your screen should be similar to Figure 1.17

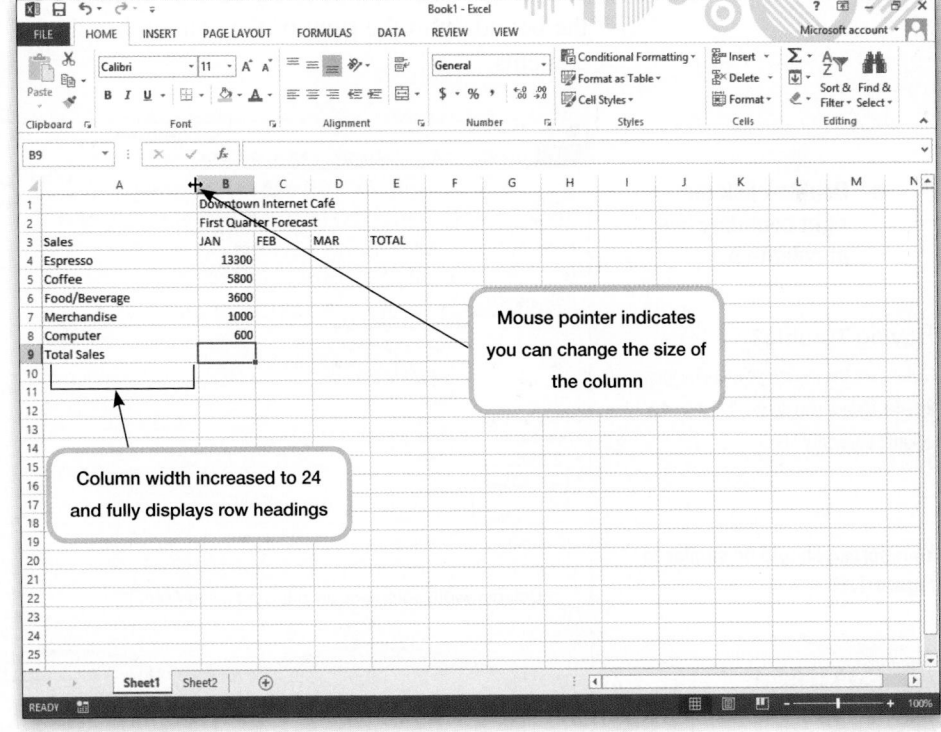

Figure 1.17

Now column A is more than wide enough to fully display all the row headings.

USING A SPECIFIED VALUE

Next, you will reduce the width of column A to 20.

- Move to any cell in column A.

- Click [📋 Format ▾] in the Cells group and choose Column Width.

- Type **20** in the Column Width text box and click [OK].

Your screen should be similar to Figure 1.18

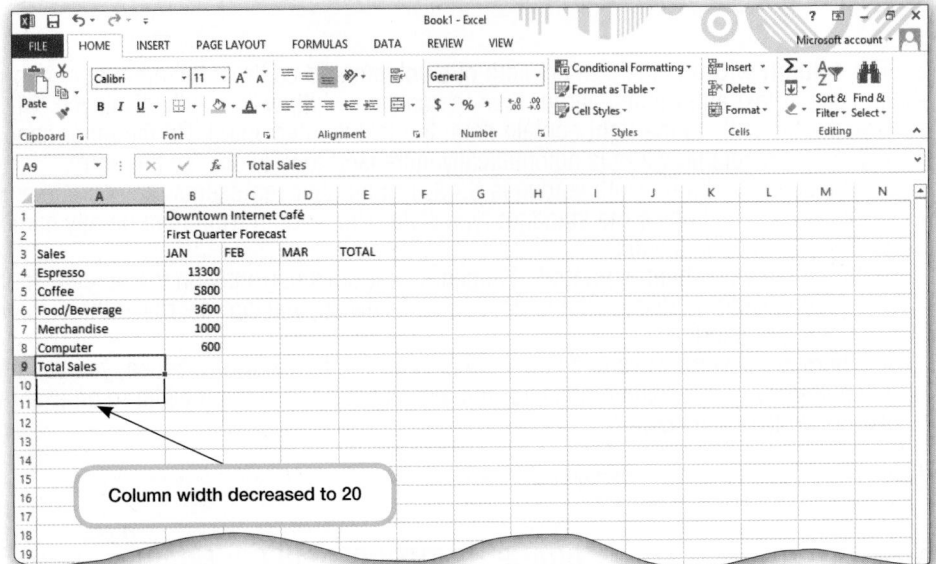

Column width decreased to 20

Figure 1.18

Although this is close, you would like to refine it a little more.

Additional Information

You can quickly return the column width to the default width setting using [📋 Format ▾]/Default Width.

USING AUTOFIT

Another way to change the column width is to use the **AutoFit** feature to automatically adjust the width to fit the column contents. When using AutoFit, double-click the boundary to the right of the column heading of the column you want to fit to contents.

- Double-click the right boundary line of column A.

Having Trouble?

Make sure the mouse pointer changes to ↔ before you double-click on the column boundary line.

Your screen should be similar to Figure 1.19

Another Method

You also can use [📋 Format ▾]/AutoFit Column Width.

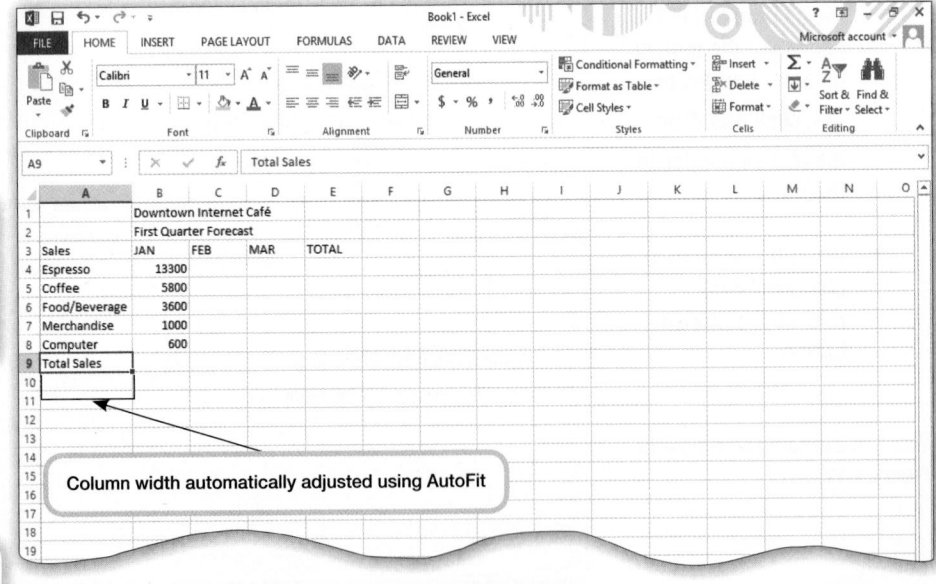

Column width automatically adjusted using AutoFit

Figure 1.19

The column width is sized to just slightly larger than the longest cell contents.

Saving, Closing, and Opening a Workbook File

You have a meeting you need to attend shortly, so you want to save the work you have completed so far on the workbook to a file and then close the file. You will name the file Cafe Forecast and use the default file type settings of Excel Workbook (*.xlsx). The file extension .xlsx identifies the file as an Excel 2007–2013 workbook.

Excel 2003 and earlier versions used the .xls file extension. If you plan to share a file with someone using Excel 2003 or earlier, you can save the file using the .xls file type; however, some features may be lost. Otherwise, if you save it as an .xlsx file type, the recipient may not be able to view all the features.

Having Trouble?

Refer to the section "Saving a File" in the Introduction to Office 2013 to review this feature.

New file name

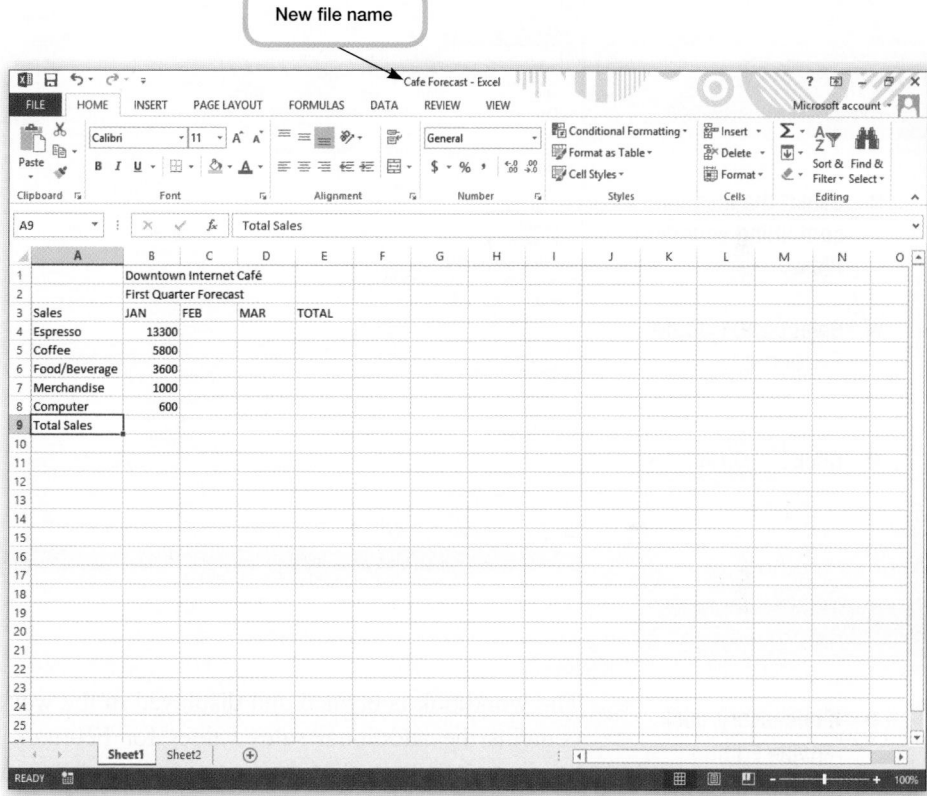

- Click 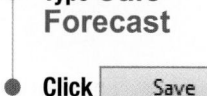 Save in the Quick Access Toolbar.

- Select the location where you want to save your file.

- If necessary, click in the File Name text box to highlight the proposed file name, or triple-click on the file name to select it.

- Type **Cafe Forecast**

- Click [Save] or press [←Enter].

Your screen should be similar to Figure 1.20

Figure 1.20

Additional Information

The file name in the title bar may display the workbook file extension, .xlsx, depending on your Windows Folder settings.

The new file name is displayed in the application window title bar. The worksheet data that was on your screen and in the computer's memory is now saved at the location you specified in a new file called Cafe Forecast.

You are now ready to close the workbook file.

- Click the File tab to open Backstage and choose Close.

Because you did not make any changes to the workbook after saving it, the workbook file is closed immediately and the Excel window displays an empty workbook window. If you had made changes to the file before closing it, you would have been prompted to save the file to prevent the accidental loss of data.

After attending your meeting, you continued working on the Café forecast. To see what has been done so far, you will open the workbook file named ex01_CafeForecast1.

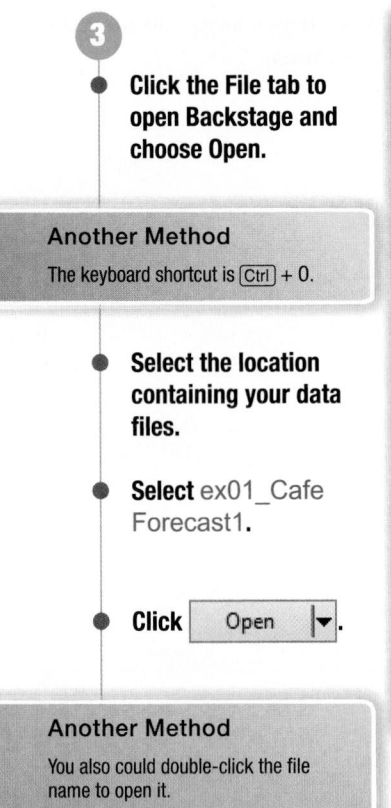

3

- **Click the File tab to open Backstage and choose Open.**

- **Select the location containing your data files.**

- **Select** ex01_Cafe Forecast1.

- **Click** Open ▼.

- **If necessary, click** Enable Editing **and maximize the workbook window.**

Your screen should be similar to Figure 1.21

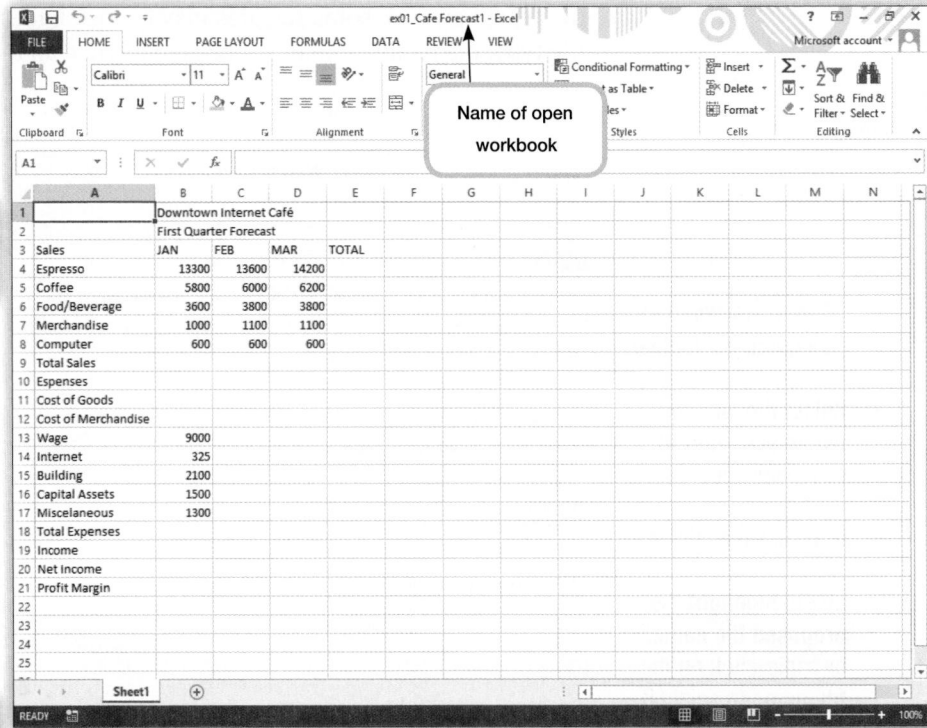

Figure 1.21

The workbook is opened and displayed in the workbook window. The workbook contains the additional sales values for February and March, the expense row headings, and several of the expense values for the month of January.

Using Proofing Tools

When entering information into a worksheet, you are likely to make spelling and typing errors. To help locate and correct these errors, the spelling checker feature can be used. Additionally, you may find that the descriptive headings you have entered may not be exactly the word you want. The thesaurus can suggest better words to clarify the meaning of the worksheet.

CHECKING SPELLING

In your rush to get the row headings entered you realize you misspelled a few words. For example, the Expenses label is spelled "Espenses." Just to make sure there are no other spelling errors, you will check the spelling of all text entries in this worksheet.

Concept  4 Spelling Checker

The **spelling checker** locates misspelled words, duplicate words, and capitalization irregularities in the active worksheet and proposes the correct spelling. This feature works by comparing each word to a dictionary of words, called the **main dictionary**, that is supplied with the program. You also can create a **custom dictionary** to hold words you commonly use but that are not included in the main dictionary. If the word does not appear in the main dictionary or in a custom dictionary, it is identified as misspelled.

When you check spelling, the contents of all cell entries in the entire active sheet are checked. If you are in Edit mode when you check spelling, only the contents of the text in the cell are checked. The spelling checker does not check spelling in formulas or in text that results from formulas.

Excel begins checking all worksheet entries from the active cell forward.

1

- If necessary, move to A1.

- Open the Review tab.

- Click ✓ ABC Spelling in the Proofing group.

Another Method
The keyboard shortcut is F7.

Your screen should be similar to Figure 1.22

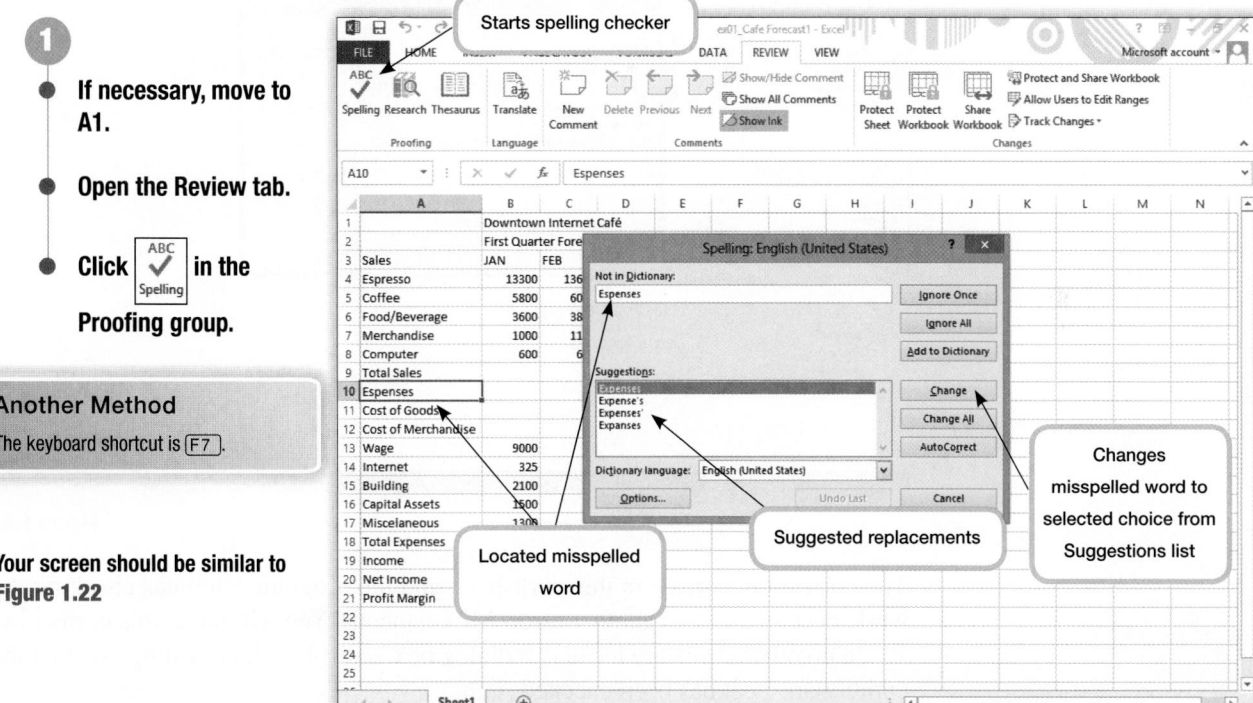

Figure 1.22

Additional Information

Spell-checking operates the same way in all Office 2013 programs. The dictionaries are shared among Office applications.

The spelling checker immediately begins checking the worksheet for words that it cannot locate in its main dictionary. The first cell containing a misspelled word, in this case Espenses, is now the active cell and the Spelling dialog box is displayed. The word it cannot locate in the dictionary is displayed in the Not in Dictionary text box. The Suggestions text box displays a list of possible replacements. If the selected replacement is not correct, you can select another choice from the suggestions list or type the correct word in the Not in Dictionary text box.

The option buttons shown in the table below have the following effects:

Option	Effect
Ignore Once	Leaves selected word unchanged.
Ignore All	Leaves this word and all identical words in worksheet unchanged.
Add to Dictionary	Adds the word in the Not in Dictionary box to a custom dictionary so Excel will not question this word during subsequent spell-checks.
Change	Changes selected word to word highlighted in Suggestions box.
Change All	Changes this word and all identical words in worksheet to word highlighted in Suggestions box.
AutoCorrect	Adds a word to the AutoCorrect list so the word will be corrected as you type.

You want to accept the suggested replacement, Expenses.

2

● Click  .

Your screen should be similar to Figure 1.23

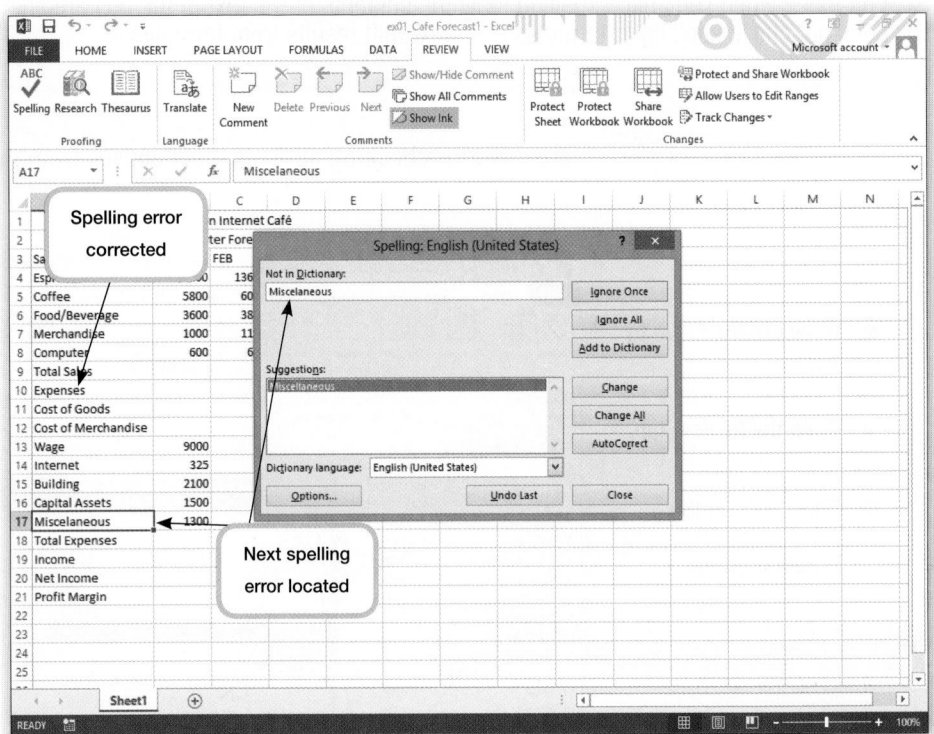

Figure 1.23

The correction is made in the worksheet, and the program continues checking the worksheet and locates another error, Miscelaneous. You will make this correction. When no other errors are located, a dialog box is displayed, informing you that the entire worksheet has been checked.

3

● **Change this word to Miscellaneous.**

● **Click** OK **to end spell-checking.**

The worksheet is now free of spelling errors.

USING THE THESAURUS

The next text change you want to make is to find a better word for "Wage" in cell A13. To help find a similar word, you will use the thesaurus tool.

Concept  Thesaurus

The **thesaurus** is a reference tool that provides synonyms, antonyms, and related words for a selected word or phrase. **Synonyms** are words with a similar meaning, such as "cheerful" and "happy." **Antonyms** are words with an opposite meaning, such as "cheerful" and "sad." Related words are words that are variations of the same word, such as "cheerful" and "cheer." The thesaurus can help to liven up your documents by adding interest and variety to your text.

To use the thesaurus, first move to the cell containing the word you want to change. If a cell contains multiple words, you need to select the individual word in the cell.

1

● Move to A13.

● Click [Thesaurus] in the Proofing group.

Another Method

You also can hold down Alt while clicking on the cell containing the word you want looked up to access the thesaurus in the Research task pane.

Your screen should be similar to Figure 1.24

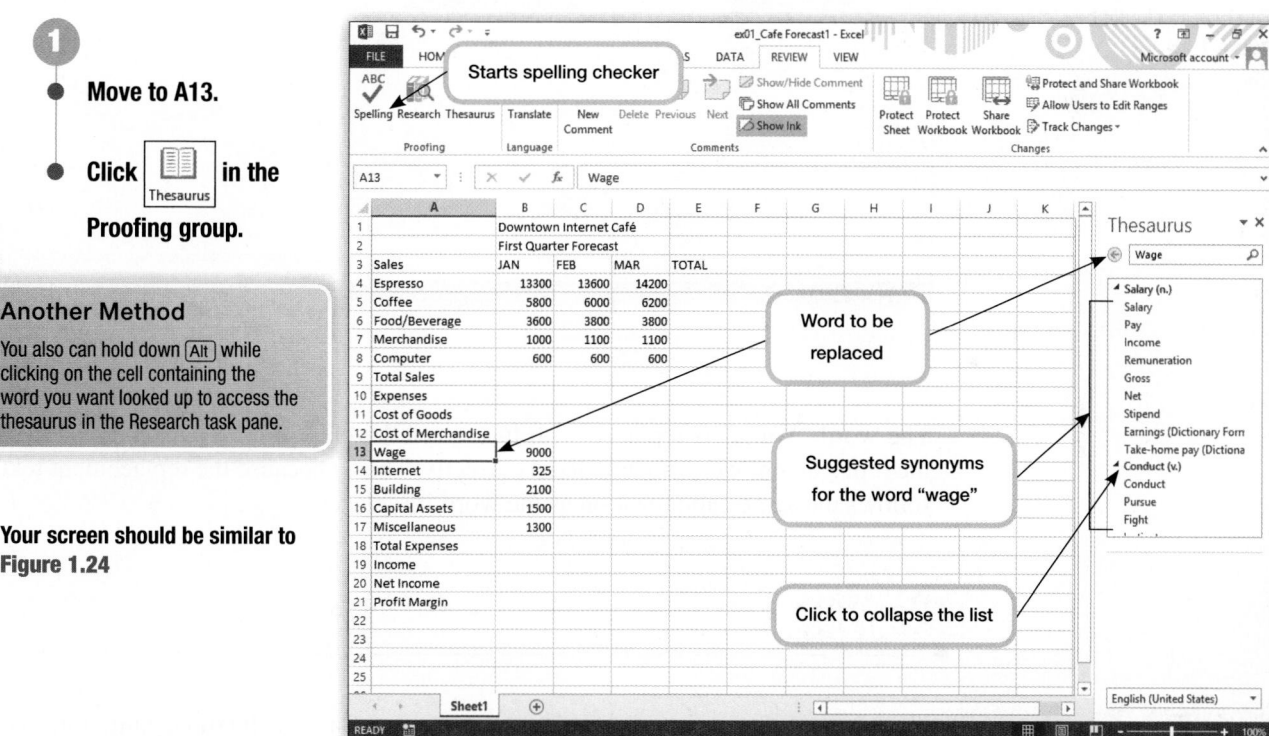

Figure 1.24

The Thesaurus task pane opens. The word in the active cell, Wage, is entered in the text box and the list box displays words in the thesaurus that have similar meanings for this word. The list contains synonyms for "wage" used as a noun or as a verb. The first word at the top of each group is the group heading and is closest in meaning. It is preceded by a ◢ collapse symbol, and the word is bold. The ◢ indicates the list of synonyms is displayed. Clicking this button will hide or collapse the list of synonyms. After collapsing a list the ◢ collapse symbol changes to an ▷ expand symbol. Clicking this symbol redisplays the list.

When you point to a word in the list, a drop-down list of two menu options, Insert and Copy, becomes available. The Insert option inserts the word into the active cell. The Copy option is used to copy and then paste the word into any worksheet cell. Clicking a word in the list looks up that word in the thesaurus. You decide to use the word "Pay" and will insert the word into cell A13 in place of "Wage."

2

● Point to "Pay" and click ▼ to display the menu.

● Choose Insert.

● Click ✕ in the title bar of the Thesaurus task pane to close it.

Your screen should be similar to Figure 1.25

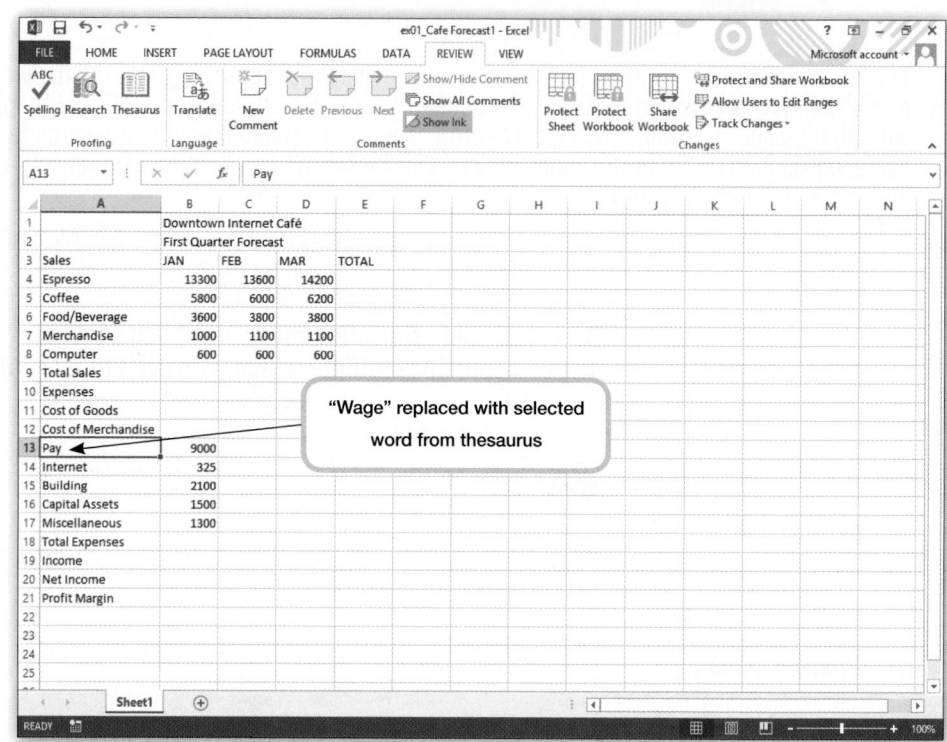

Figure 1.25

The word "Wage" is replaced with the selected word from the thesaurus. Notice the replacement word is capitalized correctly. This is because the replacement text follows the same capitalization as the word it replaces.

Copying and Pasting Cell Contents

Having Trouble?

Refer to the section "Copying and Moving Selections" in the Introduction to Microsoft Office 2013 to review this feature.

Next, you want to enter the estimated expenses for pay, Internet, building, and miscellaneous for February and March. They are the same as the January expense numbers. Because these values are the same, instead of entering the same number repeatedly into each cell you can quickly copy the contents of one cell to another. You also want to move information from one location in the worksheet to another.

COPYING AND PASTING DATA

To use the Copy command, you first select the cell or cells in the source containing the data to be copied. This is called the **copy area**. You will copy the Pay value in cell B13 into cells C13 and D13.

Move to B13.

Open the Home tab.

Click 📋 Copy in the Clipboard group.

Your screen should be similar to Figure 1.26

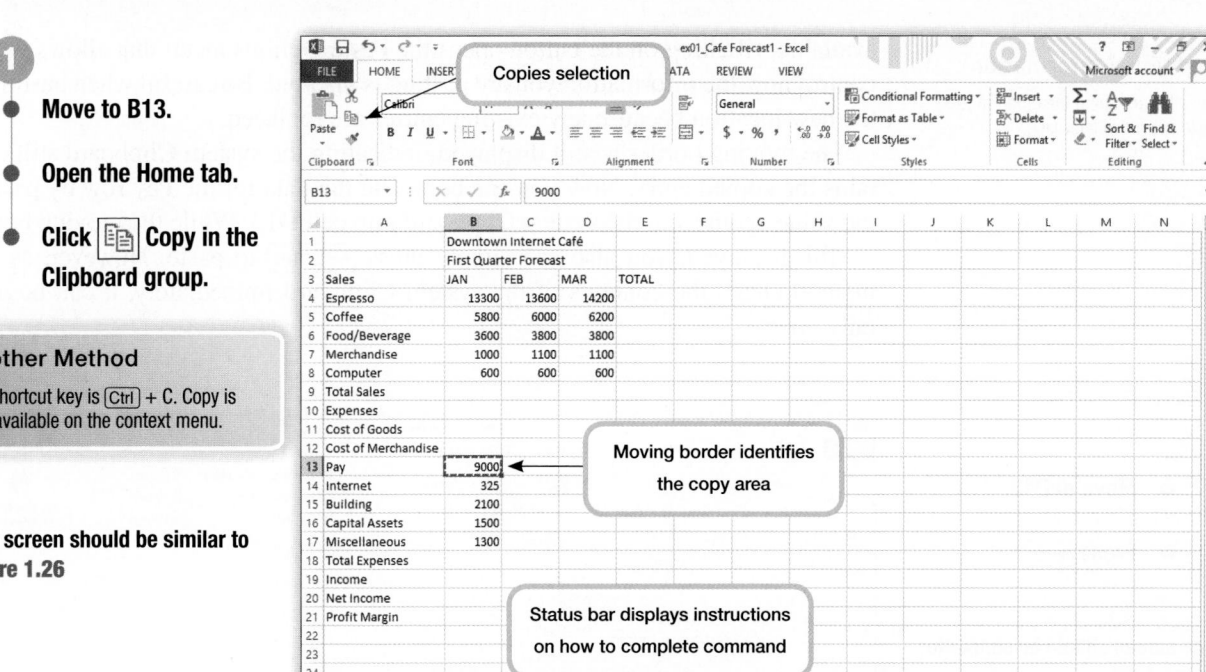

Figure 1.26

A moving border identifies the copy area and indicates that the contents have been copied to the system Clipboard. The instructions displayed in the status bar tell you to select the destination, called the **paste area**, where you want the contents copied. You will copy them to cell C13.

Move to C13.

Click the top part of the 📋 button.
Paste

Your screen should be similar to Figure 1.27

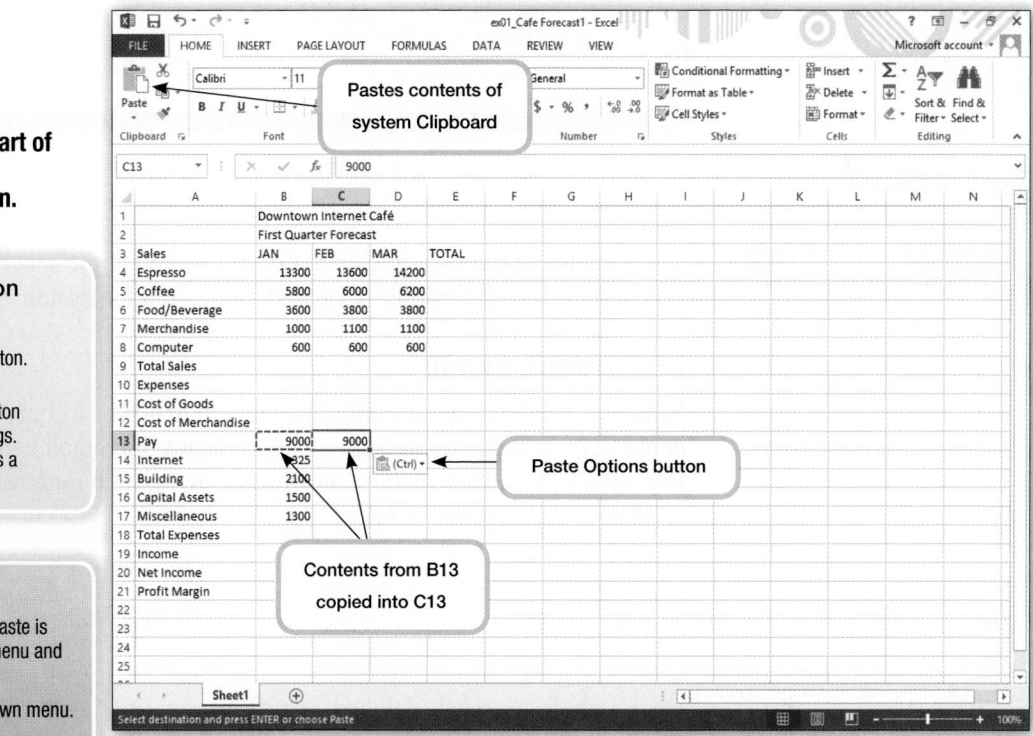

Figure 1.27

The contents of the system Clipboard are inserted at the specified destination location. Each time the Paste command is used, the 📋 (Ctrl) ▾ Paste Options button is

Copying and Pasting Cell Contents   **EX1.29**

available. Clicking on the button opens the Paste Options menu that allows you to control how the information you are pasting is inserted. Be careful when pasting to the new location because any existing entries are replaced.

The moving border is still displayed, indicating the system Clipboard still contains the copied entry. Now you can complete the data for the Pay row by pasting the value again from the system Clipboard into cell D13. While the moving border is still displayed, you also can simply press ←Enter to paste. However, as this method clears the contents of the system Clipboard immediately, it can be used only once.

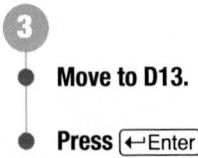

3

● **Move to D13.**

● **Press** ←Enter.

Your screen should be similar to Figure 1.28

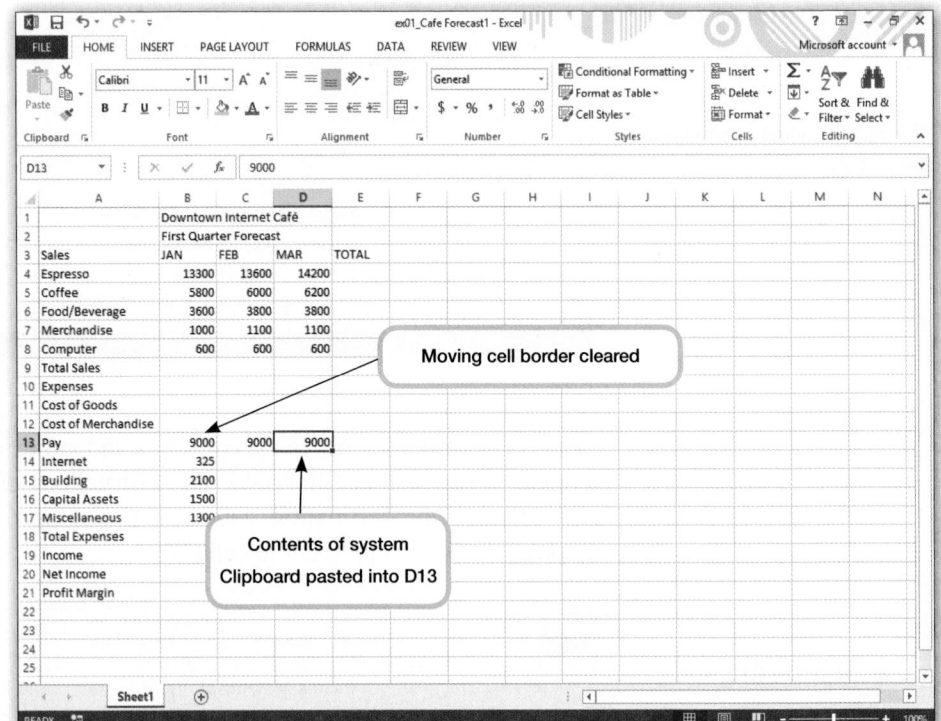

Figure 1.28

The contents of the system Clipboard are inserted at the specified destination location and the moving border is cleared, indicating the system Clipboard is empty.

SELECTING A RANGE

Now you need to copy the Internet value in cell B14 to February and March. You could copy and paste the contents individually into each cell as you did with the Pay values. A quicker method, however, is to select a range and paste the contents to all cells in the range at once.

Concept 6 Range

A selection consisting of two or more cells on a worksheet is a **range**. The cells in a range can be adjacent or nonadjacent. An **adjacent range** is a rectangular block of adjoining cells. A **nonadjacent range** consists of two or more selected cells or ranges that are not adjoining. In the example shown below, the shaded areas show valid adjacent and nonadjacent ranges. A **range reference** identifies the cells in a range. A colon is used to separate the first and last cells of an adjacent range reference. For example, A2:C4 indicates the range consists of cells A2 through C4. Commas separate the cell references of a nonadjacent range. For example, A10, B12, C14 indicates the range consists of cells A10, B12, and C14 of a nonadjacent range.

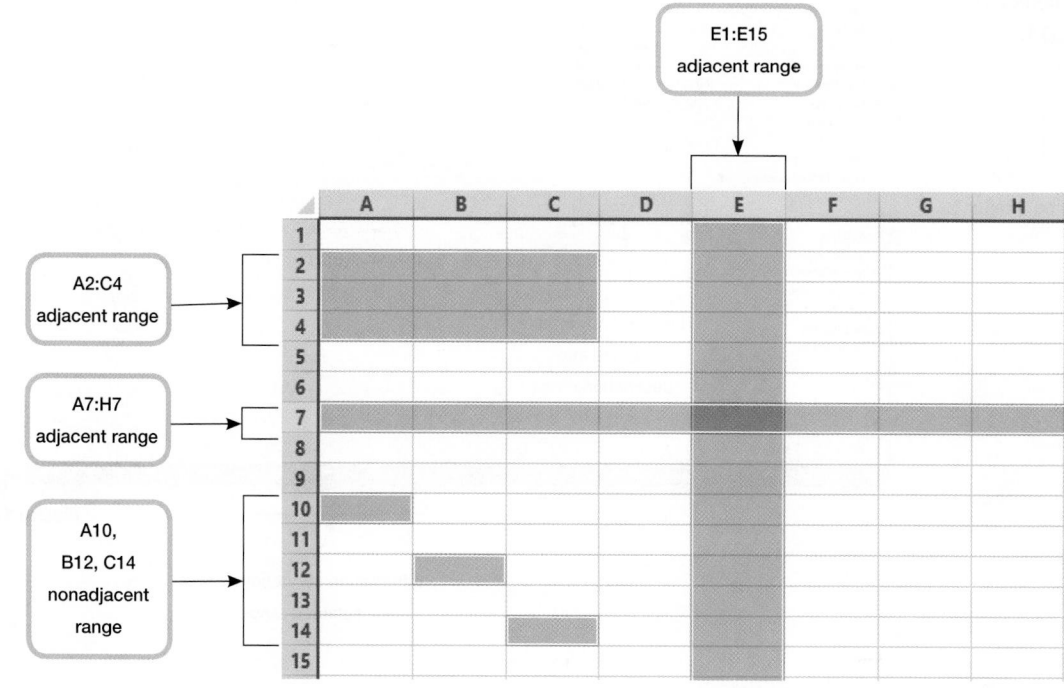

Additional Information

Selecting a range identifies the cells to be included in the selection, rather than the specific text within the cells.

You can select a range using the mouse procedures shown in the following table. You also can select using the keyboard by moving to the first cell of the range, holding down ⇧Shift or pressing F8 and using the navigational keys to expand the highlight. Using the F8 key turns on and off Extend mode. When this mode is on, Extend Selection appears in the status bar.

Touch Tip

To select a range on a touch screen, tap a cell and drag the selection handle to the extent of the range you want.

To Select	Mouse
A range	Click first cell of range and drag to the last cell.
A large range	Click first cell of range, hold down ⇧Shift, and click last cell of range.
All cells on worksheet	Click the ◣ All button located at the intersection of the row and column headings.
Nonadjacent cells or ranges	Select first cell or range, hold down Ctrl while selecting the other cell or range.
Entire row or column	Click the row number or column letter heading.
Adjacent rows or columns	Drag across the row number or column letter headings.
Nonadjacent rows or columns	Select first row or column, hold down Ctrl, and select the other rows or columns.

To complete the data for the Internet row, you want to copy the value in cell B14 to the system Clipboard and then copy the system Clipboard contents to the adjacent range of cells C14 through D14.

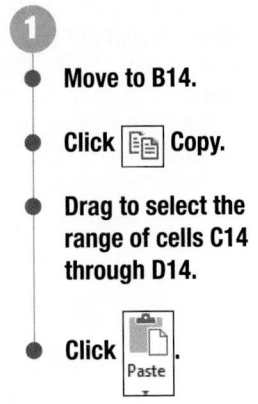

Move to B14.

Click 📋 Copy.

Drag to select the range of cells C14 through D14.

Click 📋 Paste.

Your screen should be similar to Figure 1.29

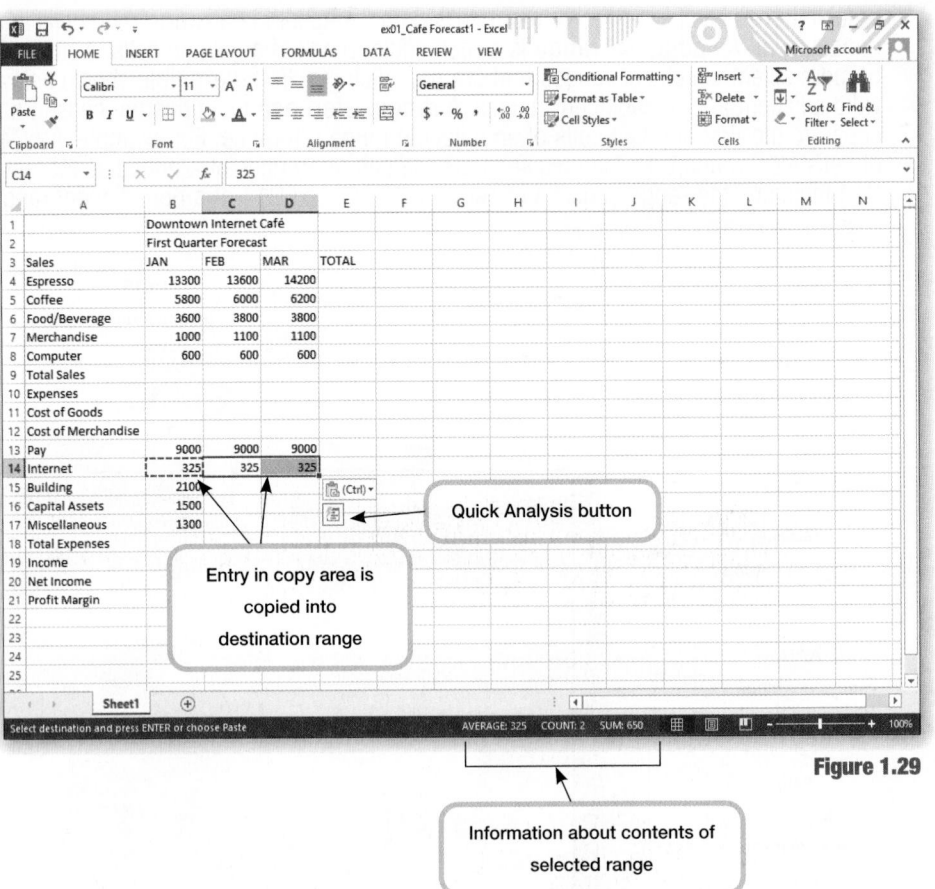

Figure 1.29

Quick Analysis button

Entry in copy area is copied into destination range

Information about contents of selected range

The destination range is highlighted and identified by a dark border surrounding the selected cells. The source entry was copied from cell B14 and pasted into the selected destination range. In addition to the ▼ Paste Options button, the 📋 Quick Analysis button is displayed. This button appears whenever a range is selected that contains data that can be formatted or analyzed. You will learn about this feature shortly. Also notice the status bar now displays the average, count, and sum of values in the selected range.

USING THE FILL HANDLE

Next, you will copy the January Building expenses to cells C15 through D15, the Capital Assets expenses to cells C16 through D16, and the Miscellaneous expenses to cells C17 through D17. You can copy all values at the same time across the row by first specifying a range as the source. Another way to copy is to select the cells that contain the data you want to copy and drag the **fill handle**, the green box in the lower-right corner of a selection across or down the cells you want to fill.

1

- Press Esc to clear the moving border.

- Drag to select cells B15 through B17.

- Point to the fill handle and when the mouse pointer is a +, drag the mouse to extend the selection to cells D15 through D17.

- Release the mouse button.

Your screen should be similar to Figure 1.30

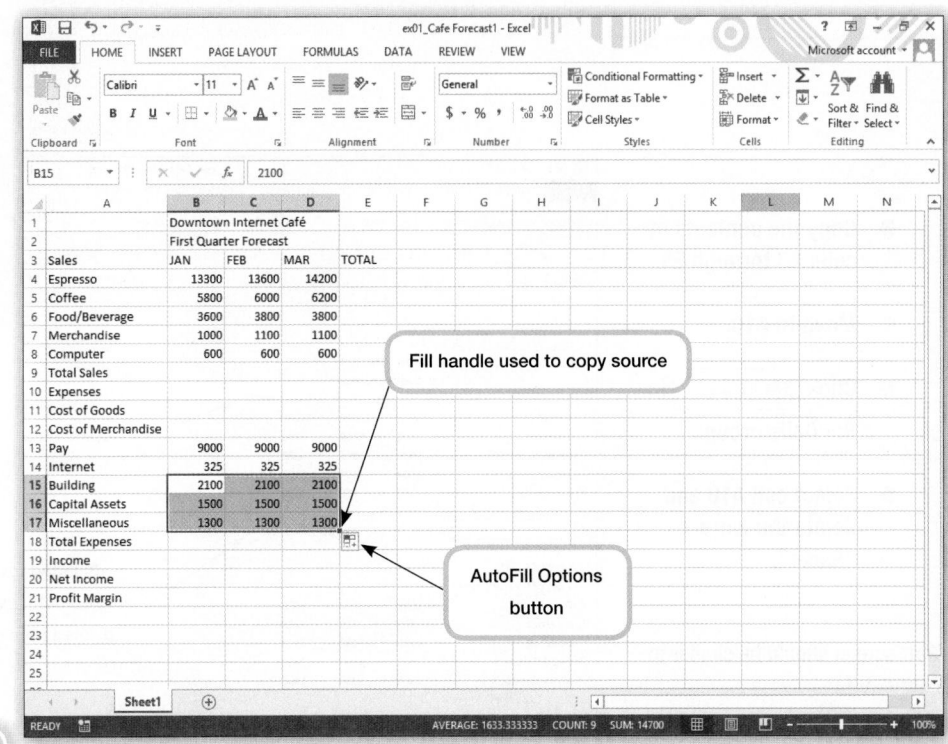

Figure 1.30

The range of cells to the right of the source is filled with the same values as in the source range. Using this method does not copy the source to the system Clipboard and therefore you cannot paste the source multiple times. When you copy by dragging the fill handle, the [⬛▾] AutoFill Options button appears. Its menu commands are used to modify how the fill operation was performed. It will disappear as soon as you make an entry in the worksheet.

INSERTING COPIED CELL CONTENT

You also decide to include another row of month headings above the expenses to make the worksheet data easier to read. To do this quickly, you can insert copied data between existing data. To indicate where to place the copied content, you move the cell selector to the upper-left cell of the area where you want the selection inserted.

The column headings you want to copy are in cells B3 through E3. You will also copy cell A3, and clear the text in column A of the new row when you paste the contents.

1

- Copy the contents of cells A3 through E3.

- Move to A10.

- Click [Insert ▾] in the Cells group.

- Select cell A10 and delete the word "Sales".

Your screen should be similar to Figure 1.31

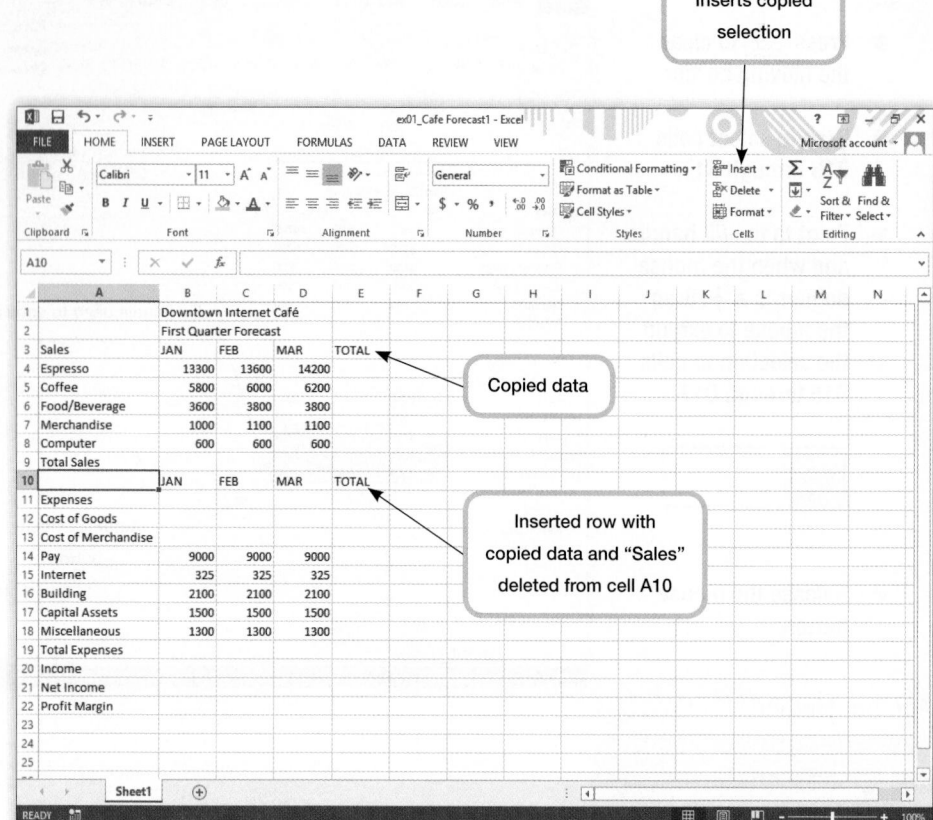

Copied data

Inserted row with copied data and "Sales" deleted from cell A10

Figure 1.31

Additional Information

You also can insert cut selections between existing cells by choosing Insert Cut Cells from the

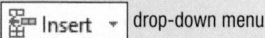 drop-down menu.

The copied data is inserted into the existing row (10) and all entries below are moved down one row.

CUTTING AND PASTING DATA

Next, you decide the Income, Net Income, and Profit Margin rows of data would stand out more if a blank row separated them from the expenses. Also, the Profit Margin row of data would be better separated from the Net Income row by a blank row. You will first remove the cell contents of the three cells using ✂ Cut and then paste the contents from the system Clipboard into the new location. The pasted content will copy over any existing content. You will use the keyboard shortcuts for these commands to complete this process.

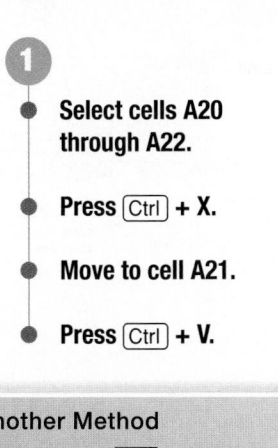

1

- Select cells A20 through A22.

- Press Ctrl + X.

- Move to cell A21.

- Press Ctrl + V.

Another Method

You also can click  Cut followed by in the Clipboard group. These commands are also available on the shortcut menu.

Your screen should be similar to **Figure 1.32**

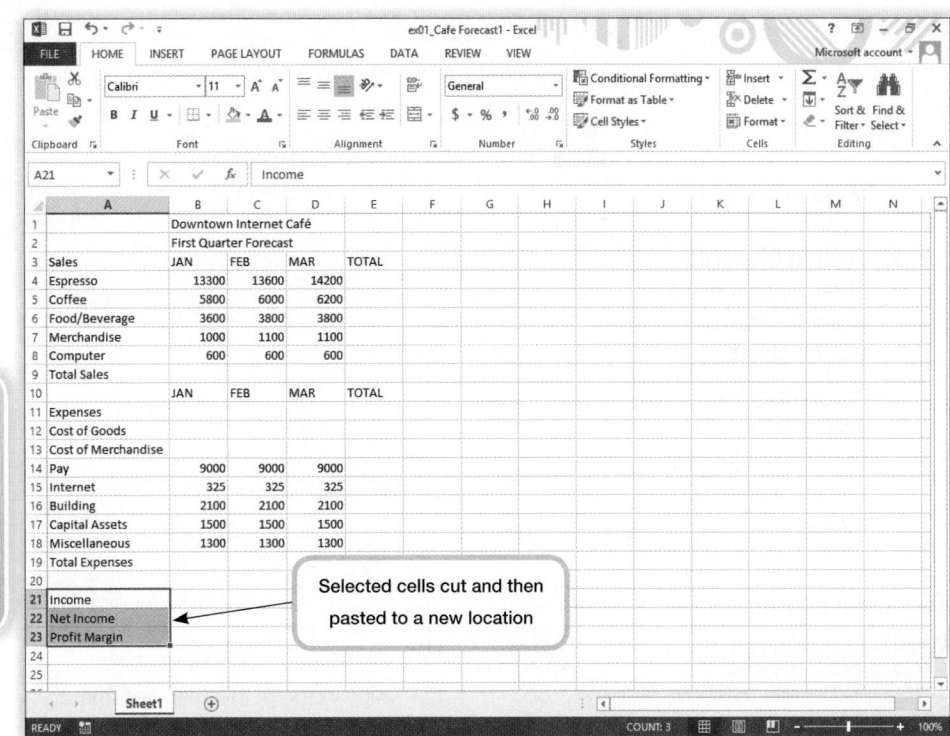

Figure 1.32

The contents of the three selected cells are copied to the system Clipboard. Then, when you paste, the cell contents are removed and inserted at the new location, copying over any existing content.

Another way you can cut and paste is to use drag and drop to move the cell contents. This method is quickest and most useful when the distance between cells is short and they are visible within the window, whereas cut and paste is best for long-distance moves. You will use this method to move the Profit Margin entry down one cell.

Additional Information

You also can hold down Ctrl and drag a selection to copy it to a new location. The mouse pointer appears as you drag when copying.

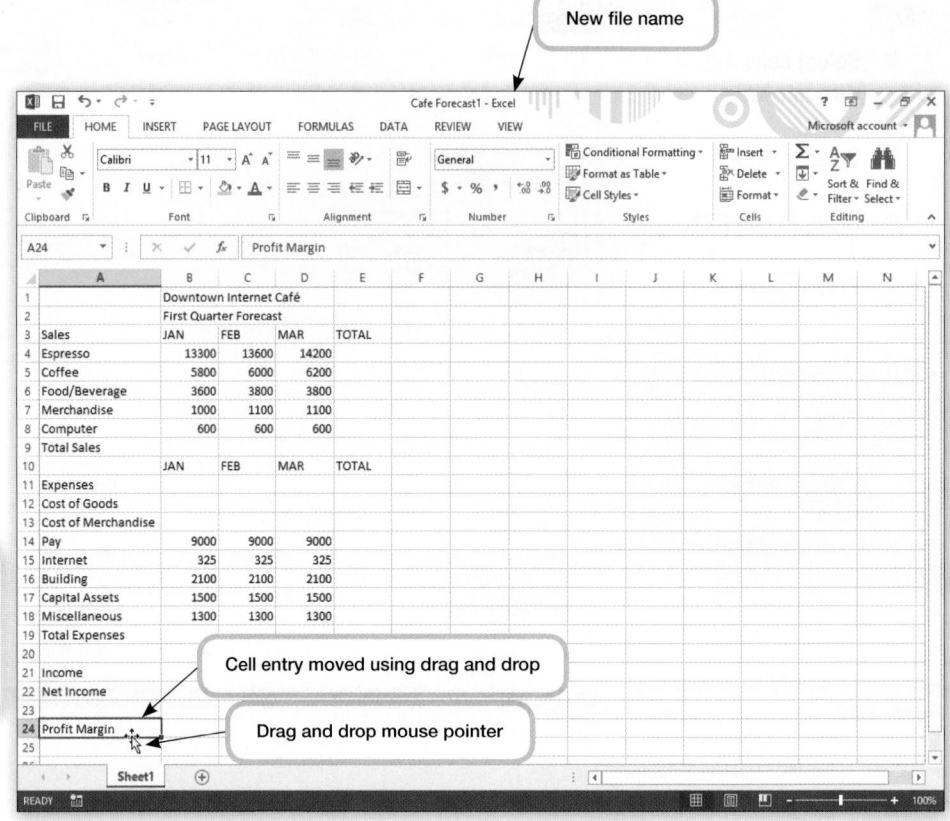

New file name

Figure 1.33

Step 2

Move to cell A23.

Point to the border of the selection and when the mouse pointer shape is ✛⇖, drag the selection down one row to cell A24 and release the mouse button.

Additional Information

As you drag, an outline of the cell selection appears and the mouse pointer displays the cell reference to show its new location in the worksheet.

Open the File tab and choose Save As.

Save the changes you have made to the workbook as Cafe Forecast1 to your solution file location.

Your screen should be similar to Figure 1.33

The cell contents were moved into cell A24 and cleared from the original cell.

When you use the Copy and Cut commands, the contents are copied to the system Clipboard and can be copied to any location in the worksheet, another workbook, or a document in another application multiple times. When you use ⬇ Fill or drag the fill handle, the destination must be in the same row or column as the source, and the source is not copied to the system Clipboard. Dragging the cell border to move or copy also does not copy the source to the system Clipboard.

NOTE If you are running short on lab time, this is an appropriate place to end your session. When you begin again, open the file Cafe Forecast1.

Working with Formulas

The remaining entries that need to be made in the worksheet are formula entries.

Concept 7 Formula

A **formula** is an equation that performs a calculation on data contained in a worksheet. A formula always begins with an equal sign (=) and uses arithmetic operators. An **operator** is a symbol that specifies the type of numeric operation to perform. Excel includes the following operators: + (addition), − (subtraction), / (division), * (multiplication), % (percent), and ^ (exponentiation). The calculated result from a formula is a **variable** value because it can change if the data it depends on changes. In contrast, a number entry is a **constant** value. It does not begin with an equal sign and does not change unless you change it directly by typing in another entry.

In a formula that contains more than one operator, Excel calculates the formula from left to right and performs the calculation in the following order: percent, exponentiation, multiplication and division, and addition and subtraction (see Example A). This is the **order of operations, that determines which operations take precedence before other operations**. If a formula contains operators with the same precedence (for example, addition and subtraction), they are again evaluated from left to right. The order of precedence can be overridden by enclosing the operation you want performed first in parentheses (see Example B). When there are multiple sets of parentheses, Excel evaluates them working from the innermost set of parentheses out.

Example A: =5*4−3   Result is 17 (5 times 4 to get 20, and then subtract 3 for a total of 17)
Example B: =5*(4−3)   Result is 5 (4 minus 3 to get 1, and then 1 times 5 for a total of 5)

The values on which a numeric formula performs a calculation are called **operands**. Numbers or cell references can be operands in a formula. Usually cell references are used, and when the numeric entries in the referenced cell(s) change, the result of the formula is automatically recalculated.

ENTERING FORMULAS

The first formula you will enter will calculate the total Espresso sales for January through March (cell E4) by summing the numbers in cells B4 through D4. You will use cell references in the formula as the operands and the + arithmetic operator to specify addition. A formula is entered in the cell where you want the calculated value to be displayed. As you enter the formula, Excel helps you keep track of the cell references by identifying the referenced cell with a colored border and using the same color for the cell reference in the formula.

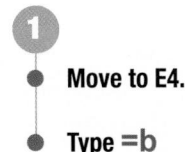

1
● Move to E4.

● Type =b

Your screen should be similar to Figure 1.34

Figure 1.34

A drop-down list of function names that begin with the letter "b" is displayed. Functions are a type of formula entry that you will learn about shortly.

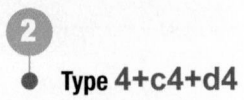

2

● Type **4+c4+d4**

Additional Information

Cell references can be typed in either uppercase or lowercase letters. Spaces between parts of the formula are optional.

Your screen should be similar to Figure 1.35

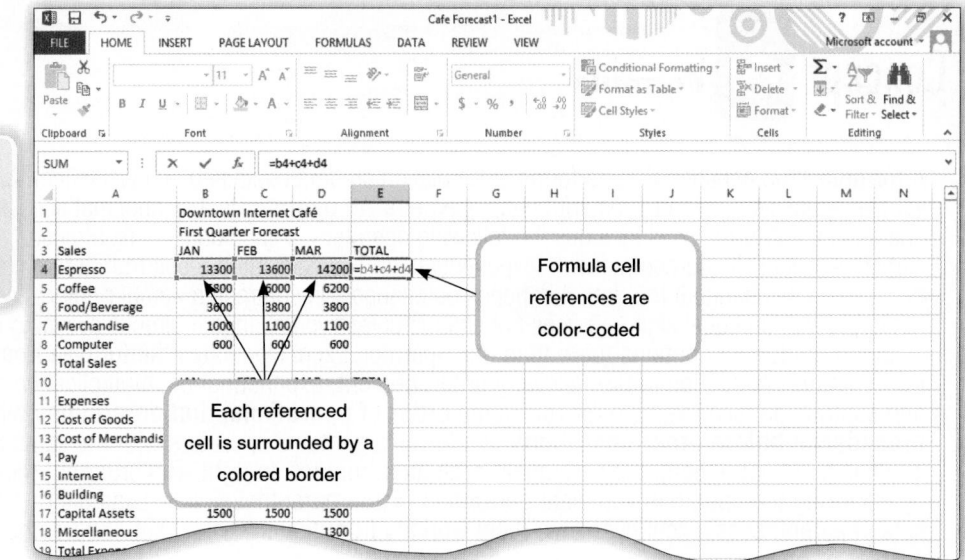

Figure 1.35

As you enter the formula, each cell that is referenced in the formula is surrounded by a colored box that matches the color of the cell reference in the formula.

3

● Press ⌃Ctrl + ←Enter or click ✓ **Enter** in the formula bar.

Your screen should be similar to Figure 1.36

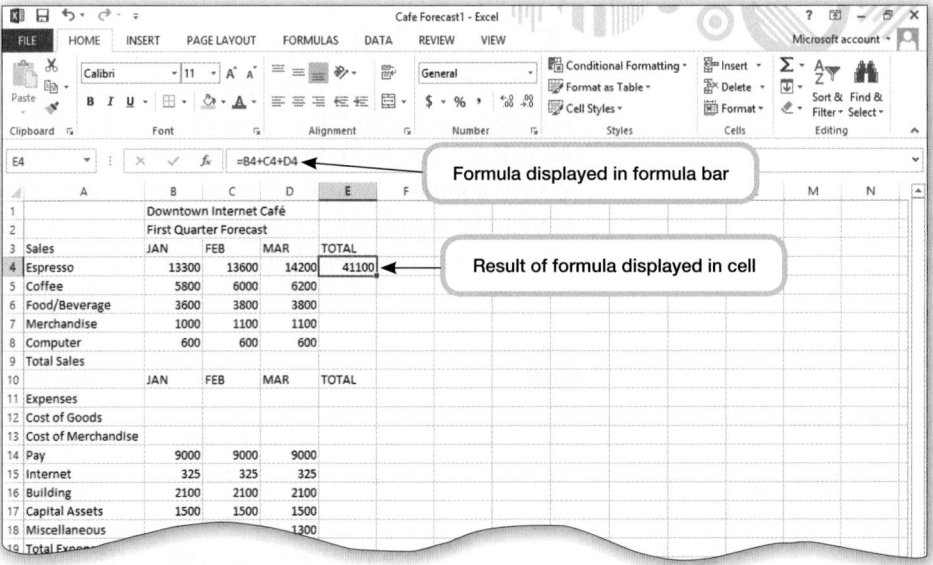

Figure 1.36

The number 41100 is displayed in cell E4, and the formula that calculates this value is displayed in the formula bar.

COPYING FORMULAS WITH RELATIVE REFERENCES

The formulas to calculate the total sales for rows 5 through 8 can be entered next. Just as you can with text and numeric entries, you can copy formulas from one cell to another.

1

- Copy the formula in cell E4 to cells E5 through E8 using any of the copying methods.

- Move to E5.

- If necessary, press Esc to clear the moving border.

Your screen should be similar to Figure 1.37

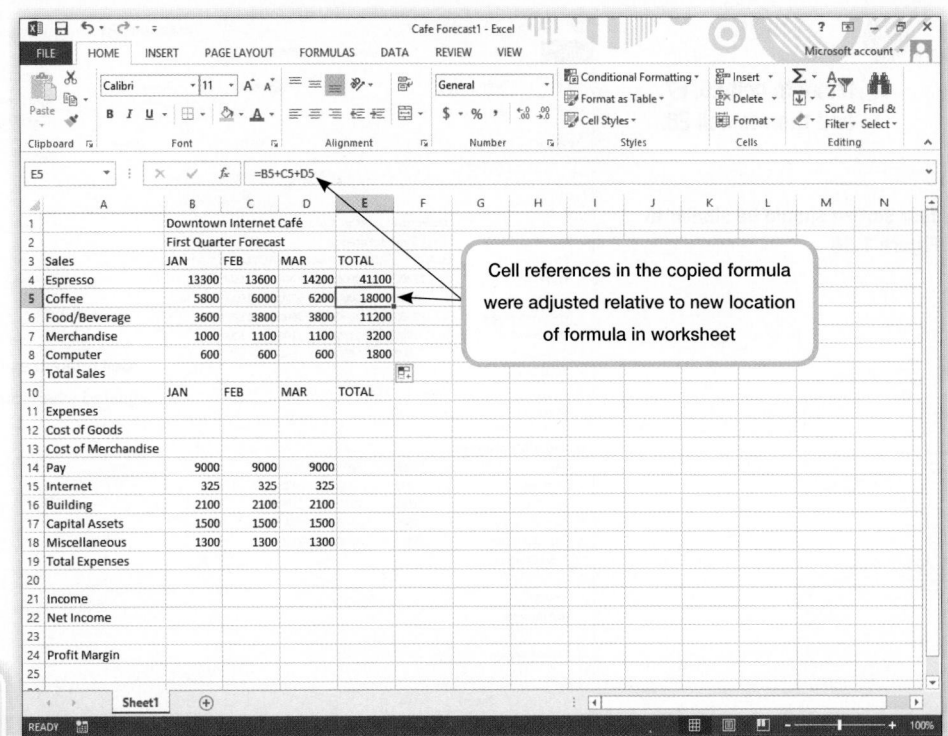

Cell references in the copied formula were adjusted relative to new location of formula in worksheet

Figure 1.37

The calculated result, 18000, is displayed in the cell. The formula displayed in the formula bar is =B5+C5+D5. The formula to calculate the Coffee total sales is not an exact duplicate of the formula used to calculate the Espresso total sales (=B4+C4+D4). Instead, the cells referenced in the formula have been changed to reflect the new location of the formula in row 5. This is because the references in the formula are relative references.

Concept 8 Relative Reference

A **relative reference** is a cell or range reference in a formula whose location is interpreted by Excel in relation to the position of the cell that contains the formula. When a formula is copied, the referenced cells in the formula automatically adjust to reflect the new worksheet location. The relative relationship between the referenced cell and the new location is maintained. Because relative references automatically adjust for the new location, the relative references in a copied formula refer to different cells than the references in the original formula. The relationship between cells in both the copied and the pasted formulas is the same although the cell references are different.

For example, in the figure here, cell A1 references the value in cell A4 (in this case, 10). If the formula in A1 is copied to B2, the reference for B2 is adjusted to the value in cell B5 (in this case, 20).

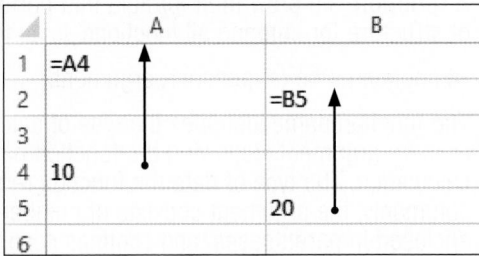

Move to cell E6, E7, and then to cell E8.

Your screen should be similar to Figure 1.38

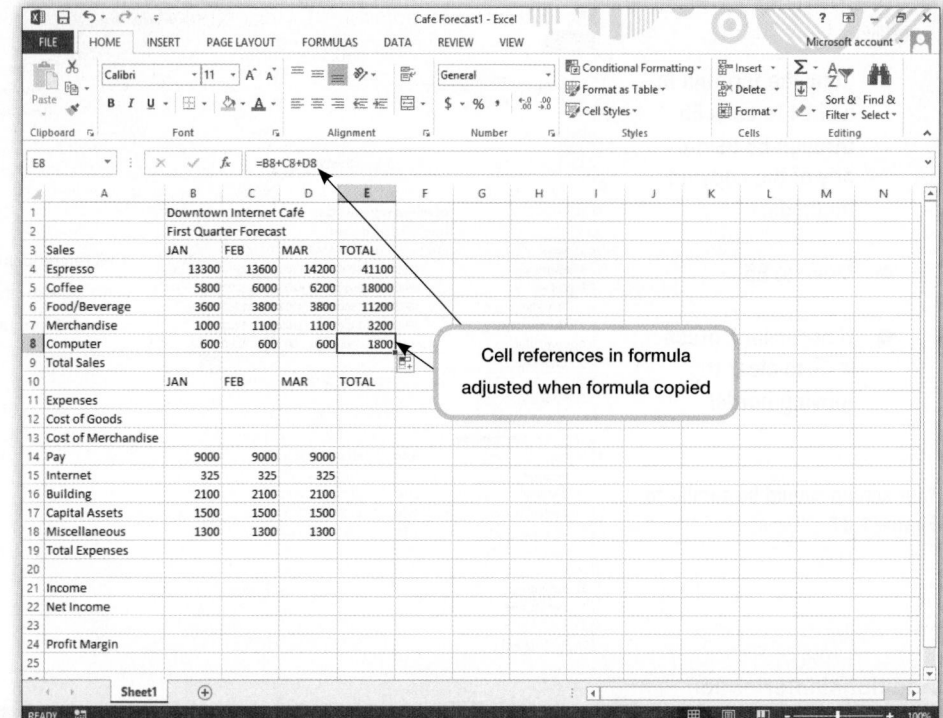

The callout in the figure reads: "Cell references in formula adjusted when formula copied"

The formula bar shows: =B8+C8+D8

Figure 1.38

The formulas in these cells also have changed to reflect the new row location and to appropriately calculate the total based on the sales.

SUMMARIZING DATA

Next, you will calculate the monthly total sales. The formula to calculate the total sales for January needs to be entered in cell B9 and copied across the row. You could use a formula similar to the formula used to calculate the category sales in column E. The formula would be =B4+B5+B6+B7+B8. However, it is faster and more accurate to use a function.

Concept ⑨ Function

A **function** is a prewritten formula that performs certain types of calculations automatically. The **syntax,** or rules of structure for entering all functions, is as follows:

=Function name (argument1, argument2, . . .)

The function name identifies the type of calculation to be performed. Most functions require that you enter one or more arguments following the function name. An **argument** is the data the function uses to perform the calculation. The type of data the function requires depends upon the type of calculation being performed. Most commonly, the argument consists of numbers or references to cells that contain numbers. The argument is enclosed in parentheses, and commas separate multiple arguments. The beginning and ending cells of a range are separated with a colon.

Some functions, such as several of the date and time functions, do not require an argument. However, you still need to enter the opening and closing parentheses; for example, =NOW(). If a function starts the formula, enter an equal sign before the function name; for example, =SUM(D5:F5)/25.

Excel includes several hundred functions divided into 11 categories. Some common functions from each category and the results they calculate are shown in the following table.

Category	Function	Calculates
Financial	PMT	Calculates the payment for a loan based on constant payments and a constant interest rate.
	PV	Returns the present value of an investment—the total amount that a series of future payments is worth now.
	FV	Returns the future value of an investment—the total amount that a series of payments will be worth.
Date & Time	TODAY	Returns the serial number that represents today's date.
	DATE	Returns the serial number of a particular date.
	NOW	Returns the serial number of the current date and time.
Math & Trig	SUM	Adds all the numbers in a range of cells.
	ABS	Returns the absolute value of a number (a number without its sign).
Statistical	AVERAGE	Returns the average (arithmetic mean) of its arguments.
	MAX	Returns the largest value in a set of values; ignores logical values and text.
	MIN	Returns the smallest value in a set of values; ignores logical values and text.
	COUNT	Counts the number of cells in a range that contain numbers.
	COUNTA	Counts the number of cells in a range that are not empty.
Lookup & Reference	COLUMNS	Returns the number of columns in an array or reference.
	HLOOKUP	Looks for a value in the top row of a table and returns the value in the same column from a row you specify.
	VLOOKUP	Looks for a value in the leftmost column of a table and returns the value in the same row from a column you specify.
Database	DSUM	Adds the numbers in the field (column) or records in the database that match the conditions you specify.
	DAVERAGE	Averages the values in a column in a list or database that match conditions you specify.
Text	PROPER	Converts text to proper case in which the first letter of each word is capitalized.
	UPPER	Converts text to uppercase.
	LOWER	Converts text to lowercase.
	SUBSTITUTE	Replaces existing text with new text in a text string.
Logical	IF	Returns one value if a condition you specify evaluates to TRUE and another value if it evaluates to FALSE.
	AND	Returns TRUE if all its arguments are TRUE; returns FALSE if any arguments are FALSE.
	OR	Returns TRUE if any arguments are TRUE; returns FALSE if all arguments are FALSE.
	NOT	Changes FALSE to TRUE or TRUE to FALSE.
	IFERROR	Returns value-if-error if expression is an error and the value of the expression itself otherwise.
Information	ISLOGICAL	Returns TRUE if value is a logical value, either TRUE or FALSE.
	ISREF	Returns TRUE if value is a reference.
Engineering	BIN2DEC	Converts a binary number to decimal.
	CONVERT	Converts a number from one measurement system to another.
Cube	CUBESETCOUNT	Returns the number of items in a set.

You will use the SUM function to calculate the total sales for January. Because the SUM function is the most commonly used function, it has its own command button.

Move to B9.

Click Σ ▾ Sum in the Editing group.

Your screen should be similar to Figure 1.39

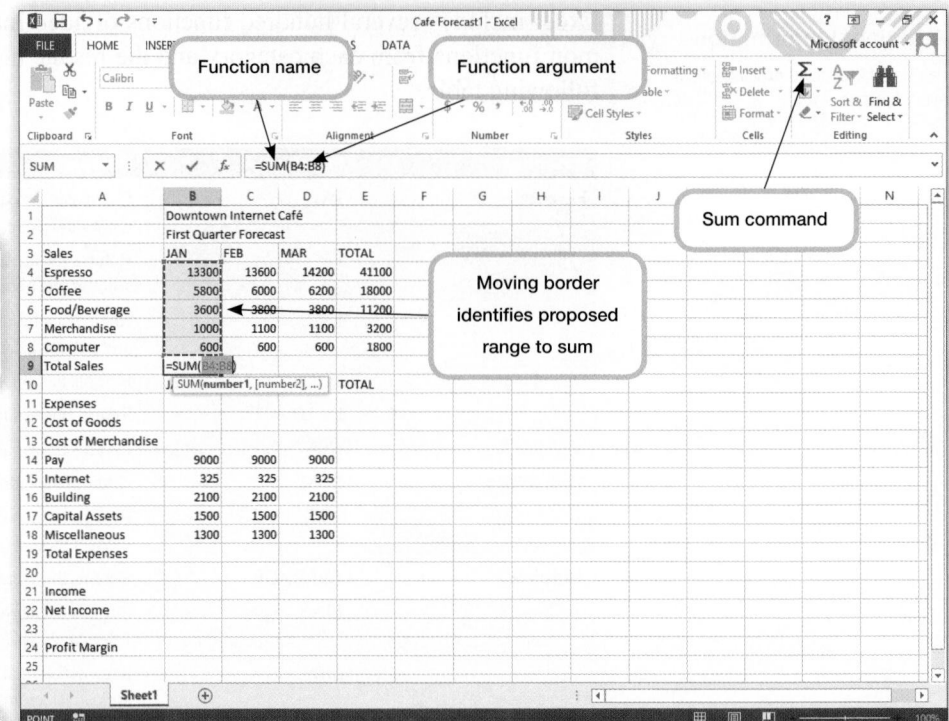

Figure 1.39

Excel automatically proposes a range based upon the data above or to the left of the active cell. The formula bar displays the name of the function followed by the range argument enclosed in parentheses. You will accept the proposed range and enter the function.

Click ✓ Enter.

Your screen should be similar to Figure 1.40

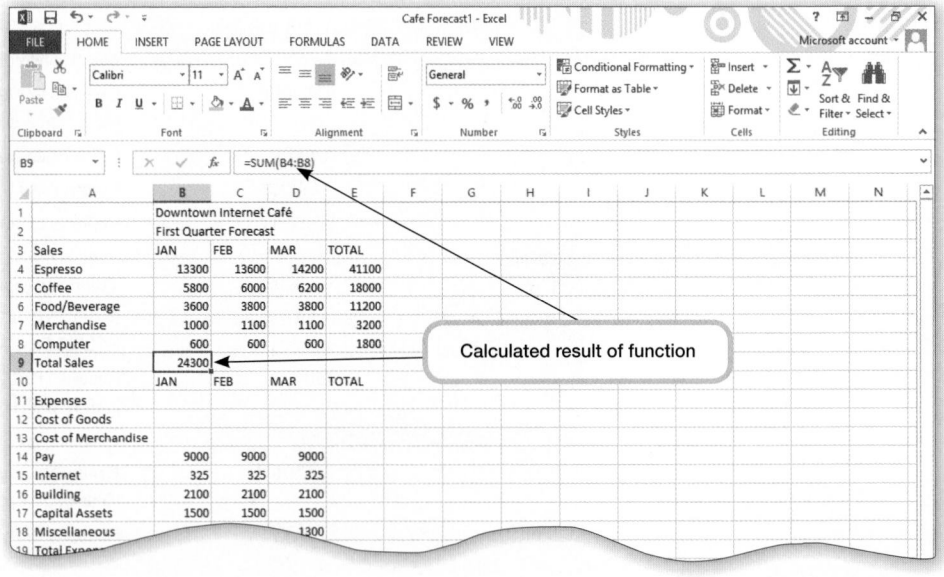

Figure 1.40

The result, 24300, calculated by the SUM function is displayed in cell B9.

USING THE QUICK ANALYSIS TOOL

Next, you need to calculate the total sales for February and March and the Total column. You will use the **Quick Analysis tool** to insert the SUM function for this range. The 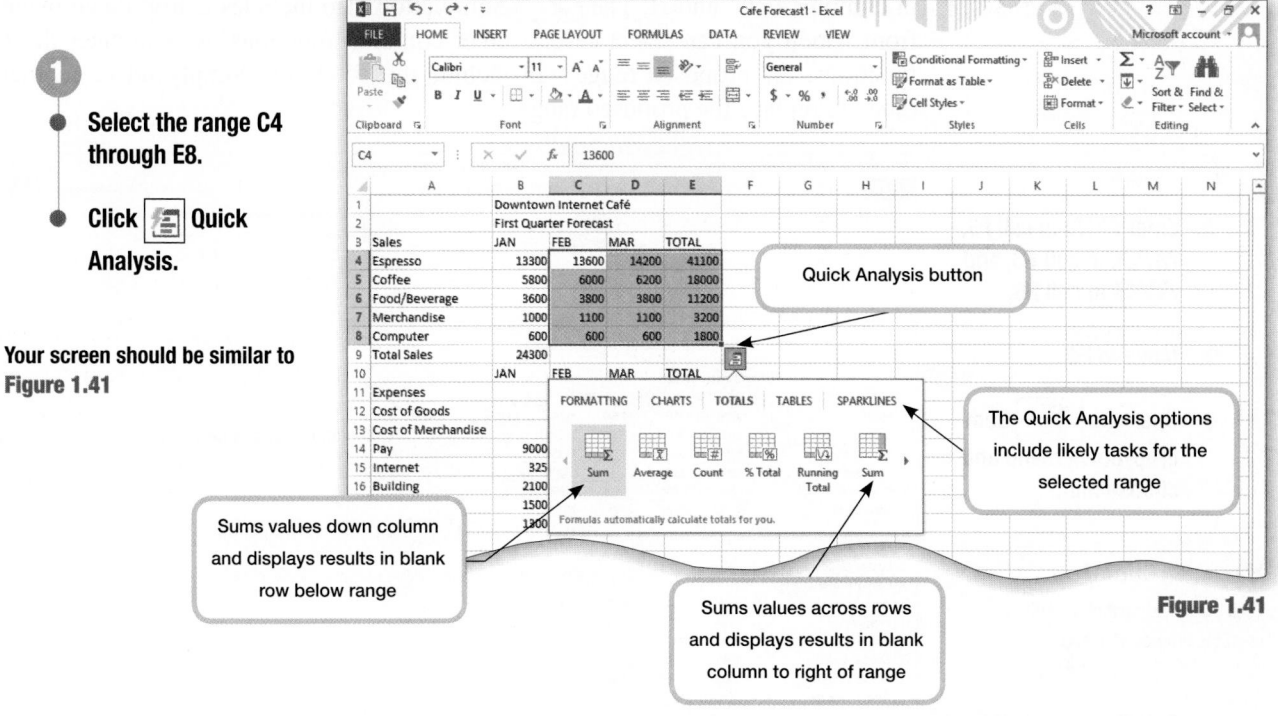 Quick Analysis button appears in the bottom-right corner of the selection when you select a range of cells for which there are several likely actions.

1

- Select the range C4 through E8.

- Click Quick Analysis.

Your screen should be similar to Figure 1.41

Quick Analysis button

FORMATTING CHARTS TOTALS TABLES SPARKLINES

The Quick Analysis options include likely tasks for the selected range

Sum Average Count % Total Running Total Sum

Formulas automatically calculate totals for you.

Sums values down column and displays results in blank row below range

Sums values across rows and displays results in blank column to right of range

Figure 1.41

The Quick Analysis gallery displays five tabs. Each tab contains several options for the most likely action suited to the selected data. Pointing to an option displays a preview of the results in the worksheet.

2

- Click the Totals tab.

- Point at 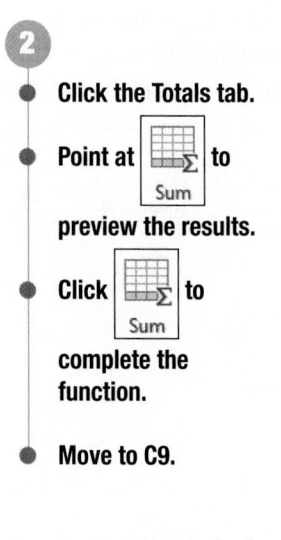 to preview the results.

- Click to complete the function.

- Move to C9.

Your screen should be similar to Figure 1.42

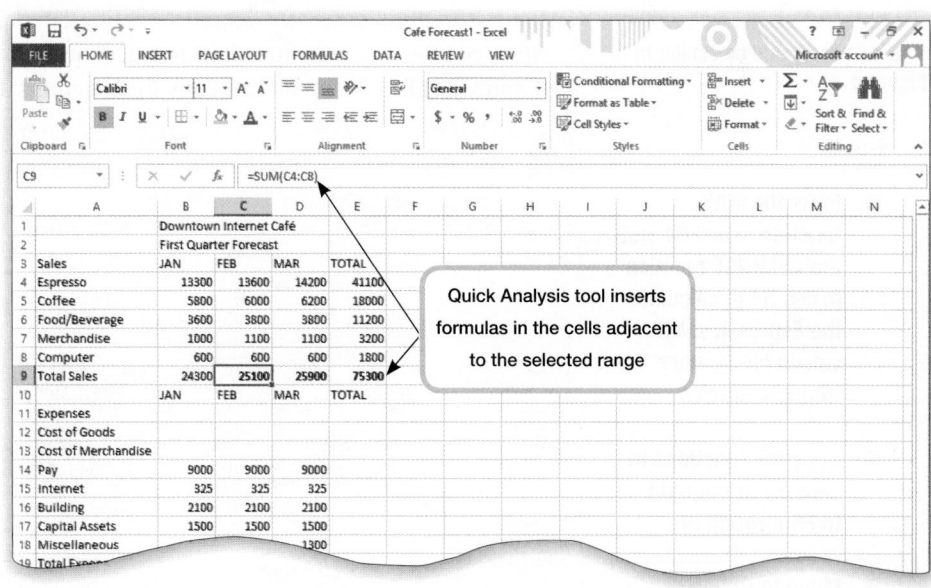

Quick Analysis tool inserts formulas in the cells adjacent to the selected range

Figure 1.42

The results calculated by the SUM function are displayed in bold in the blank row (9) below the range. You will adjust the display of these values shortly. The Totals functions in the Quick Analysis tool can be used only when the range to be calculated is adjacent to the range where the function will be entered.

USING THE MIN, MAX, AND AVERAGE FUNCTIONS

You also decide to calculate the minimum, maximum, and average sales for each sales category. You will add appropriate column headings and enter the functions in columns F, G, and H. The Σ Sum button also includes a drop-down menu from which you can select several other common functions. As you enter these functions, the proposed range will include the Total cell. Simply select another range to replace the proposed range.

1

- Enter **MIN** in cell F3, **MAX** in cell G3, and **AVG** in cell H3.

- Move to F4.

- Open the Σ Sum drop-down menu and choose Min.

Having Trouble?

Click ▼ to the right of the button to open the drop-down menu.

- Select the range B4 through D4 to specify the January through March sales values and click ✓ Enter.

Your screen should be similar to Figure 1.43

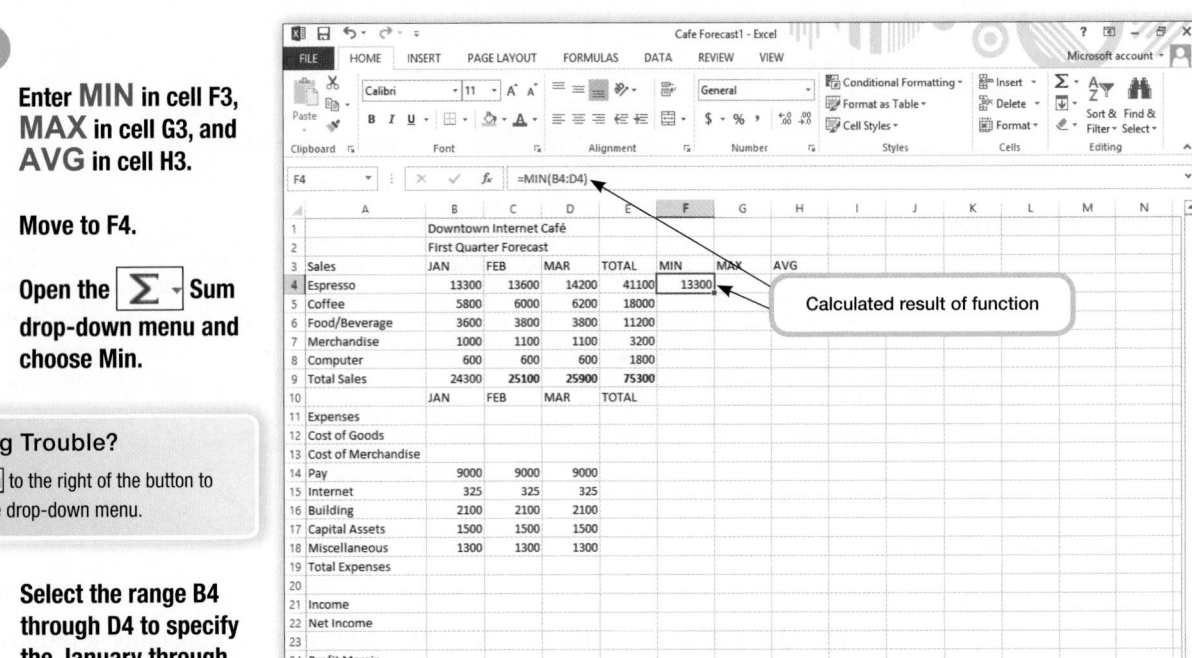

Calculated result of function

Figure 1.43

The MIN function correctly displays 13300, the smallest value in the range.

Next, you will enter the functions to calculate the maximum and average values for the Espresso sales. Then you will copy the functions down the column through row 8.

2

- Enter the MAX function in cell G4 and the AVERAGE function in cell H4 to calculate the Espresso sales values for January through March.

- Copy the functions in cells F4 through H4 to F5 through H8.

- Move to H8.

Your screen should be similar to Figure 1.44

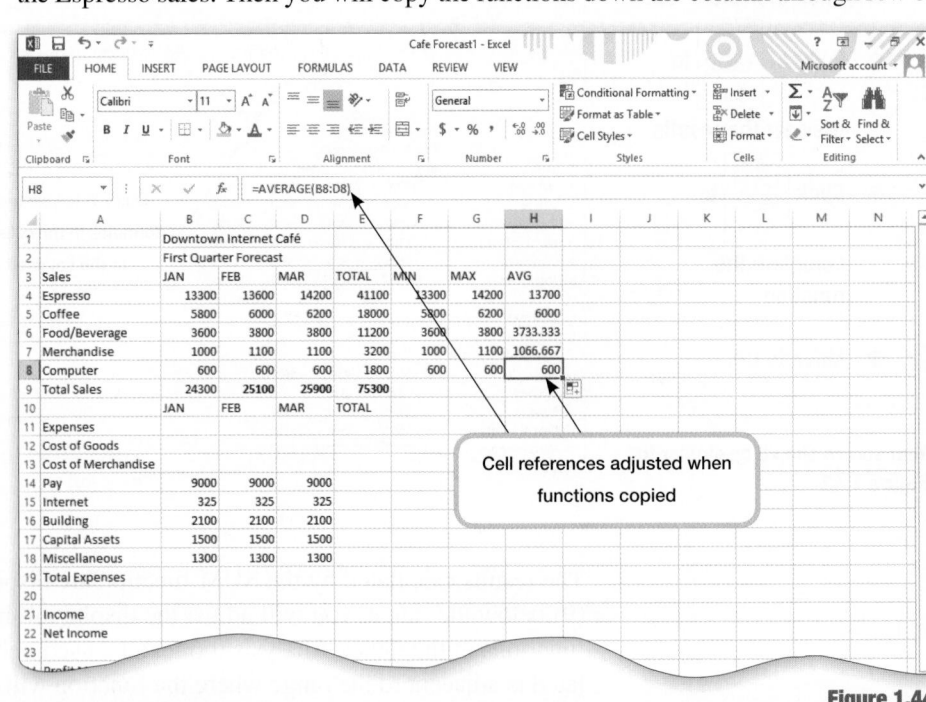

Cell references adjusted when functions copied

Figure 1.44

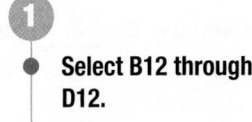

Additional Information

The Quick Analysis tool does not include the MIN or MAX functions.

The minimum, maximum, and average values for the five sales categories have been calculated. The Average column displays as many decimal places as cell space allows.

USING POINTING TO ENTER A FORMULA

Next, you will enter the formula to calculate the cost of goods for espresso, coffee, and food and beverages sold. These numbers are estimated by using a formula to calculate the number as a percentage of sales. Evan suggested using estimated percents for this worksheet so he could get an idea of what to expect from the first three months after the remodel. He wants you to calculate espresso expenses at 25 percent of espresso sales, coffee expenses at 30 percent of coffee sales, and food and beverage expenses at 60 percent of food sales.

Rather than typing in the cell references for the formula, you will enter them by selecting the worksheet cells. In addition, to simplify the process of entering and copying entries, you can enter data into the first cell of a range and have it copied to all other cells in the range at the same time by using ⌐Ctrl⌐ + ⌐←Enter⌐ to complete the entry. You will use this feature to enter the formulas to calculate the beverage expenses for January through March. This formula needs to calculate the beverage cost of goods at 25 percent first and add it to the food cost of goods calculated at 50 percent.

1

- **Select B12 through D12.**

- **Type =**

- **Click cell B4.**

Additional Information

Even when a range is selected, you can still point to specify cells in the formula. You also can use the direction keys to move to the cell.

Your screen should be similar to Figure 1.45

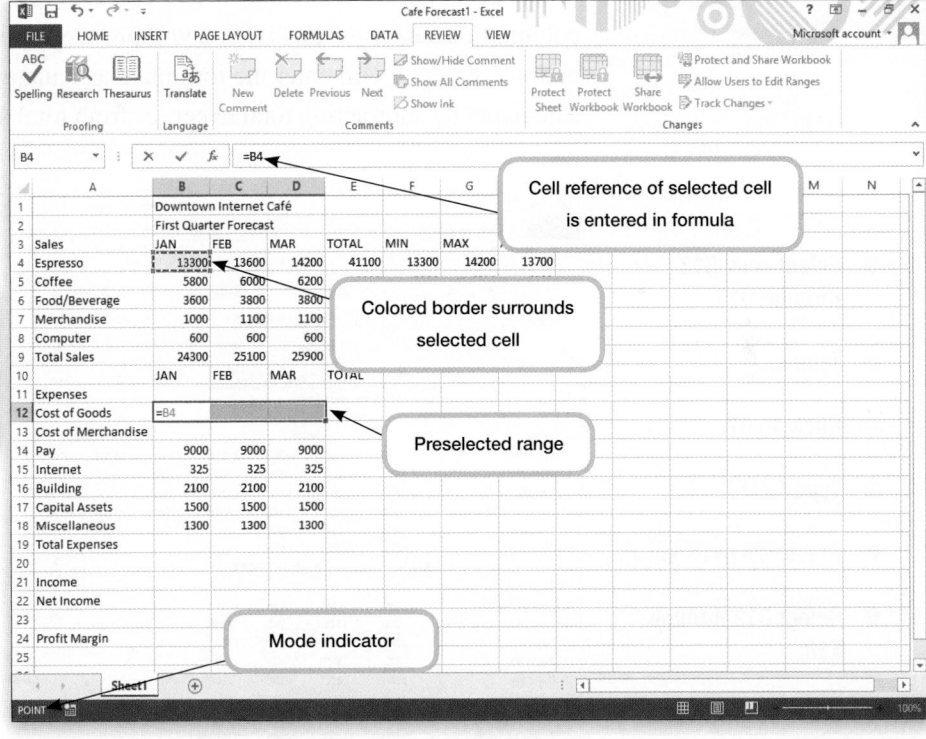

Figure 1.45

Additional Information

While entering the formula in Point mode, if you make an error, edit the entry like any other error and then continue entering the remainder of the formula.

Notice that the status bar displays the current mode as Point. This tells you that the program is allowing you to select cells by highlighting them. The cell reference, B4, is entered following the equal sign. You will complete the formula by entering the percentage value to multiply by and adding the Food percentage to the formula.

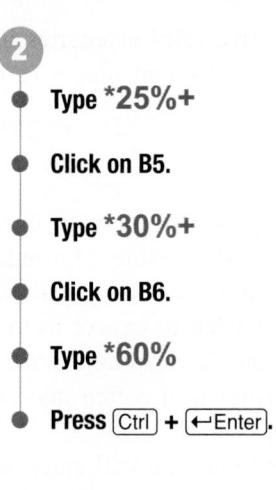

2

● Type ***25%+**

● Click on **B5.**

● Type ***30%+**

● Click on **B6.**

● Type ***60%**

● Press Ctrl + ←Enter.

Your screen should be similar to Figure 1.46

Figure 1.46

Having Trouble?

If you made an error in the formula, edit the entry in the formula bar and then press Ctrl + ←Enter again to copy it to the selected range.

The formula to calculate the January Cost of Goods expenses was entered in cell B12 and copied to all cells of the selected range.

Now you will enter the Cost of Merchandise expenses by multiplying the value in B8 by 70 percent. Then you will calculate the total expenses in row 19 and column E. To do this quickly, you will preselect the range and use the ∑ ▾ Sum button. Then you will enter the formula to calculate the net income. Net income is calculated by subtracting total expenses from total sales.

3

● Select cells **B13 through D13.**

● Type **=**

● Click on **B7.**

● Type ***70%**

● Press Ctrl + ←Enter.

● Select **B12 through E19.**

● Click ∑ ▾ **Sum.**

● Select **B22 through E22.**

● Enter the formula **=B9-B19** and press Ctrl + ←Enter.

Your screen should be similar to Figure 1.47

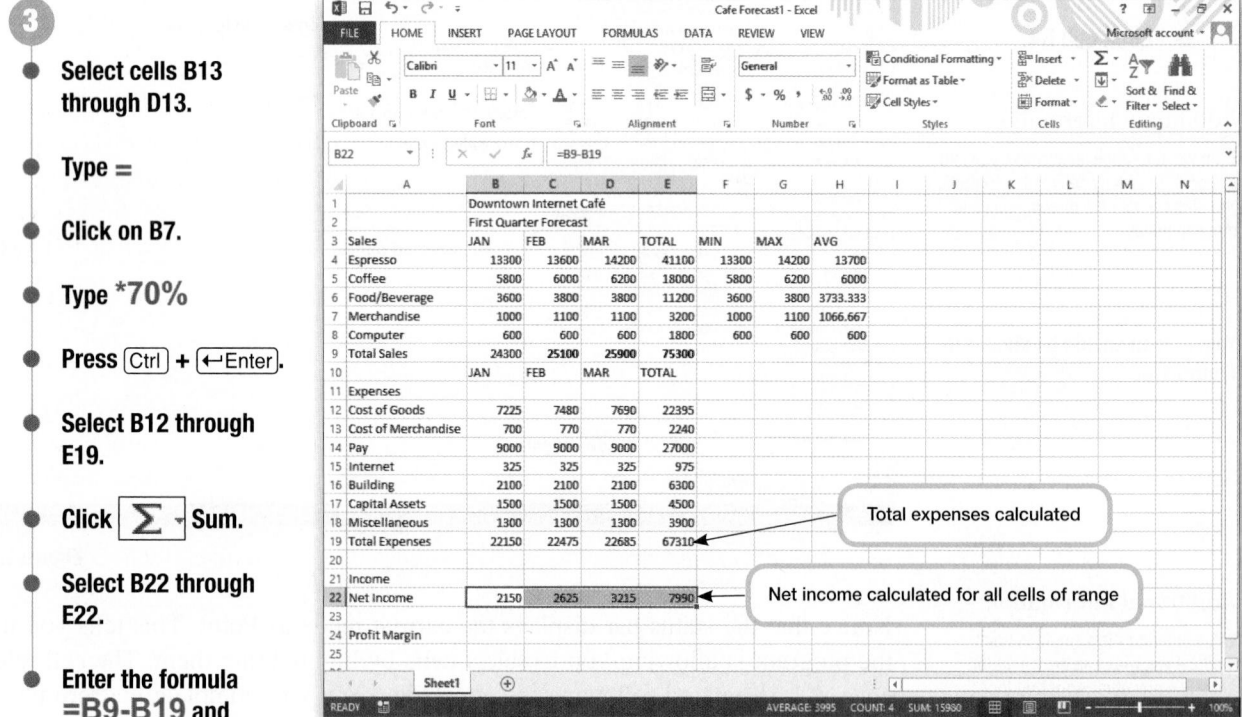

Figure 1.47

The formulas were quickly entered into all cells of the specified ranges.

Finally, you will enter the formula to calculate the profit margin. Profit margin is calculated by dividing net income by total sales.

4

- Select B24 through E24.

- Enter the formula **=B22/B9** and press Ctrl + ⏎Enter.

Your screen should be similar to Figure 1.48

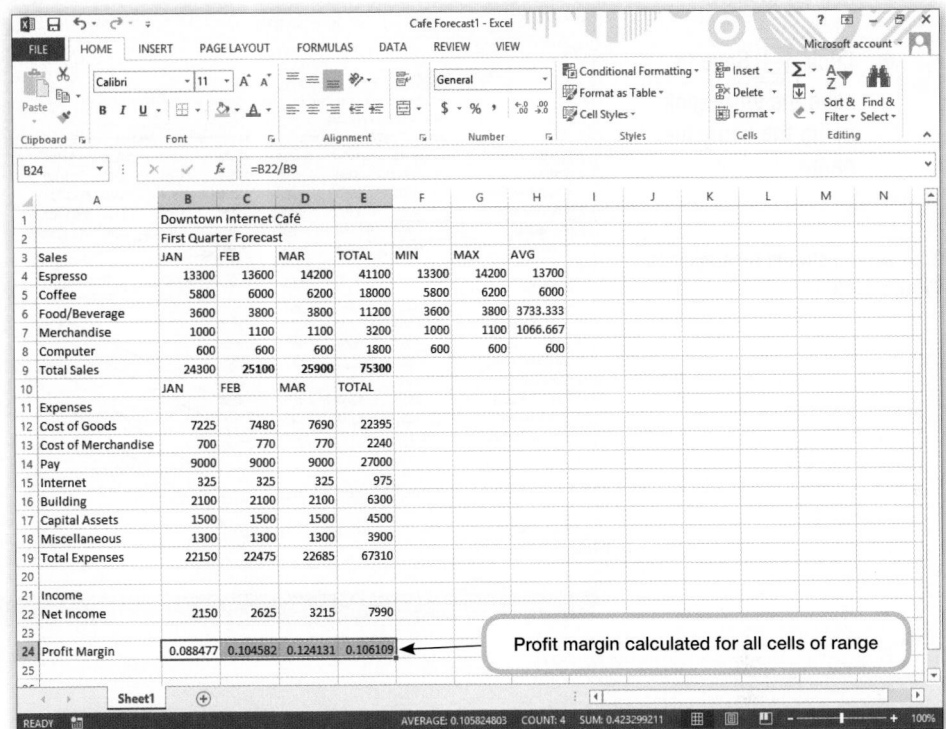

	A	B	C	D	E	F	G	H
1		Downtown Internet Café						
2		First Quarter Forecast						
3	Sales	JAN	FEB	MAR	TOTAL	MIN	MAX	AVG
4	Espresso	13300	13600	14200	41100	13300	14200	13700
5	Coffee	5800	6000	6200	18000	5800	6200	6000
6	Food/Beverage	3600	3800	3800	11200	3600	3800	3733.333
7	Merchandise	1000	1100	1100	3200	1000	1100	1066.667
8	Computer	600	600	600	1800	600	600	600
9	Total Sales	24300	25100	25900	75300			
10		JAN	FEB	MAR	TOTAL			
11	Expenses							
12	Cost of Goods	7225	7480	7690	22395			
13	Cost of Merchandise	700	770	770	2240			
14	Pay	9000	9000	9000	27000			
15	Internet	325	325	325	975			
16	Building	2100	2100	2100	6300			
17	Capital Assets	1500	1500	1500	4500			
18	Miscellaneous	1300	1300	1300	3900			
19	Total Expenses	22150	22475	22685	67310			
20								
21	Income							
22	Net Income	2150	2625	3215	7990			
23								
24	Profit Margin	0.088477	0.104582	0.124131	0.106109			
25								

Profit margin calculated for all cells of range

Figure 1.48

The net income and profit margins are calculated and displayed in the worksheet.

RECALCULATING THE WORKSHEET

Now that you have created the worksheet structure and entered some sample data for the forecasted sales for the first quarter, you want to test the formulas to verify that they are operating correctly. A simple way to do this is to use a calculator to verify that the correct result is displayed. You can then further test the worksheet by changing values and verifying that all cells containing formulas that reference the value are appropriately recalculated.

Concept 10 Recalculation

When a number in a referenced cell in a formula changes, Excel automatically **recalculates** all formulas that are dependent upon the changed value. Because only those formulas directly affected by a change in the data are recalculated, the time it takes to recalculate the workbook is reduced. Without this feature, in large worksheets it could take several minutes to recalculate all formulas each time a number is changed in the worksheet. Recalculation is one of the most powerful features of electronic worksheets.

After considering the sales estimates for the three months, you decide that the estimated sales generated from Computer usage for January are too high and you want to decrease this number from 600 to 400.

- **Change the entry in cell B8 to 400**

- **Click [ ] Save to save the workbook using the same file name.**

Your screen should be similar to Figure 1.49

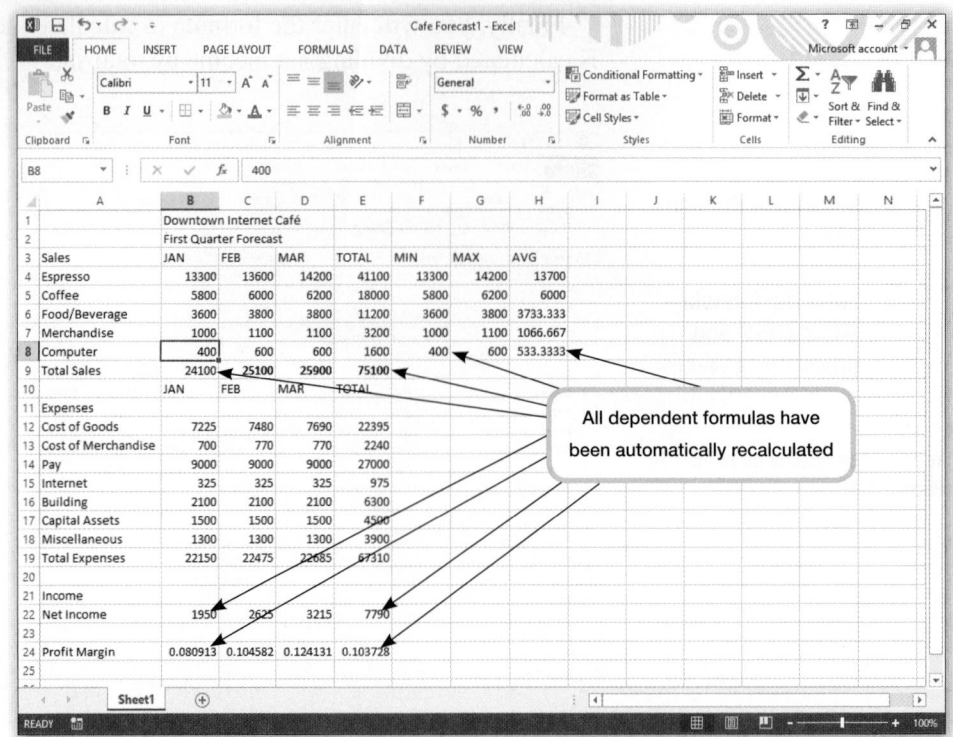

All dependent formulas have been automatically recalculated

Figure 1.49

The Computer total in cell E8 has been automatically recalculated. The number displayed is now 1600. The MIN and AVG values in cells F8 and H8 have been recalculated to 400 and 533.3333, respectively. Likewise, the January total in cell B9 of 24100 and the grand total in cell E9 of 75100 each decreased by 200 from the previous totals to reflect the change in cell B8. Finally, the Net Income and Profit Margin values also have adjusted appropriately.

The formulas in the worksheet are correctly calculating the desired result. The Sales portion of the worksheet is now complete.

Inserting and Deleting Rows and Columns

As you are developing a worksheet, you may realize you forgot to include information or decide that other information is not needed. To quickly add and remove entire rows and columns of information, you can insert and delete rows and columns. A new blank row is inserted above the active cell location and all rows below it shift down a row. Similarly, you can insert blank cells and columns in a worksheet. Blank cells are inserted above or to the left of the active cell, and blank columns are inserted to the left of the active cell. Likewise, you can quickly delete selected cells, rows, and columns, and all information in surrounding cells, rows, or columns automatically shifts appropriately to fill in the space.

Additionally, whenever you insert or delete cells, rows, or columns, all formula references to any affected cells adjust accordingly.

INSERTING ROWS

You realize that you forgot to include a row for the Advertising expenses. To add this data, you will insert a blank row above the Capital Assets row.

- Move to A17.

- Open the ⊞ Insert ▾ drop-down menu in the Cells group and choose **Insert Sheet Rows.**

Another Method

You also can choose Insert from the active cell's context menu.

- Enter the heading **Advertising** in cell A17 and the value **600** in cells B17 through D17.

- If necessary, copy the function from cell E16 to E17 to calculate the total advertising expense.

- Move to cell B20.

Your screen should be similar to Figure 1.50

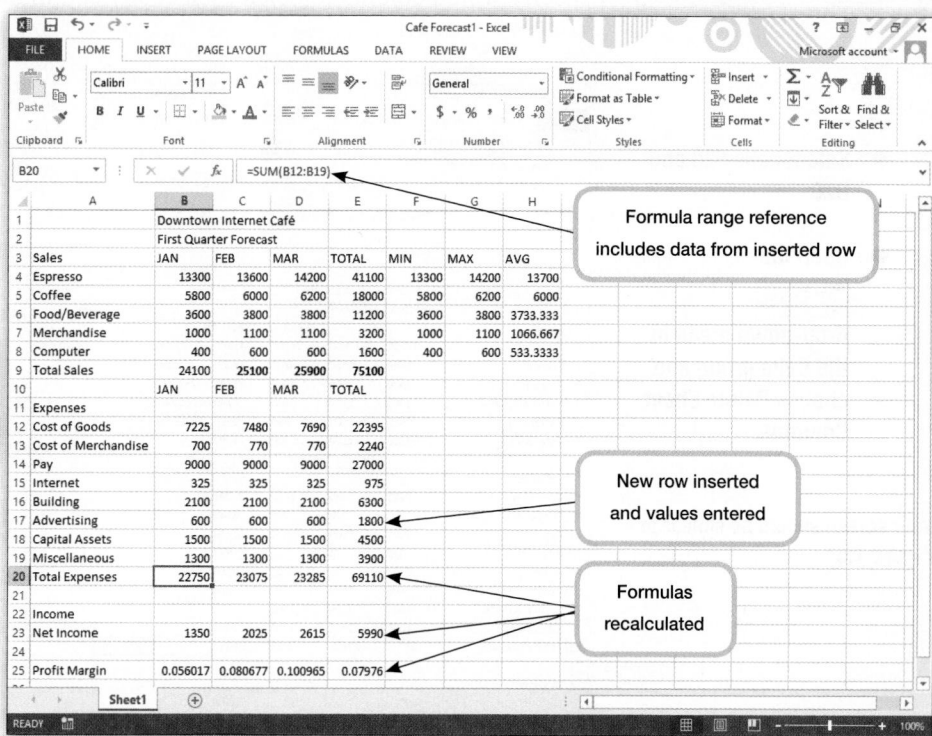

Figure 1.50

Additional Information

Click ⊞ Insert ▾ to insert blank cells, shifting existing cells down, and ⊞ Insert ▾/Sheet Columns to insert blank columns, shifting existing columns right.

A blank row was inserted in the worksheet and the cell references in all formulas and functions below the inserted row adjusted appropriately. The range in the formula to calculate monthly total expenses in row 20 has been adjusted to include the data in the inserted row, and the total expense for the first quarter is 69110. Additionally, the net income in row 23 and the profit margin in row 25 have been recalculated to reflect the change in data.

DELETING COLUMNS

As you look at the worksheet data, you decide the minimum and maximum values are not very useful since this data is so easy to see in this small worksheet. You will delete these two columns from the worksheet to remove this information. To specify which column to delete, select any cell in the column.

● **Select cells F20 and G20.**

● **Open the**

   Delete ▾

   drop-down menu in the Cells group and choose Delete Sheet Columns.

Your screen should be similar to Figure 1.51

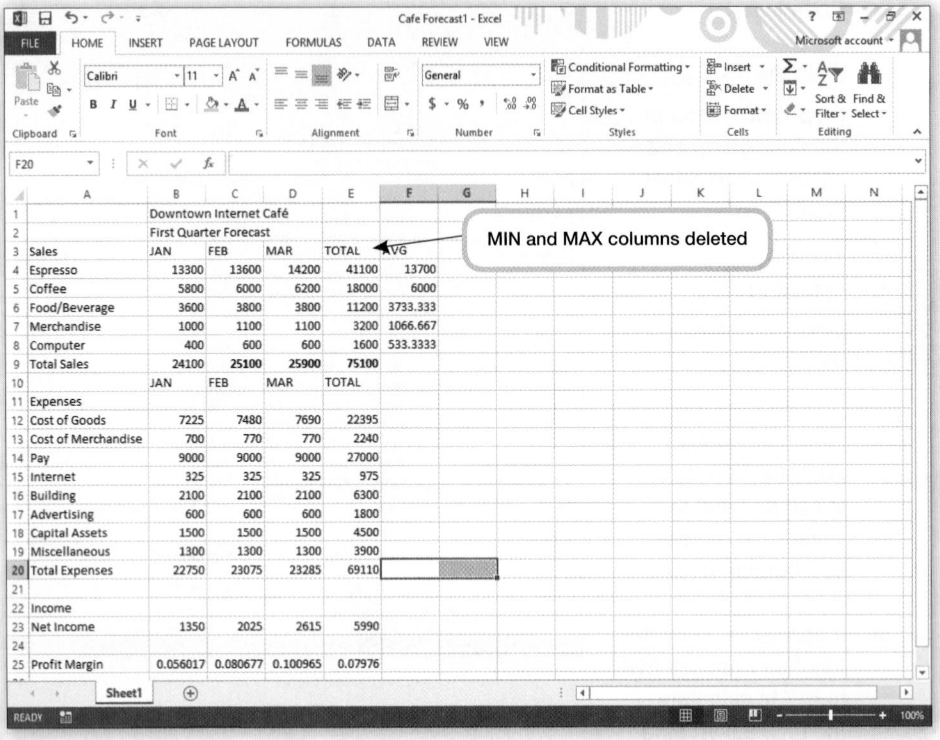

	A	B	C	D	E	F	G	H	I	J	K	L	M	N
1		Downtown Internet Café												
2		First Quarter Forecast												
3	Sales	JAN	FEB	MAR	TOTAL	AVG								
4	Espresso	13300	13600	14200	41100	13700								
5	Coffee	5800	6000	6200	18000	6000								
6	Food/Beverage	3600	3800	3800	11200	3733.333								
7	Merchandise	1000	1100	1100	3200	1066.667								
8	Computer	400	600	600	1600	533.3333								
9	Total Sales	24100	25100	25900	75100									
10		JAN	FEB	MAR	TOTAL									
11	Expenses													
12	Cost of Goods	7225	7480	7690	22395									
13	Cost of Merchandise	700	770	770	2240									
14	Pay	9000	9000	9000	27000									
15	Internet	325	325	325	975									
16	Building	2100	2100	2100	6300									
17	Advertising	600	600	600	1800									
18	Capital Assets	1500	1500	1500	4500									
19	Miscellaneous	1300	1300	1300	3900									
20	Total Expenses	22750	23075	23285	69110									
21														
22	Income													
23	Net Income	1350	2025	2615	5990									
24														
25	Profit Margin	0.056017	0.080677	0.100965	0.07976									

MIN and MAX columns deleted

Figure 1.51

The two columns have been removed and the columns to the right of the deleted columns automatically shifted to the left.

Formatting Cells and Cell Content

Now that the worksheet data is complete, you want to improve the appearance of the worksheet. Applying different formatting to text and numbers can greatly enhance the appearance of the document. In Excel, formats control how entries are displayed in a cell and include such features as the position of data in a cell, character font and color, and number formats such as commas and dollar signs.

You want to change the appearance of the row and column headings and apply formatting to the numbers. Applying different formats greatly improves both the appearance and the readability of the data in a worksheet.

CHANGING CELL ALIGNMENT

You decide the column headings would look better if they were right-aligned in their cell spaces, so that they would appear over the numbers in the column. Alignment is a basic format setting that is used in most worksheets.

Concept  Alignment

Alignment settings allow you to change the horizontal and vertical placement and the orientation of an entry in a cell.

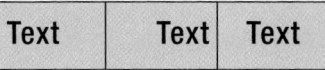

Horizontal placement allows you to left-, right-, or center-align text and number entries in the cell space. Entries also can be indented within the cell space, centered across a selection, or justified. You also can fill a cell horizontally with a repeated entry.

Vertical placement allows you to specify whether the cell contents are displayed at the top, the bottom, or the center of the vertical cell space or justified vertically.

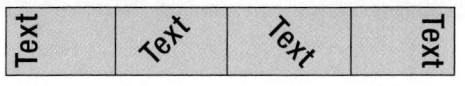

You also can change the orientation or angle of text in a cell by varying the degrees of rotation.

The default workbook horizontal alignment settings left-align text entries and right-align number entries. The vertical alignment is set to Bottom for both types of entries, and the orientation is set to zero degrees rotation from the horizontal position. You want to change the horizontal alignment of the month headings in rows 3 and 10 to right-aligned.

The Alignment group contains commands to control the horizontal and vertical placement of entries in a cell. You can quickly apply formatting to a range of cells by selecting the range first. A quick way to select a range of filled cells is to hold down ⇧Shift and double-click on the edge of the active cell in the direction in which you want the range expanded. For example, to select the range to the right of the active cell, you would double-click the right border. You will use this method to select and right-align these entries.

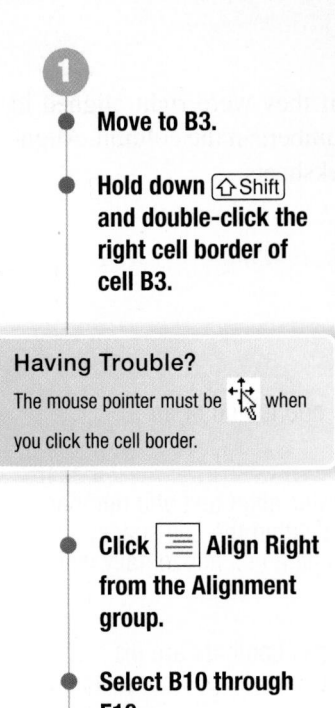

①

● Move to B3.

● Hold down ⇧ Shift and double-click the right cell border of cell B3.

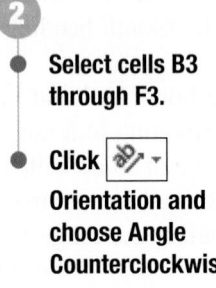

Having Trouble?

The mouse pointer must be ↔ when you click the cell border.

● Click ☰ **Align Right** from the Alignment group.

● Select B10 through E10.

● Click ☰ **Align Right.**

Your screen should be similar to Figure 1.52

Aligns text to right side of cell

Cell entries right-aligned in cell space

Figure 1.52

The entries in the selected ranges are right-aligned in their cell spaces. You notice the month labels do not stand out well and decide to try rotating them.

②

● Select cells B3 through F3.

● Click ⬢ ▼ **Orientation** and choose **Angle Counterclockwise.**

Your screen should be similar to Figure 1.53

Cell entries angled counterclockwise

Figure 1.53

Notice how the row height increased automatically to accommodate the change in size.

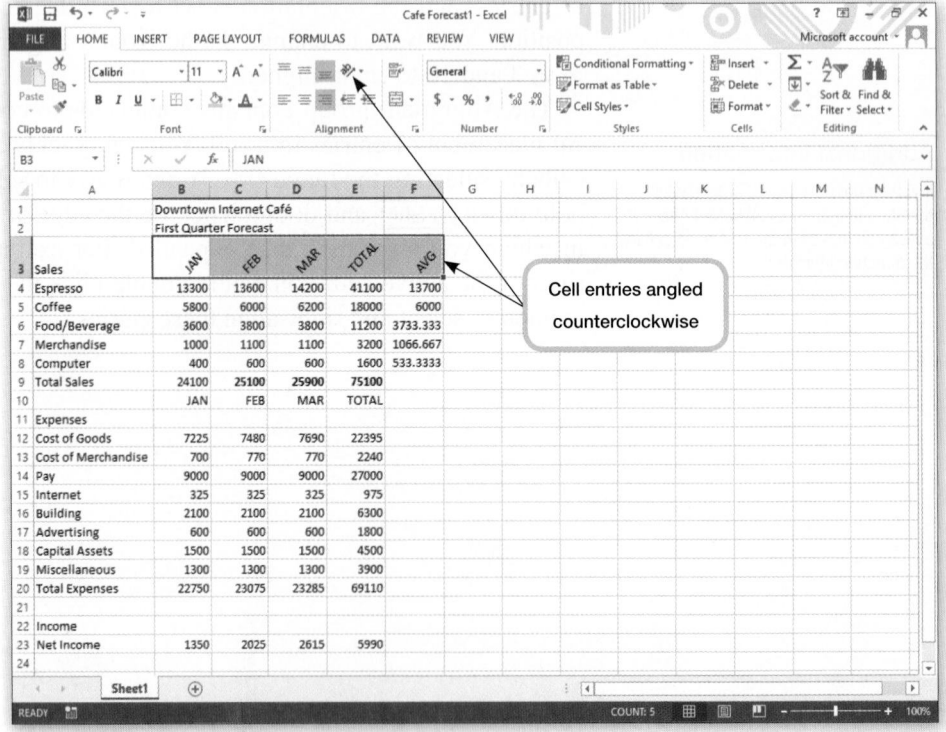

CHANGING ROW HEIGHT

You do not like the way it looks rotated and decide to undo the change, add height to the row manually to help identify the month label row better, and center-align the labels. You also decide to move the month labels in row 10 down a row to match the first row of month labels.

Concept  12 Row Height

The **row height** is the size or height of a row measured in points. The default row height is 15.00 points which is larger than the default font point size of 11. The row height can be any number from 0 to 409. If it is set to 0, the row is hidden. The row height automatically adjusts to changes in the character size, style, and orientation.

The row height can also be changed manually using methods that are similar to those used to change the column width. The difference is that you drag or click the boundary below the row heading to adjust the row height.

- Click ↶ Undo.

- Move the entries in cells B10 through E10 into the same columns in row 11.

- Drag the bottom boundary of rows 3 and 11 to increase the row height to 22.50.

- Select cells B3 through F3 and click ≡ Center.

- Center-align the labels in cells B11 through E11.

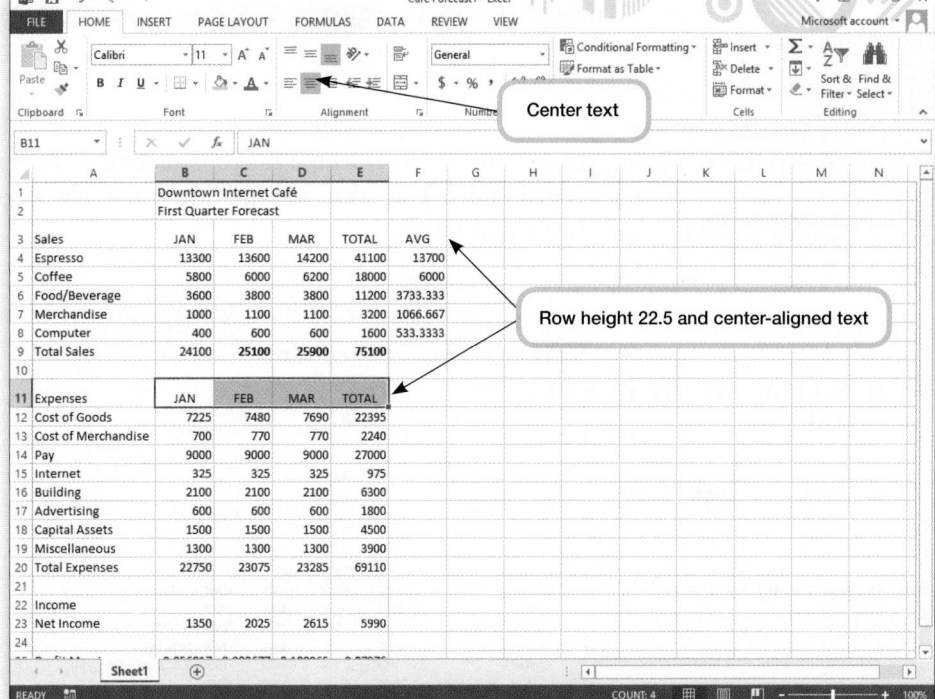

Figure 1.54

Your screen should be similar to Figure 1.54

Increasing the row height of the month labels visually separates the labels from other worksheet entries.

INDENTING CELL CONTENT

Next, you would like to indent the row headings in cells A4 through A8 and A12 through A19 to show that the entries are subtopics below the Sales and Expenses headings. You want to indent the headings in both ranges at the same time. To select nonadjacent cells or cell ranges, after selecting the first cell or range, hold down Ctrl while selecting each additional cell or range.

1

- Select A4 through A8.

- Hold down Ctrl.

- Select A12 through A19.

- Release Ctrl.

- Click ⬛ Increase Indent in the Alignment group.

- AutoFit the width of column A.

Your screen should be similar to Figure 1.55

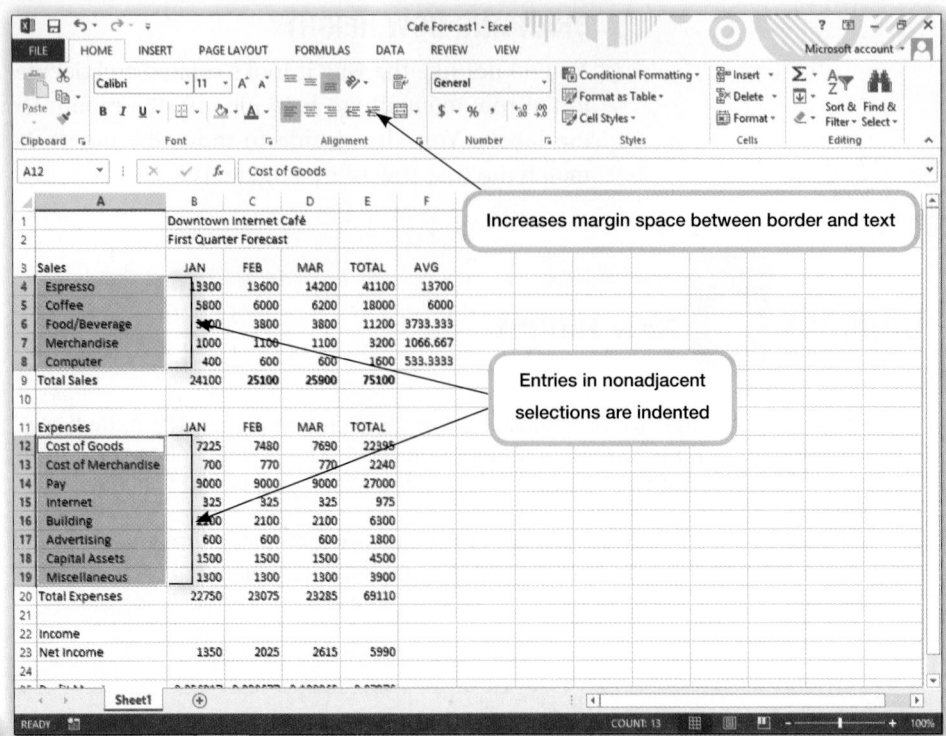

Figure 1.55

Each entry in the selected range is indented two spaces from the left edge of the cell. Finally, you want to right-align the Total Sales, Total Expenses, and Net Income headings.

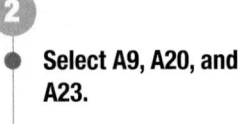

2

- Select A9, A20, and A23.

- Click ⬛ Align Right.

Your screen should be similar to Figure 1.56

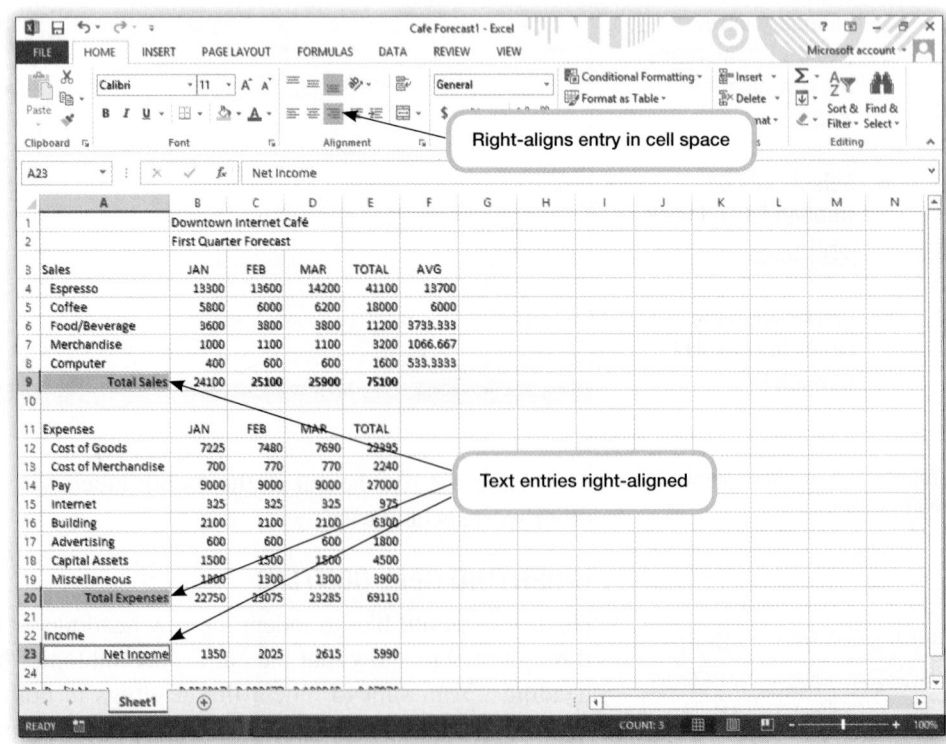

Figure 1.56

MERGING CELLS

Next, you want to center the worksheet titles across columns A through F so they are centered over the worksheet data. To do this, you will merge or combine the cells in the range over the worksheet data (A1 through F1) into a single large **merged cell** and then center the contents of the range in the merged cell.

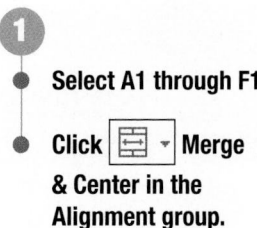

1
- Select A1 through F1.
- Click Merge & Center in the Alignment group.

Your screen should be similar to Figure 1.57

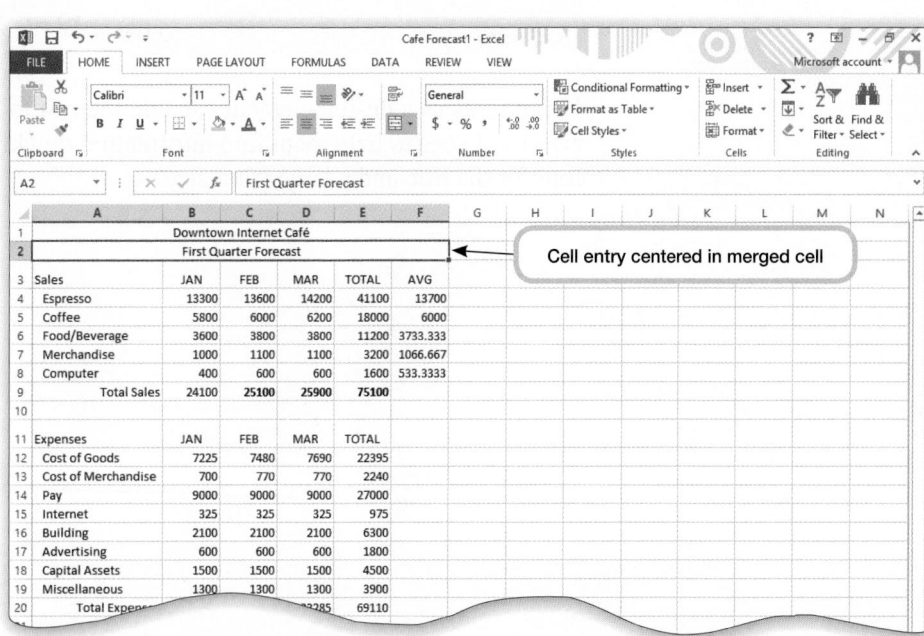

Figure 1.57

The six cells in the selection have been combined into a single large cell, and the entry that was in cell B1 is centered within the merged cell space. Only the contents of the first cell containing an entry in the upper-leftmost section of the selected range are centered in the merged cell. If other cells to the right of that cell contain data, they will be deleted. The cell reference for a merged cell is the upper-left cell in the original selected range, in this case A1.

2
- Merge and center the second title line across columns A through F.

Your screen should be similar to Figure 1.58

Figure 1.58

You also can use the commands in the [☰▾] Merge & Center drop-down menu shown in the following table to control a merge. You can merge cells horizontally and vertically.

Merge Menu	Action
[☰▾] Merge & Center	Merges cells and centers entry
[☰] Merge Across	Merges cells horizontally
[☰] Merge Cells	Merges cells horizontally and vertically
[☰] Unmerge Cells	Splits cells that have been merged back into individual cells

CHANGING FONTS AND FONT SIZES

Having Trouble?

Refer to the section "Formatting Text" in the Introduction to Microsoft Office 2013 to review fonts.

Finally, you want to improve the worksheet appearance by enhancing the appearance of the title. One way to do this is to change the font and font size used in the title. There are two basic types of fonts: serif and sans serif. **Serif** fonts have a flare at the base of each letter that visually leads the reader to the next letter. Two common serif fonts are Roman and Times New Roman. Serif fonts generally are used in paragraphs. **Sans serif** fonts do not have a flare at the base of each letter. Arial and Helvetica are two common sans serif fonts. Because sans serif fonts have a clean look, they are often used for headings in documents. It is good practice to use only two types of fonts in a worksheet, one for text and one for headings. Too many styles can make your document look cluttered and unprofessional.

Here are several examples of the same text in various fonts and sizes.

Typeface	Font Size (12 pt/18 pt)
Calibri (Sans Serif)	This is 12 pt. This is 18 pt.
Comic Sans MS (Sans Serif)	This is 12 pt. This is 18 pt.
Book Antiqua (Serif)	This is 12 pt. This is 18 pt.

Using fonts as a design element can add interest to your document and give readers visual cues to help them find information quickly. First you will try a different font for the title and a larger font size.

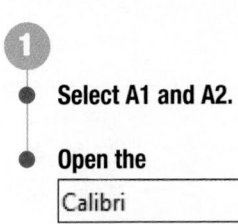

● Select **A1** and **A2**.

● Open the

Calibri ▼

Font drop-down list box in the Font group.

Your screen should be similar to Figure 1.59

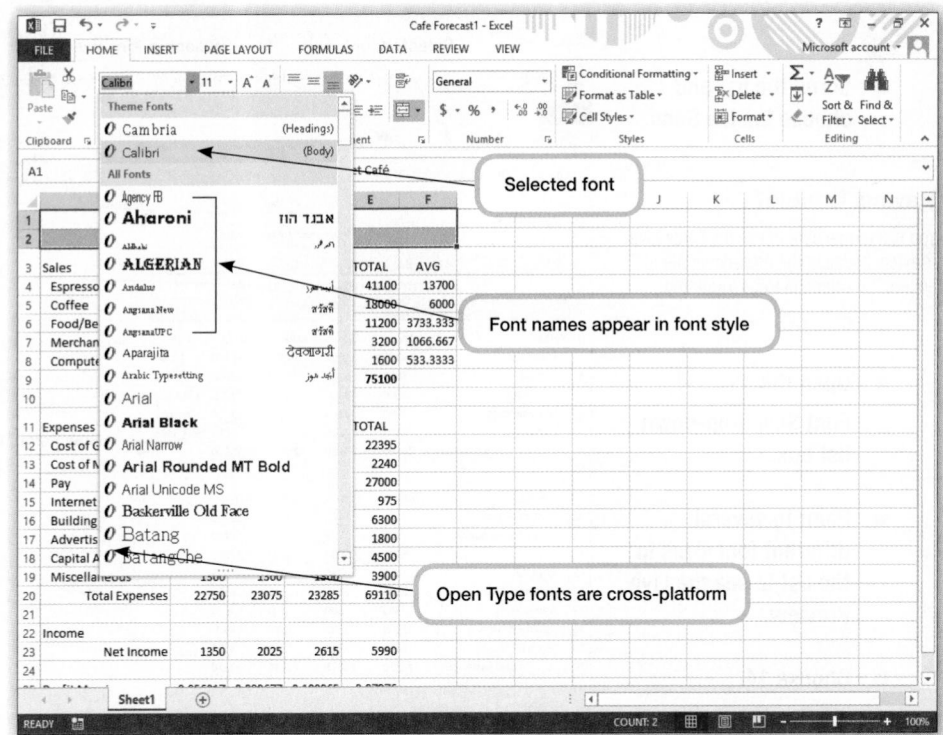

Figure 1.59

The Font drop-down list displays examples of the available fonts on your system in alphabetical order. The default worksheet font, Calibri, is highlighted. Notice the $\boxed{O}$ preceding the font name. This indicates the font is an Open Type font, a standard font format developed by Adobe Systems and Microsoft. Open Type fonts can be used by almost any application and can display many more characters than previous font formats. Other font names are preceded with a $\boxed{\mathbf{T}}$. This indicates the font is a TrueType font. TrueType fonts appear onscreen as they will appear when printed. They are installed when Windows is installed. You will change the font and increase the font size to 14. As you point to the font options, Live Preview will show how it will appear if chosen.

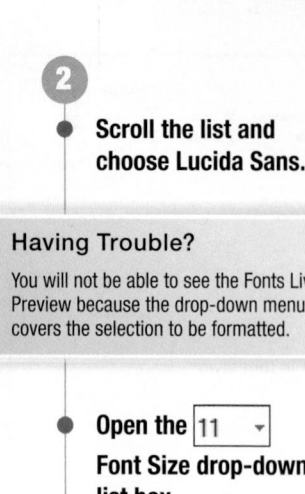

2

● **Scroll the list and choose Lucida Sans.**

Having Trouble?

You will not be able to see the Fonts Live Preview because the drop-down menu covers the selection to be formatted.

● **Open the** `11` **Font Size drop-down list box.**

● **Point to several different font sizes in the list to see the Live Preview.**

● **Choose 14.**

Your screen should be similar to Figure 1.60

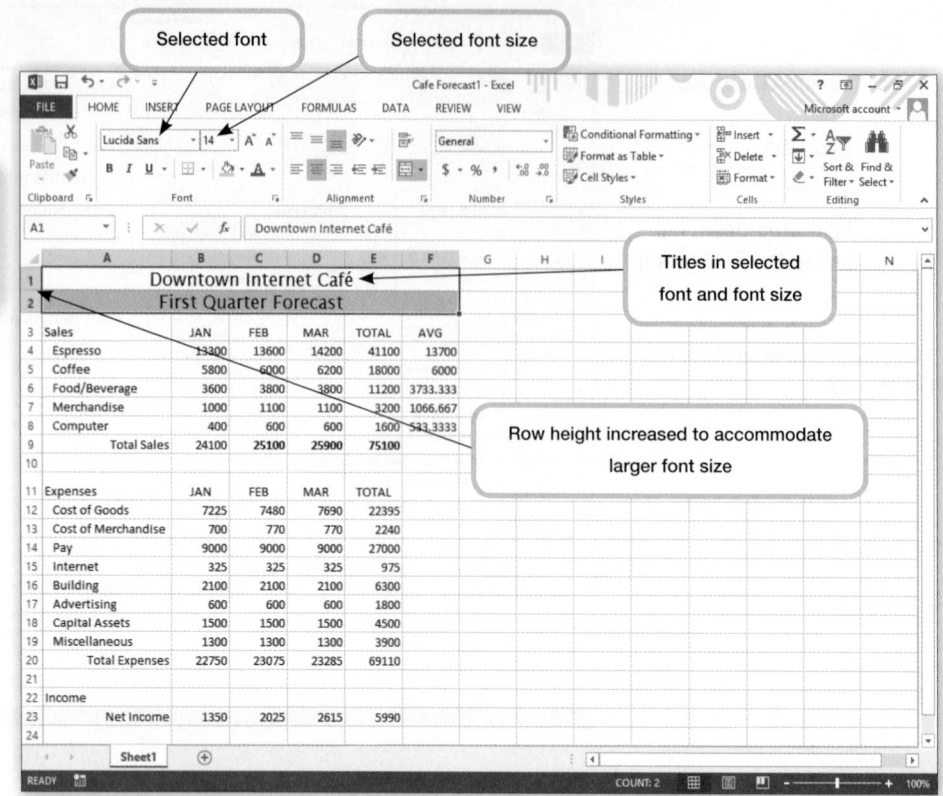

Figure 1.60

Another Method

The Font and Font Size commands are also available on the Mini toolbar.

The title appears in the selected typeface and size, and the Font and Font Size buttons display the name of the font and the size used in the active cell. Notice that the height of the row has increased to accommodate the larger font size of the heading.

APPLYING TEXT EFFECTS

Having Trouble?

Refer to the section "Formatting Text" in the Introduction to Microsoft Office 2013 to review text effects.

In addition to changing font and font size, you can apply different text effects to enhance the appearance of text. The table below describes some of the text effects and their uses.

Format	Example	Use
Bold	**Bold**	Adds emphasis.
Italic	*Italic*	Adds emphasis.
Underline	<u>Underline</u>	Adds emphasis.
Strikethrough	~~Strikethrough~~	Indicates words to be deleted.
Superscript	"To be or not to be."[1]	Used in footnotes and formulas.
Subscript	H_2O	Used in formulas.
Color	Color Color Color	Adds interest.

First you want to enhance the appearance of the column headings by increasing the font size and adding bold, italic, and underlines.

1

- Select B3 through F3.

- Increase the font size to 12.

- Click **B** Bold.

- Click **U** ▾ Underline.

Your screen should be similar to **Figure 1.61**

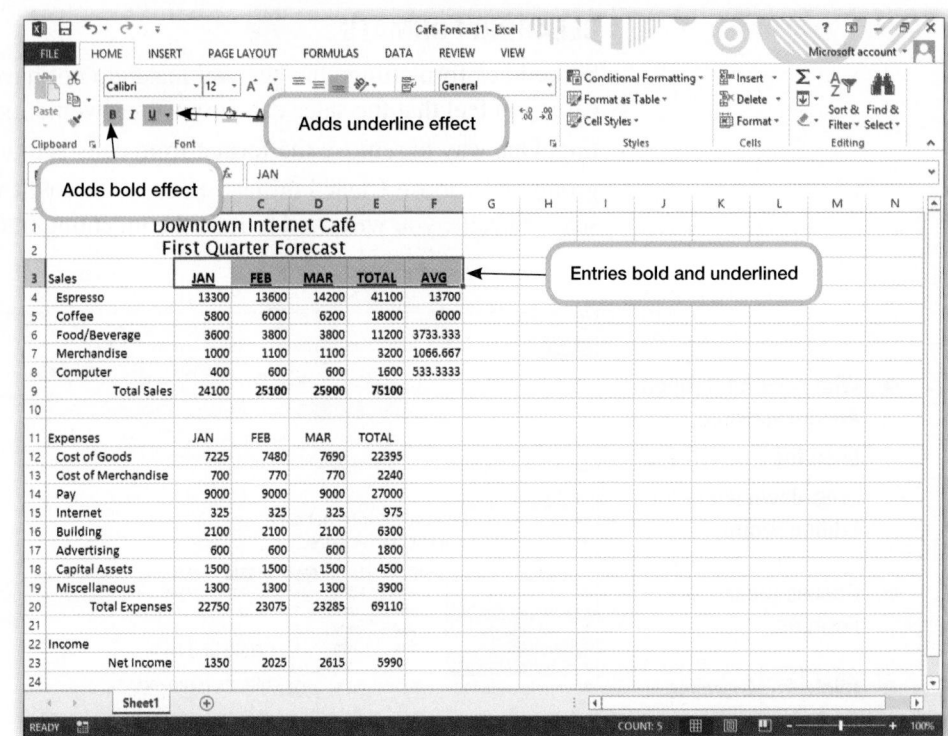

Figure 1.61

Having Trouble?

Refer to the section "Formatting Text" in the Introduction to Microsoft Office 2013 to review using the Mini toolbar.

Many of the formatting commands are also available on the Mini toolbar. In Excel, you must right-click on a cell to display the Mini toolbar and the shortcut menu. The selected formatting is applied to the entire cell contents. If you select text in a cell, the Mini toolbar appears automatically and the formatting is applied to the selected text only.

2

- Select A4 through A8.

- Right-click on the selection to display the Mini toolbar.

- Click **B** Bold.

- Click **I** Italic.

Another Method

The keyboard shortcut for bold is Ctrl + B; for italic, it is Ctrl + I; and for underline, it is Ctrl + U.

Your screen should be similar to **Figure 1.62**

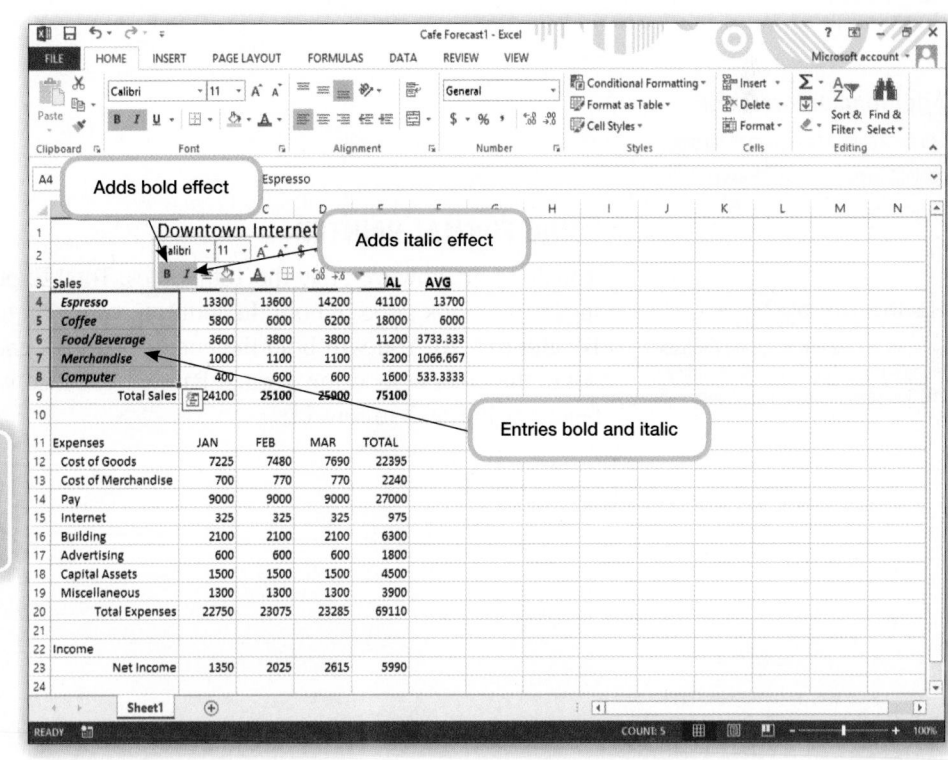

Figure 1.62

Formatting Cells and Cell Content   **EX1.59**

CLEARING FORMATS

Sometimes formatting changes you make do not have the expected result. In this case, you feel that the sales category names would look better without the formatting. One way to remove the format from cells is to use [eraser icon] ▼ Clear in the Editing group and choose Clear Formats. Because this will remove all formatting in the selected cells, you will need to redo the indenting in those cells.

1

- With cells A4 through A8 still selected, open the [eraser icon] ▼ Clear drop-down list in the Editing group.

- Choose Clear Formats.

- Click [indent icon] Increase Indent.

Another Method

You could also use [undo icon] Undo to remove the formats by reversing your last actions.

Your screen should be similar to Figure 1.63

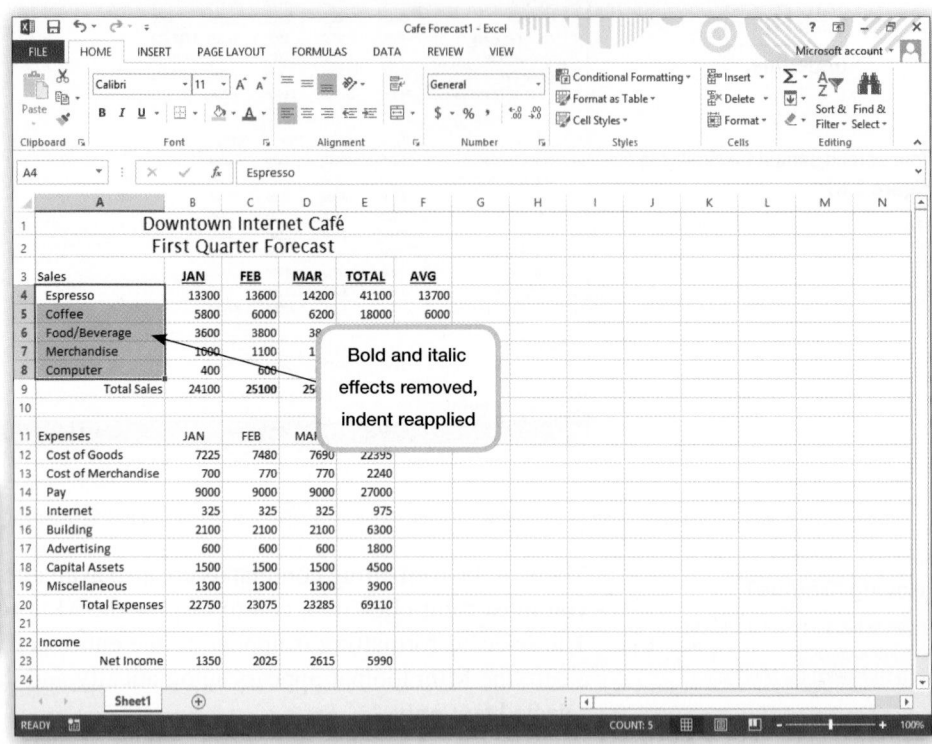

Figure 1.63

Additional Information

You can remove both formatting and content using [eraser icon] ▼ Clear/Clear All.

USING FORMAT PAINTER

Having Trouble?

Refer to the section "Copying Formats" in the Introduction to Microsoft Office 2013 to review the Format Painter.

You do think, however, that the Total Sales, Total Expenses, and Net Income headings would look good in bold. In addition, you want to bold the total values in cell B9 and row 20. You will bold the entry in cell A9 and then copy the format from A9 to the other cells using Format Painter. You also will copy the format from the headings in row 3 to row 11.

1

- Apply bold to cell A9.

- With cell A9 selected, double-click 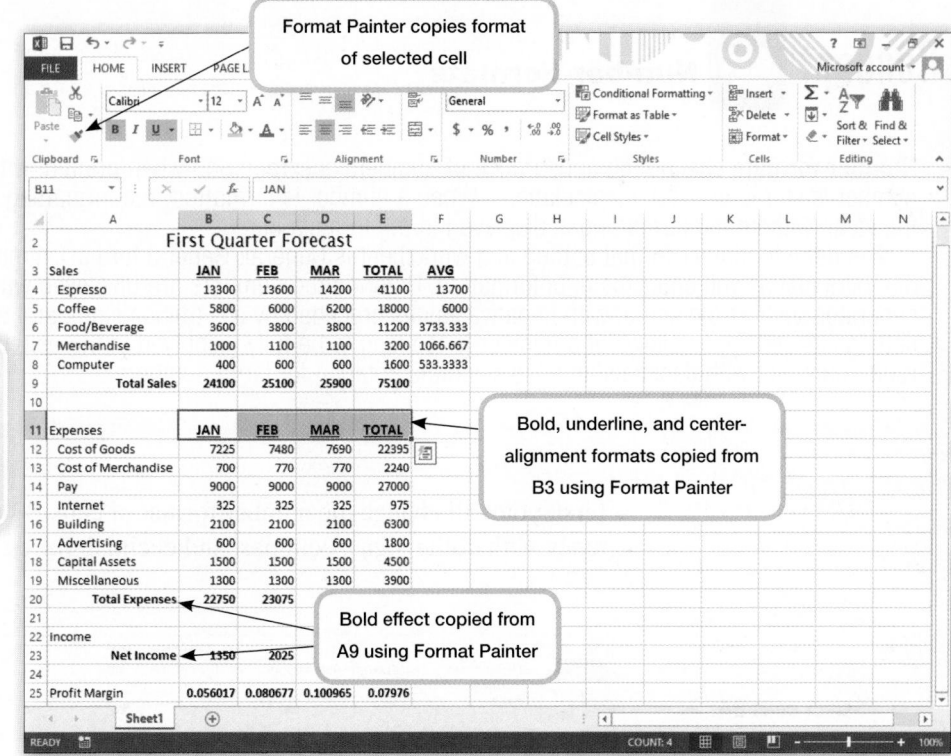 Format Painter in the Clipboard group.

- Click B9.

- Select A20:E20.

- Select A23:E23.

- Select B25:E25

- Click [icon] Format Painter to turn it off.

- Use Format Painter to copy the format from cell B3 to cells B11 through E11.

Your screen should be similar to Figure 1.64

Figure 1.64

The formatting was quickly added to each cell or range as it was selected.

FORMATTING NUMBERS

You also want to improve the appearance of the numbers in the worksheet by changing their format.

Concept ⓭ Number Formats

Number formats change the appearance of numbers onscreen and when printed, without changing the way the number is stored or used in calculations. When a number is formatted, the formatting appears in the cell, while the value without the formatting is displayed in the formula bar.

The default number format setting in a worksheet is General. General format, in most cases, displays numbers just as you enter them, unformatted. Unformatted numbers are displayed without a thousands separator such as a comma, with negative values preceded by a – (minus sign), and with as many decimal place settings as cell space allows. If a number is too long to be fully displayed in the cell, the General format will round numbers with decimals and use scientific notation for large numbers.

First, you will change the number format of cells B4 through F9 to display as currency with dollar signs, commas, and decimal places.

1

- **Select cells B4 through F9.**

- **Open the**

  General ▼

  Number Format drop-down list in the Number group.

- **Choose Currency.**

Your screen should be similar to Figure 1.65

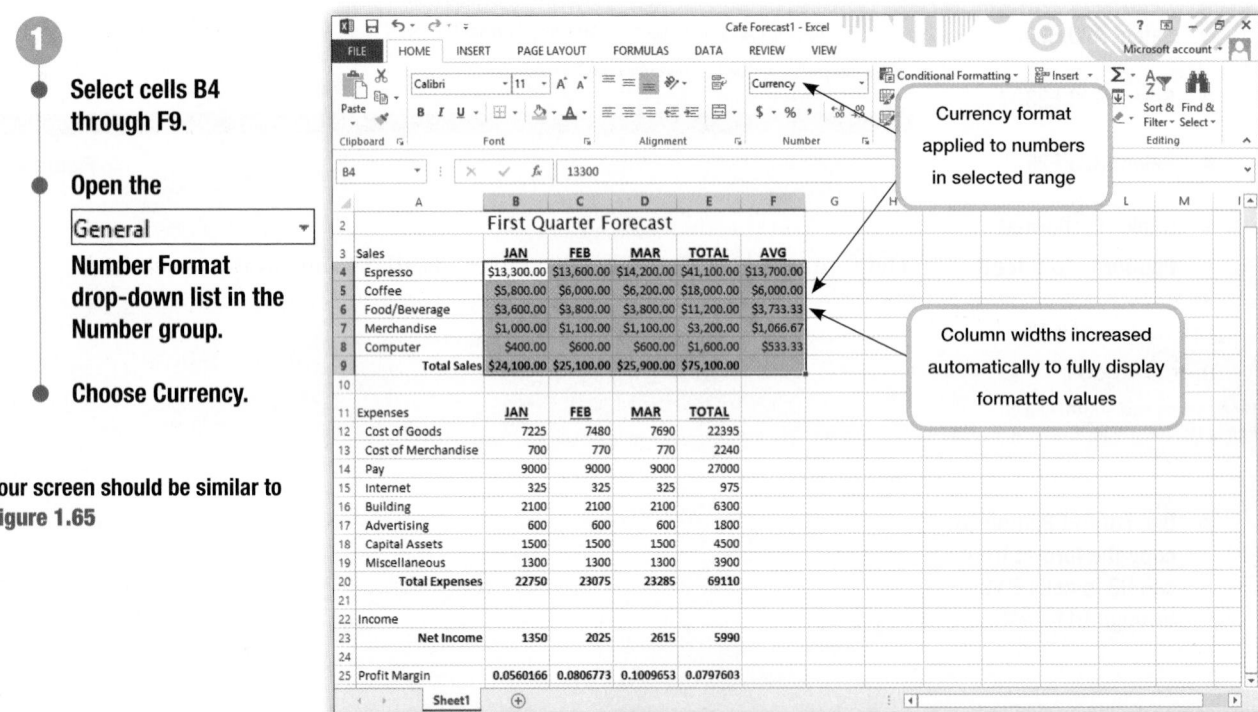

Figure 1.65

Another Method

Excel will also automatically apply a format to a cell based on the symbols you use when entering the number. For example, entering 10,000 in a cell formats the cell to Comma format, and entering $102.20 formats the cell to Currency with two decimal places.

The number entries in the selected range appear with a currency symbol, comma, and two decimal places. The column widths increased automatically to fully display the formatted values.

A second format category that displays numbers as currency is Accounting. You will try this format next on the same range. Additionally, you will specify zero as the number of decimal places because most of the values are whole values. To specify settings that are different than the default setting for a format, you can use the Format Cells dialog box.

2

● Make sure you still have cells B4 through F9 selected.

● Click in the Number group to open the Format Cells: Number dialog box.

Another Method

The keyboard shortcut to open the Format Cells dialog box is Ctrl + 1.

● From the Category list box, choose Accounting.

● Reduce the decimal places to 0.

● Click **OK**.

Your screen should be similar to Figure 1.66

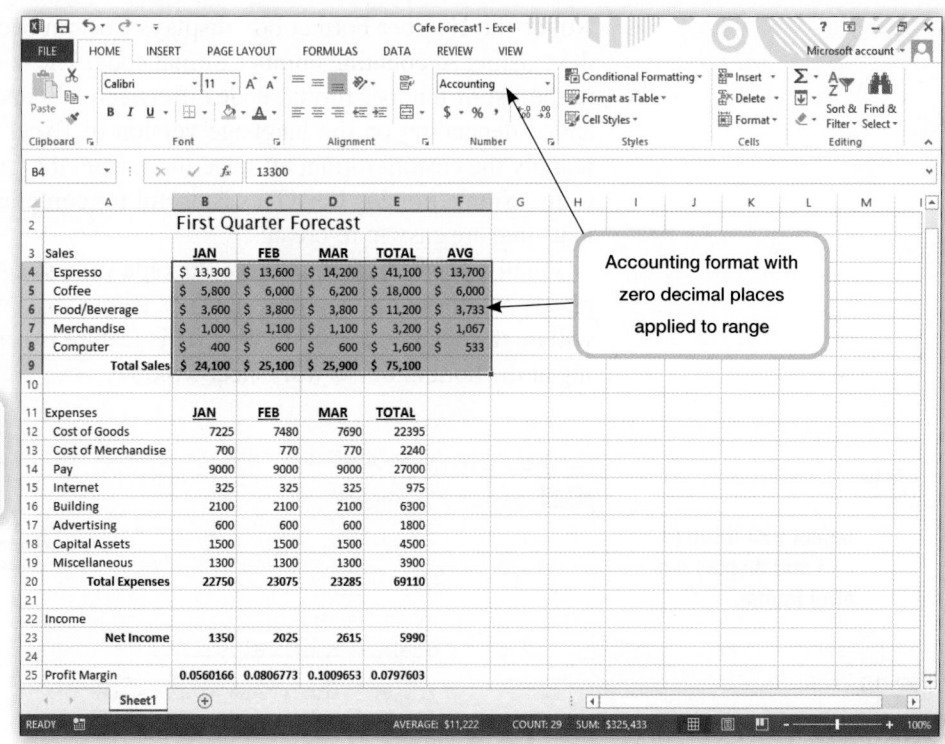

Figure 1.66

The numbers now appear in Accounting format. The primary difference between the Accounting and the Currency formats is that the Accounting format aligns numbers at the decimal place and places the dollar sign in a column at the left edge of the cell space. In addition, it does not allow you to select different ways of displaying negative numbers but displays them in black in parentheses.

You decide the Accounting format will make it easier to read the numbers in a column and you will use this format for the rest of the worksheet. An easier way to apply the Accounting format with 0 decimals is to use the commands in the Number group.

3

● Select the range B12 through E20.

● Click $ ▾ Accounting Number Format in the Number group.

● Click Decrease Decimal twice.

Your screen should be similar to Figure 1.67

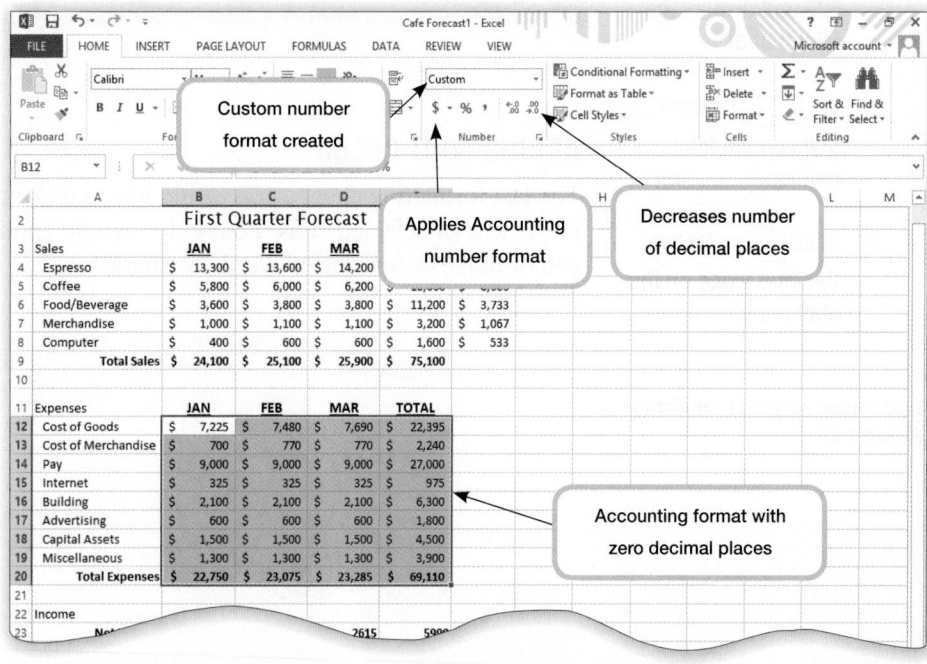

Figure 1.67

Notice the Number Format box displays Custom because you modified a copy of the existing Accounting number format code. The custom number format is added to the list of number format codes. Between 200 and 250 custom formats can be added depending on the language version of Excel you are using. You can then reapply the custom format by selecting it from the Custom category of the Format Cells: Number dialog box. This is useful for complicated formats, but not for formats that are easy to re-create.

Finally, you will format the Net Income values as Accounting with zero decimal places and the Profit Margin values as percentages with two decimal places. You will do this using the Mini toolbar. This feature is particularly helpful when working at the bottom of the worksheet window.

4

- Select B23 through E23 and display the Mini toobar.

Having Trouble

Right-click on the selection to display the Mini toolbar.

- Click $ ▾ Accounting Number Format on the Mini toolbar.

- Click .00→.0 Decrease Decimal twice on the Mini toolbar.

- Select B25 through E25 and display the Mini toobar.

- Click % Percent Style on the Mini toolbar.

- Click ←.0.00 Increase Decimal twice on the Mini toolbar.

Your screen should be similar to Figure 1.68

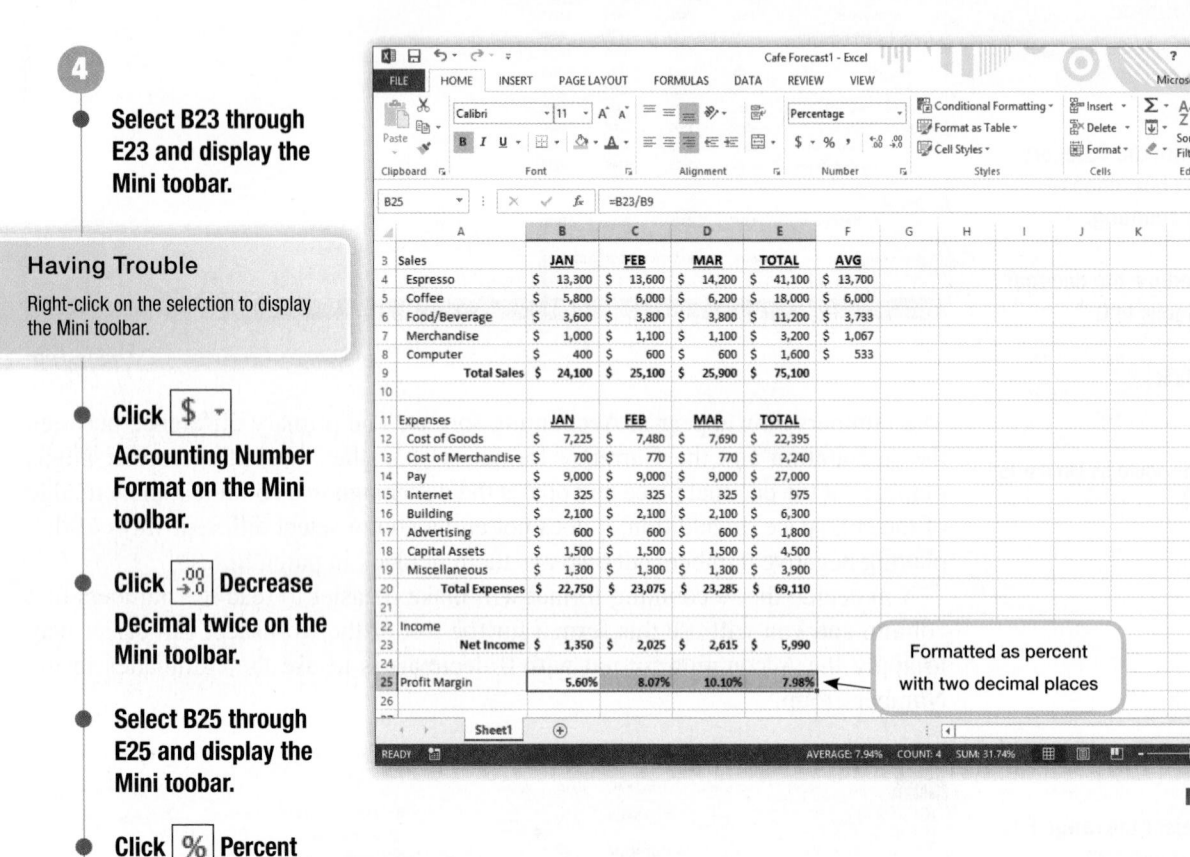

Figure 1.68

ADDING FONT COLOR

The last formatting change you would like to make to the worksheet is to add color to the text of selected cells. Font color can be applied to all the text in a selected cell or range or to selected words or characters in a cell.

1

Select A1 through A2.

Open the 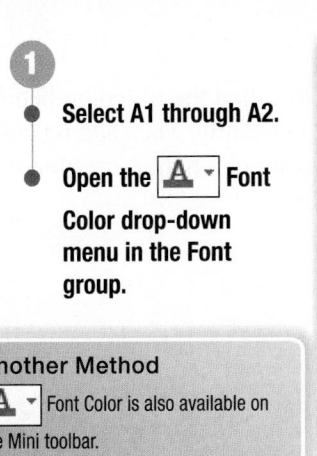 Font

Color drop-down
menu in the Font
group.

Another Method

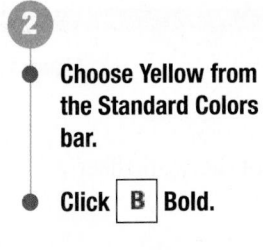 Font Color is also available on
the Mini toolbar.

Your screen should be similar to
Figure 1.69

Figure 1.69

Additional Information

You will learn about using themes
in Lab 2.

A palette of colors is displayed. Automatic is the default text color setting. This
setting automatically determines when to use black or white text. Black text is
used on a light background and white text on a dark background. The center area
of the palette displays the theme colors. Theme colors are a set of colors that are
associated with a **theme**, a predefined set of fonts, colors, and effects that can be
applied to an entire worksheet. If you change the theme, the theme colors change.
The Standard Colors bar displays 10 colors that are always the same.

As you point to a color, the entry in the selected cell changes color so you can
preview how the selection would look. A ScreenTip displays the name of the standard color or the description of the theme color as you point to it.

2

Choose Yellow from
the Standard Colors
bar.

Click **B** Bold.

Your screen should be similar to
Figure 1.70

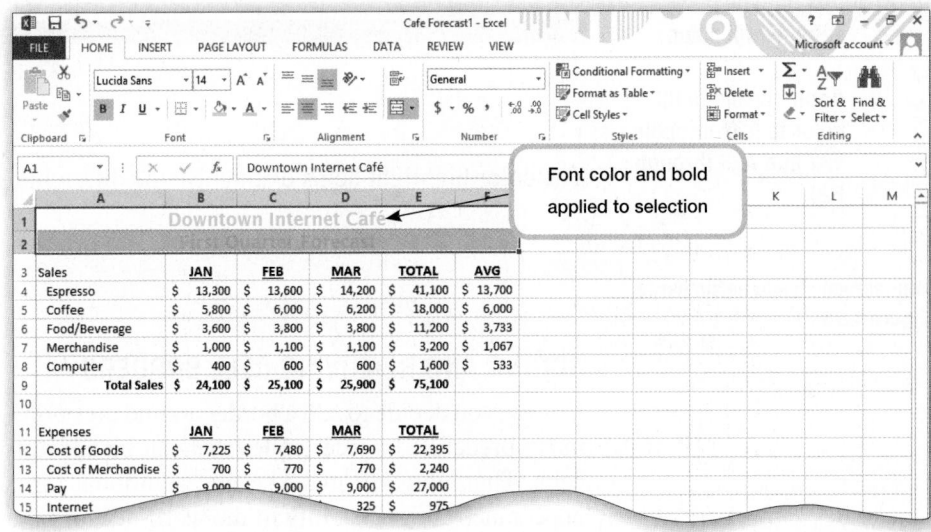

Figure 1.70

The font color of all the text in cells A1 and A2 has changed to the selected color
and bold. The selected color appears in the button and can be applied again simply
by clicking the button.

ADDING FILL COLOR

Next, you will change the cell background color, also called the fill color, behind the titles and in several other areas of the worksheet. Generally, when adding color to a worksheet, use a dark font color with a light fill color or a light font color with a dark fill color.

1

- Select cells A1 through F3.

- Open the Fill Color drop-down color palette.

- Point to several colors to see a Live Preview.

- Select Red Accent 2 (from the Theme Colors bar).

- Select cells A11 through F11 and click Fill Color to apply the last selected fill color.

- Apply the same fill color to A22 through F22 and A25 through F25.

Your screen should be similar to Figure 1.71

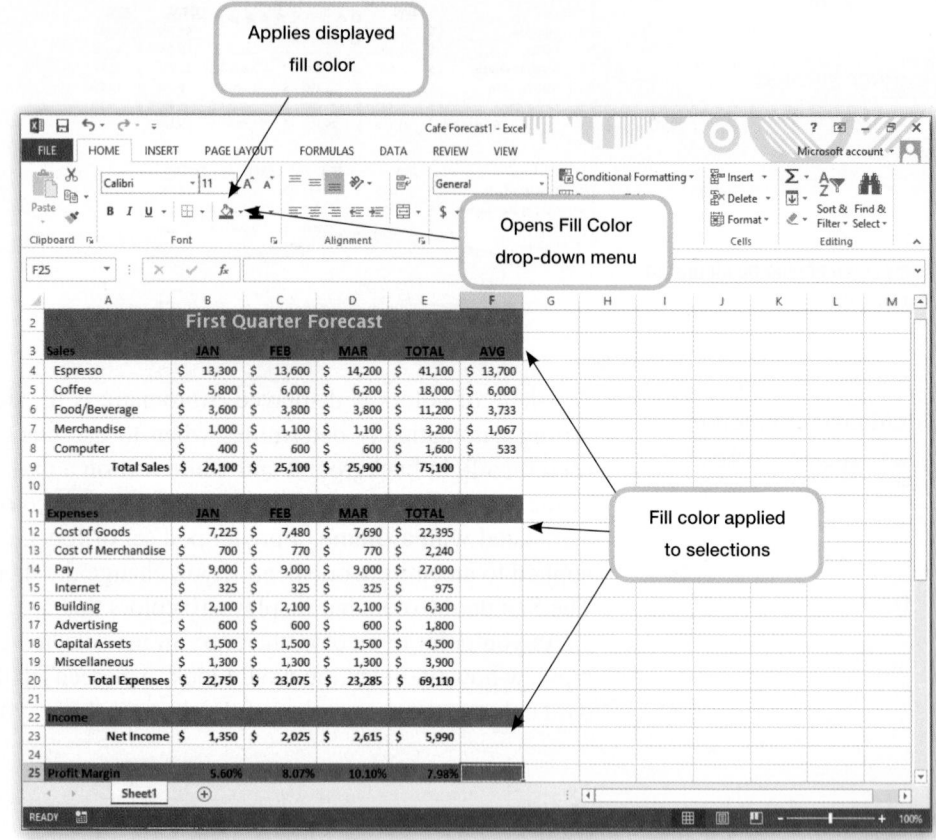

Figure 1.71

The color highlight helps distinguish the different areas of the worksheet.

ADDING AND REMOVING CELL BORDERS

Finally, you decide to add a border around the entire worksheet area. Excel includes many predefined border styles that can be added to a single cell or to a range of cells. Then you will make several additional formatting changes to improve the appearance and readability of the worksheet.

1

- Select the range A1 through F25.

- Open the 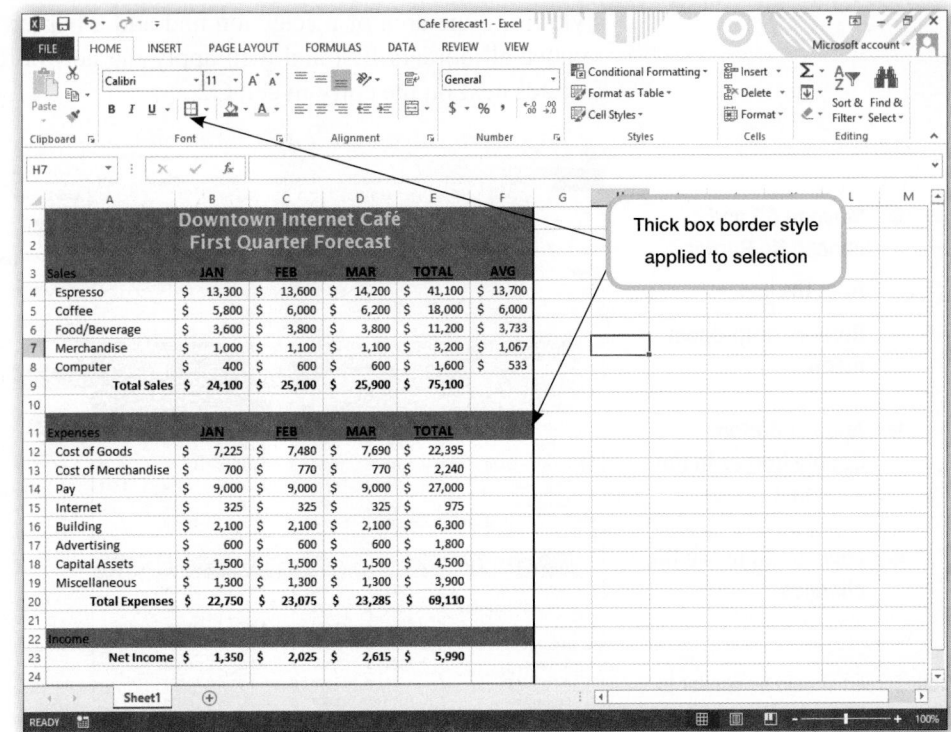 Borders drop-down menu in the Font group and choose the Thick Box Border style.

- Click outside the range to see the border.

Your screen should be similar to Figure 1.72

Figure 1.72

The range is considered a single block of cells, and the box border surrounds the entire worksheet selection.

When adding borders, the border also is applied to adjacent cells that share a bordered cell boundary. In this case, cells G1 through G25 acquired a left border and cells A26 through F26 acquired a top border. When pasting a cell that includes a cell border, the border is included unless you specify that the paste does not include the border. To see how this works, you will first copy a cell and its border, and then you will copy it again without the border.

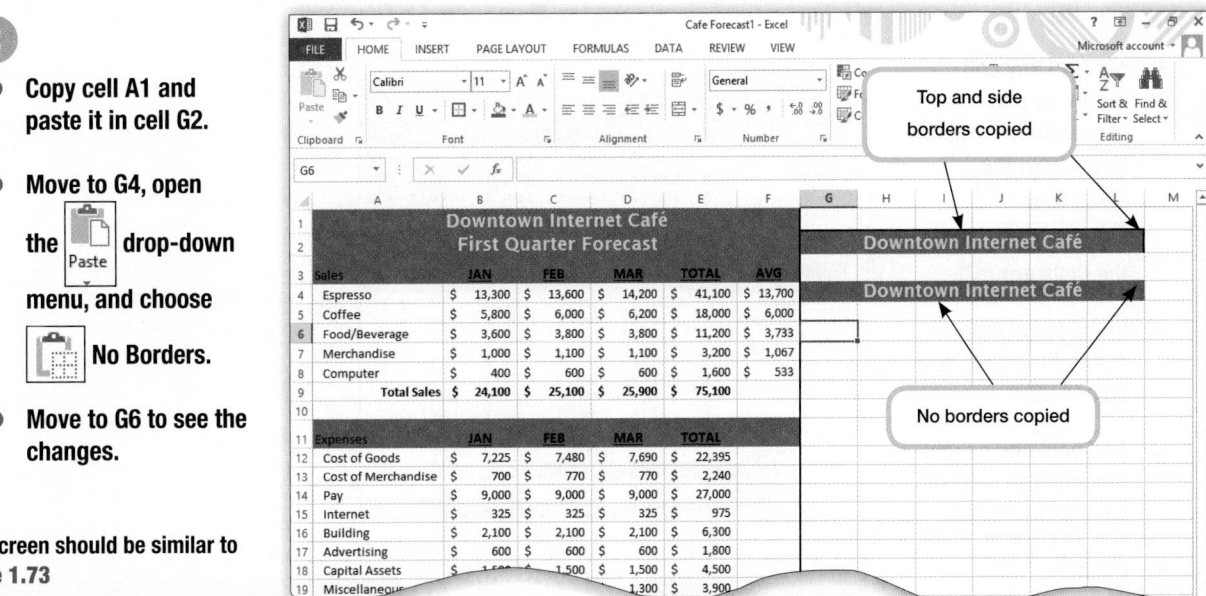

2

- Copy cell A1 and paste it in cell G2.

- Move to G4, open the Paste drop-down menu, and choose No Borders.

- Move to G6 to see the changes.

Your screen should be similar to Figure 1.73

Figure 1.73

If you want to add additional borders or replace an existing border with another, select the range and then add the border. However, if you want to remove a border style from one area of a selection and add a border to another area, you need to remove all borders first and then apply the new border styles. You will try these features next on the entry in cell G2.

3

- Move to G2 and choose No Border from the Borders drop-down menu.

- Apply a Bottom Double Border to the selection.

- Move to G6 to see the changes.

Your screen should be similar to Figure 1.74

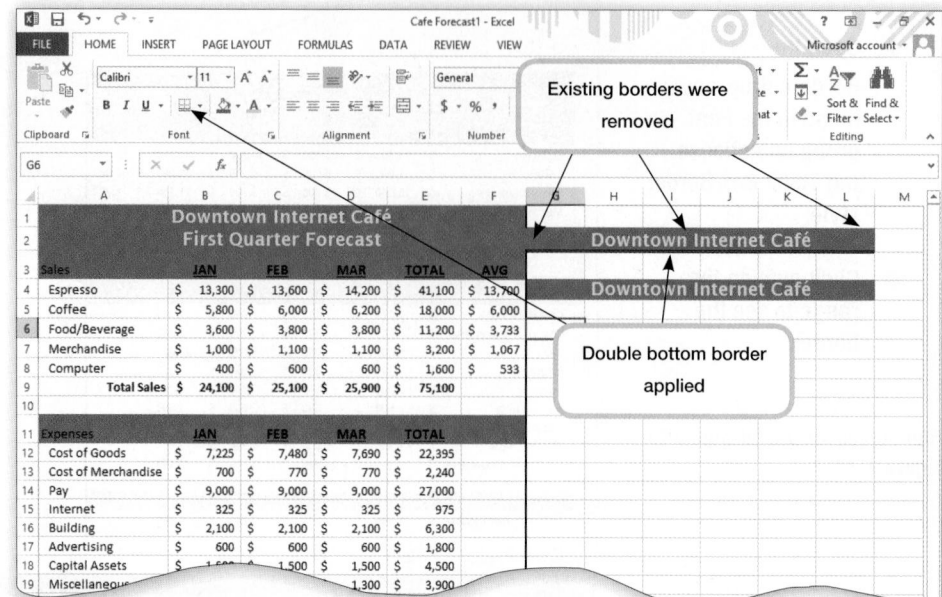

Figure 1.74

All existing borders were removed, including those that share a cell boundary, and the new double bottom border is applied to the selection. You will restore the worksheet to how it was prior to copying the title using Undo and then make some final adjustments to the worksheet.

4

- Undo your last four actions to remove the copied data.

- Move to any cell in row 10 and choose Delete Sheet Rows from the Delete drop-down menu in the Cells group.

- In the same manner, delete the blank rows 20 and 22.

- Add bold and yellow font color to cells A3, A10, A20, and A22.

- Click Save to save the worksheet changes.

Your screen should be similar to Figure 1.75

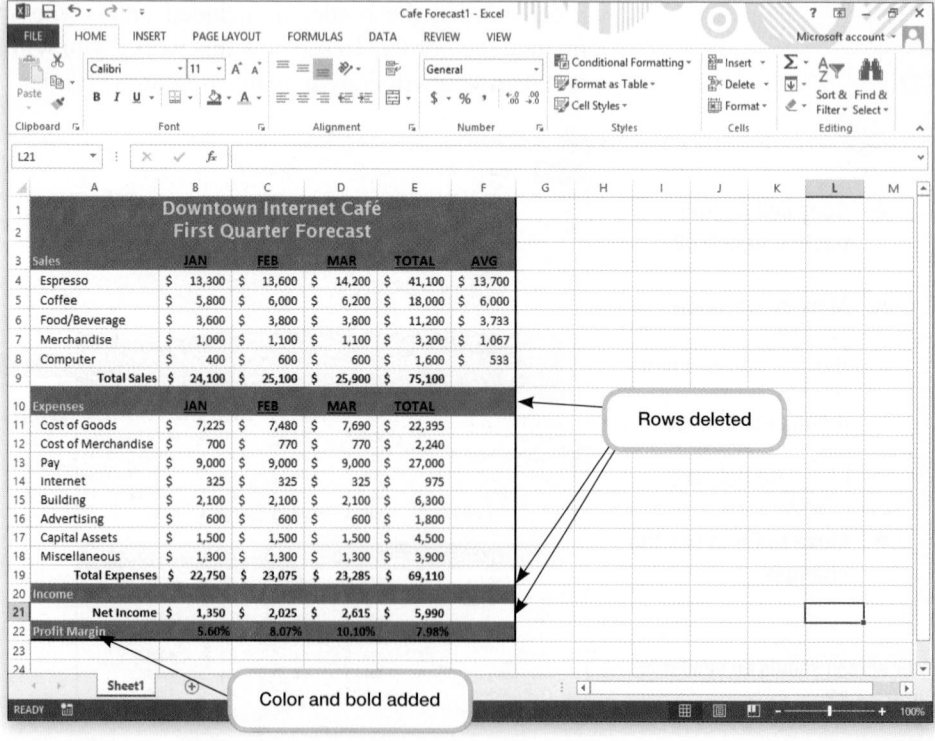

Figure 1.75

Hide and Unhide Rows and Columns

Now that the worksheet is nicely formatted, you want to focus on the data. One way to do this is to hide areas of data that you do not want to see in order to emphasize others. You will use this method to emphasize the total data.

1

- **Select columns B through D.**

- **Open the**

  Format

  drop-down menu in the Cells group and select Hide & Unhide.

- **Choose Hide Columns.**

Your screen should be similar to Figure 1.76

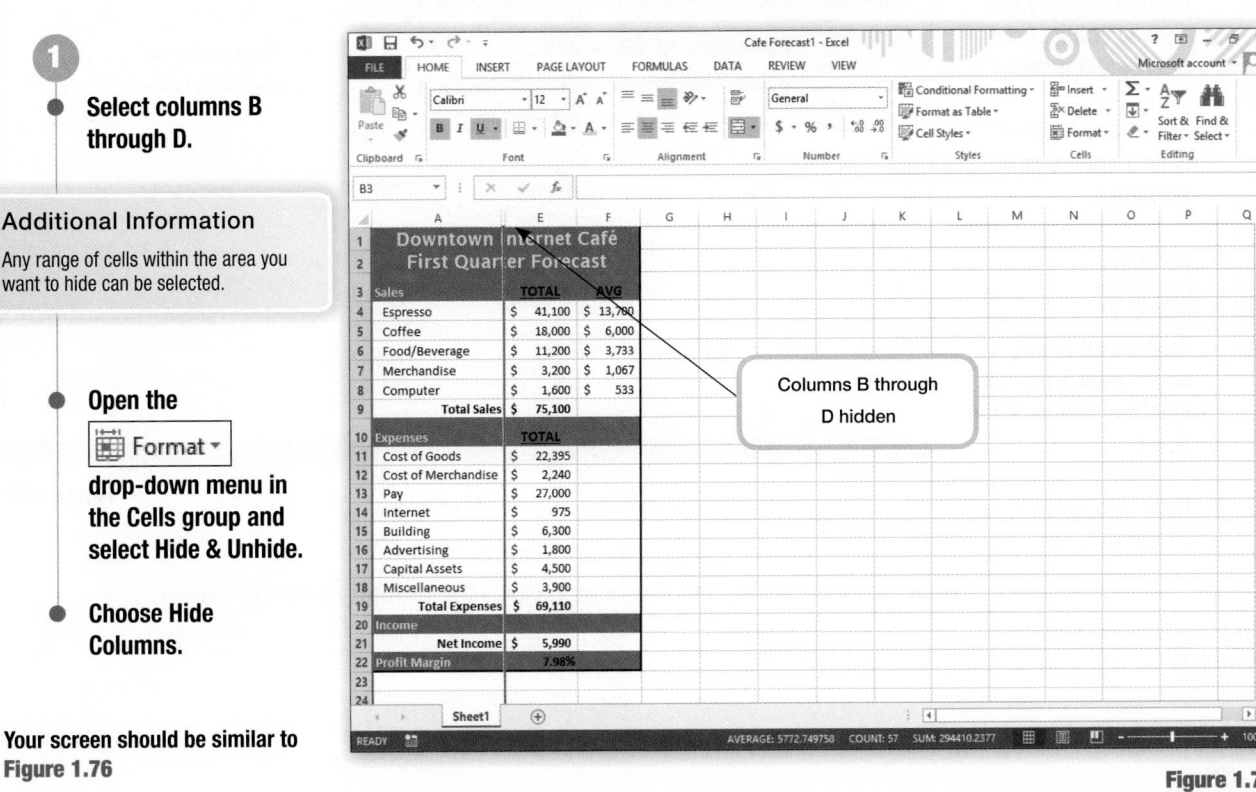

Figure 1.76

Now the worksheet focus is on the monthly total values, not the monthly values. The columns were hidden by reducing their column width to zero. Instead, you want to hide the rows.

2

- Click on column A heading and drag to select columns A and E.

- Right-click either column heading and choose Unhide from the context menu.

- Select any range of cells within rows 4 through 8.

- Open the
   Format ▾

  drop-down menu, select Hide & Unhide, and then choose Hide Rows.

- Repeat to hide rows 11 through 18.

Your screen should be similar to Figure 1.77

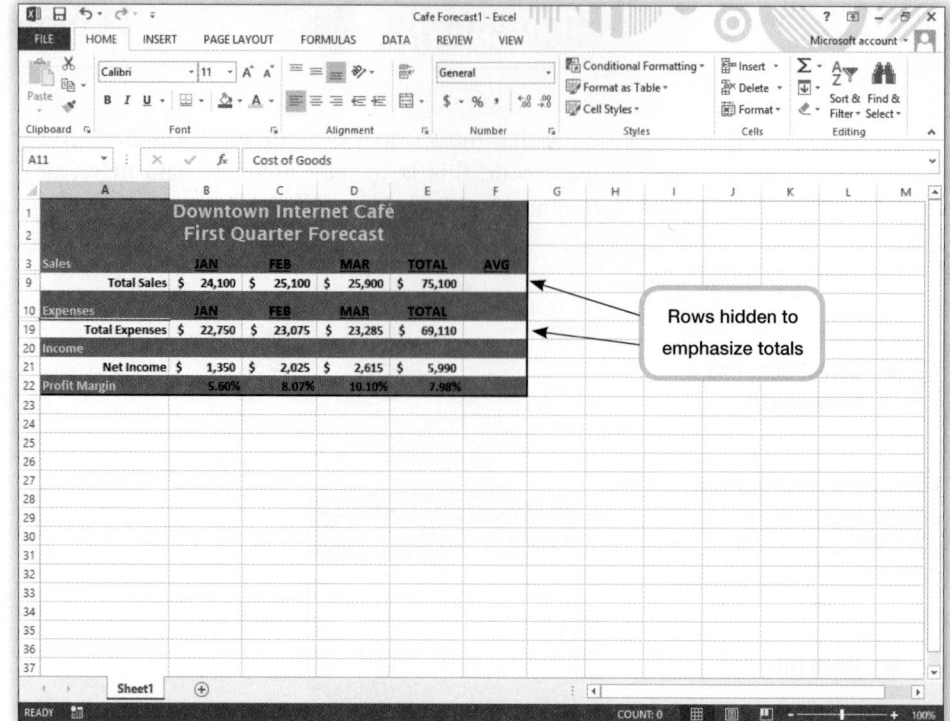

Figure 1.77

Notice how hiding the rows emphasizes the monthly totals by category.

3

- Click ↺ Undo twice to unhide the rows.

Creating a Simple Chart

Another way to better understand the data in a worksheet is to create a chart. A **chart** is a visual representation of data that is used to convey information in an easy-to-understand and attractive manner. You decide to create a chart of the sales data for the three months.

SPECIFYING DATA TO CHART

To tell Excel what data to chart, you need to select the range containing the data you want to appear in the chart plus any row or column headings you want used in the chart.

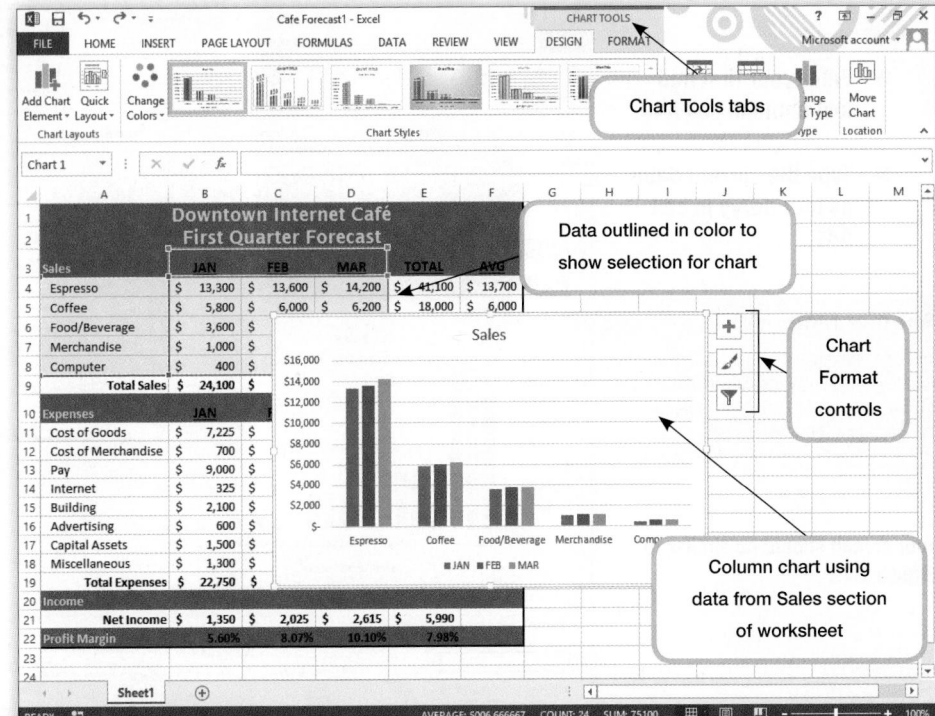

Figure 1.78

1

- Select cells A3 through D8.

- Click the Quick Analysis button.

- Click the Charts tab.

- Point to the five chart options to see a preview of each.

- Click Clustered Column.

- Click on Chart Title in the chart.

- With the mouse pointer as an I-beam, drag to select the text in the box.

- Type Sales

Your screen should be similar to **Figure 1.78**

A column chart showing the sales for the five items over three months was quickly created.

2

- Click on the edge of the chart object and drag to move it below the worksheet to cover rows 24 to 38.

- Click outside the chart object to deselect it.

Formatting Values as a Date

Now that the worksheet is complete, you want to include your name and the date in the worksheet as documentation. There are many ways to enter the date. For example, you could type the date using the format mm/dd/yy or as month dd, yyyy. When a date is entered as text, Excel converts the entry to a numeric entry that allows dates to be used in calculations. Excel stores all dates as **serial values** with each day numbered from the beginning of the 20th century. The date serial values are consecutively assigned beginning with 1, which corresponds to the date January 1, 1900, and ending with 2958465, which is December 31, 9999.

1

- Enter your first and last name in cell A40.

- Type the current date as mm/dd/yy in cell A41.

Your screen should be similar to Figure 1.79

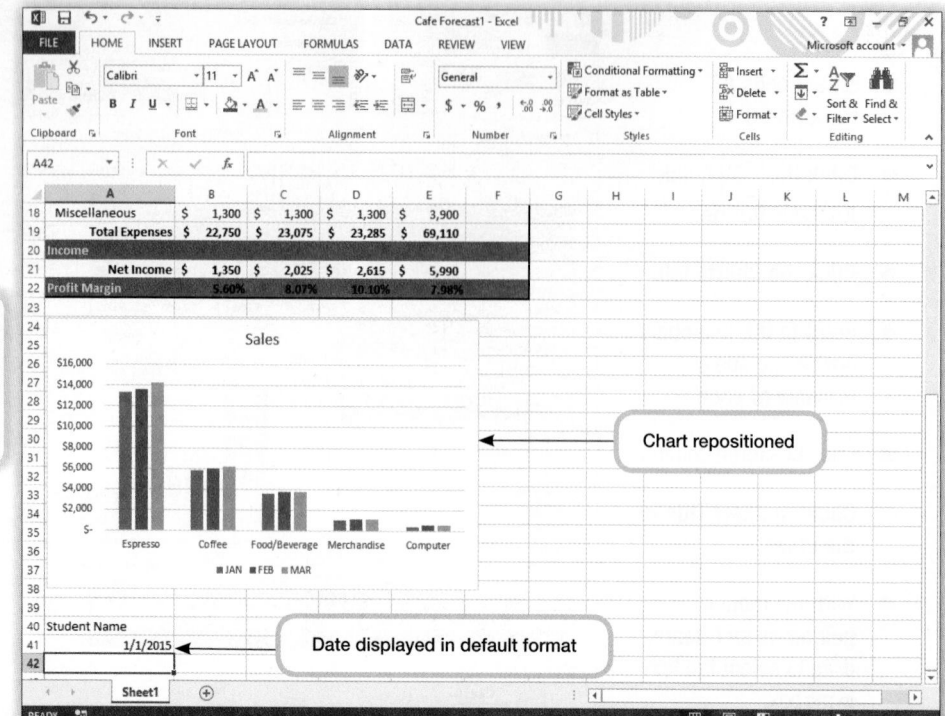

Figure 1.79

The date is displayed using the default date format, which is based on the settings in Windows. It is right-aligned in the cell because it is a numeric entry. You can change the date format in the worksheet without changing the Windows settings using the Format Cells: Number dialog box.

2

- If necessary, move to cell A41.

- Click ⌐ in the Number group to open the Format Cells dialog box.

- Choose the month xx, xxxx (March 14, 2012) date format from the Type list.

- Click OK.

Your screen should be similar to Figure 1.80

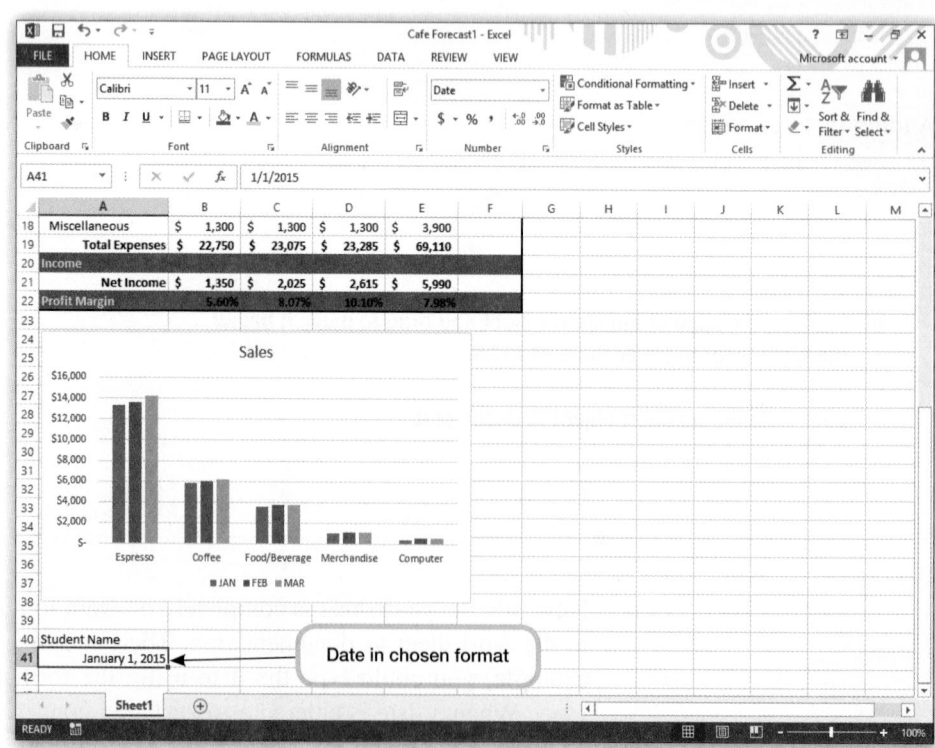

Figure 1.80

The date appears in the specified format.

Documenting a Workbook

Having Trouble?

Refer to the section "Specifying Document Properties" in the Introduction to Microsoft Office 2013 to review this feature.

You are finished working on the worksheet for now and want to save the changes you have made to the file. In addition, you want to update the file properties to include your name as the author, a title, and keywords.

1

- Press [Ctrl] + [Home].

- Open the File tab.

- In the Backstage Info window, enter the following information in the appropriate boxes.

Title	Downtown Internet Cafe
Tags	Sales Projections
Author	Your Name

Additional Information

The Author text box may be blank or may show your school or some other name. Clear the existing contents first if necessary.

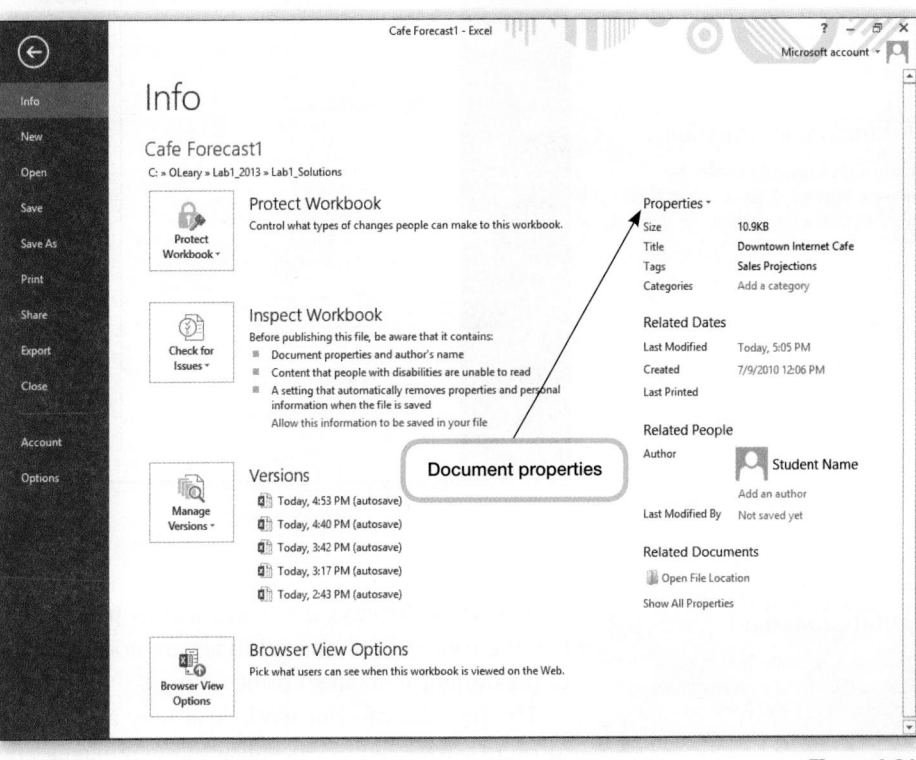

Figure 1.81

Your screen should be similar to Figure 1.81

Previewing and Printing a Worksheet

Although you still plan to make more changes to the worksheet, you want to print a copy of the estimated first quarter forecast for the owner to get feedback regarding the content and layout.

1

● **Choose Print and view the preview in the right pane.**

Your screen should be similar to Figure 1.82

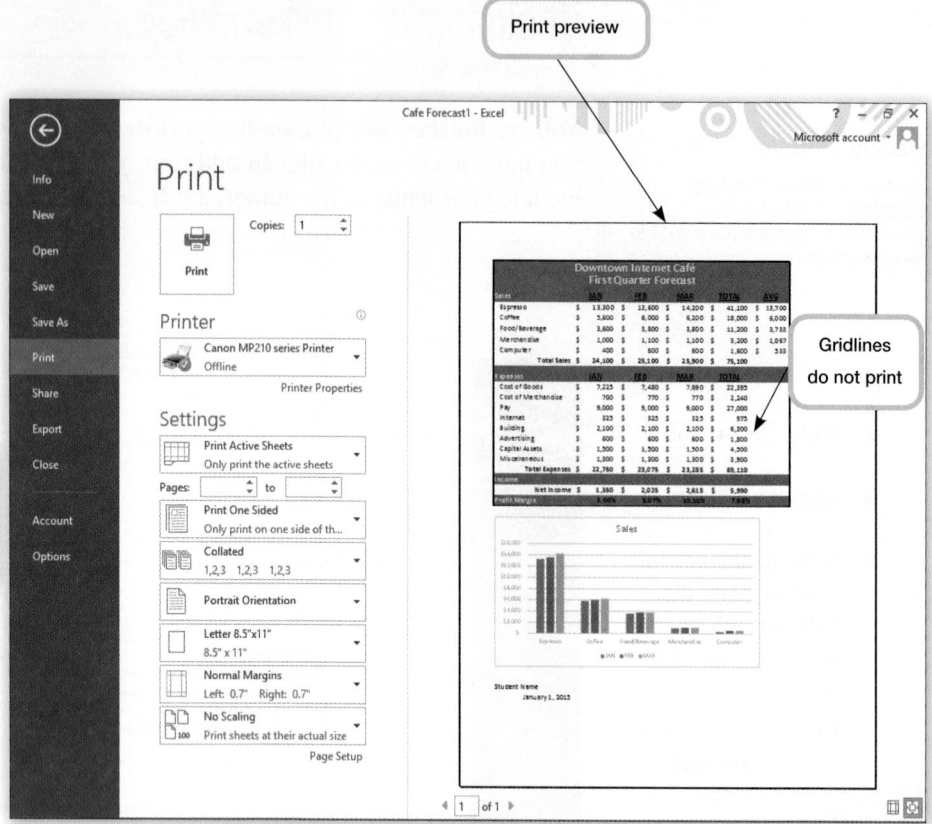

Figure 1.82

The preview displays the worksheet as it will appear on the printed page. Notice that the row and column gridlines are not displayed and will not print. This is one of the default worksheet print settings.

The preview of your worksheet may appear slightly different from that shown in Figure 1.82. This is because the way pages appear in the preview depends on the available fonts, the resolution of the printer, and the available colors. If your printer is configured to print in black and white, the preview will not display in color.

The Excel print settings let you specify how much of the worksheet you want printed. The options are described in the following table.

Option	Action
Print Active Sheets	Prints the active worksheet (default).
Print Entire Workbook	Prints all worksheets in the workbook.
Print Selection	Prints selected range only.
Pages	Prints pages you specify by typing page numbers in the text box.

The worksheet looks good and does not appear to need any further modifications immediately. Now you are ready to print the worksheet using the default print settings.

NOTE Please consult your instructor for printing procedures that may differ from the following directions.

- If necessary, make sure your printer is on and ready to print.

- If you need to change the selected printer to another printer, open the Printer drop-down list box and select the appropriate printer.

- Click .

The printed copy should be similar to the document shown in the preview area.

When printing is complete, Backstage view is automatically closed. A dotted line may appear between columns G and H. This is the automatic page break line that shows where one printed page ends and the next begins.

DISPLAYING AND PRINTING FORMULAS

Often, when verifying the accuracy of the data in a worksheet, it is helpful to display all the formulas in a worksheet rather than the resulting values. This way you can quickly verify that the formulas are referencing the correct cells and ranges.

- **Open the Formulas tab.**

- **Click** 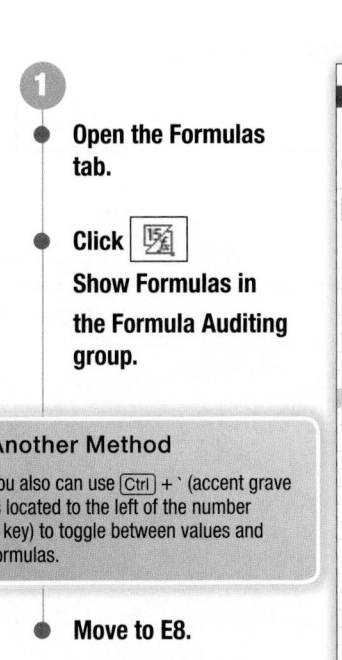 **Show Formulas in the Formula Auditing group.**

Another Method

You also can use Ctrl + ` (accent grave is located to the left of the number 1 key) to toggle between values and formulas.

- **Move to E8.**

Your screen should be similar to Figure 1.83

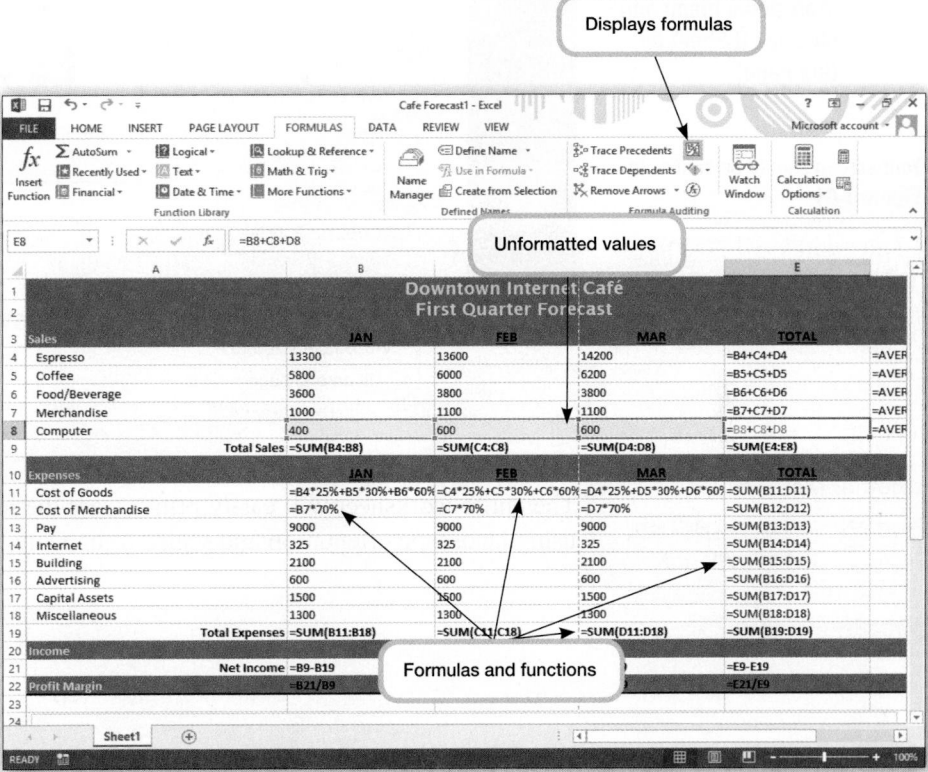

Figure 1.83

The display of the worksheet has changed to display unformatted values and the formulas and functions. It has automatically increased the column widths so the formulas and text do not overflow into the adjacent cells.

CHANGING WORKSHEET ORIENTATION AND SCALING CONTENT

Next, you will print the worksheet with formulas. Because the worksheet is so much wider, you will need to change the orientation to landscape, which prints across the length of the paper. Then you will reduce the scale of the worksheet so it fits on one page. The **scaling** feature will reduce or enlarge the worksheet contents by a percentage or fit them to a specific number of pages by height and width. You want to scale the worksheet to fit on one page.

- Open the File tab and choose Print.

- Change the orientation setting to Landscape Orientation.

- Open the 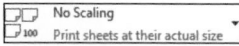 drop-down menu and choose Fit Sheet on One Page.

Your screen should be similar to Figure 1.84

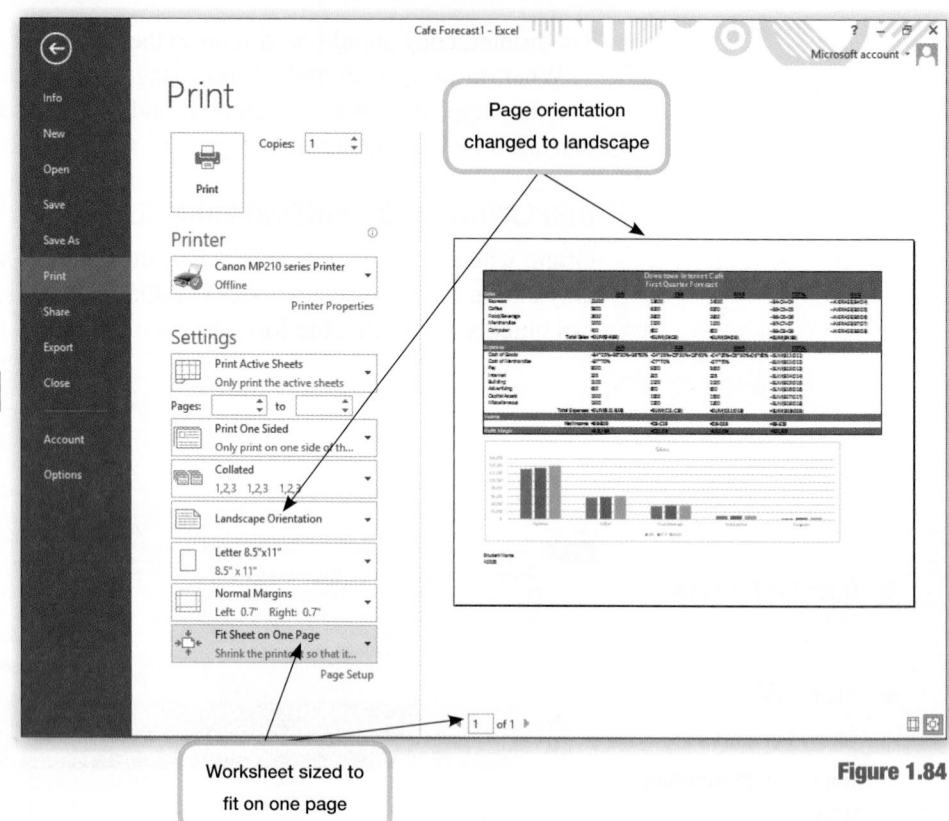

Page orientation changed to landscape

Worksheet sized to fit on one page

Figure 1.84

The entire worksheet will easily print across the length of the page when printed using landscape orientation and scaled to fit a single page.

2

- Print the worksheet.

- Press Ctrl + ` (accent grave is located to the left of the number 1 key) to return the display to values.

Having Trouble?

Refer to the "Closing a File" and "Exiting an Office 2013 Application" sections in the Introduction to Microsoft Office 2013 to review these features.

You are now ready to exit the Excel application. If you attempt to close the application without first saving the workbook, Excel displays a warning asking whether you want to save your work. If you do not save your work and you exit the application, all changes you made from the last time you saved will be lost.

1

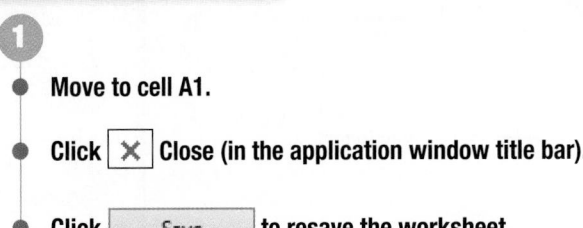

- Move to cell A1.

- Click ☒ Close (in the application window title bar).

- Click [Save] to resave the worksheet.

Additional Information

Excel saves the file with the cell selector in the same cell location it is in at the time it is saved.

Because you made several edits since last saving the worksheet, you were prompted to save it again before closing it.

CUS ON CAREERS

EXPLORE YOUR CAREER OPTIONS

Event Marketing Representative

Did you know that 40 percent of the advertised positions in sports are for marketing and promotion? A marketing graduate hired as a basketball event marketing representative would use Excel to keep track of the income and expenses for coordinated halftime activities at professional sporting events. These worksheets would provide valuable information for promoting sponsors' products and services at games. An event marketing representative might start out as an unpaid intern, but after graduation could expect to earn from $40,000 to $50,000.

Data (EX1.12)

Basic information or data you enter in a cell can be text, numbers, dates, or times.

AutoCorrect (EX1.18)

The AutoCorrect feature makes some basic assumptions about the text you are typing and, based on these assumptions, automatically corrects the entry.

Column Width (EX1.21)

The column width is the size or width of a column and controls the amount of information that can be displayed in a cell.

Spelling Checker (EX1.25)

The spelling checker locates misspelled words, duplicate words, and capitalization irregularities in the active worksheet and proposes the correct spelling.

Thesaurus (EX1.27)

The thesaurus is a reference tool that provides synonyms, antonyms, and related words for a selected word or phrase.

Range (EX1.31)

A selection consisting of two or more cells on a worksheet is a range.

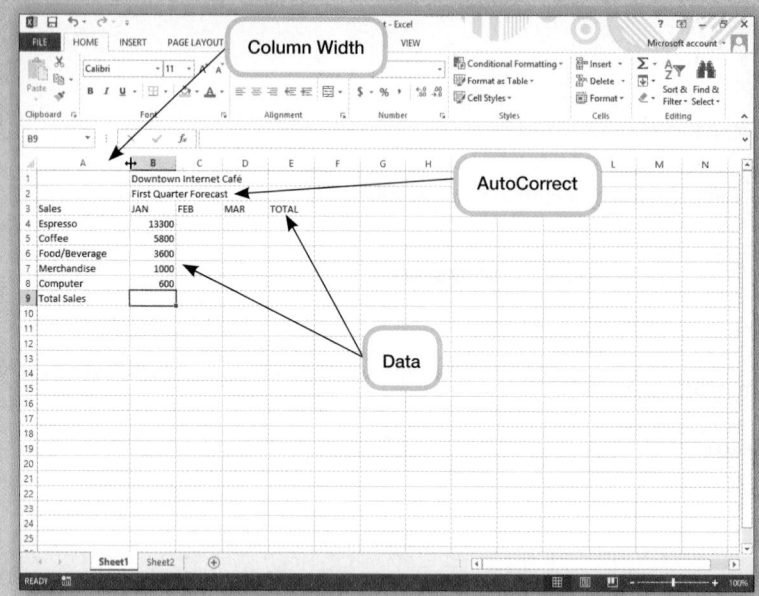

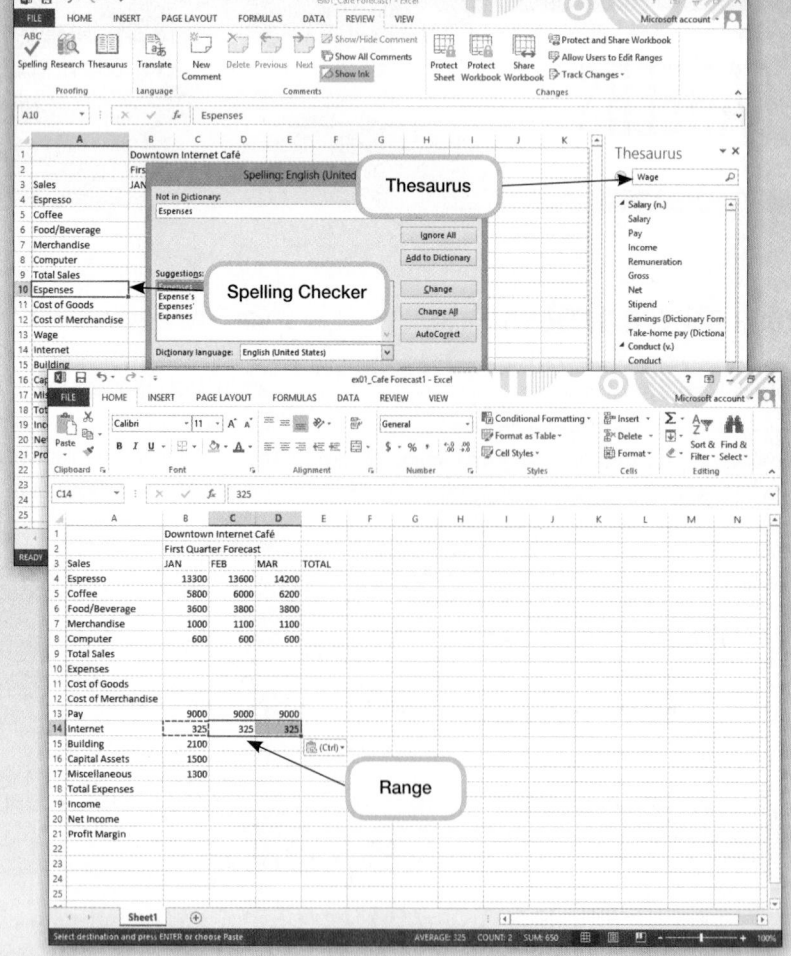

Formula (EX1.37)

A formula is an equation that performs a calculation on data contained in a worksheet.

Relative Reference (EX1.39)

A relative reference is a cell or range reference in a formula whose location is interpreted by Excel in relation to the position of the cell that contains the formula.

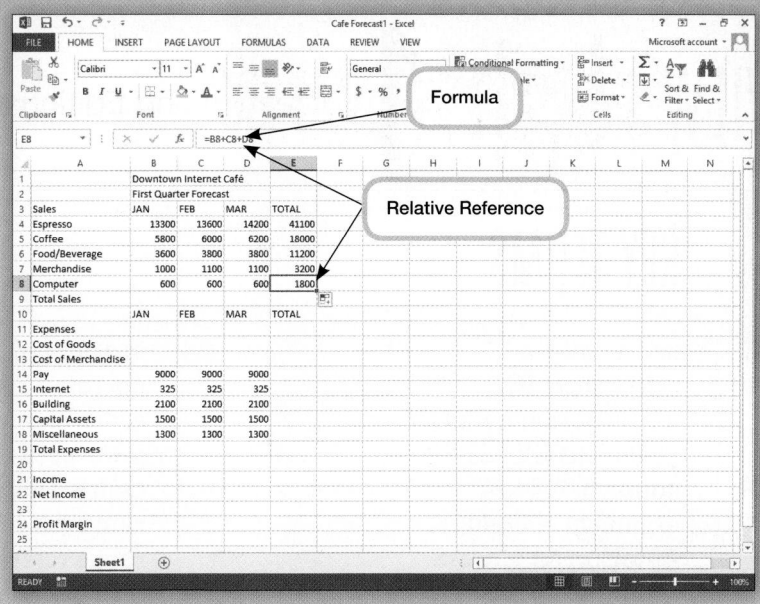

Function (EX1.40)

A function is a prewritten formula that performs certain types of calculations automatically.

Recalculation (EX1.47)

When a number in a referenced cell in a formula changes, Excel automatically recalculates all formulas that are dependent upon the changed value.

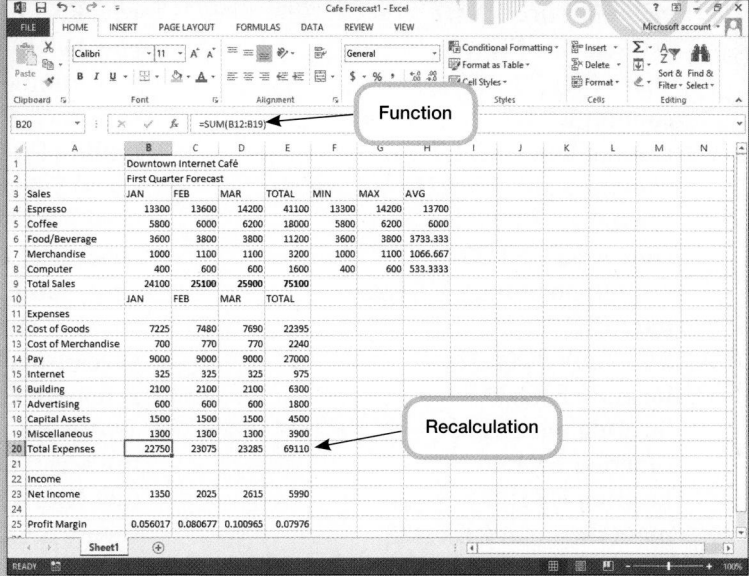

Alignment (EX1.51)

Alignment settings allow you to change the horizontal and vertical placement and the orientation of an entry in a cell.

Row Height (EX1.53)

The row height is the size or height of a row measured in points.

Number Formats (EX1.62)

Number formats change the appearance of numbers onscreen and when printed, without changing the way the number is stored or used in calculations.

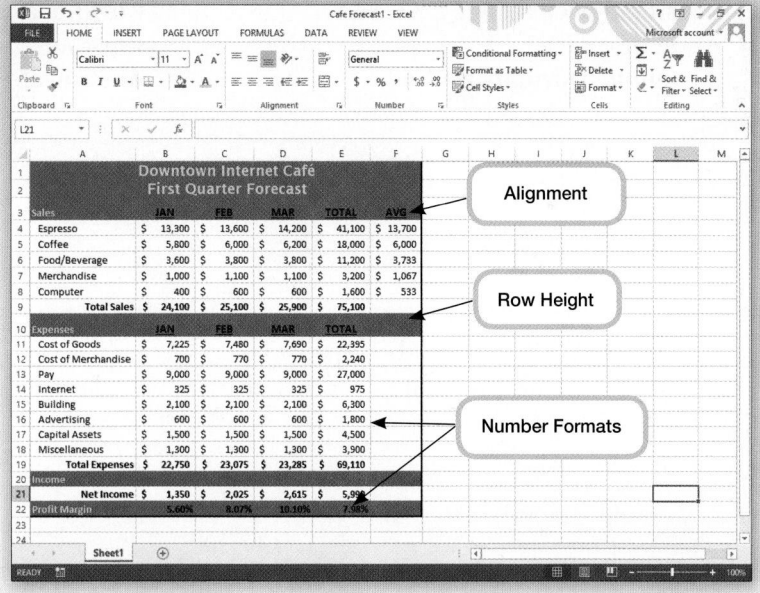

KEY TERMS

active cell EX1.7
active sheet EX1.7
adjacent range EX1.31
alignment EX1.51
antonym EX1.27
argument EX1.40
AutoCorrect EX1.18
AutoFit EX1.22
cell EX1.7
cell reference EX1.7
cell selector EX1.7
chart EX1.70
column EX1.6
column letter EX1.7
column width EX1.21
constant EX1.37
copy area EX1.28
custom dictionary EX1.25
data EX1.12
fill handle EX1.32
formula EX1.37
formula bar EX1.5
function EX1.40
heading EX1.12
main dictionary EX1.25
merged cell EX1.55
Name box EX1.5
nonadjacent range EX1.31
number EX1.12
number formats EX1.62

operand EX1.37
operator EX1.37
order of operations EX1.37
paste area EX1.29
Quick Analysis tool EX1.42
range EX1.31
range reference EX1.31
recalculation EX1.47
relative reference EX1.39
row EX1.6
row height EX1.53
row number EX1.7
sans serif EX1.56
scaling EX1.76
serial value EX1.71
serif EX1.56
sheet EX1.6
sheet tab EX1.7
spelling checker EX1.25
spreadsheet EX1.6
synonym EX1.27
syntax EX1.40
tab scroll buttons EX1.8
text EX1.12
theme EX1.65
thesaurus EX1.27
variable EX1.37
workbook EX1.5
workbook window EX1.5
worksheet EX1.6

COMMAND SUMMARY

Command	Shortcut	Action
File tab		
Open	Ctrl + O	Opens an existing workbook file
Save	Ctrl + S	Saves file using same file name
Save As	F12	Saves file using a new file name
Close	Ctrl + F4	Closes open workbook file
New	Ctrl + N	Opens a new blank workbook
Print / [Print icon] Print	Ctrl + P	Prints a worksheet
Print / [No Scaling - Print sheets at their actual size] / Fit sheet on one page		Scales worksheet to fit on a single page
Quick Access Toolbar		
[Save icon] Save	Ctrl + S	Saves document using same file name
[Undo icon] Undo	Ctrl + Z	Reverses last editing or formatting change
[Redo icon] Redo	Ctrl + Y	Restores changes after using Undo
Home tab		
Clipboard group		
[Paste icon] Paste	Ctrl + V	Pastes selections stored in system Clipboard
[Cut icon] Cut	Ctrl + X	Cuts selected data from the worksheet
[Copy icon] Copy	Ctrl + C	Copies selected data to system Clipboard
[Format Painter icon] Format Painter		Copies formatting from one place and applies it to another
Font group		
Calibri ▼ Font		Changes text font
11 ▼ Font Size		Changes text size
B Bold	Ctrl + B	Bolds selected text
I Italic	Ctrl + I	Italicizes selected text

COMMAND SUMMARY (CONTINUED)

Command	Shortcut	Action
U ▾ Underline	Ctrl +U	Underlines selected text
▦ ▾ Borders		Adds border to specified area of cell or range
🪣 ▾ Fill Color		Adds color to cell background
A ▾ Font Color		Adds color to text
Alignment group		
≡ Align Left		Left-aligns entry in cell space
≡ Center		Center-aligns entry in cell space
≡ Align Right		Right-aligns entry in cell space
⋮≡ Increase Indent		Indents cell entry
≡⋮ Decrease Indent		Reduces the margin between the left cell border and cell entry
▦ ▾ Merge & Center		Combines selected cells into one cell and centers cell contents in new cell
Number group		
General ▾ Number Format		Applies selected number formatting to selection
$ ▾ Accounting Number Format		Applies Accounting number format to selection
% Percent Style		Applies Percent Style format to selection
⬅.0 .00 Increase Decimal		Increases number of decimal places
.00 ➡.0 Decrease Decimal		Decreases number of decimal places
Cells group		
🔢 Insert ▾ /Insert Cells		Inserts blank cells, shifting existing cells down
🔢 Insert ▾ /Insert Cut Cells		Inserts cut row of data into new worksheet row, shifting existing rows down
🔢 Insert ▾ /Insert Copied Cells		Inserts copied row into new worksheet row, shifting existing rows down
🔢 Insert ▾ /Insert Sheet Rows		Inserts blank rows, shifting existing rows down
🔢 Insert ▾ /Insert Sheet Columns		Inserts blank columns, shifting existing columns right
🔢 Insert ▾ /Insert Sheet		Inserts a new blank worksheet in workbook

COMMAND SUMMARY (CONTINUED)

Command	Shortcut	Action
Delete ▾ /Delete Sheet Rows		Deletes selected rows, shifting existing rows up
Delete ▾ /Delete Sheet Columns		Deletes selected columns, shifting existing columns left
Delete ▾ /Delete Sheet		Deletes the active worksheet
Format ▾ /Row Height		Changes height of selected row
Format ▾ /AutoFit Row Height		Changes row height to match the tallest cell entry
Format ▾ /Column Width		Changes width of selected column
Format ▾ /AutoFit Column Width		Changes column width to match widest cell entry
Format ▾ /Default Width		Returns column width to default width
Editing group		
Σ ▾ Sum		Calculates the sum of the values in the selected cells
Σ ▾ Sum/Average		Calculates the average of the values in the selected range
Σ ▾ Sum/Min		Returns the smallest of the values in the selected range
Σ ▾ Sum/Max		Returns the largest of the values in the selected range
▾ Fill/Right	Ctrl + R	Continues a pattern to adjacent cells to the right
▾ Clear		Removes both formats and contents from selected cells
▾ Clear/Clear Formats		Clears formats only from selected cells
▾ Clear/Clear Contents	Delete	Clears contents only from selected cells
Formulas tab		
Formula Auditing group		
Show Formulas	Ctrl + `	Displays and hides worksheet formulas
Review tab		
Proofing group		
ABC ✓ Spelling	F7	Spell-checks worksheet
Thesaurus		Opens the thesaurus for the selected word in the Research task pane

LAB EXERCISES

SCREEN IDENTIFICATION

1. In the following Excel 2013 screen, letters identify important elements. Enter the correct term for each screen element in the space provided.

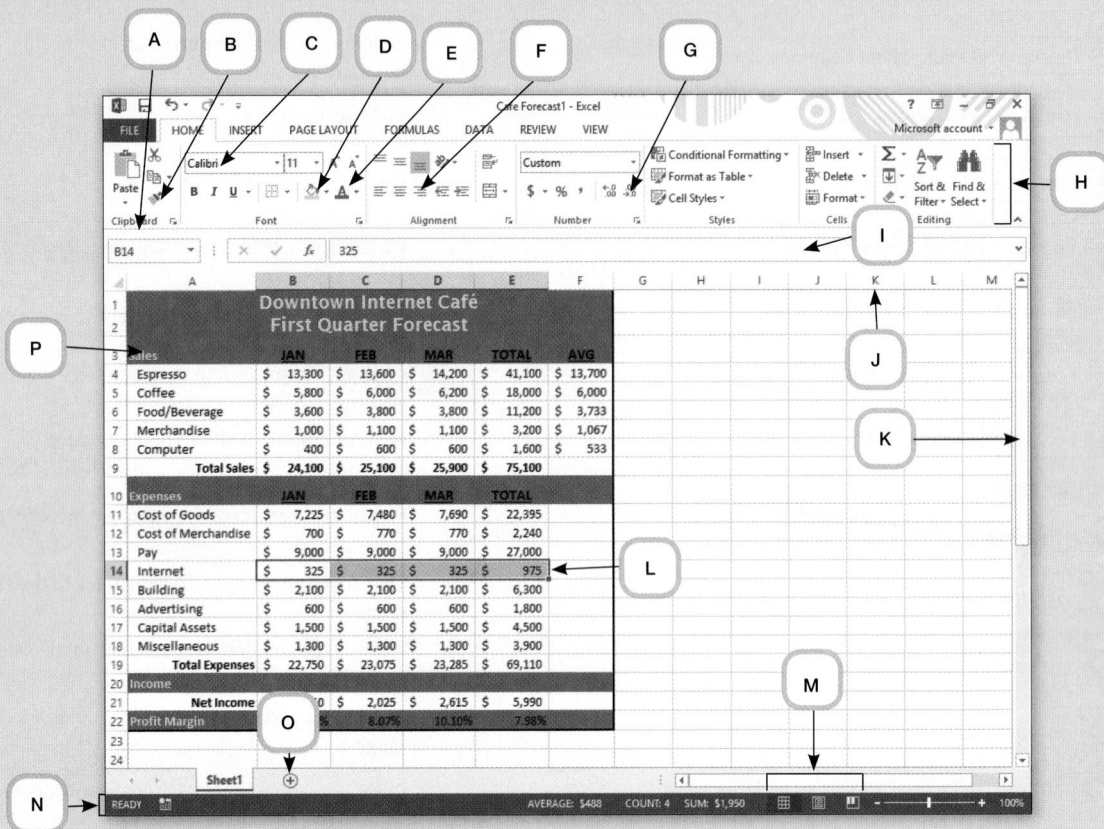

Possible answers for the screen identification are:

Active sheet	Name box	A. _____	I. _____
Align Right	New sheet	B. _____	J. _____
Chart title	Quick Analysis	C. _____	K. _____
Column label	Range	D. _____	L. _____
Fill color	Ribbon	E. _____	M. _____
Font	Row	F. _____	N. _____
Font color	Scroll bar	G. _____	O. _____
Format Painter	Status bar	H. _____	P. _____
Formula bar	Text label		
Increase Decimal	View buttons		

MATCHING

Match the lettered item on the right with the numbered item on the left.

1. 🔲▾   _____a. an arithmetic operator
2. .xlsx   _____b. pointer shape for AutoFit
3. 🔢   _____c. a graphic representation of data
4. chart   _____d. Excel workbook file name extension
5. /   _____e. two or more worksheet cells
6. 🔲   _____f. enters a SUM function
7. =C19*A21   _____g. increases decimal places shown in a cell
8. D11   _____h. merges cells and centers entry
9. range   _____i. a formula multiplying the values in two cells
10. Σ ▾   _____j. a cell reference
11. ↔   _____k. Quick Analysis

TRUE/FALSE

Circle the correct answer to the following questions.

1.	A function is a preset formula that performs a calculation.	**True**	**False**
2.	When a formula containing relative references is copied the cell references in the copied formula are adjusted based on their new location in the worksheet.	**True**	**False**
3.	The Quick Analysis tool appears when you select data for a chart.	**True**	**False**
4.	An Excel chart is a visual display of data in a worksheet.	**True**	**False**
5.	Number formats affect the way in which those values are used in calculations.	**True**	**False**
6.	When a value in a referenced formula cell is edited, Excel recalculates the formula.	**True**	**False**
7.	You can hide columns or rows in a worksheet to prohibit the data from being used in calculations.	**True**	**False**
8.	Excel's spelling checker identifies a word as misspelled if that word is not in the main dictionary.	**True**	**False**
9.	Cell alignment allows you to change the horizontal and vertical placement and the orientation of an entry in a cell.	**True**	**False**
10.	A date is a value.	**True**	**False**

LAB EXERCISES

FILL-IN

Complete the following statements by filling in the blanks with the correct key terms.

1. In a worksheet, _____ entries are right-aligned and text entries are _____-aligned.
2. Selected cells are combined into a single cell when you use the _____ command.
3. A new Excel workbook includes _____ worksheet(s).
4. When you double-click a cell with an entry, Excel changes to _____ mode.
5. Excel includes several categories of prewritten _____ to perform various arithmetic, financial, or statistical calculations.
6. In Excel, dates are stored as integers known as _____ values so that they can be used in calculations.
7. To perform an arithmetic calculation, key your own _____ in the cell.
8. When you click the File command tab, Excel changes to _____ view.
9. The values in a range of cells can be added by using the _____ function.
10. To display values with a monetary symbol and decimal places, you can use the Currency or the _____ format.

MULTIPLE CHOICE

Circle the correct response to the questions below.

1. The Excel file that stores data is a _____ .
   a. worksheet
   b. workbook
   c. workspace
   d. spreadsheet
2. To display more or less information in a cell, you can adjust the _____ .
   a. column letter
   b. row depth
   c. column width
   d. row number
3. A _____ entry can contain a combination of letters, numbers, spaces, and other special characters.
   a. number
   b. variable
   c. constant
   d. text

4. The small green square located in the lower-right corner of a cell or a selection is the _____.
   a. sheet tab
   b. fill handle
   c. scroll box
   d. sizing handle

5. Which of the following is a properly entered Excel formula as it is shown here?
   a. =(5 + 8)(2 + 1)
   b. {5 + 8*2 + 1}
   c. [5 + 8(2 + 1)]
   d. =(5 + 8)*(2 + 1)

6. Referenced cells are automatically adjusted in a copied formula if those references are _____.
   a. absolute
   b. fixed
   c. relative
   d. variable

7. Excel's _____ feature automatically inserts proper capitalization in the names of months and weekdays.
   a. AutoName
   b. AutoCorrect
   c. CorrectWords
   d. Word Wrap

8. If a worksheet does not fit on a single printed page, you can _____ it to fit.
   a. rearrange
   b. scale
   c. merge
   d. wrap

9. When a value in a cell is changed, existing formulas that refer to that cell are _____ .
   a. recalculated
   b. reformatted
   c. relooped
   d. rescaled

10. Before creating a chart, you must first _____ the data that is to be illustrated in the chart.
    a. style
    b. calculate
    c. select
    d. hide

STEP-BY-STEP

SMARTPHONE ACTIVITIES ANALYSIS ★

1. Mary Collins works for a wireless service provider. She is analyzing data gathered in a survey of 1,200 smartphone users from ages 14 to 19 for use in marketing campaigns. After you follow the directions to complete the worksheet, your solution should look similar to that shown here.

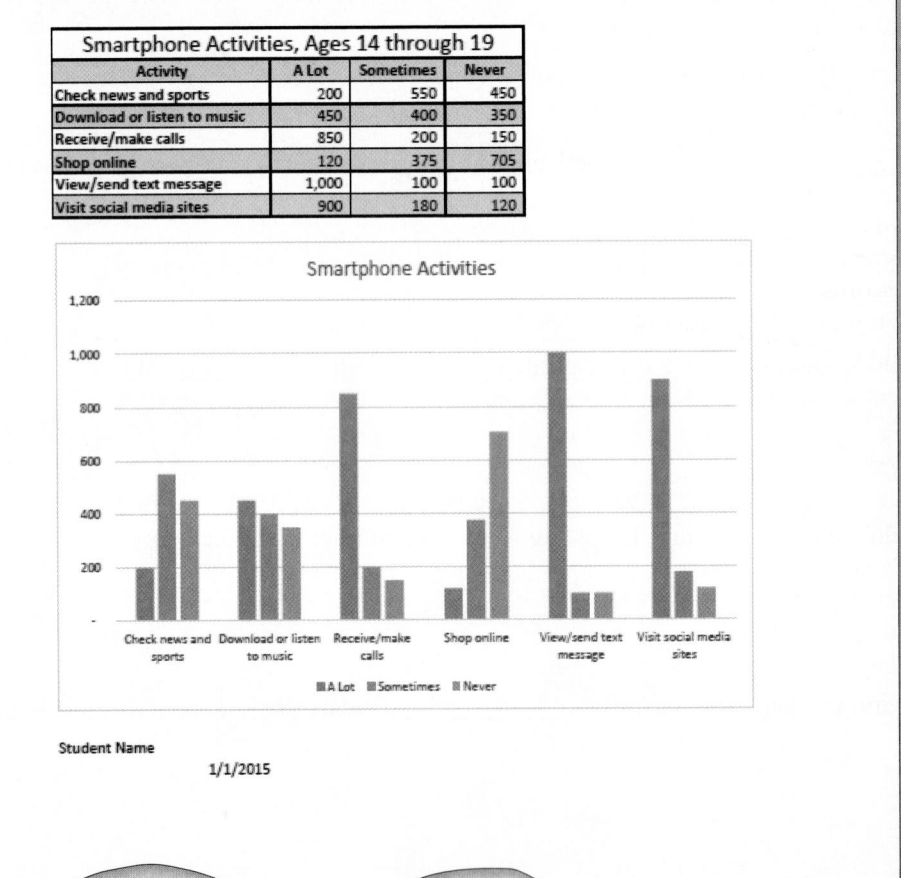

Smartphone Activities, Ages 14 through 19			
Activity	A Lot	Sometimes	Never
Check news and sports	200	550	450
Download or listen to music	450	400	350
Receive/make calls	850	200	150
Shop online	120	375	705
View/send text message	1,000	100	100
Visit social media sites	900	180	120

a. Open a new blank Excel 2013 workbook.

b. Enter the data shown here into the worksheet. Save the workbook as Smartphone Activities to your solution file location.

Row	Column A	Column B	Column C	Column D
1	Activity	A Lot	Sometimes	Never
2	Check news and sports	200	550	450
3	Download or listen to music	450	400	350
4	Receive/make calls	850	200	150
5	Shop online	120	375	705
6	View/send text message	1000	100	100
7	Visit social media sites	900	180	120

c. AutoFit the widths of columns A and C. Insert a row above row 1.

d. In cell A1, enter the title **Smartphone Activities, Ages 14 through 19**.

e. Merge and center this title across columns A through D. Set the font to 16 points.

f. Bold the column labels in row 2, and center them. Apply bold to the labels in column A.

g. Add all borders to cells A2 through D8. Add an outside border to cell A1. AutoFit columns as needed.

h. Apply the Comma number format with no decimal places to the values.

i. Create a clustered column chart using the worksheet data. Move the chart to row 10, and size it to reach cell G30. Edit the chart title to **Smartphone Activities**.

j. Add a light fill color of your choice that complements the chart to row 2. Apply the same fill to every other row up to and including row 8.

k. Enter your name in cell A32 and the date in cell A33.

l. Move to cell A1. Save the workbook again. Preview and print the worksheet.

LAB EXERCISES

ANIMAL RESCUE FOUNDATION HOUSING COST ANALYSIS ★

2. Edward Corwin, an employee at the Animal Rescue Foundation, analyzes data about major shelters in the metropolitan area. He is currently working on costs for the past two years and estimating two additional years. After you follow the directions to complete the worksheet, your solution should look similar to that shown here.

a. Open ex01_Animal Housing.

b. Widen column A to display the longest shelter name. Spell-check the worksheet.

c. Edit the titles in cells A2 and A3 so that the first letter of each word except "to" is capitalized. Increase the font size to 16 points for both titles. Merge and center each title across columns A through E.

d. Bold and center the labels in row 5.

e. In row 16, enter a function to total the values. Format the values in rows 6 and 16 with the Accounting number format and no decimal places. Format the values in rows 7 through 15 with Comma style, no decimal places.

f. Select cells B5 and C5, and use the Fill handle to enter the following two years in cells D5 and E5.

Animal Angels Housing Cost Analysis
Total Expenses to Shelter Animals

Shelter Name	2011	2012	2013	2014
Nobody's Pets	$ 127,000	$ 154,200	$ 142,600	$ 152,800
Pets Unlimited	154,500	251,000	213,500	220,300
ASPCA	129,100	154,300	148,500	142,400
FOCAS	14,500	19,200	12,500	14,700
Wood Green Animal Shelter	2,300	2,500	2,200	4,200
Pet Where Shelter	1,200	1,500	1,400	1,600
New River Animal Shelter	11,200	1,530	11,700	10,500
New Pet Shelter	19,300	19,900	18,900	25,300
City of Dogs Shelter	10,200	11,500	14,200	13,500
Humane World	29,100	12,500	26,700	29,900
Total	$ 500,411	$ 630,142	$ 594,213	$ 617,214

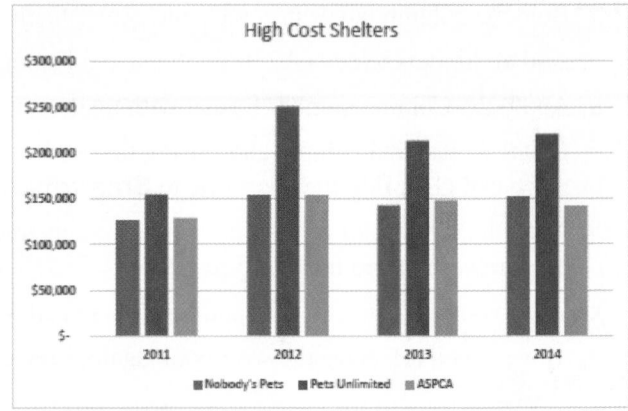

High Cost Shelters

Student Name
January 1, 2015

g. Enter the data shown here for the following two years into the worksheet. Save the workbook as Animal Housing Analysis to your solution file location.

Row	Column D	Column E
6	142600	152800
7	213500	220300
8	12500	14700
9	2200	4200
10	1400	1600
11	148500	142400
12	11700	10500
13	18900	25300
14	14200	13500
15	26700	29900

h. Copy the formula in row 16.

i. Move the ASPCA row/data so that it is above the "FOCAS" data.

j. Edit the label in cell A5 to show "Shelter Name."

k. Add all borders to cells A5 through E16. Add an outside border to cells A1 through E4.

l. Create a clustered column chart for the three shelters with the highest costs. Move the chart to cell A18, and size it to reach cell E35. Edit the chart title to **High Cost Shelters**.

m. In cells A1 through E4, apply a fill color of your choice to complement the chart. Then apply the same fill to row 16.

n. Enter your name in cell A36 and the current date in cell A37. Format the date to display the month spelled out, the date, and a four-digit year (March 14, 2012).

o. Move to cell A1. Save the workbook. Preview and print the worksheet.

p. Display formulas, and change to landscape orientation. Print the worksheet so that it fits on one page.

q. Remove the formula display.

LAB EXERCISES

WORK MILEAGE ANALYSIS ★★

3. Mary Ellen works for an insurance agency and is reviewing average miles driven to work. This data is available in a recent national study and is used to categorize drivers and rates. After you follow the directions to complete the worksheet, your solution should look similar to that shown here.

a. Open ex01_Work_Mileage.

b. Widen column A to display the longest mileage item. Spell-check the worksheet, and correct any words not found by the speller.

c. For cells A1:A2, increase the font size to 16 points. Enter the label **Number** in cell B3. Bold and center the labels in row 3.

d. Insert a column at column B. Enter the label **Percent** in cell B3.

e. Insert a row above row 1, and insert a row above row 4. Make row 4 the same height as row 1.

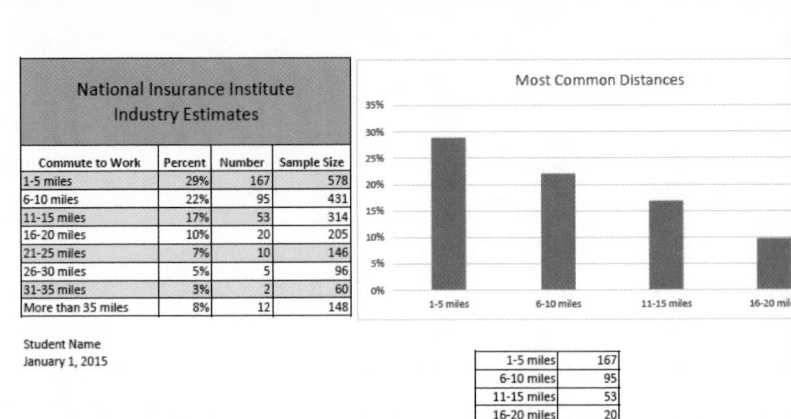

f. In cell B6, enter the formula **=c6/d6**. Format the result as Percent with zero decimal places. Copy the formula to cells B7 through B13. AutoFit column B. Save the workbook as Work Mileage Analysis to your solution file location.

g. Merge and center the labels in cells A2 and A3 across columns A through D. Add all borders to cells A5 through D13. Add an outside border to cells A1 through D4. Make row 5 slightly taller than row 6.

h. Create a clustered column chart for the four mileage categories with the highest percentages. Move the chart to cell E1. Edit the chart title to **Most Common Distances**.

i. Copy cells A6 through A9 to cells G16 through G19. Then copy cells C6 through C9 to cells H16 through H19. Right-align the categories in cells G16 through G19, and make column G wide enough to show the border on the left edge.

j. In cells A1 through D4, add a fill color of your choice to complement the chart. Then apply the same or a lighter fill to every other row of the data in columns A through D.

k. Enter your name in cell A15 and the current date in cell A16. Format the date to display the month spelled out, the date, and a four-digit year (March 14, 2012). Left-align the date.

l. Move to cell A1 and save the workbook.

m. Preview the worksheet. Change to landscape orientation, and set the scaling so that the worksheet fits on one page. Print the worksheet.

U.S. MEDIAN HOUSEHOLD INCOME WORKSHEET ★★★

4. Terrence Lewis works for an employment agency and is researching information about household income in various states. He has used data from the U.S. Census to build a worksheet. After you follow the directions to complete the worksheet, your solution should look similar to that shown here.

    a. Open ex01_Household Income.

    b. Edit the title in cell A1 to capitalize each word except "by." Delete the comma. Increase the font size to 20 points.

    c. Widen column A to show the longest state or district. Make the labels in row 2 bold.

    d. Enter the labels **$ Change** in cell E2, **% Change** in cell F2, and **Average** in cell G2. Bold and center these labels. Save the workbook as Household Income to your solution file location.

Median Household Income by State

Current Dollars	2011	2010	2009	$ Change	% Change	Average		2011	2010	2009	$ Change	% Change	Average
United States	50,054	49,445	49,777	277	0.56%	49,759	Nebraska	55,616	52,728	49,595	6,021	12.14%	52,646
Alabama	42,590	40,976	39,980	2,610	6.53%	41,182	Nevada	47,043	51,525	51,434	(4,391)	-8.54%	50,001
Alaska	57,431	58,198	61,604	(4,173)	-6.77%	59,078	New Hampshire	65,800	66,707	64,131	1,749	2.73%	65,573
Arizona	48,621	47,229	45,739	2,882	6.30%	47,213	New Jersey	62,338	63,540	64,777	(2,439)	-3.77%	63,552
Arkansas	41,302	38,571	36,538	4,764	13.04%	38,804	New Mexico	41,982	45,098	43,542	(1,560)	-3.58%	43,541
California	53,367	54,459	56,134	(2,767)	-4.93%	54,653	New York	50,636	49,826	50,216	420	0.84%	50,226
Colorado	58,629	60,442	55,930	2,699	4.83%	58,334	North Carolina	45,206	43,753	41,906	3,300	7.87%	43,622
Connecticut	65,415	66,452	64,851	564	0.87%	65,573	North Dakota	56,361	51,380	50,075	6,286	12.55%	52,605
Delaware	54,660	55,269	52,114	2,546	4.89%	54,014	Ohio	44,648	46,093	45,879	(1,231)	-2.68%	45,540
District of Columbia	55,251	55,528	53,141	2,110	3.97%	54,640	Oklahoma	48,455	43,400	45,878	2,577	5.62%	45,911
Florida	45,105	44,243	45,631	(526)	-1.15%	44,993	Oregon	51,526	50,526	49,098	2,428	4.95%	50,383
Georgia	45,973	44,108	43,340	2,633	6.08%	44,474	Pennsylvania	49,910	48,460	48,172	1,738	3.61%	48,847
Hawaii	59,047	58,507	55,649	3,398	6.11%	57,734	Rhode Island	49,033	51,914	51,634	(2,601)	-5.04%	50,860
Idaho	47,459	47,014	46,778	681	1.46%	47,084	South Carolina	40,004	41,709	41,101	(1,017)	-2.47%	40,965
Illinois	50,637	50,761	52,870	(2,233)	-4.22%	51,423	South Dakota	47,223	45,669	45,826	1,397	3.05%	46,259
Indiana	44,445	46,322	44,305	140	0.32%	45,024	Tennessee	42,279	38,686	40,517	1,762	4.35%	40,494
Iowa	50,219	49,177	50,721	(502)	-0.99%	50,039	Texas	49,047	47,464	47,475	1,572	3.31%	47,995
Kansas	46,147	46,229	44,717	1,430	3.20%	45,698	Utah	55,493	56,787	58,491	(2,998)	-5.13%	56,924
Kentucky	39,856	41,236	42,664	(2,808)	-6.58%	41,252	Vermont	51,862	55,942	52,318	(456)	-0.87%	53,174
Louisiana	40,658	39,443	45,433	(4,775)	-10.51%	41,845	Virginia	62,616	60,363	60,501	2,115	3.50%	61,160
Maine	49,693	48,133	47,502	2,191	4.61%	48,443	Washington	56,650	56,253	60,392	(3,542)	-5.87%	57,832
Maryland	68,876	64,025	64,186	4,690	7.31%	65,696	West Virginia	41,821	42,839	40,490	1,331	3.29%	41,717
Massachusetts	63,313	61,333	59,373	3,940	6.64%	61,340	Wisconsin	52,058	50,522	51,237	821	1.60%	51,272
Michigan	48,879	46,441	45,994	2,885	6.27%	47,105	Wyoming	54,509	52,359	52,470	2,039	3.89%	55,113
Minnesota	57,820	52,554	56,090	1,730	3.08%	55,488							
Mississippi	41,090	37,985	35,078	6,012	17.14%	38,051							
Missouri	45,774	46,184	48,769	(2,995)	-6.14%	46,909							
Montana	40,277	41,467	40,437	(160)	-0.40%	40,727							

U.S. Department of Commerce, Census Bureau

Student Name
January 1, 2015

    e. In cell E3, enter the formula **=b3-d3**. In cell F3, enter the formula **=(b3-d3)/d3** to calculate the percentage of change from 2009 to 2011.

    f. Format the results in cell F3 as Percent with two decimal places. Format cells B3 through E54 as Comma style with zero decimal places.

    g. In cell G3, calculate an average income for the three years using the formula **=average(b3:d3)**.

    h. Copy the three formulas in row 3 down to row 54. AutoFit columns B through G.

    i. Add all borders to cells A2 through G54.

    j. Cut cells A31 through G54 and paste them in cell I3. Copy cells B2 through G2 to cells J2 through O2. Widen column I to show the longest state name. Set the width of column H to 3. AutoFit columns J through O.

    k. Find the state with the highest positive change, and apply a light green fill color to the data. Apply a light red fill color to the state data that shows the worst negative change.

    l. Move the data in cell A56 to cell A32.

    m. Enter your name in cell A34 and the current date in cell A35. Format the date to display the month spelled out, the date, and a four-digit year (March 14, 2012). Left-align the date.

    n. Insert a row above row 1. Insert a row above row 3. Merge and center the label in cell A2 across columns A through O. Add an outside border to cells A1 through O3.

    o. Move to cell A1 and save the workbook.

LAB EXERCISES

p. Preview the worksheet. Change to landscape orientation, and set the scaling so that the worksheet fits on one page. Print the worksheet.

q. Display the formulas, and print the worksheet. Hide the formulas.

r. Save the workbook with the same file name.

PECAN GROVES HOMEOWNERS ASSOCIATION ★★★

5. The Pecan Groves Homeowners Association has several building projects coming up for next year, and it must analyze the amount of cash available in its budget for the work. Using last year's budget data, you can prepare estimates for next year. After you follow the directions to complete the worksheet, your solution should look similar to that shown here.

a. Open ex01_Pecan Groves. Spell-check the worksheet, and check for consistent use of uppercase where needed. Save the workbook as Pecan Groves Budget to your solution file location.

b. Widen column A to show the longest income or expenditure. Center the labels in cells A6 and A11. Right-align and bold the labels in cells A10 and A23.

c. Increase the indent one time for cells A17 through A20. Delete row 21.

d. In cell C10, sum the income items. In cell C22, sum all expenditures.

e. Insert a row at row 23. In cell A23, key **Net Income** and left-align it.

f. In cell C23, enter a formula to determine net income (income – expenditures). In cell C26, enter a formula to calculate the ending cash balance (net income + cash on hand + reserves).

g. Format cell B7 as Accounting number format with zero decimal places. Apply the same format to each value in column C. Then format the remaining values as Comma style with zero decimal places.

The table below shows the projected budget:

Pecan Groves Homeowners Association
Projected Budget

	This Year		Next Year	
Income				
Assessment Fees	$ 219,500		$ 232,670	
Rentals	1,700		1,802	
Earned Interest	1,200		1,272	
Total Income		$ 222,400		$ 235,744
Expenditures				
Administration	120,000		129,600	
Insurance	16,000		17,280	
Audit & Tax Preparation	12,000		12,960	
Attorney and Legal Fees	14,000		15,120	
Maintenance				
Street Repair	2,700		2,916	
Street Cleaning	1,582		1,709	
Snow Removal	550		594	
Property Signage	4,985		5,384	
Miscellaneous	3,000		3,240	
Total Expenditures		$ 174,817		$ 188,802
Net Income		$ 47,583		$ 46,942
Cash on Hand	16,701		16,701	
Reserves	23,000		23,000	
Ending Cash Balance		$ 87,284		$ 86,643

Student Name
January 1, 2015

h. Add a bottom border to cells B9, B21, and B25. Add a bottom double border to cells C10, C22, and C26.

i. Each of the income items for next year is projected to increase by 6 percent for next year. Enter a formula in cell D7 to calculate 106 percent of this year's assessment fees. Then copy the formula for the other income items. Apply the same number formats and bottom border.

j. In cell E10, enter a formula to calculate the total income for next year. Apply the same formatting as that used for this year.

k. Each of the expenditure items is expected to increase by 8 percent for next year. Enter the formula in cell D12, and copy it as needed. Delete a copied formula in cell D16. In cell E22, sum the expenditures for next year. Make sure the formatting matches that used for this year.

l. In cell E23, calculate net income for next year. In cells D24 and D25, enter the same values as those for this year. In cell E26, calculate the ending cash balance for next year.

m. Review and adjust number and border formatting as necessary.

n. Merge and center the contents of cell B5 across columns B through C. Make the label bold, and add a bottom border.

o. Insert a blank column at column D, and make it 3 spaces wide. Then merge and center the contents of cell E5 across columns E through F; add bold and a bottom border.

p. Increase the font size for cells A1:A2 to 16 points. Then merge and center these labels across the worksheet data.

q. Add a bottom border to cells A3 through F3. Apply a fill color to cells D6 through D26. Apply the same or complementary fill color to cells A5 through F5 and cells A27 through F27.

r. Insert a new row at row 1, and apply a fill color to cells A1 through F1. Delete row 5.

s. Widen column A to 26. Widen columns B through C and E through F so that the worksheet data appears centered on the page. Make sure, though, that these four columns are the same width.

t. Enter your name in cell A30 and the current date in cell A31. Format the date to display the month spelled out, the date, and a four-digit year. Left-align the date.

u. Move to cell A1. Save the workbook using the same file name. Print the worksheet.

v. Display the formulas, and print the worksheet using landscape orientation, fit to a single page. Hide the formulas.

ON YOUR OWN

TRACKING YOUR CALORIES ★

1. A worksheet can be used to track your calories for the day. Design and create a worksheet to record the food you consume and the exercise you do on a daily basis. The worksheet should include your food consumption for all meals and snacks and the activities you performed for a week. Use the Web as a resource to find out the caloric values for the items you consumed (or refer to the calorie information on the product packaging) and to find out the caloric expenditure for the exercises you do. Include an appropriate title, row and column headings, and formulas to calculate your total calorie intake and expenditure on a daily basis. Include a formula to calculate the percent deviation from your recommended daily calorie intake. Format the worksheet appropriately using features presented in this lab. Enter real or sample data. Include your name and date above the worksheet. Spell-check the worksheet. Save the workbook as Calorie Tracking and print the worksheet.

LAB EXERCISES

CREATING A PERSONAL BUDGET ★

2. In a blank Excel 2013 workbook, create a personal three-month budget. Enter an appropriate title and use descriptive labels for your monthly expenses (food, rent, car payments, insurance, credit card payments, etc.). Spell-check your worksheet. Enter your monthly expenses (or, if you prefer, any reasonable sample data). Use formulas to calculate total expenses for each month and the average monthly expenditures for each expense item. Add a column for projection for the next year showing a 2.5 percent increase in the cost of living. Enhance the worksheet using features you learned in this lab. Enter your name and the current date on separate rows just below the worksheet. Save the workbook as Personal Budget. Preview and print the worksheet.

TRACKING PROJECT HOURS ★★

3. Samantha Johnson is the project manager for a small publishing company. She has four part-time employees (Melanie, Bob, Vanessa, and Rudy). Using the steps in the planning process, plan and create a worksheet for Samantha that can be used to record and analyze the hours each employee works per day during the month on two projects: magazine and brochure. Hours-worked data for each employee will be entered into the worksheet. Using that data, the worksheet will calculate the total number of hours for each person per project. Additionally, it will calculate the total weekly hours for each project. Write a short paragraph describing how you used each of the planning steps. Enter sample data in a worksheet. Include your name and the current date on separate rows just below the worksheet. Spell-check the worksheet. Save the workbook as Project Hours. Preview and print the worksheet.

MUSIC ANALYSIS ★★★

4. Use the library and/or the Web to locate information on trends in CD sales versus music downloads on the Internet. Create a worksheet to display information relating to the increasing usage by country, age group, or any other trend you locate. Calculate totals or averages based on your data. Enhance the worksheet using features you learned in this lab. Enter your name and the current date on separate rows just below the worksheet. Spell-check the worksheet. Save the workbook as Music Analysis. Preview and print the worksheet.

HOME ELECTRONICS ANALYSIS ★★★

5. A national electronics retailer wants to analyze the trend in home electronics sales and usage for the past three years. Design and create a worksheet to record the number of households (one-person, two-person, and four-person) that have computers, Internet access, televisions, and cable and satellite TV access. Include an appropriate title, row and column headings, and formulas to calculate average by category and by year. Include a formula to calculate the percentage of growth over the three years. Format the worksheet appropriately using features presented in this tutorial. Enter sample data for the three years. Include your name and date above the worksheet. Spell-check the worksheet. Save the workbook as Home Electronics Analysis and print the worksheet.

Enhancing the Worksheet with Graphics and Charts

Objectives

After completing this lab, you will know how to:

1. Insert and size a graphic.

2. Use cell styles.

3. Apply and customize themes.

4. Create a column chart.

5. Move, size, and format a chart.

6. Change the type of chart.

7. Create a combo chart.

8. Create, explode, and rotate a pie chart.

9. Apply patterns and color to a chart.

10. Size and align a sheet on a page.

11. Add predefined headers and footers.

CASE STUDY

Downtown Internet Café

Evan is impressed with how quickly you were able to create the first quarter sales forecast for the Downtown Internet Café. He made several suggestions to improve the appearance of the worksheet, including applying different formats and adding a graphic. Evan also expressed concern that the sales values seem a little low and has asked you to contact several other Internet cafés to inquire about their start-up experiences.

While speaking with other Internet café managers, you heard many exciting success stories. Internet connections attract more customers, and the typical customer stays longer at an Internet café than at a regular café. As a result, the customers spend more money.

You would like to launch an aggressive advertising campaign to promote the new Internet aspect of the Café. The new Café features include free WiFi connection, computer rentals, and printing and copying services. You believe that the campaign will lead to an increase in customers and subsequently to an increase in sales. To convince Evan, you need an effective way to illustrate the sales growth you are forecasting. You will use Excel 2013's chart-creating and formatting features to produce several different charts of your sales estimates, as shown on the following page.

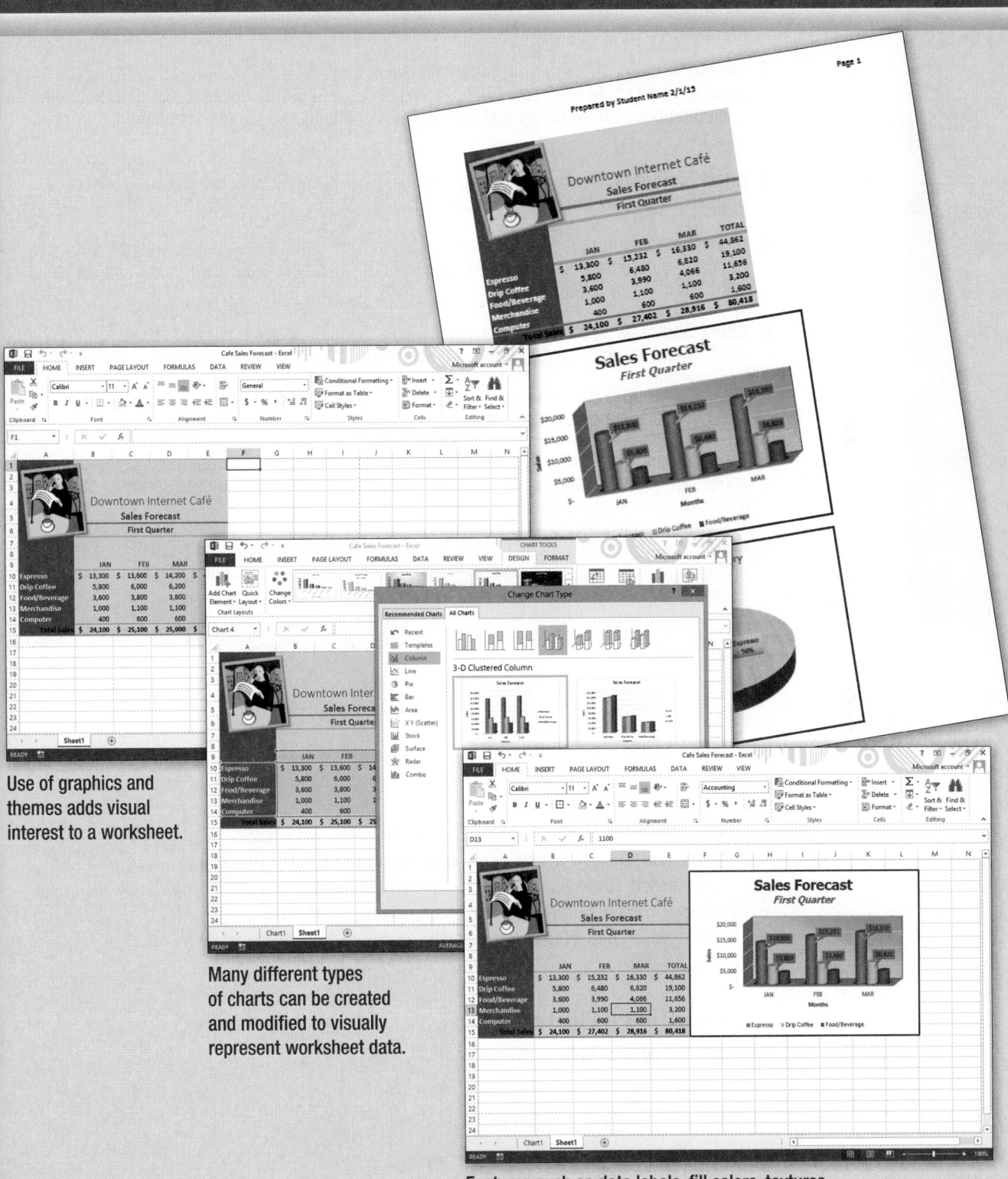

Use of graphics and themes adds visual interest to a worksheet.

Many different types of charts can be created and modified to visually represent worksheet data.

Features such as data labels, fill colors, textures, and shadows add a professional appearance to your charts.

The following concepts will be introduced in this lab:

1 Graphics A graphic is a nontext element or object such as a drawing or picture that can be added to a document.

2 Quick Style A quick style is a named group of formatting characteristics that allows you to quickly apply a whole group of formats to a selected object in one simple step.

3 Theme A theme is a set of formatting choices that can be applied to an entire worksheet in one simple step. A theme consists of a set of theme colors, a set of theme fonts (including heading and body text fonts), and a set of theme effects (including line and fill effects).

4 Chart Elements Chart elements are the different parts of a chart that are used to graphically display the worksheet data.

5 Chart Types Different chart types are used to represent data in different ways. The type of chart you create depends on the type of data you are charting and the emphasis you want the chart to impart.

6 Chart Object A chart object is a graphic object that is created using charting features. A chart object can be inserted into a worksheet or into a special chart sheet.

7 Group A group is two or more objects that behave as a single object when moved or sized. A chart is a group that consists of many separate objects.

8 Data Labels Data labels provide additional information about a data point in the data series. They can consist of the value of the point, the name of the data series or category, a percentage value, or a bubble size.

9 Headers and Footers Headers and footers provide information that typically appears at the top and bottom of each page and commonly include information such as the date and page number.

Inserting and Formatting Illustrations

To focus Evan's attention solely on the sales values for the Downtown Internet Café, you created a new worksheet containing only those values. Although you have added some formatting to the worksheet already, you still want to improve its appearance by adding a graphic, changing the theme, and applying different cell styles. Then you will create the charts to help Evan visualize the sales trends better.

INSERTING A PICTURE FROM A COMPUTER

You saved the sales portion of the worksheet in a new workbook file.

- **Start Excel 2013.**

- **If necessary, maximize the Excel application window.**

- **Open the file** ex02_ Cafe Sales.

- **If necessary, click**

  Enable Editing

  in the message bar.

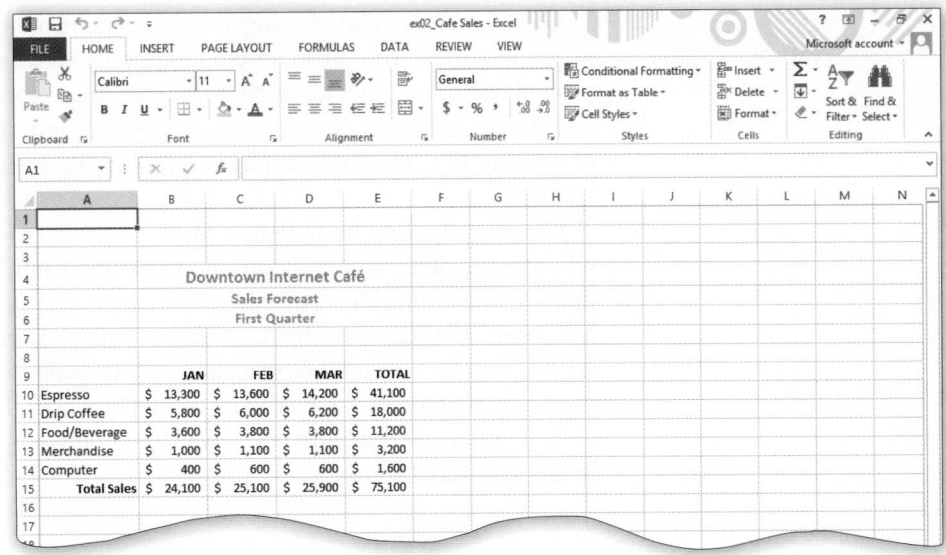

Your screen should be similar to Figure 2.1

Figure 2.1

First you want to add a graphic next to the worksheet title to add interest.

Concept  Graphics

A **graphic** is a nontext element or object such as a drawing or picture that can be added to a document. An **object** is an item that can be sized, moved, and manipulated.

A graphic can be a simple **drawing object** consisting of shapes, such as lines and boxes, that can be created using the Shapes tool. A drawing object is part of the Excel workbook. A **picture** is an illustration such as a graphic illustration or a scanned photograph. Pictures are graphics that were created from another program and are inserted in the worksheet as embedded objects. An **embedded object** becomes part of the Excel workbook and can be opened and edited using the **source program**, the program in which it was created. Any changes made to the embedded object are not made to the original picture file because they are independent. Several examples of drawing objects and pictures are shown below.

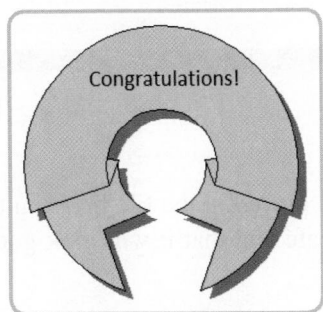
Drawing object

Graphic illustration

Photograph

Add graphics to your worksheets to help the reader understand concepts, to add interest, and to make your worksheet stand out from others.

Digital images created using a digital camera are one of the most common types of graphic files. You also can create graphic files using a scanner to convert any printed document, including photographs, to an electronic format. **Clip art** graphics, simple drawings created using a graphics program, are another common type of graphic file. The most common graphic file formats are JPG, TIF, PNG, GIF, and BMP.

Graphic files can be obtained from a variety of sources, including files stored on your computer or a computer network and from Internet websites. All types of graphics, including clip art, photographs, and other types of images, can be found on Microsoft's Office.com Clip Art website, which offers royalty-free graphics. Graphics that you locate on other websites may be protected by copyright and should be used only with permission. You also can purchase CDs containing graphics.

You will insert a picture you have stored on your computer to the left of the title in the worksheet.

1

● **Open the Insert tab.**

● **Click** [Pictures] **in the Illustrations group.**

Having Trouble?

If necessary, first click [Illustrations] to open the Illustrations group.

● **Change to the location of your data files.**

● **Select** ex02_Cafe .png.

Having Trouble?

Depending on your Windows setup, the file extension may or may not be displayed.

● **If a thumbnail image of the selected graphic is not displayed, open the** [▼] **View drop-down menu and choose Large Icons.**

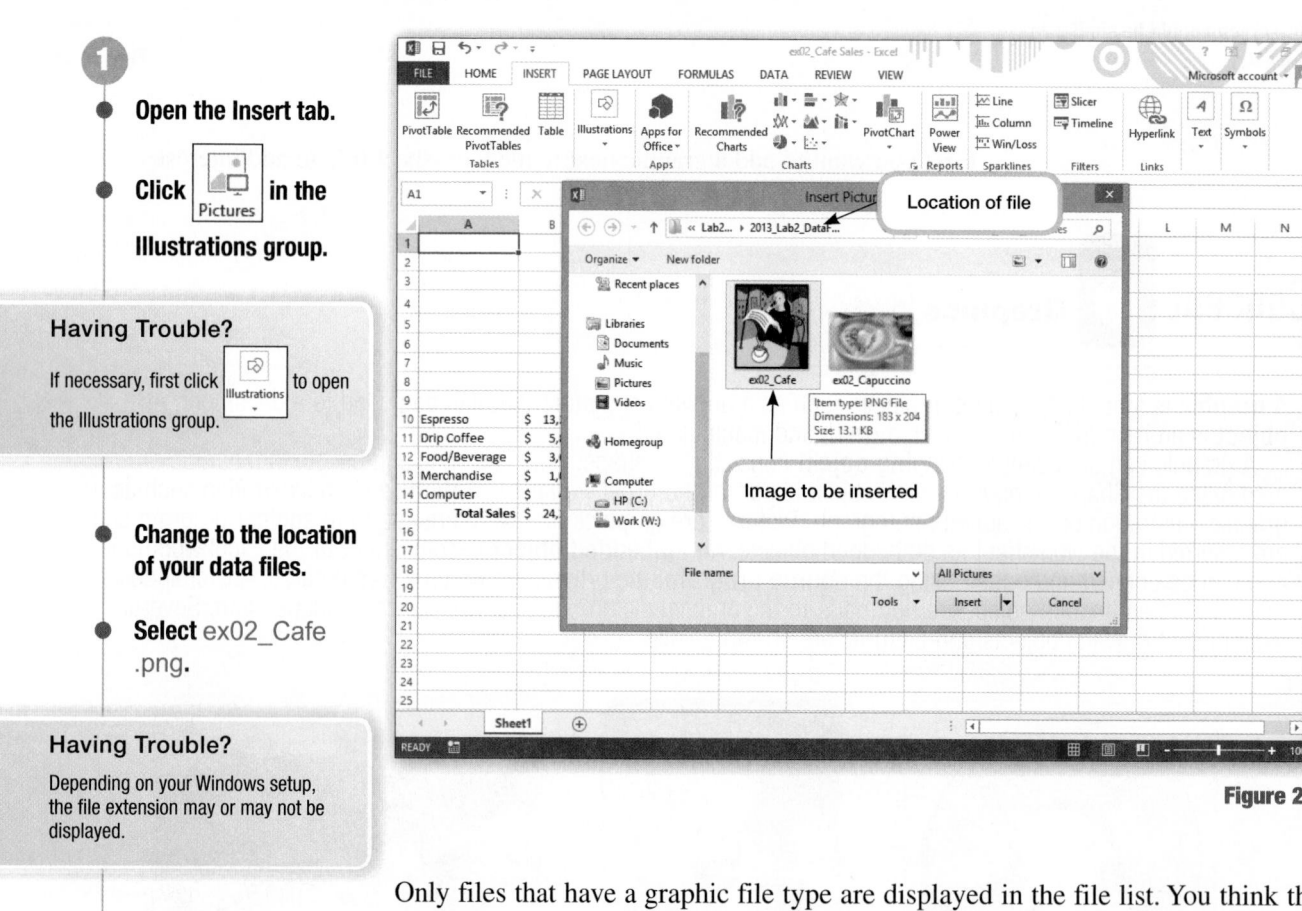

Figure 2.2

Only files that have a graphic file type are displayed in the file list. You think the selected picture illustrates the concept of a café and that it will look good in the worksheet.

Your screen should be similar to Figure 2.2

2

● Click [Insert ▼].

Your screen should be similar to Figure 2.3

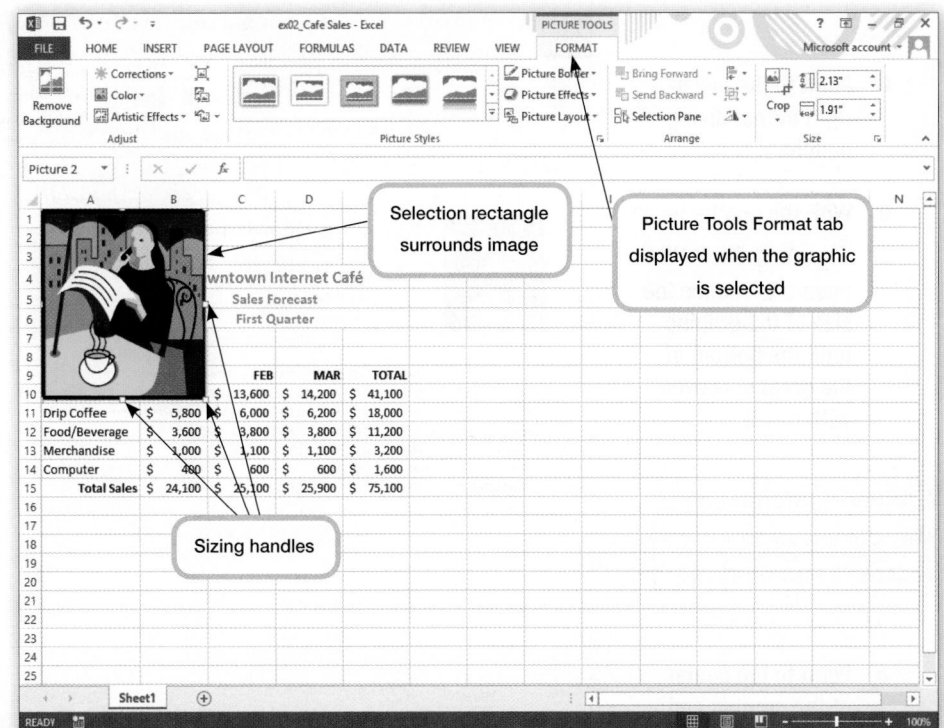

Figure 2.3

The picture is inserted in the worksheet at the location of the cell selector. It is inserted in a separate drawing layer and covers some of the worksheet data. The picture is surrounded by a **selection rectangle** and eight squares called **sizing handles**, indicating it is a selected object and can now be deleted, sized, moved, or modified. The Picture Tools Format tab is automatically displayed and can be used to modify the selected picture object.

SIZING AND MOVING A GRAPHIC

Usually, when a graphic is inserted, its size will need to be adjusted. To size a graphic, you select it and drag a sizing handle to increase or decrease the size of the object. The mouse pointer changes to 🢅 when pointing to a corner handle and ⟷ or ↕ when pointing to a side handle. The direction of the arrow indicates the direction in which you can drag to size the graphic. Dragging a corner handle maintains the scale of the picture by increasing both the width and length of the graphic equally. You also can move a graphic object by pointing to the graphic and dragging it to the new location. The mouse pointer changes to 🢄 when you can move the graphic.

1

- **Point to the lower-right corner sizing handle.**

- **With the pointer as a** 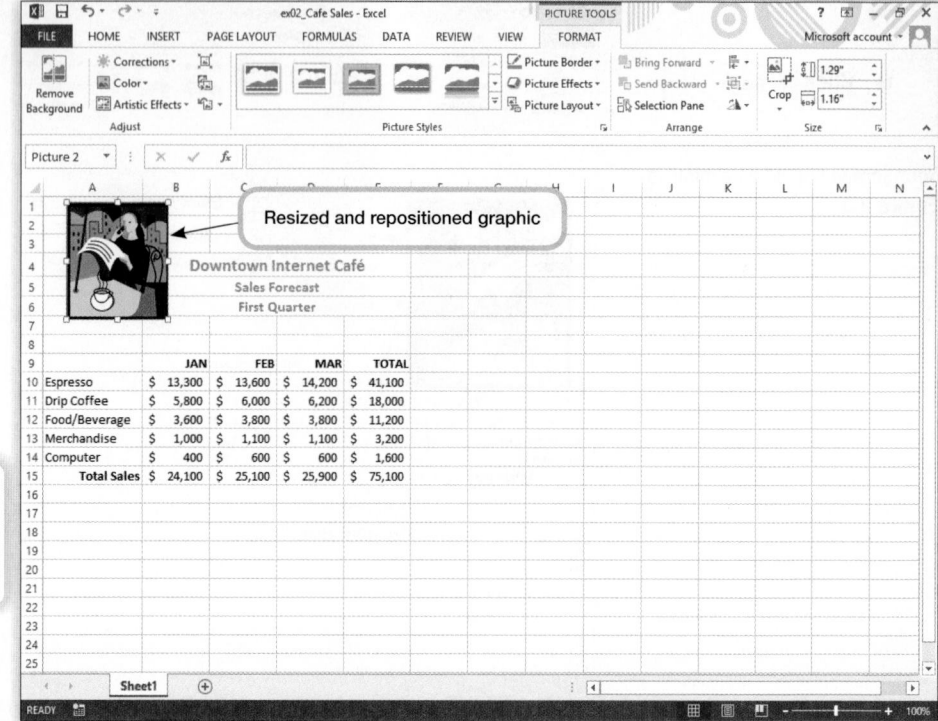**, drag the mouse inward to reduce the size of the graphic until the bottom of the graphic is even with row 6.**

Additional Information

When you drag to size the graphic, the mouse pointer shape changes to a ┼.

- **Point to the center of the graphic and, when the mouse pointer is ✛, drag the graphic to position it as in Figure 2.4.**

Your screen should be similar to Figure 2.4

Figure 2.4

The graphic is smaller and moved to the left of the title as you want it.

INSERTING A PICTURE FROM ONLINE SOURCES

Although you like the graphic, you decide to search the online sources for pictures that show the use of a computer in a café environment.

Having Trouble?

If you do not have an Internet connection, you cannot complete this section. Insert the picture ex02_Laptop from your data file location. Skip to the next section, "Deleting a Graphic."

1

- Move to cell F1 to deselect the graphic and choose the location where you want a new picture inserted.

- Open the Insert tab.

- Click [Online Pictures] in the Illustrations group.

Your screen should be similar to Figure 2.5

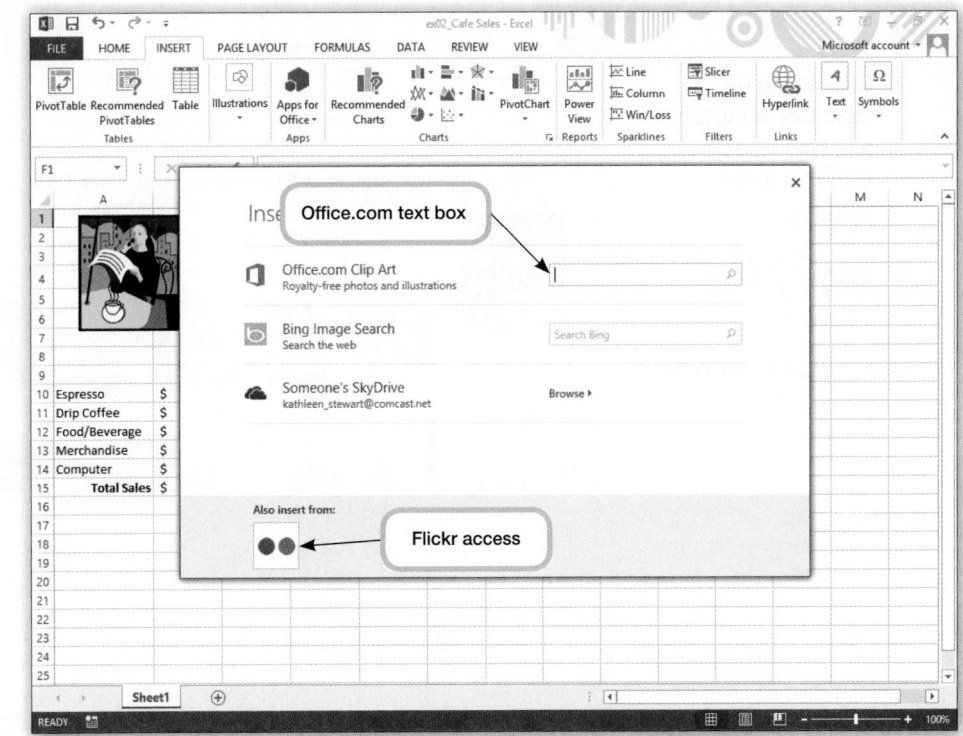

Figure 2.5

The Insert Pictures dialog box provides several methods to locate online graphics. The first is to use Microsoft's Office.com Clip Art website. The second is to use Microsoft's search engine, Bing, to search the web. A third is to access your Sky-Drive account to locate pictures you have stored at that location. Finally, you can access Flickr, an online photo management and sharing website, for pictures you have uploaded to an account with the website.

You will use the Office.com website to search for pictures by entering a word or phrase that is representative of the type of picture you want to locate. You can search files at Office.com or use the Bing search tool. You want to find pictures of laptop computers and coffee.

2

- Click in the Office .com Clip Art text box and type **laptop, coffee** in the text box.

- Click 🔍 **Search**.

Your screen should be similar to Figure 2.6

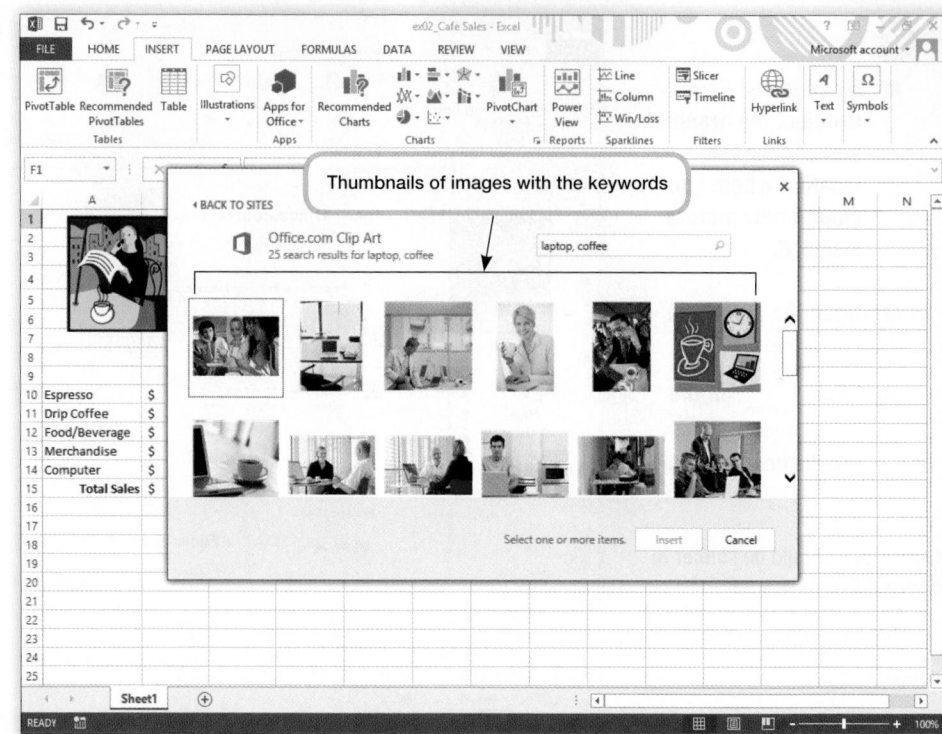

Figure 2.6

Your screen should be similar to Figure 2.6

Having Trouble?

Your results may display different pictures than those shown in Figure 2.6.

The program searches the Office.com Clip Art website for clip art and graphics that match your search terms and displays **thumbnails**, miniature representations of pictures, of all located graphics. Pointing to a thumbnail displays a ScreenTip containing the description or **keywords** associated with the picture and the 🔍 View Larger button. The bottom of the dialog box shows keywords and the size of the picture in pixels.

- Scroll the list to view additional pictures.

- Point to the thumbnail shown in Figure 2.7 to see a ScreenTip.

- Click on View Larger.

Your screen should be similar to Figure 2.7

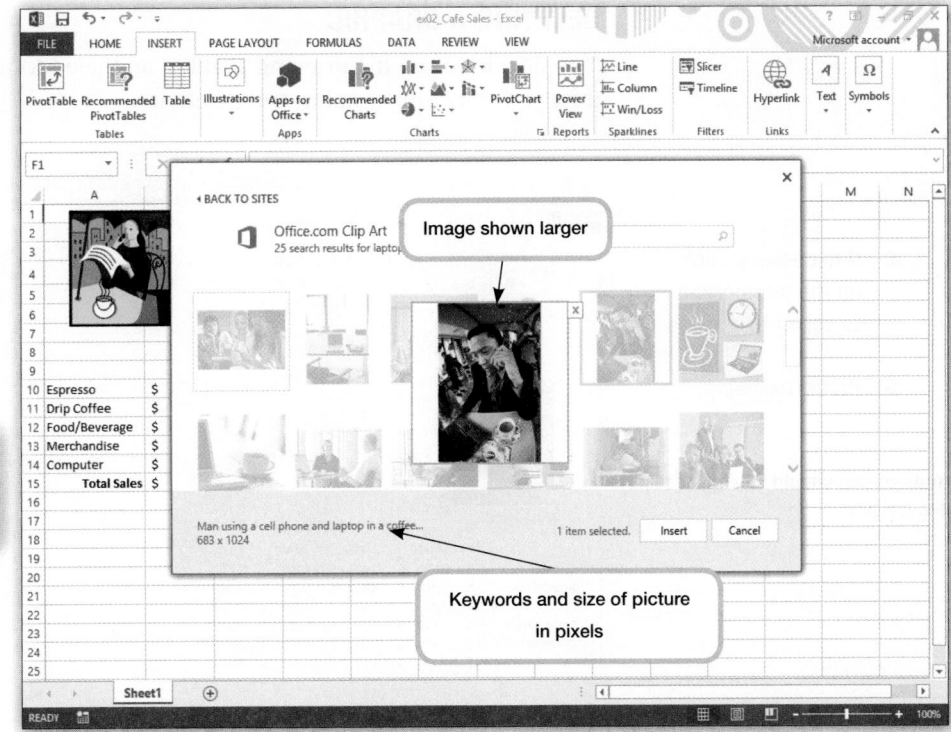

Figure 2.7

The selected graphic is displayed larger so it is easier to see. The ScreenTip displays the description of the selected picture. You think this looks like a good choice and will insert it into the worksheet.

- Double-click on the graphic to insert it into the worksheet.

Your screen should be similar to Figure 2.8

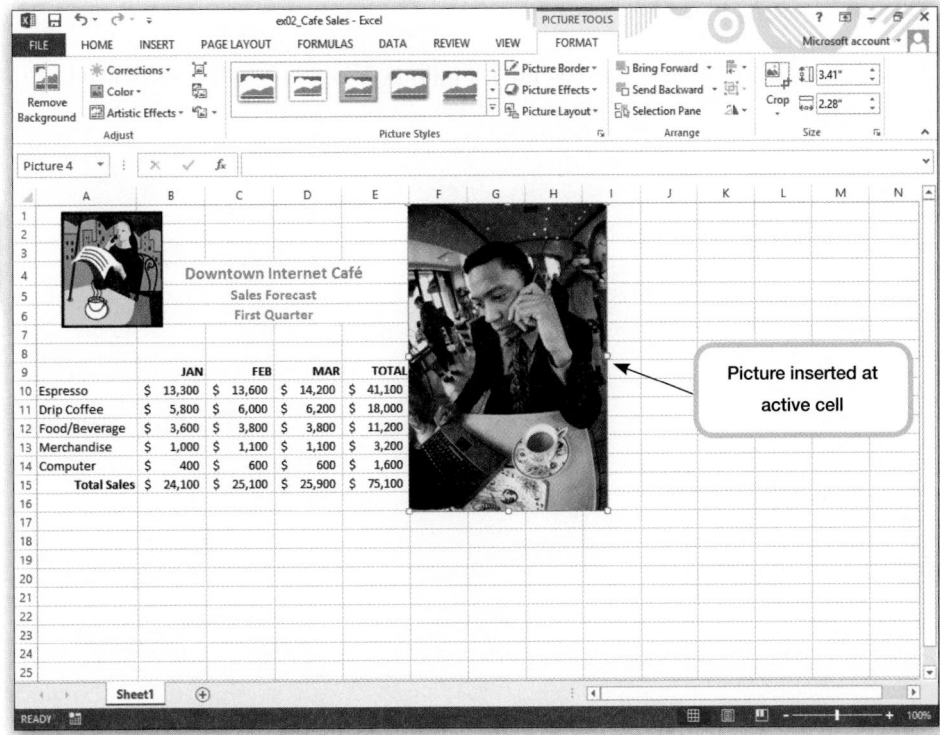

Figure 2.8

The picture is downloaded and inserted in the worksheet at the location of the cell selector. It is the selected object. You now have two graphic objects in the worksheet, a drawing and a photograph.

DELETING A GRAPHIC

You decide to use the drawing graphic and need to remove the photograph. To do this, you select the graphic and delete it.

- **If necessary, click on the photograph to select it.**

- **Press** [Delete].

Your screen should be similar to Figure 2.9

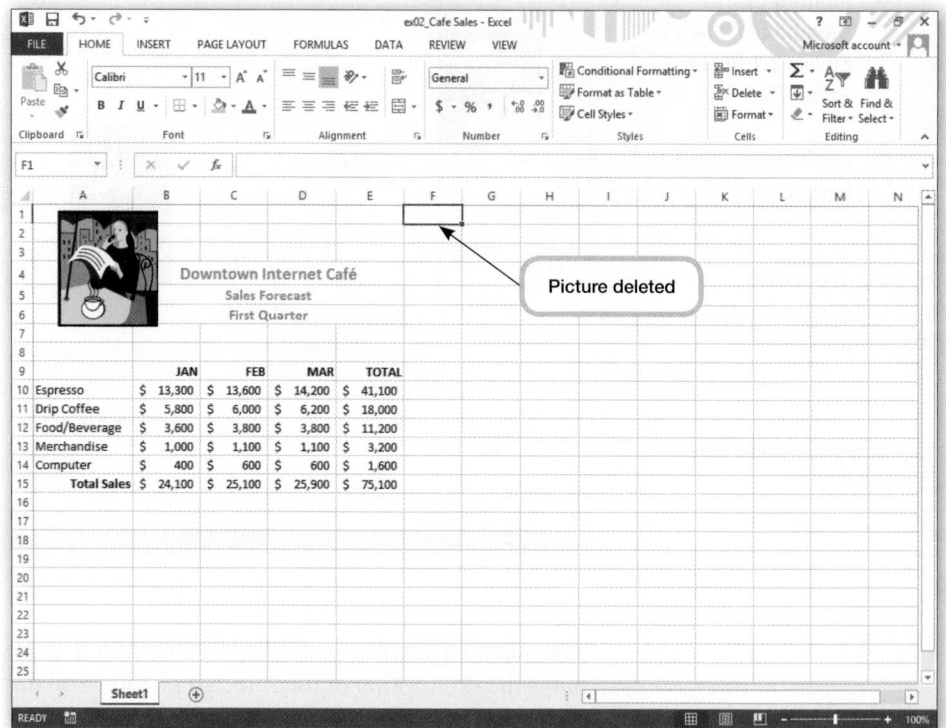

Figure 2.9

The photograph is deleted from the worksheet.

APPLYING AND MODIFYING A PICTURE QUICK STYLE

Next, you want to enhance the graphic by applying a quick style to it.

Concept 2 Quick Style

A **quick style** is a named group of formatting characteristics that allows you to quickly apply a whole group of formats to a selected object in one simple step. The formatting options associated with the different quick styles vary depending upon the type of object. For example, a line quick style may consist of a combination of color, shadows, gradients, and three-dimensional (3-D) perspectives options, whereas a shape quick style may consist of a combination of fill color, line color, and line weight options.

Many quick styles are automatically applied when certain features, such as charts, are used. Others must be applied manually to the selected object. You also can create your own custom styles.

Quick styles are available for cell selections as well as many different types of objects. Some of the most common are described in the following table.

Type of Quick Style	Description
Cell style	Affects selected cells by applying effects such as fill color, text and number formatting, and bold and underline formats.
Shape style	Affects all aspects of a shape object's appearance, including fill color, outline color, and other effects.
Chart style	Provides a consistent look to charts by applying color, shading, line, and font effects.
Picture style	Adds a border around a graphic object that consists of combinations of line, shadow, color, and shape effects.

You will use a picture quick style to add a border around the picture to make it stand out more. You also can create your own picture style effects by selecting specific style elements such as borders and shadow individually using the  Picture Border,  Picture Effects, and Picture Layout commands.

1

- Select the graphic.

- Click ☑ More in the Picture Styles group of the Format tab to open the Picture Styles gallery.

- Point to several styles to see the Live Preview.

Your screen should be similar to Figure 2.10

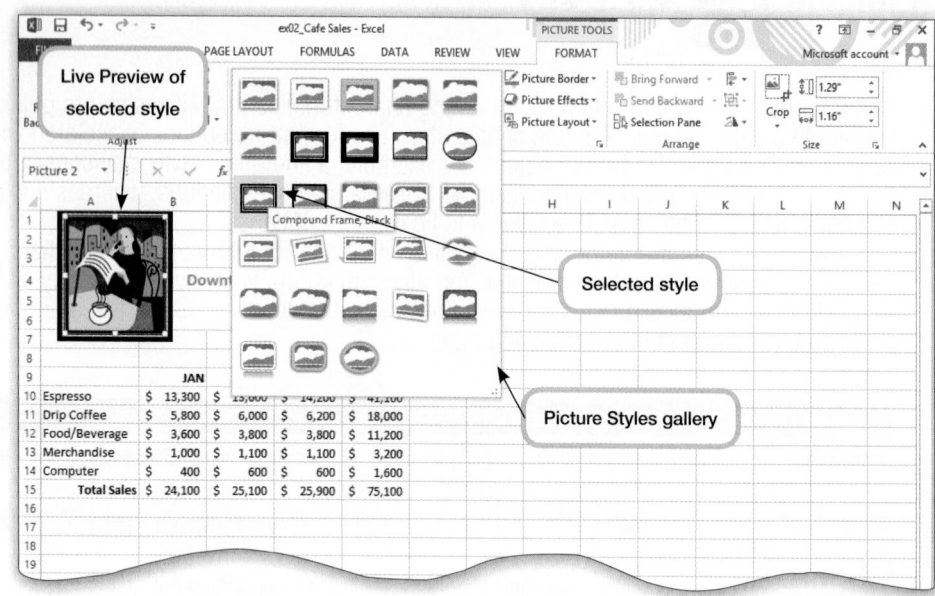

Figure 2.10

When you point to a style, the style name appears in a ScreenTip and the Live Preview shows how the selected picture style will look with your graphic. As you can see, many are not appropriate. However, you decide that the rotated style with a white border will enhance the graphic and the worksheet.

2

- Choose 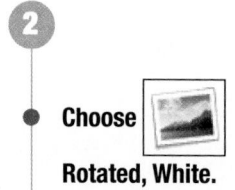 Rotated, White.

- Size and position the graphic as in Figure 2.11.

- Click outside the graphic to deselect the object.

Your screen should be similar to Figure 2.11

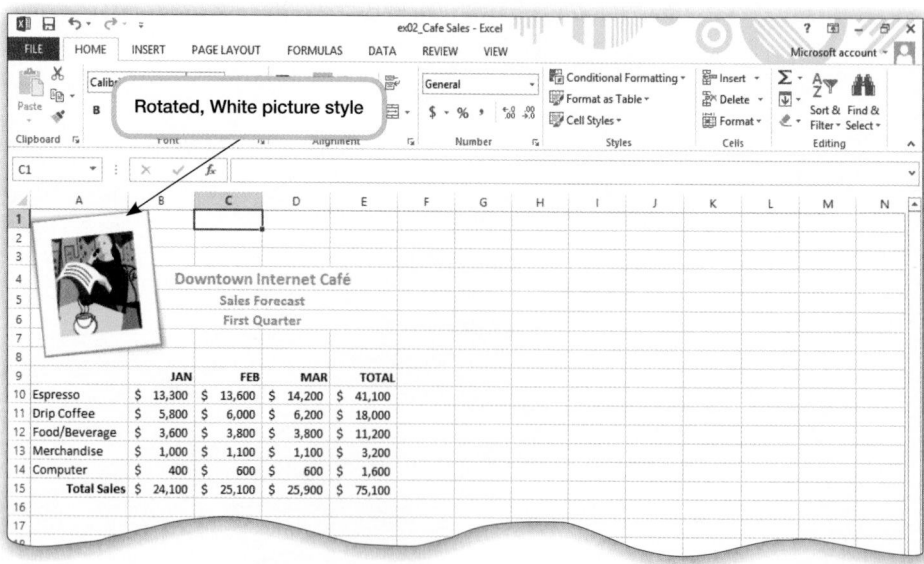

Figure 2.11

After seeing how the graphic looks with the selected picture style, you decide to modify the quick style by adding color to and changing the weight of the border.

3

- Click on the graphic to select it again.

- Click 🖉 Picture Border ▼ in the Picture Styles group of the Format tab.

- Choose the Orange Accent 2 color from the Theme Colors category.

- Click 🖉 Picture Border ▼, select Weight, and choose 4½ points.

- Click outside the graphic to deselect the object.

- Document the workbook by adding your name as author and the workbook title of **Sales Forecast**

- Save the revised workbook as Cafe Sales Forecast to your solution file location.

Your screen should be similar to Figure 2.12

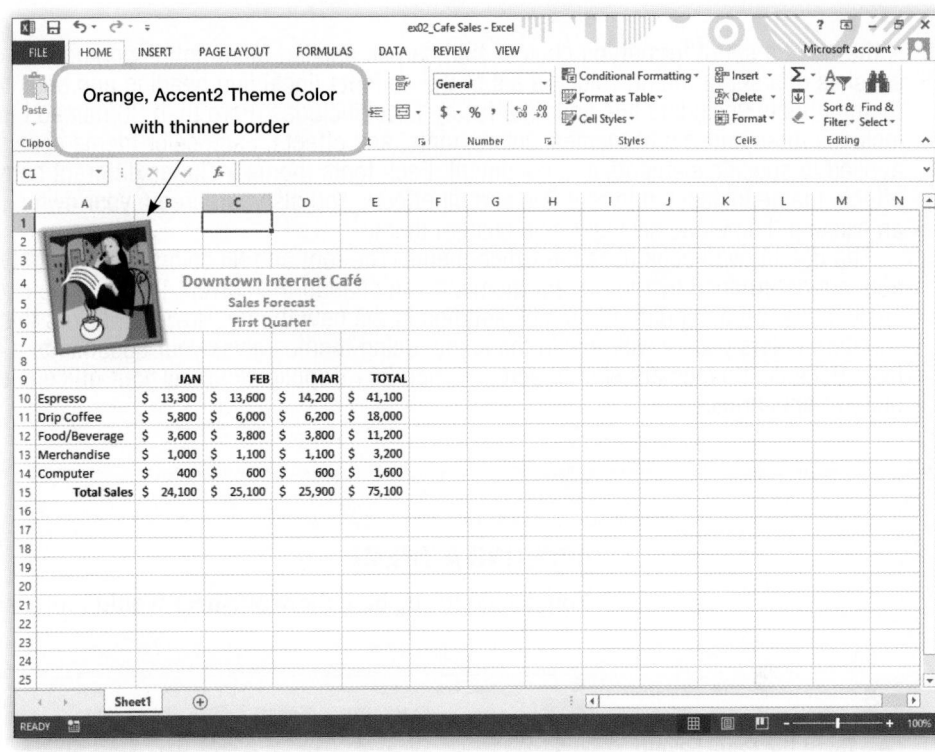

Figure 2.12

Using Themes

The addition of a graphic adds a nice touch to the worksheet title. Now, you want to continue to improve the worksheet appearance by selecting a different theme.

Concept 3 Theme

A **theme** is a set of formatting choices that can be applied to an entire workbook in one simple step. A theme consists of a set of theme colors, a set of theme fonts (including heading and body text fonts), and a set of theme effects (including line and fill effects). Excel includes more than 20 named built-in themes. Each theme includes three subsets of themes: colors, fonts, and effects. Each color theme consists of 12 colors that are applied to specific elements in a document. Each fonts theme includes different body and heading fonts. Each effects theme includes different line and fill effects. You also can create your own custom themes by modifying an existing theme and saving it as a custom theme.

The default workbook uses the Office theme. The font and fill colors and quick style effects that are available are determined by the current theme. If you change the current theme, style choices that you've previously made will be updated to match settings in the new theme. However, colors that you've selected from the standard colors gallery will remain the same. Using themes gives your documents a professional and modern look. Because themes are shared across Office 2013 applications, all your office documents can have the same uniform appearance.

APPLYING A THEME

You decide to see how the worksheet would look using a different theme.

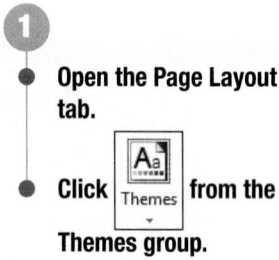

● Open the Page Layout tab.

● Click [Themes] from the Themes group.

Your screen should be similar to Figure 2.13

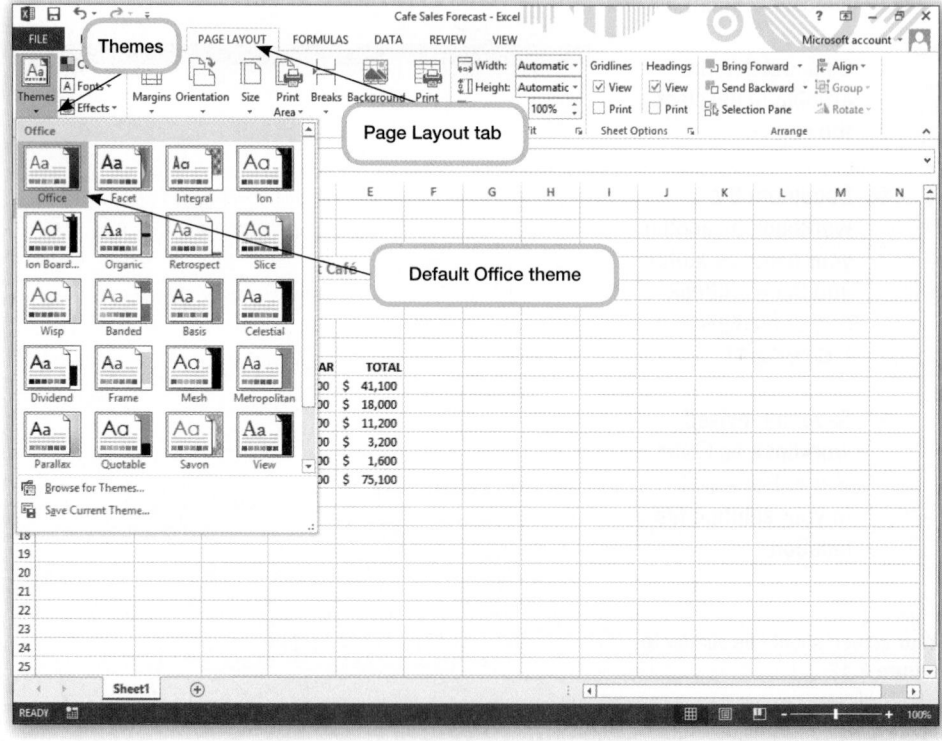

Figure 2.13

A gallery of built-in named themes is displayed. A sample shows the color and font effects included in each theme. The Office theme is highlighted because it is the default theme. Pointing to each theme will display a Live Preview of how it will appear in the worksheet.

2

● Point to several themes to preview them.

● Scroll through the selections and choose the Retrospect theme.

Your screen should be similar to Figure 2.14

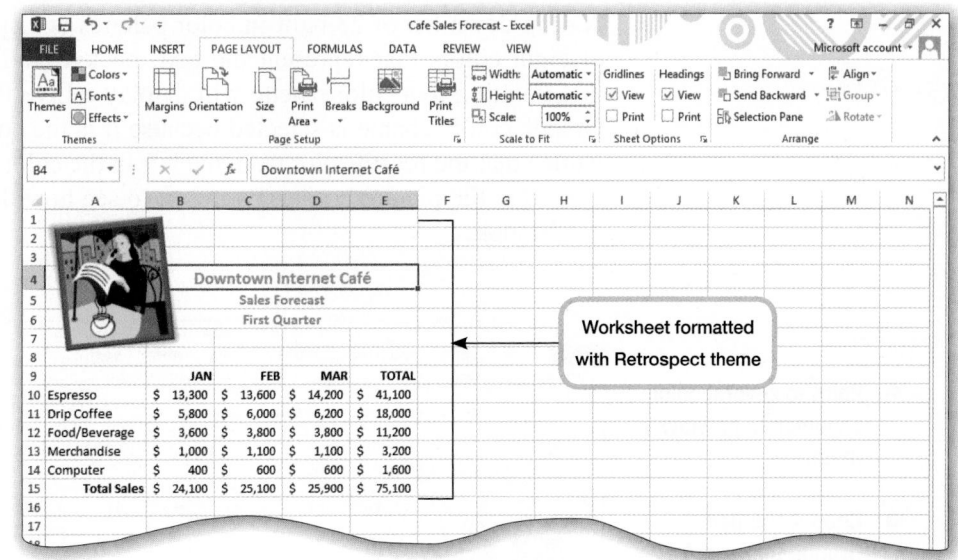

Figure 2.14

Additional Information

If the border and font colors were colors on the Standard Colors bar, the color is updated to the new theme design.

The formatting settings associated with the selected theme have been applied to the worksheet. Most noticeable is the color change of the picture border and titles. This is because the colors in the theme category have been updated to the Retrospect theme colors. Consequently the available picture quick style colors and font colors have been updated to the new theme colors.

As you add other features to the worksheet, they will be formatted using the Retrospect theme colors and effects. The same theme will be applied to the other sheets in the workbook file.

Additional Information

Only one theme can be used in a workbook.

CUSTOMIZING A THEME

Sometimes, you cannot find just the right combination of design elements in a built-in theme. To solve this problem, you can customize a theme by changing the color scheme, fonts, and effects. Each theme has an associated set of colors that you can change by applying a different color palette to the selected theme.

Additional Information

The colors you see in the

[Colors ▾] Theme Colors button

represent the current text and background colors.

1

● Click [Colors ▾] in the Themes group.

Your screen should be similar to Figure 2.15

Built-in color schemes

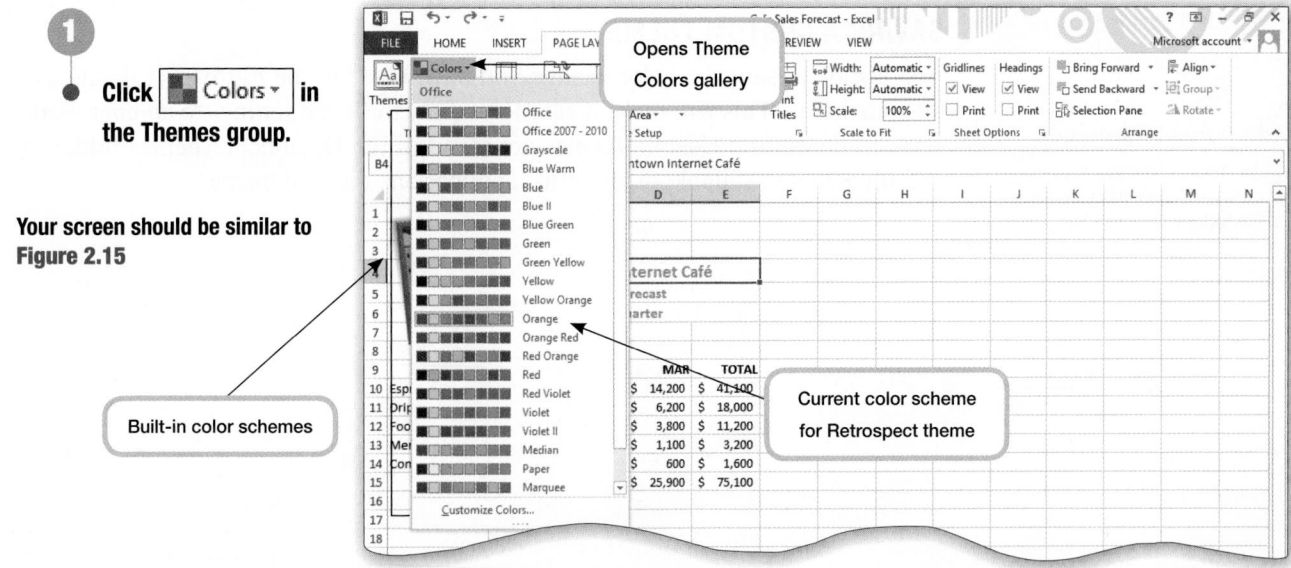

Figure 2.15

A drop-down list of 23 built-in color palettes is displayed. Each palette consists of eight colors that represent the text, background, accent, and hyperlink colors. Pointing to a color palette will display a Live Preview of the selection. The Orange color scheme is selected because it is the color scheme currently in use. Notice that the fourth color from the left in the color bar is the Accent2 color that is used in the picture border. You want to see how the Red Orange color scheme would look.

2

● **Point to several color schemes to preview them.**

● **Choose the Red Orange theme color scheme.**

Your screen should be similar to Figure 2.16

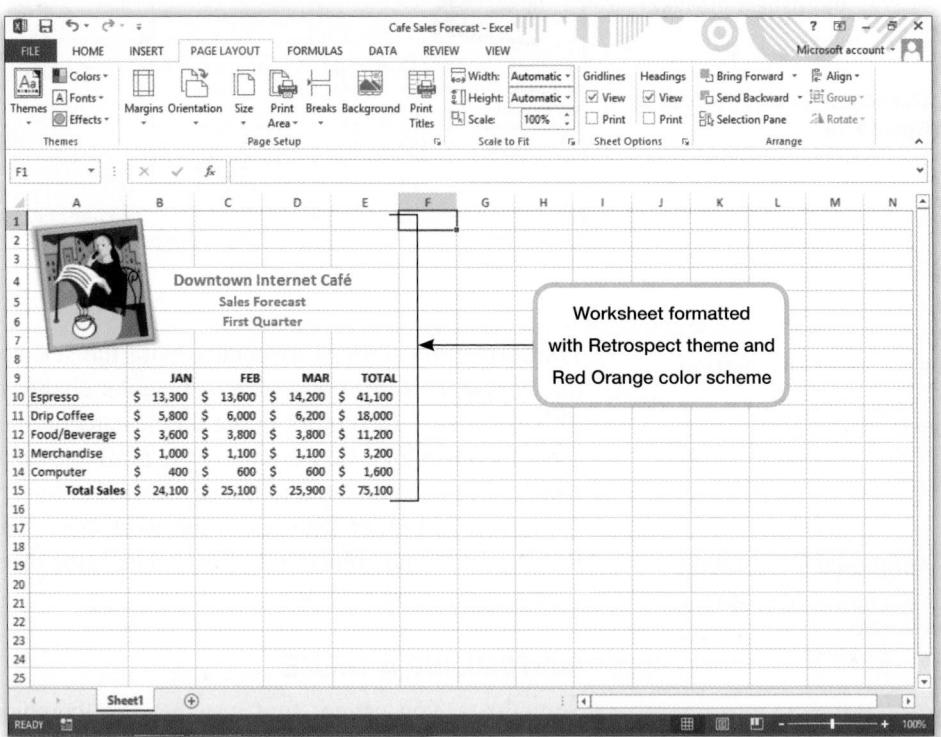

Worksheet formatted with Retrospect theme and Red Orange color scheme

Figure 2.16

The new color scheme has been applied to the picture border and font color used in the worksheet titles. All other aspects of the Retrospect theme are unchanged.

SAVING A CUSTOM THEME

You decide to save the color change you have made to the Retrospect theme as a custom theme. This will make it easy to reapply the same settings to another workbook in the future. Custom themes are saved in the Document Themes folder by default and are available in all Office applications that use themes.

1

- **Click** 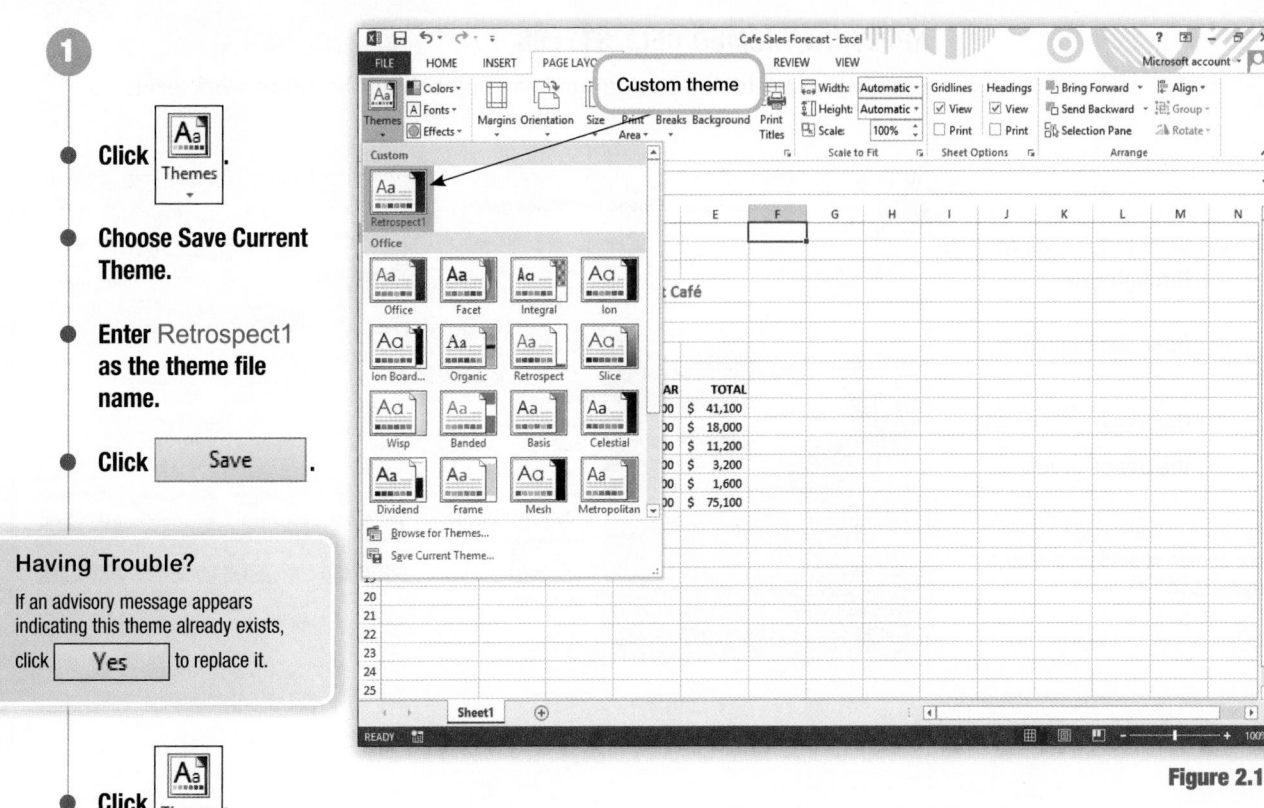 .

- **Choose Save Current Theme.**

- **Enter** Retrospect1 **as the theme file name.**

- **Click** Save .

Having Trouble?

If an advisory message appears indicating this theme already exists, click Yes to replace it.

- **Click** Themes .

Your screen should be similar to Figure 2.17

Additional Information

To remove a custom theme, choose Delete from the theme's shortcut menu.

Figure 2.17

The custom theme you created and saved appears at the top of the Themes gallery. Now you can quickly reapply this entire theme in one step to another workbook, just like the built-in themes, or to any other Office document.

Using Cell Styles

Next, you want to enhance the worksheet more by adding background cell shading to define areas of the worksheet. You will also use a heading style for the title, and change the format of the Food/Beverage, Merchandise, and Computer values to display commas only, without dollar signs.

Although you could make these changes using individual formatting commands, a quicker way is to use a predefined **cell style** to apply several formats in one step. Excel includes 47 predefined cell styles, or you can create your own custom styles. Using cell styles helps ensure that cells have consistent formatting. Cell styles are based on the theme that is applied to the entire workbook. When you switch to another theme, the cell styles are updated to match the new theme.

APPLYING THEMED CELL STYLES

First, you want to add background shading behind the entire worksheet.

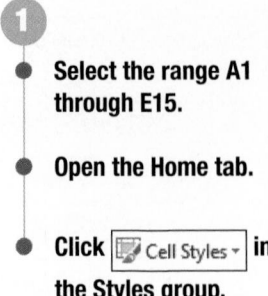

- **Select the range A1 through E15.**

- **Open the Home tab.**

- **Click** Cell Styles ▾ **in the Styles group.**

Your screen should be similar to Figure 2.18

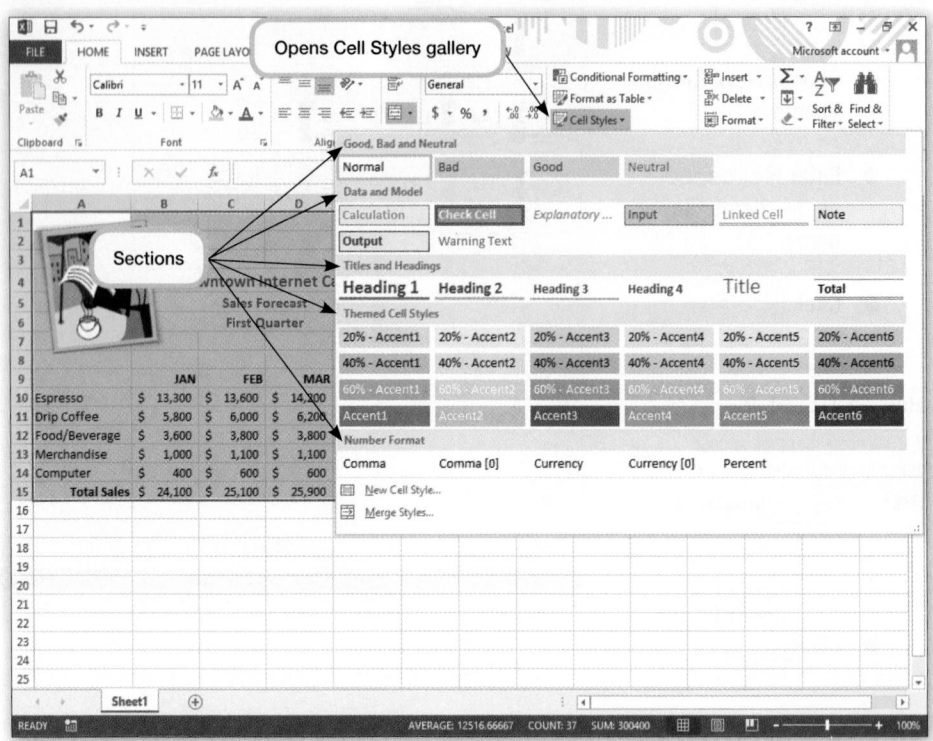

Figure 2.18

The Cell Styles gallery is divided into five sections. The styles in each section are designed to identify different areas of a worksheet and types of cell entries, as explained in the following table:

Section	Identifies
Good, Bad and Neutral	Data trends or outcomes; for example, selecting Bad would be used to identify a bad outcome
Data and Model	Worksheet areas; for example, calculations and warning notes
Titles and Headings	Worksheet titles and headings
Themed Cell Styles	Basic worksheet data
Number Format	Number formats

You will use a cell style in the Themed Cell Styles section. These cell styles consist of background fill colors and either white or black text color. The colors are associated with the theme colors. Pointing to a cell style displays a Live Preview of the cell style.

②
- Point to several cell styles to see the Live Preview.

- Choose 40%–Accent5 in the Themed Cell Styles section.

- Click on the worksheet to clear the selection.

Your screen should be similar to Figure 2.19

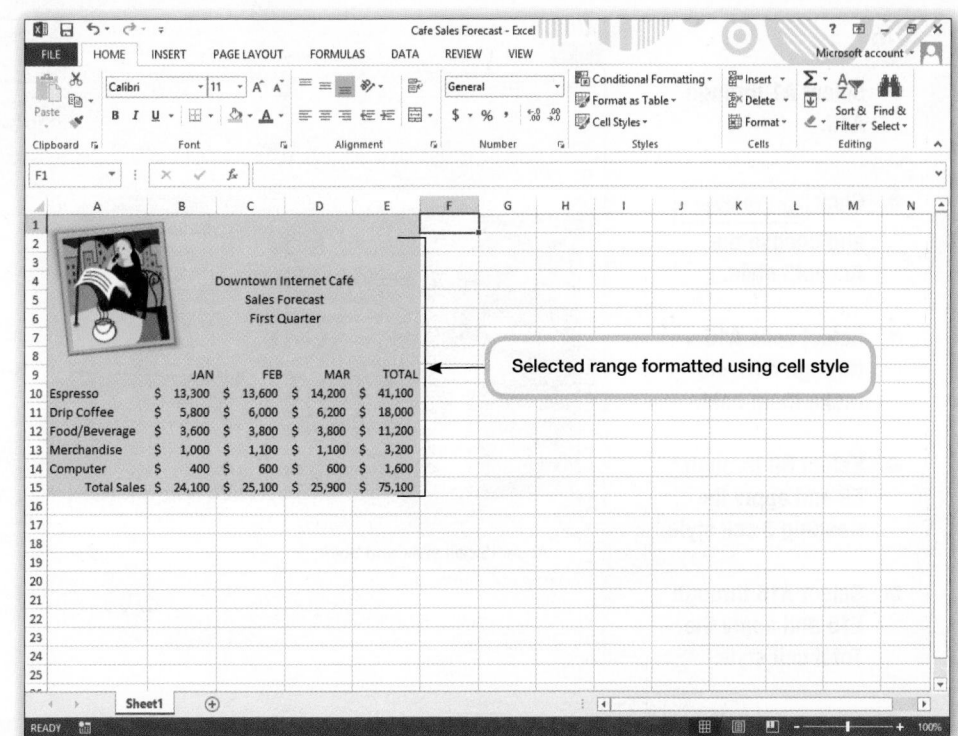

Figure 2.19

The selected range has been formatted using the selected cell style. It consists of a gold fill color for the cell background and black font color. The previous font color used in the titles was replaced with the font color associated with the cell style.

APPLYING HEADING AND TOTAL CELL STYLES

Next you will define the row headings area of the worksheet by selecting a different style from the Themed Cell Styles section. Then you will use two cell styles from the Titles and Headings section that will format the month column headings and the Total Sales row of data.

1

- Select A1 through A15.

- Click ![Cell Styles] and choose the Accent3 style.

- Select cells A10 through A15 and make them bold.

- Select B9 through E9 and apply the Heading 3 cell style.

- Select A15 through E15 and apply the Total cell style.

- Click outside the selection to see the formatting changes.

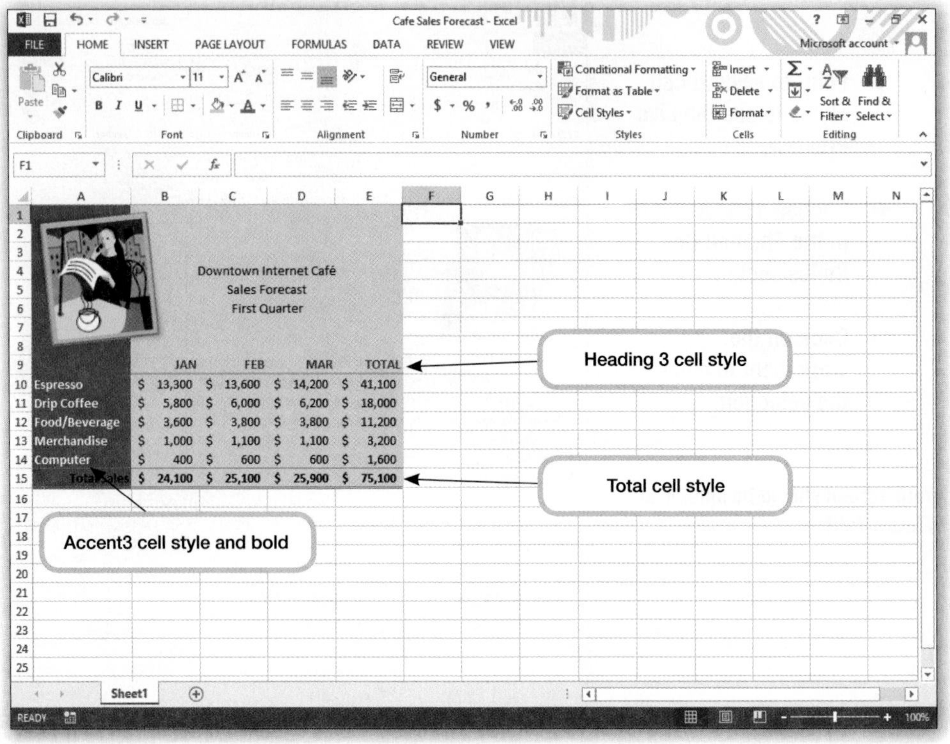

Your screen should be similar to Figure 2.20

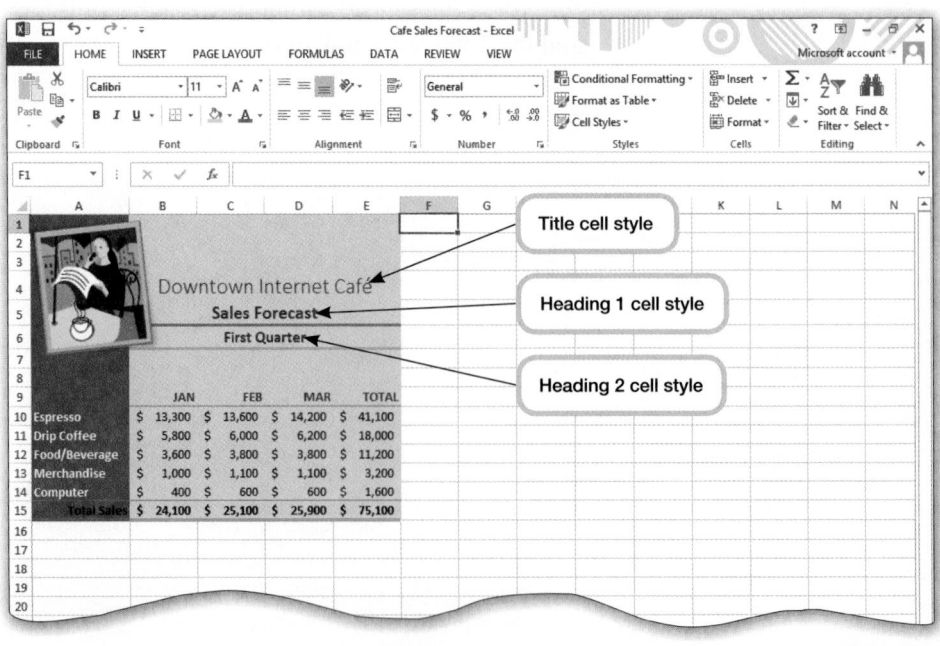

Figure 2.20

The Accent3 cell style uses a white font color with a dark red fill color. The Heading 3 style includes a dark gray font color and a bottom border. The Total cell style applies a black font color, bold text effect, and a top and bottom border.

Next, you will add formatting to the worksheet titles by applying a Title style to the first title line, a Heading 1 style to the second line, and a Heading 2 style to the third line.

2

- Apply the Title cell style to cell B4.

- Apply the Heading 1 cell style to cell B5.

- Apply the Heading 2 cell style to cell B6.

- Click outside the selection to see the formatting changes.

- Resize and reposition the graphic as needed to show the full title text.

Figure 2.21

Your screen should be similar to Figure 2.21

MODIFYING CELL STYLES

Although you like the font size change and the colored bottom border line, you feel the titles could be improved by changing the font color to a color similar to the fill color used in column A. Instead of changing the font color for each cell containing the titles, you will modify the cell styles so that the color changes to these styles will be easily available again.

- Click [Cell Styles ▾] and right-click on the Title cell style.

- Choose Modify from the shortcut menu.

- Click [Format...] and if necessary, open the Font tab.

- Open the Color gallery and choose **Dark Red, Accent 6 from the Theme Colors category.**

- Click [OK] twice.

- Modify the Heading 1 and Heading 2 cell styles in the same manner.

Your screen should be similar to Figure 2.22

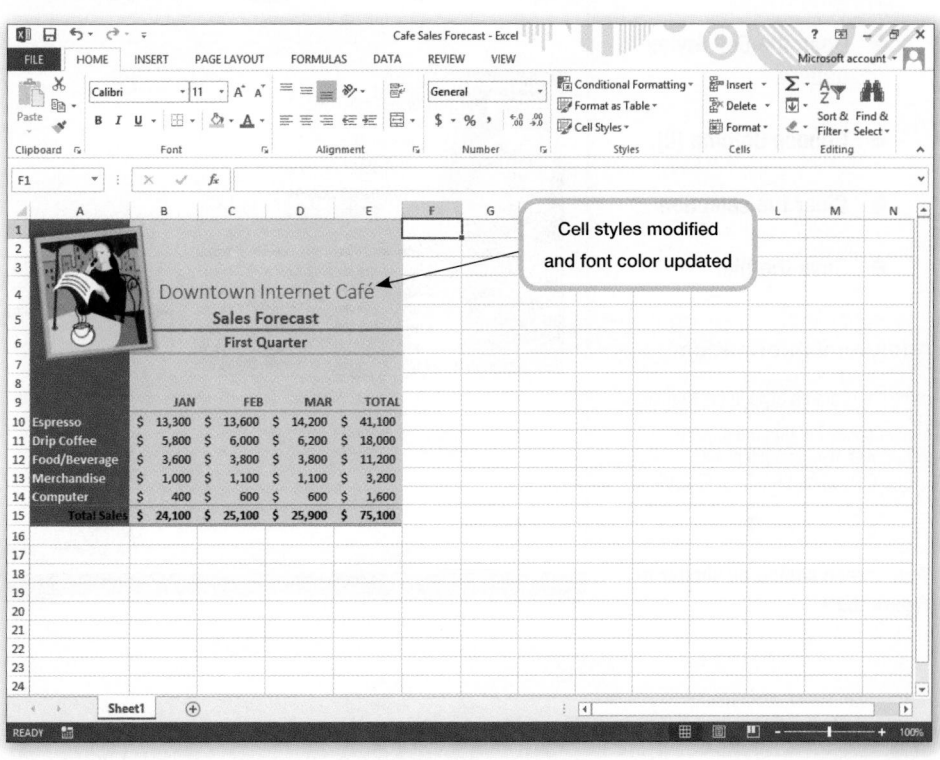

Figure 2.22

The three title lines have been updated to the new color associated with the three cell styles you modified. The changes to cell styles are saved with the current workbook file only.

APPLYING A NUMBER CELL STYLE

The final change you want to make is to change the format of some of the worksheet values. Currently all the values are formatted using the Accounting style with zero decimal places. The Cell Styles gallery also includes five predefined number format styles. Examples of the five predefined number styles are shown below.

Style	Example
Comma	89,522.00
Comma [0]	89,522
Currency	$89,522.00
Currency [0]	$89,522
Percent	89.52200%

You will use the Comma [0] style for the four rows of sales values below Espresso Sales.

- **Select B11 through E14.**

- **Open the Cell Styles gallery.**

- **Choose Comma [0].**

- **Clear the selection.**

- **Save the file.**

Your screen should be similar to Figure 2.23

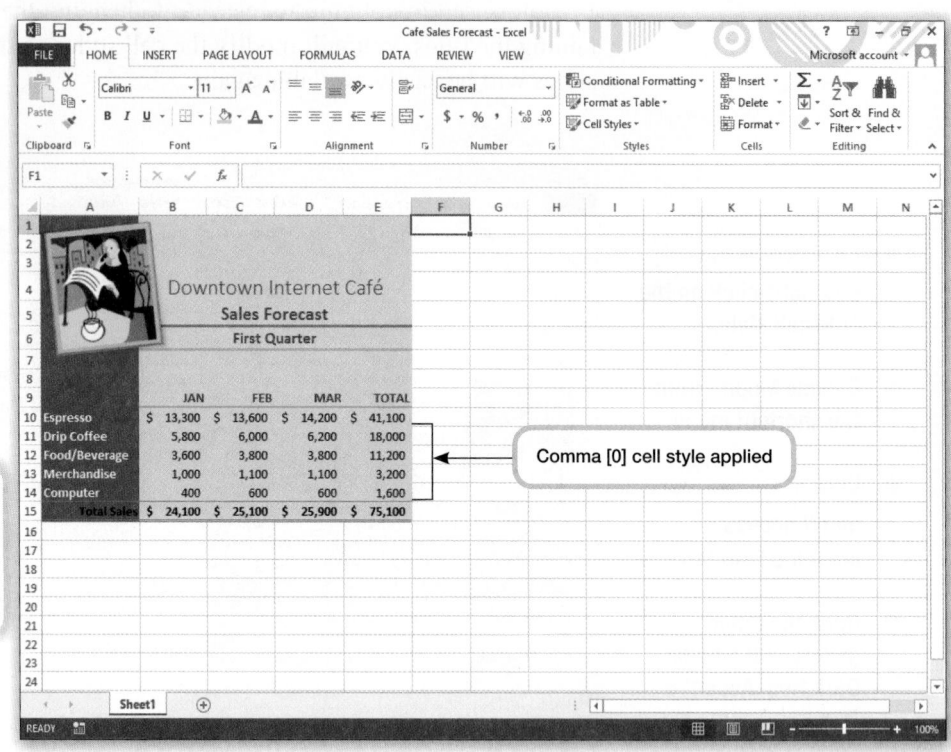

Figure 2.23

The Comma [0] style applies the Comma number format with zero decimal places and does not display a currency symbol. Using a style applies many formats in one easy step, making it quicker to apply formats to cells.

Creating Charts

Although the worksheet shows the sales data for each category, it is difficult to see how the different categories change over time. To make it easier to see the sales trends, you decide to create a chart of this data.

SELECTING THE CHART DATA

As you learned in Lab 1, a **chart** is a visual representation of data in a worksheet. Because all charts are drawn from data contained in a worksheet, the first step in creating a new chart is to select the worksheet range containing the data you want displayed as a chart plus any row or column headings you want used in the chart. Excel then recommends the chart types best suited to the selected data based upon the shape and contents of the worksheet selection.

A chart consists of a number of parts or elements that are important to understand so that you can identify the appropriate data to select in the worksheet.

Concept 4 Chart Elements

Chart elements are the different parts of a chart that are used to graphically display the worksheet data. The entire chart and all its elements is called the **chart area**.

The basic elements of a two-dimensional chart are described in the following table.

Element	Description
Plot area	Area within the X- and Y-axis boundaries where the chart data series appears.
Axis	The lines bordering the chart plot area used as a frame of reference for measurement. The **Y axis**, also called the **value axis**, is usually the vertical axis and contains data. The **X axis**, also called the **category axis**, is usually the horizontal axis and contains categories.
Data series	Related data points that are distinguished by different colors or patterns, called **data markers**, and displayed in the plot area.
Data labels	Labels that correspond to the data points that are plotted along the X axis.
Chart gridlines	Lines extending from the axis line across the plot area that make it easier to read the chart data.
Legend	A box that identifies the chart data series and data markers.
Chart title	A descriptive label displayed above the charted data that explains the contents of the chart.
Category-axis title	A descriptive label displayed along the X axis.
Value-axis title	A descriptive label displayed along the Y axis.

The basic parts of a two-dimensional chart are shown in the figure below.

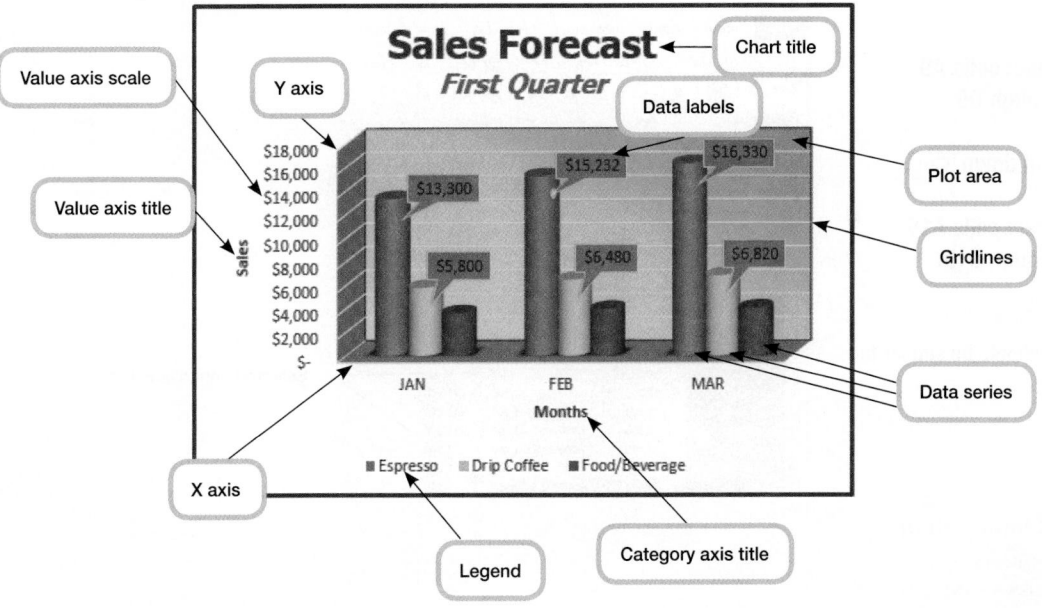

3-D column, 3-D cone, or 3-D pyramid charts have a third axis, the **depth axis** (also known as the **series axis** or **Z axis**), so that data can be plotted along the depth of a chart. Radar charts do not have horizontal (category) axes, and pie and doughnut charts do not have any axes.

The first chart you want to create will show the total sales pattern over the three months. This chart will use the month headings in cells B9 through D9 to label the X axis. The numbers to be charted are in cells B15 through D15. In addition, the heading "Total Sales" in cell A15 will be used as the chart legend, making the entire range A15 through D15.

Notice that the two ranges, B9 through D9 and A15 through D15, are not adjacent and are not the same size. When plotting nonadjacent ranges in a chart, the selections must form a rectangular shape. To do this, you will include the blank cell A9 in the selection. You will specify the range and create the chart.

Additional Information

If you select only one cell, Excel automatically plots all cells that contain data adjacent to that cell into a chart.

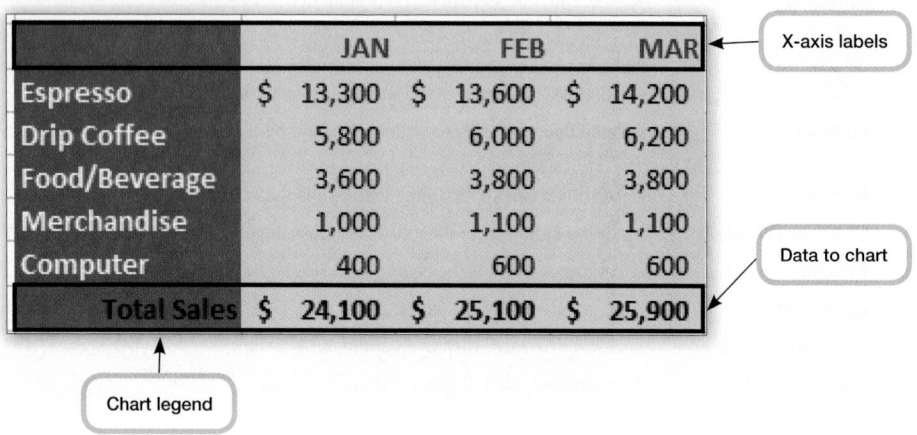

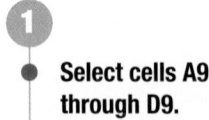

- Select cells A9 through D9.

- Hold down Ctrl.

- Select cells A15 through D15.

Your screen should be similar to Figure 2.24

Additional Information

When the selected cells are not adjacent, the Quick Analysis tool is not available.

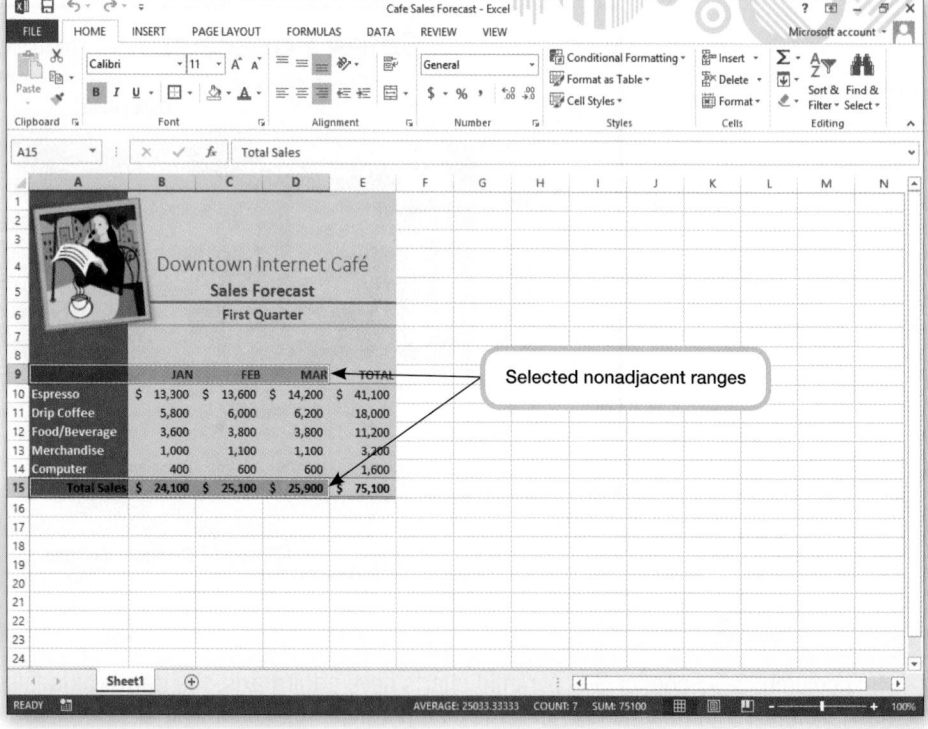

Figure 2.24

SELECTING THE CHART TYPE

The next step is to select the chart type. There are many different types of charts that can be used to convey the information in a worksheet in an attractive and easy-to-understand manner.

Concept 5 Chart Types

Different **chart types** are used to represent data in different ways. The type of chart you create depends on the type of data you are charting and the emphasis you want the chart to impart.

Excel 2013 can produce many standard types of graphs or charts, with different subtypes for each standard type. In addition, Excel includes professionally designed, built-in custom charts that include additional formatting and chart refinements. The basic chart types and how they represent data are described in the following table.

Type	Description	Type	Description
Area Charts	**Area charts** show the magnitude of change over time by emphasizing the area under the curve created by each data series.	Pie or Doughnut Charts	**Pie charts** display data as slices of a circle or pie. They show the relationship of each value in a data series to the series as a whole. Each slice of the pie represents a single value in the series. **Doughnut charts** are similar to pie charts except that they can show more than one data series.
Bar Charts	**Bar charts** display data as evenly spaced bars. The categories are displayed along the Y axis and the values are displayed horizontally, placing more emphasis on comparisons and less on time.	Stock, Surface, or Radar Charts	**Stock charts** illustrate fluctuations in stock prices or scientific data. They require three to five data series that must be arranged in a specific order. **Surface charts** display values in a form similar to a rubber sheet stretched over a 3-D column chart. These are useful for finding the best combination between sets of data. **Radar charts** display a line or area chart wrapped around a central point. Each axis represents a set of data points.
Column Charts	**Column charts** display data as evenly spaced bars. They are similar to bar charts, except that categories are organized horizontally and values vertically to emphasize variation over time.	Scatter (X, Y) or Bubble Charts	**Scatter (X, Y) charts** are used to show the relationship between two ranges of numeric data. **Bubble charts** compare sets of three values. They are similar to a scatter chart with the third value displayed as the size of bubble markers.
Line Charts	**Line charts** display data along a line. They are used to show changes in data over time, emphasizing time and rate of change rather than the amount of change.	Combo Charts	**Combo charts** display data as two different chart types. They are used when the range of values in the chart vary widely or have mixed data types.

Each type of chart includes many variations. The Charts group in the Insert tab contains commands to create the most commonly used types of charts. In addition, it includes the button, which lists the most likely chart types for your worksheet selection. You also can open the Charts group dialog box to have access to all the available chart types. You think a column chart may best represent this data.

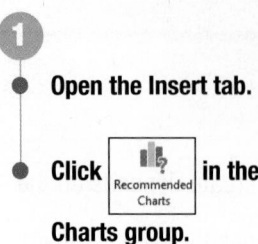

1

● Open the Insert tab.

● Click [Recommended Charts] in the Charts group.

Your screen should be similar to
Figure 2.25

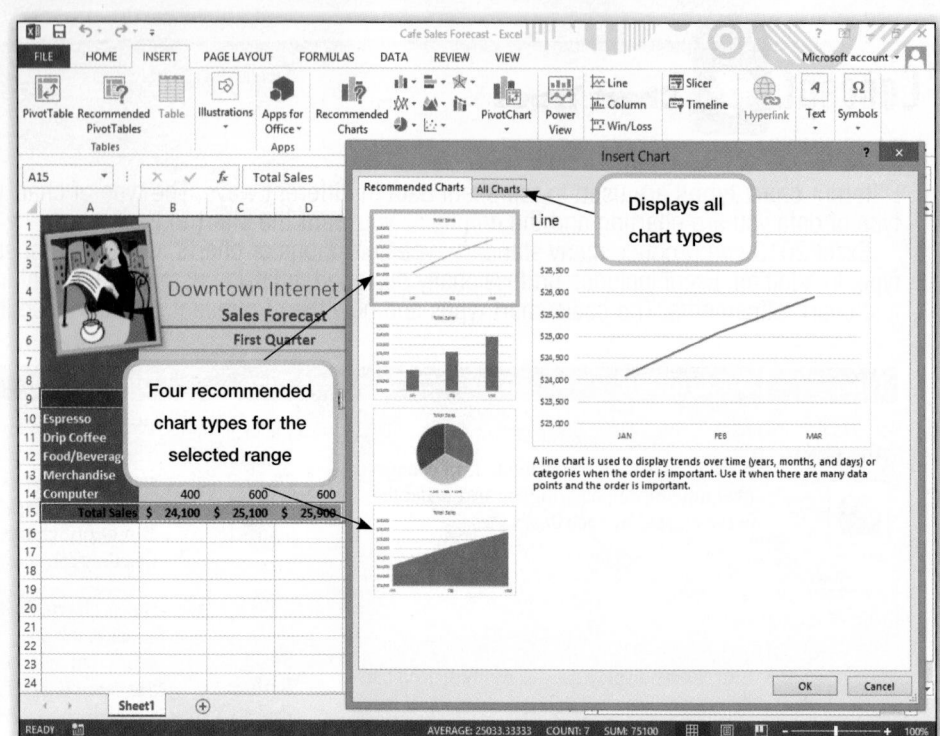

Figure 2.25

Based on the selected data, the recommended charts include a line chart, a column chart, a pie chart, and an area chart. The preview area displays a large preview of the data in the selected chart type. You can choose one of the recommended chart types, or you can click the All Charts tab to see how the selected data looks in all available chart types.

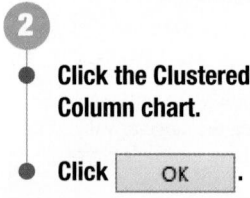

2

● Click the Clustered Column chart.

● Click [OK].

Your screen should be similar to
Figure 2.26

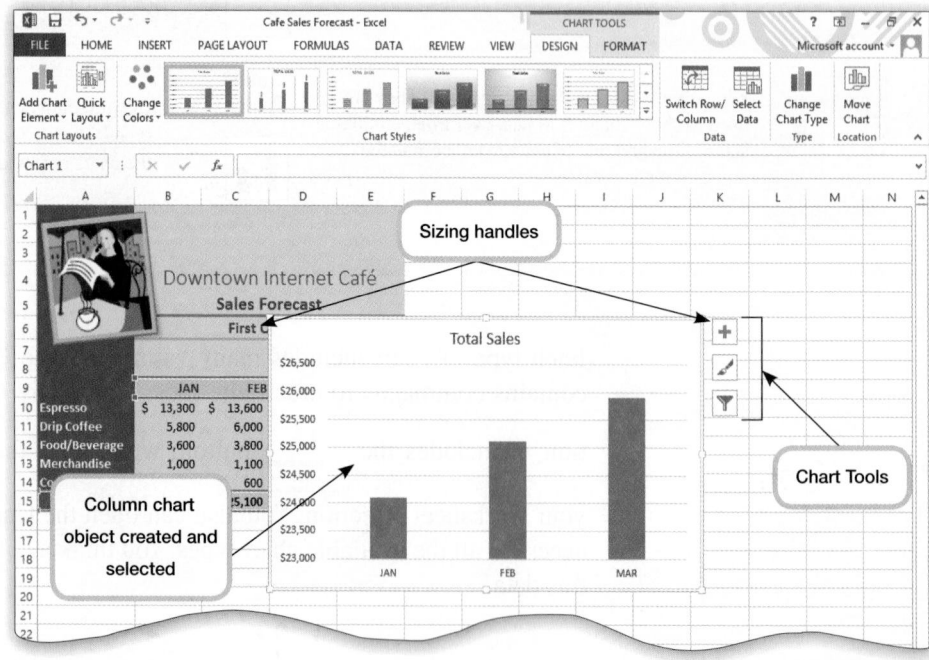

Figure 2.26

The column chart is created using the data from the worksheet and displayed as a chart object in the worksheet.

Concept 6 Chart Object

A **chart object** is a graphic object that is created using charting features. A chart object can be inserted into a worksheet or into a special chart sheet. By default, Excel inserts the chart object into the worksheet. Charts that are inserted into a worksheet are embedded objects. An **embedded chart** becomes part of the sheet in which it is inserted and is saved as part of the worksheet when you save the workbook file. Like all graphic objects, an embedded chart object can be sized and moved in a worksheet. A worksheet can contain multiple charts.

A chart that is inserted into a separate chart sheet also is saved with the workbook file. Only one chart can be added to a chart sheet, and it cannot be sized or moved.

Excel decides which data series to plot along the X and Y axes based on the type of chart selected and the number of rows and columns defined in the series. The worksheet data range that has the greater number of rows or columns appears along the X axis, and the smaller number is charted as the Y data series. When the data series is an equal number of rows and columns as it is in this case, the default is to plot the rows. The first row defines the X-axis category labels and the second row the plotted data. The content of the first cell in the second row is used as the chart title and legend text.

MOVING AND SIZING A CHART

Notice that the new chart is on top of the worksheet data. As objects are added to the worksheet, they automatically **stack** in individual layers. The stacking order is apparent when objects overlap. Stacking allows you to create different effects by overlapping objects. Because you can rearrange the stacking order, you do not have to add or create the objects in the order in which you want them to appear.

First you want to move the chart so that it is displayed to the right of the worksheet data. In addition, you want to increase the size of the chart. A chart is moved by dragging the chart border and sized just like a graphic object. If you hold down [Alt] while dragging to move and size a chart object, the chart automatically snaps into position or aligns with the closest worksheet cell when you release the mouse button. Release the mouse button before you release [Alt].

1

- Point to the chart border and drag the chart object so the upper-left corner is in cell F1.

- Point to the bottom-center sizing handle, hold down Alt, and drag the chart border line down until it is even with the bottom of row 15.

Your screen should be similar to Figure 2.27

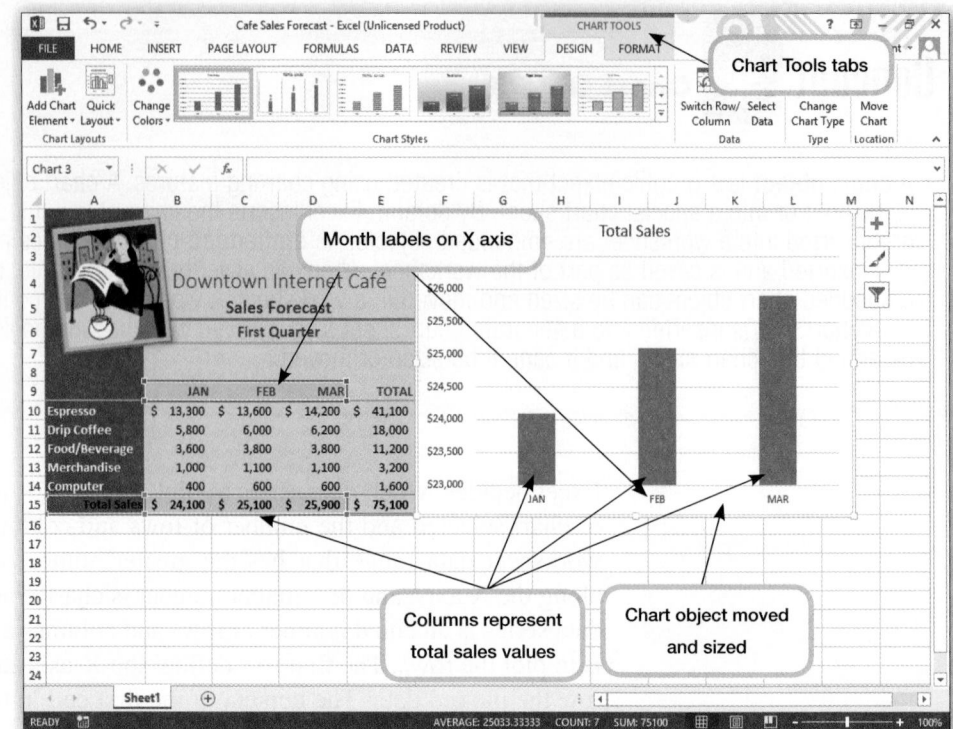

Figure 2.27

It is now easy to see how the worksheet data you selected is represented in the chart. Each column represents a value or data point in the data series (row 15) and provides a visual representation of the total sales for each month. The month labels in row 9 have been used to label the X-axis category labels. The range or scale of values along the Y axis is determined from the data in the worksheet. The upper limit is the maximum value in the worksheet rounded upward to the next highest interval. The row label in cell A15 is the chart title.

The two new Chart Tools tabs on the Ribbon contain options to modify the chart. The Design tab is used to change the layout, colors, and chart style. You can also redefine the source data, change the chart type, or move the chart to another sheet. The Format tab is used to enhance the appearance of chart elements by adding fill color, borders, and special effects. You can also add and format lines and and other shapes on the chart.

In addition, next to the upper-right corner of the chart are three buttons, ⊞, ✐, and ▼. These buttons allow you to quickly access the most commonly used features on the Chart Tools tab.

APPLYING CHART LAYOUTS

Next, you want to improve the appearance of the chart. To help you do this quickly, Excel includes many chart layouts (also called quick layouts) and quick styles from which you can select. A **chart layout** is a predefined set of chart elements that can be quickly applied to a chart. The elements include chart titles, a legend, a data table, or data labels. These elements are displayed in a specific arrangement in the chart. Each chart type includes a variety of layouts. You can then modify or customize these layouts further to meet your needs. However, the custom layouts cannot be saved.

Chart Tools Design tab is open

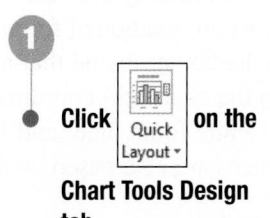

1

Click on the

Chart Tools Design tab.

Your screen should be similar to
Figure 2.28

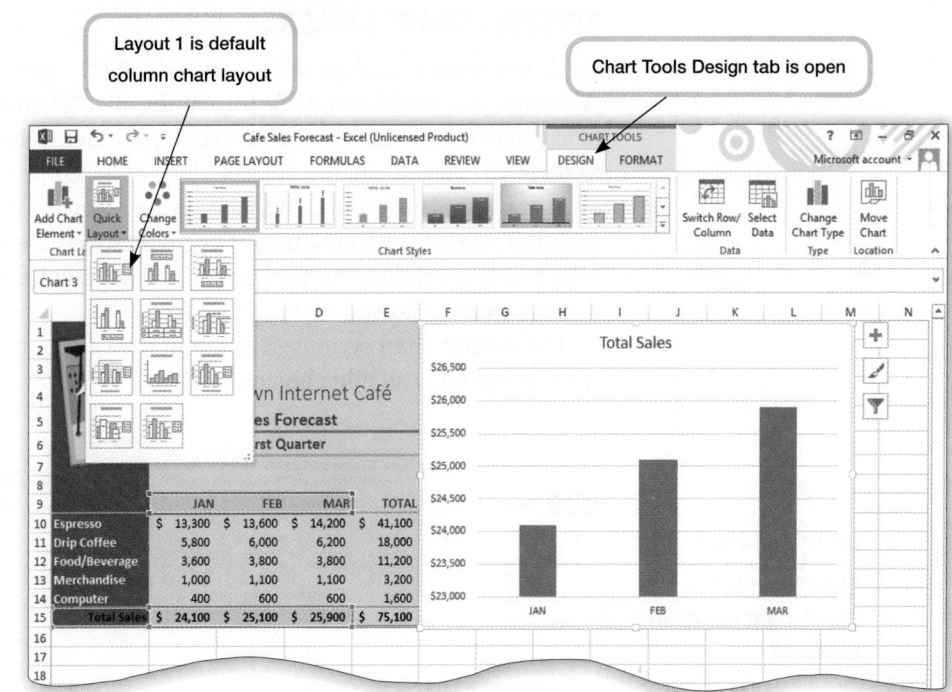

Figure 2.28

The chart layout gallery displays the 11 chart layouts for a column chart. The default chart layout is Layout 1. Pointing to a chart layout displays a Live Preview on your chart.

Default chart style

2

Point to several chart layouts to see the Live Preview.

Choose

Layout 10.

Additional Information

A ScreenTip of the chart layout name appears when you point to the layout.

Your screen should be similar to
Figure 2.29

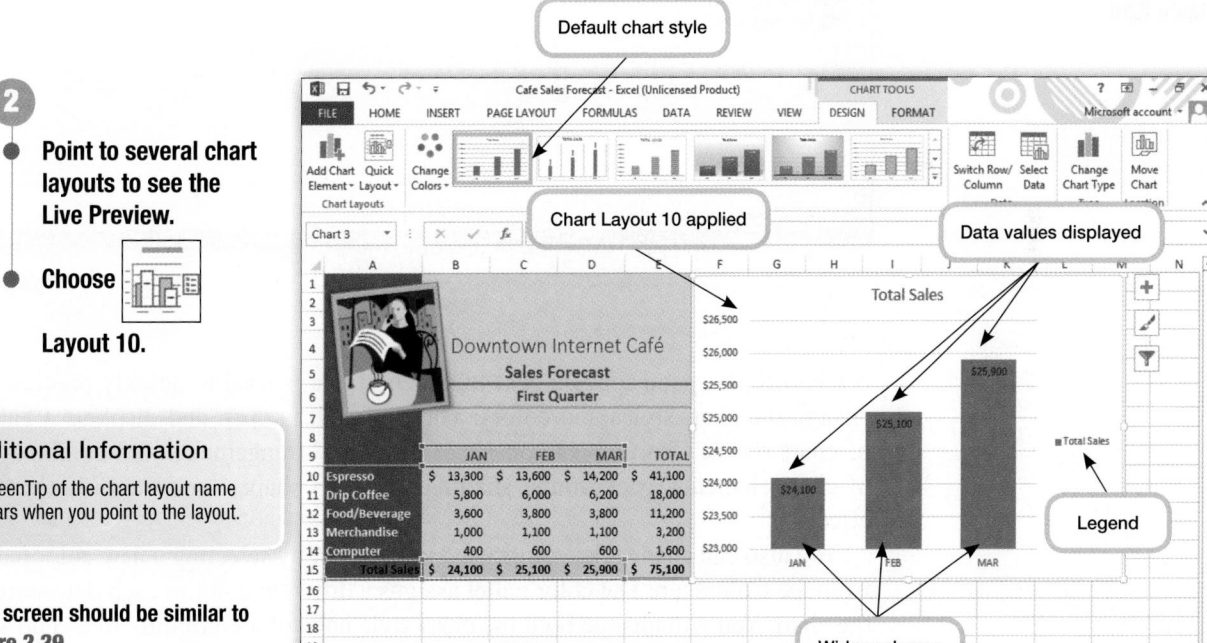

Chart Layout 10 applied

Data values displayed

Legend

Wider columns

Figure 2.29

The columns are wider and include the data values. Additionally, a legend is displayed to the right of the chart.

APPLYING CHART STYLES

Next, you want to change the visual style of the chart and the color of the columns. Although you could manually format the chart elements individually, it is quicker to use one of the predefined **chart styles** to quickly apply a combination of formats to the chart. The available chart styles are based on the document theme that has been applied. This ensures that the formats you apply to the chart will coordinate with the worksheet formatting. The chart styles use the same fonts, line, and fill effects that are defined in the theme. The chart color choices are also based on the current theme colors.

The default chart style is selected in the Chart Styles group in the Ribbon. You want to see all available choices.

1

● Click [icon] Chart Styles next to the upper-right corner of the chart.

Another Method

You could also click [icon] More in the Chart Styles group to open the gallery of chart styles.

Your screen should be similar to Figure 2.30

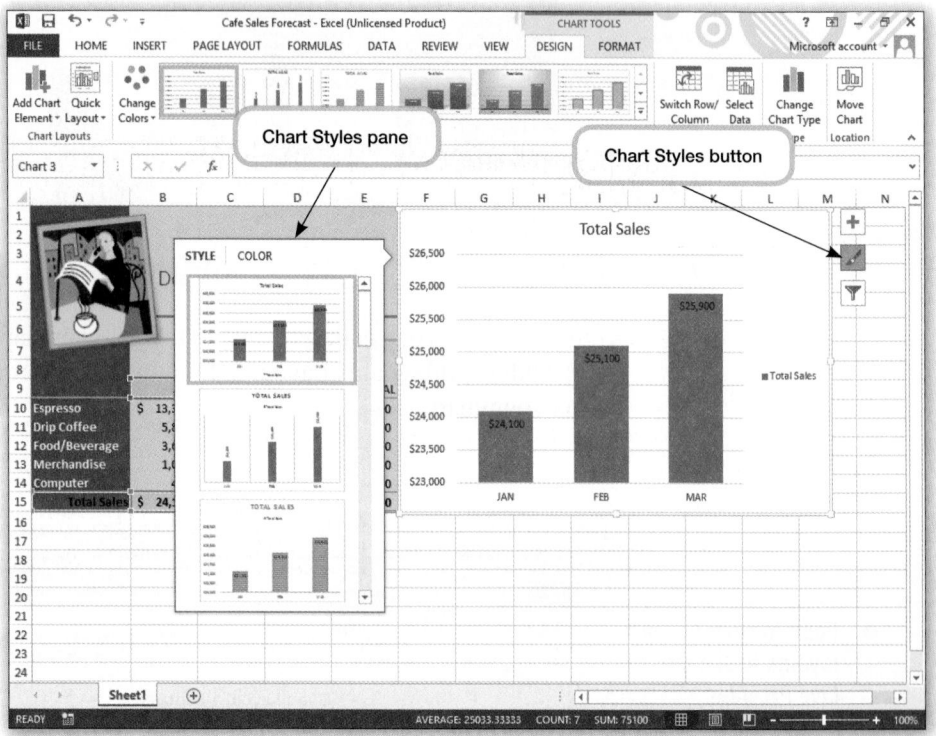

Figure 2.30

A Chart Styles pane appears next to the chart that is used to quickly preview and change the chart styles and colors. The Style tab is open and displays a gallery of chart styles. Chart styles consist of different arrangements and combinations of chart elements, background shadings, column shapes, and three-dimensional effects.

You also can change the colors used in the chart by selecting a new color palette from the Colors tab. The color pallet assigns a different color to each data series in the chart. You will change both the chart style and colors. Pointing to a chart style or color displays a Live Preview of the selection.

- Point to several chart styles to see the Live Preview.

- Click  Style 5.

- Click the Color tab in the Chart Styles pane to open it.

- Point to several colors to see the Live Preview.

- Choose Color 3.

Your screen should be similar to Figure 2.31

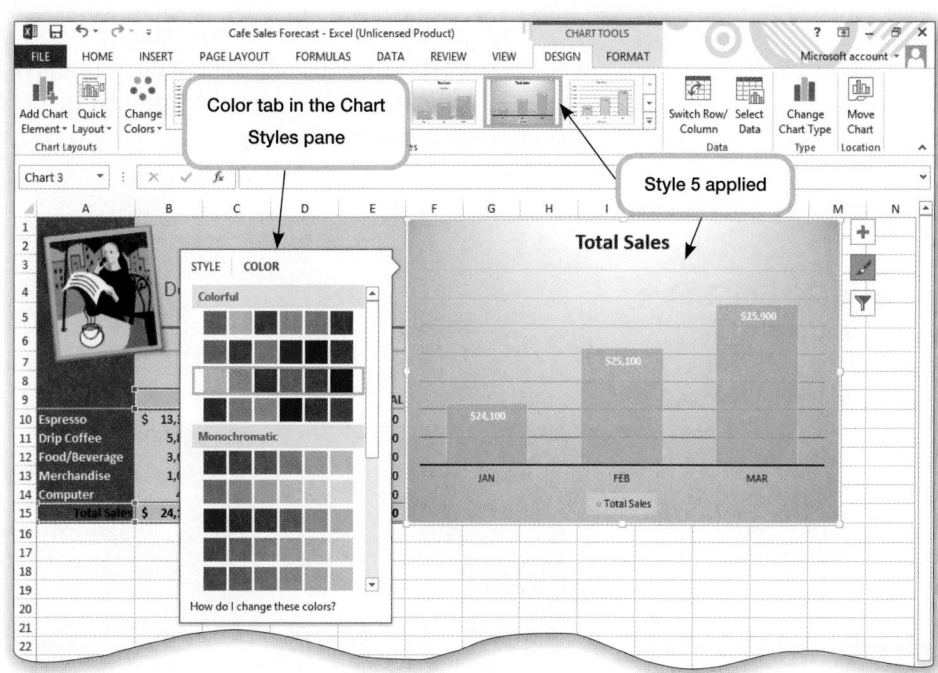

Figure 2.31

The chart style selection removed the vertical axis labels, moved the legend to the bottom of the chart, and added a shaded background in the plot area. The new color palette changed the column color to gold.

ADDING AND REMOVING CHART LABELS

Finally, you want to clarify the data in the chart by displaying the vertical axis values again, adding labels along both chart axes, removing the legend, and adding a more descriptive chart title.

- Click 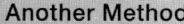 Chart Elements.

- Point to Axes and click ▶ to display a submenu.

- Choose Primary Vertical.

- Click the Axis Titles check box to turn on this feature.

Another Method

You also can click [Add Chart Element] in the Chart Layouts group of the Chart Tools Design tab to add and remove chart elements.

Your screen should be similar to Figure 2.32

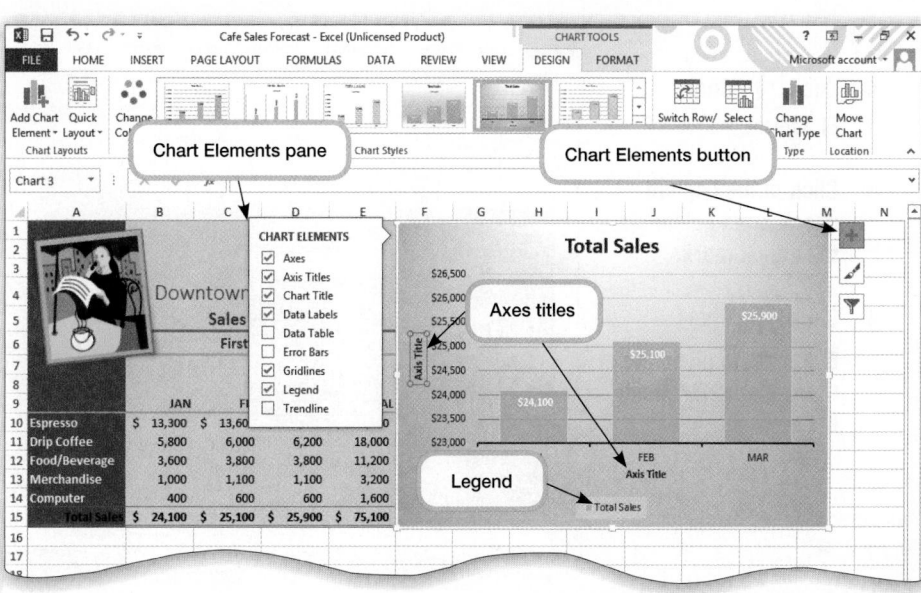

Figure 2.32

The vertical axis values are displayed again, and two axis title text boxes were inserted. The Y-axis title text box is a selected object and displays the sample text, Axis Title. A **text box** is a graphic element that is a container for specific types of information. In this case, it is designed to contain text for the axis title. You will replace the sample text with the axis title.

To replace the text in a text box, simply select the text box and type the new text. As you type, the label appears in the formula bar. After you press (Enter) it will appear in the text box. You also can edit text in a text box using the same features that are used to edit a cell entry.

2

- Type **Total Sales** and press (Enter).

- Click on the X-axis title text box to select it.

- Type **Months** and press (Enter).

Your screen should be similar to Figure 2.33

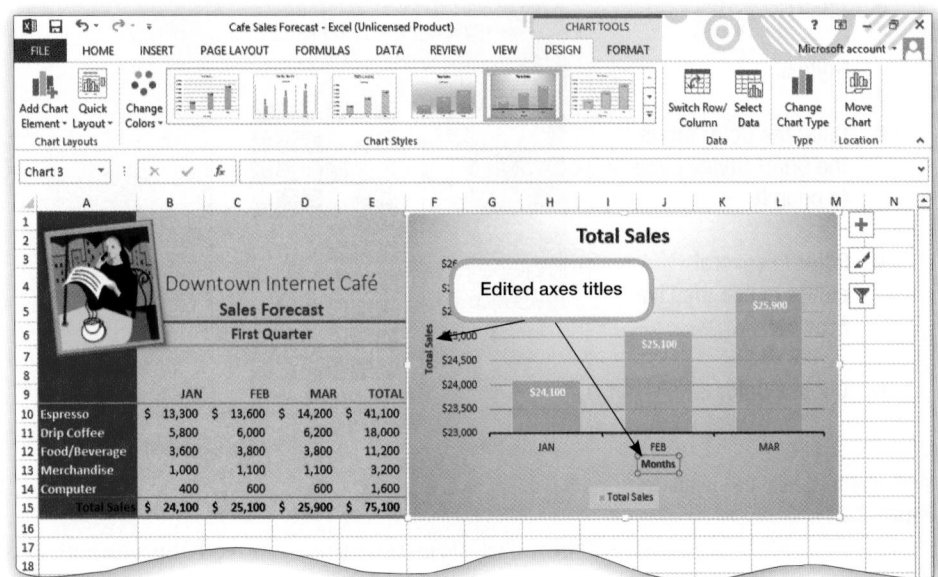

Figure 2.33

The sample text in the text boxes was replaced by the text you typed. The titles clearly describe the information displayed in the chart. Now, because there is only one data range and the horizontal category labels fully explains this data, you will remove the display of the legend.

3

- Click 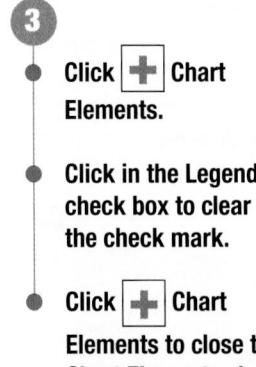 Chart Elements.

- Click in the Legend check box to clear the check mark.

- Click ⊞ Chart Elements to close the Chart Elements check list box.

Your screen should be similar to Figure 2.34

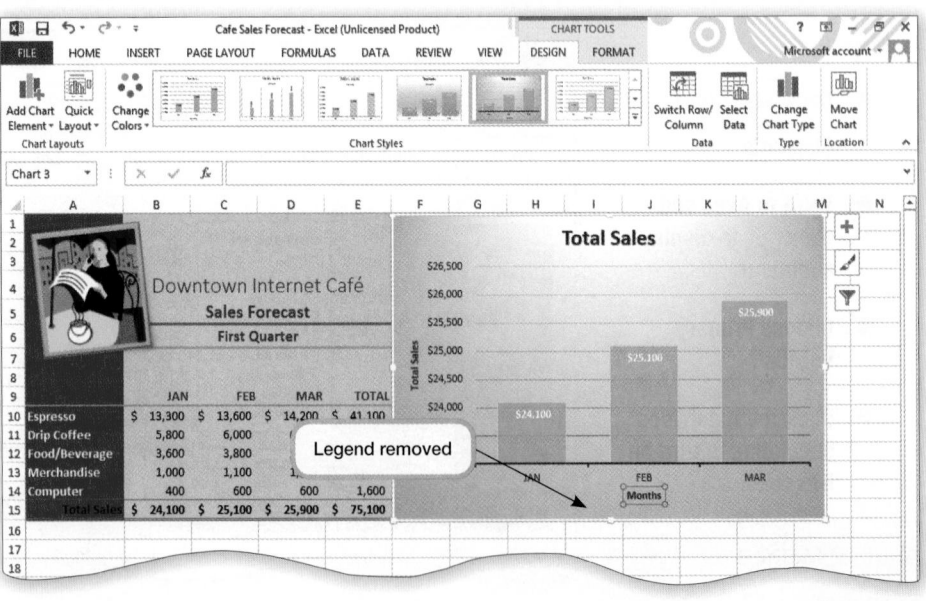

Figure 2.34

The legend is removed and the chart area resized to occupy the extra space. All chart labels can be removed in the same manner.

Finally, you want to add a more descriptive title to the chart and improve its appearance. Because this element already exists on the chart, you just need to change the text, by editing and formatting the text in the text box. When you point to different areas in the chart, a chart ScreenTip appears that identifies the chart element that will be affected by your action.

4

- Point to the chart title to see the ScreenTip.

- Click on the chart title to select it.

- Double-click on the word "Total" to select it and type **Downtown Internet Cafe**

- Select all the text in the text box and point to the Mini toolbar.

- Change the font color to Dark Red, Accent 6.

- Click anywhere in the chart to clear the selection.

Your screen should be similar to Figure 2.35

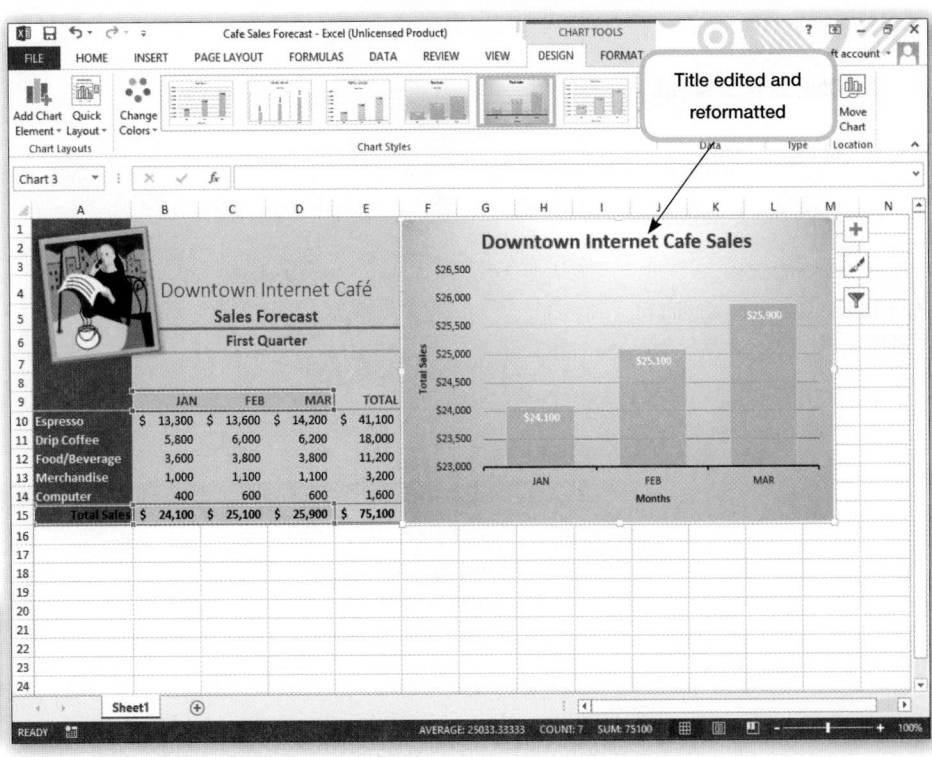

Figure 2.35

CHANGING THE CHART LOCATION

Although this chart compares the total sales for the three months, you decide you are more interested in seeing a comparison for the sales categories. You could delete this chart simply by pressing Delete while the chart area is selected. Instead, however, you will move it to a separate worksheet in case you want to refer to it again.

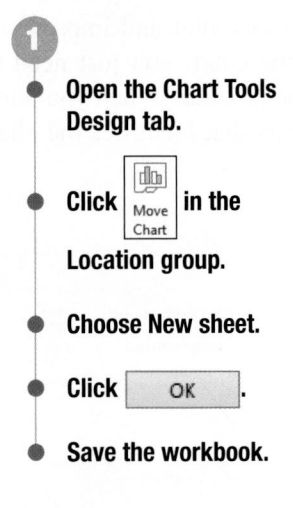

1

- Open the Chart Tools Design tab.

- Click 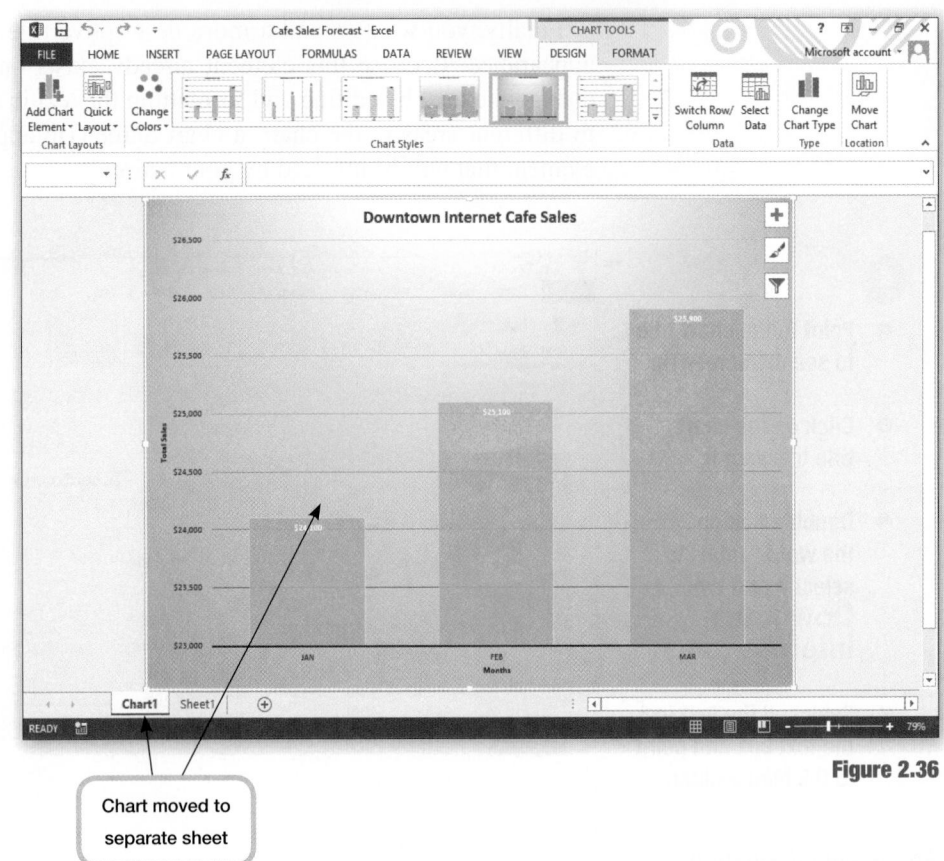 in the Location group.

- Choose New sheet.

- Click **OK**.

- Save the workbook.

Your screen should be similar to Figure 2.36

Figure 2.36

Chart moved to separate sheet

Additional Information

You also can create a chart using the default chart type (column) in a new chart sheet by selecting the data range and pressing F11.

The column chart is now an object displayed in a separate chart sheet. Generally, you display a chart in a chart sheet when you want the chart displayed separately from the associated worksheet data. The chart is still automatically linked to the worksheet data from which it was created. The new chart sheet, named Chart1, was inserted to the left of the worksheet, Sheet1. The chart sheet is the active sheet, or the sheet in which you are currently working.

Creating a Multiple Data Series Chart

Now you are ready to continue your analysis of sales trends. You want to create a second chart to display the sales data for each category for the three months. You could create a separate chart for each category and then compare the charts; however, to make the comparisons between the categories easier, you will display all the categories on a single chart.

The data for the three months for the four categories is in cells B10 through D14. The month headings (X-axis data series) are in cells B9 through D9, and the legend text is in the range A10 through A14.

1

- Click the **Sheet1** tab.

- Select **A9** through **D14**.

- Open the **Insert** tab.

- Click Recommended Charts

- Open the **All Charts** tab.

- Choose **3-D Clustered Column** from the row of column chart types.

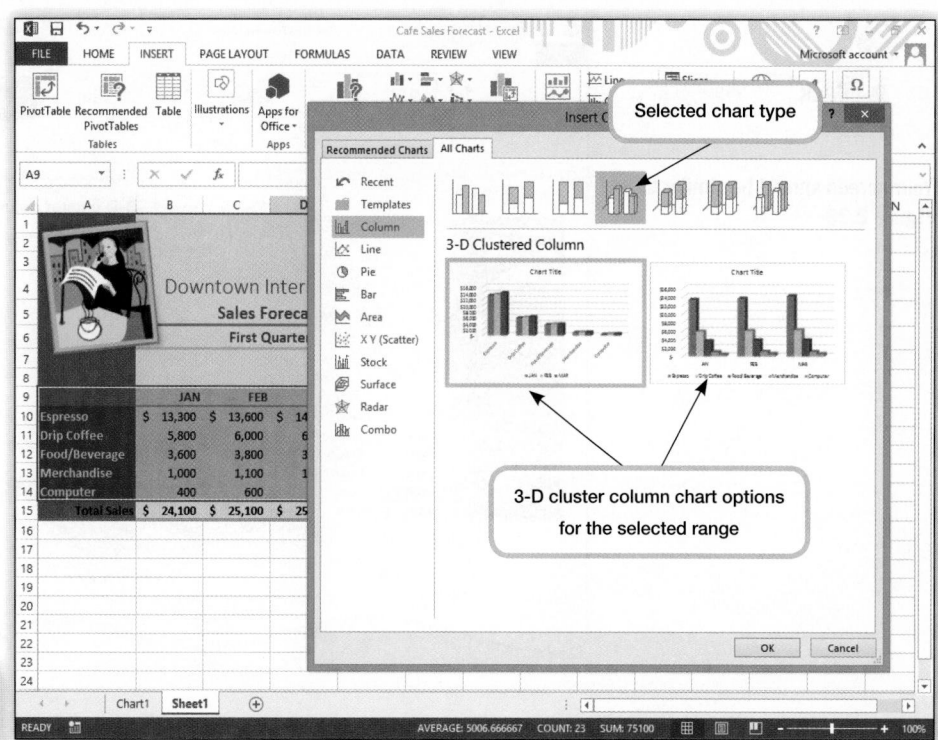

Figure 2.37

Your screen should be similar to Figure 2.37

The two 3-D clustered column chart variations display the total sales by category or by month.

You will insert the default chart showing the sales by category in the worksheet shown in the preview on the left.

2
● Click [OK].

Your screen should be similar to Figure 2.38

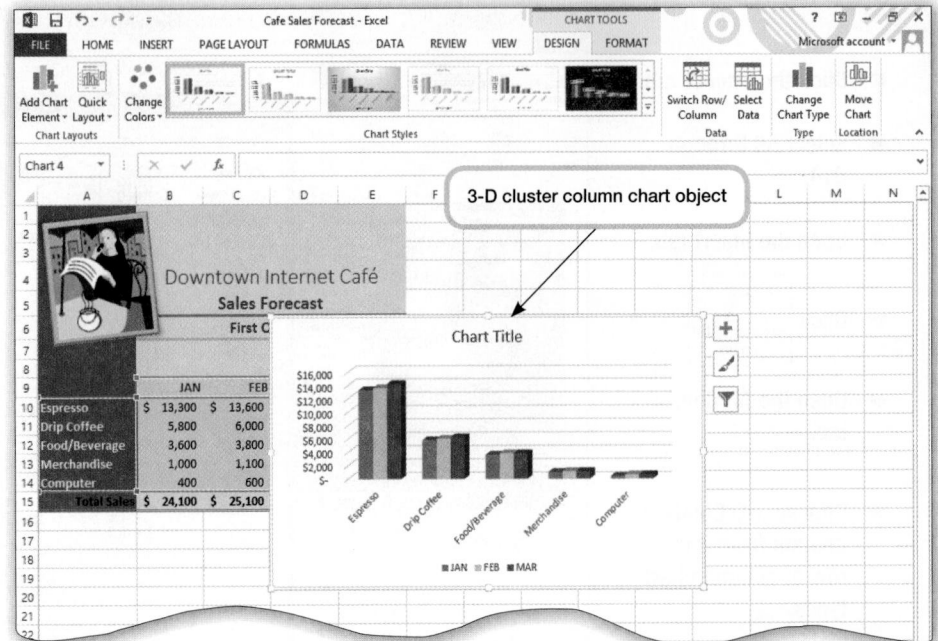

3-D cluster column chart object

Figure 2.38

A different column color identifies each data series, and the legend identifies the months. When plotting the data for this chart, Excel plotted the three months as the data series because the data range has fewer columns than rows. This time, however, you want to change the data series so that the months are along the X axis.

3
● Click 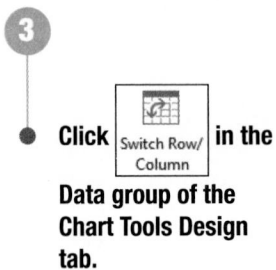 Switch Row/Column in the **Data group of the Chart Tools Design tab.**

Your screen should be similar to Figure 2.39

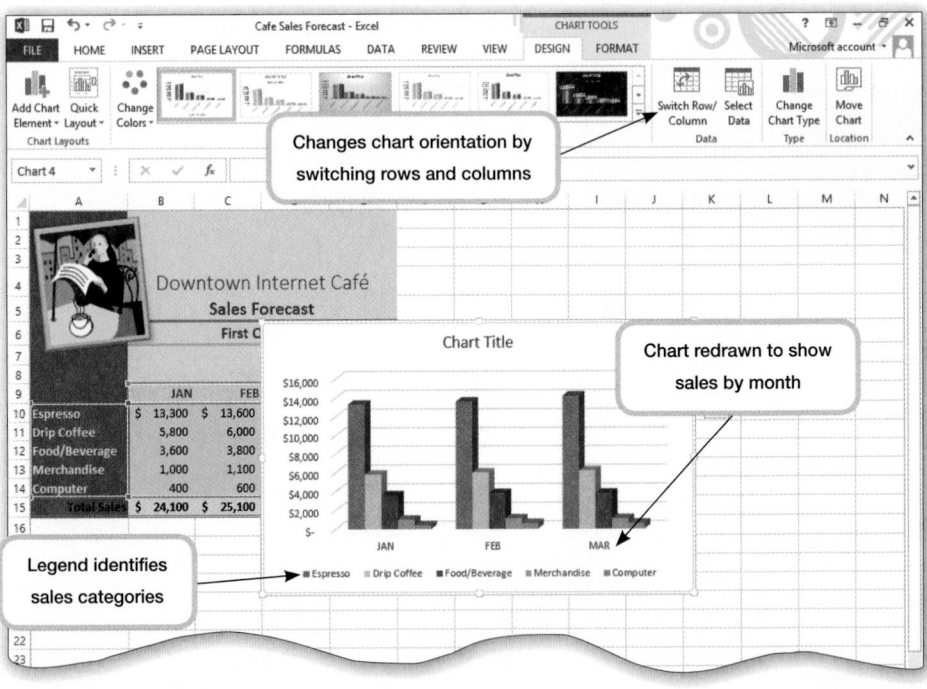

Changes chart orientation by switching rows and columns

Chart redrawn to show sales by month

Legend identifies sales categories

Figure 2.39

The chart is redrawn with the new orientation. The column chart now compares the sales by month rather than by category. The legend at the bottom of the chart displays the names of the sales categories.

Next, you will specify the chart titles and finish the chart.

4

● Change the chart style to Style 5.

● Change the chart layout to Layout 9.

● Replace the axis and title text box sample text with the titles shown below:

Title	Entry
Chart title	Sales Forecast
Horizontal Axis	Months
Vertical Axis	Sales

● Move and size the chart until it covers cells F2 through L15.

Your screen should be similar to Figure 2.40

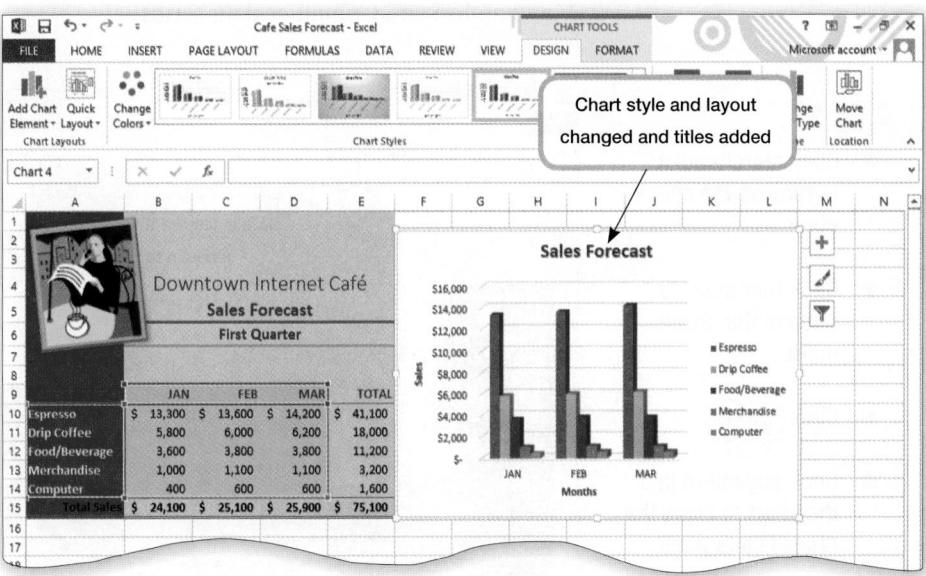

Figure 2.40

The column chart shows that sales in all categories are increasing, with the greatest increase occurring in espresso sales.

CHANGING THE DATA SOURCE

As you look at the chart, you see that the Merchandise and Computer sales values are inconsequential to the forecast because they are so small and do not change much. You will remove these data series from the chart.

1

● Click ▼ Chart Filters to the right of the chart.

Another Method

You can also click Select Data from the Data group of the Design tab for the same commands.

Your screen should be similar to Figure 2.41

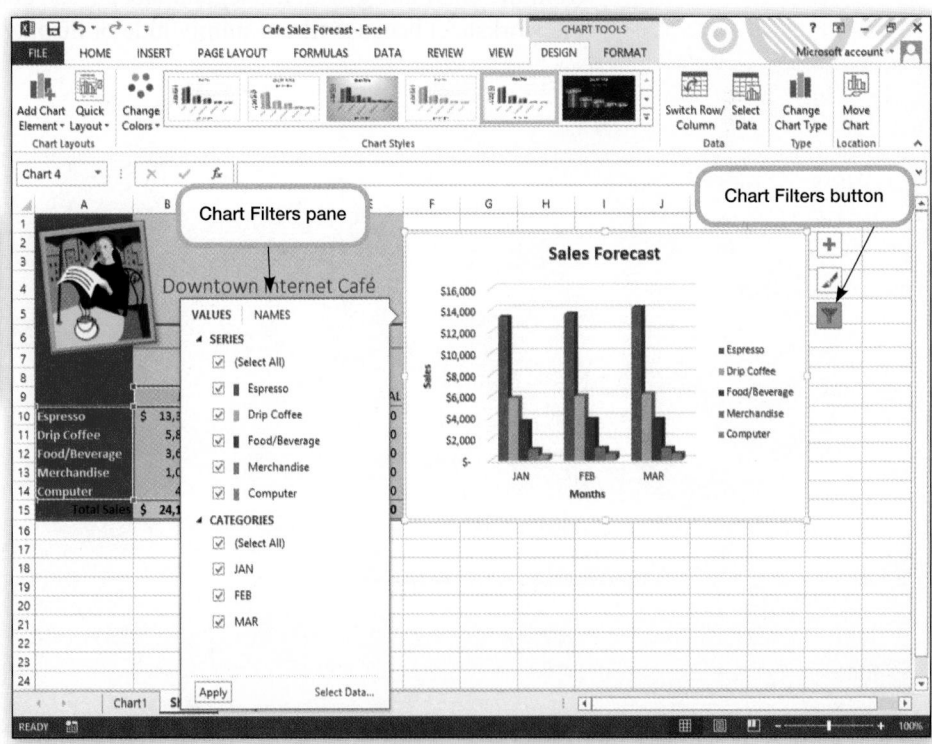

Figure 2.41

A Chart Filters pane opens next to the chart. It is used to show or hide data series and categories and set how the series names are displayed. You will remove the Merchandise and Computer data series.

2

● **Click Merchandise to remove the check mark.**

● **Click Computer to remove the check mark.**

● **Click** Apply .

● **Click anywhere in the chart to close the Chart Filters pane.**

Your screen should be similar to Figure 2.42

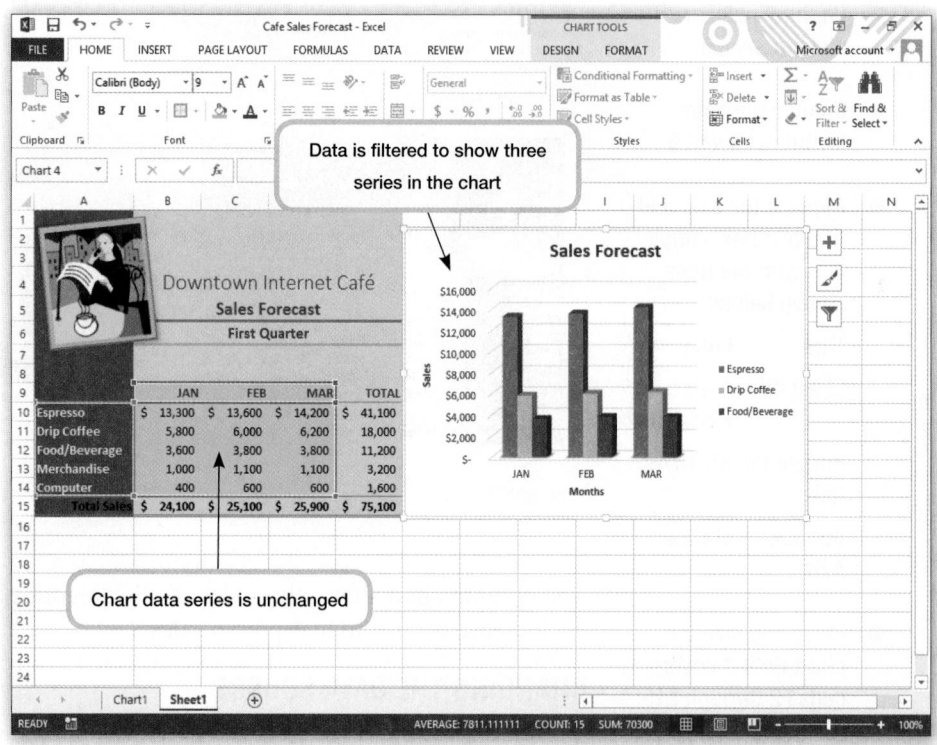

Figure 2.42

The columns representing the Merchandise and Computer series were removed from the chart along with the legend labels. The chart data series is unchanged in the worksheet because filters simply hide or display the data.

CHANGING THE CHART TYPE: LINE, BAR, AREA, STACKED

Next, you would like to see how the same data displayed in the column chart would look as a line chart. A line chart displays data as a line and is commonly used to show trends over time. You can change the chart type easily using the 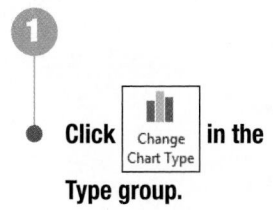 button on the Design tab.

1

Click 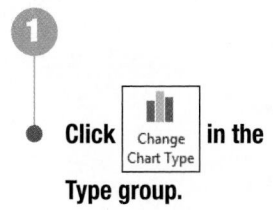 in the Type group.

Your screen should be similar to Figure 2.43

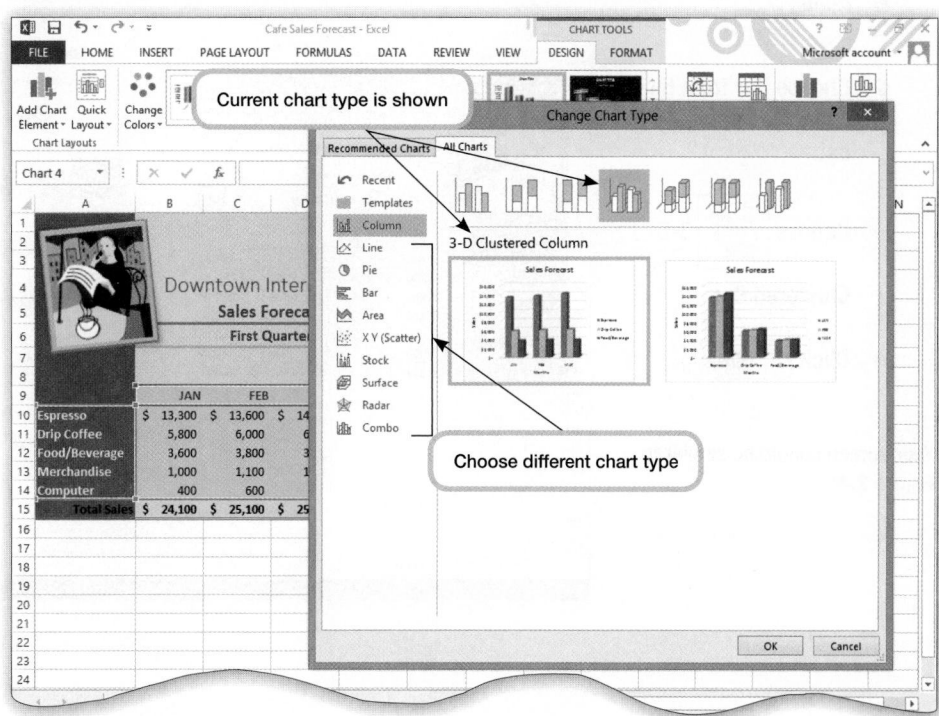

Figure 2.43

The Change Chart Type box displays all the available chart types just as in the Insert Chart dialog box. The current selection, 3-D Clustered Column, is highlighted. You want to change it to a line chart.

2

Choose Line from the chart type category list.

Choose 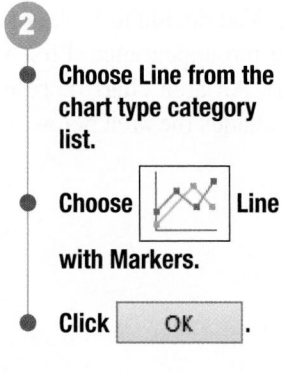 Line with Markers.

Click ☐ OK ☐.

Your screen should be similar to Figure 2.44

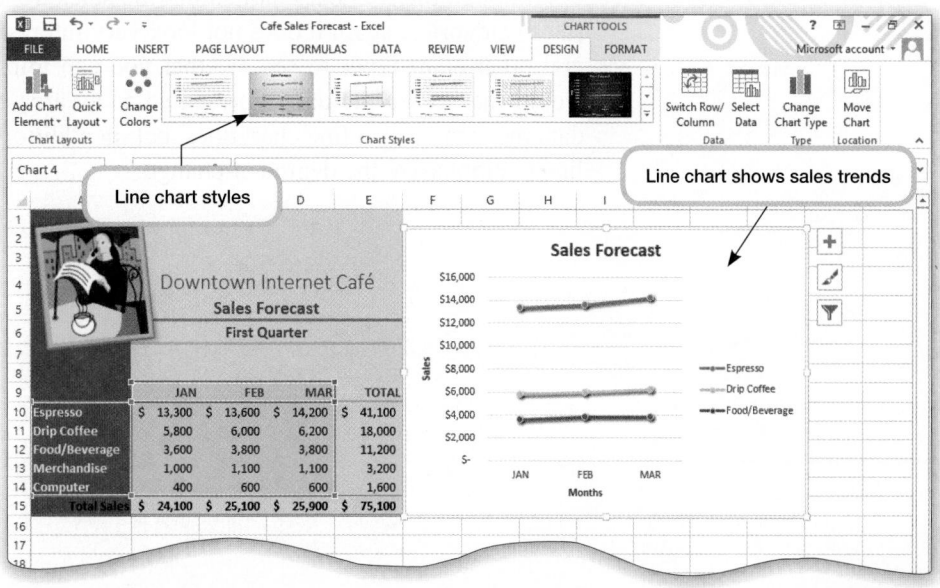

Figure 2.44

The line chart shows the sales trends from month to month. Notice the chart styles in the Ribbon reflect styles that are available for line charts.

You do not find this chart very interesting, so you will change it to a 3-D bar chart next.

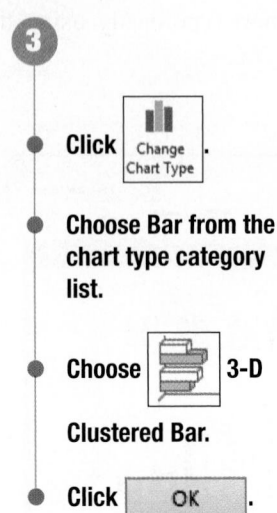

3

● **Click** [Change Chart Type]

● **Choose Bar from the chart type category list.**

● **Choose** [3-D] **3-D Clustered Bar.**

● **Click** [OK]

Your screen should be similar to Figure 2.45

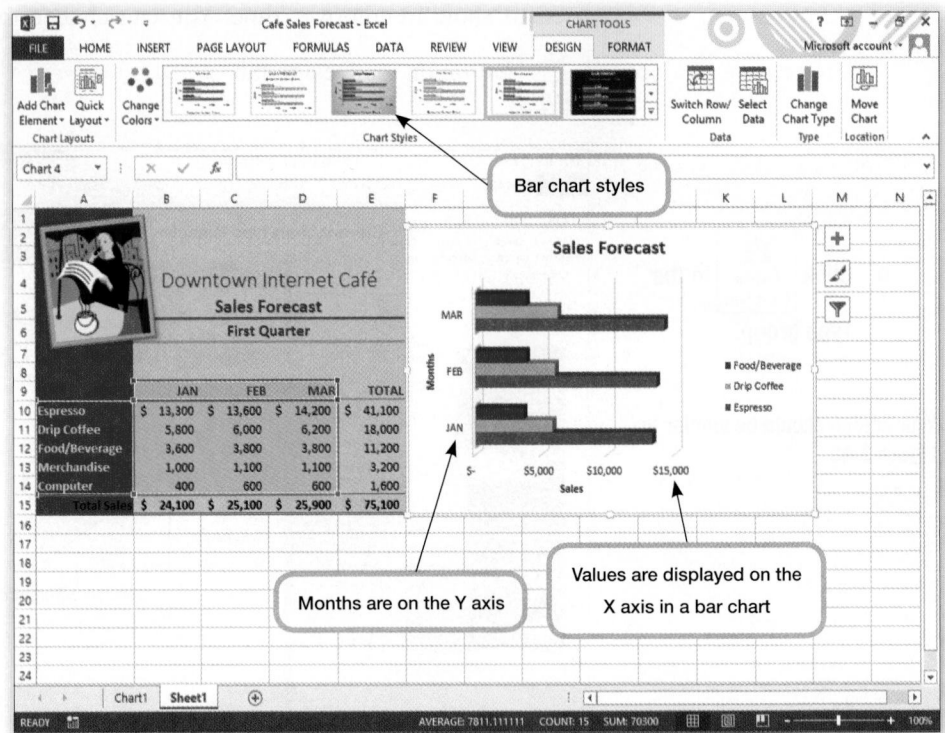

Figure 2.45

The 3-D bar chart reverses the X and Y axes and displays the data series as three-dimensional bars. As you can see, it is very easy to change the chart type and format after the data series are specified. The same data can be displayed in many different ways. Depending upon the emphasis you want the chart to make, a different chart style can be selected.

Although the 3-D bar chart shows the sales trends for the three months for the sales categories, again it does not look very interesting. You decide to look at several other chart types to see whether you can improve the appearance. First you would like to see the data represented as an area chart. An area chart represents data the same way a line chart does, but, in addition, it shades the area below each line to emphasize the degree of change.

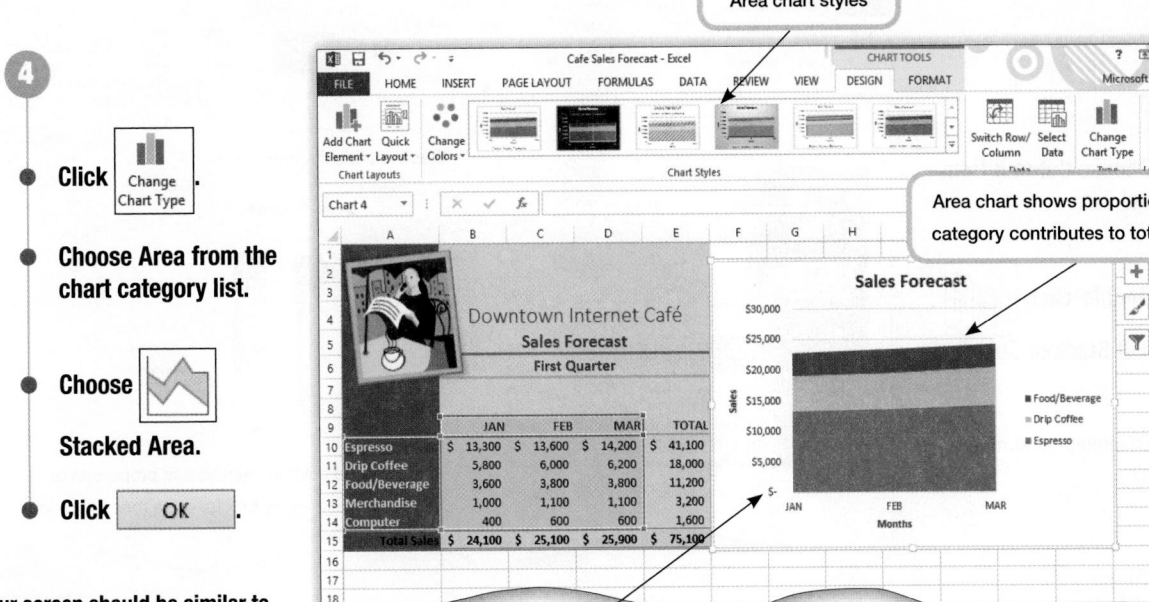

4

- Click [Change Chart Type] .

- **Choose Area from the chart category list.**

- **Choose** [icon] **Stacked Area.**

- Click [OK] .

Your screen should be similar to Figure 2.46

Area chart styles

Area chart shows proportion each category contributes to total sales

Y scale begins at 0

Figure 2.46

The Y-axis scale has changed to reflect the new range of data. The new Y-axis range is the sum of the four categories or the same as the total number in the worksheet. Using this chart type, you can see the magnitude of change that each category contributes to the total sales each month.

Again, you decide that this is not the emphasis you want to show and will continue looking at other types of charts. You want to see how this data will look as a stacked column chart. You also can double-click a chart type to insert it with the default selection.

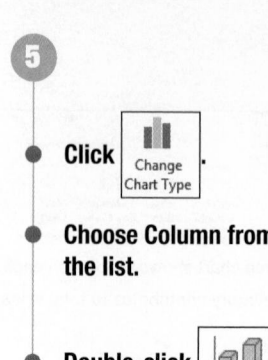

⑤

- **Click** Change Chart Type ▾

- **Choose Column** from the list.

- **Double-click** **3-D Stacked Column.**

Your screen should be similar to Figure 2.47

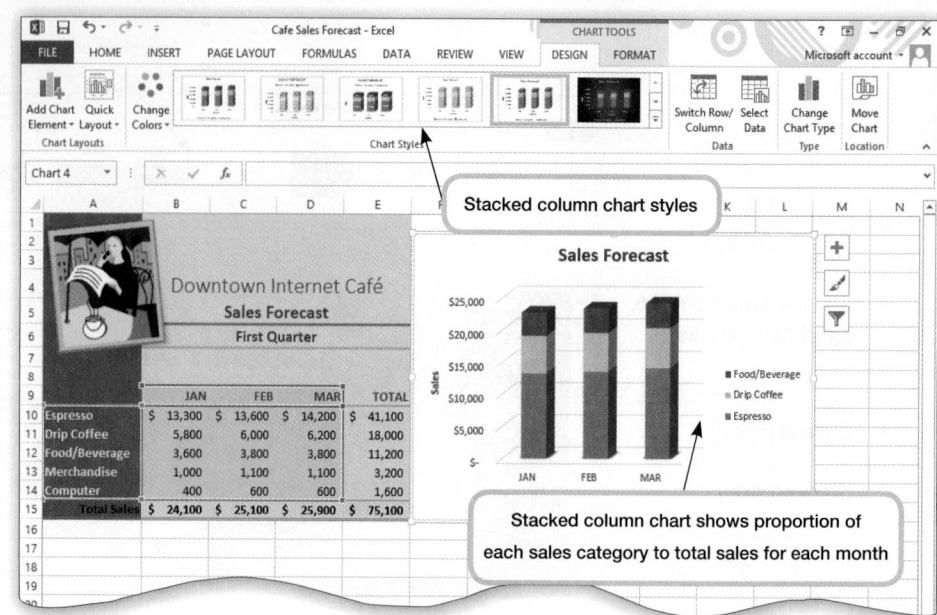

Stacked column chart styles

Stacked column chart shows proportion of each sales category to total sales for each month

Figure 2.47

The chart is redrawn showing the data as a **stacked column chart**. This type of chart also shows the proportion of each sales category to the total sales.

Although this chart is interesting, you feel that the data is difficult to read and want to see how the data will be represented in several other chart types.

⑥

- **Choose several other chart types** to see how the data appears in the chart.

- **Change the chart to** 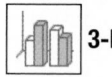 **3-D Clustered** in the Column category.

Your screen should be similar to Figure 2.48

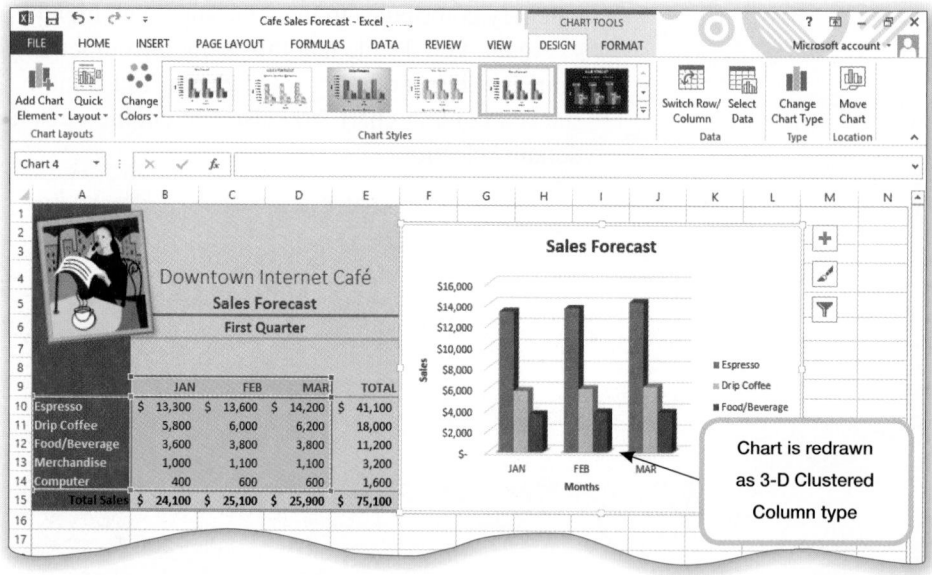

Chart is redrawn as 3-D Clustered Column type

Figure 2.48

You like how the 3-D clustered columns chart represents the data best.

MOVING THE LEGEND

While looking at the chart, you decide to move the legend below the X axis.

- Click ✚ Chart Elements.

- Point to Legend and click ▶.

- Choose Bottom from the submenu.

- Close the Chart Elements pane.

Your screen should be similar to Figure 2.49

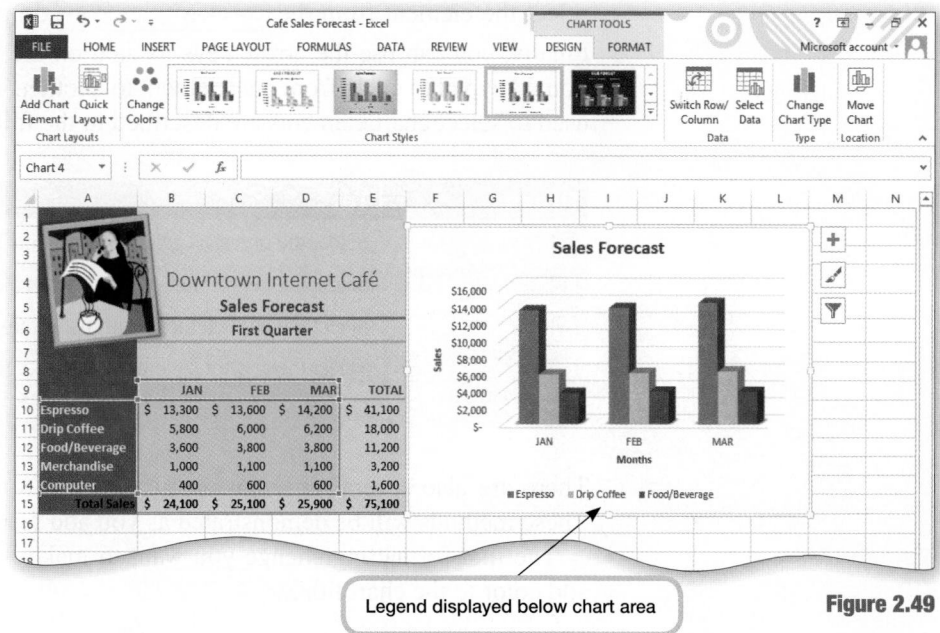

Legend displayed below chart area

Figure 2.49

The legend is displayed below the plot area of the chart.

FORMATTING CHART ELEMENTS

Next, you want to further improve the appearance of the chart by applying additional formatting to the chart titles and by changing the shape of the columns to cylinders. The chart is an object made up of many different objects or chart elements. Each element of a chart can be enhanced individually to create your own custom style chart. Because a chart consists of many separate objects, it is a group.

Concept ⑦ Group

A **group** is two or more objects that behave as a single object when moved or sized. A chart object is a group that consists of many separate objects. For example, the chart title is a single object within the chart object. Some of the objects in a chart are also groups that consist of other objects. For example, the legend is a group object consisting of separate items, each identifying a different data series.

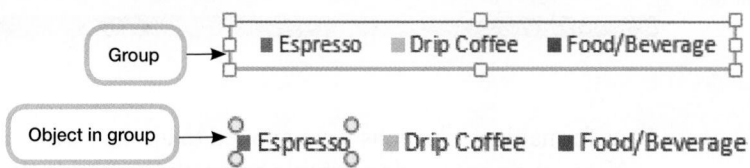

Other objects in a chart are the axis lines, a data series, a data marker, the entire plot area, or the entire chart.

There are several methods you can use to select chart elements. One, as you have learned, is to click on the element. To help you select the correct chart element, the element name displays when you point to a chart element. Another method is to select the element from the `Chart Area ▾` drop-down list in the Format tab. Finally, you can use the arrow keys located on the numeric keypad or the directional keypad to cycle from one element to another. The keyboard directional keys used to select chart elements are described in the following table.

Press	To
↓	Select the previous group of elements in a chart.
↑	Select the next group of elements in a chart.
→	Select the next element within a group.
←	Select the previous element within a group.
Esc	Cancel a selection.

There are also several different methods you can use to format chart elements. These methods will be demonstrated as you add formatting to the chart.

The first formatting change you want to make is to increase the font size and add color to the chart title.

1

- Click on the chart title to select it.

- Triple-click on the title to select all the text.

- From the Mini toolbar, choose Tahoma as the font type.

- Change the font size to 20.

- Select the Gold, Accent 5, Darker 50% theme font color.

Your screen should be similar to Figure 2.50

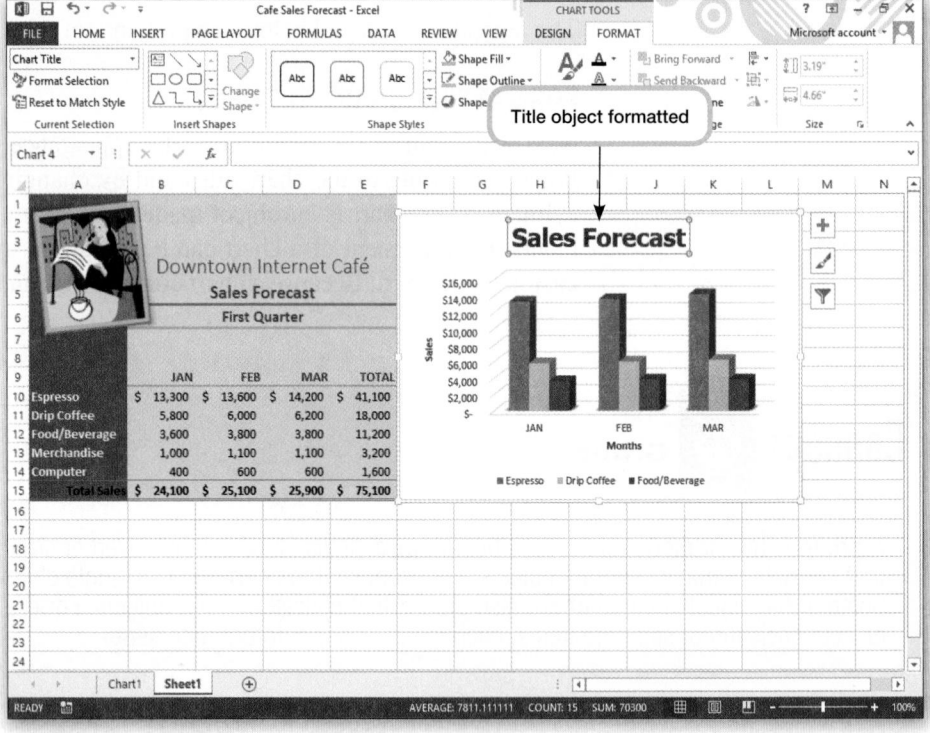

Figure 2.50

Your formatting selections were applied to all the text in the selected object.

Next, you want to add a subtitle below the main title. It will be in a smaller font size and italicized. You also can select individual sections of text in an object and apply formatting to them just as you would format any other text entry.

2

- Click at the end of the title to place the insertion point.

- Press (←Enter).

- Type **First Quarter**

- Triple-click on the second title line to select it.

- Use the Mini toolbar to italicize the selection.

- Change the font size to 14.

- Apply the Gold, Accent 5, Darker 25% theme color to the subtitle.

- Click anywhere in the chart to clear the selection.

Your screen should be similar to Figure 2.51

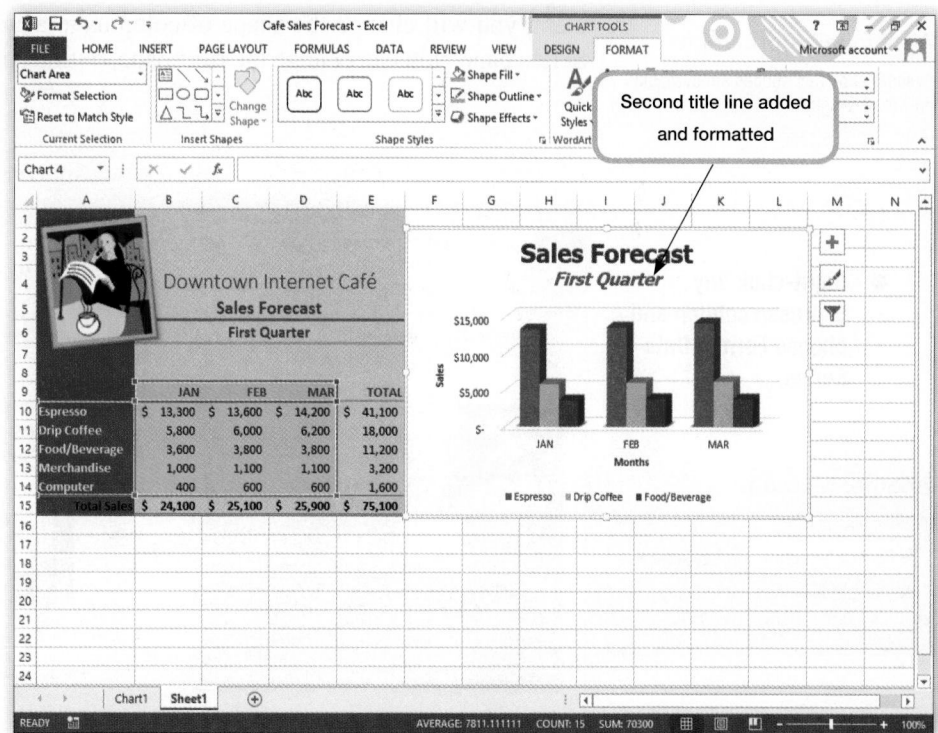

Figure 2.51

Next, you will change the shape of columns to a cylinder. From the Format Data Series pane, you can change the fill, shape, outline, and effects for each data series.

● **Right-click any Espresso column and choose Format Data Series.**

● **From the Column shape section of the Series Options list, choose Cylinder.**

● **Click the Series Options drop-down arrow ▼ and choose "Series Drip Coffee."**

● **Choose Cylinder.**

● **In a similar manner, change the Food/ Beverage series to a cylinder.**

● **Close the Format Data Series pane.**

Your screen should be similar to Figure 2.52

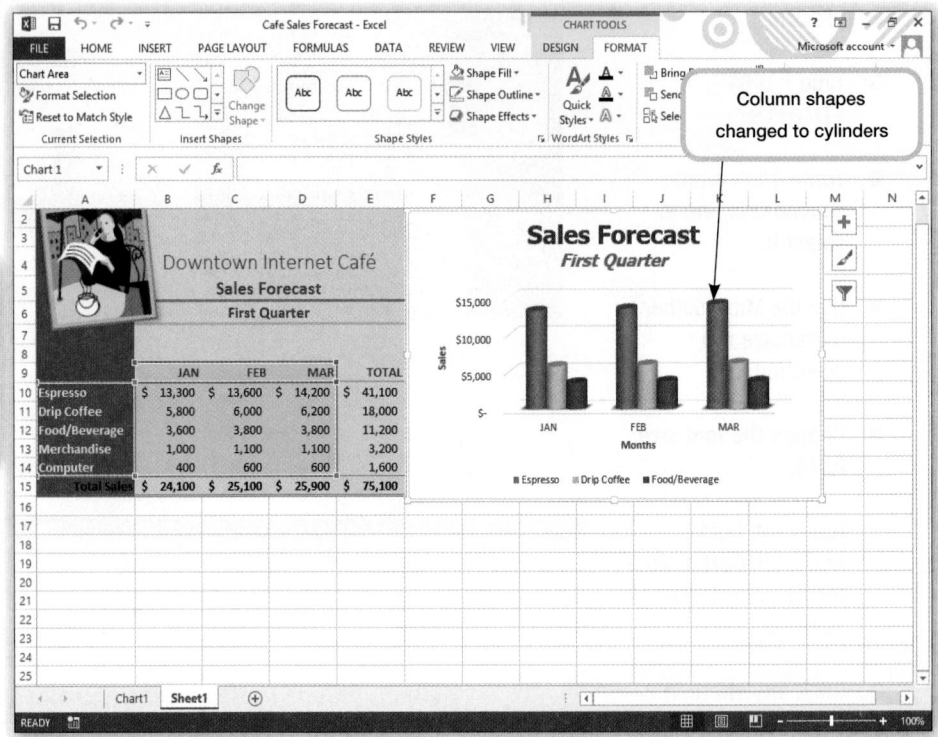

Figure 2.52

Next, you decide to add some formatting enhancements to the chart walls and floor.

4

● **Open the**

  Chart Area ▼

  Chart Elements drop-down list in the Current Selection group.

● **Choose Back Wall.**

● **Click**

  🖉 **Format Selection**

  in the Current Selection group.

● **If necessary, click Fill in the Format Wall task pane to expand the group.**

Your screen should be similar to Figure 2.53

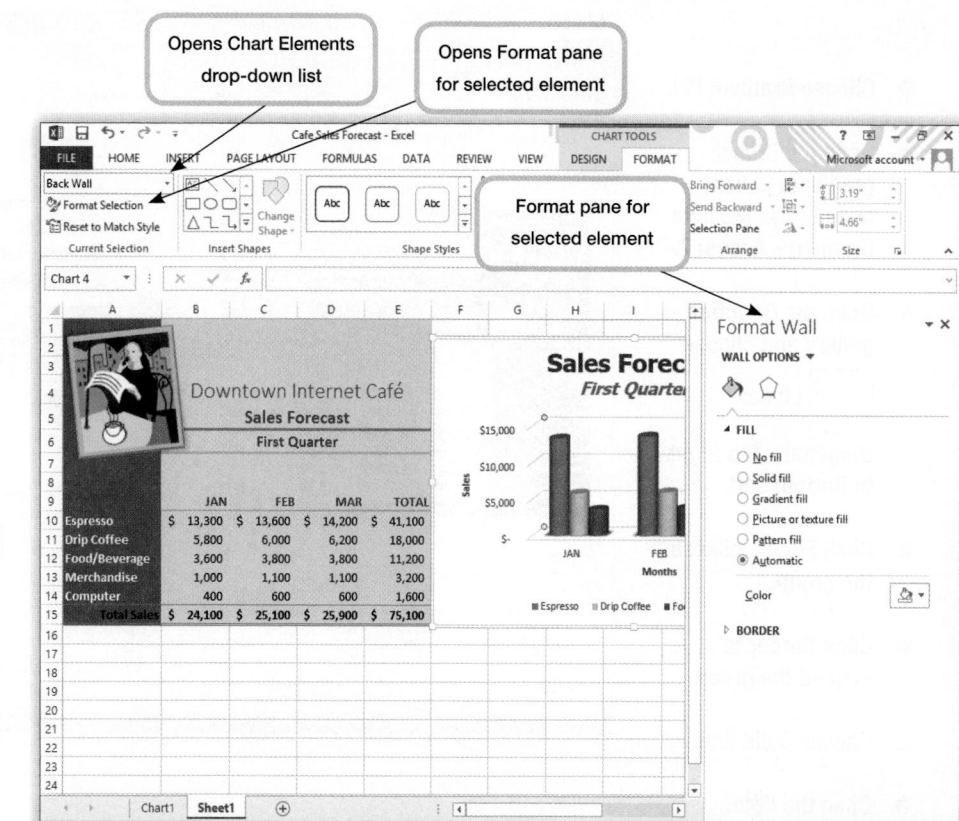

Opens Chart Elements drop-down list

Opens Format pane for selected element

Format pane for selected element

Figure 2.53

Additional Information

The corners of the selected element are marked with circles.

From the Format Wall pane, you can change the wall fill colors, outside border, and style, and add shadow, 3-D format, and rotation effects. Automatic is the currently selected fill and uses the default fill color based on the current theme colors. You decide to add a gradient fill to the background and a solid line around the chart wall. A **gradient** is a gradual progression of colors and shades that can be from one color to another or from one shade to another of the same color. Excel includes several preset colors that include combinations of gradient fills.

5

- Choose Gradient Fill.

- Open the Preset gradients gallery and choose Medium Gradient - Accent 2.

- Open the Direction gallery and choose Linear Diagonal - Top Right to Bottom Left.

- Click Fill to collapse the group.

- Click Border to expand the group.

- Choose Solid line.

- Open the Color gallery and choose Gold, Accent 5, Darker 50%.

- Close the Format Wall pane.

Your screen should be similar to Figure 2.54

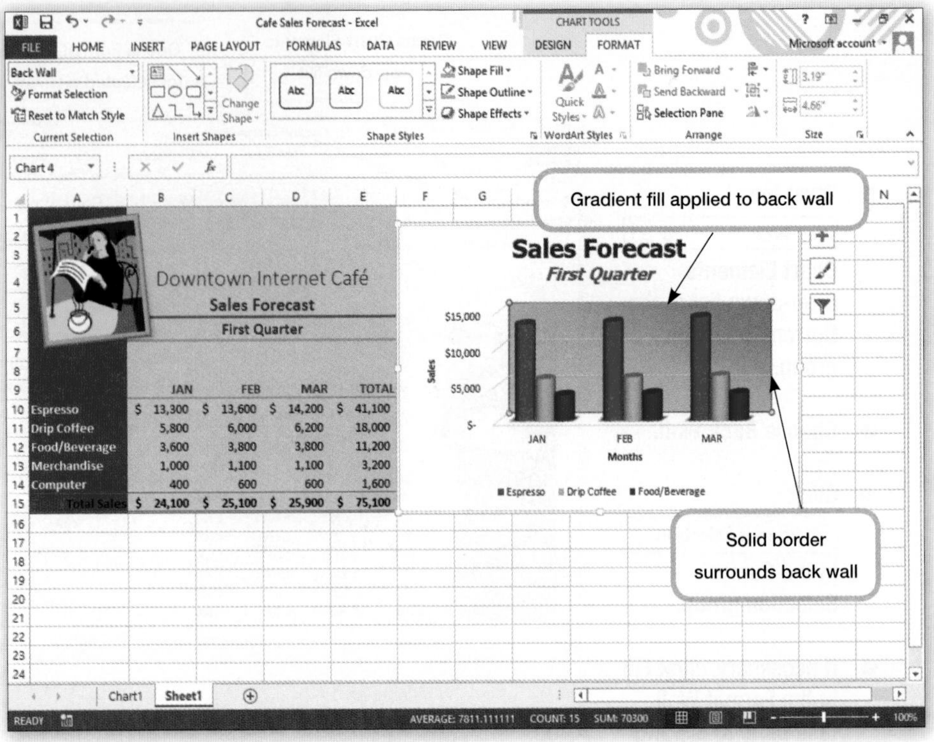

Figure 2.54

Next, you will format the side wall and floor using a solid fill color with a slight transparency.

6

- Press ← to select the chart side wall.

Additional Information

The Chart Elements box displays the name of the selected element.

- Click
  [✎ Format Selection].

- Click Fill to expand the group.

- Choose Solid Fill, and select the Dark Red, Accent 6 fill color.

- Increase the Transparency to 40%.

Having Trouble?

Drag the transparency slider, use the scroll arrows, use the ↑ and ↓ keys, or type the percentage value to change the transparency percentage.

- Choose Floor from the Chart Elements box to select it.

- Change the chart floor to the same color and transparency as the side wall.

- Close the Format Floor pane.

Your screen should be similar to Figure 2.55

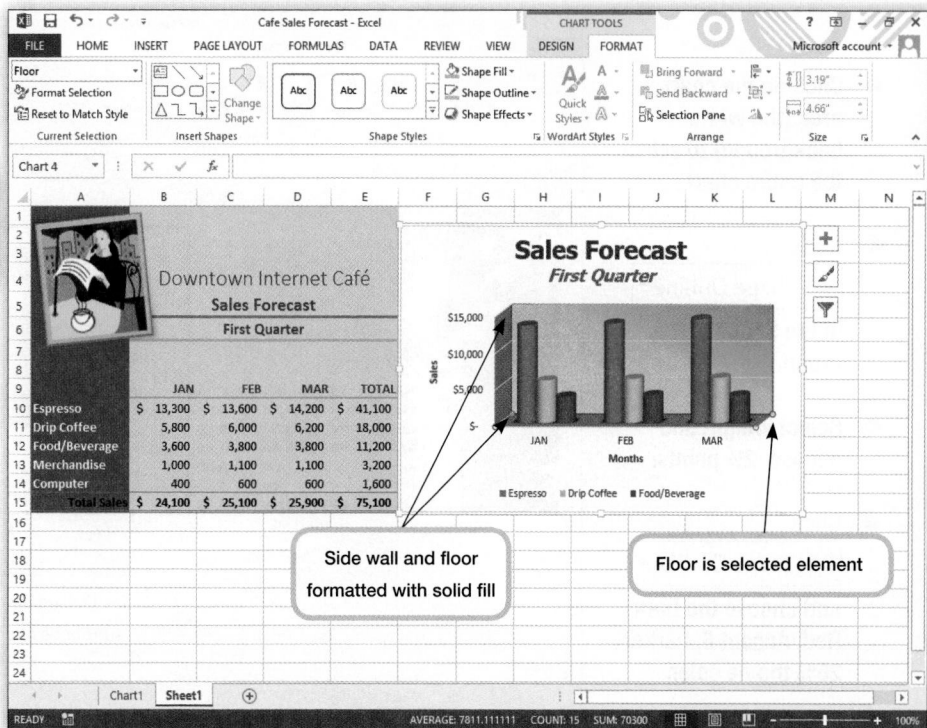

Figure 2.55

The last formatting change you will make is to modify the border line around the entire chart object.

7

- Click on the chart area (the white background) to select the entire chart.

- Click

   Shape Outline ▾

  in the Shape Styles group.

- Select Weight and choose 2¼ points.

- Click

  Shape Outline ▾

  and choose the Dark Red, Accent 6, Darker 25% theme color.

- Click outside the chart to deselect it.

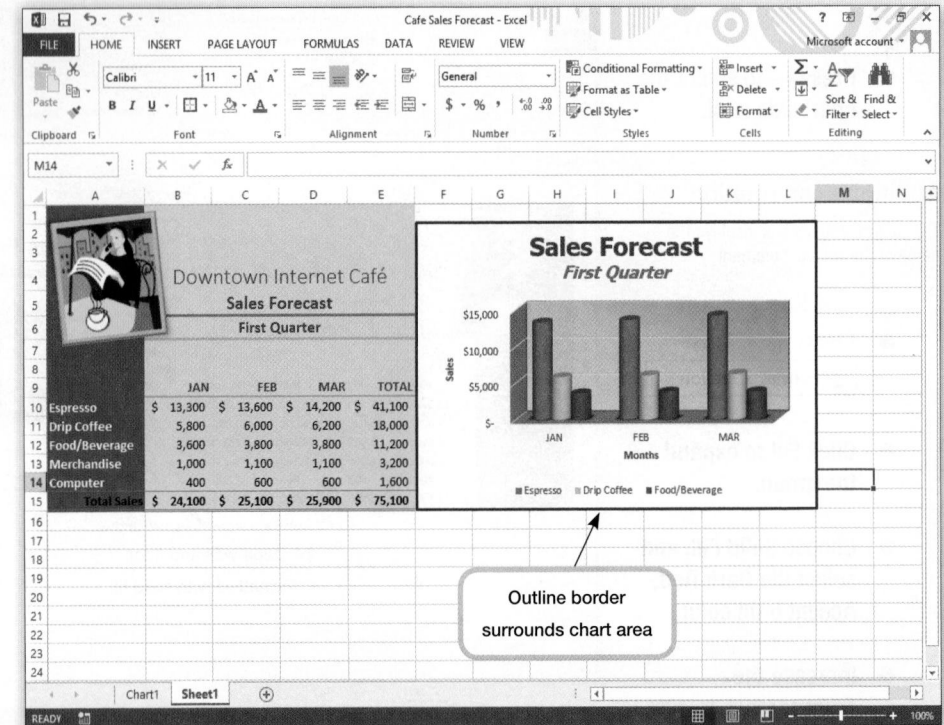

Figure 2.56

Your screen should be similar to Figure 2.56

You have modified and enhanced many of the chart elements individually, creating a unique, professional-looking chart.

ADDING AND FORMATTING DATA LABELS

Finally, to make sure that Evan sees your projected increase in espresso and coffee sales, you will include data labels containing the actual numbers plotted on the column chart.

Concept  Data Labels

Data labels provide additional information about a data point in the data series. They can consist of the value of the point, the name of the data series or category, a percentage value, or a bubble size. The different types of data labels that are available depend on the type of chart and the data that is plotted.

Value data labels are helpful when the values are large and you want to know the exact value for one data series. Data labels that display a name are helpful when the size of the chart is large and when the data point does not clearly identify the value. The percentage data label is used when you want to display the percentage of each series on charts that show parts of the whole. Bubble size is used on bubble charts to help the reader quickly see how the different bubbles vary in size.

You want to display the Espresso and Drip Coffee values as data labels for the three months. By default data labels are displayed as plain text entries. To enhance their appearance, you can show data labels inside a text bubble, and add fill and text colors and other effects to make them stand out more.

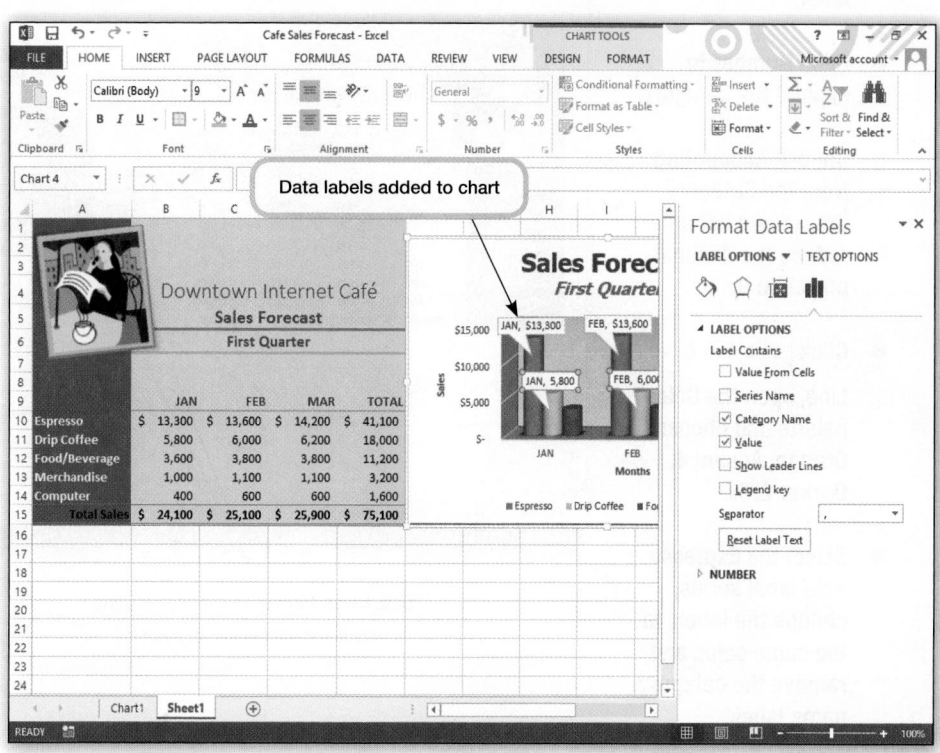

- Click on any Espresso data column to select the series.

- Click ➕ Chart Elements and choose Data Labels to insert the default data label.

- Open the Data label submenu and choose Data Callout to display the data label in a text bubble.

- Select the Drip Coffee series and choose Data Labels.

- Choose Data Callout from the Data Labels submenu.

- Choose More Options from the Data Labels submenu.

Your screen should be similar to Figure 2.57

Figure 2.57

Data labels containing the category name and actual values for Espresso and Drip Coffee sales are displayed in a text bubble callout. The values use the same formatting as the values in the worksheet. You will use the Format Data Labels task pane to change the number format of the Drip Coffee data label to display the currency symbol and add color to the labels.

Another Method

You also can choose Data Labels from the data series shortcut menu.

2

- **Click Category Name in the Label Options group to remove this label.**

- **Click Number to expand the category.**

- **Choose Accounting from the Category drop-down list and reduce the decimal places to 0.**

- **Click** 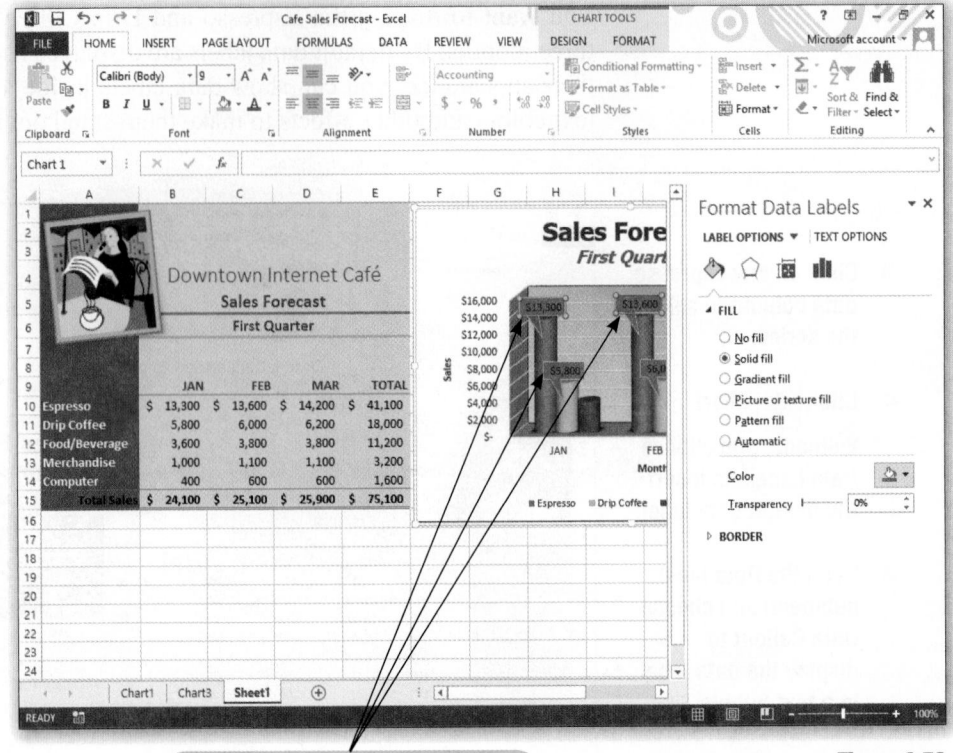 **Fill & Line, open the Color palette and choose Orange, Accent 4, Darker 25%.**

- **Select the Espresso data label series, change the labels to the same color, and remove the category name label.**

Your screen should be similar to Figure 2.58

Data labels formatted with Accounting style and zero decimal places

Figure 2.58

Next, you will reposition all the data labels so that they appear to the right of each column. Each data label needs to be selected and moved individually. Dragging the callout rectangle moves the rectangle but not the leader line. You can resize and reposition the leader line by dragging the yellow sizing square. Then rather than moving the other data labels individually, you can copy the format, including the size and location, of the selected data label to all the other data labels in the series.

3

- Click on the January Drip Coffee data label to select it and drag to position it as in Figure 2.59.

Having Trouble?

To select an individual data label, first click on a data label to select the entire series, and then click on the individual label.

- Click [icon] Label Options in the task pane and click Clone Current Label.

- In the same manner, select the January Espresso data label, position it as in Figure 2.59, and clone it to the other data labels in the series.

- Close the task pane.

Your screen should be similar to Figure 2.59

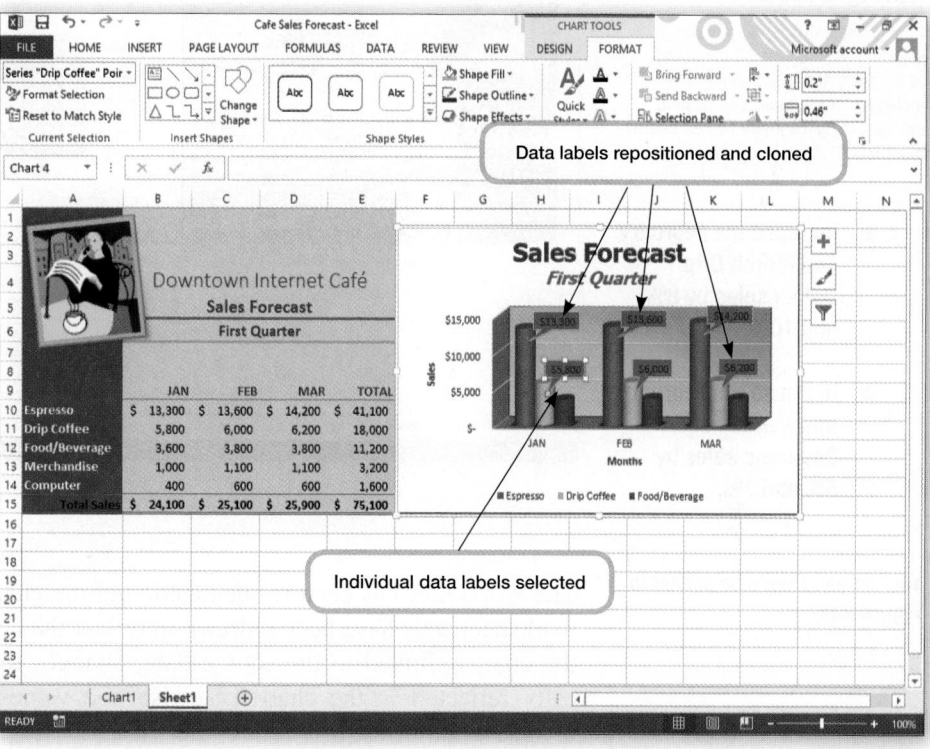

Figure 2.59

Additional Information

You can delete individual data labels or the entire series by selecting the data label or series and pressing Delete or choosing Delete from the shortcut menu.

The data label callouts are positioned to the top right of each column and make it easier to see the entire chart data.

CHANGING WORKSHEET DATA

So far, the charts you have created reflect your original sales estimates for the quarter. You are planning to heavily promote the new Internet aspect of the Café and anticipate that Espresso, Drip Coffee, and Food/Beverage sales in February and March will increase dramatically and then level off in the following months. You want to change the worksheet to reflect these increases.

1

- Increase the February and March Espresso sales by 12% and 15%, respectively.

Having Trouble?

Change the entry to a formula by inserting an = sign at the beginning of the entry and then multiply by 1 + increase; for example, a 12 percent increase in the February Espresso sales is =13600*1.12.

- Increase the February and March Drip Coffee sales by 8% and 10%.

- Increase the February and March Food/ Beverage sales by 5% and 7%.

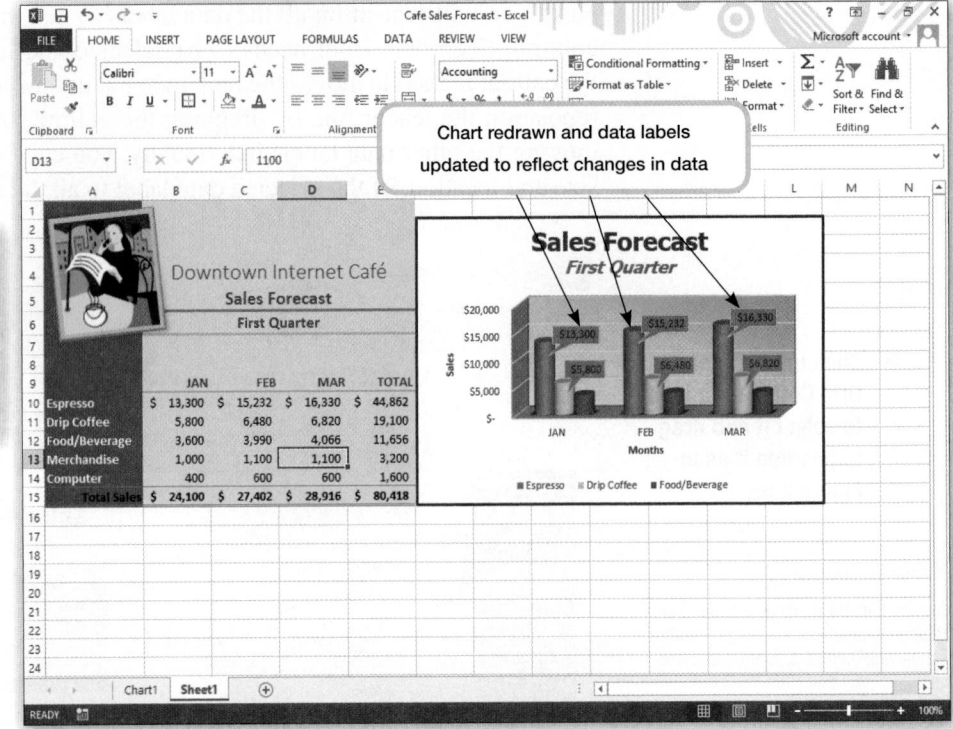

Figure 2.60

Your screen should be similar to Figure 2.60

The worksheet has been recalculated, and the chart columns that reference those worksheet cells have been redrawn to reflect the change in the sales data. Because the chart is linked to the source data, changes to the source data are automatically reflected in the chart. Likewise, the values in the data labels reflect the revised data.

2

- Move the chart to its own chart sheet.

- Make Sheet1 active again.

- Save the workbook.

Creating a Combo Chart

Next, you want to create a chart to show how much Espresso Sales contribute toward Total sales. When you have two types of data or data whose values vary widely, as is the case with monthly sales and total sales, you can use a combo (combination) chart to illustrate how these values are related. A combo chart combines two of more chart types to make comparisons easy. A common type of combo chart uses a line chart for one of the data series and a column for the other.

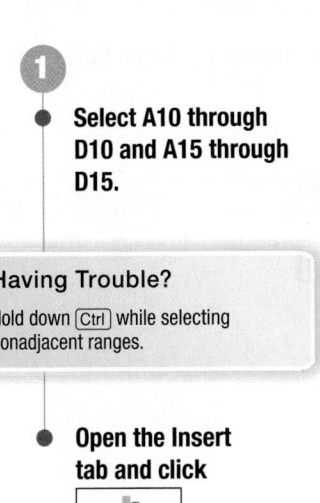

1

- Select A10 through D10 and A15 through D15.

Having Trouble?

Hold down Ctrl while selecting nonadjacent ranges.

- Open the Insert tab and click

  Recommended Charts .

Your screen should be similar to Figure 2.61

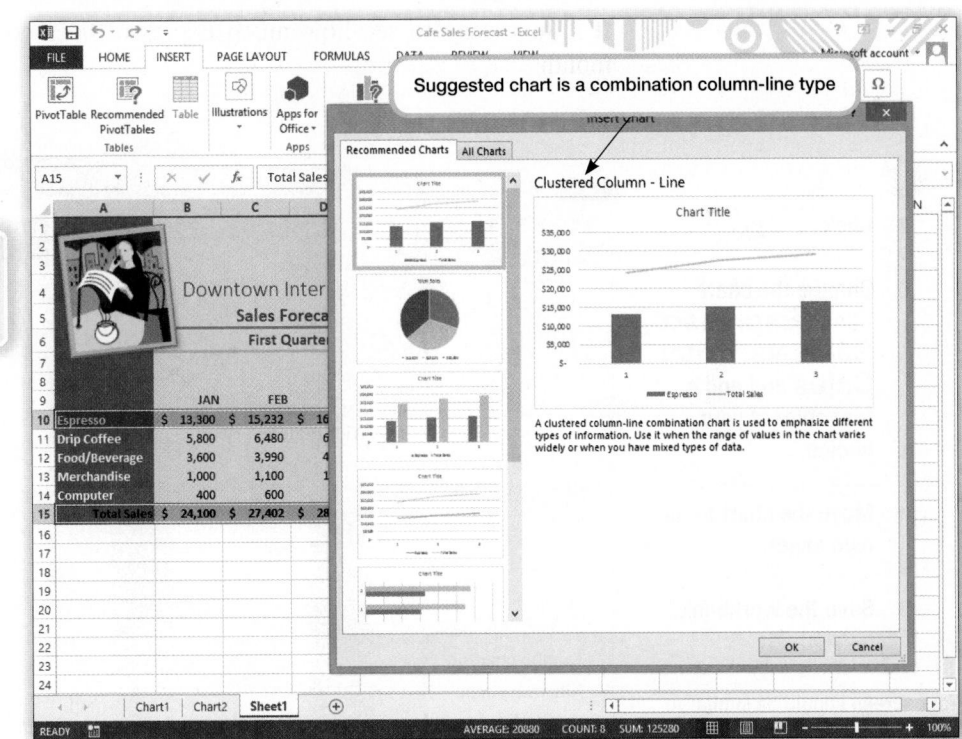

Suggested chart is a combination column-line type

Figure 2.61

Excel has recognized the mixed data values and proposes a Clustered Column–Line chart. The Total Sales values are plotted with the line chart and the Espresso Sales with the column chart. You want to reverse the chart types for the data series.

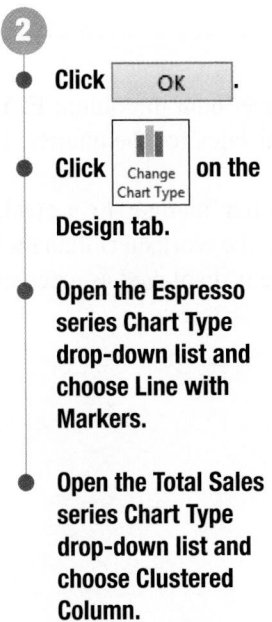

2

- Click **OK** .

- Click Change Chart Type on the Design tab.

- Open the Espresso series Chart Type drop-down list and choose Line with Markers.

- Open the Total Sales series Chart Type drop-down list and choose Clustered Column.

Your screen should be similar to Figure 2.62

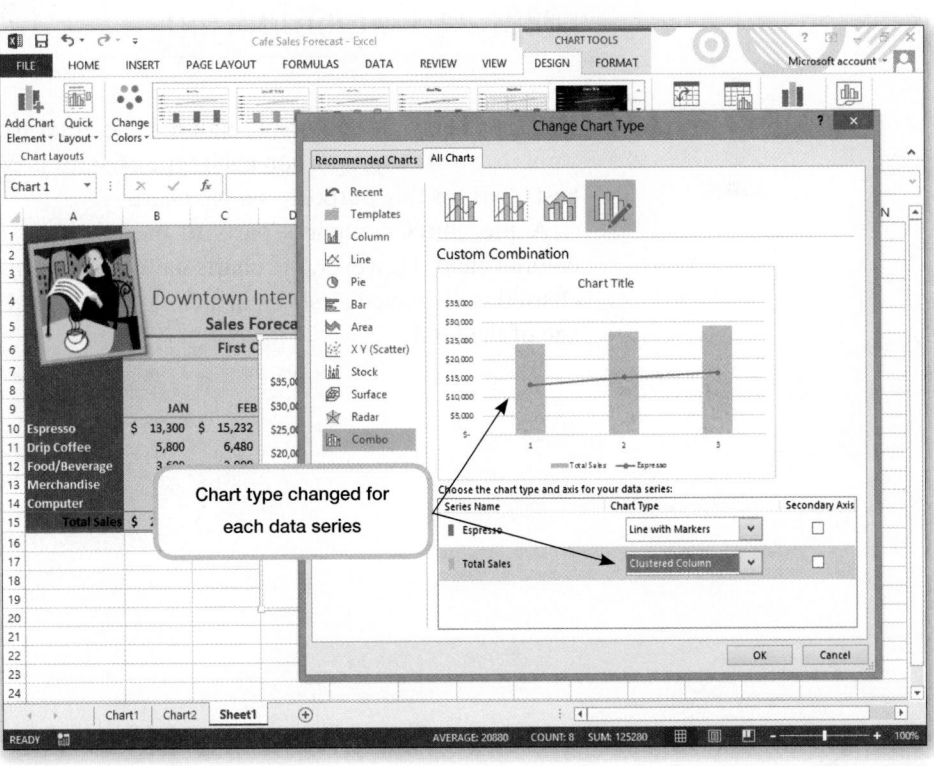

Chart type changed for each data series

Figure 2.62

It is now easy to see how much Espresso Sales contribute to Total Sales each month.

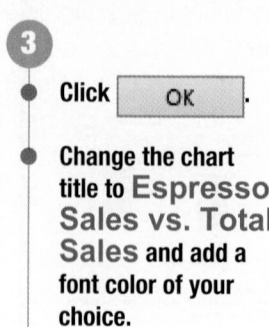

3

● Click **OK** .

● Change the chart title to **Espresso Sales vs. Total Sales** and add a font color of your choice.

● Move the chart to its own sheet.

● Save the workbook.

Your screen should be similar to Figure 2.63

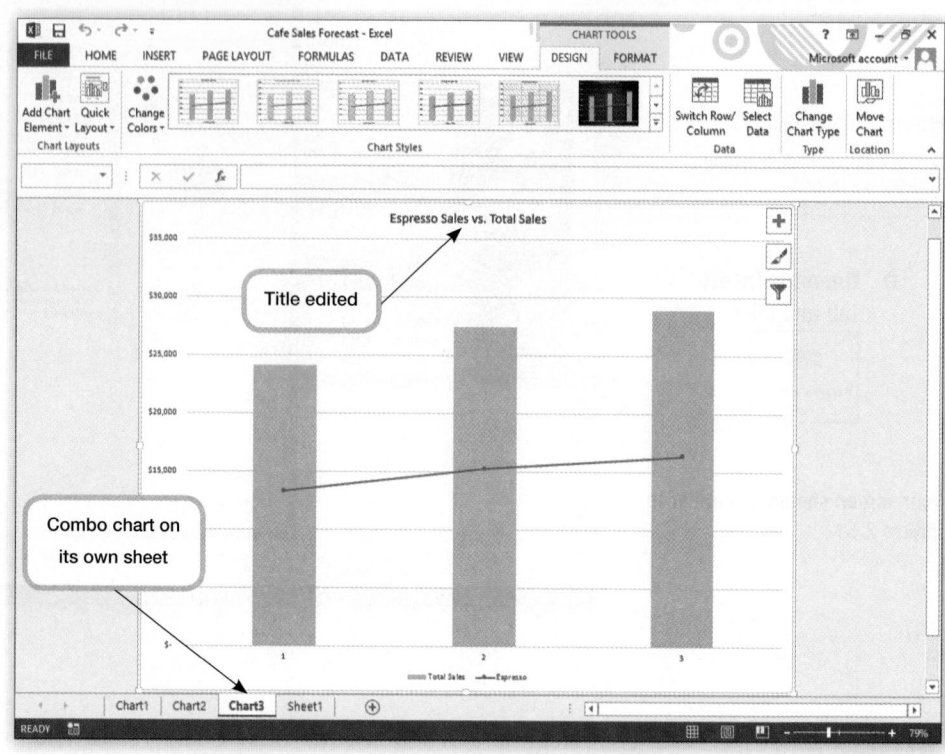

Title edited

Combo chart on its own sheet

Figure 2.63

Creating and Formatting a Pie Chart

The last chart you will create will use the Total worksheet data in column E. You want to see what proportion each type of sales is of total sales for the quarter. The best chart for this purpose is a pie chart.

A **pie chart** compares parts to the whole in a similar manner to a stacked column chart. However, pie charts have no axes. Instead, the worksheet data that is charted is displayed as slices in a circle or pie. Each slice is displayed as a percentage of the total.

SELECTING THE PIE CHART DATA

The use of X (category) and data series settings in a pie chart is different from their use in a column or line chart. The X series labels the slices of the pie rather than the X axis. The data series is used to create the slices in the pie. Only one data series can be specified in a pie chart.

The row labels in column A will label the slices, and the total values in column E will be used as the data series.

1

- **Make Sheet1 active again.**

- **Select A10 through A14 and E10 through E14.**

- **Open the Insert tab.**

- **Click [icon] and choose [icon] 3-D Pie.**

- **Move and size the pie chart to be displayed over cells F1 through L15.**

Additional Information

Hold down (Alt) while sizing to snap the chart to the cells.

Your screen should be similar to Figure 2.64

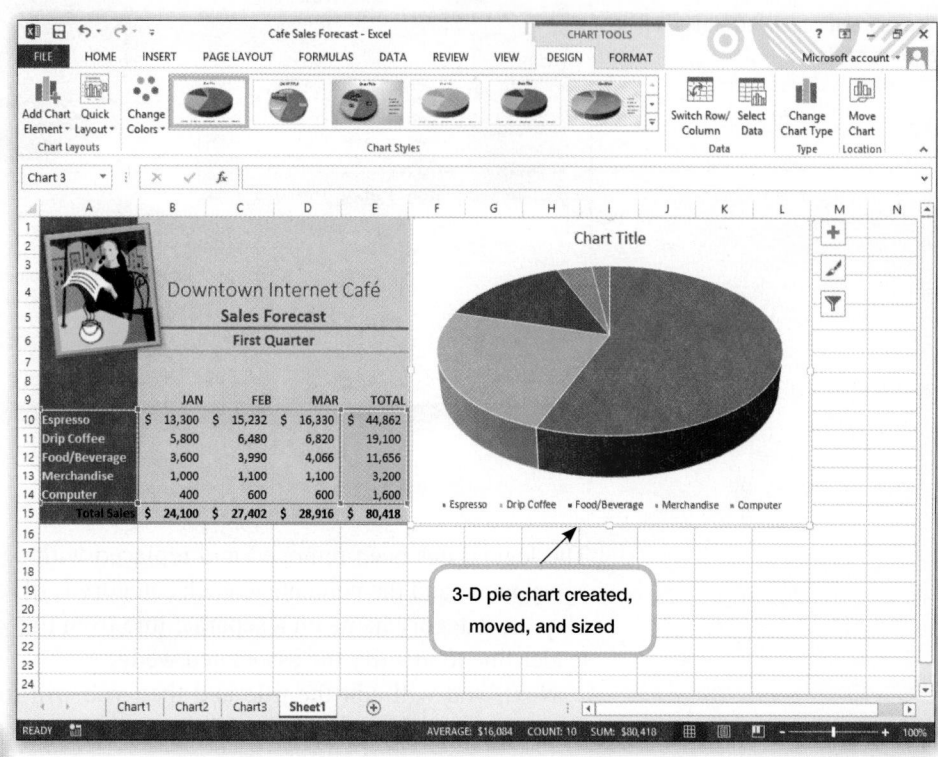

Figure 2.64

A three-dimensional pie chart is drawn in the worksheet. Each value in the data series is displayed as a slice of the pie chart. The size of the slice represents the proportion of total sales that each sales category represents.

ADDING TITLES AND DATA LABELS

To clarify the meaning of the chart, you need to edit the chart title. In addition, you want to remove the legend and display data labels to label the slices of the pie instead. You will take a look at the predefined chart layouts to see if there is a layout that will accomplish all these things in one step.

1

- Click [Quick Layout] in the **Charts Layout group of the Design tab and choose Layout 1.**

Your screen should be similar to Figure 2.65

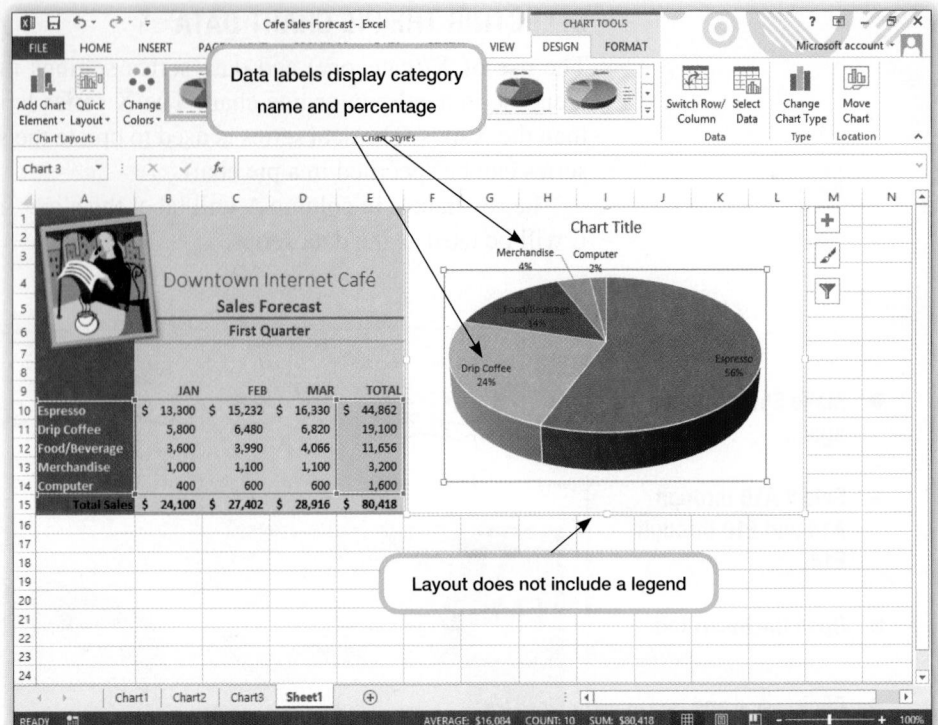

Figure 2.65

The legend has been removed and replaced with data labels that display the category name and the percentage each category is of total sales. The data labels display the category name on a separate line from the value and, if needed, include a leader line to identify the associated wedge.

Next, you will edit the title and then you will improve the appearance of the data labels by adding a gradient fill to them.

2

- Enter the chart title **Total Sales by Category**

- Add the subtitle **First Quarter**

- Change the first title line to Tahoma with the Gold, Accent 5, Darker 25% color.

- Change the subtitle line to Tahoma, with the Gold, Accent 5, Darker 50% color, and italic.

- Double-click on one of the data labels to select the data label series and open the Format Data Labels task pane.

- Click 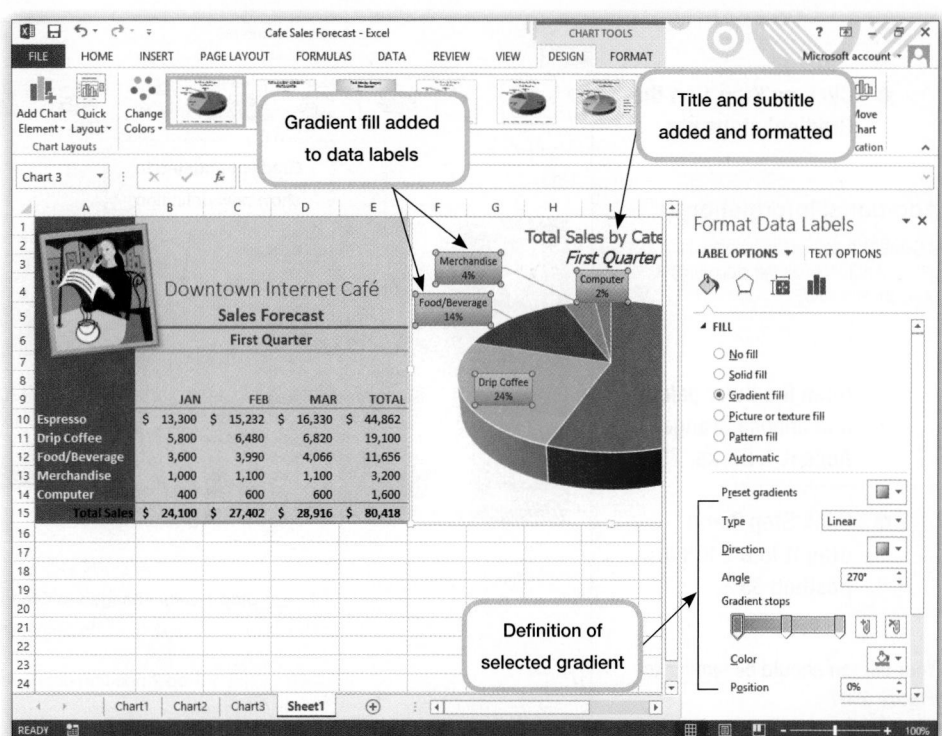 Fill & Line in the task pane, expand the Fill group if necessary, and choose Gradient Fill.

- Open the Preset gradients gallery and choose Medium Gradient - Accent 2.

Your screen should be similar to Figure 2.66

Additional Information

The maximum number of stops is 12 and the minimum is 2.

Figure 2.66

The selected gradient fill has been added to each data label. It consists of a range of dark gold fading to yellow. The Gradient stops bar shows this gradient fill is made of three "**stops**," or specific points where the blending of two adjacent colors in the gradient ends. The Stop 1 fill color is dark gold, Stop 2 is a lighter gold, and Stop 3 is yellow. You will change the Stop 1 color to orange.

Click on Stop 1 on the Gradient stops bar.

Open the Color palette and choose Orange, Accent 4, Darker 25%.

Click Stop 2 and drag it to the left to position 35%.

Your screen should be similar to Figure 2.67

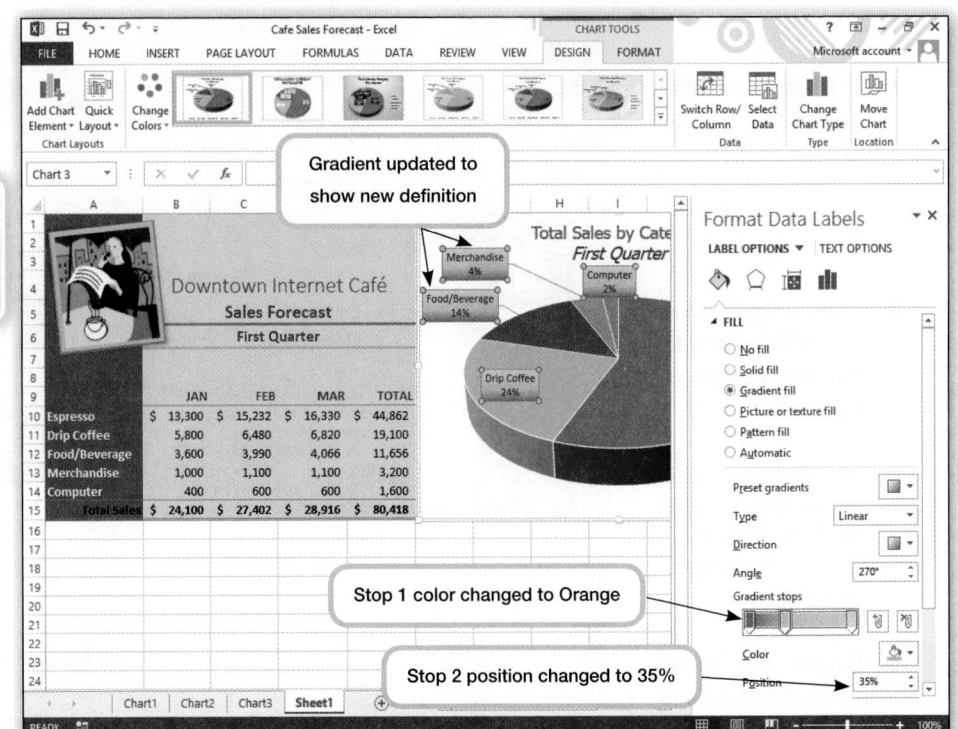

Figure 2.67

The data labels now include a gradient fill background that coordinates well with the chart colors. The pie chart clearly shows the percentage each category is of the total sales.

EXPLODING AND ROTATING THE PIE

Next, you want to separate slightly or **explode** the slices of the pie to emphasize the data in the categories.

Click on the pie chart to display the Format Data Series task pane.

Click 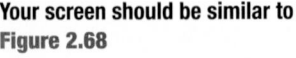 **Series Options and set the Pie Explosion to 10%.**

Your screen should be similar to Figure 2.68

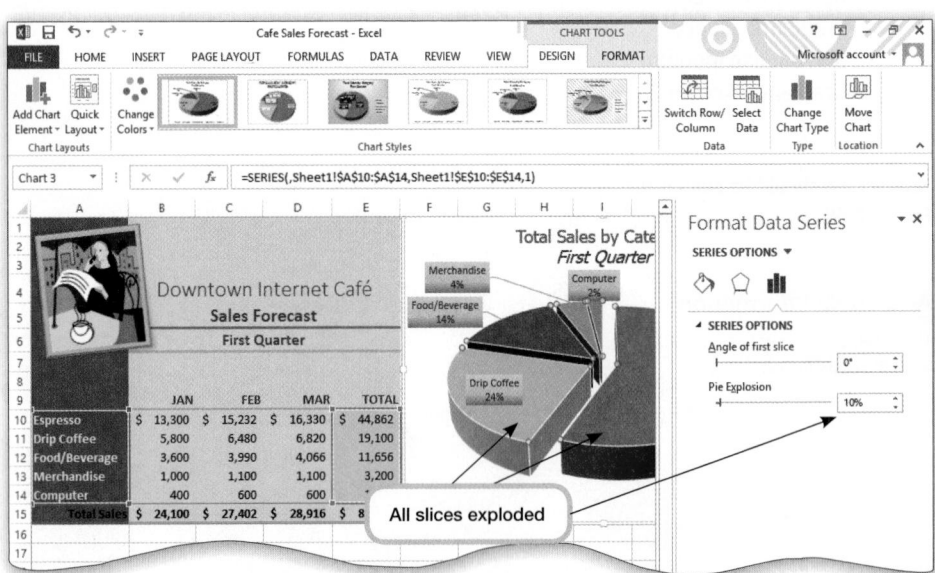

Figure 2.68

All slices are exploded from the center of the pie chart. However, you do not like how this looks. Instead, you decide you want to explode only the Espresso slice to give emphasis to the increase in sales in that category.

2

- **Set the Pie Explosion back to 0%.**

- **Click on the Espresso slice to select it.**

Your screen should be similar to Figure 2.69

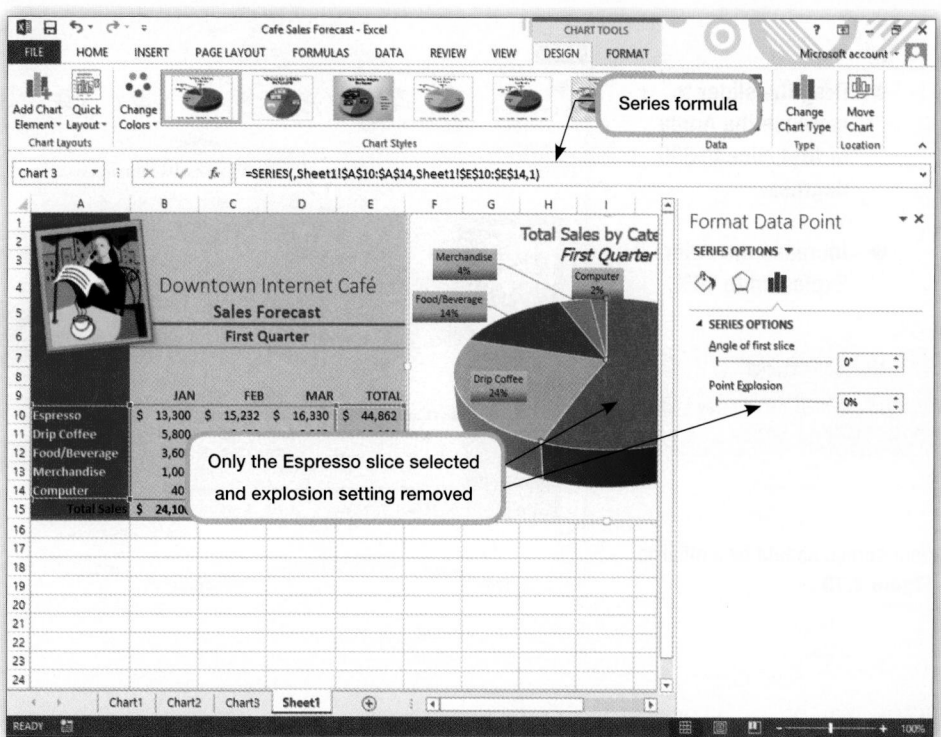

Figure 2.69

Notice that the formula bar displays a **series formula**. A series formula links the chart object to the source worksheet, in this case, Sheet1. The formula contains four arguments: a reference to the cell that includes the data series name (used in the legend), references to the cells that contain the categories (X-axis numbers), references to the numbers plotted, and an integer that specifies the number of data series plotted.

The Format Data Point task pane options rotate the pie and control the amount of explosion of the slices. You want to rotate the pie approximately 330 degrees so that the Espresso slice is more to the right side of the pie. When a pie chart is created, the first data point is placed to the right of the middle at the top of the chart. The rest of the data points are placed in order to the right until the circle is complete. To change the angle of the first slice, you rotate the pie chart. Then you will explode the Espresso slice.

3

- Drag the slider to increase the Angle of first slice to 330 degrees.

- Increase the Point Explosion to 10%.

Your screen should be similar to Figure 2.70

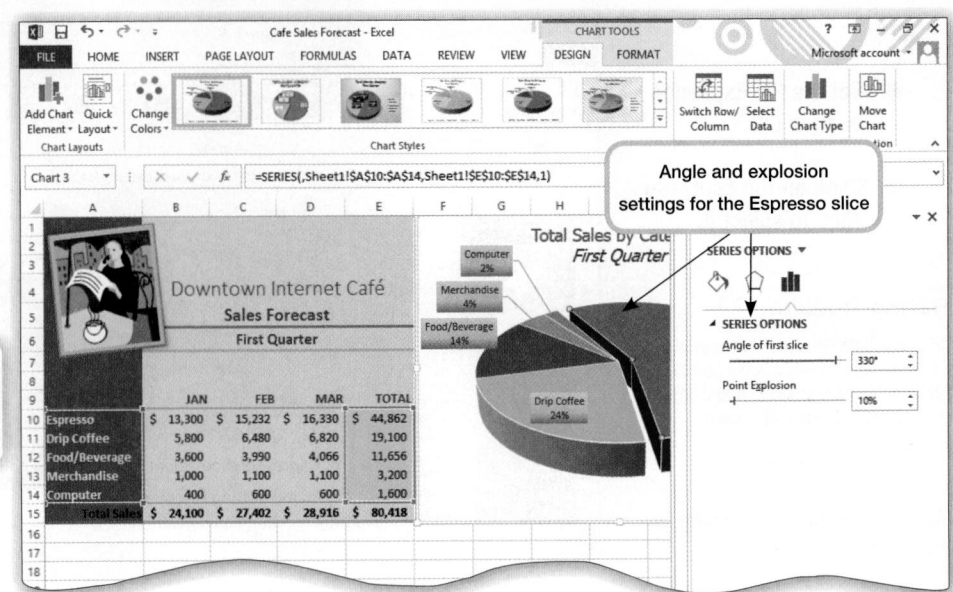

Figure 2.70

Although Excel tries to determine the best position for data labels, you can try several settings. You will try another label position to see its effects, and then move individual labels.

4

- Select the data label series.

- Click Label Options in the task pane and choose Outside End from the Label Position area.

- Choose Best Fit.

- Close the task pane.

- If necessary, drag the Espresso and then the Drip Coffee label to position them as in Figure 2.71.

Your screen should be similar to Figure 2.71

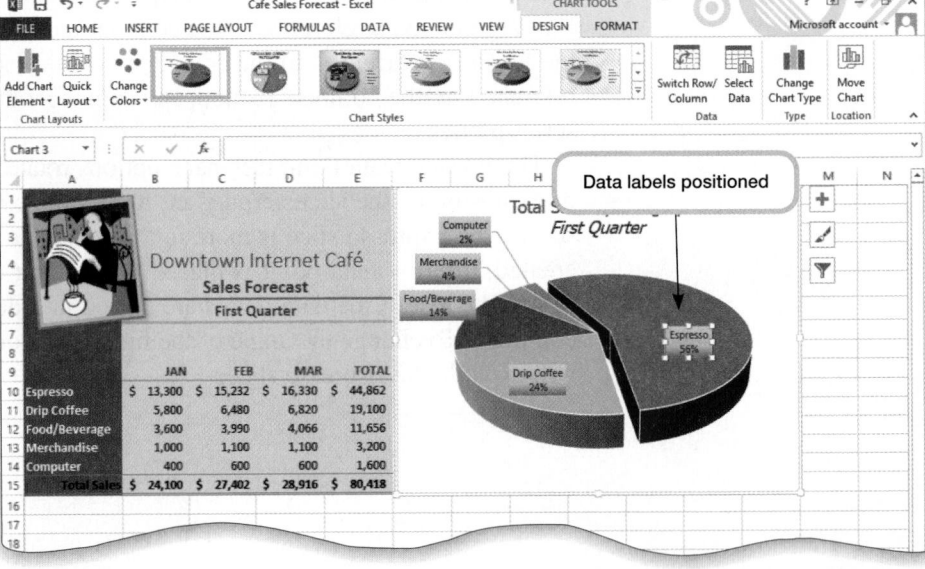

Figure 2.71

The industry standard for a successful espresso café generates 60 percent of sales from espresso-based drinks. With your suggested advertising campaign, your sales forecast is very close to this standard.

APPLYING COLOR AND TEXTURE

The last change you would like to make is to change the color of the Drip Coffee slice and add a fill to the Espresso slice to make it stand out even further. First, you will enhance the Espresso slice by adding a texture.

1

- Select the Espresso slice.

- Choose Format Data Point from the context menu.

- Click ⬧ Fill & Line.

- Choose Picture or texture fill from the Fill group.

- Open the Texture gallery.

Your screen should be similar to Figure 2.72

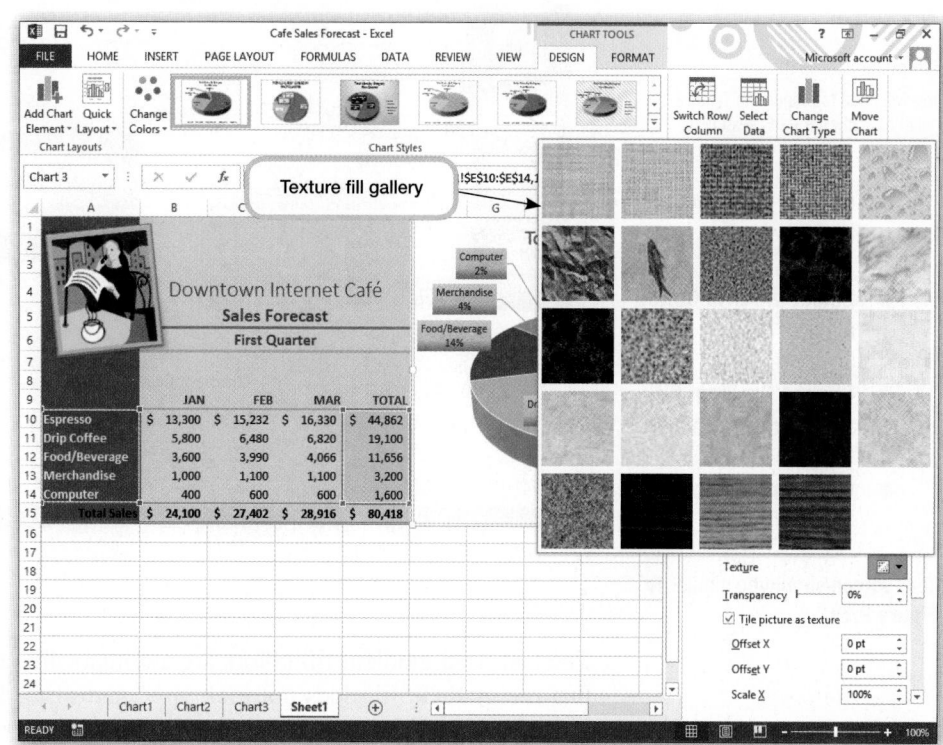

Figure 2.72

A variety of pictures and textures is displayed in the gallery. The Papyrus texture is applied by default. If none of the provided choices is suitable, you could use a picture from a file or clip art as the fill. Although you like how the Papyrus texture looks, you want to see how several other textures would look instead.

2

● Choose several texture designs to see how they will look.

Having Trouble?

You will need to reopen the Texture gallery again after each selection.

● Choose the Papyrus texture.

● Select the Drip Coffee slice.

● Choose Gradient fill from the Fill group.

● Close the task pane.

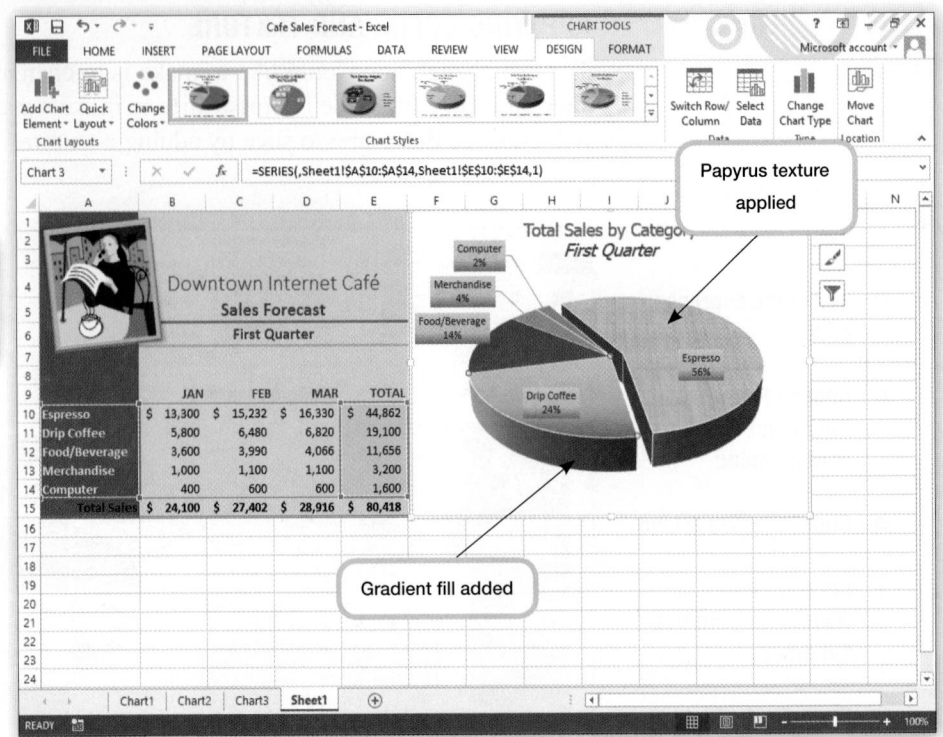

Figure 2.73

Your screen should be similar to Figure 2.73

The last-used gradient fill colors are automatically applied. You decide, however, that the gradient fill does not look good and instead will try using a shape style. **Shape styles** consist of predefined combinations of fills, outlines, and effects much like chart styles. Shape styles affect only the selected element.

③

- If necessary, select the Drip Coffee slice.

- Open the Chart Tools Format tab.

- Open the Shape Styles gallery in the Shape Styles group and point to several styles to see their effect on the slice.

- Choose the Subtle Effect - Red, Accent 1 Shape Style (4th row, 2nd column).

Your screen should be similar to Figure 2.74

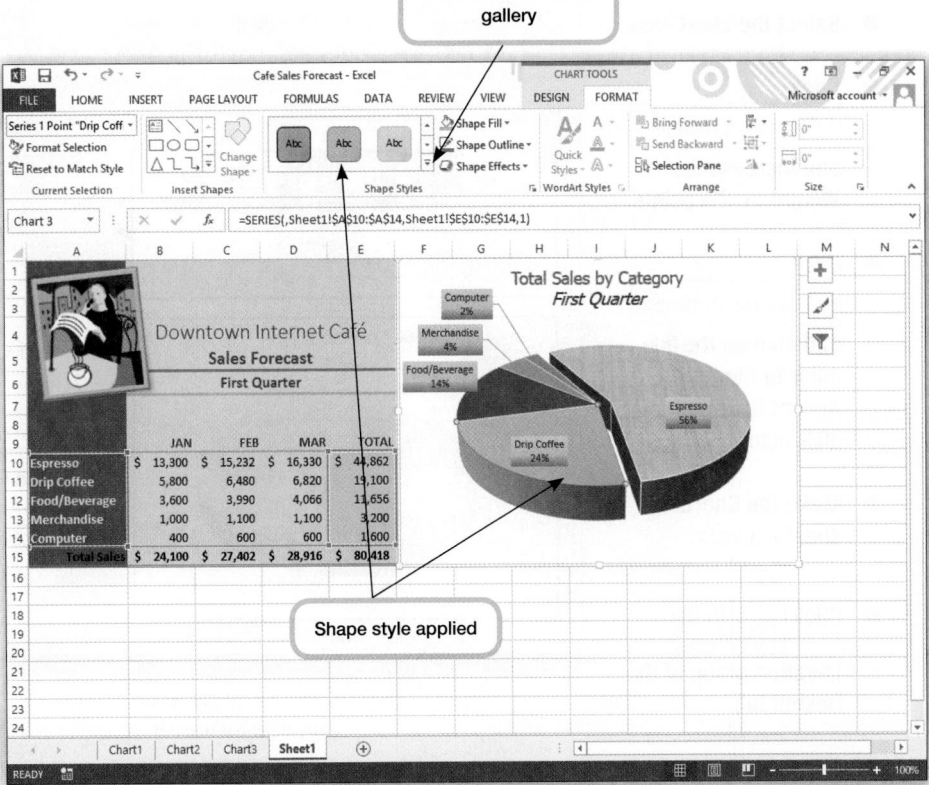

Figure 2.74

Finally, you will add a colored outline border around the entire chart, like the one you used in the column chart. Then you will move the column chart from the chart sheet back into the worksheet.

● Select the chart area.

● Click
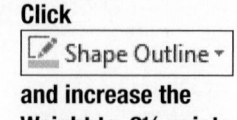
and increase the Weight to 2¼ points.

● Click
Shape Outline ▾
and change the line color to the Gold, Accent 5, Darker 50% color.

● Make the Chart2 sheet active.

● Click [Move Chart] in the Location group of the Design tab.

● Choose Object in and choose Sheet1 from the drop-down menu.

● Click OK.

● Move and size the column chart to fit A17 through F33.

● Move and size the pie chart to fit A35 through F50.

● Deselect the chart.

● Save the workbook.

Your screen should be similar to Figure 2.75

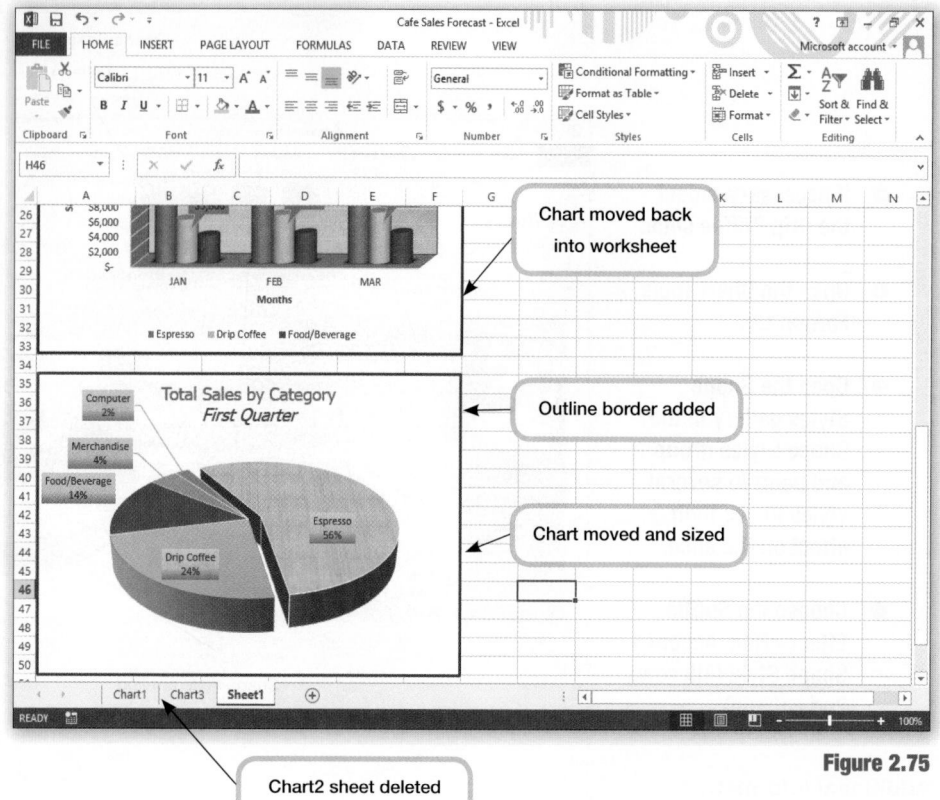

Figure 2.75

The column chart was moved back into the sheet as an embedded object, and the chart sheet it occupied was deleted.

Before printing a large worksheet or a worksheet that contains charts, you can quickly fine-tune it in Page Layout view. Using this view, you can change the layout and format of data just as in Normal view, but, in addition, you can adjust the layout of the data on the page by changing the page orientation, page margins, scaling, and alignment. Additionally, you can easily add headers and footers.

SCALING THE WORKSHEET

To get the worksheet ready for printing, you will first make several adjustments to the layout in Page Layout view. While in this view, you also will zoom out on the worksheet to see more information in the workbook window by adjusting the zoom percentage.

Having Trouble?

Refer to the section "Using the Zoom Feature" in the Introduction to Microsoft Office 2013 for information on using this feature.

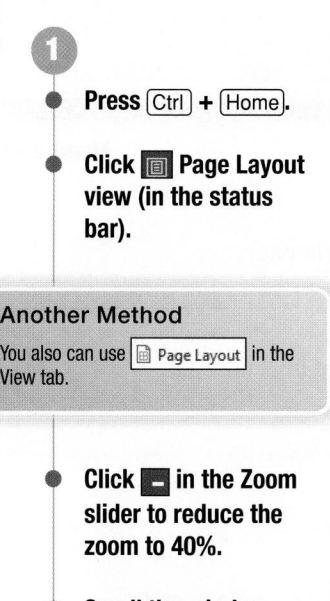

● Press Ctrl + Home.

● Click ▣ Page Layout view (in the status bar).

Another Method

You also can use ▣ Page Layout in the View tab.

● Click ▬ in the Zoom slider to reduce the zoom to 40%.

● Scroll the window up slightly to see the bottom of the pie chart.

Your screen should be similar to Figure 2.76

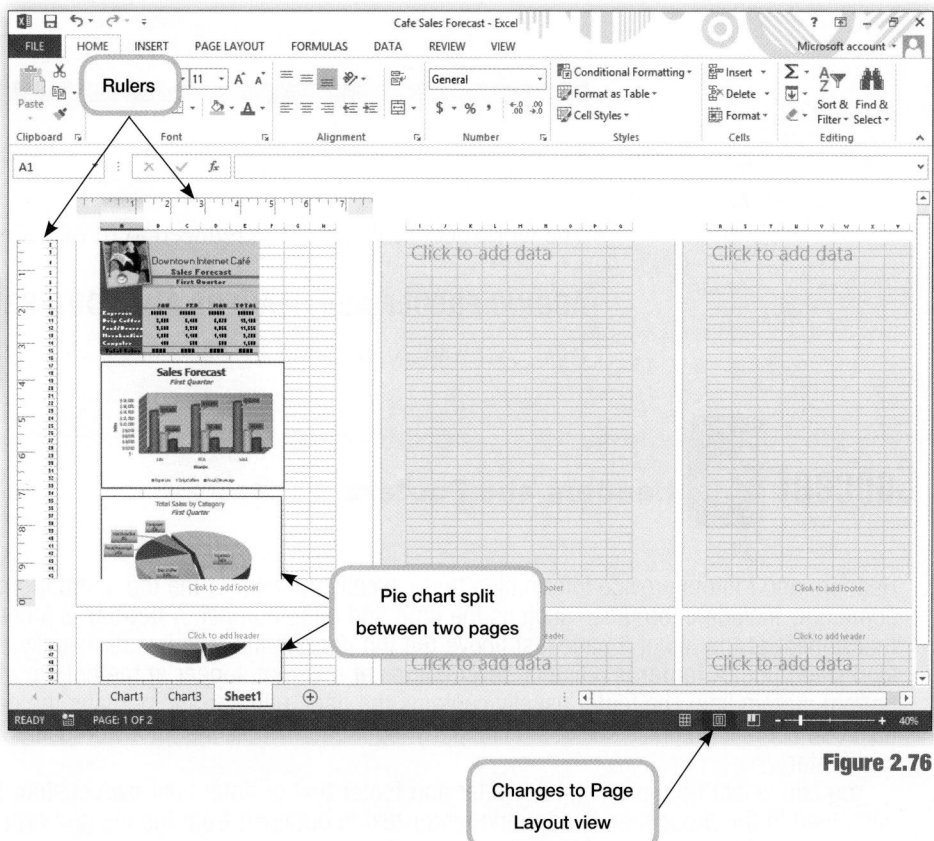

Rulers

Pie chart split between two pages

Changes to Page Layout view

Figure 2.76

This view shows how the data and charts lay out on each page of the worksheet. Because you reduced the zoom, you can quickly see that the pie chart is divided between two pages. You also notice that the worksheet and charts are not centered on the page. In Page Layout view, horizontal and vertical rulers are displayed so you can make exact measurements of cells, ranges, and objects in the worksheet. You will make several changes to the layout of the page to correct these problems.

First you will reduce the scale of the worksheet until all the data fits on one page. Because the width is fine, you will scale only the height.

2

- Open the Page Layout tab.

- Open the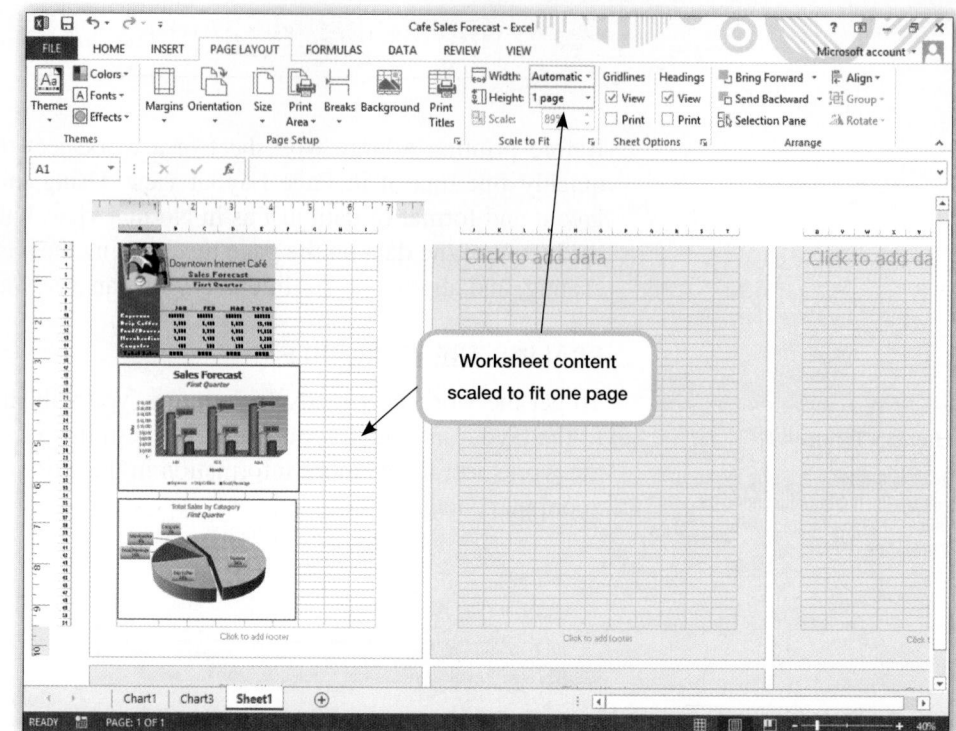

  Height: Automatic ▾

  drop-down menu and choose 1 page.

Your screen should be similar to Figure 2.77

Worksheet content scaled to fit one page

Figure 2.77

The worksheet scale has been reduced to fit on a single page.

ADDING PREDEFINED HEADERS AND FOOTERS

Next, you want to include your name and the date in a header.

Concept ⑨ Headers and Footers

Headers and footers provide information that typically appears at the top and bottom of each page and commonly include information such as the date and page number. A **header** is a line or several lines of text that appear at the top of a page just above the top margin line. The header usually contains the file name or worksheet title. A **footer** is a line or several lines of text that appear at the bottom of a page just below the bottom margin line. The footer usually contains the page number and perhaps the date. Headers and footers also can contain graphics such as a company logo. Each worksheet in a workbook can have a different header and footer.

You can select from predefined header and footer text or enter your own custom text. The information contained in the predefined header and footer text is obtained from the file properties associated with the workbook and from the program and system settings.

Header and footer text can be formatted like any other text. In addition, you can control the placement of the header and footer text by specifying where it should appear: left-aligned, centered, or right-aligned in the header or footer space.

Additional Information

If the computer you are using has your name as the user name, you will not need to add your name as the author in the document properties.

You will add a predefined header to the worksheet that displays your name, the date, and page number. To have your name appear in a predefined header, you will need to first add your name as the author to the file properties.

1

- Open the File tab and in the Info window, enter your name in the Author box.

- Open the Home tab and increase the zoom to 90%.

- Click in the center section of the Header area to activate the header.

- Click 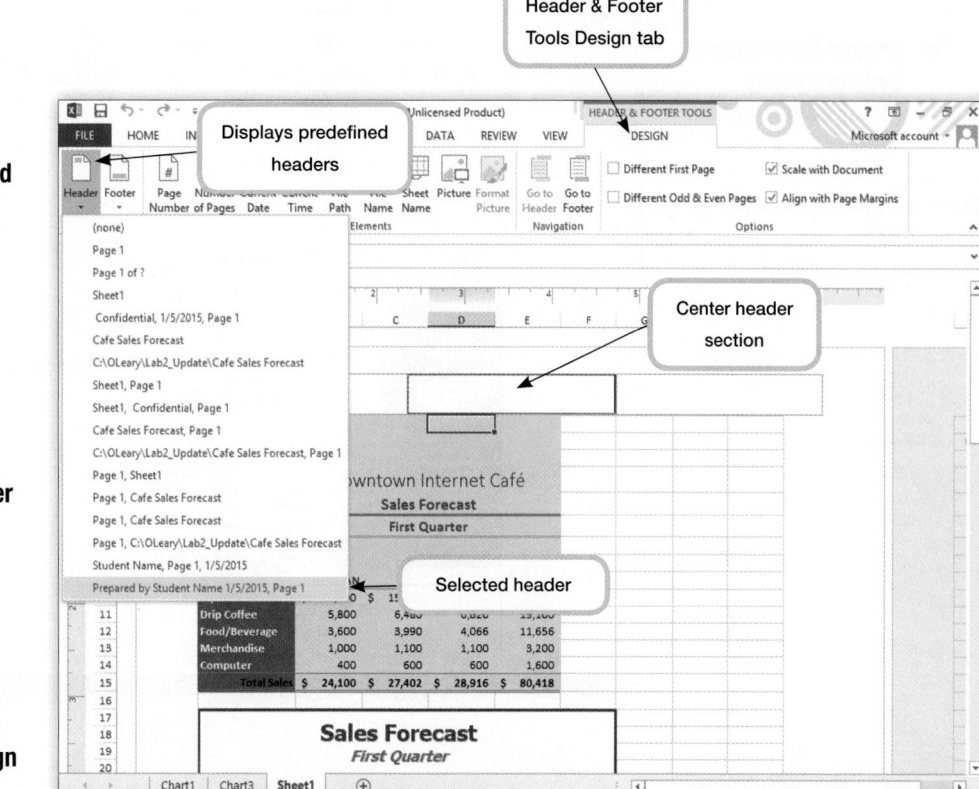 in the Header and Footer group of the Header & Footer Tools Design tab.

Your screen should be similar to Figure 2.78

Figure 2.78

Activating the worksheet header displays the Header & Footer Tools Design tab. It contains commands to add elements to, format, or navigate between a header or footer. The ⟨Header⟩ drop-down list includes many predefined headers that can be quickly inserted into the header. Notice that several of the predefined headers include information that was entered in the document properties.

● **Choose the Prepared by [your name] [date], Page 1 option.**

Your screen should be similar to Figure 2.79

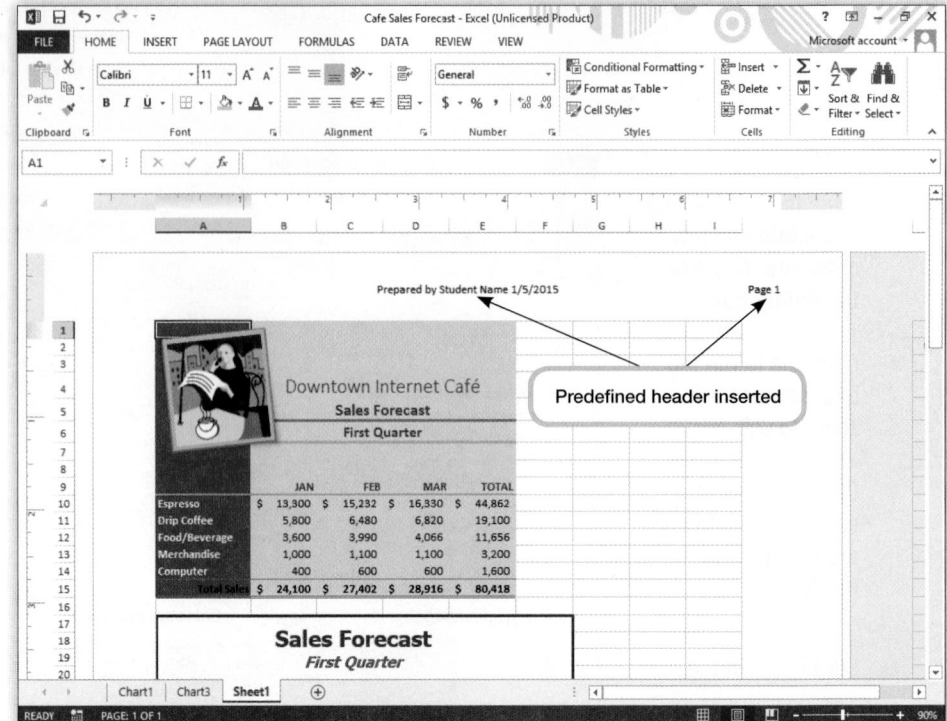

Figure 2.79

The selected header is displayed in the header area of the worksheet. It can be edited or formatted to meet your needs.

PRINTING THE ENTIRE WORKBOOK

Finally, you are ready to print the workbook. Because it includes a chart sheet and a worksheet, you first need to change the print setting to print the entire workbook.

①

- **Open the File tab and choose Print.**

- **Click**

  | Print Active Sheets | ▼ |
  | Only print the active sheets | |

  and choose Print Entire Workbook.

- **If necessary, select the printer you will use from the Printer list box.**

Your screen should be similar to Figure 2.80

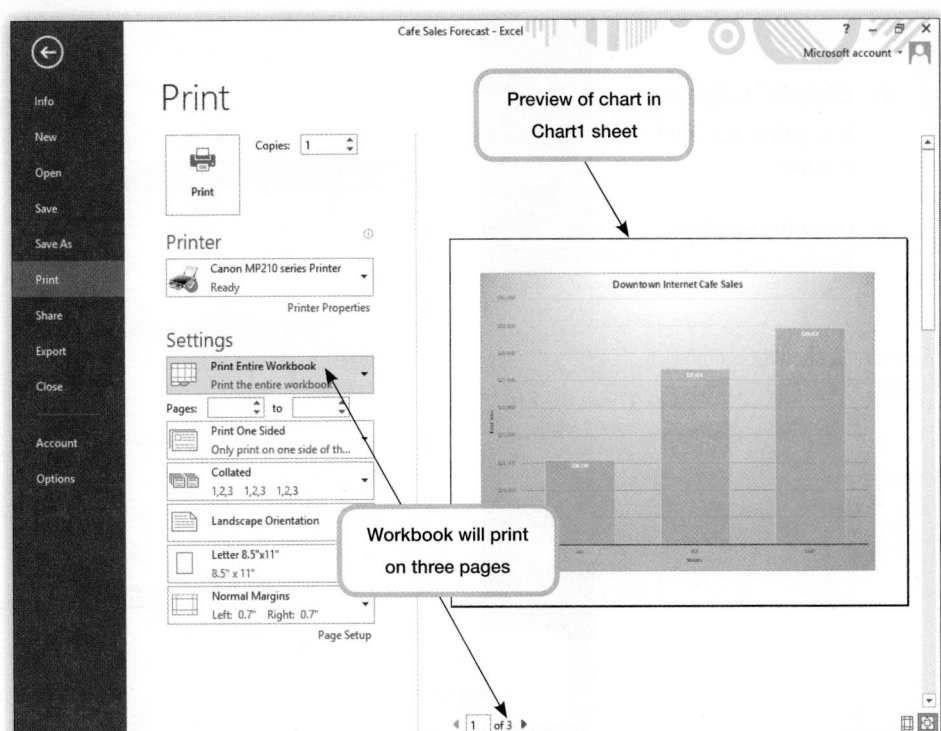

Figure 2.80

Because the Chart1 sheet containing the column chart is the first sheet in the workbook, it is displayed in the preview area. It will be printed on a separate page by itself in landscape orientation. The page indicator shows that the workbook will print on three pages. The combo chart will print on the second page and the worksheet will print on page 3. In addition, if you are not using a color printer, the preview displays the chart colors in shades of gray as they will appear when printed on a black-and-white printer.

You decide to add a footer to the column chart sheet. Each sheet can have its own header and footer definitions.

2

● Click the Page Setup link below the Print options.

● Open the Header/Footer tab.

Your screen should be similar to Figure 2.81

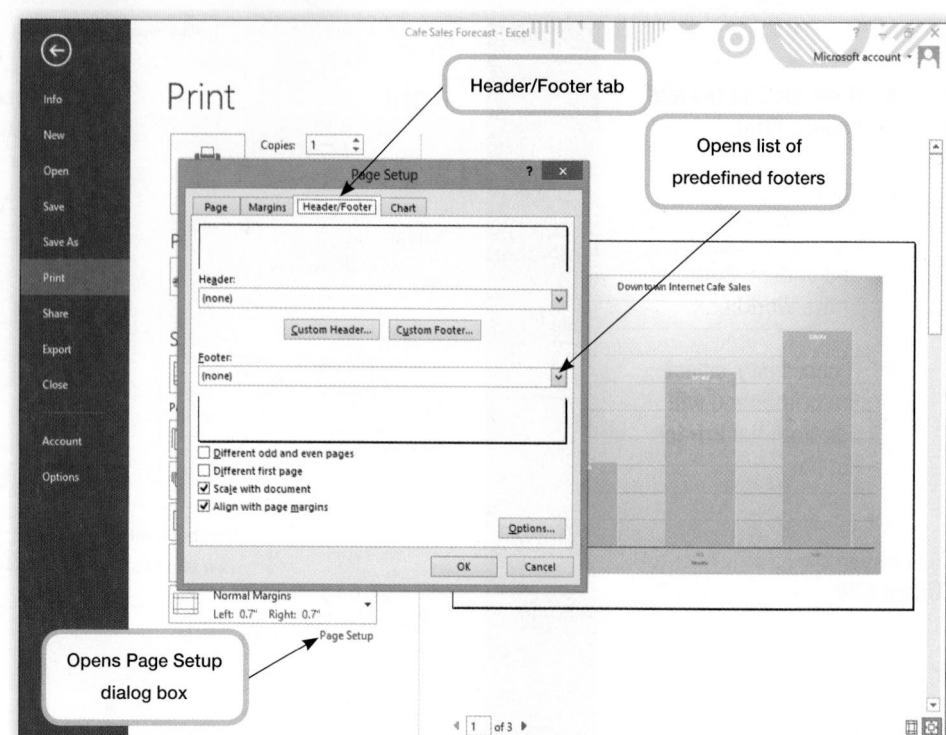

Header/Footer tab

Opens list of predefined footers

Opens Page Setup dialog box

Figure 2.81

Many of the same elements that were available when adding a header in Page Layout view are available in the Page Setup dialog box. You will add a predefined footer to the chart sheet.

3

● Click ✓ More in the Footer section to open the list of predefined footers.

● Scroll the list and choose the footer that displays your name, Page 1, and date.

● Click OK.

Your screen should be similar to Figure 2.82

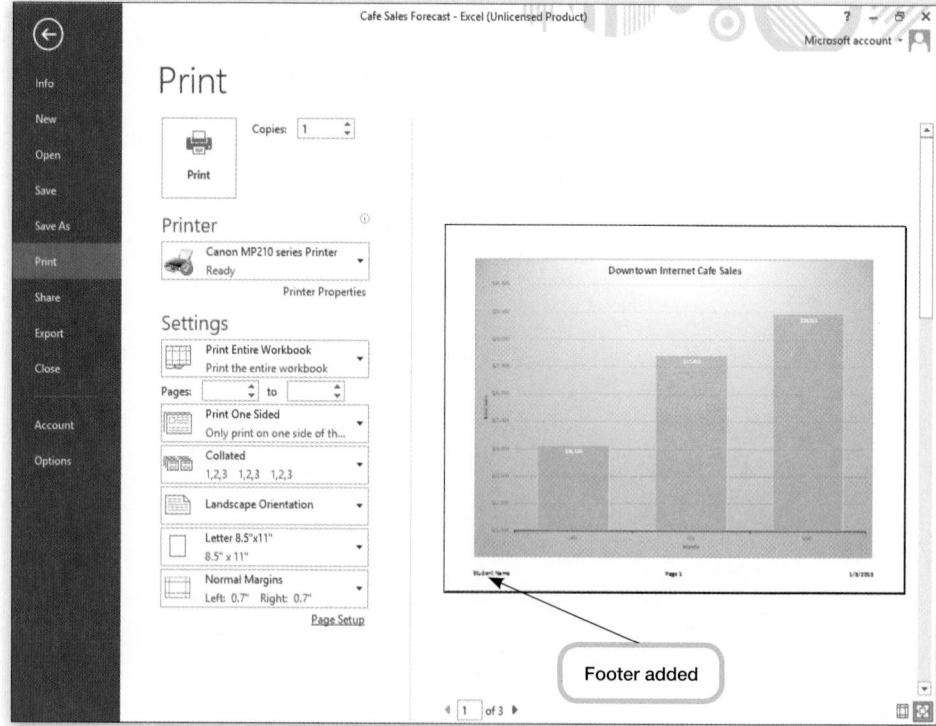

Footer added

Figure 2.82

The preview shows the selected footer.

Next, you will preview the worksheet.

● Click ▶ at the
  bottom of the
  Preview pane to see
  the combo chart and
  the worksheet and
  charts in Sheet1.

Your screen should be similar to
Figure 2.83

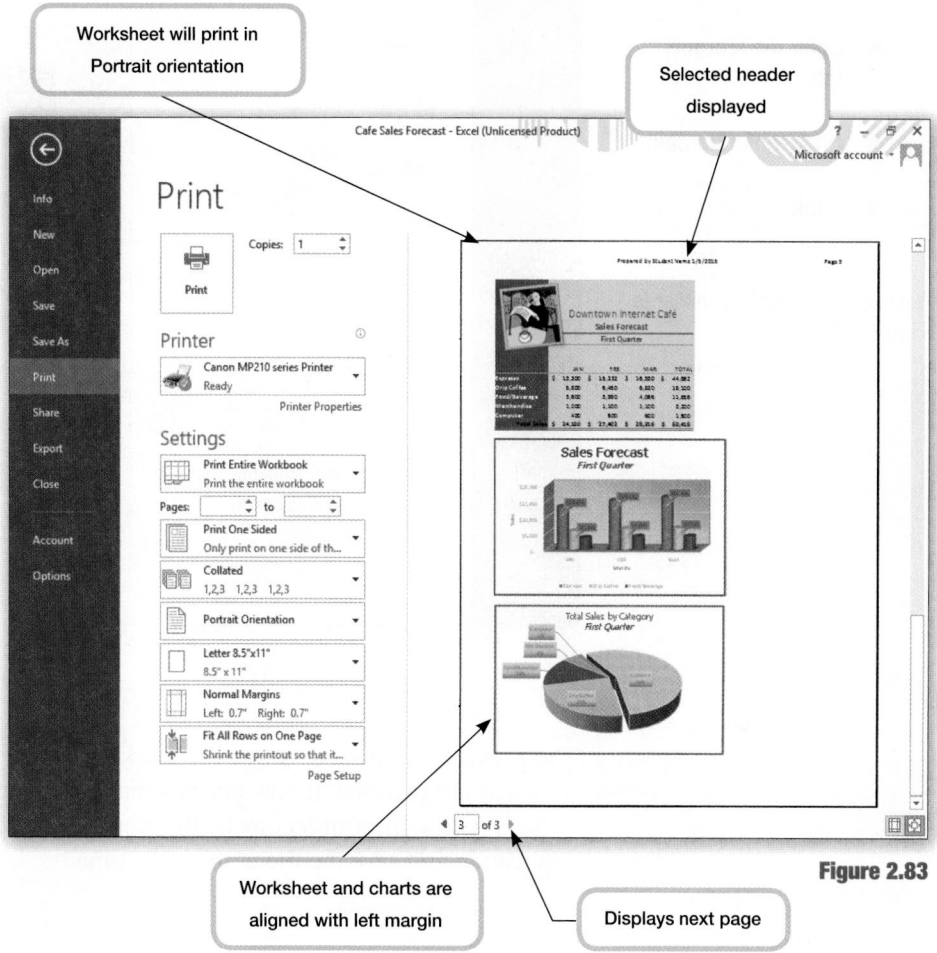

Worksheet will print in
Portrait orientation

Selected header
displayed

Worksheet and charts are
aligned with left margin

Displays next page

Figure 2.83

The preview shows the header you added to the worksheet and because the worksheet was scaled vertically, all the data fits on a single page in portrait orientation.

ALIGNING A SHEET ON A PAGE

However, in the print preview, you can see that the worksheet and charts are all aligned with the left margin. You would like to center the worksheet horizontally on the page. The default worksheet margin settings include 0.7-inch top and bottom margins and 0.75-inch right and left margins. The **margins** are the blank space outside the printing area around the edges of the paper. The worksheet contents appear in the printable area inside the margins. You want to center the worksheet data horizontally within the existing margins.

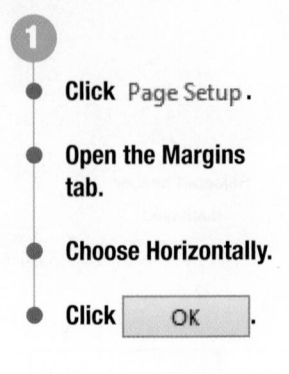

- ● **Click** Page Setup.

- ● **Open the Margins tab.**

- ● **Choose Horizontally.**

- ● **Click** OK .

Your screen should be similar to Figure 2.84

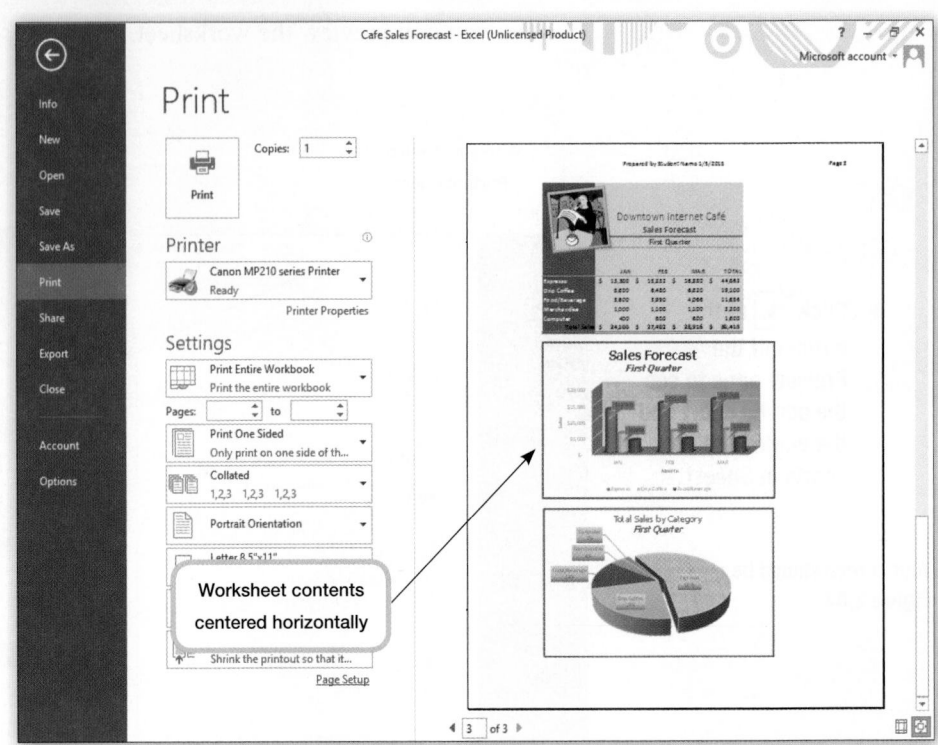

Worksheet contents centered horizontally

Figure 2.84

The preview window displays the worksheet centered horizontally between the right and left margins. It now appears the way you want it to look when printed.

Next, you will print a copy of the worksheet and chart. Then you will exit the application and save the file at the same time.

2

● Click 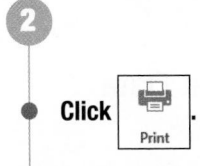.

● Change to Normal view and move to cell A9 of Sheet1.

Additional Information

The dotted line between columns H and I shows the page margin.

● Exit Excel, saving the workbook again.

The page layout settings you specified have been saved with the workbook file.

CUS ON CAREERS

EXPLORE YOUR CAREER OPTIONS

Financial Advisor

With the stock market fluctuations in the last few years, investors are demanding more from their financial advisors than ever before. An advisor needs to promote each company's potential and growth in order to persuade investors to buy stock. One way to do this is to create a worksheet of vital information and to chart that information so the investor can see why the stock is a good investment. The position of financial advisor usually requires a college degree and commands salaries from $40,000 to $60,000, depending on experience.

Graphics (EX2.5)

A graphic is a nontext element or object such as a drawing or picture that can be added to a document.

Quick Style (EX2.13)

A quick style is a named group of formatting characteristics that allows you to quickly apply a whole group of formats to a selected object in one simple step.

Theme (EX2.16)

A theme is a set of formatting choices that can be applied to an entire workbook in one simple step. A theme consists of a set of theme colors, a set of theme fonts (including heading and body text fonts), and a set of theme effects (including line and fill effects).

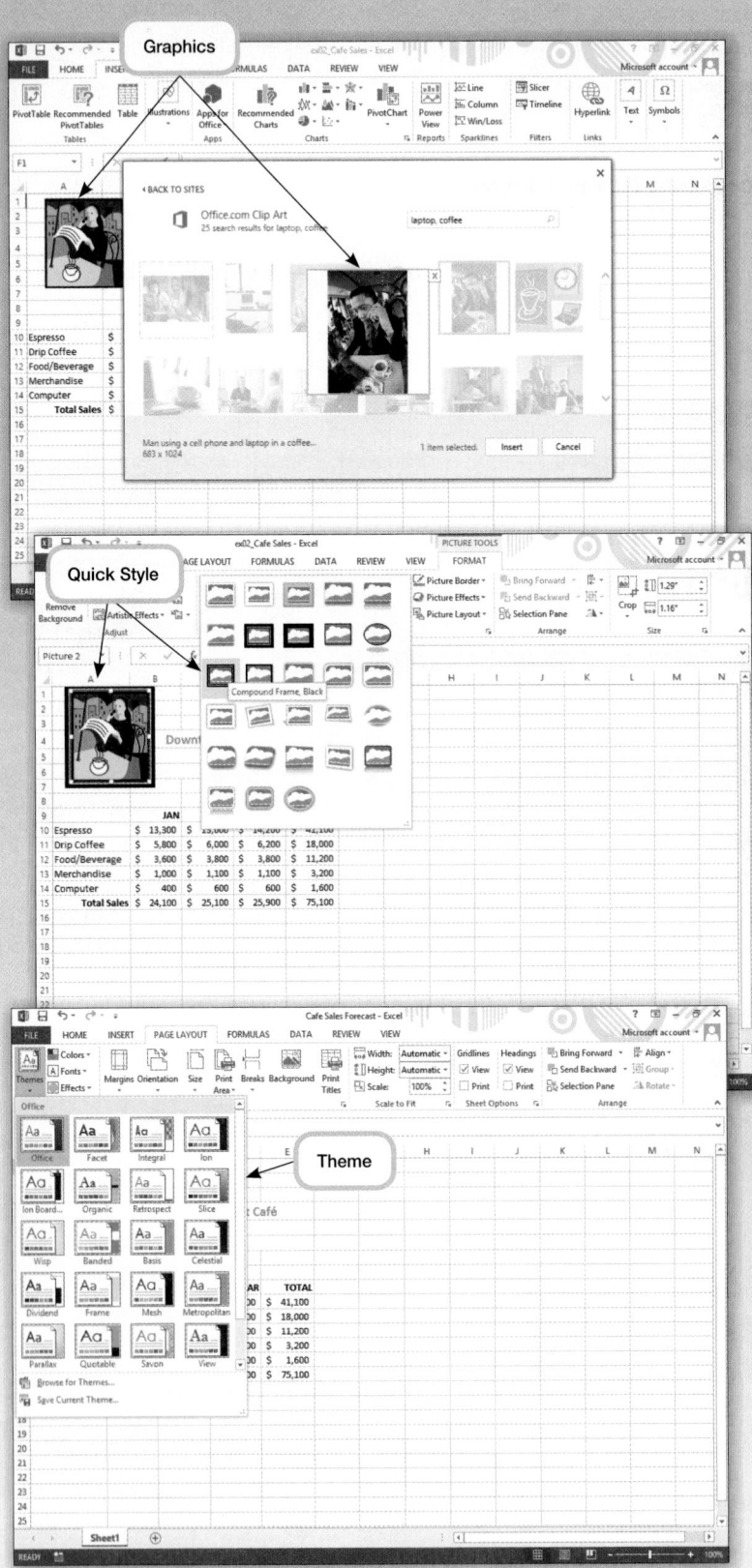

Chart Elements (EX2.25)

Chart elements are the different parts of a chart that are used to graphically display the worksheet data.

Chart Types (EX2.27)

Different chart types are used to represent data in different ways. The type of chart you create depends on the type of data you are charting and the emphasis you want the chart to impart.

Chart Object (EX2.29)

A chart object is a graphic object that is created using charting features. A chart object can be inserted into a worksheet or into a special chart sheet.

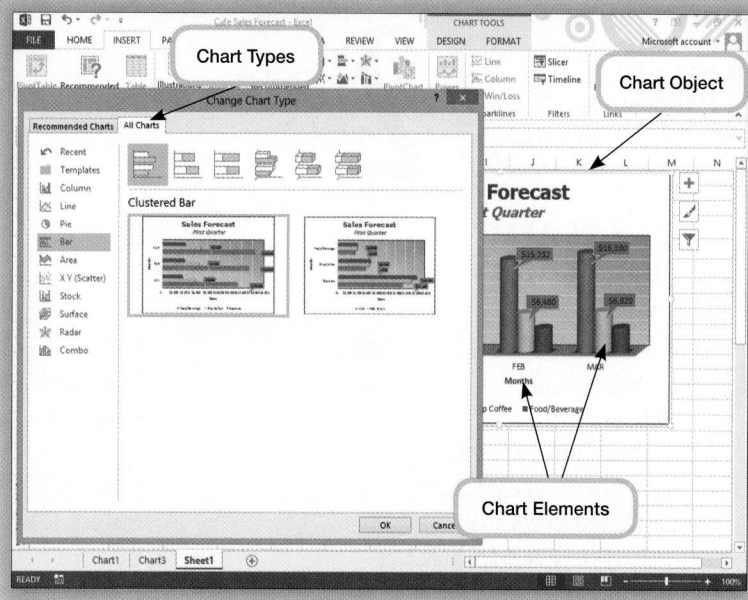

Group (EX2.45)

A group is two or more objects that behave as a single object when moved or sized. A chart is a group that consists of many separate objects.

Data Labels (EX2.52)

Data labels provide additional information about a data point in the data series. They can consist of the value of the point, the name of the data series or category, a percentage value, or a bubble size.

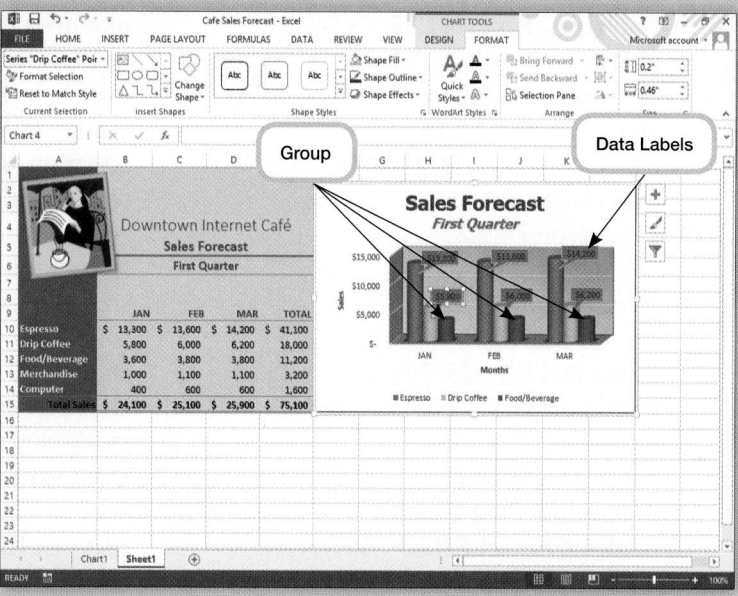

Headers and Footers (EX2.70)

Headers and footers provide information that typically appears at the top and bottom of each page and commonly include information such as the date and page number.

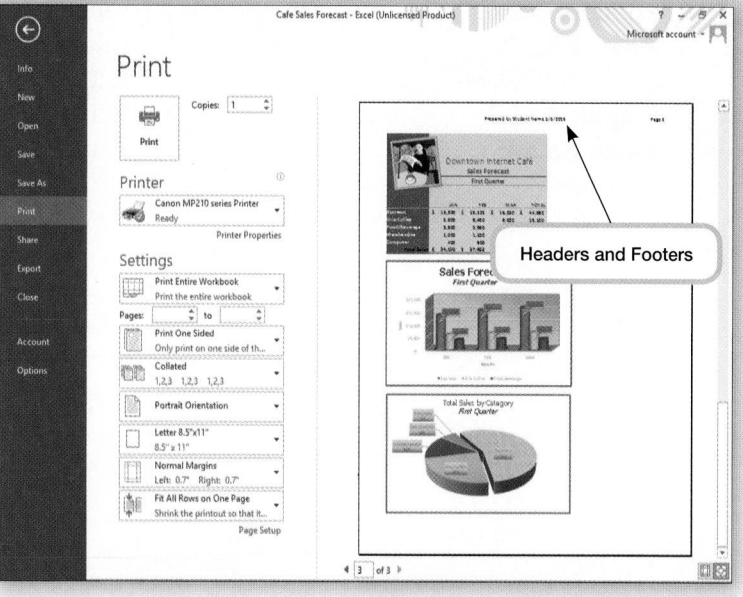

KEY TERMS

area chart EX2.27, EX2.43
axis EX2.25
bar chart EX2.27, EX2.42
bubble chart EX2.27
category axis EX2.25
category-axis title EX2.25
cell style EX2.13, EX2.19
chart EX2.24
chart area EX2.25
chart elements EX2.25
chart gridlines EX2.25
chart layout EX2.30
chart object EX2.29
chart style EX2.13, EX2.32
chart title EX2.25
chart type EX2.27
clip art EX2.6
column chart EX2.27
combo chart EX2.27, EX2.56
data label EX2.25, EX2.52
data marker EX2.25
data series EX2.25
depth axis EX2.25
doughnut chart EX2.27
drawing object EX2.5
embedded chart EX2.29
embedded object EX2.5
explode EX2.62
footer EX2.70
gradient EX2.49
graphic EX2.5
group EX2.45

header EX2.70
keyword EX2.10
legend EX2.25
line chart EX2.27, EX2.41
margin EX2.75
object EX2.5
picture EX2.5
picture style EX2.13
pie chart EX2.27, EX2.58
plot area EX2.25
quick style EX2.13
radar chart EX2.27
scatter (XY) chart EX2.27
selection rectangle EX2.7
series axis EX2.25
series formula EX2.63
shape style EX2.13, EX2.66
sizing handle EX2.7
source program EX2.5
stack EX2.29
stacked column chart EX2.44
stock chart EX2.27
stops (gradient stops) EX2.61
surface chart EX2.27
text box EX2.33
theme EX2.16
thumbnail EX2.10
value axis EX2.25
value-axis title EX2.25
X axis EX2.25
Y axis EX2.25
Z axis EX2.25

COMMAND SUMMARY

Command	Action
File tab	
Print/Settings/ ▦ Print Active Sheets / Only print the active sheets ▾ Print Entire Workbook	Prints all sheets in workbook file
Page Setup	Opens Page Setup dialog box
Home tab	
Styles group	
📋 Cell Styles ▾	Applies predefined combinations of colors, effects, and formats to selected cells
📋 Cell Styles ▾ /Modify	Modifies existing cell style
Insert tab	
Illustrations group	
🖼 Pictures	Inserts a picture from a file on your computer or local network
🖼 Online Pictures	Inserts a graphic from online sources
Charts group	
📊 Recommended Charts	Shows suggested charts to use with selected data
📊 ▾	Inserts a column chart
🥧 ▾	Inserts a pie chart
📊 ▾	Inserts a combo chart
Text group	
📄 Header & Footer	Adds header or footer to worksheet
Page Layout tab	
Themes group	
🅰 Themes	Applies selected theme to worksheet

LAB REVIEW

COMMAND SUMMARY (CONTINUED)

Command	Action
Aa Themes /Save Current Theme	Saves modified theme settings as a custom theme
Colors ▾	Changes colors for the current theme
Scale to Fit group	
Width:	Scales worksheet width to specified number of pages
Height:	Scales worksheet height to specified number of pages
Scale:	Scales worksheet by entering a percentage
Picture Tools Format tab	
Picture Styles group	
Picture Border ▾	Specifies color, width, and line style for outline of shape
Picture Effects ▾	Adds glow, shadow, and other effects to pictures
Chart Tools Design tab	
Chart Layouts	
Add Chart Element ▾	Adds chart elements such as titles and legend
Quick Layout ▾	Changes overall layout of chart
Chart Styles	
Change Colors ▾	Changes colors associated with chart styles

COMMAND SUMMARY (CONTINUED)

Command	Action
Data group	
[Switch Row/Column]	Swaps the data over the axes
[Select Data]	Changes the data range included in chart
Type group	
[Change Chart Type]	Changes to a different type of chart
Location group	
[Move Chart]	Moves chart to another sheet in the workbook
Chart Tools Format tab	
Current Selection group	
Chart Area	Selects an element on the chart
Format Selection	Opens Format dialog box for selected element
Shape Styles group	
Shape Fill ▾	Adds selected fill to shape
Shape Outline ▾	Specifies color, weight, and type of outline
Shape Effects ▾	Adds selected effect to shape
View tab	
Zoom group	
[Zoom]	Changes the magnification of the worksheet

LAB EXERCISES

MATCHING

Match the lettered item on the right with the numbered item on the left.

1. category ranges   _____ a. bottom boundary line of the chart
2. chart sheet   _____ b. identifies each number represented in a data series
3. column chart   _____ c. numbered scale along the left boundary line of the chart
4. data marker   _____ d. area of chart bounded by X and Y axes
5. explode   _____ e. applies a set of colors, fonts, and effects
6. gradient   _____ f. separate location that holds only one chart
7. legend   _____ g. a chart that displays data as vertical columns
8. plot area   _____ h. identifies the chart data series and data markers
9. scaling   _____ i. to separate a slice slightly from other slices of the pie
10. theme   _____ j. identifies the data along the X axis
11. value axis   _____ k. a gradual progression of colors and shades
12. X axis   _____ l. adjusting print size to fit on the selected number of pages

TRUE/FALSE

Circle the correct answer to the following questions.

1. An object in an Excel worksheet is an element that can be sized, moved, and formatted.   **True**   **False**
2. Before selecting any chart data, click the Recommended Charts button for suggested chart types.   **True**   **False**
3. A chart style is a predefined set of colors, styles, and effects for a chart.   **True**   **False**
4. A chart title can be modified to use a larger font size.   **True**   **False**
5. A line chart is used to illustrate trends in data over a period of time.   **True**   **False**
6. The X-axis title is also referred to as the category-axis title.   **True**   **False**
7. A header is one or more lines of text at the bottom of each page above the bottom margin.   **True**   **False**
8. A combo chart is best suited for data that compares parts to the whole.   **True**   **False**
9. Worksheet data can be horizontally centered on the printed page from the Page Setup dialog box.   **True**   **False**
10. You can explode a column in a column chart or a slice in a pie chart to emphasize that data series.   **True**   **False**

FILL-IN

Complete the following statements by filling in the blanks with the correct key terms.

1. Small circles or squares that surround a selected object in a worksheet are called _____.

2. A(n) _____ is a set of colors, fonts, and effects that is applied to the entire workbook.

3. The axis of a column chart with values is known as the _____ or _____ axis.

4. A(n) _____ uses two types of charts to illustrate mixed types of data.

5. To provide an explanation of the colors used for each data series in a chart, you can display a(n) _____.

6. A large worksheet can be fit to a single page by adjusting the _____.

7. A chart is automatically redrawn when you edit its source data because the data is _____ to the chart.

8. You can use Office.com to insert royalty-free _____ in an Excel worksheet.

9. _____ are combinations of formatting styles such as font, border, shadow, and shape effects that can be applied to a graphic in a worksheet.

10. A(n) _____ is a predefined set of elements such as a title, legend, data labels, and data table that is applied to a selected chart.

LAB EXERCISES

MULTIPLE CHOICE

Circle the correct response to the questions below.

1. A graphic can be placed in an Excel worksheet from the _____ tab.
    a. Home
    b. Insert
    c. Layout
    d. Style

2. Column, bar, and line are Excel chart _____.
    a. elements
    b. groups
    c. styles
    d. types

3. A 3-D chart includes a third axis known as the _____.
    a. W axis
    b. X axis
    c. Y axis
    d. Z axis

4. A(n) _____ is the chart object that identifies each data series.
    a. X axis
    b. legend
    c. Y axis
    d. chart title

5. A company logo, the page number, or the current date might be shown in the _____ for an Excel worksheet.
    a. chart
    b. drawing
    c. footing
    d. header

6. A chart that is included in the worksheet with its data is a(n) _____ chart.
    a. attached
    b. embedded
    c. enabled
    d. inserted

7. To change the appearance of the bars in an Excel bar chart, use the _____ task pane.
   a. Format Bars
   b. Format Data Series
   c. Modify Chart
   d. Modify Data Point

8. From the _____ dialog box, you can change margins as well as the header or footer for a worksheet.
   a. Format Page
   b. File Print
   c. Page Layout
   d. Page Setup

9. An Excel _____ chart shows the relationship of each value in a data series to the series as a whole.
   a. line
   b. bar
   c. pie
   d. bubble

10. _____ are shared across Office 2013 applications so that all your documents can have a uniform style and appearance.
    a. Masks
    b. Formats
    c. Themes
    d. Styles

STEP-BY-STEP

U.S. PATENTS BY TECHNOLOGY ★

1. Max's research paper is about patents in the technology sector. He has downloaded some data from the Science and Engineering Indicators to get started. You'll be helping him chart data for the top four categories and to format the worksheet. A completed worksheet with a bar chart is shown here, but you will change the bar chart to a column chart. Your solution may look different depending upon your format choices.

    a. Open the workbook ex02_Patent Data. Save the workbook as Patent Data to your solution file location.

    b. Change to a different document theme. Use cell styles, font and fill color, alignment, row height, number formats, borders, and other formatting effects to enhance the appearance of the data.

    c. Insert a graphic of your choice. Size and position it; apply a picture style that complements the rest of your design.

    d. Select A3 through D3 and the other required cells to build a clustered bar chart, using the Recommended Charts command. Build a chart that illustrates the top four technology areas for patents. Move the chart below the worksheet data, and size it to the same width as the data.

    e. Edit the chart title to show **Top Patent Activity**.
    Choose a chart style, or make other formatting choices to design your chart.

    f. Change the chart type to clustered column. Display and format data labels for the 2010 values.

    g. Move to cell A1. Preview the worksheet, and scale it to fit on a single page.

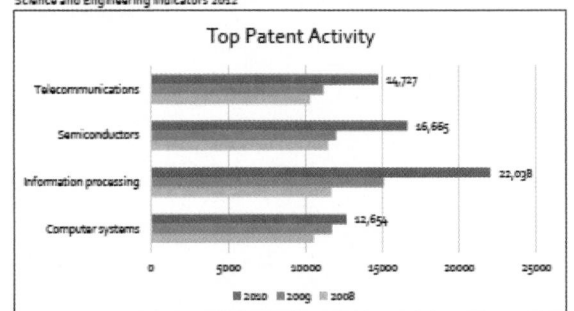

USPTO[1] Patent Activity
By Technology Area[2]

Area or Field	2008	2009	2010
Aerospace and defense	1434	1679	2098
Automation and control	2773	3225	3951
Biotechnology	5940	5826	8206
Computer systems	10506	11680	12654
Information processing	11672	15075	22038
Materials	3658	3582	5193
Measurement techniques and instrumentation	9478	9790	10918
Medical electronics	2439	2565	3489
Medical equipment	4582	4691	7424
Networking	4859	6921	9861
Optics	6597	6683	6875
Pharmaceuticals	3835	4275	5471
Semiconductors	11440	11974	16665
Telecommunications	10264	11138	14727
Total Activity	91485	101113	131580

[1] United States Patent and Trademark Office
[2] Technologies classified by the Patent Board™
Source: The Patent Board™, Proprietary Patent database, special tabulations (2011)
Science and Engineering Indicators 2012

Top Patent Activity

Telecommunications — 14,727

Semiconductors — 16,665

Information processing — 22,038

Computer systems — 12,654

(axis: 0, 5000, 10000, 15000, 20000, 25000)

■ 2010 ■ 2009 ■ 2008

Student Name   1   2/1/15

h. Add a predefined footer to the worksheet to display your name, the page number, and the date. Center the worksheet horizontally.

i. Document the workbook to include your name as the author. Save the workbook. Preview and print the worksheet.

AIRLINE BAGGAGE FEES ★★

2. Larissa works for the Department of Transportation Statistics. She's preparing a report on the amount of revenue attributable to airline baggage fees. She has assembled data for four years and plans to develop the worksheet with two charts that will illustrate the trends. Your solution should resemble the sample completed worksheets, but you may make your own format choices.

a. Open the workbook ex02_ Baggage Fees. Save the workbook as Baggage Fees to your solution file location.

b. Apply a different document theme. Change the colors associated with the theme, and save your custom theme.

c. Use cell styles, alignment, font and fill color, and other formatting features to enhance the appearance of the data.

d. Insert a graphic of your choice. Size and position it; apply a picture style, if desired, that complements the worksheet design.

e. Create a column chart for the data from the four carriers listed. Move the chart to a separate chart sheet. Enter an

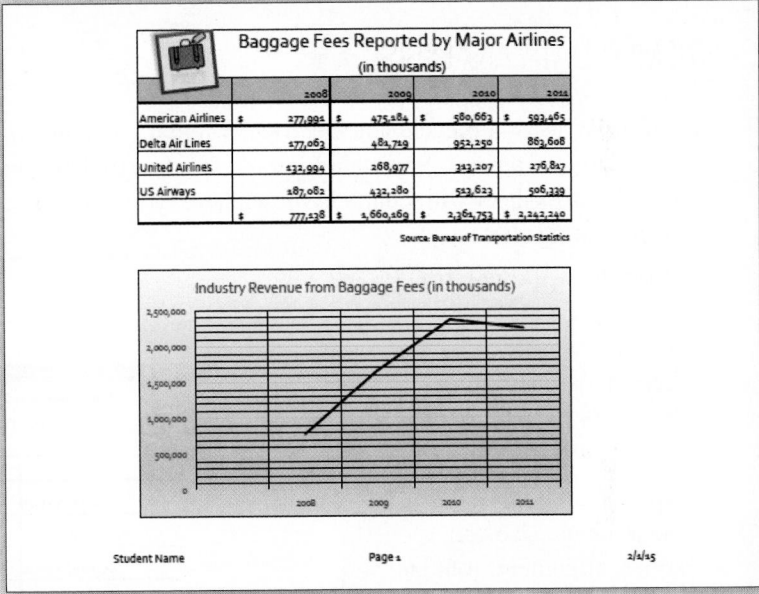

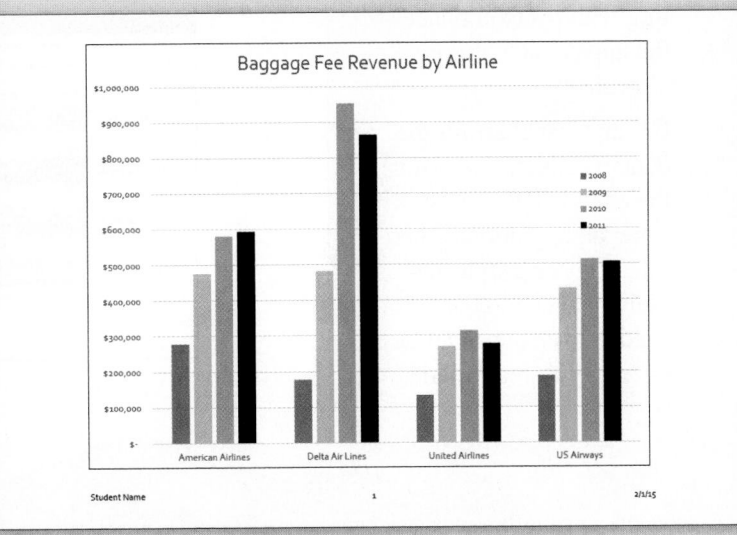

LAB EXERCISES

appropriate chart title. Choose a style, and edit individual chart elements as needed to create an attractive, easy-to-read chart.

f. Create a line chart with markers for the yearly totals. Edit and format an appropriate title. Format the chart area with a gradient fill of your choice. Show the data labels, and format and position them. Do not show a legend. Move this chart below the worksheet data.

g. Move to cell A1. Preview the worksheet, and fit the chart and data on a single page, if necessary.

h. Add a predefined footer to the worksheet and the chart sheet to display your name, the page number, and the date. Center the worksheet horizontally.

i. Document the workbook to include your name as the author. Save the workbook. Preview and print the workbook.

CUSTOMER DATA ANALYSIS ★★

3. Greenline Wheels, a bicycle and electric car rental company, has collected data about customers to help analyze future offerings. You want to graph the data to determine customer interests and purchases. The completed worksheet with charts is shown here; your worksheet may be slightly different depending on your formatting choices.

a. Open the workbook ex02_ Greenline Customers. Save the workbook as Greenline Customers Analysis to your solution file location.

b. Apply a different document theme. Use cell styles, alignment, font and fill color, or other formatting features to enhance the appearance of your worksheet.

c. Create a bar chart for the data in cells B5:D9. Move the chart below the data. Enter an appropriate chart title. Choose a style and edit individual chart elements as needed to create an attractive, easy-to-read chart.

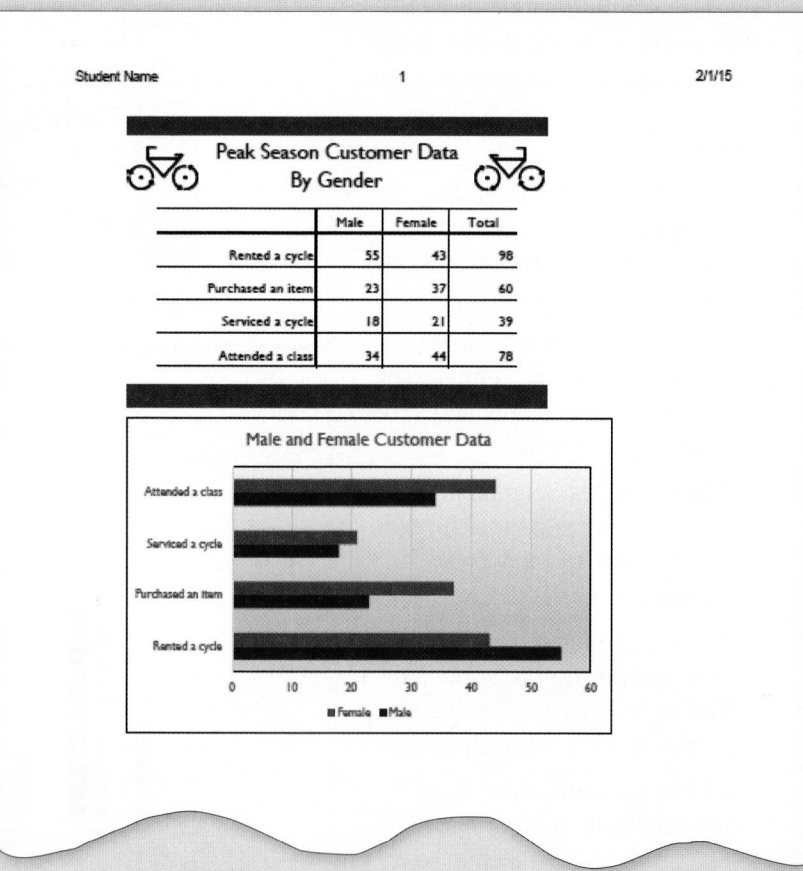

d. Insert a graphic of your choice. Size and position it; apply a picture style, if desired, that complements the worksheet design.

e. Create a column chart for the totals data. Move this chart to a separate chart sheet. Enter an appropriate chart title, and do not show a legend. Choose a style, and add and edit chart elements as needed.

f. You realize that the male and female data for the "Serviced a cycle" item is transposed. Reenter those two values.

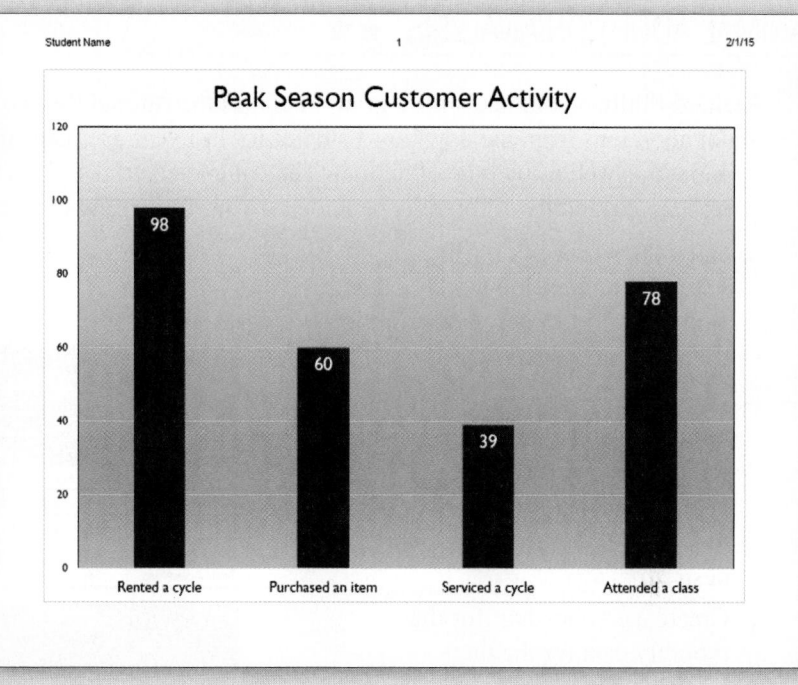

g. Move to cell A1. Preview the worksheet to determine if the data and chart fit on a single page. Scale the worksheet if necessary.

h. Add a predefined header to the worksheet to display your name, the page number, and the date. Center the worksheet horizontally. Add the same header to the chart sheet. Print both sheets.

i. Document the workbook to include your name as the author. Save the workbook.

LAB EXERCISES

ANIMAL ADOPTION ANALYSIS ★★

4. Richard Phillipe volunteers for a group that aids the Animal Rescue Foundation. He has compiled data about adoptions from the downtown shelter for last year. He plans to create charts that show adoptions by month as well as by type of animal. The completed worksheet with charts is shown here; your worksheet may be slightly different depending on your formatting choices.

   a. Open the workbook ex02_ Adoptions. Save the workbook as Animal Adoptions to your solution file location.

   b. Find and insert an image in the top-left or top-right area of the worksheet. Size and position the image. Use the Picture Tools Format tab to recolor or adjust the image if desired.

   c. Create a combo chart for the monthly data for the three categories. Show the dogs and cats categories by a clustered column chart; show the other animals category in a line chart. Edit the title to display **Adoptions by Month**.

   d. Choose a chart style; show a legend at the bottom. Move the chart below the worksheet data and size it. Add a value (Y) axis title that shows **Number of Animals**.

   e. Create a 3-D pie chart for the total adoptions by animal group for the year. Move this chart below the column chart. Choose a style that works well with your data and the column chart. Enter **Animal Adoptions by Category** as the chart title.

   f. Explode the Dogs slice slightly.

   g. Change the June value for Other Animals to **3**; change the October value for Dogs to **22**.

   h. Move to cell A1. Preview the worksheet. Scale it so that the data and charts fit on a single page.

   i. Add a predefined header to the worksheet to display your name, the page number, and the date. Center the worksheet horizontally.

   j. Document the workbook to include your name as the author. Save the workbook. Preview and print the worksheet.

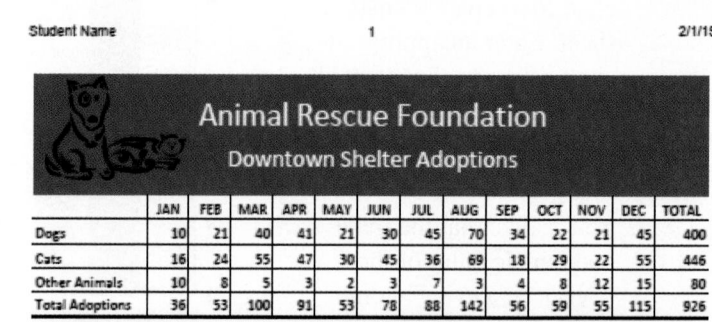

Student Name   1   2/1/15

Animal Rescue Foundation
Downtown Shelter Adoptions

	JAN	FEB	MAR	APR	MAY	JUN	JUL	AUG	SEP	OCT	NOV	DEC	TOTAL
Dogs	10	21	40	41	21	30	45	70	34	22	21	45	400
Cats	16	24	55	47	30	45	36	69	18	29	22	55	446
Other Animals	10	8	5	3	2	3	7	3	4	8	12	15	80
Total Adoptions	36	53	100	91	53	78	88	142	56	59	55	115	926

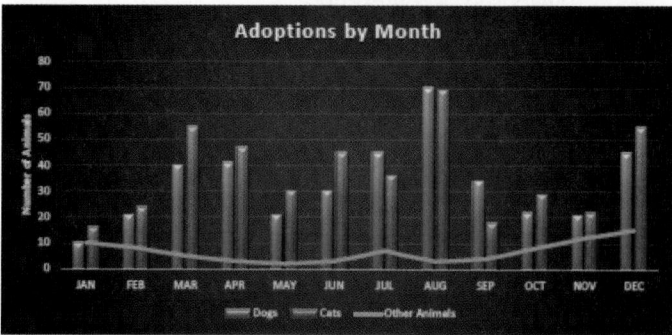

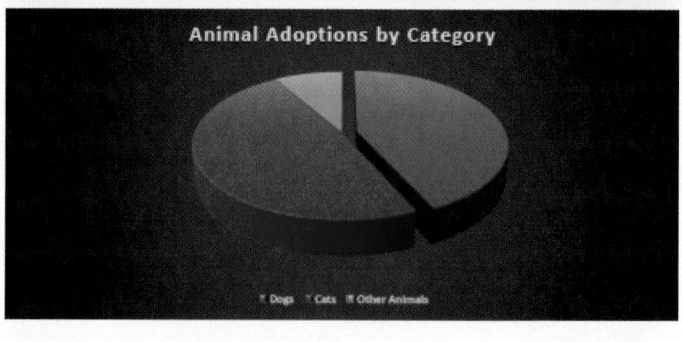

FOOD PANTRY EXPERIENCE ★★★

5. Wendy Murray is working at the local food pantry and has been asked to assemble and analyze volunteer data gathered at a recent street fair. She plans to organize the data by task and age group. She will share this data with the organization so it can better plan food distribution events. The completed worksheet with charts is shown here; your worksheet may be slightly different depending on your formatting choices.

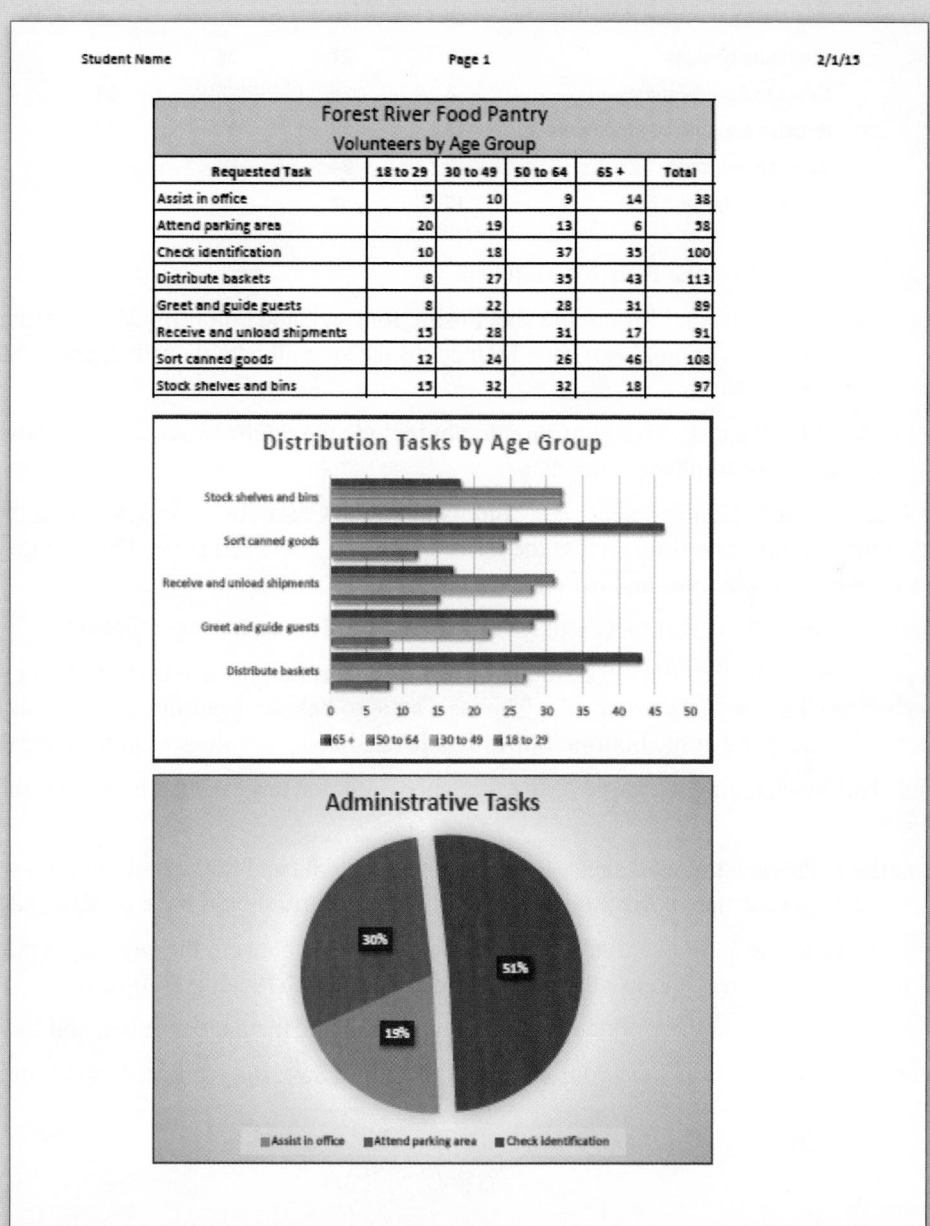

LAB EXERCISES

a. Create a worksheet using the data shown here. Save the workbook as Food Pantry to your solution file location.

FOREST RIVER FOOD PANTRY				
	Volunteers by Age Group			
Requested Task	18 to 29	30 to 49	50 to 64	65+
Assist in office	5	10	9	14
Attend parking area	20	19	13	6
Check identification	10	18	37	35
Distribute baskets	8	27	35	43
Greet and guide guests	8	22	28	31
Receive and unload shipments	15	28	31	17
Sort canned goods	12	24	26	46
Stock shelves and bins	15	32	32	18

b. Add a column to total the volunteers for each task.

c. Choose a document theme, and format the sheet using font size and color, fill color, borders, cell styles, or other formatting options you have learned. Make sure all data is visible, and set the columns with values at the same width.

d. Create a bar chart for the tasks by age group; do not include the totals. Move the chart below the data. Choose a chart style to complement the data.

e. With the chart selected, use the Select Data command on the Chart Tools Design tab. In the dialog box, switch the columns and rows so that the tasks are shown in the left pane. Then remove the first three tasks. Switch the columns and rows back to the original setting.

f. Add a chart title above the chart that displays Distribution Tasks by Age Group.

g. Create a pie chart for the first three task totals. Move this chart below the bar chart. Enter Administrative Tasks as the chart title. Choose a style to balance your other choices for the worksheet. Show a legend at the bottom. Show data labels inside the slices as percentages.

h. Rotate the chart by changing the angle of the first slice until the largest slice is at the right side of the pie. Explode this slice slightly.

i. Move to cell A1. Preview the worksheet. Scale it so that the data and both charts fit on a single portrait page, and center the data horizontally. If you think the charts should have borders, add them.

j. If you would like to use an image, find and insert one that contributes to the worksheet appearance. Size and position the image, and use the Picture Tools Format tab to adjust it if desired.

k. Add a predefined header to the worksheet to display your name, the page number, and the date.

l. Document the workbook to include your name as the author. Save the workbook and print the worksheet.

ON YOUR OWN

JOB MARKET SEMINAR ★

1. Nancy Fernandez is preparing for an upcoming job market seminar she is presenting. She has collected data comparing the mean hourly pay rate for several computer and mathematical jobs in the Midwest and Northeast to the U.S. average rates. Open the workbook ex02_Job Market. Calculate the percentage difference between the Midwest states and U.S. average in column E. Calculate the percentage difference between the Northeast states and U.S. average in column F. Add appropriate fill and font colors to the worksheet. Add a graphic to the top-left corner of the worksheet. Nancy thinks the information would be much more meaningful and have greater impact if it were presented in a chart. Create an appropriate chart of the average hourly wage for computer programmers, computer support specialists, computer systems analysts, and database administrators on a separate chart sheet. Include appropriate chart titles. Add a pattern to the data series and change the plot area fill color. Enhance the chart in other ways using different font sizes and font colors. Position the legend at the bottom of the chart. Add a predefined header to the chart sheet that displays your name, page number, and date. Save the workbook as Seminar and print the chart.

GRADE TRACKING ★

2. Create a worksheet that tracks your GPA for at least four semesters or quarters. (If necessary, use fictitious data to attain four grading periods.) Create a chart that best represents your GPA trends. Use the formatting techniques you have learned to change the appearance of the worksheet and the chart. Save the workbook as Grades. Include a header or footer that displays your name and the current date in the worksheet. Print the worksheet with the chart.

STOCK MARKET WORKBOOK ★★

3. You are interested in the stock market. Use Help to learn more about the Stock chart type. Pick five related mutual funds and enter data about their performance over a period of time. Create a stock chart of the data. Save the worksheet with the chart as Mutual Funds. Include a header or footer that displays your name and the current date in the worksheet. Print the worksheet and the chart.

LAB EXERCISES

GRADUATE SCHOOL DATA ★★★

4. Andrew Romine is considering graduate school at Ohio State and has gathered some data to present to his parents to make a case for paying part of his tuition and fees. Open the file ex02_Graduate School, which has two worksheets, one that shows earnings and the other payback data if Andrew chooses Ohio State. Using what you learned in the lab, create two charts from the data on the Earnings worksheet. One chart should represent the lifetime earning potential of people based on their level of education and the other should represent median earning by level. On the Payback worksheet, create a combo chart that compares the estimated earning and salary difference amounts. Use the features you have learned to enhance the appearance of the worksheets and charts. Include a header on both worksheets that displays your name and the current date. Save the worksheet as Graduate School2. Print the worksheet with the charts.

INSURANCE COMPARISONS ★★★

5. Roberto Sanchez is thinking about purchasing a new car. However, he is concerned about the insurance rates. Before purchasing, he wants to find out the insurance rates on the cars he is evaluating. Select three different car manufacturers and models. Use the web and select three different comparable insurance companies to get the insurance premium cost information for different amounts of coverage (minimum required). Use your own personal information as the basis for the insurance quotes. Create a worksheet that contains the cost of minimum coverage, cost of optional coverage, deductibles available, and insurance premium quotes for each vehicle. Create a chart of the data that shows the coverage and premiums. Enhance the chart appropriately. Add pictures of the cars. Include a header or footer that displays your name and the current date in the worksheet. Save the workbook as Insurance. Print the worksheet and chart.

Objectives

After completing this lab, you will know how to:

1 Use absolute references.

2 Copy, move, name, and delete sheets.

3 Use AutoFill.

4 Reference multiple sheets.

5 Use Find and Replace.

6 Zoom the worksheet.

7 Split windows and freeze panes.

8 Use what-if analysis and Goal Seek.

9 Create Sparklines.

10 Control page breaks.

11 Add custom headers and footers.

12 Print selected sheets and areas.

Downtown Internet Café

You presented your new, more-optimistic, first quarter sales forecast for the Downtown Internet Café to Evan. He was impressed with the charts and the projected increase in sales if an aggressive advertising promotion is launched. However, because the Café's funds are low due to the cost of the recent renovations, he has decided to wait on launching the advertising campaign.

Evan wants you to continue working on the Café forecast using the original, more-conservative projected sales values for the first quarter. In addition, he asks you to include an average calculation and to extend the forecast for the next three quarters.

After discussing the future sales, you agree that the Café will likely make a small profit during the first quarter of operations. Then the Café should show increasing profitability. Evan stresses that the monthly profit margin should reach 20 percent in the second quarter.

As you develop the Café's financial forecast, the worksheet grows in size and complexity. You will learn about features of Office Excel 2013 that help you manage a large workbook efficiently. You also will learn how you can manipulate the data in a worksheet to reach a goal using the what-if analysis capabilities of Excel. The completed annual forecast is shown here.

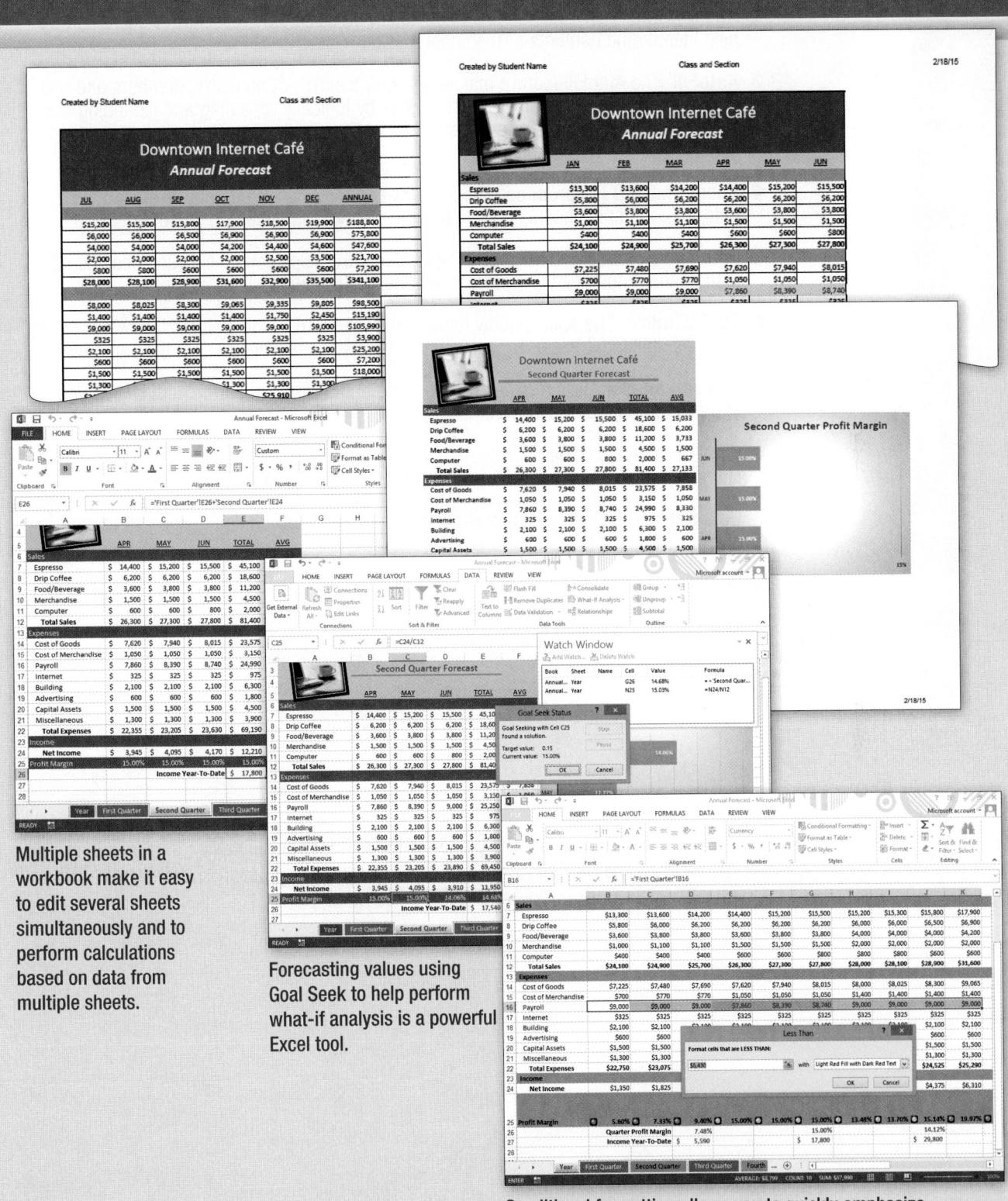

Multiple sheets in a workbook make it easy to edit several sheets simultaneously and to perform calculations based on data from multiple sheets.

Forecasting values using Goal Seek to help perform what-if analysis is a powerful Excel tool.

Conditional formatting allows you to quickly emphasize worksheet data based on specified conditions.

The following concepts will be introduced in this lab:

1 Absolute Reference An absolute reference is a cell or range reference in a formula whose location does not change when the formula is copied.

2 Sheet Name Each sheet in a workbook can be assigned a descriptive sheet name to help identify the contents of the sheet.

3 AutoFill The AutoFill feature makes entering a series of numbers, numbers and text combinations, dates, or time periods easier by logically repeating and extending the series. AutoFill recognizes trends and automatically extends data and alphanumeric headings as far as you specify.

4 Sheet and 3-D References Sheet and 3-D references in formulas are used to refer to data from multiple sheets and to calculate new values based on this data.

5 Find and Replace The Find and Replace feature helps you quickly find specific information and automatically replace it with new information.

6 Split Window The split window feature allows you to divide a worksheet window into sections, making it easier to view different parts of the worksheet at the same time.

7 Freeze Panes Freezing panes prevents the data in the pane from scrolling as you move to different areas in a worksheet.

8 What-If Analysis What-if analysis is a technique used to evaluate the effects of changing selected factors in a worksheet.

9 Goal Seek The Goal Seek tool is used to find the value needed in one cell to attain a result you want in another cell.

10 Conditional Formatting Conditional formatting changes the appearance of a range of cells based on a condition that you specify.

Correcting Formulas

After talking with Evan, the owner of the Café, about the first quarter forecast, you are ready to begin making the changes he suggested. Evan returned the workbook file to you containing several changes he made to the format of the worksheet.

1

- **Start Excel 2013.**

- **Open the workbook** ex03_First Quarter Forecast.

- **If necessary, maximize the application and workbook windows.**

- **If necessary, scroll to see row 25.**

Your screen should be similar to Figure 3.1

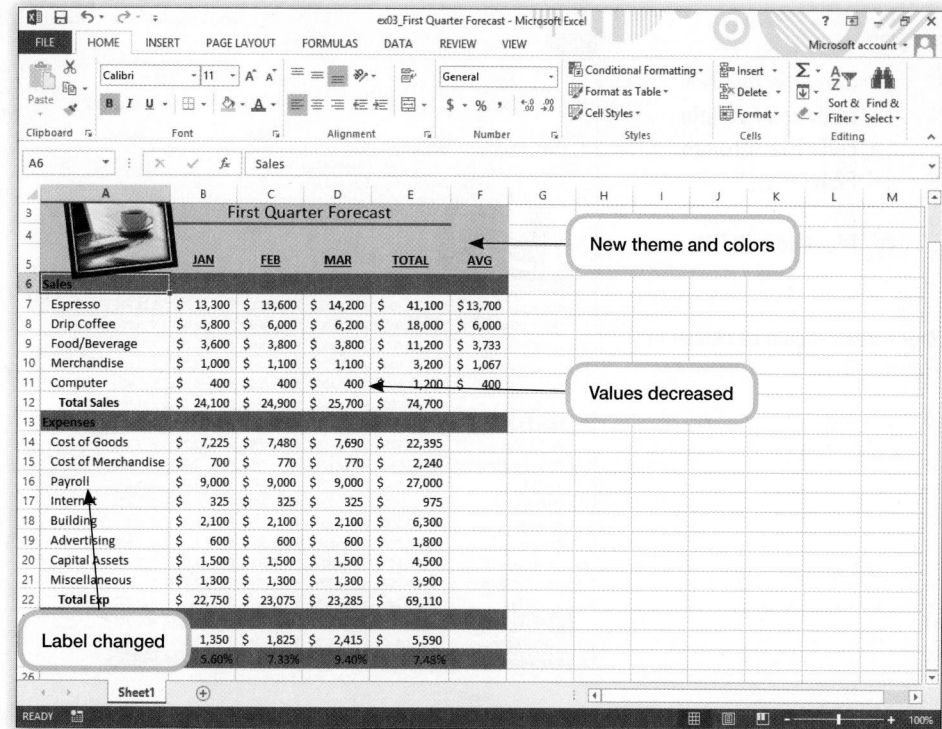

Figure 3.1

As you can see, Evan made several formatting changes to the worksheet. He added a graphic; changed the theme, fill, and text colors; and made several changes to the row headings. For example, the Pay heading has been changed to Payroll. Evan also decided to decrease the computer sales values to $400 for February and March.

IDENTIFYING FORMULA ERRORS

Now you are ready to enter the average formula for the expense values. To do this, you will copy the function down column F.

1

● Copy the function from cell F11 into cells F12 through F24.

● Move to cell F13.

Your screen should be similar to Figure 3.2

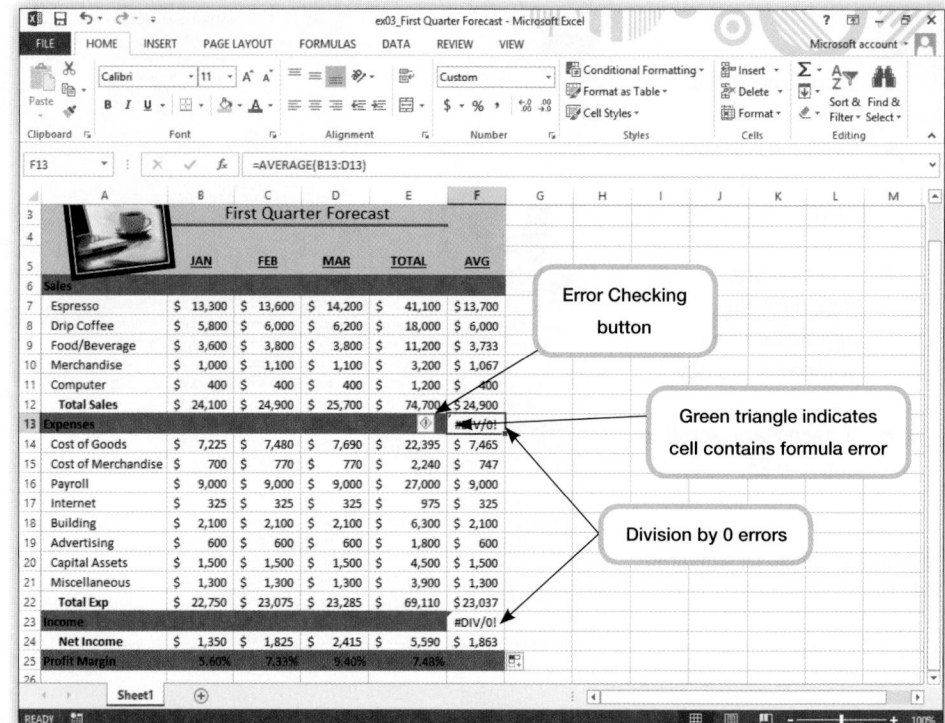

Figure 3.2

The average value has been correctly calculated for each row. Notice, however, that two cells display the error value #DIV/0!, indicating the cells contain a formula error. When a formula cannot properly calculate a result, an error value may be displayed and a green triangle appears in the upper-left corner of the cell. In addition, the ⟨!⟩ Error Checking button appears when you select a cell containing an error.

Each type of error value has a different cause, as described in the following table.

Error Value	Cause
#####	Column not wide enough to display result, or negative date or time is used
#VALUE!	Wrong type of argument or operand is used
#DIV/0!	Number is divided by zero
#NAME?	Text in formula not recognized
#N/A	Value not available
#REF!	Cell reference is not valid
#NUM!	Invalid number values
#NULL!	Intersection operator is not valid

Excel 2013 includes several tools to help you find and correct errors in formula entries. These tools provide the capability to display the relationships between formulas and cells and to identify and suggest corrections to potential problems in formulas.

To correct this problem, you need to find out the cause of the error. Pointing to the ⚠ Error Checking button displays a ScreenTip identifying the cause of the error. Clicking the ⚠ Error Checking button displays a list of options for error checking the worksheet. In this case, the formula is attempting to divide by zero or empty cells.

2

- Point to ⚠ Error Checking to see the ScreenTip.

- Click ⚠ Error Checking.

- Choose Edit in Formula Bar from the list of options.

Your screen should be similar to Figure 3.3

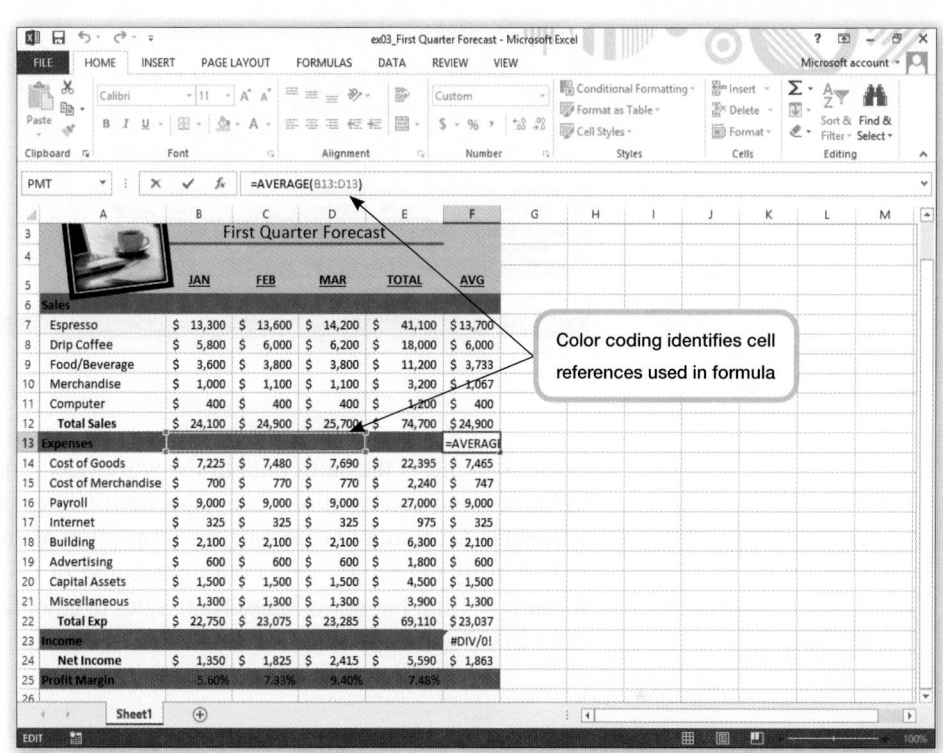

Figure 3.3

In Edit mode, the formula references are color-coded to the referenced worksheet cells and you can now easily see the error is caused by references to blank cells when the function was copied.

Since you do not need this formula, you will delete it. Likewise, you need to delete the function that was copied into cell F23.

3

- Press Esc to exit Edit mode.

- Press Delete.

- Move to cell F23.

- Delete the formula.

Your screen should be similar to Figure 3.4

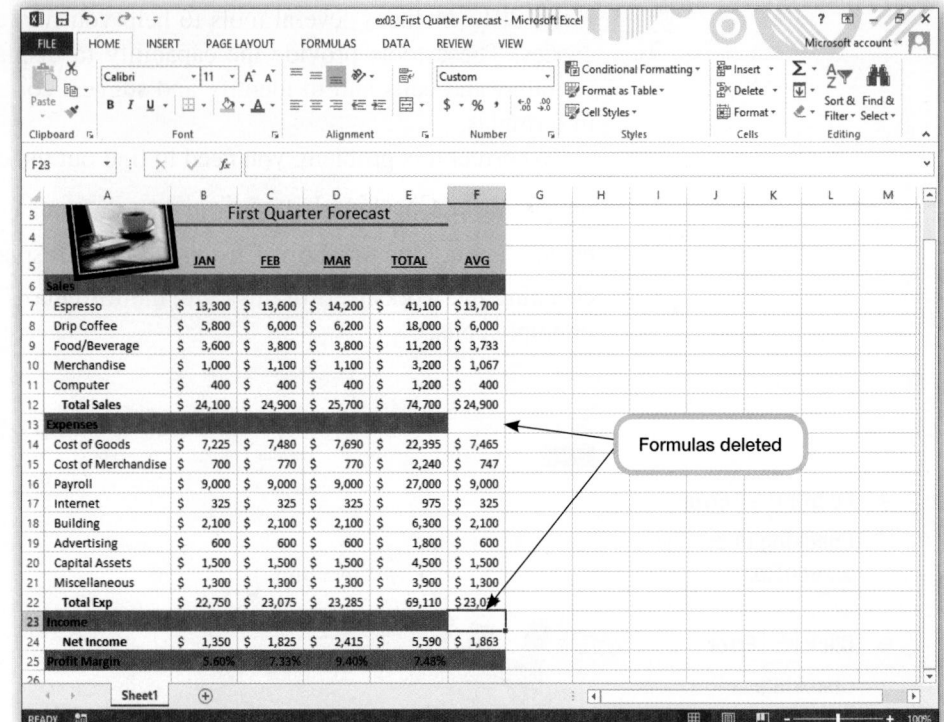

Figure 3.4

While looking at the sales data in the worksheet, you decide it may be interesting to know what contribution each sales item makes to total sales. To find out, you will enter a formula to calculate the proportion of sales by each in column G. You will start by entering a new column heading in cell G5. Then you will enter the formula = Total Espresso Sales/Total Sales to calculate the proportion for Espresso sales in G7 and copy it to G8 to calculate the proportion for Drip Coffee sales.

4

● Enter the heading **Proportion** in cell G5.

● Enter the formula **=E7/E12** in cell G7.

● Drag the fill handle to copy the formula in cell G7 to G8.

Your screen should be similar to Figure 3.5

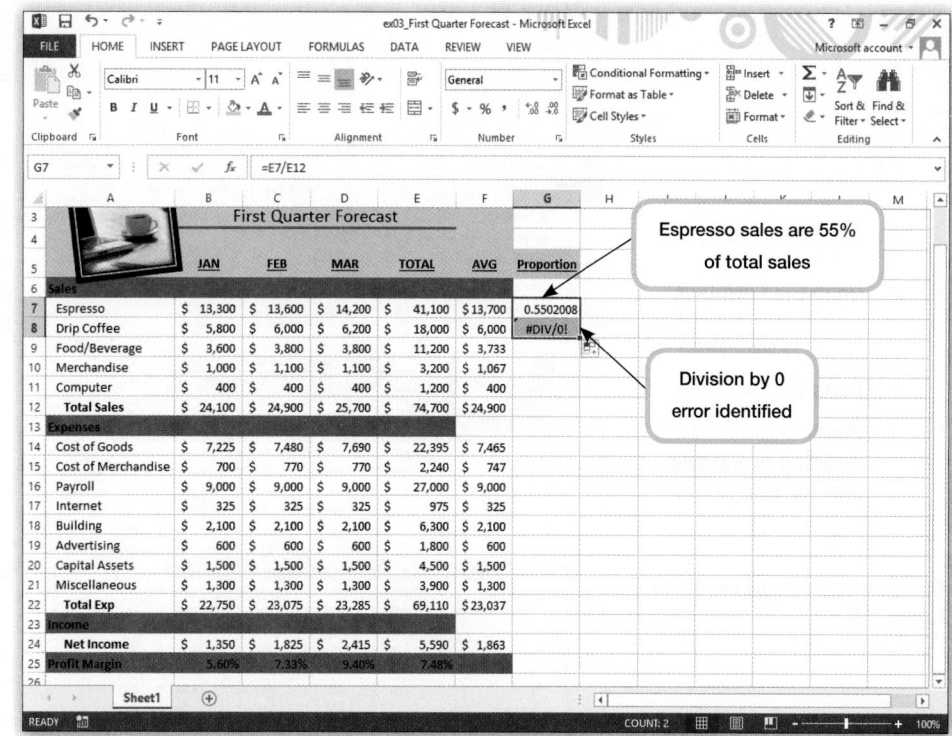

Figure 3.5

The value 0.5502008 is correctly displayed in cell G7. This shows that the Espresso sales are approximately 55 percent of Total Sales. However, a division by zero error has occurred in cell G8.

Another way to check a formula to locate errors or to confirm that the correct cell references are being used is to use the features in the Formula Auditing group of the Formulas tab.

- **Move to G8.**

- **Open the Formulas tab.**

- **Open the** 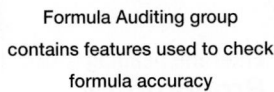 **menu in the Formula Auditing group and choose Trace Error.**

Your screen should be similar to Figure 3.6

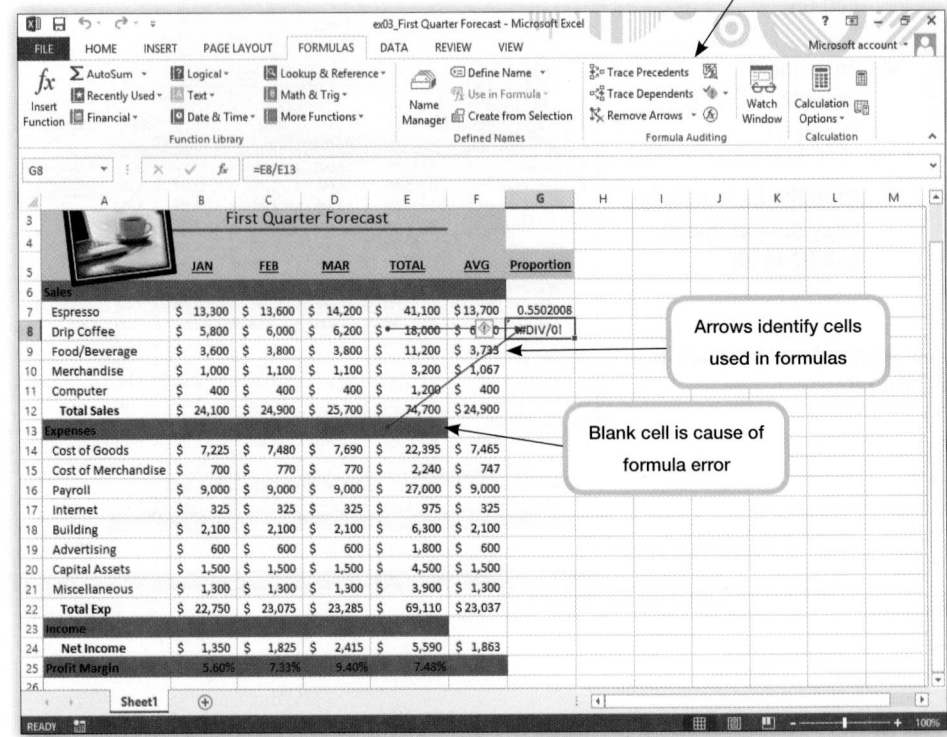

Formula Auditing group contains features used to check formula accuracy

Arrows identify cells used in formulas

Blank cell is cause of formula error

Figure 3.6

Additional Information

You also can use

Trace Precedents or

Trace Dependents to show relationships between formulas and cells.

Excel displays arrows from each cell that affects the value in the current cell. You can now see the error occurred because the relative reference to cell E12 adjusted correctly to the new location when the formula was copied and now references cell E13, a blank cell.

USING ABSOLUTE REFERENCES

The formula in G7 needs to be entered so that the reference to the Total Sales value in cell E12 does not change when the formula is copied. To do this, you need to make the cell reference absolute.

Concept 1 Absolute Reference

An **absolute reference** is a cell or range reference in a formula whose location does not change when the formula is copied.

To stop the relative adjustment of cell references, enter a $ (dollar sign) character before the column letter and the row number. This changes the cell reference to absolute. When a formula containing an absolute cell reference is copied to another row and column location in the worksheet, the cell reference does not change. It is an exact duplicate of the cell reference in the original formula.

A cell reference also can be a **mixed reference**. In this type of reference, either the column letter or the row number is preceded with the $. This makes only the row or the column absolute. When a formula containing a mixed cell reference is copied to another location in the worksheet, only the part of the cell reference that is not absolute changes relative to its new location in the worksheet.

The table below shows examples of relative and absolute references and the results when a reference in cell G8 to cell E8 is copied to cell H9.

Cell Contents of G8	Copied to Cell H9	Type of Reference
E8	E8	Absolute reference
E$8	F$8	Mixed reference
$E8	$E9	Mixed reference
E8	F9	Relative reference

You will change the formula in cell G7 to include an absolute reference for cell E12. Then you will copy the formula to cells G8 through G10.

You can change a cell reference to absolute or mixed by typing in the dollar signs directly or by using the ABS (Absolute) key, F4. To use the ABS key, the program must be in Edit mode and the cell reference that you want to change must be selected. If you continue to press F4, the cell reference will cycle through all possible combinations of cell reference types.

1

● **Click**
  ⫯ Remove Arrows in
  the Formula Auditing
  group to remove the
  trace arrows.

● **Move to G7.**

● **Click anywhere in
  the reference to E12
  in the formula bar to
  enter Edit mode.**

● **Press F4 four times
  to cycle through all
  reference types.**

● **Press F4 again to
  display an absolute
  reference.**

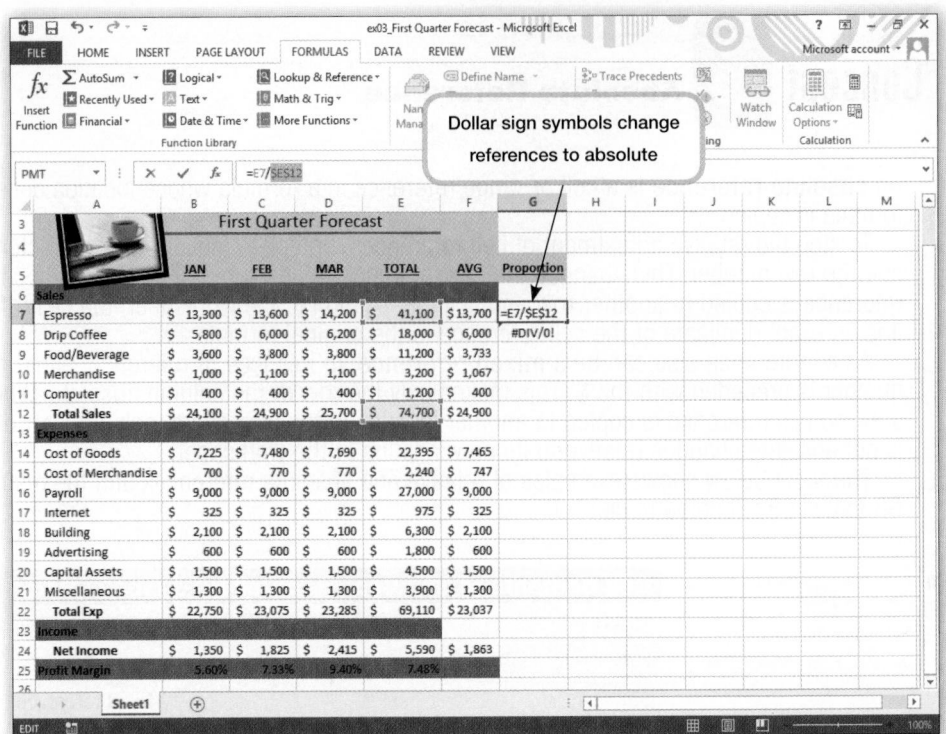

Figure 3.7

Your screen should be similar to
Figure 3.7

The cell reference now displays $ characters before the column letter and row
number, making this cell reference absolute. Leaving the cell reference absolute,
as it is now, will stop the relative adjustment of the cell reference when you copy
it again.

2

- Click ☑ **Enter** or press ⏎Enter.

- **Copy the revised formula to cells G8 through G11.**

- **Move to G8 and click ⛶ Trace Precedents in the Formula Auditing group.**

Your screen should be similar to Figure 3.8

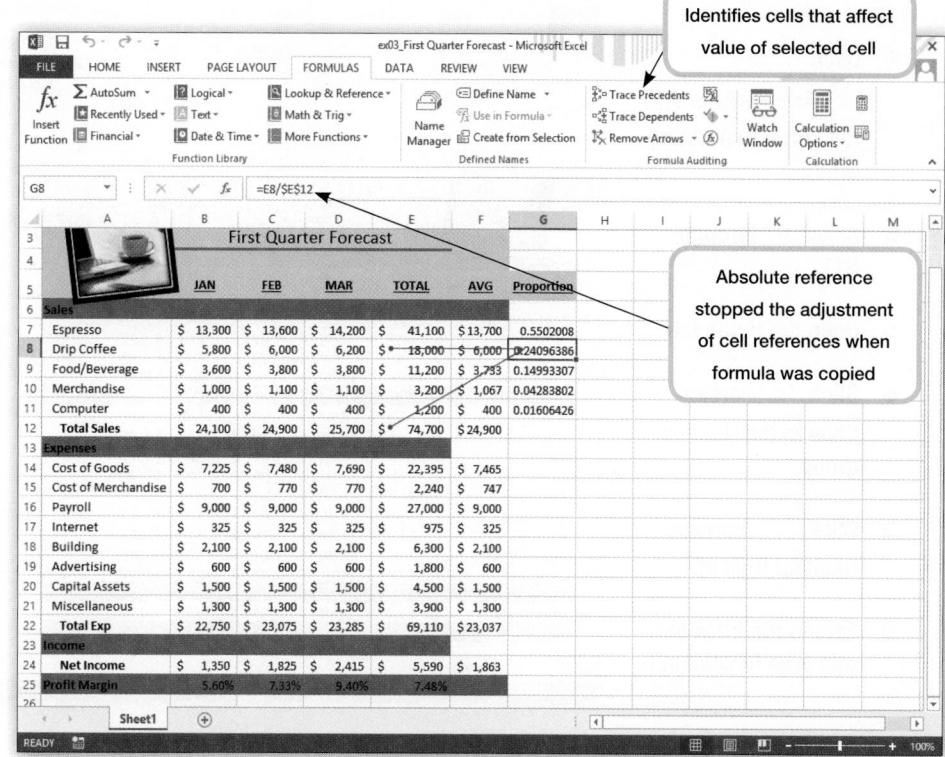

Identifies cells that affect value of selected cell

Absolute reference stopped the adjustment of cell references when formula was copied

Figure 3.8

The trace arrows show that when the formula was copied it correctly adjusted the relative cell reference to Drip Coffee sales in cell E8 and did not adjust the reference to E12 because it is an absolute reference.

The last change you need to make to the proportion data is to format it to the Percent style.

- **Click** ⟨🔍 Remove Arrows⟩ in the Formula Auditing group.

- **Select G7 through G11.**

- **Open the Home tab.**

- **Click** ⟨%⟩ **Percent Style in the Number group.**

- **Click** ⟨←.0 .00⟩ **Increase Decimal (twice).**

- **Extend the fill in the title area to column G.**

- **Extend the fill in rows 6, 13, 23, and 25 to column G.**

- **Move to cell A6 and save the workbook as** Forecast3 **to your solution file location.**

Your screen should be similar to Figure 3.9

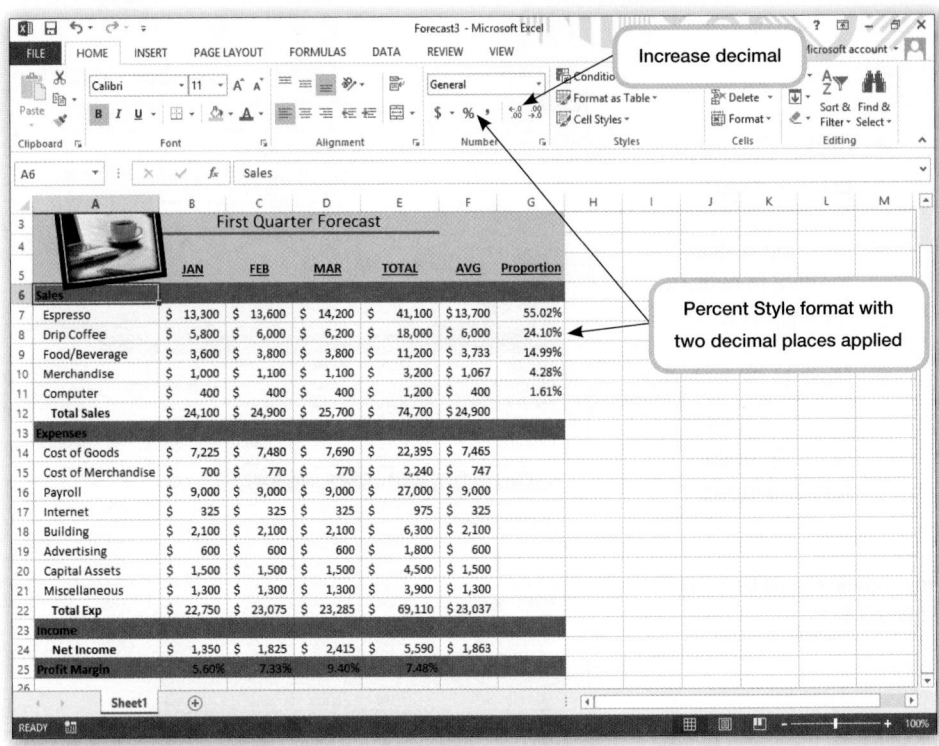

Figure 3.9

The calculated proportion shows the same values that a pie chart of this data would show.

Creating a Second-Quarter Worksheet

Next, you want to add the second-quarter forecast to the workbook. You want this data in a separate sheet in the same workbook file. To make it easier to enter the forecast for the next quarter, you will copy the contents of the first quarter forecast in Sheet1 into another sheet in the workbook. Then you will change the month headings, the title, and the number data for the second quarter. Finally, you want to include a formula to calculate a year-to-date total for the six months.

COPYING WORKSHEETS

You want to copy the worksheet data from Sheet1 to Sheet2. You can quickly make a duplicate of a worksheet including all data, objects, and formatting with the Move or Copy Sheet command.

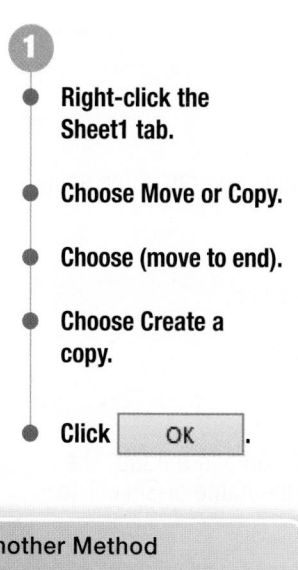

- **Right-click the Sheet1 tab.**

- **Choose Move or Copy.**

- **Choose (move to end).**

- **Choose Create a copy.**

- **Click** OK **.**

Another Method

You also can use Format /Move or Copy Sheet in the Cells group of the Home tab.

Your screen should be similar to Figure 3.10

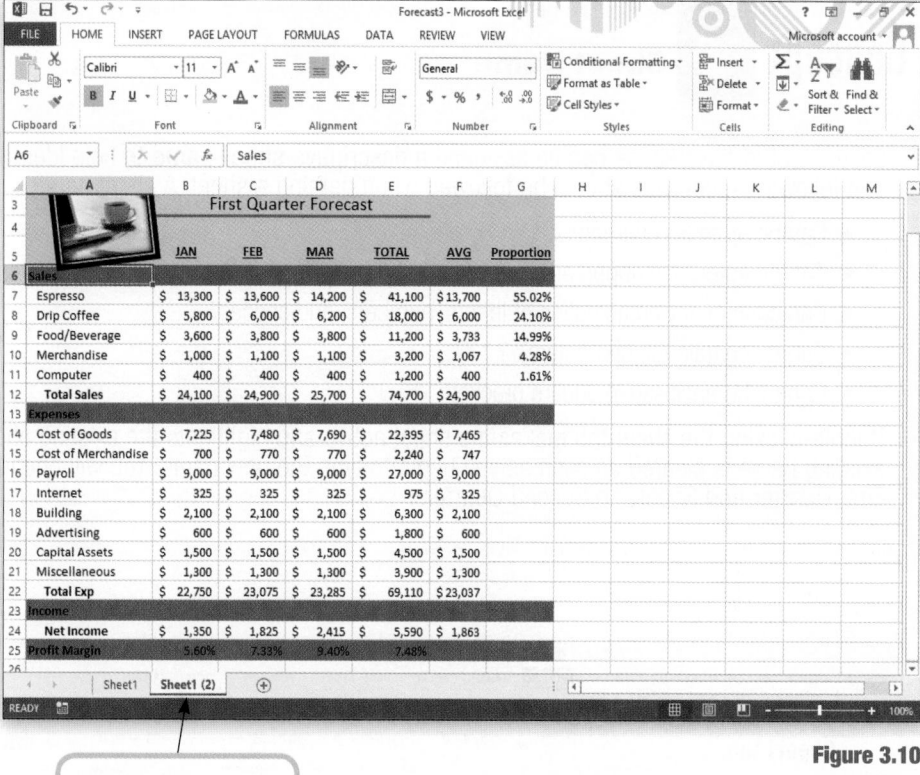

Copied sheet is active

Figure 3.10

Another Method

You also can select all the data and copy it to a new blank worksheet. With this method, you often need to resize column widths and objects.

An exact duplicate of the contents and formatting of the Sheet1 worksheet is displayed in the newly inserted sheet. It is currently named Sheet1 (2).

RENAMING SHEETS AND COLORING SHEET TABS

As more sheets are added to a workbook, remembering what information is in each sheet becomes more difficult. To help clarify the contents of the sheets, you can rename the sheets.

Concept  Sheet Name

Each sheet in a workbook can be assigned a descriptive **sheet name** to help identify the contents of the sheet. The following guidelines should be followed when naming a sheet. A sheet name

- Can be up to 31 characters.
- Can be entered in uppercase or lowercase letters or a combination (it will appear as entered).
- Can contain any combination of letters, numbers, and spaces.
- Cannot contain the characters : ? * / \.
- Cannot be enclosed in square brackets [ ].

Double-clicking the sheet tab makes the sheet active and highlights the existing sheet name in the tab. The existing name is cleared as soon as you begin to type the new name. You will change the name of Sheet1 to First Quarter and Sheet2 to Second Quarter.

- **Double-click the Sheet1 tab.**

- **Type First Quarter**

- **Press ←Enter.**

- **Change the name of the Sheet1(2) tab to Second Quarter**

Another Method

You also can use Format ▾ / Rename Sheet in the Cells group of the Home tab.

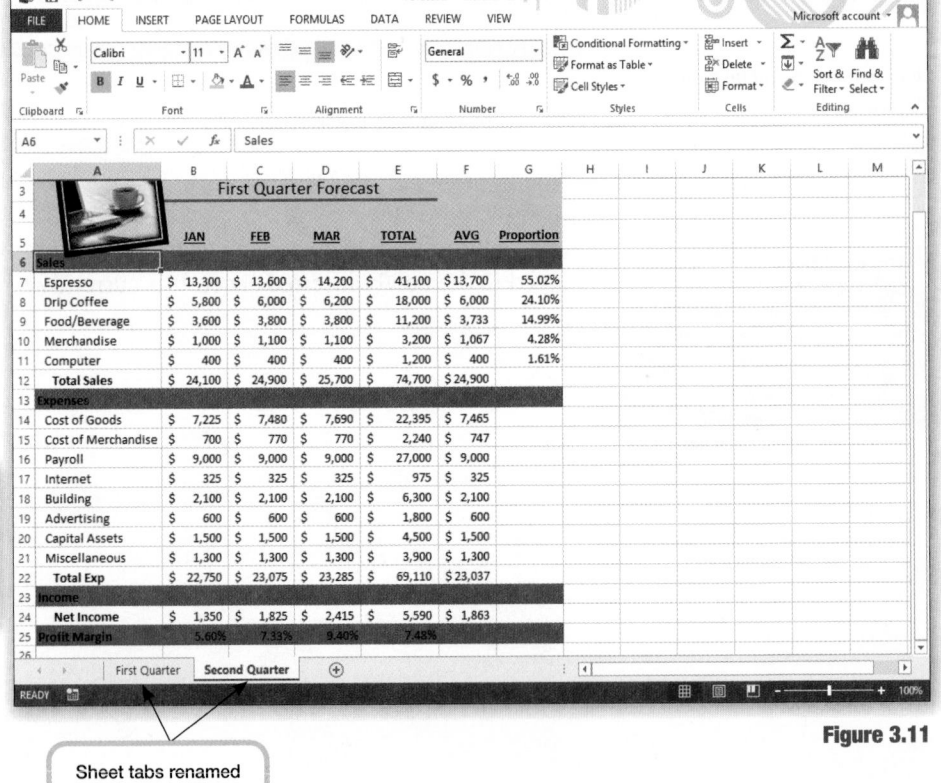

Your screen should be similar to Figure 3.11

Sheet tabs renamed

Figure 3.11

To further differentiate the sheets, you can add color to the sheet tabs.

2

- **Right-click on the First Quarter tab.**

- **Select Tab Color from the shortcut menu.**

- **Choose the Brown, Accent 3 theme color from the color palette.**

- **In the same manner, change the color of the Second Quarter sheet tab to the Orange, Accent 1 theme color.**

Your screen should be similar to Figure 3.12

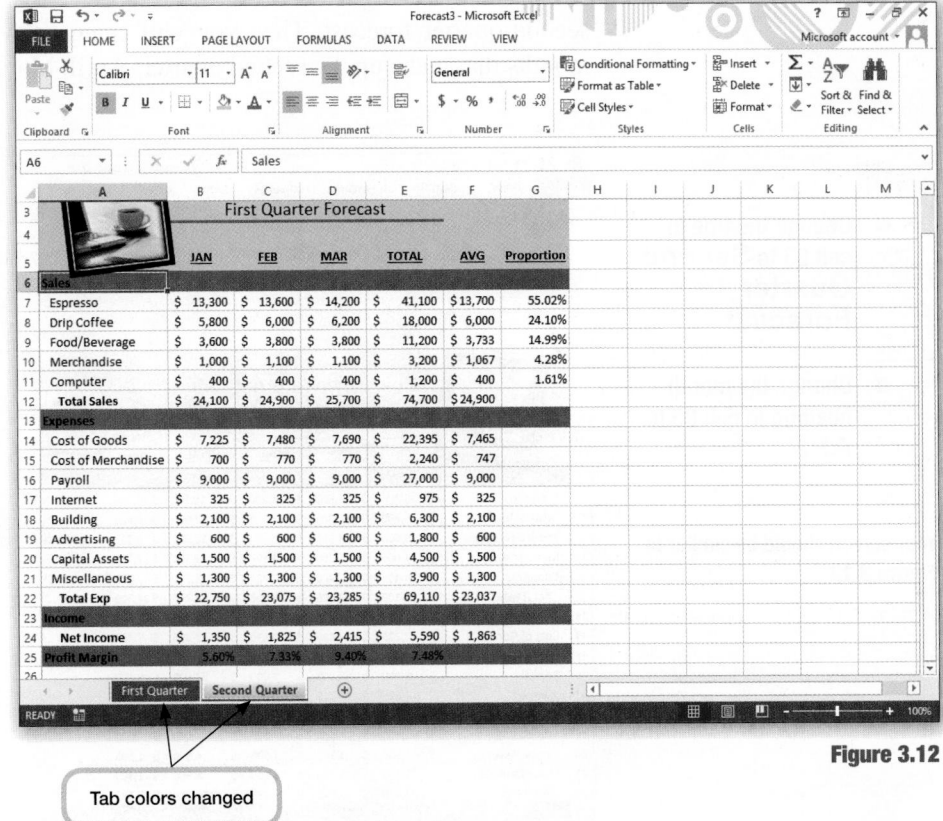

Figure 3.12

Tab colors changed

Another Method

You also can use ▦ Format ▾ /Tab Color in the Cells group.

The sheet tab name of the selected sheet is underlined in the tab color of orange and the First Quarter sheet tab is brown. When a sheet is not selected, the sheet tab is displayed with the background color.

FILLING A SERIES

Now you can change the worksheet title and data in the Second Quarter sheet. First you will change the worksheet title to identify the worksheet contents as the second-quarter forecast. Then you will change the month headings to the three months that make up the second quarter: April, May, and June.

1

● Change the title in cell B3 to Second Quarter Forecast

● Change the month heading in cell B5 to APR

Your screen should be similar to Figure 3.13

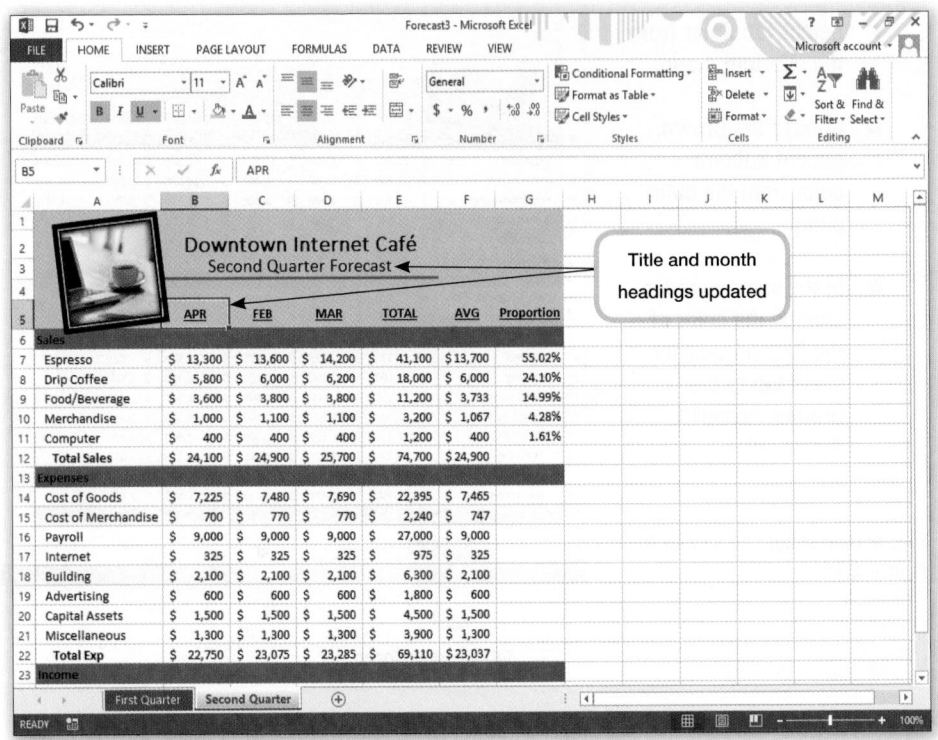

Figure 3.13

Now you need to change the remaining month headings to MAY and JUN. You will use the AutoFill feature to enter the month headings.

Concept ③ AutoFill

The **AutoFill** feature makes entering a series of numbers, numbers and text combinations, dates, or time periods easier by logically repeating and extending the series. AutoFill recognizes trends and automatically extends data and alphanumeric headings as far as you specify.

Dragging the fill handle activates the AutoFill feature if Excel recognizes the entry in the cell as an entry that can be incremented. When AutoFill extends the entries, it uses the same style as the original entry. For example, if you enter the heading for July as JUL (abbreviated with all letters uppercase), all the extended entries in the series will be abbreviated and uppercase. Dragging down or right increments in increasing order, and up or left increments in decreasing order. A linear series increases or decreases values by a constant value, and a growth series multiplies values by a constant factor. Examples of how AutoFill extends a series are shown in the table below.

Initial Selection	Extended Series
Qtr1	Qtr2, Qtr3, Qtr4
Mon	Tue, Wed, Thu
Jan, Apr	Jul, Oct, Jan

A starting value of a series may contain more than one item that can be incremented, such as JAN-15, in which both the month and year can increment. You can specify which value to increment by selecting the appropriate option from the 🔳 AutoFill Options menu.

The entry in cell B5, APR, is the starting value of a series of months. You will drag the fill handle to the right to increment the months. The mouse pointer displays the entry that will appear in each cell as you drag.

2
- Drag the fill handle of cell B5 to extend the range from cell B5 through cell D5.

- Save the workbook.

Your screen should be similar to Figure 3.14

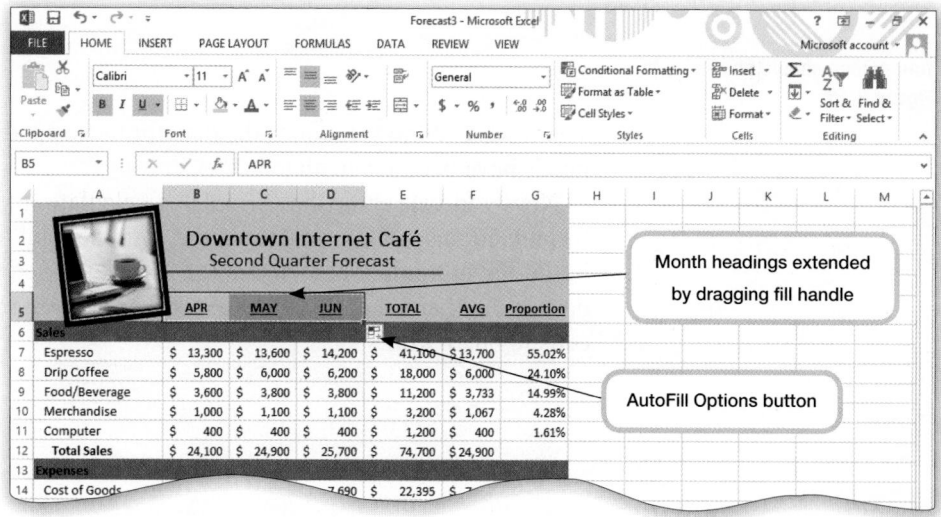

Figure 3.14

Additional Information

If you do not want a series created when you drag the fill handle, hold down Ctrl as you drag and the entries will be copied, not incremented. Alternatively, you can choose Copy Cells from the 🔳 AutoFill Options menu.

The month headings now correctly reflect the three months for the second quarter. This is because the entry in cell B5 was a month that was recognized as an entry that can be incremented. Additionally, the months appear in uppercase characters, the same as the starting month. This is because AutoFill copies formatting when extending the series.

USING A 3-D REFERENCE

Additional Information

To speed up the process of entering the following data, use [Tab] to move to the cell to the right. Alternatively, for each item, first select the range, then enter the first value, and press [Enter] to move to the next cell in the selection.

Finally, you need to update the forecast to reflect the April through June sales. You anticipate that sales will increase in all areas, except food and beverage sales, which will remain the same. Then you will enter a formula to calculate the year-to-date income total using data from both sheets.

● **Enter the following values in the specified cells.**

Sales	Cell	Number
Espresso	B7	14400
	C7	15200
	D7	15500
Drip Coffee	B8	6200
	C8	6200
	D8	6200
Merchandise	B10	1500
	C10	1500
	D10	1500
Computer	B11	600
	C11	600
	D11	600

Your screen should be similar to Figure 3.15

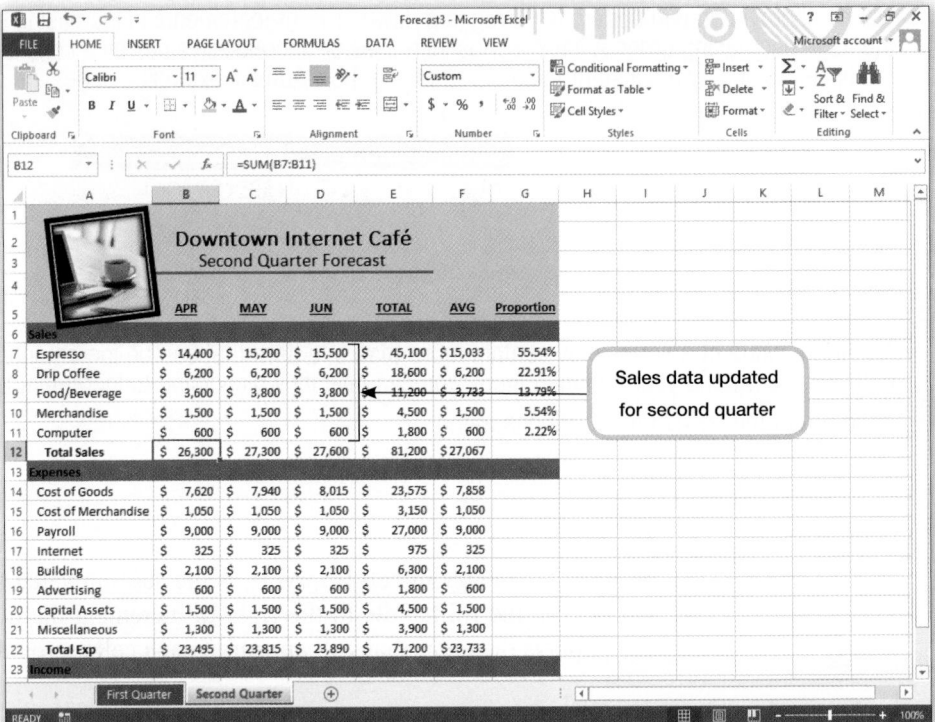

Figure 3.15

The worksheet now contains the data for the second quarter and all dependent formulas have been recalculated.

Now you can enter the formula to calculate a year-to-date income total. The formula to make this calculation will sum the total income numbers from cell E24 in the First Quarter sheet and cell E24 in the Second Quarter sheet. To reference data in another sheet in the same workbook, you enter a formula that references cells in other worksheets.

Concept  4 Sheet and 3-D References

Sheet and 3-D references in formulas are used to refer to data from multiple sheets and to calculate new values based on this data. A **sheet reference** in a formula consists of the name of the sheet, followed by an exclamation point and the cell or range reference. If the sheet name contains nonalphabetic characters, such as a space, the sheet name (or path) must be enclosed in single quotation marks.

If you want to use the same cell or range of cells on multiple sheets, you can use a **3-D reference**. A 3-D reference consists of the names of the beginning and ending sheets enclosed in quotes and separated by a colon. This is followed by an exclamation point and the cell or range reference. The cell or range reference is the same on each sheet in the specified sheet range. If a sheet is inserted or deleted, the range is automatically updated. 3-D references make it easy to analyze data in the same cell or range of cells on multiple worksheets.

Reference	Description
=Sheet2!B17	Displays the entry in cell B17 of Sheet2 in the active cell of the current sheet
=Sheet1!A1 + Sheet2!B2	Sums the values in cell A1 of Sheet1 and B2 of Sheet2
=SUM(Sheet1:Sheet4!H6:K6)	Sums the values in cells H6 through K6 in Sheets 1, 2, 3, and 4
=SUM(Sheet1!H6:K6)	Sums the values in cells H6 through K6 in Sheet1
=SUM(Sheet1:Sheet4!H6)	Sums the values in cell H6 of Sheets 1, 2, 3, and 4

Just like a formula that references cells within a sheet, a formula that references cells in multiple sheets is automatically recalculated when data in a referenced cell changes.

You will enter a descriptive text entry in cell D26 and then use a 3-D reference in a SUM function to calculate the year-to-date total in cell E26.

The SUM function argument will consist of a 3-D reference to cell E24 in the First and Second Quarter sheets. Although a 3-D reference can be entered by typing it using the proper syntax, it is much easier to enter it by pointing to the cells on the sheets. To enter a 3-D reference, select the cell or range in the beginning sheet and then hold down ⇧Shift and click on the sheet tab of the last sheet in the range. This will include the indicated cell range on all sheets between and including the first and last sheets specified.

2

- **In cell D26, enter and right-align the entry Income Year-to-Date**

- **Move to E26.**

- **Click Σ ▾ Sum.**

- **Click cell E24.**

- **Hold down ⇧Shift and click the First Quarter tab.**

- **Release ⇧Shift.**

- **Press ←Enter.**

- **Move to E26.**

Your screen should be similar to Figure 3.16

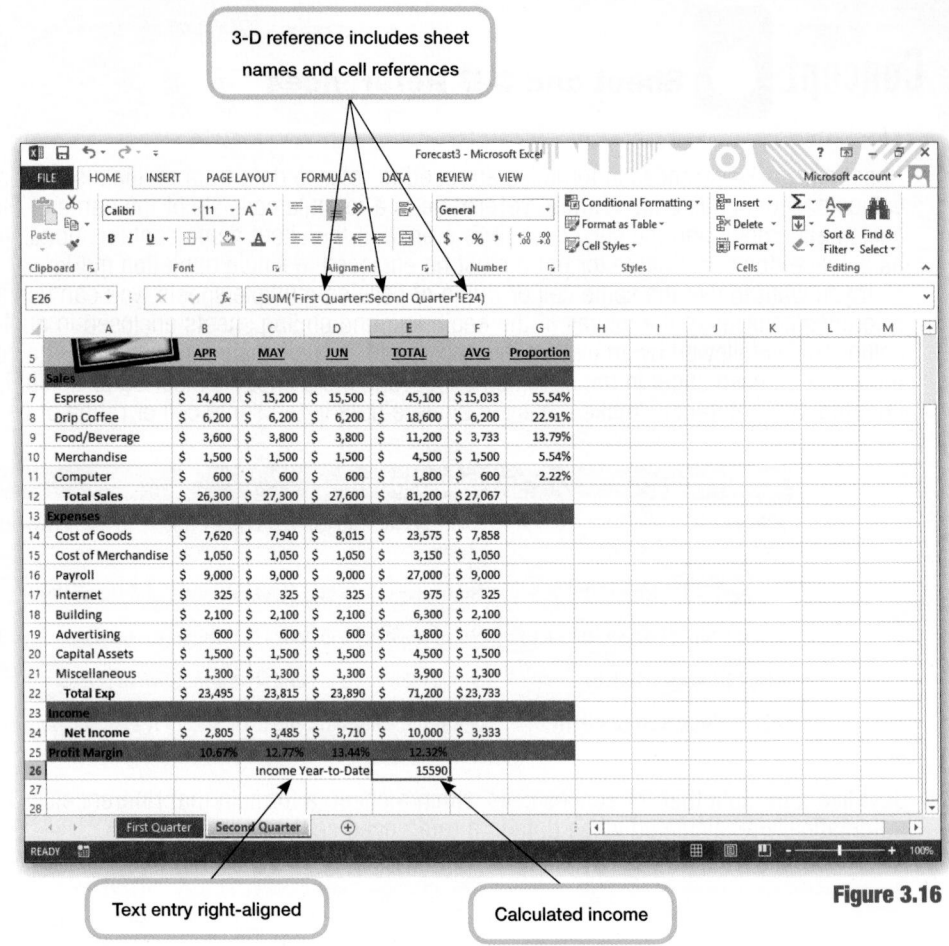

3-D reference includes sheet names and cell references

Text entry right-aligned

Calculated income

Figure 3.16

The calculated number 15590 appears in cell E26, and the function containing a 3-D reference appears in the formula bar.

HIDING GRIDLINES AND HEADINGS

Just as you completed the forecast for the first half of the year, Evan, the Café owner, stopped in and you decide to show him the forecast. To simplify the screen display while showing Evan the worksheet, you will hide the gridlines and column and row headings.

1

- **Move to cell A1 and open the View tab.**

- **Choose** ☑ Gridlines **from the Show group to clear the selection.**

- **Choose** ☑ Headings **from the Show group to clear the selection.**

Your screen should be similar to Figure 3.17

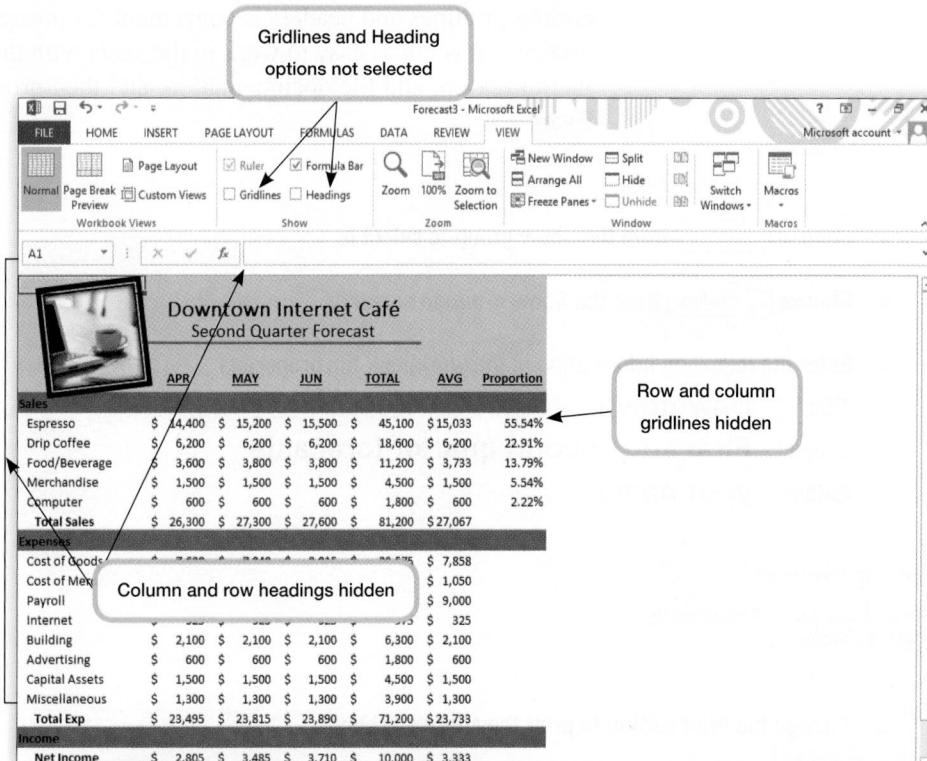

Gridlines and Heading options not selected

Row and column gridlines hidden

Column and row headings hidden

Figure 3.17

While these features are off, you will format the year-to-date income value to Accounting with zero decimal places. Rather than opening the Home tab to access these features, you will copy the format from another cell. The Paste Special menu option, Formatting, will do this quickly for you.

2

- **Select any cell that is formatted in the Accounting format and choose Copy from the context menu.**

- **Right-click on cell E26 and choose** [icon] **Formatting from the Paste Options section of the context menu.**

Your screen should be similar to Figure 3.18

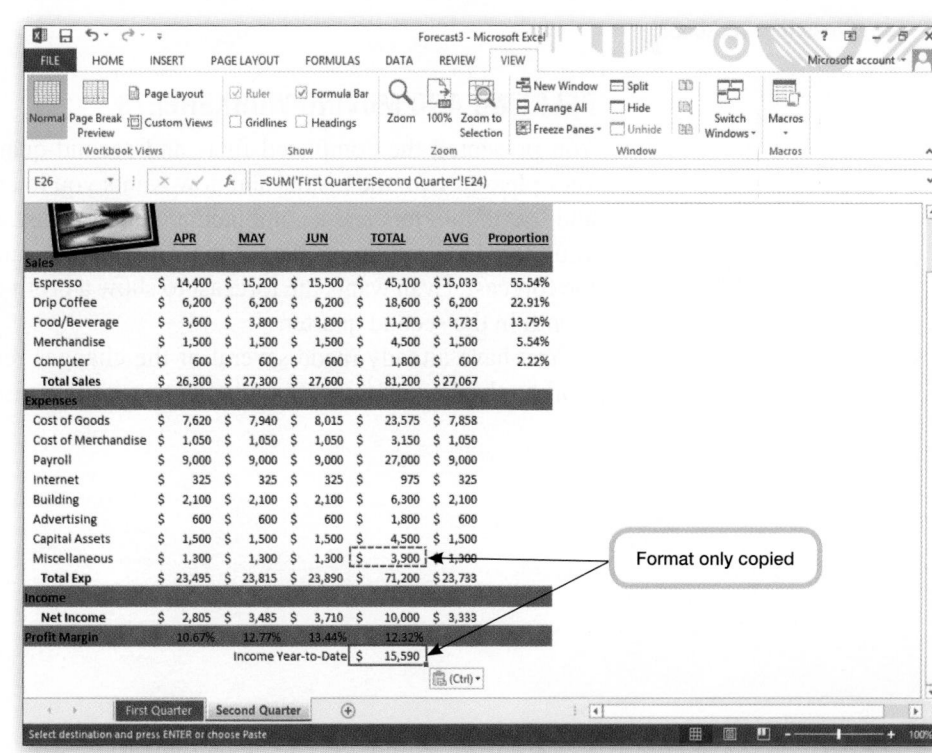

Format only copied

Figure 3.18

Creating a Second-Quarter Worksheet **EX3.23**

Hiding gridlines and headers is convenient for presenting the worksheet to others; however, it is not as easy to work in the sheet with these features off. You will turn them back on, add file documentation, and then print a copy of the workbook for Evan.

3

● Choose ☐ Gridlines from the Show group to select it.

● Choose ☐ Headings from the Show group to select it.

● Enter the following information in the workbook file properties:

Title   **Downtown Internet Cafe**

Subject   **First and second quarter forecasts**

Author   **your name**

> **Having Trouble?**
>
> If needed, click Show All Properties to display the Subject box.

● Change the Print setting to print the entire workbook.

● Preview both worksheets and scale each sheet to fit on a single page.

● Add a predefined header containing your name, page number, and the date to both worksheets.

● Print the workbook.

● Move to cell A6 in both worksheets and save the workbook.

● Close the workbook.

DELETING AND MOVING WORKSHEETS

You presented the completed first- and second-quarter forecasts to Evan. He is very pleased with the results and now wants you to create worksheets for the third and fourth quarters and a combined annual forecast. Additionally, Evan has asked you to include a column chart of the data for each quarter. Finally, after looking at the forecast, Evan wants the forecast to show a profit margin of 15 percent for each month in the second quarter.

You have already made several of the changes requested and saved them as a workbook file. You will open this file to see the revised and expanded forecast.

1

Open the workbook
file ex03_Annual
Forecast.

Your screen should be similar to
Figure 3.19

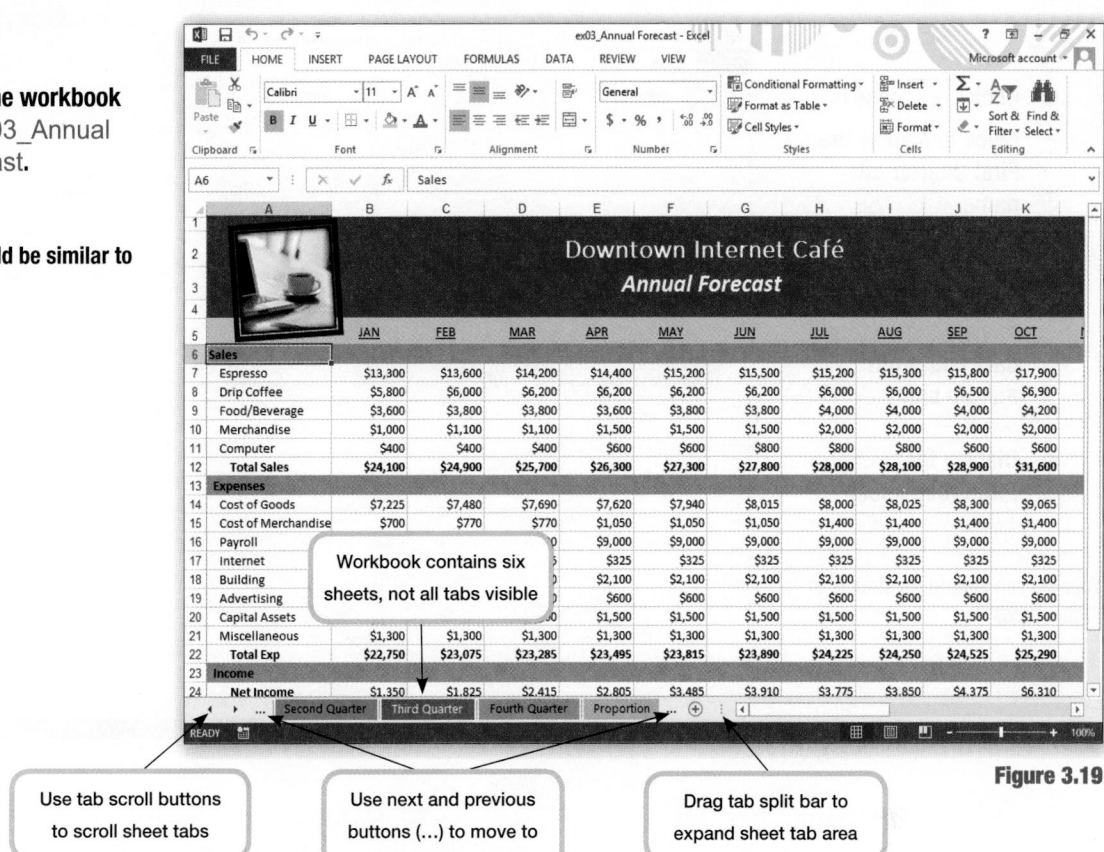

Workbook contains six
sheets, not all tabs visible

Use tab scroll buttons
to scroll sheet tabs

Use next and previous
buttons (...) to move to
next or previous sheet

Drag tab split bar to
expand sheet tab area

Figure 3.19

The workbook file now contains six sheets: First Quarter, Second Quarter, Third
Quarter, Fourth Quarter, Proportion, and Year. The Proportion sheet contains the
proportion of sales values from the first and second quarters. The Year sheet contains the forecast data for the entire 12 months. Each quarter sheet also includes a
chart of the profit margin for that quarter.

Notice also that not all the sheet tab names are visible. This is because there is
not enough space in the sheet tab area to display all the tabs. To see the tabs, you
can drag the tab split bar located at the right edge of the sheet tab area to expand
the area or use the sheet tab scroll buttons to scroll the tabs into view.

2

● Click ◄ once or twice to display the First Quarter tab name.

● Click on each of the Quarter sheet tabs to view the quarterly data and profit margin chart.

● Display the Proportion sheet.

Your screen should be similar to Figure 3.20

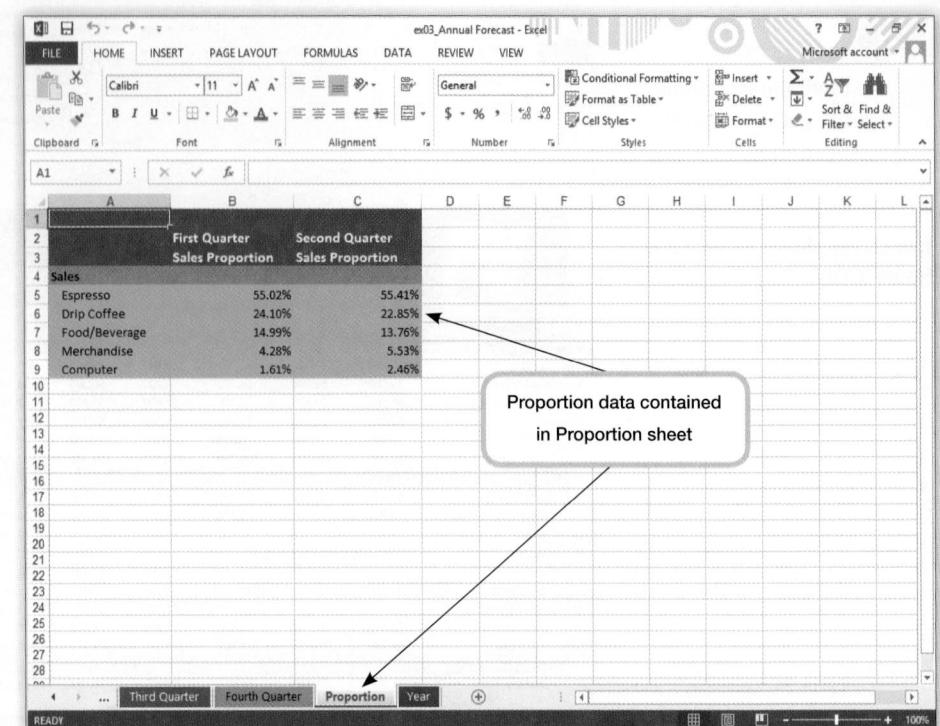

Figure 3.20

You decide this data, although interesting, is not needed in the forecast workbook and want to delete the entire sheet.

3

● In the Cells group of the Home tab, open the 🗑 Delete ▾ menu and choose Delete Sheet.

● Click Delete to confirm that you want to permanently remove the sheet.

Another Method

You also can choose Delete from the sheet tab's shortcut menu to delete a sheet.

Your screen should be similar to Figure 3.21

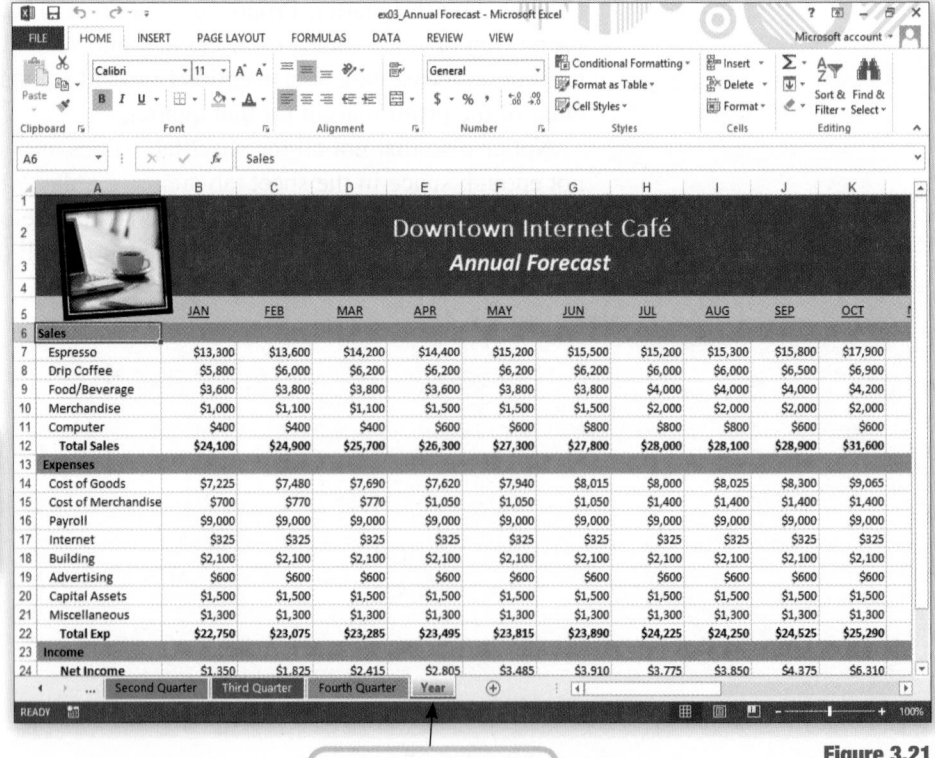

Figure 3.21

The entire sheet is deleted, and the Year sheet is now the active sheet. Next you want to move the Year sheet from the last position in the workbook to the first. You can quickly rearrange the order of sheets in a workbook by dragging the selected sheet tab along the row of sheet tabs to the new location.

Additional Information

You can insert a blank new sheet using [Insert ▾] and choosing Insert Sheet. It is inserted to the left of the active sheet.

4

Drag the Year tab to the left of the First Quarter tab.

Additional Information

The mouse pointer appears as and the symbol ▾ indicates the location where the sheet will be moved.

Another Method

You also can use Move or Copy from the sheet tab's shortcut menu to move a sheet to another location in the workbook.

Your screen should be similar to Figure 3.22

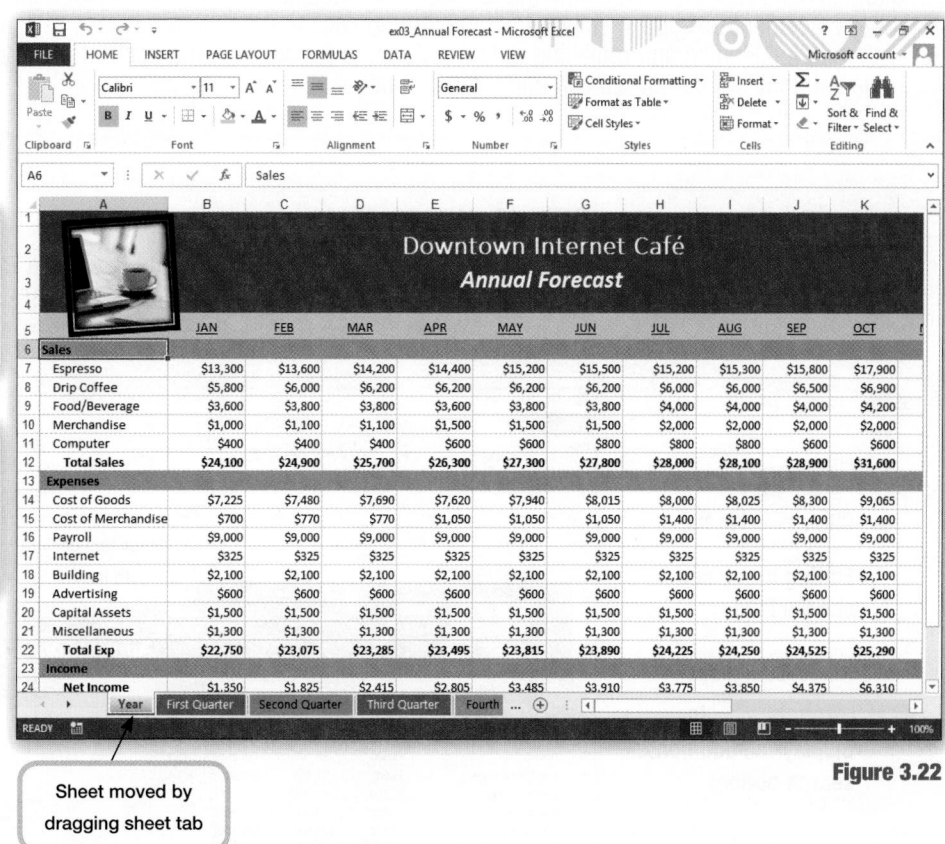

Sheet moved by dragging sheet tab

Figure 3.22

The Year sheet is now the first sheet in the workbook.

Finding and Replacing Information

As you look over the worksheets, you notice that the only abbreviation used in the entire workbook is for expenses in the Total Exp row heading. You want to change it to "Expenses" in all worksheets in the workbook.

You could change the word in each sheet by changing the text directly on the worksheet cells. However, the larger your workbook becomes, the more difficult it will be to find the data you want to modify. Therefore, you will use the Find and Replace feature to quickly locate the word and make the change.

Concept ⑤ Find and Replace

The **Find and Replace** feature helps you quickly find specific information and automatically replace it with new information. The Find command locates all occurrences of the text or numbers you specify. The Replace command is used with the Find command to locate the specified entries and replace the located occurrences with the replacement text you specify. You also can find cells that match a format you specify and replace the format with another. Finding and replacing data and formats is both fast and accurate, but you need to be careful when replacing that you do not replace unintended matches.

FINDING INFORMATION

First, you will locate and correct the abbreviation using the Find command. This command can be used to locate data in any type of worksheet.

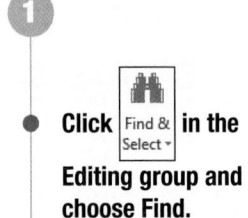

- **Click** Find & Select ▾ **in the Editing group and choose Find.**

- **If necessary, click** Options >> **to display the additional search options.**

Another Method

The keyboard shortcut is Ctrl + F.

Your screen should be similar to Figure 3.23

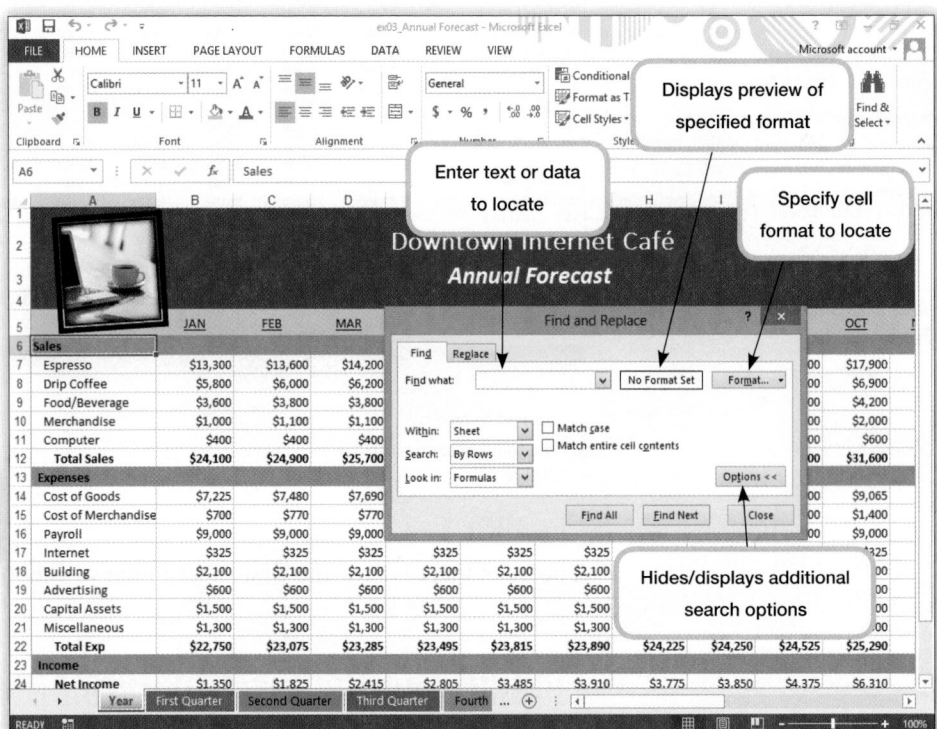

Figure 3.23

In the Find and Replace dialog box, you enter the information you want to locate in the Find what text box. It must be entered exactly as it appears in the worksheet. The additional options in the dialog box can be combined in many ways to help locate information. They are described in the table below.

Option	Effect
Within	Searches the active worksheet or workbook.
Search	Specifies the direction to search in the worksheet: By Columns searches down through columns and By Rows searches to the right across rows.
Look in	Looks for a match in the specified worksheet element: formulas, values, comments.
Match case	Finds words that have the same pattern of uppercase letters as entered in the Find what text box. Using this option makes the search case sensitive.
Match entire cell contents	Looks for an exact and complete match of the characters specified in the Find what text box.
Format	Used to specify a cell format to locate and replace. A sample of the selected format is displayed in the preview box.

You will enter the text to find, "exp," and will search using the default options.

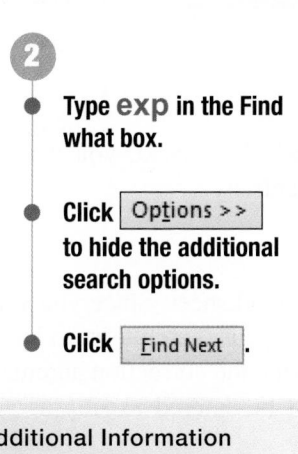

● **Type exp in the Find what box.**

● **Click** Options >> **to hide the additional search options.**

● **Click** Find Next .

Additional Information

Because the Match case option is not selected, Find looks for an exact match regardless of whether the characters are uppercase or lowercase.

Your screen should be similar to Figure 3.24

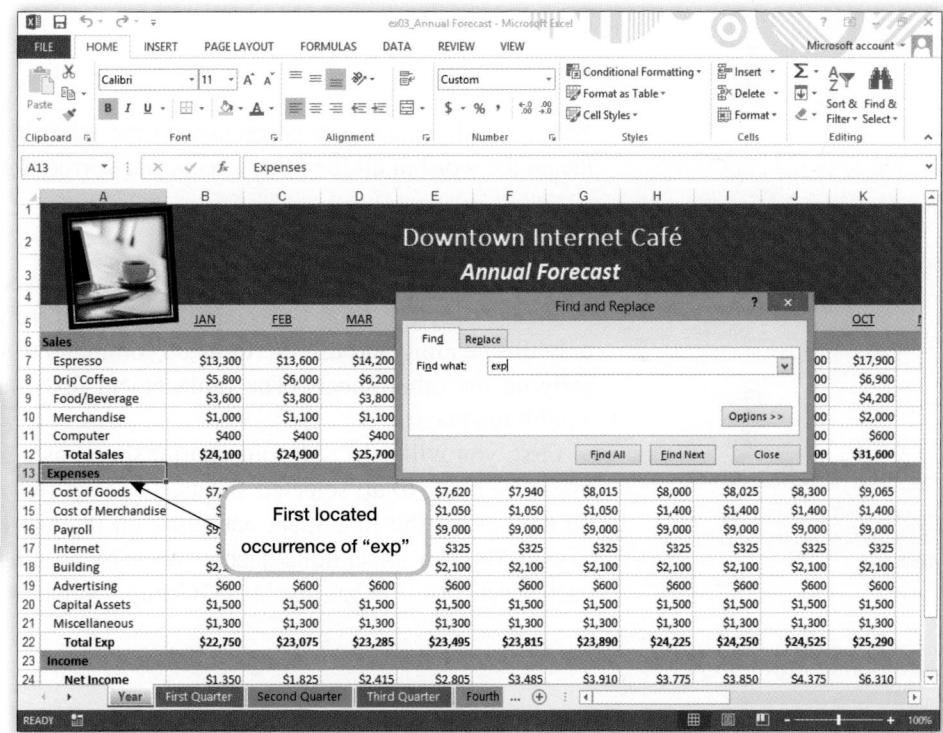

Figure 3.24

Additional Information

Clicking Find All displays all text or format matches in a list. Selecting an item from the list moves the cell selector to the cell containing the entry.

The cell selector jumps to the first occurrence of "exp," in cell A13, which contains the word "Expenses." It located this word because the first three letters match. However, this is not the entry you are trying to locate. You will continue the search to locate the next occurrence. Then you will edit the cell to display the word "Expenses."

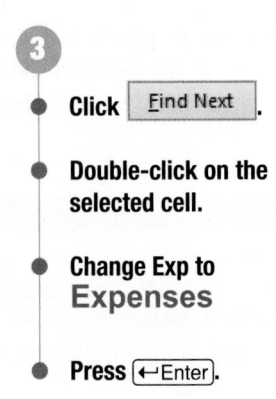

3

- Click [Find Next].

- Double-click on the selected cell.

- Change Exp to **Expenses**

- Press [←Enter].

Your screen should be similar to Figure 3.25

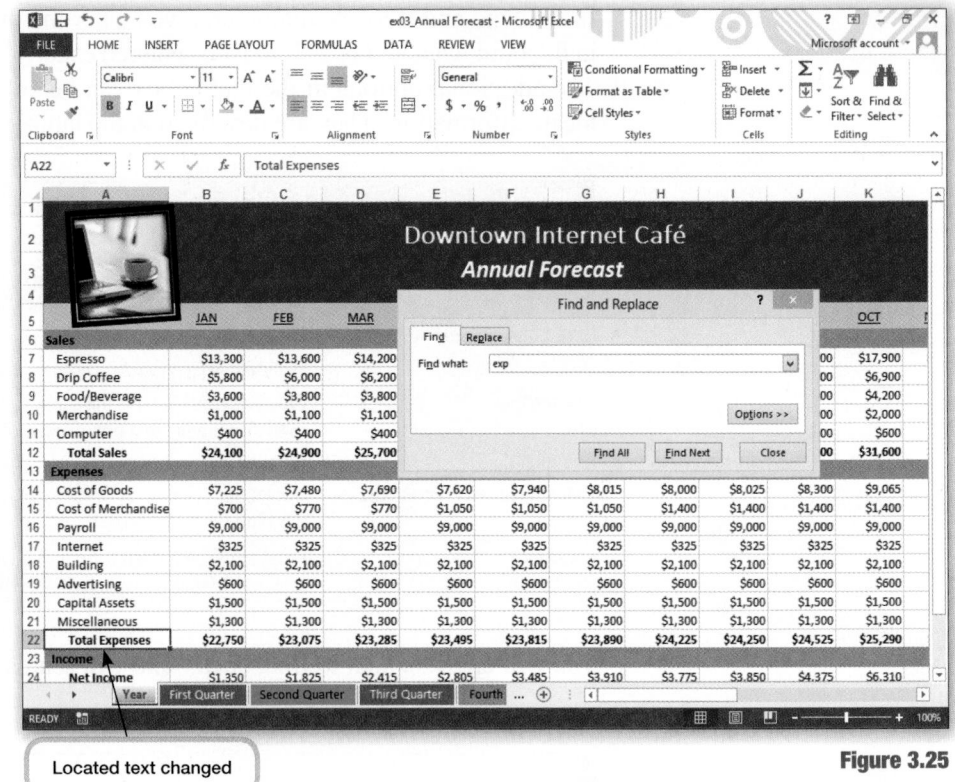

Located text changed

Figure 3.25

You manually made the correction to the label in cell A22. Next, you want to locate the word in all the other sheets and correct the entries.

REPLACING INFORMATION

You realize that "exp" will be located twice in every worksheet. Since you want to change only the Total Exp headings, you will refine your search term to locate only this heading and use the Replace command to make the correction automatically on the other sheets. The replacement text must be entered exactly as you want it to appear.

First, you will select all four quarter sheets as a group so that any changes you make are made to all selected sheets. To select two or more adjacent sheets, click on the tab for the first sheet and click on the last sheet tab while holding down [⇧ Shift]. You can select nonadjacent sheets by holding down [Ctrl] while clicking on each sheet. The title bar displays "[Group]" whenever multiple sheets are selected.

Additional Information

You can select all sheets using Select All Sheets from the sheet tab shortcut menu.

Additional Information

The tabs of all sheets appear with a white top, indicating they are selected; the active sheet tab name is bold.

- **Click on the First Quarter sheet tab,** hold down ⬆Shift, and click on the **Fourth Quarter tab.**

- **Change the entry in the Find what box to** total exp

- **Open the Replace tab.**

- **Type Total Expenses in the Replace with box.**

- **Click** Find Next.

- **Click** Replace All.

Your screen should be similar to Figure 3.26

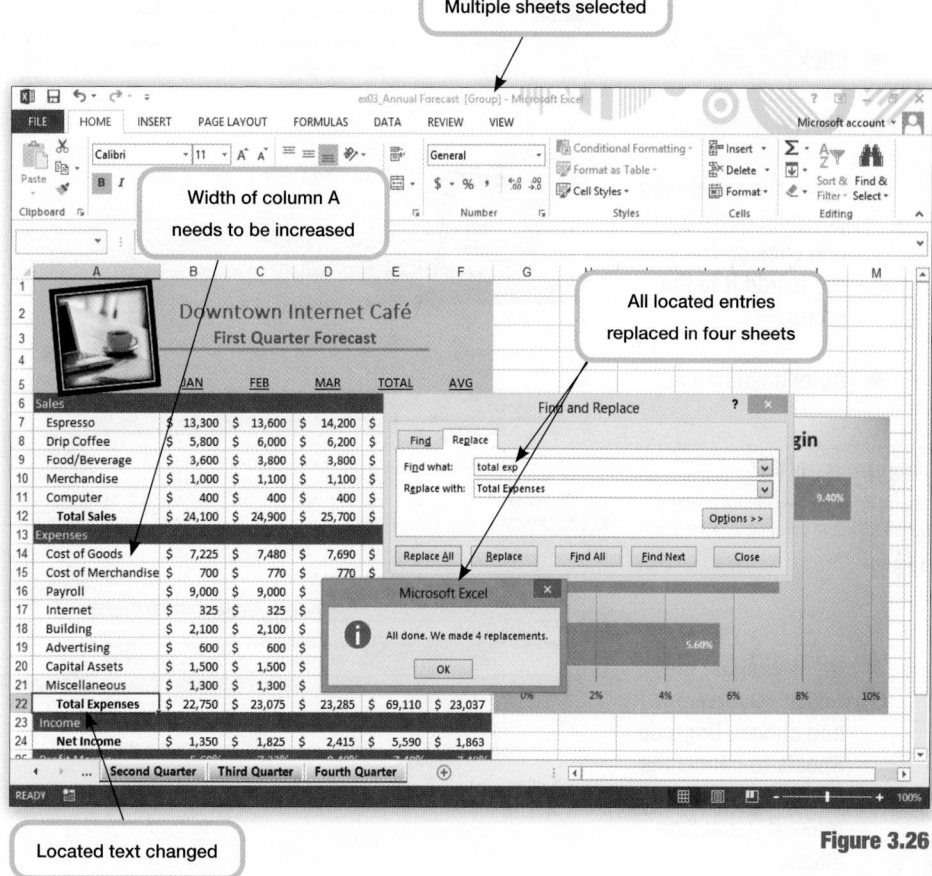

Multiple sheets selected

Width of column A needs to be increased

All located entries replaced in four sheets

Located text changed

Figure 3.26

Another Method

You also can use Find & Select /Replace; the keyboard shortcut is Ctrl + H.

Four replacements were made, indicating that the heading was corrected on all four sheets. It is much faster to use Replace All than to confirm each match separately. However, exercise care when using Replace All because the search text you specify might be part of another word and you may accidentally replace text you want to keep.

Now, you also notice that the labels in column A are not fully displayed, so you need to increase the column width. You will expand the group selection to include the Year sheet and adjust the width of column A on all worksheets at the same time.

②

- Click [OK].

- Click [Close].

- Scroll the sheet tabs and hold down `Ctrl` and click on the Year tab to add it to the group.

- AutoFit column A.

Having Trouble?

Double-click on the column border of column A when the mouse pointer is a ┿.

- Right-click on the Second Quarter tab and choose Ungroup Sheets to cancel the group selection and make it the active sheet.

Another Method

You also can click on any unselected sheet tab to cancel a group selection.

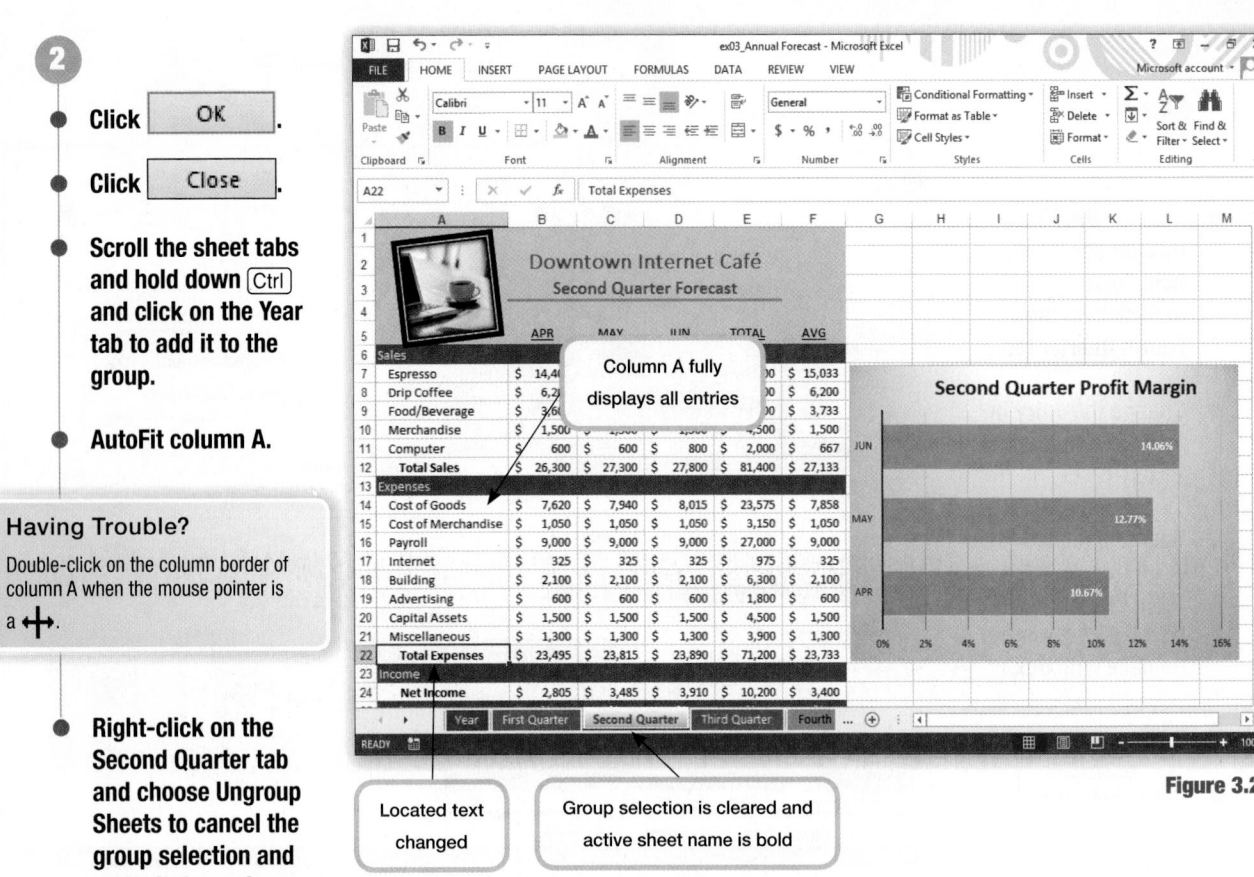

Column A fully displays all entries

Located text changed

Group selection is cleared and active sheet name is bold

Figure 3.27

You can now see that the width of column A has been adjusted and that the Total Exp label has been replaced with Total Expenses, as it has in all other sheets. When multiple sheets are selected, be careful when making changes, as all selected sheets are affected.

Your screen should be similar to Figure 3.27

Saving to a New Folder

You have made several changes to the workbook, and before continuing, you want to save it. Since the workbook is for projected forecasts, you decide to save it in a separate folder from the rest of the Café's financial workbooks. You will save the file to a new folder named Cafe Forecasts.

1

- **Display the Year sheet.**

- **Open the File tab and choose Save As.**

- **Change to the location where you save your files.**

- **Enter Annual Forecast as the file name.**

- **Click** New folder **in the Save As dialog box.**

Your screen should be similar to Figure 3.28

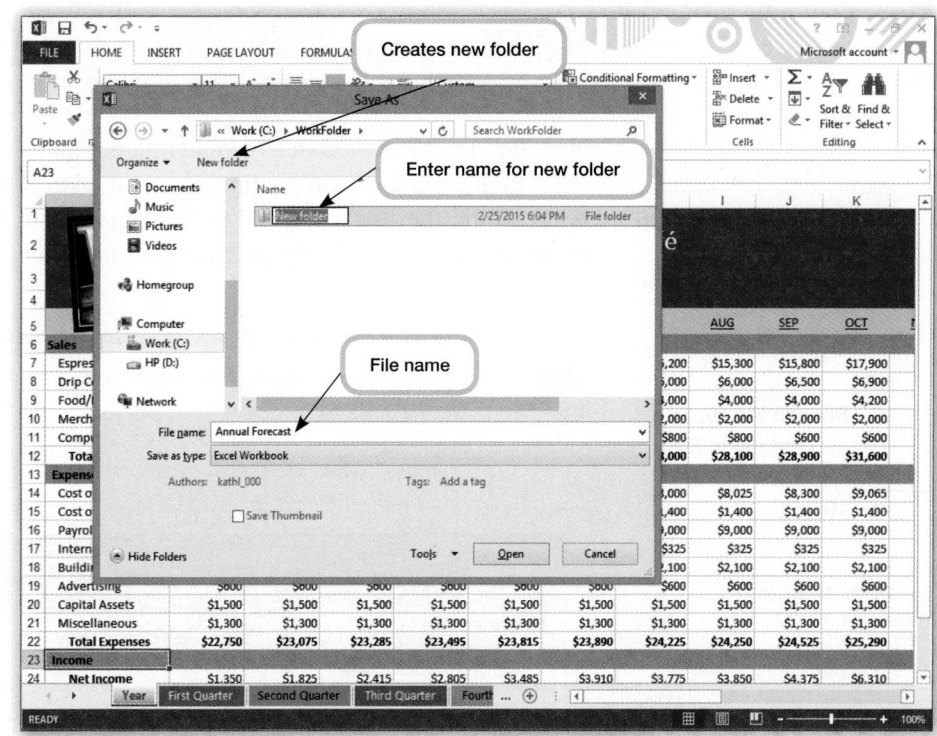

Figure 3.28

The file list displays a new folder with the default folder name, New folder. You need to replace the default folder name with a descriptive folder name. Then you will open the new folder and save the file in it.

Additional Information

You also can rename an existing folder from the Save As dialog box by choosing Rename from the folder's shortcut menu and entering the new name.

2

- **Type Cafe Forecasts in place of New folder.**

- **Press ⏎Enter to complete the folder name.**

- **Double-click on the Cafe Forecasts folder to open it.**

- **Click** Save **.**

Additional Information

If you are running short on lab time, this is an appropriate place to end this session and begin again at a later time. Open the Annual Forecast workbook and the Year sheet.

The Annual Forecast workbook is saved in the new Cafe Forecasts folder.

Now that the Year worksheet is much larger and you cannot see the entire worksheet in the window, you are finding that it takes a lot of time to scroll to different areas within the worksheet. To make managing large worksheets easier, you can zoom a worksheet, split the workbook window, and freeze panes.

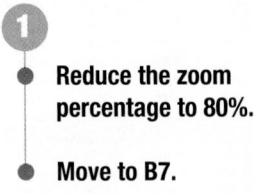

● Reduce the zoom percentage to 80%.

● Move to B7.

Another Method

You also can use  Zoom in the Zoom group on the View tab or click the zoom percentage in the status bar to open the Zoom dialog box and set the magnification.

Your screen should be similar to Figure 3.29

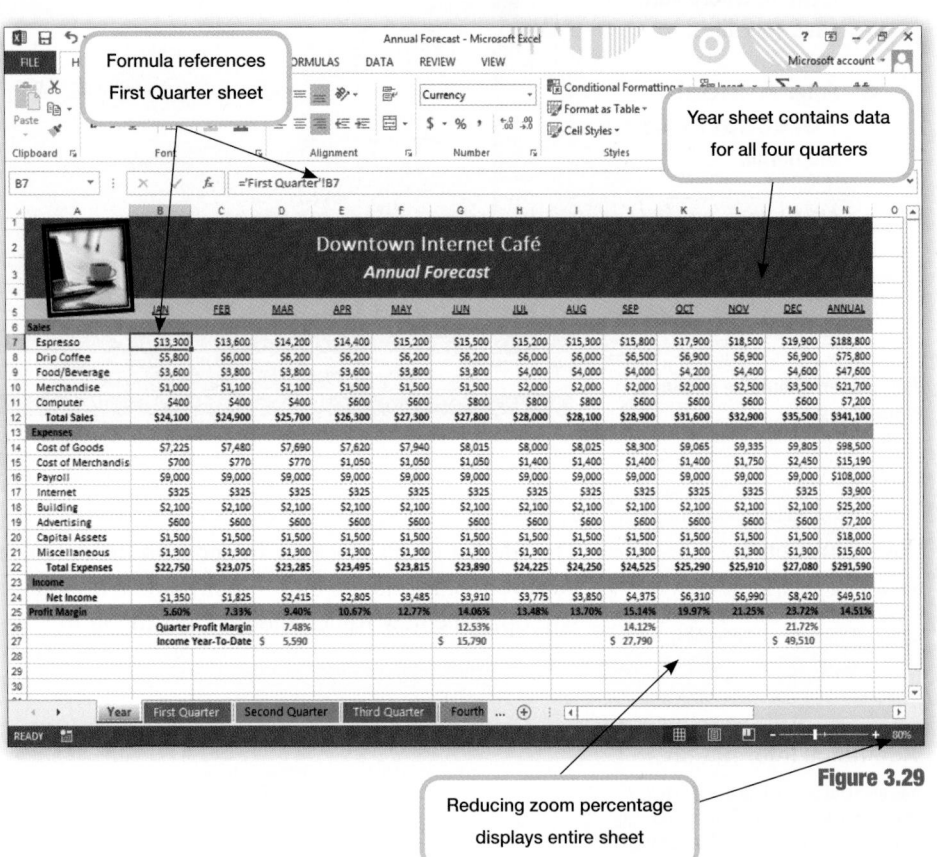

Figure 3.29

You can now see the entire worksheet. Most of the monthly values in the Year sheet, such as cell B7, contain linking formulas that reference the appropriate cells in the appropriate quarter sheets.

GOING TO A SPECIFIC CELL

The only formulas that do not reference cells outside the Year worksheet are those in the Annual column, N. Because you reduced the zoom, it is easy to see the values in column N and to move to a cell by clicking on the cell. However, when the worksheet is at 100 percent zoom, you would need to scroll the worksheet first. You will return the zoom to 100 percent and then use the Go To feature to quickly move to a cell that is not currently visible in the window.

1

● **Return the zoom to 100%.**

Additional Information

Click on the vertical line in the center of the zoom scale to jump to 100%.

● **Click in the Name box and type N16**

Having Trouble?

The Name box is located at the left end of the formula bar.

● **Press (←Enter).**

Another Method

You also can use [Find & Select ▾] and choose

Go To or the keyboard shortcut Ctrl + G.

Your screen should be similar to Figure 3.30

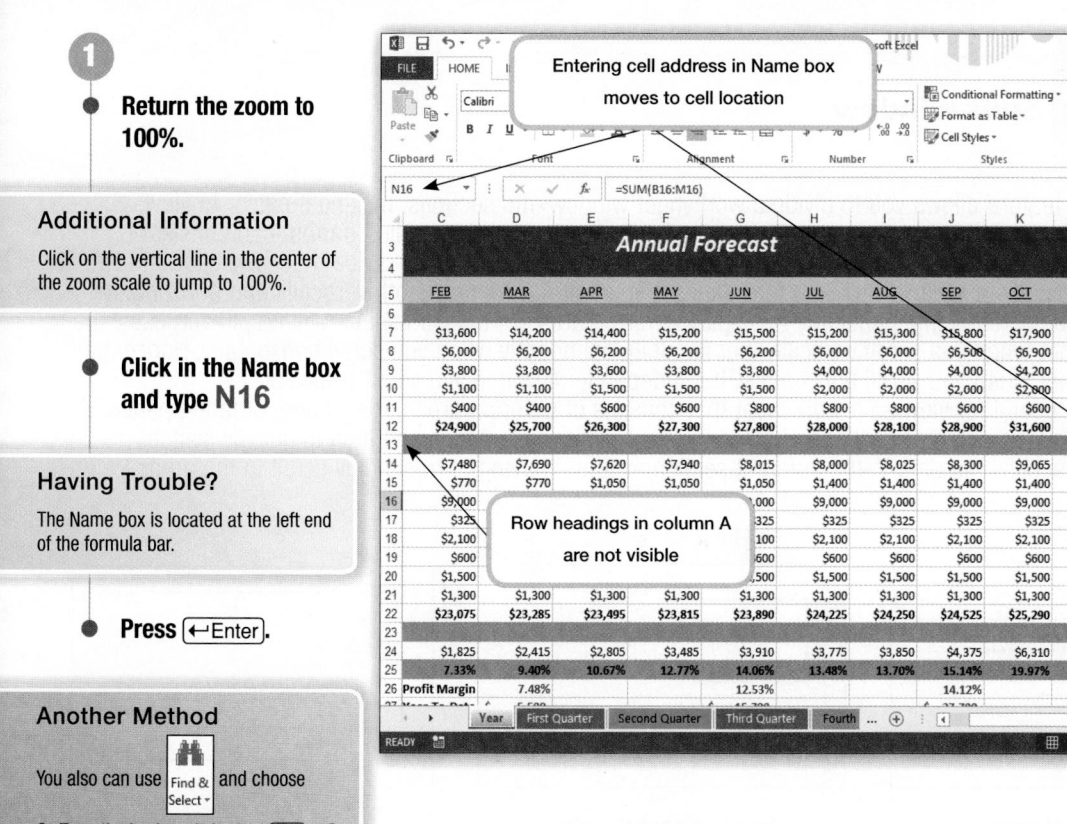

Figure 3.30

The cell selector jumps directly to cell N16 in the Annual column. The formula in this cell calculates the total of the values in row 16 and does not reference another sheet. However, it is difficult to know what the numbers represent in this row because the row headings are not visible. For example, is this number the total for the lease expenses, advertising expenses, or miscellaneous expenses? Without scrolling back to see the row headings, it is difficult to know.

SPLITTING WINDOWS

Whenever you scroll a large worksheet, you will find that information you may need to view in one area scrolls out of view as you move to another area. Although you could reduce the zoom percentage to view more of a worksheet in the window, you still may not be able to see the entire worksheet if it is very large. And as you saw, continuing to reduce the zoom makes the worksheet difficult to read. To view different areas of the same worksheet at the same time, you can split the window.

Concept 6 Split Window

The **split window** feature allows you to divide a worksheet window into sections, making it easier to view different parts of the worksheet at the same time. The sections of the window, called **panes**, can consist of any number of columns or rows along the top or left edge of the window. You can divide the worksheet into two panes either horizontally or vertically, or into four panes if you split the window both vertically and horizontally.

Each pane can be scrolled independently to display different areas of the worksheet. When split vertically, the panes scroll together when you scroll vertically, but scroll independently when you scroll horizontally. Horizontal panes scroll together when you scroll horizontally, but independently when you scroll vertically.

Panes are most useful for viewing a worksheet that consists of different areas or sections. Creating panes allows you to display the different sections of the worksheet in separate panes and then to quickly switch between panes to access the data in the different sections without having to repeatedly scroll to the areas.

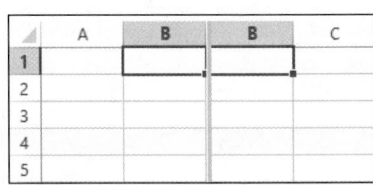

Two vertical panes

Two horizontal panes

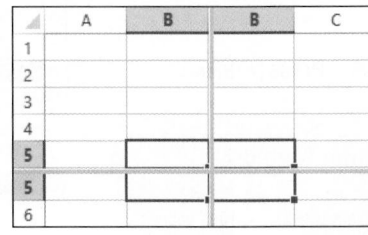

Four panes

Another Method

You also could click on a cell in row 1 of the column or in column A of the row where you want to create the split.

To split the window vertically, select a column to the right of where you want the split. To split it horizontally, select the row below the row where you want it to appear. Then use the ▦ Split command in the View tab. To create a four-way split, select a cell below and to the right of where you want the split to occur.

You will split the window into two vertical panes. This will allow you to view the headings in column A at the same time as you are viewing data in column N.

1

- Position the window to display row 4 at the top of the window. Select column E.

Having Trouble?

Click the column letter to select the entire column.

- Open the View tab.

- Click [▦ Split] in the Window group.

Having Trouble?

If you accidentally create a four-way split, double-click the unwanted split bar to remove it.

- Click cell F16 in the right pane.

Your screen should be similar to Figure 3.31

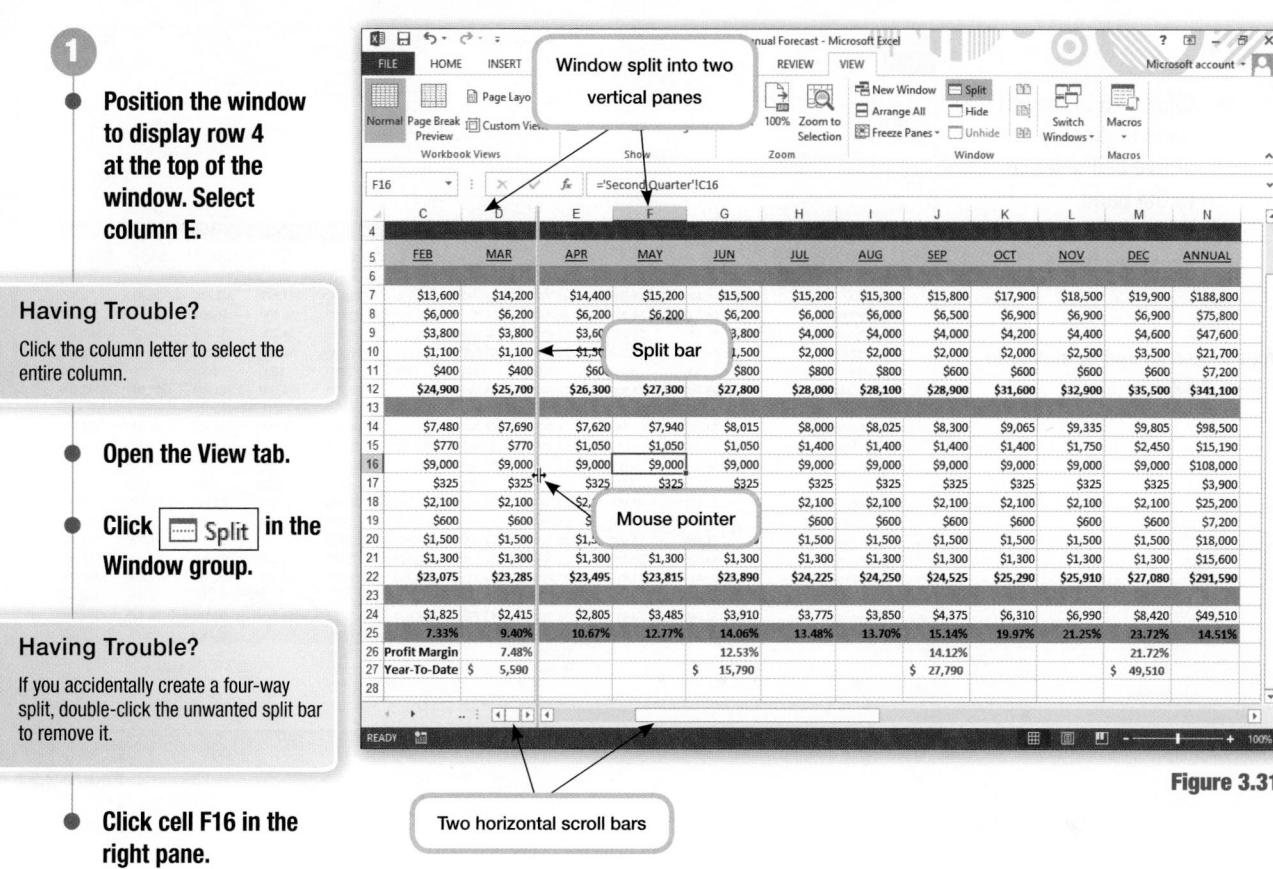

Figure 3.31

There are now two vertical panes with two separate horizontal scroll bars. The highlighted cell selector is visible in the right pane. The left pane also has a cell selector in cell F16, but it is not visible because that area of the worksheet is not displayed in the pane. When the same area of a worksheet is visible in multiple panes, the cell selector in the panes that are not active is highlighted whereas the cell selector in the active pane is clear. The active pane will be affected by your movement horizontally. The cell selector moves in both panes, but only the active pane scrolls.

You will scroll the left pane horizontally to display the month headings in column A.

- **Click C16 in the left pane to display the active cell selector in the pane.**

- **Press ⬅ twice.**

Your screen should be similar to Figure 3.32

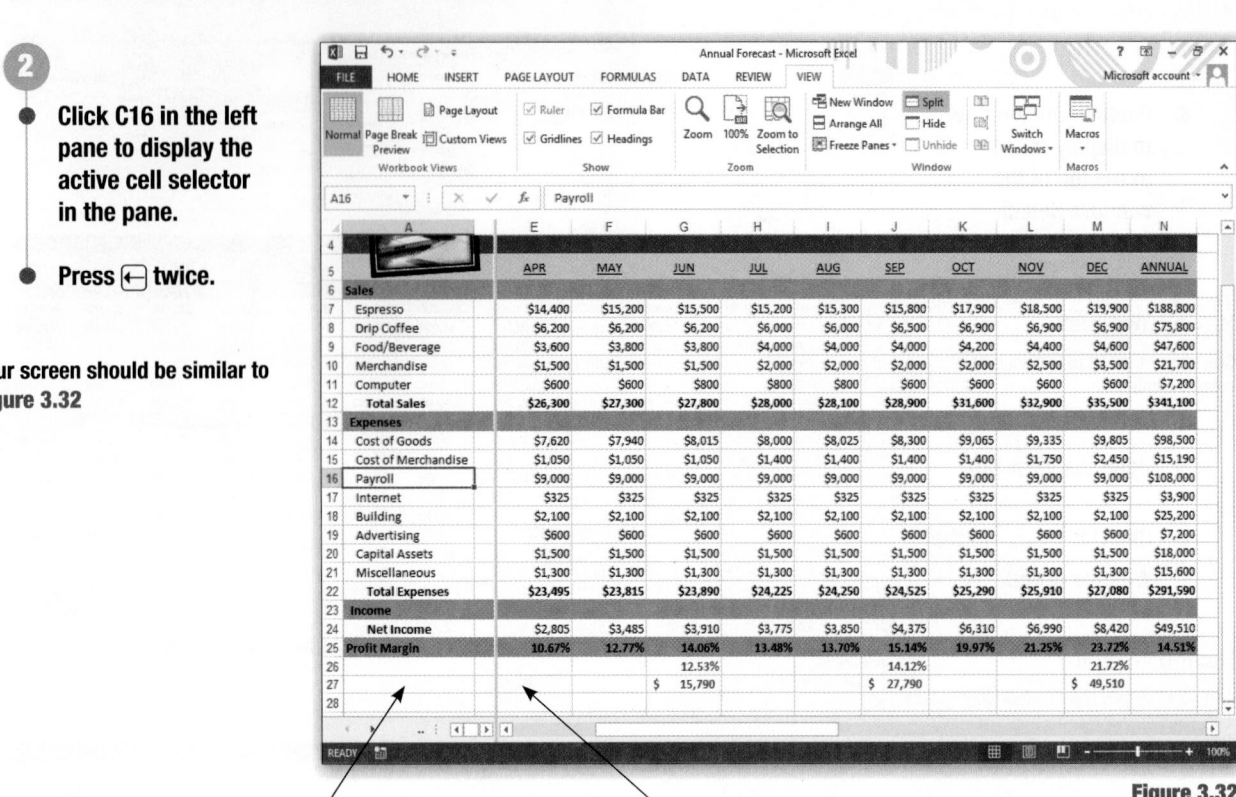

Figure 3.32

Left pane active and scrolled

Right pane not active and fixed

The right pane did not scroll when you moved horizontally through the left pane to display the row headings. The cell selector in the right pane is in the same cell location as in the left pane (A16), although it is not visible. You want to change the location of the split so that you can view an entire quarter in the left pane in order to more easily compare quarters. You can reposition a split bar by dragging it to any location in the worksheet.

3

- Drag the split bar to the right three columns.

- Click cell K16 in the right pane.

- Scroll the right pane until column K appears next to the split bar.

Your screen should be similar to Figure 3.33

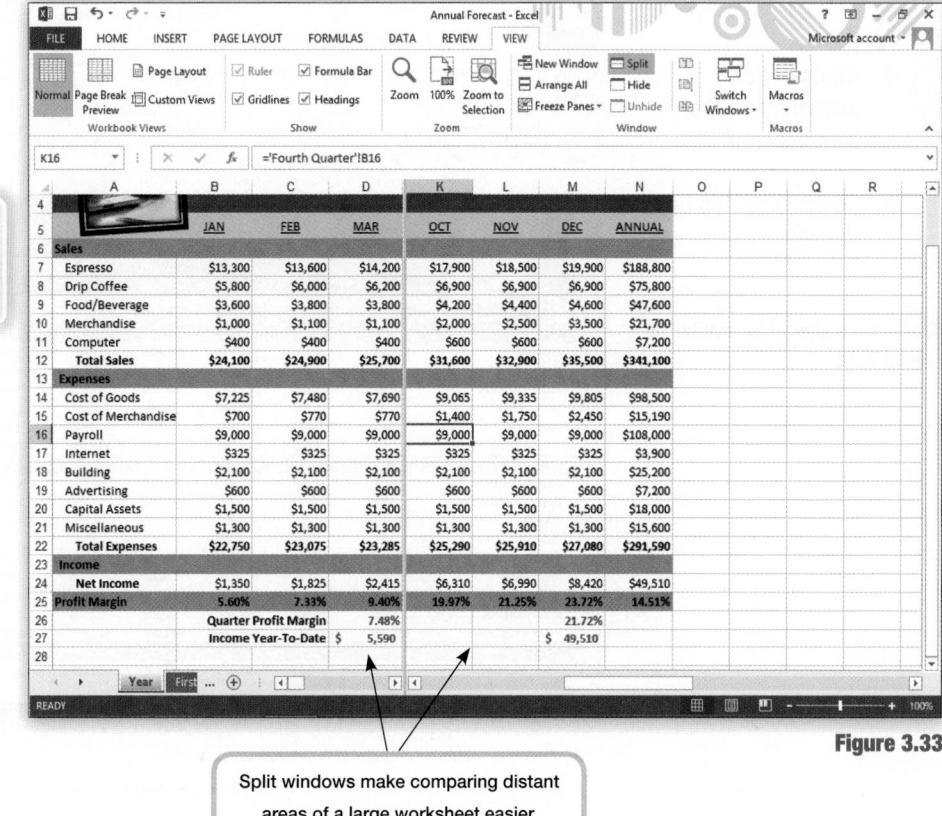

Figure 3.33

Split windows make comparing distant areas of a large worksheet easier

Now you can easily compare the first quarter data to the last-quarter data. As you can see, creating panes is helpful when you want to display and access distant areas of a worksheet quickly. After scrolling the data in the panes to display the appropriate worksheet area, you can then quickly switch between panes to make changes to the data that is visible in the pane. This saves you the time of scrolling to the area each time you want to view it or make changes to it. You will clear the vertical split from the window.

4

- **Double-click anywhere on the split bar.**

- **Scroll to the top of the window.**

Your screen should be similar to Figure 3.34

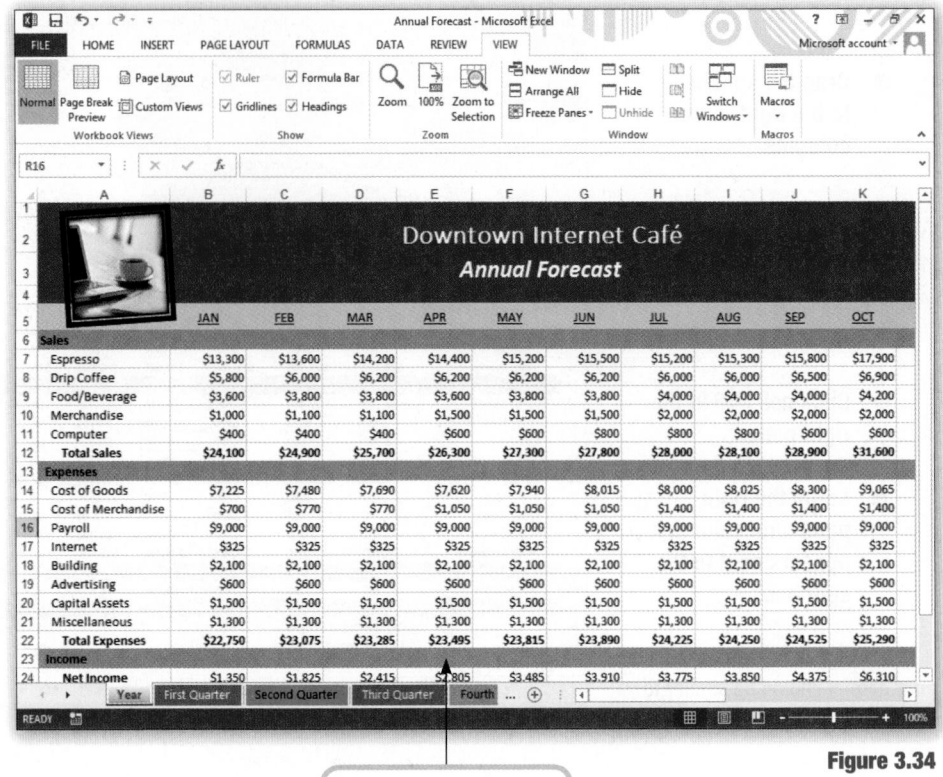

Double-clicking on split bar removes vertical split

Figure 3.34

FREEZING PANES

Another way to manage a large worksheet is to freeze panes.

Concept ⑦ Freeze Panes

Freezing panes prevents the data in the pane from scrolling as you move to different areas in a worksheet. You can freeze rows at the top and columns on the left side of the worksheet only. This feature is most useful when your worksheet is organized using row and column headings. It allows you to keep the titles on the top and left edge of your worksheet in view as you scroll horizontally and vertically through the worksheet data.

You want to keep the month headings in row 5 and the row headings in column A visible in the window at all times while looking at the Income and Profit Margin data beginning in row 22. To do this, you will create four panes with the upper and left panes frozen.

When creating frozen panes, first position the worksheet in the window to display the information you want to appear in the top and left panes. This is because data in the frozen panes cannot be scrolled like data in regular panes. Then move to the location specified in the following table before using the Freeze Panes command in the Window group on the View tab to create and freeze panes.

To Create	Cell Selector Location	Example
Two horizontal panes with the top pane frozen	Move to the leftmost column in the window and to the row or rows that you want to keep visible when you scroll.	Top pane frozen
Two vertical panes with the left pane frozen	Move to the top row of the window and to the column to or columns that you want to keep visible when you scroll.	Left pane frozen
Four panes with the top and left panes frozen	Move to the cell below and to the right of the rows and columns that you want to keep visible when you scroll.	Top and left panes frozen

You want to split the window into four panes with the month column headings at the top of the window and the row headings in column A at the left side of the window.

1

Move to B6.

Click

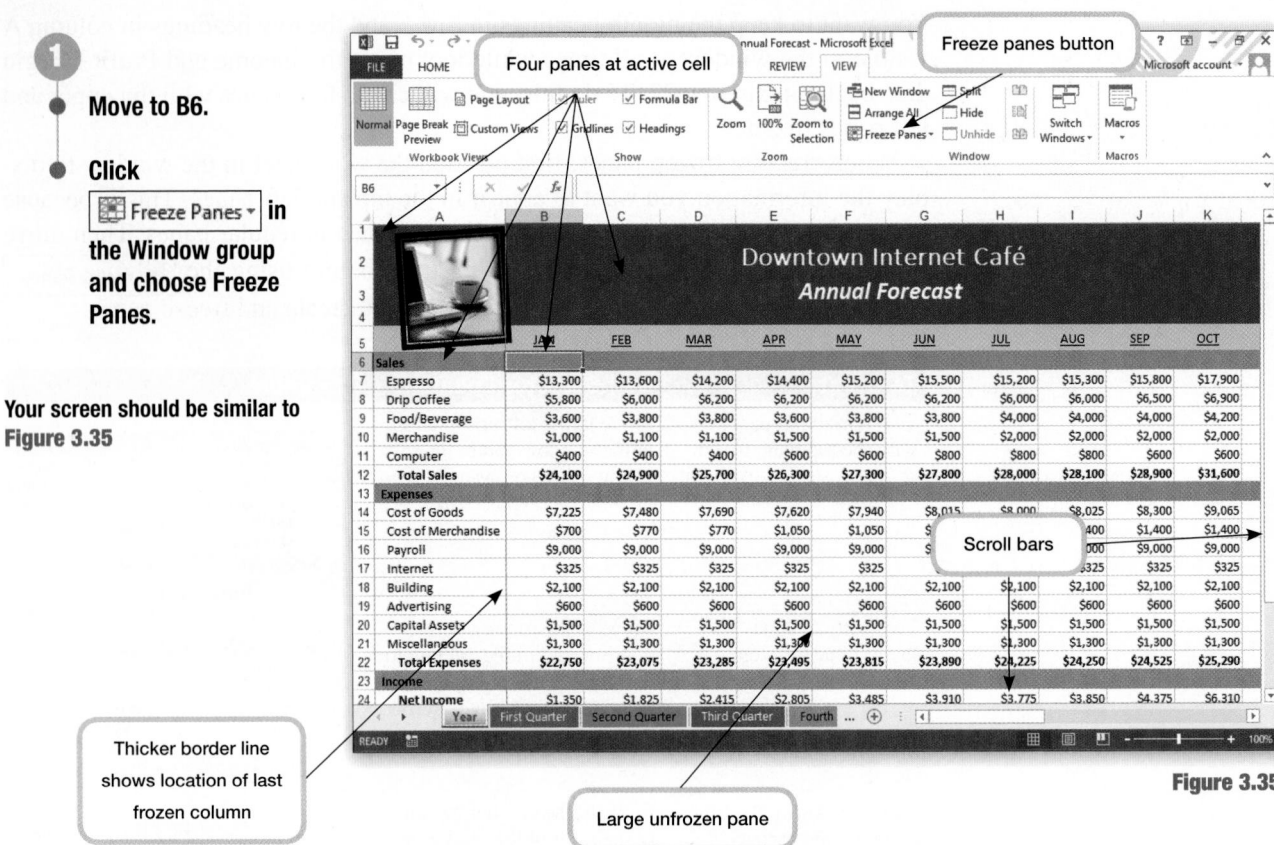

Figure 3.35

Freeze Panes ▾ in the Window group and choose Freeze Panes.

Your screen should be similar to Figure 3.35

The window is divided into four panes at the cell selector location. A slightly thicker border line appears below the last frozen row and to the right of the last frozen column. Only one set of scroll bars is displayed because the only pane that can be scrolled is the larger lower-right pane. You can move the cell selector into a frozen pane, but the data in the frozen panes will not scroll. As you move the cell selector within the worksheet it moves from one pane to another over the pane divider, making it unnecessary to click on a pane to make it active before moving the cell selector into that pane.

Because Evan has asked you to adjust the Profit Margin values, you want to view this area of the worksheet only.

2

- Use the vertical scroll bar to scroll the window until row 25 is below row 5.

- Move to cell G25.

Your screen should be similar to Figure 3.36

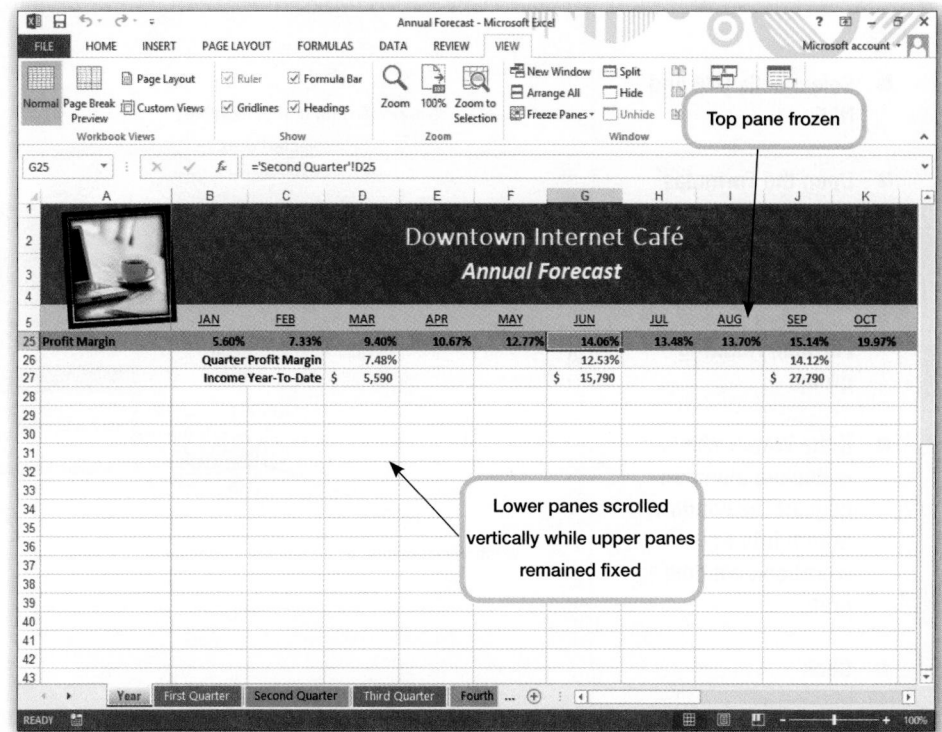

Figure 3.36

Now the Income and Profit Margin data are displayed immediately below the month headings in row 5. The data in rows 6 through 24 is no longer visible, allowing you to concentrate on this area of the worksheet.

WATCHING CELLS

While using a workbook with large worksheets and/or multiple sheets, you may want to keep an eye on how changes you make to values in one area affect cells in another. For example, if you change a value in one sheet that is referenced in a formula in another sheet, you can view the effect on the calculated value using the Watch Window toolbar.

You will be changing values in the Second Quarter sheet next and want to be able to see the effect on the second-quarter profit margin (G26) and annual profit margin (N25) in the Year sheet at the same time.

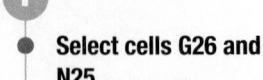

1

- Select cells G26 and N25.

- Open the Formulas tab.

- Click  in the Formula Auditing group.

- If the Watch Window is docked along an edge of the window, drag it into the workbook window area.

- Click  from the Watch Window toolbar.

Your screen should be similar to Figure 3.37

The Add Watch dialog box is used to specify the cells you want to see in the Watch Window list. The currently selected cells are identified with a moving border. You will add these cells to the Watch Window list.

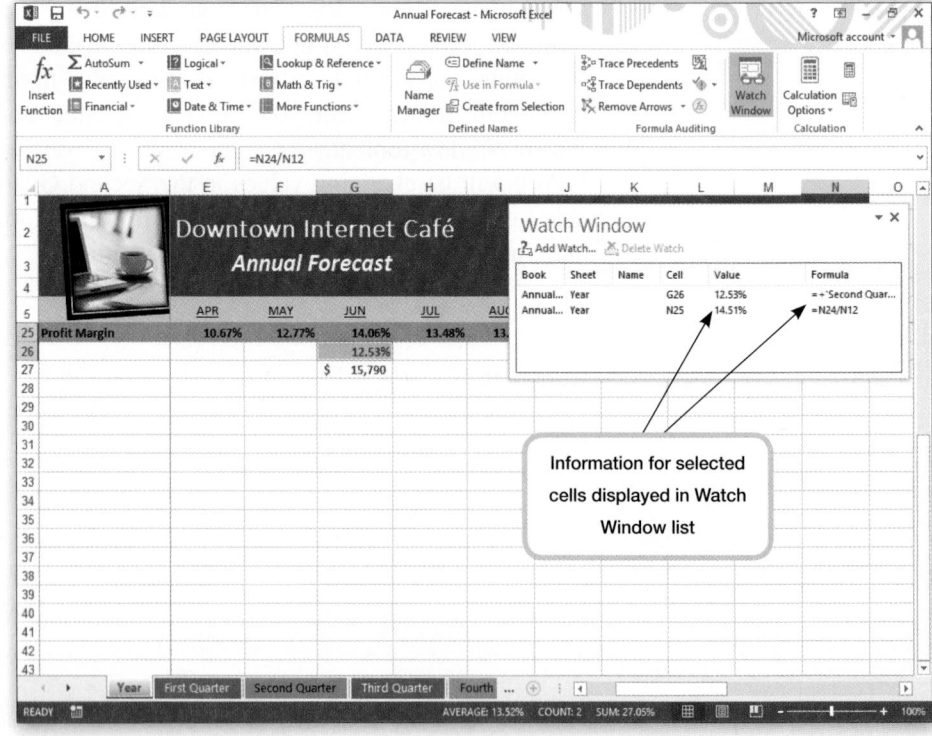

2

- Click **Add**.

- If necessary, move the Watch Window to the upper-right corner of the worksheet window below the column headings.

Your screen should be similar to Figure 3.38

The values in the selected cells as well as the formula and location information are displayed in the Watch Window list. The Watch Window will remain open on top of the worksheet as you move from one sheet to another.

Forecasting Values

Evan has asked you to adjust the forecast for the second quarter to show a profit margin of at least 15 percent for each month. After some consideration, you decide you can most easily reduce monthly payroll expenses by carefully scheduling the hours employees work during these three months. Reducing the monthly expense will increase the profit margin for the quarter. You want to find out what the maximum payroll value you can spend during that period is for each month to accomplish this goal. The process of evaluating what effect changing the payroll expenses will have on the profit margin is called what-if analysis.

Concept  What-If Analysis

What-if analysis is a technique used to evaluate the effects of changing selected factors in a worksheet. This technique is a common accounting function that has been made much easier with the introduction of spreadsheet programs. By substituting different values in cells that are referenced by formulas, you can quickly see the effect of the changes when the formulas are recalculated.

You can perform what-if analysis by manually substituting values or by using one of the what-if analysis tools included with Excel.

PERFORMING WHAT-IF ANALYSIS MANUALLY

To do this, you will enter different payroll expense values for each month and see what the effect is on that month's profit margin. You will adjust the April payroll value first.

1

- **Display the Second Quarter sheet.**

- **Type 7000 in cell B16.**

- **Press ⏎Enter.**

- **Scroll the window to see row 25.**

Your screen should be similar to Figure 3.39

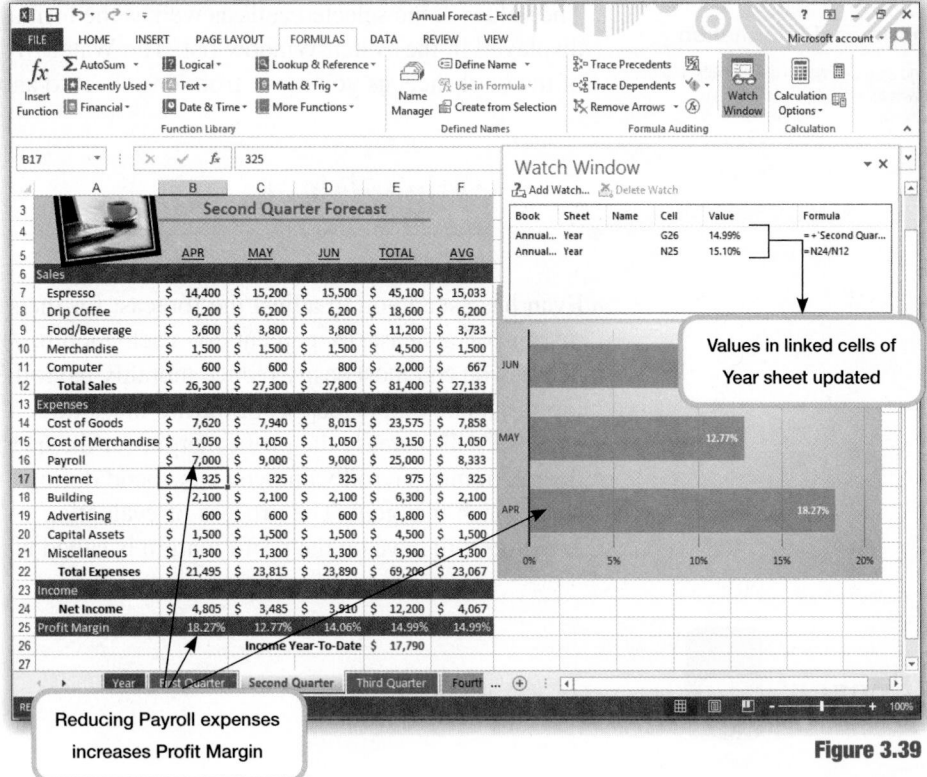

Reducing Payroll expenses increases Profit Margin

Values in linked cells of Year sheet updated

Figure 3.39

Now by looking in cell B25, you can see that decreasing the payroll expenses has increased the profit margin for the month to 18.27 percent. This is more than you need. Also notice the chart has changed to reflect the change in April's profit margin. The Watch Window shows that the values in the two linked cells in the Year sheet were updated accordingly.

You will continue to enter payroll values until the profit margin reaches the goal.

2

- Type **7900** in cell B16.

- Click ☑ Enter.

- Type **7850** in cell B16.

- Click ☑ Enter.

- Type **7860** in cell B16.

- Click ☑ Enter.

- Save the workbook.

Your screen should be similar to Figure 3.40

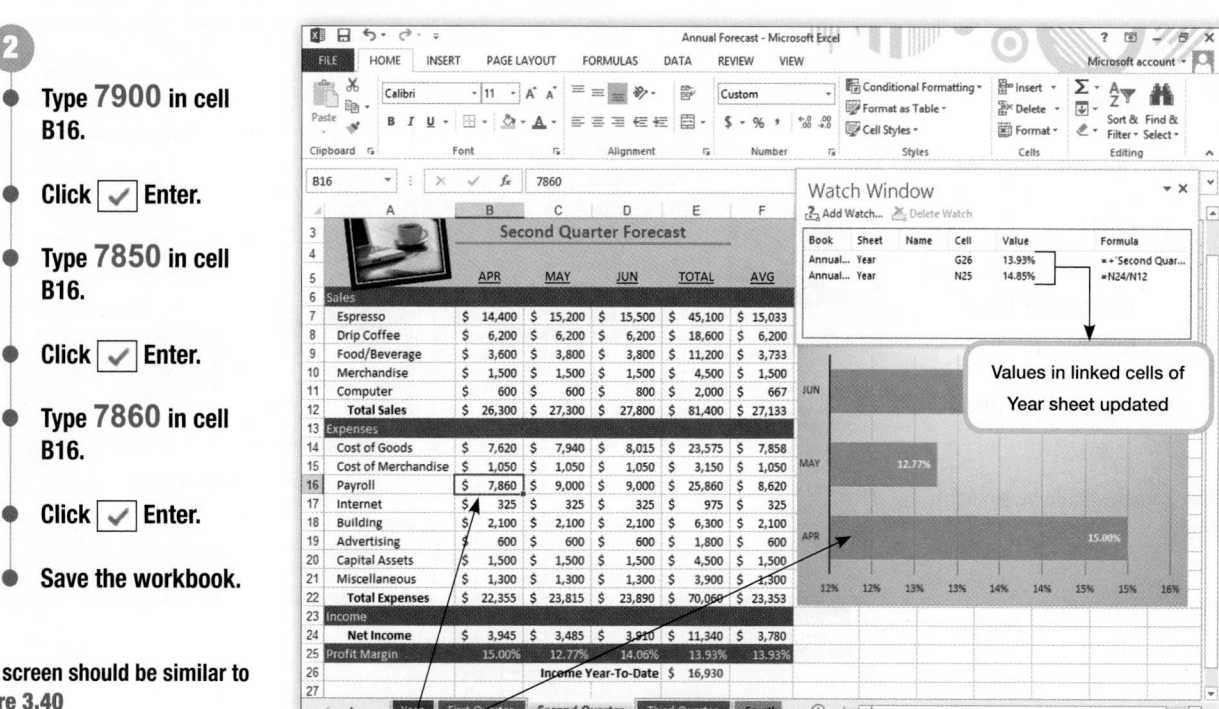

Reducing April Payroll to 7860 achieved the 15% Profit Margin

Figure 3.40

That's it! Reducing the payroll value from 9000 to 7860 will achieve the 15 percent profit margin goal for the month. Also notice that the column chart reflects the change in the April profit margin.

USING GOAL SEEK

It usually takes several tries to find the appropriate value when manually performing what-if analysis. A quicker way is to use the what-if analysis Goal Seek tool provided with Excel.

Concept 9 Goal Seek

The **Goal Seek** tool is used to find the value needed in one cell to attain a result you want in another cell. Goal Seek varies the value in the cell you specify until a formula that is dependent on that cell returns the desired result. The value of only one cell can be changed.

You will use this method to find the payroll value for May that will produce a 15 percent profit margin for that month. The current profit margin value is 12.77 percent in cell C25.

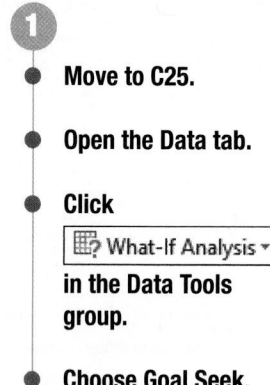

1

- Move to **C25**.

- Open the **Data** tab.

- Click

  [📊 What-If Analysis ▾]

  in the **Data Tools** group.

- Choose **Goal Seek**.

Your screen should be similar to Figure 3.41

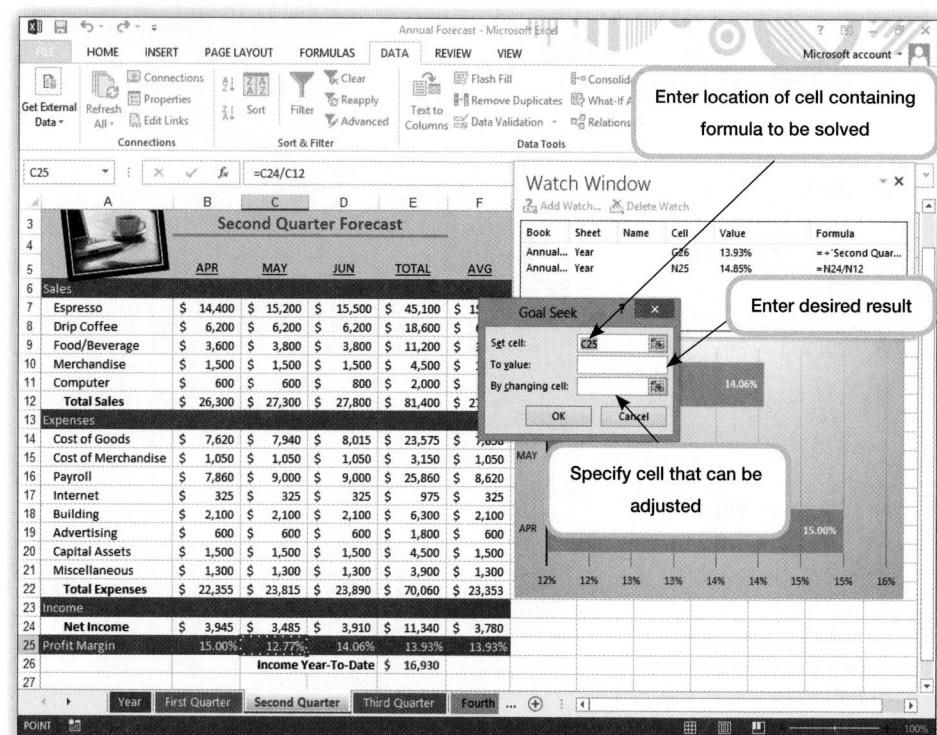

Enter location of cell containing formula to be solved

Enter desired result

Specify cell that can be adjusted

Figure 3.41

In the Goal Seek dialog box, you need to specify the location of the cell containing the formula to be solved, the desired calculated value, and the cell containing the number that can be adjusted to achieve the result. You want the formula in cell C25 to calculate a result of 15 percent by changing the payroll number in cell C16. The Set cell text box correctly displays the current cell as the location of the formula to be solved. You will enter the information needed in the Goal Seek dialog box.

2

- Click in the **To value** text box and enter **15.00%**

- Click in the **By changing cell** text box and then click on cell **C16** in the worksheet to enter the cell reference.

- Click [OK].

Your screen should be similar to Figure 3.42

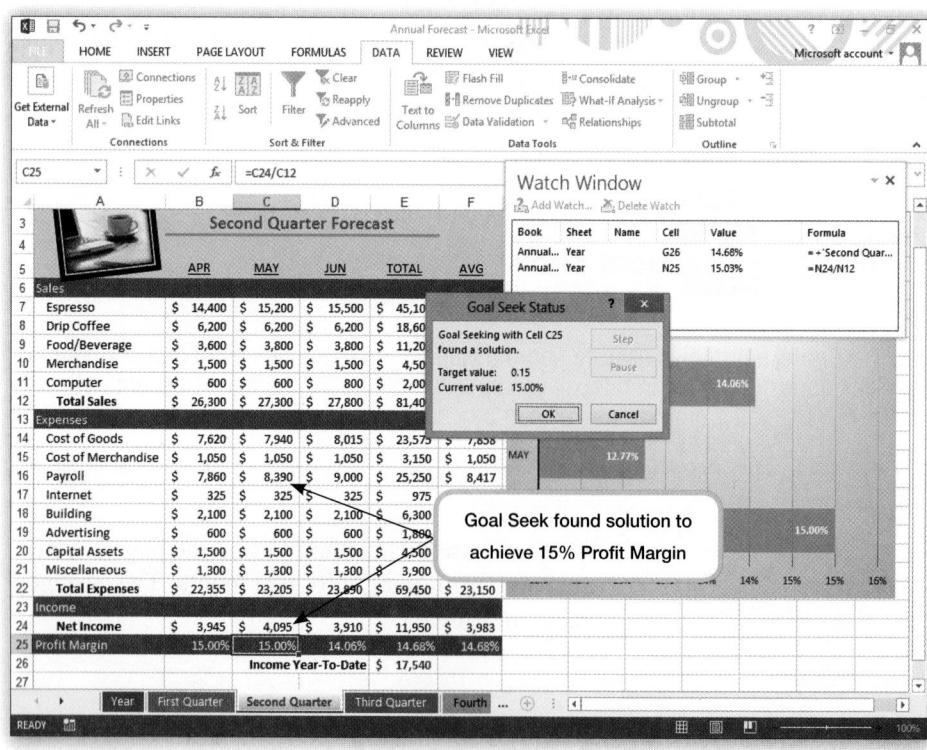

Goal Seek found solution to achieve 15% Profit Margin

Figure 3.42

The Goal Seek dialog box tells you it found a solution that will achieve the 15 percent profit margin. The payroll value of 8390 that will achieve the desired result has been temporarily entered in the worksheet. You can reject the solution and restore the original value by choosing [Cancel]. In this case, however, you want to accept the solution.

3

Click [OK].

Your screen should be similar to Figure 3.43

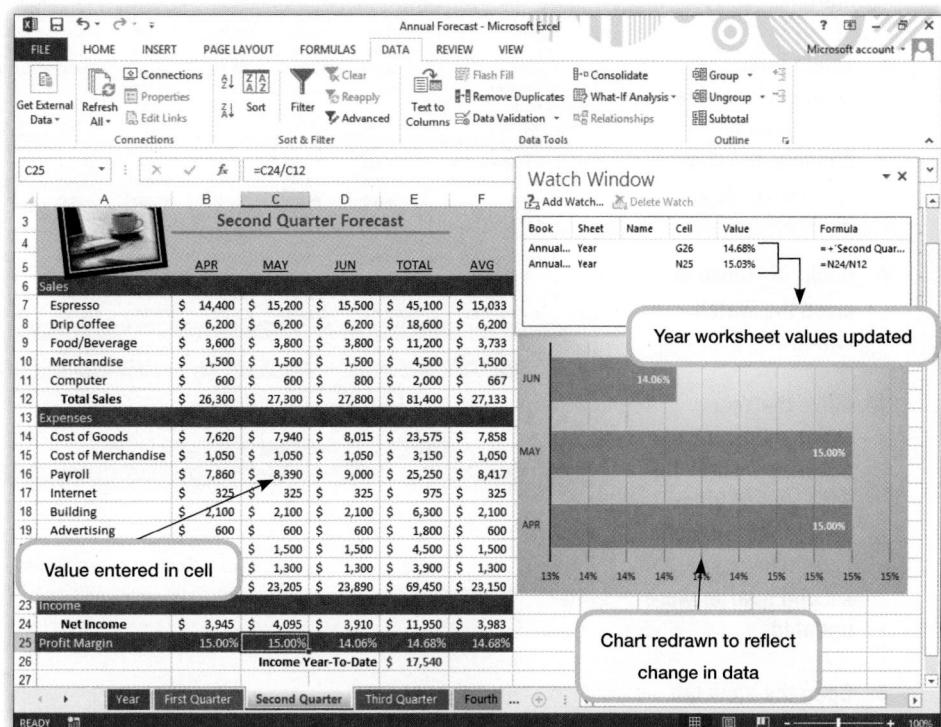

Figure 3.43

The payroll value is permanently updated and the chart redrawn to reflect the change in the May profit margin. Finally, you will adjust the June payroll value. When you are finished, you will close the Watch Window and unfreeze the Year sheet window.

4

- In a similar manner, use Goal Seek to adjust the June payroll value to achieve a 15% profit margin.

- Select both watch cell entries in the Watch Window and click Delete Watch.

- Click ☒ Close to close the Watch Window.

- Make the Year sheet active and, if necessary, scroll the window to further verify that the profit margin values for the second quarter were updated.

- Open the View tab.

- Click ☷ Freeze Panes ▾ in the Window group and choose Unfreeze Panes.

- Save the workbook file again.

Your screen should be similar to Figure 3.44

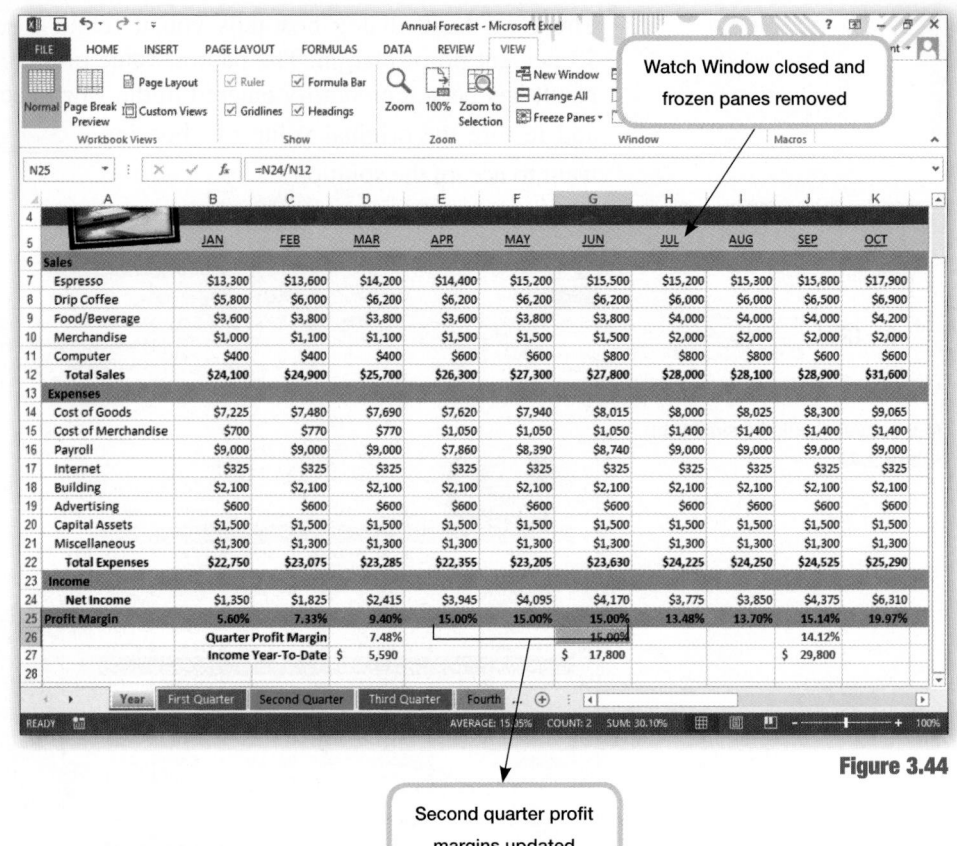

Figure 3.44

The second-quarter values are now at the 15 percent profit margin objective.

Using Conditional Formatting

Next, you want to highlight or emphasize certain values in the worksheet to help visualize the data and quickly analyze information in a worksheet. To do this, you can use conditional formatting.

Concept 10 Conditional Formatting

Conditional formatting changes the appearance of a range of cells based on a condition that you specify. If the cells in the range meet the conditions (the condition is true), they are formatted. If they do not meet the conditions (the condition is false), they remain unformatted. There are several different ways you can apply conditional formatting as described in the following table.

Conditional Formatting	Description
Highlight Cells Rules	Highlights cells based on rules you specify, such as greater than or less than, between, or equal to. It also can highlight cells that contain certain text, dates, and duplicate values.
Top/Bottom Rules	Highlights the highest and lowest values in a range by number, percentage, or average based on a cutoff value that you specify.
Data Bars	Displays a color bar in a cell to help you see the value of a cell relative to other cells. The length of the bar represents the value in the cell. A longer bar is a higher value and a shorter bar, a lower value.
Color Scales	Applies a two- or three-color graduated scale to compare values in a range. A two-color scale uses two different colors to represent high or low values and a three-color scale uses three colors to represent high, mid, and low values.
Icon Sets	Displays different color icons in the cell to classify data into three to five categories. Each icon represents a range of values.

CREATING CELL RULES

You will use the cell rules conditional formatting to highlight the payroll values that are less than $9,000 a month.

1

- Select cells B16 through M16.

- Open the Home tab.

- Click
  ![Conditional Formatting] Conditional Formatting ▾
  in the Styles group.

- Select Highlight Cells Rules.

- Choose Less Than.

Your screen should be similar to Figure 3.45

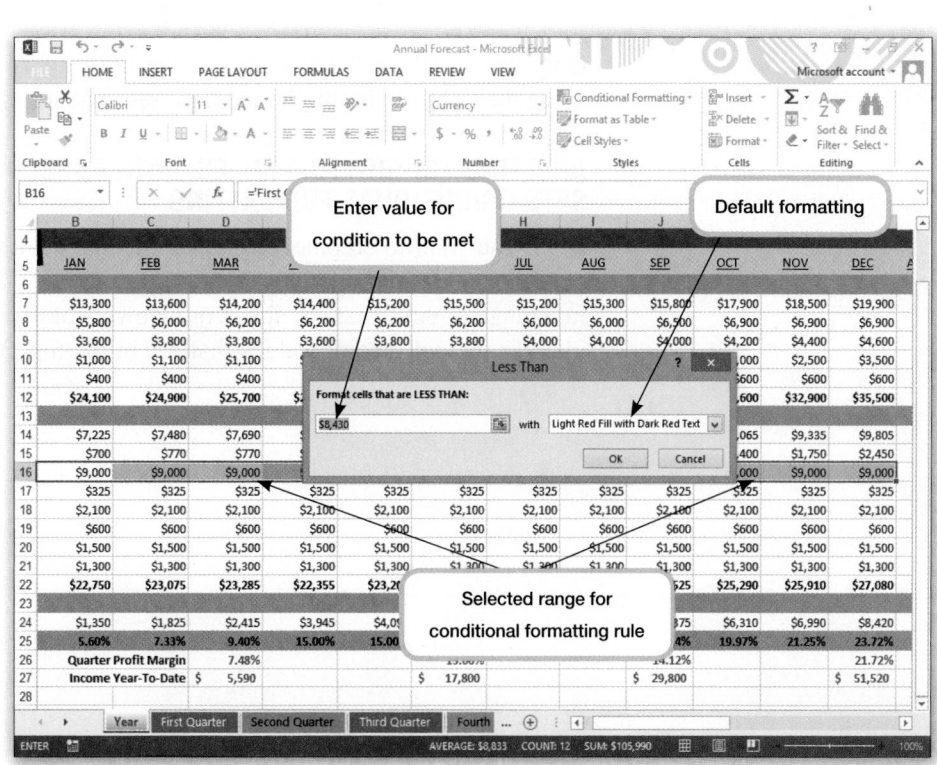

Figure 3.45

In the Less Than dialog box, you enter the value that will be used to determine which cells to highlight. In this case, you will enter the value 9000 so that all values below this amount in the selected range will be highlighted. It also lets you select the formatting to apply to those cells meeting the condition. The default formatting, a light red fill with dark red text, is acceptable.

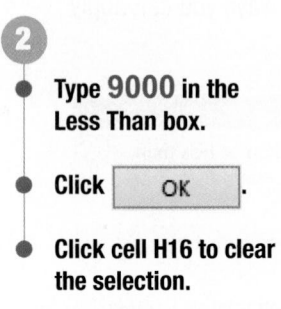

- Type **9000** in the Less Than box.
- Click **OK**.
- Click cell H16 to clear the selection.

Your screen should be similar to Figure 3.46

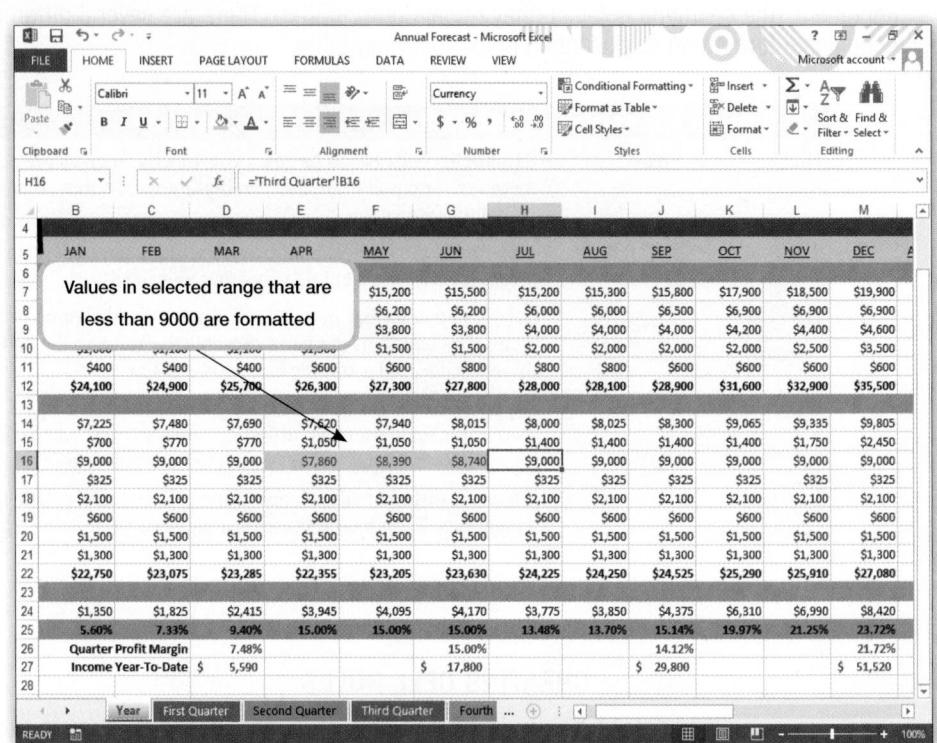

Figure 3.46

Only those cells in the Payroll row whose value is less than 9,000 are formatted using the light-red highlight and dark-red font color.

APPLYING TOP/BOTTOM RULES, DATA BARS, COLOR SCALES, AND ICON SETS CONDITIONAL FORMATTING

Next, you want to emphasize the Net Income values using the Top/Bottom Rules conditional formatting. This formatting identifies the highest and lowest values in a range of cells that are above or below a cutoff value you specify. You want to identify the net income values that are in the top 50 percent of the values in the range.

- **Select the Net Income data in cells B24 through M24.**

- **Click** 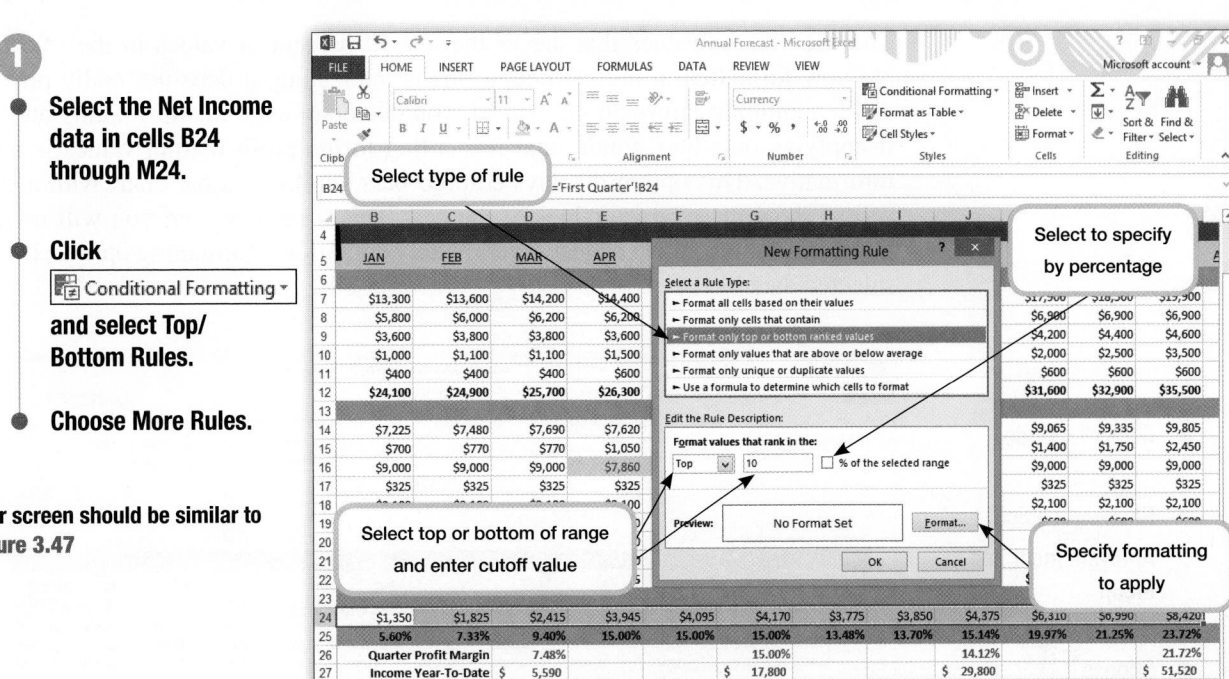 **Conditional Formatting ▾ and select Top/ Bottom Rules.**

- **Choose More Rules.**

Your screen should be similar to Figure 3.47

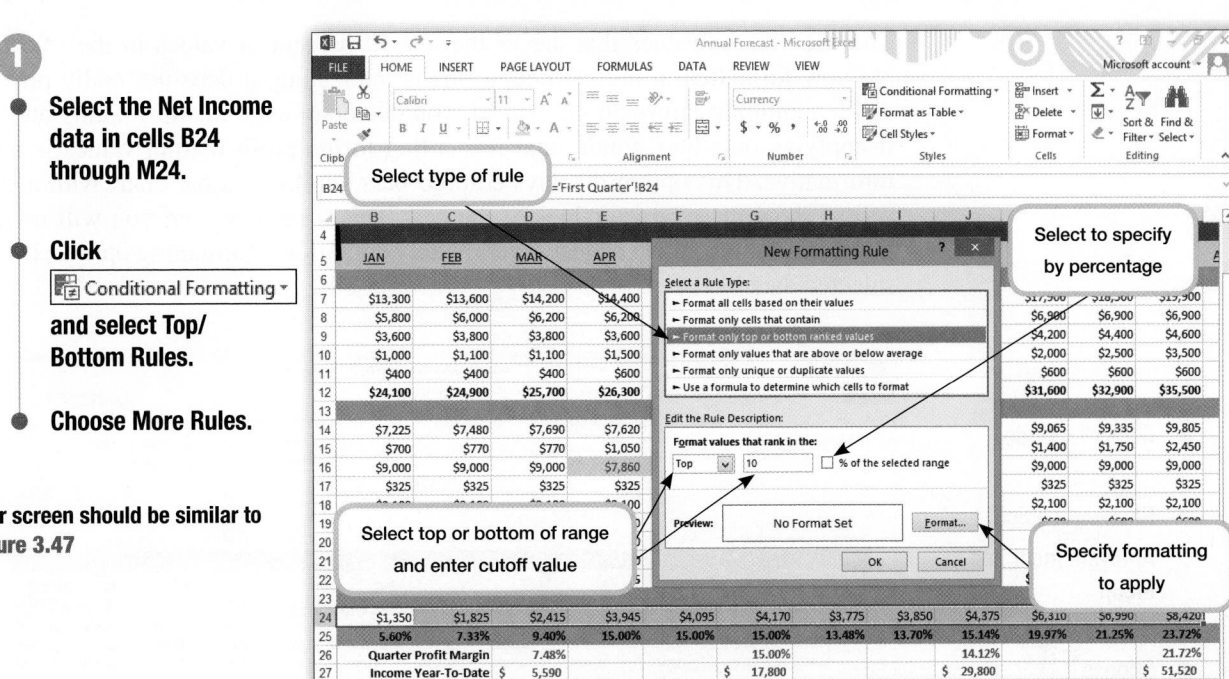

Figure 3.47

In the New Formatting Rule dialog box, you select the type of rule to apply and the rule conditions. The current type of rule is already correctly specified. In the Edit the Rule Description you will specify to format values that are in the top 50 percent of values in the range using red font color.

- **Enter 50 in the value text box.**

- **Click in the check box for % of the selected range to select it.**

- **Click Format... and choose red for the font color.**

- **Click OK twice to exit the dialog boxes.**

Your screen should be similar to Figure 3.48

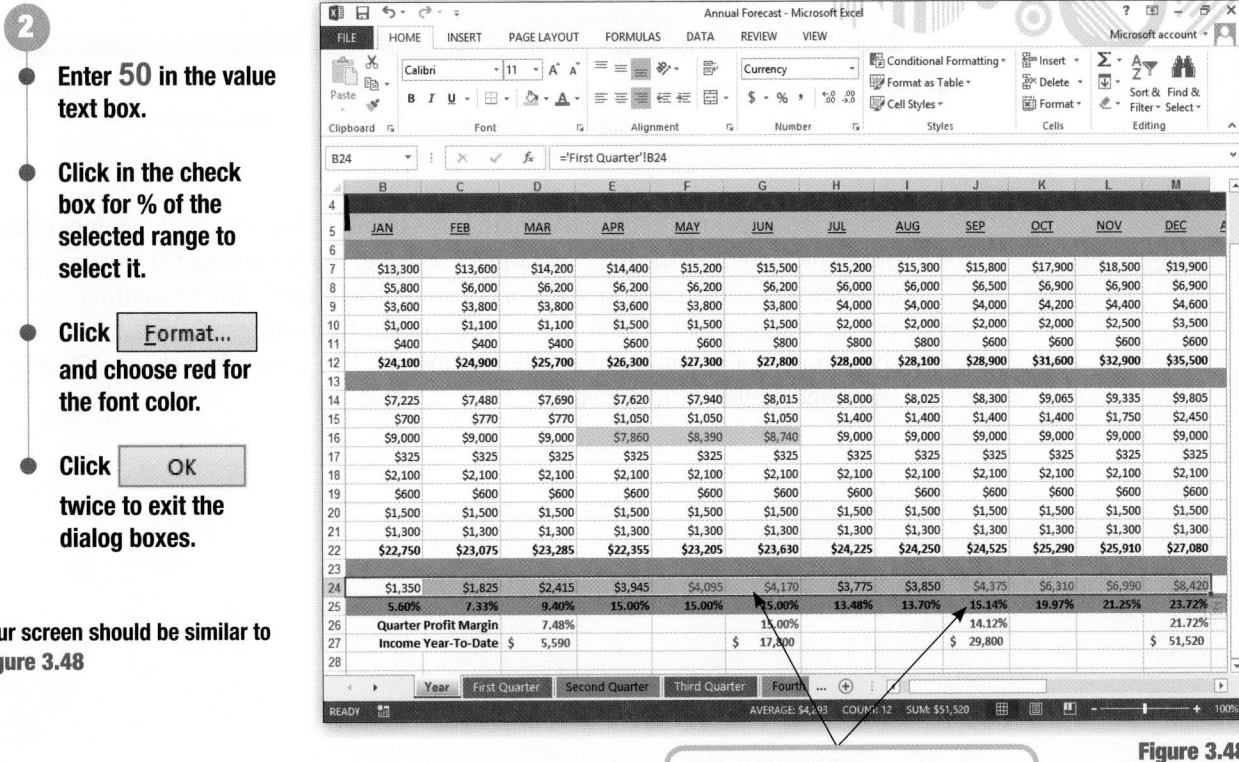

Values in selected range that are in the top 50% are formatted in red

Figure 3.48

The net income values that are in the top 50 percent of values in the selection are now formatted in red. Although this is interesting, it does not really provide much additional information. Instead, you decide to undo this formatting and see if applying data bars conditional formatting to the profit margin values is more informative. This option displays colored bars similar to a bar chart within each cell to show the relative values of the cell. This time, however, you will use the Quick Analysis tool to suggest several likely conditional formatting options for the selected data.

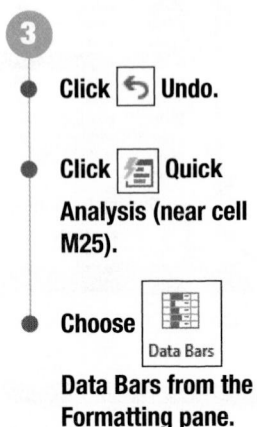

- Click � Undo.

- Click 🔳 Quick Analysis (near cell M25).

- Choose 🔲 Data Bars from the Formatting pane.

Your screen should be similar to Figure 3.49

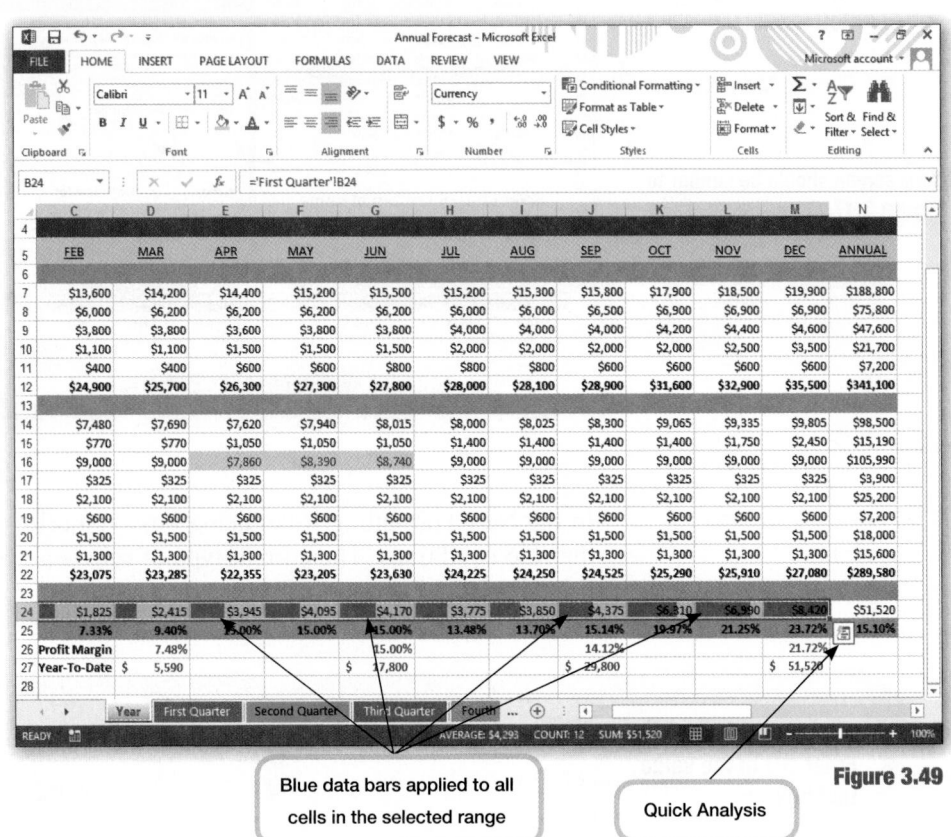

Blue data bars applied to all cells in the selected range

Quick Analysis

Figure 3.49

Color bars appear in each cell containing a number. The size of the number determines the length of the bar; the larger the value, the longer the bar. Again, you do not feel this adds much to the worksheet and will undo this formatting. Instead, you decide to try the Color Scales conditional formatting, which applies a scale consisting of a gradation of two colors to cells in a range. The shade of the color represents higher or lower values.

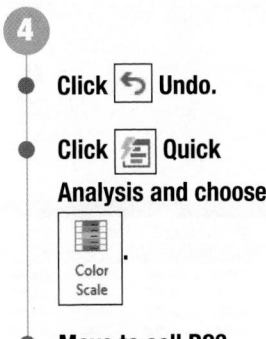

4

- Click ↶ Undo.

- Click 🔲 Quick Analysis and choose

  📊
  Color
  Scale

- Move to cell B23.

Your screen should be similar to Figure 3.50

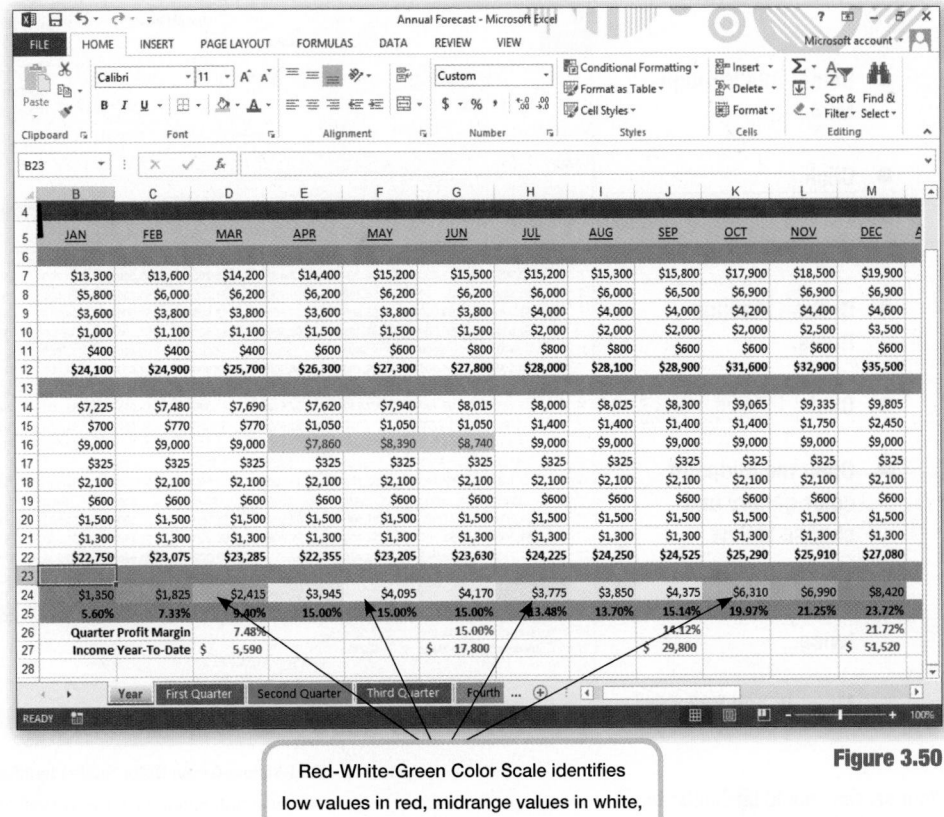

	B	C	D	E	F	G	H	I	J	K	L	M
5	JAN	FEB	MAR	APR	MAY	JUN	JUL	AUG	SEP	OCT	NOV	DEC
7	$13,300	$13,600	$14,200	$14,400	$15,200	$15,500	$15,200	$15,300	$15,800	$17,900	$18,500	$19,900
8	$5,800	$6,000	$6,200	$6,200	$6,200	$6,200	$6,000	$6,000	$6,500	$6,900	$6,900	$6,900
9	$3,600	$3,800	$3,800	$3,600	$3,800	$3,800	$4,000	$4,000	$4,000	$4,200	$4,400	$4,600
10	$1,000	$1,100	$1,100	$1,500	$1,500	$1,500	$2,000	$2,000	$2,000	$2,000	$2,500	$3,500
11	$400	$400	$400	$600	$600	$800	$800	$800	$600	$600	$600	$600
12	$24,100	$24,900	$25,700	$26,300	$27,300	$27,800	$28,000	$28,100	$28,900	$31,600	$32,900	$35,500
14	$7,225	$7,480	$7,690	$7,620	$7,940	$8,015	$8,000	$8,025	$8,300	$9,065	$9,335	$9,805
15	$700	$770	$770	$1,050	$1,050	$1,050	$1,400	$1,400	$1,400	$1,400	$1,750	$2,450
16	$9,000	$9,000	$9,000	$7,860	$8,390	$8,740	$9,000	$9,000	$9,000	$9,000	$9,000	$9,000
17	$325	$325	$325	$325	$325	$325	$325	$325	$325	$325	$325	$325
18	$2,100	$2,100	$2,100	$2,100	$2,100	$2,100	$2,100	$2,100	$2,100	$2,100	$2,100	$2,100
19	$600	$600	$600	$600	$600	$600	$600	$600	$600	$600	$600	$600
20	$1,500	$1,500	$1,500	$1,500	$1,500	$1,500	$1,500	$1,500	$1,500	$1,500	$1,500	$1,500
21	$1,300	$1,300	$1,300	$1,300	$1,300	$1,300	$1,300	$1,300	$1,300	$1,300	$1,300	$1,300
22	$22,750	$23,075	$23,285	$22,355	$23,205	$23,630	$24,225	$24,250	$24,525	$25,290	$25,910	$27,080
23												
24	$1,350	$1,825	$2,415	$3,945	$4,095	$4,170	$3,775	$3,850	$4,375	$6,310	$6,990	$8,420
25	5.60%	7.33%	9.40%	15.00%	15.00%	15.00%	13.48%	13.70%	15.14%	19.97%	21.25%	23.72%
26	Quarter Profit Margin		7.48%			15.00%			14.12%			21.72%
27	Income Year-To-Date	$ 5,590				$ 17,800			$ 29,800			$ 51,520

Year | First Quarter | Second Quarter | Third Quarter | Fourth ...

READY

Red-White-Green Color Scale identifies low values in red, midrange values in white, and high values in green.

Figure 3.50

This formatting applies a color scale to the data in those cells, with the darkest red identifying the lowest values and the darkest green identifying the highest values. This is a red-white-green scale, so the middle values appear to be unshaded.

You will change the color scale color selection to another to show color in all cells in the range.

5

- Select B24 through M24.

- Click 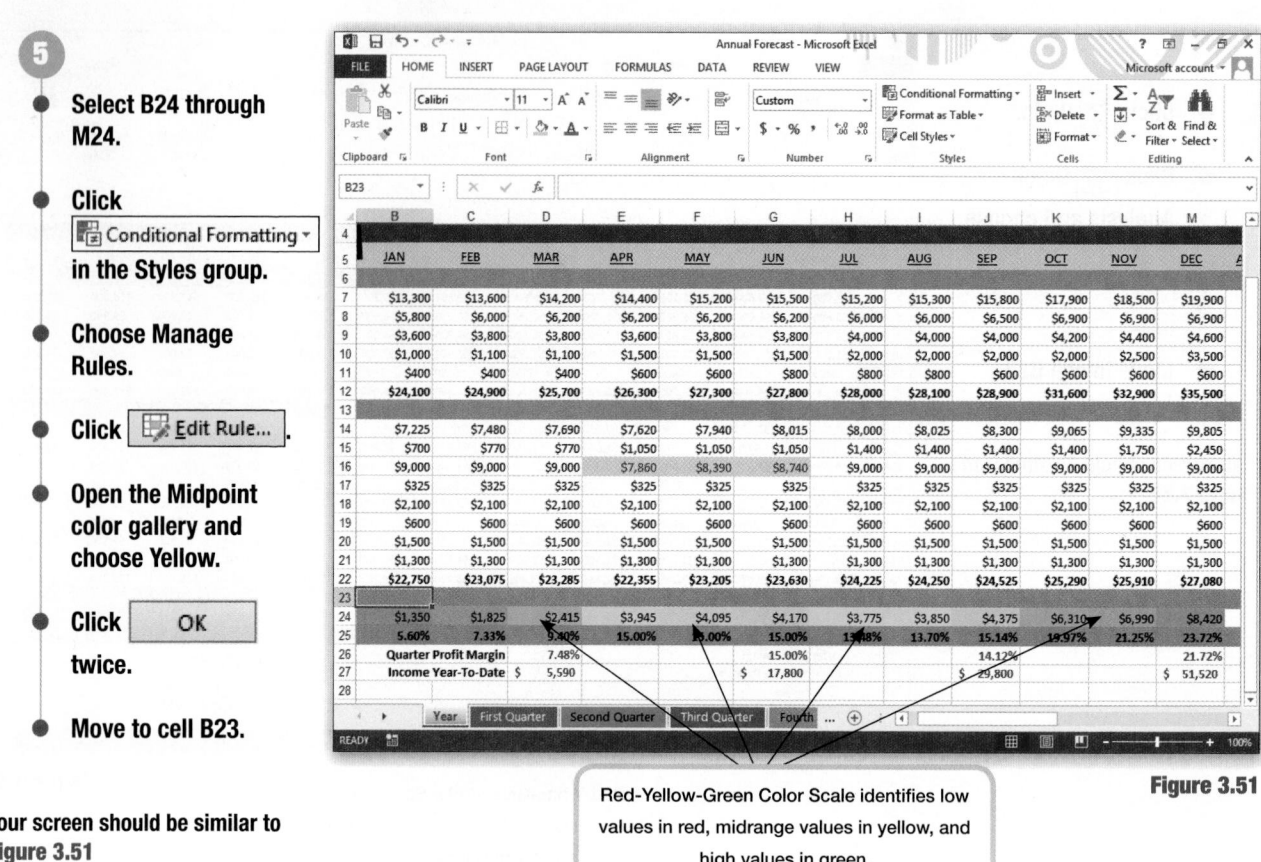 Conditional Formatting ▾ in the Styles group.

- Choose Manage Rules.

- Click 🔲 Edit Rule... .

- Open the Midpoint color gallery and choose Yellow.

- Click OK twice.

- Move to cell B23.

Your screen should be similar to Figure 3.51

	B	C	D	E	F	G	H	I	J	K	L	M
4												
5	JAN	FEB	MAR	APR	MAY	JUN	JUL	AUG	SEP	OCT	NOV	DEC
6												
7	$13,300	$13,600	$14,200	$14,400	$15,200	$15,500	$15,200	$15,300	$15,800	$17,900	$18,500	$19,900
8	$5,800	$6,000	$6,200	$6,200	$6,200	$6,200	$6,000	$6,000	$6,500	$6,900	$6,900	$6,900
9	$3,600	$3,800	$3,800	$3,600	$3,800	$3,800	$4,000	$4,000	$4,000	$4,200	$4,400	$4,600
10	$1,000	$1,100	$1,100	$1,500	$1,500	$1,500	$2,000	$2,000	$2,000	$2,000	$2,500	$3,500
11	$400	$400	$400	$600	$600	$800	$800	$800	$600	$600	$600	$600
12	$24,100	$24,900	$25,700	$26,300	$27,300	$27,800	$28,000	$28,100	$28,900	$31,600	$32,900	$35,500
13												
14	$7,225	$7,480	$7,690	$7,620	$7,940	$8,015	$8,000	$8,025	$8,300	$9,065	$9,335	$9,805
15	$700	$770	$770	$1,050	$1,050	$1,050	$1,400	$1,400	$1,400	$1,400	$1,750	$2,450
16	$9,000	$9,000	$9,000	$7,860	$8,390	$8,740	$9,000	$9,000	$9,000	$9,000	$9,000	$9,000
17	$325	$325	$325	$325	$325	$325	$325	$325	$325	$325	$325	$325
18	$2,100	$2,100	$2,100	$2,100	$2,100	$2,100	$2,100	$2,100	$2,100	$2,100	$2,100	$2,100
19	$600	$600	$600	$600	$600	$600	$600	$600	$600	$600	$600	$600
20	$1,500	$1,500	$1,500	$1,500	$1,500	$1,500	$1,500	$1,500	$1,500	$1,500	$1,500	$1,500
21	$1,300	$1,300	$1,300	$1,300	$1,300	$1,300	$1,300	$1,300	$1,300	$1,300	$1,300	$1,300
22	$22,750	$23,075	$23,285	$22,355	$23,205	$23,630	$24,225	$24,250	$24,525	$25,290	$25,910	$27,080
23												
24	$1,350	$1,825	$2,415	$3,945	$4,095	$4,170	$3,775	$3,850	$4,375	$6,310	$6,990	$8,420
25	5.60%	7.33%	9.40%	15.00%	5.00%	15.00%	15.58%	13.70%	15.14%	19.97%	21.25%	23.72%
26	Quarter Profit Margin		7.48%			15.00%			14.12%			21.72%
27	Income Year-To-Date	$	5,590			$ 17,800			$ 29,800			$ 51,520
28												

Red-Yellow-Green Color Scale identifies low values in red, midrange values in yellow, and high values in green.

Figure 3.51

The color scale now shows yellow highlight identifying the middle values in the range. Next, you decide to add icons as a visual indicator to the profit margin values.

Select cells B25 through M25.

Click

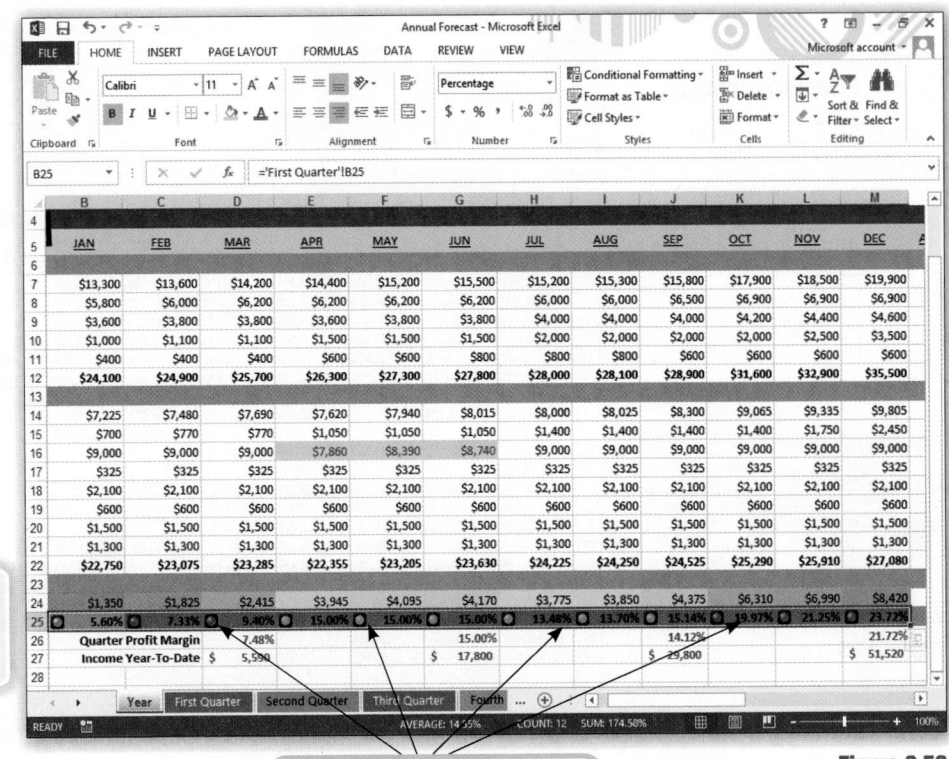

Figure 3.52

Select Icon Sets and point to the different icon sets to see the live preview.

Choose 3 Traffic Lights (Rimmed) in the Shapes group.

Your screen should be similar to Figure 3.52

Traffic light icons identify the lower third in red, the middle third in yellow, and the upper third in green.

The icons give a better indication of which months had a higher or lower profit margin. Red shows where the profit margin value was in the lower third, yellow indicates a profit margin in the middle third, and green shows values in the upper third. These icons reflect the same trends as the color scale used in the net income row of data.

CLEARING CONDITIONAL FORMATTING

Because the icon set formatting really duplicates the information provided by the conditional formatting in the Net Income row, you decide to just keep the Profit Margin formatting. This time you cannot use Undo to remove the conditional formatting from the Net Income row because it also would remove the formatting from the Profit Margin row. To remove conditional formatting, you will need to clear the rules from the range.

1

- Select B24 through M24.

- Click 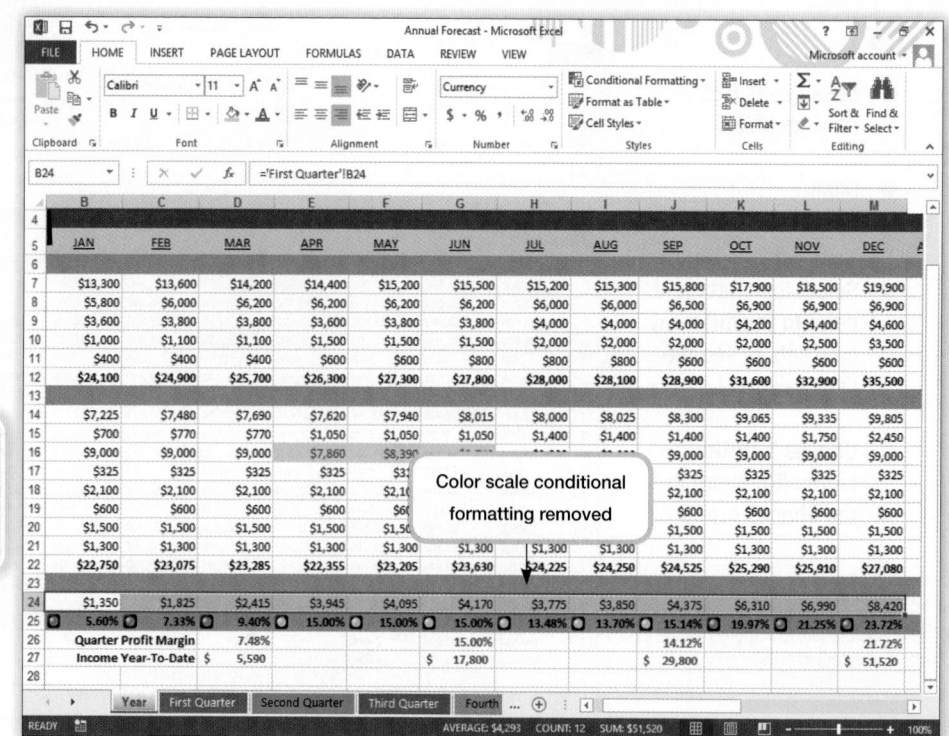 Quick

  Analysis and choose

  Clear Format

Another Method

You also can click Conditional Formatting, select Clear Rules, and choose Clear Rules from Selected Cells.

Your screen should be similar to Figure 3.53

Figure 3.53

The conditional formatting rules for the specified range were cleared and the formatting removed.

Using Sparklines

Although the icon set conditional formatting in the profit margin row identifies variances in a range, the trend is not entirely obvious. To show the data trends more clearly, you decide to create a sparkline. A **sparkline** is a tiny chart of worksheet data contained in the background of a single cell. Generally, a sparkline is positioned close to the data it represents, to have the greatest impact.

CREATING A SPARKLINE

You want to display the sparkline in cell O25, to the right of the profit margin row.

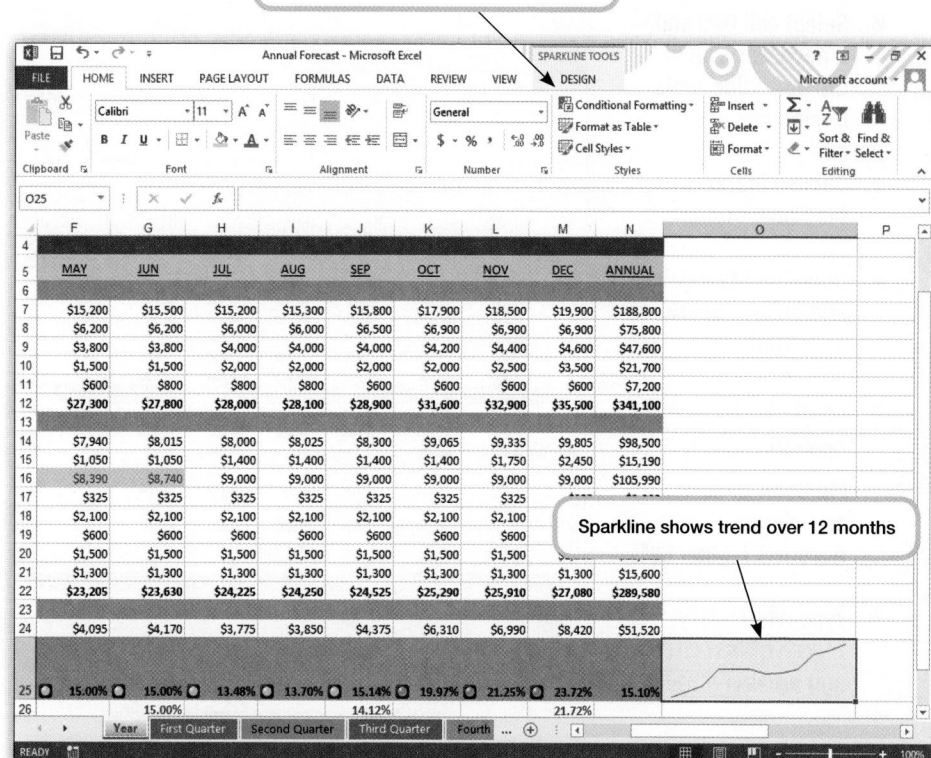

1

- Select cells B25 through M25.

- Open the Insert tab.

- Click ∿ Line in the Sparklines group.

- Enter O25 as the cell location to display the chart.

- Click OK.

- Increase the width of column O to 30, and the height of row 25 to 50.

Your screen should be similar to Figure 3.54

Figure 3.54

Sparkline Tools Design tab is available

Sparkline shows trend over 12 months

Another Method

The Quick Analysis tool will insert a sparkline chart in the cell immediately to the right of the selected range.

A simple line chart of the profit margin values clearly shows the increase in profit margin over the year.

ENHANCING A SPARKLINE

Next you want to improve the appearance of the sparkline by adding data markers and color. Then you will enter a descriptive label in the cell to clarify the meaning of the sparkline.

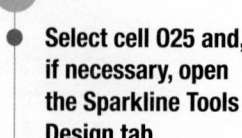

1

● Select cell O25 and, if necessary, open the Sparkline Tools Design tab.

● Choose Markers in the Show group.

● Open the Style gallery and choose Sparkline Style Dark #1.

● Open the Home tab, open the 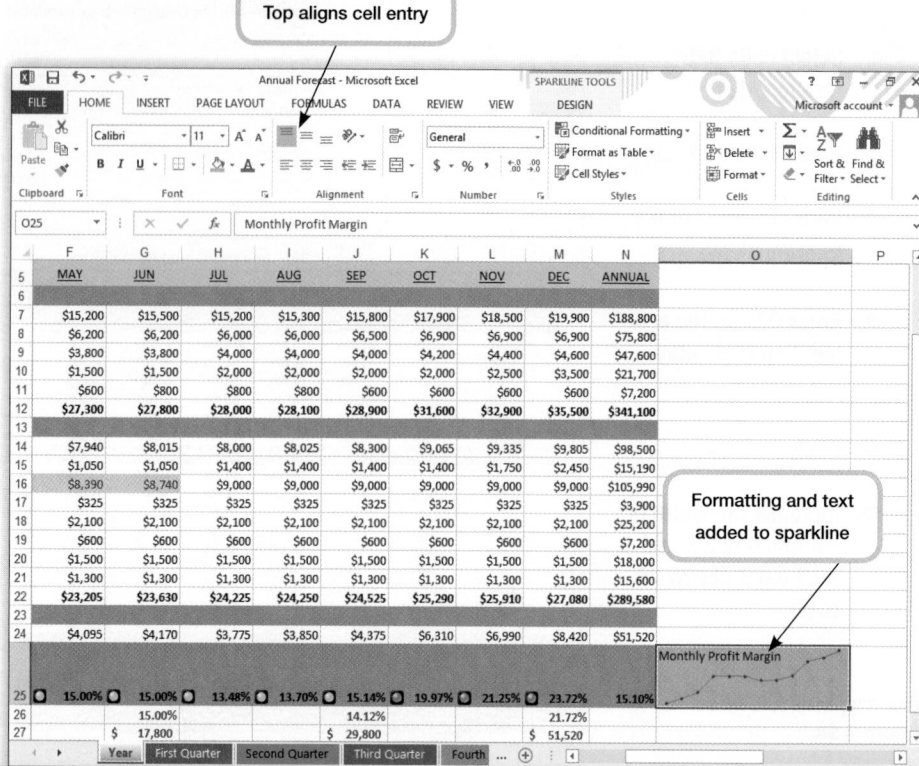 Fill Color gallery, and choose Brown, Accent 3, Lighter 60%.

● Type Monthly Profit Margin and press ←Enter.

Having Trouble?

The line chart will not display as you enter the text.

● Top-align the entry in cell O25.

● Save the workbook.

Your screen should be similar to Figure 3.55

Additional Information

To delete a sparkline, select the cell containing the sparkline and choose ✎ Clear ▾ in the Group group of the Sparkline Tools Design tab.

Figure 3.55

The addition of the sparkline helps clarify the profit margin trend for the year. Just like a chart, if the data in a referenced cell changes, the sparkline will automatically update to reflect the change.

Customizing Print Settings

Now you are ready to print the workbook. Just because your worksheet looks great on the screen, this does not mean it will look good when printed. Many times you will want to change the default print and layout settings to improve the appearance of the output. Customizing the print settings by controlling page breaks, changing the orientation of the page, centering the worksheet on the page, hiding gridlines, and adding custom header and footer information are just a few of the ways you can make your printed output look more professional.

CONTROLLING PAGE BREAKS

First you want to preview the Year sheet.

1

- Open the File tab and choose Print.

- Display page 2 of the worksheet.

Your screen should be similar to Figure 3.56

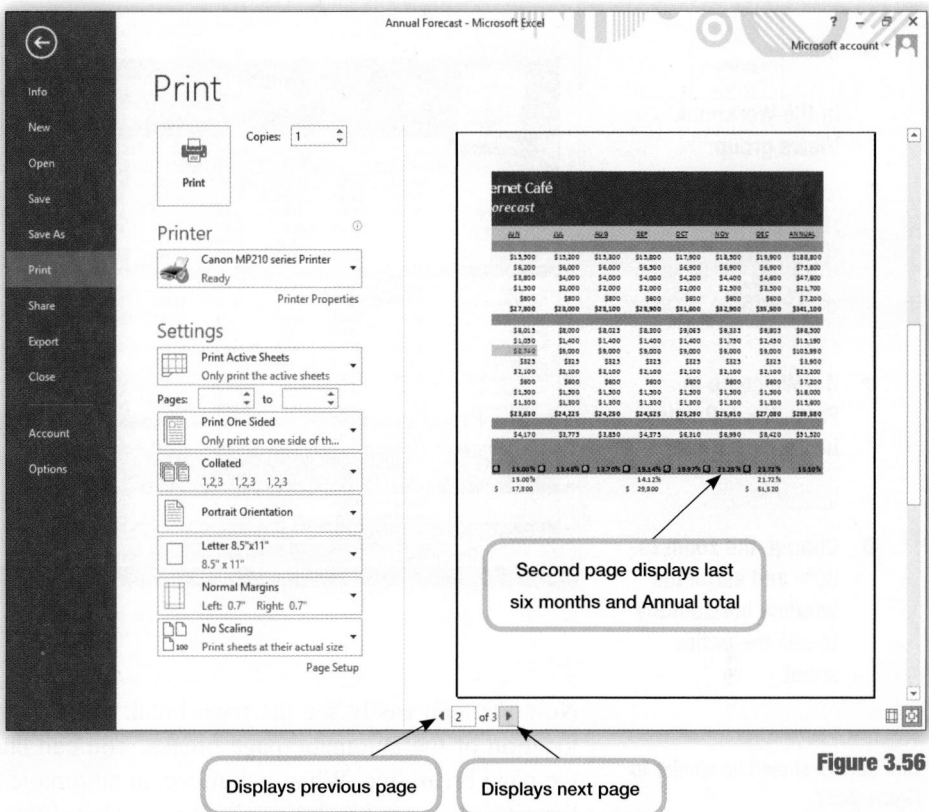

Second page displays last six months and Annual total

Displays previous page

Displays next page

Figure 3.56

The first page of the Year worksheet displays the first six months, and the second page, the remaining months and the annual total. The sparkline is by itself on a third page. Although you could change the orientation to landscape and use the Fit To feature to compress the worksheet to a single page, this would make the data small and difficult to read. Instead, you decide to fit the printout on two pages, with the sparkline on the second page.

To do this, you will change the location of the **page break**, the place where one printed page ends and another starts. Excel inserts automatic page breaks based on the paper size, margin settings, and orientation when the worksheet exceeds the width of a page. You can change the location of the automatic page break by inserting a manual page break location. To help you do this, Page Break Preview is used to adjust the location of page breaks.

- **Close the File tab and open the View tab.**

- **Click** 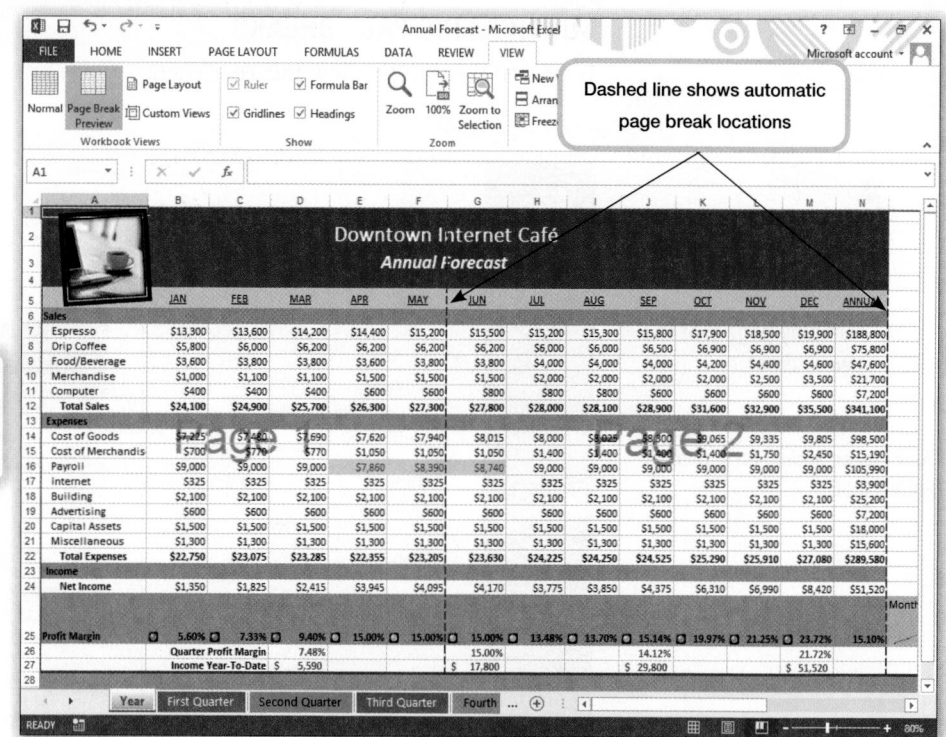 Page Break Preview **in the Workbook Views group.**

- **If a Welcome to Page Break Preview box appears, click** OK.

- **Change the zoom to 80% and scroll the window horizontally to see the entire sheet.**

Your screen should be similar to Figure 3.57

Figure 3.57

Now you can easily see the page break locations. The dashed line indicates the location of the automatic page breaks. You can change the location by dragging the page break line. When you move an automatic page break location to another location, the page break line changes to a solid line, indicating it is a manual page break. To include the sparkline on page 2, you will move the second page break to the right of column O.

Additionally, you realize that the worksheet title will be split between the two pages. You will fix the title by unmerging the cells, moving the title to the left on page 1, and copying the title to page 2.

3

- Point to the page break line after column N, and drag it to the right of column O.

Additional Information

The mouse pointer appears as ↔ when you can move the page break line.

- In a similar manner, drag the first page break line to after the June column.

- Select the two merged cells containing the titles.

- Open the Home tab.

- Open the 🔲 ▾ Merge & Center drop-down menu and choose Unmerge Cells.

- Copy the contents of D2 through D3 to K2 through K3.

- Press (Esc) to clear the selection and move to cell K4.

Your screen should be similar to Figure 3.58

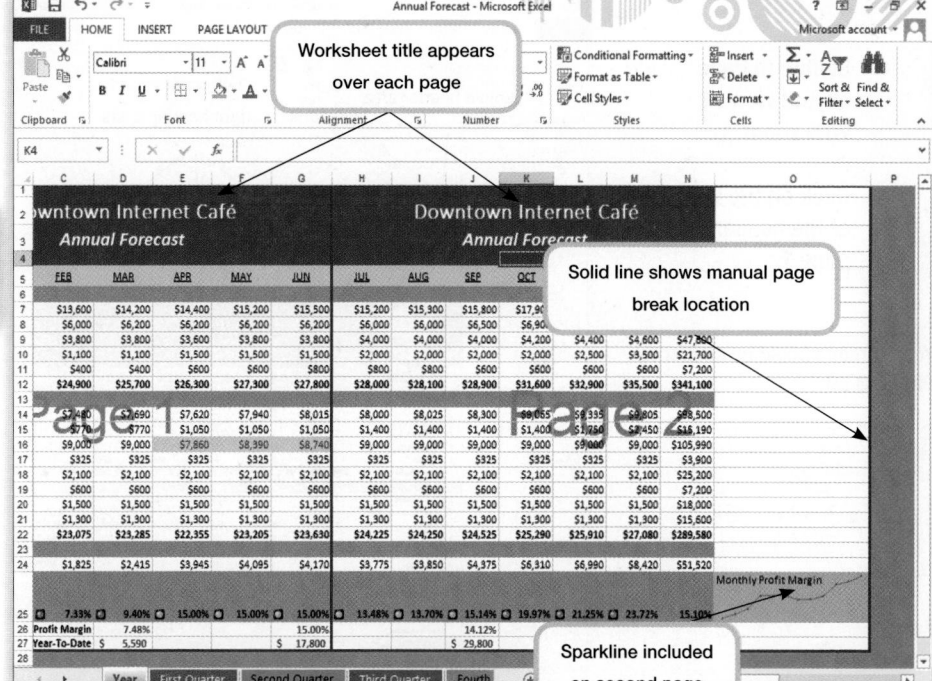

Figure 3.58

The entire worksheet will now print on two pages. Unmerging the cells split the merged cell into its original cells and moved the contents into the upper-left cell of the range of split cells. The center formatting was not removed. Now both pages of the worksheet printout will display a worksheet title.

ADDING A CUSTOM HEADER AND FOOTER

Additional Information

You also can add a custom footer by clicking in the footer area of the page.

You also would like to add a custom header to this worksheet. You will do this in Page Layout view because you can add the header simply by clicking on the header area of the page and typing the header text.

1

- **Switch to Page Layout view at 70% zoom.**

- **Click on the left end of the header area of page 1.**

Your screen should be similar to Figure 3.59

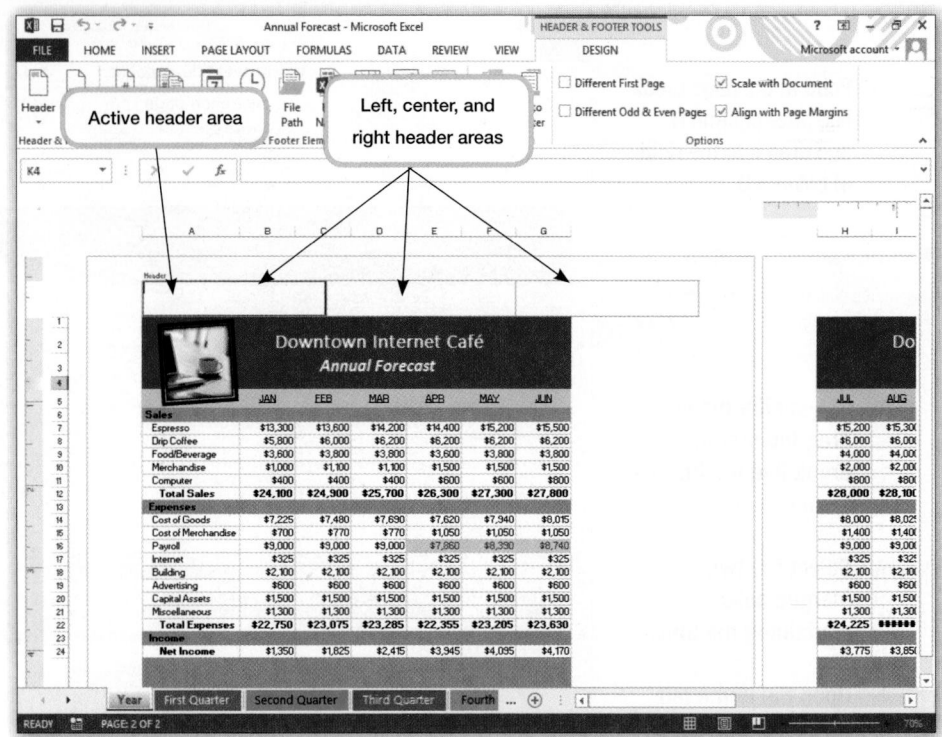

Figure 3.59

The header area is divided into three sections. The left section text box will display the text you enter aligned with the left margin; the center section will center the text; and the right section will right-align the text. You want to enter your name in the left section, class in the center, and the date in the right section. You will enter your name and class information by typing it directly in the box. You will enter the current date using the Current Date feature on the Header & Footer Tools Design tab.

- **Type Created by Your Name**

- **Press** ⌨️ Tab.

- **Enter the name of your class and the section or time.**

- **Press** ⌨️ Tab.

- **Click** [7] Current Date **in the Header & Footer Elements group.**

Your screen should be similar to Figure 3.60

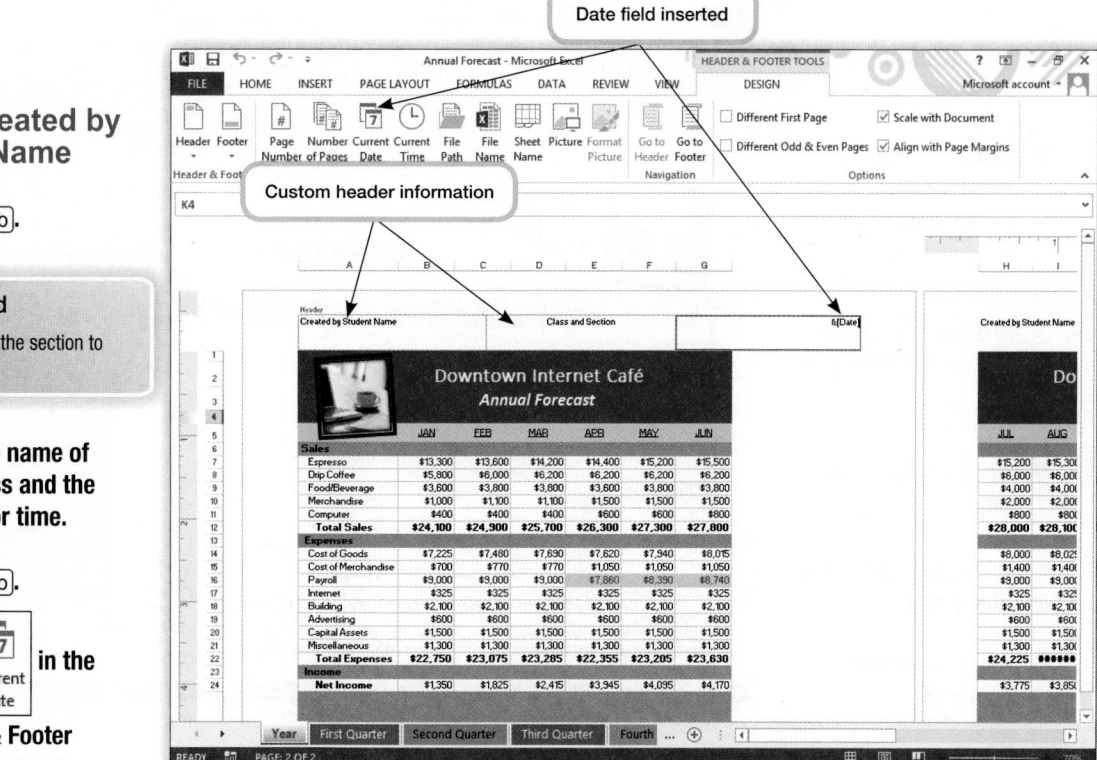

Date field inserted

Custom header information

Figure 3.60

The Date field is entered in the header. It will enter the current date whenever the worksheet is opened. The actual date will display when you leave the header area.

Next, you want to add footers to the quarter sheets. It is faster to add the footer to all sheets at the same time. If you make changes to the active sheet when multiple sheets are selected, the changes are made to all sheets in the group.

Display the First Quarter sheet.

Select the four quarter sheets to group them.

Having Trouble?

Click the First Quarter sheet tab, hold down Ctrl and click the Fourth Quarter sheet tab.

Open the Page Layout tab.

Open the Page Setup dialog box.

Open the Header/Footer tab.

Click Custom Footer... .

Your screen should be similar to Figure 3.61

Additional Information

The quarter sheets are displayed in Normal view. The view you are using applies only to the individual sheet.

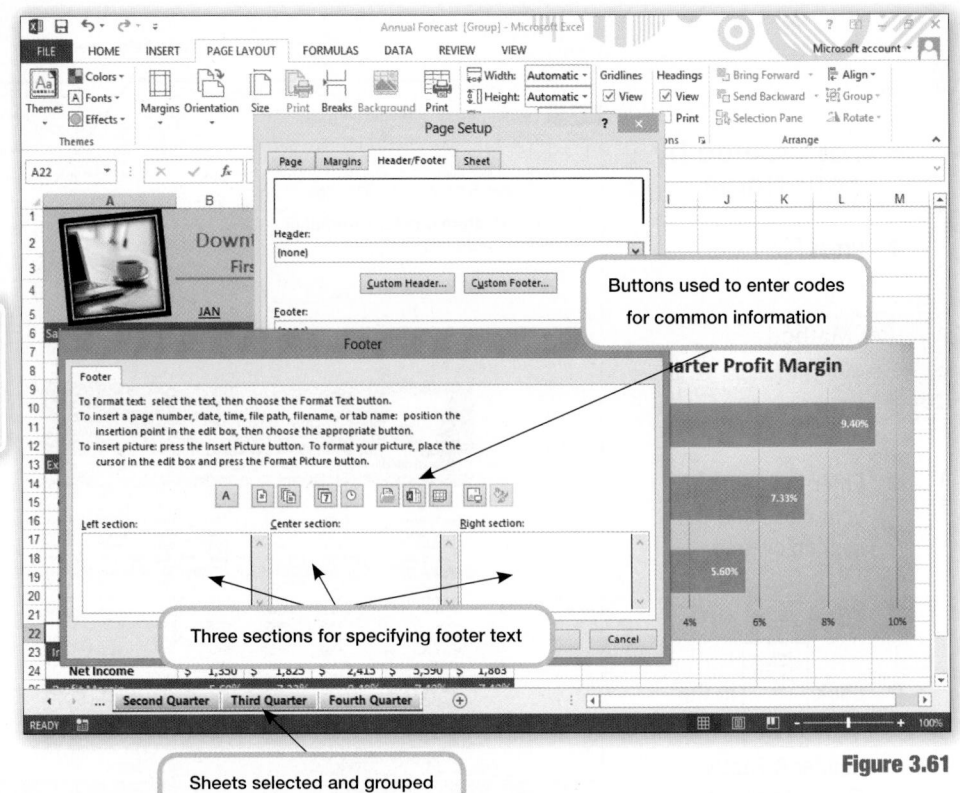

Buttons used to enter codes for common information

Three sections for specifying footer text

Sheets selected and grouped

Figure 3.61

Just like in Page Layout view, the footer area consists of three sections. The buttons above the section boxes are used to enter the codes for common header and footer information. The cursor is currently positioned in the Left section text box.

You will enter your name in the left section, the file name in the middle section, and the date in the right section.

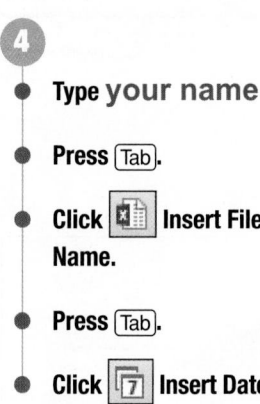

- Type **your name**

- Press Tab.

- Click 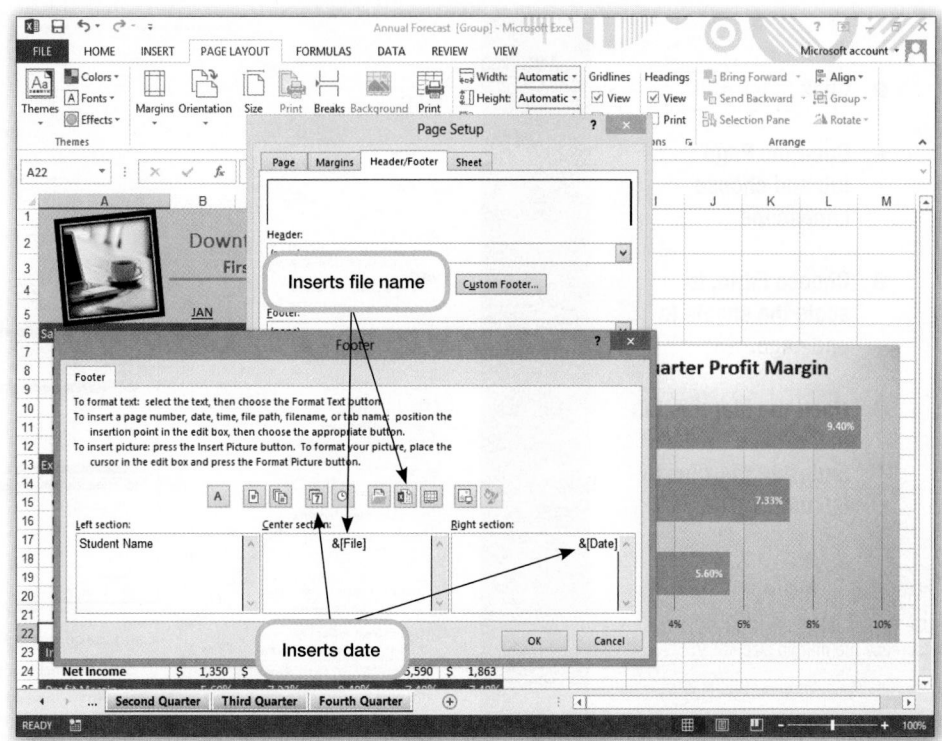 Insert File Name.

- Press Tab.

- Click Insert Date.

Your screen should be similar to Figure 3.62

Figure 3.62

Next you will change the orientation of the four sheets to landscape, change the margins to 0.5 inch, and scale the sheets to fit the page. Then you want to make one final check to see how the worksheets will look before printing the workbook.

- Click [OK].

- **Open the Page tab and choose Landscape.**

- **Choose Fit to, to scale the sheets to one page.**

- **Open the Margins tab and reduce the left and right margins to 0.5 inch.**

Having Trouble?

Use the scroll buttons to increase or decrease the margin size.

- Click [Print Preview].

- **Look at the four sheets to confirm that the footer and orientation changes were added to all the quarter sheets.**

Your screen should be similar to Figure 3.63

Additional Information

You also could drag the right or left border of the margin area in the ruler while in Page Layout view to adjust the size of the margins.

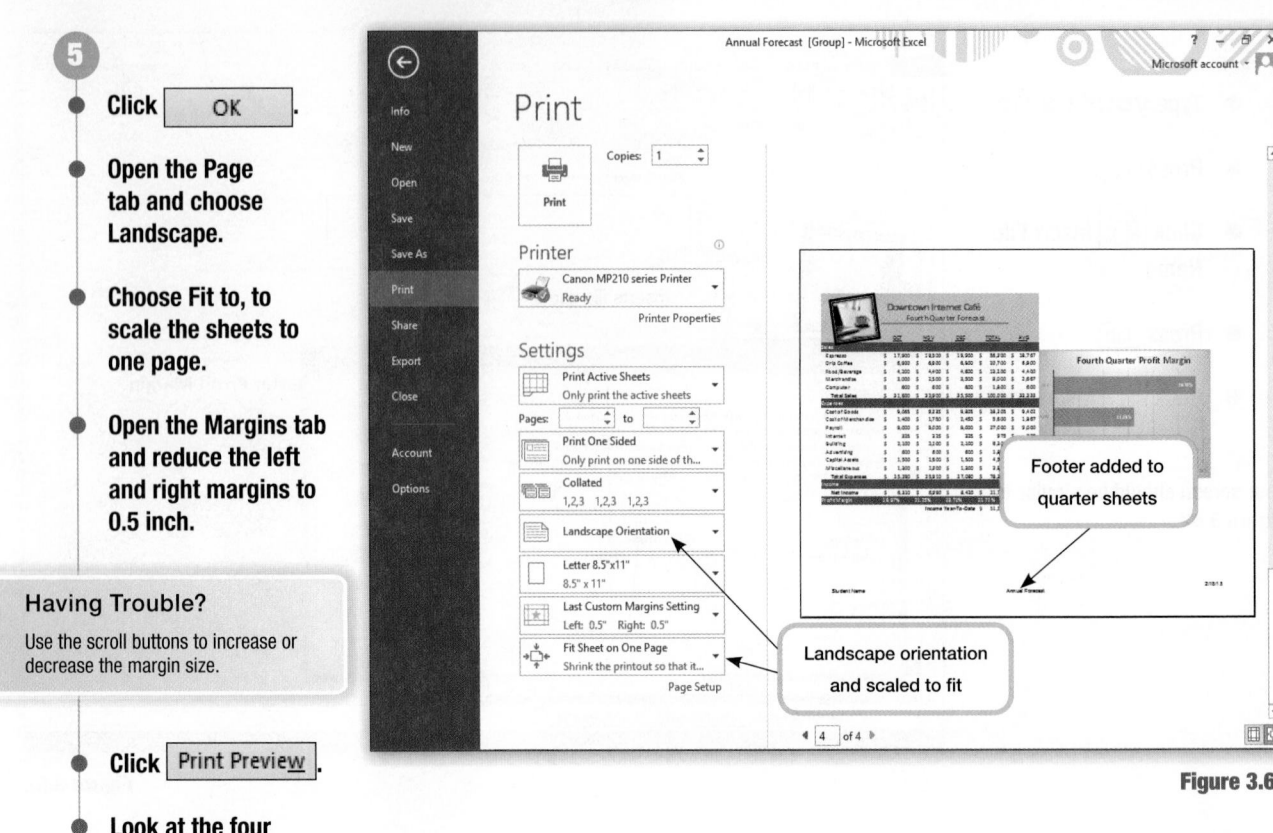

Figure 3.63

The footer as you entered it appears on all selected worksheets and the page layout changes were made as well.

PRINTING SELECTED SHEETS

You want to print the Year and Second Quarter worksheets only. Because the annual worksheet is large, you also feel the worksheet may be easier to read if the row and column gridlines were printed. Although gridlines are displayed in Page Layout view and Normal view, they do not print unless you turn on this feature.

1

- Close the File tab and open the Home tab.

- Right-click on a sheet tab and choose Ungroup Sheets.

- Make the Year sheet active.

- Open the Page Layout tab and choose Print in the Gridlines section of the Sheet Options group.

- Save the workbook again.

- Hold down Ctrl and click the Second Quarter sheet tab to add it to the selection of sheets to print.

- Open the File tab and choose Print.

- Preview the three pages and then print the worksheets.

Another Method

You also can print gridlines by choosing Gridlines from the Page Setup dialog box.

Your printed output should look like that shown in the Case Study at the beginning of the lab.

PRINTING SELECTED AREAS

You are finished printing the Year and Second Quarter sheets and you have the information Evan requested. However, you think Evan also would like a printout of the First Quarter worksheet without the chart displayed. To print a selected area, you first select the cell range that you want to print.

1

- If necessary, close the File tab.

- Make the First Quarter sheet active.

- Select cells A1 through F26.

- Open the Page Layout tab.

- Click Print Area ▾ in the Page Setup group and choose Set Print Area.

Your screen should be similar to Figure 3.64

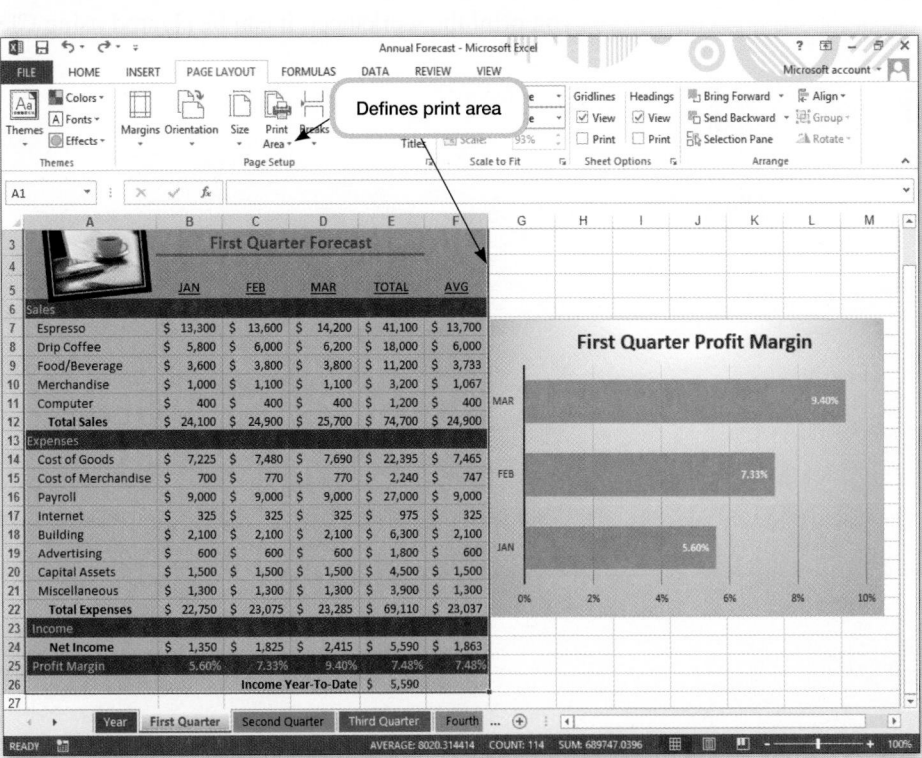

Figure 3.64

The area you selected, called the **print area**, is surrounded with a heavy line that identifies the area.

2

● **Open the File tab and choose Print.**

● **Change the orientation to Portrait Orientation.**

Your screen should be similar to Figure 3.65

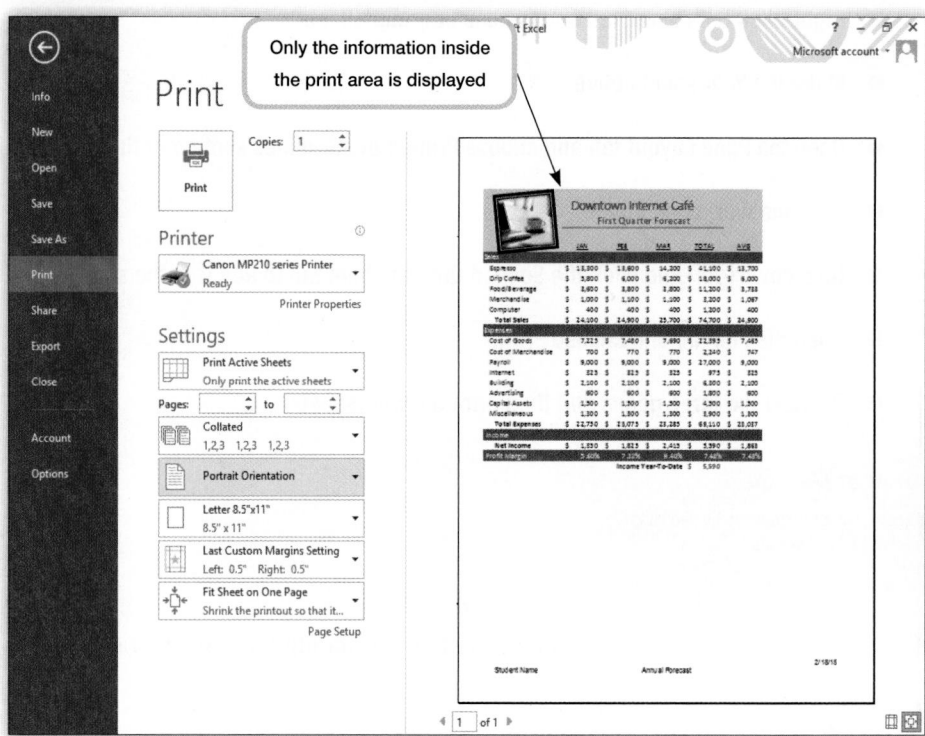

Figure 3.65

The Preview displays only the information contained in the defined print area. The print area is saved with the worksheet and will be used automatically whenever you print the worksheet. It can be cleared using Clear Print Area in the [Print Area ▾] menu.

3

- If necessary, specify any printer settings.

- Print the worksheet.

- Change the Year sheet to Normal view and move to cell A6 in the First Quarter sheet.

- Close and save the workbook and exit Excel.

)CUS ON CAREERS

EXPLORE YOUR CAREER OPTIONS

Medical Sales Account Manager

Medical sales account managers visit doctors and clinics to promote the pharmaceuticals and supplies made by the company they represent. The account managers usually specialize in a few pharmaceuticals or products so that they can help the doctor understand the benefits and risks associated with their products. Medical sales account managers must keep careful and complete records of the samples they have in inventory and what they have delivered to doctors. An Excel workbook is a useful tool to keep track of the many doctors and the deliveries made. A career as a medical sales account manager can start with a salary of $35,000 and go up to over $90,000 plus car and travel benefits.

Absolute Reference (EX3.11)

An absolute reference is a cell or range reference in a formula whose location does not change when the formula is copied.

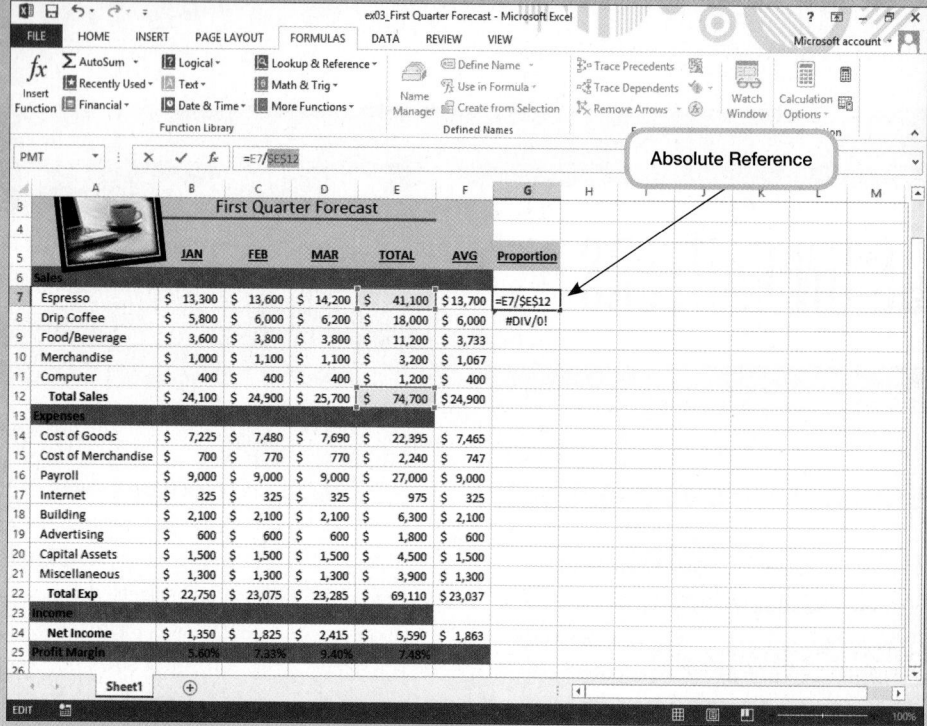

Sheet Name (EX3.16)

Each sheet in a workbook can be assigned a descriptive sheet name to help identify the contents of the sheet.

AutoFill (EX3.19)

The AutoFill feature makes entering a series of numbers, numbers and text combinations, dates, or time periods easier by logically repeating and extending the series. AutoFill recognizes trends and automatically extends data and alphanumeric headings as far as you specify.

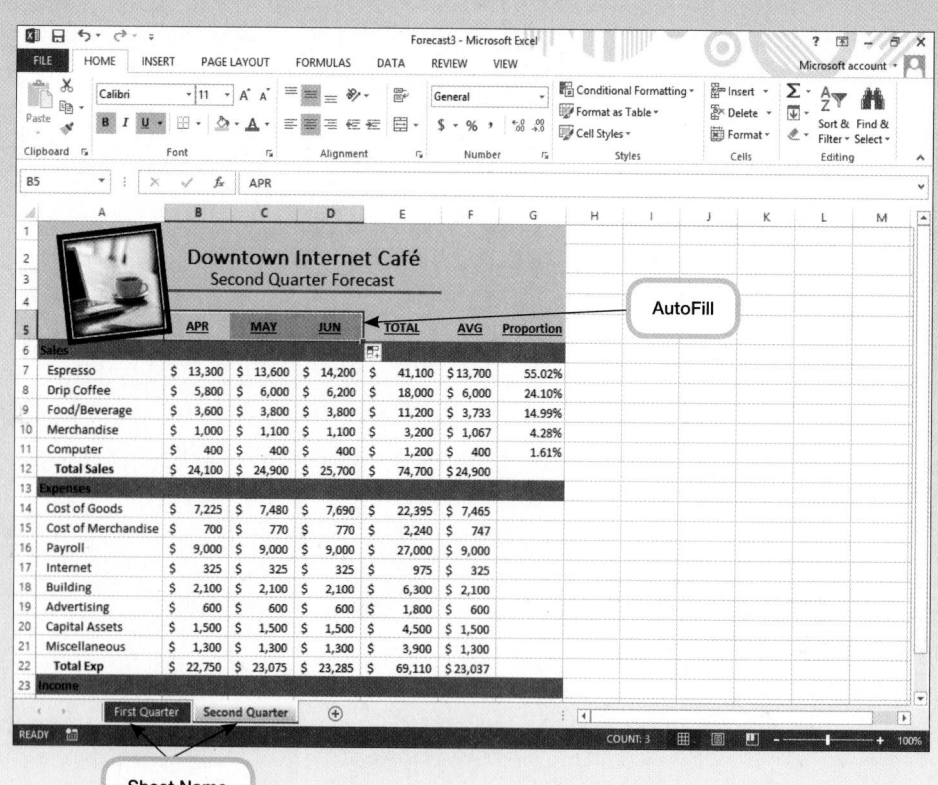

Sheet and 3-D References (EX3.21)

Sheet and 3-D references in formulas are used to refer to data from multiple sheets and to calculate new values based on this data.

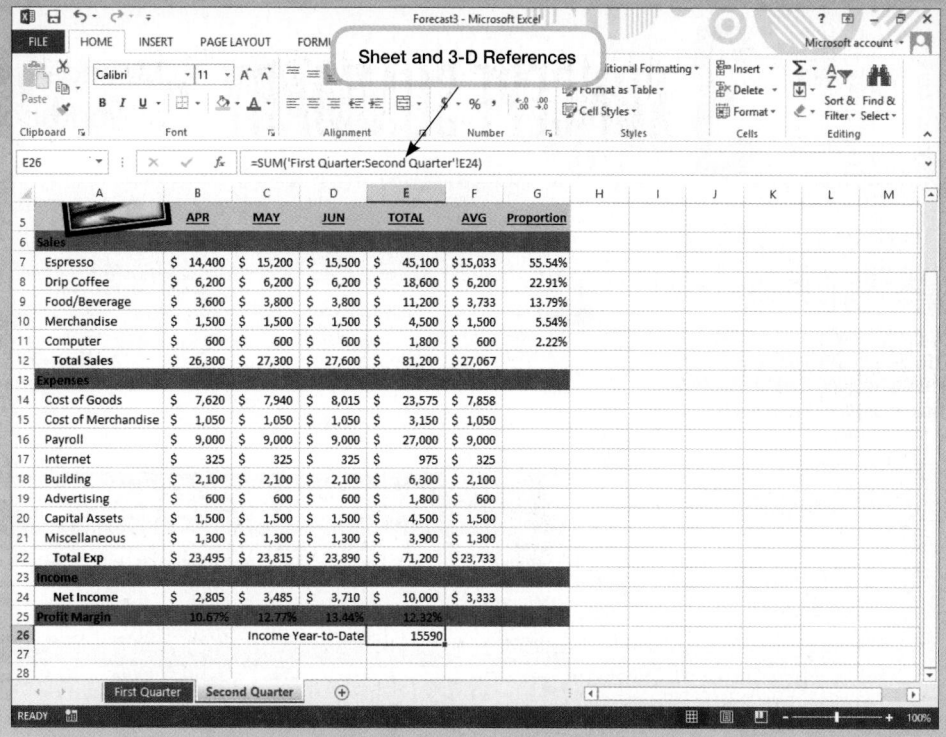

Find and Replace (EX3.28)

The Find and Replace feature helps you quickly find specific information and automatically replace it with new information.

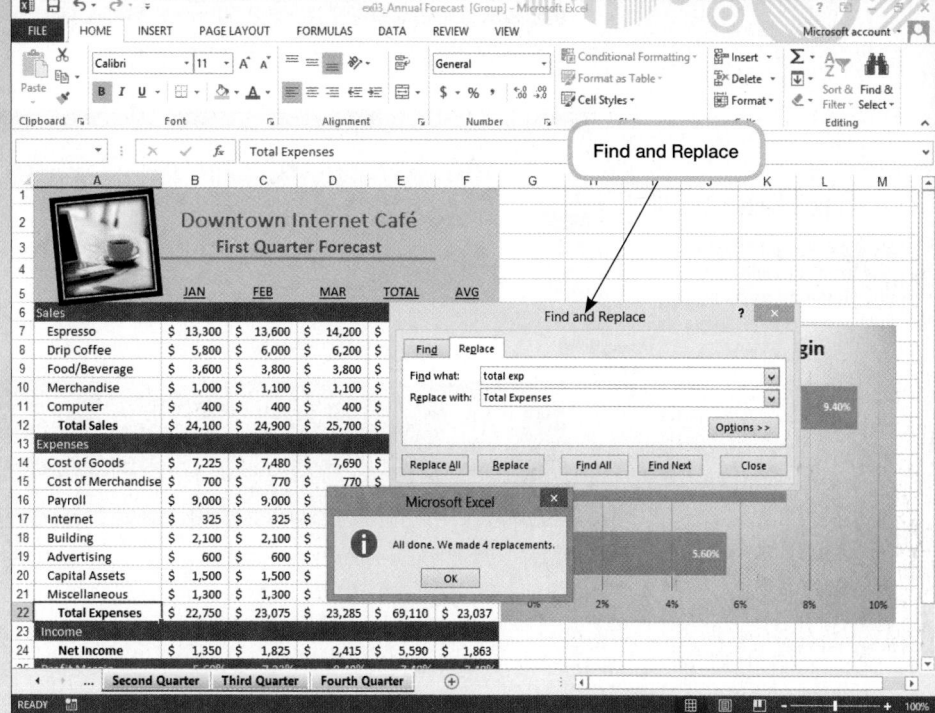

Split Window (EX3.36)

The split window feature allows you to divide a worksheet window into sections, making it easier to view different parts of the worksheet at the same time.

Freeze Panes (EX3.40)

Freezing panes prevents the data in the pane from scrolling as you move to different areas in a worksheet.

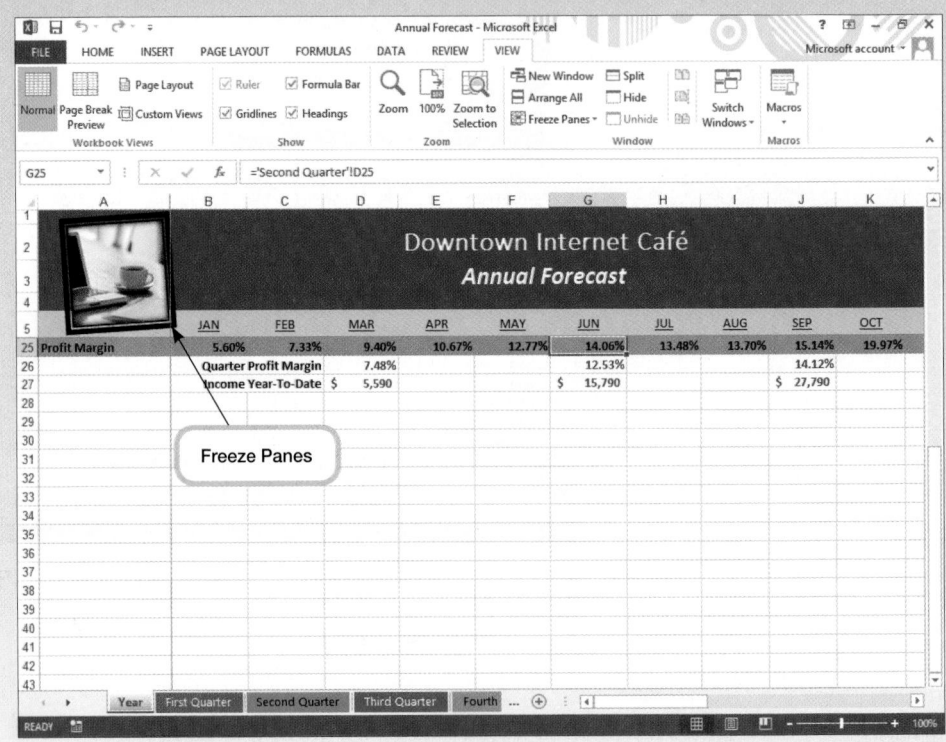

What-If Analysis (EX3.45)

What-if analysis is a technique used to evaluate the effects of changing selected factors in a worksheet.

Goal Seek (EX3.47)

The Goal Seek tool is used to find the value needed in one cell to attain a result you want in another cell.

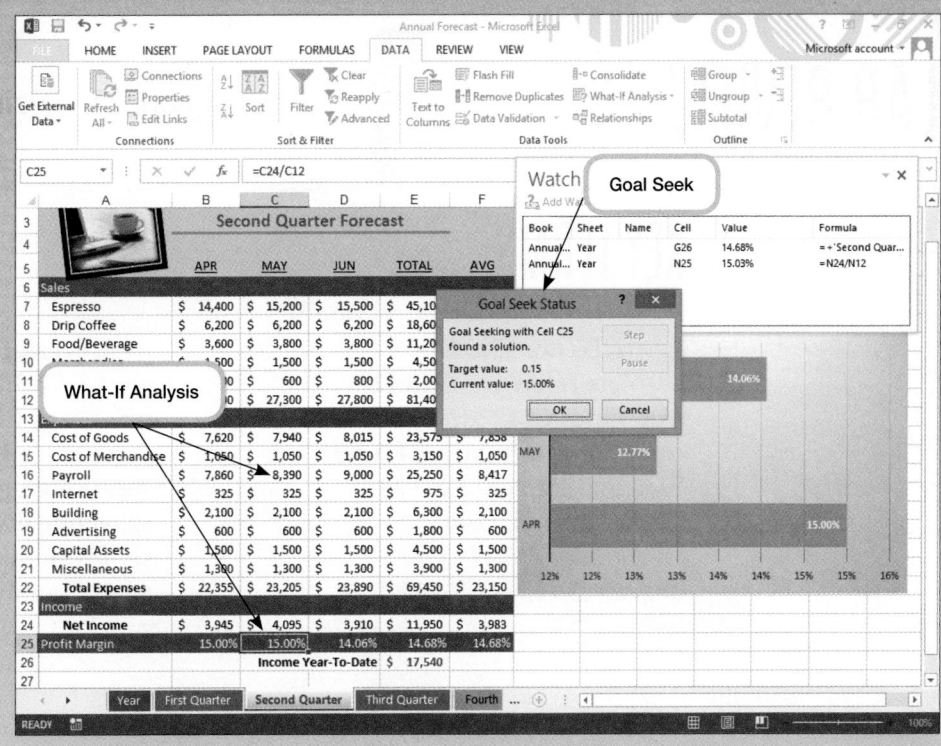

Conditional Formatting (EX3.51)

Conditional formatting changes the appearance of a range of cells based on a condition that you specify.

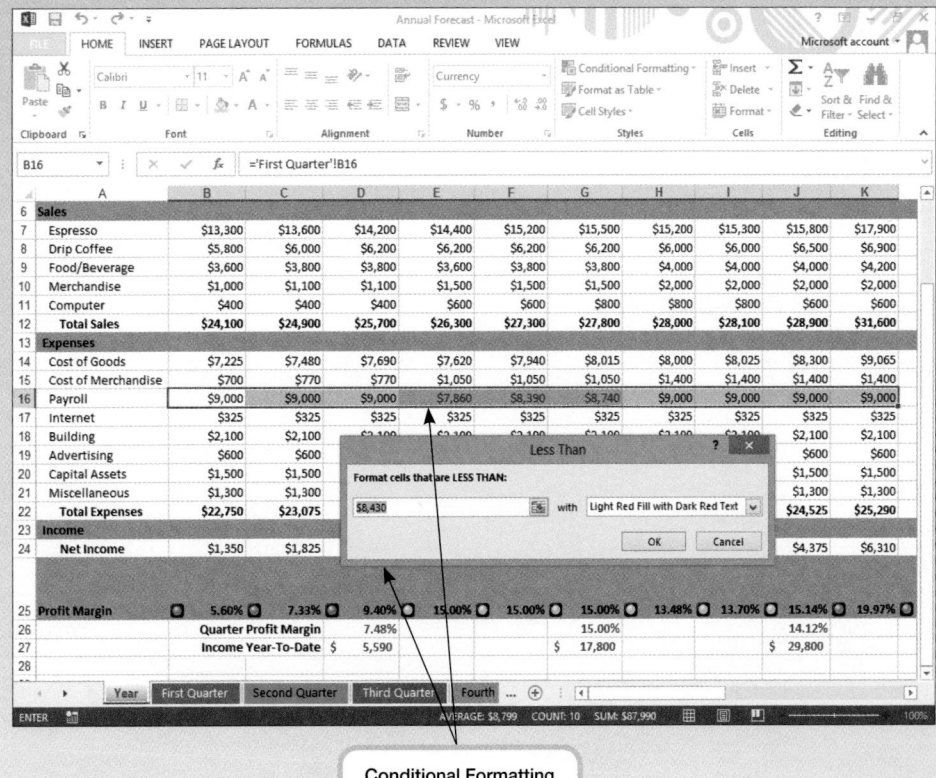

KEY TERMS

3-D reference EX3.21
absolute reference EX3.11
AutoFill EX3.19
conditional formatting EX3.51
Find and Replace EX3.28
freeze panes EX3.40
Goal Seek EX3.47
mixed reference EX3.11

page break EX3.61
pane EX3.36
print area EX3.70
sheet name EX3.16
sheet reference EX3.21
sparkline EX3.58
split window EX3.36
what-if analysis EX3.45

COMMAND SUMMARY

Command	Shortcut	Action
Home tab		
Styles group		
📊 Conditional Formatting ▾	📋 Quick Analysis, Conditional Formatting	Applies Highlight Cells Rules, Top/Bottom Rules, Data Bars, Color Scales, and Icons Sets to selected cells based on criteria
Cells group		
🗑 Delete ▾ /Delete Sheet		Deletes entire sheet
📋 Format ▾ /Rename Sheet		Renames sheet
📋 Format ▾ /Move or Copy Sheet		Moves or copies selected sheet
📋 Format ▾ /Tab Color		Changes color of sheet tabs
Editing group		
🔍 Find & Select ▾ /Find	Ctrl + F	Locates specified text, numbers, and/or formats
🔍 Find & Select ▾ /Replace	Ctrl + H	Locates specified characters or formats and replaces them with specified replacement characters or format
🔍 Find & Select ▾ /Go To	Ctrl + G	Goes to a specified cell location in worksheet
Insert tab		
Sparklines group		
📈 Line	📋 Quick Analysis, Sparkline	Inserts sparkline
Sparklines Tool Design tab		
Style group		
📈		Applies pictured style to sparkline
🧹 Clear ▾		Removes sparkline

COMMAND SUMMARY (CONTINUED)

Command	Shortcut	Action
Page Layout tab		
Page Setup group		
Margins/Narrow		Changes margin settings
Margins/Custom Margins/Horizontally		Centers worksheet horizontally on page
Margins/Custom Margins/Vertically		Centers worksheet vertically on page
Print Area/Set Print Area		Sets print area to selected cells
Breaks/Insert Page Break		Inserts page break at cell pointer location
Breaks/Remove Page Break		Removes page break at cell pointer location
Breaks/Reset all Page Breaks		Restores automatic page breaks
Scale to Fit group		
Height:/1 page		Scales worksheet vertically to fit one page
Sheet Options group		
Print Gridlines		Displays/hides gridlines for printing
Formulas tab		
Formula Auditing group		
Error Checking		Checks worksheet for formula errors
Watch Window		Opens Watch Window

COMMAND SUMMARY (CONTINUED)

Command	Shortcut	Action
Data tab		
Data Tools group		
What-If Analysis ▾ /Goal Seek		Adjusts value in specified cell until a formula dependent on that cell reaches specified result
View tab		
Workbook Views group		
Normal		Changes worksheet view to Normal
Page Layout		Displays worksheet as it will appear when printed
Page Break Preview		Displays where pages will break when a worksheet is printed
Show group		
☑ Gridlines		Turns on/off display of gridlines
☑ Headings		Turns on/off display of row and column headings
Zoom group		
Zoom		Changes magnification of window
Window group		
Freeze Panes ▾ /Freeze Panes		Freezes top and/or leftmost panes
Freeze Panes ▾ /Unfreeze Panes		Unfreezes window panes
Split		Divides window into four panes at active cell or removes split

LAB EXERCISES

MATCHING

Match the lettered item on the right with the numbered item on the left.

1. $B12   _____ a. technique used to evaluate the effects of changing selected factors in a worksheet
2. M34   _____ b. 3-D reference
3. #DIV/0!   _____ c. a what-if analysis tool
4. active pane   _____ d. mixed cell reference
5. conditional formatting   _____ e. applies formatting based on cell rules
6. freeze panes   _____ f. pane that contains the cell selector
7. Goal Seek   _____ g. the sections of a divided window
8. panes   _____ h. sheet reference
9. Sheet1:Sheet3!H3:K5   _____ i. absolute cell reference
10. sparkline   _____ j. indicates division by zero error
11. 'Third Quarter'!A23   _____ k. prevents data in pane from scrolling
12. what-if analysis   _____ l. a tiny chart of worksheet data contained in a single cell

TRUE/FALSE

Circle the correct answer to the following questions.

1.	A relative reference is a cell or range reference in a formula whose location does not change when the formula is copied	True	False
2.	A sparkline is a miniature chart contained in a single cell.	True	False
3.	B$7 is an absolute reference.	True	False
4.	Dragging the sizing handle activates the AutoFill feature and recognizes the cell entry as one that can be incremented.	True	False
5.	Icon Sets conditional formatting applies a two- or three-color graduated scale to compare values in a range.	True	False
6.	The sheet reference consists of the name of the sheet separated from the cell reference by a question mark.	True	False
7.	The Trace Errors formula auditing command outlines the cells causing the error with a colored border.	True	False
8.	To create two horizontal panes with the left pane frozen, move the cell selector in the top row of the window and select the column to the right of where you want the split to appear.	True	False
9.	What-if analysis varies the value in the cell you specify until a formula that is dependent on that cell returns the desired result.	True	False
10.	You can freeze the information in the top and right panes of a window only.	True	False

FILL-IN

Complete the following statements by filling in the blanks with the correct key terms.

1. A technique used to evaluate what effect changing one or more values in formulas has on other values in the worksheet is called _____.

2. A worksheet window can be divided into _____, either horizontal or vertical, through which different areas of the worksheet can be viewed at the same time.

3. A $ character in front of either the column or the row reference in a formula creates a(n) _____ reference.

4. A(n) _____ reference is created when the reference is to the same cell or range on multiple sheets in the same workbook.

5. _____ consist of the name of the sheet enclosed in quotes, and are separated from the cell reference by an exclamation point.

6. _____ formatting changes the appearance of a range of cells based on a set of conditions you specify.

7. The _____ feature logically repeats and extends a series.

8. The _____ tool is used to find the value needed in one cell to attain a result you want in another cell.

9. Use a(n) _____ to show the incremental change in data over time in one cell.

10. When specified rows and columns are _____, they are fixed when you scroll.

LAB EXERCISES

MULTIPLE CHOICE

Circle the correct response to the questions below.

1. A cell or range reference in a formula whose location does not change when the formula is copied is a(n) _____.
   a. absolute reference
   b. frozen cell
   c. mixed reference
   d. relative reference

2. A division of the worksheet window that allows different areas of the worksheet to be viewed at the same time is called a _____.
   a. pane
   b. part
   c. section
   d. window

3. A formula that contains references to cells in other sheets of a workbook is a(n) _____.
   a. Average formula
   b. 3-D formula
   c. Sheet formula
   d. Sparkline formula

4. _____ is used to evaluate the effects of changing selected factors in a worksheet.
   a. AutoCalculate
   b. AutoFill
   c. Value analysis
   d. What-if analysis

5. The cell reference that will adjust row 8 without adjusting column E when it is copied is _____.
   a. E8
   b. E$8
   c. $E8
   d. E8

6. The _____ error value indicates that the wrong type of argument or operand was used.
   a. #####
   b. #DIV/0
   c. #N/A
   d. #VALUE!

7. The _____ feature enters a series of numbers, numbers and text combinations, dates or time periods by logically repeating and extending the series.
   a. AutoFill
   b. AutoRepeat
   c. ExtendFill
   d. ExtendSelect

8. The _____ function key will change a selected cell reference to absolute.
   a. F3
   b. F4
   c. F7
   d. F10

9. The information in the worksheet can be _____ in the top and left panes of a window only.
   a. adjusted
   b. aligned
   c. fixed
   d. frozen

10. The number 32534 displayed with the Currency style would appear as _____ in a cell.
    a. 32,534
    b. $32534
    c. $32,534
    d. $32,534.00

11. Which of the following is NOT a valid sheet name?
    a. 3/12/12
    b. Qtr 1
    c. Second Quarter
    d. Week 8–10

12. To determine a cell value that calculates a desired result in a dependent formula, use the _____ command.
    a. Cell Rule
    b. Goal Seek
    c. Trace Dependent
    d. Trace Precedent

STEP-BY-STEP

GLOBALCOMM INCOME FORECAST ★

1. Leah Miller owns several GlobalComm franchises. She has recorded first quarter results in a worksheet and is ready to project second-quarter income. Your completed worksheet should look similar to the one shown here.

a. Open the workbook ex03_ GlobalComm. Save the workbook as GlobalComm to your solution file location.

b. Select the cells with values, and clear the conditional formatting.

c. Calculate total income by location and by month.

d. Right-click the Sheet1 tab, and make a copy of the sheet at the end. Rename Sheet1 as **First Quarter**. Rename the copied sheet as **Second Quarter**. Choose a color for each sheet tab.

e. In the Second Quarter sheet, change the label in cell B5 to **April**. Then use AutoFill to add labels for May and June. Change the label in cell A3 to **Second Quarter**.

f. Enter the following projected sales values for April.

Location	April
Bellevue Square	8600
Southcenter	15610
The Galleria	12030
Northgate	9580
Alderwood	6740
South Hill	8700
Pacific Place	10980

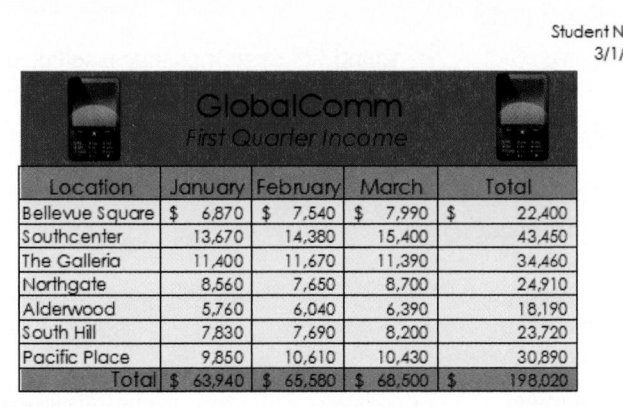

Student Name
3/1/2015

GlobalComm
First Quarter Income

Location	January	February	March	Total
Bellevue Square	$ 6,870	$ 7,540	$ 7,990	$ 22,400
Southcenter	13,670	14,380	15,400	43,450
The Galleria	11,400	11,670	11,390	34,460
Northgate	8,560	7,650	8,700	24,910
Alderwood	5,760	6,040	6,390	18,190
South Hill	7,830	7,690	8,200	23,720
Pacific Place	9,850	10,610	10,430	30,890
Total	$ 63,940	$ 65,580	$ 68,500	$ 198,020

Student Name
3/1/2015

GlobalComm
Second Quarter Income

Location	April	May	June	Total
Bellevue Square	$ 8,600	$ 9,460	$ 10,879	$ 28,939
Southcenter	15,610	17,171	19,747	52,528
The Galleria	12,030	13,233	15,218	40,481
Northgate	9,580	10,538	12,119	32,237
Alderwood	6,740	7,414	8,526	22,680
South Hill	8,700	9,570	11,006	29,276
Pacific Place	10,980	12,078	13,890	36,948
Total	$ 72,240	$ 79,464	$ 91,384	$ 243,088
			Year-to-Date Income $	441,108

g. May income is estimated at 10 percent more than April income; June income is expected to be 15 percent higher than May income. Enter formulas to calculate these amounts.

h. Group the worksheets, and change the number format for cells B7:E12 to Comma Style with zero decimal places and ungroup the sheets. Set the font for the label in cell A3 to italic.

i. In the Second Quarter sheet, enter the label **Year-to-Date Income** in cell D14. Right-align the label, and match the font size to the body of the data. In cell E14, enter a formula to calculate total income for the first six months by summing cells E13 on both sheets. Apply Accounting Number format with zero decimal places, and remove fill and borders if needed.

j. Group the sheets again. In Page Layout view, add a custom header to display your name and the date on separate lines in the right section. Center the worksheets horizontally. Ungroup the sheets.

k. Document the workbook to include your name as the author. Save the workbook. Preview and print the workbook.

FORECASTING SALES ★★

2. The La Delice Cookies bakery has decided to add brownies to its offerings and wants to know the impact on sales. You are in the process of creating a worksheet of the cookie sales for the last six months. In addition, you want to add brownies to the items for sale and project how much of this item you would need to sell to increase the net income to $2,000 a month. Then, you want to set up a second sheet that you will use to enter the sales information for the second six months when it is available. When you are done, your completed worksheets should be similar to those shown here.

a. Open the workbook ex03_La Delice. Use AutoFill to complete the month headings. Save the workbook as La Delice.

b. Add a blank row below row 15 for brownies. Add the row heading **Brownies** in A16.

c. Edit the formula in B17 to include B16, and copy it across the row through column G.

Student Name
3/1/15

La Delice Cookies
Sales Analysis

	January	February	March	April	May	June	Total	Average
INCOME								
Chocolate Chip	$ 728.03	$ 678.43	$ 712.49	$ 655.51	$ 562.12	$ 622.31	$ 3,956.89	$ 659.48
Peanut Butter	$ 325.22	$ 330.13	$ 308.40	$ 440.14	$ 370.59	$ 519.08	$ 2,293.56	$ 382.26
Ginger Snaps	$ 617.07	$ 697.64	$ 653.71	$ 692.27	$ 538.59	$ 692.26	$ 3,891.54	$ 648.59
Oatmeal Raisin	$ 391.34	$ 389.67	$ 377.76	$ 324.88	$ 279.75	$ 330.00	$ 2,093.40	$ 348.90
Shortbread	$ 949.41	$ 993.30	$ 866.49	$ 893.01	$ 831.29	$ 844.02	$ 5,377.52	$ 896.25
Molasses	$ 606.33	$ 624.96	$ 619.70	$ 613.18	$ 503.40	$ 589.91	$ 3,557.48	$ 592.91
Chocolate Sandwich	$ 331.63	$ 299.84	$ 311.29	$ 408.95	$ 352.23	$ 445.76	$ 2,149.70	$ 358.28
Black & White	$ 576.82	$ 558.03	$ 560.16	$ 535.35	$ 474.15	$ 557.47	$ 3,258.98	$ 543.16

Student Name
3/1/15

La Delice Cookies
Sales Analysis

	July	August	September	October	November	December	Annual Total	Annual Average
INCOME								
Chocolate Chip							$ 3,956.89	$ 728.03
Peanut Butter							$ 2,293.56	$ 325.22
Ginger Snaps							$ 3,891.54	$ 617.07
Oatmeal Raisin							$ 2,093.40	$ 391.34
Shortbread							$ 5,377.52	$ 949.41
Molasses							$ 3,557.48	$ 606.33
Chocolate Sandwich							$ 2,149.70	$ 331.63
Black & White							$ 3,258.98	$ 576.82
Date Nut Bars							$ 4,340.96	$ 741.13
Lemon Bars							$ 1,731.78	$ 317.12
Brownies							$ 2,411.31	$ 336.88
Total Income	$ -	$ -	$ -	$ -	$ -	$ -	$ 35,063.12	$ 2,960.49
EXPENSES								
Payroll							$ 9,450.78	$ 1,589.94
Cost of Goods							$ 6,112.34	$ 1,081.04
Overhead							$ 7,500.00	$ 1,250.00
Total Expenses	$ -	$ -	$ -	$ -	$ -	$ -	$ 23,063.12	$ 1,960.49
INCOME	$ -	$ -	$ -	$ -	$ -	$ -	$ 12,000.00	$ 1,000.00

LAB EXERCISES

d. Increase the cost of goods for each month by 12 percent to account for the added goods needed to make the brownies.

e. Enter the formulas to calculate the Total Expenses in row 23.

f. Correct all the formula errors in row 25.

g. Enter the functions to calculate the Total and Average values in cells H6:I6. Copy the functions down the columns through row 25. Clear the formulas from all cells that reference blank cells, except for row 16.

h. Freeze the window with the titles in column A and above row 5 frozen so you can scroll to see the Income values in row 25 while working on the brownie sales next.

i. Assuming other cookie sales remain the same, you want to know how much brownie sales would be necessary to generate a monthly net income of $2,000. Use Goal Seek to answer these questions and calculate the brownie sales figures for all months. (*Hint:* Net income is displayed in row 25.)

j. Unfreeze the window.

k. Using conditional formatting, create a cell rule that will highlight those cookies that have total sales greater than $3,000. Use a highlight color of your choice.

l. You will soon be working on the sales figures for the second six months and want to set up a second sheet to hold this information when it is available. Make a copy of Sheet1 at the end. Change the month headings using AutoFill for the second six months (July to December).

m. Rename Sheet1 to **January-June Sales**. Rename Sheet2 to **July-December Sales**. Add tab colors of your choice.

n. In the July-December Sales sheet, delete the contents only in cells B6:G16 and B20:G22. In cell H6, enter a formula that adds the total from January through June with the monthly figures from July through December. Copy the formula down the column. Change the average formula to average the 12 months. Clear the formula from all cells that reference blank cells. Clear the conditional formatting from all cells in the July-December Sales sheet. Check the formulas by entering (and then removing) some sample data. Change the label in H4 to **Annual Total** and I4 to **Annual Average**. Best fit both columns.

o. In the January-June Sales sheet, add a line sparkline in cell J16 using the monthly sales numbers for brownies in row 16. Type **Brownie Sales** in the cell, and top-align the text. Increase the row height and column width to show the sparkline. Display markers, and choose a style of your choice. Add a thick box border to J16.

p. Use the Find and Replace command to change "bars" to "Bars" in both sheets. In Document Properties, type your name in the Author text box. Add a custom header with your name and the date left-aligned to both sheets.

q. Preview the workbook. Change the print orientation to landscape. Make the necessary adjustments to print each worksheet on a single page. Print both worksheets.

r. Save the workbook.

SPRING BREAK TOUR COST ANALYSIS ★★

3. Colleen, a travel analyst for Adventure Travel Tours, is evaluating the profitability of a proposed trip to Rome for spring break. She has determined that a cost of $5,000 is adequate and will attract a number of students and others. Colleen has started a worksheet to assess the break-even point at which the gross revenue equals the total costs (net income = 0). With that information, she can approximate how many travelers are necessary to reach certain profit levels ($5,000 and $10,000). She has set these package costs:

Air transportation	$1,400 per person
Ground transportation	$460 per person
Hotels	$1,475 per person
Included meals	$900 per person
Included admissions	$250 per person
Local tour guides	$3,000
Administrative expense	$2,000

Your completed worksheets will look similar to those shown here.

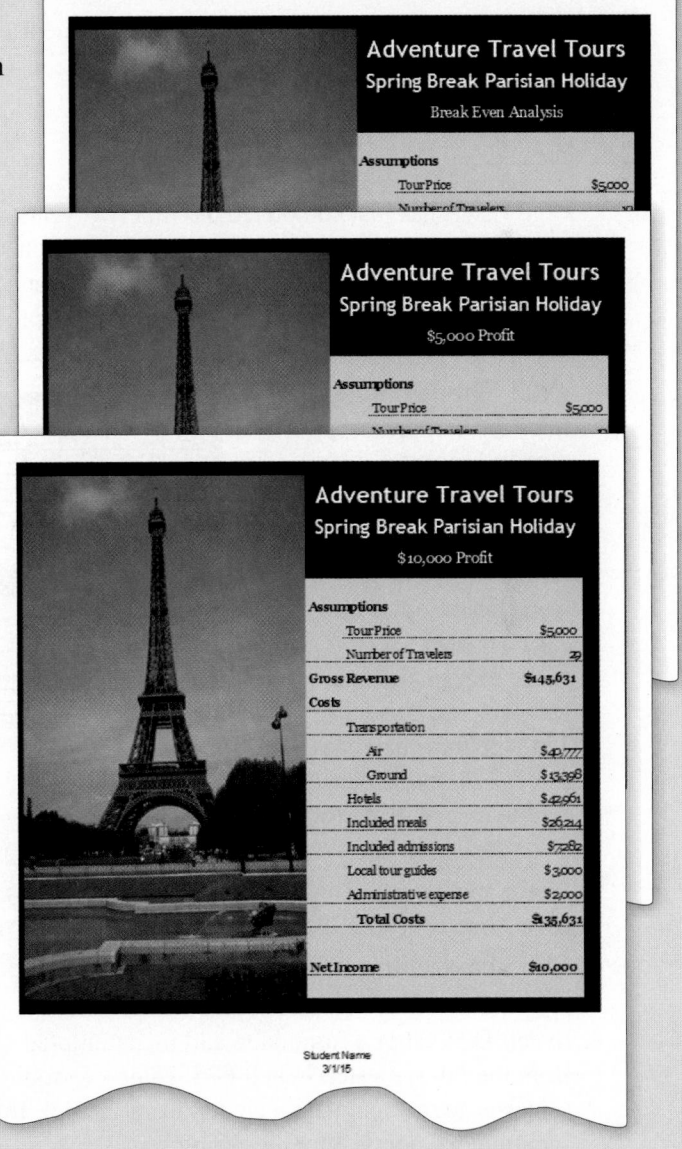

a. Open the workbook ex03_Roman Holiday. Save the workbook as Roman Holiday to your solution file location.

b. In cell E10, enter a formula to calculate revenue using the sample values. Set the result to be right-aligned, black, and bold.

c. In cell E13, enter a formula to multiple the number of travelers times $1,400. Enter similar formulas for cells E14:E17. Enter the values shown in the table above for the tour guides and administrative expense. Format these values as Currency with zero decimal places.

d. Calculate total costs in cell E20. Calculate net income in cell E22, and right-align the result. Make both cells bold.

e. Use Goal Seek to determine the number of travelers for break even, when the result for cell E22 is zero (0).

f. Make a copy of Sheet1 tab at the end. Rename Sheet1 as **BreakEven**. Rename the copied sheet as **$5,000 Profit**. Choose a color for each sheet tab.

g. Edit the label in cell C4 of the $5,000 Profit sheet to **$5,000 Profit**. Use Goal Seek again to find the number of travelers required to meet this income goal.

LAB EXERCISES

h. Make another copy of either sheet, name it **$10,000 Profit**, and use Goal Seek to find the number of travelers.

i. Group the sheets, and use Find and Replace to replace all occurrences of "Meals" with "meals." Then do the same for "Admissions."

j. With the sheets grouped, set the left and right margins at 0.5 inch and center the page horizontally. Scale it to fit one portrait page.

k. With the sheets grouped, use Page Layout view to add a footer that displays your name and the date, each on a separate line, in the center section. Ungroup the sheets.

l. Document the workbook to include your name as the author. Save the workbook. Preview and print the workbook.

GRADE POINT AVERAGE ANALYSIS ★★★

4. George Lewis has just completed the first two years of his undergraduate program in architecture. He has built a workbook that shows his grades for each semester on a separate worksheet. He has asked you to help him move all the data to a single worksheet so that he can view his two-year record on a single sheet. Your completed worksheet will look similar to the one shown here.

a. Open the workbook ex03_Grade Report. Save the workbook as Grade Report to your solution file location.

b. Clear the conditional formatting from the Fall1 worksheet. Copy cells A1:F3 to start in cell A13. Make row 13 the same height as row 1. Set row 15 to the same height as row 3. Edit the label in cell A13 to display **Spring Grades, Year 1**.

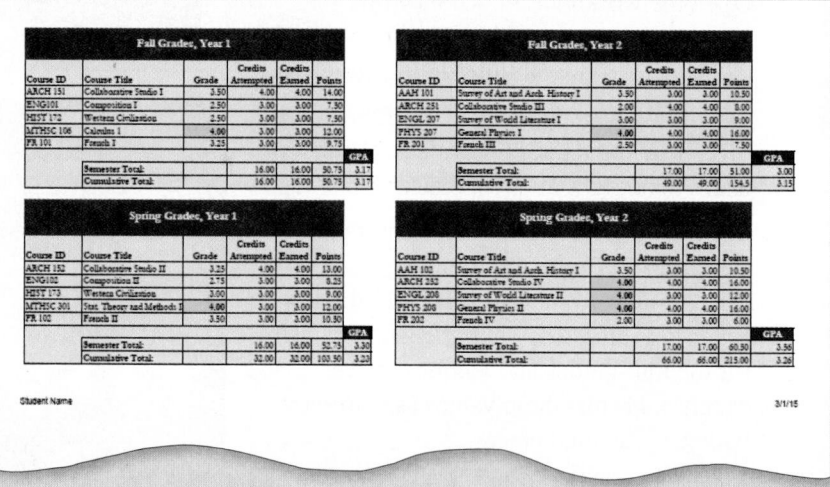

c. Select and copy cells A7:F11 on the Spring1 sheet to start in cell A16 on the Fall1 sheet. Then copy cells A9:G11 on the Fall1 sheet to cells A21:G23 on the same sheet.

d. Clear the conditional formatting from the spring data. Delete the values/formulas shown for the cumulative total for the spring data.

e. In cell D23, enter a formula to add the attempted credit hours from the spring semester to the hours from the fall semester. In cell E23, enter a formula to add the credit hours earned from the spring semester to the cumulative credits from the fall. In cell F23, enter a formula to calculate the total accumulated points after the spring semester.

f. Copy the formula in cell G22 to cell G23. Format all values to show two decimal places.

g. Copy cells A1:F3 to start in cell I1, keeping the same column widths. Edit the label in cell I1 to display **Fall Grades, Year 2**.

h. Select and copy cells A7:F11 on the Fall2 sheet to start in cell I4 on the Fall1 sheet. Clear the conditional formatting and adjust column widths to display all the data. Then copy cells A9:G15 on the Fall1 sheet to cells I9:O15 on the same sheet.

i. Delete the values in cells L11:O11. In cell L11, enter a formula to add the attempted credit hours from this semester to the cumulative hours from the previous spring semester. Enter similar formulas for the credit hours and points, and copy the formula for the GPA. Format all values to show two decimal places.

j. Complete the final section for the worksheet by copying the data from the Spring2 sheet, clearing the conditional formatting, and adjusting the formulas. Edit the title for the final semester.

k. Increase decimals where needed so that the grades, points, and GPA values all display two places. Check that all data is visible. Make column H about half its current width.

l. Select and delete the Spring1, Fall2, and Spring2 worksheets. Rename the Fall1 sheet as **Grades**.

m. Select all the grade values, and create a highlight cells rule that displays 4.0 grades in black, bold font color with yellow fill.

n. Set landscape orientation, and center the sheet horizontally. Scale the sheet to fit one page.

o. Add a footer that displays your name in the left section and the date in the right section.

p. Document the workbook to include your name as the author. Save the workbook. Preview and print the sheet.

DOGGIE DAY CARE INCOME ANALYSIS ★★★

5. Mei Liao owns Doggie Day Care Center which offers full- and half-day care for dogs as well as grooming and training services. She has prepared a worksheet with figures for January through June but still needs to complete several formulas. She will then create the worksheet for July through December and compile the year's results. Your completed worksheet will look similar to the one shown here.

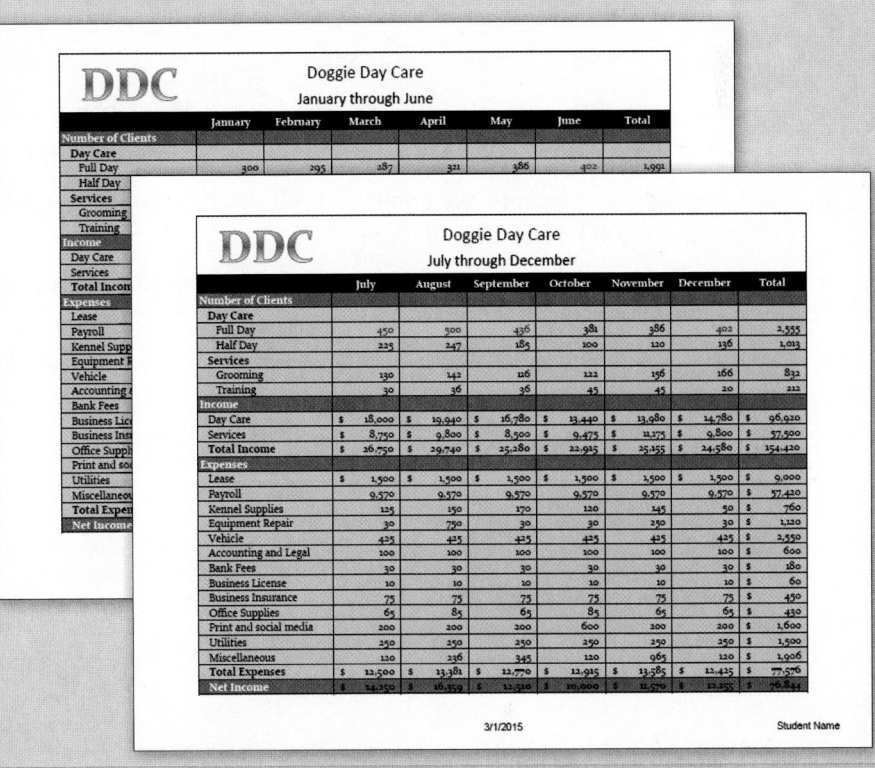

LAB EXERCISES

a. Open the workbook ex03_Doggie Day Care. Save the workbook as Doggie Day Care to your solution file location.

b. Set the zoom size so that you can see all the data. Find and correct formula errors.

c. Use SUM in cells H10:H11 as well as cells H17:H30.

d. Review the formula in cell B14; it calculates the income from grooming and training using the prices shown on the Prices worksheet. Build a similar formula in cell B13 for full- and half-day care. Use absolute references so that you can copy the formula to cells B13:G13. You can key the formula or point to enter it. Enter the SUM function in column H for these rows.

e. Calculate net income in row 31.

f. Set landscape orientation, and center the sheet horizontally. Scale the sheet to fit one page.

g. Add a footer that displays your name in the right section and the date in the center section.

h. Make a copy of the Jan-June sheet that is placed before the Prices sheet. Rename the copied sheet as **Jul-Dec**. Choose tab colors for each sheet in the workbook.

i. On the Jul-Dec sheet, edit the label in cell B3 to show the proper month names. Then key **July** in cell B4, ignoring the AutoComplete suggestion. Use AutoFill to complete the other month names.

j. Delete the values in cells B7:G8 and cells B10:G11. Select cells B31:G31, and add them to the Watch Window.

k. Enter the following values to complete the data for the second half of the year.

	July	August	September	October	November	December
Full day	450	500	436	321	386	402
Half day	225	247	185	100	120	136
Grooming	130	142	116	122	156	166
Training	30	36	36	45	45	20

l. Delete the watches in the Watch Window, and then close the Watch Window.

m. Use Goal Seek to determine the number of full-day care clients needed to increase the net income for October to $10,000. Keep the solution.

n. On each sheet, apply a conditional format to the full-day client numbers that are greater than 400. Build a custom format that you think emphasizes the values.

o. Group the Jan-Jun and Jul-Dec sheets, and replace Marketing (it has one indent space) with **Print and social media**.

p. Document the workbook to include your name as the author. Save the workbook. Preview and print the income sheets.

ON YOUR OWN

EXPANDING BUDGET PROJECTIONS ★

1. In On Your Own exercise 2 of Lab 1, you created a Personal Budget workbook for a three-month budget. Extend the worksheet to add three more months for a total of six months. Add two additional sheets. One sheet will contain a budget for the next six months. The final sheet will present a full year's summary using 3-D references to the values in the appropriate sheets. You need to budget for a vacation. On a separate line below the total balance in the summary sheet, enter the amount you would need. Subtract this value from the total balance. If this value is negative, reevaluate your expenses and adjust them appropriately. Format the sheets using the features you have learned in the first three labs. Add your name in a custom header on all sheets. Preview, print, and save the workbook as Personal Budget2.

COMPANY EXPENSE COMPARISONS ★

2. Using the Internet or the library, obtain yearly income and expense data for three companies in a related business. In a workbook, record each company's data in a separate sheet. In a fourth sheet, calculate the total income, total expenses, and net income for each company. Also in this sheet, calculate the overall totals for income, expense, and net income. Format the sheets using the features you have learned in the first three labs. Add your name in a custom header on all sheets. Preview, print, and save the workbook as Company Expenses in a folder named Business.

HOUSE ANALYSIS ★★

3. Select three cities in which you would consider living after you graduate. Using the Internet or the library, select one price point of housing and determine each house's asking price, square footage, acreage, number of bedrooms, and number of bathrooms. In a workbook containing four sheets, record each city's housing prices and statistics in separate worksheets. In the fourth sheet, calculate the average, maximum and minimum for each city. Include a chart showing the average data for the three cities. Format the sheets using the features you have learned in the first three labs. Add your name in a custom header on all sheets. Preview, print, and save the workbook as House Analysis in a folder named Housing.

LAB EXERCISES

INVENTORY TRACKING ★★★

4. It's a good idea to have an inventory of your personal items for safe keeping. Design a worksheet that will keep track of your personal items divided by category; for example, living room, dining room, bedroom, and so forth. Each category may have as many detail lines as needed to represent the items. For example, sofa, vases, art, and so on. The worksheet should keep track of the number of items; the price paid for each item; the extended price (items * price), if applicable; and the replacement value. Determine the percentage increase in replacement value. Sum the price paid and replacement value in each category and the total value. Format the sheet using the features you have learned in the first three labs. Add your name in a custom header on all sheets. Change the worksheet orientation if necessary; preview, print, and save the workbook as Inventory Tracking.

START YOUR OWN BUSINESS ★★★

5. Owning and managing a small business is a dream of many college students. Do some research on the web or in the library, and choose a business that interests you. Create a projected worksheet for four quarters in separate worksheets. In a fifth sheet, show the total for the year. Include a year-to-date value in each quarterly sheet. In the last-quarter sheet, depending on the business you select, determine how many customers or sales you need in the last quarter to break even and to end the year with a 10 percent profit. Format the sheets using the features you have learned in the first three labs. Add your name in a custom header on all sheets. Preview, print, and save the workbook as My Business.

Working Together: Linking and Embedding between Word 2013 and Excel 2013

CASE STUDY

Downtown Internet Café

Your analysis of the sales data for the first quarter of operations for the Downtown Internet Café projects a small, steady increase in sales each month. If an advertising campaign promoting the new Internet aspect of the Café is mounted, you forecast that coffee and food sales in that quarter will increase sharply.

Evan, the ĉafe owner, is still trying to decide if he should advertise and has asked you to send him a report containing the worksheet data showing the expected sales without an advertising campaign and the chart showing the projected sales with an advertising campaign. Additionally, Evan wants a copy of the second-quarter forecast showing the 15 percent profit margins for each month. He also wants a copy of the workbook file so that he can play with the sales values to see their effects on the profit margin.

You will learn how to share information between applications while you create these reports. Your completed documents will look like those shown below.

NOTE This lab assumes that you know how to use Word 2013 and that you have completed Labs 2 and 3 of Excel 2013.

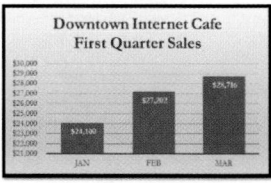

Sharing Information between Applications

All Microsoft Office 2013 applications have a common user interface such as similar Ribbon commands and galleries. In addition to these obvious features, they have been designed to work together, making it easy to share and exchange information between applications. For example, the same commands and procedures to copy information within an Excel 2013 worksheet are used to copy information to other Office 2013 applications such as Word. The information can be pasted in many different formats such as a worksheet object, a bitmap, a picture, a linked object, or an embedded object. How you decide to paste the object depends on what you want to be able to do with the data once it is inserted in the Word document.

COPYING BETWEEN EXCEL AND WORD

The report to Evan about the analysis of the sales data has already been created using Word 2013 and saved as a document file.

1

- **Start Word 2013 and open the document** exwt_Sales Forecast Report.

- **Replace Student Name with your name.**

- **Save the file as** Sales Forecast Report **to your solution file location.**

Your screen should be similar to Figure 1

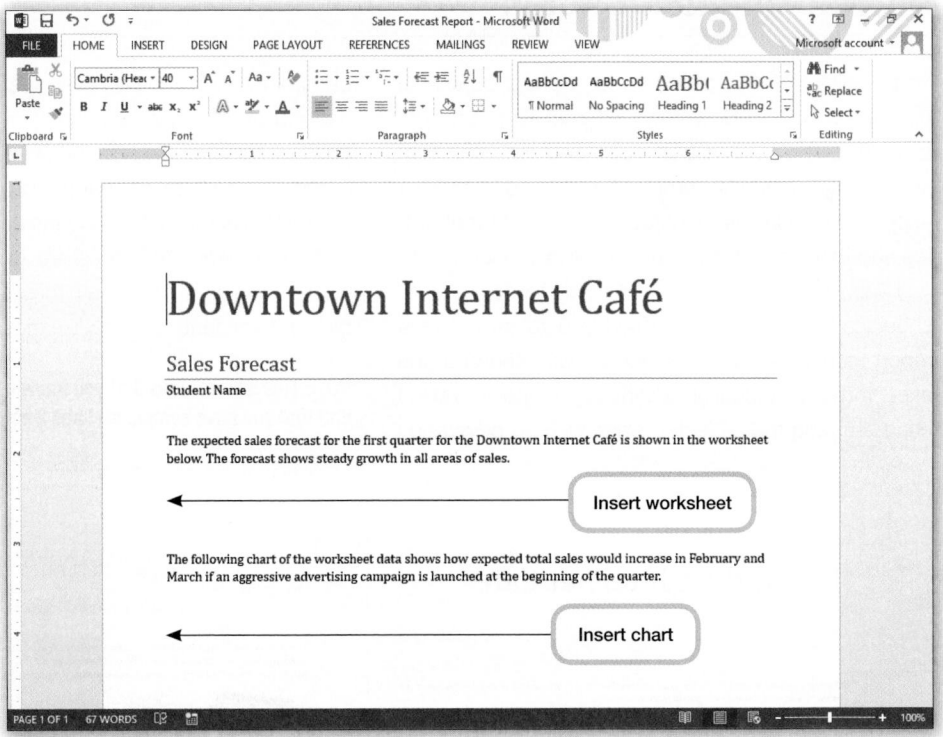

Figure 1

As you can see, you still need to add the Excel worksheet data and chart to the report. To insert the information from the Excel workbook file into the Word report, you need to open the workbook.

2

- Start Excel 2013 and open the workbook exwt_Sales Charts.

- If necessary, enable content

Your screen should be similar to Figure 2

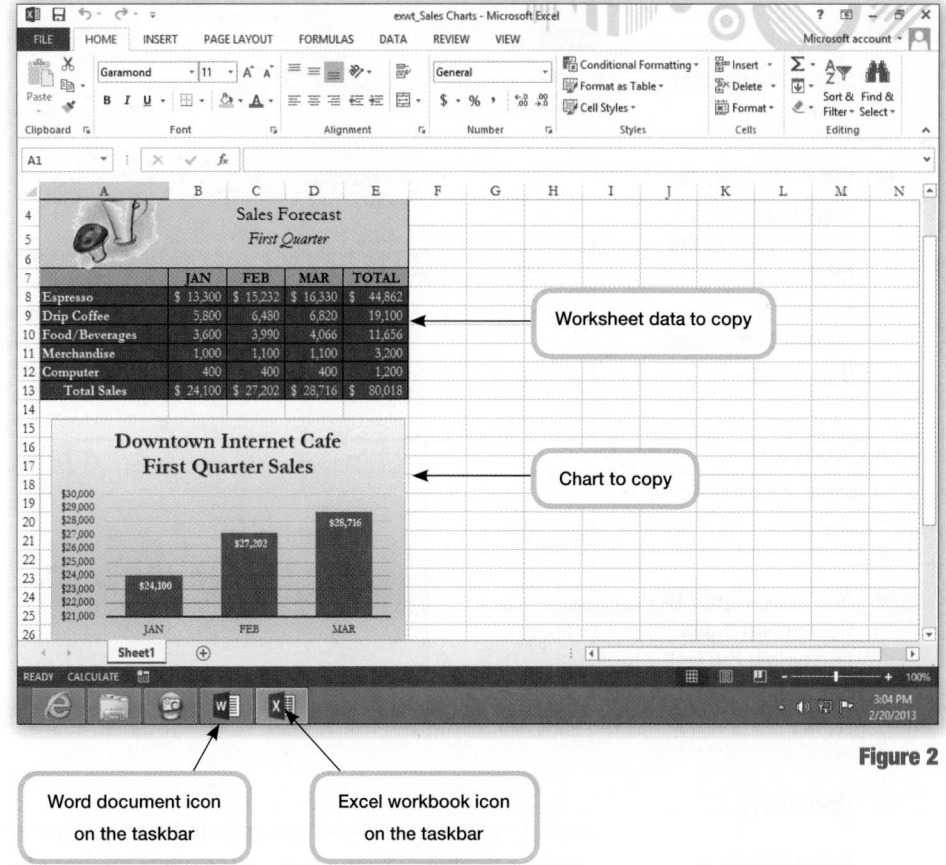

Worksheet data to copy

Chart to copy

Figure 2

Word document icon on the taskbar

Excel workbook icon on the taskbar

There are now two open applications, Word and Excel. You will insert the worksheet data of the first-quarter sales forecast below the first paragraph. Below the second paragraph, you will display the chart.

You will begin by copying the chart from Excel into the Word document. While using Excel, you have learned how to use cut, copy, and paste to move or copy information within and between worksheets. You also can perform these operations between files in the same application and between files in different Office applications. You want to insert the chart as a picture object that can be edited using the Picture Tools commands in Word.

3

- Select the column chart.

- Click 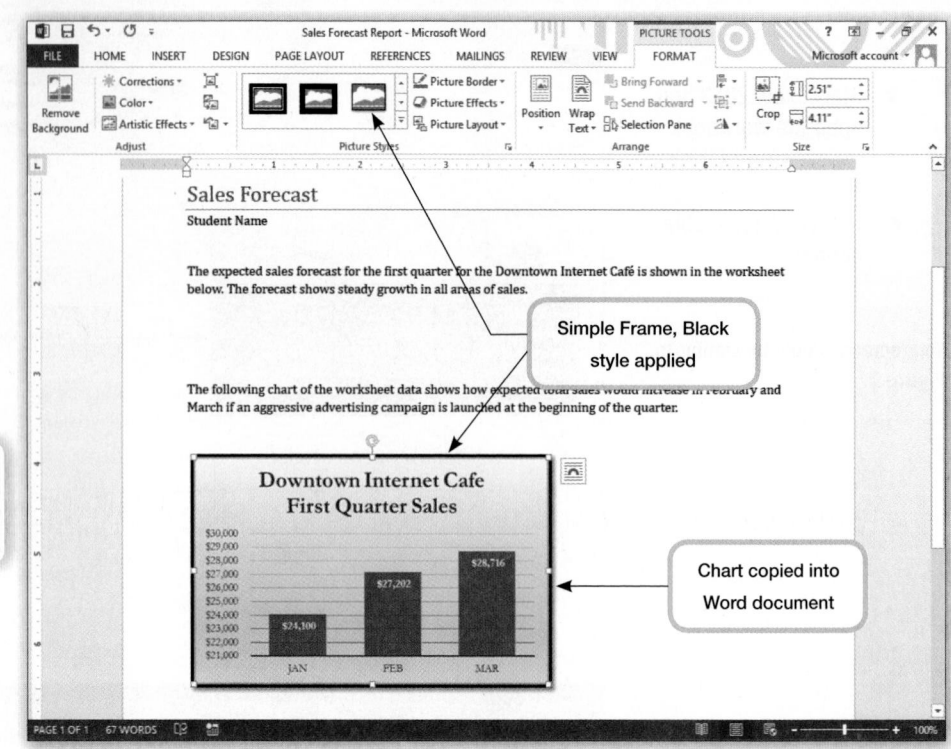 Copy to copy the selected chart object to the Clipboard.

- Switch to the Word document.

Having Trouble?

Click the Word document button in the taskbar.

- Move the cursor to the second blank line below the last paragraph of the report.

- Open the Paste menu and choose Picture.

- Open the Picture Tools Format tab.

- Open the Picture Styles gallery and choose Simple Frame, Black.

- Adjust the size of the chart and position it as in Figure 3.

Your screen should be similar to Figure 3

Simple Frame, Black style applied

Chart copied into Word document

Figure 3

A copy of the chart has been inserted as a picture object into the Word document. Adding the black frame around the chart picture object makes it stand out better. It can be formatted, sized, and moved like any other picture object.

Linking between Applications

Next, you want to copy the worksheet showing the sales trends to below the first paragraph in the report. You will insert the worksheet into the report as a **linked object**. Information created in one application also can be inserted as a linked object into a document created by another application. When an object is linked, the data is stored in the **source file** (the document in which it was created). A graphic representation or picture of the data is displayed in the **destination file** (the document in which the object is inserted). A connection between the information in the destination file to the source file is established by the creation of an **external reference**, also called a **link**. The link contains references to the location of the source file and the selection within the document that is linked to the destination file.

When changes are made in the source file that affect the linked object, the changes are reflected automatically in the destination file when it is opened. This is called a **live link**. When you create linked objects, the date and time on your computer should be accurate. This is because the program refers to the date of the source file to determine whether updates are needed when you open the destination file.

You will copy the worksheet as a linked object so that it will be updated automatically if the source file is edited. To make it easier to work with the two applications, you will display the two open application windows side-by-side.

1

- Right-click on a blank area of the taskbar and choose **Show windows side by side** from the shortcut menu.

- Click in the Excel window and select cells A7 through E13.

- Click ⬛ **Copy**.

- Click in the Word document and move to the center blank line between the paragraphs of the report.

- Open the ⬛ **Paste** menu and choose **Paste Special**.

- Choose **Paste link** from the Paste Special dialog box.

Your screen should be similar to Figure 4

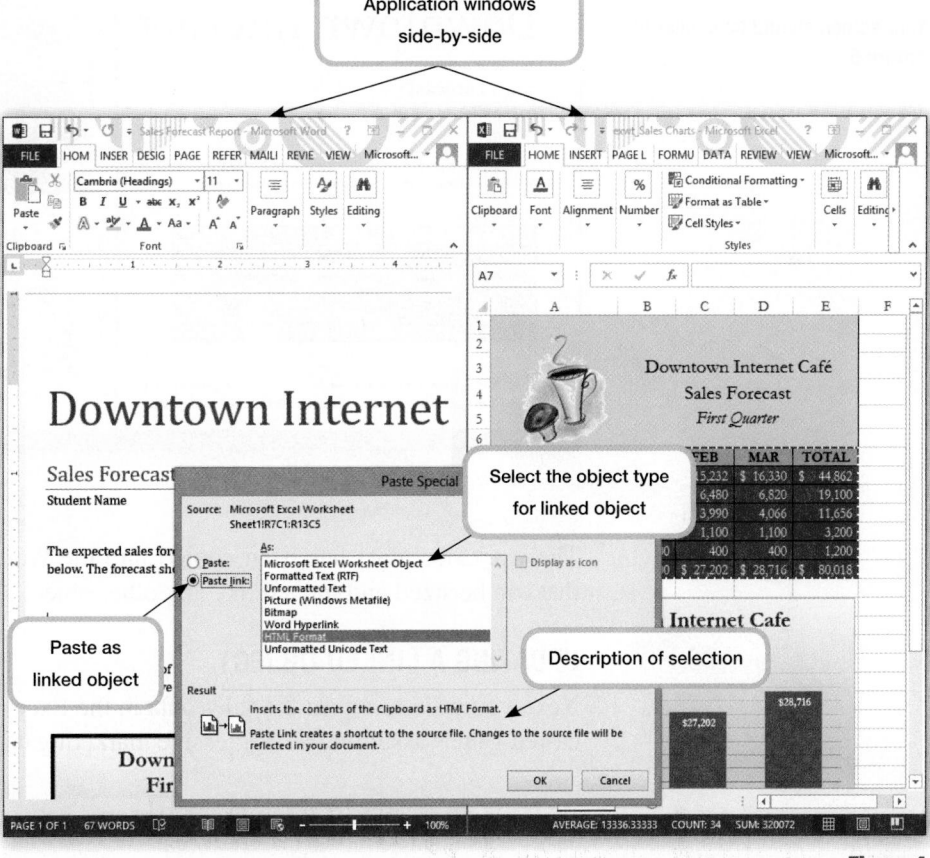

Figure 4

The Paste Special dialog box displays the type of object contained in the Clipboard and its location in the Source area. From the As list box, you select the type of format for the object you want inserted into the destination file. There are many different object types from which you can select. It is important to select the appropriate object format so that the link works correctly when inserted in the destination. In this case, you want to use the Microsoft Office Excel Worksheet Object format.

The Result area describes the effect of your selections. In this case, the object will be inserted as a picture, and a link will be created to the worksheet in the source file. Selecting the Display as Icon option changes the display of the object in the destination file from a picture to an icon. When inserted in this manner, double-clicking the icon displays the object picture.

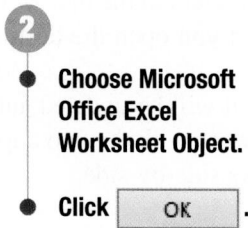

- **Choose Microsoft Office Excel Worksheet Object.**

- **Click** OK .

Your screen should be similar to Figure 5

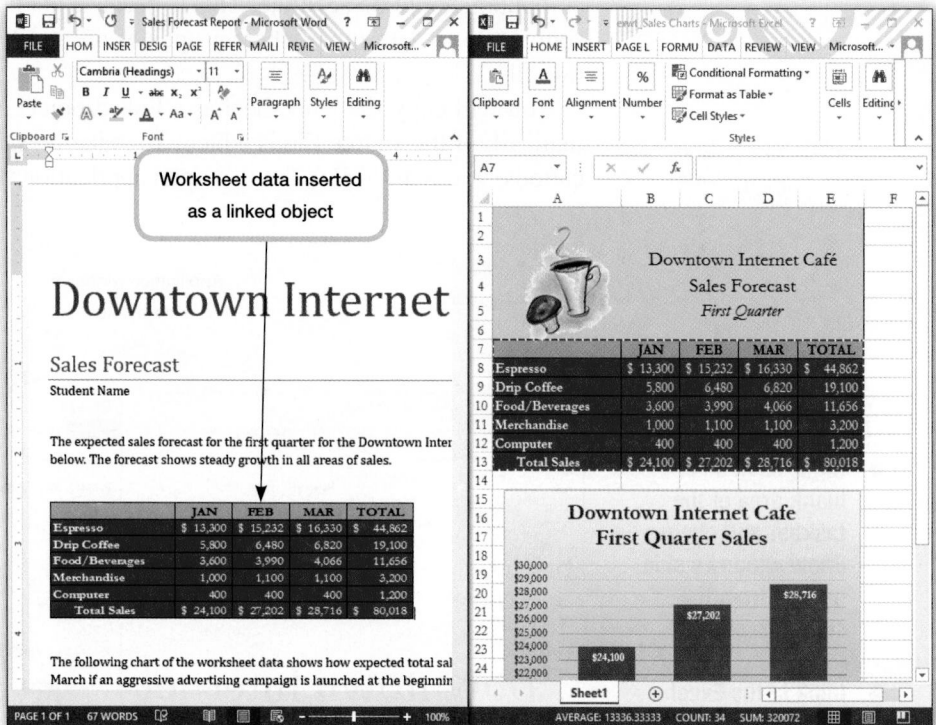

Figure 5

The worksheet data has been copied into the Word document as a linked object that can be sized and moved like any other object.

UPDATING A LINKED OBJECT

Next, you want to return the sales data in the Excel worksheet to the original fore-casted values assuming an aggressive marketing campaign is not mounted.

1

- Switch to the Excel window.

- Press `Esc` to clear the selection border.

- Change the entry in C8 to 13600 (you are removing the formula).

- In the same manner, replace the formulas in the following cells with the values shown.

Cell	Value
D8	14,200
C9	6,000
D9	6,200
C10	3,800
D10	3,800

Your screen should be similar to Figure 6

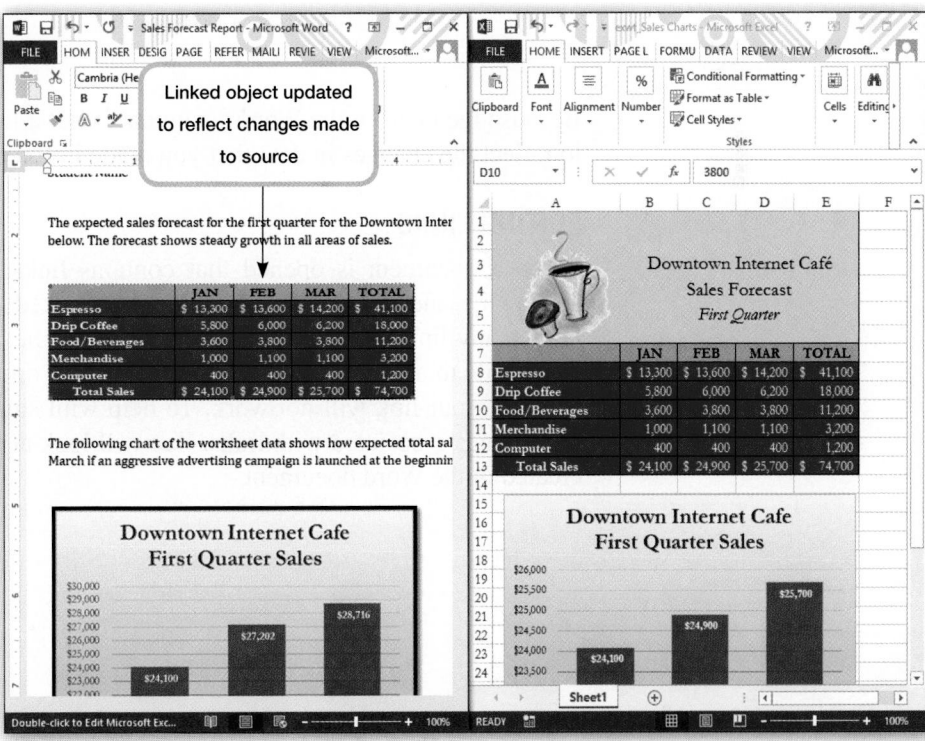

Worksheet data and chart unchanged

Worksheet data changed and chart updated

Figure 6

The Excel worksheet and chart have been updated; however, the worksheet data and chart in the Word document still reflect the original values. You will update the worksheet in the Word document next.

2

- Switch to the Word window.

- Select the worksheet object.

- Press `F9` to update the linked object.

Another Method

You also can choose Update Link from the linked object's shortcut menu.

Your screen should be similar to Figure 7

Linked object updated to reflect changes made to source

Figure 7

The linked worksheet object in the report now reflects the changes you made in Excel for the sales data. This is because any changes you make in Excel will be reflected in the linked object in the Word document. Next, you will see if the chart has been updated also.

3

- If necessary, scroll the report to see the entire chart.

- Click on the chart and press [F9].

- Deselect the chart.

- Save the document.

Additional Information

The chart may have moved to the next page when the worksheet data was inserted. If this happened, reduce the size of the chart object.

Your screen should be similar to **Figure 8**

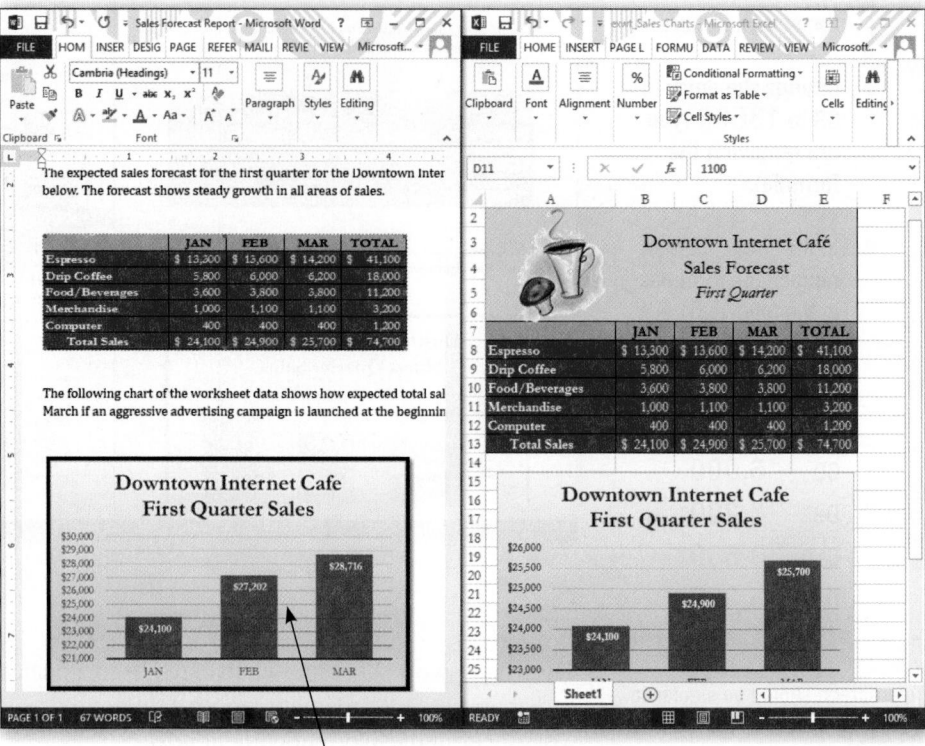

Chart does not update because it is not a linked object

Figure 8

Because the chart in the Word document is not a linked object, it does not update to reflect the changes in data that you made in Excel.

EDITING LINKS

When a document is opened that contains links, the application looks for the source file and automatically updates the linked objects. If the document contains many links, updating can take a lot of time. Additionally, if you move the source file to another location or perform other operations that may interfere with the link, your link will not work. To help with situations like these, you can edit the settings associated with links. You will look at the links to the worksheet data created in the Word document.

1

- Open the taskbar shortcut menu and choose Undo Show all windows side by side.

- If necessary, maximize the Word window.

- Right-click the worksheet object and select Linked Worksheet Object.

- Choose Links from the submenu.

Your screen should be similar to Figure 9

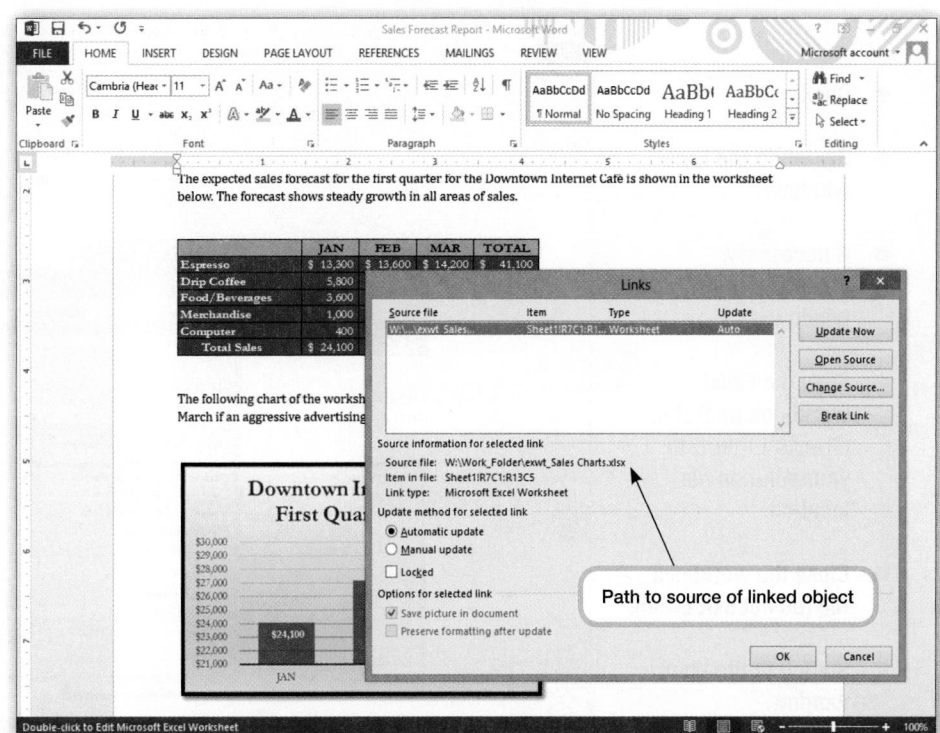

Figure 9

The Links dialog box displays the object path for all links in the document in the list box. This includes the path and name of the source file, the range of linked cells or object name, the type of file, and the update status. Below the list box, the details for the selected link are displayed.

The other options in this dialog box are described in the table below.

Option	Effect
Automatic update	Updates the linked object whenever the destination document is opened or the source file changes. This is the default.
Manual update	The destination document is not automatically updated and you must use the Update Now command button to update the link.
Locked	Prevents a linked object from being updated.
Update Now	Updates the linked object.
Open Source	Opens the source document for the selected link.
Change Source	Used to modify the path to the source document.
Break Link	Breaks the connection between the source document and the active document.

The links in the Word document are to the exwt_Sales Charts workbook file. Next, you will save the Excel workbook file using a new file name. Then you will recheck the link settings.

2

● Click [OK].

● **Switch to the Excel window.**

● **If necessary, maximize the window.**

● **Save the Excel workbook as** Sales Charts Linked **to your solution file location.**

● **Close the workbook file (do not exit Excel).**

● **Switch to the Word window.**

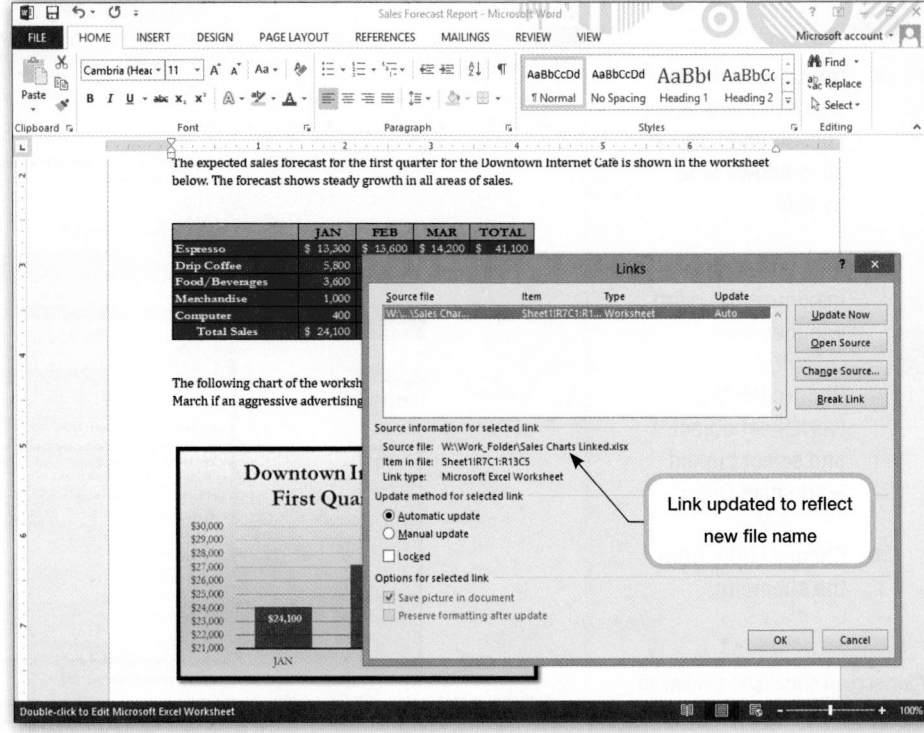

Figure 10

Having Trouble?

Click the application taskbar button to switch between windows.

You can now see that the link has been updated to reflect the new workbook file name.

● **From the worksheet object's shortcut menu, select Linked Worksheet Object and choose Links.**

Your screen should be similar to Figure 10

3

● Click [OK].

● **Increase the size of the worksheet object to the same width as the chart object.**

● **Open the File tab and choose Print.**

● **Check the layout of the document in the preview and if necessary return to the document and make any needed adjustments.**

● **Print and then close the Word document, saving any changes if needed.**

EMBEDDING AN OBJECT

The last thing you need to send Evan is a report that describes and shows the second-quarter forecast. To do this, you will open the Word document and embed the worksheet containing the second-quarter data that Evan wants in the appropriate location. An **embedded object** is stored in the destination file and becomes part of that document. The entire file, not just the selection that is displayed in the destination file, becomes part of the document. This means that you can modify it without affecting the source document where the original object resides.

1

- **Open the Word document** exwt_ Second Quarter Report **and enable content if necessary.**

- **Replace Student Name with your name in the last line of the document.**

- **Save the document as** Second Quarter Report **to your solution file location.**

- **Switch to Excel and open the workbook file** exwt_Second Quarter **and enable content if necessary.**

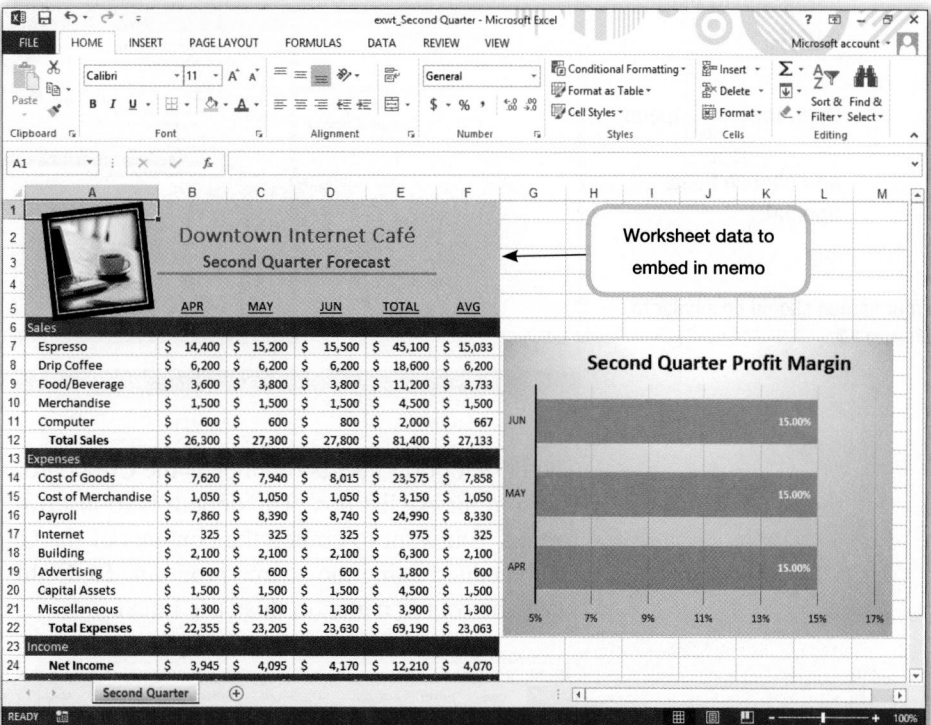

Figure 11

Your screen should be similar to Figure 11

This workbook file contains a copy of the second-quarter worksheet from the Annual Forecast workbook. You will embed the second-quarter forecast worksheet in the Word document.

2

- Copy the range A1 through F25.

- Switch to the Word window.

- Move to the blank line below the first paragraph of the report.

- Open the 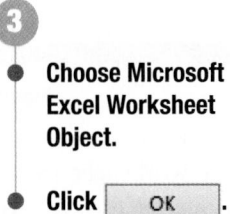 menu and choose Paste Special.

Your screen should be similar to Figure 12

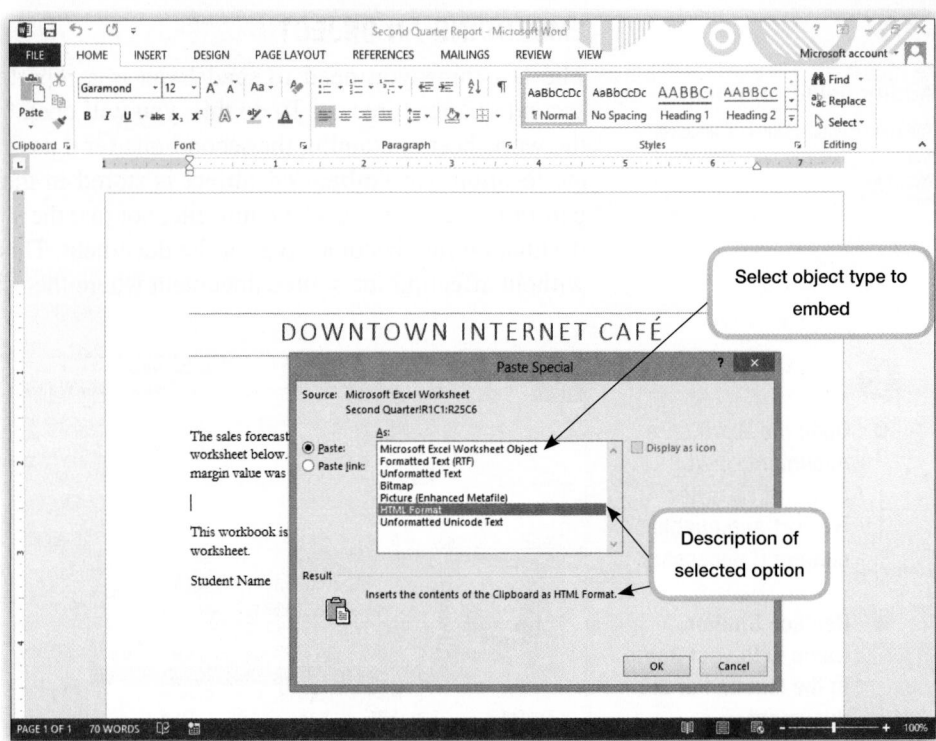

Figure 12

The Paste option inserts or embeds the Clipboard contents in the format you specify from the As list box. The default is to insert the Clipboard contents in HTML format. You want to embed the contents of the Clipboard into the document so it can be edited using the source program. To do this, you select the option that displays the source name, in this case Excel.

3

- Choose Microsoft Excel Worksheet Object.

- Click OK.

Your screen should be similar to Figure 13

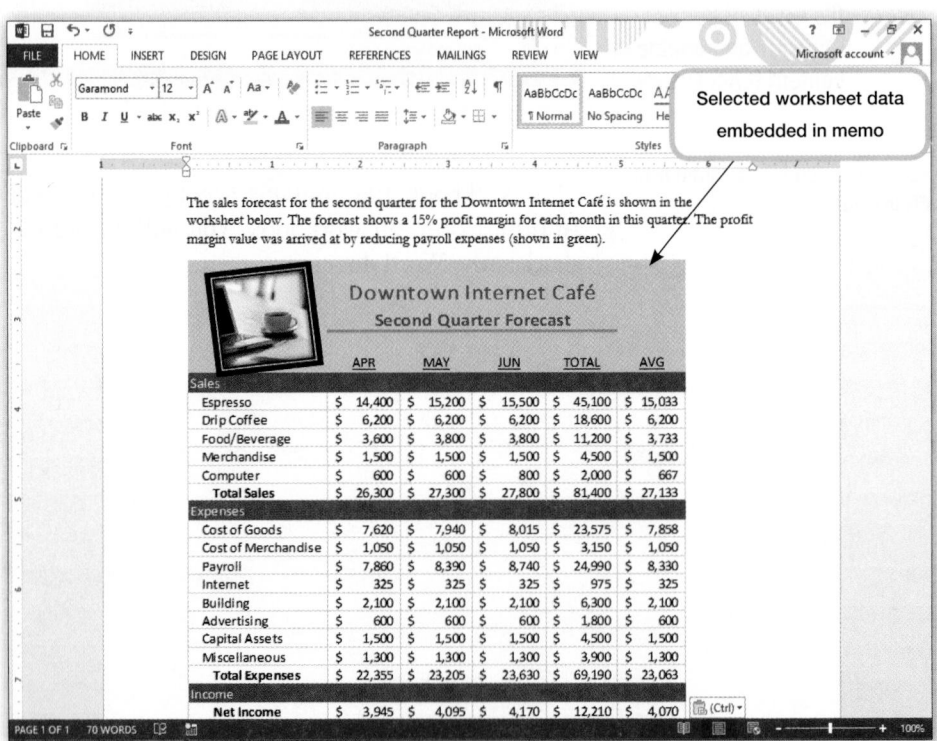

Figure 13

The selected portion of the worksheet is displayed in the report at the location of the insertion point.

UPDATING AN EMBEDDED OBJECT

You want to add color to the payroll range of cells you adjusted to arrive at the 15 percent profit margin. Because the worksheet is embedded, you can do this from within the Word document. The source program is used to edit data in an embedded object. To open the source program and edit the worksheet, you double-click the embedded object.

● **Double-click the worksheet object in Word.**

Having Trouble?

If the worksheet does not fully display the numbers, click outside the worksheet to return to the document, make the worksheet object larger, and then open the source program again.

Your screen should be similar to Figure 14

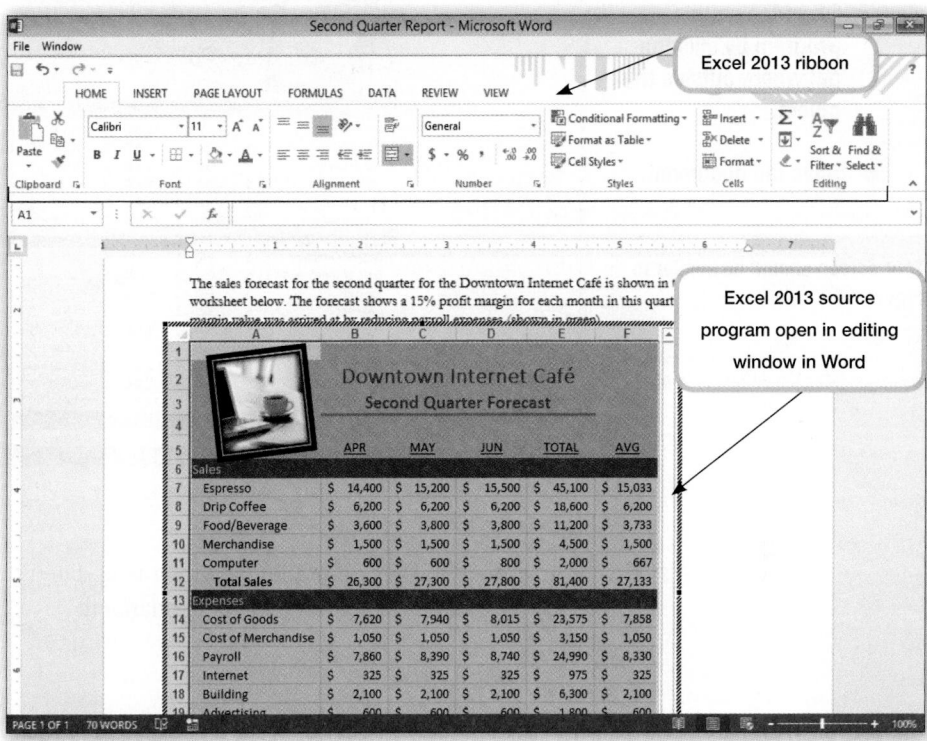

Figure 14

Additional Information

The source program must be installed on the computer system to be able to open and edit the embedded object.

The source program, in this case Excel 2013, is opened. The Excel Ribbon replaces the Word Ribbon, and the embedded object is displayed in an editing worksheet window. Now you can use the source program commands to edit the object.

2

- Change the font color of cells B16 through D16 to Green on the Standard colors bar color.

- Close the source program by clicking anywhere outside the object.

- Save the document.

Your screen should be similar to Figure 15

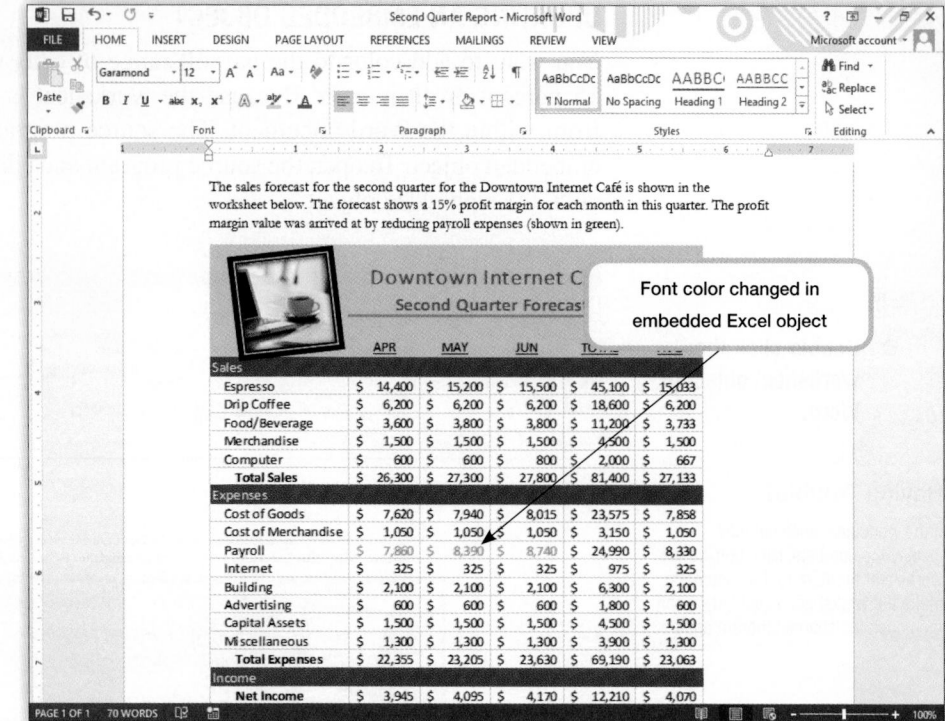

The sales forecast for the second quarter for the Downtown Internet Café is shown in the worksheet below. The forecast shows a 15% profit margin for each month in this quarter. The profit margin value was arrived at by reducing payroll expenses (shown in green).

Font color changed in embedded Excel object

Downtown Internet C
Second Quarter Forecas

	APR	MAY	JUN	TO...	
Sales					
Espresso	$ 14,400	$ 15,200	$ 15,500	$ 45,100	$ 15,033
Drip Coffee	$ 6,200	$ 6,200	$ 6,200	$ 18,600	$ 6,200
Food/Beverage	$ 3,600	$ 3,800	$ 3,800	$ 11,200	$ 3,733
Merchandise	$ 1,500	$ 1,500	$ 1,500	$ 4,500	$ 1,500
Computer	$ 600	$ 600	$ 800	$ 2,000	$ 667
Total Sales	$ 26,300	$ 27,300	$ 27,800	$ 81,400	$ 27,133
Expenses					
Cost of Goods	$ 7,620	$ 7,940	$ 8,015	$ 23,575	$ 7,858
Cost of Merchandise	$ 1,050	$ 1,050	$ 1,050	$ 3,150	$ 1,050
Payroll	$ 7,860	$ 8,390	$ 8,740	$ 24,990	$ 8,330
Internet	$ 325	$ 325	$ 325	$ 975	$ 325
Building	$ 2,100	$ 2,100	$ 2,100	$ 6,300	$ 2,100
Advertising	$ 600	$ 600	$ 600	$ 1,800	$ 600
Capital Assets	$ 1,500	$ 1,500	$ 1,500	$ 4,500	$ 1,500
Miscellaneous	$ 1,300	$ 1,300	$ 1,300	$ 3,900	$ 1,300
Total Expenses	$ 22,355	$ 23,205	$ 23,630	$ 69,190	$ 23,063
Income					
Net Income	$ 3,945	$ 4,095	$ 4,170	$ 12,210	$ 4,070

PAGE 1 OF 1   70 WORDS

Figure 15

The embedded object in the document is updated to reflect the changes you made. However, the Excel worksheet is unchanged.

3

- If necessary reduce the size of the worksheet object to fit the entire report on a single page.

- Preview and print the report.

- Exit Word.

- Look at the Excel worksheet to confirm that the worksheet has not changed.

- Exit Excel.

Linking documents is a very handy feature, particularly in documents whose information is updated frequently. If you include a linked object in a document that you are giving to another person, make sure the user has access to the source file and application. Otherwise the links will not operate correctly.

Keep the following in mind when deciding whether to link or embed objects.

Use linking when:	Use embedding when:
File size is important.	File size is not important.
Users have access to the source file and application.	Users have access to the application but not to the source file.
The information is updated frequently.	The data changes infrequently.
	You do not want the source data to change.

LAB REVIEW Working Together

KEY TERMS

destination file EXWT.4
embedded object EXWT.11
external reference EXWT.5
link EXWT.5
linked object EXWT.4
live link EXWT.5
source file EXWT.4

COMMAND SUMMARY

Command	Shortcut	Action
Home tab		
Clipboard group		
Paste/Paste Special/Paste		Inserts object as an embedded object
Paste/Paste Special/Paste Link		Inserts object as a linked object
Linked Object shortcut menu (Word)		
Update Link	F9	Updates linked object
Linked Worksheet Object/Links		Modifies selected link

STEP-BY-STEP

RESCUE FOUNDATION INCOME REPORT ★★

1. The Animal Rescue Foundation's agency director has asked you to provide her with information about income for 2015. She is particularly interested in the two pet show fund-raising and membership drive events that are held in April and October. You will create a report that will include a copy of the worksheet analysis of this data. Your completed report will be similar to that shown here.

    a. Start Word and open the document exwt_ Rescue Report.docx.

    b. Replace Student Name with your name at the bottom of the document.

    c. Start Excel and open the workbook exwt_ Contributions.

    d. Insert both worksheets as Microsoft Excel Worksheet Object links below the first paragraph in the Word report. Reduce the size of the worksheets until the report fits on one page.

    e. You notice the April raffle ticket sales value looks low, and after checking your records, you see it was entered incorrectly. In Excel, change the April raffle ticket sales income to $3,120.

    f. In the report, update the linked worksheet.

    g. Save the Excel workbook as Contributions. Exit Excel.

    h. Save the Word document as Rescue Report Linked. Preview and print the document.

Animal Rescue Foundation

Income Analysis

Below is the completed income analysis for 2015. As you can see, the income for Fall/Winter is much higher due to corporate donations.

Animal Rescue Foundation

	March	April	May	June	July	August	Total
Annual Memberships	$ 9,200	$ 18,783	$ 8,595	$ 9,934	$ 5,684	$ 5,781	$ 57,977
Private Donations	625	1,400		1,225			3,250
Corporate Donations		17,000	15,000		4,000	9,000	45,000
Raffle Tickets		3,120					3,120
Pet Show		8,000					8,000
Other	3,000	3,000	3,000	3,000	3,000	3,000	18,000
Total	$ 12,825	$ 51,303	$ 26,595	$ 14,159	$ 12,684	$ 17,781	$ 135,347

Animal Rescue Foundation

	September	October	November	December	January	February	Total	Annual Total
Annual Memberships	$ 6,740	$ 23,723	$ 10,595	$ 22,134	$ 11,584	$ 10,781	$ 85,557	$ 143,534
Private Donations	800	2,200	5,600	79,900	1,900	3,000	93,400	96,650
Corporate Donations		15,000		312,000		10,000	337,000	382,000
Raffle Tickets		3,294					3,294	6,414
Pet Show		11,000					11,000	19,000
Other	3,000	3,000	3,000	3,000	3,000	3,000	18,000	36,000
Total	$ 10,540	$ 58,217	$ 19,195	$ 417,034	$ 16,484	$ 26,781	$ 548,251	$ 683,598

Also, the pet show fundraising events have been very successful in boosting income during the slow periods of each year.

Student Name

1

LAB EXERCISES

STUDENT RETENTION REPORT ★★

2. As part of your job at the State College, you keep track of the number of students who return each year and how many of those students graduate in four or five years. You record this data in a worksheet and are preparing to include the results for the class of 2014 in a report. Your completed report will be similar to that shown here.

   a. Start Word and open the exwt_Student Retention.docx document. Replace Student Name with your name at the end of the report.

   b. Start Excel and open the exwt_College Student Retention workbook.

   c. Copy the worksheet as a linked object to below the paragraph of the report.

   d. In Excel, enter the fourth-year graduation data for 2014 of **1495** in cell E10 and the fifth-year graduation rate for 2014 of **67** in E12.

   e. In Word, update the linked worksheet object.

   f. Save the workbook as Student Retention to your solution file location. Exit Excel.

   g. Save the Word document as Student Retention Rates to your solution file location. Print the report.

State College

Student Retention Analysis

The rate of student retention for four years is displayed in the worksheet below. The number of students who return to State College every year and finish their degrees in four years is laudable, but there is growing concern at the increasing number of students who either do not return for the fourth year, or don't graduate after four years. There is a meeting scheduled for next week to discuss this issue and possible ways to decrease the rate of change. Please review this information prior to the meeting.

State College
Student Retention Rates

	2011	2012	2013	2014	Average
Enrolled First Year Students	1537	1579	1670	1700	1622
Returning Second Year Students	1397	1433	1571	1598	1500
Returning Third Year Students	1285	1398	1520	1562	1441
Returning Fourth Year Students	1221	1324	1484	1555	1396
Graduating Fourth Year Students	1211	1312	1461	1495	1370
Percent Graduate in Four Years	79%	83%	87%	88%	84%
Graduating Fifth Year Students	44	55	62	67	57
Percent Graduate in Five Years	82%	87%	91%	92%	88%

Student Name

HOME SALE PRICE REPORT ★★

3. Jennifer works in the marketing department for a local real estate company. She has recently researched the median home prices and number of days on the market over the last three years for existing homes in the local market area. She has created a worksheet and column charts of the data. Now Jennifer wants to send a report containing the information to her supervisor. The completed report will be similar to that shown here.

a. Start Word and open the document exwt_Home Price Report.docx.

b. Replace Student Name with your name.

c. Start Excel and open the workbook exwt_Real Estate Prices. Copy the worksheet and each chart as embedded objects below the first paragraph in the Word document. Size the charts so that everything fits on one page.

d. Open the embedded worksheet object in Word, and change the chart title from Average Price to Median Price.

e. Change the Days on Market chart to a 3-D clustered bar.

f. Click within the paragraph text to close the embedded object.

g. Save the Word document as Home Price Report to your solution file location. Preview and print the document.

MEDIAN EXISTING HOME PRICES

Below is a chart showing the median existing home prices over the past three years. As you can see, existing home sale prices increased slightly in 2013 and also in 2014. Another dramatic change has been the decrease in the number of days on the market for homes since 2012 which shows a marked upturn in real estate market demand. This workbook is embedded in this memo and can be viewed in its entirety by double-clicking on the object.

Median Price Existing Single Family Homes 2012 - 2014			
	2012	2013	2014
Average Price	$ 135,000	$ 158,000	$ 166,000
Days on Market	45	32	28

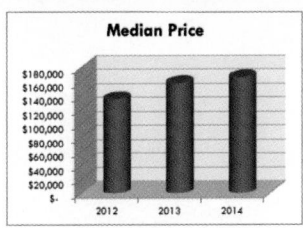

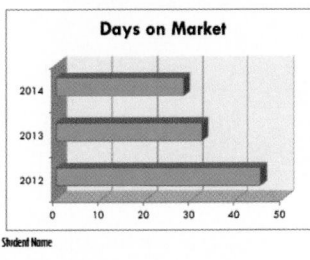

Student Name

1

Objectives

After completing this lab, you will know how to:

1. Plan, create, and modify a database.

2. Create and save a table structure.

3. Define field names, data types, field properties, and primary key fields.

4. Enter and edit data.

5. Add attachments.

6. Change views.

7. Adjust column widths.

8. Use the Best Fit feature.

9. Create a second table.

10. Navigate among records.

11. Add, copy, and move fields.

12. Add and delete records.

13. Document a database.

14. Preview and print a table.

15. Change page orientation.

16. Close and open a table and database.

CASE STUDY

Lifestyle Fitness Club

You have recently accepted a job as a human resources administrator with Lifestyle Fitness Club. Like many fitness centers, Lifestyle Fitness Club includes exercise equipment, free weights, aerobics classes, tanning and massage facilities, a swimming pool, a steam room and sauna, and child-care facilities. In addition, it promotes a healthy lifestyle by including educational seminars on good nutrition and proper exercise. It also has a small snack bar that serves healthy drinks, sandwiches, and snacks.

The Lifestyle Fitness Clubs are a franchised chain of clubs that are individually owned. You work at a club owned by Felicity and Ryan Albright, who also own two others in California. Accounting and employment functions for all three clubs are handled centrally at the Landis location.

You are responsible for maintaining the employment records for all employees, as

well as records for traditional employment activities such as hiring and benefits. Currently the club employment records are maintained on paper forms and are stored in file cabinets organized alphabetically by last name. Although the information is well organized, it still takes time to manually look through the folders to locate the information you need and to compile reports from this data.

The club has recently purchased new computers, and the owners want to update the employee record-keeping system to an electronic database management system. The software tool you will use to create the database is the database application Microsoft Access 2013. In this lab, you will create a database for the club while learning about entering data, editing, previewing, and printing information from the database.

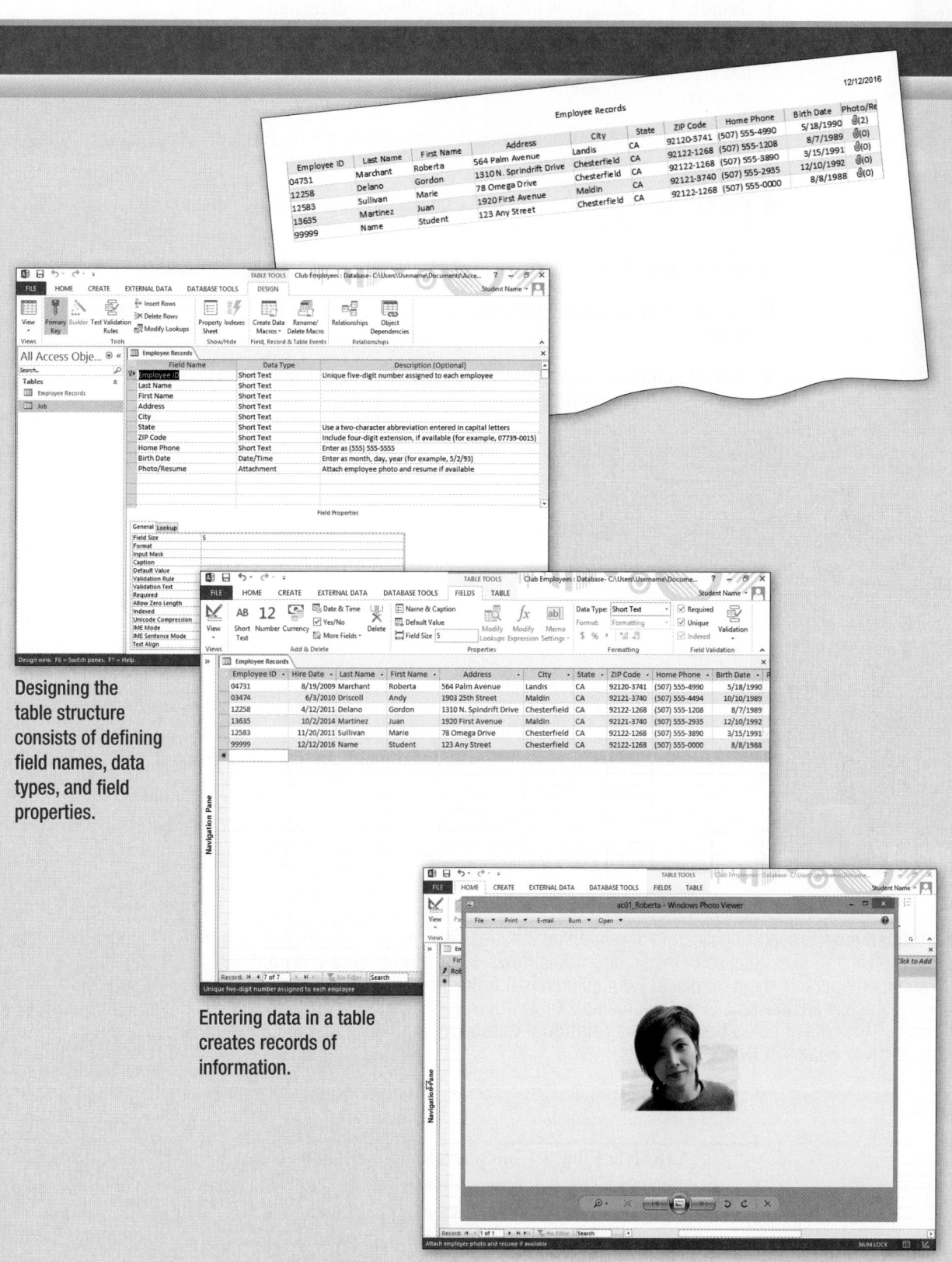

Designing the table structure consists of defining field names, data types, and field properties.

Entering data in a table creates records of information.

Fields can contain attachments such as pictures or files.

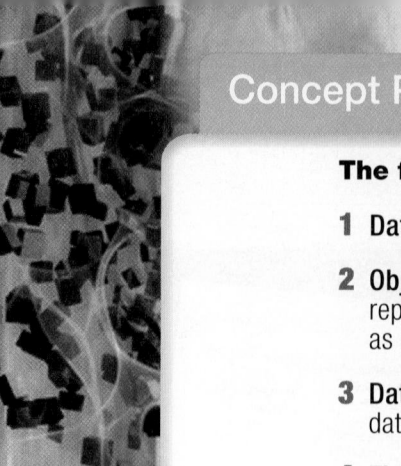

The following concepts will be introduced in this lab:

1 Database A database is an organized collection of related information.

2 Object An Access database is made up of several types of objects, such as a table or report, consisting of many elements. An object can be created, selected, and manipulated as a unit.

3 Data Type The data type defines the type of data the field will contain. Access uses the data type to ensure that the right kind of data is entered in a field.

4 Field Property A field property is a characteristic that helps define the appearance and behavior of a field.

5 Primary Key A primary key is a field that uniquely identifies each record.

6 Relationship A relationship establishes the association between common fields in two tables.

7 Subdatasheet A subdatasheet is a data table nested within a main data table; it contains information that is related or joined to the main table.

Designing a New Database

The Lifestyle Fitness Club recently purchased the 2013 Microsoft Office System software suite. You are very excited about learning to use the Access 2013 database management system to store and maintain the club's records.

Concept  Database

A **database** is an organized collection of related information. Typically, the information in a database is stored in a **table** consisting of vertical columns and horizontal rows. Each row contains a **record**, which is all the information about one person, thing, or place. Each column is a **field**, which is the smallest unit of information about a record. Access databases can contain multiple tables that can be linked to produce combined output from all tables. This type of database is called a **relational database**. Read more about relational databases in the Introduction to Microsoft Office 2013.

The Lifestyle Fitness Club plans to use Access to maintain several different types of databases. The database you will create will contain information about each club employee. Other plans for using Access include keeping track of members and inventory. To keep the different types of information separate, the club plans to create a database for each group.

Good database design follows two basic principles: Do not include duplicate information (also called redundant data) in tables, and enter accurate and complete information. Redundant data wastes space, wastes the time that is required to enter the same information multiple times, and consequently increases the possibility of errors and inconsistencies between tables. The information that is stored in a database may be used to make business decisions, and if the information is inaccurate, any decisions that are based on the information will be misinformed.

To attain these principles, the database design process is very important and consists of the following steps: plan, design, develop, implement, and refine and review. You will find that you will generally follow these steps in order as you create your database. However, you will probably retrace steps as the final database is developed.

Step	Description
Plan	The first step in the development of a database is to define the purpose of the database in writing. This includes establishing the scope of the database, determining its feasibility, and deciding how you expect to use it and who will use it.
Design	Using the information gathered during the planning step, you can create an implementation plan and document the functional requirements. This includes finding and organizing the information required for the database and deciding how this information should be divided into subject groups. You also need to think about the types of questions you might want the database to answer and determine the types of output you need such as reports and mailings.
Develop	Using the design you created, you are ready to create tables to hold the necessary data. Create separate tables for each of the major subjects to make it easier to locate and modify information. Define fields for each item that you want to store in each table. Determine how tables are related to one another, and include fields to clarify the relationships as needed. Try not to duplicate information in the different tables.
Implement	After setting up the tables, populate the tables by entering sample data to complete each record. Then work with the data to make sure it is providing the information you need.
Refine and Review	Refine the design by adding or removing fields and tables and continue to test the data and design. Apply the data normalization rules to see if the tables are structured correctly. Periodically review the database to ensure that the initial objectives have been met and to identify required enhancements.

As you develop the employee database for the Lifestyle Fitness Club, you will learn more about the details of the design steps and how to use Access 2013 to create a well-designed and accurate database.

PLANNING THE CLUB DATABASE

Your first step is to plan the design of your database tables: the number of tables, the data they will contain, and the relationship between the tables. You need to decide what information each table in the employee database should contain and how it should be structured or laid out.

You can obtain this information by analyzing the current record-keeping procedures used in the company. You need to understand the existing procedures so that your database tables will reflect the information that is maintained by different departments. You should be aware of the forms that serve as the basis for the data entered into the department records and of the information that is taken from the records to produce periodic reports. You also need to determine whether there is information that the department heads would like to be able to obtain from the database that may be too difficult to generate with current procedures.

After looking over the existing record-keeping procedures and the reports that are created from the information, you decide to create several separate tables of data in the database file. Each table should only contain information about the subject of the table. Additionally, try not to duplicate information in different tables. If this occurs, create a separate table for this information. Creating several smaller tables of related data rather than one large table makes it easier to use the tables and faster to process data. This is because you can join several tables together as needed.

The main table will include the employee's basic information, such as employee number, name, birth date, and address. Another will contain the employee's job title and work location only. A third will contain data on pay rate and hours worked each week. To clarify the organization of the database, you sketched the structure for the employee database as shown below.

Club Records Database

Employee Records Table

Emp #	Last Name	First Name	Street	City	State	Zipcode	Phone	Birth Date
7721	Brown	Linda	—	—	—	—	—	—
7823	Duggan	Michael	—	—	—	—	—	—
•	•	•	•	•	•	•	•	•

link on common field

link on common field

Clubs Table

Emp #	Location	Position
7721	Iona	Greeter
7823	Fort Myers	Server
•	•	•

Pay Table

Emp #	Pay	Hours
7721	8.25	30
7823	7.50	20
•	•	•

Creating and Naming the Database File

Now that you have decided what information you want to include in the tables, you are ready to create a new database for the employee information using the Microsoft Access 2013 database management program.

When creating a new Access database, you must first decide where the database will be stored: locally on the hard drive of a computer or a local network; or externally on the web in a SkyDrive or on a SharePoint server. This decision determines whether you use a desktop database template or a web database template to create the new database.

Once this decision is made, then you can choose from several methods to create a new database. One method is to start with a blank desktop or web database that contains the basic database objects and then add your own content. Another method is to use one of the many custom desktop or web templates that are provided by

Microsoft as the basis for your new database. A custom database template generally includes the data structure, tables, queries, forms, and reports for the selected type of database. Although using a template is sometimes the fastest way to create a database, it often requires a lot of work to adapt the template to suit the needs of the existing data. A third option is to copy or import data from another source into an Access database file. Finally, you can use a custom template that you created and saved as the basis for your new database.

You will store the Club database on your computer and will create it using the Blank desktop database. Unlike many of the custom database templates, the blank database simply consists of the basic database structure and is not designed for a specific type of database.

1

- **Start the Access 2013 application.**

- **Click** .

Having Trouble?

See the Introduction to Microsoft Office 2013 for information about starting an Office application and for a discussion of features that are common to all Office 2013 applications.

Your screen should be similar to Figure 1.1

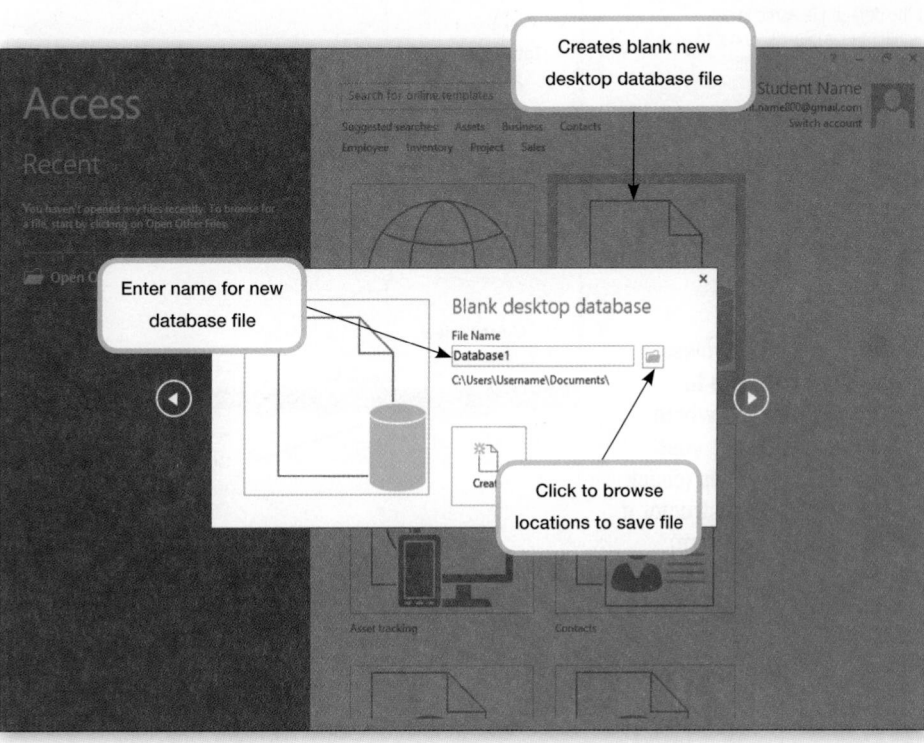

Figure 1.1

Additional Information

Depending on your Windows settings, your screens may not display file extensions.

Having Trouble?

For information on how to save a file, refer to the Saving a File section in the Introduction to Microsoft Office 2013 lab.

When creating a new database, you need to enter a file name and specify the location on your computer where you want it saved. The File Name box displays Database1, the default database file name. After you specify the file name you want to use and the location to which it should be saved, Access will display the file extension .accdb after the file name. This identifies the file as an Access 2007 to 2013 database.

2

- **Replace the text in the File Name text box with Club Employees**

Having Trouble?

If the default file name is not highlighted, triple-click on it to select the entire file name.

Additional Information

You do not need to type the file extension, as Access will add it automatically for you.

- **Click** 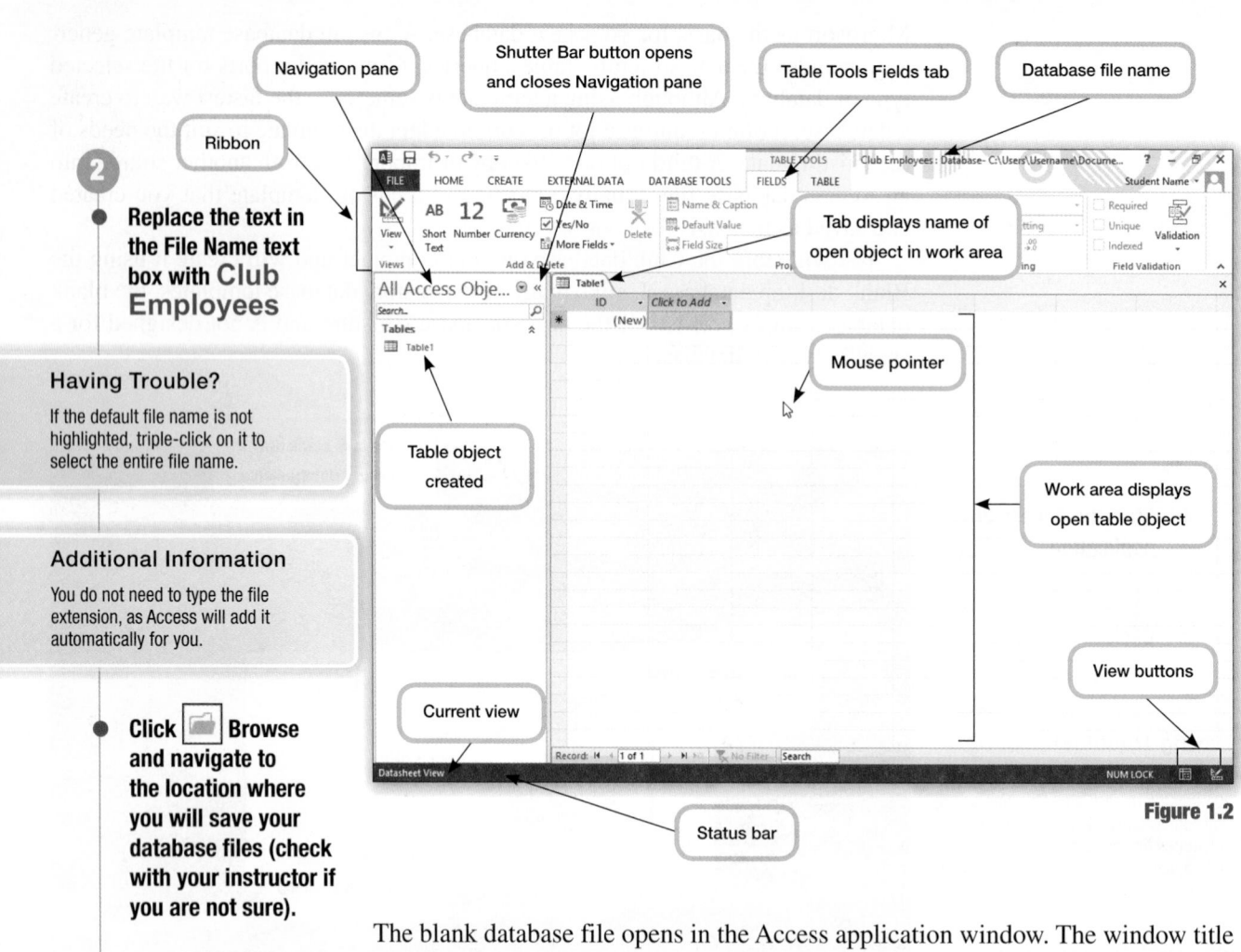 **Browse and navigate to the location where you will save your database files (check with your instructor if you are not sure).**

- **Click** `OK` .

- **Click** `Create` .

Your screen should be similar to Figure 1.2

Having Trouble?

If your screen looks slightly different, this is because Access remembers settings that were on when the program was last used.

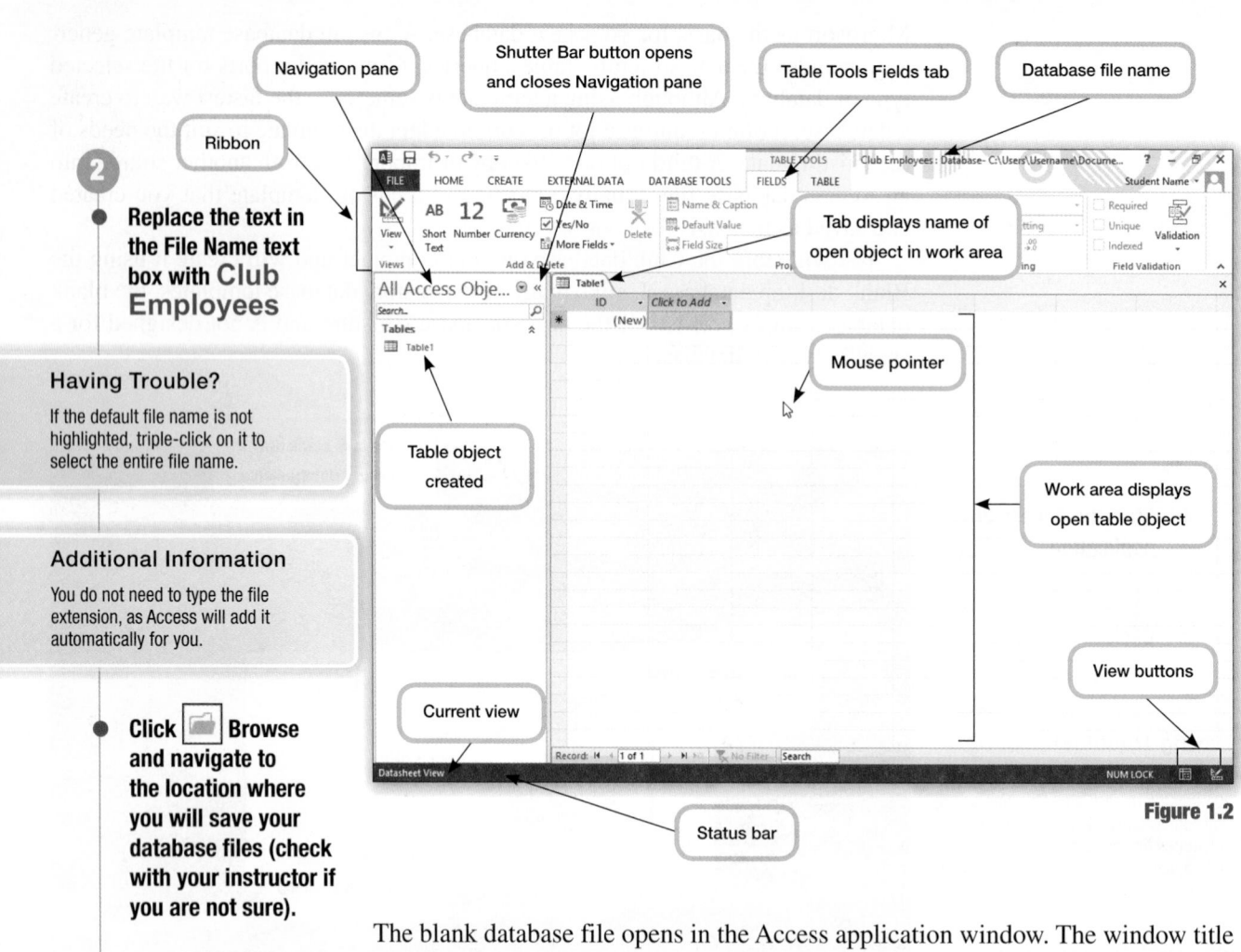

Ribbon • Navigation pane • Shutter Bar button opens and closes Navigation pane • Table Tools Fields tab • Database file name • Tab displays name of open object in work area • Mouse pointer • Work area displays open table object • View buttons • Current view • Status bar • Table object created

Figure 1.2

The blank database file opens in the Access application window. The window title bar displays the name of the database, Club Employees, followed by the file path where the file is stored.

EXPLORING THE ACCESS WINDOW

Additional Information

Read "Common Interface Features" in the Introduction to Microsoft Office 2013 lab for more information about the File tab, Ribbon, galleries, and other features that are common to all Office 2013 applications.

Located below the title bar is the Access 2013 Ribbon, which contain the commands and features you will use to create and modify database objects. The Access Ribbon always has four main tabs available: Home, Create, External Data, and Database Tools. Additional contextual tabs will appear as you perform different tasks and open various windows. In this case, the Table Tools Fields and Table contextual tabs are available to help you create a new table. The Table Tools Fields tab is currently open and contains command buttons that are used to perform basic database functions specifically relating to the fields within the table.

The mouse pointer appears as ⇖ on your screen. The mouse pointer changes shape depending upon the task you are performing or where the pointer is located in the window.

The large area below the Ribbon is the work area where different Access components are displayed as you are using the program. When a new database file is created, it includes one empty table named Table1. A **table,** is the main structure in a database that holds the data. It is one of several different database components or objects that can be included within the database file.

Concept 2 Object

An Access database is made up of several types of objects, such as a table or report, consisting of many elements. An **object** is a database component that can be created, selected, and manipulated as a unit. The basic database objects are described below.

Object	Use
Table	Store data.
Query	Find and display selected data.
Form	View, add, and update data in tables.
Report	Analyze and print data in a specific layout.

The table object is the basic unit of a database and must be created first, before any other types of objects are created. Access displays each different type of object in its own window. You can open multiple objects from the same database file in the work area; however, you cannot open more than one database file at a time in a single instance of Access. To open a second database file, you need to start another instance of Access and open the database file in it.

Additional Information

You will learn more about tables and the different database views shortly.

The work area displays a tab containing the table name for the open table. It is used to switch between open objects in the work area. There is currently just one tab because only one object is open.

Just below the work area, the status bar provides information about the task you are working on and about the current Access operation. Currently, the left end of the status bar displays Datasheet view and the right end displays two buttons that are used to change the view. In addition, the status bar displays messages such as instructions to help you use the program more efficiently.

USING THE NAVIGATION PANE

The **Navigation pane** along the left edge of the work area displays all the objects in the database and is used to open and manage the objects. Because your database only contains one object, Table1, that is the only object listed in the pane. When there are many different objects, the pane organizes the objects into categories and groups within each category. It is used to quickly access the different objects.

The Navigation pane is always displayed, but it can be collapsed to a bar to provide more space in the work area. The Shutter Bar close button « , located in the upper-right corner of the pane, is used to show or hide the pane.

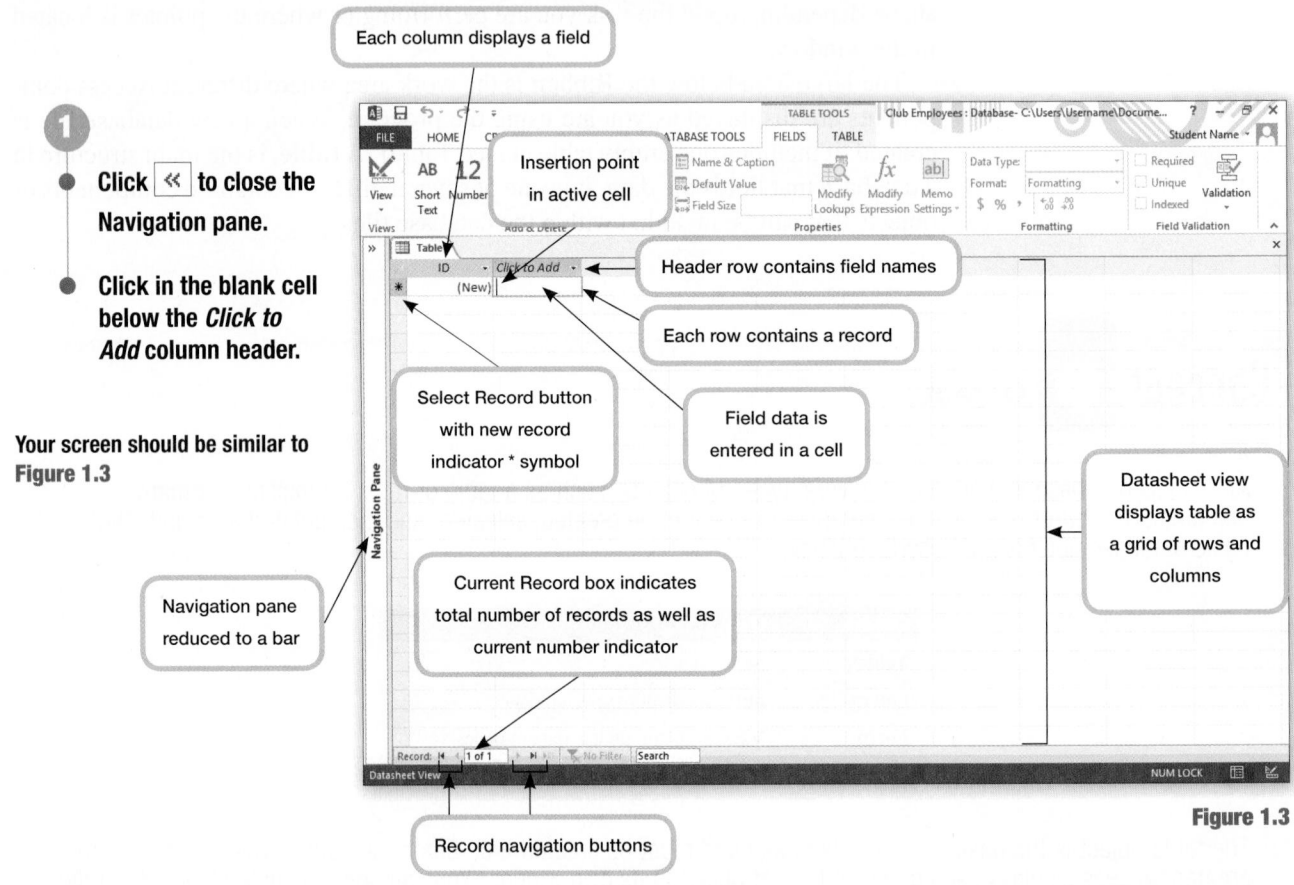

- Click « to close the Navigation pane.

- Click in the blank cell below the *Click to Add* column header.

Your screen should be similar to Figure 1.3

Each column displays a field

Insertion point in active cell

Header row contains field names

Each row contains a record

Select Record button with new record indicator * symbol

Field data is entered in a cell

Datasheet view displays table as a grid of rows and columns

Navigation pane reduced to a bar

Current Record box indicates total number of records as well as current number indicator

Record navigation buttons

Figure 1.3

Another Method

You also can press F11 to open/close the Navigation pane.

The Navigation pane is reduced to a bar along the left side of the window, and the work area expands to fill the space. The pane can be easily displayed again by clicking » . You will learn more about using the Navigation pane throughout the labs.

Creating a Table

In anticipation of your entering information in the table, Access displays the blank table in Datasheet view, one of several different window formats, called **views**, that are used to display and work with the objects in a database. Each view includes its own Ribbon tab that contains commands that are designed to work with the object in that view. The available views change according to the type of object you are using. For example, when working with reports the available views are Report view, Print Preview, Layout view, and Design view; yet when working with datasheets the viewing options are Design view and Datasheet view. The basic views are described in the following table.

View	Purpose
Datasheet view	Provides a row-and-column view of the data in tables or query results.
Form view	Displays the records in a form.
Report view	Displays the table data in a report layout.
Design view	Used to create a table, form, query, or report. Displays the underlying design structure, not the data.
Layout view	Displays the object's data while in the process of designing the object.
Print Preview	Displays a form, report, table, or query as it will appear when printed.

Datasheet view is a visual representation of the data that is contained in a database table. It consists of a grid of rows and columns that is used to display each field of a table in a column and each record in a row. The field names are displayed in the **header row** at the top of the datasheet.

Below the header row is a blank row. The intersection of the row and column creates a **cell** where you will enter the data for the record. The square to the left of each row is the **Select Record** button and is used to select an entire record. The record containing the insertion point is the **current record** and is identified by the gold color in the Select Record button. The * in the Select Record button signifies the end of the table or where a new record can be entered.

The bottom of the work area displays a Current Record box and record navigation buttons. The **Current Record box** shows the number of the current record as well as the total number of records in the table. Because the table does not yet contain records, the indicator displays "Record: 1 of 1" in anticipation of your first entry. On both sides of the record number are the **record navigation buttons**, which are used to move through records with a mouse. In addition, two buttons that are used to filter and search for data in a table are displayed. You will learn about using all these features throughout the text.

DEFINING TABLE FIELDS

Now you are ready to begin defining the fields for the table. You have already decided that the main table in this database will include the employee's basic information such as employee number, name, birth date, and address. Next, you need to determine what information you want to appear in each column (field) about the subject recorded in the table. For example, you know you want to include the employee's name. However, should the entire name be in a single column or should it appear as two separate columns: first name and last name? Because you may want to sort or search for information based on the employee's name, it is better to store the information in separate columns. Similarly, because the address actually consists of four separate parts—address, city, state, and zip code—it makes sense to store them in separate columns as well.

Generally, when deciding how to store information about a subject in a table, break down the information into its smallest logical parts. If you combine more than one kind of information in a field, it is difficult to retrieve individual facts later.

After looking at the information currently maintained in the personnel folder for each employee, you have decided to include the following fields in the table: Employee #, Hire Date, Last Name, First Name, Address, City, State, Zip Code, Home Phone, Birth Date, and Photo. The data for the first employee record you will enter is shown below.

Field Name	Data
Employee #	04731
Hire Date	August 19, 2009
Last Name	Marchant
First Name	Roberta
Address	564 Palm Avenue
City	Landis
State	CA
Zip Code	92120-3741
Home Phone	(507) 555-4990
Birth Date	May 18, 1990
Photo/Resume	Roberta.jpg

ADDING A FIELD BY ENTERING DATA

Notice that the first field in the table, ID, is already defined. The ID field is always included in a table when it is first created. It automatically assigns a number to each record as it is added to a table and is useful for maintaining record order. The second column header displays *Click to Add* and is used to add a new field in the table.

In Datasheet view, you can enter data for a record and create a new field at the same time. The first field of data you will enter is the employee number, which is assigned to each employee when hired. Each new employee is given the next consecutive number, so that no two employees can have the same number. Each number is a maximum of five digits.

When you enter data in a record, it should be entered accurately and consistently. The data you enter in a field should be typed exactly as you want it to appear. This is important because any printouts of the data will display the information exactly as entered. It is also important to enter data in a consistent form. For example, if you decide to abbreviate the word "Avenue" as "Ave." in the Address field, then it should be abbreviated the same way in every record where it appears. Also be careful not to enter a blank space before or after a field entry. This can cause problems when attempting to locate information.

Having Trouble?

For more information on moving through, entering, and editing text, refer to the section Entering and Editing Text in the Introduction to Microsoft Office 2013.

Having Trouble?

If you make an error while typing an entry, use the ⬅Backspace key to delete the characters back to the error and retype the entry.

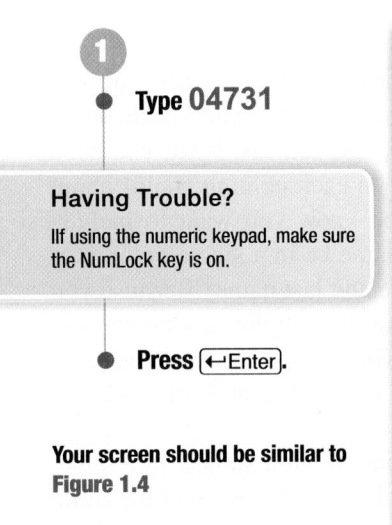

● **Type 04731**

Having Trouble?

IIf using the numeric keypad, make sure the NumLock key is on.

● **Press ↵Enter.**

Your screen should be similar to Figure 1.4

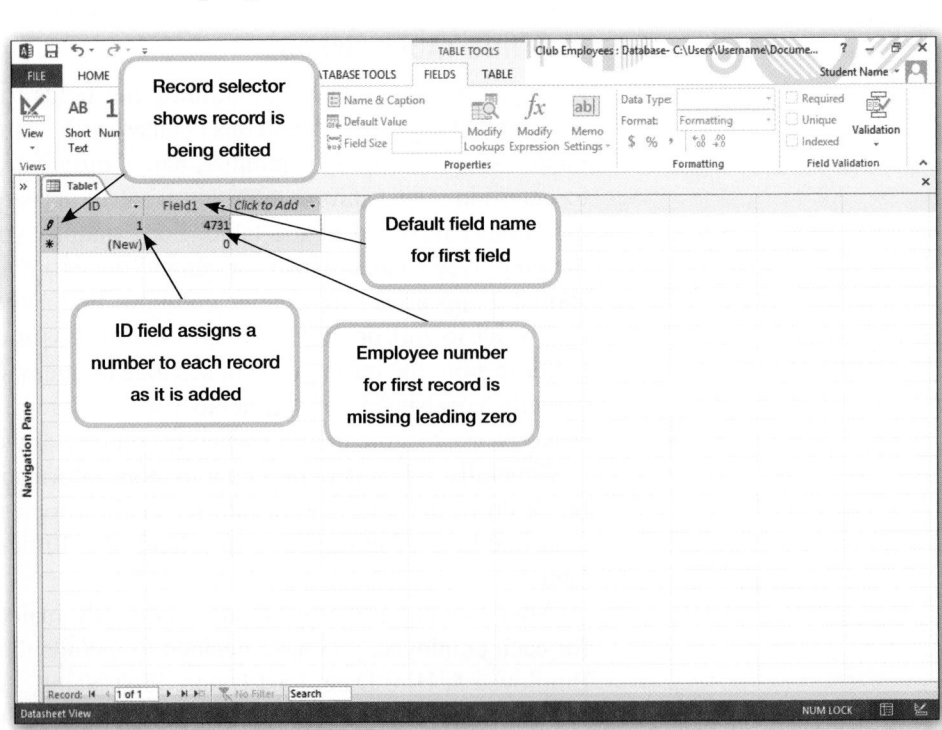

Record selector shows record is being edited

Default field name for first field

ID field assigns a number to each record as it is added

Employee number for first record is missing leading zero

Figure 1.4

The employee number for the first record is entered in the table and Access is ready for you to enter the data for the next field. However, notice the leading zero is no longer displayed in the employee number you just typed. You will learn the reason for this and how to correct it shortly.

The new field has been assigned the default field name of Field1. Also notice that the ID field displays the number 1 for the first record entered in the table.

CHANGING FIELD NAMES

Before entering more data, you want to replace the default field name with a more descriptive field name. A **field name** is used to identify the data stored in the field. A field name should describe the contents of the data to be entered in the field. It can be up to 64 characters long and can consist of letters, numbers, spaces, and special characters, except a period, an exclamation point (!), an accent grave (`), brackets ([]), or the double quotation mark ("). You also cannot start a field name with a space. It is best to use short field names to make the tables easier to manage.

Additional Information

The record selector appears as ✐ when a record is in the process of being edited.

Additional Information

Although spaces can be included in field names as well as names of objects or controls, it is better not to use spaces in order to reduce the chance of naming conflicts if you will be using Microsoft Visual Basic for Applications.

①
- **Double-click on the Field1 column header.**

- **Type Employee # (be sure to include a space before the #).**

Another Method

You also can choose Rename Column from the column header's shortcut menu.

Additional Information

The field name can be typed in uppercase or lowercase letters. It will be displayed in your database table exactly as you enter it.

Your screen should be similar to Figure 1.5

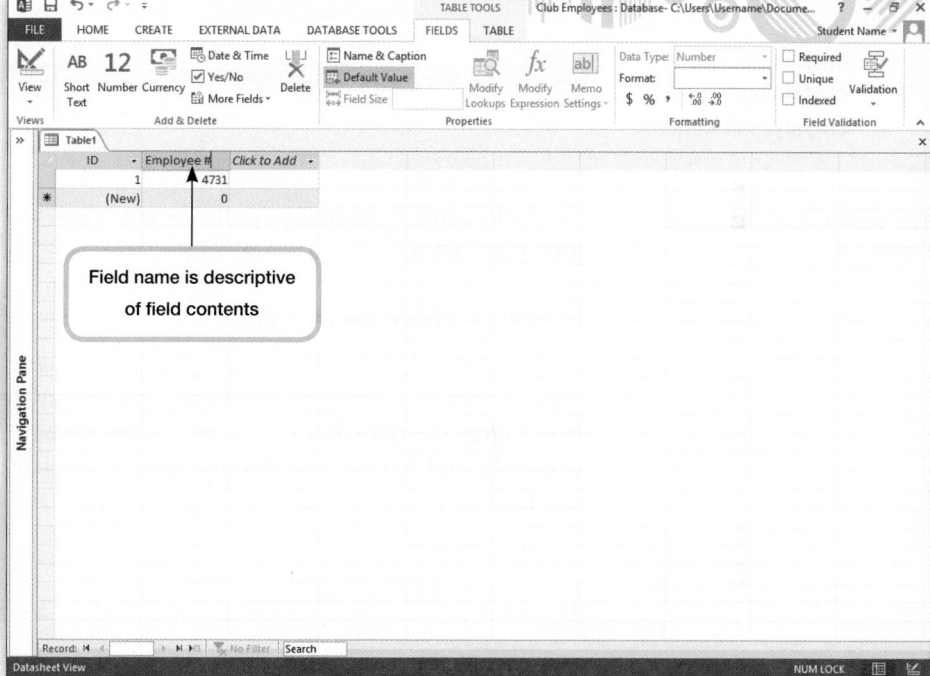

Field name is descriptive of field contents

Figure 1.5

The highlighted text is deleted and replaced by the new field name you typed. You realize that "Employee ID" is the more common term used on company forms, so you decide to use this as the field name instead. As you enter text, you are bound to make typing errors that need to be corrected. You also may want to edit or update information. In this case, you want to edit the field name you are currently working on. The insertion point is already in the correct position and you just need to delete the character to the left of it.

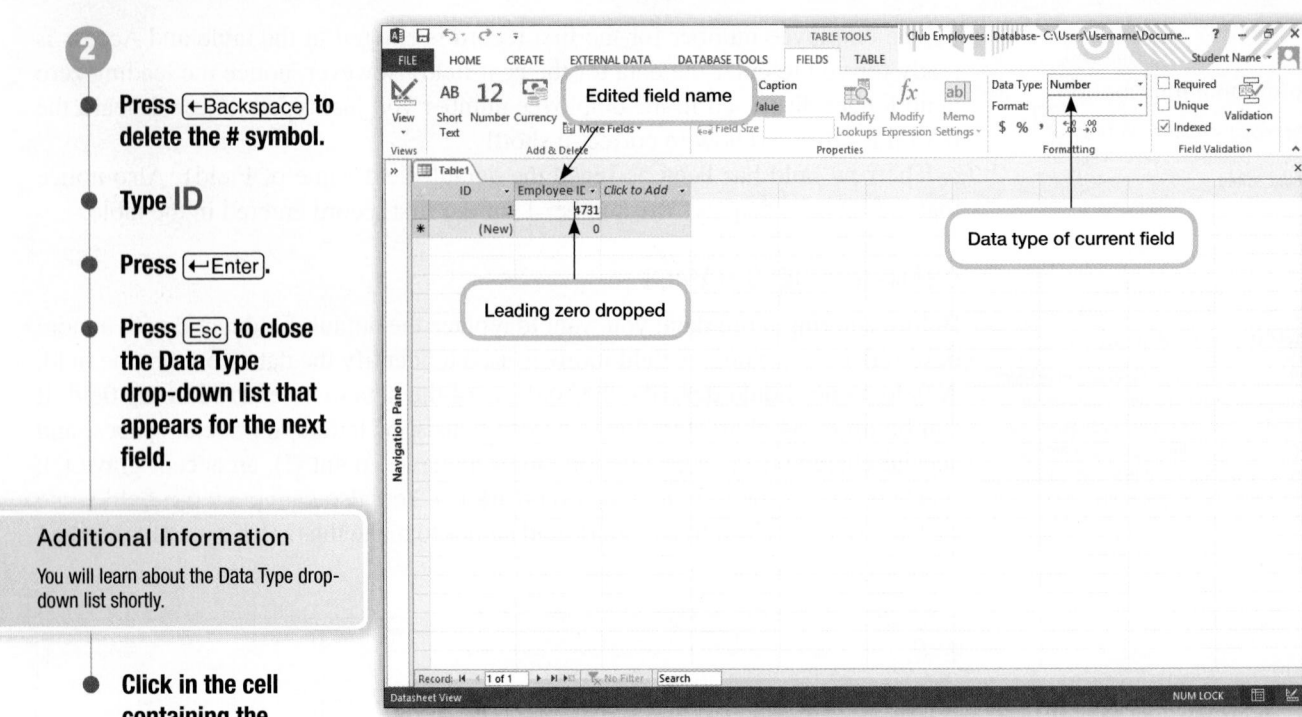

②

- Press ←Backspace to delete the # symbol.

- Type **ID**

- Press ←Enter.

- Press Esc to close the Data Type drop-down list that appears for the next field.

Additional Information

You will learn about the Data Type drop-down list shortly.

- Click in the cell containing the Employee ID number.

Figure 1.6

Your screen should be similar to Figure 1.6

The field name is complete, and it is now easy to know what the data in that column represents.

DEFINING FIELD DATA TYPE

As you noticed, the leading zero of the Employee ID number has been dropped. This is because Access automatically detects and assigns a data type to each field based upon the data that is entered. In this case, the field entry consisted of numbers only, and Access assigned the field a Number data type. This data type drops any leading zeros.

Concept ③ Data Type

The **data type** defines the type of data the field will contain. Access uses the data type to ensure that the right kind of data is entered in a field. It is important to choose the right data type for a field before you start entering data in the table. You can change a data type after the field contains data, but if the data types are not compatible, such as a text entry in a field whose data type accepts numbers only, you may lose data. The data types are described in the following table.

Data Type	Purpose
Short Text	Use in fields that contain alphanumeric data (words, combinations of words and numbers, and numbers that are not used in calculations). Short Text field entries can be up to 255 characters in length. Names and phone numbers are examples of Short Text field entries. Short Text is the default data type.
Long Text	Use in fields where you want to store more than 255 characters of alphanumeric data. A Long Text field holds up to 1 GB of characters or 2 GB of storage, of which 64,000 characters can be displayed. Text in this field can be formatted.
Number	Use in fields that contain numeric data only and that will be used to perform calculations on the values in the field. Number of units ordered is an example of a Number field entry. Leading zeros are dropped. Do not use in fields involving money or that require a high degree of accuracy because Number fields round to the next highest value. Fields that contain numbers only but will not be used in calculations are usually assigned a Short Text data type.
Date/Time	Use in fields that will contain dates and times. Access allows dates from AD January 1, 1900, to December 31, 9999. Access correctly handles leap years and checks all dates for validity. Even though dates and times are formatted to appear as a date or time, they are stored as **serial values** so that they can be used in calculations. The date serial values are consecutively assigned beginning with 1, which corresponds to the date January 1, 1900, and ending with 2958465, which is December 31, 9999.
Currency	Use in number fields that are monetary values or that you do not want rounded. Numbers are formatted to display decimal places and a currency symbol.
AutoNumber	Use when you need a unique, sequential number that is automatically incremented by one whenever a new record is added to a table. After a number is assigned to a record, it can never be used again, even if the record is deleted.
Yes/No	Use when the field contents can only be a Yes/No, True/False, or On/Off value. Yes values are stored as a 1 and No values as 0 so that they can be used in expressions.
OLE Object	Use in fields to store an object from another Microsoft Windows program, such as a document or graph. Stores up to 2 GB. The object is converted to a bitmap image and displayed in the table field, form, or report. An OLE server program must be on the computer that runs the database in order to render the object. Generally, use the Attachment field type rather than OLE Object field type because the objects are stored more efficiently and doing so does not require the OLE server.
Hyperlink	Use when you want the field to store a link to an object, document, web page, or other destination.
Attachment	Use to add multiple files of different types to a field. For example, you could add a photograph and set of resumes for each employee. Unlike OLE Object fields, the files are not converted to bitmap images and additional software is not needed to view the object, thereby saving space. Attachments also can be opened and edited from within Access in their parent programs. Size limit is 256 MB per individual file, with a total size limit of 2 GB.
Calculated	Use this data type to create a calculated field in a table. For example, you could calculate the units on hand by the cost to determine the inventory value. You can then easily display or use the results of the calculation throughout your database. Whenever a record is edited, Access automatically updates the Calculated fields, thereby constantly maintaining the correct value in the field. Note that a Calculated field cannot refer to fields in other tables or queries.

Additional Information

If Access does not have enough information to determine the data type, it sets the data type to Short Text.

Notice in Figure 1.6 that the Data Type box in the Formatting group shows the current data type for the field is Number. Access accurately specified this data type because the Employee ID field contains numbers. However, unless the numbers are used in calculations, the field should be assigned the Short Text data type. This designation allows other characters, such as the parentheses or hyphens in a telephone number, to be included in the entry. Also, by specifying the type as Short Text, leading zeros will be preserved.

You need to override the data type decision and change the data type for this field to Short Text.

Open the

Data Type: Number ▾

drop-down menu in the Formatting group of the Table Tools Fields tab.

Choose Short Text.

Click at the beginning of the Employee ID entry to place the insertion point and type 0

Press End **to move to the end of the entry.**

Press → **to move to the next column.**

Your screen should be similar to Figure 1.7

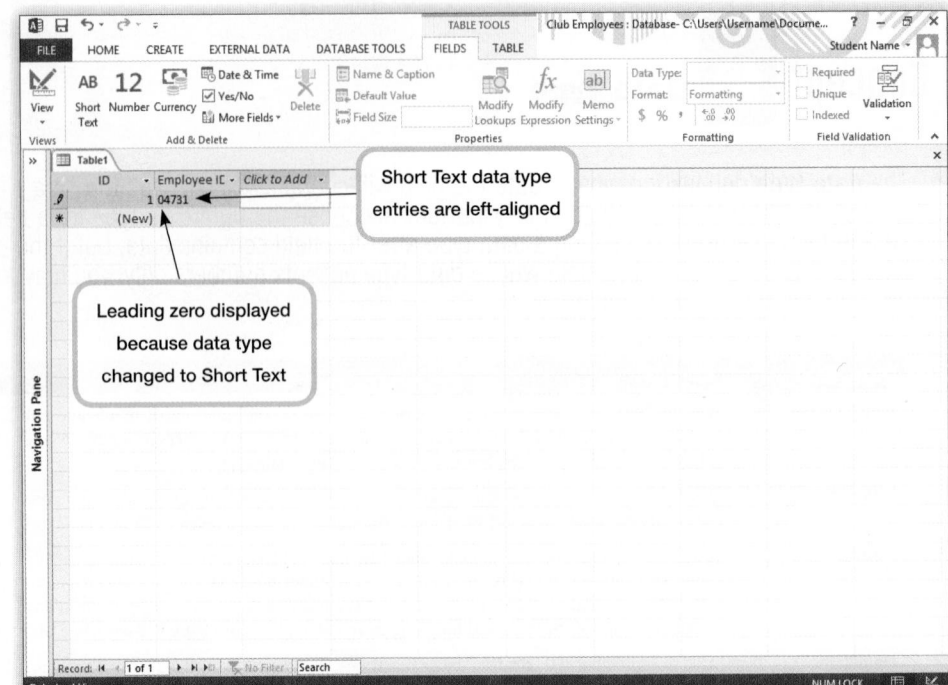

Short Text data type entries are left-aligned

Leading zero displayed because data type changed to Short Text

Figure 1.7

The leading zero is now correctly displayed. Also notice that the entry is now left-aligned in the cell space whereas it was right-aligned when the data type was set to Number. Many data types also include formatting settings that control the appearance of the data in the field. In this case, the Short Text field format is to align the text with the left edge of the cell space. You will learn more about formatting later in the lab.

Now you are ready to enter the data for the next field, Hire Date.

Type Aug 19, 2009

Press ←Enter**.**

Right-click the Field1 column name and choose Rename Field from the shortcut menu.

Type Hire Date

Press ←Enter**.**

Press Esc **to close the Data Type drop-down list that appears for the next field.**

Click on the hire date.

Your screen should be similar to Figure 1.8

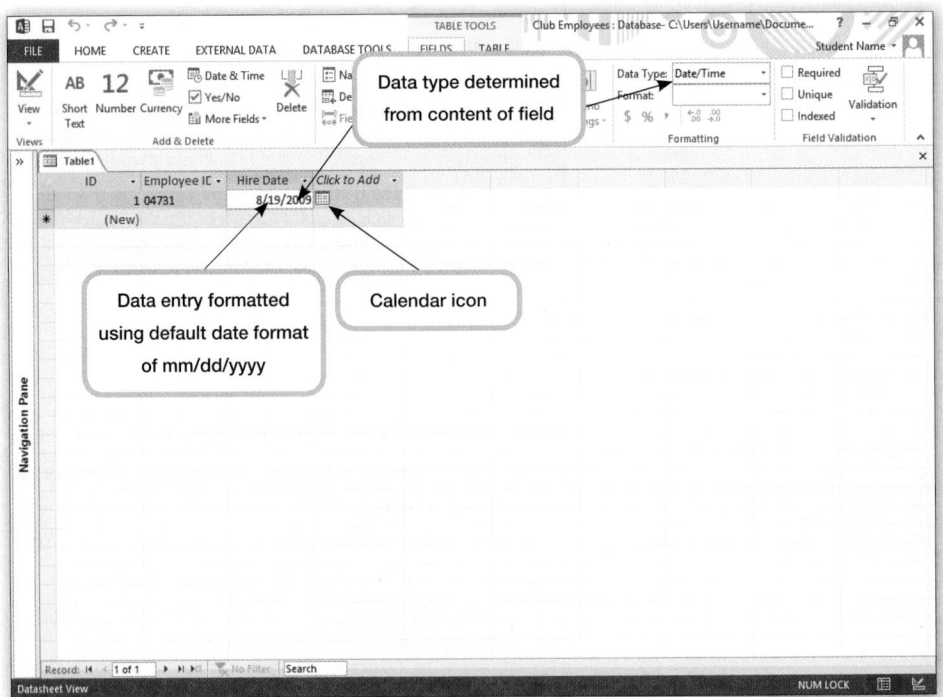

Data type determined from content of field

Data entry formatted using default date format of mm/dd/yyyy

Calendar icon

Figure 1.8

Access correctly determined that the entry is a Date type and displays the date using the default date format of mm/dd/yyyy.

Additional Information

The  calendar icon displays the month calendar for that date when you click on it.

ADDING A FIELD USING CLICK TO ADD

You will add the Last Name and First Name fields using the Click to Add feature. This feature first displays the Data Type drop-down list, and then, after the data type selection is made, it highlights the default field name in preparation for you to enter a new field name.

The next few fields you need to enter include employee name and address information.

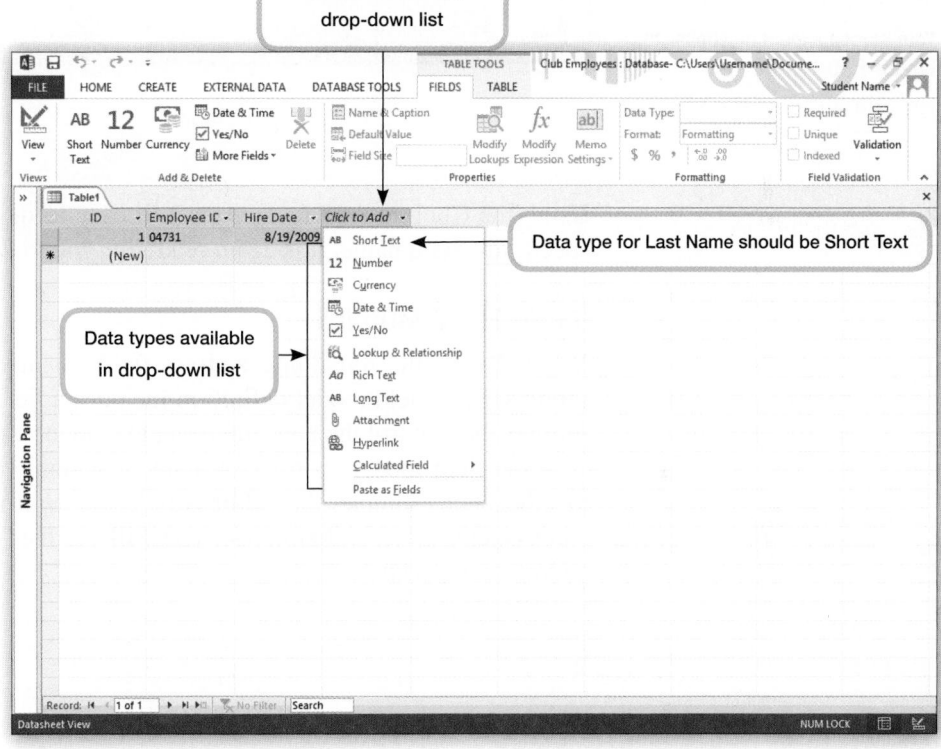

1

● Click on *Click to Add.*

Your screen should be similar to Figure 1.9

Figure 1.9

The Data Type drop-down list displays available data types as well as formatting that can be used. For example, the Rich Text option is really the Long Text data type with the format property set to Rich Text.

Additional Information

Rich text allows formatting such as color, bold, and italics.

You will set the Last Name field data type to Short Text and then enter the field name. Upon completion of the field name, the Data Type drop-down list will open for the next field in preparation for your defining the next field. You will define the same data type for the First Name field and enter the field name.

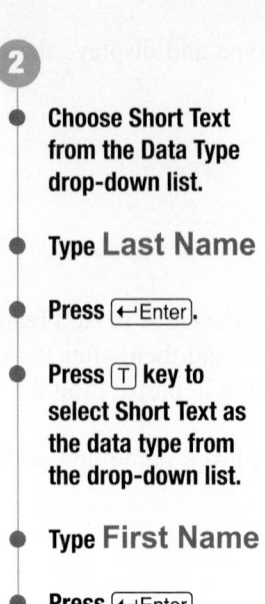

- Choose **Short Text** from the Data Type drop-down list.

- Type **Last Name**

- Press ⏎Enter.

- Press ⊤ key to select Short Text as the data type from the drop-down list.

- Type **First Name**

- Press ⏎Enter.

Your screen should be similar to Figure 1.10

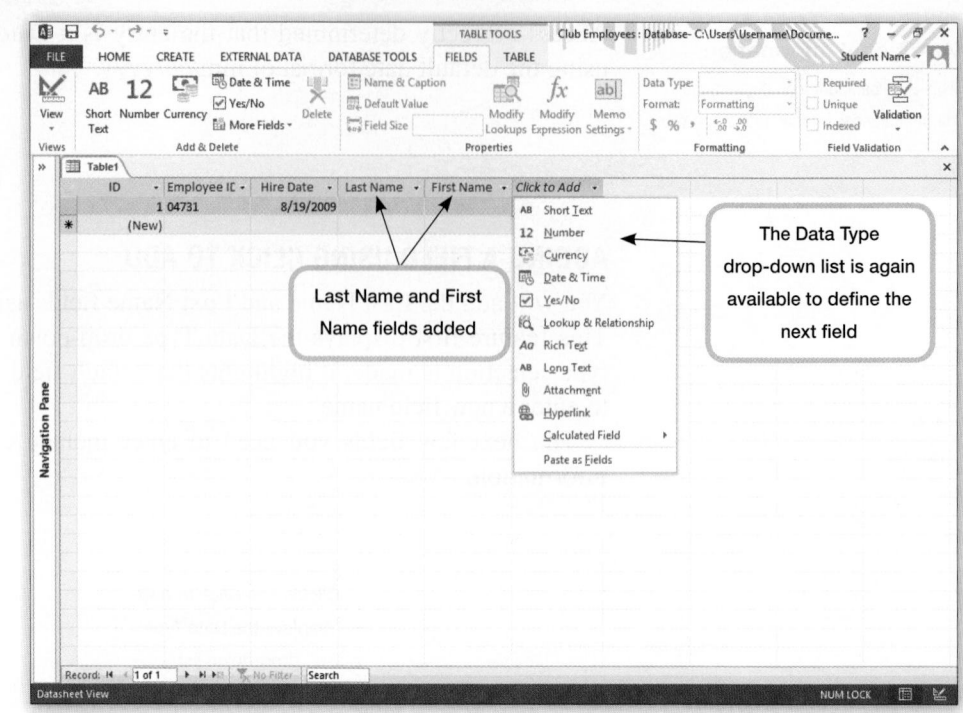

Last Name and First Name fields added

The Data Type drop-down list is again available to define the next field

Figure 1.10

Using the Click to Add feature made it easy to quickly define the data type and specify the field name. It is again ready for you to define the next field.

USING FIELD MODELS

You will add the remaining address fields using predefined fields called **field models**. Each field model definition includes a field name, a data type, and other settings that control the appearance and behavior of the field.

Some field models consist of a set of several fields that are commonly used together. For example, the Address field model comes with a field for the street address, city, state, and zip code. You will use the Address field model to add the address fields next.

Click

More Fields ▾

in the Add & Delete group of the Table Tools Fields tab.

Scroll the menu until you see the Quick Start section.

Choose Address.

Your screen should be similar to Figure 1.11

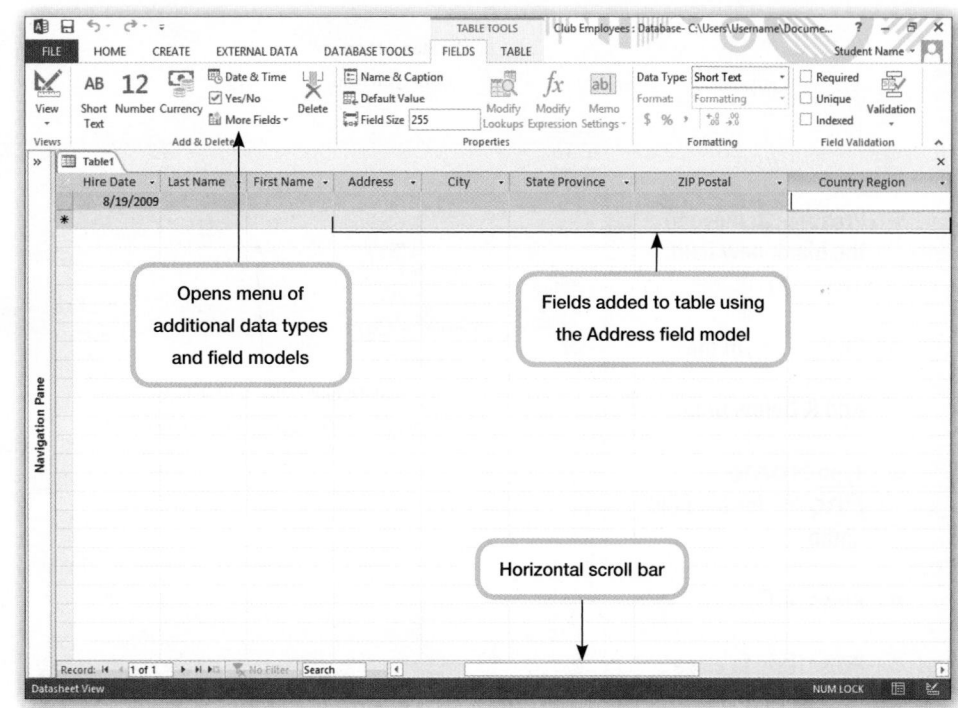

Opens menu of additional data types and field models

Fields added to table using the Address field model

Horizontal scroll bar

Figure 1.11

The Address, City, State Province, ZIP Postal, and Country Region fields were inserted to the right of the existing fields. Using field models saves time and provides the basis from which you can start. Once inserted, the field name and data type can be modified like any other fields.

A horizontal scroll bar may display at the bottom of the work area. This means there are more fields in the datasheet than can be viewed in the currently visible work space.

The last remaining field to add is Home Phone. You might have noticed the Phone option in the More Fields menu of Quick Start Field Models. Because the Phone field model contains four fields (Business Phone, Home Phone, Mobile Phone, and Fax Number), it would not be the best option to use for this table. Instead, you will add the Home Phone field using the Add & Delete group.

2

- Press → to move to the blank new field.

- Click 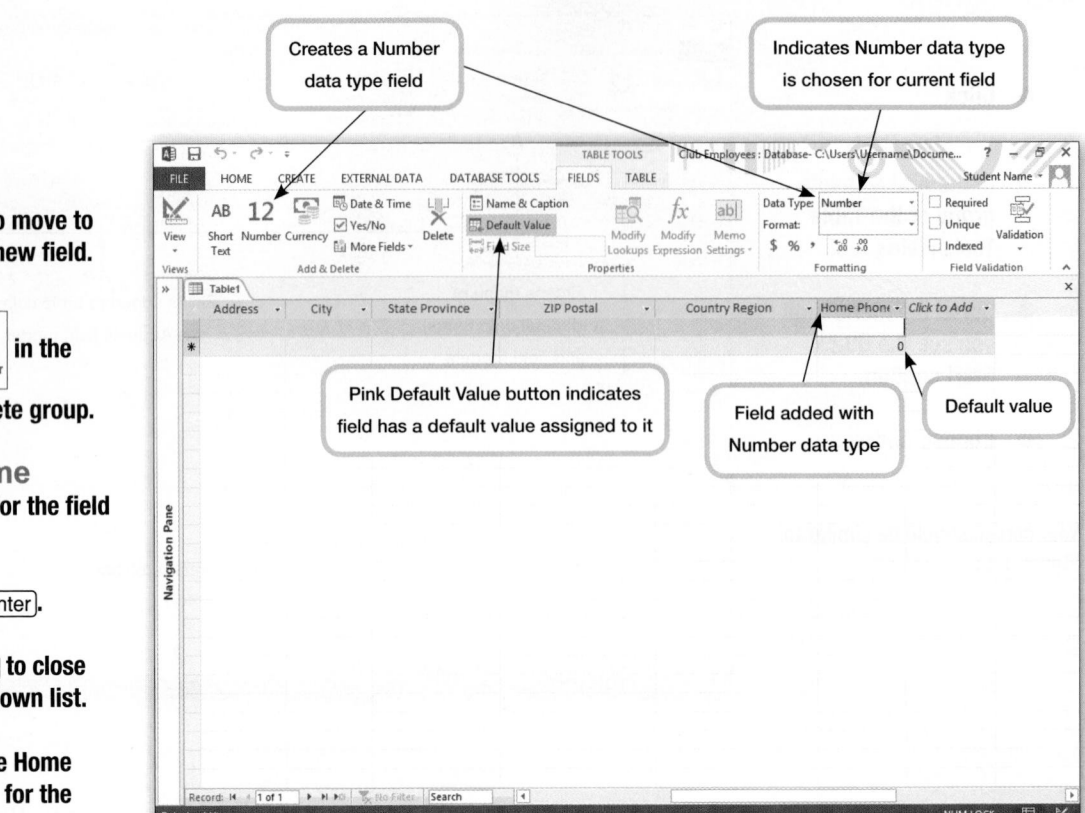 **12** **Number** in the Add & Delete group.

- Type **Home Phone** for the field name.

- Press ←Enter.

- Press Esc to close the drop-down list.

- Click in the Home Phone cell for the first record.

Creates a Number data type field

Indicates Number data type is chosen for current field

Pink Default Value button indicates field has a default value assigned to it

Field added with Number data type

Default value

Figure 1.12

Your screen should be similar to Figure 1.12

The new number data type field was automatically inserted to the right of the current field. Also, as with the Click to Add feature, you were automatically prompted to enter a field name. Notice the Home Phone cell in the new record row displays a zero. This is the default value that will appear in this cell if no other value is entered.

DELETING A FIELD IN DATASHEET VIEW

The Country Region field that was added as part of the Address field model is not needed, so you will delete it. Deleting a field permanently removes the field column and all the data in the field from the table.

- Click in the Country Region field.

- Click 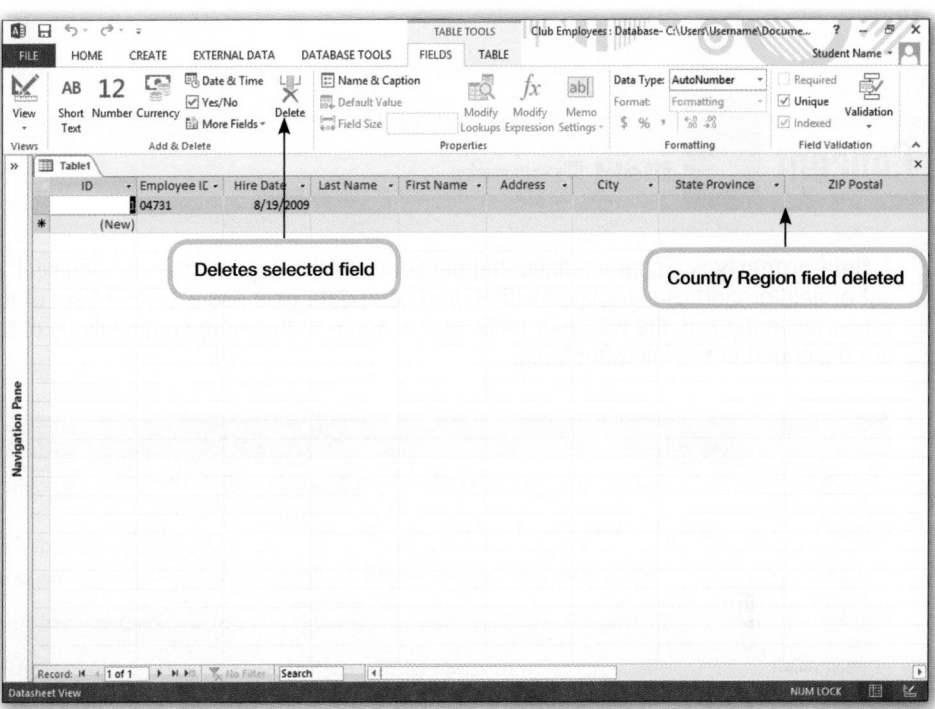 in the Add & Delete group.

- Click **Yes** in response to the message to confirm that you want to permanently delete the field.

Your screen should be similar to Figure 1.13

Figure 1.13

Another Method

You also can delete a field in Datasheet view by choosing Delete Column from the shortcut menu for the field column you want to delete.

The field is permanently removed from the table.

In addition to data type, there are many other field properties associated with a field.

Concept 4 Field Property

A **field property** is a characteristic that helps define the appearance and behavior of a field. Each field has a set of field properties associated with it, and each data type has a different set of field properties. Setting field properties enhances the way your table works. Some of the more commonly used properties and their functions are described in the following table.

Field Property	Description
Field Size	Sets the maximum number of characters that can be entered in the field.
Format	Specifies the way data displays in a table and prints.
Input Mask	Simplifies data entry by controlling the data that is required in a field and the way the data is to be displayed.
Caption	Specifies a field label other than the field name that is used in queries, forms, and reports.
Default Value	Automatically fills in a certain value for this field in new records as you add to the table. You can override a default value by typing a new value into the field.
Validation Rule	Limits data entered in a field to values that meet certain requirements.
Validation Text	Specifies the message to be displayed when the associated Validation Rule is not satisfied.
Required	Specifies whether a value must be entered in a field.
Allow Zero Length	Specifies whether an entry containing no characters is valid. This property is used to indicate that you know no value exists for a field. A zero-length string is entered as "" with no space between the quotation marks.
Indexed	Sets a field as an index field (a field that controls the order of records). This speeds up searches on fields that are searched frequently.

To view and change the field properties, you use Design view.

SWITCHING VIEWS

You can easily switch between views using the  button in the Table Tools

Fields tab. The graphic in the button changes to indicate the view that will be displayed when selected. Currently the button displays the graphic for Design view. If the view you want to change to is displayed in the button, you can simply click on the upper part of the button to change to that view. Otherwise, you can click on the lower part of the button to open the button's drop-down menu and select the view you want to use. Before you can change views, you will be asked to save the table.

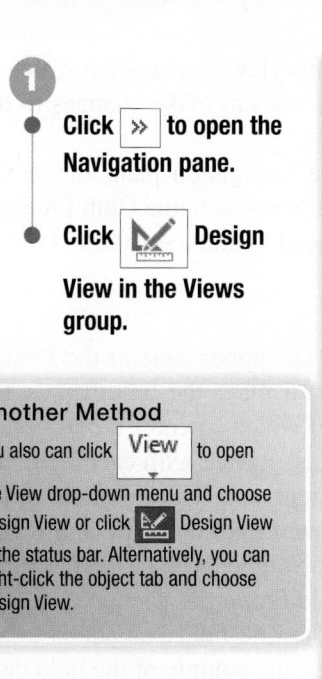

1

● Click » to open the Navigation pane.

● Click 📐 Design View in the Views group.

Another Method

You also can click [View] to open the View drop-down menu and choose Design View or click 📐 Design View in the status bar. Alternatively, you can right-click the object tab and choose Design View.

Your screen should be similar to Figure 1.14

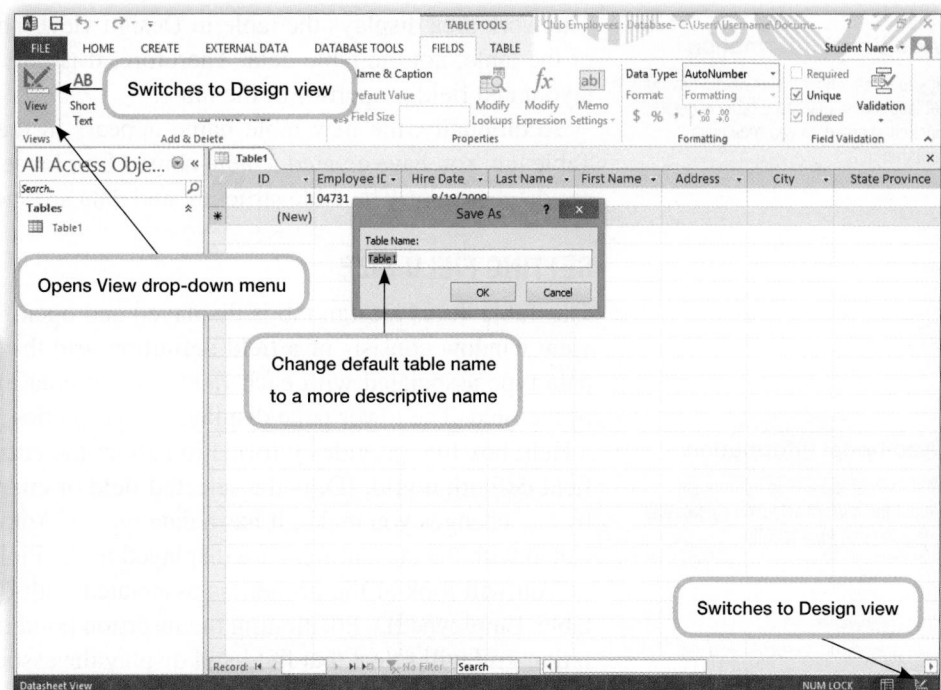

Figure 1.14

Additional Information

You also could click 💾 Save in the Records group of the Home tab, or use the keyboard shortcut ⇧ Shift + ← Enter, or click 💾 Save in the Quick Access Toolbar to save changes to the table at any time.

When you first create a new table and switch views, you are asked to save the table by replacing the default table name, Table1, with a more descriptive name. A table name follows the same set of standard naming conventions or rules that you use when naming fields. It is acceptable to use the same name for both a table and the database, although each table in a database must have a unique name. You will save the table using the table name Employee Records.

2

● Type **Employee Records**

● Click [OK].

Your screen should be similar to Figure 1.15

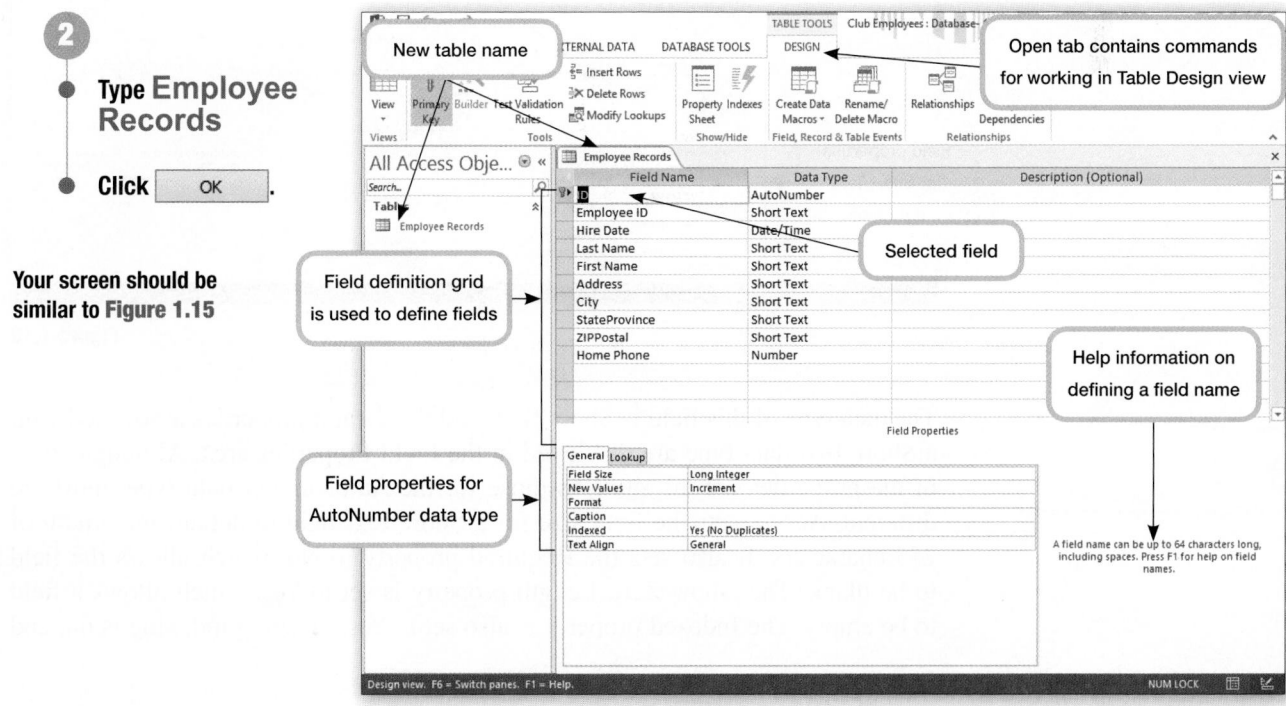

Figure 1.15

Modifying Field Properties   **AC1.23**

The work area displays the table in Design view. This view displays the structure of the table, not the table data. Therefore, it is only used to make changes to the layout and field properties of the table.

Additionally, the new table name appears in the Navigation pane and in the Table tab. You have created a table named Employee Records in the Club Employees database file. The table structure and data are saved within the database file.

SETTING FIELD SIZE

The Table Tools Design tab is displayed and open. The upper pane of the Design view window consists of a field definition grid that displays the field names, the data type associated with each field, and an area in which to enter a description of the field. The lower pane displays the properties associated with each field and a Help box that provides information about the current task. The first field in the field definition grid, ID, is the selected field or **current field** and will be affected by any changes you make. It has a data type of AutoNumber. The properties associated with the current field are displayed in the Field Properties section.

You will look at the properties associated with the first field you added to the table, Employee ID. Positioning the insertion point in any column of the field definition grid will select that field and display the associated field properties.

1

● Click on the **Employee ID field name.**

Your screen should be similar to Figure 1.16

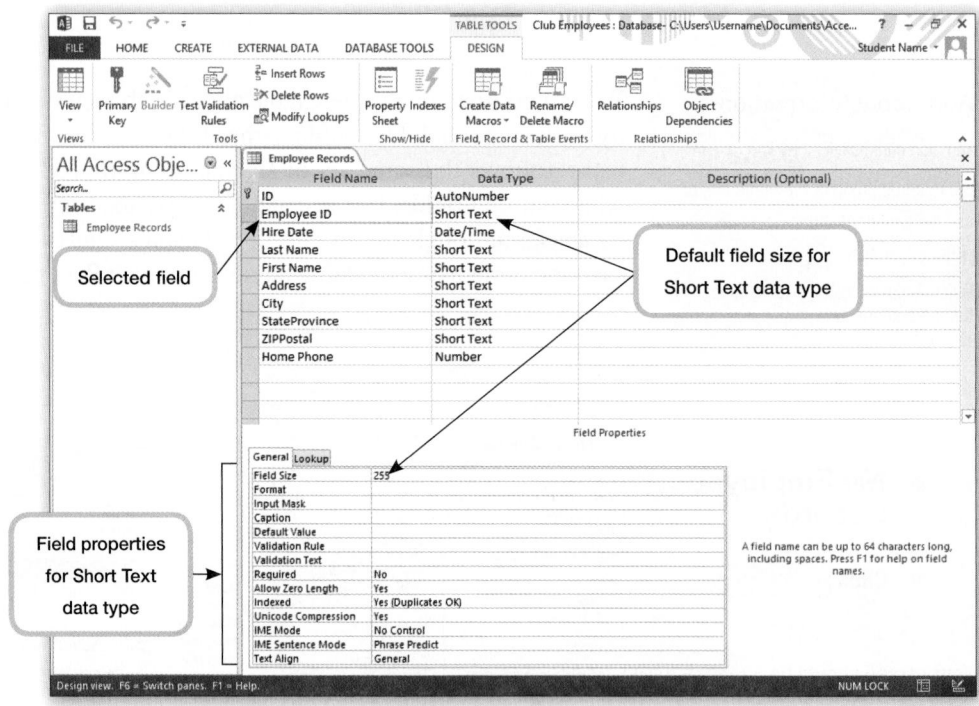

Figure 1.16

The data type of this field is Short Text, and the default properties associated with a Short Text data type are displayed in the Field Properties area. Although some of the properties are the same as those for the AutoNumber data type, most are different. Access sets the field size for a Short Text field to default maximum of 255 characters. It also sets the Required property to No, which allows the field to be blank. The Allow Zero Length property is set to Yes, which allows a field to be empty. The Indexed property is also set to Yes, meaning indexing is on, and duplicate entries are allowed in the field, as, for example, the same name could be entered in the Name field of multiple records. All these settings seem appropriate, except for the field size, which is much too large.

Although Access uses only the amount of storage space necessary for the text you actually store in a Short Text field, setting the field size to the smallest possible size can decrease the processing time required by the program. Additionally, if the field data to be entered is a specific size, setting the field size to that number restricts the entry to the maximum number.

Because the employee number will never be more than five digits long, you will change the field size from the default of 255 to 5.

2

● **Click the Field Size property text box.**

Another Method

You also can press [F6] to cycle forward between the Design view panes, the Navigation pane, the Ribbon, and Zoom controls the Design window.

● **Click the words Field Size in the row header to automatically select its contents of 255.**

Another Method

You can select text (highlight by dragging or double-clicking) and then press the [Delete] key to erase the selection.

● **Type 5 to replace the default entry.**

Additional Information

You can cancel changes you are making in the current field at any time before you move on to the next field. Just press [Esc] and the original entry is restored.

Your screen should be similar to Figure 1.17

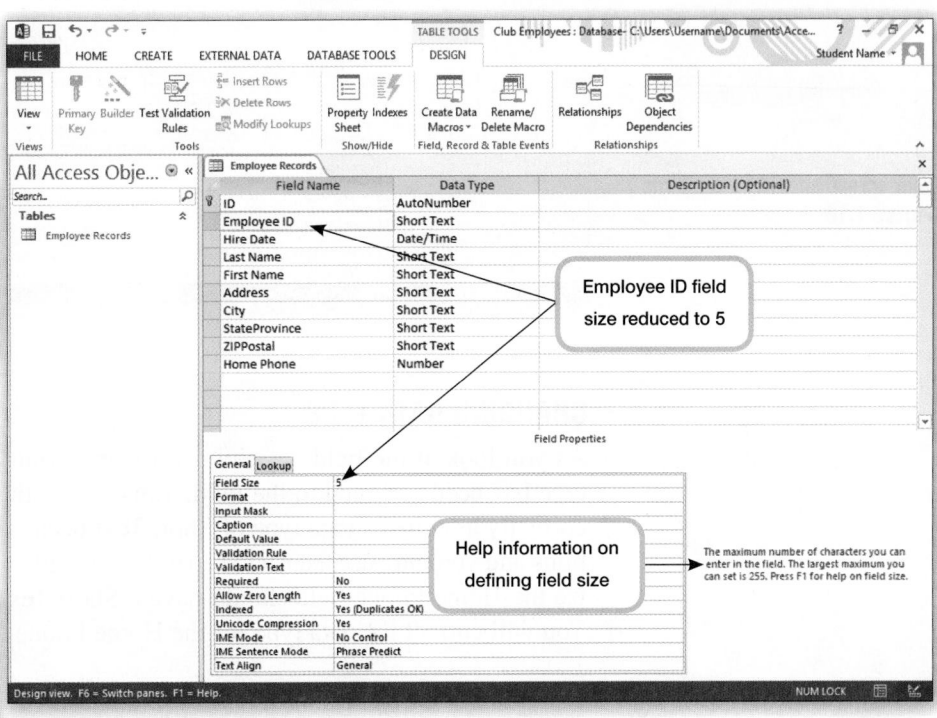

Figure 1.17

The maximum number of characters that can be entered in this field is now restricted to 5. Notice the Help box displays a brief description of the selected property.

Likewise, you will adjust the field sizes of several other fields.

3

- Change the field sizes to those shown for the fields in the following table.

Field	Size
Last Name	25
First Name	25
Address	50
City	25
StateProvince	2
ZIPPostal	10

Your screen should be similar to Figure 1.18

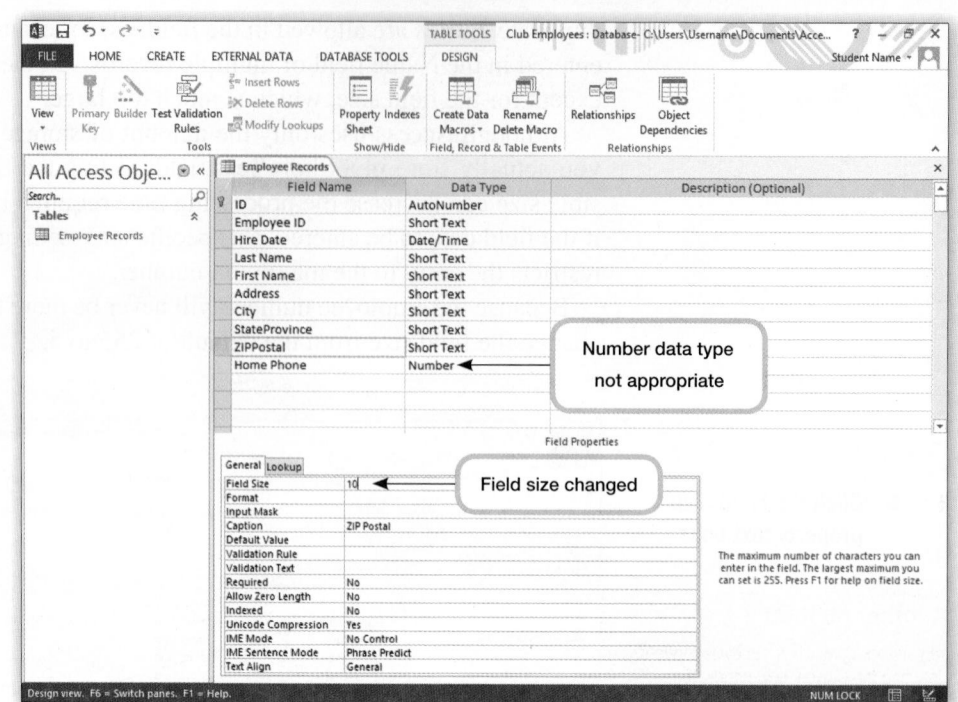

Figure 1.18

CHANGING DATA TYPE

As you look at the field definitions, it is important to make sure the correct data type has been assigned to the field. You can see that the ZIPPostal field has been correctly assigned a data type of Short Text because it will not be used in calculations and you may use a dash to separate the digits. For the same reasons, you realize the Home Phone field should have a Short Text data type instead of Number. You will correct the data type for the Home Phone field.

1

- Click in the Data Type column for the Home Phone field.

- Click ⌄ to open the drop-down list and choose Short Text.

- Change the field size for Home Phone to **15**

Your screen should be similar to Figure 1.19

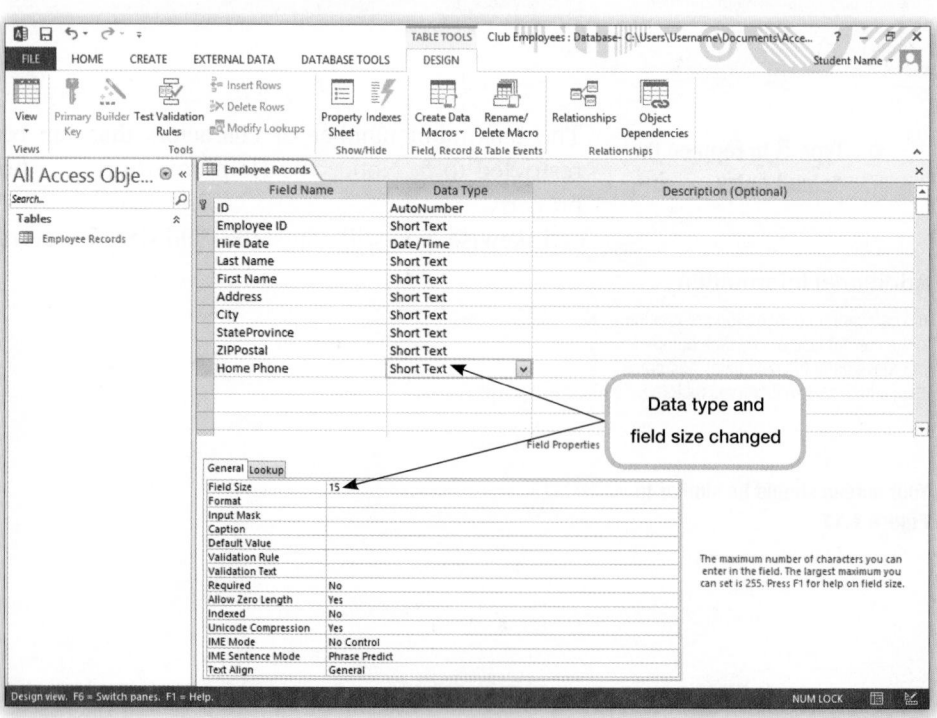

Figure 1.19

EDITING FIELD NAMES

As you continue to look over the fields, you decide to change the field names for the StateProvince and ZIPPostal fields that were assigned when you selected the Address field model.

● **Click on the StateProvince field.**

Your screen should be similar to Figure 1.20

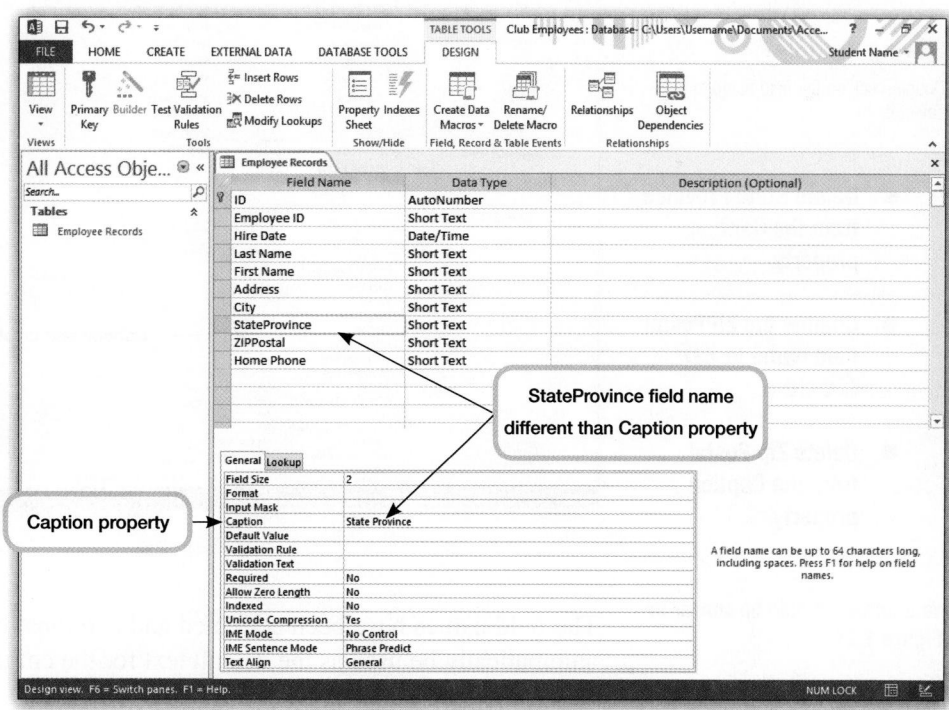

Figure 1.20

Notice that the StateProvince field name appears spelled with no space between the words, while the Caption property displays the State Province with a space. A **caption** is the text that displays in the column heading while in Datasheet view. It is used when you want the label to be different from the actual field name. If there is no text in the Caption field property, the field name will appear as the column heading in Datasheet view. You will change the field name to State and remove the caption for this field. Likewise, you will change the ZIPPostal field name to ZIP Code and clear the caption.

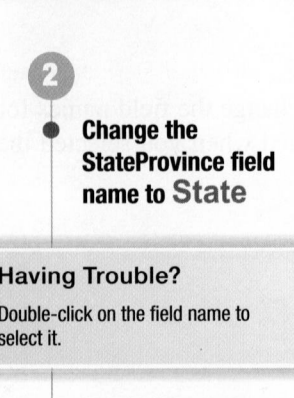

- **Change the StateProvince field name to State**

Having Trouble?

Double-click on the field name to select it.

- **Delete State Province from the Caption property.**

- **Change the ZIPPostal field name to ZIP Code**

- **Delete Zip Postal from the Caption property.**

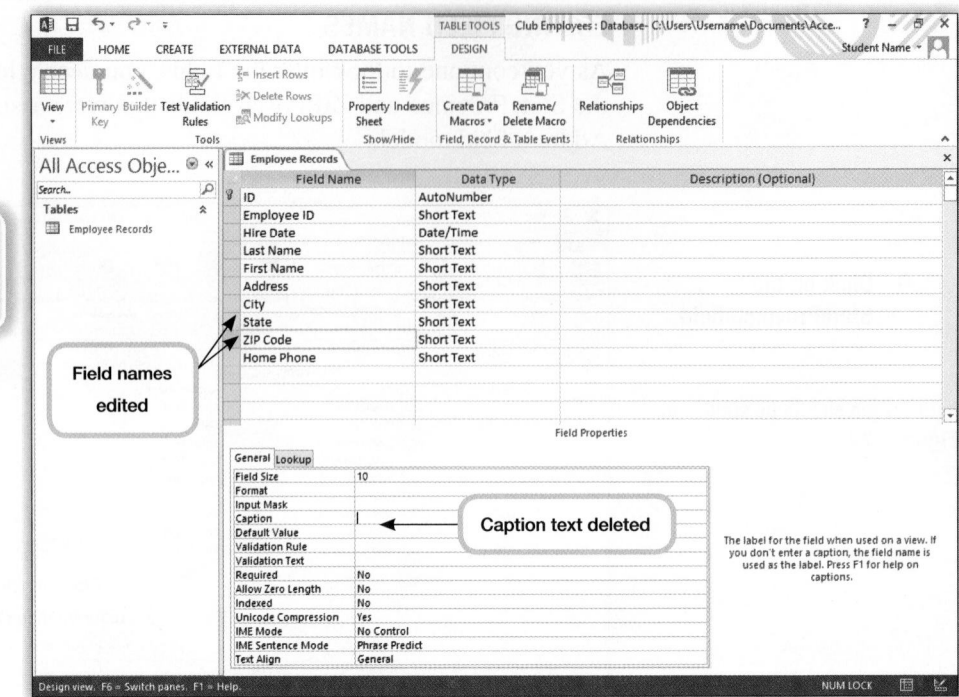

Figure 1.21

Your screen should be similar to Figure 1.21

The field names have been corrected and captions removed. The field names will automatically be used as the default text for the column headings.

DEFINING A FIELD AS A PRIMARY KEY

The next change you want to make is to define the Employee ID field as a primary key field.

Concept  Primary Key

A **primary key** is a field that uniquely identifies each record and is used to associate data from multiple tables. To qualify as a primary key field, the data in the field must be unique for each record. For example, a Social Security Number field could be selected as the primary key because the data in that field is unique for each employee. Other examples of primary key fields are part numbers or catalog numbers. (One example of a field that should not be used as the primary key is a name field because more than one person can have the same last or first name.) A second requirement is that the field can never be empty or null. A third is that the data in the field never, or rarely, changes.

A primary key prevents duplicate records from being entered in the table and is used to control the order in which records display in the table. This makes it faster for databases to locate records in the table and to process other operations.

Most tables have at least one field that is selected as the primary key. Some tables may use two or more fields that, together, provide the primary key of a table. When a primary key uses more than one field, it is called a **composite key**.

Notice the 🔑 icon that is displayed to the left of the ID field. This indicates that this field is a primary key field. You want to define the Employee ID field so that duplicate employee ID numbers will not be allowed.

1

- Click on the **Employee ID field name.**

- Click [Primary Key] in the **Tools group.**

Your screen should be similar to **Figure 1.22**

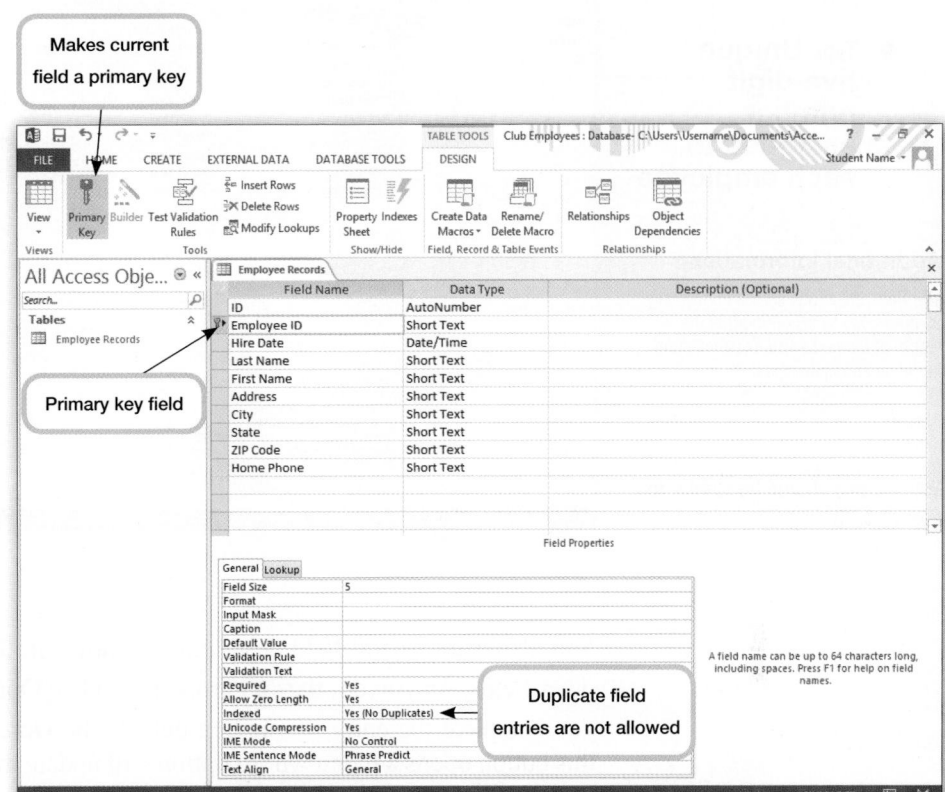

Figure 1.22

Notice the Indexed property setting for this field has changed to Yes (No Duplicates) because the field is defined as the primary key field. This setting prohibits duplicate values in a field. Also, the primary key status has been removed from the default ID field.

ENTERING FIELD DESCRIPTIONS

To continue defining the Employee ID field, you will enter a brief description of the field. Although it is optional, a field description makes the table easier to understand and update because the description is displayed in the status bar when you enter data into the table.

1

- **Click the Description text box for the Employee ID field.**

- **Type Unique five-digit number assigned to each employee**

Additional Information

The Description box scrolls horizontally as necessary to accommodate the length of the text entry. The maximum length is 255 characters.

Your screen should be similar to Figure 1.23

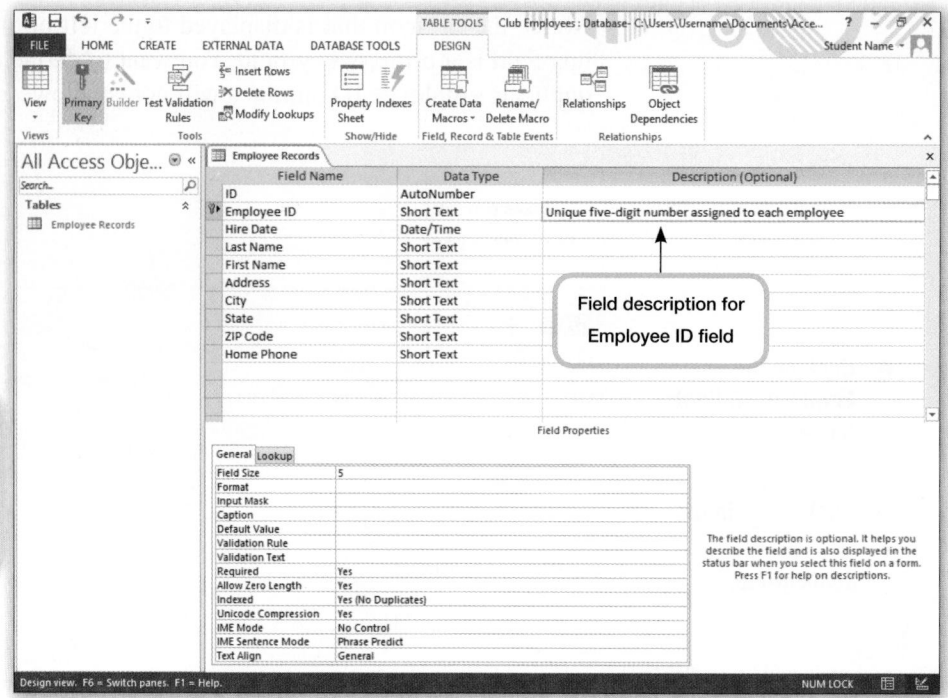

Figure 1.23

You also want to add field descriptions (shown in the following table) to several other fields. As you do, the Property Update Options button will appear when you complete the entry by moving outside the Description text box. Clicking on this button opens a menu whose option will update the description in the status bar everywhere the field is used. Because this database only contains one table, there is no need to update the description anyplace else. The button will disappear automatically when you continue working.

Field Name	Description
Hire Date	Enter as month, day, year (for example, 3/2/06)
State	Use a two-character abbreviation entered in capital letters
Zip Code	Include a four-digit extension, if available (07739-0015)
Home Phone	Enter as (555) 555-5555

2

- **Add descriptions to the fields as shown in the table above.**

Your screen should be similar to Figure 1.24

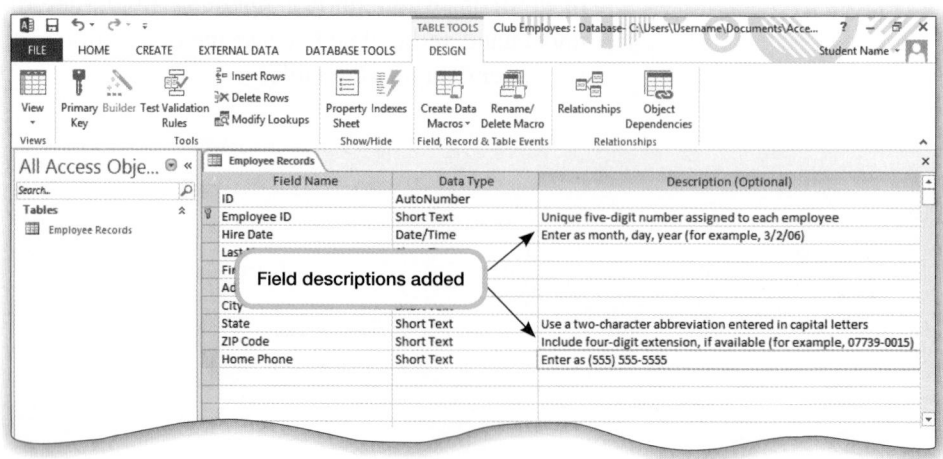

Figure 1.24

Additional Information

In a table that contains a lot of data, it is a good idea to create a backup copy of the table before you delete a field in case you need to recover the deleted data.

DELETING A FIELD IN DESIGN VIEW

Because the ID field essentially duplicates the purpose of the Employee ID field, you will delete the ID field. Just like deleting a field in Datasheet view, deleting a field in Design view permanently removes the field column and all the data in the field from the table.

1

- Click in the ID field.

- Click

  ☒ Delete Rows in
  the Tools group.

- Click [Yes]
  in response to
  the message to
  confirm you want to
  permanently delete
  the field.

Your screen should be similar to
Figure 1.25

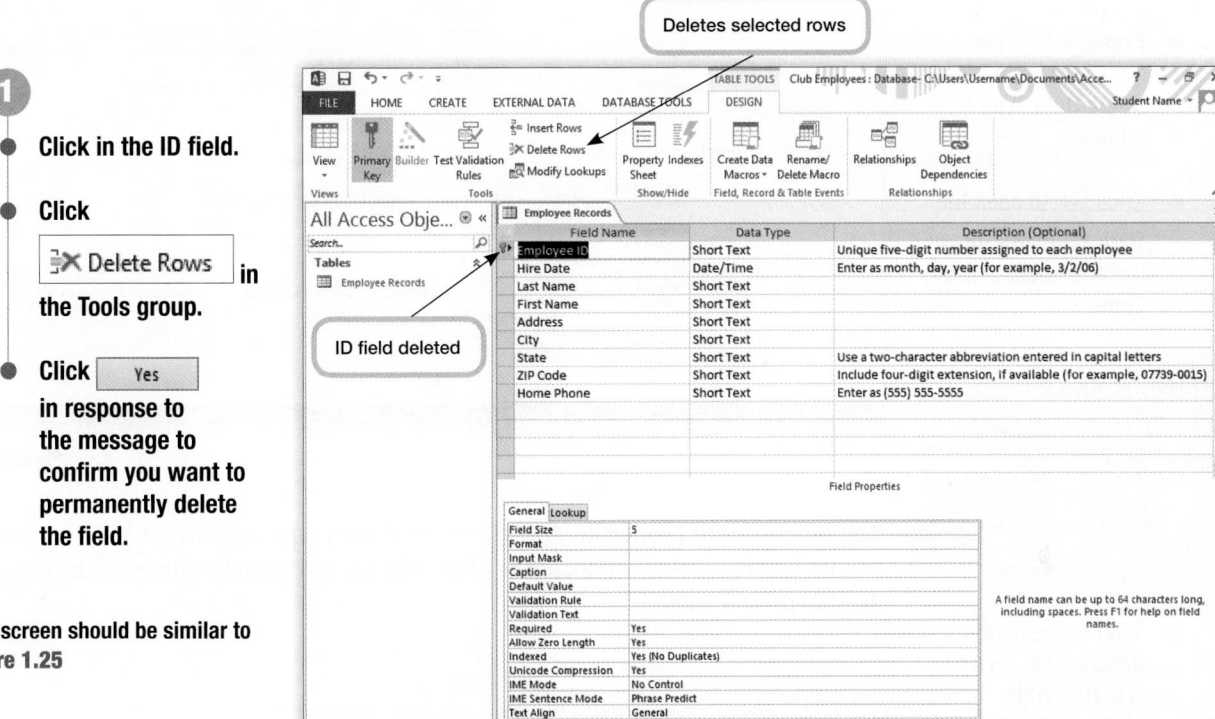

Figure 1.25

The field is permanently removed from the table.

CREATING A FIELD IN DESIGN VIEW

You still need to add two fields to the table: one for the employee's date of birth and the other to display the employee's photo. You will add the new fields and define their properties in Design view.

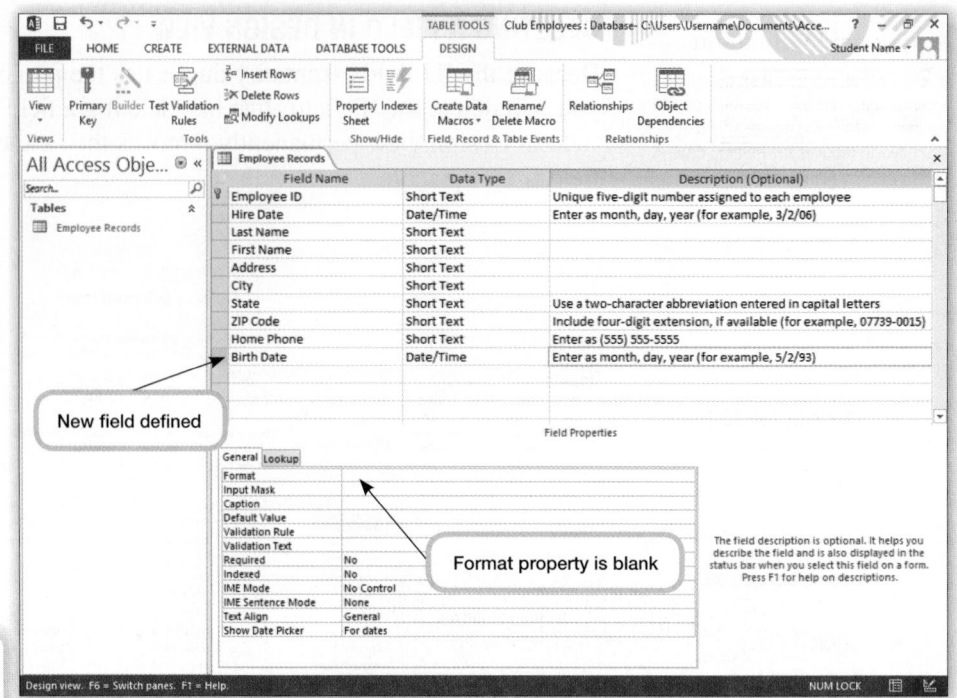

Figure 1.26

1

- Click in the blank Field Name row below the Home Phone field name.

- Type **Birth Date**

- Press ⏎Enter or Tab⇥ or → to move to the Data Type column.

- Click ⌄ to open the Data Type drop-down list and choose Date/Time.

Another Method

You also can enter the data type in Design view by typing the first character of the type you want to use. For example, if you type D, the Date/Time data type will be automatically selected and displayed in the field.

- Type in the field description: **Enter as month, day, year (for example, 5/2/93)**

Your screen should be similar to Figure 1.26

The default field properties for the selected data type are displayed. Because the format line is blank, you decide to check the format to make sure that the date will display as you want.

2

● Click in the Format property box.

● Click  to open the drop-down list of format options.

Your screen should be similar to Figure 1.27

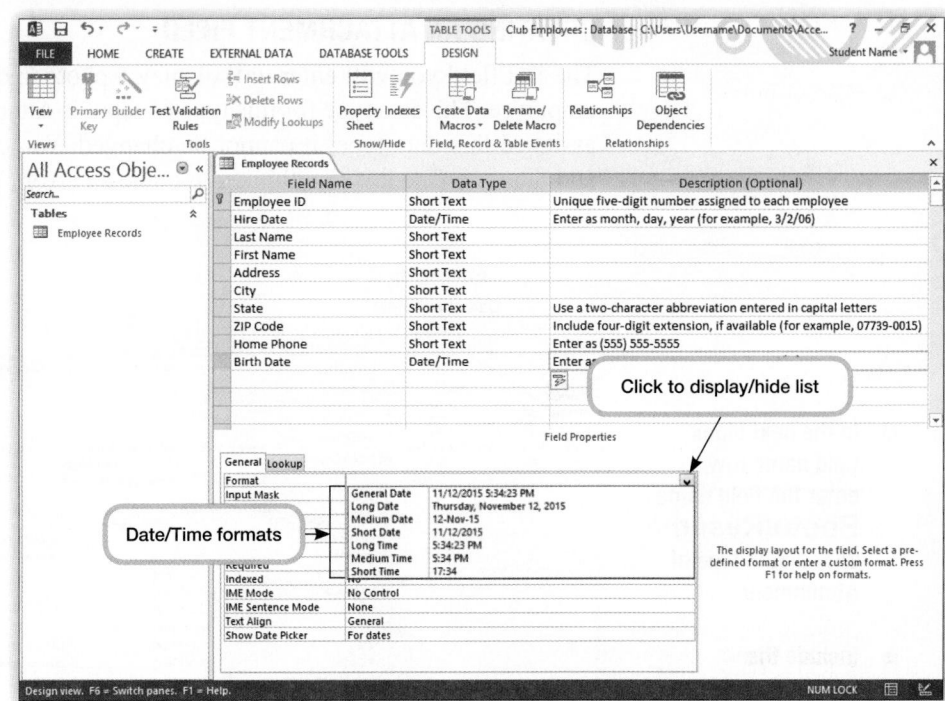

Figure 1.27

Seven Date/Time field type formats along with examples of each are displayed in the list. Although not displayed in the Format property box, the General Date format is the default format. It displays dates using the Short Date format. If a time value is entered, it will display the time in the Long Time format. You will choose the General Date format so that the setting will be displayed in the Format property box.

3

● Choose General Date.

Your screen should be similar to Figure 1.28

Additional Information

Access automatically assumes the first two digits of a year entry. If you enter a year that is between /30 and /99, Access reads this as a 20th century date (1930 to 1999). A year entry between /00 and /29 is assumed to be a 21st century date (2000 to 2029).

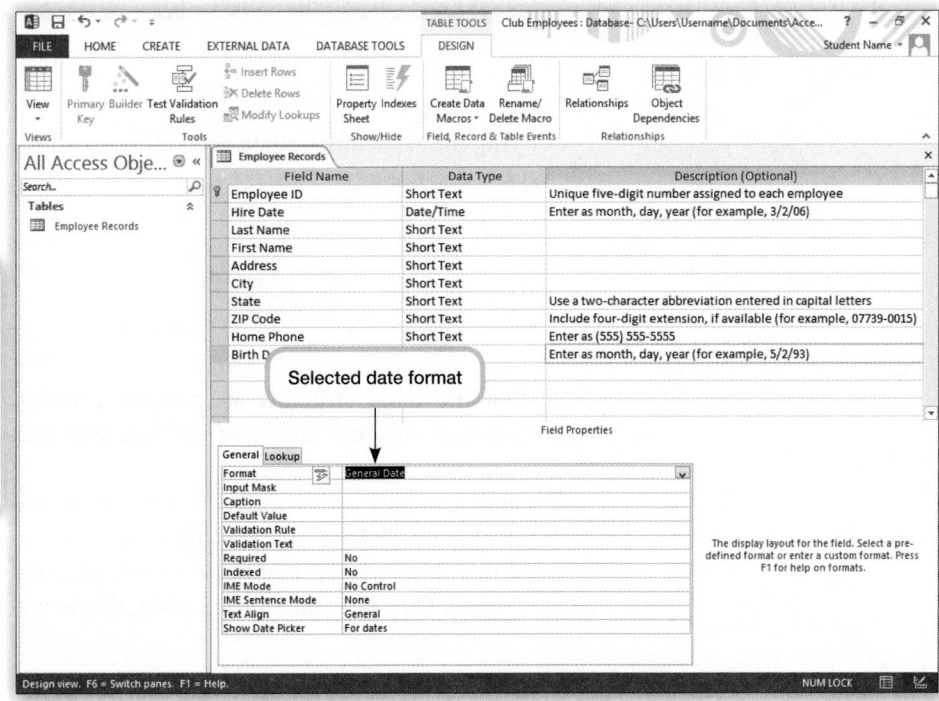

Figure 1.28

The Date/Time property setting is now displayed in the Format text box.

CREATING AN ATTACHMENT FIELD

The last field you will enter will display a photo and resume if available for each employee. The data type for this type of input is Attachment. Once a field has been assigned this data type, it cannot be changed. You can, however, delete the field and then redefine it if you think you made an error.

1

- In the next blank field name row, enter the field name **Photo/Resume** with a data type of Attachment.

- Include the description Attach employee photo and resume if available

Your screen should be similar to Figure 1.29

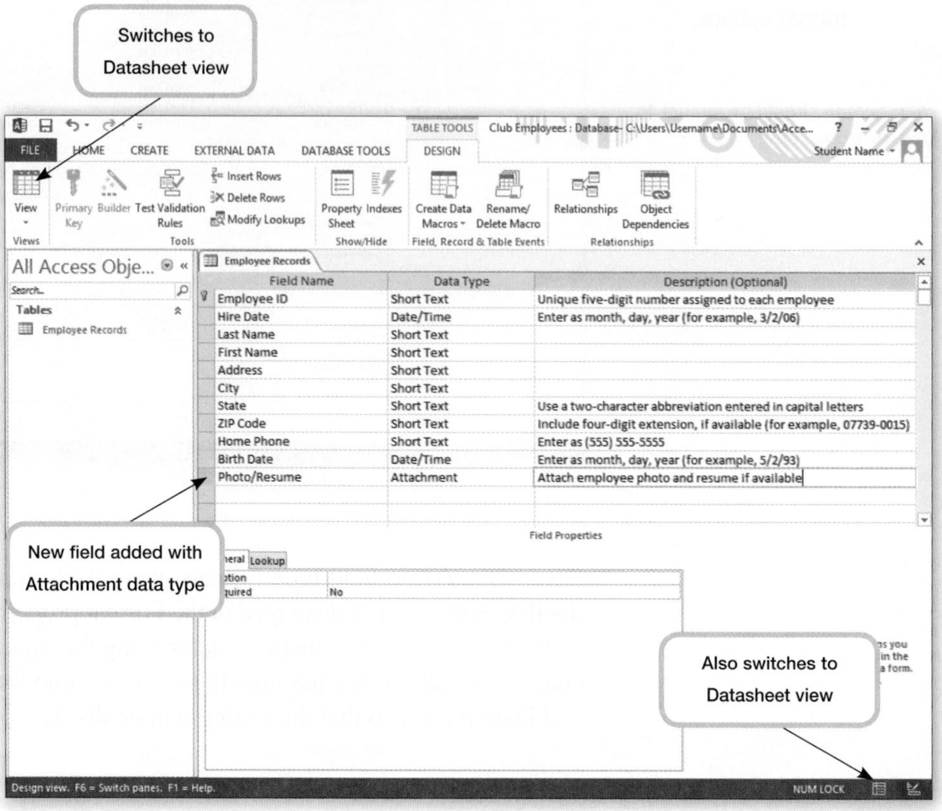

Figure 1.29

Specifying the Attachment data type allows you to store multiple files of different file types in a single field.

Entering and Editing Records

Now that the table structure is complete, you want to continue entering the employee data into the table. To do this, you need to switch back to Datasheet view.

Because you have made many changes to the table design, you will be asked to save the changes before Access will allow you to switch views. You also will be advised that data may be lost because you decreased field sizes in several fields. Since there is very little data in the table, this is not a concern.

- Click 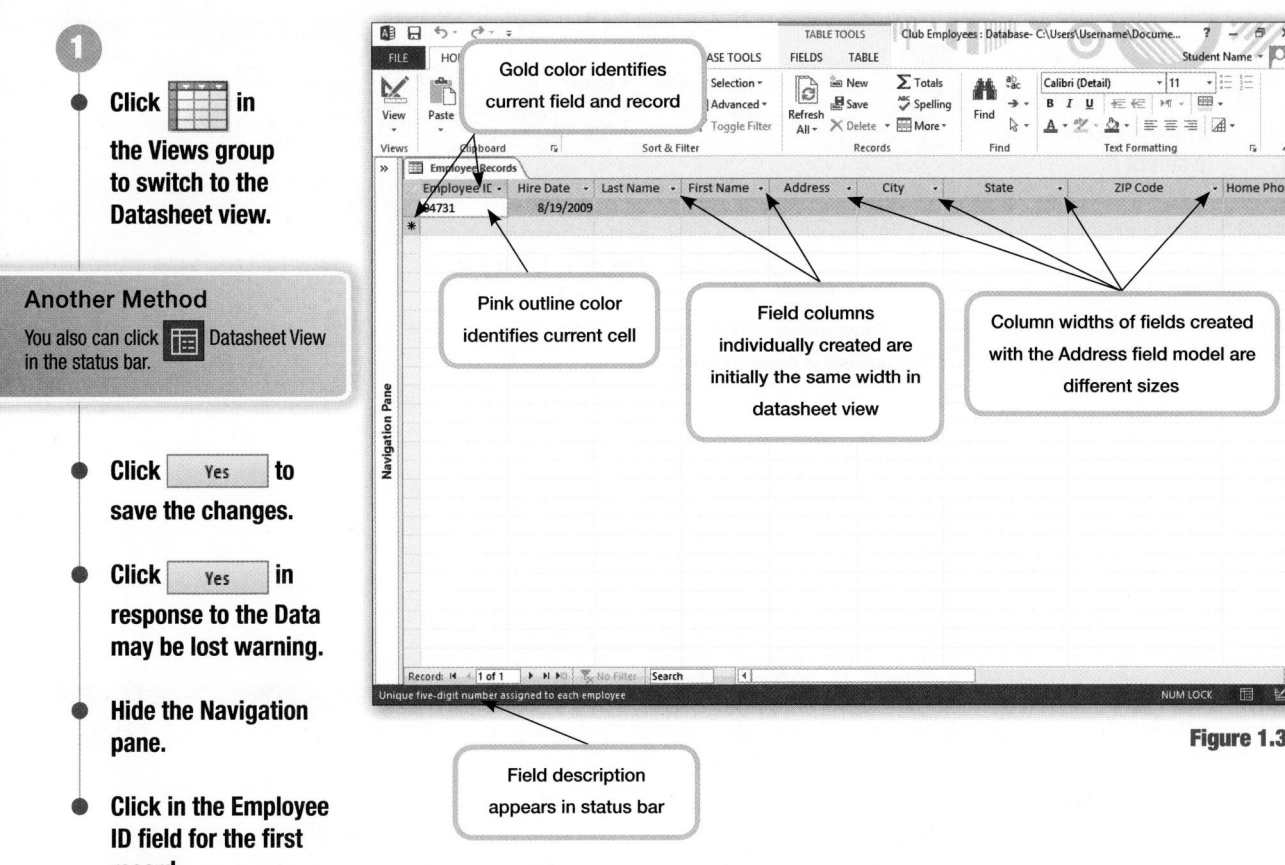 in the Views group to switch to the Datasheet view.

- Click Yes to save the changes.

- Click Yes in response to the Data may be lost warning.

- Hide the Navigation pane.

- Click in the Employee ID field for the first record.

Your screen should be similar to Figure 1.30

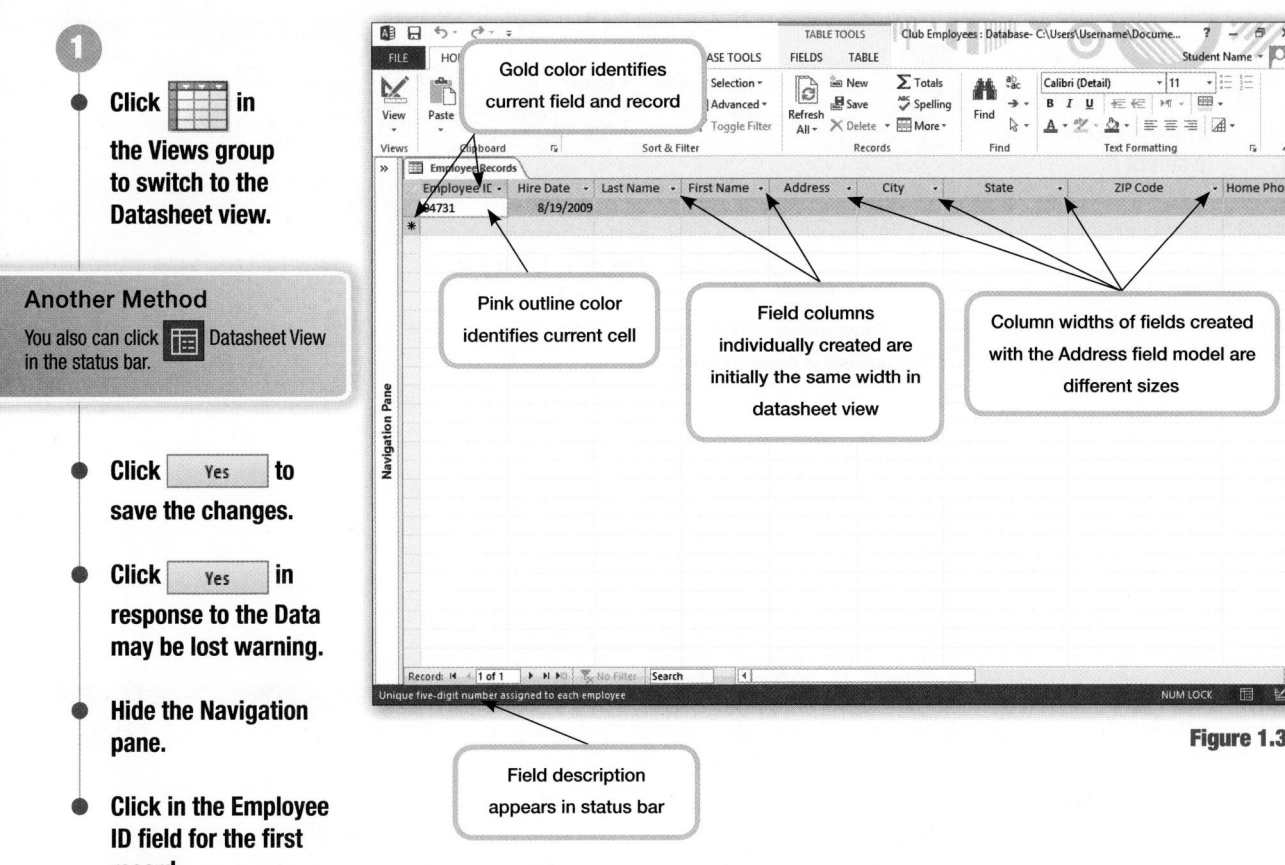

Figure 1.30

- Gold color identifies current field and record
- Pink outline color identifies current cell
- Field columns individually created are initially the same width in datasheet view
- Column widths of fields created with the Address field model are different sizes
- Field description appears in status bar

Because you deleted the ID field, it is no longer displayed and the new fields you defined are ready for you to enter the remaining data for the first record. The first cell of the first record is outlined in pink, indicating that the program is ready to accept data in this field. The field name and Select Record button are highlighted in gold to identify the current field and current record. The status bar displays the description you entered for the field.

Notice also in this view that the column widths for the fields you created individually are all the same, even though you set different field sizes in the Table Design window. This is because the Table Datasheet view has its own default column width setting. The column widths of the fields that were created using the Address field model were sized to fit the original field name for each column.

VERIFYING DATA ACCURACY AND VALIDITY

To see how field properties help ensure data accuracy, you will reenter the employee number for the first record and try to enter a number that is larger than the field size of five that you defined in Table Design view.

1

● Double-click on the Employee ID number to select it.

● Type **047310**

Your screen should be similar to Figure 1.31

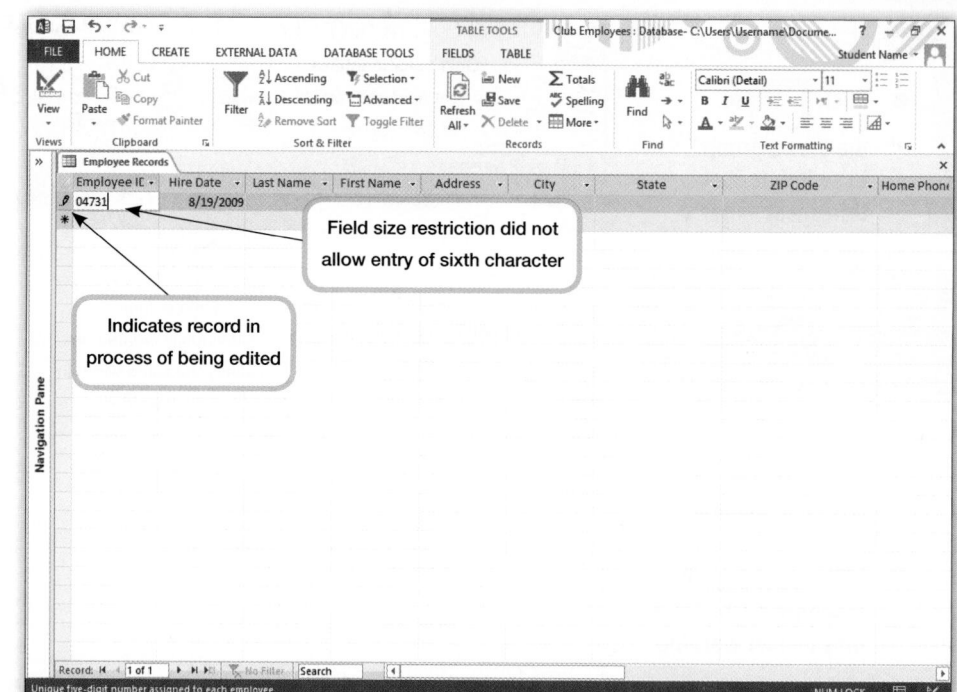

> Field size restriction did not allow entry of sixth character

> Indicates record in process of being edited

Figure 1.31

The program beeped to alert you of a problem and would not let you type a sixth character. The field size restriction helps control the accuracy of data by not allowing an entry larger than has been specified. Notice also that the current record symbol has changed to 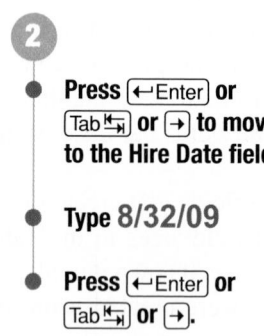. The pencil symbol means the record is in the process of being entered or edited and has not yet been saved.

Next, you will intentionally enter an invalid date to see what happens.

2

● Press ←Enter or Tab⇥ or → to move to the Hire Date field.

● Type **8/32/09**

● Press ←Enter or Tab⇥ or →.

Your screen should be similar to Figure 1.32

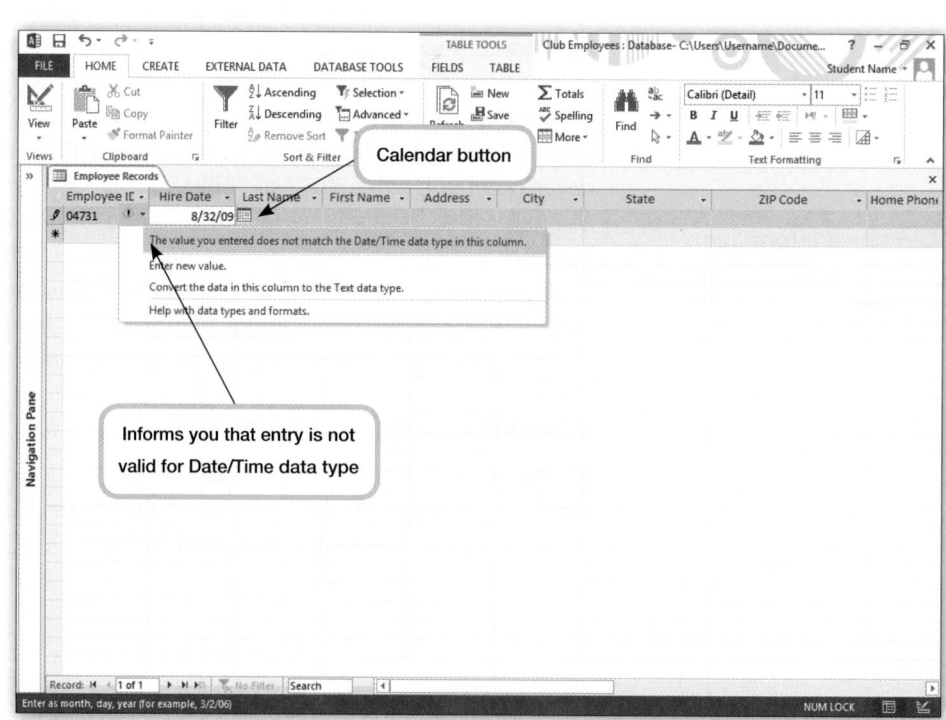

> Calendar button

> Informs you that entry is not valid for Date/Time data type

Figure 1.32

An informational message box is displayed advising you that the entry is not valid. In this case, the date entered (8/32/09) could not be correct because a month cannot have 32 days. Access automatically performs some basic checks on the data as it is entered based upon the field type specified in the table design. This is another way that Access helps you control data entry to ensure the accuracy of the data.

You will need to edit the date entry to correct it.

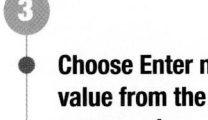

Additional Information

The calendar button appears automatically whenever a Date data type field is active. Clicking it displays a calendar for the current month from which you can quickly find and choose a date.

3
- Choose Enter new value from the message box.

- Double-click on 32 to select it.

- Type **19**

- Press Tab⇥.

Your screen should be similar to Figure 1.33

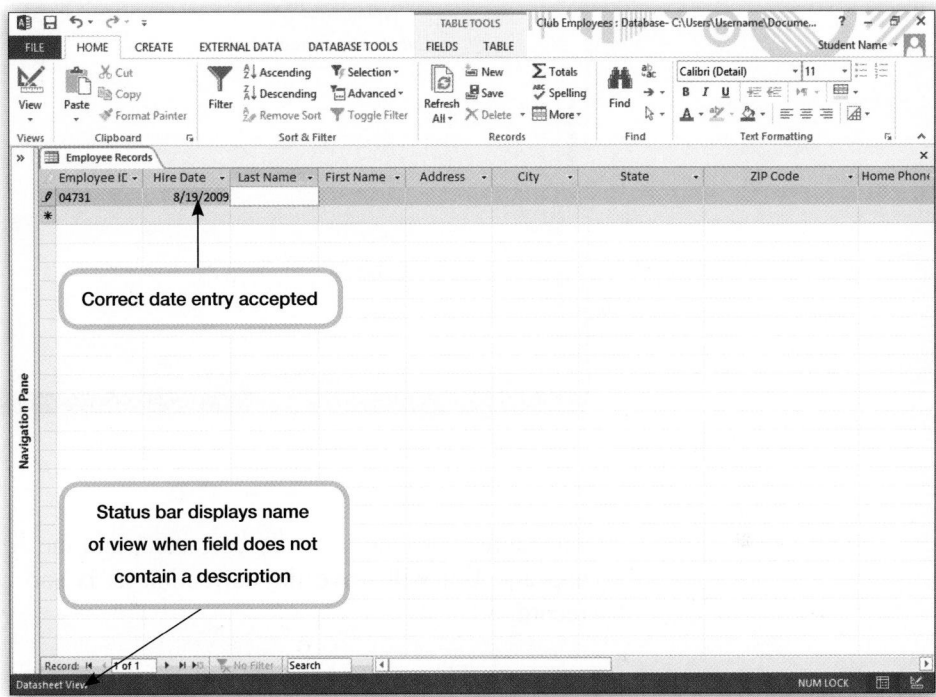

Figure 1.33

The corrected date is accepted, and the insertion point moves to the Last Name field. The year in the date changed to four digits, which reflects the date format you specified in the field's property.

Because you did not enter a description for the Last Name field, the status bar displays "Datasheet View," the name of the current view, instead of a field description.

USING AUTOCORRECT

Now you are ready to continue entering the data for the first record. As you are typing, you may make errors and they may be corrected automatically for you. This is because the AutoCorrect feature automatically corrects obvious errors such as not capitalizing names of days, the first letter of sentences, and other common typing errors and misspellings such as words starting with two initial capital letters. The AutoCorrect Options button ⚡ will appear next to any text that was corrected. You have the option of undoing the correction or leaving it as is. Most of the time, the typing error is not corrected, and you will need to fix it manually.

To see how this works, you will enter the last name incorrectly by typing the first two letters using capital letters.

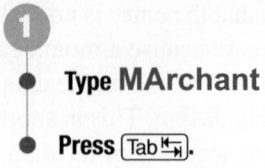

1

● Type **MArchant**

● Press Tab.

Your screen should be similar to Figure 1.34

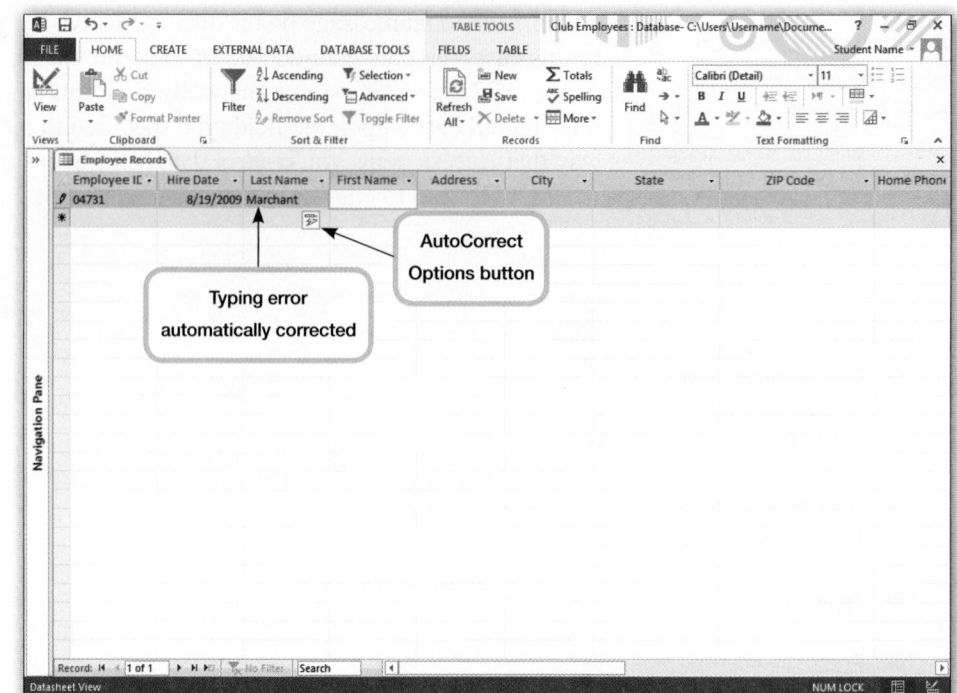

Figure 1.34

The name was automatically corrected, and the AutoCorrect Options button 彡 appears. You will leave the correction as is and continue to enter data for this record.

2

● Enter the data shown in the table on the next page for the remaining fields, typing the information exactly as it appears. Press Tab after each entry.

Additional Information

The fields will scroll in the window as you move to the right in the record.

Your screen should be similar to Figure 1.35

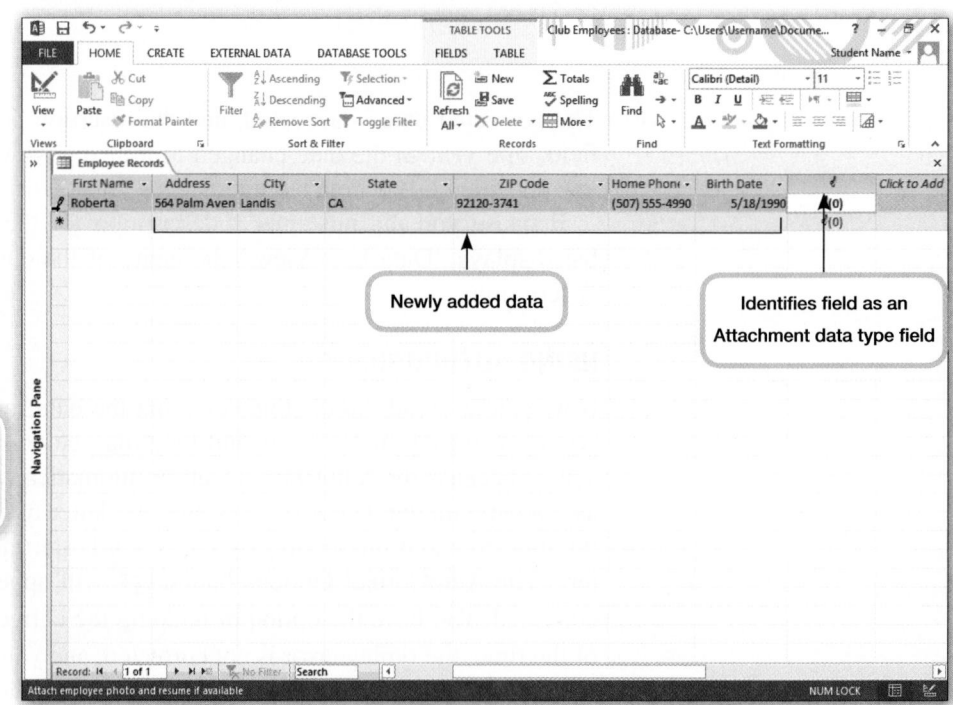

Figure 1.35

Field Name	Data
First Name	Roberta
Address	564 Palm Avenue
City	Landis
State	CA
ZIP Code	92120-3741
Home Phone	(507) 555-4990
Birth Date	May 18, 1990

All the information for the first record is now complete, except for the last field for the employee photo and resume.

ATTACHING FILES TO RECORDS

Notice that the field name in the header for this field is not Photo/Resume, as you defined in Design view. This is because Access does not use the field name for Attachment data types. Instead it displays a paper clip icon in the field header to show that the field has an Attachment data type. However, you can specify a caption for this field that will display as the field name. Before making this change, you want to add the data for this field.

You plan to attach the employee photo and a copy of the employee's resume if it is available. A photo is one of several different types of graphic objects that can be added to a database table. A **graphic** is a nontext element or object. A graphic can be a simple **drawing object** consisting of shapes such as lines and boxes that can be created using a drawing program such as Paint, or it can be a picture. A **picture** is a visual representation of an image such as a scanned photograph. A resume is a text document that is typically created using a word processor application.

Because you have not organized all the employees' badge photographs yet, you will only insert the photo for Roberta Marchant to demonstrate this feature to the club owners. You also will attach a sample resume that was created using Word 2013.

1

Double-click on the (0) Attachment field cell for this record.

Your screen should be similar to Figure 1.36

Figure 1.36

The Attachments dialog box is used to manage the items that are in an Attachment field. Because there are currently no attachments associated with this field, it is empty. You will select the photo and resume files you want to add to the field.

2

- Click [Add...].

- If necessary, specify the location of your data files in the Choose File dialog box.

- Select ac01_Roberta **and** ac01_Resume **from the file list box.**

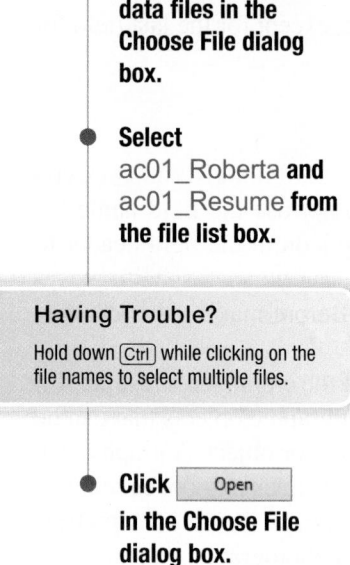

Having Trouble?

Hold down [Ctrl] while clicking on the file names to select multiple files.

- Click [Open] in the Choose File dialog box.

Your screen should be similar to Figure 1.37

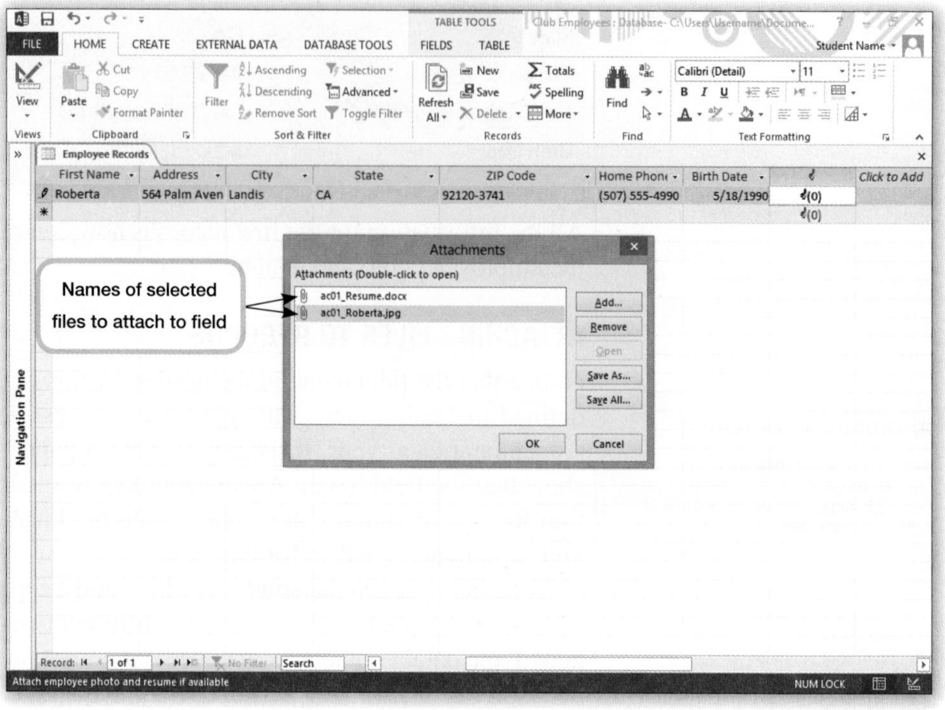

Figure 1.37

The Attachments dialog box is displayed again and now displays the names of the selected files.

Additional Information

To remove a file from the Attachment field, select the file name from the list and click [Remove].

3

● Click [OK] in the Attachments dialog box.

Your screen should be similar to Figure 1.38

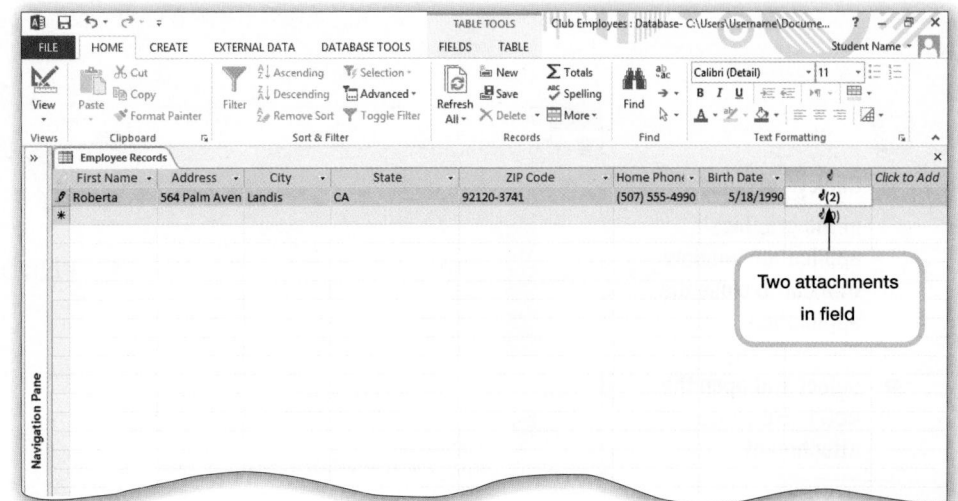

Two attachments in field

Figure 1.38

The selected files are inserted as attachments and identified with the number 2 in the cell. The number indicates how many attachments have been added to the field. You will now display the photograph from the Attachment field to check that it has been inserted properly.

4

● Double-click the cell containing the attachments for Roberta.

● Select the ac01_ Roberta file from the Attachments dialog box.

● Click [Open].

Another Method
You also can double-click the file to both select and open it.

Your screen should be similar to Figure 1.39

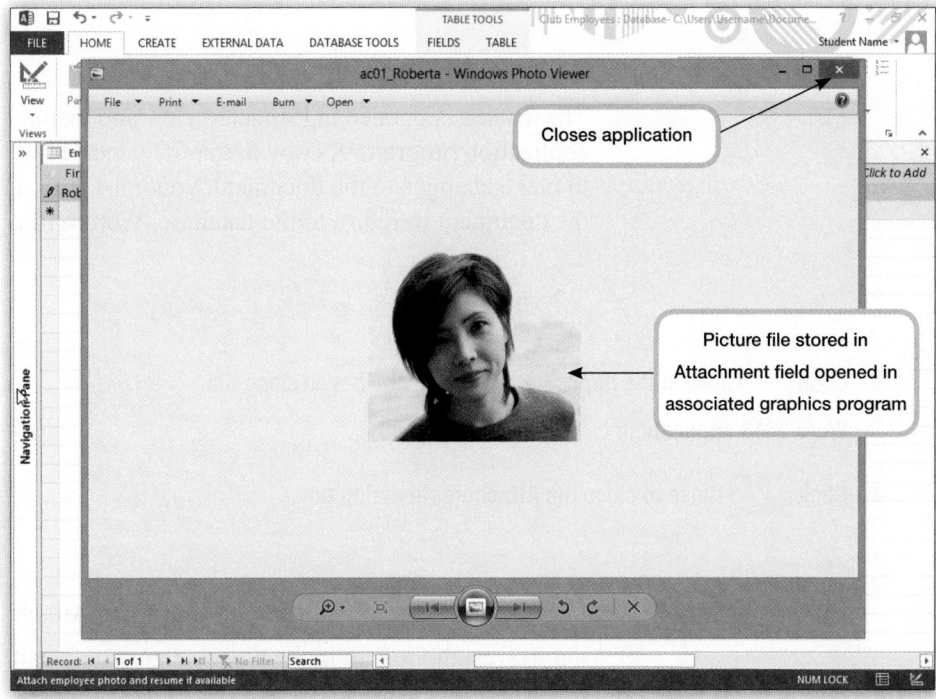

Closes application

Picture file stored in Attachment field opened in associated graphics program

Figure 1.39

The picture object is opened and displayed in the graphics program that is associated with this type of file—in this case, Windows Photos Viewer. Yours may open and display in a different graphics program such as Paint. The application that opens is not necessarily the application in which the file was created. If the application in which it opens includes features that can be used to edit the file, you will be prompted to save any changes before closing the Attachments dialog box. If you do not save them, the changes will be lost.

5

● Click [×] Close in the graphics application window title bar to close the application.

● Select and open the ac01_Resume attachment.

● If necessary, maximize the Word application window.

Your screen should be similar to Figure 1.40

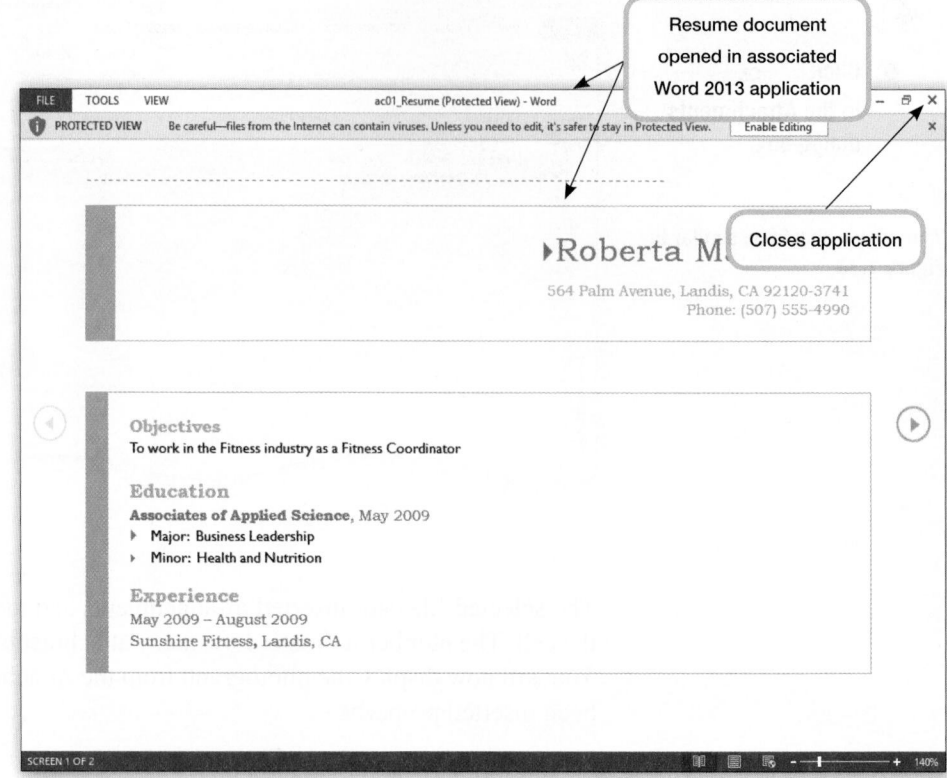

Resume document opened in associated Word 2013 application

Closes application

▸Roberta M

564 Palm Avenue, Landis, CA 92120-3741
Phone: (507) 555-4990

Objectives
To work in the Fitness industry as a Fitness Coordinator

Education
Associates of Applied Science, May 2009
▸ Major: Business Leadership
▸ Minor: Health and Nutrition

Experience
May 2009 – August 2009
Sunshine Fitness, Landis, CA

SCREEN 1 OF 2   140%

Figure 1.40

The resume is opened in Protected view and displayed in the associated Word 2013 application program. A copy of the file is placed in a temporary folder. If you want to make changes to the document, you must click Enable Editing. When you close the document to return to the database, Word will prompt you to save the changes.

6

● Click [×] Close in the application window title bar to close the Word 2013 application.

● Click [×] Close to close the Attachments dialog box.

Finally, you want to add the caption for the Attachment field. Rather than switching to Design view to make this change, you can use the [▤ Name & Caption] button in the Properties group of the Table Tools Fields tab.

7

- Click
  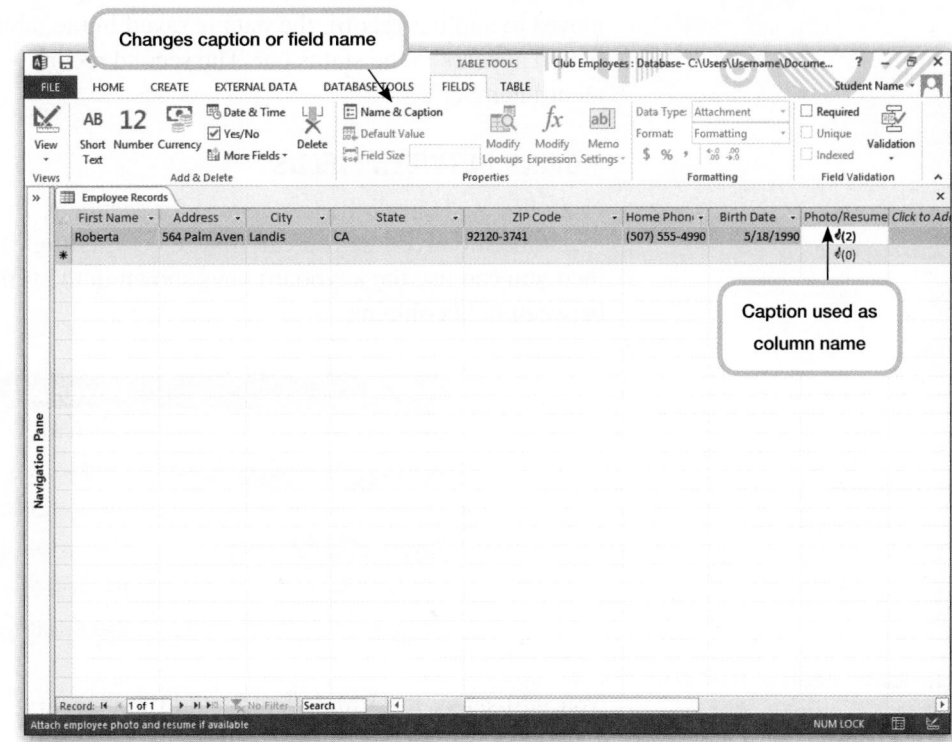 [≔ Name & Caption] in
  the Properties group
  of the Table Tools
  Fields tab.

- In the Caption text
  box of the Enter Field
  Properties dialog
  box, type Photo/
  Resume

- Click [OK].

Your screen should be similar to
Figure 1.41

Changes caption or field name

*Caption used as
column name*

Figure 1.41

The field column now displays the caption associated with the field. This clarifies
the field contents and makes it much easier for others to understand.

8

- Click in the
  Attachment field for
  the first record and
  then press [←Enter]
  to move to the
  beginning of the next
  record.

Your screen should be similar to
Figure 1.42

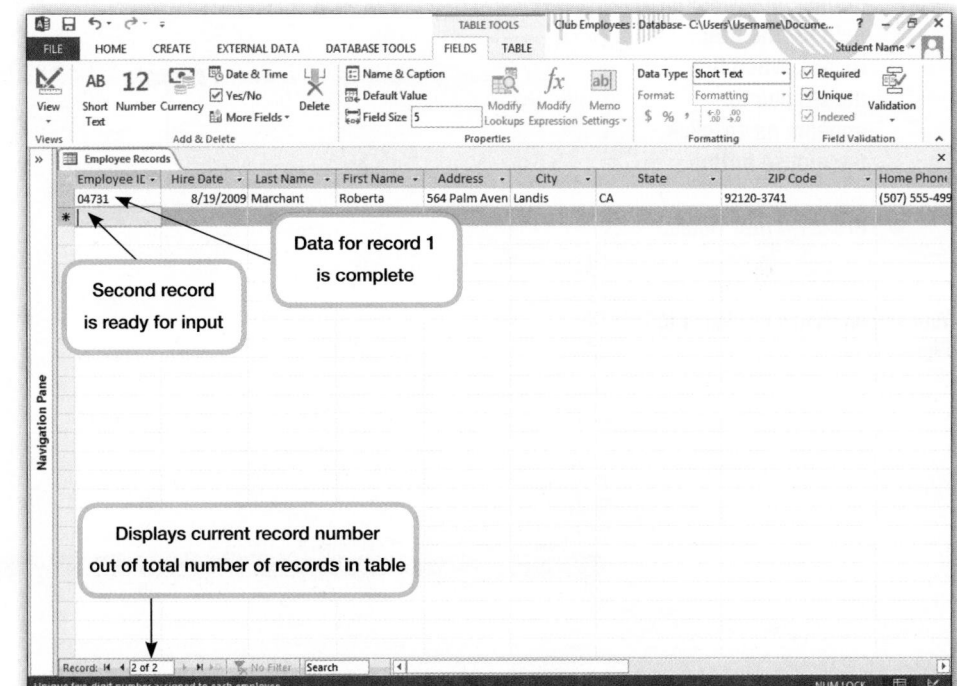

*Data for record 1
is complete*

*Second record
is ready for input*

*Displays current record number
out of total number of records in table*

Figure 1.42

The information for the first record is now complete. After pressing [Enter] in the
last field, the insertion point moves to the first field in the next row and waits for
input of the employee number for the next record. As soon as the insertion point

moves to another record, the data is saved in the table and the number of the new record appears in the status bar. The second record was automatically assigned the record number 2.

MOVING BETWEEN FIELDS

Next, you will check the first record for accuracy. To quickly move from one field to another in a record, you can first select (highlight) the entire field contents and then you can use the keyboard keys shown in the following table to move quickly between field columns.

Key	Movement
→ or Tab ⇥	Next field
← or ⇧ Shift + Tab ⇥	Previous field
↑	Current field in previous record
↓	Current field in next record
Home	First field in record
End	Last field in record

You will select the Employee ID field for the first record and then move to the Address field to check its contents.

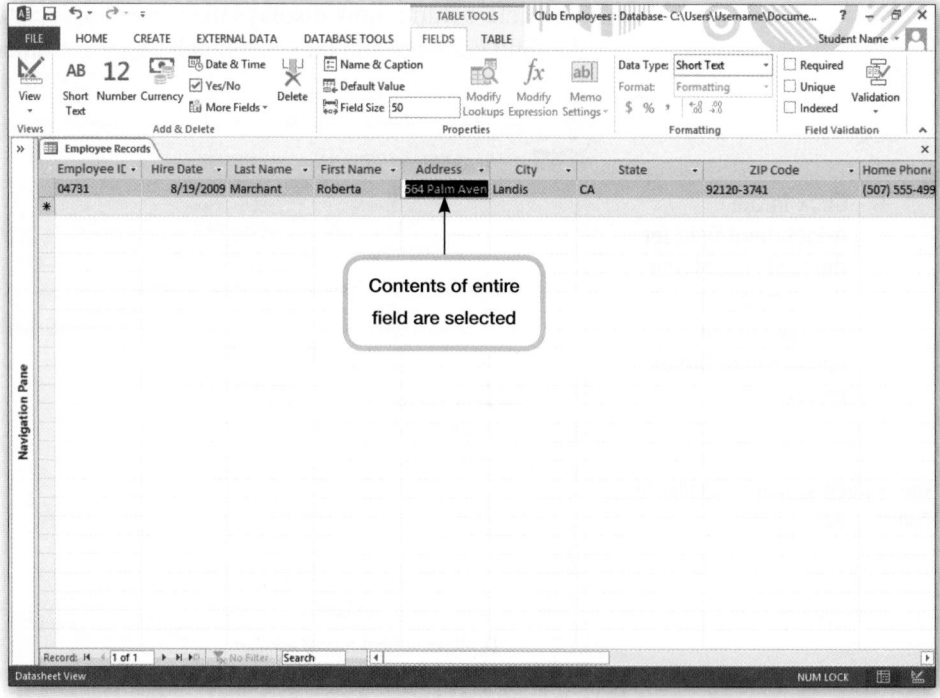

Figure 1.43

①
- **Point to the left end of the Employee ID field for the first record. When the mouse pointer appears as ⊕, click the mouse button.**

- **Press → four times.**

Your screen should be similar to Figure 1.43

Contents of entire field are selected

Additional Information

If you press Delete or ←Backspace while the entire field is selected, the entire field contents will be deleted.

Because the entire field contents are selected, you need to be careful that you do not type a character, as that will delete the selection and replace it with the new text. To switch back to editing, you need to display the insertion point in the field and then edit the entry.

2 ● Point to anywhere in the address of the Address field and when the mouse displays as an I-beam, click to place the insertion point.

Your screen should be similar to Figure 1.44

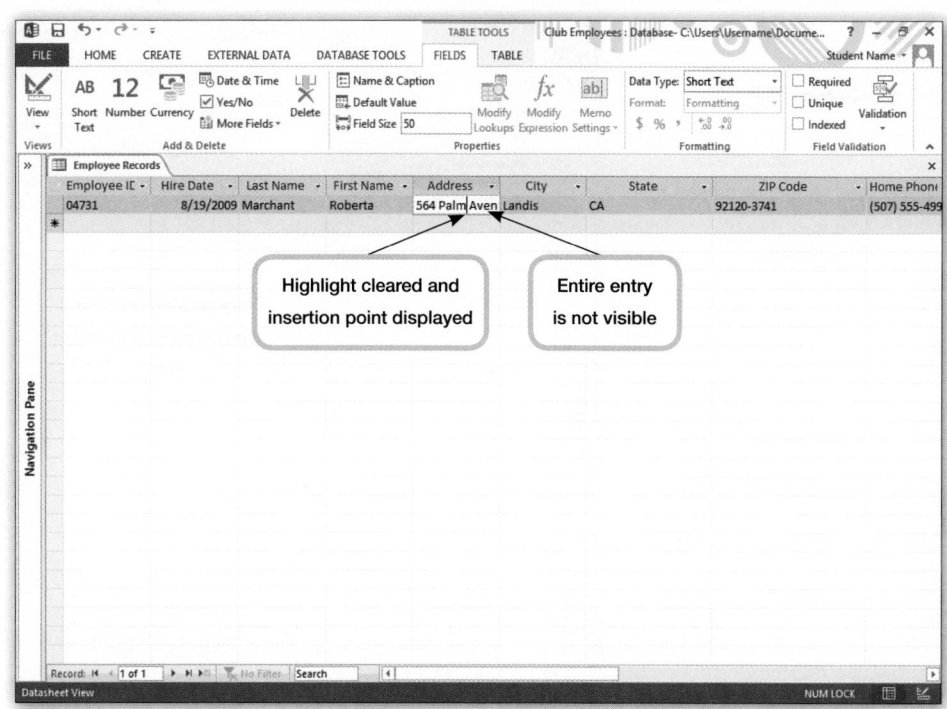

Highlight cleared and insertion point displayed

Entire entry is not visible

Figure 1.44

Additional Information

You can press F2 to switch between editing an entry (the insertion point is displayed) and navigating (the field is selected) through the datasheet.

The highlight is cleared and the insertion point is visible in the field. Now, using the directional keys moves the insertion point within the field, and you can edit the field contents if necessary.

ZOOMING A FIELD

The beginning of the field looks fine, but because the column width is too narrow, you cannot see the entire entry. You will move the insertion point to the end of the address so you can check the rest of the entry.

1

● **Press** End.

Your screen should be similar to Figure 1.45

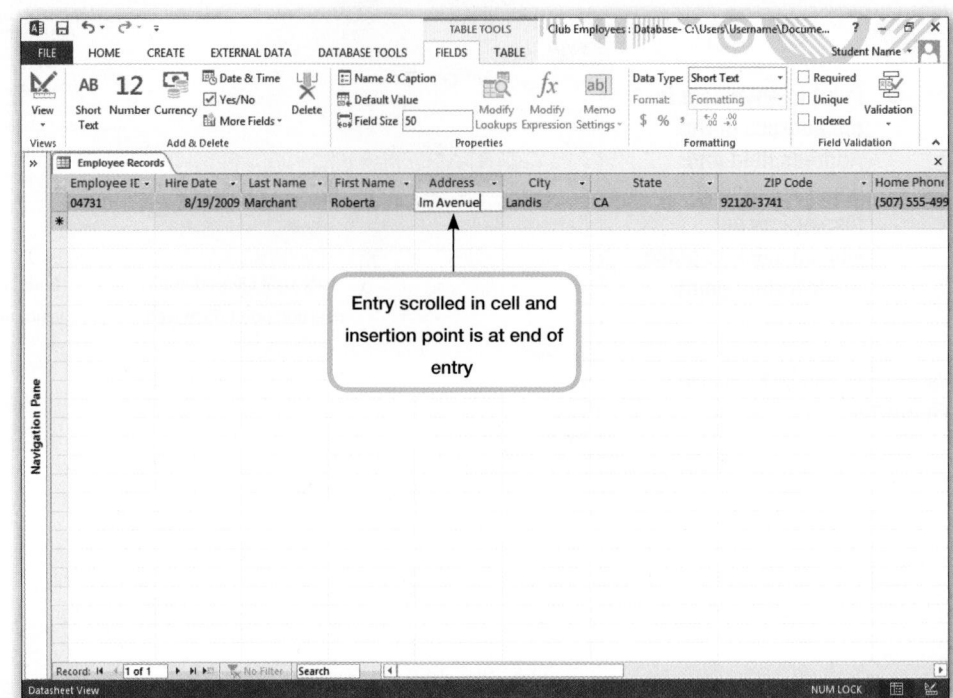

Entry scrolled in cell and insertion point is at end of entry

Figure 1.45

The text scrolled in the field, and the insertion point is positioned at the end of the entry. However, now you cannot see the beginning of the entry, which makes it difficult to edit. Another way to view the field's contents is to expand the field.

2

● **Press** ⇧Shift + F2.

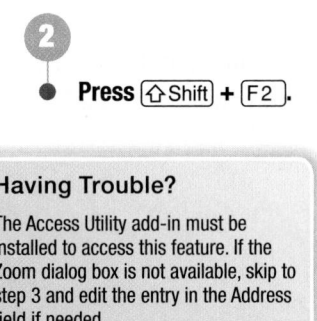

Having Trouble?

The Access Utility add-in must be installed to access this feature. If the Zoom dialog box is not available, skip to step 3 and edit the entry in the Address field if needed.

Your screen should be similar to Figure 1.46

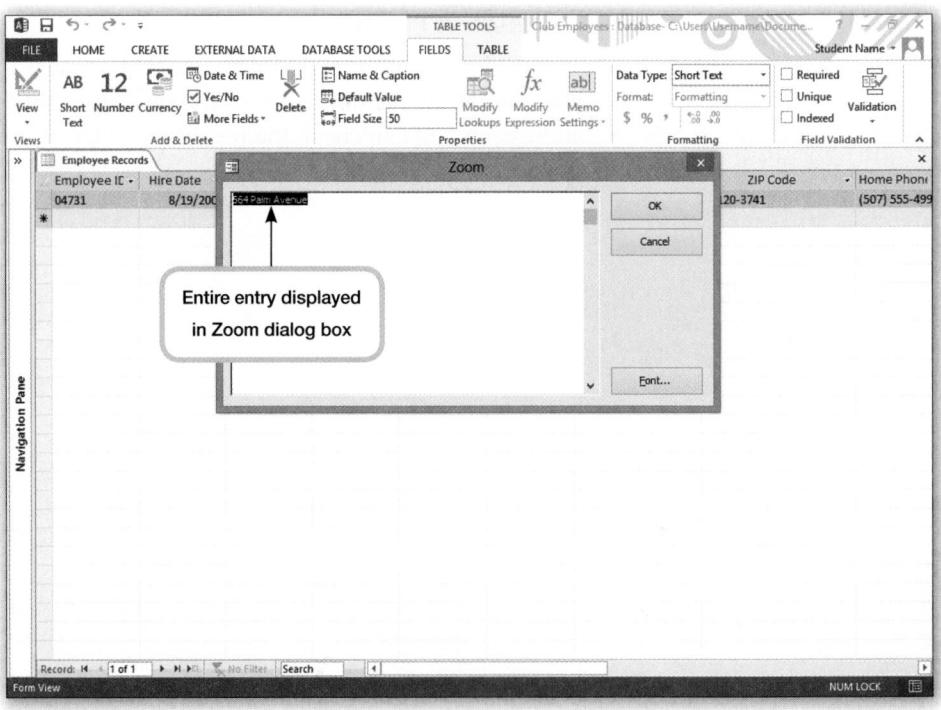

Entire entry displayed in Zoom dialog box

Figure 1.46

The entry is fully displayed in the Zoom dialog box. You can edit in the dialog box just as you can in the field.

3

- If the entry contains an error, correct it.

- Click [OK] to close the Zoom dialog box.

- Press Tab ⇥ to move to the next field.

Additional Information

You also can use the horizontal scroll bar to scroll the window and check fields that are not currently visible.

- Continue to check the first record for accuracy and edit as needed.

- Enter the data for the second record shown in the table to the right (leave the Attachment field empty).

- Check the second record for accuracy and edit it if necessary.

- Move to the first field of the blank record row.

Your screen should be similar to Figure 1.47

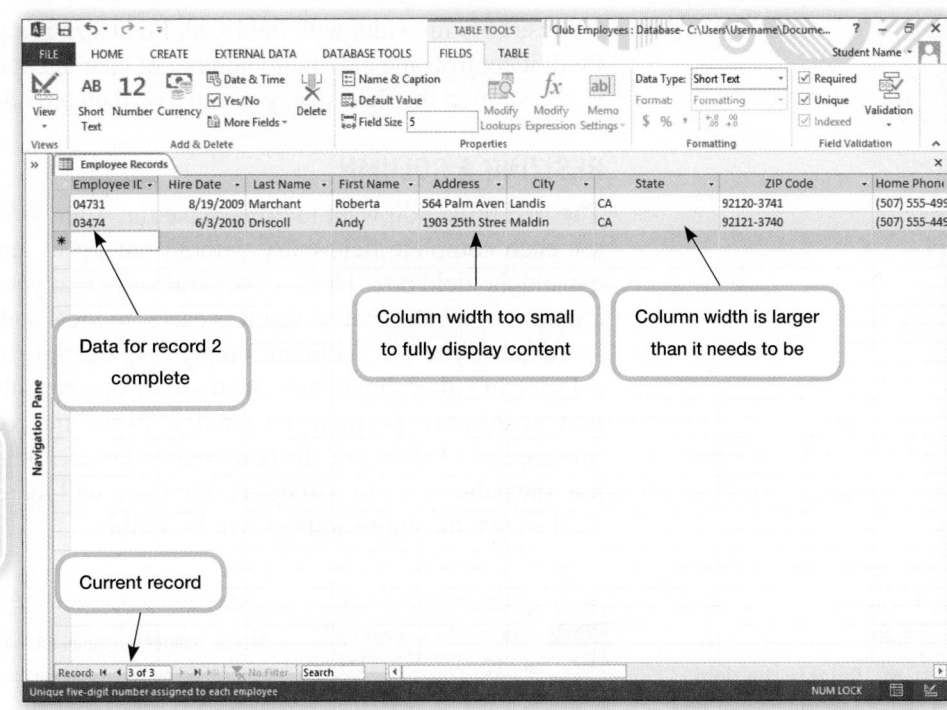

Figure 1.47

Field Name	Data
Employee ID	03474
Hire Date	June 3, 2010
Last Name	Driscoll
First Name	Andy
Address	1903 25th Street
City	Maldin
State	CA
ZIP Code	92121-3740
Home Phone	(507) 555-4494
Birth Date	October 10, 1989

The record indicator in the status bar tells you that record 3 is the current record of a total of three records.

Changing Column Width

Additional Information

The default datasheet column width is one inch and the number of characters it can display varies with your screen settings as well as the font and font size. Generally the default column width displays 12 to 15 characters.

As you have noticed, some of the fields (such as the Address field) do not display the entire entry, while other fields (such as the State field) are much larger than the field's column heading or contents. This is because the default width of a column in the datasheet is not the same size as the field sizes you specified in Design view. **Column width** refers to the size of a field column in a datasheet. The column width does not affect the amount of data you can enter into a field, but it does affect the data that you can see.

You can adjust the column width to change the appearance of the datasheet. Usually you should adjust the column width so that the column is slightly larger than the column heading or longest field contents, whichever is longer. Do not confuse column width with field size. Field size is a property associated with each field; it controls the maximum number of characters that you can enter in the field. If you shorten the field size, you can lose data already entered in the field.

RESIZING A COLUMN

The first thing you want to do is make the Address column wider so that you can see each complete field entry without having to move to the field and scroll or expand the field box. There are several ways that you can manipulate the rows and columns of a datasheet so that it is easier to view and work with the table data.

To quickly resize a column, simply drag the right column border line in the field selector in either direction to increase or decrease the column width. The mouse pointer shape is ↔ when you can drag to size the column. As you drag, a column line appears to show you the new column border. When you release the mouse button, the column width will be set. First you will increase the width of the Address field so that the entire address will be visible.

1

- Point to the right column border line for the Address field.

- When the mouse pointer shape is ↔, click and drag to the right until you think the column width will be wide enough to display the field contents.

- Adjust the column width again if it is too wide or not wide enough.

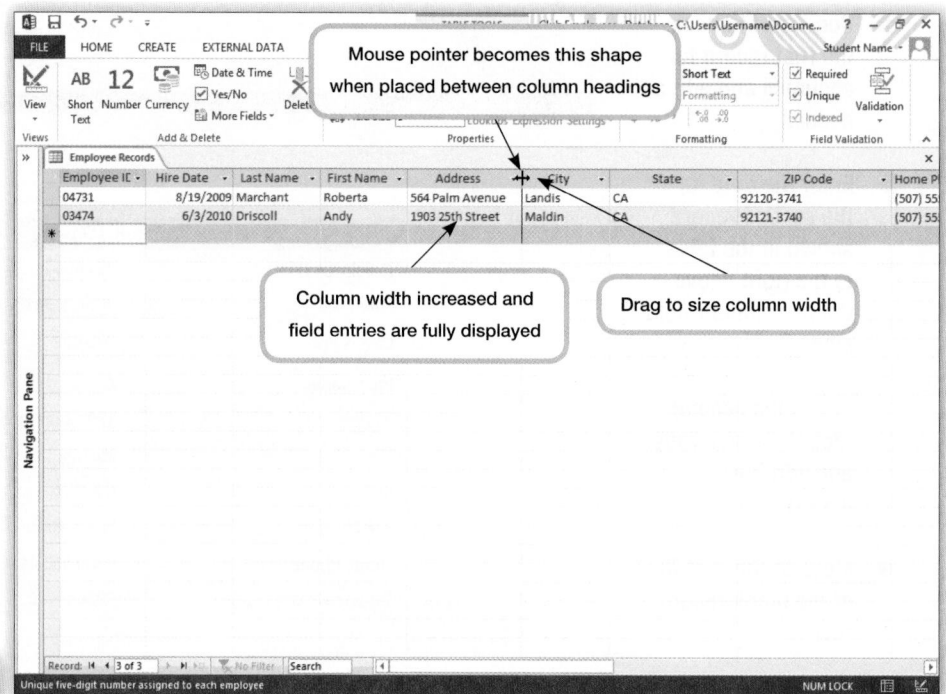

Figure 1.48

Another Method

You also can adjust the column width to a specific number of characters using ⊞ More ▾ in the Records group of the Home tab and choosing Field Width. This command is also on the shortcut menu when an entire column is selected.

Your screen should be similar to Figure 1.48

USING BEST FIT

Rather than change the widths of all the other columns individually, you can select all columns and change their widths at the same time using the **Best Fit** feature. To select multiple columns, point to the column heading in the header row of the first or last column you want to select. Then, when the mouse pointer changes to ↓, click, and without releasing the mouse button, drag in either direction across the column headings. You also can quickly select the entire table by clicking the ⬜ Select All button to the left of the first field name.

- Point to the Employee ID field column heading and when the mouse pointer appears as ↓, drag to the right to select the first four column headings.

- Click the ⬜ Select All button to select the entire table.

Your screen should be similar to Figure 1.49

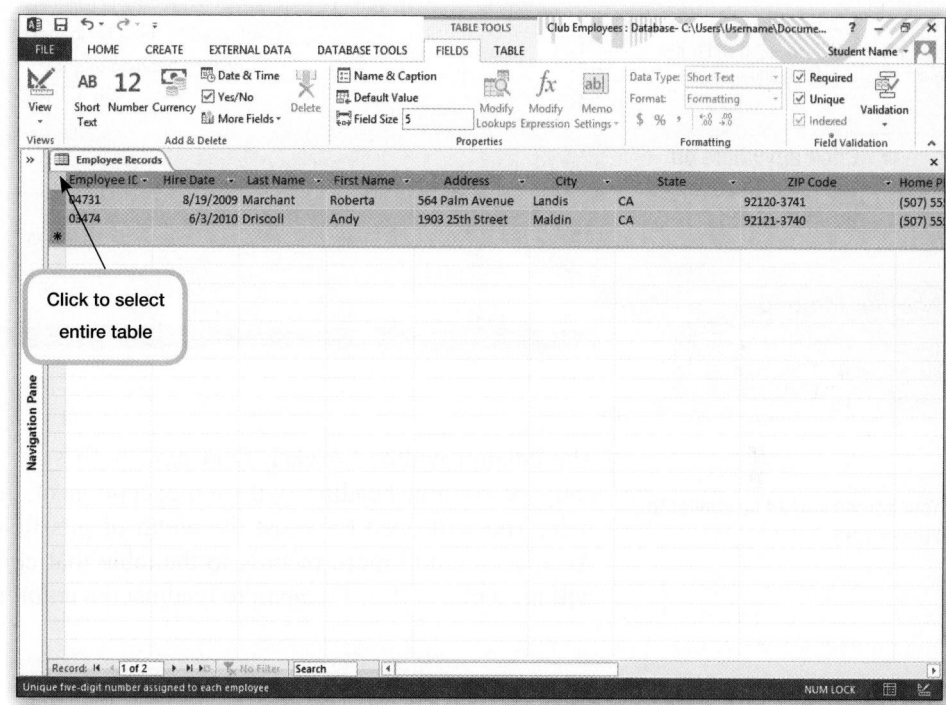

Figure 1.49

All the table columns are highlighted. Now, if you were to drag the column border of any selected column, all the selected columns would change to the same size. However, you want the column widths to be adjusted appropriately to fit the data in each column. To do this, you can double-click the column border to activate the Best Fit feature. The Best Fit feature automatically adjusts the column widths of all selected columns to accommodate the longest entry or column heading in each of the selected columns.

2

- Point to any column border line (in the field name row) and double-click when the mouse pointer shape is ↔.

Having Trouble?

If the *Click to Add* menu opens while trying to adjust the column width, just press Esc to close it and try again.

- Click anywhere on the table to deselect the datasheet.

Another Method

You also can use ⊞ More ▾ in the Records group of the Home tab and choose Field Width/Best Fit.

Your screen should be similar to Figure 1.50

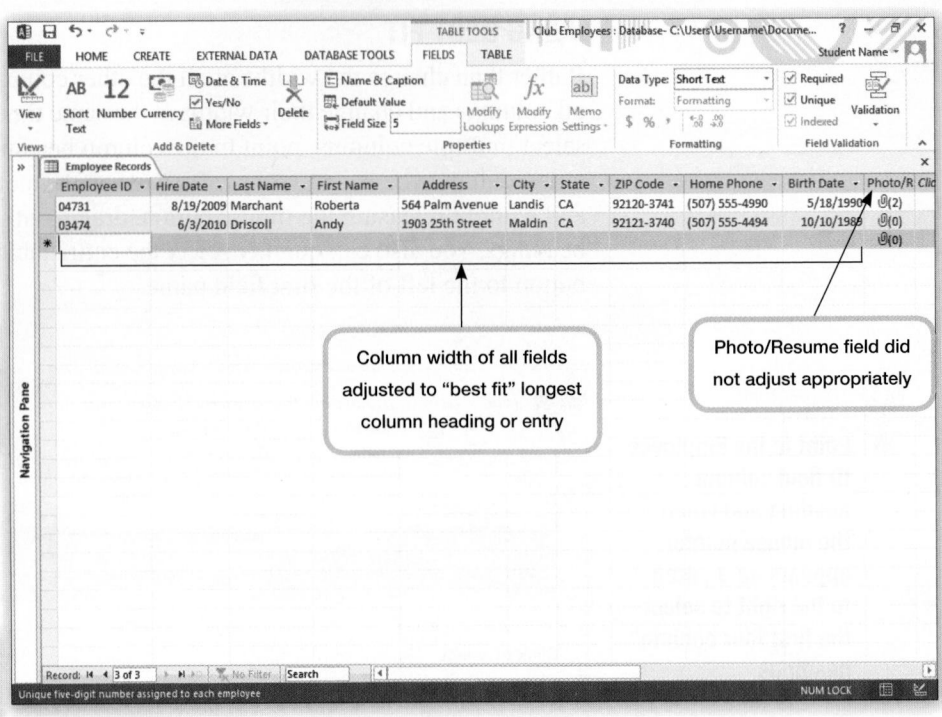

Column width of all fields adjusted to "best fit" longest column heading or entry

Photo/Resume field did not adjust appropriately

Figure 1.50

The column widths for each field have been sized to accommodate the longest entry or column heading, with the exception of the Photo/Resume Attachment field. You will need to adjust the width of this field separately from the others. Also, as you add more records to the table that contain longer field entries, you will need to use Best Fit again to readjust the column widths.

3

- Best fit the Photo/ Resume field.

- Check each of the records again and edit any entries that are incorrect.

- Add the data shown in the following table as record 3.

- Press ⏎Enter twice to skip the Photo/ Resume field and complete the record.

Your screen should be similar to Figure 1.51

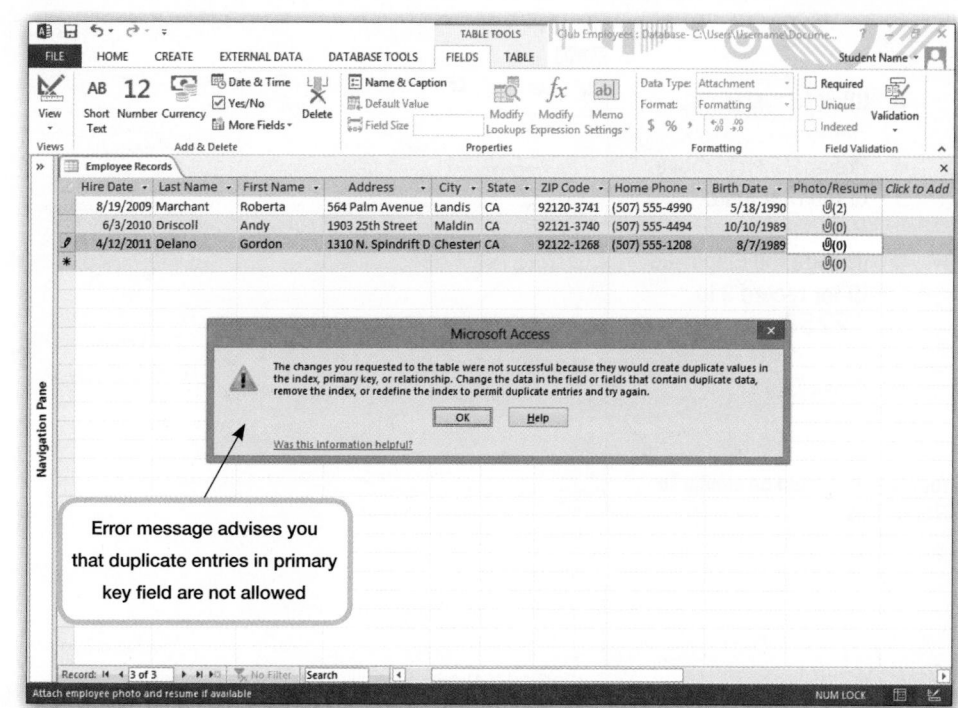

Error message advises you that duplicate entries in primary key field are not allowed

Figure 1.51

Field Name	Data
Employee ID	04731
Hire Date	April 12, 2011
Last Name	Delano
First Name	Gordon
Address	1310 N. Spindrift Drive
City	Chesterfield
State	CA
ZIP Code	92122-1268
Phone	(507) 555-1208
Birth Date	August 7, 1989

As soon as you complete the record, an error message dialog box appears indicating that Access has located a duplicate value in a primary key field. The key field is Employee ID. You realize you were looking at the employee number from Roberta Marchant's record when you entered the employee number for this record. You need to clear the message and enter the correct number.

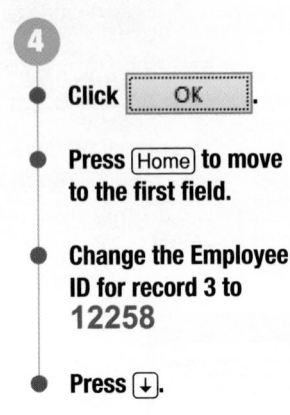

- Click [OK].

- Press [Home] to move to the first field.

- Change the Employee ID for record 3 to **12258**

- Press [↓].

Your screen should be similar to Figure 1.52

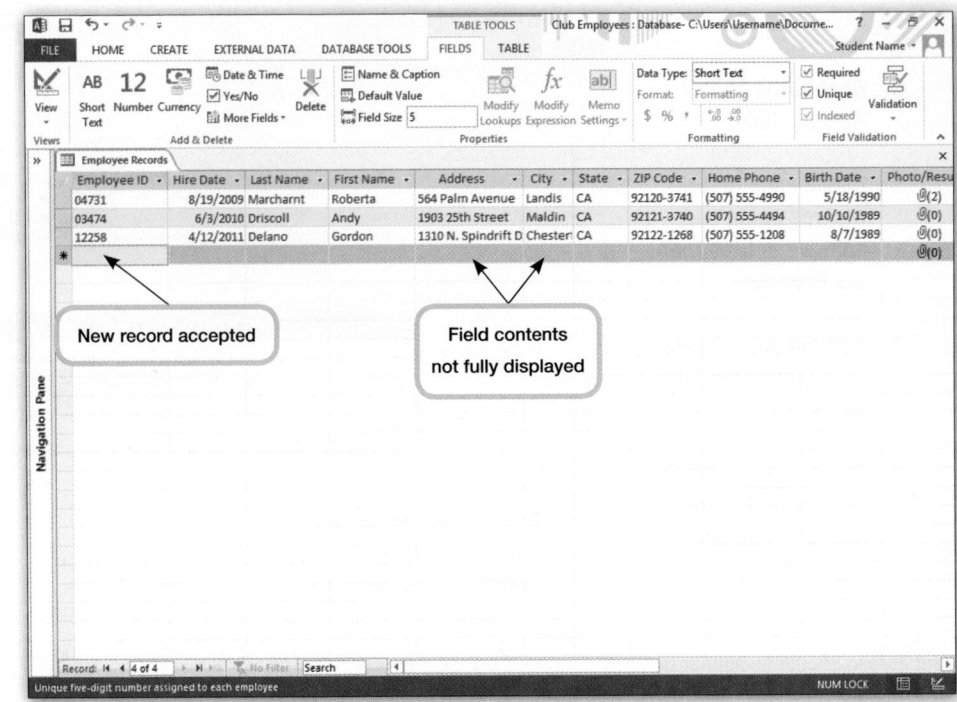

Figure 1.52

The record is accepted with the new employee number. However, you notice that the address and city for this record are not fully displayed in the fields.

- Best fit the Address and City fields.

Your screen should be similar to Figure 1.53

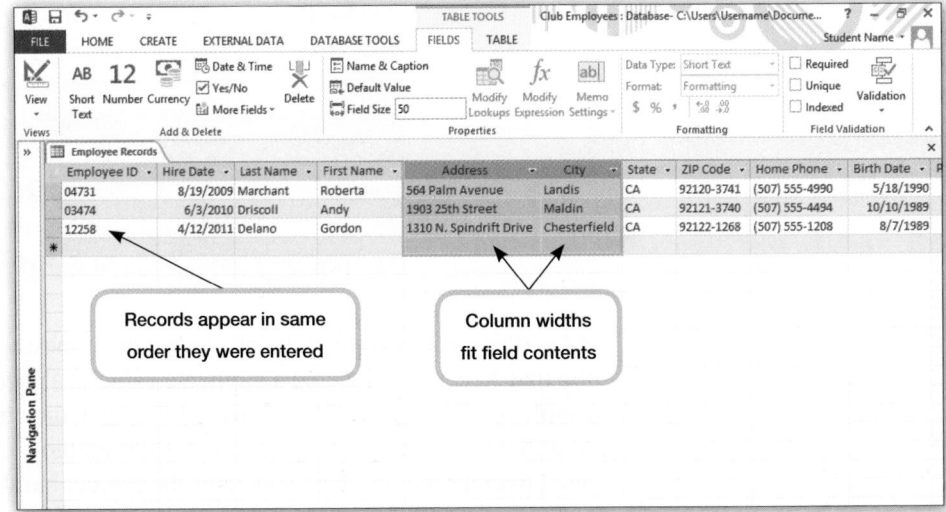

Figure 1.53

When you add new records in a datasheet, the records are displayed in the order in which you enter them. However, they are stored inside the database file in order by the primary key field.

You will add three more records to the table (shown in the following table). If data for some fields, such as the City, State, or ZIP Code, is the same from record to record, you can save yourself some typing by copying the data from one of the other records. Just select the field contents and click [Copy] in the Clipboard group on the Home tab. Then move to the field where you want the copy to appear and click [Paste] in the Clipboard group.

Field	Record 4	Record 5	Record 6
Employee ID	13635	12583	99999
Hire Date	October 2, 2014	November 20, 2011	Current date
Last Name	Martinez	Sullivan	Your last name
First Name	Juan	Marie	Your first name
Address	1920 First Avenue	78 Omega Drive	Any address
City	Maldin	Chesterfield	Chesterfield
State	CA	CA	CA
ZIP Code	92121-3740	92122-1268	92122-1268
Phone	(507) 555-2935	(507) 555-3890	Any phone number
Birth Date	December 10, 1992	March 15, 1991	Any birth date

6

- Click in the Employee ID field for the next blank record (record 4).

- Enter the data for record 4 and record 5 shown in the table.

- Enter record 6 using the data shown in the table. The information you enter in the Address, Home Phone, and Birth Date fields can be fictitious.

- Check each of the records and correct any entry errors.

Your screen should be similar to Figure 1.54

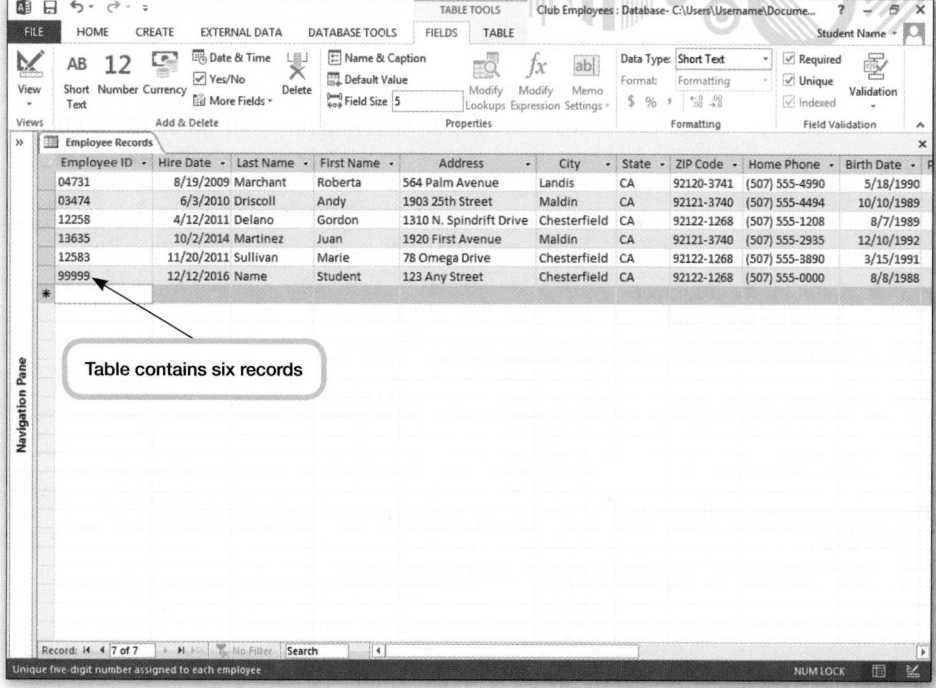

Figure 1.54

There are now a total of six records in the table.

You have found that with the addition of records, it takes longer to move around in the datasheet. Typical database tables are very large and consequently can be cumbersome to navigate. Learning how to move around in a large table will save time and help you get the job done faster.

MOVING USING THE KEYBOARD

In a large table, there are many methods you can use to quickly navigate through records in Datasheet view. You can always use the mouse to move from one field or record to another. However, if the information is not visible in the window, you must scroll the window using the scroll bar first. The following table presents several keyboard methods that will help you move around in the datasheet.

Keys	Effect
Page Down	Down one window
Page Up	Up one window
Ctrl + Page Up	Left one window
Ctrl + Page Down	Right one window
Ctrl + End	Last field of last record
Ctrl + Home	First field of first record
Ctrl + ↑	Current field of first record
Ctrl + ↓	Current field of last record

Currently, records 1 through 6 of the Employee Records table are displayed in the work area. You will use many of these methods to move around the datasheet.

Click in the Employee ID field of the first record.

Press Page Down.

Your screen should be similar to Figure 1.55

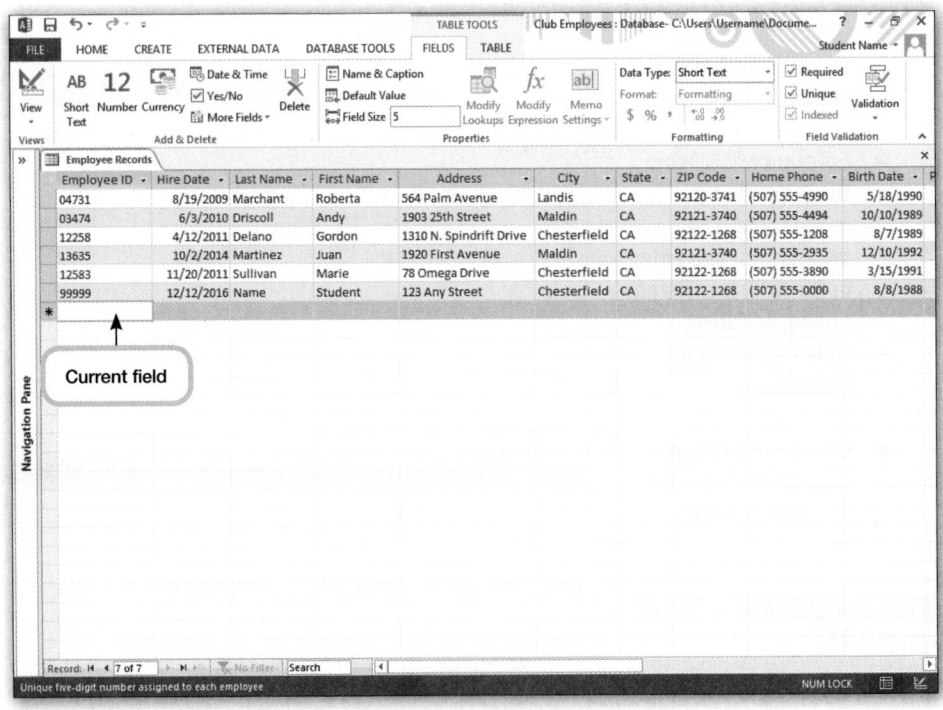

Current field

Figure 1.55

If you were working on a very large table, the next page of records would display, with the first record in the window being the current record. Because this table is small, pressing Page Down moved the insertion point to the last position in the window, the row to add a new record. To see an example of moving in a wide table, you will expand the Navigation pane. Because there are numerous fields of various widths, not all of the fields are able to display in the window at the same time. Rather than scrolling the window horizontally to see the additional fields, you can quickly move to the right one window at a time.

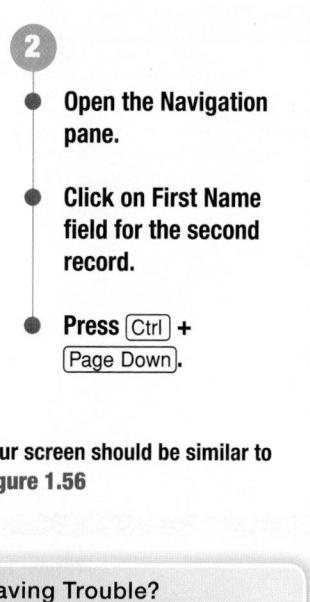

2

- **Open the Navigation pane.**

- **Click on First Name field for the second record.**

- **Press Ctrl + Page Down.**

Your screen should be similar to Figure 1.56

Having Trouble?

Your screen may display more or fewer fields depending on your screen size.

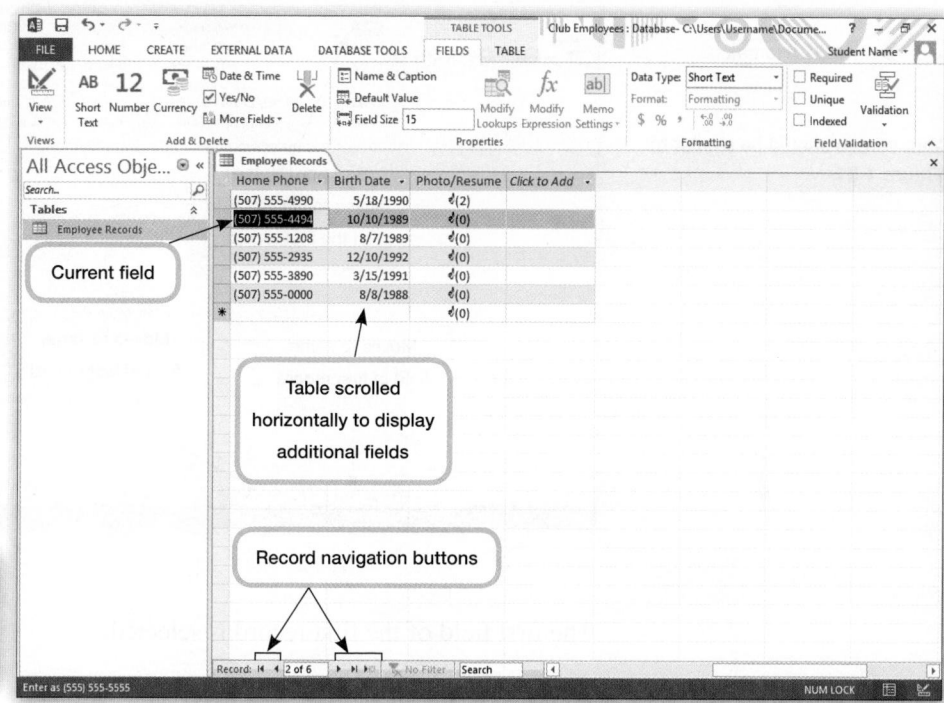

Figure 1.56

The table scrolled horizontally one window to the right, and the last three field columns in the table are now visible. The current field is the first field of this screen, but on the second record's row.

MOVING USING THE RECORD NAVIGATION BUTTONS

Another Method

You also can use ➡ ▾ Go To in the Find group of the Home tab to access the record navigation buttons.

The record navigation buttons in the status bar also provide navigation shortcuts. These buttons are described in the following table.

Button	Effect
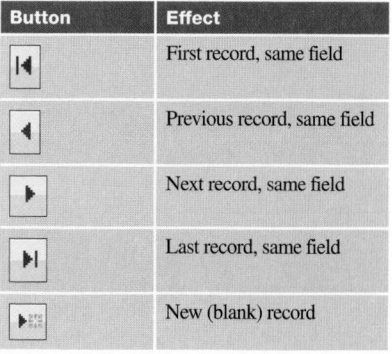	First record, same field
	Previous record, same field
	Next record, same field
	Last record, same field
	New (blank) record

You will use the record navigation buttons to move to the same field that is currently selected in the last record, and then back to the same field of the first record. Then you will move to the first field of the first record.

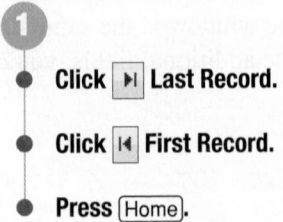

● Click ▶ᴵ **Last Record.**

● Click ᴵ◀ **First Record.**

● Press Home.

Your screen should be similar to Figure 1.57

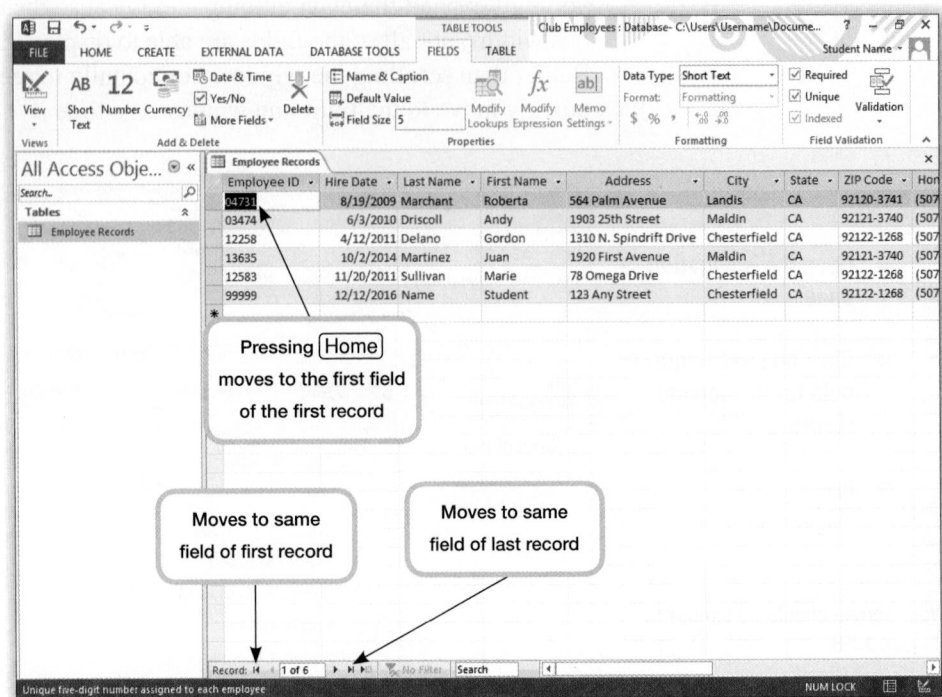

Figure 1.57

The first field of the first record is selected.

MOVING TO A SPECIFIC RECORD

You have moved the location of the insertion point to the first record by using the record navigation buttons. You can also quickly move to a specific record by simply typing the record number into the Current Record box in the record navigation bar. This method is especially helpful when navigating around a large table when you know the record number you are looking for. Now you will practice moving to a specific record number.

1

- Click in the **Current Record box.**

- Press ←Backspace or Delete to delete the number 1.

- Type in **5** and press ←Enter.

Your screen should be similar to Figure 1.58

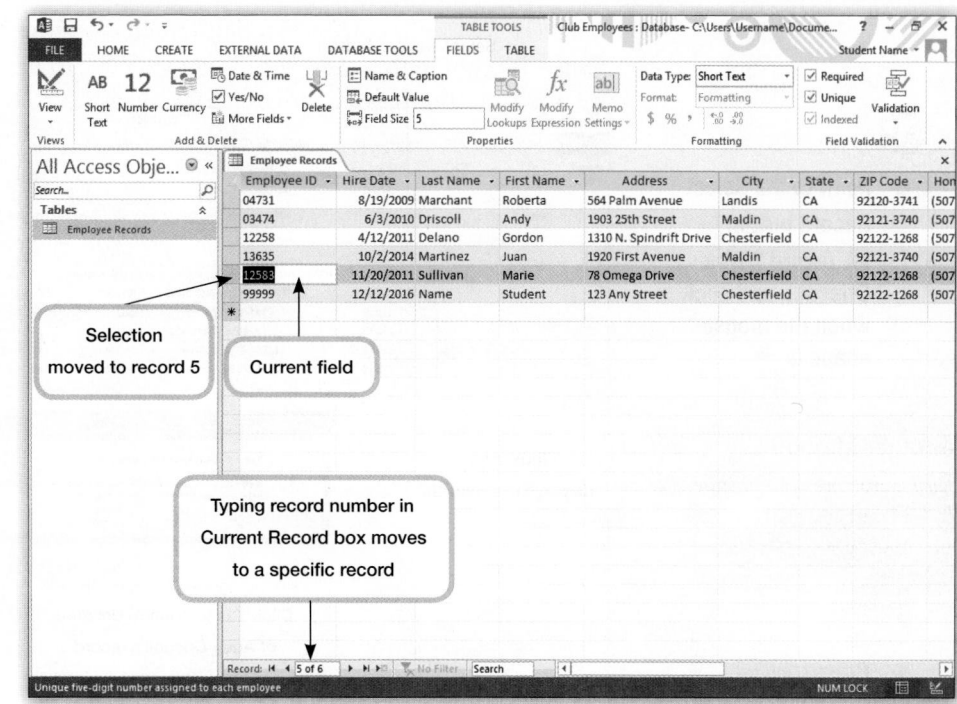

Figure 1.58

The specified record is now selected.

Deleting Records

While you are entering the employee records, you find a memo from one of your managers stating that Andy Driscoll is no longer working at the club and asking you to remove his record from the employee files.

You can remove records from a table by selecting the entire record and pressing the Delete key. After pressing Delete, you will be asked to confirm that you really want to delete the selected record. This is because this action cannot be reversed.

Select Record button

1

- Point to the **Select Record button**  for record 2 (Andy Driscoll), and click when the mouse shape is ➔.

Another Method

You also can move to the record and choose Select from the ⬚ ▾ Select drop-down list in the Find group of the Home tab.

- Press [Delete].

Another Method

You also can use ✂ Cut in the Clipboard group to delete a selected record.

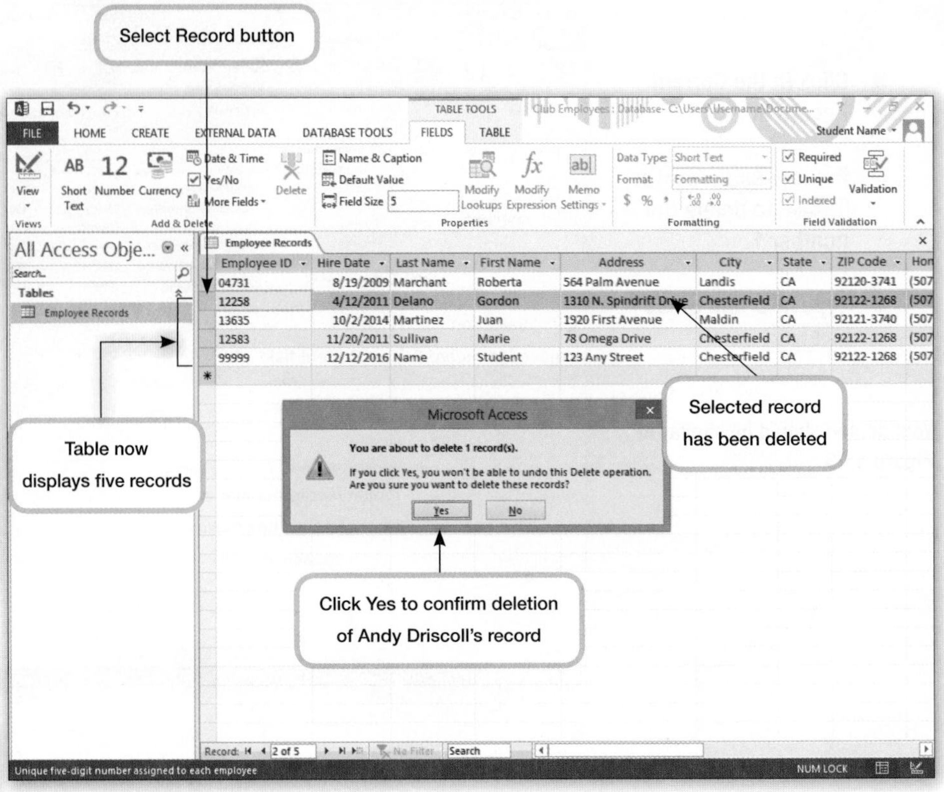

Your screen should be similar to Figure 1.59

Table now displays five records

Employee ID	Hire Date	Last Name	First Name	Address	City	State	ZIP Code	Hon
04731	8/19/2009	Marchant	Roberta	564 Palm Avenue	Landis	CA	92120-3741	(507
12258	4/12/2011	Delano	Gordon	1310 N. Spindrift Drive	Chesterfield	CA	92122-1268	(507
13635	10/2/2014	Martinez	Juan	1920 First Avenue	Maldin	CA	92121-3740	(507
12583	11/20/2011	Sullivan	Marie	78 Omega Drive	Chesterfield	CA	92122-1268	(507
99999	12/12/2016	Name	Student	123 Any Street	Chesterfield	CA	92122-1268	(507

Selected record has been deleted

Microsoft Access

⚠ You are about to delete 1 record(s).

If you click Yes, you won't be able to undo this Delete operation. Are you sure you want to delete these records?

[Yes] [No]

Click Yes to confirm deletion of Andy Driscoll's record

Record: 2 of 5   No Filter   Search

Unique five-digit number assigned to each employee   NUM LOCK

Figure 1.59

Although Andy Driscoll's record has been removed from the table, it will not be permanently deleted from the database until you confirm the deletion. If you change your mind, you can click [No] to restore the record.

2

- Click [Yes] to confirm that you want to delete the record.

Another Method

You also can choose Delete Record from the ✕ Delete ▾ drop-down list in the Records group of the Home tab. The current record is both selected and deleted at the same time.

The record has been permanently deleted and the table now consists of five employee records.

Creating a Table in Design View

Following your plan for the employee database, you will add another table to the database file. This table will hold information about the employee's work location and job title.

There are several ways to create a new table in an existing database. You can insert a blank table and define the fields in Datasheet view as you already have done, or you can create a table based on a table model. You also can import from or link to data from another source, such as another database, an Excel worksheet, or a SharePoint list. Finally, you can create a new table starting in Design view. You will use this last method to define the two fields in the table, Location and Job Title.

1
- **Open the Create tab and click** 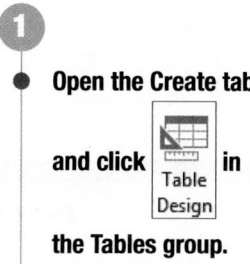 **in the Tables group.**

- **Define the fields using the settings shown in the following table.**

Your screen should be similar to Figure 1.60

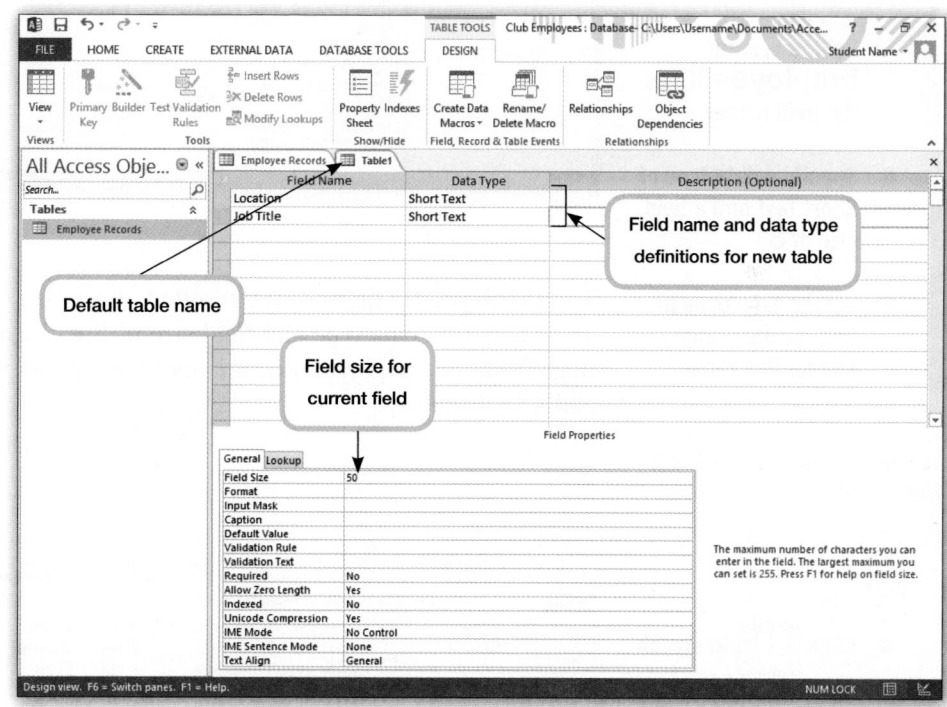

Figure 1.60

Field Name	Data Type	Field Size
Location	Short Text	20
Job Title	Short Text	50

The new table has a default table name of Table1.

INSERTING A FIELD

As you look at the table you realize you need a field to identify which employee the information belongs to. You want this field to be the first field in the table. To do this, you will insert the new field above the Location field.

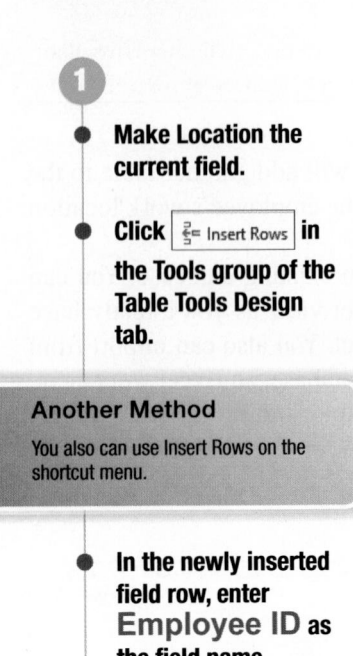

1

- Make Location the current field.

- Click ▐ Insert Rows ▌ in the Tools group of the Table Tools Design tab.

Another Method

You also can use Insert Rows on the shortcut menu.

- In the newly inserted field row, enter **Employee ID** as the field name.

- Specify a data type of Short Text and a field size of **5**

- Set the Employee ID field as the primary key for this table.

Your screen should be similar to Figure 1.61

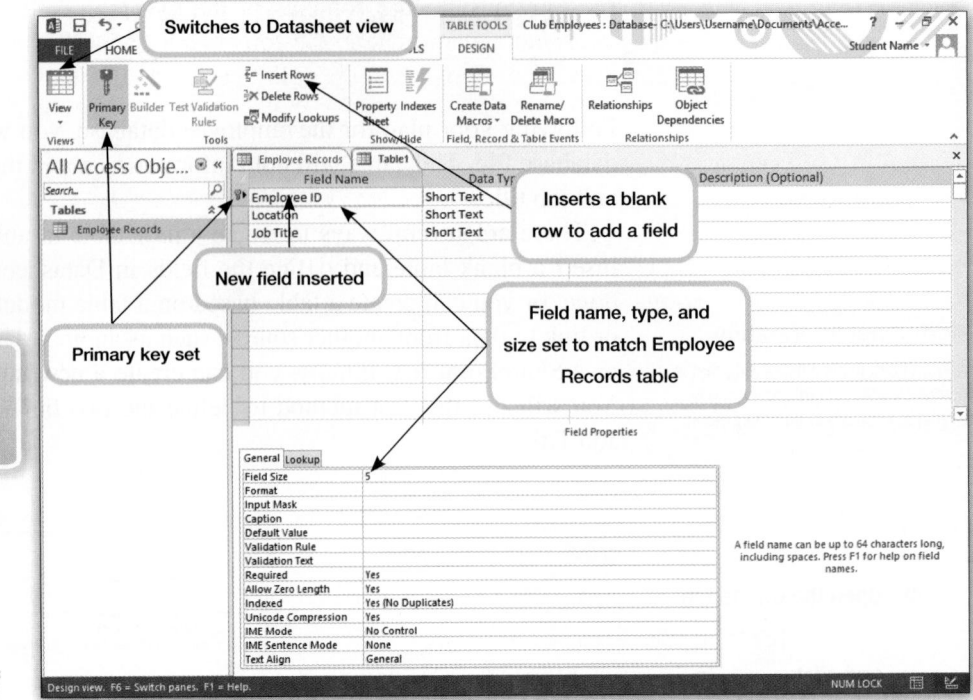

Figure 1.61

The Employee ID field is now inserted above the Location field in Design view. The Short Text data type and field size of 5 will match the existing property settings from the Employee Records table. Now you will switch to Datasheet view and save the table.

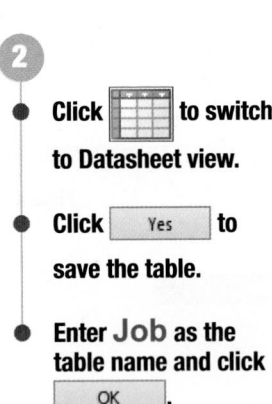

2

- Click [icon] to switch to Datasheet view.

- Click [Yes] to save the table.

- Enter **Job** as the table name and click [OK].

Your screen should be similar to Figure 1.62

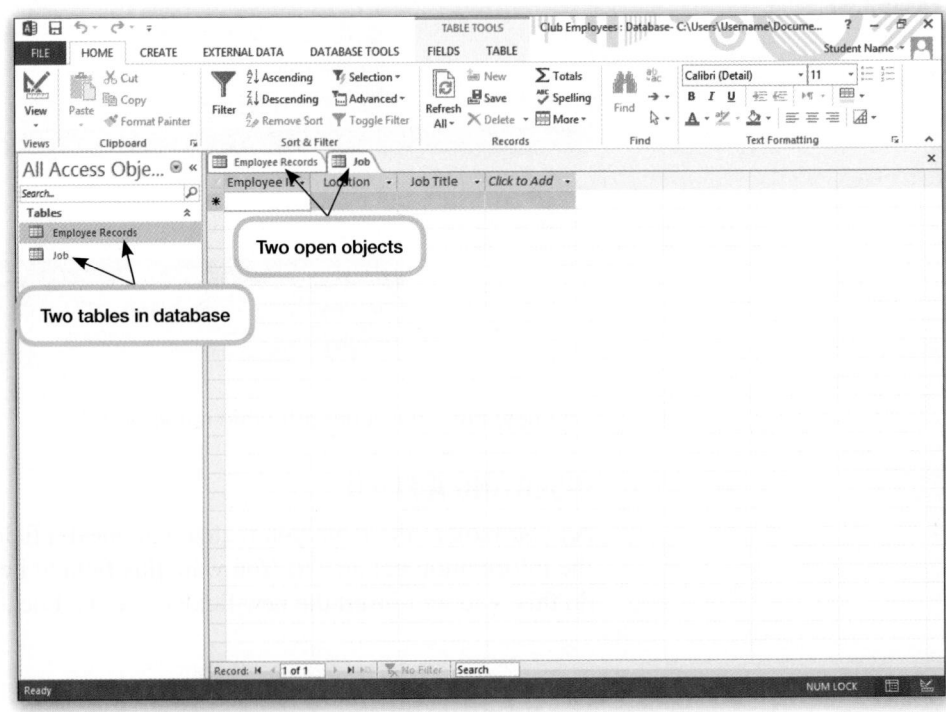

Figure 1.62

As you consider the contents of the two tables, you realize that the Hire Date information should be in the Job table because the subject matter is related to the employee's job, not to his or her personal information.

3

- Click in the Job Title field.

- Click [Date & Time] in the Add & Delete group of the Table Tools Fields tab to insert a blank field column with a Date data type to the right of the current column.

- Name the field Hire Date

- Open the

  [Format: ▼]

  drop-down menu in the Formatting group and choose Short Date.

- Click in the Hire Date field to confirm your settings.

Your screen should be similar to Figure 1.63

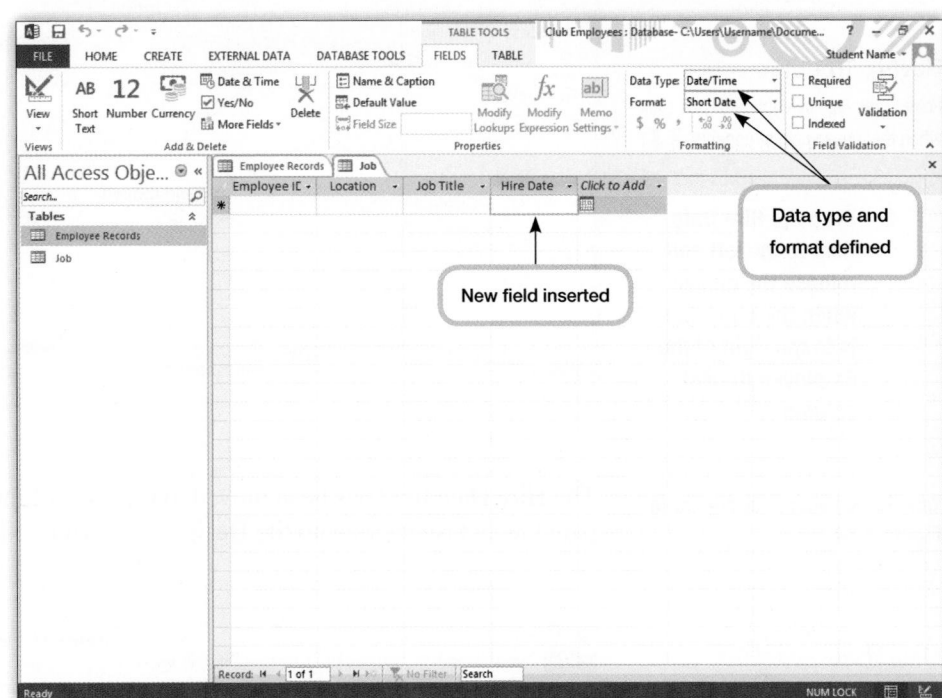

Figure 1.63

The new field has been inserted and defined.

MOVING A FIELD

The Hire Date field was inserted as the last field in the Job table. While in Datasheet view, you decide to move the Hire Date field next to the Employee ID field. To move a field column, select the column and then drag the selected column to the new location. As you drag, a heavy black bar shows where the column will be placed when you stop dragging.

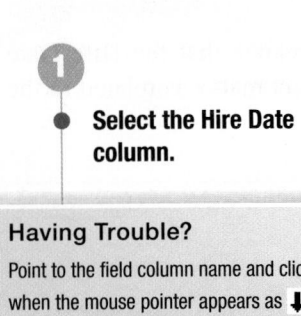

1

● Select the Hire Date column.

Having Trouble?

Point to the field column name and click when the mouse pointer appears as ↓.

● Drag the Hire Date field to the left and release the mouse when the black bar is to the right of the Employee ID field column.

Field moved

Figure 1.64

Your screen should be similar to Figure 1.64

The Hire Date field has been moved to the right of the Employee ID field. To compare the Datasheet view to the Design view, you will switch back to Design view.

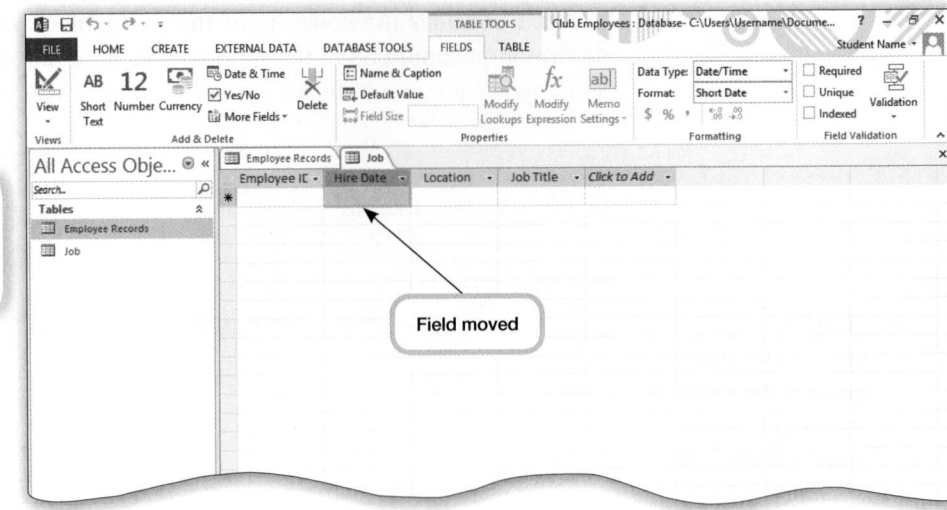

2

● Click 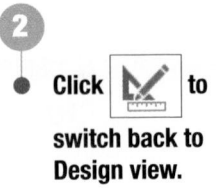 to switch back to Design view.

Your screen should be similar to Figure 1.65

Hire Date field still in last position, even though moved in Datasheet view

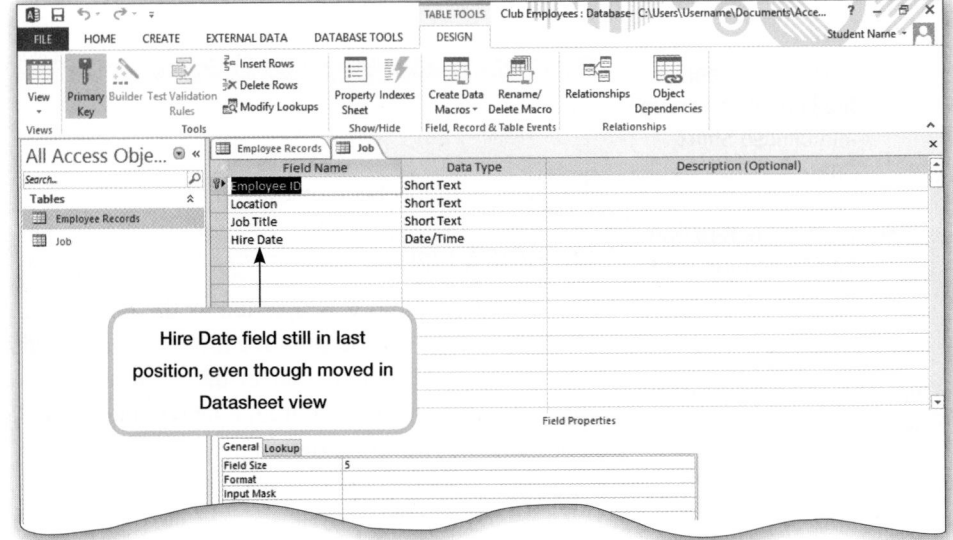

Figure 1.65

Notice the Hire Date field is still last in the list of field names in Design view, even though you moved it to the second position in Datasheet view. The order in which the fields display can differ between the two views. This enables you to aesthetically display the order of the fields in the table and yet be able to arrange them in a specific structural order in Design view.

Usually it is best for the field order to be the same in both views. You want to move the Hire Date below the Employee ID to match the placement in the datasheet. Moving a field in Design view is similar to doing so in Datasheet view, except that a row rather than a column is selected.

3

- Position the mouse in the gray row selector button next to Hire Date.

- Click when the mouse symbol changes to ➡ to select the Hire Date field row.

- While pointing to the row selector for the Hire Date row, drag up until the black move indicator line is below the Employee ID field.

- Release the mouse to place the Hire Date field row in its new position in Design view.

Your screen should be similar to Figure 1.66

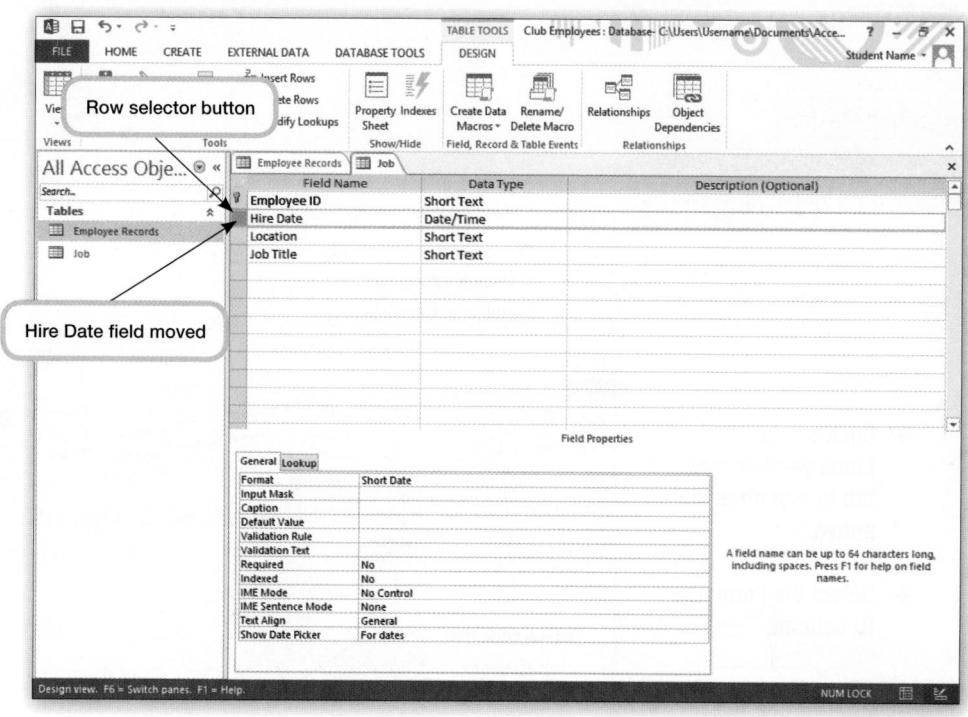

Figure 1.66

The field order in Design view now matches the order in which the fields are displayed in the datasheet.

4

- Click 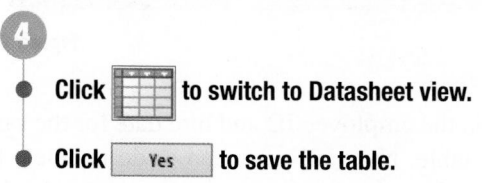 to switch to Datasheet view.

- Click [Yes] to save the table.

The Job table is now ready for you to input the data.

COPYING FIELD CONTENT

To save yourself time and prevent possible errors in typing, you will copy the data from the Employee ID and Hire Date fields in the Employee Records table into the new fields in the Job table. To switch between open tables, simply click on the table's tab. It then becomes the active table, or the table you can work in.

Having Trouble?

To review how to copy and paste, refer to the Copying and Moving Selections section in the Introduction to Microsoft Office 2013 lab.

Another Method

You can also press Ctrl + F6 to cycle between open table windows.

- Click on the Employee Records tab to make the table active.

- Select the Employee ID column.

- Click 🖹 Copy in the Clipboard group of the Home tab.

- Click on the Job tab to make the table active.

- Select the Employee ID column.

- Click 📋 in the Clipboard group of the Home tab.

- Click Yes to confirm the paste operation.

- Repeat these steps to copy the Hire Date field information from the Employee Records table into the Job table.

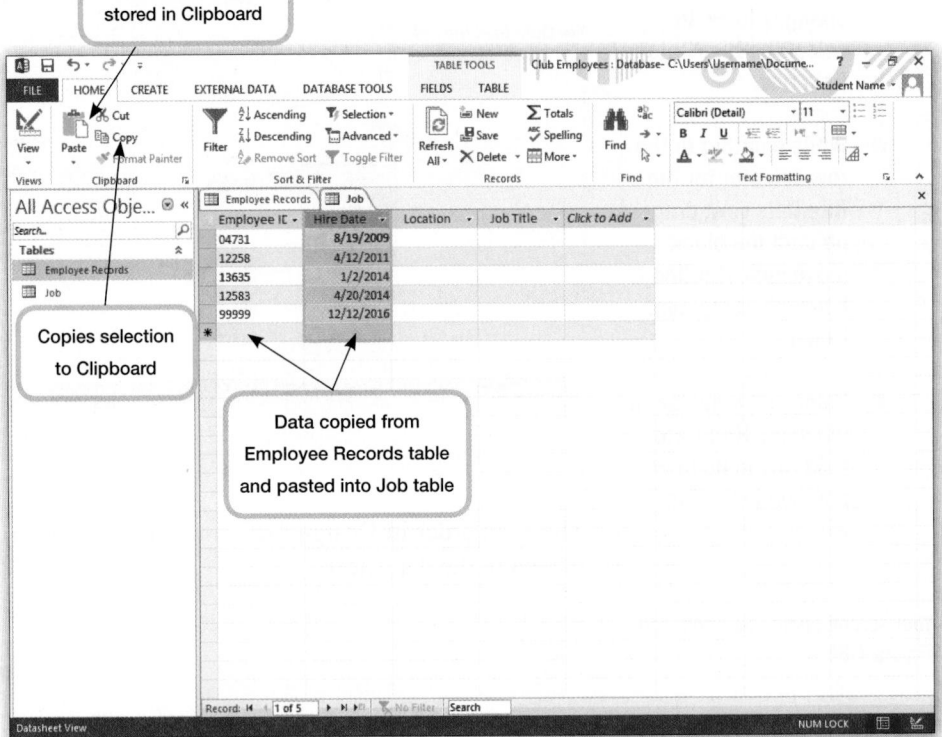

Figure 1.67

The table now includes information on the employee ID and hire date for the same records as in the Employee Records table. Now, all you need to do is delete the Hire Date field in the Employee Records table and then enter the rest of the data for the employees' job locations and titles.

Your screen should be similar to Figure 1.67

2

- Make the Employee Records table active.

- Press ⟨Delete⟩ and click ⟨ Yes ⟩ to remove the still-selected Hire Date field from the Employee Records table.

- Add the information shown below to the appropriate records in the Job table.

- Best fit the columns.

Your screen should be similar to Figure 1.68

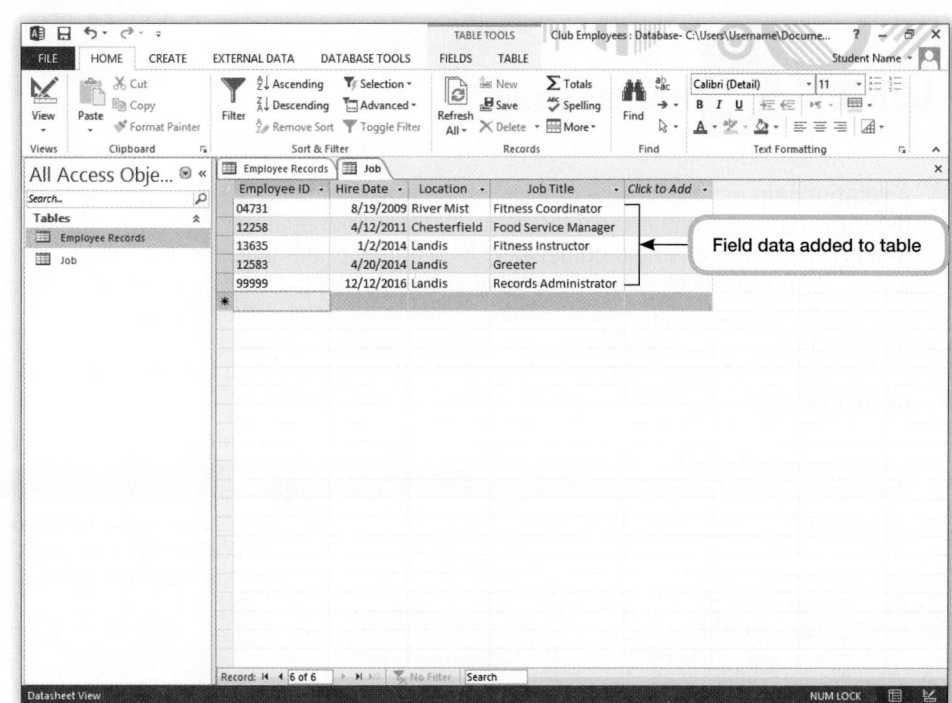

Figure 1.68

Employee ID	Location	Job Title
04731	River Mist	Fitness Coordinator
12258	Chesterfield	Food Service Manager
12583	Landis	Greeter
13635	Landis	Fitness Instructor
99999	Landis	Records Administrator

Now the Employee Records table only contains the employee's personal information, and the Job table contains information about the employee's job.

Creating Relationships

Now that the database contains two tables, a relationship needs to be created between the tables to link the data together.

Concept 6 Relationship

A **relationship** establishes the association between common fields in two tables. The related fields must be of the same data type and contain the same kind of information but can have different field names. The exception to this rule occurs when the primary key field in one of the tables is the AutoNumber type, which can be related to another AutoNumber field or to a Number field, as long as the field size property is the same for both. This is also the case when both fields are AutoNumber or Number—they always have to be the same field size in order to be related.

There are three types of relationships that can be established between tables: one-to-one, one-to-many, and many-to-many.

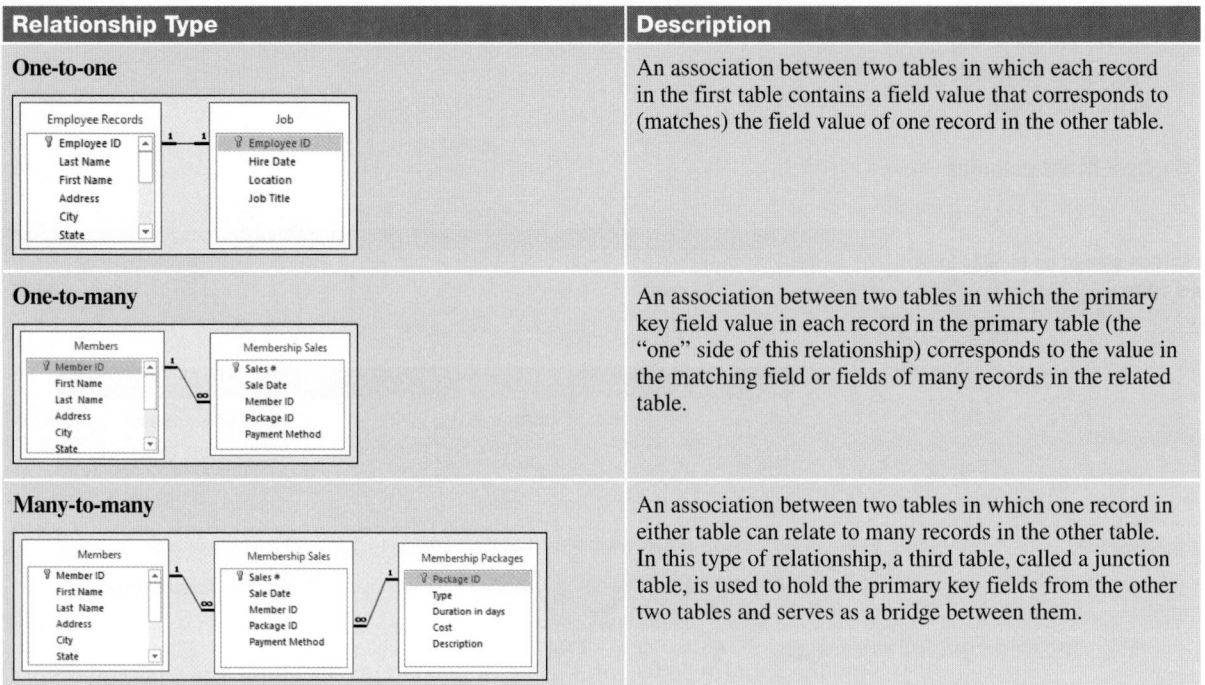

Relationship Type	Description
One-to-one	An association between two tables in which each record in the first table contains a field value that corresponds to (matches) the field value of one record in the other table.
One-to-many	An association between two tables in which the primary key field value in each record in the primary table (the "one" side of this relationship) corresponds to the value in the matching field or fields of many records in the related table.
Many-to-many	An association between two tables in which one record in either table can relate to many records in the other table. In this type of relationship, a third table, called a junction table, is used to hold the primary key fields from the other two tables and serves as a bridge between them.

Once relationships are established, rules can be enforced, called the rules of **referential integrity**, to ensure that relationships between tables are valid and that related data is not accidentally changed or deleted. The rules ensure that a record in a primary table cannot be deleted if matching records exist in a related table, and a primary key value cannot be changed in the primary table if that record has related records.

The Employee ID field is the field that the two tables have in common in this database and on which you will establish a relationship to link the tables together. To be able to create or edit relationships, you must close all open objects.

CLOSING TABLES

You close a table by closing its window and saving any layout changes you have made. Because you changed the column widths of the table, you will be prompted to save the layout changes before the table is closed. If you do not save the table, your column width settings will be lost.

1

- Click ☒ in the datasheet window to close the Job table.

- If necessary, click Yes in response to the prompt to save the table.

- In a similar manner, close the Employee Records table, saving when prompted.

Your screen should be similar to Figure 1.69

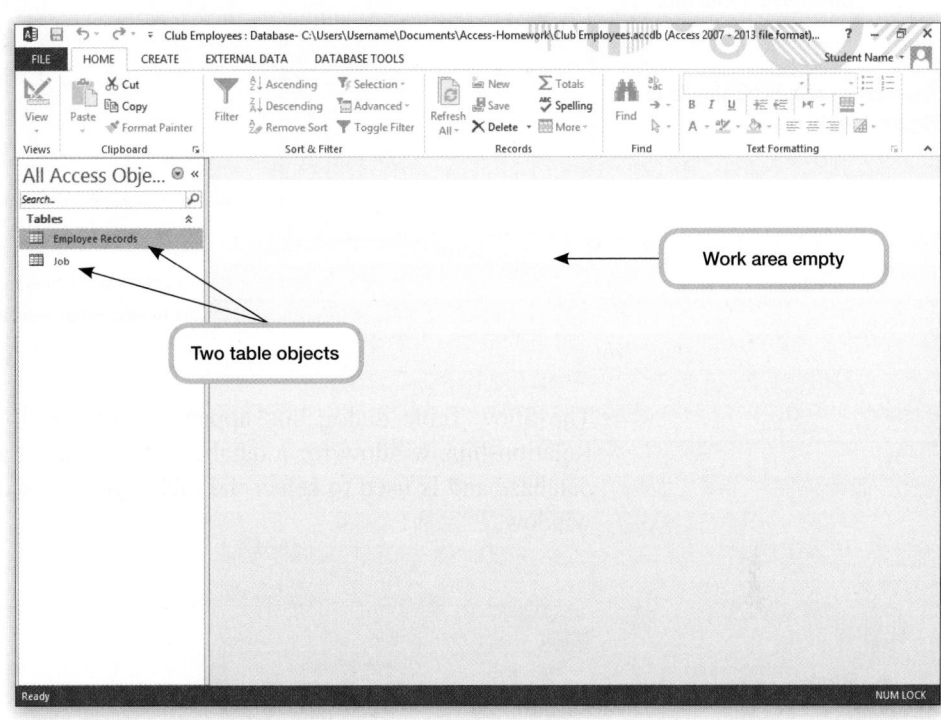

Figure 1.69

Both tables are closed and the work area is empty. The Navigation pane continues to display the names of the two table objects.

VIEWING RELATIONSHIPS

The Relationships window is used to create and edit relationships. It displays a field list for each table in the database and identifies how the tables are associated with relationship lines. However, the first time you open the Relationships window for a database, you need to select the tables to display in the window and then establish the relationship between the tables.

1

● Click [Relationships] in the Relationships group of the Database Tools tab.

Your screen should be similar to Figure 1.70

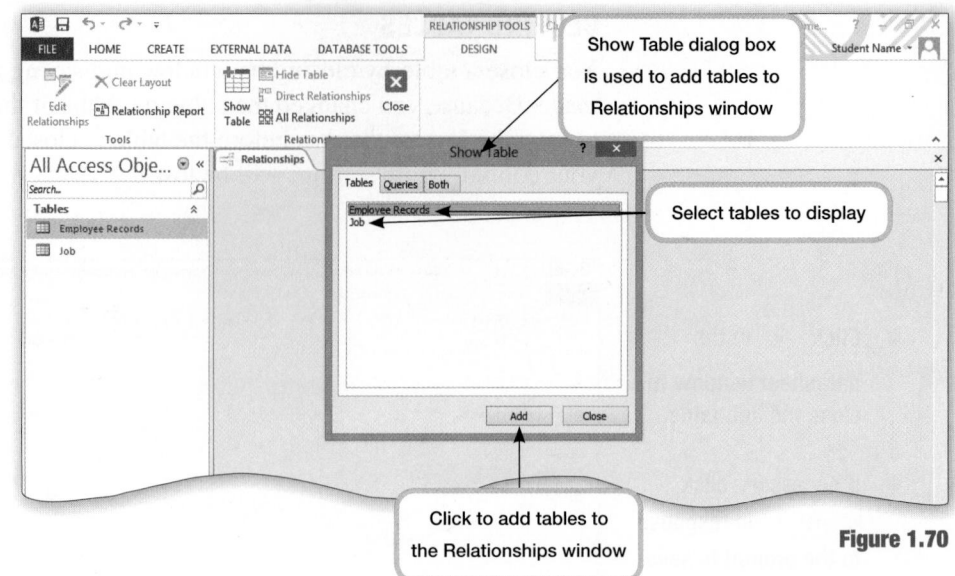

Show Table dialog box is used to add tables to Relationships window

Select tables to display

Click to add tables to the Relationships window

Figure 1.70

The Show Table dialog box appears automatically the first time you open the Relationships window for a database. It displays the names of both tables in the database and is used to select the tables you want displayed in the Relationships window.

2

● Click [Add] to add the selected table, Employee Records, to the Relationships window.

● Click Job in the Tables list to select the table and then click [Add].

● Click [Close].

Field list displays field names from each table

Figure 1.71

Your screen should be similar to Figure 1.71

As you selected each table, a field list box displaying the field names from the table was added to the Relationships window. Next, you need to establish the relationship between the tables.

DEFINING RELATIONSHIPS

When creating relationships between the tables, study them first to determine what field the two tables have in common, and then determine which table is the main table. The common field in the lesser table, called a **foreign key** field, will be used to refer back to the primary key field of the main table. The field names of these two fields do not have to match, although their data types must be the same. As we have established, the Employee ID field is the common field between the two tables in this database. The Employee Records table is the main table, as it contains the main information about the employee. The Employee ID field in the Job table is the foreign key field.

Now you must connect the Employee Records' Employee ID field to its related field in the Job table. To create the relationship, you drag the field from the field list of one table to the common field in the field list of the other table. As you point to the foreign key field, the mouse pointer will appear as ![pointer], indicating a relationship is being established.

1

Click on the Employee ID field in the Employee Records table and drag to the same field in the Job table.

Your screen should be similar to Figure 1.72

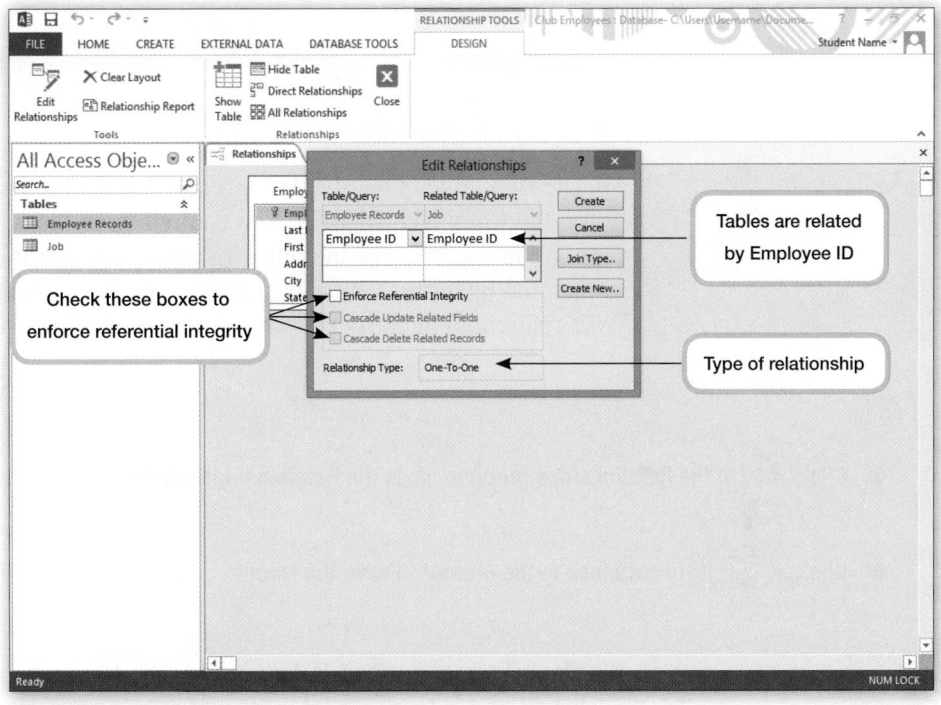

Figure 1.72

The Edit Relationships dialog box appears and shows how the tables will be related. You also want to enforce referential integrity between the tables. Selecting this option will make the Cascade Update and Cascade Delete options available. Again, you will select these options to ensure that if you change a primary key or delete a record, all fields that reference the primary key of that record are likewise updated or deleted in both tables. This prevents inconsistent and **orphaned records** (records that do not have a matching primary key record in the associated table). In addition, you can see that Access has correctly defined the type of relationship as one-to-one.

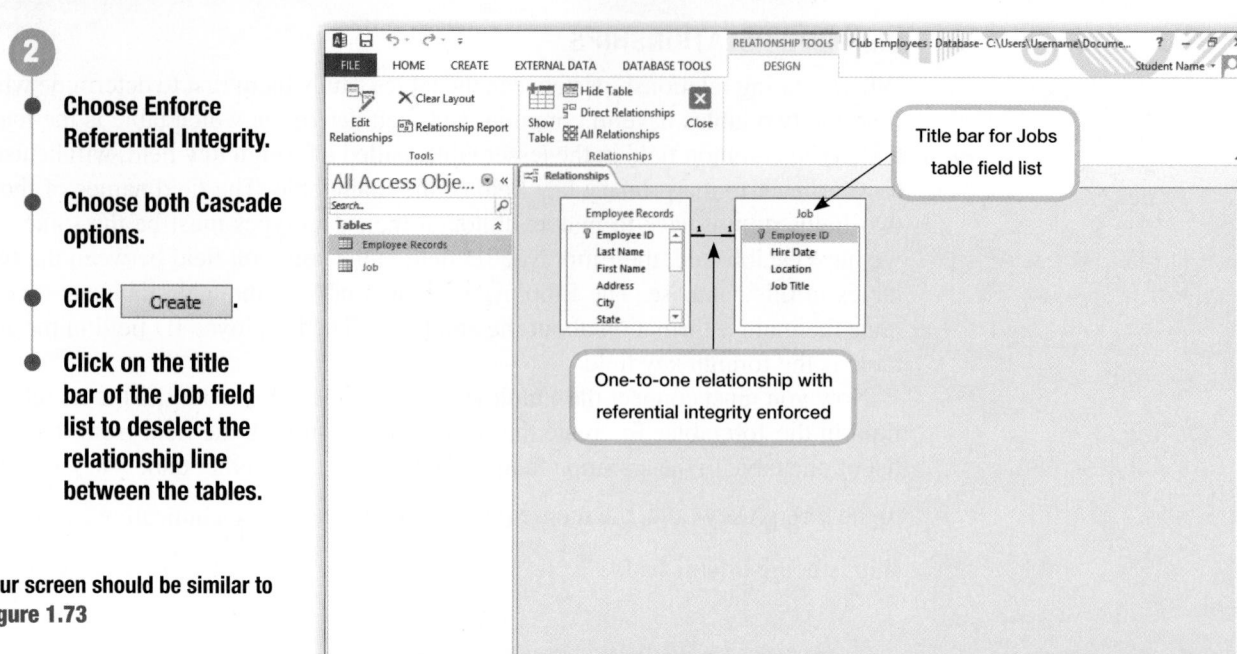

2

- Choose **Enforce Referential Integrity**.

- Choose both **Cascade** options.

- Click [Create].

- Click on the title bar of the Job field list to deselect the relationship line between the tables.

Your screen should be similar to Figure 1.73

Title bar for Jobs table field list

One-to-one relationship with referential integrity enforced

Figure 1.73

The two tables now display a relationship line that shows the tables are related on the Employee ID field. You can tell from the number 1 above each end of the relationship line that the relationship type is one-to-one. You can also tell that referential integrity is enforced because the relationship line is thicker near each end. If referential integrity were not enforced, the line would not be thicker at the ends.

3

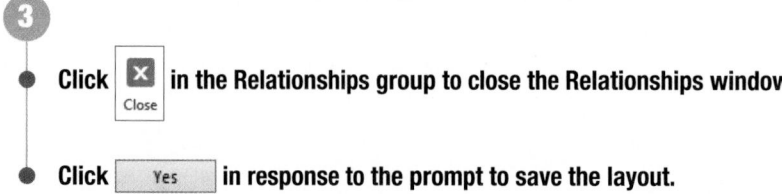

- Click [X Close] in the Relationships group to close the Relationships window.

- Click [Yes] in response to the prompt to save the layout.

The relationships and layout are saved. Now that a relationship has been established and referential integrity enforced, a warning message will automatically appear if one of the rules is broken, and you will not be allowed to complete the action you are trying to do.

OPENING TABLES

Now that you have established relationships between the tables, you will open the Employee Records table to see how it has been affected by this change. To open a table object, double-click on the name in the Navigation pane.

1

- **Double-click Employee Records in the Navigation pane.**

Another Method

You also can drag the object from the Navigation pane to the work area to open it, or right-click the object name in the Navigation pane and choose Open.

Your screen should be similar to Figure 1.74

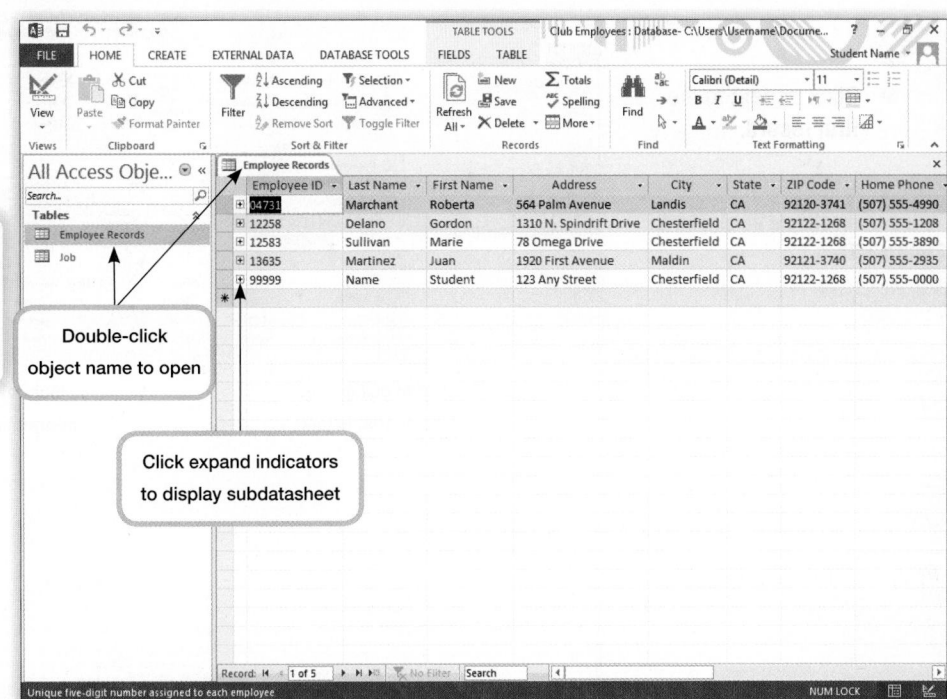

Double-click object name to open

Click expand indicators to display subdatasheet

Figure 1.74

The Employee Records table is open in the work area. Notice the records are no longer in the same order they were entered, but are now in ascending order by the primary key, Employee ID. There are also expand indicators ⊞ at the beginning of each row. This indicates there is a subdatasheet linked to the records in this table.

Concept  Subdatasheet

A **subdatasheet** is a data table nested within a main data table that contains information that is related or joined to the main table. A subdatasheet allows you to easily view and edit related data. Subdatasheets are created automatically whenever relationships are established between tables.

In this case, the subdatasheet is the Job table. Clicking ⊞ will expand the table to show the information in the subdatasheet table, Job.

2

● Click ⊞ next to the first record.

Your screen should be similar to Figure 1.75

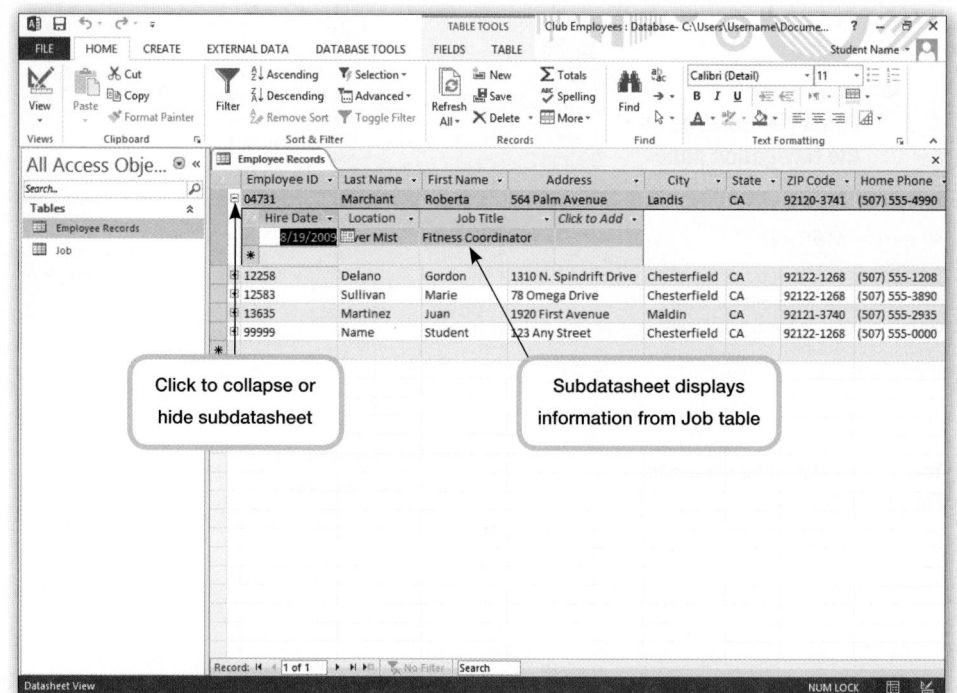

Employee ID	Last Name	First Name	Address	City	State	ZIP Code	Home Phone
⊟ 04731	Marchant	Roberta	564 Palm Avenue	Landis	CA	92120-3741	(507) 555-4990

Hire Date	Location	Job Title	Click to Add
8/19/2008	ver Mist	Fitness Coordinator	

⊞ 12258	Delano	Gordon	1310 N. Spindrift Drive	Chesterfield	CA	92122-1268	(507) 555-1208
⊞ 12583	Sullivan	Marie	78 Omega Drive	Chesterfield	CA	92122-1268	(507) 555-3890
⊞ 13635	Martinez	Juan	1920 First Avenue	Maldin	CA	92121-3740	(507) 555-2935
⊞ 99999	Name	Student	123 Any Street	Chesterfield	CA	92122-1268	(507) 555-0000

Click to collapse or hide subdatasheet

Subdatasheet displays information from Job table

Figure 1.75

Additional Information

You will learn more about relationships and subdatasheets in later labs.

A subdatasheet appears and displays the location and job title information contained in the Job table for Roberta Marchant. Similarly, the Job table will display a subdatasheet to the Employee Records table.

Then, to hide or collapse the subdatasheet again, you click the collapse indicator ⊟.

3

● Click ⊟ next to the first record.

● Close the table.

You have created a database file that contains two tables and follows the two basic principles of database design: Do not include redundant information in tables, and enter accurate and complete information. Although you may think the employee number is redundant data, it is the only way the information in the two tables can be associated. The database attains the goals of **normalization**, a design technique that identifies and eliminates redundancy by applying a set of rules to your tables to confirm that they are structured properly.

Closing and Opening a Database

It is always a good idea to close all open objects in the work area before closing the database. Since you have already closed the tables, the work area is empty and there are no open objects. Next, you will close the database, but not the Access program.

CLOSING A DATABASE

When closing a database file, unlike other types of files, you do not need to save first, as each time changes are made to the data they are automatically saved as part of the process. Changes to an object's design, however, need to be saved for the changes to be permanent.

Additional Information

To review file types, refer to the Saving a File section in the Introduction to Microsoft Office 2013 lab.

If you plan to share an Access 2007, 2010, or 2013 .accdb file with someone using Access 2003 or earlier, before closing the database open the Save As tab and choose the appropriate database file type from the Save Database As list. A copy of the file will be saved using the selected database file type. Be aware some features may be lost when saving to an older version of Access.

- Open the File tab and click **Close**.

- Open the File tab again and click **Open**.

Your screen should be similar to Figure 1.76

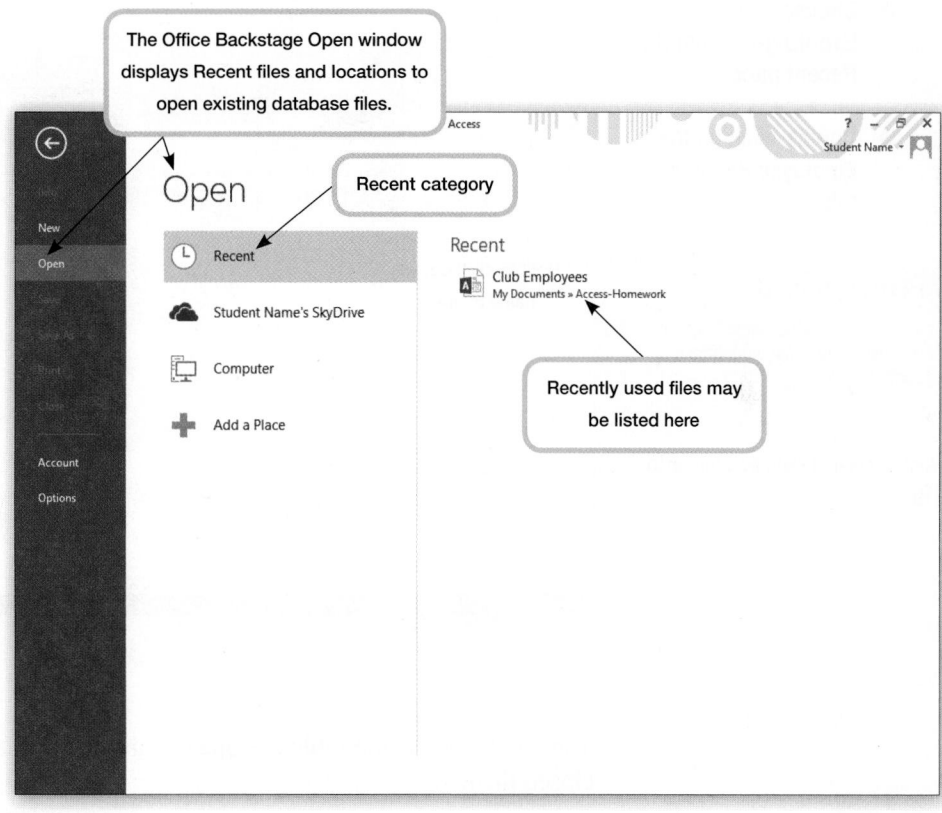

The Office Backstage Open window displays Recent files and locations to open existing database files.

Recent category

Recently used files may be listed here

Figure 1.76

When you closed the database, a blank gray Access window displayed, and most of the Ribbon commands were grayed out and unavailable.

OPENING A DATABASE

Additional Information

See the section Opening a File in the Introduction to Microsoft Office 2013 to review the basics on how to open a file.

Just as there are several methods to create a new database, there are several methods you can use to open an existing database. From the Open window you can select from a list of recently used database files listed in the Recent pane of the window. If the file you want to open was not recently used, click another option in the Open list, such as Computer to access files stored on your computer, and browse to locate the file you want to open.

You also can open database files that were created in previous versions of Access that used the .mdb file extension. These older file types must be converted to the Access 2013 file format if you want to take advantage of the new features in Access 2013.

Additional Information

Items can be removed from the Recent list by right-clicking the file name and choosing Remove from list.

The Recent pane by default displays up to 25 names of recently used database files on the computer you are using. Because the Club Employees database file was the last-used database file, it appears at the top of the Recent pane. The file names listed, however, are not always accurate as files may have been moved or deleted since they were last accessed.

1

- **Choose** Club Employees **from the Recent pane.**

- **Double-click on the Employee Records table.**

Another Method

You also can drag the object from the Navigation pane to the work area to open it.

Your screen should be similar to Figure 1.77

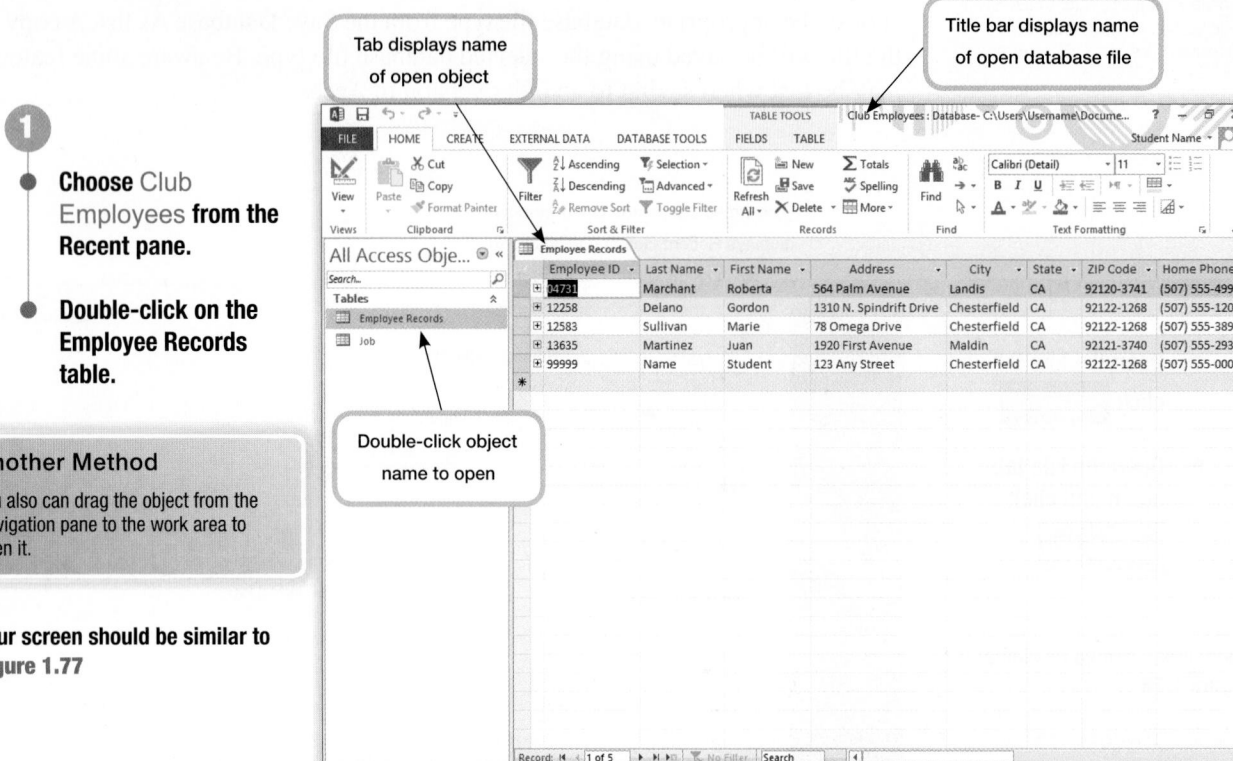

Figure 1.77

The database file and table are open again and appear just as they were when you closed them.

Setting Database and Object Properties

Now, you want to look at the file properties or settings that are associated with the database file. Some of these properties are automatically generated. These include statistics such as the date the file was created and last modified. Others such as a description of the file are properties you can add.

DOCUMENTING A DATABASE

Having Trouble?

See Specifying Document Properties in the Introduction to Microsoft Office 2013 for more information about this feature.

The information you can associate with the file includes a title, subject, author, keywords, and comments about the file. You will look at the file properties and add documentation to identify you as the author and a title for the database.

- **Open the File tab and, if necessary, click** `Info` **.**

- **Click on the View and edit database properties link, located on the right side of the screen.**

- **Open each tab in the Properties dialog box and look at the recorded information.**

- **Open the Summary tab.**

- **Enter the following information in the Summary tab.**

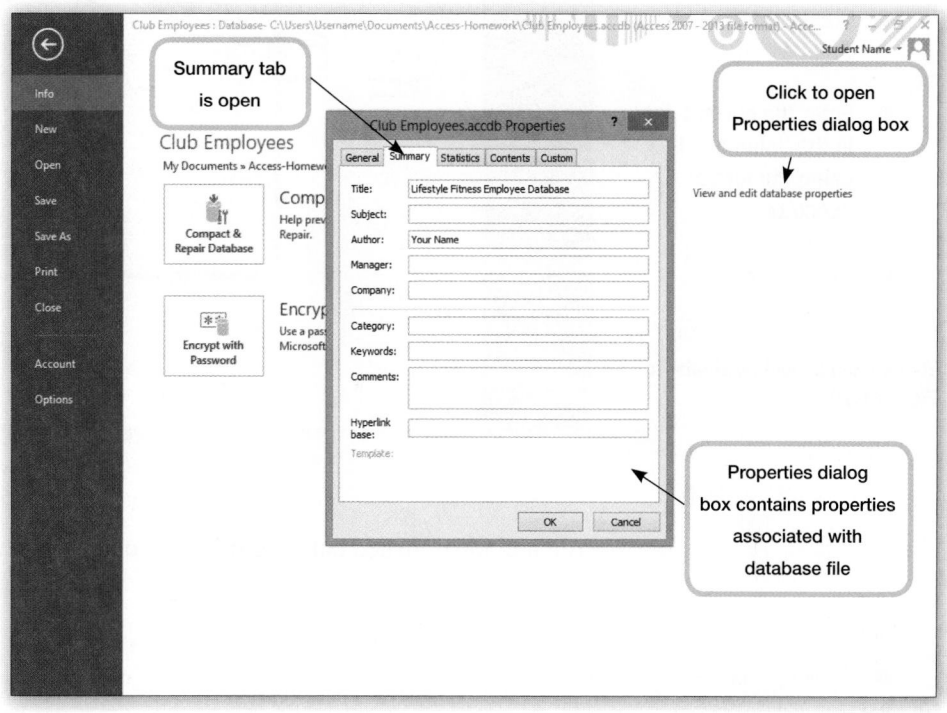

Figure 1.78

Title	Lifestyle Fitness Employee Database
Author	Your Name

You also want to create a custom property to identify the completion date.

Having Trouble?

The Title and Author text boxes may be blank or may already show information. Clear the existing contents first if necessary.

Your screen should be similar to Figure 1.78

- **Open the Custom tab.**

- **Choose Date completed from the Name list.**

- **Choose Date as the Type.**

- **Enter the current date in the Value text box using the format xx/xx/xx.**

- **Click** Add .

Your screen should be similar to Figure 1.79

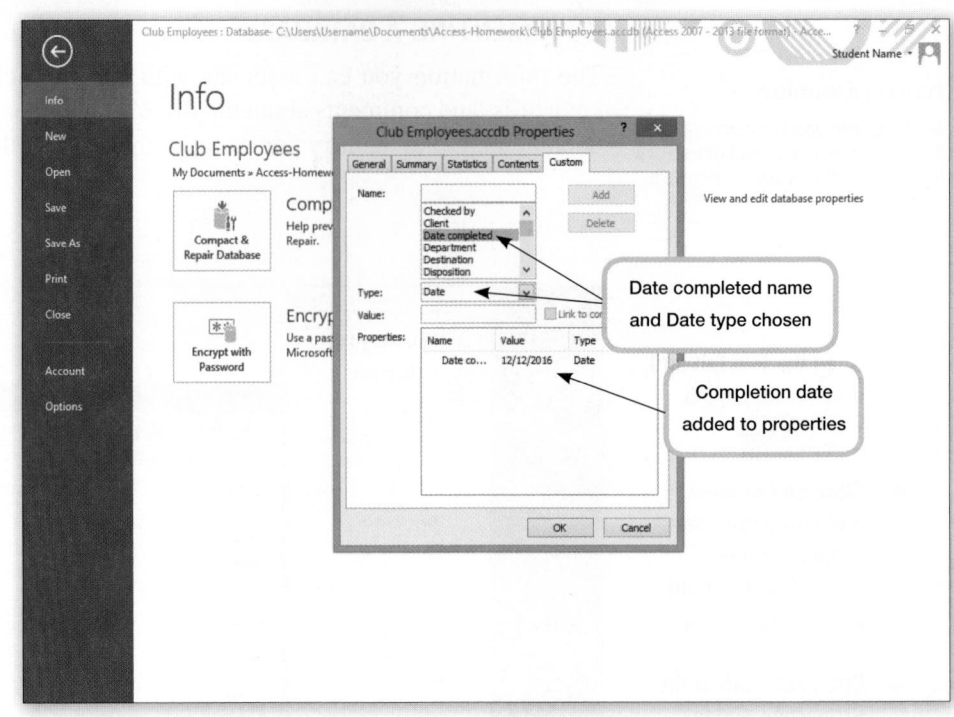

Figure 1.79

You are now finished entering information in the Database properties.

- **Click** OK .

- **Click the** ⬅ **to display the database again.**

DOCUMENTING A TABLE OBJECT

You have completed adding the properties to the file. You also can add limited documentation to each object in a database. You will add documentation to the Employee Records table object.

- **Right-click the Employee Records table object in the Navigation pane.**

- **Choose Table Properties from the drop-down menu.**

- **In the Description text box, type This table is under construction and currently contains 5 records**

Your screen should be similar to Figure 1.80

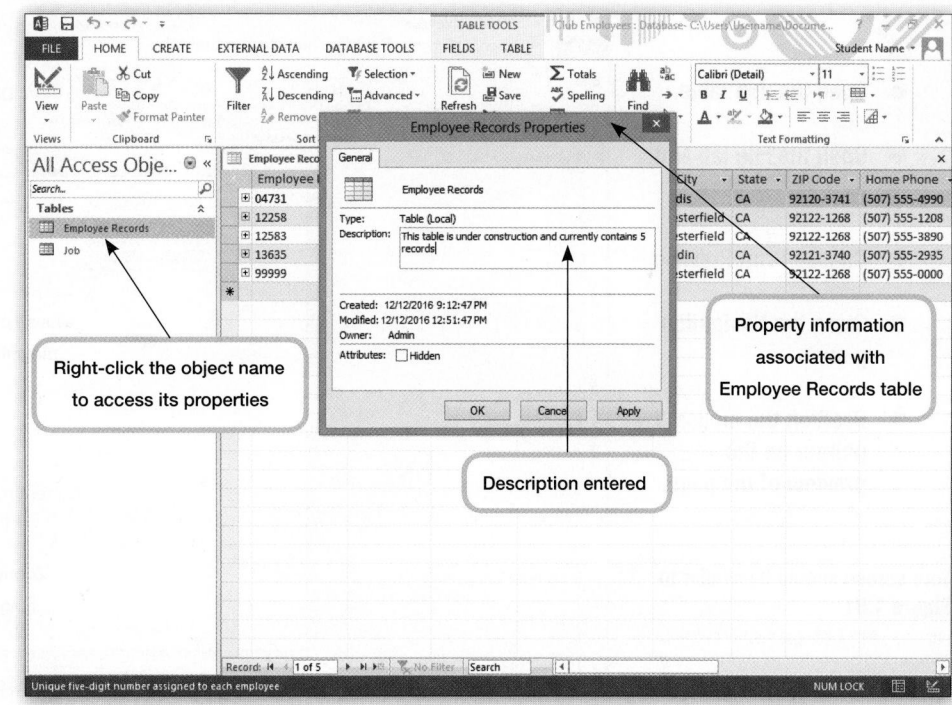

Figure 1.80

You have added property information to both the database file and the Employee Records table.

- **Click** OK **to close the Properties dialog box.**

Previewing and Printing a Table

Now that you have completed designing and entering some sample data in the two tables, you want to print a copy of the tables to get your manager's approval before you begin entering more employee records. Before printing the tables, you will preview them onscreen to see how they will look when printed.

PREVIEWING THE TABLE

Previewing a table displays each page in a reduced size so you can see the layout. Then, if necessary, you can make changes to the layout before printing to save time and avoid wasting paper.

1

- Open the Job table.

- Open the File tab and click **Print**.

- Choose Print Preview.

- Close the Navigation pane.

- Position the mouse pointer on the preview of the page.

Your screen should be similar to Figure 1.81

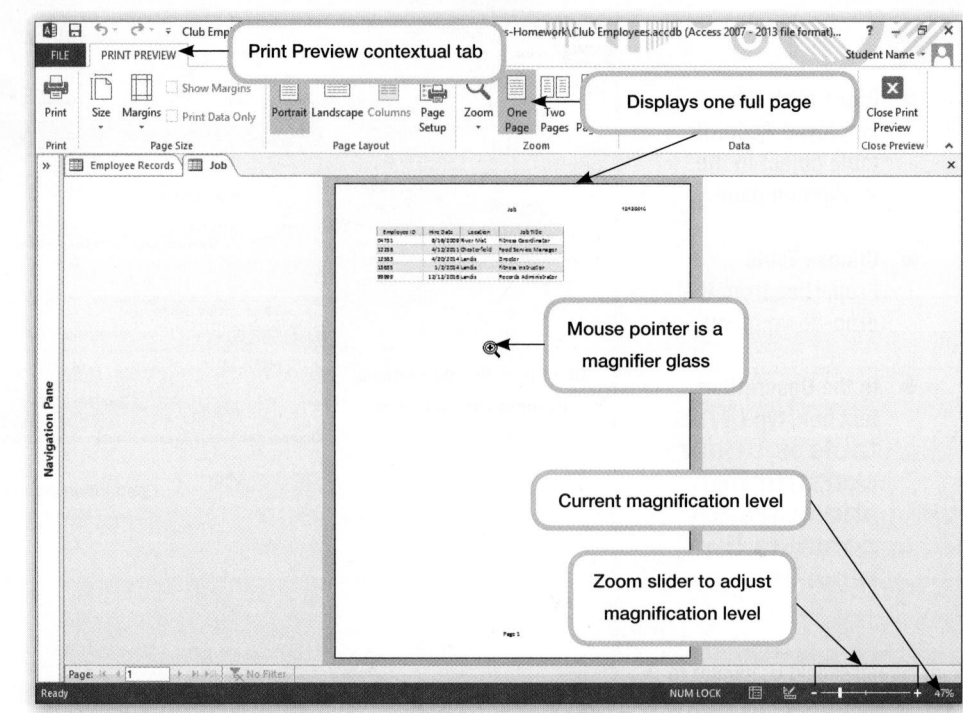

Figure 1.81

Additional Information

The current magnification level is displayed in the status bar.

The Print Preview window displays how the table will appear when printed. The Print Preview contextual tab is open and includes commands that are used to modify the print settings. Notice the mouse pointer appears as . Clicking on the preview will toggle the preview between the current zoom percentage and 100% zoom percentage.

2

- Click on the top of the table.

Additional Information

The location where you click will determine the area that is displayed initially.

Your screen should be similar to Figure 1.82

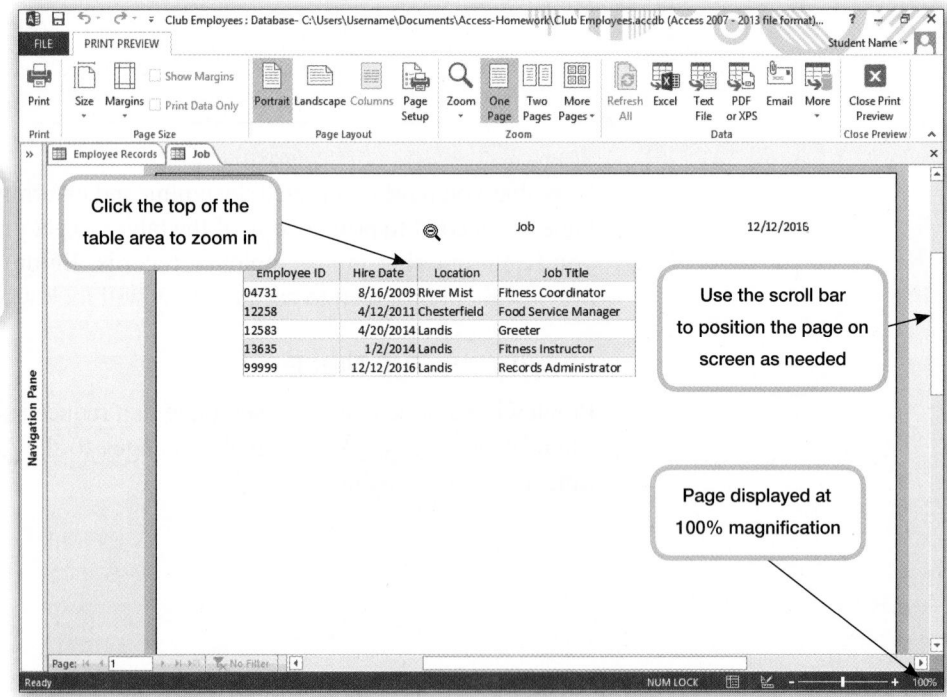

Figure 1.82

The preview now appears in 100 percent magnification. This is the size it will appear when printed.

PRINTING A TABLE

The 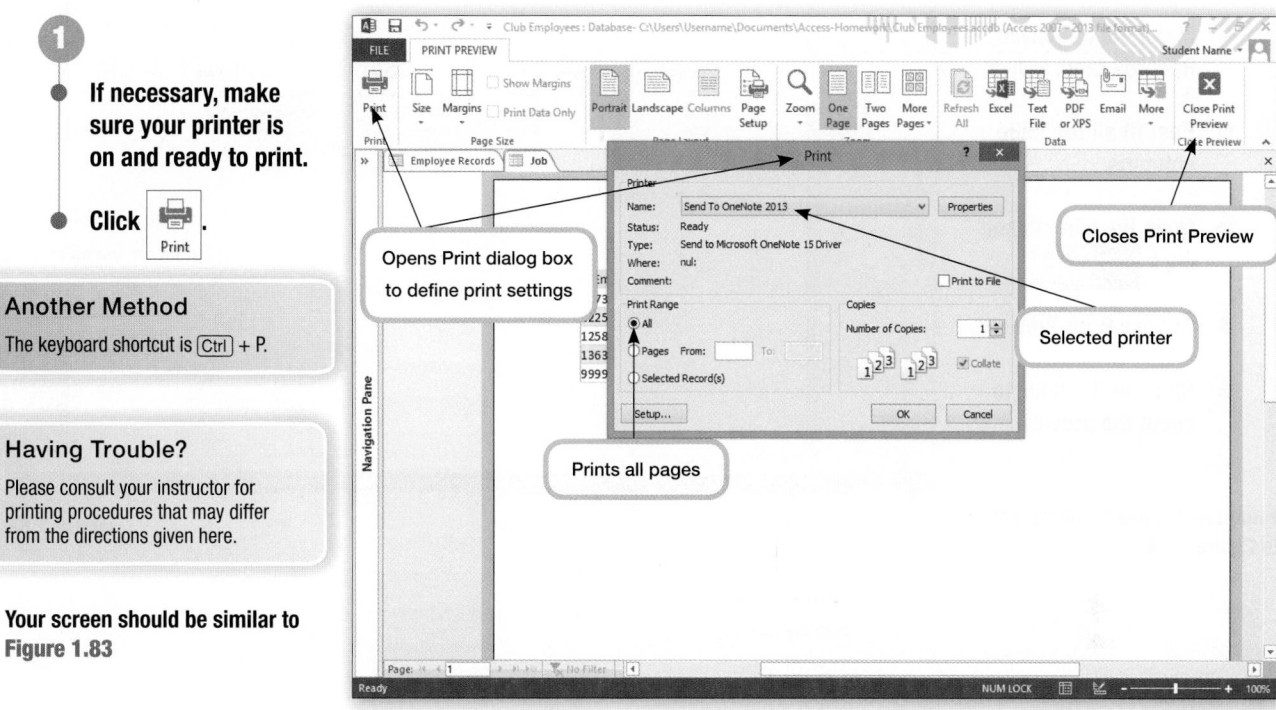 button in the Print group of the Print Preview tab is used to define the printer settings and print the document.

1

- **If necessary, make sure your printer is on and ready to print.**

- **Click** [Print].

Another Method

The keyboard shortcut is Ctrl + P.

Having Trouble?

Please consult your instructor for printing procedures that may differ from the directions given here.

Your screen should be similar to Figure 1.83

Figure 1.83

The Print Range area of the Print dialog box is used to specify the amount of the document you want printed. The range options are described in the following table.

Option	Action
All	Prints the entire document.
Pages	Prints pages you specify by typing page numbers in the text box.
Selected Records	Prints selected records only.

You will print the entire document.

2

- **If you need to change the selected printer to another printer, open the Name drop-down list box and select the appropriate printer (your instructor will tell you which printer to select).**

- **Click** [OK].

A status message box is displayed briefly, informing you that the table is being printed.

CHANGING THE PAGE ORIENTATION AND MARGINS

Next, you will preview and print the Employee Records table.

1

- Click [Close Print Preview] in the **Close Preview group.**

- **Make the Employee Records table active.**

- **Best fit all the table columns.**

- **Open the File tab and click [Print].**

- **Choose Print Preview.**

- **Click on the table to zoom the preview.**

Your screen should look similar to Figure 1.84

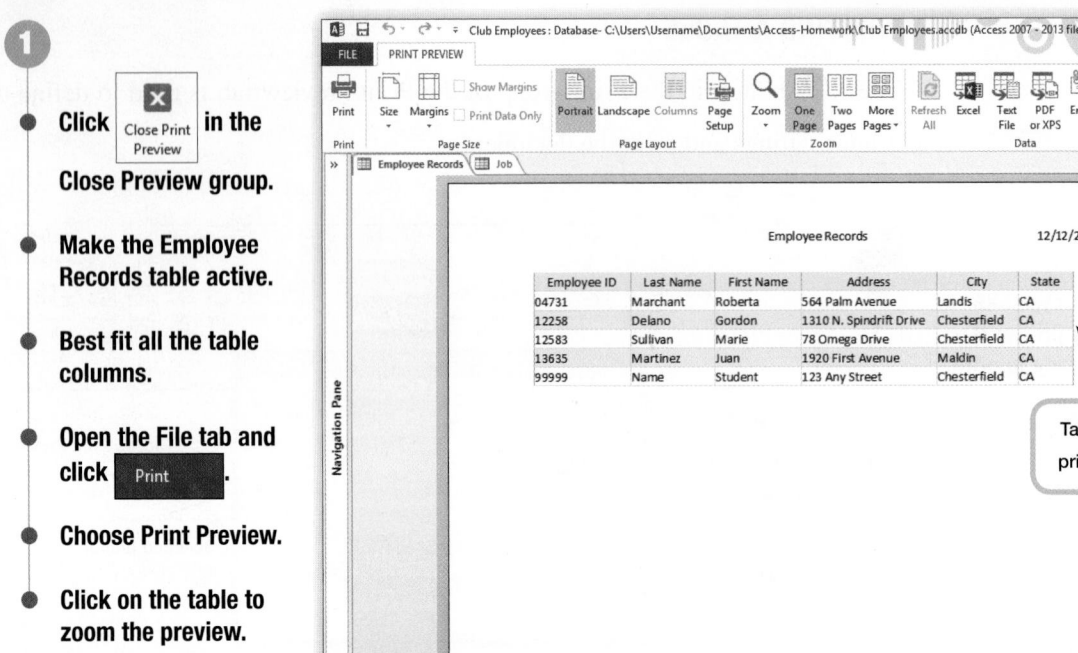

Table too wide to print on one page

Indicates more than one page

Figure 1.84

Notice that because the table is too wide to fit across the width of a page, only the first six fields are displayed on the page. Tables with multiple columns are typically too wide to fit on an 8½- by 1 1-inch piece of paper in portrait orientation. You would like to see both pages displayed onscreen.

Current page orientation

Displays two pages in Preview window

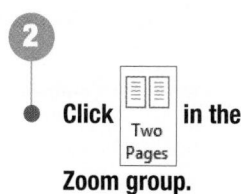

2

Click [Two Pages] in the Zoom group.

Your screen should be similar to Figure 1.85

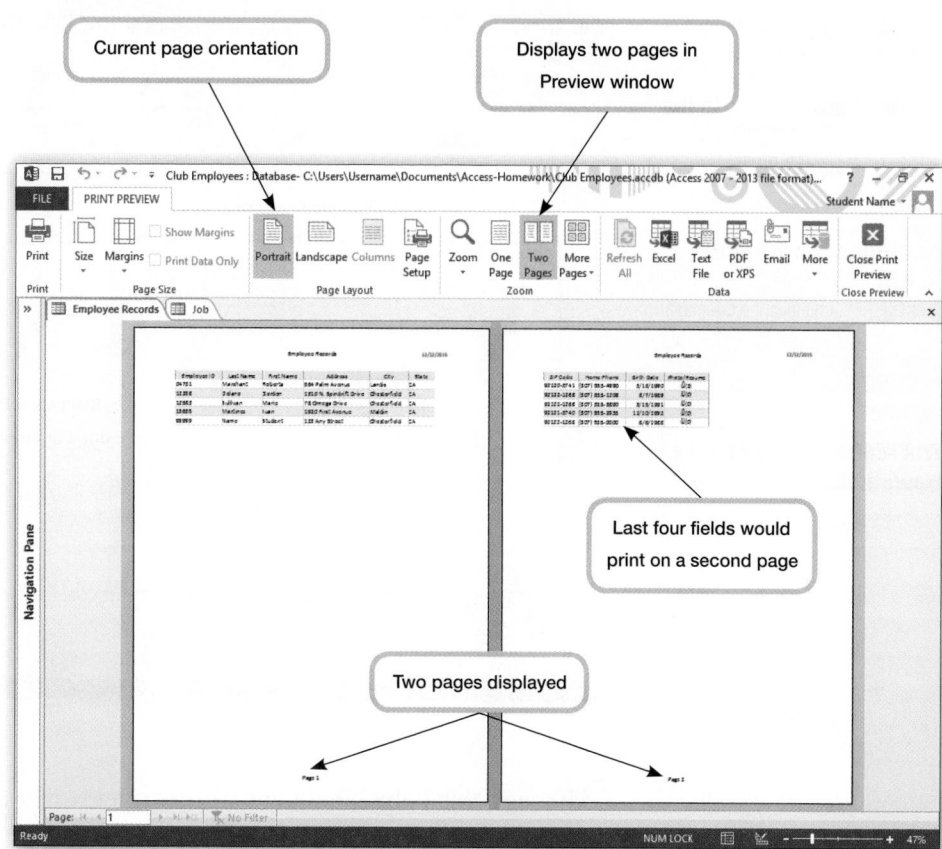

Last four fields would print on a second page

Two pages displayed

Figure 1.85

Having Trouble?

Refer to the section Printing a Document in the Introduction to Microsoft Office 2013 lab to review page orientation.

Rather than print the table on two pages, you decide to see whether changing the page orientation from portrait to landscape will allow you to print the table on one page.

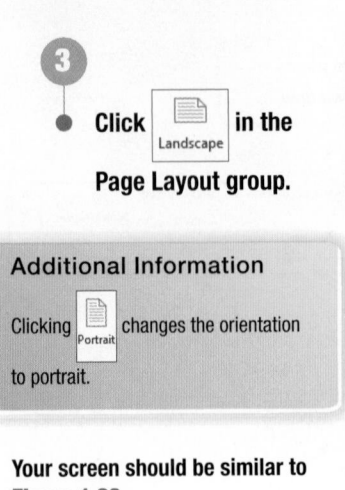

3
● Click [Landscape] in the
   Page Layout group.

**Your screen should be similar to
Figure 1.86**

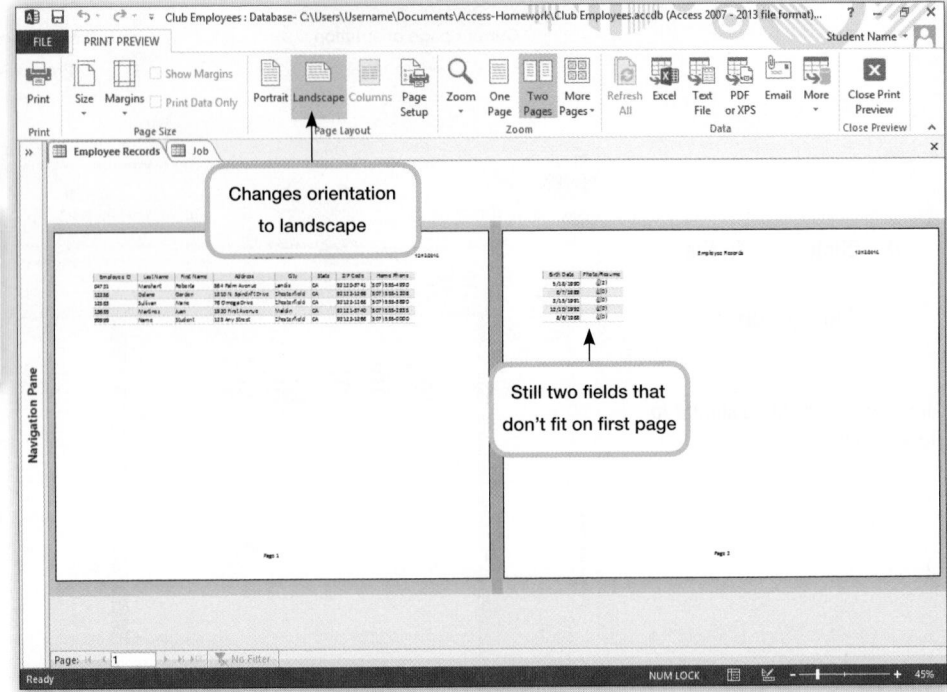

Changes orientation
to landscape

Still two fields that
don't fit on first page

Figure 1.86

Although this helps, there are still two fields that do not fit on the page. To fix
this, you will try reducing the size of the page margins. The **margin** is the blank
space around the edge of a page. The default margin setting is 1 inch margins on
all sides. You can choose from several standard margin formats or customize your
own. You will use the Normal margin format which will decrease the right and left
margin settings to 0.35 inch to see if this allows all fields to fit on one page.

4
● Click [Margins] in the
   **Page Size group of
   the Print Preview tab.**

● **Choose Normal.**

● Click [One Page].

● **Change the
   magnification level
   to 90%.**

**Your screen should be similar to
Figure 1.87**

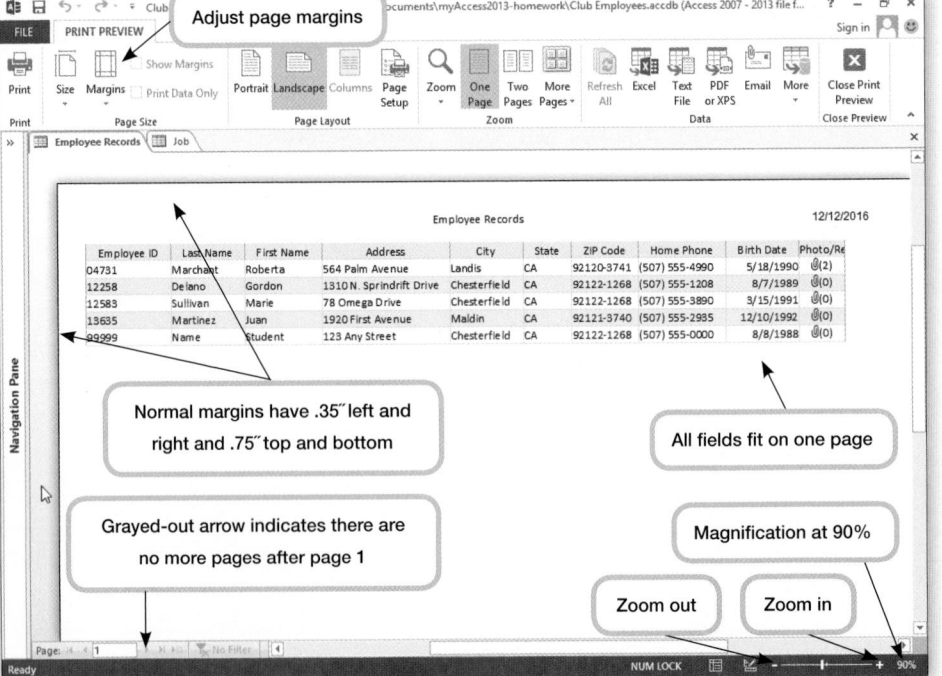

Adjust page margins

Normal margins have .35″ left and
right and .75″ top and bottom

All fields fit on one page

Grayed-out arrow indicates there are
no more pages after page 1

Magnification at 90%

Zoom out   Zoom in

Figure 1.87

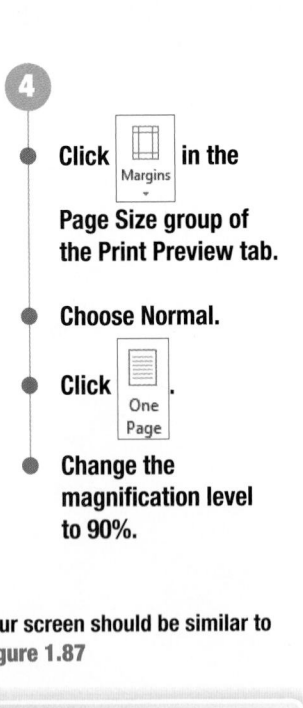

You can now see that all the fields will print on one page.

5

● Print the table.

● Close the Print Preview window.

Exiting Access

You will continue to build and use the database of employee records in the next lab. Until then, you can exit Access.

1

● Click ☒ **Close in the Access window title bar and click** [Yes] **to save the layout changes.**

Notice that this time you were not prompted to save the tables because you did not made any layout changes to them since opening them. If you had made layout changes, you would be prompted to save the tables before exiting Access.

CUS ON CAREERS

EXPLORE YOUR CAREER OPTIONS

Admitting Nurse
Can you imagine trying to organize the information of hundreds of patients in a busy emergency room? This is the job of an admitting nurse, who must be able to enter, edit, and format data; add and delete records; and so on. This information is used by all departments of the hospital, from the doctors, to the pharmacy, and to the billing department. Without a proper understanding of database software, a hospital cannot run efficiently. The average salary of an admitting nurse is in the $37,000 to $52,000 range. The demand for nurses is expected to remain high.

Database (AC1.4)

A database is an organized collection of related information.

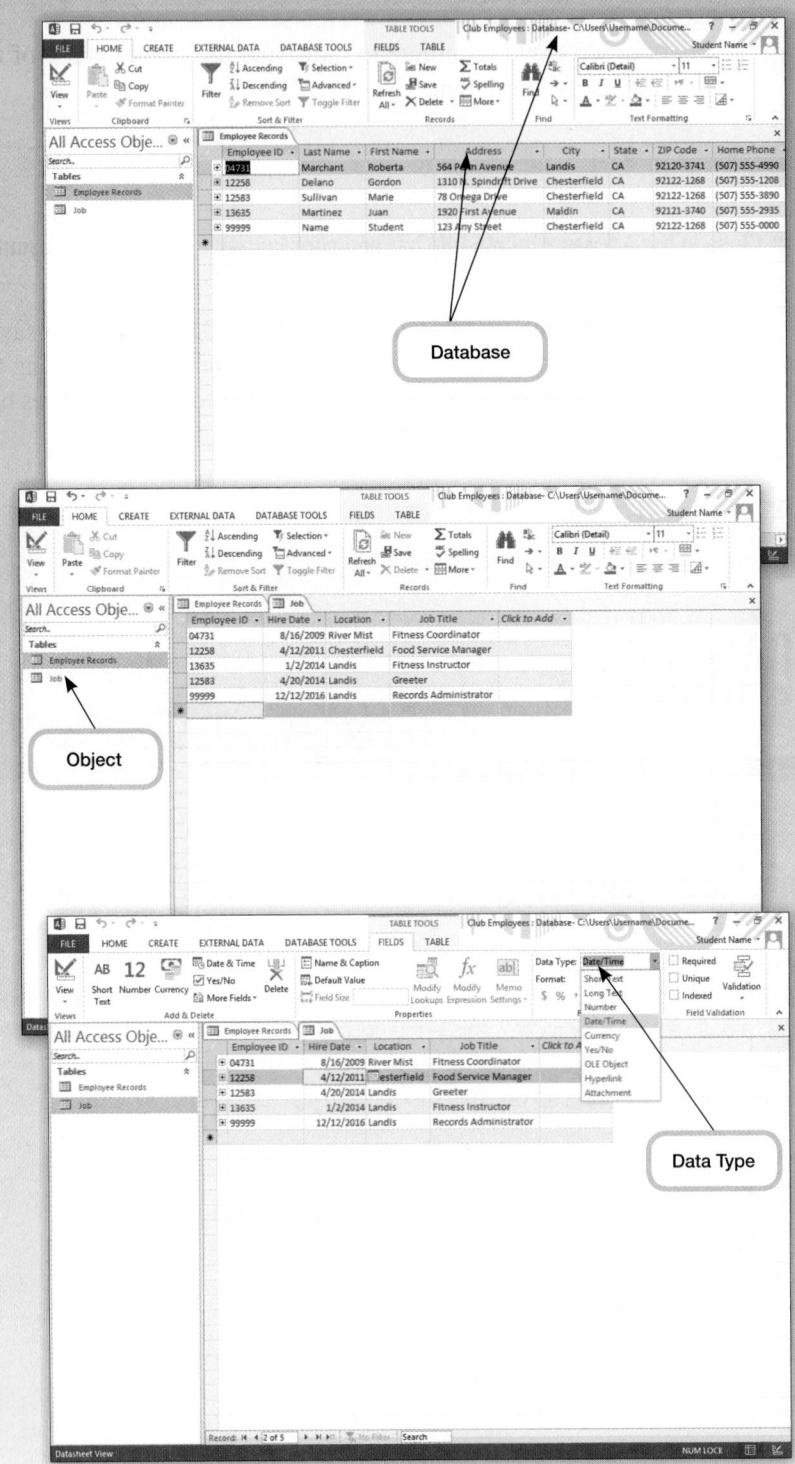

Database

Object (AC1.9)

An Access database is made up of several types of objects, such as a table or report, consisting of many elements. An object can be created, selected, and manipulated as a unit.

Object

Data Type (AC1.15)

The data type defines the type of data the field will contain. Access uses the data type to ensure that the right kind of data is entered in a field.

Data Type

Field Property (AC1.22)

A field property is a characteristic that helps define a field. A set of field properties is associated with each field.

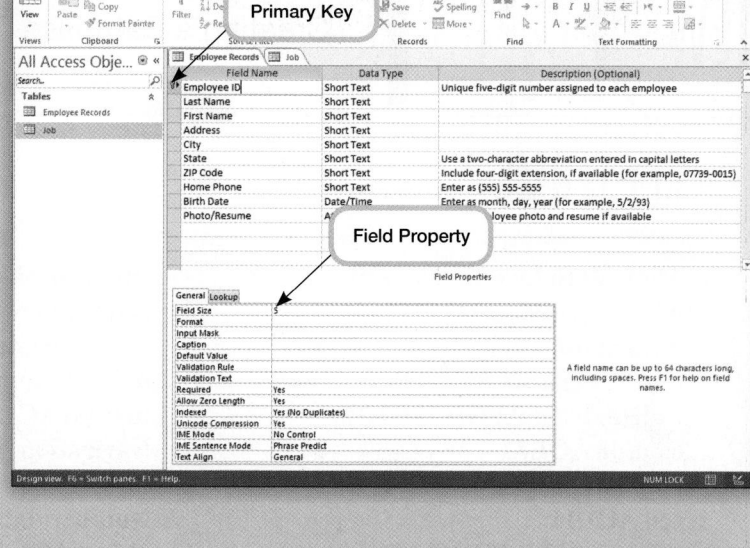

Primary Key (AC1.28)

A primary key is a field that uniquely identifies each record.

Relationship (AC1.66)

A relationship establishes the association between common fields in two tables.

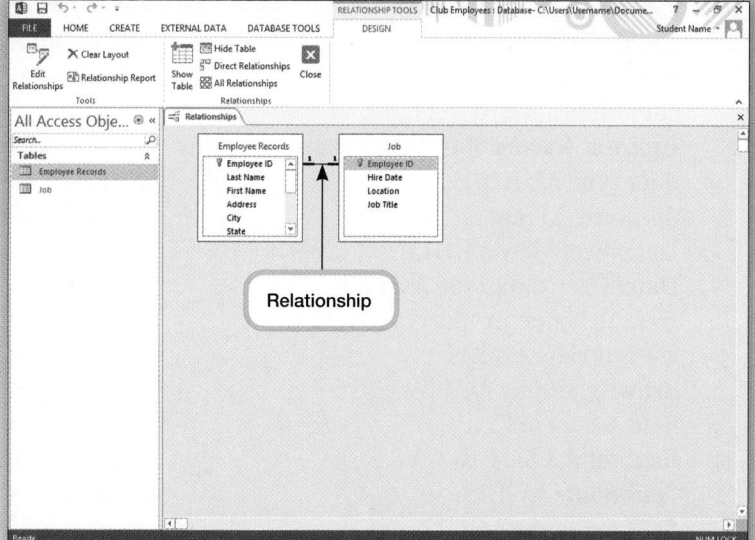

Subdatasheet (AC1.71)

A subdatasheet is a data table nested within a main data table; it contains information that is related or joined to the main table.

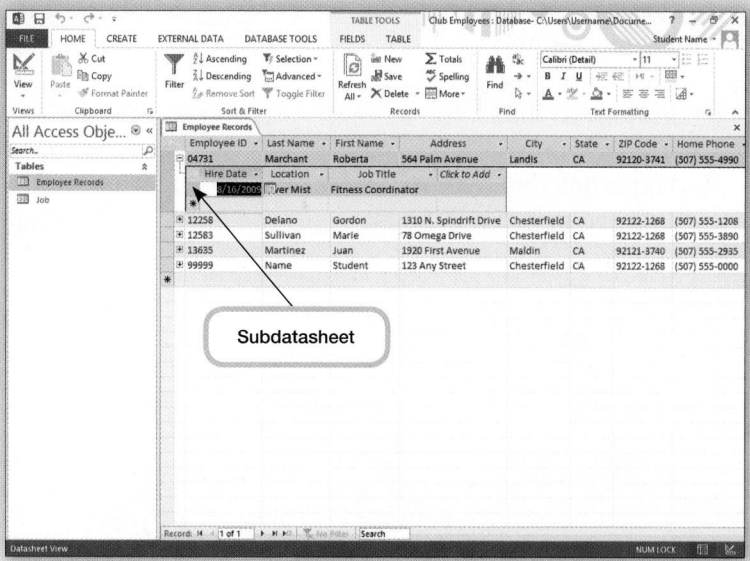

KEY TERMS

Allow Zero Length property AC1.22
Attachment data type AC1.15
AutoNumber data type AC1.15
Best Fit feature AC1.49
Calculated data type AC1.15
caption AC1.27
Caption property AC1.22
cell AC1.11
column width AC1.47
composite key AC1.28
Currency data type AC1.15
current field AC1.24
current record AC1.11
Current Record box AC1.11
data type AC1.15
database AC1.4
Datasheet view AC1.11
Date/Time data type AC1.15
Default Value property AC1.22
Design view AC1.11
drawing object AC1.39
field AC1.4
field model AC1.18
field name AC1.13
field property AC1.22
Field Size property AC1.22
foreign key AC1.69
form AC1.9
Form view AC1.11
Format property AC1.22
graphic AC1.39
header row AC1.11
Hyperlink data type AC1.15
Indexed property AC1.22

Input Mask property AC1.22
Layout view AC1.11
Long Text data type AC1.15
many-to-many AC1.66
margin AC1.82
Navigation pane AC1.10
normalization AC1.72
Number data type AC1.15
object AC1.9
OLE Object data type AC1.15
one-to-many AC1.66
one-to-one AC1.66
orphaned records AC1.69
picture AC1.39
primary key AC1.28
Print Preview AC1.11
query AC1.9
record AC1.4
record navigation buttons AC1.11
referential integrity AC1.66
relational database AC1.4
relationship AC1.66
report AC1.9
Report view AC1.11
Required property AC1.22
Select Record button AC1.11
serial value AC1.15
Short Text data type AC1.15
subdatasheet AC1.71
table AC1.9
Validation Rule property AC1.22
Validation Text property AC1.22
view AC1.10
Yes/No data type AC1.15

COMMAND SUMMARY

Command	Shortcut	Action
File Tab		
⬅		Closes File tab and returns to currently open database
New	Ctrl + N	Opens the New window where you can create a new database
Open	Ctrl + O	Displays the Open window, where you can open an existing database
Save	Ctrl + S	Saves database object
Save As	F12	Creates a copy of the database with a different file name and/or type
Print /Print	Ctrl + P	Opens the Print dialog box, where you can specify print settings, and prints current database object
Print /Print Preview		Displays current database object as it will appear when printed
Close		Closes the open database file
Home Tab		
Views group		
Design View		Displays object in Design view
Datasheet View		Displays object in Datasheet view
Clipboard group		
Paste	Ctrl + V	Inserts copy of item from Clipboard
✂ Cut	Ctrl + X	Removes selected item and copies it to the Clipboard
📋 Copy	Ctrl + C	Duplicates selected item and copies it to the Clipboard
Records group		
💾 Save	Ctrl + S or Shift + Enter	Saves record changes
✕ Delete ▾	Delete	Deletes current record
More ▾ /Field Width		Adjusts width of selected column

LAB REVIEW

COMMAND SUMMARY (CONTINUED)

Command	Shortcut	Action
Find group		
→ ▾ Go To		Accesses navigation buttons
▷ ▾ Select/Select		Selects current record
Create Tab		
Tables group		
Table Design		Creates a new table in Design view
Table Tools Fields Tab		
Views group		
Design View		Displays table in Design view
Add & Delete group		
12 Number		Inserts a new numeric field
Date & Time		Inserts a new date/time field
More Fields ▾		Opens a drop-down list of fields
Delete	Delete	Removes selected field column
Properties group		
Name & Caption		Renames selected field
Formatting group		
Data Type: Number ▾		Changes the data type for current field
Format: ▾		Sets the display format of the selected field
Table Tools Design Tab		
Views group		
Datasheet View		Displays table in Datasheet view

COMMAND SUMMARY (CONTINUED)

Command	Shortcut	Action
Tools group		
Primary Key		Makes current field a primary key field
Insert Rows		Inserts rows above selection
Delete Rows	Delete	Deletes selected field row
Database Tools Tab		
Relationships group		
Relationships		Opens relationships window
Print Preview Tab		
Print group		
Print	Ctrl + P	Prints displayed object
Page Size group		
Margins		Sets margin settings for entire document
Page Layout group		
Portrait		Changes print orientation to portrait
Landscape		Changes print orientation to landscape
Zoom group		
One Page		Displays one entire page in Print Preview
Two Pages		Displays two entire pages in Print Preview
Close Preview group		
Close Print Preview	Esc	Closes Print Preview window

LAB EXERCISES

SCREEN IDENTIFICATION

1. On the following Access screen, several items are identified by letters. Enter the correct term for each item in the spaces provided. One answer may be used twice. Not all possible answers may necessarily be needed.

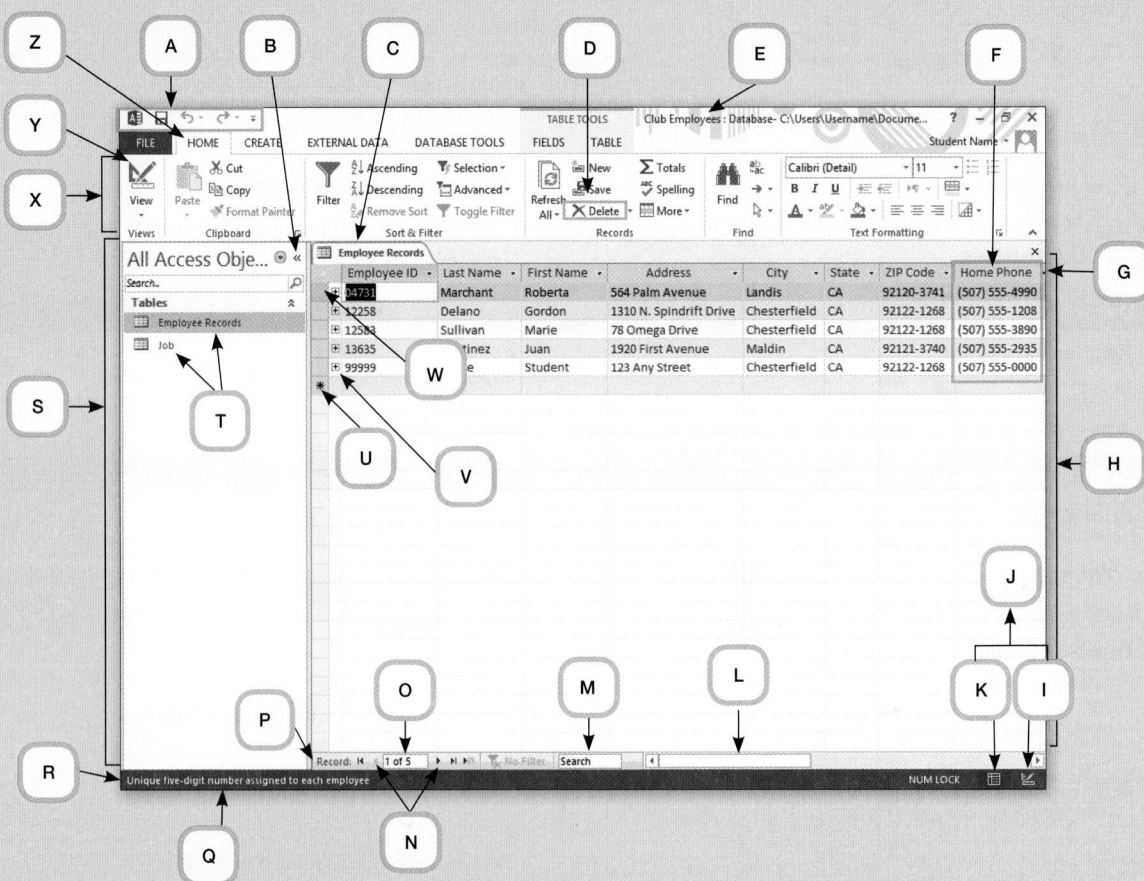

Possible answers for the screen identification are:

Current Record box
Database file name
Datasheet View button
Delete record
Design view
Field
Field description
Home tab
Navigation pane
New Record/End of
   Table marker
Objective
Open object tab
Primary key
Quick Access Toolbar

Record
Record navigation buttons
Record navigation bar
Ribbon
Scroll bar
Search
Record/Row selector
button
Status bar
Subdatasheet indicator
Table objects
Shutter bar to open/close
   Navigation pane
View buttons
Work area

A. _____
B. _____
C. _____
D. _____
E. _____
F. _____
G. _____
H. _____
I. _____
J. _____
K. _____
L. _____
M. _____

N. _____
O. _____
P. _____
Q. _____
R. _____
S. _____
T. _____
U. _____
V. _____
W. _____
X. _____
Y. _____
Z. _____

MATCHING

Match the numbered item with the correct lettered description.

1. Attachment
2. data type
3. Datasheet view
4. Design view

5. field size
6. Navigation pane
7. object
8. primary key

9. record
10. relational database

_____ a. contains multiple tables linked by a common field
_____ b. used to define the table structure
_____ c. used to open and manage database objects
_____ d. a data type that stores multiple files of different file types in a single field
_____ e. field that uniquely identifies each record
_____ f. displays table in row and column format
_____ g. defines the type of data the field will contain
_____ h. controls the maximum number of characters that can be entered in a field
_____ i. collection of related fields
_____ j. a unit of a database

TRUE/FALSE

Circle the correct answer to the following statements.

1. A field contains information about one person, thing, or place.	**True**	**False**
2. A field description is a required part of the field definition.	**True**	**False**
3. Caption text can be different from the field's name.	**True**	**False**
4. A table is a required object in a database.	**True**	**False**
5. A foreign key is a field in one table that refers to the primary key field in another table and indicates how the tables are related.	**True**	**False**
6. Changing the column width in the datasheet changes the field size.	**True**	**False**
7. Interactive databases define relationships between tables by having common data in the tables.	**True**	**False**
8. Tables and queries are two types of database objects.	**True**	**False**
9. You can format the text in a Long Text field.	**True**	**False**
10. The data type defines the information that can be entered in a field.	**True**	**False**

LAB EXERCISES

FILL-IN

Complete the following statements by filling in the blanks with the correct terms.

1. The _____ data type can be used to store a graphic file in a field.
2. You use the _____ located at the left of the work area to select the type of object you want to work with.
3. A(n) _____ is used to create a preformatted field or a set of several fields commonly used together.
4. An Access database is made up of several types of _____.
5. A(n) _____ is a data table nested in another data table that contains data that is related or joined to the table where it resides.
6. The field property that limits a Short Text data type to a certain size is called a(n) _____.
7. Using _____ orientation prints across the length of the paper.
8. The _____ data type restricts data to digits only.
9. A field name is used to identify the _____ stored in a field.
10. The _____ field property specifies how data displays in a table.

MULTIPLE CHOICE

Circle the letter of the correct response.

1. _____ view is only used to modify the table structure.
   a. Datasheet
   b. Design
   c. Query
   d. Report

2. The basic database objects are _____.
   a. forms, reports, data, and files
   b. panes, tables, queries, and reports
   c. portraits, keys, tables, and views
   d. tables, queries, forms, and reports

3. Graphics can be inserted into a field that has a(n) _____ data type.
   a. Attachment
   b. Graphic
   c. Long Text
   d. Short Text

4. Another way to create fields is to select from a list of predefined fields called _____.
   a. attachment fields
   b. data types
   c. field models
   d. value fields

5. A _____ is a field in one table that refers to the primary key field in another table and indicates how the tables are related.
   a. common key
   b. data key
   c. foreign key
   d. related key

6. _____ affects the amount of data that you can enter into a field.
   a. Column width
   b. Description size
   c. Field size
   d. Format

7. You may lose data if your data and _____ are incompatible.
   a. data type
   b. default value
   c. field name
   d. field size

8. A _____ is often used as the primary key.
   a. catalog number
   b. first name
   c. last name
   d. phone number

9. _____ is a design technique that identifies and eliminates redundancy by applying a set of rules to your tables.
   a. Database development
   b. Normalization
   c. Orientation
   d. Validation

10. The last step of database development is to _____.
    a. design
    b. develop
    c. review
    d. plan

STEP-BY-STEP

SAGE VIEW SCHOOL PARENT CONTACT DATABASE ★

1. Sage View Elementary School has decided to set up a database with the contact information for all students. As a parent, you have volunteered to do the initial database creation and teach the secretary at the school to maintain it. The database table you create will have the following information: student's last name, student's first name, guardian's name, home address, and home phone number. When you have finished, a printout of your completed database table should look similar to the one shown here.

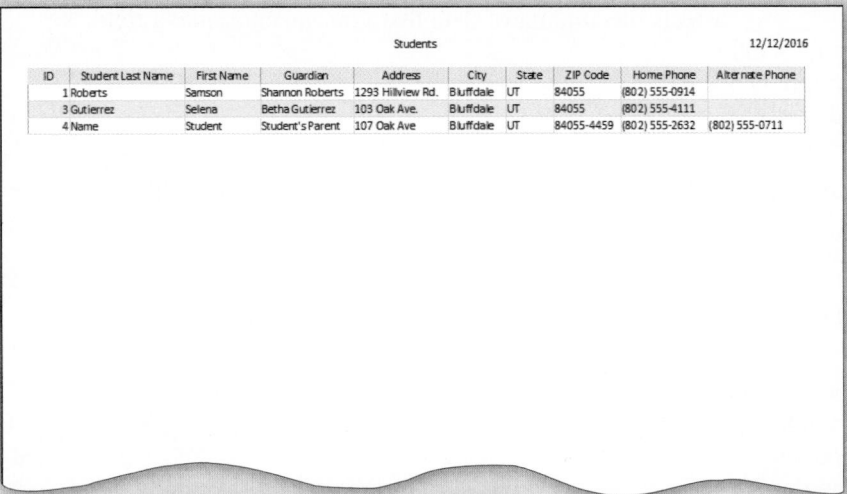

   a. Create a new blank desktop database named Sage View Elementary. Create a table in Datasheet view using the following field information. When creating the address fields, use the Quick Start Address field model to create the Address, City, State, and ZIP Code fields. Switch to Design view and save the table as **Students**. The ID field should be the primary key field. Delete the Country Region field generated from the Address field model and then modify the field names and properties to match those shown below.

Field Name	Data Type	Description	Field Size/Format
ID	AutoNumber		Long Integer
Student Last Name	Short Text	Student's legal last name	25
First Name	Short Text	Include student's nickname in parentheses	25
Guardian	Short Text	First and last names of primary guardian	55
Use the Quick Start Address field model to create these fields:			
Street Address	Short Text		75
City	Short Text		20
State	Short Text	Two-letter abbreviation	2
ZIP Code	Short Text		5
Home Phone	Short Text		15

b. In Datasheet view, enter the following records into the table, using copy and paste for fields that have the same data (such as the city):

	Record 1	Record 2	Record 3
Student Last Name	Roberts	Whitney	Gutierrez
First Name	Samson	Avette	Selena
Guardian	Shannon Roberts	Rita Whitney-Carter	Betha Gutierrez
Street Address	1293 Hillview Rd.	102 4th Street	103 Oak Ave.
City	Bluffdale	Bluffdale	Bluffdale
State	UT	UT	UT
ZIP Code	84055	84055	84055
Home Phone	(802) 555-0914	(802) 555-3375	(802) 555-4411

c. Adjust the column widths appropriately.

d. Delete record 2. Add another record with the following data:

[Your last name]

[Your first name]

[Your parent's name]

107 Oak Ave.

Bluffdale

UT

84055

(802) 555-2632

e. Add a new field after the Home Phone field with the following definitions:

Field Name: Alternate Phone

Data Type: Text

Field Size: 15

f. Change the ZIP Code field size to 10

g. Enter the Alternate Phone number of (802) 555-0711 and update the ZIP Code to 84055-4459 for the record with ID number 4

h. Best fit all columns.

i. Add the description Exercise 1 in Access Lab 1 to the table properties. In the database properties, add your name as the author and Sage View Elementary School as the title.

LAB EXERCISES

j. View the table in Print Preview; change the page orientation to landscape and margins to Normal. If the table does not all fit on one page then you may need to further adjust the column widths.

k. Print, save, and close the table.

REAL ESTATE RENTALS DATABASE ★★

2. You manage a real estate rental business and decide to implement a database to track the rental properties. A database will be useful to look up any information about the rental, including its location, how many bedrooms and bathrooms, the square feet of living space, and date available. This will help you find rentals within the desired home size and price range of your clients. When you are finished, your printed database table should be similar to the one shown here.

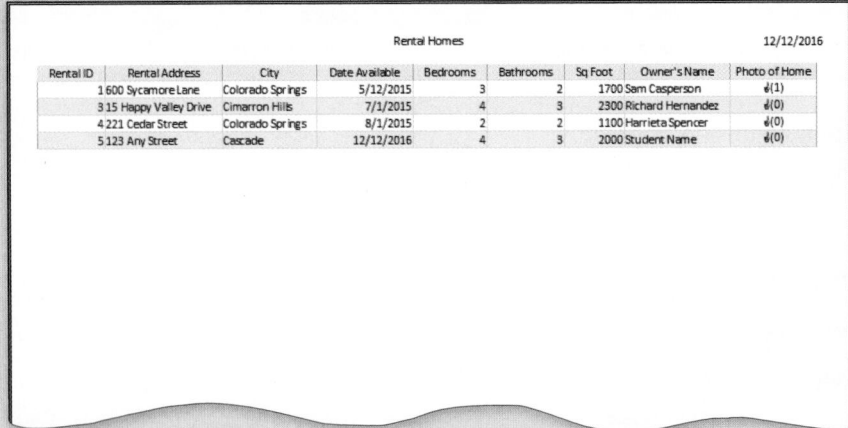

Rental ID	Rental Address	City	Date Available	Bedrooms	Bathrooms	Sq Foot	Owner's Name	Photo of Home
1	600 Sycamore Lane	Colorado Springs	5/12/2015	3	2	1700	Sam Casperson	(1)
3	15 Happy Valley Drive	Cimarron Hills	7/1/2015	4	3	2300	Richard Hernandez	(0)
4	221 Cedar Street	Colorado Springs	8/1/2015	2	2	1100	Harrieta Spencer	(0)
5	123 Any Street	Cascade	12/12/2016	4	3	2000	Student Name	(0)

Rental Homes — 12/12/2016

a. Create a new blank desktop database named Rocky Mountain Rentals

b. Add the following fields to the new table using the data types shown:

Field Name	Data Type
Rental Address	Short Text
City	Short Text
Date Available	Date
Bedrooms	Number
Bathrooms	Number
Sq Foot	Number
Owner's Name	Short Text

c. Switch to Design view. Save the table as **Rental Homes**

d. Change the ID field name to **Rental ID**

e. Add an Attachment field and name it **Photo of Home**. Use this name for the Caption property as well.

f. Change the field size of the Address and Owner's Name fields to **40**

g. Change the field size of the City field to **20**

h. Set the Date Available data type to Date, Short format.

i. Make sure the data type for Bedrooms, Bathrooms, and Sq Foot is Number.

j. Return to Datasheet view. Add the following records to the table:

Address	600 Sycamore Lane	8509 Eagle View Circle	15 Happy Valley Drive	221 Cedar Street
City	Colorado Springs	Cascade	Cimarron Hills	Colorado Springs
Date Available	5/12/2015	6/1/2015	7/1/2015	8/1/2015
Bedrooms	3	2	4	2
Bathrooms	2	1	3	2
Sq Foot	1700	840	2300	1100
Owner's Name	Sam Casperson	Betty Rosettas	Richard Hernandez	Harrieta Spencer

k. Insert the image file ac01_600_SycamoreLane in the Attachment field of the first record.

l. Adjust the column widths using the Best Fit feature.

m. Delete the record for the address 8509 Eagle View Circle. Add a new record with fictional information, City of Cascade, your name in the Owner's Name field, and the current date in the Date Available field.

n. In the database properties, add **your name** as the author and **Rocky Mountain Real Estate Rentals** as the title. Add the description **Exercise 2 in Access Lab 1** to the table properties.

o. Preview and print the table in landscape orientation with normal margins. If the table does not fit on one page, then you may need to further adjust the column widths in the table.

p. Save and close the table. Exit Access.

LAB EXERCISES

CAR CLUB MEMBERSHIP DATABASE ★★

3. You are a member of the local car club. Even though the club was founded only last year, the membership has grown considerably. Because of your computer skills, you have been asked to create a database with the membership number, membership date, first name, last name, address, city, state, zip, phone number, car year, and car model. This will help the club president contact members about events, the treasurer to mail out dues notices, and the events coordinator to mail out newsletters. Your printed database tables should be similar to those shown here.

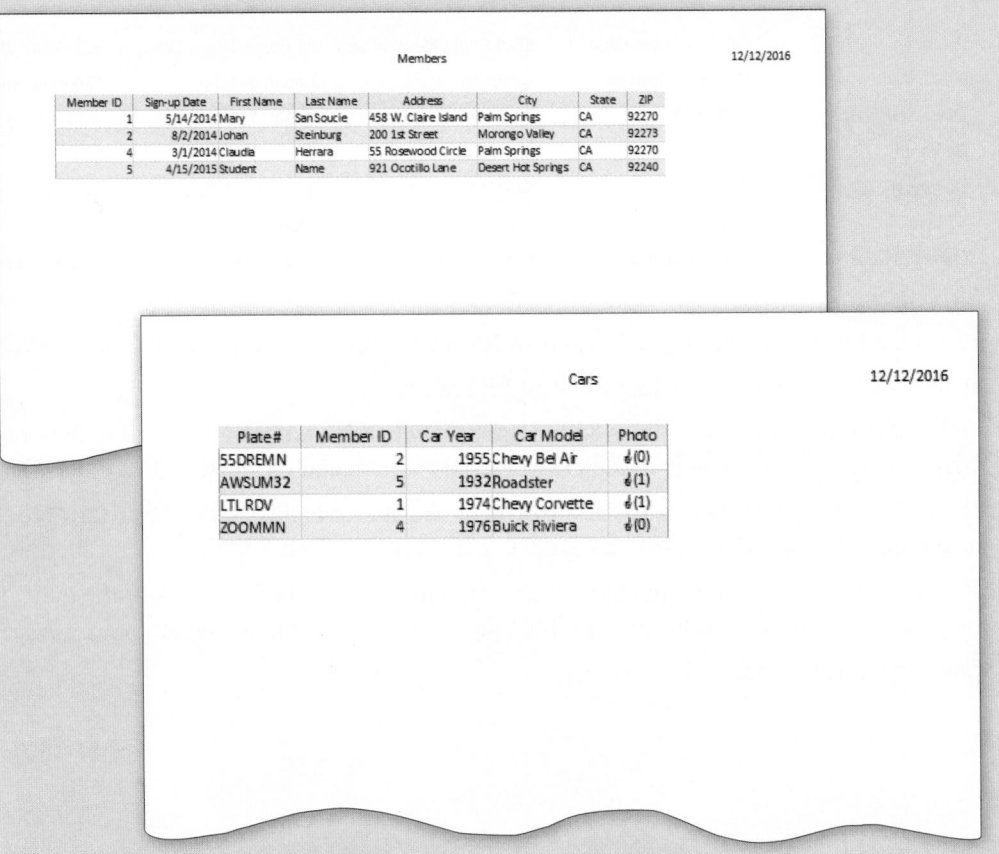

a. Create a new blank desktop database named Desert Heat Car Club

b. Add the following fields to the new table with the data types as shown:

Field Name	Data Type
Sign-up Date	Date
Member Name	Short Text

Address (use the Address field model)

c. Switch to Design view. Save the table as **Members**

d. Edit the field properties using the following information:

Field Name	Data Type	Description	Field Size/Format
Change ID to Member #	AutoNumber		
Sign-up Date	Date/Time	Date member joined club	Short Date
Change Member Name to First Name	Short Text	Member's first name	25
Address	Short Text	Mailing address	50
Change State Province to State	Short Text	Two-letter state abbreviation	2
Change ZIP Postal to ZIP	Short Text	ZIP code, ex: 99999 or 99999-1234	10

e. Insert a row above the Address field and add the following field there:

Field Name	Data Type	Description	Field Size
Last Name	Short Text	Member's last name	25

f. Delete the Country Region field that was created as part of the Address field model.

g. Switch to Datasheet view and enter the following records into the table:

	Record 1	Record 2	Record 3	Record 4
Membership date	5/14/2014	8/2/2014	12/20/2014	3/1/2014
First Name	Mary	Johan	Frank	Claudia
Last Name	San Soucie	Steinburg	Blaney	Herrera
Address	458 W. Claire Island	200 1st Street	890 Lakeside Dr.	55 Rosewood Circle
City	Palm Springs	Morongo Valley	Indio	Palm Springs
State	CA	CA	CA	CA
ZIP	92270	92273	92275	92270

h. Best fit all column widths.

i. Create a second table named **Member's Cars** with the following fields:

Field Name	Data Type	Description	Field Size
Plate #	Short Text	Enter plate # of car	7
Member #	Number	Member's ID #	Long Integer
Car Year	Number	Car's year of manufacture	Integer
Car Model	Short Text	Car's make and model (e.g., Ford Mustang)	50
Vehicle Photo	Attachment	Photo of car in Classics Car show	

j. Change the Caption property for the Vehicle Photo to read **Photo**

Since you need a way to link the two tables together, you will obtain the member information from the Members table and paste it into the Cars table.

k. Switch to Datasheet view. Make the Members table active. Copy the Member # column.

l. Make the Cars table active. Right-click the Member # field name and choose Paste to complete the copy process, bringing the Member # information into the Cars table.

LAB EXERCISES

m. Enter the following records into the Cars table:

Member ID	1	2	3	4
Plate #	LTL RDV	55DREMN	30STYLN	ZOOMMN
Car Year	1974	1955	1930	1970
Car Model	Chevy Corvette	Chevy Bel Air	Studebaker	1976 Buick Riviera
Photo	ac01_1974Corvette			

n. Best fit all column widths.

o. Make the Plate # the primary key field.

p. Close the tables, saving your changes. Establish the relationship between the Members table and the Cars table (*hint*: one member can have many cars). Enforce referential integrity and check the Cascade delete and update options. Close and save the relationship.

q. Open the Members table. Delete the record for Member 3. Add a new record with the following data:

Membership Date:	**4/15/2015**
First Name:	**Your first name**
Last Name:	**Your last name**
Address:	**921 Ocotillo Lane**
City:	**Desert Hot Springs**
State:	**CA**
Zip:	**92240**

r. Open the Cars table and add your car information as a new record. (Your Member # should be 5.)

Plate #:	**AWSUM32**
Car Year:	**your favorite car year** or use **1932**
Car Model:	**your favorite car model** or use **Roadster**
Photo:	attach photo of your car or use ac01_1932Roadster

s. Check the tables in Print Preview. Print the Members table in portrait orientation with normal margins; print the Cars table with wide margins. Save and close both tables. Exit Access.

DOWNTOWN INTERNET CAFÉ INVENTORY DATABASE ★★★

4. The Downtown Internet Café, which you helped get off the ground, is an overwhelming success. The clientele is growing every day, as is the demand for the beverages the café serves. Up until now, the information about the vendors has been kept in an alphabetical card file. This has become quite unwieldy, however, and Evan, the owner, would like a more sophisticated tracking system. He would like you to create a database containing each supply item and the contact information for the vendor that sells that item. When you are finished, your database tables should be similar to those shown here.

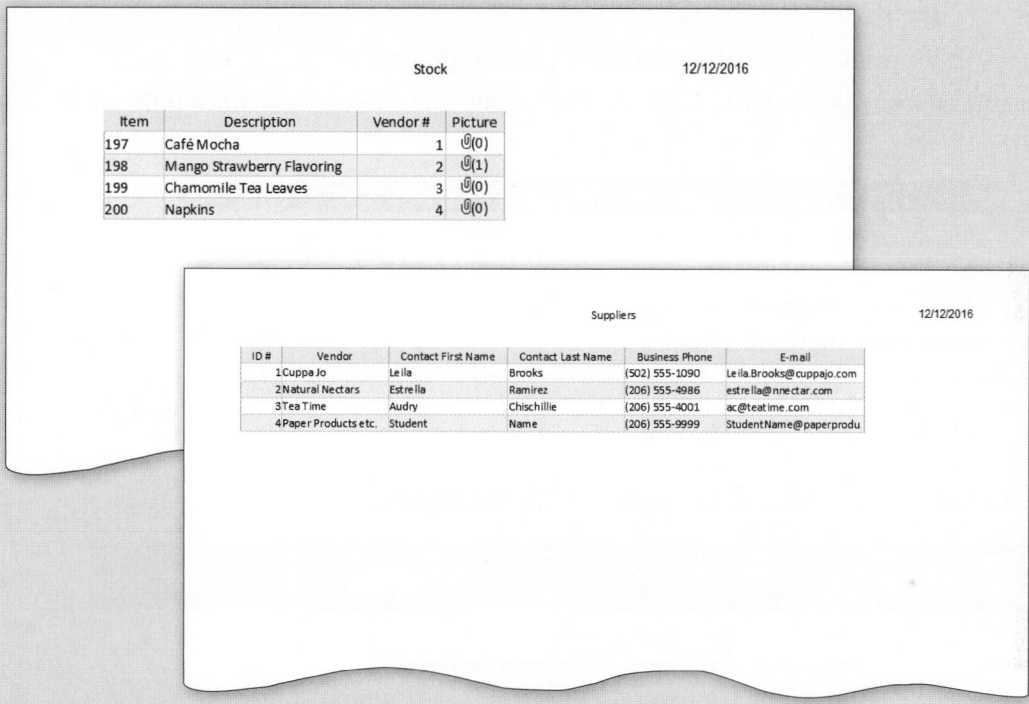

a. Create a new blank desktop database named Cafe Inventory

b. Using the Quick Add menu, choose Short Text as the data type and add fields named **Item** and **Description** to the new table.

c. Switch to Design view. Save the table as **Stock**

d. Delete the ID field. Make Item the primary key field.

e. Add the the information below to the field properties. When finished, switch back to datasheet view, saving your changes.

Field Name	Data Type	Description	Field Size
Item	Short Text	Unique three-digit product number	3
Description	Short Text	Name of product	50
Vendor #	Number	ID # of company that supplies product	Long Integer

LAB EXERCISES

f. Using the Table Design button, create a second table. Enter the following field names, each with the data type of Short Text:

ID #

Company

First Name

Last Name

Business Phone

E-mail Address

g. Make the ID the primary key field. Save the table as **Suppliers**

h. Edit the field properties as shown here, and then switch to datasheet view when finished, saving your changes.

Field Name	Data Type	Description	Field Size
ID #	Autonumber		
Change Company to Vendor	Short Text	Company name of supplier	50
Change First Name to Contact First Name	Short Text		50
Change Last Name to Contact Last Name	Short Text		50
Business Phone	Short Text	Include the area code in parentheses: (800) 555-5555	15
Change E-mail Address to E-mail	Short Text	E-mail address of contact person	50

i. Enter the following records into the Stock and Suppliers tables:

Stock table		
Record 1	**Record 2**	**Record 3**
197	198	199
Café Mocha	Mango Strawberry Flavoring	Chamomile Tea Leaves

Suppliers table			
Record 1	**Record 2**	**Record 3**	**Record 4**
Cuppa Jo	Natural Nectars	Tea Time	Paper Products etc.
Leila	Estrella	Audry	Enter your first name
Brooks	Ramirez	Chischillie	Enter your last name
(502) 555-1090	(206) 555-4986	(206) 555-4001	(206) 555-9999
lbrooks@cuppajo.com	estrella@nnectar.com	ac@teatime.com	Yourname@paperproducts.com

j. In the Stock table, type the ID # that represents Cuppa Jo as the vendor for the first record, Natural Nectars for the second record, and Tea Time for the third record.

k. In the Suppliers table, edit the record for ID 1 by changing the e-mail address to **Leila.Brooks@ cuppajo.com**

l. Add a new attachment data type field to the Stock table. Assign the new field the name and caption of **Picture**. For the attachment field of item number 198 insert the file ac01_Flavoring.

m. Add the following new item to the Stock file.

Item:	200
Description:	Napkins
Vendor:	Paper Products etc.

n. Adjust the column widths in both tables using Best Fit.

o. Create a relationship connecting the Suppliers table ID # field to the Stock table Vendor # field. Enforce referential integrity, and the cascade update and delete options.

p. Preview the Suppliers table. Change to landscape orientation. Change the margins to wide and print the table.

q. Preview the Stock table. Change to portrait orientation. Print the table.

r. Close the database. Exit Access.

LIFESTYLE FITNESS CLUB MEMBERSHIP DATABASE ★★★

5. Lifestyle Fitness Club would like you to create a database to track its members and membership packages. You will create a table for each and add a few records to test the functionality of the database before presenting it to the club owners for their approval. When you are finished, your tables should be similar to those shown here.

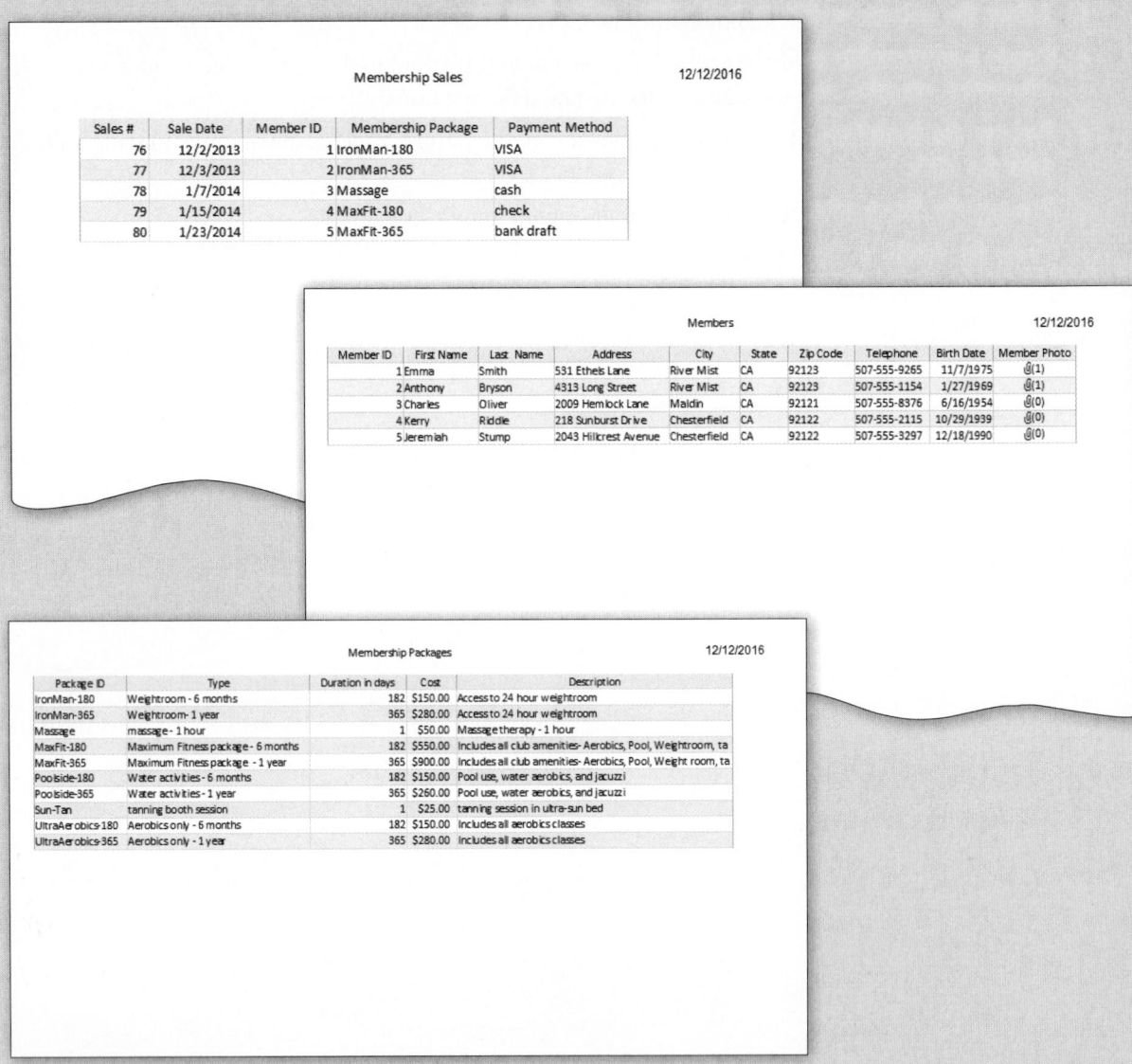

Membership Sales   12/12/2016

Sales #	Sale Date	Member ID	Membership Package	Payment Method
76	12/2/2013	1	IronMan-180	VISA
77	12/3/2013	2	IronMan-365	VISA
78	1/7/2014	3	Massage	cash
79	1/15/2014	4	MaxFit-180	check
80	1/23/2014	5	MaxFit-365	bank draft

Members   12/12/2016

Member ID	First Name	Last Name	Address	City	State	Zip Code	Telephone	Birth Date	Member Photo
1	Emma	Smith	531 Ethels Lane	River Mist	CA	92123	507-555-9265	11/7/1975	(1)
2	Anthony	Bryson	4313 Long Street	River Mist	CA	92123	507-555-1154	1/27/1969	(1)
3	Charles	Oliver	2009 Hemlock Lane	Maldin	CA	92121	507-555-8376	6/16/1954	(0)
4	Kerry	Riddle	218 Sunburst Drive	Chesterfield	CA	92122	507-555-2115	10/29/1939	(0)
5	Jeremiah	Stump	2043 Hillcrest Avenue	Chesterfield	CA	92122	507-555-3297	12/18/1990	(0)

Membership Packages   12/12/2016

Package ID	Type	Duration in days	Cost	Description
IronMan-180	Weightroom - 6 months	182	$150.00	Access to 24 hour weightroom
IronMan-365	Weightroom- 1 year	365	$280.00	Access to 24 hour weightroom
Massage	massage- 1 hour	1	$50.00	Massage therapy - 1 hour
MaxFit-180	Maximum Fitness package - 6 months	182	$550.00	Includes all club amenities- Aerobics, Pool, Weightroom, ta
MaxFit-365	Maximum Fitness package - 1 year	365	$900.00	Includes all club amenities- Aerobics, Pool, Weight room, ta
Poolside-180	Water activities - 6 months	182	$150.00	Pool use, water aerobics, and jacuzzi
Poolside-365	Water activities - 1 year	365	$260.00	Pool use, water aerobics, and jacuzzi
Sun-Tan	tanning booth session	1	$25.00	tanning session in ultra-sun bed
UltraAerobics-180	Aerobics only - 6 months	182	$150.00	Includes all aerobics classes
UltraAerobics-365	Aerobics only - 1 year	365	$280.00	Includes all aerobics classes

a. Create a blank desktop database named Lifestyle Fitness Memberships

b. Add the following fields, selecting Short Text as the data type for each one (*hint*: use the Address model to quickly add the Address, City, State, and Zip fields):

> **First Name**
>
> **Last Name**
>
> **Address**
>
> **City**
>
> **State**
>
> **Zip**
>
> **Telephone**

c. Save the table as **Members** and switch to Design view.

d. Change the ID field name to **Member ID**, and change its data type to Number.

e. Delete the Country Region field created when you used the Address model to create the address fields.

f. Add field descriptions and make changes to the field properties as shown in the following table:

Field Name	Description	Field Size
First Name	First name of member	25
Last Name	Last name of member	25
Address	Mailing address	50
City	Member's city	50
State	Use two-digit abbreviation	2
ZIP Code	Enter 10-digit code, if available	10
Telephone	Enter phone as ###-###-####	12

g. Switch to Datasheet view, saving the changes you made to the Members table.

h. Add a new field named **Birth Date** to the end of the table. Set the format to Short Date.

i. Switch to Design view and add a new field named **Member Photo** with an Attachment data type as the last field in the table. Include the description **Attach member photo**

j. Switch to Datasheet view and change the caption for the Attachment field to **Member Photo**

k. Enter the following five records for the Members table.

Member ID	1	2	3	4	5
First Name	Emma	Anthony	Charles	Kerry	Jeremiah
Last Name	Smith	Bryson	Oliver	Riddle	Stump
Address	531 Ethels Lane	4313 Long Street	2009 Hemlock Lane	218 Sunburst Drive	2043 Hillcrest Avenue
City	River Mist	River Mist	Maldin	Chesterfield	Chesterfield
State	CA	CA	CA	CA	CA
ZIP Code	92123	92123	92121	92122	92122
Telephone	507-555-9265	507-555-1154	507-555-8376	507-555-2115	507-555-3297
Birth Date	11/7/1975	1/27/1969	6/16/1954	10/29/1939	12/18/1990
Member Photo	Attach ac01_Emma	Attach ac01_Anthony			

l. Create a second table in Design view named **Membership Packages**, using the following field names, data types, descriptions, and field sizes:

Field Name	Data Type	Description	Field Size
Package ID	Short Text	Club's assigned package ID	20
Type	Short Text	Membership category and length of subscription	100
Duration in days	Number	Length of membership in days	
Cost	Currency	Price of membership	
Description	Long Text	Detailed description of membership amenities	

m. Switch to Datasheet view and add the following membership package information:

Package ID	Type	Duration in Days	Cost	Description
IronMan-180	Weight room - 6 months	182	$150	Access to 24-hour weight room
IronMan-365	Weight room - 1 year	365	$280	Access to 24-hour weight room
Massage	massage - 1 hour	1	$50	Massage therapy - 1 hour
MaxFit-180	Maximum fitness package - 6 months	182	$550	Includes all club amenities - aerobics, pool, weight room, tanning, and massage
MaxFit-365	Maximum fitness package - 1 year	365	$900	Includes all club amenities - aerobics, pool, weight room, tanning, and massage
Poolside-180	Water activities - 6 months	182	$150	Pool use, water aerobics, and jacuzzi
Poolside-365	Water activities - 1 year	365	$260	Pool use, water aerobics, and jacuzzi
Sun-Tan	Tanning booth session	1	$25	Tanning session in ultra-sun bed
UltraAerobics-180	Aerobics only - 6 months	182	$150	Includes all aerobics classes
UltraAerobics-365	Aerobics only - 1 year	365	$280	Includes all aerobics classes

n. Create a third table named **Membership Sales** using the field information shown below.

Field Name	Data Type	Description	Field Size	Format
Sales #	Number	Automatically assigned number		
Sale Date	Date/Time	Enter date membership was purchased		Short Date
Member ID	Number	Enter the Member's ID #		
Package ID	Short Text	Enter the Package ID name	20	
Payment Method	Short Text	Use payment method of VISA, check, cash, or bank draft	15	

o. In Datasheet view, enter the following information in the Membership Sales table:

Sales #	Sale Date	Member ID	Package ID	Payment Method
76	12/2/2013	1	IronMan-180	VISA
77	12/3/2013	2	IronMan-365	VISA
78	1/7/2014	3	Massage	Cash
79	1/15/2014	4	MaxFit-180	Check
80	1/23/2014	5	MaxFit-365	Bank draft

p. Establish relationship between the tables: Create a relationship between the Member ID of the Membership table and the Member ID of the Membership Sales table. Create another relationship between the Package ID of the Membership Packages table and the Package ID of the Membership Sales table. Enforce referential integrity.

q. Best fit all fields in all tables.

r. Preview and print the Members table and the Membership Packages table in landscape orientation with normal margins.

s. Print the Membership Sales table in portrait orientation with wide margins.

t. Save and close all tables and exit Access.

LAB EXERCISES

ON YOUR OWN

MUSIC COLLECTION DATABASE ★

1. You have just purchased a 200-disc CD carousel, and now you would like to organize and catalog your CDs. You realize that without an updatable list, it will be difficult to maintain an accurate list of what is in the changer. To get the most out of your new purchase, you decide a database is in order. Create a new database called Music Collection and a table called **CD Catalogue**. The table you create should include Artist's Name, Album Title, Genre, and Position Number fields. Make the Position Number field the primary key (because you may have multiple CDs by a given artist). Enter at least 15 records. Include an entry that has your name as the artist. Preview and print the table when you are finished.

VISTA HEIGHTS NEWSLETTER ADVERTISING DATABASE ★

2. Your homeowner's association distributes a monthly newsletter, *Vista Heights News,* to keep residents up to date with neighborhood news. In the past year, there has been rapid growth in building, including more houses and small office complexes. There are also plans to build an elementary school, fire station, and shopping center in the community. Consequently, the newsletter is now the size of a small newspaper, and the homeowners' dues are not covering the expense of publishing it.

    The editorial staff has already begun selling ad space in the newsletter to local businesses, and, based on your background in database management, they have asked you to set up a database to keep track of the advertiser contact information. You agree to design such a database, called Vista Heights News, and tell them you will have something to show them at the next meeting. Your finished database should include each advertiser's billing number, business name and address, and contact name and phone number in a table named **Advertisers**. Enter 10 records and include a record that has your name as the contact name. Preview and print the table when you are finished.

PATIENT DATABASE ★

3. You are the manager of a newly opened dental office. As one of your first projects, you need to create a patient database. Create a database called Dental Patients and a table named **Patient Information**. The database table you set up should contain patient identification numbers, last and first names, addresses, and phone numbers. Also include a field named "Referred by" and another field named "Patient since." Use appropriate field sizes and make the ID number field the primary key. Enter at least 10 records, adjusting the column widths as necessary. Include a record that contains your name as the patient. Preview and print the table.

OLD WATCH DATABASE USING THE WEB ★★

4. You have a small online business, Timeless Treasures, that locates and sells vintage wrist and pocket watches. Your business and inventory have grown large enough now that you have decided to use a database to track your inventory. Create a simple database named Timeless Treasures with a table named Watches that contains identification numbers, manufacturer (Waltham, Hamilton, Melrose), category (pocket watch, wrist watch), description, price, and quantity on hand. Size the fields appropriately and assign a primary key to one of them. Enter at least 10 records in the table. To obtain data about watches to include in your table, do a web search on "old watches." Use the information you locate to complete the data for the records in your table. Adjust column widths as necessary. Include your name as the manufacturer in one of the records. Preview and print the table.

EXPENSE TRACKING DATABASE ★★★

5. You work in the accounting department at a start-up company called AMP Enterprises. One of your duties is to reimburse employees for small, company-related expenses, which up until now has been a simple task of having the employees fill out a form that they submit to you for payment. You then cut checks for them that are charged to the general expense fund of the company. However, the company has grown tremendously in the last year, adding employees and departments at a rapid rate, and the executive team has decided that it is time to start managing the income and expenses on a much more detailed level. To this end, you need to create a database that includes the employee ID, employee name, submission date, expense type, and expense amount for each expense report that is turned in. Name the database AMP Enterprises. Create two tables, one for the employee information named Employee Info and the other for employee expenses named Employee Expenses. Include the Employee ID, First Name, and Last Name fields in the Employee Info table. Include the Employee ID, Submission Date, Expense Type, and Expense Amount fields in the Employee Expenses table. Use the Currency data type for the Expense Amount field, and appropriate data types for all other fields. Size the fields appropriately. Delete the ID field from the Employee Info table and make the Employee ID field the primary key. Enter at least 15 records. Adjust the column widths as necessary. Delete one of the records you just entered, and then edit one of the remaining records so it contains your name as the employee. Enter 10 records in the Employee Expenses table (one should be an expense record for the record containing your name). Preview and print both tables.

Modifying and Filtering a Table and Creating a Form

Objectives

After completing this lab, you will know how to:

1. Change field format properties.

2. Set default field values.

3. Define validation rules.

4. Hide and redisplay fields.

5. Create a lookup field.

6. Search, find, and replace data.

7. Sort records.

8. Format a datasheet.

9. Filter a table.

10. Create and use a form.

11. Modify the layout of a form.

12. Add a record using a form.

13. Organize the Navigation pane.

14. Preview, print, close, and save a form.

15. Identify object dependencies.

CASE STUDY

Lifestyle Fitness Club

Lifestyle Fitness Club owners, Ryan and Felicity, are very pleased with your plans for the organization of the database and with your progress in creating the two tables containing the employees' personal and job information. They did point out, however, that you forgot to include a field for the employee's gender. As you have seen, creating a database takes planning and a great deal of time to set up the structure and enter the data. Even with the best of planning and care, errors occur and the information may change. You will see how easy it is to modify the database structure and to customize field properties

to provide more control over the data that is entered in a field.

Even more impressive, as you will see in this lab, is the program's ability to locate information in the database. This is where all the hard work of entering data pays off. With a click of a button, you can find data that might otherwise take hours to locate. The result saves time and improves the accuracy of the output.

You also will see how you can make the data you are looking at onscreen more pleasing and easier to read by creating and using a form.

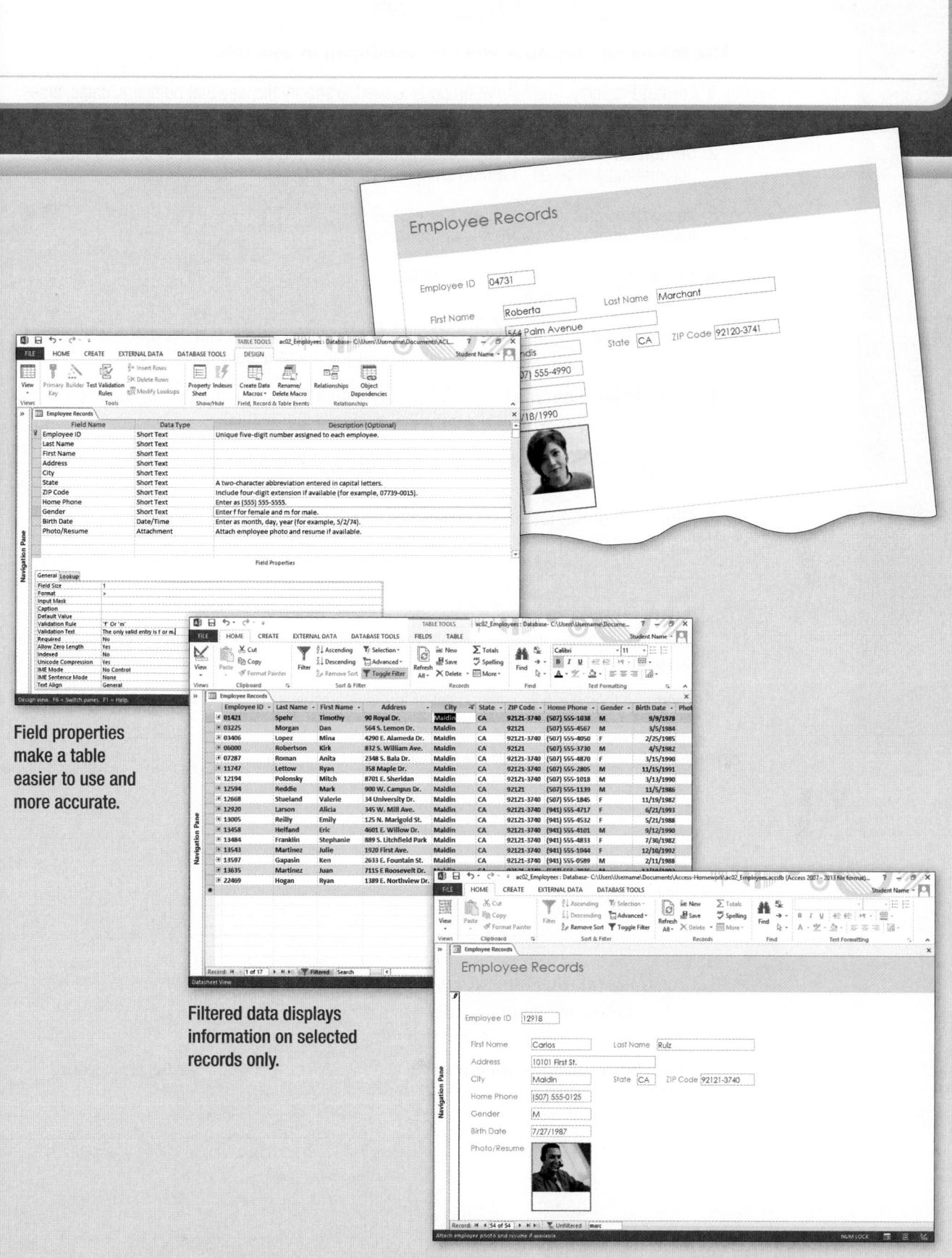

Field properties make a table easier to use and more accurate.

Filtered data displays information on selected records only.

Forms can be used to display information in an easy-to-read manner and make data entry easier.

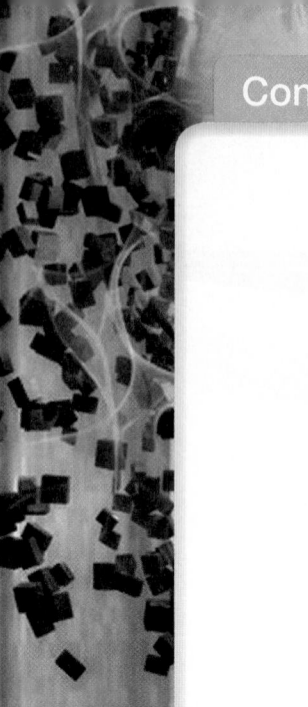

The following concepts will be introduced in this lab:

1 **Format Property** The Format property is used to specify the way that numbers, dates, times, and text in a field are displayed and printed.

2 **Default Value Property** The Default Value property is used to specify a value that is automatically entered in a field when a new record is created.

3 **Validation Rule** Validation rules are used to control the data that can be entered in a field by defining the input values that are valid or allowed.

4 **Expression** An expression is a formula consisting of a combination of symbols that will produce a single value.

5 **Lookup Field** A lookup field provides a list of values from which the user can choose to make entering data into that field simpler and more accurate.

6 **Find and Replace** The Find and Replace feature helps you quickly find specific information and automatically replace it with new information.

7 **Sorting** Sorting rearranges the order of the records in a table based on the value in each field.

8 **Filter** A filter is a restriction placed on records in the open table or form to quickly isolate and display a subset of records.

9 **Form** A form is a database object used primarily to display records onscreen to make it easier to enter new records and to make changes to existing records.

10 **Controls** Controls are objects that display information, perform actions, or enhance the design of a form or report.

11 **Theme** A theme is a predefined set of formatting choices that can be applied to all the objects in a database in one simple step.

Customizing Fields

After the Lifestyle Fitness Club owners approved the design of the database, you continued to add more records to the employee tables. You will open the expanded database to continue working on and refining the Employee Records table.

NOTE Before you begin, you may want to create a backup copy of the ac02_Employees **file by copying and renaming it.**

1

- **Start Microsoft Access 2013.**

- **Open the database file ac02_Employees.**

- **If necessary, click** **in the Security Warning bar below the Ribbon.**

- **Open the Employee Records table.**

Your screen should be similar to Figure 2.1

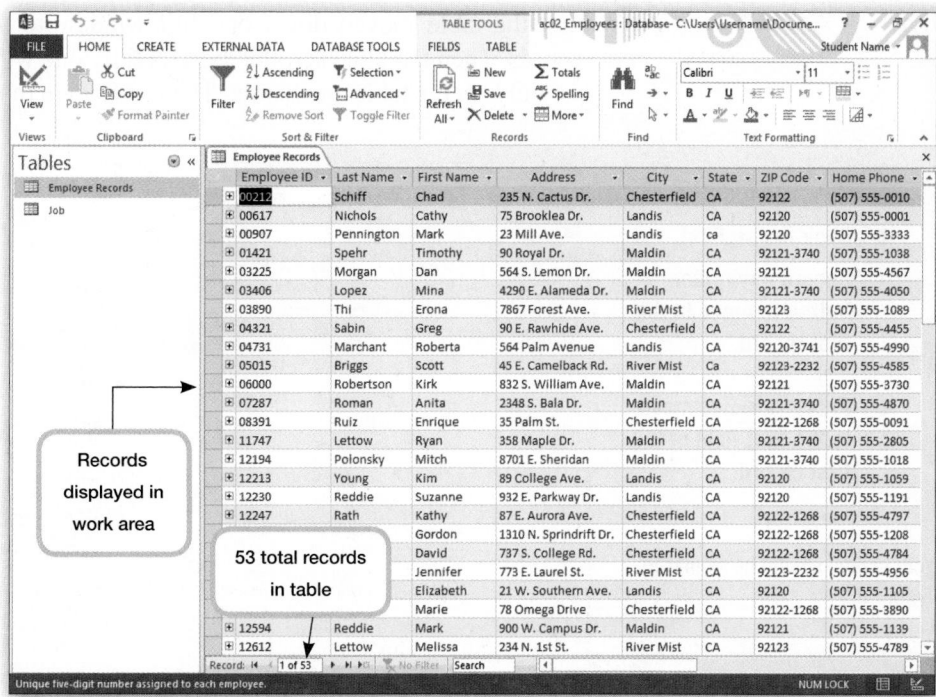

Figure 2.1

Having Trouble?

Your screen may display more or fewer records, depending upon your monitor settings.

As you can see from the record number indicator, the updated table now contains 53 records. To see the rest of the records, you will move about the table using the keyboard and the record navigation buttons.

2

- **Press Page Down to look at the next page of records.**

- **Press Ctrl + End to move to the last field of the last record.**

Your screen should be similar to Figure 2.2

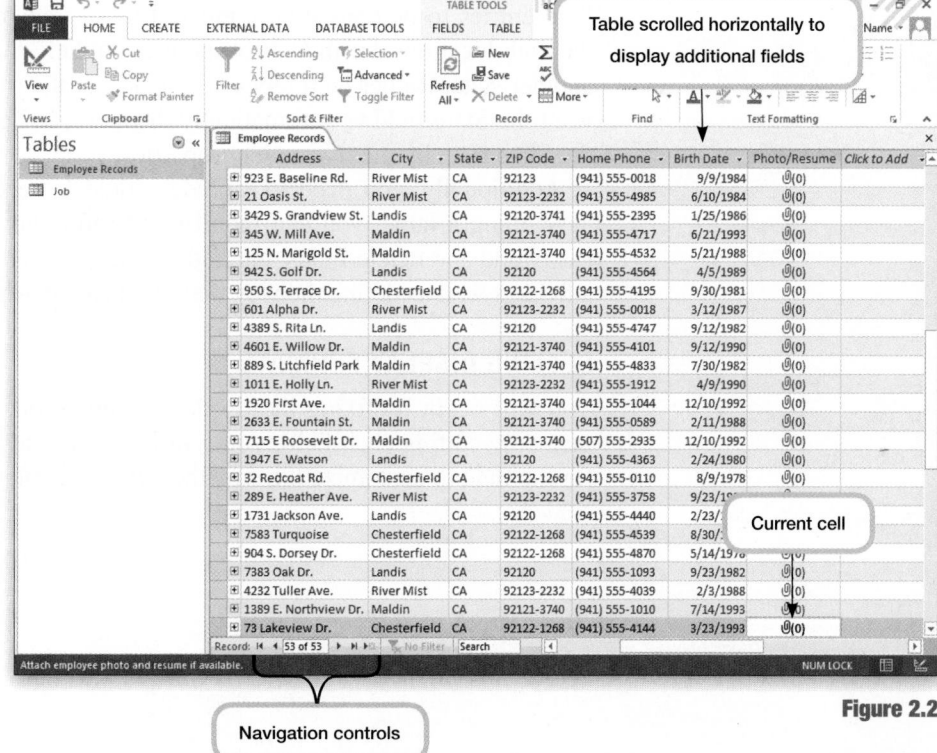

Figure 2.2

First the table moved down one full window to display a second page full of records. Then the table scrolled horizontally one window to the right, and now the last fields in the table are visible. The last field in the last record is currently active.

3

- Click the ◄ First Record navigation button to move to the first record.

- Press [Home] to move to the first field of the first record.

Your screen should be similar to Figure 2.3

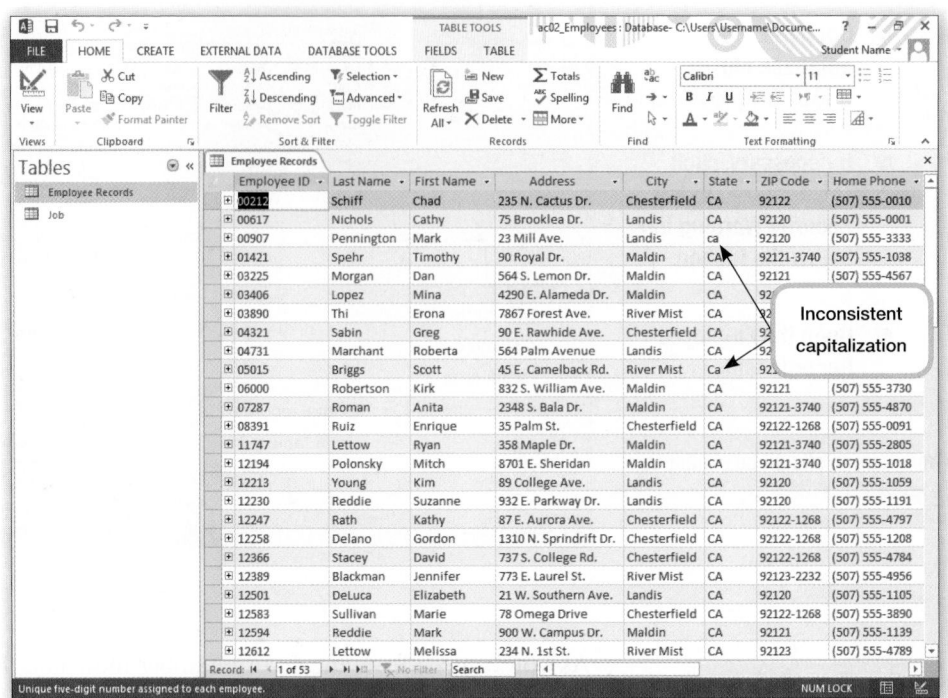

Figure 2.3

As you look through the records, you notice that record 3 has a lowercase entry in the State field and that record 10 has a mixed-case entry. You want all the State field entries to be consistently entered in all uppercase letters. Also, because all the club locations are in California, it is unlikely that any club employees live in another state. Rather than repeatedly entering the same state for each record, you want the State field to automatically display CA. You will make these changes to the State field by modifying its properties.

Additionally, you need to include a field for each employee's gender. While developing a table, you can modify and refine how the table operates. You can easily add and delete fields and add restrictions on the data that can be entered in a field as well as define the way that the data entered in a field will be displayed.

SETTING DISPLAY FORMATS

You will begin by fixing the display of the entries in the State field. Instead of manually editing each field, you will fix the entries by defining a display format for the field to customize the way the entry is displayed.

Concept 1 Format Property

The **Format property** is used to specify the way that numbers, dates, times, and text in a field are displayed and printed. Format properties do not change the way Access stores data, only the way the data is displayed. To change the **format** of a field, you can select from predefined formats or create a custom format by entering different symbols in the Format text box. For example, four common format symbols used in Short Text and Long Text data types are shown in the following table.

Symbol	Meaning	Example
@	Requires a text character or space	@@@-@@-@@@@ would display 123456789 as 123-45-6789. Nine characters or spaces are required. If the entry has fewer than nine characters, the text is left-aligned with the missing characters as leading blank spaces. For example 1234567 would display as 1-23-4567.
>	Forces all characters to uppercase	> would display SMITH whether you entered SMITH, smith, or Smith.
<	Forces all characters to lowercase	< would display smith whether you entered SMITH, smith, or Smith.
&	Allows an optional text character	@@-@@& would display 12345 as 123-45 and 1234 as 12-34. Four out of five characters are required, and a fifth is optional. Any missing characters appear as leading blank spaces.

You want to change the format of the State field to display the entries in all uppercase characters.

1

- Click 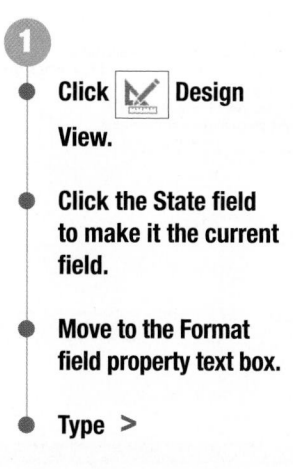 **Design View.**

- Click the **State field** to make it the current field.

- Move to the **Format** field property text box.

- Type **>**

Your screen should be similar to
Figure 2.4

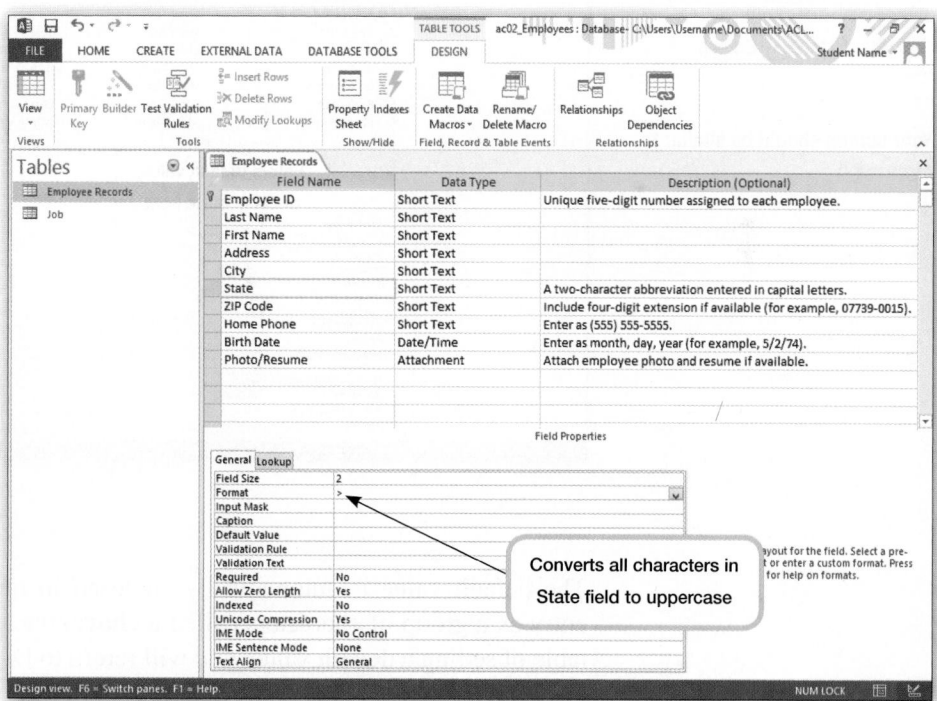

Converts all characters in State field to uppercase

Figure 2.4

SETTING DEFAULT VALUES

Next, you want to change the State field for new records to automatically display CA. To do this, you specify a Default Value property.

Concept **2** **Default Value Property**

The **Default Value property** is used to specify a value that is automatically entered in a field when a new record is created. This property is commonly used when most of the entries in a field will be the same for the entire table. That default value is then displayed automatically in the field. When users add a record to the table, they can either accept this value or enter another value. This saves time while entering data.

You will set the State field's default value to display CA.

- Click in the Default Value property text box.

- Type **CA**

- Press ⏎Enter.

Your screen should be similar to Figure 2.5

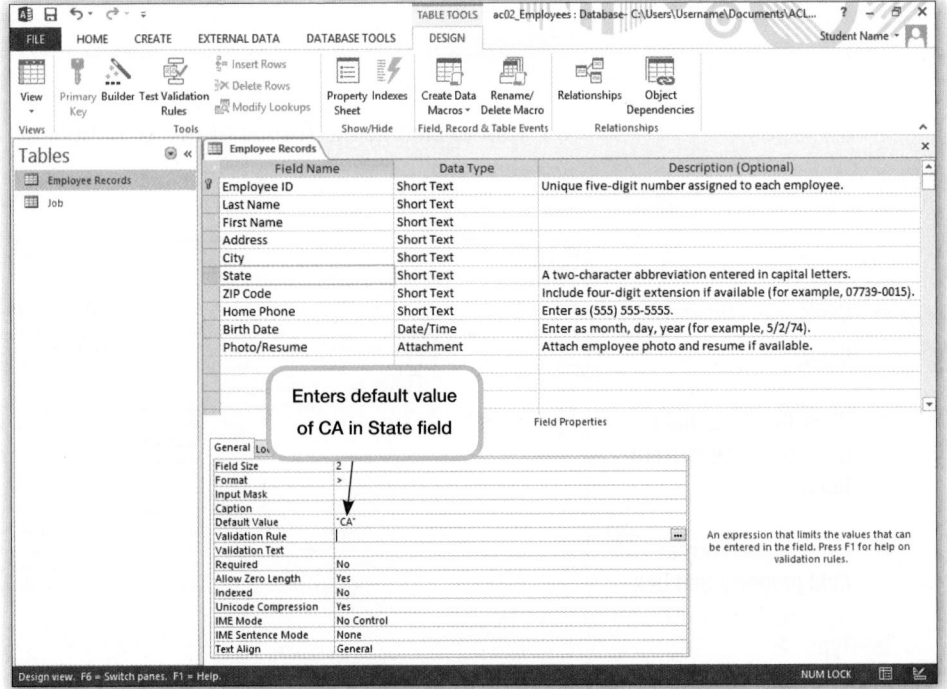

Figure 2.5

The default value is automatically enclosed in quotation marks to identify the entry as a group of characters called a **character string**. To see the effect on the table of setting a default value, you will return to Datasheet view and look at a new blank record.

First, you want to see the effect of the modifications to the State field's properties on the table.

2

- Click 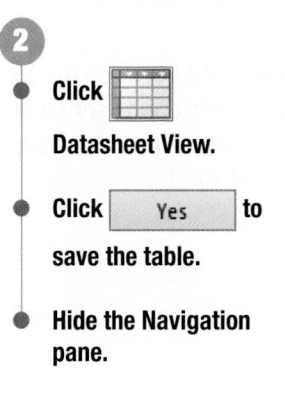 Datasheet View.

- Click [Yes] to save the table.

- Hide the Navigation pane.

Your screen should be similar to Figure 2.6

Converted to uppercase

Figure 2.6

You can see that records 3 (Mark Pennington) and 10 (Scott Briggs) now correctly display the state in capital letters. Setting the format for the field will prevent this type of error from occurring again.

3

- Click  New (blank) record on the navigation bar to move to a new record.

Your screen should be similar to Figure 2.7

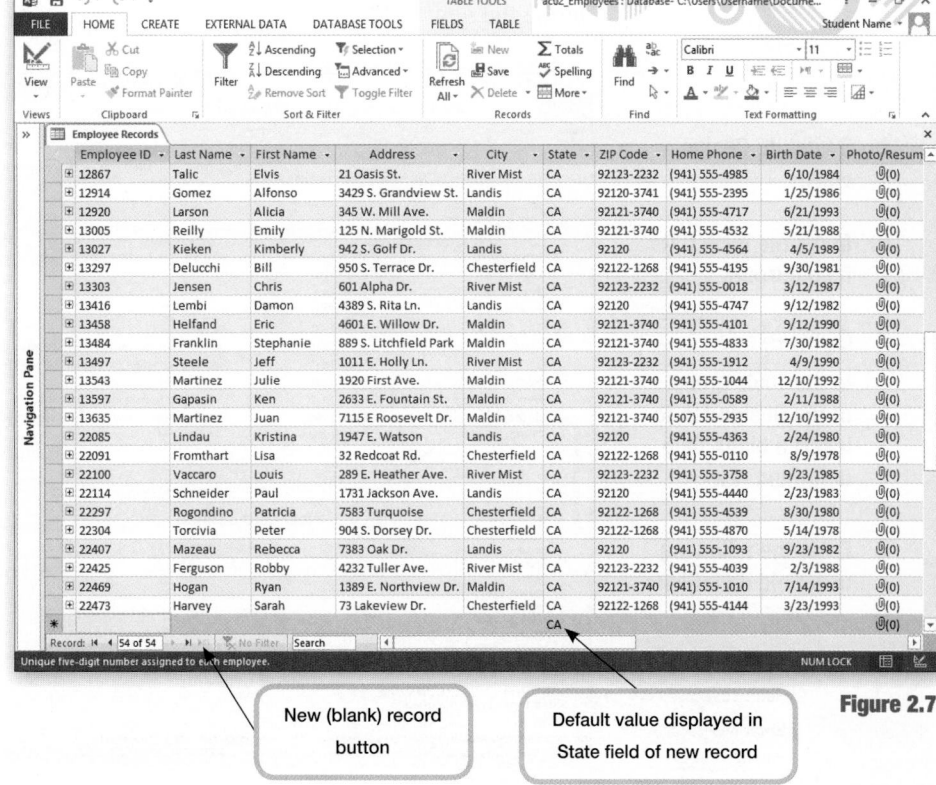

New (blank) record button

Default value displayed in State field of new record

Figure 2.7

The new blank record at the end of the table displays CA as the default value for the State field. If you did need to enter a different state, it would display in all capital letters because of the Format property setting associated with the field.

DEFINING VALIDATION RULES

After looking at the fields, you decide to add the Gender field between the Home Phone and Birth Date fields. The field will need to have restrictions set so that it only accepts a single character, either "f" or "m," and formats it for uppercase. To add this restriction, you will create a validation rule for the field.

Concept ③ Validation Rule

A **validation rule** is used to control the data that can be entered in a field by defining the input values that are valid or allowed. Certain checks on the validity of the data that is entered in a field are performed automatically based on the field's data type and size. For example, in a field whose data type is Number and size is five, the type of data that can be entered in the field is restricted to a maximum of five numeric entries. You can further refine these basic restrictions by adding a validation rule to the field's properties that defines specific restrictions for the type of data that can be entered in the field.

You also can include a validation text message. **Validation text** is an explanatory message that appears if a user attempts to enter invalid information in a text field for which there is a validity check. If you do not specify a message, Access will display a default error message, which may not clearly describe the reason for the error.

To create this customized field, you will switch to Design view to insert and define the new field.

• **Switch to Design view.**

• **Make the Birth Date field current.**

• **Click** 🔲 Insert Rows **in the Tools group of the Design tab to insert a blank field definition row.**

• **Enter the following new field definitions**

Field Name	Gender
Data Type	Short Text
Description	Enter f for female and m for male.
Field Size	1
Format	>

Your screen should be similar to Figure 2.8

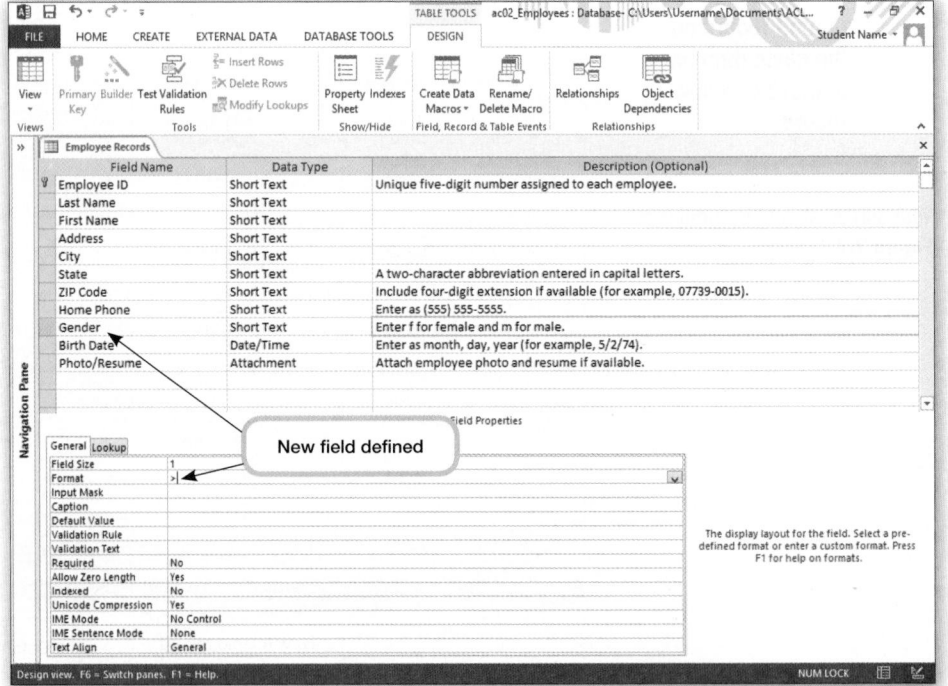

Figure 2.8

The only two characters you want the Gender field to accept are F for female and M for male. You will create a validation rule for the Gender field to restrict the data entry to the two valid characters. A validation rule is specified by entering an expression in the **Validation Rule property** that limits the values that can be entered in the field.

Concept 4 Expression

An **expression** is a formula consisting of a combination of symbols that will produce a single value. You create an expression by combining identifiers, operators, constants, and functions to produce the desired results. An **identifier** is an element that refers to the value of a field, a graphical object, or a property. In the expression [Sales Amount] + [Sales Tax], [Sales Amount] and [Sales Tax] are identifiers that refer to the values in the Sales Amount and Sales Tax fields. Each identifier is surrounded by square brackets and may be separated by an exclamation point if the expression needs to refer to the source of the values, as in Reports![Sales Report]![Sales Amount].

An **operator** is a symbol or word that indicates that an operation is to be performed. Common mathematical operators are + for addition, - for subtraction, * for multiplication, and / for division. A **comparison operator** is a symbol that allows you to make comparisons between two items. The following table describes the comparison operators:

Operator	Meaning
=	Equal to
< >	Not equal to
<	Less than
>	Greater than
<=	Less than or equal to
>=	Greater than or equal to

In addition, the OR and AND operators allow you to enter additional criteria in the same field or different fields.

Constants are numbers, dates, or character strings. Character strings such as "F", "M", or "Workout Gear" are enclosed in quotation marks. Dates are enclosed in pound signs (#), as in #1/1/99#. **Functions** are built-in formulas that perform certain types of calculations automatically. Functions begin with the function name, such as SUM, and are followed by the function **argument**, which specifies the data the function should use. Arguments are enclosed in parentheses.

The following table shows some examples of possible expressions.

Expression	Result
[Sales Amount] + [Sales Tax]	Sums values in two fields.
"F" OR "M"	Restricts entry to the letters F or M only.
>= #1/1/99# AND <= #12/31/99#	Restricts entries to dates greater than or equal to 1/1/99 and less than or equal to 12/31/99.
"Workout Gear"	Allows the entry Workout Gear only.
SUM([Pay])	Totals the values in the Pay field.

You will learn much more about entering expressions in Lab 3.

You will enter the expression to restrict the data entry in the Gender field to the letter "f" or "m." As you do, a drop-down list of available functions that begin with the character you are typing, in this case f or m, will be displayed. The context-sensitive menu appears anytime you can enter an expression and suggests identifiers and functions that could be used. This is the **IntelliSense** feature, which is designed to help you quickly type expressions and ensure their accuracy. You can continue typing to narrow the list of functions or identifiers, or you can select an item from the list and press ⏎Enter or Tab⇆ to have the highlighted suggestion entered for you. By continuing to type or by pressing an arrow key to move on, you can continue entering the expression and ignore the IntelliSense suggestions. You will also enter text in the **Validation Text property** to display a message to the user if data is entered incorrectly.

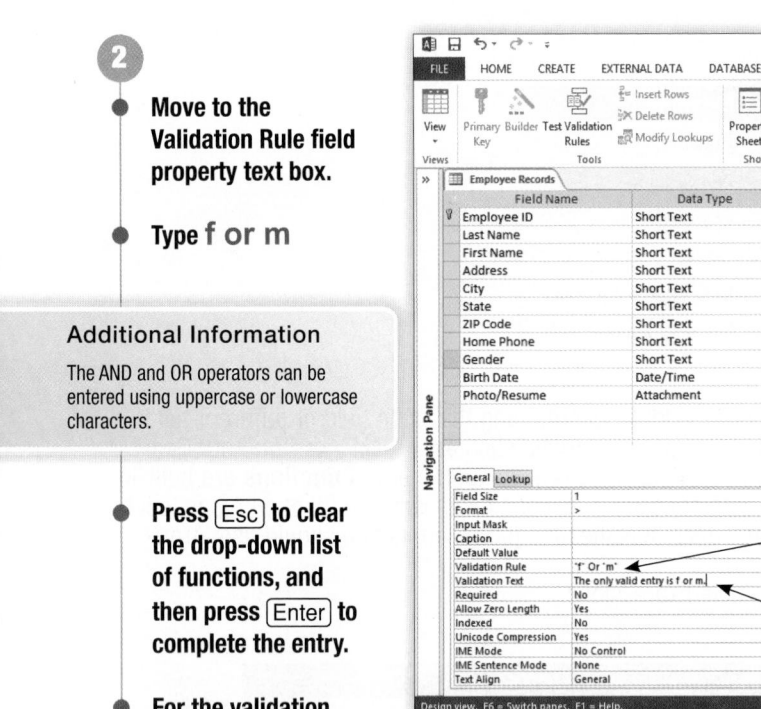

2
- Move to the Validation Rule field property text box.
- Type f or m

Additional Information
The AND and OR operators can be entered using uppercase or lowercase characters.

- Press Esc to clear the drop-down list of functions, and then press Enter to complete the entry.
- For the validation text, type The only valid entry is f or m.

Your screen should be similar to Figure 2.9

Figure 2.9

The expression you entered for the validation rule states that the only acceptable data values for this field must be equal to an F or an M. Notice that when you finished typing the validation rule, Access automatically added quotation marks around the two character strings and changed the "o" in "or" to uppercase. Because the Format property has been set to convert all entries to uppercase, a lowercase entry of f or m is as acceptable as the capitalized letters F or M.

Next, you will switch back to Datasheet view to test the validation rule by entering data for the Gender field. In addition to a message box asking whether you want to save the design changes, another message box will appear to advise you that the data integrity rules have been changed. When you restructure a table, you often make changes that could result in a loss of data. Changes such as shortening field sizes, creating validation rules, or changing field types can cause existing data to become invalid. Because the field is new, it has no data values to verify, and a validation check is unnecessary at this time.

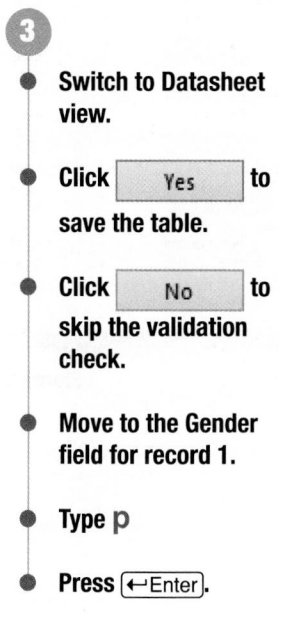

3

- Switch to Datasheet view.

- Click **Yes** to save the table.

- Click **No** to skip the validation check.

- Move to the Gender field for record 1.

- Type **p**

- Press **←Enter**.

Your screen should be similar to Figure 2.10

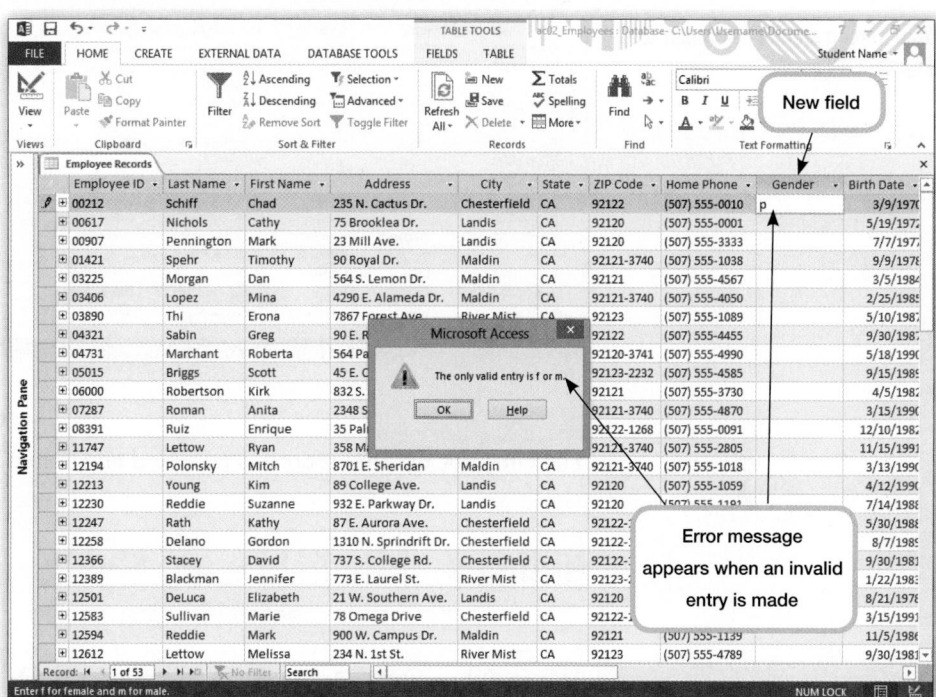

Figure 2.10

The new field was added to the table between the Home Phone and Birth Date fields. Because the letter p is not a valid entry, Access displays the error message you entered as the validation text for the field. You will clear the error message and correct the entry.

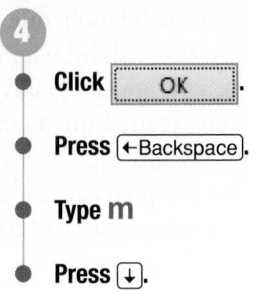

4

● Click [OK].

● Press [←Backspace].

● Type **m**

● Press [↓].

Your screen should be similar to Figure 2.11

Employee ID	Last Name	First Name	Address	City	State	ZIP Code	Home Phone	Gender	Birth Date
⊞ 00212	Schiff	Chad	235 N. Cactus Dr.	Chesterfield	CA	92122	(507) 555-0010	M	3/9/1970
⊞ 00617	Nichols	Cathy	75 Brooklea Dr.	Landis	CA	92120	(507) 555-0001		5/19/1972
⊞ 00907	Pennington	Mark	23 Mill Ave.	Landis	CA	92120	(507) 555-3333		7/7/1977
⊞ 01421	Spehr	Timothy	90 Royal Dr.	Maldin	CA	92121-3740	(507) 555-1038		9/9/1978
⊞ 03225	Morgan	Dan	564 S. Lemon Dr.	Maldin	CA	92121	(507) 555-4567		3/5/1984
⊞ 03406	Lopez	Mina	4290 E. Alameda Dr.	Maldin	CA	92121-3740	(507) 555-4050		2/25/1985
⊞ 03890	Thi	Erona	7867 Forest Ave.	River Mist	CA	92123	(507) 555-1089		5/10/1987
⊞ 04321	Sabin	Greg	90 E. Rawhide Ave.	Chesterfield	CA	92122	(507) 555-4455		9/30/1987
⊞ 04731	Marchant	Roberta	564 Palm Avenue	Landis	CA	92120-3741	(507) 555-4990		5/18/1990
⊞ 05015	Briggs	Scott	45 E. Camelback Rd.	River Mist	CA	92123-2232	(507) 555-4585		9/15/1989
⊞ 06000	Robertson	Kirk	832 S. William Ave.	Maldin	CA	92121	(507) 555-3730		4/5/1982
⊞ 07287	Roman	Anita	2348 S. Bala Dr.	Maldin	CA	92121-3740	(507) 555-4870		3/15/1990
⊞ 08391	Ruiz	Enrique	35 Palm St.	Chesterfield	CA	92122-1268	(507) 555-0091		12/10/1982
⊞ 11747	Lettow	Ryan	358 Maple Dr.	Maldin	CA	92121-3740	(507) 555-2805		11/15/1991
⊞ 12194	Polonsky	Mitch	8701 E. Sheridan	Maldin	CA	92121-3740	(507) 555-1018		3/13/1990
⊞ 12213	Young	Kim	89 College Ave.	Landis	CA	92120	(507) 555-1059		4/12/1990
⊞ 12230	Reddie	Suzanne	932 E. Parkway Dr.	Landis	CA	92120	(507) 555-1191		7/14/1988
⊞ 12247	Rath	Kathy	87 E. Aurora Ave.	Chesterfield	CA	92122-1268	(507) 555-4797		5/30/1988
⊞ 12258	Delano	Gordon	1310 N. Sprindrift Dr.	Chesterfield	CA	92122-1268	(507) 555-1208		8/7/1989
⊞ 12366	Stacey	David	737 S. College Rd.	Chesterfield	CA	92122-1268	(507) 555-4784		9/30/1981
⊞ 12389	Blackman	Jennifer	773 E. Laurel St.	River Mist	CA	92123-2232	(507) 555-4956		1/22/1983
⊞ 12501	DeLuca	Elizabeth	21 W. Southern Ave.	Landis	CA	92120	(507) 555-1105		8/21/1978
⊞ 12583	Sullivan	Marie	78 Omega Drive	Chesterfield	CA	92122-1268	(507) 555-3890		3/15/1991
⊞ 12594	Reddie	Mark	900 W. Campus Dr.	Maldin	CA	92121	(507) 555-1139		11/5/1986
⊞ 12612	Lettow	Melissa	234 N. 1st St.	River Mist	CA	92123	(507) 555-4789		9/30/1981

Entry accepted and converted to uppercase

Record: I◄ 2 of 53 ►H►I No Filter Search

Enter f for female and m for male.

Figure 2.11

The entry for the first record is accepted and displayed as an uppercase M.

Hiding and Redisplaying Fields

To enter the gender data for the rest of the fields, you will use the First Name field as a guide. Unfortunately, the First Name and Gender fields are currently on opposite sides of the screen and will require you to look back and forth across each record. You can eliminate this problem by hiding the fields you do not need to see, and then redisplaying them when you have finished entering the gender data.

HIDING FIELDS

A quick way to view two fields side by side (in this case, the First Name and Gender fields) is to hide the fields that are in between (the Address through Home Phone fields).

Select the Address field through the Home Phone field.

Additional Information

Drag along the column headings when the mouse pointer is ↓ to select the fields.

Right-click on the selection.

Choose Hide Fields from the shortcut menu.

Another Method

You also can click More ▾ in the Records group of the Home tab and choose Hide Fields.

Your screen should be similar to Figure 2.12

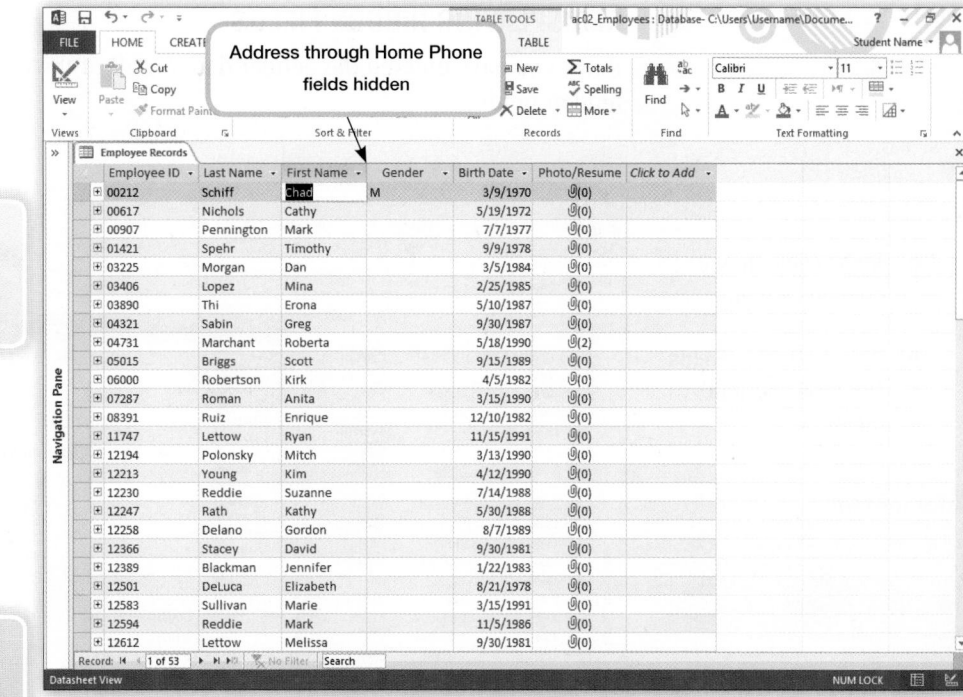

Figure 2.12

Now that the First Name and Gender columns are next to each other, you can refer to the first name in each record to enter the correct gender data.

Enter the Gender field values for the remaining records by looking at the First Name field to determine whether the employee is male or female.

Reduce the size of the Gender column using the Best Fit command.

Having Trouble?

Remember, to best fit data in a column, you double-click its right border.

Your screen should be similar to Figure 2.13

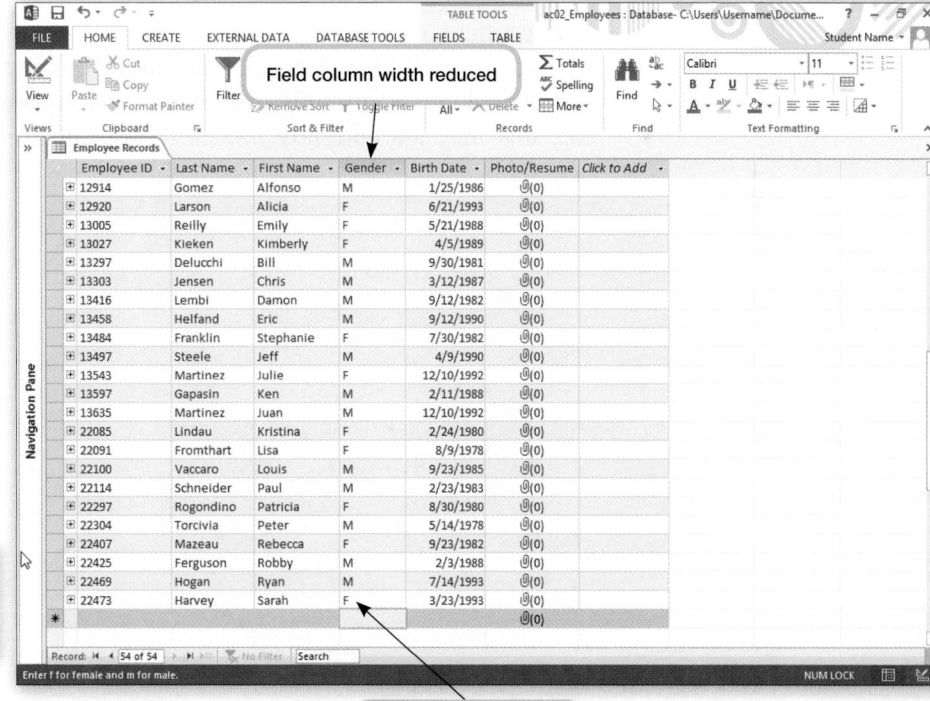

Gender data entered for all records

Figure 2.13

REDISPLAYING HIDDEN FIELDS

After you have entered the gender data for all of the records, you can redisplay the hidden fields.

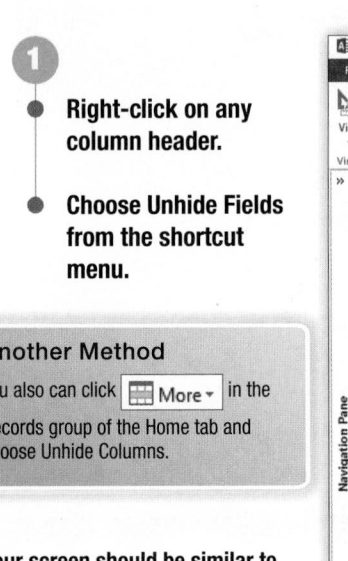

● **Right-click on any column header.**

● **Choose Unhide Fields from the shortcut menu.**

Another Method

You also can click ▦ More ▾ in the Records group of the Home tab and choose Unhide Columns.

Your screen should be similar to Figure 2.14

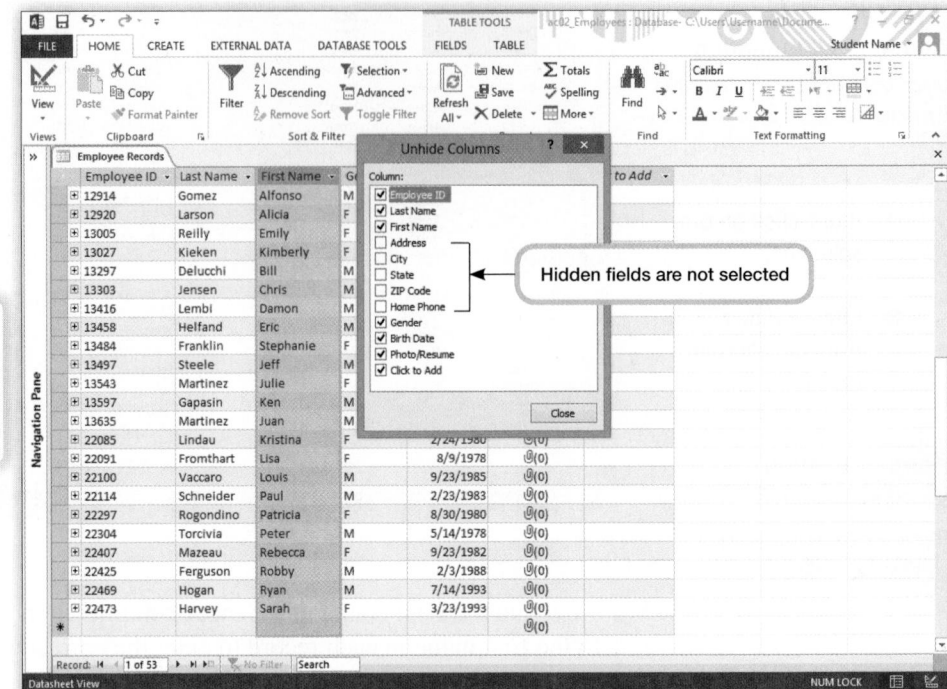

Hidden fields are not selected

Figure 2.14

You use the Unhide Columns dialog box to select the currently hidden columns you want to redisplay. A check mark in the box next to a column name indicates that the column is currently displayed; column names with no check marks indicate that they are currently hidden. You want to unhide all hidden columns in your table.

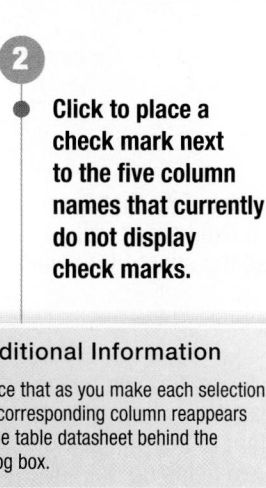

2

● **Click** to place a
   check mark next
   to the five column
   names that currently
   do not display
   check marks.

Additional Information

Notice that as you make each selection,
the corresponding column reappears
in the table datasheet behind the
dialog box.

● **Click** [Close] .

**Your screen should be similar to
Figure 2.15**

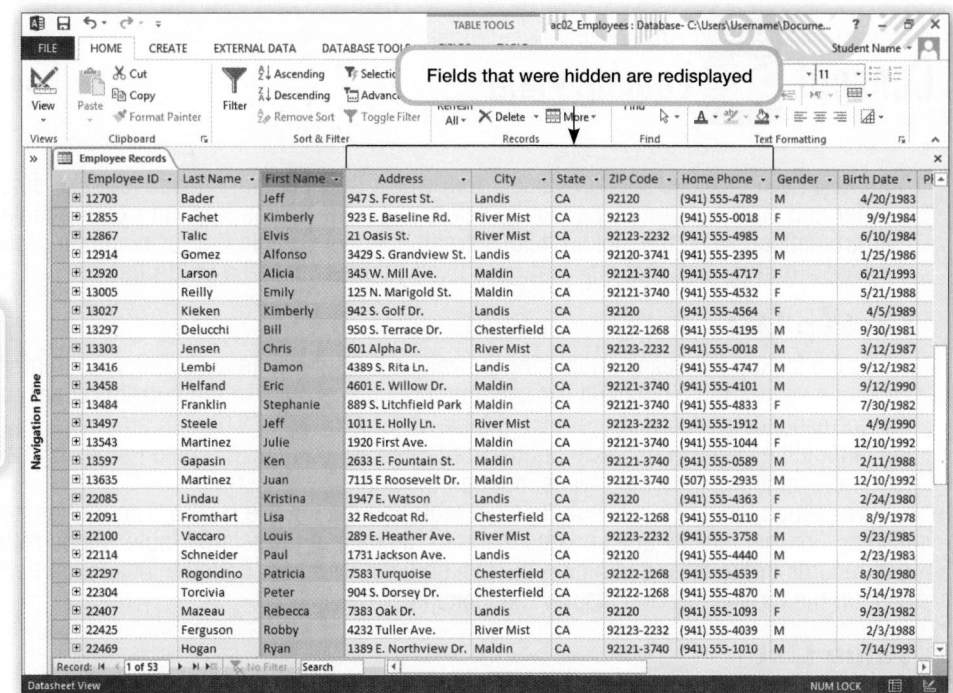

Figure 2.15

All of the fields are displayed again.

Creating a Lookup Field

Next you decide to change the Location field in the Job table to a lookup field that
will make entering the location information easier, faster, and less prone to errors.

Concept 5 Lookup Field

A **lookup field** provides a list of values from which the user can choose to make entering data into that field simpler and more accurate. The lookup field can get the values from an existing table or a fixed set of values that are defined when the lookup field is created. A lookup field that uses another table as the source for values is called a **lookup list**, and one that uses fixed values is called a **value list**.

Lookup List

When the lookup field uses a table for the values it displays, an association is created between the two tables. Picking a value from the lookup list sets the foreign key value in the current record to the primary key value of the corresponding record in the related table. A foreign key is a field in one table that refers to the primary key field in another table and indicates how the tables are related. The field names of these two fields do not have to match, although their data types must be the same.

The related table displays but does not store the data in the record. The foreign key is stored but does not display. For this reason, any updates made to the data in the related table will be reflected in both the list and records in the table containing the lookup field. You must define a lookup list field from the table that will contain the foreign key and display the lookup list.

Value List

A lookup field that uses a fixed list of values looks the same as a lookup field that uses a table, except the fixed set of values is entered when the lookup field is created. A value list should be used only for values that will not change very often and do not need to be stored in a table. For example, a list for a Salutation field containing the abbreviations Mr., Mrs., or Ms. would be a good candidate for a value list. Choosing a value from a value list will store that value in the record—it does not create an association to a related table. For this reason, if you change any of the original values in the value list later, they will not be reflected in records added before this change was made.

There are three club locations: Landis, Chesterfield, and River Mist. You want the club locations to be displayed in a drop-down list so that anyone entering a new employee record can simply choose from this list to enter the club location.

USING THE LOOKUP WIZARD

The **Lookup Wizard** is used to create a lookup field that will allow you to select from a list of values. A **wizard** is a feature that guides you step by step through the process to perform a task. You will use the Lookup Wizard to change the existing Location field to a lookup field that uses fixed values.

1

- Close the Employee Records table, saving any changes.

- Display the Navigation pane and open the Job table.

- Hide the Navigation pane and switch to Design view.

- Make the Location field active.

- Open the Data Type drop-down menu and choose Lookup Wizard.

Having Trouble?

If a security notice appears, click Open to continue.

Your screen should be similar to Figure 2.16

Additional Information

In Datasheet view, you can use 📄 More Fields ▾ in the Add & Delete group of the Table Tools Fields tab and choose Lookup & Relationship to create a new field column and start the Lookup Wizard.

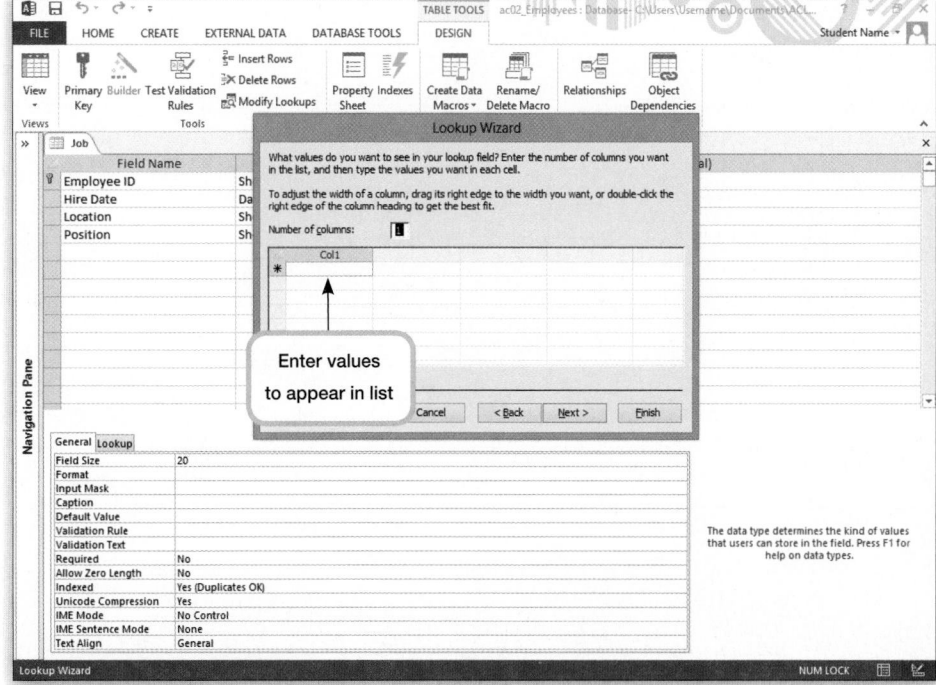

Figure 2.16

In the first Lookup Wizard dialog box, you specify the source for the values for the lookup field. You will enter your own values, the club locations, for this field.

2

- Choose "I will type in the values that I want."

- Click Next > .

Your screen should be similar to Figure 2.17

Figure 2.17

The next step is to enter the values you want listed in the lookup field. You also can add columns and adjust their widths to fit the values you enter, if necessary. You only need one column, and the current width is sufficient for the values you will enter.

Your screen should be similar to Figure 2.18

3

- Click the cell under Col1.

- Type Landis

- Press Tab↹.

- Enter Chesterfield in the second cell and River Mist in the third cell.

Having Trouble?

You can correct these entries the same way you do when entering data into any other field.

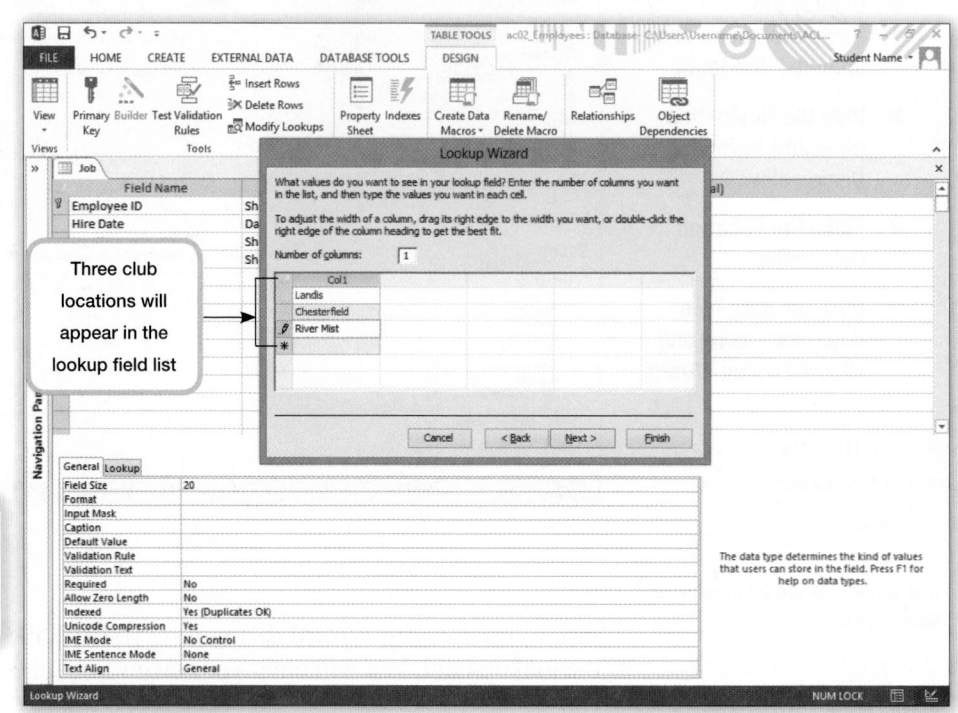

Three club locations will appear in the lookup field list

Figure 2.18

After entering the field values, you will move to the next step to enter a label for the lookup field and finish the wizard. You will leave the field name label as Location. Then you will check the field property settings established for this field to see whether any changes are necessary.

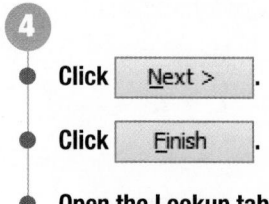

Click | Next > |.

Click | Finish |.

Open the Lookup tab in the Field Properties section.

Your screen should be similar to Figure 2.19

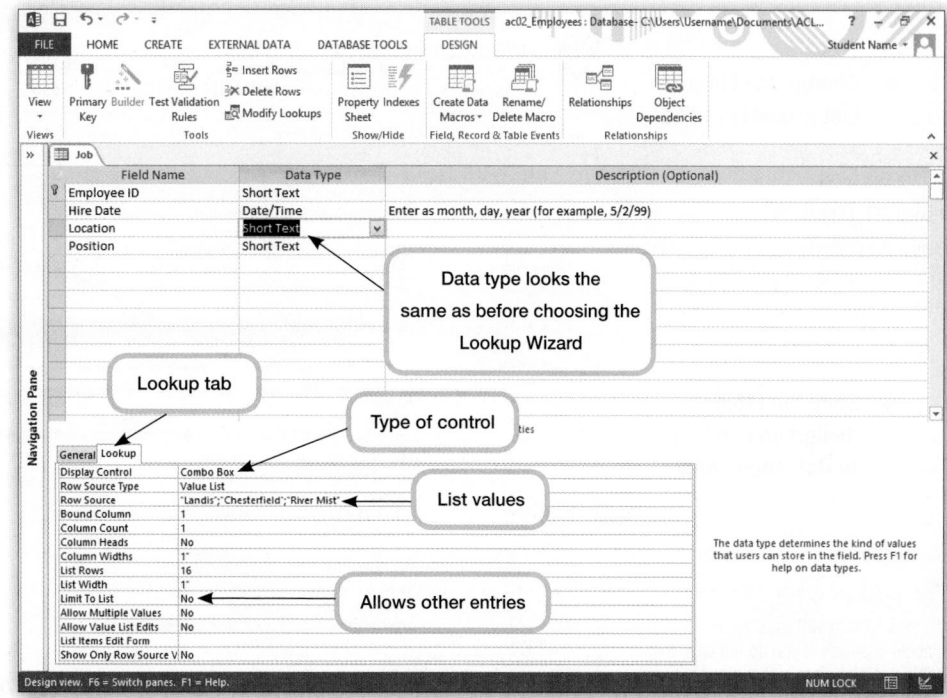

Figure 2.19

Before you clicked on the Lookup tab, you may have noticed that the property settings for the Location field looked like nothing had changed; the data type is still Short Text. By clicking the Lookup tab, you can see the values you typed in the Lookup Wizard listed in the Row Source property box. The Row Source Type is a value list and will display in a Combo Box (drop-down list) control when in Datasheet view, as well as on any forms where this field is used. The other properties are set to the defaults for lookup fields. The only change you want to make is to restrict the data entry in that field to values in the lookup list. Then you will test that the Location field is performing correctly by entering a location that is not in the list.

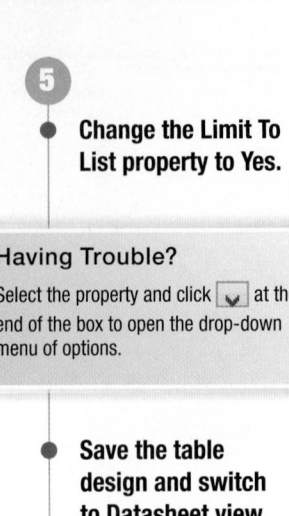

⑤

Change the Limit To List property to Yes.

Having Trouble?

Select the property and click 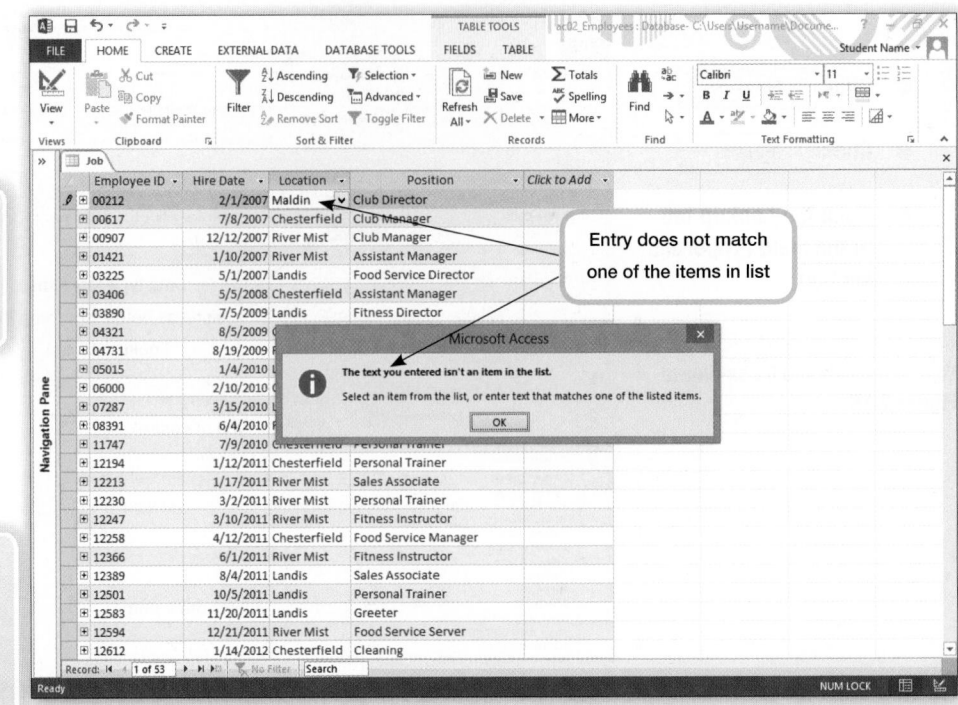 at the end of the box to open the drop-down menu of options.

Save the table design and switch to Datasheet view.

Additional Information

The 🖫 Save button in the Quick Access Toolbar will save the table design changes. If you do not save the table design before switching views, Access will prompt you to save it.

Click in the Location field of the first record.

Select and replace the current entry by typing Maldin and pressing ⏎Enter.

Your screen should be similar to Figure 2.20

Figure 2.20

A warning box advises you that the entry is not one of the listed items because you restricted the field entries in the Location field to the lookup values you specified.

Notice the field displays a ⌄, indicating a drop-down list of options is available. Clicking this button will open the list. After typing in an invalid entry, the list will open automatically for you.

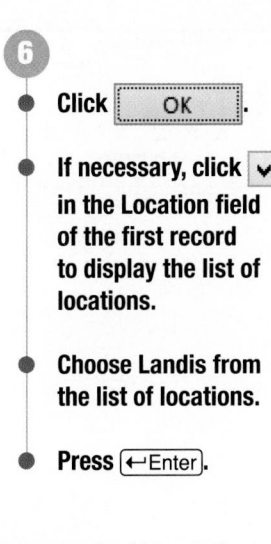

6

- Click [OK].

- If necessary, click ✓ in the Location field of the first record to display the list of locations.

- Choose Landis from the list of locations.

- Press ←Enter.

Your screen should be similar to Figure 2.21

Figure 2.21

The Location lookup field is working correctly. Using a lookup field makes entering repetitive information faster and more accurate.

Searching for, Finding, and Replacing Data

Over the past few days, you have received several change request forms to update the employee records and a request to know how many fitness instructors there are in the company. Rather than scrolling through all the records to locate the ones that need to be modified, you can use various methods to search for, find, and/or replace the data.

SEARCHING FOR DATA

While working in the Job table, you decide to find out how many fitness instructors are employed in the company first. One way to do this is to use the Search box to locate this information. The Search box is a useful tool to find any character(s) anywhere in the database. For example, it could be used to quickly locate a particular Employee ID number in order to update an address change. When you type in the Search box, Access will simultaneously highlight any possible fields that match. The more characters you type in the Search box, the more accurate the search response will be. Additionally, this feature is not case-sensitive.

You want to search for "Fitness Instructor."

1

Click in the Search box in the record navigation bar.

Type in fi

Your screen should be similar to Figure 2.22

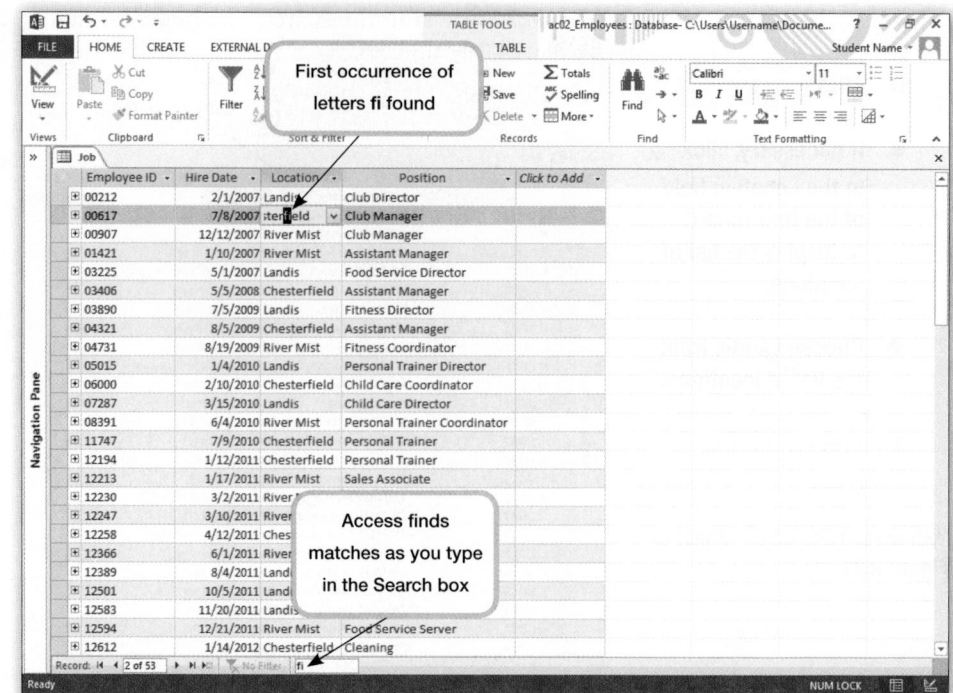

Figure 2.22

Notice that Access highlighted the "fi" in Chester**fi**eld. You will continue to type the word "Fitness" in the Search box, and notice that as you enter more text, the search is refined to more closely locate what you are looking for.

2

Continue to type the word fitness in the Search box (Fitness Director is located)

Press Spacebar **and type in to locate the first record containing the text Fitness Instructor.**

Press ←Enter **to move to the next record containing the search text.**

Your screen should be similar to Figure 2.23

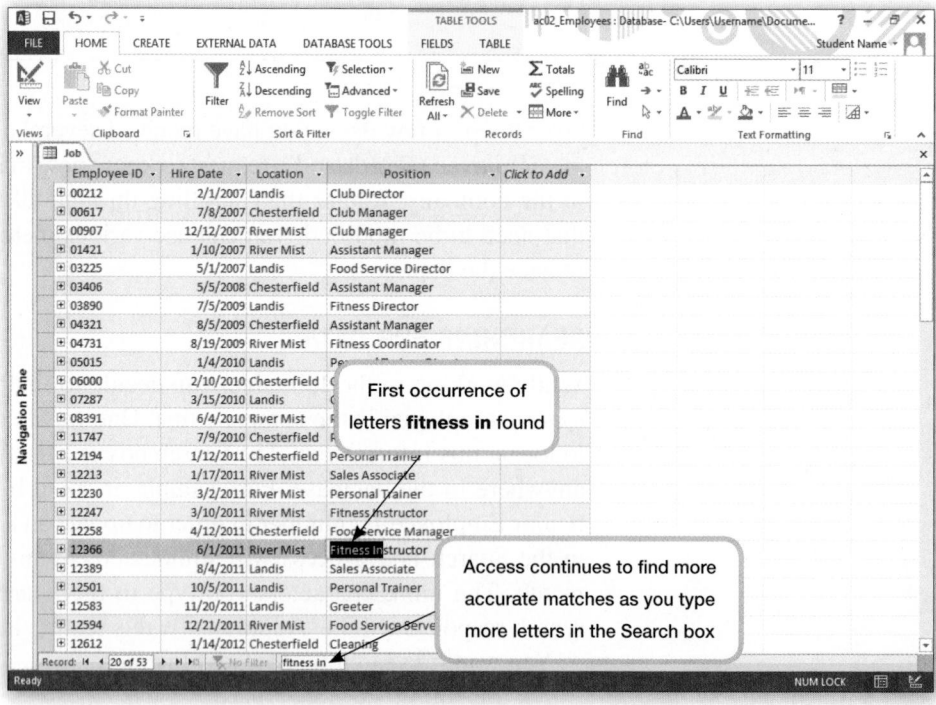

Figure 2.23

The next record in the search that matches the characters "fitness in" is selected. Because it is now locating the information you want to find, you do not need to complete the word "instructor." Notice that each time the ←Enter key is pressed, the selection moves to the next record until it reaches the last matching set of characters.

● **Continue pressing** ←Enter **to locate all fitness instructor records.**

When the last field matching the search text is selected, it will remain highlighted and Access will go no further; no message will appear telling you there are no more matches. If you were counting, there were seven fitness instructors. Although this method worked to find out the number of fitness instructors, you will learn later in this lab about another, more effective way to gather this information.

FINDING DATA

Now you will work on making the changes to update the employee records from the change request forms you have received. Rather than use the Search box to locate the records to change, you will use the Find and Replace feature.

Concept 6 Find and Replace

The **Find and Replace** feature helps you quickly find specific information and automatically replace it with new information. The Find command will locate all specified values in a field, and the Replace command will both find a value and automatically replace it with another. For example, in a table containing supplier and item prices, you may need to increase the price of all items supplied by one manufacturer. To quickly locate these items, you would use the Find command to locate all records with the name of the manufacturer and then update the price appropriately. Alternatively, you could use the Replace command if you knew that all items priced at $11.95 were increasing to $15.99. This command would locate all values matching the original price and replace them with the new price.

Finding and replacing data is fast and accurate, but you need to be careful when replacing not to replace unintended matches.

The first change request is for Melissa Lettow, who recently married and has both a name and address change. To quickly locate the correct record, you will use the Find command. This information is in the Last Name field of the Employee Records table.

1

- **Close the Job table.**

- **Open the Navigation pane and then open the Employee Records table.**

- **Close the Navigation pane.**

- **Click in the Last Name field of record 1 in the Employee Records table.**

- **Click**  **in the Find group of the Home tab.**

Another Method

The keyboard shortcut is Ctrl + F.

Your screen should be similar to Figure 2.24

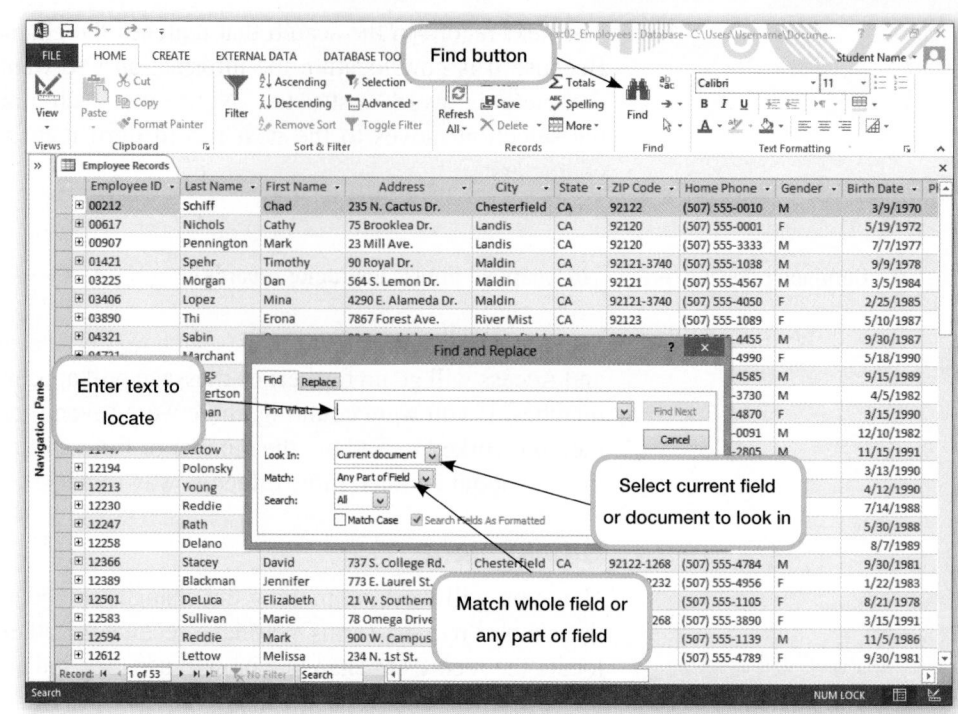

Figure 2.24

You use the Find and Replace dialog box to specify the information you are looking for and the way that you want Access to search the table. In the Find What text box, you specify the **criteria**, or a set of limiting conditions, records must meet by entering the text you want to locate. You can enter a specific character string or use wildcards to specify the criteria. **Wildcards** are symbols that are used to represent characters. The * symbol represents any collection of characters and the ? symbol represents any individual character. For example, ?ar will locate any three-letter text such as bar, far, and car. In contrast, *ar will locate the same text, but in addition will expand the criteria to locate any text ending with ar, such as star, popular, and modular.

Access defaults to search the entire current document, and matches any part of the field. You can change these settings and further refine your search by using the options described in the following table.

Option	Effect
Look In	Searches the current field or the entire table for the specified text.
Match	Locates matches to the whole field, any part of the field, or the start of the field.
Search	Specifies the direction in which the table will be searched: All (search all records); Down (search down from the current insertion point location in the field); or Up (search up from the current insertion point location in the field).
Match Case	Finds words that have the same pattern of uppercase letters as entered in the Find What text box. Using this option makes the search case sensitive.
Search Fields as Formatted	Finds data based on its display format.

With the cursor in the field you want to search, you will change the Look In location to search only that field. If you wanted to search on a different field, you could click on the field you want in the datasheet without closing the dialog box. You also will change it to match the whole field. The other default option to search all records is appropriately set.

Once your settings are as you want them, you will use the * wildcard to find all employees whose last names begin with "L."

2

- **Change the Look In setting to Current field.**

- **Change the Match setting to Whole Field.**

- **Type** L* **in the Find What text box.**

- **Click** Find Next **eight times to move from one located record to the next.**

Your screen should be similar to Figure 2.25

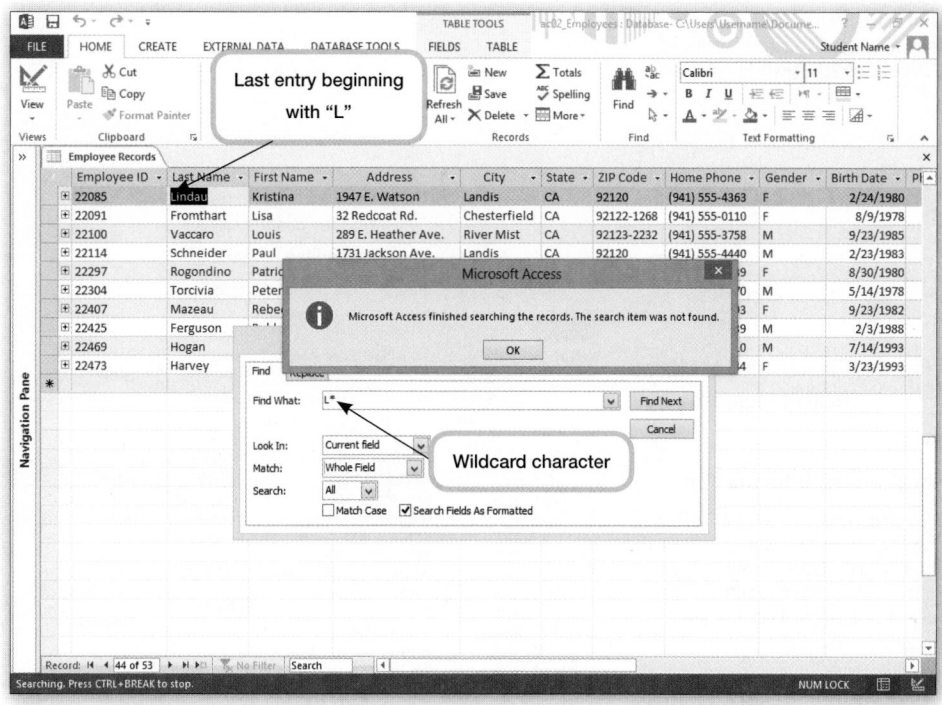

Figure 2.25

Using the wildcard located seven employees whose last names start with the letter "L." The more specific you can make your criteria, the more quickly you can locate the information you want to find. In this case, you want to find a specific last name, so you will enter the complete name in the Find What text box.

3

- **Click** OK **to close the finished searching informational box.**

- **Select the entry in the Find What text box and type** lettow

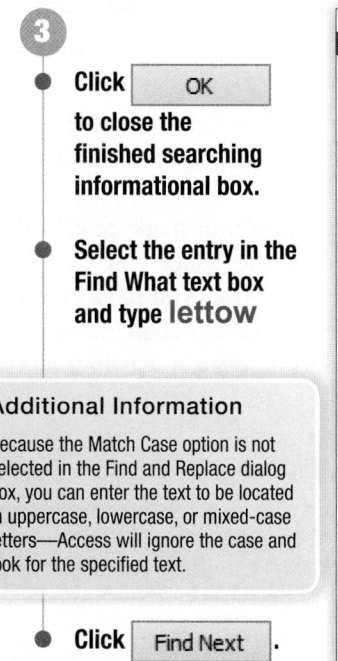

Additional Information

Because the Match Case option is not selected in the Find and Replace dialog box, you can enter the text to be located in uppercase, lowercase, or mixed-case letters—Access will ignore the case and look for the specified text.

- **Click** Find Next **.**

Your screen should be similar to Figure 2.26

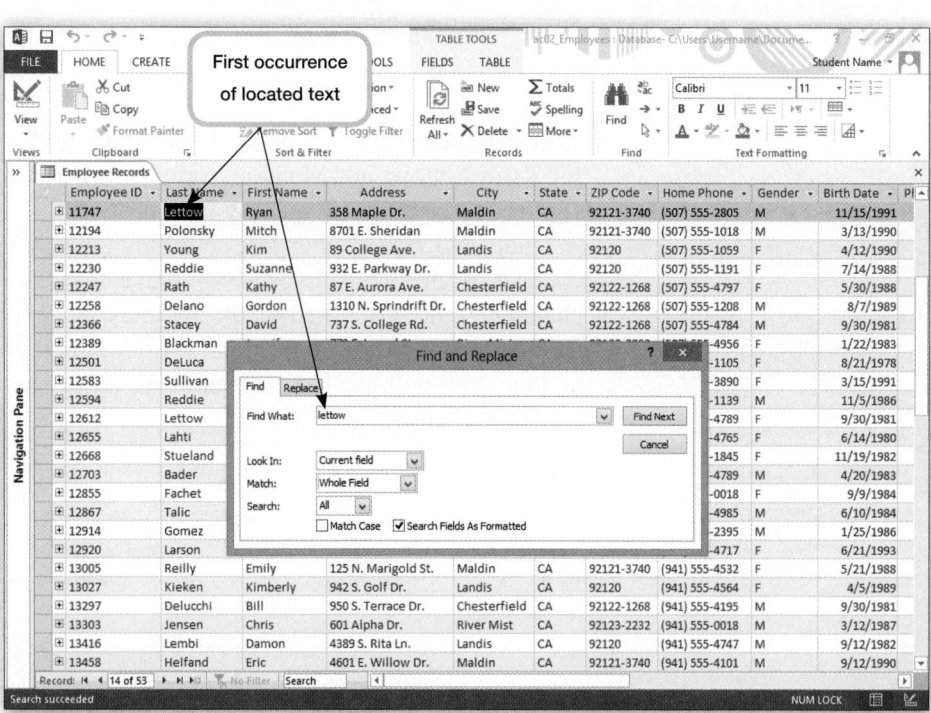

Figure 2.26

Having Trouble?

If the Find command did not locate this record, try it again. Make sure that you entered the name "lettow" (uppercase or lowercase) correctly and that Last Name is the selected field in the Look In box.

Access searches the table and moves to the first located occurrence of the entry you specified. The Last Name field is highlighted in record 14. You need to change the last name from Lettow to Richards.

4

● **Click in the Last Name field of record 14.**

Additional Information

You do not need to close the Find and Replace dialog box before you make a change to the table. You will be using this dialog box again to perform more searches, so leave it open for now.

● **Double-click Lettow to select the entry.**

● **Type Richards**

● **Press ⏎Enter.**

Your screen should be similar to Figure 2.27

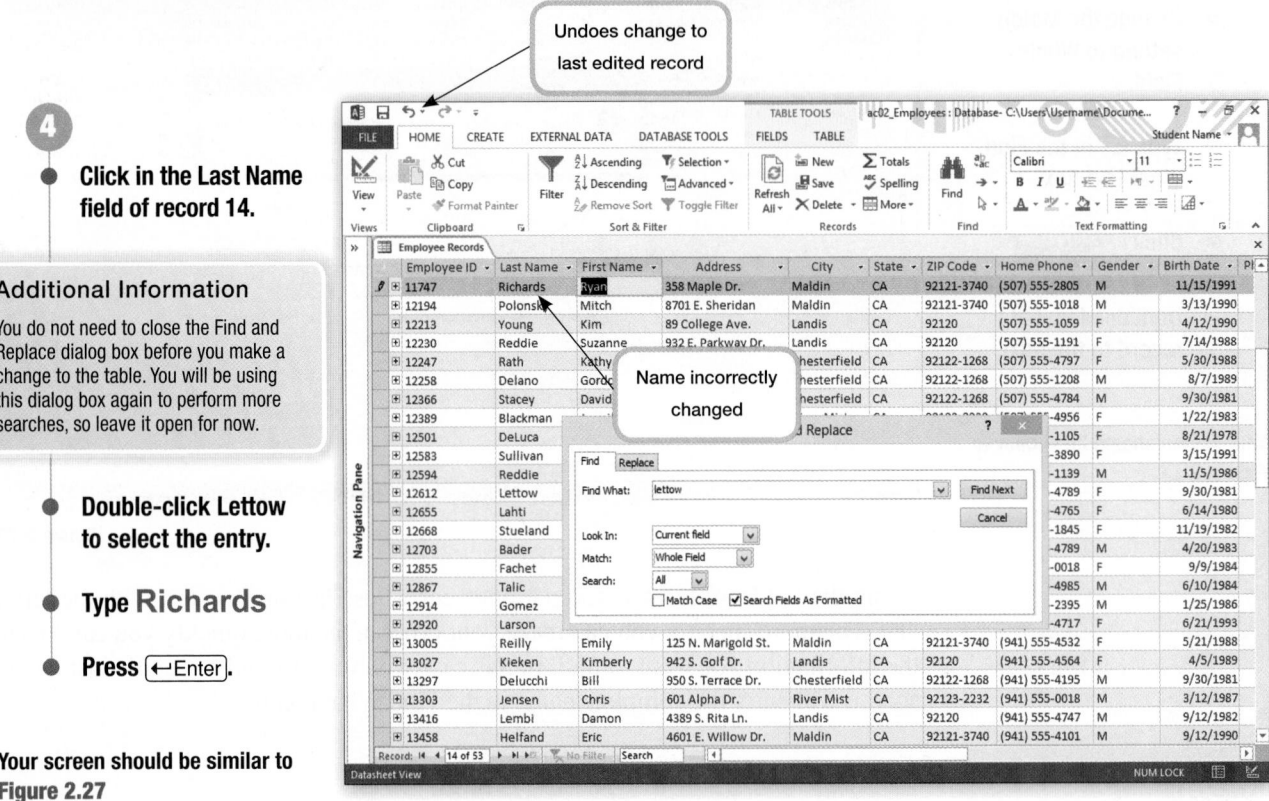

Figure 2.27

Now that the highlight is on the First Name field, you notice that this is the record for Ryan Lettow, not Melissa. You changed the wrong record. You will use the Undo command next to quickly fix this error.

Additional Information

Refer to the section Undoing and Redoing Editing Changes in the Introduction to Microsoft Office 2013 to review the Undo feature.

Undo will cancel your last action as long as you have not made any further changes to the table. Even if you save the record or the table, you can undo changes to the last edited record by clicking ↶ Undo. After you have changed another record or moved to another window, however, the earlier change cannot be undone. You will use Undo to return Ryan's record to the way it was before you made the change.

5 Click ↶ Undo.

Another Method

The keyboard shortcut is Ctrl + Z.

Your screen should be similar to
Figure 2.28

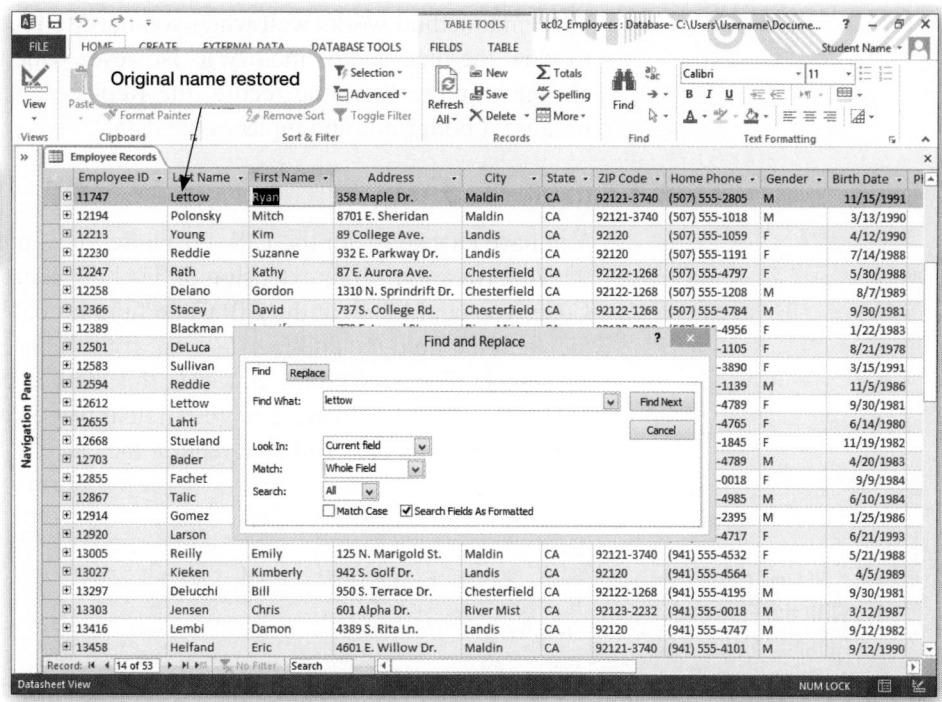

Figure 2.28

The original field value of Lettow is restored. Now you want to continue the search
to locate the next record with the last name of Lettow.

6

● Move back to the
  Last Name field of
  record 14.

● Click **Find Next**
  in the Find and
  Replace dialog box.

● When Access locates
  the record for Melissa
  Lettow (record 25),
  change her last name
  to **Richards** and
  the address to **5522
  W. Marin Lane**

Having Trouble?

If necessary, move the Find and Replace
dialog box.

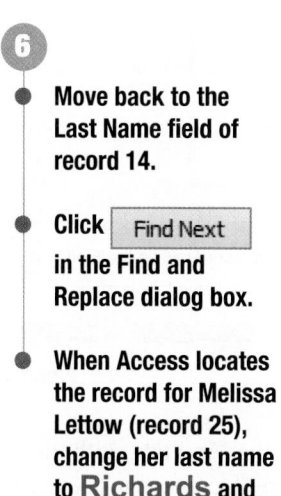

Your screen should be similar to
Figure 2.29

Figure 2.29

The Find method works well when you need to locate an individual field in order to view the data and/or modify it. However, when you need to make the same change to more than one record, the Replace command is the quicker method because it both finds and replaces the data.

REPLACING DATA

You have checked with the U.S. Postal Service and learned that all ZIP Codes of 92120 have a four-digit extension of 3741. To locate all the records with this ZIP Code, you could look at the ZIP Code field for each record to find the match and then edit the field to add the extension. If the table is small, this method would be acceptable. For large tables, however, this method could be quite time-consuming and more prone to errors. A more efficient way is to search the table to find specific values in records and then replace the entry with another.

1

- **With the Find and Replace dialog box still open, scroll to the top of the Employee Records table.**

- **Click in the ZIP Code field for record 1.**

- **Open the Replace tab of the Find and Replace dialog box.**

Another Method

You can use 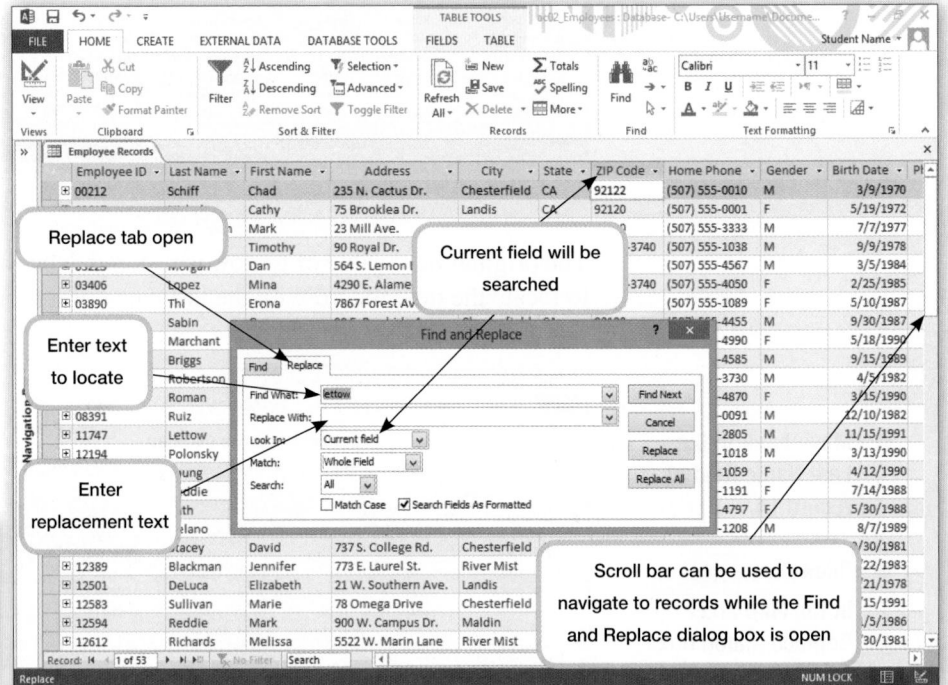 in the Find group, or the keyboard shortcut of Ctrl + H, to open the Find and Replace dialog box and display the Replace tab.

Your screen should be similar to Figure 2.30

Figure 2.30

The options in the Replace tab are the same as those in the Find tab, with the addition of a Replace With text box, where you enter the replacement text exactly as you want it to appear in your table.

2

● In the Find What text box, type **92120**

● Press Tab ⇥ to move to the Replace With text box.

● Type **92120-3741**

● Click [Find Next]

Your screen should be similar to Figure 2.31

Having Trouble?

If necessary, move the dialog box so you can see the highlighted entry.

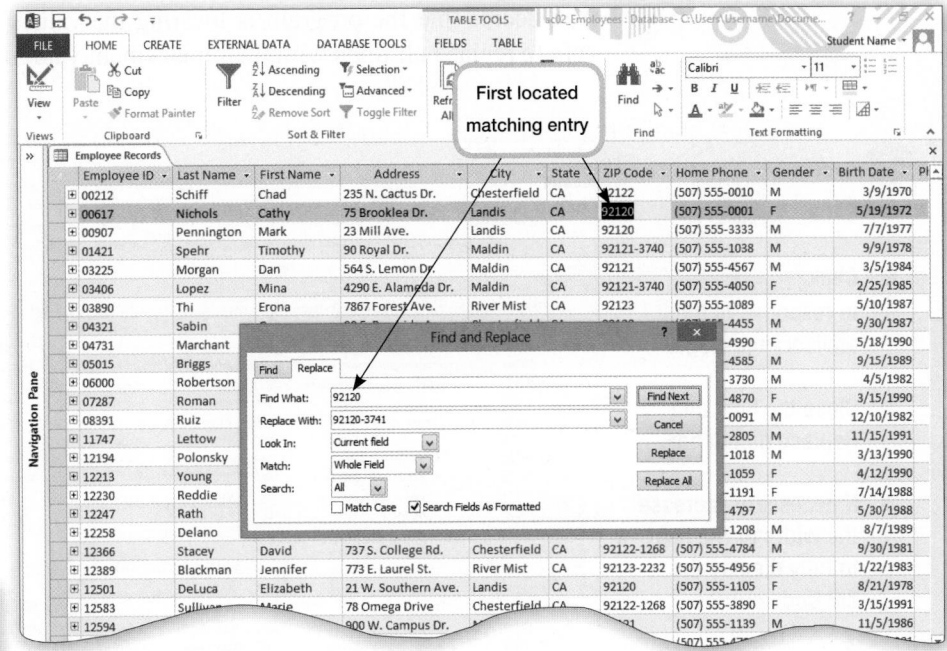

Figure 2.31

Immediately, the highlight moves to the first occurrence of text in the document that matches the Find What text and highlights it. You can now replace this text with the click of a button.

3

● Click [Replace]

Your screen should be similar to Figure 2.32

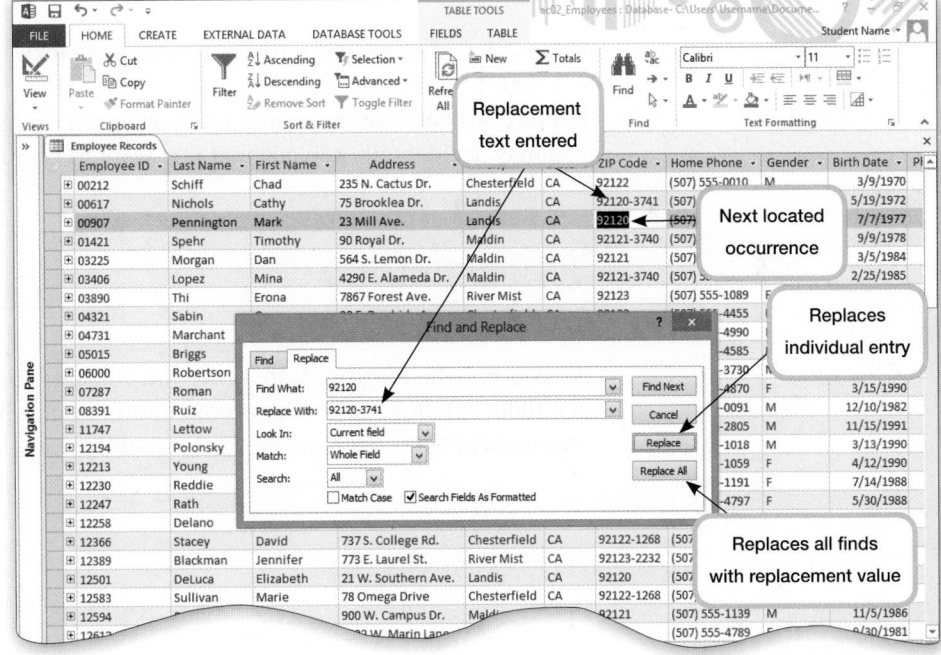

Figure 2.32

The original ZIP Code entry is replaced with the new ZIP Code. The program immediately continues searching and locates a second occurrence of the entry.

You decide that the program is locating the values accurately and that it will be safe to replace all finds with the replacement value.

4

- Click [Replace All].

- Click [Yes] in response to the advisory message.

- Close the Find and Replace dialog box.

- If necessary, increase the width of the field to fully display the ZIP Code entries.

Your screen should be similar to Figure 2.33

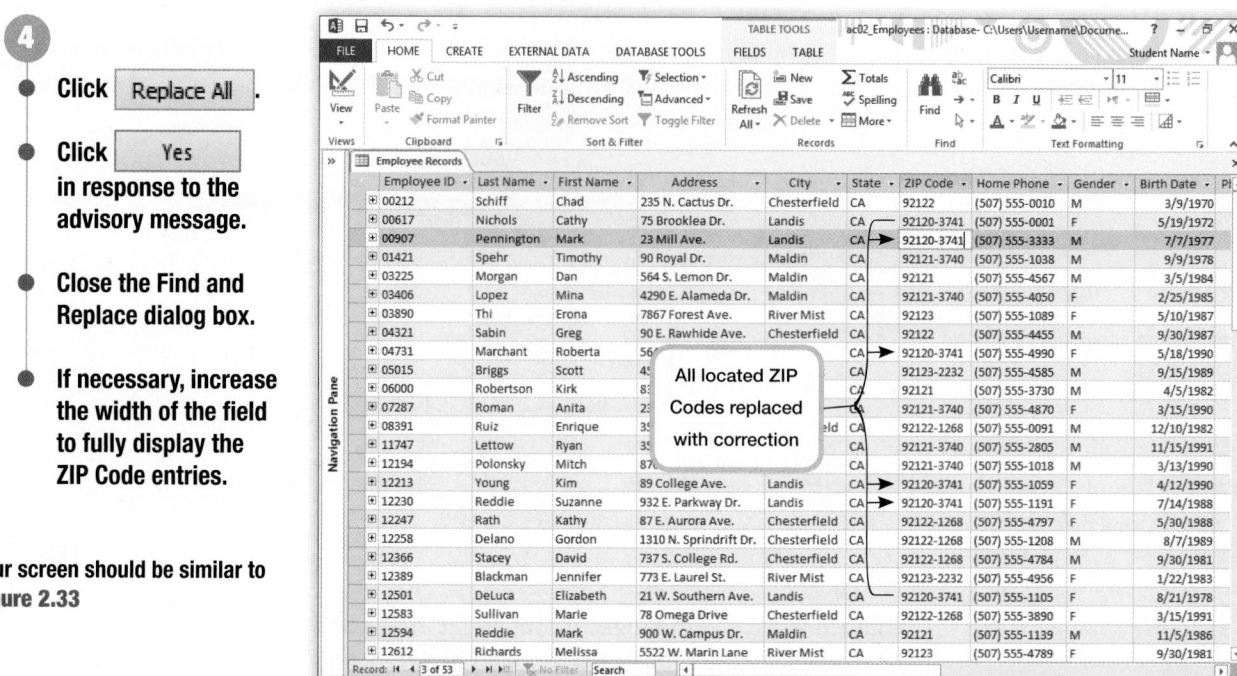

Figure 2.33

All matches are replaced with the replacement text. It is much faster to use Replace All than to confirm each match separately. However, exercise care when using Replace All because the search text you specify might be part of another field and you may accidentally replace text you want to keep.

Sorting Records

As you may recall from Lab 1, the records are ordered according to the primary key field, Employee ID. The accounting manager, however, has asked you for an alphabetical list of all employees. To do this, you will sort the records in the table.

Concept **7** Sorting

Sorting rearranges the order of the records in a table based on the value in each field. Sorting data helps you find specific information more quickly without having to browse the data. You can sort data in **ascending sort order** (A to Z or 0 to 9) or **descending sort order** (Z to A or 9 to 0).

You can sort all records in a table by a single field, such as State, or you can select adjacent columns and sort by more than one field, such as State and then City. When sorting on multiple fields, you begin by selecting the columns to sort. Access sorts records starting with the column farthest left (the outermost field) and then moves to the right across the selected columns to sort the innermost fields. For example, if you want to sort by state, and then by city, the State field must be to the left of the City field. The State field is the outermost field and the city field is the innermost field.

Access saves the new sort order with your table data and reapplies it automatically each time you open the table. To return to the primary key sort order, you must remove the temporary sort.

SORTING ON A SINGLE FIELD

You will sort the records on a single field, Last Name. To perform a sort on a single field, you move to the field on which you will base the sort and click the button that corresponds to the type of sort you want to do. In this case, you will sort the Last Name field in ascending alphabetical order.

1

- **Move to the Last Name field of any record.**

- **Click** ⬆A↓ **Ascending in the Sort & Filter group of the Home tab.**

Additional Information

Clicking ⬇Z↓ Descending arranges the data in descending sort order.

Your screen should be similar to Figure 2.34

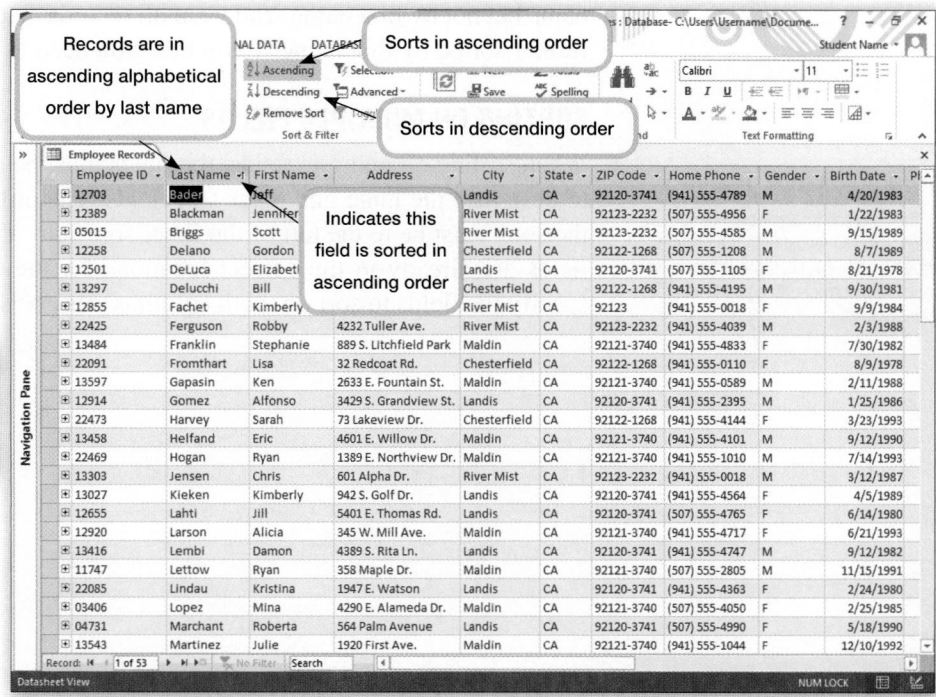

Figure 2.34

The employee records are displayed in alphabetical order by last name. The Last Name field header displays a ⬆↓ to show that the field is in ascending sorted order. Next, you want to check the rest of the table to see if there is anything else you need to do.

2

Use the scroll box to scroll down to record 25.

Additional Information

As you drag the scroll box, the record location is displayed in a ScreenTip (for example, "Record 25 of 53"). When you release the mouse, the record for the record # that was displayed in the ScreenTip will be at the top of the work area.

Your screen should be similar to Figure 2.35

	Employee ID	Last Name	First Name	Address	City	State	ZIP Code	Home Phone	Gender	Birth Date
⊞	13543	Martinez	Julie	1920 First Ave.	Maldin	CA	92121-3740	(941) 555-1044	F	12/10/1992
⊞	13635	Martinez	Juan	7115 E Roosevelt Dr.	Maldin	CA	92121-3740	(507) 555-2935	M	12/10/1992
⊞	22407	Mazeau	Rebecca	7383 Oak Dr.	Landis	CA	92120-3741	(941) 555-1093	F	9/23/1982
⊞	03225	Morgan	Dan	564 S. Lemon Dr.	Maldin	CA	92121	(507) 555-4567	M	3/5/1984
⊞	00617	Nichols	Cathy	75 Brooklea Dr.	Landis	CA	92120-3741	(507) 555-0001	F	5/19/1972
⊞	00907	Pennington	Mark	23 Mill Ave.	Landis	CA	92120-3741	(507) 555-3333	M	7/7/1977
⊞	12194	Polonsky	Mitch	8701 E. Sheridan	Maldin	CA	92121-3740	(507) 555-1018	M	3/13/1990
⊞	12247	Rath	Kathy	87 E. Aurora Ave.	Chesterfield	CA	92122-1268	(507) 555-4797	F	5/30/1988
⊞	12230	Reddie	Suzanne	932 E. Parkway Dr.	Landis	CA	92120-3741	(507) 555-1191	F	7/14/1988
⊞	12594	Reddie	Mark	900 W. Campus Dr.	Maldin	CA	92121	(507) 555-1139	M	11/5/1986
⊞	13005	Reilly	Emily	125 N. Marigold St.	Maldin	CA	92121-3740	(941) 555-4532	F	5/21/1988
⊞	12612	Richards	Melissa	5522 W. Marin Lane	River Mist	CA	92123	(507) 555-4789	F	9/30/1981
⊞	06000	Robertson	Kirk	832 S. William Ave.	Maldin	CA	92121	(507) 555-3730	M	4/5/1982
⊞	22297	Rogondino	Patricia	7583 Turquoise	Chesterfield	CA	92122-1268	(941) 555-4539	F	8/30/1980
⊞	07287	Roman	Anita	2348 S. Bala Dr.	Maldin	CA	92121-3740	(507) 555-4870	F	3/15/1990
⊞	08391	Ruiz	Enrique	35 Palm St.	Chesterfield	CA	92122-1268	(507) 555-0091	M	12/10/1982
⊞	04321	Sabin	Greg	90 E. Rawhide Ave.	Chesterfield	CA	92122	(507) 555-4455	M	9/30/1987
⊞	00212	Schiff	Chad	235 N. Cactus Dr.	Chesterfield	CA	92122	(507) 555-0010	M	3/9/1970
⊞	22114	Schneider	Paul	1731 Jackson Ave.	Landis	CA	92120-3741	(941) 555-4440	M	2/23/1983
⊞	01421	Spehr	Timothy	90 Royal Dr.	Maldin	CA	92121-3740	(507) 555-1038	M	9/9/1978
⊞	12366	Stacey	David	737 S. College Rd.	Chesterfield	CA	92122-1268	(507) 555-4784	M	9/30/1981
⊞	13497	Steele	Jeff	1011 E. Holly Ln.	River Mist	CA	92123-2232	(941) 555-1912	M	4/9/1990
⊞	12668	Stueland	Valerie	34 University Dr.	Maldin	CA	92121-3740	(507) 555-1845	F	11/19/1982
⊞	12583	Sullivan	Marie	78 Omega Drive	Chesterfield	CA	92122-1268	(507) 555-3890	F	3/15/1991
⊞	12867	Talic	Elvis	21 Oasis St.	River Mist	CA	92123-2232	(941) 555-4985	M	6/10/1984

Records with same last name not sorted by first name

Figure 2.35

Now you can see that the records for Julie and Juan Martinez are sorted by last name but not by first name. You want all records that have the same last name to be further sorted by first name. To do this, you need to sort using multiple sort fields.

SORTING ON MULTIPLE FIELDS

Additional Information

If the columns to sort were not already adjacent, you would hide the columns that are in between. If the columns were not in the correct order, you would move the columns.

When sorting on multiple fields, the fields must be adjacent to each other in order to designate the inner and outer sort fields. The **outer sort field** (primary field in the sort) must be to the left of the inner sort field. The Last Name and First Name fields are already in the correct locations for the sort you want to perform. To specify the fields to sort on, both columns must be selected.

1

- Select the Last Name and First Name field columns.

- Click $^{A}_{Z}$↓ Ascending .

- Scroll down to record 25 again.

Your screen should be similar to Figure 2.36

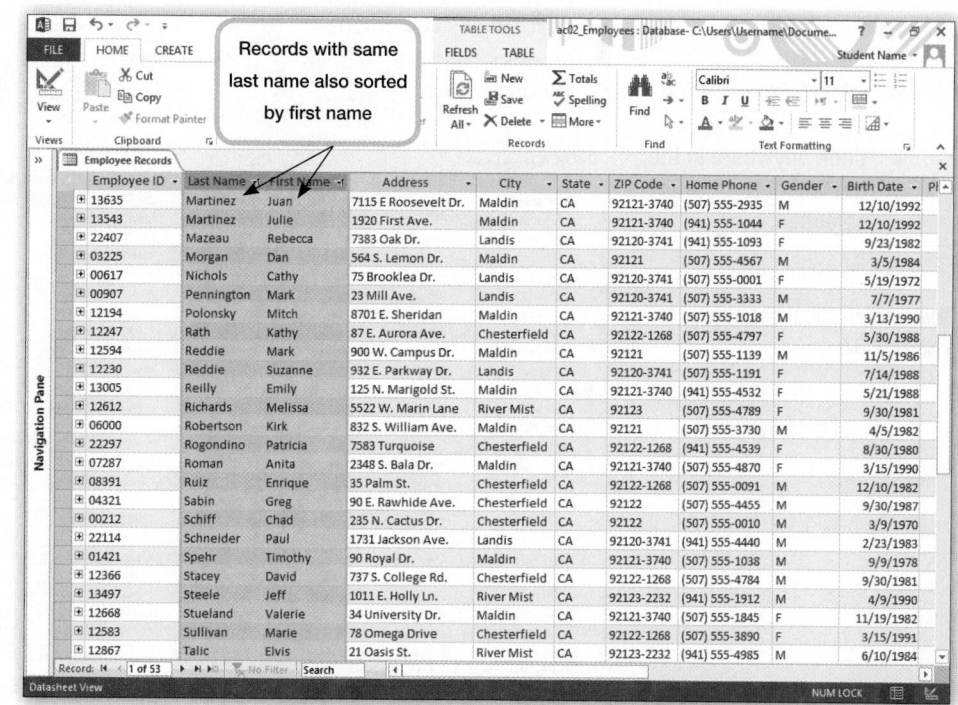

Figure 2.36

The record for Juan Martinez now appears before the record for Julie Martinez. As you can see, sorting is a fast, useful tool. The sort order remains in effect until you remove the sort or replace it with a new sort order. Although Access remembers your sort order even when you exit the program, it does not actually change the table records.

You can remove the sort at any time to restore the records to the primary key sort order. You decide to return to primary key sort order and re-sort the table alphabetically for the Accounting department later, after you have finished making changes to it.

2

● Click 🔠 Remove Sort.

● **Click anywhere in the datasheet to clear the selection.**

Your screen should be similar to Figure 2.37

Records sorted by primary key value

Clears sort order

Employee ID	Last Name	First Name	Address	City	State	ZIP Code	Home Phone	Gender	Birth Date
00212	Schiff	Chad	235 N. Cactus Dr.	Chesterfield	CA	92122	(507) 555-0010	M	3/9/1970
00617	Nichols	Cathy	75 Brooklea Dr.	Landis	CA	92120-3741	(507) 555-0001	F	5/19/1972
00907	Pennington	Mark	23 Mill Ave.	Landis	CA	92120-3741	(507) 555-3333	M	7/7/1977
01421	Spehr	Timothy	90 Royal Dr.	Maldin	CA	92121-3740	(507) 555-1038	M	9/9/1978
03225	Morgan	Dan	564 S. Lemon Dr.	Maldin	CA	92121	(507) 555-4567	M	3/5/1984
03406	Lopez	Mina	4290 E. Alameda Dr.	Maldin	CA	92121-3740	(507) 555-4050	F	2/25/1985
03890	Thi	Erona	7867 Forest Ave.	River Mist	CA	92123	(507) 555-1089	F	5/10/1987
04321	Sabin	Greg	90 E. Rawhide Ave.	Chesterfield	CA	92122	(507) 555-4455	M	9/30/1987
04731	Marchant	Roberta	564 Palm Avenue	Landis	CA	92120-3741	(507) 555-4990	F	5/18/1990
05025	Briggs	Scott	45 E. Camelback Rd.	River Mist	CA	92123-2232	(507) 555-4585	M	9/15/1989
06000	Robertson	Kirk	832 S. William Ave.	Maldin	CA	92121	(507) 555-3730	M	4/5/1982
07287	Roman	Anita	2348 S. Bala Dr.	Maldin	CA	92121-3740	(507) 555-4870	F	3/15/1990
08391	Ruiz	Enrique	35 Palm St.	Chesterfield	CA	92122-1268	(507) 555-0091	M	12/10/1982
11747	Lettow	Ryan	358 Maple Dr.	Maldin	CA	92121-3740	(507) 555-2805	M	11/15/1991
12194	Polonsky	Mitch	8701 E. Sheridan	Maldin	CA	92121-3740	(507) 555-1018	M	3/13/1990
12213	Young	Kim	89 College Ave.	Landis	CA	92120-3741	(507) 555-1059	F	4/12/1990
12230	Reddie	Suzanne	932 E. Parkway Dr.	Landis	CA	92120-3741	(507) 555-1191	F	7/14/1988
12247	Rath	Kathy	87 E. Aurora Ave.	Chesterfield	CA	92122-1268	(507) 555-4797	F	5/30/1988
12258	Delano	Gordon	1310 N. Sprindrift Dr.	Chesterfield	CA	92122-1268	(507) 555-1208	M	8/7/1989
12366	Stacey	David	737 S. College Rd.	Chesterfield	CA	92122-1268	(507) 555-4784	M	9/30/1981
12389	Blackman	Jennifer	773 E. Laurel St.	River Mist	CA	92123-2232	(507) 555-4956	F	1/22/1983
12501	DeLuca	Elizabeth	21 W. Southern Ave.	Landis	CA	92120-3741	(507) 555-1105	F	8/21/1978
12583	Sullivan	Marie	78 Omega Drive	Chesterfield	CA	92122-1268	(507) 555-3890	F	3/15/1991
12594	Reddie	Mark	900 W. Campus Dr.	Maldin	CA	92121	(507) 555-1139	M	11/5/1986
12612	Richards	Melissa	5522 W. Marin Lane	River Mist	CA	92123	(507) 555-4789	F	9/30/1981

Record: 1 of 53   No Filter   Search

Unique five-digit number assigned to each employee.   NUM LOCK

Figure 2.37

All the sorts are cleared, and the data in the table is now in order by the primary key field, Employee ID.

FORMATTING THE DATASHEET

Finally, you want to format or enhance the appearance of the datasheet on the screen to make it more readable or attractive by applying different effects. Datasheet formats include settings that change the appearance of the cell, gridlines, background and gridline colors, and border and line styles. In addition, you can change the text color and add text effects such as bold and italics to the datasheet. Datasheet formats affect the entire datasheet appearance and cannot be applied to separate areas of the datasheet.

> **Additional Information**
>
> Refer to the section Formatting Text in the Introduction to Microsoft Office 2013 to review formatting features.

CHANGING BACKGROUND AND GRIDLINE COLORS

The default datasheet format displays alternate rows in white and light gray backgrounds with a gridline color of blue-gray. The text color is set to black. You want to see the effect of changing the color of the alternate rows and gridlines in the datasheet.

1

● Click ⬚ **Datasheet Formatting** in the Text Formatting group of the Home tab to open the Datasheet Formatting dialog box.

Your screen should be similar to Figure 2.38

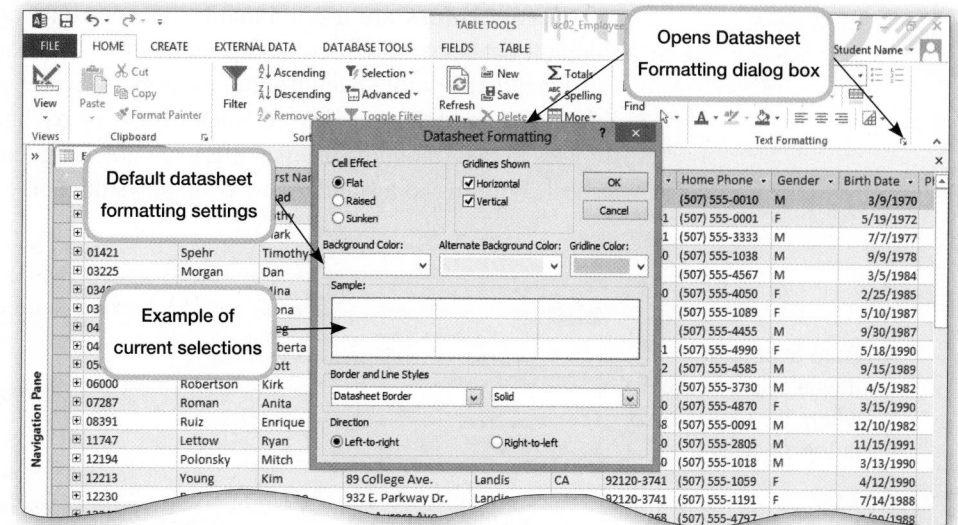

Figure 2.38

The default datasheet formatting settings are displayed in the dialog box, and the Sample area shows how the settings will appear in the datasheet. You will leave the background color white and change the color of the alternate rows.

2

● Open the Alternate Background Color drop-down menu.

Your screen should be similar to Figure 2.39

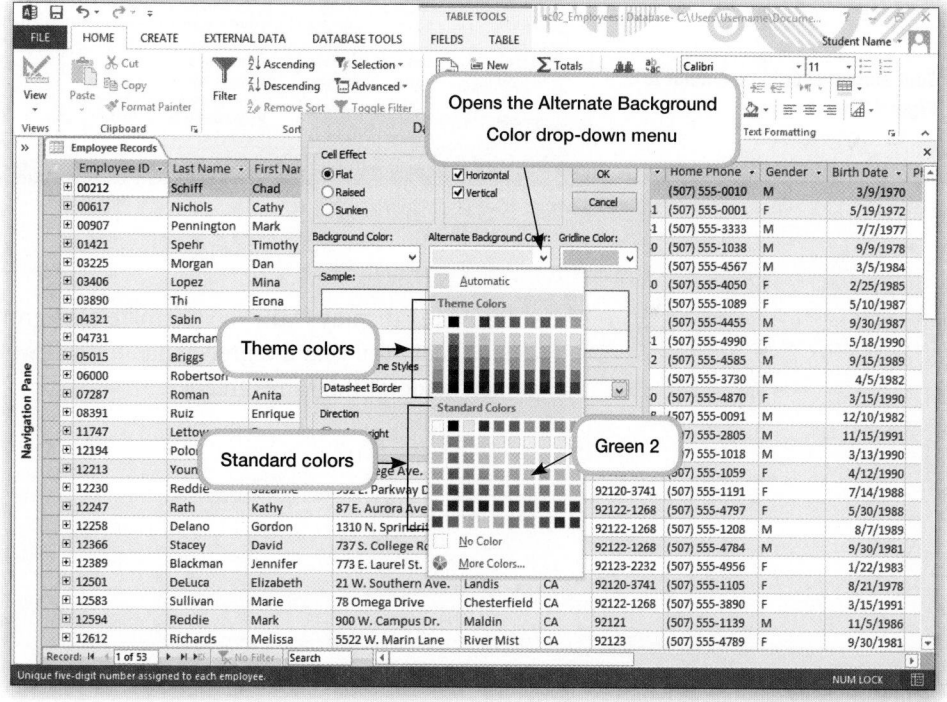

Figure 2.39

The color gallery displays the Access theme colors in the upper section and standard colors in the lower section.

Theme colors are a combination of coordinating colors that are used in the default datasheet. Each color is assigned to a different area of the datasheet, such as label text or table background. Pointing to a theme color identifies the name of the color and where it is used, such as text or background, in the ScreenTip. The colors in the Standard Colors gallery are not assigned to specific areas on the datasheet. Pointing to a standard color displays the name assigned to the color.

3

• **Point to several theme colors to see where they are used in the datasheet.**

• **Click on the Green 2 color in the Standard Colors area.**

Another Method

You also can use [icon] Alternate Row Color in the Text Formatting group to change the color.

Your screen should be similar to Figure 2.40

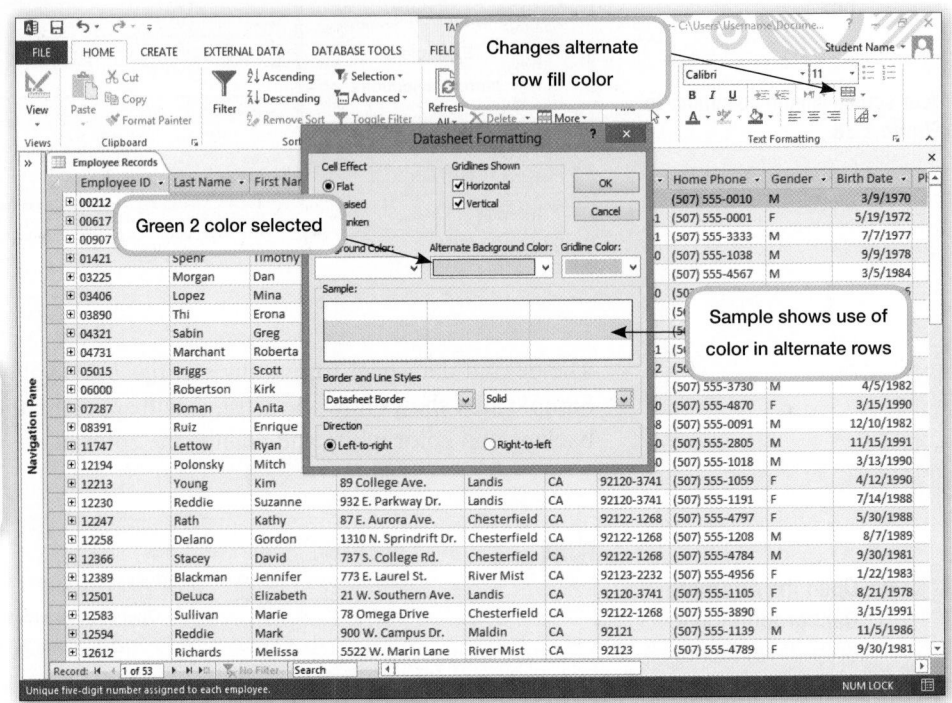

Figure 2.40

The sample area displays how the alternate background color selection will appear in the datasheet. You like the green shading and want to change the gridline color to a darker shade of the same green.

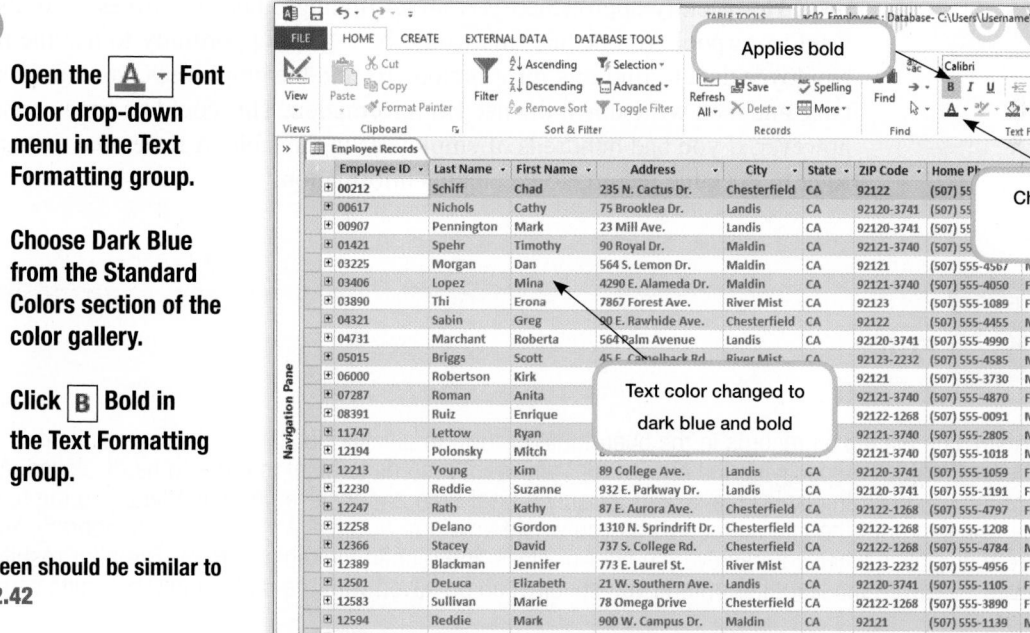

4
- Open the Gridline Color drop-down menu.

- Choose Green 5 from the Standard Colors area.

- Click [OK].

Your screen should be similar to Figure 2.41

Datasheet formatted with alternating Green 2 row color and Green 5 gridlines

Figure 2.41

Additional Information
You can use [🔲 ▾] Gridlines in the Text Formatting group to change the display of the gridlines.

The selected alternating row and gridline color formatting has been applied to the datasheet.

CHANGING THE TEXT COLOR

Although the addition of color makes it easier to read across the rows, you think the text is a little light. You will change the text color to a dark blue and bold.

1
- Open the [A ▾] Font Color drop-down menu in the Text Formatting group.

- Choose Dark Blue from the Standard Colors section of the color gallery.

- Click [B] Bold in the Text Formatting group.

Your screen should be similar to Figure 2.42

Applies bold

Changes color of text

Text color changed to dark blue and bold

Figure 2.42

You do not like how the blue text color looks and want to change it back to the default color. You cannot use Undo to remove formatting, so you will need to select the text color again.

2

- Open the [A ▾] Font Color drop-down menu.

- Choose Automatic to restore the default font color.

Your screen should be similar to Figure 2.43

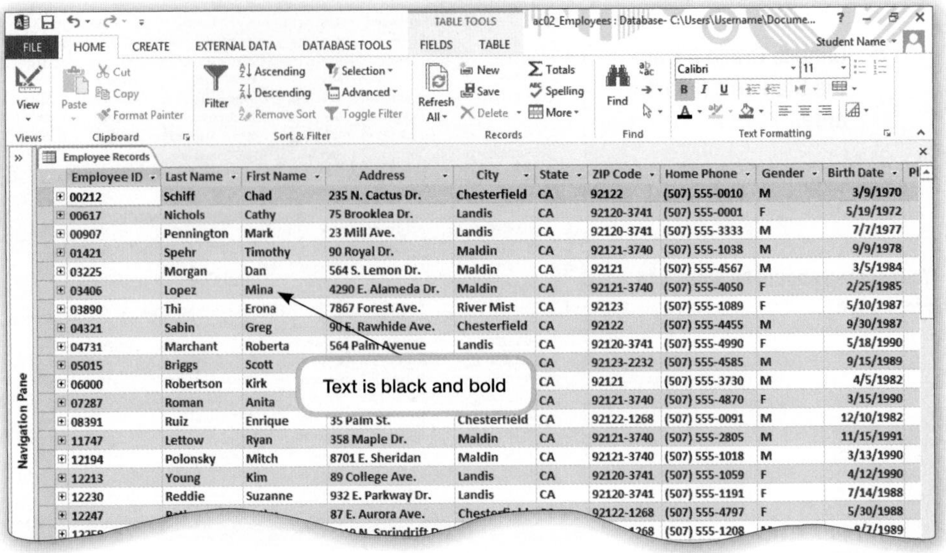

Text is black and bold

Figure 2.43

The black text color is restored. The text is still bolded and is easier to read.

Filtering a Table

Juan Martinez, an employee at the Landis location, is interested in forming a car pool. He recently approached you about finding other employees who also may want to carpool. You decide this would be a great opportunity to use the table of employee data to find this information. To find the employees, you could sort the table and then write down the needed information. This could be time-consuming, however, if you had hundreds of employees in the table. A faster way is to apply a filter to the table records to locate this information.

Concept **8** Filter

A **filter** is a restriction placed on records in the open table or form to quickly isolate and display a subset of records. A filter is created by specifying the criteria that you want records to meet in order to be displayed. A filter is ideal when you want to display the subset for only a brief time and then return immediately to the full set of records. You can print the filtered records as you would any form or table. A filter is only temporary, and all records are redisplayed when you remove the filter or close and reopen the table or form. The filter results cannot be saved. However, the last filter criteria you specify can be saved with the table, and the results can be quickly redisplayed.

USING FILTER BY SELECTION

Juan lives in Maldin and works at the Lifestyle Fitness Club located in Landis. You can locate other employees who live in Maldin quite easily by using the Filter by Selection feature. Filter by Selection displays only records containing a specific value. This method is effective when the table contains only one value that you want to use as the criterion for selecting and displaying records.

Additional Information

If the selected part of a value starts with the first character in the field, the subset displays all records with values that begin with the same selected characters.

The process used to select the value determines the results that will be displayed. Placing the cursor in a field selects the entire field's contents. The filtered subset will include all records containing an exact match. Selecting part of a value in a field (by highlighting it) displays all records containing the selection. For example, in a table for a book collection, you could position the cursor anywhere in a field containing the name of the author Stephen King, choose the Filter by Selection command, and only records for books whose author matches the selected name, "Stephen King," would be displayed. Selecting just "King" would include all records for authors Stephen King, Martin Luther King, and Barbara Kingsolver.

You want to filter the table to display only those records with a City field entry of Maldin. To specify the city to locate, you select an example of the data in the table.

1
- Move to the City field of record 4.

- Click 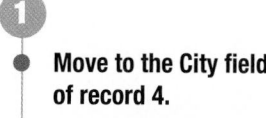 in the Sort & Filter group of the Home tab.

Your screen should be similar to Figure 2.44

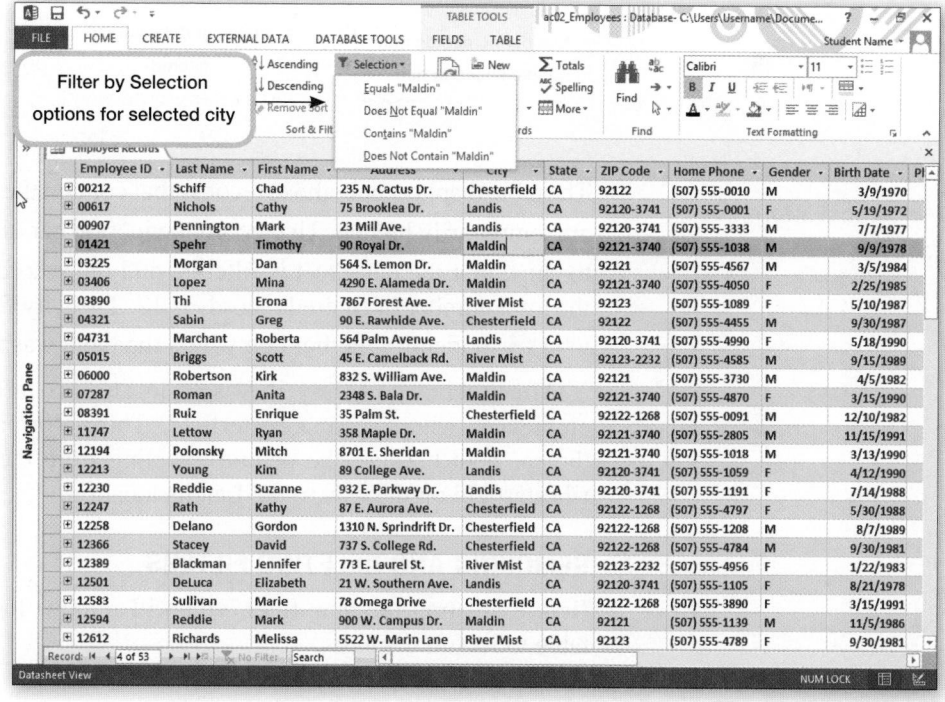

Figure 2.44

The drop-down menu of commands contains the current selected value in the field. The commands that appear will vary depending on the data type of the selected value. Also, the commands will vary depending on how much of the value is selected. If the selection is a partial selection, the commands allow you to specify a filter using the beginning, middle, or end of a field value. In this case, the entire value is selected and the four commands allow you to specify whether you want the selection to equal, not equal, contain, or not contain the value.

2
● **Choose Equals "Maldin".**

Another Method

You also can display the Filter by Selection commands using the selection's shortcut menu.

Your screen should be similar to Figure 2.45

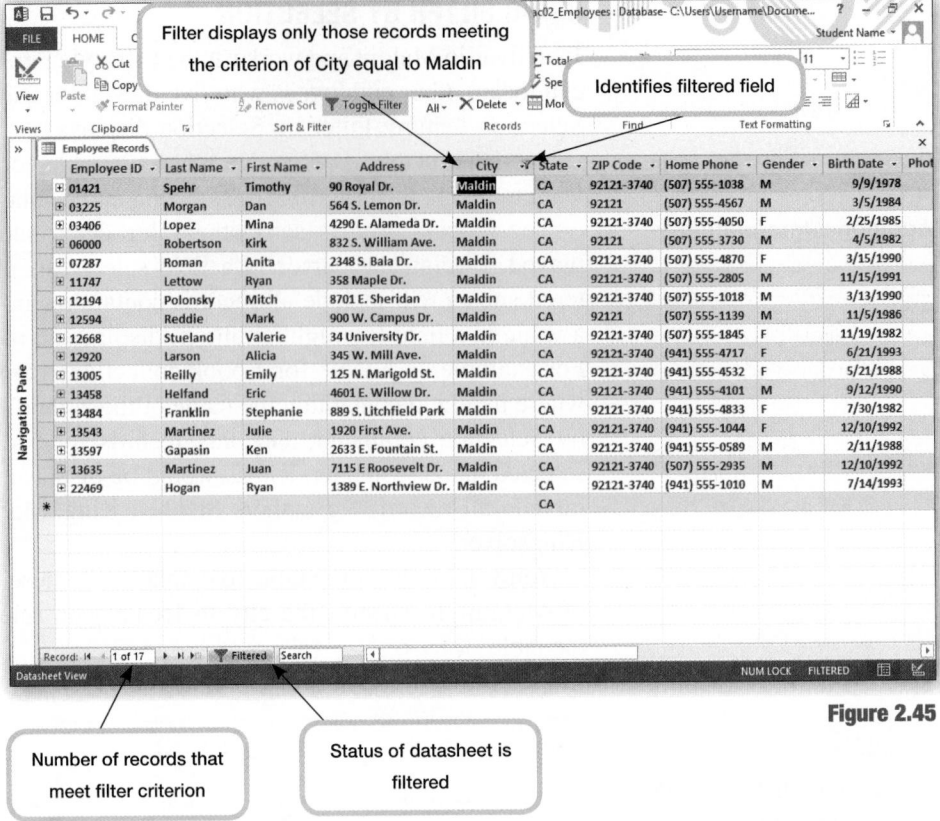

> Filter displays only those records meeting the criterion of City equal to Maldin

> Identifies filtered field

> Number of records that meet filter criterion

> Status of datasheet is filtered

Figure 2.45

Additional Information

You can print a filtered datasheet just like any other table.

The table displays only those records that contain the selected city. All other records are temporarily hidden. The record navigation bar displays the ▼ Filtered button to show that the datasheet is filtered, and the record number indicator shows that the total number of filtered records is 17. The City field name also displays a filter icon ▼ to identify the field on which the table was filtered.

After seeing how easy it was to locate this information, you want to locate employees who live in Chesterfield. This information may help in setting up the car pool because the people traveling from the city of Maldin pass through Chesterfield on the way to the Landis location.

REMOVING AND DELETING FILTERS

Before creating the new filter, you will remove the current filter and return the table to its full display.

1

● Click  **Toggle Filter** in the Sort & Filter group.

Another Method

You also can use ▼ Filtered in the record navigator bar to apply and remove a filter.

Your screen should be similar to Figure 2.46

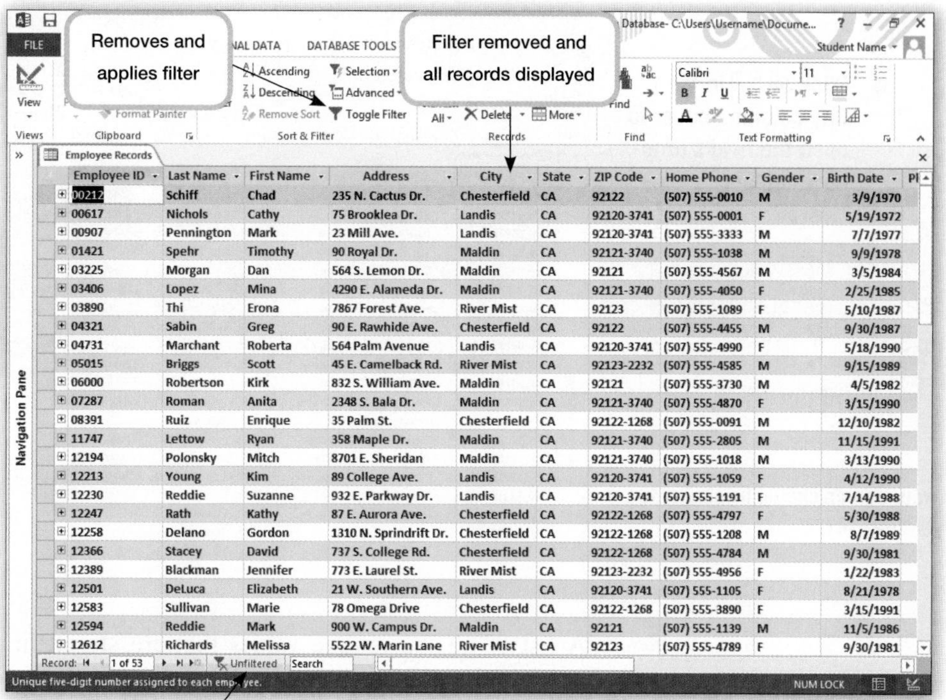

Removes and applies filter

Filter removed and all records displayed

Employee ID	Last Name	First Name	Address	City	State	ZIP Code	Home Phone	Gender	Birth Date	Pl
00212	Schiff	Chad	235 N. Cactus Dr.	Chesterfield	CA	92122	(507) 555-0010	M	3/9/1970	
00617	Nichols	Cathy	75 Brooklea Dr.	Landis	CA	92120-3741	(507) 555-0001	F	5/19/1972	
00907	Pennington	Mark	23 Mill Ave.	Landis	CA	92120-3741	(507) 555-3333	M	7/7/1977	
01421	Spehr	Timothy	90 Royal Dr.	Maldin	CA	92121-3740	(507) 555-1038	M	9/9/1978	
03225	Morgan	Dan	564 S. Lemon Dr.	Maldin	CA	92121	(507) 555-4567	M	3/5/1984	
03406	Lopez	Mina	4290 E. Alameda Dr.	Maldin	CA	92121-3740	(507) 555-4050	F	2/25/1985	
03890	Thi	Erona	7867 Forest Ave.	River Mist	CA	92123	(507) 555-1089	F	5/10/1987	
04321	Sabin	Greg	90 E. Rawhide Ave.	Chesterfield	CA	92122	(507) 555-4455	M	9/30/1987	
04731	Marchant	Roberta	564 Palm Avenue	Landis	CA	92120-3741	(507) 555-4990	F	5/18/1990	
05015	Briggs	Scott	45 E. Camelback Rd.	River Mist	CA	92123-2232	(507) 555-4585	M	9/15/1989	
06000	Robertson	Kirk	832 S. William Ave.	Maldin	CA	92121	(507) 555-3730	M	4/5/1982	
07287	Roman	Anita	2348 S. Bala Dr.	Maldin	CA	92121-3740	(507) 555-4870	F	3/15/1990	
08391	Ruiz	Enrique	35 Palm St.	Chesterfield	CA	92122-1268	(507) 555-0091	M	12/10/1982	
11747	Lettow	Ryan	358 Maple Dr.	Maldin	CA	92121-3740	(507) 555-2805	M	11/15/1991	
12194	Polonsky	Mitch	8701 E. Sheridan	Maldin	CA	92121-3740	(507) 555-1018	M	3/13/1990	
12213	Young	Kim	89 College Ave.	Landis	CA	92120-3741	(507) 555-1059	F	4/12/1990	
12230	Reddie	Suzanne	932 E. Parkway Dr.	Landis	CA	92120-3741	(507) 555-1191	F	7/14/1988	
12247	Rath	Kathy	87 E. Aurora Ave.	Chesterfield	CA	92122-1268	(507) 555-4797	F	5/30/1988	
12258	Delano	Gordon	1310 N. Sprindrift Dr.	Chesterfield	CA	92122-1268	(507) 555-1208	M	8/7/1989	
12366	Stacey	David	737 S. College Rd.	Chesterfield	CA	92122-1268	(507) 555-4784	M	9/30/1981	
12389	Blackman	Jennifer	773 E. Laurel St.	River Mist	CA	92123-2232	(507) 555-4956	F	1/22/1983	
12501	DeLuca	Elizabeth	21 W. Southern Ave.	Landis	CA	92120-3741	(507) 555-1105	F	8/21/1978	
12583	Sullivan	Marie	78 Omega Drive	Chesterfield	CA	92122-1268	(507) 555-3890	F	3/15/1991	
12594	Reddie	Mark	900 W. Campus Dr.	Maldin	CA	92121	(507) 555-1139	M	11/5/1986	
12612	Richards	Melissa	5522 W. Marin Lane	River Mist	CA	92123	(507) 555-4789	F	9/30/1981	

Record: 1 of 53 ▼ Unfiltered Search

Unique five-digit number assigned to each employee.

NUM LOCK

Figure 2.46

Datasheet not filtered

The filter is temporarily removed from the field and all the records are displayed again. The record navigation bar displays ▼ **Unfiltered**. The filter is still available and can be reapplied quickly by clicking ▼ **Toggle Filter** or ▼ **Unfiltered**.

You will reapply the filter, and then you will permanently remove these filter settings.

2

● Click ▼ **Toggle Filter** to redisplay the filtered datasheet.

● Click ▣ **Advanced** ▼ in the Sort & Filter group.

● Choose **Clear All Filters.**

The filter is removed and all the records are redisplayed. The ▼ **Toggle Filter** button is dimmed and the record navigation bar displays ▼ **No Filter** because the table does not include any filter settings.

FILTERING USING COMMON FILTERS

To filter the employee data by two cities, Chesterfield and Maldin, you can select from a list of several popular filters. Using this list allows you to perform filters on multiple criteria within a single field.

1

● **Click on** ▾ **in the City column header to open the field's drop-down menu.**

Another Method

You also can move to the field to filter on and click ▼ (Filter) in the Sort & Filter group to display the Filter list.

Your screen should be similar to Figure 2.47

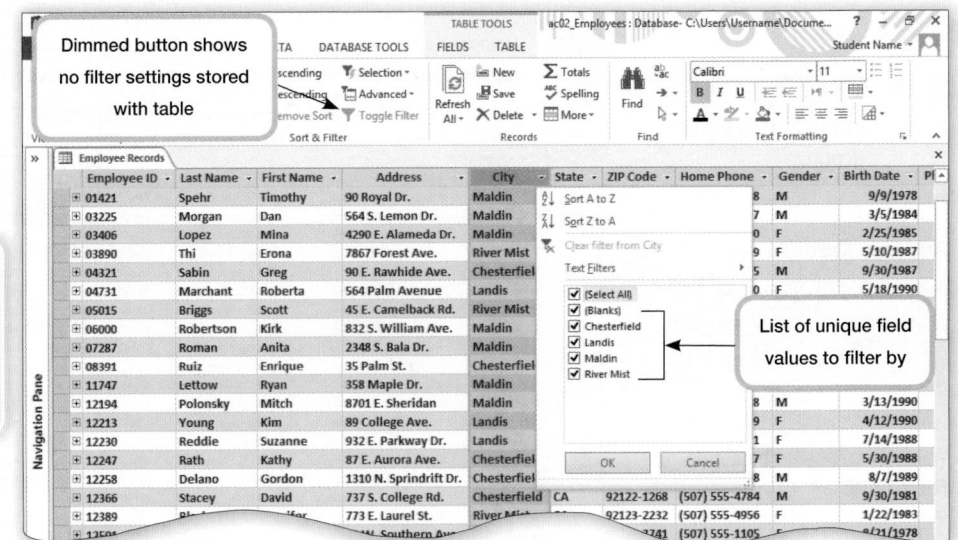

Figure 2.47

A list of all the unique values that are stored in the current field is displayed. Selecting a value from the list filters the table based on the selected value. Depending on the data type of the selected value, you may be able to filter for a range of values by clicking on a value and specifying the appropriate range. In this case, because the field is not filtered, all the values are selected. You will first clear the selection from all values, and then select the names of the two cities you want displayed in the filtered list.

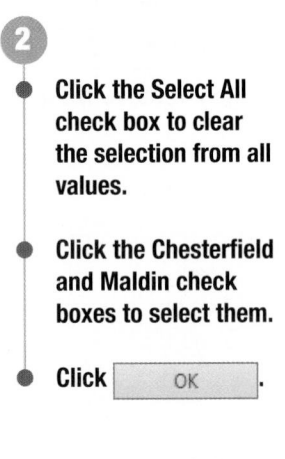

2

● **Click the Select All check box to clear the selection from all values.**

● **Click the Chesterfield and Maldin check boxes to select them.**

● **Click** OK **.**

Your screen should be similar to Figure 2.48

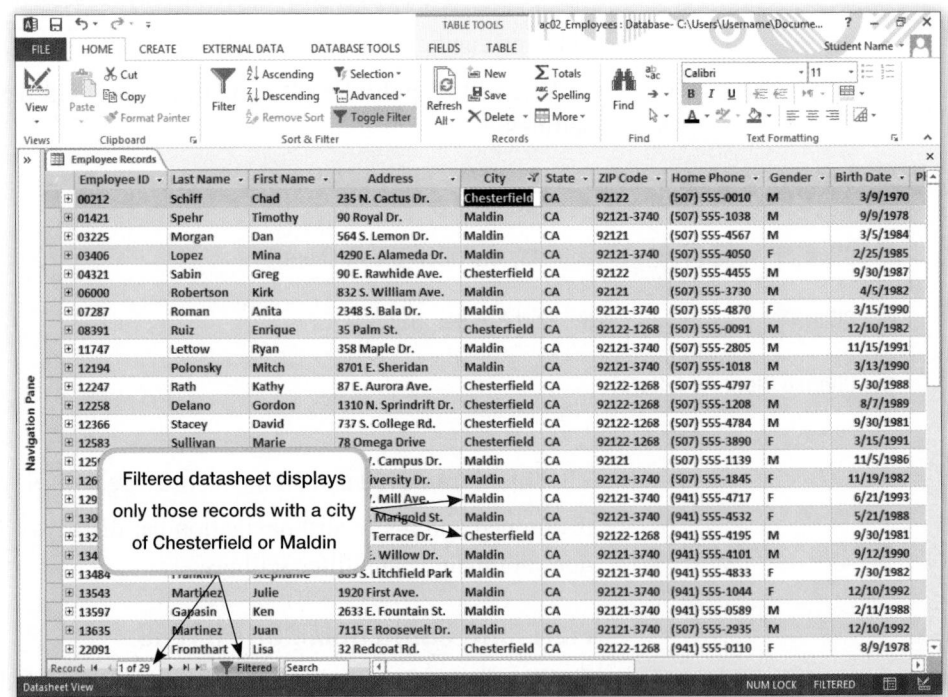

Figure 2.48

The filtered datasheet displays the records for all 29 employees who live in the cities of Chesterfield or Maldin.

FILTERING ON MULTIPLE FIELDS

As you look at the filtered results, you decide to further refine the list by restricting the results so that records with ZIP Code 92121 do not show because it is in the opposite direction from the fitness club. Although you can only specify one filter per field, you can specify a different filter for each field that is present in the view.

1

● Open the ZIP Code field's drop-down menu to display the field list.

● Clear the check mark from the 92121 value.

● Click [OK].

Your screen should be similar to Figure 2.49

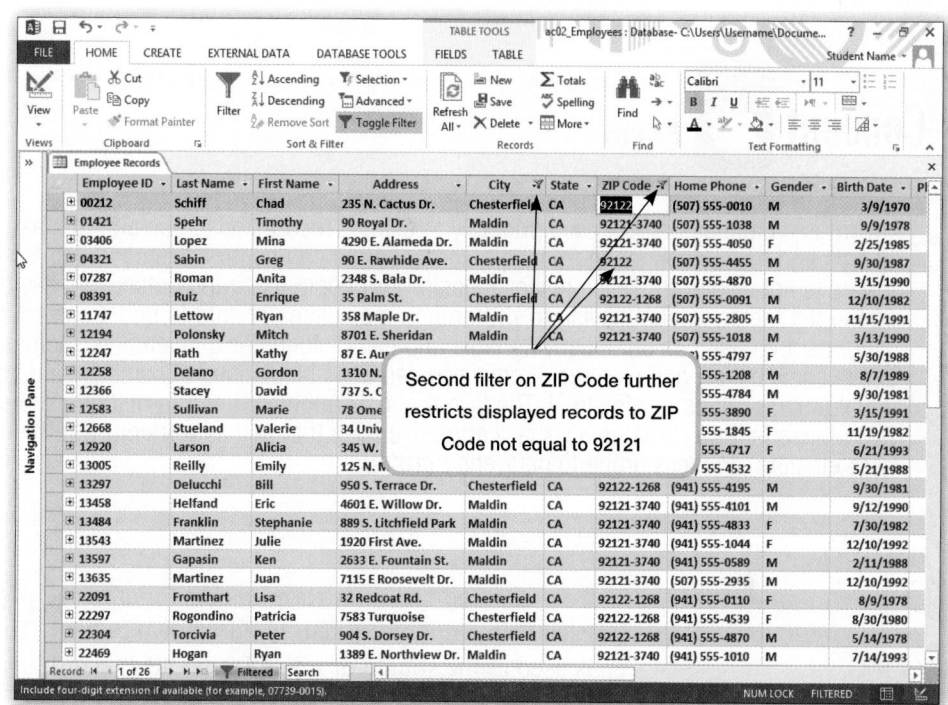

Figure 2.49

Now there are only 26 records displayed in the filtered table. Applying the second filter refined the results by removing all records from the filtered list that had a ZIP Code of 92121.

Although you would like to provide a copy of this information to Juan, you realize that it contains more information about each employee than someone would need (or should even have access to) in order to form a car pool. Also, because you are not finished adding records to the employee database, these findings may not be complete.

You will redisplay all the records in the table, but you will not clear the filter settings. If you do not clear the filters, the filter criteria you last specified are stored with the table, and the results can be redisplayed simply by applying the filter again.

2

● Click [▼ Toggle Filter] to display the unfiltered datasheet.

● Close the table, saving your design changes.

● Redisplay the Navigation pane.

NOTE If you are ending your session now, close the database file and exit Access. When you begin again, start Access and open the ac02_Employees database file.

One of your objectives is to make the database easy to use. You know from experience that long hours of viewing large tables can be tiring. Therefore, you want to create an onscreen form to make this table easier to view and use.

Concept  9 Form

A **form** is a database object used primarily to display records onscreen and to make it easier to enter new records and make changes to existing records. Forms can control access to data so that any unnecessary fields or data is not displayed, which makes it easier for people using the database. They enable people to use the data in the tables without having to sift through many lines of data to find the exact record.

Forms are based on an underlying table and can include design elements such as descriptive text, titles, labels, lines, boxes, and pictures. Forms also can use calculations to summarize data that is not listed on the actual table, such as a sales total. The layout and arrangement of information can be customized in a form. Using these features creates a visually attractive form that makes working with the database more enjoyable, more efficient, and less prone to data-entry errors.

You want the onscreen form to be similar to the paper form that is completed by each new employee when hired (shown below). The information from that form is used as the source of input for the new record that will be added to the table for the new employee.

EMPLOYEE DATA

Employee ID _____

First Name _____ Last Name _____

Street _____

City _____ State _____ Zip _____

Phone Number _____

Gender _____

Birth Date _____

There are several different methods you can use to create forms, as described in the following table. The method you use depends on the type of form you want to create.

Method	Use to
Form tool	Create a form containing all the fields in the table.
Split Form tool	Create a form that displays the form and datasheet in a single window
Blank Form tool	Build a form from scratch by adding the fields you select from the table
Datasheet tool	Create a form using all the fields in the table and display it in Datasheet view
Multiple Items tool	Create a form that displays multiple records but is more customizable than a datasheet
Form Wizard	Create a form using a wizard that guides you through the steps to create a complex form that displays selected fields, data groups, sorted records, and data from multiple tables
Modal Dialog	Creates a form that must be closed before continuing with another task in the same application.

USING THE FORM TOOL

Using the Form tool is the quickest method to create a simple form. You decide to see if the Form tool will create the form you need.

1

- If necessary, select the Employee Records table in the Navigation pane.

- Open the Create tab.

- Click [Form] in the Forms group.

Your screen should be similar to Figure 2.50

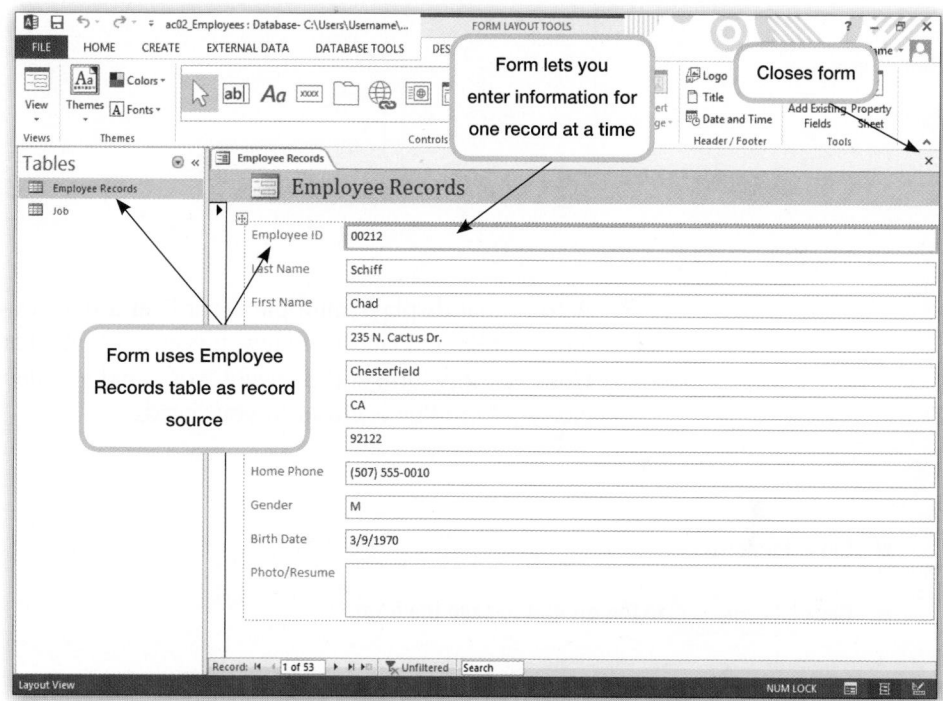

Figure 2.50

A form that allows you to enter data for one record at a time was quickly created. The fields from the Employee Records table were used to create the form because it was the selected object in the Navigation pane. The underlying table that is used to create a form is called the **record source**. The fields are in the same order as in the datasheet.

This form does not quite meet your needs, and you decide to try another method to create the form.

2

- Close the form.

- Click [No] to the prompt to save the form.

USING THE MULTIPLE ITEMS TOOL

Next, you will use the Multiple Items tool to create a form.

- Open the Create tab.

- Click [📄 More Forms ▾] in the Forms group.

- Choose Multiple Items.

Your screen should be similar to Figure 2.51

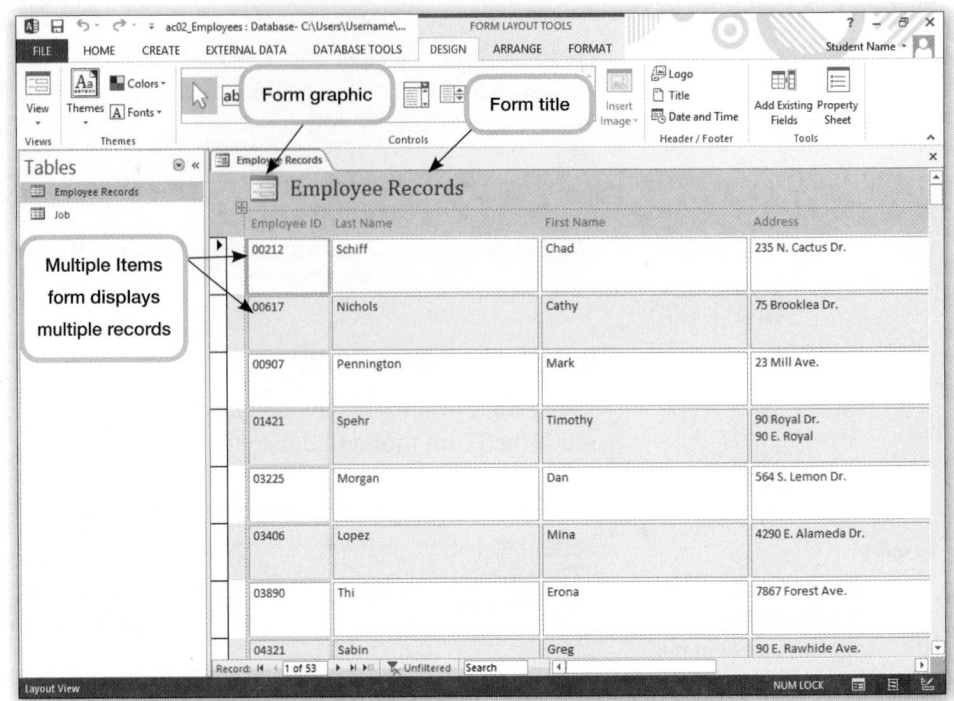

Figure 2.51

A form that displays multiple records at a time was quickly created. Although it looks similar to Datasheet view, it is easier to read and includes a title and graphic. However, this form still does not work, and you decide to use the Form Wizard to create a form that is closer to your needs.

- Close the form.

- Click [No] to the prompt to save the form.

USING THE FORM WIZARD

The **Form Wizard** will help you create a form that is closer to your needs by guiding you through a series of steps that allow you to specify different form features.

1

● Open the Create
  tab and click
  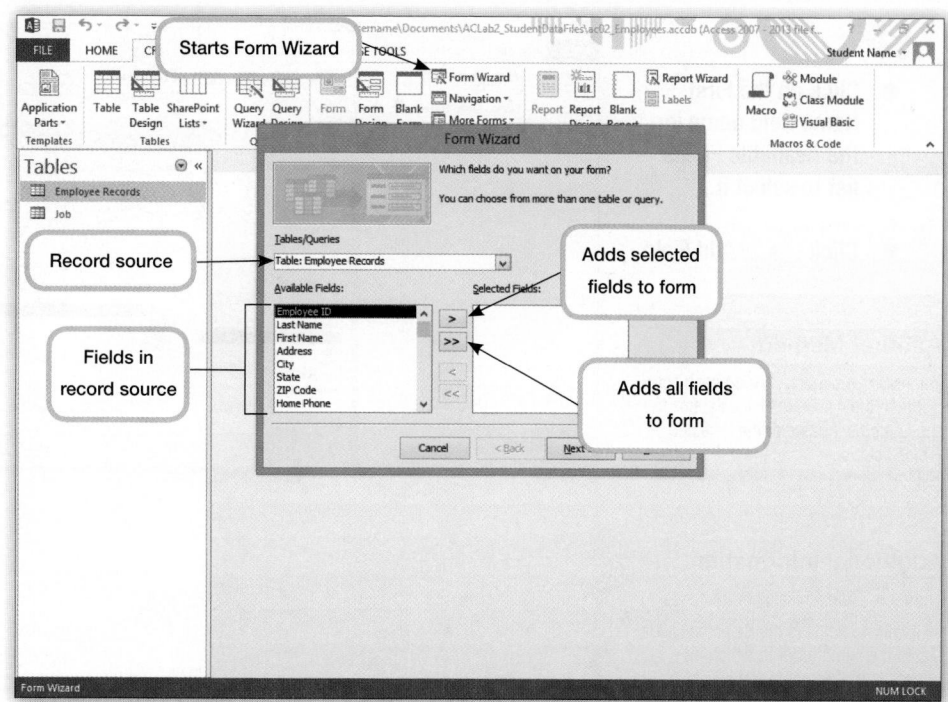 Form Wizard in
  the Forms group.

Your screen should be similar to
Figure 2.52

Figure 2.52

The Form Wizard dialog box displays the name of the current table, Employee
Records, in the Tables/Queries list box. This is the table that will be used as the
record source. If you wanted to use a different table as the record source, you
could open the Tables/Queries drop-down list to select the appropriate table.

The fields from the selected table are displayed in the Available Fields list box.
You use this box to select the fields you want included on the form, in the order in
which you want them to appear. This order is called the **tab order** because it is the
order in which the highlight will move through the fields on the form when you
press the ⟨Tab ⇆⟩ key during data entry. You decide that you want the fields to be
in the same order as they are on the paper form shown in the illustration on page
AC2.46.

Click on the First Name field name in the Available Fields list to select it.

Click > **Add Field.**

Another Method

You also can double-click on each field name in the Available Fields list box to move the field name to the Selected Fields list box.

Additional Information

The >> Add All Fields button adds all available fields to the Selected Fields list, in the same order in which they appear in the Available Fields list.

Your screen should be similar to Figure 2.53

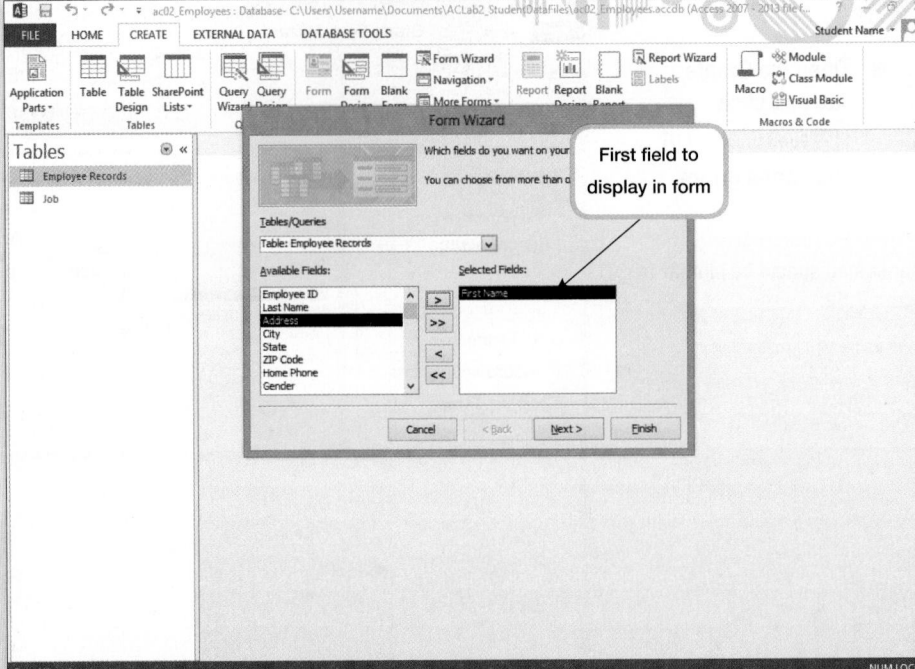

Figure 2.53

The First Name field is removed from the Available Fields list and added to the top of the Selected Fields list box. It will be the first field in the form.

In the same manner, add the following fields to the Selected Fields list in the order shown here:

Last Name

Address

City

State

ZIP Code

Home Phone

Gender

Birth Date

Employee ID

Your screen should be similar to Figure 2.54

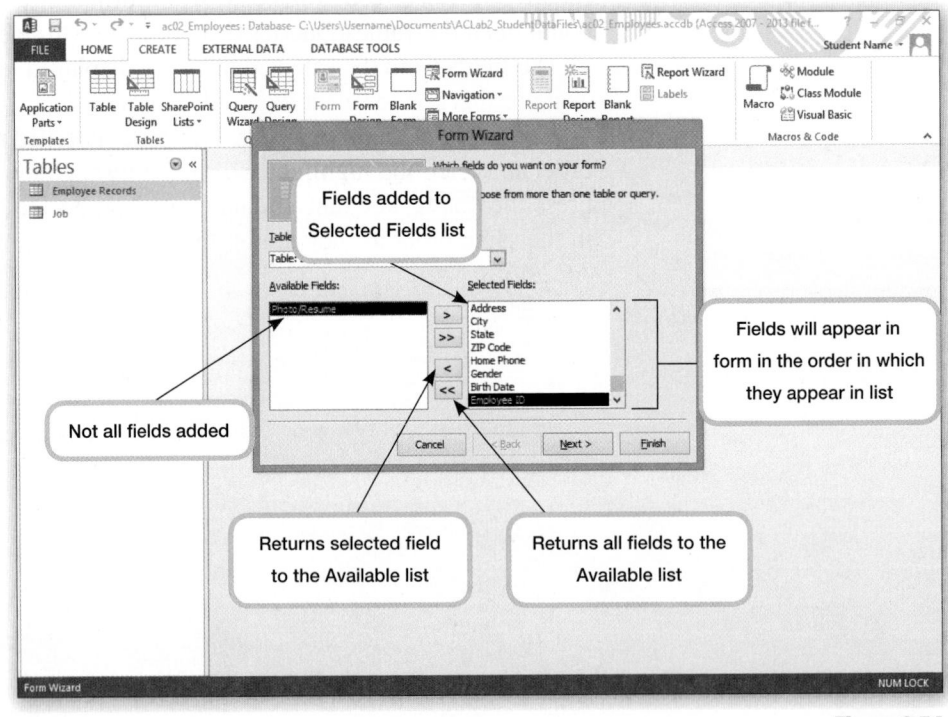

Figure 2.54

Having Trouble?

If you add a field out of the order shown you can return it to the Available Fields list by clicking on < or click << to return all the fields.

When finished, the only remaining field in the Available Fields list box is the Photo/Resume field. The Selected Fields list box contains the fields in the order in which you added them.

You are now ready to move on to the next Form Wizard screen.

Click Next >.

Your screen should be similar to Figure 2.55

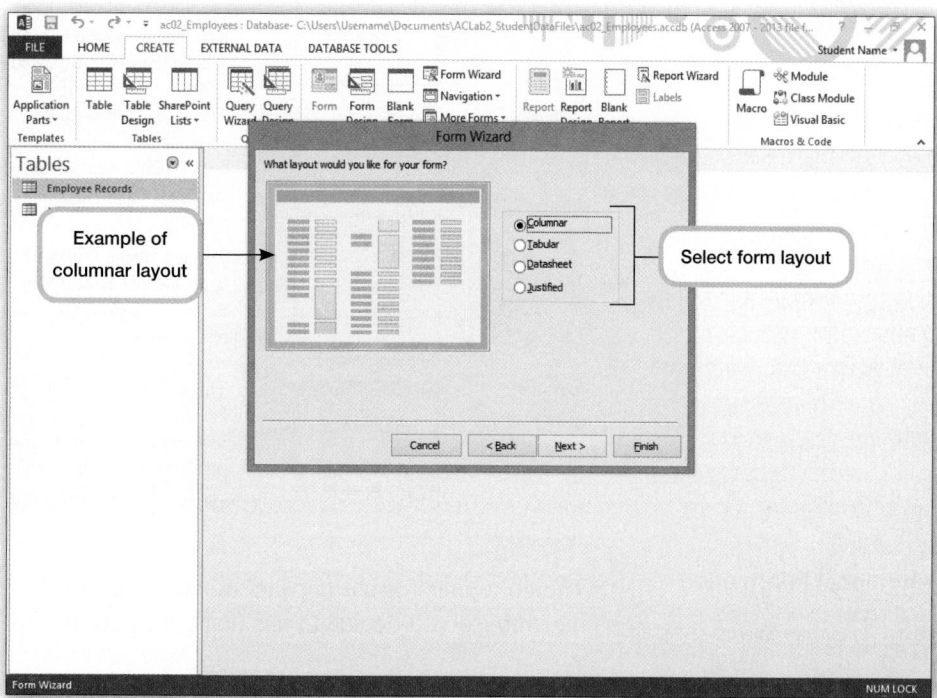

Figure 2.55

In this Form Wizard screen, you are asked to select the control layout for the form. **Layouts** determine how the data is displayed in the form by aligning the items horizontally or vertically to give the form a uniform appearance. Layouts act as a guide for the placement of items on the form.

Layouts are usually configured in a tabular or stacked format. **Tabular formats** arrange the data in rows and columns, with labels across the top. **Stacked formats** arrange data vertically with a field label to the left of the field data. A form can have both types of layouts in different sections.

The four form layouts offered by the Form Wizard are variations of the two basic layouts as described in the following table.

Format		Description
Columnar		This is a stacked format that presents data for the selected fields in columns. The field name labels are displayed in a column on the left, while the corresponding data for each field is in a column on the right. A single record is displayed in each Form window.
Tabular		This is the basic tabular format that presents data with field name labels across the top of the page and the corresponding data in columns under each heading. Multiple records are displayed in the Form window, each on a single row. All fields are displayed across the top of the Form window.
Datasheet		This is a tabular format that displays data in rows and columns similar to the table Datasheet view. It displays multiple records, one per row, in the Form window. You may need to scroll the form horizontally to see all the fields.
Justified		This is a tabular format that displays data in rows, with field name labels across the top of the row and the corresponding field data below it. A single record may appear in multiple rows in the Form window in order to fully display the field name label and data. A single record is displayed in each Form window.

Additional Information

Using 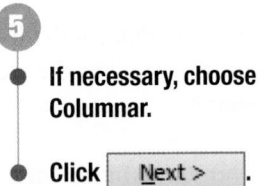 in the Forms group creates a form using the stacked layout.

The columnar format appears most similar to the paper form currently in use by the club, so you decide to use that configuration for your form.

5

● **If necessary, choose Columnar.**

● **Click** [Next >].

Your screen should be similar to Figure 2.56

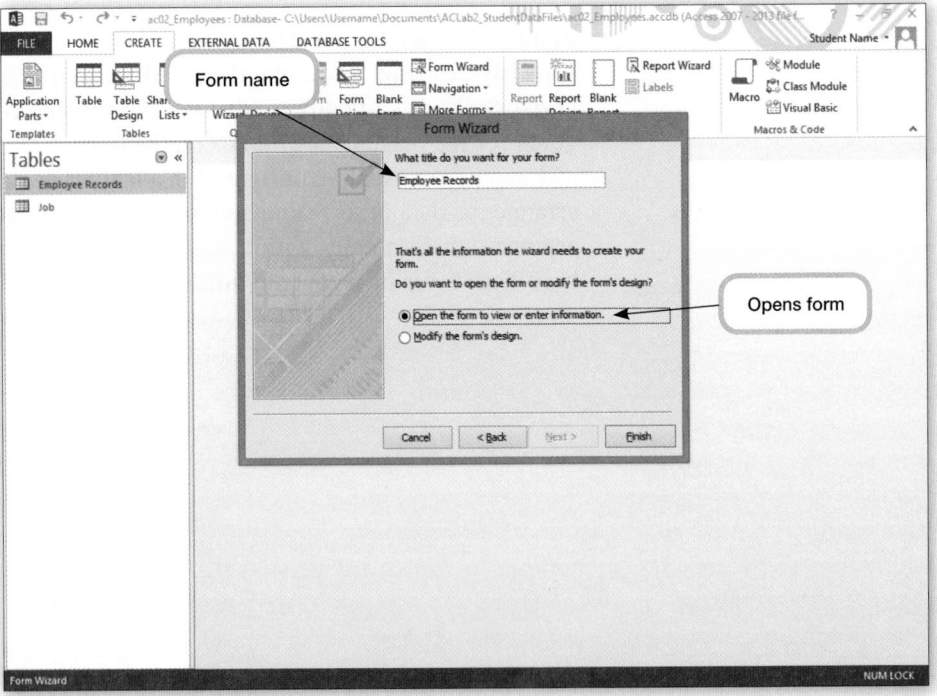

Figure 2.56

In the final Form Wizard dialog box, you can enter a form title to be used as the name of the form, and you can specify whether to open the form or to modify it. The Form Wizard uses the name of the table as the default form title. You will keep the proposed form title and the default of opening the form.

6 • Click [Finish].

Your screen should be similar to Figure 2.57

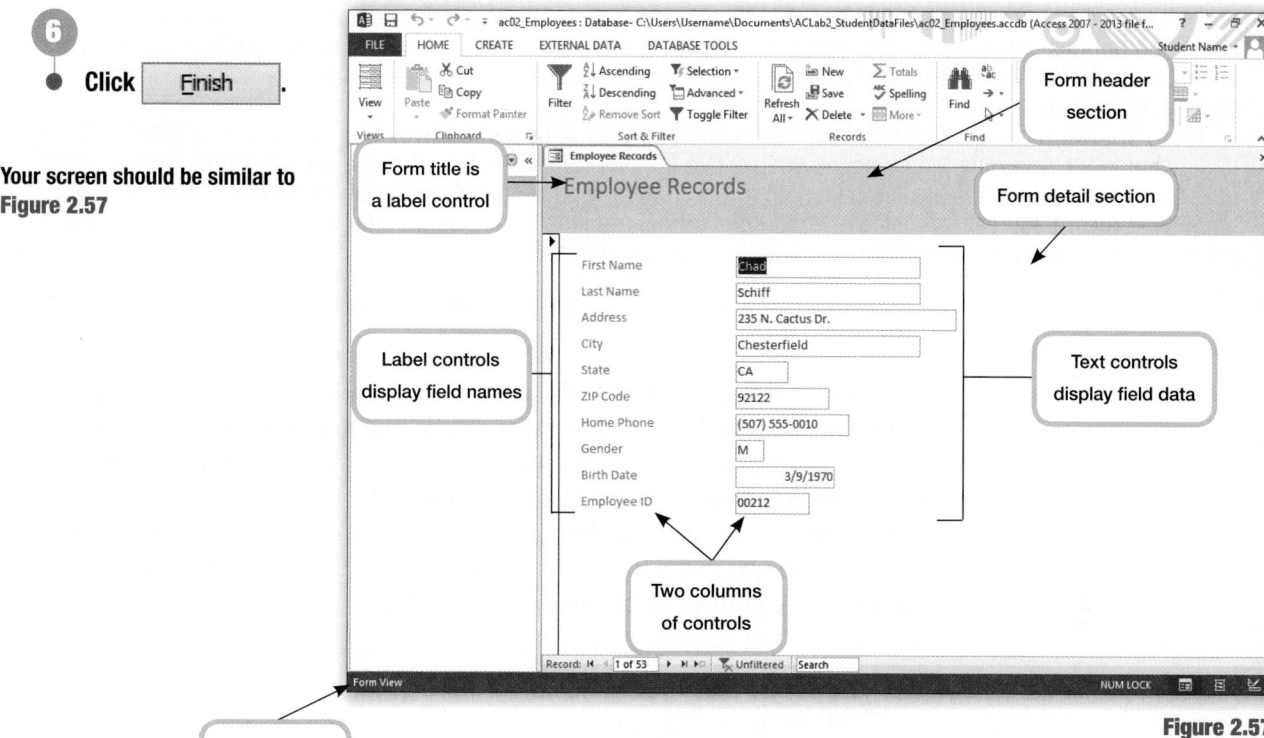

Figure 2.57

The completed form is displayed in the work area in Form view. The form title appears at the top of the form in the form header section. The employee information for Chad Schiff, the first record in the table, is displayed in the form detail section.

Additional Information

You will learn about changing the form design shortly.

The form displays the chosen fields in columnar format with the default form design. The field name labels display in a column on the left, while the data for each corresponding field is displayed in a column on the right.

Each item in the form is a separate object contained in boxes, called controls.

Concept ⑩ Controls

Controls are objects that display information, perform actions, or enhance the design of a form or report. Access provides controls for many types of objects, including labels, text boxes, check boxes, list boxes, command buttons, lines, rectangles, option buttons, and more. The most common controls are text controls and label controls. **Text controls** display the information in the field from the record source. **Label controls** display descriptive labels.

There are two basic types of controls: bound and unbound. A **bound control** is linked to a field in an underlying table. An example of a bound control is a text control that is linked to the record source (usually a field from a table) and displays the field data in the form or report. An **unbound control** is not connected to an underlying record source. Examples of unbound controls are labels such as the title of a form or elements that enhance the appearance of the form such as lines, boxes, and pictures.

This form contains two types of controls: label controls that display the form title and field names and text controls that display the field data. The text controls are bound controls. Changing information in the text controls will change the data for the record in the underlying table. Even though the label controls display the field names that are used in the underlying table, they are unbound controls. If you were to change the text in the form's label control, the field name in the table would not change. The columnar format determines the layout and position of these controls.

Modifying a Form

Although you are generally satisfied with the look of the form, there are a few changes that you want to make. You see that you accidentally placed the Employee ID field at the bottom of the form. The first change you will make is to move the Employee ID field to the top of the form and size it to more closely fit the data.

You can use the form's Layout view or Design view to modify the design and layout of a form. As in the datasheet's Design view, the Design view for a form displays the structure of the form, not the data in the form. It is used to make extensive changes to the form. The form's Layout view displays the underlying data and allows you to make many basic modifications.

USING THE FORM'S LAYOUT VIEW

You will use Layout view to make the change to the Employee ID field controls because you want to be able to see the data in the Employee ID field as you adjust the size of the control.

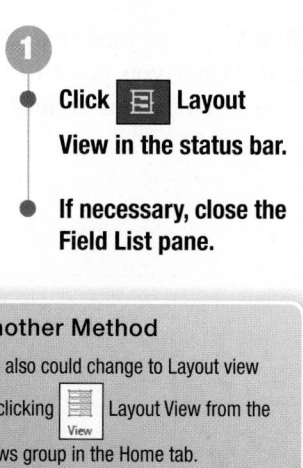

1

● Click ▦ **Layout View in the status bar.**

● **If necessary, close the Field List pane.**

Another Method

You also could change to Layout view by clicking ▦ Layout View from the Views group in the Home tab.

Your screen should be similar to Figure 2.58

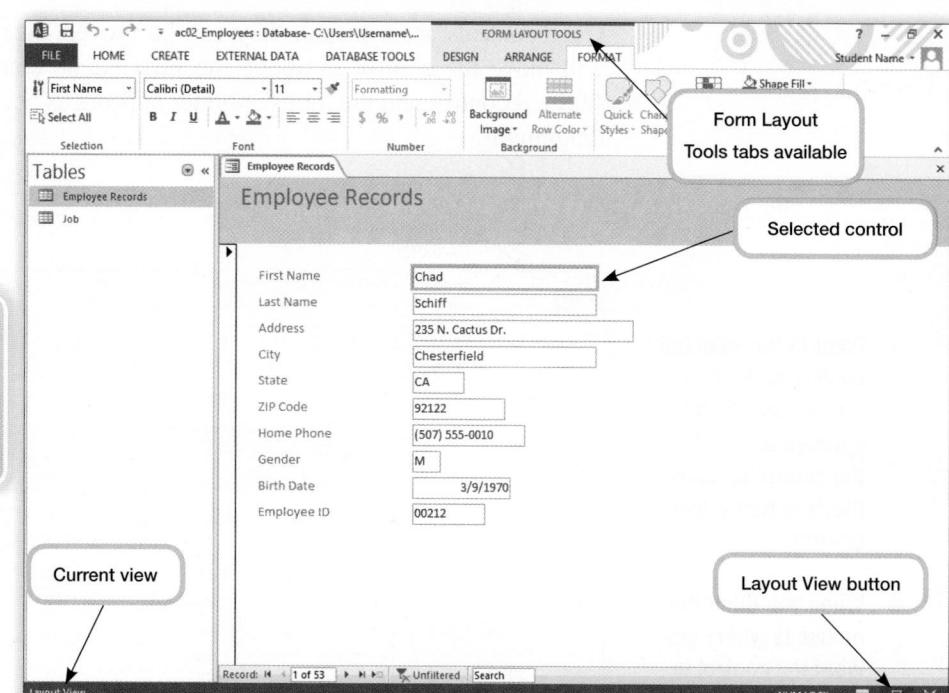

Figure 2.58

The Form Layout Tools Design, Arrange, and Format tabs are now available to help you modify the form design. Currently, the First Name text box control is surrounded with a solid orange box, indicating the control is selected and is the control that will be affected by your actions.

MOVING CONTROLS

First you will select the Employee ID control to move it.

1

● **Click on the Employee ID text control to select it.**

Your screen should be similar to Figure 2.59

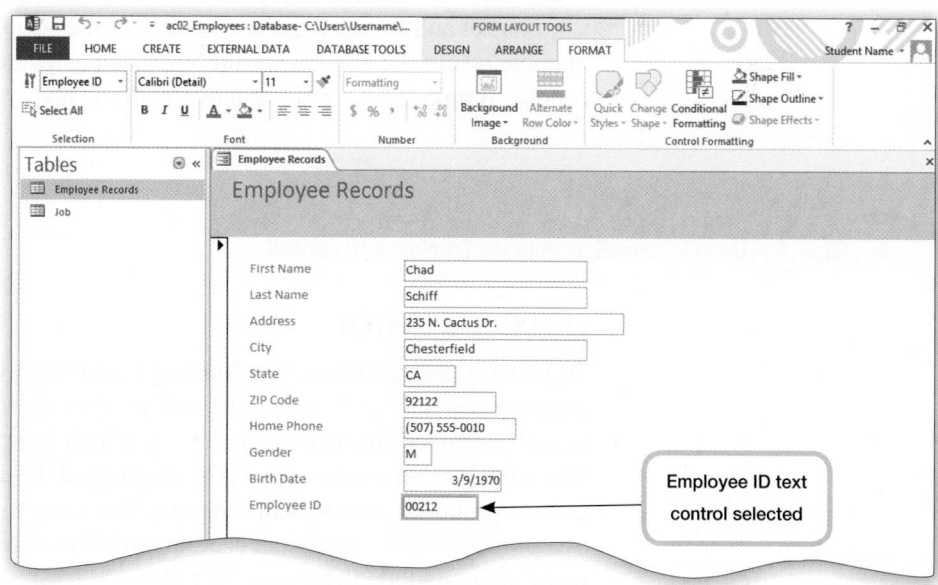

Figure 2.59

The Employee ID text control is selected and surrounded in an orange box.

Once controls are selected, they can be moved, sized, deleted, or modified. You will move the control to above the First Name control. When you point to the selected control and the mouse pointer appears as ✥, you can move the control by dragging it.

2

- **Point to the selected control, and when the mouse pointer appears as ✥, drag the control up above the First Name text control.**
- **When you think the mouse is where you want the control to appear, stop dragging and release the mouse.**

Your screen should be similar to Figure 2.60

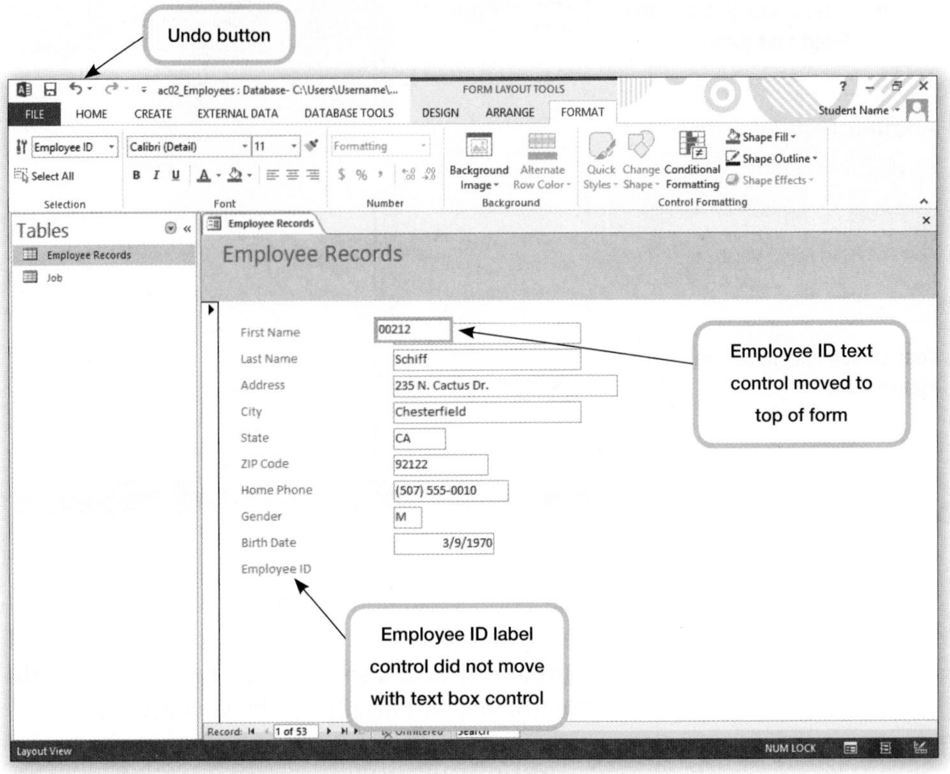

Figure 2.60

When you release the Employee ID control, it probably is on top of the First Name text control and is not aligned with any of the other controls. It also was difficult to know where the control would be placed as you dragged. In addition, the label control, Employee ID, did not move with the text control.

3

- **Click Undo to cancel moving the Employee ID control.**

APPLYING A LAYOUT

To make it easier to move and arrange controls, you will group the controls by applying the stacked layout. This will position the controls in a layout consisting of cells arranged in rows and columns, which behave much like a table in Word. When the Wizard created this form, it arranged the controls in a tabular format but did not group the controls in a layout. You want to include all the form controls except the form title in the stacked layout. You first need to select all the controls you want to include in the new layout.

- Press Ctrl + A to select all the controls on the form.

- Press Ctrl + click on the Employee Records label in the Form header to deselect it.

- Open the Arrange tab and click [Stacked] in the Table group.

Your screen should be similar to Figure 2.61

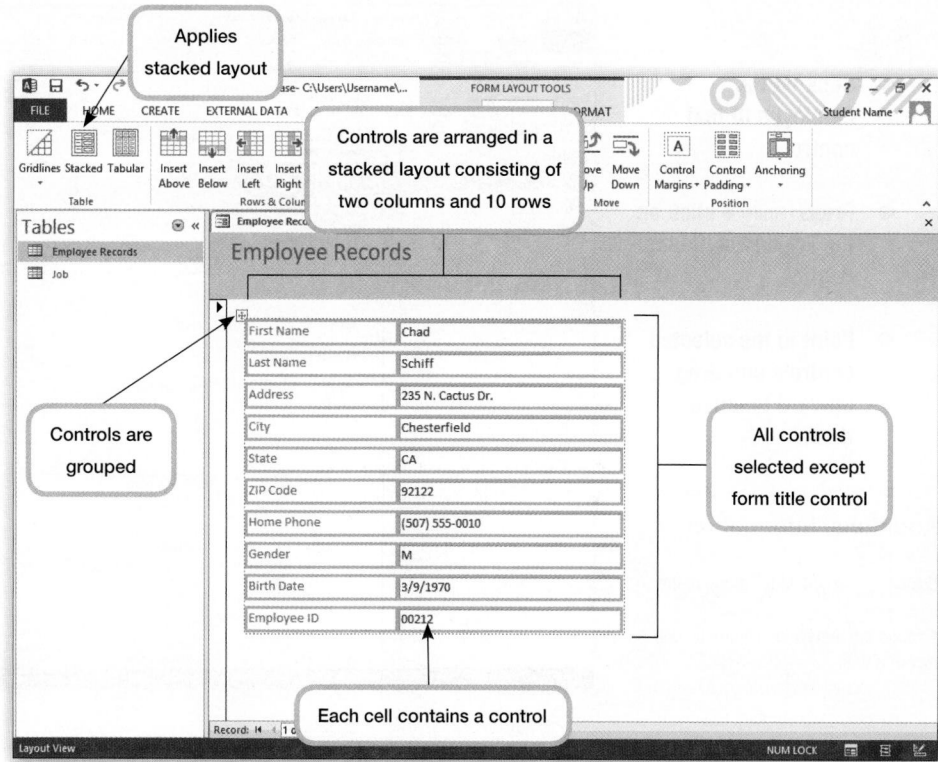

Figure 2.61

All controls in the record's detail section of the form are selected and surrounded with a solid orange border. They are grouped and arranged in the basic stacked layout with the label controls in one column to the left of the text controls. The controls in each column are now all the same size. Notice also that the group is surrounded with a dotted border with a ⊞ in the upper-left corner. This indicates the controls are grouped in the layout.

The layout is a guide that helps you align your controls horizontally and vertically. It is similar in appearance to a table, which consists of rows and columns, but the layout differs in that it only allows controls to be placed in the cells. This layout has two columns and 10 rows. Each cell contains a single control.

You will again move the Employee ID control. This time, you also will select the Employee ID label so that both controls will move together. As you move the controls in the layout, a solid pink line will appear showing you where the controls will be placed when you stop dragging.

2

• Click on the Employee ID text control.

• Press ⟨Shift⟩ + click on the Employee ID label control.

• Point to the selected controls and drag upward to move them.

Additional Information

Using 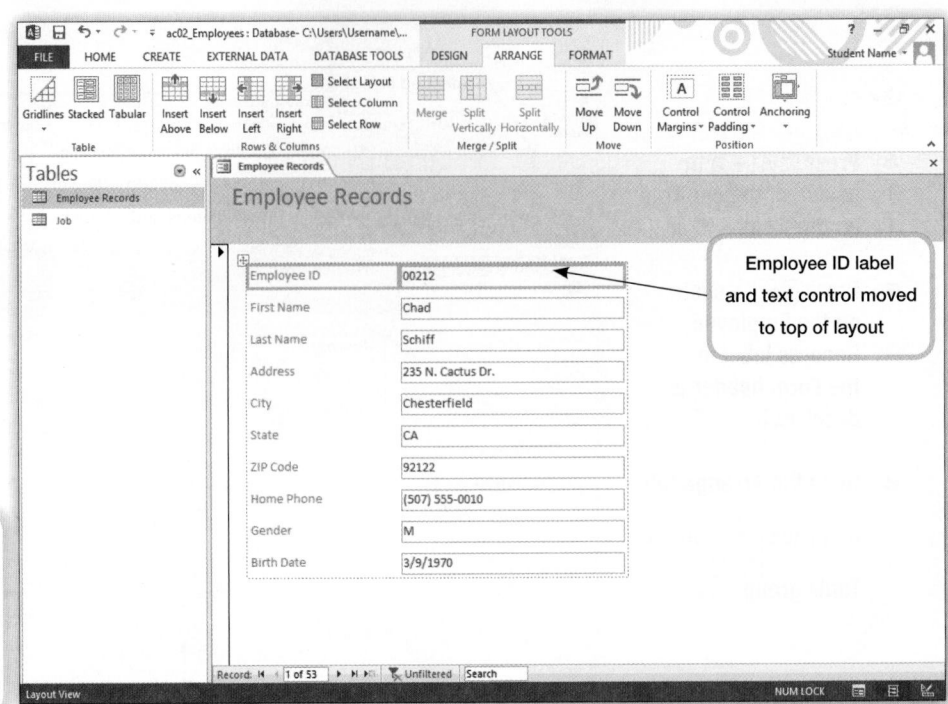 in the Move group of the Arrange tab moves the control up one row at a time.

• When the light pink line appears above the First Name control, release the mouse button to drop the controls in the new location.

Your screen should be similar to Figure 2.62

Figure 2.62

The Employee ID label and text controls have moved to the top row of the table and all other controls have moved down one row.

SIZING AND MOVING CONTROLS IN A LAYOUT

Next, you want to reduce the size of the Employee ID text control to match the size of the entry. When you position the mouse pointer on the orange box surrounding the selected control, the pointer changes to ↔ and can be used to size the control. The direction of the arrow indicates in which direction dragging the mouse will alter the shape of the object. This action is similar to sizing a window. When adjusting the size of controls, remember to size them to accommodate the longest entries. For example a ZIP Code of 92121-3740 will take up more space than a five-digit ZIP Code.

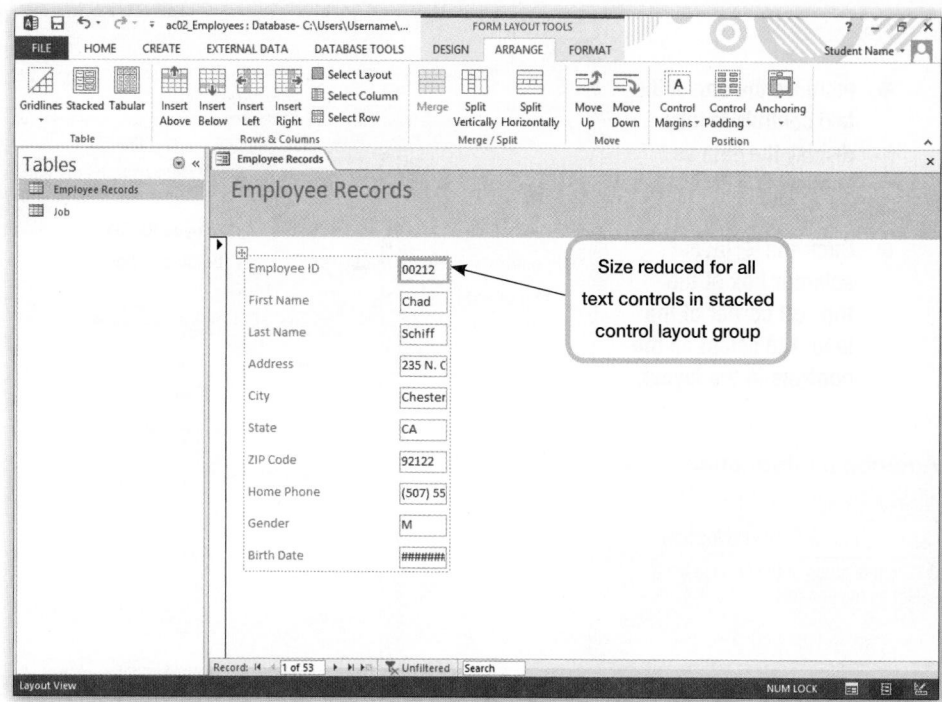

1

● Click on the
   Employee ID text
   control to select it.

● Point to the right edge
   of the control box
   and, when the mouse
   pointer is ⟷, drag
   to the left to decrease
   the size of the control
   as in Figure 2.63.

Your screen should be similar to
Figure 2.63

Figure 2.63

Unfortunately, the size of all the text box controls in the column has been reduced. This is because, in order for the stacked control layout to maintain a uniform appearance, it groups the controls so that they size as a unit. To size a control individually, it must be in its own separate column or in a separate layout group. You decide you will move the Employee ID control to a separate layout group so that it stands alone at the top of the form. Then you will size it to fit the contents.

First you will resize all the controls in the layout to fully display the information. Then you will make space at the top of the form for the Employee ID controls by moving all the controls in this layout group down. The ⊞ form layout selector will quickly select all the field controls in the layout. Then the selected controls can be moved anywhere within the form.

2

● Increase the size of the text controls to fully display the data as shown in Figure 2.64.

● Click the ⊞ layout selector box at the top-left corner of the layout to select all the controls in the layout.

Additional Information

Alternatively you can use the ▦ Select Layout button in the Rows & Columns group of the Arrange tab to select all the controls.

● Drag the selection down 2 rows.

Having Trouble?

The control layout changes to a black outline as you move it to show the new position of the object.

Your screen should be similar to Figure 2.64

Additional Information

You also can remove controls from a layout without placing them in another layout using Layout/Remove Layout on the control's shortcut menu.

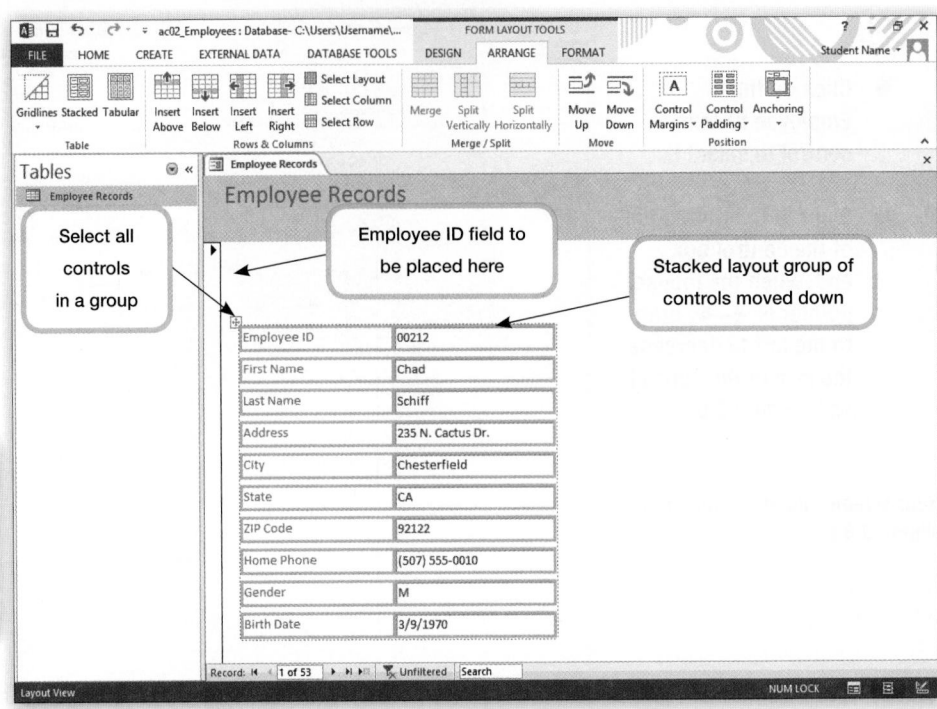

Figure 2.64

You moved the stacked layout group down to allow room for the Employee ID field to be placed at the top of the form in a separate layout group.

Although stacked layout groups can be moved anywhere in the window it is important to keep in mind the overall look of the form. If possible, all controls should be visible within the window's viewing area so that the form user does not have to scroll to see any remaining fields.

SPLITTING A LAYOUT

Now that you have space at the top of the form for the Employee ID information, you will remove the Employee ID control from the layout into a separate stacked layout and then move and size it to fit the contents.

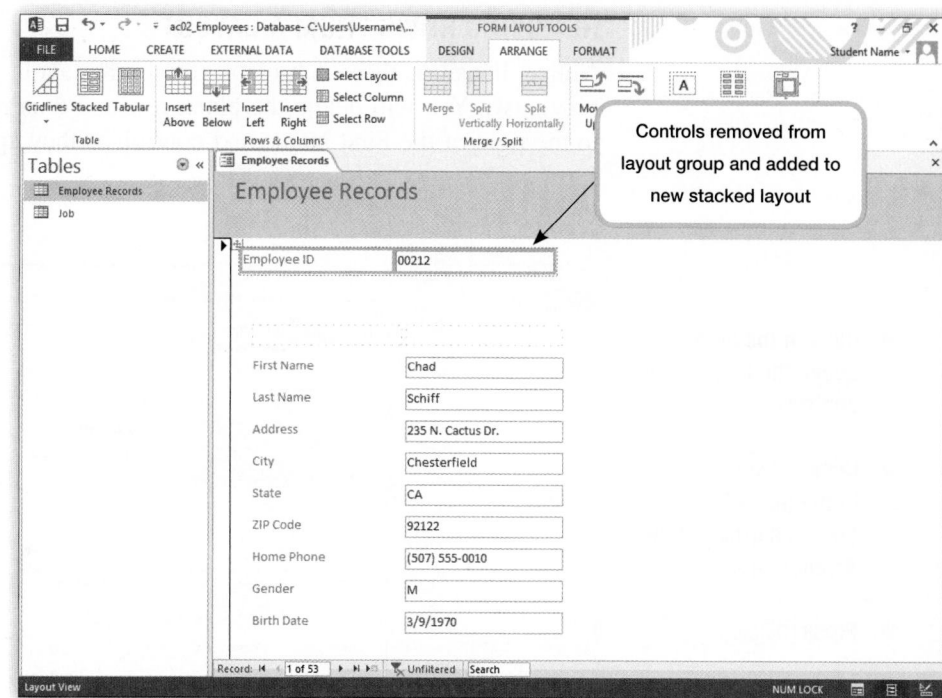

Figure 2.65

1

● Select the Employee ID text and label controls.

● Click [Stacked] in the Table group of the Arrange tab.

Your screen should be similar to Figure 2.65

The Employee ID controls have been removed from the original stacked layout and added to a separate stacked layout. There are now two stacked layouts in the form that can be sized individually. You will reposition and size the controls in both layouts next.

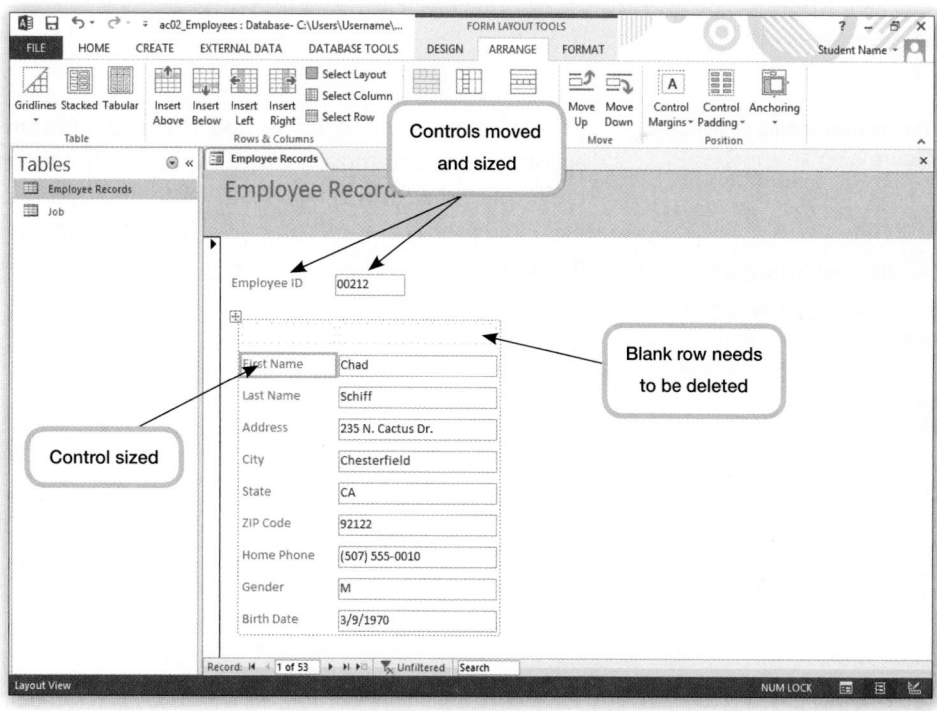

Figure 2.66

2

● Using the ⊞ layout selector, drag the Employee ID object to the position shown in Figure 2.66.

● Reduce the size of the Employee ID text and label controls as in Figure 2.66.

Having Trouble?

It may be easier to individually select and reduce the size of one control at a time.

● Click on the First Name label control to select it, and size it to match the size of the Employee ID label control.

Your screen should be similar to Figure 2.66

The Employee ID is clearly separate from the personal data on the form, and the text control has been sized to fit the data more closely.

REMOVING ROWS FROM A LAYOUT

Notice, however, there is a blank row in the layout where the Employee ID was previously. You will delete the blank row and then move the Last Name controls to the right of the First Name text control, as they appear in the company's paper form.

- Click in the blank row above the First Name controls.

- Click 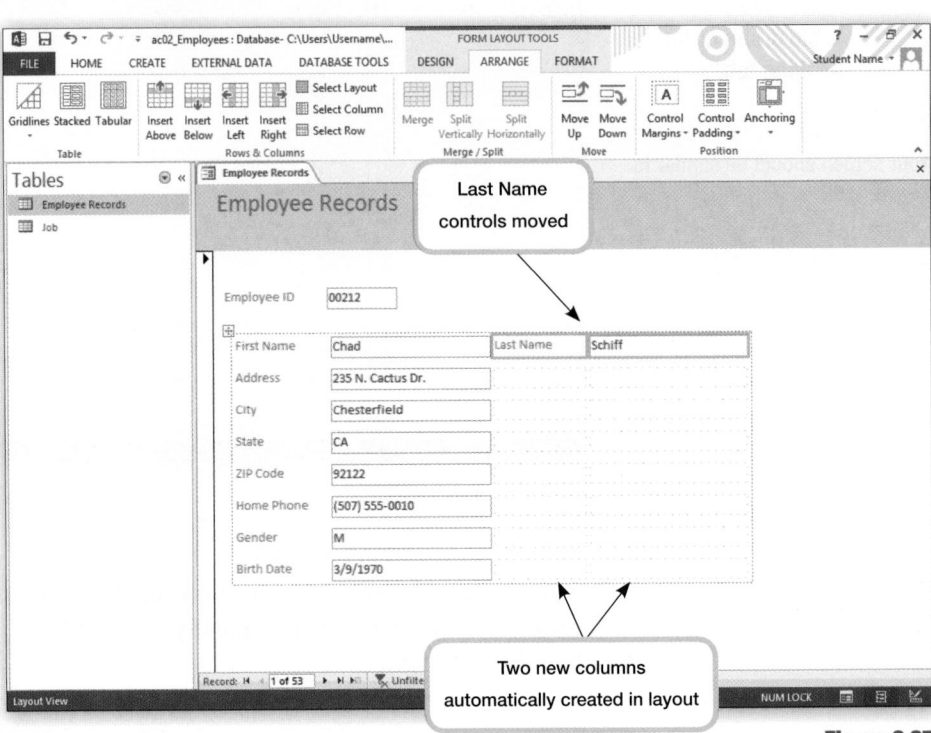 **Select Row** in the Rows & Columns group of the Arrange tab.

- Press Delete.

- Select the Last Name controls and drag them to the right of the First Name text control.

Having Trouble?

The pink indicator line should be at the right of the First Name text control when you release the mouse.

Your screen should be similar to Figure 2.67

Additional Information

You can delete a column by selecting a cell in the column, clicking **Select Column**, and pressing Delete.

The blank row was deleted, and two new columns were added to the layout to accommodate the moved controls. You will continue to arrange the elements on the form so the form appears similar to the paper form the company uses. This will make the process of entering data from the paper form into the database easier for the user.

Figure 2.67

2

- Select the State controls and drag them to the blank cell to the right of the City text control. Release the mouse when the blank cell fills with a pink shade.

- Select the ZIP Code controls and move them to the right of the State text control, releasing the mouse when the pink indicator line displays to the right of the State text control.

- Close the Navigation pane so you have more room to work.

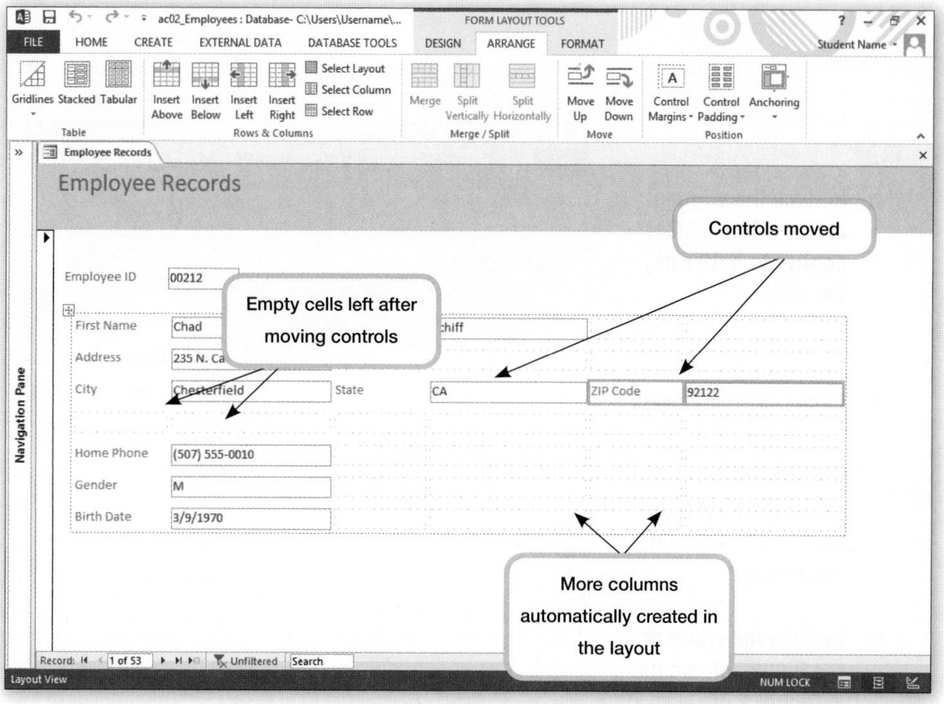

Your screen should be similar to Figure 2.68

Figure 2.68

The controls are now placed where you want them, but they need to be resized to better fit their contents. Also, you notice the Last Name and State labels are a little close to the boxes on their left and would look better with some space added between them.

INSERTING, MERGING, AND SPLITTING CELLS

Working with layouts also allows you to easily insert columns and rows, and merge and split cells to achieve the design you want for the form. The next change you want to make is to insert a narrow blank column to the left of the Last Name controls to separate the controls.

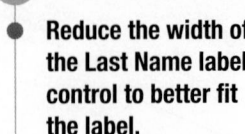

Inserts a blank column to the left of a selected cell

1

- Reduce the width of the Last Name label control to better fit the label.

- Click 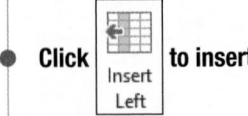 to insert a blank column to the left of the Last Name label control to add separation.

- Reduce the width of the blank column as in Figure 2.69.

- Resize the columns of the text controls in the left column so they better fit the contents of the Home Phone control.

Your screen should be similar to Figure 2.69

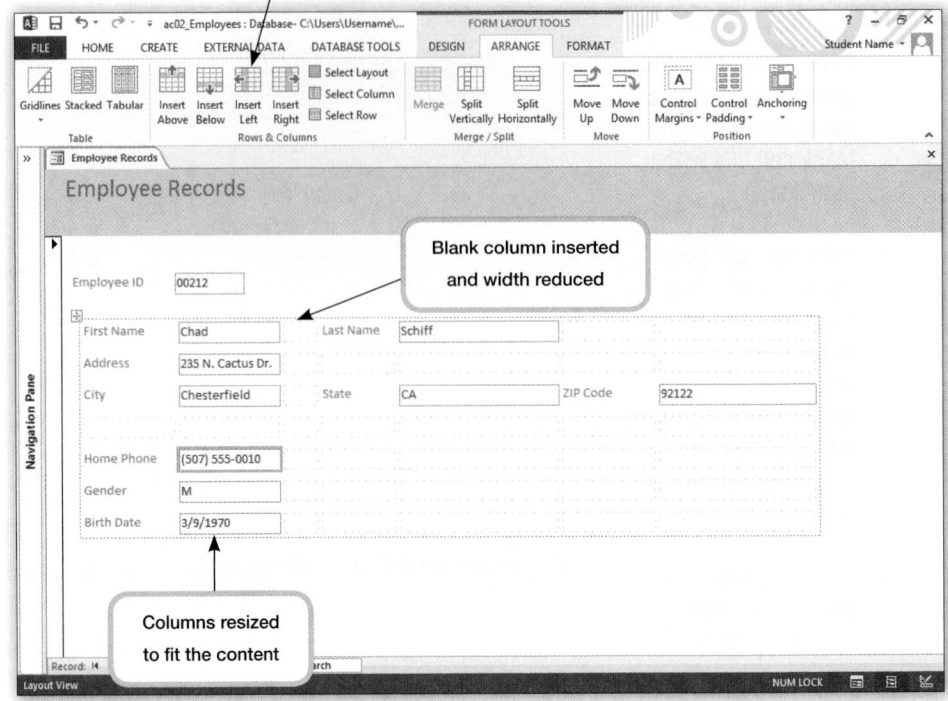

Figure 2.69

The form now has a nice visual separation between the controls on the left and those added on the right.

Now, however, you feel the Address text control could be larger. To fix this, you will merge it with the cells on the right to allow for longer address entries. When you **merge cells**, any selected adjacent cells are combined into one big cell spanning the length of the previously selected cells.

You cannot merge cells containing more than one control because each cell can contain only one control. You can merge any number of empty adjacent cells.

First you must select the cells to be merged.

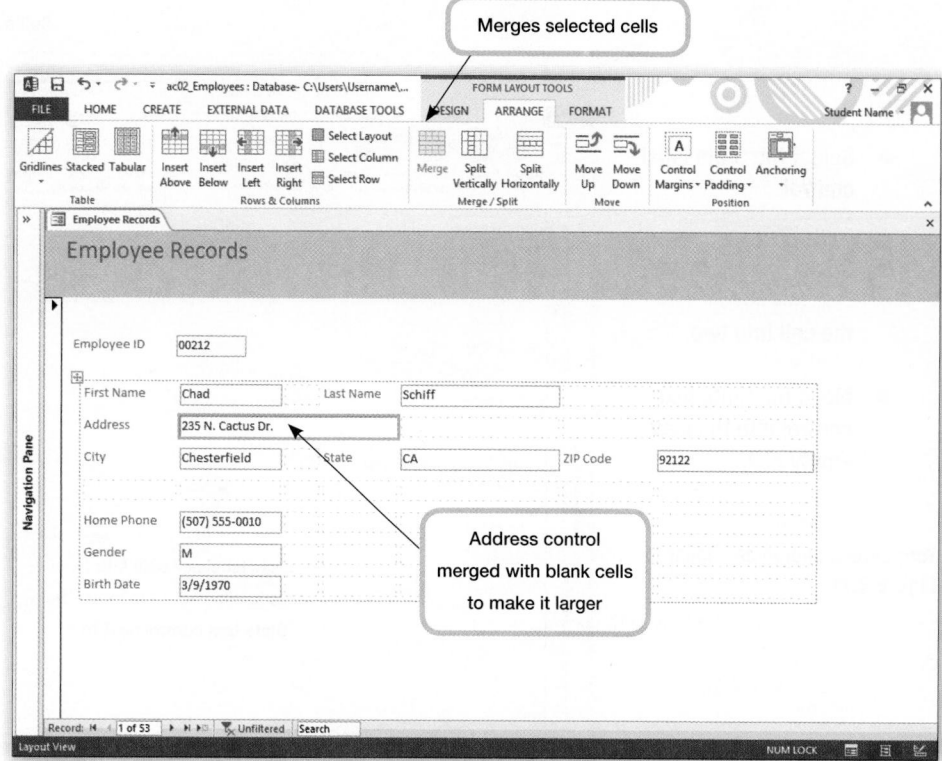

Merges selected cells

2

- Select the Address text control.

- Hold down ⇧Shift and click the two empty cells to the right of the Address control.

- Click 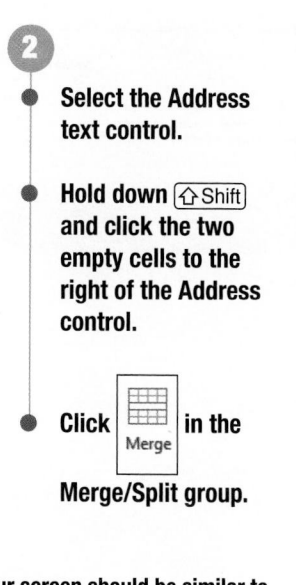 in the Merge/Split group.

Your screen should be similar to Figure 2.70

Employee Records

Employee ID	00212
First Name	Chad	Last Name	Schiff
Address	235 N. Cactus Dr.
City	Chesterfield	State	CA	ZIP Code	92122
Home Phone	(507) 555-0010
Gender	M
Birth Date	3/9/1970

Address control merged with blank cells to make it larger

Record: 1 of 53   Unfiltered   Search

Layout View

NUM LOCK

Figure 2.70

The three cells have been combined into one cell that should be large enough to display most addresses. When merging cells, it is better to adjust column sizes as much as possible before merging, as the underlying row and column structure can become complicated and make it difficult to resize just the cells you want.

To further enhance the form, the State and ZIP Code controls could be resized to better fit the text they contain. However, if you resize the State field, it will make the Last Name controls too narrow. Since the State text control only needs to be wide enough for two characters, you think it would fit next to the State label if you could utilize the extra space in the cell. To make one cell into two, you can split the cell.

You can **split cells** horizontally or vertically. Splitting a cell vertically creates a new row and splitting a cell horizontally creates a new column. Splitting can be performed on only one cell at a time. The affected cell can be an empty cell or contain a control. When splitting a cell containing a control, the control is kept in the far left box and an empty cell is created on the right side. You want to split the cell containing the State label.

3

- Select the State label control.

- Click 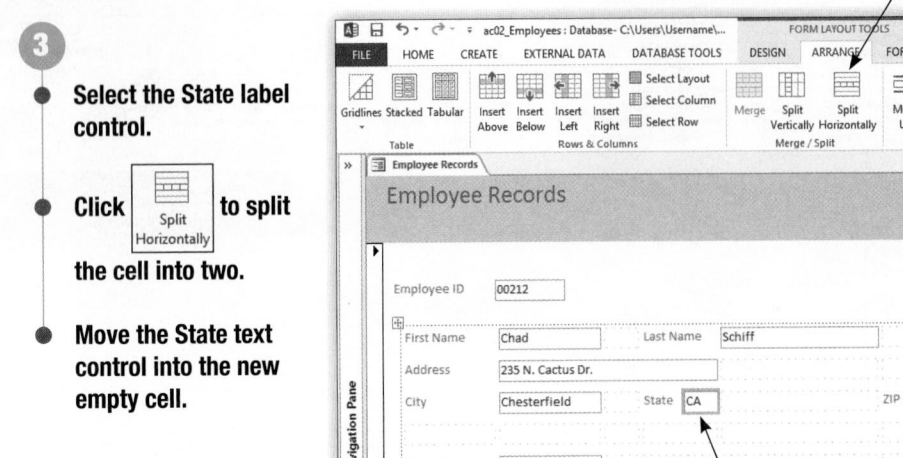 to split the cell into two.

- Move the State text control into the new empty cell.

Your screen should be similar to Figure 2.71

Splits a cell into two cells

Employee Records

Employee ID	00212
First Name	Chad	Last Name	Schiff
Address	235 N. Cactus Dr.
City	Chesterfield	State	CA	ZIP Code	92122
Home Phone	(507) 555-0010
Gender	M
Birth Date	3/9/1970

State label cell split into two cells to allow room to move the State text control next to it

Record: 1 of 53   Unfiltered   Search

Layout View   NUM LOCK

Figure 2.71

Both State controls now reside within the same column containing the last name label. You notice the Address text control also ends in this column. If you were to try and resize the State or Address text controls, it would affect the entire column, including the cell containing the Last Name label.

Your form has room for the ZIP Code label and text controls to be moved to the right of the State control. You will split the empty cell and move both ZIP Code controls into the new position.

4

- Click the empty cell to the right of the State text control.

- Click Split Horizontally.

- Select both ZIP Code controls and move them to the empty cells to the right of the State text control.

- Select the ZIP Code label control, and click ≡ Align Right in the Font group of the Format tab.

Your screen should be similar to Figure 2.72

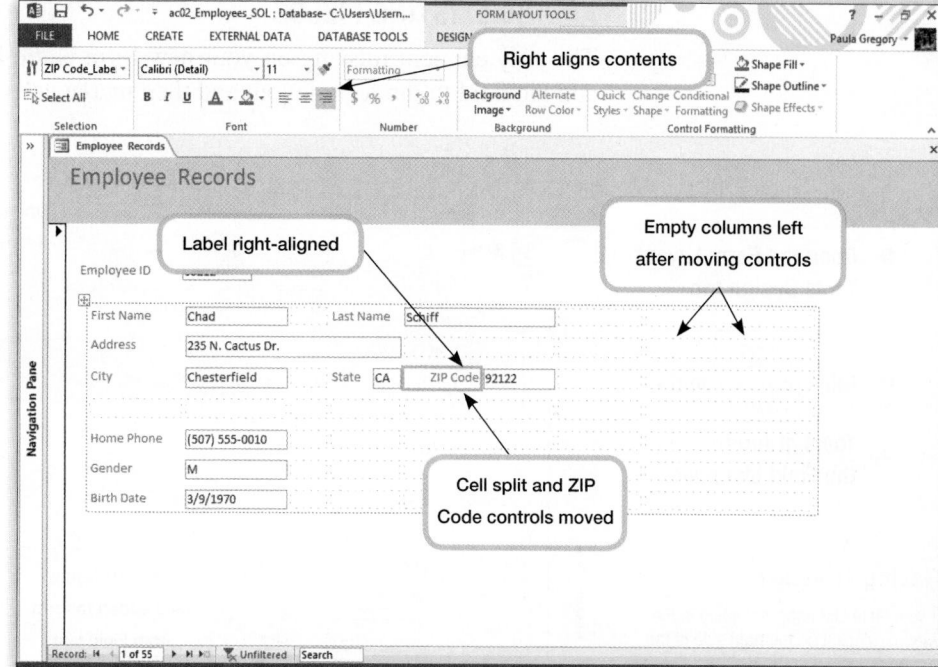

Figure 2.72

Aligning the label to the right gives the appearance of space between the label and the State text control. Now you need to delete the extra columns in the layout and move the last three fields up below the City field. To specify the column to be removed, select any cell in the column and the entire column will be deleted.

5

- Click an empty cell in the column to the right of the Last Name text control.

- Press Delete.

- In the same manner, delete the second empty column.

- Select the last three field controls by clicking on the Home Phone label control, holding down Shift, and clicking on the Birth Date text control.

- Drag the selected controls up to the blank cell under the City label.

Your screen should be similar to Figure 2.73

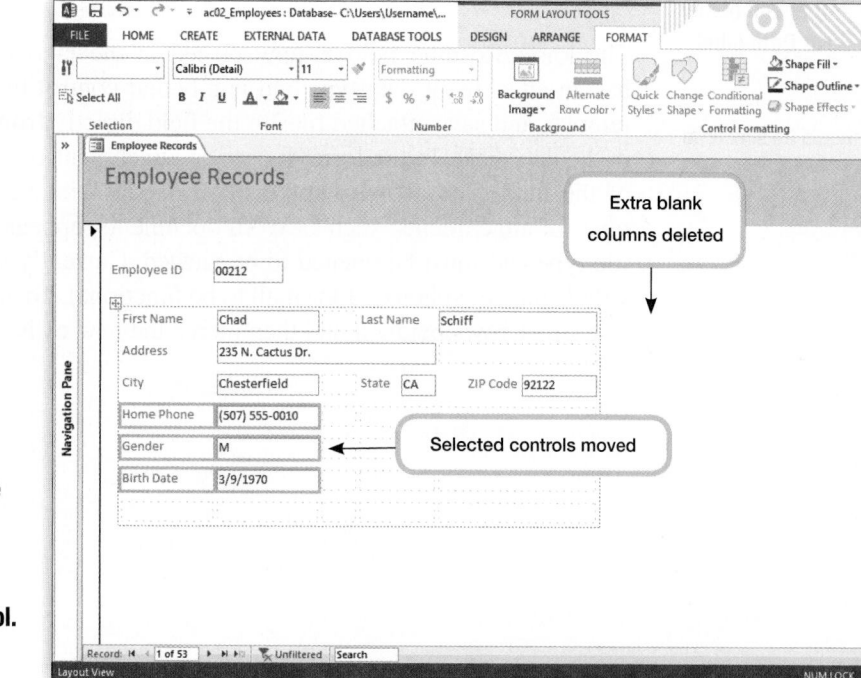

Figure 2.73

The form you have created is getting closer to matching the layout of the company's paper form.

ADDING EXISTING FIELDS

The only element missing on your new form is the Photo/Resume field. You will add the field to the form layout and then merge cells to make room for the photo.

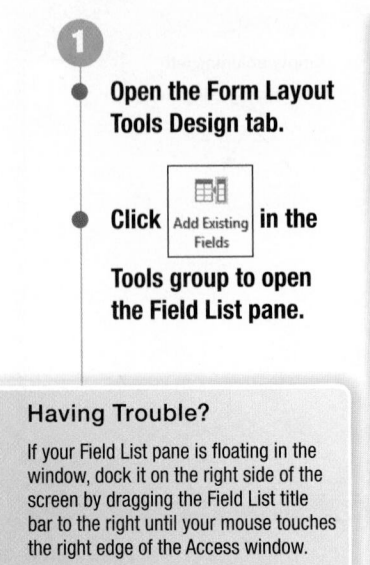

- Open the Form Layout Tools Design tab.

- Click [Add Existing Fields] in the Tools group to open the Field List pane.

Having Trouble?

If your Field List pane is floating in the window, dock it on the right side of the screen by dragging the Field List title bar to the right until your mouse touches the right edge of the Access window.

- Drag the main field name "Photo/Resume," from the Field List pane to the empty cell below the Birth Date label.

Your screen should be similar to Figure 2.74

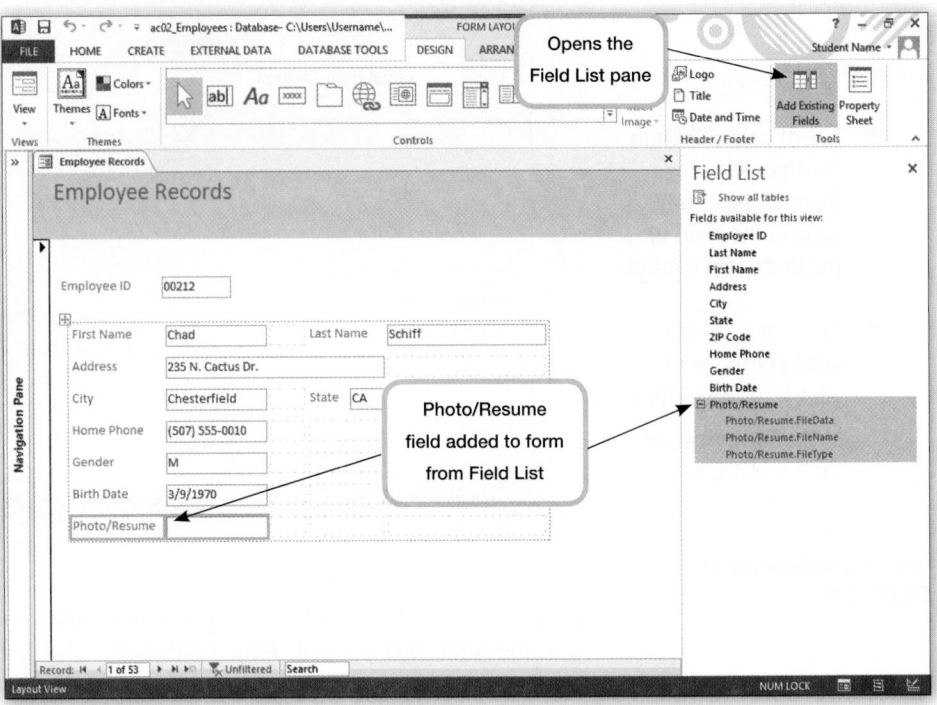

Figure 2.74

The Photo/Resume field is now placed in the layout. The Photo/Resume field has an attachment data type and is a bound control that allows you to add, edit, remove, and save attached files to the field directly from the form, just as you can in the datasheet. In the form, it uses an attachment control to display the contents of the field. The **attachment control** displays image files automatically. Other types of attachments, such as Word documents, appear as icons that represent the file type and must be opened to be viewed. Currently the attachment control that will display the photo is too small to be functional. To enlarge the control, you will insert four rows below it and then merge the new cells for the attachment control.

2

- Click on the Photo/Resume attachment control.

- Open the Arrange tab and click [Insert Below] in the Rows & Columns group four times.

- Select the Photo/Resume attachment control and the four empty cells below it.

- Click [Merge].

- Close the Field List pane.

Your screen should be similar to Figure 2.75

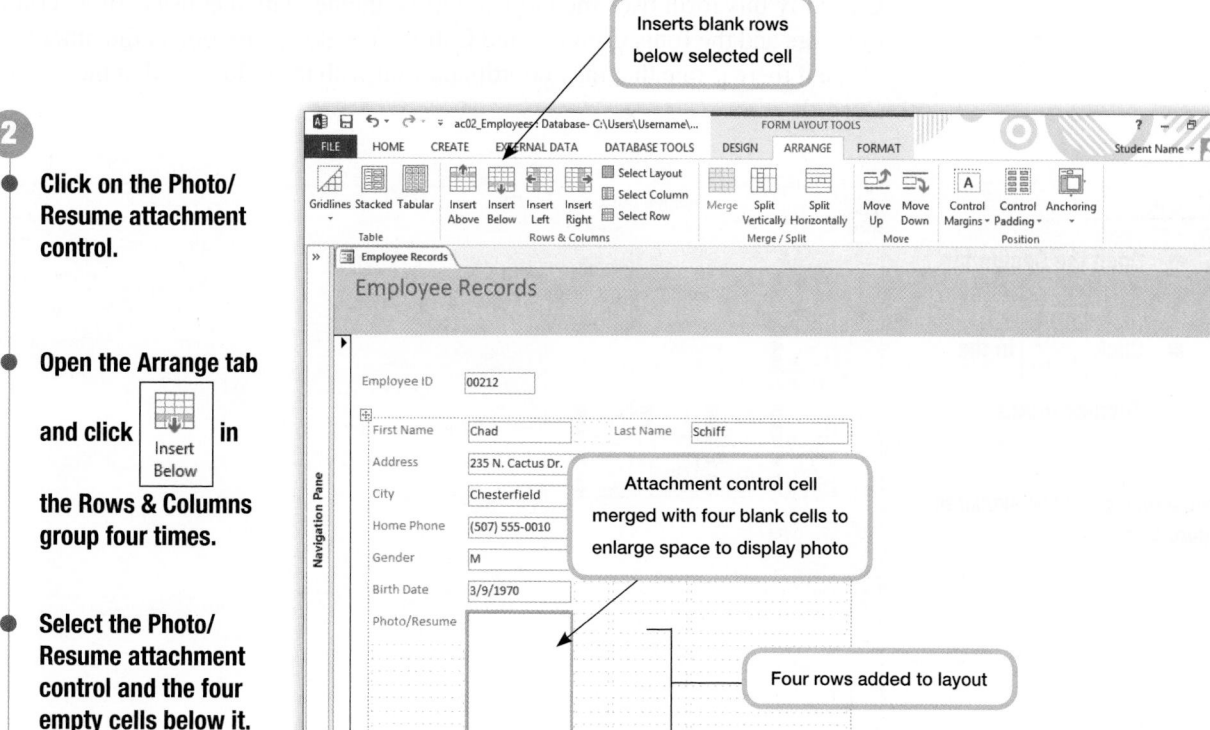

Inserts blank rows below selected cell

Attachment control cell merged with four blank cells to enlarge space to display photo

Four rows added to layout

Figure 2.75

Now the Photo/Resume attachment control is large enough to display a photo. The Photo/Resume field's control is currently empty because there are no attachments for this record.

CHANGING THE DESIGN STYLE

Next you want to enhance the form's appearance by making changes to the form colors and fonts. To make it easy to quickly change the appearance of the form, you will change the form's design theme.

Concept **11** Theme

A **theme** is a predefined set of formatting choices that can be applied to all objects in a database in one simple step. Access includes nine named, built-in themes that can be applied to forms and reports while in Design view or Layout view. The theme chosen will affect all objects in the database. Each theme includes two subsets of themes: colors and fonts. Each color theme consists of 12 colors that are applied to specific elements in the form or report. Each fonts theme includes a set of different body and heading fonts. You also can create your own custom themes by modifying an existing theme and saving it as a custom theme. The blank database file uses the default Office theme for any new objects you create.

The same themes also are available in Word 2013, Excel 2013, and PowerPoint 2013. Using themes gives your documents a professional and modern look. Because document themes are shared across Office 2013 applications, all your Office documents can have the same uniform look.

Currently this form uses the built-in Office theme, which consists of a certain set of colors and the fonts Cambria and Calibri. You decide to look at the other themes to see if there is one that may coordinate well with the colors used in the Employee Records table.

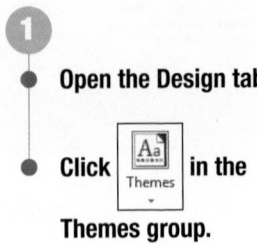

● **Open the Design tab.**

● **Click** **in the Themes group.**

Your screen should be similar to Figure 2.76

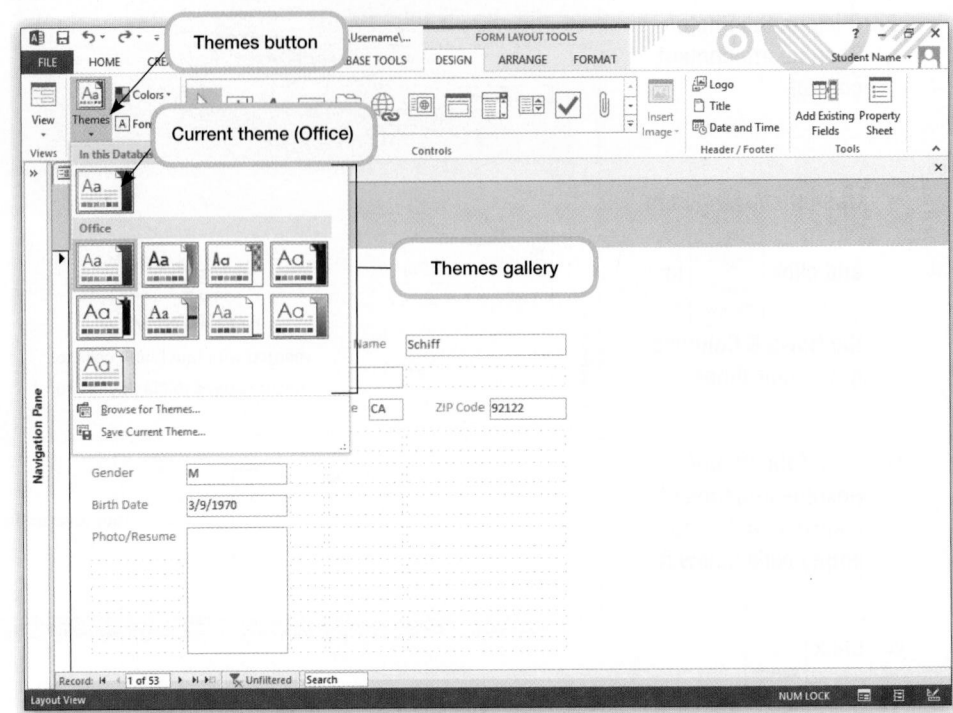

Figure 2.76

A gallery of nine built-in named themes is displayed. A sample shows the color and font used in each theme. The Office theme is the default theme and is the theme that is used in the form. When you point to each theme, the theme name appears in a ScreenTip and a live preview of how the theme's settings will look is displayed in the form. You think the Ion theme will look good.

- **Point to several themes to see the live preview for each.**

- **Choose the Ion theme.**

- **If necessary, adjust the width of any controls so the content is fully displayed and on one line.**

- **Click** 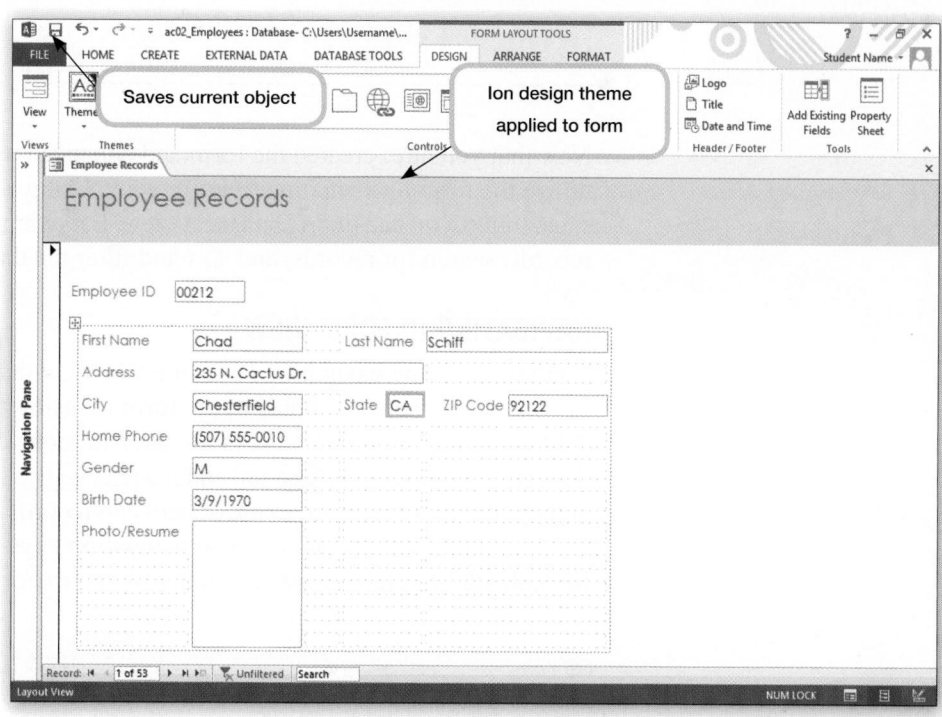 **Save in the Quick Access Toolbar to save the form design changes.**

Your screen should be similar to Figure 2.77

Figure 2.77

The formatting settings associated with the selected theme have been applied to the form. Because themes are available in the other Office applications, you can coordinate the design styles used in documents created in the other applications by choosing the same theme. The selected theme affects all other objects in the database unless the object was previously formatted using a color from the Standard colors gallery or a font other than the Heading or Detail font from the Font menu. When you create new objects, Access will apply the theme you chose for this form to the new object.

Using a Form

Now that you have created the form and enhanced its appearance, you are ready to utilize the form by switching to Form view. Using a form, you can do many of the same things you can do in Datasheet view. For example, you can update and delete records, search for records, and sort and filter the data.

NAVIGATING IN FORM VIEW

You use the same navigation keys in Form view that you used in Datasheet view. You can move between fields in the form by using the [Tab⇆], [←Enter], or [Shift] + [Tab⇆] keys. The [→] and [←] keys are used to move character by character through the entry. You can use [Page Up] and [Page Down], as well as the navigation buttons at the bottom of the form, to move between records.

You will try out several of these navigation keys as you try to locate the record for Roberta Marchant. First, you must switch to Form view.

1

Click [▦] **Form View in the status bar to change to Form view.**

Additional Information

You also can click [▦] in the Views group of the Form Layout Tools Design tab.

Press [Tab⇆] **three times.**

Press [Page Down] **two times.**

Your screen should be similar to Figure 2.78

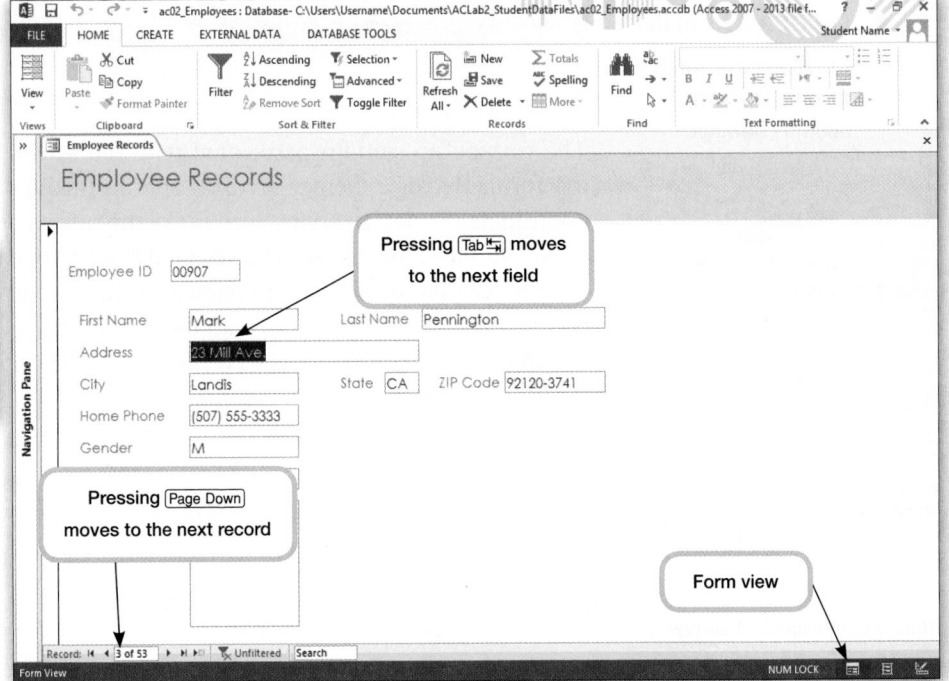

Figure 2.78

First you moved three fields to the Address field in the current record. Then you moved down two records to record 3. The field that was selected in the previous record remains the selected field when you move between records.

1

- **Click in the Search text box.**

- **Type marc**

Your screen should be similar to Figure 2.79

Searching in Form View

A quicker way to locate a record is to use the Find command or the Search feature. Both features work just as they do in Datasheet view. You will use the Search feature to locate the record for Roberta Marchant by entering the first few characters of her last name in the Search box. As you type the characters, watch how the search advances through the table and highlights matching text.

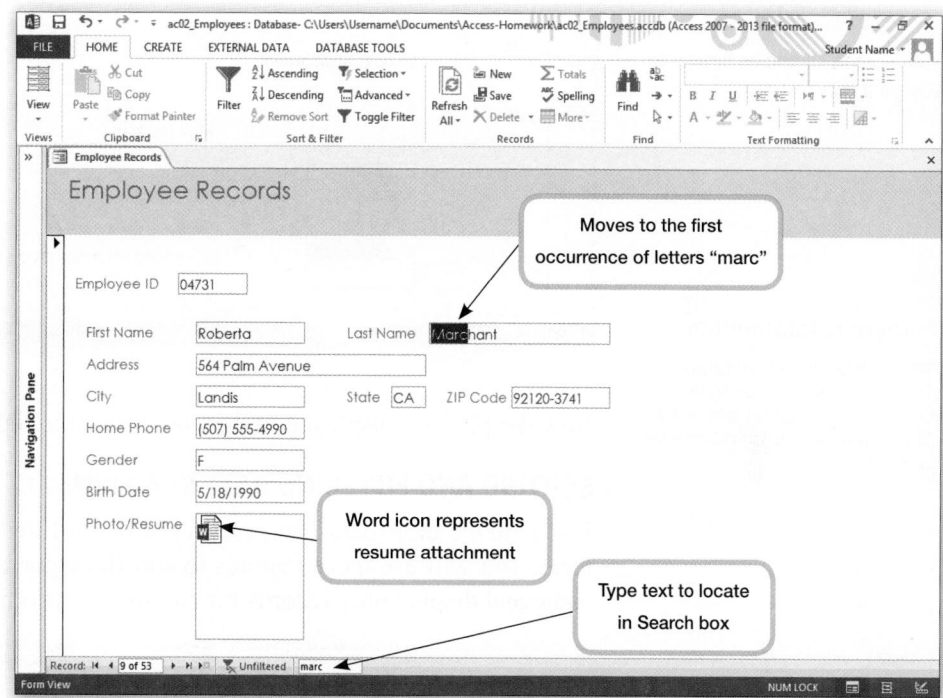

Figure 2.79

The Search feature located Roberta Marchant's record and displays it in the form. The Photo/Resume field displays a Word icon for the resume file. To open the resume file, simply double-click on the Word icon and choose [Open] from the Attachments dialog box. To display the next attachment, click on the Attachment control to make it active. This will display the Mini toolbar, which contains three buttons that are used to work with attachment controls. When the Mini toolbar first displays above the Attachment control, it will appear transparent and may be hard to discern. By pointing to the Mini Toolbar, it will become solid and easier to see. Using the Mini toolbar, you can scroll through attached files using the → and ← buttons, or you may add or view attachments using ⬚ to open the Attachments dialog box. You will use the Mini toolbar to display the photo attachment.

Additional Information

Refer to the Formatting Text section in the Introduction to Microsoft Office 2013 to review the Mini toolbar feature.

2

- Click on the Photo/Resume field to make it active.

- Point to the Mini toolbar and click → Forward to move to the next attachment.

Your screen should be similar to Figure 2.80

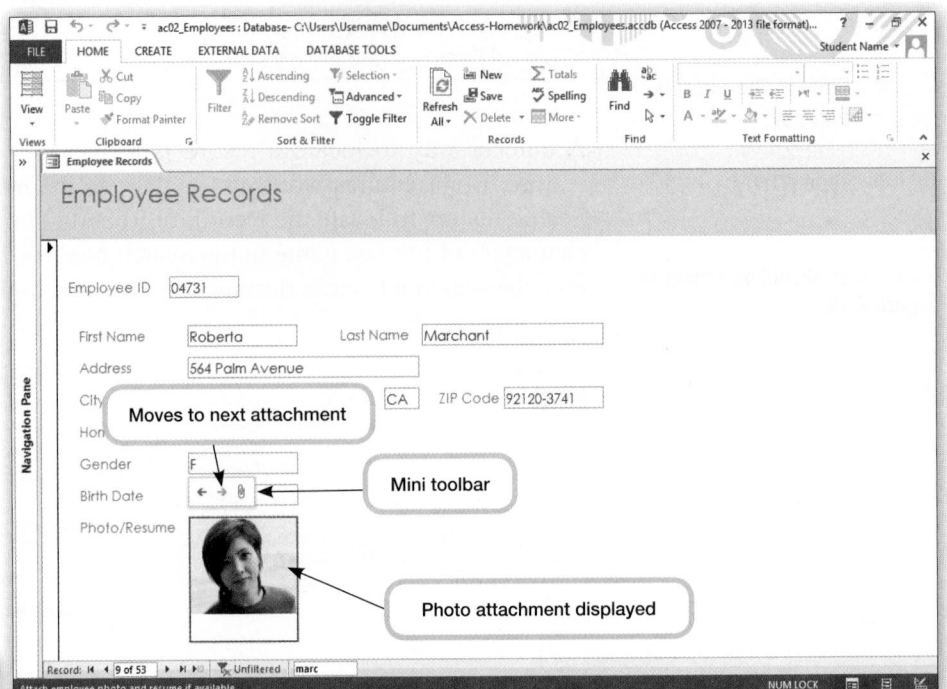

Figure 2.80

Additional Information

The files in the Attachment field are stored in alphabetical order by file name. The first object in the list is the object that will appear in the Attachment control of a form.

Now the photo is displayed in the Photo/Resume field control.

SORTING AND FILTERING DATA IN A FORM

Just as in the table datasheet, you can sort and filter the data that is displayed in a form. You will use these features to sort the records in alphabetical order by last name and display only records for employees who live in River Mist.

1

- Right-click on the Last Name field.

- Choose Sort A to Z.

- Navigate to any record that displays River Mist and right-click on the City field.

- Choose Equals "River Mist".

- Display the last record.

Your screen should be similar to Figure 2.81

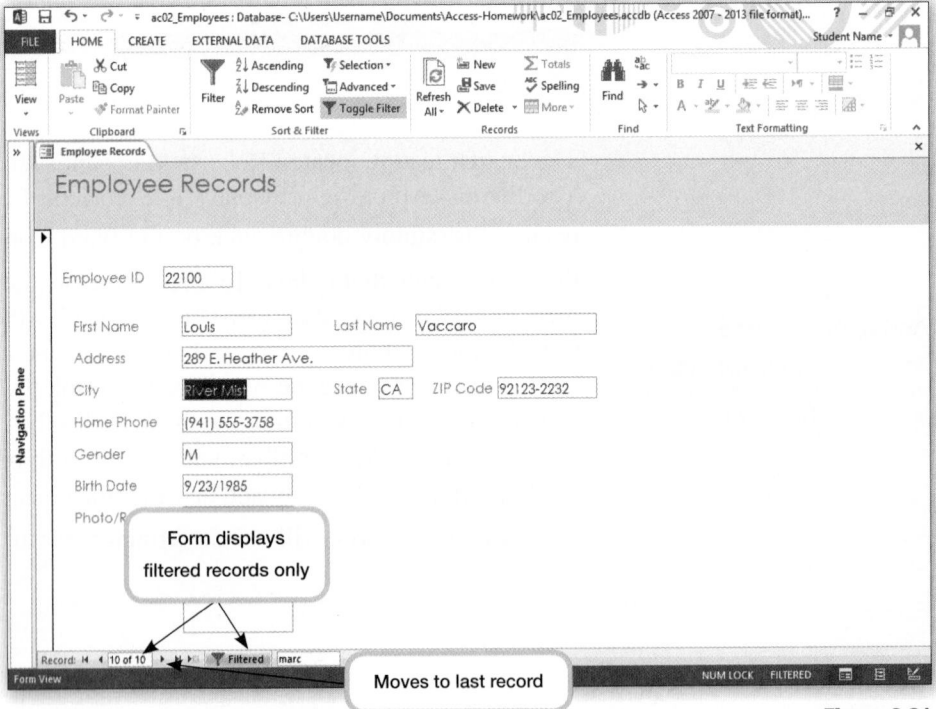

Figure 2.81

The record number indicator tells you that there are only 10 records and the table is filtered. The records are also in sorted order by last name. The sort and filter settings apply only to the object in which they were specified, in this case the form.

ADDING RECORDS USING A FORM

Additional Information

When entering data in a form, use Tab to complete the entry and quickly move to the next field control.

Now you need to add another employee record to the database whose paper employee data form is shown here. You will add the record while in Form view, using the information on the paper form to input the data into the form's fields. You also will attach a picture to the Photo/Resume field.

EMPLOYEE DATA

Employee ID   12918

First Name   Carlos   Last Name   Ruiz
Street   10101 First St.
City   Maldin   State CA   Zip Code 92121-3740
Phone Number   (507) 555-0125
Gender   M
Birth Date   July 27, 1987

①
- **Click** Filtered **in the navigation bar to remove the filter from the form.**

- **Click** ▶ **New (blank) record to display a new blank entry form.**

Another Method

You also can use ⊞ New in the Records group of the Home tab or Ctrl + + to add a new record.

- **Enter the data from the paper employee data form shown above into the new record.**

- **Double-click on the Attachment field control.**

Another Method

You also could choose Manage Attachments from the shortcut menu or click ⋓ Manage Attachments on the Mini toolbar.

- **Add the file** ac02_Carlos **from your data file location.**

Your screen should be similar to Figure 2.82

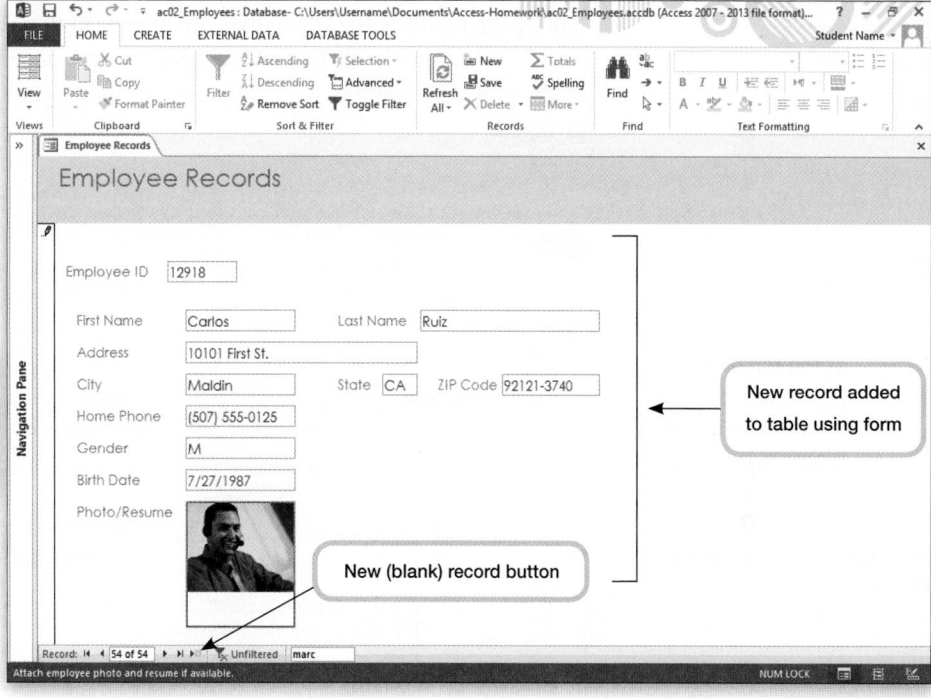

Figure 2.82

Using the form makes entering the new employee data much faster because the fields are in the same order as the information on the paper employee data form used by the personnel department.

Next, you will add a record for yourself.

2

- Enter another new record using your special Employee ID 99999 and your first and last names. Enter data in the rest of the fields for your record, using River Mist as the city and 92123-2232 as the ZIP Code. The rest of the data can be fictitious.

- Open the Navigation pane.

The form shows there are 55 records in the table. Since you added two new records to the Employee Records table, you will also need to update the Jobs table with the related information for these new records.

Organizing the Navigation Pane

Notice the name of the form does not appear in the Navigation pane. This is because initially the pane is set to display table objects only. To display other objects in the pane, you can change what objects are displayed in the pane and how they are grouped.

- Click

  Tables

  at the top of the Navigation pane to open the Tables drop-down menu.

Your screen should be similar to Figure 2.83

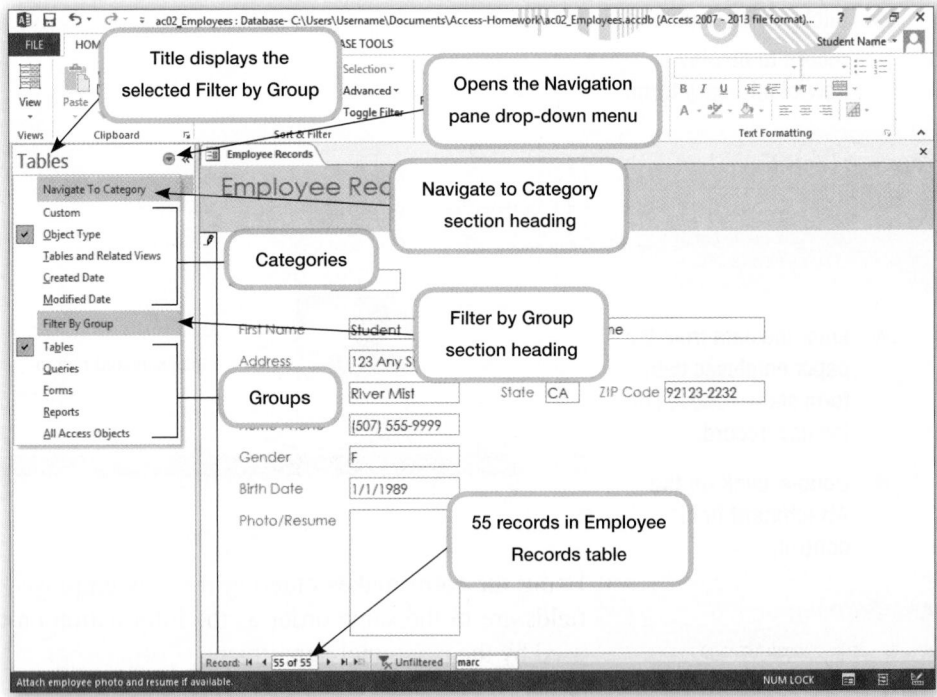

Figure 2.83

The upper section of the menu contains categories, and the lower section contains groups. The groups change as you select different categories. Currently, Object Type is the selected category and Tables is the selected group. You want to keep the category selection as Object Type but want to change the group selection to display all object types in the pane at the same time.

2

- **From the Filter By Group section, choose All Access Objects.**

- **Double-click the Job table in the Navigation pane.**

Another Method

You also can drag an object from the Navigation pane to the work area to open it.

- **Add the information for the two new records shown below to the table.**

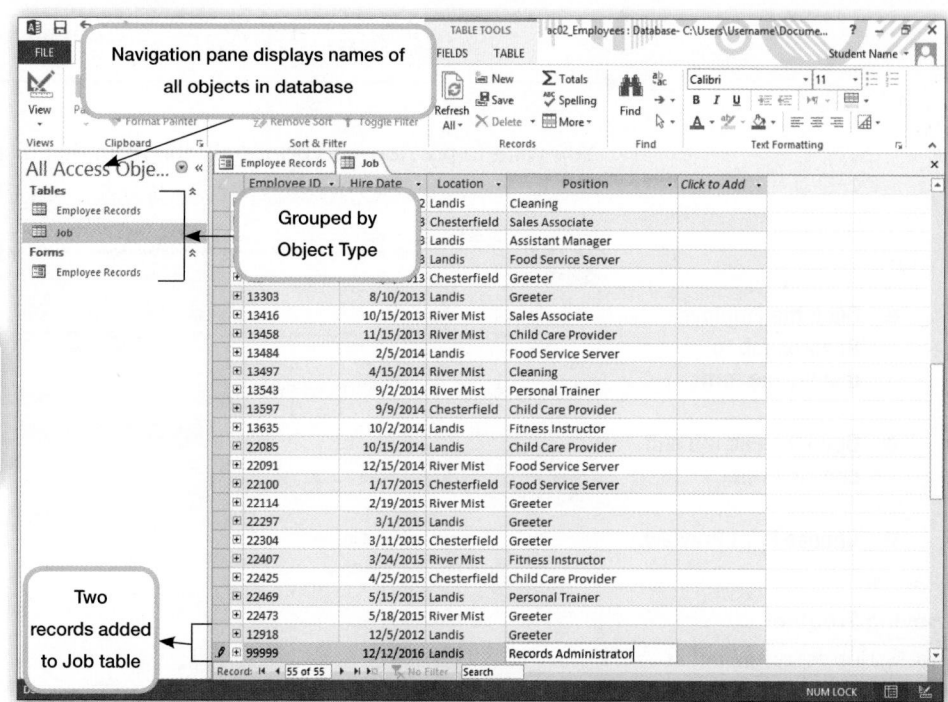

Navigation pane displays names of all objects in database

Grouped by Object Type

Two records added to Job table

Your screen should be similar to Figure 2.84

Figure 2.84

Field	Record 54	Record 55
Employee ID	12918	99999
Hire Date	12/5/2012	Today's date
Location	Landis	Landis
Position	Greeter	Records Administrator

Now both tables contain 55 records.

Previewing and Printing a Form

You want to preview and print only the form that displays your record.

- **Click the Employee Records tab to display the form.**

- **Open the File tab and choose Print.**

- **Choose Print Preview.**

> **Having Trouble?**
>
> Your form may display fewer records than in Figure 2.85.

Your screen should be similar to Figure 2.85

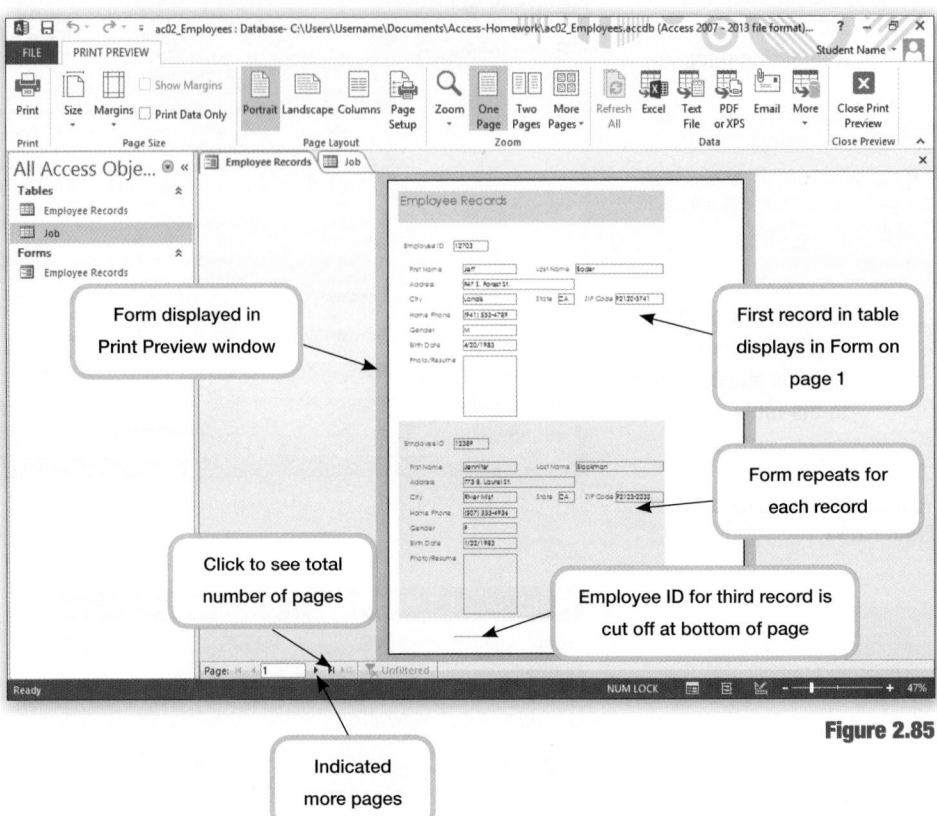

Form displayed in Print Preview window

First record in table displays in Form on page 1

Form repeats for each record

Click to see total number of pages

Employee ID for third record is cut off at bottom of page

Indicated more pages

Figure 2.85

The form object is displayed in the Print Preview window. Each page prints as many records in form layout as possible and may split a form between pages. The form title appears on the first page only. By default, all records in the table will be printed, resulting in a printout that is many pages long.

PRINTING A SELECTED RECORD

You want to print only the form displaying your record. To do this, you need to select your record first in Form view.

1

- Click [Close Print Preview]

- Display your record in the form.

- Click the Record Selector bar (the white bar along the left side of the form) to select the entire record.

Another Method

You also can use [⬚ ▾]/Select in the Find group of the Home tab to select the record.

Your screen should be similar to Figure 2.86

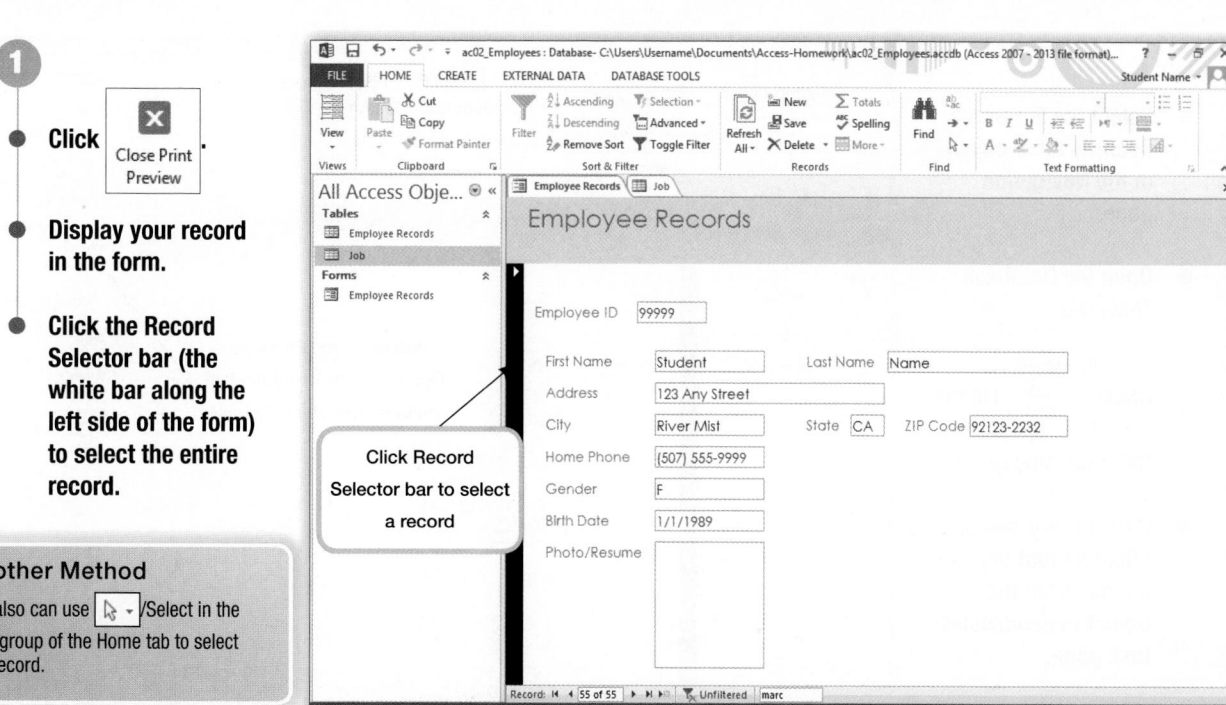

Click Record Selector bar to select a record

Figure 2.86

Now that the record is selected, you can print it.

2

- Open the File tab and choose Print.

- Choose Print.

Additional Information

You cannot preview printing a selected record.

- Choose the Selected Record(s) option from the Print dialog box.

- If necessary, make sure your printer is on and select the appropriate printer.

- Click [OK].

Identifying Object Dependencies

The form is the third database object that has been added to the file. Many objects that you create in a database have **object dependencies**, meaning they are dependent upon other objects for their content. In this case, the form is dependent upon the Employee Records database table for its content. Sometimes it is helpful to be able to find out what objects an object is dependent on or what depend on it. To help in these situations, you can display the object dependencies.

Select the Employee Records table object in the Navigation pane.

Open the Database Tools tab.

Click 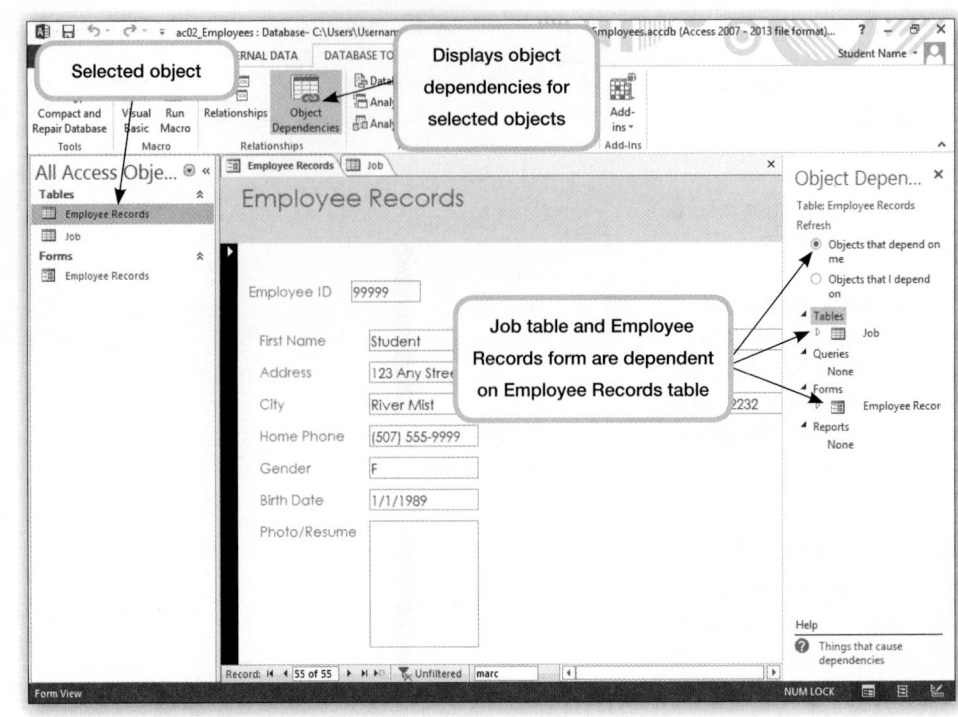 **in the Relationships group.**

If necessary, select "Objects that depend on me" from the Object Dependencies task pane.

Your screen should be similar to Figure 2.87

Figure 2.87

The Object Dependencies task pane identifies the two objects that are dependent on the table: the Job table and the Employee Records form. Next, you will see which objects depend on the Employee Records form.

Select Employee Records in the Forms category of the Navigation pane.

Click Refresh in the Object Dependencies task pane.

Your screen should be similar to Figure 2.88

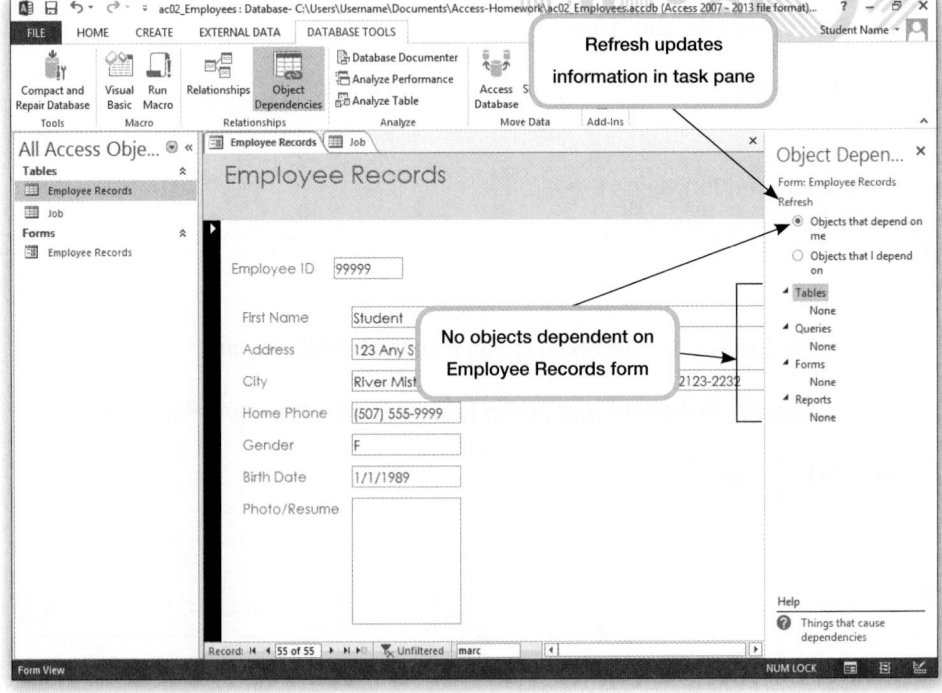

Figure 2.88

You can now see that the Employee Records form object does not have any objects dependent on it.

3

● Choose "Objects that I depend on" from the Object Dependencies task pane.

Your screen should be similar to Figure 2.89

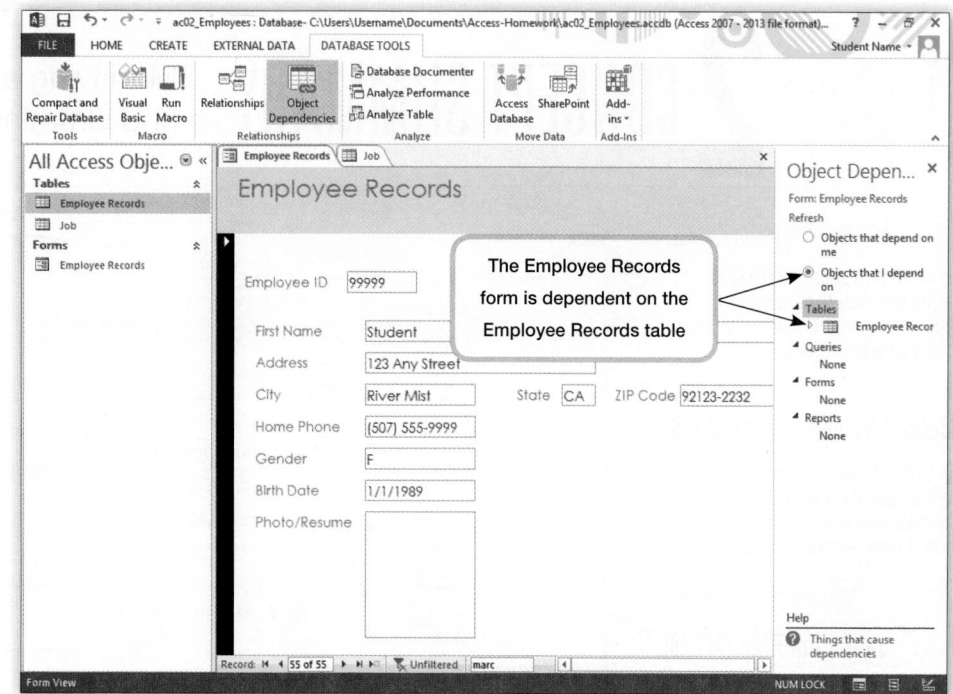

The Employee Records form is dependent on the Employee Records table

Figure 2.89

The Object Dependencies task pane identifies that the only object that the form depends on is the Employee Records table.

4

● Close the Object Dependencies task pane.

● Close the form and table objects, saving any changes.

● In the database properties, add your name as the author, and in the Comments box, add **This database contains 55 records and is still under construction.**

● Exit Access.

CUS ON CAREERS

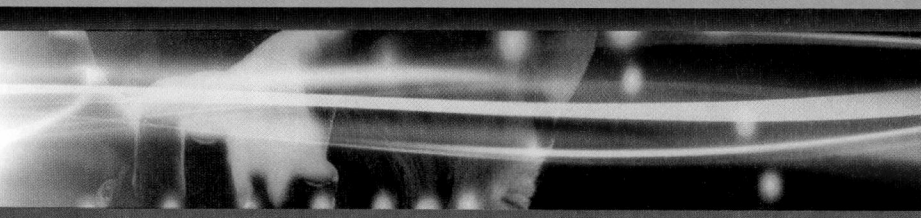

EXPLORE YOUR CAREER OPTIONS

Administrative Assistant

Administrative assistants are typically responsible for the efficient management of office operations. This position may involve conducting research, training new staff, scheduling meetings, and maintaining databases. As an administrative assistant, you could be responsible for updating an inventory or staffing database. The typical salary range of an administrative assistant is $27,000 to $64,000. Demand for experienced administrative assistants, especially in technology and health fields, is expected to increase through 2018.

Format Property (AC2.7)

The Format property is used to specify the way that numbers, dates, times, and text in a field are displayed and printed.

Default Value Property (AC2.8)

The Default Value property is used to specify a value that is automatically entered in a field when a new record is created.

Validation Rule (AC2.10)

Validation rules are used to control the data that can be entered in a field by defining the input values that are valid or allowed.

Expression (AC2.11)

An expression is a formula consisting of a combination of symbols that will produce a single value.

Lookup Field (AC2.18)

A lookup field provides a list of values from which the user can choose to make entering data into that field simpler and more accurate.

Find and Replace (AC2.25)

The Find and Replace feature helps you quickly find specific information and automatically replace it with new information.

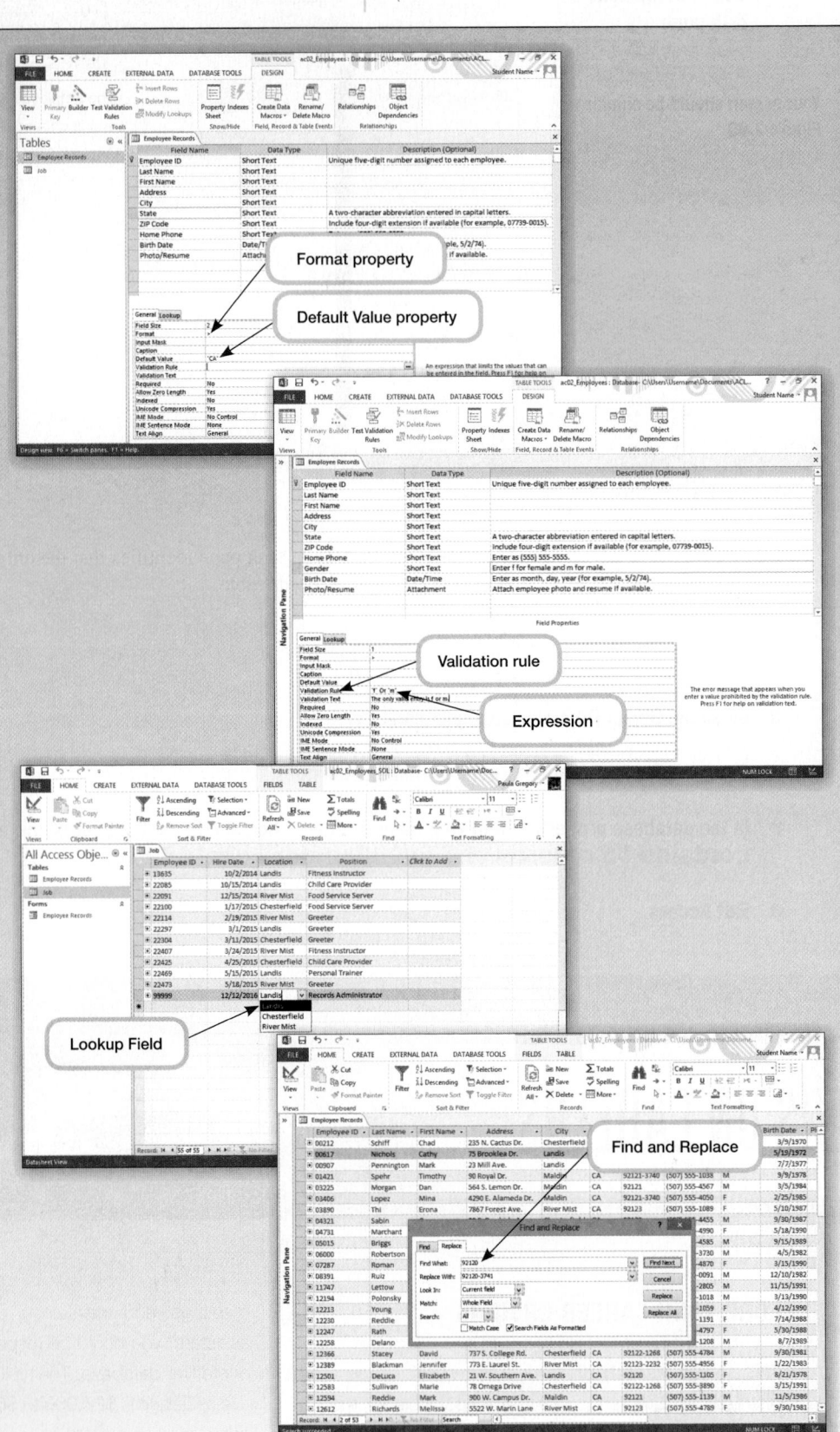

Sorting (AC2.33)

Sorting rearranges the order of the records in a table based on the value in each field.

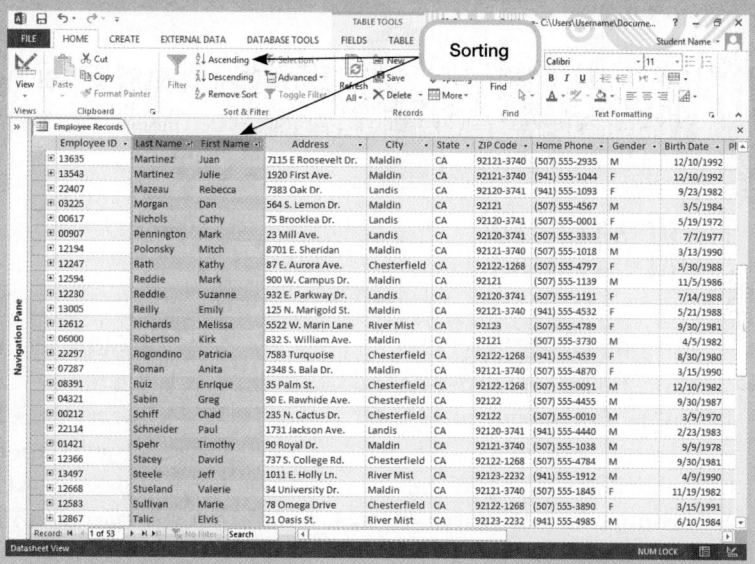

Filter (AC2.40)

A filter is a restriction placed on records in the open table or form to quickly isolate and display a subset of records.

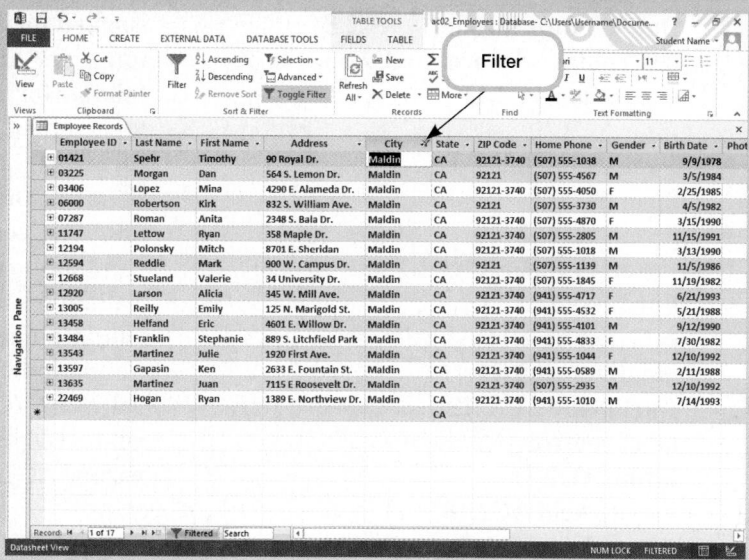

Form (AC2.46)

A form is a database object used primarily to display records onscreen to make it easier to enter new records and to make changes to existing records.

Controls (AC2.54)

Controls are objects that display information, perform actions, or enhance the design of a form or report.

Theme (AC2.69)

A theme is a predefined set of formatting choices that can be applied to all objects in a database in one simple step.

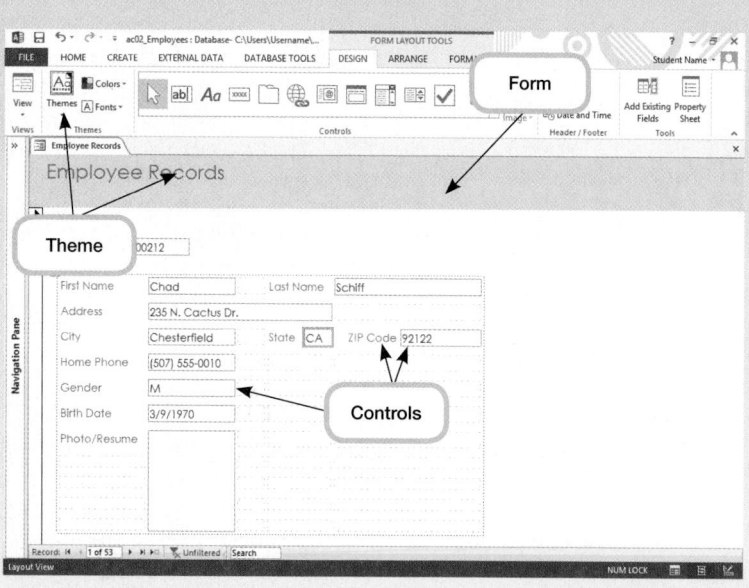

KEY TERMS

argument AC2.11	lookup list AC2.18
ascending sort order AC2.33	Lookup Wizard AC2.18
attachment control AC2.68	merge cells AC2.64
bound control AC2.54	object dependencies AC2.79
character string AC2.8	operator AC2.11
comparison operator AC2.11	outer sort field AC2.34
constant AC2.11	record source AC2.47
control AC2.54	sorting AC2.33
criteria AC2.26	split cells AC2.65
Default Value property AC2.8	stacked format AC2.51
descending sort order AC2.33	tab order AC2.49
expression AC2.11	tabular format AC2.51
filter AC2.40	text control AC2.54
Find and Replace AC2.25	theme AC2.69
form AC2.46	theme colors AC2.38
format AC2.7	unbound control AC2.54
Format property AC2.7	validation rule AC2.10
Form Wizard AC2.48	Validation Rule property AC2.10
function AC2.11	validation text AC2.10
identifier AC2.11	Validation Text property AC2.12
IntelliSense AC2.12	value list AC2.18
label control AC2.54	wildcards AC2.26
layout AC2.51	wizard AC2.18
lookup field AC2.18	

COMMAND SUMMARY

Command	Shortcut	Action
Quick Access Toolbar		
↩ Undo	Ctrl + Z	Cancels last action
💾 Save	Ctrl + S	Saves the current object
Home tab		
Views group		
/Form View		Changes to Form view
/Form Layout View		Changes to Form Layout view
Sort & Filter group		
Filter		Used to specify filter settings for selected field
A↓ Ascending		Changes sort order to ascending
Z↓ Descending		Changes sort order to descending
Remove Sort		Clears all sorts and returns sort order to primary key order
Selection ▾ /Equals		Sets filter to display only those records containing selected value
Advanced ▾ /Clear All Filters		Deletes all filters from table
Toggle Filter		Applies and removes filter from table
Records group		
New	Ctrl + +	Adds new record
Save	⇧ Shift + ↵ Enter	Saves changes to object design
More ▾ /Hide Fields		Hides selected columns in Datasheet view
More ▾ /Unhide Fields		Redisplays hidden columns
Find group		
Find	Ctrl + F	Locates specified data
Replace	Ctrl + H	Locates specified data and replaces it with specified replacement text

LAB REVIEW

COMMAND SUMMARY (CONTINUED)

Command	Shortcut	Action
→ ▼ Go To		Moves to First, Previous, Next, Last, or New record location
�▼ Select/Select		Selects current record
�▼ Select/Select All		Selects all records in database
Text Formatting group		
B Bold	Ctrl + B	Applies bold effect to all text in datasheet
A ▼ Font Color		Applies selected color to all text in datasheet
▦ ▼ Gridlines		Changes the display of gridlines in the datasheet
▦ ▼ Alternate Row Color		Changes background color of alternate rows in datasheet
Create tab		
Forms group		
Form		Creates a new form using all the fields from the underlying table
Form Wizard		Creates a new form by following the steps in the Form Wizard
More Forms ▼ /Multiple Items		Creates a form that displays multiple items
Database Tools tab		
Relationships group		
Object Dependencies		Shows the objects in the database that use the selected object
Table Tools Design tab		
Tools group		
Insert Rows		Inserts a new field in Table Design view
Table Tools Fields tab		
Add & Delete group		
More Fields ▼ Lookup & Relationship		Creates a lookup field
Form Layout Tools Design tab		
Themes group		
Aa Themes ▼		Opens gallery of theme styles

COMMAND SUMMARY (CONTINUED)

Command	Shortcut	Action
Tools group		
Add Existing Fields		Opens the Field List pane where existing fields can be selected and added to a form
Form Layout Tools Arrange tab		
Table group		
Stacked		Applies Stacked layout to the controls
Rows & Columns group		
Insert Below		Inserts a blank row below the selected cell in a layout
Insert Left		Inserts a blank column to the left of the selected cell in a layout
Select Layout		Selects entire layout
Select Column		Selects column in a layout
Select Row		Selects row in a layout
Merge/Split group		
Merge		Combines two or more layout cells into a single cell
Split Horizontally		Divides a layout cell horizontally into two cells
Move group		
Move Up		Moves selected control up
Form Layout Tools Format tab		
Font group		
Align Right		Right-aligns contents of cell

LAB EXERCISES

MATCHING

Match the numbered item with the correct lettered description.

1. * (asterisk)
2. >=
3. ="Y" Or "N"
4. ascending sort
5. character string
6. filter
7. find
8. form
9. record source
10. tab order

_____ a. rearranges records in A to Z or 0 to 9 order
_____ b. a group of characters
_____ c. operator
_____ d. temporarily displays subset of records
_____ e. order that the insertion point moves in a form when
  Tab ⇄ is used
_____ f. underlying table for a form
_____ g. an expression
_____ h. locates specified values in a field
_____ i. database object used primarily for onscreen display
_____ j. wildcard character

TRUE/FALSE

Circle the correct answer to the following statements.

1.	Values are numbers, dates, or pictures.	True	False
2.	The Default Value property determines the value automatically entered into a field of a new record.	True	False
3.	Text controls are unbound controls.	True	False
4.	An expression is a sequence of characters (letters, numbers, or symbols) that must be handled as text, not as numeric data.	True	False
5.	Filter results can be saved with the database and quickly redisplayed.	True	False
6.	A validation rule is an expression that defines acceptable data entry values.	True	False
7.	A contrast operator is a symbol that allows you to make comparisons between two items.	True	False
8.	Text controls display the data, while label controls display the field name.	True	False
9.	Not all database objects are dependent on another object.	True	False
10.	Forms are database objects used primarily for viewing data.	True	False

FILL-IN

Complete the following statements by filling in the blanks with the correct terms.

1. The upper section of the Navigation pane contains _____ , and the lower section contains _____ .

2. _____ restrict the type of data that can be entered in a field.

3. _____ is displayed when an invalid entry is entered.

4. A(n) _____ is a symbol or word that indicates that an operation is to be performed.

5. The most common controls are _____ controls and _____ controls.

6. A(n) _____ is a guide that helps you align controls in a form horizontally and vertically.

7. The two basic form layouts are _____ and _____ .

8. The _____ property changes the way data appears in a field.

9. Format _____ is used to create custom formats that change the way numbers, dates, times, and text display and print.

10. The _____ property is used to specify a value that is automatically entered in a field when a new record is created.

LAB EXERCISES

MULTIPLE CHOICE

Circle the letter of the correct response.

1. A _____ is a feature that guides you step by step through a process.
   a. dialog box
   b. gallery
   c. task pane
   d. wizard

2. _____ properties change the way that data is displayed.
   a. Data
   b. Field
   c. Format
   d. Record

3. The _____ property is commonly used when most of the entries in a field will be the same for the entire table.
   a. AutoNumber
   b. Best Fit
   c. Default Value
   d. Field Data

4. A(n) _____ control is linked to its underlying data source.
   a. bound
   b. field
   c. label
   d. unbound

5. _____ is/are an explanatory message that appears if a user attempts to enter invalid information in a text field.
   a. Expressions
   b. Validation rule
   c. Validation text
   d. Validity checks

6. The _____ is used to specify a value that is automatically entered in a field when a new record is created.
   a. Default Value property
   b. Field value
   c. Format property
   d. Sort property

7. _____ layouts arrange data vertically with a field label to the left of the field data.
   a. Datasheet
   b. Justified
   c. Stacked
   d. Tabular

8. A _____ is a temporary restriction placed on a table to display a subset of records.
   a. control
   b. filter
   c. sort
   d. wildcard

9. A form is _____ an underlying table for its content.
   a. contingent on
   b. dependent on
   c. independent of
   d. separate from

10. _____ determine(s) what information is displayed in a form.
    a. Controls
    b. Design styles
    c. Layouts
    d. Tab order

STEP-BY-STEP

NOTE **Before you begin, you may want to create a backup copy of each data file by copying and renaming it.**

ANTIQUES EMPORIUM INVENTORY DATABASE ★

1. You have already set up an inventory database for the Antiques Emporium consignment shop. It currently contains fields for the item number, description, price, and consignor last name, and it has records for the inventory currently in stock. The owner of the shop is quite pleased with the database as it stands but has asked you to change the name of the existing Price field to show that it is the original price and to add a new field for the current selling price of the item. Also, she would like you to modify some existing records, create a form to ease data entry, and print a copy of the form. Your completed table and form will be similar to those shown here.

   a. Open the database named ac02_Antiques Emporium and the table named Antiques Inventory. Examine the table, noting that the Price field has numbers and text of "contact dealer," which needs to be changed to currency.

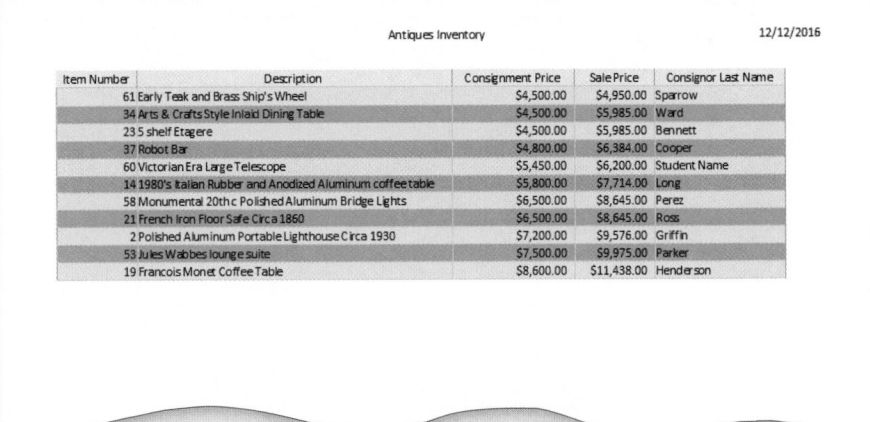

   b. In Design view, change the Price field name to **Consignment Price**. Change the data type for this field to Currency.

   c. Insert the following field before the Consignor Last Name field:

   Field Name: **Sale Price**

   Data Type: Currency

   d. Make all fields except Sale Price required. (*Hint:* Set the Required property to Yes.)
   Note that the Item Number field is automatically required because it is the primary key. Reduce the field size of the Consignor Last Name field to **25**.

e. Switch to Datasheet view and respond "yes" to all prompts and warnings when saving the design changes. (When the Consignment Price field is converted to the Currency data type, the "contact dealer" text will be deleted from the field and you will receive several error messages because of this.)

f. Update the table by entering **0** in the Consignment Price field for all records that have a blank entry in this field.

g. Enter appropriate values in the Sale Price field for each record. (Generally the sale price is 33 percent more than the consignment price.) Leave the Sale Price field blank for those items with $0.00 in the Consignment Price field.

h. Appropriately size all columns to fully display the data.

i. Find all occurrences of dates that include an apostrophe (1930's) and are preceded with the word circa. Manually delete the apostrophe s ('s) from each located item.

j. Filter the table to display all records with a consignment price greater than or equal to $4,500. Sort the filtered records in ascending sort order by consignment price.

k. Format the datasheet using alternate row fill colors of your choice. Save and close the table object.

l. Use the Form tool to create a simple form for the Antiques Inventory table.

m. In Layout view, change the theme style to another of your choice. Reduce the overall size of the controls to best fit the largest content. Then use the Split Horizontally button to make the Item Number, Consignment Price, Sale Price, and Consignor Last Name text controls smaller. Resize them further, as necessary.

n. Switch to Form view and use the new form to enter the following new records:

Field Name	Record 1	Record 2
Description	Victorian Era Large Telescope	Early Teak and Brass Ship's Wheel
Consignment Price	$5,450	$4,500
Sale Price	$6,200	$4,950
Consignor Last Name	[Your Last Name]	Sparrow

o. Print the form for the record containing your name. Close the form, saving it as **Inventory**.

p. Open the table and rerun the filter to display your record in the results. Sort in Ascending order by price. Print the filtered datasheet in landscape orientation using the wide margin setting. Close the table.

q. Display all Access objects by type in the Navigation pane.

r. Add your name to the database properties and exit Access.

LAB EXERCISES

TOP NOTCH EMPLOYMENT CLIENT DATABASE ★★

2. You work for a private employment agency as an administrative assistant. As part of your responsibilities, you maintain a client database that contains the job candidates' basic contact information: name, address, and phone number. The office manager has asked you to add to the database the date each candidate applied at your office, the date they were placed with an employer, and the employer's name. Also, because the database is getting rather large, you decide to create a form to make it easier to enter and update records. Your completed table and form will be similar to those shown here.

a. Open the database named ac02_Top Notch Employment Agency and the table named Candidates.

b. Switch to Design view. Reduce the State field size to **2**. Change the State field Format property to display all entries in uppercase. Make the default value for the State field **FL**.

c. Change the ZIP Code data type to Short Text with a field size of **10**.

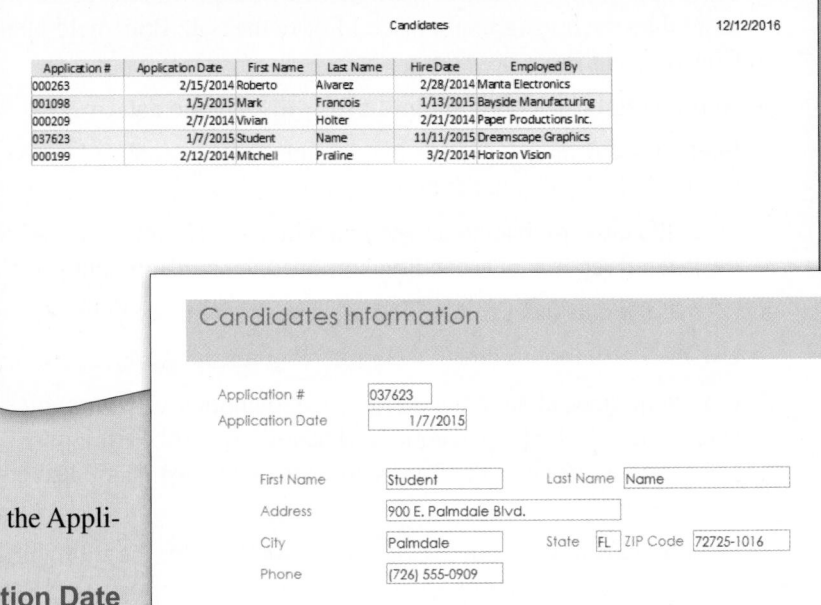

d. Insert the following field after the Application # field.

Field Name:	**Application Date**
Data Type:	Date/Time
Format:	Short Date

e. Add the following two fields to the end of the table:

Field Name:	**Hire Date**
Data Type:	Date/Time
Format:	Short Date
Field Name:	**Employed By**
Data Type:	Short Text
Description:	**Enter the name of the employer**
Field Size:	45

f. Switch to Datasheet view and save the table design changes. Click Yes if you get an error message.

g. All ZIP Codes of 72725 need to be changed to **72725-1016**. Use Find and Replace to make this change in the database. Best fit the columns.

h. Use the Form Wizard to create a form for the Candidates table. Include all the table fields in their current order. Use the columnar layout. Title the form **Candidate Information**.

i. In Form Layout view, select the label and text box controls for all the fields except the Application # and Application Date. Apply the stacked layout. Apply a theme of your choice. Close the Field List pane if it displays. Adjust the column widths so they best fit the contents in the form. (*Hint:* You will need to click elsewhere in the form to deselect the controls, then resize each column individually.)

j. Insert a column on the right side of the layout. Make the following changes to the placement of the controls:

- Move the Last Name label and control to the right of the First Name field.
- Move the State label and control to the right of the City field.
- Horizontally split the cell containing the State label and then move the State text control next to the label.
- Move the ZIP Code label to the right of the State field. Horizontally split the cell containing the ZIP Code label; then move the ZIP Code text control next to the label.
- Move the Phone label and text control underneath the City field.
- Use the layout selector to move the stacked controls so they are down and to the right about 0.5" from its current position.
- Select the Address text control and insert a blank column to the right. Make the blank column about 0.25" wide. Merge the Address control with the two blank cells on the right.
- Merge the Employed By control with the two blank cells on the right.
- Delete any empty row or column placeholders in the layout, but leave one empty row above the Hire Date. Resize all columns to best fit the contents making sure to allow enough room for the longest entries in each field, including the long ZIP Codes.

k. Switch to Form view and use the form to enter the following new records:

Application #	001098	037623
Application Date	1/5/2015	1/7/2015
First Name	Mark	Your first name
Last Name	Francois	Your last name
Address	124 Beach Front Way	900 E. Palmdale Blvd.
City	Lexington	Palmdale
State	FL	FL
ZIP Code	72724	72725-1016
Phone	(726) 555-4623	(726) 555-0909
Hire Date	1/13/2015	1/11/2015
Employed By	Bayside manufacturing	Dreamscape Graphics

l. Use the Search feature to locate the following records and update their data.

Locate	Application Date	Hire Date	Employed By
Vivian Holter	2/7/2014	2/21/2014	Paper Productions Inc.
Mitchell Praline	2/12/2014	3/2/2014	Horizon Vision
Roberto Alvarez	2/15/2014	2/28/2014	Manta Electronics

m. Display all object types in the Navigation pane.

n. Print the form for the record containing your name. Close the form.

o. Filter the Candidates table to display only those records displaying a hire date. Sort the records in ascending order by last name. Hide the Address through Phone columns.

p. Print the filtered datasheet using the wide margin setting in landscape orientation.

q. Toggle the filter off and unhide the columns.

r. Add your name to the database properties. Close all objects and exit Access.

ARF TRACKING DATABASE ★★

3. You have created a database for tracking the animals that come into and go out of the foundation. Now you need to modify the database structure and customize field properties to control the data entered by the foundation's volunteers who are assigned this task. You also want to create a form to make it easier for the volunteers to enter the necessary information. Your completed datasheet and form will be similar to those shown here.

a. Open the file ac02_ ARF Database and the table Rescues in Datasheet view.

b. Use the Replace command to change the Age field from abbreviations to spelled out information. Make Y = Young, A = Adult, and B = Baby.

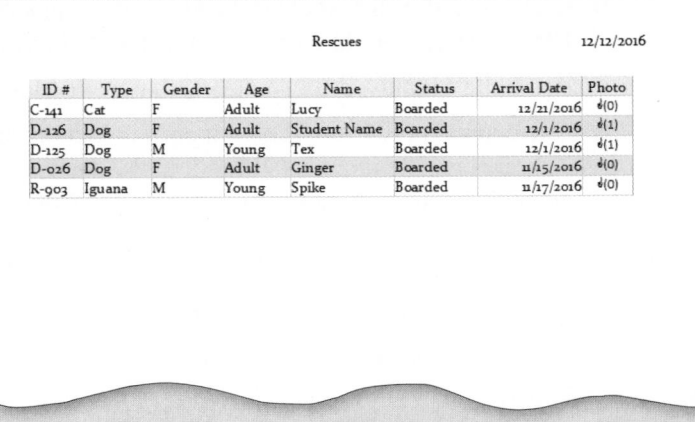

Rescues   12/12/2016

ID #	Type	Gender	Age	Name	Status	Arrival Date	Photo
C-141	Cat	F	Adult	Lucy	Boarded	12/21/2016	(0)
D-126	Dog	F	Adult	Student Name	Boarded	12/1/2016	(1)
D-125	Dog	M	Young	Tex	Boarded	12/1/2016	(1)
D-026	Dog	F	Adult	Ginger	Boarded	11/15/2016	(0)
R-903	Iguana	M	Young	Spike	Boarded	11/17/2016	(0)

c. Use Find to locate ID # R-904. Add the adoption date 6/13/2015.

d. Use Search to locate the animal named Spreckels; change the age to **Adult** and enter **12/01/2015** as the Foster Date.

e. Switch to Design view. Create a values lookup field to select Boarded, Foster Care, or Adopted. Place the field before the Arrival Date field, with the following specifications:

Field Name:	**Status**
Description:	**Select Boarded, Foster Care, or Adopted**
Field Size:	**15**

Animals

ID #	D-126	Name	Student Name
Type	Dog	Photo	
Gender	F		
Age	Adult		
Status	Boarded		
Arrival Date	12/1/2016		
Foster Date			
Adoption Date			

f. Make the following additional changes to the database structure:

- Restrict the entries in the Status field to limit to list items only. Make **Boarded** the default value for Status.
- Add a validation rule and validation text to the Gender field to accept only M or F (male or female). Format the field to display the information in uppercase.
- Change the Age field to a lookup field with the values of Baby, Young, or Adult. Change the field size to **5**. Restrict the entries to items on the list only.

g. In Datasheet view, complete the data for the Status field by entering A (if there is an adoption date), F (if there is a Foster Date but no adoption date), or B (if there is neither a foster nor adoption date). (*Hint:* A quick way to get started is to filter the table on the Adoption Date for Does Not Equal Blank and use the results to enter A for Adopted in the Status field).

h. Add formatting of your choice to the datasheet. Change the font of the datasheet to Constantia, (or a font of your choice) and increase the font size to 12 point.

i. Best fit all columns.

j. Use the Form Wizard to create a columnar form. Include all the fields except for the Photo attachment field. Add the fields in their current order and title the form **Animals**.

k. Switch to Form Layout view and make the following changes to the form:

- Choose a theme design style of your choice.
- Apply the stacked layout to all the controls except the form title.
- Insert three columns to the right. Move the Name label and text controls to the right of the ID text control, in the second empty column.
- Use the Add Existing Fields list to add the Photo attachment field under the Name label, on the right side of the form. Select the attachment control box and the four empty cells beneath it. Merge these cells together.
- Adjust the widths of the empty column and label and text controls to better fit their contents.

l. Search in Form view to locate the animal named Titus, and add the picture ac02_Titus_dog to the Attachment field.

m. Add two new records using the new form. Use the ID # **D-125** for the first record and attach the picture of ac02_Tex_dog, a young male dog. In the second record you add, use the ID # **D-126** and enter your name in the Name field. Attach the picture of ac02_Lilly_dog, who is an adult female dog, to your record. For both records, update the type, gender, name, and age according to what is deduced about the animal in these instructions. Use the current date as the arrival date, and make the status Boarded.

n. Save the form and print the record with your name as the animal name. Close the form.

o. Filter the Rescues datasheet to display only those animals with a status of Boarded. Sort the filtered datasheet in ascending order by Type. Hide the Foster Date and Adoption Date. Print the Rescues datasheet in portrait orientation using the wide margin setting.

p. Unhide all columns. Clear all sorts and toggle the filter off. Save the table.

q. Display all Access objects by type in the Navigation pane.

r. Identify object dependencies.

s. Add your name to the database properties. Close all objects and exit Access.

LAB EXERCISES

ROCKY MOUNTAIN REAL ESTATE RENTALS DATABASE ★★★

4. Rocky Mountain Rentals is a property rental business, and you recently put the rental homes into a database to track the rental properties. The database initially began with basic facts about each home, but now you see the need for more detailed information. A database will be useful to look up any information about the rental, including its location, how many bedrooms and bathrooms, square footage, and date available. You decide to make some additional changes to help with inventory control and make data entry even easier. This will help you find rentals within the desired home size and price range of your clients. When you are finished, your printed database table and form should be similar to the ones shown here.

   a. Open the database file you created in Lab1, page AC1.96, Rocky Mountain Rentals. Save the database as **Rocky Mountain Rentals-2**.

   b. Open the table Rental Homes.

   c. Add a Currency field after the Sq Footage field. Name the new field **Monthly Rent**.

   d. Add a Long Text field at the end of the table and name it **Comments**.

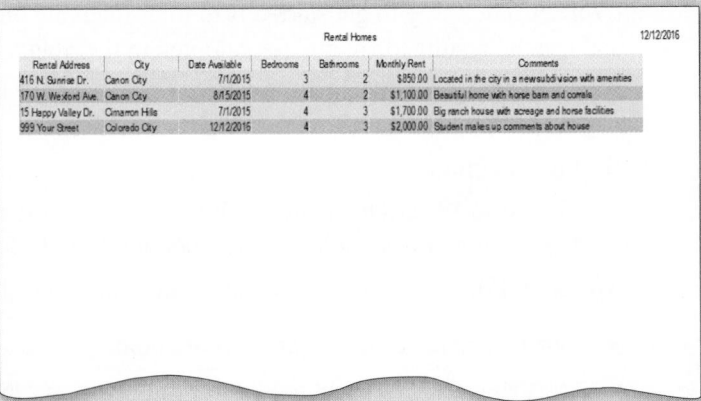

   e. Switch to Design view. You want to add a new field to show whether pets are permitted in each home. This field can only contain four possible values: Pets not okay, Pets okay, Horses and pets allowed, or Assistance animals only. Insert a new field after Sq Footage named **Animal Permission**. Use a data type of Lookup and enter the following as list values: **Pets not okay, Pets okay, Horses and pets allowed,** or **Assistance animals only**. Set the field's default value to **Pets not okay**, and limit entries to the list items.

   f. Insert a new field after the Date Available field named **Rented** with a field size of **1**, data type of Short Text. Add **Y or N** as a validation rule. Add **Must be Y or N** as the Validation text. Format the field to display in uppercase.

g. In Datasheet view, add two new records:

Rental Address:	170 W. Wexford Ave.	416 N. Sunrise Dr.
City:	Canon	Canon
Date Available:	8/15/2015	7/1/2015
Bedrooms:	4	3
Bathrooms:	2	2
Sq Foot:	2000	1500
Animal Permission:	Horses and pets allowed	Assistance animals only
Monthly Rent:	$1100	$850
Owner's Name:	Gary Malloy	Ginger Harlow
Comments:	Beautiful home with horse barn and corrals	Located in the city in a new subdivision with amenities

h. Widen the fields to best fit the data.

i. Hide the Rental ID, Bedrooms, Bathrooms, Sq Foot, Owner's Name, and Photo Attachment fields.

j. Update the other records with information for the new fields (Monthly Rent, Animal Permission, and Comments) using the information from the table below:

Record	Monthly Rent	Animal Permission	Comments
600 Sycamore Lane	$1050	Pets not okay	Townhome with homeowners association rules
15 Happy Valley Drive	$1700	Horses and pets allowed	Big ranch house with acreage and horse facilities
221 Cedar Street	$750	Pets okay	Older home close to nice parks
Your street	name your price	Pets okay	your comments

k. Unhide all fields.

l. Find all instances of Canon in the City field and replace with **Canon City**.

m. Use Search to find the record for 221 Cedar Street. The home has been rented out, so delete the entry in Date Available and type in **Y** for the Rented field. Enter **N** for the Rented field for the other records.

n. Add formatting of your choice to the datasheet. Change the font of the datasheet to one of your choice. Adjust column widths as needed.

o. Use the Form Wizard to create a form for the Rentals table. Include all of the fields except Rental ID and Photo of Home from the Rentals table, in order. Use the columnar form layout and accept the form name **Rental Homes**.

p. Switch to Layout view. Select a theme style. Select the Comments label and text control and apply the stacked layout. Resize the Comments controls so they are the same size as the controls above. Move the Comments stacked control group to the right side of the other fields. Add the Photo of Home form field within the Comments stacked control group, underneath the Comments field. Resize the height of the row containing the Photo control so the bottom of the photo box aligns with the bottom of the Owner's Name control. Resize the controls to better fit the text boxes.

q. Use the form to enter another new record for your 3-bedroom, 2-bath, 1,750-square-foot home located on 123 Any Street, Colorado Springs. The home is currently rented but will be available

8/1/2015. Pets are not okay. Monthly rent is $1200. Add Comments of your choice. Insert the picture ac02_123_Any_Street for the Photo of Home field.

r. Preview and print the form for your new record in landscape orientation. Save and close the form.

s. Filter the Rental Homes table to display only those records with Rented N and Pets okay (*hint:* select both pets okay and horses and pets allowed options). Sort in ascending order by City. Hide the Rental ID, Rented, Sq Foot, Owner Name, Animal Permission, and Attachments fields. Print the filtered datasheet in landscape orientation with normal margins (*hint:* the datasheet should preferably fit on one page). Toggle the filter off and then unhide the hidden fields. Save and close the table.

t. Display all Access objects by type in the Navigation pane.

u. Make sure your name is in the database properties as the author. Save the database and exit Access.

LIFESTYLE FITNESS CLUB MEMBERSHIP DATABASE ★★★

5. After getting approval from the Lifestyle Fitness Club owners, you continued to add records to the Lifestyle Fitness Club Membership database. You still need to make additional changes to make the database more efficient and accurate. You also want to create a form to make data entry easier. Your completed database table and form will be similar to those shown here.

a. Open the database file named ac02_Lifestyle Fitness Memberships from your data file location.

b. Open the Members table.

c. In Design view, change the State field Format property to display all entries in uppercase. Make the default value for the State field **CA**. Change the ZIP Code data type to Short Text and the field size to **10**.

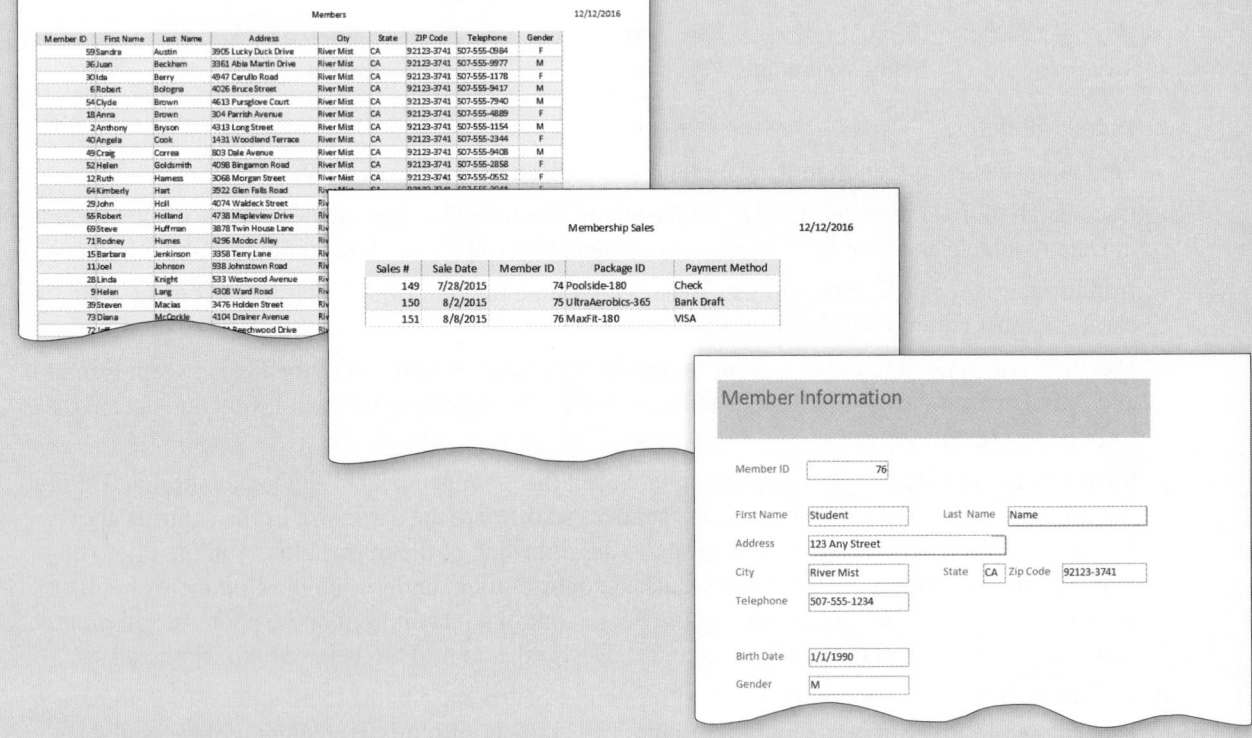

d. Insert the following field before the Birth Date field:

Field Name:	**Gender**
Data Type:	Short Text
Field Size:	**1**
Format:	**>**
Validation Rule:	**"f" or "m"**
Validation Text:	**Enter F or M**

e. Switch to Datasheet view, and enter the gender for each member using the first name as a guide.

f. All ZIP Codes of 92123 need to be updated to **92123-3741**. Use the Find and Replace to make this change in the database. Best fit the columns. Save the table.

g. Use the Form Wizard to create a form for the Members table. Include all the table fields in their current order. Use the columnar layout and theme of your choice. Title the form **Member Information**.

h. Switch to the form's Layout view; select the label and text box controls for all the fields except the Member ID field. Apply the stacked layout, and then adjust the column widths so they best fit the contents in the form.

i. Insert a column on the right side of the form layout. Make the following changes to the placement of the controls:

- Move the Last Name label and text box control to the right of the First Name field.
- Move the State label and text box control to the right of the City field.
- Horizontally split the cell containing the State label, and then move the State text box control next to the label.
- Move the ZIP Code label to the right of the State text box field. Horizontally split the cell containing the ZIP Code label; then move the ZIP Code text box control next to the label.
- Move the Telephone label and text box control underneath the City field.
- Select the Last Name label. Insert a blank row above and a blank column to the left. Adjust the blank column width so that it is about 0.25″ wide, just enough to give some space between the fields.
- Merge the Address text box control with the two blank cells on the right.
- Delete any empty row or column placeholders in the layout, but leave one empty row above the First Name and the Birth Date fields. Resize all columns to best fit the contents.

j. Switch to Form view and enter the following new records:

Field Name	New Record 1	New Record 2	New Record 3
Member ID	74	75	76
First Name	Evelyn	Wanda	Your first name
Last Name	Anderson	Rather	Your last name
Address	3547 Brownton Road	4590 Bingamon Road	123 Any Street
City	Chesterfield	River Mist	River Mist
State	CA	CA	CA
ZIP Code	92122	92123-3741	92123-3741
Telephone	507-555-6320	507-555-3488	507-555-1234
Birth Date	5/3/60	9/16/81	1/1/90
Gender	F	F	

LAB EXERCISES

k. Use the Search feature to locate the following records and update their data.

Locate	Address Correction
Emma Barajas	1686 Black Stallion Avenue
Sean Mason	2954 McVarney Road
Angela Cook	1431 Woodland Terrace

l. Display all Access objects by type in the Navigation pane.

m. Print the form for the record containing your name. Close the form.

n. Open the Members table and complete the following:

- Filter the Members table to display only those records with a city of River Mist.

- Sort in ascending order by last name.

- Hide the Birth Date field. Print the filtered Members table in landscape orientation with normal margins.

- Unhide the Birth Date field. Clear all sorts and toggle the filter off. Save and close the table.

o. Open the Membership Sales table in Design view and complete the following:

- Change the Member ID to a lookup field to obtain its values from the Members table (use the Lookup Wizard option to get the values from another table). Include the Member ID, First Name, and Last Name fields in the lookup. Sort by last name in ascending order. Uncheck the Hide key column option. Adjust the column widths of the fields in the Lookup Wizard. Choose to store the Member ID field as the value. Keep the label of Member ID for the field, and check to Enable Data Integrity.

- Change the Package ID field to a lookup for the Membership Packages table. Include the Package ID and Type fields in the lookup. Sort by Type and choose not to hide the key column. Store the Package ID as the value to store in the table.

- Make the Payment method a lookup—type in the values of **VISA, Check, Cash,** and **Bank draft.**

- Change to Datasheet view, and add the new membership sales records for the new members shown below:

Field Name	New Record 1	New Record 2	New Record 3
Sale Date	7/28/2015	8/2/2015	8/8/2015
Member	Evelyn Anderson	Wanda Rather	Your name
Membership Package	Poolside-180	UltraAerobics-365	MaxFit-180
Payment Method	Check	Bank draft	VISA

- Best fit all fields.

- Right-click the 7/28/2015 date in the Sale Date field, and choose to filter the table on or after 7/28/2015.

p. Preview and print the Membership Sales table in portrait orientation.

q. Add your name to the database properties.

r. Save and close all objects and exit Access.

ON YOUR OWN

ADVENTURE TRAVEL PACKAGES FORM ★

1. You have heard from the employees of Adventure Travel Tours that the database table you created is a bit unwieldy for them to enter the necessary data because it now contains so many fields that it requires scrolling across the screen to locate them. You decide to create a form that will make entering data not only easier but more attractive as well. Open the ac02_Adventure Travel database. Best fit the columns. Change the order of the Length and Description field columns in Design view. Apply formatting of your choice to the datasheet. Sort the table on Destination in ascending order. Use the Form Wizard to create a form called **Travel Packages** for the Packages table. Use the form to enter five new records with tour package information of your choice (use the newspaper travel section or the web for ideas). Enter your name as the contact in one of the new records. Print the form containing your name. Print the datasheet in landscape orientation.

AMP ACCOUNT TRACKING ★★

2. While creating the database table for AMP Enterprises, you learned that some employees have been receiving advances for anticipated expenses (such as for travel). You also have been informed that the CEO wants to start tracking the expenses by department. Open the database file AMP Enterprise (Lab 1, On Your Own 5). Add a new field named **Advanced Amount** with a Currency data type to the Employee Expenses table. Also add a Yes/No field named **Payment Made** to record whether or not the expense has been paid, with a corresponding validation rule and message. In the Employee Info table, add a new field named **Department** for the department's charge code number. Update both tables to include appropriate values in the new fields in the existing records. Apply formatting of your choice to the Employee Expenses datasheet. Sort the Employee Expenses table on the Expense Amount field in descending sort order. Close the table, saving the changes. Use the Form Wizard to create a form named **Expenses** for the Employee Expenses table. Include the form title **Your Name Expenses**. Modify the form in Layout view to make it more attractive and user friendly. To test the form, enter a new expense record using the employee ID number for the record containing your name in the Employee Info table. Select your record in the form and print it.

DENTAL PATIENT DATABASE UPDATE ★★

3. The dentist office for which you created a patient database has expanded to include a second dentist and receptionist. The two dentists are Dr. Jones and Dr. Smith. You now need to modify the database to identify required fields and to add a new field that identifies which patient is assigned to which dentist. You also decide that creating a form for the database would make it easier for both you and the other receptionist to enter and locate patient information. Open the Dental Patients database (Lab 1, On Your Own 3) and the Patient Information table. Make the patient identification number, name, and phone number required fields. Add a **Dentist Name** lookup list field, with the two dentists' names and an appropriate validation rule and message. Update the table to "assign" some of the patients to one of the

LAB EXERCISES

dentists and some patients to the other dentist. Assign the record containing your name to Dr. Jones. Sort the table by dentist name to see the results of your new assignments. "Reassign" one of the displayed patients and then remove the sort. Filter the table to display only those patients for Dr. Jones. Apply formatting of your choice to the datasheet. Print the filtered datasheet and then remove the filter. Create a form called **Patient Data** for the table using the Form Wizard. Modify the form in Layout view to make it more attractive and user friendly. Enter two new records, one for each of the dentists. Use the Search feature to locate the record that has your name as the patient, and then select and print the displayed record in the form.

LEWIS & LEWIS EMPLOYEE DATABASE ★★

4. You work in the Human Resource Management department at Lewis & Lewis, Inc. You recently created a simple database containing information on each employee's department and work telephone extension. Several of your co-workers also want to use the database. You decide to add a field for the employee's job title and enhance the table. You also want to create a form that will make it easier for others to update the information in the database. Open the ac02_Lewis Personnel database and Phone List table, and add the **Job Title** field after the Department field. Update the table to include information in the new field for the existing records (*hint:* use job titles such as Accounts Payable Clerk, Graphic Design Coordinator, Personnel Manager, etc.). Add a new record that includes your name and administrative assistant for the job title. Apply formatting of your choice to the datasheet. Sort the table by Department and Last Name. Use the Search feature to locate and delete the record for Anna Tai, who has left the company. Print the datasheet in landscape orientation. Remove the sort and close the table, saving the changes. Create a form called **Phone List** for the Phone List table using the Form Wizard. Modify the form using Layout view, and place the controls in a more user-friendly order (for example, place the Last Name control to the right of the First Name control.) Enter five new records. Use the Replace command to locate and change the last name for Alexa Hirsch to Alexa **Muirhead**, who has gotten married since you first created the database. Use the Search feature to locate the record form that has your name as the employee. Select and print the displayed record.

TIMELESS TREASURES INVENTORY DATABASE ★★★

5. You realize that you have left out some very important fields in the Inventory table you created in the Timeless Treasures database (Lab 1, On Your Own 4)—fields that identify the sources where you can obtain the vintage watches your customers are looking for. Repeat your web search for old watches, and note the resources (for example, online shopping services, specialty stores, or individual collectors who are offering these items at online auctions) for the watches in your table. Add a **Source Name** field, a **Source E-mail** field, and a **Source Phone** field to the table. Update the table to include this information in the existing records. Apply formatting of your choice to the datasheet. Sort the records according to the Source Name field, and adjust the column widths to accommodate the new information. Print the datasheet. Remove the sort and close the table, saving the changes. Now, to make data entry easier, create a form named **Watches** using the Form Wizard. Modify the arrangement of controls to make the form more visually appealing. Use the form to locate the record with your name as the manufacturer, and then print it.

Querying Tables and Creating Reports Lab 3

Objectives

After completing this lab, you will know how to:

1. Evaluate table design.

2. Modify relationships.

3. Enforce referential integrity.

4. Create and modify a simple query.

5. Query two tables.

6. Filter a query.

7. Find unmatched and duplicate records.

8. Create a parameter query.

9. Create reports from tables and queries.

10. Display a Totals row.

11. Modify a report design.

12. Select, move, and size controls.

13. Change page margins.

14. Preview and print a report.

15. Compact and back up a database.

CASE STUDY

Lifestyle Fitness Club

After modifying the structure of the table of personal data, you have continued to enter many more records. You also have created a second table in the database that contains employee information about locations and job titles. Again, the owners are very impressed with the database. They are eager to see how the information in the database can be used.

As you have seen, compiling, storing, and updating information in a database are very useful. The real strength of a database program, however, is its ability to

find the information you need quickly, and to manipulate and analyze it to answer specific questions. You will use the information in the tables to provide the answers to several inquiries about the club's employees. As you learn about the database's analytical features, imagine trying to do the same tasks by hand. How long would it take? Would your results be as accurate or as well presented? In addition, you will create several reports that present the information from the database attractively.

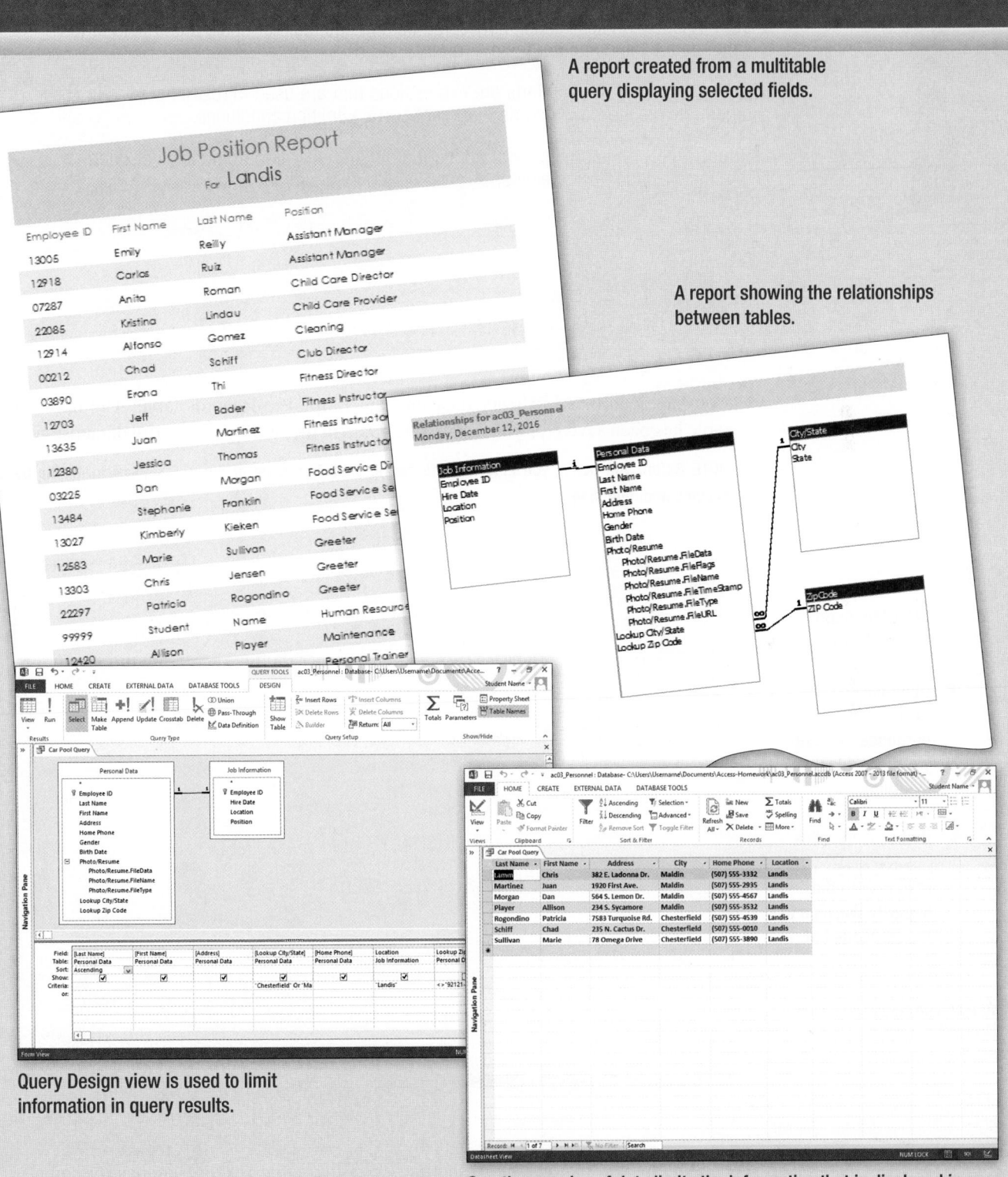

A report created from a multitable query displaying selected fields.

A report showing the relationships between tables.

Query Design view is used to limit information in query results.

Creating queries of data limits the information that is displayed in the results.

Concept Preview

The following concepts will be introduced in this lab:

1 Query A query is a request for specific data contained in a database. Queries are used to view data in different ways, to analyze data, and even to change existing data.

2 Join A join is an association between a field in one table or query and a field of the same data type in another table or query.

3 Query Criteria Query criteria are expressions that are used to restrict the results of a query to display only records that meet certain limiting conditions.

4 Report A report is professional-appearing output generated from tables or queries that may include design elements, groups, and summary information.

Refining the Database Design

You have continued to enter data into the Employee Records table. The updated table has been saved for you as Personal Data in the ac03_Personnel database file.

NOTE Before you begin, you may want to create a backup copy of the ac03_Personnel file by copying and renaming it.

1

● **Start Microsoft Access 2013.**

● **Open the ac03_Personnel database file from your data file location.**

● **If necessary, click** Enable Content **in response to the Security Warning in the message bar.**

Your screen should be similar to Figure 3.1

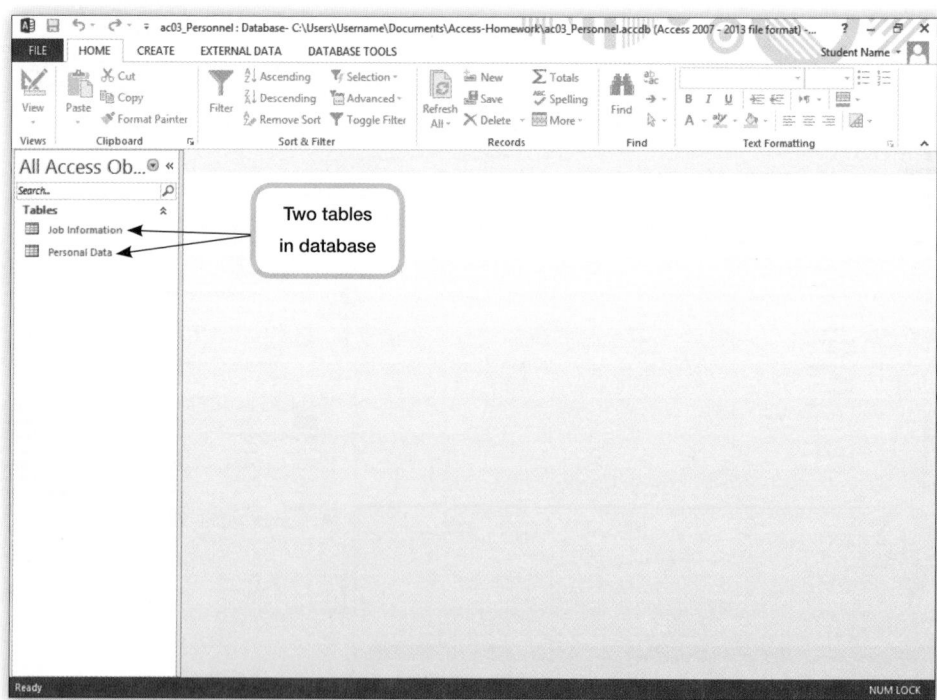

Figure 3.1

The Navigation pane displays the names of two tables in this database: Personal Data and Job Information.

AC3.4   Lab 3: Querying Tables and Creating Reports

WWW.MHHE.COM/OLEARY

Access 2013

2

- **Open the Personal Data table.**

- **Add your information as record number 70 using your special ID number 99999 and your name. Enter Maldin as the city and 92121 as the ZIP code. Fill in the remaining fields as desired.**

- **Return to the first field of the first record.**

- **Hide the Navigation pane.**

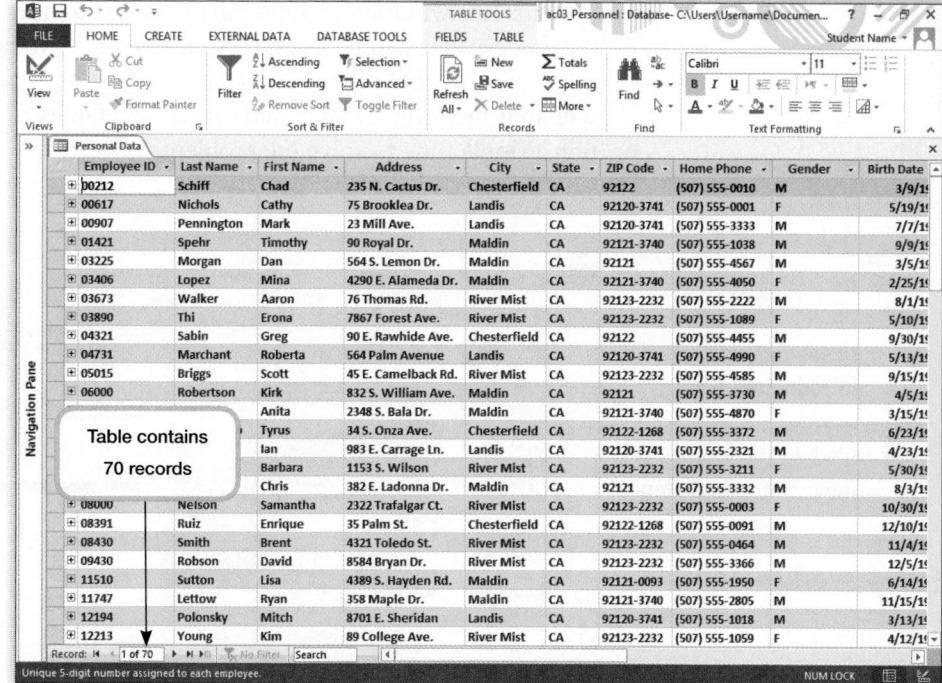

Figure 3.2

Your screen should be similar to Figure 3.2

EVALUATING TABLE DESIGN

As you continue to use and refine the database, you have noticed that you repeatedly enter the same city, state, and ZIP code information in the Personal Data table. You decide there may be a better way to organize the table information and will use the Table Analyzer tool to help evaluate the design of the Personal Data table.

1

- **Open the Database Tools tab.**

- **Click Analyze Table in the Analyze group.**

Having Trouble?

If necessary, click Open in response to the security warning message.

Your screen should be similar to Figure 3.3

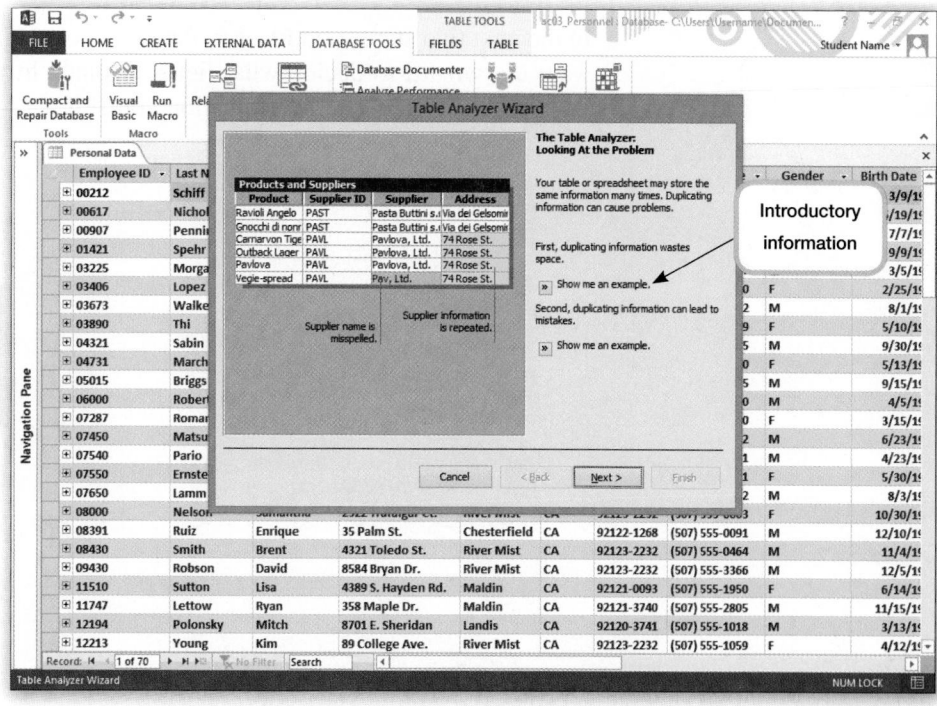

Figure 3.3

The first two windows of Table Analyzer Wizard are introductory pages that review the process that will be used. First, the wizard will analyze the information stored in the table by looking for duplicate information. Then, if duplicates are located, it will split the original table and create new tables to store the duplicated information a single time to solve the problem.

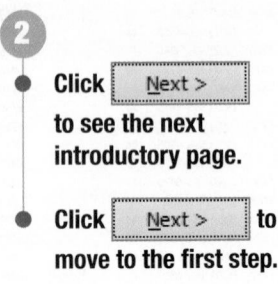

Click [Next >] to see the next introductory page.

Click [Next >] to move to the first step.

Your screen should be similar to Figure 3.4

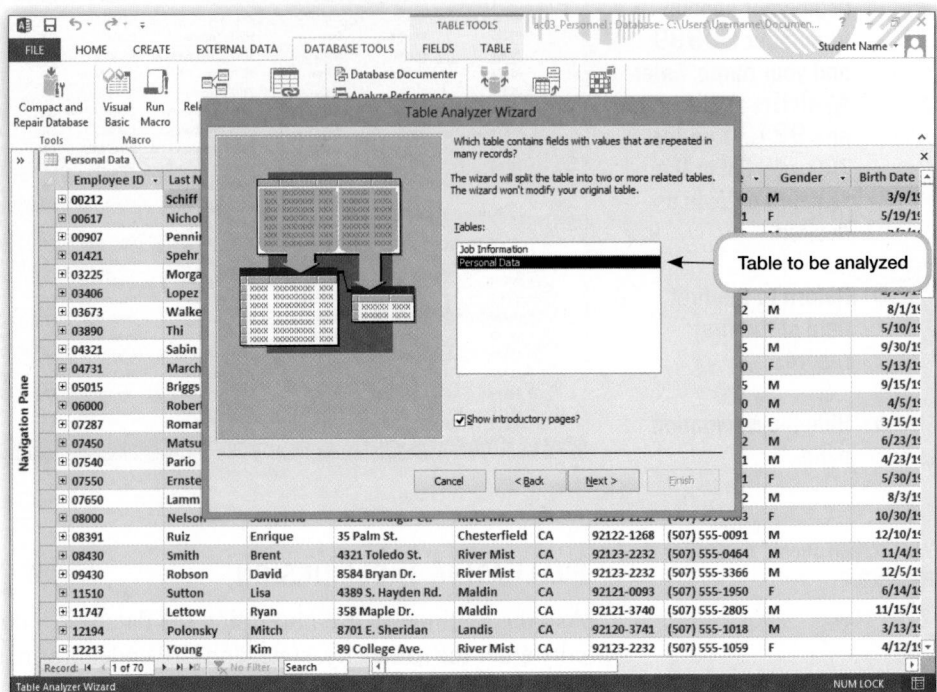

Figure 3.4

In the next two steps, you identify the table you want to evaluate and whether you want the wizard to decide what fields to place in the new table or whether you would rather make that determination yourself.

3

- Click **Next >** to accept analyzing the Personal Data table for fields that have values that are repeated.

- Click **Next >** to accept letting the wizard decide what fields go in what tables.

- If the field names in the Table2 and Table3 list boxes are not visible, increase the length and/or width of the box.

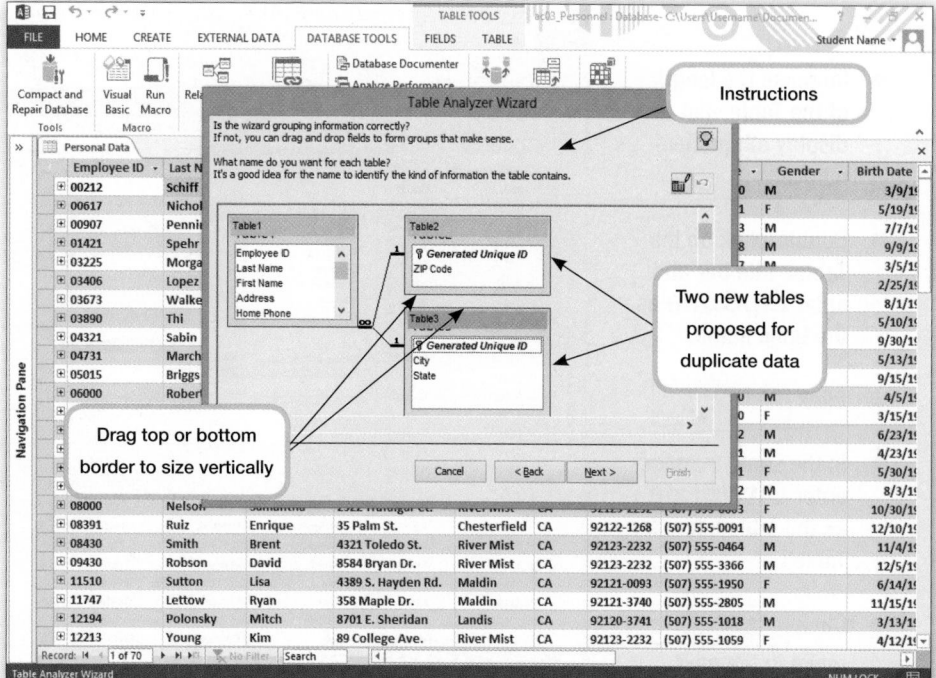

Figure 3.5

Your screen should be similar to Figure 3.5

The wizard has identified duplicate data in the ZIP Code, City, and State fields and proposes to move these fields into two additional tables—one for ZIP codes and the other for city and state—where the information would be stored only once. The instructions at the top of the Table Analyzer Wizard box ask you to revise the grouping if needed and to create names for the tables. You agree that creating the two new tables will prevent duplicate data. You will then rename the new tables and move to the next step.

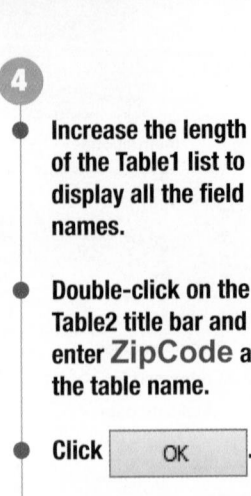

4

- Increase the length of the Table1 list to display all the field names.

- Double-click on the Table2 title bar and enter **ZipCode** as the table name.

- Click [OK].

- In the same manner, enter **City/State** as the table name for Table3.

- Click [Next >] to move to the next step.

Your screen should be similar to Figure 3.6

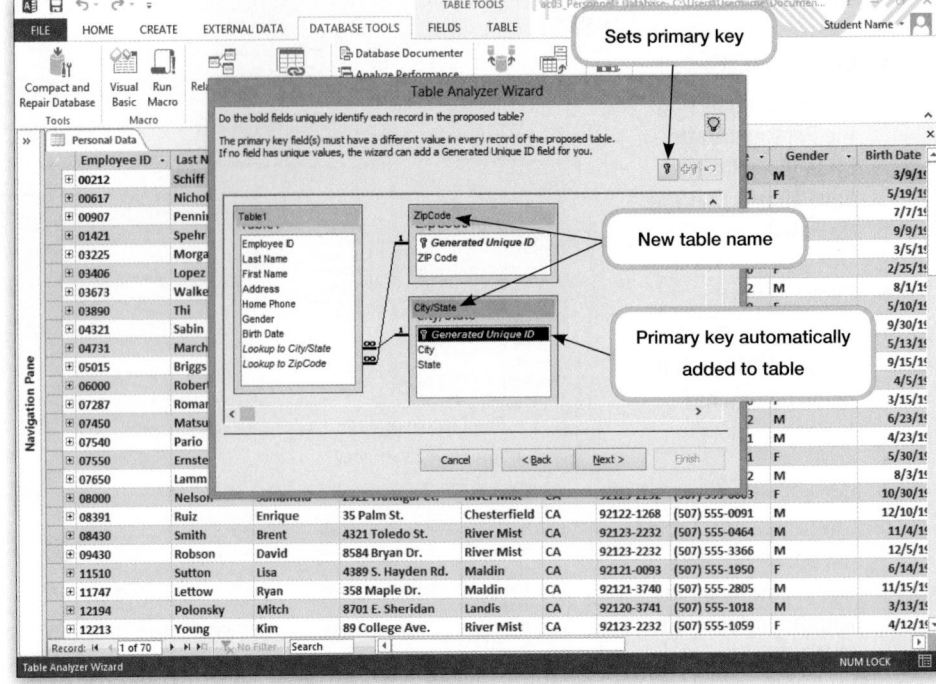

Sets primary key

New table name

Primary key automatically added to table

Figure 3.6

This step identifies the fields to use as primary keys in the new tables by bolding the field names. The wizard automatically added a Generated Unique ID field (AutoNumber) to the ZipCode and City/State tables and defined it as the primary key field. In both tables, this field is unnecessary because the values in the City and ZIP Code fields are unique and therefore can be used as the primary key fields. You will define the City and ZIP Code fields as the primary key field in each table, which will also remove the Unique ID field.

5

- Select the ZIP Code field and then click [🔑].

- In the same manner change the City field to the primary key field.

- Click [Next >] to move to the next step.

Your screen should be similar to Figure 3.7

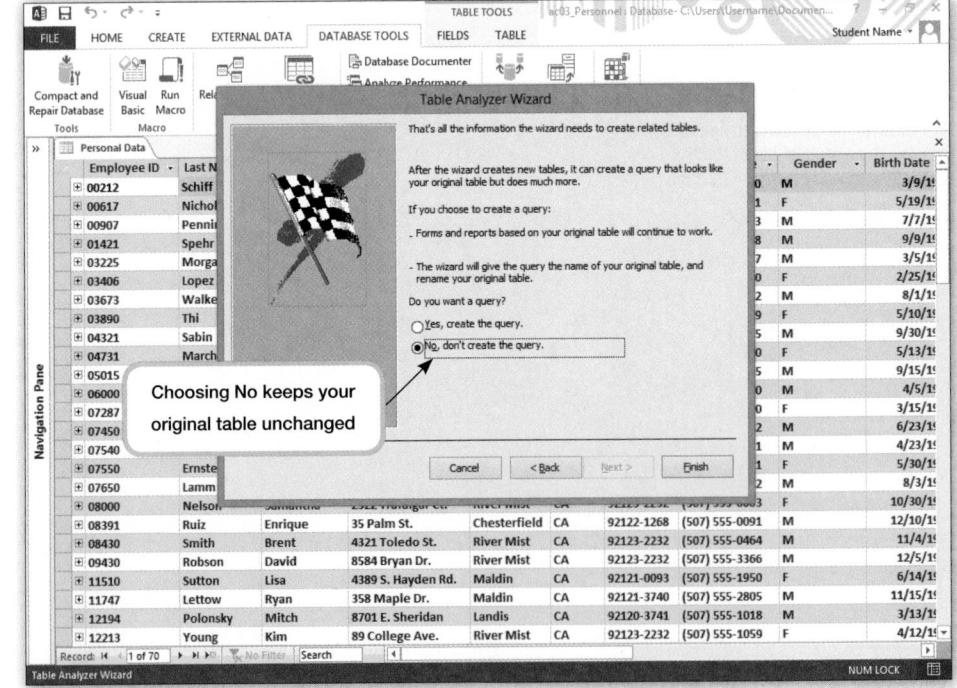

Choosing No keeps your original table unchanged

Figure 3.7

The final wizard step asks if you want to create a query. You will be learning about queries shortly, so you will not create a query at this time.

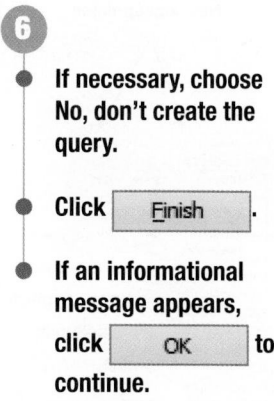

6

- If necessary, choose No, don't create the query.

- Click [Finish].

- If an informational message appears, click [OK] to continue.

Your screen should be similar to Figure 3.8

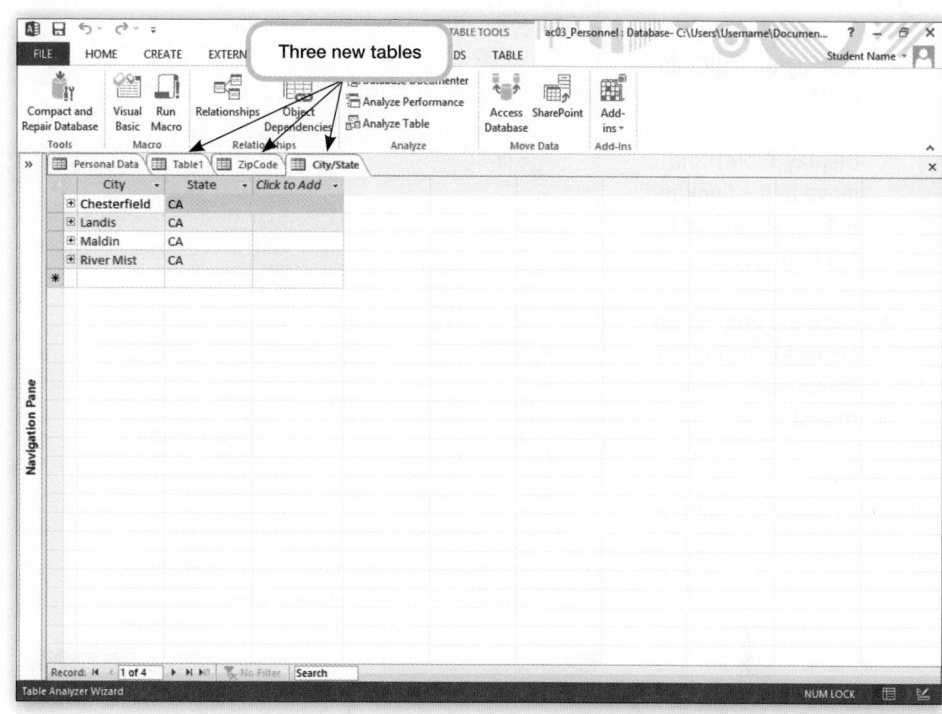

Figure 3.8

There are now three new tables open: City/State, ZipCode, and Table1. Table1 was automatically created by the Table Analyzer Wizard. It is a replica of the Personal Data table but with lookup fields for the City/State and ZipCode tables. The City/State table is currently displayed and consists of two fields, City and State, with the City field as the primary key field. You will take a look at the ZipCode table, which only contains the ZIP Code field set as the primary key, and then examine Table1. The primary key fields in the City/State and ZipCode tables have been associated with the data in the new Table1.

7

● **Display the ZipCode table.**

● **Display Table1 and move to the Lookup to City/State field for the first record.**

● **Click the drop-down arrow to display the lookup list for the record.**

Your screen should be similar to Figure 3.9

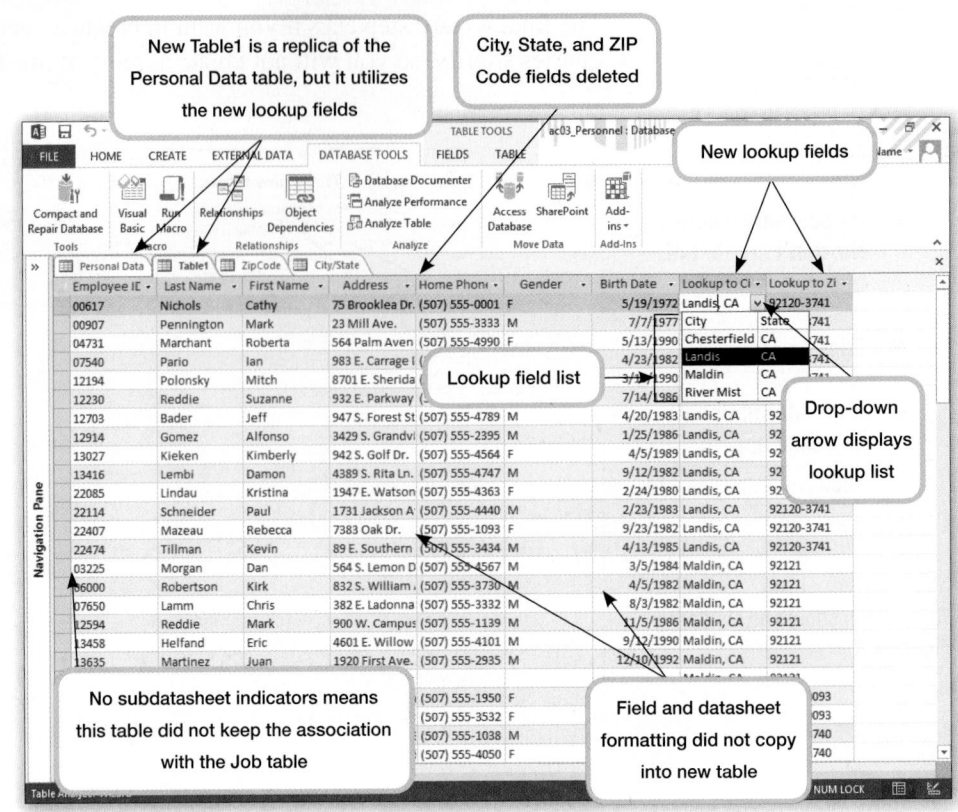

Figure 3.9

Table1 displays the ZIP code, city, and state information as lookup fields with data from their associated tables. Clicking the drop-down arrow in a lookup field displays the list of possible choices from the originating table. The individual fields that stored this information for each record have been deleted from Table1. You can now see how using separate tables to store this data saves space by not repeating the information and also makes data entry easier and more accurate.

CREATING A TABLE LIST LOOKUP FIELD

Now your database contains two tables that hold duplicate data, Table1 and Personal Data, and you need to decide which table to keep. You notice that Table1 did not maintain the association to the Job Information table and the field and datasheet formatting. Rather than make these same changes again to Table1, you decide to modify the Personal Data table by creating lookup fields that will use the values in the City/State and ZipCode tables for the lookup list.

Having Trouble?

Refer to Concept 5: Lookup Field in Lab 2 to review this feature.

1

● Display the Personal Data table.

● Scroll to the right to display the last column.

Having Trouble?

If necessary, click **Open** in response to the security warning message.

● Open the Click to Add menu and choose Lookup & Relationship.

● Use the Lookup Wizard to specify the following settings:

  ● Get the values from another table or query.

  ● Choose the City/State table.

  ● Add the City and State fields to the Selected Fields list.

  ● Specify ascending sort order by City.

  ● Clear the check mark from the Hide key column option and size the State column to best fit.

  ● Choose the City field as the value to store in the database.

  ● Enter the field name **Lookup City/State** and click **Finish**.

● Use the Lookup Wizard to add a second lookup field to get the values from the ZipCode table. Sort in ascending order. Best fit the lookup field. Name the field **Lookup Zip Code**

● Click in the Lookup City/State field for the first record and display the drop-down list.

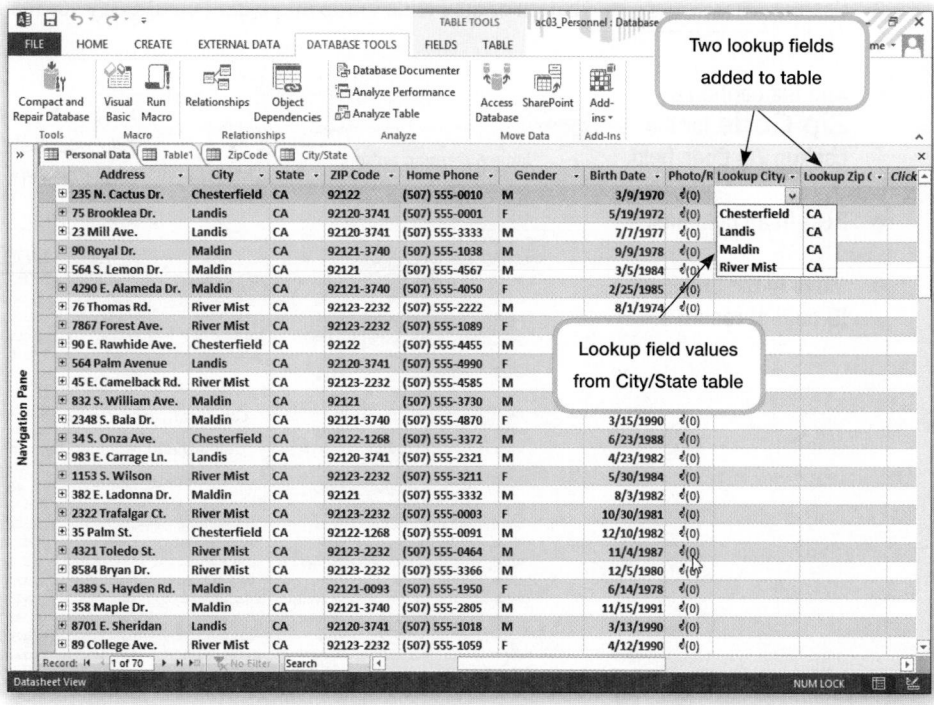

Figure 3.10

Your screen should be similar to Figure 3.10

You have added two new lookup fields to the table. Now you need to add the data for these fields. Instead of selecting the city and ZIP code for each record, you will copy the data from the existing City and ZIP Code field columns into the new lookup columns. Then, because you will no longer need them, you will delete the original City, State, and ZIP Code fields. Finally, you will move the lookup field columns after the Address field column.

2

• Copy the data in the City field column to the Lookup City/State column.

Having Trouble?
Remember: To select an entire column, click on its column heading when the mouse pointer is ↓.

• Click [Yes] in response to the advisory message.

• Copy the data in the ZIP Code field column to the Lookup Zip Code column and click [Yes] in response to the advisory message.

• Delete the original City, State, and ZIP Code columns.

• Click [Yes] twice to permanently delete the fields and their indexes.

• Select both lookup field columns and move them to the right of the Address field.

Having Trouble?
Refer to the Moving a Field topic in Lab 1 to review this feature.

• Use the [▣≡ Name & Caption] button in the Fields tab to add a caption of City for the Lookup City/State field.

• Add the caption of Zip Code for the Lookup Zip Code field.

• Best fit all columns.

• Move to the Employee ID field of record 1.

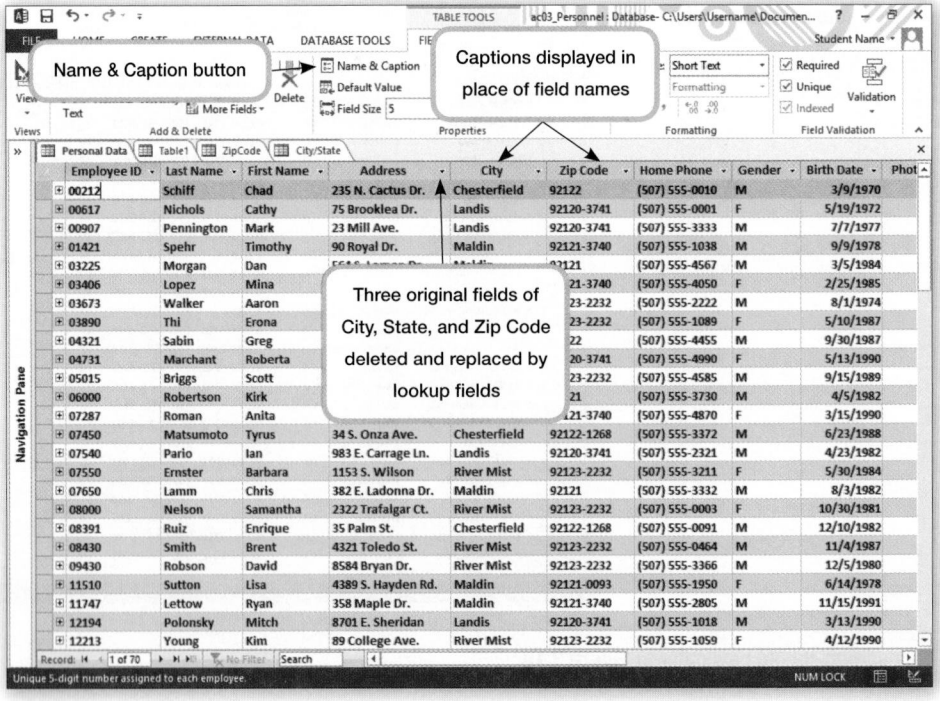

Figure 3.11

Your screen should be similar to Figure 3.11

DELETING A TABLE

Now that the Personal Data table is modified, you will delete the duplicate Table1.

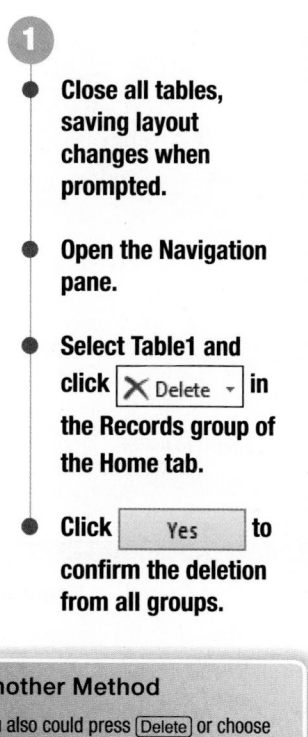

- **Close all tables, saving layout changes when prompted.**

- **Open the Navigation pane.**

- **Select Table1 and click ✕ Delete ▾ in the Records group of the Home tab.**

- **Click Yes to confirm the deletion from all groups.**

Another Method

You also could press Delete or choose Delete from the object's shortcut menu.

Your screen should be similar to Figure 3.12

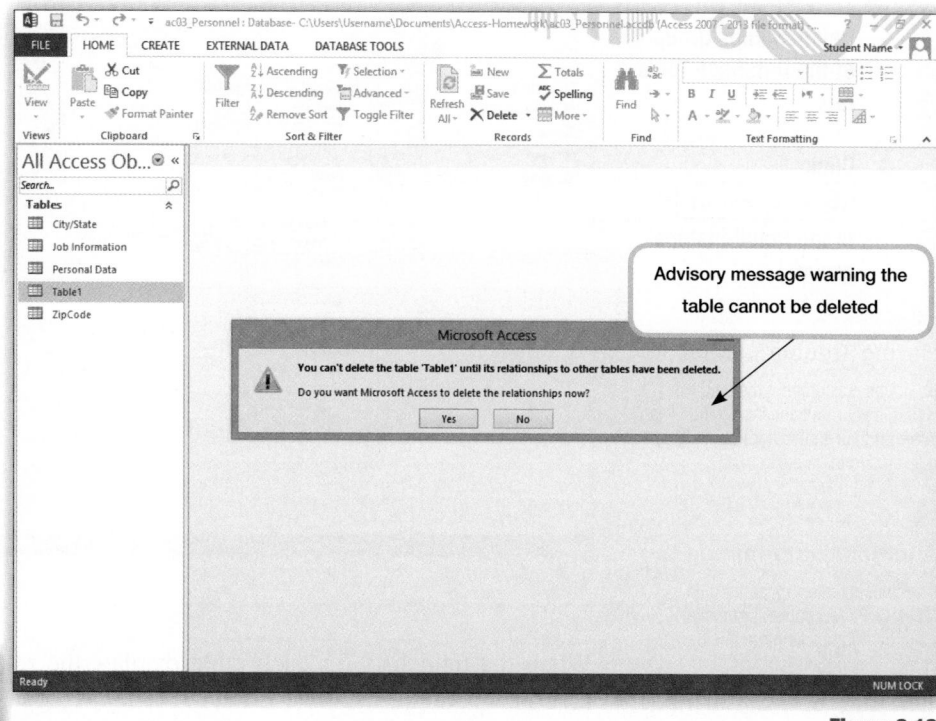

> Advisory message warning the table cannot be deleted

Figure 3.12

The advisory message warns that the table cannot be deleted until its relationships to other tables have been deleted. Rather than have the program remove the relationships for you, you will look at the relationships that have been created between all tables first.

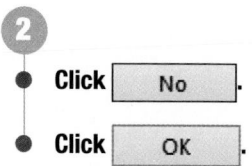

- **Click No.**
- **Click OK.**

Defining and Modifying Relationships

When you create lookup fields, Access automatically establishes relationships between the tables. You will open the Relationships window to edit these relationships.

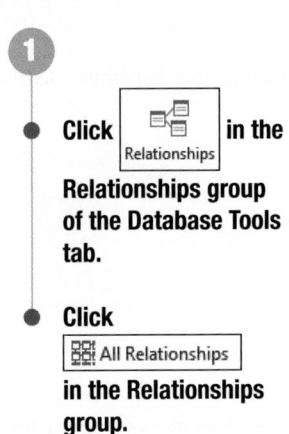

- Click 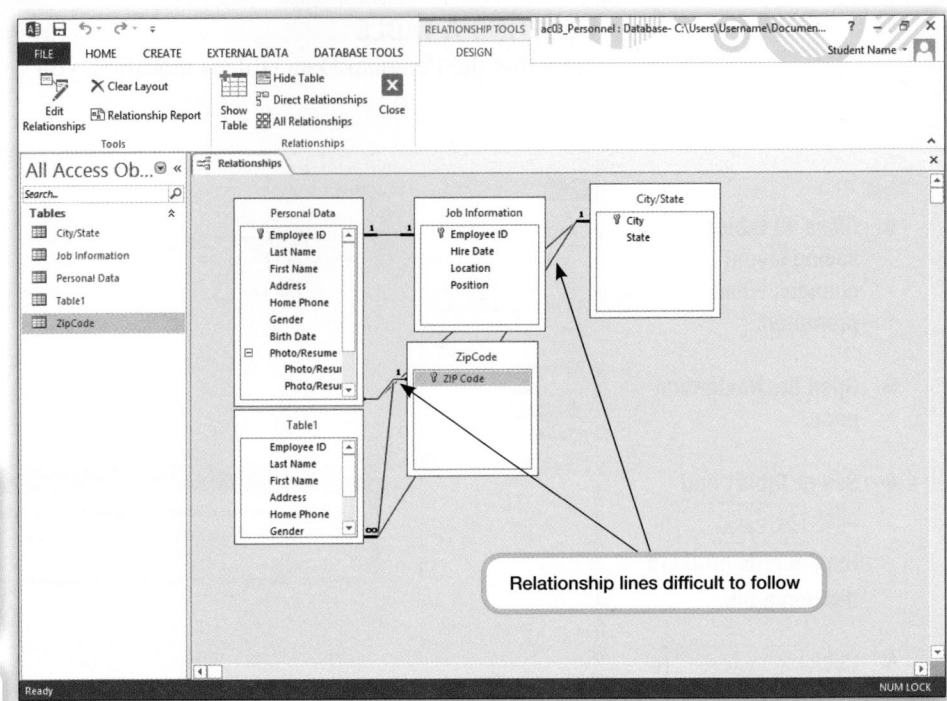 in the Relationships group of the Database Tools tab.

- Click [⊞ All Relationships] in the Relationships group.

Having Trouble?

Do not be concerned if the field list layout in your Relationships window is different than shown here. You will be rearranging them next.

Additional Information

If additional tables appear named MSysNavPaneGroups . . . remove them by right-clicking the title bar and choosing Hide Table.

Your screen should be similar to Figure 3.13

Figure 3.13

When the field lists for each table display, the relationship lines show how the tables are associated. However, the lines may appear tangled and untraceable when the tables first display. To see the relationships better, you will rearrange and size the field lists in the window. The field list can be moved by dragging the title bar and sized by dragging the border.

2

- Click on the Job Information field list title bar, and drag the field list to the left of the Personal Data field list.

- Continue to move the field lists until they are in the locations shown in Figure 3.14.

- Drag the bottom border of the Personal Data field list down so that all fields are displayed.

- Increase the length of the Table1 field list so that all fields are displayed.

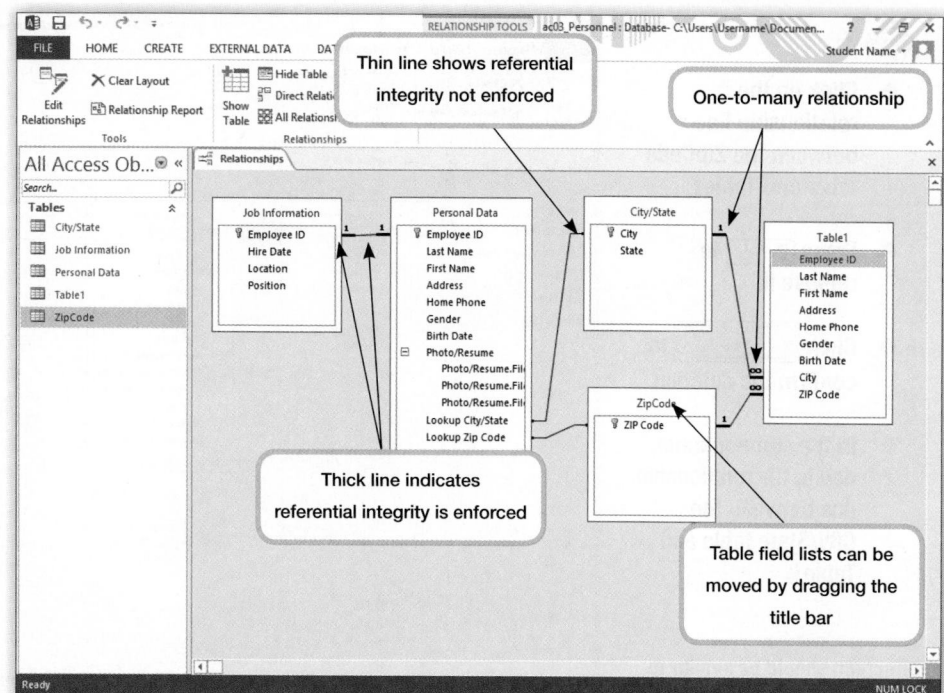

Figure 3.14

Your screen should be similar to Figure 3.14

Having Trouble?

Refer to the Creating Relationships section of Lab 1 to review this feature.

Now it is easier to follow the relationship lines. The Personal Data and Job Information tables are related by the Employee ID key fields and are connected by a relationship line indicating they have a one-to-one relationship. This relationship was established when you created the Job Information table.

There is also a relationship line between the Lookup Zip Code field in the Personal Data table and the ZIP Code field in the ZipCode table. A thin line between common fields shows that the relationship does not support referential integrity. The third relationship that exists is between the Lookup City/State field and the City field in the City/State table.

Lastly, the ZIP Code field in the ZipCode table and the City field in the City/State table connect to their matching fields in Table1. These lines are thicker at both ends, which indicates referential integrity has been enforced. It also displays a 1 at one end of the line and an infinity symbol (∞) over the other end. This tells you the relationship is a one-to-many type relationship.

DELETING RELATIONSHIPS

The first relationship changes you want to make are to remove the relationships between Table1 and the City/State and ZipCode tables so that you can delete Table1. To edit or delete a relationship, click on the relationship line to select it. It will appear thicker to show it is selected. Then it can be modified.

1

- **Click on the relationship line between the ZipCode table and Table1.**

- **Press** Delete **to remove it.**

- **Click** Yes **to confirm the deletion.**

- **In the same manner, delete the relationship line between the City/State table and Table1.**

Your screen should be similar to Figure 3.15

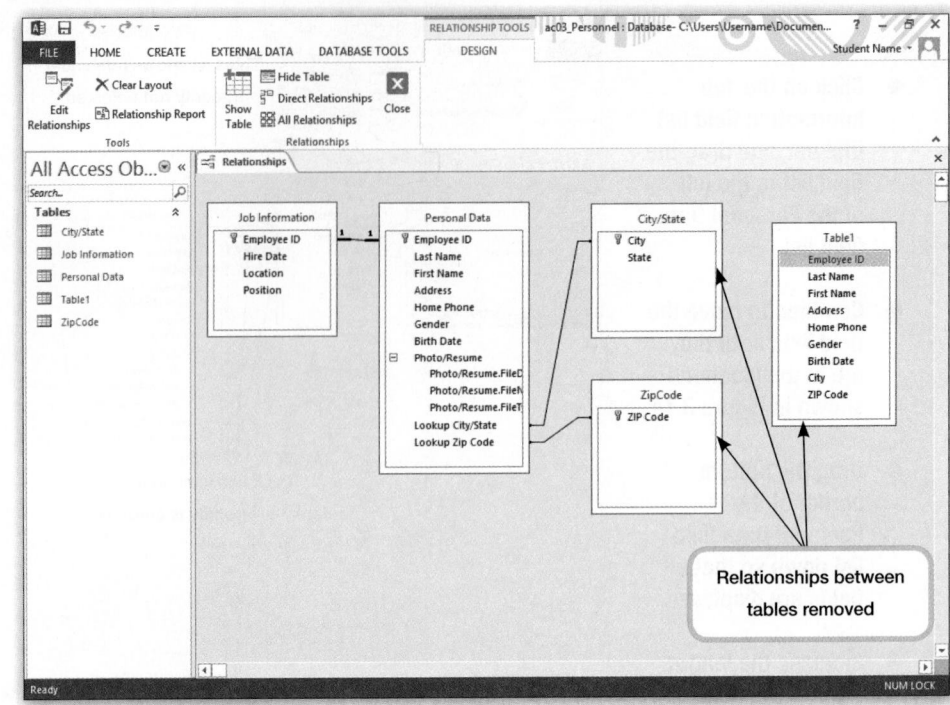

Figure 3.15

The relationship lines have been removed between the tables. Now you can delete the table.

2

- **Click on the title bar of the Table1 field list to select it and then press** Delete.

Your screen should be similar to Figure 3.16

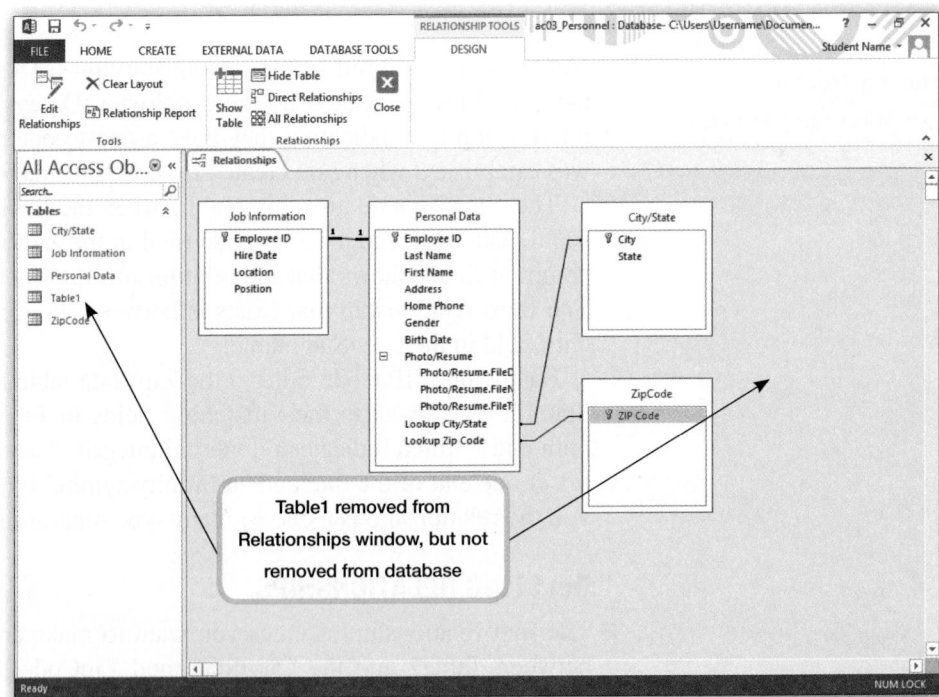

Figure 3.16

The Table1 field list is removed from the Relationships window. However, the Table1 object has not been removed from the Navigation pane, indicating that the table has not been deleted from the database. Now that the relationships have been removed from Table1, you can delete the actual table.

3

- **Right-click Table1 in the Navigation pane.**

- **Choose Delete from the shortcut menu.**

- **Click** Yes **to confirm deleting the table.**

Your screen should be similar to Figure 3.17

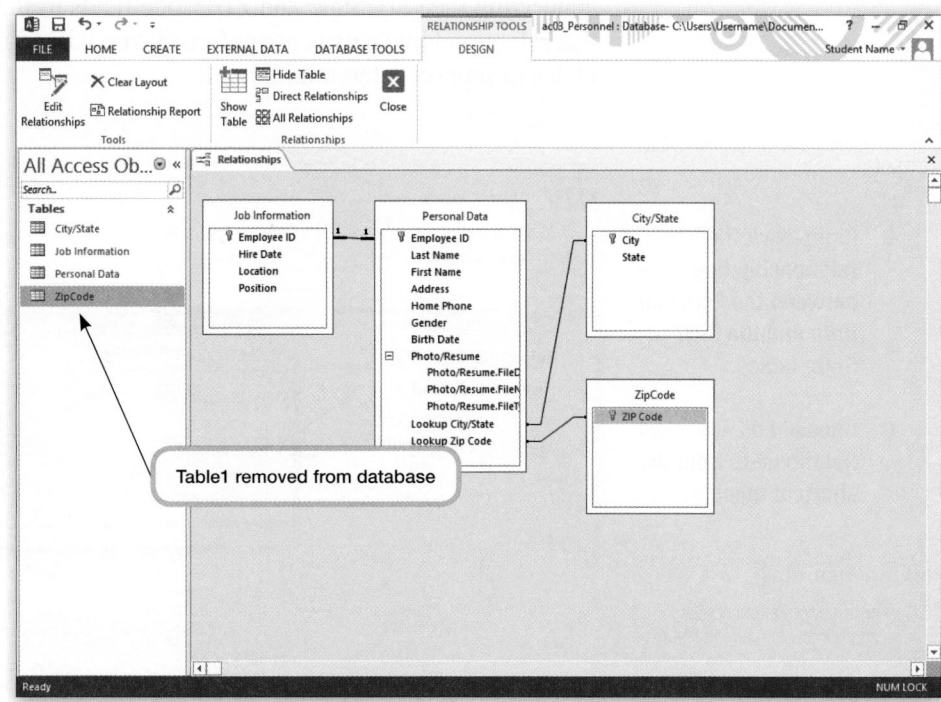

Figure 3.17

Table1 no longer appears in the Tables list in the Navigation pane, showing that it has been deleted from the database.

EDITING RELATIONSHIPS TO ENFORCE REFERENTIAL INTEGRITY

Having Trouble?

Refer to the Defining Relationships section of Lab 1 to review referential integrity.

The next change you want to make is to enforce referential integrity between the tables to ensure that the relationships are valid and that related data is not accidentally changed or deleted and end up as orphaned records. An **orphaned** has a field that refers to another record that does not exist. The thin relationship lines connecting the City/State and ZIP Code fields to the Personal Data table indicate that referential integrity is not enforced. You will edit the relationships between the tables to support referential integrity.

- **Right-click the relationship line between the Personal Data and the City/State tables.**

- **Choose Edit Relationship from the shortcut menu.**

Having Trouble?

If the wrong shortcut menu appears, click on another location on the line to try again.

Another Method

You also can double-click the relationship line or click in the Tools group to open the Edit Relationships dialog box.

Your screen should be similar to Figure 3.18

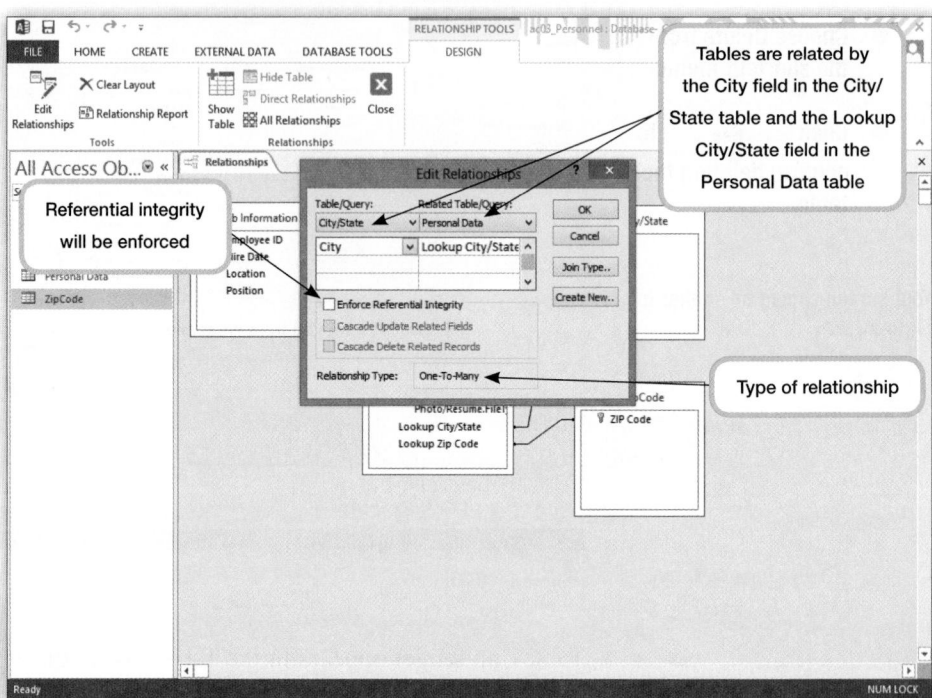

Figure 3.18

The Edit Relationships dialog box shows the City field in the City/State table is related to the Lookup City/State field in the Personal Data table. In addition, you can see the relationship type is one-to-many.

You will enforce referential integrity to prevent users from entering a city or ZIP code in the Personal Data table that is not in the associated lookup table. To enter a new city or ZIP code would require that the new city or ZIP code values be entered in the lookup tables first. This prevents cities and ZIP codes that are not in the lookup tables from being used in the Personal Data table and would maintain an accurate lookup field list.

2

- Choose **Enforce Referential Integrity.**

- Click [OK].

- In a similar manner, edit the relationship between the Personal Data table and the ZipCode table to enforce referential integrity.

- Click on the ZipCode field list to deselect the relationship line.

Your screen should be similar to Figure 3.19

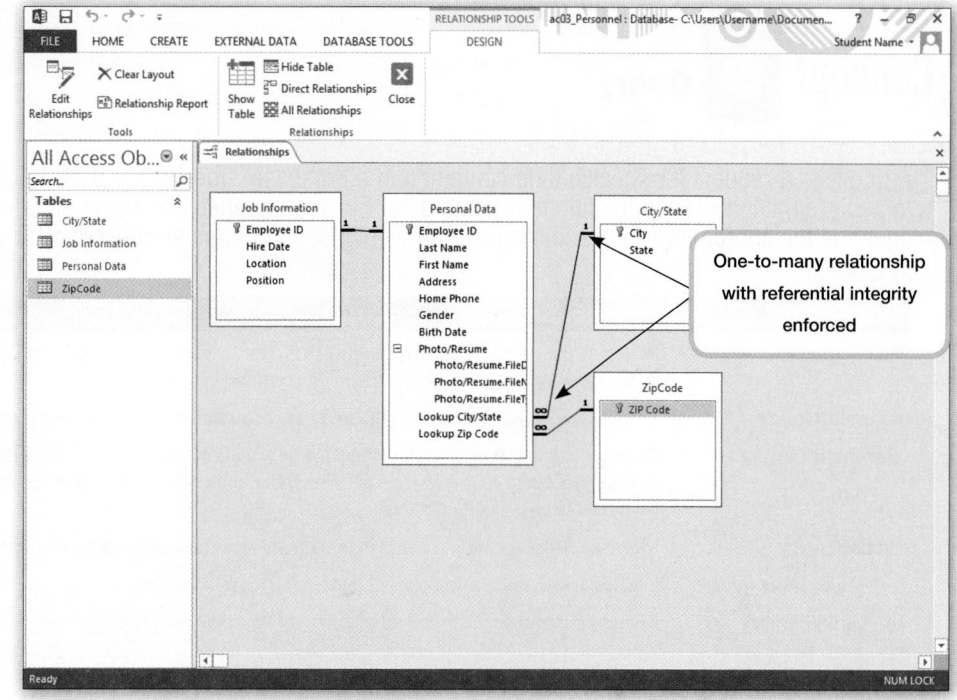

Figure 3.19

Once referential integrity is enforced, the relationship line changes and identifies the type of relationship.

3

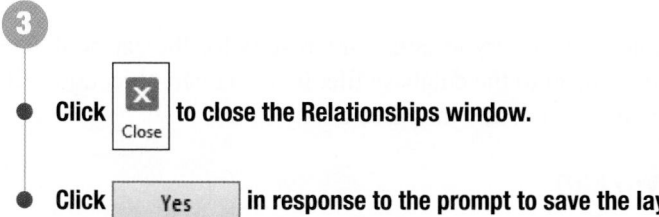

- Click [Close] to close the Relationships window.

- Click [Yes] in response to the prompt to save the layout.

The relationship and layout changes are saved. Now that referential integrity is enforced between these tables, a warning message will automatically be displayed if one of the rules is broken while entering or editing data, and you will not be allowed to complete the action you are trying to do.

Creating a Query

You are ready to start gathering information from the database. Your fellow employee, Juan, would like to create a car pool and has enlisted your help as the database expert. In Lab 2, you were able to filter the table to obtain the information needed for the car pool list, but it contained more data about each employee than someone would need, or should have access to. To obtain the exact information you need to give Juan for his car pool, you will use a query.

Concept ① Query

A **query** is a request for specific data contained in a database. Queries are used to view data in different ways, to analyze data, and even to change existing data. Because queries are based on tables, you also can use a query as the source for forms and reports. The five types of queries are described in the following table.

Query Type	Description
Select query	Retrieves the specific data you request from one or more tables, then displays the data in a query datasheet in the order you specify. This is the most common type of query.
Crosstab query	Summarizes large amounts of data in an easy-to-read, row-and-column format.
Parameter query	Displays a dialog box prompting you for information, such as the criteria for locating data. For example, a parameter query might request the beginning and ending dates, then display all records matching dates between the two specified values.
Action query	Makes changes to many records in one operation. There are four types of action queries:
Make-table query	Creates a new table from selected data in one or more tables.
Update query	Makes update changes to records, when, for example, you need to raise salaries of all sales staff by 7 percent.
Append query	Adds records from one or more tables to the end of other tables.
Delete query	Deletes records from a table or tables.
SQL query	Creates a query using SQL (Structured Query Language), an advanced programming language used in Access.

You will create a simple select query to obtain the results for the car pool. Creating a query adds a query object to the database file. It is a named object, just like a form, that can be opened, viewed, and modified at any time.

USING THE QUERY WIZARD

Query Design view or the Query Wizard can be used to create a query. The process is much like creating a table or form. You will first use the Query Wizard to guide you through the steps. Selecting the table object in the Navigation pane will help start the process in the right direction but is not a required step.

1

- **Click the Personal Data table object in the Navigation pane.**

- **Open the Create tab and click** Query Wizard **in the Queries group.**

Your screen should be similar to Figure 3.20

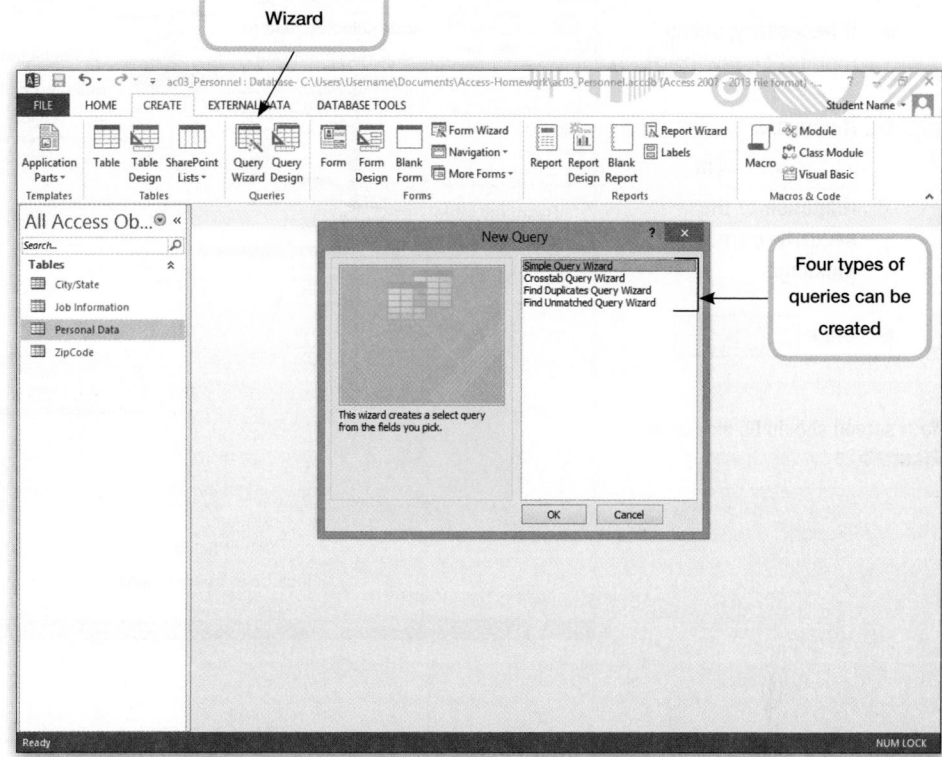

Four types of queries can be created

Figure 3.20

From the New Query dialog box, you select the type of query you want to create using the wizard.

Query Wizard	Type of Query
Simple	Select query.
Crosstab	Crosstab query.
Find Duplicates	Locates all records that contain duplicate values in one or more fields in the specified tables.
Find Unmatched	Locates records in one table that do not have records in another. For example, you could locate all employees in one table who have no hours worked in another table.

You will use the Simple Query Wizard to create a select query to see if it gives you the results you want.

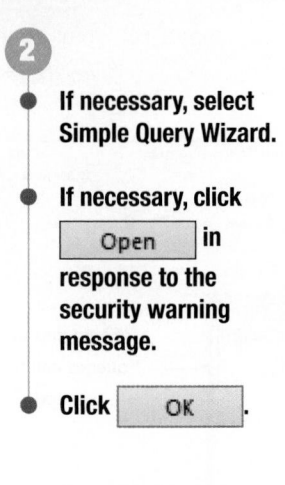

2

- If necessary, select Simple Query Wizard.

- If necessary, click ▭Open▭ in response to the security warning message.

- Click ▭OK▭.

Your screen should be similar to Figure 3.21

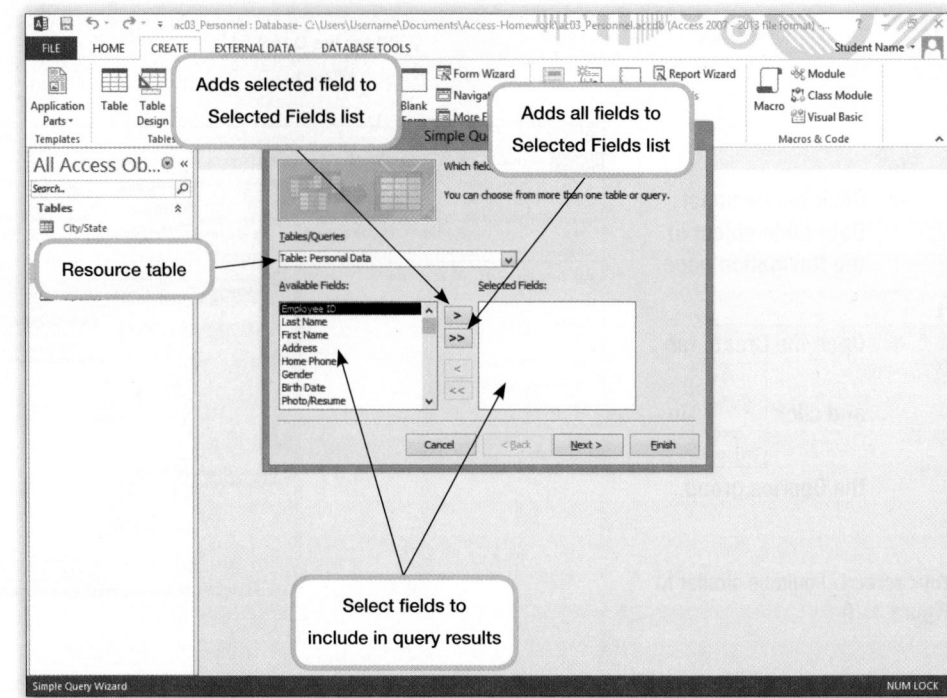

Figure 3.21

In the first Simple Query Wizard dialog box, you specify the resource table that will be used to supply the data and the fields that you want displayed in the query result, just as you did when creating a form. You will use the Personal Data table as the resource table and select the fields you want displayed in the query output.

3

- If necessary, select the Personal Data table from the Tables/Queries drop-down list.

- Add the Last Name, First Name, Address, Lookup City/State and Home Phone fields to the Selected Fields list in that order.

Additional Information

The quickest way to add a field to the Selected Fields list is to double-click its field name in the Available Fields list.

- Click ▭Next >▭.

Your screen should be similar to Figure 3.22

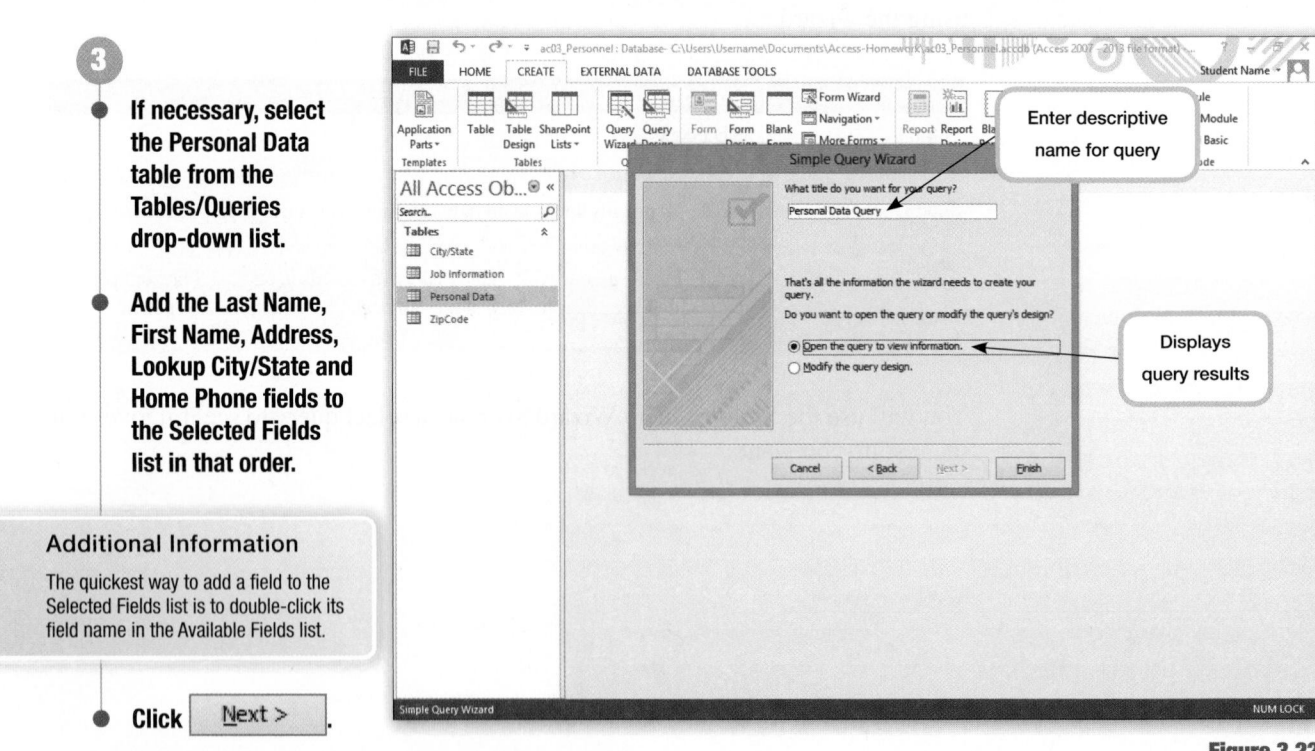

Figure 3.22

In the last Simple Query Wizard dialog box, you specify a name for your query and whether you want to open it to see the results or modify it in Design view. You decide that you just want to display the query results, and you want to give the query a name that will identify it.

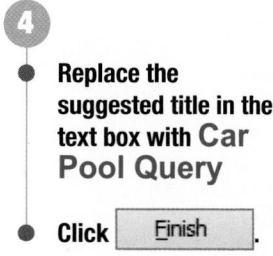

4 ● **Replace the suggested title in the text box with Car Pool Query**

● **Click** Finish **.**

Your screen should be similar to Figure 3.23

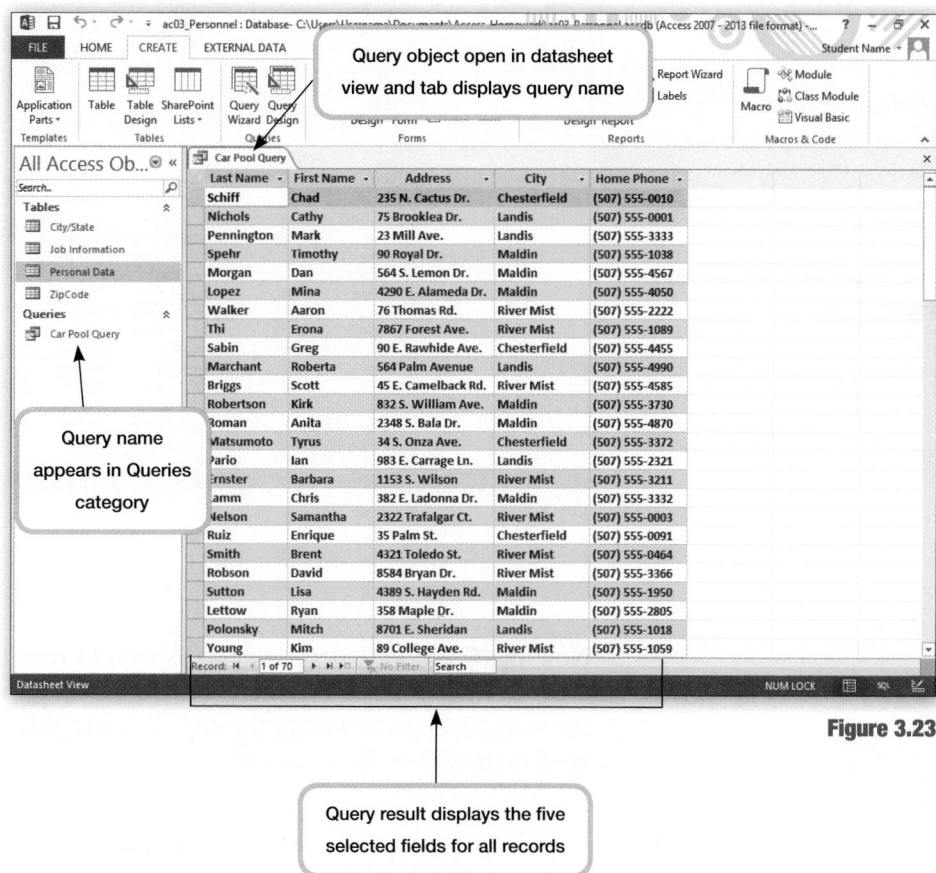

Query object open in datasheet view and tab displays query name

Query name appears in Queries category

Figure 3.23

Query result displays the five selected fields for all records

The query result displays the five specified fields for all records in the table in a new query datasheet object. The object's tab displays the query name. The Navigation pane also displays the name of the new query object in the Queries category.

FILTERING A QUERY

Although the query result displays only the fields you want to see, it includes all the records in the table. To display only those records with the cities needed for the car pool information for Juan, you will filter the query results.

1

● Filter the query to display only records with a city name of Chesterfield or Maldin.

Having Trouble?

Refer to the Filtering a Table section of Lab 2 to review this feature.

Your screen should be similar to Figure 3.24

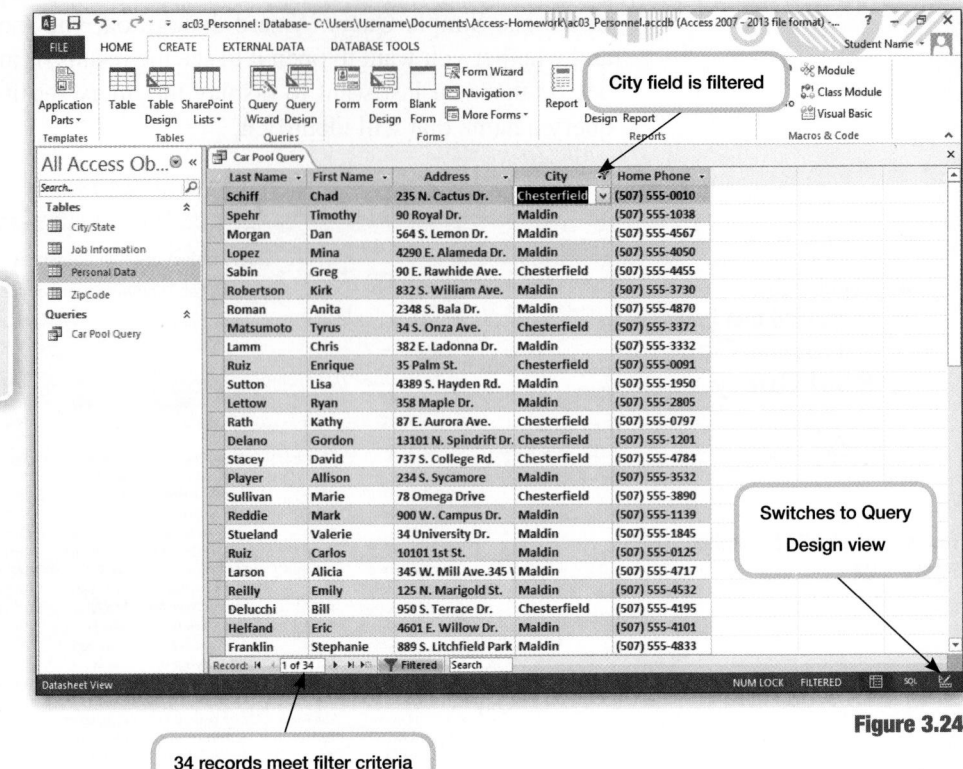

City field is filtered

Switches to Query Design view

34 records meet filter criteria

Figure 3.24

Now the Car Pool Query results display 34 records. Although these results are close to what you need, you are still not satisfied. You want the results to display the work location as well as the city. To make these refinements to the query, you need to use Query Design view.

2

● Click [icon] Design View in the status bar to switch to Query Design view.

● If necessary, click [X] Close in the upper-right corner of the Property Sheet pane to close it.

Your screen should be similar to Figure 3.25

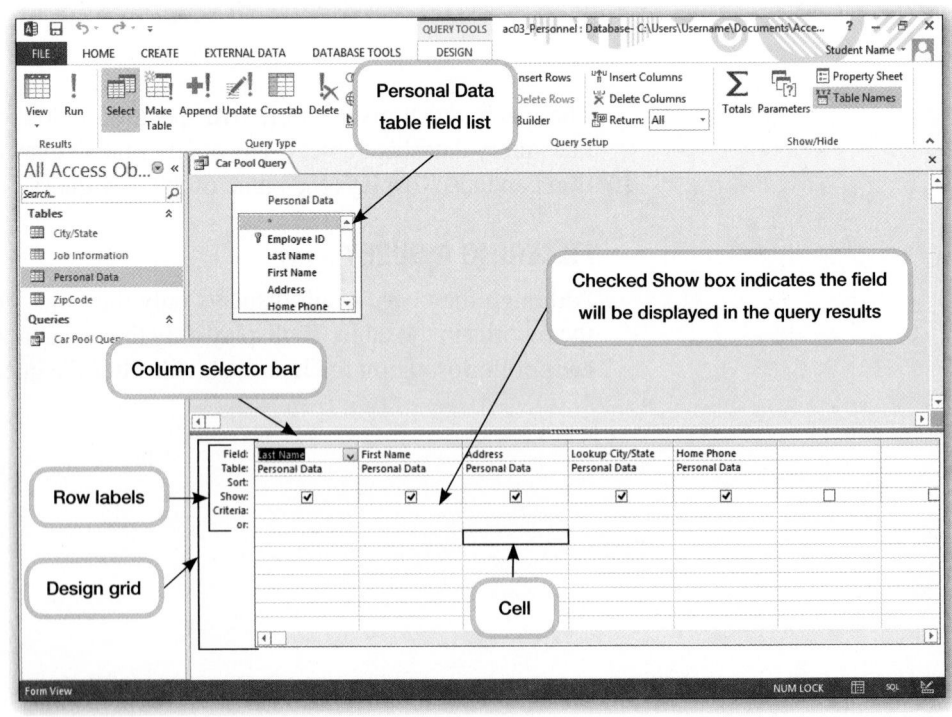

Personal Data table field list

Checked Show box indicates the field will be displayed in the query results

Column selector bar

Row labels

Design grid

Cell

Figure 3.25

USING QUERY DESIGN VIEW

Query Design view can be used to create a new query as well as modify the structure of an existing query. This view automatically displays the Query Tools Design tab, which contains commands that are used to create, modify, and run queries.

Query Design view is divided into two areas. The upper area displays a list box of all the fields in the selected table. This is called the **field list**. The lower portion of the window displays the **design grid** where you enter the settings that define the query. Each column in the grid holds the information about each field to be included in the query datasheet. The design grid automatically displays the fields that are specified when a query is created using the Query Wizard.

Above the field names is a narrow bar called the **column selector bar**, which is used to select an entire column. Each **row label** identifies the type of information that can be entered. The intersection of a column and row creates a cell where you enter expressions to obtain the query results you need.

The boxes in the Show row are called Show boxes. The **Show box** for a field lets you specify whether you want that field displayed in the query result. A checked box indicates that the field will be displayed; an unchecked box means that it will not.

ADDING A SECOND TABLE TO THE QUERY

To display the work location information for each employee in the query results, you need to add the Job Information table to the query design. A query that uses information from two or more tables to get the results is called a **multitable query**.

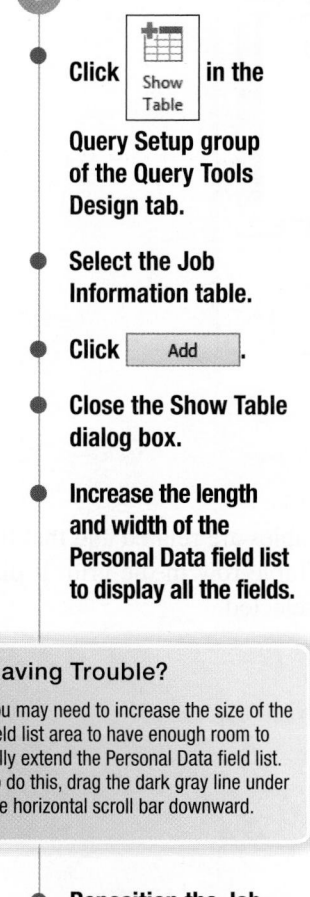

● Click [Show Table] in the **Query Setup group of the Query Tools Design tab.**

● Select the Job Information table.

● Click [Add].

● Close the Show Table dialog box.

● Increase the length and width of the Personal Data field list to display all the fields.

Having Trouble?

You may need to increase the size of the field list area to have enough room to fully extend the Personal Data field list. To do this, drag the dark gray line under the horizontal scroll bar downward.

● Reposition the Job Information field list if needed.

Your screen should be similar to Figure 3.26

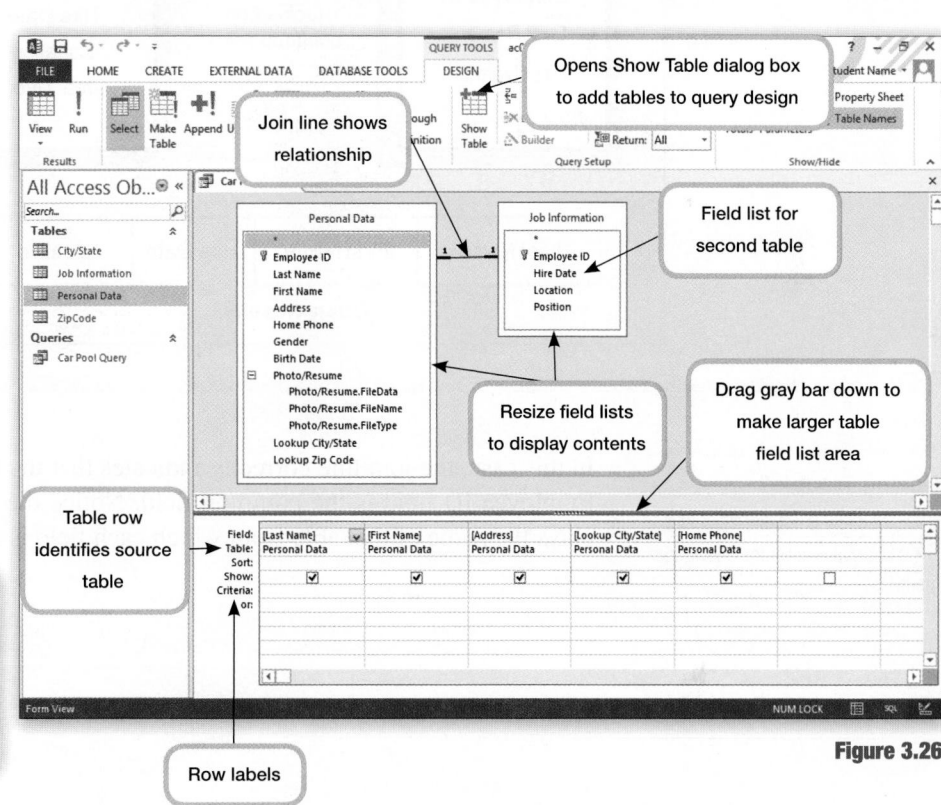

Figure 3.26

The field list for the Job Information table has been added to the Query Design window. When multiple tables are added to a query, Access automatically creates joins between the tables.

Concept 2 Join

A **join** is an association that is created in a query between a field in one table or query and a field of the same data type in another table or query. The join is based on the relationships that have already been defined between tables. A **join line** between the field lists identifies the fields on which the relationship is based.

If a table did not already have a relationship defined, a join would be created between common fields in the tables if one of the common fields is a primary key. If the common fields have different names, however, Access does not automatically create the join. In those cases, you would create the join between the tables using the same procedure that is used to create table relationships.

The difference between a relationship line and a join line in a query is that the join line creates a temporary relationship that establishes rules that the data must match to be included in the query results. Joins also specify that each pair of rows that satisfies the join conditions will be combined in the results to form a single row.

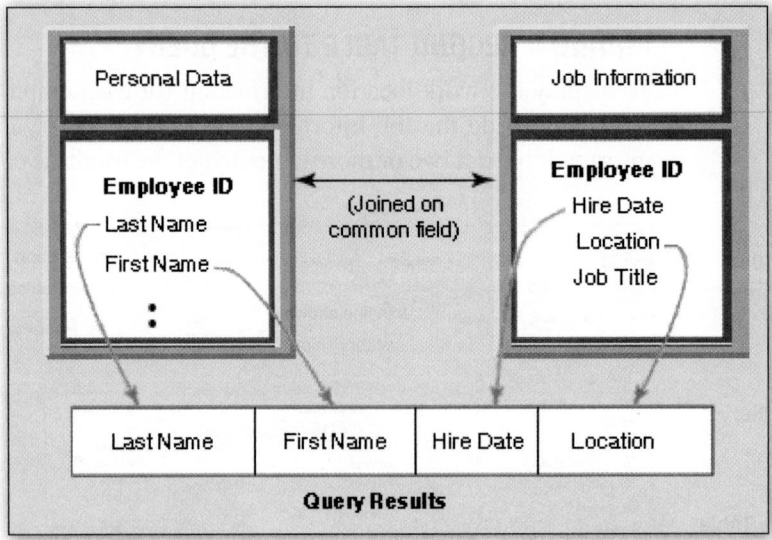

Having Trouble?

If the Table row is not displayed, click
[XYZ Table Names] in the Show/Hide group.

In this case, the join line correctly indicates that the tables are related and that the Employee ID field is the common field. Notice the Table row in the grid. It displays the name of the table from which each field is selected.

ADDING FIELDS

You want the query results to display the work location for each record. To do this, you need to add the Location field from the Job Information field list to the design grid. You can use the following methods to add fields to the design grid:

- Select the field name and drag it from the field list to the grid. To select several adjacent fields, press ⇧Shift while you click the field names. To select nonadjacent fields, press Ctrl while clicking the field names. To select all fields, double-click the field list title bar. You can then drag all the selected fields into the grid, and Access will place each field in a separate column.

- Double-click on the field name. The field is added to the next available column in the grid.

- Select the field cell drop-down arrow in the grid, and then choose the field name.

In addition, if you select the asterisk in the field list and add it to the grid, Access displays the table or query name in the field row followed by a period and asterisk. This indicates that all fields in the table will be included in the query results. Also, using this feature will automatically include any new fields that may later be added to the table and will exclude deleted fields. You cannot sort records or specify criteria for fields, however, unless you also add those fields individually to the design grid.

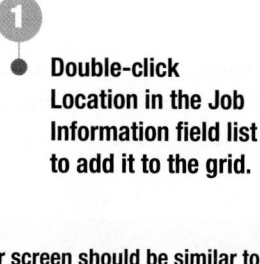

Double-click Location in the Job Information field list to add it to the grid.

Your screen should be similar to Figure 3.27

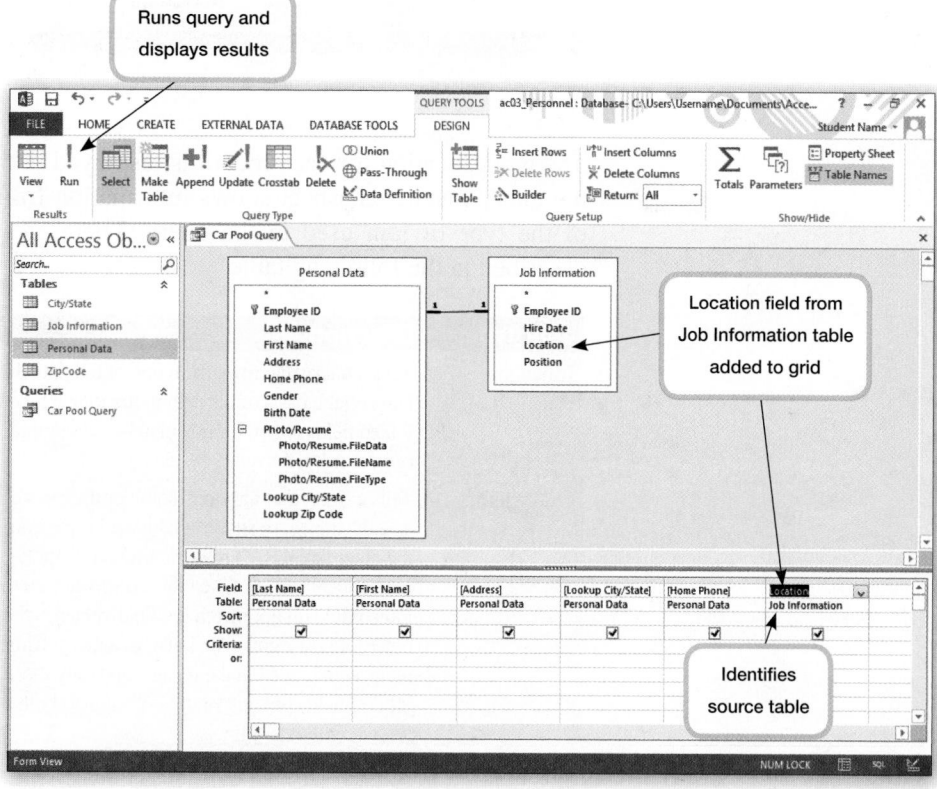

Figure 3.27

Notice the Table row displays the name of the table from which the Location field was drawn. Sometimes when multiple tables are specified in a query, they have fields with the same names. For example, two tables may have fields named Address; however, the address in one table may be a personal address and the one in the other table may be a business address. It is important to select the appropriate field from a table that contains the data you want to appear in the query. The Table row makes it clear from which table a field was drawn.

Now you want to see the query results. To do this, you run the query.

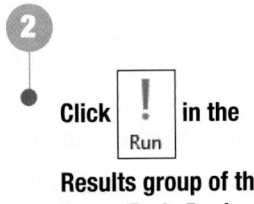

②

Click **!** **Run** in the Results group of the Query Tools Design tab.

Your screen should be similar to Figure 3.28

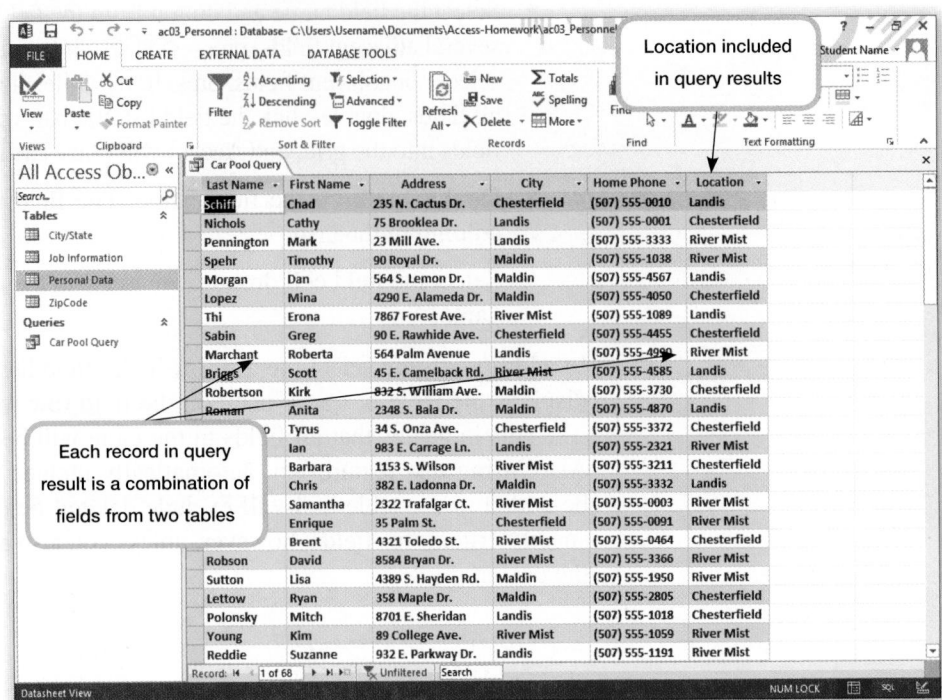

Location included in query results

Each record in query result is a combination of fields from two tables

Figure 3.28

The work location for each record is displayed in the results. Now each record in the query results datasheet shows information from both tables. This is because of the type of join used in the query. There are three basic types of joins, as described in the following table.

Join Type	Description
Inner join	Tells a query that rows from one of the joined tables correspond to rows in the other table on the basis of the data in the joined fields. Checks for matching values in the joined fields; when it finds matches, it combines the records and displays them as one record in the query results.
Outer join	Tells a query that although some of the rows on both sides of the join correspond exactly, the query should include all rows from one table even if there is no match in the other table. Each matching record from two tables is combined into one record in the query results. One table contributes all of its records even if the values in its joined field do not match the field values in the other table. Outer joins can be left outer joins or right outer joins. In a query with a left outer join, all rows in the left table are included in the results, and only those rows from the other table where the joining field contains values common to both tables are included. The reverse is true with a right outer join.
Unequal joins	Records to be included in the query results are based on the value in one join field being greater than, less than, not equal to, greater than or equal to, or less than or equal to the value in the other join field.

In a query, the default join type is an inner join. In this case, it checked for matching values in the Employee ID fields, combined matching records, and displayed them as one record in the query result.

Having Trouble?

See Concept 4, Expression, in Lab 2 to review this feature.

SPECIFYING QUERY CRITERIA

You have created a query that displays six fields from two tables for each record. However, you only want to display those with a work location in Landis. You can limit the results of a query by specifying query criteria in the query design grid.

Concept  3 Query Criteria

Query criteria are expressions that are used to restrict the results of a query to display only records that meet certain limiting conditions. In addition to comparison operators that are commonly used in expressions, other commonly used criteria are described in the following table.

Criterion	Description
Is Null	This can be used to find any records where field contents are empty, or "null."
Is Not Null	Returns records only where there is a value in the field.
Not	Returns all results *except* those meeting the Not criteria.
DateDiff	Used with Date/Time fields to determine the difference in time between dates.
Like	Returns records where there is a match in content.
Not Like	Returns records that do not contain the text string.

The Criteria row in the query design grid is used to enter the query criteria. Entering the **criteria expression** is similar to using a formula and may contain constants, field names, and/or operators. To instruct the query to locate records meeting multiple criteria, also called **compound criteria**, you use the **AND** or **OR operators**. Using AND narrows the search because a record must meet both conditions to be included. This condition is established by typing the word "and" in a field's Criteria cell as part of its criteria expression. It is also established when you enter criteria in different fields in the design grid. Using OR broadens the search because any record meeting either condition is included in the output. This condition is established by typing the word "or" in a field's Criteria cell or by entering the first criteria expression in the first Criteria cell for the field and the second expression in the Or criteria row cell for the same field.

The following table shows some sample query criteria and their results.

Criteria	Result
DateDiff ("yyyy", [BirthDate], Date()) > 40	Determines the difference between today's year and the BirthDate field. If the difference is greater than 40, the corresponding records will display.
Not Like M*	Returns records for all states whose names start with a character other than "M."
Like "*9.99"	Returns records where the price ends with "9.99," such as $9.99, $19.99, $29.99, and so on.
>= "Canada"	Returns a list of countries starting with Canada and ascending through the rest of the alphabet.
Not "Smith"	Returns all records with names other than Smith.
1 OR 2	Returns all records with either a 1 or a 2 in the selected field.
"Doctor" AND "Denver"	Returns only those records that have the text string of Doctor and Denver within the same record.
"Mi*"	Finds all words starting with the letters "Mi." Example: Michigan, Missouri, Minnesota.
"*Main*"	Finds all records that contain the text "Main" within it. Example: 590 Main Street, 11233 W. Mainland Dr.

You will enter the query criteria in the Criteria row of the Location column to restrict the query results to only those records where the location is Landis. It is not necessary to enter = (equal to) in the criteria because it is the assumed comparison operator.

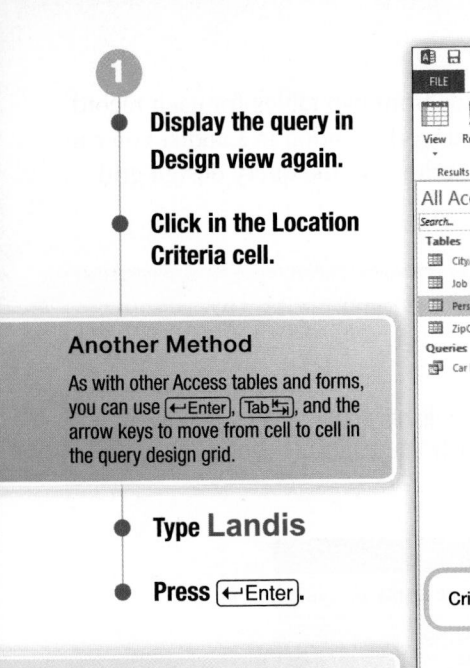

1

- Display the query in Design view again.

- Click in the Location Criteria cell.

Another Method

As with other Access tables and forms, you can use ←Enter, Tab↹, and the arrow keys to move from cell to cell in the query design grid.

- Type **Landis**

- Press ←Enter.

Additional Information

The criteria expression is not case-sensitive.

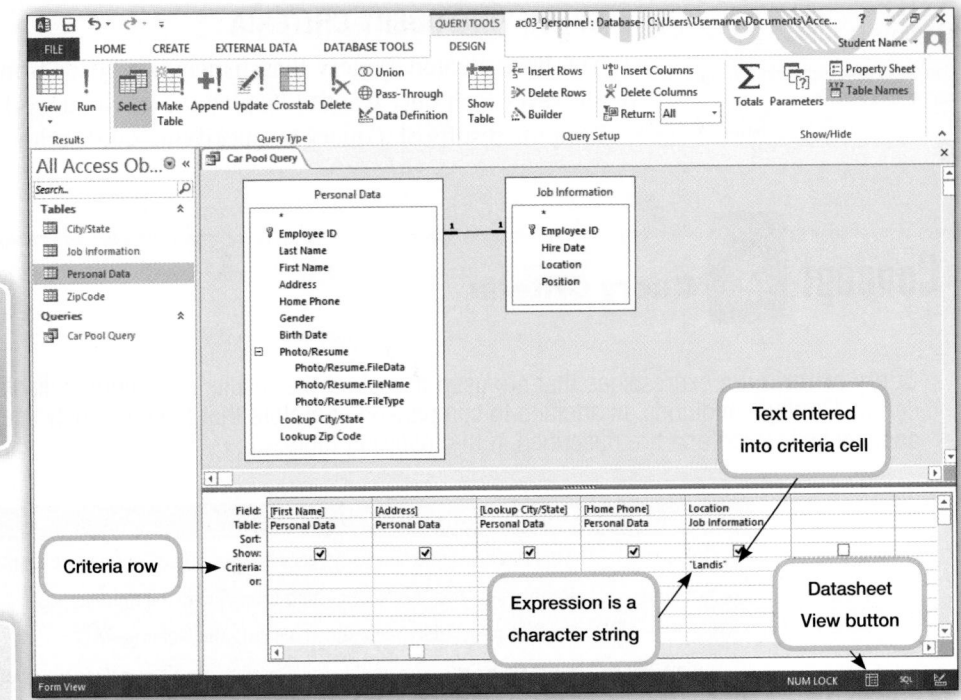

Figure 3.29

Your screen should be similar to Figure 3.29

The Landis text you typed as the query criterion is enclosed in quotation marks because it is a character string. To display the query results, you will run the query. Another way to run a query is to change to Datasheet view.

2

- Click 🔳 Datasheet View in the status bar.

Your screen should be similar to Figure 3.30

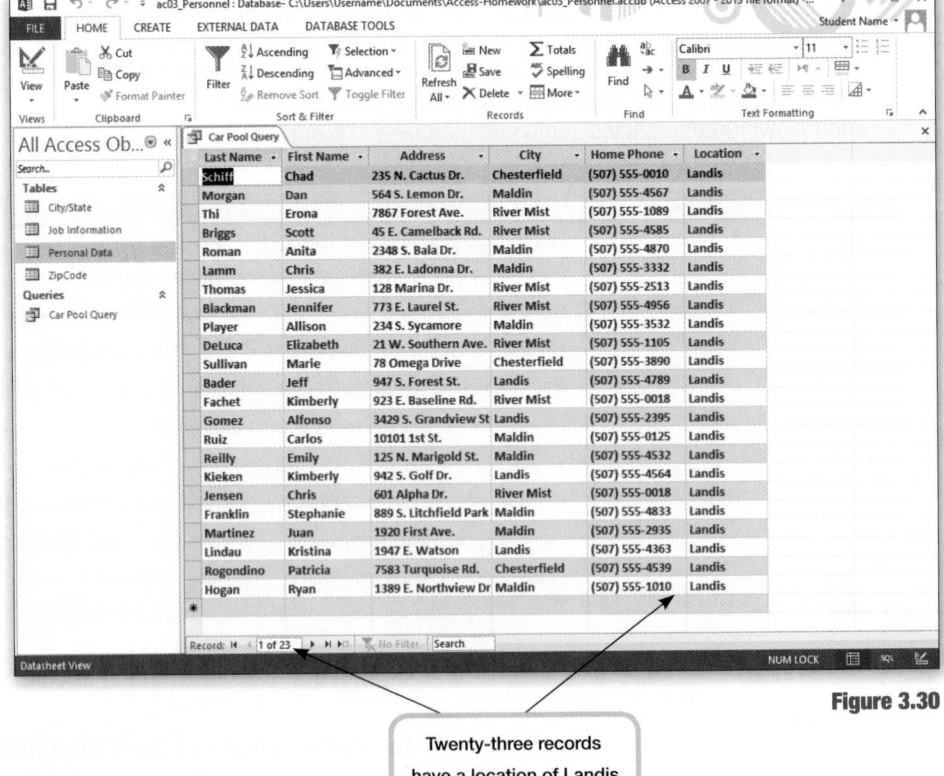

Figure 3.30

Twenty-three records have a location of Landis

Now the query datasheet displays 23 records meeting the location criterion. However, the results do not show only those who reside in Chesterfield or Maldin and commute to the Landis location. You could apply a filter for these cities, but each time you run the query, you would need to reapply the filter. Rather than do this, you decide to specify the criteria in the query design so it will automatically return the results you want each time the query is run.

To include those who live in Chesterfield and Maldin, you will add a second criterion to the City field. Because you want to display the records for employees who live in either city, you will use the OR operator.

Additional Information

The Or criteria row must be used to enter "or" criteria for different fields.

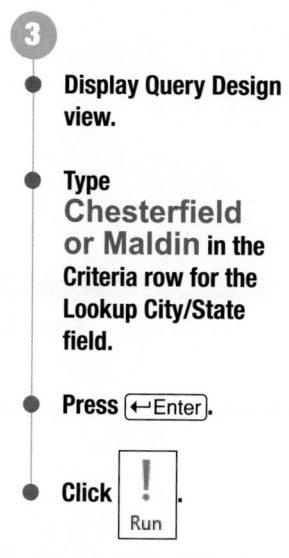

③

- **Display Query Design view.**

- **Type Chesterfield or Maldin in the Criteria row for the Lookup City/State field.**

- **Press** ←Enter.

- **Click** ! Run .

Additional Information

If an expression is entered incorrectly, an informational box that indicates the source of the error will be displayed when the query is run.

Your screen should be similar to Figure 3.31

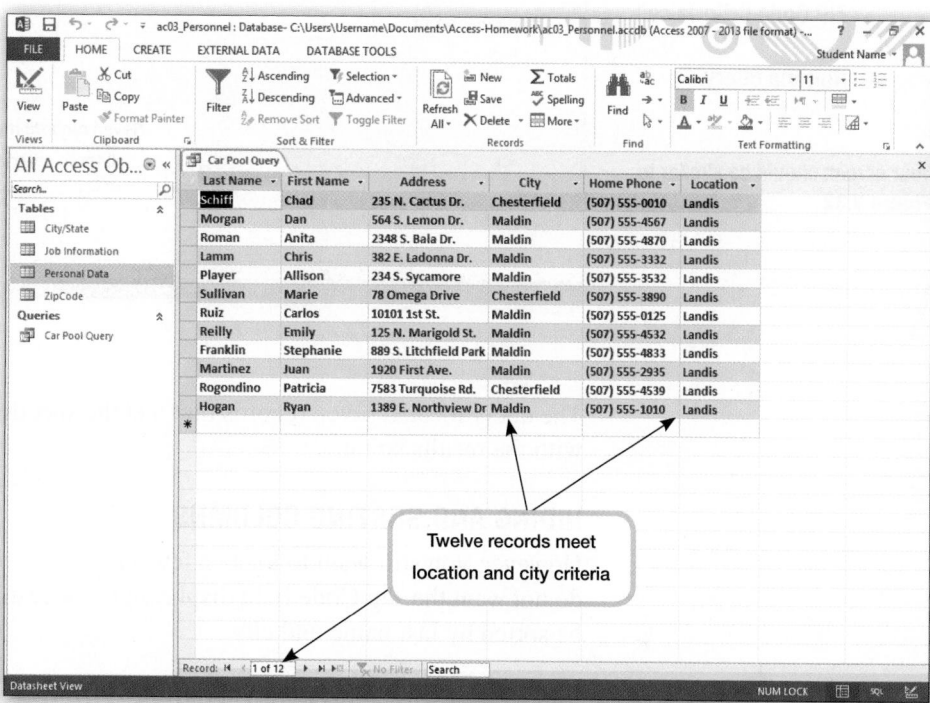

Twelve records meet location and city criteria

Figure 3.31

The results are closer to what you need to create the car pool list. The last step is to exclude those who do not need a car pool because they live close to the Landis work location, in the ZIP code 92121-3740. You will need to add the Lookup ZIP Code field to the query grid and then enter the criteria to exclude the ZIP code of 92121-3740. Then you will run the query.

4

- **Switch to Design view.**

- **Add the Lookup ZIP Code field from the Personal Data field list to the query grid.**

- **Enter <>92121-3740 in the Lookup ZIP Code Criteria cell.**

- **Run the query.**

Your screen should be similar to Figure 3.32

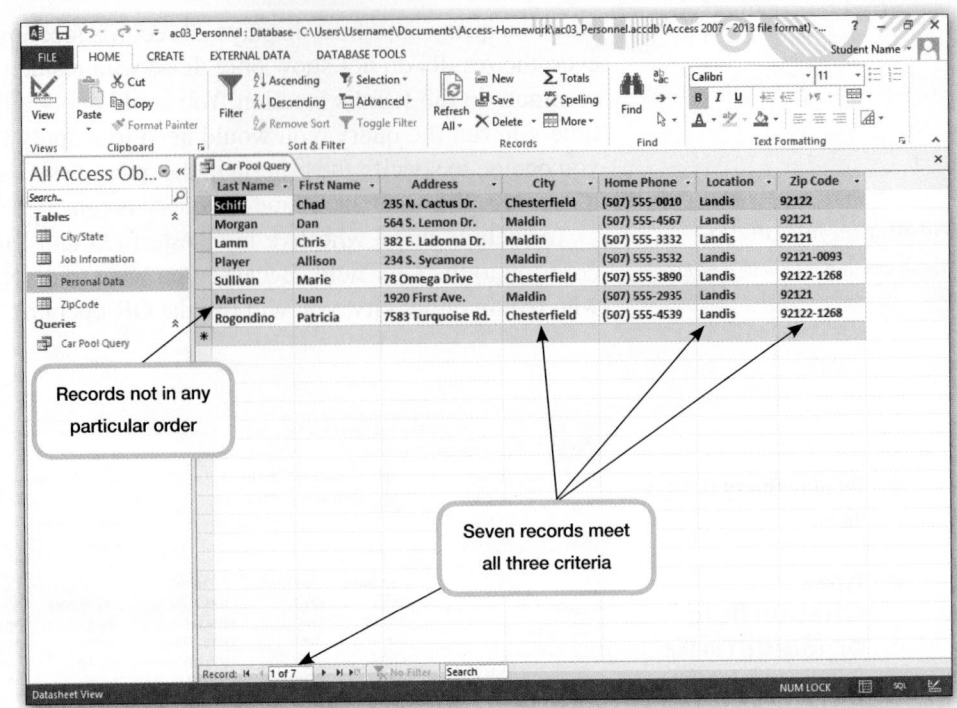

Records not in any particular order

Seven records meet all three criteria

Figure 3.32

The query located seven records that met the specified criteria, and you are pleased with the results so far.

HIDING AND SORTING COLUMNS

However, you still want to make a few additional changes to the query design. You do not want the Zip Code field displayed in the results and would like the results to be sorted by last name and city.

1

- Switch to Design view.

- Click the Show box of the Lookup Zip Code field to clear the check mark.

- If necessary, scroll to the left to see the fields on the left side of the design grid.

- Click in the Sort row of the Last Name field.

- Open the Sort drop-down menu and choose Ascending.

- Close the Navigation pane so you can see all the fields in the query grid.

Your screen should be similar to Figure 3.33

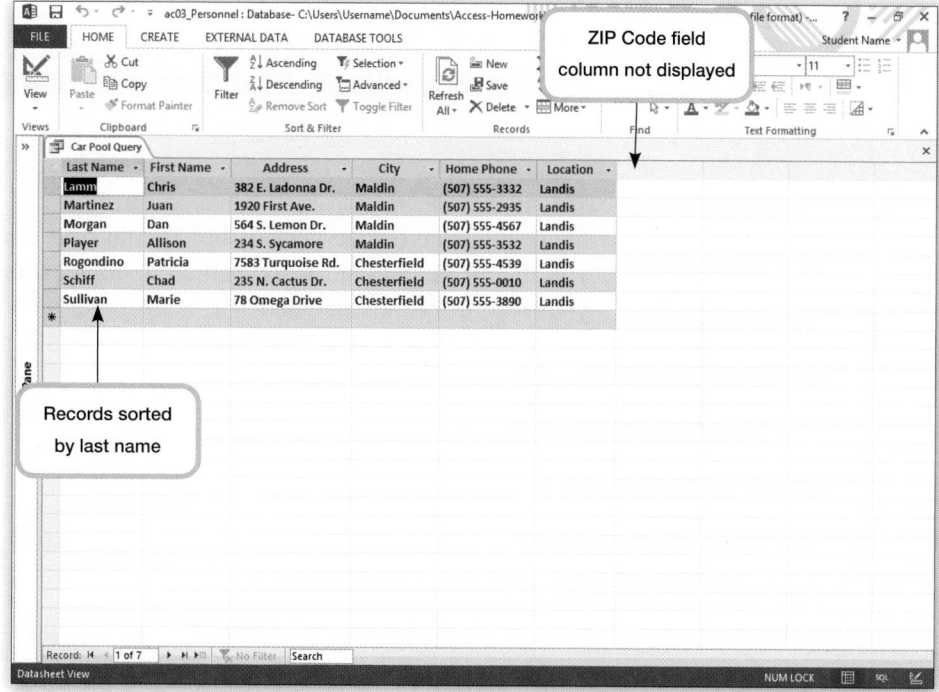

Figure 3.33

Now you can display the results.

2

- Run the query.

Your screen should be similar to Figure 3.34

Figure 3.34

The query result shows that seven employees meet all the criteria. The ZIP Code field is not displayed, and last names are sorted in ascending alphabetical order.

REARRANGING THE QUERY DATASHEET

The order of the fields in the query datasheet reflects the order in which they appear in the design grid. You think the results will be easier to read if the Last Name field column follows the First Name column.

Moving a field column in the query datasheet is the same as moving a column in a table datasheet. Changing the column order in the query datasheet does not affect the field order in the resource table, which is controlled by the table design. It also does not change the order of the fields in the query design grid.

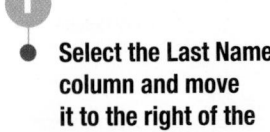

- Select the Last Name column and move it to the right of the First Name column.

Another Method

You also could move the field columns in the design grid and then run the query to obtain the same results.

Your screen should be similar to Figure 3.35

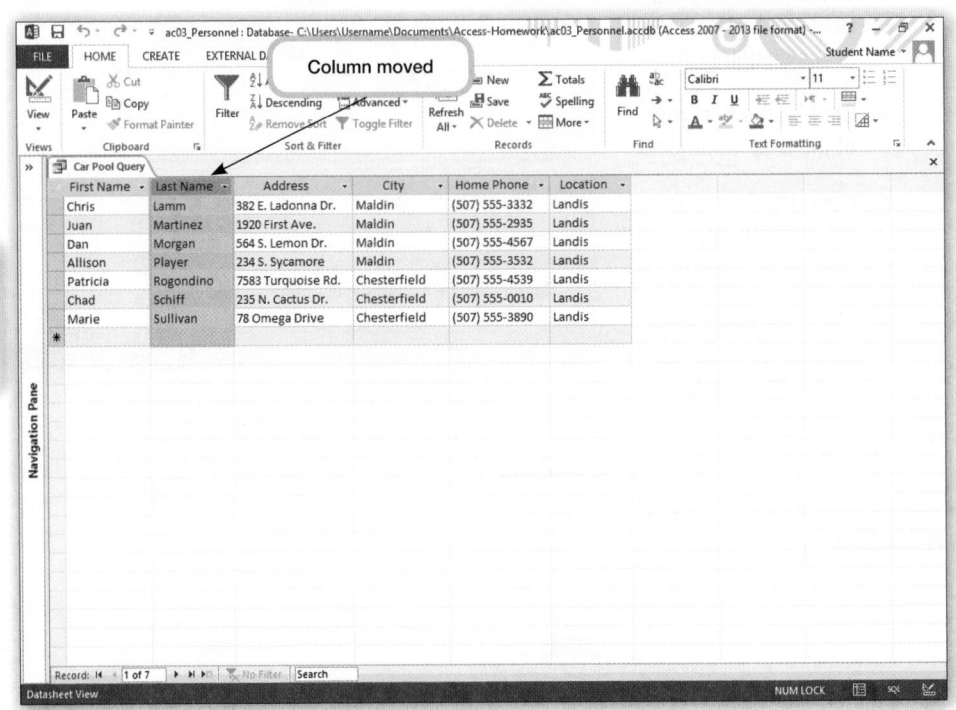

Figure 3.35

This is the information Juan needs to form his car pool. However, as you look at the results, you realize your record should have been included in the list because you live in Maldin and work at the Landis location. You need to determine why your record was not included.

FINDING UNMATCHED RECORDS

When working with a database containing several tables, occasionally a record may be created in one table without any correlating data entered into the corresponding table. This can happen accidentally (for example, when the data entry person forgets to update the related table) or on purpose (when a customer may not have an order pending). The Find Unmatched query is a helpful tool that will locate records in one table that do not have related records in another table. You will use the Find Unmatched query to locate any records that are missing corresponding information in the Job Information table. First, however, you decide to do a manual inspection of the record count in the tables, which will reveal if there are potentially missing records.

1

● Open the Navigation pane.

● Display the Personal Data table.

● Scroll to the bottom of the table to see your record.

You can see that the Personal Data table has 70 records from the record indicator and that your record is the last record. Now, however, you realize that you did not add your information to the Job Information table.

You will check the Job Information table to see how many records it contains.

2

● Open the Job Information table.

Your screen should be similar to Figure 3.36

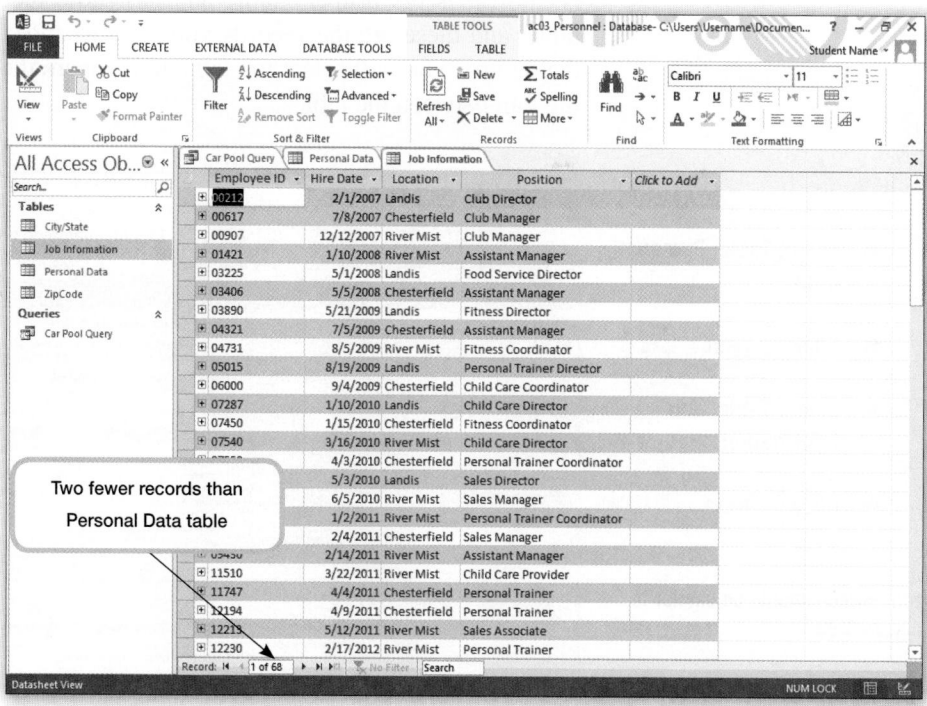

Two fewer records than Personal Data table

Figure 3.36

This table has 68 records, whereas the Personal Data table has 70. You know your record is one of the missing records, but you need to locate the other missing record. You can do this quickly using the Find Unmatched Query Wizard.

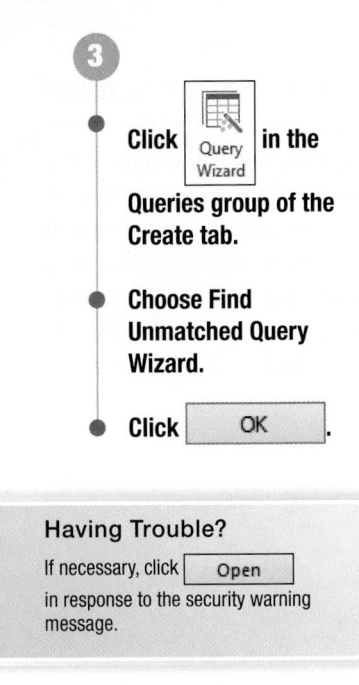

3

● **Click** [Query Wizard] **in the Queries group of the Create tab.**

● **Choose Find Unmatched Query Wizard.**

● **Click** [OK].

Having Trouble?

If necessary, click [Open] in response to the security warning message.

Your screen should be similar to Figure 3.37

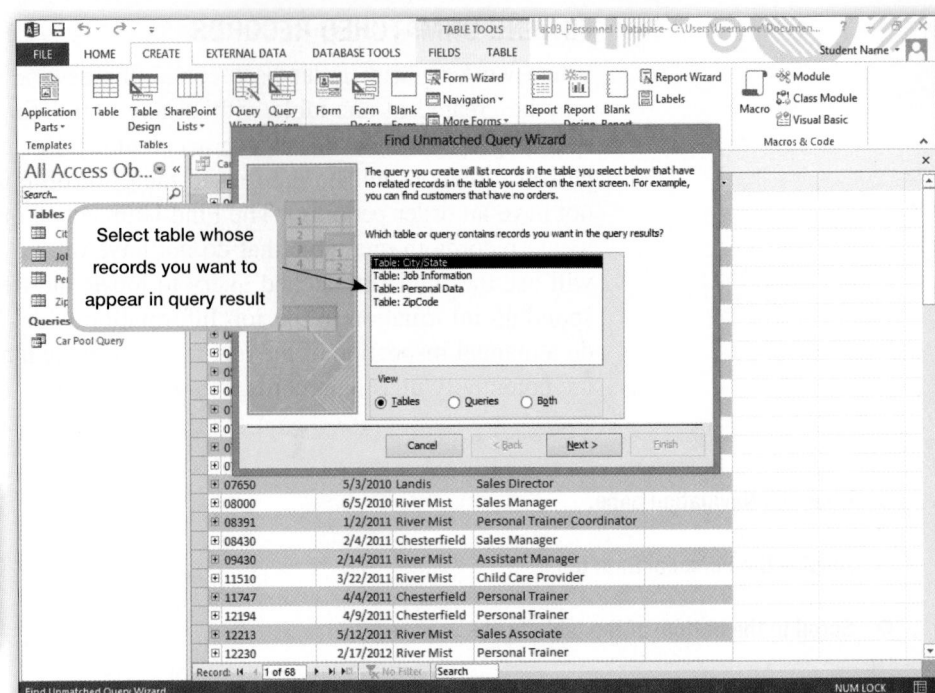

Figure 3.37

In the first wizard dialog box, you select the table that contains records you want to appear in the results. In this case, you will select the Personal Data table first because it is the primary table and has more records than the Job Information table, and these are the records you want to appear in the results. In the second dialog box, you will select the table to compare the first table to. This establishes the join between the tables.

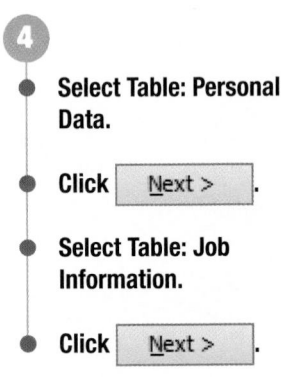

4

● **Select Table: Personal Data.**

● **Click** [Next >].

● **Select Table: Job Information.**

● **Click** [Next >].

Your screen should be similar to Figure 3.38

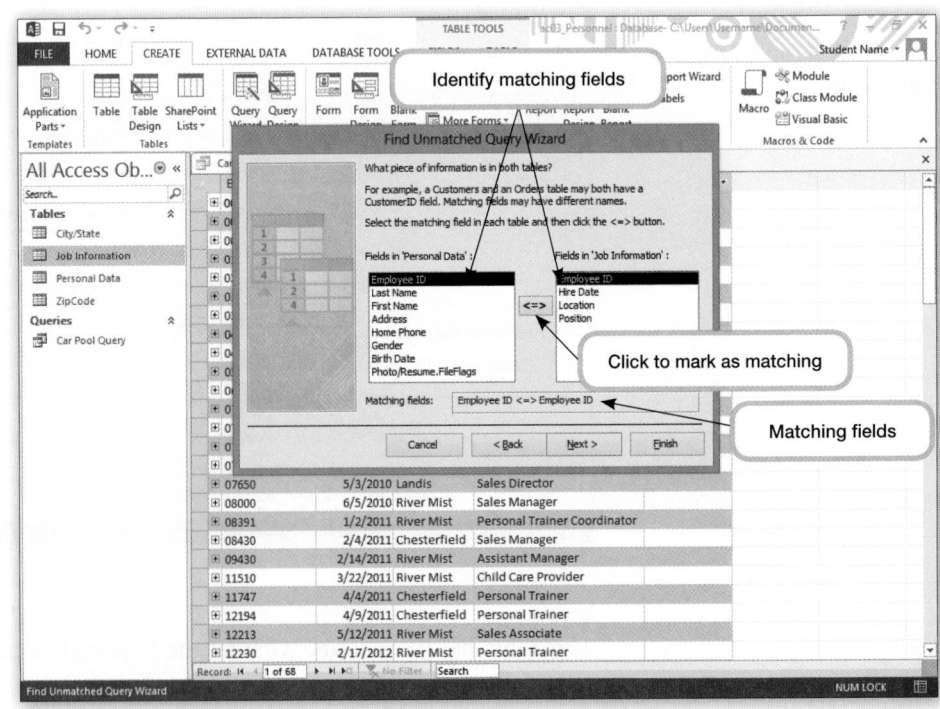

Figure 3.38

The third step is to identify the matching (common) fields. The two highlighted fields, Employee ID, in both tables are already correctly highlighted.

5

● Click <=> to mark these fields as the matching fields.

Additional Information
The field names of the selected matching fields appear in the Matching Fields text box.

● Click Next >.

Your screen should be similar to Figure 3.39

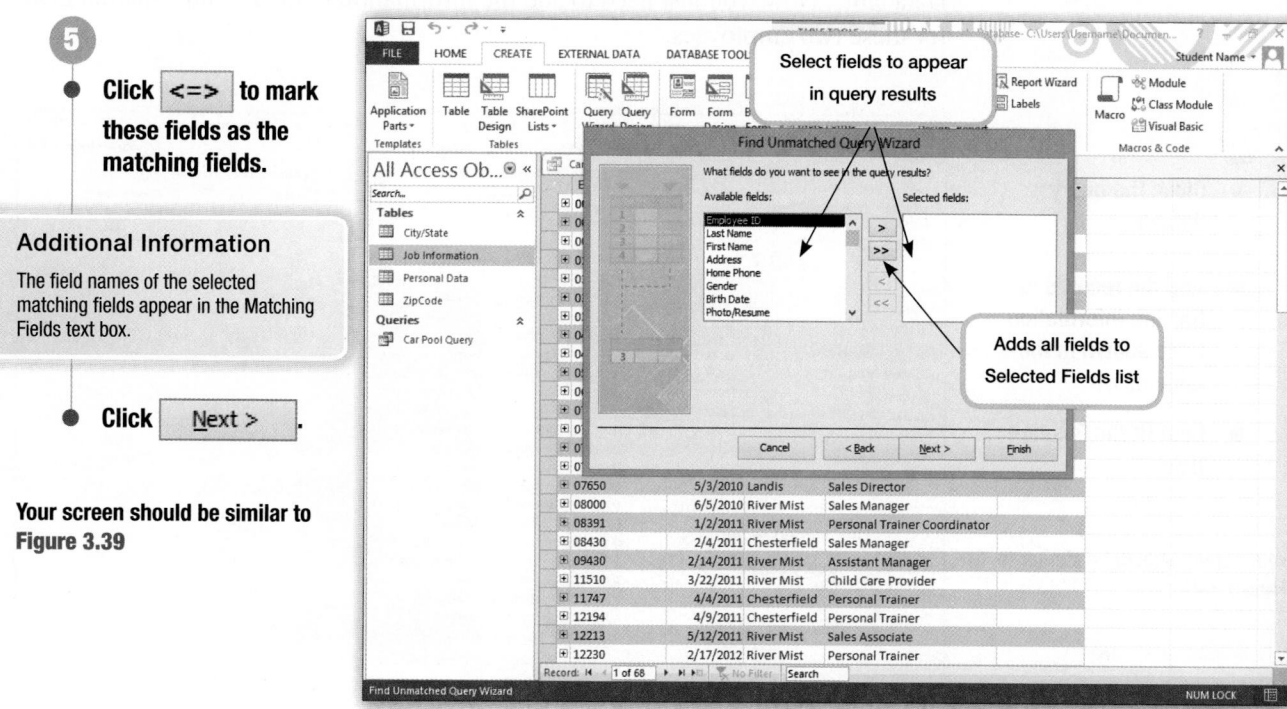

Figure 3.39

Next, you need to identify the fields you want to appear in the query results.

6

● Click >> to add all the fields to the Selected Fields list.

● Click Next >.

● Click Finish.

Your screen should be similar to Figure 3.40

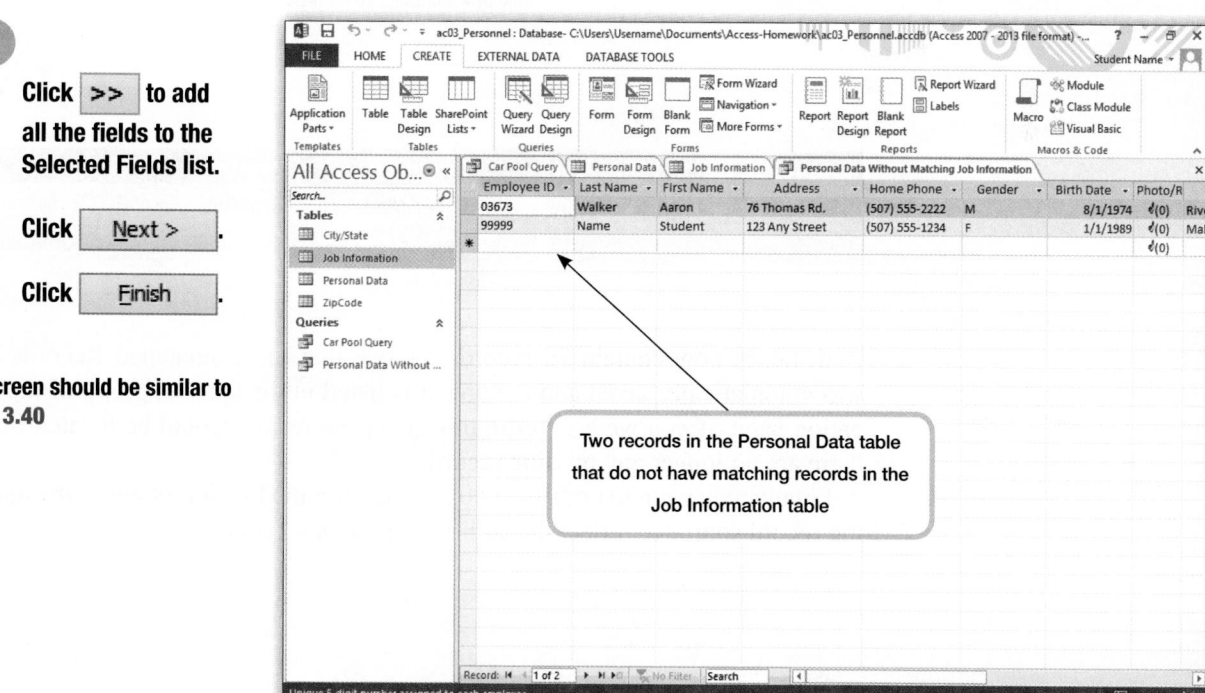

Figure 3.40

The two records in the Personal Data table that do not have matching records in the Job Information table are displayed in the query results. One record is the matching information for your own record that you added earlier to the Personal Data table. Now, you just need to add the information to the Job Information table for these two employees.

7

● Close the query datasheet.

● Add the records to the Job Information table shown in the table below.

● Best fit the Position field.

Your screen should be similar to Figure 3.41

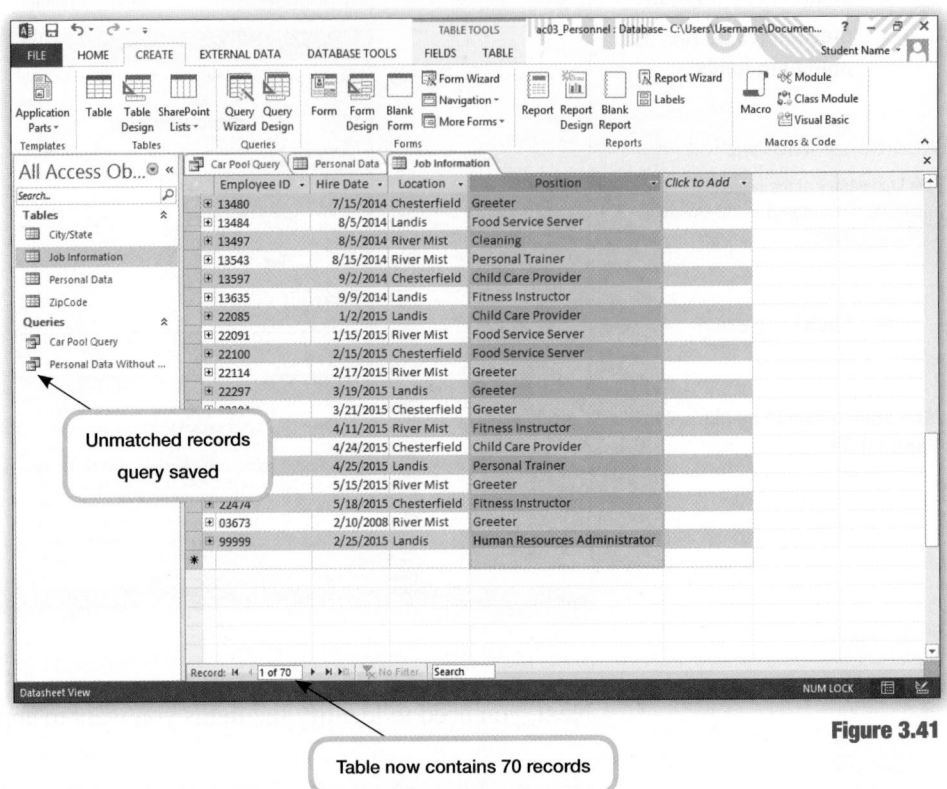

Unmatched records query saved

Table now contains 70 records

Figure 3.41

Employee ID	Hire Date	Location	Position
03673	2/10/2008	River Mist	Greeter
99999	2/25/2015	Landis	Human Resources Administrator

Both tables now contain 70 records. Notice that the Unmatched Records query was automatically saved and the object is listed in the Queries group of the Navigation pane. If you were to rerun this query, no results would be located because there are no longer any missing records.

Finally, you want to update all objects that use the Location field as the underlying record source to reflect the addition of the new records.

8

- Display the Car Pool Query datasheet.

- Click 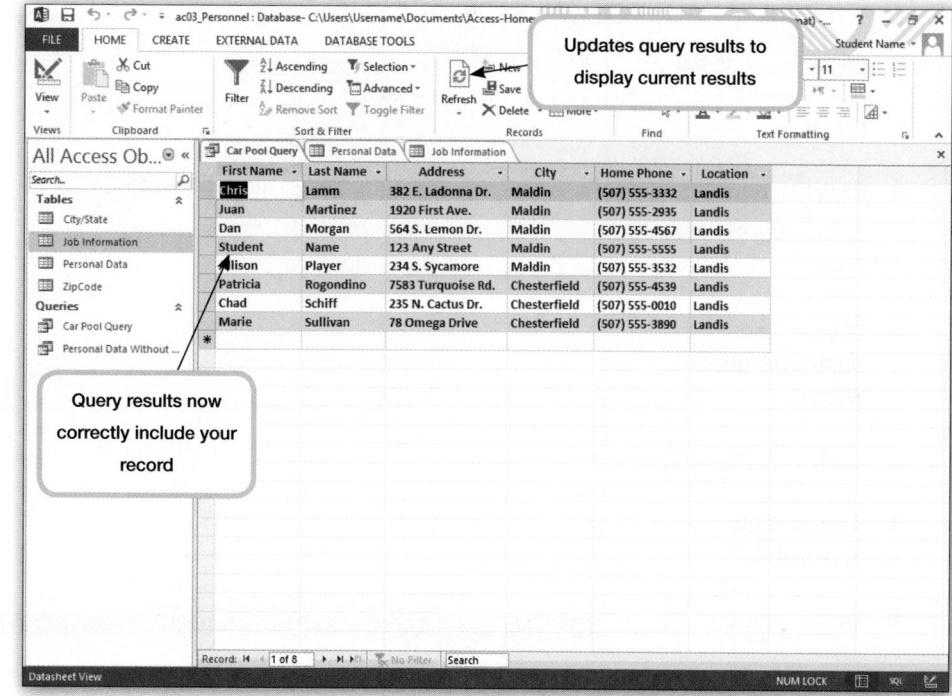 in the Records group of the Home tab to refresh the screen image with the change in data.

Your screen should be similar to Figure 3.42

Figure 3.42

The query results list eight records that meet the criteria and now correctly include your record.

FINDING DUPLICATE RECORDS

Next, you want to check the Personal Data table for possible duplicate records. Even though this table uses the Employee ID field as the primary key, it is possible to enter the same record with two different IDs. To check for duplication, you will use the Find Duplicates Query Wizard.

1

- **Click** Query Wizard **in the Create tab.**

- **Click** Yes **to save the Car Pool Query.**

- **Choose Find Duplicates Query Wizard.**

- **Click** OK **.**

- **Choose Table: Personal Data.**

- **Click** Next > **.**

Your screen should be similar to Figure 3.43

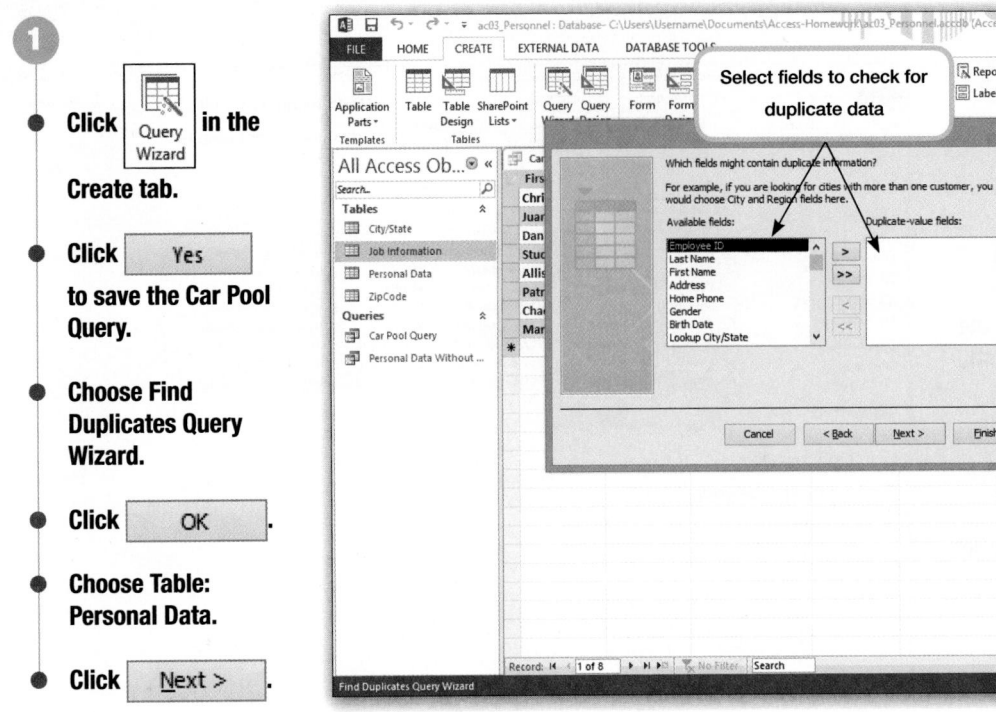

Figure 3.43

In this wizard dialog box, you identify the fields that may contain duplicate data. In this case, you will check the Last Name fields for duplicate values.

2

- **Add the Last Name field to the Duplicate-Value Fields list.**

- **Click** Next > **.**

Your screen should be similar to Figure 3.44

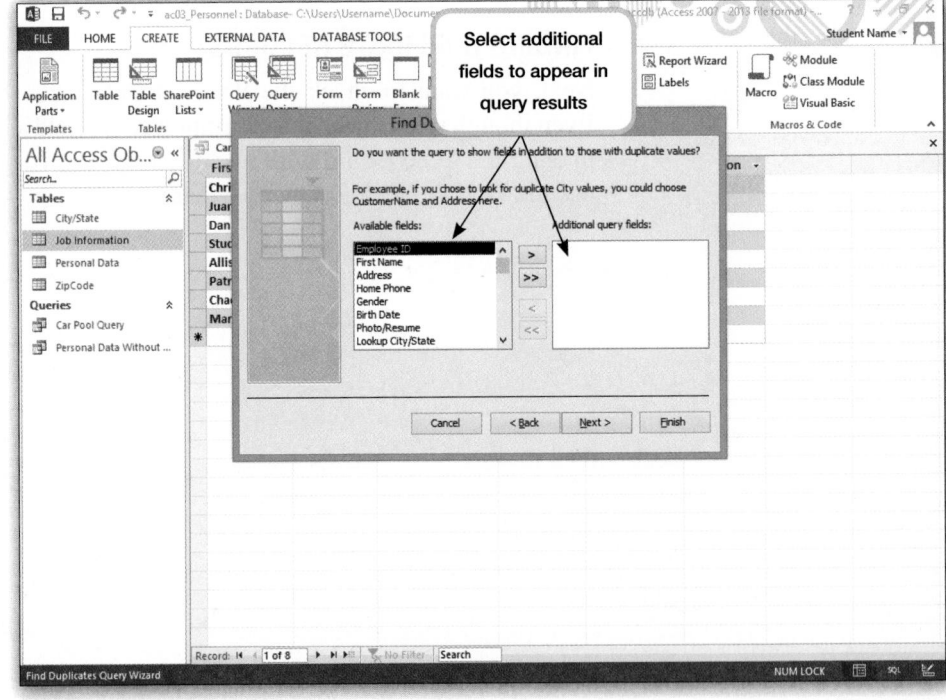

Figure 3.44

Next, you need to identify the additional fields you want to appear in the query results.

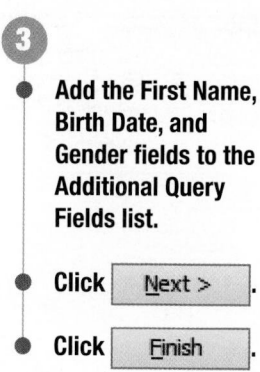

3 ● Add the First Name, Birth Date, and Gender fields to the Additional Query Fields list.

● Click [Next >].

● Click [Finish].

Your screen should be similar to Figure 3.45

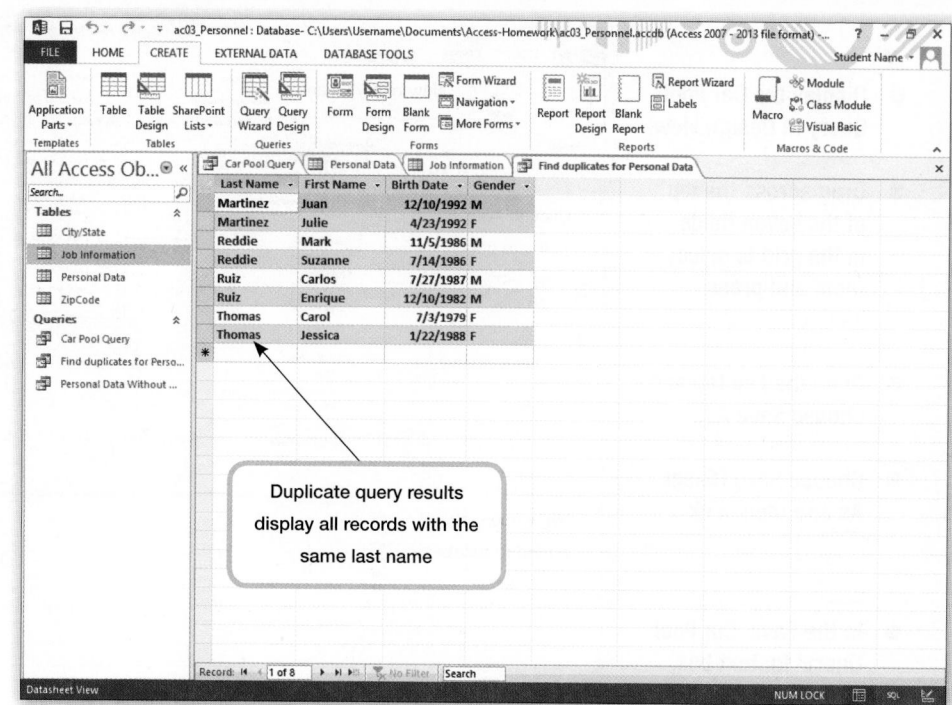

Duplicate query results display all records with the same last name

Figure 3.45

All records with the same last name are listed. These all look like valid records, so you will not make any changes.

CREATING A PARAMETER QUERY

Periodically, the club director wants to know the employee numbers and names of the employees at each club and their job positions. To find this information, you will create a simple query and sort the Location field to group the records.

To create this query, you will modify the existing Car Pool Query design, since it already includes the two tables—Personal Data and Job Information—that you need to use. You will clear the design grid and save the modified query using a new name.

Another Method

You can also use 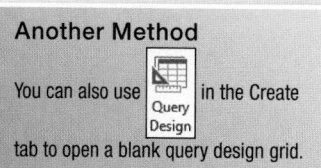 in the Create tab to open a blank query design grid.

1

- Display the Car Pool Query in Design view.

- Drag across the top of the seven fields in the grid to select them and press Delete.

- Open the File tab and choose Save As.

- Choose Save Object As and then click ![Save As]

- In the Save 'Car Pool Query' to: text box, enter Location Query and click OK.

Your screen should be similar to Figure 3.46

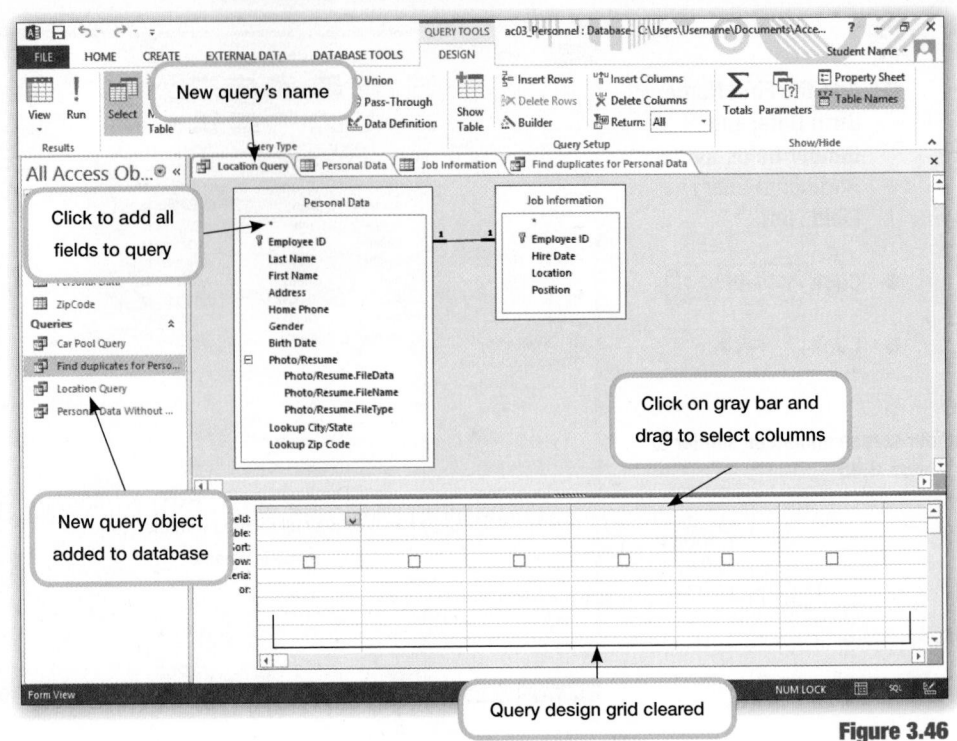

Figure 3.46

The query object is added to the Navigation pane, and you are ready to define the query. You will add all the fields from the Personal Data table to the grid, along with the Location field from the Job Information table.

❷

- **Double-click * in the Personal Data field list.**

- **Double-click Location in the Job Information table.**

- **Sort the Location field in ascending sort order.**

- **Run the query.**

- **Hide the Navigation pane.**

- **Scroll the window to the right to see the Location field.**

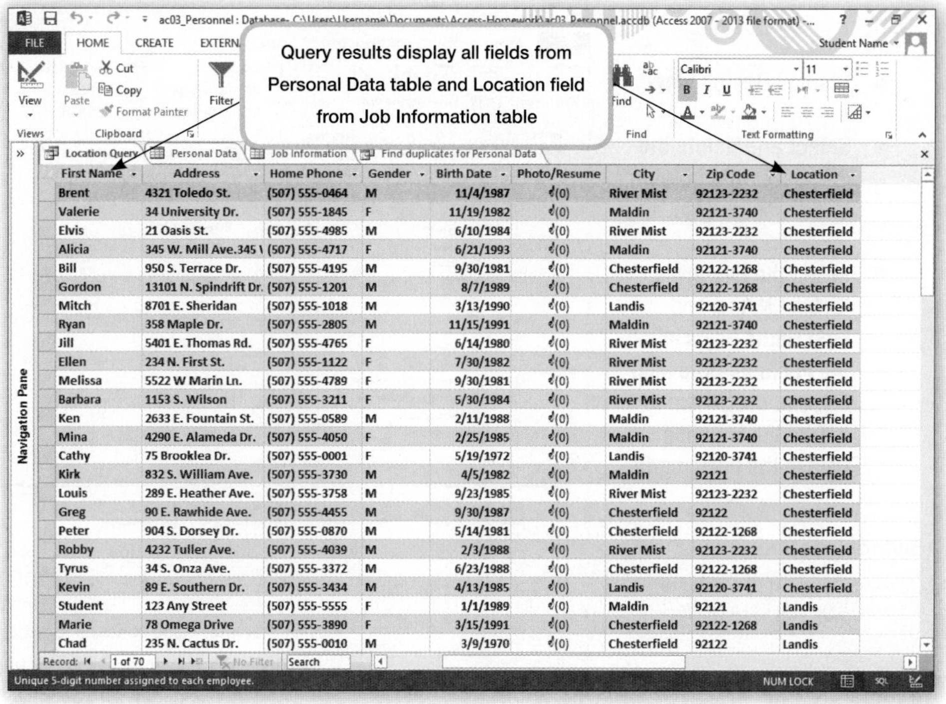

Query results display all fields from Personal Data table and Location field from Job Information table

Figure 3.47

Your screen should be similar to Figure 3.47

All the fields from the Personal Data table and the Location field are displayed. The location is in sorted order. However, because the director wants the information for each location on a separate page when printed, sorting the Location field will not work. To display only the records for a single location at a time, you could filter the Location field, or change the criteria in the Location field to provide this information, and then print the results.

Another method, however, is to create a parameter query that will display a dialog box prompting you for location information when the query is run. This saves having to change to Design view and enter the specific criteria or applying a filter. Criteria that are entered in the Criteria cell are **hard-coded criteria**, meaning they are used each time the query is run. In a parameter query, you enter a **parameter value** in the Criteria cell rather than a specific value. The parameter value tells the query to prompt you to enter the specific criteria each time the query is run.

Additionally, the director does not need all the information from the Personal Data table, so you will change the design to include only the necessary fields. First, you will change the fields in the design grid to display only the Employee ID and the First Name and Last Name fields from the Personal Data table.

3

- Display Design view.

- Select and delete the Personal Data column in the design grid.

- Select the Employee ID, Last Name, and First Name fields in the Personal Data field list, and drag them to before the Location field in the design grid.

Having Trouble?

Hold down ⇧Shift while clicking on each field name to select all three.

- Remove the Sort from the Location field.

- Type **[Enter Location]** in the Location Criteria cell.

Your screen should be similar to Figure 3.48

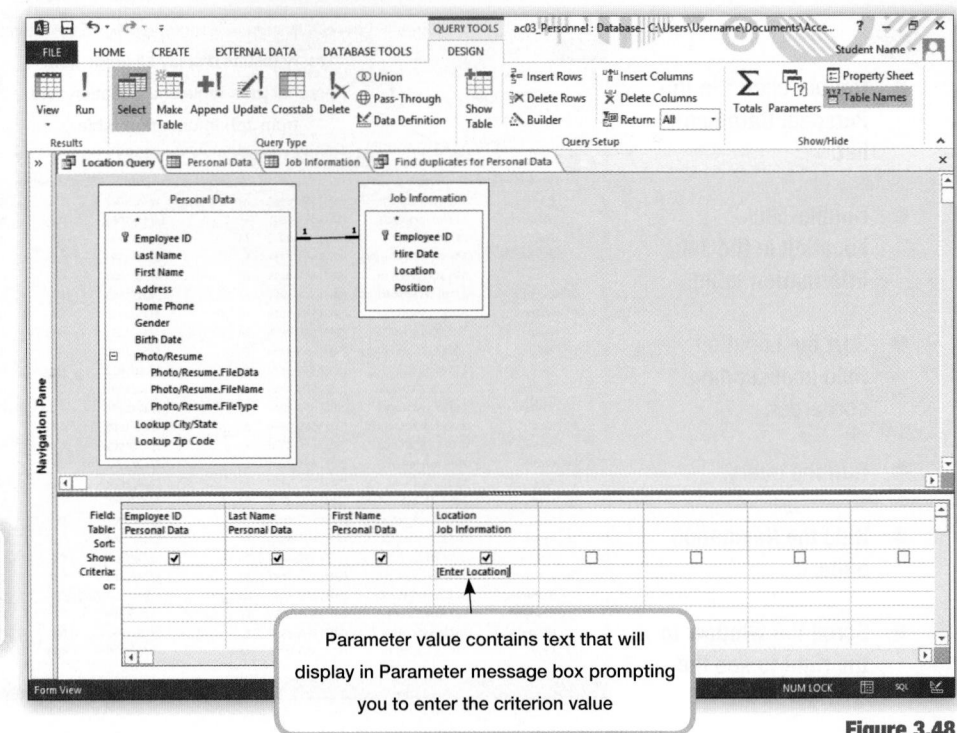

Figure 3.48

The Location criterion you entered is the parameter value. Parameter values are enclosed in square brackets and contain the text you want to appear when the parameter prompt is displayed. The parameter value cannot be a field name because Access will assume you want to use that particular field and will not prompt for input.

4

- Run the query and type **Landis** in the Enter Parameter Value dialog box.

- Click 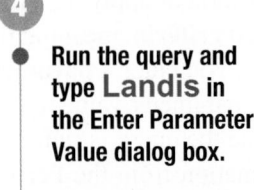.

Your screen should be similar to Figure 3.49

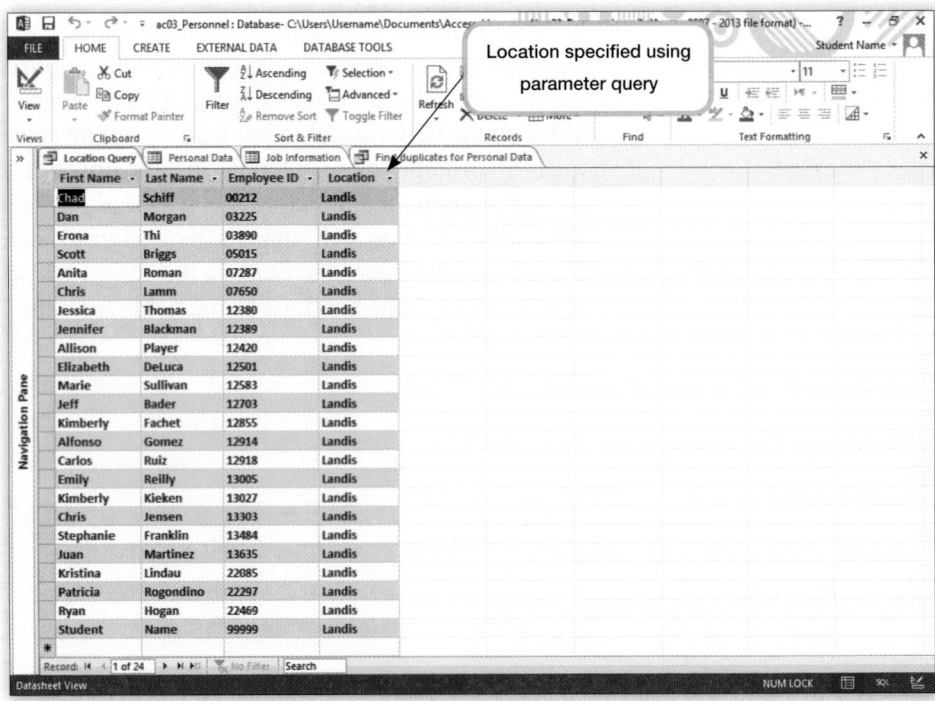

Figure 3.49

Only those records whose location is Landis are displayed. Additionally, only the fields you specified are included in the result. Now, each time you run the query, you simply need to specify the location in the Enter Parameter Value dialog box to obtain results for the different locations.

Displaying a Totals Row

As you look at the query results, you can see the record indicator tells you there are 24 records. The record indicator is a simple count of the total number of records in the table and only appears when you view the datasheet. You decide to display a Totals row in the datasheet that will display this information when you print the datasheet.

Additional Information

Some functions also can use a Date/Time data type.

In addition to count totals, the Totals row can perform other types of calculations such as averages and sums on a column of data. Calculations that are performed on a range of data are called **aggregate functions**. Because aggregate functions perform calculations, the data type in a column must be a Number, Decimal, or Currency data type. The Personal Data table does not use any of these data types. However, the Count function can be used on all data types.

You will add a Totals row and then use the Count aggregate function to display the record count. The Totals row appears at the bottom of the table, under the add new blank record row. It remains fixed on the window as you scroll up and down in the table. Clicking in a column of the Totals row selects the field to be calculated. Then you open the drop-down list to select the function you want to use. For Text data types, only the Count function is listed.

1

- Click $\sum$ Totals in the Records group of the Home tab.

- Click on the Last Name field in the Totals row.

- Open the drop-down list and choose Count.

Your screen should be similar to Figure 3.50

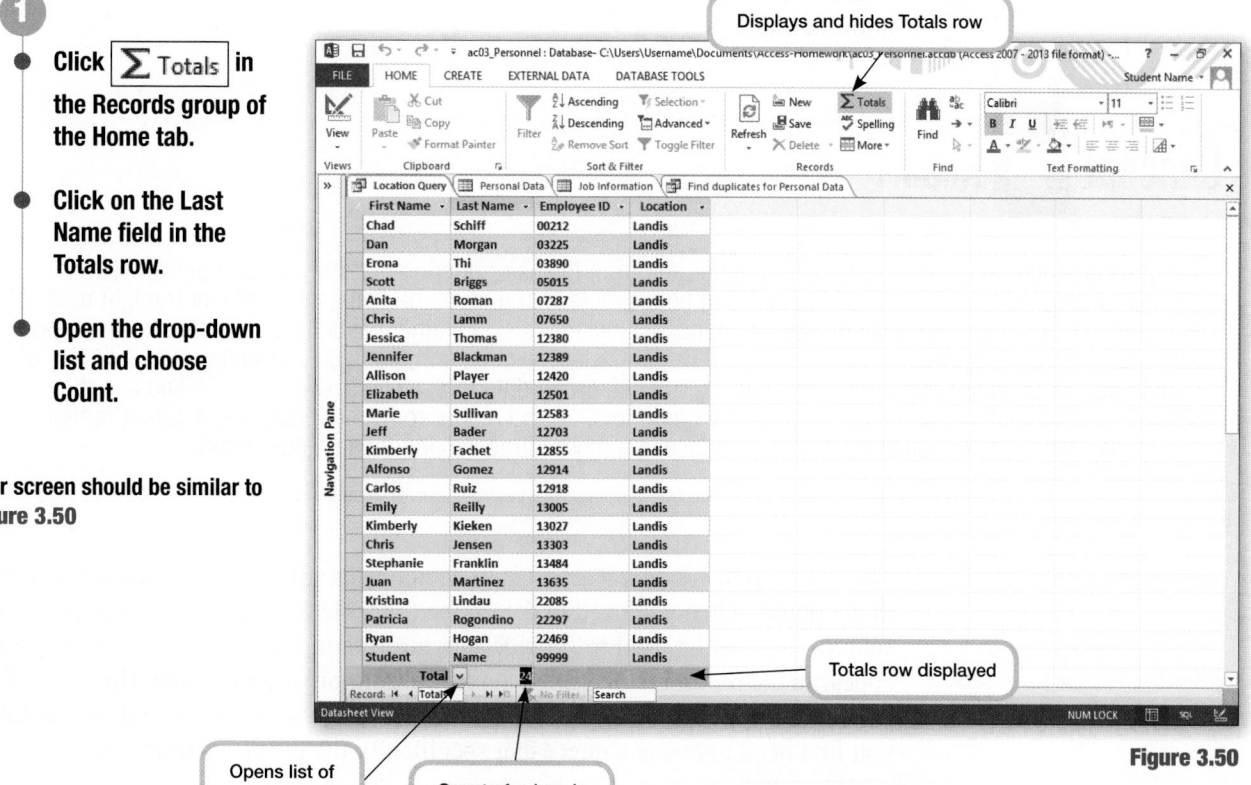

Figure 3.50

The Totals row displays 24 as the number of values in the column. The Totals label in the first column identifies the meaning of this value.

You can turn the display of the Totals row on and off any time by clicking Σ Totals . When you redisplay the row, any functions that were selected are displayed again. A Totals row also can be displayed in a table datasheet.

You will print this query datasheet and then close all open objects.

2

- Click  Save in the Quick Access Toolbar to save the query.

- Preview and then print the Location Query datasheet.

- Close the query, saving the layout changes if prompted.

- Close all remaining open objects, saving the layout when prompted.

- Open the Navigation pane.

NOTE If you are running short on time, this is an appropriate place to end your Access session. When you begin again, open the ac03_Personnel **database.**

Creating Reports

As you know, you can print the table and query datasheets to obtain a simple printout of the data. However, there are many times when you would like the output to look more professional. To do this, you can create custom reports using this information.

Concept 4 Report

A **report** is professional-appearing output generated from tables or queries that may include design elements, groups, and summary information. A report can be a simple listing of all the fields in a table, or it might be a list of selected fields based on a query. Reports generally include design elements such as formatted labels, report titles, and headings, as well as different theme design styles, layouts, and graphics that enhance the display of information. In addition, when creating a report, you can group data to achieve specific results. You can then display summary information such as totals by group to allow the reader to further analyze the data. Creating a report displays the information from your database in a more attractive and meaningful format.

The first step in creating a report is to decide what information you want to appear in the report. Then you need to determine the tables or queries (the report's record source) that can be used to provide this information. If all the fields you want to appear in the report are in a single table, then simply use that table. However, if the information you want to appear in the report is contained in more than one table, you first need to create a query that specifically fits the needs of the report.

There are several different methods you can use to create reports, as described in the following table. The method you use depends on the type of report you need to create.

Report tool	Creates a simple report containing all the fields in the table.
Blank Report tool	Builds a report from scratch in Report Layout view by adding the fields you select from the table.
Report design	Builds a report from scratch in Report Design view by adding the fields you select from the table.
Report Wizard	Guides you through the steps to create a report.

USING THE REPORT TOOL

Although you could give Juan a simple printout of the car pool query results, you decide to create a report of this information. Because the fastest way to create a report is to use the Report tool, you decide to try this method first. This tool uses the selected or displayed table or query object as the report source.

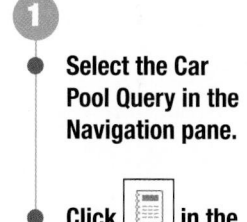

- Select the Car Pool Query in the Navigation pane.

- Click 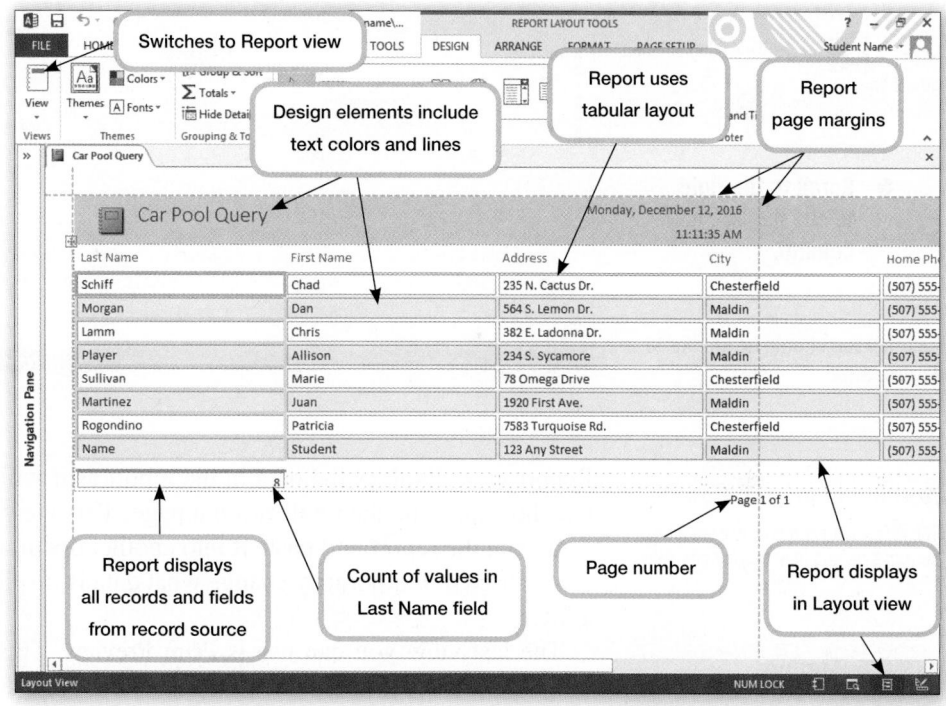 in the Reports group of the Create tab.

- Hide the Navigation pane.

Your screen should be similar to Figure 3.51

Figure 3.51

The Report tool creates a report that displays all fields and records from the record source in a predesigned report layout and style. It uses a tabular layout in which each field name appears at the top of the column and each record appears in a line, much like in Datasheet view. The fields are displayed in the order in which they appear in the query design. Notice the records are not sorted by last name as they are in the query results. This is because the query sort order is overridden by the report sort order, which defaults to ordering the records by the primary key. It also displays the object name as the report title and the current date and time in the title area. The report design elements include black font color for the report title and gray fill color behind the title. The title is also in a larger text size. The last row displays a total value of the number of records in the report. The dotted lines identify the report page margins and show that the report will be split between two pages.

VIEWING THE REPORT

The report is displayed in Layout view. As in Form Layout view, you could modify the report design if needed in this view. Instead, you will switch to Report view to see how the report will look when printed.

Having Trouble?

Do not be concerned if your report splits at a different location than shown here. You will learn how to modify reports shortly.

1

● Click **Report View** in the Views group of the Report Layout Tools Design tab.

Another Method

Click the Report View button in the status bar.

● Scroll to the right to see the last field column.

Your screen should be similar to Figure 3.52

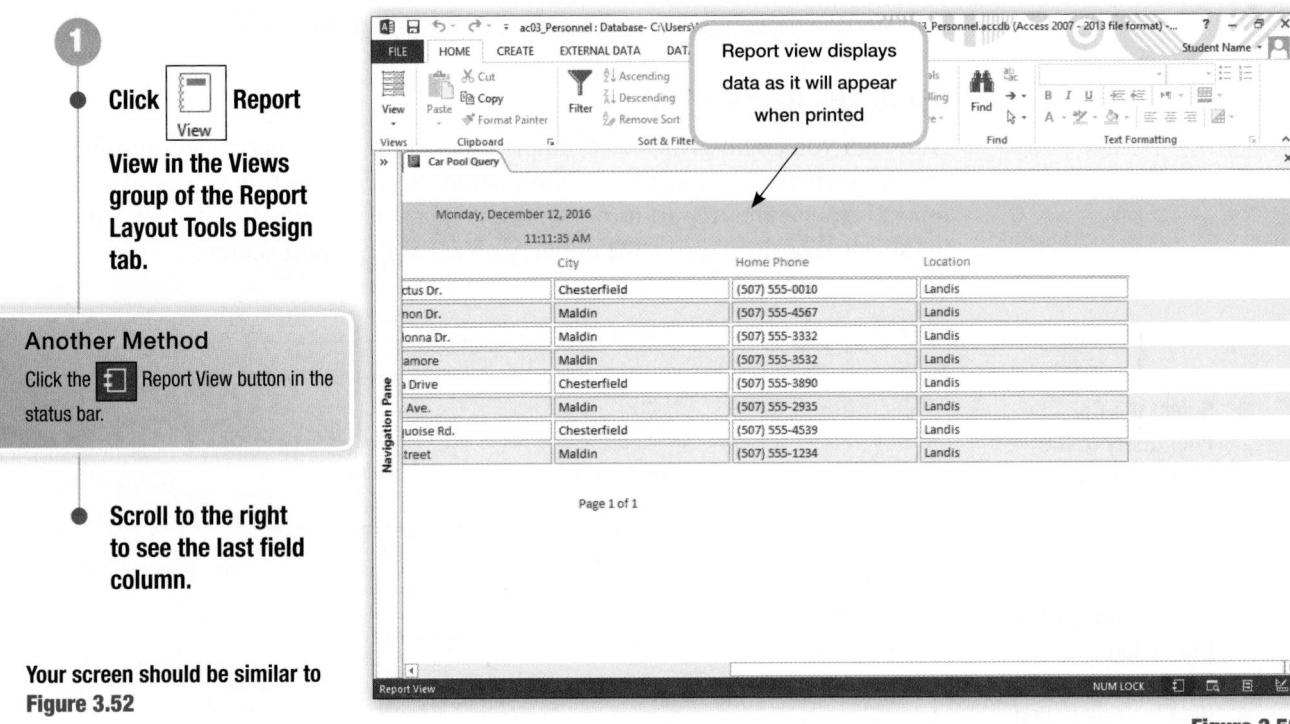

Figure 3.52

Report view displays the data in the report as it will appear when printed. It does not show how the data will fit on a page. This view is useful if you want to copy data from the report and paste it into another document such as a Word file. It also can be used to temporarily change what data is displayed in the report by applying a filter.

The last view you can use is Print Preview. This view will show you exactly how the report will look when printed and can be used to modify the page layout and print-related settings. Another way to display this view is from the object's shortcut menu.

Additional Information

The report date and time will reflect the current date and time on your computer.

Another Method

You also can use Print Preview in the status bar or choose Print Preview from the View drop-down menu.

- Right-click on the report tab or an empty area of the report and choose **Print Preview**.

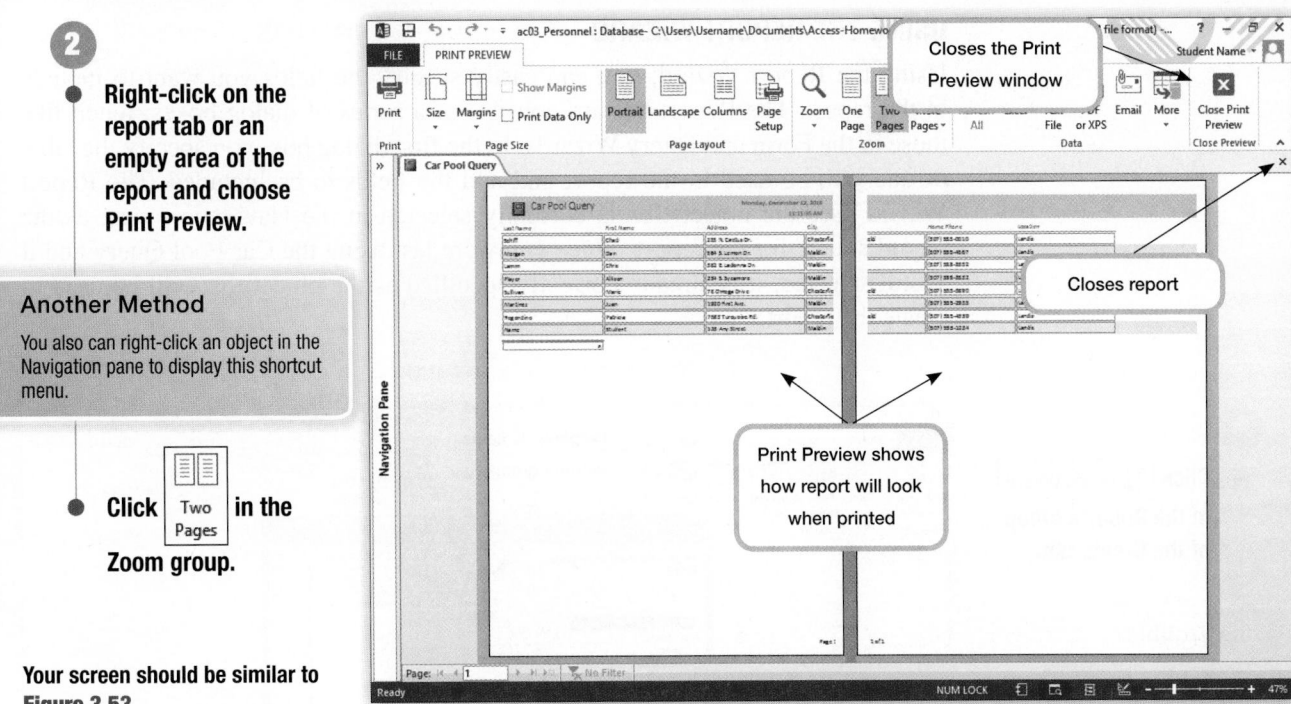

Closes the Print Preview window

Closes report

Print Preview shows how report will look when printed

Another Method

You also can right-click an object in the Navigation pane to display this shortcut menu.

- Click [Two Pages] in the **Zoom group**.

Your screen should be similar to Figure 3.53

Figure 3.53

It is now easy to see exactly how the report will look when printed. After looking over the report, you decide that although the tabular layout is appropriate for your report, you do not want the report to include all the fields from the query. Rather than modify the report design by removing the unneeded fields, you will close this report without saving it and then use the Report Wizard to create a report that is more appropriate for your needs.

3

- Click [Close Print Preview] to close Print Preview.

- Click [×] to close the report.

- Click [No] in response to the dialog box to save the report.

USING THE REPORT WIZARD

Using the Report Wizard, you can easily specify the fields you want to include in the report. The Report Wizard consists of a series of dialog boxes, much like those in the Form and Query Wizards. In the first dialog box, you specify the table or query to be used in the report and add the fields to be included. The Report Wizard uses the object that is currently selected in the Navigation pane as the record source for the report. Since you were last using the Car Pool Query and it is still selected, it is already correctly specified as the object that will be used to create the report.

1

● Click [Report Wizard] in the Reports group of the Create tab.

Having Trouble?

If necessary, click [Open] in response to the security warning message.

● Add the First Name field to the Selected Fields list.

● Add all the remaining fields to the list.

● Remove the Location field.

● Click [Next >].

Your screen should be similar to Figure 3.54

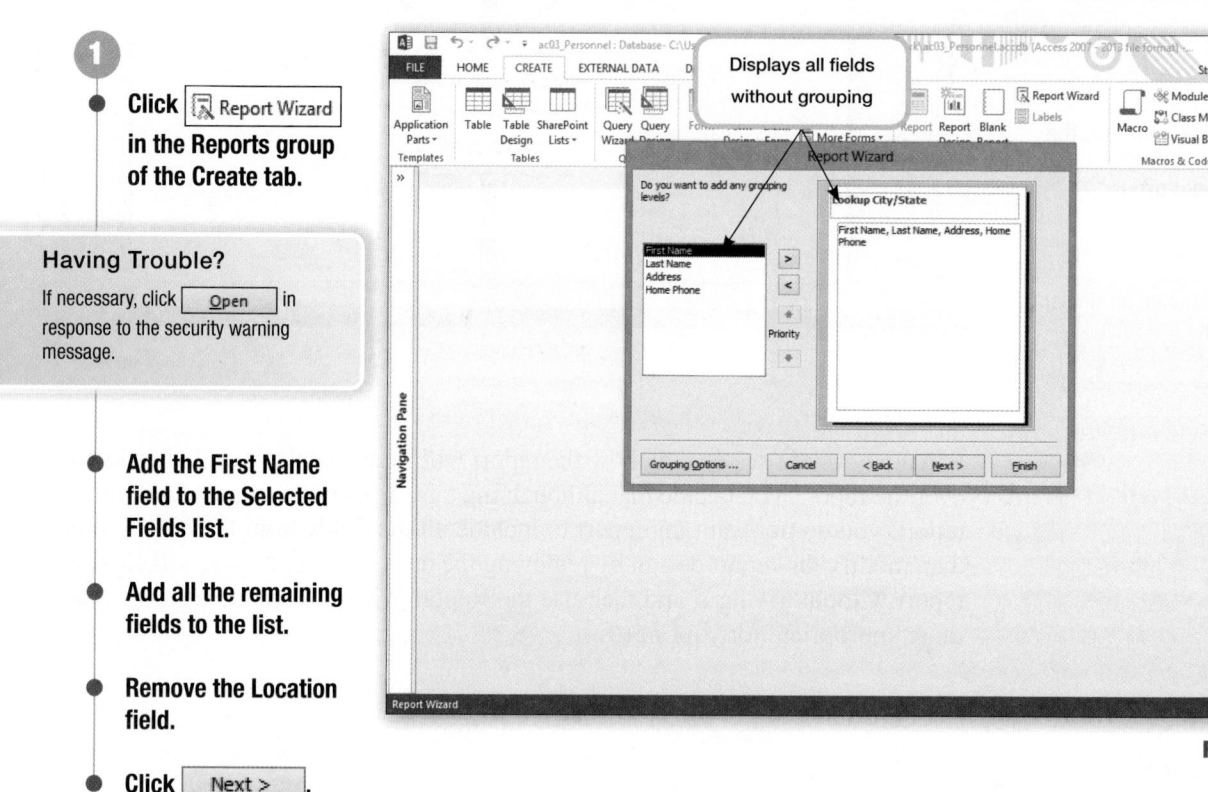

Figure 3.54

In this dialog box, you are asked if you want to add any grouping levels to the report. As suggested, you will group the report by city.

②

Click Next >.

Your screen should be similar to Figure 3.55

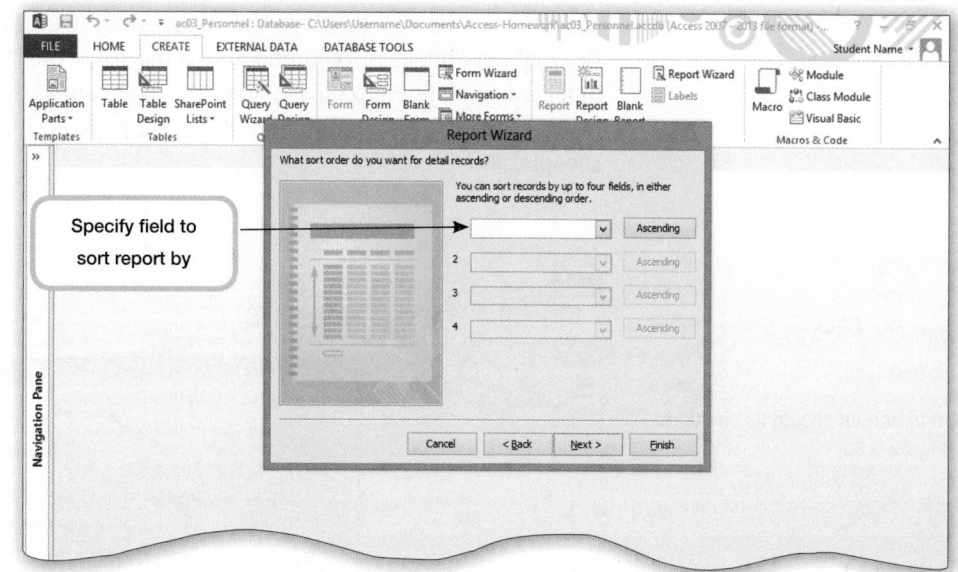

Specify field to sort report by

Figure 3.55

You can specify a sort order for the records in this dialog box. Because you want the last names sorted within each city group, you will specify to sort by last name.

③

● Open the first list box drop-down menu and choose Last Name.

● Click Next >.

Your screen should be similar to Figure 3.56

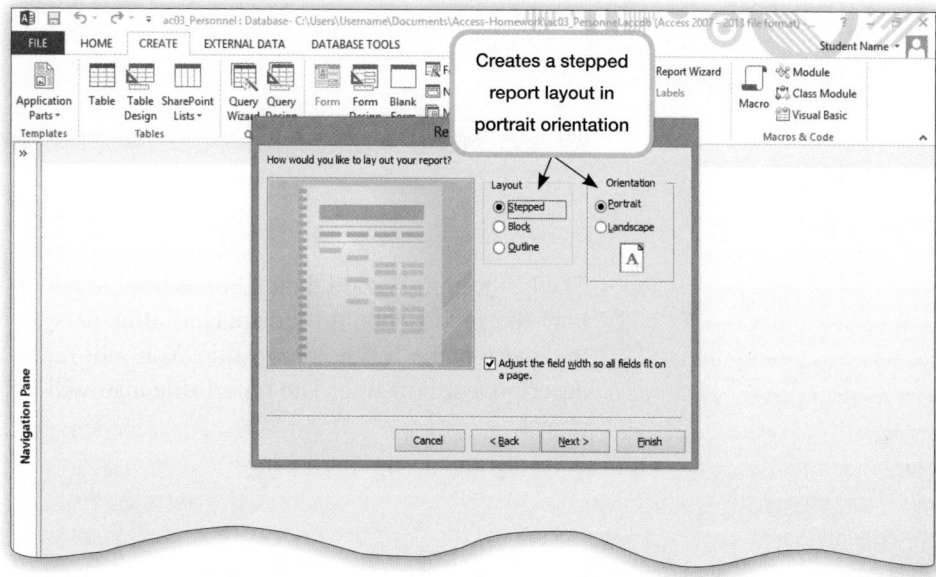

Creates a stepped report layout in portrait orientation

Figure 3.56

This dialog box is used to change the report layout and orientation. The default report settings for a grouped report use a stepped report design layout with portrait orientation.

The stepped design displays the report data using a tabular format in which the field labels appear in columns above the rows of data. The data in each group is indented or stepped to clearly identify the groups. In addition, the option to adjust the field width so that all fields fit on one page is selected. The default settings are acceptable.

Click [Next >].

Your screen should be similar to Figure 3.57

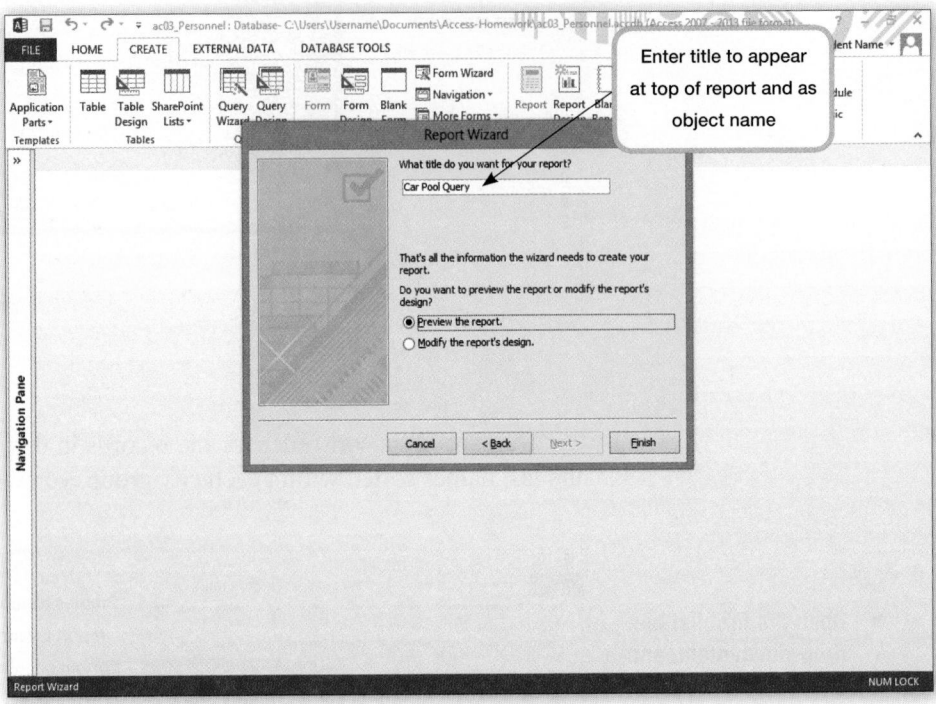

Figure 3.57

The last Report Wizard dialog box is used to add a title to the report and to specify how the report should be displayed after it is created. Access initially suggests the query name for the report title. You will replace the query name with a more descriptive report title. The report title also will be used as the name of the report object.

5 ● Enter **Car Pool Report: Maldin to Landis** as the title.

● Click Finish .

Your screen should be similar to Figure 3.58

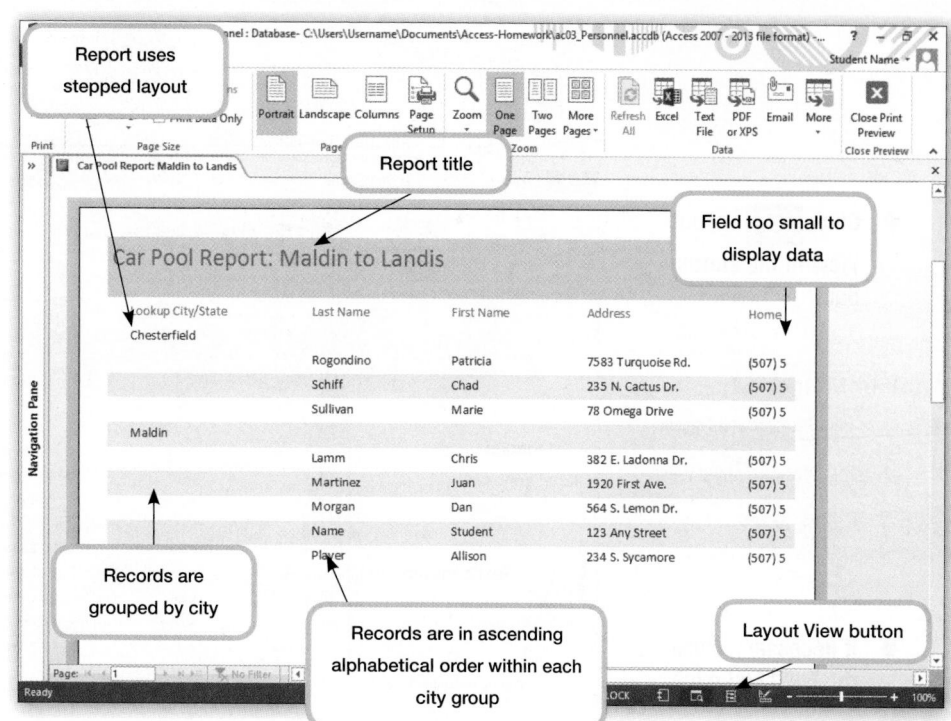

Figure 3.58

In an instant, the completed report with the data from the resource query is displayed in Print Preview. The report appears in the stepped layout, grouped by city. The title reflects the title you specified. The records appear in alphabetical order within each group, as you specified in the Report Wizard.

However, there are a few problems with the report. The most noticeable is that the city field is much larger than it needs to be; consequently, the Home Phone field is truncated. Additionally, you want to change the Lookup City/State column heading to City and to display the First Name field column before the Last Name.

MODIFYING THE REPORT IN LAYOUT VIEW

To make these changes, you need to modify the report design. You can modify a report in either Design view or Layout view. To make these simple changes, you will use Layout view.

Your screen should be similar to Figure 3.59

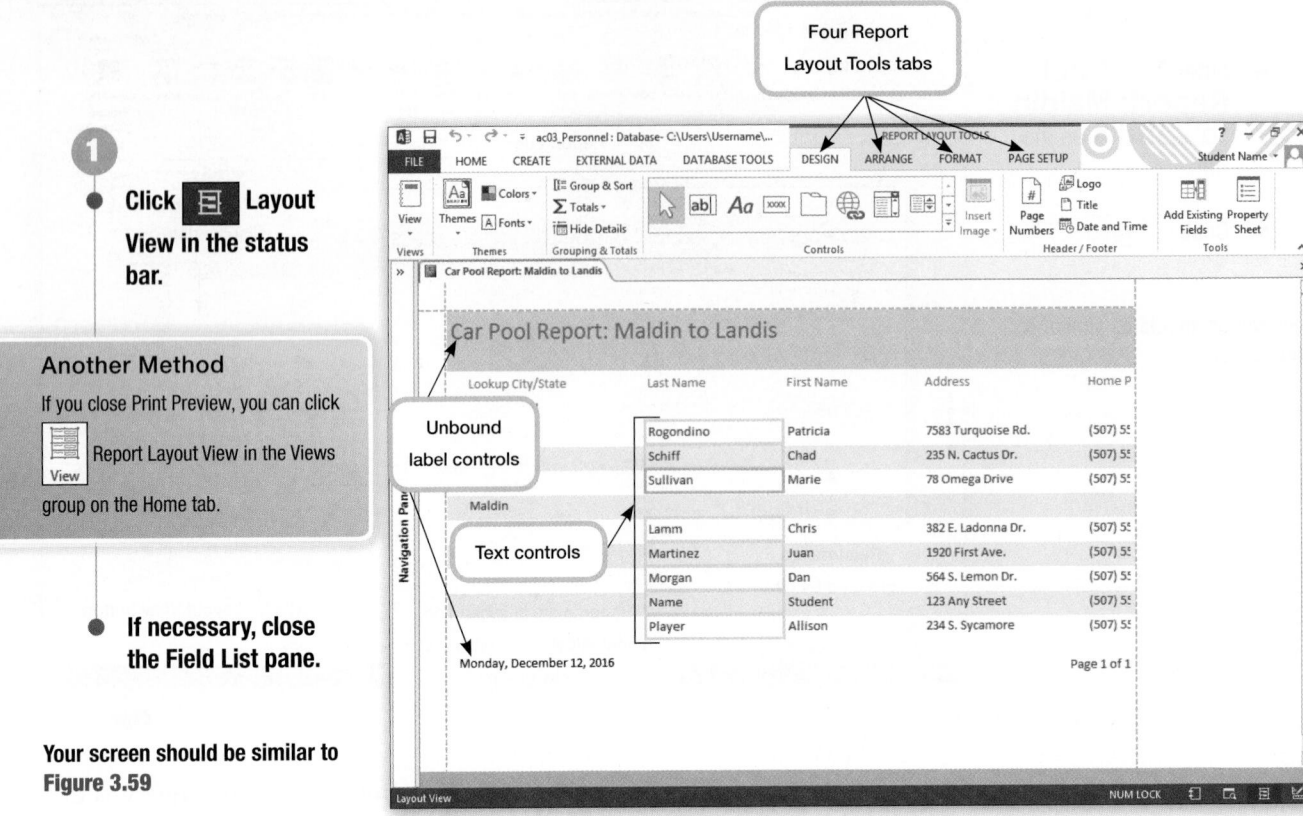

Figure 3.59

1

● Click ⊟ Layout View in the status bar.

Another Method

If you close Print Preview, you can click ⊞ Report Layout View in the Views group on the Home tab.

● If necessary, close the Field List pane.

Having Trouble?

See Concept 10: Controls in Lab 2 to review this feature.

Additional Information

The commands in the Rows & Columns group of the Arrange tab are not available until a table layout has been applied.

In Layout view, four tabs are available to help you modify the report. The Design tab features are used to add fields, controls, totals, and other elements to the report. The Arrange tab is used to modify the overall layout of the report or of individual elements. The Format tab contains commands to format shapes as well as make text enhancements such as changing the font and font color. The Page Setup tab is used to control the page layout of the report for printing purposes.

Just as in forms, each item in the report is a separate control. The field names are label controls and the field information is a text control. The text controls are bound to the data in the underlying table. The field names and report title are unbound label controls. The stepped report design controls the layout and position of these controls.

The same features you learned when working in Form Layout view are available in Report Layout view. Additionally, just like forms, reports can use a stacked or tabular table layout to make it easier to work with controls. Generally, reports use a tabular layout in which controls are arranged in rows and columns like a spreadsheet, with labels across the top. Currently, although the stepped design you selected in the Report Wizard displays the controls using a tabular design, it did not group the controls in a layout. You will apply a tabular layout to the report controls so that you can easily modify the report.

- Press **Ctrl** + **A** to select all the controls on the report.

- Hold down **Ctrl** while clicking on the title, date, and page # label controls to deselect them.

- Click in the **Tabular** Table group of the Arrange tab to group the selected controls in a tabular layout.

- Change the text in the Lookup City/State label control to City.

- Click anywhere in the First Name field and click **Select Column** in the Rows & Columns group to select the column.

- Drag the First Name field column to the left of the Last Name field column.

Having Trouble?

When you move a field column, a pink bar indicates where the column will be placed when you stop dragging.

- Adjust the size of the fields as in Figure 3.60.

Your screen should be similar to Figure 3.60

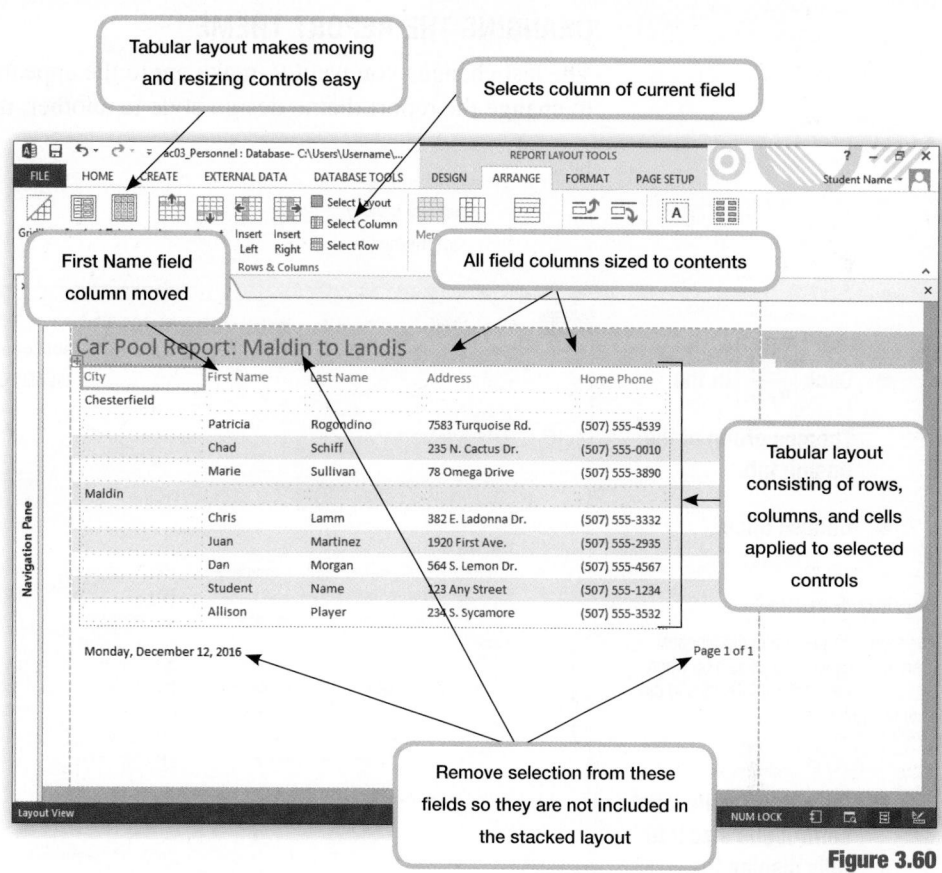

Tabular layout makes moving and resizing controls easy

Selects column of current field

First Name field column moved

All field columns sized to contents

Car Pool Report: Maldin to Landis

Tabular layout consisting of rows, columns, and cells applied to selected controls

Remove selection from these fields so they are not included in the stacked layout

Figure 3.60

Applying the tabular layout made it easy to size and move the controls. Now the report easily fits on a single page and all the fields fully display their contents.

CHANGING THE REPORT THEME

The last changes you want to make are to the appearance of the report. You decide to change the report theme design style to another, more colorful style.

1

Click **in the Themes group of the Design tab.**

Choose Slice.

Having Trouble?

The theme names are in alphabetical order and appear in a ScreenTip when you point to the different designs in the Themes gallery.

Click on the title label control and size it to fully display the text.

Resize any other label and text controls that do not fully display their contents.

Your screen should be similar to Figure 3.61

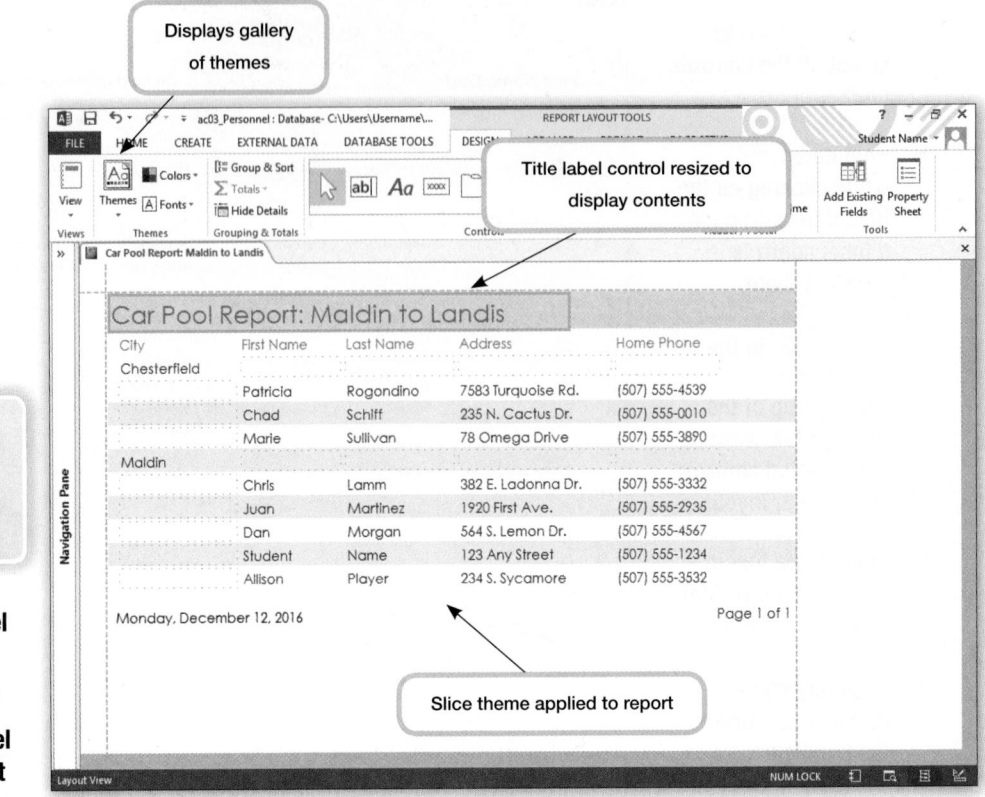

Figure 3.61

Additional Information

You can apply a theme to just the current object by right-clicking the theme choice and choosing Apply Theme to This Object Only.

The selected theme is applied to the report and all other objects that respond to themes. It includes different fonts and colors. You are finished making changes to the report and will close and save the report.

2

Close the report, saving the changes when prompted.

Open the Navigation pane.

The name of the report you created appears in the Reports category of the Navigation pane.

- Select the **Location Query** from the Queries category and click 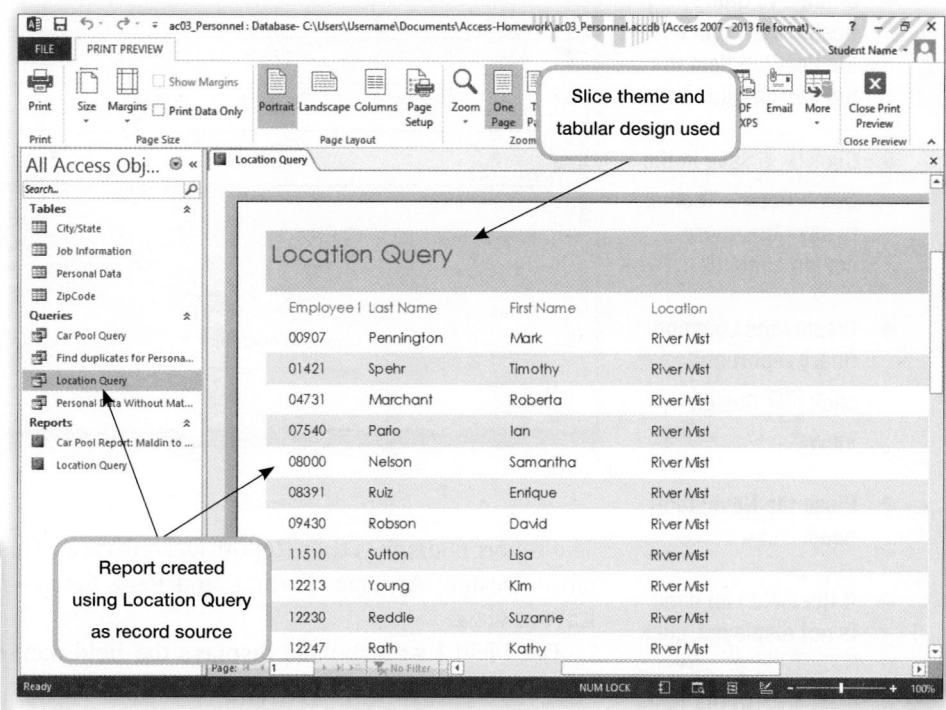 Report Wizard in the Create tab.

- Add all the fields to the report.

- Click **Finish**.

- Enter **River Mist** as the location and click **OK**.

Your screen should be similar to Figure 3.62

MODIFYING A REPORT IN DESIGN VIEW

After seeing how easy it was to create a report for the car pool information, you decide to create a custom report for the job position and location information requested by the club director. You will create the report using the Report Wizard. Then you will modify the report in Design view.

Figure 3.62

Because you knew that you would be using the default or last-used wizard settings, you were able to end the wizard without moving through all the steps. The report displays the specified fields and uses a tabular design and the Slice theme. The tabular design was used because it is the default setting for the Report Wizard and the Slice theme was used because it was the last-used theme in the database. The report title and report object name use the name of the query on which the report was based.

As you look at the report, you realize you forgot to include the Position field. You will modify the query and then add this field in Design view to the report.

2

- **Open the Location Query and enter River Mist as the location.**

- **Change to Query Design view and add the Position field to the design grid.**

- **Click** 🖫 **Save in the Quick Access Toolbar to save the query design changes.**

- **Display the Location Query report and click** 🔲 **Design View.**

- **Close the Navigation pane.**

- **If the Field List pane is not displayed, click**

in the Tools group of the Design tab.

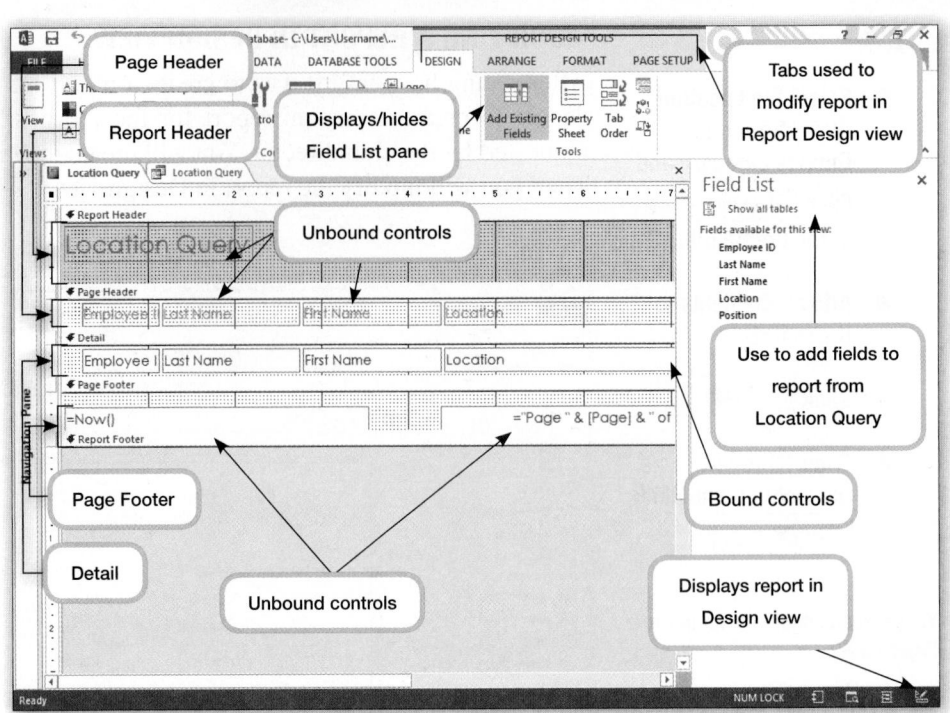

Figure 3.63

The report is displayed in Report Design view. This view displays the same four tabs—Design, Arrange, Format, and Page Setup—that were available in Report Layout view.

The Field List task pane displays the field names from the design grid of the Location Query. You will use the Field List task pane shortly to add the missing field to the report.

The Report Design window is divided into five sections: Report Header, Page Header, Detail, Page Footer, and Report Footer. The contents of each section appear below the horizontal bar that contains the name of that section. The sections are described in the following table.

Having Trouble?

If your Field List pane is floating in the window, dock it on the right side of the screen by dragging the Field List title bar to the right until your mouse touches the right edge of the Access window.

Another Method

You also can use the shortcut key [Alt] + [F8] to hide and display the Field List pane.

Section	Description
Report Header	Contains information to be printed once at the beginning of the report. The report title is displayed in this section.
Page Header	Contains information to be printed at the top of each page. The column headings are displayed in this section.
Detail	Contains the records of the table. The field column widths are the same as the column widths set in the table design.
Page Footer	Contains information to be printed at the bottom of each page such as the date and page number.
Report Footer	Contains information to be printed at the end of the report. The Report Footer section currently contains no data.

Your screen should be similar to Figure 3.63

The controls in the Page Header section are unbound label controls, whereas those in the Detail section are bound text controls. The control in the Report Header that displays the report title is also an unbound label control, while those in the Page Footer that display the date and page numbers are unbound text box controls.

First, you will group the controls in the Page Header and Detail sections together by applying a tabular layout to the selected fields. Then you will add the missing field to the report.

3

- Click in the ruler area to the left of the fields in the Page Header section to select all the controls in that section.

Additional Information

When positioning the mouse in the ruler, the pointer will appear as a selection arrow ➡ indicating that you can select all fields in the section.

- ⇧Shift click on the ruler area next to the Detail section to select all the controls in that section as well.

Having Trouble?

You can also select the controls individually by using the ⇧Shift key.

- Click ⊞ Tabular in the Table group of the Arrange tab.

- Scroll the window horizontally to view the Location controls and the right edge of the report.

- Drag the Position field from the field list to the right of the Location text control in the Detail section, and when a pink vertical bar appears, release the mouse to drop it at that location.

Another Method

You also can double-click on a field in the field list to move it into the Detail section of the report.

Your screen should be similar to Figure 3.64

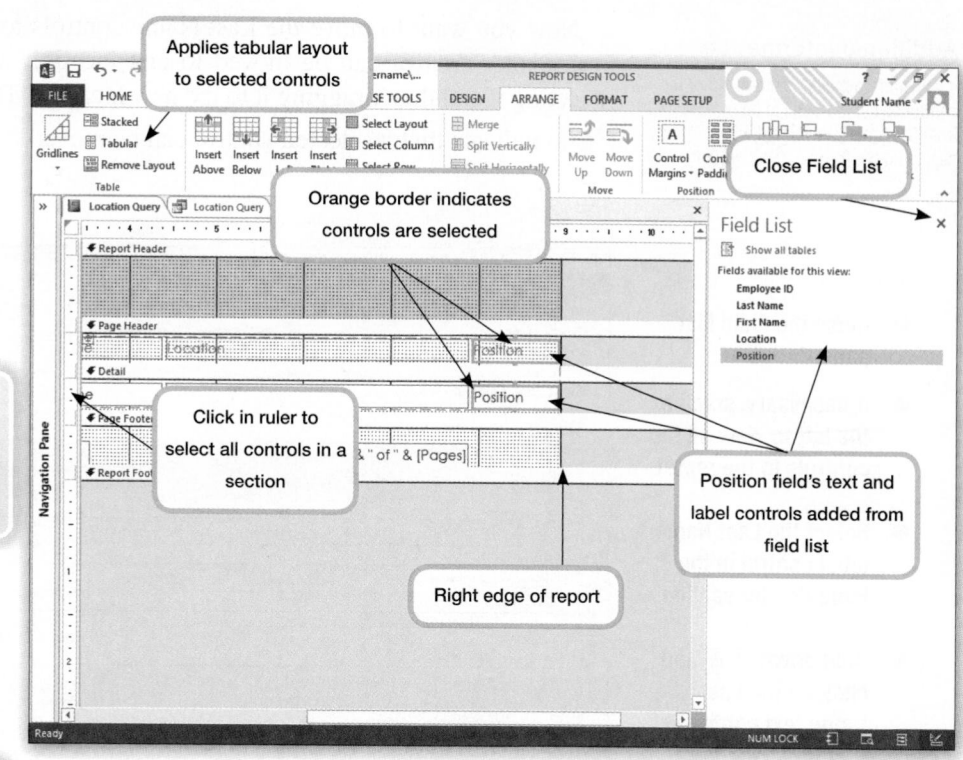

Figure 3.64

The Position field text and label controls have been added to the report. The Position label control was inserted in the Page Header section, and the Position text control was inserted in the Detail section. This is because the controls were inserted into the tabular control layout and comply with the horizontal and vertical alignment settings of the layout. The text control is a bound control that is tied to the Position field data. Both controls are surrounded by an orange border, indicating that they are selected.

Now you want to move the Last Name controls to the right of the First Name controls. A control can be moved to any location within the control layout by selecting it and then dragging it to the new location. The mouse pointer changes to to indicate that a selected control can be moved.

4

- **Close the Field List pane.**

- **If necessary, scroll to the left to view all the controls in the report.**

- **Select the Last Name label control in the Page Header section.**

- **Hold down** [Shift] **and click on the Last Name text control in the Detail section.**

- **Point to the selected controls, and when the pointer changes to , drag it to the right of the First Name controls, releasing the mouse when the pink bar appears at the desired location.**

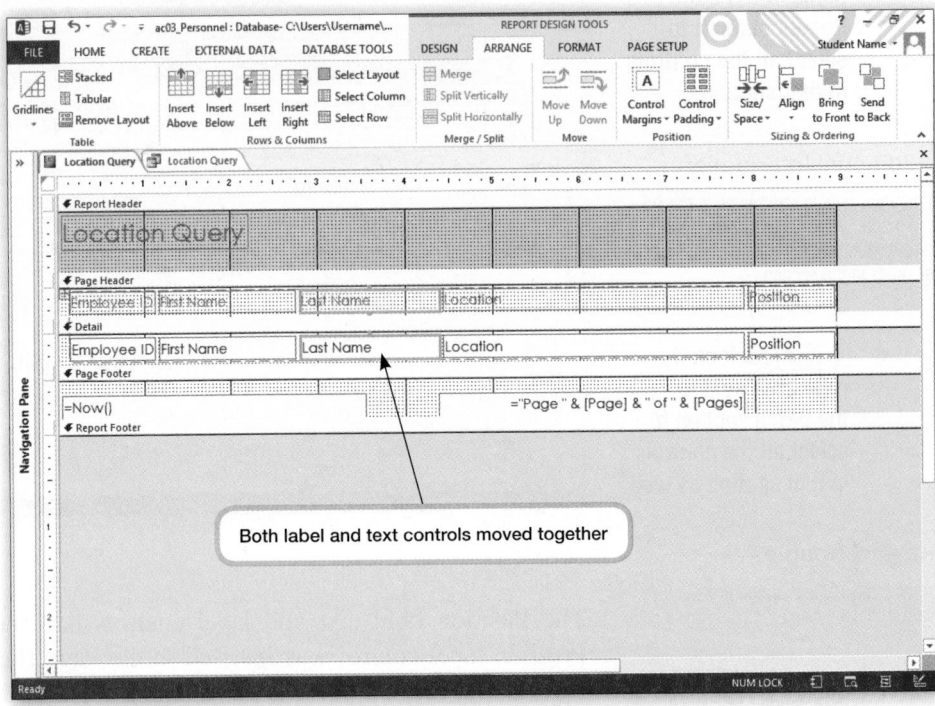

Both label and text controls moved together

Figure 3.65

Your screen should be similar to Figure 3.65

Notice that the Last Name label and text controls moved together because they were both selected. The controls in both the Page Header and Detail sections are horizontally and vertically aligned and spaced an equal distance apart.

FORMATTING CONTROLS

Next, you decide to change the text of the report title and center it over the report. First you will enlarge the Title control to extend the width of the report, and then center the text within the control.

1

- Select the report title control.

- Drag the right-middle sizing handle toward the right margin; stop at approximately 8″ on the ruler.

- Click ≡ Center in the Font group of the Report Design Tools Format tab.

- Click in the report title control and select the Location Query text.

- Type Job Position Report and then press ⏎Enter.

Your screen should be similar to Figure 3.66

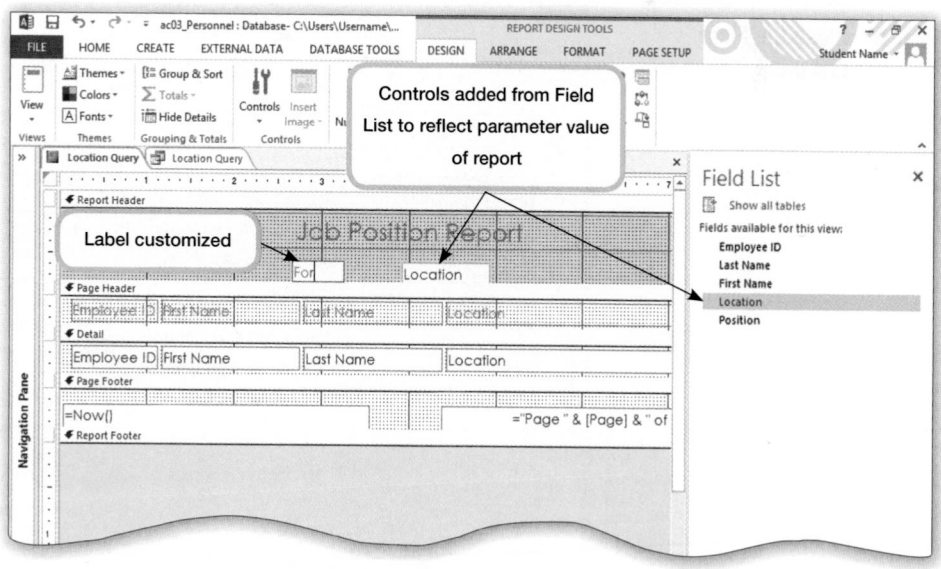

Figure 3.66

The revised title is centered over the report columns. Changing the title text does not change the name of the report object. You also want the work location to be included in the title because the report results could vary depending on what location you entered into the parameter dialog box when the report was opened. To make the title reflect the contents of the report, you will add the Location field to the Report Header area and then use the formatting tools to change its appearance.

2

- Click 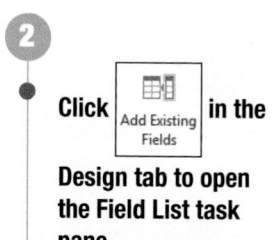 in the Design tab to open the Field List task pane.

- Drag the Location field into the Report Header section, below the title.

- Select and replace the text in the Location label control with For

Your screen should be similar to Figure 3.67

Figure 3.67

Next you will change the formatting of the Location controls by making them transparent, removing the outline border, and changing the font size and color.

- Click on the Location text control.

- Click 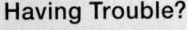 Shape Fill ▾ in the Control Formatting group of the Format tab and choose Transparent.

- Click ⬜ Shape Outline ▾ in the Control Formatting group and choose Transparent.

- Open the 11 ▾ Font Size drop-down list in the Font group and choose 18.

- Use the sizing handles to enlarge the Location text control to fully display the text.

Having Trouble?

In order to grab the corner sizing handles to increase the size of the control, you may need to expand the Report Header section. Do this by positioning the mouse on the top edge of the Page Header section bar and, when the mouse becomes ✛, dragging, the bar down slightly.

- Open the A ▾ Font Color gallery, and choose Dark Red from the Standard Colors section (last row, first column).

- Position and resize both control boxes as shown in Figure 3.68.

Having Trouble?

Use the large gray handle in the upper-left corner of a control to move each control individually.

- **Close the Field List pane.**

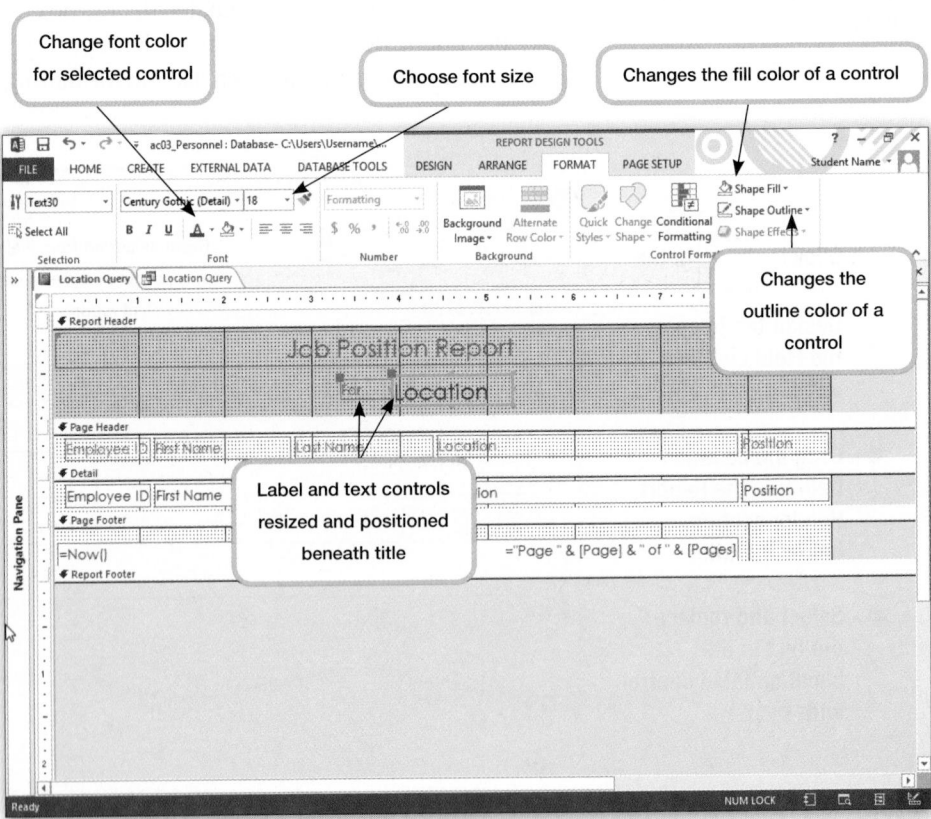

Change font color for selected control

Choose font size

Changes the fill color of a control

Changes the outline color of a control

Label and text controls resized and positioned beneath title

Figure 3.68

Your screen should be similar to **Figure 3.68**

When you were attempting to position the Location text and label controls, you may have noticed how they moved together. When the controls are associated and act as one when moved, they are called **compound controls**.

Now you want to see the effects of your changes. You will be prompted to enter the location. This time, you will enter Landis as the location, and the report title now will update to include the location information.

4
● **Switch to Layout view.**

● **Enter the location of Landis**

Your screen should be similar to Figure 3.69

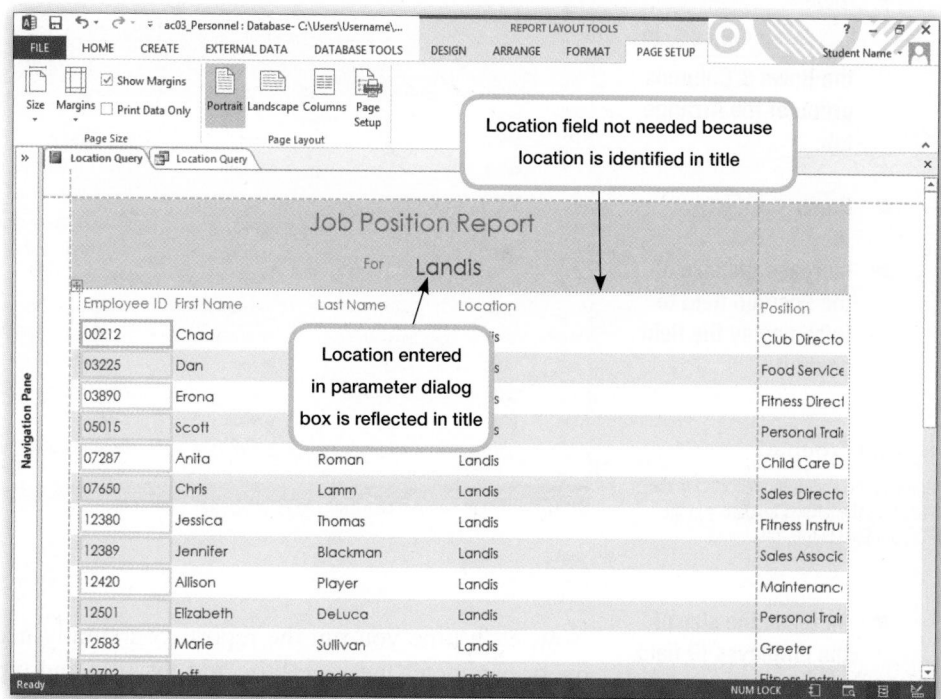

Figure 3.69

The report is really shaping up. However, there are still a few changes you need to make. You want to remove the Location field because the report title now identifies the location. Then you will adjust the sizes of the fields to make the report fill more of the width of the page.

DELETING A FIELD

You will delete the Location field and make adjustments to the other fields in Layout view so you can see the field content and layout while working with them.

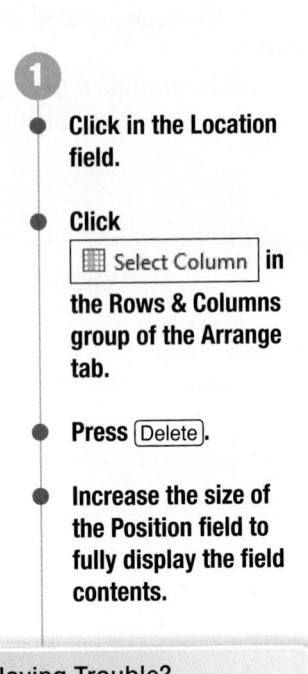

1

- Click in the Location field.

- Click 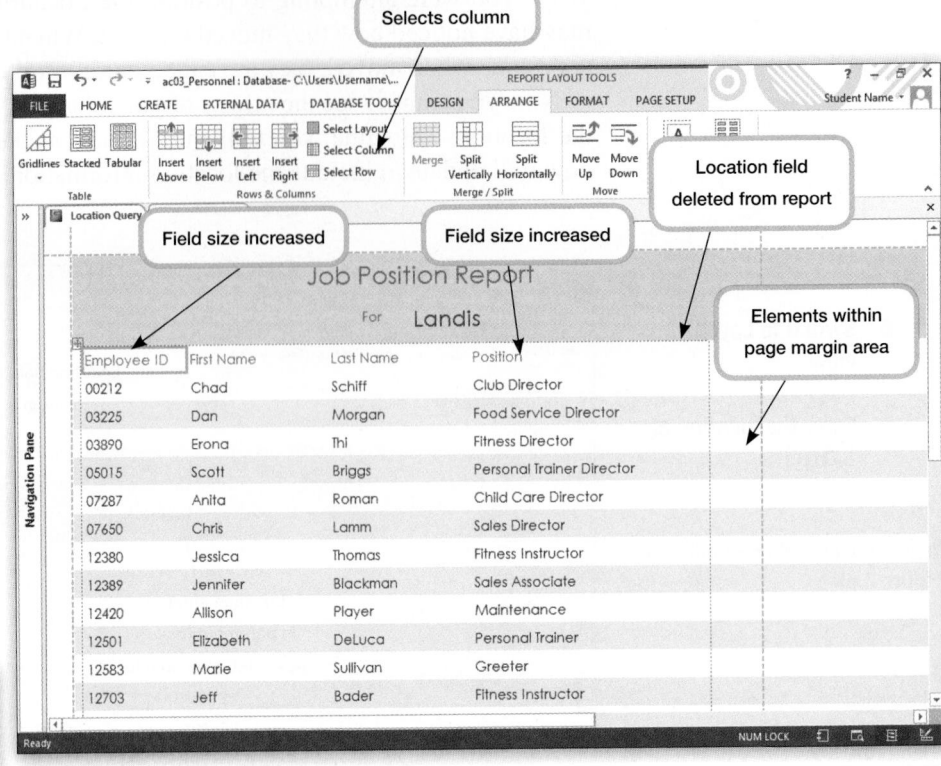 **Select Column** in the Rows & Columns group of the Arrange tab.

- Press Delete.

- Increase the size of the Position field to fully display the field contents.

Having Trouble?

Scroll to the end of the report to make sure that the largest text entry in the Position field is fully displayed.

- Increase the size of the Employee ID field slightly.

Your screen should be similar to Figure 3.70

Now, each time you run the report, you simply need to enter the location in the query parameter message box, and the title and report contents will reflect your input.

SORTING AND FILTERING DATA IN A REPORT

You also notice that the records in the report are in order by employee ID. This is because a sort order was not specified in the query or the report when they were created. Just as in a table datasheet, query, or form, you can sort and filter the data that is displayed in a report. You will use these features to sort the records in alphabetical order by last name and display only the records for employees whose job is fitness instructor.

Figure 3.70

1

- **Right-click on the Last Name field of any record.**

- **Choose Sort A to Z.**

- **Right-click on the Position field of any record that displays Fitness Instructor.**

- **Choose Equals "Fitness Instructor".**

Your screen should be similar to Figure 3.71

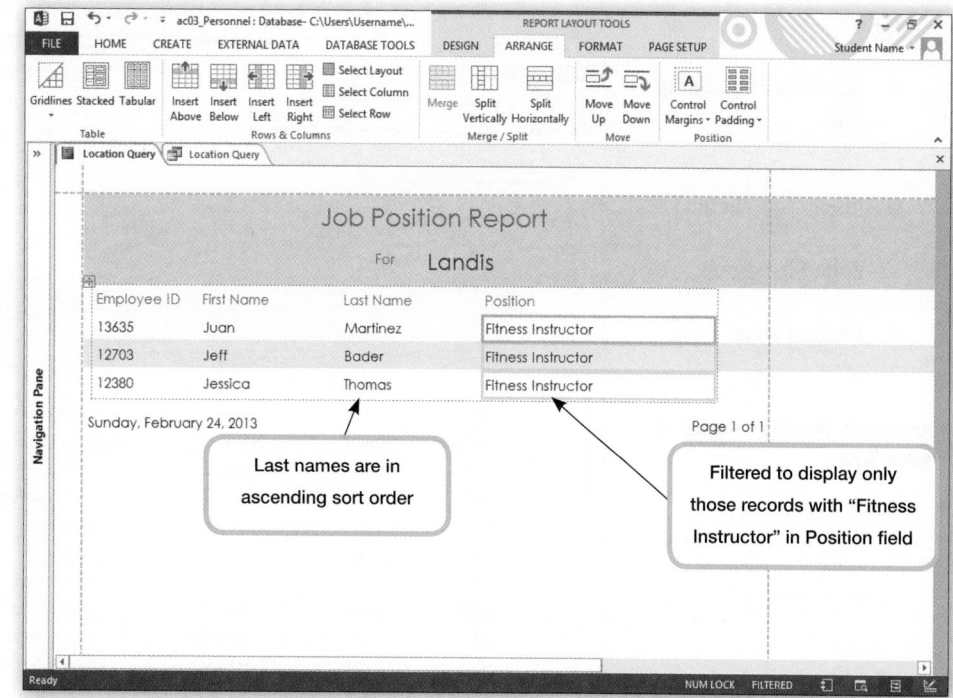

Figure 3.71

Only the three records meeting the filter requirements are displayed in the report. They are in alphabetical order by last name. You will remove the filter but maintain the sorted record order.

2

- **Right-click on the Position field of any record.**

- **Choose Clear filter from Position.**

Additional Information
You also can click ▼ Toggle Filter in the Home tab to remove the filter.

All the records are redisplayed again.

Preparing Reports for Printing

You can print the report from any view or even when the report is closed. However, unless you are sure the page settings are correct, it is a good idea to check how its elements are arranged in Layout view or Print Preview before printing. The advantage to Layout view is that you can instantly see how any changes made to the page layout will affect the printed report and you can make any needed adjustments.

MODIFYING THE PAGE SETUP

As you look at the layout of the report on the page, you see the report is not centered horizontally on the page and there is a lot of empty space to the right of the Position column. To fix this, you will increase the size of the right and left margins, from the Normal setting of 0.35 inch to the Wide setting of 0.75 inch. Then you will readjust the column widths.

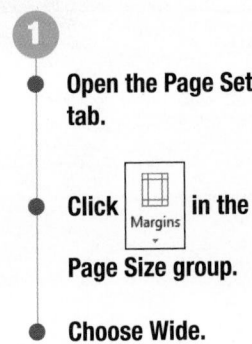

1

● Open the Page Setup tab.

● Click [Margins] in the Page Size group.

● Choose Wide.

Your screen should be similar to Figure 3.72

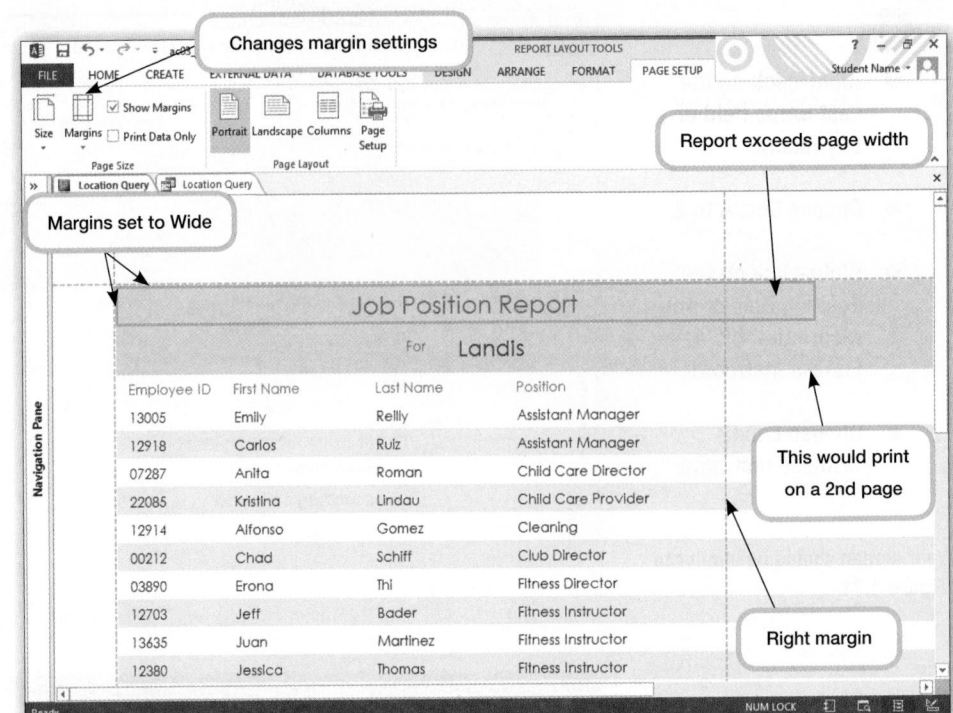

Changes margin settings

Report exceeds page width

Margins set to Wide

Job Position Report

For Landis

Employee ID	First Name	Last Name	Position
13005	Emily	Reilly	Assistant Manager
12918	Carlos	Ruiz	Assistant Manager
07287	Anita	Roman	Child Care Director
22085	Kristina	Lindau	Child Care Provider
12914	Alfonso	Gomez	Cleaning
00212	Chad	Schiff	Club Director
03890	Erona	Thi	Fitness Director
12703	Jeff	Bader	Fitness Instructor
13635	Juan	Martinez	Fitness Instructor
12380	Jessica	Thomas	Fitness Instructor

This would print on a 2nd page

Right margin

Figure 3.72

The Wide margin option increases the left and right margins to 0.75 inch. The columns now begin at 0.75 inch, and the report columns are pushed to the right making the report appear more balanced on the page; however, now the report width exceeds a single page. This is because some of the controls in the report exceed the new page margins. Additionally, the title is no longer centered because the control is wider than the new page width. These problems can be quickly fixed by reducing the size of the controls that are causing the problem. You decide to increase the margins to 1 inch and then make the adjustments to the controls to fit the new page width. To do this, you will set custom left and right margins.

②

- Click  in the **Page Layout group.**

- Enter **1** in the **Left and Right Margin text boxes.**

- Click OK.

- **Size the title control to fit the new page width.**

- **Select the Landis Location control and the For label control in the title area and move the controls so they are centered under the Job Position Report title.**

- **Move the Location control until the bottom of the text is even with the bottom of the text in the For control.**

- **Scroll to the bottom of the report and click on the Page Number control in the footer.**

- **Reduce the Page Number control size (from the right edge) until it is inside the right margin line.**

- **Adjust the sizes of the First Name and Last Name field columns until the report fits within the margins.**

- **Scroll to the top of the report.**

Your screen should be similar to Figure 3.73

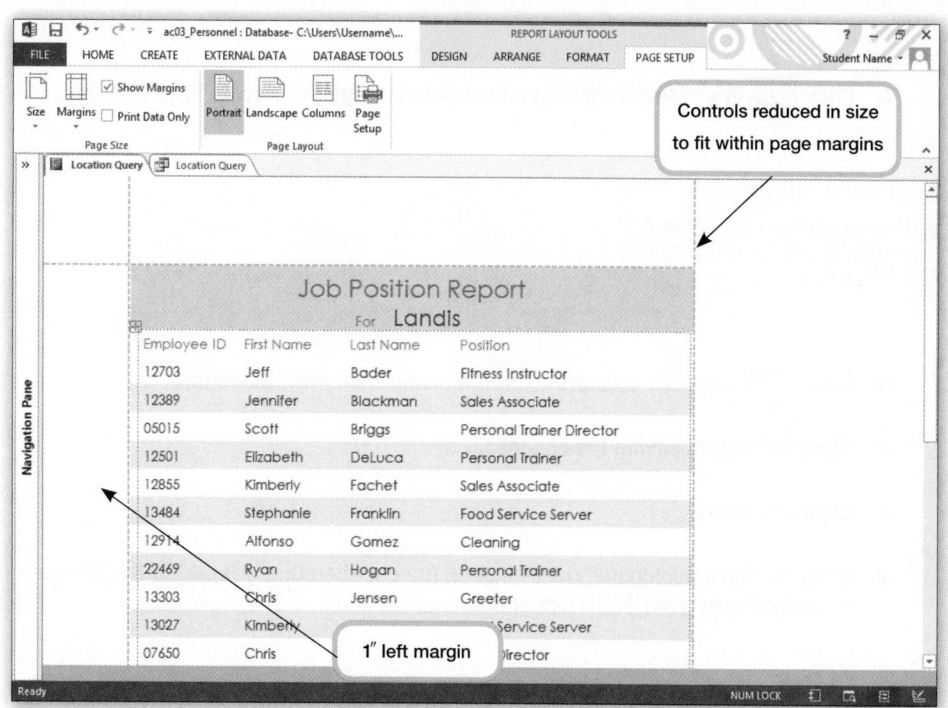

Figure 3.73

Now the columns are spaced attractively across the page. The page layout settings you specify are saved with the report, so unless you make changes to the report design, you only need to set them once.

PREVIEWING AND PRINTING REPORTS

Although you believe the report is ready to print, you will preview it first and then print it.

1

● Click **Print Preview in the status bar to change the view to Print Preview.**

Additional Information

You also can specify margins and page setup using the same features in the Print Preview ribbon.

● Click 🖶 . **Specify your printer settings and then print the report.**
  Print

● **Close the report, saving the changes.**

● **Close the query.**

● **Open the Navigation pane, right-click on the Location Query report in the Navigation pane, and choose Rename. Type in** Job Position Report **and then press** Enter **.**

Additional Information

If you do not like the default name, you can rename any objects in the Navigation pane as long as the object is not open in the work area.

Your printed report should look like the one shown in the case study at the beginning of the lab.

PRINTING A RELATIONSHIPS REPORT

Before exiting Access, you want to print a report that shows the relationships between the tables in your database.

1

● **Open the Database Tools tab.**

● Click
🖇️ *Relationships*

● **If necessary, click** 🔡 All Relationships **to show all table relationships.**

● **Click** 🖺 Relationship Report **in the Tools group.**

Having Trouble?

If necessary, click ⬜ Open ⬜ in response to the security message.

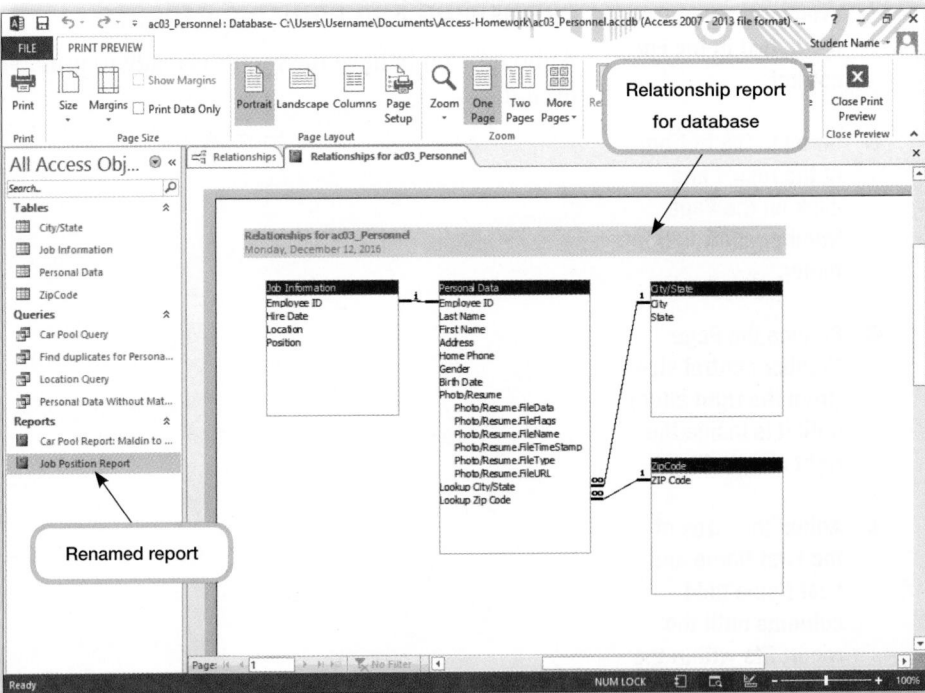

Figure 3.74

● **Print the report.**

Your screen should be similar to
Figure 3.74

A preview of how the report will look when printed is displayed. The database name and creation date are automatically used as the report header. You can print this report as well as save it for future reference.

- Close the relationship report without saving it.

- Close the Relationships window.

Compacting and Backing Up the Database

Additional Information

A file is fragmented when it becomes too large for your computer to store in a single location on your hard disk. When this happens, the file is split up and stored in pieces in different locations on the disk, making access to the data slower.

As you modify a database, the changes are saved to your disk. When you delete data or objects, the database file can become fragmented and use disk space inefficiently. To make the database perform optimally, you should **compact** the database on a regular basis. Compacting makes a copy of the file and rearranges the way that the file is stored on your disk.

- Open the File tab and if necessary, choose 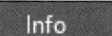.

- Click  to compact and repair the database.

Another Method

You can also use  in the Database Tools tab.

Although it appears that nothing has happened, the database file has been compacted and repaired as needed. It is also a good idea to back up your databases periodically. This will ensure that you have a copy of each database in case of a power outage or other system failure while you are working on a file, or in case you need to access a previous version of a database that you have changed.

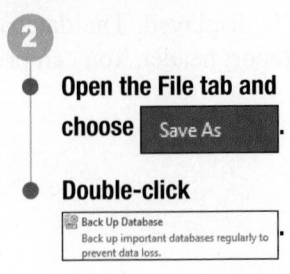

2

• **Open the File tab and choose** Save As .

• **Double-click**

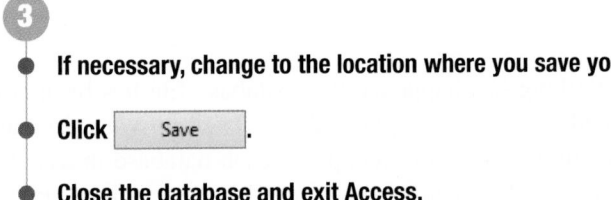

Back Up Database
Back up important databases regularly to
prevent data loss.

Your screen should be similar to Figure 3.75

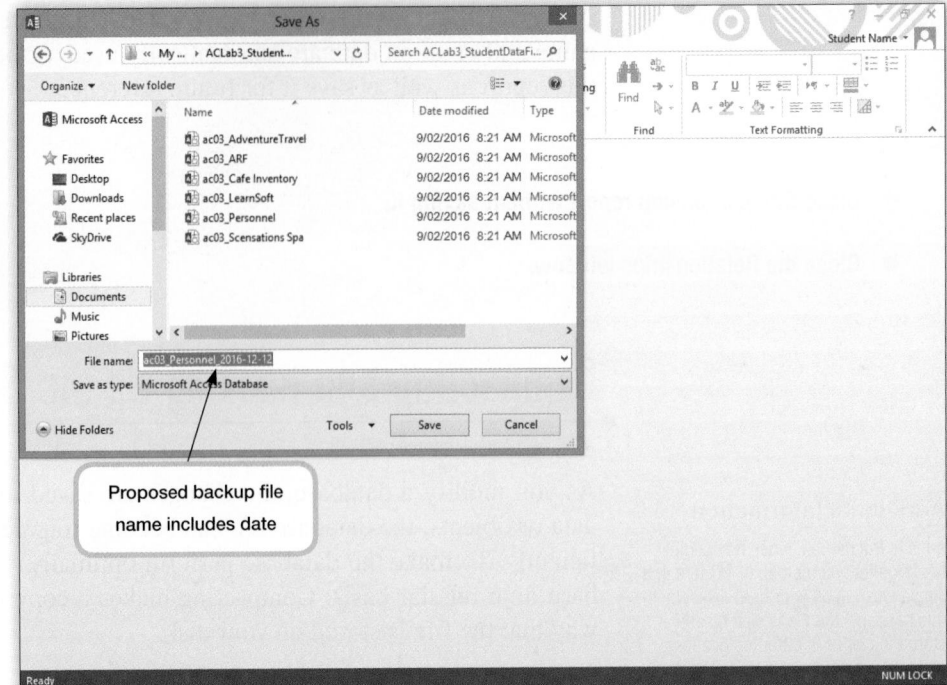

Proposed backup file
name includes date

Figure 3.75

The Save As dialog box displays the database file name (which in this case is ac03_Personnel) with the current date appended to it. This is a good way to keep track of when you performed the backup on the database, so you will not change this file name.

3

• **If necessary, change to the location where you save your solution files.**

• **Click** Save .

• **Close the database and exit Access.**

The backup database file has been saved to your solution file location. If you need to restore a backed-up database, you just change the name of the backup file (so it does not conflict with another file of the same name that you may have created since the backup) and then open it in Access.

ORE YOUR CAREER OPTIONS

base Administrator

ase administrators are responsible for organizing and aining an organization's information resources by work- th database management software to implement, ana- and organize the presentation and use of the data. The istrator usually controls user access, tests new objects, up the data, and trains new users to use the database.

As a database administrator, your position also would include safeguarding the system from threats, whether internal or via the Internet. The typical salary range of a database admin-istrator is $40,000 to $80,000, but with years of experi-ence an administrator can earn over $100,000. A bachelor's degree in computer science is typically preferred in addition to practical experience. Demand for skilled database admin-istrators is expected to make this one of the fastest-growing occupations.

Query (AC3.20)

A query is a request for specific data contained in a database. Queries are used to view data in different ways, to analyze data, and even to change existing data.

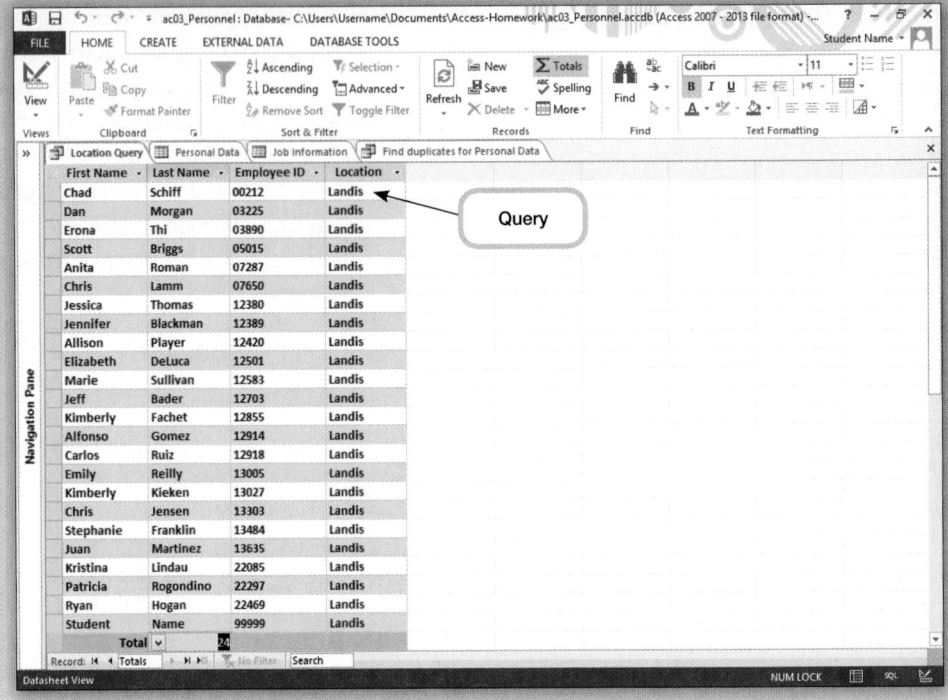

Join (AC3.26)

A join is an association that is created in a query between a field in one table or query and a field of the same data type in another table or query.

Query Criteria (AC3.29)

Query criteria are expressions that are used to restrict the results of a query to display only records that meet certain limiting conditions.

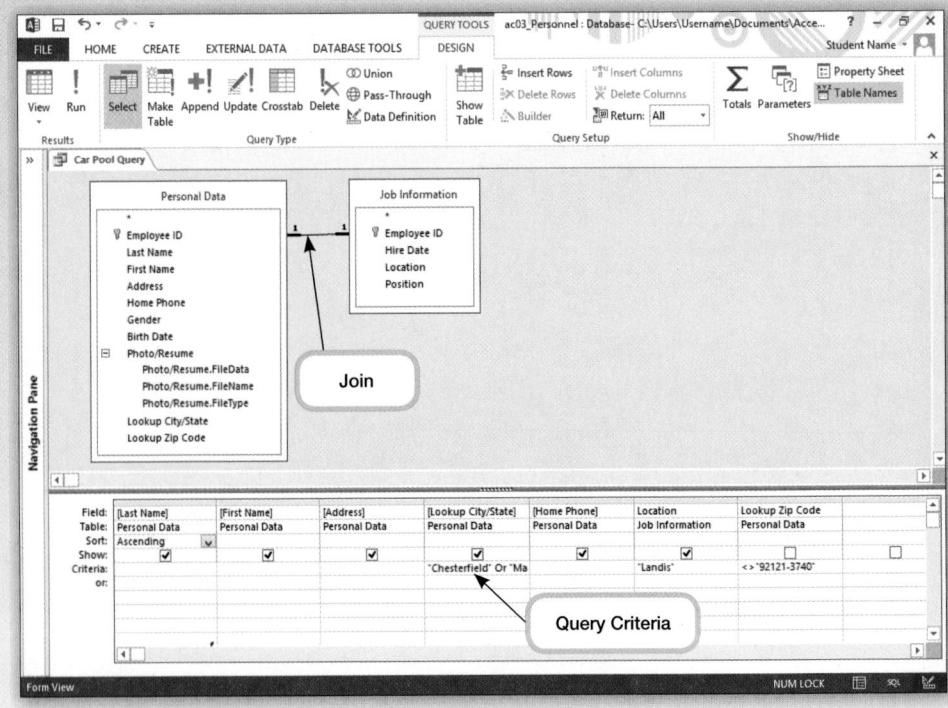

Report (AC3.46)

A report is professional-appearing output generated from tables or queries that may include design elements, groups, and summary information.

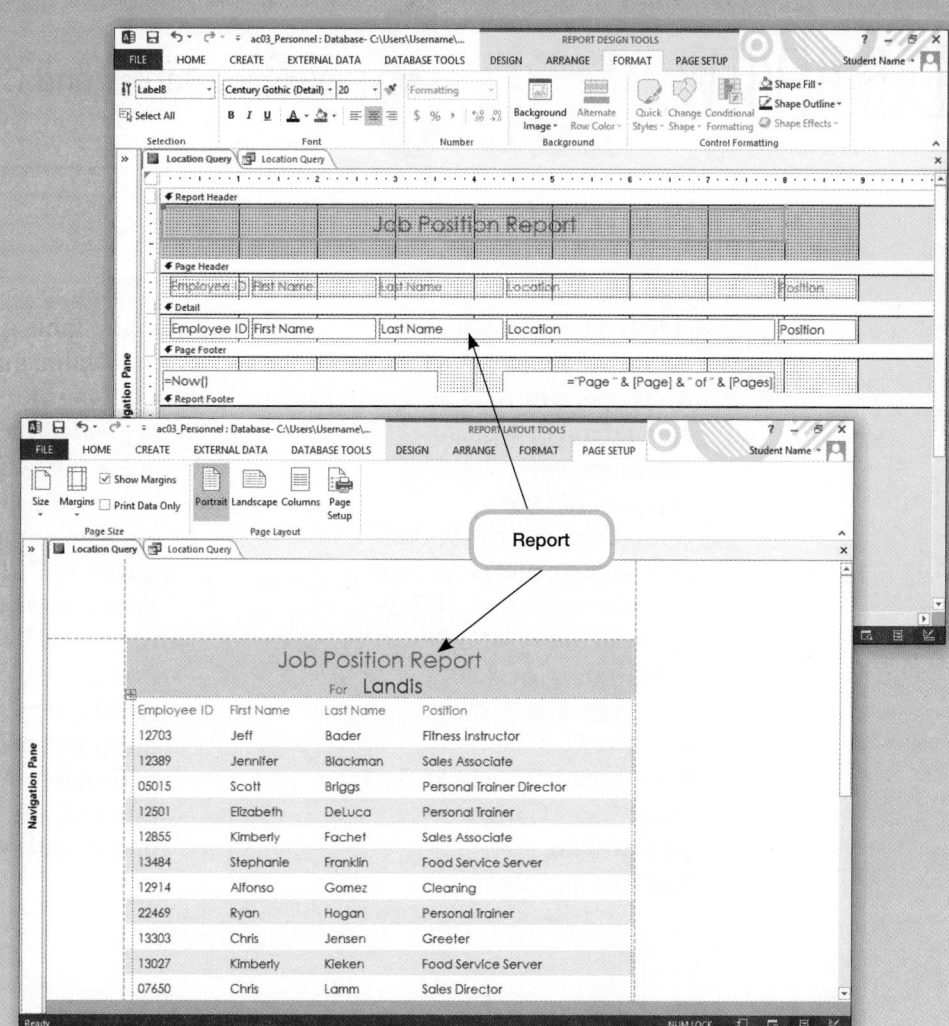

KEY TERMS

action query AC3.20	make-table query AC3.20
aggregate functions AC3.45	multitable query AC3.25
AND operator AC3.29	OR operator AC3.29
append query AC3.20	orphaned record AC3.18
column selector bar AC3.25	outer join AC3.28
compact AC3.69	parameter query AC3.20
compound control AC3.63	parameter value AC3.43
compound criteria AC3.29	query AC3.20
criteria expression AC3.29	query criteria AC3.29
crosstab query AC3.20	report AC3.46
delete query AC3.20	row label AC3.25
design grid AC3.25	select query AC3.20
field list AC3.25	Show box AC3.25
hard-coded criteria AC3.43	SQL query AC3.20
inner join AC3.28	unequal join AC3.28
join AC3.26	update query AC3.20
join line AC3.26	

COMMAND SUMMARY

Command	Shortcut	Action
File Tab		
Info / Compact & Repair Database		Compacts and repairs database file
Save As / Save Database As		Saves database with a new file name.
Save As / Save Object As		Saves database object with a new name
Save As / Back Up Database — Back up important databases regularly to prevent data loss.		Backs up database
Home tab		
Views group		
View — Report View		Displays report in Report view
View — Report Layout View		Displays report in Layout view
Records group		
Refresh All		Updates selected object
Σ Totals		Displays/hides Totals row
Create tab		
Queries group		
Query Wizard		Creates a query using the Query Wizard
Query Design		Creates a query using Query Design view
Reports group		
Report		Creates a report using all fields in current table
Report Design		Creates a report using Report Design view
Report Wizard		Creates a report using the Report Wizard

COMMAND SUMMARY (CONTINUED)

Command	Shortcut	Action
Database Tools tab		
Relationships group		
Relationships		Defines how the data in tables is related
Analyze group		
Analyze Table		Evaluates table design
Query Tools Design tab		
Results group		
! Run		Displays query results in Query Datasheet view
Query Setup group		
Show Table		Displays/hides Show Table dialog box
Show/Hide group		
Table Names		Displays/hides the Table row
Report Layout Tools Design tab		
Tools group		
Add Existing Fields	Alt + F8	Displays/hides Add Existing Fields task pane
Themes group		
Themes		Applies predesigned theme styles to report
Report Layout Tools Arrange tab		
Table group		
Tabular		Arranges controls in a stacked tabular arrangement
Rows & Columns group		
Select Column		Selects column
Report Layout Tools Format tab		
Font group		
A ▾ Font color		Changes color of text
11 ▾ Font Size		Used to change the font size of text

COMMAND SUMMARY (CONTINUED)

Command	Shortcut	Action
☰ Align Text Left		Aligns text at left edge of control
☰ Center		Centers text in selected control
Control Formatting group		
🪣 Shape Fill ▾		Changes the color fill inside a control
✏️ Shape Outline ▾		Opens menu to change the border color and line thickness
Report Layout Tools Page Setup tab		
Page Size group		
Margins ▾		Sets margins of printed report
Page Layout group		
Page Setup		Sets features related to the page layout of printed report
Relationship Tools Design tab		
Tools group		
Edit Relationships		Opens the Relationships window where you can to edit the relationships between tables
Relationship Report		Creates a report of the displayed relationships
Relationships group		
All Relationships		Displays all tables and any relationship join lines there may be
Print Preview tab		
Page Size group		
Margins		Adjusts margins in printed output

LAB EXERCISES

MATCHING

Match the numbered item with the correct lettered description.

1. [Run button icon] _____ a. set of limiting conditions

2. aggregate functions _____ b. prompts you for the specific criteria you want to use when you run the query

3. cell _____ c. query that uses data from more than one table

4. compact _____ d. runs a query and displays a query datasheet

5. multitable query _____ e. used to ask questions about database tables

6. orphaned record _____ f. calculations that are performed on a range of data

7. parameter value _____ g. the most common type of query

8. query _____ h. intersection of a column and row

9. query criteria _____ i. record that refer to a nonexistent record in an associated table

10. select query _____ j. makes a copy of the file and rearranges the way that the file is stored on your disk

TRUE/FALSE

Circle the correct answer to the following statements.

1. Values that tell Access how to filter the criteria in a query are called filter expressions. — True False

2. Reports can be generated from tables only. — True False

3. A query can be created with information from more than one table. — True False

4. A join line shows how different tables are related. — True False

5. A field cannot be added to a report without using the Report Wizard. — True False

6. Queries are used to view data in different ways, to analyze data, and to change existing data. — True False

7. A delete query is the most common type of query. — True False

8. A compound criterion is created using the AND operator. — True False

9. A compound control consists of two controls that are associated. — True False

10. Hard-coded criteria are used each time the query is run. — True False

FILL-IN

Complete the following statements by filling in the blanks with the correct terms.

1. The operator that narrows the search for records meeting both conditions is known as the _____ operator.

2. Aggregate functions perform _____ on a range of data.

3. The Page Setup tab is used to control the page layout of the report for _____ purposes.

4. A request for specific data contained in a database is called a _____.

5. In a report, a(n) _____ is not connected to a field.

6. Entering a criteria _____ is similar to using a formula and may contain constants, field names, and/or operators.

7. The _____ is where you enter the settings that define the query.

8. The _____ is used to display the results of a query.

9. To be joined, tables must have at least one _____ field.

10. In a form a(n) _____ control is used to enter multiple criteria.

LAB EXERCISES

MULTIPLE CHOICE

Circle the letter of the correct response.

1. Bound and unbound are types of _____.
   a. buttons
   b. controls
   c. forms
   d. properties

2. The _____ operator broadens the filter, because any record meeting either condition is included in the output.
   a. ALL
   b. AND
   c. MOST
   d. OR

3. _____ view can be used to view the data in a report and modify the report design and layout.
   a. Datasheet
   b. Design
   c. Layout
   d. Print Preview

4. When a file is _____, it uses disk space inefficiently.
   a. broken
   b. compacted
   c. fragmented
   d. repaired

5. _____ view is used to create and modify the structure of a query.
   a. Datasheet
   b. Design
   c. Layout
   d. Update

6. A(n) _____ query prompts the user to enter the desired criteria each time the query is run.
   a. append
   b. parameter
   c. SQL
   d. update

7. A report title is a(n) _____ control because it is not connected to a field.
   a. associated
   b. bound
   c. text
   d. unbound

8. The _____ operator is assumed when you enter criteria in multiple fields.
   a. AND
   b. BETWEEN
   c. EQUAL TO
   d. OR

9. The query _____ is where you enter the settings that define the query.
   a. design grid
   b. field list
   c. object
   d. Show box

10. A join line creates a _____ relationship that establishes rules that the data must match to be included in the query results.
    a. permanent
    b. partial
    c. temporary
    d. complete

LAB EXERCISES

Hands-On Exercises

RATING SYSTEM

★   Easy

★★   Moderate

★★★   Difficult

STEP-BY-STEP

ROCKY MOUNTAIN REAL ESTATE RENTALS ★

1. As your property rental business has grown, you've noticed that potential renters usually want to search by price and date availability. You decide to create a query to determine inventory according to these parameters. Your completed query will be similar to that shown here.

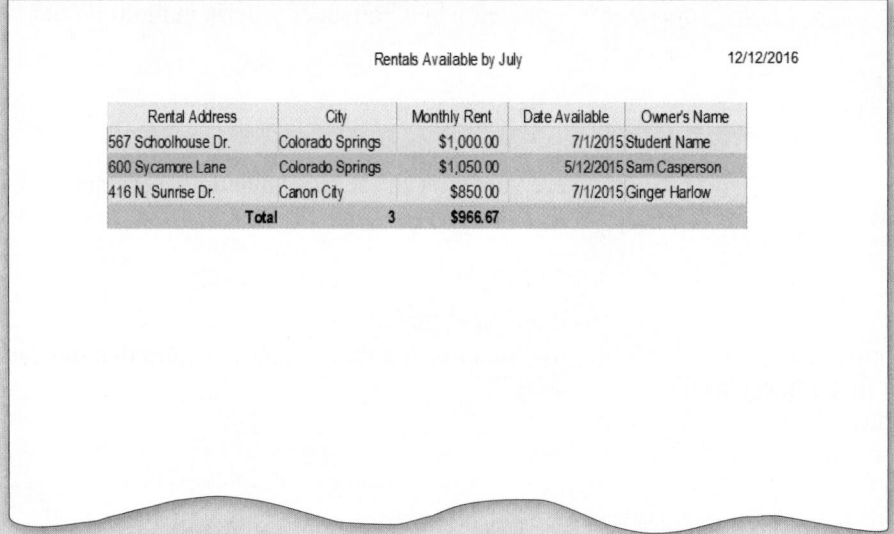

Rentals Available by July				12/12/2016
Rental Address	City	Monthly Rent	Date Available	Owner's Name
567 Schoolhouse Dr.	Colorado Springs	$1,000.00	7/1/2015	Student Name
600 Sycamore Lane	Colorado Springs	$1,050.00	5/12/2015	Sam Casperson
416 N. Sunrise Dr.	Canon City	$850.00	7/1/2015	Ginger Harlow
Total	3	$966.67		

a. Open the Rocky Mountain Rentals-2 database you modified in Lab 2, Step-by-Step Exercise 4, page AC2.98, and save the database as Rocky Mountain Rentals-3.

b. Open the Rental Homes form and add the following two new records shown below. Leave the Animal Permission at the default "Pets not okay."

Rental Address:	1661 Golden Hawk Circle	567 Schoolhouse Drive
City:	Cimmaron Hills	Colorado Springs
Rented:	Y	N
Date Available:	6/15/2015	7/1/2015
Bedrooms/Baths:	3/2	2/2
Sq Footage:	1400	1300
Monthly Rent:	$850	$1000
Owner's Name:	Kelsey McGee	Your name
Comments:	Make appointment to view	Victorian home in historic district

c. Close the form.

d. Use the Query Wizard to create a query based on the Rental Homes table. Include, in this order, the Rental Address, City, Monthly Rent, Date Available, Rented, and Owner's Name fields. Save the query as **Rentals Available by July** and then modify the query design. In Query Design view, type in criteria of **<=July 1, 2015** for the date available and **<=1100** for the monthly rent.

e. Run the query and examine the results. There should be 4 records that meet the criteria. Next, filter the query to show only the records for the homes that are not currently rented. Best fit the query datasheet columns. Hide the Rented field. Display a Totals row with a count in the City column and an Average in the Monthly Rent column. Print the query results.

f. Close all objects. Compact and repair the database. Exit Access.

SCENSATIONS SPA DATABASE ★★

2. The Scensations Salon and Day Spa offers hair and spa treatments exclusively for women. The owner of the spa is offering a new spa package that would include various anti-aging skin treatments and massages. She wants to send an announcement about this package to her clients who are over the age of 45. You will get this information for her from the client information that is stored in an Access 2013 database file. Your printed report will be similar to that shown here.

a. Open the database file named ac03_Scensations Spa and the table named Clients.

b. Find and delete any duplicate records using the Last Name field as the field to check for duplicate data. Include the Client ID, First Name, and Birth Date as the additional fields to display. Save the query as **Find duplicates for Clients**. Delete the duplicate record with the higher Client ID#. Close the query.

Clients 45+ Report

First Name	Last Name	Address	City	State/Province	ZIP/Postal Code
Lisa	Anderson	7428 S. Hill	Yerington	NV	89447
Beatrice	Arnold	369 N. Main	Yerington	NV	89447
Alma	Austin	560 E. Hickory	Smith Valley	NV	89430
Kristen	Chavez	861 S. Tenth	Smith Valley	NV	89430
Gloria	Cook	224 E. Laurel	Dayton	NV	89403
Phyllis	Foster	27984 W. Dogwood	Femley	NV	89408
Robin	Hayes	861 N. Fourth	Femley	NV	89408
Andrea	Henderson	8666 N. 9th	Dayton	NV	89403
Barbara	Jones	738 N. Eighth	Smith Valley	NV	89430
Elsie	Kelley	1008 W. 11th	Silver City	NV	89428
Erica	Matthews	738 E. Sixth	Yerington	NV	89447
Peggy	Myers	492 S. Lincoln	Femley	NV	89408
Student	Name	123 Any Street	Silver City	NV	89428
Sue	Peters	1238 E. Fourth	Silver City	NV	89428
Doris	Reed	10494 N. Forest	Dayton	NV	89403
Vanessa	Sims	784 N. Cherry	Smith Valley	NV	89430
Dawn	Sullivan	369 E. 8th	Femley	NV	89408
Dorothy	Taylor	1238 E. Fifth	Smith Valley	NV	89430
Linda	Williams	495 W. Cherry	Smith Valley	NV	89430

Monday, December 12, 2016   Page 1 of 1

c. Use the Table Analyzer Wizard to create a second table containing the city, state, and ZIP code information. Name the new table **City/State/Zip**. Make the Zip Code field the primary key in this table.

LAB EXERCISES

d. Delete the original Clients table. Close Table1 that the wizard created, and then rename it as **Clients table**. Open the table again and then move the City/State/Zip lookup field after the Address field. Best fit all the fields in the table.

e. Create a query to find clients older than 45 years of age by adding the First Name, Last Name, Address, and Birth Date fields from the Clients table to the query. Name the query **Clients 45+ Query**. Switch to Design view, show the City/State/Zip table, and add all the fields from it to the query design grid. Sort by the Last Name in ascending order. Enter criteria to find those records with a birth date before **1/1/71**. Save and run the query. If you get an error message, click OK as necessary. Best fit the columns.

f. Move the Birth Date field to the first position in the datasheet. Display a Totals row showing a count of the Last Name field. Save the query. Print the query results in portrait orientation with normal margins.

g. Use the Report Wizard to create a report with the client names and addresses, based on the Clients 45+ query. Choose landscape orientation and the tabular layout. Save the report as **Clients 45+ Report**.

h. Change the report margins to normal. Switch to Layout view. Select all the controls except those containing the title, date, and page numbering. Apply the tabular layout to the controls, and then adjust the controls to fit the report on a single page widthwise.

i. Add a new record to the Clients table that includes your name in the First Name and Last Name fields and a birth date of **2/11/65**. Enter an address and phone number of your choice.

j. Refresh the query and report to update them.

k. Print the report.

l. Compact and repair the database. Back up the database.

m. Close the database, saving as needed, and exit Access.

DOWNTOWN INTERNET CAFÉ INVENTORY ★★

3. The Inventory database you created for the Downtown Internet Café (Lab 1, Step-by-Step Exercise 4) has been in use several weeks now and is working well. During this time, you have modified the table design and added more information to the table. Evan, the owner, has asked you to submit a daily report on all low-quantity items so he can place the necessary orders. You will use the database to moni-

tor inventory levels and respond to Evan's request. First, you decide to run a query to find the low-stock items, and then you can generate the requested report from the query. Your completed report should look similar to the report below.

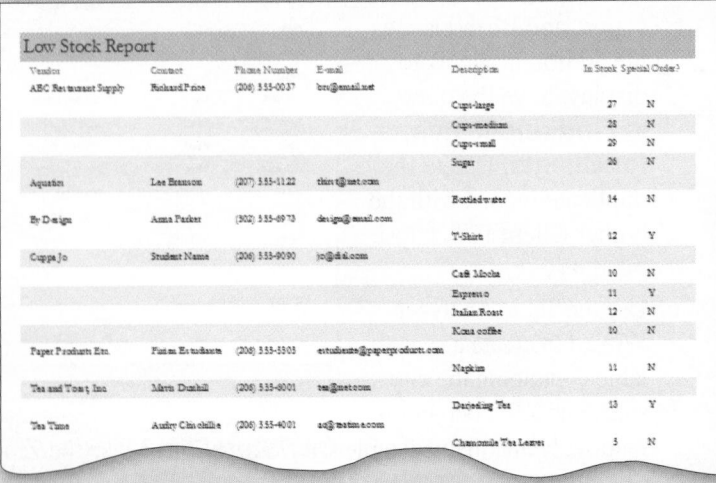

a. Open the database file named ac03_Cafe Inventory. Open the Stock table to view its contents. Open the Suppliers table, replace the contact for Cuppa Jo (Joseph Tan) with your name. Close both tables.

b. Use the Query Wizard to create a query based on the Stock table. Include all fields, except Item, in their current order. Name the query **Low Stock**.

c. In Query Design view, enter the criteria to display only those records with an In Stock value less than **30**, and run the query.

d. Upon reviewing the query results, you realize that the query needs to include the contact names, phone numbers, and e-mail addresses for Evan to use when he places orders. Switch to Design view and show the Suppliers table list. Add the Vendor, Contact, Phone Number, and E-mail fields from the Suppliers table to the query design. Uncheck the Vendor # field so that is does not show, and then run, save, and close the query.

e. Use the Report Wizard to create a report based on the Low Stock query. Include all the fields in the order listed. Choose to view the data by Suppliers, and select Description to be sorted in ascending order. Select the stepped layout and landscape orientation. Name the report **Low Stock Report**.

f. In Design view, select the label and text box controls in both the Page Header, Vendor Header, and Detail sections. Apply the tabular layout arrangement. In Report Layout view, change the theme design for the report to Organic. Resize the control box for the title, and then change the title font color to a color of your choice. Change the margin setting to normal, and then adjust the field column widths as needed to appropriately display the data. Center the data in the Special Order column. Resize or move any controls that cause the report to overlap to a second page.

g. Preview and print the report. Close the Report window, saving the changes.

h. Compact and repair the database.

i. Back up the database. Exit Access.

ADVENTURE TRAVEL TOURS ★★

4. You have continued working on the database you created for Adventure Travel Tours in Lab 2, On Your Own Exercise 1. Although you are pleased with it, it still needs some revisions to make booking trips easier, as well as a price sheet for selected packages to give to potential customers. Your finished report will appear similar to that shown below.

a. Open ac03_AdventureTravel and then open the Clients table. Add a new record with your name as Client **99999**, and fill out the remaining information for your client record, using Denver for the City and Office fields.

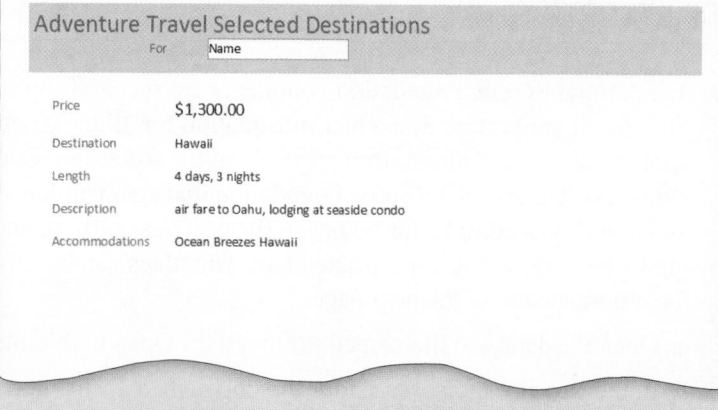

b. Create a new table named **Trip Sales**. In Design view, enter **Sale #** as an AutoNumber ID field and set it as the primary key. Create a lookup field called **Client**, based on the Client table, and use the Last Name and First Name fields sorted in ascending order. Create a lookup field called **Package**, using the Package table. Include the Destination and

LAB EXERCISES

Length fields, and sort in ascending order by destination. Make sure to adjust all column widths when prompted to do so in the wizard. Lastly, create a lookup field called **Agent**, based on the Agent table, and use the agent's last and first names, sorted in ascending order.

c. Switch to Datasheet view and assign trips to these customers:

Client	Package	Agent
Your Name	Hawaii	Mary Cook
Allen Bozin	Lake Tahoe	Mark Milligan
Torri Dunn	Caribbean, 8 days	Lynn Sims
Cindy Miller	Washington DC	Mary Cook

d. Edit the relationships for the four tables. Enforce referential integrity for all relationships. Print the relationships report.

e. Create a parameter query named **Destination Query** that displays all fields from the Package table and the Client field from the Trip Sales table. Type **[Enter Destination]** in the criteria box for the Destination field. Run and test the query using the destination of **Caribbean**. Save and close.

f. Using the Report Wizard, create a report using the Destination Query. Include the Destination, Length, Description, Accommodations, and Price fields. Sort by price in ascending order. Use the columnar layout and portrait orientation. Save the report as **Adventure Travel Selected Destinations**. Type in **Hawaii** when prompted to enter the destination.

g. Modify the report in Design view. Change the font size for the Price text box control to 14 points, and align the text to the left. Add the Client field to the report header, under the Adventure Travel Selected Destinations title. Change the Client label by deleting the word "Client" and typing in the word **For**. In Layout view, apply the stacked layout to the labels and text controls in the Detail area before adjusting the width of any controls as needed. Print the report.

h. Add your name as the author to the database properties.

i. Compact and repair the database. Save any changes and exit Access.

ARF REPORTS ★★★

5. The Animal Rescue Foundation volunteers are successfully using the database you created in Lab 2, Step-by-Step Exercise 3, to enter information for all the rescued animals. Meanwhile, you created another table containing information about the foster homes (including names, addresses, and phone numbers). The Animal Rescue Foundation management has now asked you for a report, shown below, of all animals placed in foster homes in the past year (2016), and the names and addresses of those providing foster care, so the appropriate thank-you notes can be sent. Your completed report will be similar to the report shown on the next page.

a. Open the database file named ac03_ARF. Open both tables to review their content.

b. In the Rescues table, search for the dog named Tasha, update the information for foster date to **4/15/2016**, and attach the photo ac03_Tasha. Update her status to reflect that she is being fostered.

c. In the Fosters table, add your name as a new foster parent with the ID number **F-999**. Enter an address and phone number of your choice, but use the city of **Tempe**. Close the Fosters table.

d. Use the Query Wizard to find and delete any duplicate records in the Fosters table using the Last Name field as the field to check for duplicate data. Use the Foster ID, First Name, and Street as the additional fields to help you check for duplicates. Delete the duplicate records that have the highest Foster ID number. Close the query.

e. To generate the requested information, you need to add a new field to the Rescues table that identifies the

2016 Foster Parents Report

Foster First Name	Foster Last Name	Foster Street	Foster City	Foster State	Foster Zip	Type
Nathan	Bromley	24 Broadway Rd.	Mesa	AZ	85205-0346	Cat
Fran	Calco	799 Summer St.	Tempe	AZ	86301-1268	Horse
Fran	Calco	799 Summer St.	Tempe	AZ	86301-1268	Cat
Betty	Cavender	453 Orange St.	Tempe	AZ	85201-1268	Dog
Tricia	Franko	1289 S. Hayden Rd.	Mesa	AZ	85205-0346	Cat
Judith	Gold	663 Alameda Dr.	Scottsdale	AZ	85201-6760	Cat
Lucy	Granger	61 Lincoln Blvd.	Mesa	AZ	85205-0346	Cat
Bradley	Hawkins	789 University Ave.	Tempe	AZ	85201-1268	Cat
Mark	Lemon	900 Thomas Rd.	Phoenix	AZ	82891-9999	Cat
Cathy	Lind	1271 Rawhide Circle	Chandler	AZ	83174-2311	Dog
Cathy	Lind	1271 Rawhide Circle	Chandler	AZ	83174-2311	Cat
Susan	Malik	22 Sunrise Dr.	Mesa	AZ	85205-0346	Dog
Allyn	McMurphy	111 S. Central Rd.	Phoenix	AZ	82891-9999	Cat
Student	Name	123 Any Street	Tempe	AZ	85201-1268	Horse
John	Ryan	1020 Alameda Rd.	Chandler	AZ	83174-2311	Dog
John	Ryan	1020 Alameda Rd.	Chandler	AZ	83174-2311	Cat
Roy	Smithson	2020 Main St.	Phoenix	AZ	82891-9999	Dog
Brian	Steckler	1033 First Ave.	Phoenix	AZ	82891-9999	Dog
Susannah	Troy	13 College Ave.	Tempe	AZ	86301-1268	Dog
Kurt	Valdez	44 Franklin Dr.	Phoenix	AZ	82891-9999	Dog
Alex	Vine	676 Palm Ave.	Tempe	AZ	85201-1268	Dog
Ned	Young	387 Rawhide Rd.	Chandler	AZ	83174-2311	Dog

Monday, December 12, 2016   Page 1 of 1

foster person that was assigned to the animal. Instead of checking the Fosters table to find the number and then entering the number in the Rescues table, you will make the new field a lookup field that will display values from the Fosters table.

With the Rescues table open in Design view, add the **Foster ID#** field after the Foster Date field of the Rescues table. Select Lookup Wizard from the Data Type list. Select the following options from the Lookup Wizard:

- Look up values in a table.
- Use the Fosters table.
- Display the Foster ID#, Foster Last Name, and Foster First Name fields.
- Sort by the last and first names.
- Clear the Hide key column option, and then adjust the widths as needed.
- Select Foster ID# as the value to store.
- Use the Foster ID# field name.

f. Switch to Datasheet view. You need to enter the Foster ID# for all animals that have been in a foster home but decide to use a query to help you with the process. Create a query to display only the pets that have had a foster in 2016. Display the animal's Name, Status, Foster Date, and Foster ID# columns only. Name the query **Fosters for 2016**. In Query Design view, type in **>=1/1/2016** for the Foster Date criteria. When you run the query, only the pets with a foster in 2016 should display. From the Foster ID# drop-down list, assign a foster parent to each animal (the foster list is quite long, and you can scroll to choose more names). Select your name as the foster parent for the last animal. Save the changes to the query.

g. Next you will modify the query to display the information you need in the report. Add the Fosters

LAB EXERCISES

table to the query design, and resize both table field lists to fully display their information. Delete the Foster ID# field from the grid. Add the following fields from the tables specified in the order listed below.

Rescues table

- Type

Fosters table

- Foster First Name
- Foster Last Name
- Foster Street
- Foster City
- Foster State
- Foster Zip

h. Sort the Foster Last Name column in ascending order. Run the query and review the resulting datasheet. Hide the Status field. Save the query as **2016 Foster Parents**.

i. Use the Report Wizard to create a report based on the 2016 Foster Parents query you just saved. Include the following fields in the order listed below:

- Foster First Name
- Foster Last Name
- Foster Street
- Foster City
- Foster State
- Foster Zip
- Type

j. View the data by Rescues; sort by last name in ascending order. Use the tabular layout and landscape orientation. Name the report **2016 Foster Parents Report**.

k. Change the page margin setting to .75" left and right, .5" top and bottom. Switch to Design view. Center the Report Header control at the top of the page. Change the theme to one of your choice. Apply the tabular table layout to all the controls in the Page Header and Detail sections. Use Layout view to size the controls as needed to enhance the report appearance and fit the entire report on a single page.

l. Preview and then print the report. Close the report window, saving the changes you made.

m. Compact and repair the database.

n. Back up the database and exit Access.

ON YOUR OWN

TIMELESS TREASURES REPORT ★

1. The owners of Timeless Treasures have decided to expand their offerings to include vintage clocks as well as watches. Open the database file Timeless Treasures that you worked on in Lab 2, On Your Own Exercise 5. Revisit the web to obtain information on vintage clocks. Create a second table in the database with the same fields as the Watches table to use for maintaining the clock inventory. Name this table **Clocks**. Enter 10 records in the new table. Create an inventory report called **Timeless Treasures Watches Inventory** that displays the Identification Number, Description, Price, and Quantity on Hand fields of information. Use a layout and theme of your choice. Modify the report design as needed to improve its appearance. Create the same report for the Clocks table and name it **Timeless Treasures Clocks Inventory**. Preview and print both reports. Compact and back up the database.

DENTAL OFFICE CAR POOL LIST ★

2. As the office manager at Jones & Smith Dentistry, you see a need to arrange car pooling for the employees. Open the Dental Patients database you worked with in Lab 2, On Your Own Exercise 3. Create a table named **Employees** that includes fields for the employee ID number, first and last names, and home contact information (street, city, state, ZIP code, and phone). Enter eight records in the table. For the employee's city, choose from these three cities: **Williams**, **Flagstaff**, and **Munds Park**. Include your name as the employee name in one of the records. Then use this table to create a query that includes only the employee first and last names and home address fields of information. Sort the query by city. Enter the criteria of Williams OR Munds Park for the city. Save the query as **Employees Outside of Flagstaff**. Create a report named **Employee Car Pool List** using the query as the record source. Use the tabular layout and a theme of your choice. Modify the report design as needed to improve its appearance. Compact and back up the database.

LEARNSOFT DEVELOPERS ★★

3. Learnsoft Inc. develops computer-based curricula for grades K–8. The company uses a database to track which software titles have been worked on by the project managers. The program manager for Learnsoft wants a report of this information so he can use it for employee reviews the following week. Open the database file ac03_Learnsoft and the table named Software. Add a new field named **Project Manager** before the Release Date field to include the name of the project manager for each title. Make this field a lookup list field that will look up the names of the five project managers. (Use names of your choice, but include your name as one of the project managers.) Complete the data for this field by selecting a project manager for each record. Assign your name as project manager to one of the records with a release date in 2015. Create a query named **Project Manager Query** that shows the titles, subject, and project manager names for the years 2013 through 2015. Create a report using all the fields in the Project Manager Query. Name the report **Project Manager Report**. Use a theme and layout of your choice. Modify the report design as needed to improve its appearance. Compact and back up the database.

LAB EXERCISES

AMP EXPENSE ACCOUNT REPORT ★★

4. One of the department managers at AMP Enterprises has requested a report showing who in her department has submitted an expense reimbursement request but has not yet been paid. You decide this would be a good report to generate for all departments. In the AMP Enterprises database, open the Employee Expenses table you updated in Lab 2, On Your Own Exercise 2. Create a one-to-many relationship between the Employee Info table and the Employee Expenses table based on the Employee ID fields. Enforce referential integrity and select the Cascade Update option. Create a query that displays all fields from both tables, sorted by department. View the query results. Modify the query to not show the Employee ID field and to display only those employees who have not been paid. Apply an ascending sort to the Submission Date field. Save the query as **Pending Payment**. Use the Report Wizard to create a report named **Open Expense Requests** based on the Pending Payment query. Use a theme and layout of your choice. Modify the report design as needed to improve its appearance. Preview and print the report. Compact and back up the database.

LIFESTYLE FITNESS CLUB MEMBERSHIP DATABASE ★★★

5. The membership database you created for Lifestyle Fitness Club has been very well received. The owners have requested a few changes to be made to the database. You have decided to create a query and then generate a report that shows the monthly sales. Open the ac02_Lifestyle Fitness Memberships database you modified in Lab 2. Exercise 5, and then save the database as Lifestyle Fitness Memberships3. Back up the database in case you have any trouble with this lesson and need to recover the original file. Create a parameter query named **Monthly Sales** that displays the Sale Date from the Membership Sales table and the Type and Cost fields from the Membership Packages table. Sort the Sale Date in ascending order. For the Sale Date field criteria, type in the following expression that includes two parameter questions: **Between [Enter begin date] AND [Enter ending date]**. Run the query to test it, and enter **7/1/2015** for the beginning date and **7/31/2015** for the ending date. Save the query. Create a report using the Monthly Sales query. Include all the fields from the query. Sort the report by sale date. Use the tabular layout in portrait orientation. Name the report **Monthly Sales Report**. Change the page margins to wide. In Design view, select the controls in the Page Header and Detail sections and arrange them in the tabular layout. Adjust the size of the report controls in Layout view to appropriately display the data on one page. Use the Slice theme. Preview and print the report. Create and print a relationships report, saving the report with the name **Relationships**. Compact and repair the database.

CASE STUDY

Lifestyle Fitness Club

Periodically, the club director wants to know the names of the employees at each club and their job positions. You created a parameter query to obtain this information and a custom report to display it professionally. Now you want to provide this information to the director. You also need to add the employee's pay information to the Personnel database to make it more complete.

You will learn about importing data from Excel, and how to export Access data to Excel and Word. Then you will learn how to copy and paste objects and selections between Access and Word to create a memo to the director.

Your memo containing a copy of the query results and the report generated by Access will look like the one shown here.

NOTE This tutorial assumes that you already know how to use Word 2013 and that you have completed Lab 3 of Access 2013.

Importing Data

The owners of the Lifestyle Fitness Club have asked you to include the employees' pay rate information in the Personnel database. You will create a new table to hold this information that will contain three fields of data: Employee ID, Social

Security Number, and Pay Rate. This information is currently maintained in an Excel workbook file that is used to generate payroll. Instead of reentering this data, you will **import** it from the Excel workbook. Importing can save you time and help ensure data accuracy.

Importing data creates a copy of information from an external data source, converts it into a format that can be used in Access, and inserts the data in a new table in your Access database. The file that supplies the data is the **source file** and the file that is created is the **destination file**. The source table or file is not altered in this process. You also can import database objects other than tables, such as forms or reports, from another Access database.

When importing data from another Access database, Access creates a new table with the imported data in it. You cannot add the imported data to a table that already contains records (except when importing spreadsheet or text files). After you have imported a table into an Access database, you can perform an append query to add the table's data to another table. You can import data from an Excel spreadsheet into an existing table in your Access database as long as the field names are the same.

Imported data also can be linked to the source data. This creates a table that displays the information in the source but does not actually store the data in Access. Changes made to the source are reflected in the linked table. However, you can only view, not change, the data from within Access. The linked data can be used in creating queries and reports. You may want to link rather than import when the source data changes frequently and you do not want to maintain the data in the destination Access database.

You will import the employee pay data for the Lifestyle Fitness Club from an Excel workbook file named acwt_Pay.xlxs.

Note: **Before you begin, you may want to create a backup copy of the** acwt1_Personnel **file by copying and renaming it.**

1

• **Start Access 2013 and open the** acwt_Personnel **database file.**

• **Enable the content.**

• **Open the Personal Data table.**

• **Replace Student Name with your name in the last record (70) of the table.**

Your screen should be similar to Figure 1

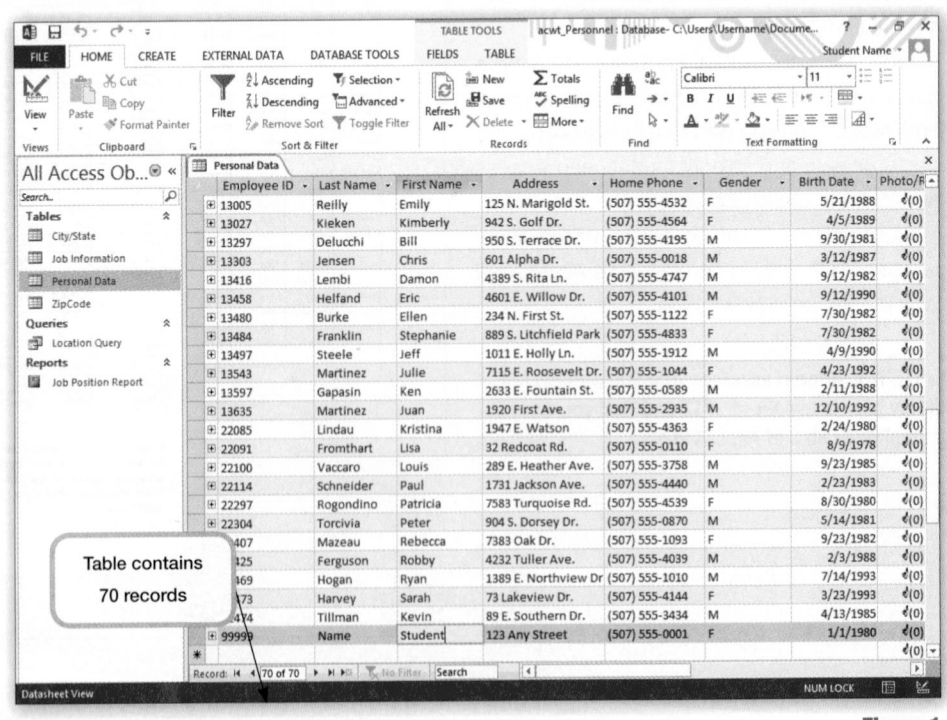

Table contains 70 records

Figure 1

There are 70 records in the Personal Data table. You will import the data from the Excel workbook file to create a table to hold the pay data for each of these records.

2

● Close the Personal Data table.

● Open the External Data tab and click [Excel icon] in the Import & Link group.

Your screen should be similar to Figure 2

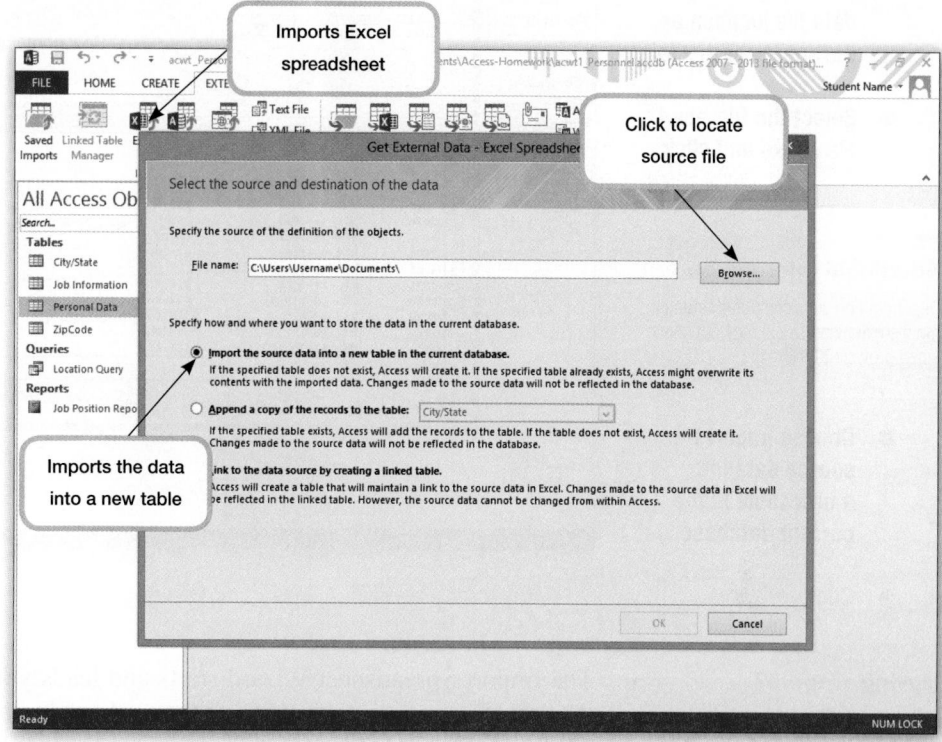

Figure 2

In the Get External Data - Excel Spreadsheet dialog box, you first need to specify the source of the data you want to import. Then you specify how and where you want to store the data.

3

- Click [Browse...] and navigate to your data file location as the source of the data.

- Select the file acwt_Pay.xlxs and click [Open].

Additional Information

Depending on your computer settings, the file extension (.xlsx) may not show when browsing for the file.

- Choose Import the source data into a new table in the current database.

- Click [OK].

Having Trouble?

If necessary, click [Open] in response to the security warning message.

Your screen should be similar to Figure 3

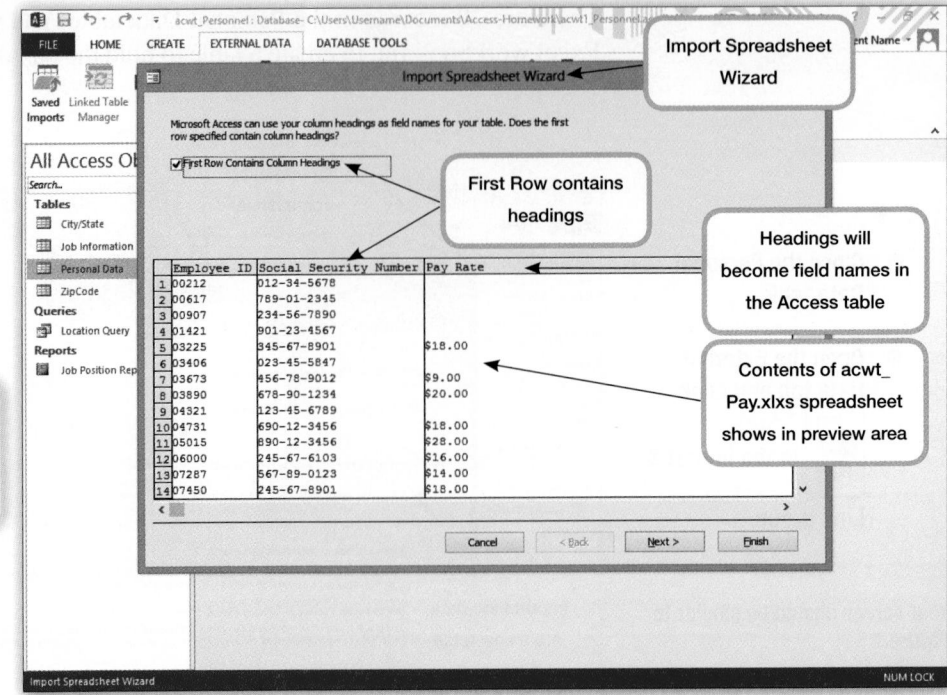

Figure 3

The Import Spreadsheet Wizard starts and leads you through the steps to import the data. First you specify whether to use the column headings in the worksheet as the field names. The preview area shows how the data in the worksheet is set up so you can easily confirm that the first row contains information you want to use as column headings.

4

- If necessary, choose First Row Contains Column Headings (a check mark should be in the check box).

- Click [Next >].

Your screen should be similar to Figure 4

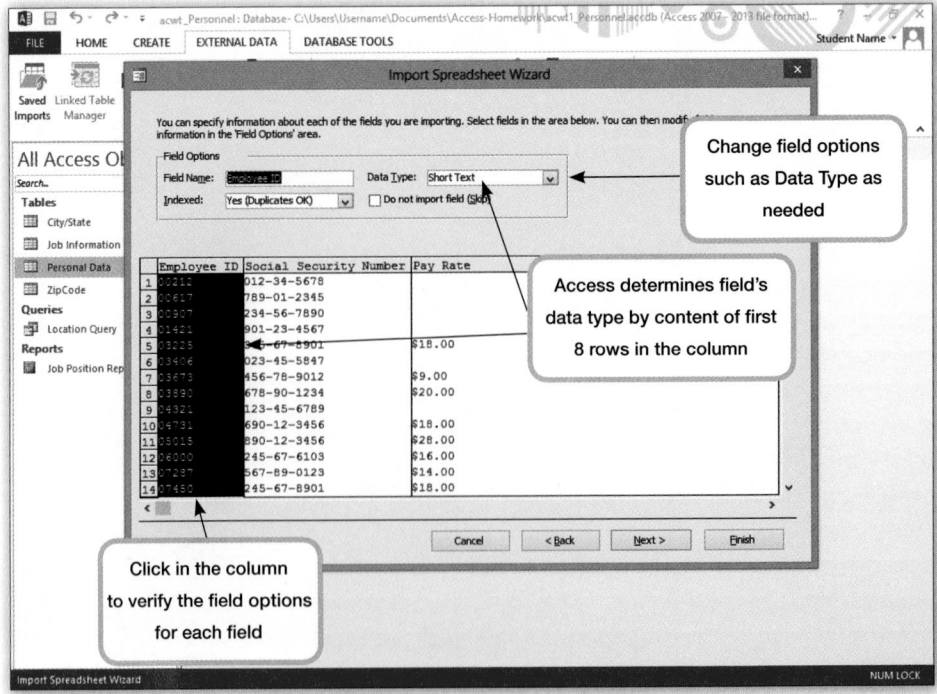

Figure 4

In this step, you can modify the field information, including the field name and data type. The Employee ID field is the selected field and is highlighted in the preview area. The field options associated with the Employee ID field are displayed in the Field Options area of the dialog box. This field will have a Short Text data type, which is correct, and the field name is appropriate. Access determines the data type by looking at the content of the first eight rows in each column and suggests an appropriate data type. Most often, this is the Short Text data type. You can choose a different data type; however, if the values are not compatible with the data type you choose, they will be ignored or converted incorrectly. You will accept the data types as suggested.

5

● **Click on the Social Security Number field in the preview area and verify that the field options are appropriate.**

● **Select the Pay Rate field and verify the options are also correct.**

● **Click Next > .**

Your screen should be similar to Figure 5

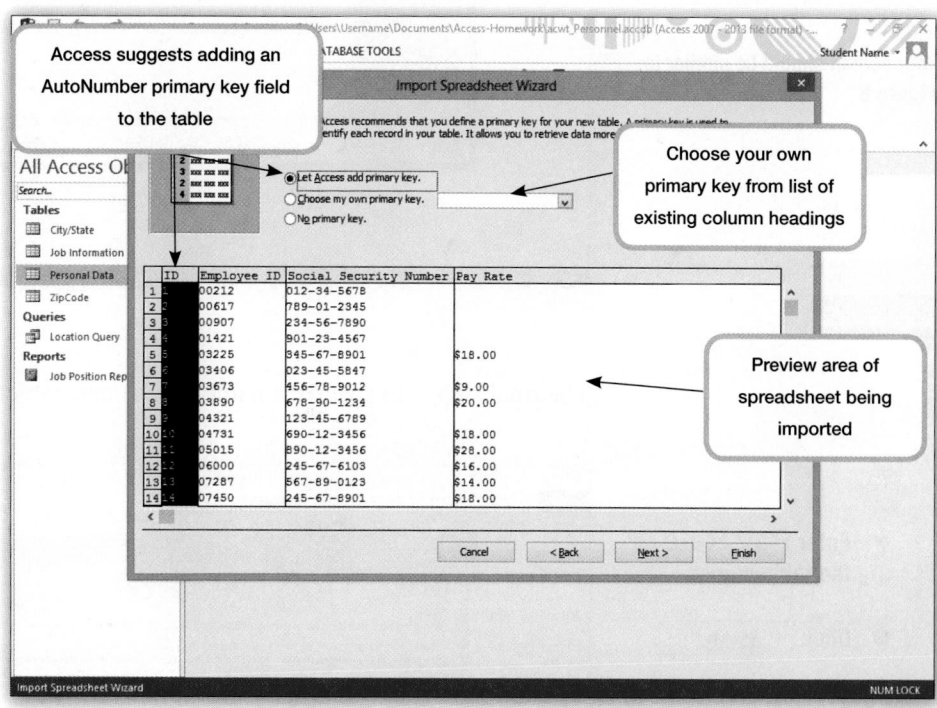

Figure 5

Next you are asked to specify a primary key field. Initially, Access adds an AutoNumber data type ID field to the table and uses it as the primary key field. You will specify your own instead.

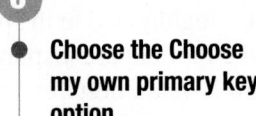

6

- Choose the **Choose my own primary key** option.

- If necessary, specify the Employee ID field from the drop-down list.

- Click [Next >].

Your screen should be similar to Figure 6

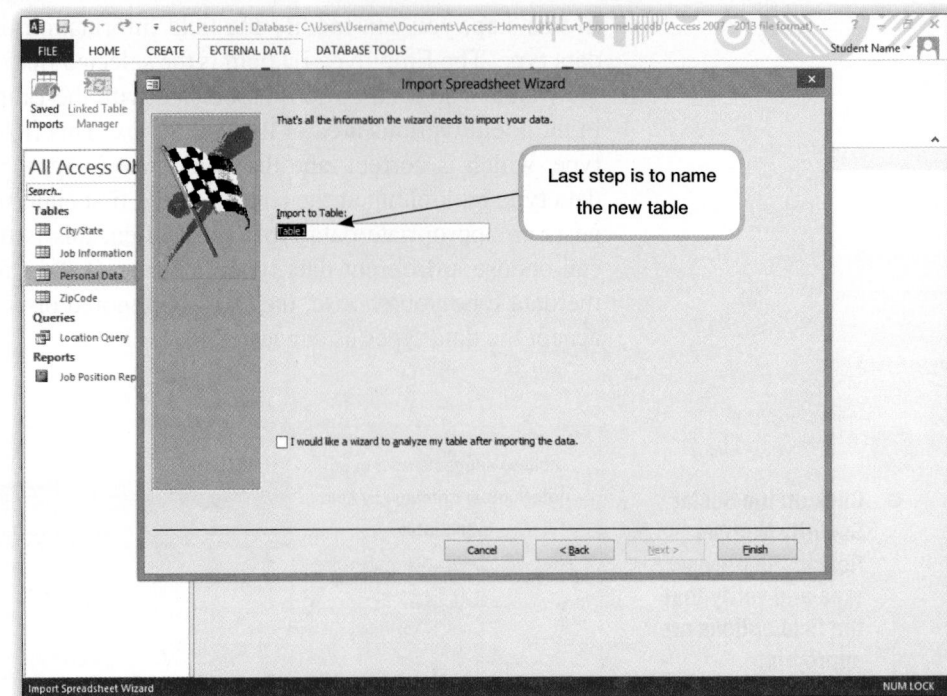

Last step is to name the new table

Figure 6

The final step is to specify a name for the new table.

7

- Enter **Pay Rate** as the table name.

- Click [Finish].

Your screen should be similar to Figure 7

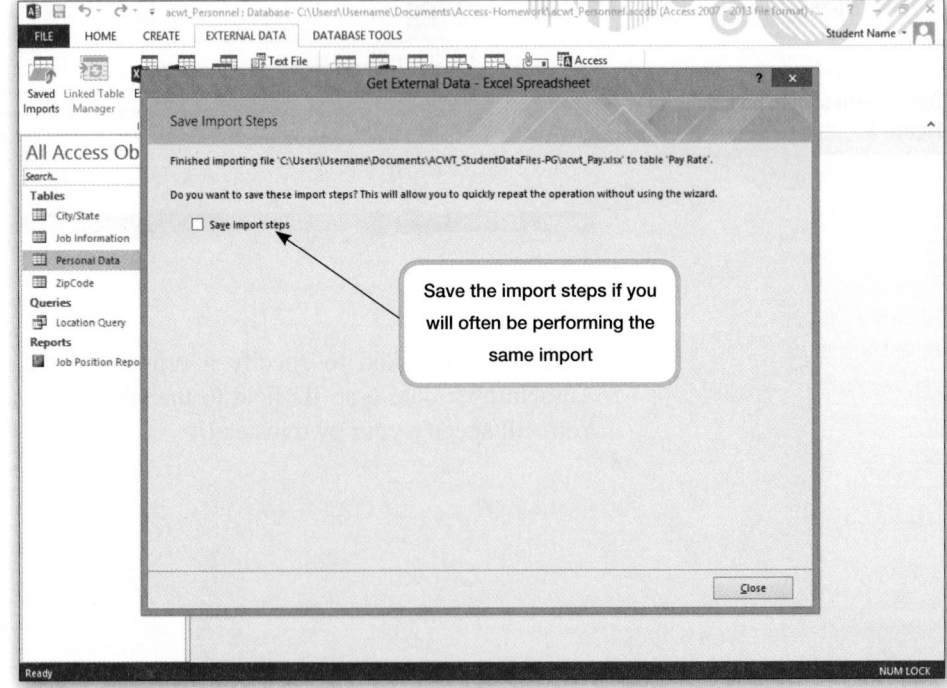

Save the import steps if you will often be performing the same import

Figure 7

The Save Import Steps dialog box informs you that the Excel data was successfully imported to the Pay Rate table and asks if you want to save the import steps. It is not necessary to save the import steps unless you will be repeating this import process frequently in the future.

You will open the new table next.

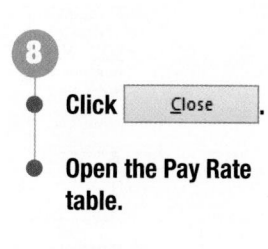

8

● Click [Close].

● Open the Pay Rate table.

Your screen should be similar to Figure 8

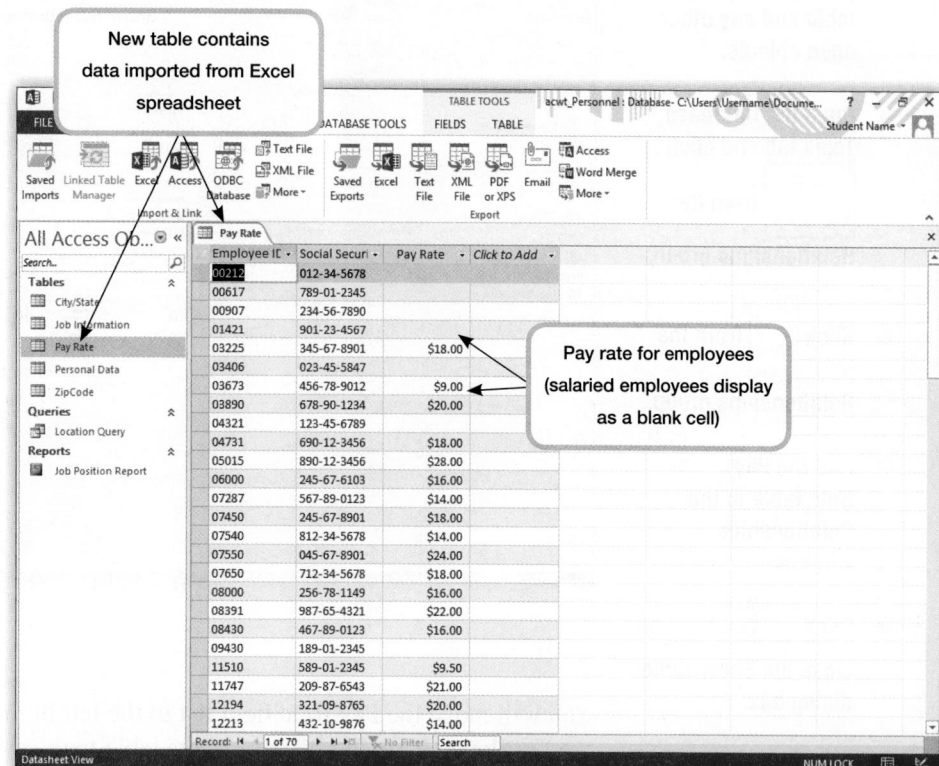

Figure 8

The Pay Rate table contains the pay rate for each employee. Salaried employees do not include a pay rate. Since you added a table to your database, you now need to add it to the relationships.

9

- Close the Pay Rate table and any other open objects.

- Open the Database Tools tab and click  from the Relationships group.

- Click from the Relationships group.

- Add the Pay Rate table to the Relationships window.

- Click `Close` to close the Show Table dialog box.

Your screen should be similar to
Figure 9

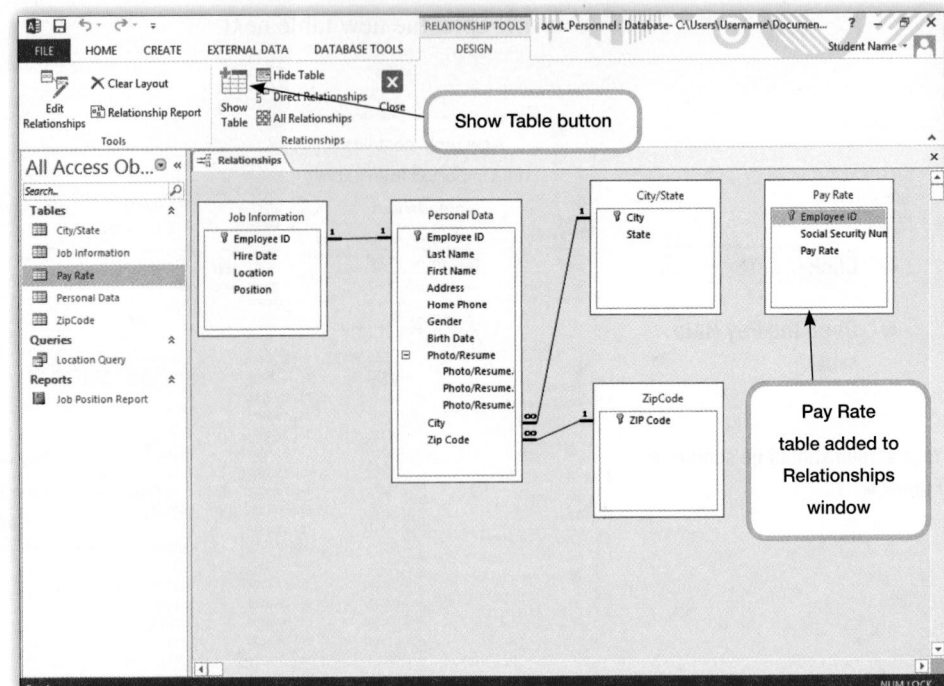

Figure 9

You will move the Pay Rate field list to the left of the Personal Data table and join the Employee ID in the Personal Data table to the same field in the Pay Rate table.

10

- Move the Pay Rate table to the left of the Personal Data table, just underneath the Job information table.

- Drag the Employee ID field from the Personal Data table to the Employee ID field in the Pay Rate table.

- Choose the Enforce Referential Integrity, Cascade Update Related Fields, and Cascade Delete Related Records options.

- Click `Create`.

Your screen should be similar to
Figure 10

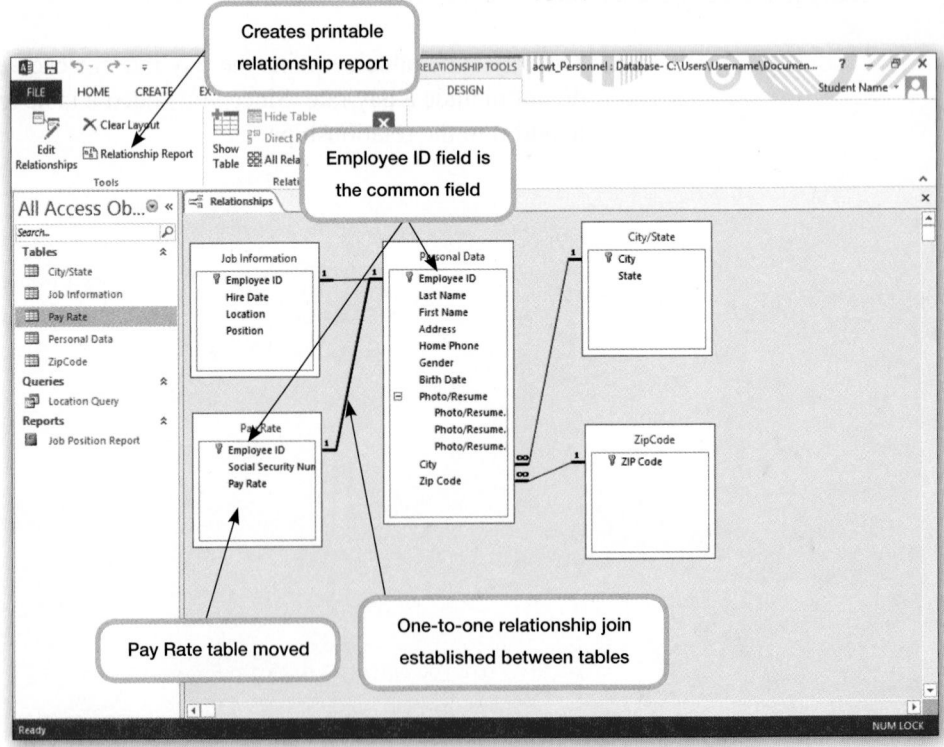

Figure 10

11

● Print a relationship report, and then close the report without saving it.

● Close the Relationships window, saving any changes.

Exporting Data

Your next project is to provide the club director with the names of the employees and their job positions at each club location. Because the director prefers to work with data in Excel, you will **export** the information to an Excel workbook for him. Exporting copies data from an Access database object to a file outside the database. There are a variety of methods you can use, depending upon the type of output needed. The most common export types are described below:

Export to	Description
Excel	Creates a copy of the selected data, table, query, or form object and stores the copy in an Excel worksheet.
Word	Creates a copy of the selected data, table, query, form, or report, including formatting, in a new rich text file (*.rtf) that can be utilized in Word.
Access database	Creates a copy of the table definition and data or just the table definition in another Access database.
Text file	Creates a copy of the selected data, table, query, form, or report, approximating formatting if possible, in a new text file (*.txt) document.
SharePoint site	Creates a copy of a table or query and stores it on a SharePoint site as a list.

The Export Wizard is used for all types of exports. In addition, in some cases, you can copy and paste an object in another application. The file that you export from is the source file and the file that is created is the destination file.

EXPORTING TO EXCEL 2013

Additional Information

If you want to export a selection, you need to open the object and select the records you want to export.

When exporting to Excel, the database file you want to copy from must be open in Access. Then you select the object you want to export. The Export Wizard can copy selected data, a table, a query, or a form object, but it cannot export a report to Excel. Because you cannot export a report, you will export the Location Query instead.

Additional Information

Only one object can be exported at a time.

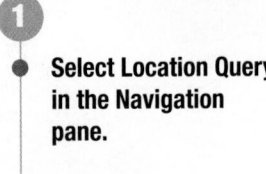

1

- Select Location Query in the Navigation pane.

- Click [Excel] in the **Export** group of the **External Data** tab.

Your screen should be similar to Figure 11

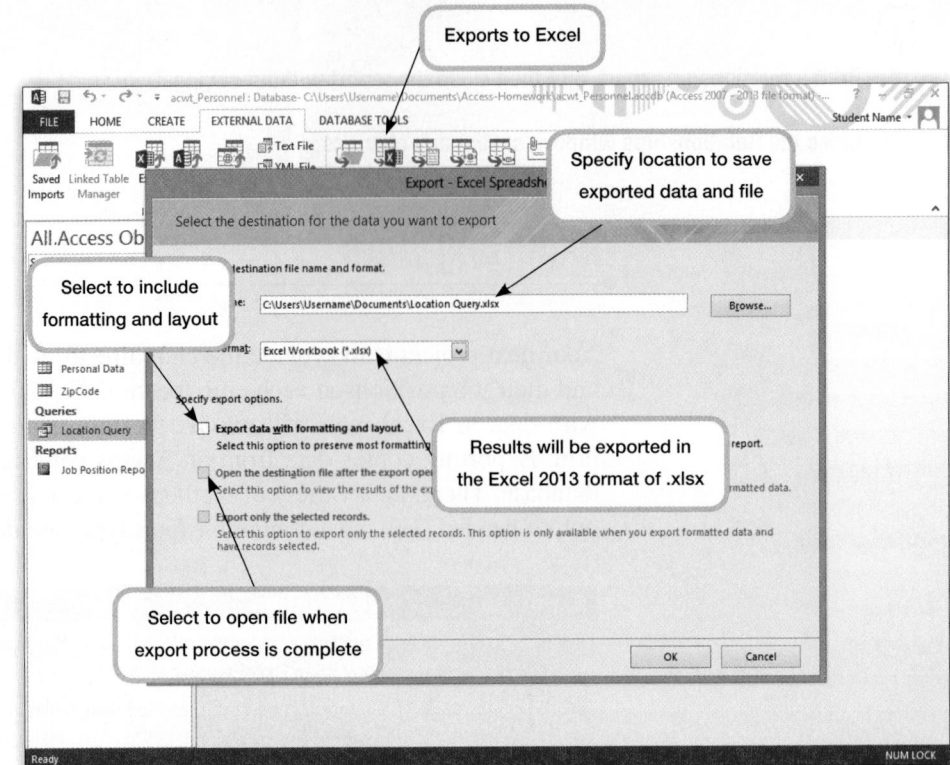

Figure 11

In the first Export - Excel Spreadsheet Wizard dialog box, you specify the name of the destination file and the file format. The default file format of an Excel 2013 workbook file (.xlsx) is acceptable; however, you need to change the file location and name. In addition, you want to include the formatting from the query object and see the new Excel workbook file after it is created. Because the query is a parameter query, you also will be asked to enter which fitness club location you want the exported query results to display.

2

- Click **Browse...** and specify the location to save the file.

- In the File Save dialog box, enter the file name **Landis Job Positions** and click **Save** .

- Choose Export data with formatting and layout.

- Choose Open the destination file after the export operation is complete.

- Click **OK** .

- Type **Landis** in the Enter Parameter Value dialog box.

- Click **OK** .

- If necessary, maximize the Excel application window.

Your screen should be similar to Figure 12

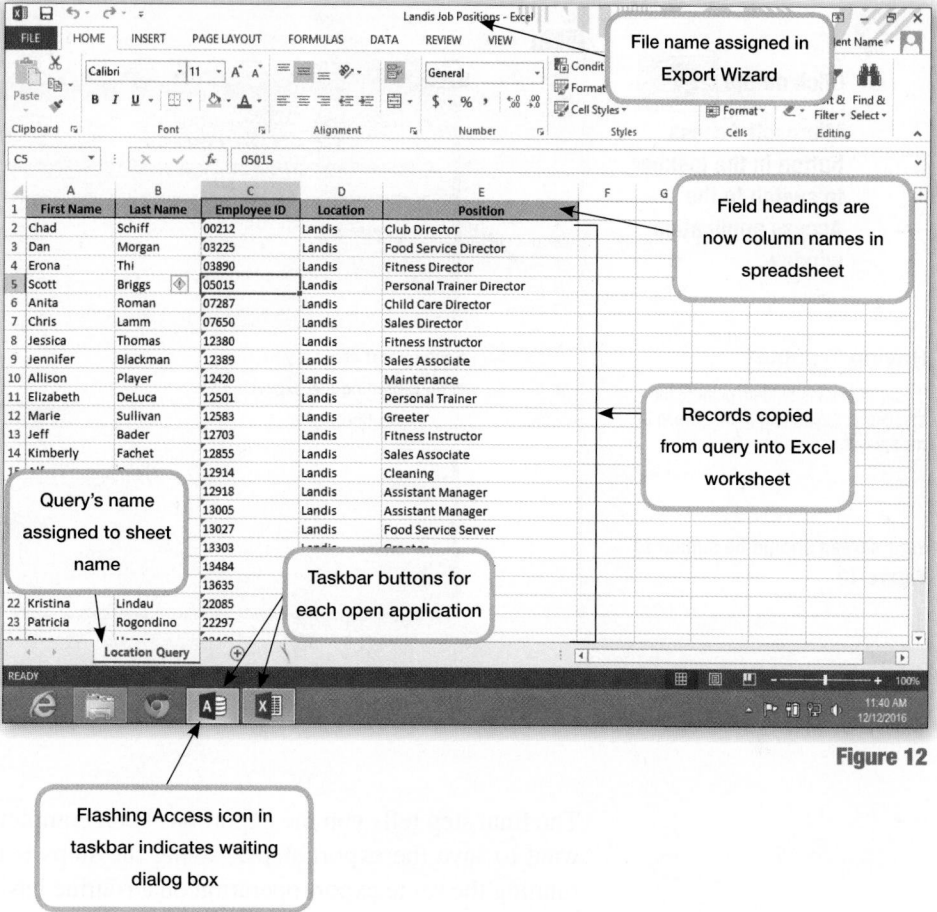

File name assigned in Export Wizard

Field headings are now column names in spreadsheet

Records copied from query into Excel worksheet

Query's name assigned to sheet name

Taskbar buttons for each open application

Location Query

Flashing Access icon in taskbar indicates waiting dialog box

Figure 12

Now there are two applications open, Excel and Access, and application buttons for both open windows are displayed in the taskbar. The Excel 2013 application window is displayed, and the exported data has been copied into a worksheet of the new workbook file. The field headings appear formatted in the first row of the worksheet, and each row that follows is a record from the query datasheet. Notice that the Microsoft Access button in the taskbar is flashing. This is to tell you that the wizard is not yet done.

3

• Click on the **Microsoft Access button in the taskbar to switch to the Access application window.**

Having Trouble?

If your taskbar is hidden, point to the thin line at the bottom of the screen to redisplay it.

Your screen should be similar to Figure 13

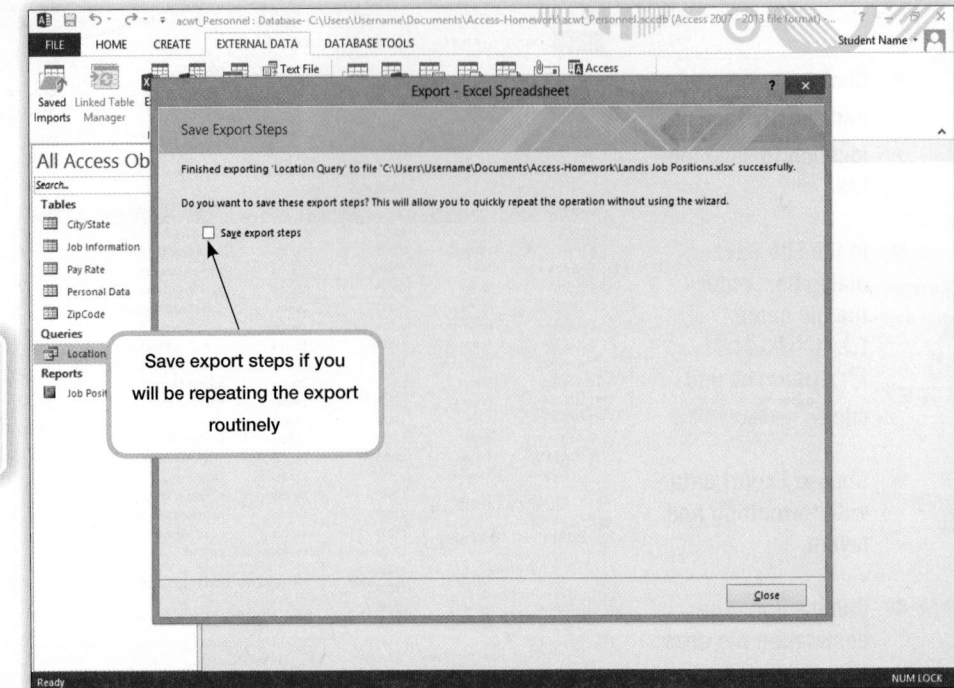

Figure 13

The final step tells you the export has been completed successfully and asks if you want to save the export steps. Saving the steps is useful if you think you will be running the same export operation on a routine basis. Since you need to repeat this operation for each location, you will save the steps using the suggested name. The wizard also can add a reminder for you in Outlook to run the export if you need to generate the results on a routine basis. You will not include this feature at this time.

Then you will use the saved export steps to export the River Mist location data.

4

- Choose Save Export Steps.

- Click `Save Export`.

- Click `Saved Exports` in the Export group to start the next export process.

Your screen should be similar to Figure 14

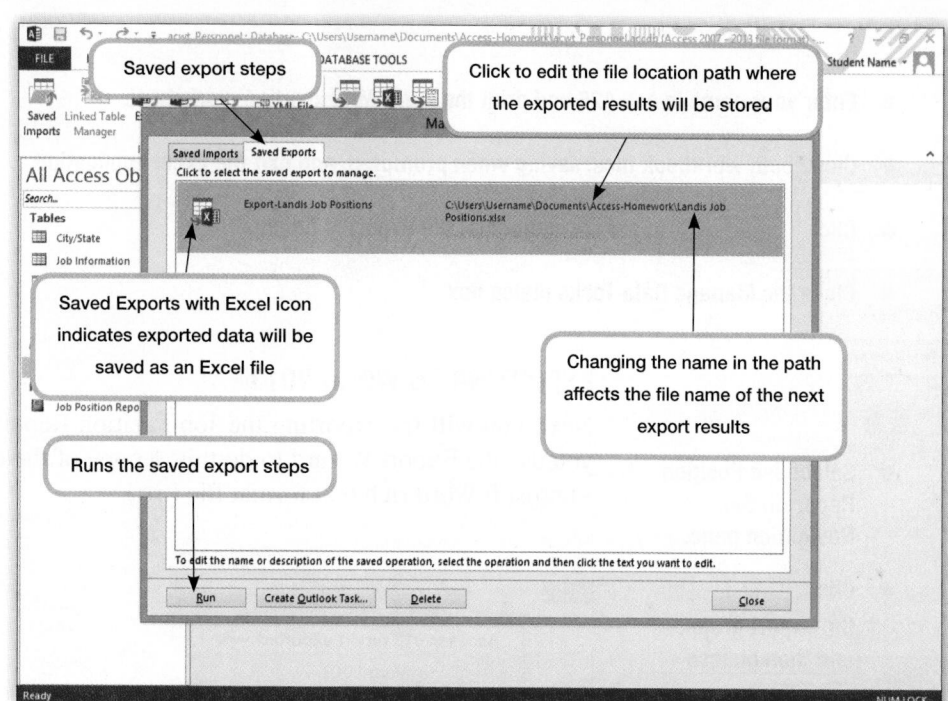

Figure 14

The Saved Exports dialog box contains options for running export steps that have been previously executed and saved. The only change you will make to the saved export is to edit the file name to reflect the River Mist location. The exported data is saved as an Excel file with the name you specify.

5

- Click on the path, select the word Landis in the file name Landis Job Positions, and change it to **River Mist**

- Press ←Enter to complete the change.

- Click `Run`.

- In the Enter Parameter Value dialog box, type **River Mist** as the location.

- Click `OK`.

Your screen should be similar to Figure 15

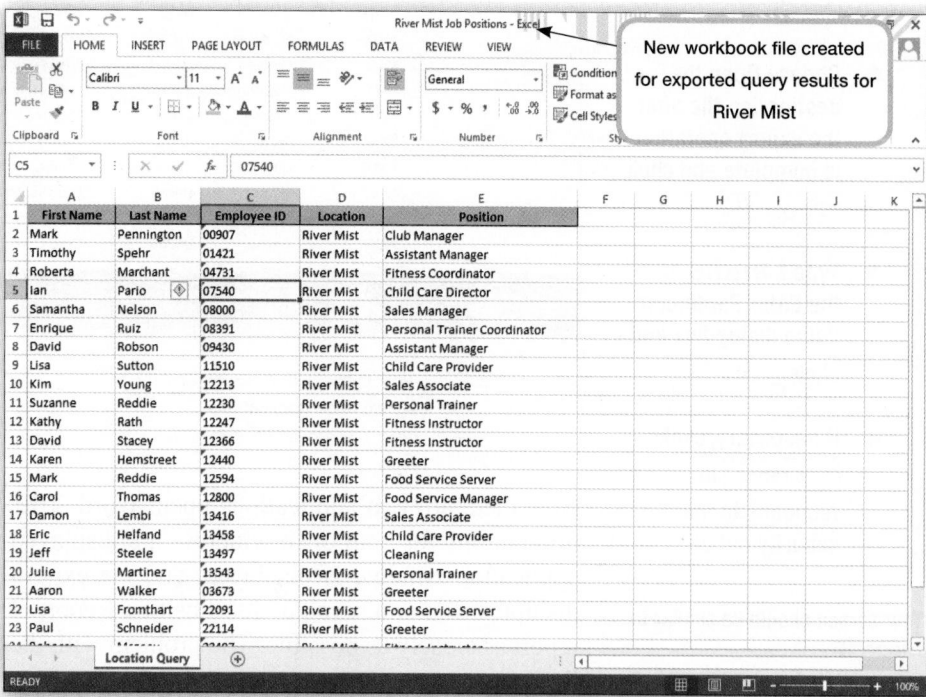

Figure 15

A separate workbook file was created and contains the data for the River Mist location. Now all the Excel features can be used to analyze the data in the worksheets. After exporting each location to a workbook, you could combine the workbooks by copying the worksheet data from each worksheet into one workbook file.

Enter your name in cell A26 and print the River Mist location worksheet.

Close both workbook files, saving when prompted, and exit the Excel application.

Click [OK] to acknowledge that the export is finished.

Close the Manage Data Tasks dialog box.

EXPORTING TO WORD 2013

Next, you will try exporting the Job Position Report to a Word document. When you use the Export Wizard to do this, a copy of the object's data is inserted into a Microsoft Word rich text format file (.rtf).

1

Select Job Position Report in the Navigation pane.

Click [More ▾] in the Export group, and then choose [Word — Export the selected object to Rich Text] .

If necessary, change to your solution file location.

> **Having Trouble?**
>
> The report will be saved using the default file name of Job Position Report.

Choose Open the destination file after the export operation is complete and click [OK] .

Type Landis in the Enter Parameter Value dialog box and click [OK] .

If necessary, click [Open] in response to the security notice.

Your screen should be similar to Figure 16

> **Having Trouble?**
>
> If WordPad is the open application, this is because your system has associated .rtf file types with this application. You could close WordPad and open the document in Word 2013.

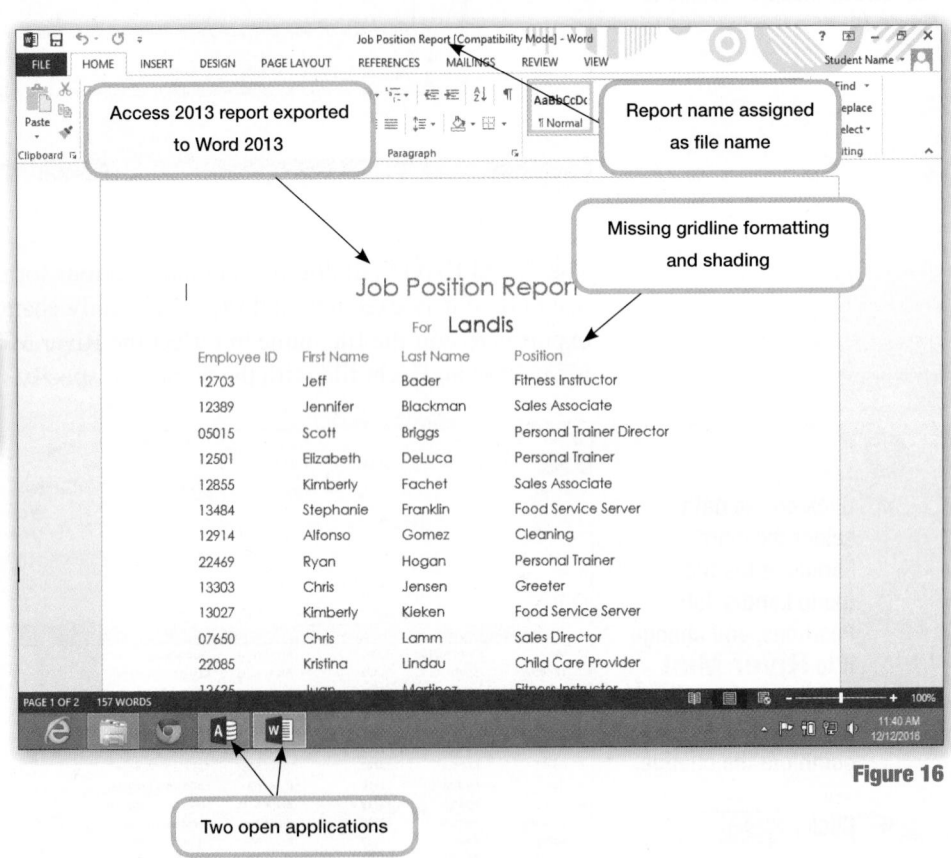

Access 2013 report exported to Word 2013

Report name assigned as file name

Missing gridline formatting and shading

Two open applications

Figure 16

Now there are two applications open, Word 2013 and Access 2013, and application buttons for both open windows are displayed in the taskbar. The Word 2013 application window is displayed, and the exported data has been copied into a document file and saved as Job Position Report. The report resembles the Access report as closely as possible. The problem with the exported report is that the gridlines and shading did not copy.

You will return to the Access application and will not save the export steps.

2
- Switch to the Access application window.
- Click [_Close_] to close the Export Wizard.

COPYING A QUERY OBJECT TO WORD 2013

Finally, you decide to try copying an Access object to an existing Word document without using the Export Wizard. To do this, you can use the Copy and Paste commands or drag and drop to copy a database object between the Access and Word applications.

You have already started a memo to the club director about the employee job position information he requested.

1
- Switch to the Word application window, and close the Job Position Report document (do not close Word).

- Open the Word document acwt_Job Positions from your data file location.

- If necessary, click [Enable Editing]

- In the memo header, replace Student Name with your name.

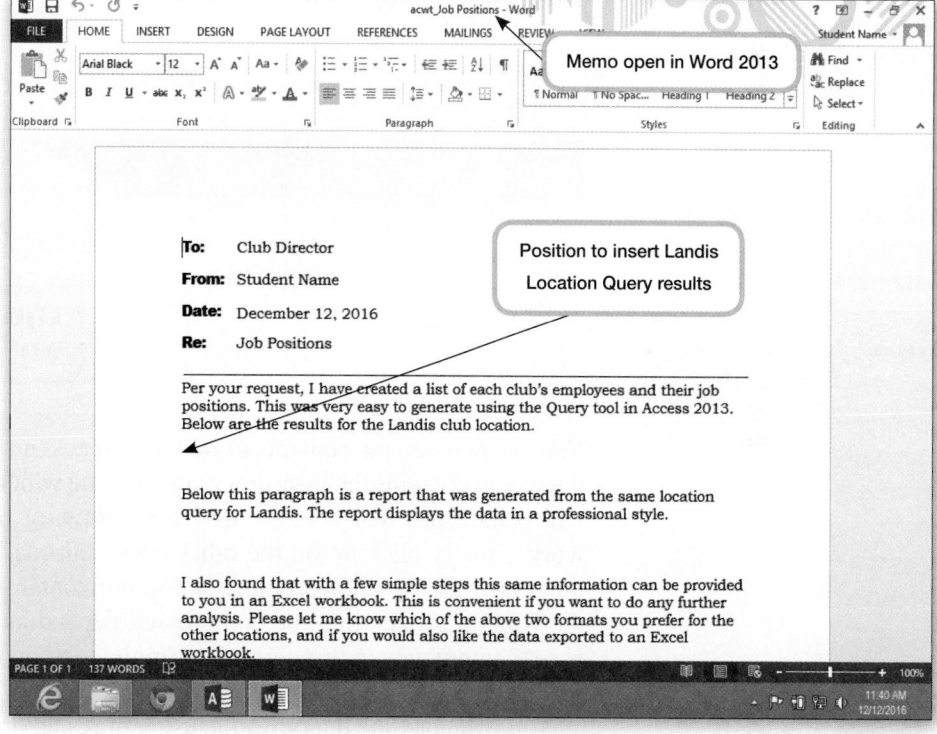

Position to insert Landis Location Query results

Memo open in Word 2013

Figure 17

This document contains the text of the memo to the director. Below the first paragraph, you want to copy the output from the Location Query using drag and drop. To do this, both applications must be open and visible, which you will do by displaying the application windows side by side.

Because the Location Query is a parameter query, Access will prompt you to enter a location before it creates the results in the Word document.

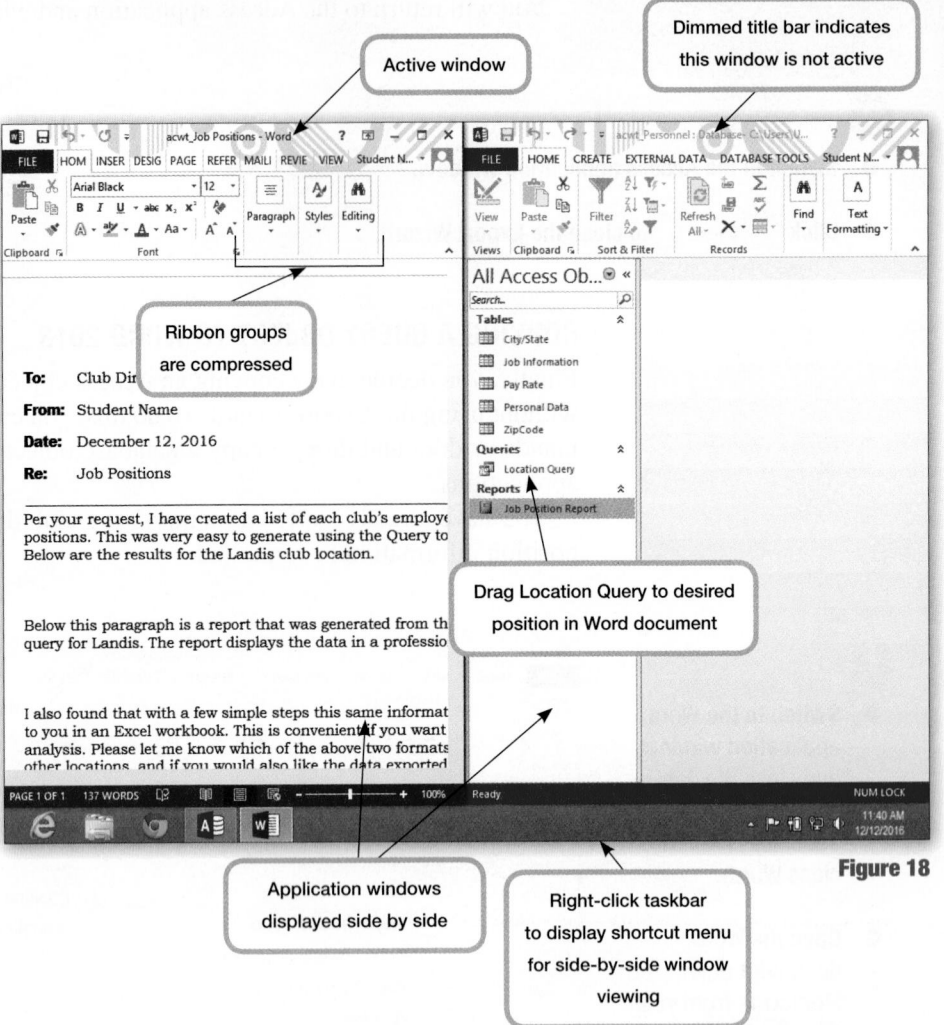

2

- **Right-click on a blank area of the taskbar to open the shortcut menu.**

- **Choose Show windows side by side.**

- **Click in the Word application window to make it the active window.**

Your screen should be similar to Figure 18

Active window

Dimmed title bar indicates this window is not active

Ribbon groups are compressed

Drag Location Query to desired position in Word document

Application windows displayed side by side

Right-click taskbar to display shortcut menu for side-by-side window viewing

Figure 18

You can now see the contents of both the Access and Word applications. The Word document contains the insertion point, and the window title bar text is not dimmed, which indicates that it is the **active window**, or the window in which you can work. Simply clicking on the other document makes it active. Because the windows are side by side and there is less horizontal space in each window some of the Ribbon groups may be compressed depending on your monitor settings. To access commands in these groups, simply click on the group button and the commands appear in a drop-down list.

You will copy the query results using drag and drop to below the first paragraph of the memo. As you drag the object you want to copy from Access into the Word document, a temporary cursor | shows the location in the document where the content will be inserted and the mouse pointer appears as ⊞.

- Select Location Query in the Access Navigation pane.

- Drag the selected object to the second blank line below the first paragraph of the memo.

Having Trouble?

Do not release the mouse until the I bar is in the desired location on the page.

- Enter **Landis** as the Location parameter and click
  OK .

- Click in the Word document to deselect the table.

- Scroll the document to see more of the table.

Your screen should be similar to Figure 19

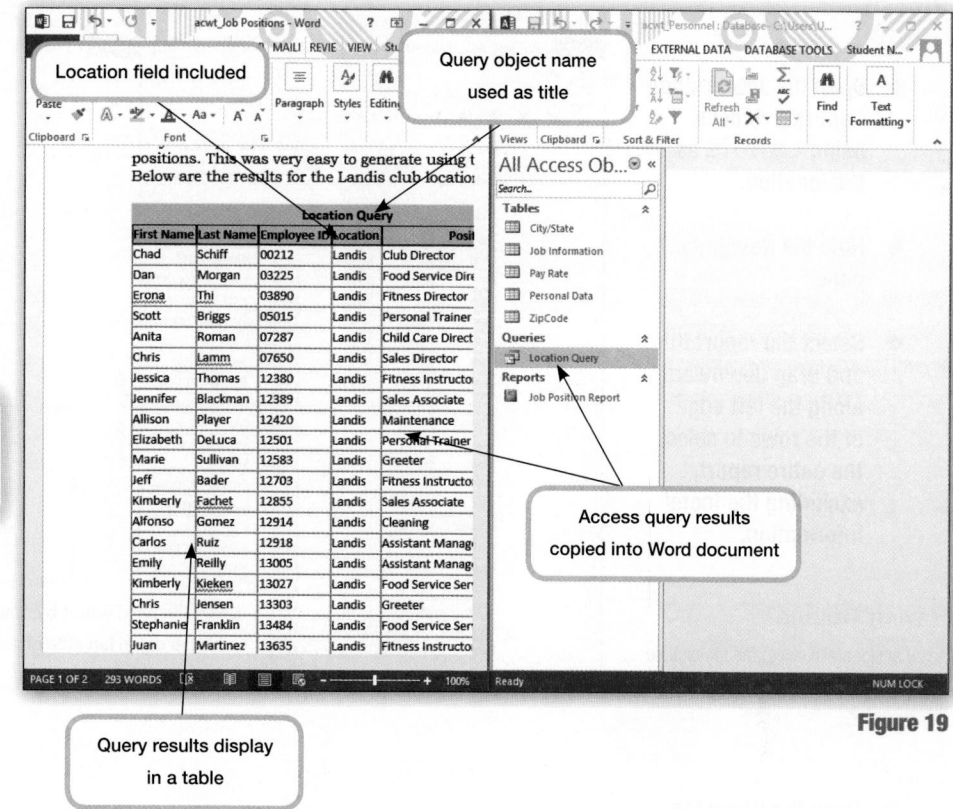

Figure 19

Callouts in figure:
- Location field included
- Query object name used as title
- Access query results copied into Word document
- Query results display in a table

The query results have been copied into the Word document as a table that can be edited and manipulated within Word. The formatting associated with the copied object also is included. However, the title is the same as the query name and the Location field is displayed. To change this, you could edit the title and then delete the table column using Word 2013.

COPYING A REPORT

Next, you will copy the report into the memo to show how it will look. To copy report data, you run the report in Access and then use the Copy and Paste commands to copy the contents to a Word document.

1

● Open the Job Position Report in Access using Landis as the location.

● Hide the Navigation pane.

● Select the report title, and drag downward along the left edge of the rows to select the entire report, excluding the footer information.

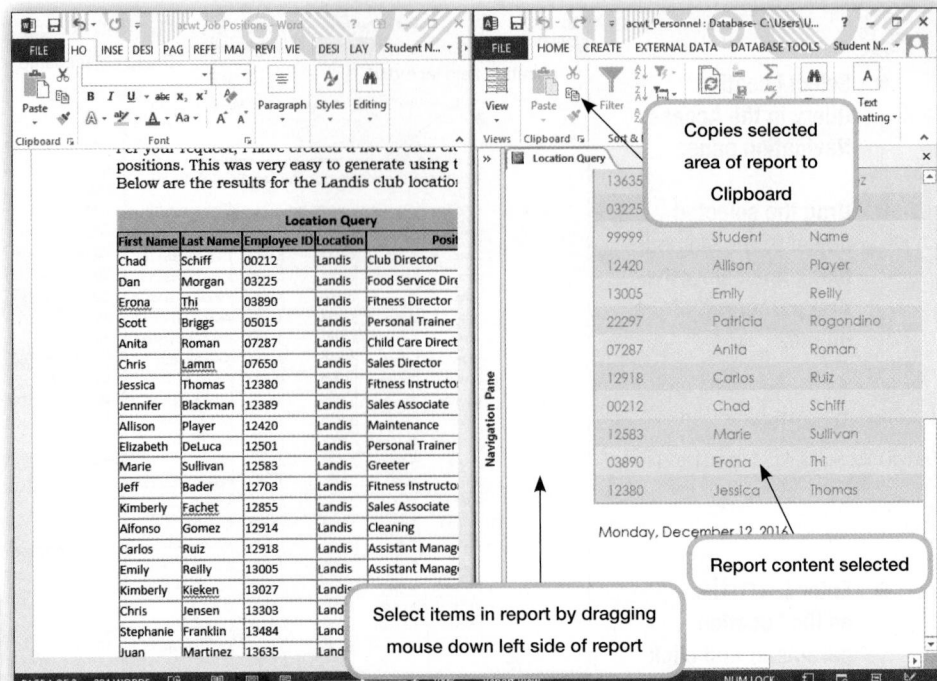

Figure 20

Having Trouble?

If you accidentally select the footer, hold down ⇧Shift and click to the left of the last record to remove the selection from the footer.

● Open the Home tab and click 🖹 Copy in the Clipboard group.

Notice the Location Query name, not the report object name is displayed in the tab. This is because the report runs the Location query to obtain the report data. Next, you need to select the location in the memo where you want the copied data inserted.

Your screen should be similar to Figure 20

2

● Scroll the Word document, and click on the second blank line between the second and third paragraphs.

● Click 🖹 in the Home tab.

● Scroll the document up to see the top of the report.

Your screen should be similar to Figure 21

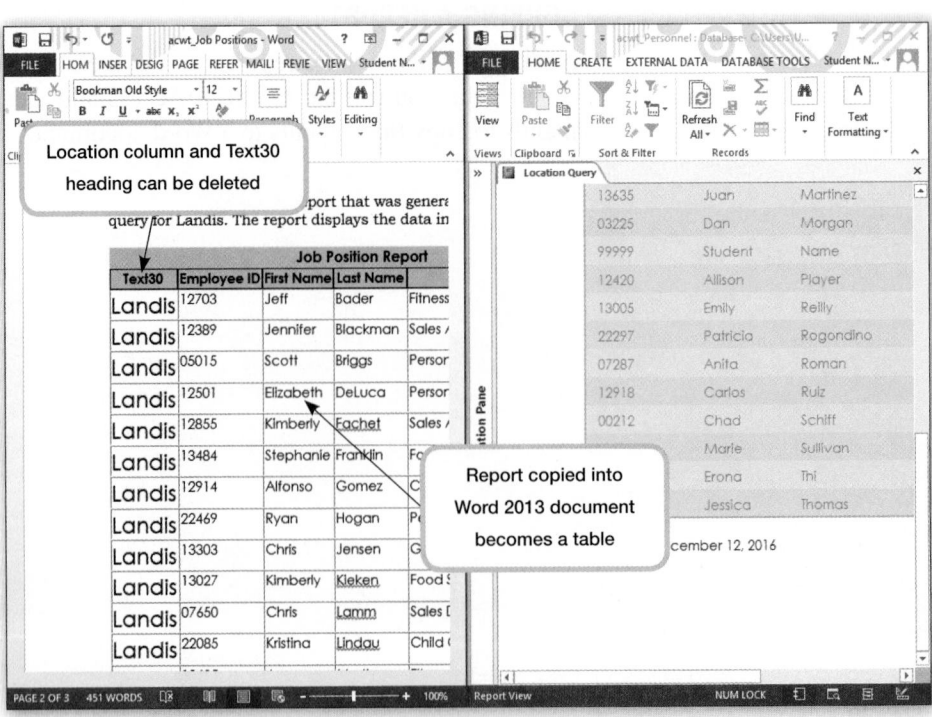

Figure 21

The report is copied into the Word document as a table. Notice the location field data is displayed in a column in the Word document, even though it was not displayed in the report. You will remove the column and add the location to the report title.

③

- **Select the cells in the column containing the heading Text30 and the Landis text underneath.**

Having Trouble?

You will have to scroll up to the previous page to select the column heading at the beginning of the table.

- **Right-click the selection and choose Delete Cells.**

- **Click** OK **to shift the cells left.**

- **In the report title, click in front of the words Job Position Report.**

- **Type Landis and press ←Enter.**

Your screen should be similar to Figure 22

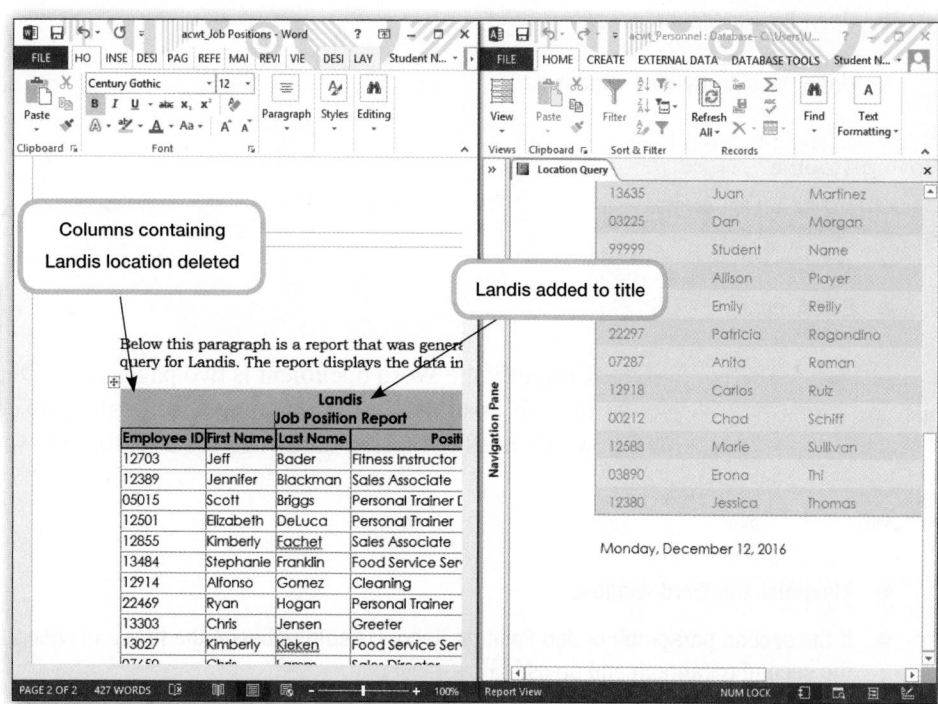

Figure 22

The Location column has been removed, and the table title is now descriptive of the table contents.

4

- Switch to Access and close the report.

- Click [No] to not save the copied data that was placed on the Clipboard.

- Open the Navigation pane.

- Undo the side-by-side windows.

Having Trouble?

Choose Undo Show Side by Side from the taskbar shortcut menu.

- Exit Access.

Currently the Word document is two pages long. Depending on your system fonts, the Job Position Report may have been split between pages. To correct this, you would need to insert a hard page break before the second paragraph.

5

- Maximize the Word window.

- If the second paragraph or Job Position Report is split between the first and second page, move to the beginning of the second paragraph and press [Ctrl] + [Enter].

- Save the memo as Landis Job Positions to your solution file location.

- Print the memo.

- Exit Word.

Your printed memo should be two pages long and look similar to the one shown in the case study at the beginning of this lab.

B REVIEW Working Together Importing and Exporting Data

KEY TERMS

active window ACWT.16
destination file ACWT.2
export ACWT.9
import ACWT.2
source file ACWT.2

COMMAND SUMMARY

Command	Shortcut	Action
External Data tab		
Import & Link group		
Excel		Imports data into an Access table from an Excel spreadsheet
Export group		
Saved Exports		Views and runs saved exports
Excel		Exports selected object to an Excel workbook
More / Word Export the selected object to Rich Text		Exports selected object to a rich text format (*.rtf) file

STEP-BY-STEP

SPA MARKETING MEMO ★

1. The Scensations Salon and Day Spa database has been used extensively. The owner asked you for a list of clients who are over the age of 45 to get an idea of how much interest there would be in an anti-aging spa package she is considering offering. You already filtered the Clients table to locate this information and now want to include the results in a memo to Latisha. The first page of the memo is shown here.

    a. Open the ac03_Scensations Spa database file that you modified in Lab 3, Step-by-Step Exercise 2. Display the results of the Clients 45+ query. Click Ok to any error messages that display.

    b. Start Word 2013 and enter the following text in a new blank document. As you enter the text, press [Tab] after typing each colon.

To:	**Latisha Pine**
From:	**[Your Name]**
Date:	**[current date]**
Re:	**Anti-aging spa package research**
	[press Enter twice]

    Here is the information you requested on the clients who are over the age of 45:
    [press Enter]

    To: Latisha Pine
    From: Student Name
    Date: December 12, 2016
    Re: Anti-aging spa package research

    Here is the information you requested on the clients who are over the age of 45:

    Clients 45+ Query

Birth Date	First Name	Last Name	Address	City	State/Province	ZIP/Postal Code
1/2/1968	Lisa	Anderson	7428 S. Hill	Yerington	NV	89447
7/15/1968	Beatrice	Arnold	369 N. Main	Yerington	NV	89447
2/9/1948	Alma	Austin	560 E. Hickory	Smith Valley	NV	89430
12/7/1960	Kristen	Chavez	861 S. Tenth	Smith Valley	NV	89430
1/6/1969	Gloria	Cook	224 E. Laurel	Dayton	NV	89403
8/15/1970	Phyllis	Foster	27984 W. Dogwood	Fernley	NV	89408
9/23/1969	Robin	Hayes	861 N. Fourth	Fernley	NV	89408
4/15/1970	Andrea	Henderson	8666 N. 9th	Dayton	NV	89403
6/4/1970	Barbara	Jones	738 N. Eighth	Smith Valley	NV	89430
4/4/1968	Elsie	Kelley	1008 W. 11th	Silver City	NV	89428
6/19/1969	Erica	Matthews	738 E. Sixth	Yerington	NV	89447
10/30/1968	Peggy	Myers	492 S. Lincoln	Fernley	NV	89408
2/11/1968	Student	Name	123 Any Street	Silver City	NV	89428
3/5/1951	Sue	Peters	1238 E. Fourth	Silver City	NV	89428
12/11/1970	Doris	Reed	10494 N. Forest	Dayton	NV	89403
1/11/1949	Vanessa	Sims	784 N. Cherry	Smith Valley	NV	89430
12/2/1968	Dawn	Sullivan	369 E. 8th	Fernley	NV	89408
12/3/1969	Dorothy	Taylor	1238 E. Fifth	Smith Valley	NV	89430
5/2/1968	Linda	Williams	495 W. Cherry	Smith Valley	NV	89430
	19					

    c. Show windows side by side, and then drag the Clients 45+ Query into the Word document below the last paragraph.

    d. Close Access and maximize Word. Save the document as 45+ Spa Clients Memo. Print the memo.

    e. Close Word.

LOW STOCK ANALYSIS ★★

2. Evan, the owner of the Downtown Internet Café, continues to be impressed with the café's inventory database (Lab 3, Step-by-Step Exercise 3). Evan has also asked you to create a new table that lists the unit costs of the inventory items. You will get this information by importing it from an Excel workbook. He has also asked you for a list of all special-order items and how many of these items are currently in stock. He wants this information as an Excel 2013 worksheet so that he can further analyze the data. You will provide this information by exporting the data from Access 2013 to Excel 2013. Your completed worksheet of this data should be similar to that shown here.

a. Open the ac03_Cafe Inventory database that you modified in Lab 3, Step-by-Step Exercise 3. Save the database as acwt_Cafe Inventory.

Item	Description	In Stock	Special Order?	Unit Price	Vendor
121	Powdered cream	31	Y	$55.00	ABC Restaurant Supply
131	T-Shirts	10	Y	$76.00	By Design
171	Decaf Viennese	33	Y	$140.00	Pure Processing
172	Decaf Sumatra	35	Y	$140.00	Pure Processing
257	Coffee mints	30	Y	$75.00	Sweet Stuff
273	French Roast	47	Y	$125.00	Café Ole
753	Guatamala coffee	45	Y	$125.00	Cuppa Jo
754	Java coffee	46	Y	$140.00	Cuppa Jo
755	Arabian coffee	47	Y	$115.00	Cuppa Jo
759	Espresso	11	Y	$185.00	Cuppa Jo
859	Darjeeling Tea	13	Y	$75.00	Tea and Toast, Inc.

b. Import the Excel file acwt_Prices to a new table. During the import wizard steps, change the data type for the Item # field to Short Text and make the Item # the primary key field. Name the new table **Inventory Prices**.

c. Open the new table in Design view. Check the field properties and adjust as needed. Make both fields required.

d. Close all tables and establish appropriate relationships between tables. Enforce referential integrity and Update Cascade for both relationships. Print, save, and close the Relationships window.

e. Create a new query named **Special Orders** and include the Item, Description, In Stock, Special Order? fields from the Stock table, Unit Price field from the Inventory Prices table, and the Vendor field from the Suppliers table (in that order). Modify the criteria so that only those with a Y in the Special Order? field will display in the query results. Run the query; then save it.

f. Export the data to Excel using the file name **Special Orders**. Include formatting, and choose Open to view the file. Close the workbook file.

g. Save the export steps.

h. In Access, with the query still open, change the data in the In Stock field for T-shirts to 10 and coffee mints to 30. Rerun the export using the saved steps, replacing the Special Orders file.

i. Print the worksheet in landscape orientation and exit Excel.

j. Save the query. Close Access.

LAB EXERCISES

FOSTER PARENTS MEMO ★★

3. The Foster Parents Report you created for the Animal Rescue Foundation needs to be sent to management. (See Lab 3, Step-by-Step Exercise 5.) You want to include a brief note with the report and decide to export the report to a memo you create using Word. Your completed memo should be similar to that shown here.

   a. Open the ac03_ARF3 database that you created in Lab 3, Step-by-Step Exercise 5. Save the database as acwt_ARF. Modify the 2016 Foster Parents query to show only the Name, Foster Date, Foster First Name, and Foster last name fields. Sort in ascending order by Last Name. Leave the criteria for the foster date at >=#1/1/2016#. Save the query as 2016 Foster Names.

   b. Open Word and create a new blank document.

   c. Enter the following text, pressing Tab after typing each colon.

   To: ARF Management
   From: [Your Name]
   Date: [current date]
   Re: Foster Parents for 2016

   As you requested, here is a list of the foster parents and pets for the year 2016.

   To: ARF Management
   From: Student Name
   Date: December 12, 2016
   Re: Foster Parents for 2016

   As you requested, here is a list of the foster parents and pets for the year 2016.

2016 Foster Names			
Name	Foster Date	Foster First Name	Foster Last Name
Puddy	4/18/2016	Nathan	Bromley
Winny	4/14/2016	Fran	Calco
Fluffy	1/25/2016	Fran	Calco
Annie	9/15/2016	Betty	Cavender
Pickles	12/3/2016	Tricia	Franko
Smokey	2/4/2016	Judith	Gold
Tiny	11/12/2016	Lucy	Granger
Tara	5/20/2016	Bradley	Hawkins
Cally	8/17/2016	Mark	Lemon
Max	12/15/2016	Cathy	Lind
Lemon	12/24/2016	Cathy	Lind
Toby	10/29/2016	Susan	Malik
Coal	7/3/2016	Allyn	McMurphy
Buck	10/12/2016	Student	Name
Lilly	5/23/2016	John	Ryan
Mira	10/1/2016	John	Ryan
King	8/20/2016	Roy	Smithson
Kramer	5/1/2016	Brian	Steckler
Rusty	2/17/2016	Susannah	Troy
Tasha	4/15/2016	Kurt	Valdez
Mandy	6/1/2016	Alex	Vine
Valentine	3/20/2016	Ned	Young

   d. Copy the 2016 Foster Names query results to the Word document, allowing an appropriate amount of space between the last paragraph and the newly insert table.

   e. Apply formatting of your choice to the table. Size and center the table appropriately.

   f. Save the document as ARF Foster Parents Memo. Print the document.

   g. Close Word and Access.

Objectives

After completing this lab, you will know how to:

1   Use a template to create a presentation.

2   View and edit a presentation.

3   Copy and move selections.

4   Move, copy, and delete slides.

5   Increase and decrease list levels.

6   Create a numbered list.

7   Check spelling.

8   Size and move placeholders.

9   Change fonts and formatting.

10   Insert, size, move, and modify graphics.

11   Run a slide show.

12   Document a file.

13   Preview and print a presentation.

Animal Rescue Foundation

You are the volunteer coordinator at the local Animal Rescue Foundation. This nonprofit organization rescues unwanted pets from local animal shelters and finds foster homes for them until a suitable adoptive family can be found. The agency has a large volunteer group called the Animal Angels that provides much-needed support for the foundation.

The agency director has decided to launch a campaign to increase community awareness about the foundation. As part of the promotion, you have been asked to create a powerful and persuasive presentation to entice more members of the community to join Animal Angels.

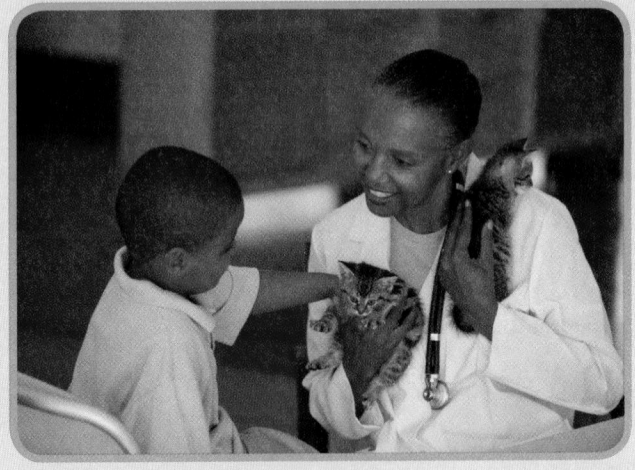

The agency director has asked you to preview the presentation at the weekly staff meeting tomorrow and has asked you to present a draft of the presentation by noon today.

To help you create the presentation, you will use Microsoft PowerPoint 2013, a graphics presentation application that is designed to create presentation materials such as slides, overheads, and handouts. In addition, your presentation can be designed to incorporate the latest high-definition (HD) and widescreen technology. Using PowerPoint 2013, you can create a high-quality and interesting onscreen presentation with pizzazz that will dazzle your audience.

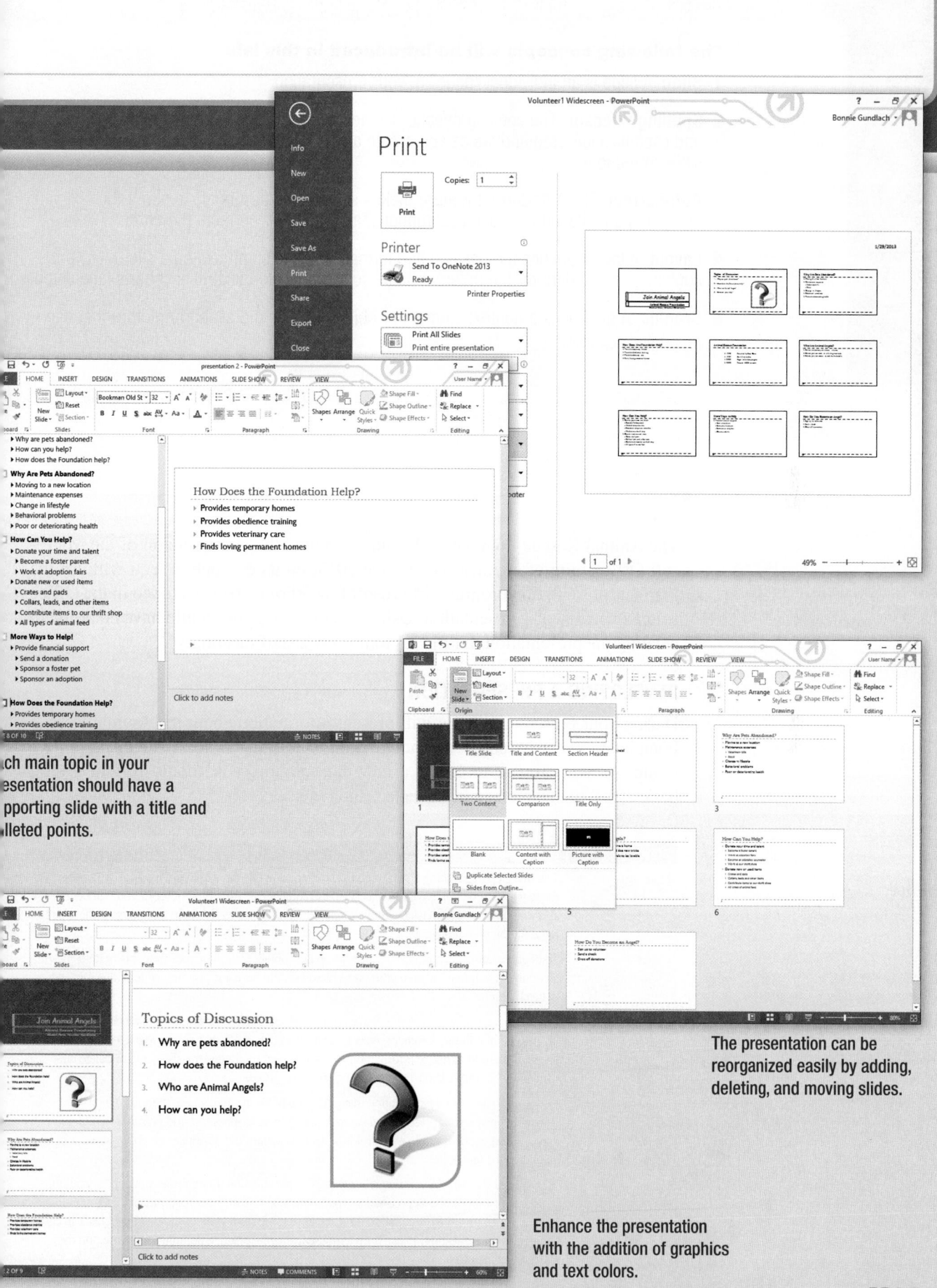

Each main topic in your presentation should have a supporting slide with a title and bulleted points.

The presentation can be reorganized easily by adding, deleting, and moving slides.

Enhance the presentation with the addition of graphics and text colors.

The following concepts will be introduced in this lab:

1 **Slide** A slide is an individual "page" of your presentation.

2 **Spelling Checker** The spelling checker locates all misspelled words, duplicate words, and capitalization irregularities as you create and edit a presentation, and proposes possible corrections.

3 **AutoCorrect** The AutoCorrect feature makes some basic assumptions about the text you are typing and, based on those assumptions, automatically corrects the entry.

4 **Layout** A layout defines the position and format for objects and text on a slide. A layout contains placeholders for the different items such as bulleted text, titles, charts, and so on.

5 **Graphic** A graphic is a nontext element or object such as a drawing or picture that can be added to a slide.

Starting a New Presentation

The Animal Rescue Foundation has just installed the latest version of the Microsoft Office suite of applications, Office 2013, on its computers. You will use the graphics presentation program, Microsoft PowerPoint 2013, included in the Office suite, to create your presentation. Using this program, you should have no problem creating the presentation in time for tomorrow's staff meeting.

DEVELOPING A PRESENTATION

During your presentation, you will present information about the Animal Rescue Foundation and why someone should want to join the Animal Angels volunteer group. As you prepare to create a new presentation, you should follow several basic steps: plan, create, edit, enhance, and rehearse.

Step	Description
Plan	The first step in planning a presentation is to understand its purpose. You also need to find out the length of time you have to speak, who the audience is, what type of room you will be in, and what kind of audiovisual equipment is available. These factors help to determine the type of presentation you will create.
Create	To begin creating your presentation, develop the content by typing your thoughts or notes into an outline. Each main idea in your presentation should have a supporting slide with a title and bulleted points.
Edit	While typing, you will probably make typing and spelling errors that need to be corrected. This is one type of editing. Another type is to revise the content of what you have entered to make it clearer, or to add or delete information. To do this, you might insert a slide, add or delete bulleted items, or move text to another location.
Enhance	You want to develop a presentation that grabs and holds the audience's attention. Choose a design that gives your presentation some dazzle. Wherever possible, add graphics to replace or enhance text. Add effects that control how a slide appears and disappears and that reveal text in a bulleted list one bullet at a time.
Rehearse	Finally, you should rehearse the delivery of your presentation. For a professional presentation, your delivery should be as polished as your materials. Use the same equipment that you will use when you give the presentation. Practice advancing from slide to slide and then back in case someone asks a question. If you have a mouse available, practice pointing or drawing on the slide to call attention to key points.

After rehearsing your presentation, you may find that you want to go back to the editing or enhancing phase. You may change text, move bullets, or insert a new slide. As you make changes, rehearse the presentation again to see how the changes affect your presentation. By the day of the presentation, you will be confident about your message and at ease with the materials.

EXPLORING THE POWERPOINT DOCUMENT WINDOW

During the planning phase, you have spoken with the foundation director regarding the purpose of the presentation and the content in general. The purpose of your presentation is to educate members of the community about the organization and to persuade many to volunteer. In addition, you want to impress the director by creating a professional presentation that will use the new widescreen and high-definition (HD) technology the organization recently purchased.

Just as in some of the other Microsoft Office 2013 applications, you can start with a blank template or use one of the predesigned templates.

1

● **Start the PowerPoint 2013 application.**

● **If necessary, maximize the window.**

Having Trouble?

See "Common Office 2013 Interface Features," page IO.14, for information on how to start the application and use features that are common to all 2013 Office applications.

Your screen should be similar to Figure 1.1

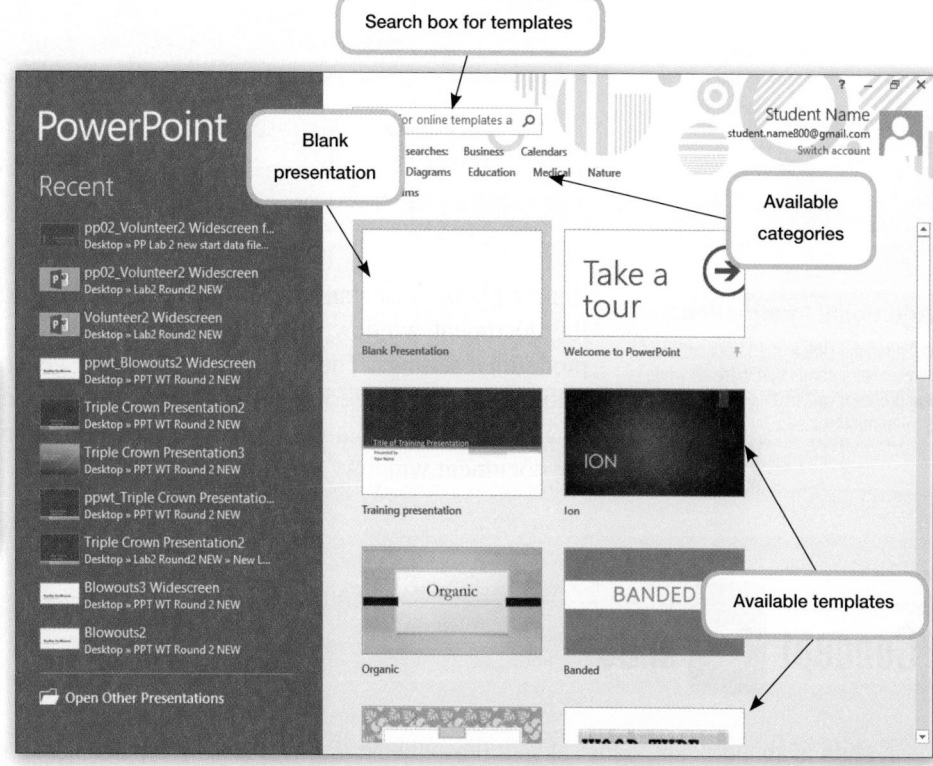

Figure 1.1

You decide to try to create your first presentation using the Blank Presentation template. It is the simplest and most generic of the templates. Because it has minimal design elements, it is good to use when you first start working with Power-Point, as it allows you to easily add your own content and design changes.

2

- Choose Blank Presentation.

- If necessary, click ⬚ NOTES in the status bar to display the notes pane.

Your screen should be similar to Figure 1.2

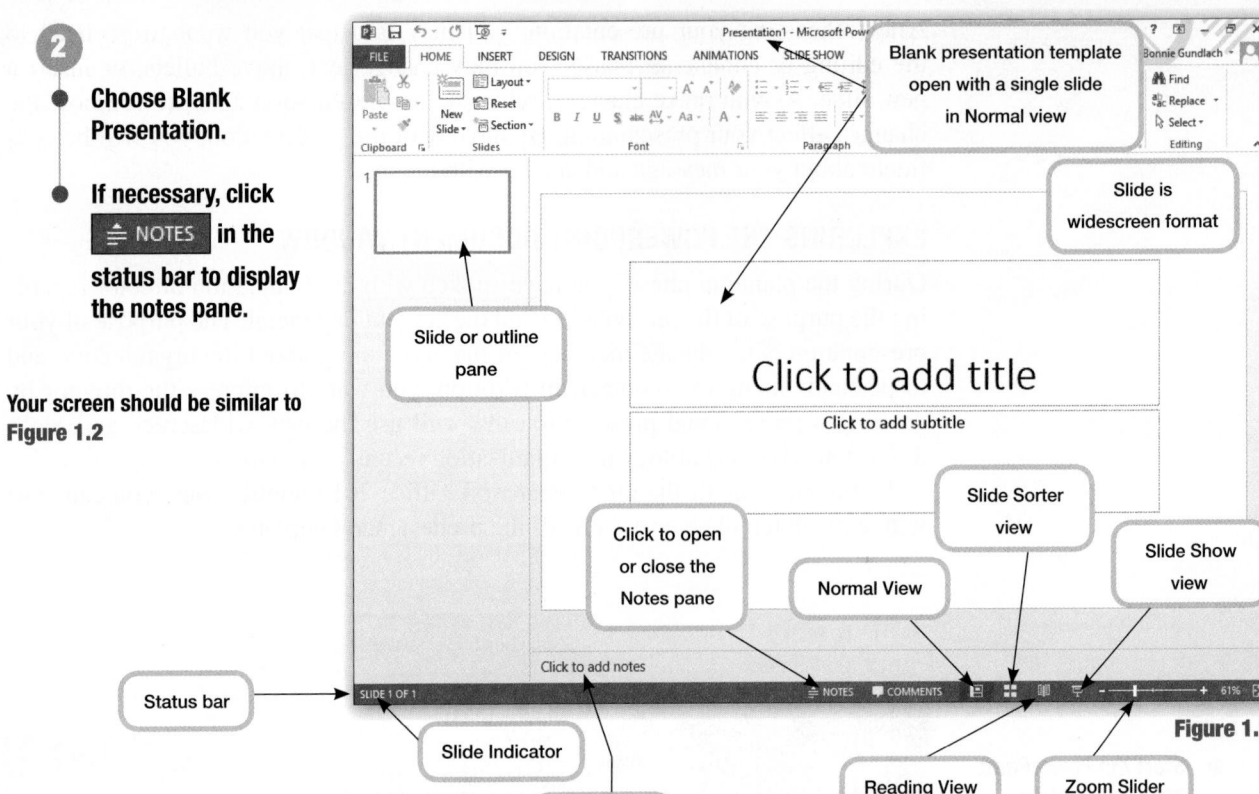

Blank presentation template open with a single slide in Normal view

Slide is widescreen format

Slide or outline pane

Click to add title

Click to add subtitle

Slide Sorter view

Click to open or close the Notes pane

Normal View

Slide Show view

Status bar

Slide Indicator

Notes pane

Reading View

Zoom Slider

Figure 1.2

A new blank presentation file, named Presentation1, is opened and displayed in the document window. It is like a blank piece of paper that already has many predefined settings. These default settings are generally the most commonly used settings and are stored in the Blank Presentation template file.

The Blank Presentation template consists of a single slide that is displayed in the document window.

Concept 1 Slide

A **slide** is an individual "page" of your presentation. The first slide of a presentation is the title slide, which is used to introduce your presentation. Additional slides are used to support each main point in your presentation. The slides give the audience a visual summary of the words you speak, which helps them understand the content and keeps them engaged. The slides also help you, the speaker, organize your thoughts and prompt you during the presentation.

When you first start PowerPoint, it opens in a view called Normal view. A **view** is a way of looking at a presentation and provides the means to interact with the presentation. PowerPoint provides several views you can use to look at and modify your presentation. Depending on what you are doing, one view may be preferable to another.

View	Button	Description
Normal		Provides three working areas of the window that allow you to work on all aspects of your presentation in one place.
Outline		Displays content of presentation in outline form in the Outline tab making it easier to focus on content rather than design.
Slide Sorter		Displays a miniature of each slide to make it easy to reorder slides, add special effects such as transitions, and set timing between slides.
Reading View		Displays each slide in final form within the PowerPoint window so you can see how it will look during a presentation but still have access to the Windows desktop.
Slide Show		Displays each slide in final form using the full screen space so you can practice or present the presentation.

Normal view is displayed by default because it is the main view you use while creating a presentation. Normal view has three working areas: Slides or outline pane, Slide window, and Notes pane. These areas allow you to work on all components of your presentation in one convenient location. The **Slides pane** displays a miniature version or **thumbnail** of each slide. When selected, the **Outline pane** displays the slide's content in outline form rather than as a slide thumbnail. The **Slide window** displays the selected slide. Notice the blank slide shape is rectangular. This is the default **widescreen** slide size (16:9) and is used to create a presentation that can take advantage of new widescreen technology, including HD features and equipment. Standard slide size (4:3) is also available. In this size, slides are squarer and are designed to be displayed on traditional-size screens. The **Notes pane,** when displayed, appears below the Slide window. It is used to enter notes that apply to the current slide and can be opened and closed by clicking ≜ NOTES on the status bar.

Below the document window is the status bar, which displays the slide indicator, messages and information about various PowerPoint settings, buttons to change the document view, and a window zoom feature. The **slide indicator** on the left side of the status bar identifies the number of the slide that is displayed in the Slide pane, along with the total number of slides in the presentation. You will learn about the other features of the status bar shortly.

ENTERING AND EDITING TEXT

Notice the blank slide contains two boxes with dotted borders. These boxes, called **placeholders**, are containers for all the content that appears on a slide. Slide content consists of text and **objects** such as, graphics, tables and charts. In this case, the placeholders are text placeholders that are designed to contain text and display standard **placeholder text** messages that prompt the user to enter a title and subtitle.

As suggested, you will enter the title for the presentation. As soon as you click on the placeholder, the placeholder text will disappear and will be replaced by the text you type.

● **Click the "Click to add title" placeholder.**

Your screen should be similar to Figure 1.3

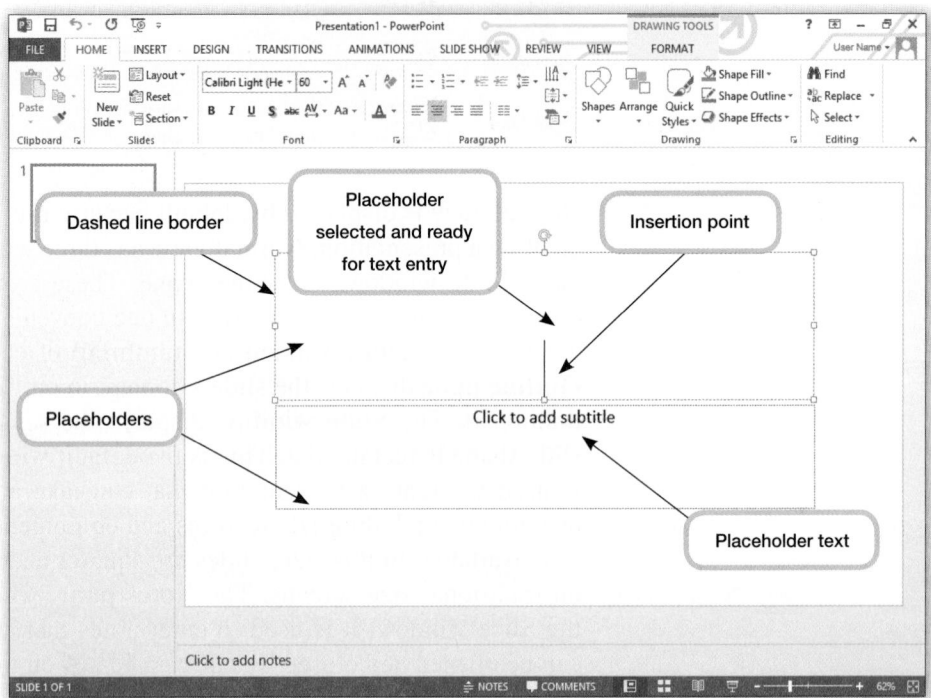

Figure 1.3

Additional Information

A solid border indicates that you can format the placeholder box itself. Clicking the dashed-line border changes it to a solid border.

Notice that the placeholder is surrounded with a dashed-line border. This indicates that you can enter, delete, select, and format the object inside the placeholder. Because this placeholder contains text, the insertion point is displayed to show your location in the text and to allow you to select and edit the text. Additionally, the mouse pointer appears as a I to be used to position the insertion point.

Next you will type the title text you want to appear on the slide. Then you will enter the subtitle.

Having Trouble?

See the section "Entering and Editing Text" on page IO.37 in the Introduction to Microsoft Office 2013 to review this feature.

Type Join Animal Angels

Click in the "Click to add subtitle" placeholder and type Animal Rescue Foundation

Your screen should be similar to Figure 1.4

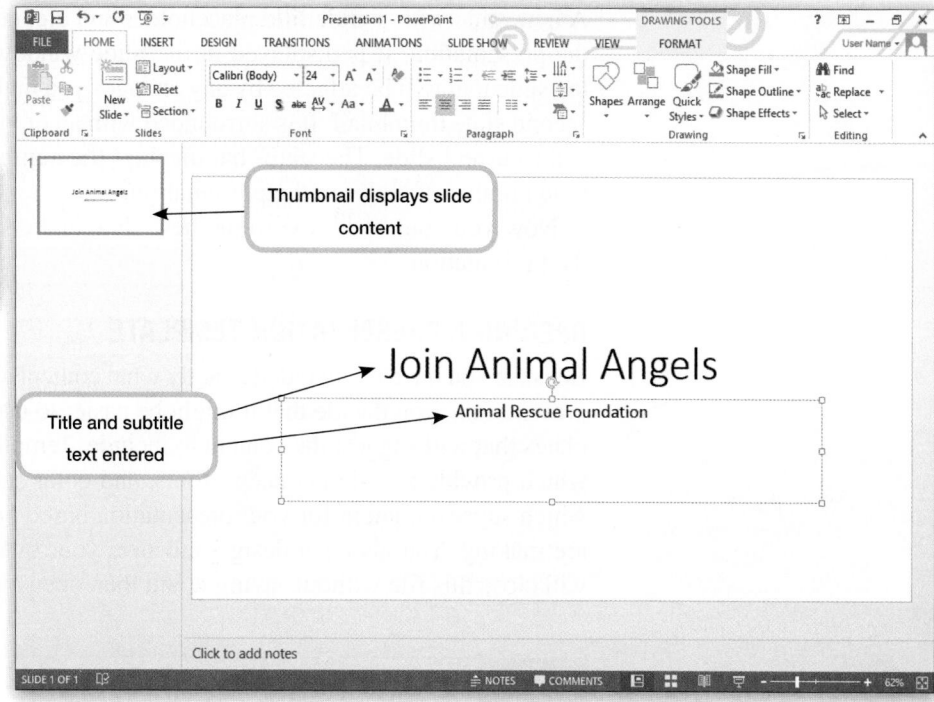

Figure 1.4

The content for the first slide is complete. Notice that the thumbnail of the slide in the Slides pane now displays the text you just entered.

INSERTING A SLIDE

Next you want to add the content for a second slide. To continue creating the presentation, you need to add another slide.

If necessary, open the Home tab.

Click the upper section of New Slide button in the Slides group.

Your screen should be similar to Figure 1.5

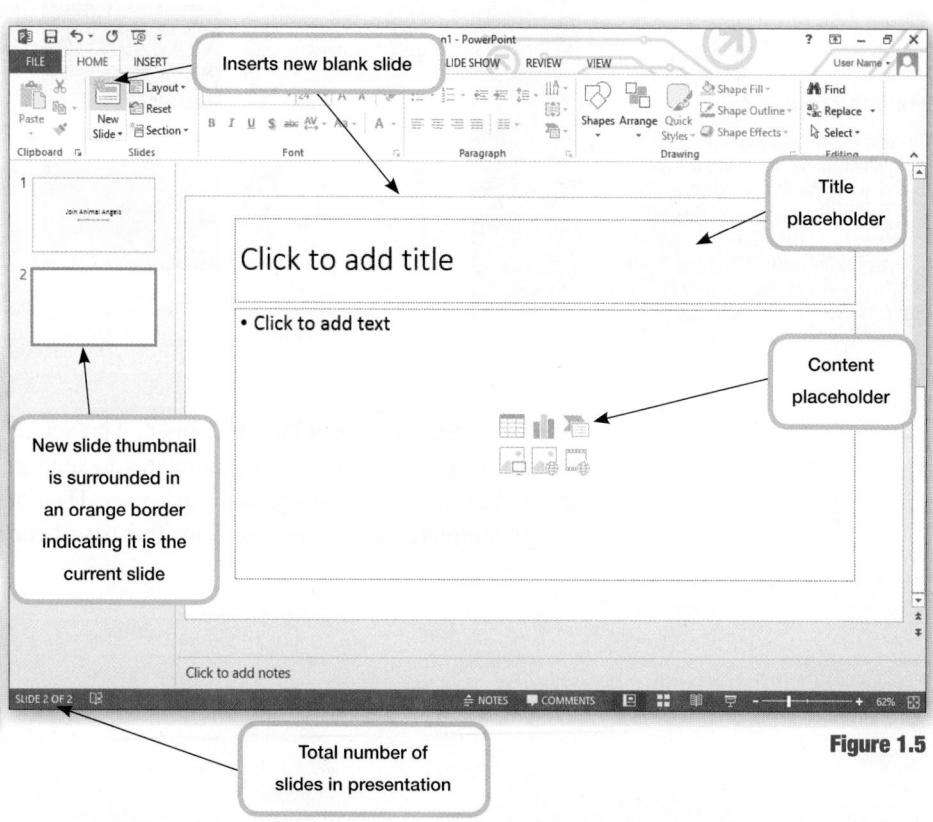

Figure 1.5

A new slide with a slide title placeholder and a content placeholder was added to the presentation. It is displayed in the Slide window and is the **current slide**, or the slide that will be affected by any changes you make. The Slides pane displays a second slide thumbnail. It is surrounded with an orange border further indicating it is the current slide. The status bar displays the number of the current slide and the total number of slides in the presentation.

Now you could add text to the new slide and continue adding slides to create the presentation.

OPENING A PRESENTATION TEMPLATE

Because you have not decided exactly what content should be presented next in the presentation, you decide that it might be easier to use one of the predesigned templates that will suggest the content to include. Templates include design templates, which provide a design concept, fonts, and color scheme; and content templates, which suggest content for your presentation based on the type of presentation you are making. You also can design and save your own presentation templates. You will close this file without saving it and then open a presentation template file.

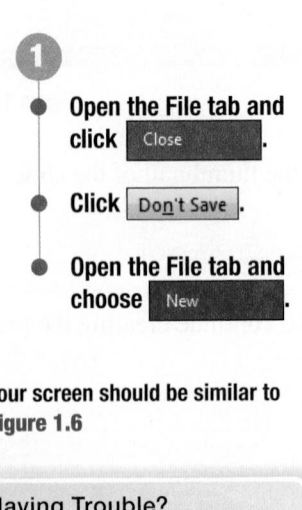

1

• Open the File tab and click `Close`.

• Click `Don't Save`.

• Open the File tab and choose `New`.

Your screen should be similar to Figure 1.6

Having Trouble?

To complete steps 2 and 3 you need an Internet connection. If you are not connected to the Internet, choose 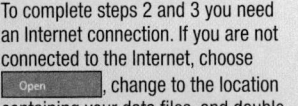, change to the location containing your data files, and double-click on the file pp01_Training. Then skip to the next section, Viewing the Presentation.

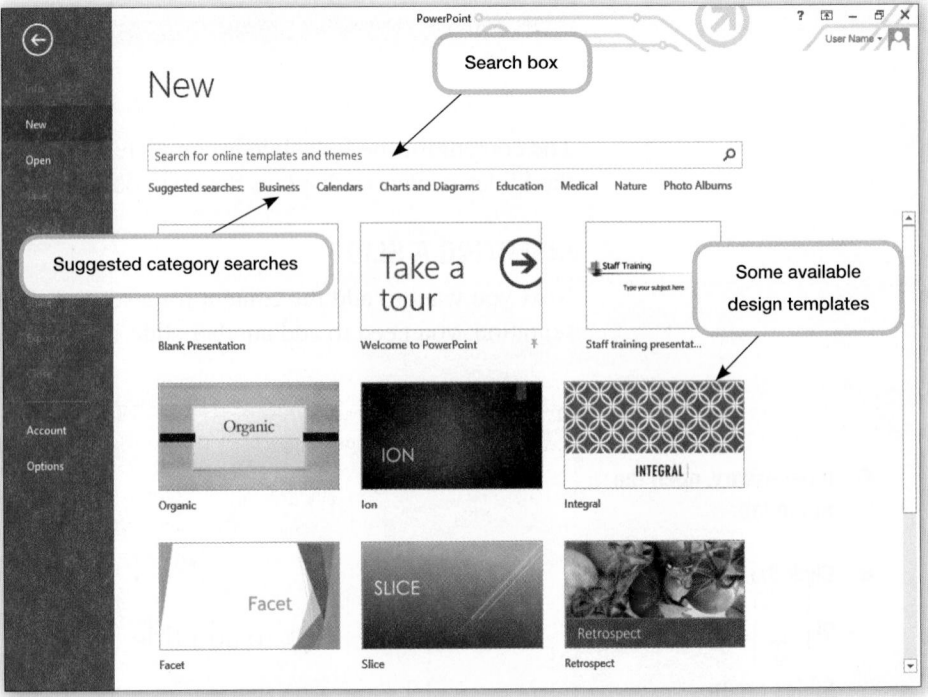

Figure 1.6

The New presentation window is open. The search box at the top of the window is used to quickly find content templates located in a specific category. Below the search box are links to suggested categories. The main window area displays several design templates as well as templates that have been recently opened.

You will look for templates in the business category that will help you create a basic business presentation. When you open a category, examples of the content and/or design templates will be displayed. Before deciding on the template you will use, you will look at some of the available templates.

2

● **Choose Business from the suggested searches list of links.**

Your screen should be similar to Figure 1.7

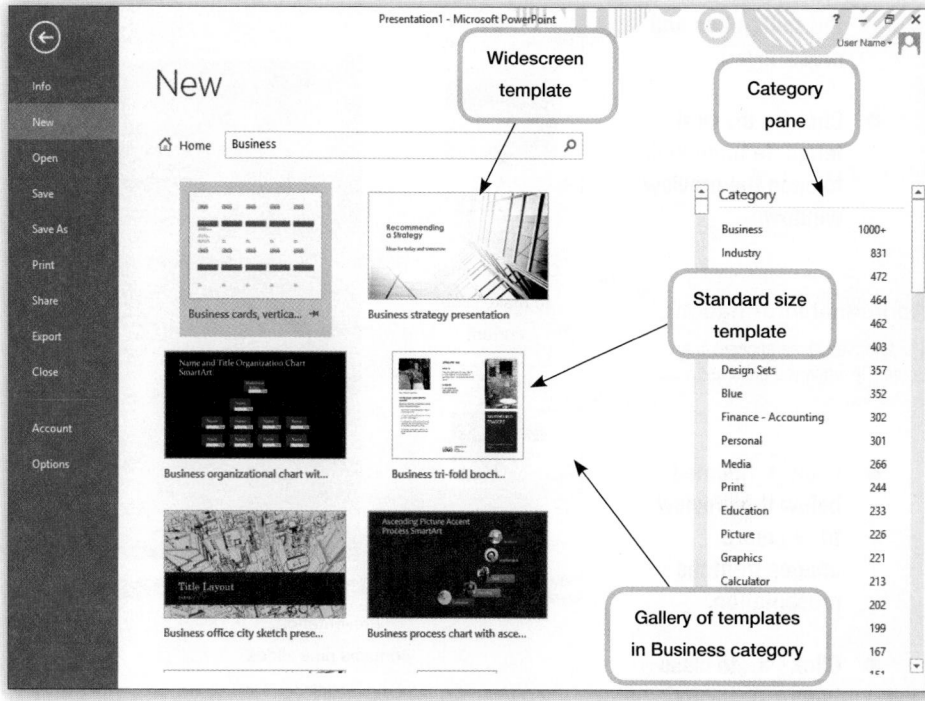

Figure 1.7

Thumbnail images representing the first slide in each template file are displayed. Notice that the thumbnails are different shapes and sizes. Templates can have either portrait or landscape orientation and can be either standard or widescreen in size.

You find the Business category contains a large number of templates. To narrow the number of selections, you can choose another more specific category from the Category pane or type a more specific search term in the search box.

Type Training **in the search box and press** Enter**.**

Click on the first template thumbnail to open the preview window.

Click ▶ **located below the preview to see more images from the presentation.**

Click ✕ **to close the preview window.**

Locate and preview the Training seminar presentation (shown in Figure 1.8).

Click .

Your screen should be similar to Figure 1.8

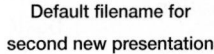
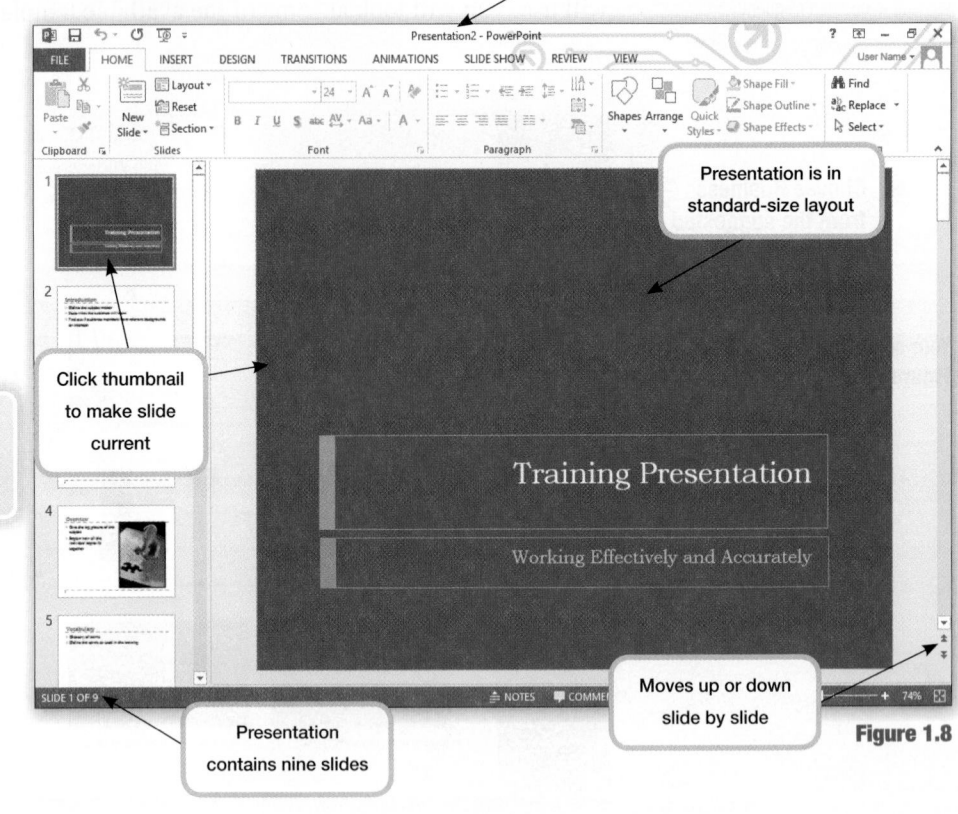

Figure 1.8

The template file is downloaded and opened in PowerPoint. It contains a total of nine slides. Because this is the second new presentation you have worked on since starting PowerPoint 2013, the default file name is Presentation2. You think the design of the template looks good and you will begin your presentation for the volunteers using the content in this template as a guide.

CHANGING SLIDE SIZE

This template uses standard-size slides in its layout. Because you know that during the meeting you will be using equipment that supports widescreen features, you will change the slide size to widescreen before adding the presentation content. This will make your editing process easier since you will already be using the correct format. If necessary, you can always convert back to standard later; however, adjustments to your slides may be required. It's always best to start in the layout that will be used in order to avoid having to make many modifications later.

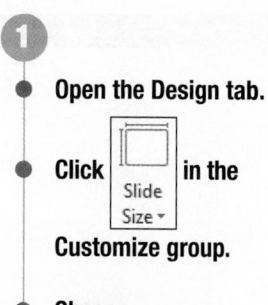

1

- Open the Design tab.

- Click [Slide Size ▾] in the Customize group.

- Choose [☐ Widescreen (16:9)].

- If necessary, click [▦] at the right end of the status bar to fit the slide to the current window.

- Point to the splitter bar between the Slide tab and the Slide pane, and when the mouse pointer is shaped as ⇔, drag to the right to increase the width of the pane to show four slides.

Your screen should be similar to Figure 1.9

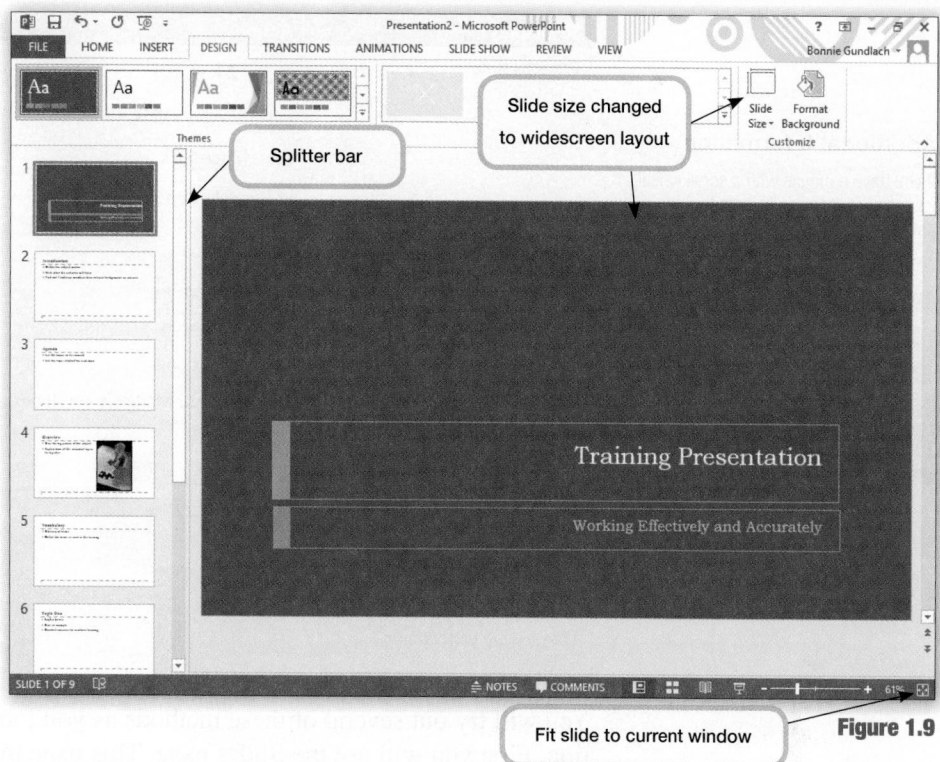

Figure 1.9

The slide size is now the rectangular shape used with widescreen equipment. Additionally, by increasing the width of the Slide tab, you can more easily see the slide content.

MOVING AMONG SLIDES

You want to look at the slides in the presentation to get a quick idea of their content. There are many ways to move from slide to slide in PowerPoint. Most often, the quickest method is to click on the slide thumbnail in the Slides pane. Clicking on a slide in the Slides pane displays it in the Slide window and makes it the current slide. However, if your hands are already on the keyboard, you may want to use the keyboard directional keys. The table on the next page shows both keyboard and mouse methods to move among slides in Normal view.

To Display	Action
Previous slide	Click [▲] Click above scroll box Press [Page Up] [↑] One slide up
Next slide	Click [▼] Click below scroll box Press [Page Down] [↓] One slide down
Any slide	Drag the Slide window's scroll box until the ScreenTip displays the slide you want to view. 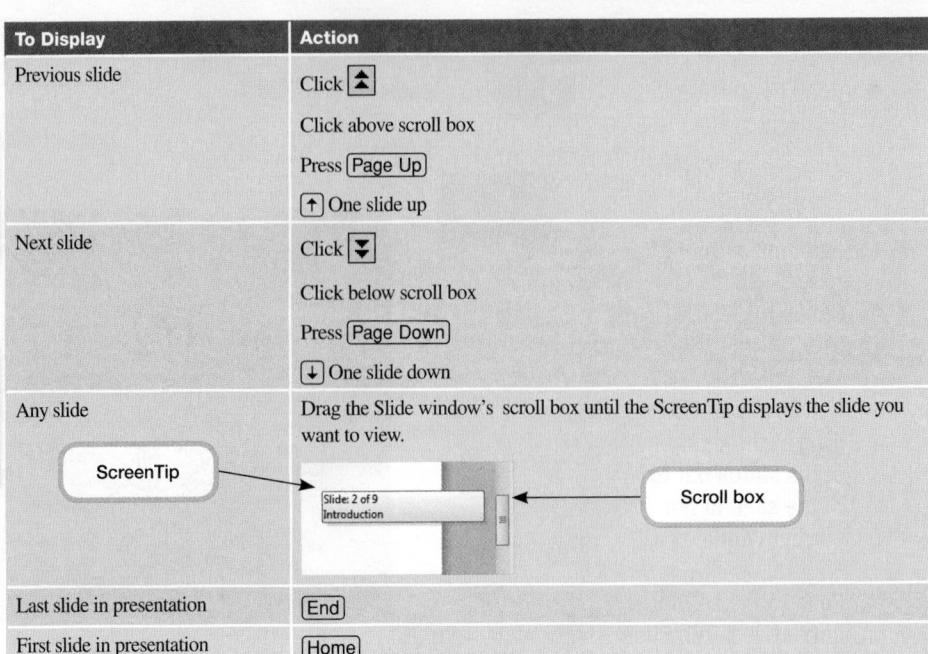
Last slide in presentation	[End]
First slide in presentation	[Home]

You will try out several of these methods as you look at the slides in the presentation. First you will use the Slides pane. This pane makes it easy to move from one slide to another.

1

- Open the Home tab.

- Press [↓] or [Page Down] to move to the next slide.

- Scroll the Slides pane to display slides 4 to 7.

- Click on slide 4.

Your screen should be similar to Figure 1.10

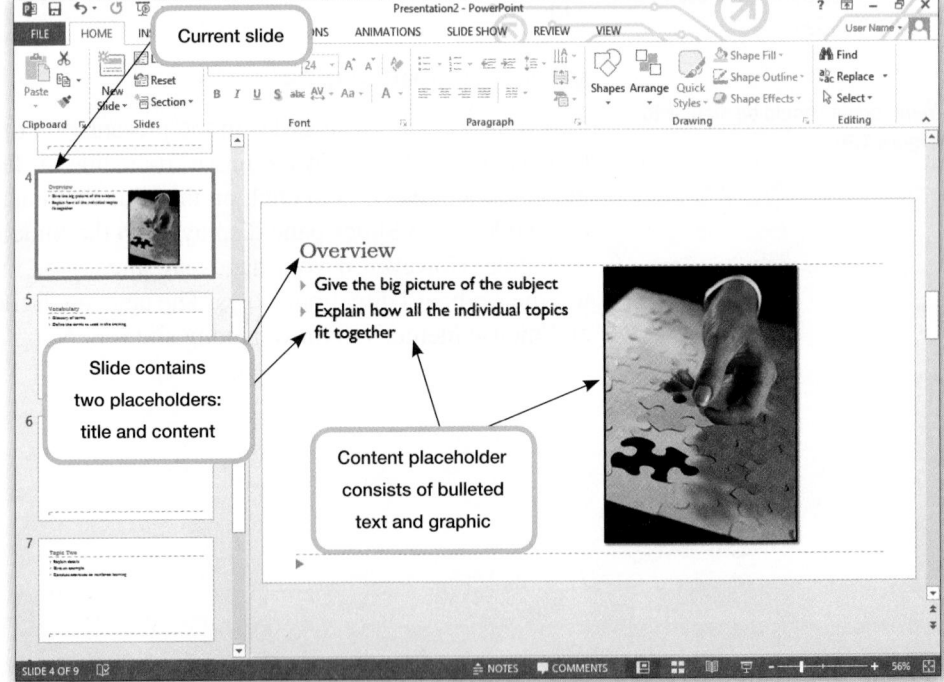

Figure 1.10

Slide 4 is the current slide and is displayed in the Slide window. This slide contains two placeholders: title and content. The content placeholder consists of two bulleted items as well as a graphic. Next you will use the Slide window scroll bar to display the next few slides.

2

● Click ▼ Next Slide to display slide 5.

Having Trouble?

The ▲ Previous Slide and ▼ Next Slide buttons are located at the bottom of the Slide window's vertical scroll bar.

● Drag the scroll box and stop when the ScreenTip displays Slide 6 of 9.

● Click below the scroll box to display slide 7.

● Press End to display the last slide.

Your screen should be similar to Figure 1.11

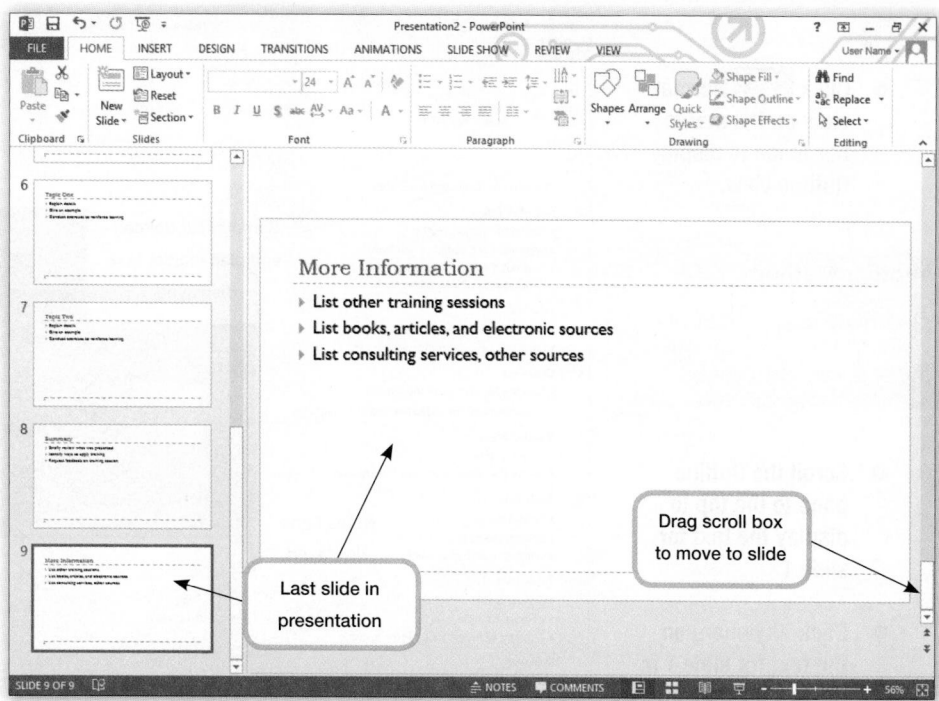

Figure 1.11

You can see this template will help you to create your presentation because the content provides some basic guidance as to how to organize a presentation.

Editing a Presentation

Now you need to edit the presentation to replace the sample content with the appropriate information for your presentation. Editing involves making text changes and additions to the content of your presentation. It also includes making changes to the organization of content. This can be accomplished quickly by rearranging the order of bulleted items on slides as well as the order of slides.

USING OUTLINE VIEW

You have already entered text in a slide in the Slide window in Normal view. Another way to make text-editing changes is to use Outline view. Outline view displays the content of the presentation in outline form in the Outline pane, making it easy to see the organization of your presentation as you enter and edit content. The first change you want to make is to enter a title for the presentation on slide 1. First, you will open Outline view and select the sample title text on the slide in the Outline pane and delete it.

1

● **Click** 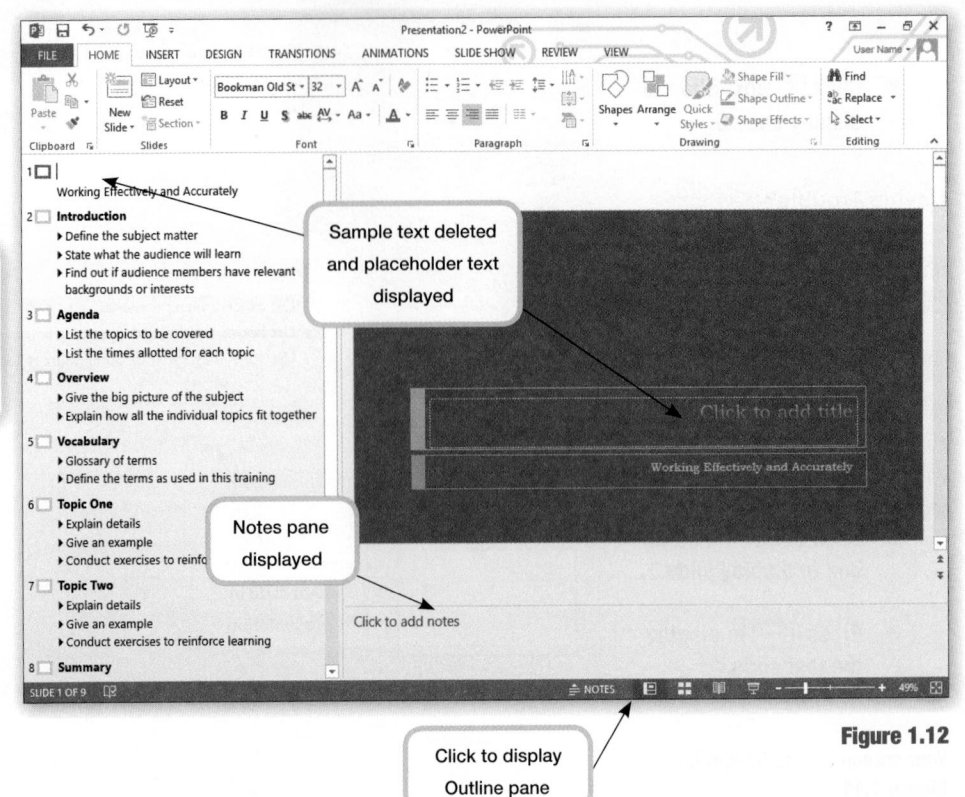 **Normal view on the status bar twice to display Outline view.**

Another Method

You also can choose ⬚ Outline View from the View tab to display the Outline tab.

● **Scroll the Outline pane to the top to display the text for slide 1.**

● **Click anywhere on the text for slide 1 in the Outline pane to make it the current slide.**

● **Select the text "Training Presentation" on slide 1 in the outline pane.**

Having Trouble?

Refer to the topic "Selecting Text" on page IO.40 in the Introduction to Microsoft Office 2013 to review these features.

Additional Information

The Mini toolbar appears automatically when you select text.

● **Press** Delete.

Your screen should be similar to Figure 1.12

Figure 1.12

When in Normal view, clicking ⬚ Normal view switches between displaying the Slides pane and the Outline pane. In Outline view, the Slides pane is replaced with the Outline pane. Unlike the Slides pane that displays a miniature version of each slide, the Outline pane displays the text on the slides only. Also notice that the Notes pane is now displayed. Changing views automatically displays the Notes pane.

The sample text is deleted. As you change the text content in the Outline pane, it also appears in the slide displayed in the Slide window. Notice that although you deleted the sample text, the slide still displays the title placeholder text.

You will enter the title and subtitle for the presentation next.

Type Join Animal Angels

Select the text "Working Efficiently and Accurately" on the second line of slide 1 in the Outline pane and type Animal Rescue Foundation

Your screen should be similar to Figure 1.13

Text entered in the Outline pane appears on the slide

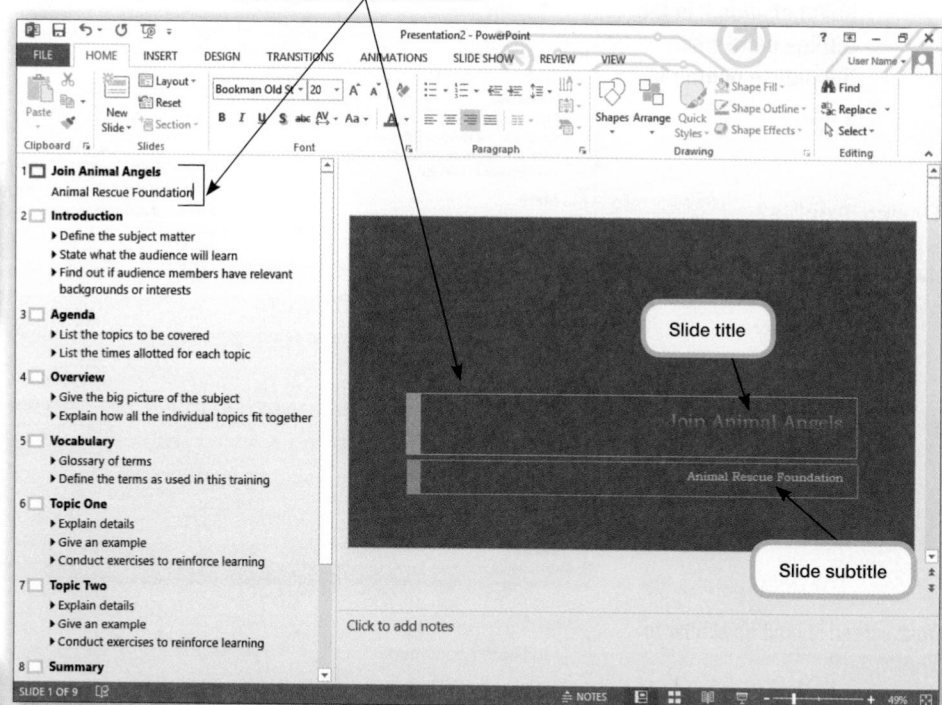

Slide title

Slide subtitle

Figure 1.13

As soon as you pressed a key, the selected text was deleted and replaced with the text you typed. When entering the title for a slide, it is a common practice to use title case, in which the first letter of most words is capitalized.

The next change you want to make is on the Introduction slide. The sample text recommends that you define the subject of the presentation and what the audience will learn. You will replace the sample text next to the first bullet with the text for your slide. In the Outline pane, you can select an entire paragraph and all sub-paragraphs by pointing to the left of the line and clicking when the mouse pointer is a .

Click on the first bullet of slide 2 in the Outline pane when the mouse pointer is a **.**

Having Trouble?

If you accidentally drag selected text, it will move. To return it to its original location, immediately click ⟲⸱ Undo on the Quick Access Toolbar.

Type Your Name, Volunter (this word is intentionally misspelled) Coordinator

Your screen should be similar to Figure 1.14

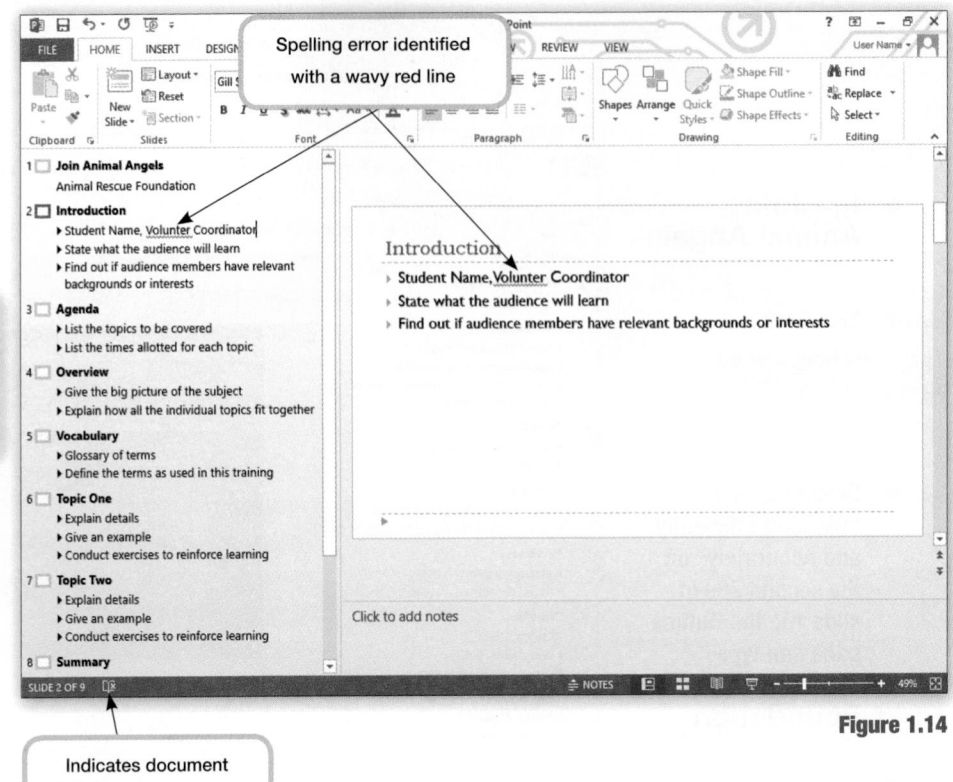

Spelling error identified with a wavy red line

Indicates document contains a spelling error

Figure 1.14

Having Trouble?

Do not be concerned if the spelling checker identifies your name as misspelled.

Having Trouble

If the Spelling indicator is not displayed, right click on the status bar and choose Spell Check from the context menu.

CORRECTING ERRORS

As you enter text, the program checks each word for accuracy. In this case, a spelling error was located. PowerPoint identified the word as misspelled by underlining it with a wavy red line. The Spelling indicator 🔲 in the status bar also shows a spelling error has been detected in the document.

Concept ❷ Spelling Checker

The **spelling checker** locates all misspelled words, duplicate words, and capitalization irregularities as you create and edit a presentation, and proposes possible corrections. This feature works by comparing each word to a dictionary of words. If the word does not appear in the main dictionary or in a custom dictionary, it is identified as misspelled. The **main dictionary** is supplied with the program; a **custom dictionary** is one you can create to hold words you commonly use, such as proper names and technical terms, that are not included in the main dictionary.

If the word does not appear in either dictionary, the program identifies it as misspelled by displaying a red wavy line below the word. You can then correct the misspelled word by editing it. Alternatively, you can display a list of suggested spelling corrections for that word and select the correct spelling from the list to replace the misspelled word in the presentation.

To quickly correct the misspelled word, you can select the correct spelling from a list of suggested spelling corrections displayed on the shortcut menu.

1

Right-click on the misspelled word in the Outline pane to display the shortcut menu.

Your screen should be similar to Figure 1.15

Additional Information

Sometimes the spelling checker cannot suggest replacements because it cannot locate any words in its dictionary that are similar in spelling. Other times the suggestions offered are not correct. If either situation happens, you must edit the word manually.

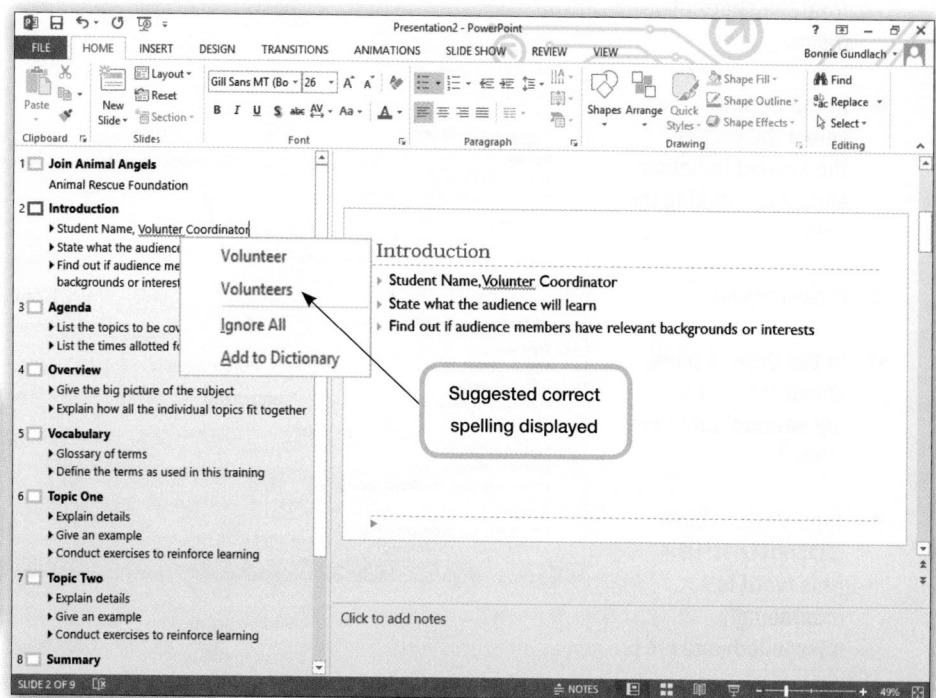

Figure 1.15

The shortcut menu displays two suggested correct spellings. The menu also includes two related menu options described below.

Additional Information

The spelling checker works just as it does in the other Microsoft Office 2013 applications.

Option	Effect
Ignore All	Instructs PowerPoint to ignore the misspelling of this word throughout the rest of this session.
Add to Dictionary	Adds the word to the custom dictionary list. When a word is added to the custom dictionary, PowerPoint will always accept that spelling as correct.

You will replace the word with the correct spelling and then enter the information for the second bullet.

2

- Choose "Volunteer" from the shortcut menu.

- In the Outline pane, select the text in the second bullet on slide 2 by clicking the bullet.

- Press Delete.

- In the Outline pane, select the text in the second bullet on slide 2.

- Type volunteer oppotunities (this word is intentionally misspelled) and press Spacebar.

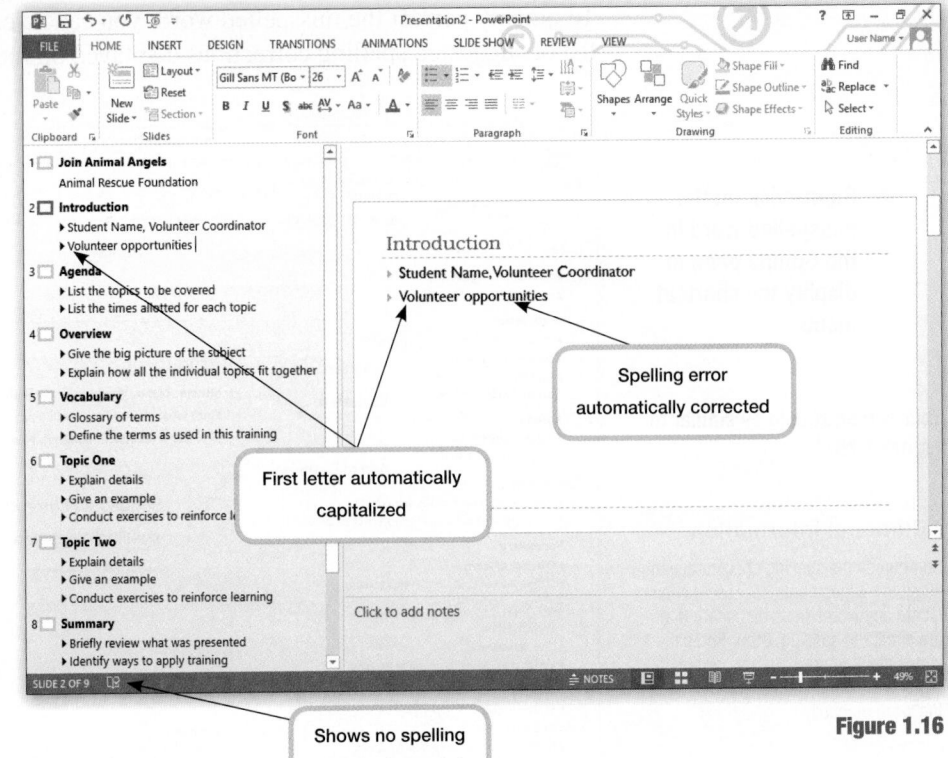

Figure 1.16

Your screen should be similar to
Figure 1.16

Additional Information

Bulleted items in a presentation are capitalized in sentence case format. Ending periods, however, are not included.

Notice that the first letter of "volunteer" was automatically capitalized. Also notice that the incorrect spelling of the word "oppotunities" was corrected. These corrections are part of the AutoCorrect feature of PowerPoint.

Concept  AutoCorrect

The **AutoCorrect** feature makes some basic assumptions about the text you are typing and, based on those assumptions, automatically corrects the entry. The AutoCorrect feature automatically inserts proper capitalization at the beginning of sentences and in the names of days of the week. It also will change to lowercase letters any words that were incorrectly capitalized due to the accidental use of the Caps Lock key. In addition, it also corrects many common typing and spelling errors automatically.

One way the program makes corrections automatically is by looking for certain types of errors. For example, if two capital letters appear at the beginning of a word, the second capital letter is changed to a lowercase letter. If a lowercase letter appears at the beginning of a sentence, the first letter of the first word is capitalized. If the name of a day begins with a lowercase letter, the first letter is capitalized.

Another way the program makes corrections is by automatically replacing a misspelled word with the correct spelling in situations where the spelling checker offers only one suggested spelling correction. AutoCorrect also checks all words against the AutoCorrect list, a built-in list of words that are commonly spelled or typed incorrectly. If it finds the entry on the list, the program automatically replaces the error with the correction. For example, the typing error "aboutthe" is automatically changed to "about the" because the error is on the AutoCorrect list. You also can add words to the AutoCorrect list that you want to be corrected automatically. Any such words are added to the list on the computer you are using and will be available to anyone who uses the machine after you.

COPYING AND MOVING SELECTIONS

You are now ready to enter the text for the next slide in your presentation by entering the three main topics of discussion. You want to enter a new slide title, Topics of Discussion, with three bulleted items describing the topics to be discussed. Two placeholder bullets with sample text are displayed. You will edit these and then add a third bulleted item.

1

- Move to slide 3.

- In the Outline pane, replace the sample title, Agenda, with **Topics of Discussion**

- Select and replace the text in the first bullet with **Why are pets abandoned?**

- Select and replace the text in the second bullet with **How can you help?**

- Press [Enter].

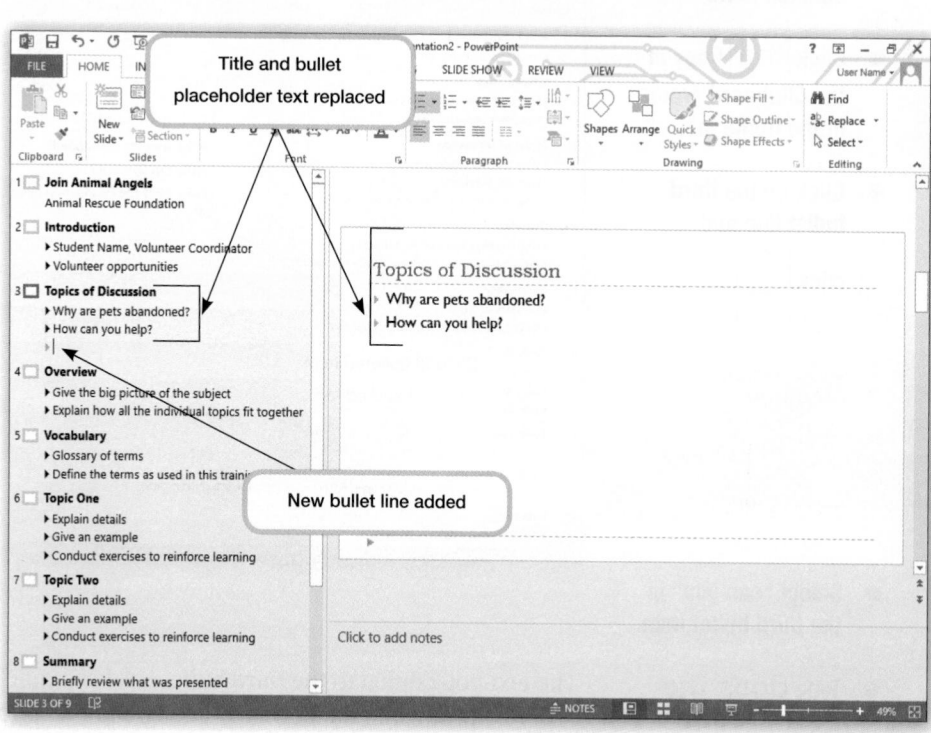

Figure 1.17

Having Trouble?

If you accidentally insert an extra bullet and blank line, press [Backspace] twice to remove them.

Your screen should be similar to Figure 1.17

Having Trouble?

Refer to "Copying and Moving Selections" on page IO.47 in the Introduction to Microsoft Office 2013 to review this feature.

A new bulleted line is automatically created whenever you press [Enter] at the end of a bulleted item. Because the text you want to enter for this bullet is similar to the text in the second bullet, you decide to save time by copying and pasting the bullet text. Then you will modify the text in the third bullet.

2

- Select the second bulleted item.

- Click 🔲 ▾ **Copy** in the Clipboard group of the Home tab.

- Click on the third bullet line and click 🔲 **Paste** ▾.

- Select "can you" in the third bullet item.

- Type **does the Foundation**

- If necessary, select and delete the fourth blank bullet line.

Your screen should be similar to Figure 1.18

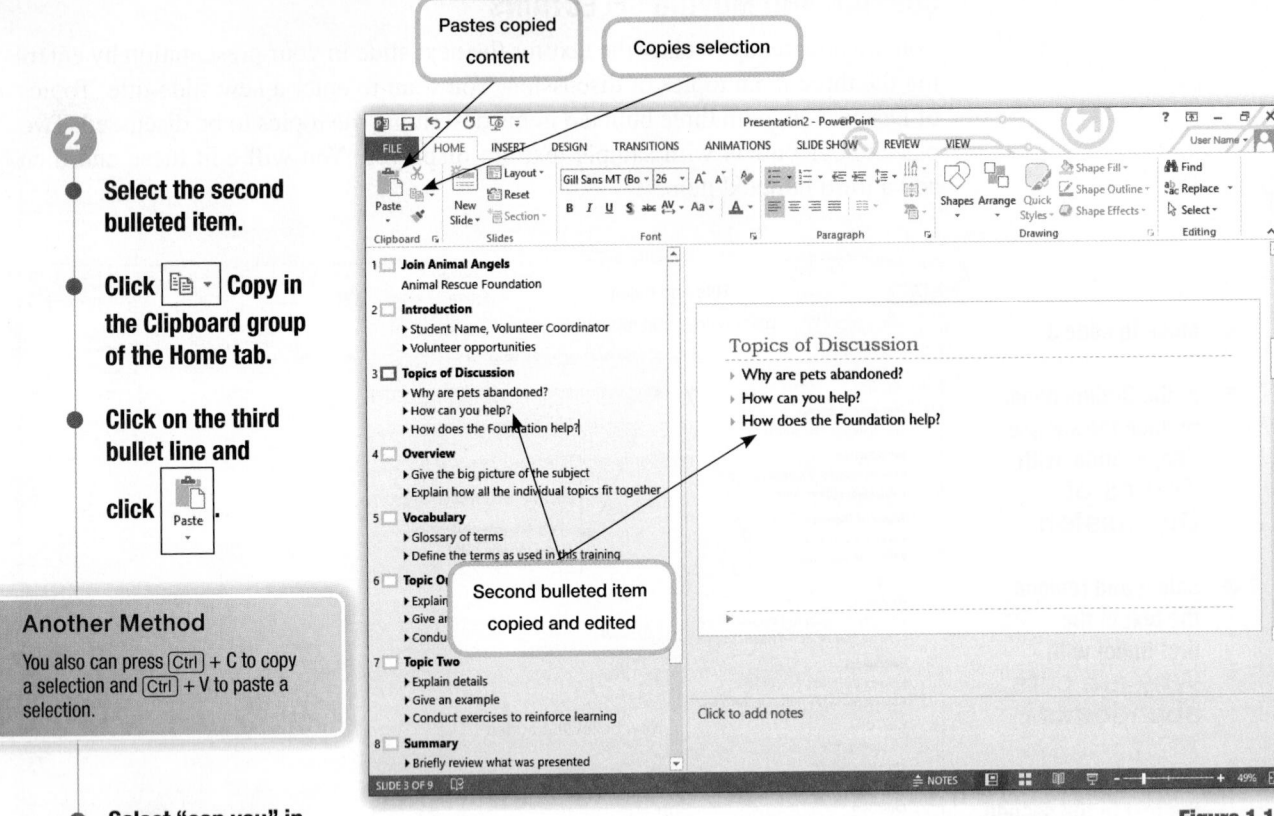

Figure 1.18

The text you copied to the third bullet has been quickly modified. Copying is especially helpful when the entries are long and complicated.

As you review what you have entered so far in your presentation, you decide that it would be better to introduce yourself on the first slide. Rather than retyping this information, you will move your introduction from slide 2 to slide 1. You will do this using drag and drop.

3

● In the Outline pane, press Enter at the end of the subtitle in slide 1 to create a blank line.

● Select the first bulleted item on slide 2.

● Drag the selection to the blank line on slide 1.

Another Method

You can also use ✂ Cut or Ctrl + X to cut a selection and then paste it to the new location.

● Move to the blank line at the end of slide 1 and press Backspace to delete it.

Your screen should be similar to **Figure 1.19**

Having Trouble?

Review saving files in the "Saving a File" section on page IO.54 in the Introduction to Microsoft Office 2013.

4

● Open the File tab and click Save As.

● Select the location where you will save your solution files.

● Replace the proposed file name in the File Name text box with **Volunteer.**

● Click Save.

Additional Information

The file extensions may or may not be displayed, depending upon your Windows folder settings.

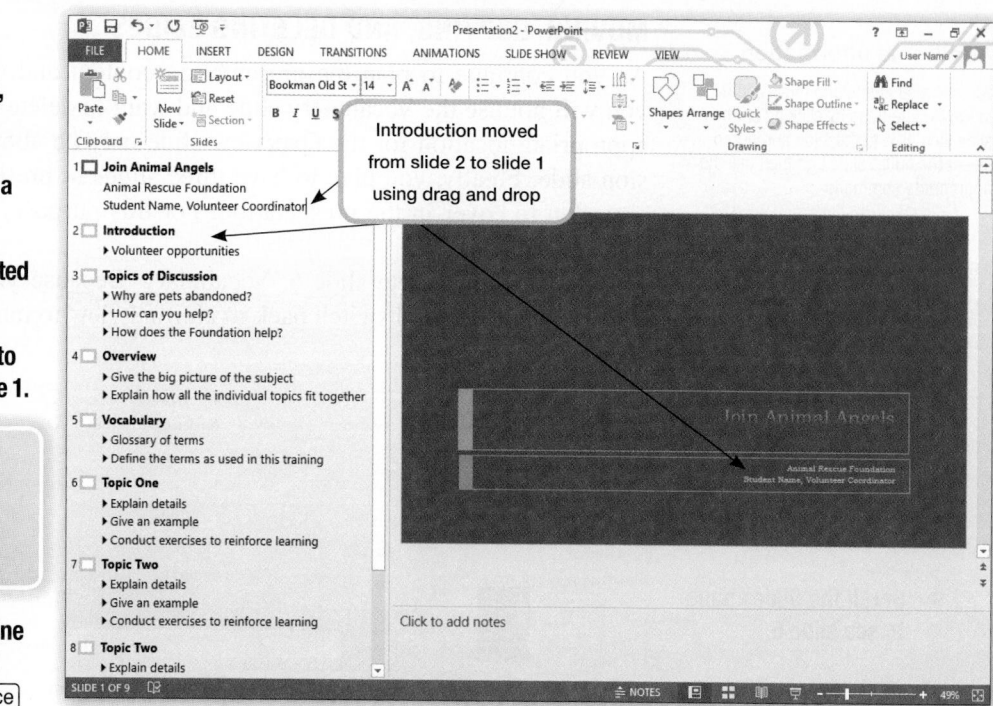

Introduction moved from slide 2 to slide 1 using drag and drop

Figure 1.19

Because the Outline pane lets you see the content in multiple slides at once, it makes it easy to see the organization of the presentation and to quickly make text changes within and between slides.

Before continuing, you will save your work to a file named Volunteer.

The presentation is now saved to the location you specified in a new file named Volunteer. The view in use at the time the file is saved also is saved with the file. The file is saved with the default file extension of .pptx. You can also save Power-Point presentations as an image file using the .gif, .tif, or .jpg file extension. When you save a presentation as an image file, you are given the choice to save the Current Slide Only or Every Slide as an image, in which case each slide will be saved as a separate image file.

Additional Information

You can also delete and move slides in the Outline pane by clicking on the slide icon next to the slide number to select the entire slide and then use the appropriate command.

As you continue to plan the presentation content and organization, you decide you will not use the Vocabulary slide and want to delete it. You also think a more appropriate location for the Overview slide may be above the Topics of Discussion slide. Finally, you plan to have three slides to present the three main topics you plan to cover in the presentation. For this purpose, you want to add a third topic slide.

First you will delete slide 5, Vocabulary. Because you are not working with slide content, you will switch back to Normal view to make these changes.

- Click Normal to display the Slides pane in Normal view.

- Scroll the Slides pane to see slide 5.

- Click on slide 5 to select the slide.

- Press Delete.

Another Method

You can also choose Delete Slide from the selected slide's context menu.

Your screen should be similar to Figure 1.20

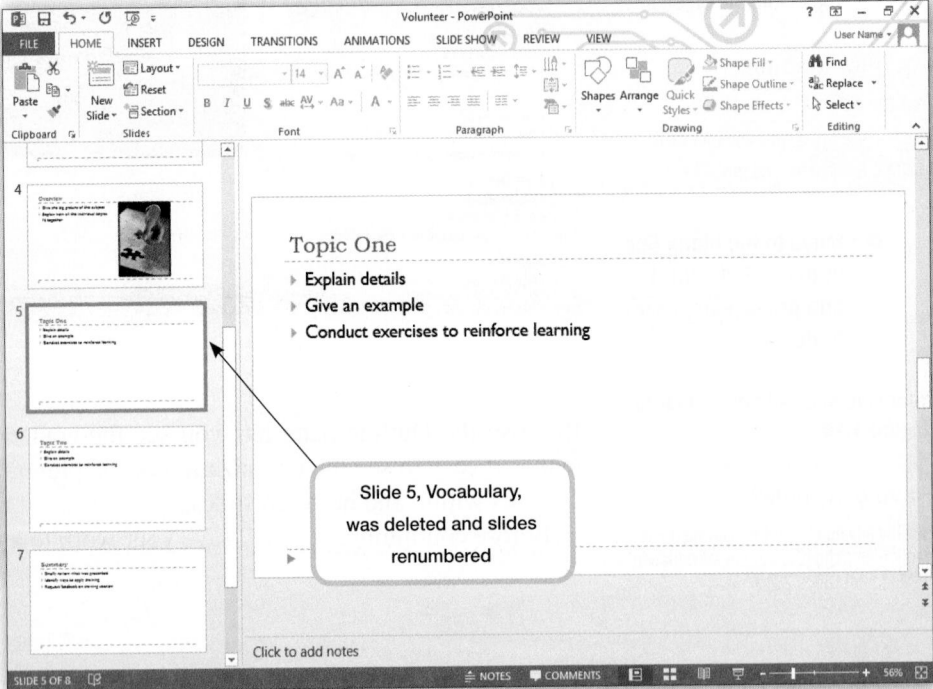

Slide 5, Vocabulary, was deleted and slides renumbered

Figure 1.20

The slide has been deleted and all subsequent slides renumbered.

Next, you will move the Overview slide (4) above slide 3 using drag and drop.

• **Select slide 4 in the Slides pane.**

• **If necessary, scroll the Slides pane to show slide 3.**

• **Drag slide 4 above slide 3 in the Slides pane.**

Additional Information

The slides will change places as you drag the slides to the new location.

Touch Tip

If you have a touch device you can tap a slide in the slide pane and drag it to its new location.

Your screen should be similar to Figure 1.21

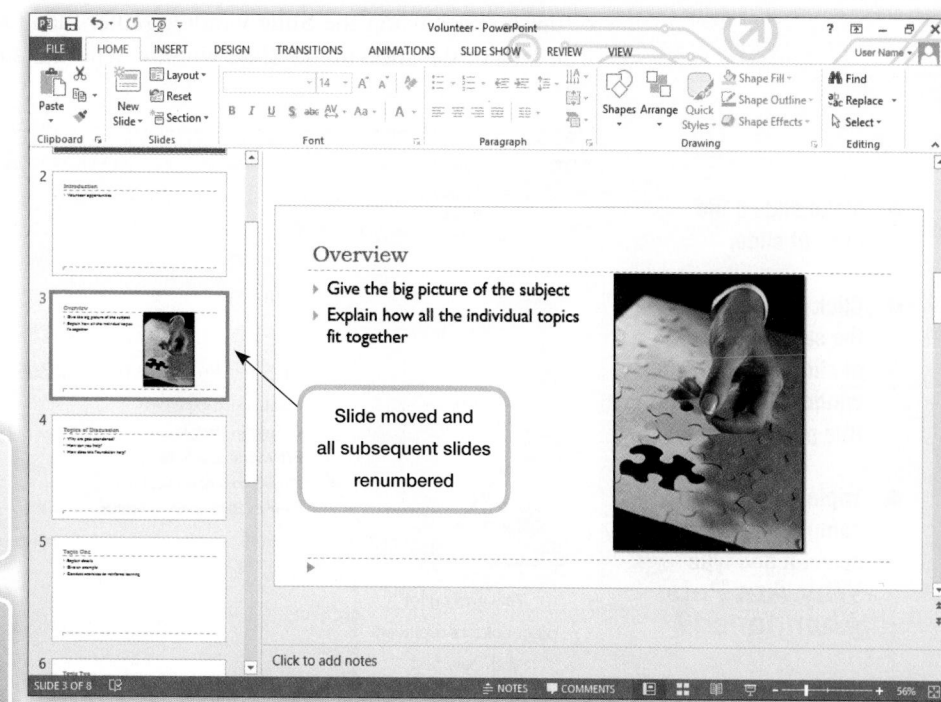

Figure 1.21

The Overview slide is now slide 3, and, again, all following slides are appropriately renumbered. Finally, you will make a copy of slide 6.

• **Select slide 6 in the Slides pane.**

• **Open the Copy drop-down menu and choose Duplicate.**

Another Method

You could also copy and paste the slide to duplicate it or use New Slide in the Slides group and choose Duplicate Selected Slides from the menu.

• **Scroll the Slides pane to see slides 5 to 7.**

Your screen should be similar to Figure 1.22

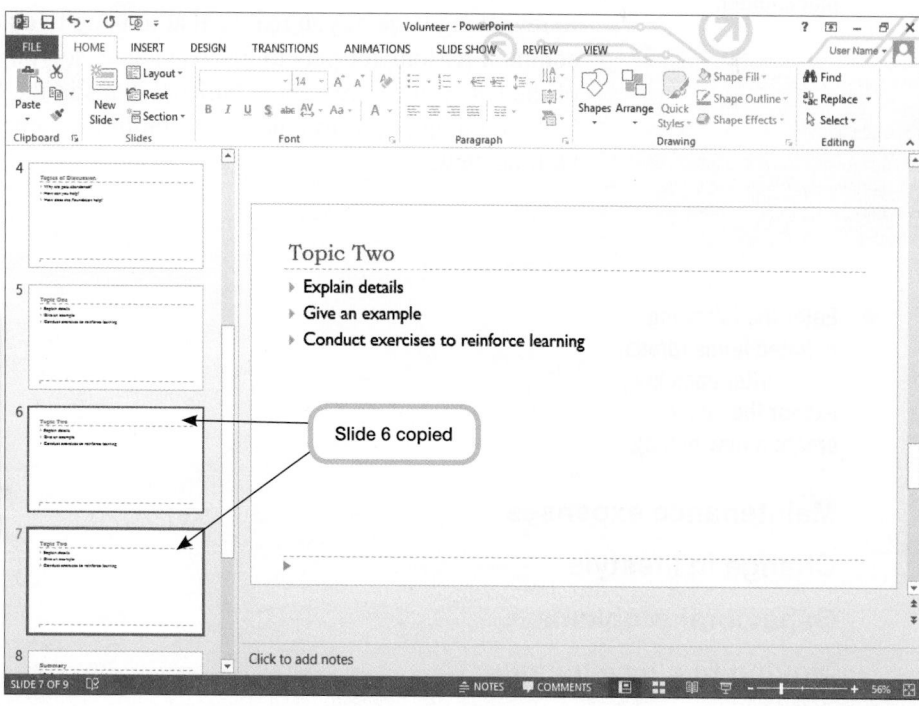

Figure 1.22

There are now three topic slides. The duplicate slide was inserted directly below the slide that was copied and is the selected slide.

Editing a Presentation   **PP1.25**

MOVING, DEMOTING, AND PROMOTING BULLETED ITEMS

Now you are ready to enter the text for the three topic slides. You will enter the text for these slides using the Slide window rather than Outline view. Simply clicking in an area of the slide in the Slide window will make it the active area.

1

- Make slide 5 the current slide.

- Click anywhere in the sample title text of slide 5 in the Slide window to select the title placeholder.

- Triple-click on the sample title to select it and type **Why Are Pets Abandoned?**

- Click anywhere on the bulleted list to select the content placeholder.

- Drag to select all the text in the content placeholder.

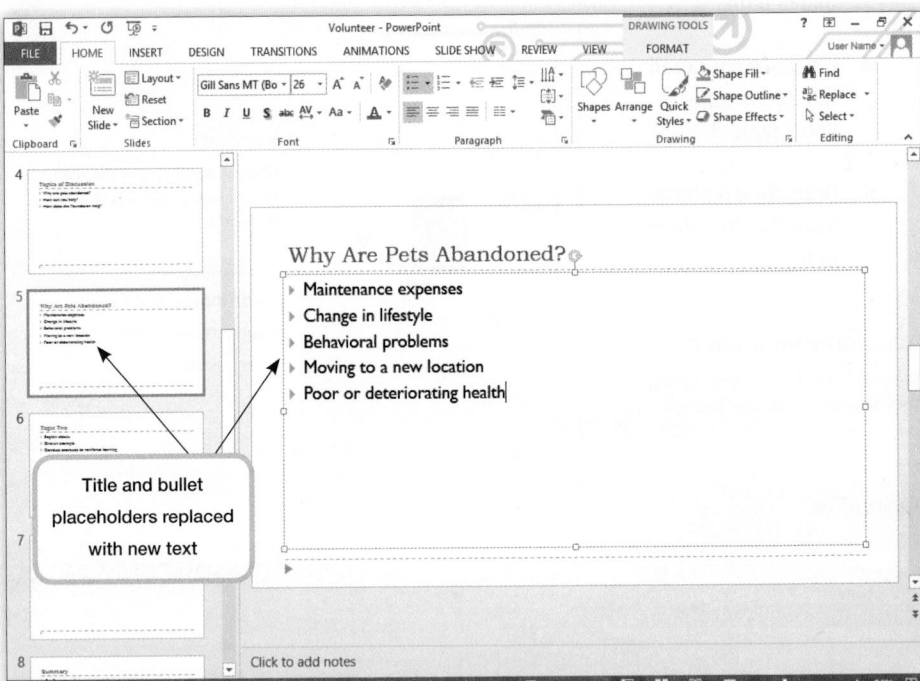

Figure 1.23

Another Method

You also can click [⬚ Select ▾] in the Editing group of the Home tab or use the shortcut key [Ctrl] + A to select everything in a placeholder box.

- Enter the following bulleted items (press [Enter] after each line, except the last, to create a new bullet):

Maintenance expenses

Change in lifestyle

Behavioral problems

Moving to a new location

Poor or deteriorating health

Your screen should be similar to Figure 1.23

In reviewing slide 5, you realize that moving to a new location is one of the most common reasons for pets to be abandoned, so you decide to move that to the top of the list. You can rearrange bulleted items in the Slide window by selecting the item and dragging it to a new location in the same way you moved selections in Outline view.

- Select all the text in the fourth bulleted item in the Slide window.

- Drag the selection to the beginning of the first bulleted item.

Your screen should be similar to Figure 1.24

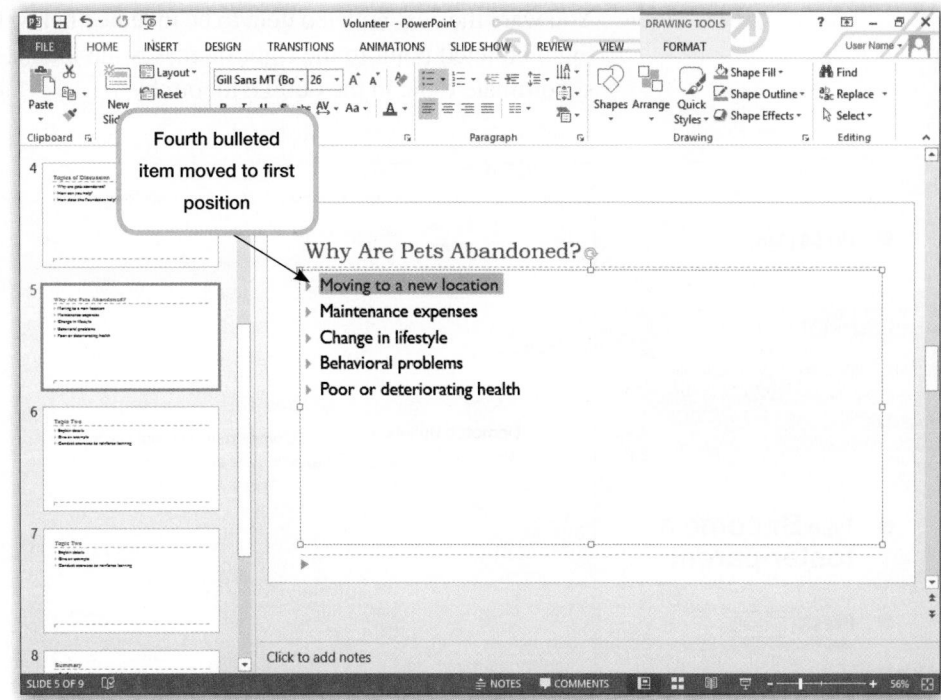

Figure 1.24

The fourth bullet is now the first bulleted item in the list.

ADJUSTING LIST LEVELS

In the next slide, you will enter information about how people can help the Animal Rescue Foundation.

- Make slide 6 the current slide.

- Replace the sample title text with **How Can You Help?**

- Select all the text in the bulleted text placeholder.

- Type **Donate your time and talent**

- Press Enter.

Your screen should be similar to Figure 1.25

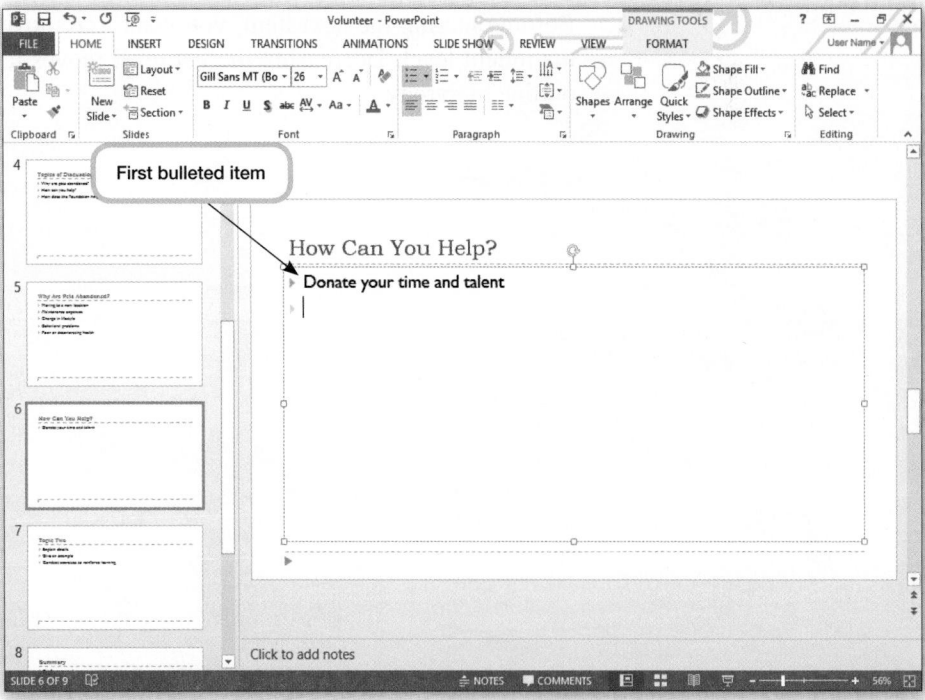

Figure 1.25

You want the next bulleted item to be indented below the first bulleted item. Indenting a bulleted point to the right increases the indent level and makes it a lower or subordinate topic in the outline hierarchy.

2

● **Press** Tab.

Another Method

You also can click ⬚ Increase List Level in the Paragraph group of the Home tab.

● **Type** Become a foster parent

● **Press** Enter.

● **Type** Work at adoption fairs

● **Press** Enter.

Your screen should be similar to Figure 1.26

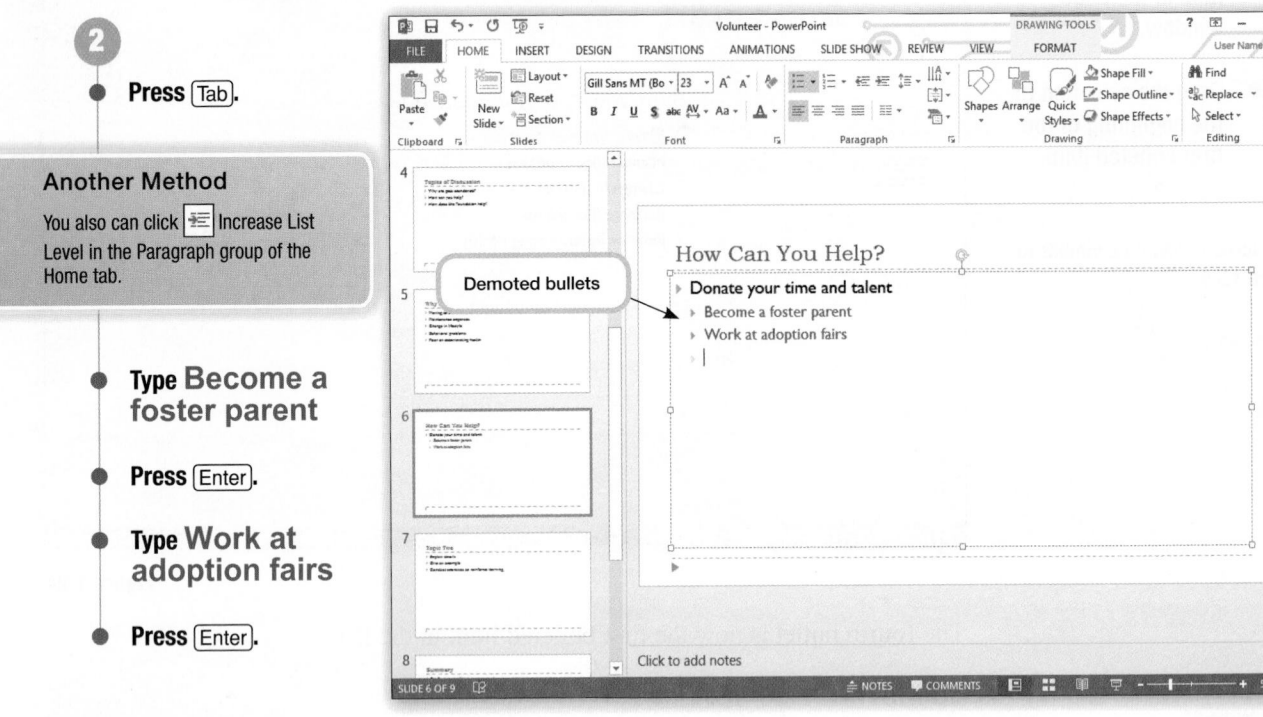

Figure 1.26

PowerPoint continues to indent to the same level until you cancel the indent. Before entering the next item, you want to remove the indentation by decreasing the indent level. Decreasing the list level moves it to the left, or up a level in the outline hierarchy.

● **Click** **Decrease List Level in the Paragraph group of the Home tab.**

Another Method

You may also use Shift + Tab to decrease the list level.

● **Type Donate new or used items**

● **Press Enter.**

● **Enter the next four bulleted items:**

Crates and pads

Collars, leads, and other items

Contribute items to our thrift shop

All types of animal feed

Your screen should be similar to Figure 1.27

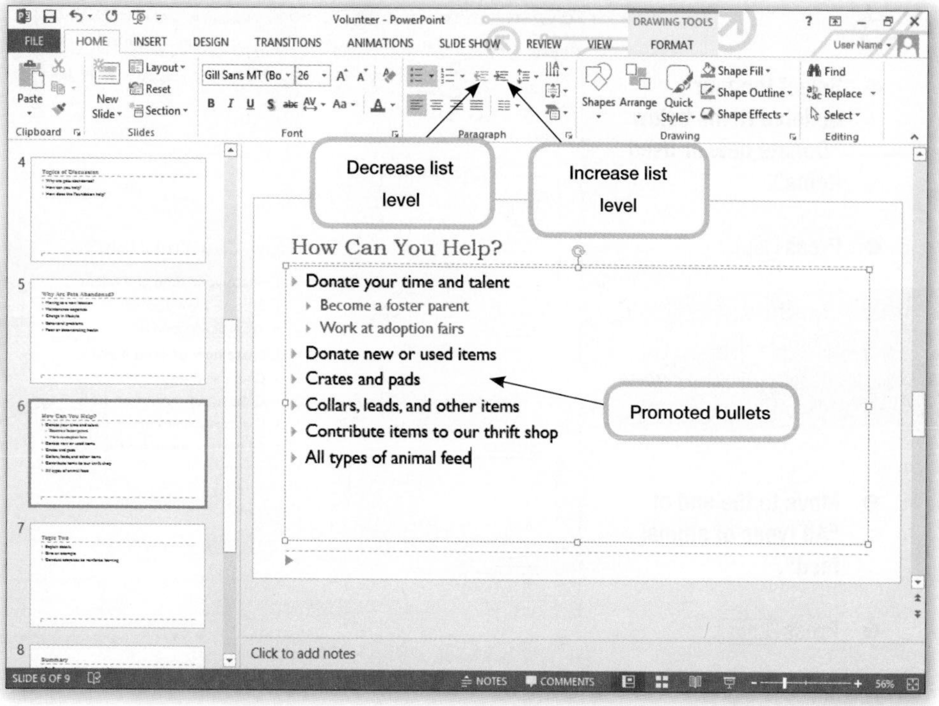

Decrease list level

Increase list level

How Can You Help?

▸ Donate your time and talent
  ▸ Become a foster parent
  ▸ Work at adoption fairs
▸ Donate new or used items
▸ Crates and pads
▸ Collars, leads, and other items   Promoted bullets
▸ Contribute items to our thrift shop
▸ All types of animal feed

Figure 1.27

You also can increase or decrease list levels after the text has been entered. The insertion point must be at the beginning of the line to be adjusted, or all the text must be selected. You will increase the level of the last four bulleted items.

4

- Select the four bulleted items below "Donate new or used items".

- Press `Tab`.

 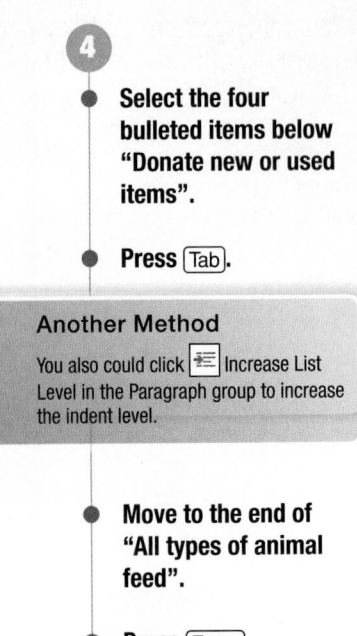
- Move to the end of "All types of animal feed".

- Press `Enter`.

Your screen should be similar to Figure 1.28

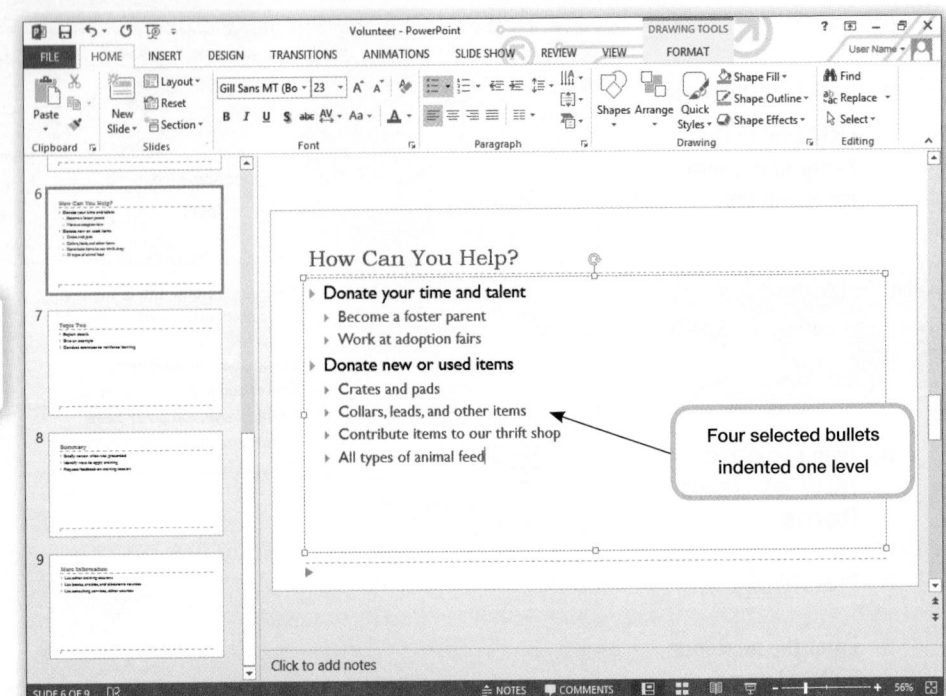

Figure 1.28

The list level of the four selected items has been indented one level. Next you will add more items to the bulleted list.

5

- Type **Provide financial support**

- Press `Enter`.

- Enter the following three bulleted items:

  Send a donation

  Sponsor a foster pet

  Sponsor an adoption (Do not press `Enter`)

- Decrease the level of the "Provide financial support" bullet.

Your screen should be similar to Figure 1.29

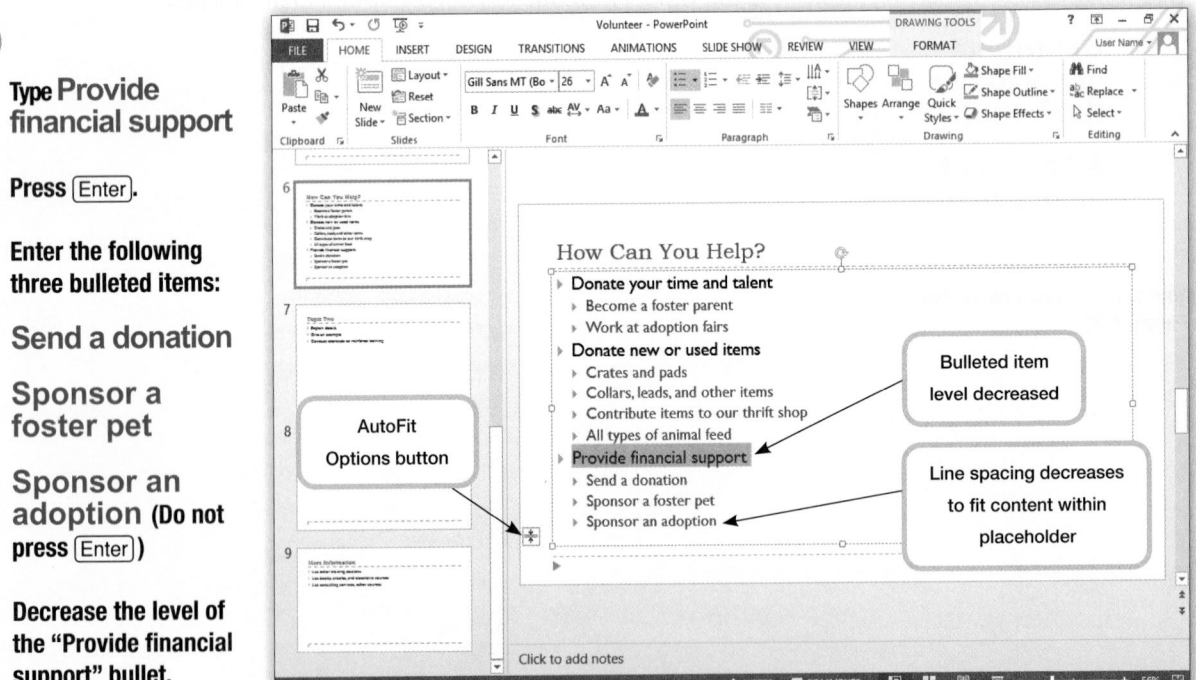

Figure 1.29

As you entered bulleted items, the line spacing of the text decreased to fit all the content in the placeholder. This feature is known as AutoFit and is "on" by default. When this adjustment occurs, an ⊟ AutoFit Options button appears at the bottom left corner of the placeholder. It provides options that allow you to turn this feature on and off or to control the AutoFit options.

SPLITTING TEXT BETWEEN SLIDES

Although using AutoFit made all the content fit inside the placeholder, you decide that 10 bulleted items are too many for a single slide. Generally, when creating slides, it is a good idea to limit the number of bulleted items on a slide to six. It also is recommended that the number of words on a line should not exceed five.

You decide to split the slide content between two slides. To make this change, you need to change to Outline view and indicate where to start a new slide by moving the insertion point to the end of the item you want to be the last item on the current slide.

1

● Change to Outline view.

● If necessary, scroll the Outline pane so that slides 6 and 7 are visible.

● Move the insertion point to the end of the item "All types of animal feed" on slide 6.

● Press Enter.

● Click ⇤ Decrease List Level twice to decrease the indent level of the blank line.

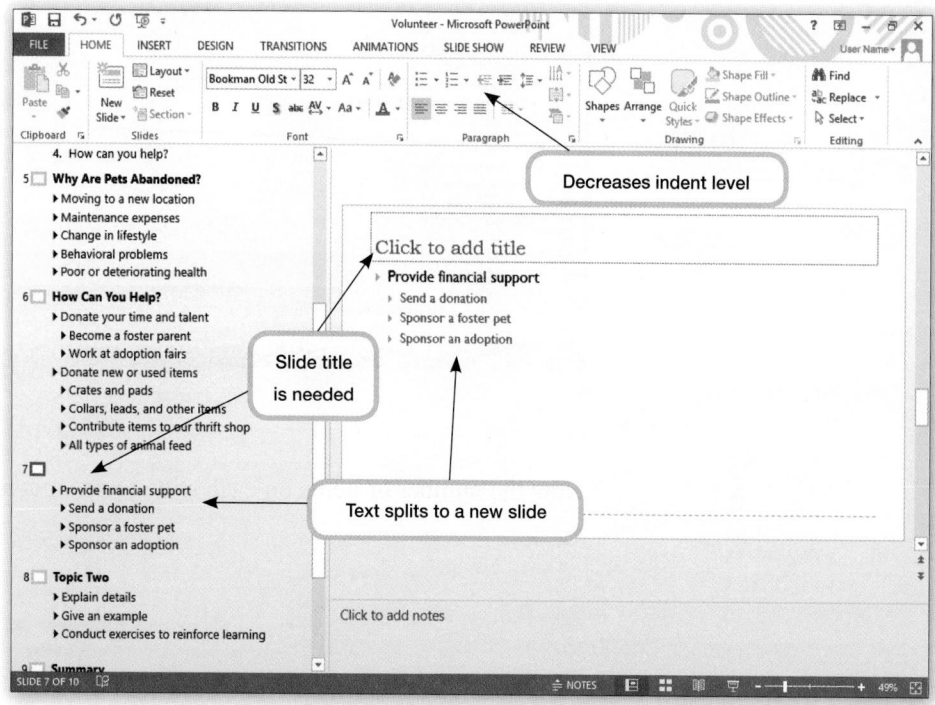

Figure 1.30

Your screen should be similar to Figure 1.30

A new slide, with a title placeholder, is inserted into the presentation. The items from the previous slide, beginning with where you positioned the insertion point, were moved to the new slide. Sometimes, when splitting text between slides, the content may not split appropriately and you may still need to make adjustments to the slides. You will add a title to the new slide.

2

On slide 7, replace the title placeholder with **More Ways to Help!**

Your screen should be similar to Figure 1.31

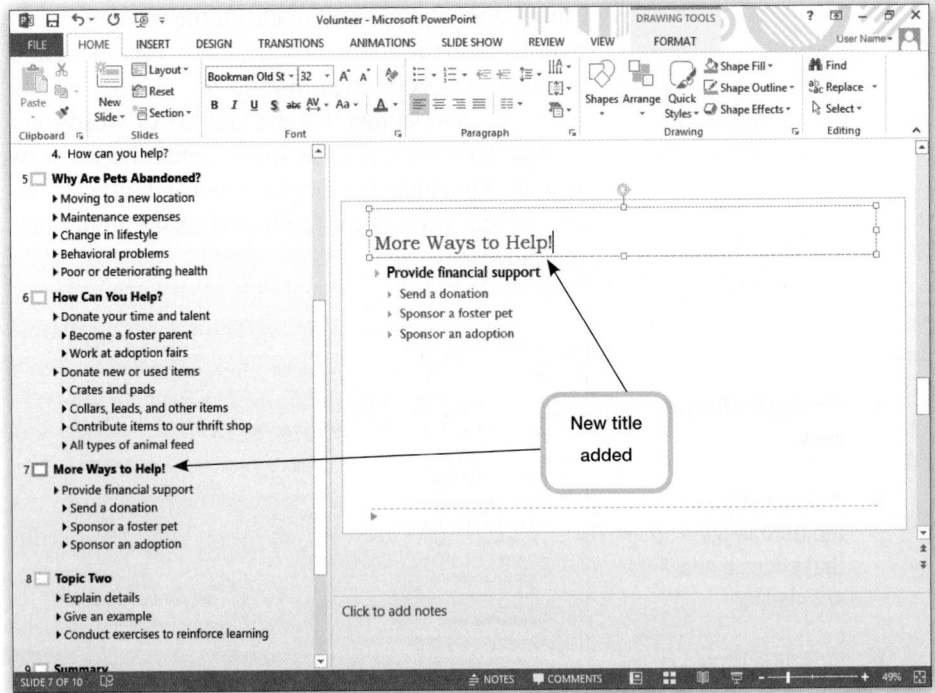

Figure 1.31

Now the number of items on each slide seems much more reasonable.

Finally, you will add the text for the third topic slide.

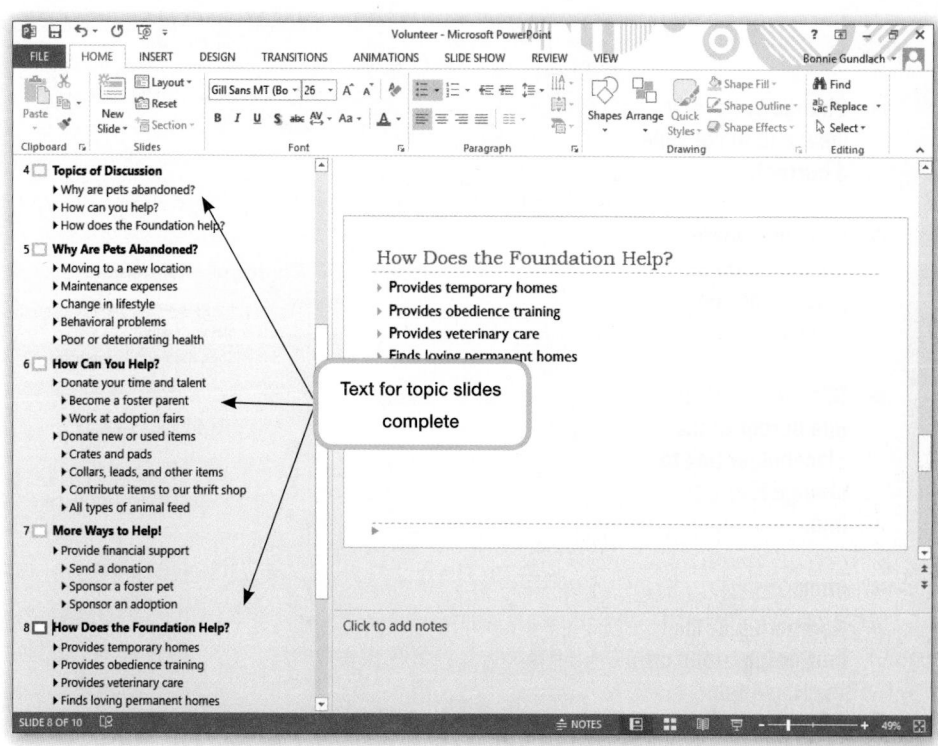

Figure 1.32

3

- Make slide 8 current.

- Enter the slide title **How Does the Foundation Help?**

- Enter the following bulleted items:

  Provides temporary homes

  Provides obedience training

  Provides veterinary care

  Finds loving permanent homes

- Scroll the Outline pane to see slides 4 through 8.

Your screen should be similar to Figure 1.32

The text for the three topic slides reflects the order of the topics in the Topics of Discussion slide.

CREATING A NUMBERED LIST

After looking at slide 4, you decide that it would be better if the topics of discussion were a numbered list. You can easily change the format of the bulleted items to a numbered list using the Numbering command in the Paragraph group on the Home tab.

1

- **Change to Normal view and make slide 4 current.**

- **Click anywhere in the bulleted items placeholder on slide 4.**

- **Click on the dashed-line border of the placeholder box to change it to a solid line.**

- **Click** ⬚ ▼ **Numbering in the Paragraph group on the Home tab.**

Your screen should be similar to Figure 1.33

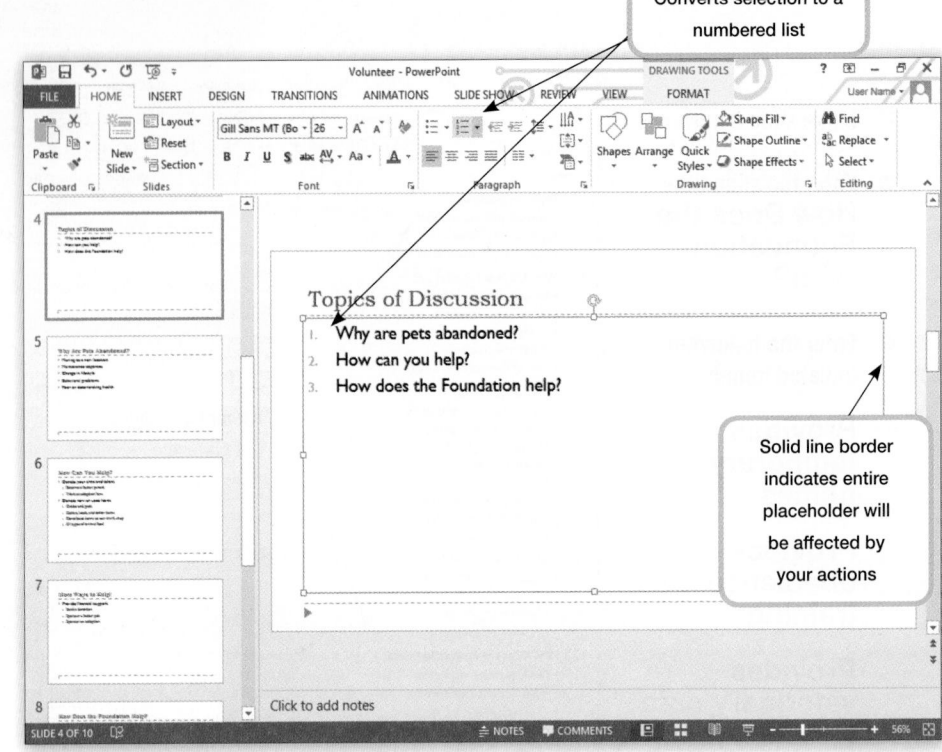

Converts selection to a numbered list

Solid line border indicates entire placeholder will be affected by your actions

Figure 1.33

Notice the insertion point does not appear in the placeholder box. This is because a solid line around the placeholder indicates your action will affect the entire placeholder rather than individual parts, such as the text, of the placeholder. The bullets have been replaced with an itemized numbered list.

CHANGING LINE SPACING

Since there are only three items in the numbered list, you decide to increase the line spacing on this slide. Even if more items are added later, the new spacing will still be appropriate. Because you want the line spacing to affect all text within the placeholder, you still want to have the entire placeholder box selected. Otherwise, only the line spacing of the line you are on would change.

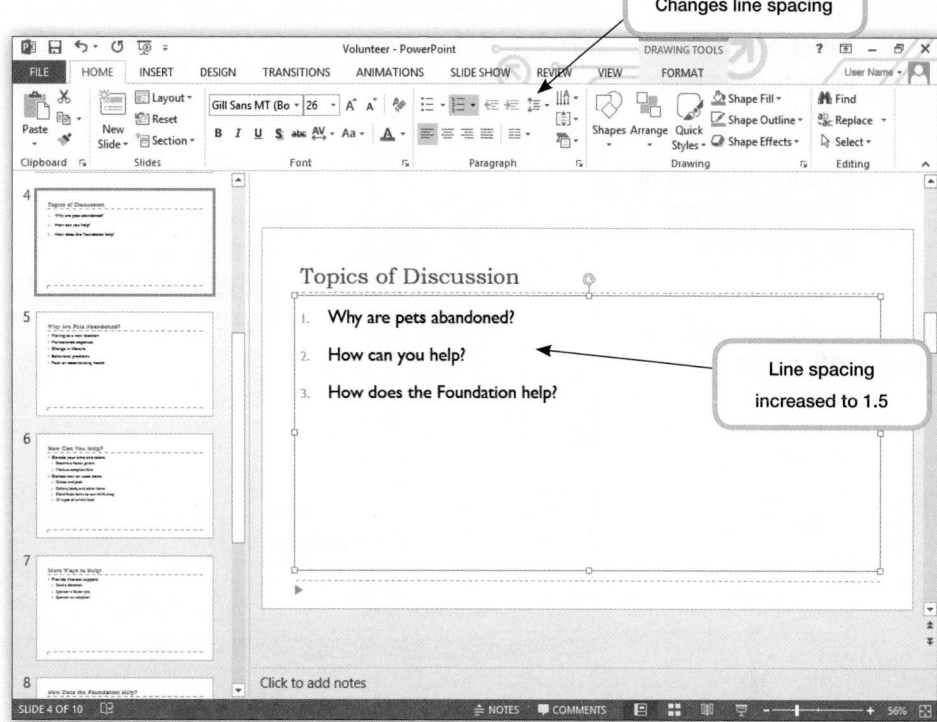

1

- If necessary, click the dashed line border of the placeholder box to change it to a solid line.

- Click ⬍≡ ▾ Line Spacing in the Paragraph group.

- Choose 1.5 from the drop-down menu.

Your screen should be similar to Figure 1.34

Figure 1.34

MOVING, DEMOTING, AND PROMOTING NUMBERED ITEMS

Now it is obvious to you that you entered the topics in the wrong order. You want to present the information about the Foundation before information about how individuals can help. Just like a bulleted item, an item in a numbered list can be moved easily by selecting it and dragging it to a new location.

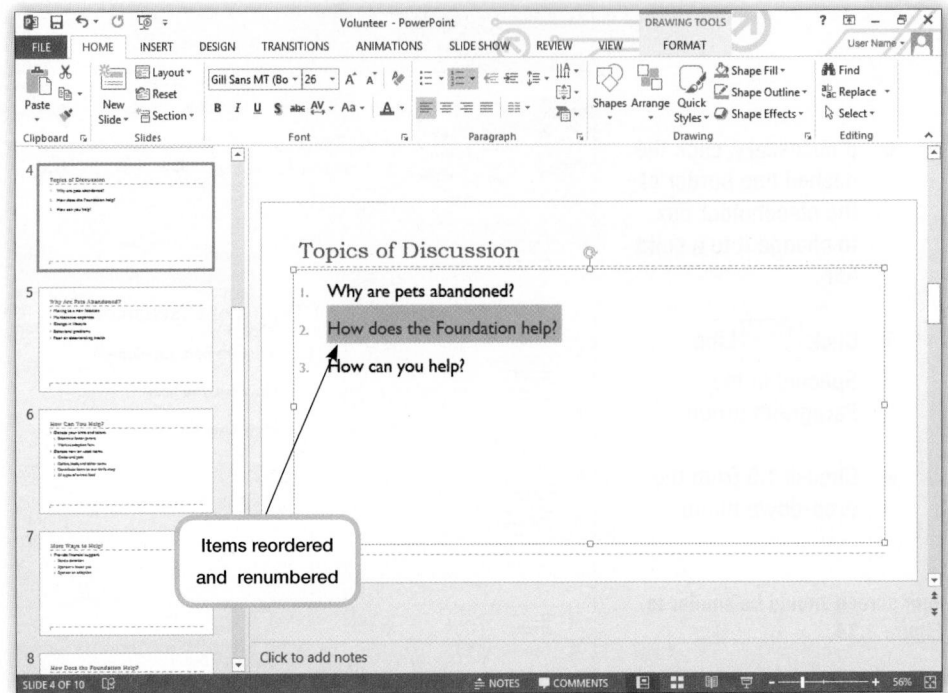

- Select the third item in the placeholder on slide 4.

- Drag the selection up to the beginning of the second line.

Your screen should be similar to Figure 1.35

Figure 1.35

As soon as you clicked inside the placeholder, the insertion point appeared and the solid-line border changed to a dashed-line border, indicating you can edit the contents of the placeholder. The third item in the numbered list is now the second item, and PowerPoint automatically renumbered the list for you.

You now realize that you forgot to include the Animal Angels volunteer group as a topic to be discussed. You will add it to the Topics of Discussion slide as a subtopic below the "How can you help?" topic.

2

- Open Outline view to review the slide content.

- In the Outline pane, click at the end of the third numbered list item on slide 4 and press Enter.

- Press Tab and type **Who are Animal Angels?**

Your screen should be similar to Figure 1.36

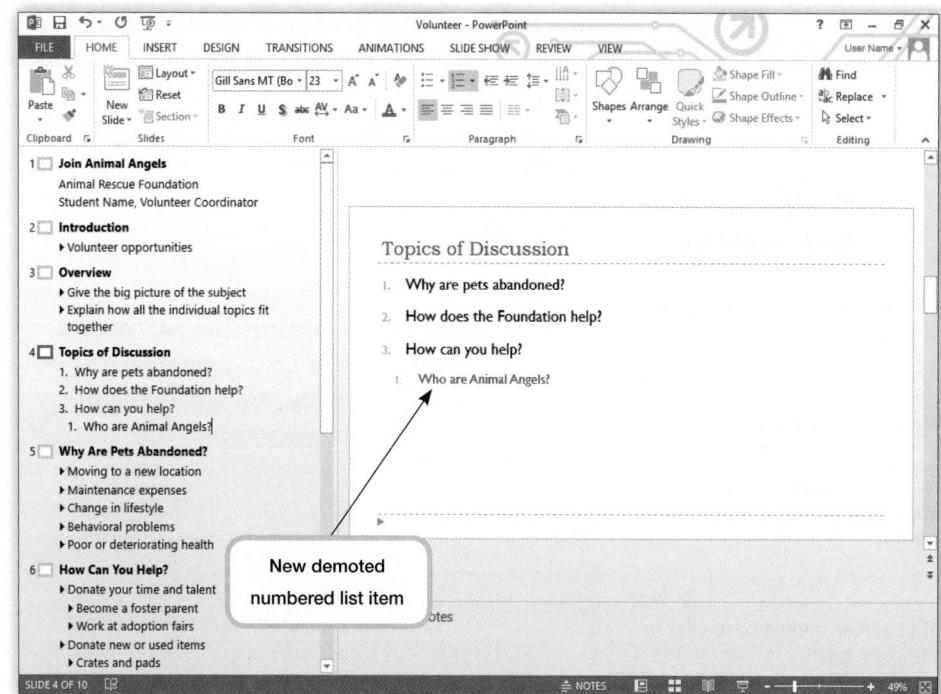

Figure 1.36

The numbering for the subtopic begins with 1 again. The new item is too important to be indented on the list, so you will decrease the list level to the same level as the other items.

3

- In the Slide window, select the entire fourth line.

- Press Shift + Tab to decrease the list level of the fourth line.

- Drag the selected item to the beginning of the third line.

Your screen should be similar to Figure 1.37

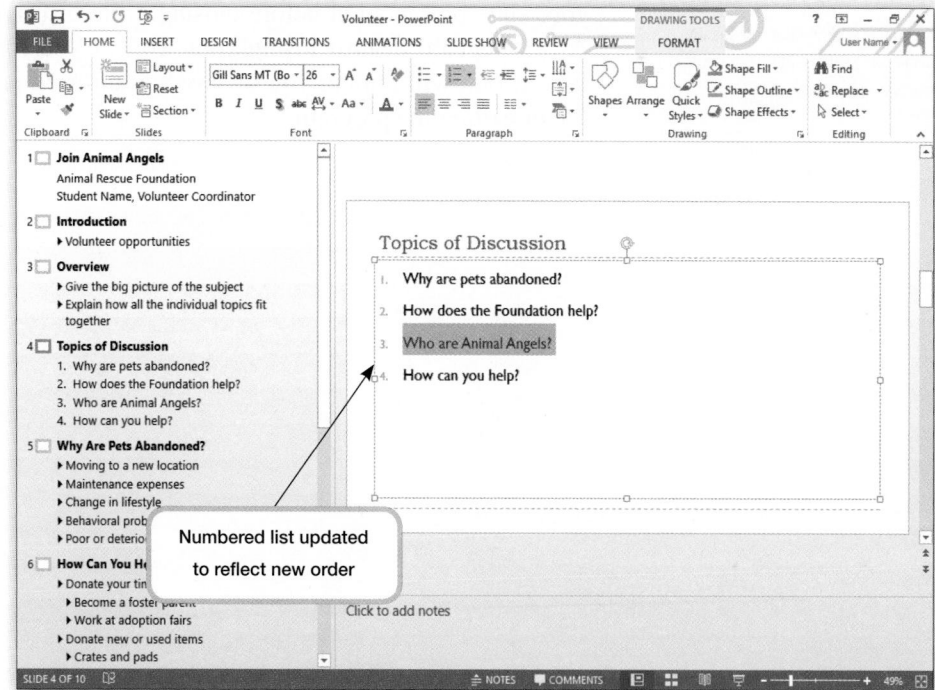

Figure 1.37

The numbered list has again been appropriately adjusted.

You have just been notified about an important meeting that is to begin in a few minutes. Before leaving for the meeting, you will save and close the presentation.

4

- Click 🖫 **Save in the Quick Access bar.**

- **Open the File tab and click** Close **.**

Having Trouble?

Review the section "Closing a File" on page IO.63 in the Introduction to Microsoft Office 2013 to review this feature.

Your screen should be similar to Figure 1.38

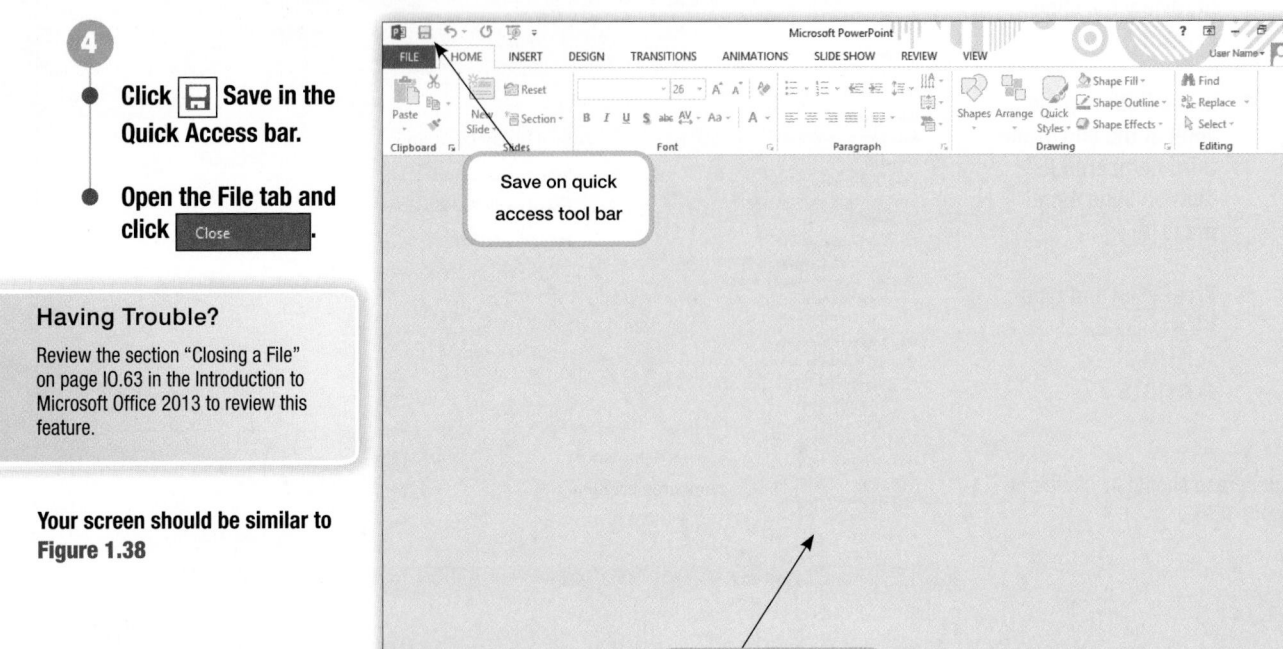

Save on quick access tool bar

File closed and blank workspace shown

Figure 1.38

Additional Information

If you are ending your lab session now, click ✕ at the upper-right corner of the window or press Alt + F4 to exit the program.

The presentation is closed, and an empty workspace is displayed. Always save your slide presentation before closing a file or leaving the PowerPoint program. As a safeguard against losing your work if you forget to save the presentation, PowerPoint will remind you to save any unsaved presentation before closing the file or exiting the program.

After returning from your meeting, you continued to work on the presentation. You revised the content of several of the slides and added information for several new slides. Then you saved the presentation using a new file name. You will open this file to see the changes and will continue working on the presentation.

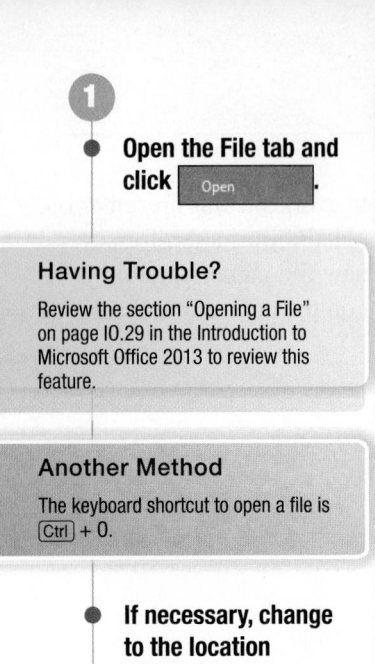

1

● **Open the File tab and click** Open .

Having Trouble?

Review the section "Opening a File" on page IO.29 in the Introduction to Microsoft Office 2013 to review this feature.

Another Method

The keyboard shortcut to open a file is Ctrl + O.

● **If necessary, change to the location containing your data files.**

● **Select** pp01_Volunteer1 Widescreen.

Additional Information

You also can quickly open a recently used file by selecting it from the Recent Presentations list.

● **Click** Save .

● **Open Outline view.**

● **Replace "Student Name" in slide 1 with your name.**

● **Scroll the Outline pane to see the additional content that has been added to the presentation.**

Your screen should be similar to Figure 1.39

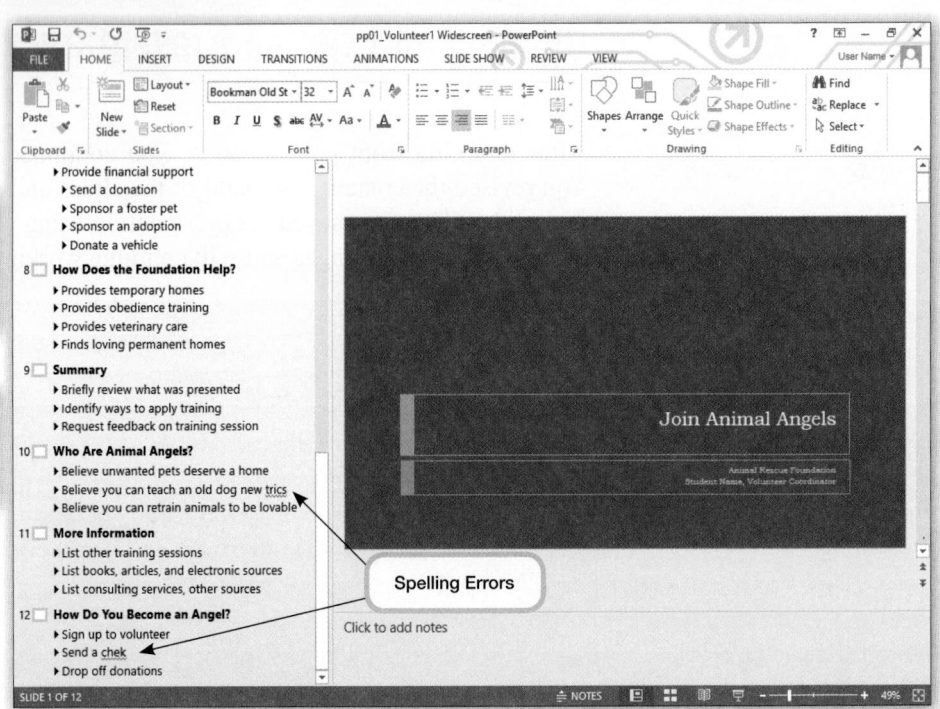

Figure 1.39

The presentation now contains 12 slides, and all the sample text has been replaced with text for the volunteer recruitment presentation, except for slides 3, 9, and 11.

Using Spelling Checker

As you entered the information on the additional slides, you left some typing errors uncorrected. To correct the misspelled words, you can use the shortcut menu to correct each individual word or error, as you learned earlier. However, in many cases, you may find it more efficient to wait until you are finished writing before you correct any spelling or grammatical errors. To do this, you can manually turn on the spelling checker to locate and correct the spelling on all slides of the presentation at once.

Additional Information

Unlike Word 2013, Powerpoint does not check for grammar errors.

1

Open the Review tab.

Click 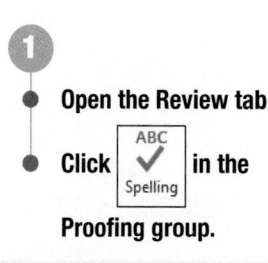 **in the Proofing group.**

Another Method

The keyboard shortcut to check spelling is F7.

Your screen should be similar to Figure 1.40

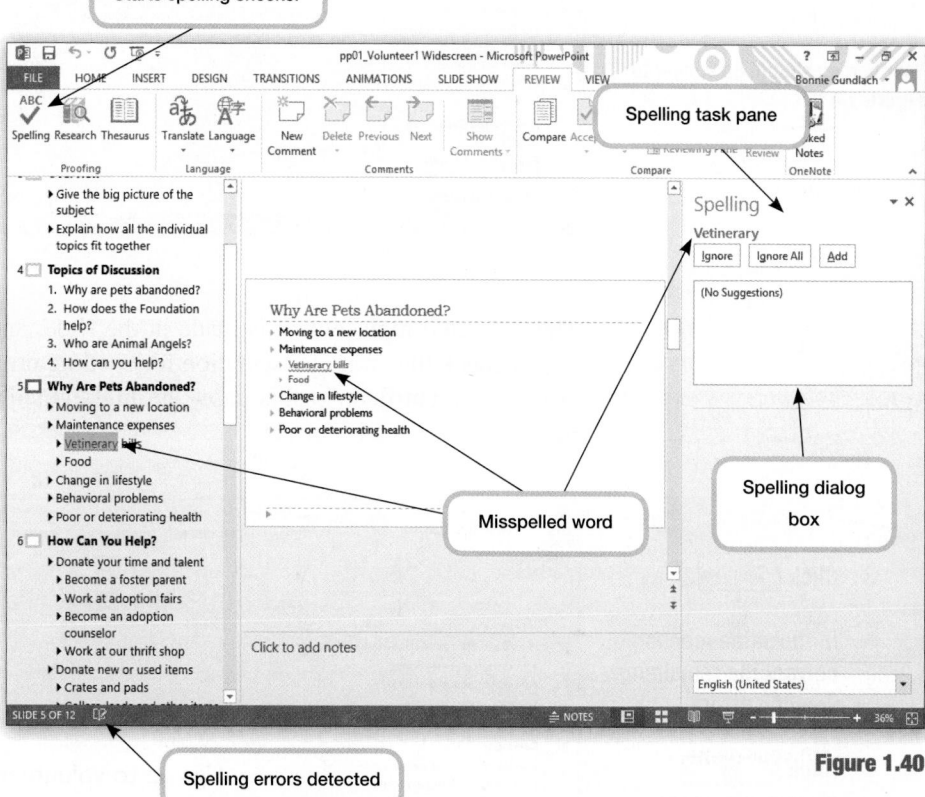

Figure 1.40

Additional Information

The spelling checker identifies many proper names and technical terms as misspelled. To stop this from occurring, use the Add option to add those names to the custom dictionary.

The program jumps to slide 5; highlights the first located misspelled word, "Vetinerary," in the Outline pane; and opens the Spelling task pane. The misspelled word is displayed at the top of the task pane. The Suggestions list box typically displays the words the spelling checker has located in the dictionary that most closely match the misspelled word.

In this case, the spelling checker does not display any suggested replacements because it cannot locate any words in the dictionaries that are similar in spelling. When there are no suggestions or none of the suggestions is correct, you must edit the word yourself by typing the correction in the slide.

Type Veterinary to make the correction.

Additional Information

The replacement text should be entered exactly as you want it to appear, including capitalization.

Click `Resume` **in the Spelling pane.**

Your screen should be similar to Figure 1.41

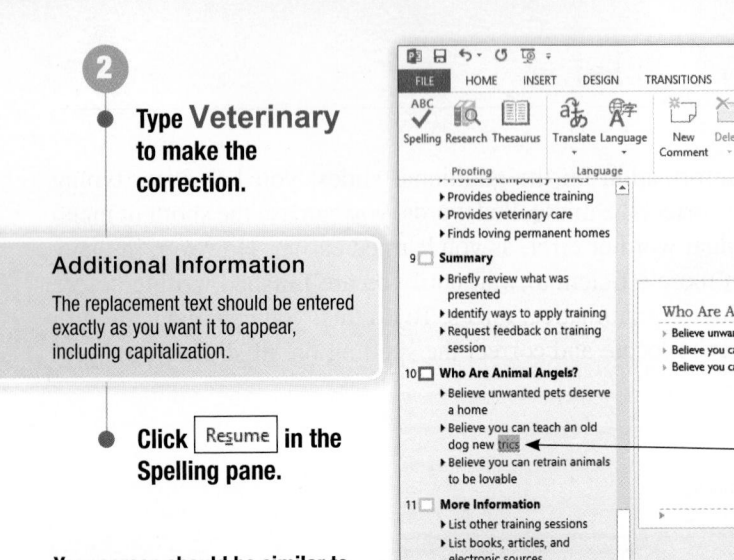

Correct replacement

Next misspelled word identified

Suggested corrections

Figure 1.41

The corrected replacement is made in the slide, and the spelling checker continues to check the entire presentation for spelling errors. The next misspelled word, "trics," is identified. In this case, the highlighted suggested replacement in the Spelling task pane is correct.

Click `Change`.

In the same manner, correct the remaining spelling errors.

Click `OK` **in response to the message telling you that the spell check is complete.**

Open the File tab, click `Save As`**, and save the revised presentation as Volunteer1 Widescreen to your solution file location.**

Your screen should be similar to Figure 1.42

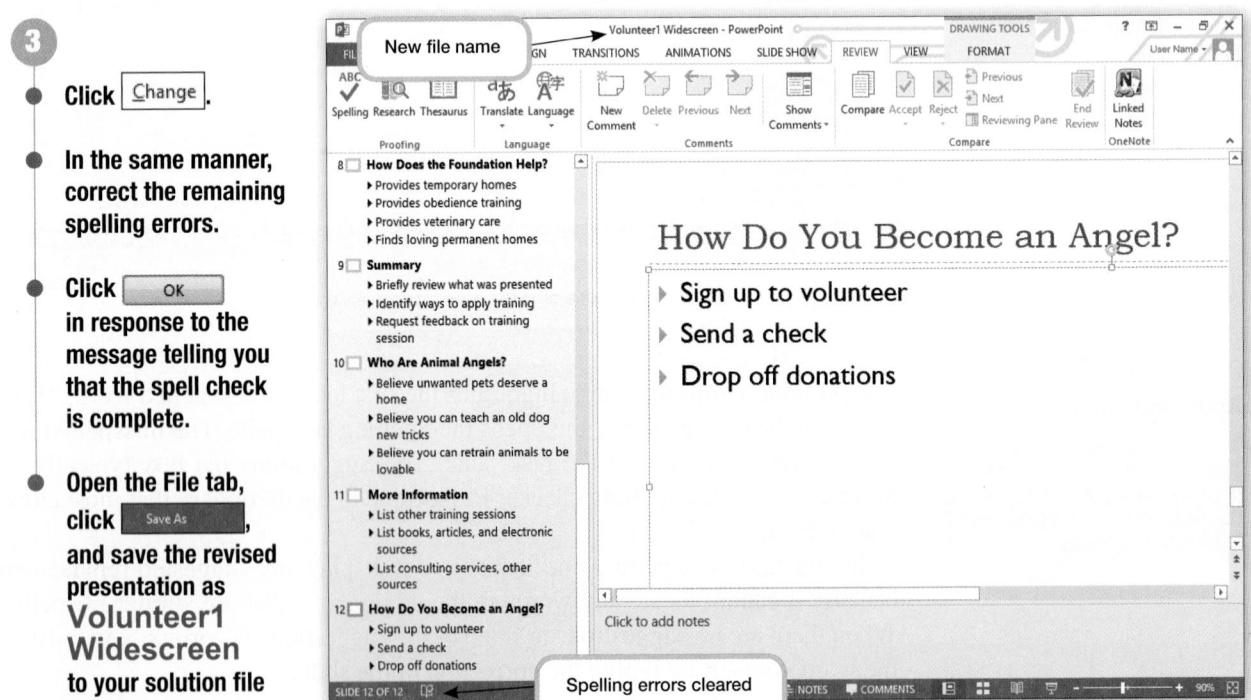

New file name

Spelling errors cleared

Figure 1.42

The Spelling indicator in the status bar shows that all spelling errors have been resolved.

Using Slide Sorter View

To get a better overall picture of the presentation, you will switch to Slide Sorter view. This view displays thumbnail images of each slide in the Slide window and is particularly useful for rearranging slides to improve the flow and organization of the presentation. Clicking on a thumbnail selects the slide and makes it the current slide.

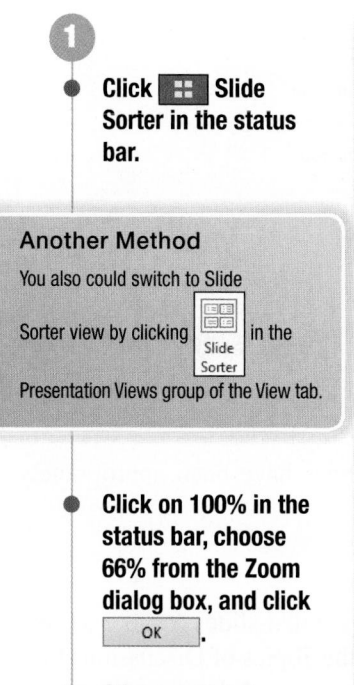

1

- Click [icon] **Slide Sorter in the status bar.**

- Click on 100% in the status bar, choose 66% from the Zoom dialog box, and click OK .

- Click on slide 1.

Your screen should be similar to Figure 1.43

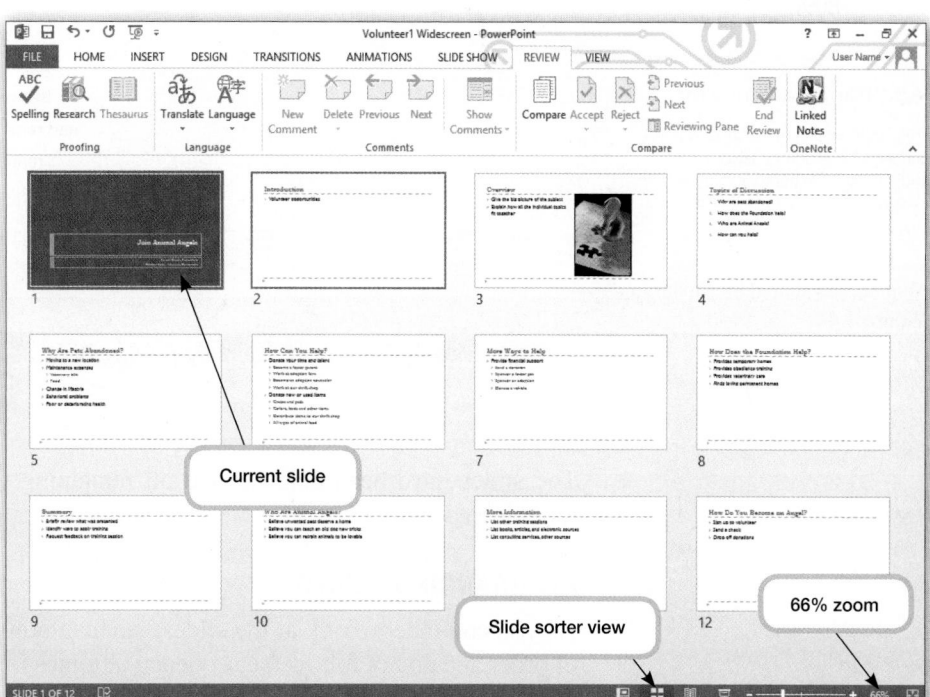

Figure 1.43

The currently selected slide, slide 1, appears with an orange border around it. Viewing all the slides side by side helps you see how your presentation flows. You realize that the second slide is no longer necessary because you added your name to the opening slide. You also decide to delete the original slides 3, 9, and 11 because you plan to add any necessary information to other slides.

SELECTING AND DELETING SLIDES

In Slide Sorter view, it is easy to select and work with multiple slides at the same time. To select multiple slides, hold down Ctrl while clicking on each slide to select it.

1

- Click on slide 2, hold down Ctrl, and click on slides 3, 9 and 11 to select them.

- Press Delete.

- Increase the zoom to 80%.

Additional Information

The zoom setting for each view is set independently and remains in effect until changed to another zoom setting.

Your screen should be similar to Figure 1.44

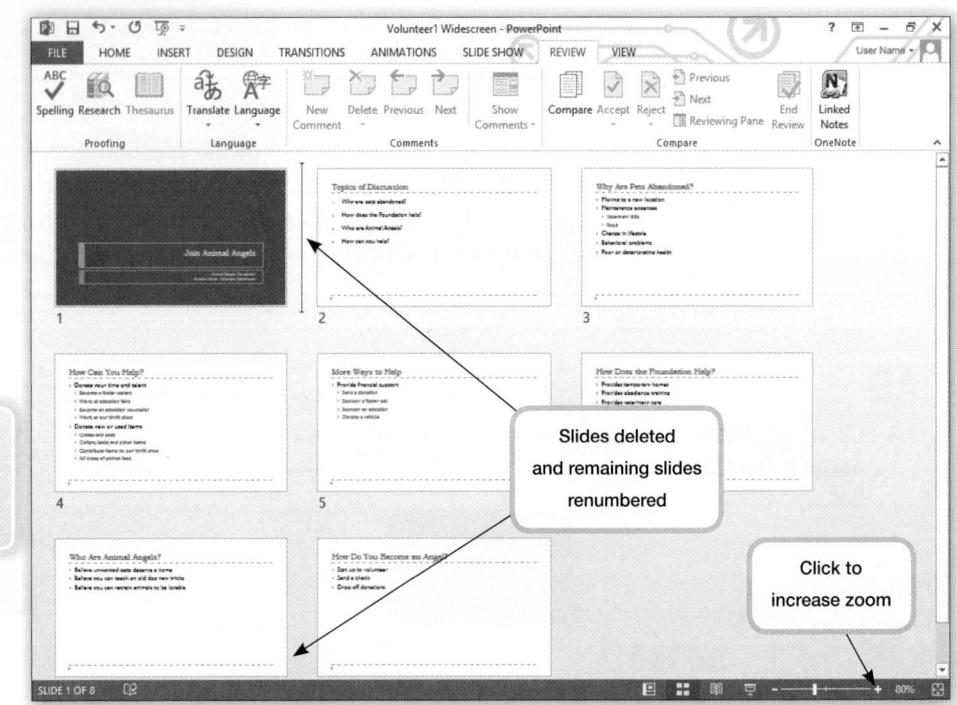

Figure 1.44

The slides have been deleted, and all remaining slides have been appropriately renumbered.

REARRANGING SLIDES

As you continue to look at the slides, you can now see that slides 6 and 7 are out of order and do not follow the sequence of topics in the Topics of Discussion slide. You will correct the organization of the slides by moving slides 6 and 7 before slide 4. To reorder a slide in Slide Sorter view, you drag it to its new location using drag and drop. As you drag the mouse, Live Preview shows you where the slide will be placed when you release the mouse button.

- Select slides 6 and 7.

- Point to either selected slide and drag the mouse until the slides are positioned before slide 4.

- Release the mouse button.

 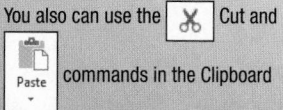
Your screen should be similar to Figure 1.45

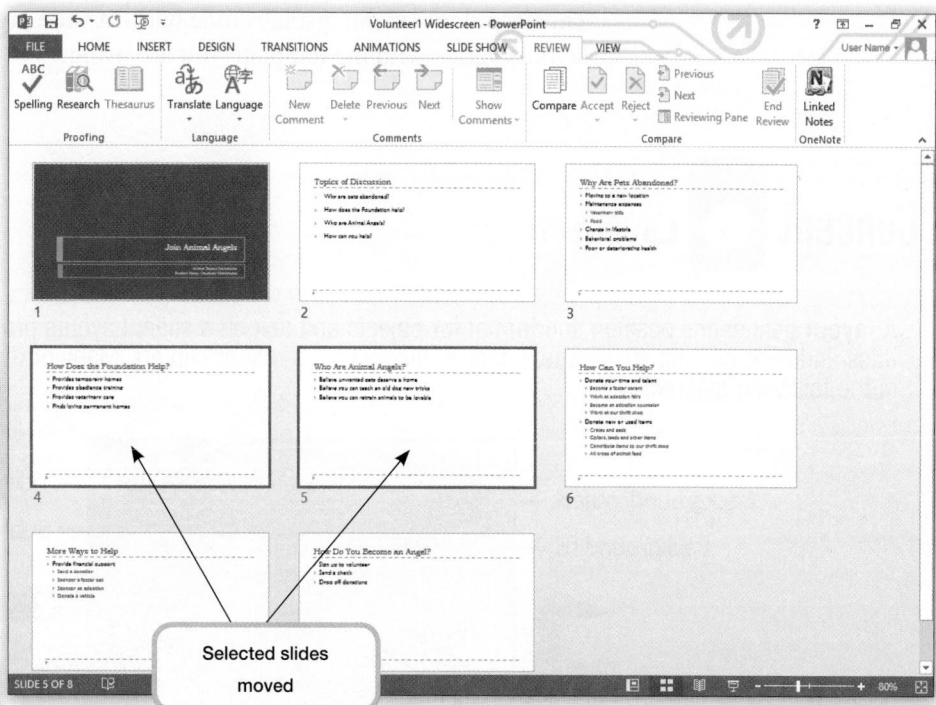

Figure 1.45

The slides now appear in the order in which you want them.

SELECTING A SLIDE LAYOUT

During your discussion with the foundation director, it was suggested that you add a slide showing the history of the organization. To include this information in the presentation, you will insert a new slide after slide 4. A new slide is inserted after the current or selected slide.

- Select slide 4.

- Open the Home tab.

- Open the New Slide ▾ drop-down menu in the Slides group.

Your screen should be similar to Figure 1.46

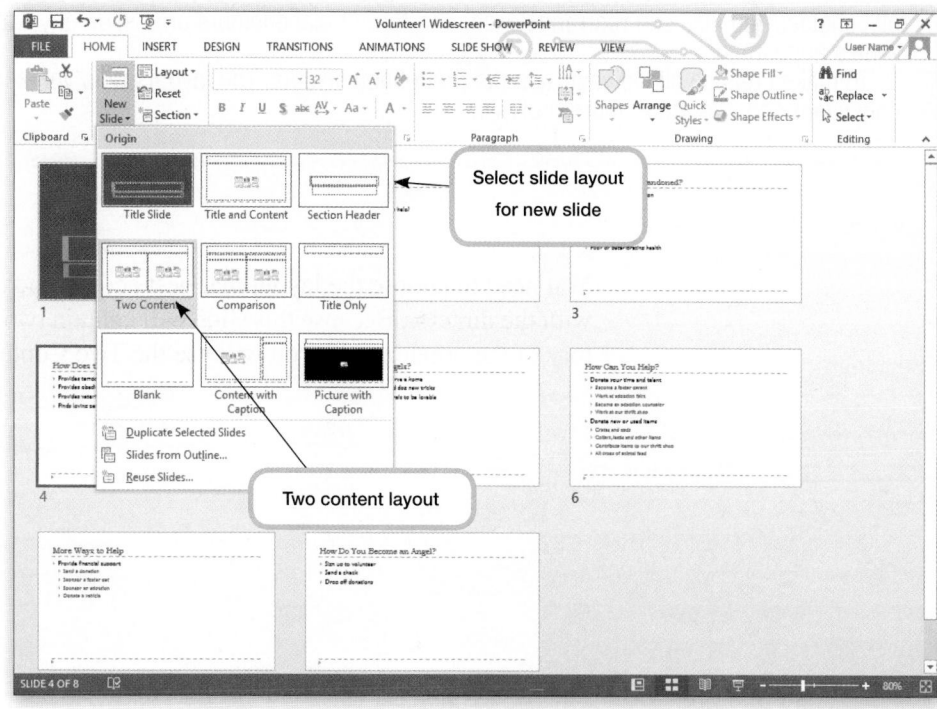

Figure 1.46

The drop-down menu displays nine built-in slide layouts. The number of available layouts varies with the template you are using.

Concept 4 Layout

A layout defines the position and format for objects and text on a slide. Layouts provide placeholders for slide titles and slide content such as text, tables, diagrams, charts, or clip art. Many of these placeholders are shown in the following diagram.

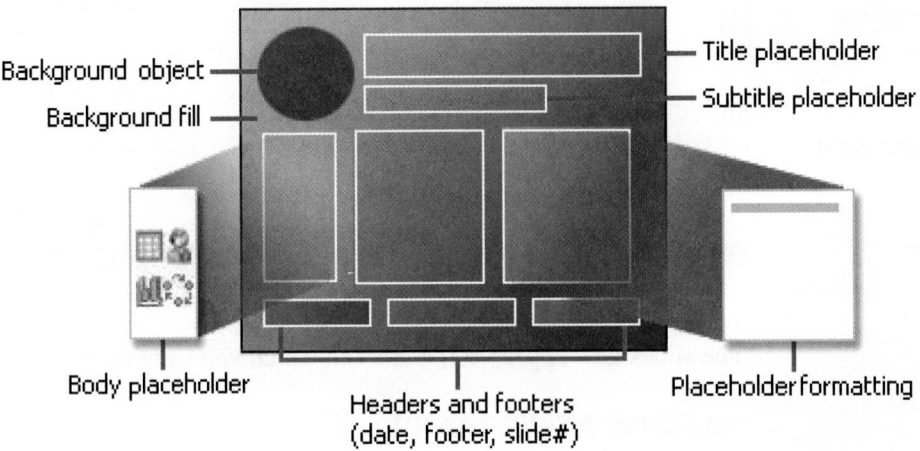

You can change the layout of an existing slide by selecting a new layout. If the new layout does not include placeholders for objects that are already on your slide (for example, if you created a chart and the new layout does not include a chart placeholder), you do not lose the information. All objects remain on the slide, and the selected layout is automatically adjusted by adding the appropriate type of placeholder for the object. Alternatively, as you add new objects to a slide, the layout automatically adjusts by adding the appropriate type of placeholder. You also can rearrange, size, and format placeholders on a slide any way you like to customize the slide's appearance.

To make creating slides easy, use the predefined layouts. The layouts help you keep your presentation format consistent and, therefore, more professional.

You need to choose the layout that best accommodates the changes you discussed with the director. Because this slide will contain two columns of text about the history of the organization, you will use the Two Content layout.

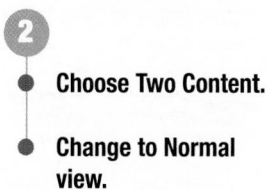

● Choose Two Content.

● Change to Normal view.

Additional Information

The current slide does not change when you switch views.

Your screen should be similar to Figure 1.47

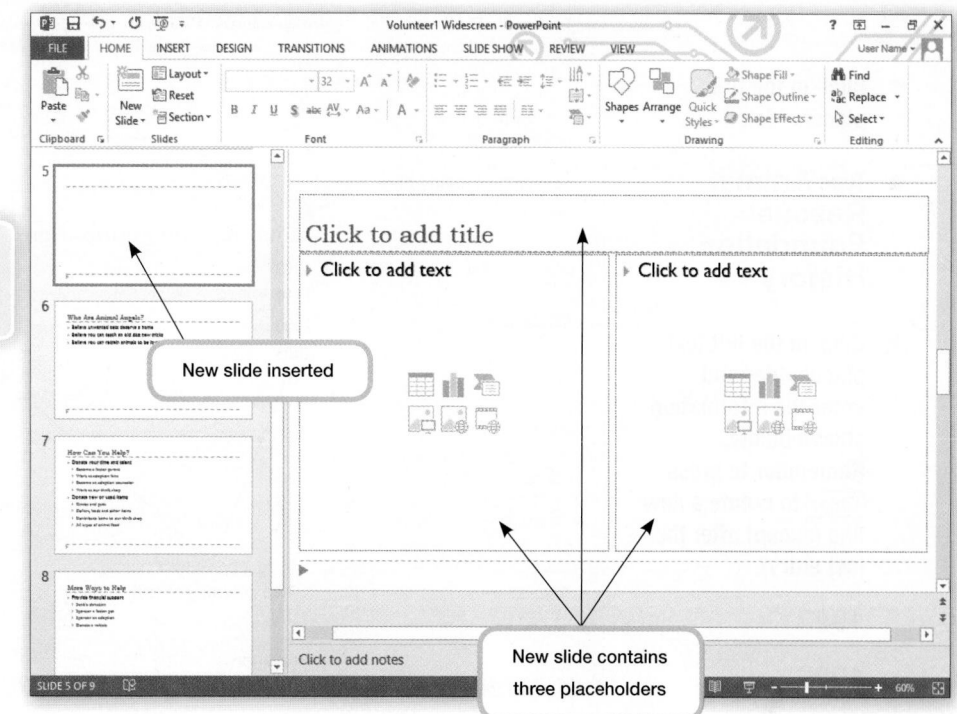

Figure 1.47

A new Two Content slide is inserted with the same design elements as the other slides in the presentation. The Two Content layout contains three placeholders, but unlike the template slides, the placeholders on the inserted slide do not contain sample text. When you select the placeholder, you can simply type in the text without having to select or delete any sample text.

CHANGING A PLACEHOLDER

You will add text to the slide presenting a brief history of the Animal Rescue Foundation. First, you will enter the slide title and then the list of dates and events.

1

- Click in the title placeholder.

- Type **Animal Rescue Foundation History**

- Click in the left text placeholder and enter the information shown below. Remember to press Enter to create a new line (except after the last entry).

  1998

  1999

  2000

  2008

- In the same manner, enter the following text in the right text placeholder:

  Founded by Steve Dow

  Built first shelter

  Began volunteer program

  Rescued 3000 animals!

Your screen should be similar to Figure 1.48

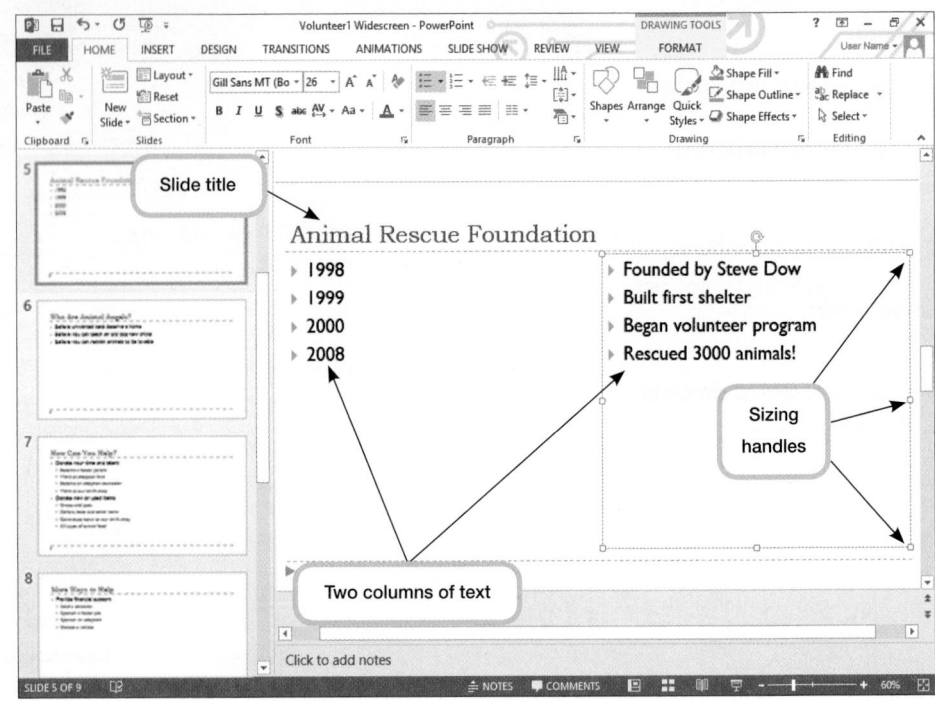

Figure 1.48

Notice that the left placeholder is much too big for the content and leaves too much space between the columns of information. To fix this, you can adjust the size of the placeholders.

SIZING A PLACEHOLDER

The four squares that appear at the corners and sides of a selected placeholder's border are **sizing handles** that can be used to adjust the size of the placeholder. Dragging the corner sizing handles will adjust both the height and width at the same time, whereas the center handles adjust the associated side borders. When you point to the sizing handle, the mouse pointer appears as ⬉, indicating the direction in which you can drag the border to adjust the size.

You will decrease the width of the left placeholder and the height of both placeholders.

1 ●

● Select the left text placeholder and drag the right-center sizing handle to the left as in Figure 1.49.

● With the left placeholder still selected, hold down (Shift) while clicking on the right placeholder to select both.

● Use the bottom-middle sizing handle of either selected placeholder to decrease the height of the placeholders as in Figure 1.49.

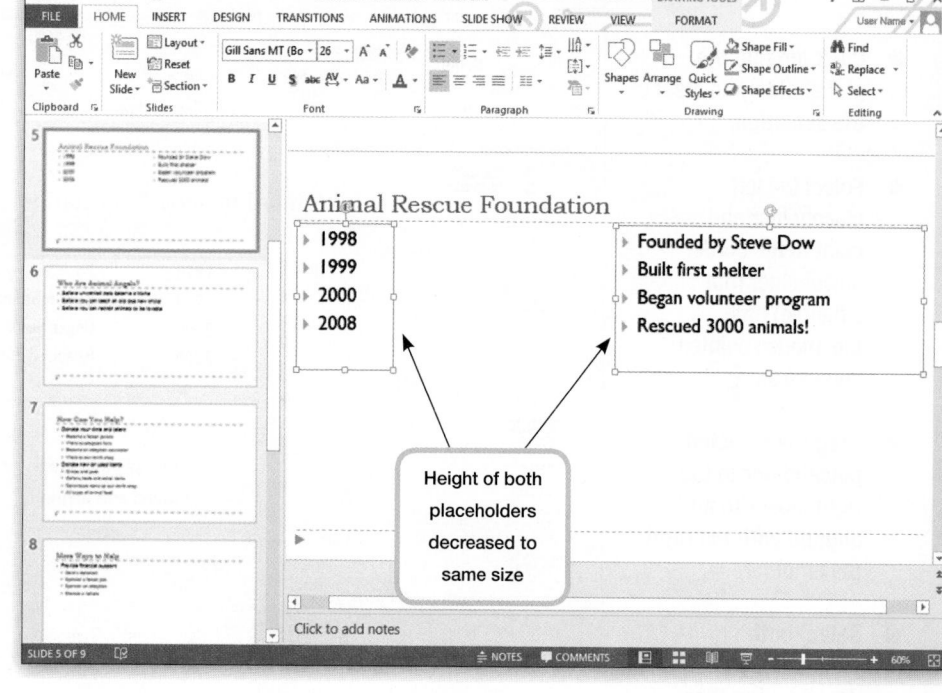

Figure 1.49

Your screen should be similar to Figure 1.49

MOVING AND ALIGNING A PLACEHOLDER

Next, you will decrease the blank space between the two columns. Then you will move both placeholders so they appear more centered in the space. An object can be moved anywhere on a slide by dragging the placeholder's border. The mouse pointer appears as ✛ when you can move a placeholder. As you drag the place-holder, red Smart Guide alignment lines appear when two objects are close to even, to help you evenly align the selected object with another. They also appear when you move an object close to the left or right margin of the slide to help you align the object with the margins.

- Click outside the placeholders to clear the selection.

- Select the left placeholder and point to the border placeholder (not a handle) until the mouse pointer appears as ⬚.

- Drag the selected placeholder to the right closer to and aligned with the right placeholder.

- Select both placeholders and drag to align them with the left margin.

- Position the placeholders as in Figure 1.50.

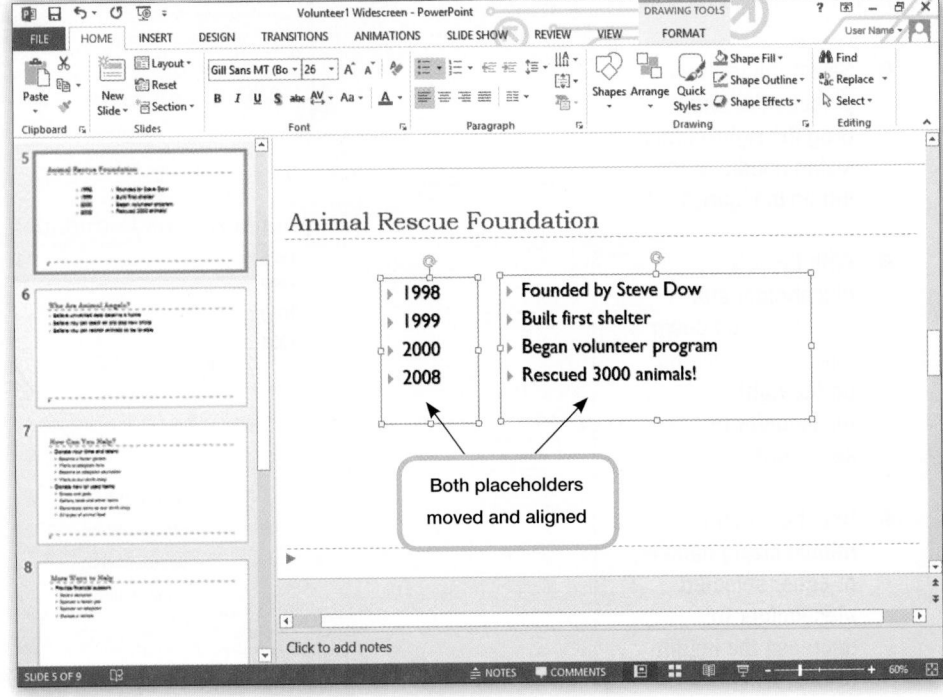

Figure 1.50

Another Method

You also can use ☰ Align ▾ Align in the Arrange group of the Format tab to evenly align two selected objects.

Your screen should be similar to Figure 1.50

ADDING AND REMOVING BULLETS

Next, you will remove the bullets from the items on the history slide. You can quickly apply and remove bullets using ☷ ▾ Bullets in the Paragraph group on the Home tab. This button applies the bullet style associated with the design template you are using. Because the placeholder items already include bullets, using this button will remove them.

1

With both text placeholders still selected, click ⊞ ▾ Bullets from the Paragraph group in the Home tab to remove all bullets.

Your screen should be similar to Figure 1.51

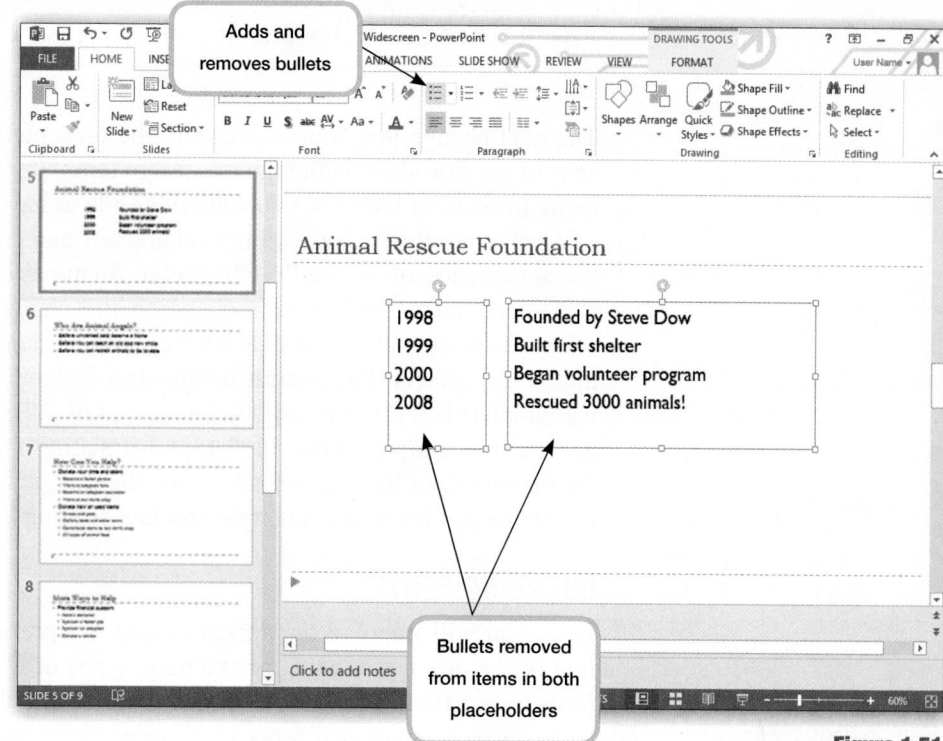

Figure 1.51

The bullets are removed from all the items in both placeholders. Now, however, you think it would look better to add bullets back to the years in the first column.

2

• Select the four years in the left column.

• Click ⊞ ▾ Bullets from the Paragraph group in the Home tab.

• Click outside the selected placeholder to deselect it.

• Save the presentation again.

Your screen should be similar to Figure 1.52

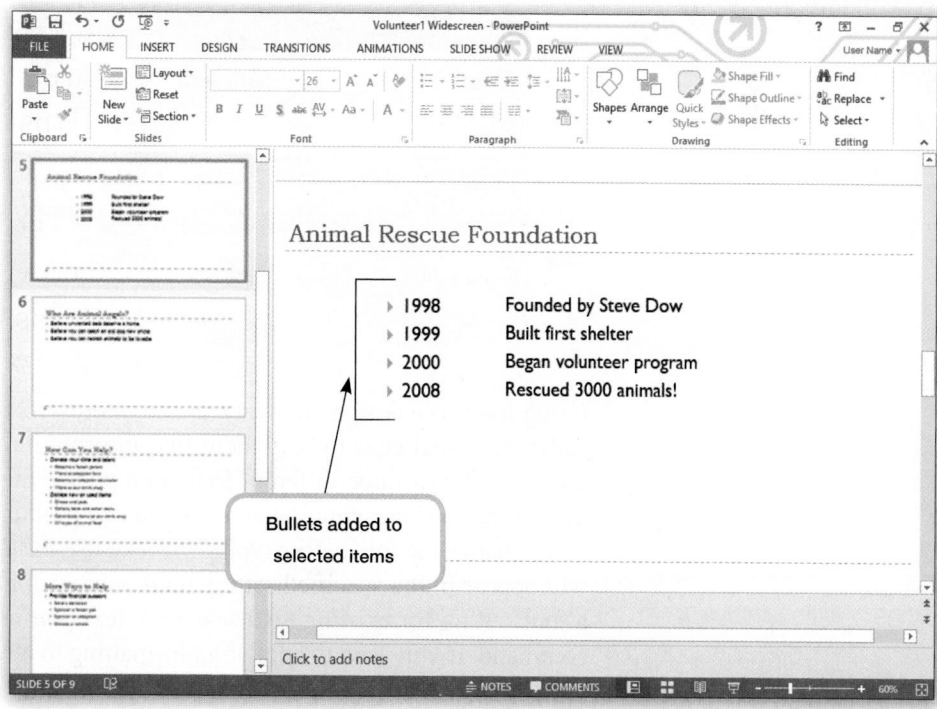

Figure 1.52

Bullets appear before the selected text items only.

Formatting Slide Text

The next change you want to make to the presentation is to improve the appearance of the title slide. Although the design template you are using already includes many formatting features, you want this slide to have more impact.

Applying different formatting to characters and paragraphs can greatly enhance the appearance of the slide. **Character formatting** features affect the selected characters only. They include changing the character style and size, applying effects such as bold and italics, changing the character spacing, and adding animated text effects. **Paragraph formatting** features affect an entire paragraph. A paragraph is text that has an ⟨Enter⟩ at the end of it. Each item in a bulleted list, title, and subtitle is a paragraph. Paragraph formatting features include the position of the paragraph or its alignment between the margins, paragraph indentation, spacing above and below a paragraph, and line spacing within a paragraph.

CHANGING FONTS

First, you will improve the appearance of the presentation title by changing the font of the title text. There are two basic types of fonts: serif and sans serif. **Serif fonts** have a flair at the base of each letter that visually leads the reader to the next letter. Two common serif fonts are Courier New and Garamond. Serif fonts generally are used for text in paragraphs. **Sans serif fonts** do not have a flair at the base of each letter. Calibri and Helvetica are two common sans serif fonts. Because sans serif fonts have a clean look, they are often used for headings in documents.

Each font can appear using a different font size. Several common fonts in different sizes are shown in the following table.

Having Trouble?

Refer to the section "Formatting Text" on page IO.43 in the Introduction to Microsoft Office 2013 to review this feature.

Font Name	Font Type	Font Size
Calibri	Sans serif	This is 10 pt. This is 16 pt.
Courier New	Serif	This is 10 pt. This is 16 pt.
Garamond	Serif	This is 10 pt. This is 16 pt.

Using fonts as a design element can add interest to your presentation and give your audience visual cues to help them find information quickly. It is good practice to use only two or three different fonts in a presentation, because too many can distract from your presentation content and can look unprofessional.

To change the font before typing the text, use the command and then type. All text will appear in the specified setting until another font setting is selected. To change a font setting for existing text, select the text you want to change and then use the command. If you want to apply font formatting to a word, simply move the insertion point to the word and the formatting is automatically applied to the entire word. To apply formatting to all the text in a placeholder, select the entire placeholder first.

Additional Information

The font used in the title is Bookman Old Style as displayed in the ⟨Bookman Old St ▾⟩ Font button. It is automatically used in all headings in this template.

The ⟨Bookman Old St ▾⟩ Font button in the Font tab or on the Mini toolbar that appears when you select text is used to change the font style. As you select a font from the drop-down menu, a live preview of how the selected font will appear is displayed in the document.

1

- Select the Title placeholder on slide 1.

- Click the border of the placeholder to change it to a solid line.

- Open the Bookman Old St Font drop-down list in the Font group of the Home tab.

- Point to several fonts to see the live preview.

Your screen should be similar to Figure 1.53

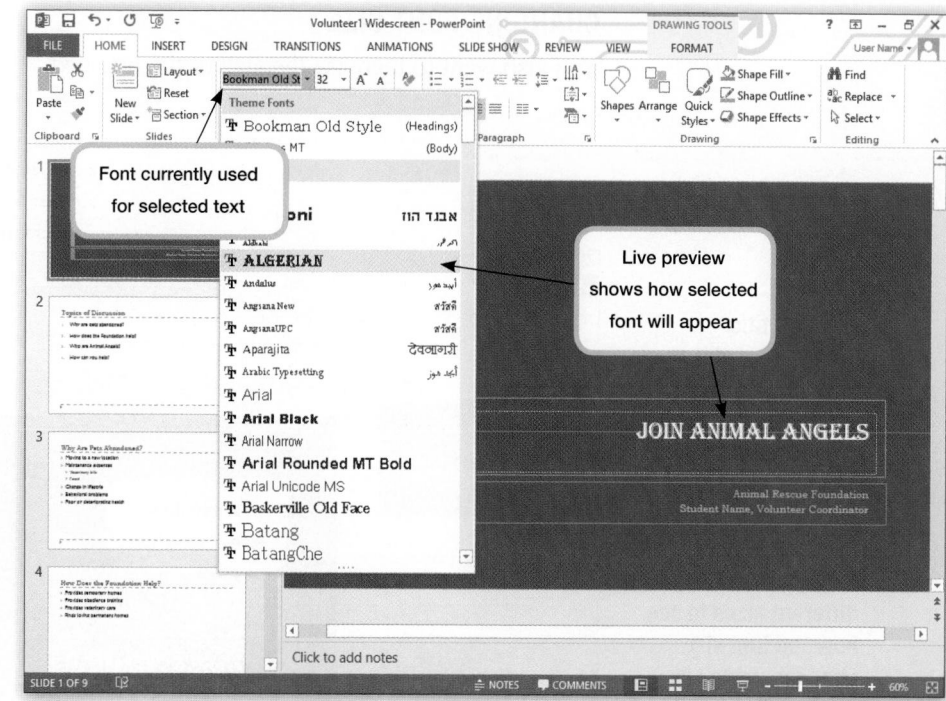

Figure 1.53

All the text in the placeholder appears in the font style selected. With Live Preview, you can see how the text will look with the selected font before you choose the one that you want. You want to change the font to a design that has a less serious appearance.

2

- Scroll the menu and choose Comic Sans MS.

Another Method

You can also select text and make format changes using the Mini toolbar.

Your screen should be similar to Figure 1.54

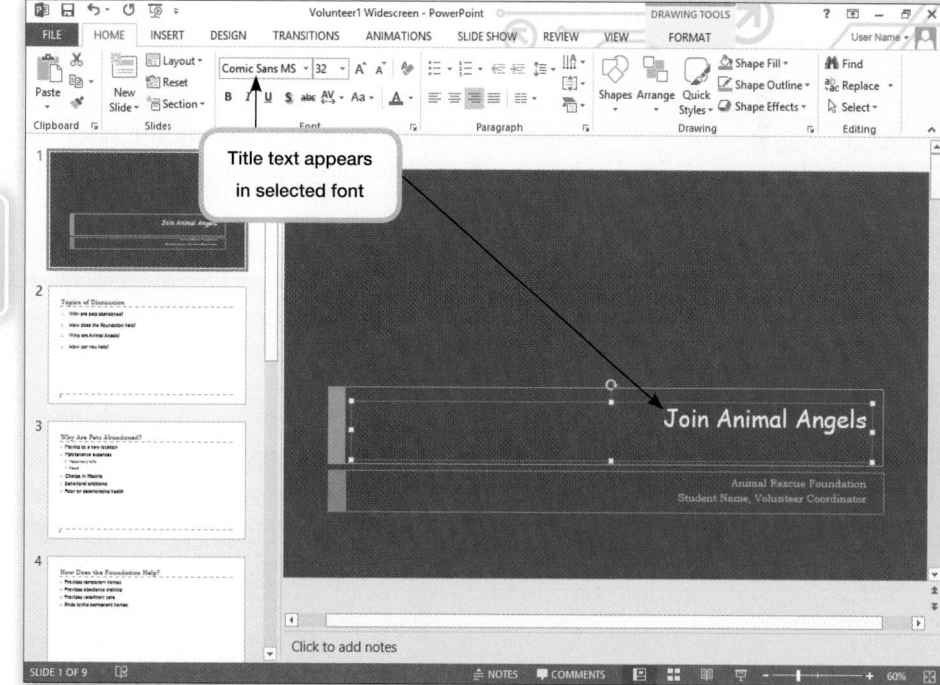

Figure 1.54

The title has changed to the new font style, and the Font button displays the font name used in the current selection.

CHANGING FONT SIZE

You also want to increase the size of the title text.

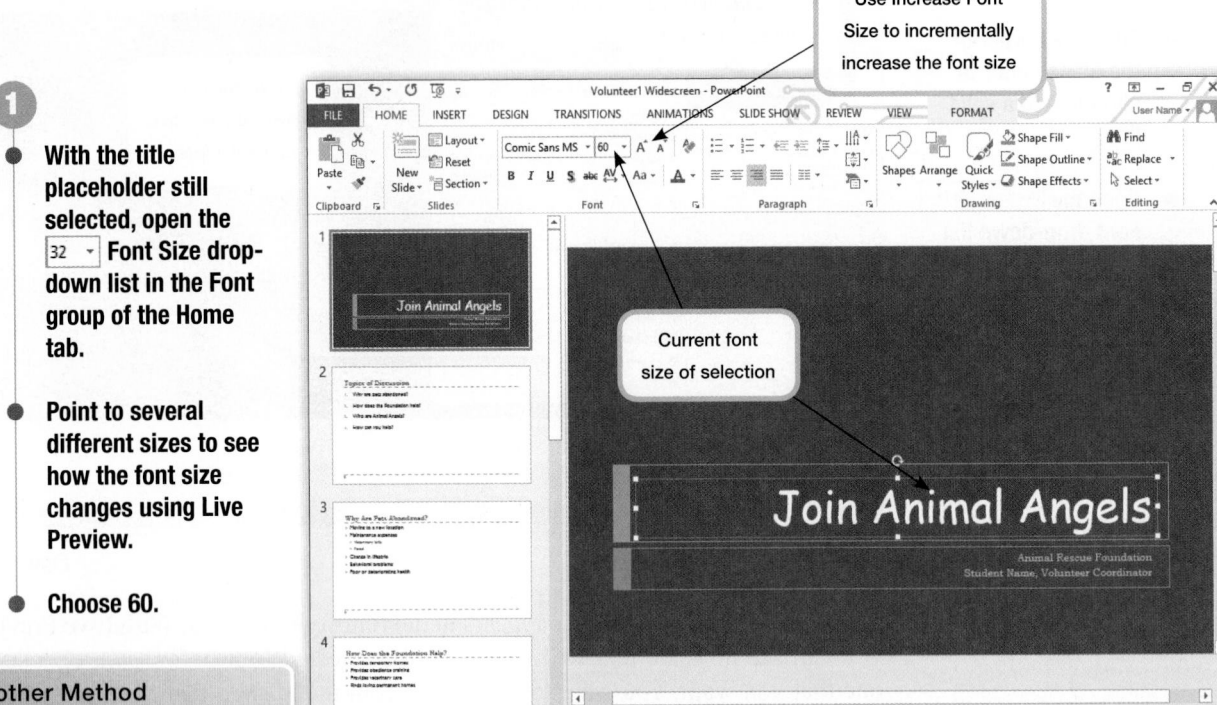

Figure 1.55

1

- **With the title placeholder still selected, open the** 32 ▾ **Font Size drop-down list in the Font group of the Home tab.**

- **Point to several different sizes to see how the font size changes using Live Preview.**

- **Choose 60.**

The font size increased from 32 points to 60 points. The Font Size button displays the point size of the current selection. If a selection includes text in several different sizes, the smallest size appears in the Font Size button followed by a plus sign.

APPLYING TEXT EFFECTS

Next, you want to further enhance the title slide by adding **text effects** such as color and shadow to the title and subtitle. The following table describes some of the effects and their uses. The Home tab and the Mini toolbar contain buttons for many of the formatting effects.

Format	Example	Use
Bold, italic	***Bold Italic***	Adds emphasis
Underline	<u>Underline</u>	Adds emphasis
Superscript	"To be or not to be."[1]	Used in footnotes and formulas
Subscript	H_2O	Used in formulas
Shadow	Shadow	Adds distinction to titles and headings
Color	**Color Color Color**	Adds interest

You decide to add color and a shadow effect to the main title first.

①

With the title placeholder still selected, click S **Text Shadow in the Font group.**

Open the A ˅ **Font Color menu to display a gallery of colors.**

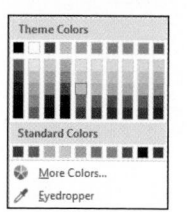

Choose Gold, Accent 1, Lighter 40% in the Theme Colors section.

Your screen should be similar to Figure 1.56

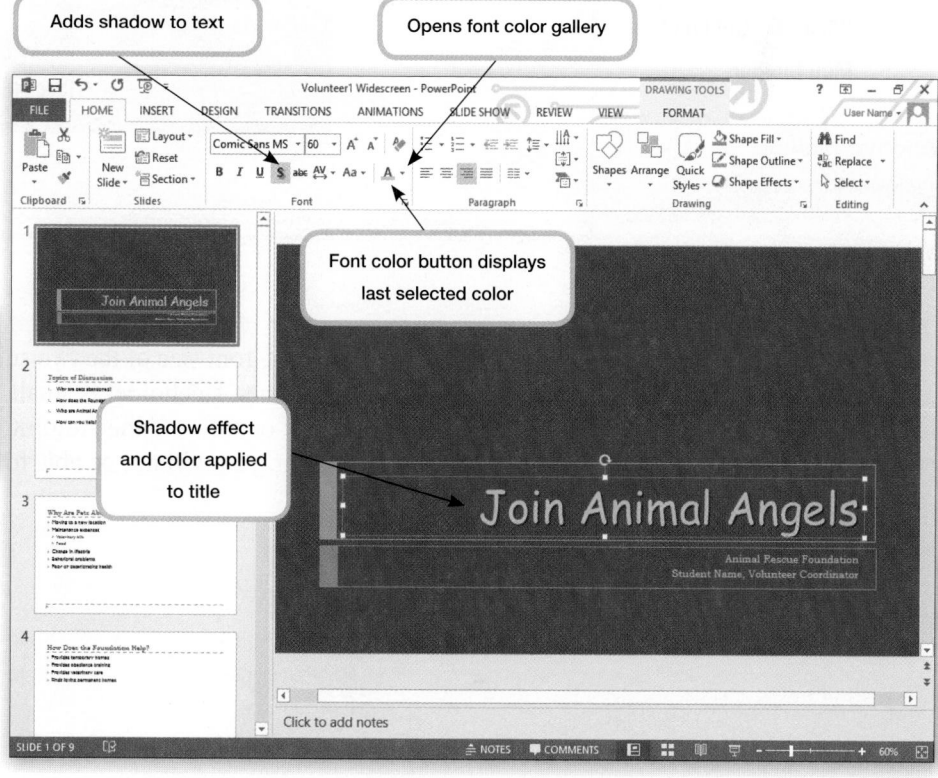

Figure 1.56

The selected color and slight shadow effect make the title much more interesting. Also notice the color in the Font Color button is the gold color you just selected. This color can be quickly reapplied to other selections now simply by clicking the button.

Next you will enhance the two lines in the Subtitle placeholder by applying a different effect to each line.

2

- Select the text "Animal Rescue Foundation".

- Open the A ▾ Font Color gallery in the Mini toolbar.

- Choose Gold, Accent 1 in the Theme Colors section.

- Click **B** Bold on the Mini toolbar.

Another Method

The keyboard shortcut is Ctrl + B.

Your screen should be similar to Figure 1.57

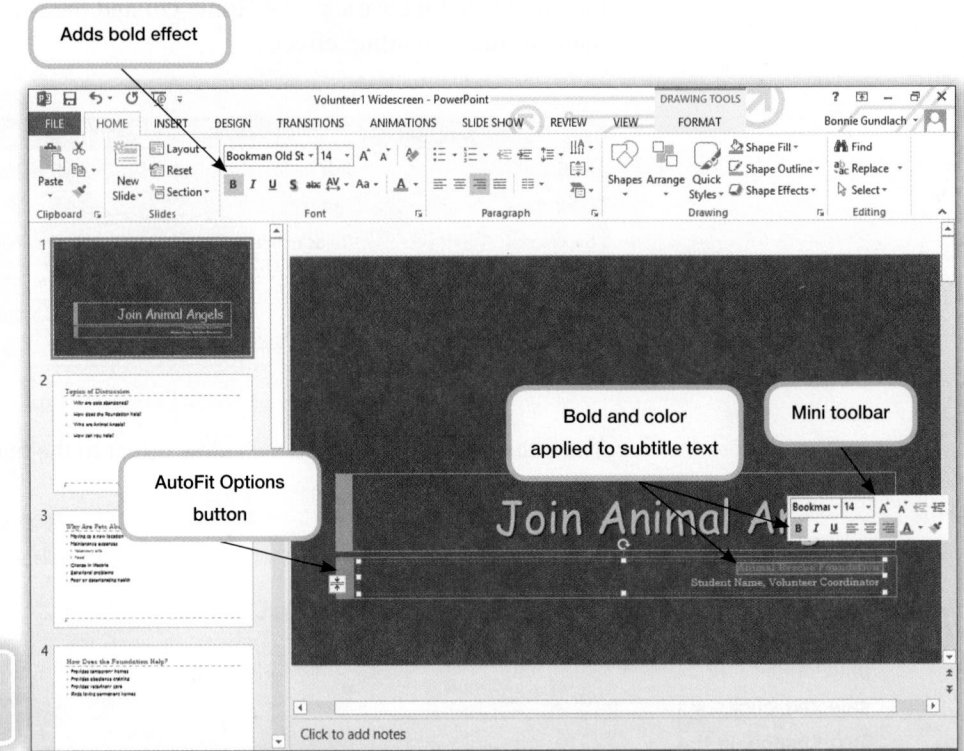

Figure 1.57

Next you want to increase the font size of the two subtitle lines and add a few additional text effects. Because the placeholder is small, you will first need to increase the size of the placeholder or turn off the AutoFit to placeholder feature. If you leave the AutoFit feature on, you will not be able to increase the font size.

3

- Click 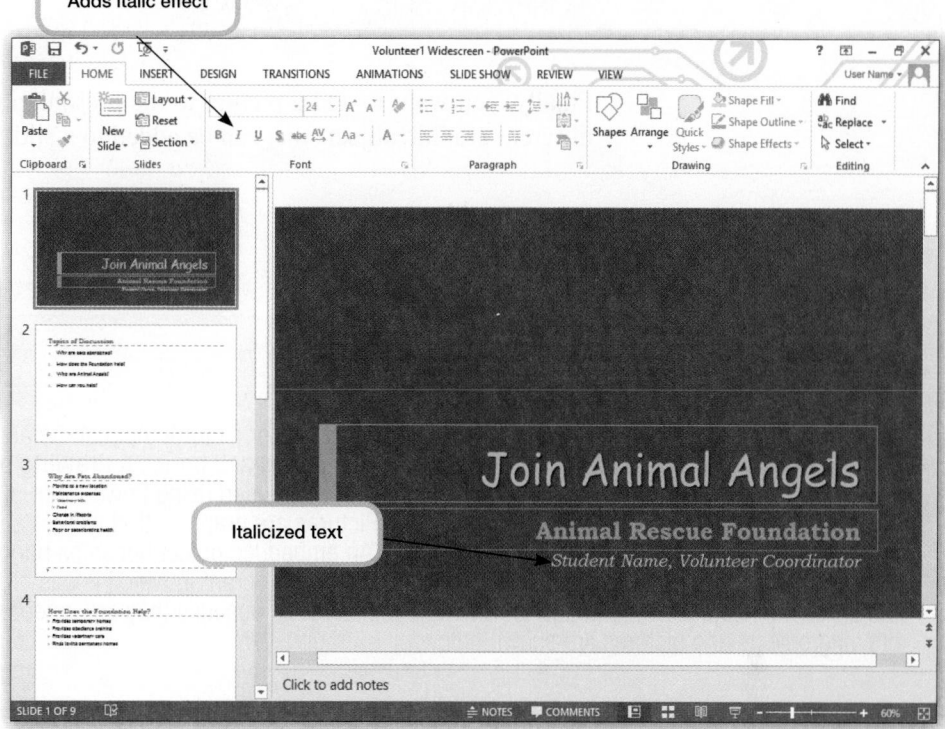 Autofit and choose **Stop Fitting Text to This Placeholder.**

Having Trouble?

If the Mini toolbar is no longer displayed, right-click on the selection to display it again.

- Change the font size to 32.

- Select the entire second line of the subtitle.

- Click I **Italic.**

- Click $A^{\uparrow}$ **Increase Font Size.**

- Click somewhere outside the placeholder.

- Save the presentation.

Your screen should be similar to Figure 1.58

Adds italic effect

Italicized text

Figure 1.58

Now the title slide has much more impact.

Working with Graphics

Finally, you want to add a picture to the presentation. A picture is one of several different graphic objects that can be added to a slide.

Concept  5 Graphics

A **graphic** is a nontext element or object, such as a drawing or picture, that can be added to a slide. A graphic can be a simple drawing object consisting of shapes such as lines and boxes. A **drawing object** is part of your presentation document. Many simple drawing objects can be created using PowerPoint. A **picture** is an image such as a graphic illustration or a scanned photograph. Pictures are graphics that were created from another program and are inserted in a slide as **embedded objects**. An embedded object becomes part of the presentation file and can be opened and edited using the **source program**, the program in which it was created. Any changes made to the embedded object are not made to the original picture file because they are independent. Several examples of drawing objects and pictures are shown below.

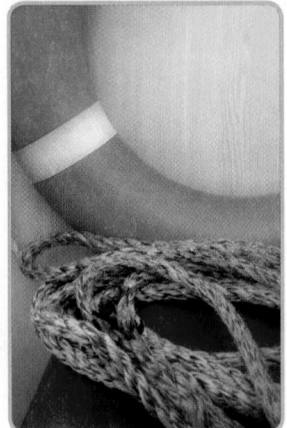
Photograph

Graphic illustration

Drawing object

Add graphics to your presentation to help the audience understand concepts and to add interest.

Digital images created using a digital camera are one of the most common types of graphic files. You also can create graphic files using a scanner to convert printed documents, including photographs, to an electronic format.

Graphic files can be obtained from your computer or a computer network and a variety of online sources. All types of graphics, including clip art, photographs, and other types of images, can be found on the Internet. **Clip art** are simple drawings created using a graphics program. Remember that any images you locate on the Internet are protected by copyright and should only be used with permission. You can also purchase CDs or access to stock image sites containing graphics.

INSERTING A PICTURE FROM YOUR COMPUTER

You want to add a graphic of a question mark you have stored on your computer to slide 2.

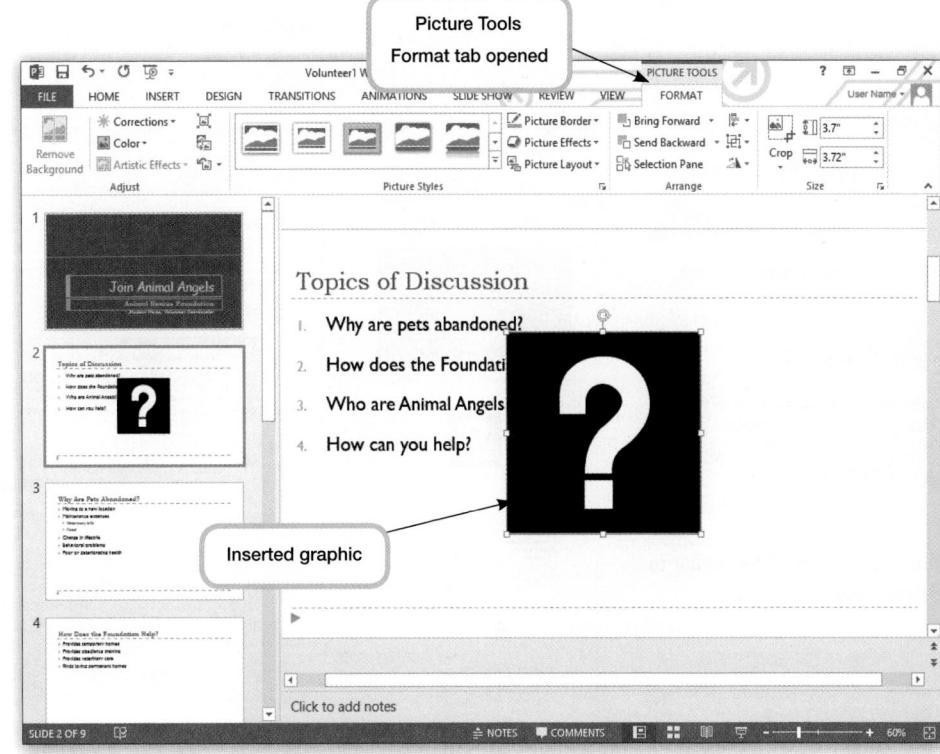

1

- Make slide 2 current.

- Open the Insert tab.

- Click [Pictures] in the Images group.

- Navigate to the location of your student files and double-click pp01_Question Mark1.

Your screen should be similar to Figure 1.59

Figure 1.59

The question mark graphic is inserted on the slide and is a selected object that can be sized and moved like any other object. Because graphic objects are inserted as **floating objects** in the **drawing layer**, a separate layer from the placeholder, it may cover some of the content in the placeholder. This allows graphics to be positioned precisely on the slide, including above and below other graphics and text. The Picture Tools Format tab automatically appears and can be used to modify the selected picture object.

INSERTING A GRAPHIC FROM ONLINE SOURCES

You decide you want to search online sources for a graphic of a question mark that might be more interesting.

1

● **Open the Insert tab.**

● **Click** Online Pictures **in the Images group.**

Your screen should be similar to Figure 1.60

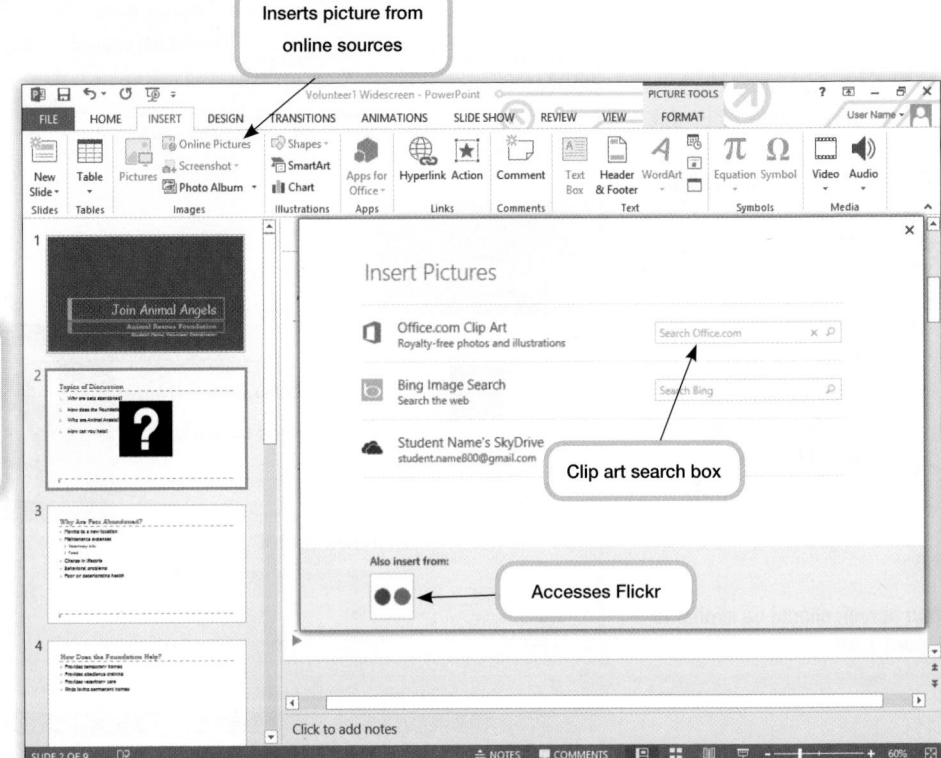

Figure 1.60

The Insert Pictures window provides several methods to locate online graphics. The first is to use Microsoft's Office.com clip art website. The second is to use Microsoft's search engine Bing to search the web. A third is to access your Sky-Drive account to locate pictures you have stored at that location. Finally, you can access Flickr, an online photo management and sharing website, for pictures you have uploaded to an account with the website.

You will use the Office.com website to search for question mark pictures by entering a word or phrase that is representative of the type of picture you want to locate in the Search Office.com text box. Enter a specific search term to get fewer results that are more likely to meet your requirements.

- In the Search For text box, type **question mark**

- Click 🔍 or press ⏎ Enter.

- Point to the first thumbnail image.

Having Trouble?

Because the online selection of clip art is continuously changing, the thumbnails displayed on your screen may not match those shown in Figure 1.61.

Your screen should be similar to Figure 1.61

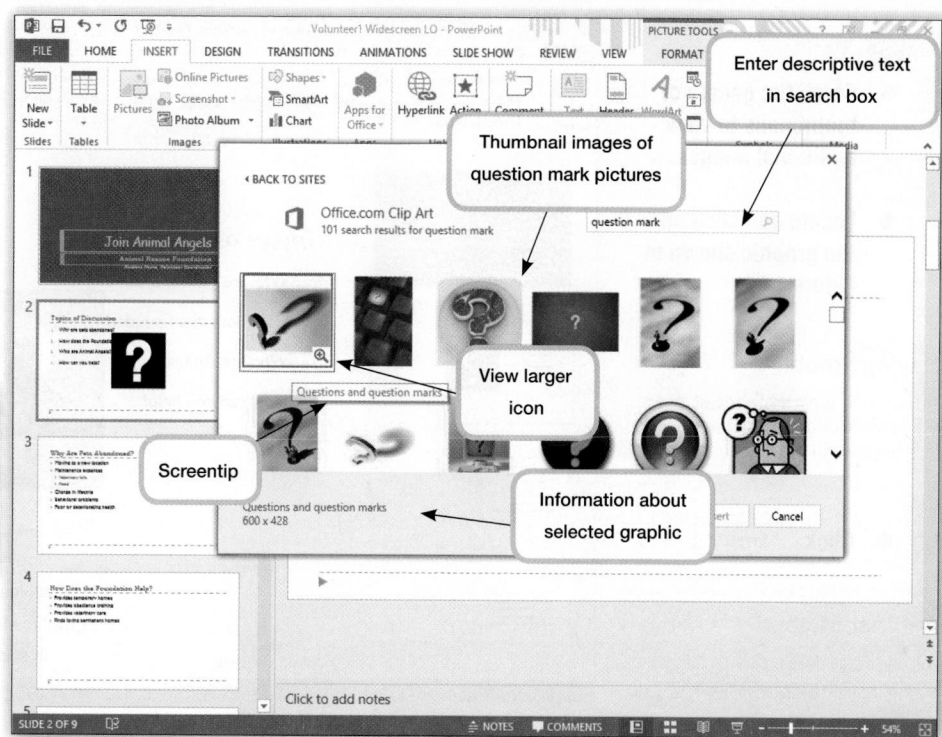

Figure 1.61

The program searches the Office.com Clip Art gallery for clip art and graphics that match your search term and displays thumbnails of all located graphics. Pointing to a thumbnail displays a ScreenTip containing a descriptive title associated with the graphic. At the bottom of the window, it displays the title and information about the picture properties. Additionally, because it is sometimes difficult to see the detail in the graphic, you can preview it in a larger size by clicking the 🔍 View Larger icon.

- **Scroll the gallery of thumbnails to view additional images.**

- **Locate and click on the graphic shown in Figure 1.62.**

Having Trouble?

If this graphic is not available just choose a question mark graphic that you like from the gallery.

- **Click** Insert .

Another Method

You could also double-click on the graphic to both select and insert it in the slide.

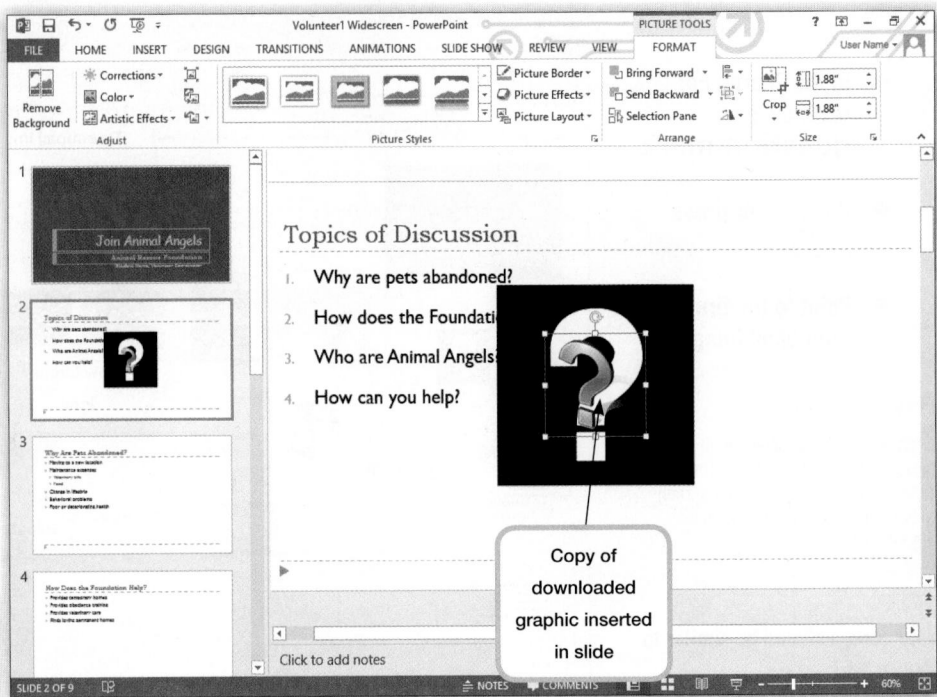

Figure 1.62

Your screen should be similar to Figure 1.62

The clip art image is downloaded and inserted in the center of the slide and may be on top of the other graphic.

DELETING, SIZING, AND MOVING A GRAPHIC

There are now two graphics in the slide. You decide to use the graphic from the online site and need to remove the original graphic. To do this, you select the graphic and delete it.

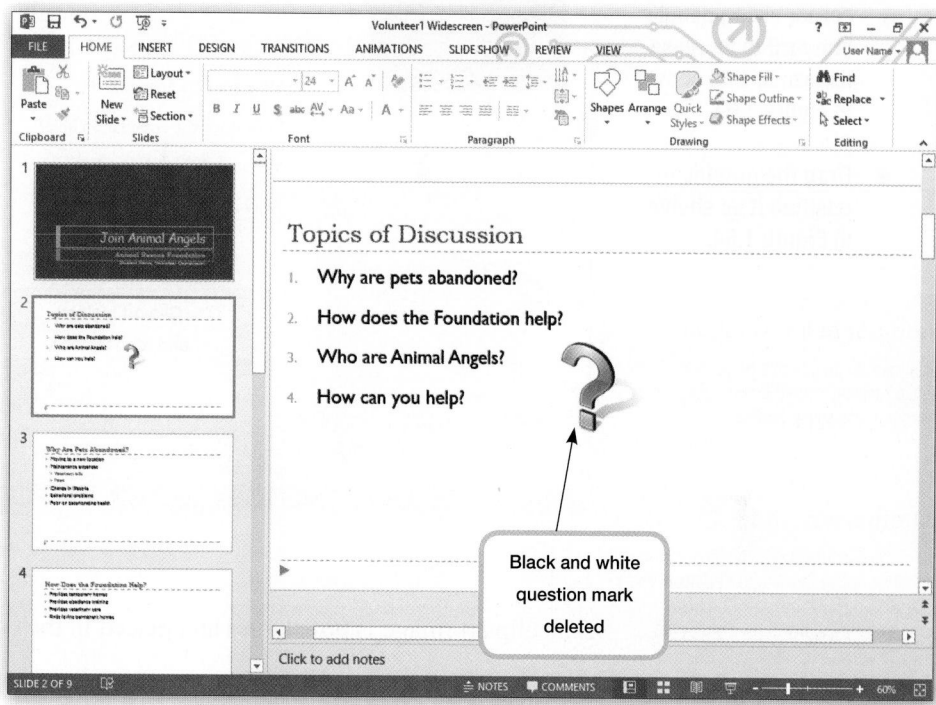

1

- **Click on the black-and-white question mark graphic to select it.**

- **Press** Delete**.**

Your screen should be similar to Figure 1.63

Figure 1.63

Next, you need to size and position the remaining graphic on the slide. A graphic object is sized and moved just like a placeholder. You want to increase the graphic size and move it to the right on the slide.

2

- Click on the graphic to select it.

- Drag the top left corner sizing handle outward to increase its size to that shown in Figure 1.64.

- Drag the graphic to position it as shown in Figure 1.64.

Additional Information

To maintain an object's proportions while resizing it, hold down [Shift] while dragging the sizing handle.

Another Method

You also can size a graphic by entering exact values in the Shape Height and Shape Width text boxes in the Size group of the Picture Tools Format tab.

Your screen should be similar to Figure 1.64

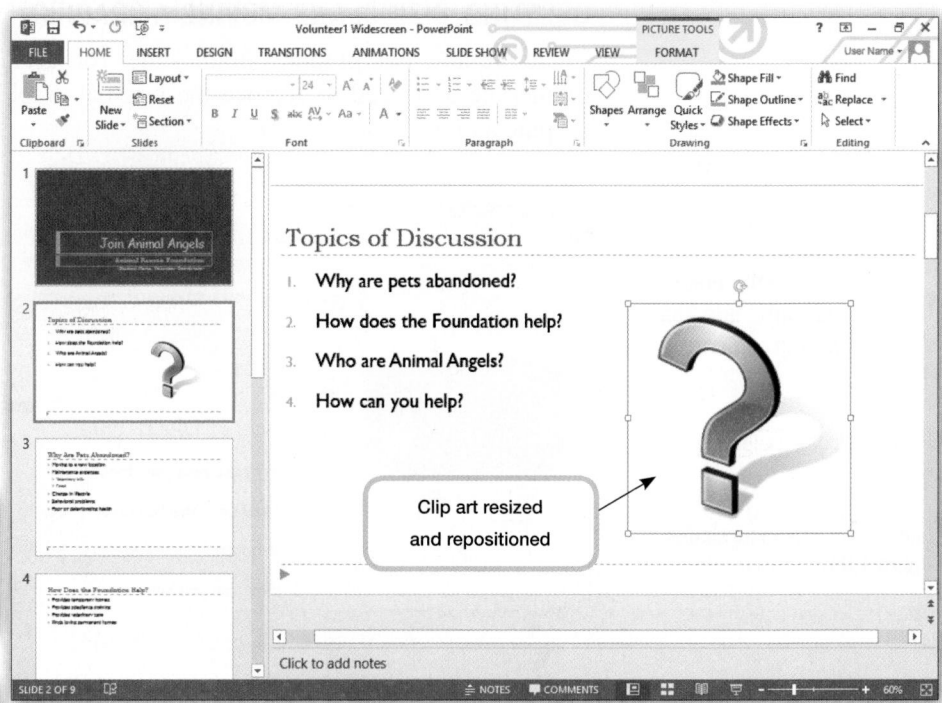

Clip art resized and repositioned

Figure 1.64

The clip art image is now larger and placed in the correct position on the slide.

ADDING GRAPHIC EFFECTS

The Picture Tools Format tab is used to customize the look of the graphic to suit your presentation. The first enhancement you would like to make is to change the color of the question mark so it coordinates with the slide design.

①

- With the clip art selected, click **Color ▾** in the Adjust group of the Picture Tools Format tab.

- Point to the choices in the Recolor gallery to see live previews.

- Choose Aqua, Accent color 2 Dark (second row, third from left).

Your screen should be similar to Figure 1.65

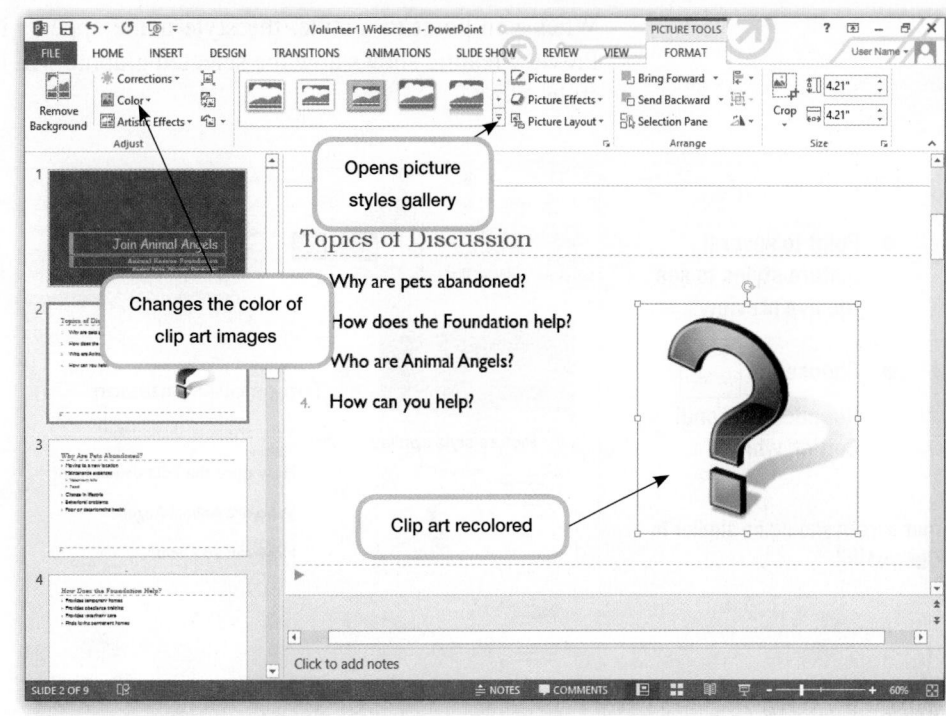

Figure 1.65

Next, you want to enhance the graphic by applying a picture style to it. A **style** is a combination of formatting options that can be applied in one easy step. In the case of **picture styles**, the combinations consist of border, shadow, and shape effects. You also can create your own picture style effects by selecting specific style elements, such as borders and shadows, individually using the ⬛ Picture Effects ▾ , ⬛ Picture Border ▾ , and ⬛ Picture Layout ▾ commands.

②

- Click ⬇ More in the Picture Styles group to open the Picture Styles gallery.

Your screen should be similar to Figure 1.66

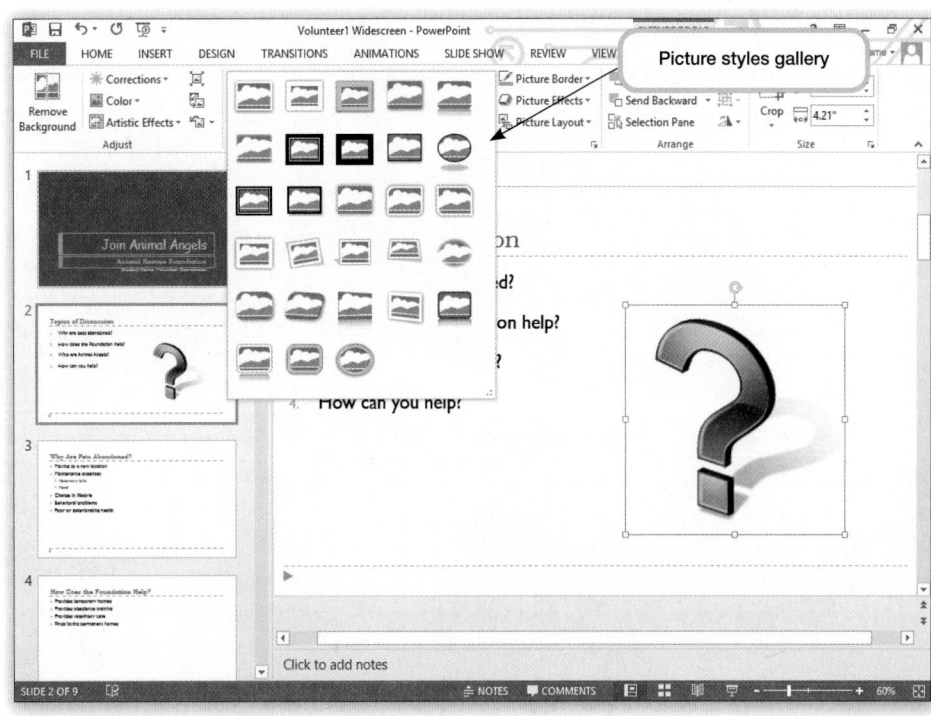

Figure 1.66

When you point to a style, the style name appears in a ScreenTip, and the Live Preview feature shows how the selected graphic will look with the selected picture style.

3

● **Point to several picture styles to see the live previews.**

● **Choose the** 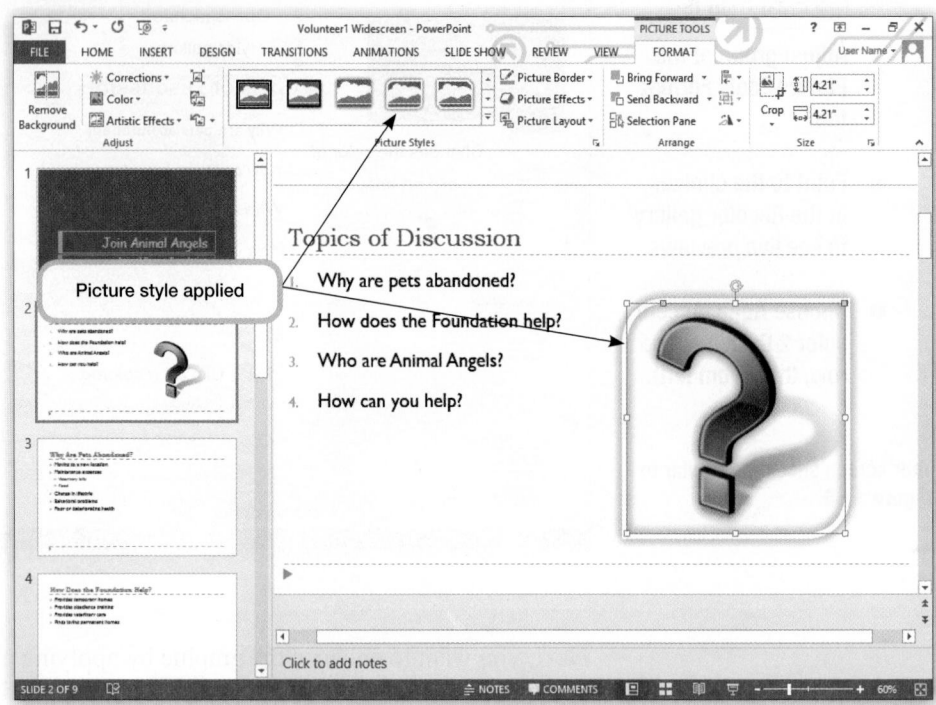 **Rounded Diagonal Corner, white.**

Your screen should be similar to Figure 1.67

Figure 1.67

As you look at the picture, you decide to change the color of the border and remove the shadow.

4

- If necessary, select the graphic and open the Picture Tools Format tab.

- Click 🖋 Picture Border ▾ in the Picture Styles group.

- Choose Gold, Accent 1 from the Theme Colors group.

- Click 📷 Picture Effects ▾ in the Picture Styles group.

- From the Shadow group, choose No Shadow.

- Click outside the graphic to deselect the object.

- Save the presentation.

Your screen should be similar to Figure 1.68

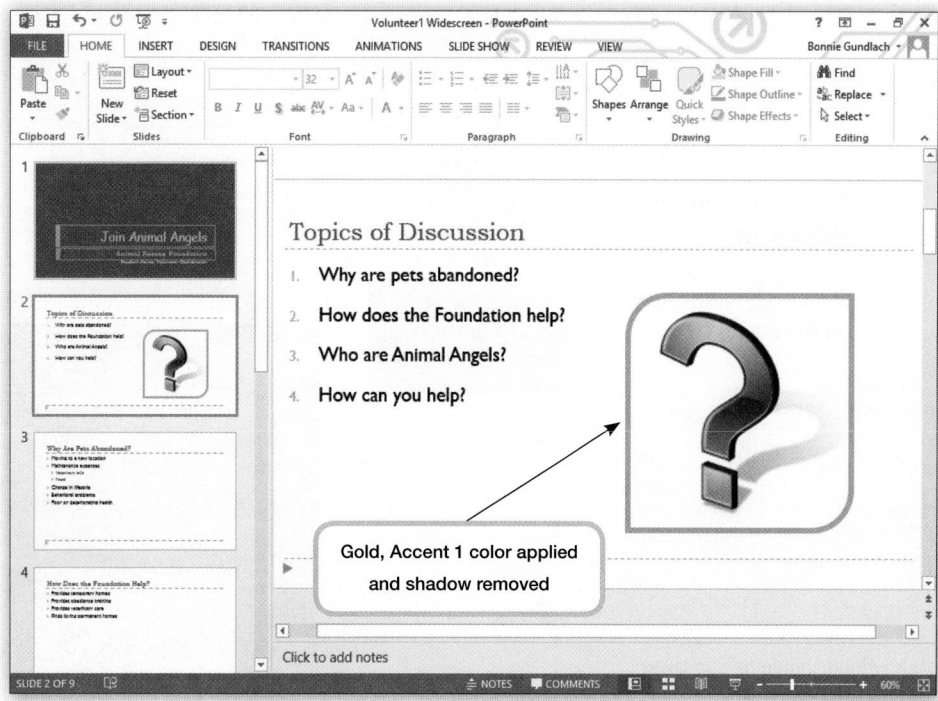

Figure 1.68

The addition of a customized graphic image gives your presentation a more polished look. Now that the slides are in the order you want and formatted, you would like to see how the presentation will look when viewed by an audience.

Rehearsing a Presentation

Rather than projecting the presentation on a large screen as you would to present it for an audience, a simple way to rehearse a presentation is to view it on your computer screen as a **slide show**. A slide show displays each slide full screen and in order. While the slide show is running during this rehearsal, you can plan what you will say while each slide is displayed.

USING SLIDE SHOW VIEW

When you view a slide show, each slide fills the screen, hiding the PowerPoint application window, so you can view the slides as your audience would. You will begin the slide show starting with the first slide.

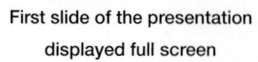

First slide of the presentation
displayed full screen

1
- Select slide 1 in the Slides pane.

- Click  Slide Show (in the status bar).

Your screen should be similar to Figure 1.69

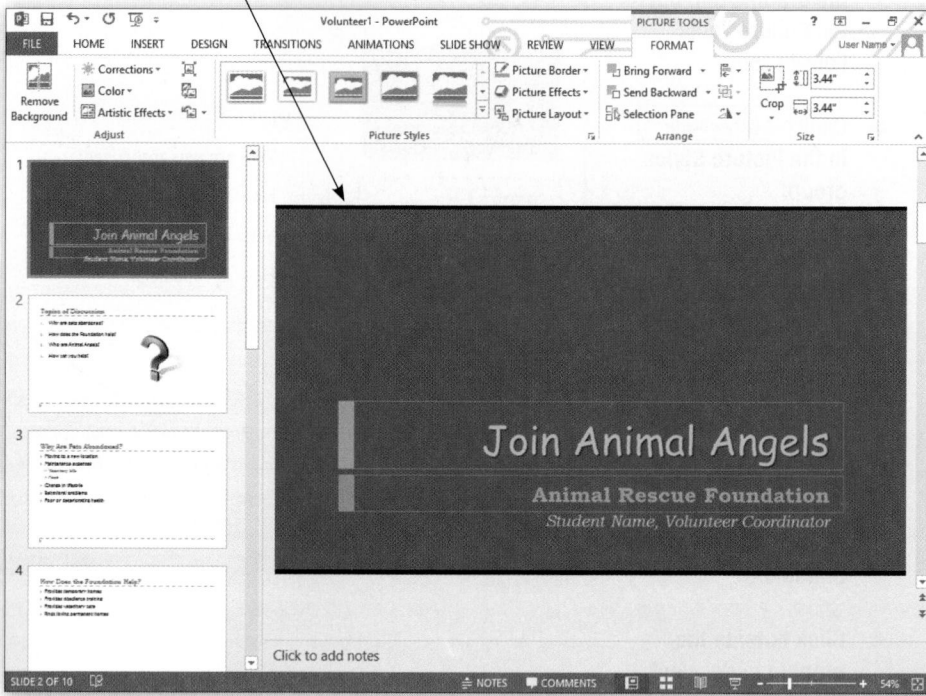

Figure 1.69

The presentation title slide is displayed full screen, as it will appear when projected on a screen using computer projection equipment. The easiest way to see the next slide is to click the mouse button. You also can use the keys shown below to move to the next or previous slide.

Next Slide	Previous Slide
Spacebar	Backspace
Enter	
→	←
↓	↑
Page Down	Page Up
N (for Next)	P (for Previous)

You also can select Next, Previous, or Last Viewed from the shortcut menu. Additionally, moving the mouse pointer to the lower-left corner of the window in Slide Show displays the Slide Show toolbar. Clicking 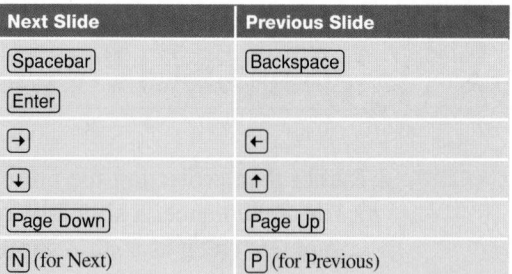 or ⊙ moves to the previous or next slide, and ⊙ opens the shortcut menu.

- **Click to display the next slide.**

- **Using each of the methods described, slowly display the entire presentation.**

- **When the last slide displays a black window, click again to end the slide show.**

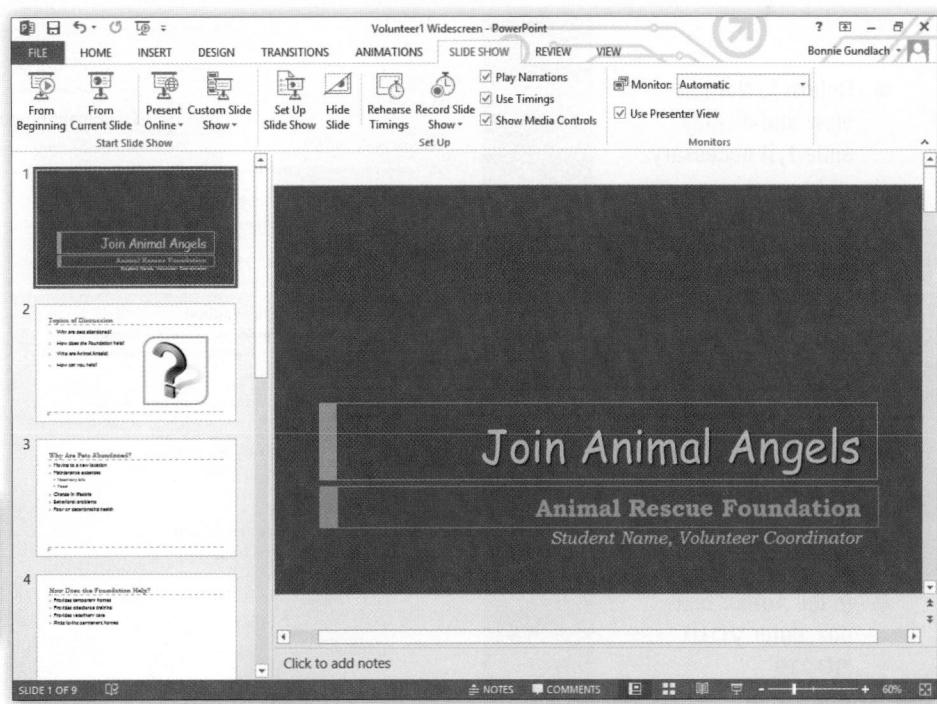

Figure 1.70

Your screen should be similar to Figure 1.70

After the last slide is displayed, the program returns to the view you were last using, in this case, Normal view.

Documenting a File

Finally, you want to update the presentation file properties by adding your name as the author, the title, and a tag.

1

- **Return to Normal view and display slide 1, if necessary.**
- **Open the File tab and, if necessary, click** Info.
- **In the Title text box, enter** Join Animal Angels
- **In the Tags text box, enter** Volunteer, Recruit
- **In the Author text box, enter** your name
- **Click anywhere outside the text box.**

Your screen should be similar to Figure 1.71

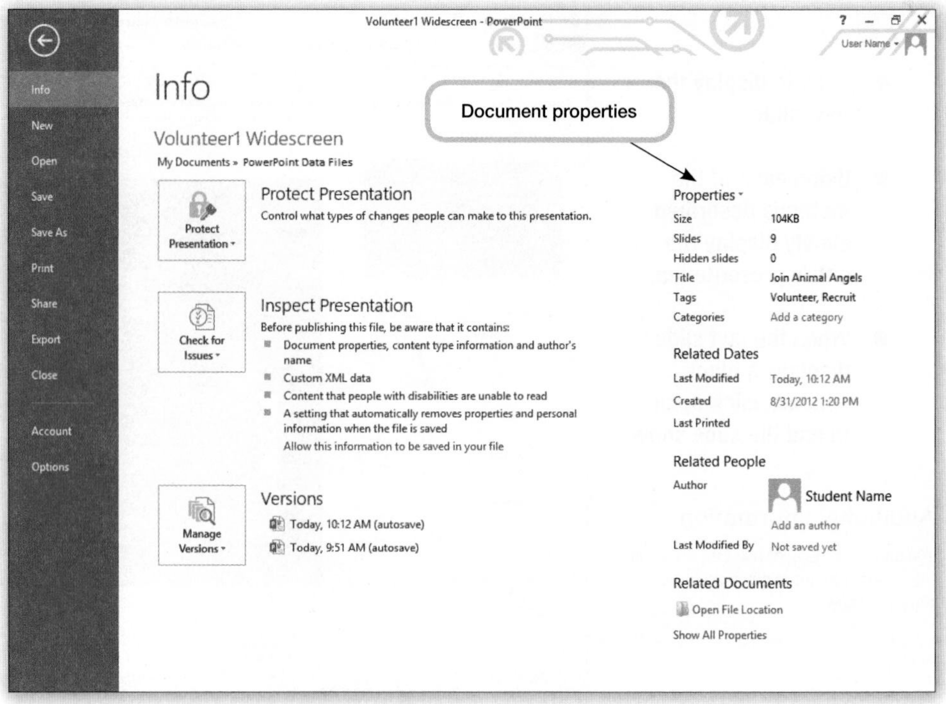

Volunteer1 Widescreen - PowerPoint
User Name
Info
New
Open
Save
Save As
Print
Share
Export
Close
Account
Options
Info
Document properties
Volunteer1 Widescreen
My Documents » PowerPoint Data Files
Protect Presentation
Protect Presentation
Control what types of changes people can make to this presentation.
Check for Issues
Inspect Presentation
Before publishing this file, be aware that it contains:
Document properties, content type information and author's name
Custom XML data
Content that people with disabilities are unable to read
A setting that automatically removes properties and personal information when the file is saved
Allow this information to be saved in your file
Manage Versions
Versions
Today, 10:12 AM (autosave)
Today, 9:51 AM (autosave)
Properties
Size 104KB
Slides 9
Hidden slides 0
Title Join Animal Angels
Tags Volunteer, Recruit
Categories Add a category
Related Dates
Last Modified Today, 10:12 AM
Created 8/31/2012 1:20 PM
Last Printed
Related People
Author Student Name
Add an author
Last Modified By Not saved yet
Related Documents
Open File Location
Show All Properties

Figure 1.71

Previewing and Printing the Presentation

Although you still plan to make many changes to the presentation, you want to provide a printed copy of the presentation to the foundation director to get feedback regarding the content and layout.

PRINTING A SLIDE

Although your presentation looks good on your screen, it may not look good when printed. Shading, patterns, and backgrounds that look good on the screen can make your printed output unreadable. Fortunately, PowerPoint displays a preview of how your printed output will appear as you specify the print settings. This allows you to make changes to the print settings before printing and reduces unnecessary paper waste.

Having Trouble?

Refer to the section "Printing a Document" on page IO.59 in the Introduction to Microsoft Office 2013 to review basic printing features.

1 Click [Print] from the File tab.

Your screen should be similar to Figure 1.72

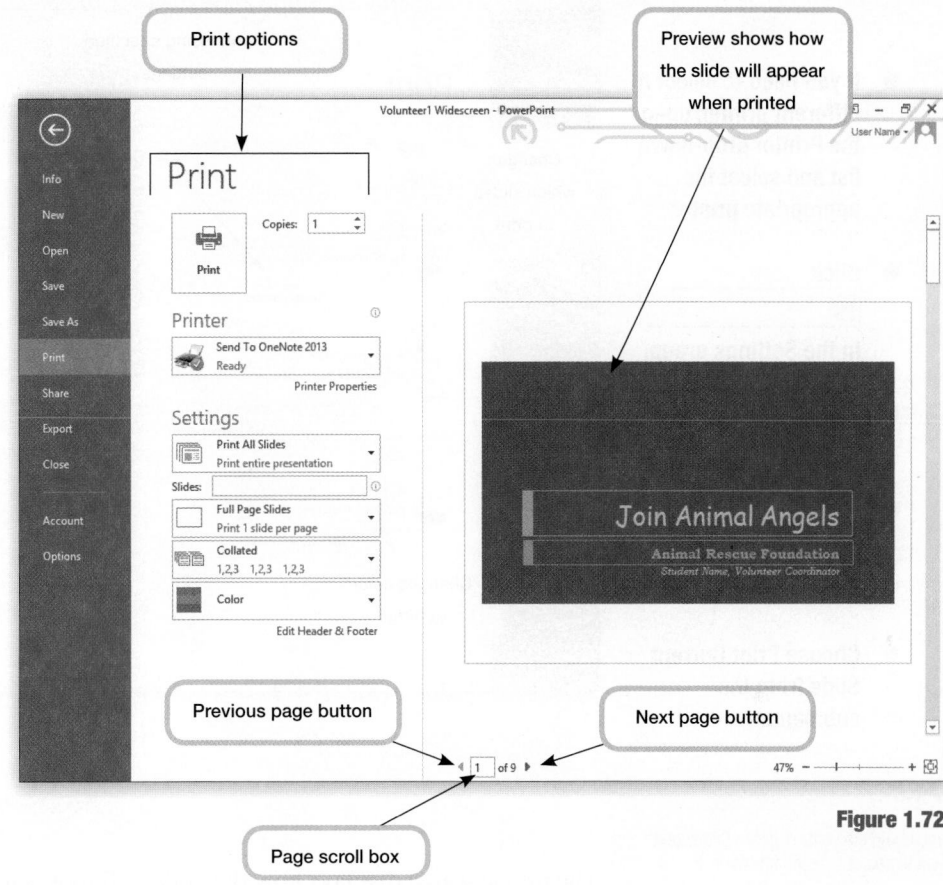

Print options

Preview shows how the slide will appear when printed

Previous page button

Next page button

Page scroll box

Figure 1.72

Additional Information

Use grayscale when your slides include patterns whose colors you want to appear in shades of gray.

The Print window displays the print options in the left pane that are used to modify the print settings. The preview area displays the first slide in the presentation as it will appear when printed using the current settings. It appears in color if your selected printer is a color printer; otherwise, it appears in grayscale (shades of gray). Even if you have a color printer, you can print the slides in grayscale or pure black and white. You want to print using the black-and-white option. The page scroll box shows the page number of the page you are currently viewing and the number of total pages. The scroll buttons on either side are used to scroll to the next and previous pages.

The other change you want to make to the print settings is to print only the first slide in the presentation. To do this, you will change the settings to print the current slide only.

2

- If you need to select a different printer, open the Printer drop-down list and select the appropriate printer.

- Click
   Color
  in the Settings group.

- Choose Pure Black and White.

- Click
  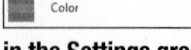 Print All Slides
  Print entire presentation
  in the Settings area.

- Choose Print Current Slide from the submenu.

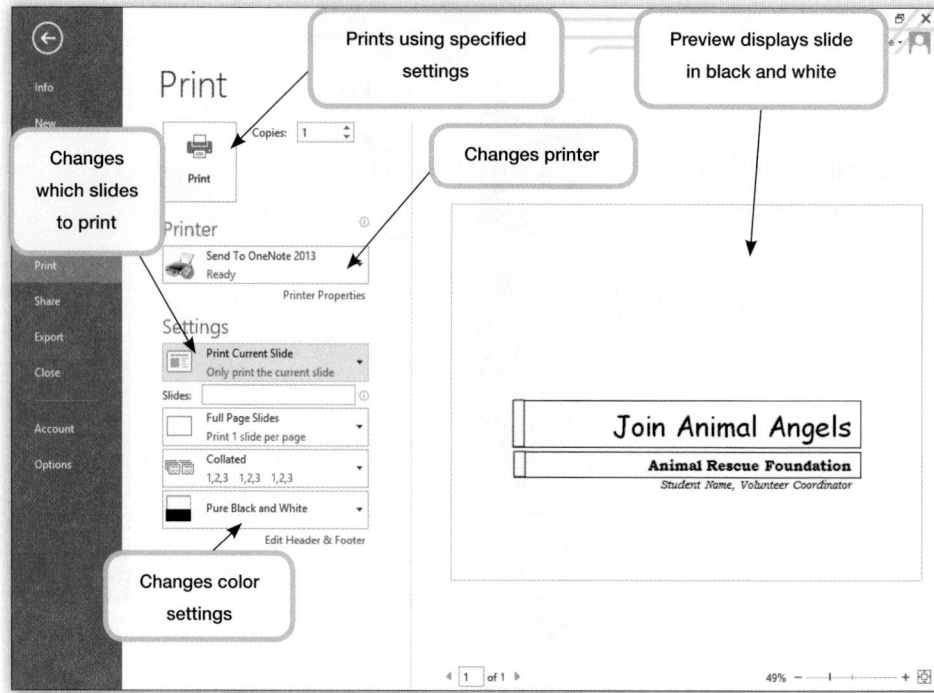

Figure 1.73

Your screen should be similar to Figure 1.73

The preview area displays how the slide will look when printed in black and white. Notice the page scroll box in the preview area now shows 1 of 1, indicating that only the first slide will be printed.

3

- If necessary, make sure your printer is on and ready to print.

- Click .

A printing progress bar appears in the status bar, indicating that the program is sending data to the printer and the title slide should be printing.

PRINTING HANDOUTS

You also can change the type of printed output from full page slides to any one of the output settings described in the table below. Only one type of output can be printed at a time.

Additional Information
You will learn about notes in Lab 2.

To help the foundation's director get a better feel for the flow of the presentation, you decide to also print out the presentation as a handout. The handout format will allow him to see each slide as it appears onscreen.

1

- **Open the File tab and click** Print **.**

- **Click** Print Current Slide / Only print the current slide **in the Settings area and choose Print All Slides.**

- **Click** Full Page Slides / Print 1 slide per page **in the Settings area and choose** 6 Slides Vertical **.**

Your screen should be similar to Figure 1.74

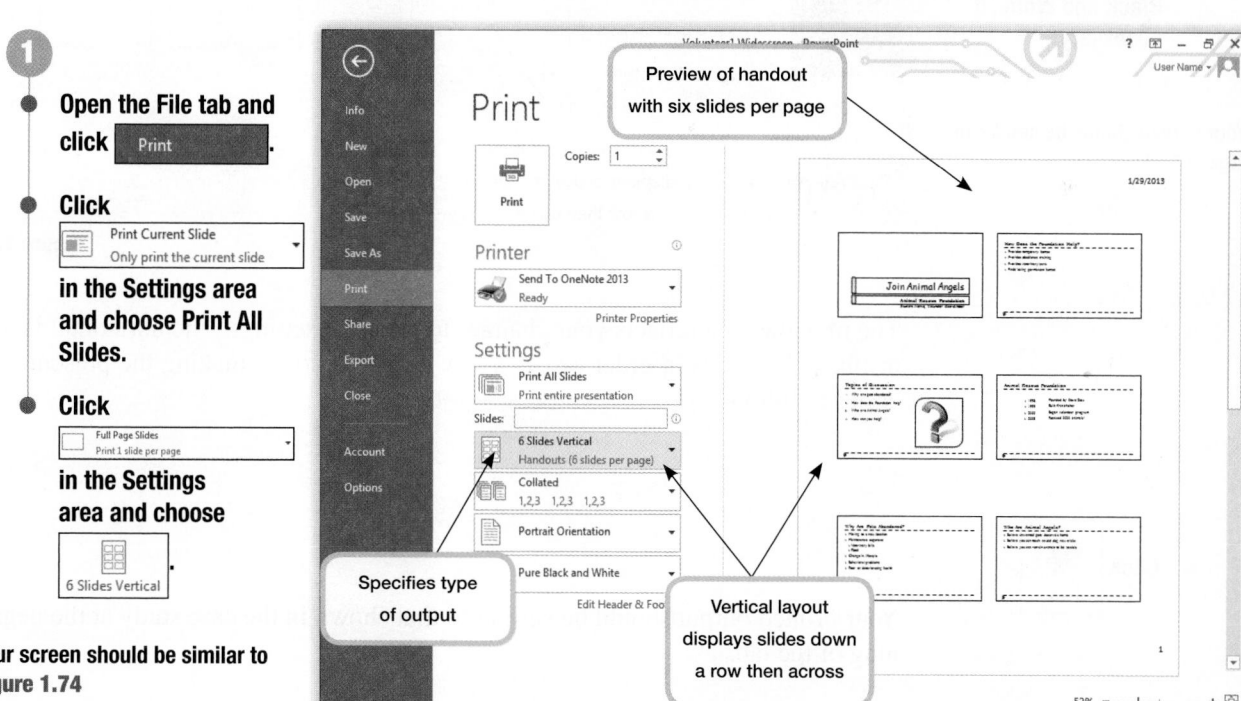

Figure 1.74

Additional Information

The Orientation setting will override the Slide Layout setting. So, even if you leave the Slide Layout setting as 6 Slides Vertical, the presentation will print horizontal to match the Orientation setting.

The preview area shows the handouts as they will print. The vertical arrangement of the slides displays the slides down a row and then across. You decide to change the orientation from the default of portrait to landscape so that the slides print across the length of the paper, to change the arrangement to horizontal, and also to increase the number of slides per page so that the entire presentation fits on one page.

2

- Click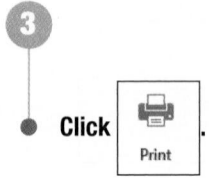

  | 6 Slides Vertical |
  | Handouts (6 slides per page) |

  and choose 9 Slides Horizontal.

- Click

  | Portrait Orientation |

  and choose Landscape Orientation.

- Change the Color setting to Pure Black and White, if necessary.

Your screen should be similar to Figure 1.75

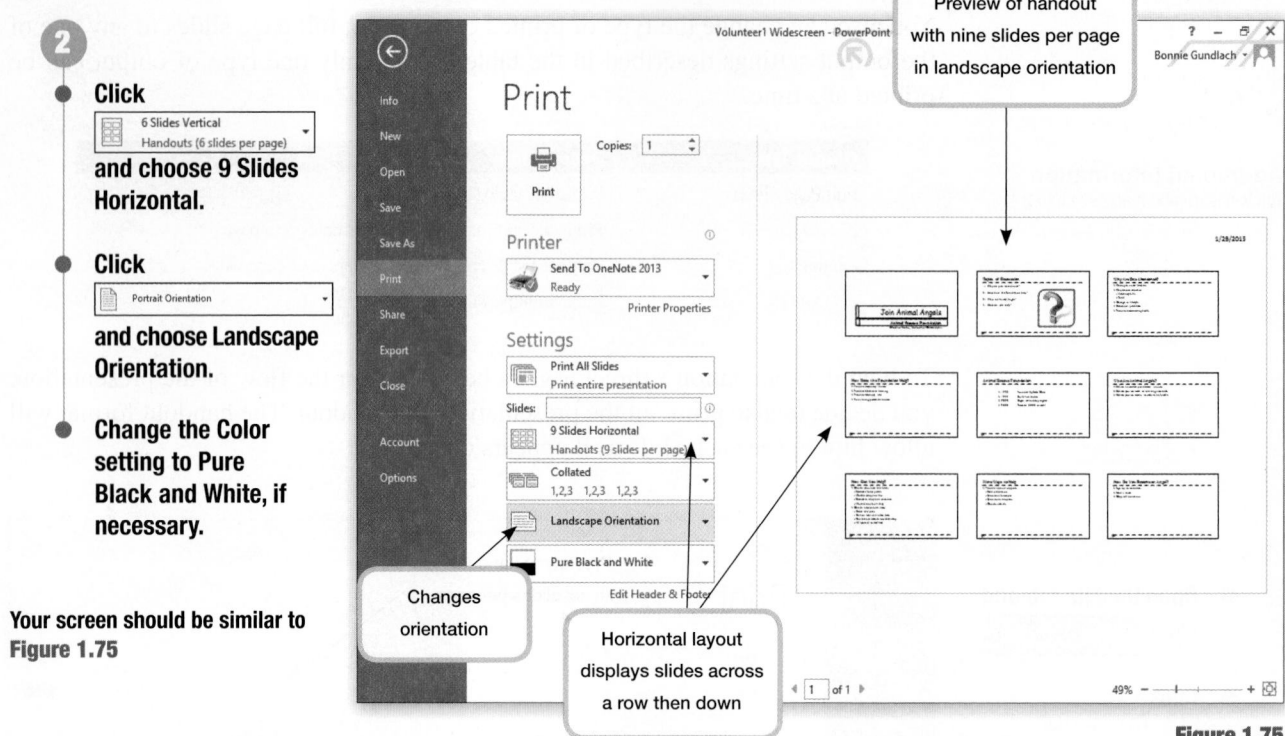

Figure 1.75

The preview area reflects your changes to the print settings. The horizontal layout displays the slides in order across a row and then down, making the presentation easier to follow.

3

- Click 🖶 Print .

Your printed output should be similar to that shown in the case study at the beginning of the lab.

PRINTING AN OUTLINE

The final item you want to print is an outline of the presentation. An outline will make it easier for the director to provide feedback on the overall organization of the presentation.

1

- Open the File tab and choose **Print**.

- Change the Color setting to Pure Black and White again, if necessary.

- Change the orientation to Portrait Orientation.

- Click 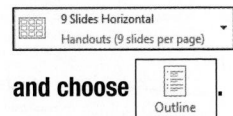 and choose **Outline**.

- Ensure that the correct printer is selected and ready.

Your screen should be similar to Figure 1.76

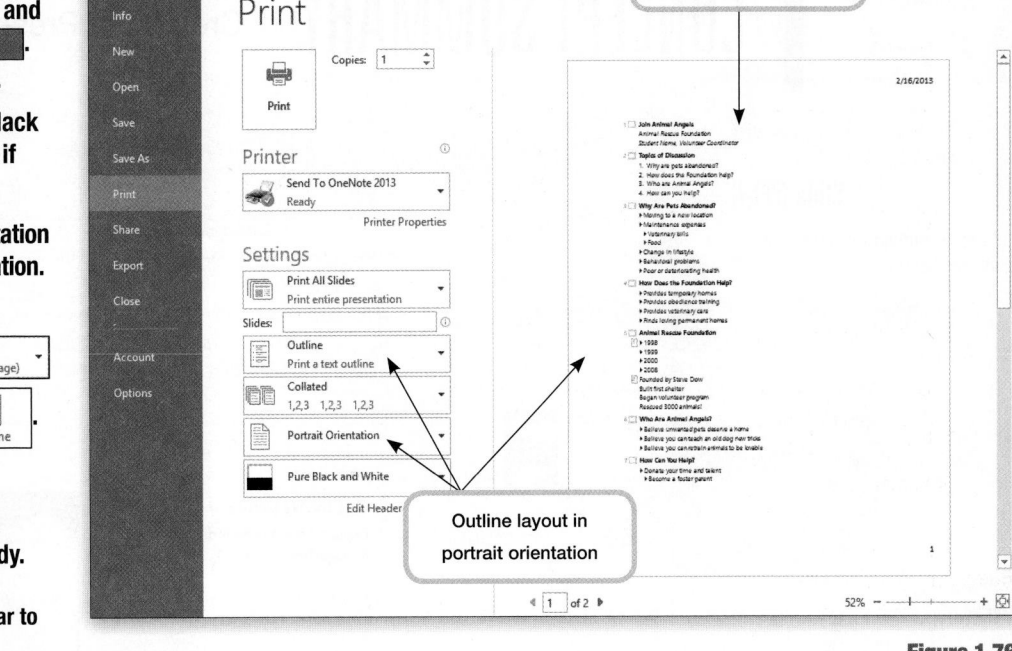

Figure 1.76

2

- Click **Print**.

The printed outline will be a two-page document that looks similar to the preview.

Exiting PowerPoint

1

- Click ☒ Close in the title bar.

- If asked to save the file again, click **Save**.

You have finished working on the presentation for now and will exit the Power-Point program.

EXPLORE YOUR CAREER OPTIONS

Account Executive

Sales is an excellent entry point for a solid career in any company. Account executive is just one of many titles that a sales professional may have; field sales and sales representative are two other titles. Account executives take care of customers by educating them on the company's latest products, designing solutions using the company's product line, and closing the deal to make the sale and earn their commission. These tasks require the use of effective PowerPoint presentations that educate and motivate potential customers. The salary range of an account executive is limited only by his or her ambition; salaries range from $30,000 to more than $120,540. To learn more about this career, visit the website for the Bureau of Labor Statistics of the U.S. Department of Labor.

Lab 1 CONCEPT SUMMARY Creating a Presentation

Slide (PP1.7)

A slide is an individual "page" of your presentation.

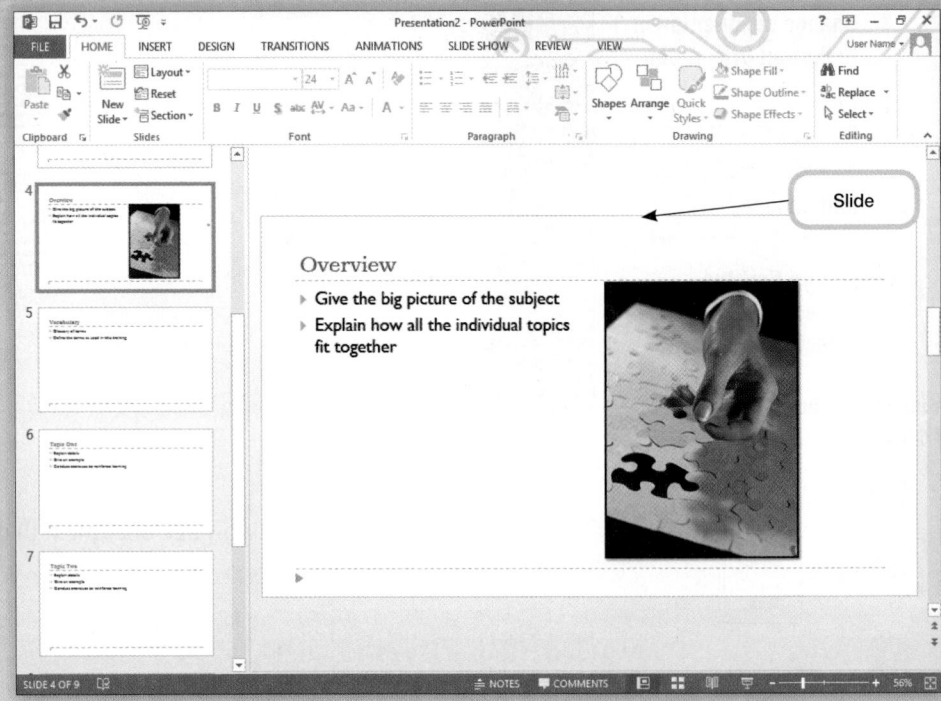

Spelling Checker (PP1.18)

The spelling checker locates most misspelled words, duplicate words, and capitalization irregularities as you create and edit a presentation, and proposes possible corrections.

AutoCorrect (PP1.20)

The AutoCorrect feature makes some basic assumptions about the text you are typing and, based on those assumptions, automatically corrects the entry.

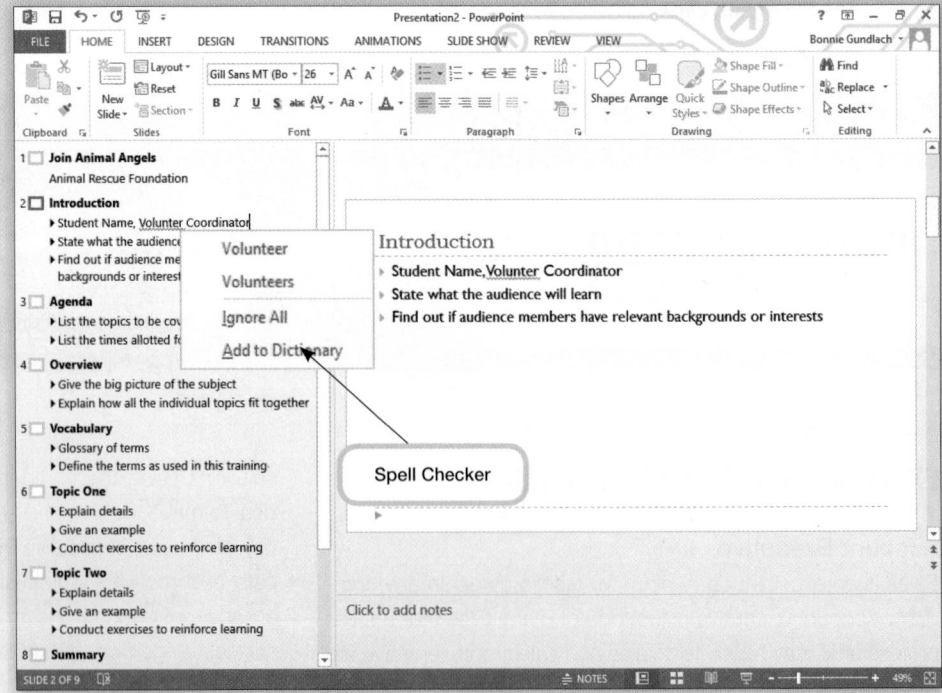

Layout (PP1.46)

A layout defines the position and format for objects and text on a slide. A layout contains placeholders for the different items such as bulleted text, titles, charts, and so on.

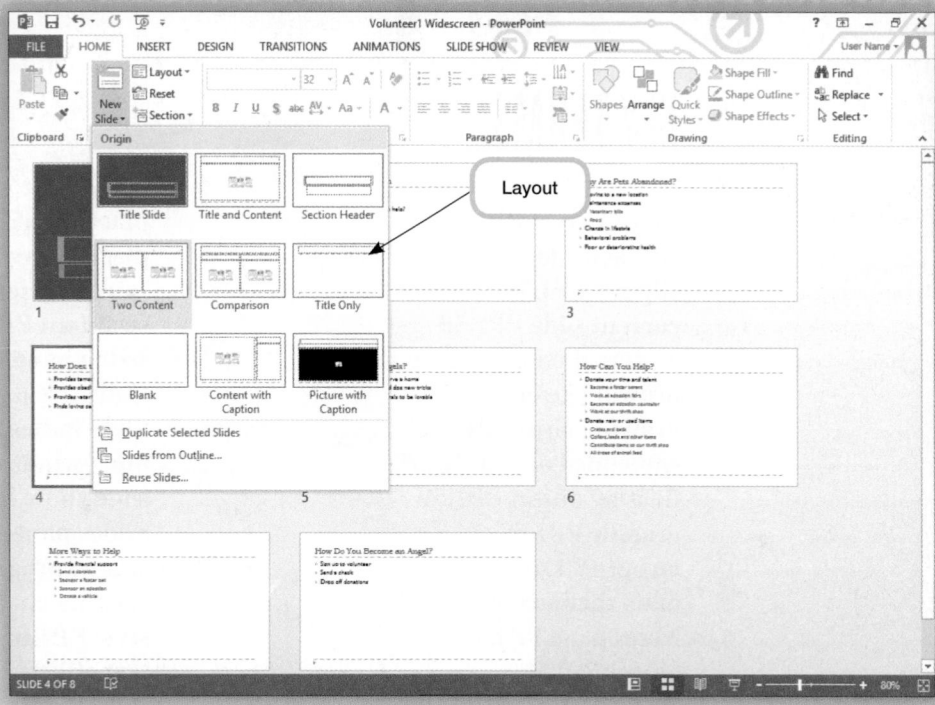

Graphic (PP1.58)

A graphic is a nontext element or object, such as a drawing or picture, that can be added to a slide.

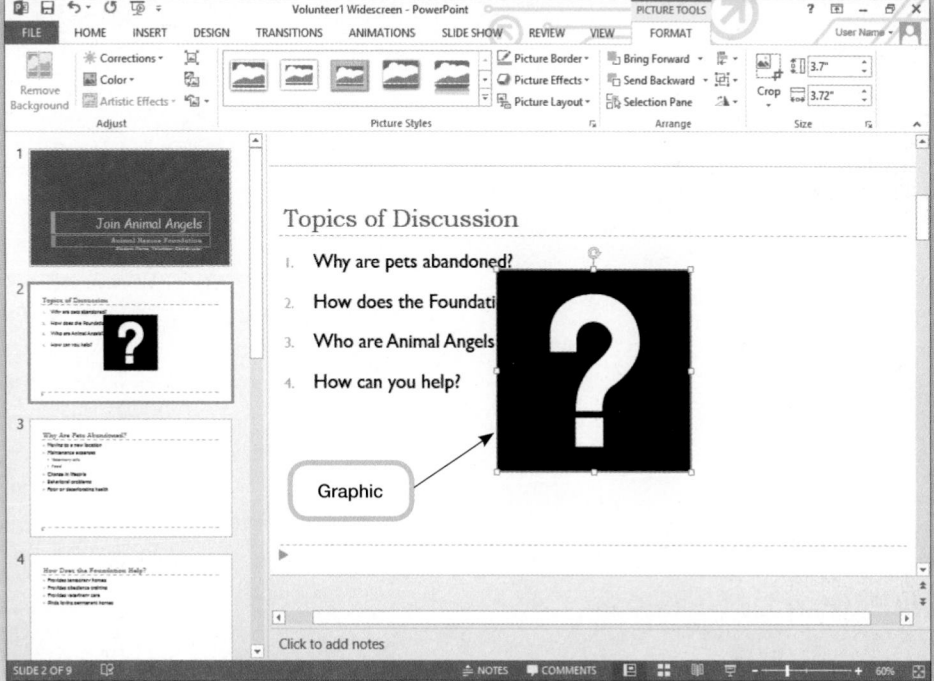

KEY TERMS

AutoCorrect PP1.20
character formatting PP1.52
clip art PP1.58
current slide PP1.10
custom dictionary PP1.18
drawing layer PP1.59
drawing object PP1.58
embedded object PP1.58
floating object PP1.59
graphic PP1.58
layout PP1.46
main dictionary PP1.18
Notes pane PP1.7
object PP1.8
Outline pane PP1.7
paragraph formatting PP1.52
picture PP1.58
picture style PP1.65

placeholder PP1.8
placeholder text PP1.8
sans serif font PP1.52
serif font PP1.52
sizing handles PP1.48
slide PP1.6
Slide indicator PP1.7
Slide window PP1.7
slide show PP1.67
Slides pane PP1.7
source program PP1.58
spelling checker PP1.18
style PP1.65
text effects PP1.54
thumbnail PP1.7
view PP1.7
widescreen PP1.7

COMMAND SUMMARY

Command	Shortcut	Action
File tab		
Save	Ctrl + S	Saves presentation
Save As	F12	Saves presentation using new file name and/or location
Open	Ctrl + O	Opens existing presentation
Close		Closes presentation
Info		Document properties
New	Ctrl + N	Opens New Presentation dialog box
Print	Ctrl + P	Opens print settings and a preview pane
× Exit		Closes PowerPoint
Quick Access Toolbar		
💾 Save	Ctrl + S	Saves presentation
↺ ▾ Undo	Ctrl + Z	Reverses last action
Home tab		
Clipboard group		
Paste ▾	Ctrl + V	Pastes item from Clipboard
✂ Cut	Ctrl + X	Cuts selection to Clipboard
📋 ▾ Copy	Ctrl + C	Copies selection to Clipboard
Slides group		
New Slide ▾	Ctrl + M	Inserts new slide with selected layout
Layout ▾		Changes layout of a slide
Font group		
Bookman Old St ▾ Font		Changes font type
32 ▾ Size		Changes font size

LAB REVIEW

COMMAND SUMMARY (CONTINUED)

Command	Shortcut	Action
A˄		Increases font size
A˅		Decreases font size
I		Italicizes text
U		Underlines text
S		Applies a shadow effect
A▾		Changes font color
Paragraph group		
Bullets/Bullets		Formats bulleted list
Numbering/Bulleted		Formats numbered lists
Decrease List Level		Decreases the indent level
Increase List Level		Increases the indent level
Editing group		
Select▾ / Select All	Ctrl + A	Selects everything in the placeholder box
Insert tab		
Images group		
Pictures		Inserts picture from your computer
Online Pictures		Finds and inserts pictures from a variety of online sources
Design tab		
Customize group		
Slide Size▾		Selects standard, widescreen, or custom slide size

COMMAND SUMMARY (CONTINUED)

Command	Shortcut	Action
Slide Show tab		
Start Slide Show group		
From Beginning	F5	Displays presentation starting with the first slide
From Current Slide	Shift + F5	Displays presentation starting with the current slide
Review tab		
Proofing group		
ABC ✓ Spelling	F7	Spell-checks presentation
View tab		
Presentation Views group		
Normal	▣	Switches to Normal view
Slide Sorter	▦	Switches to Slide Sorter view
Outline View	▣	Switches pane view to Outline
Picture Tools Format tab		
Adjust group		
Color ▾		Modifies the color of the picture
Picture Styles group		
▼ More		Opens Picture styles gallery to choose an overall visual style for a picture
Picture Layout ▾		Changes layout of a drawing
Picture Border ▾		Applies a border style to picture
Picture Effects ▾		Applies a visual effect to picture

LAB EXERCISES

SCREEN IDENTIFICATION

1. In the following PowerPoint screen, letters identify important elements. Enter the correct term for each screen element in the space provided.

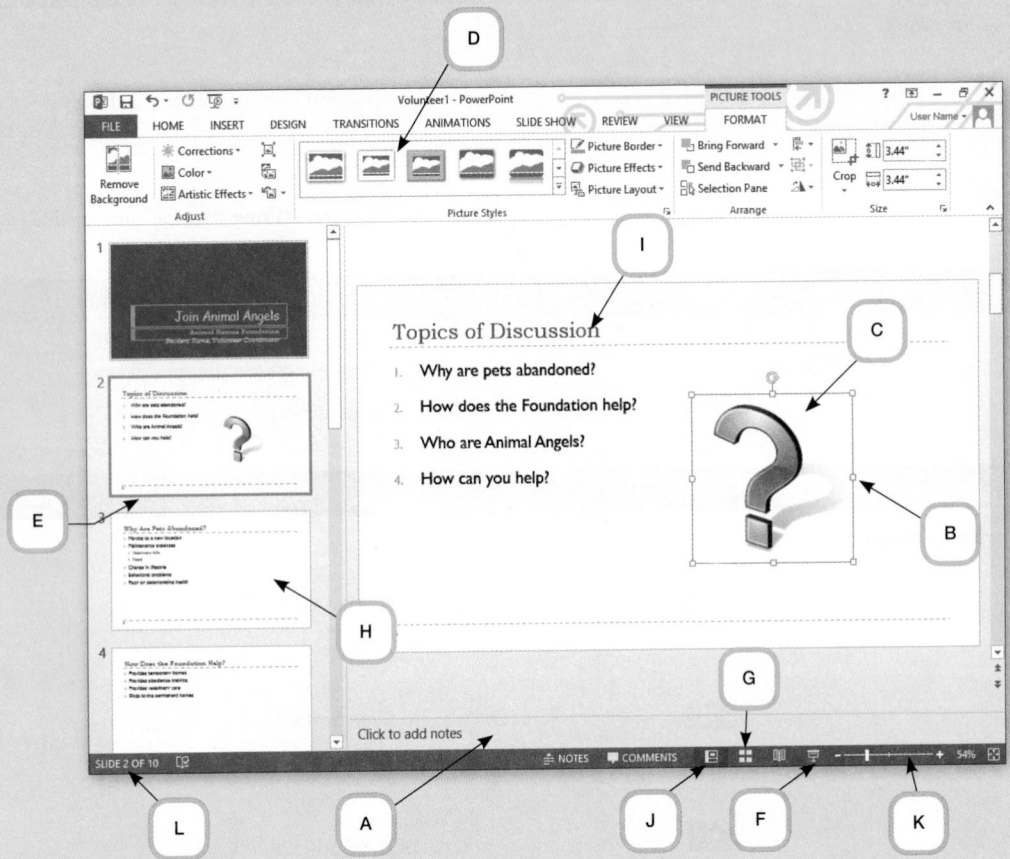

Possible answers for the screen identification are:

Graphic	Presentation template	A. _____	G. _____
Slide indicator	Zoom slider	B. _____	H. _____
Picture Styles	Sizing handle	C. _____	I. _____
Slide Show view	Slides tab	D. _____	J. _____
Slide Sorter view	Note pane	E. _____	K. _____
Slide title	Thumbnail	F. _____	L. _____
Current slide	Normal view		

MATCHING

Match the item on the left with the correct description on the right.

1. thumbnail   _____ a. small image
2. Notes pane   _____ b. sample text that suggests the content for the slide
3. slide   _____ c. moves the slide back to the previous slide in a presentation
4. placeholder text   _____ d. individual page of a presentation
5. AutoFit   _____ e. displays each slide as a thumbnail
6. Previous Slide button   _____ f. indents a bulleted point to the right
7. Slides pane   _____ g. defines the position and format for objects and text that will be added to a slide
8. template   _____ h. includes space to enter notes that apply to the current slide
9. tab   _____ i. a preset, formatted presentation on which you can base your presentation
10. layout   _____ j. tool that automatically resizes text to fit within the placeholder

TRUE/FALSE

Circle the correct answer to the following questions.

1. The Previous Slide and Next Slide buttons are located at the bottom of the horizontal scroll bar.	True	False
2. PowerPoint will continue to indent to the same level when you demote a bulleted point until you cancel the indent.	True	False
3. Content templates focus on the design of a presentation.	True	False
4. Widescreen is the default for a new, blank presentation.	True	False
5. A layout contains placeholders for different items such as bulleted text, titles, and charts.	True	False
6. PowerPoint identifies a word as misspelled by underlining it with a wavy blue line.	True	False
7. PowerPoint limits the type of output you can print from your presentation to slides only.	True	False
8. You can rely on AutoCorrect to ensure your document is error free.	True	False
9. After the final slide is displayed in Slide Sorter view, the program will return to the view you were last using.	True	False
10. Graphics are objects, such as charts, drawings, pictures, and scanned photographs, that provide visual interest or clarify data.	True	False

LAB EXERCISES

FILL-IN

Complete the following statements by filling in the blanks with the correct terms.

1. A(n) _____ is an individual "page" of your presentation.
2. A(n) _____ is a miniature of a slide.
3. _____ is a feature of PowerPoint that enables all text to fit within a placeholder.
4. _____ is a PowerPoint feature that advises you of misspelled words as you add text to a slide and proposes possible corrections.
5. A(n) _____ is a file containing predefined settings that can be used as a pattern to create many common types of presentations.
6. _____ define the position and format for objects and text that will be added to a slide.
7. When selected, a placeholder is surrounded with eight _____.
8. Use _____ to modify the level of indented items.
9. The _____ can be adjusted to increase or decrease the size of the slides on your computer screen.
10. The size of a(n) _____ can be changed by dragging its sizing handles.

MULTIPLE CHOICE

Circle the correct response to the questions below.

1. The keyboard shortcut to view a slide show is _____.
   a. F5
   b. Alt + V
   c. F3
   d. Ctrl + V

2. The step in the development of a presentation that focuses on determining the length of your speech, the audience, the layout of the room, and the type of audiovisual equipment available is _____.
   a. editing
   b. creating
   c. planning
   d. enhancing

3. If you want to provide copies of your presentation to the audience showing multiple slides on a page, you would print _____.
   a. note pages
   b. handouts
   c. slides
   d. outline area

4. The _____ feature makes some basic assumptions about the text you are typing and, based on those assumptions, automatically corrects the entry.
   a. grammar checker
   b. AutoCorrect
   c. spelling checker
   d. template

5. When the spelling checker is used, you can create a(n) _____ dictionary to hold words that you commonly use but are not included in the main dictionary.
   a. official
   b. common
   c. personal
   d. custom

6. A _____ is a nontext element or object, such as a drawing or picture, that can be added to a slide.
   a. slide
   b. template
   c. text box
   d. graphic

7. _____ view is used to work on most aspects of your presentation.
   a. Normal
   b. Outline
   c. Slide
   d. Slide Sorter

8. A _____ is a file containing predefined settings that can be used as a pattern to create many common types of presentations.
   a. presentation
   b. slide
   c. template
   d. graphic

9. A(n) _____ is an onscreen display of your presentation.
   a. slide
   b. handout
   c. outline
   d. slide show

10. _____ displays a miniature of each slide to make it easy to reorder slides, add special effects such as transitions, and set timing between slides.
   a. Slide Show view
   b. Slide Sorter view
   c. Reading view
   d. Normal view

STEP-BY-STEP

TRIPLE CROWN PRESENTATION ★

1. Kevin Mills works at Adventure Travel Tours. He is working on a presentation about lightweight hiking to be presented to a group of interested clients. Kevin recently found some new information to add to the presentation. He also wants to rearrange some slides and make a few other changes to improve the appearance of the presentation. The handouts of your completed presentation will be similar to those shown here.

   a. Open the file pp01_Triple Crown. Save the presentation as Triple Crown Presentation. Run the slide show.

   b. Enter your name in the subtitle on slide 1.

   c. Spell-check the presentation, making the appropriate corrections.

   d. Change the layout of slide 5 to Title Only.

   e. Move slide 6 before slide 5.

   f. Insert an appropriate photograph from online sources on slide 4. Size and position it appropriately.

   g. Insert a new slide using the Two Content layout after slide 4.

h. Enter the title **Less is More**. Insert an appropriate photograph on hiking from online sources in the right content placeholder. Move to slide 4 and select the second promoted bullet, "Where to cut weight:" and its subpoints. Cut this text and paste it in the left content placeholder of slide 5.

i. Change the layout of slide 7 to Title and Content layout. Add the following text in the text place-holder: **Contact Steve Johnson at Adventure Travel Tours or visit us on the web at www.AdventureTravelTours.com/hiking**.

j. Run the slide show.

k. Save the presentation. Print the slides in landscape orientation as handouts (four per page).

EMERGENCY DRIVING TECHNIQUES ★★

2. The Department of Public Safety holds monthly community outreach programs. Next month's topic is about how to handle special driving circumstances, such as driving in rain or snow. You are responsible for presenting the section on how to handle tire blowouts. You have organized the topics to be presented and located several clip art graphics that will complement the talk. Now you are ready to begin creating the presentation. Handouts of the completed presentation are shown here.

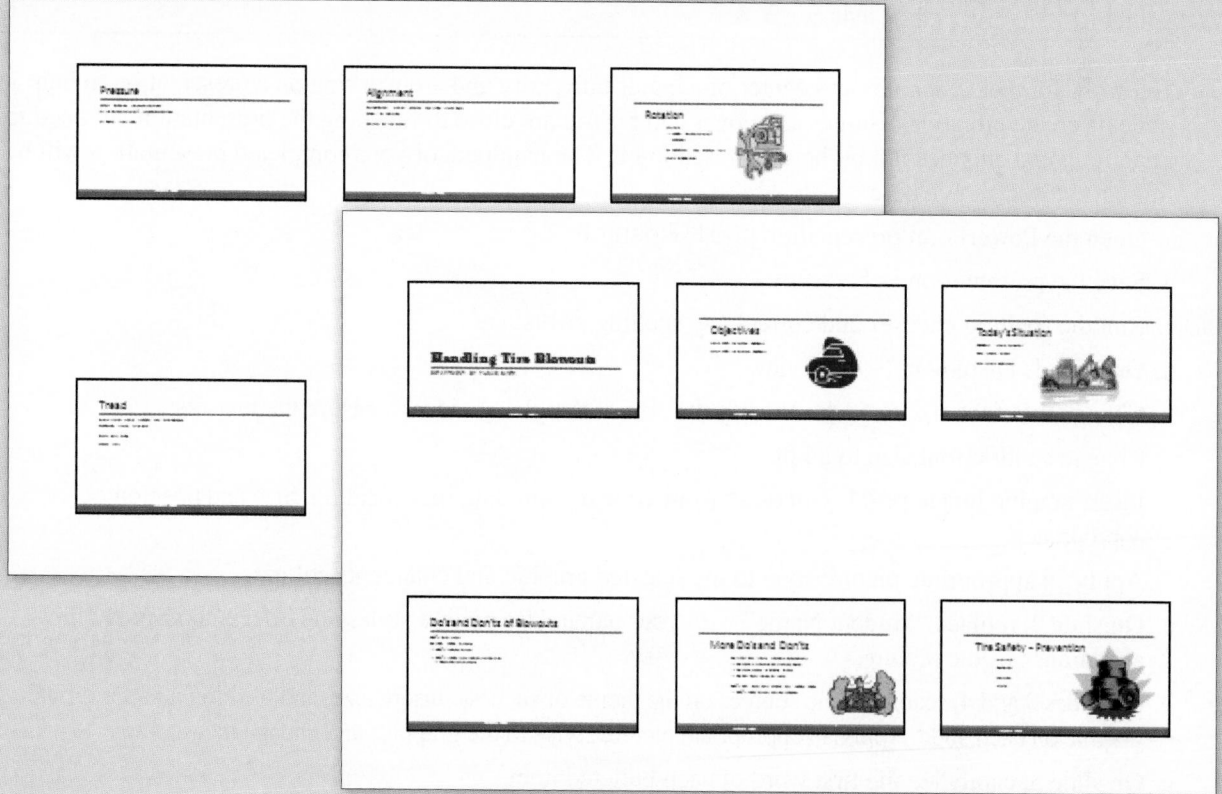

LAB EXERCISES

a. Open the PowerPoint presentation pp01_Handling Blowouts.

b. Save the presentation as Handling Blowouts.

c. Change format to widescreen.

d. Run the spelling checker and correct any errors.

e. On slide 1, replace "Student Name" with your name and increase font size to 16.

Increase the title text to 54 pt.

Change title text color to Orange, Accent 2, Darker 50%.

f. On slide 5:

Promote bullet 4.

Demote the last bullet.

Resize and reposition the graphic if necessary.

g. On slide 6, insert a graphic on the theme of tires and position it in the lower-right corner of the slide.

h. On slide 3, change the color of the clip art to Orange Accent color 1 Dark. Apply the Reflected Perspective Right picture style to the clip art image.

i. Save the presentation.

j. Run the slide show.

k. Print the slides as handouts (six per page, horizontal) and close the presentation.

WRITING EFFECTIVE RÉSUMÉS ★★

3. You work for the career services center of a major university and are working on a presentation to help students create effective résumés and cover letters. You are close to finishing the presentation but need to clean it up and enhance it a bit before presenting it. The handouts of your completed presentation will be similar to those shown here.

a. Open the PowerPoint presentation pp01_Resume.

b. Save the presentation as Resume1.

c. Run the spelling checker and correct any spelling errors.

d. On slide 1: Display in Normal view.

Change title font size to 54 pt. Modify the size of the placeholder to ensure the text fits.

Change subtitle font size to 24 pt.

Insert graphic image pp01_Success from your student data files location. Size and position appropriately.

Apply an appropriate picture style to the selected graphic and change its color.

e. On slide 2, replace "Student Name" with your name. Use picture styles and effects to improve the appearance of the picture.

f. On slides 3 and 4, search online sources on the theme of success. Insert, size, and position an appropriate graphic on each slide. Apply an appropriate picture styles to the graphics and change their colors.

g. On slide 5, capitalize the first word of each bulleted item.

h. On slide 6, split the slide content into two so slide 7 begins with the "Other" bulleted item. Add title to Slide 7: More Resume Headings.

i. On slide 10, reorganize the bulleted items so "Types of cover letters" is the first item.

j. To match the slide order with the way the topics are now introduced, move slide 13 before slide 11.

k. On slide 13: Break each bulleted item into two or three bullets each as appropriate.

Capitalize the first word of each bulleted item.

Remove any commas and periods at the end of the bullets.

l. Save the presentation.

m. Run the slide show.

n. Print the slides as handouts (nine per page, horizontal, in landscape orientation) and close the presentation.

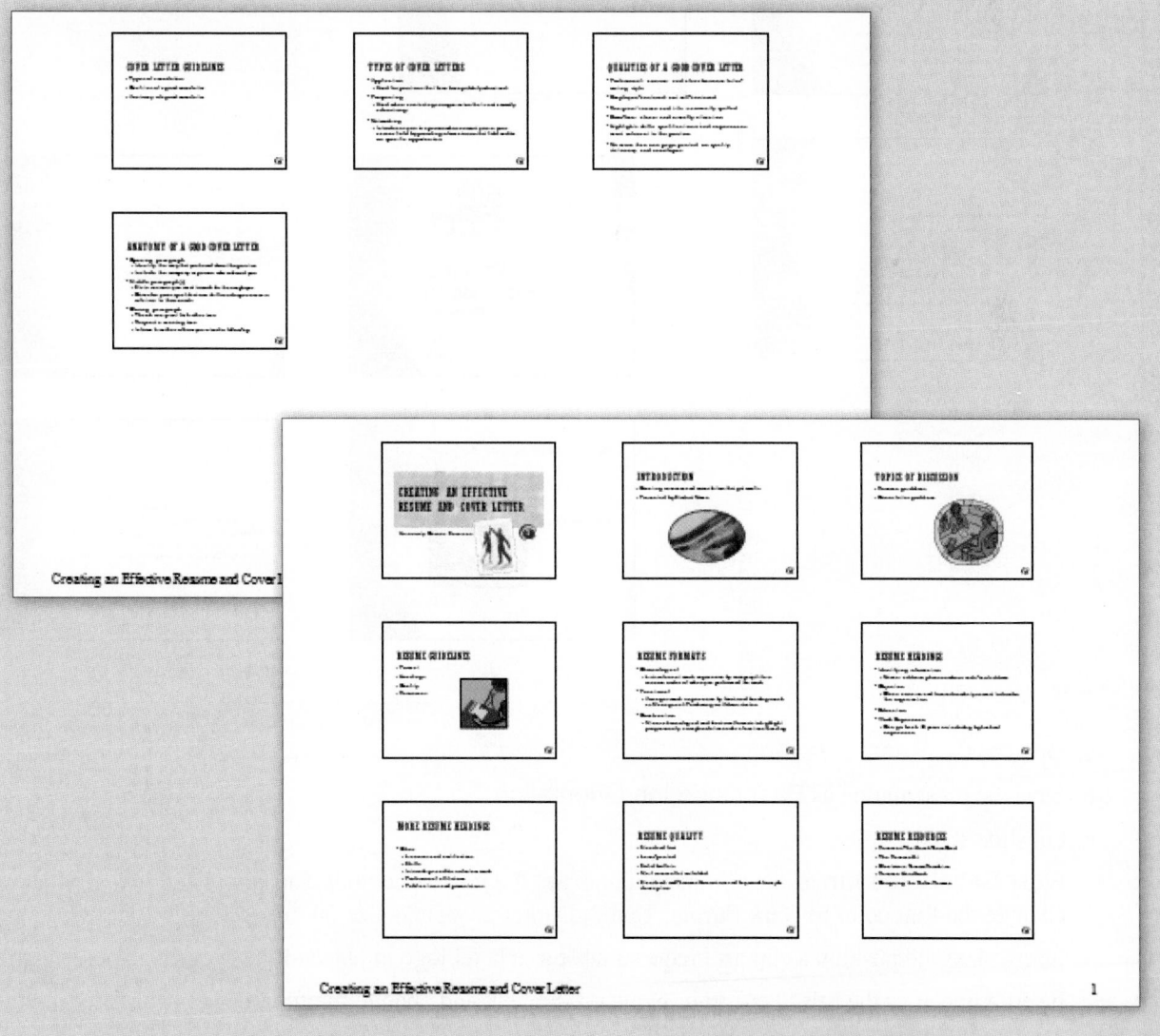

LAB EXERCISES

EMPLOYEE ORIENTATION ★★★

4. As the front desk manager of the Beachside Inn, you want to make a presentation to your new employees about the amenities your hotel offers its guests as well as information on activities and dining in the area. The purpose of this presentation is to enable employees to answer the many questions that are asked by the guests about both the hotel and the town. The handouts of your completed presentation will be similar to those shown here.

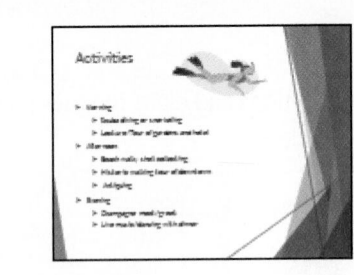
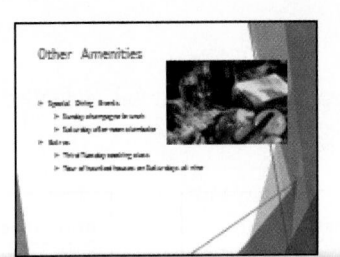
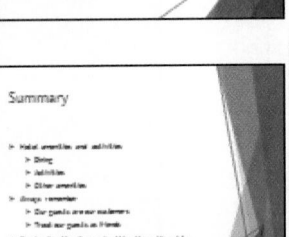

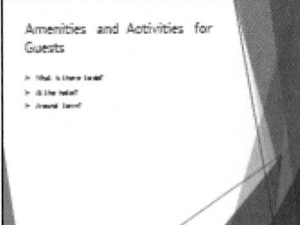

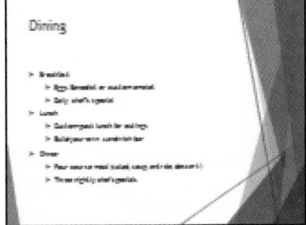

a. Open pp01_Beachside Inn.

b. Save the presentation as Beachside Inn Orientation.

c. On slide 1:

Enter **Beachside Inn** as the company name. Set the font to Lucinda Sans; apply Bold and Shadow. Change the font color to Dark Purple, Text 2, Darker 25%, and size 54.

Insert, size, and position a clip art image suitable as a hotel logo in place of the "your logo here" graphic.

Insert a line after the title. Type your name on the line, and change the font to Trebuchet MS and the font size to 20. Apply italics.

d. On slide 2:

Enter **Amenities and Activities for Guests** as the title.

Enter the sample bulleted text **What is there to do?** as the first bullet.

Enter **At the hotel?** as the second bullet.

Enter **Around town?** as the third bullet.

Remove the remaining bulleted items.

e. Insert a new slide after slide 2. In this slide:

Set the layout to Title and Content.

Enter **Hotel Amenities and Activities** as the title.

Enter **Dining** as the first bullet.

Enter **Activities** as the second bullet.

Enter **Other amenities** as the third bullet.

Insert, size, and position a clip art image suitable for a hotel at the bottom center of the slide. Apply picture styles and effects.

f. Insert a new slide after slide 3. In this slide:

Set the layout to Title and Content.

Enter **Dining** as the title.

Enter **Breakfast** as the first bullet under Dining.

Enter **Eggs Benedict or custom omelet** and demote to appear as the first bullet under Breakfast.

Enter **Daily chef's special** as the second bullet under Breakfast.

Enter **Lunch** and promote to appear as the second bullet under Dining.

Enter **Custom-pack lunch for outings** and demote to appear as the first bullet under Lunch.

Enter **Build-your-own sandwich bar** as the second bullet under Lunch.

Enter **Dinner** and promote to appear as the third bullet under Dining.

Enter **Four-course meal (salad, soup, entrée, dessert)** as the first bullet under Dinner.

Enter **Three nightly chef specials** as the second bullet under Dinner.

g. Insert a new slide after slide 4. In this slide:

Set the layout to Title and Content.

Enter **Activities** as the title.

Enter **Morning** as the first bullet under Activities.

Enter **Scuba diving or snorkeling** and demote to appear as the first bullet under Morning.

Enter **Lecture/Tour of gardens and hotel** as the second bullet under Morning.

Enter **Afternoon** and promote to appear as the second bullet under Activities.

Enter **Beach walk; shell collecting** as the first bullet under Afternoon.

Enter **Historic walking tour of downtown** as the second bullet under Afternoon.

Enter **Antiquing** as the third bullet under Afternoon.

Enter **Evening** and promote to appear as the third bullet under Activities.

Enter **Champagne meet/greet** and demote to appear as the first bullet under Evening.

Enter **Live music/dancing with dinner** as the second bullet under Evening.

Add a graphic reflecting one of the mentioned activities to this slide.

h. Insert a new slide after slide 5. In this slide:

Set the layout to Title and Content.

Enter **Other Amenities** as the title.

Enter **Special dining events** as the first bullet under Other Amenities.

Enter **Sunday champagne brunch** and demote to appear as the first bullet under Special Dining Events.

Enter **Saturday afternoon clambake** as the second bullet under Special Dining Events.

Enter **Extras** and promote to appear as the second bullet for Other Amenities.

Enter **Third Tuesday cooking class** and demote to appear as the first bullet under Extras.

Enter **Tour of haunted houses on Saturdays at nine** as the second bullet under Extras.

Insert, size, and position a clip art image suitable for a hotel at the bottom center of the slide. Apply picture styles and effects.

i. Delete slides 7 through 13.

j. On the Summary slide 7.

Enter **Hotel amenities and activities** as the first bullet under Summary.

Enter **Dining** and demote to appear as the first bullet under Hotel amenities and activities.

Enter **Activities** as the second bullet under Hotel amenities and activities.

Enter **Other amenities** as the third bullet under Hotel amenities and activities.

Enter **Always remember** and promote to appear as the second bullet under Summary.

Enter **Our guests are our customers** and demote to appear as the first bullet under Always remember.

Enter **Treat our guests as friends** as the second bullet under Always remember.

Enter **Thanks for attending and putting these ideas into practice** and promote to appear as the third bullet under Summary.

Delete any remaining bullet placeholders.

k. Save the presentation.

l. Run the slide show.

m. Print the slides as handouts (four per page, horizontal, in landscape orientation).

WORKPLACE ISSUES ★★★

5. Tim is preparing for his lecture on "Workplace Issues" for his Introduction to Computers class. He uses PowerPoint to create presentations for each of his lectures. He has organized the topics to be presented, and located several clip art graphics that will complement the lecture. He is now ready to begin creating the presentation. Several slides of the completed presentation are shown here.

   a. Open a new presentation using the Training Presentation template. If you don't have access to the Internet, you can use the file pp01_Training.

   b. Save the presentation as Workplace Issues.

   c. On slide 1:

   Change the title to **Workplace Issues - Lecture 4**. Change the font size to 54 and apply a bold effect.

   Change **Your Name** to your name. Change the font size of this line to 28.

   Insert, size, and position a graphic image suitable for the theme of an office meeting. Apply a picture style to the image.

LAB EXERCISES

   d. On slide 2:

      Enter **Topics of Discussion** as the title text.

      Enter **Ergonomics** as bullet 1.

      Enter **Ethics** as bullet 2.

      Enter **Environment** as bullet 3.

   e. On slide 3:

      Enter **Ergonomics** as the title.

      Enter **Definition** as the first bullet.

      Enter **Fit the job to the worker rather than forcing the worker to contort to fit the job** as the second bullet.

      Enter **The study of human factors related to computers** as the third bullet.

      Delete the last bullet.

   f. Change the order of bullets 2 and 3 on slide 3.

      Demote bullets 2 and 3.

   g. On slide 4:

      Change the title to **Mental Health**.

      Include two bulleted items: **Noise** and **Monitoring**.

   h. Change the title of slide 5 to **Physical Health** and include the following bulleted items:

      Bullet 1: **Eyestrain and headache**

      Bullet 2: **Back and neck pain**

      Bullet 3: **Electromagnetic fields**

      Bullet 4: **Repetitive strain injury**

      Insert, size, and position a suitable clip art image. Use the picture formatting tools to customize the image to suit the presentation.

   i. On slide 6:

      Change the title to **Ethics**.

      Include two bullets: **Definition** and **Guidelines for the morally acceptable use of computers in our society.**

      Demote bullet 2.

      Delete the third bullet.

   j. Change the title of slide 7 to **Primary Ethical Issues**.

      Enter **Privacy** as bullet 1.

      Enter **Accuracy** as bullet 2.

      Enter **Property** as bullet 3.

      Enter **Access** as bullet 4.

      Insert, size, and position a suitable clip art image. Use the picture formatting tools to customize the image to suit the presentation.

k. Insert a new Two Content layout slide between slides 7 and 8. On the new slide 8:

Enter **The Environment** as the title.

Enter **The Energy Star Program** as the first bullet.

Enter **The Green PC** as the second bullet.

In the right placeholder, insert, size, and position a suitable graphic. Use the picture formatting tools to customize the image to suit the presentation.

l. Create a duplicate of slide 8. On the new slide 9:

Enter **The Green PC** as the title.

Enter **System Unit** as the first bullet.

Enter **Display** as the second bullet.

Enter **Manufacturing** as the third bullet.

In the right placeholder, insert, size, and position an appropriate graphic.

m. Add a new slide after slide 9. Use the Title and Content layout.

Enter **Personal Responsibility** as the title.

Enter **Conserving** as the first bullet.

Enter **Recycling** as the second bullet.

Enter **Educating** as the third bullet.

n. In Slide Sorter view, move slide 5 before slide 4.

o. Delete slides 11-17.

p. Save the presentation.

q. Run the slide show.

r. Print the slides as handouts (six per page in landscape orientation).

ON YOUR OWN

INTERNET POLICY PRESENTATION ★

1. You are working in the information technology department at International Sales Incorporated. Your manager has asked you to give a presentation on the corporation's Internet policy to the new-hire orientation class. Create your presentation with PowerPoint, using the information in the Word file pp01_Internet Policy as a resource. Use a template of your choice. When you are done, run the spelling checker, then save your presentation as Internet Policy and print it.

LAB EXERCISES

TELEPHONE TRAINING COURSE ★★

2. You are a trainer with Super Software, Inc. You received a memo from your manager alerting you that many of the support personnel are not using proper telephone protocol or obtaining the proper information from customers who call in. Your manager has asked you to conduct a training class that covers these topics. Using the Word document pp01_Memo data file as a resource, prepare the slides for your class. When you are done, save the presentation as Phone Etiquette and print the handouts. Be sure to use a design theme, graphics, and widescreen format.

VISUAL AIDS ★★

3. You are a trainer with Super Software, Inc. Your manager has asked you to prepare a presentation on various visual aids that may be used in presentations. Using the pp01_VisualAids data file as a resource, create an onscreen presentation using an appropriate template. Select a widescreen template, or modify the template you like to widescreen so your presentation can be showcased with new technology. Add graphics that illustrate each type of visual aid. Include your name on the title slide. When you are done, save the presentation as Presentation Aids and print the handouts.

WEB DESIGN PROPOSAL ★★★

4. Your company wants to create a website, but it is not sure whether to design its own or hire a web design firm to do it. You have been asked to create a presentation to management relaying the pros and cons of each approach. To gather information, search the web for the topic "web design," and select some key points about designing a web page from one of the "how-to" or "tips" categories. Use these points to create the first part of your presentation, and call it something like "Creating Our Own web Page." Then search the web for the topic "web designers," and select two web design firms. Pick some key points about each firm (for example, websites they have designed, design elements they typically use, and/or their design philosophy). Finally, include at least one slide that lists the pros and cons of each approach. Include your name on the title slide. When your presentation is complete, save it as Web Design and print the slides as handouts.

   You will expand on this presentation in On Your Own Exercise 4 of Lab 2.

CAREERS WITH ANIMALS ★★★

5. You have been volunteering at the Animal Rescue Foundation. The director has asked you to prepare a presentation on careers with animals to present to local schools in hopes that some students will be inspired to volunteer at the foundation. Using the Word document pp01_Animal Careers data file as a resource, create the presentation. Add photos or other graphics where appropriate. When you are done, save the presentation as Careers with Animals and print the handouts.

Modifying and Refining a Presentation

Lab 2

Objectives

After completing this lab, you will know how to:

1. Find and replace text.

2. Create and enhance a table.

3. Crop and enhance graphic objects.

4. Create and enhance shapes.

5. Create a text box.

6. Change the theme.

7. Modify slide masters.

8. Add animation, sound, and transitions.

9. Control a slide show.

10. Add speaker notes.

11. Add and hide slide footers.

12. Use Presenter view.

13. Customize print settings.

Animal Rescue Foundation

The Animal Rescue Foundation director was very impressed with your first draft of the presentation to recruit volunteers and asked to see the presentation onscreen. While viewing it together, you explained that you plan to make many more changes to improve the appearance of the presentation. For example, you plan to use a different color theme and to include more art and other graphic features to enhance the appearance of the slides. You also explained that you will add more action to the slides using the special effects included with PowerPoint to keep the audience's attention.

The director suggested that you include more information on

ways that volunteers can help. Additionally, because the organization has such an excellent adoption rate, the director wants you to include a table to illustrate the success of the adoption program.

PowerPoint 2013 gives you the design and production capabilities to create a first-class onscreen presentation. These features include artist-designed layouts and color themes that give your presentation a professional appearance. In addition, you can add your own personal touches by modifying text attributes, incorporating art or graphics, and including animation to add impact, interest, and excitement to your presentation.

Displaying
information in tables
makes data easy to
understand.

Pictures add interest
and enhance the
appearance of
the slide.

Animations and transitions add action to a slide show.

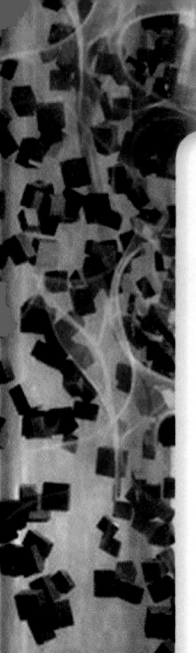

The following concepts will be introduced in this lab:

1 Find and Replace To make editing easier, you can use the Find and Replace feature to find text in a presentation and replace it with other text.

2 Table A table is used to organize information into an easy-to-read format of horizontal rows and vertical columns.

3 Alignment Alignment controls the position of text entries within a space.

4 Theme A theme is a predefined set of formatting choices that can be applied to an entire document in one simple step.

5 Master A master is a special slide or page that stores information about the formatting for all slides or pages in a presentation.

6 Animations Animations are special effects that add action to text and graphics so they move around on the screen during a slide show.

Finding and Replacing Text

After meeting with the foundation director, you want to update the content to include the additional information on ways that volunteers can help the Animal Rescue Foundation.

- **Start PowerPoint 2013.**

- **Open the file** pp02_Volunteer2 Widescreen **from your data file location.**

- **If necessary, switch to Normal view.**

- **Replace Student Name in slide 1 with your name.**

- **Scroll the Slide window to view the content of the revised presentation.**

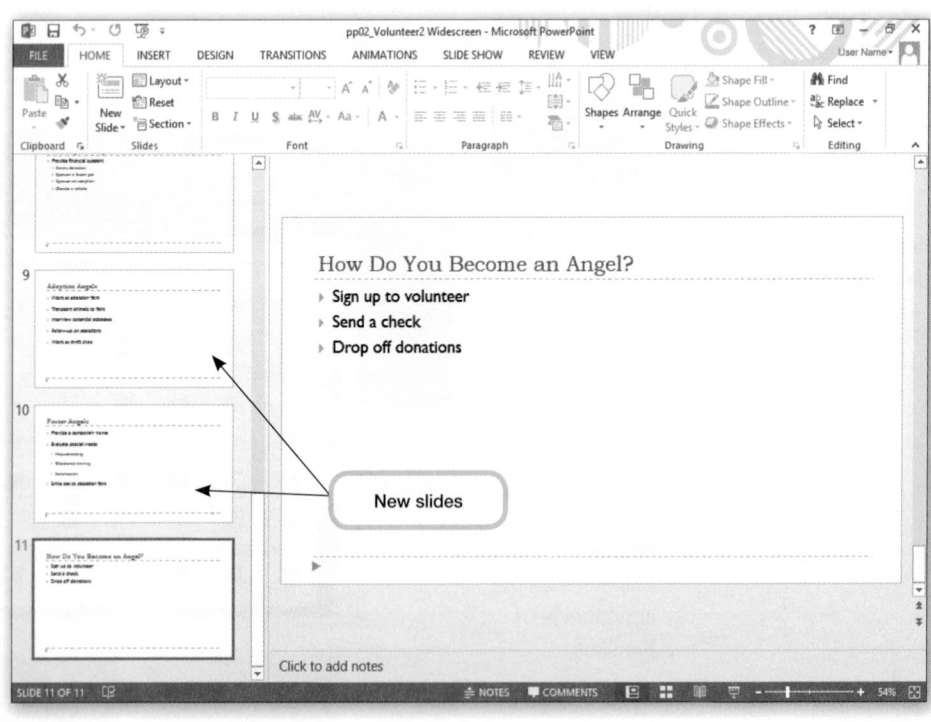

Figure 2.1

Your screen should be similar to Figure 2.1

You added two new slides, 9 and 10, with more information about the Animal Angels volunteer organization, bringing the total number of slides in the presentation to 11. As you reread the content of the presentation, you decide to edit the text by finding the word "pet" and replacing it with the word "animal." To do this, you will use the Find and Replace feature.

Concept 1 Find and Replace

To make editing easier, you can use the **Find and Replace** feature to find text in a presentation and replace it with other text. The Find feature will locate and identify any text string you specify in the presentation by highlighting it. When used along with the Replace feature, not only will the string be identified, but it will be replaced with the replacement text you specify if you choose. For example, suppose you created a lengthy document describing the type of clothing and equipment needed to set up a world-class home gym, and then you decided to change "sneakers" to "athletic shoes." Instead of deleting every occurrence of "sneakers" and typing "athletic shoes," you can use the Find and Replace feature to perform the task automatically.

The Replace feature also can be used to replace a specified font in a presentation with another. When using this feature, however, all text throughout the presentation that is in the specified font is automatically changed to the selected replacement font.

The Find and Replace feature is fast and accurate; however, use care when replacing so that you do not replace unintended matches.

FINDING TEXT

First, you will use the Find command to locate all occurrences of the word "pet" in the presentation.

- Make slide 1 active.

- If necessary, open the Home tab.

- Click ▓▓ Find in the Editing group.

Another Method
The keyboard shortcut is Ctrl + F.

Your screen should be similar to Figure 2.2

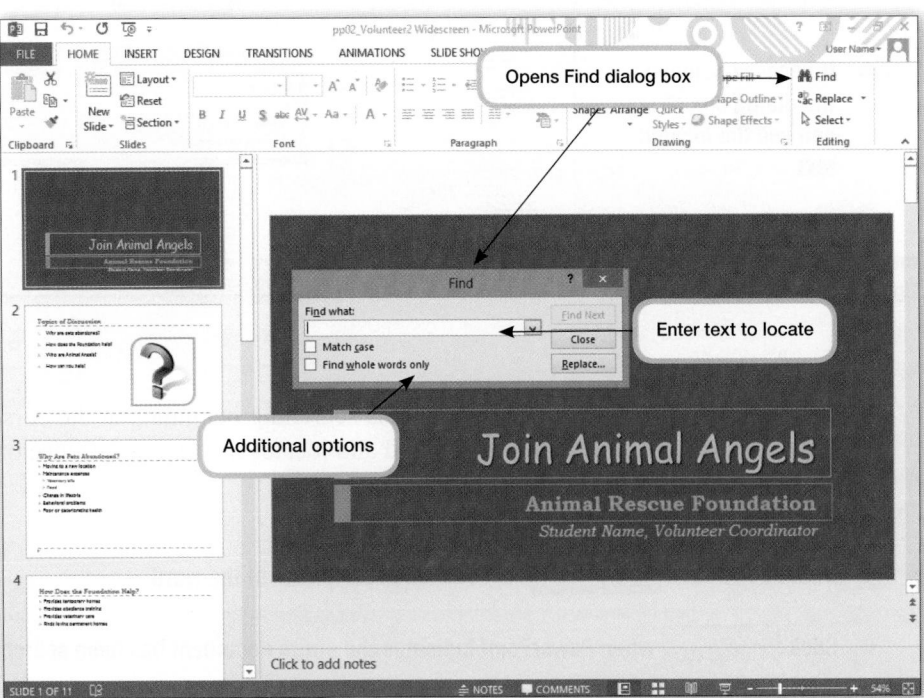

Figure 2.2

In the Find dialog box, you enter the text you want to locate in the Find what text box. The two options described in the following table allow you to refine the procedure that is used to conduct the search.

Option	Effect on Text
Match Case	Distinguishes between uppercase and lowercase characters. When selected, finds only those instances in which the capitalization matches the text you typed in the Find what box.
Find Whole Words Only	Distinguishes between whole and partial words. When selected, locates matches that are whole words and not part of a larger word. For example, finds "cat" only and not "catastrophe," too.

You want to find all occurrences of the complete word "pet." You will not use either option described above, because you want to locate all words regardless of case and because you want to find "pet" as well as "pets" in the presentation.

2

- **Type pet in the Find what text box.**

- **Click** Find Next .

Additional Information

You can also press Enter after specifying the search term to begin the search.

- **If necessary, move the dialog box so you can see the located text.**

Your screen should be similar to Figure 2.3

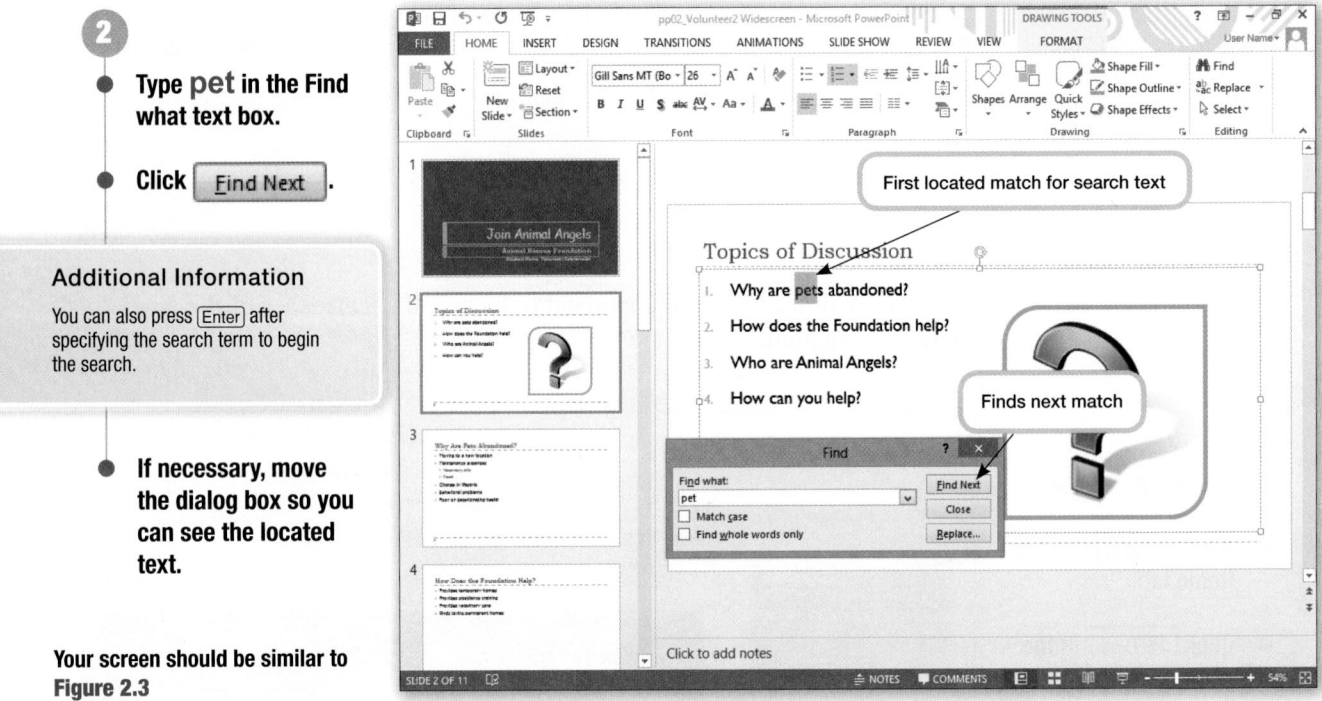

Figure 2.3

PowerPoint begins searching beginning at the cursor location for all occurrences of the text to find and locates the first occurrence of the word "pet."

3

- **Continue to click** Find Next **to locate all occurrences of the word.**

- **Click** OK **when PowerPoint indicates the entire document has been searched.**

The word "pet" is used five times in the document. Using the Find command is a convenient way to quickly navigate through a document to locate and move to specified information.

REPLACING TEXT

You want to replace selected occurrences of the word "pet" with "animal" throughout the presentation. You will use the Replace feature to specify the text to enter as the replacement text.

Click `abc Replace ▾` **in the Editing group.**

Another Method

The keyboard shortcut to replace text is Ctrl + H.

Your screen should be similar to Figure 2.4

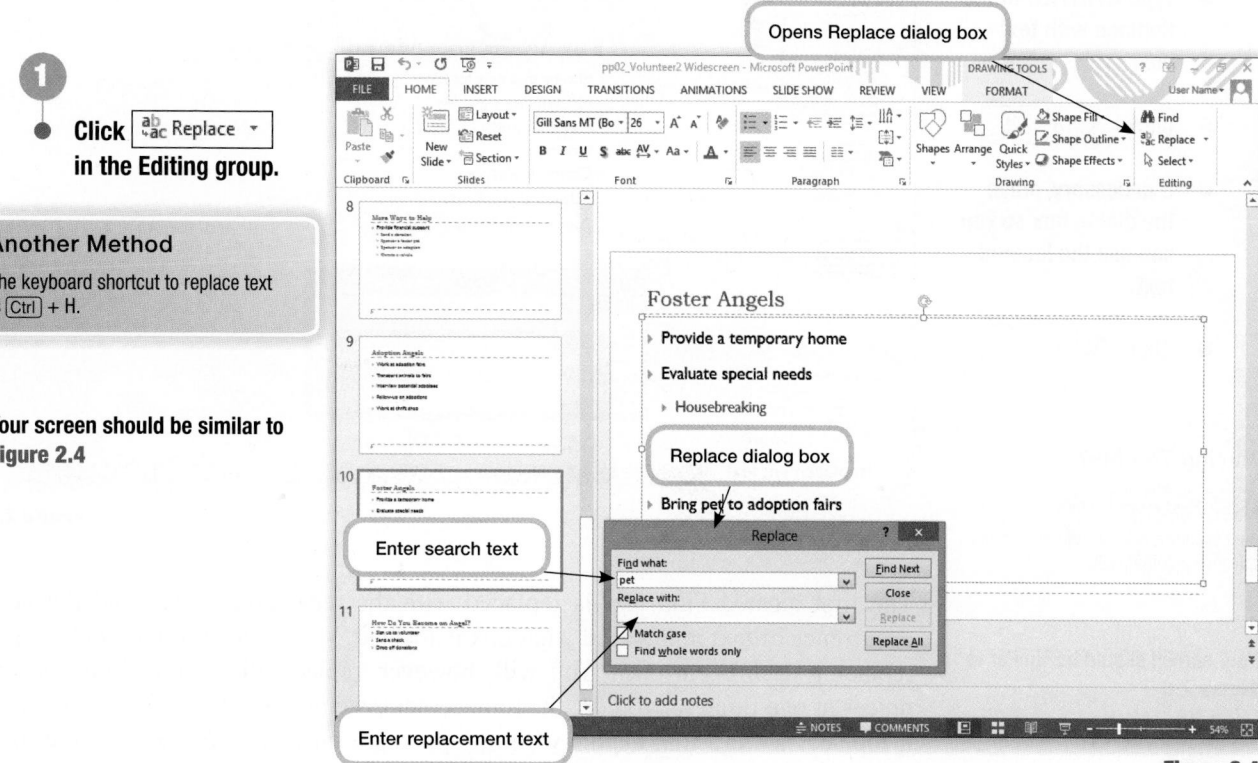

Figure 2.4

The Find dialog box changes to the Replace dialog box, and the search text you entered is still specified in the Find what text box. You can now enter the replacement text in the Replace with text box. The replacement text must be entered exactly as you want it to appear in your presentation.

2

- Press Tab or click in the Replace with text box.

- Type **animal** in the Replace with text box.

- Click Find Next.

- If necessary, move the dialog box so you can see the located text.

- Click ᵃᵇₐᵪ Replace ▾.

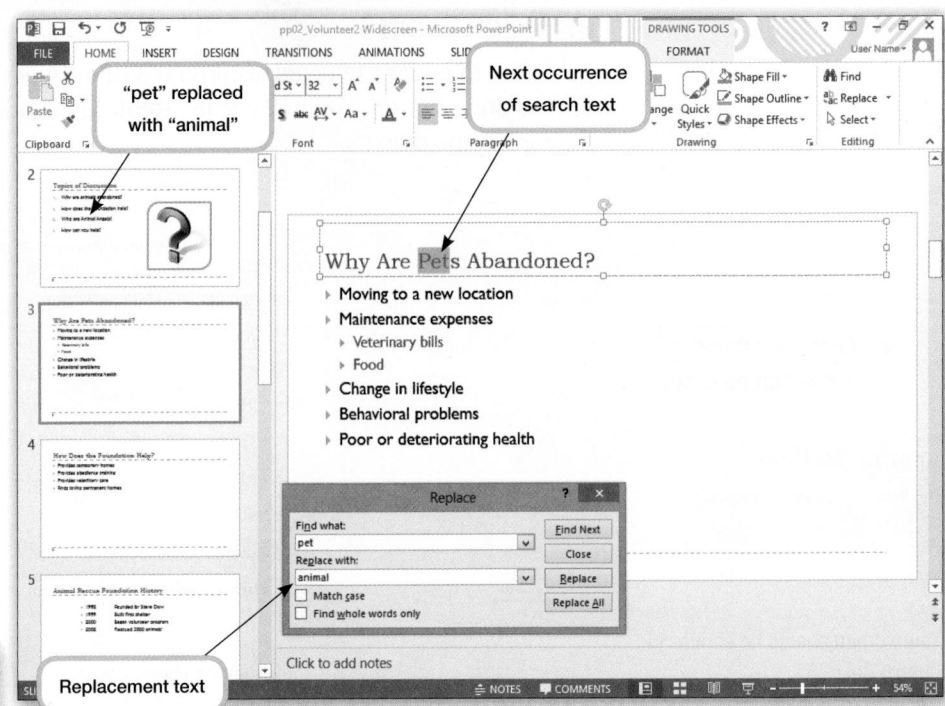
Figure 2.5

Having Trouble?

Click Find Next to move to the next occurrence if the search does not advance automatically.

Your screen should be similar to Figure 2.5

The first located Find text is replaced with the replacement text, and the next occurrence of text in the Find what box is located. You could continue finding and replacing each occurrence. You will, however, replace all the remaining occurrences at one time. As you do, the replacement is entered in lowercase even when it replaces a word that begins with an uppercase character. You will correct this when you finish replacing.

③

- Click **Replace All** to continue.

- Click **OK** in response to the finished searching dialog box.

- Click **Close** to close the Replace dialog box.

- Edit the word "animals" to "Animals" in slide 3.

- Click somewhere outside the placeholder.

- Save the presentation as Volunteer2 Widescreen to your solution file location.

Your screen should be similar to Figure 2.6

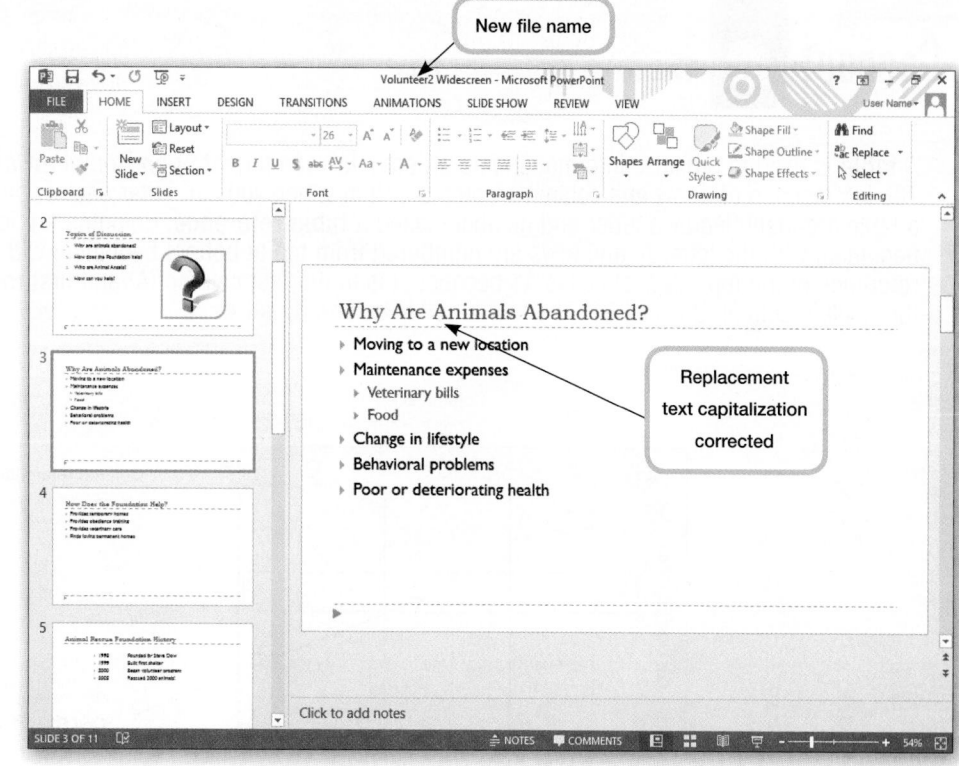

New file name

Replacement text capitalization corrected

Figure 2.6

If you plan to change all occurrences, it is much faster to use **Replace All**. Exercise care when replacing all occurrences, however, because the search text you specify might be part of another word and you may accidentally replace text you want to keep.

Creating a Simple Table

During your discussion with the director, he suggested that you add a slide containing data showing the success of the adoption program. The information in this slide will be presented using a table layout.

Concept 2 Table

A **table** is used to organize information into an easy-to-read format of horizontal rows and vertical columns. The intersection of a row and column creates a **cell** in which you can enter data or other information. Cells in a table are identified by a letter and number, called a **table reference**. Columns are identified from left to right beginning with the letter A, and rows are numbered from top to bottom beginning with the number 1. The table reference of the top-leftmost cell is A1 because it is in the first column (A) and first row (1) of the table. The third cell in column B is cell B3. The fourth cell in column C is C4.

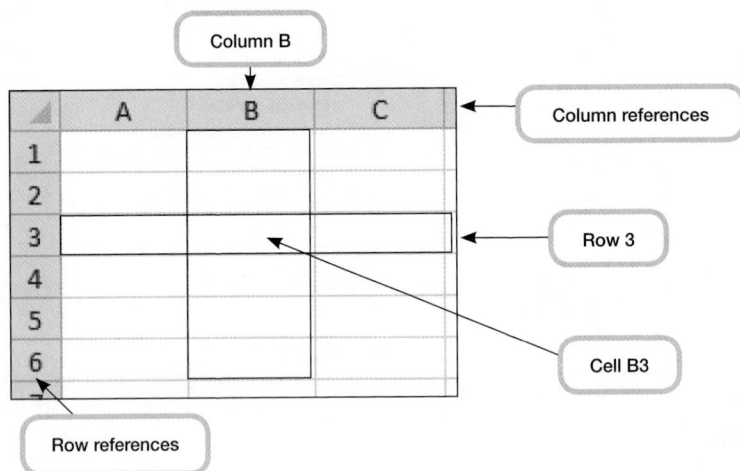

Tables are a very effective method for presenting information. The table layout organizes the information for readers and greatly reduces the number of words they have to read to interpret the data. Use tables whenever you can to make the information in your presentation easier to read.

The table you will create will display columns for the year and for the number of rescues and adoptions. The rows will display the data for the past four years. Your completed table will be similar to the one shown here.

Year	Rescues	Adoptions
2012	3759	3495
2013	3847	3784
2014	3982	3833
2015	4025	3943

CREATING A TABLE SLIDE

To include this information in the presentation, you will insert a new slide after slide 5. Because this slide will contain a table showing the adoption data, you will use the Title and Content layout.

1

- Make slide 5 current.

- Open the [New Slide ▾] drop-down menu from the Slides group on the Home tab.

- Choose the Title and Content layout.

Additional Information

PowerPoint remembers the last slide layout used while working in this presentation or during the current session and inserts it when you click the

top part of [New Slide ▾].

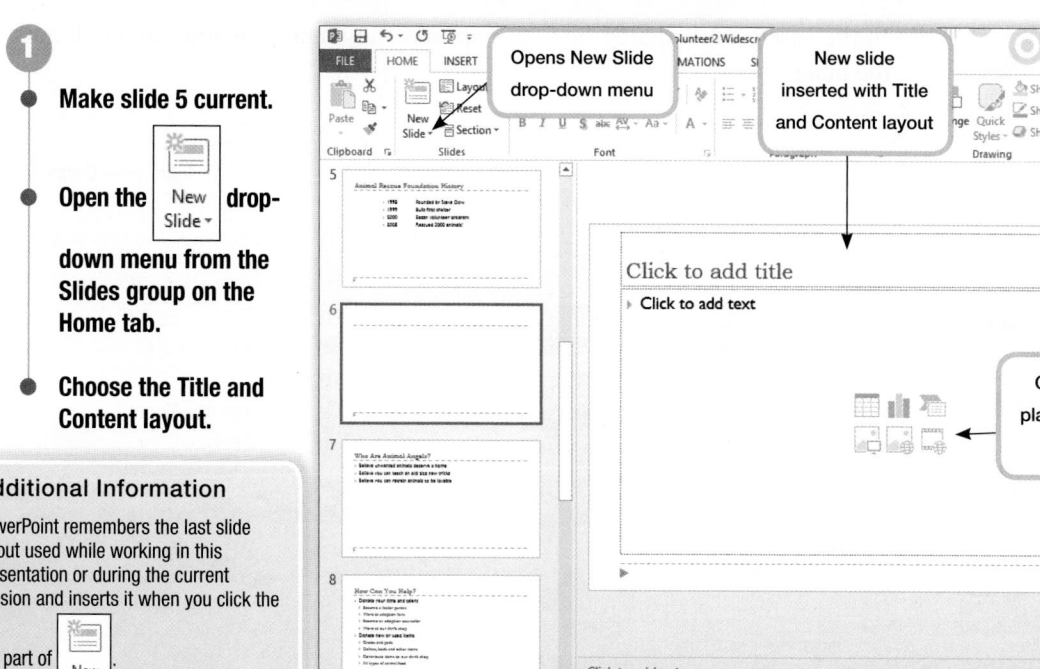

Figure 2.7

Your screen should be similar to Figure 2.7

Six icons appear inside the content placeholder, each representing a different type of content that can be inserted. Clicking an icon opens the appropriate feature to add the specified type of content.

INSERTING THE TABLE

First, you will add a slide title, and then you will create the table to display the number of adoptions and rescues.

1

- Enter the title **Success Rate** in the title placeholder.

- Click the [⊞] Insert Table icon in the center of the slide.

Your screen should be similar to Figure 2.8

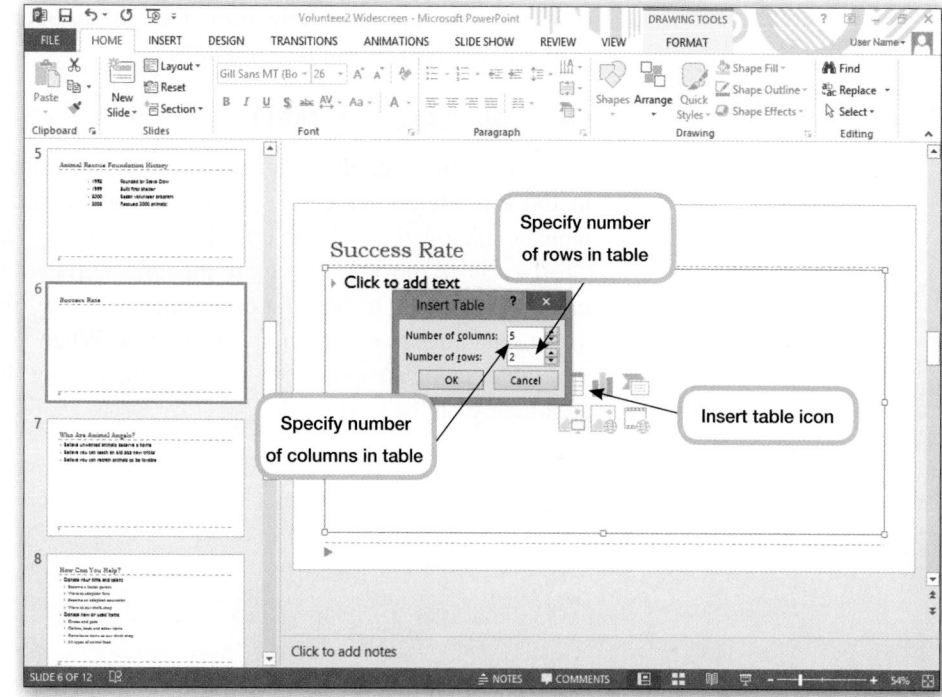

Figure 2.8

In the Insert Table dialog box, you specify the number of rows and columns for the table.

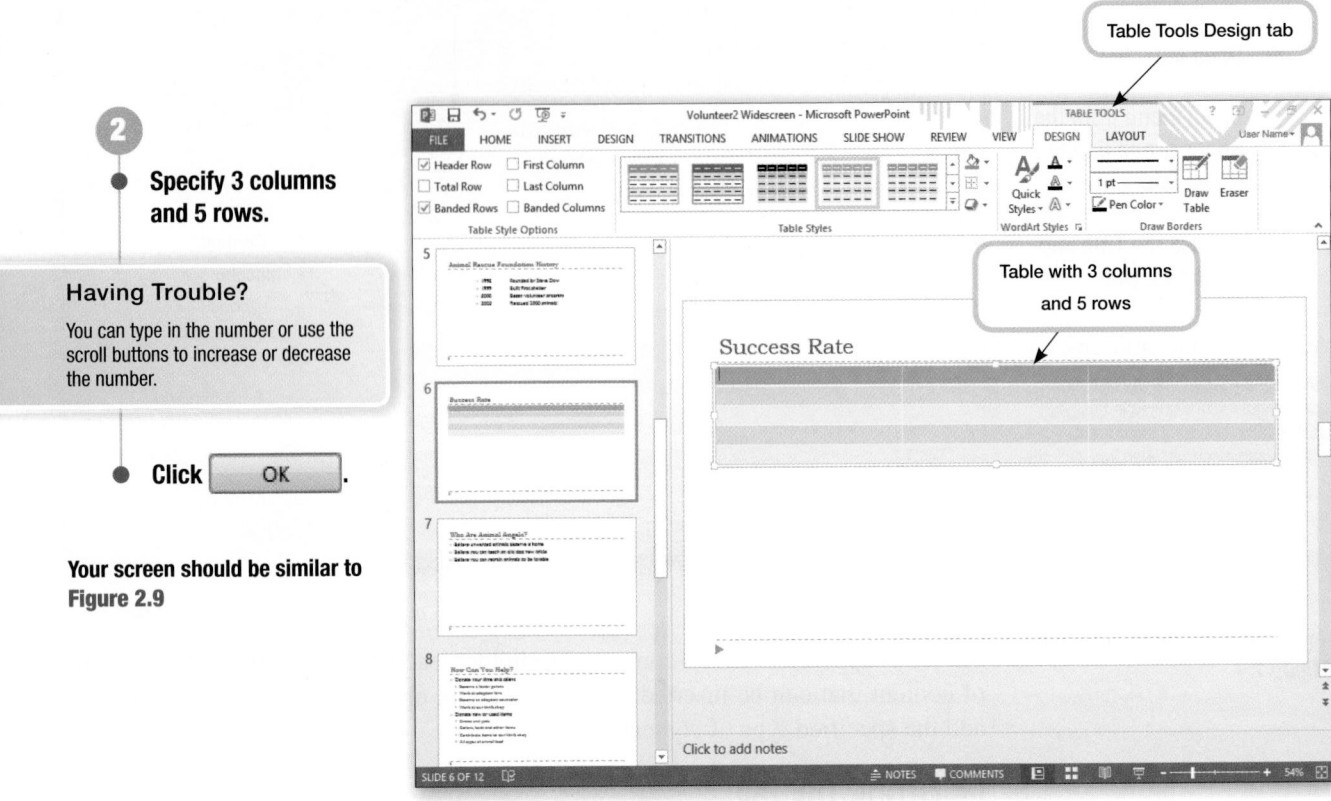

Table Tools Design tab

2

- **Specify 3 columns and 5 rows.**

Having Trouble?

You can type in the number or use the scroll buttons to increase or decrease the number.

- **Click** OK .

Your screen should be similar to Figure 2.9

Table with 3 columns and 5 rows

Success Rate

Figure 2.9

A basic table consisting of three columns and five rows is displayed as a selected object. In addition, the Table Tools Design tab opens in anticipation that you will want to modify the design of the table.

ENTERING DATA IN A TABLE

Now you can enter the information into the table. The insertion point appears in the top-left corner cell, cell A1, ready for you to enter text. To move in a table, click on the cell or use Tab to move to the next cell to the right and Shift + Tab to move to the cell to the left. If you are in the last cell of a row, pressing Tab takes you to the first cell of the next row. You also can use the ↑ and ↓ directional keys to move up or down a row. When you enter a large amount of text in a table, using Tab to move is easier than using the mouse because your hands are already on the keyboard.

- Type **Year**

- Press Tab or click on the next cell to the right.

Your screen should be similar to Figure 2.10

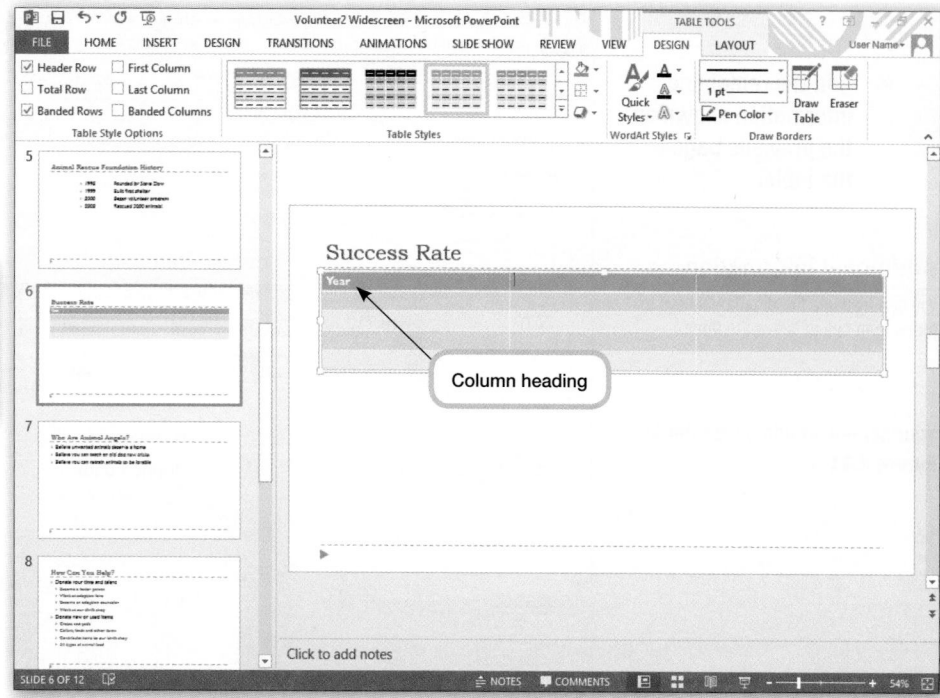

Column heading

Figure 2.10

Next, you will complete the information for the table by entering the data shown below.

	Column A	Column B	Column C
Row 1	Year	Rescues	Adoptions
Row 2	2012	3759	3495
Row 3	2013	3847	3784
Row 4	2014	3982	3833
Row 5	2015	4025	3943

2

● **Add the remaining information shown on the previous page to the table.**

Additional Information

You can also use the directional keys to move from cell to cell in the table.

Your screen should be similar to Figure 2.11

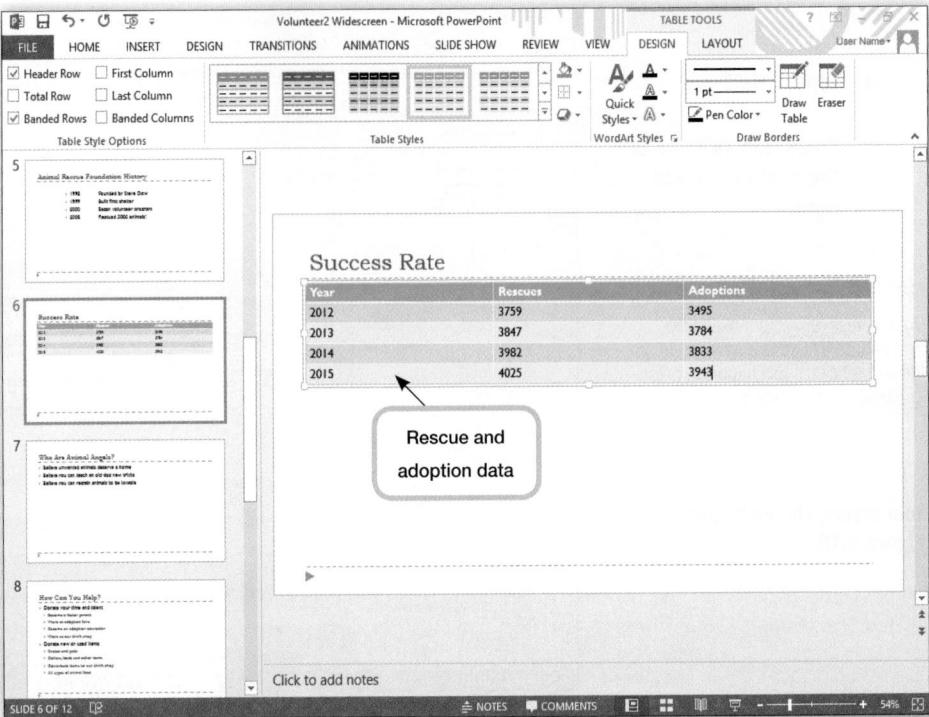

Figure 2.11

You are happy with the table but would like to increase the font size of the text to make it more readable onscreen. The size of the font in a table can be changed like any other text on a slide. However, selecting text in a table is slightly different. The following table describes how to select different areas of a table.

Area to Select	Procedure
Cell	Drag across the contents of the cell.
Row	Drag across the row or click in front of the row when the mouse pointer is a ➡.
Column	Drag down the column or click in front of the row when the mouse pointer is a ⬇.
Multiple cells, rows, or columns	Drag through the cells, rows, or columns when the mouse pointer is a ➚ or I.
	Or select the first cell, row, or column, and hold down ⇧Shift while clicking on another cell, row, or column.
Contents of next cell	Press Tab⇥.
Contents of previous cell	Press ⇧Shift + Tab⇥.
Entire table	Drag through all the cells or click anywhere inside the table and press Ctrl + A. Alternatively, select the entire table as an object first by clicking on the table border.

Because you want to increase the font size of all the text in the table, you will select the table as an object. The insertion point will not display in the table when the entire table is selected.

- **Click on the table border to select it as an object.**

- **Open the Home tab.**

- **Click** **Increase Font Size in the Font group four times.**

Your screen should be similar to Figure 2.12

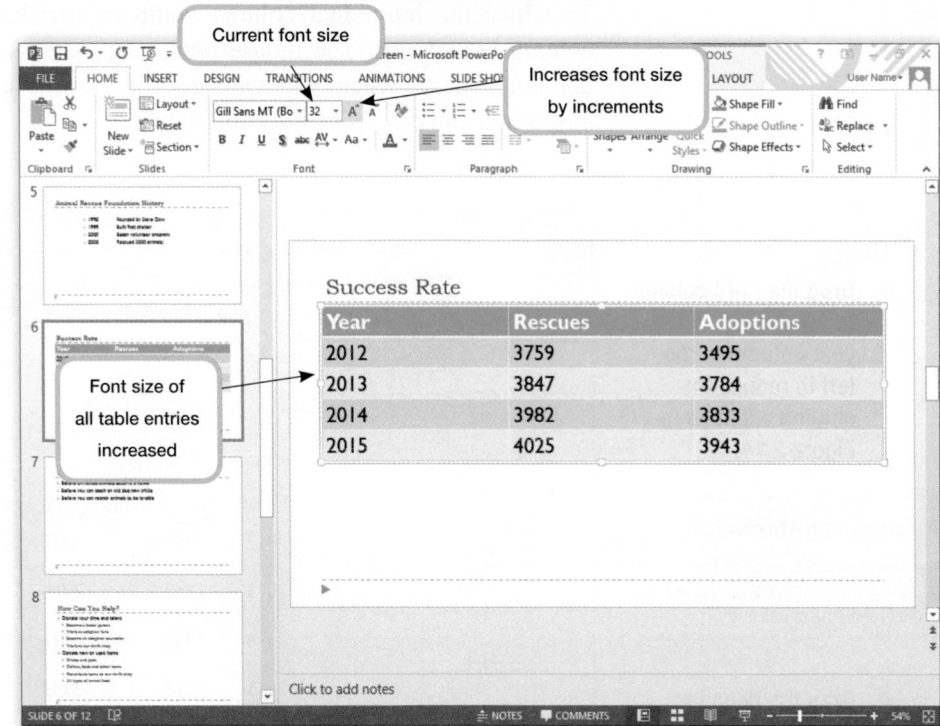

Figure 2.12

The font size has quickly been increased by four units, and at 32 points the text is much easier to read.

SIZING THE TABLE AND COLUMNS

You now want to increase the overall size of the table to better fill the space on the slide and then adjust the size of the columns to fit their contents.

1

- **Drag the lower-right corner sizing handle down to increase the table size as in Figure 2.13.**

Additional Information

The mouse pointer will appear as when you can drag the corner sizing handle and as ┼ while dragging.

Your screen should be similar to Figure 2.13

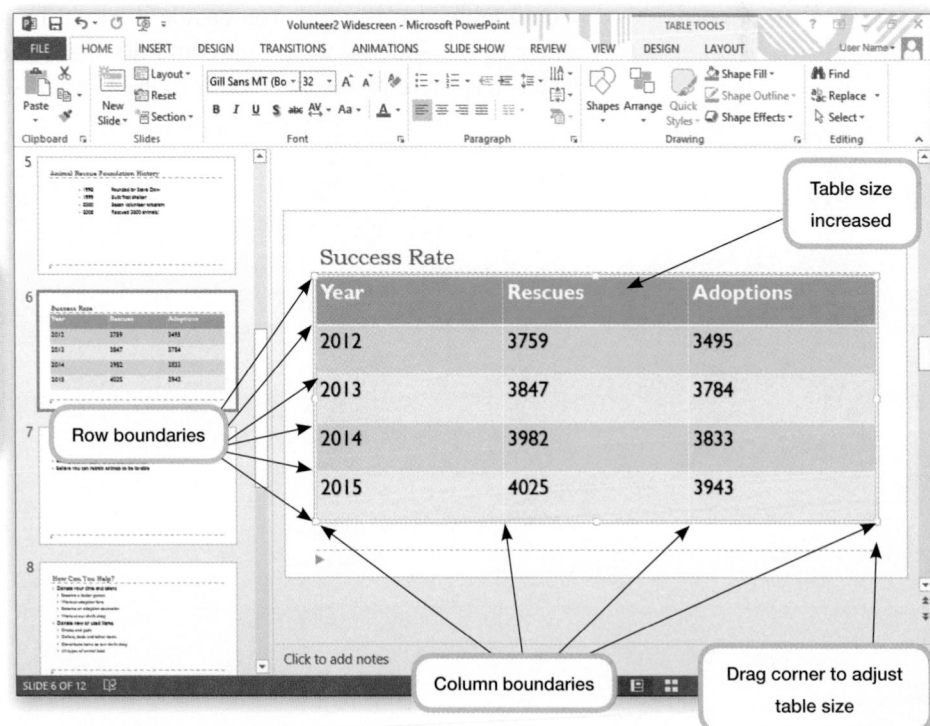

Figure 2.13

To adjust the individual column width or row height, you drag the row and column boundaries. The mouse pointer appears as a ⬌ when you can size the column and ⬍ when you can size the row. The mouse pointer appears as a ⬥ when you can move the entire table.

2

Drag the right column boundary line of the year column to the left to reduce the column width as in Figure 2.14.

Additional Information

You also can double-click on the boundary line to automatically size the width to the largest cell entry.

Drag the boundary lines of the other two columns to the left to reduce the column widths as in Figure 2.14.

Your screen should be similar to Figure 2.14

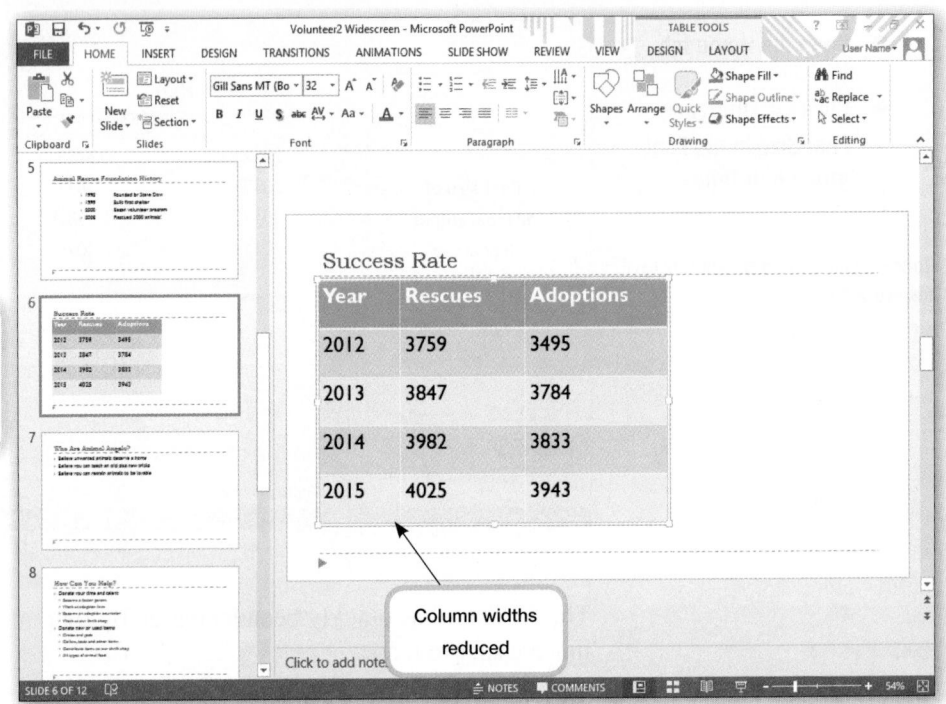

Figure 2.14

Now the columns are more appropriately sized to the data they display and the overall table size is good. You decide it would look best to align the table in the center of the slide as well. You could do this manually by moving the object to center it. A more precise method is to use the built-in alignment feature.

- Open the Table Tools Layout tab.

- Click **Align** in the Arrange group to display the drop-down menu.

Having Trouble?

You may need to click **Arrange** to open the group.

- Choose Align Center.

Your screen should be similar to Figure 2.15

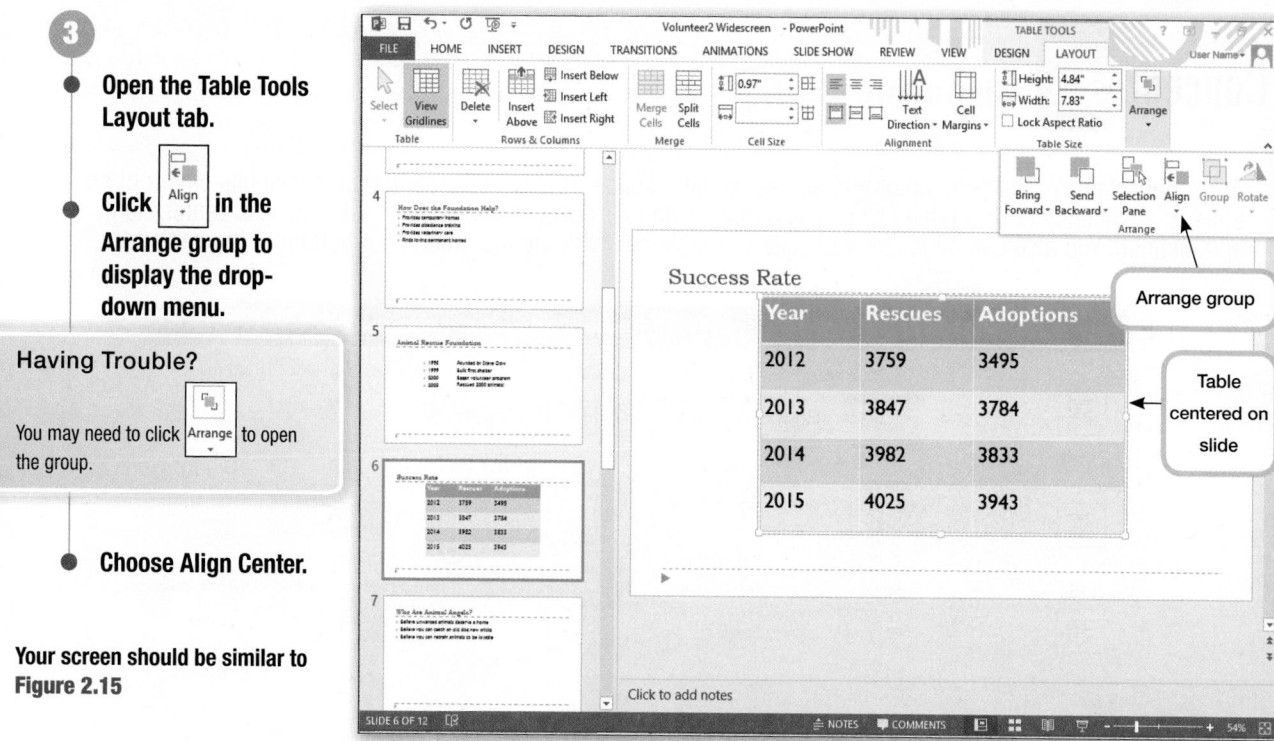

Figure 2.15

ALIGNING TEXT IN CELLS

The next change you want to make is to center the text and data in the cells. To do this, you can change the alignment of the text entries.

Concept ③ Alignment

Alignment controls the position of text entries within a space. You can change the horizontal placement of an entry in a placeholder or a table cell by using one of the four horizontal alignment settings: left, center, right, and justified. You also can align text vertically in a table cell with the top, middle, or bottom of the cell space.

Horizontal Alignment	Effect on Text	Vertical Alignment	Effect on Text
Align Left	Aligns text against the left edge of the placeholder or cell, leaving the right edge of text, which wraps to another line, ragged.	Align Top	Aligns text at the top of the cell space.
Center	Centers each line of text between the left and right edges of the placeholder or cell.	Center Vertically	Aligns text in the middle of the cell space.
Align Right	Aligns text against the right edge of the placeholder or cell, leaving the left edge of multiple lines ragged.	Align Bottom	Aligns text at the bottom of the cell space.
Justify	Aligns text evenly with both the right and left edges of the placeholder.		

The commands to change alignment are in the Paragraph group of the Home tab and in the Alignment group of the TableTools Layout tab. Additionally, you can use the shortcuts shown below or the Mini toolbar.

Alignment	Keyboard Shortcut
Left	Ctrl + L
Center	Ctrl + E
Right	Ctrl + R
Justify	Ctrl + J

The data in the table is not centered within the cells. You want to center the cell entries both horizontally and vertically in their cell spaces.

1

- If necessary, select the entire table as an object.

- Click ☰ Center in the Alignment group.

Another Method

You also could click ☰ Center in the Paragraph group of the Home tab.

- Click ☰ Center Vertically in the Alignment group.

Another Method

You can also open the ⊞▾ Align Text drop-down menu in the Paragraph group and choose Middle.

- Drag the table to position it as in Figure 2.16.

Your screen should be similar to Figure 2.16

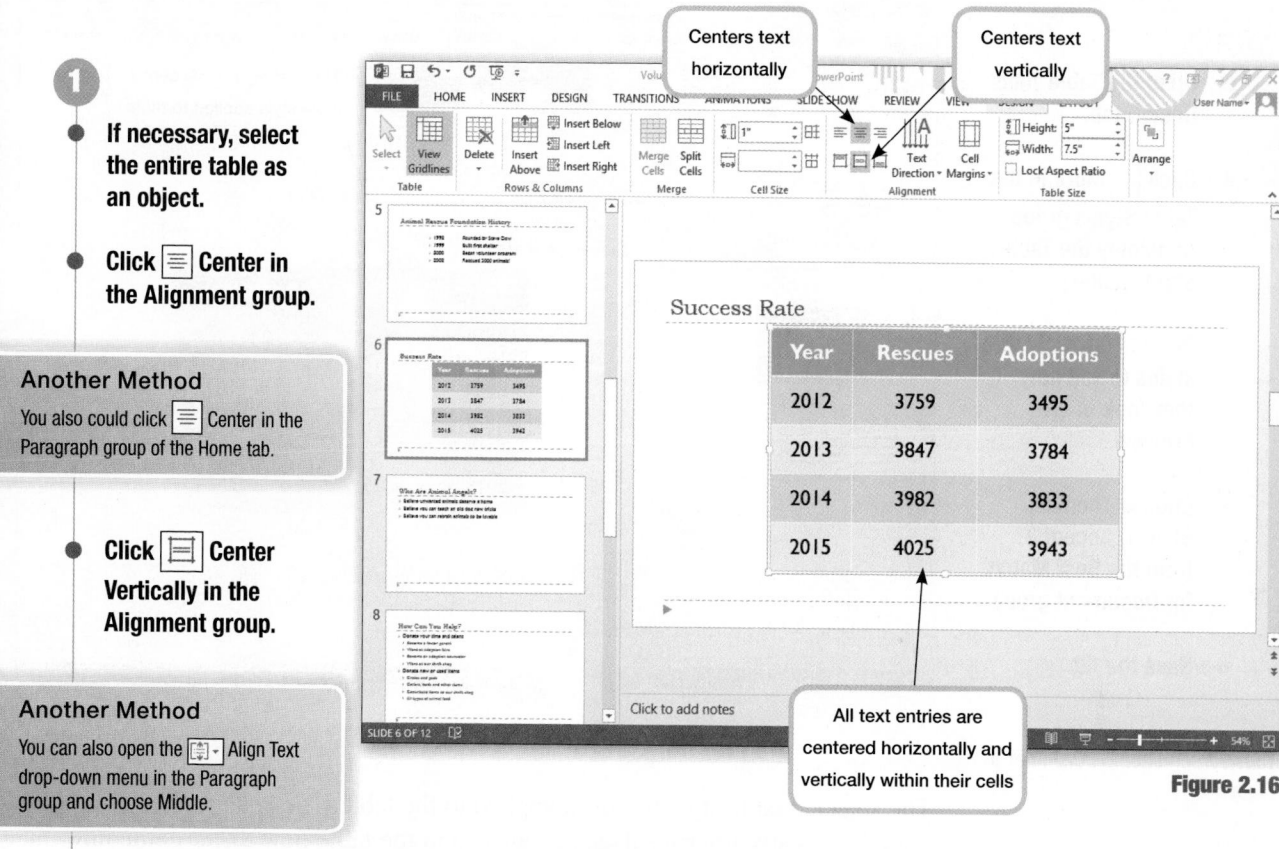

Figure 2.16

ENHANCING THE TABLE

Next, you will add color and other formatting changes to the table. To quickly make these enhancements, you will apply a table style. Like picture styles, **table styles** are combinations of shading colors, borders, and visual effects such as shadows and reflections that can be applied in one simple step. You also can create your own table style effects by selecting specific style elements such as borders and shadows individually using the ⬥▾ Shading, ⊞▾ Borders, and �𝄄▾ Effects commands from the Table Styles group on the Table Tools Design tab.

1

- **Open the Table Tools Design tab.**

- **Click ⟱ More in the Table Styles group to display the Table Styles gallery.**

- **Point to several table styles to see how they look in Live Preview.**

- **Choose Themed Style 1, Accent 2 from the Best Match for Document group.**

- **Save the file.**

Your screen should be similar to Figure 2.17

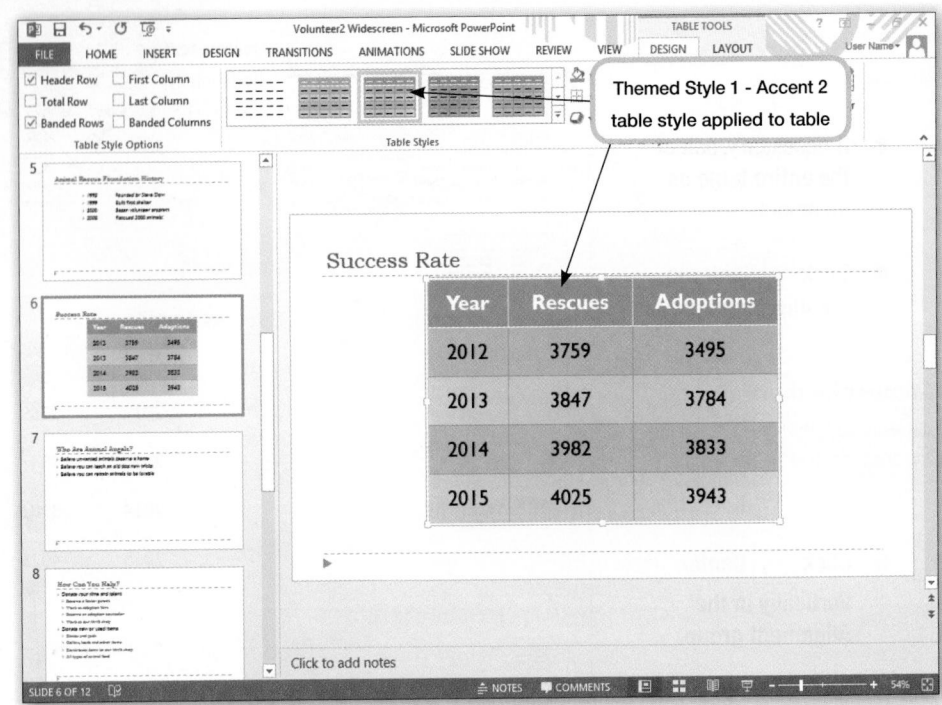

Figure 2.17

The selected table style has been applied to the table. The enhancements added to the table greatly improve its appearance, and the table now displays the information in an attractive and easy-to-read manner.

Cropping and Enhancing Pictures

Now you are ready to further enhance the presentation by adding to the title slide a picture of a dog that is up for adoption. You will improve the appearance of the picture by cropping it and enhancing it with a picture style.

INSERTING A GRAPHIC

You will first insert the picture of the dog from a file on your computer.

1

- Select slide 1.

- Open the Insert tab.

- Click 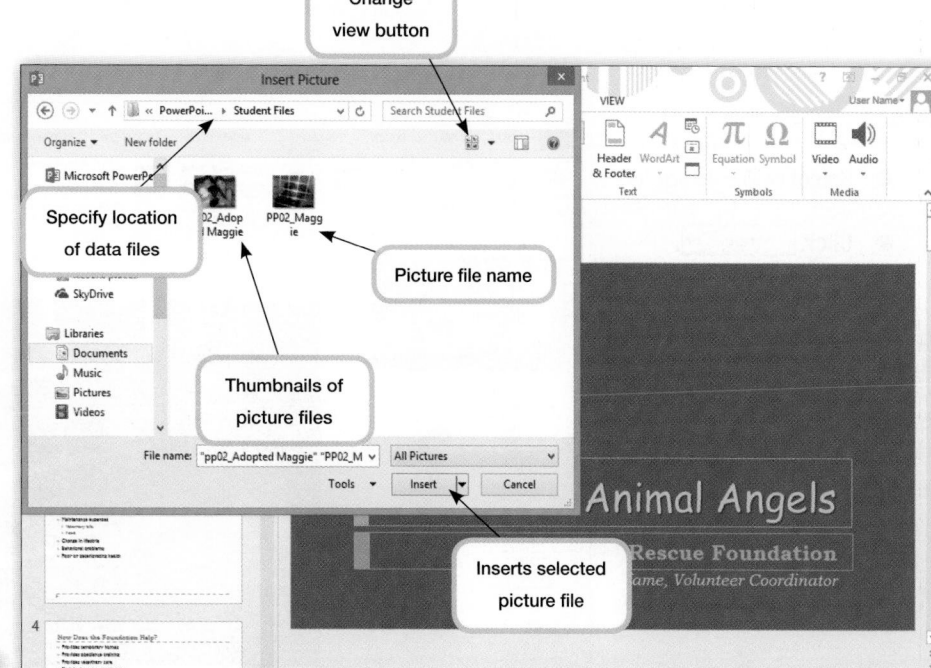 Pictures in the Images group.

- Change the location to your data file location.

- If necessary, change the view to Large Icons.

Having Trouble?

If necessary, click [icon] ▼ and choose Large Icon.

Figure 2.18

Your screen should be similar to Figure 2.18

Having Trouble?

Your screen may display additional picture files.

A thumbnail preview of each picture is displayed above the file name.

Select pp02_Maggie

Click Insert ▼.

Your screen should be similar to Figure 2.19

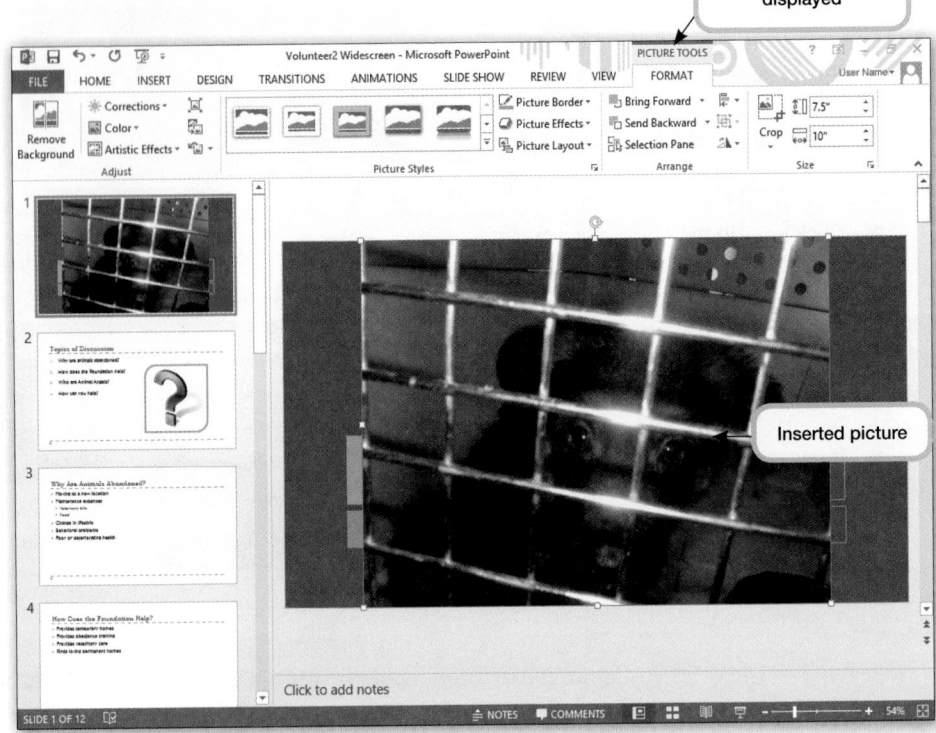

Picture Tools Format tab automatically displayed

Inserted picture

Figure 2.19

The Picture Tools Format tab is automatically displayed in the Ribbon, in anticipation that you may want to modify the graphic. You will decrease the size of the picture first.

3 ● Drag the bottom-right corner sizing handle inward to decrease its size to that shown in Figure 2.20.

Additional Information

To maintain an object's proportions while resizing it, hold down (Shift) while dragging the sizing handle.

Your screen should be similar to Figure 2.20

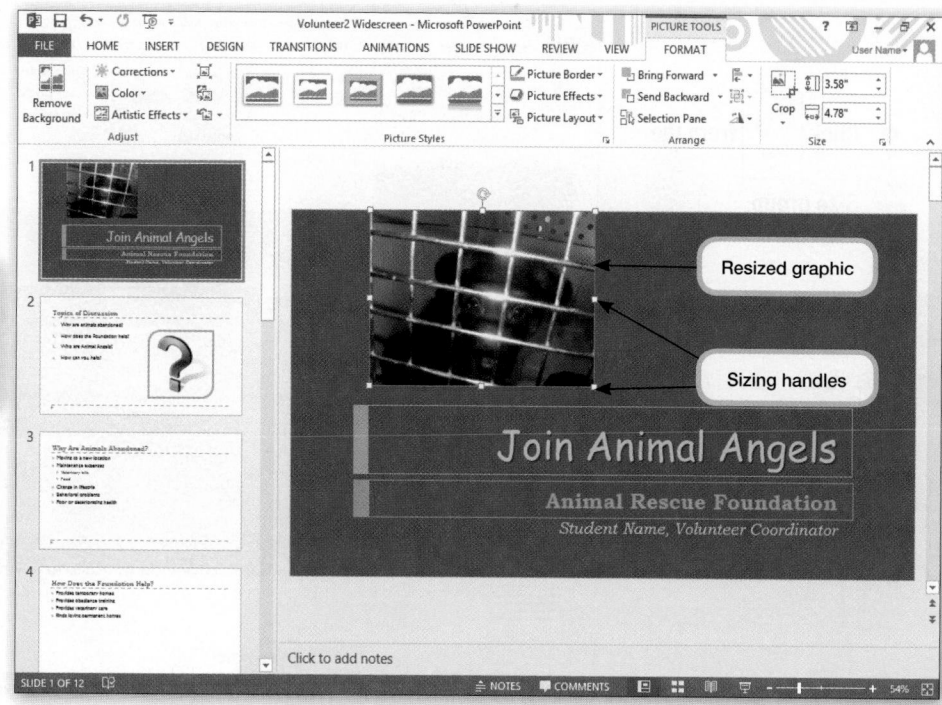

Figure 2.20

CROPPING A GRAPHIC

Next, you decide that you can draw more attention to Maggie by cropping the picture. Trimming or removing part of a picture is called **cropping**. Cropping removes the vertical or horizontal edges of a picture to help focus attention on a particular area. You will remove the upper part of the picture by cropping it to show Maggie only.

Click 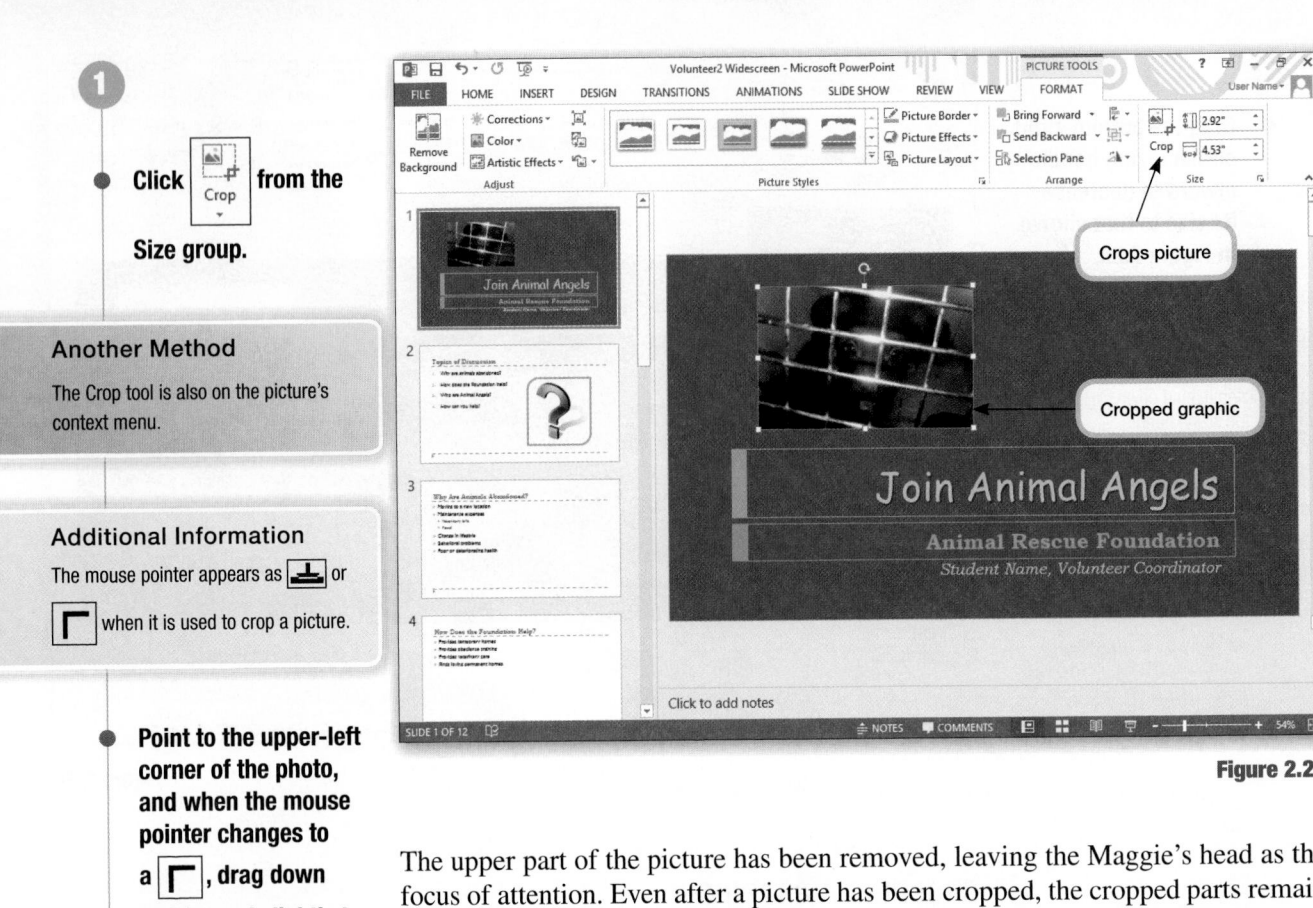 **from the**

Size group.

- **Point to the upper-left corner of the photo, and when the mouse pointer changes to a [⌐], drag down and inward slightly to just above Maggie's head.**

- **Click [⊞] from the**

Size group to turn off this feature.

Your screen should be similar to Figure 2.21

Figure 2.21

The upper part of the picture has been removed, leaving the Maggie's head as the focus of attention. Even after a picture has been cropped, the cropped parts remain as part of the picture file. This allows you to readjust how the picture was cropped. To permanently delete the cropped parts use the [⌐] Compress Pictures command in the Adjust group and save the file. This also reduces the file size and prevents others from viewing the cropped parts of the picture.

Next you want to increase the graphic's size and position it centered in the space above the title.

2

• Size the picture as in Figure 2.22 (approximately 3 by 4.75 inches).

Additional Information

The Shape Height and Shape Width buttons in the Size group display the current shape's size as you drag.

• Open the [ ] Align Objects drop-down menu in the Arrange group of the Picture Tools Format tab and choose Align Center.

• If necessary, position the graphic vertically on the slide as shown in Figure 2.22.

Your screen should be similar to Figure 2.22

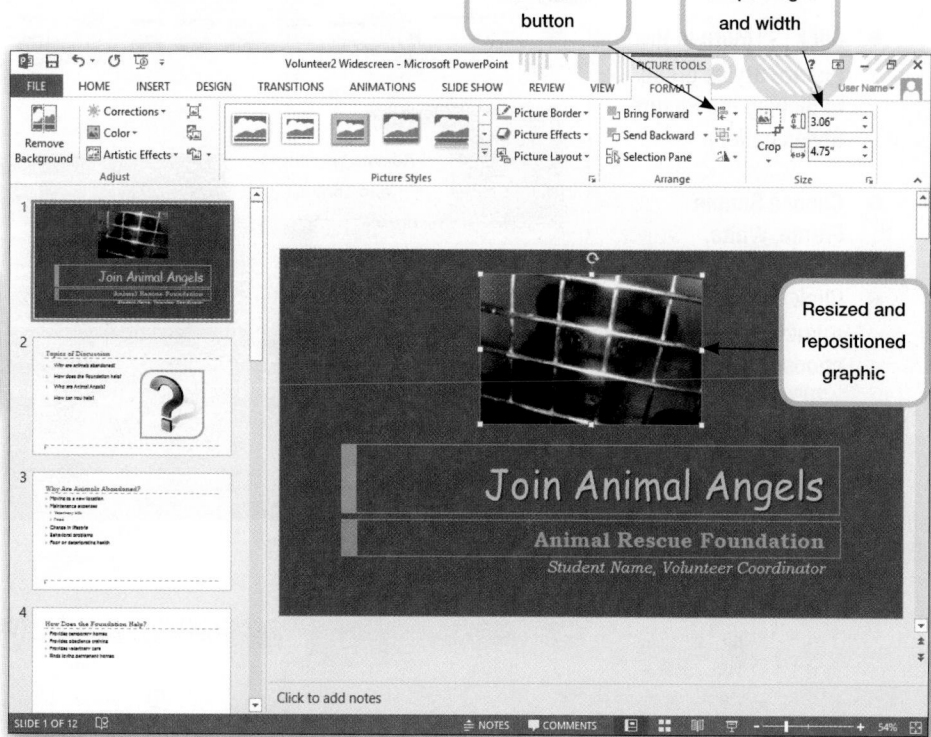

Figure 2.22

ENHANCING A PICTURE

Finally, you want to enhance the picture by selecting a picture style and then improve the brightness of the picture so that the dog stands out better.

- **Click** ⏷ **More in the Picture Styles group to display the Picture Styles gallery.**

- **Choose Simple Frame, White.**

- **Click** in the **Adjust group and choose Brightness: +20% Contrast: 0% (Normal).**

Your screen should be similar to Figure 2.23

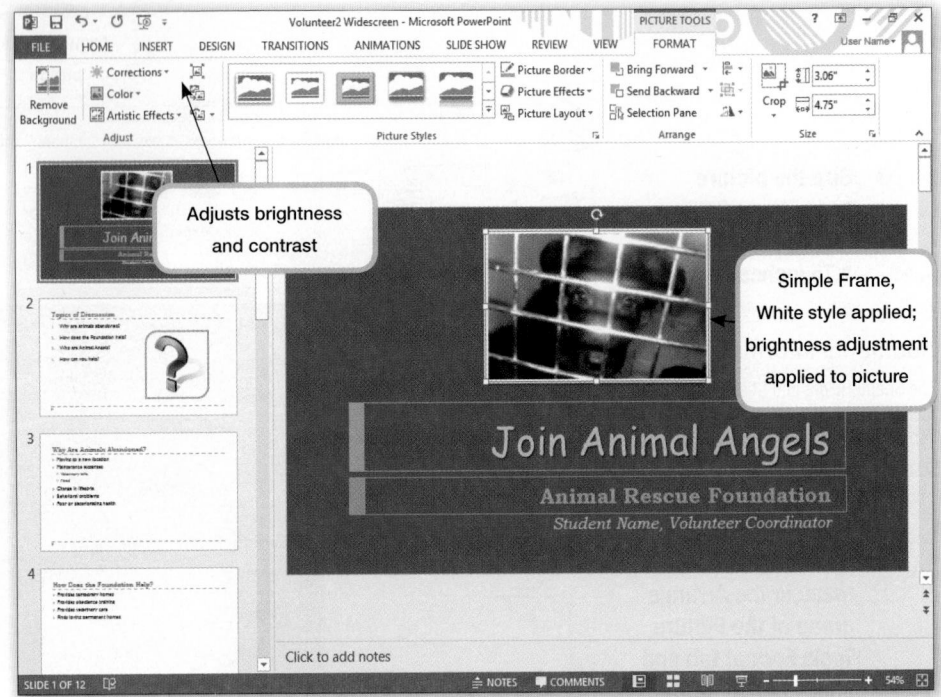

Figure 2.23

The addition of the picture style and adjustment of the brightness greatly improves the appearance of the picture and makes the title slide much more interesting and effective.

Inserting and Enhancing Shapes

At the end of the presentation, you want to add a concluding slide. This slide needs to be powerful, because it is your last chance to convince your audience to join Animal Angels.

ADDING A SHAPE

To create the concluding slide, you will duplicate slide 1 and replace the picture with another showing Maggie's adoption. You will also add a graphic of a heart that you will create using one of the ready-made shapes supplied with PowerPoint. These shapes include rectangles and circles, lines, a variety of basic shapes, block arrows, flowchart symbols, stars and banners, action buttons, and callouts.

1

- Duplicate slide 1.

- Move slide 2 to the end of the presentation.

- Select the picture and press Delete.

- Insert the picture pp02_Adopted Maggie from your student file location.

- Crop the picture as in Figure 2.24.

- Increase the brightness 20%.

- Choose the Simple Frame, White (the first choice) from the Picture Styles gallery.

- Size and position the picture as in Figure 2.24.

Your screen should be similar to Figure 2.24

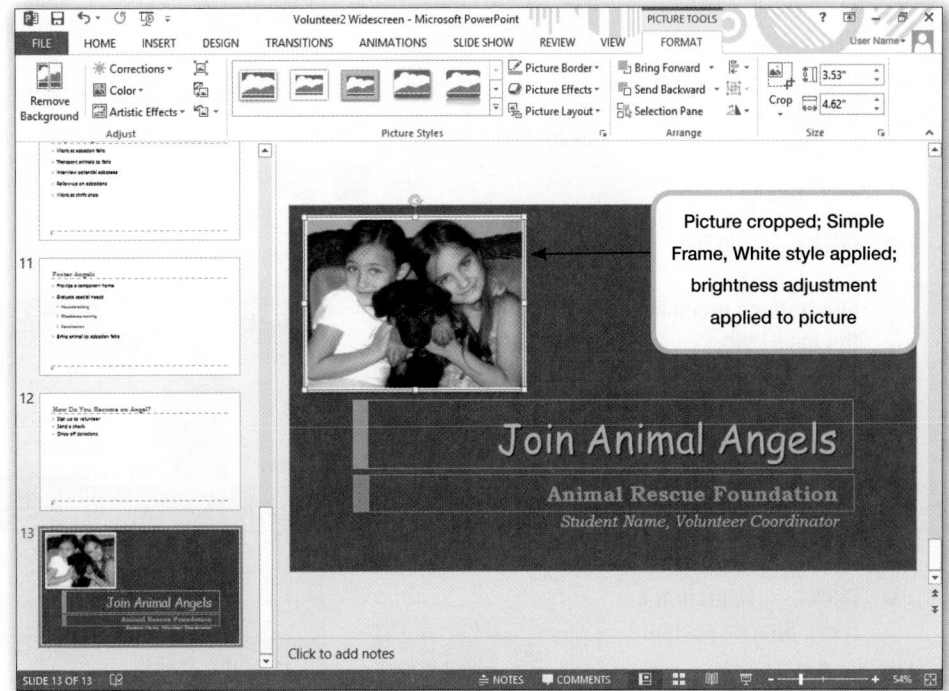

Figure 2.24

The picture is cropped, framed, sized, and positioned in the upper-left corner of the slide. In the space to the right you will insert a heart shape by selecting the shape from the Shapes gallery on the Insert tab. When inserting a shape, the mouse pointer appears as + when pointing to the slide. Then, to insert the shape, click on the slide and drag to increase the size.

● Click [Shapes] in the
Illustrations group of
the Insert tab.

Another Method

You also can access the Shapes
gallery from the Drawing group of
the Home tab.

● Click ♡ Heart in the
Basic Shapes section.

Additional Information

The selected shape will be added to the
Recently Used Shapes section of the
Shapes gallery.

● Click above the title
on the slide and drag
to insert and enlarge
the heart shape.

Another Method

To maintain the height and width
proportions of the shape, hold down
Shift while you drag.

● Size and position the
heart shape as in
Figure 2.25.

Additional Information

A shape can be sized and moved just
like any other object.

**Your screen should be similar to
Figure 2.25**

Additional Information

Many more shapes are available from
the Office.com Clip Art gallery.

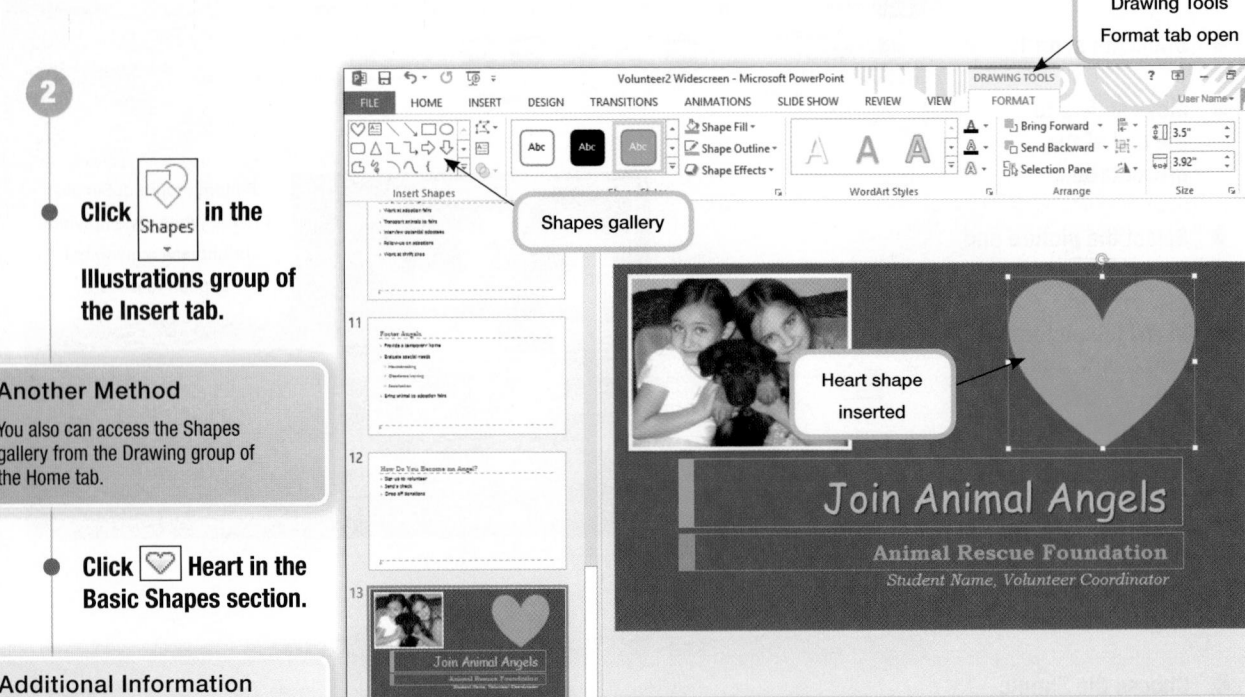

Figure 2.25

The heart shape is inserted and the Drawing Tools Format tab is available.

ENHANCING A SHAPE

Next, you will enhance the heart graphic's appearance by selecting a shape style
and adding a reflection. Just like the other styles in PowerPoint 2013, **shape styles**
consist of combinations of fill colors, outline colors, and effects.

1

- **Open the Drawing Tools Format tab.**

- **Click ⊽ More in the Shape Styles group to open the Shape Styles gallery.**

- **Choose Moderate Effect, Gold Accent 1.**

- **Click 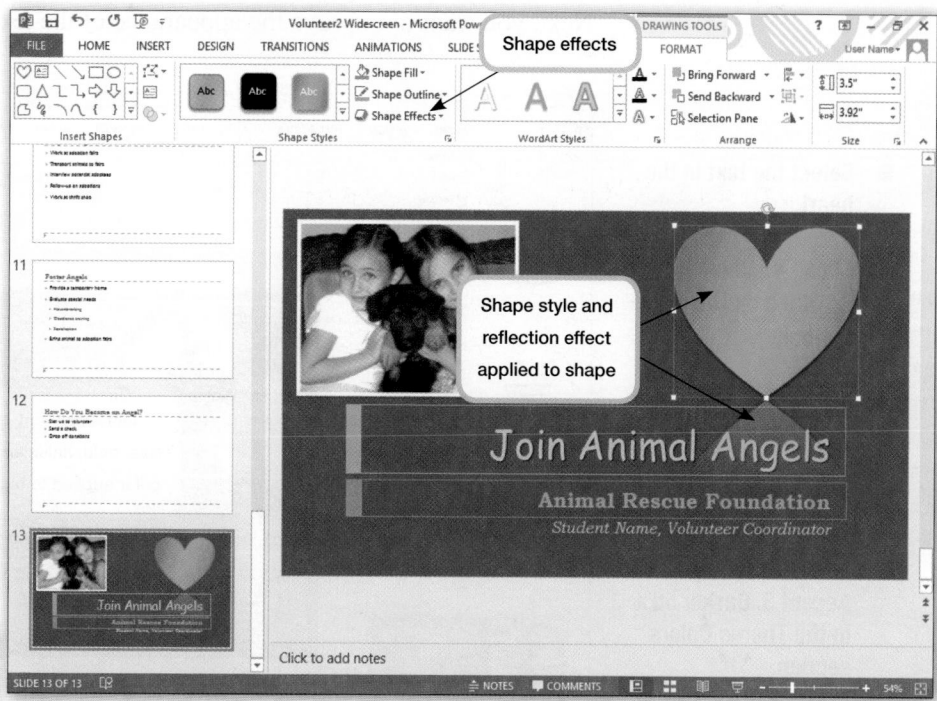 Shape Effects ▾ and choose Half Reflection, 4 pt offset from the Reflection gallery.**

Additional Information

The offset controls the amount of space between the object and the reflection.

Your screen should be similar to Figure 2.26

Figure 2.26

The addition of style and reflection effects greatly improves the appearance of the heart.

ADDING TEXT TO A SHAPE

Next, you will add text to the heart object. Text can be added to all shapes and becomes part of the shape; when the shape is moved, the text moves with it.

1

- **Right-click on the heart shape to open the context menu, and choose Edit Text.**

- **Type Open Your Heart**

Having Trouble?

If the inserted text does not fit into the heart shape, increase the size of the heart.

Your screen should be similar to Figure 2.27

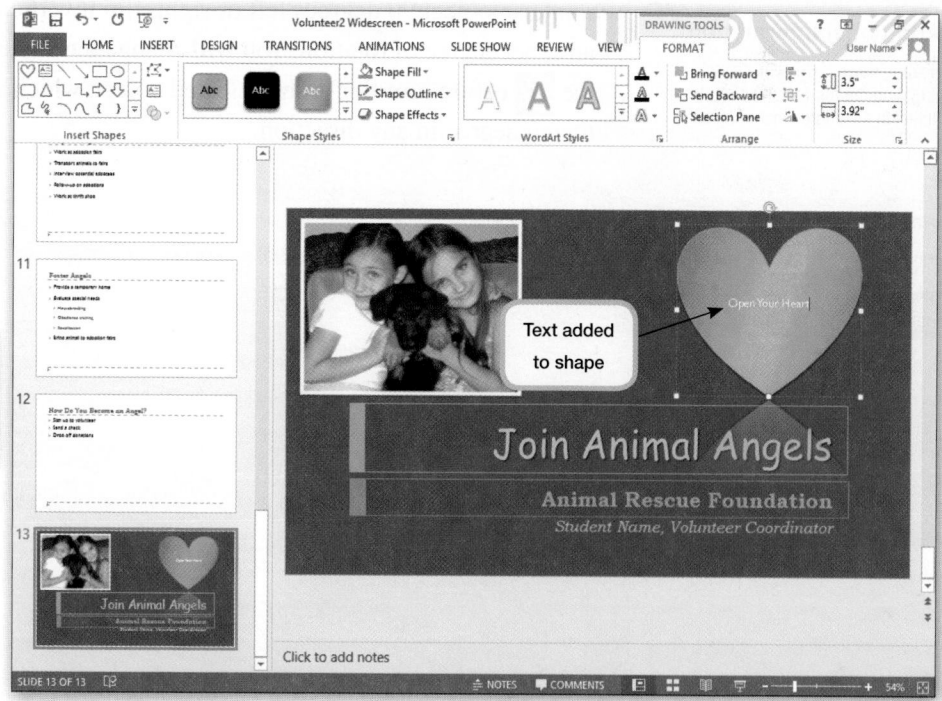

Figure 2.27

Next, you want to improve the appearance of the text using character effects.

2

- Select the text in the heart.

- Click **B** Bold and *I* Italic on the Mini toolbar.

- Increase the font size to 24 points.

- Open the [A ▾] Font Color gallery and choose Rose, Accent 3, Darker 50% in the Theme Colors section.

- Click outside the heart to deselect the shape.

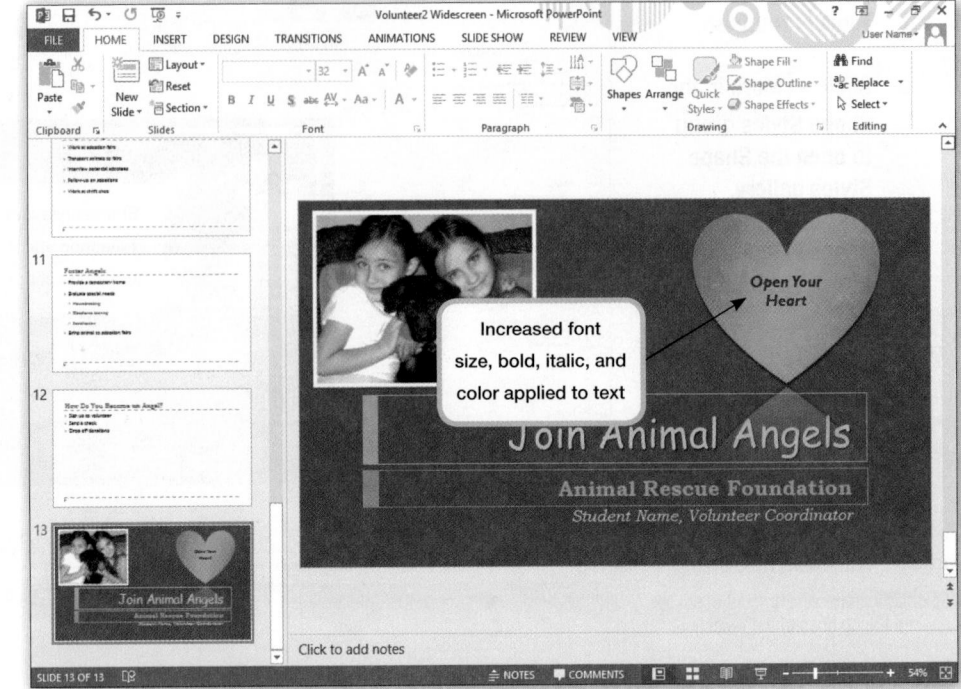

Figure 2.28

Your screen should be similar to Figure 2.28

Additional Information

Holding down [Shift] while slowly dragging the rotate handle rotates the object in 15-degree increments.

Another Method

You also can use [▾] Rotate Objects in the Arrange group of the Drawing Tools Format tab to rotate an object.

ROTATING THE OBJECT

Finally, you want to change the angle of the heart shape and the picture. You can rotate an object 90 degrees left or right, flip it vertically or horizontally, or specify an exact degree of rotation. You will change the angle of the heart to the right using the [○] **rotate handle** for the selected object, which allows you to rotate the object to any degree in any direction.

1

- Select the heart shape.

- Drag the rotate handle to the right slightly.

Additional Information

The mouse pointer appears as 🔄 when positioned on the rotate handle, and Live Preview shows how the object will look as you rotate it.

- Select the picture.

- Drag the rotate handle to the left slightly.

Having Trouble?

You may need to reposition and/or slightly resize the graphics.

Your screen should be similar to Figure 2.29

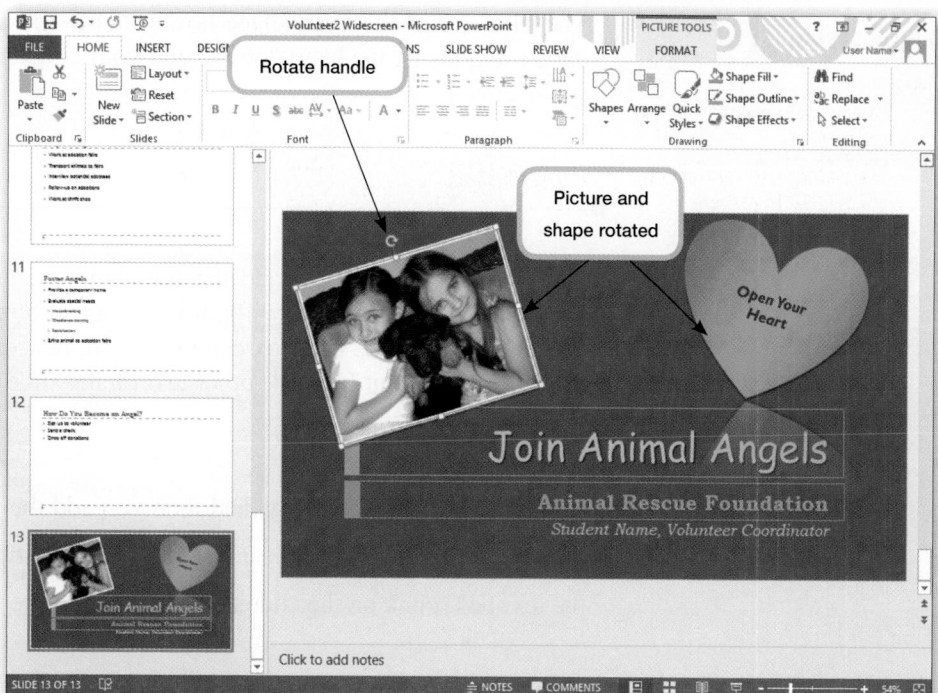

Figure 2.29

The angle of the graphics is an interesting addition to the slide.

USING COLOR MATCHING

You decide the color of the heart you added is too dark, and you'd like to match the lighter yellow in the girl's shirt. PowerPoint 2013 includes an **eyedropper tool** that makes it easy to copy a color from an object in the slide and apply it to any shape.

1

- Select the heart shape.

- Click 🎨 Shape Fill ▾ in the Drawing group of the Home tab.

- Choose Eyedropper.

Additional Information

The insertion point changes to 🎨 with a small box that shows the color you are pointing to.

- Point to the light yellow color in the girl's blouse, and when the ScreenTip displays Light Yellow, click to choose it.

Your screen should be similar to Figure 2.30

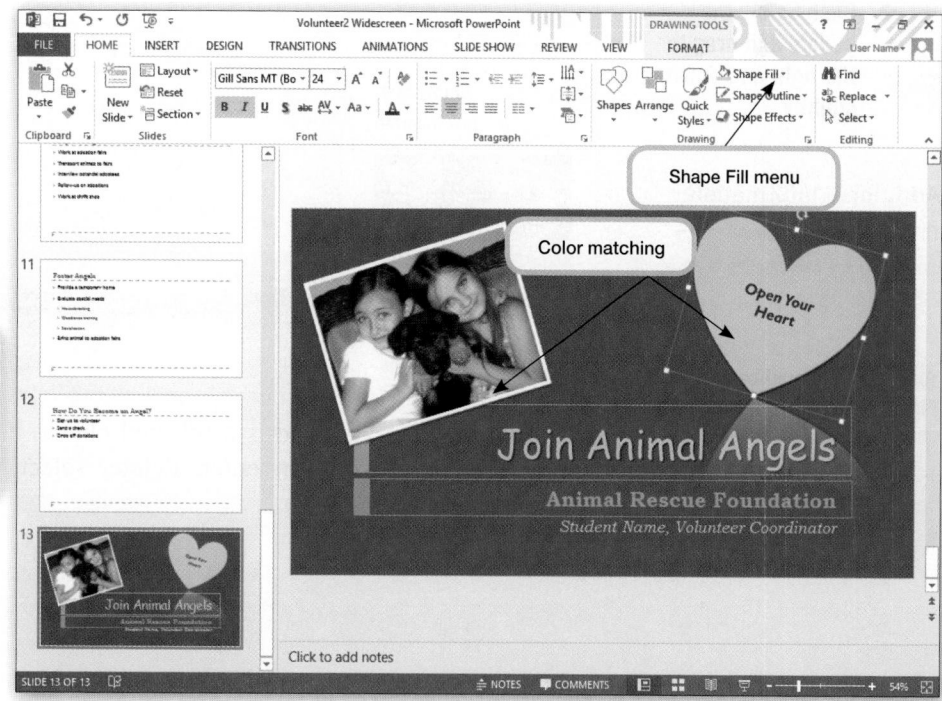

Figure 2.30

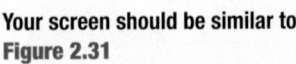
The fill color of the heart shape now matches the light yellow in the blouse. The darker text inside the heart "pops," and your concluding slide stands out.

Working with Text Boxes

On slide 12, you want to add the foundation's contact information. To make it stand out on the slide, you will put it into a text box. A **text box** is a container for text or graphics. The text box can be moved, resized, and enhanced in other ways to make it stand out from the other text on the slide.

CREATING A TEXT BOX

First you create the text box, and then you add the content. When inserting a text box, the mouse pointer appears as ↓ when pointing to the slide. Then, to create the text box, click on the slide and drag to increase the size.

1

- Display slide 12.

- Open the Insert tab.

- Click ⬛ in the Text group.

- Click below the bullets and drag to the right and down slightly.

Your screen should be similar to Figure 2.31

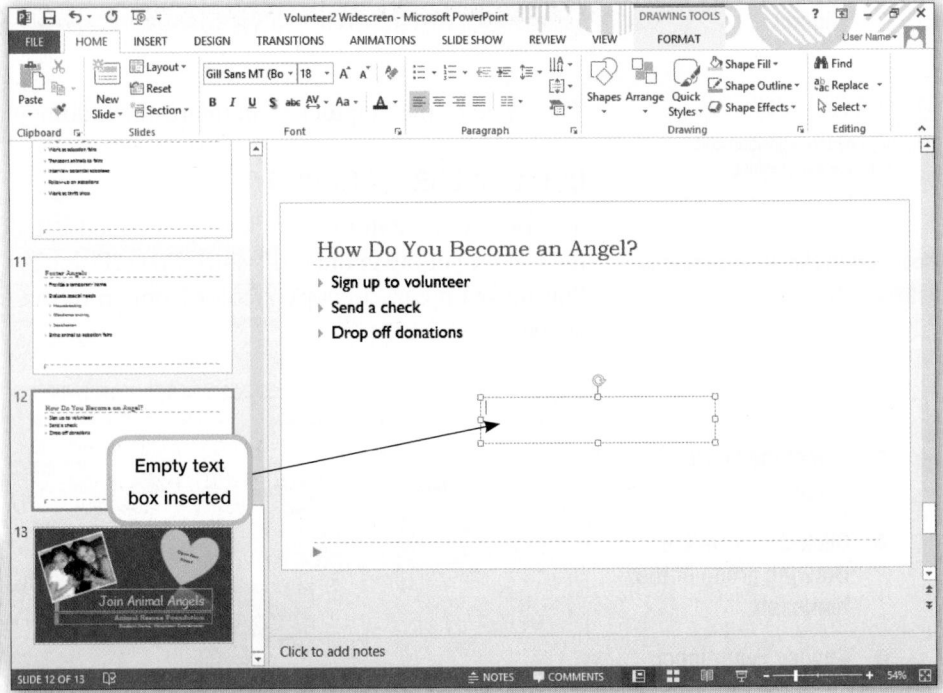

Figure 2.31

The text box is created and is a selected object. It is surrounded with a dashed border indicating you can enter, delete, select, and format the text inside the box.

ADDING TEXT TO A TEXT BOX

The text box displays an insertion point, indicating that it is waiting for you to enter the text. As you type the text, the text box will automatically resize as needed to display the entire entry.

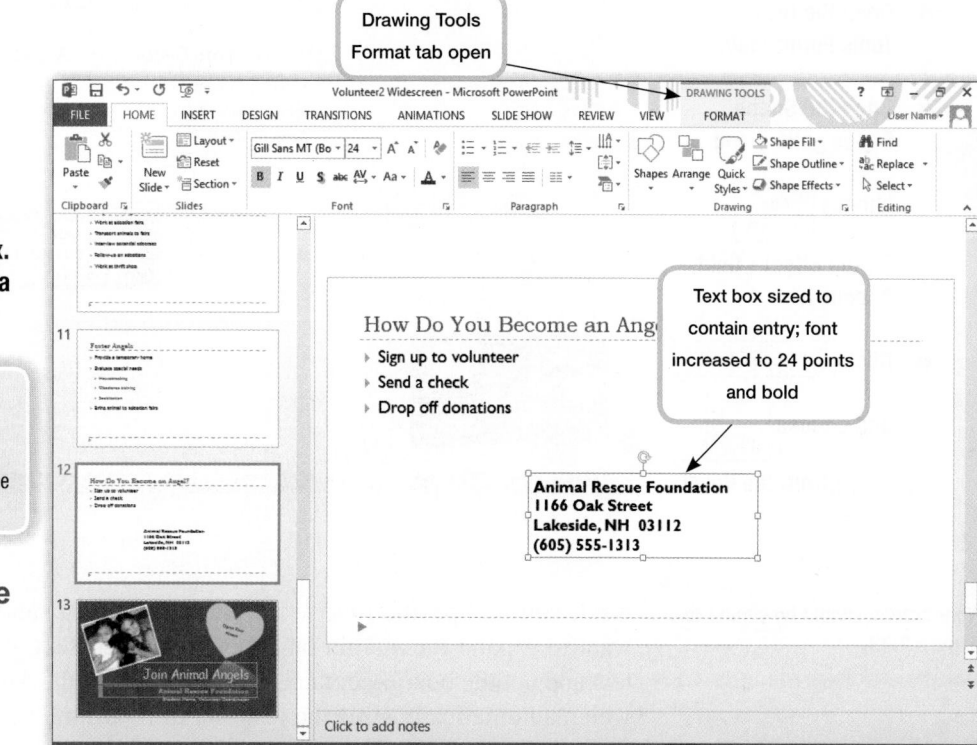

Figure 2.32

1

- **Type the organization's name and address shown below in the text box. Press [Enter] to start a new line.**

Animal Rescue Foundation

1166 Oak Street

Lakeside, NH 03112

(603) 555-1313

- **Click on the text box border to select the entire object and increase the font size to 24 points and bold.**

- **If necessary, increase the width of the text box to display the name of the foundation on a single line.**

Your screen should be similar to Figure 2.32

The text box is now more prominent and the content is easier to read.

ENHANCING THE TEXT BOX

Like any other object, the text box can be sized and moved anywhere on the slide. It also can be enhanced by adding styles and effects. You want to change the color and add a bevel effect around the box to define the space.

- If necessary, select the text box as an object (solid border).

- Open the Drawing Tools Format tab.

- Open the Shape Styles gallery and choose **Abc** Subtle Effect - Gold, Accent 1.

- Click ⬜ Shape Effects ▾ and choose ⬜ Angle from the Bevel group.

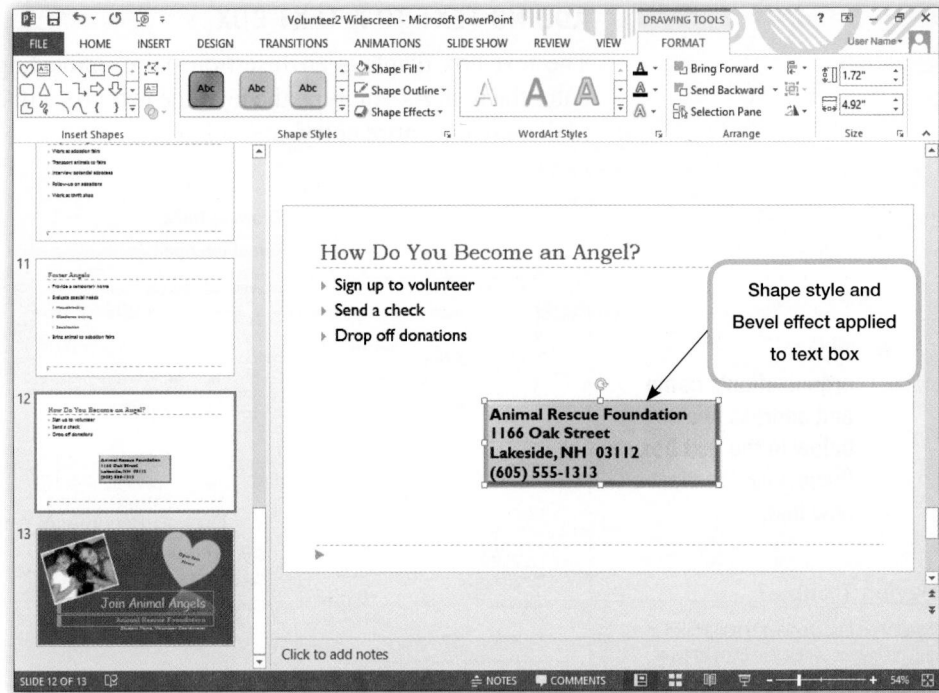

Figure 2.33

Your screen should be similar to Figure 2.33

Next, you will position the text within the text box and the box on the slide. You want to expand the margin on either side of the text to focus the attention on the text and not the box. By default, PowerPoint uses the AutoFit feature on text boxes, which automatically sizes the text box to fit around the text. You will turn off the AutoFit feature so that you control the position of the text.

- **Right-click within the text of the text box and choose Format Text Effects.**

- **Click ⬛ Textbox from the Format Shape pane and choose Do Not AutoFit.**

- **Change the left and right margins to .3.**

- **Choose Middle Centered from the Vertical Alignment drop-down box.**

- **Close the Format Shape pane.**

- **Adjust the size of the text box to display the information as in Figure 2.34.**

- **Move the text box to the position shown in Figure 2.34.**

- **Deselect the text box.**

- **Save the presentation.**

Your screen should be similar to Figure 2.34

NOTE If you are ending your session now, exit PowerPoint 2013. When you begin again, open this file.

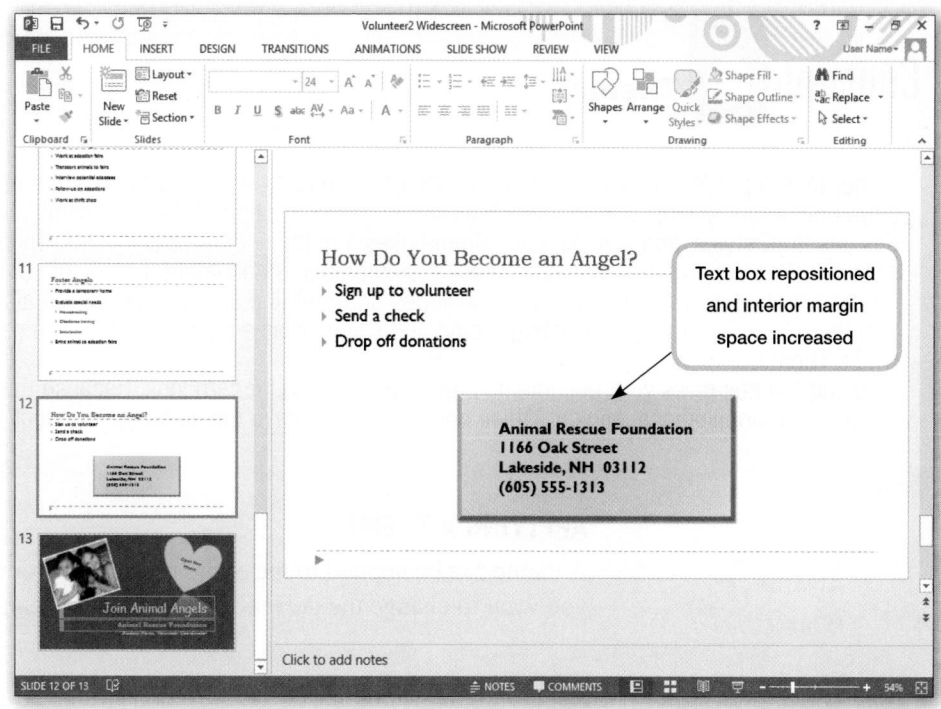

Figure 2.34

The information in the text box now stands out from the other information on the slide.

Changing the Presentation Design

When you first started this presentation, you used a PowerPoint template that included sample text as well as color and design elements. Now you are satisfied with the presentation's basic content and organization, but you would like to change its design style and appearance by applying a different theme.

Concept ④ Theme

A **theme** is a predefined set of formatting choices that can be applied to an entire document in one simple step. PowerPoint includes 29 named, built-in themes consisting of different combinations of colors, background designs, font styles, and layouts. Each theme uses a unique set of colors, fonts, and effects. Each theme consists of 12 colors that are applied to specific elements in a document. Each font component includes body and heading fonts. Each effects component includes different line and fill effects. You also can create your own custom themes by modifying an existing theme and saving it as a custom theme. The default presentation uses the Office Theme.

Using themes gives your documents a professional and modern look. Because themes are shared across Office 2013 applications, all your Office documents can have the same uniform look.

APPLYING A THEME

A theme can be applied to the entire presentation or to selected slides. In this case, you want to change the design for the entire presentation.

①
- Display slide 1.

- Open the Design tab.

- Click ▾ More in the Themes group to open the Themes gallery.

- Point to Wisp in the Office section of the gallery.

Your screen should be similar to Figure 2.35

Figure 2.35

The Themes gallery displays thumbnails of each theme in the Office section. The This Presentation area displays the Origin theme that is currently used in the presentation. This is the theme associated with the presentation template you used to start the presentation. Pointing to a thumbnail displays a Live Preview of the presentation in the selected theme. As you can see, the slide colors, background designs, font styles, and overall layout of the slide are affected by the theme.

You will preview several other themes, and then use the Facet theme for the presentation.

2

Preview several other themes.

Choose the  Facet theme.

Your screen should be similar to Figure 2.36

Facet theme
applied to all slides
in the presentation

Figure 2.36

The Facet theme has been applied to all slides in the presentation. When a new theme is applied, the text styles, graphics, and colors that are included in the design replace the previous design settings. Consequently, the layout may need to be adjusted. For example, the slide title on slide 1 will need to be repositioned and and the picture size adjusted.

However, if you had made individual changes to a slide, such as changing the font of the title, these changes are not updated to the new theme design. In this case, the title font is still the Comic Sans MS that you selected in Lab 1; however, it has a different point size.

Additional Information

To apply a theme to selected slides, preselect the slides to apply the themes to in the Slide pane, and use the Apply to Selected Slides option from the theme's shortcut menu.

3

- Select each slide and check the layout.

- Make the adjustments shown in the table below to the indicated slides.

- Switch to Slide Sorter view to see how all your changes look.

- Reduce the zoom to display all the slides in the window.

- Save the presentation.

Your screen should be similar to Figure 2.37

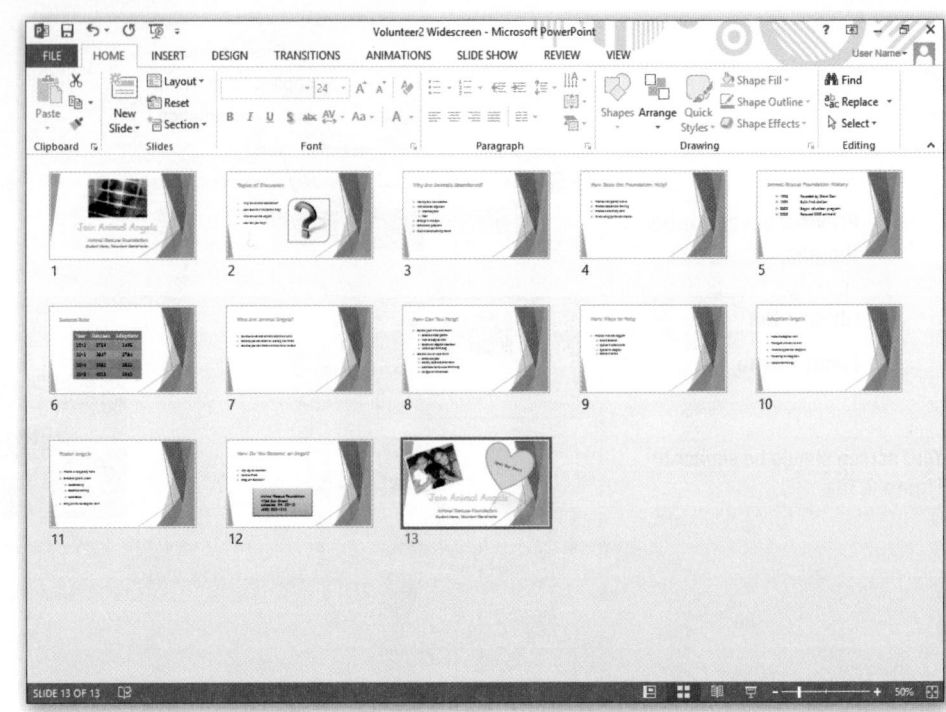

Figure 2.37

Slide	Adjustment
1	Move the title box down and the subtitle box to the left. If necessary, make the subtitle box smaller. Increase the size of the graphic slightly. Realign the graphic to the center of the slide.
2	If needed, adjust the position of the text content placeholder so the bullets align with the title text. If needed, adjust the size of the graphic and reposition it slightly.
5	If necessary, move the title placeholder down slightly to the same position on the slide as the title on the other slides. Select both content placeholders and move them slightly to the left, and increase the font size to 24 points.
6	Appropriately adjust the size and position of the table.
8	Move the content placeholder up slightly.
12	Adjust the position of the text box as needed.
13	If necessary, rotate, move, and resize both graphics to fit the slide. Reposition the title and subtitle placeholder boxes appropriately on the slide.

SELECTING THEME VARIANTS

By default, the Facet theme uses a green color palette with a white background. In addition, each theme includes a set of variations from which you can choose different color palettes and font families. You will change the variant to one that includes a more interesting background.

1

- **Display slide 1 in Normal view.**

- **Open the Design tab.**

- **Point to each of the four variants and look at the live previews.**

- **Select the last variant.**

Your screen should be similar to Figure 2.38

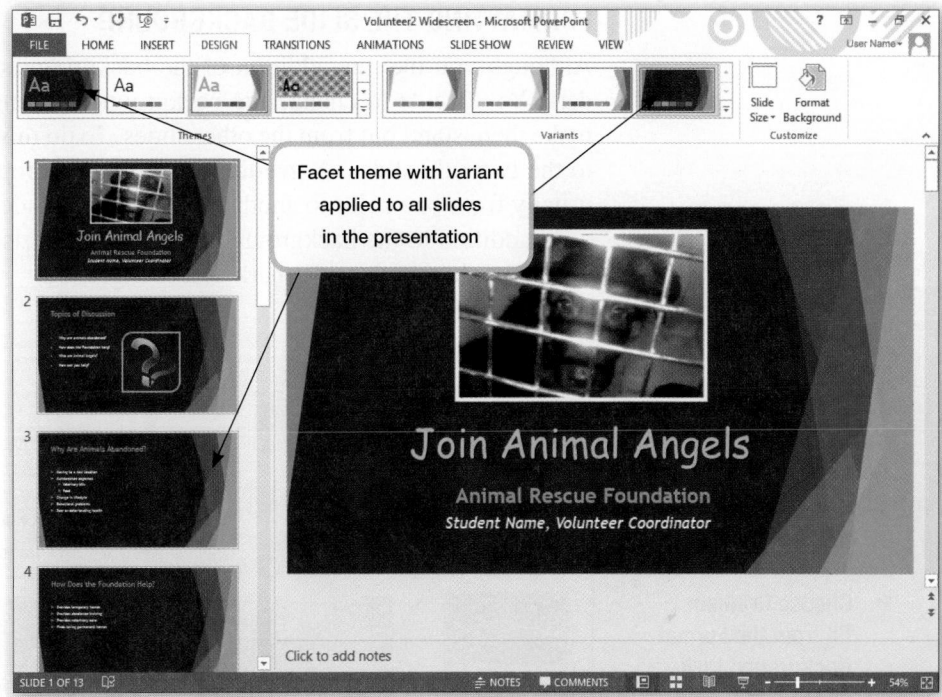

Facet theme with variant applied to all slides in the presentation

Figure 2.38

The selected variant includes light green and white text with a dark blue-gray background on all slides.

FORMATTING THE SLIDE BACKGROUND

Although you like the addition of the background color, you think it is a bit too dark. You decide to change the background shading in the first and last slide to make them stand out from the other slides. To do this, you will add a gradient color to the two title slides. A **gradient** is a gradual progression of colors and shades, usually from one color to another or from one shade to another of the same color.

In addition to the background colors, you can also use texture and pattern fills, a picture, clip art, or watermark as a background.

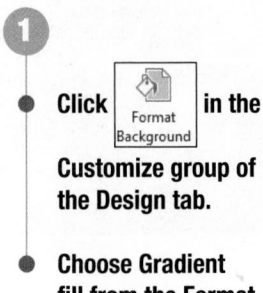

● Click [Format Background] in the **Customize group of the Design tab.**

● Choose **Gradient fill from the Format Background task pane.**

Your screen should be similar to Figure 2.39

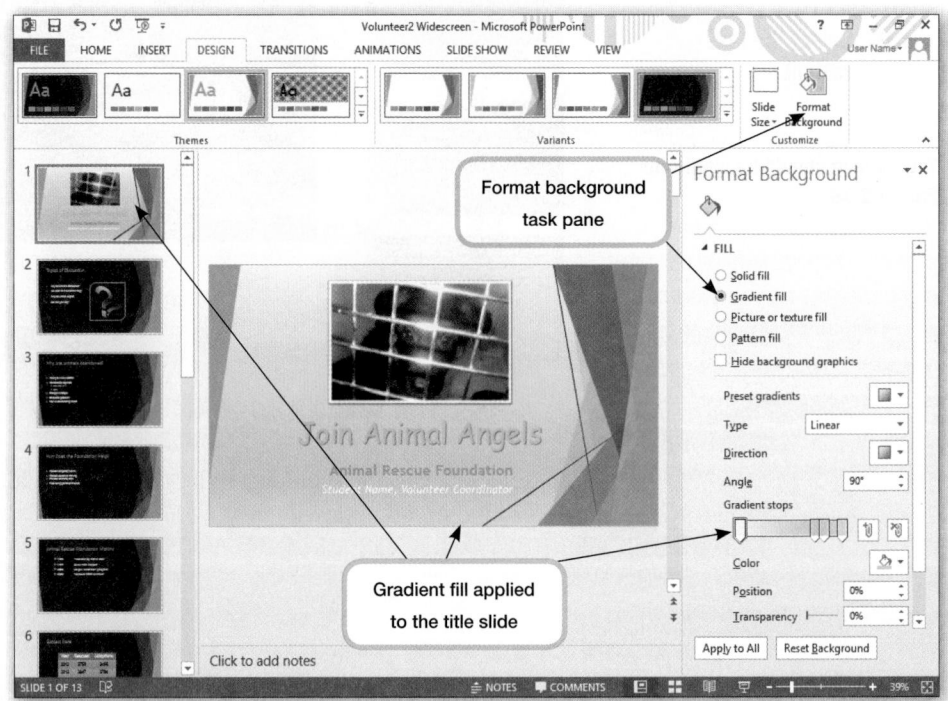

Figure 2.39

Since the original theme (Facet) uses shades of green, the gradient background shows a white to light green progression. The type of fill used by default is linear, from top to bottom. You will make a simple modification of the color so that the progression goes from blue-gray to green and from bottom to top.

2

- Click 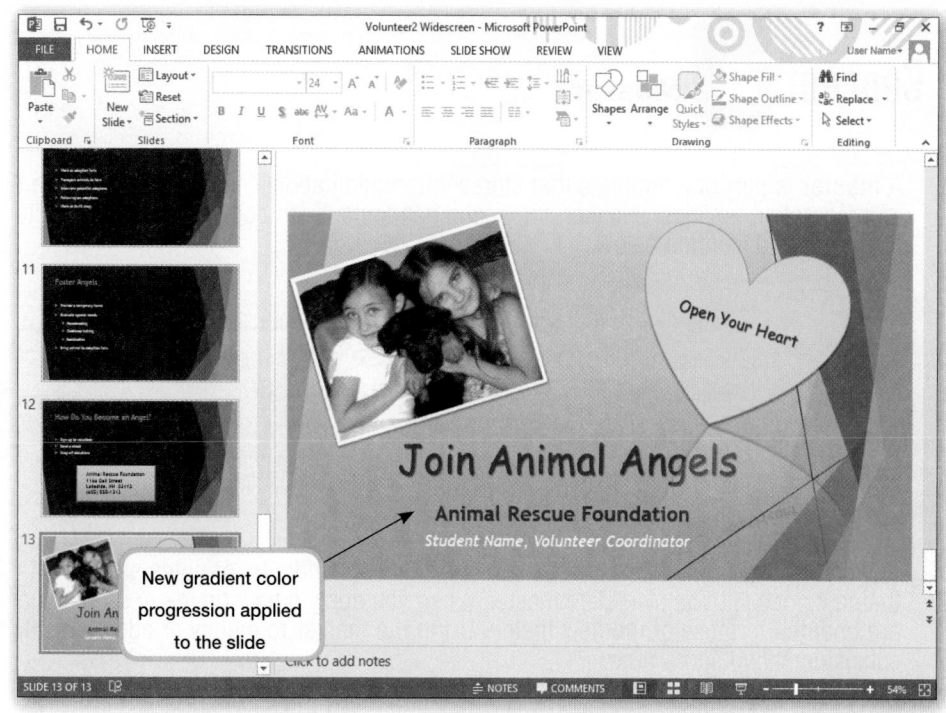 Color and choose Blue-Gray, Background 2, Lighter 60%.

- Click ⬜ ▾ Direction and choose Linear Up (second row, second item).

- Display slide 13 and choose Gradient Fill.

- Close the Format Background pane.

- Change the color of the title and first subtitle line on slides 1 and 13 to Red, Accent 5, Darker 25%.

- Save the presentation.

Your screen should be similar to Figure 2.40

Figure 2.40

When you selected Gradient Fill on the last slide, the changes you made to slide 1 automatically applied to slide 13. Now, both title slides have the same effects for consistency, and both slides stand out.

Working with Master Slides

While viewing the slides, you think the slide appearance could be further improved by changing the font color and bullet design on all slides. Although you can change each slide individually, you can make the change much faster to all the slides by changing the slide master.

Concept 5 Master

A **master** is part of a template that stores information about the formatting for the three key components of a presentation—slides, speaker notes, and handouts. Each component has a master associated with it. The masters are described below.

Slide master	Defines the format and layout of text and objects on a slide, text and object placeholder sizes, text styles, backgrounds, color themes, effects, and animation.
Handout master	Defines the format and placement of the slide image, text, headers, footers, and other elements that will appear on every handout.
Notes master	Defines the format and placement of the slide image, note text, headers, footers, and other elements that will appear on all speaker notes.

Any changes you make to a master affect all slides, handouts, or notes associated with that master. Each theme comes with its own slide master. When you apply a new theme to a presentation, all slides and masters are updated to those of the new theme. Using the master to modify or add elements to a presentation ensures consistency and saves time.

You can create slides that differ from the slide master by changing the format and placement of elements in the individual slide rather than on the slide master. For example, when you changed the font settings of the title on the title slide, the slide master was not affected. Only the individual slide changed, making it unique. If you have created a unique slide, the elements you changed on that slide retain their uniqueness, even if you later make changes to the slide master. That is the reason that the title font did not change when you changed the theme.

MODIFYING THE SLIDE MASTER

You will change the title text font color and the bullet style in the slide master so that all slides in the presentation will be changed.

- Open the View tab.

- Click [Slide Master] in the **Master Views group.**

- Scroll to the top of the slide thumbnail pane.

Your screen should be similar to Figure 2.41

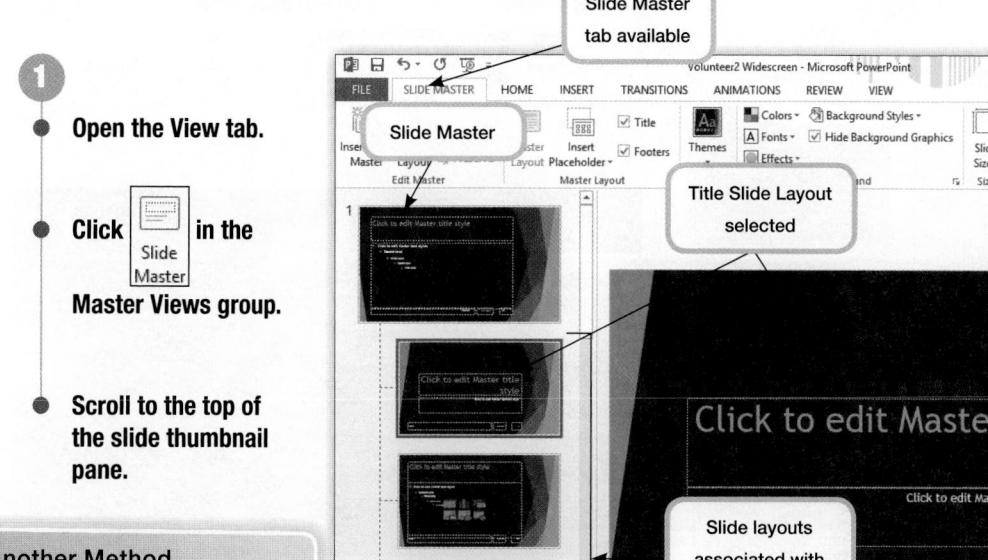

Figure 2.41

Slide Master view consists of two panes: the slide thumbnail pane on the left containing slide thumbnails for the slide master and for each of the layouts associated with the slide master and the Slide pane on the right displaying the selected slide. In the slide thumbnail pane, the slide master is the large thumbnail at the top of the pane. It stores information about the theme and slide layouts of a presentation. Below the slide master are the layouts associated with the slide master. The slide master and all supporting layouts appear in the current theme, Facet, with the color variant you selected. Each slide layout displays a different layout arrangement. The thumbnail for the Title Slide Layout is selected, and the Slide pane displays the slide.

If you modify the slide master, all layouts beneath the slide master are also changed. If you modify a slide layout, although you are essentially also modifying the slide master, the changes affect only that layout under the slide master. You want to change the slide master so that your changes affect all the associated layouts.

2

- Point to the thumbnails to see the ScreenTip.

- Click on the Facet Slide Master thumbnail to select it.

Your screen should be similar to Figure 2.42

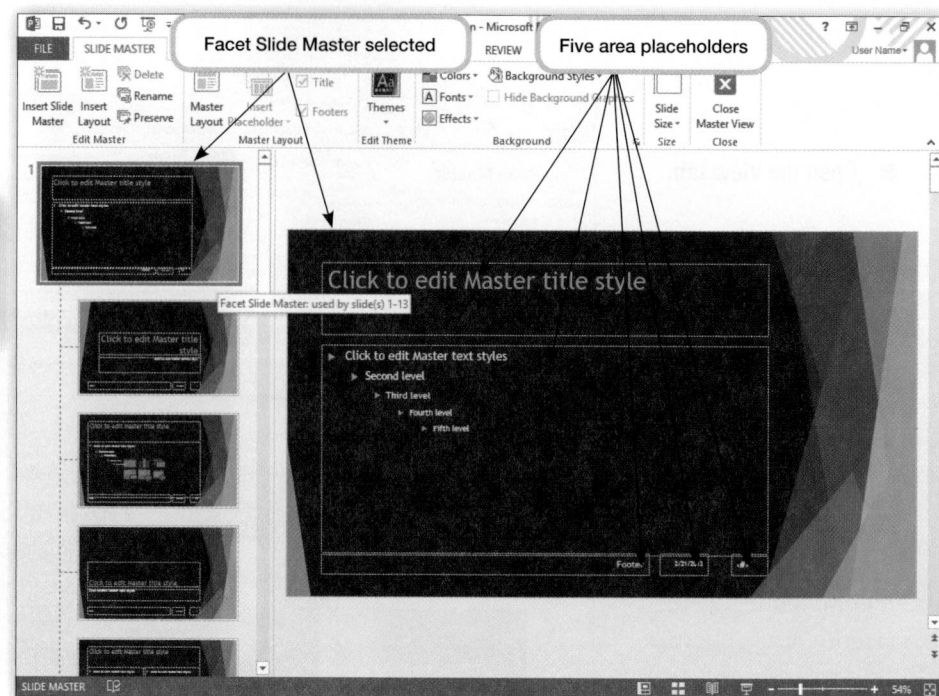

Figure 2.42

The Facet Slide Master consists of five area placeholders that control the appearance of all slides: title, content, date, slide number, and footer. The title and content areas display sample text to show you how changes you make in these areas will appear. You make changes to the slide master in the same way that you change any other slide. First you will change the font color and size for the title text throughout the presentation.

3

- Click on the title area placeholder border to select it.

- Open the Home tab.

- Change the font color to Gold, Accent 3 and bold.

Your screen should be similar to Figure 2.43

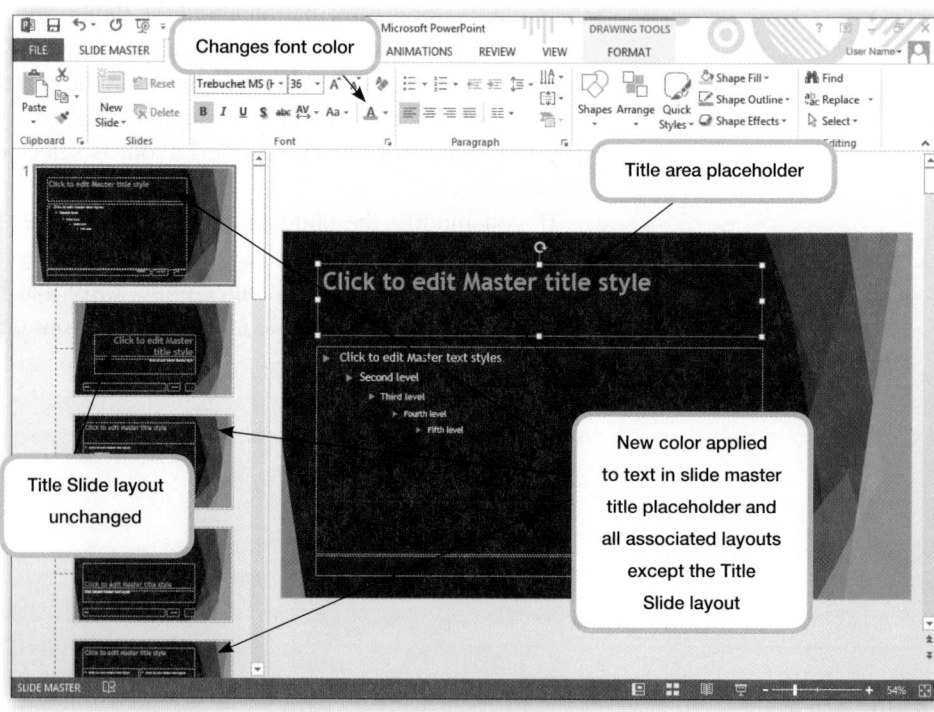

Figure 2.43

4

- Click on the content area placeholder border to select it.

- Open the Bullets drop-down menu.

- Choose Bullets and Numbering.

- Click `Picture...`.

- In the Office.com clip art search box, type **bullets** and press `Enter`.

Having Trouble?

If you do not have Internet access, select another bullet design from the basic designs provided.

Your screen should be similar to Figure 2.44

Notice that the font changes appear in all layouts below the slide master except the Title Slide layout. This is because you changed the format of the title on the individual slides which overrides the changes made to the master slide.

Next, you will modify the content area placeholder to change the bullet style, increase the font size, and modify the position of the placeholder.

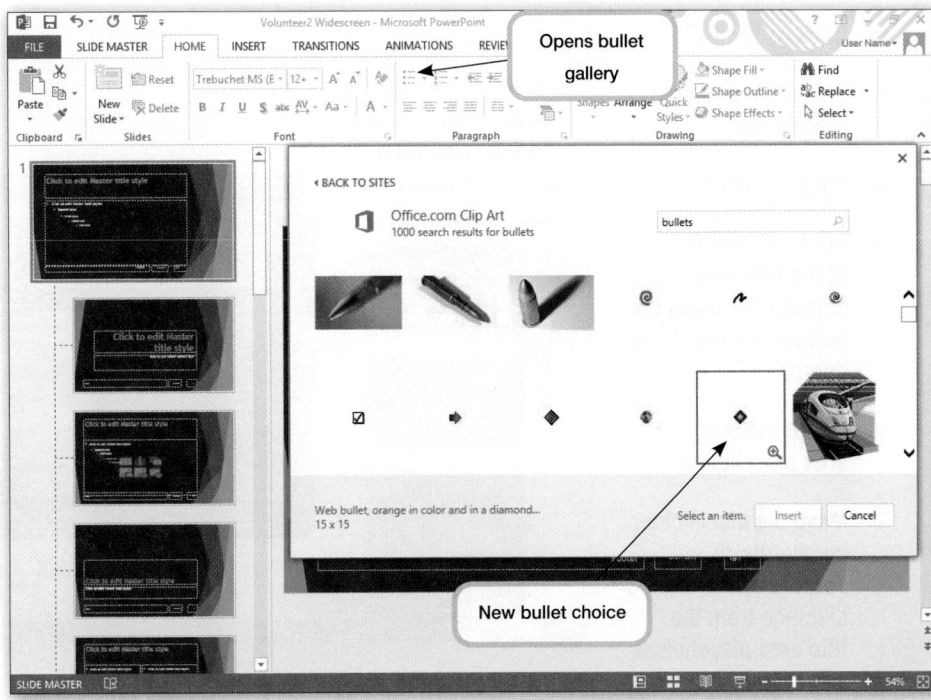

Figure 2.44

From the search results, you select the bullet design you want to use from the bullet styles listed. You will use a diamond-shaped bullet design.

5

- From the search results, choose **Web bullet, orange in color in a diamond shape.**

- Click `Insert`.

Your screen should be similar to Figure 2.45

Additional Information

You can apply different bullet styles to each level by selecting each level individually.

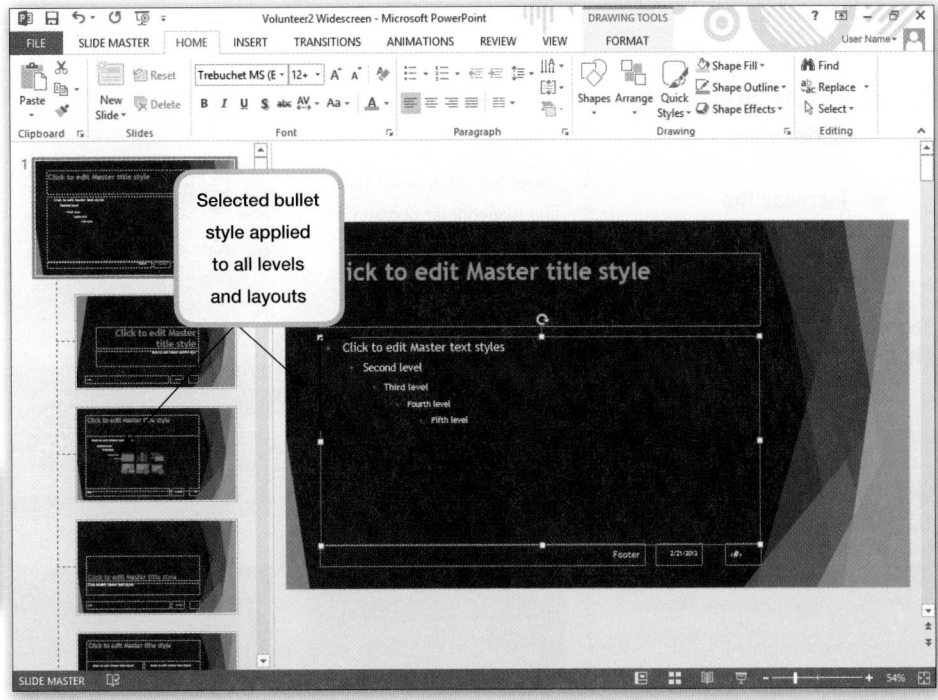

Figure 2.45

Working with Master Slides   **PP2.45**

The selected bullet style has been applied to all levels of items in the content area and to all layouts under the slide master that have bulleted items. Next, you will increase the font size and adjust the size and position of the title and content area placeholders.

6

- If necessary, select the content area placeholder.

- Click [A⌃] twice.

- Select the title area placeholder.

- Click [A⌄] once.

- Decrease the height of the title area placeholder using the bottom, middle sizing handle.

- Select the content area placeholder.

- Move the placeholder up slightly, to decrease the distance from the title area placeholder, as in Figure 2.46.

Your screen should be similar to Figure 2.46

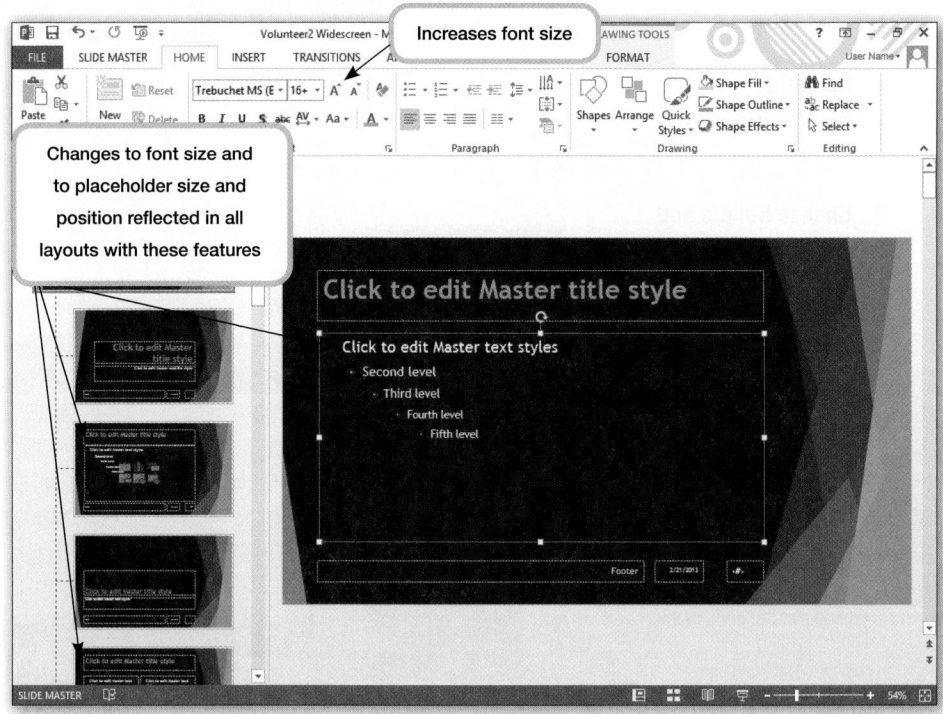

Increases font size

Changes to font size and to placeholder size and position reflected in all layouts with these features

Figure 2.46

Now you want to see how all the changes you have made to the slide master have affected the actual slides in the presentation.

7

- Click [⊞] Slide Sorter view.

- Increase the magnification to 90%.

Your screen should be similar to Figure 2.47

Having Trouble?

With the changes made to the master slide, you may need to resize or reposition a graphic.

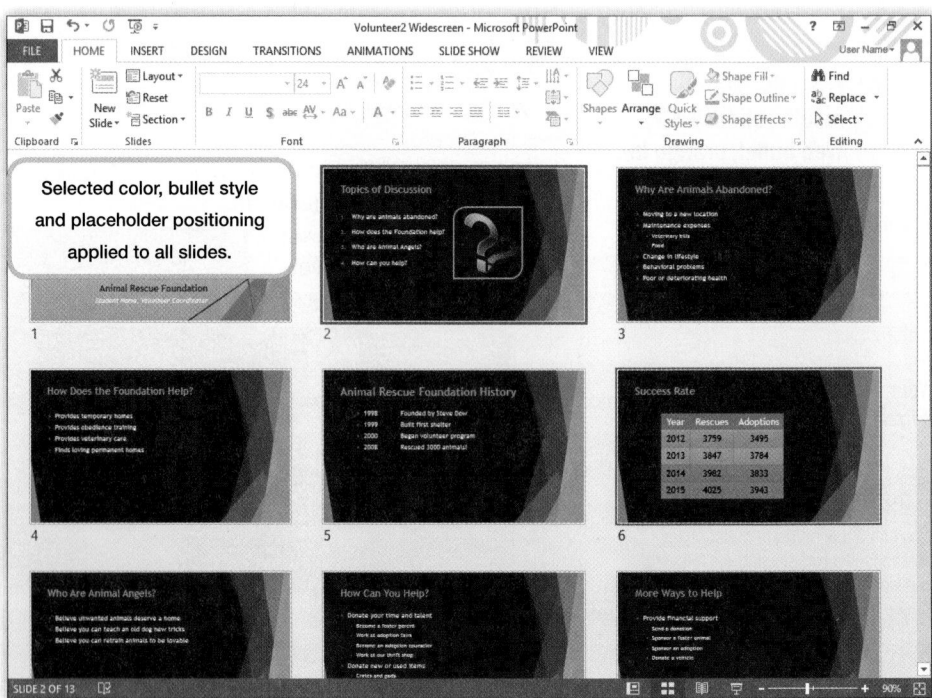

Selected color, bullet style and placeholder positioning applied to all slides.

Figure 2.47

You can now see that the changes you made to the bullet style, font color and size, and positioning of the placeholders in the slide master are reflected in all slides in the presentation with the exception of the Title Layout slides. Using the slide master allows you to quickly make global changes to your presentation.

You will run the slide show next to see how the changes you have made look full screen.

8

● **Run the slide show beginning with slide 1.**

● **Click on each slide to advance through the presentation.**

● **If necessary, fix any slides that did not display correctly.**

● **Save the presentation.**

Now that you are happy with the look of the presentation, you want to incorporate animation effects to change the way the text appears on the slides.

Animating the Presentation

You are pleased with the changes you have made to the presentation so far. However, you have several places in mind where using animation will make the presentation more interesting.

Concept  Animations

Animations are special effects that add action to text and graphics so they move around on the screen during a slide show. Animations provide additional emphasis for items or show the information on a slide in phases. There are two basic types of animations: object animations and transitions.

Object animations are used to display each bullet point, text, paragraph, or graphic independently of the other text or objects on the slide. You set up the way you want each element to appear (to fly in from the left, for instance) and whether you want the other elements already on the slide to dim or shimmer when a new element is added. For example, because your audience is used to reading from left to right, you could select animations that fly text in from the left. Then, when you want to emphasize a point, bring a bullet point in from the right. That change grabs the audience's attention.

Transitions control the way that the display changes as you move from one slide to the next during a presentation. You can select from many different transition choices. You may choose Dissolve for your title slide to give it an added flair. After that, you could use Wipe Right for all the slides until the next to the last, and then use Dissolve again to end the show. As with any special effect, use slide transitions carefully.

When you present a slide show, the content of your presentation should take center stage. You want the animation effects to help emphasize the main points in your presentation—not draw the audience's attention to the special effects.

ADDING TRANSITION EFFECTS

First, you want to add a transition effect to the slides. Although you can add transitions in Normal view, you will use Slide Sorter view so you can more easily preview the action on the slides.

- **Switch to Slide Sorter view, if necessary.**

- **Select slide 1.**

- **Open the Transitions tab.**

- **Click ⌄ More in the Transition to This Slide group to open the Transitions gallery.**

Your screen should be similar to Figure 2.48

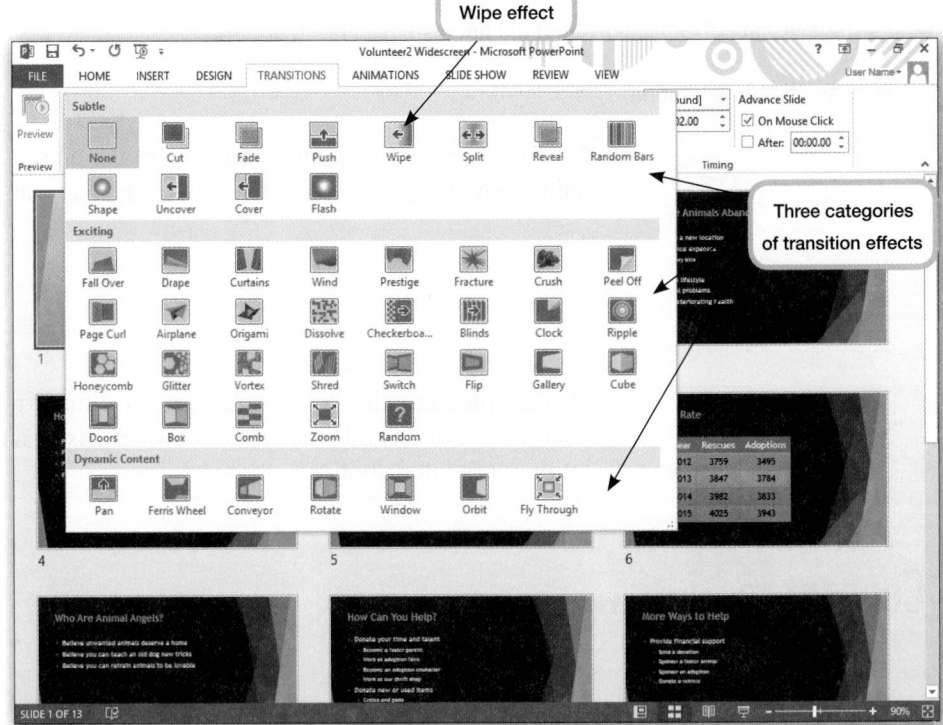

Figure 2.48

Additional Information

Use the None transition option to remove transition effects.

There are three transition categories, Subtle, Exciting, and Dynamic Content, with each containing variations on the category effect. You want to use a simple transition effect that will display as each slide appears. As you choose a transition effect a Live Preview of the effect is displayed on the selected slide.

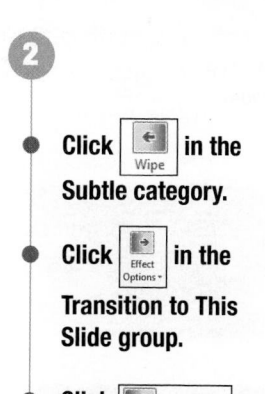

● Click [←] Wipe **in the Subtle category.**

● Click [↓] Effect Options **in the Transition to This Slide group.**

● Click [→] From Left.

Having Trouble?

If you want to see the transition effect again, click ☒ below the slide in Slide Sorter view.

Your screen should be similar to Figure 2.49

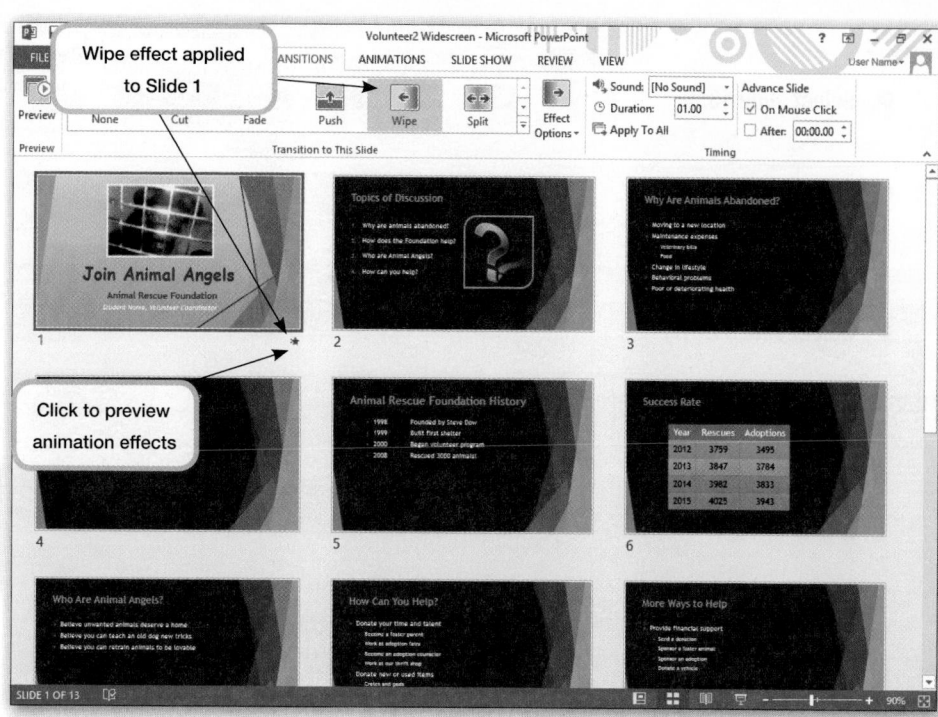

Figure 2.49

Another Method

You can also see the transition effect that is applied to a slide by selecting the slide and clicking [▶] Preview in the Preview group of the Transitions tab.

The selected slide displays the Wipe Left transition effect. This effect displays the next slide's content by wiping over the previous slide from the right with the new slide content. You will use the Wipe Right transition effect on slide 13. You also want to try different transition effects on the other slides using the Random transition effect, which randomly displays a different transition effect for each slide.

Additional Information

You also can select transition effects from the Transitions gallery by scrolling the list in the Transition to This Slide group.

- **Select slide 13.**

- **Click**  **in the Transition to This Slide group.**

- **Select slides 2–12.**

> **Having Trouble?**
>
> Select slide 2 and hold down ⇧Shift while selecting slide 12.

- **Choose** [? Random] **in the Exciting group.**

Your screen should be similar to Figure 2.50

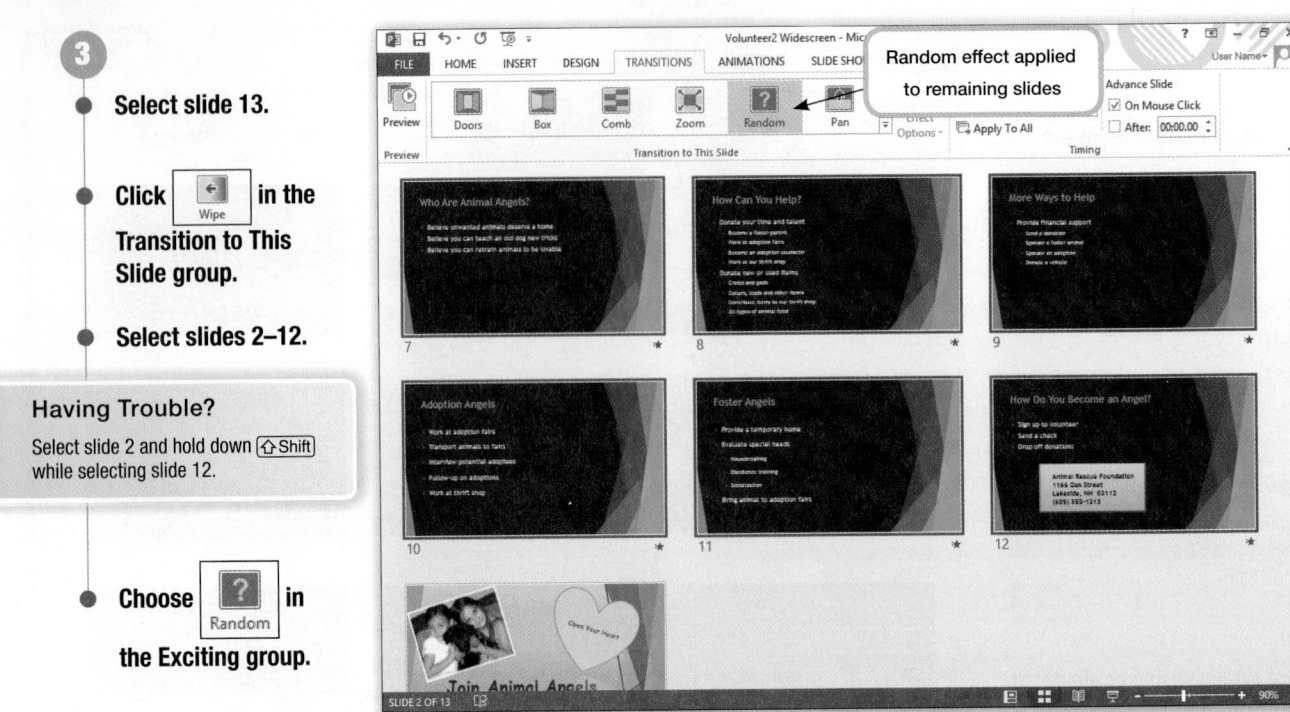

Random effect applied to remaining slides

Figure 2.50

The transition animation effects associated with the selected slides were individually previewed beginning with slide 2, and each slide now displays a transition icon.

4

- **Switch to Normal view.**

- **Save the presentation.**

Notice an animation icon appears below each slide number in the Slides pane.

ANIMATING AN OBJECT

Next, you want to add an animation effect to the heart shape on the final slide. There are four different types of animation effects, described below. Animation effects can be used by themselves or in combination with other effects.

Type	Effect
Entrance	Makes an object appear on the slide using the selected effect.
Exit	Makes an object leave the slide using the selected effect.
Emphasis	Makes an object more noticeable by applying special effects to the object such as changing the text size and colors or adding bold or underlines.
Motion Path	Makes an object move in a selected pattern such as up, down, or in a circle.

1

- Display slide 13 in Normal view.

- Select the heart shape.

- Open the Animations tab.

- Open the Animations gallery and click on several effects to see the Live Preview.

- Choose .

Your screen should be similar to Figure 2.51

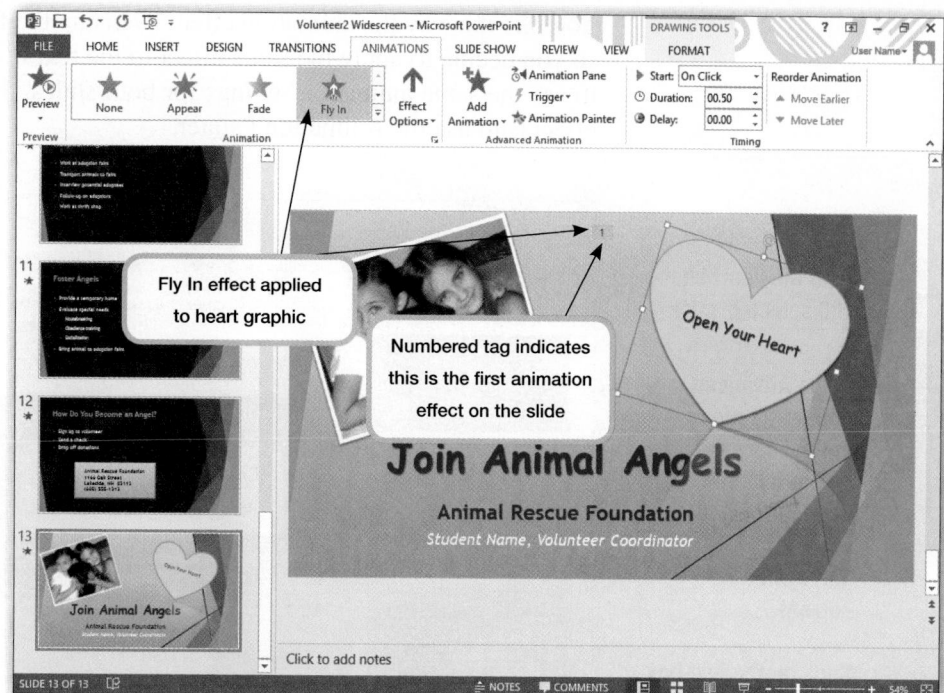

Figure 2.51

As you add animated items to a slide, each item is numbered. The number determines the order in which they display. A nonprinting numbered tag appears on the slide near each animated item that correlates to the effects in the list. This number does not appear during a slide show.

Next, you want to change the Fly In effect to come in from the left and to run slower.

2

- Click [Effect Options] and choose [→ From Left] .

- In the Duration box in the Timing group, increase the duration to 1.00.

- Click [Preview] in the Preview group to preview the new animation settings.

Your screen should be similar to Figure 2.52

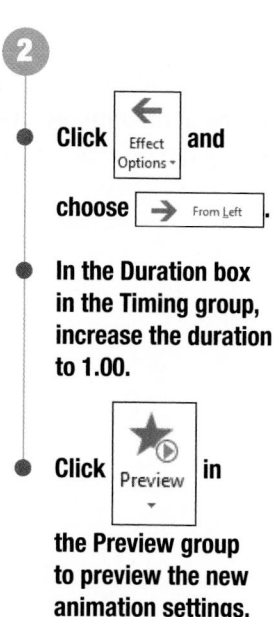

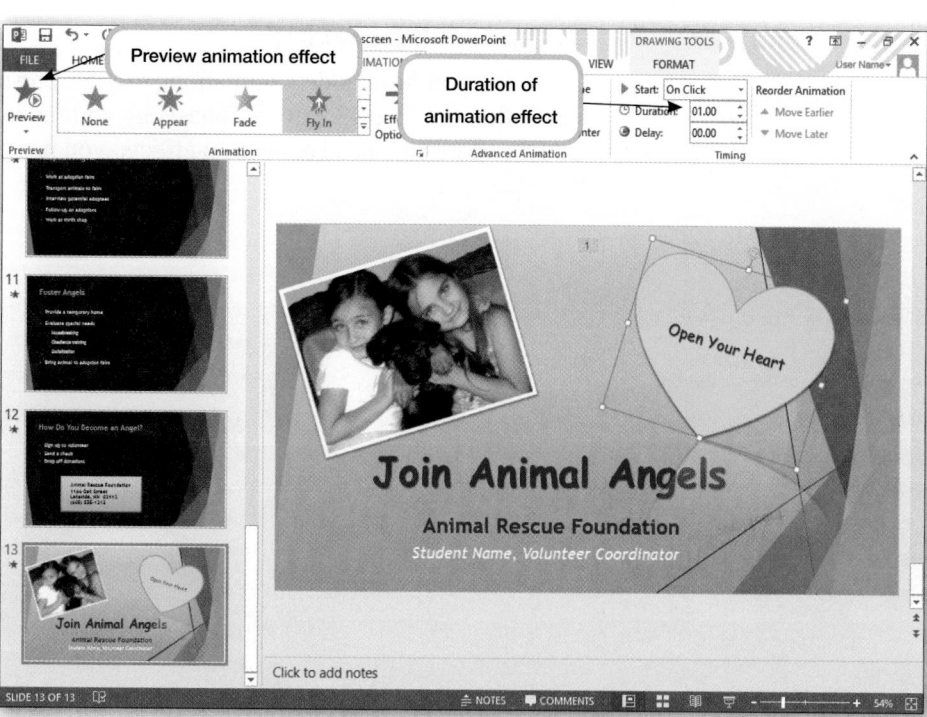

Figure 2.52

You like the way the animation effect livens up the final slide of the presentation, so you decide to apply the same effect to the text box on slide 12. Since you plan to use the same animation settings for both slides, the easiest way to duplicate an effect is to use the Animation Painter.

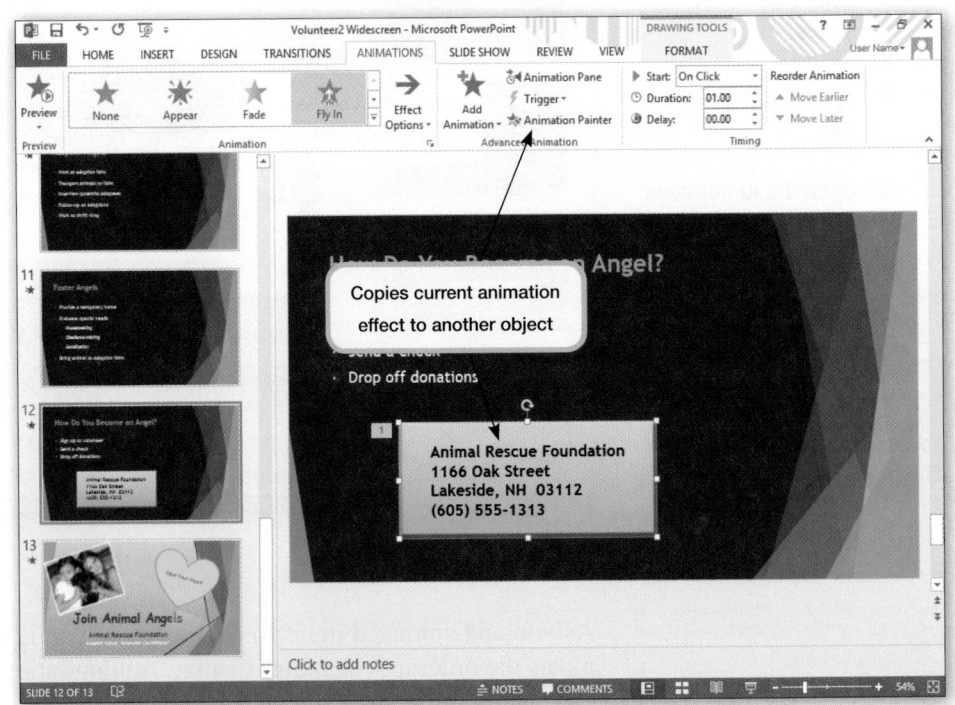

3

- With the heart shape still selected, click ⭐ Animation Painter in the Advanced Animation group to duplicate the animation effect of the heart shape.

- Make slide 12 current.

- Click on the text box to apply the copied effects.

Your screen should be similar to Figure 2.53

Figure 2.53

The Fly In animation effect is applied to the text box and previewed for you.

ADDING SOUND EFFECTS

Now that you have added animations to your presentation, you decide to give the animation on slide 13 extra emphasis by adding sound to the animation effect. To add the more advanced animation effects, you need to display the Animation pane.

- **Select the heart shape on slide 13.**

- **Click** 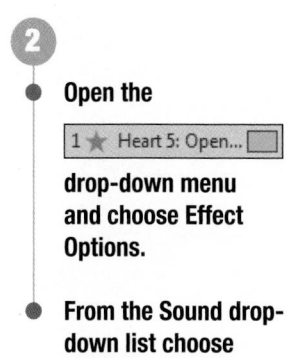 **in the Advanced Animation group.**

- **Click** ▶ Play From **in the Animation pane.**

Your screen should be similar to Figure 2.54

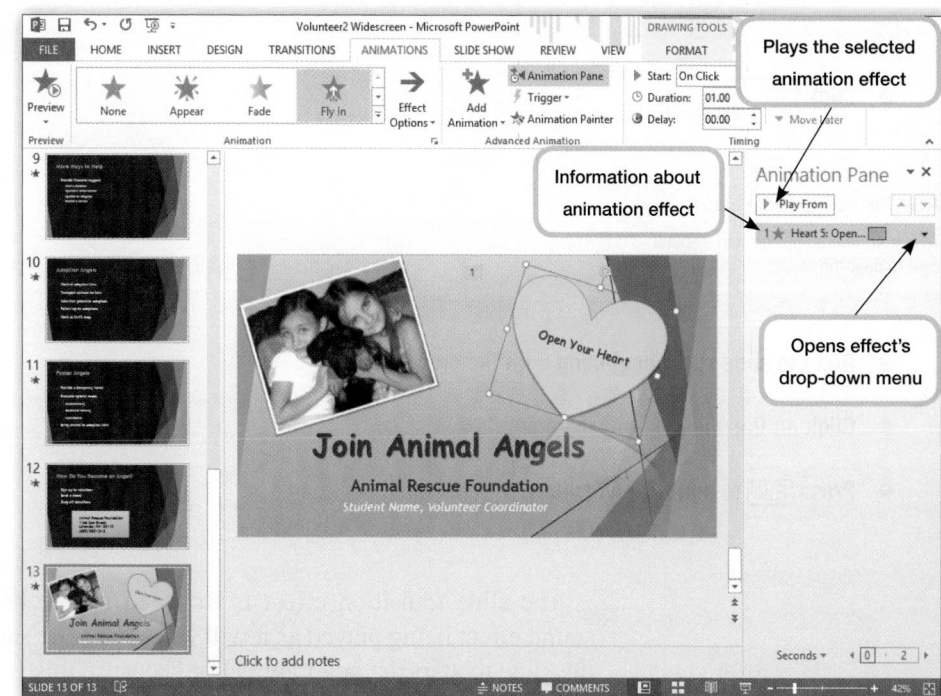

Figure 2.54

The Animation pane shows information about each animation effect on a slide. This includes the type of effect, the order of multiple effects in relation to one another, the name of the object affected, and the duration of the effect. It also is used to manage the animations and to add advanced effects to existing animations. You will use it to add a sound to the Fly In effect.

- **Open the** 1 ⭐ Heart 5: Open... **drop-down menu and choose Effect Options.**

- **From the Sound drop-down list choose Chime.**

Your screen should be similar to Figure 2.55

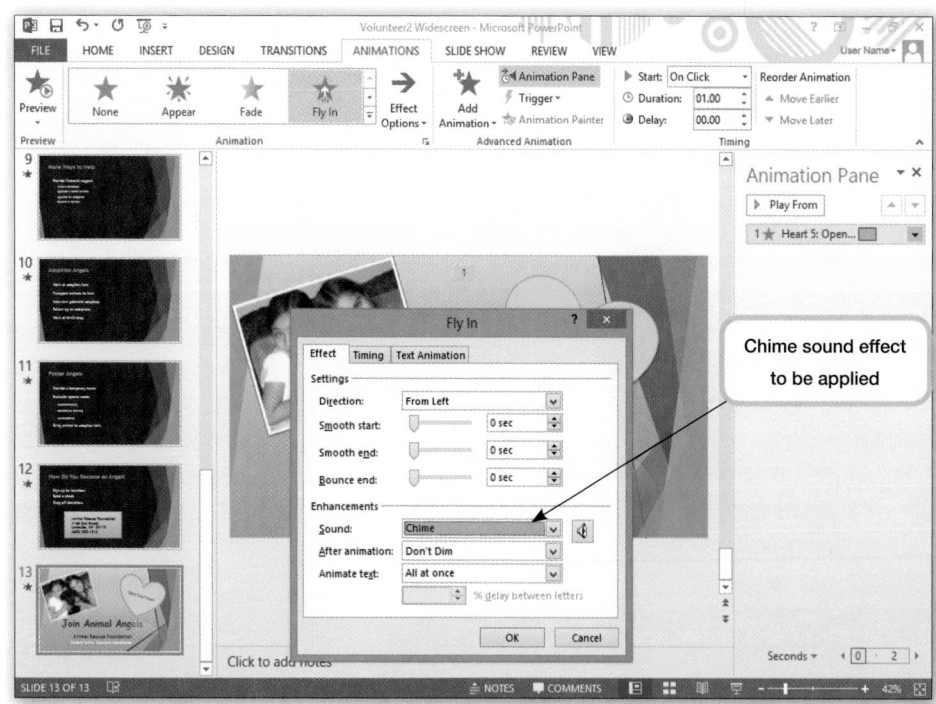

Figure 2.55

The Fly In dialog box is used to change the default settings associated with the selected effect. In this case, you are adding the Chime sound to the animation.

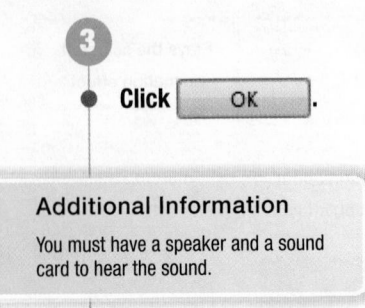

3

● Click [OK].

● Run the slide show beginning with the current slide.

● Click on the slide to start the animation.

● Press [Esc] to end the slide show.

The slide transition effect is followed by the heart fly-in animation and the sound effect being played as it will when the slide show is run. You had to click on the slide to start the heart animation, because this is the default setting to start an animation.

ANIMATING A SLIDE MASTER

The next effect you want to add to the slides is an animation effect that will display each bullet or numbered item progressively on a slide. When the animation is applied to a slide, the slide initially shows only the title. The bulleted text appears as the presentation proceeds. You want to add this effect to all the slides that have bulleted items (slides 2–4 and 7–12). However, you do not want slide 5, which contains the foundation's history, to display with an animation because you want the history to appear all at the same time.

To apply the animation to the bulleted items, you could add the effect to each slide individually. However, when there are many slides, it is faster to add the effect to the slide master so all slides based on the selected slide layout display the effect. You will move to slide 2, the first slide in the presentation to use bullets, and apply the animation effects to the associated slide layout under the slide master.

1

- Make slide 2 current.

- Change to Slide Master view.

- Point to the selected slide layout thumbnail to see the ScreenTip and confirm that the correct slides will be affected (Title and Content Layout: used by slide(s) 2 – 4, 6 – 12).

- Select the content placeholder.

- Open the Animations tab.

- Scroll the Animation gallery and click 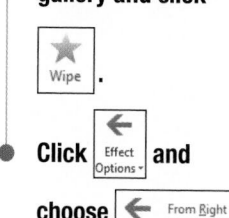.

- Click [Effect Options] and choose [From Right].

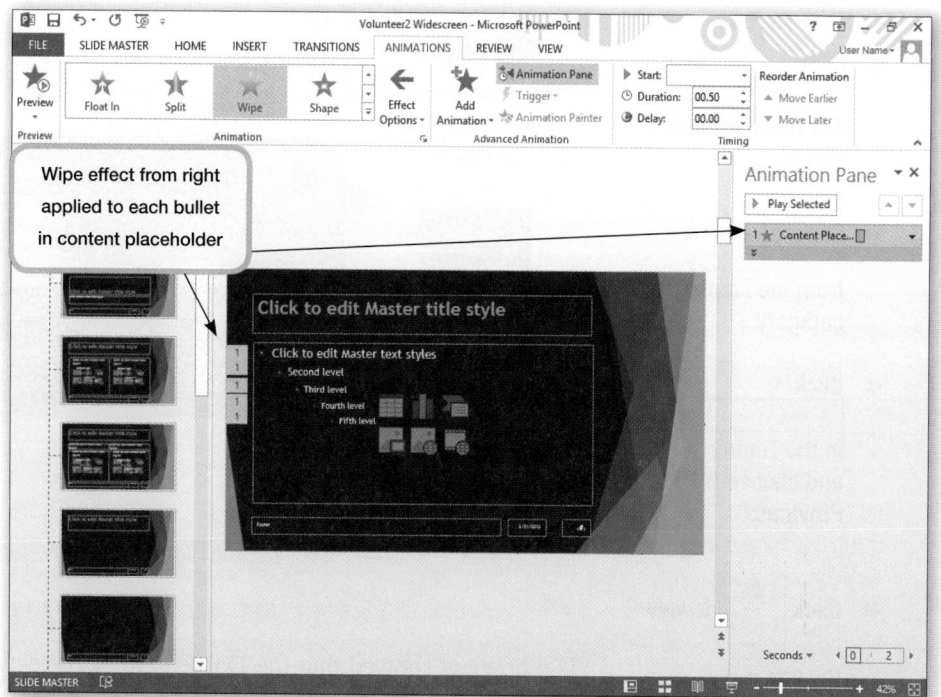

Figure 2.56

Animation icons appear next to each bulleted item in the content placeholder, and the Animation pane displays the information about the animation. The preview demonstrated how this effect will appear on the slide. Although the slide master preview does not show it, each bullet will appear individually on the slide. You can confirm this because a number tab appears next to each bullet in the content area indicating that the effect will be applied to each line.

Your screen should be similar to Figure 2.56

You also want to add a second animation effect to give more emphasis to the bulleted items. You will add the Darken animation effect and change the Start timing setting associated with the effect. The Start settings control the method used to advance the animation for each bullet item while you run the slide show. The default Start setting, On Click, means you need to click the mouse to start each animation effect. You want the Darken effect to begin automatically after the first animation effect is finished.

2

- Select the content placeholder again.

- Click **Add Animation** in the **Advanced Animation group**.

- Choose **Darken** from the Emphasis category.

- Click **Start:** in the Timing group and choose After Previous.

- Click **Preview** to view the effect.

Your screen should be similar to Figure 2.57

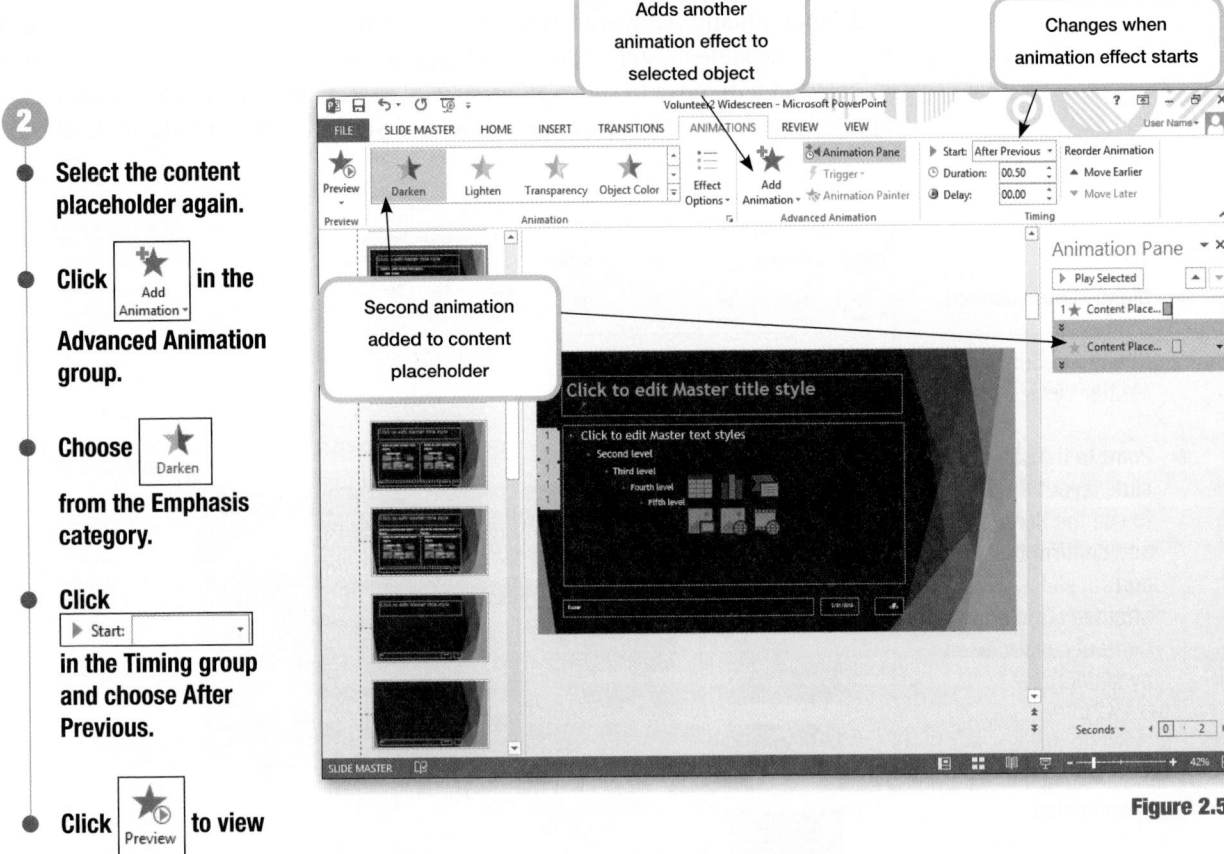

Figure 2.57

The preview showed that the Darken effect correctly started after the Wipe effect ended. You are concerned, however, that the timing for the Wipe effect is too fast and the Darken emphasis is too subtle. You will lengthen the duration for the Wipe effect and change the Darken emphasis to another.

3

- Click on  in the Animation pane to select it.

- **Increase the Duration setting in the Timing group to 3.00.**

- Click on [★ Content Place... ▾] in the Animation pane to select it.

- Choose [★ **B** / Bold Reveal] from the Emphasis group of the Animation gallery.

- Click [▶ Play Selected].

Your screen should be similar to Figure 2.58

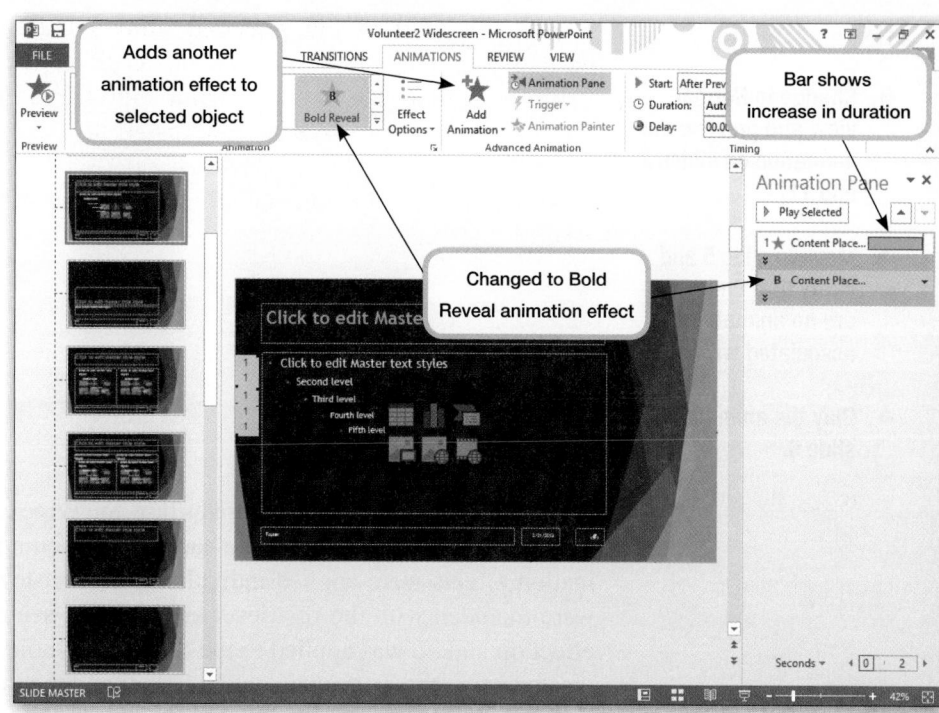

Figure 2.58

The changes in the animation effects are shown in the Animation pane and have been applied to slides 2–4 and 6–12. To check how the animation effects actually appear in a slide, you will return to Normal view and preview the animations.

Additional Information

The bar in each effect in the Animation pane indicates the length of the duration.

4

- Change to Normal view and preview the animation on slides 2 and 11.

- Move to slide 5 and verify that there are no animations associated with it.

- Play the animation on slide 6.

On slide 2, the preview demonstrates how the Wipe effect and then the Bold Reveal emphasis appears one-by-one on each bullet. You noticed on slide 11 that the animation effects were applied individually to first-level bullets, and any subbullets were included with the first-level bullets. This seems appropriate. The animation effect on slide 6 was applied to the table as a whole. This is because the slide was created using the Title and Content layout and the table is considered a single bulleted item.

CHANGING AND REMOVING ANIMATION EFFECTS

You want to remove the animation from slide 6. However, because the animation is associated with the slide master, removing it would remove it from all slides using that layout. Instead, you will change the slide layout to another layout that does not have an animation associated with it. Then you will add some other animation effects to this slide and apply these same effects to slide 5.

- Change the slide layout of slide 6 to the Title Only layout.

Having Trouble?
Open the Home tab and click

- Center the table in the slide space.

- Select the title placeholder and apply the Fly In from Left animation.

- Change the Start setting to With Previous and change the duration to 1.00.

- Apply the Random Bars animation with a duration of 2.00 to the table object.

- Preview the animations.

- Use the Animation Painter to copy the animation from the title placeholder of slide 6 to the title placeholder of slide 5.

- Use the Animation Painter to copy the table animation from slide 6 to both content placeholders on slide 5.

Additional Information

To apply the animation to multiple objects, double-click 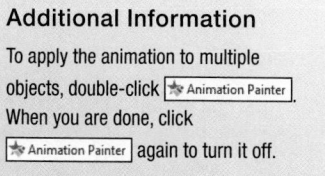. When you are done, click 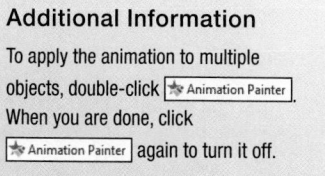 again to turn it off.

- Preview the animations on slide 5.

Your screen should be similar to Figure 2.59

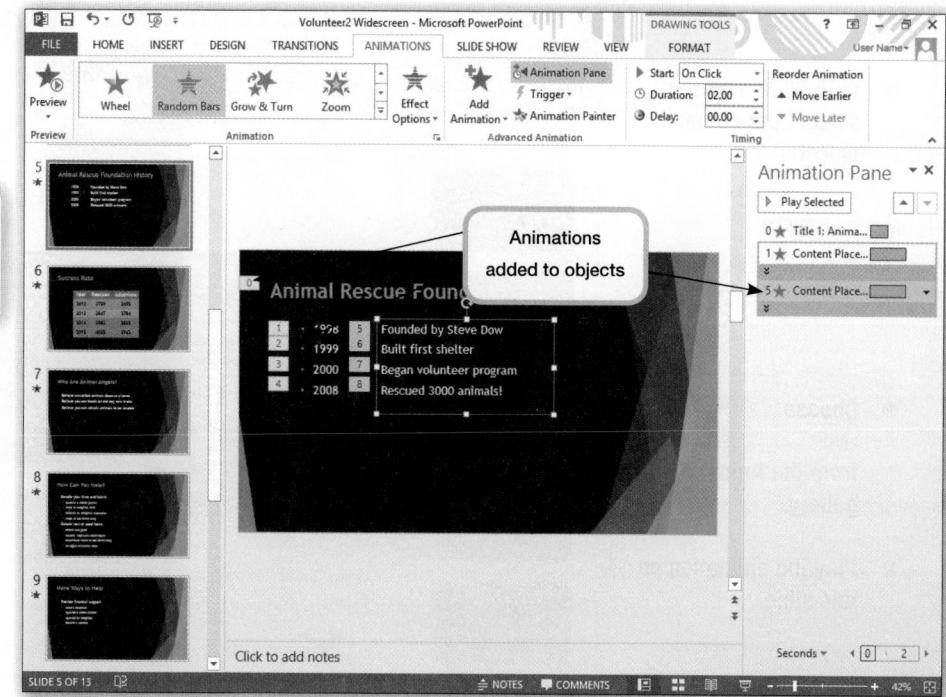

Figure 2.59

You like the title animation; however, you decide to remove the animations associated with the two content placeholders.

2

- With Slide 5 current, select both content placeholders.

- Choose [None star icon] from the Animation gallery.

- Play the animation on this slide.

Your screen should be similar to Figure 2.60

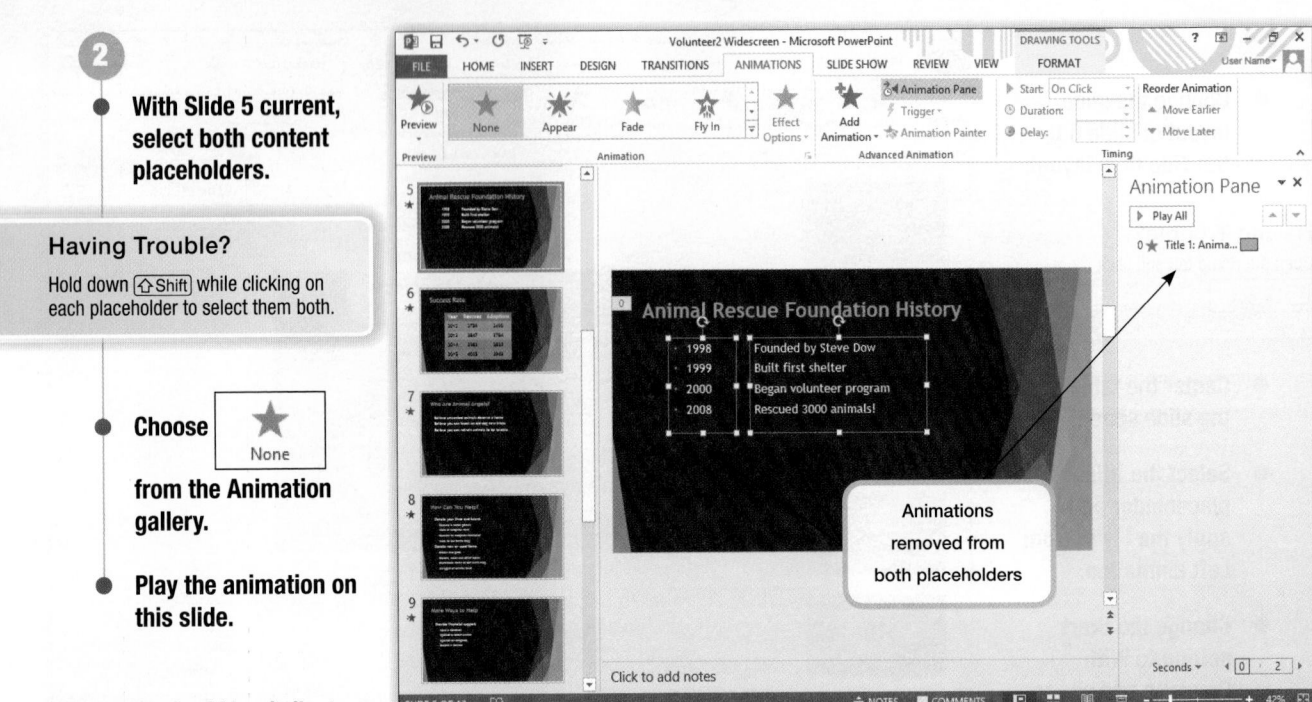

Figure 2.60

Now the only animation on this slide is the Fly In affect of the title placeholder. Be careful when using animations, as sometimes too many animation effects distract from the slide content. You think your animation changes will add interest without making the presentation appear too lively.

3

- Close the Animation pane.

- Save the presentation.

To see how the transitions and animations work together, you will run the slide show next.

As you run the slide show to see the animation effects, you will also practice preparing for the presentation. As much as you would like to control a presentation completely, the presence of an audience usually causes the presentation to change course. PowerPoint has several ways to control a slide show during the presentation.

NAVIGATING IN A SLIDE SHOW

Running the slide show and practicing how to control the slide show help you to have a smooth presentation. For example, if someone has a question about a previous slide, you can go backward and redisplay it. You will try out some of the features you can use while running the slide show.

1

- Start the slide show from the beginning.

- Click to advance to slide 2.

- Click 4 times to display the four bullets.

Your screen should be similar to Figure 2.61

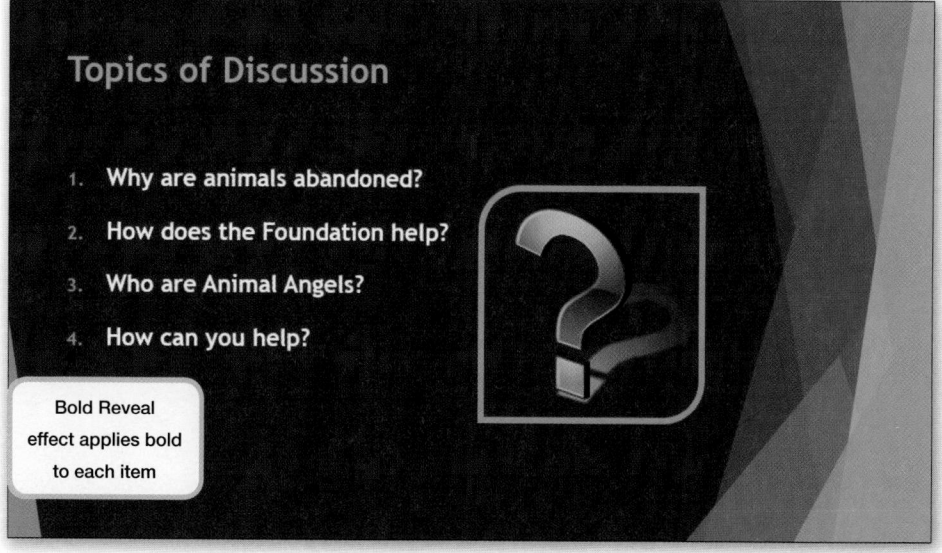

Figure 2.61

Another Method

You can also use the mouse wheel to move forward or backward through a presentation.

The first slide appeared using the Wipe From Left transition effect associated with the slide. The second slide appeared using a random transition effect. Each bulleted item on slide 2 appeared when you clicked using the Wipe animation effect, and the Bold Reveal animation effect started automatically as soon as the last bullet appeared.

When an animation is applied to the content area of a slide, the content items are displayed only when you click or use any of the procedures to advance to the next slide. This is because the default setting to start an animation is On Click. This allows the presenter to focus the audience's attention and to control the pace of the presentation. The Bold Reveal associated with slide 2 started automatically because you changed the Start setting to After Previous.

2

- Continue to click or press [Spacebar] until the title of slide 8, "How Can You Help?" appears.

- Press [Backspace] (5 times).

Additional Information

You can return to the first slide in the presentation by holding down both mouse buttons for two seconds.

Your screen should be similar to Figure 2.62

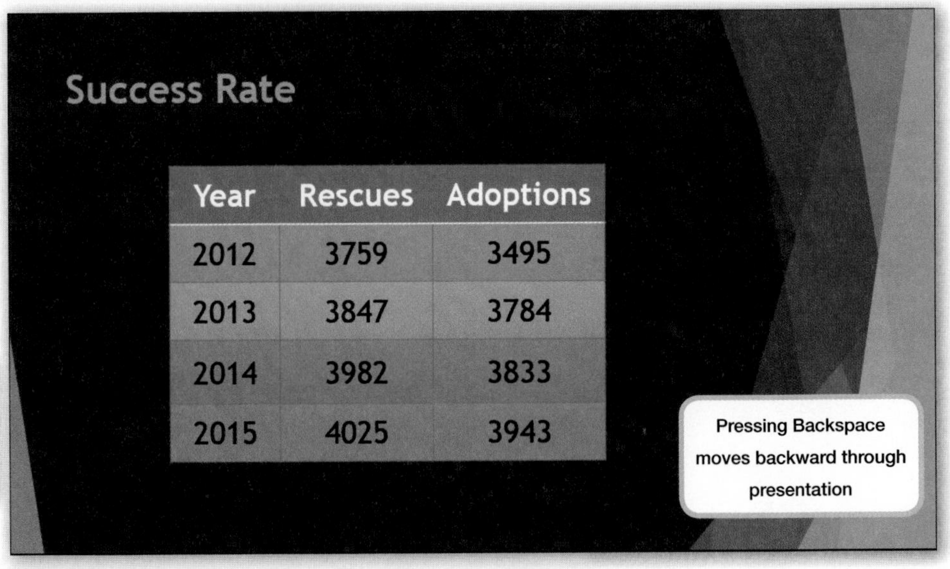

Figure 2.62

You returned the onscreen presentation to slide 6, but now, because the audience has already viewed slide 7, you want to advance to slide 8. To go to a specific slide number, you type the slide number and press [Enter].

3

- Type **8** and press [Enter].

Another Method

You also can choose Go to Slide from the shortcut menu and select a slide to display.

- Click two times to display the bulleted items.

- Click again to display slide 9.

Your screen should be similar to Figure 2.63

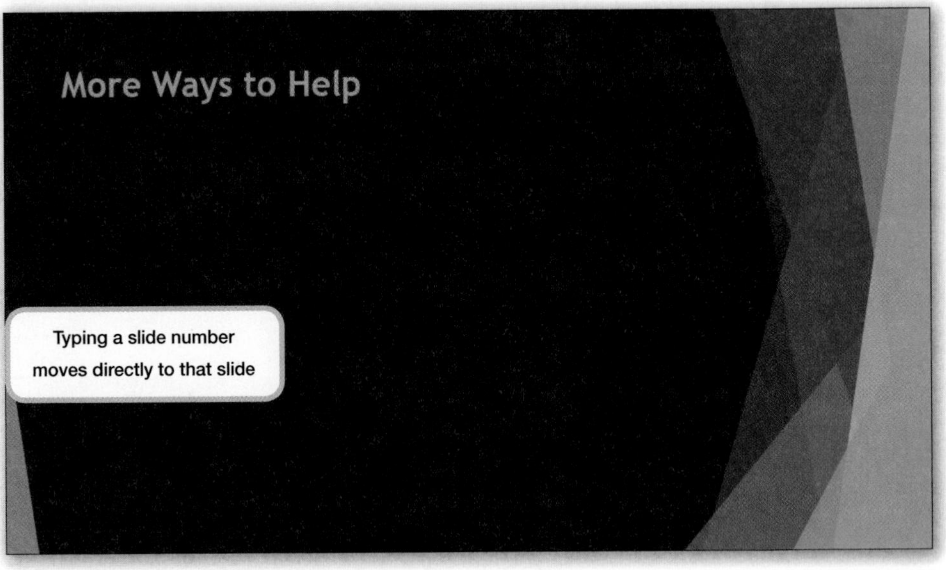

Figure 2.63

Slide 9, More Ways to Help, is displayed.

Sometimes a question from an audience member can interrupt the flow of the presentation. If this happens to you, you can black out the screen to focus attention on your response.

Press b or B.

Additional Information

You also can white out the screen by pressing W.

The screen goes to black while you address the topic. When you are ready to resume the presentation, you can bring the slide back.

5

Click, or press b.

Click to display the bulleted items on slide 9.

ADDING FREEHAND ANNOTATIONS

During your presentation, you may want to point to an important word, underline an important point, or draw check marks next to items that you have covered. To do this, you can use the mouse pointer during the presentation. When you move the mouse, the mouse pointer appears and the **Slide Show control bar** (shown on Figure 2.64) is displayed in the lower-left corner of the screen.

Icon	Description
◀	Displays the previous slide.
▶	Displays the next slide.
✎	Provides pen and laser pointer tools to add annotations to slides.
▦	Shows thumbnails of all slides, making it easy to quickly jump to any slide.
🔍	Zooms in to a portion of the slide to show greater detail.
⋯	Provides options to hide/show Presenter view, black or white out the screen, change display and arrow settings, and end the slide show.

The mouse pointer in its current shape ⟶ can be used to point to items on the slide. You also can change it to a laser pointer, a pen, or a highlighter.

1

- Move the mouse on your desktop to display the mouse pointer and the Slide Show control bar.

- Click [⊘] in the Slide Show control bar to display the Pointer Options menu.

Another Method

You also can select Pointer Options from the shortcut menu.

Your screen should be similar to Figure 2.64

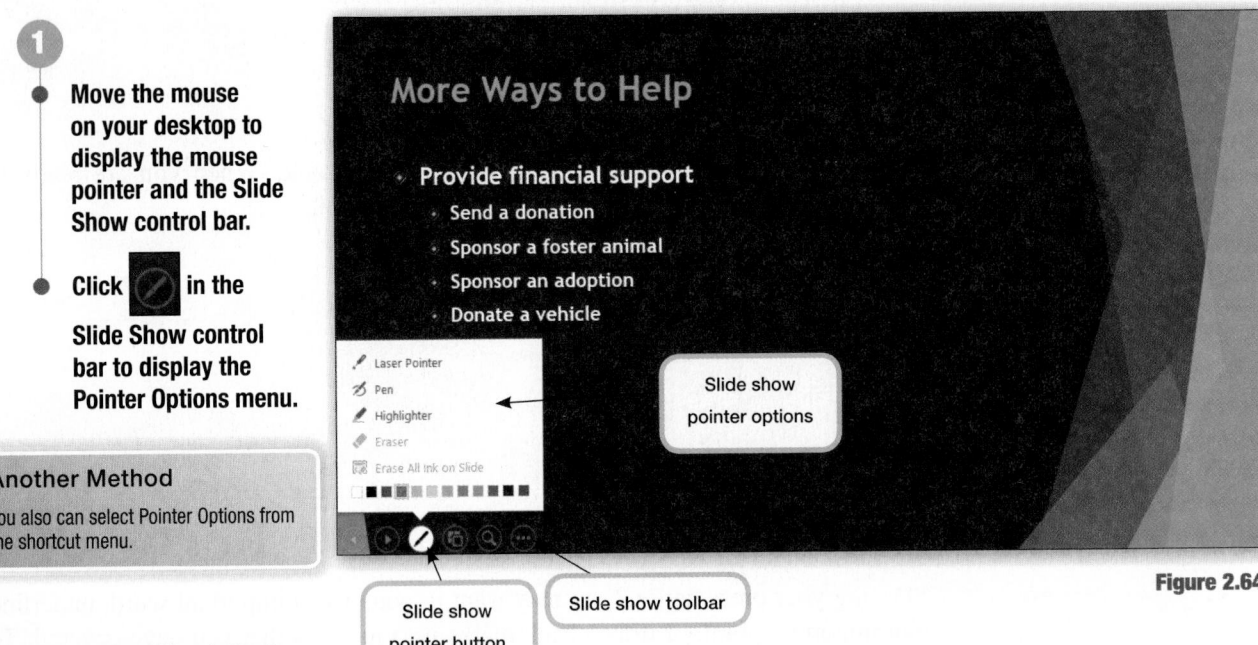

Figure 2.64

The pointer options are described in the following table.

Pointer Options	Effect
Laser Pointer	Changes the mouse pointer to a red laser tip for emphasis.
Pen	Changes the mouse pointer to a ballpoint pen for annotation.
Highlighter	Changes the mouse pointer to a highlighter.
Eraser	Changes the mouse pointer to an eraser to remove selected annotations.
Erase All Ink on Slide	Removes all annotations from the slide.

You will try out several of the freehand annotation features to see how they work. To use the slide annotation features, first select the pointer style and then drag the pointer in the direction you want to draw.

2

- Choose Pen.

Another Method
You also can use [Ctrl] + P to display the Pen.

- Point near the word "Send" and then drag until a circle is drawn around the word "Send".

- Choose Light Blue from the Colors bar of the Pointer Options menu.

- Draw three lines under the word "Help"

- Choose Highlighter from the Pointer Options menu and highlight the word "donation".

Your screen should be similar to Figure 2.65

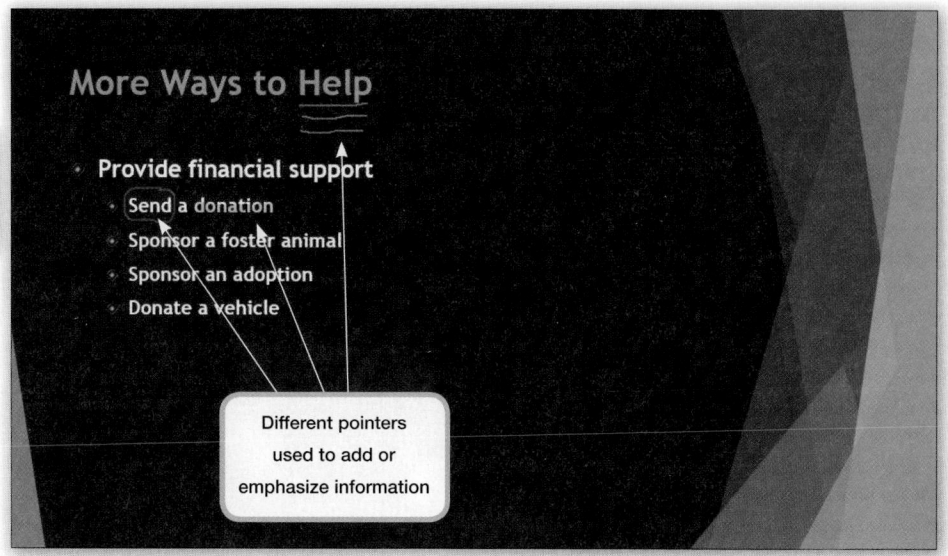

Figure 2.65

The freehand annotation feature allows you to point out and emphasize important information on a slide during the presentation.

3

- Practice using the freehand annotator to draw any shapes you want on the slide.

- To erase the annotations, choose Erase All Ink on Slide from the Pointer Options menu.

Another Method
The keyboard shortcut to erase annotations is E.

- To turn off freehand annotation, click on the tool you are using in the Pointer Options menu to toggle it off or press [Esc].

Another Method
You also can use [Ctrl] + A to display the arrow or right-click on the slide to display the shortcut menu; select Pointer Options, Arrow Options; and choose Automatic to turn off freehand annotation.

Another feature that you can use to emphasize information on a slide is to change the mouse pointer to a laser pointer.

4

- Click to display the five bulleted items on slide 10.

- Choose Laser Pointer from the Pointer Options menu.

Additional Information

You can control the color of the laser light by clicking Set Up Slideshow on the Slide Show tab. You can then click the Laser pointer color drop-down list to choose a different color.

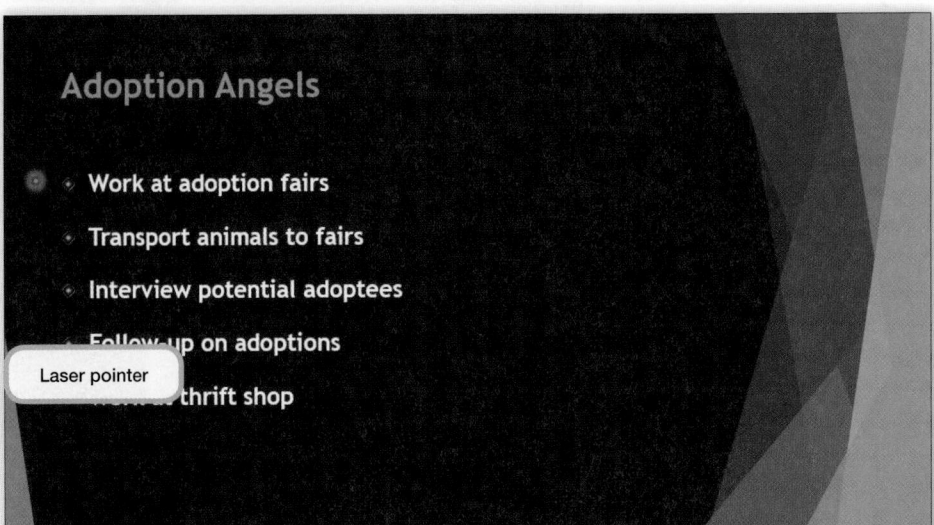

Adoption Angels

- Work at adoption fairs
- Transport animals to fairs
- Interview potential adoptees
- Follow-up on adoptions

Laser pointer

thrift shop

Figure 2.66

- Use the laser pointer to point to the first bulleted item on the slide.

Your screen should be similar to Figure 2.66

The laser pointer is much brighter than the regular mouse pointer.

If you do not erase annotations before ending the presentation, you are prompted to keep or discard the annotations when you end the slide show. If you keep the annotations, they are saved to the slides and will appear as part of the slide during a presentation.

Another Method

If you press Ctrl and hold down the left mouse button, you can temporarily turn on the laser pointer.

Adding Speaker Notes

When making your presentation, there are some critical points you want to be sure to discuss. To help you remember the important points, you can add notes to a slide and then print the **notes pages**. These pages display the notes below a small version of the slide they accompany. You can create notes pages for some or all of the slides in a presentation. You decide to add speaker notes on slide 9 to remind you to suggest foster care donations.

1

- Press Esc to end the slide show.

- Display slide 9 in Normal view.

- Increase the size of the Notes pane to that shown in Figure 2.67.

Having Trouble?

Adjust the size of the notes pane by dragging the pane splitter bar.

- Click in the Notes pane and type the following:

  Suggested foster animal donations per month

  Cat: $10

  Dog: $15/small $20/medium $25/large

Having Trouble?

Press Enter to begin a new line and Tab to separate the dollar amounts.

Your screen should be similar to Figure 2.67

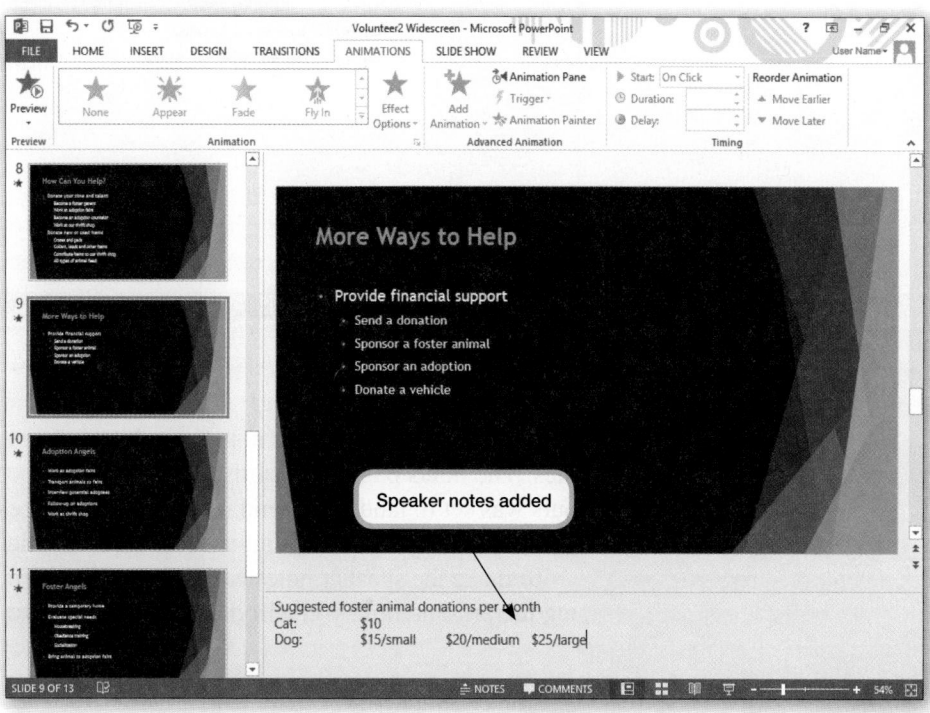

Figure 2.67

You will preview the notes page to check its appearance before it is printed.

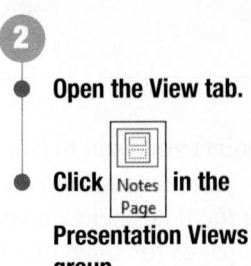

2

● Open the View tab.

● Click [Notes Page] in the Presentation Views group.

Your screen should be similar to Figure 2.68

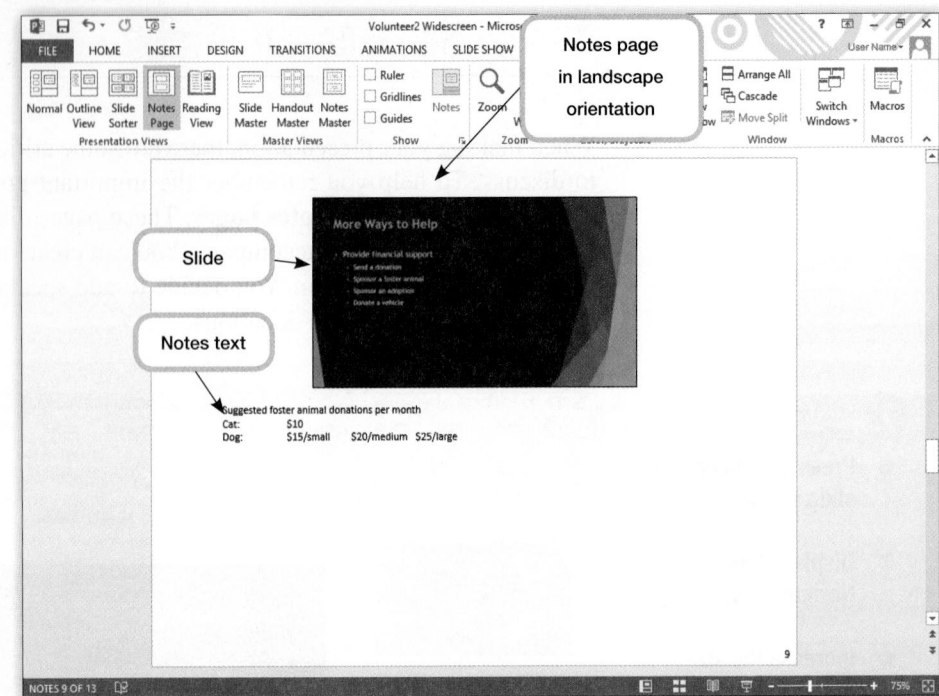

Figure 2.68

The notes pages display the note you added below the slide that the note accompanies. The notes page is in landscape orientation because the orientation for handouts was set to landscape (end of Lab 1). The page orientation setting affects both handouts and notes pages and is saved with the file.

To make the speaker notes easier to read in a dimly lit room while you are making the presentation, you will increase the font size of the note text.

3

● Click on the note text to select the placeholder.

● Click on the placeholder border to select the entire object.

● Increase the font size to 20.

● Click outside the note text border.

Your screen should be similar to Figure 2.69

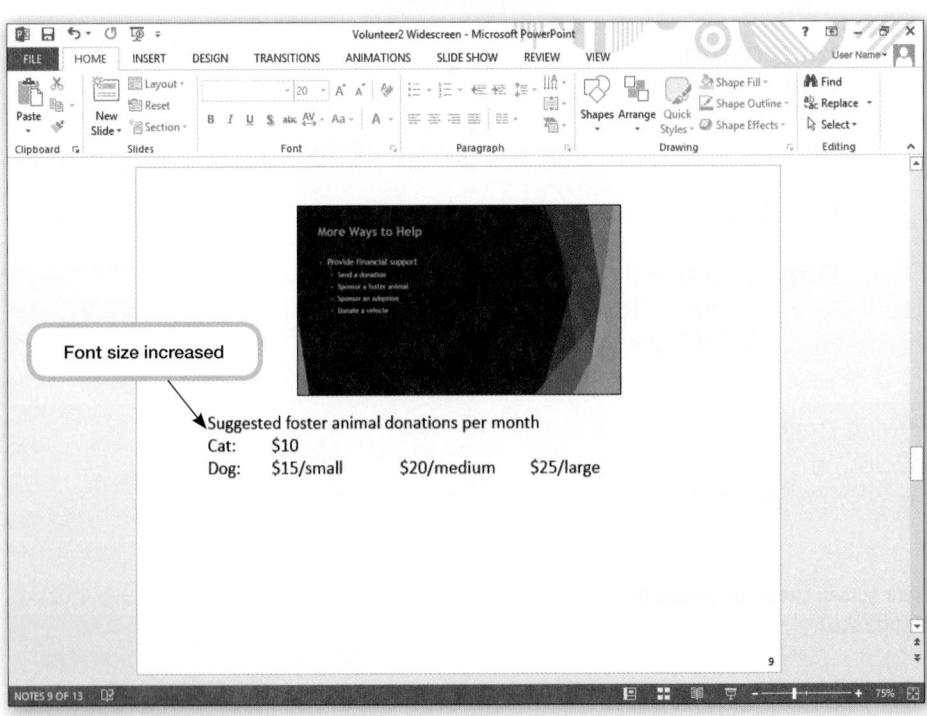

Figure 2.69

Adding Headers and Footers

Currently, the only information that appears in the footer of the notes page is the page number. You want to include additional information in the header and footer of the notes and handouts. The header and footer typically display information inside the margin space at the top and bottom of each printed page. Additionally, slides also may include header and footer information.

ADDING A HEADER TO A NOTES PAGE

You want to include the date and your name in the header of the notes pages.

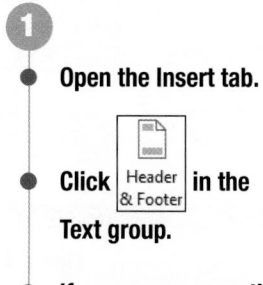

- Open the Insert tab.

- Click Header & Footer in the Text group.

- If necessary, open the Notes and Handouts tab.

Your screen should be similar to Figure 2.70

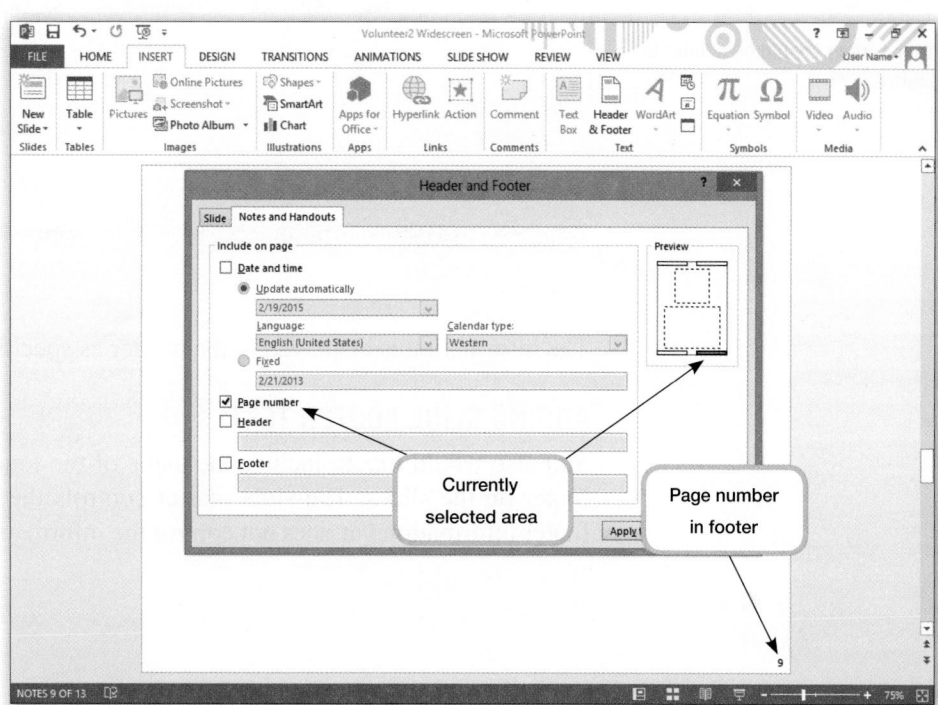

Figure 2.70

On notes and handouts, you can include header text and a page number. The Preview box identifies the four areas where this information will appear and identifies the currently selected areas, in this case page number, in bold.

2

- Choose **Date and Time** to turn on this option and, if necessary, choose **Update Automatically.**

- Choose **Header** and enter your name in the Header text box.

- Click **Apply to All**.

Your screen should be similar to Figure 2.71

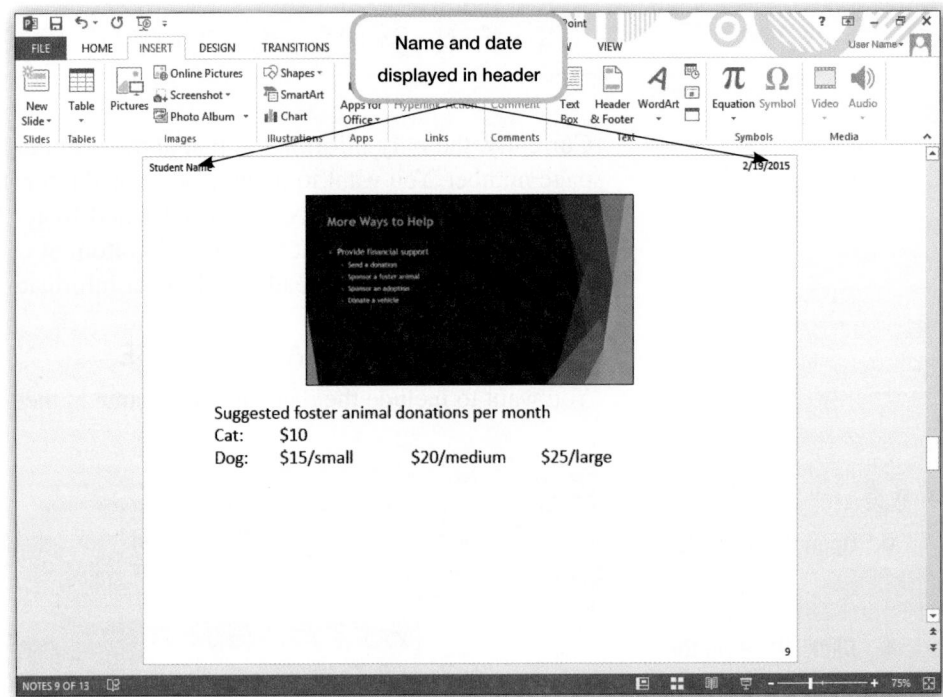

Figure 2.71

The information is displayed in the header as specified.

ADDING SLIDE FOOTER TEXT

You also would like to include the name of the foundation and slide number in a footer on the slides. The slide master controls the placement and display of the footer information but does not control the information that appears in those areas.

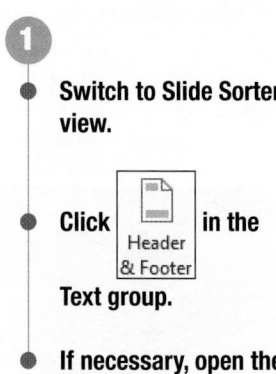

1

- Switch to Slide Sorter view.

- Click [Header & Footer] in the Text group.

- If necessary, open the Slide tab.

Your screen should be similar to Figure 2.72

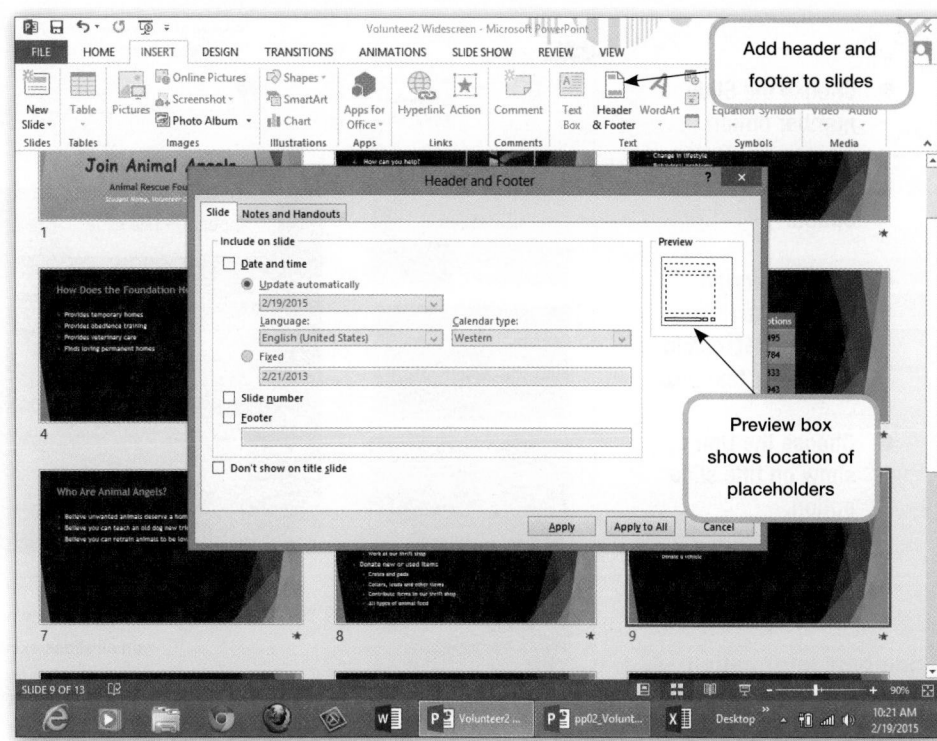

Add header and footer to slides

Preview box shows location of placeholders

Figure 2.72

Slides can display the date and time, slide number, or footer text. The Preview box shows the location of the placeholders for each of these elements on the selected slide. When specified, this information can be displayed on all slides or selected slides only. You also can turn off the display of this information in title slides only. You would like to add the foundation name in the footer and the slide number to all slides, except the title slides.

- Choose the Slide number option.

- Choose the Footer option.

- Type **Animal Rescue Foundation** in the Footer text box.

- Choose the Don't show on title slide option.

- Click Apply to All .

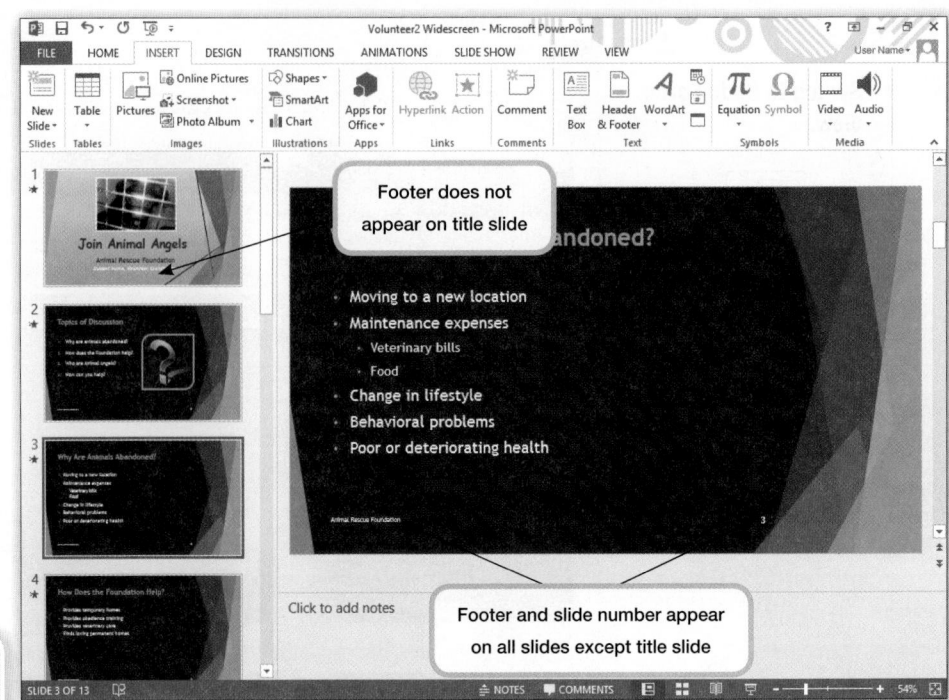

Figure 2.73

Additional Information

The Apply command button applies the settings to the current slide or selected slides only.

- Double-click slide 3.

- Scroll the Slides pane to the top.

- Save the presentation.

Your screen should be similar to Figure 2.73

Additional Information

You can also delete the footer and slide number placeholders from individual slides to remove this information.

The foundation name and slide number appear in placeholders at the bottom of the slide. No footer information is displayed on the first or last slides in the presentation because they use the Title Slide layout.

USING PRESENTER VIEW

Finally, you will check the presentation again in Slide Show view using **Presenter view.** This view shows the full-screen slide show on one monitor for the audience and a "speaker view" on another monitor. Presenter view shows the current slide, a preview of the next slide, the speaker notes, a timer, and additional features to help you present the materials. It allows you to see your notes on your screen while your audience sees only the slide. This is quite helpful as you want to remember to emphasize key points in your presentation and add pertinent information, as you did on slide 9 with the suggested donation amounts.

You will start the slideshow with slide 9, switch to Presenter view, and try out the features available. If you have two monitors, Presenter view automatically displays on the other monitor. If you have only one monitor, you can use [Alt] + [F5] to switch between views to try it out.

- Make slide 9 current and start the slide show.

- Click once to display bulleted items.

- Click ⬤ More slide show options in the Slide Show control bar.

- Choose Show Presenter View.

Having Trouble?

Press [Alt] + [F5] to switch between Slide Show and Presenter view windows.

Your screen should be similar to Figure 2.74

Figure 2.74

Presenter view opens in a separate window and consists of three sections. The current slide is displayed in the large main section, the next slide in the upper-right section, and the notes page for the current slide in the lower-right section. The top of the Presenter view window contains a taskbar providing options to display the Windows taskbar, to select display settings, and to end the slide show. Below the taskbar is the timer that shows the time elapsed since the slide show started and pause and restart timer buttons. The current time is displayed on the far right of the same line.

Below the current slide is the control bar containing the same buttons as in the Slide Show window. This allows you to control the slide show using Presenter view rather than from the Slide Show window, making it much less obtrusive. They are always visible and easy to use.

At the bottom of the Presenter view window, a slide count shows which slide you are currently viewing of the total slides in the presentation and two navigation buttons to move to the previous or next slide. Additionally, the A Increase Font Size and A Decrease Font Size buttons below the Notes section can be used to increase or decrease the size of the text in that section.

You will now try out several of the features in Presenter view.

2

- Click ▦ See all slides.

- Click on slide 6 and then click once more to show the chart.

- Click ⊙ Advance to the next slide.

- Click 3 more times to display bulleted items.

- Click ⊡ END SLIDE SHOW in the taskbar to end slide show.

As you ran the slide show, Presenter view displayed information about the animations and transitions that were running.

You have created both slides and a notes page for the presentation and have seen how Presenter view works. Now you want to print the notes page and some of the slides. Customizing the print settings by selecting specific slides to print and scaling the size of the slides to fill the page are a few of the ways to make your printed output look more professional.

PRINTING NOTES PAGES

First you will print the notes page for the slide on which you entered note text.

1

● **Make slide 9 current.**

● **Open the File tab and choose** Print .

● **If necessary, select the printer.**

● **Choose Print Current Slide as the slide to print.**

● **Choose Notes Pages as the layout.**

● **Change the orientation to Portrait Orientation.**

● **If necessary, change the color setting to Grayscale.**

Your screen should be similar to Figure 2.75

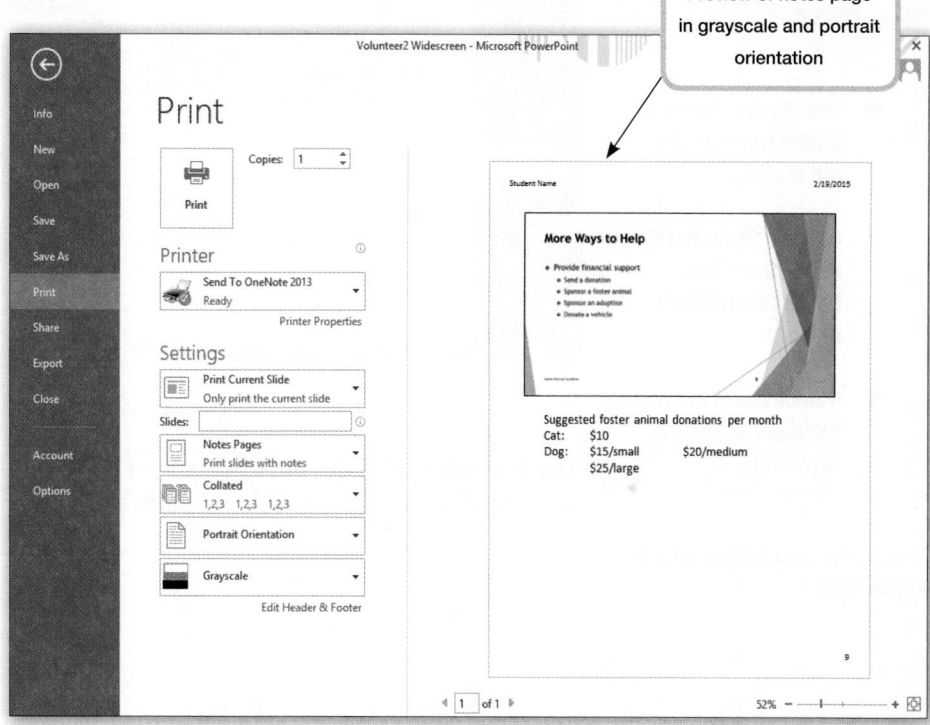

Preview of notes page in grayscale and portrait orientation

Figure 2.75

The notes page is displayed in grayscale and in portrait orientation, as it will appear when printed.

2

● **Click**  .

Additional Information

To print multiple Notes pages, enter the slide number of each slide (separated by commas) you want to print in the Slides text box.

PRINTING SELECTED SLIDES

Next you will print a few selected slides to be used as handouts. You will change the orientation to portrait and scale the slides to fit the paper size.

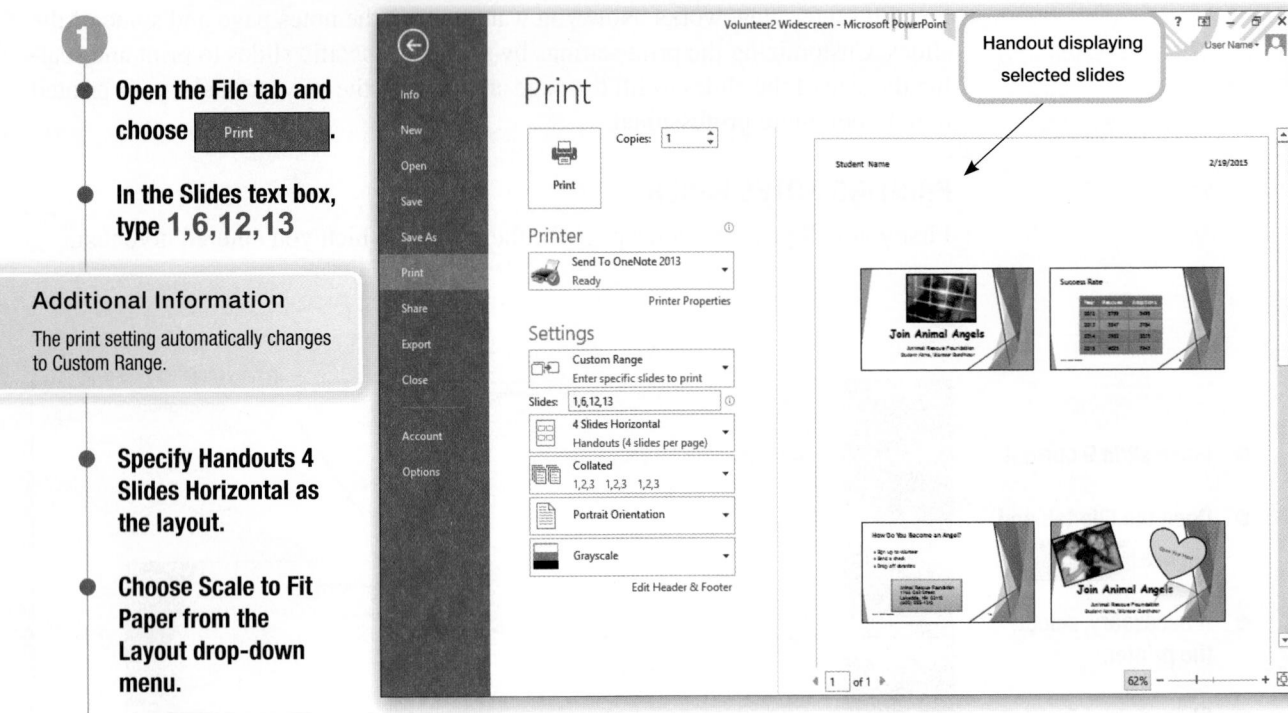

1

- Open the File tab and choose Print .

- In the Slides text box, type **1,6,12,13**

Additional Information

The print setting automatically changes to Custom Range.

- Specify Handouts 4 Slides Horizontal as the layout.

- Choose Scale to Fit Paper from the Layout drop-down menu.

- If necessary, change the color setting to Grayscale.

Your screen should be similar to Figure 2.76

Figure 2.76

The four selected slides are displayed in portrait orientation, and the slide images were sized as large as possible to fill the page.

2

- Print the handout.

- Open the File tab and if necessary, choose Info .

- In the Properties pane, enter **your name** in the Author text box.

- If necessary, in the Tags text box, enter **Volunteer, Recruit**

- Save the completed presentation.

- Exit PowerPoint.

The view you are in when you save the file is the view that will be displayed when the file is opened.

CUS ON CAREERS

EXPLORE YOUR CAREER OPTIONS

Communications Specialist

Are you interested in technology? Could you explain technology in words and pictures? Communications specialists, also known as public relations specialists, assist sales and marketing management with communications media and advertising materials that represent the company's products and services to customers. In high-tech industries, you will take information from scientists and engineers and use PowerPoint to transform the data into eye-catching presentations that communicate effectively. You also may create brochures, develop websites, create videos, and write speeches. If you thrive in a fast-paced and high-energy environment and work well under the pressure of deadlines, then this job may be for you. Typically a bachelor's degree in journalism, advertising, or communications is desirable. Typical salaries range from $38,400 to $98,000, depending on the industry. To learn more about this career, visit the website for the Bureau of Labor Statistics of the U.S. Department of Labor.

Find and Replace (PP2.5)

To make editing easier, you can use the Find and Replace feature to find text in a presentation and replace it with other text as directed.

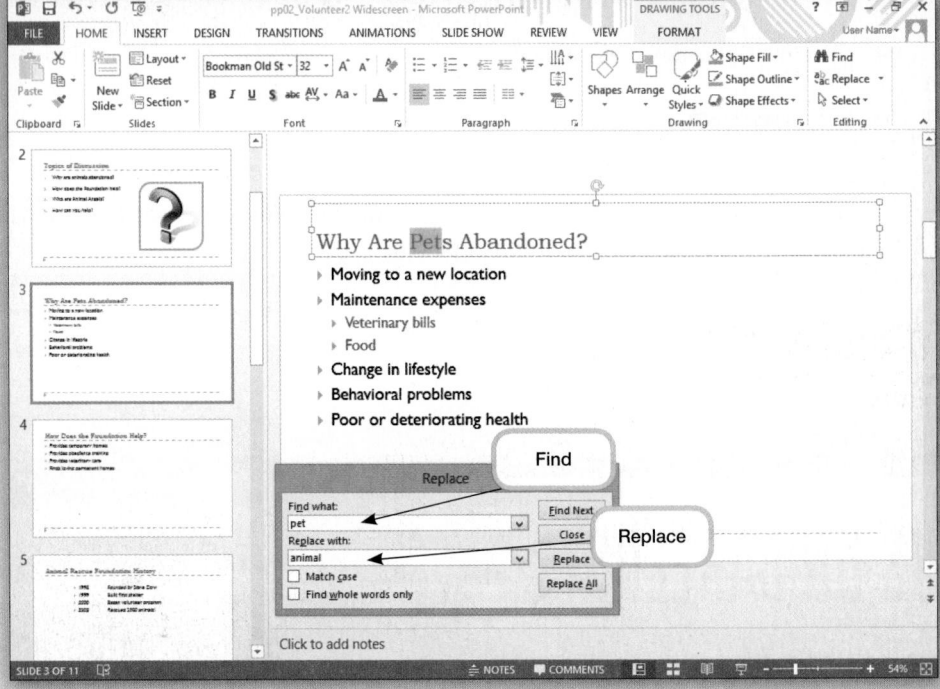

Table (PP2.10)

A table is used to organize information into an easy-to-read format of horizontal rows and vertical columns.

Alignment (PP2.18)

Alignment controls how text entries are positioned within a space.

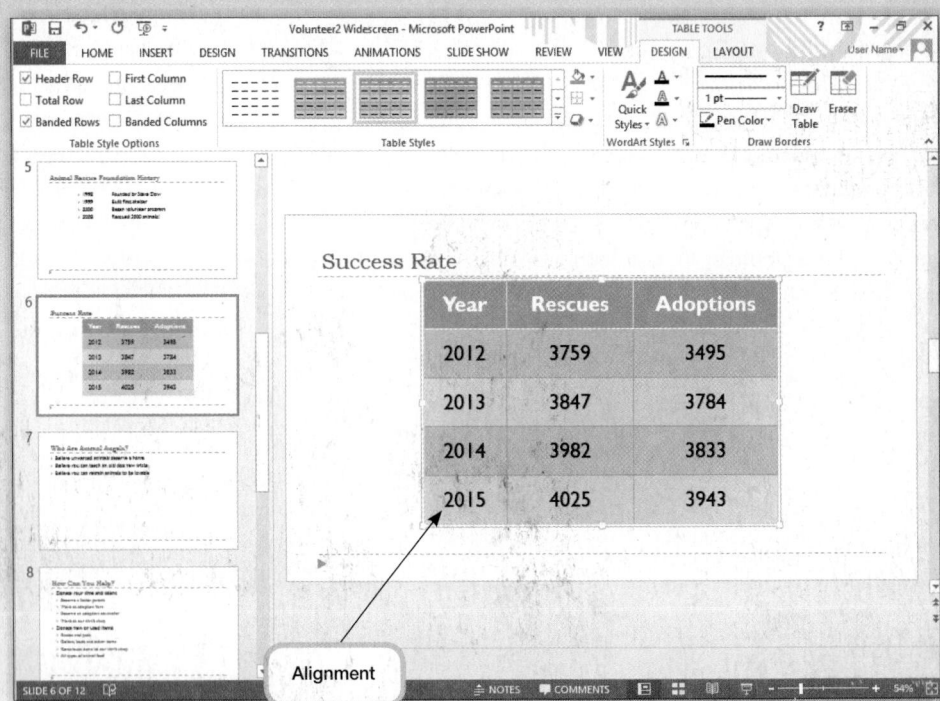

Theme (PP2.36)

A theme is a predefined set of formatting choices that can be applied to an entire document in one simple step.

Master (PP2.42)

A master is a special slide or page that stores information about the formatting for all slides in a presentation.

Animations (PP2.47)

Animations are special effects that add action to text and graphics so they move around on the screen during a slide show.

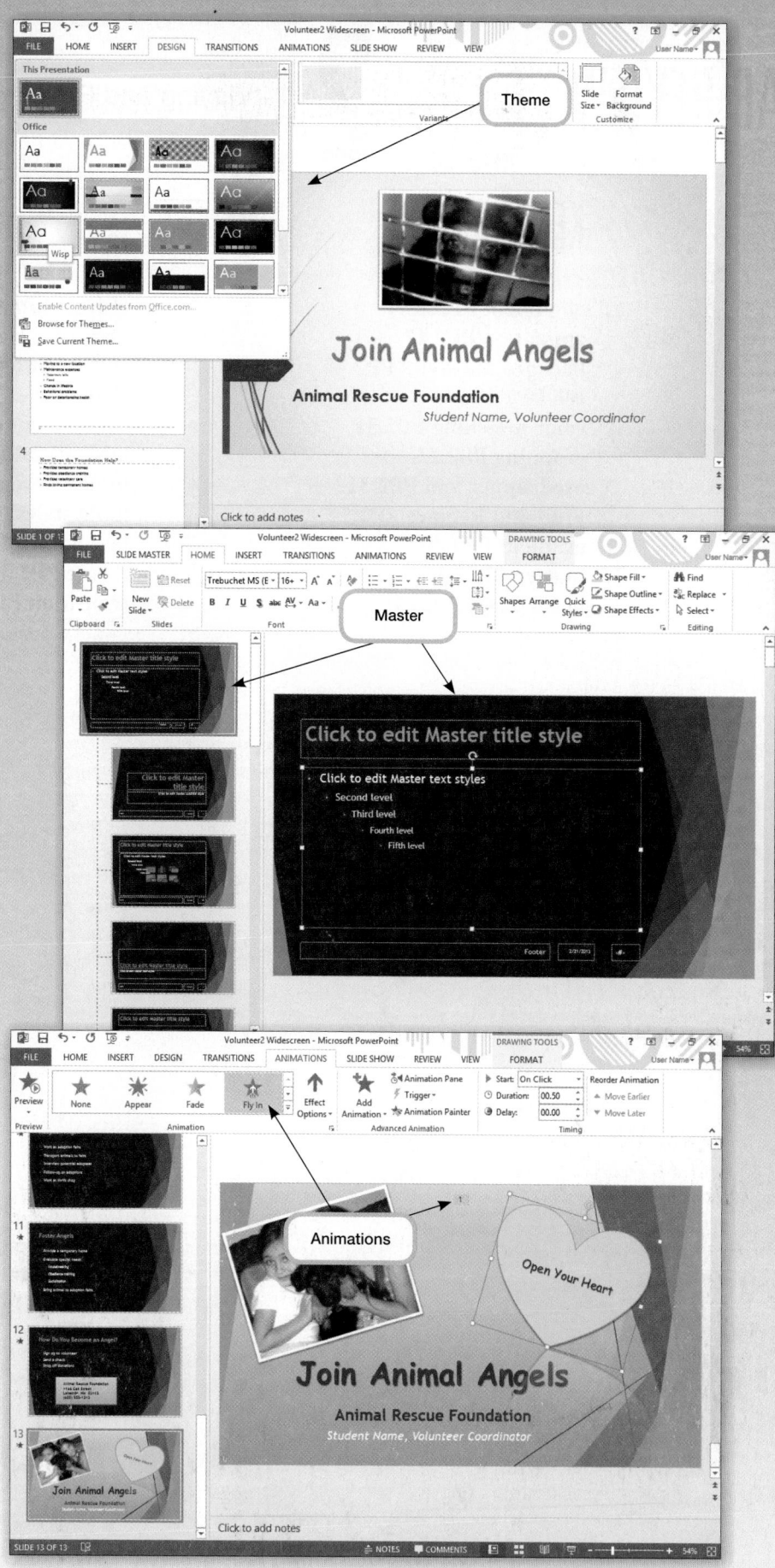

KEY TERMS

alignment PP2.18
animation PP2.47
background styles PP2.40
cell PP2.10
color matching PP2.31
cropping PP2.23
eyedropper tool PP2.31
Find and Replace PP2.5
gradient PP2.40
master PP2.42
notes pages PP2.67

object animations PP2.47
presenter view PP2.73
rotate handle PP2.30
shape styles PP2.28
slide Show control bar PP2.63
table PP2.10
table reference PP2.10
table styles PP2.19
text box PP2.32
theme PP2.36
transition PP2.47

COMMAND SUMMARY

Command	Shortcut	Action
Home tab		
Paragraph group		
▤ Align Left	Ctrl + L	Aligns text to the left
▤ Align Center	Ctrl + E	Centers text
▤ Align Right	Ctrl + R	Aligns text to the right
▤ Justify	Ctrl + J	Aligns text to both the left and right margins
▤ Align Text		Sets vertical alignment of text
Drawing group		
Shapes		Inserts a shape
Shape Fill ▾		Fills the selected shape with a solid color, gradient, picture, or texture
Shape Effects ▾		Applies a visual effect to the selected shape, such as shadow, glow, or reflection
Editing group		
Find	Ctrl + F	Finds specified text
Replace ▾	Ctrl + H	Replaces located text with replacement text
Insert tab		
Images group		
Pictures		Inserts picture from a file
Online Pictures		Finds and inserts a picture from a variety of online sources
Illustrations group		
Shapes		Inserts a shape
Text group		
Text Box		Inserts text box or adds text to selected shape
Header & Footer		Inserts a header and footer

COMMAND SUMMARY (CONTINUED)

Command	Shortcut	Action
Design tab		
Themes group		
⏷ More		Opens gallery of themes
Variants group		
⏷ More button		Customizes the look of the current theme
Transitions tab		
Preview group		
Preview		Displays the transition effect
Transition to This Slide group		
Effect Options ▾		Opens a gallery of effect options
⏷		Opens gallery of transition effects
Animations tab		
Preview group		
Preview		Displays the transition effect
Animation group		
Effect Options ▾		Opens a gallery of effect options
⏷		Opens a gallery of animation effects
Advanced Animation group		
Add Animation ▾		Adds an animation effect to an object
Animation Pane		Opens the Animation pane
Animation Painter		Copies animation effect to another object
Timing group		
▶ Start:		Sets the trigger for the animation
⏱ Duration: 01.00		Controls the amount of time for the animation to complete
View tab		
Presentation Views group		
Notes Page		Displays current slide in Notes view to edit the speaker notes

COMMAND SUMMARY (CONTINUED)

Command	Shortcut	Action
Slide Master		Opens Slide Master view to change the design and layout of the master slides
Drawing Tools Format tab		
Shapes Styles group		
More		Opens the Shape Styles gallery to select a visual style to apply to a shape
Shape Effects ▾		Applies a visual effect to a shape
Arrange group		
▾ or		Rotates or flips the selected object
Picture Tools Format tab		
Adjust group		
Color ▾		Recolors picture
Compress Pictures		Compresses pictures in the document to reduce its size; permanently deletes cropped parts of a picture
Picture Styles		
More		Opens Picture Styles gallery to select an overall visual style for picture
Picture Effects ▾		Applies a visual effect to picture
Arrange group		
▾ Align		Changes placement of selected objects on slide
Size group		
Crop		Crops off unwanted section of a picture
Table Tools Design tab		
Table Styles group		
More		Opens the Table Styles gallery to choose a visual style for a table
▾ Shading		Colors background behind selected text or paragraph
▾ Border		Applies a border style
▾ Effects		Applies a visual effect to the table such as shadows and reflections
Table Tools Layout tab		
Alignment group		
Center		Centers the text within a cell
Center Vertically		Centers the text vertically within a cell
Arrange group		
Align Align		Aligns edges of multiple selected objects

LAB EXERCISES

MATCHING

Match the item on the left with the correct description on the right.

1. object animation   _____ a. adds text to a slide as an object

2. master   _____ b. organizes information into an easy-to-read format of horizontal rows and vertical columns

3. Animation Painter   _____ c. allows you to spin an object to any degree in any direction

4. theme   _____ d. controls the way the display changes as you move from one slide to the next

5. rotate handle   _____ e. predefined set of formatting choices that can be applied to an entire document

6. gradient   _____ f. the progressive change of color

7. transition   _____ g. motion, such as clip art that flies in from the left

8. table   _____ h. special effects that add action to text and graphics

9. text box   _____ i. quickly copies an animation effect and applies it to a different object

10. animation   _____ j. slide that stores information about the formatting for all slides or pages in a presentation

TRUE/FALSE

Circle the correct answer to the following questions.

1.	Using masters, you are able to easily apply formatting changes to a selected group of slides.	True	False
2.	You cannot insert a table into PowerPoint, only graphics or other objects.	True	False
3.	Alignment controls the position of text entries in a placeholder.	True	False
4.	Find and Replace makes it difficult to locate specific words or phrases.	True	False
5.	A master is a special slide on which the formatting for selected slides or pages in your presentation is defined.	True	False
6.	When adding text to a text box in PowerPoint, the text box will lengthen automatically to display the entire entity.	True	False
7.	When you create a footer, it is automatically applied to every slide in the presentation.	True	False
8.	You can print 12 slides per page using notes pages.	True	False
9.	Tables contain rows and columns.	True	False
10.	A theme can be applied to selected slides in a presentation.	True	False

FILL-IN

Complete the following statements by filling in the blanks with the correct terms.

1. A(n) _____ is a container for text or graphics.

2. _____ provides access to a combination of different formatting options such as edges, gradients, line styles, shadows, and three-dimensional effects.

3. _____ lets you see your notes while your audience is viewing your slide.

4. _____ add action to text and graphics so they move on the screen.

5. The _____ allows you to add or highlight information on a slide during the slide show.

6. _____ controls the position of text entries within a space.

7. A(n) _____ is part of a template that stores information about the formatting for the three key components of a presentation—slides, speaker notes, and handouts.

8. Object _____ are used to display each bullet point, text, paragraph, or graphic independently of the other text or objects on the slide.

9. Use a(n) _____ or _____ on a slide to display information such as the date or slide number.

10. The _____ slide is a special slide that stores information about the formatting for all slides or pages in a presentation.

LAB EXERCISES

MULTIPLE CHOICE

Circle the letter of the correct response to the questions below.

1. To help you remember the important points during a presentation, you can add comments to slides and use _____.
   a. animation
   b. Normal view
   c. slide handouts
   d. Presenter view

2. If you want to display information in columns and rows, you would create a _____.
   a. slide layout
   b. shape
   c. table
   d. text box

3. A(n) _____ is a predefined set of formatting choices that can be applied to an entire document in one simple step.
   a. theme
   b. animation
   c. slide layout
   d. master

4. _____ add action to text and graphics so they move around on the screen.
   a. Animations
   b. Slides
   c. Transitions
   d. Masters

5. The _____ defines the format and placement of the slide image, note text, headers, footers, and other elements that will appear on all speaker notes.
   a. handouts master
   b. title master
   c. slide master
   d. notes master

6. _____ control the way that the display changes as you move from one slide to the next during a presentation.
   a. Graphics
   b. Transitions
   c. Animations
   d. Slide masters

7. You can change the horizontal placement of an entry in a placeholder or a table cell by using one of the four horizontal alignment settings: left, center, right, and _____.
   a. located
   b. marginalized
   c. highlighted
   d. justified

8. The best way to apply changes to every slide in your presentation is to _____.
   a. use slide sorter view
   b. change the title slide layout
   c. change each slide individually
   d. modify the theme slide master

9. If you wanted to add a company logo on each slide in your presentation, you would place it on the _____.
   a. notes page
   b. master
   c. handout
   d. outline slide

10. To substitute one word for another in a presentation, you would use the _____ feature.
    a. Find and Replace
    b. Duplicate
    c. Copy
    d. Locate and Move

STEP-BY-STEP

ENHANCING A STAFF TRAINING PRESENTATION ★

1. You are working on the staff training presentation for the Mountain View Inn. You have already created the introductory portion of the presentation and need to reorganize the topics and make the presentation more visually appealing. Three slides from your modified presentation will be similar to those shown here.

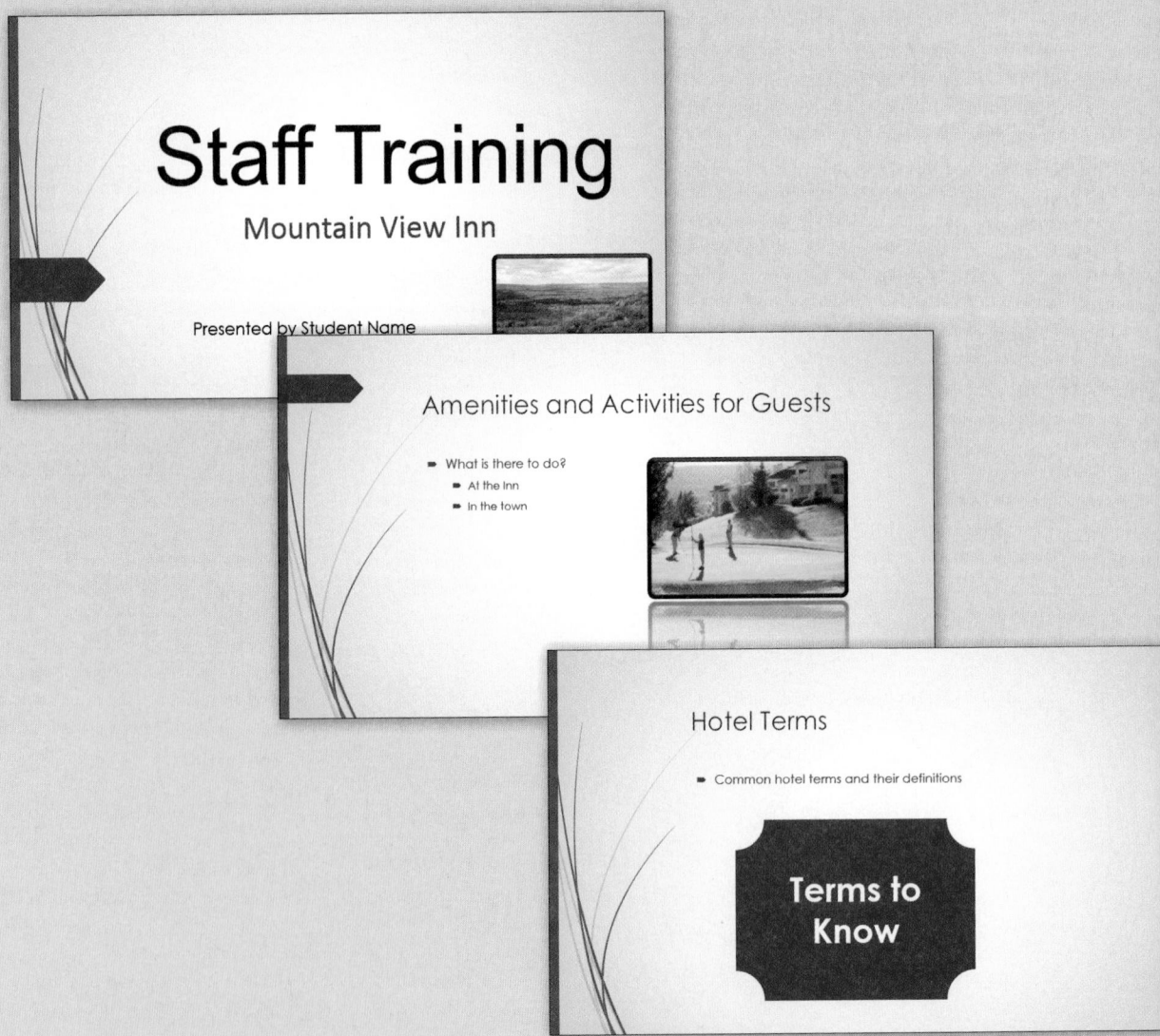

a. Open the file pp02_Mountain View Staff Training.

b. Save the file as Mountain View Training.

c. Run the slide show to see the progress so far.

d. Spell-check the presentation, making the appropriate corrections.

e. Find and replace any occurrence of "city" with the word **town**.

f. In slide 1:

Insert a text box below the subtitle.

Type **Presented by Your Name**.

Set the font size to 24 and position the text box appropriately on the slide.

Add the following speaker note: **Be sure to introduce yourself and play the name game**.

g. In slide 4:

Add a shape of your choice to emphasize the text on the inserted shape.

Enter and format the text **Terms to Know** within the inserted shape.

Position and size the shape appropriately. Add an animation effect of your choice to the shape.

h. In slide 5:

Set the Picture Style to Reflected Bevel, Black.

Set the Picture Effect to Half Reflection, 4 pt offset.

i. Move slide 4 after slide 12.

j. Change the design of the slides to one of your choice from the Themes gallery. Check all slides and make any needed adjustments.

k. Duplicate slide 1 and move it to the end of the presentation. Delete the speaker note from slide 15.

l. Add a transition effect of your choice to all slides. Add an animation effect and sound to the first slide.

m. Using the theme master slide, increase title font one increment and content font by three increments.

n. Add your name to the File properties. Save the file.

o. Print slides 1, 4, 12, and 15 as handouts (four slides horizontal in portrait orientation).

LAB EXERCISES

EMERGENCY DRIVING TECHNIQUES ★

2. To complete this problem, you must have completed Step-by-Step Exercise 2 in Lab 1. You have completed the first draft of the presentation on tire blowouts, but you still have some information to add. Additionally, you want to make the presentation look better using many of the presentation features. Several slides of the modified presentation are shown here.

   a. Open the presentation Handling Blowouts, which was saved at the end of Step-by-Step Exercise 2 in Lab 1. If necessary, switch to Normal view.

   b. Save the file as Blowouts2.

   c. In Slide Master view, make the following adjustments to the Title Slide Layout:

   Delete the page number placeholder.

   Change the font of the title and subtitle to Tahoma or a similar font. Add a shadow.

   Decrease the title text to 54 pt.

   Change title text color to Orange, Accent 2, Darker 50%.

   d. On the Title and Content Layout master slide, delete the date placeholder, and move the student name placeholder to line up with the left edge of the of the title placeholder. Left justify the student name text. Ensure the slide number placeholder is right justified and in line with the right edge of the content placeholder.

e. Make the same changes as in Step d to the Title, Text, and Content Layout master (the last one). Move the page number placeholder to line up with the right edge of the right content placeholder. If necessary, resize the page number placeholder to fit within the brown bar.

f. On slide 6, replace the = in the title with a right-facing block arrow AutoShape. Add a Fly In from the Left animation to the AutoShape. Modify slide title text as necessary to fit on one line.

g. Change the shape fill color of the arrow to Ice Blue, Background 2, Darker 75%.

h. Duplicate the title slide and move it to the end of the presentation. Add a drawing object to this slide that includes the text **Drive Safely!** Modify the shape style.

i. Select an animation scheme of your choice to add transition effects to all the slides. Run the slide show.

j. Add the following note to slide 7 in a point size of 18:

   Underinflation iṣ the leading cause of tire failure.

   Maximum inflation pressure on tire is not recommended pressure.

k. Add the following note to slide 10 in a point size of 18:

   Penny test–tread should come to top of Lincoln's head.

l. Add file documentation and save the completed presentation.

m. Print the notes page for slide 7. Print slides 1, 6, and 11 as handouts with three slides per page.

ENHANCING THE ASU PRESENTATION ★★

3. Bonnie is the Assistant Director of New Admissions at Arizona State University. Part of her job is to make presentations at community colleges and local high schools about the university. She has already created the introductory portion of the presentation and needs to reorganize the topics and make the presentation more visually appealing. Several slides of the modified presentation are shown here.

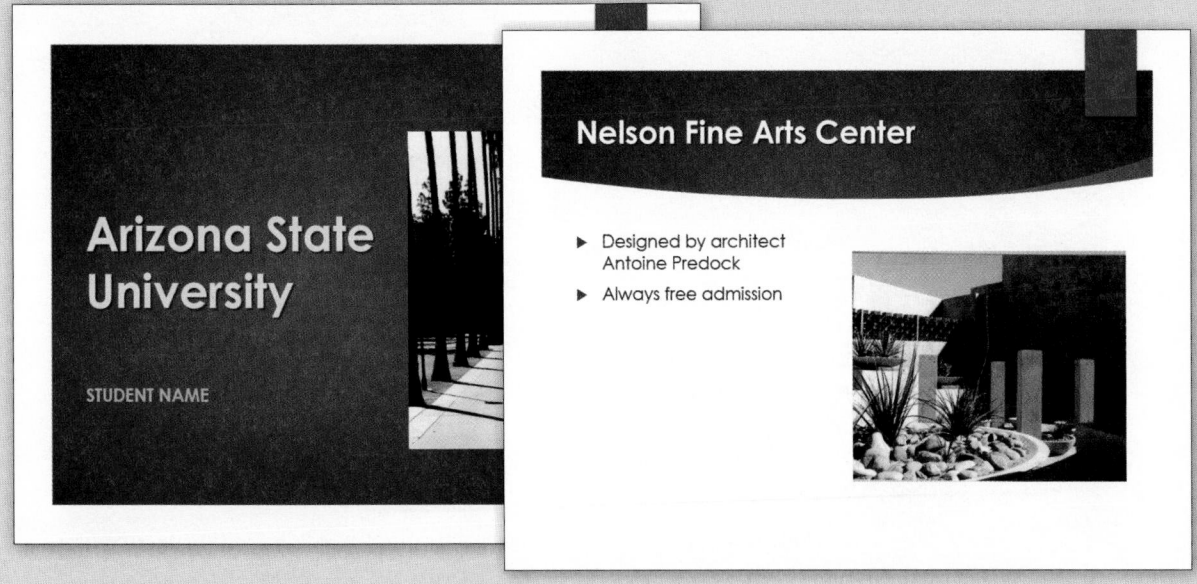

LAB EXERCISES

a. Open the file pp02_ASU Presentation.

b. Save the file as ASU Presentation1.

c. Run the slide show to see what Bonnie has done so far.

d. Spell-check the presentation, making the appropriate corrections.

e. Move slide 5 before slide 4.

f. Use the Find and Replace feature to locate all occurrences of "Arizona State University" and replace them with "ASU" on all slides except the first and second slides.

g. Enter your name as the subtitle in slide 1. Insert the picture pp02_PalmWalk on the title slide. Size the picture and position the placeholders on the slide appropriately.

h. Demote all the bulleted items on slides 8 and 9 except the first item.

i. Change the document theme to one of your choice. Choose a theme variant of your choice. If necessary, reposition graphics and change font sizes.

j. Modify the text color of all the titles in the presentation using the slide master.

k. Duplicate slide 1 and move the duplicate to the end of the presentation. Replace your name with **Apply Now!**

l. Bonnie would like to add some picture of the building at the end of presentation. Switch to Slide Sorter view and select slides 12, 13, and 14. Apply the Two Content layout. Insert the picture pp02_Student Services in slide 12, the picture pp02_Library in slide 13, and the picture pp02_Fine Arts in slide 14 from your student file location.

m. Add a custom animation and sound to the picture on the title slide.

n. Apply random transitions to all slides in the presentation.

o. Apply the Fly In From Right build effect to all slides with bullet items.

p. Run the slide show.

q. Add file documentation and save the presentation. Print slides 1, 2, and 12–15 as handouts (six per page).

4. To complete this exercise, you must have completed Step-by-Step Exercise 1 in Lab 1. Kevin's work on the Triple Crown Presentation was well received by his supervisor. She would like to see some additional information included in the presentation, including a table of upcoming qualifying hikes. Four slides from your updated presentation will be similar to those shown here.

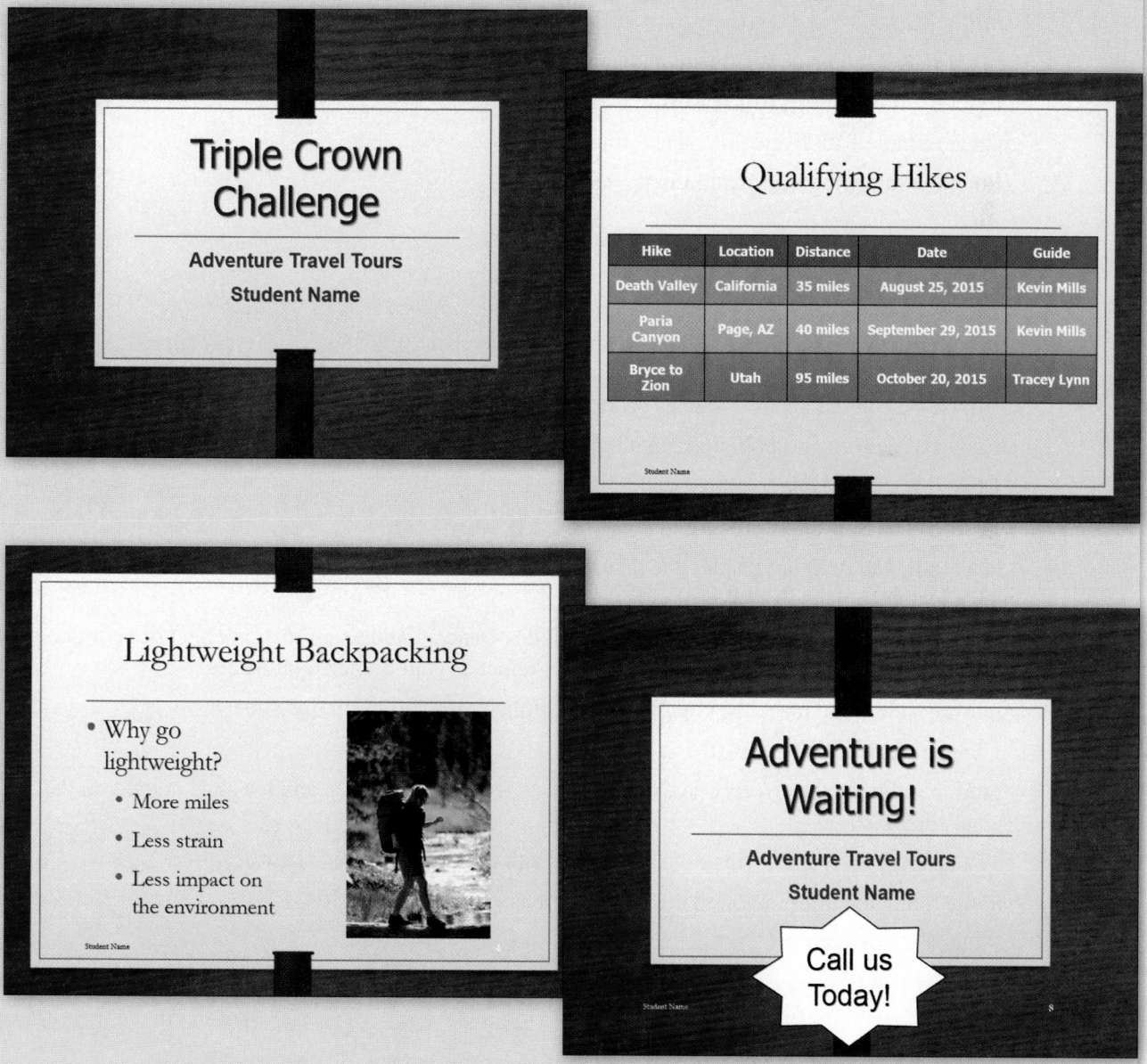

LAB EXERCISES

a. Open the file Triple Crown Presentation.

b. Save the file as Triple Crown Presentation2.

c. Change the document theme to one of your choice. Choose a theme variant of your choice. If necessary, reposition graphics and change font sizes.

d. Using the slide master, change the text color of the titles and subtitles. Change the bullet styles.

e. Use the Find and Replace command to replace any occurrence of "Paria Canyon" with **Emerald Pools**.

f. Replace slide 3 with a new Title and Content slide. In this slide:

   Enter the title **Qualifying Hikes**.

   Create a table with five columns and four rows.

   Enter the following information in the table:

Hike	Location	Distance	Date	Guide
Death Valley	California	35 miles	August 25, 2015	Kevin Mills
Paria Canyon	Page, AZ	40 miles	September 29, 2015	Kevin Mills
Bryce to Zion	Utah	95 miles	October 20, 2015	Tracey Lynn

   Adjust the column and row size as needed.

   Center the cell entries both horizontally and vertically in their cell spaces.

   Change the table style to one of your choice.

   Position the table appropriately.

g. Add a footer that does not display the date and time but does display your name and the slide number on all slides except the title slide.

h. Add the Float In animation to the graphics on slides 4 and 5. Add an animation effect of your choice to all slides that include bullets. Add a transition effect of your choice to all slides.

i. Duplicate slide 1 and place the copy at the end of the presentation. In this slide:

   Change the title to **Adventure is Waiting!**

   Add the slide footer. (*Hint:* Use Copy and Paste to copy your name and the slide number to the final slide.)

   Add a shape of your choice to the final slide with the text: **Call us Today!**

j. Add the following information to the file properties:

   Author: **Your Name**

   Title: **Triple Crown Presentation**

k. Save the file.

l. Print slides 1, 3, 5, and 8 as a handout with four slides, horizontal, on one page.

5. To complete this problem, you must have completed Step-by-Step Exercise 5 in Lab 1. Tim has completed the first draft of the presentation for his class lecture on workplace issues, but he still has some information he wants to add to the presentation. Additionally, he wants to make the presentation look better using many of the PowerPoint design and slide show presentation features. Several slides of the modified presentation are shown here.

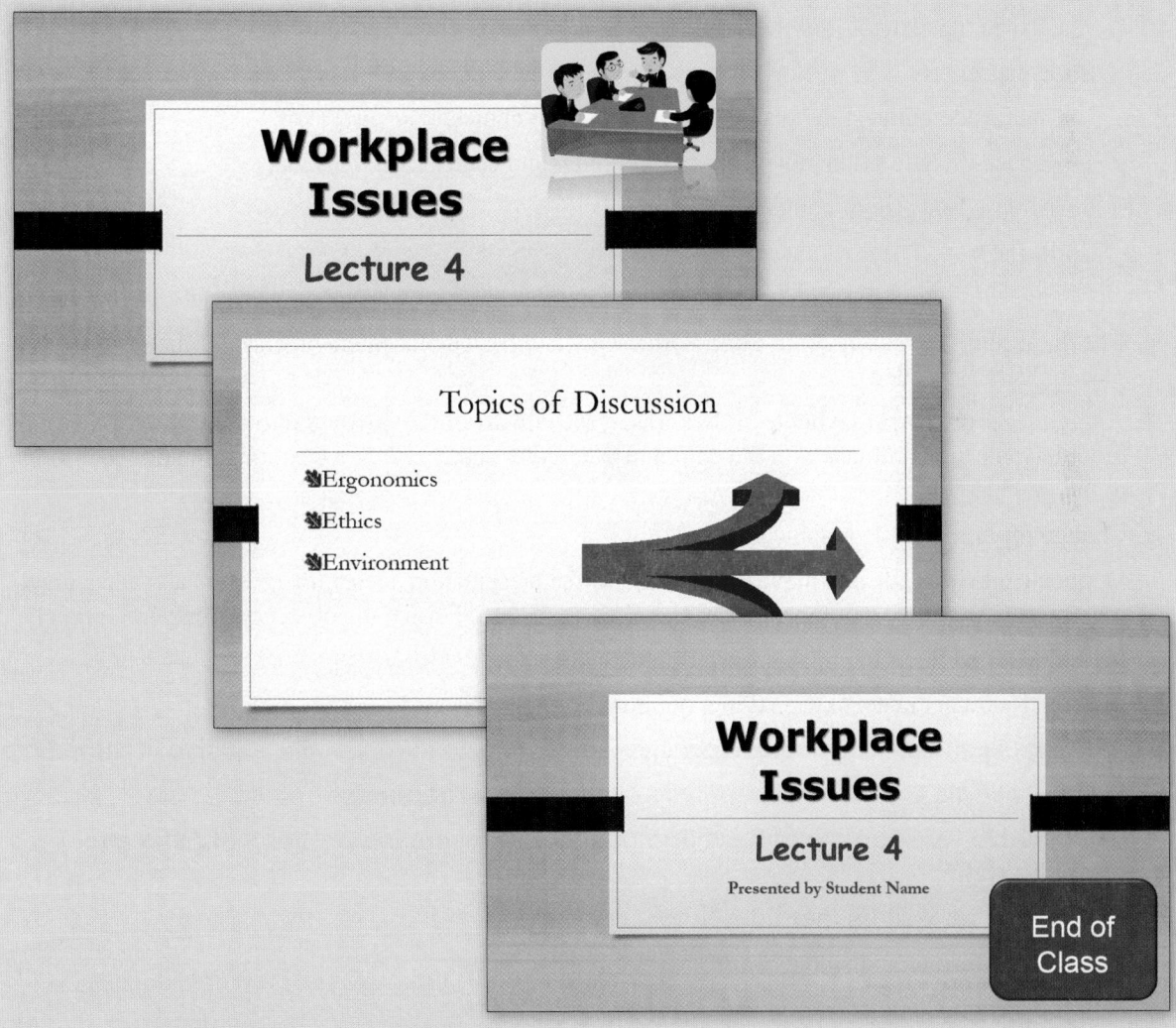

LAB EXERCISES

a. Open the presentation Workplace Issues, which was saved at the end of Step-by-Step Exercise 5 in Lab 1. If necessary, switch to Normal view.

b. Save the file as Workplace Issues2.

c. Change the design template to Organic. Change the theme variant to one of your choice. Modify fonts and graphics as appropriate.

d. Change to Slide Sorter view and check the slide layouts. Make the following adjustments:

Title Slide Layout (in Slide Master view):

Delete the date area and number area placeholders.

Change the text color of the subtitle to a color of your choice and bold it.

Slide master:

Change the bullet style to a picture style of your choice.

Reduce the size of the object area placeholder and center it on the slide.

Increase font size of content text.

Slide 1:

Change the font of the title to Verdana or a similar font. Apply the shadow effect.

e. Check the slide layouts again in Slide Sorter view and fix the placement and size of the placeholders as needed.

f. Apply the Two Content layout to slide 2. Insert the clip art pp02_Arrows into the slide. Modify the graphic color to coordinate with the colors in your color scheme. Add a custom animation and sound to the graphic.

g. Change the angle of the graphic in slide 4.

h. Duplicate the title slide and move it to the end of the presentation. Delete the graphic and add a drawing object to this slide that includes the text End of Class. Format the object and text appropriately.

i. Add transition effects to all the slides. Run the slide show.

j. Add the following notes to slide 3 in a point size of 18:

Computers used to be more expensive—focus was to make people adjust to fit computers

Now, people are more expensive—focus is on ergonomics

Objective—design computers and use them to increase productivity and avoid health risks

Physical as well as mental risks

k. Add a bullet format to the notes on slide 3.

l. Add file documentation and save the completed presentation.

m. Print the notes page for slide 3. Print slides 1, 2, 6, and 11 as handouts with four slides per page.

ON YOUR OWN

CLUTTER CONTROL ★

1. You work for a business that designs and builds custom closet solutions. You have been asked to prepare a presentation for new clients that will help them prepare for the construction phase. Clients need to organize and categorize their items before the crews arrive on-site; your presentation will serve as an organization guide. Research ideas on reducing clutter on the web. Add transitions, animations, and a theme that will catch the viewer's attention. Include your name and the current date in a slide footer. Save the presentation, early and often, as Custom Closets, and print the presentation as handouts, nine per page.

DREAM VACATION ★★

2. For a class project, you have been asked to plan your "dream vacation." Choose your destination, and do some research on the web to create a presentation illustrating key tourist attractions, fun things to do, dining experiences, hotel choices, and travel costs and arrangements. Start a new presentation and add appropriate text content. Include a table. Add transitions, graphics, animations, and a theme that will catch the viewer's attention. Include your name and the current date in the slide footer. Save the presentation, early and often, as Dream Vacation and print the handouts.

ENHANCING THE CAREERS WITH ANIMALS PRESENTATION ★★★

3. To add interest to the Careers with Animals presentation that you created in Lab 1, On Your Own Exercise 5, select a theme and color theme of your choice. Add graphics, animation, sound, and transitions that will hold your audience's interest. Add speaker notes with a header that displays your name. Include your name and the current date in a slide footer. Modify the format to widescreen; be sure to check all slides and make any necessary modifications. Add appropriate documentation to the file, save the presentation, early and often, as Careers with Animals2, print the presentation as handouts, and print the notes pages for only the slides containing notes.

ENHANCING THE INTERNET POLICY PRESENTATION ★★★

4. After completing the Internet Policy presentation you created in Lab 1, On Your Own Exercise 1, you decide it could use a bit more sprucing up. You want to add some information about personal computing security. Do some research on the web to find some helpful tips on protecting personal privacy and safeguarding your computer. Enter this information in one or two slides. Add some animated graphics and transitions to help liven up the presentation. Make these and any other changes that you think would enhance the presentation. Add a table and format it appropriately. Include speaker notes for at least one slide. Add appropriate documentation to the file. Save the file, early and often, as Internet Policy2; print the presentation as handouts, nine per page; and print the notes pages (with a header displaying your name and the current date) for only the slides containing notes.

LAB EXERCISES

ENHANCING THE WEB DESIGN PRESENTATION ★★★

5. After completing the Web Design presentation in Lab 1, On Your Own Exercise 4, you decide it needs a bit more sprucing up. First of all, it would be more impressive as an onscreen presentation with a custom design. Also, the pros and cons information would look better as a table, and a few animated clip art pictures, nonstandard bullets, builds, and transitions wouldn't hurt. Make these and any other changes that you think would enhance the presentation. Include speaker notes for at least one slide. Include your name and the current date in a slide footer. Add appropriate documentation to the file and save it, early and often, as Web Design2. Print the presentation as handouts and print the notes pages for only the slides containing notes.

Working Together: Copying, Embedding, and Linking between Applications

CASE STUDY

Animal Rescue Foundation

The director of the Animal Rescue Foundation has reviewed the PowerPoint presentation you created and has asked you to include an adoption success rate chart that was created using Excel. Additionally, the director has provided a list of dates for the upcoming volunteer orientation meetings that he feels would be good content for another slide.

Frequently you will find that you want to include information that was created using a word processing, spreadsheet, or database application in your slide show. As you will see, you can easily share information between applications, saving you both time and effort by eliminating the need to re-create information that is available in another application while you create the new slides. The new slides containing information from Word and Excel are shown here.

NOTE **The Working Together section assumes that you already know how to use Microsoft Word and Excel 2013 and that you have completed PowerPoint Lab 2.**

Information can be easily copied from a file created in another application, such as Word or Excel, and pasted into a PowerPoint slide as a linked or embedded object.

Copying between Applications

The director prepared the list of orientation meeting dates and locations in a document using Word 2013. As you have learned, all the Microsoft Office system applications have a common user interface, such as similar Ribbons and commands. In addition to these obvious features, the applications have been designed to work together, making it easy to share and exchange information between applications.

Rather than retype information, you will copy the list from the Word document into the presentation. You also can use the same commands and procedures to copy information from PowerPoint or other Office applications into a Word document.

COPYING FROM WORD TO A POWERPOINT SLIDE

First, you need to modify the PowerPoint presentation to include a new slide for the orientation meeting dates.

1

● **Start PowerPoint 2013.**

● **Open the presentation** Volunteer2 Widescreen **(saved at the end of Lab 2).**

> **Having Trouble?**
>
> If this file is not available, open ppwt_ Volunteer2 Widescreen. Be sure to change Student Name on the first slide to your name.

● **Insert a new slide using the Title Only layout after slide 12.**

● **Save the presentation as** Volunteer2 WT **to your solution file location.**

Your screen should be similar to Figure 1

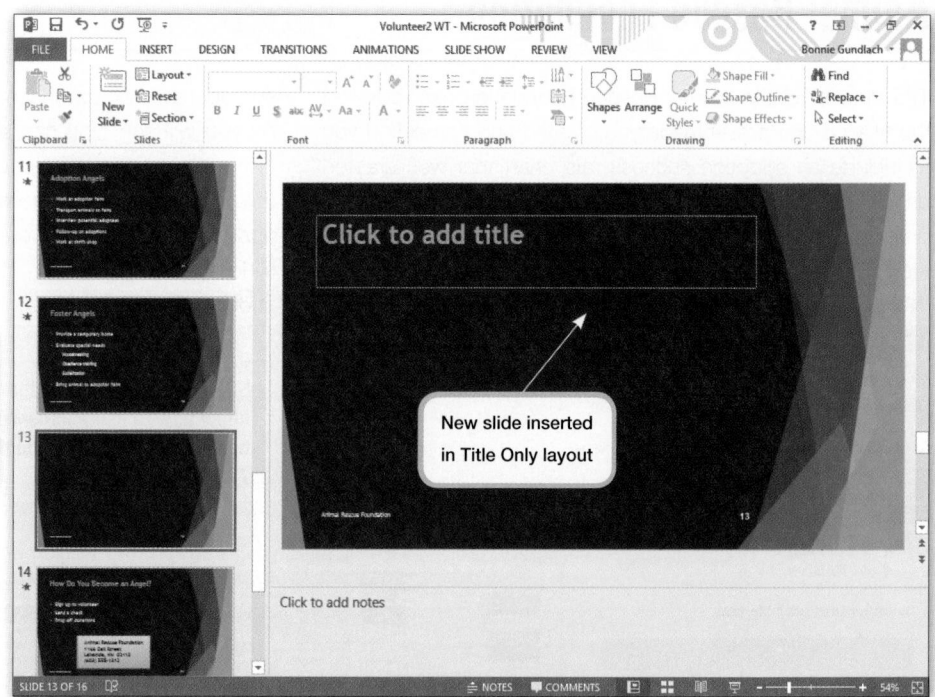

Figure 1

To copy information from the Word document file into the PowerPoint presentation, you need to open the Word document.

Start Word 2013.

Open the document ppwt_Orientation Meetings

If necessary, maximize the window, hide the rulers, and set the magnification to 100%.

Your screen should be similar to Figure 2

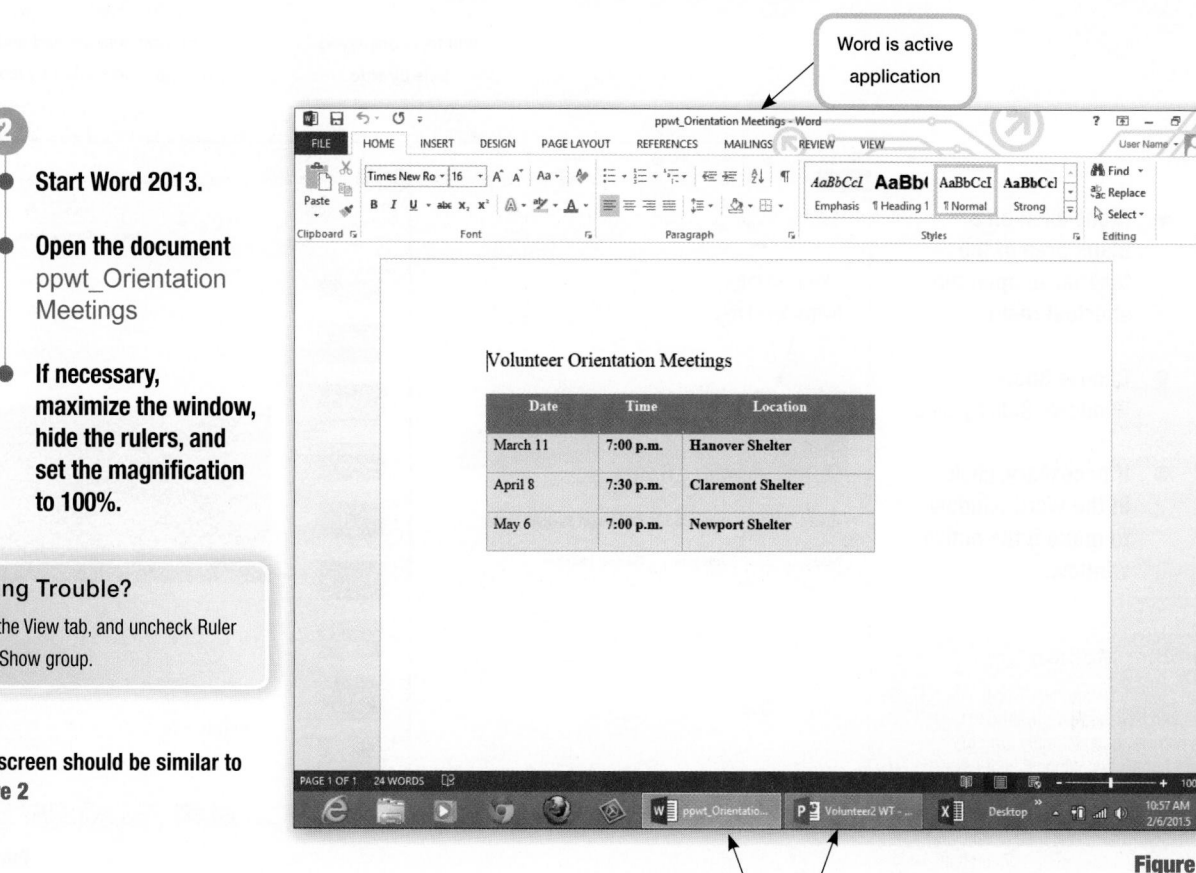

Word is active application

Two open applications

Figure 2

There are now two open applications, Word and PowerPoint. PowerPoint is open in a window behind the Word application window. Both application buttons are displayed in the taskbar. There are also two open files, ppwt_Orientation Meetings in Word and Volunteer2 WT in PowerPoint. Word is the active application, and ppwt_Orientation Meetings is the active file. To make it easier to work with two applications, you will display the windows next to each other to view both on the screen at the same time.

3

Right-click on a blank area of the taskbar to open the shortcut menu.

Choose Show Windows Side by Side.

If necessary, click in the Word window to make it the active window.

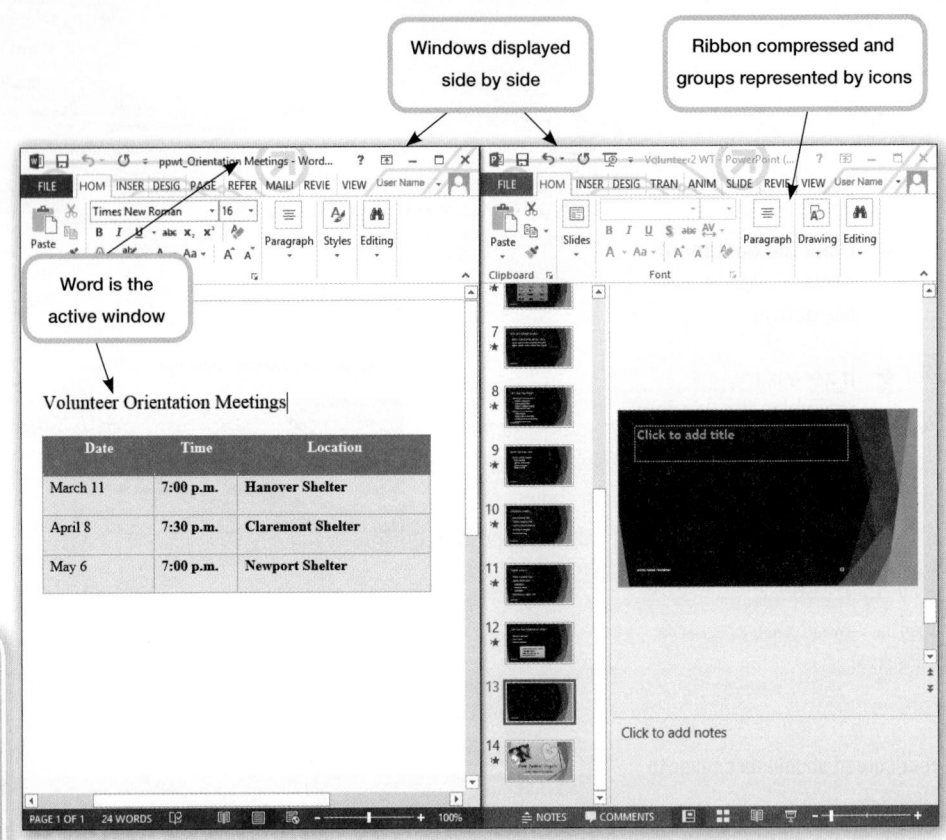

Figure 3

Another Method

With Microsoft Windows 7 or 8, you also can use the Snap feature to quickly tile your windows. Simply drag the Word application window all the way to the left side of the screen and the PowerPoint window all the way to the right. The windows will automatically resize so that they each take up half the screen.

Your screen should be similar to Figure 3

The active window is the window that displays the insertion point and does not have a dimmed title bar. It is the window in which you can work. Because the windows are side by side and there is less horizontal space in each window, the Ribbon groups are compressed. To access commands in these groups, simply click on the group button and the commands appear in a drop-down list.

First, you will copy the title from the Word document into the title placeholder of the slide. While using the Word and PowerPoint applications, you have learned how to use cut, copy, and paste to move or copy information within the same document. You can also perform these same operations between documents in the same application and between documents in different applications. The information is pasted in a format that the application can edit, if possible.

4

- Select the title "Volunteer Orientation Meetings."

- Click 📋 Copy on the Home tab in Word.

- Click on the PowerPoint window to make it the active window.

- Right-click in the title placeholder in the Slide window in PowerPoint.

- Click 📋 Use Destination Theme in the Paste Options area of the shortcut menu to apply the slide formatting to the title.

Another Method

You also could use drag and drop to copy the text to the slide.

- Click on the slide to deselect the placeholder.

Your screen should be similar to Figure 4

Additional Information

You could also click 📋 Reset in the Slides group of the Home tab to quickly convert all the text on the slide to match the presentation's theme.

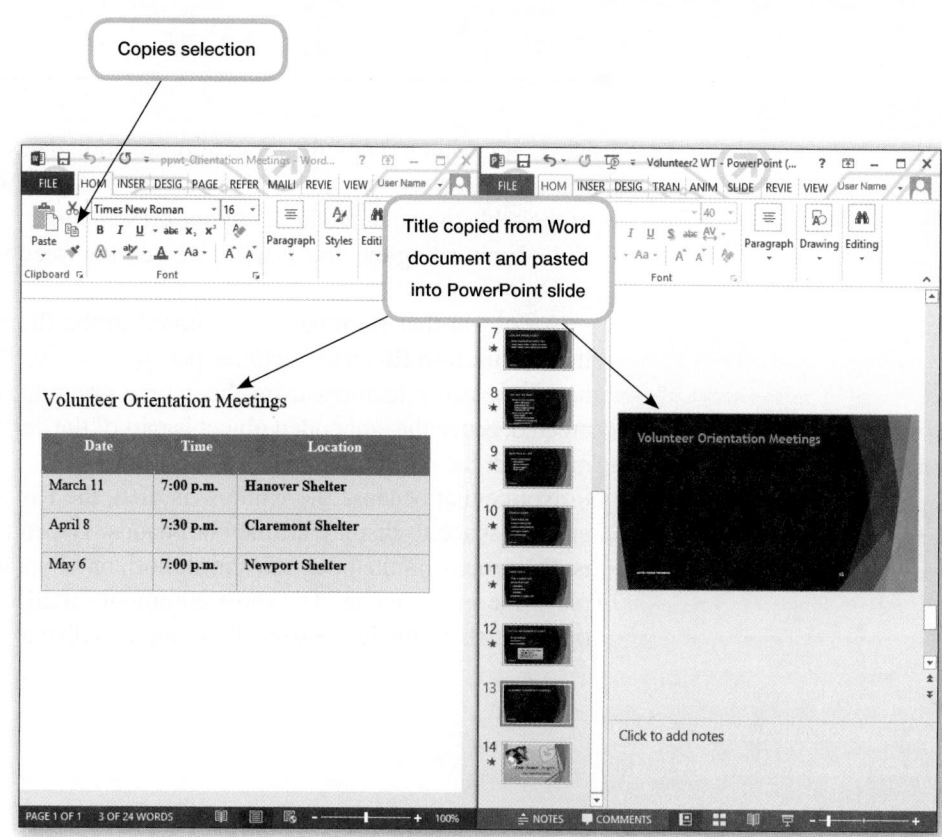

Figure 4

The title has been copied into the slide and can be edited and manipulated within PowerPoint. Because you used the Use Destination Theme paste option, the formats associated with the slide master were applied to the copied text.

Embedding a Word Table in a PowerPoint Slide

Next, you want to copy the table of orientation dates and place it below the title in the slide. Because you know that you are going to want to change the formatting of the table to match the look of your presentation, you will **embed** the table in the slide. Embedding the object will give you the freedom to modify the table's shape and appearance.

An object that is embedded is stored in the file in which it is inserted, called the **destination file**, and becomes part of that file. The embedded object can then be edited using features from the source program, the program in which it was created. Since the embedded object is part of the destination file, modifying it does not affect the original file, called the **source file**.

Notice that because the window is tiled, the Ribbon is smaller and there is not enough space to display all the commands. Depending on how small the Ribbon is, the groups on the open tab shrink horizontally and show a single icon that displays the group name. The most commonly used commands or features are left open. Clicking the icon opens the group and displays the commands.

1

● **Make the Word window active.**

● **Click within the table and open the Table Tools Layout tab.**

Having Trouble?

Use ◄ and ► located at both ends of the Ribbon tabs to scroll to see tabs that are not visible.

● **Click** Select **in the Table group and choose Select Table.**

Another Method

You can also click the ⊞ Table Selection Handle or drag to select the entire table.

● **Open the Home tab and click** ▣.

● **Click on the PowerPoint window.**

● **Open the** Paste **drop-down menu and choose** ▣ **Embed.**

Having Trouble?

See "Copying and Moving Selections," on page IO.47 in the Introduction to Microsoft Office for more information on the Paste Options feature.

Your screen should be similar to Figure 5

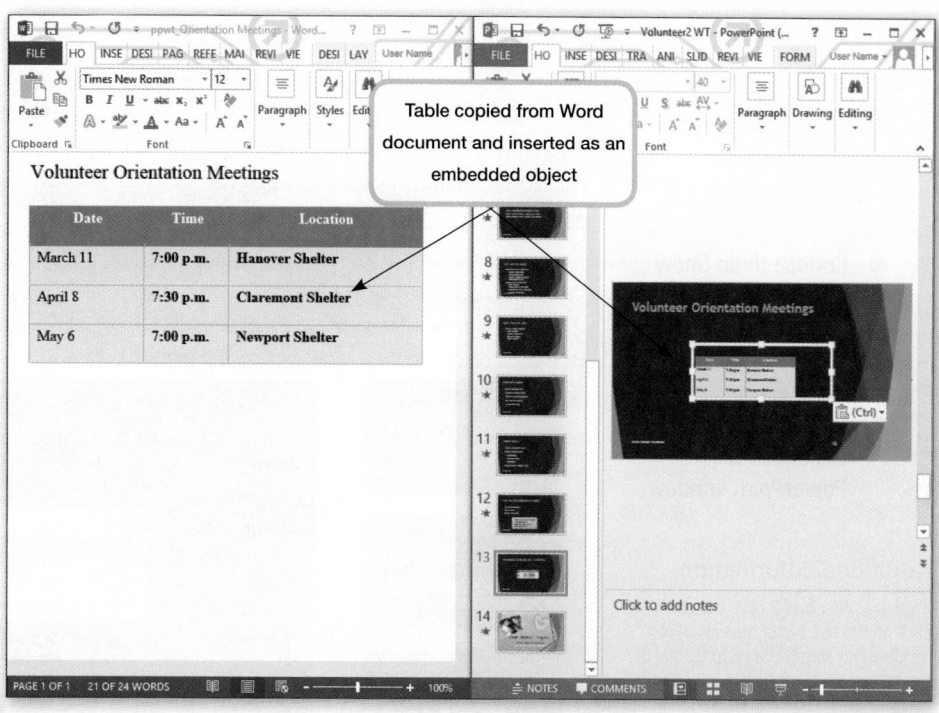

Table copied from Word document and inserted as an embedded object

Figure 5

The table, including the table formatting, is copied into the slide as an embedded object that can be manipulated. The object container is larger than the table it holds.

EDITING AN EMBEDDED OBJECT

As you look at the table, you decide to change the size and appearance of the table. To do this, you will edit the embedded object using the source program.

- **Choose Undo Show Side by Side from the taskbar shortcut menu.**

- **If necessary, maximize the PowerPoint window.**

Additional Information

If you use Windows 7 or 8, you can click on the title bar of the PowerPoint window and simply drag it to the top of the screen to maximize it.

- **Double-click the table.**

Your screen should be similar to Figure 6

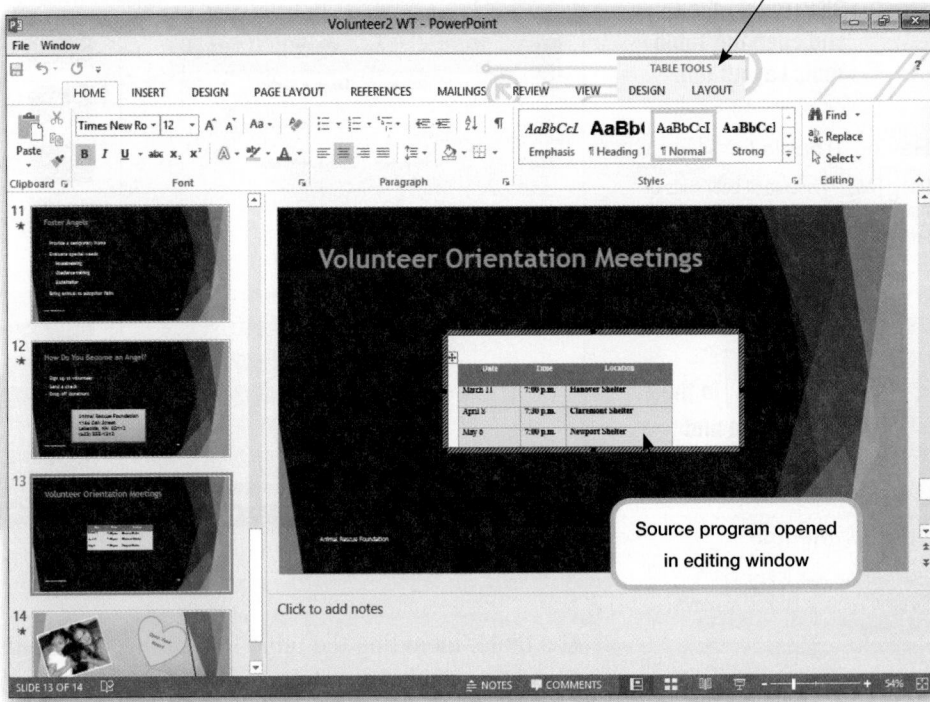

Word's Table Tools Design and Layout tabs available for editing the table

Source program opened in editing window

Figure 6

Additional Information

You must have the source program on your system to be able to open and edit an embedded object.

Additional Information

If you want to see gridlines in your table, open the Layout tab and click .

The source program, in this case Word 2013, is opened. The Word Ribbon replaces the PowerPoint Ribbon. The embedded object is displayed in an editing window. If your table does not display gridlines, this is because this feature is not on in your application. First, you will increase the size of the embedded object so that you can increase the size of the table within it.

2 Drag the sizing handle to increase the object's size as in Figure 7.

Your screen should be similar to Figure 7

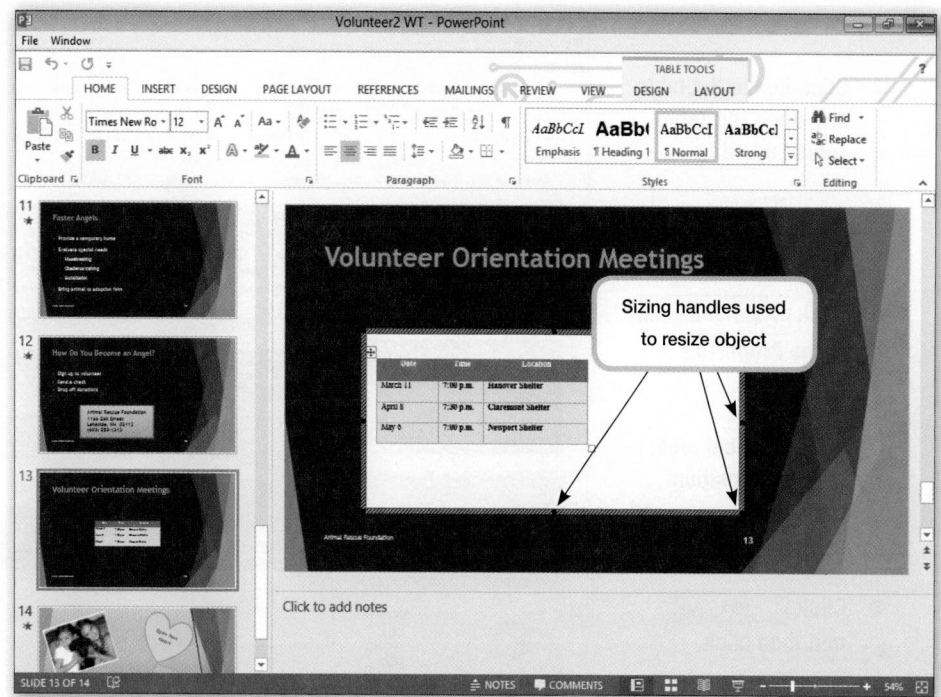

Figure 7

Now that the embedded object's container is larger, you can resize and reposition the table within the container.

3

- Click inside the table and open the Table Tools Layout tab.

- Click ☷ Properties in the Table group.

- Click Positioning... in the Properties dialog box.

- In the Vertical area, open the Position drop-down menu and choose Top.

- Click OK and then click OK.

- Scroll the window to see the entire table.

Having Trouble?

Use the directional keys or the scroll wheel to adjust it vertically.

- Slowly drag the bottom-right corner sizing handle of the table to increase the size of the table in the object's container.

Having Trouble?

If you can't see the table's bottom-right corner sizing handle, try clicking in the table and scrolling up and down until it appears.

Having Trouble?

If the table gets too large to fit in the container, click ↶ ▾ Undo to reset it and try again.

Your screen should be similar to Figure 8

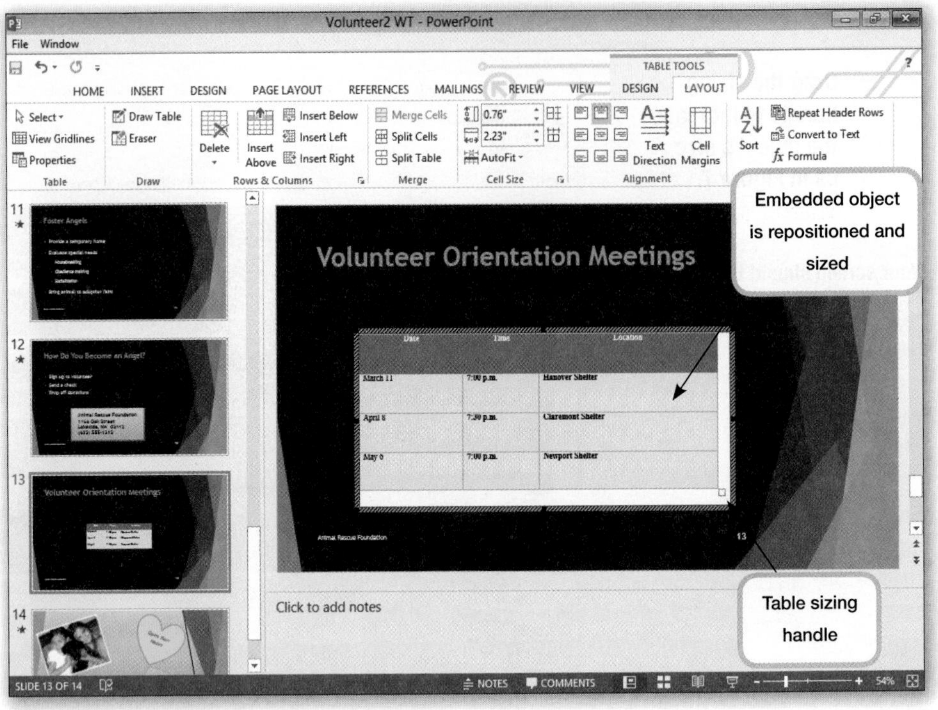

Figure 8

Next, you will use the Word commands to edit the object. You want to apply a different table design style and change the appearance of the text in the table.

4

- Open the Table Tools Design tab.

- Click ⬇ More in the Table Styles group.

- Choose ▦ Grid Table 5, Dark-Accent 2 from the Table Styles gallery (fifth row, third column).

- Drag to select the entire table and open the Table Tools Layout tab.

- In the Alignment group, choose ▤ Align Center Left.

- With the table still selected, open the Home tab and click A˄ four times to increase the font size to 20.

- Drag to select the first row of table headings and click A˄ three times to increase the font size to 26.

- Click anywhere outside the object to close the source program.

- Position the object as in Figure 9 and deselect it.

Your screen should be similar to Figure 9

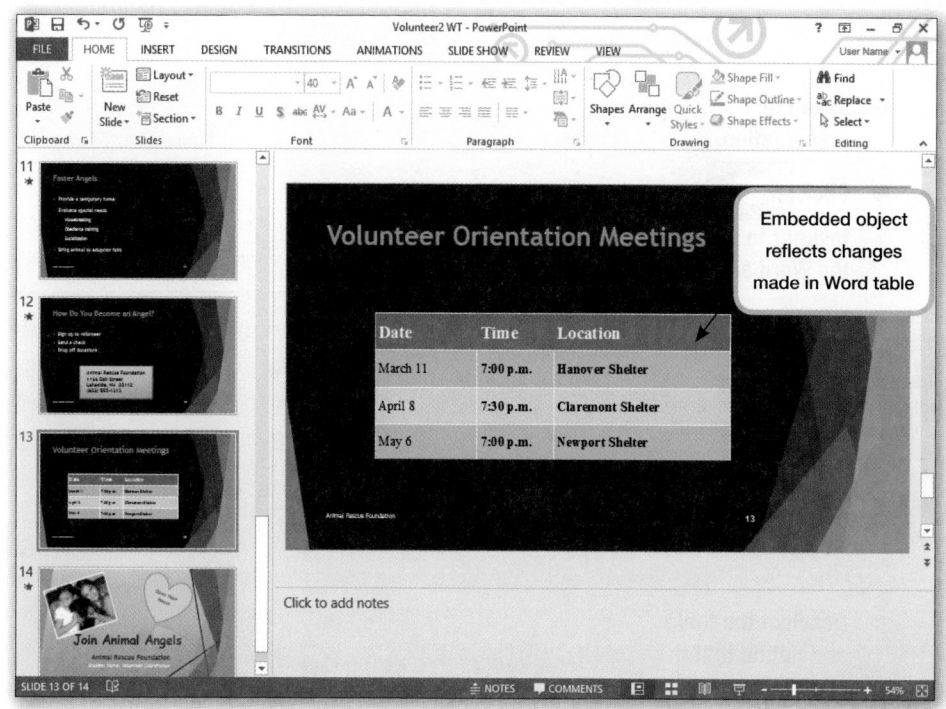

Figure 9

The embedded object in the PowerPoint slide is updated to reflect the changes you made in the Word table.

5

- Save the presentation.

- Click [w] in the taskbar to switch to the Word application.

Having Trouble?

Don't worry if your Word application taskbar image looks different than this one. Applications will look different depending on which version of Windows is installed on the computer you are using.

- Deselect the table and notice that the source file has not been affected by the changes you made to the embedded object.

- Exit Word.

Linking between Applications

Next, you want to copy the chart of the rescue and adoption data into the presentation. You will insert the chart object into the slide as a **linked object**, which is another way to insert information created in one application into a document created by another application. With a linked object, the actual data is stored in the source file (the document in which it was created). A graphic representation or picture of the data is displayed in the destination file (the document in which the object is inserted). A connection between the information in the destination file and the source file is established by creating a link. The link contains references to the location of the source file and the selection within the document that is linked to the destination file.

When changes are made in the source file that affect the linked object, the changes are automatically reflected in the destination file when it is opened. This connection is called a **live link**. When you create linked objects, the date and time on your machine should be accurate. This is because the program refers to the date of the source file to determine whether updates are needed when you open the destination file.

LINKING AN EXCEL CHART TO A POWERPOINT PRESENTATION

The chart of the rescue and adoption data will be inserted into another new slide following slide 6.

1

- Insert a new slide following slide 6 using the Title Only layout.

- Start Excel 2013 and open the workbook ppwt_Rescue Data from your data files.

- Display the application windows side by side.

Your screen should be similar to Figure 10

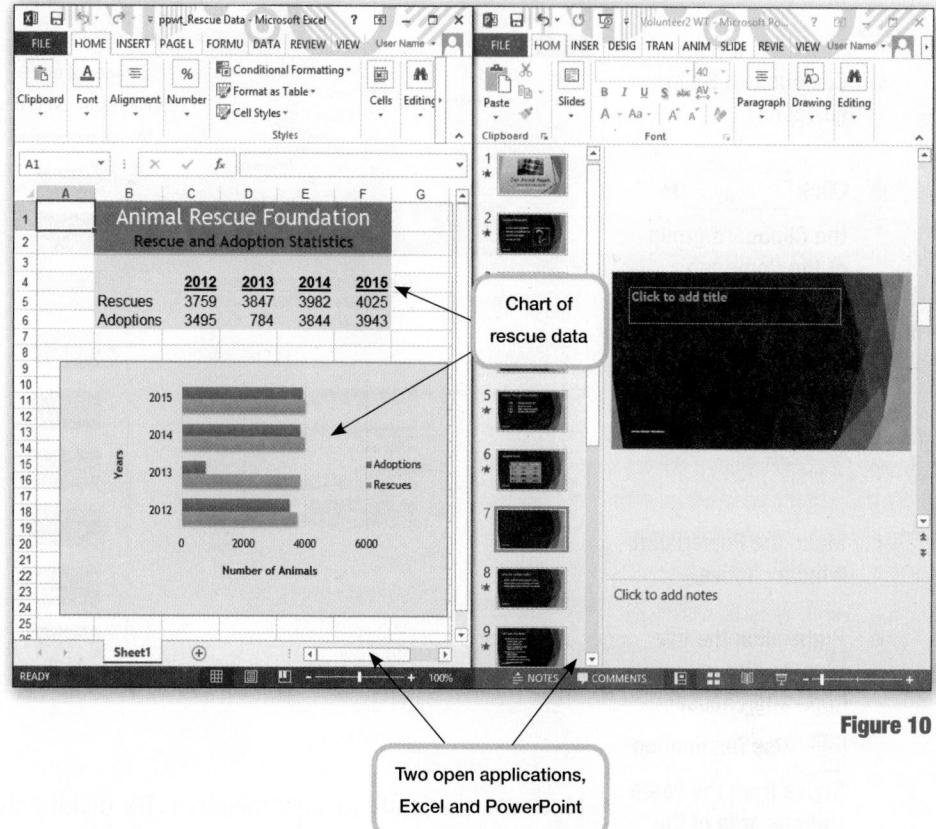

Chart of rescue data

Two open applications, Excel and PowerPoint

Figure 10

The worksheet contains the rescue and adoption data for the past four years as well as a bar chart of the data. Again, you have two open applications, PowerPoint and Excel. Next you will copy the second title line from the worksheet into the slide title placeholder.

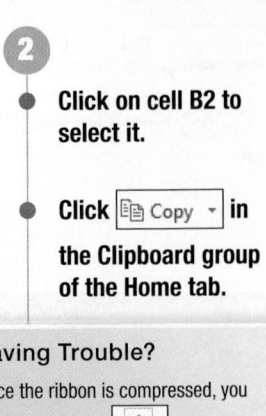

2

- Click on cell B2 to select it.

- Click [📋 Copy ▾] in the Clipboard group of the Home tab.

Having Trouble?

Since the ribbon is compressed, you may need to click [Clipboard] and then [📋 Copy ▾].

- Make the PowerPoint window active.

- Right-click the title placeholder in the slide and choose [📋] **Use Destination Styles** from the Paste Options area of the shortcut menu.

- Click on the slide to deselect the placeholder.

Your screen should be similar to Figure 11

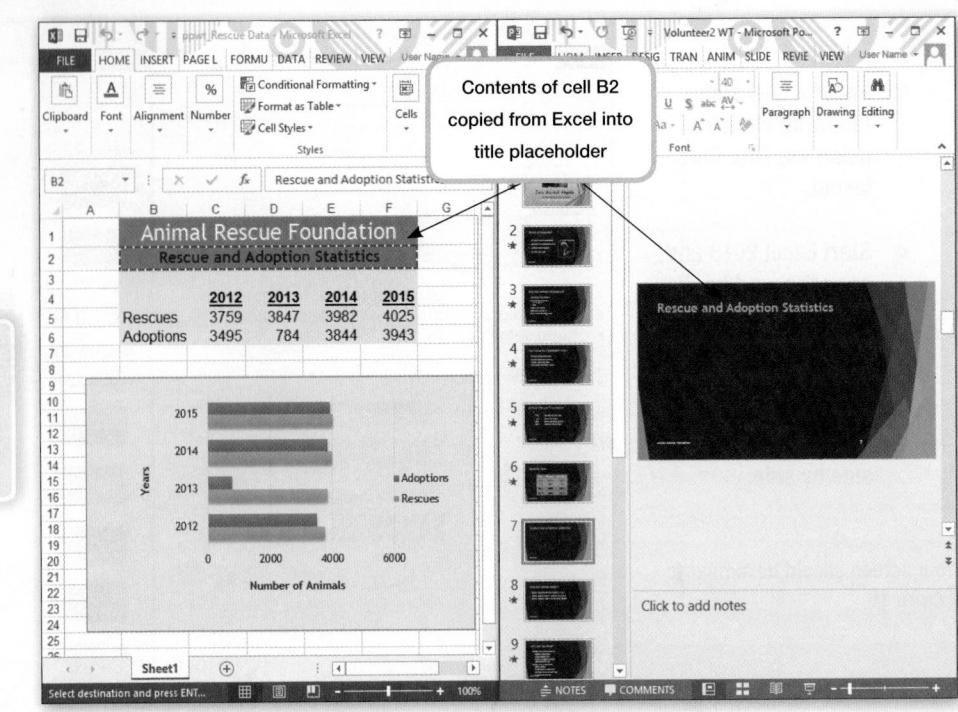

Figure 11

Now you are ready to copy the chart. By making the chart a linked object, it will be updated automatically if the source file is edited.

3

- Make the Excel window active.

- Press Esc to deselect B2 and then click on the chart object in the worksheet to select it.

Having Trouble?

Click on the chart to select it when the ScreenTip displays "Chart Area."

- Click 📋 Copy ▾ in the Clipboard group.

- Click on the slide.

- From the Home tab, open the Paste drop-down menu and choose Paste Special.

Your screen should be similar to Figure 12

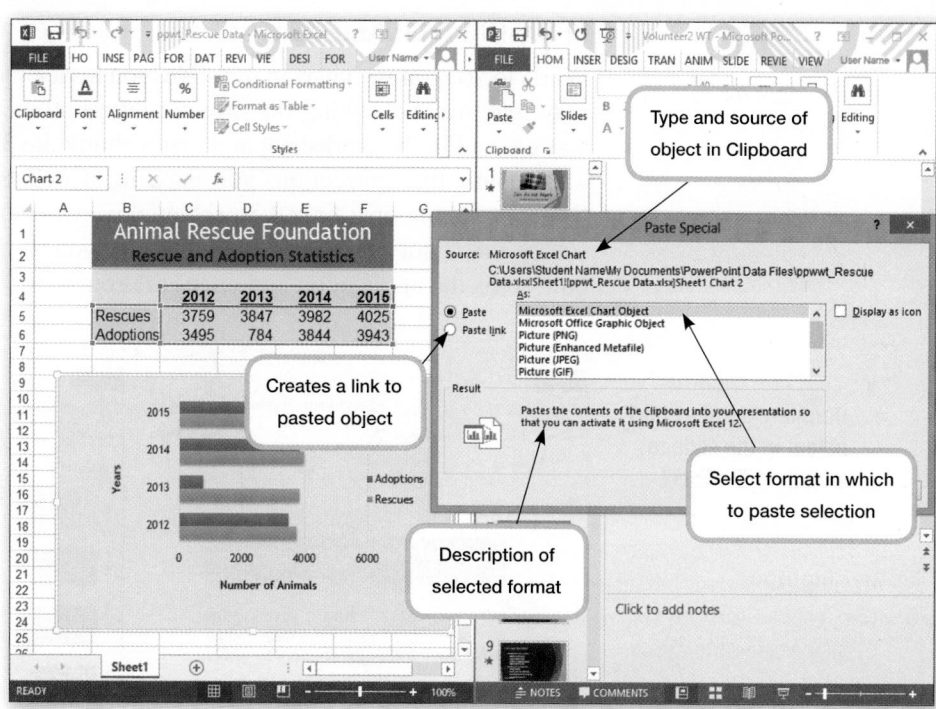

Figure 12

The Paste Special dialog box displays the type of object contained in the Clipboard and its location in the Source area. From the As list box, you select the type of format in which you want the object pasted into the destination file. The Result area describes the effect of your selections. In this case, you want to insert the chart as a linked object to Microsoft Excel.

4

- Choose Paste link.

- Click OK.

- Appropriately size and position the linked object on the slide.

Your screen should be similar to Figure 13

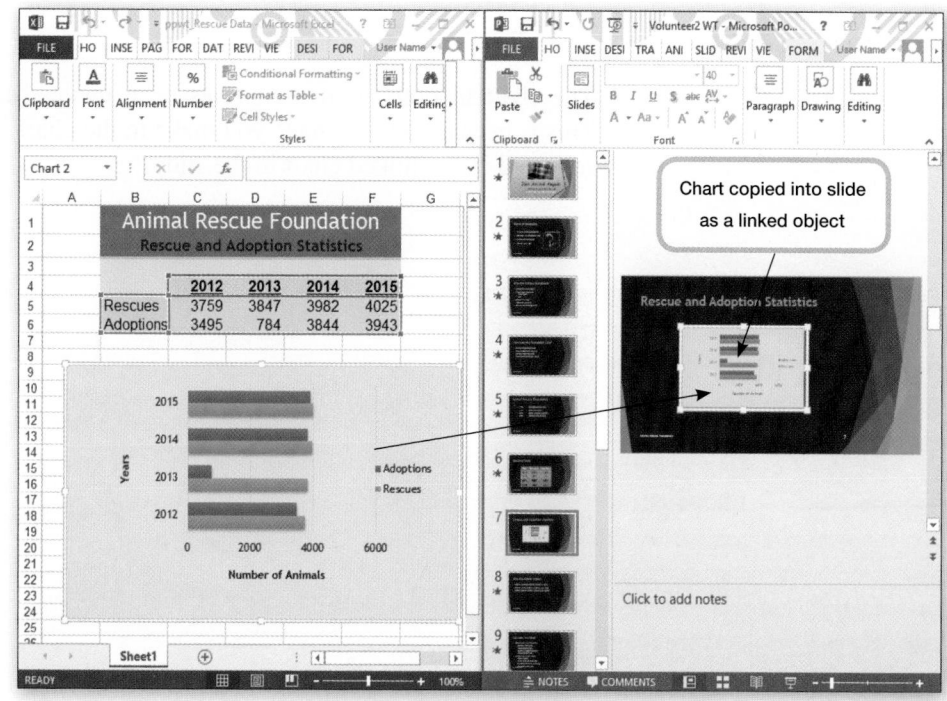

Figure 13

The chart object was inserted as a picture, and a link was created to the chart in the source file.

UPDATING A LINKED OBJECT

While looking at the chart in the slide, you notice the adoption data for 2013 looks very low. After checking the original information, you see that the wrong value was entered in the worksheet and that it should be 3784.

To make this correction, you need to switch back to the Excel application. Double-clicking on a linked object quickly switches to the open source file. If the source file is not open, it opens the file for you. If the application is not started, it both starts the application and opens the source file.

1

● **Double-click the chart object in the slide to switch to the Excel file.**

Another Method

You can also right-click the edge of the object and select Linked Worksheet Object/Edit.

● **Change the value in cell D6 to 3784 and press Enter.**

Your screen should be similar to Figure 14

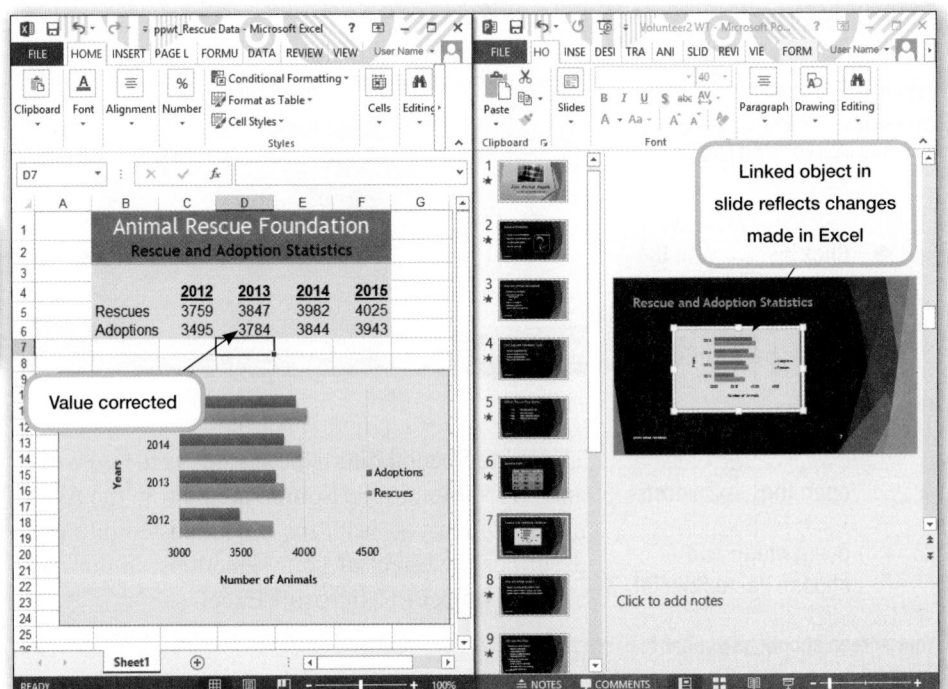

Figure 14

The chart in both applications has been updated to reflect the change in data. This is because any changes you make in the chart in Excel will be automatically reflected in the linked chart in the slide.

2

- Undo the side-by-side window display.

- Save the revised Excel workbook as Rescue Data Linked to your solution file location.

- Exit Excel.

- If necessary, maximize the PowerPoint window.

Linking documents is a very handy feature, particularly in documents whose information is updated frequently. If you include a linked object in a document, make sure the source file name and location do not change. Otherwise the link will not operate correctly.

Printing Selected Slides

Next, you will print the two new slides.

1

- Open the File tab and choose Print.

- If necessary, select the printer.

- Enter 7,14 in the Slides text box to specify the slides to print.

- Specify Handouts (2 slides) as the type of output.

- Change the color setting to Grayscale.

- If necessary, click the Edit Header & Footer link and change the header to display your name.

Your screen should be similar to Figure 15

2

- Print the page.

- Save the linked presentation as Volunteer2 Linked and exit PowerPoint.

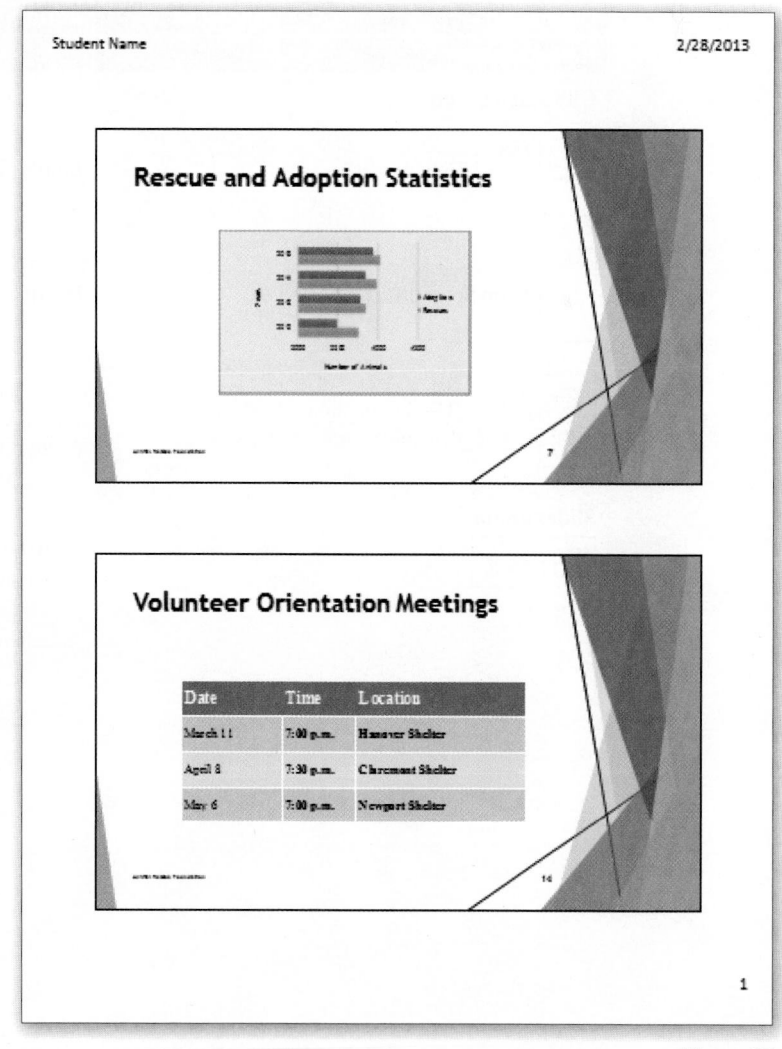

Figure 15

KEY TERMS

destination file PPWT.6
embed PPWT.6
linked object PPWT.12

live link PPWT.12
source file PPWT.6

COMMAND SUMMARY

Command	Shortcut	Action
Home tab		
Clipboard group		
Paste / Embed		Embeds an object from another application
Paste /Paste Special/Paste Link		Inserts an object as a linked object
Paste / Use Destination Theme		Uses formatting associated with presentation theme
Slides group		
Reset		Converts all the slides content to match the presentation's theme

STEP-BY-STEP

EMBEDDING A TABLE OF MASSAGE PRICES ★

1. At the Hollywood Spa and Fitness Center, you have been working on a presentation on massage therapy. Now that the presentation is almost complete, you just need to add some information to the presentation about prices for all massage services. Your manager has already given you this information in a Word document. You will copy and embed this information into a new slide. The completed slide is shown below.

   a. Start Word and open the file ppwt_Massage Prices.

   b. Start PowerPoint and open the ppwt_Massage Therapy2 presentation.

   c. Save the presentation as Massage Therapy.

   d. Add a new slide after slide 9 using the Title Only layout.

   e. Copy the title from the Word document into the slide title placeholder. Use the Keep Text Only option.

   f. Copy the table into the slide as an embedded object. Exit Word.

   g. Size and position the object on the slide appropriately.

   h. Edit the table to change the font color to an appropriate font color.

   i. Change the fill color of the table to match the slide design.

   j. If necessary, change the footer to display your name.

   k. Save the presentation.

   l. Print the new slide.

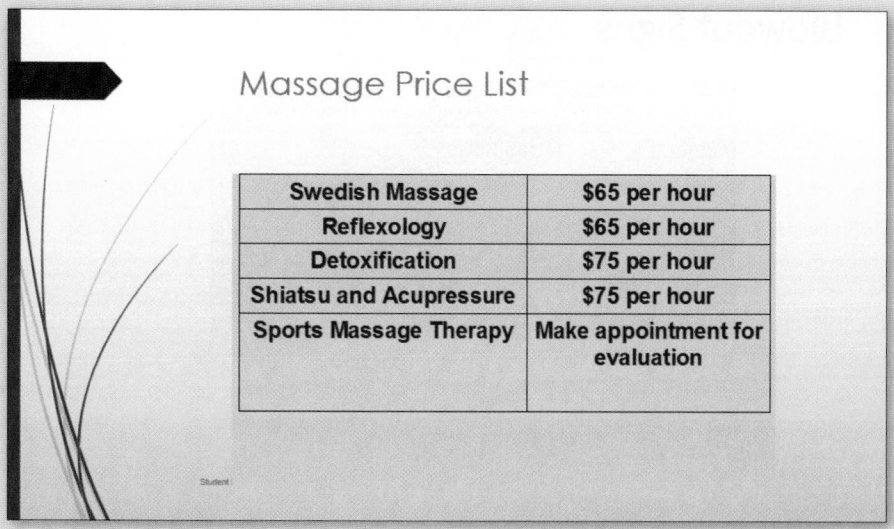

LAB EXERCISES

EMBEDDING A TABLE OF BLOWOUT INDICATORS ★★

2. To complete this problem, you must have completed Step-by-Step Exercise 2 in Lab 2. The Blowouts section for the Department of Safety presentation is almost complete. You just need to add some information to the presentation about the indicators of a flat tire. This information is already in a Word document as a table. You will copy and embed it into a new slide. The completed slide is shown below.

   a. Start Word and open the ppwt_BlowoutSigns file.

   b. Start PowerPoint and open the Blowouts2 presentation. If this file is not available, you can use ppwt_Blowouts2 Widescreen.

   c. Save the presentation as Blowouts3 Widescreen.

   d. Add a new slide after slide 3 using the Title Only layout.

   e. Copy the title from the Word document into the slide title placeholder.

   f. Copy the table into the slide as an embedded object. Exit Word.

   g. Size and position the object on the slide appropriately.

   h. Change the design of the table to suit your presentation.

   i. Change the fonts and font sizes of the table headings.

   j. If necessary, change the footer to display your name.

   k. Save the presentation.

   l. Print the new slide.

Blowout Signs

Blowout	Effect
General	Loud noise Vehicle shakes
Front tire	Vehicle pulls to side of blowout
Back tire	Vehicle fishtails

STUDENT NAME

4

LINKING A WORKSHEET ON FOREST USE ★★★

3. To complete this problem, you must have completed Step-by-Step Exercise 4 in Lab 2. Kevin has found some interesting data on the increase in Americans hiking and wants to include this information in his lecture presentation. The completed slide is shown below.

   a. Start PowerPoint and open the Triple Crown Presentation2 file. If this file is not available, you can use ppwt_Triple Crown Presentation2. Save the presentation as Triple Crown Presentation3.

   b. Start Excel and open the ppwt_Forest Use worksheet. Save the worksheet as Forest Use Linked.

   c. Add a new slide after slide 6 using the Title Only layout.

   d. Copy the worksheet cell A1 and paste it in the title placeholder using the Keep Text Only.

   e. Copy the worksheet range A2 through B6 as a linked object into slide 7. Size and position it appropriately.

   f. Format the linked data so that it blends appropriately with the presentation.

   g. Add an appropriate Shape Outline to the linked object's container in the slide.

   h. You notice that the percentage for hiking seems low. After checking the original source, you see you entered the value incorrectly. In Excel, change the value in cell B5 to 42%.

   i. Copy the text in cell A8 and paste it into the Notes for slide 7.

   j. Save the worksheet and exit Excel.

   k. Change the look of the presentation by applying the Slice theme.

   l. Check each slide to resize and reposition objects as necessary.

   m. If necessary, change the footer to display your name.

   n. Save the presentation.

   o. Print the new slide.

Sightseeing	44%
Relaxation	36%
Viewing Wildlife	37%
Hiking	**42%**
Driving	24%

MOST POPULAR FOREST ACTIVITIES

Student Name

7

COMMAND	SHORTCUT	ACTION
Quick Access Toolbar		
💾 Save	Ctrl + **S**	Saves document using same file name
↩ Undo	Ctrl + **Z**	Restores last editing change
↪ Redo	Ctrl + **Y**	Restores last Undo or repeats last command or action
File Tab		
Info/ Check for Issues /Inspect Document		Checks your document for hidden data or personal information
Info/ Check for Issues /Check Compatibility		Checks your document for features that aren't compatible with previous versions
New	Ctrl + **N**	Opens new blank document or specialized template
Open	Ctrl + **O**	Opens existing document file
Save	Ctrl + **S**	Saves document using same file name
Save As	F12	Saves document using a new file name, type, and/or location
Print		Displays document as it will appear when printed
Print / Print	Ctrl + **P**	Prints document
Share / Send as Attachment		Sends a document as an e-mail attachment
Close	Ctrl + F4	Closes document
Options		Change options for working with Word
Options /Proofing		Changes settings associated with Spelling and Grammar checking
Home Tab		
Clipboard Group		
Paste	Ctrl + **V**	Pastes items from Clipboard

WORD 2013 COMMAND SUMMARY

COMMAND	SHORTCUT	ACTION
/Paste Special/Paste Link		Pastes contents of Clipboard as a linked object
/Paste Special/Paste		Embeds contents of Clipboard as selected type of object
Cut	Ctrl + X	Cuts selection to Clipboard
Copy	Ctrl + C	Copies selection to Clipboard
Format Painter		Duplicates formats of selection to other locations
Font Group		
Calibri (Body) Font		Changes typeface
11 Font Size		Changes font size
Increase Font Size		Incrementally increase font size
Bold	Ctrl + B	Adds/removes bold effect
Italic	Ctrl + I	Adds/removes italic effect
Underline	Ctrl + U	Underlines selected text with single line
Change Case	Shift + F3	Changes case of selected text
Clear Formatting		Removes all formatting from selection
Text Highlight Color		Applies color highlight to text
Font Color		Changes text to selected color
Paragraph Group		
Bullets		Creates a bulleted list
Numbering		Creates a numbered list
Decrease Indent		Decreases indent of paragraph to previous tab stop
Increase Indent		Increases indent of paragraph to next tab stop

COMMAND	SHORTCUT	ACTION
☰ Align Left	Ctrl + L	Aligns text to left margin
☰ Center	Ctrl + E	Centers text between left and right margins
☰ Align Right	Ctrl + R	Aligns text to right margin
☰ Justify	Ctrl + J	Aligns text equally between left and right margins
‡☰ ▾ Line and Paragraph Spacing	Ctrl + 1 or 2	Changes spacing between lines of text
A↓ Z Sort		Rearranges information in a list into ascending alphabetical/numerical order
¶ Show/Hide	Ctrl + *	Displays or hides formatting marks
⌟/ Tabs...		Specifies types and positions of tab stops
⌟/Indents and Spacing/Special/First Line	Tab	Indents first line of paragraph from left margin
⌟/Indents and Spacing/Line Spacing	Ctrl + 1 or 2	Changes the spacing between lines of text
Editing Group		
🔍 Find ▾	Ctrl + F	Locates specified text
ab/ac Replace	Ctrl + H	Locates and replaces specified text
Insert Tab		
Pages Group		
📄 Cover Page ▾		Inserts a preformatted cover page
📄 Blank Page		Inserts a blank page
⊢⊣ Page Break	Ctrl + Enter	Inserts hard page break
Tables Group		
▦ Table ▾		Inserts table at insertion point
Illustrations Group		
🖼 Pictures		Inserts selected picture
🖼 Online Pictures		Inserts online clips

WORD 2013 COMMAND SUMMARY

COMMAND	SHORTCUT	ACTION
Shapes		Inserts graphic shapes
Media Group		
Online Video		Inserts online video
Header and Footer Group		
Header ▾		Inserts predesigned header style
Footer ▾		Inserts predesigned footer style
Text Group		
Explore Quick Parts		Inserts Building Blocks
Insert Date and Time		Inserts current date or time, in selected format
Design Tab		
Document Formatting Group		
Themes		Applies selected theme to document
Colors		Changes colors for current theme
Fonts		Changes fonts for current theme
Paragraph Spacing ▾		Changes the paragraph spacing for the entire document
Page Background Group		
Watermark		Inserts ghosted text behind page content
Page Borders		Inserts and customizes page borders

WWW.MHHE.COM/OLEARY

COMMAND	SHORTCUT	ACTION
Page Layout Tab		
Page Setup Group		
Margins		Sets margin sizes
Breaks		Inserts page and section breaks
References Tab		
Table of Contents Group		
Table of Contents		Generates a table of contents
Add Text		Adds selected text as an entry in table of contents
Update Table	F9	Updates the table of contents field
Footnotes Group		
AB¹ Insert Footnote	Alt + Ctrl + F	Inserts footnote reference at insertion point
Citations & Bibliography Group		
Insert Citation		Creates a citation for a reference source
Manage Sources		Displays list of all sources cited
Style: MLA		Sets the style of citations
Bibliography		Creates a bibliography list of sources cited
Captions Group		
Insert Caption		Adds a figure caption
Insert Table of Figures		Inserts a table of figures
Update Table	F9	Updates table of figures field
Cross-reference		Creates figure cross-references
Index Group		
Mark Entry		Marks an index entry
Insert Index		Inserts an index at the insertion point

WORD 2013 COMMAND SUMMARY

COMMAND	SHORTCUT	ACTION
Mailings Tab		
Create Group		
Envelopes		Prepares and prints an envelope
Review Tab		
Proofing Group		
Spelling & Grammar	F7	Opens Spelling and Grammar pane and starts Spelling and Grammar Checker
Thesaurus	Shift + F7	Opens Thesaurus tool
View Tab		
Views Group		
Read Mode		Displays document only, without application features
Print Layout		Shows how text and objects will appear on printed page
Web Layout		Shows document as it will appear when viewed in a web browser
Outline		Shows structure of document
Draft		Shows text formatting and simple layout of page
Show Group		
Ruler		Displays/hides ruler
Zoom Group		
Zoom		Opens Zoom dialog box
100%		Zooms document to 100% of normal size
One Page		Zooms document so an entire page fits in window
Page Width		Zooms document so width of page matches width of window

COMMAND	SHORTCUT	ACTION
Window Group		
Arrange All		Arranges all open windows horizontally on the screen
Split	Alt + Ctrl + S	Divides a document into two horizontal sections
View Side by Side		Displays two document windows side by side to make it easy to compare content
Synchronous Scrolling		Moves two documents together
Switch Windows		Switches between open document windows
Table Tools Design Tab		
Table Style Options Group		
Header Row		Turns on/off formats for header row
First Column		Turns on/off formats for first column
Last Column		Turns on/off formats for last column
Table Styles Group		
More		Opens Table Styles gallery
Table Tools Layout Tab		
Table Group		
View Gridlines		Displays or hides table gridlines
Rows & Columns Group		
Insert Above		Inserts a new row in table above selected row
Cell Size Group		
AutoFit		Automatically resizes column width in tables
Alignment Group		
Align Top Center		Aligns text at top center of cell space
Data Group		
Sort		Rearranges items in a selection into ascending alphabetical/numerical order
Picture Tools Format Tab		
Picture Styles Group		
Picture Border		Customizes a picture's border

WORD 2013 COMMAND SUMMARY

COMMAND	SHORTCUT	ACTION
🖼 Picture Effects ▾		Adds special effects to a picture
Arrange Group		
📄 Wrap Text ▾		Controls how text will wrap around a graphic object
Header & Footer Tools Design Tab		
Header & Footer Group		
📄 Header ▾		Inserts predesigned header style
📄 Footer ▾		Inserts predesigned footer style
📄 Page Number ▾		Inserts page number in header or footer
Insert Group		
📅 Date & Time		Inserts current date or time in header or footer
📄 Document Info ▾		Inserts document information in header or footer
📄 Quick Parts ▾ / Document Property		Inserts document property Quick Part
📄 Quick Parts ▾ / Field		Inserts selected field Quick Part
Navigation Group		
📄 Previous		Moves to previous header or footer
📄 Next		Moves to next header or footer
📄 Link to Previous		Turns on/off link to header or footer in previous section
Options Group		
☑ Different First Page		Specifies a unique header and footer for the first page
☐ Different Odd & Even Pages		Specifies different header or footer on odd and even pages
☑ Show Document Text		Shows/hides document text when working on header or footer
Drawing Tools Format Tab		
Shape Styles Group		
▾		Opens the Shape Styles gallery
🎨 Shape Fill ▾		Adds colors, gradients, and textures to shapes
🖊 Shape Outline ▾		Adds colors and other effects to a shape's outline

COMMAND	SHORTCUT	ACTION
Quick Access Toolbar		
💾 Save	Ctrl + **S**	Saves document using same file name
↶ Undo	Ctrl + **Z**	Reverses last editing or formatting change
↷ Redo	Ctrl + **Y**	Restores changes after using Undo
File Tab		
Save	Ctrl + **S**	Saves file using same file name
Save As	F12	Saves file using a new file name
Open	Ctrl + **O**	Opens an existing workbook file
Close	Ctrl + F4	Closes open workbook file
New	Ctrl + **N**	Opens a new blank workbook
Print	Ctrl + **P**	Opens Print dialog box
Print/ Scale: /Fit To		Scales the worksheet to fit a specified number of pages
Options		Displays and changes program settings
Home Tab		
Clipboard Group		
Paste	Ctrl + **V**	Pastes selections stored in system Clipboard
Paste Special/Paste		Inserts object as an embedded object
Paste Special/Paste Link		Inserts object as a linked object
✂ Cut	Ctrl + **X**	Cuts selected data from the worksheet
Copy	Ctrl + **C**	Copies selected data to system Clipboard
Format Painter		Copies formatting from one place and applies it to another
Font Group		
Calibri ▾ Font		Changes text font
11 ▾ Font Size		Changes text size
B Bold	Ctrl + **B**	Bolds selected text
I Italic	Ctrl + **I**	Italicizes selected text

EXCEL 2013 COMMAND SUMMARY

COMMAND	SHORTCUT	ACTION
U ▾ Underline	Ctrl + U	Underlines selected text
⊞ ▾ Borders		Adds border to specified area of cell or range
🖌 ▾ Fill Color		Adds color to cell background
A ▾ Font Color		Adds color to text
Alignment Group		
≣ Align Left		Left-aligns entry in cell space
≣ Center		Center-aligns entry in cell space
≣ Align Right		Right-aligns entry in cell space
⇤ Decrease Indent		Reduces the margin between the left cell border and cell entry
⇥ Increase Indent		Indents cell entry
⊞ ▾ Merge & Center		Combines selected cells into one cell and centers cell contents in new cell
Number Group		
General ▾ Number Format		Applies selected number formatting to selection
$ ▾ Accounting Number Format		Applies Accounting number format to selection
% Percent Style		Applies Percent Style format to selection
, Comma Style		Applies Comma Style format with two decimals to selection
.00 Increase Decimal		Increases number of decimal places
.00 Decrease Decimal		Decreases number of decimal places
Styles group		
🗔 Cell Styles ▾		Applies predefined combinations of colors, effects, and formats to selected cells
🗔 Cell Styles ▾ /Modify		Modifies existing cell style
🗔 Conditional Formatting ▾		Applies Highlight Cells Rules, Top/Bottom Rules, Data Bars, Color Scales, and Icon Sets to selected cells based on criteria
Cells Group		
🗔 Insert ▾ /Insert Cells		Inserts blank cells, shifting existing cells down

CEL 2013 COMMAND SUMMARY

COMMAND	SHORTCUT	ACTION
Insert ▾ /Insert Cut Cells		Inserts cut row of data into new worksheet row, shifting existing rows down
Insert ▾ /Insert Copied Cells		Inserts copied row into new worksheet row, shifting existing rows down
Insert ▾ /Insert Sheet		Inserts a new blank worksheet in workbook
Insert ▾ /Insert Sheet Rows		Inserts blank rows, shifting existing rows down
Insert ▾ /Insert Sheet Columns		Inserts blank columns, shifting existing columns right
Delete ▾ /Delete Sheet		Deletes the active worksheet
Delete ▾ /Delete Sheet Rows		Deletes selected rows, shifting existing rows up
Delete ▾ /Delete Sheet Columns		Deletes selected columns, shifting existing columns left
Delete ▾ /Delete Sheet		Deletes entire sheet
Format ▾ /Row Height		Changes height of selected row
Format ▾ /AutoFit Row Height		Changes row height to match the tallest cell entry
Format ▾ /Column Width		Changes width of selected column
Format ▾ /AutoFit Column Width		Changes column width to match widest cell entry
Format ▾ /Default Width		Returns column width to default width
Format ▾ /Rename Sheet		Renames sheet
Format ▾ /Move or Copy Sheet		Moves or copies selected sheet
Format ▾ /Tab Color		Changes color of sheet tabs

Editing Group

COMMAND	SHORTCUT	ACTION
Σ ▾ Sum		Calculates the sum of the values in the selected cells
Σ ▾ Sum/Average		Calculates the average of the values in the selected range
Σ ▾ Sum/Max		Returns the largest of the values in the selected range
Σ ▾ Sum/Min		Returns the smallest of the values in the selected range

EXCEL 2013 COMMAND SUMMARY

COMMAND	SHORTCUT	ACTION
Fill/Right	Ctrl + R	Continues a pattern to adjacent cells to the right
Clear		Removes both formats and contents from selected cells
Clear/Clear Formats		Clears formats only from selected cells
Clear/Clear Contents	Delete	Clears contents only from selected cells
/Find	Ctrl + F	Locates specified text, numbers, and/or formats
/Replace	Ctrl + H	Locates specified characters or formats and replaces them with specified replacement characters or format
/Go To	Ctrl + G	Goes to a specified cell location in worksheet

Insert Tab

Illustrations Group

Pictures		Inserts a picture from a file on your computer or a local network
Online Pictures		Finds and inserts pictures from online sources

Charts Group

Recommended Charts		Displays several recommended chart types for selected data
		Inserts a column chart
		Inserts a pie chart
		Inserts a combo chart

Sparklines Group

Line		Inserts sparkline in the selected cell

COMMAND	SHORTCUT	ACTION
Text Group		
Header & Footer		Adds header or footer to worksheet
Page Layout Tab		
Themes Group		
Themes		Applies selected theme to worksheet
Themes /Save Current Theme		Saves modified theme settings as a custom theme
Colors ▾		Changes colors for the current theme
Page Setup Group		
Margins /Narrow		Changes margin settings
Margins /Custom Margins/Horizontally		Centers worksheet horizontally on page
Margins /Custom Margins/Vertically		Centers worksheet vertically on page
Orientation /Landscape		Changes page orientation to landscape
Print Area /Set Print Area		Sets print area to selected cells
Breaks /Insert Page Break		Inserts page break at cell pointer location
Breaks /Remove Page Break		Removes page break at cell pointer location
Breaks /Reset All Page Breaks		Restores automatic page breaks
Scale to Fit Group		
Width:		Scales worksheet width to specified number of pages
Height:		Scales worksheet height to specified number of pages

EXCEL 2013 COMMAND SUMMARY

COMMAND	SHORTCUT	ACTION
↕ ⊟ Height: /1 page		Scales worksheet vertically to fit one page
⊡ Scale:		Scales worksheet by entering a percentage
⊡ Scale: /Fit To		Scales the worksheet to fit a specified number of pages
Sheet Options Group		
Gridlines ☑ View ☑ Print		Displays/hides gridlines for viewing and printing

Formulas Tab

Function Library Group		
Σ AutoSum ▾		Enters Sum, Average, Minimum, Maximum, or Count function
Formula Auditing Group		
⊞ Show Formulas	Ctrl + '	Displays and hides worksheet formulas
⚠ ▾ Error Checking		Checks worksheet for formula errors
Watch Window		Opens Watch Window toolbar

Data Tab

Data Tools Group		
⊞? What-If Analysis ▾ /Goal Seek		Adjusts value in specified cell until a formula dependent on that cell reaches specified result

Review Tab

Proofing Group		
ABC ✓ Spelling	F7	Spell-checks worksheet
Thesaurus	Shift + F7	Opens the Thesaurus for the selected word in the Research task pane

View Tab

Workbook Views Group		
Normal		Changes worksheet view to Normal
Page Break Preview		Displays where pages will break when a worksheet is printed
Page Layout		Displays worksheet as it will appear when printed

CEL 2013 COMMAND SUMMARY

COMMAND	SHORTCUT	ACTION
Show Group		
☑ Gridlines		Turns on/off display of gridlines
☑ Headings		Turns on/off display of row and column headings
Zoom Group		
Zoom		Changes magnification of window
Window Group		
Freeze Panes ▾ /Freeze Panes		Freezes top and/or leftmost panes
Freeze Panes ▾ /Unfreeze Panes		Unfreezes window panes
Split		Divides window into four panes at active cell or removes split
Picture Tools Format Tab		
Picture Styles Group		
Picture Border ▾		Specifies color, width, and line style for outline of shape
Picture Effects ▾		Adds glow, shadow, and other effects to pictures
Picture Layout ▾		Converts selected picture to a SmartArt graphic
Chart Tools Design Tab		
Chart Layouts Group		
Add Chart Element ▾ /Chart Title		Adds, removes, or positions the chart title
Add Chart Element ▾ /Axis Titles		Adds, removes, or positions the axes titles
Add Chart Element ▾ /Legend		Adds, removes, or positions the chart legend
Add Chart Element ▾ /Data Labels		Adds, removes, or positions the data labels
Quick Layout ▾		Changes the overall layout of the chart

COMMAND	SHORTCUT	ACTION
Chart Styles Group		
Change Colors ▾		Changes colors associated with chart styles
Data Group		
Switch Row/ Column		Swaps the data over the axes
Select Data		Changes the data range included in chart
Type Group		
Change Chart Type		Changes to a different type of chart
Location Group		
Move Chart		Moves chart to another sheet in the workbook
Chart Tools Format Tab		
Current Selection Group		
Chart Area ▾		Selects an element on the chart
Format Selection		Opens Format dialog box for selected element
Shape Styles Group		
More		Opens Shape Styles gallery
Shape Fill ▾		Adds selected fill to shape
Shape Outline ▾		Specifies color, weight, and type of outline
Shape Effects ▾		Adds selected effect to shape
Sparklines Tool Design Tab		
Style Group		
More		Opens sparkline style gallery
Clear ▾		Removes sparkline

COMMAND		SHORTCUT	ACTION
Quick Access Toolbar			
💾 Save		Ctrl + S	Saves the current object
↩ Undo		Ctrl + Z	Cancels last action
✕		Alt + F4	Closes Access
File Tab			
Info	Compact & Repair Database		Compacts and repairs database file
Info	/View and edit database properties		Set keywords, author name, and subject
New		Ctrl + N	Opens the New window where you can select options to create a new database
Open		Ctrl + O	Opens an existing database
Open	Recent		Displays list of recently used database files.
Save		Ctrl + S	Saves database object
Save As	Save Database As		Saves database with a new file name
Save As	Save Object As		Saves a copy of the open object
Save As	Save Object As / Back Up Database — Back up important databases regularly to prevent data loss.		Backs up database
Print	Print — Select a printer, number of copies, and other printing options before printing.	Ctrl + P	Specifies print settings and prints current database object
Print	Print Preview — Preview and make changes to pages before printing.		Displays current object in Print Preview
Close			Closes open database
←			Closes File tab and returns to currently open database
Home Tab			
Views Group			
Datasheet View		(icon)	Displays object in Datasheet view
Design View		(icon)	Displays object Design view
Form View		(icon)	Changes to Form view

ACCESS 2013 COMMAND SUMMARY

COMMAND	SHORTCUT	ACTION
Form Layout View		Changes to Form Layout view
Report View		Displays report in Report view
Report Layout View		Displays report in Layout view
Clipboard Group		
Paste or	Ctrl + **V**	Inserts copy of item from the Clipboard
Cut	Ctrl + **X**	Removes selected item and copies it to the Clipboard
Copy or	Ctrl + **C**	Duplicates selected item and copies it to the Clipboard
Sort & Filter Group		
Filter		Specifies filter settings for selected field
Ascending		Changes sort order to ascending
Descending		Changes sort order to descending
Remove Sort		Clears all sorts and returns sort order to primary key order
Selection ▾ /Equals		Sets filter to display only those records containing selected value
Advanced ▾ /Clear All Filters		Removes all filters from table
Toggle Filter		Applies and removes filter from table
Records Group		
Refresh All ▾		Updates selected object
New	Ctrl + +	Adds new record
Save	⇧Shift + ↵Enter	Saves changes to object design
Delete ▾	Delete	Deletes current record
Totals		Displays/hides Totals row

COMMAND	SHORTCUT	ACTION
More ▾ /Hide Fields		Hides selected columns in Datasheet view
More ▾ /Unhide Fields		Redisplays hidden columns
More ▾ /Field Width		Adjusts width of selected column
Find Group		
Find	Ctrl + F	Locates specified data
Replace	Ctrl + H	Locates specified data and replaces it with specified replacement text
→ ▾ Go To		Moves to First, Previous, Next, Last, or New record location
▾ Select/ Select		Selects current record
▾ Select/ Select All		Selects all records in database
Text Formatting Group		
B Bold	Ctrl + B	Applies bold effect to all text in datasheet
A ▾ Font Color		Applies selected color to all text in datasheet
▾ Gridlines		Changes display of gridlines in the datasheet
▾ Alternate Row Color		Changes background row colors of datasheet

Create Tab

Tables Group

Table		Creates a new table in Datasheet view
Table Design		Creates a new table in Design view

Queries Group

Query Wizard		Creates a query using the Query Wizard
Query Design		Creates a query using Query Design view

ACCESS 2013 COMMAND SUMMARY

COMMAND	SHORTCUT	ACTION
Forms Group		
Form		Creates a new form using all the fields from the currently selected table
More Forms ▾		Displays options for creating forms with different appearances: Multiple Items, Datasheet, Split Form, and Modal Dialog.
Form Wizard		Creates a new form by following the steps in the Form Wizard
More Forms ▾ /Multiple Items		Creates a form that displays multiple items
Reports Group		
Report		Creates a report using all fields in current table
Report Design		Creates a report using Report Design view
Report Wizard		Creates a report using the Report Wizard
External Data Tab		
Import & Link Group		
Excel		Imports data from an Excel spreadsheet
Export Group		
Saved Exports		Views and runs saved exports
Excel		Exports selected object to an Excel workbook
More ▾		Displays more export choices
More ▾ / Word Export the selected object to Rich Text		Exports selected object to a rich text format (*.rtf) file
Database Tools Tab		
Relationships Group		
Relationships		Opens relationships window
Object Dependencies		Shows the objects in the database that depend on the selected object

COMMAND	SHORTCUT	ACTION
Analyze Group		
Analyze Table		Evaluates table design
Table Tools Fields Tab		
Views Group		
Design View		Displays table in Design view
Add & Delete Group		
12 Number		Inserts a new field with Number data type
Date & Time		Inserts a new Date/time field
More Fields ▾		Displays drop-down list to create more fields
More Fields ▾ /Lookup & Relationship		Creates a lookup field
Delete	Delete	Removes selected field column
Properties Group		
Name & Caption		Displays dialog box to change field name and/or caption
Formatting Group		
Data Type: Number		Changes the data type for the current field
Format:		Sets the display format of the selected field
Table Tools Design Tab		
Views Group		
Datasheet View		Displays table in Datasheet view
Tools Group		
Primary Key		Makes current field a primary key field
Insert Rows		Inserts a new field in Table Design view
Delete Rows	Delete	Deletes selected field row
Query Tools Design Tab		
Results Group		
! Run		Displays query results in Query Datasheet view
Query Setup Group		
Show Table		Displays Show Table dialog box

COMMAND	SHORTCUT	ACTION
Show/Hide Group		
XYZ Table Names		Displays/hides the Table row
Relationship Tools Design Tab		
Tools Group		
Edit Relationships		Opens the Edit Relationships dialog box where changes can be made to selected relationship join line
Relationship Report		Creates a report of the displayed relationships
Relationships Group		
All Relationships		Shows all tables with relationships in the database.
Report Layout Tools Design Tab		
Themes Group		
Aa Themes		Applies predesigned theme styles to report
Tools Group		
Add Existing Fields		Displays/hides the Field List pane
Report Layout Tools Arrange tab		
Table Group		
Tabular		Arranges controls in a stacked tabular arrangement
Rows & Columns Group		
Select Column		Selects column
Report Layout Tools Format Tab		
Font Group		
A ▾ Font color		Changes color of text
11 ▾ Font Size		Used to change the font size of text
Align Text Left		Aligns text at left edge of control
Center		Centers text in selected control

COMMAND	SHORTCUT	ACTION
Control Formatting Group		
Shape Fill ▾		Changes the color fill inside a control
Shape Outline ▾		Opens menu to change the border color and line thickness of a selected control
Report Layout Tools Page Setup Tab		
Page Size Group		
Margins		Sets margins of printed report
Page Layout Group		
Page Setup		Sets features related to the page layout of printed report
Form Layout Tools Design Tab		
Themes Group		
Themes		Opens gallery of theme styles
Tools Group		
Add Existing Fields		Opens the Field List pane where existing fields can be selected and added to a form
Form Layout Tools Arrange Tab		
Table Group		
Stacked		Applies Stacked layout to the controls
Rows & Columns Group		
Insert Below		Inserts a blank row below the selected cell
Insert Left		Inserts a blank column to the left of the selected cell
Select Layout		Selects entire layout
Select Column		Selects column in a layout
Select Row		Selects row in a layout

ACCESS 2013 COMMAND SUMMARY

COMMAND	SHORTCUT	ACTION
Merge/Split Group		
Merge		Merges two or more layout cells into a single cell
Split Horizontally		Splits a layout cell horizontally into two cells
Form Layout Tools Format Tab		
Font Group		
/Align Right		Right-aligns contents of cell
Print Preview Tab		
Print Group		
Print	Ctrl + P	Prints displayed object
Page Size Group		
Margins		Adjusts margins in printed output
Page Layout Group		
Portrait		Changes print orientation to portrait
Landscape		Changes print orientation to landscape
Zoom Group		
One Page		Displays one entire page in Print Preview
Two Pages		Displays two entire pages in Print Preview
Close Preview Group		
Close Print Preview	Esc	Closes Print Preview window

COMMAND	SHORTCUT	ACTION
Quick Access Toolbar		
Save	Ctrl + S	Saves presentation
Undo	Ctrl + Z	Reverses last action
File Tab		
Save	Ctrl + S	Saves presentation
Save As	F12	Saves presentation using new file name and/or location
Open	Ctrl + O	Opens existing presentation
Close		Closes presentation
Info		Document properties
New	Ctrl + N	Opens New Presentation dialog box
Print	Ctrl + P	Opens print settings and a preview pane
Home Tab		
Clipboard Group		
Paste	Ctrl + V	Pastes item from Clipboard
Paste / Embed		Embeds an object from another application
Paste /Paste		Inserts the copied text or object
Paste / Use Destination Theme		Uses formatting associated with presentation theme
Paste /Paste Special/Paste Link		Inserts an object as a linked object
Cut	Ctrl + X	Cuts selection to Clipboard
Copy	Ctrl + C	Copies selection to Clipboard
Slides Group		
New Slide	Ctrl + M	Inserts new slide with selected layout
Layout		Changes layout of a slide

POWERPOINT 2013 COMMAND SUMMARY

COMMAND	SHORTCUT	ACTION
Keep Text Only		Keeps the format associated with the destination format.
Reset		Converts slide content to match the presentation's theme.
Use Destination Theme		Pastes text using presentation theme formatting
Font Group		
Bookman Old St ▾ Font		Changes font type
32 ▾ Size		Changes font size
Increase Font Size		Increases font size of selected text
Decrease font size		Decreases font size of selected text
Italicize text		Italicizes selected text
Underline text		Underlines selected text
Shadow		Applies shadow effect to selected text
Change font color		Modifies color of selected text
Paragraph Group		
Bullet list		Formats bulleted list
Numbered list		Formats numbered lists
Decrease List Level		Decreases the indent level
Increase List Level		Increases the indent level
Align Text		Sets vertical alignment of text
Align Left	Ctrl + L	Aligns text to the left
Align Center	Ctrl + E	Centers text
Align Right	Ctrl + R	Aligns text to the right
Justify	Ctrl + J	Aligns text to both the left and right margins

WERPOINT 2013 COMMAND SUMMARY

COMMAND	SHORTCUT	ACTION
Drawing Group		
Shapes		Inserts selected shape
Shape Fill ▾		Fills the selected shape with a solid color, gradient, picture or texture
Shape Effects ▾		Applies a visual effect to the selected shape, such as shadow, glow, or reflection
Editing Group		
Find	Ctrl + F	Finds specified text
Replace ▾	Ctrl + H	Replaces located text with replacement text
Select ▾ / Select All	Ctrl + A	Selects everything in the placeholder box
Insert Tab		
Images Group		
Pictures		Inserts picture from a file on your computer
Online Pictures		Finds and inserts pictures from a variety of online sources
Illustrations Group		
Shapes ▾		Inserts a shape
Text Group		
Text Box		Inserts text box or adds text to selected shape
Header & Footer		Inserts a header and footer

COMMAND	SHORTCUT	ACTION
Design Tab		
Themes Group		
More		Opens gallery of document themes
Variant Group		
More		Customizes the look of the current theme
Customize Group		
Slide Size		Selects Standard, Widescreen, or Custom slide size
Transitions Tab		
Preview Group		
Preview		Displays the transition effect
Transition to This Slide Group		
More		Opens a gallery of transition effects
Effect Options		Opens a gallery of effect options
Animations Tab		
Preview Group		
Preview		Displays the transition effect
Animation Group		
More		Opens a gallery of animation effects
Effect Options		Opens a gallery of effect options
Advanced Animation Group		
Add Animation		Adds an animation effect to an object
Animation Pane		Opens the Animation pane
Animation Painter		Copies animation effect to another object

COMMAND	SHORTCUT	ACTION
Timing Group		
▶ Start: ▾		Sets the trigger for the animation
⊙ Duration: 01.00 ⬍		Controls the amount of time for the animation to complete
Slide Show Tab		
Start Slide Show Group		
From Beginning	F5	Displays presentation starting with the first slide
From Current Slide	Shift + F5	Displays presentation starting with the current slide
Review Tab		
Proofing Group		
ABC ✓ Spelling	F7	Spell-checks presentation
View Tab		
Presentation Views Group		
Normal	▤	Switches to Normal view
Slide Sorter	▦	Switches to Slide Sorter view
Notes Page		Displays current slide in Notes view to edit the speaker notes
Outline View		Switches Slides pane to Outline pane
Master Views Group		
Slide Master		Opens Slide Master view to change the design and layout of the master slides
Picture Tools Format Tab		
Adjust Group		
🖼 Color ▾		Modifies the color of the picture
Picture Styles Group		
▽ More		Opens the Picture Styles gallery to select an overall visual style for picture

POWERPOINT 2013 COMMAND SUMMARY

COMMAND	SHORTCUT	ACTION
Picture Border ▾		Applies a border style to picture
Picture Effects ▾		Applies a visual effect to picture
Picture Layout ▾		Changes layout of a drawing
Arrange Group		
Align Objects		Opens a gallery of alignment options
Size Group		
Crop		Removes unwanted section of a picture
Drawing Tools Format Tab		
Shapes Styles Group		
More		Opens the Shape Styles gallery to select a visual style to apply to a shape
Shape Effects ▾		Applies a visual effect to a shape
Arrange Group		
		Rotates or flips the selected object
Table Tools Design Tab		
Table Styles Group		
More		Opens gallery of table designs
Shading		Colors background behind selected text or paragraph
Border		Applies a border style
Effects		Applies a visual effect to the table, such as shadows and reflections
Table Tools Layout Tab		
Alignment Group		
Center		Centers the text within a cell
Center Vertically		Centers the text vertically within a cell
Arrange Group		
Align		Opens a gallery of alignment options

b

Backstage: Contains commands that allow you to work with your document, unlike the Ribbon that allows you to work in your document; contains commands that apply to the entire document.

Buttons: Graphical elements that perform the associated action when you click on them using the mouse.

c

Character effects: Enhancements such as bold, italic, and color that are applied to a selected text.

Clipboard: Where a selection is stored when it is cut or copied.

Cloud: Any application or service hosted and run on servers connected to the Internet.

Commands: Options that carry out a selected action.

Context menu: Also called a shortcut menu; opened by right-clicking on an item on the screen.

Contextual tabs: Also called on-demand tabs; tabs that are displayed only as needed. For example, when you are working with a picture, the Picture Tools tab appears.

Cursor: The blinking vertical bar that marks your location in the document and indicates where text you type will appear; also called the insertion point.

d

Database: A collection of related data.

Default: The standard options used by Office 2013.

Destination: The new location into which a selection that is moved from its original location is inserted.

Dialog box launcher: A button that is displayed in the lower-right corner of a tab group if more commands are available; clicking opens a dialog box or task pane of additional options.

Document window: The large center area of the program window where open application files are displayed.

e

Edit: To revise a document by changing the parts that need to be modified.

Enhanced ScreenTip: Displayed by pointing to a button in the Ribbon; shows the name of the button and the keyboard shortcut.

f

Field: The smallest unit of information about a record; a column in a table.

Font: Type style; also called typeface.

Font size: Size of typeface, given in points.

Format: The appearance of a document.

g

Groups: Part of a tab that contains related items.

h

Hyperlink: Connection to information located in a separate location, such as on a website.

i

Insertion point: Also called the cursor; the blinking vertical bar that marks your location in a document and indicates where text you type will appear.

k

Keyboard shortcut: A combination of keys that can be used to execute a command in place of clicking a button.

Keyword: A descriptive word that is associated with the file and can be used to locate a file using a search.

l

Live Preview: A feature that shows you how selected text in a document will appear if a formatting option is chosen.

m

Metadata: Details about the document that describe or identify it, such as title, author name, subject, and keywords; also called document properties.

Mini toolbar: Appears automatically when you select text; displays command buttons for often-used commands from the Font and Paragraph groups that are used to format a document.

O

Office Clipboard: Can store up to 24 items that have been cut or copied.

On-demand tabs: Also called contextual tabs; tabs that are displayed only as needed.

P

Paste Preview: Shows how a Paste Option will affect a selection.

Properties: Shown in a panel along the right side of the Info tab, divided into four groups; information such as author, keywords, document size, number of words, and number of pages.

Q

Quick Access Toolbar: Located to the right of the Window button; provides quick access to frequently used commands such as Save, Undo, and Redo.

R

Records: The information about one person, thing, or place; contained in a row of a table.

Ribbon: Below the title bar; provides a centralized location of commands that are used to work in your document.

S

ScreenTip: Also called a tooltip; appears with the command name and the keyboard shortcut.

Scroll bar: Horizontal or vertical, it is used with a mouse to bring additional information into view in a window.

Selection cursor: Cursor that allows you to select an object.

Shortcut menu: A context-sensitive menu, meaning it displays only those commands relevant to the item or screen location; also called a context menu, it is opened by right-clicking on an item on the screen.

Slide: An individual page of a presentation.

Slide shows: Onscreen electronic presentations.

Source: The original location of a selection that is inserted in a new location.

S (cont.)

Status bar: At the bottom of the application window; displays information about the open file and features that help you view the file.

T

Table: A database object consisting of columns and rows.

Tabs: Used to divide the Ribbon into major activity areas.

Tag: A descriptive word that is associated with the file and can be used to locate a file using a search; also called a keyword.

Task pane: A list of additional options opened by clicking the dialog box launcher; also called a dialog box.

Template: A professionally designed document that is used as the basis for a new document.

Text effects: Enhancements such as bold, italic, and color that are applied to selected text.

Tooltip: Also called a ScreenTip; appears displaying a command name and the keyboard shortcut.

Typeface: A set of characters with a specific design; also commonly referred to as a font.

U

User interface: A set of graphical elements that are designed to help you interact with the program and provide instructions for the actions you want to perform.

V

View buttons: Used to change how the information in the document window is displayed.

W

Worksheet: An electronic spreadsheet, or worksheet, that is used to organize, manipulate, and graph numeric data.

Z

Zoom slider: Located at the far right end of the status bar; used to change the amount of information displayed in the document window by "zooming in" to get a close-up view or "zooming out" to see more of the document at a reduced view.

a

Active window: The window in which you can work.

Alignment: The positioning of text on a line between the margins or indents. There are four types of paragraph alignment: left, centered, right, and justified.

Anchor: An icon that displays near a graphic and indicates the graphic is a floating object that is attached to that location in the document.

Antonym: A word with an opposite meaning.

Attachment: A file that is sent with the e-mail message but is not part of the e-mail text.

AutoCorrect: A feature that makes some basic assumptions about the text you are typing and, based on these assumptions, automatically corrects the entry.

b

Bibliography: Located at the end of the report, it includes the complete source information for citations.

Building blocks: Reusable pieces of content or document parts included in the Quick Parts feature.

Bulleted list: A list to which bullets have been added before the items to organize information and make the writing clear and easy to read.

c

Caption: A numbered label for a figure, table, picture, or graph.

Case sensitive: In a search, this means that lowercase letters will not match uppercase letters in the text and vice versa.

Cell: The intersection of a row and column in a table.

Character formatting: Formatting features that affect selected characters only. This includes changing the character style and size, applying effects to characters, and changing the character spacing.

Citations: Parenthetical source references that give credit for specific information included in the document.

Compatibility Checker: Lists any features that aren't compatible with the previous versions of Word, and the number of occurrences in the document.

Control: A graphic element that is a container for information or objects. Controls, like fields, appear shaded when you point to them.

Cross-reference: A reference from one part of a document to related information in another part.

Custom dictionary: A list of words such as proper names, technical terms, and so on, that are not in the main dictionary and that you want the spelling checker to accept as correct. Adding words to the custom dictionary prevents the flagging as incorrect of specialized words that you commonly use. Word shares custom dictionaries with other Microsoft Office applications such as PowerPoint.

d

Default: A document's predefined settings, generally the most commonly used. The default settings include a standard paper-size setting of 8.5 by 11 inches, 1-inch top and bottom margins, and 1-inch left and right margins.

Destination file: The document in which the object is inserted.

Document theme: A predefined set of formatting choices that can be applied to an entire document in one simple step.

Document window: The large area below the Ribbon in a Word document. A vertical and horizontal ruler may be displayed along both edges of the document window.

Drawing layer: A separate layer from the text that allows graphic objects to be positioned precisely on the page.

Drawing object: A simple graphic consisting of shapes such as lines and boxes. A drawing object is part of your Word document.

e

Edit: Revising a document to correct typing, spelling, and grammar errors, as well as adding and deleting information and reorganizing it to make the meaning clearer.

Embedded object: Graphic that was created using another program and inserted in a Word document. An embedded object becomes part of the Word document and can be opened and edited from within the Word document using the source program, the program in which it was created.

Endnote: Used in documented research papers to explain or comment on information in the text, or provide source references for text in the document. Appears at the end of a document.

End-of-file marker: The solid horizontal line that marks the last-used line in a document.

f

Field: A placeholder that instructs Word to insert information into a document.

Field code: Contains the directions as to the type of information to insert or action to perform in a placeholder. Field codes appear between curly brackets { }, also called braces.

Field result: The information that is displayed as a result of the field code.

Find and Replace: A feature that finds text in a document and replaces it with other text as directed.

Floating object: Can be placed anywhere in the document, including in front of or behind other objects including the text.

Font: Also commonly referred to as a typeface, a font is a set of characters with a specific design.

Font size: The height and width of the character, commonly measured in points, abbreviated "pt."

Footer: A line or several lines of text in the margin space at the bottom of every page.

Footnote: Used in documented research papers to explain or comment on information in the text, or provide source references for text in the document. Appears at the bottom of a page containing the material that is being referenced

Format: Any effects added to a document that alters its appearance. Formatting changes can include many features such as font, font size, boldfaced text, italics, and bulleted lists.

Format Painter: Applies the formats associated with the current selection to new selections.

g

Gradient: A gradual progression of colors and shades, usually from one color to another, or from one shade to another of the same color.

Grammar checker: Advises you of incorrect grammar as you create and edit a document, and proposes possible corrections.

Graphic: A nontext element or object such as a drawing or picture that can be added to a document.

h

Hard page break: A manually inserted page break at a specific location. A hard page break instructs Word to begin a new page regardless of the amount of text on the previous page. When used, its location is never moved regardless of the changes that are made to the amount of text on the preceding page.

Header: A header is a line or several lines of text in the top margin of each page.

Heading style: Combinations of fonts, type sizes, color, bold, italics, and spacing to be applied to topic headings.

Hyperlink: A connection to a location in the current document, another document, or a website. It allows the reader to jump to the referenced location by clicking on the hyperlink text when reading the document on the screen.

i

Indent: To help your reader find information quickly, you can indent paragraphs from the margins. Indenting paragraphs sets them off from the rest of the document.

Index: Appears at the end of a long document as a list of major headings, topics, and terms with their page numbers.

Inline object: An object that is positioned directly in the text at the position of the insertion point. It becomes part of the paragraph and any paragraph alignment settings that apply to the paragraph also apply to the object.

Insert mode: Allows new characters to be inserted into the existing text by moving the existing text to the right to make space for the new characters.

l

Leader character: Solid, dotted, or dashed lines that fill the blank space between tab stops.

Line spacing: The vertical space between lines of text and paragraphs.

Linked object: Information created in one application that is inserted in a document created by another application while maintaining a link between the files.

Live link: Changes made in the source file affect the linked object. The changes are automatically reflected in the destination file when it is opened.

Live Preview: A feature of Word that displays how the selected text in the document will appear when formatting options are chosen.

m

Main dictionary: The dictionary supplied with the spelling checker; includes most common words.

Multilevel list: Displays multiple outline levels that show a hierarchical structure of the items in the list.

n

Navigation pane: When the Find feature is activated, the Navigation pane appears to the left of your document and provides a convenient way to quickly locate and move to specified text. The Search text box at the top of the pane is used to specify the text you want to locate.

Normal document template: Automatically opens whenever you start Word 2013. Settings such as a Calibri 11-point font, left-alignment, and 1-inch margin are included.

Note reference mark: A superscript number appearing in the document at the end of the material being referenced.

Note separator: The horizontal line separating the footnote text from the document text.

Numbered list: A list to which numbers have been added before the items to organize information and make the writing clear and easy to read.

O

Object: An item such as a drawing or a picture that can be added to a document. An object can be sized, moved, and manipulated.

P

Page break: A page break marks the point at which one page ends and another begins. Two types of page breaks can be used in a document: soft page breaks and hard page breaks.

Page margin: The blank space around the edge of the page. Standard single-sided documents have four margins: top, bottom, left, and right.

Paragraph formatting: Formatting that affects an entire paragraph, including how the paragraph is positioned or aligned between the margins, paragraph indentation, spacing above and below a paragraph, and line spacing within a paragraph.

Picture: A graphic such as an illustration or a scanned photograph.

Placeholder: A graphic element, usually set apart with brackets, designed to contain specific types of information.

Q

Quick Parts: A feature that includes reusable pieces of content or document parts for document building.

r

Ruler: Shows the line length in inches, and is used to set margins, tab stops, and indents and also shows your line location on the page.

S

Sans serif fonts: Fonts that don't have a flair at the base of each letter and are generally used for text in paragraphs. Arial and Calibri are two common sans serif fonts.

Section break: Identifies the end of a section and stores the document format settings associated with that section of the document.

Selection rectangle: A rectangle surrounding an object, indicating it is selected and can now be deleted, sized, moved, or modified.

Serif fonts: Fonts that have a flair at the base of each letter that visually leads the reader to the next letter. Two common serif fonts are Roman and Times New Roman.

Sizing handles: Eight squares, located on the selection rectangle surrounding an object, used to resize the selected object.

Soft page break: Word inserts a soft page break automatically when the bottom margin is reached and starts a new page. As you add or remove text from a page, Word automatically readjusts the placement of the soft page break.

Soft space: Extra space that adjusts automatically whenever an addition or deletion is made to the text when using justified alignment, created so the columns of text are even.

Sort: Word can quickly arrange or sort text, numbers, or data in lists or tables in alphabetical, numeric, or date order based on the first character in each paragraph.

Source file: The source file is the document where data was created.

Source program: The program in which an object was created.

Spelling checker: Advises you of misspelled words as you create and edit a document, and proposes possible corrections.

Split window: Splits the document window into separate viewing areas.

Style: A named group of formatting characteristics.

Synchronized: When synchronized, the documents in two windows will scroll together so you can compare text easily.

Synonyms: Words with a similar meaning.

t

Tab stop: A marked location on the horizontal ruler that indicates how far to indent text each time the Tab key is pressed.

Table: Used to organize information into an easy-to-read format of horizontal rows and vertical columns.

Table of contents: A listing of the topic headings that appear in a document and their associated page numbers.

Table of figures: A list of the figures, tables, or equations used in a document and their associated page numbers.

Table reference: A letter and number used to identify cells in a table.

Template: A document file that stores predefined settings and other elements such as graphics for use as a pattern when creating documents.

Text box: A container for text and other graphic objects that can be moved like any other object.

Text wrapping: Controls the appearance of text around a graphic object.

Theme: Predefined set of formatting choices that can be applied to an entire document in one simple step.

Thesaurus: A reference tool that provides synonyms, antonyms, and related words for a selected word or phrase.

Thumbnail: Miniature representation of a graphic object.

TrueType: Fonts that are automatically installed when you install Windows. They appear onscreen exactly as they will appear when printed.

Typeface: A font; a set of characters with a specific design.

U

URL: Uniform Resource Locator, a website's address.

W

Watermark: Text or picture that appears behind document text.

Word wrap: A feature that automatically decides where to end a line and wraps text to the next line based on the margin settings.

3-D Reference: A formula that contains references to cells in other sheets of a workbook; allows you to use data from multiple sheets and to calculate new values based on this data.

a

Absolute Reference: A cell or range reference in a formula whose location does not change when the formula is copied.

Active Cell: The cell your next entry or procedure affects, indicated by a black outline.

Active Sheet: The sheet in which you can work, the name of which appears bold.

Adjacent Range: A rectangular block of adjoining cells.

Alignment: The settings that allow you to change the horizontal and vertical placement and the orientation of an entry in a cell.

Antonym: A word with an opposite meaning.

Area Chart: Shows the magnitude of change over time by emphasizing the area under the curve created by each data series.

Argument: The data a function uses to perform a calculation.

AutoCorrect: A feature that makes some basic assumptions about the text you are typing and, based on these assumptions, automatically corrects the entry.

AutoFill: A feature that makes entering a series of headings easier by logically repeating and extending the series. AutoFill recognizes trends and automatically extends data and alphanumeric headings as far as you specify.

AutoFit: Automatically adjusts the width of the columns to fit the column contents.

AutoRecover: A feature that, when enabled, will automatically save your work and can recover data if the program unexpectedly closes.

Axis: A line bordering the chart plot area used as a frame of reference for measurement.

b

Bar Chart: Displays data as evenly spaced bars. The categories are displayed along the Y axis and the values are displayed horizontally, placing more emphasis on comparisons and less on time.

Bubble Chart: Compares sets of three values. They are similar to a scatter chart with the third value determining the size of the bubble markers.

C

Category Axis: The X axis, usually the horizontal axis; contains categories.

Category-Axis Title: Clearly describes the information on and/or format of the X axis.

Cell: The intersection of a row and a column.

Cell Reference: The column letter and row number of the active cell (e.g., A1).

Cell Selector: The black border that surrounds the active cell.

Cell Style: A defined theme-based combination of formats that have been named and that can be quickly applied to a selection.

Character Effect: Font formatting, such as color, used to enhance the appearance of the document.

Chart: A visual representation of data in a worksheet.

Chart Area: The entire chart and all its elements.

Chart Elements: The different parts of a chart that are used to graphically display the worksheet data.

Chart Gridlines: Lines extending from the axis line across the plot area that make it easier to read the chart data.

Chart Layout: A predefined set of chart elements that can be quickly applied to a chart. The elements include chart titles, a legend, a data table, or data labels.

Chart Object: A graphic object that is created using charting features. An object can be inserted into a worksheet or into a special chart sheet.

Chart Style: A predefined set of chart formats that can be quickly applied to a chart.

Chart Title: A descriptive label displayed above the charted data that explains the contents of the chart.

Chart Type: The different chart types, such as bar, area, and line, that represent data in different ways.

Clip Art: Royalty-free drawings and photographs.

Column: The vertical stacks of cells in a workbook.

Column Chart: Displays data as evenly spaced vertical columns. They are similar to bar charts, except that categories are organized horizontally and values vertically to emphasize variation over time.

Column Letter: Located across the top of the workbook window; identifies each worksheet column.

Combo Chart: Combines two or more chart types to make comparisons easy when you have two types of data or the data values vary widely.

Column Width: The size or width of a column that controls the number of characters that can be displayed in a cell.

Conditional Formatting: Changes the appearance of a range of cells based on a condition that you specify.

Constant: A value that does not begin with an equal sign and does not change unless you change it directly by typing in another entry.

Copy Area: Range of data to be copied and pasted.

Custom Dictionary: In the spelling checker, holds words you commonly use but that are not included in the main dictionary.

d

Data: The information entered in a cell. It can be text, numbers, dates or times.

Data Label: Label that corresponds to the data points (values) that are plotted along the X axis.

Data Marker: A bar, area, dot, slice, or other symbol in a chart, representing a single data point or value that originates from a worksheet cell.

Data Series: Related data markers in a chart.

Default: Predefined settings, used on new blank workbooks.

Depth Axis: The Z axis; a third axis, in a 3-D column, 3-D cone, or 3-D pyramid chart; allows data to be plotted along the depth of a chart.

Destination File: The document into which an object is inserted.

Doughnut Chart: Similar to pie chart except that it can show more than one data series.

Drawing Object: A graphic element.

e

Embedded Chart: Chart that is inserted into a worksheet; it becomes part of the sheet in which it is inserted and is saved as part of the worksheet when you save the workbook file.

Embedded Object: An object, such as a graphic, created from another program and inserted in the worksheet, becoming part of the sheet in which it is inserted; it is saved as part of the worksheet.

Explode: Separation between the slices of a pie chart to emphasize the data in the categories.

External Reference: References the location of a source file and the selection within a document that is linked to the destination file.

f

Fill Handle: The green box in the lower-right corner of a selection.

Find and Replace: A feature that helps you quickly find specific information and automatically replaces it with new information.

Footer: Provides information that appears at the bottom of each page; commonly includes information such as the date and page number.

Formula: An equation that performs a calculation on data contained in a worksheet. A formula always begins with an equal sign (=) and uses arithmetic operators.

Formula Bar: Below the Ribbon; displays entries as they are made and edited in the workbook window.

Freeze Panes: Prevents the data in the pane from scrolling as you move to different areas in a worksheet.

Function: A prewritten formula that performs certain types of calculations automatically.

g

Goal Seek: A tool used to find the value needed in one cell to attain a result you want in another cell.

Gradient: A fill option consisting of a gradual progression of colors and shades that can be from one color to another or from one shade to another of the same color.

Graphic: A nontext element or object such as a drawing or picture that can be added to a document.

Group: Two or more objects that behave as a single object when moved or sized. A chart is a group that consists of many separate objects.

h

Header: Information appearing at the top of each page.

Headings: Entries that are used to create the structure of the worksheet and describe other worksheet entries.

k

Keyword: Descriptive term associated with a graphic.

l

Legend: A box that identifies the chart data series and data markers.

Line Chart: Displays data along a line; used to show changes in data over time, emphasizing time and rate of change rather than the amount of change.

Link: Contains references to the location of a source file and the selection within a document that is linked to the destination file.

Linked Object: Information created in one application that is inserted into a document created by another application.

Live Link: A link that updates the linked object when changes are made to the source file.

m

Main Dictionary: The dictionary that is supplied with the spelling checker program.

Margin: The blank space outside the printing area around the edges of the paper.

Merged Cell: Two or more cells combined into one.

Mixed Reference: In a formula, either the column letter or the row number is preceded with the $. This makes only the row or column absolute. When a formula containing a mixed cell reference is copied to another location in the worksheet, only the part of the cell reference that is not absolute changes relative to its new location in the worksheet.

n

Name Box: Displays the cell reference.

Nonadjacent Range: Two or more selected cells or ranges that are not adjoining.

Number: The digits 0 to 9.

Number Format: Formatting that changes the appearance of numbers onscreen and when printed, without changing the way the number is stored or used in calculations.

o

Object: An element that is added to a document.

Operand: The values on which a numeric formula performs a calculation, consisting of numbers or cell references.

Operator: A symbol that specifies the type of numeric operation to perform, such as + (addition), − (subtraction), / (division), * (multiplication), % (percent), and ^ (exponentiation).

Order of Operations: In a formula that contains more than one operator, Excel calculates the formula from left to right and performs the calculation in the following order: percent, exponentiation, multiplication and division, and addition and subtraction.

p

Page Break: The place where one printed page ends and another starts.

Pane: A section of the workbook window when using the Split command.

Paste Area: Location you paste material you have copied.

Picture: A graphic element.

Picture Style: Adds a border around a graphic object that consists of combinations of line, shadow, color, and shape effects.

Pie Chart: Displays data as slices of a circle or pie; shows the relationship of each value in a data series to the series as a whole. Each slice of the pie represents a single value in the series.

Plot Area: The area within the X- and Y-axis boundaries where the chart appears.

Print Area: The area you selected for printing; surrounded by a heavy line that identifies the area.

q

Quick Analysis Tool: A feature that displays a gallery of likely formatting or analysis commands for the current selection.

Quick Style: A named group of formatting characteristics that allow the user to apply various formats to a selection.

r

Radar Chart: Displays a line or area chart wrapped around a central point. Each axis represents a set of data points.

Range: A selection consisting of two or more cells on a worksheet.

Range Reference: Identifies the cells in a range.

Recalculation: When a number in a referenced cell in a formula changes, Excel automatically recalculates all formulas that are dependent upon the changed value.

Relative Reference: A cell or range reference in a formula whose location is interpreted in relation to the position of the cell that contains the formula.

Row: Horizontal string of cells in a workbook.

Row Height: The size or height of a row measured in points.

Row Number: Along the left side of the workbook window; identifies each worksheet row.

s

Sans Serif: Fonts that do not have a flare at the base of each letter, such as Arial and Calibri.

Scaling: Reducing or enlarging the worksheet contents by a percentage or to fit it to a specific number of pages by height and width.

Scatter (XY) Chart: Used to show the relationship between two ranges of numeric data.

Selection Rectangle: Box that surrounds a selected object, indicating that it is a selected object and can now be deleted, sized, moved, or modified.

Serial Value: Data stored as consecutively assigned numbers, such as dates where each day is numbered from the beginning of the 20th century. The date serial values begin with 1.

Series Axis: The Z axis; a third axis, in a 3-D column, 3-D cone, or 3-D pyramid chart; allows data to be plotted along the depth of a chart.

Series Formula: Links a chart object to the source worksheet.

Serif: Fonts that have a flare at the base of each letter that visually leads the reader to the next letter. Two common serif fonts are Cambria and Times New Roman.

Sheet: Used to display different types of information, such as financial data or charts.

Shape Style: Predefined combinations of fills, outlines, and effects that can be applied to the selected chart element.

Sheet Name: Descriptive name that can be assigned to each sheet in a workbook. A sheet name helps identify the contents of the sheet.

Sheet Reference: The name of the sheet, followed by an exclamation point and the cell or range reference, in a formula.

Sheet Tab: Where the name of each sheet in a workbook is displayed, shown at the bottom of the workbook window.

Size: The width of a column.

Sizing Handles: Eight squares and circles located on the selection rectangle that allow the object to be resized.

Source File: The document that houses information that is referenced elsewhere.

Source Program: The program in which an object was created.

Sparkline: A tiny chart of worksheet data contained in the background of a single cell.

Spelling Checker: Locates misspelled words, duplicate words, and capitalization irregularities in the active worksheet and proposes the correct spelling.

Split Window: A feature that allows you to divide a worksheet window into sections, making it easier to view different parts of the worksheet at the same time.

Spreadsheet: A worksheet; a rectangular grid of rows and columns used to enter data.

Stacked Column Chart: Displays data as evenly spaced columns; this type of chart also shows the proportion of each category to the total.

Stock Chart: Illustrates fluctuations in stock prices or scientific data; requires three to five data series that must be arranged in a specific order.

Stops (Gradient Stops): Specific points where the blending of two adjacent colors in the gradient ends.

Surface Chart: Displays values in a form similar to a rubber sheet stretched over a 3-D column chart. These are useful for finding the best combination between sets of data.

Synonym: A word with a similar meaning.

Syntax: Rules of structure for entering all functions.

t

Tab Scroll Buttons: Located in the sheet tab area; used to scroll tabs right or left when there are more sheet tabs than can be seen.

Template: A file that contains settings that are used as the basis for a new file you are creating.

Text: Any combination of letters, numbers, spaces, and any other special characters.

Text Box: A graphic element that is designed to contain specific types of information.

Theme: A predefined set of formatting choices that can be applied to an entire worksheet in one simple step.

Thesaurus: A reference tool that provides synonyms, antonyms, and related words for a selected word or phrase.

Thumbnail: Miniature representations of graphic objects.

V

Value Axis: The Y axis, usually the vertical axis; contains data.

Value-Axis Title: Describes the information on and/or format of the Y axis.

Variable: A value that can change if the data it depends on changes.

W

What-If Analysis: A technique used to evaluate the effects of changing selected factors in a worksheet.

Workbook: An Excel file that stores the information you enter using the program.

Workbook Window: The large center area of the program window.

Worksheet: Also commonly referred to as a spreadsheet; a rectangular grid of rows and columns used to enter data.

X

X Axis: Also called the category axis; usually the horizontal axis and contains categories

Y

Y Axis: Also called the value axis; usually the vertical axis and contains data.

Z

Z Axis: Also called the depth axis or series axis; a third axis, in a 3-D column, 3-D cone, or 3-D pyramid chart; allows data to be plotted along the depth of a chart.

Access Glossary of Key Terms

a

Action query: Used to make changes to many records in one operation. There are four types of action queries.

Active window: The window in which you can work.

Aggregate functions: Calculations that are performed on a range of data; to use, the data type in the column must be a number, decimal, or currency.

Allow Zero Length property: Specifies whether an entry containing no characters is valid. This property is used to indicate that you know no value exists for a field. A zero-length string is entered as "" with no space between the quotation marks.

AND operator: Instructs the query to locate records meeting multiple criteria, narrowing the search because any record must meet both conditions included in the output.

Append query: Adds records from one or more tables to the end of other tables.

Argument: Specifies the data the function should use; enclosed in parentheses.

Ascending sort order: Data arranged A to Z or 0 to 9.

Attachment control: A bound control that allows you to add, edit, remove, and save attached files to the field directly from the form, just as you can in the datasheet.

Attachment data type: Data type that is used to add multiple files of different types to a field.

AutoNumber data type: Data type that automatically assigns a number to each record as it is added to a table; useful for maintaining record order.

b

Best Fit feature: Automatically adjusts the column widths of all selected columns to accommodate the longest entry or column heading in each of the selected columns.

Bound control: A control linked to a field in an underlying table, such as a text control that is linked to the record source and displays the field data in the form or report.

c

Calculated data type: Data type that is used to create a calculated field in a table.

Caption: The text that displays in the column heading while in Datasheet view. It is used when you want the label to be different from the actual field name.

Caption property: Specifies a field label other than the field name that is used in queries, forms, and reports.

Cell: The intersection of the row and column.

Character string: Constants such as "F" or "M"; enclosed in quotation marks.

Clipboard: A temporary storage area in memory.

Column selector bar: A narrow bar above the field names in Query Design view; used to select an entire column.

Column width: The size or width of the field column that controls the amount of data that can be seen in the field.

Common field: A field shared between two tables.

Compact: Makes a copy of the database file and rearranges the way that the file is stored on your disk.

Comparison operator: A symbol that allows you to make comparisons between two items.

Composite key: A primary key that uses more than one field.

Compound controls: The controls are associated, and the two controls will act as one when moved, indicated by both controls being surrounded by an orange border.

Compound criteria: Using more than one type of criterion in a query.

Constant: Numbers, dates, or character strings in an expression.

Control: Objects that display information, perform actions, or enhance the design of a form or report.

Criteria: Expressions that are used to restrict the results of a query to display only records that meet certain limiting conditions.

Criteria expression: Defines the query criteria in the query design grid; similar to using a formula and may contain constants, field names, and/or operators.

Crosstab query: Summarizes large amounts of data in an easy-to-read, row-and-column format.

Currency data type: Data type that is used in number fields that are monetary values or that you do not want rounded. Numbers are formatted to display decimal places and a currency symbol.

Current field: The selected field.

Current record: The record containing the insertion point.

Current Record box: Shows the number of the current record as well as the total number of records in the table.

d

Data type: Defines the type of data the field will contain. Access uses the data type to ensure that the right kind of data is entered in a field.

Database: An organized collection of related information.

Datasheet view: Provides a row-and-column view of the data in tables or query results.

Date/Time data type: Data type that is used in fields that will contain dates and times; checks all dates for validity. Even though dates and times are formatted to appear as a date or time, they are stored as serial values so that they can be used in calculations.

Default Value property: Used to specify a value that is automatically entered in a field when a new record is created.

Delete query: Deletes records from a table or tables.

Descending sort order: Data arranged Z to A or 9 to 0.

Design grid: In Query Design view, the lower portion of the window where you enter the settings that define the query.

Design view: Used to create a table, form, query, or report. Displays the underlying design structure, not the data.

Destination: The location where you paste the copied data from the Clipboard.

Destination file: The file that is created by exporting information from a database.

Drawing object: A graphic consisting of shapes such as lines and boxes that can be created using a drawing program such as Paint.

e

Export: The process of copying information to a file outside of a database.

Expression: A formula consisting of a combination of symbols that will produce a single value.

f

Field: Information that appears in a column about the subject recorded in the table.

Field list: List of fields contained in a table.

Field model: A predefined field or set of fields that includes a field name, a data type, and other settings that control the appearance and behavior of the field.

Field name: Displayed in the header row at the top of the datasheet in Datasheet view.

Field property: A characteristic that helps define the appearance and behavior of a field.

Field Size property: The maximum number of characters that can be entered in the field.

Filter: A restriction placed on records in the open datasheet or form to quickly isolate and display a subset of records.

Find and Replace: A feature that helps you quickly find specific information and automatically replace it with new information

Foreign key: A field in one table that refers to the primary key field in another table and indicates how the tables are related.

Form: A database object used primarily to display records onscreen to make it easier to enter new records and to make changes to existing records.

Form view: Displays the records in a form.

Form Wizard: Guides you through the steps to create a complex form that displays selected fields, data groups, sorted records, and data from multiple tables.

Format: The appearance of an object or data.

Format property: Used to specify the way that numbers, dates, times, and text in a field are displayed and printed.

Function: Built-in formulas that perform certain types of calculations automatically.

g

Graphic: A nontext element or object, such as a picture or shape.

h

Hard-coded criteria: Criteria that are entered in the criteria cell; they are used each time the query is run.

Header row: The row at the top of the datasheet where field names are displayed.

Hyperlink data type: Used when you want the field to store a link to an object, document, web page, or other destinations.

i

Identifier: An element that refers to the value of a field, a graphical object, or a property.

Import: The process of creating a copy of information from an external data source.

Indexed property: Sets a field as an index field (a field that controls the order of records).

Inner join: Tells a query that rows from one of the joined tables corresponds to rows in the other table on the basis of the data in the joined fields. Checks for matching values in the joined fields; when it finds matches, it combines the records and displays them as one record in the query results.

Input Mask property: Controls the data that is required in a field and the way the data is to be displayed.

IntelliSense: The context-sensitive menu that appears anytime you can enter an expression; suggests identifiers and functions that could be used.

j

Join: An association that is created in a query between a field in one table or query and a field of the same data type in another table or query.

Join line: Identifies the fields on which the relationship is based.

l

Label control: Displays descriptive labels in a form or report.

Layout: Determines how the data is displayed in a form by aligning the items horizontally or vertically to a uniform appearance.

Layout view: Displays the object's data in the process of designing the object.

Long Text data type: Data type that allows field entries greater than 255 characters of alphanumeric data.

Lookup field: Provides a list of values from which you can choose to make entering data into a field simpler and more accurate.

Lookup list: A lookup field that uses another table as the source for values.

Lookup Wizard: A feature that guides you step by step through creating a lookup field that will allow you to select from a list of values.

m

Make-table query: Creates a new table from selected data in one or more tables.

Many-to-many: An association between two tables in which one record in either table can relate to many records in the other table.

Margin: The blank space around the edge of a page.

Merge cells: Combines any selected adjacent cells into one big cell spanning the length of the previously selected cells.

Mini toolbar: Appears when the attachment control is made active; contains three buttons that are used to work with attachment controls.

Multitable query: A query that uses information from two or more tables to get results.

n

Navigation pane: Located along the left edge of the work area; displays all the objects in the database and is used to open and manage the objects.

Normalization: A design technique that identifies and eliminates redundancy by applying a set of rules to your tables to confirm that they are structured properly.

Number data type: Data type that allows field entries consisting of numbers only; this data type drops any leading zeros.

o

Object: Items that make up a database, such as a table or report, consisting of many elements. An object can be created, selected, and manipulated as a unit.

Object dependencies: An object may be dependent upon other objects for its content.

OLE Object data type: Data type that is used in fields to store an object from other Microsoft Windows programs, such as a document or graph; the object is converted to a bitmap image and displayed in the table field, form, or report.

One-to-many: An association between two tables in which the primary key field value in each record in the primary table corresponds to the value in the matching field or fields of many records in the related table.

One-to-one: An association between two tables in which each record in the first table contains a field value that corresponds to (matches) the field value of one record in the other table.

Operator: A symbol or word that indicates that an operation is to be performed.

OR operator: Instructs the query to locate records meeting multiple criteria, broadening the search because any record meeting either condition is included in the output.

Orientation: Refers to the direction that text prints on a page.

Orphaned records: Records that do not have a matching primary key record in the associated table.

Outer join: Tells a query that although some of the rows on both sides of the join correspond exactly, the query should include all rows from one table even if there is no match in the other table.

Outer sort field: The primary field in a sort; must be to the left of the inner sort field.

p

Parameter query: Displays a dialog box prompting you for information, such as the criteria for locating data.

Parameter value: Tells the query to prompt you for the specific criteria you want to use when you run the query.

Picture: A graphic such as a scanned photograph.

Primary key: A field that uniquely identifies each record and is used to associate data from multiple tables.

Print Preview: Displays a form, report, table, or query as it will appear when printed.

q

Query: Finds and displays specific data contained in a database.

Query criteria: Expressions that are used to restrict the results of a query in order to display only records that meet certain limiting conditions.

r

Record: All the information about one person, thing, or place.

Record navigation buttons: Found on the bottom of the work area on both sides of the record number; used to move through records with a mouse.

Record source: The underlying table that is used to create a form.

Referential integrity: Ensures that relationships between tables are valid and that related data is not accidentally changed or deleted.

Relational database: Databases containing multiple tables that can be linked to produce combined output from all tables.

Relationship: Establishes the association between common fields in two tables.

Report: A professional-appearing output generated from tables or queries that may include design elements, groups, and summary information; analyzes and displays data in a specific layout.

Report view: Displays the table data in a report layout.

Required property: Property that requires a value must be entered in a field.

Row label: Identifies the type of information that can be entered in the fields of a query design grid.

S

Search box: Finds any character(s) anywhere in the database.

Select query: Retrieves the specific data you request from one or more tables, then displays the data in a query datasheet in the order you specify.

Select Record button: The box to the left of each row in Datasheet view; used to select an entire record.

Serial value: Data stored as sequential numbers, such as dates and times.

Short Text data type: Data type that allows entry of up to 255 characters of alphanumeric data.

Show box: The box in the row label of a query design grid; lets you specify whether you want a field displayed in the query result.

Sorting: Rearranges the order of the records in a table based on the value in each field.

Source: The original information.

Source file: The database file from which you export information.

Split cells: Divides a cell into two or more adjacent cells.

SQL query: A query created using SQL (Structured Query Language), an advanced programming language used in Access.

Stacked format: Arranges data vertically with a field label to the left of the field data.

Subdatasheet: A data table nested in another data table that contains data related or joined to the table where it resides.

T

Tab order: The order in which the highlight will move through fields on a form when you press the [Tab ⇆] key during data entry.

Table: Organized collection of information, consisting of vertical columns and horizontal rows.

Tabular format: Arranges the data in rows and columns, with labels across the top.

Text control: Displays the information in a field from a record source.

Theme: A predefined set of font and color formats that can be applied to an entire document in one simple step.

Theme colors: A set of 12 colors that are applied to specific elements in a document.

U

Unbound control: A text control that is not connected to an underlying record source.

Unequal join: Records to be included in query results that are based on the value in one join field being greater than, less than, not equal to, greater than or equal to, or less than or equal to the value in the other join field.

Update query: Makes update changes to records.

V

Validation rule: Limits data entered in a field to values that meet certain requirements.

Validation Rule property: Specifies a validation rule, which limits the values that can be entered in the field to those that meet certain requirements.

Validation text: An explanatory message that appears if a user attempts to enter invalid information in a text field for which there is a validity check.

Validation Text property: The message to be displayed when the associated validation rule is not satisfied.

Value list: A list of options for a drop-down list.

View: Window formats that are used to display and work with the objects in a database.

W

Wildcards: Symbols that are used to represent characters. The * symbol represents any collection of characters; the ? symbol represents any individual character.

Wizard: A feature that guides you step by step through the process to perform a task.

Y

Yes/No data type: Data type that restricts the field contents to only a Yes/No, True/False, or On/Off value. A Yes value is stored as a 1 and a No value is stored as a 0 so that they can be used in expressions.

a

Alignment: Controls the position of text entries within a space.

Animation: Special effects that add action to text and graphics so they move around on the screen during a slide show.

AutoCorrect: A feature that makes some basic assumptions about the text you are typing and, based on those assumptions, automatically corrects the entry.

b

Background styles: A set of theme colors and textures that you can apply to the background of your slides.

c

Cell: The intersection of a row and a column in a table.

Character formatting: Applies changes such as color and size to the selected characters only.

Clip art: Simple drawings; available in the Clip Organizer, a Microsoft Office tool that arranges and catalogs clip art and other media files stored on the computer's hard disk.

Color matching: Uses the eyedropper tool to copy a color from an object in the slide and apply it to a selected shape or object.

Cropping: Trimming or removing part of a graphic.

Current slide: The slide that will be affected by any changes you make.

Custom dictionary: The dictionary you can create to hold words you commonly use, such as proper names and technical terms, that are not included in the spelling checker's main dictionary.

d

Destination file: The file into which an object is embedded.

Document theme: A predefined set of formatting choices that can be applied to an entire document in one simple step.

Drawing layer: A separate layer from the placeholder.

Drawing object: A graphic consisting of shapes such as lines and boxes.

e

Embed: The process of inserting an object that was created in another program in a slide. An embedded object becomes part of the presentation file and can be opened and edited using the program in which it was created.

Eyedropper tool: Used to match a color on the slide and apply it to another shape or object.

f

Find and Replace: A feature used to find text in a presentation and replace it with other text.

Floating object: How graphics are inserted in a document.

g

Gradient: A gradual progression of colors and shades.

Graphic: A nontext element or object, such as a drawing or picture, that can be added to a slide.

k

Keyword: Descriptive words or phrases associated with a graphic or figure that give information about the properties of the object.

l

Layout: Defines the position and format for objects and text that will be added to a slide. A layout contains placeholders for the different items such as bulleted text, titles, charts, and so on.

Linked object: A way to insert information created in one application into a document created by another application. With a linked object, the actual data is stored in the source file.

Live link: Connection that allows changes made in the source file that affect the linked object to be automatically reflected in the destination file when it is opened.

m

Main dictionary: The dictionary that is supplied with the spelling checker program.

Master: A special slide or page that stores information about the formatting for all slides or pages in a presentation.

Metadata: Additional data saved by PowerPoint as part of the presentation, may include author's name and other personal information.

n

Notes pages: Pages that display notes below a small version of the slide they accompany.

Notes pane: View that includes space for you to enter notes that apply to the current slide.

o

Object: A drawing, picture or shape that can be added to a slide.

Object animations: Used to display each bullet point, text, paragraph, or graphic independently of the other text or objects on the slide.

Outline pane: Displays the text content of each slide in outline format.

p

Paragraph formatting: Formatting features that affect an entire paragraph.

Picture: An image such as a graphic illustration or a scanned photograph, created in another program.

Picture style: Effects added to a picture, such as borders and shadows.

Placeholder: Boxes with dotted borders that are used to contain content such as text, graphics and other objects.

Placeholder text: Messages inside placeholders that prompt you to enter text.

Presenter view: View that shows the full-screen slide show on one monitor for the audience and a "speaker view" on another monitor. Will show all information on one screen using a single monitor.

r

Rotate handle: Allows you to rotate the selected object to any degree in any direction.

s

Sans serif font: A font without a flair at the base of each letter, such as Arial or Helvetica.

Serif font: A font that has a flair at the base of each letter, such as Roman or Times New Roman.

Shape styles: Combinations of fill colors, outline colors, and effects used to enhance the appearance of a shape.

Sizing handles: The four circles and squares that appear at the corners and sides of a selected placeholder's border.

Slide: An individual "page" of your presentation.

Slide indicator: Identifies the number of the slide that is displayed in the workspace, along with the total number of slides in the presentation.

Slide show: Displays each slide full screen and in order.

Slide show control bar: Bar that displays icons for navigating, zooming and showing and hiding slides as well as tools to add freehand annotations during a presentation.

Slides pane: Displays a miniature version, or thumbnail, of each slide.

Slide window: Workspace area that displays the selected slide.

Source file: The original file used to create an embedded object.

Source program: The program in which an object was created.

Spelling checker: Locates all misspelled words, duplicate words, and capitalization irregularities as you create and edit a presentation, and proposes possible corrections.

Standard size: Slide size (4:3) designed to be displayed on traditional-size screens.

Style: A combination of formatting options that can be applied in one easy step.

t

Table: Used to organize information into an easy-to-read format of horizontal rows and vertical columns.

Table reference: A letter and number used to identify cells in a table. Columns are identified from left to right beginning with the letter A, and rows are numbered from top to bottom beginning with the number 1.

Table styles: Combinations of shading colors, borders, and visual effects such as shadows and reflections that can be applied to a table.

Template: A file containing predefined settings that can be used as a pattern to create many common types of presentations.

Text box: A container for text or graphics.

Text effects: Enhancements to the text such as color and shadow.

Theme: A predefined set of formatting choices that can be applied to an entire document.

Thumbnail: A miniature version of a slide, picture, or object.

Transition: Controls the way that the display changes as you move from one slide to the next during a presentation.

v

View: A way of looking at a presentation that provides the means to interact with the presentation.

w

Widescreen: Default slide size (16:9) intended to take advantage of new HD features and equipment.

Credits

Word

WD1.2	Brand X Pictures/PunchStock
WD2.2	Getty Images
WD3.2	Royalty-Free/CORBIS

Excel

EX1.2	TRBfoto/Getty Images
EX2.2	BlueMoon stock/agefotostock
EX3.2	Hill Street Studios/Getty Images

Access

AC1.2	Ryan Mcvay/Getty Images
AC2.2	Jupiterimages
AC3.2	Corbis Super R/Alamy

Powerpoint

PP1.2	Blend Images/PunchStock
PP2.2	Thinkstock/PunchStock

Notes

Notes

Notes